The Complete Directory to Prime Time TV Stars

Also by Tim Brooks (with Earle Marsh)

The Complete Directory to Prime Time Network TV Shows—1946 to the Present

TV's Greatest Hits—The 150 Most Popular TV Shows of All Time

TV in the 60's—Those Wonderful Shows You Grew Up With

The Complete Directory to Prime Time TV Stars
1946–Present

Tim Brooks

Ballantine Books • New York

Library of Congress Catalog Card Number: 86-92108

ISBN: 0-345-32681-4

Cover design by James R. Harris

Cover photos (left to right): Freddie Prinz, *Movie Star News*;
Stefanie Powers, courtesy of Stefanie Powers;
Barbara Eden, *Movie Star News* and courtesy of Hanson
and Schwam Public Relations.

Manufactured in the United States of America

First Edition: September 1987

10 9 8 7 6 5 4 3 2

To three very special people who were stars of another kind—P.G., Auntie M., and "Brad."

CONTENTS

Acknowledgments   ix

Introduction   x

PRIME TIME TV STARS A–Z   1

Appendixes

    1. Extremes and Oddities   933

    2. The TV Academy Hall of Fame   938

    3. TV Stars' Birthday Calendar   939

    4. Index of Stars' Birthplaces   981

Bibliography   1049

Index   1051

ACKNOWLEDGMENTS

Actors who step to the podium to accept an award often graciously acknowledge that many people helped them get there, and wind up thanking everyone from their mother to the men who built the sets. My mother was unable to help me with this book, and there is no set, but many helping hands contributed to this volume in one way or another.

Colleagues at all three networks were generous in providing information both obvious and obscure. At NBC, my thanks to Betty Jane Reed, Tom O'Brien, Vera Mayer, Judy Friedman, Curt Block, Ron Korda, Doris Katz, Marilyn Kelly, and an indulgent Ted Frank. At CBS: John Behrens, Jim Sirmans, and Dorothy Miller. At ABC: Chris Morgan, Mike Schumm, Cynthia Vincente, Asa Hoff, and Barbara Cronin.

Two exceptional researchers deserve special credit: my friend and co-worker Earle Marsh, with whom I wrote an earlier volume on TV shows and who contributed much program information from his files; and Karen Botkin of the NBC Library, who by now must be a leading expert on the *Variety* obituaries page. In addition, thanks go to Mimi White and her trusty computer for extensive computer entry work, to actress/activist Fran Lee, and to Peter W. Lowry. At Ballantine Books, Senior Editor Ann La Farge—who not only offered encouragement from the start, but proved as patient and understanding an editor as any obsessive author could hope for.

To these and many others who supplied odd bits of information, my sincere thanks. Any errors or omissions are the author's own responsibility and he would, needless to say, be glad to hear about them.

INTRODUCTION

Edward R. Murrow once said of his television work, "All I can say I've done is agitate the air for ten or fifteen minutes and then *boom!*... It's gone."

Telly Savalas, on landing the biggest role of his career at age 49, saw it differently. "People used to say 'there goes what's-his-name,'" he cracked. "Two weeks on television as Kojak and the whole world knows you."

Television, the medium that only the people love, has created a galaxy of stars during the last four decades. Some, like Murrow and Moyers and Susskind and Serling, have used it as a vehicle for thoughtful, intelligent expression, and helped make the world a better place for us all. Most, like Telly and Lucy and Uncle Miltie and Johnny Carson, are (or were) primarily entertainers, seeking only to give us some harmless diversion at the end of a hard day. A few, like Bill Cosby and Michael Landon, God bless 'em, have successfully pursued both goals—entertaining, but at the same time leaving their viewers a little richer in life's experiences. Pay no attention to cynics who decry television as just a "vast wasteland." Quality sells.

Nearly ten years ago, while working on *The Complete Directory to Prime Time Network TV Shows, 1946–Present,* it became apparent to me that a companion volume on the performers who have populated the medium was sorely needed. Many of them, especially the supporting players and the one-shot wonders ("whatever happened to . . . ?") are ill-documented. There are volumes on movie stars, stage actors, musical performers, etc.,

but there was no remotely comprehensive single source on those in the most pervasive medium of all. The first humble attempt to assemble such a book is in your hands.

The first TV "star" has been almost completely forgotten today. Helen Parrish, a pert and pixieish young lady who had been a child performer in movies of the '20s and '30s, hosted the very first big league network TV series, a weekly NBC variety show called *Hour Glass,* in 1946. She was the sweetheart of the few thousand East Coast viewers who had sets then. Two years later a much bigger star came along and captured the attention of all America. Milton Berle is still known as "Mr. Television," and for good reason. His *Texaco Star Theater* ranked number one during the years when set ownership was spreading like wildfire, from 1% of U.S. homes in 1948 to 50% in 1953; indeed, many people bought their first black-and-white set just to see him and find out what all the fuss was about.

In the years that followed, TV welcomed many celebrities from movies, radio, music and stage—especially the stage, since in the early '50s most network shows originated live from New York. Some it rescued from foundering careers elsewhere; for example, Ed Wynn, Loretta Young, and later Robert Wagner. Most important, TV created its own superstars, celebrities who may have had careers in other fields but who are most closely associated with the video medium: Ed Sullivan, Sid Caesar, Lucille Ball, Jack Webb, Jackie Gleason, Dave Garroway, Raymond Burr, James Arness, Lorne Greene, Carol Burnett, Andy Griffith, Dean Martin, Walter Cronkite, Bill Cosby, the Smothers Brothers, Robert Young, Flip Wilson, Ronnie Howard, Carroll O'Connor, Bob Newhart, Mary Tyler Moore, Redd Foxx, Alan Alda, Lee Majors, James Garner, John Ritter, Ed Asner, Jack Lord, Larry Hagman, Joan Collins, Tom Selleck, Dick Clark, Johnny Carson, and the inimitable Mr. T.

And that's only the beginning. Within this volume I have attempted to document them all, the major stars and the supporting players—actors, singers, comics, smiling emcees, witty panelists, clever puppeteers, weighty newscasters, cartoon voices, cowboys and cops, bishops and knights, kids and grandpas—literally everyone who was ever a regular on any nighttime network series.

THE FORMAT

A few definitions, for those who want to know the "rules." Included in this volume is everyone who was a *regular* on a nighttime network series. A series regular is someone who was seen (or heard) every week, or nearly every week, in an on-screen capacity. Thus dancers, singers, puppeteers and sometimes announcers (if a principal cast member) get in, but not strictly behind-the-scenes people like writers, producers and directors.

A nighttime network series is defined as one that ran for four weeks or more (or was supposed to!) on ABC, CBS, NBC or the old DuMont television network, between the hours of 6:00 P.M. and sign-off. Therefore in addition to "prime time" performers, many early evening and late night personalities are included here. These definitions are essentially the same ones that were used in *The Complete Directory to Prime Time Network TV Shows, 1946–Present,* by Earle Marsh and myself. The reader is referred to

that book for information on the shows themselves, their plots, broadcast histories, etc.

To enrich the listings I have also included the principals in the 200 or so top syndicated programs of all time that ran predominantly in the evening hours, as well as the casts of TV's all-time top rated miniseries.

Credits: Listed for each personality are the series in which he or she appeared as a regular, what types of programs these were (drama, comedy, etc.), the name of each character played, and the years in which the performer played that character. Thus an actor's career can be traced as he or she moved from role to role. Credits have been updated through October 1986; those still on the air at that time are indicated by a dash ("—") in place of a final year.

Emmy Awards: Emmy Awards won by the performer are listed, even if they were not for nighttime series (e.g., specials, daytime programs, behind-the-scenes technical awards, etc.).

Biographical Notes: For the biggest stars, and also for many of the more interesting lesser personalities, I have included notes, descriptions, and sometimes full biographies. While nighttime series work is the main focus of this book, important guest roles, roles in daytime and on Saturday morning programs, and notable achievements in movies, onstage, and in other media are also noted.

Also, where the information is available, I have indicated date and place of birth (b), place raised if it is different (r), and date of death (d).

A WORD ON DETERMINING ACTORS' AGES

Let me pause for a moment while the laughter subsides. . .

Actually, one of the greatest inducements to an acting career, aside from the remote possibility of wealth and fame, is the prospect of recasting yourself into whatever person you want to be—and getting away with it. Got the pushing-40 blues? Tell your agent to list you as 31, and 31 will be printed everywhere. Too short? Just add a few inches, and nobody will argue. Too heavy? Same thing. Practically every male in Hollywood, with the possible exception of Herve Villechaize, seems to be six feet, 160 pounds, and golden blond, according to their official bios. They are also invariably several years younger than you thought. It is a city of biological miracles.

For the record, I have decided to become two inches taller, ten pounds lighter, ten years younger, and curly haired. Try it; all you have to do is put the perfect you "officially" in print somewhere and, believe me, it will get picked up, reprinted, and accepted as truth.

Cutting through this nonsense is one of the biographer's most difficult tasks, and one at which he can never be completely successful. Some performers have hidden their beginnings quite well. Lucille Ball was born in Wyandotte, Mich., Butte, Mont., Colvin, N.Y., or Jamestown, N.Y., on August 6 or 11, in 1910 or 1911, depending on what published source you believe! David Ragan in *Movie Stars of the '40s* tells the story of June Allyson, who was publicized by her studio as having been born in 1924 to a loving family in posh Westchester, N.Y. In fact she was born in near-poverty in the Bronx in 1917, to a father who walked out when she was six months old, and endured a decidedly hardscrabble childhood. Others lie for various reasons. Duncan *(The Cisco Kid)* Renaldo's birthplace was officially listed as Camden, N.J., to hide the fact that he was an illegal alien from somewhere in Europe. Stylish Merle Oberon, passed off as a product of cultured British society, was actually born the half-caste, illegitimate daughter of an Indian mother and a British soldier (who disappeared before her birth) in squalid Calcutta. Robin Williams first told his network's publicity department that he was born in Scotland, simply because he is unable to be serious about anything. (He is actually from Chicago—I think.)

Actors usually make themselves younger and trimmer so they can get more roles.

Compounding these felonies, most authors give no indication of the sources of their information or the degree of certainty in the dates and places they list. I have combed through thousands of "official" network and studio biographies, hundreds of actor interviews, and scores of reference books (see the bibliography) to assemble the birth dates and places given here. Where significant discrepancies occur they are footnoted; where they can be resolved I have indicated that fact (see, for example, Bing Crosby and Efrem Zimbalist, Jr.). In all cases, the date listed immediately under the actor's name is the most probable.

As for heights and weights, you're on your own!

I hope the reader will enjoy this first comprehensive "Who's Who" of the thousands of stars, big and small, who have flickered across the home screen since the 1940s. The book has been carefully researched for the scholar, but it is also written to be fun —just like TV itself. Comments and additional information (with sources, please!) are welcome, care of the publisher. If you want to quibble about someone's birth date, however, you'd better send a copy of their birth certificate!

Now turn to channel "A"—or to whatever name interests you most— and meet forty years of TV stars.

List of Abbreviations

Due to space limitations, a number of abbreviations have had to be used in identifying types of TV shows. Below is a key:

adv	adventure
aud par	audience participation
cartn	cartoon
child	children's
com	comedy
doc	documentary
drama	drama
info	information
int	interview
mag	magazine
misc	miscellaneous
music	music
news	news
police	police
pub aff	public affairs
quiz	quiz
sci fi	science fiction
sport	sportscast
talent	talent
talk	talk
var	variety
wes	western

The Complete Directory
to Prime Time
TV Stars

A

AAKER, LEE—actor

b: Sep 24, 1943, Los Angeles, Calif.

Adventures of Rin Tin Tin (wes)
.... Rusty (1954–59)

A child star who made 15 films between 1947 and 1956, including *Benji* in 1947. Later he left show business and became a carpenter.

AAMES, WILLIE—actor

b: Jul 15, 1960, Newport Beach, Calif.

We'll Get By (com)...... Kenny Platt (1975)
Swiss Family Robinson (adv)
.... Fred Robinson (1975–76)
Eight Is Enough (com)
.... Tommy Bradford (1977–81)
We're Movin' (mag) .... host (1982)
Charles in Charge (com)
.... Buddy Lembeck (1984–85)

After a series of clean-cut teenager roles in the 1970s—most notably that of middle son Tommy Bradford in the hit comedy *Eight Is Enough*—Willie Aames went on to make a number of forgettable movies, including *Hog Wild* and *Bull From the Sky*. He also appeared in the early 1980s as shady disco manager Robbie in the daytime serial *The Edge of Night*. In 1984 he landed the role of Scott Baio's pal Buddy in the short-lived *Charles in Charge*. Offscreen, Willie likes to surf, skin-dive and race speedboats.

AARON, BETSY—newscaster

r: Forest Hills, N.Y.

NBC Magazine with David Brinkley (pub aff)
.... correspondent (1980–82)

Betsy Aaron is one of a small group of newscasters who have been seen on all three networks. She began as a secretary at ABC in 1960 and soon moved into writing, producing, and reporting at local stations in Philadelphia and New York. By the mid-1970s she was a correspondent for ABC-TV (1975–76) and then for CBS-TV (1976–80). In July 1977, while covering a Ku Klux Klan rally in Plains, Ga., she was severely injured when a car rammed into the crowd in which she was standing. De-

spite the lingering effects of her injuries, in 1980, while with NBC-TV, she undertook the most strenuous and celebrated assignment of her career. Aaron and a camera crew slipped across the closed border into Afghanistan and walked 150 miles across the mountainous terrain, filming an inside report on the war between Afghan rebels and the Soviets. The story later won two awards. After two years with NBC, Aaron switched back to ABC in 1982.

Aaron is married to news correspondent Richard Threlkeld.

ABBOTT, BUD—comedian

b: Oct 2, 1895, Asbury Park, N.J. d: Apr 24, 1974

The Abbott and Costello Show (com)
.... as himself (1951–53)
The Colgate Comedy Hour (var)
.... rotating host (1951–54)

Abbott and Costello were probably the most famous slapstick comedy team in the history of American entertainment. Abbott was the tall, exasperated straight man, and Costello his chubby companion. Each had been in vaudeville and burlesque during the 1920s and 1930s; they teamed up in 1936. In 1940 they began their first radio series, and also appeared in their first motion picture, *One Night in the Tropics*, which was a sensation. For the rest of the 1940s they ranked among America's top comedy stars, with such hit films as *Buck Privates* and *In the Navy*.

When television began to catch on in the late 1940s, Abbott and Costello's knockabout comedy was perfect for the new medium. They guested on variety shows, doing such routines as their famous "Who's on First?", and were frequent hosts of NBC's big-budget *Colgate Comedy Hour*. They are probably best remembered, however, for their own syndicated comedy series, which incorporated many of their stage routines and which has been constantly rerun ever since its 52 episodes were filmed in 1951–53.

Abbott and Costello finally broke up in 1957; after that Abbott made only occasional appearances, among other things providing his own voice for a Saturday morning Abbott and Costello cartoon series in 1967. His last years were painful; after suffering throughout his life from bouts with epilepsy and alcoholism, he was reduced to near-poverty by government demands for back taxes. He died of cancer in 1974.

ABBOTT, GEORGE—host, Broadway producer
b: Jun 25, 1887, Forestville, N.Y.

The U.S. Royal Showcase (var). . host (1952)

George Abbott was one of Broadway's legendary producer/director/writers, and was responsible for such stage hits as *The Pajama Game* and *Damn Yankees.* He briefly hosted this combination variety and talent series in the early 1950s. His autobiography was published in 1963 under the title *Mister Abbott.*

ABBOTT, PHILIP—actor
b: Mar 21, 1923, Lincoln, Neb.

The F.B.I. (police) . . Arthur Ward (1965–74)
Rich Man, Poor Man—Book II (drama)
.... John Franklin (1976–77)

ABEL, WALTER—actor
b: Jun 6, 1898, St. Paul, Minn. d: Mar 26, 1987

Suspicion (drama). . . . . host (1959)

Broadway and Hollywood character actor whose film career spanned 1930–74 and included such titles as *Arise My Love, Holiday Inn,* and *Dream Girl.* One of his last roles was in the TV movie *Man without a Country* (1974).

ABELEW, ALAN—actor

Lucas Tanner (drama)
.... Jaytee Drumm (1974–75)

ABELLIRA, REMI—actor
r: Hawaii

Big Hawaii (drama) . . Kimo Kalahani (1977)

ABERLIN, BETTY—actress

The Smothers Brothers Show (var)
.... regular (1975)

ABERNETHY, ROBERT—newscaster
b: Nov 5, 1927, Geneva, Switzerland r: Washington, D.C.

NBC News Encore (doc) . . . . host (1966)
Decision '80 (news). . . . . . anchorman (1980)

This silver-haired NBC correspondent is best known for his coverage of Washington politics, science, and education. He began his career with NBC in 1952, then served as anchor for the network's Los Angeles station for 11 years in the 1960s and 1970s. He was seen on *Today* in the late 1970s. In 1966 Abernethy wrote an award-winning history book for teenagers titled *Introduction to Tomorrow.*

ACE, GOODMAN—comedian, writer
b: Jan 15, 1899, Kansas City, Mo. d: Mar 25, 1982

Easy Aces (talk) . . . . regular (1949–50)

One of the most successful and highly regarded comedy writers of the radio era, Goodman Ace made the transition to television in the 1950s writing gags for Milton Berle, Sid Caesar, Perry Como, and others. He also had his own successful radio show, *Easy Aces,* consisting of witty chatter with his wife Jane. The program was seen briefly on television in 1949–50. Despite his considerable behind-the-scenes success, he was a frequent and vociferous critic of TV's reliance on ratings, claiming they dragged the medium down into the "muck of mediocrity."

ACE, JANE—comedian
b: 1900 d: Nov 11, 1974

Easy Aces (talk) . . . . regular (1949–50)

Wife of Goodman Ace, known for her malapropisms ("You're giving me an interior complex!", "You could have knocked me down with a fender," "up at the crank of dawn").

ACE TRUCKING COMPANY, THE— improvisational comedy troupe

This Is Tom Jones (var). . regulars (1970–71)

ACKER, SHARON—actress
b: Apr 2, 1935, Toronto, Canada

The Senator (drama) . Erin Stowe (1970–71)
Perry Mason (revival) (drama)
.... Della Street (1973–74)

Executive Suite (drama)
.... Helen Walling (1976–77)

Though she is most often seen in dramatic roles, Miss Acker's film debut was in the 1958 comedy *Lucky Jim*. She has had guest roles on such series as *Quincy, M.E., Dallas, Simon & Simon* and the daytime soap *Texas*.

ACKERMAN, BETTYE—actress
b: Feb 28, 1928, Cottageville, S.C.

Ben Casey (drama)
.... Dr. Maggie Graham (1961–68)

The wife of actor Sam Jaffe, who also starred in the Casey series.

ACKERMAN, LESLIE—actress
r: New Jersey

Skag (drama) ...... Barbara Skagska (1980)

Youthful actress who played Karl Malden's overweight teenage daughter in the series *Skag*. Married to comedian Jeff Altman.

ACKROYD, DAVID—actor
b: May 30, 1940, Orange, N.J.

Dallas (drama)...... Gary Ewing (1978–79)
Little Women (drama)
.... Prof. Friedrich Bhaer (1979)
AfterMASH (com)........: Dr. Boyer (1984)

This actor worked for several years in the daytime soap operas *The Secret Storm* and *Another World* before moving into prime time in the late 1970s. Since then he has played the original Gary Ewing on *Dallas* and the feisty surgeon Dr. Boyer on *AfterMASH*, as well as appearing in the miniseries *Dark Secret of Harvest Home* and *Women in White*.

ACOVONE, JAY—actor
b: Aug 20, 1955, Mahopac, N.Y.

Hollywood Beat (police)
.... Det. Jack Rado (1985)

ACTMAN, JANE—actress
b: Apr 6, 1949, New York City, N.Y.

The Paul Lynde Show (com)
..... Barbara Simms Dickerson (1972–73)

ACUFF, ROY—country musician
b: Sep 15, 1903, Maynardville, Tenn.

Grand Ole Opry (music) .. regular (1955–56)
Hee Haw (var)........... regular (1980–85)

One of the legendary stars of country music, Roy began his career in the 1930s as leader of his own band ("The Crazy Tennesseans") and has been a top star of radio and records ever since; his familiar theme song is "The Wabash Cannonball." He is also a rather astute businessman, having cofounded Nashville's largest music publishing company, and has been quite active in politics, having run three times for governor of Tennessee during the 1940s. Though he lost those campaigns, he won a different kind of election in 1963, when he became the first living performer to be elected into the Country Music Hall of Fame.

Acuff became a regular on radio's *Grand Ole Opry* in 1940 and was with the series during its brief network television run in 1955–56.

ADAGALA, SETH—actor

The Search for the Nile (drama)
.... Bombay (1972)

ADAIR, DEBORAH—actress
b: May 23, Lynchburg, Va.

Dynasty (drama) .. Tracy Kendall (1983–84)
Finder of Lost Loves (drama)
.... Daisy Lloyd (1984–85)

A comely young actress who for several years played the role of Jill Foster on *The Young and the Restless*, then broke hearts on *Dynasty* for a season. Later she brought lovers back together as Tony Franciosa's beautiful assistant on *Finder of Lost Loves*. Deborah originally planned on a business career, earning a degree in marketing and working for four years writing and producing commercials for KIRO radio and TV in Seattle. She proved so adept at reading her work that she was soon delivering the commercials herself, which led in time to an acting career.

ADAIR, PAT—musician

School House (var)......... regular (1949)
Country Style (var)......... regular (1950)

ADAM, NOELLE—French vocalist

b: 1935, La Rochelle, France

The Keefe Brasselle Show (var)
.... regular (1963)

ADAMLE, MIKE—sportscaster

b: c. 1950, Kent, Ohio

Games People Play (sport)
.... field reporter (1980–81)

A former pro football player who spent six seasons with the Kansas City Chiefs, New York Jets, and Chicago Bears. He joined NBC Sports after a leg injury abruptly ended his career in 1977. Adamle is the son of onetime Cleveland Browns linebacker Tony Adamle.

ADAMS, BROOKE—actress

b: Feb 8, 1949, New York City, N.Y.

O. K. Crackerby (com)
.... Cynthia Crackerby (1965–66)

ADAMS, CARSWELL—sportscaster

d: Dec 9, 1957

Your Sports Special (sport)
.... reporter (1948–49)

ADAMS, CATLIN—actress

b: Oct 11, 1950, Los Angeles, Calif.

Square Pegs (com).... Ms. Loomis (1982–83)

ADAMS, CEDRIC—host

Prize Performance (var)........ host (1950)

ADAMS, DAVID—actor

S.W.A.T. (police)
.... Kevin Harrelson (1975–76)

ADAMS, DON—comedian

b: Apr 13, 1926,* New York City

Kraft Music Hall (var).... regular (1961–63)
The Bill Dana Show (com)
.... Byron Glick (1963–65)
Get Smart (com)
..... Maxwell Smart (Agent 86) (1965–70)
The Partners (com)
.... Det. Lennie Crooke (1971–72)
Don Adams' Screen Test (com).. host (1975)
Check It Out (com)
.... Howard Bannister (1985–)

*Some sources give April 19.

Emmy Awards: Best Actor in a Comedy Series, for *Get Smart* (1967, 1968, 1969)

One of the 1960s' favorite comedians, known for such *Get Smart* catchphrases as "Sorry about that, Chief," and (when some preposterous bluff of his was challenged) "Would you believe—?"

SMART to enemy agent: "You'll never get away with this . . ."
AGENT: "Oh? Why, Mr. Smart?"
SMART: "Because at this very minute, 25 of our agents are converging on this building. Would you believe it? Twenty-five agents!"
AGENT: "I find that hard to believe."
SMART: "Would you believe, two squad cars and a motorcycle cop?"
AGENT: "I don't think so."
SMART: "How about a vicious streetcleaner and a toothless police dog?"

Adams began his career as a small-time nightclub comedian in the 1950s while supporting himself as a commercial artist. He had a natural flair for impersonations, his own favorite being a greatly exaggerated version of sophisticated movie star William Powell (which later became the basis of Don's Maxwell Smart character). After winning a competition on *Arthur Godfrey's Talent Scouts,* Don teamed with young comedian Bill Dana in 1954, a partnership that lasted until both became major TV personalities in the 1960s. Dana is still one of his closest friends.

Adams' most conspicuous success, for which he will always be remembered, was as the bumbling hero on the classic secret agent parody *Get Smart,* from 1965–70. Later he hosted an odd syndicated show *(Screen Test)* in which a contestant and a guest star together acted out a scene from a famous movie, in comic fashion, with Don as "director."

ADAMS, EDIE—singer, actress

b: Apr 16, 1931*, Kingston, Pa.

Ernie in Kovacsland (var)..... singer (1951)
The Ernie Kovacs Show (var)
.... regular (1952–53)
The Ernie Kovacs Show (var)
.... regular (1956)
The Chevy Show (music) .... host (1958)

*Some sources give 1927.

4

Take a Good Look (quiz)
.... panelist (1960–61)
Edie Adams Show (var)...... host (1963–64)

Best known as the wife of comedian Ernie Kovacs, Edie appeared with him on most of his programs of the 1950s as a featured singer and sometimes supporting actress. After his death in 1962, she briefly had her own alternate-week variety show, which was nominated for an Emmy Award (she lost out to Carol Burnett). From the mid-1950s on, Edie played roles in numerous dramatic series, appeared in several movies, and was also seen on Broadway, where she won a Tony for her supporting role in *Li'l Abner*. In more recent years she has been seen mostly in nightclubs and a few offbeat films such as *Cheech and Chong's Up in Smoke* (1978) and *The Happy Hooker Goes to Washington* (1977). In 1984 she surprisingly turned up playing Mae West in the TV biography of her late husband, *Ernie Kovacs: Between the Laughter.*

ADAMS, FRANKLIN P.—columnist
b: Nov 15, 1881, Chicago, Ill. d: Mar 23, 1960

Information Please (quiz) ... panelist (1952)

Popular columnist for several New York and Chicago newspapers, known to his readers by his initials, "F.P.A." Adams was best known for his humorous column "The Conning Tower," and for his long run as the "literary expert" on the witty and literate radio series *Information Please* (1938–48). The program was revived for a short TV run in the summer of 1952.

ADAMS, JEB—actor
b: Apr 10, 1961, Hollywood, Calif.

Baa Baa Black Sheep (drama)
.... Lt. Jeb Pruitt (1978)

Blonde, blue-eyed son of the late actor Nick Adams (*The Rebel*). Young Jeb was given a role as an underage Marine pilot in *Black Sheep* by series star Robert Conrad, out of appreciation for the fact that more than 20 years earlier, Jeb's father had helped the young Conrad get his own start in Hollywood.

ADAMS, JOEY—comedian, writer
b: Jan 6, 1911, Brooklyn, N.Y.

Back That Fact (aud par) ..... emcee (1953)

Nightclub comedian, prolific writer (20 books), and frequent TV guest star, known to viewers as one of those "joke-a-minute" comics. Joey's specialty was the put-down: "His idea of an exciting night is to turn up his electric blanket."; "Stay with me, I want to be alone!"

ADAMS, JULIE—actress
b: Oct 17, 1928*, Waterloo, Iowa

Yancy Derringer (adv)
.... Amanda Eaton (1958–59)
The Jimmy Stewart Show (com)
.... Martha Howard (1971–72)
Code Red (adv) .... Ann Rorchek (1981–82)

A busy actress who has costarred in dozens of movies over the years, and in more than a hundred episodes of TV dramatic series, from *Lux Video Theatre* in 1955 to *Trapper John, M.D.* in the 1980s. Among her more notable films were the soap opera *Bright Victory* (her first major role, in 1951), the sprawling western *Bend of the River,* and the comedy *The Private War of Major Benson.* Though never the lead, she was often the love interest. On TV she seemed to specialize in the loyal wife—Jimmy Stewart's in *The Jimmy Stewart Show* and Lorne Greene's in *Code Red.* She has also been seen in the daytime serials *General Hospital* in 1969–70 and *Capitol* in the 1980s (on the latter playing the not-so-supportive wife of Sen. Mark Denning).

Julie was known early in her career as Betty Adams and Julia Adams.

ADAMS, MASON—actor
b: Feb 26, 1919, New York City, N.Y.

Lou Grant (drama)
.... Charlie Hume (1977–82)
Morningstar/Eveningstar (drama)
.... Gordon Blair (1986)

Mason Adams is best known to younger viewers as managing editor Charlie Hume, Lou Grant's boss, but he had an even more famous persona in radio in the 1940s and '50s—that of the title character on the long-

*Some sources give 1926.

running soap opera *Pepper Young's Family,* a role he played from 1945–59. Even after all these years, his nasal twang is still recognized by loyal, if aging, radio fans as that of their "Pepper." He also appeared in a number of Broadway plays and TV movies and has made a great deal of money doing commercials, most notably as the spokesman for Smucker's jams and jellies.

ADAMS, MAUD—actress
b: Feb 12, 1945, Lulea, Sweden

Chicago Story (drama)
.... Dr. Judith Bergstrom (1982)
Emerald Point N.A.S. (drama)
.... Maggie Farrell (1983–84)

A sexy Swedish fashion model who turned to acting in the mid-1970s. She appeared in a number of movies, including *Tattoo* and the James Bond films *The Man with the Golden Gun* and *Octopussy* (in the title role), as well as guest-starring in various TV series. Neither of her own shows lasted very long—in *Emerald Point* she was about to marry series star Dennis Weaver when the program was abruptly canceled. No matter, whatever else she may do she will be fondly remembered (by men at least) for those very provocative lip-gloss commercials she did in the 1970s.

ADAMS, NICK—actor
b: Jul 10, 1931, Nanticoke, Pa. d: Feb 5, 1968

The Rebel (wes) ... Johnny Yuma (1959–61)
Saints and Sinners (drama)
.... Nick Alexander (1962–63)

Compact, blond actor with a promising career in the 1950s. Although he made 30 films, including the well-received *No Time for Sergeants* and *Twilight of Honor* (for which he was nominated for an Oscar), and starred in a popular TV series, he never quite made it to the top in Hollywood. By the late 1960s he was reduced to monster movies (*Frankenstein Meets the Giant Devil Fish*) and scattered appearances on TV action shows.

He died of a drug overdose in 1968.

ADAMS, STANLEY—actor
b: 1920

How To (info).............. panelist (1951)

ADDAMS, DAWN—actress
b: Sep 21, 1930, Felixstowe, England d: May 7, 1985

The Alan Young Show (var)
.... Kay Prindall (1953)
Star Maidens (sci fi)......... Clara (1977)

Glamorous British actress Addams probably forgot that as a young starlet in Hollywood she spent two months playing Alan Young's girlfriend in a short-lived revival of *The Alan Young Show.* She was certainly better known for her many international films and for her long and stormy marriage to Italian prince Don Vittorio Massimo.

ADIARTE, PATRICK—actor

M*A*S*H (com)............ Ho-John (1972)

ADLAM, BUZZ—composer, orchestra leader
b: Dec 31, Chelmsford, England

Stage Two Revue (var) . orch. leader (1950)

Basil "Buzz" Adlam was a radio and TV conductor who was very active around 1950. Before that he had composed some forgotten pop songs of the 1930s (does anybody remember "My Galveston Gal"?) and been a saxophonist in Ozzie Nelson's big band. Later Ozzie made him musical director of his *Ozzie & Harriet* TV series.

ADLER, CLYDE—actor

Soupy Sales (child)........ assistant (1955)

ADLER, LUTHER—actor
b: May 4, 1903, New York City, N.Y. d: Dec 8, 1984

The Psychiatrist (drama)
.... Dr. Bernard Altman (1971)

Heavyset, jowly character actor who usually played villains in films of the 1940s and 1950s (including Hitler in *The Magic Face*). He also had a long career as a supporting actor on Broadway and guest starred in numerous episodes of TV dramatic series in the 1950s and '60s. His career spanned nearly 70 years (1908–76).

ADLER, WILLIAM—actor

Not for Publication (drama).. Collins (1951)

ADOLPHUS, TED, DANCERS—dancers

Ford Star Revue (var) ...... regulars (1951)

ADRIAN, IRIS—actress
b: May 29, 1913, Los Angeles, Calif.

The Ted Knight Show (com) .. Dottie (1978)

Brassy, wisecracking blonde who appeared in scores of movies from the 1930s to the 1970s, including a number of Disney films. Though she did not do much television, she did turn up, toward the end of her career, as Ted Knight's sarcastic receptionist (and sister-in-law) in this short-lived comedy in which Ted ran an escort service.

ADRIAN, JANE—actress

The Marshal of Gunsight Pass (wes)
.... Ruth (1950)

ADRIENNE (MEYERBERG)—singer

Champagne and Orchids (music)
.... hostess (1948–49)

One of TV's many early (and obscure) vocalists; a svelte brunette who specialized in torch songs sung in French, Spanish, and English.

AGRONSKY, MARTIN—newscaster
b: Philadelphia

At Issue (int)............... host (1953–54)

Though he was known in later years as a venerable and somewhat curmudgeonly interviewer of Washington politicians, Agronsky began his career in broadcasting in 1939 as an NBC war correspondent flying bombing raids over Italy and following the troops in the Pacific. During 14 years with ABC radio and TV (1943–57) he turned largely to political reporting, anchoring several interview shows, including the prime time series *At Issue*. Later he returned to NBC (1957–65) and then spent four years with CBS (1965–69). In the 1970s and '80s he was best known for his syndicated and PBS network discussion programs,

Agronsky & Company and *Evening Edition*, both of which originated in Washington.

AHN, PHILIP—actor
b: Mar 29, 1911, Los Angeles, Calif. d: Feb 28, 1978

Kung Fu (wes) .... Master Kan (1972–75)

Ahn, the son of one of the founders of the Korean republic, was one of Hollywood's favorite all-purpose Oriental character actors during the 1940s and '50s. He worked steadily, mostly in war movies, in roles such as that of the villainous Japanese, the inscrutable Chinese, or whatever other Asian was needed. He then turned to TV for many guest roles in action series of the 1950s and '60s, including several appearances in early episodes of *Hawaii Five-0*. On *Kung Fu* he played one of David Carradine's boyhood teachers, in flashback scenes. Ahn continued to appear on television up to the time of his death in 1978.

AIDMAN, CHARLES—actor, director, composer
b: Jan 31, 1925, Frankfort, Ind.

The Twilight Zone (sci fi) . narrator (1985–)

A veteran supporting actor, who coincidentally had appeared in one of the earliest—and eeriest—of the original *Twilight Zone* episodes, in 1959. In that story, titled "And When the Sky Was Opened," he played an astronaut who found himself disappearing from the minds and view of those around him. Aidman also appeared in many crime dramas over the years (*Hec Ramsey, Quincy, M.E.,* etc.) as well as in supernatural anthologies such as *Ghost Story* and *The Night Stalker*.

AIELLO, DANNY—actor
b: Jun 20, 1933, New York City, N.Y.

Lady Blue (police)
.... Chief Terry McNichols (1985–86)

Emmy Award: Best Performer in a Children's Program, for the *ABC Afterschool Special* "Family of Strangers" (1981).

AIKEN, CHARLES—juvenile actor

Friends (com) .... Pete Richards (1979)

AJAYE, FRANKLYN—comedian
b: May 13, 1949, Brooklyn, N.Y.

Keep On Truckin' (var) . . . . . . regular (1975)

A black stand-up comedian, also seen in such films as *Car Wash* and *The Jazz Singer.*

AKERLING, MYA—juvenile actress
Jennifer Slept Here (com)
. . . . Marilyn Elliot (1983–84)

AKINS, CLAUDE—actor
b: May 25, 1918, Nelson, Ga.

Movin' On (adv) . . . . Sonny Pruitt (1974–76)
Nashville 99 (police)
. . . . Det. Lt. Stonewall Huff (1977)
The Rhinemann Exchange (drama)
. . . . Walter Kendall (1977)
B.J. and the Bear (adv)
. . . . Sheriff Elroy P. Lobo (1979)
Lobo (com) . Sheriff Elroy P. Lobo (1979–81)
Legmen (drama). . . . . Tom Bannon (1984)

Burly Claude Akins is living proof that it is possible to overcome typecasting—even if it takes a decade or two. In the 1950s and '60s he was seen frequently in films, usually westerns, and almost always played the snarling bad guy. Then in 1974, in his midfifties, and after much TV work, he finally landed his own series playing a sympathetic trucker in *Movin' On.* By the spring of 1979 he had metamorphosed into the slapstick Sheriff Lobo on *B.J. and the Bear,* a role he carried over into his own successful comedy series the following fall.

AKUNE, SHUKO—actress
b: Wahoo, Nebr. r: Chicago, Ill.

E/R (com) . . . . Maria Amardo (1984–85)

ALADDIN—violinist
b: c. 1917, New York City, N.Y.

The Lawrence Welk Show (music)
. . . . regular (1955–67)

Mustachioed violinist in the Welk orchestra who also delivered florid dramatic readings. His real name (take a deep breath!) is Aladdin Abdullah Achmed An-

thony Pallante—but his friends know him as "Laddy."

ALAIMO, MICHAEL—actor
Billy (com). . . . . Norval Shadrack (1979)

ALAMO, TONY—singer
The Sammy Kaye Show (var)
. . . . regular (1950–55)

ALANN, LLOYD—actor
Joe & Valerie (com)
. . . . Frank Berganski (1979)

ALBA, JAIME—
Mulligan's Stew (drama)
. . . . Polo Polocheck (1977)

ALBEE, JOSHUA—juvenile actor
Lassie (adv) . . . . Mike Holden (1972–74)

ALBERONI, SHERRY—actress
b: Dec 1946

Ed Wynn Show (com) . . . . . Midge (1958–59)
The Tom Ewell Show (com)
. . . . Debbie Potter (1960–61)

Popular juvenile actress of the 1950s and onetime *Mickey Mouse Club* mouseketeer. She played the preteen daughter in two short-lived family comedies and also appeared in several films; in the 1970s she provided voices for *Josie and the Pussycats* and other Saturday morning cartoons.

ALBERT, EDDIE—actor
b: Apr 22, 1908, Rock Island, Ill.

Leave It to Larry (com)
. . . . Larry Tucker (1952)
Nothing But the Best (var) . . . . . . host (1953)
Saturday Night Revue (var) . . . . . host (1954)
Green Acres (com)
. . . . Oliver Wendell Douglas (1965–71)
Switch (drama). . . . Frank McBride (1975–78)

Eddie Albert's friendly smile and easygoing manner won him steady work in theater, film, radio, and TV for more than 50 years. He was originally a singer as well as an actor; in the mid-1930s he co-starred with Grace Albert on a New York radio show called *The Honeymooners* [sic]. A role in the 1936 Broadway comedy *Brother Rat* led to a Hollywood career when the play was made into a movie, and he went on to costar in more than 75 films—usually as the amiable friend of the star.

Eddie began appearing on television in the early 1950s and was frequently seen in playhouse series such as *Studio One, Schlitz Playhouse of Stars* and *Climax.* He also had his own short-lived sitcom, *Leave It to Larry* (with Ed Begley), and hosted two summer variety shows. Ten years later he landed a more durable role, as Eva Gabor's sensible husband in the long-running city-folks-go-to-the-country comedy *Green Acres.* Later he costarred with Robert Wagner in the lightweight detective show *Switch* in the mid-1970s and then turned primarily to TV miniseries and movies such as *Beulah Land, Goliath Awaits,* and *Beyond Witch Mountain.*

That trademark "aw shucks" smile served him well.

ALBERT, EDWARD—actor
b: Feb 20, 1951, Los Angeles, Calif.

The Last Convertible (drama)
.... Ron "Dal" Dalrymple (1979)
The Yellow Rose (drama)
.... Quisto Champion (1983–84)
Falcon Crest (drama)
.... Jeff Wainwright (1986–)

The son of Eddie Albert and his actresswife, Margo, who tutored young Edward in her acting workshop. Edward's big break came as Goldie Hawn's blind boyfriend in *Butterflies Are Free*; since then he has been seen in a number of films and TV series, as well as in the miniseries *The Last Convertible* (in which he got the girl). He was also the lawyer Quisto in the nighttime soap opera *The Yellow Rose.*

ALBERT, WIL—actor

The Dumplings (com)...... the prude (1976)

ALBERTSON, JACK—actor
b: Jun 16, 1907, Malden, Mass. d: Nov 25, 1981

Broadway Jamboree (var)....... host (1948)

The Thin Man (drama)
.... Lt. Harry Evans (1958–59)
Room for One More (com)
.... Walter Burton (1962)
Ensign O'Toole (com)
.... Lt. Cdr. Virgil Stoner (1962–63)
Dr. Simon Locke (drama)
.... Dr. Sellers (1971–72)
Chico and the Man (com)
.... Ed Brown (1974–78)
Grandpa Goes to Washington (com)
.... Senator Joe Kelley (1978–79)

Emmy Awards: For a guest appearance on the *Cher* series (1975); Best Actor in a Comedy Series, for *Chico and the Man* (1976)

"One nice thing about achieving success at this age is that I have fewer years to become a has-been," quipped Jack Albertson during the run of the smash hit comedy *Chico and the Man.* He was too modest. By the time he was in his sixties, Albertson was one of the most loved and honored old-time troopers in show business. In addition to his Emmys, he won a Tony Award for the Broadway production of *The Subject Was Roses* in 1965 and an Oscar for the movie version of the same play in 1968.

Albertson's career began a couple of generations before his TV heyday, as a dancer in vaudeville and a straight man for such comics as Milton Berle, Bert Lahr, and Willie Howard. At one time he was Phil Silvers' partner. Jack was on TV in the 1940s, including a brief stint as host of the early variety show *Broadway Jamboree.* Later he played the police contact on *The Thin Man,* a family friend on *Room for One More,* the nutty ship's executive officer on *Ensign O'Toole* and the wise older doctor on the cheaply made syndicated series *Dr. Simon Locke* (a role he despised). He finally hit the jackpot as the grouchy garage owner on *Chico and the Man.* His last series role was as the feisty grandpa on *Grandpa Goes to Washington,* playing the drums and yelling "Bring on the bimbo!"

Albertson was also seen in numerous films and in episodes of other TV series, both comic and serious, from the 1950s to the '80s. He was quite a character—and never a has-been.

ALBERTSON, MABEL—actress
b: 1901 d: Sep 28, 1982

That's My Boy (com)
.... Henrietta Patterson (1954–55)
Those Whiting Girls (com)
.... Mrs. Whiting (1955)
Those Whiting Girls (com)
.... Mrs. Whiting (1957)
The Tom Ewell Show (com)
.... Irene Brady (1960–61)

Character actress who was seen on television and in the movies during the 1950s and '60s, often as the wise and witty mom (as in *Those Whiting Girls*) or grandma (as in *The Tom Ewell Show*). Later she made a few appearances on *That Girl* as Don Hollinger's mother, Mildred.

ALBIN, ANDY—actor

The Bob Newhart Show (var)
.... regular (1961–62)

ALBRIGHT, LOLA—actress
b: Jul 20, 1925, Akron, Ohio

Peter Gunn (drama) ... Edie Hart (1958–61)

Sexy, sultry Lola Albright attracted a lot of attention—not to mention wolf whistles—in the late 1940s and early '50s in movies such as *The Champion* and *The Tender Trap*. She also did a fair amount of television, with her most notable role that of a nightclub singer (and Craig Stevens' girlfriend) Edie on *Peter Gunn*. For several months in 1965–66 she took over the leading role of Constance MacKenzie on *Peyton Place*, substituting for Dorothy Malone, who was ill. Semiretired in the 1970s and '80s, Lola still made occasional appearances in episodes of series such as *Medical Center* and *Switch*. She was married during the 1950s to comedian Jack Carson.

ALDA, ALAN—actor
b: Jan 28, 1936, New York City, N.Y.

That Was the Week That Was (com)
.... regular (1964)
M*A*S*H (com)
Capt. Benjamin Franklin Pierce (1972–83)

Emmy Awards: Actor of the Year (1974); Best Actor in a Comedy Series, for

M*A*S*H (1974, 1982); Best Directing in a Comedy Series, for *M*A*S*H* (1977); Best Writing in a Comedy Series, for *M*A*S*H* (1979)

Alan Alda's dry, sarcastic manner would not seem to make him a candidate to become one of TV's biggest stars, but in the right series (*M*A*S*H*) at the right time (the Vietnam War era) it clicked perfectly. *M*A*S*H* was—and is—one of the most popular and honored series in TV history. It gave Alda—as the wisecracking, antiwar Capt. "Hawkeye" Pierce—the role with which he will always be associated.

Alda's career was certainly low-key before *M*A*S*H* came along. The son of actor Robert Alda, he began as a Broadway stage actor in the 1950s and '60s. One of his plays, Ossie Davis's antiracist comedy *Purlie Victorious,* was made into a movie (as *Gone Are the Days*) in 1963, giving Alan his first film role. It also helped establish him as one of the young liberal comics of the 1960s and won him a regular spot on NBC's pioneering news satire, *That Was the Week That Was.*

Alda's TV appearances, like his movie and Broadway roles, were infrequent, however. One of his first TV guest shots was on an episode of *The Phil Silvers Show* in 1958; in the 1960s he turned up on occasional episodes of dramas such as *Route 66* and *Coronet Blue.* He also made a couple of unsuccessful pilots for proposed series (*Where's Everett,* 1966, *Higher and Higher,* 1968) before *M*A*S*H* made it to the schedule in 1972. Among his TV films and specials have been *6 Rms Riv Vu* (from the Broadway play in which he starred) and *Kill Me if You Can* (as Caryl Chessman).

In addition to acting, Alda has been very successful as a producer, director, and writer. He worked behind the scenes on numerous episodes of *M*A*S*H*—including the famous two-and-a-half hour final episode in 1983—and also created two short-lived comedies, *We'll Get By* in 1974 and *The Four Seasons* in 1984, the latter based on his hit movie of the same name.

ALDA, BEATRICE—actress
b: Aug 10, 1961

The Four Seasons (com)
.... Lisa Callan (1984)

Daughter of Alan Alda, who gave her a part in this short-lived comedy.

ALDA, ELIZABETH—actress
b: Aug 20, 1960

The Four Seasons (com)
.... Beth Burroughs (1984)

Daughter of Alan Alda.

ALDA, ROBERT—actor
b: Feb 26, 1914, New York City, N.Y. d: May 3, 1986

By Popular Demand (var)..... emcee (1950)
Personality Puzzle (quiz)...... emcee (1953)
What's Your Bid? (aud par)..... host (1953)
Secret File, U.S.A. (drama)
.... Major William Morgan (1954–55)
Can Do (quiz)................ emcee (1956)
Supertrain (drama) ... Dr. Dan Lewis (1979)

A durable actor whose career has been overshadowed by that of his famous son, Alan Alda. Pére Alda began at the top; his film debut was in *Rhapsody in Blue* (1945), the hit screen biography of George Gershwin, in which he played Gershwin. Six years later he won a Tony Award for his portrayal of Sky Masterson in the original Broadway production of *Guys and Dolls.*
Nothing afterward quite equaled those heady early days. His TV career began in the 1950s hosting variety and game shows, including the rather bizarre *What's Your Bid?,* in which contestants were supposed to bring their own money to the studio to bid on prizes. By the 1960s, his career in decline, Alda moved to Italy with his actress-wife Flora Marino and appeared in several European films. He returned to the states in the 1970s and began doing an increasing amount of TV work on series as diverse as *Quincy, M.E.* and *The Facts of Life.* He turned up as Valerie Harper's swinging father-in-law on *Rhoda,* and even appeared on number-one son's program *M*A*S*H.* He also landed his first regular role in 23 years, but, unfortunately, it was on NBC's disastrous *Supertrain.*

ALDEN, NORMAN—actor
b: Sep 13, 1924, Fort Worth, Texas

Not for Hire (drama) ..... regular (1959–60)

Hennesey (com)......... Pulaski (1960–62)
Rango (com) .... Capt. Horton (1967)
Fay (com) .... Al Cassidy (1975–76)

A character actor who did a fairly large amount of TV in the 1960s and '70s. His first principal role was in the syndicated detective series *Not for Hire* in 1959, followed by regular supporting roles in the comedies *Hennesey, Rango* (as Tim Conway's nemesis), and later *Fay* (as the attorney). His Saturday morning TV credits include *Electra Woman & Dyna Girl* in 1976 and *The Godzilla Power Hour* in 1978. In addition, Alden appeared in episodes of dozens of series over the years, from *Mr. Lucky* to *Mary Hartman, Mary Hartman* (as Leroy Fedders).

ALDERSON, BROOKE—actress

Condo (com)........ Kiki Kirkridge (1983)

ALDRIDGE, SHEILA AND SHERRY— singers

The Lawrence Welk Show (music)
.... regulars (1977–82)

ALETTER, FRANK—actor
b: Jan 14, 1926, College Point, Long Island, N.Y.

Bringing Up Buddy (com)
.... Buddy Flower (1960–61)
The Cara Williams Show (com)
.... Frank Bridges (1964–65)
It's About Time (com) ...... Mac (1966–67)
Nancy (com)......... Tom Daily (1970–71)

Broadway actor of the 1950s who came to TV in 1960 as the star of the comedy *Bringing Up Buddy,* in which he played a young executive who was much put-upon by his meddlesome aunts. This was followed by costarring roles on *The Cara Williams Show* (as Cara's husband), *It's About Time* (as the astronaut Mac), and finally *Nancy.* By the 1970s Aletter had turned to guest roles on episodes of numerous series, among them *Ironside, Marcus Welby,* and *Police Woman.*

ALEXANDER, BEN—actor
b: May 26, 1911, Goldfield, Nev. d: Jul 5, 1969

Party Time at Club Roma (var)
.... emcee (1950–51)

Dragnet (police)
.... Off. Frank Smith (1953–59)
Take a Good Look (quiz) ... panelist (1960)
Felony Squad (police)
.... Desk Sgt. Dan Briggs (1966–69)

Although he is probably best remembered as Jack Webb's genial but worrywart partner on *Dragnet* in the 1950s, beefy Ben Alexander spent practically his entire life in front of the camera. He was a child star in silent films, first appearing at age three as Cupid in *Each Pearl a Tear*. He made many more silents, and in the 1930s continued to average three to four movies per year. In the 1940s he moved into radio, starring in quiz, comedy, and chatter shows. When television came along he was recruited to host a short-lived variety/talent show called *Party Time at Club Roma*, liked the medium, and promptly went on to his famous role in *Dragnet*.

Alexander continued to appear on TV sporadically in the 1960s, on Ernie Kovacs' nighttime quiz *Take a Good Look* and on his own daytime game show *About Faces*. Later he became the paunchy desk sergeant and mother hen to the young detectives on *Felony Squad*, which lasted until the year of his death.

ALEXANDER, BOB—actor

The Powers of Matthew Star (sci fi)
.... Chip Frye (1982)

ALEXANDER, JASON—actor

E/R (com) .... Harold Stickley (1984–85)

ALEXANDER, JOAN—actress
b: St. Paul, Minn. r: Butte, Mont.

The Name's the Same (quiz)
.... panelist (1951–55)

ALEXANDER, ROD—dancer

See Linn, Bambi, & Rod Alexander

ALEXANDER, SHANA—journalist
b: Oct 6, 1925, New York City, N.Y.

60 Minutes (pub aff) ..... debater (1975–79)

The liberal side of *60 Minutes*' campy "Point-Counterpoint" political debates in the late 1970s; her opponent was conserva-tive James J. Kilpatrick. *NBC's Saturday Night Live* mercilessly parodied these set-piece exchanges as little more than name-calling brawls ("Shana, you slut!") and they were eventually dropped. Actually, Miss Alexander had a long career as a writer and editor for such esteemed magazines as *Harper's Bazaar, Life, McCall's,* and *Newsweek* and was a founder of the National Women's Political Caucus.

ALEXANDER, TERRY—actor
b: Mar 11, 1923, London, England

Behind the Screen (drama)
.... Tony, the director (1981–82)

ALEXANDER, VAN—orchestra leader
b: May 2, 1915, New York City, N.Y.

The Gordon MacRae Show (music)
.... orch. leader (1956)
The Guy Mitchell Show (var)
.... orch. leader (1957–58)
The Wacky World of Jonathan Winters (var)
.... orch. leader (1972–74)

A veteran arranger of the big band era who scored tunes for Benny Goodman and Paul Whiteman as well as for his own orchestra. One of his most famous arrangements was Ella Fitzgerald's million-selling record, "A-Tisket, A-Tasket." In the 1950s he turned to movie and television work, conducting for Gordon MacRae (with whom he had long been associated) and Guy Mitchell. Later he provided the background music for such popular comedy series as *Hazel, Julia, The Jimmy Stewart Show,* and *The Wacky World of Jonathan Winters*.

ALEXANDRA, TIANA—actress

Pearl (drama) .... Holly (1978)

ALFORD, ANN—actress

The Patty Duke Show (com)
.... Eileen (1965–66)

ALICIA, ANA—actress
b: Dec 12, 1956, Mexico City, Mexico. r: El Paso, Texas

Falcon Crest (drama)
.... Melissa Agretti Cumson (1982–)

This young starlet was born Ana Alicia Ortiz, of Italian and Mexican parents. Her first break was on the daytime soap *Ryan's Hope* as Alicia Nieves, after which she moved on to TV movies and episodes of prime time series and miniseries (including *The Sacketts* and *Roughnecks*) in the late 1970s.

ALLAN, JED—actor
b: The Bronx, N.Y.

Lassie (adv) .... Scott Turner (1968–70)
Love, American Style (com)
.... repertory player (1973–74)

An actor best known for his daytime roles on *Love of Life, The Secret Storm,* and especially *Days of Our Lives,* on which he played attorney Don Craig for some 12 years. He also hosted the syndicated *Celebrity Bowling* series in the 1970s.

ALLBRITTON, LOUISE—actress
b: Jul 3, 1920, Oklahoma City, Okla. r: Wichita Falls, Tex d: Feb 16, 1979

The Stage Door (drama) . Celia Knox (1950)
I've Got a Secret (quiz) ..... panelist (1952)

A classy blond movie starlet with a gift for comedy who was touted in the 1940s as "the new Lombard." She might have been, too, but she gradually gave up her career after marrying young CBS news correspondent Charles Collingwood in 1946. Her TV career was brief and confined to the early and mid 1950s (including a year starring in the daytime serial *Concerning Miss Marlowe* in 1954–55). She spent her later years mostly living in London, where her husband became CBS' chief European correspondent. She died of cancer in 1979.

ALLDREDGE, MICHAEL—actor
Alice (com) .... Ralph (1979–81)

ALLEN, BYRON—comedian, actor
b: Apr 22, 1961, Detroit, Mich. r: Los Angeles, Calif.

Real People (aud par) .... regular (1979–84)

Black comic Byron Allen landed his breakthrough role as cohost of *Real People* while he was still a high school student.

Producer George Schlatter spotted him making his debut on *The Tonight Show* and signed him immediately. Byron was already a veteran of sorts; while in his midteens he wrote material for Jimmie Walker and Freddie Prinze and practiced his own stand-up comedy act under Walker's guidance at Los Angeles area improvisational clubs. He pursued his college education (in film studies) while appearing on the hit NBC show—a unique work-study program that must have made him the envy of his classmates.

ALLEN, CHAD—juvenile actor
b: Jun 5, 1974, Cerritos, Calif.

Our House (drama)
.... David Witherspoon (1986–)

ALLEN, CHET—actor
b: Aug 17, 1932, Chickasha, Okla. d: Jun 17, 1984

Bonino (com) .... Jerry (1953)
The Troubleshooters (adv) .. Slats (1959–60)

A young actor-director of part Cherokee Indian extraction who appeared briefly as one of Ezio Pinza's sons on *Bonino* and later as one of the crew members on *The Troubleshooters.*

ALLEN, DAYTON—comedian
b: Sep 24, 1919, New York City. r: Mt. Vernon, N.Y.

Adventures of Oky Doky (child)
.... voice of Oky Doky (1948–49)
The Steve Allen Show (var)
.... regular (1958–61)

Dayton Allen labored for many years in the show business vineyards before two words brought him national notoriety. He was the tall comic who looked into the camera each week on *The Steve Allen Show* and boomed an incredulous "WHY NOT?" Despite this bit of on-camera nonsense, Dayton was known throughout most of his career as the man of a thousand voices on dozens of cartoon and puppet shows. He was the voice of Oky Doky, of Mr. Bluster on *The Howdy Doody Show,* and of Heckle and Jeckle and Deputy Dawg (among others) in the Terry-Toons cartoons; on camera, he was the bungling Mr. Bungle on *Winky Dink and You.*

ALLEN, DEBBIE—black dancer, actress
b: Jan 16, 1950, Houston, Texas

3 Girls 3 (var).............. regular (1977)
Roots: The Next Generations (drama)
.... Nan Branch Haley (1979)
Fame (drama)........ Lydia Grant (1982–)

Emmy Awards: Best Choreography, for *Fame* (1982, 1983)

Glamorous dancer Debbie Allen burst onto the scene in the late 1970s as one of the three young discoveries on NBC's innovative "inside show biz" series *3 Girls 3* (the other two: Mimi Kennedy and Ellen Foley). She was later seen in the dramatic role of Alex Haley's wife in the *Roots* sequel, but real fame came with *Fame* —on which she played the hard-driving dance instructor Lydia. Miss Allen's flashy choreography for the series won her two Emmy Awards, and she was also nominated for Best Actress for her role as Lydia.

Debbie is the younger sister of actress Phylicia Rashad (*The Cosby Show*).

ALLEN, DEBORAH—country singer
b: Sep 30, 1953, Memphis, Tenn.

The Jim Stafford Show (var).. regular (1975)

ALLEN, DENNIS—comedian
b: Jul 10, Kansas City, Mo.

The Leslie Uggams Show (var)
.... regular (1969)
What's It All About, World? (var)
.... regular (1969)
Rowan & Martin's Laugh-In (var)
.... regular (1970–73)

ALLEN, ELIZABETH—actress
b: Jan 25, 1934, Jersey City, N.J.

Bracken's World (drama)
.... Laura Deane (1969–70)
The Paul Lynde Show (com)
.... Martha Simms (1972–73)
C.P.O. Sharkey (com)
.... Capt. Quinlan (1976–77)

A young actress who began as a high fashion model (she was once an assistant to designer Givenchy) but became best known for her work in the musical theater in the late 1950s and '60s. In the 1970s, as youth began to fade, she moved into television, first as the studio talent head on *Bracken's World,* and then in comedy —Paul Lynde's wife on *The Paul Lynde Show* and Don Rickles' commanding officer on *C.P.O. Sharkey.* "It helps," she was quoted as saying, "to have a good sense of humor." In the 1980s she appeared for a time on the daytime soap *Texas.*

ALLEN, FRED—comedian
b: May 31, 1894, Cambridge, Mass. d: Mar 17, 1956

Colgate Comedy Hour (var)
.... rotating host (1950)
Chesterfield Sound Off Time (var)
.... star (1951–52)
Judge for Yourself (quiz) ... emcee (1953–54)
What's My Line (quiz)... panelist (1954–56)

One of the biggest names of the radio era, who failed to make the transition to television. He was an extremely witty and intelligent man, and his nasal delivery and cast of imaginary characters (Mrs. Nussbaum, Titus Moody, Senator Claghorn) were fascinating to hear on radio. However, on television it all seemed wrong: Allen's low-key style, his caustic humor and his gaunt, baggy-eyed appearance were out of place in the high energy, frothy world of early TV.

Allen certainly tried to make it on TV. He was seen as host of two big budget variety shows but lasted only a few months on each; he had his own quiz/talent show in 1953–54, but it failed after trying two different formats. (He was also supposed to star in *Two for the Money,* but Herb Shriner got the role, and TV fame, when Allen became ill before the first telecast). Perhaps his most successful telecast was the special "Fred Allen's Sketchbook," presented on *Armstrong Circle Theatre* in 1954. Later he became a panelist on *What's My Line,* remaining until his death in 1956.

His first autobiography, sarcastically titled *Treadmill to Oblivion,* was published in 1954. A second, *Much Ado About Me,* came out in 1956.

ALLEN, GARY—actor

When the Whistle Blows (com)
. . . . Ted Hanrahan (1980)
Harper Valley P.T.A. (com)
. . . . Norman Clayton (1981)

ALLEN, GRACIE—comedian

b: Jul 26, 1902*, San Francisco, Calif. d: Aug 28, 1964

The George Burns and Gracie Allen Show (com). . . . . as herself (1950–58)

The pretty, scatterbrained wife of George Burns, with whom she had one of the longest-running husband and wife acts in show business history. George was the cigar flicking, endlessly patient husband, and Gracie the sweet simpleton who cheerily delivered a steady stream of malapropisms and saw things with a logic all her own.

They met in the mid-1920s and quickly became stars of vaudeville and then of radio in the 1930s and '40s. Their gentle family comedy show moved intact to television in 1950 (at first, telecast live) and was successful there for eight years, until Gracie decided to retire.

George and Gracie's union was not only professional but one of true love. As Gracie's health deteriorated badly in the 1960s, she became increasingly depressed. She—and George—knew she was dying, but to lift her spirits he surprised her one day with a new fur coat. Why would he have bought her such an expensive gift, he told her, if he didn't think she was going to get better?

ALLEN, HERB—producer, host

Hail the Champ (child) . . . . emcee (1951–52)

ALLEN, JONELLE—black actress

b: Jul 18, 1944, New York City, N.Y.

Palmerstown, U.S.A. (drama)
. . . . Bessie Freeman (1980–81)
Berrengers (drama). . . Stacey Russell (1985)

A black performer who began as a child actress in the theater and on television in the 1950s; among the video productions in which she appeared was the *Hallmark Hall of Fame* TV play "Green Pastures."

*Some sources give 1906.

After dropping out of sight during her adolescent years she returned to show business in the late 1960s to do theater as well as scattered TV series episodes. She had a recurring role as Booker T.'s mother on the gentle drama about race relations, *Palmerstown, U.S.A.*

ALLEN, KAREN—actress

b: Oct 5, 1951, Maryland

East of Eden (drama). . . . . Abra (1981)

ALLEN, MARK—actor

The Travels of Jaimie McPheeters (wes)
. . . . Matt Kissel (1963–64)

ALLEN, MARTY—comedian

b: Mar 23, 1922, Pittsburgh, Pa.

$1.98 Beauty Show (com)
. . . . frequent panelist (1978–80)

Bug-eyed nightclub comedian who was partnered with Steve Rossi in the 1960s, as Allen and Rossi.

ALLEN, MEL—sportscaster

b: Feb 14, 1913, Birmingham, Ala.

Thursday Night Basketball (sport)
. . . . sportscaster (1949)
Sports Spot (sport) . . . . host (1951–54)
Jackpot Bowling Starring Milton Berle (sports). host (1959–61)

One of the grand old men of sportscasting, Mel Allen began as a radio sportscaster in the late 1930s after abandoning a law career in his home state of Alabama. For nearly 30 years beginning in 1939 he was the voice of the New York Yankees. He won so many fans that the team once gave him a "Mel Allen Day" at Yankee Stadium. His friendly southern drawl and enthusiastic style ("How *about* that?") was heard covering numerous TV sports events from the 1940s to the '70s, as well as on Movietone newsreels from 1946–64. Mel continued to do radio sports coverage in the 1970s and '80s.

ALLEN, PHILLIP R.—actor

b: Mar 26, 1939, Pittsburgh, Pa.

The Hardy Boys Mysteries (adv)
. . . . Harry Gibbon (1978–79)

The Bad News Bears (com)
.... Roy Turner (1979–80)
Alice (com) .... Mitch Aames (1981–82)

TV supporting actor who has been seen in a variety of series and miniseries (*Washington Behind Closed Doors, Friendly Fire*), as well as in three recurring roles: a federal agent in *The Hardy Boys,* the coach of the rival kids' baseball team in *The Bad News Bears,* and one of the many regular customers of Alice's restaurant.

ALLEN, RAYMOND—actor

Sanford and Son (com)
.... Woody Anderson (1976–77)
The Sanford Arms (com)
.... Woody Anderson (1977)

ALLEN, REX—cowboy actor, singer
b: Dec 31, 1922*, Wilcox, Ariz.

Frontier Doctor (wes)
.... Dr. Bill Baxter (1958)
Five Star Jubilee (var) .... host (1961)

Cowboy actor who made his name as a singer on radio's *National Barn Dance* in the late 1940s, then went on to star in numerous grind-'em-out western B movies in the 1950s (he made 32 of them between 1950 and 1957 alone). Rex was certainly one of the more authentic cowboy stars, having been a ranch hand and bronco rider on the rodeo circuit in his younger days. His TV career consisted mostly of guest appearances on variety shows such as *The Red Skelton Show*; however, he also starred in the short-lived syndicated western *Frontier Doctor* and was one of the hosts of the summer variety series *Five Star Jubilee* in 1961. He had an active recording career, with two major country/pop hits: "Crying In the Chapel" in 1953 and "Don't Go Near the Indians" in 1962.

After some final films in the 1960s, including several for Disney, he "retired" to the personal appearance circuit in the 1970s with his trick pony Koko, Jr., son of the steed who had so often carried him across the silver screen.

ALLEN, REX, JR.—country singer
b: Aug 23, 1947, Chicago, Ill.

*Some sources give 1924.

CBS Newcomers (var) .... regular (1971)
Nashville on the Road (music)
.... regular (1981–83)

This "Junior" is one of four children of the cowboy star of the '50s, and the only one to follow in his father's show-biz boots. He had a successful career as a Nashville recording artist in the '70s and '80s and has appeared on various country series, including radio's *Grand Ole Opry* and TV's widely syndicated *Nashville on the Road.*

ALLEN, RICKY—actor

My Three Sons (com)
.... Sudsy Pfeiffer (1961–63)

ALLEN, STEVE—comedian, actor, musician
b: Dec 26, 1921, New York City, N.Y.

The Steve Allen Show (var).. host (1950–52)
Songs for Sale (music) ..... emcee (1951–52)
Talent Patrol (talent) .... emcee (1953)
What's My Line (quiz)... panelist (1953–54)
Tonight (talk) .... host (1954–57)
The Steve Allen Show (var).. host (1956–61)
The Steve Allen Show (var).. host (1962–64)
I've Got a Secret (quiz)
.... moderator (1964–67)
The Steve Allen Comedy Hour (var)
.... host (1967)
The Steve Allen Show (var).. host (1967–69)
I've Got a Secret (quiz)
.... moderator (1972–73)
Rich Man, Poor Man—Book I (drama)
.... Nichols (1976)
Steve Allen's Laugh-Back (com)
.... host (1976)
Meeting of Minds (pub aff)
.... moderator (1977–81)
The Steve Allen Comedy Hour (var)
.... host (1980–81)
Life's Most Embarrassing Moments (com)
.... host (1985)

Steve Allen can't seem to make up his mind what he wants to do—he's dabbled in just about every area of show business. First, in the late '40s, he was a radio disc jockey and talk show host in Los Angeles. Then he broke into movies via an obscure 1949 feature titled *Down Memory Lane,* in which he played a TV host [sic] introducing clips from old silent films. A few years later he scored a major success in films

16

playing the title role in the 1956 hit *The Benny Goodman Story*. At the same time Steve was playing Benny on screen he had himself diversified into the music field; he has since written and recorded hundreds of songs, including the jazz-flavored standards "This Could Be the Start of Something" (1956) and "Gravy Waltz" (a Grammy Award winner in 1963).

Allen writes prolifically, too. At last count he had authored nearly 30 books, mostly about the art of comedy (although one was a touching account of his reconciliation with his estranged, dropout son).

It is from television, however, that most Americans know this entertainer-of-many-parts. He is a true TV "personality"—all his series have featured Steve as himself, usually as a host or panelist, always with his intelligent, verbal humor. His first network series was a half-hour early evening variety show carried five nights a week on CBS in the winter of 1950. Steve played the piano, chatted with guests, and ad-libbed funny interviews with members of the studio audience, setting a pattern that would become familiar on many of his later shows. The show moved to daytime and then back to nighttime for a summer run in 1952. Meantime, Steve began yet another career on game and talent shows, starting with *Songs for Sale*, then *Talent Patrol*, then the long-running *What's My Line?* (on which he coined the famous phrase designed to quickly guess the size of an object: "Is it bigger than a breadbox?"). Later he did two stints as host of the equally popular *I've Got a Secret*.

This frenzy of activity did not seem to keep him busy enough, so in June 1953 he agreed to host a local late-night talk show in New York. A year later the program was picked up by the NBC-TV network, and Steve thereby became the first host of the legendary *Tonight Show*. Even greater success—probably the height of his career—came in the late '50s when he hosted his own Sunday night variety hour, which gave Ed Sullivan a run for his money from 1956–59. It was for this series that Steve assembled a resident troupe of young comics who developed some of TV's most memorable bits: Louis Nye as suave, smug Gordon Hathaway, Tom Poston as an incredibly forgetful man, Don Knotts as the extremely nervous and fidgety Mr. Morrison, Dayton Allen as the "WHY NOT?" man, Bill Dana as the shy Jose Jimenez. Man-in-the-street interviews, funny phone calls and guest stars (including young Elvis Presley, before he appeared on Sullivan's show) were all part of the mix.

Nothing Steve was to do in later years quite matched the freshness and creativity of those glorious days. During the 1960s and '70s he hosted two syndicated late-night talk shows (1962–64 and 1967–69), a CBS summer show in 1967, the syndicated *Steve Allen's Laugh-Back* (in which he reminisced and showed clips from his earlier series), and the innovative PBS series *Meeting of Minds* (in which he moderated a serious discussion between four or five historical figures, played by actors). This last-named program won an Emmy Award. Steve himself, strangely enough, has never won an Emmy, although he was often nominated.

In 1980 Steve hosted yet another variety hour (one of NBC's frequent and futile efforts to revive variety shows in prime time). He has guested on innumerable series over the years, hosted award shows and specials beyond counting, and even appeared in a few dramatic roles.

Steve has long been married to actress Jayne Meadows, who appeared with him in several of his series.

ALLEN, VERA—actress

The O'Neills (drama)
.... Peggy O'Neill (1949–50)

A veteran soap opera actress who got her start in the theater in the 1920s and '30s, then turned to radio and continuing roles on at least half a dozen tear-stained daily dramas (including *Young Doctor Malone*), mostly in the 1940s. When television came along she became a soap opera favorite there as well. First she was seen as the lead on the early prime time serial *The O'Neills* and later she appeared in daytime on *Search for Tomorrow, From These Roots*, and finally *Another World* (fittingly, by then, in the role of Grandma).

ALLEN, VERNETT, III—actor

The Travels of Jaimie McPheeters (wes)
.... Othello (1963–64)

ALLENDE, FERNANDO—actor
b: Mexico

Flamingo Road (drama)
.... Julio Sanchez (1981–82)
Master of the Game (drama)
.... George Mellis (1984)

A dark, handsome young actor and singer who was a fast-rising star in his native Mexico during the 1970s, in music, movies, and TV. His first major U.S. role was opposite Joanne Woodward in the 1979 TV film *Streets of Los Angeles.* Later he invaded *Flamingo Road* as the fiery and proud young Cuban, Julio, and had a role in the miniseries *Master of the Game,* melting ladies' hearts there, too.

ALLEY, KIRSTIE—actress
b: Jan 12, 1955, Wichita, Kans.

Masquerade (drama)
.... Casey Collins (1983–84)
North and South (drama)
.... Virgilia Hazard (1985)

Beautiful young Kirstie Alley landed several juicy roles shortly after she arrived in Hollywood from Kansas in 1981. Among them were the half-Vulcan Lt. Saavik in the movie *Star Trek II,* the continuing role of Casey in the short-lived spy series *Masquerade,* and that of the buxom Virgilia in the 1985 miniseries *North and South.* She has also played opposite her husband, actor Parker Stevenson, in several productions.

ALLEY, PAUL—newscaster

The War as It Happens (news)
.... narrator (1944–45)

A newsreel announcer of the 1930s and '40s who became a TV pioneer when he produced and announced the very first regular network newscast, on NBC during World War II. Alley was not seen on camera, but rather read the stories as film clips were shown to a small but fascinated audience of home viewers in three interconnected East Coast cities. When interviewed by this writer in the late 1970s, Alley remarked on how much TV news had changed since that dim, distant time. "We never envisioned the day," he said, "when commentators reading news bulletins would become bigger than the news they broadcast."

ALLISON, ALLEGRA—actress

The Richard Pryor Show (var)
.... regular (1977)

ALLISON, BETSI—vocalist

Three About Town (music)... hostess (1948)

ALLISON, FRAN—actress, singer
b: Nov 20, 1907, LaPorte City, Iowa

Kukla, Fran & Ollie (child)
.... hostess (1948–57)
Don McNeill TV Club (var)
.... regular (1950–51)
Down You Go (quiz)
.... regular panelist (1954)
It's About Time (quiz) ...... panelist (1954)
Let's Dance (music) ..... interviewer (1954)
Kukla, Fran & Ollie (child)
.... hostess (1969–71)
Kukla, Fran & Ollie (child)
.... hostess (1975–76)

A sweet, gentle lady who will always be remembered by kids of the '50s as the host of the popular puppet show *Kukla, Fran & Ollie.* Though she seemed youthful at the time, she was actually in her forties, having had a long career on radio before *Kukla* came along. She worked out of Chicago and was a singer on various network series originating from that city in the 1930s and '40s. Her best-known radio role was that of the gossipy Aunt Fanny on *Don McNeill's Breakfast Club* for many years.

Fran joined Burr Tillstrom's puppet show when it began on local Chicago TV in 1947 as the human friend and foil for the puppets. She meshed so naturally with Burr's whimsical creations on the live, unscripted program that they seemed like a human family. Fran appeared elsewhere on early TV as well. She followed the *Breakfast Club* to TV for its brief, unsuccessful run, was a panelist on quiz shows, and did celebrity interviews (from Chicago) on the short-lived 1954 series *Let's Dance.* She was frequently seen as the commercial spokeswoman for Whirlpool appliances.

Fran appeared infrequently after the 1950s, except for occasional revivals of

Kukla, Fran & Ollie (on PBS in 1969, in syndication in 1975). From 1967–77 Fran and her puppet friends hosted *The CBS Children's Film Festival* on Saturday or Sunday mornings. In the 1980s Los Angeles viewers could see her hosting a local program for senior citizens.

ALLISON, JACK, SINGERS—chorus

The Kate Smith Evening Hour (var)
.... regulars (1951–52)

ALLMAN, ELVIA—actress
b: 1905, Spencer, N.C.

Blondie (com)......... Cora Dithers (1957)
Petticoat Junction (com)
.... Selma Plout (1965–70)
The Beverly Hillbillies (com)
.... Elverna Bradshaw (1969–71)

A feisty older actress much in demand to play pushy old broads on comedy shows of the 1950s and '60s. Most of her earlier career had been on radio; in the late 1930s and '40s she was a familiar voice on such series as *The Burns and Allen Show* (as Gracie's friend), *Bob Hope* (as a scatterbrained socialite), *Abbott and Costello,* and *Mazie.* She made the transition to TV easily, and was seen as the boss's wife on *Blondie,* Bea Benederet's archrival on *Petticoat Junction,* and, toward the end of her career, as Granny's nemesis on *The Beverly Hillbillies.* She also turned up occasionally on many other series, including *The Dick Van Dyke Show* (Rose Marie's boyfriend's domineering mother), *The People's Choice* (Jackie Cooper's boss), and *Abbott and Costello* (Mrs. Crumbcake, the neighbor).

ALLMAN, SHELDON—actor
b: Jun 8, 1924, Chicago, Ill.

Harris Against the World (com)
.... Norm Miller (1964–65)

ALLYSON, JUNE—actress
b: Oct 7, 1917, The Bronx, N.Y.

DuPont Show with June Allyson (drama)
.... hostess (1959–61)

Pert, sexy "All American Girl" June Allyson was one of Hollywood's major stars during the 1940s and '50s, playing the loyal girlfriend or wife opposite Van Johnson, Jimmy Stewart, and others. Born in poverty in the Bronx, New York, she worked her way up as a chorus girl in the 1930s and had her first starring role in *Best Foot Forward* in 1943. She came to television as her film career began to decline—wholesomeness was on its way out in movies, but it was alive and well on TV. She hosted, and sometimes starred in, her own big budget anthology series on CBS from 1959–61, and appeared several times between 1960–63 on husband Dick Powell's two series, *Zane Grey Theater* and *The Dick Powell Show.* After that, June was seen only occasionally. Among her appearances were roles in the TV movie pilot for the series *Vegas,* the Gary Coleman film *The Kid with the Broken Halo,* and, inevitably, *The Love Boat.*

June was married to Dick Powell from 1945 until his death in 1963.

ALMANZAR, JAMES—actor

Doctors' Hospital (drama)
.... Dr. Anson Brooks (1975–76)

ALTAY, DERIN—actress

The Baxters (com).. Naomi Baxter (1979–80)

ALTMAN, JEFF—comedian

Cos (var) .... regular (1976)
The Starland Vocal Band Show (var)
.... regular (1977)
Pink Lady (var) .... host (1980)
Solid Gold (music) .... regular (1982–83)

A young comic whose most memorable assignment, without doubt, was trying to interpret for American audiences the two sexy, Japanese-speaking stars of the *Pink Lady* show in 1980.

ALVAREZ, ABRAHAM—actor

Archie Bunker's Place (com)
.... Jose (1979–83)

The Puerto Rican busboy at Archie Bunker's bar.

AMATO, TOMMY—comedian

Bobby Darin Show (var)..... regular (1973)

AMECHE, DON—actor

b: May 31, 1908, Kenosha, Wisc.

Take a Chance (quiz) . . . . emcee (1950)
Holiday Hotel (var)
. . . . the manager (1950–51)
Coke Time with Eddie Fisher (music)
. . . . host (1953)
International Showtime (var)
. . . . host (1961–65)

Don Ameche was a dapper Hollywood leading man of the 1930s and '40s who came to television when his film career began to decline. One of eight children of a Wisconsin barkeep, he broke into radio in the 1930s as the suave host of such dramatic series as *Grand Hotel* and *The First Nighter*. Hollywood stardom followed, as he made more than three dozen features between 1936 and 1945, among them *The Story of Alexander Graham Bell, Down Argentine Way* and *Heaven Can Wait*. When his movie roles became less frequent in the late 1940s he returned initially to radio, starring with Frances Langford as the bickering husband and wife, *The Bickersons*.

Don entered television with two series running simultaneously on two networks in the fall of 1950—the NBC quiz show *Take a Chance* and the ABC variety stanza *Holiday Hotel* (later renamed *Don Ameche's Musical Playhouse*). Later he costarred with Langford on a daytime series from 1951–52, and hosted Eddie Fisher's original *Coke Time* show in 1953.

He also appeared in a number of TV plays and musical specials, notably "High Button Shoes" in 1956 and the *Climax* dramatization of the life of gangster Albert Anastasia in 1958. In 1961 he was recruited to become the traveling host of *International Showtime*, which presented circuses and ice shows taped on location in Europe. Although he knew little of circuses before this, he quickly became a self-proclaimed expert on the subject and enjoyed the assignment immensely.

After *Showtime* he was seen less frequently, although he did turn up on those refuges of old stars, *The Love Boat* and *Fantasy Island* in 1979–80. Then in the early '80s, quite unexpectedly, his movie career began to revive with character roles in the hit films *Trading Places* (1983) and *Cocoon* (1985), for which he won an Oscar.

AMECHE, JIM—actor

b: c. 1914 d: Feb 4, 1983

Festival of Stars (drama) . . . . host (1957)

Sound-alike brother of Don Ameche, whose career was concentrated mostly on radio in the 1930s and '40s. His most notable role was that of *Jack Armstrong, All American Boy*. He hosted a collection of reruns of *The Loretta Young Show* on NBC-TV during the summer of 1957.

AMELIO, PHILIP J., II—juvenile actor

b: Nov 3, Sharon, Conn.

Life with Lucy (com)
. . . . Kevin McGibbon (1986–)

AMENDOLIA, DON—actor

b: Feb 1, Glassboro, N.J.

Mama Malone (com) . . Dino Forresti (1984)

AMES, ED—singer, actor

b: Jul 9, 1927, Malden, Mass.

Daniel Boone (wes) . . . . Mingo (1964–68)

Ed Ames has had two distinct careers, both of them very successful. The first was as a pop singer. Ed and his three brothers began harmonizing in high school, and by the late 1940s they had signed their first recording contract. The Ames Brothers soon became one of the biggest-selling acts in popular music, with million-selling hits such as "Sentimental Me"/"Rag Mop" (two sides of one record), "You, You, You" and "The Naughty Lady of Shady Lane"— melodious tunes that can still be heard today on adult oldies radio stations. The brothers appeared frequently on television variety shows. With the advent of rock 'n' roll their career began to falter, however; their last top ten hit was "Melodie D'Amour" in 1957. In 1959 they broke up.

Ed then studied acting for a year in New York and began appearing in off-Broadway plays. His success in *The Fantastiks* led to a revival of his singing career, via his solo recording of a tune from the show called "Try to Remember" (this was followed by several more best-sellers in the late 1960s, including the smash hit "My Cup Runneth Over"). But acting was now his goal. In addition to stage productions he appeared in a number of TV series episodes and in 1964 was cast as the Oxford-educated Cherokee Indian Mingo in *Daniel Boone.* The role was inspired by that of the schizophrenic Indian he had portrayed the previous year in the Broadway production of *One Flew over the Cuckoo's Nest.*

After his four years on *Daniel Boone* Ed made additional appearances on TV, but the glory days were over and he pursued his singing and acting career primarily in theaters and supper clubs in the Los Angeles area.

AMES, FLORENZ—actor

Adventures of Ellery Queen (drama)
...... Inspector Richard Queen (1950–52)
Adventures of Ellery Queen (drama)
.... Inspector Richard Queen (1954)
Blondie (com)......... J. C. Dithers (1957)

A Broadway character actor who appeared in many successful plays of the 1920s, '30s and '40s, including *Of Thee I Sing* and *I'd Rather Be Right.* In the 1950s he turned to supporting roles in movies and television, portraying Ellery Queen's somewhat dense father in two versions of the oft-revived TV detective series. Later he was Dagwood's blustering boss in the first incarnation of the *Blondie* situation comedy series.

AMES, JOYCE—

Dean Martin Presents the Golddiggers (var)
.... regular (1969)

AMES, LEON—actor

b: Jan 20, 1903, Portland, Ind.

Life with Father (com)
.... Clarence Day, Sr. (1953–55)
Frontier Judge (wes)
.... Judge John Cooper (1956)
Father of the Bride (com)
.... Stanley Banks (1961–62)
Mr. Ed (com)... Gordon Kirkwood (1963–65)

Dapper, mustachioed supporting actor who had a very long career in movies, spanning nearly 50 years (1932–79) and about 100 features. He specialized in the slightly harassed father, a role he continued in his first two television series, *Life with Father* (one of the first live color series) and *Father of the Bride.* Younger

viewers probably remember him better as the next door neighbor during two seasons of *Mr. Ed.* In addition to these continuing roles, Ames brought his dignified presence to episodes of many comedy and drama series, from *Lux Video Theatre* in the 1950s to *The Beverly Hillbillies* and *My Three Sons* in the 1960s and *The Jeffersons* in the 1970s. He then retired comfortably in Studio City, California, on the continuing profits from the Ford automobile dealership he had had the foresight to buy.

AMES, NANCY—singer

b: 1937, Washington, D.C.

That Was the Week That Was (com)
.... regular (1964–65)

Nancy Ames was the "TW3 Girl," the blonde singer who belted out the opening number that satirized the week's news events at the beginning of each edition of NBC's *That Was the Week That Was.* She was born Nancy Hamilton Alfaro, the daughter of a prominent Washington physician and granddaughter of a former president of Panama. After her *TW3* days she did some theatrical work and made an abortive attempt to launch a recording career in the mid-1960s, then disappeared from view.

AMES, RACHEL—actress

b: Nov 2, Portland, Ore.

The Lineup (police)
.... Off. Sandy McAllister (1959–60)

Rachel Ames was best known for her long run as the character Audrey on the daytime soap opera *General Hospital,* from 1964 to the 1980s. She was born the daughter of two highly successful Hollywood character actors, Dorothy Adams and Byron Foulger. While mom and dad were working steadily in films of the 1940s and '50s, Rachel learned the trade and made her own debut in the 1951 sci-fi film *When Worlds Collide.* Her career then stalled, however, and her next major role did not come until eight years later when she played a policewoman during the last season of TV's *The Lineup.* When the role on *General Hospital* came along a few years later she grabbed it—and found a home.

AMES, TRUDI—actress

Karen (com) . . . . Candy (1964–65)

AMORY, CLEVELAND—writer

b: Sep 2, 1917, Nahant, Mass.

One Minute Please (quiz)
. . . . panelist (1954–55)

Grumpy-looking writer and critic of the TV scene who is probably less known for this short stint in front of the cameras than for his long tenure as *TV Guide*'s chief reviewer of programs in the 1960s and '70s. In the latter capacity, he didn't seem to like much of anything the commercial networks put on. Perhaps that was the result of his own experiences in the medium, such as his participation in this silly DuMont game show in which panelists were supposed to talk for one minute on a subject they knew nothing about; or his role as co-creator of Burl Ives' disastrous sitcom *O. K. Crackerby*, which was canceled after 13 weeks in 1965. No wonder he was mad.

AMOS, JOHN—black actor

b: Dec 27, 1941, Newark, N.J. r: Orange, N.J.

The Mary Tyler Moore Show (com)
. . . . . . Gordon (Gordy) Howard (1970–73)
The Funny Side (var) . . . . regular (1971)
Maude (com). . . . . . . Henry Evans (1973–74)
Good Times (com). . . James Evans (1974–76)
Roots (drama)
. . . . Kunta Kinte/Toby (adult) (1977)
Hunter (police) . . . . . . Capt. Dolan (1984–85)

A heavyset actor who began his career as a stand-up comedian in New York's Greenwich Village, then branched into comedy writing for such programs as *The Leslie Uggams Show*. He was also at one time part of a variety act in Chicago called "Amos and Annie." By the early 1970s John was winning on-camera parts, including the role of Gordy the weatherman on *The Mary Tyler Moore Show* and that of Esther Rolle's ne'er-do-well husband on *Maude* and its spin-off, *Good Times*. After his *Good Times* character was killed off in a car crash (how comedies had changed!) he appeared in a 1977 comedy pilot called *Future Cop* on ABC. Perhaps his most notable role—which won him an Emmy nom-

ination—was that of the rebellious slave Kunta Kinte in the enormously successful miniseries *Roots*.

John Amos continued to be seen in TV movies and series episodes during the late 1970s and 1980s, including a short run as the uncooperative police captain in *Hunter*.

AMSTERDAM, MOREY—comedian, actor

b: Dec 14, 1912*, Chicago, Ill.

Stop Me If You've Heard This One (quiz)
. . . . panelist (1948)
The Morey Amsterdam Show (var)
. . . . host (1948–50)
Broadway Open House (talk). . . . host (1950)
Battle of the Ages (talent). . . . . emcee (1952)
Who Said That? (quiz). . . . . . panelist (1954)
Keep Talking (quiz) . . . . . . regular (1958–60)
The Dick Van Dyke Show (com)
. . . . Buddy Sorrell (1961–66)
Can You Top This? (com)
. . . . panelist (1969–70)

"Many personalities witnessed the birth of television comedy," wrote one observer, "but Morey Amsterdam practically delivered the baby."** Morey had in fact been in show business for twenty years when TV arrived in its diapers. His father was a concert violinist with the Chicago Opera and the San Francisco Symphony and wanted his son to pursue a classical music career as a cellist. Instead, young Morey used the bulky instrument as a prop in his comedy routines. He did vaudeville, nightclubs, and finally radio in the 1930s, where he was heard on several network series. Will Rogers was an early mentor. Morey also branched into songwriting, producing such deathless classics as "Why Oh Why Did I Ever Leave Wyoming?", "Yuk-A-Puk" (his catchphrase), and the million-selling "Rum and Coca-Cola." That last one got him into a lot of trouble when it was proven to be a cleaned up version of an old, ribald Trinidad song. The original authors demanded, and got, a hefty settlement.

In June 1948 Morey began a CBS radio series which moved to television in the fall. He wowed the early TV audiences with his

*Some sources give 1914.
**Joe Franklin, in *Joe Franklin's Encyclopedia of Comedians* (Bell, 1979)

22

rapid-fire gags and one-liners ("TV," he cracked, "just stands for tired vaudeville.") The show was set in a fictional Times Square nightclub and costarred young Art Carney as the waiter and Jacqueline Susann as the cigarette girl. Before long Morey was recruited to host the late-night talk show *Broadway Open House*, the predecessor of *The Tonight Show*, and to deliver gags on a succession of quiz and talent shows. He also appeared on episodes of various situation comedies, including *The Danny Thomas Show* and *Oh, Susanna!*

Even after all that he was probably not very well known to younger viewers until he took the role of Buddy Sorrell, Dick Van Dyke's wisecracking friend and co-worker on the comedy classic *The Dick Van Dyke Show*. It was the role of a lifetime, and it capped his long career. Morey was seen only occasionally afterward, appearing several times on ABC's late night "Honeymoon Suite" specials in 1973 and on *The Love Boat* (where else?) in 1978.

Of his diverse activities, Morey remarked, "I'm a songwriter when my songs are sung, a gag writer when people tell my jokes, a comedian when people laugh. Otherwise, it's straight drama."

ANACANI—female Latin singer

The Lawrence Welk Show (music)
.... regular (1972–82)

ANDERS, LAURIE—comedienne
b: Goose Egg, Wyoming [sic]

The Ken Murray Show (var)
.... regular (1950–53)

Sexy comedienne who was a momentary sensation in the early 1950s with her skimpy cowgirl outfit and her western drawl ("Ah love the waahd open spaces!"). She disappeared completely when Murray's show left the air.

ANDERS, MERRY—actress
b: 1932

The Stu Erwin Show (com)
.... Joyce Erwin (1954–55)
It's Always Jan (com)
.... Val Marlowe (1955–56)
How to Marry a Millionaire (com)
.... "Mike" McCall (1957–59)

A classy-looking actress who appeared young enough to play Stu Erwin's teenage daughter in the early 1950s (though she was 22) but was perhaps a bit more credible as Janis Paige's actress-roommate in *It's Always Jan* and the ringleader of the gold-digging lovelies in *How to Marry a Millionaire.* Merry also made quite a few B films in the 1950s and early '60s. Her career petered out thereafter.

ANDERSON, BARBARA—actress
b: Nov 27, 1945, Brooklyn, N.Y.

Ironside (police).... Eve Whitfield (1967–71)
Mission: Impossible (drama)
.... Mimi Davis (1972–73)

Emmy Award: Best Supporting Actress, for *Ironside* (1968)

Barbara Anderson made it in Hollywood the hard way, working at clerical jobs, playing local theaters and trooping to auditions for six years before she landed a contract with Universal Studios and began appearing in series TV in 1966. Her first major role was her most successful. It was that of Officer Eve, one of Raymond Burr's loyal detectives on *Ironside,* and it won her an Emmy in 1968 and nominations twice thereafter.

Barbara brought her combination of beauty and brains to many other action series in the late 1960s and '70s, among them *Star Trek* ("Conscience of the King"), *Mission: Impossible* (as an occasionally seen IMF agent), *Night Gallery,* and *Hawaii Five-0.*

ANDERSON, BOB—actor

Wichita Town (wes)
.... Aeneas MacLinahan (1959–60)

ANDERSON, BRIDGETTE–child actress

Gun Shy (Com) ....,... Celia (1983)

ANDERSON, DARYL—actor
b: Jul 1, 1951, Seattle, Wash.

Lou Grant (drama)
.... Dennis "Animal" Price (1977–82)

Daryl Anderson is a lanky (6'4") young man who says that he decided to become an actor at age five, when he realized that

23

"guys on television didn't really die when they got shot." After studying drama at the University of Washington, he arrived in Hollywood in 1976 and promptly landed a part in his first film, *Sweet Revenge*. A year later he was cast as the scruffy but dedicated newspaper photographer in *Lou Grant*—the role for which he is best known.

Oddly enough, the role got Daryl interested in serious photography, to the extent that a picture he took of a fire near a location film site was picked up and distributed nationwide by the Associated Press—thus marking his debut as a real-life professional photographer.

ANDERSON, DAVID—actor

The Growing Paynes (com)
.... regular (1948–49)
Major Dell Conway of the Flying Tigers (adv)
.... regular (1951)

ANDERSON, DONNA—juvenile actress

The Travels of Jaimie McPheeters (wes)
.... Jenny (1963–64)

ANDERSON, EDDIE "ROCHESTER"— black actor

b: Sep 18, 1905, Oakland, Calif. d: Feb 28, 1977

The Jack Benny Show (com)
.... himself (1950–65)

It is said that luck, as well as talent, plays a large part in the great show business success stories. One day in 1937 Jack Benny needed a bit player to play a pullman porter on a single episode of his radio show. Eddie Anderson, an obscure 31-year-old actor, got the part. He was such a hit on that one-night stand that he was invited back—and stayed for the next 28 years!

Rochester, as Benny's long-suffering valet and straight man, was one of the most beloved comic creations in American broadcasting history. To be sure, he was an outrageous stereotype, with his subservient "Yes, Boss," his rubber face, and rolling eyes. But in many ways he was smarter than Benny, and it was always apparent that there was real affection between them. Then there was his incredible voice. "His voice is his trademark," wrote one

observer, "a grinding rasp that sounds like a crosscut saw biting through a knot in a hardwood log . . . Rochester parlayed a cement-mixer voice into fame and fortune."

Anderson was the son of circus and vaudeville parents. He joined an all-black revue while still in his teens, and eventually played the Roxy, the Cotton Club, and the Apollo in Harlem. By the early 1930s he was in Hollywood breaking into films, mostly in the subservient, stereotyped roles reserved for blacks in those days. Among his notable performances were those of Noah in *Green Pastures* (1936), Uncle Peter in *Gone with the Wind* (1939), and the lead in *Cabin in the Sky* (1943).

After the mid-1940s he concentrated almost exclusively on the Benny show, for which he had become best known, following it to TV in 1950 and staying on (on a reduced schedule) even after he suffered a heart attack in 1958. Family troubles began to dog him in the 1950s, including the death of his wife, the imprisonment of his son on marijuana charges, and the aftereffects of his heart attack, which impaired his speech and sight. The death of his beloved boss, "Mr. Benny," was a heavy blow in 1974. "It was more than just being an employee or just a member of the cast," he said of their 37-year friendship. "There was a warmth, a closeness. There was a love between us."

ANDERSON, HARRY—actor

b: Oct 14, 1952, Newport, R.I.

Night Court (com)
.... Judge Harry Stone (1984–)
Our Time (var).............. regular (1985)

Harry Anderson took up magic as a youngster, to escape the pressures of an unhappy childhood. One of three children raised by his divorced mother, he was shuffled between parents and moved constantly until he was 18, by which time he was good enough at his hobby to begin performing in amateur and professional productions. His youthful good looks and glib, comic patter won him appearances on local TV, and then on network series such as *NBC's Saturday Night Live* and *The Billy Crystal Show*. Gradually the comedy supplanted the magic. Three memorable appearances on *Cheers* (as a neighborhood con man) led in 1984 to his first starring role, that of the offbeat young judge on *Night Court*.

ANDERSON, HERBERT—actor
b: 1917

Dennis the Menace (com)
.... Henry Mitchell (1959–63)

Hollywood character actor of the 1940s and '50s, who was best known as the bumbling sidekick in films, and—of course—as Dennis's owlish, long-suffering dad on television.

ANDERSON, INGRID—actress

Cover Up (drama)...... Gretchen (1984–85)

ANDERSON, JANE—comedienne

The Billy Crystal Comedy Hour (var)
.... regular (1982)

ANDERSON, JOHN—actor
b: Oct 20, 1922, Clayton, Ill.

The Life and Legend of Wyatt Earp (wes)
.... Virgil Earp (1959–61)
Rich Man, Poor Man—Book II (drama)
.... Scotty (1976–77)
Backstairs at the White House (drama)
.... Pres. Franklin D. Roosevelt (1979)

A tall, thin, craggy-faced character actor who is said to have appeared in over 500 television productions, 30 movies, and innumerable stage plays. He did considerable television work during the 1960s and '70s, mostly on dramas, TV movies, and miniseries.

ANDERSON, LARRY—actor
b: Sep 22, Minneapolis, Minn.

Brothers and Sisters (com)
.... Harlan Ramsey (1979)
Life with Lucy (com)
.... Ted McGibbon (1986–)

ANDERSON, LONI—actress
b: Aug 5, 1945, St. Paul, Minn.

WKRP in Cincinnati (com)
.... Jennifer Marlowe (1978–82)
Partners in Crime (drama)
.... Sydney Kovak (1984)
Easy Street (com) ... L. K. McGuire (1986–)

Blonde, buxom Loni Anderson plugged away in minor roles in the theater and TV for ten years before she suddenly became the Sex Symbol of 1978—thanks to her role as the curvaceous but intelligent receptionist on *WKRP in Cincinnati*. There were Loni posters, bosom gags, and contract squabbles (befitting her sudden star-status), but Loni did not fade from view as many overnight sensations have done. During and after the run of *WKRP* she appeared on many TV specials (she was a particular favorite of Bob Hope's), and starred as the sex goddess of an earlier era in the TV film *The Jayne Mansfield Story* (1980). In 1984 she was briefly paired with ex–Wonder Woman Lynda Carter in the inept detective series *Partners In Crime*. We will likely see more of Loni in the future.

ANDERSON, LYNN—country singer
b: Sep 26, 1947, Grand Forks, N.D.

The Lawrence Welk Show (music)
.... regular (1967–68)
Dean Martin Presents Music Country (var)
.... regular (1973)

Pretty country singer Lynn Anderson was still in her teens when she was signed to be a regular on *The Lawrence Welk Show* in 1967, though she had already scored her first minor success on the country record charts. She left the show after only a year, to marry, and soon became one of the top-selling artists in the country field.

Oddly enough, her mother, Liz Anderson, a successful country songwriter, also began achieving success as a singer at about the same time. Mother and daughter each had many hits on the country charts during the late 1960s and '70s. It was Lynn who had the biggest of all, however—"I Never Promised You a Rose Garden," which sold more than a million copies in 1970–71, was a major pop hit, and made her a national celebrity. Lynn went on to appear on many network telecasts, including *The Tonight Show, Kraft Music Hall, The Johnny Cash Show, Hee Haw* and Dean Martin's *Music Country*.

ANDERSON, MELISSA SUE—actress
b: Sep 26, 1962, Berkeley, Calif.

Little House on the Prairie (adv)
.... Mary Ingalls Kendall (1974–81)

Emmy Award: For her performance in the *ABC Afterschool Special "Which Mother Is Mine?"* (1980)

Golden-haired Melissa Sue Anderson was barely 11 years old when she made her first TV appearances on episodes of *The Brady Bunch* and *Shaft.* The following season she was cast as Michael Landon's eldest daughter on the long-running *Little House on the Prairie,* where she proceeded to grow up before viewers' eyes. Her character eventually went blind and married her braille instructor, a nice young man named Adam Kendall.

ANDERSON, MELODY—actress
b: Dec 3, 1955, Edmonton, Alberta, Canada

Manimal (police).. Brooke McKenzie (1983)

Canadian Melody Anderson worked briefly as a radio correspondent and a model before getting into television in 1977. She appeared in episodes of a number of adventure series, then landed the role of the beautiful but not-too-believable police officer in *Manimal.*

ANDERSON, MICHAEL, JR.—actor
b: Aug 6, 1943, London, England

The Monroes (wes)
.... Clayt Monroe (1966–67)

A young British actor who made a dozen or so films in the late 1950s and early '60s while he was a juvenile (or could pass for one). On *The Monroes* he was the eldest son in an orphaned family of youngsters who were trying to homestead in the old west. He was seen occasionally in later years in films such as *Logan's Run* (1976) and *The Martian Chronicles* (1980). Michael is the son of British film director Michael Anderson (*Around the World in Eighty Days, Logan's Run,* etc.), who sometimes included Junior in his movies.

ANDERSON, MICKEY—musician (female)

The Ina Ray Hutton Show (var)
.... regular (1956)

ANDERSON, RICHARD—actor
b: Aug 8, 1926, Long Branch, N.J. r: Los Angeles

Mama Rosa (com).......... the son (1950)
Bus Stop (drama).. Glenn Wagner (1961–62)
The Lieutenant (drama)
.... Col. Hiland (1963–64)
Perry Mason (drama)
.... Lt. Steve Drumm (1965–66)
Dan August (police)
..... Chief George Untermeyer (1970–71)
The Six Million Dollar Man (adv)
.... Oscar Goldman (1974–78)
The Bionic Woman (adv)
.... Oscar Goldman (1976–78)
Pearl (drama)................ North (1978)
Cover Up (drama). Henry Towler (1984–85)

A solid—one might say stolid—authoritative actor who (on TV at least) usually played wise, middle-aged officials. He was the district attorney on *Bus Stop,* the colonel on *The Lieutenant,* a senior police officer on *Perry Mason* and *Dan August,* and the government agent to whom both the Six Million Dollar Man and the Bionic Woman reported. That last role, incidentally, gave Anderson the unique distinction of being the first actor in TV history to play the same regular character on two different series simultaneously.

On *Cover Up* Anderson was again a government official, this time sending Mac and Danielle off on their globe-trotting missions. In addition to his regular roles, he was seen many, many times on other dramatic series of the 1960s, '70s, and '80s, including multiple appearances on *Big Valley, The F.B.I.,* and *Ironside.* Prior to his TV career Anderson had been quite active as a supporting actor in movies, appearing in several dozen films of the '50s—among them *Paths of Glory* and *The Long Hot Summer.* He was married at one time to the daughter of screen legend Norma Shearer.

ANDERSON, RICHARD DEAN—actor
b: Jan 23, 1950, Minneapolis, Minn.

Seven Brides for Seven Brothers (adv)
.... Adam McFadden (1982–83)
Emerald Point N.A.S. (drama)
.... Lt. Simon Adams (1983–84)
MacGyver (drama) ..... MacGyver (1985–)

Richard Dean Anderson is an athletic young actor who planned to become a professional hockey player before he broke both of his arms playing varsity hockey in high school. Taking a hint, he went into acting, at first as a street mime and jester in an Elizabethian-style cabaret in Los Angeles. His big break came with the part of Dr. Jeff Webber on the daytime soap *General Hospital,* from 1976–81. Then, in quick succession, came juicy, macho roles in prime time—the eldest brother on *Seven Brides for Seven Brothers,* the "good son" in a bad family on *Emerald Point, N.A.S.,* and finally the lead in his own adventure series, *MacGyver.*

Anderson continues to maintain an intense interest in athletics, as well as in his second love, music (his father is a jazz musician). He made a number of appearances with his own rock band, called Ricky Dean and Dante.

ANDERSON, ROBERT—actor

Court of Last Resort (drama)
.... Park Street, Jr. (1957–58)

ANDERSON, SAM—actor

Mama Malone (com) .... Stanley (1984)

ANDERSON, SHEILA—actress
b: Jul 10, New York City, N.Y.

The New Odd Couple (com)
.... Cecily Pigeon (1982–83)

ANDERSON, WARNER—actor
b: Mar 10, 1911, Brooklyn, N.Y. d: Aug 26, 1976

The Doctor (drama) ... the doctor (1952–53)
The Lineup (police)
.... Det. Lt. Ben Guthrie (1954–60)
Peyton Place (drama)
.... Matthew Swain (1964–65)

A solid, if unexceptional, character actor who had a busy career in movie supporting roles from the mid-1940s to the mid-1950s. He began to shift to television in the early 1950s, first with a short run as host of a long-forgotten medical anthology series and then with a very long one as hard-nosed detective Ben Guthrie on *The Lineup.* A few years later he was back as the gaunt, silver-haired editor of *The Clar-*

ion during the first season of *Peyton Place.*

Anderson appeared in a few more episodes of dramatic series after that, including an *Ironside* episode as late as 1973.

ANDES, KEITH—actor
b: Jul 12, 1920, Ocean City, N.J.

This Man Dawson (police)
.... Col. Frank Dawson (1959)
Glynis (com)....... Keith Granville (1963)
Search (adv)........... Dr. Barnett (1973)

This likable, young-looking actor appeared in approximately 20 movies (mostly in the 1950s) and did a lot of television work (in the 1950s, '60s, and '70s), but none of his roles are particularly well remembered. He was first seen in such 1950s series as *Ford Theatre* and *The Loretta Young Show,* then starred in his own syndicated police show, *This Man Dawson,* in 1959. In the 1960s and early '70s he appeared in episodes of many series, both comedy and drama, including several episodes each of *The Lucy Show, I Spy,* and *Cannon.* He costarred (with Glynis Johns) as the harried husband in the comedy-detective series *Glynis* in 1963 and also tried daytime soap operas via the leading role in NBC's new *Paradise Bay* in 1965–66. Neither show lasted long. Later, Andes was seen briefly in the equally unsuccessful sci-fi/adventure series *Search* in 1973.

His appearances became less frequent after the mid-1970s.

ANDES, OLIVER—actor

Bonino (com) .... Carlo (1953)

ANDOR, PAUL—actor
b: Germany

Claudia, The Story of a Marriage (drama)
.... Fritz (1952)

A journeyman actor who played minor German roles in many films, plays, and TV shows over the years. He began his movie career in Hollywood in 1928 using the name Wolfgang Zilzer. After appearing in several anti-Nazi films during World War II, including *Hitler's Madman* and *Appointment In Berlin,* he changed his name to Andor. In the 1950s and '60s Andor worked mostly on Broadway. His only regular TV series was the short-lived comedy-drama *Claudia, The Story of a Marriage* in 1952.

ANDRE, E. J.—actor

b: c. 1908, Detroit, Mich. d: Sep 6, 1984

Dallas (drama) . . . Eugene Bullock (1982–83)

ANDREWS, DANA—actor

b: Jan 1, 1909, Collins, Miss.

Ike (drama) . . . Gen. George Marshall (1979)

Dana Andrews was a major movie star of the 1940s and '50s who did a fair amount of television, starting at the top and, unfortunately, working his way down. He was born the son of a Mississippi Baptist minister who preached to his congregations against the sinfulness of movies. Father's advice seemed to have had little effect, since both Dana and one of his brothers went on to become successful movie and TV actors (the brother under the name Steve Forrest). After struggling through the 1930s in Hollywood, Dana finally hit it big in the mid-1940s in such films as *The Ox-Bow Incident, The Best Years of Our Lives,* and the fondly remembered mystery classic, *Laura.* Square-jawed and handsome, he often played a flawed hero and often didn't get the girl.

Dana's years at the top were waning by the mid-1950s (though he continued to make films), and he began to be seen periodically on TV. At first it was in prestige showcases such as *Playhouse 90* and *The DuPont Show of the Month*—he was, after all, still a big name. By 1969 he was reduced to headlining a new NBC daytime soap called *Bright Promise,* which failed after a couple of years. After that there were a few TV films and appearances on episodes of series such as *Get Christie Love* and *The Hardy Boys.* A more prestigeous appearance, perhaps, was in the 1979 miniseries *Ike,* as General George C. Marshall.

ANDREWS, EDWARD—actor

b: Oct 9, 1915*, Griffin, Ga. d: Mar 9, 1985

Broadside (com)
 . . . . Cmdr. Rogers Adrian (1964–65)
Supertrain (drama)
 . . . . conductor Harry Flood (1979)

*Some sources give 1914.

A beaming, hearty character actor who did not break into movies or television until he was in his forties—following a 20 year career in the theater—but who did much work in both media in the years that followed. In addition to his regular roles as the much put-upon C.O. in *Broadside* and the genial conductor on *Supertrain,* he appeared as a guest star in such series as *The Phil Silvers Show, The Doris Day Show* (as Doris' publisher) and the 1971 *Don Rickles Show* (as Don's boss).

ANDREWS, JOHNNY—singer

b: Apr 1, 1917, Boston, Mass.

Songs at Twilight (music) . . . . host (1951)

ANDREWS, JULIE—actress

b: Oct 1, 1935, Walton-on-Thames, England

The Julie Andrews Hour (var)
 . . . . hostess (1972–73)

Emmy Award: As host of *The Julie Andrews Hour* (1973)

Julie Andrews, who seems to be cursed with the image of the ultimate "Miss Sweetness and Light," has had a roller-coaster career. She made her debut in a London revue at age 12, and by age 18 was on stage in New York. Shortly thereafter she starred in two of the biggest musical hits Broadway has ever seen, *My Fair Lady* in 1956 and *Camelot* in 1960. She was seen on television during this period in the big-budget musical specials "High Tor" (1956) and "Cinderella" (1957), among other appearances.

Passed over by the moguls at Warner Brothers Studios for the lead in the film version of *My Fair Lady* (they chose Audrey Hepburn instead), she made her film debut in Disney's *Mary Poppins* (1964)—which not only became a bigger hit than the Hepburn film, but won her an Academy Award for best actress. *Mary Poppins* and *The Sound of Music* the following year were megahits that established Julie as the number-one box office attraction in the world. Several successful films followed, but by the end of the decade her career was already in decline (sweetness and light were "out"). She began making more frequent appearances on television, mostly in big, glossy specials such as *Julie and Carol at Carnegie Hall* (with Carol Burnett),

An Evening With Julie Andrews and Harry Belafonte, and *Julie Andrews' Invitation to the Dance with Rudolf Nureyev.* In addition, she starred in her own hour-long variety show on ABC in 1972–73, which was a ratings failure but won her an Emmy.

Julie has been married to director Blake Edwards since 1968.

ANDREWS, NORMAN J.—

The Jerry Reed When You're Hot You're Hot Hour (var) .... regular (1972)

ANDREWS, STANLEY—actor
b: 1891* d: Jun 23, 1969

Death Valley Days (wes)
.... the Old Ranger (host) (1952–65)

This kindly, older actor with the trim mustache and friendly manner will be remembered by TV audiences chiefly for his long tenure as host of *Death Valley Days,* from 1952–65. He had been in show business for many years before that, however, on radio in the 1930s (including a stint as Daddy Warbucks on *Little Orphan Annie*) and in movies from the mid-1930s to the mid-1950s. Among his many film roles were those of the captain in *Alexander's Ragtime Band,* of Weston in *Meet John Doe,* and of the villainous Jeffries in the 1938 *Lone Ranger* serial.

ANDREWS, TIGE—actor
b: Mar 19, 1923, Brooklyn, N.Y.

The Detectives, Starring Robert Taylor (police) .... Lt. John Russo (1959–62)
The Mod Squad (police)
.... Capt. Adam Greer (1968–73)

Square-jawed, authoritative-looking actor who fit perfectly the role of a tough police officer, although he apparently never played one until he was cast in *The Detectives* in 1959. Born of Lebanese-American parents (his real name is Tiger Androwaous), he did much theatrical work in the late 1940s and early '50s, then had a minor career in movies (he was in both the stage and film versions of *Mr. Roberts*). He did principally TV work after the mid-1950s, including the occasional role of Private Gander on *The Phil Silvers Show.*

*Some sources give 1892.

ANDREWS, TINA—black actress
b: Apr 23, Chicago, Ill.

The Sanford Arms (com)
.... Angie Wheeler (1977)
The Contender (drama)
.... Missy Dinwittie (1980)
Falcon Crest (drama) ..... Valerie (1983–84)

This young actress was first seen in the early 1970s in episodes of *Room 222* and *Sanford and Son* (as Fred's niece), as well as in the controversial 1974 TV movie *Born Innocent.* She then played the role of Valerie Grant on the daytime soap opera *Days of Our Lives* for a time before moving on to regular supporting roles in several prime time series.

ANDREWS, TOD—actor
b: 1920, Buffalo, N.Y. d: Nov 6, 1972

The Gray Ghost (adv)
.... Maj. John Singleton Mosby (1957)
Counterthrust (drama) .... agent (1959)

A burly actor with a scattering of credits in the theater, movies, and TV during the 1940s and '50s, mostly in action stories. During the early years of his career he was known as Michael Ames. His last known appearance, shortly before his death, was in the daytime soap opera *Bright Promise,* c. 1970.

ANDRONICA, JAMES—actor

Gangster Chronicles (drama)
.... Frank Costello (1981)

ANDROSKY, CAROL—actress

Diana (com) .... Holly Green (1973–74)

ANGAROLA, RICHARD—actor

How the West Was Won (miniseries) (drama)
.... Chief Claw (1977)

ANGELA, JUNE—juvenile actress

Mr. T and Tina (com) .... Sachi (1976)

ANGELOU, MAYA—black writer, actress
b: Apr 4, 1928, St. Louis, Mo.

Roots (drama)............ Nyo Boto (1977)

Maya Angelou is a rather intense writer and poet who spent five years of her childhood as a voluntary mute—not speaking to anyone, but cultivating a "love for written words" that helped her master six languages and develop a deep awareness of the human condition. She is best known for her autobiographical book about growing up in Arkansas, *I Know Why the Caged Bird Sings*, which later became a successful Broadway play and was produced as a TV movie in 1979. Though she is known primarily as a writer, Maya has been seen in a number of plays and TV specials, including *Roots* and the 1977 *Richard Pryor Special*.

ANGLIM, PHILIP—actor, producer

b: Feb 11, 1953, San Francisco, Calif.

The Thorn Birds (drama)
.... Dane O'Neill (1983)

Young actor best known for his role as John Merrick in *The Elephant Man* on Broadway and television (in January 1982). He was also seen in *The Adams Chronicles* and *The Thorn Birds* miniseries.

ANGUSTAIN, IRA—actor

b: Aug 6, Glendale, Calif.

The White Shadow (drama)
.... Ricky Gomez (1978–80)

Young Ira Angustain began as a child actor on such series as *Pete and Gladys* (at age three), *Dan August,* and *Ironside.* He bears a striking resemblance to the late comedian Freddie Prinze, a fact that helped win him the leading role in the 1979 TV movie about Prinze's life, *Can You Hear the Laughter?—The Freddie Prinze Story.*

ANHOLT, TONY—actor

The Protectors (adv). Paul Buchet (1972–73)
The Strauss Family (drama)..... Edi (1973)
Space 1999 (sci fi)
...... First Off. Tony Verdeschi (1976–77)

A handsome young actor who appeared in several series produced in Europe during the 1970s.

ANKRUM, DAVID—actor

Tabitha (com).... Adam Stephens (1977–78)

ANONYMOUS

The Invisible Man (drama)
.... Dr. Peter Brady (1958–60)

Here's a trivia question for you: what was the only series in network history whose star has to this day remained deliberately anonymous? A lot of actors in some of TV's more dreadful flops probably wish they *could* have been anonymous, but only one series lead actually was. That was the actor who played Dr. Peter Brady in the original 1958 version of *The Invisible Man*. He was, of course, never seen on the show (although his clothes moved about, and his voice was heard).

The series was filmed in England. Perhaps someday the producer, Ralph Smart, will reveal who really was inside that empty overcoat.

Incidentally, you get half a point if your answer to the above question was John Beresford Tipton of *The Millionaire*. His face was never seen either, but his voice was supplied by veteran announcer Paul Frees, and his hand (seen on the arm of the chair) probably by several actors over the years.

ANSARA, MICHAEL—actor

b: Apr 15, 1922, Lowell, Mass.

Broken Arrow (wes)..... Cochise (1956–58)
Law of the Plainsman (wes)
   Dep. U.S. Marshal Sam Buckhart (1959–60)
Centennial (drama). Lame Beaver (1978–79)
Buck Rogers in the 25th Century (sci fi)
.... Kane (1979–80)

Swarthy actor who became known for his Indian roles, thanks largely to his two 1950s series, *Broken Arrow* (in which he played an Apache chief) and *Law of the Plainsman* (in which he was an Anglicized Apache). Asked if this might typecast him, he replied at the time, "It will give us all a chance to find out." Evidently it did, because twenty years later he was still playing Indian roles, as on the miniseries *Centennial*. Ansara did have many other roles on various series, from a 1950 episode of *The Lone Ranger* to *CHiPs* and *Fantasy Island* in the 1980s. He was an especially familiar face on westerns such as *Rawhide* and *Gunsmoke* and on crime dramas such as *The Name of the Game* and *McMillan* and Wife. In *Buck Rogers* he played the evil henchman of Princess Ardala.

Ansara appeared in several dozen movies from 1950 onward, earning early notice for his brief role as Judas in *The Robe* (1953). He actually has no Indian blood. "I'm Lebanese," he says. "I guess it's my size [6'3"] and dark complexion that makes me suitable for the Indian role." Ansara was married to actress Barbara Eden from 1958 until 1973.

ANSBRO, GEORGE—announcer

Manhattan Maharaja (var)
.... host/maharaja (1950–51)

Network radio announcer of the 1940s, especially familiar for his long association with *Young Widder Brown*. He also handled a number of announcing and host assignments for ABC in the early days of television, including that of network TV's only "maharaja."

ANSPACH, SUSAN—actress
b: 1939, New York City, N.Y.

The Yellow Rose (drama)
.... Grace McKenzie (1983)

ANTHONY, LEROY—musician

The Ray Anthony Show (var)
.... regular (1956–57)

Saxophone-playing brother of orchestra leader Ray Anthony.

ANTHONY, RAY—orchestra leader
b: Jan 20, 1922, Bentleyville, Pa. r: Cleveland, Ohio

TV's Top Tunes (music)
.... orch. leader (1953–54)
The Ray Anthony Show (var)
.... host (1956–57)
The Ray Anthony Show (var) ... host (1962)
The Ray Anthony Show (var) ... host (1968)

A very popular bandleader of the 1950s who bore a striking resemblance to actor Cary Grant. Born Raymond Antonini, he began playing trumpet at age five in his father's "Antonini Family Orchestra." By the late 1930s, while still in his teens, he had become a top professional in the field, playing with the big bands of Jimmy Dor-

sey and Glenn Miller. His first appearance on-screen was with Miller in *Sun Valley Serenade* (1941); he later took acting lessons and played minor roles in several films of the 1950s. After the war Ray formed his own band, which became extremely popular. Two of his biggest record hits came from television: the themes from *Dragnet* in 1953 and from *Peter Gunn* in 1959. Another of his hits, which he co-wrote, was the dance craze "The Bunny Hop."

The handsome bandleader broke into TV in the early 1950s, appearing on variety shows. He hosted the summer replacement for Perry Como in 1953 and 1954 and had his own Friday night variety hour in 1956–57. He also hosted two syndicated variety shows in the 1960s, featuring his orchestra and a pair of beautiful young girls called The Bookends.

Ray found a new goal in later years. Dismayed at the decline of big band music, in 1980 he began organizing like-minded friends into a nonprofit organization called Big Bands 80s. Its purpose was to keep the sound alive by publicizing the surviving bands, sending big band LPs to radio stations, and selling them to the public by mail (since many record stores no longer carried them). It is credited with helping spark the revival of big band music on many local radio stations.

Ray was married at one time to actress Mamie Van Doren.

ANTILLE, LISA—actress

The Ted Knight Show (com)
.... Lisa Flores (1986)

ANTON, SUSAN—actress
b: Oct 12, 1950, Oak Glen, Calif.

Presenting Susan Anton (var)
.... hostess (1979)
Stop Susan Williams (drama)
.... Susan Williams (1979)

Susan Anton was the 1979 discovery of television mogul Fred Silverman. So sure was he that she would be a major star that he headlined her on not one but two NBC series that spring—her own variety show and a campy adventure called *Stop Susan Williams* (which ran as part of the *Cliffhangers* series). Both flopped, and little has been heard from Susan since.

Prior to her three months in the sun, the statuesque blonde did nightclub work and appeared with Mel Tillis in a short-lived 1977 summer variety show. She was perhaps best known, however, for her sexy Muriel Cigars commercials (from 1976 on).

ANTONACCI, GREG—actor
b: Feb 2, New York City

Busting Loose (com)
.... Vinnie Mordabito (1977)
Makin' It (adv)....... Tony Manucci (1979)

ANTONINI, ALFREDO—conductor
b: May 31, 1901, Alessandria, Italy d: Nov 3, 1983

Jane Froman's U.S.A. Canteen (var)
.... orch. leader (1952–53)

Emmy Award: Musical Direction, for "And David Wept" (religious program) (1972)

Antonini was a longtime musical director for the CBS radio and television networks, responsible for the music on many of the network's offerings from the 1940s to the '70s. He studied in Italy in the 1930s, where he played organ and celeste in La Scala Opera under Arturo Toscanini. He joined CBS in 1941.

ANTONIO, LOU—actor, director
b: Jan 23, 1934, Oklahoma City, Okla.

The Snoop Sisters (drama)
.... Barney (1973–74)
Dog and Cat (police)
.... Det. Sgt. Jack Ramsey (1977)
Makin' It (adv)...... Joseph Manucci (1979)

Lou Antonio is one of the more successful actor-directors in the television medium, his amiable but persistent style working equally well on both sides of the camera. He began his career in supporting roles in the New York theater and in movies in the late 1950s. One of his more notable roles was that of Koko in *Cool Hand Luke* (1967). Moving into television, he began to pursue a dual career. As a director, he was responsible for numerous episodes of *McCloud, Owen Marshall, Counselor At Law, McMillan and Wife,* and other se-

ries, and was twice nominated for the Emmy Award for his deft direction of the tearjerkers *Something for Joey* (1978) and *Silent Victory: The Kitty O'Neill Story* (1979). As one critic put it, "If we must have tearjerkers, Antonio is the man to make them."

As an actor he appeared in various series and specials, as well as playing the legman for Helen Hayes and Mildred Natwick in *The Snoop Sisters,* police partner to sexy Kim Basinger in *Dog and Cat,* and David Naughton's blue collar dad on *Makin' It.*

APLON, BORIS—actor

Stand By for Crime (police)
.... Inspector Webb (1949)

APOLLONIA—

See Kotero, Patricia

APPLEGATE, CHRISTINA—juvenile actress
b: Nov 25, Hollywood, Calif.

Heart of the City (drama)
.... Robin Kennedy (1986–)

APPLEGATE, EDDIE—actor
b: Oct 4, 1935, Wyncote, pa.

The Patty Duke Show (com)
.... Richard Harrison (1963–66)
Nancy (com).............. Willie (1970–71)

APPLEGATE, FRED—actor

Newhart (com)................ J. J. (1985–)

APREA, JOHN—actor

The Montefuscos (com)
.... Father Joseph Montefusco (1975)
Matt Houston (drama)
.... Lt. Vince Novelli (1982–83)

Italian-American actor who had a minor career on stage and in movies from the 1960s on. He also appeared in various TV series episodes, as well as in the regular (though short-lived) roles of the second son in *The Montefuscos* and Lee Horsley's homey police contact during the first season of *Matt Houston.*

ARAGONES, SERGIO—satirical cartoonist

Laugh-In (revival) (var) ... regular (1977–78)
Speak Up, America (aud par)
.... regular (1980)

ARBUS, ALAN—actor

b: Feb 15, 1918, New York City, N.Y.

M*A*S*H (com)
   Dr. Sidney Freedman (occasional) (1972–83)
Working Stiffs (com)
.... Mitch Hannigan (1979)
The Gangster Chronicles (drama)
.... Goodman (1981)
The Four Seasons (com) . Boris Elliot (1984)

Wiry, somewhat scruffy-looking older actor who was little noticed until, in his late fifties, he appeared in a few episodes of *M*A*S*H* as an understanding psychiatrist passing through the 4077th (which certainly needed one). Perhaps his best remembered appearance was in the 1983 final episode of the series, in which he calmly helped Alan Alda recover from a very realistic nervous breakdown. Presumably in appreciation, Alda cast him as the attorney in his subsequent (but unsuccessful) series *The Four Seasons*.

ARCHER, ANNE—actress

b: Aug 25, 1947, Los Angeles, Calif.

Bob & Carol & Ted & Alice (com)
.... Carol Sanders (1973)
Seventh Avenue (drama)
.... Myrna Gold (1977)
The Family Tree (drama)
.... Annie Benjamin Nichols (1983)
Falcon Crest (drama)
.... Cassandra Wilder (1985)

Pretty Anne Archer could hardly help but follow a theatrical career. Her mother is actress Marjorie Lord, her father actor John Archer, and her stepfather producer Randolph Hale. She is married to producer/director Terry Jastrow. Anne's film career began in 1970 and progressed from minor to costarring roles; none of the films have been particularly notable, however (anyone recall *Hero at Large* with John Ritter or *Naked Faces* with Roger Moore?). She also starred in, and co-produced with her husband, a film called *Waltz Across Texas* and made her stage debut in the off-Broadway production *A Couple of White Chicks Sitting Around Talking.*

Anne's television work has been steady but unspectacular. *Bob & Carol & Ted & Alice* lasted only a few weeks; *Seventh Avenue* was a none-too-successful miniseries; and *The Family Tree* was a January tryout that didn't make it to the fall schedule. In *Falcon Crest,* at last, she joined a hit series.

ARCHER, BEVERLY—actress

b: July 19, 1948, Oak Park, Ill.

The Nancy Walker Show (com)
.... Lorraine (1976)
We've Got Each Other (com)
.... Judy Hibbard (1977–78)
Spencer (com)......... Miss Spier (1984–85)
Under One Roof (com).... Miss Spier (1985)
Mama's Family (com) .... Iola (1986)

Lanky, schoolmarmish actress who played the hypochrondriac daughter on *The Nancy Walker Show* and the working wife on *We've Got Each Other.*

ARCHER, GENE—singer

Capitol Capers (music) ..... vocalist (1949)

ARDEN, EVE—actress

b: Apr 30, 1912, Mill Valley, Calif.

Our Miss Brooks (com)
.... Connie Brooks (1952–56)
Eve Arden Show (com)
.... Liza Hammond (1957–58)
The Mothers-in-Law (com)
.... Eve Hubbard (1967–69)

Emmy Award: Best Actress, for *Our Miss Brooks* (1953)

Few major television stars have ever been as closely identified with a single character as Eve Arden. She will always be Our Miss Brooks, the sarcastic, wisecracking, and thoroughly delightful English teacher from Madison High.

Eve was born near San Francisco, and was already trying to crash Hollywood by the time she was a teenager. After some lean years, and a couple of minor roles under her real name, Eunice Quedens, she began to attract notice as a sketch comedian in the *Ziegfeld Follies* onstage in the mid-1930s. (Along the way, she says, she invented her new name from the labels on a couple of cosmetic bottles: "Evening in Paris" and "Elizabeth Arden"). Her big break came in a 1937 film called *Stage Door*, in which she was supposed to have a small part, but improvised her way to a comedy performance that almost stole the show. After that she became Hollywood's favorite wisecracking best friend of the star, never the lead, but almost always a comic highlight of any film she was in. Her quick ripostes were famous; for example, her memorable crack about Joan Crawford's horrible daughter in *Mildred Pierce* ("Veda's convinced me that alligators have the right idea. They eat their young.")

Eve also appeared in a number of radio series in the 1940s, playing her patented character, but it was not until *Our Miss Brooks* began on CBS radio in 1948 that she found the perfect character—and supporting cast—for her unique talents. Connie Brooks was a logical extension of the roles she had been playing for years. The show was an immediate hit and moved successfully to television in 1952 while continuing on radio.

After that famous series ended, Eve was much in demand and immediately starred in another sitcom as writer/lecturer Liza Hammond, but this failed. She made pilots for some proposed series in the 1960s (*Careful, It's My Art* in 1963, *He's All Yours* in 1964) but none sold until *The Mothers-in-Law* made it on to the NBC schedule in 1967 for a two year run. In this, she was the "straight" mother-in-law, while Kaye Ballard was the unconventional one. From the late '60s on she turned up often as a guest on other shows, as well as making more pilots for proposed series of her own. She appeared on *The Love Boat* in 1980. But it will not be for those roles, or Liza Hammond, or Eve Hubbard, that she will be fondly remembered. She will always be Our Miss Brooks.

As her amiable young student Walter Denton would put it when he met her each morning, "Greetings, fairest of all possible English teachers." (To which Connie would invariably reply, "Well good morning, most observant of all possible pupils.")

Eve's autobiography was titled *Three Phases of Eve* (1985).

ARDEN, ROBERT—actor
b: 1921

Saber of London (drama)
.... Bob Page (1958–60)

ARDEN, SUZI—country singer

Ozark Jubilee (music)..... regular (1958–59)

ARESCO, JOEY—actor

Baa Baa Black Sheep (drama)
.... Hutch (1976–77)
Supertrain (drama) .. Wayne Randall (1979)

ARGO, ALLISON—actress
b: Dec 23, Richmond, Va.

Ladies' Man (com) .... Susan (1980–81)

ARGOUD, KARIN—actress

Mama's Family (com)
.... Sonja Harper (1983–84)

ARKIN, ADAM—actor
b: Aug 19, 1956, Brooklyn, N.Y.

Busting Loose (com)
.... Lenny Markowitz (1977)
Pearl (drama)............. Zylowski (1978)
Teachers Only (com)
.... Michael Dreyfus (1982)
Tough Cookies (com)
.... Danny Polchek (1986)

The son of actor Alan Arkin. Adam debuted at age 13 in one of his father's productions and appeared occasionally on TV and in minor film roles during the years that followed.

ARKIN, DAVID—actor

Storefront Lawyers (drama)
.... Gabriel Kaye (1970–71)

ARLEN, DAVID—actor

CBS Newcomers (var) .... regular (1971)

ARLEN, ROXANNE—hostess
b: c. 1935, Detroit, Mich.

Beat the Clock (quiz) ... assistant (1950–55)

Roxanne was the shapely blonde "photographer" and assistant to emcee Bud Collyer who snapped pictures of the contestants as they finished their comic stunts on this popular show. She became something of a minor celebrity due to her exposure on the program, appearing in fashion magazine articles and making personal appearances. Her real name is Dolores Rosedale.

ARLISS, DIMITRA—actress
b: Oct 23, 1932

Rich Man, Poor Man—Book II (drama)
.... Marie Falconetti (1976–77)

ARMEN, KAY—singer
b: Chicago, Ill.

Love & Marriage (com) ... Sophie (1959–60)

A pleasant-voiced singer of the 1940s and '50s, Kay recorded widely but never had a major hit. She was frequently heard on radio (including a stint on *Stop the Music*) and made many appearances on TV variety shows. On *Love & Marriage* she played the singing secretary.

ARMITRAJ, VIJAY—actor

The Last Precinct (com)
Shivaramanbhai Poonchwalla ("Alphabet") (1986)

ARMS, RUSSELL—singer
b: Feb 3, 1929, Berkeley, Calif.

School House (var).......... regular (1949)
Fifty-Fourth Street Revue (var)
.... regular (1949–50)
Chance of a Lifetime (quiz)
.... vocalist (1950–51)
Your Hit Parade (music) . vocalist (1952–57)

A ballad singer of the 1950s who is best remembered for his long run singing other people's hits on the weekly countdown show *Your Hit Parade*. Russell originally aimed for a movie career and played bit parts in a few films of the early 1940s while he was under contract to Warner Brothers Studios. When his movie career stalled he turned to singing on radio and TV, where he won spots on several early variety shows. It was *Your Hit Parade* that made him famous, however, and he eventually scored a record hit of his own in 1957 called "Cinco Robles." In later years little

was heard from him; he did some road shows, narrated industrial films, and emceed talent shows and beauty pageants.

ARMSTRONG, BESS—actress
b: Dec 11, 1953, Baltimore, Md.

On Our Own (com)... Julia Peters (1977–78)
All Is Forgiven (com) .. Paula Russell (1986)

ARMSTRONG, BILL—host

Liar's Club (quiz)........... host (1976–77)

ARMSTRONG, R. G.—actor
b: Apr 7, 1917, Birmingham, Ala.

T.H.E. Cat (adv)
.... Capt. MacAllister (1966–67)

Tough-looking, husky actor who struggled for years to become a playwright, then finally drifted into acting in the 1950s doing supporting roles on stage and screen. He appeared in a great many episodes of TV series over the years. On *T.H.E. Cat* he was the one-armed police captain.

ARMSTRONG, TODD—actor
b: 1939

Manhunt (police)
.... Det. Carl Spencer (1960–61)

Todd was one of six young actors discovered during a talent search conducted by the producers of *Manhunt*, and given his first major exposure on that syndicated series. He went on to appear in a number of successful movies of the 1960s *(Jason and the Argonauts, King Rat)*, but his career never took off as expected.

ARMSTRONG, VALORIE—actress

Funny Face (com) ... Alice McRaven (1971)

ARNAZ, DESI—actor
b: Mar 2, 1917, Santiago, Cuba d: Dec 2, 1986

I Love Lucy (com) . Ricky Ricardo (1951–57)
The Lucy-Desi Comedy Hour (specials) (com)
.... Ricky Ricardo (1957–60)
Westinghouse Desilu Playhouse (drama)
.... host (1958–60)

Cuban bandleader and showman who achieved video immortality as Lucille

Ball's harried husband in one of TV's all-time classic comedies, *I Love Lucy*. The stuffy executives at CBS in 1951 didn't want him on the show, arguing that no one would believe that red-haired Lucy was married to this crazy Cuban (which, in fact, she was). However, she insisted, they relented, and the rest is history. Many of the plots involved housewife Lucy trying to break into show business or into Desi's nightclub act, with hilarious results.

Desi was born Desiderio Alberto Arnaz y de Archa III, the only child of a wealthy Cuban landowner. He grew up spoiled and rich on his father's estates until the Batista revolution swept the island in 1933. Within a few hours the family property was confiscated, his father was imprisoned, and Desi and his mother forced to flee to Miami, nearly penniless. Cut adrift from the world he had known, young Desi decided to try show business. He was only an indifferent musician, but his Latin good looks and effervescent good humor quickly got him work, first with the Xavier Cugat band in 1937 and later with his own rhumba band. In 1940 Desi went to Hollywood to appear in the movie *Too Many Girls* (he had already been in the stage version the year before). A young starlet named Lucille Ball was also in the film; she and Desi hit it off at once, had a whirlwind courtship, and were married in November, 1940.

Their marriage proved stormy, as Lucy pursued her movie career and Desi was often on the road with his band during the following years (he also made a few more films). Finally, in a last attempt to save their marriage, they fought for the chance to do *I Love Lucy* together.

Desi proved to be not only a superb comedian, but an astute producer and businessman. He founded the couple's own Desilu Productions to handle the show, and quickly built it into a major independent studio, responsible for such hits as *Our Miss Brooks, December Bride,* and *The Untouchables.* Desi himself hosted the studio's *Westinghouse Desilu Playhouse,* which presented many notable hour-long dramas and comedies during the late 1950s.

After Lucy and Desi divorced in 1960, Lucy took control of Desilu. Desi concentrated on an independent producing career; from 1967–69 he was executive pro-ducer of the Eve Arden series *The Mothers-in-Law* (on which he sometimes appeared as the bullfighter Raphael del Gado). He was mostly inactive after that, turning up rarely in the 1970s (on *Ironside* in 1973, on *Alice* in 1978).

Desi's autobiography was published in 1976, titled *A Book.*

ARNAZ, DESI, JR.—actor

b: Jan 19, 1953, Los Angeles, Calif.

Here's Lucy (com)... Craig Carter (1968–71)
Automan (police)
.... Walter Nebicher (1983–84)

Desi, Jr., was probably television's most famous baby. His mother, Lucille Ball, incorporated her pregnancy as a story line in her hit series *I Love Lucy* during the fall of 1952 and gave birth on the very night (January 19, 1953) that CBS ran the episode in which her character, Lucy Ricardo, did the same. It was the most watched episode in TV history up to that time, and Lucy and her baby were one of the most highly publicized media events of the year.

Little Desi appeared only once in that classic series. He and sister Lucie were in a crowd scene in the final episode of the series, in 1957, watching the unveiling of a statue in a public park—the statue was impersonated by their mother! Desi began appearing on TV regularly in the late '60s, appearing in a couple episodes of his producer-father's series, *The Mothers-in-Law* in 1968, and then as a regular on his mother's show from 1968–71.

At about the same time Desi joined with Dean Martin's son and a school chum to form a bubble-gum rock band called Dino, Desi and Billy, which had some success on the record charts from 1965–68. Lucy was no fan of this venture. She later told a reporter, "I had a problem with Desi because he started this thing when he was ten. That was a big mistake—Sinatra [helped him], and I, like a fool, let it happen." Despite helpful friends like Sinatra and Dennis and Brian Wilson of the Beach Boys, Dino, Desi and Billy's musical career was short-lived. (Dino and Desi were later part of another musical group called The Beverly Hills Blues Band.)

During the 1970s and '80s Desi appeared in a scattering of TV series, from *The Brady Bunch* to *Fantasy Island,* and also in a number of forgettable TV movies (does anybody remember *The Night the Bridge Fell Down* or *The Great American Traffic Jam*?). He had a brief run as the star of his own series, *Automan,* in 1983–84.

ARNAZ, LUCIE—actress
b: Jul 17, 1951, Los Angeles, Calif.

Here's Lucy (com).... Kim Carter (1968–74)
The Lucie Arnaz Show (com)
.... Dr. Jane Lucas (1985)

The eldest child of Desi Arnaz and Lucille Ball, Lucie made several appearances on her mother's series *The Lucy Show* in the mid-1960s before becoming a regular on *Here's Lucy* from 1968–74. In the 1970s she turned mostly to stage work, starring in productions of *Cabaret, Once Upon a Mattress* and the Neil Simon Broadway hit *They're Playing Our Song* (1979).

Lucie also made a number of TV movies, including *Who Is the Black Dahlia?* in 1975, and had her own series briefly in 1985. She is married to actor Laurence Luckinbill, with whom she appeared in several productions, including the TV movie *The Mating Season* (1980).

ARNER, GWEN—actress

The New Land (adv)
.... Molly Lundstrom (1974)

ARNESS, JAMES—actor
b: May 26, 1923, Minneapolis, Minn.

Gunsmoke (wes)
.... Marshal Matt Dillon (1955–75)
How the West Was Won (miniseries) (drama)
.... Zeb Macahan (1977)
How the West Was Won (wes)
.... Zeb Macahan (1978–79)
McClain's Law (police)
.... Det. Jim McClain (1981–82)

James Arness has the unique distinction of having starred in the longest-running dramatic series in network history. For 20 years he was Matt Dillon on *Gunsmoke*—the most popular TV program ever—and the very image of stern, compassionate justice on the American frontier.

The tall, strapping (6'6") actor did have a career outside of *Gunsmoke,* hard as that may be to believe. Movie buffs will remember his B films of the late 1940s and early '50s, especially the 1951 sci-fi classic *The Thing* (in which he played the towering monster uncovered from beneath the arctic ice) and 1954's equally scary *Them.*

Jim grew up in Minneapolis, a withdrawn and uneasy lad due in part to his size. He fought in World War II as a combat infantryman and was wounded at Anzio in 1943. After the war he drifted to Hollywood, picking up odd jobs and bit parts in films (his first was in 1947), while leading a rather wild life with some buddies. He appeared on television a few times in the early 1950s, including an episode of *The Lone Ranger* in 1950 and *Lux Video Theatre* in 1954. The movie roles gradually began to get better, and when his friend and mentor John Wayne recommended him for the *Gunsmoke* role in 1955 Jim at first turned it down.

Wayne was furious at this ingratitude, so the story goes, and asked the young actor over to his house to talk about it. The two big men sat across a table, with a bottle between them, arguing into the night. Jim was afraid that a role in a TV western, which would probably flop (westerns weren't very popular then), would finish his budding film career. But Duke finally talked him into it and even agreed to appear on camera to introduce the first episode himself—guaranteeing a large tune-in for the first night.

Throughout the long years of *Gunsmoke*'s run, Arness was a dynamo on the set, having a raucous good time. Off the set he became known as one of Hollywood's most famous recluses, never appearing in public or on other programs of any kind. "Aloneness is absolutely essential to my life," he said at one point. "I can't see how people don't need it occasionally. I feel a need for it regularly." He bore tragedy silently—a divorce from his wife of many years in 1963, the suicide of his daughter in 1975.

By the time *Gunsmoke* was finally canceled in 1975, Jim was a wealthy man (he by then owned part of the show). Nevertheless he returned a few months later as Zeb Macahan in the TV movie *The Macahans* (January 1976), which led to the miniseries and series *How the West Was Won.* Later he played an older cop who had returned to the force on *McClain's Law.*

Jim is the brother of actor Peter Graves.

ARNETTE, JEANNETTA—actress
b: Jul 29, Washington, D.C.

Head of the Class (com)
.... Bernadette Meara (1986–)

ARNGRIM, ALISON—juvenile actress
b: 1962, New York City, N.Y. r: Los Angeles, Calif.

Little House on the Prairie (adv)
.... Nellie Oleson Dalton (1974–81)

ARNGRIM, STEFEN—juvenile actor
b: 1955

Land of the Giants (sci fi)
.... Barry Lockridge (1968–70)

Alison and Stefen are brother and sister.

ARNO, SIG—actor
b: 1895, Hamburg, Germany d: Aug 17, 1975

My Friend Irma (com)
.... Professor Kropotkin (1952–53)

German born actor who was best known for his comic roles as the haughty butler, the blustery waiter, or the blundering foreigner. He began his film career in Germany in the late 1920s, but left when the Nazis came to power in 1933. He was in many Hollywood movies in the 1940s and did some television work in the 1950s, including the role of Marie Wilson's nutty violin-playing neighbor in *My Friend Irma.*

ARNOLD, EDDY—country singer
b: May 15, 1918, near Henderson, Tenn.

The Eddy Arnold Show (var)
.... regular (1952–53)
Eddy Arnold Time (var) ..... host (1954–56)
The Eddy Arnold Show (var).... host (1956)
The Kraft Music Hall (var)...... host (1968)

A fabulously successful country crooner, sometimes known as the "Country Crosby," who dominated the field in the late 1940s and early '50s with hits like "Bouquet of Roses," "Any Time," and "That's How Much I Love You." He was the son of a Tennessee sharecropper and billed himself as The Tennessee Plowboy. Eddy was seen frequently on television variety shows during the 1950s, due no doubt in part to the efforts of his colorful man-

ager, Colonel Tom Parker (who later guided Elvis Presley to superstardom). Eddy made his network debut on Milton Berle's *Texaco Star Theater* in 1949. He hosted summer shows in 1952, 1953, and 1956 and starred in his own syndicated series from 1954–56.

Eddy's career declined somewhat with the advent of rock 'n' roll and its country counterpart, rockabilly. He came back strong in the 1960s, however, with an updated Nashville sound that often crossed over into the pop field; his biggest hit, in 1965, was "Make the World Go Away." Eddy continued to be seen on television during the 1960s and '70s, hosting specials, appearing on numerous telecasts of *The Kraft Music Hall* and even subbing for Johnny Carson on *The Tonight Show.*

He was elected to the Country Music Hall of Fame in 1966.

ARNOLD, JEANNE—actress

Cara Williams Show (com)
.... Mary Hammilmeyer (1964–65)

ARNOLD, MURRAY—pianist

Freddy Martin Show (var) ... pianist (1951)

ARNOLD, PAUL—folk singer, guitarist

America Song (music) .... host (1948–49)
The Paul Arnold Show (music)
.... host (1949–50)

ARQUETTE, CLIFF—comedian
b: Dec 28, 1905, Toledo, Ohio d: Sep 23, 1974

The RCA Victor Show (com)
.... Charley Weaver (1952–54)
Do It Yourself (com)
.... Charley Weaver (1955)
The Jack Paar Show (talk)
.... Charley Weaver (1958–62)
Hobby Lobby (com)
.... Charley Weaver (1959–60)
The Roy Rogers & Dale Evans Show (var)
.... Charley Weaver (1962)
Hollywood Squares (quiz)
.... Charley Weaver (1968)
The Jonathan Winters Show (var)
.... Charley Weaver (1968–69)

Cliff Arquette spent practically his entire TV career as someone else: folksy Charley

Weaver, the pudgy, yarn-spinning old-timer from Mount Idy. It was a character developed from years of experience playing old folks on radio. Arquette was born of show business parents. He started out to be a musician in the early 1920s, then moved into vaudeville, then broke into big time radio in the mid-1930s. Producers immediately recognized that he had a perfect "old" voice—though he was barely 30—and gave him many spots on popular variety and comedy shows over the next 15 years. He invariably played the comical old man or sometimes woman (e.g., the forgetful Mrs. Wilson on *The Dick Haymes Show*).

In early 1952 Cliff switched to television with a 15-minute daytime show called *Dave and Charley*, costarring Dave Willock. Cliff was now playing Charley Weaver, the bespectacled old-timer reading his letters from mom that told about the colorful characters back home. Charley was such a hit that Cliff took him to the nighttime *RCA Victor Show* in the fall—where he became Dennis Day's janitor—and later to a whole series of prime time comedy and quiz shows. Charley was probably best known for his appearances on Jack Paar's late-night show (aka *The Tonight Show*) from 1958–62, and for his long run in the 1960s and '70s on the daytime quiz *Hollywood Squares*, which was also seen at night for a time in 1968.

ARQUETTE, LEWIS—actor

The Marilyn McCoo and Billy Davis, Jr. Show (var) .... regular (1977)
The Waltons (drama)
.... J. D. Pickett (1978–81)

The son of comedian Cliff Arquette.

ARQUETTE, ROSANNA—actress
b: Aug 10, 1959, New York City, N.Y.

Shirley (com) .... Debra Miller (1979–80)

Petite daughter of actor Lewis Arquette and granddaughter of Cliff Arquette ("Charley Weaver"). Besides playing the teenage daughter on *Shirley*, Rosanna appeared in adolescent and young adult roles on a number of series episodes and TV movies in the late 1970s and '80s. She was nominated for an Emmy Award for her per-

formance in the TV movie *The Executioner's Song* in 1983.

ARRANGA, IRENE—actress

Welcome Back, Kotter (com)
.... Mary Johnson (1978–79)
Secrets of Midland Heights (drama)
.... Sue (1980–81)

ARTHUR, ALAN—reporter

Entertainment Tonight (news)
.... host/reporter (1983–84)

ARTHUR, BEATRICE—actress
b: May 13, 1923*, New York City, N.Y. r: Cambridge, Md.

Caesar's Hour (var) ...... regular (1956–57)
All in the Family (com)
.... Maude Findlay (occasional) (1971–72)
Maude (com)..... Maude Findlay (1972–78)
Amanda's (com)
.... Amanda Cartwright (1983)
Golden Girls (com)
.... Dorothy Zbornak (1985–)

Emmy Award: Best Actress in a Comedy Series, for *Maude* (1977)

Bea Arthur became an "overnight sensation" on television after 25 years on the New York stage. Her booming voice and forceful personality—which was perfect for reaching the back rows in a large theater—led naturally to the outspoken, abrasive, but always funny character that made her famous, Maude Findlay. Bea made her Broadway debut in a play called *Dog Beneath the Skin* in 1947. She gradually progressed from small parts to larger ones until, in the 1960s, she was starring in hits such as *Fiddler on the Roof* and *Mame*. The latter performance won her a Tony Award in 1966 and also a role in the movie version in 1973.

Bea had done some television work in the 1950s, including a season as a regular on Sid Caesar's comedy-variety show in 1956–57. However, it was not until she made some very funny guest appearances as Edith Bunker's loud, liberal cousin on *All in the Family* in 1971–72 that TV audiences suddenly discovered her. These guest shots led to her own series, *Maude*, which immediately became a top ten hit.

*Some sources give 1924 or 1926.

After its run, Bea continued to appear in TV specials and in 1983 she starred in another series, *Amanda's* (based on the British hit, *Fawlty Towers*). That one was short-lived, but two years later she was back, loud as ever, in the 1985 hit *Golden Girls*

ARTHUR, CAROL—actress

Dom DeLuise Show (var) .... regular (1968)

The wife of Dom DeLuise. She appeared in a few plays and movies over the years; for example, the 1975 film *The Sunshine Boys*.

ARTHUR, JEAN—actress
b: Oct 17, 1905, New York City, N.Y.

The Jean Arthur Show (com)
.... Patricia Marshall (1966)

This petite, throaty actress was a favorite in movie comedies of the 1930s and '40s. Her last film, *Shane*, was made in 1953. Twelve years later she came out of retirement to do a single episode of *Gunsmoke* and liked it so much she agreed to do her own situation comedy the following year (in which she donned a blonde wig to cover her snow-white hair). It's a wonder she turned up on TV at all. Though many of her films were box office and critical successes, she was always terribly uncertain of her own abilities and backed out of many commitments over the years. After her series she taught for a few years at Vassar College, then retired again to her California home which overlooks the sea.

ARTHUR, MAUREEN—actress
b: c. 1934, St. Louis, Mo.

Tonight (talk) .... regular (1956–57)
Holiday Lodge (com)
.... Dorothy Jackson (1961)
What's It All About, World? (var)
.... regular (1969)
Empire (com) .... Peg (1984)

ARVAN, JAN—actor
b: c. 1912 d: May 24, 1979

Zorro (wes) .... Nacho Torres (1957–59)
The Red Skelton Show (var)
.... regular (1970–71)

ASH, GLEN—actor

The New Andy Griffith Show (com)
.... Buff MacKnight (1971)

ASHBROOK, DAPHNE—actress
b: Jan 30, Long Beach, Calif.

Our Family Honor (drama)
.... Officer Liz McKay (1985–86)
Fortune Dane (police)
.... Kathy "Speed" Davenport (1986)

ASHBY, ALVAN—singer

The Lawrence Welk Show (music)
.... regular (1957–59)

ASHFORD, EMMETT—sports commentator

The Jacksons (var) .... regular (1977)

ASHLEY, JOHN—actor
b: Dec 25, 1934, Kansas City, Mo.

Straightaway (adv)
.... Clipper Hamilton (1961–62)

Handsome young actor who costarred in this series about racing drivers. He also appeared in a number of teen movies of the 1960s (*Beach Party, How to Stuff a Wild Bikini*).

ASHMORE, FRANK—actor

V (movie) (sci fi) .... Martin (1983)

ASHTON, JOHN—actor

Dallas (drama)... Willie Joe Garr (1978–79)
Breaking Away (com)....... Roy (1980–81)

Actor who appeared in both the movie and TV versions of *Breaking Away* as Roy, the young campus cop.

ASHTON, LAURA—actress

Berrengers (drama).... Laurel Hayes (1985)

ASKIN, LEON—actor
b: Sep 8, 1907, Vienna, Austria

The Charlie Farrell Show (com)
.... Pierre (1956)

Rotund character actor who came to the U.S. in 1940, did some theatrical work, then played foreign roles (evil and comic) in films of the 1950s and '60s. On *The Charlie Farrell Show* he was the chef, Pierre. Younger viewers may remember him for his occasional appearances on *Hogan's Heroes* as Burkhalter, the German General who was always trying to marry his sister Gertrude off to Colonel Klink.

ASNER, EDWARD—actor

b: Nov 15, 1929, Kansas City, Kan.

Slattery's People (drama)
.... Frank Radcliff (1964–65)
The Mary Tyler Moore Show (com)
.... Lou Grant (1970–77)
Rich Man, Poor Man—Book I (drama)
.... Axel Jordache (1976)
Roots (drama)......... Capt. Davies (1977)
Lou Grant (drama) .... Lou Grant (1977–82)
Off the Rack (com) ... Sam Waltman (1985)

Emmy Awards: Best Supporting Actor in a Comedy, for *The Mary Tyler Moore Show* (1971, 1972, 1975); Best Actor, Single Performance, for *Rich Man, Poor Man* (1976); Best Actor, Single Performance, for *Roots* (1977); Best Actor in a Drama Series, for *Lou Grant* (1978, 1980)

For gruff, paunchy Ed Asner, television fame did not come until he was into his forties, an expanding waistline, and his second series role. But when success came, it came in a big way. Asner won a shelf full of Emmys as one of the finest actors of the 1970s.

Born the youngest of five children, Ed was at first torn between drama and sports (he was an All-City tackle in high school) —finally, in college, drama won. He made his stage debut as Thomas à Becket in a college production of *Murder in the Cathedral* and after graduation pursued a stage career in Chicago (1953–55) and then New York. He appeared in a number of off-Broadway and Shakespearean Festival productions in the late '50s.

Broadway fame seemed elusive, however, so in 1961 Ed packed up and moved to Hollywood, beginning a busy career as a character actor in TV episodes and an occasional movie (his first being *The Satan Bug* in 1965). During the '60s he was seen in numerous episodes of *The Defenders, The Fugitive, The F.B.I.,* and other dramatic series. He also landed his first continuing role, that of the veteran political reporter (shades of things to come!) in the Richard Crenna series *Slattery's People*. The program lasted only about a year.

In 1970 grumpy Ed decided to try a different tack. Though he had been seen mostly in dramas up to this time, he was perfect as the hard-boiled but sentimental boss surrounded by the slightly daft newsroom crew at WJM-TV; the comedy role made him a star and brought three Emmys. By the time *The Mary Tyler Moore Show* ended its run, Ed could have his pick of roles. He chose to make a very unusual transition, taking the same character, editor Lou Grant, from a half-hour situation comedy to an hour-long dramatic show; Lou was now managing editor of a Los Angeles newspaper. *Lou Grant* proved to be a hit, too, and won additional honors both for himself and for the way the show dealt with important social issues. The series was finally canceled amid controversy. Its audience was undeniably declining, but Asner had by the early 1980s become publicly outspoken on behalf of liberal political causes. Some felt the real reason for the show's cancellation was that CBS believed Asner was using his fictional, TV-built image of an honest, crusading newspaperman to promote his own political views. Where did fiction end and reality begin?

Ed himself certainly had no qualms about exploiting his image. He was a leading activist in the actor's strike of 1980 and in 1981 was elected president of the Screen Actors Guild (the same position that launched Ronald Reagan on his political career). He was an outspoken and controversial leader, and there was much turmoil in the union.

After he became a star in the early 1970s, Ed's appearances outside his own series were limited mostly to TV movies and miniseries. Two of them, as the Jordache father in *Rich Man, Poor Man* and as the slave ship captain in *Roots,* won additional Emmys. In 1985 he starred as the grouchy (of course) boss in a small garment factory, but *Off the Rack* was well below the standards of his earlier efforts and quickly disappeared.

ASTAIRE, FRED—actor, dancer
b: May 10, 1899, Omaha, Neb. d: Jun 22, 1987

Alcoa Premiere (drama)
.... host/occasional star (1961–63)
It Takes a Thief (drama)
.... Alister Mundy (1969–70)

Emmy Awards: Best Single Performance by an actor, for the special *An evening with Fred Astaire* (1959); Best Performance in a Variety Program, for the special *Astaire Time* (1961); Best Actor in a Drama Special, for *A Family Upside Down* (1978)

This legendary Hollywood star of the '30s and '40s appeared in some very classy TV productions over the years. Television came relatively late in Fred Astaire's long career. He debuted on stage with his sister Adele at the age of ten, and the young brother and sister act went on to become a top dancing team on Broadway and in vaudeville from the late 1910s to the early 1930s. When Adele retired in 1931 to marry an English Lord, Fred decided to try Hollywood. The now-famous report on his 1933 screen test read: "Can't act . . . can't sing . . . can dance a little." Despite this classic bit of misjudgment, Astaire quickly became one of the most popular and best-loved stars Hollywood has ever known, with a string of smash hit musicals including *Flying Down to Rio* and *Swing Time*.

Fred's first television appearance was in February 1954, on Ed Sullivan's *Toast of the Town*. He made his dramatic debut in 1957 on *General Electric Theater* (two years before his first dramatic movie role, in *On the Beach*), and from 1961–63 he was the debonair host and occasional star of *Alcoa Premiere*. For a truly memorable evening, however, nothing could surpass his October 1958 NBC special "An Evening With Fred Astaire." Joined by dancing partner Barrie Chase and the Jonah Jones Quartet, Fred and producer Bud Yorkin spun an hour of pure magic that won nine Emmy Awards and led to two similar specials in 1959 and 1960.

Astaire was seen occasionally in the 1960s. Among his appearances were a multipart story on *Dr. Kildare* in 1965, another well-received musical special in 1968, and a season as Robert Wagner's seldom-seen father on *It Takes a Thief*. In the '70s he turned entirely to acting and was rarely seen on TV, except for such notable programs as the award-winning TV movie *A Family Upside Down* in 1978.

He was a longtime horse racing enthusiast and owner of several prizewinners. In 1980 he made headlines when he married a lady jockey half his age (Robyn Smith, 36). His two children—who were older than their new stepmother—were by his first wife, Phyllis, who died in 1954.

Fred's autobiography, *Steps in Time,* was published in 1959.

ASTIN, JOHN—actor, director
b: Mar 30, 1930, Baltimore, Md.

I'm Dickens—He's Fenster (com)
.... Harry Dickens (1962–63)
The Addams Family (com)
.... Gomez Addams (1964–66)
The Pruitts of Southampton (com)
.... Rudy Pruitt (1967)
Operation Petticoat (com)
... Lt. Cmdr. Matthew Sherman (1977–78)
Mary (com).......... Ed LaSalle (1985–86)

A tall, smiling comic actor whose chief claim to fame is his role as husband Gomez in the hit 1960s situation comedy *The Addams Family.* He began on the New York stage in the '50s in *The Three Penny Opera, Major Barbara,* and other plays, then broke into movies in the early '60s. His greatest success was on TV, however. In addition to his regular series roles, he appeared during the '60s and '70s in scores of episodes of other programs, mostly comedies. One of his more notable appearances was on *Batman* as The Riddler. Astin is also a director, responsible for episodes of *Night Gallery, Holmes and Yoyo, CHiPs,* and other series.

He was formerly married to actress Patty Duke Astin.

ASTIN, MACKENZIE—juvenile actor
b: 1973

The Facts of Life (com)
.... Andy Moffet (1985–)

The son of John and Patty Duke Astin.

ASTIN, PATTY DUKE—actress
b: Dec 14, 1947, New York City, N.Y.

The Patty Duke Show (com)
.... Patty/Cathy Lane (1963–66)

Captains and the Kings (drama)
.... Bernadette Hennessey Armagh (1976)
It Takes Two (com) . Molly Quinn (1982–83)
Hail to the Chief (com)
.... Pres. Julia Mansfield (1985)

Emmy Awards: Best Single Performance by an Actress, for *My Sweet Charlie* (1970); Best Actress in a Limited Series, for *Captains and the Kings* (1977); Best Actress in a Special, for *The Miracle Worker* (1980)

This onetime child actress has been a star of stage, film, and television. She made her film debut at age eight; she was an extra in *I'll Cry Tomorrow* (1955) and *Somebody Up There Likes Me* (1956). By 1957 she was appearing on TV playhouse series such as *Kraft Television Theatre, Armstrong Circle Theatre,* and (in 1958) *The U.S. Steel Hour.* Little Patty also did TV commercials and appeared briefly in the 1958 daytime serial *Kitty Foyle.*

The role that made her a star—at 12— was that of young Helen Keller in the Broadway play *The Miracle Worker;* three years later she won an Academy Award for the film version. Although most of her success to this point had been in dramas, young Patty decided in 1963 to try TV comedy, with an unusual dual role as teenage twins. *The Patty Duke Show* ran for three years and won her an Emmy nomination.

After a relatively dry period during the late 1960s, Patty became active again in the '70s, with increasingly frequent appearances in TV series episodes and especially in TV movies. She received her first Emmy for the 1970 TV film *My Sweet Charlie* and garnered others for the 1976 miniseries *Captains and the Kings* and a 1979 TV version of *The Miracle Worker* (this time she played Helen Keller's adult teacher and friend Anne Sullivan). Other notable appearances in *Having Babies* (1978), *The Women's Room* (1980), *Please Don't Hit Me, Mom* (about child abuse, 1981) and the miniseries *George Washington* (as Martha, 1984). She continued to try situation comedy, but with less success; neither *It Takes Two* in 1982 nor *Hail to the Chief* in 1985 (in which she played the first woman President of the U.S.) lasted long.

ATELL, ANTOINETTE (TOAD)—actress

Laugh-In (revival) (var) ... regular (1977–78)

ATES, ROSCOE—actor
b: Jan 20, 1892*, Grange, Miss. d: Mar 1, 1962

The Marshal of Gunsight Pass (wes)
.... Dep. Roscoe (1950)

Dopey-faced, bug-eyed comic sidekick who made many films in the 1930s and '40s —especially westerns. Though he cured himself of a real-life stutter as a youngster, he found stammering a useful device in many of his comedy roles. He appeared in episodes of various TV shows (including several times on *Alfred Hitchcock Presents*) during the 1950s.

ATHERTON, WILLIAM—actor
b: Jul 30, 1947, New Haven, Conn.

Centennial (drama)..... Jim Lloyd (1978–79)

ATKIN, HARVEY—actor
b: Canada

Cagney & Lacey (police)
...... Desk Sgt. Ronald Coleman (1982–)

ATKINS, CHET—guitar player
b: Jun 20, 1924, Luttrell, Tenn.

Grand Ole Opry (music) .. regular (1955–56)
Eddy Arnold Show (var) ..... regular (1956)

Chet Atkins is one of the legends of the country music field, as an artist, producer, and recording executive. He picked guitar for practically every big name that recorded in Nashville, from Hank Williams to Perry Como and Elvis Presley, and also had many best-selling LPs of his own. Early in his career he recorded as a singer; he later tried to locate and destroy the master recordings from these sessions! A shy man on camera, Chet made infrequent TV appearances, mostly on country music shows.

ATKINS, CHRISTOPHER—actor
b: Feb 21, 1961, Rye, N.Y.

Dallas (drama).... Peter Richards (1983–84)
Rock 'n' Roll Summer Action (var)
.... host (1985)

Young, blond-haired Adonis who got his first big break as the teen heartthrob play-

*Some sources give 1894 or 1895.

ing opposite Brooke Shields in the 1980 movie *The Blue Lagoon*.

ATKINS, TOM—actor
b: Nov 13, Pittsburgh, Pa.

The Rockford Files (drama)
.... Lt. Alex Diehl (1974–76)
Serpico (police) .... Tom Sullivan (1976–77)

ATTERBURY, MALCOLM—actor
b: Feb 20, 1907, Philadelphia, Pa.

Thicker Than Water (com)
.... Jonas Paine (1973)
Apple's Way (drama)
.... Grandfather Aldon (1974–75)

ATWATER, EDITH—actress
b: Aug 22, 1911, Chicago, Ill. d: Mar 14, 1986

Love on A Rooftop (com)
.... Phyllis Hammond (1966–67)
The Hardy Boys Mysteries (adv)
.... Aunt Gertrude (1977–78)
Kaz (drama) .... Illsa Fogel (1978–79)

Wife of character actor Kent Smith.

AUBERJONOIS, RENÉ—actor
b: Jun 1, 1940, New York City, N.Y.

Benson (com)
.... Clayton Endicott III (1980–86)

A supporting actor who did mostly stage work during the 1960s (winning a Tony Award for his supporting role in *Coco*), then began appearing in TV movies and series episodes in the 1970s. On *Benson* he played the tall, officious governor's aide. A descendant of French aristocrats—his mother would be a princess if the French still had such titles—René taught drama at several colleges, in addition to pursuing his own acting career.

AUBUCHON, JACQUES—actor

Paris 7000 (adv)....... Jules Maurois (1970)

AUERBACH, ARTIE—comedian

The Jack Benny Show (com)
.... regular (1950–65)

An old-time comedian who was for many years featured on Benny's radio show as the word-garbling Jewish man, Mr. Kitzel.

AUNT GRACE—hostess

Birthday Party (child) .... host (1948)

One of the minor mysteries of early TV, this unknown lady for a time cohosted an early-evening birthday party for children on the DuMont network.

AUSTIN, AL—actor

The Investigators (drama)
.... Bill Davis (1961)

AUSTIN, BOB—

Country Style (var)......... regular (1950)

AUSTIN, KAREN—actress
b: Oct 24, Welch, W. Va.

The Quest (adv)....... Carrie Welby (1982)
Night Court (com)
.... Court Clerk Lana Wagner (1984)

AUSTIN, NANCY—

The Jimmie Rodgers Show (var)
.... regular (1969)

AUSTIN, TERI—actress
b: Apr 17, 1959, Toronto, Canada

Knots Landing (drama)
.... Jill Bennett (1985–)

AUTRY, GENE—actor, singer
b: Sep 29, 1907, Tioga, Texas

Gene Autry Show (wes)
.... as himself (1950–56)

The famous cowboy star of the 1930s and '40s was a fixture on television in the 1950s. Like several other screen cowboys (Roy Rogers, Hopalong Cassidy), he realized that his young fans were abandoning the Saturday afternoon matinees to watch television at home, so he followed them there. *The Gene Autry Show* was the video version of his long-running radio series *Gene Autry's Melody Ranch* (1940–56), and it stressed the same Ten Commandments of Good Behavior for boys and girls.

After it left the air, Gene retired from

performing (except for a brief syndicated series in 1966) and began multiplying his accumulated wealth into a veritable business empire. His Flying A Productions, founded to produce his own show, turned out such popular western fare as *The Range Rider, Annie Oakley,* and *The Adventures of Champion* (his horse). He assembled a chain of radio and television stations, with the flagship being giant KTLA-TV in Los Angeles, started a record label (Challenge), a hotel chain, and in 1962 cofounded the Los Angeles Angels (later California Angels) pro baseball team. An astute businessman, he was by 1980 rated as one of the ten richest men in California.

His TV sidekick, Pat Buttram, once reminisced about his 15 years with Gene Autry as follows: "We made over 100 westerns together. At the end of each picture Gene would ride off into the sunset. Now he owns it."

Ina, his wife of 48 years, died in 1980; Gene (age 74) then married a 39-year-old lady banker. His autobiography is titled *Back in the Saddle Again* (1978).

AVALON, FRANKIE—singer
b: Sep 18, 1939*, Philadelphia, Pa.

Easy Does It . . . Starring Frankie Avalon (var)
.... host (1976)

During the late '50s and early '60s, Frankie Avalon had many hit records which might be classified as "soft rock" (or "wimp rock," depending on your point of view). He was on television long before that, however, appearing fairly frequently from the early '50s on. At first it was as a child-prodigy trumpet player on variety shows, including those of Jackie Gleason, Ray Anthony and Paul Whiteman. Then, during his years as a teenage record star, he was seen frequently on Dick Clark's shows and other pop music showcases. The story goes that he created the unique nasal effect on his first hit, "Dede Dinah," by holding his nose during the recording session. There is no record of how he recreated this effect on camera.

In the later '60s and '70s Frankie turned to acting, in movies and in episodes of some TV series—*Burke's Law, It Takes a Thief,* and *Love, American Style* among

*Some sources give 1940.

them. By the 1980s he was seen primarily on the supper club circuit.

AVALOS, LUIS—actor
b: Sep 2, Havana, Cuba r: New York City

Highcliffe Manor (com) . Dr. Sanchez (1979)
Condo (com) .... Jesse Rodriguez (1983)
E/R (com) .. Dr. Thomas Esquivel (1984–85)
I Had Three Wives (drama)
.... Lt. Gomez (1985)

A Hispanic actor well-known to kids as Dr. Doolots and Pedro (among others) on the PBS children's series *The Electric Company,* on which he appeared for ten years. He began concentrating on commercial TV in the 1980s.

AVEDON, DOE—actress
b: 1926, Old Westbury, N.Y.

Big Town (drama) . Diane Walker (1955–56)

AVERA, TOM—actor

Admiral Broadway Revue (var)
.... regular (1949)
Your Show of Shows (var) ... regular (1950)

AVERBACK, HY—producer, director, actor
b: 1920*, Minneapolis, Minn. r: Los Angeles

Tonight (talk) .... regular (1955)
Our Miss Brooks (com) . Mr. Romero (1956)
NBC Comedy Hour (var)..... regular (1956)

Hy Averback began his career as a radio announcer in the 1940s, with Bob Hope, Jack Benny, Jack Paar, and other top stars. He later worked as an actor in a few TV series and films (including *The Benny Goodman Story*) before changing careers and becoming one of TV's most successful comedy directors. Among his many directing credits are numerous episodes of *The Real McCoys, F Troop, The Brothers,* and *M*A*S*H* (for which he was twice nominated for an Emmy Award for best directing).

AVERY, PHYLLIS—actress
b: Nov 14, 1924, New York City, N.Y.

*Some sources give 1925, though this would have made him one of the youngest network radio announcers ever known!

The Ray Milland Show (com)
...... Peggy McNutley/McNulty (1953–55)
George Gobel Show (var) ... Alice (1958–59)
Mr. Novak (drama)
.... Ruth Wilkinson (1964–65)

Following her retirement, Ray Milland's and George Gobel's TV "wife" became a real estate agent in Los Angeles.

AVERY, TOL—actor
d: 1973

The Thin Man (drama)
.... Lt. Steve King (1957–58)
Slattery's People (drama)
.... Speaker Bert Metcalf (1964–65)

AVRAMO, PETER—juvenile actor

A Date with Judy (com)
.... Randolph Foster (1952–53)

AXTON, HOYT—singer, actor
b: Mar 25, 1938, Duncan, Okla.

The Rousters (adv)
.... Cactus Jack Slade (1983–84)
Domestic Life (com) ...... Rip Steele (1984)

Prior to the 1970s burly Hoyt Axton was known primarily as a folksinger and songwriter; among his compositions was Three Dog Night's 1971 hit "Joy to the World." (He came from a musical family—his mother Mae co-wrote Elvis Presley's 1956 multimillion-seller "Heartbreak Hotel.") In the late 1970s Hoyt began appearing in supporting roles in films such as *The Black Stallion* and on TV.

AYERS-ALLEN, PHYLICIA—black actress
b: June 19, 1948, Houston, Texas

The Cosby Show (com)
.... Clair Huxtable (1984–)

The older sister of actress Debbie Allen. She was formerly a regular on the daytime serial *One Life to Live*, in 1983–84. In 1986 she married athlete Amad Rashad and changed her professional billing to Phylicia Rashad.

AYKROYD, DAN—comedian, writer
b: Jul 1, 1952, Ottawa, Canada

NBC's Saturday Night Live (com)
.... regular (1975–79)

Emmy Award: Best Writing for a Comedy Series, for *NBC's Saturday Night Live* (1977)

During the heyday of *Saturday Night Live*, Danny Aykroyd was known primarily as John Belushi's offscreen buddy and on-screen partner in such sketches as "The Blues Brothers," and "The Bees," and in several of Belushi's movies. Always the more thoughtful and disciplined of the two, he remained in Belushi's shadow until the latter's untimely death. Aykroyd's considerable individual talents have since become apparent, especially as co-writer and costar of the smash hit 1984 movie *Ghostbusters*. He is an alumnus of the Toronto Second City comedy troupe and starred in the Canadian TV series *Coming Up Rosie* before joining *Saturday Night Live*.

AYRES, LEAH—actress
b: May 28, Baltimore, Md.

9 to 5 (com)........ Linda Bowman (1983)

Leah was a regular on the daytime serial *The Edge of Night* in the early 1980s.

AYRES, LEW—actor
b: Dec 28, 1908, Minneapolis, Minn.

Frontier Justice (wes).......... host (1958)
Lime Street (drama)
.... Henry Wade Culver (1985)

A veteran Hollywood actor who first came to fame as the sensitive young soldier with pacifist leanings in *All Quite on the Western Front* in 1930 and later starred as young Dr. Kildare in the *Kildare* movie series of the 1930s. Lew's own strong antiwar feelings made headlines and seriously hurt his career when he refused to fight in World War II—a very unpopular stand at the time (he spent the war as a medic and assistant chaplain). He made a few more films in the late 1940s and early '50s, then turned to television. He acted in many series episodes over the years, but never in a continuing role until *Lime Street* in 1985.

A deeply religious man, Lew produced and narrated a number of religious films, including *Altars of the East* (1955). Appropriately enough, he portrayed Noah in the

1978 TV production *Greatest Heroes of the Bible.*

AYRES, MITCHELL—orchestra leader
b: Dec 24, 1910, Milwaukee, Wisc. r: New York City, N.Y. d: Sep 5, 1969

The Chesterfield Supper Club (var)
.... orch. leader (1948–50)
The Perry Como Show (var)
.... orch. leader (1950–61)
TV's Top Tunes (music)
.... orch. leader (1951)
TV's Top Tunes (music)
.... orch. leader (1955)
The Julius La Rosa Show (var)
.... orch. leader (1957)
Perry Presents (var) .... orch. leader (1959)
Kraft Music Hall (var)
.... orch. leader (1961–63)
The Hollywood Palace (var)
.... orch. leader (1964–69)
The King Family Show (var)
.... orch. leader (1965–66)
The John Gary Show (var)
.... orch. leader (1966)

The Milton Berle Show (var)
.... orch. leader (1966–67)

Although Mitchell Ayres was one of TV's busiest conductors in the 1950s and '60s, he was best known as Perry Como's orchestra leader on radio, TV, and records. He began as a violinist in the 1930s and fronted his own "sweet" band in the late 1930s and early '40s, before linking up with Como in the late 1940s. They were a perfect match: Ayres' tasteful, melodious, full orchestra backing and Como's smooth crooning. After Como left series television, Mitch continued on other family-oriented variety shows. He was struck and killed by a car in Las Vegas in 1969.

AZZARA, CANDY—actress
b: May 18, 1947, Brooklyn, N.Y.

Calucci's Department (com)
.... Shirley Balukis (1973)
Rhoda (com) .... Alice Barth (1974–75)
Soap (com) .... Millie (1979)

B

BABCOCK, BARBARA—actress
b: Feb 27, 1937

Dallas (drama)........ Liz Craig (1978–82)
Hill Street Blues (police)
.... Grace Gardner (1981–85)
The Four Seasons (com)
.... Lorraine Elliot (1984)
Mr. Sunshine (com)
.... Mrs. June Swinford (1986)

Emmy Award: Best Actress in a Drama Series, for "Fecund Hand Rose" episode of Hill Street Blues (1981)

Barbara Babcock has been active in television since the mid-1960s, but did not really come into her own until she began playing mature woman roles 15 years later —especially that of Sergeant Esterhaus' passionate love interest in Hill Street Blues. She also appeared in a few films (including Bang the Drum Slowly) and Broadway plays (Auntie Mame) in the 1970s and '80s.

BABSON, THOMAS—actor

240-Robert (adv) .... Terry (1979–80)

BACCALA, DONNA—actress

The Survivors (drama)
.... Marguerita (1969–70)

BACH, CATHERINE—actress
b: Mar 1, 1954, Warren, Ohio

The Dukes of Hazzard (com)
.... Daisy Duke (1979–85)

Sexpot actress whose character on Dukes of Hazzard was rather obviously patterned on Li'l Abner's skimpily clad Daisy Mae. She also had a few minor roles decorating TV series episodes and films in the 1970s and '80s—including Burt Reynolds' Hustle and Cannonball Run II.

BACKES, ALICE—actress
b: May 17, Salt Lake City, Utah

Bachelor Father (com)..... Vickie (1957–58)

BACKUS, HENNY—actress

Blondie (com)...... Cora Dithers (1968–69)

Wife of Jim Backus, who starred as Mr. Dithers in this version of Blondie.

BACKUS, JIM—actor
b: Feb 25, 1913, Cleveland, Ohio

Hollywood House (var) ... regular (1949–50)
I Married Joan (com)
.... Judge Bradley Stevens (1952–55)
The Jim Backus Show (com)
.... Mike O'Toole (1960)
Talent Scouts (talent)........... host (1962)
Famous Adventures of Mr. Magoo (cartn)
.... voice of Mr. Magoo (1964–65)
Gilligan's Island (com)
.... Thurston Howell III (1964–67)
Continental Showcase (var)..... host (1966)
Blondie (com)....... J. C. Dithers (1968–69)

Jim Backus had one of the most famous voices on television. For millions of kids he will always be the ever-incredulous, incredibly nearsighted Mr. Magoo, as well as the pompous Thurston Howell III of Gilligan's Island.

His comic voice served him well during a long career in radio, television, and films. He began on stage, none too successfully, then hit his stride on radio in the mid-1930s, where he became a favorite for his many (mostly comic) voices. Probably his most famous radio creation, on The Alan Young Show, was Hubert Updyke, a man so unbelievably rich he once sold his Cadillac because it was headed in the wrong direction.

Backus came to television in the late 1940s as cohost of a short-lived variety show Hollywood House, then scored his first major hit as Joan Davis' husband on I Married Joan. Thereafter he was frequently seen, on series ranging from Studio One in the 1950s to a delectable episode of Maverick in 1961 (in which he parodied Lorne Greene in a hilarious takeoff on Bonanza) to Fantasy Island in the 1980s. Along the way he did a number of Magoo Christmas (and other) specials and assorted revivals and cartoon versions of Gilligan's Island. He also had his own syndicated comedy series in 1960—The Jim Backus Show (aka Hot off the Wire)—in which he played the editor of a failing newspaper.

Occasionally, for a change of pace, he would turn up in a serious role. Perhaps the most notable was that of James Dean's worried father in the classic 1955 film *Rebel Without a Cause.*

Jim's memoirs were published in 1965 with the title *Only When I Laugh.*

BADDELEY, HERMIONE—actress
b: Nov 13, 1906, Broseley, Shropshire, England
d: Aug 19, 1986

Camp Runamuck (com)
.... Eulalia Divine (1965–66)
The Good Life (com)
.... Grace Dutton (1971–72)
Maude (com)
.... Mrs. Nell Naugatuck (1974–77)

Ribald British comedienne who was seen mostly on stage until the 1940s, but made many films and did a fair amount of television after that in both England and the United States. Her rubber features have long delighted audiences. George Bernard Shaw, upon seeing her perform, once advised: "Change your name from Baddeley to Goodeley."

On TV she played an assortment of roles, including the stuffy girls' camp owner on *Camp Runamuck*, the stuck-up boss's sister on *The Good Life*, and Bea Arthur's hard-drinking maid on *Maude.* She also did a two-part *Batman* episode in 1968.

Her sister, Angela Baddeley, is familiar to TV viewers as Mrs. Bridges, the cook on PBS's *Upstairs, Downstairs.*

BADEL, ALAN—actor
b: Sep 11, 1923, Manchester, England d: Mar 9, 1982

Shogun (drama) .... Father Dell'Aqua (1980)

BADLER, JANE—actress
r: Long Island, N.Y.

V (movie) (sci fi) .... Diana (1983)
V: The Final Battle (miniseries) (sci fi)
.... Diana (1984)
V (sci fi)................. Diana (1984–85)

Jane Badler, the deliciously evil alien commander on *V*, was a onetime winner of the Miss New Hampshire pageant (at age 17) and an actress in commercials. She came to national attention as the neurotic Melinda on the daytime soap opera *One Life to Live,* and she was also seen on daytime's *The Doctors* for a time. She then tried out for a role on *The A-Team,* lost out, but got the juicy part in *V* instead. Too bad. An episode in which the *A-Team's* heroes met the snarling, gerbil-swallowing lizard Diana would have been something to see!

BAER, MAX, JR.—actor
b: Dec 4, 1937, Oakland, Calif.

The Beverly Hillbillies (com)
.... Jethro Bodine (1962–71)
The Beverly Hillbillies (com)
.... Jethrene Bodine (1962–63)

Son of the heavyweight boxing champion of the 1930s. Max, Jr., achieved national fame as the big, dumb Jethro on the number-one hit comedy of the 1960s, *The Beverly Hillbillies* (he also played Jethro's sister Jethrene during the first season). Finding himself typecast after the series ended its run, he later turned to producing and directing, with the films *Ode to Billy Joe* (1976) and *Hometown U.S.A.* (1979) among his credits.

BAER, PARLEY—actor

The Adventures of Ozzie & Harriet (com)
.... Darby (1955–61)
The Andy Griffith Show (com)
.... Mayor Stoner (1962–63)
Double Life of Henry Phyfe (com)
.... Mr. Hamble (1966)

Parley Baer was a character actor who was very active in radio in the 1940s and '50s; perhaps his best-known role was that of Chester in the radio version of *Gunsmoke,* from 1952 to 1961. He also played small parts in several dozen films of the 1950s and '60s and was seen in a variety of occasional television roles. Among the latter were the insurance agent on *The Addams Family,* Mayor Stoner on *The Andy Griffith Show,* Don Rickles' boss on *The Don Rickles Show,* and Simon Legree in the PBS production of "The Plot to Overthrow Christmas" in 1971.

BAGDASARIAN, ROSS—actor, songwriter

b: Jan 27, 1919, Fresno, Calif. d: Jan 16, 1972

The Alvin Show (cartn)
voices of David Seville and the Chipmunks (1961–62)

This talented young man had a varied but minor career in show business prior to one fateful day in 1958. A first cousin of playwright William Saroyan, he had coauthored (with Saroyan) the 1951 song hit "Come On-a My House" and had some supporting roles in films (he played the songwriter in *Rear Window*).

That all changed one day in 1958 when he began fiddling with the controls on his tape recorder, trying to come up with a new sound for a novelty record. The result was a series of speeded-up voices on a tune he called "The Witch Doctor," which, to everyone's surprise, was a smash hit. He then decided to try a follow-up Christmas record with *three* speeded-up voices—which he called the "Chipmunks"—together with his own natural voice as the little fellows' harried manager. He called himself David Seville on these recordings.

From such foolery sprang the rest of his life's work. Chipmunk novelties, comics, and eventually an animated TV series all followed. Twenty years later, in the 1980s, the imaginary little creatures also provided a living for Ross's son, Ross, Jr., in a new Saturday morning series called *Alvin & the Chipmunks* and some rather bizarre Chipmunk LPs of disco, punk rock, and other music.

BAGGETTA, VINCENT—actor

b: Dec 7, 1947, Paterson, N.J.

Eddie Capra Mysteries (drama)
.... Eddie Capra (1978–79)
Chicago Story (drama)
.... Lou Pellegrino (1982)

A dark, intense actor whose first major television role was that of Dr. Peter Chernak on the daytime soap opera *Love Is a Many Splendored Thing* in the early 1970s. He later moved on to occasional prime time and stage work.

BAILEY, BILL—host

Cactus Jim (child) .... Cactus Jim (1951)
Old American Barn Dance (music)
.... emcee (1953)

BAILEY, DAVID—actor

Temperatures Rising (com)
.... Dr. David Amherst (1972–73)

BAILEY, F. LEE—lawyer, host

b: June 10, 1933, Waltham, Mass.

Good Company (int)............ host (1967)
Whodunnit? (quiz).......... panelist (1979)
Lie Detector (aud par) .... host (1983)

Celebrated trial lawyer and author *(The Defense Never Rests)* F. Lee Bailey appeared fairly frequently on television from the 1960s on. He also offered legal advice on *Good Morning, America* and lent himself to some rather diverse entertainment formats—as a celebrity interviewer on *Good Company,* a crime-guessing panelist on *Whodunnit?,* and an inquisitor trying to determine if well-known people were lying on *Lie Detector.*

BAILEY, G. W.—actor

b: Aug 27, Port Arthur, Texas

*M*A*S*H* (com)
.... Sgt. Luther Rizzo (1981–83)
St. Elsewhere (drama)
.... Dr. Hugh Beale (1982–83)
Goodnight, Beantown (com)
.... Albert Addelson (1983–84)

BAILEY, HILLARY—actress

b: Boston, Mass.

No Soap, Radio (com) .... Karen (1982)

BAILEY, JACK—host

b: Sep 15, 1907, Hampton, Iowa d: Feb 1, 1980

Place the Face (quiz) ...... emcee (1953–54)
Truth or Consequences (quiz)
.... emcee (1954–56)

Jack Bailey was a popular game show host on both radio and television in the 1940s and '50s. He is probably best remembered for his long association with the daytime show *Queen for a Day,* beginning on radio in 1945 and including its TV run from 1956–64.

BAILEY, PEARL—black singer
b: Mar 29, 1918, Newport News, Va.

The Pearl Bailey Show (var)
.... hostess (1971)
Silver Spoons (com) .. Lulu Baker (1984–85)

Emmy Award: Best Actress in a Children's Special, for the *ABC Afterschool Special* "Cindy Eller: A Modern Fairy Tale" (1986)

A preacher's daughter, Pearl Bailey became an earthy, witty jazz singer who was a familiar face on television from the late 1940s on. An early appearance was as a guest on the very first telecast of Milton Berle's *Texaco Star Theater* in June 1948. She is known for her quips. Her famous response to a question about how it felt to have been both up and down in show business: "Honey, I've been rich and I've been poor, and rich is better!"

Pearlie Mae started her career in cabarets and onstage in the 1940s and also made a few movies over the years. In 1968 she won a Tony Award for her role in the all-black stage revival of *Hello Dolly*. In 1984 she turned up in a rare acting role as Lulu on the comedy *Silver Spoons*. Her autobiography, published in 1968, is titled *The Raw Pearl*.

BAILEY, RAYMOND—actor
b: 1904, San Francisco, Calif. d: Apr 15, 1980

My Sister Eileen (com)
.... Mr. Beaumont (1960–61)
The Many Loves of Dobie Gillis (com)
.... Dean Magruder (1961–63)
The Beverly Hillbillies (com)
.... Milton Drysdale (1962–71)

BAIN, BARBARA—actress
b: Sep 13, 1931, Chicago, Ill.

Richard Diamond, Private Detective (drama)
.... Karen Wells (1959)
Mission: Impossible (drama)
.... Cinnamon Carter (1966–69)
Space 1999 (sci fi)
.... Dr. Helena Russell (1975–77)

Emmy Award: Best Actress in a Dramatic Series, for *Mission: Impossible* (1967, 1968, 1969)

Barbara Bain broke into TV in the late 1950s and was seen fairly regularly during the early and mid 1960s on episodes of series such as *Perry Mason, Hawaiian Eye, Wagon Train,* and *The Dick Van Dyke Show* (where she played, in a flashback, Dick's pushy girlfriend before he met Mary Tyler Moore). Her considerable success on *Mission: Impossible* seemed to spoil her, however. After quitting the show (together with her actor-husband Martin Landau) in a contract dispute, she was seen only occasionally in subsequent years.

BAIN, CONRAD—actor
b: Feb 4, 1923, Lethbridge, Alberta, Canada

Maude (com).. Dr. Arthur Harmon (1972–78)
Diff'rent Strokes (com)
.... Philip Drummond (1978–86)

Sometimes it pays to happen to have the right person in your audience. Conrad Bain was an obscure Canadian actor who had been playing small roles on the stage for 20 years when producer Norman Lear noticed him in a New York production and remembered him. Subsequently, Lear cast him as Bea Arthur's next-door neighbor in his new comedy, *Maude,* and Bain suddenly became a famous face to viewers across America. Prior to this, Bain's TV appearances had been infrequent, limited to a few dramatic shows such as *Studio One* and *The Defenders. Maude* lasted six years, and when it ended, Lear—obviously a fan —gave him another plum part, that of Gary Coleman's understanding father in *Diff'rent Strokes,* a series that lasted even longer.

The smiling, friendly Bain claims he is not really like Phil Drummond, although he is a dedicated family man ("Nothing in life compares to raising my three kids"). A rather different role for him was that of the head of a group of Arizona polygamists in the 1981 TV movie *Child Bride of Short Creek.*

BAIO, JIMMY—actor
b: Mar 15, 1963, Brooklyn, N.Y.

Joe and Sons (com)... Nick Vitale (1975–76)
Soap (com) .... Billy Tate (1977–81)

Chubby younger brother of Joey Baio. Jimmy played teenage roles in the '70s.

BAIO, JOEY—actor

The Hero (com) ... Burton Gilman (1966–67)

Brother of Jimmy. After a brief career playing juvenile roles in the 1960s, Joey studied law and became an attorney in Manhattan in the 1980s.

BAIO, SCOTT—actor
b: Sep 22, 1961, Brooklyn, N.Y.

Blansky's Beauties (com)
.... Anthony DeLuca (1977)
Happy Days (com)
.... Chachi Arcola (1977–84)
Who's Watching the Kids? (com)
.... Frankie "the Fox" Vitola (1978)
We're Movin' (mag) .... host (1981)
Joanie Loves Chachi (com)
.... Chachi Arcola (1982–83)
Charles in Charge (com). Charles (1984–85)

A cousin of juvenile actors Jimmy and Joey Baio, Scott started out as a model in children's clothing ads. Older cousin Joey (by then a law student) got the handsome youngster an agent who began lining up acting roles. Scott's specialty became that of the cocky, wisecracking young operator who was perhaps not so sure of himself as he seemed. He played this type of character on *Blansky's Beauties* and on *Who's Watching the Kids?*, but it was on *Happy Days* that he perfected it —and became a teen idol—as the young cousin who idolized Fonzie (Henry Winkler). Scott later had his own short-lived spin-off series, *Joanie Loves Chachi,* and appeared on numerous specials, including several with social messages for youngsters—*The Boy Who Drank Too Much,* 1980; *Stoned,* 1980 (for which he received an Emmy Award nomination); and *Run, Don't Walk,* about a youthful paraplegic, in 1981.

BAIRD, BIL—puppeteer
b: Aug 15, 1904, Grand Island, Neb. d: Mar 18, 1987

The Jack Paar Show (talk)
.... semiregular (1957–58)

BAKALYAN, DICK—actor

Dean Martin Presents Bobby Darin (var)
.... regular (1972)

The Bobby Darin Show (var)
.... regular (1973)

BAKEN, BONNIE—actress

Mixed Doubles (drama)
.... Elaine Coleman (1949)

BAKER, ANN—juvenile actress
b: c. 1932, Sedalia, Mo.

Meet Corliss Archer (com)
.... Corliss Archer (1954–55)

BAKER, ART—host
b: Jan 7, 1898, New York City, N.Y. d: Aug 26, 1966

You Asked for It (aud par) ... host (1950–58)
The End of the Rainbow (aud par)
.... emcee (1958)

Genial, silver-haired Art Baker lost one big chance for fame, but then got another just a few years later. The son of a woman who ran a settlement house for the poor on New York's Bowery, Art became a traveling evangelical worker in the 1920s, touring the country for ten years. He then tried his hand at selling refrigerators during the Depression, and when that failed went to work as a tour guide and lecturer at Los Angeles' gaudy Forest Lawn Cemetery. He moved into radio in the late 1930s and became successful as a host and announcer on a succession of talk and variety shows (including Bob Hope's).

Art lost his first big chance for fame in the early 1940s; he was named the first host of radio's *People Are Funny* but was fired after a year in favor of a young announcer named Art Linkletter, who rode the show to fame and fortune while Baker faded into the radio background. However, a few years later, in 1950, Art got a second chance when a new TV show, also based on stunts, was launched. *You Asked for It* became a TV standby of the 1950s, and Baker, with his windbreaker, cheery smile, and willingness to go anywhere to bring the viewers the sights they wanted to see, finally found his niche in broadcasting history.

BAKER, BLANCHE—actress
b: Dec 20, 1956, New York City, N.Y.

Holocaust (drama) ..... Anna Weiss (1978)

Emmy Award: Best Supporting Actress in a Single Performance in a Drama, for *Holocaust* (1978)

The daughter of actress Carroll Baker and director Jack Garfein, who was himself an inmate at Auschwitz concentration camp during World War II.

BAKER, CATHY—actress
b: c. 1947

Hee Haw (var)............ regular (1969–)

BAKER, DAVID LAIN—actor
b: Jun 12, Long Beach, Calif.

Call to Glory (drama)
.... airman Tom Bonelli (1984–85)

BAKER, DIANE—actress
b: Feb 25, 1938, Hollywood, Calif.

Here We Go Again (com)
.... Susan Evans (1973)
The Blue and the Gray (drama)
.... Evelyn Hale (1982)

BAKER, DON—host
Sportsman's Quiz (sport).. regular (1948–49)

BAKER, DON "RED"—actor
Little House on the Prairie (adv.)
.... Larrabee (1978–79)

BAKER, JAY—actor
The Best Times (drama)
.... Tony Younger (1985)

BAKER, JIM B.—actor
b: Jul 12, Great Falls, Mont. r: Conrad, Mont.

Flo (com).......... Farley Waters (1980–81)

BAKER, JOBY—actor
Good Morning, World (com)
.... Dave Lewis (1967–68)

BAKER, JOE—comedian
Kraft Music Hall Presents the Des O'Connor Show (var)................. regular (1971)
ABC Comedy Hour (com).... regular (1972)
The Rich Little Show (var)... regular (1976)

The Big Show (var)......... regular (1980)
The Steve Allen Comedy Hour (var)
.... regular (1980–81)

Short, plump comedian who also did voices for Saturday morning cartoons in the late 1970s and '80s.

BAKER, JOE DON—actor
b: Feb 12, 1943*, Groesbeck, Texas

Eischied (police)
.... Chief Earl Eischied (1979–80)

A burly, squint-eyed, imposing Southerner who gained fame as tough-as-nails Sheriff Buford Pusser in the original *Walking Tall* movie (1973). Baker made quite a few TV appearances during the late 1960s and early '70s, in such action series as *Gunsmoke, Lancer,* and *Bonanza* but was seen less often—mostly in TV movies—after his Hollywood film career took off. His arrival in series TV as *Eischied* was heralded, but the show quickly died opposite *Dallas* on Friday nights, and Joe Don went back to Hollywood.

BAKER, PHIL—comedian
b: Aug 24, 1896, Philadelphia, Pa. d: Nov 30, 1963

Who's Whose (quiz)......... emcee (1951)

Phil Baker was an old-time vaudevillian who was popular on radio in the 1930s with his own comedy show and in the '40s as the host of the quiz *Take It or Leave It,* which was the precursor of TV's *$64,000 Question* (the radio version originated the idea of doubling winnings up to "the $64 Question"). His career on television was brief, however. *Who's Whose* was canceled after exactly one telecast in the summer of 1951.

BAKEWELL, WILLIAM—actor
b: May 2, 1908, Los Angeles, Calif.

The Pinky Lee Show (com)
.... the stage manager (1950)

BAL, JEANNE—actress
b: May 3, 1928, Santa Monica, Calif.

Love & Marriage (com)
.... Pat Baker (1959–60)

*Some sources give 1936.

NBC Playhouse (drama) . . . . . hostess (1960)
Bachelor Father (com)
. . . . Suzanne Collins (1961)
Mr. Novak (drama) . . Jean Pagano (1963–64)

BALDAVIN, BARBARA—actress

Medical Center (drama)
. . . . Nurse Holmby (1971–76)

BALDING, REBECCA—actress
b: Sept 21, Little Rock, Ark.

Lou Grant (drama) . Carla Mardigian (1977)
Soap (com) . . . . Carol David (1978–81)
Makin' It (adv) . . . . . . Corky Crandall (1979)

BALDWIN, ALEC—actor
b: Apr 3, 1958, Amityville, N.Y.

Cutter to Houston (drama)
. . . . Dr. Hal Wexler (1983)
Knots Landing (drama)
. . . . Joshua Rush (1984–85)

BALDWIN, BILL—announcer
b: c. 1913 d: Nov 17, 1982

Mayor of Hollywood (var)
. . . . campaign manager (1952)

BALDWIN, CURTIS—black actor
b: Nov 25, 1967, Los Angeles, Calif.

227 (com) . . . . Calvin Dobbs (1985–)

BALENDA, CARLA—actress
b: 1925

The Mickey Rooney Show (com)
. . . . Pat (1954–55)
The Adventures of Fu Manchu (drama)
. . . . Betty Leonard (1955–56)

BALFOUR, MICHAEL—actor
b: 1918

The Vise (Mark Saber) (drama)
. . . . Barney O'Keefe (1955–56)

BALL, LUCILLE—actress
b: Aug 6, 1911, Jamestown, N.Y.

I Love Lucy (com) . . Lucy Ricardo (1951–57)
The Lucy-Desi Comedy Hour (specials) (com)
. . . . Lucy Ricardo (1957–60)
The Lucy Show (com)
. . . . Lucy Carmichael (1962–68)

Here's Lucy (com) . . . . Lucy Carter (1968–74)
Life with Lucy (com) . . Lucy Barker (1986–)

Emmy Awards: Best Comedienne (1952), Best Actress in a Continuing Series, for *I Love Lucy* (1955); Best Actress in a Comedy Series, for *The Lucy Show* (1967, 1968)

The first lady of television comedy had a 20-year career in movies and on radio before finding real fame on television. She first tried to crash show business in New York in the 1920s, as a teenager, but was told that she was too shy, too skinny, and generally had little future in the business. That didn't stop her, though; she made her way to Hollywood and by 1933 was getting bit parts in dozens of films, usually as a wacky ingenue. By the later 1930s her name was beginning to appear in the credits of some of these films—albeit at the bottom of the list.

After she married Cuban bandleader Desi Arnaz in 1940 she continued to try to build her film career (at one point she was supposed to be the "new Harlow") but by 1948 stardom was as elusive as ever and she decided to give radio a try. The result was the role of the nutty housewife in *My Favorite Husband*, which ran for a respectable three years.

Notwithstanding her radio success, Lucille Ball was in 1951 still one of many second-line names in show business; not unknown, but hardly a household name. Then she began *I Love Lucy*.

The show made history. It was the number-one rated program on TV for most of its original run and is probably the most often repeated series in television history. It also made Lucy so rich she was able to achieve the actor's ultimate revenge for all those years as a second stringer on the RKO movie lot: she bought the studio. (It was used for her own production company, Desilu.)

Lucy and Desi gave up the weekly grind in 1957 while their series was still number one, and continued to do specials until 1960, when they were divorced. Lucy then took a two-year hiatus from the small screen, during which she scored a personal triumph in her first—and only—starring role on Broadway, in *Wildcat* (1960). She married comedian Gary Morton in 1961. From 1962 to 1974 she once again starred in weekly series, and these shows too placed in the top ten. All of these series—*I Love Lucy, The Lucy Show, Here's Lucy*—ran on Monday nights at either 8:30 or 9:00 P.M., a 20-plus-year Monday night anchor of the CBS schedule and of American's viewing habits.

Lucy's acting appearances in other series were rare, aside from a few episodes of sitcoms in 1959 (*The Danny Thomas Show, The Phil Silvers Show, The Ann Sothern Show,* all in that year). From 1974 to 1977 she appeared in occasional specials, and in 1979 it was announced amid great fanfare that she had ended her 30-year relationship with CBS and would develop new comedy shows for NBC. This resulted in a "Lucy Moves to NBC" special in 1980, but little else. A new series in 1986, complete with a doddering old Gale Gordon (her nemesis in her '60s shows), was not very successful. By the 1980s Lucy was essentially a monument to TV's past, granted eternal life as the young and energetic Lucy Ricardo in black and white prints of the classic series that would seemingly run forever.

Her two children, Lucie Arnaz and Desi Arnaz, Jr., have also had TV careers. Biographies of Lucy include *Lucy: The Bittersweet Life of Lucille Ball* by Joe Morella and E.Z. Epstein (1973), *The Lucille Ball Story* by James Gregory (1974), and *Loving Lucy* by Bart Andrews and Thomas Watson (1982).

BALL, SUE—actress

Leo & Liz in Beverly Hills (com)
.... Mitzi Green (1986)

BALLANTINE, CARL—actor, comedian
r: Chicago, Ill.

McHale's Navy (com)
.... Lester Gruber (1962-66)
The Queen and I (com) ...... Becker (1969)
One in a Million (com)
.... Max Kellerman (1980)

BALLANTINE, EDDIE—orchestra leader
b: Jan 26, 1907, Chicago, Ill.

Don McNeill TV Club (var)
.... orch. leader (1950-51)

BALLARD, KAYE—actress, singer
b: Nov 20, 1926, Cleveland, Ohio

Henry Morgan's Great Talent Hunt (var)
.... regular (1951)
Kraft Music Hall (var).... regular (1961-63)
The Mothers-in-Law (com)
.... Kaye Buell (1967-69)
The Doris Day Show (com)
.... Angie Palucci (1970-71)
The Steve Allen Comedy Hour (var)
.... regular (1980-81)

A nightclub singer and impressionist with an offbeat sense of humor reminiscent of Carol Burnett. After getting her start as a comic singer with the Spike Jones band in the late 1940s, Kaye appeared fairly frequently on TV variety and talk shows of the 1950s and '60s, including those of Mel Torme (she was a regular on his daytime show in 1951-52), Perry Como, Johnny Carson, and Merv Griffin. She turned increasingly to acting in the 1960s and had roles in a number of TV comedies, as well as appearing in a few films and stage plays. Notable among the plays was the off-Broadway production of *The Decline and Fall of the Entire World As Seen Through the Eyes of Cole Porter* (1965). She continued to appear in episodes of various series in the 1970s and '80s, including *Love, American Style, The Love Boat,* and *Trapper John, M.D.*

BALLARD, MICHAEL—actor

Alice (com) .... Mike (1979-80)

BALSAM, MARTIN—actor
b: Nov 4, 1919, New York City, N.Y.

Archie Bunker's Place (com)
.... Murray Klein (1979-81)

Martin Balsam is one of those familiar actors who appeared in hundreds of TV productions over the years without ever being identified with any one famous role. He entered the medium in 1948 and was seen throughout the 1950s in playhouse series such as *Philco Playhouse, Goodyear Playhouse,* and *Alfred Hitchcock Presents.* During the 1960s he worked steadily, mostly in drama series—*The Naked City, Route 66, Dr. Kildare, The Untouchables, Name of the Game,* and many others. By the 1970s he had turned mostly to TV movies and miniseries, including *Raid on Entebbe* (1977), for which he received an

Emmy Award nomination. Since Balsam was known primarily as a dramatic "guest star," it came as a surprise to see him in a regular role in a comedy series from 1979–81—as Archie Bunker's Jewish business partner in *Archie Bunker's Place*.

Balsam also had a busy career as a supporting actor on stage and in films from the 1950s onward. Some of his more notable film roles have been in *Twelve Angry Men*, *Psycho* (as the ill-fated detective), *The Carpetbaggers*, and *A Thousand Clowns*.

BALSON, ALLISON—juvenile actress

The Life and Times of Eddie Roberts (com)
.... Chrissy Roberts (1980)
Little House on the Prairie (adv)
.... Nancy Oleson (1981–83)

BALTZELL, DEBORAH—actress
b: c. 1956 d: Oct 24, 1981

I'm a Big Girl Now (com)
.... Karen Hawks (1980–81)

BAMBER, JUDY—actress

Anybody Can Play (quiz) .. assistant (1958)

BAMBOSCHEK, GUISEPPE—conductor

Opera Cameos (music).... conductor (1954)

BANAS, BOB—choreographer
b: Sep 20, 1933, New York City, N.Y.

Malibu U (music)........... regular (1967)
The Jonathan Winters Show (var)
.... regular (1967–68)

BANCROFT, GRIFFING—journalist

Capitol Cloak Room (pub aff)
.... moderator (1949–50)

BANFIELD, BEVER-LEIGH—actress
b: Oct 5, New York City, N.Y.

Curse of Dracula (adv) .... Christine (1979)
Roots: The Next Generations (drama)
.... Cynthia Harvey Palmer (1979)
Open All Night (com)
.... Officer Edie (1981–82)

BANGERT, JOHNNY—juvenile actor

Margie (com) .... Cornell Clayton (1961–62)

BANGHART, KEN—announcer

Gillette Summer Sports Reel (sport)
.... commentator (1953)

BANHAM, RUSS—actor

Joe's World (com) .. Brad Hopkins (1979–80)

BANK, FRANK—juvenile actor
b: Apr 12, 1942, Hollywood, Calif.

Leave It to Beaver (com)
.. Clarence "Lumpy" Rutherford (1958–63)

Frank Bank was a Los Angeles kid who found work in television in the 1950s mostly because he was overweight—there were lots of handsome youngsters answering casting calls, but few of them were so chunky. After some appearances on *The Jack Benny Show* he was cast as Wally's oafish buddy Lumpy on *Leave It to Beaver*, a role that brought him a cult following—and a new Cadillac.

Unfortunately, it also typecast him and made it difficult to get subsequent work, so he drifted out of show business and into a very lucrative career as an investment counselor in Southern California. He is still heavyset but is now very well off.

BANKHEAD, TALLULAH—actress
b: Jan 31, 1903*, Huntsville, Ala. d: Dec 12, 1968

All Star Revue (var)
.... alternating host (1952–53)

Tallulah was one of the truly outrageous characters of American show business—her gravelly voice, her theatrical manner ("Thank you, dahling"), her sarcastic, rapier wit made her a favorite guest on radio variety shows of the 1930s and '40s and on TV in the 1950s.

Her principal career was in the theater; she appeared in dozens of Broadway productions from the 1920s to the '60s, scoring triumphs in everything from *The Skin of Our Teeth* (1942) and *Private Lives* (1948) to *Midgie Purvis* (1961). She made only a scattering of films, perhaps the best-known being Hitchcock's *Lifeboat* in 1944. Only a year before her death she appeared as the villainous Black Widow on *Batman* (March 1967).

*Some sources give 1902.

Her autobiography, *Tallulah,* was published in 1952.

BANKS, C. TILLERY—actor

Harris and Company (drama)
.... Angie Adams (1979)

BANKS, DAVID—actor

The Richard Pryor Show (var)
.... regular (1977)

BANKS, EMILY—actress

The Tim Conway Show (com)
.... Becky Parks (1970)

BANKS, JOAN—actress

Private Secretary (com).... Sylvia (1953–57)

One of the busiest actresses on radio in the late '30s and '40s—she seemed to be in every soap opera that was launched (*John's Other Wife, Valiant Lady,* etc.) as well as in many general dramas. On television she is principally remembered as Ann Sothern's man-hungry girlfriend on *Private Secretary.*

BANKS, JONATHAN—actor

Gangster Chronicles (drama)
.... Dutch Schultz (1981)
Otherworld (sci fi)
.... Kommander Nuveen Kroll (1985)

BANKS, TYLER—juvenile actor

Dallas (drama)
.... John Ross Ewing III (1980–83)

BANNER, JOHN—actor

b: Jan 28, 1910, Vienna, Austria d: Jan 28, 1973

Hogan's Heroes (com)
.... Sgt. Hans Schultz (1965–71)
Chicago Teddy Bears (com)
.... Uncle Latzi (1971)

Paunchy, dim-witted Sergeant Schultz of *Hogan's Heroes* had been a romantic lead early in his career as a stage actor in prewar Austria and Germany. He came to the U.S. in 1939—unable to speak a word of English—and landed supporting roles (at first speaking phonetically) in a number of films, usually playing the explosive foreigner. His greatest fame came late in his career as Sergeant Schultz; he died shortly after the series ended its run.

BANNISTER, JEFF—actor

At Ease (com)............. Maurice (1983)

BANNON, JACK—actor

b: Jun 14, 1940, Los Angeles, Calif.

Lou Grant (drama) . Art Donovan (1977–82)
Trauma Center (drama)
.... Buck Williams (1983)

The son of actress Bea Benaderet and actor Jim Bannon. Jack had a minor career on television in the 1960s in episodes of such series as *Daniel Boone, Green Acres,* and his mother's *Petticoat Junction.* He tried the New York stage in the early and mid 1970s, then returned to Los Angeles, where he got his major break as the tall, soft-spoken assistant city editor on *Lou Grant.*

BANNON, JIM—actor

b: 1911, Kansas City, Mo.

Adventures of Champion (adv)
.... Sandy North (1955–56)

A lanky, amiable actor whose one regular television role was on a series starring a horse (Gene Autry's Champion). In the 1940s he was known primarily as a radio announcer (for *The Great Gildersleeve,* among other series), and he also appeared in movies. For a time in the 1950s he starred in the Red Ryder B western film series. He is the father of actor Jack Bannon.

BAR-YOTAM, REUVEN—actor

Casablanca (drama)........ Ferrari (1983)

BARA, FAUSTO—actor

b: Jan 21, Mexicali, Baja California, Mexico

Renegades (police) .... Gaucho (1983)

BARA, NINA—actress

b: May 3, 1925, Buenos Aires, Argentina

Space Patrol (child) .... Tonga (1951–52)

BARAL, EILEEN—actress

Nanny and the Professor (com)
.... Francine Fowler (1970–71)

BARASH, OLIVIA—juvenile actress
b: Jan 11, 1965, Miami, Fla.

In the Beginning (com)....... Willie (1978)
Out of the Blue (com)
.... Laura Richards (1979)

BARBEAU, ADRIENNE—actress
b: Jun 11, 1947, Sacramento, Calif.

Maude (com).............. Carol (1972–78)

A pretty actress who got her first major break as Maude's divorced daughter on *Maude,* then went on to a series of mostly forgettable TV movies and miniseries (e.g., *Having Babies, Valentine Magic on Love Island*). She won a Tony Award nomination in 1972 for her role in the Broadway production of *Grease.*

BARBER, AVA—country singer
b: Jun 28, 1954, Knoxville, Tenn.

The Lawrence Welk Show (music)
.... regular (1974–82)

BARBER, BOBBY—actor

The Abbott and Costello Show (com)
.... various roles (1951–53)

BARBER, GLYNIS—actress

Dempsey and Makepeace (pol)
.... Det. Sgt. Harriet (Harry)
Makepeace (1984–)

BARBER, RED—sportscaster
b: Feb 17, 1908, Columbus, Miss.

Red Barber's Clubhouse (sport)
.... reporter (1949–50)
Peak of the Sports News (sport)
.... reporter (1953)
Red Barber's Corner (sport)
.... reporter (1954–58)

"The Ol' Redhead" of sports (not to be confused with The Ol' Redhead of Entertainment, Arthur Godfrey) was born Walter L. Barber. He had a long career on radio and TV, primarily doing baseball play-by-play. He was the voice of the Cincinnati Reds from 1934–39, the Brooklyn Dodgers from 1939–54, and the New York Yankees from 1954–66. After 32 years covering major league games he was abruptly fired by the Yankees for reporting that stadium attendance was down and directing the cameras to scan the empty seats. The Yanks evidently didn't want that much objectivity from their announcers. Red subsequently did some free-lance work and then retired around 1970.

BARBOUR, JOHN—host
b: Apr 24, 1934, Toronto, Canada

Real People (aud par) .... regular (1979–82)

Smiling, friendly John Barbour was as well-known for his work behind the camera as in front of it. In the 1960s he wrote for the series *Gomer Pyle* and *My Mother the Car*; later he became a producer (he was co-producer of *Real People*). On camera he was a stand-up comedian, an entertainment critic, and for many years a Los Angeles–area TV personality and host of several local talk shows.

BARBOUR, WILLIAM P.—golf pro

Practice Tee (info) .... Golf Pro (1949)

BARBUTTI, PETE—comedian
B: May 4, 1934, Scranton, Pa.

The Garry Moore Show (var)
.... regular (1966–67)
The John Davidson Show (var)
.... regular (1976)

BARDETTE, TREVOR—actor
b: 1902 d: Nov 28, 1977

The Life and Legend of Wyatt Earp (wes)
.... Old Man Clanton (1959–61)

BARGY, JEAN—singer, pianist

Blues by Bargy (music) ... hostess (1949–50)

The daughter of veteran orchestra leader Roy Bargy.

BARGY, ROY—orchestra leader
b: Jul 31, 1894, Newaygo, Mich. r: Toledo, Ohio
d: Jan 15, 1974

The Jimmy Durante Show (var)
.... orch. leader (1954–56)

58

Pianist and composer Roy Bargy had a career in the music business stretching back to the early 1920s. He had made many popular records of his own (solo piano and orchestra) and also been a pianist and arranger for the Paul Whiteman orchestra. In the 1930s he appeared with Whiteman on radio, while in the 1940s and '50s he was associated principally with Jimmy Durante, first on radio and later on TV. He retired in 1963.

BARI, LENNY—actor

Fish (com) .... Mike (1977–78)

BARI, LYNN—actress
b: Dec 18, 1913*, Roanoke, Va.

Detective's Wife (com)
.... Connie Conway (1950)
Boss Lady (com) ..... Gwen F. Allen (1952)

This forceful, worldly wise lady with a resounding voice had a busy career in Hollywood in the 1930s and '40s, when she was known as "The Queen of the Bs" (B grade films) at 20th Century-Fox. Never able to break out of roles such as the nasty "other woman" or the lady with a gun in her purse, she decided to try television, starring in two summer replacement shows in the early 1950s—*Detective's Wife* in 1950 and *Boss Lady* in 1952 (the latter was unusual for the time in that she starred as a woman executive rather than as a housewife). She appeared in many TV playhouse productions during the rest of the decade (*Pulitzer Prize Playhouse, Science Fiction Theater,* etc.), but was less frequently seen after that. The stylish brunette had a stormy marital life and was involved in a well-publicized custody battle for her son in the 1950s. She did some stage work in the 1960s and '70s and then retired.

BARKER, BOB—host
b: Dec 12, 1923, Darrington, Wash. r: Rosebud Indian Reservation, S.D.

The End of the Rainbow (aud par)
.... emcee (1958)
Truth or Consequences (quiz)
.... emcee (1966–74)
That's My Line (com)........ host (1980–81)
The Price Is Right (quiz)...... emcee (1986)

*Some sources give 1915, 1917, or 1919.

Emmy Award: Best Host of a Daytime Game Show, for *The Price Is Right* (1982, 1984)

This energetic emcee made a life's work out of two of television's noisier game shows, seen mostly in daytime. For 18 years he was the host of *Truth or Consequences,* first in daytime (1956–65) and then in nighttime syndication (1966–74). Even before that venerable series ended production he began hosting the daytime revival of *The Price Is Right* (1972) and stayed with that show into the '80s.

Barker began as a local radio announcer and disc jockey in the late 1940s. Beginning in 1966 he was the annual emcee for both the Miss U.S.A. Pageant and the Miss Universe Pageant, as well as a frequent commentator for the Rose Bowl Parade and other similar events.

BARKLEY, ALBEN W.—Vice President of the U.S.
b: Nov 24, 1877, Graves County, Ky. d: Apr 30, 1956

Meet the Veep (info) .... regular (1953)

Former Senator and Vice President under Harry Truman (1949–53) who reminisced about his career on this discussion program telecast shortly after he left office. He was reelected to the Senate in 1954. His autobiography is titled *That Reminds Me* (1954).

BARLOW, HOWARD—conductor
b: May 1, 1892, Plain City, Ohio d: Jan 31, 1972

The Voice of Firestone (music)
.... conductor (1949–59)
The Voice of Firestone (music)
.... conductor (occasional) (1962–63)

BARNARD, PAT—

Adventures of Oky Doky (child)
.... regular (1948–49)

BARNES, ANN—child actress

Blondie (com)..... Cookie Bumstead (1957)

BARNES, C. B.—juvenile actor
b: Nov 7, 1972, Portland, Me.

Starman (adv) ...... Scott Hayden (1986–)

BARNES, EMILY—

Country Style (var)......... regular (1950)

BARNES, GEORGE, TRIO—guitarist
b: Jul 17, 1921, Chicago Heights, Ill.

Sing-co-pation (music)....... regular (1949)
The Skip Farrell Show (music)
.... regular (1949)

BARNES, GEORGENE—actress

The Jonathan Winters Show (var)
.... regular (1968–69)

BARNES, JOANNA—actress
b: Nov 15, 1934, Boston, Mass.

21 Beacon Street (drama)...... Lola (1959)
The Trials of O'Brien (drama)
........................Katie (1965–66)

BARNES, PRISCILLA—actress
b: Dec 7, 1955, Fort Dix, N.J.

The American Girls (adv)
.... Rebecca Tomkins (1978)
Three's Company (com)
.... Terri Alden (1981–84)

An alluring blonde who was a frequent beauty contest winner as a teenager; even earlier, at age 13, she was a member of a five-girl dance troupe called "The Vivacious Vixens" that performed in the Los Angeles area. Priscilla began doing TV movies and series episodes in the mid-1970s and subsequently had a regular role in *The American Girls* and was one of Suzanne Somers' replacements in *Three's Company.*

BARNES, WALTER—actor

Tales of the Vikings (adv)..... Finn (1960)
Walking Tall (police).... Carl Pusser (1981)

BARNSTABLE, CYB AND TRICIA—
actresses (twins)

Quark (com)......... Betty I and II (1978)

BARON, JEFFREY—

Marie (var)............. regular (1980–81)

BARON, SANDY—comedian, actor
b: c. 1938 r: Brooklyn, N.Y.

That Was the Week That Was (com)
.... regular (1964)
Hey Landlord (com)
.... Chuck Hookstratten (1966–67)

BARR, DOUGLAS—actor
b: May 1, 1949, Cedar Rapids, Iowa

When the Whistle Blows (com)
.... Buzz Dillard (1980)
The Fall Guy (adv)
.... Howie Munson (1981–86)
The Wizard (adv)..... Alex Jagger (1986–)

BARR, LEONARD—actor
b: c. 1903 d: Nov 22, 1980

Szysznyk (com) . Leonard Kriegler (1977–78)

BARR, RAY—pianist
b: Jul 16, 1912, New York City, N.Y.

Vincent Lopez (var)...... regular (1949–50)

BARRAT, MAXINE—hostess

Photographic Horizons (info).. model (1949)
And Everything Nice (var)
.... hostess (1949–50)

BARRETT, LYNNE—singer

Melody, Harmony & Rhythm (music)
.... regular (1949–50)

BARRETT, MAJEL—actress
b: Feb 23, Columbus, Ohio

Star Trek (sci fi)
.... Nurse Christine Chapel (1966–69)

One of the less-remembered crew members of the Starship Enterprise, Barrett had earlier been seen (in occasional appearances) as Lumpy Rutherford's mother on *Leave It to Beaver.*

BARRETT, RAY—sportscaster
b: 1907 d: Jan 16, 1973

Harness Racing (sport)
.... host, quiz segment (1950)
Gillette Summer Sports Reel (sport)
.... commentator (1953)
Gillette Summer Sports Reel (sport)
.... commentator (1955)

BARRETT, RONA—gossip columnist
b: Oct 8, 1936, New York City, N.Y.

The Tomorrow Show (talk)
.... cohost (1980–81)
Television: Inside and Out (mag)
.... hostess (1981–82)

Hollywood has to have someone like Rona Barrett. The petite blonde, who knows all and, worse yet, tells all, was a precocious graduate of New York University (at age 18) and by the time she was in her early twenties was writing a nationally circulated column called "Young Hollywood" for *Motion Picture Magazine.* In the early 1960s this was syndicated to more than one hundred newspapers.

Rona was first seen on-camera during the '60s and by 1969 was hosting a nationally syndicated report that was carried on many stations. Her first novel, *The Lovemaniacs,* was a best-seller in 1972 and her autobiography, *Miss Rona* (1974), was also highly successful. In 1976 she began contributing reports to ABC's *Good Morning, America.* In 1980 NBC stole her away to cohost (from Hollywood) Tom Snyder's late night *Tomorrow Show,* a move not at all appreciated by Snyder. The two fought and Rona soon quit. Later she briefly had her own prime time magazine show on NBC (*Television: Inside and Out*), before returning to ABC.

BARRIE, BARBARA—actress
b: May 23, 1931, Chicago, Ill.

Diana (com) ..... Norma Brodnik (1973–74)
Barney Miller (com)
.... Elizabeth Miller (1975–76)
79 Park Avenue (drama)
.... Kaati Fludjicki (1977)
Backstairs at the White House (drama)
.... Mamie Eisenhower (1979)
Breaking Away (com)
.... Evelyn Stohler (1980–81)
Tucker's Witch (drama)
.... Ellen Hobbes (1982–83)
Reggie (com)....... Elizabeth Potter (1983)
Double Trouble (com)
.... Aunt Margo (1984–85)

This fine-featured, understanding woman looks like she was born to play somebody's mother on a TV sitcom. In fact she has had many such roles, but none of them lasted long enough to become closely identified with her. In fact, of the half-dozen series in which she has been a regular, all but one have been short-lived. The exception was *Barney Miller,* in which *she* was short-lived (as Barney's wife).

Barbara started her career as a stage actress in the 1950s and soon began picking up work in TV. In the 1960s she was seen in episodes of *Naked City, Ben Casey, The Defenders,* and *The Twilight Zone* (in a "lost" episode called "Miniatures," which was not repeated until the 1980s). In the 1970s and '80s she branched into TV movies and miniseries, including *79 Park Avenue* and *Backstairs at the White House.* A highlight of her career was her role as David's mother in both the movie and TV versions of *Breaking Away.*

BARRIE, WENDY—actress, hostess
b: Apr 18, 1912*, Hong Kong d: Feb 2, 1978

Adventures of Oky Doky (child)
.... hostess (1948–49)
Picture This (cartn)....... hostess (1948–49)
The Wendy Barrie Show (talk)
.... hostess (1949–50)

Bright, breezy British actress who had an up-and-down career. After gaining notice in British films in the early 1930s, she came to Hollywood in 1935 and appeared in more than three dozen features (many of them Bs) over the next eight years. She was one of the most popular eligible young ladies in town and her career looked promising. Then everything came to a crashing halt due to her friendship with mobster Bugsy Siegel; the studios suddenly wanted nothing to do with her. A few years later, still vivacious if not quite so young, she moved to New York and got into TV on the ground floor, appearing in a series of children's programs and women's chatter shows (her cheery sign-off: "Be a good bunny!"). Later she hosted local talk shows in New York and was the Revlon spokesperson in commercials on *The $64,000 Question.* However, her TV career never really ignited.

In the 1960s she had a nationally syndicated radio interview show, *The Wendy Barrie Celebrity Parade,* but few on-screen roles. She died alone, in a nursing home, in 1978.

Her stage name, incidentally, was from J. M. Barrie's *Peter Pan;* "Wendy" for the

*Some sources give 1913.

61

little girl in the story, and "Barrie" from the author's last name.

BARRIS, CHUCK—producer, host
b: Jun 3, 1929, Philadelphia, Pa.

The Gong Show (com) . . . . host (1977–80)
The Chuck Barris Rah Rah Show (var)
. . . . host (1978)

The curly-haired "King of Bad Taste" whose gaudy game shows were lambasted by critics but nevertheless attracted large followings. A onetime network executive, Chuck began producing programs in the 1960s and scored major hits with *The Dating Game* (1965) and *The Newlywed Game* (1966). In 1976 he launched the ultimate daytime talent show—for people with no talent. This was the infamous *Gong Show*, which he decided to host himself (a year later he began hosting the nighttime syndicated version as well). Apparently "Chucky Baby" liked the limelight, as he later fronted his own prime time variety show in 1978. Among his other series (as producer) were *How's Your Mother-in-Law?* (1967), *Operation Entertainment* (1968), and *The $1.98 Beauty Show* (1978).

BARRIS, MARTY—comedian

Comedy Tonight (var) . . . . regular (1970)
The Late Summer Early Fall Bert Convy Show
(var) . . . . regular (1976)

BARRY, DONALD—actor
b: Jan 11, 1912, Houston, Texas d: Jul 17, 1980

Surfside Six (drama)
. . . . Lt. Snedigar (1960–61)
Mr. Novak (drama) . . . . . Mr. Gallo (1963–64)

BARRY, GENE—actor
b: Jun 14, 1921, New York City, N.Y.

Our Miss Brooks (com)
. . . . Gene Talbot (1955–56)
Bat Masterson (wes)
. . . . Bat Masterson (1959–61)
Burke's Law (police)
. . . . Capt. Amos Burke (1963–66)
The Name of the Game (adv)
. . . . Glenn Howard (1968–71)
The Adventurer (drama)
. . . . Steve Bradley (1972)
Aspen (drama) . . . . Carl Osborne (1977)

"I may not have been the fastest gun in the West, but I was neat," quipped Gene Barry recently. Barry became famous playing rather similar natty heroes on three hit series of the '50s and '60s. On *Bat Masterson* he was a dapper western hero with a derby and cane; on *Burke's Law* the dapper and very rich police detective who arrived at the scene of the crime in his Rolls; and in *The Name of the Game* the still dapper, flamboyant head of a huge publishing conglomerate who also solved crimes.

Gene arrived at this string of TV hits after twenty years in show business. In the 1940s he worked primarily on the New York stage, and in the 1950s he became one of TV's busiest supporting actors. He appeared in all sorts of dramas, including multiple episodes of *The Loretta Young Show*, *Science Fiction Theater*, *Alfred Hitchcock Presents*, and *Ford Theatre*. He briefly played the object of Eve Arden's affections in *Our Miss Brooks*, but was bumped when Robert Rockwell—as Mr. Boynton—rejoined the cast.

After his great hits of the 1960s he could pretty much name his roles, at least on TV (his film career never got off the ground). He worked primarily in big-budget TV movies and miniseries (including *Aspen*) and also appeared a number of times in the late 1970s and early '80s in those homes for yesterday's stars, *The Love Boat* and *Fantasy Island*.

BARRY, HAROLD—host

Versatile Varieties (var) . . . emcee (1949–50)

BARRY, IVOR—actor

Mr. Deeds Goes to Town (com)
. . . . George, the butler (1969–70)
Bridget Loves Bernie (com)
. . . . Charles, the butler (1972–73)

BARRY, J. J.—actor

The Corner Bar (com)
. . . . Fred Costello (1972–73)

BARRY, JACK—producer, emcee
b: Mar 20, 1918, Lindenhurst, N.Y. d: May 2, 1984

Juvenile Jury (quiz) . . . . emcee (1947)
Life Begins at Eighty (talk)
. . . . emcee (1950–56)

Juvenile Jury (quiz) .... emcee (1951–54)
Wisdom of the Ages (info)
.... moderator (1952–53)
The Big Surprise (quiz) .... emcee (1955–56)
Twenty-One (quiz) .... emcee (1956–58)
High-Low (quiz) .... emcee (1957)
Concentration (quiz) .... emcee (1958)
The Generation Gap (quiz) .... emcee (1969)
Juvenile Jury (quiz) .... emcee (1970–71)
The Reel Game (quiz) .... emcee (1971)
Break the Bank (quiz) .... host (1976)
The Joker's Wild (quiz) ...... host (1976–84)

Jack Barry had one of television's most unusual careers; a top kids' show host and producer of the 1950s, he was practically run out of the business due to his involvement with the quiz show scandals, only to be "rehabilitated" ten years later and become successful all over again.

Jack first gained fame as a man who had a special way with kids and old folks. While working as an announcer on the *Uncle Don* radio show in 1945 he and his partner Dan Enright got to thinking about how interesting these kids might be to a general audience. They recruited some of Uncle Don's little fans to make a test program one day, after the regular show, and the result was the network hit *Juvenile Jury* (1946)—in which bright kids talked about how they would deal with life's little problems. That was followed by *Life Begins at Eighty* in 1948, in which oldsters did the same thing, and then by a whole string of Barry and Enright–produced game shows in the 1950s. Barry also created and hosted one of the most fondly remembered—and certainly one of the most participatory—kids shows ever. *Winky Dink and You* (daytime, 1953–57) encouraged kids to put a piece of clear plastic over the TV screen and then use crayons to draw along with the show's characters, right on the screen!

Barry and Enright got in on the fad for big-money quiz shows in the mid-1950s with such hits as *The Big Surprise* and *Twenty-One*, but that proved to be their undoing. *Twenty-One* was revealed to be one of the leading culprits in the rigged quiz show scandals of the late 1950s. All of Barry's shows were canceled and he was unable to sell anything to the networks for the next ten years.

Finally, in the late 1960s, he was able to start working again on a succession of daytime and nighttime shows, the most successful of which was *The Joker's Wild*; he hosted it in daytime from 1972–75 and in syndication from 1976 until his death in 1984. Not forgetting the kids who had given him his start, Barry also produced a children's version called *Joker! Joker! Joker!* from 1979–81.

BARRY, MATTHEW—actor

Ivan the Terrible (com) ...... Sascha (1976)

BARRY, NORMAN—host

Portrait of America (int) .... host (1949)

BARRY, PATRICIA—actress
b: Nov 16, 1930, Davenport, Iowa

Harris Against the World (com)
.... Kate Harris (1964–65)

BARRY, ROBERT—juvenile actor

The Aldrich Family (com)
.... Homer Brown (1951–52)

BARRYMORE, JOHN, JR.—actor
b: Jun 4, 1932, Beverly Hills, Calif.

Pantomime Quiz (quiz) ... regular (1953–54)

This scion of the famous acting family, who was also known as John Drew Barrymore, was the son of John Barrymore and the nephew of Ethel and Lionel Barrymore. He was the only one of the Barrymores to have much of an acting career on television. A handsome young man, with his father's famous profile, he appeared in a number of playhouse series of the 1950s (*Climax, Matinee Theater, Playhouse 90*, etc.) as well as in scattered series episodes during the 1960s (*Rawhide, Gunsmoke*). In 1974–75, as a favor to his close friend David Carradine, he appeared in several episodes of *Kung Fu*.

Barrymore has led a tumultuous life, in and out of trouble with the law, and at times as a recluse. He is the father of 1980s child star Drew Barrymore.

BARSTOW, EDITH—choreographer
b: 1907 d: Jan 6, 1960

Frankie Laine Time (var) ... dancers (1956)

BARTH, EDDIE—actor
b: Sep 29, 1931, Philadelphia, Pa.

Shaft (drama) . . . . Lt. Al Rossi (1973–74)
Rich Man, Poor Man—Book I (drama)
. . . . Papadakis (1976)
Husbands, Wives & Lovers (com)
. . . . Harry Bellini (1978)
Number 96 (drama)
. . . . Lou Sugarman (1980–81)
Simon & Simon (drama)
. . . . Myron Fowler (1981–83)
Mickey Spillane's Mike Hammer (drama)
. . . . Ritchie (1984–)

BARTH, ISOLDE—actress
Holocaust (drama) . . . . Eva (1978)

BARTLETT, BONNIE—actress
Little House on the Prairie (adv)
. . . . Grace Edwards (1976–77)
St. Elsewhere (drama)
. . . . Mrs. Ellen Craig (1982–)

Emmy Award: Best Supporting Actress in
a Drama Series, for *St. Elsewhere* (1986).

The wife of actor William Daniels, also
an Emmy winner for *St. Elsewhere*

BARTLETT, DIANA—actress
The Beverly Hillbillies (com)
. . . . Joy Devine (1970–71)

BARTOLD, NORMAN—actor
Adam's Rib (com)
. . . . District Attorney Donahue (1973)
Teachers Only (com) . . . . . Mr. Brody (1982)

BARTON, DAN—actor
r: Chicago

Dan Raven (police)
. . . . Det. Sgt. Burke (1960–61)

BARTON, EARL—
Broadway Open House (talk)
. . . . regular (1951)

BARTON, EILEEN—singer
b: Nov 24, 1929, Brooklyn, N.Y.

The Swift Show (var) . . . . regular (1948)
Broadway Open House (talk)
. . . . regular (1951)

Pop singer known primarily for her million-
selling novelty hit, "If I Knew You Were
Comin' I'd've Baked a Cake," in 1950. The
daughter of vaudeville parents, Eileen was
a performer herself since childhood. She
appeared on many radio and TV variety
shows of the 1940s and '50s, especially Milton Berle's programs.

BARTON, JOAN—comedienne
A Couple of Joes (var) . . . . regular (1949–50)

BARTON, PETER—actor
b: Jul 19, Valley Stream, Long Island,
N.Y.

Shirley (com) . . . . Bill Miller (1979–80)
The Powers of Matthew Star (sci fi)
. . . . Matthew Starr (1982–83)

"There were two people ahead of me in
line when I was registering for my third
year in pharmacy school," said young
Peter Barton when asked how he got
started. "I had the check in my hand and
was about to pay for registration when I
decided to take my sister's advice and try
for a modeling career."
Smart move. The handsome youth immediately landed several assignments and
barely a month later won the role of Shirley Jones's teenage son in *Shirley*, beating
out 300 other applicants. In 1981 he was
slated to begin his own science-fiction series *The Powers of Matthew Star,* but was
badly burned in an accident on the set. He
recovered and the series did go on the air
the following year, but it lasted only a single season.

BARTON, TOD—actor
The Lineup (police)
. . . . Inspector Charlie Summers (1959–60)

BARTY, BILLY—actor
b: Oct 25, 1924, Millsboro, Pa.

Ford Festival (var) . . . . regular (1951–52)
The Spike Jones Show (var) . . regular (1954)
Circus Boy (adv)
. . . . Little Tom, the midget (1956–58)
The Spike Jones Show (var) . . regular (1957)
Club Oasis (var) . . . . regular (1958)
Ace Crawford, Private Eye (com)
. . . . Inch (1983)

He was only 3'9" and weighed 80 pounds, but he had a 50-year career in show business. Billy Barty's big grin and infectious personality made him a favorite midget in comedies and kids' shows. He began in films at the age of three and had been in over 120 movies by the time he was in his teens; among them were *Footlight Parade* and *Golddiggers of 1933.* He was also Mickey Rooney's kid brother in the Mickey McGuire shorts of the late 1920s.

Barty got into television almost at the beginning, appearing as Billy Bitesize on *Your Pet Parade* (daytime, 1951) and Little Tom in *Circus Boy* (1956). From 1952–60 he was a member of Spike Jones' City Slickers, and he was regularly seen on Spike's own shows (including *Club Oasis* and others). Some of his best known bits were developed with Jones' lunatic musicians, particularly Billy's seltzer water and exploding candelabra-filled impersonation of Liberace.

Billy continued to be active in the 1960s and '70s, turning increasingly to children's shows. He was in *The Bugaloos, The Krofft Superstars,* and *The Bay City Rollers* Saturday morning shows in the 1970s and from 1973–75 was Sigmund, the lovable, six-armed creature on *Sigmund and the Sea Monsters.* He was back in 1981 in the movie *Under the Rainbow* and in 1983 in the short-lived Tim Conway comedy, *Ace Crawford, Private Eye* (as Inch, the diminutive bartender).

Concerned with the treatment of others of small stature, he founded two organizations to assist them: The Little People of America (1957) and, in later years, The Billy Barty Foundation.

BARUCH, ANDRÉ—announcer
b: c. 1906, Paris, France

Masters of Magic (misc) . . . . host (1949)
Your Hit Parade (music)
. . . . announcer (1950–57)

BASCH, HARRY—actor

Falcon Crest (drama)
. . . . Vince Caproni (1982–84)

BASEHART, RICHARD—actor
b: Aug 31, 1914, Zanesville, Ohio d: Sep 17, 1984

Voyage to the Bottom of the Sea (sci fi)
. . . . Adm. Harriman Nelson (1964–68)
W.E.B. (drama). . . . . Gus Dunlap (1978)

Emmy Award: Best Narration, for *Let My People Go* (1965)

A thoughtful, subdued actor who had a solid but unspectacular career for nearly 30 years before becoming identified with the role of Admiral Nelson in *Voyage to the Bottom of the Sea* in the 1960s. He was a stage actor in local productions in the 1930s, finally making it to Broadway in 1943. In the late 1940s he moved to Hollywood. Although he attracted critical acclaim for a number of his films over the years (*He Walked By Night,* 1948; *La Strada,* 1954; *Moby Dick,* 1956); he never reached star status.

Basehart began appearing on television in the late 1950s on some of the medium's most prestigious dramatic showcases, including *Playhouse 90, Studio One,* and *The Hallmark Hall of Fame.* More dramatic appearances followed in the 1960s, including episodes of *The Alfred Hitchcock Hour, Arrest and Trial,* and *The Twilight Zone,* before he became the authoritative commander on *Voyage.*

Basehart continued to appear in the 1970s and '80s, largely in TV movies. He was also honored for his narration on a number of literate specials.

BASILE, LOUIS—actor
b: c. 1935 d: Mar 2, 1984

The Super (com) . . . . Louie (1972)

BASINGER, KIM—actress
b: Dec 8, 1953, Athens, Ga.

Dog and Cat (police)
. . . . Officer J. Z. Kane (1977)
From Here to Eternity (drama)
. . . . Lorene Rogers (1979–80)

BASS, EMORY—actor

Angie (com). . . . Phipps, the butler (1979–80)

BASS, TOD—juvenile actor
b: Apr 26, 1964, Los Angeles, Calif.

Rowan & Martin's Laugh-In (var)
. . . . regular (1972–73)

BASSETT, WILLIAM—actor

Nancy (com)............ Turner (1970–71)

BASTEDO, ALEXANDRA—actress
b: 1946

The Champions (adv)
.... Sharon Macready (1968)

BATEMAN, CHARLES—actor

Manhunt (police)
.... Det. George Peters (1959–60)
Two Faces West (wes)
..... Ben/Rick January (dual role) (1961)

BATEMAN, JASON—juvenile actor
b: Jan 14, 1969, Rye, N.Y.

Little House on the Prairie (adv)
.... James Cooper (1981–82)
Silver Spoons (com)
.... Derek Taylor (1982–84)
It's Your Move (com)
.... Matthew Burton (1984–85)
Valerie (com)....... David Hogan (1986–)

Jason Bateman, who specializes in young schemers, was introduced to TV viewers during the 1980–81 season as a young waif adopted by Michael Landon on *Little House on the Prairie;* the following fall he became a regular. He was later seen as Ricky Schroder's mischief-making pal on *Silver Spoons* and as a teenage con artist on *It's Your Move.*

He is the brother of Justine Bateman.

BATEMAN, JUSTINE—juvenile actress
b: Feb 19, 1966, Rye, N.Y.

Family Ties (com). Mallory Keaton (1982–)

Jason Bateman's better-behaved older sister.

BATES, BARBARA—actress
b: Aug 6, 1925, Denver, Colo. d: Mar 18, 1969

It's a Great Life (com)
.... Kathy Morgan (1954–56)

BATES, JEANNE—actress

Ben Casey (drama).. Nurse Wills (1961–68)

BATES, JIM, DANCERS—

The Mac Davis Show (var).. regulars (1976)

BATES, JIMMY—actor

Father Knows Best (com)
.... Claude Messner (1954–59)

BATES, JOHN—

Marie (var)............. regular (1980–81)

BATES, LULU—singer

Gay Nineties Revue (var)
.... regular (1948–49)

BATES, RHONDA—actress
r: Evansville, Ind.

Keep On Truckin' (var)...... regular (1975)
Blansky's Beauties (com) .. Arkansas (1977)
The Roller Girls (com)
.... Mongo Sue Lampert (1978)
Speak Up, America (aud par)
.... regular (1980)

Towering (6'2") actress with a booming voice who played Amazon-like comedy roles beginning in the late 1970s. She found happiness in real life by marrying a man who was 6'5".

BATTISTE, HAROLD—orchestra leader

The Sonny and Cher Show (var)
.... orch. leader (1976–77)

Black orchestra leader who was a very active producer of funky rock and rhythm and blues records in New Orleans in the 1950s and '60s ("You Talk Too Much," "Ya Ya," etc.) before migrating to the West Coast. He was an old friend of Sonny's from the music business.

BAUER, CHARITA—actress
b: Dec 20, 1923, Newark, N.J. d: Feb 28, 1985

The Aldrich Family (com)
.... Mary Aldrich (1949–50)

A soap opera actress of the 1940s who appeared briefly in *The Aldrich Family* comedy in 1949–50, then found lasting fame—and a lifelong career—as Bert on the daytime serial *The Guiding Light.* She joined *The Guiding Light* in 1950 while it was still on radio, followed it to TV in 1952, and remained with it until 1984—a feat of endurance that led the Academy of Television Arts and Sciences to bestow upon her a "Lifetime Achievement Award" in 1983.

BAUER, DR. LOUIS H.—physician, host

Horizon (info) .... host (1954–55)

BAUER, JAIME LYN—actress
b: Mar 9, 1949, Phoenix, Ariz.

Bare Essence (drama)
.... Barbara Fisher (1983)

Jamie is perhaps best known as Laurie Brooks, a leading heroine on the daytime serial The Young and the Restless in the '70s and '80s.

BAUKHAGE, H. R.—newscaster

News and Views (news)
.... anchorman (1948–52)

BAUMAN, JON "BOWSER"—host, singer
b: Sep 14, 1947, Queens, N.Y.

Sha Na Na (var) .... emcee (1977–81)
The Pop 'n' Rocker Game (quiz)
.... host (1983)

Bowser was the greasy-haired, muscle-flexing leader of the Sha Na Na singing group, which specialized in vintage rock 'n' roll and 1950s comedy. He later tried to build a solo career, hosting a syndicated music quiz show in 1983 and a revival of the Hollywood Squares (as part of The Match Game/Hollywood Squares Hour) in daytime in 1983–84. Neither was particularly successful.

BAUMANN, KATHRINE—comedienne

Keep On Truckin' (var) ...... regular (1975)

BAUR, ELIZABETH—actress
b: Dec 11, 1948, Los Angeles, Calif.

Lancer (wes)..... Teresa O'Brien (1968–70)
Ironside (police)..... Fran Belding (1971–75)

BAVAAR, TONY—singer

Club Seven (music).......... host (1950–51)

BAVIER, FRANCES—actress
b: 1905, New York City, N.Y.

It's a Great Life (com)
.... Mrs. Amy Morgan (1954–56)
The Eve Arden Show (com)
.... Nora (1957–58)
The Andy Griffith Show (com)
.... Aunt Bee Taylor (1960–68)
Mayberry R.F.D. (com) . Aunt Bee (1968–70)

Emmy Award: Best Supporting Actress in a Comedy, for The Andy Griffith Show (1967)

This grandmotherly woman played the Widow Morgan on It's a Great Life and Eve Arden's mother on The Eve Arden Show; sharp-eyed movie fans may remember her for her supporting roles in a number of minor movies of the 1950s, '60s, and '70s (The Day the Earth Stood Still, 1951; Benji, 1974). However, she is best known, by far, as kindly Aunt Bee, who looked after Ronnie Howard on The Andy Griffith Show.

BAXTER, ANNE—actress
b: May 7, 1923, Michigan City, Ind. r: Bronxville, N.Y. d: Dec 12, 1985

Marcus Welby, M.D. (drama)
.... Myra Sherwood (1969–70)
East of Eden (drama)......... Faye (1981)
Hotel (drama)..... Victoria Cabot (1983–86)

Anne Baxter seems to have been one step behind Bette Davis at several points in her career. One of Baxter's best films was All About Eve (1950), in which she played a scheming young actress determined to climb to the top over Davis's fading star; 21 years later in Applause (the stage version of All About Eve) she was in the Davis role herself; and 12 years after that she was called in to replace Davis as the grand dame of the TV series Hotel when the older actress had to bow out due to illness.

Notwithstanding these coincidences, Anne Baxter had a long career of her own on both the large and small screens. Born of wealthy parents (her grandfather was the famous architect Frank Lloyd Wright), she attended the finest schools and became a child actress on Broadway at age 13. Her movie debut was in 1940, and she later starred in a number of notable films, one of which—The Razor's

Edge—earned her an Academy Award.

She entered television in the late 1950s as her movie career began to decline. Her dramatic debut was on *General Electric Theater* in 1957, followed by appearances on *Playhouse 90, Lux Video Theater, The U.S. Steel Hour,* and similar showcases. She retired to a remote corner of Australia with her second husband for a few years in the early 1960s, but then returned to pick up her TV career. More dramas followed *(Alfred Hitchcock, Dr. Kildare, Ironside, The Name of the Game),* interspersed with occasional comedies, including *Batman*—on which she camped it up as Zelda the Great.

In later years Anne was seen primarily in TV movies (including the *Marcus Welby* pilot) and miniseries such as *East of Eden.* Her agreement to appear in *Hotel* was a coup for that series, bringing a veteran star to the cast.

Anne Baxter's autobiography, *Intermission,* was published in 1977.

BAXTER, CAROL—actress

Curse of Dracula (adv)
.... Mary Gibbons (1979)

BAXTER, DR. FRANK—host, English professor

Telephone Time (drama) ..... host (1957–58)

BAXTER-BIRNEY, MEREDITH—actress
b: Jun 21, 1947, Los Angeles, Calif.

Bridget Loves Bernie (com)
.... Bridget Fitzgerald Steinberg (1972–73)
Family (drama)
..... Nancy Lawrence Maitland (1976–80)
Family Ties (com)... Elyse Keaton (1982–)

Meredith Baxter is a thoughtful, blonde-haired young actress who moved quickly into television once she had decided on an acting career. Shortly after graduating from Michigan's Interlochen Arts Academy, she landed her first two TV roles, in episodes of *The Interns* and *The Young Lawyers*—which aired within a week of each other in January 1971. More guest appearances followed and in 1972 she was cast opposite David Birney in a new CBS comedy about a Jewish boy who marries an Irish girl, *Bridget Loves Ber-*

nie. The series was rather controversial and was soon canceled, but Bridget really did fall in love with Bernie—Meredith and David were married in real life, in 1973.

She then went on to do more episode work and several TV movies, beginning with *The Cat Creature* in 1973. After making a number of pilots for proposed new series, she was offered a plum role on *Family,* playing the daughter around whom many of the stories revolved. In 1982 she was seen in a slightly more mature role as Michael J. Fox's mom in the hit comedy *Family Ties.*

Meredith is the daughter of actress Whitney Blake, who also had a TV career. Meredith and her mother played opposite each other in the 1974 TV movie *The Stranger Who Looks Like Me.*

BAYER, GARY—actor
b: Jun 25, North Hollywood, Calif.

Me & Mrs. C. (com)
.... Ethan Conklin (1986–)

BAYLOR, HAL—actor

The Life and Legend of Wyatt Earp (wes)
.... Bill Thompson (1955–56)

BAZLEN, BRIGID—juvenile actress
b: Jun 9, 1944, Fond du Lac, Wis.

Too Young to Go Steady (com)
.... Pam Blake (1959)

BEACHAM, STEPHANIE—actress
b: Feb 28, 1947*, Hertfordshire, England

Dynasty II: The Colbys (drama)
.... Sable Scott Colby (1985–)

BEAIRD, BARBARA—juvenile actress
b: c. 1948, Waco, Texas

Fibber McGee and Molly (com)
.... Teeny (1959–60)

Cute, pigtailed cousin of child actress Pamela Beaird. In 1959 11-year-old Barbara was asked how long she would stay in show business. "Maybe five years," she replied. "Then I'd like to become a teacher."

*Some sources give 1949.

BEAIRD, BETTY—actress
b: c. 1939, El Paso, Texas r: Houston, Texas

Julia (com).... Marie Waggedorn (1968–71)

BEAIRD, PAMELA—juvenile actress
b: c. 1942

My Friend Flicka (adv)
.... Hildy Broeberg (1956)

Cousin of Barbara Beaird.

BEAN, ORSON—comedian
b: Jul 22, 1928, Burlington, Vt.

I've Got a Secret (quiz) ..... panelist (1952)
The Blue Angel (var) .... host (1954)
Keep Talking (quiz) ...... regular (1959–60)
To Tell the Truth (quiz).. panelist (1964–67)
Mary Hartman, Mary Hartman (com)
.... Reverend Brim (1977–78)

A bright young New England comic who first gained attention in the early 1950s with his comedy monologues, which were originally part of his magic act. (He adopted the stage name Orson as a tribute to another actor who was fascinated with magic, Orson Welles.) Bean became a favorite guest on TV variety shows of the 1950s and '60s and a frequent panelist on game shows. He also appeared regularly in Broadway and off-Broadway revues during this period.

In addition to doing comedy, Bean was a legitimate actor and appeared in many episodes of live TV dramas during the 1950s and early '60s (*Broadway Television Theatre, U.S. Steel Hour,* etc.). He was the eccentric Mr. Bevis in a 1960 episode of *The Twilight Zone.* Bean was seen less often in later years, although he did turn up in an episode of *Ellery Queen* in 1975 and on *Mary Hartman, Mary Hartman* in 1977–78.

BEANE, REGINALD—pianist
b: c. 1921 d: Apr 14, 1985

Starlit Time (var) ...... regular (trio) (1950)
Once Upon a Tune (music)... regular (1951)

BEARD, JAMES—cooking expert

I Love to Eat (misc) .... host (1946–47)

BEASLEY, ALLYCE—actress
b: Jul 6, 1954 Brooklyn, N.Y.

Moonlighting (drama)
.... Agnes Dipesto (1985–)

BEATTY, MORGAN—newsman
b: Sep 6, 1902, Little Rock, Ark. d: 1975

DuMont Evening News (news)
.... anchorman (1954–55)

Although he briefly anchored the *DuMont Evening News* (which was seen by hardly anyone), Beatty was best-known as a radio commentator for NBC from 1941 until his retirement in 1967. Before that, he had been an Associated Press reporter for 14 years (1927–41).

BEATTY, NED—actor
b: Jul 6, 1937, Lexington, Ky.

Szysznyk (com) ... Nick Szysznyk (1977–78)

BEATTY, WARREN—actor
b: Mar 30, 1937, Richmond, Va.

The Many Loves of Dobie Gillis (com)
.... Milton Armitage (1959–60)

Even big-league movie stars have to start somewhere, and for boyishly handsome Warren Beatty it was on TV productions of the late 1950s—*Kraft Television Theatre, Studio One, Suspicion.* Those with keen memories will recall him as the goodlooking ladies' man Milton Armitage during part of the first season of *Dobie Gillis.* He left the series in February 1960 to go to Hollywood and never came back.

Beatty is the younger brother of actress Shirley MacLaine.

BEAUCHAMP, RICHARD—actor

C.P.O. Sharkey (com).. Rodriguez (1976–78)
Zorro and Son (com) . Sgt. Sepulveda (1983)

BEAUDINE, DEKA—actor

The Paper Chase (drama)
.... Asheley Brooks (1978)

BEAUMONT, CHRIS—actor

Here We Go Again (com)....... Jeff (1973)

BEAUMONT, HUGH—actor
b: Feb 16, 1909, Lawrence, Kan. d: May 3, 1982

Leave It to Beaver (com)
.... Ward Cleaver (1957–63)

Beaumont is warmly remembered as the "perfect father" (of Beaver and Wally Cleaver) on TV's *Leave It to Beaver*. Actually, he didn't like the role much at all, feeling that it had typecast him and had all but obliterated recall of his many other roles in movies and on TV. He had been in films since 1941, usually as a supporting player in action films, but also starred as detective Michael Shayne in several. In the 1950s he was a frequent actor in TV dramas, with multiple appearances on *Four Star Playhouse, Cavalcade Theatre,* and *The Loretta Young Show.*

After *Beaver,* Beaumont appeared in a scattering of series episodes *(Mannix, The Virginian, Petticoat Junction),* continuing to act until he suffered a stroke in 1972. His death ten years later was a blow to many viewers' memories of childhood, as well as to the producers of the 1983 TV film *Still the Beaver.* In that bittersweet reunion of the series regulars, his TV wife June spent a good deal of time beside Ward's gravestone thinking aloud about her grown sons' problems and asking, "Ward, what would *you* do?"

BEAVERS, LOUISE—black actress
b: Mar 8, 1902*, Cincinnati, Ohio d: Oct 26, 1962

Beulah (com) .... Beulah (1952–53)

Joyous, corpulent actress who played cooks and housekeepers almost exclusively throughout her long career. She began in films in the 1920s (having been spotted by a talent scout and signed for a role in *Uncle Tom's Cabin*) and was in many features of the 1930s, '40s, and '50s. She is known to TV viewers as the housekeeper who looked after an inept white middle-class family on *Beulah.* This was one of the earliest TV comedies to star a black.

She continued to make occasional appearances on TV in later years, including a role in Disney's *Swamp Fox* in 1959.

*Some sources give 1898.

BECK, BILLY—actor
Lou Grant (drama) .. photo editor (1979–81)

BECK, JACKSON—announcer
b: New York City, N.Y.

Charade Quiz (quiz)..... panelist (1947–49)
Lifeline (doc) .... narrator (1978)

BECK, JOHN—actor
b: Jan 28, c. 1944, Chicago, Ill.

Nichols (wes)......... Ketcham (1971–72)
Flamingo Road (drama)
.... Sam Curtis (1981–82)
Dallas (drama)...... Mark Graison (1983–)

BECK, KIMBERLY—actress
b: Jan 9, 1956, Glendale, Calif.

Peyton Place (drama).. Kim Schuster (1965)
Lucas Tanner (drama)
.... Terry Klitsner (1974–75)
Rich Man, Poor Man—Book II (drama)
.... Diane Porter (1976–77)

The stepdaughter of singer Tommy Leonetti. She has been an actress since age two, when she played Glenn Ford's little daughter in the film *Torpedo Run.* Later she was the deaf-mute child on TV's *Peyton Place.* In the 1980s, as Kimberly Beck-Hilton, she originated the role of Julie Clegg on the daytime soap opera *Capitol.*

BECK, MICHAEL—actor
b: Feb 4, 1949, Memphis, Tenn.

Holocaust (drama) ..... Hans Helms (1978)

BECKER, BARBARA—actress
Wayne King (music)...... regular (1951–52)

BECKER, GEORGE, SINGERS
Garry Moore Show (var)
.... regulars (1959–64)

BECKER, SANDY—announcer
b: 1922, New York City, N.Y.

Armstrong Circle Theatre (drama)
.... host-narrator (1954–55)
Win with a Winner (quiz)..... emcee (1958)

BECKER, TERRY—actor

Voyage to the Bottom of the Sea (sci fi)
.... Chief Sharkey (1965–68)

BECKER, TONY—juvenile actor

The Texas Wheelers (com)
.... T. J. Wheeler (1974–75)
The Oregon Trail (wes)
.... William Thorpe (1977)
For Love and Honor (drama)
.... Pvt. Utah Wilson (1983)

BECKHAM, BRICE—juvenile actor
b: Feb 11, 1976, Long Beach, Calif.

Mr. Belvedere (com)
.... Wesley Owens (1985–)

BECKLEY, WILLIAM—actor

Dynasty (drama) .... Gerard (1984–)

BECKMAN, HENRY—actor

I'm Dickens—He's Fenster (com)
.... Yel Mulligan (1962–63)
The Lieutenant (drama)
.... Maj. Barker (1963–64)
Peyton Place (drama)
.... George Anderson (1964–65)
McHale's Navy (com)
.... Col. Harrington (1965–66)
Here Come the Brides (adv)
.... Capt. Charley Clancey (1968–70)
Funny Face (com) ...... Pat Harwell (1971)
Bronk (police)....... Harry Mark (1975–76)
Check It Out (com)..... Alf Scully (1985–)

BEDELIA, BONNIE—actress
b: Mar 25, 1946, New York City, N.Y.

The New Land (adv) .. Anna Larsen (1974)

BEDFORD, BRIAN—actor
b: Feb 16, 1935, Morley, Yorkshire, England

Coronet Blue (drama)...... Anthony (1967)

BEDFORD-LLOYD, JOHN—actor
b: Jan 2, New Haven, Conn.

Hometown (drama).... Peter Kincaid (1985)

BEER, JACQUELINE—actress
b: c. 1932, France

77 Sunset Strip (drama)
.... Suzanne Fabray (1958–63)

Miss France of 1954.

BEERS, FRANCINE—actress

One of the Boys (com)... Mrs. Green (1982)

BEERY, NOAH, JR.—actor
b: Aug 10, 1913*, New York City, N.Y. r: California

Circus Boy (adv) . Joey, the clown (1956–58)
Riverboat (adv) .... Bill Blake (1960–61)
Hondo (wes) .... Buffalo Baker (1967)
Doc Elliot (drama) ... Barney Weeks (1974)
The Rockford Files (drama)
...... Joseph "Rocky" Rockford (1974–80)
The Quest (adv)........ Art Henley (1982)
The Yellow Rose (drama)
.... Luther Dillard (1983–84)

Easygoing Noah Beery was a grizzled old-timer by the time he achieved his greatest fame on television. He had been in front of the cameras since the days of silent films. His father, Noah Beery, Sr. (who died in 1946), was one of the screen's great villains, and his uncle, Wallace Beery, was also a famous film star. Young Noah first appeared in one of his father's films in 1920; then, after a few years, launched his own solo career, which eventually totaled more than 125 features. Many of them were westerns and action thrillers in which Noah loyally supported the hero. "I established an image long ago of being the brother of the girl or the friend of the leading man," he said in the 1970s. "If you want to keep busy, don't be a Romeo."

Noah used this laid-back approach through most of his long TV career as well. In the 1950s he was the kindly clown who cared for young Mickey on *Circus Boy*; in the 1960s, the pilot on *Riverboat* and a colorful scout on *Hondo*; and in the 1970s the owner of the general store on *Doc Elliot* and Jim Garner's dad on *The Rockford Files*—the latter role being his most famous and the one that brought him two Emmy Award nominations. Noah continued to be in demand in the 1980s, with regular roles on *The Quest* and *The Yellow Rose*.

His interest in the old west was genuine.

*Some sources give 1915 or 1916.

A collector of western paintings and sculptures, he spent much of his time in later years on his large ranch north of Los Angeles.

BEGA, LESLIE—actress
b: Apr 17, Los Angeles, Calif.

Head of the Class (com)
.... Maria Tomlinson (1986–)

BEGLEY, ED—actor
b: Mar 25, 1901, Hartford, Conn. d: Apr 28, 1970

Roller Derby (sport) ...... announcer (1951)
Leave It to Larry (com).. Mr. Koppel (1952)

A hearty, barrel-chested character actor who excelled at playing corrupt politicians and other aggressive types. His career built rather slowly. He was a radio and stage actor in local productions in the 1930s, finally making it to Broadway in 1943 (once there he scored some considerable successes over the next 25 years). He was quite active in network radio drama series of the 1940s, most notably as Charlie Chan, and in 1947 began a film career as well.

Begley was seen on television beginning in the early, live days, in literally hundreds of dramas (one estimate is that he was in some 250 shows). One of his most famous roles was in "Patterns" on *Kraft Television Theatre* in 1955, a drama about a corporate power struggle which was later made into a movie (also with Begley). He continued to be very active through the 1960s, mostly in dramas and westerns (*Bonanza, Gunsmoke, The Fugitive, Burke's Law*) with an occasional comedy thrown in (*My Three Sons, The Dick Van Dyke Show*). One of his finest performances of this period was in "Inherit the Wind" (1965), the TV adaptation of a Broadway play in which he had starred. His appearances continued right up until the time of his death; an episode of *The Name of the Game* in which he appeared aired the month he died.

BEGLEY, ED, JR.—actor
b: Sep 16, 1949, Los Angeles, Calif.

Roll Out (com)
.... Lt. Robert W. Chapman (1973–74)

St. Elsewhere (drama)
.... Dr. Victor Erlich (1982–)

The sandy-haired son of actor Ed Begley, whose style was as laid-back as his father's was forceful. The elder Begley did not try to push his son into show business, but young Ed would have nothing else, hammering away until he finally wrangled a guest spot on *My Three Sons* when he was 17. He later had some parts in other series, including a recurring role as a basketball player on *Room 222,,* before landing the regular role of a young lieutenant in a mostly black World War II army unit on *Roll Out.*

Real success continued to be elusive, however, until eight years later, when he joined the cast of *St. Elsewhere.* His performance there as the dedicated, unassuming young Dr. Erlich won him two Emmy nominations.

BEL GEDDES, BARBARA—actress
b: Oct 31, 1922, New York City, N.Y.

Dallas (drama).. Miss Ellie Ewing (1978–84)
Dallas (drama)... Miss Ellie Ewing (1985–)

Emmy Award: Best Actress in a Drama Series, for *Dallas* (1980)

The kindly Miss Ellie, who kept the peace among the scheming members of the Ewing clan, had an active career in the 1940s and '50s but was infrequently seen after that, until she began her role on *Dallas.* The daughter of one of Broadway's most illustrious scenic designers (Norman Bel Geddes), Barbara was primarily a stage actress during her earlier career; like many New York stage actors, she also appeared on live television on many of the playhouse series of the early days (*Robert Montgomery Presents, Schlitz Playhouse of Stars,* etc.). Later she did a few episodes of *Alfred Hitchcock Presents,* but after 1960 her appearances became quite infrequent, whether on television, in movies, or on-stage.

She left *Dallas* in 1984 to recuperate from a heart operation but returned a year later in 1985.

BELACK, DORIS—actress
b: Feb 26, New York City, N.Y.

Baker's Dozen (com)
.... Capt. Florence Baker (1982)

BELAFONTE, HARRY—black singer
b: Mar 1, 1927, Harlem, New York City, N.Y. r: Jamaica, West Indies

Sugar Hill Times (var)....... regular (1949)

Emmy Awards: Best Performance in a Variety Program, for "Tonight with Belafonte" (1960)

Though known to TV viewers primarily for his big, glossy musical specials in the late 1950s and '60s, Harry Belafonte did appear as a regular in one early series— the short-lived black musical revue *Sugar Hill Times,* in 1949. He was a virtually unknown cabaret performer at the time, doing ordinary pop songs. He began to attract attention as a folk singer on Broadway in 1953–54 (his first film was made at the same time) and scored his first major triumph singing folk songs on the CBS special "Three for Tonight" in June 1955. His recording career took off with several huge calypso hits in 1956–57, and for the rest of the decade he made guest appearances on the top variety shows of the day *(Colgate Comedy Hour, The Ed Sullivan Show).*

In 1959 he began his own musical specials, including one, in December 1959, which won him an Emmy Award—the first ever awarded to a black performer (he had been nominated for his 1955 performances).

Belafonte was deeply involved in the Civil Rights struggle of the 1960s and was not immune from controversy himself. A 1968 appearance with Petula Clark drew complaints when Petula touched Belafonte's arm during a love duet—the sight of a black man and a white woman touching was still considered unacceptable to some at that time. In the same year he took part in a televised debate on racism in America, as part of an ABC documentary series; and a segment he taped for *The Smothers Brothers Comedy Hour,* showing him singing in front of a filmed montage of riots at the Democratic National Convention, was censored by CBS.

Belafonte's appearances were less frequent in later years, although he continued to be seen on occasional variety shows and specials. In 1981 he portrayed a football coach in the well-received TV movie *Grambling's White Tiger.*

BELAFONTE-HARPER, SHARI—black actress
b: Sep 22, 1954, New York City, N.Y.

Hotel (drama)........ Julie Gillette (1983–)

The daughter of Harry Belafonte, who got her start in Calvin Klein jeans commercials.

BELASCO, LEON—actor
b: Oct 11, 1902, Odessa, Russia

My Sister Eileen (com)
.... Mr. Appopoplous (1960–61)

BELFORD, CHRISTINE—actress
b: Jan 14, 1949, Amityville, N.Y.

Banacek (drama). Carlie Kirkland (1973–74)
Married: The First Year (drama)
.... Emily Gorey (1979)
Empire (com) .... Jackie Willow (1984)

BELGARD, MADELINE—juvenile actress
One Man's Family (drama)
.... Teddy Lawton (1951–52)

BELL, EDWARD—actor
Knots Landing (drama)
.... Mitchell Casey (1983)

BELL, MICHAEL—actor
Dallas (drama)...... Les Crowley (1980–81)

BELL, REX—cowboy star
b: Oct 16, 1905, Chicago, Ill. d: Jul 4, 1962

Cowboys & Injuns (child) .... host (1950)

BELL, TITA—actress
Happy Days (com) .... Trudy (1974–75)

BELL, TOM—actor
b: 1933*, Liverpool, England

Holocaust (drama) . Adolf Eichmann (1978)

BELLAMY, RALPH—actor
b: Jun 17, 1904, Chicago, Ill.

*Some sources give 1932.

Man Against Crime (drama)
.... Mike Barnett (1949–54)
To Tell the Truth (quiz).. panelist (1957–59)
Frontier Justice (wes).......... host (1961)
The Eleventh Hour (drama)
.... Dr. L. Richard Starke (1963–64)
The Survivors (drama)
.... Baylor Carlyle (1969–70)
The Most Deadly Game (drama)
.... Mr. Arcane (1970–71)
Hunter (drama) .... Gen. Baker (1977)
Wheels (drama)...... Lowell Baxter (1978)
The Winds of War (drama)
.... Pres. Franklin D. Roosevelt (1983)

Ralph Bellamy was one of those older actors for whom television came along at just the right time. Beginning as a stage actor in the 1920s, he moved to Hollywood in 1931 and appeared in scores of films over the next 15 years. Most of them were B films; he starred in a series of *Ellery Queen* mystery films of the period. With his movie roles becoming less frequent in the mid-1940s (as he entered *his* forties) he turned to TV and immediately scored with one of the most popular crime series of the medium's early days: *Man Against Crime*. After that, his television work was steady for the next 30-plus years. He appeared in a great many dramatic shows, from *The U.S. Steel Hour* and *Philco Playhouse* in the 1950s to *Alcoa Premiere, Death Valley Days,* and *Twelve O'Clock High* in later years. He was also a regular in several series in the 1960s and '70s, though none was as successful as *Man Against Crime*. By the 1970s he was appearing mostly in TV movies and miniseries (including *Wheels*); his craggy, distinguished features were perfect for powerful businessmen and politicians.

Bellamy reprised one of his best known roles, that of F.D.R., in the 1983 miniseries *Winds of War*. Twenty-five years earlier he had scored his greatest triumph on stage as F.D.R. in *Sunrise at Campobello,* and had repeated the role to acclaim in a 1960 movie.

Bellamy was active politically, serving 20 years on the California Arts Commission and 12 years (1952–64) as president of Actor's Equity. His autobiography, published in 1979, was titled *When the Smoke Hits the Fan.*

BELLAND, BRUCE—singer
b: Oct 26, 1936, b: Chicago, Ill. r: Los Angeles, Calif.

The Tim Conway Comedy Hour (var)
.... regular (1970)

A onetime member of the 1950s singing group The Four Preps and co-writer of some of their biggest hits ("26 Miles," "Big Man"). In the 1960s Belland became a TV script writer and actor, appearing for four years in occasional roles on *The Adventures of Ozzie & Harriet* and other series. He then moved to the business side of TV, becoming a network program executive.

On the Conway show Belland teamed with another member of a popular 1950s group, Dave Sommerville of The Diamonds, in a vocal duo.

BELLAVER, HARRY—actor
b: Feb 12, 1905

Naked City (police)
.... Ptlm./Sgt. Frank Arcaro (1958–63)

BELLER, KATHLEEN—actress
b: Feb 10, 1955, Queens, N.Y.*

The Blue and the Gray (drama)
.... Kathy Reynolds (1982)
Dynasty (drama) .... Kirby (1982–84)

BELLER, MARY LINN—actress

A Date with Judy (com)
.... Judy Foster (1952–53)

BELLFLOWER, NELLIE—actress

The Kelly Monteith Show (var)
.... regular (1976)
East of Eden (drama).... Mrs. Trask (1981)

BELLI, MELVIN—lawyer
b: July 29, 1907, Sonora, Calif.

Whodunnit? (quiz)......... panelist (1979)

A famed criminal attorney who was occasionally seen on television, including a short run as a regular panelist on this unusual game show.

BELLINI, CAL—actor

Diagnosis: Unknown (drama)
.... Dr. Motilal Mookerji (1960)

*Some sources give Westchester, N.Y.

BELLSON, LOUIS—orchestra leader

b: Jul 26, 1924, Rock Falls, Ill.

The Pearl Bailey Show (var)
.... orch. leader (1971)

The husband of Pearl Bailey and her frequent accompanist. An accomplished jazz drummer in his own right, and veteran of the Goodman, Dorsey, and Ellington big bands, he was a member of Doc Severinsen's *Tonight Show* orchestra in the 1970s.

BELLWOOD, PAMELA—actress

b: Jun 26, 1951, New York City, N.Y.

W.E.B. (drama).... Ellen Cunningham (1978)
Dynasty (drama)
.... Claudia Blaisdel (1981–86)

BELTRAN, ALMA—actress

Berrengers (drama)... Mami Morales (1985)

BELUSHI, JIM—actor

b: June 15, 1954, Chicago, Ill. r: Wheaton, Ill.

Who's Watching the Kids? (com)
.... Bert Gunkel (1978)
Working Stiffs (com)
.... Ernie O'Rourke (1979)
NBC's Saturday Night Live (com)
.... regular (1983–85)

Look-alike younger brother of comedian John Belushi.

BELUSHI, JOHN—actor

b: Jan 24, 1949, Chicago, Ill. r: Wheaton, Ill.
d: Mar 5, 1982

NBC's Saturday Night Live (com)
.... regular (1975–79)

Emmy Award: Best Comedy Writing, for *NBC's Saturday Night Live* (1977)

"He could have given us a lot more laughs, but nooooooo."

So reads an anonymous sign at the lonely grave of John Belushi on Martha's Vineyard, off the coast of Massachusetts. Belushi's career was spectacular and short. An alumnus of Chicago's famed Second City improvisational comedy troupe (1971–72) and the off-Broadway revue *Lemmings* (1973), he got his big break in 1975 as one of the bright young comics in the original cast of *NBC's Saturday Night Live.* The show was a sensation, and so was Belushi (and his buddy Dan Aykroyd) in such skits as the Samurai warrior, the Blues Brothers, and the bees (which he hated). In 1978 Belushi crashed into movies as the gross Bluto in the smash hit film *Animal House.* However, none of his subsequent films were nearly as successful, including one with Aykroyd based on their *SNL* creation, The Blues Brothers. John's career became a frenzied swirl of drugs and deals as he desperately tried to regain the momentum of the late '70s. Heavily into drugs, his personal life out of control, he died of an overdose of cocaine mixed with heroin in a Hollywood bungalow in early 1982. The woman who gave him the fatal injection, Cathy Smith, was charged with murder; she later pleaded guilty to a reduced charge of manslaughter.

Belushi's drug-filled life was recounted in sensationalized fashion in the best-selling 1984 biography, *Wired: The Short Life and Fast Times of John Belushi,* by Bob Woodward.

BELVEDERES—

The Ray Anthony Show (var)
.... regulars (1956–57)

BELZER, RICHARD—comedian

Thicke of the Night (talk)
.... regular (1983–84)

BENADERET, BEA—actress

b: Apr 4, 1906, New York City, N.Y. d: Oct 13, 1968

The George Burns and Gracie Allen Show (com)........... Blanche Morton (1950–58)
The George Burns Show (com)
.... Blanche Morton (1958–59)
Peter Loves Mary (com) .. Wilma (1960–61)
The Flintstones (cartn)
.... Betty Rubble (voice) (1960–64)
The Beverly Hillbillies (com)
.... Cousin Pearl Bodine (1962–63)
Petticoat Junction (com)
.... Kate Bradley (1963–68)

Bea Benaderet was a matronly woman who was quite popular playing a wife or next-door neighbor on radio and TV. She worked steadily in both media for nearly

30 years. In the 1940s, on radio, she was a regular on *Ozzie and Harriet* (as their maid), *A Date with Judy* (Judy's mom), and *My Favorite Husband* (Lucille Ball's best friend), among many others. On television she was seen as a regular on one series or another almost every year from 1950 until her death in 1968. Her best-known roles were those of next-door neighbor Blanche on *The George Burns and Gracie Allen Show* for eight years and the mother of three gorgeous girls on *Petticoat Junction* for five.

Kids may also recall her for her voice work on cartoons, including *The Flintstones* and *Sylvester & Tweety*. She was married to cowboy actor Jim Bannon and was the mother of *Lou Grant*'s Jack Bannon.

BENARD, FRANÇOIS-MARIE—actor
b: Madagascar

Scruples (drama) .... Edouard (1980)

Also known as Frank M. Benard.

BENBEN, BRIAN—actor
b: Jun 18, Winchester, Va. r: Marlboro, N.Y.

The *Gangster Chronicles* (drama)
.... Michael Lasker (1981)
Kay O'Brien (drama)
.... Dr. Mark Doyle (1986–)

BENCH, JOHNNY—sportscaster

Games People Play (sport)
.... field reporter (1980–81)

Former all-star catcher for baseball's Cincinnati Reds. He also hosted the syndicated sports talk shows *M.V.P.* in 1971 and *The Baseball Bunch* in the early 1980s.

BENDIX, WILLIAM—actor
b: Jan 14, 1906, New York City, N.Y. d: Dec 14, 1964

The Life of Riley (com)
.... Chester A. Riley (1953–58)
The Overland Trail (wes)
.... Frederick Thomas Kelly (1960)

"What a revolting' development this is," he would groan, and audiences never failed to howl at the latest predicament of TV's favorite bumbler. Pug-faced, gravel-voiced

William Bendix, with his born-in-Brooklyn accent, was a very popular blue-collar type (and sometime villain) in the '40s and '50s. He got into acting rather late, having been born the son of a violinist and conductor of the Metropolitan Opera Orchestra who wanted him to be a musician. Instead, Bendix tried careers as a pro baseball player and grocery store manager. Neither worked out, so he turned to acting in the '30s, reaching Broadway in William Saroyan's *The Time of Your Life* in 1939. He appeared in a great many films, mostly war movies and adventures, from 1941 on. His most famous character, however, originated in 1943 when he began the radio version of *The Life of Riley*. This popular series had two TV versions, the first (1949–50) starring Jackie Gleason. Bendix fought clear of his heavy movie commitments long enough to do the second (1953–58) himself, and it made Chester A. Riley one of the favorite comic characters of early TV.

Bendix also made many guest appearances on other series, including *Lights Out* (in 1952), *Fireside Theatre, Wagon Train,* and *The Dick Powell Theater.* He was active up until the time of his death of pneumonia in 1964; an episode of *Burke's Law* in which he appeared aired only two months before he died, and a film on which he was working, *Young Fury,* was released posthumously in 1965.

BENEDICT, DIRK—actor
b: Mar 1, 1944, Helena, Mont. r: White Sulphur Springs, Mont.

Chopper One (police) .. Off. Gil Foley (1974)
Battlestar Galactica (sci fi)
.... Lt. Starbuck (1978–79)
The A-Team (adv)
.... Lt. Templeton Peck (1983–)

This actor was so handsome he was nicknamed "The Face" on *The A-Team,* his usual assignment being to charm his way past adversaries (especially females) or smoothly talk them out of the information the team needed to complete its mission. Benedict was born Dick Niewoehner; he claims he adopted his stage name from a plate of eggs he was eating one day. After roles in a few very forgettable movies of the early 1970s (including *SSSSSSS,* in which he was a scientist transformed into a king cobra), he moved into television and found rather steady work in regular series and guest appearances.

Benedict survived a bout with cancer by assiduously following a macrobiotic diet, and now plays gung-ho hero roles. A private pilot, he frequently flies back to his native Montana to spend time at a cabin he maintains in a remote area of the "Big Sky" country.

BENEDICT, GREG—actor

No Time for Sergeants (com)
.... Pvt. Blanchard (1964–65)

BENEDICT, PAUL—actor
b: Sep 17, 1938, Silver City, N.M. r: Boston, Mass.

The Jeffersons (com)
.... Harry Bentley (1975–81)
The Blue and the Gray (drama)
.... Arbuthnot (1982)
The Jeffersons (com)
.... Harry Bentley (1983–85)

The long-faced Englishman of *The Jeffersons.* His background was primarily in the theater.

BENIADES, TED—actor

Andros Targets (drama)
.... Wayne Hillman (1977)

BENJAMIN, JULIA—juvenile actress

Hazel (com) .... Susie Baxter (1965–66)

BENJAMIN, RICHARD—actor
b: May 22, 1938, New York City, N.Y.

He & She (com) .... Dick Hollister (1967–68)
Quark (com) .... Adam Quark (1978)

Although Richard Benjamin is known primarily for his offbeat movie roles of the 1960s and '70s *(Goodbye Columbus, Catch-22)*, he had a somewhat quirky TV career as well. After graduating from New York's High School for the Performing Arts (the school immortalized in *Fame*), he struggled to establish himself in the theater during the early and mid 1960s, picking up occasional TV work along the way—including a role on *Dr. Kildare* in 1964. He began to attract attention on Broadway in

late 1966, in *Star Spangled Girl,* and the following year costarred with his wife (since 1961) Paula Prentiss in the critically acclaimed TV comedy *He & She.* The show was not a hit with viewers, however, and Benjamin turned to movies, where he became a major star.

He was lured back to TV in the late 1970s for one of the strangest comedies ever, called *Quark,* in which he played the captain of an intergalactic garbage scow! Viewers apparently did not know what to make of this melange of high camp and space parody, and it—along with Benjamin —disappeared from television after a short run.

BENJAMIN, SUE—
See Bennett, Sue

BENJAMIN, SUSAN—juvenile actress
b: Feb 22, 1959

Accidental Family (com)
.... Tracy Kramer (1967–68)

BENNETT, DONN—host, producer
b: c. 1910, Ashtabula, Ohio d: Aug 20, 1986

The Big Idea (info) .... host (1952–53)

BENNETT, ELIZABETH—actress
b: Jul 20, Yorkshire, England

You Again? (com) .. Enid Tompkins (1986–)

This English television actress had the unique distinction of appearing in the same series in the U.S. and England—simultaneously. She played the housekeeper Enid in *You Again?,* starring Jack Klugman, and the same role in the British series on which it was based, called *Home to Roost,* jetting back and forth between continents to meet the production schedules of both shows.

Good servants are hard to find, even on TV.

BENNETT, JOAN—actress
b: Feb 27, 1910, Palisades, N.J.

Too Young to Go Steady (com)
.... Mary Blake (1959)

Joan Bennett, the movie queen of the '30s and '40s, made a fair number of guest appearances on television over the years, in playhouse series of the 1950s *(Somerset Maugham Theatre, Ford Theatre, Shower of Stars)* and in a few dramas and TV movies thereafter (including 1981's *This House Possessed)*. She had only two regular series roles: as the mom in *Too Young to Go Steady* in 1959, and as Elizabeth Stoddard in the campy daytime soap opera *Dark Shadows* in the late 1960s.

Her memoirs were titled *The Bennett Playbill* (1970).

BENNETT, MARJORIE—actress
b: c. 1895 d: Jun 14, 1982

The Many Loves of Dobie Gillis (com)
.... Mrs. Blossom Kenney (1959–61)

BENNETT, MICHELLE—juvenile actress

The Yellow Rose (drama)
.... L. C. Champion (1983–84)

BENNETT, PETER—actor
b: Sep 17, 1917, London, England

Adventures of Sir Lancelot (adv)
.... Leonides (1956–57)

BENNETT, SUE—singer

Teen Time Tunes (music) .... hostess (1949)
Kay Kyser's Kollege of Musical Knowledge (quiz).................. vocalist (1949–50)
Your Hit Parade (music) . vocalist (1951–52)

BENNETT, TONY—singer
b: Aug 3, 1926, Queens, N.Y.

Songs for Sale (music) .... regular (1950)
The Tony Bennett Show (var) ... host (1956)
Perry Presents (var) .... cohost (1959)

Tony Bennett was virtually unknown when he won a spot as one of the staff singers on the 1950 summer series *Songs for Sale*. He left after a month and soon became one of the hottest names in popular music, with early '50s hits such as "Because of You" and "Cold, Cold Heart." He was a guest on many shows in subsequent years, generally singing adult, jazz-flavored material. He also served as the summer replacement for Perry Como twice in the '50s.

BENNY, JACK—comedian
b: Feb 14, 1894, Waukegan, Ill. d: Dec 26, 1974

The Jack Benny Show (com)
.... as himself (1950–65)
Shower of Stars (var)
.... regular star (1955–58)

Emmy Awards: Best Series Performance By a Person Who Essentially Plays Himself, for *The Jack Benny Show* (1957); Trustees Award, for His Contributions to Television (1958); Best Actor in a Comedy, for *The Jack Benny Show* (1959).

Probably no one brought old-fashioned character comedy to early television quite as successfully as Jack Benny. His array of stock characteristics—his stinginess, his terrible violin playing, his mild but continual exasperation over his slightly batty friends (Don Wilson, Mary Livingstone, Dennis Day)—had been ingrained on the American consciousness via radio for 20 years, and they made a big hit in television as well. Long before Benny died (of cancer, in 1974) he was a show business legend.

Jack actually did begin as a violinist, in vaudeville before World War I, but soon took to joking about it. At first he called himself Ben K. Benny; he had to change the name to avoid confusion with popular bandleader Ben Bernie. Jack really hit his stride on radio, beginning in 1932. His program ranked as one of the top (or *the* top) show on the air for as long as the medium lasted. He also branched into movies in the 1930s and '40s, and although some of his films were minor gems, his main success was on the air.

Jack tiptoed into TV. From 1950 to 1953 he was seen approximately once a month, then from 1953 until 1960 every other week, always on Sunday nights. Finally, in the 1960s, his show became a weekly series. It was a comfortable, friendly half hour, always done with good taste and good humor, and it was highly rated for most of its run. Eternally 39, and eternally vain, Benny himself was the main butt of the show's jokes, and the viewer knew he didn't mind. One of the classic gags had tightwad Benny confronted by a burglar:

BURGLAR: "Your money or your life!"
BENNY: (long silence, as audience starts to giggle)
BURGLAR: "Well?"

BENNY (finally): "I'm thinking, I'm thinking!"

Jack continued to appear in the late
1960s and early '70s, on specials and other
programs, guesting a number of times on
Lucille Ball's series between 1965 and 1971.
He was active until his death, appearing in
the special "Annie and the Hoods" (as
Anne Bancroft's psychiatrist) in November
1974, and in a Dean Martin celebrity roast
which aired posthumously in 1975.

Jack was married to Mary Livingstone in
1927 and appeared with her throughout his
career (she always portrayed his girlfriend, not his wife). Though he played the
skinflint, he was in reality one of Hollywood's most generous and self-effacing
stars.

BENOIT, PATRICIA—actress
b: Feb 21, Fort Worth, Texas

Mr. Peepers (com)
.... Nancy Remington (1952–55)

BENSON, BARBARA—

The Sammy Kaye Show (var)
.... regular (1951–52)

BENSON, CORT—actor

Young Mr. Bobbin (com)
.... Mr. Willis (1951–52)

BENSON, IRVING—comedian

The Milton Berle Show (var)
.... Sidney Sphritzer (1966–67)

BENSON, LUCILLE—actress
b: July 17, 1922*, Scottsboro, Ala. d: Feb 17,
1984

Nashville 99 (police)..... Birdie Huff (1977)
Bosom Buddies (com)
.... Lilly Sinclair (1980–81)

BENSON, PAT—actress

Joe & Valerie (com).. Stella Sweetzer (1978)

BENSON, RED—host
b: 1917, Columbus, Ohio r: Philadelphia, Pa.

Name That Tune (quiz) .... emcee (1953–54)

*Some sources give 1914.

BENSON, ROBBY—actor
b: Jan 21, 1956, Dallas, Texas

Tough Cookies (com)
.... Det. Cliff Brady (1986)

Having made his name in juvenile roles in
movies, especially tearjerkers such as *Ode
to Billy Joe, Tribute,* and *The Death of Richie,* Robby turned to television to establish a more mature image for himself. In
Tough Cookies he played a hard-driving
police detective, but the audience didn't
buy the change of character.

Robby's previous small screen appearances had been mostly in TV films, usually
as somebody's son (Jack Warden's in *Remember When,* Arthur Hill's in *Death Be
Not Proud*) or grandson (George Burns'
in *Two of a Kind*). In the early 1970s,
while still in his teens, he played the
continuing role of Mary Stuart's adopted
son on the daytime serial *Search for
Tomorrow.*

BENTLEY, BEVERLY—actress

Beat the Clock (quiz) ... assistant (1955–58)

BENTON, BARBI—actress
b: Jan 28, 1950, Sacramento, Calif.

Hee Haw (var).......... regular (1971–76)
Sugar Time! (com)........ Maxx (1977–78)

Perhaps it is her first name, perhaps her
sexy but featherheaded roles, but Barbi
Benton has been typed as TV's ultimate
bimbo. Her credits reflect it: a sexpot on
Hee Haw, a naive hatcheck girl on *Sugar
Time!,* and similar roles on episodes of
quite a few series from the late 1960s onward (including *Laugh-In*). She was seen
on *Playboy After Dark* in 1969 and has
even starred in a special called "A Barbi
Doll for Christmas."

BENTON, EDDIE—actress

Rafferty (drama) ... Nurse Koscinski (1977)
Doctors' Private Lives (drama)
.... Nurse Diane Cooper (1979)

BENTON, LEE—actress

Mickey Spillane's Mike Hammer (drama)
.... Jenny the bartender (1984–)

BERADINO, JOHN—actor

b: May 1, 1917, Los Angeles, Calif.

I Led Three Lives (drama)
.... special agent Steve Daniels
(occasional) (1953–56)
The New Breed (police)
.... Sgt. Vince Cavelli (1961–62)

John Beradino is probably the only person to have combined major careers in sports and soap operas. As a child he was bitten by the show business bug, which led to appearances in several of the *Our Gang* comedies. Then a love of sports took over; he became a star athlete in college and went on to a ten-year career in major league baseball (1939–53, interrupted by service in World War II). He played first with the St. Louis Browns and then with the Cleveland Indians and was second baseman with the Indians when they won the 1948 World Series.

After a leg injury ended his baseball career, Beradino turned to acting, appearing as a commie-chasing F.B.I. agent in *I Led Three Lives* and as a seasoned cop in *The New Breed*. Then, on April 1, 1963, he found a permanent home on daytime TV, originating the central role of Dr. Steve Hardy on ABC's brand new soap opera *General Hospital*. He stayed with the show for the next 20-plus years, winning several Emmy nominations along the way.

BERDIS, BERT—comedian

b: Mar 23, 1939, Pittsburgh, Pa.

The Tim Conway Show (var)
.... regular (1980–81)

A onetime comedy writer and ad agency man, Bert came to prominence in commercials of the 1970s as one-half of the comedy team of Dick and Bert (with Dick Orkin). Among their greatest hits: *Time* magazine and Lancer ads.

BERG, GERTRUDE—actress

b: Oct 3, 1899, Harlem, New York City, N.Y. d: Sep 14, 1966

The Goldbergs (com)
.... Molly Goldberg (1949–55)
Gertrude Berg Show (com)
.... Sarah Green (1961–62)

Emmy Award: Best Actress (1950)

Gertrude Berg was America's favorite Jewish mother for more than 25 years. Beginning in 1929, with *The Rise of the Goldbergs,* her character of Molly Goldberg was a solid hit, first on radio and then on television. She wrote and researched the show herself, spending days walking through New York City's Lower East Side, shopping and talking and picking up vignettes from the largely Jewish immigrant population that made her series all the more authentic (she herself was raised in an upper-class home). Her scripts were full of family turmoil, always soothed by homilies—"Better a crust of bread and enjoy it than a cake that gives you indigestion"— and a great deal of love.

She became so identified with her character that fans on the street always called her "Molly." When *The Goldbergs* finally ended its TV run in 1955 she could do little else. After a few dramatic appearances in the late 1950s *(The U.S. Steel Hour, The Elgin TV Hour),* she made a stab at another series, *The Gertrude Berg Show* (aka *Mrs. G. Goes to College*), but it lasted less than a year.

Her autobiography was titled, appropriately, *Molly and Me* (1961).

BERGAN, JUDITH-MARIE—actress

Maggie (com) .... Buffy Croft (1981–82)
Domestic Life (com) ... Candy Crane (1984)
All Is Forgiven (com)
.... Cecile Porter-Lindsey (1986)

BERGEN, BILL—singer

The Polly Bergen Show (var)
.... regular (1957–58)

Polly Bergen's father.

BERGEN, EDGAR—comedian

b: Feb 16, 1903, Chicago, Ill. d: Sep 30, 1978

Do You Trust Your Wife? (quiz)
.... emcee (1956–57)

Ostensibly (and originally) a ventriloquist, Edgar Bergen became one of the brightest stars on radio through his witty repartee with his dummies Charlie McCarthy and Mortimer Snerd. He was seen on television mostly as a guest star, primarily on variety shows, but also as a straight actor on such series as *The Dick Powell Show* and *Burke's Law.* In 1956–57 he hosted the prime time quiz show *Do You Trust Your Wife?* He later donated Charlie McCarthy to the Smithsonian Institution.

He was the father of film star Candice Bergen.

BERGEN, FRANCES—actress

Yancy Derringer (adv)
.... Madame Francine (1958–59)

BERGEN, JERRY—comedian

Buzzy Wuzzy (var)............ host (1948)

BERGEN, POLLY—singer, actress
b: Jul 14, 1930, Knoxville, Tenn.

Pepsi-Cola Playhouse (drama)
.... hostess (1954–55)
To Tell the Truth (quiz).. panelist (1956–61)
The Polly Bergen Show (var)
.... hostess (1957–58)
79 Park Avenue (drama)
.... Vera Keppler (1977)
The Winds of War (drama)
.... Rhoda Henry (1983)

Emmy Award: Best Actress in a Single Performance, for "The Helen Morgan Story" (1957)

A pert young brunette with a pleasant voice and personality. Polly began her career in several media simultaneously in the early 1950s, and though she had some success in each, none led to real stardom. As a singer, she recorded several LPs, appeared in musical stage revues and on TV variety shows (including *Your Hit Parade*). Her own *Polly Bergen Show* in 1957–58 was primarily a musical variety series. As an actress, she appeared in more than a score of movies and was fairly frequently seen on TV playhouse series of the 1950s, among them *Schlitz Playhouse of Stars, The Elgin TV Hour,* and *General Electric Theater.* By far her most famous role was that of the ill-starred singer Helen Morgan in the *Playhouse 90* production of "The Helen Morgan Story," in April 1957.

She continued to appear in the early 1960s but then gradually downplayed her performing career to concentrate on her business ventures, which included fashion books and the successful Oil of the Turtle cosmetics line. She returned to the limelight—part time—in the mid-1970s, primarily in TV movies and miniseries, among them *79 Park Avenue* and *The Winds of War.*

BERGER, ANNA—actress

Seventh Avenue (drama)
.... Celia Blackman (1977)

BERGER, HELMUT—actor
b: May 29, 1944, Salzburg, Austria

Dynasty (drama) .. Peter de Vilbis (1983–84)

BERGERE, LEE—actor
b: Apr 10, New York City, N.Y.

Hot L Baltimore (com)....... George (1975)
Dynasty (drama) .. Joseph Anders (1981–83)

BERGMAN, PETER—actor
b: Jun 11, Guantanamo Bay, Cuba

The Starland Vocal Band Show (var)
.... regular (1977)

Peter Bergman is known to daytime viewers as the idealistic Dr. Cliff Warner of *All My Children* (1979–87).

BERGMAN, RICHARD—actor
b: Plymouth, Ind.

Father Murphy (drama)
.... Father Joe Parker (1981–82)

BERGMEIER, JANE—

The Ken Murray Show (var)
.... regular (1951–52)

BERLE, MILTON—comedian
b: Jul 12, 1908, Harlem, N.Y.

The Milton Berle Show (var)
.... host (1948–56)
Milton Berle in the Kraft Music Hall (var)
.... host (1958–59)
Jackpot Bowling Starring Milton Berle (sports) .... host (1960–61)
The Milton Berle Show (var)
.... host (1966–67)

Emmy Awards: Outstanding Personality (1949); Special Emmy to "Mr. Television" (1979)

"Ladies and Gentlemen, I give you the five-star-general of all the armies of funny men, *still* Mr. Television, Milton Berle." With those words, Gregory Peck introduced Milton Berle in 1978 on one of the innumerable tribute shows devoted to him in the '70s and '80s. Berle was an object of TV veneration almost longer than he was a star performer. The important fact seems to have been that Berle was there at the very beginning and was the first superstar that TV could call its own—thereby providing the medium in later years with living evidence of its own historical roots.

Berle's career was almost unbelievably long. A hustler from day one, he began appearing in silent movies (then made in New Jersey) at the tender age of five; among them were *Tillie's Punctured Romance* and *The Perils of Pauline* in 1914. He played vaudeville in the 1920s and broke into radio in the 1930s, but by the mid-1940s—after half a dozen radio shows and several movies—it looked as if his career was never really going to ignite.

Then, in the summer of 1948, NBC signed him to make four appearances on its new variety show, *The Texaco Star Theater*, which was intended to have a variety of hosts. To everyone's surprise, this slightly shopworn but very energetic trooper caused a sensation among the small fraternity of TV-set owners around the country (only 1% of Americans had TV sets then). In September he was made permanent host, and Berle—and television—became the talk of the country.

TV ownership skyrocketed while Berle was number one, and many credited him, at least in part, for the rapid growth. His loud, brash comedy, outrageous puns, constant breakups during sketches, and outlandish costumes (women's dresses were a favorite) were perfect for a new visual medium, and there was very little serious competition in any event. In 1951, recognizing his immense popularity, NBC signed him to an unheard-of 30 year contract. TV really was here to stay!

By the early 1950s his popularity was already beginning to slip, however, as a great deal of new talent—some of it considerably more sophisticated—flooded into TV. In 1951–52 his show was nudged out of the number-one spot by Arthur Godfrey; by 1954–55 it had slipped out of the top ten. There was frantic tinkering and later attempts at revivals, but Uncle Miltie's salad days were over.

Milton hung around the medium for many years thereafter, making guest appearances and occasionally displaying unsuspected talent as a dramatic actor. During the 1960s he appeared on *The Dick Powell Show, Bob Hope's Presents the Chrysler Theatre* ("Murder at NBC"), *Kraft Suspense Theatre,* and *The Defenders,* among others. But he was best with a twinkle in his eye—as Wise Owl (ugh!) on *F Troop,* or Louie the Lilac on *Batman.*

NBC released him from that 30-year contract and he sailed away on *The Love Boat* not once but several times. Finally, in the 1980s, he was deposited, still spewing jokes, into the TV Hall of Fame.

Berle wrote several autobiographies, the most recent being *Milton Berle, An Autobiography* (1974).

BERLINGER, WARREN—actor
b: Aug 31, 1937, Brooklyn, N.Y.

The Joey Bishop Show (com)
.... Larry Barnes (1961–62)
The Funny Side (var)....... regular (1971)
A Touch of Grace (com)
.... Walter Bradley (1973)
Operation Petticoat (com)
.... chief engineer Dobritch (1978–79)
Small & Frye (com).......... Eddie (1983)

Warren Berlinger has been a busy TV actor since he was a child, appearing in more than 300 roles in live shows of the 1950s and for three years as trouble-prone teenager Jerry Ames on *The Secret Storm* (1954–57). His best work was in comedy, however, including many appearances in the 1960s and '70s; he was practically a semiregular on *Love, American Style* and later a favorite on *CHiPs.* In 1983 he turned up as the proprietor of Darren McGavin's hangout, Eddie's Bar and Grill, on *Small & Frye.*

BERMAN, SHELLEY—comedian
b: Feb 3, 1926, Chicago, Ill.

Mary Hartman, Mary Hartman (com)
.... Mel Beach (1977–78)

BERNARD, CRYSTAL—actress
b: Sep 30, Dallas, Texas

Happy Days (com)
.... K. C. Cunningham (1982–83)
It's a Living (com).. Amy Tompkins (1985–)

BERNARD, DOROTHY—actress
b: c. 1890 d: Dec 21, 1955

Life with Father (com)
.... Margaret, the maid (1953–55)

BERNARD, ED—black actor
b: Jul 4, 1939, Philadelphia, Pa.

Cool Million (drama)
.... Tony Baylor (1972–73)
Police Woman (police)
.... Det. Joe Styles (1974–78)
The White Shadow (drama)
.... Jim Willis (1978–80)

A black actor who appeared in a number of daytime soap operas before making it to prime time.

BERNARD, JASON—actor

The White Shadow (drama)
.... Jim Willis (first episode) (1978)
Cagney & Lacey (police)
... Deputy Inspector Marquette (1982–83)
High Performance (adv) ...... Fletch (1983)

BERNARD, TOMMY—juvenile actor

The Ruggles (com)
.... Chuck Ruggles (1949–52)

BERNARDI, HERSCHEL—actor
b: Oct 30, 1923*, New York City, N.Y. d: May 9, 1986

Peter Gunn (drama) ... Lt. Jacoby (1958–61)
The Jetsons (cartn) . various roles (1962–63)
Arnie (com).......... Arnie Nuvo (1970–72)
Seventh Avenue (drama).. Joe Vitelli (1977)
Hail to the Chief (com)
.... Helmut Luger (1985)

In addition to his roles on Broadway (*Fiddler on the Roof*, etc.) and in films (usually as a cop or a thug), this burly character actor often lent his deep bass voice to cartoons. Among other things, he was Charlie the Tuna and the Jolly Green Giant in commercials.

As a supporting actor, he was a TV standby for many years, appearing in a
*Some sources give Oct. 20.

great many dramatic series of the 1960s and '70s (*Naked City, The Defenders, Route 66,* etc.).

BERNER, SARA—actress

The Hank McCune Show (com)
.... regular (1950)

BERNHARDT, SANDRA—

The Richard Pryor Show (var)
.... regular (1977)

BERNIE, AL—comedian

Fifty-Fourth Street Revue (var).. host (1949)

BERNS, BILL—commentator, producer
b: c. 1919 d: Aug 9, 1972

Television Screen Magazine (mag)
.... regular (1948–49)

BERNSEN, CORBIN—actor
b: Sep 7, North Hollywood, Calif.

L.A. Law (drama) .... Arnie Becker (1986–)

A former daytime serial actor *(Ryan's Hope)*—and the son of daytime soap opera queen Jeanne Cooper. His mother has long played Kay Chancellor on *The Young and the Restless.*

BERRY, FRED—black actor
b: March 13, 1951, St. Louis, Mo.

What's Happening! (com).. Rerun (1976–79)
What's Happening Now!! (com)
...... Freddie ("Rerun") Stubbs (1985–86)

BERRY, KEN—actor
b: Nov 3, c. 1930, Moline, Ill.

The Ann Sothern Show (com)
.... Woody (1960–61)
The Bob Newhart Show (var)
.... regular (1962)
F Troop (com)
.... Capt. Wilton Parmenter (1965–67)
Mayberry R.F.D. (com)
.... Sam Jones (1968–71)
The Ken Berry "Wow" Show (var)
.... host (1972)
Mama's Family (com)
.... Vinton Harper (1983–)

Amiable Ken Berry is one of the most relaxed—and relaxing—comedy actors on television. He was perfect at the friendly snail's pace of *Mayberry R.F.D.*, and as a counterpoint to the antics of the lunatic cast on *F Troop*. Of the latter assignment he once said, "I loved the show and I loved the guys. It was like two years of recess."

Ken had been around show business for about fifteen years, not making much of a fuss, before he hit the big time in the 1960s. As a teenager in the 1940s he toured the country for more than a year with Horace Heidt's Youth Opportunity caravan. His television debut was on Arlene Francis' *Talent Patrol* in the mid-1950s, and that was followed by a spot on *The Ed Sullivan Show* but not by much else until he began landing small roles in TV comedies in the late 1950s.

After his great success as the befuddled Captain on *F Troop* and the loving dad on *Mayberry*, he made an abortive attempt to launch his own variety show (if Jim Nabors could, why couldn't he?) and then was seen in occasional appearances on other series for the rest of the 1970s. His most frequent appearances were on *Love, American Style, The Love Boat,* and *Fantasy Island*. In the 1980s he returned, still wide-eyed and a bit naive, in the underrated comedy series *Mama's Family*.

BERTHRONG, DEIRDRE—actress

James at 15 (drama)
.... Kathy Hunter (1977–78)

BERTI, DEHL—actor

Operation Neptune (sci fi)
.... Mersennus (1953)
Born to the Wind (adv)
.... One Feather (1982)

BERTINELLI, VALERIE—actress
b: Apr 23, 1960, Wilmington, Del.

One Day at a Time (com)
.... Barbara Cooper Royer (1975–84)

The daughter of a General Motors executive, Valerie began her acting career while she was still in grade school, appearing in commercials and in an episode of *Apple's Way* in 1974. Almost immediately she won the part of younger daughter Barbara on *One Day at a Time,* a role that lasted so long she literally grew up on the series—from age 15 to 24. She also starred in a number of TV movies, including 1985's *Silent Witness*.

In April 1981 Valerie married rock star Eddie Van Halen.

BERWICK, BRAD—actor

Window on Main Street (com)
.... Arny Logan (1961–62)

BESCH, BIBI—actress
b: Feb 1, 1942, Vienna, Austria r: Westchester County, N.Y.

Secrets of Midland Heights (drama)
.... Dorothy Wheeler (1980–81)
The Hamptons (drama)
.... Adrienne Duncan Mortimer (1983)

BESSELL, TED—actor
b: Mar 20, 1935*, Flushing, N.Y.

It's a Man's World (com)
.... Tom-Tom DeWitt (1962–63)
Gomer Pyle, U.S.M.C. (com)
.... Frankie Lombardi (1966)
That Girl (com) ... Don Hollinger (1966–71)
Me and the Chimp (com)
.... Mike Reynolds (1972)
Good Time Harry (com)
.... Harry Jenkins (1980)
Hail to the Chief (com)
.... Gen. Oliver Mansfield (1985)

Ted Bessell had a fairly active career in the 1960s and early '70s, though he is known primarily for one role—that of Marlo Thomas's boyfriend on the trendsetting *That Girl*.

As a child, Ted was a musical prodigy, performing in a piano recital at Carnegie Hall at age 12. After graduating from college in 1958, however, he turned to acting. Besides his well-known role on *That Girl* (for which he received an Emmy nomination), he had a short tenure as one of Jim Nabors' barracks buddies on *Gomer Pyle* and starred or costarred in a couple of flops of his own.

He drifted from sight in the mid-1970s, turning up in an occasional above-average TV movie (*Breaking Up Is Hard to Do,* 1979, *The Acorn People,* 1981) and in some

*Some sources give 1926.

fairly offbeat series. One was the obscure but rather good 1980 comedy *Good Time Harry,* and another 1985's equally short-lived *Hail to the Chief.*

BESSER, JOE—comedian

The Ken Murray Show (var)
.... regular (1950–51)
The Abbott and Costello Show (com)
.... Stinky (1951–52)
The Joey Bishop Show (com)
.... Mr. Jillson (1962–65)

One of the Three Stooges during their final days in the '50s. His autobiography is titled *Not Just a Stooge.*

BEST, JAMES—actor

b: July 26, 1926, Powderly, Ky. r: Corydon, Ind.

The Dukes of Hazzard (com)
..... Sheriff Roscoe P. Coltrane (1979–85)

BEST, WILLIE—black actor

b: May 27, 1916, Mississippi d: Feb 27, 1962

The Stu Erwin Show (com)
.... Willie (1950–55)
My Little Margie (com)... Charlie (1952–55)
Waterfront (adv).. Willie Slocum (1953–56)

A young black actor whose entire career was spent playing stereotyped Negroes—wide-eyed, dim-witted, lazy, and scared stiff at the least provocation. Earlier in his career Willie even adopted a professional name that described his speciality, "Sleep 'n' Eat." He made many films in the 1930s and '40s, then turned to TV for his last few active years, as the handyman for the white folks on *The Stu Erwin Show* and *My Little Margie* and a deckhand on *Waterfront.*

BESTWICK, MARTINE—actress

b: 1941

Aspen (drama)...... Joan Carolinian (1977)

BETHUNE, IVY—actress

Father Murphy (drama)
.... Miss Tuttle (1981–82)

The mother of young actress Zina Bethune.

BETHUNE, ZINA—juvenile actress

b: Feb 17, 1946, New York City, N.Y.

The Nurses (drama) ... Gail Lucas (1962–65)

A precocious young actress who was quite active in the 1950s and '60s. Her principal career was on daytime soap operas—*The Guiding Light* (1956–58), *Young Doctor Malone* (1959), and *Love of Life* (1965–71) —but she also made many appearances in prime time. Besides her role as the young nurse on *The Nurses* in the early 1960s, she appeared as a teenager in playhouse series such as *Kraft Television Theatre* and *The U.S. Steel Hour* and in dramas such as *Route 66.*

She continued to act in the '70s and '80s, but her appearances were, by then, infrequent.

BETTGER, LYLE—actor

b: Feb 13, 1915, Philadelphia, Pa.

Court of Last Resort (drama)
.... Sam Larson (1957–58)
The Grand Jury (drama)
.... Harry Driscoll (1959)

After ten indifferent years in the theater in the 1930s and '40s, Lyle Bettger was about to give up acting when Hollywood discovered that he made a perfect villain—tall and good-looking, but with a crooked smile and a slightly sinister charm. Beginning in 1950, in one feature after another, he kicked dogs, slapped women, knocked old people out of wheelchairs, and once, in a bit of inspired villainy, coaxed an elephant into planting a heavy foot on the face of the leading lady.

Lyle brought his menacing good looks to television in the late 1950s, appearing in many dramatic productions and westerns (*Laramie, Tales of Wells Fargo,* etc.). On the two series on which he was a regular, he played a good guy, but audiences evidently liked him better the other way, as neither lasted very long. In later years he was seen mostly on police shows, including numerous appearances on *Hawaii Five-O.*

BETTS, JACK—actor

b: Miami, Fla.

Checkmate (drama)..... Chris Devlin (1962)

85

BETZ, BETTY—journalist

Going Places with Betty Betz (info)
.... moderator (1951)

BETZ, CARL—actor

b: Mar 9, 1920, Pittsburgh, Pa. d: Jan 18, 1978

The Donna Reed Show (com)
.... Dr. Alex Stone (1958–66)
Judd, for the Defense (drama)
.... Clinton Judd (1967–69)

Emmy Award: Best Actor in a Dramatic Series, for *Judd, for the Defense* (1969)

Dark-haired, handsome Carl Betz began his career in the theater, reaching Broadway in the early 1950s. He tried movies in 1953, playing supporting roles in half a dozen features in that one year, but this was a false start. Television showed more promise, and soon he was working fairly steadily in dramatic shows such as *The Millionaire* and *Alfred Hitchcock Presents;* he also had a very early role in the daytime serial *Love of Life. The Donna Reed Show* made him a favorite with America's kids. In it he played the perfect professional father (TV son Paul Petersen even recorded a best-selling tribute to him: "My Dad"). However his two years starring in *Judd, for the Defense* must have been more satisfying professionally, earning him the industry's highest honor—an Emmy Award.

After *Judd,* Betz was much in demand and worked steadily in drama series such as *The F.B.I., Mission: Impossible,* and *Police Story,* as well as making several TV movies. He was active until shortly before his death in 1978.

BEUTEL, BILL—newscaster

b: Cleveland, Ohio

ABC Weekend News (news)
.... anchorman (1976–77)

BEXLEY, DON—black actor

Sanford and Son (com)
.... Bubba Hoover (1972–77)
The Sanford Arms (com)
.... Bubba Hoover (1977)

BEYER, TROY—black actress

Dynasty (drama) .. Jackie Deveraux (1986–)

BEYERS, BILL—actor

b: Lake Success, N.Y. r: Babylon, N.Y.

Joe & Valerie (com)
.... Frank Berganski (1978)

BEYMER, RICHARD—actor, director

b: Feb 21, 1939, Avoca, Iowa

Paper Dolls (drama)... David Fenton (1984)

Beymer did much work as a youthful actor from the mid-1950s to the mid-1960s, both in films *(West Side Story)* and on television. He then became a TV director and thereafter was rarely seen on-screen—an exception being the 1984 drama *Paper Dolls.*

BIBERMAN, ABNER—actor, director

b: Apr 1, 1909, Milwaukee, Wis. d: June 20, 1977

Kodiak (police)
.... Abraham Lincoln Imhook (1974)

Husband of actress Joanna Barnes and a very active director of TV westerns and dramas from the 1950s to the '70s. In the 1940s he was a supporting actor in movies, and in his later years he occasionally played a role as an old-timer on TV.

BICE, ROBERT—actor

b: c. 1914 d: 1968

Mysteries of Chinatown (drama)
.... regular (1949–50)

BICKFORD, CHARLES—actor

b: Jan 1, 1889, Cambridge, Mass. d: Nov 9, 1967

The Man Behind the Badge (police)
.... narrator (1955)
The Virginian (wes)
.... John Grainger (1966–67)

A rugged, intense, principled actor who was the terror of the Hollywood establishment in the 1930s and '40s, while making scores of fine pictures. He was quite active in television from the early 1950s on, with numerous appearances on *Playhouse 90, Ford Theatre,* and later *The Virginian* (in 1962–63). In the year before his death, he became a regular on the latter series, as the owner of the Shiloh Ranch.

His typically combative autobiography was titled *Bulls, Balls, Bicycles and Actors* (1965).

BIEHN, MICHAEL—actor
b: 1957, Arizona

The Runaways (drama)
.... Mark Johnson (1978–79)

BIENER, TOM—

The Jim Stafford Show (var).. regular (1975)
The Jacksons (var) .... regular (1977)

BIERI, RAMON—actor

Sarge (drama)..... Barney Verick (1971–72)
Joe's World (com) ... Joe Wabash (1979–80)
Bret Maverick (wes). Elijah Crow (1981–82)

BIGELOW, PROF. DONALD N.—History Professor

Columbia University Seminar (info)
.... instructor (1952–53)

BILL, TONY—producer, actor
b: Aug 23, 1940, San Diego, Calif.

What Really Happened to the Class of '65 (drama)............ Sam Ashley (1977–78)

BILLINGSLEY, BARBARA—actress
b: Dec 22, 1922, Los Angeles, Calif.

Professional Father (com)
.... Helen Wilson (1955)
Leave It to Beaver (com)
.... June Cleaver (1957–63)

A pleasant, somewhat proper woman who gained her greatest fame as the idealized mom on *Leave It to Beaver*. Earlier she had played a very similar role, but with less winsome kids, on *Professional Father*.

Barbara made a number of minor films in the early 1950s *(Shadow on the Wall, Pretty Baby)*, and did a good deal of TV work on 1950s drama series such as *Schlitz Playhouse of Stars* and *Four Star Playhouse*. She also made a few appearances on the comedy *The Brothers*, as Gale Gordon's girlfriend, the year before *Beaver* premiered.

After *Beaver* left the air she was seen only rarely, turning up infrequently in series episodes (e.g., *The F.B.I.*), in movies

(Airplane), and of course in the *Beaver* revival in the 1980s. She has two sons of her own and lives quietly with her physician husband in Malibu. Often recognized by fans of her classic series, she has fond memories of those days.

BILLINGSLEY, KELLY—

Hee Haw (var)........... regular (1984–)

BILLINGSLEY, PETER—juvenile actor, host
b: 1972, New York City, N.Y.

Real People (aud par) .... regular (1982–84)

Great-nephew of Stork Club impresario Sherman Billingsley and the brother of child actress Melissa Michaelsen. He was seen frequently in commercials of the 1970s, with his favorite role being "Messy Marvin" in a chocolate syrup commercial.

BILLINGSLEY, SHERMAN—host
b: Mar 10, 1900, Enid, Okla. d: Oct 4, 1966

The Stork Club (talk)........ host (1950–55)

Well-known New York impresario and owner of the chic Stork Club.

BILLINGTON, MICHAEL—actor
b: Dec 24, Blackburn, Lancashire, England r: London

UFO (sci fi)........ Col. Paul Foster (1970)
The Quest (adv)
.... Count Louis Dardinay (1982)

BINKLEY, LANE—actress

Roots (drama).............. Martha (1977)

BINNS, EDWARD—actor
b: 1916, Pennsylvania

Brenner (police)
.... Det. Lt. Roy Brenner (1959)
The Nurses (drama)
.... Dr. Anson Kiley (1962–64)
Brenner (police)
.... Det. Lt. Roy Brenner (1964)
It Takes a Thief (drama)
.... Wallie Powers (1969–70)

BIRCH, PAUL—actor
b: 1908, d: May 24, 1969

Court of Last Resort (drama)
.... Erle Stanley Gardner (1957–58)
Cannonball (adv)...... Mike Malone (1958)

BIRCH, PETER—choreographer
b: Dec 11, 1922, Bronx, N.Y.

Jane Froman's U.S.A. Canteen (var)
.... dancers (1952–55)

BIRD, BILLIE—actress
b: Feb 28, Pocatello, Idaho

It Takes Two (com) .... Mama (1982–83)
Benson (com) ...... Mrs. Cassidy (1984–86)

BIRMAN, LEN—actor
Dr. Simon Locke (drama)
..... Chief/Det. Lt. Dan Palmer (1971–73)

BIRNEY, DAVID—actor
b: Apr 23, 1939, Washington, D.C.

Bridget Loves Bernie (com)
.... Bernie Steinberg (1972–73)
Serpico (police) ... Frank Serpico (1976–77)
St. Elsewhere (drama)
.... Dr. Ben Samuels (1982–83)
Master of the Game (drama)
.... David Blackwell (1984)
Glitter (drama)....... Sam Dillon (1984–85)

Though he is not from a theatrical family (his father was an F.B.I. agent), David Birney set his sights on acting at an early age, earned a degree in it, and plunged into the theater as soon as he was out of college. This single-minded determination won him stage roles with the Lincoln Center Repertory Theatre and the New York Shakespeare Festival in the late 1960s and then the break he had been working for—the role of heartthrob Mark Elliott on the daytime soap opera *Love Is a Many Splendored Thing,* in 1969–70. After a short run on another soap, *A World Apart,* in 1970–71, he began appearing more frequently in prime time. He landed his best role yet—and met his future wife, actress Meredith Baxter—in the controversial 1972 comedy *Bridget Loves Bernie.*

After that he found TV roles plentiful, especially on police shows (*Police Story, Bronk, Streets of San Francisco,* etc.). In the spring of 1976 he played detective Frank Serpico in the TV movie *The Deadly Game,* and this led to his own series the

following fall. In the following years he concentrated more on TV movies and miniseries, including *Master of the Game.* Further regular series roles were those of a charming, promiscuous doctor on *St. Elsewhere* and an aggressive reporter on *Glitter.*

Though his most popular roles have capitalized on his youthful and vaguely sexy good looks, Birney himself counts as his favorites two of his meatier parts: as John Quincy Adams in *The Adams Chronicles* (1976) and as the idealistic doctor on *Testimony of Two Men* (1978).

BISHOP, ED—actor
UFO (sci fi) .... Cdr. Edward Straker (1970)

BISHOP, JENNIFER—
Hee Haw (var).......... regular (1969–71)

BISHOP, JOEY—comedian
b: Feb 3, 1919, Bronx, N.Y. r: Philadelphia, Pa.

Keep Talking (quiz) ...... regular (1958–60)
The Jack Paar Show (talk)
.... semiregular (1958–62)
The Joey Bishop Show (com)
.... Joey Barnes (1961–65)
The Joey Bishop Show (talk)
.... host (1967–69)
Liar's Club (quiz)........ panelist (1976–78)

Joey Bishop has that look of an ordinary schlump who meets life's endless aggravation with one wisecrack after another. "Ya know whadda mean?" He was for many years strictly a small-time lounge comic working in the Northeast; by his own admission, he did not even play a "class club" until 1952. When he did it was thanks to Frank Sinatra, who caught his act in some dive and finally got him booked into the right places (Joey was Sinatra's buddy, and a member of his "Rat Pack," ever after).

Joey remained a local celebrity until he took a cut in pay to do a TV panel show, *Keep Talking,* in 1958. This brought him to a national audience for the first time. Viewers liked his deadpan, throwaway humor and he soon found himself in demand, doing guest spots on talk shows, some parts in situation comedies, and then his own successful comedy series in the early 1960s.

He was the number one substitute host for Johnny Carson in the mid-1960s, a fact that led ABC to give him his own late-night talk show in competition with Carson from 1967–69. That eventually failed, and, in later years, Joey returned to what he did best, stand-up comedy and panel show work.

BISHOP, JOHN—actor

The Life and Times of Grizzly Adams (adv)
.... Robbie Cartman (1977–78)

BISHOP, JULIE—actress
b: Aug 30, 1914, Denver, Colo.

My Hero (com).... Julie Marshall (1952–53)

This leading lady of the 1930s and '40s began making films as a child in the 1920s (in later years she preferred to avoid discussing just how long she had been in the business, commenting, "It does tend to date one"). She had a short career on television in the 1950s, including a costarring role in Robert Cummings's first series, before retiring in 1957. She devoted her later years to painting, philanthropy, and doting on her children, including actress Pamela Shoop.

BISHOP, MEL—

The Rich Little Show (var)... regular (1976)

BISHOP, WILLIAM—actor
b: Jul 16, 1917, Oak Park, Ill. d: Oct 3, 1959

It's a Great Life (com)
.... Steve Connors (1954–56)

BISOGLIO, VAL—actor
b: May 7, 1926, New York City, N.Y.

Roll Out (com)
.... Capt. Rocco Calvelli (1973–74)
Police Woman (police)
.... Lt. Paul Marsh (1974–76)
Quincy, M.E. (police)
.... Danny Tovo (1976–83)
Working Stiffs (com) .... Al Steckler (1979)

BISSEL, WHIT—actor
b: Oct 25, 1909*, New York City, N.Y. d: 1981

*Some sources give 1914 or 1919.

The Time Tunnel (sci fi)
.... Gen. Heywood Kirk (1966–67)

BIVIANO, JOSEPH—orchestra leader

Chance of a Lifetime (quiz)
.... orch. leader (1950–51)
Manhattan Maharaja (var)
.... orch. leader (1950–51)

BIXBY, BILL—actor
b: Jan 22, 1934, San Francisco, Calif.

The Joey Bishop Show (com)
.... Charles Raymond (1962)
My Favorite Martian (com)
.... Tim O'Hara (1963–66)
The Courtship of Eddie's Father (com)
.... Tom Corbett (1969–72)
The Magician (adv)
.... Anthony Blake (1973–74)
Masquerade Party (quiz)
.... regular panelist (1974–75)
Rich Man, Poor Man—Book I (drama)
.... Willie Abbott (1976)
The Incredible Hulk (drama)
.... David Bruce Banner (1978–82)
The Book of Lists (var) .... host (1982)
Goodnight, Beantown (com)
.... Matt Cassidy (1983–84)

Bill Bixby's first break in Hollywood was not quite what he expected. While he was a struggling young actor in the '50s, working part time as a lifeguard at a Hollywood pool, he was spotted by a Detroit auto executive who recruited him to travel to the Midwest for his first screen roles—in some industrial films. The credits helped, however, and before long Bill was back on the West Coast picking up small parts in episodes of TV series, beginning with a bit part on *The Many Loves of Dobie Gillis*. In January, 1962 he landed his first continuing role, as Joey Bishop's boss on *The Joey Bishop Show* (Bixby replaced another actor who was fired in the middle of the season). His big break—and the first of his three hit series—came the following year, as the reporter on *My Favorite Martian*. This was followed by rather steady TV work and several more series, including the well-remembered *Courtship of Eddie's Father* (for which he received his first Emmy Award nomination) and *The Incredible Hulk*. Following his series *The*

Magician in 1973–74 he took to hosting occasional magic specials as well.

Bixby began a parallel career as a TV director in the 1970s and was responsible for some episodes of *Rich Man, Poor Man*, among other things.

BLACK, FISCHER—editor

Better Living TV Theatre (doc)
.... host (1954)

Mr. Black was the editor of *Electrical World* magazine.

BLACK, GERRY—actor

Hill Street Blues (police)
.... Det./Lt. Alf Chesley (1981–82)

BLACK, KAREN—actress

b: Jul 1, 1942, Park Ridge, Ill.

The Second Hundred Years (com)
.... Marcia Garroway (1967–68)

BLACK, MARIANNE—actress

Sugar Time! (com)........ Maggie (1977–78)

BLACKBURN, DOROTHY—actress

Robert Montgomery Presents (summer) (drama)........... repertory player (1955)

BLACKMAN, JOAN—actress

b: 1938

Peyton Place (drama)
.... Marian Fowler (1965–66)

BLACKMORE, STEPHANIE—actress

Dallas (drama).......... Serena (1983–85)

BLACKTON, JAY—orchestra leader

b: Mar 25, 1909, New York City, N.Y.

Inside U.S.A. with Chevrolet (var)
.... orch. leader (1949–50)

One of Broadway's top musical directors and arrangers, responsible for such all-time hits as *Oklahoma!, Annie Get Your Gun*, and *George M.*

BLACQUE, TAUREAN—black actor

b: May 10, Newark, N.J.

Hill Street Blues (police)
.... Det. Neal Washington (1981–)

Taurean Blacque was a mailman for ten years before he enrolled in an acting school and began to pick up parts in New York theatrical productions. He moved to Los Angeles in 1976 and five years later won his first continuing role, that of detective Neal Washington on *Hill Street Blues*.

BLADE, JIMMY—pianist

Diane Doxee Show (music)... pianist (1950)

BLAINE, JIMMY—singer, host

b: c. 1924 d: Mar 18, 1967

Stop the Music (quiz).... vocalist (1949–52)
Hold That Camera (quiz) ..... emcee (1950)
Jimmy Blaine's Junior Edition (music)
.... host (1951)
The Billy Daniels Show (music)
.... host (1952)
Music at the Meadowbrook (var)
.... host (1953)
Music at the Meadowbrook (var)
.... host (1956)

Jimmy Blaine was a pleasant young vocalist who was a TV personality in the early days of live, New York–originated programs. In the late '50s he hosted one of the earliest Saturday morning cartoon shows, *Ruff & Ready*. He then disappeared from sight.

BLAINE, VIVIAN—actress, singer

b: Nov 21, 1921*, Newark, N.J.

Those Two (com)........ regular (1951–52)

Movie actress of the 1940s who did occasional TV work in the 1950s, then generally dropped out of sight until the late 1970s, when she turned up (briefly) as Mary Hartman's neighbor on *Mary Hartman, Mary Hartman*, Blaine also made a few TV movies in the late 1970s. By far her best-known role was as Adalaide in the stage and film versions of *Guys and Dolls.*

BLAIR, FRANK—newscaster

b: 1915, Yemassee, S.C.

Heritage (music) .... host (1951)

*Some sources give 1924.

Georgetown University Forum (pub aff)
.... moderator (1951–53)

Frank Blair was a longtime NBC newsman who began his career on local radio in South Carolina in 1935 and gradually worked his way up. Although he hosted a number of television public affairs shows in the 1950s, he is best-known as the sober-looking news reader on *Today* from 1953 until his retirement in 1975. In the early 1980s he returned to TV briefly to cohost *Over Easy,* a PBS series for older Americans.

BLAIR, JANET—actress
b: Apr 23, 1921, Altoona, Pa.

Leave It to the Girls (talk)
.... panelist (1949–54)
Caesar's Hour (var) .. Jane Victor (1956–57)
The Chevy Show (music) .... host (1958–59)
The Smith Family (drama)
.... Betty Smith (1971–72)

The vivacious "strawberry blonde" movie actress of the 1940s was seen fairly frequently on television dramatic series and variety shows in the 1950s and early '60s. One of her specials, in 1959, was in fact called "Strawberry Blonde." On *Caesar's Hour,* she was one of several actresses to play Sid Caesar's wife in sketches. After the early 1960s she did little TV work, except for one season, 1971–72, when she returned to play the wife of Hollywood veteran Henry Fonda on *The Smith Family.*

BLAIR, JUNE—actress
b: c. 1936

The Adventures of Ozzie & Harriet (com)
...... June (Mrs. David) Nelson (1961–66)

Real-life wife of David Nelson. She also had a short film career.

BLAIR, LIONEL—choreographer
b: Dec 12, 1931, Montreal, Canada

Spotlight (var) .... dancers (1967)

BLAIR, NICKY—actor
Saints and Sinners (drama)
.... Charlie (1962–63)

BLAIR, PATRICIA—actress
b: c. 1938, Fort Worth, Tex r: Dallas

The Rifleman (wes) . Lou Mallory (1962–63)
Daniel Boone (wes)
.... Rebecca Boone (1964–70)

BLAIR AND DEANE—dancers
For Your Pleasure (music) .. dancers (1948)

BLAISDELL, BRAD—actor
Three's Company (com)
Mike the bartender (occasional) (1981–84)

BLAKE, AMANDA—actress
b: Feb 20, 1927*, Buffalo, N.Y.

Gunsmoke (wes) .... Kitty Russell (1955–74)

BLAKE, GEOFFREY—actor
Paper Dolls (drama).......... Steve (1984)

BLAKE, JONATHAN—host
The Web (drama) .. host/narrator (1950–54)

BLAKE, MADGE—actress
b: 1900 d: 1969

The Real McCoys (com)
.... Flora MacMichael (1957–63)
The Joey Bishop Show (com)
.... Mrs. Barnes (1961–62)
Batman (adv)
.... Aunt Harriet Cooper (1966–68)

BLAKE, OLIVER—actor
b: 1905, Centralia, Ill.

The Brothers (com)..... Carl Dorf (1956–57)

BLAKE, ROBERT—actor
b: Sep 18, 1934, Nutley, N.J.

The Richard Boone Show (drama)
.... regular (1963–64)
Baretta (police)
.... Det. Tony Baretta (1975–78)
Hell Town (drama)
... Father Noah "Hardstep" Rivers (1985)

Emmy Award: Best Actor in a Drama Series, for *Baretta* (1975)

Asked to compare his roles as policeman Baretta and priest Hardstep, Robert Blake

*Some sources give 1921 or 1929.

91

replied: "There are more similarities than differences. They both care a lot about people and they both get impatient with the system if the system seems to be keeping them from doing their jobs. And they both ain't afraid to do a little scuffling to get the job done."

Blake could have been talking about himself. The short, chunky, combative actor caused ulcers for more than one Hollywood producer over the years, but his intense performances attracted a loyal following. He started out as a child actor, beginning at age five (using his real name, Mickey Gubitosi) in a long series of *Our Gang* movie shorts; he also played Little Beaver in 32 of the *Red Ryder* cowboy films and had juvenile roles in a number of other movies in the '40s, including that of a Mexican boy in the classic *Treasure of the Sierra Madre.*

His career declined during his teenage years, both because of his hell-raising (he says he was Los Angeles' first "assigned risk" high school student, thrown out of five schools in two years) and a bout with drugs. After military service he returned to movies, at first finding work as a stuntman. By then calling himself Bobby Blake, he appeared in a number of television dramas and westerns during the 1950s and early '60s, among them *Fireside Theatre; Have Gun, Will Travel; Bat Masterson*; and *The Rebel* (an episode called "He's Only a Boy"). He was one of the repertory players on *The Richard Boone Show* in 1963–64, but real fame was not to come for another decade, when he became the pugnacious Detective Baretta.

Blake took only occasional roles in the years following his big hit, in carefully selected dramas—three *Joe Dancer* private eye TV movies in 1981–82, John Steinbeck's *Of Mice and Men* (which he also produced) in 1981, and *Blood Feud* (as Jimmy Hoffa) in 1983. In 1985 he returned to series television as feisty Father Hardstep in *Hell Town.* Once again network executives knew they were taking a chance, and once again he gave them grief, insisting that the show be done *his* way; but once again his screen character was compelling and committed, pure Blake.

"It's all a matter of luck in this society," he told a reporter. "I say the winners are the individualists."

BLAKE, WHITNEY—actress
b: Los Angeles, Calif.

Hazel (com) ..... Dorothy Baxter (1961–65)
The David Frost Revue (com)
.... regular (1971–73)

BLAKELY, SUSAN—actress
b: Sep 7, 1948, Frankfurt, Germany

Rich Man, Poor Man—Book I (drama)
.... Julie Prescott Abbott Jordache (1976)

BLAKENEY, OLIVE—actress
b: c. 1903 d: 1959

Dr. Hudson's Secret Journal (drama)
.... Mrs. Grady (1955–57)

BLANC, MEL—actor
b: May 30, 1908, San Francisco, Calif.

The Jack Benny Show (com)
.... regular (1950–65)
Musical Chairs (quiz)...... panelist (1955)
The Bugs Bunny Show (cartn)
.... voices (1960–62)
The Flintstones (cartn)
.... Barney Rubble (voice) (1960–66)
The Flintstones (cartn)
.... Dino the dinosaur (1960–66)
The Jetsons (cartn) . various roles (1962–63)
Where's Huddles? (cartn)
.... Bubba McCoy (voice) (1970)
The Bugs Bunny/Roadrunner Show (prime time) (cartn) .... voices (1976)
Buck Rogers in the 25th Century (sci fi)
.... Twiki (voice) (1979–81)

A holdover from radio days, Mel Blanc was extremely popular in the television era—even though many of the viewers in his audience never saw his face and didn't know his name. He was one of the voices behind *Bugs Bunny, The Flintstones,* and *The Jetsons* in prime time and was the voice of dozens of Saturday morning favorites: The Road Runner, Sylvester the cat, Tweetie Pie, Porky Pig, Yosemite Sam, Daffy Duck, Woody Woodpecker, Speedy Gonzales, Heathcliffe the cat, Speed Buggy, and so many more, in old Warner Brothers cartoons and in modern Hanna-Barbera productions. It was Mel who delivered Bugs's "What's up, Doc?", Tweetie Pie's "I taut I taw a puddy tat" and the Road Runner's "Beep Beep!" He was, in short, a human sound effects machine.

Mel Blanc began as a musician, playing the tuba in various bands in the Northwest. He crashed Hollywood in 1935 and soon became a radio and movie cartoon standby. A small, mousey-looking man, he began to be seen occasionally when TV came along, mostly on Jack Benny's program, on which he played Jack's long-suffering violin teacher, Professor LeBlanc. However, even on that show he was better heard—as the sound of Benny's sputtering, coughing, ancient Maxwell automobile.

Thirty years later he was still sputtering along, voicing Twiki in *Buck Rogers in the 25th Century*. He once estimated he had done more than 400 different voices in some 3,000 cartoons—closing many of them with Porky Pig's immortal line, "That's all, folks!"

BLANCHARD, MARI—actress
b: Apr 13, 1927, Long Beach, Calif. d: 1970

Klondike (adv).... Kathy O'Hara (1960–61)

BLANCHARD, SUSAN—actress

Mr. T and Tina (com) .... Tina Kelly (1976)
Young Maverick (wes)
.... Nell McGarrahan (1979–80)

The wife of *Young Maverick* star Charles Frank, with whom she also appeared in the daytime soap opera *All My Children* in the early 1970s.

BLANKFIELD, MARK—comedian
b: May 8, Pasadena, Tex.

Fridays (var)............ regular (1980–82)

BLATTNER, BUDDY—sportscaster
Baseball Corner (sport)........ host (1958)

BLEDSOE, TEMPESTT—black juvenile actress
b: Aug 1, 1973, Chicago, Ill.

The Cosby Show (com)
.... Vanessa Huxtable (1984–)

BLEIWEISS, NANCY—comedienne
Laugh-In (revival) (var) ... regular (1977–78)

BLENDERS, THE—vocal quartet
The Lawrence Welk Show (music)
.... regular (1965–67)

BLESSING, JACK—actor
b: Jul 29, Baltimore, Md.

Small & Frye (com)...... Chip Frye (1983)

BLEYER, ARCHIE—orchestra leader
b: June 12, 1909, Corona, N.Y.

Arthur Godfrey's Talent Scouts (talent)
.... orch. leader (1948–54)
Arthur Godfrey and His Friends (var)
.... orch. leader (1949–54)

Archie Bleyer was a music business veteran who had recorded with his own orchestra in the 1930s, then became closely associated with Arthur Godfrey in the 1940s and '50s—until Godfrey abruptly fired him in 1954. Not to worry. Archie had just formed a record company (Cadence), which proceeded to sell millions of copies of records by two other acts who had also been fired by Godfrey, Julius LaRosa and the Chordettes, as well as millions more by other new performers that Bleyer later discovered (Andy Williams, the Everly Brothers). Archie retired in 1964, a wealthy man indeed.

BLOCK, DAVID A.—actor
Masada (drama) .... Reuben (1981)

BLOCK, HAL—gag writer
b: Chicago, Ill.

What's My Line (quiz)... panelist (1950–53)
Tag the Gag (quiz) .... moderator (1951)

BLOCK, HUNT—actor
b: Feb 16, Washington, D.C. r: New England

Knots Landing (drama)
.... Peter Hollister (1985–)

BLOCK, MARTIN—announcer
b: 1903 d: Sep 19, 1967

The Chesterfield Supper Club (var)
.... announcer (1948–50)

A pioneer radio disc jockey whose "Make Believe Ballroom" in New York was enormously popular in the 1930s and '40s. He was also an announcer on many network radio shows. On television he was Perry Como's first announcer on *The Chesterfield Supper Club* and later had his own daytime variety show on ABC-TV in 1956–57.

BLOCK, RAY—orchestra leader
b: Aug 3, 1902, Alsace-Lorraine, France

The Gay Nineties Revue (var)
.... orch. leader (1948–49)
The Ed Sullivan Show (var)
.... orch. leader (1948–71)
Toni Twin Time (var)... orch. leader (1950)
Sing It Again (quiz).. orch. leader (1950–51)
Songs for Sale (music)
.... orch. leader (1950–52)
The Jackie Gleason Show (var)
.... orch. leader (1952–55)
Blind Date (aud par).... orch. leader (1953)
The Larry Storch Show (var)
.... orch. leader (1953)
Summertime U.S.A. (music)
.... orch. leader (1953)
The Jackie Gleason Show (var)
.... orch. leader (1956–59)

Ray, who got his start in radio as a CBS staff conductor in the 1930s, was a busy man during the heyday of TV variety shows in the 1950s. He is perhaps best-remembered for his 23 years with Ed Sullivan, providing music for all manner of variety, comedy, and musical acts, but he also had time for Jackie Gleason and many others.

Born in Germany, he immigrated to the U.S. during World War I and worked as a pianist in the 1920s.

BLOCKER, DAN—actor
b: Dec 10, 1932*, Bowie County, Texas
r: O'Donnell, Texas d: May 13, 1972

Cimarron City (wes)
.... Tiny Budinger (1958–59)
Bonanza (wes)
.... "Hoss" Cartwright (1959–72)

Dan Blocker was a mountain of a man who, at birth, was said to have been the largest baby ever born in his Texas county —14 pounds. When he entered Texas Military Institute at age 12 he was 6′ tall and 200 pounds, and by the time he reached college, 6′4″ and 275. Fortunately, he

*Some sources give 1929.

stopped growing then, in time to be pursued by every football coach in the Southeast.

Dan discovered acting while in college (they needed somebody with enough strength to carry the bodies out of the basement in *Arsenic and Old Lace*) and graduated with bachelor and master's degrees in drama. Nevertheless, he went into teaching at first in the public schools of Carlsbad, N.M., from 1954–56. He then moved to Los Angeles to work on his Ph.D., but was sidetracked when he found how much money he could earn doing small roles in television westerns such as *The Restless Gun, Jefferson Drum,* and *Gunsmoke.* He soon landed his first continuing role in *Cimarron City* and a year later became the gentle Hoss on *Bonanza*—a role he continued for the rest of his days.

His son, Dirk Blocker, is also an actor.

BLOCKER, DIRK—actor
b: Jul 31, 1957, Los Angeles, Calif.

Baa Baa Black Sheep (drama)
.... Lt. Jerry Bragg (1976–78)
Ryan's Four (drama)
.... Dr. Norman Rostov (1983)

Son of Dan Blocker, and almost equally hefty.

BLONDELL, GLORIA—actress

The Life of Riley (com)
.... Honeybee Gillis (1953–58)

Sister of actress Joan Blondell.

BLONDELL, JOAN—actress
b: Aug 30, 1909*, New York City, N.Y. d: Dec 25, 1979

The Real McCoys (com)
.... Winifred Jordan (1963)
Here Come the Brides (adv)
.... Lottie Hatfield (1968–70)
Banyon (drama).... Peggy Revere (1972–73)

This delightful, gum-chewing, wisecracking golddigger of so many Hollywood films of the 1930s and '40s did a lot of television work in the 1950s and '60s—everything from *The U.S. Steel Hour* to *The Twilight Zone* and *The Lucy Show.* She was twice

*Some sources give 1906 or 1912.

nominated for an Emmy Award for her portrayal of saloon keeper Lottie on *Here Come the Brides*. She continued to work until shortly before her death, appearing in an episode of *Fantasy Island* and the miniseries *The Rebels* in mid-1979.

Her sister Gloria Blondell was also an actress. In 1972 Joan published a semiautobiographical novel called *Center Door Fancy*

BLOOM, CHARLES—actor

The Waverly Wonders (com)
.... John Tate (1978)
Number 96 (drama)... Lyle Bixler (1980–81)

BLOOM, CLAIRE—actress
b: Feb 15, 1931, London, England

Backstairs at the White House (drama)
.... Edith Galt Wilson (1979)

BLOOM, LINDSAY—actress
b: c. 1952, Omaha, Neb.

Dallas (drama).... Bonnie Robertson (1982)
Mickey Spillane's Mike Hammer (drama)
.... Velda (1984–)

A former Miss U.S.A. (1973), Lindsay entered show business as one of the "Ding-a-Ling Girls" on the *Dean Martin Show*.

BLOOMGARDEN, HANK—

High-Low (quiz)........... panelist (1957)

BLUE, BEN—actor, comedian
b: Sep 12, 1901, Montreal, Canada d: Mar 7, 1975

The Frank Sinatra Show (var)
.... regular (1950–51)
Saturday Night Revue (var).. regular (1954)
Accidental Family (com)
.... Ben McGrath (1967–68)

BLUESTONE, ED—comedian
b: 1949

Laugh-In (revival) (var)... regular (1977–78)

BLYDEN, LARRY—actor, emcee
b: 1925, Houston, Tex. d: June 6, 1975

Joe & Mabel (com) ...... Joe Sparton (1956)
Harry's Girls (com).. Harry Burns (1963–64)

What's My Line (quiz)
.... moderator (1972–75)

Larry Blyden was one of those actors who was all over television in the 1950s, '60s, and '70s, but never scored a big enough hit to become firmly identified with any one role. Besides his two short-lived comedy roles—on *Joe & Mabel* as Joe the cabby and *Harry's Girls* as a song and dance man chaperoning a bevy of beauties—he was (1) a game show host (*Personality, You're Putting Me On, The Movie Game, What's My Line*), (2) a frequent guest on *The Tonight Show* and other talk programs, and (3) an actor of some versatility, often in comic roles, in dozens of anthology series such as *Playhouse 90, Play of the Week, The Loretta Young Show,* and *The U.S. Steel Hour*. In two appearances on *The Twilight Zone* he played a small-time hustler who dies and goes to heaven (or is it?); and a temperamental cowboy star who gets his comeuppance when he meets some *real* old west varmints.

Blyden's greatest success was in still another arena—on Broadway. He was three times nominated for a Tony Award, winning in 1972 for *A Funny Thing Happened on the Way to the Forum*. He died in 1975, just before starting work on still another game show (*Showoffs*), of injuries sustained in an auto accident in Morocco.

BLYE, MAGGIE—actress

Kodiak (police)............. Mandy (1974)

BOARDMAN, ERIC—comedian

The Tim Conway Show (var)
.... regular (1980)

BOARDMAN, NAN—actress

This is the Life (drama)
.... Mrs. Fisher (1952–56)

BOATANEERS, THE—

The Nat "King" Cole Show (var)
.... regulars (1956)

BOB AND RAY—comedians
Bob Elliott—b: Mar 26, 1923, Boston, Mass. r: Winchester, Mass.
Ray Goulding—b: Mar 20, 1922, Lowell, Mass.

Bob and Ray (var)...... regulars (1951–53)
Club Embassy (var) .... cohosts (1952)
The Name's the Same (quiz) . emcees (1955)
Happy Days (var) .... regulars (1970)

Although they are known primarily as radio satirists, Bob and Ray have appeared on a number of television series, including their own sketch comedy show (with Audrey Meadows and Cloris Leachman in the supporting cast) in 1951–52. Both Bob and Ray are from the Boston area; they met when both were hired by Boston radio station WHDH in 1946, Bob as a morning DJ and Ray as a newscaster. They began trading quips on the air and soon were in great demand as a team.

After a few years in local radio, they moved to the NBC radio network in July of 1951 and to NBC television that November (while a teenager, Bob had been an NBC page, serving as an usher for studio audiences there). Among their later shows was *Happy Days*, a 1970 summer variety series (not the famous situation comedy). In addition to their comedy shows, Bob and Ray used their intelligent, satirical humor in numerous commercials over the years; among the best-remembered were the Piels Beer ads of the 1950s and '60s.

BOBATOON, STAR-SHEMAH—actress

Palmerstown, U.S.A. (drama)
.... Diana Freeman (1980–81)

BOBO, NATASHA—black juvenile actress
b: Feb 11, 1980, Watsonville, Calif.

Together We Stand (com).... Sally (1986–)

BOBO, WILLIE—jazz drummer, bandleader
b: Feb 28, 1934, New York City, N.Y. d: Sep 15, 1983

Cos (var) .... regular (1976)

BOCHNER, HART—actor
b: 1956, Toronto, Canada r: Los Angeles, Calif.

East of Eden (drama) .... Aron Trask (1981)

The son of actor Lloyd Bochner.

BOCHNER, LLOYD—actor
b: Jul 29, 1924, Toronto, Canada

One Man's Family (drama)
.... Capt. Nicholas Lacey (1952)
Hong Kong (adv).. Neil Campbell (1960–61)
The Richard Boone Show (drama)
.... regular (1963–64)
Dynasty (drama) ..... Cecil Colby (1981–82)

This distinguished-looking Toronto native was quite active in Canadian radio, TV, and stage productions in the 1950s. He moved to Hollywood in 1960 to costar as Hong Kong Police Commissioner Neil Campbell in the ABC series *Hong Kong*. In subsequent years he played a wide range of guest roles on a great many TV dramatic series, including *The Man from UNCLE, Mission: Impossible, Mannix, Charlie's Angels,* and several times on *Daniel Boone*. He was best known in later years as power broker Cecil Colby on *Dynasty*, who died of a cardiac arrest while having passionate sex with seductress Joan Collins.

BOEN, EARL—actor
b: Aug 8, Pueblo, Colo.

It's a Living (com)
.... Dennis Hubner (1981–82)

BOGERT, WILLIAM—actor

Miss Winslow and Son (com)
.... Mr. Joseph X. Callahan (1979)

BOHAN, DENNIS—actor

The Fashion Story (misc) . regular (1948–49)

BOHAY, HEIDI—actress
b: Dec 15, 1959, Somerset County, N.J.

Hotel (drama)...... Megan Kendall (1983–)

BOHRER, CORINNE—actress
b: Camp LeJeun, N.C.

E/R (com) ..... Nurse Cory Smith (1984–85)

BOKENO, CHRIS—host

The Music Scene (music)
.... rotating host (1969)

BOLAND, BONNIE—actress

Turn-On (var) .... regular (1969)
The Tim Conway Comedy Hour (var)
.... regular (1970)
Chico and the Man (com) .. Mabel (1974–75)

BOLAND, JOE—emcee

Ask Me Another (quiz) .... emcee (1952)

BOLES, JIM—actor

b: Feb 28, 1914, Lubbock, Texas d: May 26, 1977

One Man's Family (drama)
.... Joe Yarbourogh (1950–52)
Kraft Music Hall Presents: The Dave King
Show (var)................. regular (1959)

BOLGER, RAY—actor, dancer

b: Jan 10, 1904, Dorchester, Mass. d: Jan 15, 1987

The Ray Bolger Show (com)
.... Raymond Wallace (1953–55)

Ray Bolger is fondly remembered as the understuffed happy/sad scarecrow in the 1939 movie fantasy The Wizard of Oz. The telecast of this classic has been an annual event on television since 1956. Bolger's major career was on the stage, however, where he began in the early 1920s; he reached Broadway in 1926 and had a long string of hit shows during the following years. One of the biggest was the 1948 musical Where's Charley?, which gave him his trademark song "Once in Love with Amy." The show was made into a movie in 1952, and the title was used for Bolger's TV comedy series during its first season (1953–54). There and in Bolger's later TV appearances during the 1950s he was basically a song and dance man whose long face and infectious smile always reminded viewers of the famous scarecrow.

Ray made relatively few appearances in the 1960s and '70s. Then in the late 1970s he started turning up again in specials and lightweight series such as The Love Boat, Aloha Paradise, and Fantasy Island. He received an Emmy nomination for the special The Entertainer in 1976.

BOLLING, TIFFANY—actress

r: Hendersonville, N.C.

The New People (drama)
.... Susan Bradley (1969–70)

BOLTON, ELAINE—actress

Blansky's Beauties (com)
.... Bridget Muldoon (1977)
Who's Watching the Kids (com)
.... Bridget (1978)

BONADUCE, DANNY—juvenile actor

b: Aug 13, 1959

The Partridge Family (com)
.... Danny Partridge (1970–74)

After his years as the pint-sized con artist on The Partridge Family and its Saturday morning cartoon spin-offs, Danny appeared occasionally in TV movies and series episodes (e.g., CHiPs, California Fever).

BONAR, IVAN—actor

Adventures of Ozzie & Harriet (com)
.... Dean Hopkins (1964–66)
Dynasty II: The Colbys (drama)
.... Henderson Palmer (1985–)

BOND FORD—announcer

Cities Service Band of America (music)
.... announcer (1949–50)
Prime Time Football (sport)
.... announcer (1953)

Veteran radio announcer and sportscaster of the 1930s and '40s.

BOND, J. BLASINGAME, & THE DIXIELAND QUARTET—

The Sammy Kaye Show (var)
.... regulars (1958–59)

BOND, RALEIGH—actor

Alice (com) .... Raleigh (1979–81)

BOND, SHEILA—actress

b: 1928, New York City, N.Y.

Inside U.S.A. with Chevrolet (var)
.... regular (1949–50)

BOND, SUDIE—actress

b: Jul 13, 1923, Louisville, Ky. d: Nov 10, 1984

Temperatures Rising (com)
.... Martha Mercy (1973–74)
Flo (com)
...... Mama Velma Castleberry (1980–81)

BOND, WARD—actor
b: Apr 9, 1903, Denver, Colo.* d: Nov 5, 1960

Wagon Train (wes)
.... Major Seth Adams (1957–61)

Movie tough-guy Ward Bond had a long career in Hollywood, playing supporting roles in some 200 features, often as a villain or a soft-hearted cop. He got into films in the late 1920s when he was a student on the football team at the University of Southern California; Ward and fellow teammate John Wayne were recruited together to appear in some westerns. The two remained lifelong friends.

Bond appeared in an assortment of television dramas in the 1950s (*Schlitz Playhouse, Ford Theatre,* etc.), but it was as the gruff, leather-skinned Major Adams on the hit western *Wagon Train* that he finally found real fame. The show was number two in the ratings (behind *Gunsmoke*) when Bond died suddenly of a heart attack in 1960 while preparing for a personal appearance.

BONERZ, PETER—actor
b: Aug 6, 1938, Portsmouth, N.H. r: Milwaukee, Wis.

Bob Newhart Show (com)
.... Jerry Robinson (1972–78)
9 To 5 (com) ...... Franklin Hart (1982–83)

A lanky comic actor who played the unorthodox dentist on *The Bob Newhart Show* and later the overbearing boss on *9 To 5*. He is also active as a director of TV comedies.

BONET, LISA—black actress
b: Nov 16, 1967, San Francisco, Calif.

The Cosby Show (com)
.... Denise Huxtable (1984–   )

BONKETTES, THE—dancers

Bonkers (com) .... dancers (1978–79)

*Some sources give Bendelman, Neb.

98

BONNE, SHIRLEY—actress
b: c. 1934, Inglewood, Calif.

My Sister Eileen (com)
.... Eileen Sherwood (1960–61)

BONNER, FRANK—actor
b: Feb 28, 1942, Little Rock, Ark.

WKRP in Cincinnati (com)
.... Herb Tarlek (1978–82)
Sidekicks (adv)
.... Det. P. J. Mooney (1986–   )

BONO, CHASTITY—juvenile performer
b: March 4, 1969

The Sonny and Cher Comedy Hour (var)
.... regular (1973–74)
The Sonny and Cher Show (var)
.... regular (1976–77)

Daughter of singers Cher and Sonny Bono.

BONO, CHER
See Cher

BONO, SONNY—singer
b: Feb 16, 1935, Detroit, Mich.

The Sonny and Cher Comedy Hour (var)
.... cohost (1971–74)
The Sonny Comedy Revue (var)
.... host (1974)
The Sonny and Cher Show (var)
.... cohost (1976–77)

Sonny, the mousey, nasal-voiced guy who often seemed overpowered by his formidable wife Cher, was actually the brains of the pair when the two began in the music business. A hustler from the start, he was selling songs to recording artists while he was still in his teens and talked himself into a job as a producer and A&R man for Specialty Records in the 1950s. He also doubled as a singer and was a favored background vocalist on producer Phil Spector's big hits in the early 1960s. It was at one of these Spector recording sessions that Sonny met another unknown background singer, Cher LaPierre; they were married and formed a recording act of their own, at first called Caesar and Cleo. But it was as Sonny and Cher that they hit it big, with a string of million sellers (including their theme "I Got You Babe") from 1965–

67. How big? It is said that in one year, their income jumped from under $10,000 (1964) to around $2 million (1965).

Sonny and Cher made frequent appearances on variety and talk shows during the late 1960s, attracting attention both for their outlandish fashions and their music. Their career was beginning to decline when CBS signed them to do a youth-oriented summer variety show in 1971. It was popular enough to win them a regular berth the following December, and after that their husband and wife put-down comedy really caught on, eventually taking them into the TV top ten. However, all was not well behind the scenes; their often stormy marriage ended in divorce in 1974, whereupon each tried to continue in a separate show (Sonny's *Sonny Comedy Revue* flopped). They were back together, professionally at least, the following year, but the comeback was unsuccessful.

Sonny continued to guest star on various series in later years, including multiple episodes of *Fantasy Island* and *The Love Boat*.

BOOKE, SORRELL—actor
b: Jan 4, 1930, Buffalo, N.Y.

Rich Man, Poor Man—Book II (drama)
.... Phil Greenberg (1976–77)
The Dukes of Hazzard (com)
... Jefferson Davis "Boss" Hogg (1979–85)

BOOMER, LINWOOD—actor
b: Oct 9, 1955, Vancouver, Canada r: San Francisco

Little House on the Prairie (adv)
.... Adam Kendall (1978–81)

BOONE, BRENDON—actor
Garrison's Gorillas (drama)
.... Chief (1967–68)

BOONE, PAT—singer
b: Jun 1, 1934, Jacksonville, Fla. r: Nashville, Tenn.

Arthur Godfrey and His Friends (var)
.... singer (1955–57)
The Pat Boone-Chevy Showroom (var)
.... host (1957–60)

Pat Boone was the establishment's answer to rock 'n' roll in the 1950s. Clean-cut, easygoing, and an obvious white, middle-class achiever (while at the height of his fame he went back to college and graduated magna cum laude from Columbia), he was the perfect antidote to the greasy, sexual rock 'n' rollers who were capturing teenagers' attention then. Surprisingly, a lot of teenagers liked him.

A descendant of frontiersman Daniel Boone, Pat was the son of a building contractor who moved several times while Pat was young. He was a star athlete and student leader in high school and had his own radio show while still in his teens. At 20 he won a competition on *Arthur Godfrey's Talent Scouts,* which resulted both in a recording contract and a regular spot on Godfrey's variety show the following year.

The recording contract led to a spectacularly successful career in pop music—Pat was second only to Elvis Presley in record sales in the late 1950s—while the Godfrey spot led to his own ABC-TV variety show, which ran for three wholesome years. As Pat's career finally cooled off in the 1960s he was seen less often, but in the 1970s he made a comeback of sorts on talk shows, in commercials (for milk), and on religious programs. A deeply religious man, he has written two books designed to help teens deal with their problems through faith.

Pat was married in the early 1950s to his school sweetheart Shirley Foley, the daughter of country star Red Foley. In later years he appeared with Shirley, his daughter Debbie (also a singer), and his other daughters in Christmas and other specials.

BOONE, RANDY—actor
b: Jan 17, 1942, Fayetteville, N.C.

It's a Man's World (com)
.... Vern Hodges (1962–63)
The Virginian (wes) ...... Randy (1963–66)
Cimarron Strip (wes)
.... Francis Wilde (1967–68)

Handsome young Randy Boone was something of a teen heartthrob in the 1960s as the easygoing, guitar-strumming ranch hand on *The Virginian.* Unfortunately, he was unable to handle professional success (or two marriages) very well, and after an unsuccessful try at a recording career in the early 1970s he drifted out of show business. He is now an easygoing guitar-strumming handyman in Los Angeles.

BOONE, RICHARD—actor

b: Jun 18, 1917, Los Angeles, Calif. d: Jan 10, 1981

Medic (drama)
.... Dr. Konrad Styner (1954–56)
Have Gun Will Travel (wes)
.... Paladin (1957–63)
The Richard Boone Show (drama)
.... host (1963–64)
Hec Ramsey (wes) .. Hec Ramsey (1972–74)

Richard Boone was, like singer Pat, a descendent of frontiersman Daniel Boone. There the resemblance ended. A craggy, serious, even menacing actor, Richard was most frequently cast as a heavy until starring roles on television allowed him a wider range.

The son of a lawyer, Richard studied acting on the GI Bill after World War II. His methodical, serious approach to his craft led to minor stage, film, and TV roles in the late 1940s and early '50s and to his first regular series, *Medic,* a pioneer in TV realism. Though critically acclaimed, it was not a major hit; his next series was, however, and *Have Gun Will Travel* made Richard Boone a star. He followed this with another more serious effort, a dramatic anthology that he hosted, often starred in, and sometimes directed. *The Richard Boone Show* got half the audience of its CBS competition, *Petticoat Junction.* Boone left television to live in Hawaii for the next seven years and spend time with his young son.

He returned in the early 1970s with a periodic series (part of the *Sunday Mystery Movie* rotation) about a frontier detective, Hec Ramsey. After that he was seen infrequently. He died of cancer in 1981.

BOOTH, BILLY—juvenile actor

Dennis the Menace (com)
.... Tommy Anderson (1959–63)

BOOTH, SHIRLEY—actress

b: Aug 20, 1907, New York City, N.Y.

Hazel (com) .... Hazel Burke (1961–66)
A Touch of Grace (com)
.... Grace Simpson (1973)

Emmy Award: Best Actress, for *Hazel* (1962, 1963)

Shirley Booth was a frumpy, cheerful woman who achieved her greatest fame in middle age. She was a stage actress in the late '20s and '30s, then scored a hit on radio as the Brooklynese daughter on *Duffy's Tavern* (which starred and was produced by her husband, Ed Gardner). Even greater success came a few years later with the role of the frowsy wife in *Come Back, Little Sheba,* which brought her a Tony Award for the Broadway play (1950) and an Oscar for the movie version (1952).

Her TV debut did not come until 1957, when she played Pearl Mesta on a *Playhouse 90* production, and she did little TV work thereafter until *Hazel* premiered in 1961. That role, the cheerful housekeeper, won her an Emmy Award, making her one of the few actresses to receive all three of acting's top awards—Tony, Oscar, and Emmy.

Shirley made a few appearances on specials and in TV movies in the late 1960s and had one more series in 1973. She was mostly inactive after that.

BOOTHE, POWERS—actor

b: 1949, Snyder, Texas

Skag (drama) .... Whalen (1980)

Emmy Award: Best Actor in a Single Appearance, for *Guyana Tragedy: The Story of Jim Jones* (1980).

BORDEN, ALICE—actress

That Girl (com) .... Ruth Bauman (1969–71)

BORDEN, LYNN—actress

b: c. 1935, Detroit, Mich.

Hazel (com) ..... Barbara Baxter (1965–66)

BORELLI, CARLA—actress

r: San Francisco, Calif.

Falcon Crest (drama)
.... Connie Giannini (1985)

BORGE, VICTOR—comedian

b: Jan 3, 1909, Copenhagen, Denmark

The Victor Borge Show (var).... host (1951)

This famous humorist, who has been called "The Danish Noel Coward," was a child prodigy concert pianist and a top comedy star in his native Denmark before World War II. In 1940 he fled to America to escape the Nazis (who might not be expected to appreciate his jokes about them) and quickly established himself as a radio favorite with his witty mix of music and patter, often making fun of the classics.

Borge was a frequent guest on TV variety shows in the 1950s, and had his own show for a few months in 1951. Seated at a grand piano, and looking very dignified, he would start straight but constantly interrupt himself, and soon whatever he was playing would be in a shambles. Probably his most famous and clever routine was "Phonetic Punctuation," in which he carefully explained how conversation would be made simpler if each comma, period, and dash were replaced with a different little noise. He then demonstrated with a rapid-fire paragraph loaded with "ffftt's," "sscht's," and "phutts" which would leave the audience in hysterics.

BORGNINE, ERNEST—actor
b: Jan 24, 1917*, Hamden, Conn.

McHale's Navy (com)
..... Lt. Cmdr. Quinton McHale (1962–66)
Airwolf (adv) .... Dominic Santini (1984–86)

Ernest Borgnine was another one of the screen "heavies" who was able to change his image completely for his greatest television success. He didn't take up acting until he was in his midthirties, after ten years as a gunner's mate in the Navy. However, his gruff, scowling manner and beefy appearance got him many movie roles as a bad guy; among other things, he was the sadistic sergeant who beat Frank Sinatra to death in *From Here to Eternity*.

Borgnine also did a good deal of television in the 1950s and early '60s on anthologies such as *Zane Grey Theater, Wagon Train, Laramie,* and *General Electric Theater,* but his great success was as boisterous Capt. McHale in the service comedy *McHale's Navy.* There his beady eyes and gap teeth seemed comic, not menacing. He made only infrequent TV appearances afterward (including a notable performance in the 1979 TV production of *All Quiet on the Western Front*), until he was recruited to be Jan Michael Vincent's experienced partner on *Airwolf* in 1984.

*Some sources give 1915 or 1918.

BORN, DAVID AND STEVEN—infants
Happy (com)............. Happy (1960–61)

BORN, ROSCOE—actor
b: Nov 24, Topeka, Kan.

Paper Dolls (drama).... Mark Bailey (1984)

BORREGO, JESSE—actor
Fame (drama).... Jesse Valesquez (1984–   )

BOSLEY, TOM—actor
b: Oct 1, 1927, Chicago, Ill.

That Was the Week That Was (com)
.... regular (1964)
The Debbie Reynolds Show (com)
.... Bob Landers (1969–70)
The Dean Martin Show (var)
.... regular (1971–72)
The Sandy Duncan Show (com)
.... Bert Quinn (1972)
Wait Till Your Father Gets Home (cartn)
.... Harry Boyle (voice) (1972–74)
Happy Days (com)
.... Howard Cunningham (1974–84)
That's Hollywood (doc).. narrator (1976–82)
Murder, She Wrote (drama)
.... Sheriff Amos Tupper (1984–   )

This rotund, cherubic actor began his career in local theater shortly after graduating from college in the late 1940s and spent the 1950s slowly working his way up on the New York stage. His stage career culminated with a major success in the title role in the musical *Fiorello!* in 1959, for which he won several awards, including a Tony.

He continued active on Broadway until the mid-1960s, but his success there and his talent for comedy began landing him an increasing number of good TV roles as well. He was one of the repertory players on NBC's satirical revue *That Was the Week That Was* in 1964 and a regular on a series starring Debbie Reynolds (as her brother-in-law), Dean Martin, and Sandy Duncan. He also appeared on numerous episodes of other series, including *Bonanza; Love, American Style,* and *Get Smart.* There's nothing like a regular role on a hit series to make an actor famous, however, and for Bosley it was the part of the understanding dad on a seemly innocuous comedy called *Happy Days*; the show shot to the top of the ratings in the late 1970s. Ironically, his previous regular role had been as a less agreeable father, one patterned closely on Archie Bunker, on the syndicated cartoon series *Wait Till Your Father Gets Home*.

During and after the long run of *Happy Days*, Tom appeared fairly regularly in TV movies, miniseries, and specials, with an occasional cruise on *The Love Boat* thrown in. He was also seen incessantly on comercials for garbage bags, happily taking out the trash from the house that *Happy Days* had built. Why shouldn't he be cheerful?

BOSSON, BARBARA—actress
b: Nov 1, 1939, Belle Vernon, Pa.*

Richie Brockelman, Private Eye (drama)
.... Sharon Deterson (1978)
Hill Street Blues (police)
.... Fay Furillo (1981–)

Actress-wife of *Hill Street Blues* producer Steven Bochco. She was once a Playboy bunny ("only to earn a lot of money") and had a minor film career before *Hill Street*.

BOSTOCK, BARBARA—actress
Love on a Rooftop (com)
.... Carol Parker (1966–67)

BOSTWICK, BARRY—actor
b: Feb 24, 1945, San Mateo, Calif.

Scruples (drama)...... Spider Elliott (1980)
Foul Play (drama)
.... Det. Tucker Pendleton (1981)

BOSWELL, CHARLES—actor
MacGruder & Loud (police)
.... Zacharias (1985)

BOSWELL, CONNEE—singer
b: Dec 3, 1907, New Orleans, La. d: Oct 10, 1976

Pete Kelly's Blues (drama)
.... Savannah Brown (1959)

An uncommonly good, jazz-oriented pop singer who was a major star in the 1930s with her sisters, as The Boswell Sisters.

*Some sources give Charleroi, Pa., which is across the river.

102

She had a long and successful career in music despite being crippled by polio (she was usually seen seated, so her audiences never knew). Her TV appearances were relatively few; on *Pete Kelly's Blues* she played a singer in one of the clubs frequented by the star.

BOTKIN, PERRY, JR.—orchestra leader
b: Apr 16, 1933, New York City, N.Y.

The Late Summer Early Fall Bert Convy Show (var).................. orch. leader (1976)

BOTTOMS, JOSEPH—actor
b: Apr 22, 1954, Santa Barbara, Calif.

Holocaust (drama) ...... Rudi Weiss (1978)

Joseph, Sam, and Timothy Bottoms are brothers.

BOTTOMS, SAM—actor
b: Oct 17, 1955, Santa Barbara, Calif.

East of Eden (drama)..... Cal Trask (1981)

BOTTOMS, TIMOTHY—actor
b: Aug 30, 1950*, Santa Barbara, Calif.

East of Eden (drama)... Adam Trask (1981)

BOTWINICK, AMY—actress
Lobo (com) .... Peaches (1980–81)

BOUCHER, BOB—orchestra leader
b: Jan 16, 1919, Kent, Ohio

Music on Ice (var)...... orch. leader (1960)

BOUCHER, SHERRY—actress
Lassie (adv) .... Sue Lambert (1973–74)

BOURNE, HAL—orchestra leader
The Tony Martin Show (music)
.... orch. leader (1954–55)

BOUTON, JIM—actor
b: March 8, 1939, Newark, N.J.

Ball Four (com) .... Jim Barton (1976)

This major league pitcher's book about behind-the-scenes life in baseball was a hit,

*Some sources give 1949 or 1951.

but his TV series based on the book was not. Little has been seen of him since.

BOUTSIKARIS, DENNIS—actor

Nurse (drama) .... Joe Calvo (1981–82)

BOWEN, DENNIS—actor

Welcome Back, Kotter (com)
.... Todd Ludlow (1975–77)

BOWEN, ROGER—actor

b: May 25, Attleboro, Mass. r: Providence, R.I.

Arnie (com).. Hamilton Majors, Jr. (1970–72)
The Brian Keith Show (com)
.... Dr. Austin Chaffee (1973–74)
At Ease (com)........... Col. Clapp (1983)
Suzanne Pleshette Is Maggie Briggs (com)
.... Donny Bauer (1984)

BOWER, ROGER—director, emcee

b: c. 1903, New York City, N.Y. d: May 17, 1979

Stop Me If You've Heard This One (quiz)
.... emcee (1948)

A successful radio director of the 1930s and '40s, who followed one of his radio shows to television for a brief run.

BOWER, TOM—actor

b: Jan 3, Denver, Colo.

The Waltons (drama)
.... Dr. Curtis Willard (1976–78)

BOWERS, KENNY—actor

School House (var)......... regular (1949)

BOWES, GEOFFREY—actor

The Comedy Factory (var) ... regular (1985)

BOWMAN, LEE—actor

b: Dec 28, 1914, Cincinnati, Ohio d: Dec 25, 1979

Adventures of Ellery Queen (drama)
.... Ellery Queen (1951–52)
What's Going On? (quiz).. moderator (1954)
Masquerade Party (quiz)
.... panelist (1958–60)
Miami Undercover (drama)
.... Jeff Thompson (1961)

Suave, dark-haired (it was a toupee) Lee Bowman had an active career in B films in the late 1930s and '40s, then moved to television when movie roles became harder to get in the 1950s. He was one of several actors who played Ellery Queen, and he also appeared in various playhouse series, including numerous productions on *Robert Montgomery Presents*. After the cheaply made syndicated crime show *Miami Undercover* folded in 1961, his TV career folded as well, and he turned to an unusual line of work that made good use of his years of acting experience—coaching politicians and corporate executives for their on-air appearances. Asked if he missed being on-screen, he replied "not a bit."

BOWMAN, PATRICIA—dancer

The Patricia Bowman Show (music)
.... hostess (1951)

BOWREN, DON—actor

Paper Dolls (drama)..... Chris York (1984)

BOXLEITNER, BRUCE—actor

b: May 12, 1950, Elgin, Ill. r: Mt. Prospect, Ill.

How the West Was Won (miniseries) (drama)
.... Luke Macahan (1977)
How the West Was Won (wes)
.... Luke Macahan (1978–79)
The Last Convertible (drama)
.... George Virdon (1979)
East of Eden (drama). Charles Trask (1981)
Bring 'Em Back Alive (adv)
.... Frank Buck (1982–83)
Scarecrow and Mrs. King (adv)
..... Lee Stetson ("Scarecrow") (1983–)

Tall, handsome Bruce Boxleitner was a Chicago kid who plunged into acting as soon as he finished high school, skipping college altogether. His good looks and friendly manner got him small acting roles, and, after he moved to Los Angeles in 1972, bit parts on a number of TV series (his first was on *The Mary Tyler Moore Show* in December 1973). A small part in a *Gunsmoke* episode caught the eye of producer John Mantley, who later cast him as James Arness' trouble-prone nephew in the 1976 TV movie *The Macahans* and its sequel

How the West Was Won. He then had prominent roles in the miniseries *The Last Convertible* and *East of Eden,* before starring in his own light-action series: the unsuccessful *Bring 'Em Back Alive* and the very successful *Scarecrow and Mrs. King.*

A health enthusiast, he particularly enjoys horseback riding and hiking.

BOYD, JIMMY—actor, singer
b: Jan 9, 1940, McComb, Mo.

Date with the Angels (com)
.... Wheeler (1957–58)
Bachelor Father (com)
.... Howard Meechim (1958–61)
Broadside (com)
machinist's mate Marion Botnik (1964–65)

Jimmy Boyd tried hard to get his show business career back on track after one spectacular success as a child, but without much luck. A precocious youngster, he won a number of talent contests as a singer and made an appearance on Frank Sinatra's TV variety show in the early 1950s. That led to a Columbia records contract and a cute little novelty song called "I Saw Mommy Kissing Santa Claus," which, to everyone's amazement, was a mammoth hit at Christmas 1952, eventually selling about ten million copies.

Thus catapulted into the limelight, Jimmy branched into acting, playing juvenile roles in TV productions (including "Huck Finn" on *The U.S. Steel Hour*) and some B movies in the late 1950s. He later had regular roles on three TV comedies, but then drifted out of sight.

BOYD, TANYA—actress

The Ted Knight Show (com)
.... Philadelphia Phil Brown (1978)

BOYD, WILLIAM—cowboy star
b: Jun 5, 1895*, Cambridge, Ohio** d: Sep 12, 1972

Hopalong Cassidy (wes)
.... Hopalong Cassidy (1949–51)

This cowboy star is so famous as Hopalong Cassidy that it is hard to believe he

*Some sources give 1898.
**Some sources give Hedrysburg, Ohio, wherever that is.

ever played anything else. In fact, for 15 years before Hoppy loped onto the screen in 1935, Boyd was a leading man in many dramatic films, scoring great success in Cecil B. DeMille silent films of the 1920s. His career was in decline when Hoppy came along, however, so though he hated horses he learned to ride to get the part. He never had to worry about finding work again.

Boyd was wise enough to buy the television rights to the Hopalong Cassidy movies in the 1940s, before the new medium took off. He went into debt up to his stetson to do it, but the gambit paid off; Hopalong Cassidy was a TV sensation in the early 1950s, with a whole new generation of youngsters. The movies, the TV show (which included new episodes and old footage), a comic strip, toys, and other Hopalong products grossed an estimated $70 million in 1952, the height of the boom.

The white-haired, dark-suited star hardly needed to do anything after that—TV, not movies, had made him a millionaire. In the late 1950s he sold out all his interests for an enormous profit. He lived out the rest of his years quietly in California, making only occasional personal appearances for his young fans. Kids were never charged admission.

BOYER, CHARLES—actor
b: Aug 28, 1899, Figeac, France d: Aug 26, 1978

Four Star Playhouse (drama)
.... costar (1952–56)
Alcoa Theatre (drama)
.... recurring star (1957–58)
The Rogues (com)
.... Marcel St. Clair (1964–65)

This suave, romantic screen star of the 1930s, '40s and '50s was one of the cofounders of the Four Star Television production company (with Dick Powell, Joel McCrea and Rosalind Russell). It was a foresighted gamble on the new medium that earned him a great deal of money as well as providing a TV showcase for the famous actor in the mid-1950s. Boyer made occasional appearances on other high-class TV dramatic productions of the late 1950s and early '60s as well, but he was not without a sense of humor about his famous romantic charm. He hilariously lampooned himself in a 1956 *I Love Lucy* episode which had Lucy nonchalantly peeling an orange while Boyer tried to make love to her (when she realized who it was, she almost choked on the fruit!).

In 1964 Boyer was lured back to series TV as costar of the international mystery *The Rogues,* with Gig Young and David Niven. Subsequent appearances were few. In 1978, two days after the death of his wife of 44 years from cancer, he committed suicide (their only child, Michael, had also committed suicide in 1965).

BOYETT, WILLIAM—actor

Adam 12 (police)
.... Sgt. MacDonald (1968–75)

BOYLAN, BARBARA—dancer

The Lawrence Welk Show (music)
.... regular (1961–67)

BOYLE, PETER—actor
b: Oct 18, 1933, Philadelphia, Pa.

Comedy Tonight (var) .... regular (1970)
From Here to Eternity (drama)
.... Fatso Judson (1979)
Joe Bash (com)........ Off. Joe Bash (1986)

BRACKEN, EDDIE—actor, comic
b: Feb 7, 1920, Astoria, Queens, N.Y.

I've Got a Secret (quiz) ..... panelist (1952)
Make the Connection (quiz). panelist (1955)
Masquerade Party (quiz)...... emcee (1957)

BRACKETT-ZIKA, CHRISTIAN—juvenile actor

Domestic Life (com) ... Harold Crane (1984)

BRADDOCK, MICKEY—

See Dolenz, Mickey

BRADEN, KIM—actress

Laugh-In (revival) (var) ... regular (1977–78)

BRADFORD, JOHNNY—singer
b: Jul 2, 1919, Long Branch, N.J.

The Ransom Sherman Show (var)
.... regular (1950)

BRADFORD, RICHARD—actor

Man in a Suitcase (drama)... McGill (1968)

BRADLEY, ED—black newscaster
b: Jun 22, 1941, Philadelphia, Pa.

CBS Weekend News (news)
.... anchorman (1976–81)
60 Minutes (pub aff)
.... correspondent (1981–)

Emmy Awards: correspondent on various CBS news reports (1980, 1981, 1982). Best News Segment, for the *60 Minutes* Report "Schizophrenia."

As a co-anchor of *60 Minutes,* Ed Bradley was one of the most visible black reporters on network television in the 1980s. It was no token assignment on the part of the network; Bradley had worked his way up through the ranks as a local radio reporter in Philadelphia and New York from 1963–71 and as a CBS-TV field correspondent in the 1970s (including two tours in Vietnam, where he was wounded while on assignment in Cambodia). He has won many awards for his reports, which have ranged from a profile of singer Lena Horne to an investigation into the use of heroin for terminally ill patients in Britain.

BRADLEY, JESSE, TRIO—

Van Camp's Little Show (music)
.... regulars (1950–51)

BRADLEY, TRUMAN—host, announcer
b: c. 1905 d: Jul 28, 1974

Science Fiction Theater (sci fi)
.... narrator (1955–57)

Truman Bradley was a top sportscaster and announcer on radio in the 1930s and '40s for *The Red Skelton Show* and *Suspense,* among other programs. He is best-known to TV audiences as host of the much-rerun *Science Fiction Theater.*

BRADY, PAT—actor
b: Dec 31, 1914, Toledo, Ohio d: Feb 27, 1972

The Roy Rogers Show (wes)
.... as himself (1951–57)

The Roy Rogers & Dale Evans Show (var)
.... regular (1962)

Roy Rogers' curly-haired comic sidekick in movies and on TV. Like Roy, Pat got his start as a member of The Sons of the Pioneers western singing group in the 1930s.

BRADY, SCOTT—actor
b: Sep 13, 1924, Brooklyn, N.Y. d: Apr 16, 1985

Shotgun Slade (wes)
.... Shotgun Slade (1959–61)
The Winds of War (drama)
.... Red Tully (1983)

Movie tough guy Scott Brady, who was a lumberjack in his youth and a lightweight boxing champion during his service in the navy in the 1940s, was frequently seen in supporting roles on television dramas from the 1950s on. During the 1950s he was practically a semiregular on *Ford Theatre* and *Schlitz Playhouse of Stars*; in 1959 he starred in his own rather violent western. He was seen in many action shows of the 1960s and '70s, including numerous episodes of *Police Story*.

BRAEDEN, ERIC—
See Gudegast, Hans

BRAKE, PATRICIA—actress
b: 1942

The Ugliest Girl in Town (com)
.... Julie Renfield (1968–69)

BRAMLEY, RAYMOND—actor
Doorway to Danger (drama)
.... John Randolph (1953)

BRAND, JACK—host
Action Autographs (doc) .... host (1949)
Sing-co-pation (music) .... host (1949)

BRAND, JOLENE—actress
b: c. 1935, Los Angeles, Calif.

Zorro (wes)
.... Anna Maria Verdugo (1958–59)
Take a Good Look (quiz) . regular (1959–61)
GuestwardHo! (com).. Pink Cloud (1960–61)

BRAND, NEVILLE—actor
b: Aug 13, 1921, Kewanee, Ill.

Laredo (wes)...... Reese Bennett (1965–67)

"Listen," he growled at the reporter, "with this kisser I knew early in the game I wasn't going to make the world forget Clark Gable." Maybe not, but Neville Brand's deep, rutted features and tough manner made him one of the busiest actors in television, playing hundreds of roles in the 1950s, '60s, '70s, and '80s. TV (and movies) always need a good villain. On *The Untouchables* he was Al Capone; on *Bonanza*, Hoss's ruthless uncle who kidnapped Little Joe; on the TV movie *Deathstalk*, an escaped convict who terrorized two couples on a camping trip; and on *Rawhide*, a hired hand out to kill the entire cast.

Before all this villainy began, Brand was a real-life World War II hero—reportedly the fourth most decorated GI of the war. Once in a while, during his long TV career, he would change pace and turn up in a comedy. His only starring series, *Laredo*, was a western done with a light touch. However, his bread and butter was his scowl. As he put it, "the creepy characters are more interesting." You want to argue with him?

BRAND, OSCAR—folksinger
b: Feb 7, 1920, Winnipeg, Canada

Draw Me a Laugh! (quiz) .... regular (1949)

BRANDO, MARLON—actor
b: Apr 3, 1924, Omaha, Neb.

Roots: The Next Generations (drama)
.... George Lincoln Rockwell (1979)

Emmy Award: Best Supporting Actor in a Limited Series, for *Roots: The Next Generations* (1979)

This is one famous movie actor who has practically avoided TV altogether. Almost. On January 9, 1949, just after his first Broadway success in *A Streetcar Named Desire* and before his first film, he appeared in a live drama called "I'm No Hero" on ABC's obscure *Actor's Studio* series. Thirty years later, with considerably more fanfare, he made one more TV acting appearance, on *Roots*, as Nazi leader George Lincoln Rockwell. The industry was so awed it gave him an Emmy Award.

In between, Brando was seen, very rarely, on talk and variety shows such as *Ed Sullivan* and *Person to Person* in the 1950s and *The Dick Cavett Show* in the '70s. And that's about all.

BRANDON, CLARK—actor
b: Dec 30, 1958, New York City, N.Y.

The Fitzpatricks (drama)
.... Sean Fitzpatrick (1977–78)
Out of the Blue (com)
.... Chris Richards (1979)
Mr. Merlin (com)
.... Zachary Rogers (1981–82)

BRANDON, MICHAEL—actor
b: Brooklyn, N.Y.

Emerald Point N.A.S. (drama)
.... David Marquette (1983–84)
Dempsey and Makepeace (police)
.... Lt. James Dempsey (1984–)

BRANDS, X.—actor
b: c. 1926, Kansas City r: Los Angeles, Calif.

Yancy Derringer (adv)
.... Pahoo-Ka-Ta-Wah (1958–59)

Yes, that's his real name, inherited from a long line of forebears also named "X." Guess how he signs his checks?

BRANDT, HANK—actor

Julia (com)...... Len Waggedorn (1968–71)

BRANDT, JANET—actress
b: New York City, N.Y.

The Super (com) .... Mrs. Stein (1972)

BRANDT, MEL—actor, announcer
b: Jun 18, 1919, Brooklyn, N.Y.

Faraway Hill (drama) .... regular (1946)

BRANDT, VICTOR—actor
b: Sep 19, Los Angeles, Calif.

Nobody's Perfect (com).. Det. Jacobi (1980)

The son of actress Janet Brandt.

BRASFIELD, ROD—country comedian
b: 1910, Smithville, Miss. d: 1958

Grand Ole Opry (music) .. regular (1955–56)

BRASFIELD, UNCLE CYP & AUNT SAP—comedians

Ozark Jubilee (music).... regulars (1956–60)

BRASSELLE, KEEFE—actor, emcee
b: Feb 7, 1923, Elyria, Ohio d: Jul 7, 1981

Keep It in the Family (quiz)
.... emcee (first telecast) (1957)
Be Our Guest (var)............ host (1960)
The Keefe Brasselle Show (var)
.... host (1963)

This wavy-haired actor never quite achieved stardom on-screen, but he did cause something of an uproar in the industry in the 1960s. Brasselle began his career in movies, with appearances in about two dozen films (mostly Bs) between 1945 and the late '50s. His most notable film role was as Eddie Cantor in *The Eddie Cantor Story* (1953). He branched into television in the mid-1950s, appearing in various dramatic series and occasionally as a host, then founded his own production company in the 1960s. Through a still unexplained connection with hard-driving CBS-TV President James T. Aubrey ("the Smiling Cobra"), Brasselle managed to wrangle a summer variety show of his own on CBS in 1963. Then, without benefit of any of the testing or lengthy consultation that normally accompanies the development of prime time series, Brasselle sold Aubrey three major programs for the fall 1964 CBS schedule, all sight unseen. Many felt this reeked of an "inside deal," and both CBS and the Federal Communications Commission conducted investigations. All three shows—*The Baileys of Balboa, The Cara Williams Show* and *The Reporter*—were flops, and the once powerful Aubrey was fired in early 1965 amid allegations of scandal.

Brasselle thereupon retired from television and wrote a scathing, best-selling exposé of the business, called *The CanniBalS,* which was a thinly disguised account of his days at CBS (note the capitalized letters). He later wrote a similar novel, *The Barracudas.* He made further news in the 1970s due to his arrest for attempted murder during a bar brawl (the charges were later dropped) and a messy lawsuit alleging unpaid alimony to his former wife. He died in 1981.

BRAUN, BOB—singer
b: Apr 20, 1929, Ludlow, Ky

Dotty Mack Show (music)
.... regular (1952–56)

BRAUNER, ASHER—actor
b: Oct 25, Chicago, Ill.

B.A.D. Cats (police)
.... Off. Nick Donovan (1980)

BRAVERMAN, BART—actor
b: Feb 1, 1946, Los Angeles, Calif.

Vega$ (drama)
.... Bobby Borso (Binzer) (1978–81)
The New Odd Couple (com).. Roy (1982–83)

BRAVO, DANNY—actor

Jonny Quest (cartn)
.... Hadji (voice) (1964–65)

BRAY, ROBERT—actor
b: Oct 23, 1917, Kalispell, Mont. d: Mar 7, 1983

Stagecoach West (wes)
.... Simon Kane (1960–61)
Lassie (adv) .... Corey Stuart (1964–69)

BRAY, THOM—actor
b: Apr 30, Camden, N.J.

Breaking Away (com)....... Cyril (1980–81)
Riptide (drama)
.... Murray "Boz" Bozinsky (1984–86)

BRAZZI, ROSSANO—actor
b: Sep 18, 1916, Bologna, Italy

The Survivors (drama)
.... Antaeus Riakos (1969–70)

A graying, distinguished Italian romantic actor with a booming baritone voice who appeared in films of the 1950s (e.g., *South Pacific*). He appeared in a scattering of television dramatic shows over the years, from *The June Allyson Show* in the 1960s to *Fantasy Island* in the '80s. His only regular role was as Lana Turner's old

flame (and Jan Michael Vincent's father) on *The Survivors*. He returned to Italy in the late 1960s and continued to make films there.

BRECHT, SUSAN—actress
Dorothy (com) .... Meredith (1979)

BRECK, PETER—actor
b: 1929, Rochester, N.Y.

Black Saddle (wes)
.... Clay Culhane (1959–60)
The Big Valley (wes)
.... Nick Barkley (1965–69)
The Secret Empire (drama)
.... Jess Keller (1979)

A dark, handsome actor who was supposed to be catapulted to stardom by the 1959 western *Black Saddle,* but wasn't. Four years as the brawling young son Nick on *Big Valley* didn't turn the trick either (although it did for his "sister" and "brother" on the show, Linda Evans and Lee Majors), and Breck reverted to occasional guest roles.

BREEDING, LARRY—actor
b: Sep 28, 1946, Winchester, Ill. d: Sep 28, 1982

Who's Watching the Kids? (com)
.... Larry Parnell (1978)
The Last Resort (com)
.... Michael Lerner (1979–80)

BREEN, PROF. ROBERT—panelist
Short Story Playhouse (drama)
.... narrator (1951)
Down You Go (quiz)
.... regular panelist (1951–54)

BREESE, LOU—orchestra leader
The Jack Carter Show (var)
.... orch. leader (1950)

BREEZE, SYD—emcee
Stump the Authors (talk)...... editor (1949)

BREGMAN, BUDDY—orchestra leader, arranger
b: Jul 9, 1930, Chicago, Ill.

The Eddie Fisher Show (var)
.... orch. leader (1957–59)
The Music Shop (var) .... host (1959)

Youthful Buddy Bregman, a nephew of composer Jule Styne, was a very busy composer and arranger for television variety shows from the 1950s on (beginning at age 19 when he orchestrated a 1949 Jack Haley special on NBC). He has provided jazz-flavored, big band backing for such artists as Judy Garland, Ella Fitzgerald, Sammy Davis, Jr., and Fred Astaire, on TV and on records.

BRENDAN, GAVIN—actor

Marcus Welby, M.D. (drama)
.... Phil Porter (1975–76)

BRENNA, BETTINA—actress

The Beverly Hillbillies (com)
.... Gloria Buckles (1969–71)

BRENNAN, EILEEN—actress
b: Sep 3, 1937*, Los Angeles, Calif.

Rowan & Martin's Laugh-In (var)
.... regular (1968)
All That Glitters (com) ... Ma Packer (1977)
13 Queens Boulevard (com)
.... Felicia Winters (1979)
A New Kind of Family (com)
.... Kit Flanagan (1979–80)
Private Benjamin (com)
.... Capt. Doreen Lewis (1981–83)
Off the Rack (com) ... Kate Halloran (1985)

Emmy Award: Best Supporting Actress in a Comedy Series, for *Private Benjamin* (1981)

Eileen Brennan perfected her persona as a brassy, scowling, neurotic dame in movies and TV shows of the 1970s and '80s. Ironically, her first major success had been in the title role of the off-Broadway musical *Little Mary Sunshine* in 1959. This was followed by more plays, until she was spotted in one by producers Norman Lear and Bud Yorkin, who brought her to Hollywood for a small role in their 1967 film *Divorce: American Style*. More movie roles and guest shots on TV episodes followed, as well as a brief stint on *Laugh-In*. Lear and Yorkin, who obviously liked her,

*Some sources give 1935.

gave her guest roles in *All in the Family* and the syndicated comedy *All That Glitters,* and finally a starring role in *13 Queens Boulevard.* Eileen's first real hit, however, was as the frustrated, sarcastic Captain Doreen Lewis in the 1980 Goldie Hawn movie *Private Benjamin,* a role she repeated for the popular TV version the following year.

Just when her career seemed to be taking off, Brennan was critically injured in a 1983 automobile accident and then had to fight a long battle to overcome a dependency on prescription painkillers. She eventually recovered and was back on-screen in the mid-1980s.

BRENNAN, WALTER—actor
b: Jul 25, 1894, Swampscott, Mass.* d: Sep 21, 1974

The Real McCoys (com)
.... Grandpa Amos McCoy (1957–63)
The Tycoon (com)
.... Walter Andrews (1964–65)
The Guns of Will Sonnett (wes)
.... Will Sonnett (1967–69)
To Rome with Love (com)
.... Grandpa Andy Pruitt (1970–71)

Walter Brennan was another one of TV's patented characters, the wheezy, gosh-darnin', con-sarnin' old-timer who was perfect for the role of Grandpa—which is in fact what he played on all four of his regular series. He was the grandfather of Richard Crenna on *The Real McCoys,* of Pat McNulty on *Tycoon,* of Dack Rambo on *The Guns of Will Sonnett,* and of John Forsythe's three young daughters on *To Rome with Love.*

Brennan was actually young once, though it was hard to tell, since he had perfected his movie characterization of a toothless old codger while he was still in his thirties (after losing his own teeth in a riding accident). He had a long career in Hollywood, beginning in the 1920s, and was the first actor ever to win three Academy Awards, between 1936 and 1940. He did a good deal of television work in the 1950s, in dramas, and continued to be a familiar face on the small screen, mainly in his one-after-another series. Another bit of perfect casting was in the 1969 TV movie *The Over the Hill Gang,* and its 1970 sequel.

*Some sources give Lynn, Mass.

"Never wanted to be a star," he snorted. "Just wanted to be good at what I was doin'." He certainly was.

BRENNER, DORI—actress
b: Dec 16, New York City r: Lawrenceville, N.Y.

Seventh Avenue (drama)
.... Rhoda Gold (1977)
Cassie & Company (drama)
.... Meryl Foxx (1982)

BRENT, GEORGE—actor
b: Mar 15, 1904, Dublin, Ireland* d: May 26, 1979

Wire Service (drama)
.... Dean Evans (1956–57)

BRESLER, JERRY—orchestra leader
b: May 29, 1914, Chicago, Ill.

Arthur Godfrey and His Friends (var)
.... orch. leader (1954–55)
Arthur Godfrey's Talent Scouts (talent)
.... orch. leader (1954–55)

BRESLIN, JIMMY—New York newspaper columnist
b: Oct 17, 1930, Queens, New York City, N.Y.

Jimmy Breslin's People (talk)... host (1986–)

BRESLIN, PAT—actress
b: c. 1930, New York

The People's Choice (com)
.... Amanda "Mandy" Peoples Miller (1955–58)

Jackie Cooper's girlfriend (and later wife) on *The People's Choice* had an active career in television dramas of the 1950s and early '60s. She was a particular favorite on *Perry Mason* and on *Alfred Hitchcock Presents*, which featured her at least five times, usually as the loyal wife. In one *Hitchcock* episode she was not so loyal, though; conspiring to murder her boyfriend's wife, she bumped off the woman herself, then posed as her temporarily to answer the door—only to get shot by a hitman hired to do the same job.

Breslin later went into daytime soap operas, appearing briefly on *Peyton Place*

*Some sources give Shannonsbridge, Ireland.

and then for a longer run on *General Hospital* (1966–69).

BRESSLER, BRIAN—comedian
b: Jan 6, Vancouver, B.C., Canada

Rowan & Martin's Laugh-In (var)
.... regular (1972–73)

BRESTOFF, RICHARD—actor

Operation Petticoat (com)
.... Yeoman Hunkle (1977–79)

BREWER, BETTY—singer

Captain Billy's Mississippi Music Hall (var)
.... regular (1948)
Holiday Hotel (var)
.... regular (1950–51)

BREWER, TERESA—singer
b: May 7, 1931, Toledo, Ohio

Summertime U.S.A. (music) .. cohost (1953)
Perry Presents (var) .... cohost (1959)

A petite singer with a booming voice who was quite popular in the 1950s with hits such as "Music, Music, Music" and "Ricochet Romance." Teresa made many appearances on television variety shows of the day, including those of Ed Sullivan and Perry Como, and she was Como's summer replacement in 1959.

BREWSTER, DIANA—announcer

The Ina Ray Hutton Show (var)
.... announcer (1956)

BREWSTER, DIANE—actress
b: 1931, Kansas

Leave It to Beaver (com)
.... Miss Canfield (1957–58)
Maverick (wes)
.... Samantha Crawford (1958–59)
The Islanders (adv)
.... Wilhelmina Vandeveer (1960–61)

BREWTON, MAIA—juvenile actress
b: Sep 30, c. 1977, Los Angeles, Calif.

Lime Street (drama)
.... Margaret Ann Culver (1985)

BRIAN, DAVID—actor
b: Aug 5, 1914, New York City, N.Y.

Mr. District Attorney (police)
.... D. A. Paul Garrett (1954)
The Immortal (adv)
.... Arthur Maitland (1970–71)

BRICKELL, BETH—actress
b: c. 1941, Camden, Ark.

Gentle Ben (adv) . . . Ellen Wedloe (1967–69)

BRIDGE, LOIE—actress

Life with Elizabeth (com)
Mrs. Chlorine "Chloe" Skinridge (1953–55)

BRIDGES, BEAU—actor
b: Dec 9, 1941, Hollywood, Calif.

Ensign O'Toole (com)
.... Seaman Howard Spicer (1962–63)
United States (com) . Richard Chapin (1980)

Lloyd Bridges seems to have done everything possible to get his two sons, Jeff and Beau, into acting. Young Beau had roles in films made by his father's friends when he was between the ages of four and eight; he was also on stage at age six and was given parts in his father's series *Sea Hunt, The Lloyd Bridges Show,* and *The Loner* when he was in his teens and early twenties. Beau also appeared in episodes of other series of the 1960s, and had a regular role as baby-faced Seaman Spicer on *Ensign O'Toole.* However, his principal success, like that of younger brother Jeff, has been in movies.

BRIDGES, LLOYD—actor
b: Jan 15, 1913, San Leandro, Calif.

Sea Hunt (adv) ...... Mike Nelson (1957–61)
The Lloyd Bridges Show (drama)
.... Adam Shepherd/other roles (1962–63)
The Loner (wes). . William Colton (1965–66)
San Francisco International Airport (drama)
.... Jim Conrad (1970–71)
Joe Forrester (police)
.... Joe Forrester (1975–76)
Roots (drama).......... Evan Brent (1977)
East of Eden (drama)
.... Samuel Hamilton (1981)
The Blue and the Gray (drama)
.... Ben Geyser (1982)
Paper Dolls (drama) . . . Grant Harper (1984)

Beefy Lloyd Bridges transcended a role that could have typecast another actor—

that of underwater diver Mike Nelson in the 1950s hit *Sea Hunt*—to play many other types of characters during a long and busy television career.

After stage experience in the 1930s, Lloyd broke into movies in 1941 and played supporting roles in many action films. Two of his best were as the calculating deputy in *High Noon* (1952) and in the Marilyn Monroe allegory *The Goddess* (1958). He was also quite busy on television from its start, appearing in many of the live playhouses of the 1950s, and was nominated for an Emmy Award for a 1956 performance on *Alcoa Playhouse.*

Following the success of *Sea Hunt* the roles got even better, and Bridges alternated between his own series and guest appearances on such shows as *Zane Grey Theater* and *The Eleventh Hour.* By the late 1960s he was doing mostly TV movies and miniseries, among the latter *Roots, East of Eden,* and *The Blue and the Gray.* After *Joe Forrester,* he swore he'd never do another weekly series, but the soap-operish *Paper Dolls* somehow lured him back in 1984 to play the powerful patriarch Grant Harper.

Always an outspoken member of the Hollywood community, Bridges was in the early 1950s a key witness at the hearings of the House Un-American Activities Committee, after affirming his own onetime membership in the Communist Party. By the 1980s he was much more interested in talking about the success of his actor sons, Jeff and Beau, of whom he was quite proud.

BRIDGES, TODD—black actor
b: May 27, 1965, San Francisco, Calif.

Fish (com) .... Loomis (1977–78)
Diff'rent Strokes (com)
.... Willis Jackson (1978–86)

Todd Bridges has grown up on TV. A child actor from the age of six, he was the young black kid on *Fish,* in which adults patted him on the head and said "Aren't you cute?" By the time he was in his teens, on *Diff'rent Strokes,* teenage girls were screaming when he walked onto the set. "I hope that means they like my acting," he said.

BRIGHT, JACK—host

Try and Do It (var)............ host (1948)

BRIGHT, PATRICIA—hostess, actress

Movieland Quiz (quiz)..... assistant (1948)
Fifty-Fourth Street Revue (var)
.... regular (1949)
Draw Me a Laugh! (quiz) ..... emcee (1949)
It's Always Jan (com)
.... Pat Murphy (1955–56)

BRILES, CHARLES—actor

The Big Valley (wes)
... Eugene Barkley (occasional) (1965–66)

BRILL, CHARLIE—actor

Rowan & Martin's Laugh-In (var)
.... regular (1968–69)
Supertrain (drama)
.... Robert the hairdresser (1979)

BRILL, MARTY—actor
r: Chicago, Ill.

The New Dick Van Dyke Show (com)
.... Bernie Davis (1971–73)

BRIMLEY, WILFORD—actor
b: Sep 27, 1934, Salt Lake City r: Santa Monica,
Calif.

Our House (drama)
.... Gus Witherspoon (1986–   )

Barrel-chested, walrus-mustached Wilford Brimley got into acting rather late, dislikes the Hollywood rat race (he lives on a ranch in Utah), and doesn't mind being habitually cast as grumpy old-timers much older than himself. "Those are just circumstances created by writers," he snorts. "I know my real age."

A onetime blacksmith, ranch hand, and racehorse trainer, Brimley began in movies as an extra and stunt man. By the late 1970s he was winning supporting roles, attracting notice as a company man in *The China Syndrome,* a baseball manager in *The Natural,* a no-nonsense lawyer in *Absense of Malice,* and especially as the leader of the spunky senior citizens in 1985's *Cocoon.* In *Our House* he played a gruff (of course) 65-year-old (of course) widower who opened his home to his wid-

owed daughter-in-law and her cute kids. Harrrumph!

BRINEGAR, PAUL—actor

The Life and Legend of Wyatt Earp (wes)
.... Jim "Dog" Kelly (1956–58)
Rawhide (wes)........ Wishbone (1959–66)
Lancer (wes)....... Jelly Hoskins (1969–70)
Matt Houston (drama)
.... Lamar Pettybone (1982–83)

BRINKLEY, DAVID—newscaster
b: Jul 10, 1920, Wilmington, N.C.

The Huntley-Brinkley Report (news)
.... anchorman (1956–71)
David Brinkley's Journal (doc)
.... commentator (1961–63)
NBC Evening News (news)
.... anchorman (1976–79)
NBC Magazine with David Brinkley (pub aff)
.... anchorman (1980–81)

"Huntley, Brinkley, Huntley, Brinkley, one is solemn, the other is twinkly," went a bit of '60s doggerel. David Brinkley was of course the "twinkly" one, a veteran newsman who after years on the beat was still able to deliver analyses with a sly smile and a wry sense of humor.

He started writing for his local newspaper while still a high school student and worked briefly for United Press before serving in World War II. Upon his discharge in 1943 he joined NBC as a White House correspondent and stayed with the network for the next 38 years. Brinkley's star really began to rise in 1956 when he was paired with Chet Huntley (the "solemn" one) for coverage of that year's political conventions. They were so popular that they were named co-anchors of NBC's principal evening newscast, replacing John Cameron Swayze; *The Huntley-Brinkley Report* was the number-one newscast in America in the late 1950s and early '60s. Despite the fame this brought him, Brinkley avoided celebrity, always adhering to high professional standards.

When Huntley retired in 1970, Brinkley was briefly teamed with other correspondents, then left the anchor position to become a commentator and to work on news specials. Desperately looking for a way to compete with CBS's Walter Cronkite, NBC brought Brinkley back to the anchor chair in 1976, this time paired with John Chancellor, then shunted him aside once again in 1979 when the ratings didn't improve. Understandably miffed by this kind of treatment, and at odds with NBC news management, Brinkley left the network in 1981 and joined ABC. Signing a newsman of Brinkley's stature was considered a major coup for ABC. However, they chose not to use him on their evening news, instead giving him an expanded Sunday public affairs program, *This Week with David Brinkley*, which proved quite popular in its time period.

During his long career Brinkley has reported on practically every major national news event, including the Apollo 11 landing on the moon, the Watergate scandal, and the funerals of presidents Eisenhower and Johnson. He has won enough awards to fill a room. And he still has a twinkle.

BRISEBOIS, DANIELLE—actress
b: Jun 28, 1969, Brooklyn, N.Y.

All in the Family (com)
. . . . Stephanie Mills (1978–83)
Knots Landing (drama)
. . . . Mary-Frances Sumner (1983–84)

Archie Bunker's streetwise niece, Stephanie, was played by a New York child actor who had been spotted by the producers of the show in the cast of the Broadway musical *Annie*. An old trooper by that time, she had been doing commercials since age four and later made appearances on a number of series, including the daytime soap operas *All My Children* and *As the World Turns*. She aspires to a career as an opera singer.

BRISSETTE, TIFFANY—juvenile actress
b: Dec 26, 1974

Small Wonder (com)
. . . . Vicki (Victoria Ann Smith) (1985–   )

BRITT, ELTON—country singer
b: Jul 7, 1917, Marshall, Ark. d: Jun 23, 1972

Saturday Night Jamboree (music)
. . . . emcee (1948)

BRITTANY, MORGAN—actress
b: Dec 5, 1951, Hollywood, Calif.

Dallas (drama)
. . . . Katherine Wentworth (1981–84)
Glitter (drama). . . . . Kate Simpson (1984–85)

BRITTON, BARBARA—actress
b: Sep 26, 1920*, Long Beach, Calif. d: Jan 17, 1980

Mr. & Mrs. North (drama)
. . . . Pamela North (1952–54)

Screen star Barbara Britton appeared in television playhouse productions of the early 1950s (*Robert Montgomery Presents, Ford Theatre,* etc.) and the *Mr.-& Mrs. North* series before retiring from acting in the mid-1950s. She was known in later years primarily for her Revlon cosmetics commercials, though she also appeared sporadically in plays.

BRITTON, PAMELA—actress
b: 1923, Milwaukee, Wis. d: Jun 17, 1974

Blondie (com). . . . . Blondie Bumstead (1957)
My Favorite Martian (com)
. . . . Mrs. Lorelei Brown (1963–66)

BROCK, JIMMY—actor
The College Bowl (com) . . regular (1950–51)

BROCK, LOU—sportscaster
Monday Night Baseball (sport)
. . . . sportscaster (1980)

BROCK, STAN—
Wild Kingdom (doc). . . . assistant (1968–71)

BROCK, STANLEY—actor
b: Jul 7, Brooklyn, N.Y. r: Bronx, N.Y.

He's the Mayor (com) . . Ivan Bronski (1986)

BRODERICK, JAMES—actor
b: Mar 7, 1930, Charleston, N.H. d: Nov 1, 1982

Brenner (police). . . Off. Ernie Brenner (1959)
Brenner (police). . . Off. Ernie Brenner (1964)
Family (drama) . . Doug Lawrence (1976–80)

The father of Matthew Broderick.

*Some sources give 1919 or 1921.

BRODERICK, MALCOLM—actor

The Marriage (com)
.... Pete Marriott (1954)

BRODIE, STEVE—actor

b: Nov 25, 1919, Eldorado, Kan.

The Life and Legend of Wyatt Earp (wes)
.... Sheriff Johnny Behan (1959–61)

BROEKMAN, DAVID—musician, panelist

b: May 13, 1902, Leiden, Holland d: Jan 1, 1958

Think Fast (quiz)........ panelist (1949–50)

BROGAN, JIMMY—comedian, actor

b: Sep 18, Boston, Mass.

Out of the Blue (com)...... Random (1979)

BROKAW, TOM—newscaster

b: Feb 6, 1940, Yankton, S.D.

NBC Weekend News (news)
.... anchorman (1975–76)
NBC Nightly News (news)
.... anchorman (1982–)

"I couldn't have picked a worse time for the republic, a better time for a reporter," says Tom Brokaw of his breakthrough assignment covering the Watergate scandal at the White House. Brokaw is seen as a beneficiary of the networks' attempts to give their evening newscasts a younger look after years of distinguished older anchormen such as Cronkite, Chancellor, and Reasoner. He was by no means a neophyte when he acceded to the top spot on the *NBC Nightly News* in 1982, however—he had been in the business for 20 years.

Tom started out on local TV, and residents of Omaha and Atlanta may remember seeing him on their local newscasts between 1962–66. He quickly moved on to bigger things: a top spot at KNBC-TV in Los Angeles in 1966, White House correspondent for NBC in 1973, and host of the early morning *Today* show in 1976. Though he was never as contentious as his CBS counterpart, Dan Rather (who argued with the president at press conferences), or as sardonic as David Brinkley, he projected a calm, competent, in-charge image that led NBC to choose him over several others for its top news position in the early 1980s,

first as co-anchor with Roger Mudd, and then on his own.

BROKENSHIRE, NORMAN—announcer, host

b: 1898 d: May 4, 1965

The Better Home Show (info)
.... regular (1951–52)
Four Square Court (info).. moderator (1952)

An old-time radio announcer, famous for his exaggerated opening ("How *do* you do?"). A kindly old gent, he hosted a fix-it show called *The Better Home Show* on ABC in the early 1950s, as well as a similar syndicated show called *Handyman* in 1955.

BROLIN, JAMES—actor

b: Jul 18, 1940*, Los Angeles, Calif.

Marcus Welby, M. D. (drama)
.... Dr. Steven Kiley (1969–76)
Hotel (drama).... Peter McDermott (1983–)

Emmy Award: Best Supporting Actor in a Drama, for *Marcus Welby, M.D.* (1970)

A tall (6'4"), handsome actor who, as the young, apprentice doctor, provided youthful counterpoint to Robert Young in the *Welby* series. Brolin crashed Hollywood around 1960, doing odd jobs at the studios and getting small roles in series episodes, beginning with a *Bus Stop* episode in 1961. He appeared several times on *The Monroes* in 1966–67 before getting his big break on *Welby* in 1969. He was seen mostly in films during the late 1970s and early '80s (including the role of Clark Gable in 1976's *Gable and Lombard*), then turned up on *Hotel* in 1983.

BROMFIELD, JOHN—actor

b: Jun 11, 1922, South Bend, Ind.

The Sheriff of Cochise (police)
. Sheriff/Marshal Frank Morgan (1956–60)

BROMFIELD, VALRI—comedienne, actress

b: Feb 10, Toronto, Canada

Bobbie Gentry Show (var) ... regular (1974)
Angie (com)......... Mary Mary (1979–80)

*Some sources give 1942.

Best of the West (com)
.... Laney Gibbs (1981–82)
The New Show (var) .... regular (1984)

This somewhat offbeat stand-up comedienne once gave one-woman shows with titles like "You're Eating out of the Dog's Dish" and "Cultural Phunque," in her native Canada. She was a writer-performer on several Canadian TV series and a member of the fertile Second City comedy troupe there before coming to the U.S. She claims to be working on a movie called *Housewives Behind Bars.*

BROMLEY, SHEILA—actress
b: 1911

I Married Joan (com)
.... Janet Tobin (1954–55)
Hank (com)..... Mrs. Ethel Weiss (1965–66)

BRONSON, CHARLES—actor
b: Nov 3, 1921*, Ehrenfield, Pa.

Man with a Camera (drama)
.... Mike Kovac (1958–60)
Empire (wes) .... Paul Moreno (1963)
The Travels of Jaimie McPheeters (wes)
.... Linc Murdock (1963–64)

Hatchet-faced tough guy Charles Bronson is today known for his booming movie career, but in the 1950s and early '60s he was quite active on television, both in guest roles and as a regular on three series.

Before starting his acting career in the early 1950s he had what could only be described as a hard life. He was born one of 15 children in a poor coal-mining family and worked in the mines himself for several years before seeing hair-raising action as a tail-gunner during World War II. Swearing he would never go back to the mines, he enrolled in acting school after the war and began getting bit parts in films and TV shows in the early 1950s, at first under his real name Charles Buchinski (or Buchinsky).

Bronson appeared on numerous live and filmed TV dramas, including multiple appearances on *Treasury Men in Action, Crusader, Have Gun Will Travel,* and *General Electric Theater,* receiving an Emmy nomination for a 1961 role on the

*Some sources give 1922.

last-named series. He usually played a villain, and a terrifying one at that. Twice on *Alfred Hitchcock* he portrayed a murderous thug who gets his due just when he thinks he has it made. His own series presented him in only a slightly softer light: on *Man with a Camera* he was a rough-edged photographer/detective, on *Empire* a ranch hand originally accused of murder, and on *The Travels of Jaimie McPheeters* a powerful but troubled wagonmaster.

After steadily building his movie career in action films of the 1960s *(The Great Escape, The Dirty Dozen),* he left Hollywood —and TV—for Europe in 1968, where he became a major star. By the 1970s he was a star in the U.S. as well, in violent films such as *Death Wish.* Bronson is married to actress Jill Ireland.

BRONSON, LILLIAN—actress
b: Oct 21, 1902, Lockport, N.Y.

Kings Row (drama)..... Grandma (1955–56)
Date with the Angels (com)
.... Mrs. Drake (1957–58)

BRONSON, MILT—actor

Abbott and Costello Show (com)
.... various roles (1951–53)

BROOK, FAITH—actress
b: Feb 16, 1922, York, England

Claudia, The Story of a Marriage (drama)
.... Julia Naughton (1952)

Daughter of actor Clive Brook.

BROOKE, HILLARY—actress
b: Sep 8, 1914, Astoria, N.Y.

The Abbott and Costello Show (com)
.... as herself (1951–52)
My Little Margie (com)
.... Roberta Townsend (1952–55)

After a 20-year career in B films (1937–57) and ten active years on television in the 1950s, both in comedies and dramas, Hillary married an MGM executive and retired in the early 1960s. Asked years later about how she managed to stay away from acting so long, she replied simply, "I don't want to work anymore."

115

BROOKE, WALTER—actor
b: c. 1915 d: Aug 20, 1986

One Man's Family (drama)
.... Bill Herbert (1950–52)
The Green Hornet (drama)
. District Attorney F. P. Scanlon (1966–67)

For Walter, fame came late in life with one word spoken in the movie *The Graduate*. He is the actor who whispered the word "plastics" into Dustin Hoffman's ear.

BROOKES, JACQUELINE—actress
b: Jul 24, 1930, Montclair, N.J.

Jack and Mike (drama) ...... Nora (1986–)

BROOKS, ALBERT—comedian, director, writer
b: Jul 22, 1947, Los Angeles, Calif.

Dean Martin Presents the Golddiggers (var)
.... regular (1969)
NBC's Saturday Night Live (com)
.... regular (1975–76)

The son of well-known radio comedian Parkyakarkus, who worked with Eddie Cantor for many years; Albert is also the brother of comedian Bob Einstein.

BROOKS, AVERY—black actor
b: Oct 2, Evansville, Ind. r: Gary, Ind.

Spenser: For Hire (drama) .. Hawk (1985–)

The tall, ominous, rather enigmatic "enforcer" on *Spenser: For Hire*. Before joining that series in 1985, Brooks spent 13 years as a professor of theater at Rutgers University in New Jersey.

BROOKS, ELISABETH—actress
r: Toronto, Canada

Doctors' Hospital (drama)
...... Nurse Connie Kimbrough (1975–76)

BROOKS, FOSTER—comedian
b: May 11, 1912, Louisville, KY.

The New Bill Cosby Show (var)
.... regular (1972–73)
Mork & Mindy (com)
.... Mr. Miles Sternhagen (1981)

Foster Brooks gained fame rather late in life with a single characterization—the inebriated oldster trying hard to get a sentence out straight. After a long, minor career in films and on TV, he literally became an overnight celebrity via *Dean Martin's Celebrity Roasts* in the 1970s, where he was introduced as a fictional "friend" of the star being roasted. Later he was Mindy's boss on *Mork & Mindy*.

BROOKS, GERALDINE—actress
b: Oct 29, 1925, New York City, N.Y. d: Jun 19, 1977

Faraday and Company (drama)
.... Lou Carson (1973–74)
The Dumplings (com)
.... Angela Dumpling (1976)

BROOKS, HELEN—actress

The Steve Allen Comedy Hour (var)
.... regular (1980–81)

BROOKS, JOE—actor

F Troop (com)
.... Trooper Vanderbilt (1965–67)

BROOKS, JOEL—actor
b: Dec 10, New York City, N.Y.

Private Benjamin (com)
.... Lt. Billy Dean (1982)
Teachers Only (com)
.... Barney Betelman (1983)
Hail to the Chief (com) ...... Randy (1985)
My Sister Sam (com) ... J. D. Lucas (1986–)

BROOKS, MARTIN E.—actor

Medical Center (drama)
.... Lt. Samuels (1971–76)
The Six Million Dollar Man (adv)
.... Dr. Rudy Wells (1975–78)
The Bionic Woman (adv)
.... Dr. Rudy Wells (1976–78)
Dallas (drama)... Edgar Randolph (1983–84)

BROOKS, NED—newscaster

Meet the Press (int) ... moderator (1953–65)

BROOKS, PETER—actor

My Three Sons (com)
.... Hank Ferguson (1961–63)

BROOKS, RAND—actor
b: Sep 21, 1918, Los Angeles, Calif.

Adventures of Rin Tin Tin (wes)
.... Cpl. Boone (1954–59)

This wavy-haired actor got his best role early in his career—perhaps too early—playing Scarlett O'Hara's ill-fated first husband in *Gone with the Wind* (1939). Thereafter he slipped back into B films and then TV work in the 1950s. Among other roles, he was Hopalong Cassidy's sidekick Lucky in a number of the Cassidy features of the late 1940s and Corporal Boone on TV's *Rin Tin Tin*. In later years Rand retired from show business and operated the Professional Ambulance Service in Glendale, California.

BROOKS, RANDI—actress
b: Nov 8, New York City, N.Y. r: France and Calif.

Wizards and Warriors (adv)
.... Witch Bethel (1983)
The Last Precinct (com)
.... Off. Mel Brubaker (1986)

BROOKS, RANDY—black actor
b: Jan 30, The Bronx, N.Y.

Brothers and Sisters (com)
.... Ronald Holmes III (1979)
Renegades (police) .... Eagle (1983)
Rituals (drama)
.... Lucky Washington (1984–85)

A young actor who had some stage experience, including a role in the road company of *Hair*, before breaking into television in the late 1970s. Besides his regular roles on a short-run college comedy (*Brothers and Sisters*, two-and-a-half months) and an even shorter-run action show (*Renegades*, one month), he appeared in the syndicated soap opera *Rituals* in 1984–85.

BROOKS, ROXANNE—actress

Richard Diamond, Private Detective (drama)
.... "Sam" (1959–60)

BROOKS, STEPHEN—actor
b: 1942, Columbus, Ohio

The Nurses (drama)
.... Dr. Ned Lowry (1963–64)

The F.B.I. (police)
..... Special Agent Jim Rhodes (1965–67)
The Interns (drama)
.... Dr. Greg Pettit (1970–71)

BROOKSHIER, TOM—sportscaster
b: 1931, Roswell, N.M.

Celebrity Challenge of the Sexes (sport)
.... host/commentator (1978)

This onetime defensive back for the Philadelphia Eagles football team (1953–61) turned to sportscasting when a leg injury ended his playing days. In addition to covering NFL contests for CBS for more than 20 years beginning in 1964, he hosted *CBS Sports Spectacular*, two syndicated sports series (*This Is the NFL* and *Sports Illustrated*), and CBS's prime time series *Celebrity Challenge of the Sexes*, which filled an important gap in sports coverage by presenting such riveting contests as Barbi Benton and Reggie Jackson in a bicycle race and Karen Black and Don Adams playing Ping-Pong.

BROPHY, KEVIN—actor

Lucan (adv)............... Lucan (1977–78)

BROPHY, SALLIE—actress
b: Dec 14, Phoenix, Ariz.

Buckskin (wes)
.... Mrs. Annie O'Connell (1958–59)

BROSNAN, PIERCE—actor
b: May 16, 1952, County Meath, Ireland

Remington Steele (drama)
.... Remington Steele (1982–86)

Dashing Irish actor Pierce Brosnan, who is sometimes said to look a bit like Cary Grant ("It's a lot of twaddle," Pierce modestly replies), entered acting in 1976 in London. He appeared in several British TV productions, including *The Manions of America* in 1981. He landed the plum role of Remington Steele while on a visit to America the following year. To the dismay of his many female admirers, he is married and has three children.

BROTHER THEODORE—

See Gottlieb, Theodore

BROTHERS, DR. JOYCE—psychologist
b: Sep 20, 1928, New York City, N.Y.

The Gong Show (com) ... panelist (1976–80)

TV's best-known shrink became nationally famous overnight, in a rather unusual way. In addition to her obvious knowledge of psychology (she has a Ph.D. from Columbia), the petite blonde happened to have an encyclopedic knowledge of boxing —a fact that won her a total of $134,000 as a contestant on *The $64,000 Question* and *The $64,000 Challenge* in 1955–56.

That moment in the limelight proved to be a springboard to a long career in show business. Her first TV venture was as co-host of NBC's *Sports Showcase.* Dr. Brothers then began a counseling program on radio and TV in the late '50s; she has since written newspaper columns and books and hosted a variety of radio and TV counseling programs (e.g., *Consult Dr. Brothers, Ask Dr. Brothers, Tell Me, Dr. Brothers*).

Obviously enjoying show biz, she has also lent her talents (sometimes in self-parody) to such diverse series as *Beggarman, Thief, Captain Kangaroo, Sha Na Na, Just Our Luck,* and *The Gong Show* (as a regular panelist). She even appeared in 1972 on *One Life to Live,* providing psychological counseling for one of the soap's tormented characters.

Brothers, who has also taught at several universities, comes from a professional family; her mother and father were both lawyers, and her husband is a physician.

BROUGH, CANDI—actress

B.J. and the Bear (adv)
.... Terri Garrison (1981)

BROUGH, RANDI—actress

B.J. and the Bear (adv)
.... Geri Garrison (1981)

BROWN, A. WHITNEY—writer, comedian

NBC's Saturday Night Live (var)
.... regular (1986–)

BROWN, ALLAN—host

Melody Street (music) .... host (1953)

BROWN, BLAIR—actress
b: 1952, Washington, D.C.

Captains and the Kings (drama)
...... Elizabeth Healey Hennessey (1976)
Wheels (drama)...... Barbara Lipton (1978)

A young actress who has appeared mostly in miniseries and in a few regular series episodes. She married actor Richard Jordan, whom she met during the filming of *Captains and the Kings.*

BROWN, BOB (1940s)—host

Science Circus (info) .... host (1949)

Chicago-based radio and TV announcer, known for his long association with the radio series *Vic and Sade.*

BROWN, BOB (1970s–80s)—newscaster

20/20 (mag)........ correspondent (1980–)

Emmy Awards: For *20/20* profiles of Ray Charles (1981), George Burns (1981) and Mel Torme (1984); Best News Segment for "Wall of Tears, Wall of Hope" (1985)

Bob Brown joined ABC news in 1977. Before that, during the 1970s, he was a local TV newsman in Texas and Oklahoma.

BROWN, BRYAN—actor
b: 1950, Sydney, Australia

The Thorn Birds (drama)
.... Luke O'Neill (1983)

BROWN, CANDY ANN—black actress
b: San Rafael, Calif.

The Roller Girls (com).. J. B. Johnson (1978)

BROWN, CHARLES—black actor
b: Jan 15, Talladega, Ala.

Today's F.B.I. (police) (pilot only)
.... Dwayne Thompson (1981)

BROWN, CHELSEA—black actress
b: Dec 6, Chicago, Ill. r: Los Angeles, Calif.

Rowan & Martin's Laugh-In (var)
.... regular (1968–69)
Matt Lincoln (drama)....... Tag (1970–71)

BROWN, CHRISTOPHER J.—actor

Operation Petticoat (com)
.... Ensign Stovall (1977–78)

BROWN, DORIS—hostess

Lucky Pup (child) .... hostess (1948–51)

BROWN, DWIER—actor

The Thorn Birds (drama)
.... Stuart Cleary (1983)

BROWN, EARL—composer, orchestra leader

b: Dec 25, 1928, Salt Lake City, Utah

The Danny Kaye Show (var)
.... singers (1964–67)
The Jonathan Winters Show (var)
.... orch. leader (1968–69)
The Sonny and Cher Comedy Hour (var)
.... singers (1971–74)
The Diahann Carroll Show (var)
.... orchestra leader (1976)

BROWN, ERIC—actor

b: Dec 17, 1964, New York City, N.Y.

Mama's Family (com)
..... Vinton "Buzz" Harper, Jr. (1983–84)

BROWN, GEORG STANFORD—black actor, director

b: Jun 24, 1943, Havana, Cuba r: Harlem, N.Y.

The Rookies (police)
.... Off. Terry Webster (1972–76)
Roots (drama)................. Tom (1977)
Roots: The Next Generations (drama)
.... Tom Harvey (1979)
North and South (drama) ..... Grady (1985)

Emmy Award: Best Directing for a Drama Series for *Cagney & Lacey* (1986)

Moody, afro-ed actor who had stage experience in the 1960s, mainly in New York Shakespeare Festival productions, then gained fame as one of the three rookie cops in the 1970s action series *The Rookies*. In the mid-1970s he turned to directing, with his growing list of credits in that field including episodes of *Charlie's Angels*, *Starsky and Hutch*, the TV movie *Grambling's White Tiger*, *Roots* (in which he also acted), *Dynasty*, and *Hill Street Blues* (for which he received an Emmy nomination for best director). He has also directed episodes of *Cagney & Lacey*, which stars his wife Tyne Daly.

BROWN, HARRY JOHN—conductor

The Voice of Firestone (music)
.... conductor (occasional) (1962–63)

BROWN, HY—panelist

Q.E.D. (quiz).............. panelist (1951)

BROWN, JAMES—actor

b: Mar 22, 1920, Desdemona, Texas

The Adventures of Rin Tin Tin (wes)
.... Lt. Rip Masters (1954–59)

A onetime teenage tennis star, James "Lefty" Brown broke into movies in the 1940s in action B films. *Rin Tin Tin* provided what was by far his best-remembered TV role, so much so that he was brought back 20 years later to film new introductions to the old black-and-white shows (as storytelling Lt. Rip Masters) in an attempt to re-syndicate the aging property. By that time, however, he had found a new and far more profitable career outside of acting—manufacturing body-building equipment. He eventually sold out his business and retired, but was back in front of the cameras again for a small role in the 1975 film *Whiffs*.

Brown remembers the *Rin Tin Tin* days fondly, and many a child of that era remembers him as the strong, firm father figure. "Our stories simply taught that right was right and wrong was wrong," he says. "You don't get those kinds of values on television anymore."

BROWN, JIM ED—country singer

b: Mar 1, 1934, Sparkman, Ark.

Nashville on the Road (music)
.... host (1975–81)

BROWN, JOE E.—comedian

b: Jul 28, 1892, Holgate, Ohio d: Jul 6, 1973

Buick Circus Hour (drama)
.... the clown (1952–53)

Joe Evans Brown had one of the most distinctive faces in show business—impish, happy, and with a cavernous mouth that seemed to stretch from ear to ear, usually in a broad grin. He was a top star in movies in the 1930s and '40s and did a fair amount of television in the 1950s, primarily on variety shows. He substituted for Arthur Godfrey on *Talent Scouts,* for Warren Hull on *Strike It Rich,* and starred in *The Buick Circus Hour,* a once-a-month musical comedy that alternated with Milton Berle. (Appropriately, Joe E. had worked in a circus for several years as a youth, as a trapeze artist.) A big-hearted, unfailingly kind man (itself a rarity in show business), he was perfectly cast in the *Circus Hour* as a gentle and loving clown trying to help a young girl win her true love, the circus manager.

Joe E. was semiretired by the end of the decade, making one of his last appearances in the 1959 movie *Some Like It Hot.* His autobiography, published in 1956, was titled *Laughter Is a Wonderful Thing.*

BROWN, JOHN—actor

The Life of Riley (com)
.... Digby "Digger" O'Dell (1949–50)
The George Burns and Gracie Allen Show (com)................. Harry Morton (1951)

A very active radio actor of the 1940s, especially on comedies such as *Ozzie and Harriet* and *My Friend Irma.* He also played Digger O'Dell on the radio version of *The Life of Riley.*

BROWN, JOHN MASON—drama critic
b: Jul 3, 1900, Louisville, Ky.

Americana (quiz)...... moderator (1947–48)
Critic at Large (pub aff)
.... moderator (1948–49)
Tonight on Broadway (int) ... host (1948–49)
Who Said That? (quiz)...... panelist (1955)

BROWN, JOHNNY—black comedian
b: Jun 11, 1937, St. Petersburg, Fla.

The Leslie Uggams Show (var)
.... Lamar (1969)
Rowan & Martin's Laugh-In (var)
.... regular (1970–72)
Good Times (com)
.... Nathan Bookman (1977–79)

BROWN, LES—orchestra leader
b: Mar 14, 1912, Reinerton, Pa.

The Steve Allen Show (var)
.... orch. leader (1959–61)
The Hollywood Palace (var)
.... orch. leader (1964)
The Dean Martin Show (var)
.... orch. leader (1965–74)
The Dean Martin Summer Show (var)
.... orch. leader (1966–67)
Dean Martin Presents the Golddiggers (var)
.... orch. leader (1968–69)

Les Brown was one of the more popular bandleaders of the big band era, starting out in the mid-1930s fronting the Duke Blue Devils (in college) and continuing through the 1940s. His biggest hits came in the mid and late 1940s, and some of them have become all-time classics, including "Sentimental Journey" and "I've Got My Love to Keep Me Warm." In 1947 Les began a long association with Bob Hope on radio, television, and tours; later his "Band of Renown" was used regularly by Steve Allen and Dean Martin as well.

BROWN, LES, JR.—actor

Baileys of Balboa (com)
.... Jim Bailey (1964–65)

BROWN, LOU—orchestra leader
b: May 4, 1912, Brooklyn, N.Y.

The Jerry Lewis Show (talk)
.... orch. leader (1963)
The Jerry Lewis Show (var)
.... orch. leader (1967–69)

BROWN, MITCH—actor
b: Dec 23, the Bronx, N.Y.

The Cowboys (wes) .... Hardy (1974)

The son of actor Jed Allan.

BROWN, OLIVIA—black actress
b: Apr 10, Frankfurt, West Germany r: Sacramento

Miami Vice (police)
.... Det. Trudy Joplin (1984–)

BROWN, PENDLETON—actor

Mama Malone (com) .... Ken (1984)

BROWN, PEPE—comedian

Pat Paulsen's Half a Comedy Hour (var)
.... regular (1970)

BROWN, PETER—actor

b: Oct 5, c. 1935, New York, N.Y.

The Lawman (wes)
.... Deputy Johnny McKay (1958–62)
Laredo (wes)...... Chad Cooper (1965–67)

Boyishly handsome Peter Brown got into acting as a way to occupy his spare time —indoors—while stationed in Alaska with the army; he organized a base theater group. He went on to study acting at U.C.L.A. following his discharge and began getting roles in TV westerns as well as in a few action-oriented movies. His big break was the role of John Russell's young deputy on *The Lawman*; later he had a similar role on *Laredo* (this time with Neville Brand as the father figure). After working out a seven-year contract with Universal Studios (1965–72), he switched to daytime soap operas and has enjoyed steady employment ever since— a seven-year run as Dr. Greg Peters on *Days of Our Lives* (1972–79) followed by stints on *The Young and The Restless* and *Loving* in the 1980s.

BROWN, PHILIP—actor

b: Mar 26, Coalinga, Calif.

Doris Day Show (com)
.... Billy Martin (1968–71)
When the Whistle Blows (com)
.... Randy Hartford (1980)
Dynasty II: The Colbys (drama)
.... Neil Kittredge (1985–)

Nephew of actor Peter Brown. As a child actor, Philip was Doris Day's TV son for three seasons. Later he appeared in occasional prime time series episodes and (like his uncle) found his way into daytime soap operas with roles on *Days of Our Lives* and *Search for Tomorrow*.

BROWN, R. G.—comedian

The Andy Williams Show (var)
.... regular (1962–63)
The John Byner Comedy Hour (var)
.... regular (1972)
The Rich Little Show (var)... regular (1976)

BROWN, RENEE—black actress

Harris and Company (drama)
.... Liz Harris (1979)

BROWN, ROBERT—actor

b: 1927, Hebrides Islands, Scotland r: New York City

Ivanhoe (adv).......... the monk (1957–58)
Here Come the Brides (adv)
.... Jason Bolt (1968–70)
Primus (adv)......... Carter Primus (1971)

BROWN, RUTH—black singer, actress

b: Jan 30, 1928, Portsmouth, Va.

Hello, Larry (com).. Leona Wilson (1979–80)
Checking In (com)............. Betty (1981)

Yes, it *is* the same Ruth Brown. Probably more than a few 1980s viewers who had been kids in the 1950s wondered if the sharp-tongued black actress who began turning up on comedies around 1980 was in fact the singer who 25 years before had produced such hard-driving rhythm and blues hits as "Mama, He Treats Your Daughter Mean" and "Lucky Lips."

Born the daughter of a church choir director, Ruth got her start as a singer in the late 1940s, but just when she was about to make her big debut—at New York's Apollo Theater—she was critically injured in an automobile accident. In time she recovered, landed a recording contract, and started turning out hits in the early 1950s, at first for black record buyers and later, when rock 'n' roll began to spread, for the pop market at large. Frankie Laine gave her the nickname "Miss Rhythm."

When her hits gradually trailed off in the 1960s she turned increasingly to the jazz circuit, appearing in festivals and on tour. Then in 1976 she made her acting debut in a local theater production on the West Coast. Producer Norman Lear saw her and cast her in *Hello Larry* as McLean Stevenson's neighbor. This was followed by more roles and a new career for an old rock 'n' roller.

BROWN, TED—announcer, emcee

b: Collingwood, N.J.

Birthday Party (child) .... King Cole (1949)
The Paul Winchell-Jerry Mahoney Show (var)................. announcer (1951–54)

The Greatest Man on Earth (quiz)
.... emcee (1952–53)

As a young announcer, Ted Brown was heard and seen on a number of New York–originated TV series of the 1950s. Among other things, he was Buffalo Bob's replacement (as "Bison Bill") on *Howdy Doody* when Smith was off the show during the 1954–55 season due to a heart attack. Later Ted became a leading New York disc jockey, a career which he continued into the 1980s.

BROWN, TIMOTHY—black actor
b: 1937, Chicago, Ill.

*M*A*S*H* (com)
.... Spearchucker Jones (1972)

BROWN, TOM—actor
b: Jan 6, 1913, New York City, N.Y.

Gunsmoke (wes) ... Ed O'Connor (1955–75)
Mr. Lucky (adv)....... Lt. Rovacs (1959–60)

Though hardly a major name in show business annals, Tom Brown had a remarkably long and varied career. The son of actor parents, he worked in vaudeville as a small child, then on stage in the 1920s, then in movies in the '30s—where he gained his first major fame portraying clean-cut all-American boys. After service in World War II and Korea, he added television to his repertoire, appearing in a variety of supporting roles, including the occasional one of rancher O'Connor on *Gunsmoke* and Mr. Lucky's helpful police contact. In the 1970s he had a long run as crusty Al Weeks on the daytime soap opera *General Hospital*.

BROWN, VANESSA—actress
b: Mar 24, 1928, Vienna, Austria

Leave It to the Girls (talk)
.... panelist (1949–54)
My Favorite Husband (com)
.... Liz Cooper (1955)
All That Glitters (com)
.... Peggy Horner (1977)

Vanessa Brown was a pert and pretty young ingenue who made her first film at age 16 and several more in the late 1940s and early '50s. She did a good deal of television work in the 1950s as well, including

dramas (*Climax, The Millionaire*), comedy (*My Favorite Husband*), and a long run on the chatter show *Leave It to the Girls*. She went into semiretirement after marrying TV director Mark Sandrich, Jr., concentrating on her writing. She has published newspaper and magazine articles, a novel, and a book on national labor policy and was also a free-lance reporter for the Voice of America for eight years. Vanessa returns to the screen occasionally for guest roles, recently on the syndicated soap opera parody *All That Glitters* in 1977.

BROWN, WALLY—actor
b: Oct 9, 1904, Malden, Mass. d: Nov 13, 1961

Cimarron City (wes).... Jed Fame (1958–59)

BROWN, WARREN—panelist

Ask Me Another (quiz) ..... panelist (1952)

BROWN, WOODY—actor
b: Feb 21, Dayton, Ohio

Flamingo Road (drama)
.... Skipper Weldon (1981–82)
The Facts of Life (com)...... Cliff (1983–84)

BROWNE, CORAL—actress
b: Jul 23, 1913, Melbourne, Australia

Time Express (drama)...... Margaret (1979)

The actress-wife of Vincent Price, who co-starred with her husband in this rather eerie but short-lived drama. Mr. and Mrs. Price escorted folks back in time in order to allow them to alter mistakes made earlier in their lives.

BROWNE, KATHIE—actress

Slattery's People (drama)
.... Liz Andrews (1965)
Hondo (wes)............ Angie Dow (1967)

BROWNE, ROBERT ALAN—actor

Heart of the City (drama).. Stanley (1986–)

BROWNE, ROSCOE LEE—black actor
b: May 2, 1925, Woodbury, N.J.

McCoy (drama) .... Gideon Gibbs (1975–76)

Miss Winslow and Son (com)
.... Harold Devore Neistadter (1979)
Soap (com) .... Saunders (1980–81)

Emmy Award: Best Guest Performer in a Comedy, for an episode of *The Cosby Show* (1986)

This distinguished-looking, now balding actor has become familiar to television viewers primarily via guest roles from the 1960s on, though he has also been a regular in three series—as Tony Curtis' partner in *McCoy*, the sarcastic neighbor in *Miss Winslow and Son*, and the butler (replacing Benson) on *Soap*. Among his many other TV credits have been roles in the miniseries *King*, *The Name of the Game*, *All in the Family*, and *Barney Miller* (he was nominated for an Emmy Award for the last-named appearance). Generally he plays a snobbish, intellectual type—which is not inappropriate considering the actor's "other" lives.

What most viewers don't know is that Browne has also achieved notable success in several fields quite unrelated to acting. In the late 1940s and early '50s he was an international track champion and twice All-American; then a salesman for several years; a professor of comparative literature and French at two universities; and a published poet and short story author.

BROWNING, DOUG—announcer, moderator

Q.E.D. (quiz) .... moderator (1951)

BROWNING, SUSAN—actress
b: Feb 25, 1941, Baldwin, N.Y.

Mary Hartman, Mary Hartman (com)
.... Pat Gimble (1976–77)

BRUBAKER, ROBERT—actor

The Sheriff of Cochise (police)
.... Deputy Blake (1958)

BRUCE, CAROL—singer, actress
b: Nov 15, 1919, Great Neck, N.Y.

WKRP In Cincinnati (com)
.... Lillian "Mama" Carlson (1979–82)

BRUCE, DAVID—actor
b: Jan 6, 1914, Kankakee, Ill. d: May 3, 1976

Beulah (com) .. Harry Henderson (1952–53)

BRUCE, ED—actor

Bret Maverick (wes)
.... Tom Guthrie (1981–82)

BRUHL, HEIDI—

Continental Showcase (var).. regular (1966)

BRULL, PAMELA—actress
b: Aug 25, Monterey Park, Calif.

The Secret Empire (drama) ... Maya (1979)
Off the Rack (com)
.... Brenda Patagorski (1985)

BRUNDIN, BO—actor
b: Apr 25, 1937, Stockholm, Sweden

The Rhinemann Exchange (drama)
.... Heinrik Stoltz (1977)

BRUNEAU, LAURA—actress

Bare Essence (drama) .... Cathy (1983)

BRUNS, MONA—actress

Wesley (com)........ Mrs. Eggleston (1949)
One Man's Family (drama)
.... Mrs. Roberts (1950–51)

The mother of actor Frankie Thomas (*Tom Corbett—Space Cadet*) and wife of actor Frank Thomas, Sr., with whom she starred in *Wesley*. Bruns was a longtime actress in TV soap operas. Among her credits are *A Woman to Remember* (1949), *Three Steps to Heaven* (1953–54), *The Brighter Day* (1954–62, as Aunt Emily), and *Paradise Bay* (1965–66). She was also known by her married name, Mona Thomas. Her autobiography: *By Emily Possessed* (1973).

BRUNS, PHILIP—actor

The Jackie Gleason Show (var)
.... regular (1964–66)
Mary Hartman, Mary Hartman (com)
.... George Shumway (1976–77)

BRY, ELLEN—actress

The Amazing Spider-Man (adv)
.... Julie Mason (1978–79)
St. Elsewhere (drama)
.... Nurse Shirley Daniels (1982–85)

BRYAN, ARTHUR Q.—actor, host
b: c. 1900 d: 1959

Movieland Quiz (quiz)........ emcee (1948)
The Hank McCune Show (com)
.... regular (1950)

In addition to radio work and occasional films, Bryan was the voice of Elmer Fudd in the Bugs Bunny cartoons of the 1940s and '50s. He was quite active on radio in the 1940s, on such series as *Fibber McGee and Molly, The Great Gildersleeve,* and *Major Hoople* (as Hoople).

BRYANT, ANITA—singer
b: Mar 25, 1940, Barnsdall, Okla.

The George Gobel Show (var)
.... regular (1959–60)

A former Miss Oklahoma (1958), Anita is best known to television viewers as a pop singer of the early 1960s ("Paper Roses," "Til There Was You," etc.) and later as commercial spokesperson for the Florida Citrus Commission. She made headlines in the 1980s due to her outspoken views on social issues, which caused the orange juice folks to drop her as too controversial.

BRYANT, JOSHUA—actor
Behind the Screen (drama)
.... Gerry Holmby (1981–82)

BRYANT, LEE—actress
T. J. Hooker (police)
.... Fran Hooker (1982–83)
The Lucie Arnaz Show (com)..... Jill (1985)

BRYANT, MARDI—
The Ted Steele Show (music)
.... regular (1948–49)

BRYANT, MEL—actor
Archie Bunker's Place (com)
.... Ed Swanson (1980–81)

BRYANT, NANA—actress
b: 1888, Cincinnati, Ohio d: Dec 24, 1955

Our Miss Brooks (com).. Mrs. Nestor (1955)

BRYANT, WILLIAM—actor
b: Detroit, Mich. r: Bogalusa, La.

The Web (drama) .... narrator (1957)

Hondo (wes)............. Col. Crook (1967)
Switch (drama)........ Lt. Shilton (1976–78)

BRYANT, WILLIE—black singer, emcee
b: Aug 30, 1908, New Orleans, La. d. Feb 9, 1964

Sugar Hill Times (var)....... regular (1949)

A onetime big band vocalist, this entertainer is perhaps best known as an emcee at Harlem's legendary Apollo Theater. On television he hosted two early black variety shows, *Sugar Hill Times* and the 1954 syndicated series *Showtime at the Apollo.*

BRYAR, CLAUDIA—actress
The Manhunter (drama)
.... Mary Barrett (1974–75)

BRYCE, EDWARD—actor
Tom Corbett, Space Cadet (child)
.... Capt. Steve Strong (1951–55)

This actor is more familiar to viewers for his long run as Bill Bauer on *The Guiding Light.* His son Scott is also a soap opera actor (*As the World Turns*).

BRYNE, BARBARA—actress
b: London, England

Love, Sidney (com). Mrs. Gaffney (1982–83)

BRYNES, BURKE—actor
Dallas (drama)...... Pete Adams (1984–85)

BRYNNER, YUL—actor
b: Jul 11, 1915*, Sakhalin Island, Japan d: Oct 10, 1985

Anna and the King (com)
.... King of Siam (1972)

Although this famous actor was best known for his stage and screen roles, he was deeply involved in early, New York–based live television, both as an actor and director. In addition to acting on various playhouse series, he directed episodes of such varied series as *Danger, Studio One,* and *Life with Snarky Parker.* Brynner's life changed dramatically in 1951, when he

*Some sources give 1917, 1920, or 1922. The mystery continues.

was chosen for the lead role in a new Rodgers and Hammerstein Broadway musical called *The King and I*. The role of the fiery, intense king with a shaven head became Brynner's trademark, and he was identified with it for the rest of his life. He made a hit movie version in 1956 and brought it to television in 1972—though the TV version was not successful.

Brynner's past was intentionally shrouded in mystery, but the facts appear to be that he was born on Sakhalin Island, north of Japan, of part gypsy parentage (this came out in the 1970s when he became active on behalf of gypsy rights). He migrated to Paris in his teens and became a circus trapeze artist and musician; he came to the U.S. in 1940 and established himself here in the theater and later in movies and as a guest on TV dramas and specials.

In the late 1960s and early '70s Brynner lived in Switzerland, becoming a Swiss citizen and making several European films. He later returned to America, where he scored his last great success in a series of revivals of *The King and I*.

BRYSON, DR. LYMAN—educator
b: Jul 11, 1888, Valentine, Neb. d: Nov 24, 1959

Presidential Straws in the Wind (pub aff)
..............................host (1948)
U.N. Casebook (doc)... moderator (1948–49)
We Take Your Word (quiz) . panelist (1950)

BUCHANAN, EDGAR—actor
b: Mar 20, 1903*, Humansville, Mo. d: Apr 4, 1979

Hopalong Cassidy (wes)
.... Red Connors (1949–51)
Judge Roy Bean (wes)
.... Judge Roy Bean (1956)
Petticoat Junction (com)
.... Uncle Joe Carson (1963–70)
Cade's County (police)
.... J. J. Jackson (1971–72)

This familiar television old-timer began adult life as a dentist and was at one time head of oral surgery at an Oregon hospital. Finding little satisfaction in his work, however, he moved to Los Angeles in the late 1930s and gradually phased out his dental

*Some sources give 1902.

practice in favor of acting. His new career was good to him. He played rascals and kindly old men in scores of movie westerns and eventually became Hopalong Cassidy's sidekick on TV. A later generation found him lovable as Uncle Joe on the 1960s hit *Petticoat Junction*.

BUCHANON, KIRBY—singer

The Roy Rogers & Dale Evans Show (var)
.... regular (1962)

BUCHWALD, ART—humorist
b: Oct 20, 1925, Mount Vernon, N.Y.

The Entertainers (var) .... regular (1964)
The American Parade (pub aff)
.... correspondent (1984)

Art Buchwald was a World War II GI who had a yen to see Paris after the war (he had been in the Pacific), liked it, and stayed to write humorous tidbits about Parisian life for English language newspapers there. His column, begun in 1949, was soon being published in the U.S. as well. In 1962 he finally returned to America and began writing a political satire column, which has continued into the 1980s. His pudgy countenance turns up occasionally on television to poke fun at the foibles of whoever is in power. As long as political humor is his subject, he will never have to worry about having enough material.

BUCKLEY, BETTY—actress
b: Jul 3, 1947, Big Springs, Texas

Eight Is Enough (com) .. Sandra Sue Abbott "Abby" Bradford (1977–81)

Although she starred for five years as the mom on *Eight Is Enough*, Betty Buckley's heart seems to be primarily in stage work. Among her Broadway hits, from the 1960s to the '80s: *1776, Pippin, Cats*, and *Drood*. Betty was born in Texas, where she used her singing and dancing talents to compete in numerous talent shows and beauty pageants. She generally didn't win, but that may have been a blessing in disguise, as she was invited to appear in a network TV special that featured "all of the losers who never made it to Atlantic City" (i.e., the Miss America pageant). From that she won her first big role, as Martha Jefferson in *1776*.

BUCKLEY, HAL—actor
b: c. 1936 d: Mar 17, 1986

O. K. Crackerby (com)
.... St. John Quincy (1965–66)

BUCKLEY, KEITH—actor
The Search for the Nile (drama)
.... Henry Stanley (1972)

BUCKMAN, TARA—actress
Lobo (com) .... Brandy (1980–81)

BUCKNER, SUSAN—actress
b: Jan 28, Seattle, Wash. r: Burien, Wash.

The Hardy Boys Mysteries (adv)
.................George Fayne (1977–78)
The Nancy Drew Mysteries (adv)
.................George Fayne (1977–78)
When the Whistle Blows (com)
.... Lucy Davis (1980)

Susan was a former beauty queen who won the title of Miss Washington and was a finalist in the 1971 Miss America Pageant. That led to a spot as one of Dean Martin's Golddiggers troupe, and later the role of Pamela Sue Martin's buddy "George" on *The Nancy Drew Mysteries*. She is also a songwriter.

BUDKIN, CELIA—actress
The O'Neills (drama) .. Mrs. Levy (1949–50)

BUENO, DELORA—Latin singer
b: c. 1924, Dubuque, Iowa r: Brazil

Delora Bueno (music)........ hostess (1949)
Flight to Rhythm (music).... vocalist (1949)

BUFANO, VINCENT—actor
b: Apr 9, New York City, N.Y.

Flatbush (com)....... Turtle Romero (1979)
Eischied (police) ..... Rick Alessi (1979–80)

BUFFANO, JULES—pianist, songwriter
b: Nov 18, 1897, St. Louis, Mo. d: Sep 12, 1960

The Jimmy Durante Show (var)
.... regular (1954–56)

BUFFERT, KENNY—
The College Bowl (com) .. regular (1950–51)

BUFFINGTON, SAM—actor
Whispering Smith (wes)
.... Chief John Richards (1961)

BUKTENICA, RAY—actor
b: Aug 6, 1943, Greenwich Village, New York City, N.Y.

Rhoda (com)..... Benny Goodwin (1977–78)
House Calls (com)
.... Dr. Norman Solomon (1979–82)

BULIFANT, JOYCE—actress
b: Dec 16, 1937, Newport News, Va.

Tom, Dick and Mary (com)
.... Mary Gentry (1964–65)
The Bill Cosby Show (com)
.... Mrs. Marsha Peterson (1969–71)
The Mary Tyler Moore Show (com)
.... Marie Slaughter (1971–77)
Love Thy Neighbor (com)
.... Peggy Wilson (1973)
Flo (com).... Miriam Willoughby (1980–81)

A perky, pug-nosed comedienne who turned up often as a wife or best friend on comedies of the 1960s, '70s, and '80s. She got her start on the New York stage in the late 1950s but quickly moved into television, at first as a dancer on *The Arthur Murray Dance Party*. In addition to her continuing roles, she has been seen on episodes of westerns (*Wide Country, The Virginian*), dramas (*Perry Mason, Police Story*), and comedies (*Love, American Style; Lobo*).

She was first married to actor James MacArthur and later to TV producer William Asher.

BULL, RICHARD—actor
Voyage to the Bottom of the Sea (sci fi)
.... Doctor (1964–68)
Little House on the Prairie (adv)
.... Nels Oleson (1974–83)

BULLOCK, JM J.—actor
b: Feb 9, Casper, Wyoming r: Texas

Too Close for Comfort (com)
.... Monroe Ficus (1980–85)

The Ted Knight Show (com)
.... Monroe Ficus (1986)

BULOT, CHUCK—

The Nashville Palace (var)
.... regular (1981–82)

BUNCE, ALAN—actor
b: Jun 28, 1903, Westfield, N.J. d: Apr 27, 1965

Ethel and Albert (com)
.... Albert Arbuckle (1953–56)

This mousy little man began his career on the New York stage in the 1920s, then moved into radio, where he scored substantial success: six years as *Young Doctor Malone* followed by five as Albert on *Ethel and Albert.* He also played Albert on the television version of the latter show, which was first seen as a continuing sketch within *The Kate Smith Hour* in 1952–53 and then as a separate series. Bunce also appeared as a supporting actor in many TV dramatic series of the 1950s and early '60s, including *The Web, Kraft Television Theatre,* and *The Defenders.*

BUNTROCK, BOBBY—juvenile actor
b: Aug 4, 1952, Denver, Colo.

Hazel (com) ...... Harold Baxter (1961–66)

BUONO, VICTOR—actor
b: 1938, San Diego, Calif. d: Jan 1, 1982

Man from Atlantis (adv)
.... Mr. Schubert (1977–78)
Backstairs at the White House (drama)
.... Pres. William Howard Taft (1979)

This hefty (300-pound) actor was a favorite supporting character on dramas of the 1960s and '70s, usually as a villain. Among his many credits were multiple episodes of *The Untouchables, Perry Mason, Night Gallery, Batman* (as King Tut), and *The Wild Wild West* (twice as the evil magician Count Manzeppi). Later he branched into comedies, including *The Odd Couple* and *Barney Miller.* On *The Man from Atlantis,* however, he reverted to type as the diabolical scientist who made Patrick Duffy's life miserable.

Probably Buono's most famous role was as the suitably nasty Edwin Flagg in the 1962 film *Whatever Happened to Baby Jane,* which earned him a nomination for an Academy Award.

BURDICK, HAL—actor

Night Editor (drama) .... host (1949–54)

BURGESS, BOBBY—dancer

The Lawrence Welk Show (music)
.... regular (1961–78)

A former *Mickey Mouse Club* mouseketeer (1955–59).

BURGHOFF, GARY—actor
b: May 24, 1940, Bristol, Conn.

Don Knotts Show (var) ... regular (1970–71)
M*A*S*H (com)
.... Cpl. Walter O'Reilly (1972–79)

Emmy Award: Best Supporting Actor in a Comedy, for *M*A*S*H* (1977)

Pint-sized actor Gary Burghoff has been perfectly cast at least twice during his career, first as Charlie Brown in the off-Broadway hit *You're a Good Man, Charlie Brown,* and then as prescient company clerk "Radar" O'Reilly in the movie and television versions of *M*A*S*H.*

Gary started out as a musician, joining the Bud Wilber Orchestra as a singer, dancer, and entertainer while he was still in high school in Wisconsin. He later moved to New York to study acting and made his TV debut in the early 1960s, practically unnoticed, on *The CBS Television Workshop.* Gary's big breaks came a few years later, first with *Charlie Brown* in 1967, then the role of Radar in the movie *M*A*S*H* in 1970, and a regular spot on Don Knotts' TV variety show that fall. When *M*A*S*H* was brought to TV in 1972 Burghoff was the only principal to recreate his movie role (Timothy Brown was also in both movie and series—briefly—but in different roles).

Seven years on *M*A*S*H* brought Gary national fame. He left in 1979 and has since occupied himself with a variety of activities: TV movies, a few guest spots on series such as *The Love Boat* and *Fantasy Island,* and a nightclub act in which he sings, dances, and plays drums. He also spends time in Hawaii, where he has business interests.

BURGUNDY STREET SINGERS—

The Jimmie Rodgers Show (var)
.... regulars (1969)
The Red Skelton Show (var)
.... regulars (1970–71)

BURKE, ALAN—talk show host

The Alan Burke Show (talk)
.... host (1966–70)

BURKE, BILLIE—actress
b: Aug 7, 1885, Washington, D.C. d: May 14, 1970

Doc Corkle (com) .... Melinda (1952)

Stage and screen legend Billie Burke, at age 67, for some reason agreed to make her TV series debut in this flimsy situation comedy, which was canceled after only three weeks. She never starred in another series and appeared only infrequently in TV dramas and specials. Her last recorded TV acting appearance was in an episode of *77 Sunset Strip* in 1960.

Burke will no doubt be longer remembered for her delightfully fluttery movie roles, especially as the good witch Glinda in *The Wizard of Oz* and for her long marriage to flamboyant showman Florenz Ziegfeld. Her autobiographies were titled *With a Feather on My Nose* (1949) and *With Powder on My Nose* (1959).

BURKE, DELTA—actress
b: Jul 30, 1956, Orlando, Fla.

The Chisholms (wes)
.... Bonnie Sue Chisholm (1980)
Filthy Rich (com).. Kathleen Beck (1982–83)
Designing Women (com)
.... Suzanne Sugarbaker (1986–)

BURKE, JAMES—actor
b: 1886 d: May 28, 1968

Mark Saber (drama)
.... Sgt. Tim Maloney (1951–54)

BURKE, JERRY—pianist, organist
b: c. 1911 d: Feb 13, 1965

The Lawrence Welk Show (music)
.... regular (1955–65)

BURKE, PAUL—actor
b: Jan 21, 1926*, New Orleans, La.

Noah's Ark (drama)
.... Dr. Noah McCann (1956–57)
Harbourmaster (adv)
.... Jeff Kittridge (1957–58)
Five Fingers (drama) .. Robertson (1959–60)
Naked City (police)
.... Det. Adam Flint (1960–63)
Twelve O'Clock High (drama)
Capt./Major/Colonel Joe Gallagher (1964–67)
Dynasty (drama)
.... Cong. Neal McVane (1982–84)
Hot Shots (drama)
.... Nicholas Broderick (1986–)

Paul Burke is one of those TV standbys who, despite considerable exposure over the years, has yet to become closely identified with any one famous role. He entered the medium in the early 1950s, after some experience in local theater, appearing in dramas and adventures such as *Big Town* and *Superman*. His roles during his "young" period were generally heroic—the young veterinarian on *Noah's Ark,* Barry Sullivan's helper at the boatyard in *Harbourmaster,* David Hedison's contact in the spy series *Five Fingers.* Burke's major success came in the 1960s, three years as a young detective on *Naked City* and three more as a brash young flyer (advancing rapidly in rank) on *Twelve O'Clock High.*

After the last-named series, Burke, exhausted, moved to Europe for four years. When he returned in 1970, it was to play a greater variety of roles, sometimes as heavies, on such series as *Medical Center* (several appearances), *Owen Marshall, Police Story,* and *Trapper John, M.D..* By 1982 he was a leading character on *Dynasty,* as the murderous congressman Neal McVane, and, after that, for a short time in daytime as the calculating millionaire C. C. Capwell on *Santa Barbara.*

BURKHARDT, BOB—

Campus Corner (music)...... regular (1949)

BURKLEY, DENNIS—actor
b: Sep 10, Van Nuys, Calif.

The Texas Wheelers (com) .. Bud (1974–75)

*Some sources give 1929.

Mary Hartman, Mary Hartman (com)
.... Mac Slattery (1977–78)
Hanging In (com)....... Sam Dickey (1979)
Sanford (com)......... Cal Pettie (1980–81)

BURMESTER, LEO—actor
b: Feb 1, Louisville, Ky.

Flo (com) .... Randy Stumphill (1980–81)
Chiefs (drama) ...... Emmett Spense (1983)

BURNETT, CAROL—comedienne
b: Apr 26, 1933*, San Antonio, Texas r: Los
Angeles

Stanley (com) .... Celia (1956–57)
Pantomime Quiz (quiz) ... regular (1958–59)
The Garry Moore Show (var)
.... regular (1959–62)
The Entertainers (var) ..... costar (1964–65)
The Carol Burnett Show (var)
.... hostess (1967–79)
Mama's Family (com)
.... Eunice Higgins (occasional) (1983–84)

Emmy Awards: Best Performance on a Variety Program, for *The Garry Moore Show*
(1962); same, for the specials *Julie and
Carol at Carnegie Hall* and *Carol and
Company* (1963); Best Musical Variety Series, for *The Carol Burnett Show* (1972,
1974, 1975)

Carol Burnett is one of the brightest stars
of the television era and one whose career
is solidly rooted in the TV medium. It is
easy to forget how humble her beginnings
were. In fact, some of her early jobs sound
like comedy sketches from her later series
—girlfriend to a wooden dummy, frantic
young panelist on a rather hoary pantomime show, skinny nightclub singer belting out ridiculous songs.

Carol originally intended to be a journalist, editing the school paper at Hollywood
High and entering U.C.L.A. to study journalism. But her ability to crack people up
with her mobile features and outrageous
gags soon pushed her into Theater Arts.
She and her boyfriend were doing a routine at a society party when a wealthy on-
looker staked her $1,000 to go to New York
and launch her professional career (the
money was later, gratefully, repaid).

She arrived in New York in 1954, but no
one noticed. After a lot of odd jobs and

*Some sources give 1934 or 1936.

auditions she finally landed her first regular television role in December 1955—13
weeks as dummy Jerry Mahoney's "girlfriend" on the Saturday morning Paul Winchell-Jerry Mahoney kids' show. The fall of
1956 brought more substantive work, a
spot on Garry Moore's daytime variety
show and the role of Buddy Hackett's girlfriend on the short-lived prime time situation comedy *Stanley* (which, scheduled
opposite *Arthur Godfrey's Talent Scouts*,
was seen by hardly anyone). More live TV
followed, as her 1957 nightclub debut led to
guest spots with Jack Paar and Ed Sullivan.
Carol sang her newly introduced cabaret
hit, "I Made a Fool of Myself Over John
Foster Dulles" and audiences howled.

After a season with *Pantomime Quiz*,
she joined Garry Moore's prime time variety show as a regular in 1959, and began to
attract a lot of fans. One of them was CBS
itself, which offered its rising star a $1 mil-
lion ten-year contract for her exclusive services. The first result was a rather ill-conceived variety series, *The Entertainers*,
which teamed her, peculiarly, in a sort of
semi-rotation with Bob Newhart and
Catarina Valente. The second was better.
The Carol Burnett Show, premiering in
1967, was a long-distance champ that
played Carol's offbeat comic style against
a superb supporting cast. The show was
produced by none other than her husband,
Joe Hamilton. One of the many regular
sketches on the series featured a noisy,
squabbling family; it gave rise to a separate series in the 1980s, *Mama's Family*, in
which Carol sometimes appeared.

Carol made some notable appearances
outside her own series during the 1960s
and '70s, too. She starred in a number of
highly rated and critically acclaimed specials, often paired with other stars (Julie
Andrews, Dolly Parton, Beverly Sills), and
in two TV adaptations of her 1959 Broadway hit, *Once Upon a Mattress*. She
guested several times on Lucille Ball's series, as well as on Jack Benny's. She even
made a well-remembered appearance on
The Twilight Zone as a klutzy usherette
whose life is turned upside down when a
bungling apprentice angel tries to help her
out.

In 1979 Carol, the clown, surprised viewers with a dramatic triumph as an anguished mother in the Vietnam movie
Friendly Fire. Her TV appearances be-

came less frequent in the 1980s, as she finally began to turn primarily to theatrical films (e.g., *The Four Seasons, Annie*).

She has published a memoir, *Once Upon a Time* (1986).

BURNETT, DON—actor

Northwest Passage (adv)
.... Ensign Langdon Towne (1958–59)

BURNETT, RAMONA—singer

This Is Music (music)..... regular (1958–59)

BURNETT, SANDI—

Music Hall America (music) . regular (1976)

BURNETTE, SMILEY—cowboy actor
b: Mar 18, 1911, Summum, Ill. d: Feb 16, 1967

Ozark Jubilee (music)........ regular (1959)
Petticoat Junction (com)
.... Charlie Pratt (1963–67)

Gene Autry's roly-poly movie sidekick of the 1930s and '40s officially "retired" from acting in 1953. Nevertheless he made a few TV acting appearances after that date, including a four-year run (until his death) as the hayseed railroad engineer on *Petticoat Junction.*

BURNIER, JEANNINE—comedienne

Keep On Truckin' (var)...... regular (1975)

BURNS, BART—actor

Mickey Spillane's Mike Hammer (drama)
.... Capt. Pat Chambers (1957–59)

BURNS, DAVID—actor
b: Jun 22, 1902, New York City, N.Y. d: Mar 12, 1971

The Imogene Coca Show (var)
.... Harry Milliken (1955)
My Favorite Husband (com)
.... Uncle Norman Fildew (1955)
The Trials of O'Brien (drama)
.... The Great McGonigle (1965–66)

Emmy Award: Best Supporting Actor in a Drama, for the *Hallmark Hall of Fame* production *"The Price"* (1971)

David Burns was a veteran stage actor (*The Music Man; Hello, Dolly;* etc.) who also did some television work. He won critical acclaim for the 1968 Broadway production of Arthur Miller's play *The Price* and an Emmy Award for his acting in its television adaptation, which was telecast the year he died.

BURNS, GEORGE—comedian
b: Jan 20, 1896, New York City, N.Y.

The George Burns and Gracie Allen Show (com)................. as himself (1950–58)
The George Burns Show (com)
.... as himself (1958–59)
Wendy and Me (com) . as himself (1964–65)
The George Burns Comedy Week (com)
.... host (1985)

A reporter asked 90-year-old George Burns how long he would continue performing as a comedian. "Until I'm the last one left," came the snappy reply. Indeed, George never seems to have heard the word "retire" during his extraordinary career. He began performing in 1903 and had adopted his famous cigar as a prop by 1910 (at age 14). Seventy-five years later he was still at it, hosting a brand new network series.

George was born Nathan Birnbaum in the tenements of New York's Lower East Side. He broke into vaudeville, where he met his future wife and professional partner, Gracie Allen, in 1923. They were married three years later. Their gentle comedy banter was a major hit on radio in the 1930s and '40s, as well as on television in the 1950s. After Gracie retired in 1958, George continued on his own with unsuccessful situation comedies in 1958 and 1964 (the latter costarring Connie Stevens). Then he seemed to drift out of the limelight, making only occasional appearances on specials and on Lucille Ball's series.

What appeared to be a well-earned retirement after a long and successful career was only an interlude, however. Beginning in 1975, at age 79, George was suddenly back in a series of hit movies, beginning with *The Sunshine Boys* (he got the part at the last minute when Jack Benny, the intended star, passed away). That was followed by *Oh God!* (with George playing guess who), *Going in Style,* and others. His television appearances picked up as well and in 1985 he hosted, but did not act in, his first regular series in 20 years, *George Burns' Comedy Week*. Was this hard work, at his advanced age? "People think that all I do is stand up and tell a few jokes," he remarked. "The jokes are easy. It's the standing up that's hard."

All of which goes to show, you can't keep a man with a cigar and a funny story to tell down.

George's autobiographies are *I Love Her, That's Why* (with Cynthia Lindsay, 1955) and *Living It Up, or They Still Love Me in Altoona!* (1976).

BURNS, JACK—actor, comedian
b: Nov 15, 1933, Boston, Mass.

The Andy Griffith Show (com)
.... Warren Ferguson (1965–66)
Our Place (var) .... regular (1967)
Getting Together (com)
.... Off. Rudy Colcheck (1971–72)
Wait Till Your Father Gets Home (cartn)
.... Ralph (voice) (1972–74)
The Burns and Schreiber Comedy Hour (var)
.... costar (1973)

"Let it suffice to say that I am a legend in my own mind," cracks ruddy-cheeked Jack Burns, the thin, serious half of the Burns and Schreiber comedy team, when asked about the pair's place in TV history. Indeed, much of their career might be characterized by the word "almost."

The son of an air force officer, Jack started out as a radio announcer and reporter in the '50s. Finding that comedy was more fun than straight news interviews with the likes of Fidel Castro, he teamed with another young announcer, George Carlin, to do a humorous morning show in Los Angeles. Eventually he dumped his radio career altogether and joined the Second City comedy troupe in Chicago in 1962, where he bumped into portly Avery Schreiber. The two formed an act and within a few years were appearing on network shows, including the 1967 summer variety show *Our Place*. Along the way Jack began acting, spending a season as Don Knotts' replacement on *The Andy Griffith Show*.

Then Burns and Schreiber split, leaving Jack to pursue a solo career as a comedy actor on the Bobby Sherman series *Getting Together* and writer for such hit shows as *The Kraft Music Hall, Hee Haw,* and *The*

Flip Wilson Show (he invented Geraldine for Flip). In 1972 he reunited with Schreiber and the following summer they headlined their own variety series. Jack has also continued as a top TV writer and producer, his later credits including *Fridays* (head writer) and *We've Got Each Other* (producer).

BURNS, MICHAEL—actor
b: Dec 30, 1947, Mineola, Long Island, N.Y.

It's a Man's World (com)
.... Howie Macauley (1962–63)
Wagon Train (wes)
.... Barnaby West (1963–65)

Michael Burns, the son of a TV technician, got his start playing a youthful entrepreneur on an episode of *Dobie Gillis* in 1958, at age ten. He was a popular child actor for the next several years, guesting on many series, including *Alfred Hitchcock Presents, General Electric Theater, Lassie, The Lone Ranger,* and *Bonanza*. He had a regular role for a season as Glenn Corbett's kid brother on *It's a Man's World*; then, a number of guest appearances on *Wagon Train* led to a regular role on that series from 1963–65, as an orphan who joined the caravan.

Some child actors find it hard to find work once they are in their teens, but Michael's youthful good looks continued to win him parts through his teens and twenties, with appearances on *Gunsmoke*; *The F.B.I.*; *Love, American Style*; and *The Streets of San Francisco,* among others.

BURNS, RONNIE—actor
b: Jul 9, 1935, Evanston, Ill.

The George Burns and Gracie Allen Show (com)................ as himself (1955–58)
The George Burns Show (com)
.... as himself (1958–59)
Happy (com)......... Chris Day (1960–61)

The adopted son of George Burns and Gracie Allen. Later he became a businessman.

BURNS, STEPHAN—actor
b: Elkins Park, Pa. r: Chew's Landing, N.J.

240-Robert (adv)
.... Deputy Brett Cueva (1981)

The Thorn Birds (drama)
.... Jack Cleary (1983)

BURR, ANNE—actress

City Hospital (drama)
.... Dr. Kate Morrow (1952–53)

This obscure radio and television actress of the 1940s and '50s is notable for having portrayed one of the first woman doctors seen as a regular on TV. In fact, she played two such roles, first on the prime time series *City Hospital* and then in 1954–55 as the leading character on the short-lived daytime soap opera *The Greatest Gift.* She had a somewhat longer run in the late 1950s on *As the World Turns.*

BURR, RAYMOND—actor
b: May 21, 1917, New Westminster, B.C., Canada

Perry Mason (drama)
.... Perry Mason (1957–66)
Ironside (police).. Robert Ironside (1967–75)
Kingston: Confidential (drama)
.... R. B. Kingston (1977)
79 Park Avenue (drama)
.... Armand Perfido (1977)
Centennial (drama).... Bockweiss (1978–79)

Emmy Award: Best Actor in a Dramatic Series, for *Perry Mason* (1959, 1961)

This dark, stocky actor with a magnetic personality gained TV fame via two very popular and long-running series, *Perry Mason* (nine years) and *Ironside* (eight). Interestingly, although he is always instantly identified with the Perry Mason role, it did not typecast him. Perhaps his personality is simply too forceful to be typecast.

Burr was born in Canada and he began his acting career onstage there and in England in the late '30s and '40s. He served in the U.S. Navy during World War II, returning after the war to begin an active career in movies. As might be expected, he was cast mostly as a villain (Hollywood always went for the obvious), though his intensity and charisma often made his roles more interesting than they had any right to be. He was particularly memorable in *A Place in the Sun* (1951) and the Hitchcock classic *Rear Window* (1954, as the maniacal Thorwald). Trivia buffs may also remember him

in such camp classics as *Godzilla* and *Gorilla at Large* (in 3-D!).

Burr was fairly busy on radio in the late '40s and early '50s and on television practically from the beginning. Among other things, he was on *Guild Playhouse, Climax, Stars over Hollywood,* as well as the very first episode of *Dragnet* ("The Human Bomb") in 1951. He was still considered a supporting player when he auditioned for the role of detective Paul Drake on the planned *Perry Mason* series in 1957, but he won the lead instead.

Twenty years and three series later, Burr finally settled down to a less strenuous schedule of periodic TV movies and miniseries (including the top-rated *79 Park Avenue* and *Centennial*). He also found time to raise orchids at his home in Los Angeles and tend his copra plantation in the Fiji Islands.

BURRELL, JIMMY—singer

American Minstrels of 1949 (var)
.... singer (1949)

BURRELL, MARYEDITH—comedienne
b: May 20, Oakland, Calif. r: Gilroy, Calif.

Fridays (var)............. regular (1980–82)

BURRELL, RUSTY—actor

The People's Court (misc).. bailiff (1981–)

BURRIS, NEAL—country singer

The Pee Wee King Show (var)
.... regular (1955)

BURROWS, ABE—composer, director
b: Dec 18, 1910, Brooklyn, N.Y. d: May 17, 1985

This Is Show Business (var)
.... panelist (1949–51)
Abe Burrows' Almanac (var).... host (1950)
We Take Your Word (quiz)
.... panelist (1950–51)
The Name's the Same (quiz)
.... panelist (1951–52)
This Is Show Business (var)
.... panelist (1956)
What's It For? (quiz) .... panelist (1957–58)

This famous Broadway composer/director was a familiar figure on early live television. Jovially styled as "the bald-headed baritone from Brooklyn," he was well-known in show biz circles as the life of any party. Although he was host or panelist on a number of New York–originated quiz and variety shows, he will probably be longer-remembered for his stage and movie hits *(Guys and Dolls, How to Succeed in Business Without Really Trying, The Solid Gold Cadillac)*—if not for his rather offbeat songs, such as "The Girl with the Three Blue Eyes" and "I Looked Under a Rock and Found You."

BURRUD, BILL—producer, host
b: Jan 12, 1925, Hollywood, Calif.

Animal World (doc) . . . . host (1968–76)
Safari to Adventure (doc)
. . . . narrator (1969–75)

Bill Burrud is a man who turned a natural wanderlust into a lifelong career; he is one of television's leading producers of travelogue, outdoor, and animal films. A onetime child actor (he was in a dozen Hollywood features between 1936–38), he formed Bill Burrud Productions in the early 1950s and began traveling the country and the world, turning out a steady stream of syndicated specials and series, including *Assignment America, Vagabond, Wanderlust, The American West* and *The Wonderful Women of the World*. Most of these he hosted himself. Probably his best-known series were the long running *Safari to Adventure* (syndicated) and *Animal World*, which was on NBC from 1968–72 and syndicated from 1972–76. Burrud's shows, with their beautiful flora and fauna, served as many a local station's standby films to fill time in odd corners of the schedule.

BURSKY, ALAN—actor

The Partridge Family (com)
. . . . Alan Kinkaid (1973–74)

BURSTYN, ELLEN—actress
b: Dec 7, 1932, Detroit, Mich.

The Iron Horse (wes)
. . . . Julie Parsons (1967–68)
The Ellen Burstyn Show (com)
. . . . Ellen Brewer (1986–)

BURT, HARDY—moderator
Answers for Americans (pub aff)
. . . . moderator (1953–54)

BURTON, LEVAR—black actor
b: Feb 16, 1957, Landsthul, Germany

Roots (drama)
. . . . Kunta Kinte (as a boy) (1977)

This young actor skyrocketed to fame on the strength of one brief role, in the spectacularly successful miniseries *Roots* in 1977. He and four other actors from the same miniseries were all nominated for the best actor Emmy that year (Lou Gossett won). Burton's subsequent career has been noticeably less successful, thus far. He has appeared in a number of TV movies, including *Billy: Portrait of a Street Kid* (as Billy), *The Ron LeFlore Story* (as Ron), *Grambling's White Tiger,* and *Dummy,* among others.

BURTON, NORMANN—actor
The New Adventures of Wonder Woman (adv) . . . . Joe Atkinson (1977)
The Ted Knight Show (com)
. . . . Burt Dennis (1978)

BURTON, RICHARD—actor
b: Nov 10, 1925, Pontrhydyfen, South Wales, England d: Aug 5, 1984

Winston Churchill—The Valiant Years (doc)
. . . . narrator (1960–61)

Celebrated film star Richard Burton was an infrequent guest on television, appearing in a few dramas and specials over the years. Among them were TV productions of *Wuthering Heights* (his TV acting debut, 1958), *The Twilight* (1960), and *Brief Encounter* (1974). With his once and future wife Elizabeth Taylor he costarred in one odd little TV movie, *Divorce His/Divorce Hers* in 1973, but probably a more famous appearance of the pair was on *Here's Lucy* in 1970, together with the famous giant diamond ring Richard had given his lady. Burton's last appearance was on the lumbering miniseries *Ellis Island,* telecast in November 1984. As he himself was once quoted as saying, "I've done the most awful rubbish in order to have somewhere to go in the morning."

BURTON, ROBERT—actor
b: Aug 13, 1895 d: Sep 29, 1964

Kings Row (drama)... Dr. Gordon (1955–56)

BURTON, SHELLEY—actor

Car 54, Where Are You? (com)
.... Off. Murdock (1961–62)

BURTON, SKIP—juvenile actor

Lassie (adv) .... Ron Holden (1972–74)

BURTON, WENDELL—actor
b: Jul 21, 1947, San Antonio, Texas

The New Dick Van Dyke Show (com)
.... Lucas Preston (1973)
East of Eden (drama)
.... Tom Hamilton (1981)

BUSE, KATHLEEN—actress

The Hamptons (drama)
.... Karen Harper (1983)

BUSEY, GARY—actor
b: Jun 29, 1944, Goose Creek, Texas

The Texas Wheelers (com)
.... Truckie Wheeler (1974–75)

BUSFIELD, TIMOTHY—actor
b: Jun 12, East Lansing, Mich.

Reggie (com).......... Mark Potter (1983)
Trapper John, M.D. (drama)
.... Dr. John (J.T.) McIntyre, Jr. (1984–86)

BUSH, OWEN—actor

Sirota's Court (com)
.... Bailiff John Bellson (1976–77)

BUSH, TOMMY—actor

Bret Maverick (wes)
.... Dep. Sturgess (1981–82)

BUSHKIN, JOE—jazz pianist
b: Nov 7, 1916*, New York City, N.Y.

A Couple of Joes (var) ..... costar (1949–50)

BUTKUS, DICK—actor
b: Dec 9, 1942, Chicago, Ill.

*Some sources give November 6 or November 17.

Rich Man, Poor Man—Book I (drama)
.... Al Fanducci (1976)
Blue Thunder (police)
.... Richard "Ski" Butowski (1984)
Half Nelson (drama).......... Kurt (1985)

A beefy former football superstar, with the Chicago Bears. He later did beer commercials and scattered acting assignments, often with his buddy from football days Bubba Smith.

BUTLER, DAWS—voice specialist
b: Nov 16, 1916, Toledo, Ohio r: Oak Park, Ill.

The Jetsons (cartn)
.... Elroy Jetson (voice) (1962–63)

This diminutive gentleman was one of Hollywood's leading "voice men," spending more than 40 years providing the voices for such cartoon favorites as Yogi Bear, Huckleberry Hound, and Quick Draw McGraw. He was the original Beany on the *Beany and Cecil* puppet show in the 1950s and was heard in hundreds of Saturday morning cartoons (especially those of Hanna-Barbera Productions) in the 1960s and '70s. Of course he was always heard, and never seen, a kind of anonymity that Butler seemed to take philosophically. "There was a time in my early career," he reminisced, "when I resented the prospect of going through life known only as Yogi Bear. I got over the resentment long ago. After all, Yogi is still a star, long after hundreds of others have faded away." "And he needs me," Butler added. "To Yogi Bear, at least, I am indispensable."

BUTLER, DEAN—actor
b: May 20, 1956, Prince George, B.C., Canada
r: San Francisco

Little House on the Prairie (adv)
.... Almanzo Wilder (1979–83)

BUTLER, JOHNNY—choreographer
b: Greenwood, Miss.

The Kate Smith Evening Hour (var)
.... regular (1951–52)

BUTLER, LOIS—actress

The RCA Victor Show (com)
.... Lois Sterling (1952–53)

BUTLER, PAUL—black actor

Crime Story (police)
.... Det. Walter Clemmens (1986–)

BUTRICK, MERRITT—actor

b: Sep 3, Gainesville, Fla. r: California

Square Pegs (com).. Johnny Slash (1982–83)

BUTTERFIELD, HERB—actor

b: 1896 d: 1957

The Halls of Ivy (com)
.... Clarence Wellman (1954–55)

BUTTERFIELD, WALLY—sportscaster

Thursday Night Fights (sport)
.... sportscaster (1952)

BUTTERWORTH, SHANE—juvenile actor

b: Oct 3, 1969, Riverside, Calif. r: Simi Valley, Calif.

The Bad News Bears (com)
.... Timmy Lupus (1979–80)

BUTTONS, RED—comedian

b: Feb 5, 1919, The Bronx, N.Y.

The Red Buttons Show (var)
.... host (1952–55)
The Double Life of Henry Phyfe (com)
.... Henry Wadsworth Phyfe (1966)

Comic Red Buttons was a sensation on television, rather briefly, in the early '50s. He was born Aaron Chwatt, of immigrant parents, on New York's Lower East Side. His stage name supposedly came from the gaudy uniform he wore while he was working as a bellboy and singer at Dinty Moore's Tavern in the Bronx, when he was a teenager. Red worked his way up slowly in burlesque and at Catskill Mountain resorts and had roles in several Broadway revues during the 1940s. Then, in the early '50s, he was pegged as one of television's comedy "finds," appearing with Milton Berle and on other variety shows and winning his own variety series in 1952. *The Red Buttons Show* began with a great deal of fanfare, and initially did well, but Red's silly, slapstick antics soon wore thin and the ratings slid. Writers were hired and fired with alarming rapidity, the format was changed to a situation comedy, and

the show changed networks, but all to no avail.

Thereafter Red appeared sporadically, in both comic and serious roles, on regular series such as *Studio One* and *General Electric Theater,* and big budget specials such as *Hansel and Gretel* and *George M.* He attempted a comeback in 1966 with the comedy *The Double Life of Henry Phyfe,* but this was a failure. Red was not seen much for a time after that, but in the late 1970s started working more frequently again in such lightweight series as *Vegas, The Love Boat,* and *Fantasy Island.*

BUTTRAM, PAT—cowboy actor

b: c. 1917, Addison, Ala.

Gene Autry Show (wes)
.... as himself (1950–56)
Green Acres (com) .... Mr. Haney (1965–71)

Most viewers know affable Pat Buttram as the grizzled sidekick on *The Gene Autry Show* or the bucolic Bilko on *Green Acres.* However, Pat had another highly successful career, as one of Hollywood's favorite toastmasters at testimonial dinners for some of show biz's leading stars. Some of his quips:

On Milton Berle: "You know, Milton recently switched from comedy to drama. Unfortunately, it happened while he was still doing comedy."

On Mae West: "Do you realize that she went through her life without once having a man say to her, 'You remind me of my mother'?"

On Johnny Carson: "He's an Episcopalian—that's an Off-Broadway Catholic."

On Dean Martin: "Dean would eat hay if you dipped it in gin."

On Roy Rogers and Dale Evans: "The Lunt and Fontanne of the fertilizer set."

On Ed McMahon: "It's good we honor Ed, because I understand that next week a group of Texas businessmen are going to buy him, tear him down, and put up a Ramada Inn."

On Hugh O'Brian: "Hugh is going to get married as soon as he finds a girl who loves him as much as he does."

On the TV industry: "Television is the only profession where you can be discovered, starred, and forgotten in one year."

What does Pat say about his own career? "I started back in the old days in Hollywood when everybody knew where Howard Hughes was and nobody cared . . . I finally got my footprints in front of Grauman's Chinese Theatre. I was sitting on a curb and a bus ran over my feet." Ask Pat how he feels being famous, though, and he'll ruefully pull out a real-life clipping from a day in 1950 when he was gravely injured in an accident on a movie set. The headline: GENE AUTRY ALMOST HURT IN EXPLOSION.

BUTTS, K. C.—actor

Our Man Higgins (com)
.... Dinghy MacRoberts (1962–63)

BUWEN, JOE—singer

Melody Street (music) .... regular (1953–54)

BUX, KUDA—mystic

b: c. 1905, Akhnur, Kashmir, India d: Feb 5, 1981

I'd Like to See (info)........ regular (1949)
Kuda Bux, Hindu Mystic (misc) . star (1950)

Early TV had its freak show annex, and one of its most popular denizens was this sideshow performer who was billed as "The man with the X-ray eyes." His peculiar talent was an ability to see through blindfolds, bandages, lead foil, and just about any other concealing medium one might think of—onstage, and in front of a live audience! Though his background was a little murky, he was supposedly born in Kashmir, India (real name: Khudah Bukhsh). He had performed in Europe for a number of years before coming to the U.S., where he found his way into television history, and this book.

BUZBY, ZANE—

Our Time (var)............. regular (1985)

BUZZI, RUTH—comedienne

b: Jul 24, 1936, Westerly, R.I. r: Wequetequock, Conn.

The Entertainers (var) .... regular (1964–65)
The Steve Allen Comedy Hour (var)
.... regular (1967)
That Girl (com)
.... Margie "Pete" Peterson (1967–68)

Rowan & Martin's Laugh-In (var)
.... regular (1968–73)

Fading actress Blossom LaVerne, the Friendly Lady with her lamppost, Flicker Farkle, the Etiquette Lady, the stewardess of Burbank Airlines, the fat dowager, and the dowdy Gladys Ormphby—all of these favorites from *Rowan and Martin's Laugh-In* were one and the same, comedienne Ruth Buzzi. It seems that she has not been able to live them down, either. Her once booming career has been back in second gear ever since that famous series left the air.

Ruth started out to be a dancer, and, failing that, turned to comedy, graduating in 1957 from the Pasadena Playhouse. A good deal of stage work followed in the late 1950s and '60s, supplemented by television appearances on such series as *The Entertainers,* Steve Allen's 1967 summer show, and a season on *That Girl.* Her major break, though, was on *Laugh-In,* which made her—and Gladys—a star. Ruth was one of the few cast members to remain for the series' entire run.

It was a hard act to follow. Ruth made guest shots on variety and comedy shows for a number of years afterward and appeared on a couple of Saturday morning kids' shows (*Lost Saucer* in 1975, *Baggy Pants and the Nitwits* in 1977—the latter a cartoon version of her Gladys character from *Laugh-In*). By 1979 she was turning up on such things as an episode of *CHiPs* titled "CHiPs Goes Roller Disco." In 1983 she made a brief appearance on the daytime soap opera *Days of Our Lives.*

BYINGTON, SPRING—actress

b: Oct 17, 1886*, Colorado Springs, Colo. d: Sep 7, 1971

December Bride (com)
.... Lily Ruskin (1954–59)
Laramie (wes) ..... Daisy Cooper (1961–63)

Spring Byington's first name was appropriate considering the kinds of characters she played—sunny, cheerful, young in spirit, and usually somebody's mom. It was a characterization she played all her life (as well as a reflection of her own personality), and it brought her great success on television in the 1950s in the long running,

*Some sources give 1893.

136

oft repeated comedy *December Bride.*

Spring had been an actress since she was in her teens, a very long time before. She traveled the far west with local theater troupes, made it to New York and Broadway in the 1920s, and moved into films in the 1930s in a long succession of warm, motherly roles. By the early 1950s her film career was winding down, and, like many of her contemporaries, she began doing TV, at first in theater series like *Ford Theatre. December Bride* was made for her special talents and it was a major hit. Later she continued to do some television work, though she accepted only a fraction of the offers she received. In addition to a two-year run on *Laramie* as a surrogate mother to the cowboys, she appeared in an *Alfred Hitchcock Presents* episode in 1960, a four-part story on *Dr. Kildare* in 1965, *Batman* in 1966, and *I Dream of Jeannie* in 1967.

BYNER, JOHN—actor

The Garry Moore Show (var)
.... regular (1966–67)
The Steve Allen Comedy Hour (var)
.... regular (1967)
The Kraft Music Hall (var)... regular (1968)
Something Else (var) .... cohost (1970)
The John Byner Comedy Hour (var)
.... host (1972)
The Practice (com)
.... Dr. Roland Caine (1976–77)
Soap (com) ... Detective Donahue (1978–80)

This stand-up comedian and impressionist enjoyed some popularity on variety shows in the 1960s and '70s and had his own brief summer show in 1972. He also appeared as an actor on a number of situation comedies, including regular roles on *Soap* and *The Practice* (whose star, Danny Thomas, had once advised him to get out of show business and become a plumber). His impressionist's ability with voices also brought him work on Saturday morning kids' shows, including a long run in the 1970s on "The Ant and the Aardvark" segment of *The Pink Panther Show.*

BYRD, DAVID—actor

Highcliffe Manor (com) ... Dr. Lester (1979)
Mary (com) .... Vincent Tully (1985–86)

BYRD, DICK—

The Ted Mack Family Hour (var)
.... regular (1951)

BYRD, RALPH—actor

b: Apr 22, 1909, Dayton, Ohio d: Aug 18, 1952

Dick Tracy (police)... Dick Tracy (1950–51)

BYRD, RICHARD—actor

3 Girls 3 (var).............. regular (1977)

BYRD, TOM—actor

Boone (drama) .... Boone Sawyer (1983–84)

BYRD-NETHERY, MIRIAM—actress

Mr. T and Tina (com)
.... Miss Llewellyn (1976)

BYRNE, BOBBY—orchestra leader

b: Oct 10, 1918, Columbus, Ohio

Club Seven (music).. orch. leader (1948–49)

BYRNES, EDD—actor

b: Jul 30, 1933, New York City, N.Y.

77 Sunset Strip (drama)
.... Gerald Lloyd ("Kookie")
Kookson III (1958–63)
$weepstake$ (drama) .... emcee (1979)

Edd Byrnes had five very good years as an actor in the late 1950s and early '60s and has been trying to regain the momentum of those years ever since. He was a virtual unknown when he won the role of the laid-back, jive-talking young parking lot attendant "Kookie" in *77 Sunset Strip.* The role made him a star and also resulted in a million-selling novelty record called "Kookie, Kookie, Lend Me Your Comb" (Kookie was always combing his luxuriant hair).

Even though he had graduated to full-fledged detective by later in the series run, Byrnes was seen as something of a flash-in-the-pan novelty and found it difficult to get substantial parts afterward. After some secondary roles in some secondary movies (e.g., *Beach Ball,* 1965), he moved to Europe and began appearing in "spaghetti westerns." He was back in the U.S. in the 1970s, resigned to his fate, appearing in episodes of numerous action series such as

137

The Hardy Boys, Police Woman, California Fever, and B.J. and the Bear. In 1979 he briefly starred as the lottery emcee in the short-lived $weepstake$.

BYRON, CAROL—actress
b: c. 1937, Los Angeles, Calif.

Window on Main Street (com)
.... Peggy Evans (1961–62)
Oh, Those Bells (com)
.... Kitty Matthews (1962)

BYRON, JEAN—actress

Mayor of the Town (com)
.... Minnie, the secretary (1954–55)
The Many Loves of Dobie Gillis (com)
.... Mrs. Ruth Adams (1959–60)
The Many Loves of Dobie Gillis (com)
.... Dr. Burkhart (1961–63)
The Patty Duke Show (com)
.... Natalie Masters (1963–66)
Pat Paulsen's Half a Comedy Hour (var)
.... regular (1970)

C

CABAL, ROBERT—actor

Rawhide (wes). Hey Soos Patines (1961–64)

CABOT, SEBASTIAN—actor
b: Jul 6, 1918, London, England d: Aug 22, 1977

The Three Musketeers (adv)
.... Count de Brisemont (1956)
Checkmate (drama). . . . Carl Hyatt (1960–62)
The Beachcomber (adv)
.... Commissioner Crippen (1962)
Suspense (drama) .... host (1964)
Family Affair (com)
.... Mr. (Giles) French (1966–71)
Ghost Story (drama)
.... Winston Essex (host) (1972)

Portly, *veddy* English actor Sebastian
Cabot was known to a generation of young
TV fans as the slightly stuffy but lovable
Mr. French of *Family Affair* and to older
ones as the teller of scary stories on *Ghost
Story* and *Suspense*. Youngsters seemed
to have a special liking for Cabot, even
though he spent much of his career playing
rather adult roles.

Born in London, Cabot left school at 14
to find odd jobs and get his start in the
theater. He was appearing in British films
by the time he was 18 and during World
War II was for a time an expert dialecti-
cian for the British Broadcasting Corporation. After the war he began to travel to
America for occasional stage and film
roles, and, beginning in the mid-1950s, for
television appearances as well. These included early episodes of *Gunsmoke* and
Alfred Hitchcock Presents. He became
better-known through U.S. syndication of
the British series *The Three Musketeers*.
His appeal to children began to evidence
itself in repeat appearances on *The World
of Disney* and *Shirley Temple's Storybook*. His first real hit, however, was as the
debonair criminologist (with the now-fa-
miliar beard) on *Checkmate* from 1960–62.

After considerable TV series success in
the 1960s, Cabot was seen less often in the
1970s. His rolling tones were still familiar
to kids, though, on the popular *Winnie the
Pooh* TV specials and records, for which
he served as narrator.

"Sabbie" Cabot, as he was known to his
friends, died of a stroke in Canada in 1977.

CADORETTE, MARY—actress
b: Mar 31, 1957, East Hartford, Conn.

Three's a Crowd (com)
.... Vicky Bradford (1984–85)

CADY, FRANK—actor
b: 1915, Susanville, Calif.

Adventures of Ozzie & Harriet (com)
.... Doc Williams (1954–65)
Petticoat Junction (com)
.... Sam Drucker (1963–70)
Green Acres (com) . Sam Drucker (1965–71)

CAESAR, DAVE—

Caesar's Hour (var) ...... regular (1955–57)

CAESAR, JIMMY—comedian

The Keane Brothers Show (var)
.... regular (1977)

CAESAR, SID—comedian
b: Sep 8, 1922, Yonkers, N.Y.

Admiral Broadway Revue (var)
.... regular (1949)
Your Show of Shows (var)
.... regular (1950–54)
Caesar's Hour (var) .. Bob Victor (1954–57)
Caesar's Hour (var) ....host (1954–57)
Sid Caesar Invites You (var) . cohost (1958)
The Sid Caesar Show (var) .. host (1963–64)

Emmy Awards: Best Actor (1951); Best Comedian, for *Caesar's Hour* (1956)

The tall, lanky comedian, alone on the
stage, begins slowly. With just his gestures
and his mobile features he begins to con-
vey the building momentum of an aerial
battle, the bursts of machine gun fire, the
heroic American pilot (always smiling),
quickly to the dastardly German (always
scowling), fast cut for the obligatory love
scene, back to the ferocious assault on a
machine gun nest, then suddenly the
smoke clears, and John Wayne is triumphant!—it has all been a hilarious parody
of every Hollywood war movie ever made,
packed into a couple of minutes, with no
props at all. There is no doubt that Sid
Caesar was one of the comic geniuses of

early TV, able to carry off such a frenzied one-man tour de force in ingenious fashion. The man could become a punching bag, a seltzer bottle, a dial telephone, a gum dispensing machine, or an entire cattle stampede. His simple miming of a woman getting dressed in the morning (how many zippers *are* there?) would have audiences on the floor.

Surprisingly, Caesar was not particularly glib as a host. However, put him in a sketch, or have him embellish upon a story (he rarely followed the script), and he could paint a funny and true picture of human foibles that everyone could recognize.

Sid's father owned a restaurant in Yonkers, N.Y., and his son picked up his knowledge of dialects and accents listening to the foreign clientele there while he was a teenager. He didn't intend to become a comedian at the time, pursuing music instead. He studied saxophone at the Juilliard School and played with such famous bands as those of Charlie Spivak, Claude Thornhill, and Shep Fields (he even recorded with Fields in 1942).

When World War II began, Sid joined the Coast Guard and was assigned as a musician to take part in the service show *Tars and Spars*. A soft-spoken producer who was working on the show, Max Liebman, overheard Sid breaking up the other band members with his improvised routines and switched him to comedy. Sid went on to do his "war" routine in both the stage and movie versions of the revue. Liebman continued to guide Sid's career after the war, casting him in the Broadway revue *Make Mine Manhattan* in 1948 and bringing him to television in 1949 for a new, big-budget variety show called the *Admiral Broadway Revue* (later called *Your Show of Shows*). Teamed with a first-rate cast, including Imogene Coca, Carl Reiner, and Howard Morris, Caesar became one of TV's top satirical comedians.

After five years of some of the most creative comedy the medium has ever known, *Your Show of Shows* had its final telecast in 1954, a big, nostalgic farewell complete with the president of NBC onstage. Sid then starred in his own variety hour for three years, as well as in two subsequent series, but by the mid-1960s he was seen only in occasional guest appearances. He continued to turn up from time to time in the '70s and '80s on such diverse series as *The Big Show, The Misadventures of Sheriff Lobo,* the TV film *Curse of the Black Widow,* and Steven Spielberg's *Amazing Stories.*

His autobiography: *Where Have I Been?* (with Bill Davidson, 1983).

CAHILL, CATHY—

Dean Martin Presents Bobby Darin (var) .... regular (1972)

CAILLOU, ALAN—actor

Quark (com) .... The Head (1978)

CAIN, JESS/JEFF—actor

Marge and Jeff (com) .... Jeff (1953–54)

CAIN, MADELYN—actress

Whiz Kids (drama) ... Irene Adler (1983–84)

CAINE, HOWARD—actor
b: Jan 2, 1928, Nashville, Tenn.

The Californians (wes) ... Schaab (1957–58)

CAINE DANCERS—

Polka-Go-Round (music) .. regular (1958–59)

CALDER, KING—actor
b: c. 1900 d: Jun 28, 1964

Martin Kane, Private Eye (drama) .... Lt. Grey (1952–54)

CALDWELL, JIM—host

Tic Tac Dough (quiz) .... host (1985–86)

CALFA, DON—actor

Park Place (com) .... Howard "Howie" Beech (1981)
Legmen (drama).. Oscar Armismendi (1984)

CALHOUN, RORY—actor
b: Aug 8, 1918*, Los Angeles r: Santa Cruz, Calif.

The Texan (wes) .... Bill Longley (1958–60)
The Blue and the Gray (drama) .... Gen. George Meade (1982)

*Some sources give 1922 or 1923.

This rugged, handsome star of numerous Hollywood westerns and other action films of the 1950s made many appearances on television, often in roles similar to those he played on the big screen. In the 1950s he was seen on such shows as *Ford Theatre* and *Screen Director's Playhouse*, and he produced and starred in his own CBS western, *The Texan*. In the 1960s and '70s he was a fairly frequent guest star, at first on westerns (*Wagon Train, Death Valley Days, Gunsmoke*) and later on crime dramas and in TV movies. In 1982 Rory joined the cast of the new daytime serial *Capitol* as Judson Tyler, the patriarch of the McCandless family. He was also seen that year in the miniseries *The Blue and the Gray*.

Rory's background was rather rough. Raised by his mother and stepfather in poor circumstances, he was often in trouble with the law and served time in reformatories and prison until a caring chaplain set him straight. He later worked at a succession of blue-collar jobs. A chance encounter with Alan Ladd in the mid-1940s put him on the trail to Hollywood stardom.

CALI, JOSEPH—actor
b: Mar 30, New York City, N.Y.

Flatbush (com)
.... Presto Prestopopolos (1979)
Today's F.B.I. (police)
.... Nick Frazier (1981–82)

CALIFORNIANS, THE—singers

CBS Newcomers (var) ...... regulars (1971)

CALIRI, JON—actor
b: Jan 28, c. 1960, Providence, R.I.

Square Pegs (com)
.... Vinnie Pasetta (1982–83)
Double Trouble (com)
.... Michael Gillette (1984)

CALLAHAN, BILL—dancer

The Jack Carter Show (var)
.... dancer (1950–51)

CALLAHAN, JAMES—actor

Wendy and Me (com)
.... Danny Adams (1964–65)
Convoy (drama).. Lt. Dick O'Connell (1965)

The Governor & J.J. (com)
.... George Callison (1969–70)
The Runaways (drama)
.... Sgt. Hal Grady (1979)

CALLAHAN, JOHN—actor
b: Dec 23, Brooklyn, N.Y. r: Long Island, N.Y.

Falcon Crest (drama)
.... Eric Stavros (1986–   )

CALLAN, K—actress
b: Jan 9, Dallas, Texas

Married: The First Year (drama)
.... Cathy Baker (1979)
Joe's World (com) . Katie Wabash (1979–80)
Cutter to Houston (drama)
.... Nurse Connie Buford (1983)

CALLAN, MICHAEL—actor
b: Nov 22, 1935, Philadelphia, Pa.

Occasional Wife (com)
.... Peter Christopher (1966–67)
Scruples (drama) .... Alan Wilton (1980)

This bright comic and former dancer has been appearing in lightweight films and TV episodes since the late 1950s. He had his own NBC situation comedy in 1966–67, playing a young bachelor who had to persuade his neighbor (Patricia Harty) to pose as his "wife" in order to impress his boss. The characters did not get married on the series, but Callan and Harty did in fact fall in love during the series' run and were married in real life. (They later divorced).

In subsequent years Callan was seen in other similarly fluffy television guest roles, including multiple appearances on *Love, American Style* and *Fantasy Island*. He had a somewhat heavier part in the 1980 miniseries *Scruples*.

CALLAS, CHARLIE—comedian
b: Dec 20, Brooklyn, N.Y.

The Andy Williams Show (var)
.... regular (1970–71)
ABC Comedy Hour (com) .... regular (1972)
Switch (drama)... Malcolm Argos (1975–78)

A pint-sized comic of the 1960s who had an off-and-on career in TV series of the '70s, including the regular role of the ex-con man who sometimes helped Eddie Albert and Robert Wagner carry off their scams on *Switch*.

Charlie began in show business as a drummer, then later became a stand-up comedian. His first real break was on *The Merv Griffin Show* in 1966, followed by a role in the Jerry Lewis movie *Big Mouth* in 1967.

CALLAWAY, BILL—actor

Love, American Style (com)
.... repertory player (1969–71)

Bill Callaway spent most of the 1970s and '80s doing voices for Saturday morning cartoons produced by Hanna-Barbera (*The Drak Pack, Cattanooga Cats, Richie Rich,* etc.). He was also Charlie the Owl on *The New Zoo Revue*.

CALLAWAY, CHERYL—actress

Dr. Hudson's Secret Journal (drama)
.... Kathy Hudson (1955–57)

CALLAWAY, THOMAS—actor

Falcon Crest (drama).. Dr. Foster (1983–84)

CALMER, NED—host, writer
b: c. 1907 d: Mar 9, 1986

In the First Person (int)......... host (1950)

CALVERT, BILL—actor

Fast Times (com)......... the surfer (1986)

CALVERT, HENRY—actor

Hot L Baltimore (com)....... Gordon (1975)

CALVIN, HENRY—actor
b: 1918 d: Oct 6, 1975

Zorro (wes)......... Sgt. Garcia (1957–59)

CALVIN, JOHN—actor
b: Nov 29, Staten Island, N.Y.

The Paul Lynde Show (com)
.... Howie Dickerson (1972–73)
From Here to Eternity (drama)
.... Lt. Kenneth Barrett (1980)
Tales of the Gold Monkey (adv)
.... Rev. Willie Tenboom (1982–83)

CAMACHO, CORINNE—actress

Medical Center (drama)
.... Dr. Jeanne Bartlett (1969–71)

CAMARATA, TUTTI—arranger, orchestra leader
b: May 11, 1913, Glen Ridge, N.J.

The Vic Damone Show (var)
.... orch. leader (1956)

Salvador "Toots" Camarata was a veteran of the big band era who spent many years as Jimmy Dorsey's arranger, and providing Dorsey fans with such memorable arrangements as "Green Eyes," "Tangerine," and "Yours." He later became an orchestra leader and musical director for Decca Records and in the 1950s and '60s was musical director for a number of TV series as well as for Walt Disney films.

CAMERON, DEAN—actor
b: Dec 25, 1962, Morrison, Ill. r: Oklahoma

Spencer (com)...... Herbie Bailey (1984–85)
Under One Roof (com)
.... Herbie Bailey (1985)
Fast Times (com)........ Jeff Spicoli (1986)

A gawky young actor who often plays awkward juveniles; he has co-authored a screenplay called "Geek's Lost Weekend."

CAMERON, KIRK—juvenile actor
b: Oct 12, 1970, Panorama City, Calif.

Two Marriages (drama)
.... Eric Armstrong (1983–84)
Growing Pains (com)
.... Mike Seaver (1985–)

CAMERON, ROD—actor
b: Dec 7, 1910* , Calgary, Alta. Canada d: Dec 21, 1983

City Detective (police)
.... Det. Lt. Bart Grant (1953–55)
State Trooper (police)
.... Trooper Rod Blake (1956–59)
Coronado 9 (drama) .... Don Adams (1959)

Rod Cameron was a rugged, handsome actor who found steady work in Hollywood B films of the 1940s and then carved out a career in television B series as well.

*Some sources give 1912.

A lanky (6'4"), likable fellow, he got into acting rather late, after ten years as a construction worker. From the late 1930s on he was seen in numerous action films, especially westerns, first as a stuntman or double and later as a lead.

In 1953 he starred in the first of three action-packed syndicated TV series, *City Detective.* This was followed in quick succession by the similarly action-oriented *State Trooper* and *Coronado 9* (as a detective). During and after the runs of his own shows Rod appeared in episodes of many other series, including *The Loretta Young Show, Bonanza,* and *Alias Smith and Jones.* He was a favorite outlaw (often with a sympathetic side) on *Laramie,* with at least six appearances on that western between 1959 and 1963. Among his last TV roles were a number of guest shots on *Adam-12* in the early and mid 1970s.

Cameron attracted a certain amount of gossip-column notoriety in 1960 when he divorced his wife of ten years, Anela, and married her mother Dorothy. Whatever Anela may have thought about her husband becoming her father-in-law, the new union lasted for many years.

CAMMANN, DR. SCHUYLER—professor of anthropology

What in the World (quiz)... panelist (1953)

CAMP, HAMILTON—actor

b: Oct 30, 1934, London, England.

He & She (com)
.... Andrew Hummel (1967–68)
Turn-On (var).............. regular (1969)
Co-ed Fever (com)...... Mr. Peabody (1979)
Too Close for Comfort (com)
.... Arthur Wainwright (1981)
The Nashville Palace (var)
.... regular (1981–82)
Just Our Luck (com) ... Professor Bob (1983)

Diminutive former child actor and folksinger who has played comic roles on a number of short-lived series over the years. He is a former member of the Second City comedy troupe.

CAMP, HELEN PAGE—actress

13 Queens Boulevard (com)
.... Mildred Capestro (1979)

CAMPANELLA, FRANK—actor

Skag (drama) .... Paczka (1980)

CAMPANELLA, JOSEPH—actor

b: Nov 21, 1927, New York City, N.Y.

The Nurses (drama)
.... Dr. Ted Steffen (1964–65)
Mannix (drama)
.... Lou Wickersham (1967–68)
The Lawyers (drama)
.... Brian Darrell (1969–72)
The Undersea World of Jacques Cousteau (doc) .... narrator (1974–)
This Is Your Life (misc)........ host (1983)

Joseph Campanella's hard-edged features have been a familiar sight on TV dramas since the early 1950s; he is perfect as an authority figure, on either side of the law. The son of an Italian immigrant, Campanella served in the navy during World War II (as one of its youngest landing-craft skippers), then studied acting under Lee Strasberg in the late 1940s. He began his career however, as a radio announcer, doing sportscasts in Pennsylvania and broadcasting for the foreign language section of the Voice of America. He also tried out for the New York Giants (he is an excellent athlete) but abandoned that career when he learned that he might be farmed out and have to leave his beloved New York.

Campanella's first television appearance was on an episode of *Suspense* in the early 1950s, followed by roles on many other New York–based live playhouse series. He finally began commuting to Hollywood for roles in series being filmed there. He was a busy actor indeed during the 1960s, with credits including multiple episodes of *Combat, The Virginian, The Fugitive, Mission: Impossible, Name of the Game,* and *Ironside.* He was Mike Connors' detective-agency boss during the first season of *Mannix* and costarred in *The Lawyers* segment of the Sunday night *Bold Ones* anthology from 1969–72.

He continued to be seen frequently in the 1970s and '80s (*Night Gallery, Owen Marshall, Quincy, M.E.,* etc.) and was heard as narrator of the National Geographic and Jacques Cousteau specials.

CAMPBELL, ALAN—actor
b: Apr 22, Homestead, Fla.

Three's a Crowd (com)
.... E. Z. Taylor (1984–85)

CAMPBELL, ARCHIE—country comedian
b: Nov 17, 1914, Bullsgap, Tenn.

Hee Haw (var).......... regular (1969–)

CAMPBELL, BEVERLY—actress

Mama Rosa (com)...... the daughter (1950)

CAMPBELL, DEAN—singer

Campus Corner (music)...... regular (1949)

CAMPBELL, DUANE R.—actor

Alice (com).............. Chuck (1978–85)

CAMPBELL, FLORA—actress
b: c. 1911 d: Nov 6, 1978

Faraway Hill (drama)
.... Karen St. John (1946)
A Date with Judy (com)
.... Dora Foster (1952–53)

She is almost completely forgotten today, but Flora Campbell deserves at least a small plaque in TV's Hall of Fame (perhaps in the shape of a teardrop) for starring in the very first network soap opera, Du-Mont's *Faraway Hill*. She was the city woman who moved to the country and fell in love with a handsome farmboy—who, unfortunately, was in love with someone else.

Miss Campbell's principal career was on the New York stage, where she appeared in numerous productions from the mid-1930s to the mid-1960s. She also made a career out of soap operas, on radio in the 1940s, and then on TV in the '50s. Her longest TV run was as the "valiant lady" on *Valiant Lady* from 1954–57; others included *The Seeking Heart, Love of Life, The Edge of Night*, and *The Secret Storm*.

CAMPBELL, GLEN—singer
b: Apr 22, 1935*, Delight, Ark.

Shindig (music) ... frequent guest (1964–66)

*Some sources give March 22, 1936 or April 10, 1938.

The Summer Smothers Brothers Show (var)
.... host (1968)
The Glen Campbell Goodtime Hour (var)
.... host (1969–72)
The Glen Campbell Music Show (music)
.... host (1982–83)

Although pop singer Glen Campbell is best known for his television appearances and hit records in the late 1960s, his career began many years before that. His birthplace and date are a bit muddled; he talks of being born in tiny Delight, Arkansas (pop. 446), but some sources claim it was Billstown, Arkansas, a place so obscure it isn't even on maps. Young Glen started pickin' on a guitar before he got to grade school and was a child prodigy at age six. He played with a traveling band in the Southwest for a few years in his teens, then landed in California in 1960, where he found steady work as a studio guitarist backing such stars as Frank Sinatra and Elvis Presley.

Glen's own recording career began in the early 1960s and produced some fine solo guitar LP's and a few minor vocal hits. He was seen on TV music shows, including *Shindig*. However, it was not until 1967–68 that he hit the big time with hits like "By the Time I Get to Phoenix," "Wichita Lineman," and "Gentle on My Mind" (his theme). These folkish ballads—something of an antidote to the psychedelic rock of the day—won him guest spots on top variety shows, including that of the Smothers Brothers, who liked him so much they made him host of their summer replacement series in 1968. Glen's easygoing, ingratiating style went over well, and he was given his own CBS series the following January, which ran for three-and-a-half years.

Glen retired from series TV after that (except for a briefly syndicated music show in 1982) but has continued active in the music business. He often turns up on TV specials, costarring with Bob Hope, Johnny Cash, and various country artists.

CAMPBELL, NICHOLAS—actor
b: Mar 24, 1952, Toronto, Canada

The Insiders (drama) ... Nick Fox (1985–86)

CAMPBELL, TONI—actress

Mama (com)........... Dagmar (1956–57)

CAMPBELL, WILLIAM—actor
b: Oct 30, 1926, Newark, N.J.

Cannonball (adv).... Jerry Austin (1958–59)
Dynasty (drama) ..... Luke Fuller (1984–85)
Crime Story (police)
.... Det. Joey Indelli (1986–)

CAMPO, PUPI—orchestra leader
The Jack Paar Program (var)
.... orch. leader (1954)

CAMPOS, RAFAEL—actor
b: May 13, 1936, Santiago, Dominican Republic d: Jul 9, 1985

Rhoda (com) ..... Ramon Diaz, Jr. (1977–78)
Centennial (drama)........ Nacho (1978–79)
V (movie) (sci fi) .... Sancho (1983)

CAMPOS, VICTOR—actor
b: Jan 15, New York City, N.Y.

Cade's County (police)
.... Rudy Davillo (1971–72)
Doctors' Hospital (drama)
.... Dr. Felipe Ortega (1975–76)

CANARY, DAVID—actor
b: Aug 25, 1938, Elwood, Ind. r: Massilon, Ohio

Peyton Place (drama)
.... Dr. Russ Gehring (1965–66)
Bonanza (wes) .... Candy (1967–70)
Bonanza (wes) .... Candy (1972–73)

Emmy Award: Best Actor in a Daytime Drama, for *All My Children* (1986)

David Canary claims to be a descendant of the Old West's most notorious hell-raiser, Calamity Jane (real name: Martha Jane Canary). The tall, rugged actor originally intended to play football but turned to acting after a gridiron injury in college left him with a smashed nose. As he delicately puts it, "I have a face that looks like a bowl of oatmeal thrown against a kitchen wall."

David broke into the New York theater in the 1960s, detoured for a couple of years in the army (where he won the 1963 All-Army Entertainment Contest as a singer), then got his big break as Dr. Russ Gehring on *Peyton Place*. That was followed by a long run as ranch hand Candy on *Bonanza*,

as well as guest shots on a number of other westerns and police series. By the mid-1970s his TV work had slacked off and he was devoting most of his time to the theater.

The actor began a new TV career in daytime soap operas in 1981, first with two years as Stephen Frame on *Another World* and then as wealthy, unpredictable Adam Chandler on *All My Children*.

CANDY, JOHN—comedian
b: Oct 31, 1950, Newmarket, Ontario, Canada

Second City TV (com)
.... Johnny LaRue (1977–79)
SCTV Network 90 (com) .. regular (1981–83)

Emmy Award: Best Comedy Writing, for *SCTV Network 90* (1982, 1983)

Chubby John Candy, who played inept features man Johnny LaRue (among other roles) on *Second City TV*, is a product of the Second City comedy workshops in Chicago and Toronto. He originally auditioned for the troupe in 1973, along with his friends Dan Aykroyd and Valerie Bromfield, and he has appeared with them and other Second City alumni in many projects since, including the movies *1941, The Blues Brothers*, and *Stripes*. His relative lack of solo fame is probably due in part to the fact that he submerges himself so thoroughly in his roles you see only the character, not the actor. Watch for the fat man.

CANFIELD, MARY GRACE—actress
b: Sep 3, Rochester, N.Y.

The Hathaways (com)
.... Amanda Allison (1961–62)
Green Acres (com)
.... Ralph Monroe (1966–71)
Family (drama) ..... Mrs. Hanley (1976–78)

Blonde actress with stage experience in the 1940s and '50s who is best known as Ralph the lady carpenter on *Green Acres*.

CANNING, TOM—orchestra leader
Thicke of the Night (talk)
.... orch. leader (1983–84)

CANNON, DYAN—actress
b: Jan 4, 1937, Tacoma, Wash.

Master of the Game (drama)
.... Kate Blackwell (1984)

Movie actress and onetime wife of Cary Grant, who appeared fairly frequently on television in the early and mid 1960s (mostly in westerns and police shows) before her film career took off with *Bob and Carol and Ted and Alice* in 1969. She has returned occasionally in prestigious TV productions such as the 1984 miniseries *Master of the Game.*

CANNON, GLENN—actor

Hawaii Five-O (police)
.... Att. Gen. John Manicote (1975–77)

CANNON, J. D.—actor

b: Apr 24, 1922, Salmon, Idaho

McCloud (police)
.... Peter B. Clifford (1970–77)
Ike (drama)
.... Gen. Walter Bedell Smith (1979)
Call to Glory (drama)
.... General Hampton (1984–85)

Tough-looking J. D. Cannon grew up among the mountains and ranches of Idaho, dreaming of becoming an actor. It proved to be a harder climb than he imagined, as he spent many lean years in the 1950s and '60s playing minor New York stage roles, including many in Shakespearean plays. He did scattered TV work along the way *(The Fugitive, The Defenders, Profiles in Courage)* but it was not until 1970 and the continuing role of Dennis Weaver's tough-talking boss on *McCloud* that he finally achieved financial security as an actor. In the years since, he has appeared mostly in TV movies and miniseries (including *Ike*) and returned to his first love, the stage.

CANNON, JIMMY—New York Post columnist

Are You Positive? (quiz) .... panelist (1952)
What's the Story? (quiz) . panelist (1952–55)
ABC's Nightlife (talk)........ regular (1965)

CANNON, KATHERINE—actress

b: Sep 6, 1953, Hartford, Conn.

The Survivors (drama)..... Shelia (1969–70)

Baa Baa Black Sheep (drama)
.... Capt. Dottie Dixon (1977–78)
The Contender (drama) ... Jill Sindon (1980)
Father Murphy (drama)
...... Mae Woodward Murphy (1981–82)

CANNON, MAUREEN—singer

School House (var).......... regular (1949)
Broadway Open House (talk)
.... regular (1951)
Paul Whiteman's Goodyear Revue (var)
.... regular (1951–52)

CANNON, MICHAEL AND WILLIAM— infant actors

Too Close for Comfort (com)
.... Andrew Rush (1983–84)

CANOVA, DIANA—actress

b: Jun 1, 1953, West Palm Beach, Fla. r: Hollywood, Calif.

Dinah and Her New Best Friends (var)
.... regular (1976)
Soap (com) .... Corrine Tate (1977–80)
I'm a Big Girl Now (com)
.... Diana Cassidy (1980–81)
Foot in the Door (com).. Harriet Foot (1983)

When asked why she went into show business, Diana Canova replies, "Growing up in Hollywood and being around my mother, my attitude was 'What else is there?' " Her mother, of course, was popular movie and radio singer/comedienne Judy Canova, whose earsplitting rustic yodels woke up many a comedy sketch over the years.

With mom's encouragement, Diana took music and acting lessons at an early age. She began doing television work in 1973 (an episode of *Ozzie's Girls*) and was a regular on Dinah Shore's summer show in 1976. Her big break was the role of the sexy daughter of Jessica and Chester Tate on *Soap* in 1977. She left that series in 1980 to costar in Danny Thomas's *I'm a Big Girl Now*, followed by other series work in the 1980s. She has also pursued her singing career, but she does not yodel.

CANTOR, CHARLIE—actor

b: c. 1898 d: Sep 11, 1966

The Ray Bolger Show (com)
.... Artie Herman (1954–55)

146

CANTOR, EDDIE—comedian
b: Jan 31, 1892, New York City, N.Y. d: Oct 10, 1964

The Colgate Comedy Hour (var)
.... rotating host (1950–54)
Eddie Cantor Comedy Theatre (com)
.... host (1954–55)

Show business legend Eddie Cantor was a familiar—if somewhat old fashioned—performer on television in the 1950s. A slender man with a frantic manner and bulging ("banjo") eyes, he was born and raised in vaudeville, and by the time TV came along his slapstick jokes and endless renditions of old chestnuts like "If You Knew Susie," "Makin' Whoopee," and "You'd Be Surprised" (which he had first recorded in 1919) seemed just a little out of date.

Still, TV provided a warm welcome and a successful coda to his long career, which had included vaudeville in the 1910s, hit Broadway shows in the 1920s, movies in the 1930s, and a hugely successful radio career in the 1930s and '40s. He was one of the big name stars of TV's *Colgate Comedy Hour* and had his own syndicated comedy-variety series in 1954.

Cantor's tenure on the *Colgate* show was temporarily interrupted by a heart attack following a telecast in 1952, after which declining health forced the old trooper to gradually slow down. He was seen after 1955 mostly on tribute shows and specials. Ida, his beloved wife of 48 years, and the subject of many of his gags and of his most famous song ("Ida, sweet as Apple Cider"), passed away in 1962. Eddie himself followed two years later.

Cantor wrote several autobiographies, among them *Take My Life* (1957), *The Way I See It* (1959), and *As I Remember Them* (1962).

CANTOR, NATE—
The Robbins Nest (var) ...... regular (1950)

CAPOSELLA, FRED—sportscaster
Sportsreel (sport) ... commentator (1954–55)

CAPP, AL—host, cartoonist
b: Sep 28, 1909, New Haven, Conn. d: Nov 5, 1979

Anyone Can Win (quiz) ... moderator (1953)
What's the Story? (quiz) .. moderator (1953)

Cartoonist famous for "Li'l Abner" and "Fearless Fosdick," and for his conservative political opinions. He turned up periodically over the years on TV talk shows and briefly hosted his own 90-minute syndicated show in 1968.

CAPPY, TED, DANCERS—
The Guy Mitchell Show (var)
.... regulars (1957–58)

CARA, IRENE—black actress, singer
b: Mar 18, 1959, The Bronx, N.Y.

Roots: The Next Generations (drama)
.... Bertha Palmer Haley (1979)

CARBONE, ANTHONY—actor
Rich Man, Poor Man—Book I (drama)
.... Lou Martin (1976)

CARD, KATHRYN—actress
b: 1893 d: 1964

The Charlie Farrell Show (com)
.... Mrs. Papernow (1956)

CARDI, PAT—actor
It's About Time (com) ...... Breer (1966–67)

CARERE, CHRISTINE—actress
b: 1930, France

Blue Light (drama)
.... Suzanne Duchard (1966)

CAREY, MACDONALD—actor
b: Mar 15, 1913, Sioux City, Iowa

Dr. Christian (drama)
.... Dr. Mark Christian (1956)
Lock Up (drama)
.... Herbert L. Maris (1959–61)
Roots (drama)........ Squire James (1977)

Emmy Awards: Best Actor in a Daytime Drama, for *Days of Our Lives* (1974, 1975)

Amiable, mild-mannered Macdonald Carey has been a fixture in dramas since the late 1930s, first in radio, then movies, and for the last 30-plus years on TV. Born the son of a judge, his early ambition was

147

to become a doctor—which is ironic since he has played doctors for much of his acting career. Despite the Depression, he managed to get a good education, including a master's degree in drama, then broke into radio in the late 1930s. Roles in popular shows like *First Nighter* and *Stella Dallas* did not bring major fame, so Carey tried Broadway *(Lady in the Dark)* and then moved to Hollywood, where he became a contract player for Paramount. He has appeared in more than 50 films since 1940's *Dr. Broadway,* but none could be called classics. (His own favorite is *The Lawless,* a 1950 film about bigotry against Mexican-American fruit pickers in Southern California.)

Carey worked steadily in television, beginning with a *Studio One* episode in 1950 and continuing through scores of appearances on drama series of the 1950s through the '80s. Among these were multiple episodes of *Ford Theatre, Climax, The U.S. Steel Hour, Amos Burke, Run for Your Life,* and *Alfred Hitchcock Presents.* He had two syndicated series of his own in the 1950s, *Dr. Christian* and *Lock Up,* but neither was a major hit, so in 1965 he agreed to headline a new daytime soap opera. His role as Dr. Tom Horton, the kindly patriarch on *Days of Our Lives,* will no doubt go down as his most famous, lasting more than 20 years. It is Carey who intones one of daytime's most famous lines at the beginning of each episode: "Like sands through the hourglass, so are the days of our lives."

Since *Days* began Carey has continued to make periodic appearances in TV movies, miniseries (including *Roots*), and episodes of prime time shows—the latter ranging from *Fantasy Island* to *Buck Rogers in the 25th Century.* He has also found time to write a book of poetry, *A Day in the Life.*

CAREY, MICHELE—actress

A Man Called Sloane (drama)
.... Effie (voice) (1979–80)

CAREY, OLIVE—actress
b: c. 1896

Mr. Adams and Eve (com) .. Elsie (1957–58)
Lock Up (drama) .... Casey (1959–61)

The widow of screen star Harry Carey, and no relation to Macdonald. A onetime silent movie actress, she returned to the screen and also began a TV career playing character parts following the death of her husband in 1947. She was also known as Olive Golden and Olive Deering.

CAREY, PHILIP—actor
b: Jul 15, 1925, Hackensack, N.J.

Tales of the 77th Bengal Lancers (adv)
.... Lt. Michael Rhodes (1956–57)
Philip Marlowe (drama)
.... Philip Marlowe (1959–60)
Laredo (wes)
.... Capt. Edward Parmalee (1965–67)
Untamed World (doc) ... narrator (1968–75)

"Rugged" and "virile" seem to be the words that pop up most often in descriptions of this strapping (6'4") actor, who was a standby in action films and TV series from the early 1950s on. After seeing real-life combat in World War II as a marine, he had his first major film role opposite John Wayne in the war movie *Operation Pacific* in 1951. He later appeared in many action-oriented TV shows of the 1950s and '60s, including his own series *Tales of the 77th Bengal Lancers* and *Philip Marlowe.* In addition, he was seen in numerous episodes of *Ford Theatre* from 1953–57 and in *Cheyenne* and *The Virginian* and other westerns during the 1960s.

In 1979, his hard-riding days over, he assumed the somewhat more sedate role of Texas tycoon Asa Buchanan on the daytime serial *One Life to Live.*

CAREY, RON—actor
b: Dec 11, 1935, Newark, N.J.

The Melba Moore-Clifton Davis Show (var)
.... regular (1972)
The Corner Bar (com)
.... Donald Hooten (1973)
The Montefuscos (com)
.... Frank Montefusco (1975)
Barney Miller (com)
.... Officer Carl Levitt (1976–82)

One of the running gags on *Barney Miller* was pint-sized patrolman Levitt who wanted to become a detective but was "too short." Actually, Ron Carey was not *that* short (he's 5'7"), but his ebullient, little-guy humor made him practically a mascot for the detectives in the squad room.

Carey began as a stand-up (so they could see him?) comic in the 1960s, doing clubs, commercials, and spots on talk shows such as *The Tonight Show,* Merv Griffin, and Mike Douglas. After a stint on the Melba Moore-Clifton Davis summer variety show in 1972, he had roles in two short-lived comedies before his big break on *Barney Miller* in 1976. Little guys sometimes win out in the end, too; on the last episode of that series, eager patrolman Levitt was finally promoted to sergeant.

CARHART, MRS. GEORGIANA—panelist

Life Begins at Eighty (talk)
.... panelist (1950–56)

CARIDI, CARMINE—actor

Phyllis (com)........ Dan Valenti (1976–77)
Fame (drama).... Angelo Martelli (1982–83)

CARL, JANN—newscaster

Eye on Hollywood (pub aff).. host (1985–86)

CARLE, FRANKIE—pianist, orch. leader
b: Mar 25, 1903, Providence, R.I.

The Golden Touch of Frankie Carle (music)
.... host (1956)

CARLETON, CLAIRE—actress
b: 1913, New York City, N.Y. d: Dec 11, 1979

The Mickey Rooney Show (com)
.... Mrs. Mulligan (1954–55)
Cimarron City (wes).. Alice Purdy (1958–59)

CARLIN, GEORGE—comedian
b: May 12, 1937, The Bronx, N.Y.

The Kraft Summer Music Hall (var)
.... regular (1966)
That Girl (com) .... George Lester (1966–67)
Away We Go (var).......... regular (1967)
Tony Orlando and Dawn (var)
.... regular (1976)

George Carlin started as a clean-cut young comic doing Kennedy impressions in the early 1960s but attracted little notice until he suddenly changed his entire approach —to sex, drugs, long hair, and dirty jeans.

The looser image worked ("I discovered a much better character for me—myself," he claims) and Carlin—minus the dirty words —was soon doing guest shots on variety and talk shows. Besides appearing as a regular on a couple of summer shows in 1966 and 1967, he had the regular role of Marlo Thomas's agent on *That Girl* for a season.

One of his more notable later appearances was as host of the very first episode of *NBC's Saturday Night Live,* in October 1975. Why him? Quoth producer Lorne Michaels: "I like George Carlin first and foremost because he's punctual. Most comedians are very disorganized and not willing to spend their time filling out all the forms you need to fill out in order to host a major television show. George's application, however, was very neat and his writing was very legible. Also, George has been around enough to know that it's NBC policy to go with the comedian with the earliest postmark."

CARLIN, LYNN—actress
b: Jan 31, 1930, Los Angeles, Calif.

James at 15 (drama)
.... Mrs. Joan Hunter (1977–78)

CARLISLE, KEVIN, DANCERS—

What's It All About, World? (var)
.... regular (1969)

Emmy Award: Best Choreography, for *The Third Barry Manilow Special* (1979)

CARLISLE, KITTY—panelist
b: Sep 3, 1914, New Orleans, La.

I've Got a Secret (quiz) .. panelist (1952–53)
What's Going On? (quiz).... panelist (1954)
To Tell the Truth (quiz).. panelist (1956–67)
To Tell the Truth (quiz).. panelist (1969–77)

Kitty Carlisle is best known to television viewers for her long run as one of the witty and urbane panelists on *To Tell the Truth,* but she had some other rather different careers as well. In her twenties she was an opera singer, attracting notice in several Hollywood musicals of 1934–35. Later she concentrated on stage appearances. She had virtually faded from view until TV panel shows in the '50s brought her back to prominence. After many years on camera, she retired in the mid-1970s and became chairman of the New York State Council on the Arts.

Kitty is the widow of playwright Moss Hart.

CARLON, FRAN—actress

The Hamptons (drama) . . . . Ada (1983)

CARLSON, KAREN—actress

Here Come the Brides (com)
. . . . one of the brides (1968–70)
American Dream (drama)
. . . . Mrs. Donna Novak (1981)
Two Marriages (drama)
. . . . Ann Daley (1983–84)

The wife of actor David Soul, whom she met during the filming of *Here Come the Brides.*

CARLSON, LINDA—actress

b: May 12, 1945, Knoxville, Tenn. r: Sioux Falls, S.D.

Westside Medical (drama)
. . . . Dr. Janet Cottrell (1977)
Kaz (drama) . . . . . Katie McKenna (1978–79)
Newhart (com) . . . . Bev Dutton (1984–)

CARLSON, RICHARD—actor, writer, director

b: Apr 29, 1912, Albert Lea, Minn. d: Nov 25, 1977

I Led Three Lives (drama)
. . . . Herbert Philbrick (1953–56)
Mackenzie's Raiders (wes)
. . . . . Col. Ranald S. Mackenzie (1958–59)

This soft-spoken, intelligent-looking young man—a Phi Beta Kappa graduate of Minnesota University—was brought to Hollywood as a writer in 1938 by David O. Selznick. When Selznick saw the young man, he put him in front of the cameras instead, beginning a long screen career for Carlson in minor films of the late 1930s to the '50s.

Carlson became very active in television in the 1950s, appearing on many of the leading playhouse series, including *Studio One, Schlitz Playhouse of Stars,* and *Climax.* He also starred in two syndicated series of his own, the very popular *I Led Three Lives* (hunting Communists under

our noses) and *Mackenzie's Raiders.* He was active offscreen as well, writing short stories for national magazines and writing or directing numerous TV episodes and several feature films. Carlson continued to appear in dramas in the 1960s and early '70s (*Perry Mason, The Virginian, Owen Marshall,* etc.), remaining semiactive until shortly before his death in 1977.

CARLYLE, RICHARD—actor

Crime Photographer (drama) . . Casey (1951)

CARMEL, ROGER C.—actor

b: 1932, Brooklyn, N.Y. d: Nov 11, 1986

The Mothers-in-Law (com)
. . . . Roger Buell (1967–68)
Fitz and Bones (com)
. . . . Lawrence Brody (1981)

CARMEN, JULIE—actress

b: Apr 4, 1954, Millburn, N.J.*

Condo (com) . . . . Linda Rodriguez (1983)
Falcon Crest (drama)
. . . . Sofia Stavros (1986–)

CARMICHAEL, HOAGY—songwriter, actor

b: Nov 22, 1899, Bloomington, Ind. d: Dec 27, 1981

Saturday Night Revue (var) . . . . . host (1953)
Laramie (wes) . . . . Jonesy (1959–60)

Hoagland Howard Carmichael will no doubt be longest remembered for writing some of the most popular and enduring songs of the twentieth century, among them "Georgia on My Mind," "In the Still of the Night," "The Nearness of You," and "In the Cool, Cool, Cool of the Evening." Oh, and a little number written one sentimental evening in 1927 while he was visiting his alma mater in Indiana, a song which may well be the most widely recorded tune ever written—"Star Dust."

As if that wasn't enough, Hoagy branched into acting in the 1940s and to everyone's surprise proved an engaging supporting player. His twinkle and lopsided grin brightened many a movie. He appeared in a few TV dramatic productions in the 1950s, but he is known to TV

*Some sources give Mt. Vernon, N.Y.

viewers primarily as the easygoing ranch hand Jonesy during the first season of *Laramie.* Later he appeared in a few other series, including a couple of episodes of *Burke's Law,* and he provided one of the voices for an episode of *The Flintstones* called "The Hit Song Writers."

His autobiographies are *The Stardust Road* (1946) and *Sometimes I Wonder* (with Stephen Longstreet, 1965).

CARMICHAEL, RALPH—orchestra leader
b: May 27, 1927, Quincy, Ill.

The Roy Rogers & Dale Evans Show (var)
.... orch. leader (1962)
The King Family Show (var)
.... orch. leader (1969)

CARNE, JUDY—actress
b: Apr 27, 1939, Northhampton, England

Fair Exchange (com)
.... Heather Finch (1962–63)
Baileys of Balboa (com)
.... Barbara Wyntoon (1964–65)
Love on a Rooftop (com)
.... Julie Willis (1966–67)
Rowan & Martin's Laugh-In (var)
.... regular (1968–70)
Kraft Music Hall Presents Sandler & Young (var)....................... regular (1969)

There is a notion out there that the cast of *Laugh-In* was made up entirely of bright young comics who were "discovered" on the show and who later went on to show business fame. Wrong. Exhibit #1: Judy Carne, who costarred in no fewer than three different situation comedies and appeared in other series episodes and several movies before she became the "Sock It to Me" girl.

Moreover, for Judy, *Laugh-In* was something less than a ticket to future stardom. She appeared in the Broadway production of *The Girl Friend* in 1970 and made a few more television appearances during the early and mid 1970s, including several on *Love, American Style.* She was seen in a 1975 episode of *Get Christie Love* that featured a virtual reunion of the *Laugh-In* cast. Then she dropped from sight.

CARNEY, ALAN—actor
b: Dec 22, 1911, Brooklyn, N.Y. d: May 2, 1973

Take It from Me (com) ... Herbie (1953–54)

CARNEY, ART—actor
b: Nov 4, 1918, Mount Vernon, N.Y.

The Morey Amsterdam Show (var)
.... regular (1948–50)
Cavalcade of Stars (var).. regular (1950–52)
Henry Morgan's Great Talent Hunt (var)
.... regular (1951)
The Jackie Gleason Show (var)
.... regular (1951–55)
The Honeymooners (series) (com)
.... Ed Norton (1955–56)
The Jackie Gleason Show (var)
.... regular (1956–57)
The Jackie Gleason Show (var)
.... regular (1966–70)
Lanigan's Rabbi (police)
.... Chief Paul Lanigan (1977)

Emmy Awards: Best Supporting Actor, for *The Jackie Gleason Show* (1953, 1954) and for *The Honeymooners* (1955); Best Individual Achievement, for performances on *The Jackie Gleason Show* (1967, 1968); Best Supporting Actor in a Special, for *Terrible Joe Moran* (1984)

Friendly, affable Art Carney hasn't given an interview in 30 years in which he hasn't been asked about Jackie Gleason and *The Honeymooners.* Constant references to his famous costar don't seem to bother him, though. Unlike Gleason, the self-proclaimed "Great One," Carney hides his many Emmy Awards (he has six to Gleason's none) in a closet and just plays the regular guy. His incredible range of achievements speak for themselves. As Alfred Lunt once remarked after seeing him in a *Kraft Theatre* drama: "There is practically nothing this man can't do."

As a kid Art did impressions, specializing in the famous political figures of the day. However, his first break (at age 19) was as a singer with the Horace Heidt Orchestra. He toured with the band, made a few records with them (including "Piggy Wiggy Woo"), and even had a small part in Heidt's 1941 film *Pot o' Gold*—Art's first screen appearance. He also did some radio work on Heidt's show and on *The March of Time*—for the latter doing straight impersonations of politicians in the news (his specialty was F.D.R.).

Then World War II intervened and Art was drafted. He suffered a leg wound during the Normandy invasion, which left him with a slight limp thereafter. Emerging from the service, he picked up his radio career and worked on a number of shows; he was with Morey Amersterdam in 1948 when Amsterdam's show, set at the Golden Goose Café, moved to CBS-TV. Art played Charlie the doorman, and his laid-back style caught the eye of Jackie Gleason, who signed him for his new DuMont variety series, *Cavalcade of Stars*. In the very first live "Honeymooners" sketch on *Cavalcade*, Art played a neighborhood cop who is hit in the face with a pie Alice intended for Ralph. Thereafter, Art was Ed Norton, the sewer worker, Ralph's loyal if not-too-bright sidekick through thick and thin.

Ed Norton was unquestionably Art's most famous character, one he continued to play for years on various Gleason shows. But it was by no means his only role. Throughout the 1950s the versatile comic made numerous appearances outside the Gleason show, on prestige showcases such as *Studio One*, *Kraft Theatre*, and *Playhouse 90*. After leaving Gleason for a time in 1957 he starred in some highly popular specials, including TV productions of *Peter and the Wolf* and *Harvey* in 1958 and *Our Town* in 1959. He was the villainous "Archer" on *Batman* and an unemployed department store Santa Claus with a wondrous bag of gifts on a classic Christmas episode of *The Twilight Zone*. He also began a Broadway career, during which he originated the role of Felix Unger (opposite Walter Matthau's Oscar Madison) in the Neil Simon stage hit *The Odd Couple* (1965).

Art returned to movies in the mid-1960s and scored one of his greatest individual triumphs with the 1974 film *Harry and Tonto*, for which he won an Academy Award. He began turning up more often on TV in the mid-1970s and played his only non-Gleason regular series role as the small town police chief in *Lanigan's Rabbi* in 1977. His projects since then have consisted mostly of specials (including several *Honeymooners* reunions) and TV movies, including a 1985 film with Gleason called *Izzy and Moe*.

Despite the Emmies, the Oscar, and many other awards filling his closet, Art remains a self-effacing man. He has said of his most famous character, "Ed is the

kind of person even dogs and cats like." That could be said of Art Carney as well.

CARNEY, BARBARA—actress

Lanigan's Rabbi (police)
.... Bobbie Whittaker (1977)

Daughter of Art Carney.

CARNEY, GRACE—actress

Rocky King, Inside Detective (police)
.... Mabel King (1950–54)

CARON, LESLIE—actress, dancer
b: Jul 1, 1931, Paris, France

Master of the Game (drama)
.... Solange (1984)

This famous movie star has done very little television work.

CARPENTER, KEN—announcer
b: c. 1900, Avon, Ill. d: Oct 16, 1984

Lux Video Theatre (drama)
.... announcer (1950–57)

CARPENTER, THELMA—black actress
b: Jan 15, 1922, Brooklyn, N.Y.

Barefoot in the Park (com)
.... Mabel Bates (1970–71)

CARPENTERS, THE—vocal duo
Karen Carpenter: b: Mar 2, 1950, New Haven, Conn. d: Feb 4, 1983
Richard Carpenter: b: Oct 15, 1946, New Haven, Conn.

Make Your Own Kind of Music (var)
.... regulars (1971)

This popular brother and sister recording act, which had many hit records in the early 1970s, headlined their own summer variety show in 1971 when they were at the peak of their success. Karen died tragically in 1983, of anorexia.

CARR, BETTY ANN—actress
b: c. 1947, r: Joplin, Mo.

Cade's County (police)
.... Betty Ann Sundown (1971–72)

CARR, CLARK—

The Sonny and Cher Comedy Hour (var)
.... regular (1971–72)

CARR, DARLEEN—actress
b: 1950, Chicago, Ill.

The John Forsythe Show (com)
.... Kathy (1965–66)
Dean Martin Presents the Golddiggers (var)
.... regular (1969)
The Smith Family (drama)
.... Cindy Smith (1971–72)
Once an Eagle (drama)
...... Tommy Caldwell Damon (1976–77)
The Oregon Trail (wes)
.... Margaret Devlin (1977)
Miss Winslow and Son (com)
.... Susan Winslow (1979)
Bret Maverick (wes)
.... Mary Lou Springer (1981–82)

A perky actress who has had a busy career since the mid-1960s, although her one starring vehicle—*Miss Winslow and Son*—was a flop. An innovative flop, though. The CBS comedy cast Darleen as a middle-class unwed mother of a baby boy who had decided *not* to marry the child's father but rather to raise it by herself. TV comedy was not quite ready for that.

Miss Carr began her television career as a teenager in somewhat more conventional roles, first as a schoolgirl on *The John Forsythe Show* and later as Henry Fonda's daughter on *The Smith Family*. She was also seen irregularly as Karl Malden's daughter on *The Streets of San Francisco* in the mid-1970s, and she made guest appearances on many other series as well. In the early 1980s she was the feisty editor of the local newspaper who gave James Garner grief (didn't everyone!) on *Bret Maverick*.

CARR, DIDI—actress

Sugar Time! (com)........ Diane (1977–78)

CARR, GERALDINE—actress
b: c. 1916 d: 1954

I Married Joan (com) ...... Mabel (1953–54)

CARR, LARRY—singer, pianist
b: 1914 d: Jan 7, 1987

Flight to Rhythm (music)..... regular (1949)

CARR, NANCY—singer

This Is Music (music)..... regular (1951–52)

CARR, PAUL—actor
b: New Orleans, La.

Scruples (drama)...... Pat O'Byrnne (1980)
Buck Rogers in the 25th Century (sci fi)
.... L. Devlin (1981)

CARR, VIKKI—singer
b: Jul 19, 1941*, El Paso, Texas r: Rosemead, Calif.

The Ray Anthony Show (var)
.... regular (1962)
The Ray Anthony Show (var)
.... regular (1968)

CARRADINE, DAVID—actor
b: Oct 8, 1936**, Hollywood, Calif.

Shane (wes) .... Shane (1966)
Kung Fu (wes)
.... Kwai Chang Caine (1972–75)
North and South (drama)
.... Justin LaMotte (1985)

The moody, eccentric son of an equally eccentric father (John Carradine), David was television's reflection of the spaced out, hippy generation of the psychedelic '60s. A gaunt, sad-eyed young man, he spent much of his youth working as a laborer and experimenting with drugs before entering films, in minor parts, in the mid-1960s. He also did some television at about the same time, including one of the last *Alfred Hitchcock Presents* episodes (as a strangler). He won the starring role of the brooding gunfighter in the TV adaptation of the movie *Shane* in 1966, but the series proved short-lived and David went back to appearing in episodes of other series, including a number of times on *Ironside*.

Then in 1972 he was cast in the role that would make him famous. Again it was in character, inasmuch as the mystic Oriental philosophy of the fugitive Caine was not far from that of the actor who played him. Carradine's later roles were infrequent but similarly individual. Among other things, he played the title role in the western mini-

*Some sources give 1938 or 1942.
**Sources vary; either Oct. 8 or Dec. 8, and either 1936 or 1940.

series *Mr. Horn* in 1979, the role of Gaugin in *Gaugin the Savage* in 1980, and Justin in *North and South* in 1985.

CARRADINE, JOHN—actor
b: Feb 5, 1906, Greenwich Village, New York City, N.Y.

My Friend Irma (com)
.... Mr. Corday (1953–54)

Emmy Award: Best Performer in a Children's Program, for the special *Umbrella Jack* (1985)

The father of actors David, Keith, and Robert Carradine, and surely one of Hollywood's most colorful character actors. A man of gaunt, menacing appearance, with a deep, rich, Shakespearean voice to match, John was born of well-educated but unconventional parents and spent some years as a painter, sculptor, and drifter before working his way into films in the early 1930s. He soon became one of the busiest character actors Hollywood has ever known (more than 170 films in over 50 years), often playing psychopaths or mad doctors but in other roles as well. He has played Count Dracula at least three times on screen and has also been Bluebeard, Hitler's vicious General Heydrich, and Abraham Lincoln.

Carradine began doing television around 1950 and has been just as prolific there. During the medium's first 30 years he was seen constantly in dramas of all kinds —for example *Lights Out, Climax,* and *Suspicion* in the 1950s; *Thriller, Bonanza,* and *The Twilight Zone* (as a monk who captures the Devil himself) in the 1960s; and on *Ironside* and son David's *Kung Fu* in the 1970s. Not all of his roles have been horrific. His only regular role was that of an eccentric actor-friend on *My Friend Irma,* and he also lent his lush tones to a number of children's shows, including *Beany and Cecil* and *The Misunderstood Monsters.*

CARRADINE, KEITH—actor, singer
b: Aug 8, 1949, San Mateo, Calif.

Chiefs (drama) ... Foxy Funderburke (1983)

Son of John Carradine. He has been seldom seen on television except for occasional TV movies (including the pilot for *Kung Fu,* as a younger Caine) and mini-series (including *Chiefs*).

CARRADINE, ROBERT—actor
b: Mar 24, 1954, Los Angeles, Calif.

The Cowboys (wes) .... Slim (1974)

Son of John Carradine, also not often seen on television.

CARRAHER, HARLEN—juvenile actor
b: c. 1960

The Ghost and Mrs. Muir (com)
.... Jonathan Muir (1968–70)

CARRELL, LORI—actress

The Four Seasons (com)
.... Sharon Hogan (1984)

CARRERA, BARBARA—actress
b: c. 1945, Managua, Nicaragua

Centennial (drama) .. Clay Basket (1978–79)
Masada (drama) .... Sheva (1981)
Dallas (drama) .... Angelica Nero (1985–   )

CARREY, JIM—actor
b: Jan 17, 1962, Jacksons Point, Ontario, Canada

The Duck Factory (com)
.... Skip Tarkenton (1984)

CARRI, ANNA—actress

Room for One More (com)
.... Mary Rose (1962)

CARRICART, ROBERT—actor
b: c. 1917, Bordeaux, France

T.H.E. Cat (adv) .... Pepe (1966–67)

CARRILLO, LEO—actor
b: Aug 6, 1881*, Los Angeles, Calif. d: Sep 10, 1961

The Cisco Kid (wes) ...... Pancho (1950–56)

Plump, cheerful Pancho, the loyal Latin sidekick of the Cisco Kid, was a favorite comic character with children in the '50s. His fractured English was a trademark ("Ceesco? Less went! Ze shereef he ees get-

*Some sources give 1880.

154

ting closer!"). Though he mostly provided comic relief, he was also handy with a bull-whip when the need arose.

Carrillo's most famous role came late in life—he was in his seventies when the series was filmed—but the hard riding and fights didn't seem to bother him. Born to one of California's oldest Spanish families and descended from the state's first governor, he first appeared onstage doing dialect comedy in the 1910s and launched a long and prosperous movie career in the late 1920s.

CARROLL, BEESON—actor

Palmerstown, U.S.A. (drama)
.... W. D. Hall (1980–81)

CARROLL, BOB—singer, actor
b: June 18, 1918

Stage Two Revue (var) ...... regular (1950)
Songs at Twilight (music) .... host (1951)
Judge for Yourself (quiz) .... vocalist (1954)
The Stranger (drama)
.... the stranger (1954–55)

CARROLL, DAVID-JAMES—actor

Ball Four (com) .... Bill Westlake (1976)

CARROLL, DIAHANN—black actress, singer
b: Jul 17, 1935, The Bronx, N.Y.

Julia (com)........... Julia Baker (1968–71)
The Diahann Carroll Show (var)
.... hostess (1976)
Dynasty (drama)
.... Dominique Deveraux (1984–)

Glamorous actress Diahann Carroll is best known as the star of the comedy *Julia*—a pioneering show in raising the visibility of blacks on TV in the late 1960s—but she has been active in several other areas as well. The daughter of a New York City subway conductor, she showed an early aptitude for music and studied at the city's High School of Music and Art. She was a model in her teenage years, and a singer as well; her first TV exposure was on the Dennis James talent show *Chance of a Lifetime* in the early 1950s, where she won first place. Her prize was a week's engagement at the Latin Quarter nightclub, which was ex-

tended to a month. This led to further club work and to the leading role in the Broadway musical *House of Flowers* in 1954. Movies followed *(Carmen Jones, Porgy and Bess)* as well as television appearances, the latter including a dramatic role on *Naked City* in 1962 that won her an Emmy nomination.

Following the success of *Julia*, Diahann was seen only occasionally in specials and TV movies, until *Dynasty* lured her back to series TV in 1984 as the stylish and scheming businesswoman Dominique Deveraux.

In private life, one of the actress's key interests is helping teenagers in trouble (she has a degree in child psychology, which she earned as a "backup career" in case acting didn't work out). She often visits Los Angeles–area schools and detention homes to counsel young people. She recently married singer Vic Damone. Her autobiography: *Diahann!* (with Ross Firestone, 1986).

CARROLL, EDDIE—

Don Knotts Show (var) ... regular (1970–71)

CARROLL, HELENA—actress

Backstairs at the White House (drama)
.... Annie (1979)

CARROLL, JANET—actress

Double Dare (police)
.... Lt. Samantha Warner (1985)

CARROLL, JEAN—comedienne

Take It from Me (com) ..... wife (1953–54)

CARROLL, JIMMY—singer, pianist
b: Dec 13, 1913, New York City, N.Y. d: 1972

The Most Important People (var)
.... cohost (1950–51)
Frankie Laine Time (var)
.... orch. leader (1955)

CARROLL, LEO G.—actor
b: 1892, Weedon, Northants, England d: Oct 16, 1972

Topper (com) ..... Cosmo Topper (1953–55)
Going My Way (com)
.... Father Fitzgibbon (1962–63)
The Man From U.N.C.L.E. (drama)
.... Mr. Alexander Waverly (1964–68)

The Girl From U.N.C.L.E. (drama)
.... Alexander Waverly (1966–67)

Leo G. Carroll, one of television's (and movies') favorite Englishmen, gained his greatest fame when he was in his sixties and seventies. He was originally a stage actor, making his London debut in 1911 and appearing in many New York productions of the 1920s and '30s. He began appearing in movies in 1934 and is remembered as the dignified, aloof Britisher in quite a few films, including several Hitchcock classics (*Rebecca, Suspicion, Spellbound, North by Northwest,* etc.).

Leo began doing occasional TV work around 1950 and first became famous in the CBS series *Topper,* as the prim and proper banker Cosmo G. Topper whom the ghostly Kerbys were always trying to loosen up. More guest appearances followed, and also the one-season series *Going My Way.* Then, at age 72, he delighted a whole new generation as the dapper boss of U.N.C.L.E. on both *The Man From U.N.C.L.E.* and *The Girl From U.N.C.L.E..* His last recorded appearance was in 1970 on an episode of *Ironside.*

CARROLL, NANCY—actress
b: Nov 19, 1904*, New York City, N.Y. d: Aug 6, 1965

The Aldrich Family (com)
.... Mrs. Alice Aldrich (1950–51)

A movie beauty of the 1930s who did little television. Biography: *The Films of Nancy Carroll,* by Paul M. Nemcek (1969).

CARROLL, PAT—actress
b: May 5, 1927, Shreveport, La. r: Los Angeles, Calif.

The Red Buttons Show (var)
.... regular (1952–53)
Saturday Night Revue (var) .. regular (1954)
Caesar's Hour (var)
.... Alice Brewster (1956–57)
Masquerade Party (quiz).... panelist (1958)
Keep Talking (quiz) ...... regular (1958–60)
You're in the Picture (quiz).. panelist (1961)
The Danny Thomas Show (com)
.... Bunny Halper (1961–64)
Getting Together (com)
.... Rita Simon (1971–72)

*Some sources give 1905 or 1906.

Busting Loose (com)
.... Pearl Markowitz (1977)
The Ted Knight Show (com)
.... Hope Stinson (1986)

Emmy Award: Best Supporting Actress, for *Caesar's Hour* (1956)

This pert, ash-blonde comedienne was seen quite a bit on live, New York–originated variety and panel shows of the 1950s, including stints as Red Buttons' girlfriend and Howard Morris's wife, Alice (on *Caesar's Hour*).

Pat got her start as a child performer in local productions, then became a stage and nightclub performer after she graduated from college in 1947. She also spent some time touring with U.S. Army productions as a "civilian actress technician" in the late 1940s. During the summers from 1951–53 she starred at a famous launching pad for comic talent—the Tamiment resort in Pennsylvania (where Sid Caesar, Imogene Coca, and Dick Shawn got their starts)—while simultaneously beginning her career on early television. In later years she played a succession of wives and landladies in series of the 1960s and '70s.

CARROLL, RITA—hostess

The Most Important People (var)
.... cohost (1950–51)

Wife of pianist Jimmy Carroll, with whom she appeared on her one series.

CARROLL, VICTORIA—actress

Alice (com) .... Marie Massey (1978–80)
Small & Frye (com)
.... Vicki, the waitress (1983)

CARSON, JACK—comedian
b: Oct 27, 1910, Carmen, Manitoba, Canada d: Jan 2, 1963

All Star Revue (var)
.... alternating host (1950–52)
The U.S. Royal Showcase (var).. host (1952)

Although he is not now well-remembered, this chubby, wisecracking comedian was popular on radio and in movies during the 1940s and moved easily into television in the 1950s as one of its early stars. His most popular persona was that of the loud-mouthed, not-too-bright character who always gets shown up in the end, but he also essayed more serious roles, including many on *The U.S. Steel Hour.* His other series appearances included *Alcoa Theatre, Playhouse 90,* and *The Twilight Zone* (as a used-car dealer who inexplicably finds himself blurting out the truth!).

When asked in the mid-1940s what he would like to be doing at age 60, Carson cracked "breathing." Though he worked steadily until the end of his days, he unfortunately missed this goal. He died of cancer at age 52.

CARSON, JEAN—actress
b: 1925, Charleston, W. Va.

The Betty Hutton Show (com)
.... Rosemary (1959–60)

Tall, blonde American actress, not to be confused (although she often is) with British comedienne Jeannie Carson.

CARSON, JEANNIE—comedienne, actress
b: May 23, 1928, Yorkshire, England

Hey Jeannie (com)
.... Jeannie MacLennan (1956–57)

A petite British comedienne who began in London stage productions in the late 1940s and was brought to America in 1954 to appear in producer Max Liebman's TV "Spectaculars." Considered a fresh new comedy discovery, she soon won her own starring vehicle, *Hey Jeannie,* in which she played a Scottish lass just arrived in the U.S. and befuddled by its customs. However the series fizzled, and so did Miss Carson's career. Later she made a few films (*I Married a Monster from Outer Space*) and appeared in road productions of some musical plays.

CARSON, JOHNNY—host, comedian
b: Oct 23, 1925, Corning, Iowa r: Norfolk, Neb.

Earn Your Vacation (quiz) .... emcee (1954)
The Johnny Carson Show (var)
.... host (1955–56)
The Tonight Show Starring Johnny Carson (talk) .... host (1962–)

Emmy Awards: Special Award for Individual Achievement, for *The Tonight Show* (1976, 1977, 1978, 1979)

Here is one superstar who belongs entirely to television; practically his entire career has been spent in the TV medium, and it has made him both wealthy and something of an American institution. Johnny has been host of *The Tonight Show* so long that many viewers cannot imagine anyone else delivering their bedtime monologue. His show has been one of NBC's most reliable hits through good times and lean years for the network. When NBC's prime time schedule finally started to gain audience in the 1980s, network head Grant Tinker remarked, "It's nice to see the rest of the network getting in step with Johnny."

The career of the boyish-looking kid from the Midwest is fairly familiar, since he has joked about it for years on *The Tonight Show.* He began doing a magic act in his Nebraska hometown at the age of 14, billed as "The Great Carsoni." Norfolk was a bit limiting for his talents, however, and after World War II service in the navy (where, as an ensign, he entertained the enlisted men) he had a series of jobs in local radio and TV: KFAB, Lincoln, Nebraska; WOW and WOW-TV in Omaha; and then KNXT-TV in Los Angeles, in 1950. While at the latter station he started his own sketch comedy show, *Carson's Cellar* (1951–53), which attracted the attention of Hollywood. He then became a staff writer for Red Skelton's network variety show and had an early break during a live 1954 telecast when Skelton was injured backstage and Johnny was pushed in front of the cameras (did he have to be pushed?) to take his place. It was probably Johnny's first monologue before a network audience.

Recognized as an up-and-coming young comic, Johnny was tried in various formats—on the prime time summer quiz show *Earn Your Vacation* in 1954, in his own variety show, which began in daytime in early 1955 and moved to prime time for the 1955–56 season; and then in the daytime game show *Who Do You Trust?* from 1957–62 (where, in 1958, he was joined for the first time by his longtime sidekick Ed McMahon). Johnny also tried a few acting roles, once on *Play-*

house 90 in 1957, twice on *The U.S. Steel Hour* in 1960, and once in a pilot for a prime time series called *Johnny Come Lately* (1960)—which didn't make it to the regular schedule.

In 1958 Johnny was asked to sit in for Jack Paar on *The Tonight Show*. Four years later, when Paar left the show for good, Johnny was NBC's choice to become his replacement. He took a while to catch on; at first the show declined from Paar's rating levels. But soon audiences warmed to Carson's friendly, quick-witted style and that boyish grin that could make even slightly "blue" jokes seem all right. He became a media phenomenon, making headlines when he got into one of his periodic contractual spats with NBC and when a minor novelty singer named Tiny Tim was married on his show (in 1969).

By the late 1970s the industry had begun to recognize Johnny's incredible staying power, and awards began to pile up, including four Emmys in a row (after a number of earlier nominations). His annual anniversary specials, consisting of clips from earlier shows, first appeared in prime time in 1979, and a 1982 prime time special *Johnny Goes Home* (to Nebraska) was a ratings hit.

Besides his long and famous run on *The Tonight Show*, Carson has turned up elsewhere as TV's most famous emcee. He was the host of the Academy Awards ceremonies repeatedly after 1979 (even though he has otherwise had little to do with the movie industry), and he has made many personal appearances in Las Vegas and Atlantic City. Once in a while he would pop up unexpectedly on another series; for example, as a suspicious conductor eyeing Don Adams on a 1965 episode of *Get Smart*. He founded his own production company, Carson Productions, which miraculously managed to sell quite a few of its pilots to a grateful NBC (one of these, *TV's Bloopers and Practical Jokes*, became a hit).

In the 1980s Johnny was said to be the highest-paid performer in the history of TV, making a reported $5 million a year for *The Tonight Show* alone. The show, which had been declining in ratings, began to pick up again and after two decades was still the undisputed late-night champ. Did Carson foresee such a run? "I thought it might last five or six years," he recently commented. "No one could have predicted . . ."

CARSON, KEN—singer
b: Nov 14, 1914, Coalgate, Okla.

The Garry Moore Show (var)
.... regular (1950–51)

CARSON, MINDY—singer
b: July 16, 1927, New York City, N.Y.

Ford Star Revue (var) .... regular (1951)
Club Embassy (var) ..... vocalist (1952–53)

CARTER FAMILY, WITH MOTHER MAYBELLE—
Mother Maybelle Carter: b: May 10, 1909, Nickelsville, Va. d: Oct 23, 1978

The Johnny Cash Show (var)
.... regulars (1969–71)

This legendary family of country singers was one of the first major stars of commercial country music in the late 1920s and '30s. The original group consisted of A. P. and Sara Carter and A. P.'s sister-in-law Maybelle. In the early television era the group was still performing on country music shows, by then composed of Maybelle and her daughters June, Helen, and Anita.

The Carter Family disbanded in the late 1950s but was reunited a decade later to become regulars on the prime time variety show hosted by June's husband, Johnny Cash. One wonders how many TV viewers realized what a historic moment it was when "Mother" Maybelle, one of the authentic pioneers of country music, once again played her famous "Wildwood Flower" on the autoharp—for her largest audience ever.

CARTER, CONLAN—actor
b: 1936, Arkansas

The Law and Mr. Jones (drama)
.... C. E. Carruthers (1960–62)
Combat (drama)............ Doc (1963–65)

CARTER, DIXIE—actress
b: May 25, 1939, McLemoresville, Tenn.

On Our Own (com).. April Baxter (1977–78)
Out of the Blue (com)... Aunt Marion (1979)

Filthy Rich (com)... Carlotta Beck (1982–83)
Diff'rent Strokes (com)
.... Maggie McKinney (1984–85)
Designing Women (com)
.... Julia Sugarbaker (1986–)

CARTER, GAYLORD, TRIO—

Sawyer Views Hollywood (var)
.... regulars (1951)

CARTER, JACK—comedian
b: Jun 24, 1923, Brooklyn, N.Y.

American Minstrels of 1949 (var)
.... emcee (1949)
Cavalcade of Stars (var)... emcee (1949–50)
The Jack Carter Show (var)
.... host (1950–51)

Jack Carter was one of television's first generation of "rising young comedians," but his time in the limelight was rather brief. He began appearing on early, live TV almost at the same time he was launching his career as a nightclub and stage comic in the late 1940s. He was one of the original rotating hosts of the *Texaco Star Theater* in the summer of 1948, before Milton Berle got the permanent assignment; had his own series of specials on the fledgling ABC network (called *Jack Carter and Company)* in early 1949; and was host of a short-lived minstrel show. An important break came in the summer of 1949, when he became host of Dumont's Saturday night *Cavalcade of Stars* (later the launching pad for Jackie Gleason's career). An obviously impressed NBC stole him away in early 1950 to host the first hour of its own Saturday night variety extravaganza, calling his segment *The Jack Carter Show* (later in the evening viewers got Sid Caesar in *Your Show of Shows*).

Carter was one of the slapstick, mugging, gag-a-minute comics who made early TV look like a vaudeville stage, and his appeal soon wore thin in the intimate medium. His series failed to sustain its initial popularity and was canceled at the end of the 1950–51 season. Thereafter Jack was a frequent guest on other variety and talk shows, including *Stage Show* in 1956, *The Tonight Show* in 1962, and a syndicated old-time vaudeville series in 1975. He has also appeared in supporting roles in numerous TV movies since the 1960s, including *Sex Sym-*

bol in 1974 and *Rainbow* (as George Jessel) in 1978.

CARTER, JOHN—actor
b: Nov 26, 1927, Center Ridge, Ark.

The Smith Family (drama)
.... Sgt. Ray Martin (1971–72)
Barnaby Jones (drama)
.... Lt. John Biddle (1974–80)
The Winds of War (drama)
.... Col. William Forrest (1983)
Falcon Crest (drama)
.... Max Hartman (1984–85)

CARTER, JUNE—singer
b: Jun 23, 1929, Maces Spring, Va.

Grand Ole Opry (music) .. regular (1955–56)
The Johnny Cash Show (var)
.... regular (1969–71)
The Johnny Cash Show (var)
.... regular (1976)

As a member of the famous Carter Family singers, June appeared both with her family and as a solo act in the 1950s and was on the *Grand Ole Opry* during its network run in 1955–56. It was backstage at the *Opry* in 1956 that she met young Johnny Cash, and by the 1960s she was performing with his musical entourage. She became far more important to Cash than just a backup singer, however; she helped the mercurial singer survive his dark, drug-filled days of the early 1960s, and the two were married in 1968. She has performed with him ever since, appearing regularly on both his 1969 and 1976 network variety shows. "I've gotten more pleasure out of John's career than I ever did from my own," she modestly admits.

CARTER, LYNDA—actress
b: Jul 24, 1951, Phoenix, Ariz.

Wonder Woman (adv)
   Yeoman Diana Prince (Wonder Woman) (1976–79)
Partners in Crime (drama)
.... Carole Stanwyck (1984)

Lynda Carter crashed show business rather young, singing with a rock band in the Southwest while she was in her mid-teens. A statuesque beauty, she began entering talent contests and in 1973 won the title of Miss World–U.S.A. Shortly thereafter she landed the television role that made her famous—Wonder Woman —first in a series of specials in 1975–76, and then in the series that ran for several years.

Lynda's subsequent TV career has been a bit uneven, consisting of specials, TV movies, and a failed 1984 detective series with Loni Anderson called *Partners in Crime.*

CARTER, NELL—black actress
b: Sep 13, 1948, Birmingham, Ala.

Lobo (com) . . . . . . Sgt. Hildy Jones (1980–81)
Gimme a Break (com)
. . . . Nell Harper (1981–)

Emmy Award: Best Performance in a Special, for *Ain't Misbehavin'* (1982)

Short (4'11") and portly actress Nell Carter started out to be a singer, in the jazz/blues shouter tradition. She sang in New York cabarets and off-Broadway revues in the early 1970s and scored her first major success in the hit Broadway musical *Ain't Misbehavin'* (based on the music of Fats Waller), for which she won a Tony Award in 1978.

Following some early appearances on *Today* and similar programs, Nell landed an acting role in the daytime soap opera *Ryan's Hope* in 1979 and another in the prime time comedy *Lobo* in 1980. The following year she began her role as the boisterous housekeeper in *Gimme a Break,* and stardom was assured.

CARTER, RALPH—black actor
b: May 30, 1961, New York City, N.Y.

Good Times (com)
. . . . Michael Evans (1974–79)

CARTER, RAY—orchestra leader
b: Nov 24, 1908, Chicago, Ill.

Arthur Murray Party (var)
. . . . orch. leader (1953–60)

CARTER, T. K.—black actor
b: Dec 14, 1956, Los Angeles, Calif.

Just Our Luck (com) . . . . Shabu (1983)
Punky Brewster (com)
. . . . Mike Fulton (1985–86)

CARTER, TERRY—black actor
b: Dec 16, Brooklyn, N.Y.

McCloud (police)
. . . . Sgt. Joe Broadhurst (1970–77)
Battlestar Galactica (sci fi)
. . . . Col. Tigh (1978–79)

Terry Carter, Dennis Weaver's longtime sidekick on *McCloud,* had been playing minor supporting roles on television for at least 15 years prior to *McCloud's* premiere. He can be seen in many episodes of the old *Phil Silvers Show* from the late 1950s as a black member of Sergeant Bilko's platoon (he was Private Sugarman). Later, in the mid-1960s, he was a newscaster for WBZ-TV in Boston and a commercial spokesperson for Standard Oil.

CARTER, THOMAS—black actor
b: Jul 17, Naples, Italy

Szysznyk (com) . . . . Ray Gun (1977–78)
The White Shadow (drama)
. . . . James Hayward (1978–80)

CARTWRIGHT, ANGELA—juvenile actress
b: Sep 9, 1952, Cheshire, England

The Danny Thomas Show (com)
. . . . Linda Williams (1957–64)
Lost in Space (sci fi)
. . . . Penny Robinson (1965–68)
Make Room for Granddaddy (com)
. . . . Linda Williams (1970–71)

British-born Angela Cartwright starred in two prominent kid's roles in the 1950s and '60s—as Danny Thomas's cute stepdaughter in *The Danny Thomas Show* and as teenager Penny in *Lost in Space.* In between those two series, she was seen as one of the kids in the 1965 movie hit *The Sound of Music.*

Angela's career since those days has been rather low-key, though she has continued to act. She made occasional series appearances *(Room 222, Adam-12, Logan's Run),* as well as returning as Linda in the revival of the Thomas show in 1970–71. She has also had minor roles in several films, including, in the 1980s, two TV movies which featured child stars of the past in roles as parents: *Scout's Honor* (1980) and *High School U.S.A.* (1983). Angela and Veronica Cartwright are sisters.

CARTWRIGHT, VERONICA—juvenile actress
b: 1949, Bristol, England

Daniel Boone (wes)
.... Jemima Boone (1964–66)

CARUSO, CARL—host, announcer

Spin the Picture (quiz)....... emcee (1949)
Back That Fact (aud par) .. assistant (1953)

CARVEN, MICHAEL—actor

Emerald Point N.A.S. (drama)
.... Lt. Alexi Gorichenko (1983–84)

CARVER, MARY—actress
b: May 3, 1924, Los Angeles, Calif.

Simon & Simon (drama)
.... Cecilia Simon (1981–)

CARVER, RANDALL—actor
b: May 25, Fort Worth, Texas

Mary Hartman, Mary Hartman (com)
.... Jeffrey DeVito (1977–78)
Taxi (com)........... John Burns (1978–79)

CARVER, ZEBE—emcee

Village Barn (var)............ emcee (1948)

CARVEY, DANA—actor
b: Jun 6, 1955, Missoula, Mont., r: San Carlos, Calif.

One of the Boys (com)
.... Adam Shields (1982)
Blue Thunder (police)
.... Clinton "Jafo" Wonderlove (1984)
NBC's Saturday Night Live (var)
.... regular (1986–)

CARY, CHRISTOPHER—actor

Garrison's Gorillas (drama)
.... Goniff (1967–68)

CASADOS, ELOY PHIL—actor
b: Sept 28, Long Beach, Calif.

Young Dan'l Boone (adv) ... Tsiskwa (1977)

CASE, ALLEN—actor
b: c. 1935, Dallas, Texas d: Aug 25, 1986

The Deputy (wes) .. Clay McCord (1959–61)
The Legend of Jesse James (wes)
.... Frank James (1965–66)

CASE, NELSON—announcer, host
b: Feb 3, 1910, Long Beach, Calif d: Mar 24, 1976

Armstrong Circle Theatre (drama)
.... host/narrator (1950–51)
Trash or Treasure (misc) .. emcee (1952–53)
Summer Playhouse (drama)..... host (1954)
Sneak Preview (misc).......... host (1956)

A prominent network radio announcer of the 1940s who was quite active on television in the 1950s.

CASE, RUSS—orchestra leader
b: Mar 19, 1912, Hamburg, Iowa d: Oct 10, 1964

The Eddy Arnold Show (var)
.... orch. leader (1952)
The Julius La Rosa Show (music)
.... orch. leader (1955)
Upbeat (music)......... orch. leader (1955)
Frankie Laine Time (var)
.... orch. leader (1956)

CASEY, ANGEL—actress

Stump the Authors (talk)..... author (1949)

A local Chicago radio and television personality.

CASEY, BERNIE—black actor
b: Jun 8, 1939, Wyco, W. Va.

Harris and Company (drama)
.... Mike Harris (1979)
Bay City Blues (drama)
.... Ozzie Peoples (1983)

This former pro football player (with the San Francisco 49ers and the L.A. Rams) began his acting career in the late 1960s with supporting roles in several films and episodes of TV series. Among other things, he appeared in *Brian's Song* (1971), *Ring of Passion* (as Joe Louis, 1978), and *Sophisticated Gents* (1981). Another TV movie in which he appeared, *Love Is Not Enough* (1978), became the basis for a short-lived NBC series called *Harris and Company*. It was an unusual attempt to build a TV drama around a loving, caring black family, but unfortunately it did not attract much of an audience.

CASEY, LAWRENCE—actor

The Rat Patrol (adv)
.... Pvt. Mark Hitchcock (1966–68)

CASEY, ROBERT—juvenile actor
b: Jun 27, 1927, Rochester, N.Y.

The Aldrich Family (com)
.... Henry Aldrich (1949–50)

CASH, JOHNNY—singer, actor
b: Feb 26, 1932, Kingsland, Ark. r: Dyess, Ark.

The Johnny Cash Show (var)
.... host (1969–71)
The Johnny Cash Show (var).... host (1976)
North and South (drama)
.... John Brown (1985)

Johnny Cash's life story is the stuff of which movies are made. Born to a poor cotton farming family in rural Arkansas; rocketed to sudden wealth and fame in the early rock 'n' roll era; plunged into the depths of drug abuse and self-destruction in the 1960s; saved by a strong-willed woman who cared about him; back on top as a major music and television star in the 1970s.

The tall, Lincolnesque Cash spent his youth picking cotton and doing manual labor. After four years in the air force in the early 1950s he formed a trio with two auto mechanics, Luther Perkins and Marshall Grant, playing one-night stands and eventually making a few records for a small label. One of these, "I Walk the Line," became an enormous hit and Johnny suddenly found himself one of the top recording artists in America.

Fame and fortune took its toll, however, as the pressures of touring led to more and more self-abuse and troubles with the law (by his own account he was jailed seven times for drunkenness and drugs; the last time the sheriff gave him back his pills and said "Go ahead, kill yourself"). Through the efforts of family and friends, and the woman who would become his wife—June Carter—he was eventually pulled out of his darkest period to achieve even greater success in the '70s. An ABC summer show in 1969 did so well it was added to the regular schedule the following winter and ran for a year and a half. He hosted another music-comedy hour in 1976 on CBS and made many appearances on specials and other shows.

Through it all Johnny has not forgotten his roots. The 1969–71 series in particular was an unusual blend of popular and traditional country music, incorporating "Ride This Train" segments that traced America's musical heritage in semidocumentary fashion. Johnny has also made some acting appearances, including *The Pride of Jesse Hallam* in 1981 (about illiteracy), *Murder in Coweta County* in 1983 and the miniseries *North and South* in 1985. His autobiography, detailing his turbulent career and his renewed commitment to Christianity, is titled *Man in Black* (1975).

CASH, JUNE CARTER—
See Carter, June

CASH, NORM—sportscaster

Monday Night Baseball (sport)
.... sportscaster (1976)

Former pro baseball player and veteran of 15 seasons with the Detroit Tigers; known by baseball fans as "Stormin' Norman."

CASHELL, JEANINE—actress

It's a Man's World (com)
.... Alma Jean Dobson (1962–63)

CASNOFF, PHIL—actor
b: Philadelphia, Pa.

The Hamptons (drama)
.... David Landau (1983)
North and South (drama)
.... Elkanah Bent (1985)

CASON, BARBARA—actress
b: Nov 15, 1933, Memphis, Tenn.

Comedy Tonight (var) .... regular (1970)
Temperatures Rising (com)
.... Miss Tillis (1973–74)
Carter Country (com)
.... Cloris Phebus (1977–79)

CASS, PEGGY—actress
b: May 21, 1924, Boston, Mass.

Keep Talking (quiz) ...... regular (1958–60)
The Jack Paar Show (talk)
.... semiregular (1958–62)
The Hathaways (com)
.... Elinore Hathaway (1961–62)
To Tell the Truth (quiz).. panelist (1964–67)
To Tell the Truth (quiz).. panelist (1969–77)

"I'm really an actress, but this year all I do is talk," commented Peggy Cass in 1959, when asked about her many appearances on Jack Paar's show. In the years that followed the plump actress found herself talking more and more and acting hardly at all, quite a change from her earlier career on the stage.

Peggy began in the theater in the late 1940s after her family gave up trying to push her into a secretarial career. She made her Broadway debut in *Touch and Go* in 1949, then worked up to better roles until she scored her greatest success as the nutty secretary Agnes Gooch in both the stage (1956) and movie (1958) versions of *Auntie Mame*. She also had occasional acting roles on television, including the part of an undertaker's wife in a 1959 episode of *Alfred Hitchcock Presents*. But talk shows seemed to suit her best, and after a brief fling in a situation comedy co-starring a bunch of chimpanzees (*The Hathaways*), she was seen almost exclusively on daytime and nighttime game and panel shows, including eleven years on *To Tell the Truth*.

CASSAVETES, JOHN—actor, director
b: Dec 9, 1929, New York City, N.Y.

Johnny Staccato (drama)
.... Johnny Staccato (1959–60)

Before his film career took off in the late 1960s, actor John Cassavetes did a great deal of television work. A lean, intense young man, he often portrayed disillusioned youths on playhouse series of the 1950s such as *The Elgin TV Hour, Armstrong Circle Theatre, Climax,* and *Danger*. In 1959, when he was beginning work on *Johnny Staccato* (about an individualistic jazz pianist and part-time detective), an NBC press release estimated that he had already appeared in more than 100 live TV dramas.

Cassavetes continued to be frequently seen after his single season on *Staccato*,

with multiple appearances on *Burke's Law, Alfred Hitchcock Presents,* and others. However, with his success in the movies *The Dirty Dozen* and *Rosemary's Baby* in 1967–68, he shifted mostly to film work, both as an actor and as a director of rather controversial experimental films. He has been married since 1954 to actress Gena Rowlands, with whom he has appeared in many of his films.

CASSELL, ARTHUR—actor

One Man's Family (drama)
.... Jack Barbour (1949–50)

CASSELL, MALCOLM—actor

Life with Father (com).. John Day (1954–55)

CASSEY, CHUCK—choral director
b: Jul 22, 1933, Chicago, Ill.

The Jimmy Dean Show (var)
.... singers (1963–66)

CASSIDY, DAVID—actor
b: Apr 12, 1950, New York City, N.Y.

The Partridge Family (com)
.... Keith Partridge (1970–74)
David Cassidy—Man Undercover (police)
.... Officer Dan Shay (1978–79)

"I had to stop performing because I was overworked. I was putting in 18 hours a day, seven days a week ... I finally said, 'Enough!' " That comment, made in 1978, helps explain David Cassidy's three-year disappearance from show business, between his initial fame as a teenage heart-throb on *The Partridge Family* and his re-emergence as an adult actor.

Acting seemed to be preordained for the handsome youngster; he was the only son of actor Jack Cassidy and actress-singer Evelyn Ward (who had a minor TV career), and his father's second wife was Academy Award winner Shirley Jones. Phase one of his career was filled with screaming teenage girls, gold records, and high visibility on one of the most popular shows of the early 1970s. He had played some supporting roles on other series during the 1969–70 season (*The Survivors, Adam-12, Bonanza*), but it was the simultaneous debut of *The Partridge Family* and of the group's first record ("I Think I

Love You") in September 1970 that brought him instant fame.

The next few years were chaotic. Fans even invaded his hospital room after a gall bladder operation; he finally shocked them all with a nude photo layout for *Rolling Stone* magazine in 1972. By 1974 it was all too much, and David simply retreated from the limelight to his tranquil Hawaiian estate and a horse ranch in Santa Barbara. In 1977 he married actress Kay Lenz.

In 1978 he was lured out for a guest appearance as a young detective on *Police Story*, a role that won him an Emmy Award nomination. The character was spun off into the short-lived series *Man Undercover*. David made a number of TV appearances in the years that followed, in TV movies and on series.

CASSIDY, JACK—actor

b: Mar 5, 1927, Richmond Hill, Queens, N.Y. d: Dec 12, 1976

He & She (com) ..... Oscar North (1967–68)

The father of young actors David, Patrick, and Shaun Cassidy. The debonair Jack had a lengthy stage career beginning in the 1940s and also appeared in many television productions from the 1950s on, both comedies and dramas. His only regular role was in the 1967 comedy *He & She,* as the egotistical star of an imaginary TV show created by cartoonist Richard Benjamin. Cassidy continued much in demand during the 1970s, in programs ranging from *The Mary Tyler Moore Show* to the TV movie *Death Among Friends.* He died in a fire that swept his West Hollywood apartment after he fell asleep while smoking a cigarette.

CASSIDY, JOANNA—actress

b: Aug 2, 1944, Haddonfield, N.J.

Shields and Yarnell (var)
.... regular (1977)
The Roller Girls (com)
.... Selma "Books" Cassidy (1978)
240-Robert (adv)
... Deputy Morgan Wainwright (1979–80)
The Family Tree (drama)
.... Elizabeth Nichols (1983)
Buffalo Bill (com) .... Jo Jo White (1983–84)
Codename: Foxfire (drama)
.... Elizabeth "Foxfire" Towne (1985)

CASSIDY, PATRICK—actor

Bay City Blues (drama)
.... Terry St. Marie (1983)

Brother of David and Shaun; his and Shaun's mother is actress Shirley Jones.

CASSIDY, SHAUN—actor

b: Sep 27, 1958, Los Angeles, Calif.

The Hardy Boys Mysteries (adv)
.... Joe Hardy (1977–79)
Breaking Away (com)
.... Dave Stohler (1980–81)

Another teenybopper sensation from the Cassidy clan. Shaun, like his half-brother David Cassidy, shot to stardom via a program that was very popular with younger viewers *(The Hardy Boys)* and also used the exposure as a launching pad for a brief but spectacular singing career (his biggest hit: a remake of the old rock 'n' roll standard "Da Do Ron Ron").

Unlike David, Shaun did not find it necessary to retreat from it all and instead went quickly into a second series, *Breaking Away.* However, he has been seen infrequently since then. Such are the perils of being a teen sensation.

CASSIDY, TED—actor

b: 1932*, Pittsburgh, Pa. d: Jan 16, 1979

The Addams Family (com)
.... Lurch and "Thing" (1964–66)
The New Adventures of Huck Finn (adv)
.... Injun Joe (1968–69)

This towering actor was a favorite with kids in the 1960s and '70s as the butler Lurch in *The Addams Family* ("You rang?" he would ghoulishly intone) and also as the voice of numerous Saturday morning cartoon characters—including Meteor Man and Godzilla. He died following open heart surgery in 1979.

CASSINI, IGOR—columnist ("Cholly Knickerbocker")

The Igor Cassini Show (int) .. host (1953–54)

CASSISI, JOHN—actor

Fish (com) .... Victor Kreutzer (1977–78)

*Some sources give 1933.

CASSITY, KRAIG—actor

Operation Petticoat (com)
.... Seaman Dooley (1977–78)

CASSMORE, JUDY—actress

The Don Rickles Show (com)
.... Audrey (1972)

CASSON, MEL—cartoonist
b: c. 1920, Boston, Mass. r: New York City,
N.Y.

Draw Me a Laugh! (quiz) .... regular (1949)

CAST, TRICIA—juvenile actress
b: Nov 16, 1966, Medford, N.Y.

The Bad News Bears (com)
.... Amanda Whirlitzer (1979–80)
It's Your Move (com)
.... Julie Burton (1984–85)

CASTELLANO, MARGARET—actress

The Super (com) ...... Joanne Girelli (1972)

Daughter of Richard Castellano, the star of
The Super.

CASTELLANO, RICHARD—actor
b: Sep 4, 1933, The Bronx, N.Y.

The Super (com) .... Joe Girelli (1972)
Joe and Sons (com).... Joe Vitale (1975–76)
Gangster Chronicles (drama)
. Giuseppe "Joe the Boss" Masseria (1981)

This enormous actor was perfect for a certain kind of role—the big, beer-guzzling,
blue-collar working stiff (or gangster) with
a heavy Bronx accent. "Hey, Paulie, close
da fridge." Or, "Ya cross me, Paulie, and
youse sleep wit da fishes tonight."
He got into acting rather late, after running a construction company. From 1963 on
he appeared on the New York stage and
later in the decade he began getting movie
roles as well. His most memorable performance, no doubt, was as the gangster
Clemenza in *The Godfather* (1972). On television, Castellano played a number of
roles, including the lead in two tailor-made
series—as the beer-guzzling building super
in *The Super* and as the beer-guzzling Joe
of *Joe and Sons.* Later he was Joe da Boss
in *The Gangster Chronicles.*

CASTELLARI, ENZO—actor

The Winds of War (drama)
.... Benito Mussolini (1983)

CASTLE SINGERS, THE—

Glenn Miller Time (music) . regulars (1961)

CASTLE, JO ANN—ragtime pianist

The Lawrence Welk Show (music)
.... regular (1959–69)

CASTLE, NICK—choreographer
b: Mar 21, 1910, Brooklyn, N.Y. d: Aug 28, 1968

The Dinah Shore Chevy Show (var)
.... regular (1962–63)
The Judy Garland Show (var)
.... regular (1963)
The Andy Williams Show (var)
.... regular (1963–66)
The Jerry Lewis Show (var)
.... regular (1967–69)

CASTLE, PEGGY—actress
b: Dec 22, 1926*, Appalachia, Va. d: Aug 11,
1973

The Lawman (wes)... Lily Merrill (1959–62)

Also known as Peggie Castle.

CASTRO, RON—actor

Search (adv)............ Carlos (1972–73)

CATES SISTERS, THE—

Nashville on the Road (music)
.... regulars (1975–76)

CATES, GEORGE—orchestra director
b: Oct 19, 1911, New York City, N.Y.

The Lawrence Welk Show (music)
.... musical director (1955–82)

CATLETT, MARY JO—actress
r: Denver, Colo.

Semi-Tough (com)......... Big Barb (1980)
Foul Play (drama)........... Stella (1981)
Diff'rent Strokes (com)
.... Pearl Gallagher (1982–86)

*Some sources give 1927.

165

CATLIN, JOAN—actress

A Woman to Remember (drama)
.... Carol Winstead (1949)

CATTRALL, KIM—actress
b: Aug 21, 1956, Liverpool, England

Scruples (drama).... Melanie Adams (1980)

CATUSI, JIM—actor

The David Frost Revue (com)
.... regular (1971–73)

CAULDWELL, ALAN—actor

Ivan the Terrible (com) ...... Nikolai (1976)

CAULFIELD, JOAN—actress
b: Jun 1, 1922, East Orange, N.J.

My Favorite Husband (com)
.... Liz Cooper (1953–55)
Sally (com) ...... Sally Truesdale (1957–58)

This demure blonde film star of the late 1940s did some television in the 1950s, including two series—*My Favorite Husband,* as a scatterbrained wife, and *Sally,* as the traveling companion of a slightly wacky widow. In these, as in her films, Joan played rather lightweight characters; she is perhaps best remembered for her wholesome, cover-girl beauty (she was, in fact, a former model and cover girl). By the 1960s, Joan's services were not much in demand by either movies or TV and she was seen in only a few series episodes *(Burke's Law, The Magician)* and TV movies *(The Hatfields and the McCoys).* Otherwise, she has kept active mostly in summer stock.

CAULFIELD, MAXWELL—actor
b: Nov 23, Derbyshire, England

Dynasty II: The Colbys (drama)
.... Miles Colby (1985–)

The husband of actress Juliet Mills.

CAVANAUGH, MICHAEL—actor
b: Nov 21, New York City r: San Francisco, Calif.

Starman (adv) .... George Fox (1986–)

CAVELL, MARC—actor

Pistols 'n Petticoats (com)
.... Gray Hawk (1966–67)

CAVETT, DICK—host
b: Nov 19, 1936, Kearney, Neb.

The Dick Cavett Show (talk)
.... host (1969–72)
ABC Late Night (certain weeks) (talk)
.... host (1973–74)
The Dick Cavett Show (var).... host (1975)
The Dick Cavett Show (talk) .. host (1986–)

Emmy Award: Best Talk Series, for *The Dick Cavett Show* (1972, 1974)

Dick Cavett is Nebraska's *other* gift to the talk show world. Like Johnny Carson, he was raised in the Corn Husker state, got his start as a writer-comedian, and graduated to hosting a nighttime network talk show. There the similarity ends. Whereas Carson's regular-guy humor appealed to the mass audience, the urbane and witty Cavett was the darling of the intelligentsia. When he referred to a guest's "Mephistophelian beard," the TV audience had no idea what he was talking about, but critics loved it.

Cavett is a Yale graduate who crashed New York as a copy boy for *Time* magazine. One day, so he says, he noticed an item reporting that Jack Paar was worried about his opening monologue on *The Tonight Show.* Cavett wrote one, slipped it to the surprised Paar, and managed to wrangle himself a job on the *Tonight* writing staff.

Cavett continued to write for the show after Paar left, but soon turned to doing his own material in nightclubs around the country. He appeared on a number of TV variety shows, including Merv Griffin's, Ed Sullivan's and his old habitat, *The Tonight Show.* Then, in early 1968, ABC signed him to do his own 90-minute daytime show. This failed to attract a large audience, so the indulgent network tried him in a prime time summer show in 1969 and then as host of its late-night show (opposite *Tonight*) from the fall of 1969 until 1972. None of these rocked the Nielsen ratings, but Cavett had built up a very vocal following—not to mention having the critics on his side—and rather than cancel him ABC cut his appearances to a few times a month in

1973–74. In 1975 Cavett moved briefly to CBS to do a prime time summer variety show. From 1977–82 he was a fixture on PBS.

CAWDRON, ROBERT—actor

From a Bird's Eye View (com)
.... Uncle Bert Quigley (1971)

CAZENOVE, CHRISTOPHER—actor
b: Dec 17, 1945, Winchester, England

Dynasty (drama) ... Ben Carrington (1986–)

CELLA, LEN—cohost

TV's Bloopers & Practical Jokes (com)
.... regular (1984–86)

CELLINI, KAREN—actress
b: May 13, Philadelphia, Pa.

Dynasty (drama)
.... Amanda Carrington (1986–)

CELLINO, CATARINA—actress

Welcome Back, Kotter (com)
.... Maria (1975–76)

CERF, BENNETT—publisher
b: May 25, 1898, New York City, N.Y. d: Aug 27, 1971

What's My Line (quiz)... panelist (1951–67)

CERF, PHYLLIS—panelist

Down You Go (quiz)
.... regular panelist (1955)

CERUSICO, ENZO—actor
b: c. 1943, Rome, Italy

My Friend Tony (drama)
.... Tony Novello (1969)

Does anybody remember Enzo? This young Italian actor was spotted by producer Sheldon Leonard while the latter was on location in Rome filming an episode of *I Spy* in 1966. Leonard not only gave him a part in the episode but brought him to America to costar with James Whitmore in another series he was developing, *My Friend Tony.* Enzo set about learning English, had his brief run in prime time, made a couple of movies (one of which,

Don't Push—I'll Charge When I'm Ready sat on the shelf for eight years), and then disappeared. One hopes he at least learned English.

CERVANTES, DON—actor

Greatest American Hero (adv)
.... Rodriguez (1981–83)

CERVERA, JORGE, JR.—actor

Viva Valdez (com) .... Jerry Ramirez (1976)

Also known as George Cervera.

CESANA, RENZO—host
b: Oct 30, 1907*, Rome, Italy d: 1970

First Date (int) .... host (1952)
The Continental (talk) .... host (1952–53)

Though he only had a short run on network TV (four months on CBS, four on ABC), this oily Italian made a remarkable impression on television with his late-night romantic monologues in which he purred sweet nothings into the ears of the ladies in his audience. He was promoted as an Italian count. Well, in the soft candlelight, the ladies might believe just about anything.

Cesana appeared in a number of films over the years, most notably *Stromboli* with Ingrid Bergman (1950). He briefly hosted the syndicated *First Date* and later had small parts in such series as *Mission: Impossible, Bewitched* and, what else, *To Rome with Love.* Late in life he lamented the typecasting that his accent, and more specifically *The Continental,* had forced upon him, calling his most famous role his "Frankenstein's monster."

CHADWICK, JUNE—actress
b: Warwickshire, England

V (sci fi) .... Lydia (1984–85)
Riptide (drama) .... Lt. Joanna Parisi (1986)

CHAGRIN, JULIAN—actor, mime
b: Feb 22, 1940, London, England

Dean Martin Presents the Golddiggers (var)
.... regular (1970)

*Some sources give 1917.

CHAKIRIS, GEORGE—actor, dancer
b: Sep 16, 1933, Norwood, Ohio

Dallas (drama).......... Nicholas (1985–)

The Oscar-winning actor-dancer (for *West Side Story* in 1961) has done relatively little television over the years, appearing only occasionally in dramas of the '60s and '70s, including *Medical Center* and *Hawaii Five-O. Dallas* represented his first regular series role.

CHAMBERLAIN, RICHARD—actor
b: Mar 31, 1935, Beverly Hills, Calif.

Dr. Kildare (drama)
.... Dr. James Kildare (1961–66)
Centennial (drama)
.... Alexander McKeag (1978–79)
Shogun (drama)
.... John Blackthorne (Anjin) (1980)
The Thorn Birds (drama)
.... Father Ralph de Bricassart (1983)

Boyishly handsome Richard Chamberlain has had two major careers in television—as the heartthrob *Dr. Kildare* in the 1960s and as the king of the miniseries in the late '70s and '80s. Born in the heart of Hollywood, he studied to be a painter but turned instead to acting, beginning with small roles in various filmed series of the late 1950s. His first major role was in an episode of *Gunsmoke,* followed by appearances on *Thriller, The Deputy, Alfred Hitchcock Presents,* and others. His major break came in 1961 when he was cast as the earnest young Kildare (he had previously been considered for a comedy series, but chose drama instead).

Following a very successful five-year run, which included his own popular recording of the *Kildare* theme song ("Three Stars Will Shine Tonight"), Chamberlain was anxious to counter the "pretty boy" image he had built up. He essayed some fairly heavyweight stage and screen acting roles, including parts in *Hamlet, Julius Caesar,* and *The Three Musketeers.* When he returned to television in the 1970s it was in similarly high-class productions, including *The Lady's Not for Burning* (1974), *The Count of Monte Cristo* (1975), and *The Man in the Iron Mask* (1977). However, his greatest success came with his leading roles in several of the most popular TV movies and miniseries of the late '70s and

'80s—*Centennial, Shogun, The Thorn Birds,* and *Wallenberg,* among others. Today he is in his fifties, and, according to many women, still gorgeous.

CHAMBERLIN, LEE—black actress
b: Feb 14, New York City, N.Y.

All's Fair (com) .... Lucy Daniels (1976–77)
Paris (police) ...... Barbara Paris (1979–80)

CHAMBERS, HENNEN—

Marie (var) .... regular (1980–81)

CHAMBERS, PHIL—actor

The Gray Ghost (adv) ... Lt. St. Clair (1957)

CHAMBLIS, WOODY—actor
b: c. 1914, Texas d: Jan 8, 1981

Gunsmoke (wes) .... Mr. Lathrop (1966–75)

CHAMPION, MARGE AND GOWER— dancers
Marge: b: Sep 2, 1919*, Los Angeles, Calif.
Gower: b: Jun 22, 1919**, Geneva, Ill. d: Aug 25, 1980

Admiral Broadway Revue (var)
.... dancers (1949)
The Marge and Gower Champion Show (com)
.... as themselves (1957)

Emmy Award (Marge): Best Choreography, for the special *Queen of the Stardust Ballroom* (1975)

Hollywood's most famous husband-and-wife dance team of the 1950s was featured on some of the splashiest television variety shows and specials of that era, as well as in their own biweekly comedy series (which included plenty of dancing) in the spring of 1957.

Marge and Gower met in high school but pursued separate careers until after World War II, when they formed a dance team. They were married in 1947 and subsequently appeared together in a string of movie musicals (*Show Boat, Lady in the Dark,* etc.). Gower began to concentrate on choreographing and directing Broadway shows, including some of

*Some sources give 1921, 1923, or 1925.
**Some sources give 1920 or 1921.

the top hits of the '60s *(Bye, Bye Birdie, Hello, Dolly);* Marge became a character actress as well as a choreographer. They were divorced in 1971.

CHAMPLIN, IRENE—actress

Flash Gordon (sci fi). . Dale Arden (1953–54)

CHANCELLOR, JOHN—newscaster
b: Jul 14, 1927, Chicago, Ill.

NBC Evening News (news)
.... anchorman (1970–82)

Fatherly-looking John Chancellor has been one of the stalwarts of NBC news for more than 30 years and was the network's evening anchorman for 12 of those years.

He started out as a copyboy and reporter for the Chicago *Sun-Times* in the late 1940s and joined NBC's Chicago affiliate, WMAQ-TV, in 1950. He was soon made the network's Midwest correspondent, and then a national political reporter, serving as a floor reporter at the Republican and Democratic political conventions of the 1950s and '60s. In 1961–62, NBC tried him out as host of *Today,* succeeding Dave Garroway, but his style was a little too stolid for that time in the morning and Hugh Downs eventually got the job instead.

Chancellor returned to reporting for a time before receiving a unique and prestigious honor—he was asked by President Lyndon Johnson in 1965 to become head of the Voice of America, the first working journalist to do so. He served for two years. Three years after returning to NBC, his career received another substantial boost when he took over the coveted anchor position on the network's evening newscast, following the demise of the long-running Huntley-Brinkley report. Although he was teamed for various periods with other co-anchors, including David Brinkley, Chancellor remained in the anchor chair until 1982, when NBC—perennially in second place—decided to go for more youth appeal with Tom Brokaw. Chancellor then shifted to the position of regular commentator on the newscast.

CHANDLER, CHICK—actor
b: Jan 18, 1905, Kingston, N.Y.

Soldiers of Fortune (adv)
.... Toubo Smith (1955–56)
One Happy Family (com)
.... Barney Hogan (1961)

CHANDLER, GEORGE—actor
b: Jun 30, 1898, Waukegan, Ill. d: Jun 10, 1985

Lassie (adv) . Uncle Petrie Martin (1958–59)
Ichabod and Me (com)
.... Ichabod Adams (1961–62)

CHANDLER, LORETTA—actress

Fame (drama).............. Dusty (1985–)

CHANDLER, ROBIN—hostess
b: c. 1921

Who's Whose (quiz)........ panelist (1951)
Quick on the Draw (quiz).... hostess (1952)
Revlon Mirror Theatre (drama)
.... hostess (1953)
Take a Guess (quiz)........ panelist (1953)

CHANEY, LON, JR.—actor
b: Feb 10, 1906, Oklahoma City, Okla. d: Jul 12, 1973

Hawkeye (wes) ...... Chingachgook (1957)
Pistols 'n' Petticoats (com)
.... Chief Eagle Shadow (1966–67)

Chaney was one of the movie's favorite monsters, just as his father, "The Man of a Thousand Faces," had been in the 1920s. A big, hulking brute of a man, he made quite a few television appearances in the 1950s and early '60s, mostly on playhouse series and westerns. He was seen a number of times in the '60s in *Route 66.* His last major TV role was in a comedy, however—the recurring character Chief Eagle Shadow in *Pistols 'n Petticoats.*

CHANG, HARRY—actor

The Mackenzies of Paradise Cove (adv)
.... Barney (1979)

CHANNING, STOCKARD—actress
b: Feb 13, 1944, New York City, N.Y.

Stockard Channing in Just Friends (com)
.... Susan Hughes (1979)
The Stockard Channing Show (com)
.... Susan Goodenow (1980)

CHAO, ROSALIND—actress
b: Los Angeles r: Orange County, Calif.

Diff'rent Strokes (com)
.... Miss Chung (1982–83)
*M*A*S*H* (com).......... Soon-Lee (1983)
AfterMASH (com)
.... Soon-Lee Klinger (1983–84)

CHAPEL, BETTE—singer
b: c. 1925

Garroway at Large (var).. regular (1949–51)

CHAPEL, LOYITA—actress

The Life and Times of Eddie Roberts (com)
.... Vivian Blankett (1980)
Behind the Screen (drama)
.... Dory Ranfield Holmby (1981–82)

CHAPIN, LAUREN—juvenile actress
b: May 23, 1945, Los Angeles, Calif.

Father Knows Best (com)
.... Kathy (Kitten) Anderson (1954–60)

Impish little Lauren Chapin was one of television's child stars who seemed to have had no show business career, to speak of, after her one famous series. She came from a show business family; her brothers Michael and Billy both played juvenile roles in minor films of the early 1950s. *Father Knows Best* was Lauren's first professional role. During the run of the series she made guest appearances on a number of other shows, including *Fireside Theatre* and *General Electric Theater*.

Viewers next saw her in the *Father Knows Best* reunion special in 1977, at age 31. "I hope they'll like me grown up," she remarked.

CHAPMAN, GRAHAM—comedian
b: 1940, Leicester, England

The Big Show (var)......... regular (1980)

One of the founding members of Britain's Monty Python comedy troupe.

CHAPMAN, JEAN ANNE—

The Jim Stafford Show (var).. regular (1975)

CHAPMAN, JOSEPH—actor

Knots Landing (drama)
.... Mark St. Claire (1984)

CHAPMAN, LONNY—actor
b: Oct 1, 1920, Tulsa, Okla. r: Joplin, Mo.

The Investigator (drama)... Jeff Prior (1958)
For the People (police)
.... Frank Malloy (1965)

CHAPMAN, ROBERT—actor

Father Knows Best (com)
.... Ralph Little (1957–58)

CHAPPELL, JOHN—actor

AfterMASH (com)
.... Mike D'Angelo (1983–84)

CHAPTER 5—singers

The Peter Marshall Variety Show (var)
.... regulars (1976)

CHARLES, LEWIS—actor
b: Nov 2, 1920, New York City, N.Y. d: Nov 9, 1979

The Feather and Father Gang (drama)
.... Lou (1977)

CHARLES, RAY—orchestra and choral director
b: Sep 13, 1918, Chicago, Ill.

The Perry Como Show (var)
.... singers (1950–61)
The Kraft Music Hall (var)
.... singers (1961–63)
The John Byner Comedy Hour (var)
.... orch. leader (1972)

Emmy Awards: Achievement in Music, Lyrics and Special Material, for the NBC Special "The First Nine Months Are the Hardest" (1971); same award, for an episode of *The Funny Side* (1972)

The white Ray Charles was one of television's most familiar choral directors in the 1950s, principally through his long association with Perry Como. Ray began his career as a radio singer around 1940 and soon branched into arranging and writing special material for various shows. After World War II he conducted the orchestra for the Broadway hit *Finian's Rainbow,* then met Mr. C, who made him a fixture on his television shows. Besides conducting the chorus, Ray composed such familiar Como material as "Letters, We Get

Letters" and "Sing to Me, Mr. C" for the show.

He was also associated with other series and specials over the years, from *Your Hit Parade* in the early 1950s to—believe it or not—*Sha Na Na* in the '70s.

CHARLES, RAY—R&B singer
b: Sep 23, 1930, Albany, Ga.

Three's Company (com)
.... sang theme (1977–84)

The black Ray Charles, a major recording artist for many years, has appeared on numerous television specials and variety shows—including Flip Wilson's on which he sometimes took part in skits with Flip. He was heard singing the theme song over the credits of the hit comedy *Three's Company* during the late 1970s and early '80s.

CHARLESON, IAN—actor
b: Aug 11, 1949, Edinburgh, Scotland

Master of the Game (drama)
.... Jamie McGregor (1984)

CHARMOLI, TONY—choreographer, director
b: Jun 11, 1922, Mountain Iron, Minn.

NBC Comedy Hour (var).... dancers (1956)
The Dinah Shore Chevy Show (var)
.... dancers (1957–62)
The Danny Kaye Show (var)
.... dancers (1963–67)
The Jonathan Winters Show (var)
.... dancers (1968)
The Julie Andrews Hour (var)
.... dancers (1972–73)
Cher (var) .... dancers (1975)
The Big Show (var)........ dancers (1980)

Emmy Awards: Best Choreography, for *Your Hit Parade* (1954); for the Special *Mitzi . . . A Tribute to the American Housewife* (1974); for the Shirley MacLaine special *Gypsy In My Soul* (1976)

CHARNEY, JORDAN—actor

Andros Targets (drama)
.... Ted Bergman (1977)
Falcon Crest (drama)
.... Norton Crane (1983–84)

A veteran daytime soap opera actor, on *Love of Life, Another World, One Life to Live,* etc., since the mid-1960s.

CHARO—actress
b: Jan 15, 1951, Murcia, Spain

Chico and the Man (com)
.... Aunt Charo (1977–78)

Real name: Maria Rosario Pilar Martinez.

CHARTOFF, MELANIE—comedienne
b: Dec 15, New Haven, Conn.

Fridays (var)............ regular (1980–82)

CHASE, BUD—singer

This Is Music (music)..... regular (1958–59)

CHASE, CHARLIE—host

This Week in Country Music (news)
.... host (1983–)

CHASE, CHEVY—comedian
b: Oct 8, 1943*, New York City, N.Y.

NBC's Saturday Night Live (com)
.... regular (1975–76)

Emmy Awards: Best Supporting Actor in a Variety Show, for *Saturday Night Live* (1976); Best Writing for a Comedy Show, for *Saturday Night Live* (1976); Best Writing, for *The Paul Simon Special* (1978)

No, Chevy Chase is not his real name, but it's close—Cornelius Crane Chase. He began as a comedy writer and sometimes on-screen performer for several shows in the early and mid 1970s, including PBS's *Great American Dream Machine,* an Alan King special, and the 1975 version of *The Smothers Brothers Show.* He was also in National Lampoon's 1973 off-Broadway comedy, *Lemmings,* which is where he first met John Belushi and other members-to-be of the *Saturday Night Live* cast.

Chevy was the first major "discovery" of NBC's avant-garde late-night comedy, becoming the show's major star during the first season as the cool, buttoned-down yuppy in the midst of the craziness. His most popular role was as the newscaster in "Weekend Update" ("Hello. I'm Chevy

*Some sources give (somewhat optimistically!) 1949.

Chase, and you're not"). Chevy left *SNL* after a single season to capitalize on his sudden fame, but at first success seemed slow in coming. His first TV special was a disappointment, and his movies uneven. In the 1980s he began to find his stride in youth-oriented slapstick films such as *Caddyshack* and *National Lampoon's Vacation*. He is only occasionally seen on television now.

CHASE, ERIC—actor

Here Come the Brides (adv)
.... Christopher Pruitt (1969–70)

CHASE, ILKA—actress, writer

b: Apr 8, 1903*, New York City, N.Y. d: Feb 22, 1978

Celebrity Time (quiz).... panelist (1949–50)
Glamour-Go-Round (int) .... host (1950)
Masquerade Party (quiz)
.... panelist (1952–57)
Keep Talking (quiz) ...... regular (1958–59)
The Trials of O'Brien (drama)
.... Margaret (1965–66)

Autobiography: *Past Imperfect.*

CHASE, MARY, MARIONETTES—

Fearless Fosdick (cartn) .... puppets (1952)

CHASE, SYLVIA—newscaster

b: Feb 23, 1938, Northfield, Minn.

ABC Weekend News (news)
.... anchor (1977–79)
20/20 (mag) .... correspondent (1978–86)

Emmy Awards: Outstanding Achievement in Broadcast Journalism for the *20/20* segments "Exploding Gas Tanks" (1978) and "VW Beetle: The Hidden Danger" (1980)

CHASTAIN, DON—actor

b: Sep 2, Oklahoma City, Okla.

The Edie Adams Show (var)
.... regular (1963–64)
The Debbie Reynolds Show (com)
.... Jim Thompson (1969–70)

CHEEK, MOLLY—actress

b: Mar 27, Bronxville, N.Y.

*Some sources give 1900 or 1905.

Chicago Story (drama)
.... Megan Powers (1982)

CHEERLEADERS, THE—singers

Party Time at Club Roma (var)
.... regulars (1950–51)
Garroway at Large (var)
.... regulars (1953–54)
The College of Musical Knowledge (quiz)
.... regulars (1954)
Musical Chairs (quiz)....... regulars (1955)
The Gordon MacRae Show (music)
.... regulars (1956)
The Nat "King" Cole Show (var)
.... regulars (1957)

This busy vocal group of the 1950s was founded in 1949 at an impromptu singing party and had a changing membership of four or five over the following years—usually two men and two women. The leader and only continuing member was a young accountant named Tom Roddy, who was in his twenties at the time the group was popular. When asked to explain his abrupt change of careers, he replied, "After all, I'm still in a business where figures count."

CHEONG, GEORGE LEE—actor

Bring 'Em Back Alive (adv)
.... Chaing, the bartender (1982–83)

CHER—singer

b: May 20, 1946, El Centro, Calif.

The Sonny and Cher Comedy Hour (var)
.... cohost (1971–74)
Cher (var) .... hostess (1975–76)
The Sonny and Cher Show (var)
.... cohost (1976–77)

Rock singer Cher, of the booming voice and daring wardrobe, was born Cherilyn Sarkisian LaPierre to a show business family (her mother was an actress) and studied acting and singing as a youngster. In the early 1960s her family moved to New York City and teenager Cherilyn began getting work as a backup singer at recording sessions; at one of these she met Sonny Bono, something of an experienced hand around the studios. The two were married and formed their own act. As "Caesar and Cleo" they didn't do much, but in 1964 they switched to Sonny and Cher and in 1965 came up with their first hit recording, Sonny's composition "I Got You Babe."

Their soft rock songs, psychedelic fashions, and irreverent style was perfect for the times and they became major stars, making many television appearances. In 1971 they landed their own CBS variety show, which began as a summer replacement and turned into a major regular season hit. It ended when the couple divorced in 1974, but Cher was back the following February with her own series, *Cher*. This did well enough at first but then started to slip, so the two were reunited—professionally at least (Cher had in the meantime married rock star Greg Allman). The new *Sonny & Cher Show* never recaptured the momentum of the original and was canceled at the end of the 1976–77 season.

Cher has since been active in TV specials and talk shows and has appeared in several films, including *Mask* (as the mother).

CHERNE, LEO—commentator
b: c. 1912

Our Secret Weapon—The Truth (info)
.... panelist (1951)
All Star News (news)
.... correspondent (1952–53)
Wisdom of the Ages (info)
.... panelist (1952–53)

CHERRY, BYRON—actor
b: Apr 17, Atlanta, Ga.

The Dukes of Hazzard (com)
.... Coy Duke (1982–83)

CHERRY, DON—singer
b: Jan 11, 1924, Wichita, Texas

Penthouse Party (var)..... regular (1950–51)
The Dean Martin Summer Show (var)
.... regular (1967)

Popular singer and recording artist of the 1950s whose biggest hit was "Band of Gold"; he made frequent appearances on music and variety shows.

CHERRY, HUGH—actor, emcee
b: Nashville, Tenn.

Midwestern Hayride (var) . emcee (1955–56)

CHESHIRE, ELIZABETH—juvenile actress
b: Mar 3, 1967, Burbank, Calif.

The Family Holvak (drama)
.... Julie Mae Holvak (1975)
Sunshine (com)................. Jill (1975)

CHESIS, EILEEN—juvenile actress
The Tom Ewell Show (com)
.... Sissie Potter (1960–61)

CHESNEY, DIANA—actress
Fair Exchange (com) . Sybil Finch (1962–63)

CHESTER, COLBY—actor
Sword of Justice (adv) ... Buckner (1978–79)

CHI, CHOU-LI—actor
b: Apr 5, Taiyuan, Shansi, China

Falcon Crest (drama)...... Chou-Li (1981–)

CHILDRE, LEW—
Ozark Jubilee (music)........ regular (1960)

CHILDRESS, ALVIN—black actor
b: c. 1907, Meridian, Miss. d: Apr 19, 1986

Amos 'n' Andy (com)
.... Amos Jones (1951–53)

Alvin Childress's career in later years consisted largely of interviews in which he was asked to explain why *Amos 'n' Andy* was not offensive to blacks and how it felt to be an actor in one of television's most famous suppressed series. He was very candid. It provided work for black actors when there was little else available for them in television, and it showed them in all kinds of professional roles—doctors, lawyers, store owners—something unheard of at the time. "I didn't feel it harmed the Negroes at all," he said.

Although Amos is unquestionably his most famous role, Childress also played many others. He began his career on stage in the 1930s and appeared in a number of Broadway plays of the 1930s and '40s (including *Brown Sugar* and *Anna Lucasta*). He was the first actor cast for the projected TV version of the famous *Amos 'n' Andy* radio series, and he helped recruit others during a lengthy and well-publicized talent hunt.

In later years he continued to act, usually in minor supporting roles, including a part in the 1959 movie version of *Anna Lucasta*. After a period of relative inactivity in the '60s he became busy again in the '70s in occasional TV movies (including the *Banyon* pilot in 1971, *Sister, Sister* in 1982) and episodes of series such as *Sanford and Son*, *Good Times*, and *The Jeffersons*. His regular job was as an employment counselor for Los Angeles County.

CHILDS, SUZANNE—

That's My Line (com).... reporter (1980–81)

CHILES, LINDEN—actor
b: St. Louis, Mo., r: Barrington, Ill.

Convoy (drama)
...... Chief Officer Steve Kirkland (1965)
James at 15 (drama)
.... Mr. Paul Hunter (1977–78)

CHILES, LOIS—actress
b: 1950, Alice, Texas

Dallas (drama)... Holly Harwood (1982–84)

CHING, WILLIAM—actor
b: 1912

Our Miss Brooks (com)
.... Clint Albright (1955–56)

CHODER, JILL—actress

Number 96 (drama)
.... Sandy Galloway (1980–81)

CHORDETTES, THE—vocal group
Virginia "Jinny" Osborne (Lockard), b: Seattle r: Sheboygan, Wis.
Dorothy Schwartz, b: Sheboygan, Wis.
Janet Ertel (Bleyer), b: Sheboygan, Wis.
Carol Hagendorn (Bushman), b: Sheboygan, Wis.

Arthur Godfrey and His Friends (var)
.... singers (1949–53)

This very popular vocal group was formed in 1946 as a girl's barbershop quartet in their hometown of Sheboygan, Wis. Jinny Osborne, the organizer, was the daughter of the president of the SPEBQSA, the national barbershop singing club. The four attracted attention beyond the barbershop world, however, with their smooth, close harmonies and good looks. In September 1949 they entered and won the competition on *Arthur Godfrey's Talent Scouts* as barbershop singers.

Godfrey promptly hired them for his Wednesday night variety show, and for the next four years they received national exposure on his top-rated series. Then without explanation they were suddenly fired by the unpredictable Godfrey—a fate that also befell several of his other TV "friends."

Orchestra leader Archie Bleyer, who had also been fired by Godfrey, signed them for his newly founded Cadence record label; he also married one of them. In 1954 their Cadence recording of "Mr. Sandman," a bouncy pop number vaguely reminiscent of barbershop, shot to the top of the music charts and established them as top recording artists. They appeared on numerous music and variety shows and for a time right after leaving Godfrey were regulars on Robert Q. Lewis's daytime show. They never had an unkind word to say about their celebrated ex-boss. Asked in 1955 "How do you feel about Mr. Godfrey *now?*", they chorused "Who's Mr. Godfrey?" The group remained successful until the early '60s, through several personnel changes.

Much misinformation has been published about the composition of this group. Those listed above were the original members who made up the quartet during its years on the Godfrey show (Dorothy was replaced by Lynn Evans during the last three months on the show); married names are given in parentheses.

CHRISTIAN, CLAUDIA—actress

Berrengers (drama).. Melody Hughes (1985)

CHRISTIAN, MICHAEL—actor

Peyton Place (drama)...... Joe Rossi (1968)

CHRISTIE, AUDREY—actress
b: Jun 27, 1912, Chicago, Ill.

Joey Faye's Frolics (var) ..... regular (1950)
Guess What (quiz) .... panelist (1952)
Fair Exchange (com)
.... Dorothy Walker (1962–63)

The Cara Williams Show (com)
.... Agnes (1964–65)

CHRISTIE, DICK—actor

Ace Crawford, Private Eye (com)
.... Lt. Fanning (1983)
Small Wonder (com) . Ted Lawson (1985–)

CHRISTIE, DINAH—actress

Check It Out (com).. Edna Moseley (1985–)

CHRISTIE, KEN, SINGERS—

Musical Comedy Time (com)
.... regulars (1950–51)

CHRISTINE, VIRGINIA—actress
b: Mar 5, 1920*, Stanton, Iowa

Tales of Wells Fargo (wes) . Ovie (1961–62)

This actress is probably better known for her 15 years as "Mrs. Olson" in Folger's coffee commercials during the '60s and '70s.

CHRISTMAS, ERIC—actor

The Sandy Duncan Show (com)
.... Ben Hampton (1972)

CHRISTOPHER, ANDY—actor

Mr. Black (drama)........ Mr. Black (1949)

CHRISTOPHER, JORDAN—actor
b: Oct 23, 1942**, Youngstown, Ohio

Secrets of Midland Heights (drama)
.... Guy Millington (1980–81)

CHRISTOPHER, THOM—actor

Buck Rogers in the 25th Century (sci fi)
.... Hawk (1981)

CHRISTOPHER, WILLIAM—actor
b: Oct 20, 1932, Evanston, Ill.

Gomer Pyle, U.S.M.C. (com)
.... Pvt. Lester Hummel (1964–69)
M*A*S*H (com)
...... Father Francis Mulcahy (1972–83)
AfterMASH (com)
...... Father Francis Mulcahy (1983–84)

*Some sources give 1917.
**Some sources give 1938 or 1940.

The gentle padre of *M*A*S*H* started out as a stage actor in the '50s and early '60s, mostly in regional and off-Broadway theater. A role with the touring company of *Beyond the Fringe* brought him to Los Angeles in 1963, where he began to pick up work in episodes of television series, often as a hayseed or cowpoke (e.g., in *The Andy Griffith Show, The Men From Shiloh, Alias Smith and Jones,* and a recurring role on *Gomer Pyle*). In 1972 he was cast as Father Mulcahy on *M*A*S*H,* replacing another actor who had the part in the pilot; he played the role for the next twelve years and was one of only three cast members to remain with the original series for its entire run (the others: Alan Alda and Loretta Swit).

Christopher has appeared in small roles in a number of movies over the years, including Doris Day's most recent film, *With Six You Get Eggroll,* which also had Jamie Farr and *Alice's* Vic Tayback in small parts.

CHRISTY, JULIE—actress

Faraway Hill (drama) .... regular (1946)

CHUNG, BYRON—actor

Search (adv)............. Kuroda (1972–73)
Baa Baa Black Sheep (drama)
.... Capt. Tommy Harachi (1977–78)

CHUNG, CONNIE—newscaster
b: Aug 20, 1946, Washington, D.C.

NBC Weekend News (news)
.... anchor (1983–)
1986 (pub aff) .... anchor (1986)

Pretty Connie Chung has become one of the more prominent female reporters on network television and one of the few of Asian extraction. After graduating with a journalism degree from the University of Maryland in the late 1960s, she worked briefly for local Washington, D.C., stations and then became a political reporter for CBS in 1971. Five years later she made news when, after a relatively short time in the business, she was signed by one of the country's largest TV stations, KNXT in Los Angeles, to become the principal co-anchor on both its early and late evening newscasts. She also began filling in on CBS network newscasts. She won multiple awards for her work during this period.

Seen as a rising star, Connie was hired away by NBC in 1983 and given wide exposure as anchor of that network's weekend newscast, of its early morning *News At Sunrise,* and as a contributor to its prime time newsmagazines.

CHURCH, ELAINE—actress

Doctors' Hospital (drama)
.... Nurse Wilson (1975–76)

CIAMPA, CHRIS—actor

Mulligan's Stew (drama)
.... Adam Friedman (1977)

CIANNELLI, EDUARDO—actor
b: Aug 30, 1887*, Island of Ischia, Italy (near Naples) d: Oct 8, 1969

Johnny Staccato (drama).. Waldo (1959–60)

Although he had only one regular series role, as the restaurant owner on *Johnny Staccato,* Eduardo Ciannelli was a very busy supporting actor on television in the 1950s and '60s. His etched features and sinister eyes made him fine as a villain (as he had been in many films), but he also played many other roles calling for a mature Italian. He was seen on numerous episodes of *Climax* in the 1950s ("The Shadow of Evil," "The Disappearance of Daphne," etc.) and on *Dr. Kildare, The Man From U.N.C.L.E., Alfred Hitchcock Presents, The Fugitive,* and others in later years. He could also play comedy: on *I Love Lucy* he was the owner of a pizza parlor where Lucy, trying to make her first pizza, wreaked havoc.

Ciannelli studied medicine as a young man in Naples, but dumped that career to head for America and seek fame as an opera singer (those were the days of Caruso, when "Golden Age" tenors and baritones were becoming famous and wealthy). He drifted into acting, first on stage and then in films in the 1930s, where he became a favorite character villain.

CIARDI, JOHN—critic, host

Accent on an American Summer (doc)
.... host (1962)

*Some sources give 1889.

176

CIMINO, LEONARD—actor

V (movie) (sci fi) .... Abraham (1983)

CIOFFI, CHARLES—actor
b: 1935

Assignment Vienna (drama)
.... Maj. Caldwell (1972–73)
Get Christie Love (police)
.... Lt. Matt Reardon (1974)

CIRILLO, AL—announcer

Bowling Headliners (sport)
.... announcer (1949)

CIRILLO, JOE—actor

Eischied (police) .. Det. Malfitano (1979–80)

CISAR, GEORGE—actor

Stand By for Crime (police)
.... Sgt. Kramer (1949)
Dennis the Menace (com)
.... Sgt. Theodore Mooney (1961–63)

CIVITA, DIANE—actress

Misfits of Science (adv)
.... Miss Nance (1985–86)

CLAIR, DICK—comedian
b: Nov 12, San Francisco, Calif.

What's It All About, World? (var)
.... regular (1969)
The Funny Side (var)....... regular (1971)

Emmy Awards: Best Writing for a Variety Show, for *The Carol Burnett Show* (1974, 1975, 1978)

One half of the comedy team of Clair and (Jenna) McMahon, which became popular on the club circuit in the mid-1960s. They also appeared on TV variety shows and as a team wrote for quite a few series, including *The Don Knotts Show, The Carol Burnett Show,* and *Soap.*

CLAIR, RICHARD—actor

The Many Loves of Dobie Gillis (com)
.... Lt. Merriweather (1961)

CLAIRE, DOROTHY—singer
b: Jun 5, 1925, LaPorte, Ind.

Henry Morgan's Great Talent Hunt (var)
.... regular (1951)

The Paul Winchell-Jerry Mahoney Show (var)................... regular (1951–52)

CLARE, DIANE—actress

Court-Martial (drama) ... Sgt. Wendy (1966)

CLARIDGE, SHAARON—police radio operator
b: Santa Monica, Calif.

Adam 12 (police)
.... voice of dispatcher (1968–75)

Leave it to Jack Webb! The voice of the radio dispatcher on Webb's hit police series, *Adam-12*, the authoritative female voice that regularly summoned officers Martin Milner and Kent McCord to action. ("One Adam-12, One Adam-12!") belonged to a *real* police radio operator. Shaaron Claridge had filled such a position for nine years in the Van Nuys division of the Los Angeles Police Department when Webb, with the approval of her superiors, recruited her to work part-time on the show. He wanted "authenticity."

Shaaron, who was married in real life to a motorcycle officer, was more appreciative of the money. She made $112 per hour for her television work, compared to $3.30 an hour for her regular job.

CLARK, ALEX—actor

Claudia, The Story of a Marriage (drama)
.... Harley Naughton (1952)

CLARK, CLIFF—actor

Combat Sergeant (drama)
.... Gen. Harrison (1956)

CLARK, DANE—actor
b: Feb 18, 1913, Brooklyn, N.Y.

Wire Service (drama). Dan Miller (1956–57)
Bold Venture (adv) ... Slate Shannon (1959)
Perry Mason (revival) (drama)
.... Lt. Arthur Tragg (1973–74)

Wiry Dane Clark is one of those actors who never quite made it to the top in either movies or television, but never lacked for work in either medium. The scrappy, tough leads he portrayed grew out of his own disappointments in life. He was born the son of a sporting goods dealer and as a young man set out to make baseball his career. He played semipro but failed to make the cut for the majors, tried boxing and fared little better there, then finally enrolled in law school. He got his degree, but in the depths of the Depression could find no work, so he began picking up odd jobs as a stage actor. He made little progress in that profession either until, after nearly a decade of small parts, walk-ons and understudy roles, he crashed Hollywood in 1942. There he slowly worked his way up to more substantial roles in second features, many of them war films.

Dane entered TV virtually at its outset and worked steadily, if unspectacularly, from the early 1950s onward. At first he was seen in live TV playhouse dramas, then in filmed series including *Wagon Train, The Untouchables, Ben Casey, Ironside, Mannix, Police Story*, and many others. He starred in two syndicated series of the '50s, *Wire Service* and *Bold Venture*, and years later played a continuing role on the abortive revival of *Perry Mason*.

CLARK, DICK—host
b: Nov 30, 1929, Mt. Vernon, N.Y.

American Bandstand (prime time) (music)
.... host (1957)
The Dick Clark Show (music)
.... host (1958–60)
Dick Clark's World of Talent (var)
.... host (1959)
Dick Clark Presents the Rock and Roll Years (music) .... host (1973–74)
Dick Clark's Live Wednesday (var)
.... host (1978)
The Krypton Factor (quiz) ...... host (1981)
The $50,000 Pyramid (quiz)...... host (1981)
Inside America (mag).......... host (1982)
TV's Bloopers & Practical Jokes (com)
.... host (1984–86)
The $100,000 Pyramid (quiz).. host (1985–)
Dick Clark's Nighttime (var)
.... host (1985–86)

Emmy Awards: Best Host of a Game Show, for *The $25,000 Pyramid* (1979, 1985, 1986); Best Children's Entertainment Special (Executive Producer), for *The Woman Who Willed a Miracle* (1983); Outstanding Program Achievement (Executive Producer), for *American Bandstand* (1983)

Dick Clark is something of a one-man band in the field of light television entertainment—he creates, produces, and emcees the shows, and owns and sells them as well. Though he is most closely associated with rock music programs, his own tastes as a youth ran to jazz (there was no rock 'n' roll then). He landed his first job at a local radio station during his college years in the late 1940s, and by 1952 he had become a staff announcer at WFIL radio and TV in Philadelphia. Among other things, he read the Tootsie Roll commercials on *Paul Whiteman's TV Teen Club,* an ABC network show that originated at the station.

Dick's first real break came in 1956, under unfortunate circumstances. Bob Horn, the host of WFIL's popular afternoon TV dance party, *Bandstand,* was abruptly fired in a drunk-driving scandal. Desperate to refurbish its image, the station put clean-cut young Dick Clark in charge of the show, and its popularity reached new heights. By August, 1957, Dick had persuaded the ABC network to carry the newly renamed *American Bandstand* nationwide. For a time in the fall of 1957 it was also seen in prime time; in 1958 Dick launched a separate Saturday night popular music show on ABC.

Dick's ability to give new records national TV exposure gave him tremendous power in the music business—the young entrepreneur was not slow to capitalize on. He had interests in record companies, owned publishing rights, and packaged tours. Remarkably, many of the songs he had an interest in managed to get played on his shows and go on to become best-selling hits. This apparent conflict of interest did not escape the notice of congressional investigators a couple of years later during the payola scandals, and Dick's future was for a time seriously in doubt. While other careers were ruined in the scandals, Dick survived however. He had apparently done nothing illegal (i.e., he had paid his taxes and taken no bribes); to eliminate any possible conflict in the future he agreed to sell off all his outside interests.

Dick remained on *Bandstand* and in 1964 moved his base of operations to Los Angeles. Gradually he began to expand his activities into new areas, producing and even acting in a few movies and producing other music-related television shows such as *Where the Action Is, Swingin' Country,* and *Happening.* In 1973 he began hosting a daytime game show, *The $10,000 Pyramid,* which, like *American Bandstand,* went on to a very long run on CBS and ABC. He also hosted a number of prime time variety and quiz shows, the most successful of which was *TV's Bloopers and Practical Jokes.* And, of course, whenever there was a rock 'n' roll nostalgia special in prime time, odds were that Dick Clark would be the host—and creator, producer, and owner.

Dick's candid autobiography is titled *Rock, Roll and Remember* (1976).

CLARK, DORAN—actress
b: Aug 8, New Orleans, La.

Secrets of Midland Heights (drama)
.... Ann Dulles (1980–81)
King's Crossing (drama) ...... Jillian (1982)
Emerald Point N.A.S. (drama)
.... Ensign Leslie Mallory (1983–84)

The granddaughter of World War II general Mark Clark.

CLARK, ERNEST—actor
b: Feb 12, 1912, Maida Vale, London, England

Doctor in the House (com)
.... Prof. Geoffrey Loftus (1970–73)

CLARK, EUGENE—actor

Night Heat (police)
.... Det. Colby Burns (1985–)

CLARK, FRED—actor
b: Mar 9, 1914, Lincoln, Calif. d: Dec 5, 1968

The George Burns and Gracie Allen Show (com)............. Harry Morton (1951–53)
The Double Life of Henry Phyfe (com)
.... Gerald B. Hannahan (1966)

CLARK, GAGE—actor

The Hartmans (com)
.... The man next door (1949)
Mr. Peepers (com)
.... Superintendent Bascom (1952–55)
Date with the Angels (com)
.... Dr. Gordon (1957–58)

CLARK, GORDON—actor

Secrets of Midland Heights (drama)
.... Max Bormann (1980–81)

CLARK, HARRY, TRIO—

Mohawk Showroom (music)
.... regulars (1949–51)

CLARK, JACK—host

Kodak Request Performance (drama)
.... host (1955)
100 Grand (quiz) .... emcee (1963)
Dealer's Choice (quiz) .... host (1974–75)
Cross-Wits (quiz)........... host (1975–80)

CLARK, MARLENA—black actress

Sanford and Son (com)
.... Janet Lawson (1976–77)

CLARK, MATT—actor

Dog and Cat (police)
.... Lt. Arthur Kipling (1977)

CLARK, OLIVER—actor
b: Jan 4, Buffalo, N.Y.

Karen (com) .... Jerry Siegel (1975)
The Bob Newhart Show (com)
.... Mr. Herd (1976–77)
3 Girls 3 (var).............. regular (1977)
We've Got Each Other (com)
.... Stuart Hibbard (1977–78)
The Two of Us (com)
.... Cubby Royce (1981–82)

CLARK, PATTY—singer

Glenn Miller Time (music) ... regular (1961)

CLARK, PHILIP—actor

The Young Lawyers (drama)
.... Chris Blake (1971)

CLARK, ROY—country singer, actor
b: Apr 15, 1933, Meherrin, Va.

Hee Haw (var).............. host (1969–)
The Kallikaks (com)
.... theme song singer (1977)

CLARK, SUSAN—actress
b: Mar 8, 1940, Sarnia, Ont., Canada

Webster (com)
.... Katherine Calder-Young Papadapolis
.... (1983–)

Emmy Award: best actress in a special, for *Babe* (1976)

Canadian-born Susan Clark began as a child actor in local and regional plays, then went on to study at England's Royal Academy of Dramatic Arts. Onstage in London in her teens, she later returned to Canada to appear in CBC productions in the 1960s. In the late 1960s she was signed to an exclusive contract by Universal Studios and began appearing in the studio's films and TV productions. Probably her most famous role was in the TV movie *Babe* in 1975, portraying the famous athlete Babe Didrickson Zaharias. The role won her an Emmy Award and introduced her to her future husband, Alex Karras, who played opposite her as Babe's husband, George Zaharias.

The following year Susan starred in the TV film *Amelia Earhart;* later she and Alex began producing TV films as well. The couple starred as husband and wife in the 1983 comedy *Webster.*

CLARK, THOMAS—panelist
b: c. 1870

Wisdom of the Ages (info)
.... panelist (1952–53)

CLARKE, BRIAN PATRICK—actor
b: Aug 1, 1952, Gettysburg, Pa.

Delta House (com) . Greg Marmalard (1979)
Eight Is Enough (com)
... Merle "The Pearl" Stockwell (1979–81)

CLARKE, GARY—actor
b: Aug 16, 1936, Los Angeles, Calif.

Michael Shayne (drama)
.... Dick Hamilton (1960–61)
The Virginian (wes) .... Steve (1962–64)
Hondo (wes)......... Capt. Richards (1967)

CLARKE, JOHN—actor

The New Breed (police)
.... Ptlmn. Joe Huddleston (1961–62)

This actor may be better known for his long run (since 1965) as Mickey Horton on the daytime soap opera *Days of Our Lives.*

CLARKE, VAN NESSA—actress

Teachers Only (com)
.... Gwen Edwards (1982)

CLARKE, WARREN—actor

Masada (drama) .... Plinius (1981)

CLARY, ROBERT—actor
b: Mar 1, 1926, Paris, France

Pantomime Quiz (quiz) ... regular (1954–57)
Hogan's Heroes (com)
.... Louis LeBeau (1965–71)

Pint-sized actor Robert Clary started out as a singer, first in France (as a child he was on French radio in the late 1930s), and, after the war, in America. He gradually turned to acting, appearing on stage and in a few films in the 1950s; in addition, he was an early regular on TV's *Pantomime Quiz.* Prime time viewers may remember him best for his long run as Corporal Louis Le-Beau on *Hogan's Heroes.* In daytime, he had an even longer run in the 1970s and early '80s as nightclub singer Robert Le Clair on *Days of Our Lives.*

Clary appeared as himself in *Remembrance of Love,* a 1982 TV movie about the real-life gathering of survivors of the Holocaust in Israel in 1981. He had in fact been in Nazi concentration camps for 31 months during World War II, and he lectures extensively on the subject. Clary is married to a daughter of Eddie Cantor.

CLAUSEN, ALF—orchestra leader
b: Mar 28, 1941, Minneapolis, Minn.

Mary (var)............. orch. leader (1978)

CLAWSON, CONNIE—hostess

Live Like a Millionaire (talent)
.... assistant (1951–52)

CLAWSON, CYNTHIA—gospel singer

CBS Newcomers (var) .... regular (1971)

CLAYTON, JAN—actress
b: Aug 26, 1917, Tularosa, N.M. d: Aug 28, 1983

Pantomime Quiz (quiz) ... regular (1953–54)
Lassie (adv) .... Ellen Miller (1954–57)
Pantomime Quiz (quiz) ... regular (1962–63)

CLEMMON, DAVID—actor

Rafferty (drama) .... Dr. Calvin (1977)

CLENNON, DAVID—actor

Park Place (com)......... Jeff O'Neil (1981)

CLERK, CLIVE—actor

Happy Days (var) .... regular (1970)

CLEVELAND, GEORGE—actor
b: 1883*, Sydney, Nova Scotia, Canada d: Jul 15, 1957

Lassie (adv) .... "Gramps" Miller (1954–57)

CLEVELAND, ODESSA—actress

*M*A*S*H* (com). Lt. Ginger Ballis (1972–74)

CLIFF QUARTET—

Capitol Capers (music)
.... instrumental group (1949)

CLINGER, DEBRA—actress
b: June 8, Salt Lake City, Utah

The American Girls (adv)
.... Amy Waddell (1978)

CLOHESSY, ROBERT—actor

Hill Street Blues (drama)
.... Off. Flaherty (1986–)

CLOONEY, BETTY—singer
b: Apr 12, c. 1930, Maysville, Ky.

The Jack Paar Program (var)
.... regular (1954)

The younger sister of Rosemary Clooney, with whom she sang in a sister act in the 1940s. Later, Betty had a minor career as a single, including stints with Robert Q. Lewis and Jack Paar on television.

CLOONEY, GEORGE—actor

E/R (com) .... Ace (1984–85)
The Facts of Life (com)
.... George Burnett (1985–86)

*Some sources give 1885 or 1886.

The son of popular Los Angeles news-caster Nick Clooney and nephew of singer Rosemary Clooney.

CLOONEY, ROSEMARY—singer
b: May 23, 1928, Maysville, Ky.

Songs for Sale (music).... regular (1950–51)
The Rosemary Clooney Show (var)
.... hostess (1956–57)
The Lux Show Starring Rosemary Clooney (var)..................... hostess (1957–58)

Television played a major role in launch-ing Rosemary Clooney's career. In the 1940s, together with her sister Betty, she had sung on local radio and toured with the Tony Pastor band; then, in 1949, she decided to go solo. Her first major break was on *Arthur Godfrey's Talent Scouts* in early 1950, where she won first place; that led to a spot on the 1950 CBS summer se-ries *Songs for Sale* and another in early 1951 on the short-lived daytime series *The Johnny Johnston Show* (whatever hap-pened to him?). By February, 1951, she had her first charted record, and in the summer of that year she recorded the million-sell-ing song about oranges and pomegranates that was to make her famous: "Come on-a My House." It was followed by many more top hits.

Rosemary continued to be very active on television throughout the 1950s—in numer-ous guest appearances and as host of a syndicated show in 1956–57 and an NBC network series in 1957–58. However, all was not well in her private life. She went through a tumultuous marriage to José Fer-rer (off and on from 1954 to 1967), a com-plete mental breakdown and confinement to a psychiatric ward, and eventual recov-ery. All of this was described in her 1977 autobiography, *This for Remembrance* and was dramatized in the 1982 TV movie *Rosie: The Rosemary Clooney Story,* star-ring Sondra Locke. On the wave of public-ity it generated, Rosemary became familiar to TV viewers once again, on talk shows, specials, and in numerous commercials.

CLOUGH, APRIL—actress
T. J. Hooker (police) .... Vicki Taylor (1982)

CLOWER, JERRY—country comedian
b: Sep 28, 1926, Amite County, Miss.

Nashville on the Road (music)
.... regular (1975–81)

CLUTE, SIDNEY—actor
b: Apr 21, 1916, Brooklyn, N.Y. d: Oct 2, 1985

Lou Grant (drama)
.... national editor (1977–79)
Cagney & Lacey (police)
.... Det. Paul La Guardia (1982–85)

CLYDE, ANDY—actor
b: Mar 25, 1892, Blairgowrie, Scotland d: May 18, 1967

The Real McCoys (com)
.... George MacMichael (1957–63)
Lassie (adv) .... Cully Wilson (1958–64)
No Time for Sergeants (com)
.... Grandpa Jim Anderson (1964–65)

Andy Clyde, who played Hopalong Cas-sidy's grizzled old sidekick "California" in so many oaters of the 1940s, proved equally successful as a television old-timer in the 1950s and '60s. Young viewers first saw him in edited versions of those '40s westerns during TV's Hopalong Cassidy boom of the early '50s. Later he was famil-iar as next-door-neighbor George on *The Real McCoys,* Timmy's elderly friend Cully on *Lassie,* and, briefly, "Grandpa" on *No Time for Sergeants.*

COATES, PAUL—columnist
b: Mar 10, 1921, New York City, N.Y.

Tonight! America After Dark (talk)
.... regular (1957)

COATES, PHYLLIS—actress
The Adventures of Superman (adv)
.... Lois Lane (1951)
The Duke (com)............. Gloria (1954)
Professional Father (com)
.... Nurse Madge Allen (1955)
This Is Alice (com)
.... Mrs. Holliday (1958–59)

COBB, BUFF—actress
b: Oct 19, 1928, Florence, Italy

All Around the Town (int)
.... cohost (1951–52)
Masquerade Party (quiz)
.... panelist (1953–55)

The granddaughter of humorist Irvin S. Cobb and onetime wife of TV newsman Mike Wallace, with whom she cohosted several local and network interview shows in the early 1950s. She and Mike were married in 1949 and divorced in 1954. After a rather minor acting career in films and onstage, she turned to producing in the 1960s and then went into retirement.

COBB, JULIE—actress
b: Los Angeles, Calif.

The D.A. (drama)
   Public Defender Katherine Benson (1971–72)
A Year at the Top (com) . . . . Trish (1977)
Charles in Charge (com)
   . . . . Jill Pembroke (1984–85)

The daughter of actor Lee J. Cobb.

COBB, LEE J.—actor
b: Dec 8, 1911, New York City, N.Y. d: Feb 11, 1976

The Virginian (wes)
   . . . . Judge Henry Garth (1962–66)
The Young Lawyers (drama)
   . . . . Attorney David Barrett (1970–71)

Veteran movie actor Lee J. Cobb played many a tough, middle-aged character in films during his long career, but he is best known for a stage and a TV role: that of Willie Lohman in the original Broadway production of Arthur Miller's *Death of a Salesman* in 1949 (also staged as a TV special, with Cobb, in 1966); and that of Judge Henry Garth, one of the rugged men who opened up the American West, in *The Virginian.*
   Cobb also appeared in a number of prestigious television dramatic productions of the 1950s, on *Playhouse 90, The DuPont Show of the Month,* and similar showcases. In later years he was seen mainly in TV movies, the last being a heist comedy called *The Great Ice Rip-Off* in 1974.

COBURN, JAMES—actor
b: Aug 31, 1928, Laurel, Nebr.

Klondike (adv) . . . . Jeff Durain (1960–61)
Acapulco (adv) . . . . Gregg Miles (1961)
Darkroom (drama) . . . . host (1981–82)

Film star James Coburn did quite a bit of television in the 1950s and early '60s, before Hollywood fame came his way in movies like *Charade* and *Our Man Flint.*
   Coburn's family moved to California when he was five, after his father's garage business was wiped out in the Depression. James began appearing in local stage productions around 1950, trekked to New York for several years of minor roles in early live TV drama series, and then returned to Los Angeles when live TV died out. Thereafter he worked steadily in filmed series, most of them westerns—*Restless Gun, The Californians, Lawman,* etc. Tall, craggy, and lithe, he could be alternately menacing and comic. One of his appearances was in a dramatization of the classic story "Occurrence at Owl Creek Bridge" on *Alfred Hitchcock Presents* in 1959. He had two regular roles—as the conniving Jeff Durain on *Klondike* and as the more sympathetic beachcomber Gregg Miles on *Acapulco*—but neither lasted long. If they had, he might have stayed in television.
   After a long absence, Coburn returned to the small screen in the 1978 miniseries *The Dain Curse.* Later he hosted the spooky anthology *Darkroom* and appeared in some rather sub-par TV movies, including *Jacqueline Susann's Valley of the Dolls, Malibu,* and *Draw.*

COCA, IMOGENE—comedienne
b: Nov 18, 1908*, Philadelphia, Pa.

Buzzy Wuzzy (var) . . . . host (1948)
Admiral Broadway Revue (var)
   . . . . regular (1949)
Your Show of Shows (var)
   . . . . regular (1950–54)
The Imogene Coca Show (var)
   . . . . Betty Crane (1954–55)
Sid Caesar Invites You (var) . cohost (1958)
Grindl (com) . . . . Grindl (1963–64)
It's About Time (com) . . . . . . Shad (1966–67)

Emmy Award: Best Actress (1951)

Imogene Coca was performing in television earlier than most; owners of the first, small-screen sets could see her on experimental telecasts in 1939. And she was a show-business veteran even then. The daughter of a musician father and performer mother (a magician's assistant),

*Some sources give 1909.

Imogene was writing and acting in amateur plays while in grade school. In her first appearance she was clad in white for her portrayal of "An Evil Germ." Later, at the ripe old age of nine, she was tap-dancing in vaudeville. She never did finish high school, going straight into a career as a dancer. However, her first real break came as a comedienne, in *New Faces of 1934* on Broadway.

Throughout the 1930s and '40s Imogene performed in the New York area, onstage and in cabarets, and at that breeding ground for future talent, the Tamiment resort in Pennsylvania's Pocono Mountains. Her first regular TV spot was in the fall of 1948 on a short-lived variety show called *Buzzy Wuzzy,* starring a now-forgotten actor named Jerry Bergen. The show that would make her famous premiered the following January. Max Liebman's big-budget variety spectacular *Admiral Broadway Revue* teamed Imogene with a young comic (14 years her junior) named Sid Caesar. The two of them made comedy magic. As wide-ranging and preposterous as Caesar's characterizations could be, she matched him at every turn with her rubber features and pixieish lunacy. She could be the perfect wife/girlfriend/salesgirl/movie star or whatever else their skit called for. Caesar and Coca were together for the next five years, on the *Revue* and its successor series *Your Show of Shows.*

Many feel that Imogene's best work (as well as Caesar's) was in those heady days of the early '50s, when television was still, to some extent, a comedy workshop. In any event, *Your Show of Shows* made her a major star, and she went on to headline her own NBC series in 1954–55, which alternated between situation comedy and variety formats. She made many guest appearances in the late 1950s and was reunited briefly with Caesar in 1958, but by the '60s she was in danger of becoming a star of yesteryear. That cued a new career in situation comedy, including regular roles in *Grindl* (as a maid) and *It's About Time* (as Shad the cave dweller).

After a number of appearances in *Love, American Style; Bewitched;* and similar series in the early 1970s, Imogene—by then nearing 70 ("No lady in her right mind ever tells the truth about her age," she cracked) —went into semiretirement. She has made

only occasional appearances since, one of them as 100-year-old "Granny's Maw" on *The Return of the Beverly Hillbillies* in 1981.

COCHRAN, RON—newscaster, host
b: 1912, Saskatchewan, Canada r: Fairfield, Iowa

Man of the Week (int).... moderator (1954)
Armstrong Circle Theatre (drama)
.... host/narrator (1961–62)
ABC Late News (news)
.... anchorman (1961–63)
ABC News Reports: 1963 Civil Rights Crisis (doc) .... reporter (1963)
ABC Evening News (news)
.... Anchorman (1963–65)

Back in the days when ABC's newscasts were viewed by hardly anyone, the network's anchor for a time was veteran newsman Ron Cochran. He had begun in local radio in the 1930s, detoured for a few years in the mid-1940s to work as an FBI agent, then from 1951–61 was heard on CBS's local stations in Washington and New York and occasionally on the network. His early TV appearances included hosting *Man of the Week,* the predecessor of CBS's *Face the Nation.*

After a short stint as a television drama host, he joined ABC in 1961 and became its leading anchorman, until he was supplanted by Peter Jennings in 1965.

COCHRANE, ROBERT—host
The Johns Hopkins Science Review (info)
.... host (1949)

COCO, JAMES—actor
b: Mar 21, 1929*, The Bronx, N.Y. d: Feb 25, 1987

Calucci's Department (com)
.... Joe Calucci (1973)
The Dumplings (com).. Joe Dumpling (1976)

Emmy Award: Best Supporting Actor, for an episode of *St. Elsewhere* (1983)

James Coco said of his childhood, "My life was like a soap opera. We were very, very poor. We grew most of our food in the backyard, and we could never afford a tel-

*Some sources give 1928 or 1930.

ephone. My father made shoes, and I shined them."

Determined to escape such humble beginnings, the chubby youngster sought a career on the stage; he was hardly a romantic lead, but a gift for comedy won him roles in summer stock and off-Broadway plays. The road to fame was a long one, however. He worked in scattered television productions of the 1960s (mainly those originating in New York) and finally scored his first major success in the 1969 Broadway hit *Last of the Red Hot Lovers.* In the '70s, by now portly and balding, he starred in two tailor-made but short-lived situation comedies, *Calucci's Department* and *The Dumplings.* He also guested on other series, including *Marcus Welby* and *Flip Wilson.* In later years Coco appeared mostly in films. And, yes, he was seen briefly on two soap operas along the way: *Search for Tomorrow* and *The Doctors.*

COE, BARRY—actor
b: 1934

Follow the Sun (adv)
.... Ben Gregory (1961–62)

COE, GEORGE—actor

Goodnight, Beantown (com)
.... Dick Novak (1983)

COFFIELD, PETER—actor
b: c. 1946, Illinois d: Nov 19, 1983

W.E.B. (drama)............. Kevin (1978)

COFFIN, TRIS—actor

Washington Report (info) . moderator (1951)
26 Men (wes)
.... Capt. Tom Rynning (1957–59)

COGAN, SHAYE—singer

Face the Music (music)..... vocalist (1948)
Spin the Picture (quiz).... regular (1949–50)
The Vaughn Monroe Show (var)
.... regular (1950–51)

COHEN, EVAN—juvenile actor
b: Mar 31, Los Angeles, Calif.

The Ropers (com) . David Brookes (1979–80)
It's Not Easy (com)..... Johnny Long (1983)

COHEN, JILL—actress

Knots Landing (drama) ..... Amy (1981–83)

COHEN, MARTY—comedian

The Jacksons (var) .... regular (1976)
Solid Gold (music) .... regular (1980–81)

COHN, MINDY—actress
b: May 20, 1966, Los Angeles, Calif.

The Facts of Life (com)
.... Natalie Green (1979–   )

Mindy Cohn, the chubby girl in the *Facts of Life* boarding school, was discovered by series star Charlotte Rae while Rae was visiting a private school in Los Angeles where Mindy was a student. The two started talking, hit it off, and before she knew it the 13-year-old schoolgirl had been offered her first professional job. "I give her credit for changing my life," she says of Rae.

Though Mindy became famous overnight, she continued to study for her degree and plans to become a television newscaster.

COHOON, PATTI—juvenile actress
b: Jan 27, 1959, Whittier, Calif.

Here Come the Brides (adv)
.... Molly Pruitt (1969–70)
Apple's Way (drama)
.... Cathy Apple (1974–75)
The Runaways (drama)
.... Debbie Shaw (1979)

COLASANTO, NICHOLAS—director, actor
b: Jan 19, 1924, Providence, R.I. d: Feb 12, 1985

Cheers (com)
.... Ernie "Coach" Pantusso (1982–85)

The beloved, absentminded "coach" on *Cheers* started out as an accountant, then switched to acting and directing in the 1950s. From the mid-1960s on he was known in Hollywood primarily as a director and was responsible for approximately 100 episodes of such series as *Run for Your Life* (his first), *Bonanza, Starsky and Hutch, Streets of San Francisco, Today's F.B.I.,* and many others. He acted occasionally, including roles in Hitchcock's film *The Family Plot* and as the mafia chief in *Raging Bull*, but it was in *Cheers* in the '80s that he became an on-screen celebrity. He had a history of heart trouble and died of a heart attack in early 1985. "As an actor I will miss him very much," said series star Ted Danson. "As Sam Malone, I miss him as I would a father."

COLBERT, ROBERT—actor
b: Jul 26, Long Beach, Calif. r: Santa Barbara, Calif.

Maverick (wes) ..... Brent Maverick (1961)
The Time Tunnel (sci fi)
.... Dr. Doug Phillips (1966–67)

Colbert later played Stuart Brooks on *The Young and the Restless* for ten years (1973–83).

COLBIN, ROD—actor

The Ropers (com) .... Hubert (1979–80)

COLBY, ANITA—fashion model, actress, writer
b: Aug 5, 1914, Washington, D.C.

Pepsi-Cola Playhouse (drama)
.... hostess (1954)

COLBY, CARROLL "KIB"—cartoonist

Billy Boone and Cousin Kib (child)
.... host (1950)

COLBY, MARION—dancer, singer

Broadway Open House (talk)
.... regular (1951)
Doodles Weaver (var) .... regular (1951)
The Henny and Rocky Show (var)
.... vocalist (1955)

COLE, CAROL—black actress
b: Oct 17, 1944, West Medford, Mass.

Grady (com)
.... Ellie Wilson Marshall (1975–76)

The daughter of Nat "King" Cole.

COLE, DENNIS—actor
b: Jul 19, 1940,* Detroit, Mich.

Felony Squad (police)
.... Det. Jim Briggs (1966–69)
Bracken's World (drama)
.... Davey Evans (1969–70)
Bearcats (adv) .... Johnny Reach (1971)

COLE, HARRY—

Hee Haw (var) .... regular (1972–76)

COLE, MICHAEL—actor
b: 1945, Madison, Wis.

The Mod Squad (police)
.... Pete Cochran (1968–73)

COLE, NAT "KING"—black singer
b: Mar 17, 1919**, Montgomery, Ala. d: Feb 15, 1965

The Nat "King" Cole Show (var)
.... host (1956–57)

Nat "King" Cole started out as a jazz artist in the '40s and moved into the mainstream of popular music late in that decade with lush ballad hits such as "Nature Boy" and "Mona Lisa." He was a major singing star in the '50s, a popular guest on early variety shows, and he almost made TV history—as the first major black star of the medium. Unfortunately, his 1956 variety show on NBC was widely ignored by viewers, who preferred to watch *Robin Hood* instead. Despite a loyal network and widespread support from other star performers, many of whom appeared on his show for minimal fees, the show was eventually canceled due to lack of audience—and therefore of a national sponsor. Cole himself, a genteel and not normally vindictive man, laid the blame at the feet of Madison Avenue, which, he said, never tried very hard to sell his program. "Their big clients didn't want their products associated with Negroes," he wrote bitterly in *Ebony* magazine. In the last analysis, he said, "racial prejudice is more finance than romance."

COLE, OLIVIA—black actress
b: Nov 26, 1942, Memphis, Tenn. r: New York City

Roots (drama)............. Mathilda (1977)
Szysznyk (com) .... Ms. Harrison (1977–78)

*Some sources give July 1 as his birthday.
**Some sources give 1917.

Backstairs at the White House (drama)
.... Maggie Rogers (1979)
Report to Murphy (com) .... Blanche (1982)
North and South (drama)
.... Maum Sally (1985)

Emmy Award: Best Supporting Actress in a Single Performance, for *Roots* (1977).

COLE, ROCKY—pianist

The Patti Page Olds Show (var)
.... pianist (1958–59)

COLE, TINA—actress, singer
b: 1943, Hollywood, Calif.

My Three Sons (com)
.... Katie Miller Douglas (1967–72)

COLEMAN, CAROLE—singer
b: c. 1922 d: Aug 31, 1964

Face the Music (music) .. vocalist (1948–49)

COLEMAN, CHARLES H.—orchestra leader

The Melba Moore-Clifton Davis Show (var)
.... orch. leader (1972)

COLEMAN, CY—orchestra leader, composer
b: Jun 14, 1929, New York City, N.Y.

Starlit Time (var) .... trio (1950)
ABC's Nightlife (talk)... orch. leader (1965)

Emmy Award: Best Writing for a Comedy or Music Special, for *Shirley MacLaine: If They Could See Me Now* (1975); Best Comedy or Musical Special (Producer), for *Gypsy in My Soul* with Shirley MacLaine (1976).

Coleman is a Broadway composer who is known for such songs as "Witchcraft," "The Best Is Yet to Come," and "Hey, Look Me Over."

COLEMAN, DABNEY—actor
b: Jan 2, 1932, Austin, Texas r: Corpus Christi, Texas

That Girl (com)
.... Dr. Leon Bessemer (1966–67)
Mary Hartman, Mary Hartman (com)
.... Merle Jeeter (1976–78)

Apple Pie (com)
.... "Fast Eddie" Murtaugh (1978)
Buffalo Bill (com) ... Bill Bittinger (1983–84)

Unctuous character actor Dabney Coleman has certainly had some offbeat roles in series TV. First seen as Marlo Thomas's neighbor Dr. Bessemer in *That Girl,* he later turned up as the mayor of Fernwood on the wacky *Mary Hartman,* as "Fast Eddie" on the fleeting comedy *Apple Pie* (which lasted two weeks), and most recently as self-centered talk show host Bill Bittinger on *Buffalo Bill*— the latter being perhaps the most despicable leading character ever seen in a situation comedy. Coleman's movie career also spans 20 years. After a number of obscure supporting roles beginning with 1965's *The Slender Thread,* his work in *Nine to Five, Tootsie,* and *On Golden Pond* suddenly made him a hot property in the '80s.

Originally, Coleman was a law school student, but decided to pursue acting instead. He first played dramatic roles and went virtually unnoticed until he switched to comedy in the 1960s.

COLEMAN, EMIL—orchestra leader
b: Jun 19, 1894 d: 1965

Arthur Murray Party (var)
.... orch. leader (1951–52)

COLEMAN, GARY—black juvenile actor
b: Feb 8, 1968, Zion, Ill.

Diff'rent Strokes (com)
.... Arnold Jackson (1978–86)

Gary Coleman was one of America's favorite TV kids during the '70s and '80s and an inspiring story of success over handicap. Born with a defective kidney, his growth was stunted from childhood and he always appeared younger than his years. His mother allowed him to become a child model at age five, because it was an activity in which her son could excel without fear of injury.

An uncommonly intelligent youngster, Gary quickly developed acting ability and was a favorite child actor in commercials for Chicago area stores and banks during the mid-1970s. He won several awards for these commercials. A talent scout for producer Norman Lear saw them and brought him to Hollywood to appear in the pilot for a proposed series based on the Little Rascals. That show did not make it to the schedule, but Lear kept Gary under contract and featured him in episodes of *America 2-Night, Good Times,* and *The Jeffersons* during the 1977–78 season. Lear then developed *Diff'rent Strokes* for him during 1978. It turned into a major hit, and Gary, at age ten, was a star.

Despite his medical condition, the young actor was extremely active, making at least one TV movie during each hiatus from the series—*The Kid from Left Field* in 1979, *Scout's Honor* in 1980, *The Kid with the Broken Halo* in 1981, *The Kid with the 200 I.Q.* in 1982, *The Fantastic World of D. C. Collins* in 1983, and *Playing With Fire* in 1984 among them.

Gary had received a kidney transplant at age six, and in 1982 the kidney began to fail, forcing him to rely on portable dialysis equipment. In November 1984 he received a second transplant. He returned to his series two months later with the words, "Let's go to work!"

COLEMAN, JACK—actor
b: Feb 21, 1958, Easton, Pa.

Dynasty (drama)
.... Steven Carrington (1982–)

COLEMAN, JAMES—actor
S.W.A.T. (police)
.... Off. T. J. McCabe (1975–76)

COLEN, BEATRICE—actress
Happy Days (com) ...... Marsha (1974–76)
Wonder Woman (adv)
.... Corp. Etta Candy (1976–77)

COLICOS, JOHN—actor
b: Dec 10, 1928, Toronto, Ontario, Canada

Battlestar Galactica (sci fi)
.... Count Baltar (1978–79)

Colicos will be remembered by daytime viewers as the mad scientist Mikkos Cassadine on *General Hospital,* who threatened to destroy Luke, Laura, and the entire world during the series' hugely successful "Ice Princess" adventure story in 1981.

COLIN, MARGARET—actress
b: c. 1957 r: New York City, N.Y.

Foley Square (com)
...... Asst. D.A. Alex Harrigan (1985–86)

COLLETT, VERNE—actor
The Witness (drama)
.... court reporter (1960–61)

COLLEY, DON PEDRO—black actor
Daniel Boone (wes) ...... Gideon (1968–69)
The Dukes of Hazzard (com)
.... Sheriff Little (1981–84)

COLLIER, DICK—announcer
The Singing Lady (child).. announcer (1949)
Chance of a Lifetime (quiz)
.... regular (1950–51)

COLLIER, DON—actor
b: c. 1928, Inglewood, Calif.

The Outlaws (wes)
..... Dep. Marshal Will Forman (1960–62)
The High Chaparral (wes)
.... Sam Butler (1967–71)

COLLIER, LOIS—actress
b: Mar 21, 1919, Salley, South Carolina

Boston Blackie (drama)
.... Mary Wesley (1951–53)

COLLIER, MARIAN—actress
Mr. Novak (drama)
.... Miss Marilyn Scott (1963–65)

COLLIER, RICHARD—actor
Many Happy Returns (com)
.... Harry Price (1964–65)

COLLINGWOOD, CHARLES— newscaster
b: Jun 4, 1917, Three Rivers, Mich. d: Oct 3, 1985

The Big Question (news).. moderator (1951)
Adventure (doc)........... narrator (1953)
Person to Person (int)....... host (1959–61)
Eyewitness to History (news)
.... anchorman (1962–63)
Portrait (int) .... host (1963)
Chronicle (doc) .... host (1963–64)

Charles Collingwood, one of CBS's classiest and most experienced foreign correspondents, was a foundation of the network's reputation as TV's premier news organization. A law and philosophy graduate of Cornell University, he studied at Oxford on a Rhodes scholarship in the late 1930s and remained in England to become a London reporter for United Press in 1939. As war clouds gathered over Europe, the American radio networks began to establish European branches, and Collingwood was recruited by Edward R. Murrow in 1941 to join CBS. The young reporter covered the major battles of the European theater, and, after the war, became CBS' first United Nations correspondent.

In the 1950s and '60s CBS used Collingwood's expertise on a number of public affairs series and specials, including two years as host of *Person to Person* (succeeding Murrow) and as host of the highly publicized 1962 special *A Tour of the White House with Mrs. John F. Kennedy.* In 1964 Collingwood was named the network's chief foreign correspondent. He became one of the most familiar reporters on and analysts of the Vietnam War and was the first American network reporter admitted into North Vietnam (in 1968).

Collingwood returned to the U.S. on a permanent basis in 1975 and appeared on many telecasts dealing with foreign and domestic affairs. By this time he was considered one of the grand old men of CBS News, and received numerous honors—including an appointment by Queen Elizabeth II as Commander in the Order of the British Empire (a title that earned him the nickname around CBS of "Lord Collingwood"). He retired in 1982.

Collingwood was married to actress Louise Allbritton from 1945 until her death in 1979.

COLLINS, AL "JAZZBO"—disc jockey
b: Jan 4, 1919, New York City, N.Y.

Tonight! America After Dark (talk)
.... host (1957)

COLLINS, DOROTHY—singer
b: Nov 18, 1926, Windsor, Ontario, Canada

Your Hit Parade (music) . vocalist (1950–59)

The singing sweetheart of *Your Hit Parade* started on local radio as a child and in the mid-1940s—while still a teenager—began appearing with Raymond Scott's orchestra and on his radio shows. When Scott became musical director of *Your Hit Parade* he brought Dorothy with him; she made her TV debut singing the sponsor's "Be happy, go Lucky" jingles in the middle of the Lucky Strike bull's-eye.

For most of the rest of the 1950s Dorothy sang the weekly top hits on America's first popular "countdown" show. With its demise in 1959 (cause of death: rock 'n' roll), she began appearing in clubs and was a frequent guest on *Candid Camera.* Her role there was to set up the "victims" in hilarious fashion. In one of her best remembered bits, she was the demure motorist who pulled into a filling station and complained of engine trouble; the mechanic opened the hood to reveal—no motor! "I think it was there when I left the house," Dorothy would murmur innocently.

In later years she worked mostly onstage, including a role in the Broadway production *Follies.* She was married to her mentor, Raymond Scott, from 1952 until 1965.

COLLINS, GARY—actor, host
b: Apr 30, 1938, Venice, Calif.

The Wackiest Ship in the Army (adv)
.. Lt. (j.g.) Richard "Rip" Riddle (1965–66)
The Iron Horse (wes)
.... Dave Tarrant (1966–68)
The Sixth Sense (drama)
.... Dr. Michael Rhodes (1972)
Born Free (adv) ... George Adamson (1974)
Roots (drama)................. Grill (1977)

Emmy Award: Best Host of a Daytime Talk Show, for *Hour Magazine* (1984)

Easygoing Gary Collins first attracted attention as an actor in the 1960s. He was the youthful commander of *The Wackiest Ship in the Army,* Dale Robertson's right-hand man on *The Iron Horse,* the parapsychology expert on *The Sixth Sense,* and a caring young game warden on *Born Free,* as well as a guest star on numerous other series.

None of these roles resulted in major stardom, however, and by the early 1980s Gary had turned to hosting, at which he proved particularly adept. He has been host of the popular *Hour Magazine* syndicated daytime series since 1980 and of the annual *Miss America Pageant* since 1982. He is married, coincidentally, to actress Mary Ann Mobley, Miss America of 1959.

COLLINS, JACK—actor

The Milton Berle Show (var)
.... regular (1953–55)
Occasional Wife (com)
.... Max Brahms (1966–67)

COLLINS, JOAN—actress

b: May 23, 1933, London, England

Dynasty (drama)
.... Alexis Carrington Colby (1981–)

If there was ever proof positive that life begins at 40, Joan Collins is it. She has been playing sultry, alluring women all her life, but not until the 1980s and the fabulous success of *Dynasty* did she suddenly become a superstar.

The British-born actress trained at the Royal Academy of Dramatic Arts and made her stage debut at age nine as a boy in Ibsen's *A Doll's House.* Thereafter she was cast mostly as wayward young girls in British plays and films; her first American movies, in 1954, were *Land of the Pharoahs* and *The Virgin Queen* (the title referred to Bette Davis' Queen Elizabeth I, not to Joan!).

After years of mostly forgettable films, she began turning up on television in the 1960s in series such as *Run for Your Life, Batman* (as the Siren), and *Star Trek* (in "City on the Edge of Forever"). She was a man-eater, figuratively, in the 1976 miniseries *The Moneychangers*— and literally in a 1975 episode of *Space: 1999.* Then she brushed aside her veil to reveal herself as Blake Carrington's vengeful former wife on *Dynasty* in 1981, and her career was made. In 1983 she posed seminude (at age 50) for *Playboy,* and the issue was a sellout. In 1985 *TV Guide* named her the most beautiful woman on television. Eat your hearts out, all you young bimbos!

Joan's autobiography, *Past Imperfect,* was originally published in 1978 and became a best-seller when updated in 1984. Joan is the sister of sex-and-sleaze novelist Jackie Collins, two of whose works have been made into Joan Collins films—*The Stud* and *The Bitch.*

COLLINS, JOHNNIE, III—juvenile actor

The Tim Conway Show (com)
.... Ronnie Crawford (1970)

COLLINS, PAT—panelist

I've Got a Secret (quiz) ..... panelist (1976)

COLLINS, PATRICK—actor

Supertrain (drama) .... Dave Noonan (1979)
Checking In (com)...... Earl Bellamy (1981)
Gimme a Break (com)
.... Tim Donovan (1986–)

COLLINS, RAY—actor

b: 1890*, Sacramento, Calif. d: Jul 11, 1965

The Halls of Ivy (com)
.... Dr. Merriweather (1954)
Perry Mason (drama)
.... Lt. Arthur Tragg (1957–65)

Ray Collins is probably best remembered by television viewers as the craggy, everfrustrated police inspector on *Perry Mason,* but that was merely the culmination of a long and notable career. Originally a stage actor in the 1910s and '20s, he entered radio in the '30s. There he met an ambitious young producer named Orson Welles, who began to feature him in his *Mercury Theatre* productions. One of these was the 1938 drama that has become perhaps the most famous in radio history, *War of the Worlds* (Collins provided the dying voice of the last human reporter as the Martians took over the world).

In the 1940s, Welles brought Collins to Hollywood with him and used him in such classic films as *Citizen Kane* and *The Magnificent Ambersons.* Collins did many more movies, too, before branching into television in the '50s with roles on many of the dramatic series of the day. In "Conversation over a Corpse" on *Alfred Hitchcock Presents* he was the not-so-dead corpse. In 1957, in his late sixties, he took the role of Lt. Tragg on *Perry Mason* and played it for the rest of his days.

*Some sources give 1888 or 1889.

COLLINS, STEPHEN—actor

b: Oct 1, 1949, Des Moines, Iowa

The Rhinemann Exchange (drama)
.... David Spaulding (1977)
Tales of the Gold Monkey (adv)
.... Jake Cutter (1982–83)
Chiefs (drama)... Billy Lee (as adult) (1983)

COLLINS, TED—pianist, announcer

b: c. 1900, New York City, N.Y. d: Mar 29, 1964

The Kate Smith Evening Hour (var)
.... host (1951–52)

Kate Smith's longtime mentor, manager, and accompanist.

COLLYER, BUD—emcee

b: Jun 18, 1908, Manhattan, N.Y. d: Sep 8, 1969

Winner Take All (quiz) .... emcee (1948–50)
Talent Jackpot (talent)..... assistant (1949)
Break the Bank (quiz) .... cohost (1949–53)
Beat the Clock (quiz) ...... emcee (1950–58)
Say It with Acting (quiz)
.... team captain (1951)
Masquerade Party (quiz)..... emcee (1952)
Talent Patrol (talent) .... emcee (1953)
Quick As a Flash (quiz)
.... moderator (1953–54)
On Your Way (quiz)....... emcee (1953–54)
To Tell the Truth (quiz).... emcee (1956–67)

Clayton "Bud" Collyer was one of the friendliest and most familiar voices in America for nearly 40 years, on radio in the '30s and '40s and on television in the '50s and '60s. He had started out to be a lawyer, receiving his degree from Fordham in 1933, but switched to singing and acting instead. He soon carved out a very busy career on network radio as a straight man on comedy shows, an actor on soap operas, and an announcer on others. His most famous role was at first kept a deep, dark secret, however—no one was supposed to know that Bud was the voice of . . . Superman! Finally the truth leaked out (Superman couldn't lie). Bud played the role for nine years altogether, from 1940–49.

He was also active on radio game shows, and it was in that field that he made his mark in television. Natty in his bow tie, he hosted more than a dozen on daytime and nighttime TV, probably the most famous being *Beat the Clock* in the '50s and *To Tell the Truth* in the '50s and '60s. He also provided the voices for Saturday morning cartoon characters and, in the late 1960s, just before his retirement, was heard as the cartoon voice of *Batman*.

COLLYER, JUNE—actress

b: Aug 19, 1907, New York City, N.Y. d: Mar 16, 1968

The Stu Erwin Show (com)
.... June Erwin (1950–55)

The wife of Stu Erwin and sister of TV host Bud Collyer. A former debutante who had a brief film career in the late '20s and early '30s, June came out of retirement to do this TV series with her husband.

COLMAN, BOOTH—actor

b: Mar 8, Portland, Ore.

The Planet of the Apes (sci fi). Zaius (1974)

COLMAN, RONALD—actor

b: Feb 9, 1891, Richmond-Surrey, England d: May 19, 1958

The Halls of Ivy (com)
.... Dr. William Todhunter Hall (1954–55)

This suave British leading man, who fairly radiated intelligence and good manners, was a major Hollywood star for 25 years before television came on the scene. He appeared several times on *Four Star Playhouse,* as well as in his own series, *The Halls of Ivy* (based on a radio series in which he had starred). His biography, *A Very Private Person,* was written by his daughter Juliet Benita Colman and published in 1975.

COLOMBY, SCOTT—actor

b: Sept 19, 1952, Brooklyn, N.Y.

Sons and Daughters (drama) .. Stash (1974)
Szysznyk (com) ... Tony La Placa (1977–78)

COLONNA, JERRY—comedian

b: Oct 17, 1904*, Boston, Mass. d: Nov 21, 1986

The Jerry Colonna Show (var)
.... emcee (1951)

*Some sources give 1903 or 1905.

This famous comedian with the bellowing voice, walrus moustache, and bulging eyes was much more famous on radio (with Bob Hope) and in movies than on TV. He was seen mostly in guest shots, although he had his own variety series briefly and was the ringmaster on *Super Circus* for a season in 1955–56. He became inactive following a stroke in 1966.

COLORADO, HORTENSIA—actress
b: Nov 8, Blue Island, Ill.

Nurse (drama)
.... Nurse Betty LaSada (1981–82)

COLPITTS, CISSY—actress
The Ted Knight Show (com)
................···.... Graziella (1978)

COLT, MACKENZIE—
Hee Haw (var).......... regular (1978–82)

COLT, MARSHALL—actor
b: Oct 26, c. 1948, New Orleans, La.

McClain's Law (police)
.... Det. Harry Gates (1981–82)
Lottery (drama) .... Eric Rush (1983–84)

COLVIN, JACK—actor
b: Oct 13, Lyndon, Kans.

The Incredible Hulk (drama)
.... Jack McGee (1978–82)

COMBS, GEORGE HAMILTON—host
b: c. 1899 d: Nov 29, 1977

Through the Curtain (pub aff)
.... host (1953–54)

COMEGYS, KATHLEEN—actress
b: 1895

Jamie (com)
.... Aunt Ella (occasional) (1953–54)

COMI, PAUL—actor
Two Faces West (wes)
.... Dep. Johnny Evans (1960–61)
Ripcord (adv) .... Chuck Lambert (1961–62)

COMO, PERRY—singer
b: May 18, 1912, Canonsburg, Pa.

The Chesterfield Supper Club (var)
.... host (1948–50)
·*The Perry Como Show* (var).. host (1950–61)
The Kraft Music Hall (var)... host (1961–63)

Emmy Awards: Best Male Singer (1954, 1955); Best Emcee (1955); Best Male Personality (1956); Best Actor in a Musical or Variety Show (1959)

Perry Como is probably the most popular singer in the history of television. He certainly takes the prize for longevity, having been seen practically every year since 1948, either in a series or specials. His casual, relaxed style has worn very well over the years.

Perry was born Pierino Como, and used the name Nick Perido for a time before settling on something closer to his real name. He was a barber in the late 1920s and early '30s, and a rather successful one, until a local bandleader lured him into show business in 1933. From 1936–42 he was a vocalist with the nationally popular Ted Weems Orchestra, but the pressures of life on the road very nearly drove him back to barbering in the early 1940s—until offers of a solo career with minimum traveling brought him to network radio. At about the same time his recording career began to take off, with some of the biggest hits of the mid-1940s—"Till the End of Time," "Prisoner of Love," and "If I Loved You" among them.

Perry's first television series premiered in 1948 as a simple adaptation of his popular radio show, *The Chesterfield Supper Club*. In fact, cameras were simply wheeled into the radio studio, with music stands and radio microphones remaining in full view. Two years later (now dressed up for TV) the series became a three-a-week 15-minute show, and in 1955 it became a full-fledged prime time variety hour, which ran for eight very successful years. Perry's easygoing manner was the hallmark of all his shows and probably contributed to the 1950s being such a mellow decade. His sleepy manner eventually became the butt of jokes ("Wake up, Perry!").

After 1963 Perry cut back on his schedule to do only a few specials per year. These always included his Christmas special (which continued into the 1980s), on which he often traveled to such faraway spots as the Bahamas, Paris, and Guadalajara.

COMPTON, FORREST—actor
b: Sep 15 1925, Reading, Pa.

Gomer Pyle, U.S.M.C. (com)
.... Col. Gray (1964–69)

This prime time actor of the 1960s subsequently had a long run in daytime as Mike Karr on *The Edge of Night* (1971–84).

COMPTON, GAIL—host
Pet Shop (misc) .... host (1951–53)

COMPTON, GAY—assistant
Pet Shop (misc) .... regular (1951–53)

The young daughter of Gail Compton, and his assistant on this Chicago-originated pet show.

COMPTON, JOHN—actor
b: Jun 21, 1923, Lynchburg, Tenn.

The D.A.'s Man (police).... Shannon (1959)

COMPTON, WALTER—newscaster
b: c. 1912, Charleston, S.C. d: Dec 9, 1959

DuMont Evening News (news)
.... anchorman (1947–49)

COMSTOCK, FRANK—arranger,
orchestra leader
b: Sep 20, 1922, San Diego, Calif.

The Jimmie Rodgers Show (var)
.... orch. leader (1969)

CONAWAY, JEFF—actor
b: Oct 5, 1950, New York City, N.Y.

Taxi (com)....... Bobby Wheeler (1978–81)
Wizards and Warriors (adv)
.... Prince Erik Greystone (1983)
Berrengers (drama)..... John Higgins (1985)

CONDON, EDDIE—jazz guitarist,
bandleader
b: Nov 16, 1904*, Goodland, Ind. d: Aug 4, 1973

Eddie Condon's Floor Show (music)
.... host (1949–50)

*Some sources give 1905 or 1906.

Autobiography: *We Called It Music* (1947).

CONIFF, FRANK—emcee
Are You Positive? (quiz) ...... emcee (1952)

CONKLIN, HAL—actor
Captain Video and His Video Rangers (child)
.... Dr. Pauli (1949–55)
Operation Neptune (sci fi)... Kebeda (1953)

CONLEY, JOE—actor
b: Mar 3, Buffalo, N.Y.

The Waltons (drama)
.... Ike Godsey (1972–81)

CONN, DIDI—actress
b: Jul 13, 1951, Brooklyn. N.Y.

Keep On Truckin' (var) ...... regular (1975)
The Practice (com) .... Helen (1976–77)
Benson (com)
.... Denise Stevens Downey (1981–85)

This squeeky-voiced comedienne was particularly good at Betty Boop–type voices. Among other things, she was the voice of Cupcake on the Saturday morning cartoon *Fonz and The Happy Days Gang* and of Raggedy Ann in the animated feature *Raggedy Ann and Andy* (1977).

CONNELL, JANE—actress
b: Oct 27, 1925, Oakland, Calif.

Stanley (com)............. Jane (1956–57)
The Dumplings (com)
.... Bridget McKenna (1976)

CONNELL, JIM—actor
Run Buddy Run (com) ..... Junior (1966–67)
Donny and Marie (var) ... regular (1976–79)

CONNELLY, CHRISTOPHER—actor
b: 1941

Peyton Place (drama)
.... Norman Harrington (1964–69)
Paper Moon (com)
.... Moses (Moze) Pray (1974–75)

CONNELLY, MARC—playwright
b: Dec 13, 1890, McKeesport, Pa. d: Dec 21, 1980

Actors Studio (drama) .... host (1948–50)
Droodles (quiz)............ panelist (1954)
One Minute Please (quiz)
.... panelist (1954–55)

The famous author of *The Green Pastures*, which was adapted several times on television. He also acted in a number of TV dramas, including two appearances on *The Defenders* in 1963.

CONNELLY, PEGGY—comedienne
b: Shreveport, La. r: Texas

Take a Good Look (quiz) . regular (1959–61)

CONNER, BETTY—actress

Gidget (com) .... Anne Cooper (1965–66)

CONNOR, WHITFIELD—actor
b: 1916

Willy (drama)....... Charlie Bush (1954–55)

CONNORS, CHUCK—actor
b: Apr 10, 1921, Brooklyn, N.Y.

The Rifleman (wes)
.... Lucas McCain (1958–63)
Arrest and Trial (drama)
.... Att. John Egan (1963–64)
Branded (wes) .... Jason McCord (1965–66)
Cowboy in Africa (adv)
.... Jim Sinclair (1967–68)
Thrill Seekers (doc)
.... host/narrator (1972–74)
Roots (drama).......... Tom Moore (1977)
The Yellow Rose (drama)
.... Jeb Hollister (1983–84)

Rugged Chuck Connors is probably the most successful of the many professional athletes who have turned to television acting. He excelled in many sports as a youngster and was reported to have had his choice of 27 athletic scholarships when he was ready to enter college. He played infield with the Chicago Cubs and the Los Angeles Angels in the 1940s, and was known even then for his colorful, crowd-pleasing antics. When his baseball career ended in the early '50s he moved easily into acting, in action films and in television dramatic series, particularly westerns. Occasionally he did a situation comedy, such as *My Favorite Husband* or *The Gale*

Storm Show. One of his earliest roles was in a hilarious 1954 episode of *Superman*, as country bumpkin Sylvester J. Superman, who rode into Metropolis on a mule and caused great confusion among the citizenry, who all wondered if he could possibly be the real McCoy!

Connors' real fame came in the *Rifleman*, a highly popular father-and-son western costarring Johnny Crawford. He followed it with several other series in the 1960s and then in the '70s and '80s was seen primarily in TV movies and miniseries.

CONNORS, HAROLD "HOOT"—actor

Mickie Finn's (var) .... bartender (1966)

CONNORS, MIKE—actor
b: Aug 15, 1925, Fresno, Calif.

Tightrope (police) .... Nick (1959–60)
Mannix (drama)...... Joe Mannix (1967–75)
Today's F.B.I. (police) . Ben Slater (1981–82)

Mike Connors made his acting debut on stage as a lawyer—the profession he studied for—but most of his career since then has been spent in action dramas and murder mysteries. Born Kreker Ohanian, his first order of business as an actor was to change his name, and he entered films in 1952 as "Touch" Connors. He began doing television at about the same time, appearing in anthology dramas such as *Schlitz Playhouse* and in filmed series such as *Maverick* and *Cheyenne*. His first big break was the starring role of the undercover agent in *Tightrope* in 1959. Real fame came several years later as the two-fisted hero of *Mannix*, one of the most violent series of the late 1960s and early '70s. He was nominated four times for the Emmy Award for this series.

In later years Mike turned mostly to TV movies, except for a single season in the '80s when he was the father figure who kept the young hot shots under control on *Today's F.B.I.* Mannix must have mellowed.

CONRAD, MICHAEL—actor
b: Oct 16, 1921, Washington Heights, New York City, N.Y. d: Nov 22, 1983

Delvecchio (police) .. Lt. Macavan (1976–77)

193

Hill Street Blues (police)
.... Sgt. Phil Esterhaus (1981–84)

Emmy Award: Best Supporting Actor in a Drama, for *Hill Street Blues* (1981, 1982)

Michael Conrad scored his greatest success with his last role. As tall, fatherly Sgt. Esterhaus on *Hill Street Blues,* he was an anchor in the chaotic stationhouse, always ending his roll call with the same words: "And hey, let's be careful out there."

Conrad's imposing height (6'4") limited his earlier roles mainly to action dramas, including many westerns. "It's held me back more often than it's helped me," he once remarked. "I can play more than just physical parts. . . . I work carefully at not intimidating people with my size," he added. "That is, I do the best I can."

Despite this limitation Conrad worked steadily from the 1950s on, first onstage and then (in the '60s) in supporting roles in films and on television. Among the many series in which he appeared were *Gunsmoke* (several times), *The Virginian, Mannix,* and *Silent Force.* He also was seen in a few comedies as well as in an occasional offbeat role; in the *Twilight Zone* episode "Black Leather Jackets" he was the sheriff who came to take away the aliens, only to be revealed as an alien himself.

On *Delvecchio* Conrad was Judd Hirsch's (and Charles Haid's) boss. A few years later, on another cop show, he began the role that capped his career. Conrad died of cancer in the middle of the 1983–84 season and was remembered in a special tribute telecast in early 1984.

CONRAD, NANCY—actress

Baa Baa Black Sheep (drama)
.... Nurse Nancy Gilmore (1977–78)

The daughter of *Baa Baa Black Sheep*'s star, Robert Conrad.

CONRAD, ROBERT—actor
b: Mar 1, 1935, Chicago, Ill.

Hawaiian Eye (drama)
.... Tom Lopaka (1959–63)
The Wild Wild West (wes)
.... James T. West (1965–69)

The D.A. (drama)
.... Deputy D.A. Paul Ryan (1971–72)
Assignment Vienna (drama)
.... Jake Webster (1972–73)
Baa Baa Black Sheep (drama)
.... Maj. Gregory "Pappy" Boyington
.... (1976–78)
Centennial (drama)..... Pasquinel (1978–79)
The Duke (drama)
.... Oscar "Duke" Ramsey (1979)
A Man Called Sloane (drama)
.. Thomas Remington Sloane III (1979–80)

Robert Conrad is 5'10", 160 pounds, and all muscle. One of television's leading "macho" types, he also knows what he wants. "I've lasted longer than most actors because I'm honest and I'm talented," he says. "Sometimes I'm abrasive, but more actors should be that honest. Sometimes I'll say, 'Gee, I wish I hadn't said that.' It may not be right, but I've always been outspoken because I'm honest."

Faced with that kind of determination, producers could hardly say no. Conrad has worked steadily in TV since he crashed Hollywood in the late 1950s, following a brief career as a singer and an amateur boxer. With a helping hand from actor Nick Adams (of *The Rebel*), who introduced him to the right people, Conrad almost immediately landed a costarring role in *Hawaiian Eye.* This was followed by even greater success in the 1960's hit *The Wild Wild West.*

A hard worker, and always pitching ideas to the networks, Conrad has had several subsequent series as well, although none have been as successful as his first two. He does much of his own stunt work, a fact that has caused him a number of serious injuries over the years (including neck injuries while filming *Assignment Vienna* and multiple injuries when he fell from a chandelier in a *Wild Wild West* sequence). But he continues to live an energetic life and considers as his hobbies "running, boxing, skiing, swimming, and bicycling." Paunchy producers, watch out!

CONRAD, WILLIAM—actor, director
b: Sep 27, 1920, Louisville, Ky. r: Calif.

The Bullwinkle Show (cartn)
.... narrator of *Bullwinkle* (1961–62)
The Fugitive (drama) .... narrator (1963–67)

Cannon (drama)... Frank Cannon (1971–76)
The Wild, Wild World of Animals (doc)
.... narrator (1973–78)
Tales of the Unexpected (drama)
.... narrator (1977)
How the West Was Won (miniseries) (drama)
.... narrator (1977)
Buck Rogers in the 25th Century (sci fi)
.... narrator (1979–80)
Nero Wolfe (drama)..... Nero Wolfe (1981)

Believe it or not, television's favorite fat man, William Conrad, was a fighter pilot during World War II. Since that time he has moved through several careers, making use of his magnificent, menacing voice, his sharp eye as a director, and finally his abilities as an on-screen actor.

He began as a radio announcer on local California stations in the mid-1930s and turned to acting after his military service. He had a particularly auspicious film debut in the 1946 thriller *The Killers;* however, his rapidly expanding waistline limited future roles mostly to villains. So he made use of that commanding voice to do a great deal of radio work in the late 1940s and '50s. He was particularly good as host and actor on dramatic series such as *Escape* and *CBS Radio Workshop,* but his most famous role by far was as Matt Dillon on the long-running radio version of *Gunsmoke* (1952–61). All told, he says, he was in approximately 7,500 radio productions over the years.

Television, like movies, seemed to offer him limited acting opportunities, so in the late 1950s he began a major career as a producer/director. His first important series was *Bat Masterson,* from 1957–59; later, he produced *Klondike* and directed the Jack Webb anthology *General Electric True* (Conrad had been closely associated with Webb since their radio days together). Other series in which he had a key role behind the cameras included *Naked City, 77 Sunset Strip, Temple Houston* and, appropriately, *Gunsmoke.*

Conrad continued to do some acting during the 1960s, in westerns and crime series, but it was not until 1971 that a role came along that fit his portly frame perfectly— that of Frank Cannon. He was a major hit as the heavyweight detective. Aside from that series, and a brief run as *Nero Wolfe* in the '80s, however, Conrad has been heard as much as he has been seen on tele-

vision. He was the narrator of several popular series and specials, and in the early 1980s, even while appearing as the fastidious detective Nero Wolfe, he doubled as the voice of the Lone Ranger on Saturday morning.

CONRIED, HANS—actor

b: Apr 15, 1917, Baltimore, Md d: Jan 5, 1982

Pantomime Quiz (quiz) ... regular (1950–52)
Take a Guess (quiz)........ panelist (1953)
Pantomime Quiz (quiz) ... regular (1955–57)
What's It For? (quiz) .... panelist (1957–58)
The Danny Thomas Show (com)
.... Uncle Tonoose (1958–64)
Take a Good Look (quiz)
.... panelist (1959–61)
The Jack Paar Show (talk)
.... semiregular (1959–62)
The Bullwinkle Show (cartn)
...... Snidley Whiplash (voice) (1961–62)
Pantomime Quiz (quiz) ... regular (1962–63)
Made in America (quiz)...... emcee (1964)
Make Room for Granddaddy (com)
.... Uncle Tonoose (1970–71)
The Tony Randall Show (com)
.... Wyatt Franklin (1977–78)
American Dream (drama)
.... Abe Berlowitz (1981)

Tall, acerbic Hans Conried was a fixture on TV game shows of the '50s and '60s, although he is even better remembered as Danny Thomas's sharp-tongued Uncle Tonoose on *The Danny Thomas Show.* In addition to this and other series roles and many guest appearances, he also did quite a bit of voice work. He was delightful as Snidley Whiplash on *The Bullwinkle Show* ("heh, heh"), and he also narrated the *Dr. Seuss* specials in the early 1970s. In 1980–81, just before his death, he was both the family friend on *American Dream* and the voice of Dr. Dred on *The Drak Pack* on Saturday mornings.

Before television, Conried's clipped diction had made him a favorite comic support in films of the '40s and '50s, and on radio. He was a regular in the '40s on such hit radio series as *My Friend Irma, Burns and Allen,* and *The Great Gildersleeve.*

CONSIDINE, BOB—newscaster, writer

b: Nov 4, 1906 d: Sep 25, 1975

On the Line with Considine (news)
.... host (1951–54)
Who Said That? (quiz)...... panelist (1955)
Tonight! America After Dark (talk)
.... regular (1957)

CONSIDINE, TIM—actor
b: Dec 10, 1941, Louisville, Ky.

My Three Sons (com)
.... Mike Douglas (1960–65)

The nephew of newscaster Bob Considine. After a career as a juvenile actor (which included appearances in several Disney productions), Tim became a TV writer and director.

CONSTANTINE, MICHAEL—actor
b: May 22, 1927, Reading, Pa.

Hey Landlord (com)
.... Jack Ellenhorn (1966–67)
Room 222 (drama)
.... Seymour Kaufman (1969–74)
Sirota's Court (com)
.... Judge Matthew J. Sirota (1976–77)
79 Park Avenue (drama)
.... Ben Savitch (1977)

Emmy Award: Best Supporting Actor in a Comedy, for *Room 222* (1970)

This Greek-American actor has been active on television since 1956; at the time of his first series, in 1966, he estimated that he had already appeared in more than 200 episodes of different shows, mostly unbilled. "I had done so many different roles on TV that people recognized the face from somewhere," he was quoted as saying. "They'd ask if I had a furniture store in Ohio or a hat cleaning establishment in South Bend, but if I suggested that they must have seen me on TV they were sure that wasn't it at all."

Constantine finally became recognizable with his role as the cool, slightly sarcastic principal in the hit *Room 222*.

CONTE, JOHN—actor, host
b: Sep 15, 1915, Palmer, Mass. r: Los Angeles

Van Camp's Little Show (music)
.... host (1950–51)
Mantovani (music) .... host (1958–59)

This handsome heartthrob was also the host of *Matinee Theater*, an early and ambitious color anthology series that aired in daytime from 1955–58. He now runs a television station in Palm Springs.

CONTE, RICHARD—actor
b: Mar 24, 1910, Jersey City, N.J. d: Apr 15, 1975

Four Just Men (adv) ...... Jeff Ryder (1959)
The Jean Arthur Show (com)
.... Richie Wells (1966)

CONTI, VINCE—actor
Kojak (police)......... Det. Rizzo (1974–77)

CONTRERAS, ROBERTO—actor
The High Chaparral (wes) . Pedro (1967–70)

CONVERSE, FRANK—actor
b: May 22, 1938, St. Louis, Mo.

Coronet Blue (drama)
.... Michael Alden (1967)
N.Y.P.D. (police)
.... Det. Johnny Corso (1967–69)
Movin' On (adv) .. Will Chandler (1974–76)
The Family Tree (drama)
.... Kevin Nichols (1983)

CONVY, BERT—actor, host
b: Jul 23, 1933*, St. Louis, Mo.

The Snoop Sisters (drama)
.... Lt. Steve Ostrowski (1973–74)
The Late Summer Early Fall Bert Convy Show (var).......................... host (1976)
It's Not Easy (com).. Neal Townsend (1983)
People Do the Craziest Things (aud par)
.... host (1984–85)

Emmy Award: Best Host of a Game Show, for *Tattletales* (1977)

Bert Convy has had more careers than you can shake a friendly smile at. First, and dearest to his heart, was baseball. One day after his graduation from high school, teenager Convy signed with the Philadelphia Phillies and was sent to their farm club in Klamath Falls, Oregon. Two years later, after a chance meeting with Mickey Mantle, "Bert realized the physical and economic realities of the sport" (as a later

*Some sources give 1934 or 1935.

press release delicately put it), and got out.

Next came music. In 1954 young Bert linked up with an ambitious songwriting and producing team named Jerry Leiber and Mike Stoller, who were in the process of forming a pop group called The Cheers. Bert joined as a singer. During 1954–55 The Cheers had several best-selling records, the biggest being a hard-driving, rather rebellious song in the James Dean mold, called "Black Leather Jacket and Motorcycle Boots." However, they disbanded in 1956 and Bert began to actively pursue career number three: acting.

His first real success was on the stage, in the musical *The Billy Barnes Revue*, which had a long run in Los Angeles before moving to Broadway in 1959. During the following ten years Bert starred in several major Broadway hits, including *Fiddler on the Roof, Cabaret,* and *The Front Page.* At the same time his stage career was beginning Bert began appearing as an actor in episodes of TV series, including roles in *77 Sunset Strip, Perry Mason, Father of the Bride,* and, later, *Love, American Style* and *The Partridge Family.* He launched still another career in the 1960s (are we up to number four or number five?), which became his most successful of all—that of a TV talk and game show host. He became a frequent guest host on *The Tonight Show* and in 1974 began his own daytime game show, *Tattletales,* which has run off and on ever since. He also began hosting the daytime *Super Password* in 1984 and even had his own prime time variety show in the summer of 1976.

Still boyish-looking and glib in his fifties, he has doubtless just begun.

CONWAY, CAROLYN—singer

Sing Along with Mitch (var)
.... regular (1962–63)

CONWAY, GARY—actor
b: Feb 4, 1936, Boston, Mass.

Burke's Law (police)
.... Det. Tim Tilson (1963–65)
Land of the Giants (sci fi)
.... Capt. Steve Burton (1968–70)

CONWAY, PAT—actor

Tombstone Territory (wes)
.... Sheriff Clay Hollister (1957–60)

CONWAY, PATRICIA—hostess

The Ken Murray Show (var)
.... regular (1951–52)
The Greatest Man on Earth (quiz)
.... assistant (1952–53)

CONWAY, RUSS—actor
b: Apr 25, 1913, Brandon, Manitoba, Canada

Richard Diamond, Private Detective (drama)
.... Lt. Kile (1959–60)

CONWAY, SHIRL—actress
b: 1916, Franklinville, N.Y.

Joe & Mabel (com) . Dolly Armstrong (1956)
Caesar's Hour (var)
................:...... Betty Hansen (1956–57)
The Nurses (drama) .. Liz Thorpe (1962–65)

CONWAY, TIM—comedian
b: Dec 15, 1933, Willoughby, Ohio

The Steve Allen Show (var).. regular (1961)
McHale's Navy (com)
.... Ensign Charles Parker (1962–66)
Rango (com) .... Rango (1967)
The Tim Conway Show (com)
.... Spud Barrett (1970)
The Tim Conway Comedy Hour (var)
.... host (1970)
The Carol Burnett Show (var)
.... regular (1975–79)
The Tim Conway Show (var)
.... host (1980–81)
Ace Crawford, Private Eye (com)
.... Ace Crawford (1983)

Emmy Awards: Best Supporting Performance in a Music or Variety Show, for *The Carol Burnett Show* (1973, 1977, 1978); Best Writing for a Comedy Series, for *The Carol Burnett Show* (1978)

Mousey Tim Conway has long been a favorite comic second-banana on television, but attempts to star him in a series of his own have not been successful. He began on local TV in Cleveland in the 1950s doing, among other things, comedy spots on the station's late movie. Comedienne Rose Marie saw him there and arranged an audition for *The Steve Allen Show,* which proved to be his first network break. Later, he scored a hit as the bumbling ensign on *McHale's Navy,* which led to several series of his own—all as bumblers of one kind or another (a bumbling Texas ranger, a bumbling pilot, a bumbling detective). However, none of these seemed to click. His greatest success in later years was as a regular on *The Carol Burnett Show.*

CONWAY, TOM—actor
b: Sep 15, 1904, St. Petersburg, Russia d: Apr 22, 1967

Mark Saber (drama)
.... Mark Saber (1951–54)
The Betty Hutton Show (com)
.... Howard Seaton (1959–60)

The brother of film star George Sanders, and equally suave.

CONWELL, PATRICIA—actress
The Duke (drama)...... Dedra Smith (1979)

COOGAN, JACKIE—actor
b: Oct 26, 1914, Los Angeles, Calif. d: Mar 1, 1984

Pantomime Quiz (quiz) ... regular (1950–55)
Cowboy G-Men (wes)
.... Stoney Crockett (1952)
McKeever & The Colonel (com)
.... Sgt. Barnes (1962–63)
The Addams Family (com)
.... Uncle Fester (1964–66)

One of the most famous child stars of early movies. Jackie debuted in films at 18 months and had his first starring role—one that would be identified with him for the rest of his life—at age six in *The Kid,* with Charlie Chaplin. Jackie remained active for the next 60 years, playing many roles on television from the 1950s through the '70s. He once estimated that he had appeared in approximately 1,400 TV shows over the years. Probably best remembered was his role as the bald, gnomelike Uncle Fester on *The Addams Family.* Other appearances included *Playhouse 90* (several times), *The Loretta Young Show, The Shirley Temple Show, Perry Mason, The Lucy Show, Love, American Style, The Wild Wild West, Police Story,* and, as late as 1979, *Sweepstakes.*

COOGAN, RICHARD—actor
b: Apr 4, Short Hills, N.J.

Captain Video and His Video Rangers (child)
.... Captain Video (1949–50)
The Californians (wes)
.... Matthew Wayne (1957–59)

The original Captain Video. Richard Coogan was a veteran of the Broadway stage and of radio (*Abie's Irish Rose, Young Doctor Malone,* etc.) in the 1940s. He was fortunate not to have been so completely typecast by the Captain Video role as his successor, Al Hodge; Coogan continued to have a minor career as a TV and film actor through the '50s, including a starring role as the marshal in *The Californians.*

COOK, BOB—sportscaster
Fight Talk (sport) .. commentator (1954–55)

COOK, DONALD—actor
b: Sep 26, 1901*, Portland, Ore. d: Oct 1, 1961

Plymouth Playhouse (misc)...... host (1953)
Too Young to Go Steady (com)
.... Tom Blake (1959)

COOK, ELISHA—actor
b: Dec 26, 1906**, San Francisco, Calif.

Magnum, P.I. (drama)
... Francis (Ice Pick) Hofstetler (1983–)

A small, wiry character actor, long in movies (since 1929) and often on TV as the sniveling villain who gets killed in the end. On *Magnum* he played the recurring role of a crime czar.

COOK, NATHAN—black actor
b: Apr 9, 1950, Philadelphia, Pa.

The White Shadow (drama)
.... Milton Reese (1978–80)
Hotel (drama)........ Billy Griffin (1983–)

COOK, PETER—actor, producer
b: Nov 17, 1937, Torquay, England

The Two of Us (com)
.... Robert Brentwood (1981–82)

Emmy Award: Producer, Best Limited Series for *American Playhouse:* "Concealed Enemies" (1984)

*Some sources give 1900.
**Some sources give 1902, but that appears to be incorrect.

198

The former partner with Dudley Moore in the *Beyond the Fringe* English comedy troupe.

COOKE, ALISTAIR—host
b: Nov 20, 1908, Manchester, England

Omnibus (misc) .... host (1952–61)
Masterpiece Theatre (drama)
.... host (1971–)
America (doc).............. host (1972–73)

Emmy Awards: Outstanding Achievement in a Documentary Program, as narrator and writer of *America* (1973); Outstanding Individual Achievement, as host of *Masterpiece Theatre* (1975); Governor's Award (1985)

Though known to Americans as the ever-charming, often witty host of PBS's *Masterpiece Theatre,* Alistair Cooke has another reputation in England: as that country's leading America-watcher for nearly 50 years. He first came to the U.S. in 1932 to become an actor, but found the country itself "as exciting as a nine-ring circus." So, after a few years, he began reporting back to his fellow Britons on the endless variety of the American scene, via a column in *The Manchester Guardian* and the long-running BBC radio series *Letters from America,* which has been heard continuously since 1945.
Cooke became a U.S. citizen in 1941.

COOKE, JENNIFER—actress
V (sci fi).............. Elizabeth (1984–85)

COOKE, SARAH PALFREY—tennis champion
Sportswoman of the Week (sport)
.... hostess (1948)

COOKSEY, DANNY—juvenile actor
b: Nov 2, 1975, Moore, Okla.

Diff'rent Strokes (com)
.... Sam McKinney (1984–86)

COOKSEY, DARRYL—actor
Emerald Point N.A.S. (drama)
.... Scott Farrell (1983–84)

COOKSON, GARY—actor
Delta House (com)
.... Doug Neidermayer (1979)

The son of actress Beatrice Straight.

COOLIDGE, PHILIP—actor
b: 1909 d: May 23, 1967

The Farmer's Daughter (com)
.... Cooper, the butler (1963–64)

COON, DR. CARLETON—professor of anthropology
b: Jun 23, 1904 d: Jun 3, 1981

What in the World (quiz) ... panelist (1953)

COOPER, ANN—actress
Blue Thunder (police)... J. J. Douglas (1984)

COOPER, BUZZ—actor
Love, American Style (com)
.... repertory player (1969–70)

COOPER, CATHY—actress
Sanford (com)............ Clara (1980–81)

COOPER, CHARLES—actor
Father Murphy (drama).... sheriff (1981–82)

COOPER, GLADYS—actress
b: Dec 18, 1888, Lewisham, England d: Nov 17, 1971

The Rogues (com)
.... Margaret St. Clair (1964–65)

Autobiography: *Without Veils* (1953).

COOPER, JACKIE—actor, producer, director
b: Sep 15, 1921*, Los Angeles, Calif.

The People's Choice (com)
.... Socrates "Sock" Miller (1955–58)
Hennesey (com)
... Charles J. "Chick" Hennesey (1959–62)
The Dean Martin Comedy World (var)
.... host (1974)
Mobile One (adv) ... Peter Campbell (1975)

Emmy Awards: Best Directing for a Comedy, for the "Carry On, Hawkeye" Episode
*Some sources give 1922.

of *M*A*S*H* (1974); Best Directing for a Drama, for the pilot episode of *The White Shadow* (1979)

For Jackie Cooper, the curly-haired, pug-nosed child star of the 1930s, television has represented something of a second career. Adulthood, in the 1940s (after World War II service), had proven a bitter experience for the onetime superstar, with few roles available to him. He turned to the stage late in the decade, to try to gain adult experience, and scored considerable success—and a much-craved "comeback"—in the 1950 Broadway hit *Mr. Roberts.* However, television soon became his principal medium, with numerous appearances on playhouse series and dramas such as *Robert Montgomery Presents* (multiples), *Studio One,* and *Ford Theatre.*

Jackie also began a very successful career as a TV producer and director. He produced his own two series, *The People's Choice* and *Hennesey,* then left acting altogether from 1964–69 to become head of TV production at one of Hollywood's largest studios, Columbia Pictures.

He returned to acting and independent directing after that. On-screen he was seen in numerous dramas (*Ironside, Police Story, The Rockford Files,* etc.), and off-screen he directed many episodes of various series. Jackie won Emmy Awards for his work on *M*A*S*H* and *The White Shadow.* Meanwhile, observant viewers could continue to see him as a kid in black-and-white reruns of those old *Our Gang* comedy shorts made so long ago.

Jackie's autobiography is titled *Please Don't Shoot My Dog* (1981).

COOPER, JEANNE—actress
b: Oct, Taft, Calif.

Bracken's World (drama)
.... Grace Douglas (1970)

Since 1973 Miss Cooper has played Kay Chancellor on the daytime soap opera *The Young and the Restless.*

COOPER, JED—actor

Studs Lonigan (drama).... Phil Rolfe (1979)

COOPER, JEFF—actor

Dallas (drama)........ Dr. Ellby (1979–81)

COOPER, MAGGIE—actress
Falcon Crest (drama)
.... Lori Stevens (1982–83)
I Had Three Wives (drama)
.... Mary Parker (1985)

COOPER, MELVILLE—actor
b: Oct 15, 1896, Birmingham, England d: Mar 29, 1973

I've Got a Secret (quiz)..... panelist (1952)

COOPER, ROY—actor
b: Jan 22, London, England

Beacon Hill (drama).. Trevor Bullock (1975)

COOPER, WYLLIS—radio director, writer
b: Jan 26, 1899, Pekin, Ill. d: Jun 22, 1955

Volume One (drama)....... narrator (1949)

COOTE, ROBERT—actor
b: Feb 4, 1909, London, England d: Nov 26, 1982

Who's There? (quiz)........ panelist (1952)
The Rogues (com)
.... Timmy St. Clair (1964–65)
Nero Wolfe (drama)
.... Theodore Horstman (1981)

COPAGE, MARC—black juvenile actor
b: Jun 21, 1962, Los Angeles, Calif.

Julia (com).......... Corey Baker (1968–71)

COPELAND, ALAN—singer, orchestra leader
b: Oct 6, 1926, Los Angeles, Calif.

Your Hit Parade (music). vocalist (1957–58)
Happy Days (var).......... regular (1970)
The Peter Marshall Variety Show (var)
.... orch. leader (1976)
The Keane Brothers Show (var)
.... orch. leader (1977)

COPELAND, JOANNE—hostess
Video Village (quiz)....... assistant (1960)

COPELAND, MAURICE—actor
b: c. 1911, Rector, Ark. d: Oct 3, 1985

Those Endearing Young Charms (com)
.... Ralph Charm (1952)

COPLEY, TERI—actress
b: c. 1961, r: Las Vegas and Covina, Calif.

We Got It Made (com)
.... Mickey McKenzie (1983–84)
I Had Three Wives (drama)
.... Samantha (1985)

COPPOLA, FRANK—actor

Joe's World (com) .... Andy (1979–80)

CORBETT, GLENN—actor
b: 1929*, El Monte, Calif.

It's a Man's World (com)
.... Wes Macauley (1962–63)
Route 66 (adv) .... Linc Case (1963–64)
The Road West (wes)
.... Chance Reynolds (1966–67)
Dallas (drama)...... Paul Morgan (1983–84)

CORBETT, GRETCHEN—actress
b: Aug 13, 1947, Camp Sherman, Ore.

The Rockford Files (drama)
.... Beth Davenport (1974–78)
Otherworld (sci fi)...... June Sterling (1985)

CORBIN, BARRY—actor

The Thorn Birds (drama) .... Pete (1983)
Boone (drama) ..... Merit Sawyer (1983–84)

CORBY, ELLEN—actress
b: Jun 3, 1913, Racine, Wisc., r: Philadelphia, Pa.

Please Don't Eat the Daisies (com)
.... Martha O'Reilly (1965–67)
The Waltons (drama)
..... Esther (Grandma) Walton (1972–79)

Emmy Awards: Best Supporting Actress in a Drama, for *The Waltons* (1973, 1975, 1976)

Grandma of *The Waltons* was a busy character actress in films of the 1940s and '50s. Her pinched features and busybody manner made her perfect for a certain kind of minor role, and occasionally a larger one: among the latter was the role of Aunt Trina in the 1947 film version of *I Remember Mama,* which brought her an Academy Award nomination.

Television used her in similar parts, often small ones. In the 1960s, for example,

*Some sources give 1934.

she was Mother Lurch on *The Addams Family,* and, for two years, played the maid on *Please Don't Eat the Daisies.* However, *The Waltons* was her major vehicle, and she was with it through most of the '70s (aside from 18 months in 1976–77, when she was sidelined by a stroke). She was also seen in *The Waltons* reunions in the early 1980s.

Ellen had originally come to Hollywood as a young girl in the early 1930s, intending to become an actress. Instead, she was offered a job as a script girl and remained in that capacity for nearly 12 years before finally turning to acting in the 1940s.

CORCORAN, BRIAN—juvenile actor
b: c. 1953, California

O. K. Crackerby (com)
.... O. K. Crackerby, Jr. (1965–66)

One of eight Corcoran children who appeared in movies and on television; probably the most famous were sister Noreen (of *Bachelor Father*) and brother Kevin (in several Disney productions).

CORCORAN, KELLY—juvenile actor
b: 1958, California

The Road West (wes) .. Kip Pride (1966–67)

Another member of the Corcoran family.

CORCORAN, NOREEN—juvenile actress
b: Oct 14, 1943, Quincy, Mass. r: California

Bachelor Father (com)
.... Kelly Gregg (1957–62)

Another Corcoran sibling. She made several films, including 1965's *The Girls on the Beach,* but has since retired from acting—as have most of her brothers and sisters.

CORD, ALEX—actor
b: Aug 3, 1931*, Floral Park, N.Y.

W.E.B. (drama)........... Jack Kiley (1978)
Cassie & Company (drama)
.... Mike Holland (1982)
Airwolf (adv) . Michael Archangel (1984–86)

A onetime rodeo horseback rider in films and on television since the 1960s. He or-

*Some sources give 1935.

iginally acted under the name Alex Viespi.

CORDAY, PEGGY—model
b: c. 1925

Photographic Horizons (info) .. model (1949)

CORDEN, HENRY—

The Kelly Monteith Show (var)
.... regular (1976)

CORE, NATALIE—actress
b: Ford City, Pa.

Herbie, The Love Bug (com)
.... Mrs. Bigelow (1982)
Hell Town (drama) .. Mother Maggie (1985)

COREY, IRWIN—actor, comedian
b: Jan 29, 1912, Brooklyn, N.Y.

The Andy Williams Show (var)
.... regular (1969–70)
Doc (com) .... "Happy" Miller (1975–76)

Famous since the 1940s for his "Professor Irwin Corey" comedy double-talk routines.

COREY, JEFF—actor, director
b: Aug 10, 1914, New York City, N.Y.

Hell Town (drama) ..... Lawyer Sam (1985)
Morningstar/Eveningstar (drama)
.... Bill McGregor (1986)

A gaunt, worried-looking character actor who has been much in films since the early 1940s. A victim of political blacklisting in the '50s, and unable for a time to find roles, he founded an acting school and became one of Hollywood's leading dramatic coaches. He has also been a busy TV director for series including *Night Gallery, Police Story,* and *The Bob Newhart Show.*

COREY, JILL—singer
b: Sep 30, 1935, Avonmore, Pa.

Garroway at Large (var) .. regular (1953–54)
The Johnny Carson Show (var)
.... vocalist (1955–56)
Your Hit Parade (music) . vocalist (1957–58)

COREY, JOE—actor
b: c. 1927 d: 1972

Dear Phoebe (com)
.... Humphrey Humpsteader (1954–55)

COREY, WENDELL—actor
b: Mar 20, 1914, Dracut, Mass. d: Nov 8, 1968

Harbor Command (police)
.... Capt. Ralph Baxter (1957–58)
Peck's Bad Girl (com) ... Steve Peck (1959)
Westinghouse Playhouse (com)
.... Dan McGovern (1961)
The Eleventh Hour (drama)
.... Dr. Theodore Bassett (1962–63)

Wendell Corey generally played sober, rather colorless types both in films and on television, and, though he appeared in many TV drama series of the '50s and '60s, little remains that is particularly memorable today—including his four short-lived regular series roles. The son of a clergyman, Wendell began as a stage actor in the 1930s but had little success until he suddenly scored a Broadway hit in *Dream Girl* in 1945; that provided entree to Hollywood and many roles over the next 23 years, but never real stardom.

His greatest impact on Hollywood was probably political. He was president of the Academy of Motion Picture Arts and Sciences in the 1950s and active in governing the Screen Actors Guild and the Academy of Television Arts and Sciences as well. In 1966 he sought the Republican nomination for congressman from his district, but lost. He continued active in films and on TV until his death in 1968. His last TV acting appearance was in an episode of *The Wild Wild West* early that year, in which he played a madman plotting to assassinate President Grant, seize control of California, and secede from the Union.

CORI, LISA—actress

California Fever (com) .... Sue (1979)

CORLEY, AL—actor
b: May 22, 1956, Wichita, Kans.

Dynasty (drama)
.... Steven Carrington (1981–82)

CORLEY, MARJORIE—actress

Mr. Novak (drama)
.... Miss Rosemary Dorsey (1964–65)

CORLEY, PAT—actor
b: Texas, r: California

Bay City Blues (drama)... Ray Holtz (1983)
He's the Mayor (com)
.... Chief Walter Padget (1986)

CORNELIUS, HELEN—country singer
b: Dec 6, 1941, near Hannibal, Mo.

Nashville on the Road (music)
.... regular (1977–81)

CORNELL, LYDIA—actress
b: Jul 23, El Paso, Texas

Too Close for Comfort (com)
.... Sara Rush (1980–85)

CORNTHWAITE, ROBERT—actor
b: Apr 28, 1917, St. Helens, Ore.

The Adventures of Jim Bowie (wes)
.... John James Audubon (1956–58)

CORRELL, CHARLES—actor
b: Feb 3, 1890, Peoria, Ill. d: Sep 26, 1972

Calvin and the Colonel (cartn)
.... Calvin (voice) (1961–62)

A white actor famous as the co-creator (with Freeman Gosden) of radio's most famous comedy series, *Amos 'n' Andy*. He played the dim-witted Andy on radio but could not continue the role on television, since the cast was all black. Instead, ten years later, Correll and Gosden created a thinly disguised (to allay racial complaints) cartoon version of their famous show, centering on a group of animals who had moved to the big city. It was not a success.

CORRELL, RICHARD—actor

Leave It to Beaver (com)
.... Richard (1960–63)

The son of Charles Correll.

CORRIGAN, LLOYD—actor
b: Oct 16, 1900, San Francisco, Calif. d: Nov 5, 1969

Willy (drama)....... Papa Dodger (1954–55)
The Life and Legend of Wyatt Earp (wes)
..... Ned Buntline (occasional) (1955–61)

Happy (com)...... Charlie Dooley (1960–61)
Hank (com)....... Prof. McKillup (1965–66)

CORRIGAN, RAY (CRASH)—cowboy actor
b: Feb 14, 1902*, Milwaukee, Wis. d: Aug 10, 1976

Crash Corrigan's Ranch (child).. host (1950)

CORSAUT, ANETA—actress
b: Nov 3, 1933, Hutchinson, Kans.

The Gertrude Berg Show (com)
.... Irma Howell (1961–62)
The Andy Griffith Show (com)
.... Helen Crump (1964–68)
House Calls (com)
.... Head Nurse Bradley (1979–82)

CORT, BILL—actor
b: El Paso, Texas

Dusty's Trail (com)........... Andy (1973)
The Montefuscos (com).. Jim Cooney (1975)
A.E.S. Hudson Street (com)
.... Dr. Mackler (1978)

COSBY, BILL—black actor, comedian
b: Jul 12, 1937, Philadelphia, Pa.

I Spy (adv) ..... Alexander Scott (1965–68)
The Bill Cosby Show (com)
.... Chet Kincaid (1969–71)
The New Bill Cosby Show (var)
.... host (1972–73)
Cos (var) .... host (1976)
The Cosby Show (com)
. Dr. Heathcliff (Cliff) Huxtable (1984–)

Emmy Awards: Best Actor in a Drama Series, for *I Spy* (1966, 1967, 1968); Best Performance in a Variety Program, for *The Bill Cosby Special* (1969); Best Performance in a Children's Program, for *The New Fat Albert Show* (1981)

Anyone who feels that television offers nothing worthwhile for children has obviously not seen Bill Cosby. His career has been mostly spent on TV, where he has been a star in the '60s, '70s, and '80s. In the latter decade he proved once again that a TV comedy does not have to be gimmicky or "inappropriate for family viewing" to become a smash hit.

Cosby was born to a lower-class family

*Some sources give 1903 or 1907.

203

in North Philadelphia and became a high school dropout when he joined the navy in the early 1950s. However, he earned his diploma through correspondence school and, upon his discharge, entered Temple University on an athletic scholarship. He first gained national attention in the early 1960s as a nightclub comedian and a recording artist. His comedy LPs, with titles such as "Why Is There Air?" and "Wonderfulness," told of everyday life, and particularly of children, in a natural yet hilarious way. They were enormous sellers; Cosby is said to be the biggest-selling comedy artist ever on record. Nevertheless, producer Sheldon Leonard took an enormous chance when he cast the young comedian in his new spy series, *I Spy,* in 1965. Cosby was not an actor, and, in addition, no network drama series had ever starred or costarred a black.

To everyone's relief and delight, *I Spy* was a major hit and one of the great breakthroughs of television history (many series starring blacks followed in its wake). Cosby went on to work on many more TV projects, many of them aimed at, and beneficial to, children. A prime time special in 1969 based on his own childhood experiences, called "Hey, Hey, Hey, It's Fat Albert," was a hit and led in 1972 to the long-running Saturday morning cartoon series, *Fat Albert and the Cosby Kids* (later called *The New Fat Albert Show*). Bill also turned up in the '70s on PBS's acclaimed *The Electric Company* (as the milkman), and in the early '80s on *Captain Kangaroo* (hosting the Picturepages segment).

Bill's prime time series in the '70s were not nearly as successful. *The Bill Cosby Show,* featuring him as an athletic instructor, did well in its first season but dropped far behind *The F.B.I.* in its second; *The New Bill Cosby Show,* a 10 P.M. variety show, never got off the ground; and *Cos,* a frenetic nighttime variety show aimed at two to twelve year olds, lasted only eight weeks. Cosby then left nighttime TV for eight years to pursue other activities, including the completion of his Ph.D. degree in education, which he received in 1977. He was seen mostly in Jell-O commercials. In 1984 he was lured back with the promise of a program over which he would have complete creative control; the result was *The Cosby Show,* a smash hit in the mid-1980s.

Disliking Hollywood, Cosby lives on a farm in Shelburne, Mass., and tapes his show in Brooklyn, N.Y.

Steve Allen, in his perceptive book *Funny People,* summed up Cosby's special genius as follows: "Bill Cosby is the child that each of us was, the child that still lives within us, the Thurber-esque innocent in a dangerous world."

COSELL, HOWARD—sportscaster

b: Mar 21, 1920*, Winston-Salem, N.C.

Sports Focus (sport) . . . . . reporter (1957–58)
Prime Time Football (sport)
. . . . announcer (1959)
Monday Night Football (sport)
. . . . announcer (1970–83)
Saturday Night Live with Howard Cosell (var). . . . . host (1975–76)
Monday Night Baseball (sport)
. . . . sportscaster (1977–85)

Emmy Award: Outstanding Achievement in Sports Journalism, as producer of *ABC SportsBeat* (1983, 1986)

Howard Cosell is the sort of sportscaster fans love to hate—loud, outrageous, opinionated, but a seasoned pro. He began his career as a lawyer, then in 1953 was asked to host an ABC radio show on which New York–area Little Leaguers were introduced to baseball stars. The show lasted five years and led to other ABC sports assignments. In the late 1960s, Howard attracted considerable attention championing Muhammad Ali's right to become a conscientious objector during the Vietnam War; later he took on practically anybody and everybody, often decrying the rapid commercialization of sports. While his opinions sometimes had wide support, his abrasive, stentorian way of propounding them on every forum he was given (including *Monday Night Football*) often did not. An attempt to broaden his appeal in the mid-1970s, including his own Saturday night variety show, was a resounding flop.

Howard nevertheless remained the most famous sportscaster in the business and guested on many specials (often on the Dean Martin roasts). He was also known for his active support of charitable activities. He ended his career in 1985 on a rather sour note with the book *I Never Played the Game,* in which he lambasted

*Some sources give 1918.

204

many of his former on-camera colleagues for their perceived inadequacies.

COSSART, VALERIE—actress
b: Jun 27, 1907, London, England

The Hartmans (com) .... regular (1949)

COSTA, COSIE—actor
b: Jun 22, Grass Valley, Calif.

California Fever (com)........ Bobby (1979)

COSTA, JOE—photographer

Photographic Horizons (info).... host (1949)

The President of the National Press Photographer's Association.

COSTA, MARY—actress, singer
r: Knoxville, Tenn.

Climax (drama) .... cohost (1956–58)

COSTANZO, ROBERT—actor

Joe & Valerie (com).. Vincent Pizo (1978–79)
The Last Resort (com) .... Murray (1979–80)
Checking In (com).... Hank Sabatino (1981)

COSTELLO, LOU—comedian
b: Mar 6, 1906, Paterson, N.J. d: Mar 3, 1959

For career details, see Abbott, Bud.

COSTELLO, MARICLARE—actress
b: Feb 3, Peoria, Ill.

The Waltons (drama)
 .... Rosemary Hunter Fordwick (1973–77)
Sara (wes)............. Julia Bailey (1976)
The Fitzpatricks (drama)
 .... Maggie Fitzpatrick (1977–78)

COSTER, NICOLAS—actor
b: Dec 30, 1934, London, England

Our Private World (drama)
 .... John Eldredge (1965)
Lobo (com) .... Chief J.C. Carson (1980–81)
Ryan's Four (drama)
 .... Dr. Morris Whitford (1983)

COTLER, JEFF—juvenile actor
b: Nov 20, 1967, Long Beach, Calif.

Struck by Lightning (com)...... Brian (1979)

The brother of child actress Kami Cotler.

COTLER, KAMI—juvenile actress
b: Jun 17, 1965, Long Beach, Calif.

Me and the Chimp (com)
 .... Kitty Reynolds (1972)
The Waltons (drama)
 .... Elizabeth Walton (1972–81)

COTTEN, JOSEPH—actor
b: May 15, 1905, Petersburg, Va.

The 20th Century-Fox Hour (drama)
 .... host (1955–56)
The Joseph Cotten Show (drama)
 .... host/star (1956–57)
Hollywood and the Stars (doc)
 .... host (1963–64)

This famous film star appeared in many television dramas of the '50s, '60s, and '70s, and also hosted two anthology series and the documentary *Hollywood and the Stars*. He made his TV debut in 1954 in the *General Electric Theater* production "The High Green Wall," the story of Evelyn Waugh.

COTTEN, SUSAN—actress

Brothers and Sisters (com)
 .... Isabel St. Anthony (1979)

COUGHLIN, FRANCIS—Chicago radio editor

Down You Go (quiz)
 .... regular panelist (1951–56)

COUGHLIN, KEVIN—actor
b: 1945 d: Jan 19, 1976

Mama (com)......... T. R. Ryan (1952–57)

A child actor of the 1950s who remained active in TV through the '60s and early '70s, including several appearances on *Gunsmoke*.

COULTON, JIM, AND REX—

Kraft Music Hall Presents The Des O'Connor Show (var)................ regulars (1970)

COUNTRY LADS, THE—
Leader: Dick Flood, b: 1932, Philadelphia, Pa.

The Jimmy Dean Show (var)
.... regulars (1957)

Country group under the leadership of singer-bandleader Dick Flood.

COUNTY BRIAR HOPPERS—square dancers

Midwestern Hayride (var)
.... regulars (1951–52)

COURT, HAZEL—actress
b: 1926, Sutton Coldfield, England

Dick and the Duchess (com)
.... Jane Starrett (1957–58)

COURTNEY, ALEX—actor, director
d: Dec 2, 1985

Sword of Justice (adv)
.... Arthur Woods (1978–79)

COUSIN JODY—country comedian
b: Possum Hollow, Tenn. (sic)

Grand Ole Opry (music) .. regular (1955–56)

A longtime *Grand Old Opry* regular whose incredibly square, squashed face added to his "hick" appeal. Real name: James C. Summey.

COUSTEAU, CAPT. JACQUES-YVES— documentary producer, host
b: Jun 11, 1910, Saint Andre, France

The Undersea World of Jacques Cousteau (doc) .... regular (1968–)
Those Amazing Animals (doc)
.... regular (1980–81)

Emmy Award: Outstanding Achievement in Cultural Programming, as executive producer of *The Undersea World of Jacques Cousteau* (1972); Producer and Host, Best Informational Special, for *Cousteau's Mississippi* (1985).

Television's most famous producer of undersea documentaries. As a French naval officer in the 1930s, he developed a fascination with undersea life and was partly responsible for the invention of the aqualung. He began underwater filmmaking in the '40s and has produced many award-winning documentaries since then, often utilizing his famous exploration vessel, the Calypso.

COVAN, DEFOREST—actor

That's My Mama (com)...... Josh (1974–75)

COVER, FRANKLIN—actor
b: Nov 20, 1928, Cleveland, Ohio

The Jeffersons (com).. Tom Willis (1975–85)

COWAN, JEROME—actor
b: Oct 6, 1897, New York City, N.Y. d: Jan 24, 1972

Not for Publication (drama)
.... Collins (1951–52)
The Tab Hunter Show (com)
.... John Larsen (1960–61)
The Tycoon (com)
.... Herbert Wilson (1964–65)

COWLING, SAM—comedian

Don McNeill TV Club (var)
.... regular (1950–51)

COX, COURTENEY—actress
b: Jun 15, Birmingham, Ala.

Misfits of Science (adv)
.... Gloria Dinallo (1985–86)

A bright and bouncy young actress who got her big break when she jumped up out of the audience and danced with Bruce Springsteen in his hit music video "Dancing in the Dark."

COX, RICHARD—actor
b: May 6, 1948, New York City, N.Y.

Executive Suite (drama)
.... Mark Desmond (1976–77)

COX, RONNY—actor
b: Jul 23, 1938, Cloudcroft, N.M.

Apple's Way (drama)
.... George Apple (1974–75)
Spencer (com).... George Winger (1984–85)

COX, RUTH—actress

The Hardy Boys Mysteries (adv)
.... Bess (1977–78)

The Nancy Drew Mysteries (adv)
.... Bess (1977–78)
The Runaways (drama)
.... Susan Donovan (1978)

COX, WALLY—actor
b: Dec 6, 1924, Detroit, Mich. d: Feb 15, 1973

School House (var)......... regular (1949)
Mr. Peepers (com)
.... Robinson Peepers (1952–55)
The Adventures of Hiram Holiday (com)
.... Hiram Holiday (1956–57)
Hollywood Squares (quiz).... regular (1968)

Wally Cox was perhaps the most perfectly cast one-role actor in television history. A shy, bespectacled little man, he played the part of shy, bespectacled *Mr. Peepers* in the mid-1950s and was identified with it for the rest of his life. He had similar roles in *Hiram Holiday,* in a number of films, and in numerous TV specials and guest appearances over the years.

Wally had originally been a shy, bespectacled jeweler in New York who told exceedingly funny stories at parties. Theatrical friends, including onetime schoolmate Marlon Brando, encouraged him to go into show business and in 1948 he made his debut at the Village Vanguard nightclub to rave reviews. Television appearances followed, including variety shows and dramas (*Goodyear Playhouse,* etc.). Then, in 1952, he was cast in a live summer replacement show that had been developed especially for him, *Mr. Peepers.* It was such a hit that NBC brought it back in the fall.

After its run, Wally continued to appear on many series, ranging from *The Beverly Hillbillies* to *Bonanza.* He was a regular on the daytime game show the *Hollywood Squares* for many years, including its prime time run in 1968, and was the voice of *Underdog* on Saturday mornings from 1964–73.

When not on-screen, he enjoyed rock collecting and birdwatching. Of course.

COY, WALTER—actor
b: 1913 d: 1974

Frontier (wes).......... narrator (1955–56)

CRAIG, COL. JOHN D.—documentary producer, host
b: Apr 28, 1903, Cincinnati, Ohio

Kingdom of the Sea (doc)... narrator (1957)
Danger Is My Business (doc).... host (1958)
Expedition (doc) .... host (1960–62)
Of Lands and Seas (doc)....... host (1967)

A world-class adventurer/photographer who stalked tigers and terrorists with his lenses in the '20s, dove to the long-sunken wreck of the Lusitania in the '30s, and earned a caseful of medals for heroism as a combat photographer during World War II (whence the "Colonel"). In the '50s he brought his accumulated store of knowledge and love of adventure in exotic locales to TV viewers via a series of network and syndicated shows. Alas, he lamented of the TV generation, "we get a little soft. You don't hear of many lads beating around the world on a tramp steamer anymore."

CRAIG, DON, CHORUS—
Holiday Hotel (var) ..... regulars (1950–51)

CRAIG, HELEN—actress
b: May 13, 1912, San Antonio, Texas d: Jul 20, 1986

Rich Man, Poor Man—Book I (drama)
.... Martha (1976)

CRAIG, YVONNE—dancer, actress
b: 1941, Taylorville, Ill.

Batman (adv)
...... Barbara (Batgirl) Gordon (1967–68)

CRAMER, MARC—producer, host
Youth Takes a Stand (info)
.... moderator (1953)

CRAMPTON, CYDNEY—actress
Lobo (com) ... Rose Lobo Perkins (1979–80)

CRANE, BOB—actor
b: Jul 13, 1929*, Waterbury, Conn. d: Jun 29, 1978

The Donna Reed Show (com)
.... Dr. Dave Kelsey (1963–65)
Hogan's Heroes (com)
.... Col. Robert Hogan (1965–71)
The Bob Crane Show (com)
.... Bob Wilcox (1975)

*Some sources give 1928.

Sometimes, unfortunately, the shocking nature of an actor's death overshadows his work in life, and so it has been with Bob Crane. Crane started out as a drummer in bands in the Northeast and then became a disc jockey and talk show host on local radio. Eventually, in 1956, his easy, ingratiating manner won him a spot on KNX radio in Los Angeles, where he held forth interviewing celebrities for several years.

The contacts he made helped land him small roles on various TV series, including *General Electric Theater, The Lucy Show,* and *Alfred Hitchcock Presents.* By 1963 he had a regular role on *The Donna Reed Show,* as Donna's next door neighbor. He left after two years when given the opportunity to star in his own series, a comedy based on the rather unlikely premise of fun and games in a World War II prisoner-of-war camp. Despite the premise, *Hogan's Heroes* was a major hit, and Crane was, in his late thirties, a star.

After *Hogan* he made numerous guest appearances (*Love, American Style, Tenafly,* etc.) and had another short-lived series in 1975. Then, still quite popular, he decided to work for a while in regional theater. He was in Scottsdale, Arizona, just finishing an engagement, when someone quietly entered his room late at night and bludgeoned him to death with a crowbar while he slept. The intruder then tied an electrical cord around Crane's neck and just as quietly left. Occupants of neighboring rooms heard nothing.

Suspects were questioned. Crane was in the middle of divorce proceedings with his wife, actress Sigrid Valdis (who had been a regular on *Hogan's Heroes*), but she had been nowhere near Scottsdale. A video equipment dealer in Los Angeles was later brought in for questioning, but he was released for lack of evidence. The authorities were certain it was a well-planned murder. But to this day, it remains unsolved.

CRANE, BRANDON—actor

Otherworld (sci fi).... Smith Sterling (1985)

CRANE, LES—talk show host
b: c. 1935

ABC's Nightlife (talk)........ host (1964–65)

CRANE, NORMA—actress
b: c. 1931 d: Sep 28, 1973

Mr. Peepers (com)..... Rayola Dean (1952)

CRANE, RICHARD—actor
b: Jun 6, 1918, Newcastle, Ind. d: Mar 9, 1969

Surfside Six (drama)
.... Lt. Gene Plehan (1961–62)

CRANSHAW, PAT—actor

On the Rocks (com) ...... Gabby (1975–76)
Alice (com) .... Andy (1976–78)
AfterMASH (com).. Bob Scannell (1983–84)

CRAVEN, MATT—actor

Tough Cookies (com)
.... Richie Messina (1986)

CRAWFORD, BOBBY, JR.—juvenile actor
b: May 13, 1944, Quantico, Va.

Laramie (wes) .... Andy Sherman (1959–61)

The older brother of Johnny Crawford (of *The Rifleman*).

CRAWFORD, BRODERICK—actor
b: Dec 9, 1911, Philadelphia, Pa. d: Apr 26, 1986

Highway Patrol (police)
.... Chief Dan Matthews (1955–59)
King of Diamonds (drama)
.... John King (1961–62)
The Interns (drama)
.... Dr. Peter Goldstone (1970–71)

Gruff, beefy Broderick Crawford looked and sounded like a gangster, and that is exactly what he played in many films of the late '30s and '40s, as well as on television—at first. The son of an actor father and comedienne mother (Helen Broderick), he was brought up in show business. However, his mother strongly discouraged his acting ambitions. She was not won over, it is said, until he won the Academy Award in 1949—for his role as the ruthless politician in *All the King's Men.*

Beginning in the early '50s he appeared on such TV anthology series as *Schlitz*

Playhouse and *Lux Video Theatre.* His fame was assured with the role of Chief Dan Matthews on *Highway Patrol,* a cheaply made, syndicated cops-and-robbers show that enjoyed enormous popularity. He could hardly top that, but he continued to be active in the '60s, mostly in dramas *(Burke's Law, The Name of the Game)* and occasionally in comedy, such as a 1969 episode of *Get Smart* called "The Treasure of C. Errol Madre." He was less active after 1976, though he did turn up occasionally in undemanding roles such as those on *Fantasy Island* (1981).

He once answered the inevitable question about the secret of his success with a quotable quote: "The guys with the ugly mugs are working."

CRAWFORD, EDWARD—juvenile actor
b: c. 1963

Sanford and Son (com)
.... Roger Lawson (1976–77)

CRAWFORD, JOHN—actor
b: 1926

Take a Guess (quiz) .... panelist (1953)
The Waltons (drama)
.... Sheriff Ep Bridges (1972–81)

CRAWFORD, JOHNNY—juvenile actor
b: Mar 26, 1946, Los Angeles, Calif.

The Rifleman (wes)
.... Mark McCain (1958–63)

Johnny was onstage before he was old enough to enter first grade and had fairly numerous child roles in the mid and late 1950s on such series as *Cavalcade Theatre* ("The Boy Nobody Wanted"), *The Loretta Young Show,* and *Wild Bill Hickok.* His first major break was as one of the *Mickey Mouse Club* Mouseketeers from 1955–56. Two years later he became Chuch Connors' son in *The Rifleman,* the role for which is he best remembered.

In the early 1960s Johnny capitalized on his *Rifleman* fame by launching a recording career. He had several best-selling records with the teenybopper set, including "Cindy's Birthday" and a minor pop classic called "Your Nose Is Gonna Grow." He continued to act for a few more years, but as he entered his twen-

ties roles became fewer and further between. Among them have been appearances on *Star Trek* in 1967, *The Invisible Man* in 1975, and in the Kenny Rogers TV movie *The Gambler—The Adventure Continues* in 1983.

Johnny is the son of Hollywood film editor Robert Crawford and the brother of juvenile actor Bobby Crawford, Jr.

CRAWFORD, KATHERINE—actress
b: Mar 2, 1944, Los Angeles, Calif.

Captains and the Kings (drama)
.... Moira/Mary Armagh (1976)
Gemini Man (adv)... Abby Lawrence (1976)

Katherine was possibly one of the best-connected actresses in Hollywood in the 1970s; she was the wife of Universal Television president Frank Price and the daughter of top TV producer Roy Huggins.

CRAWFORD, MICHAEL—actor
b: Jan 19, 1942, Salisbury, England

The Adventures of Sir Francis Drake (adv)
.... John Drake (1962)

CRAWFORD, REV. PERCY—clergyman

Youth on the March (misc)... host (1949–53)

CRAWFORD, ROBERT—actor

Manhunt (police).. Det. Phil Burns (1960–61)

CREATORS, THE—

The Benny Rubin Show (com)
.... regulars (1949)

CRENNA, RICHARD—actor
b: Nov 30, 1926*, Los Angeles, Calif.

Our Miss Brooks (com)
.... Walter Denton (1952–55)
The Real McCoys (com)
.... Luke McCoy (1957–63)
Slattery's People (drama)
.... James Slattery (1964–65)
All's Fair (com)
.... Richard C. Barrington (1976–77)
Centennial (drama)
.... Col. Frank Skimmerhorn (1978–79)
It Takes Two (com)
.... Dr. Sam Quinn (1982–83)

*Some sources give 1927.

Emmy Award; Best Actor in a Special, for *The Rape of Richard Beck* (1985)

Few actors were able to sustain their success in juvenile roles quite as long as Richard Crenna. Beginning in radio as a squeaky-voiced real-life teenager, he quickly became one of the busiest youthful actors in the medium during the '40s, with regular roles on *The Great Gildersleeve, Burns and Allen, A Date with Judy* (as boyfriend Oogie Pringle), and *Our Miss Brooks.*

When *Our Miss Brooks* moved to television in 1952, Richard moved with it, in his role as Eve Arden's dim-witted student Walter Denton. His still-cracking teenage voice and gawky manners made him a perfect foil for her wisecracks, but by the time he left the series he was pushing 30 and the "teenage" persona was becoming a bit hard to believe (of course, Walter *was* dim-witted, so maybe he just hadn't graduated yet). Along the way he portrayed teenagers elsewhere as well, including a memorable 1952 episode of *I Love Lucy* in which Lucy tried to get Crenna and his girlfriend back together by teaching the awkward teenager how to dance; she and Desi then had to masquerade as their own grandparents to get rid of the two kids.

In 1957, Crenna was back in series TV, all grown up, as the young husband Luke on *The Real McCoys.* This was followed by a somewhat more dignified role as an idealistic politician on *Slattery's People.* Since that series ended in 1965, he has appeared mostly in TV movies, with occasional detours into series comedy. He has also worked as a director.

CRESPI, TODD—actor
b: Oct 24, 1951, Frankfurt, Germany

The Magician (adv)
.... Dennis Pomeroy (1973–74)

CREWSON, WENDY—actress

Night Heat (police)
.... Dorothy Fredericks (1985)

CRIBBINS, BERNARD—actor
b: Dec 29, 1928, Oldham, Lancs., England

The Val Doonican Show (var)
.... regular (1971)

CRICHTON, DON—dancer, choreographer

The Entertainers (var) .... regular (1964)
The Jimmie Rodgers Show (var)
.... regular (1969)
The Tim Conway Show (var)
.... dancers (1980–81)

CRISCUOLO, LOU—actor

Popi (com)................. Maggio (1976)
Stockard Channing in Just Friends (com)
.... Milt D'Angelo (1979)

CRISTAL, LINDA—actress
b: Feb 24, 1935*, Buenos Aires, Argentina

The High Chaparral (west)
.... Victoria Cannon (1967–71)

CRITTENDEN, JAMES—actor

Code Red (adv) ..... Rags Harris (1981–82)

CROCKETT, JAN—

The Jimmy Dean Show (var)
.... regular (1957)

CROFT, MARY JANE—actress

Our Miss Brooks (com)
.... Miss Daisy Enright (1952–54)
The People's Choice (com)
.... voice of Cleo (dog) (1955–58)
The Adventures of Ozzie & Harriet (com)
.... Clara Randolph (1956–66)
I Love Lucy (com)..... Betty Ramsey (1957)
The Lucy Show (com)
.... Mary Jane Lewis (1965–68)
Here's Lucy (com)
.... Mary Jane Lewis (1968–74)

This radio actress of the 1940s and '50s went on to a long career in television, specializing in supporting roles on comedies. In the early seasons of *Our Miss Brooks* she was Eve Arden's snooty rival for the affections of Mr. Boynton (Robert Rockwell); later she had long runs as a friend of the Nelsons on *Ozzie and Harriet* (10 years), and as Lucille Ball's chief cohort, after the departure of Vivian Vance, on *The Lucy Show* and *Here's Lucy* (nine years).

*Some sources give 1934 or 1936.

CROMWELL, JAMES—actor
b: Jan 27, Los Angeles, Calif.

All in the Family (com)
.... Stretch Cunningham (1974)
Hot L Baltimore (com).... Bill Lewis (1975)
The Nancy Walker Show (com)
.... Glen (1976)
Easy Street (com)
.... Quentin Standard (1986–)

CRONIN, PATRICK J.—actor

Alice (com).............. Jason (1978–79)

CRONKITE, KATHY—actress
b: Sept 5, 1950

Hizzonner (com) ...... Annie Cooper (1979)

The daughter of CBS newsman Walter
Cronkite.

CRONKITE, WALTER—newscaster
b: Nov 4, 1916, St. Joseph, Mo. r: Houston,
Texas

Open Hearing (doc) ...... moderator (1951)
CBS Weekend News (news)
.... anchorman (1951–62)
Pick the Winner (pub aff)....... host (1952)
Man of the Week (int)
.... moderator (1952–53)
You Are There (drama)
.... anchorman (1953–57)
It's News to Me (quiz).... moderator (1954)
Pick the Winner (pub aff)....... host (1956)
Air Power (doc)........ narrator (1956–57)
The 20th Century (doc) .. narrator (1957–70)
Presidential Countdown (pub aff)
.... anchorman (1960)
Eyewitness to History (news)
.... anchorman (1961–62)
CBS Evening News (news)
.... anchorman (1962–81)
Campaign Countdown (news)
.... anchorman (1980)
Universe (doc)....... anchorman (1980–82)

Emmy Awards: For coverage of the following events—*Man on the Moon, The Epic
Journey of Apollo XI* (1970), space coverage (1971), the Watergate affair and the
shooting of Governor George Wallace
(1973), the Agnew resignation (1974), Watergate (1974), *CBS Reports: The Rock-
efellers* (1974), interview with Solzhenit-
syn (1974); Special Academy Governors'
Award (1979); Special Trustees' Award,
for Distinguished Service to Television and
the Public (1982).

"Uncle Walter," or "Old Iron Bottom" as
he was sometimes known around CBS
News (for his ability to continuously anchor seemingly endless political events),
was one of the most familiar faces on television for more than 30 years. A onetime
United Press correspondent, he had his
own syndicated radio news program in the
1940s before joining CBS in July, 1950. CBS
quickly made him one of its principal on-
air reporters on all sorts of news and public affairs telecasts. His first widespread
recognition came as host of two very popular documentary series, *You Are There,* in
which CBS correspondents covered a historical event as if they were on the scene,
and *The 20th Century,* half-hour documentaries about major events of the past and
future. One of his least-remembered assignments during this period was as host of
a celebrity quiz show called *It's News to
Me,* in the summer of 1954.

In 1962 Cronkite took over the anchor
position on CBS's evening newscast, succeeding Douglas Edwards. He remained
there for 19 years, eventually surpassing in
audience NBC's top-rated *Huntley-Brinkley Report.* His avuncular style and imper-
turbability made him—according to many
polls—the most trusted man in America
during the turbulent 1960s. Though studi-
ously impartial, he was not cold. His occasional displays of genuine emotion, as
when he wept during coverage of the
Kennedy assassination, endeared him all
the more to viewers. Only once was his
reputation for fairness tarnished. That was
during the chaotic 1968 Democratic National Convention when he allowed an "interview" with Chicago Mayor Richard
Daley to turn into a self-serving forum for
the controversial politician. Uncle Walter
later allowed as how that had been a mistake, and America forgave him.

During later years, as the political scene
calmed down, Cronkite showed increasing
interest in science and space, anchoring
virtually all of CBS's telecasts of space
launches and the lunar landing. He was the
obvious choice to anchor the marathon,
flag-waving coverage of the nation's bicentennial in 1976. He finally relinquished his

nightly anchor position to Dan Rather in 1981 and concentrated on the summer science series *Universe*, as well as on other special reports for the network. Among the latter were on-location retrospectives on the fortieth anniversaries of D-Day (1984) and VE-Day (1985).

He is, appropriately, enshrined in the Television Academy's Hall of Fame, along with Milton Berle, Lucille Ball, and other icons of the television age.

CRONYN, HUME—actor

b: Jul 18, 1911, London, Ontario, Canada

The Marriage (com) .... Ben Marriott (1954)

While Cronyn is known primarily as a leading Broadway stage actor, he appeared on television as early as 1939 and was seen fairly frequently during the 1950s in live, New York–originated playhouse productions (on *Omnibus, Studio One, Alcoa Hour,* etc.). He and his wife, Jessica Tandy, appeared together in a 1954 summer series which bears one notable distinction—it was the first series regularly telecast in color.

CROOK, LORIANNE—hostess

This Week in Country Music (news)
.... host (1983–)

CROSBIE, ANNETTE—actress

b: 1934, England

The Six Wives of Henry VIII (drama)
.... Catherine of Aragon (1971)

CROSBY, BING—singer, actor

b: May 3, 1903*, Tacoma, Wash. r: Spokane, Wash. d: Oct 14, 1977

The Bing Crosby Show (com)
.... Bing Collins (1964–65)
The Hollywood Palace (var)
.... frequent host (1964–70)

*There has always been a great deal of uncertainty regarding Bing's birth date, with published years ranging from 1901 to 1904. Even Bing himself gave different dates in the U.S. and British editions of his autobiography. There is apparently no birth certificate in existence; however, in 1978 researchers from the British Bing Crosby society turned up a baptismal certificate from May 1903 that confirms that the correct date was, in fact, May 3, 1903. The matter was covered in some detail in the society's magazine, *Bing*, in March 1978.

Although he was the most popular American singer of the first half of the twentieth century and an Oscar-winning movie actor, Bing Crosby had only moderate success on television. Perhaps he waited too long to make the transition. Bing was *so* identified with the 1930s and '40s that by the time he tried series TV in the 1960s he seemed like the superstar of another generation. Then too, unlike some of his contemporaries (Jack Benny, Burns and Allen, Red Skelton), he simply didn't work very hard at conquering the video medium.

Nevertheless, Bing did appear on some of the big, glossy musical specials of the 1950s and '60s, as well as doing occasional unexpected walk-ons on programs such as *I Married Joan* and *The Phil Silvers Show*. His television debut was on a special Red Cross program in February 1951. He did not appear in the 1962 TV version of his most famous movie, *Going My Way* (Gene Kelly assumed his role), but he did launch his own situation comedy in 1964, playing a family man; it was not successful. Six years later he was approached about starring in an offbeat detective show, but turned it down, reportedly because it would interfere with his golf game. How different *Columbo* would have been if he had accepted!

From 1964 to 1970 Bing was a frequent host on *The Hollywood Palace*. A highlight of this series was his annual Christmas show, sometimes with his family; these were continued as specials after the series ended, up until the time of Crosby's death. They almost always ended with snow gently falling outside the window and Bing crooning, in his reassuring baritone, "White Christmas." And that was how the last one ended in November 1977; it had been taped just a few weeks before he died.

Bing was the father of actors Gary and Mary Crosby and the brother of bandleader Bob Crosby. His autobiography was titled *Call Me Lucky* (1953); a more up-to-date "authorized" biography, by Charles Thompson, was published in 1976 under the title *Bing*.

CROSBY, BOB—orchestra leader

b: Aug 23, 1913, Spokane, Wash.

The Bob Crosby Show (var).... host (1958)

Bandleader brother of Bing Crosby. He also hosted a daytime show on CBS from 1953–57.

CROSBY, CATHY LEE—actress
b: Dec 2, 1948, Los Angles, Calif.

That's Incredible (aud par)... host (1980–84)

Blonde actress who began appearing on television in the early 1970s and later in a few films. She is no relation to Bing Crosby.

CROSBY, GARY—actor
b: Jun 25, 1933, California

The Bill Dana Show (com). Eddie (1963–64)
Adam 12 (police)... Off. Ed Wells (1968–75)
Chase (police)...... Off. Ed Rice (1973–74)

The eldest son of Bing Crosby; according to Bing he was named after the crooner's close friend Gary Cooper. Gary made his first show business splash in 1950 with a best-selling duet recording with his dad ("Play a Simple Melody" and "Sam's Song"). His TV debut came five years later on *The Jack Benny Show*. Once seen mostly as part of a musical act with his three brothers Dennis, Phillip, and Lindsay, Gary later found work as a supporting actor on several series—often as a uniformed cop.
Autobiography: *Going My Own Way* (1983).

CROSBY, LOU—announcer
b: 1911, Lawton, Okla. d: Jan 27, 1984

Mayor of Hollywood (var)
.... campaign manager (1952)

Not related to Bing Crosby.

CROSBY, MARY—actress
b: Sep 14, 1959, Los Angeles, Calif.

Brothers and Sisters (com)
.... Suzi Cooper (1979)
Dallas (drama)... Kristin Shepard (1979–81)

The daughter of Bing Crosby by his second wife, Katherine Grant. Also known as Mary Francis Crosby. Mary began appearing with her actress mother in stage productions in the late 1970s and then moved into a solo career on television with supporting roles in TV movies and series episodes. Her most famous role to date has been that of Kristin, the woman who shot J.R. on *Dallas*. No longer worried about being forever identified as Bing Crosby's daughter, she says, "Now I've got to prove that I'm something more than the sexpot who shot J.R."

CROSBY, MARY (1950s)—singer

Jimmy Blaine's Junior Edition (music)
.... regular (1951)

The wife of New York radio/TV critic John Crosby.

CROSBY, NORM—comedian
b: Sep 15, 1927, Boston, Mass.

The Beautiful Phyllis Diller Show (var)
.... regular (1968)
Liar's Club (quiz)....... panelist (1976–78)
The Comedy Shop (com)....... host (1978)

CROSS, DENNIS—actor

The Blue Angels (adv)
.... Cmdr. Arthur Richards (1960)

CROSS, MILTON J.—announcer
b: Apr 16, 1897, New York City, N.Y. d: Jan 3, 1975

Metropolitan Opera Auditions of the Air (talent) .... commentator (1952)

CROSS, MURPHY—actress
b: Jun 22, 1950, Havre de Grace, Md. r: Laurel, Md.

Phyl & Mikhy (com)
.... Phyllis ("Phyl") Wilson (1980)

CROSSE, RUPERT—black actor
b: Nov 29, 1927, New York City, N.Y. d: 1973

The Partners (com)
.... Det. George Robinson (1971–72)

CROTHERS, SCATMAN—black actor
b: May 23, 1910, Terre Haute, Ind. d: Nov 26, 1986

Chico and the Man (com).. Louie (1974–78)
Roots (drama).............. Mingo (1977)

One of the Boys (com)
.... Bernard Solomon (1982)
Casablanca (drama).......... Sam (1983)
Morningstar/Eveningstar (drama)
.... Excell Dennis (1986)

Talk about paying your dues! This old trooper had been a small-time performer in various media for nearly 50 years before TV suddenly made him nationally known in the late 1970s. In the '20s, '30s, and '40s he was a jazz musician and singer, playing small clubs and radio. His first television appearance was in 1948, and in the 1950s he was seen in small roles on *The Colgate Comedy Hour* with Donald O'Connor, as well as in a few films. By the '70s he was playing character parts, often as a gullible, slow-witted black, in such series as *The Governor and J.J.*, *Kojak*, and *Toma*. However, the role of Louie the garbageman on *Chico and The Man* finally made his name. In the years that followed he had similar roles on other series; perhaps truest to his roots was the one on *One of the Boys*, where he played a cheerful old jazzman who sometimes jammed down at the club with series star Mickey Rooney.

Scatman also provided voices for a number of Saturday morning cartoons in the 1970s and '80s, including *Hong Kong Phooey* and *The Harlem Globetrotters*.

CROUGH, SUZANNE—juvenile actress
The Partridge Family (com)
.... Tracy Partridge (1970–74)
Mulligan's Stew (drama)
.... Stevie Friedman (1977)

CROW, CARL—juvenile actor
National Velvet (adv) ..... Teddy (1960–62)

CROWE, TONYA—actress
b: Jan 24, Long Beach, Calif.
Knots Landing (drama)
.... Olivia Cunningham (1980–)

CROWLEY, KATHLEEN—actress
b: 1931, Green Bank, Egg Harbor, N.J.
Waterfront (adv)
.... Terry Van Buren (1953–56)

CROWLEY, PATRICIA—actress
b: Sep 17, 1933*, Olyphant, Pa.
Please Don't Eat the Daisies (com)
.... Joan Nash (1965–67)
Joe Forrester (police)
.... Georgia Cameron (1975–76)

Pat Crowley landed her first major TV role when she was barely out of high school and for a time seemed likely to become an important juvenile star of the 1950s. The role was the lead in the 1951–52 version of *A Date with Judy*, which was adapted from the popular radio series and telecast on Saturday mornings. When it moved to prime time in 1952 another actress took over the part. However, Patricia continued to be seen on series such as *Armstrong Circle Theatre*, *The Loretta Young Show*, and *General Electric Theater*. She worked steadily in the 1960s, too, in comedies and dramas, and from 1965 to 1967 had her second chance at series stardom in the leading role on *Please Don't Eat the Daisies*—this time as a harried mother of four.

That series was only moderately successful, and Pat went back to supporting roles, remaining active—if not especially famous—in the 1970s and '80s. Her later work included several appearances on *Police Story*.

CRUIKSHANK, RUFUS—actor
The Adventures of Robin Hood (adv)
.... Little John (1955–56)

CRUTCHFIELD, PAUL—rodeo announcer
Texas Rodeo (sport)... commentator (1959)

CRUTCHLEY, ROSALIE—actress
b: 1921, England
The Six Wives of Henry VIII (drama)
.... Catherine Parr (1971)

CRUZ, BRANDON—juvenile actor
b: May 28, 1962, Bakersfield, Calif.
The Courtship of Eddie's Father (com)
.... Eddie Corbett (1969–72)

As the freckle-faced Eddie on *The Courtship of Eddie's Father*, Brandon Cruz was

*Some sources give 1929.

one of the cutest, and most famous, kids on television. He had no prior acting experience, having been cast on the basis of an audition tape submitted by his mother when he was five. By all reports he enjoyed being on the show immensely and was very attached to his TV "dad," Bill Bixby, offscreen as well as on (Brandon's own parents were divorced). Unfortunately, once he reached his teens, further roles were hard to come by. Brandon guested in a number of series from 1972–76, including *Kung Fu, Gunsmoke,* and *Police Story,* and had small parts in a few films (including 1976's *The Bad News Bears*), but since then has been seldom seen. In recent years he has performed with his own local rock group, The Eddys, and hopes to get back into acting.

CRYSTAL, BILLY—comedian, actor
b: Mar 14, 1947, Long Beach, Long Island, N.Y.

Soap (com) . . . . Jodie Dallas (1977–81)
The Billy Crystal Comedy Hour (var)
. . . . host (1982)
NBC's Saturday Night Live (com)
. . . . regular (1984–85)

Billy Crystal grew up in musical surroundings. His father produced jazz concerts and his uncle, Milt Gabler, was a longtime record producer and founder of Commodore, one of America's leading jazz labels. While growing up Billy met many performers and knew he wanted to get into show business—as a comic. He denies, however, that he was the class clown in school. "I was the class comedian," he says. "There's a difference. The class clown is the guy who drops his pants and runs across the field at halftime. The class comedian is the guy who talked him into doing it."

After graduating from college, Billy teamed up with two friends and did stand-up comedy in coffee houses and on campuses for four years in the early 1970s. He also landed some guest spots as a solo act on *The Tonight Show, The Mike Douglas Show,* and similar programs, but his major break was in the role of the gay son Jodie on the hit comedy *Soap.*

After leaving *Soap* Billy continued to perform for younger audiences, making several campus tours. He scored a major

hit in the mid-1980s as a regular for a season on NBC's *Saturday Night Live.*

CUERVO, ALMA—actress
b: Aug 13, Tampa, Fla.

a.k.a. Pablo (com) . . . . . Sylvia Rivera (1984)

CUEVAS, NELSON D.—actor
Viva Valdez (com) . . Ernesto Valdez (1976)

CUFF, SIMON—actor
Doctor in the House (com)
. . . . Dave Briddock (1970–73)

CUGAT, XAVIER—Latin bandleader
b: Jan 1, 1900, Barcelona, Spain r: Havana, Cuba

The Xavier Cugat Show (music)
. . . . host (1957)

Married to singer Abbe Lane in the 1950s and later to actress Charo. Desi Arnaz once played in Cugat's band, which was extremely popular during the 1930s and '40s. Cuggie was mostly inactive after suffering a stroke in 1971. His autobiography was titled *Rhumba Is My Life* (1948).

CULEA, MELINDA—actress
b: May 5, Western Springs, Ill.

The A-Team (adv). . . . . . . Amy Allen (1983)
Glitter (drama). . . Terry Randolph (1984–85)

CULLEN, BILL—host
b: Feb 18, 1920, Pittsburgh, Pa.

Who's There (quiz) . . . . panelist (1952)
I've Got a Secret (quiz) . . panelist (1952–67)
Where Was I? (quiz) . . . . panelist (1953)
Why? (quiz) . . . . assistant (1953)
Bank on the Stars (quiz) . . . . . . emcee (1954)
Name That Tune (quiz) . . . . emcee (1954–55)
Place the Face (quiz) . . . . . . emcee (1954–55)
Down You Go (quiz) . . . . emcee (1956)
The Price Is Right (quiz) . . . emcee (1957–64)
To Tell the Truth (quiz) . . panelist (1969–77)
The $25,000 Pyramid (quiz). . . host (1974–79)
I've Got a Secret (quiz) . . . moderator (1976)
The Joker's Wild (quiz) . . . . . . host (1984–)

"It's great to be witty and funny, but a host should never distract a contestant from winning money," says Bill Cullen. Perhaps that supportive attitude is what has made him such a successful emcee for so many years. It has certainly kept him busy. Cullen modestly admits, "I've not been unemployed since 1939."

Life was not always so kind to Bill. As a child he was stricken with polio, which left him with a prominent limp. Determined to lead an active life despite this, he took boxing lessons from a pro, earned a pilot's license at age 15, and competed in various sports. He began his broadcasting career as a disc jockey at age 19, went on to network announcing, and in 1946 got the fateful assignment that set the pattern for the rest of his career—hosting the radio quiz show *Winner Take All*. Since then, he estimates, he has appeared on at least 25 different series, radio and television, daytime and nighttime, and taken part in at least 5,000 half-hour games. During one season in the mid-1960s he could be seen on all three networks—on *Eye Guess* on NBC, *The Price Is Right* on ABC, and *I've Got a Secret* on CBS.

For a time in the '50s Bill had a second career as a football and hockey play-by-play announcer and a third as operator of his own charter flying service. He remained an ardent pilot until the mid-1970s.

Once asked if he would like to have all the money he's given away over the years on all those shows, he replied, "No. I would rather have all the answers to the questions I've asked. As the smartest guy in the world, all the rest would follow."

CULLEN, BRETT—actor
b: Aug 26, Houston, Texas

The Chisholms (wes)
.... Gideon Chisholm (1980)
The Thorn Birds (drama)
.... Bob Cleary (1983)

CULLEN, PETER—comedian

The Sonny and Cher Comedy Hour (var)
.... regular (1971–74)
The Sonny Comedy Revue (var)
.... regular (1974)

CULLEN, WILLIAM KIRBY—actor
b: Mar 9, 1952, Santa Ana, Calif.

How the West Was Won (miniseries) (drama)
.... Josh (1977)

How the West Was Won (wes)
.... Josh Macahan (1978–79)

CULLY, ZARA—black actress
b: Jan 26, Worcester, Mass.

The Jeffersons (com)
.... Mother Olivia Jefferson (1975–78)

CULP, ROBERT—actor, writer, director
b: Aug 16, 1930, Berkeley, Calif.

Trackdown (wes)... Hoby Gilman (1957–59)
I Spy (adv) ...... Kelly Robinson (1965–68)
The Greatest American Hero (adv)
.... Bill Maxwell (1981–83)

Lean, athletic Robert Culp has been a TV standby since the mid-1950s. He often plays slightly cynical types, and, though he has had three successful series, this lack of warmth may have prevented him from becoming a superstar. Culp came to New York in 1951 to get his start (New York was then the television and theatrical capital of the world). He appeared in a number of off-Broadway plays and in some live TV dramas, then went back to Los Angeles to star in his first series—the CBS western *Trackdown*. This did not lead immediately to another series, but it did result in a great deal of work on other shows: *Zane Grey Theater, Ben Casey, The Outer Limits, 87th Precinct*, etc. After a while Culp called himself "the highest paid actor still doing difficult character parts in other people's TV series."

Finally, in 1965, he was cast with Bill Cosby in the adventure series *I Spy*, which became a major hit. As the more experienced actor of the two, Culp helped Cosby learn the trade, a fact that the black comic remembered appreciatively for many years thereafter.

In the late 1960s Culp became quite active in the civil rights movement and invested a year of his time and his own money to film *Operation Breadbasket*, a documentary about black economics that was aired twice on ABC. He also scored his first major motion picture success in the film *Bob and Carol and Ted and Alice*. He was seen fairly often in guest roles in the 1970s, on *The Name of the Game, Police Story, Columbo* (and *Mrs. Columbo*), and other series. In 1981 he returned to series TV in the role of the jaded F.B.I. agent on *The Greatest American Hero.* He has also been active as a writer and sometime director over the years, contributing scripts to *Trackdown, The Rifleman, I Spy,* and *Cain's Hundred,* among others; one of his scripts for *I Spy* was nominated for an Emmy.

CULPEPPER, STUART—actor

Chiefs (drama) . . . . Grady Butts (1983)

CULVER, HOWARD—actor
b: c. 1918, Colorado r: Los Angeles, Calif. d: Aug 5, 1984

Gunsmoke (wes) . . . . Howie (1955–75)

CUMBUKA, JI-TU—black actor
b: Mar 4, Helena, Ala. r: Johnstown, Pa.

Roots (drama) . . . . the wrestler (1977)
Young Dan'l Boone (adv) . . . . . Hawk (1977)
A Man Called Sloane (drama)
. . . . Torque (1979–80)

CUMMINGS, QUINN—juvenile actress
b: Aug 13, 1967, Los Angeles, Calif.

Big Eddie (com) . . . . Ginger Smith (1975)
Family (drama) . . . . Annie Cooper (1978–80)
Hail to the Chief (com)
. . . . Lucy Mansfield (1985)

CUMMINGS, ROBERT—actor
b: Jun 9, 1910*, Joplin, Mo.

My Hero (com)
. . . . Robert S. Beanblossom (1952–53)
The Bob Cummings Show (com)
. . . . Bob Collins (1955–59)
The Bob Cummings Show (adv)
. . . . Bob Carson (1961–62)
My Living Doll (com)
. . . . Dr. Robert McDonald (1964–65)

Emmy Award: Best Actor in a Single Performance, for the *Studio One* production "Twelve Angry Men" (1954)

Eternally boyish Robert Cummings has several secrets for staying young, among them health foods and astrology. They certainly worked for him. He remains fit and healthy in his seventies, appropriate for a man who once wrote a book

*Some sources give 1908.

called *How to Stay Young and Vital.*

Cummings' on-screen image was similarly radiant. He began on stage in the early 1930s and at first passed himself off as Englishman "Blade Stanhope-Conway" because only English actors seemed to be getting roles then. (He even went to London and bribed a stagehand to take his picture standing under a phony marquee, on which his name was temporarily affixed, to establish his "credentials"). Later he posed as "Brice Hutchens," and, still later, when western he-men were getting parts, he affected a Texas drawl. By the late 1930s he was able to find roles under his real name, appearing in numerous movies through the '40s and '50s. Many of them were light comedies, but there were also some more serious parts (in *King's Row, Dial M for Murder,* etc.).

Bob was on television beginning in the early 1950s, both on dramatic playhouses and in his own situation comedies. The original *Bob Cummings Show* from 1955–59 (also known as *Love That Bob*) was a hit, and probably the closest thing to a sex comedy on 1950s TV. Bob continued to be quite active in the '60s and did not begin to reduce his activities until the early 1970s, after a flurry of appearances on *Love, American Style* and in some TV movies.

Though retired now, he still follows a rigorous health program and is amused when people remember him as Hollywood's leading "health food nut." "I'd tell all those critics how well I feel today because of my diet," he says. "But they're all dead."

CUNNINGHAM, BILL—newscaster

Meet the Boss (int) . . . . host (1952)

CUNNINGHAM, BOB—host

Crisis (drama) . . . . the "director" (1949)

CUNNINGHAM, RONNIE—

Admiral Broadway Revue (var)
. . . . regular (1949)

CUNNINGHAM, SARAH—actress
b: c. 1918, Greenville, S.C. d: Mar 24, 1986

Trapper John, M.D. (drama)
. . . . Nurse Andrews (1981–86)

CUNNINGHAM, ZAMAH—actress
b: c. 1893 d: Jun 2, 1967

Menasha the Magnificent (com)
.... Mrs. Davis (1950)

CURB, MIKE, CONGREGATION— singers
Mike Curb b: Dec 24, 1944, Savannah, Ga.

The Glen Campbell Goodtime Hour (var)
.... regulars (1971–72)

Curb, a top recording executive, was elected lieutenant governor of California in 1979.

CURFEW BOYS, THE—dancers

The Gisele MacKenzie Show (var)
.... dancers (1957–58)

CURRAN, BRIAN—actor

Number 96 (drama)
.... Dr. Robert Leon (1980–81)

CURRERI, LEE—actor
b: Jan 4, New York City, N.Y.

Fame (drama)..... Bruno Martelli (1982–84)

CURTAIN CALLS, THE—

The Beautiful Phyllis Diller Show (var)
.... singer/dancers (1968)

CURTIN, JANE—actress
b: Sep 6, 1947, Cambridge, Mass.

NBC's Saturday Night Live (com)
.... regular (1975–80)
Kate & Allie (com) .. Allie Lowell (1984–)

Emmy Award: Best Actress in a Comedy Series, for *Kate & Allie* (1984, 1985)

CURTIN, VALERIE—actress, writer
b: Mar 31, Jackson Heights, New York City, N.Y.

The Jim Stafford Show (var).. regular (1975)
9 to 5 (com)......... Judy Bernly (1982–83)
9 to 5 (com)......... Judy Bernly (1986–)

Valerie is the daughter of Joseph Curtin, a popular radio actor who costarred in *Mr. & Mrs. North* and other radio series of the 1940s. After a brief period of stage experi-ence in New York, Valerie moved to the West Coast in the early 1970s and began appearing in films (including *Alice Doesn't Live Here Anymore* and *All The President's Men*) and episodes of TV series. She has also authored scripts for movies and TV, including *The Mary Tyler Moore Show*. Valerie and Jane Curtin are cousins.

CURTIS, BARRY—juvenile actor
b: c. 1943

Adventures of Champion (adv)
.... Ricky North (1955–56)

CURTIS, BOB—pianist

Jack Leonard (music)........ pianist (1949)

CURTIS, BOB—actor

Falcon Crest (drama) . Father Bob (1985–)

CURTIS, DICK—actor

The Jonathan Winters Show (var)
.... regular (1967–69)
Andy Williams Presents Ray Stevens (var)
.... regular (1970)

CURTIS, DONALD—actor
b: 1915, Eugene, Ore.

Detective's Wife (com)
.... Adam Conway (1950)

CURTIS, HELEN—

The Jackie Gleason Show (var)
.... regular (1964–66)

CURTIS, JAMIE LEE—actress
b: Nov 22, 1958, Los Angeles, Calif.

Operation Petticoat (com)
.... Lt. Barbara Duran (1977–78)

The daughter of Janet Leigh and Tony Cur-tis launched her acting career while still a teenager, with guest roles on TV series of the mid-1970s, before she plunged full-time into horror movies. Her first appearance, arranged during a school vacation, con-sisted of two lines on a *Quincy, M.E.*, epi-sode; this was followed by guest roles on *The Nancy Drew Mysteries, The Love Boat,* and *Buck Rogers in the 25th Century* (in which she and series hunk Gil Girard had to escape from an interplanetary prison while handcuffed together). She also had a regular role on *Operation Petticoat.* Jamie Lee has since starred in a number of TV movies, including *Death of a Centerfold: The Dorothy Stratton Story* in 1981.

CURTIS, JANET LYNN—actress

Lobo (com) .... Margaret Ellen (1979–80)

CURTIS, KEENE—actor
b: Feb 15, 1923, Salt Lake City, Utah

The Magician (adv)
.... Max Pomeroy (1973–74)
One in a Million (com) . Mr. Cushing (1980)
Amanda's (com)....: Clifford Mundy (1983)

CURTIS, KEN—actor
b: Jul 2, 1916, Lamar, Colo.

Ripcord (adv) .... Jim Budkley (1961–63)
Gunsmoke (wes) .. Festus Haggen (1964–75)
The Yellow Rose (drama)
.... Hoyt Coryell (1983–84)

Most viewers who knew Ken Curtis as the twangy, scruffy deputy Festus on *Gunsmoke* in the 1960s and '70s would probably have been surprised to learn about the actor's previous career—as a big band singer, crooning ballads such as "Love Sends a Little Gift of Roses" (with Tommy Dorsey in 1941) or World War II flag-wavers such as "This Is Worth Fighting For" (with the Shep Fields Orchestra).

After his big band days Ken continued to sing with the Sons of the Pioneers western group. He also began an acting career in the late 1940s, starring in low-budget westerns and appearing as a supporting player in some A films (including *Mr. Roberts*). On television, he costarred as a sky diver in *Ripcord* in 1961, before replacing Dennis Weaver as Matt Dillon's deputy on *Gunsmoke.*

CURTIS, LIANE—actress

The Best Times (drama)
.... Annette Dimetriano (1985)

CURTIS, MINNIE JO—comedienne

Starlit Time (var) .... regular (1950)

CURTIS, TONY—actor
b: Jun 3, 1925, The Bronx, New York

The Persuaders (adv)
.... Danny Wilde (1971–72)
McCoy (drama) .... McCoy (1975–76)
Vegas$ (drama) ...... Philip Roth (1978–81)

Hollywood leading man Tony Curtis was seldom seen on television during his peak film years in the '50s and '60s; an occasional appearance on *General Electric Theater* or *Ford Star Time* was the most small-screen viewers got. In the '70s, however, he brought his virile charm and his famous Bronx accent to TV in no fewer than three series—he was a playboy adventurer in the British-made *The Persuaders,* a conman with a heart of gold in *McCoy,* and a casino owner in *Vegas$.* Tony was later seen in occasional TV movies (e.g., *The Million Dollar Face*) and miniseries *(Moviola).*

In 1985, as he was about to appear with Susan Lucci in the TV movie *Mafia Princess,* he explained why he hadn't been seen much lately. "The truth is I'm a recovering alcoholic and an ex–dope adict. I'm not ashamed of it. I did it all. I was stupid. But that's over with; I've beaten all that down. I'm healthy now and working, and for me, that's the greatest therapy in the world."

Tony is also an accomplished painter, whose canvases have been sold for as much as half-a-million dollars each.

CURTIS, VIRGINIA—actress

Caesar's Hour (var)
.... Betty Hansen (1954–55)

CUSACK, JOAN—comedienne
b: Oct 11, 1962, Evanston, Ill.

NBC's Saturday Night Live (var)
.... regular (1985–86)

CUTLER, JON—actor

Brothers and Sisters (com)
.... Stanley Zipper (1979)

CUTLER, WENDY—

People Do The Craziest Things (aud par)
.... assistant (1984–85)

CUTTER, LISE—actress
b: Jul 31, Los Angeles, Calif.

Perfect Strangers (com)
.... Susan Campbell (1986–   )

CUTTS, PATRICIA—actress
b: 1926, England d: 1974

Down You Go (quiz)
.... regular panelist (1955–56)

CYPHER, JON—actor

Hill Street Blues (police)
...... Chief Fletcher P. Daniels (1981–   )
Knots Landing (drama)
.... Jeff Munson (1982–83)

CYPHERS, CHARLES—actor

The Betty White Show (com)
.... Hugo Muncy (1977–78)

D

DABNEY, AUGUSTA—actress
b: Oct 23, Berkeley, Calif.

Robert Montgomery Presents (summer) (drama)............. repertory player (1955)

This actress is known primarily for her stage work and for her many years on various daytime soap operas—from *Young Doctor Malone* in the '50s to *Loving* in the '80s. She is married to actor William Prince.

D'ABO, MARYAM—actress

Master of the Game (drama)
.... Dominique (1984)

DAGMAR—actress
b: Nov 29, 1926, Huntington, W. Va.

Broadway Open House (talk)
.... regular (1950–51)
Dagmar's Canteen (var)...... hostess (1952)
Masquerade Party (quiz)
.... panelist (1955–56)

Blonde, busty Jennie Lewis—"Dagmar"—was one of the favorite sights on early television. And what a sight she was, even on a ten-inch black-and-white screen! Her statuesque figure and ample endowment (bust estimates ranged from 39 to 42) made her television's first parody of that Hollywood staple, the sexy dumb blonde.

Prior to 1950 she had been an obscure bit player on the New York stage. Her first exposure was as a stooge in Olsen and Johnson's stage hit *Laffin' Room Only* in the mid-1940s; later she was seen on an early Bob Hope TV special. Then, in 1950, fast-talking comic Jerry Lester, something of a runt, hired her to decorate his late-night show, *Broadway Open House*. "You just sit there next to the orchestra and look dumb," he told her. However, her deadpan "poetry readings" and garbled English, delivered with wide-eyed innocence, soon made her the hit of the show. Some sample Dagmarisms:

Mushroom–"A place where you make love."
Isolate–"That's when you admit that you are tardy."

Source–"Skin wounds."
Languish–"What people speak."
Singular–"Musically inclined."
Martial–"Swampy?"

Lester, a borsch-belt hustler, realized that his comic creation was becoming more popular than he was, and the friction between them grew. Finally, Jerry left the show. Dagmar took advantage of the resulting publicity (she was even on the cover of *Life* magazine) to launch a solo career with her own late-night series in early 1952. Later she was a regular on *Masquerade Party,* but her brief moment of celebrity was by then over. She was seen infrequently in later years in an occasional guest spot and in local stage productions. An attempt to launch a Broadway career closed out of town.

Dagmar was married several times over the years, once (in 1951) to actor Danny Dayton. She now lives in retirement, still glamorous and still remembering those heady days of the early 1950s.

DAHL, ARLENE—actress
b: Aug 11, 1924, Minneapolis, Minn.

Pepsi-Cola Playhouse (drama)
.... hostess (1953–54)
Opening Night (drama) ...... hostess (1958)

This red-haired movie beauty of the 1950s was seen on daytime's *One Life to Live* for several years in the early 1980s.

DAHL, ROALD—writer
b: 1916, Norway

Way Out (drama) .... host (1961)

DAILEY, DAN—actor
b: Dec 14, 1914*, New York City, N.Y. d: Oct 16, 1978

Four Just Men (adv) ...... Jim Collier (1959)
The Governor & J.J. (com)
...... Gov. William Drinkwater (1969–70)
Faraday and Company (drama)
.... Frank Faraday (1973–74)

DAILEY, FRANK—orchestra leader, host
b: c. 1901 d: Feb 27, 1956

*Some sources give 1915.

Music at the Meadowbrook (var)
.... regular (1953)
Music at the Meadowbrook (var)
.... regular (1956)

DAILY, BILL—actor
b: Aug 30, 1928, Des Moines, Iowa

I Dream of Jeannie (com)
.... Capt. Roger Healey (1965–70)
The Bob Newhart Show (com)
.... Howard Borden (1972–78)
Aloha Paradise (com).... Curtis Shea (1981)
Small & Frye (com)..... Dr. Hanratty (1983)

Bill Daily began his professional career in the 1950s as a TV writer and director in Chicago. He eventually began doing on-camera comedy routines and was spotted by Steve Allen, who brought him to Hollywood to work on his show. A few years later Daily landed the two comedy supporting roles for which he is best known; as Larry Hagman's buddy on *I Dream of Jeannie* and then as Bob Newhart's nutty, aviator neighbor on *The Bob Newhart Show.*

DAKER, DAVID—actor
Holocaust (drama) .... Hoess (1978)

DALE, ALAN—singer
b: July 9, 1925, Brooklyn, N.Y.

The Alan Dale Show (music)
.... host (1948–51)
Sing It Again (quiz)....... regular (1950–51)

DALE, DICK—singer, saxophonist
b: c. 1926, Iowa

The Lawrence Welk Show (music)
.... regular (1955–82)

DALE, JIMMY—orchestra leader
b: Jun 18, 1901, The Bronx, N.Y.

The Sonny and Cher Comedy Hour (var)
.... orch. leader (1971–73)
The Ken Berry "Wow" Show (var)
.... orch. leader (1972)
Cher (var) .... orch. leader (1975)
The Bobby Vinton Show (var)
.... orch. leader (1975–78)

DALIO, MARCEL—actor
b: Jul 17, 1900, Paris, France d: Nov. 20, 1983

Casablanca (drama)
.... Capt. Renaud (1955–56)

DALLESANDRO, JOE—actor
b: Dec 31, 1948, Pensacola, Fla. r: New York City, N.Y.

Fortune Dane (police)
.... Perfect Tommy (1986)

A young actor associated with Andy Warhol's mildly pornographic "art films" of the 1970s.

DALLIMORE, MAURICE—actor
d: 1973

Fair Exchange (com)
.... Willie Shorthouse (1962–63)

DALTON, ABBY—actress
b: Aug 15, 1932, Las Vegas, Nev. r: Los Angeles

Hennesey (com)
.... Nurse Martha Hale (1959–62)
The Joey Bishop Show (com)
.... Ellie Barnes (1962–65)
The Jonathan Winters Show (var)
.... regular (1967–69)
Barney Miller (com)
.... Elizabeth Miller (pilot) (1975)
Falcon Crest (drama)
.... Julia Cumson (1981–)

Abby Dalton has been a familiar face for longer than she has been a familiar name. As a teenager in the 1950s she was a model, appearing on magazine covers and record album jackets. Her movie debut was in a 1957 Roger Corman quickie called *Rock All Night,* followed by such late '50s B films as *Stakeout on Dope Street* and *Girls on the Loose.*

Abby's TV debut was at about the same time, as the youthful Belle Starr in a *Schlitz Playhouse* production. Later, she had roles on *Maverick, Have Gun Will Travel,* and *Rawhide* (as a stranded showgirl) before landing the regular role of Jackie Cooper's girlfriend on *Hennesey.* No sooner had she and Jackie been "married" on a May 1962 episode, however, than *Hennesey* was canceled and Abby went on to become Joey Bishop's TV wife on *The Joey Bishop Show.* There, in 1963, her character gave birth to a baby—which was played by Abby's own real life infant son, Matthew.

In later years Abby was a regular on *The Jonathan Winters Show,* where she played Jonathan's wife Margaret in sketches, and she *almost* became Mrs. Barney Miller as well (Barbara Barrie took over the role for the series' first season). Lately, Abby has been seen as a wife of a different kind, as the mentally disturbed, murderous Julia Cumson on *Falcon Crest.*

DALTON, DARREN—actor

The Best Times (drama)
.... Chris Henson (1985)

DALTON, SUSANNA—actress

Delta House (com)
.... Mandy Pepperidge (1979)

DALTON, TIMOTHY—actor

b: Mar 21, 1944, Colwyn Bay, Wales

Centennial (drama)
.... Oliver Seccombe (1978–79)

DALY, JAMES—actor

b: Oct 23, 1918, Wisconsin Rapids, Wis. d: Jul 3, 1978

Foreign Intrigue (drama)
.... Michael Powers (1953–54)
Medical Center (drama)
.... Dr. Paul Lochner (1969–76)

Emmy Award: Best Supporting Actor in a Drama, for the *Hallmark Hall of Fame* production "Eagle In a Cage" (1966)

James Daly was a New York stage actor who made a great many appearances in television dramas, beginning as early as 1945. In the '50s he was practically a repertory player on *Studio One* (more than a dozen appearances), *The Web,* and *Omnibus.* He also starred for a season as the globetrotting correspondent on *Foreign Intrigue.* In the 1960s he continued for a time on anthologies such as *Hallmark Hall of Fame* and *The DuPont Show of the Month,* and when playhouse series began to die out he moved on to regular series, including *Dr. Kildare, Felony, Squad* and *Mission: Impossible.* His last and best remembered principal role was as the experienced older doctor on *Medical Center;* after that he was seldom seen, except

for a small part in *Roots: The Next Generations,* which aired in 1979, after his death.

Following Daly's death, a self-professed former male lover of the actor sued for a portion of his estate, one of the earlier court cases of that kind.

DALY, JOHN—newscaster, host

b: Feb 20, 1914, Johannesburg, South Africa

Celebrity Time (quiz).... panelist (1949–50)
The Front Page (drama)
.... Walter Burns (1949–50)
CBS Weekend News (news)
.... anchorman (1950)
We Take Your Word (quiz)
.... wordmaster (1950–51)
What's My Line (quiz)
.... moderator (1950–67)
It's News to Me (quiz)
.... moderator (1951–53)
America's Town Meeting (pub aff)
.... moderator (1952)
ABC Evening News (news)
.... anchorman (1953–60)
Open Hearing (pub aff)
.... host/moderator (1954)
Who Said That? (quiz)........ emcee (1955)
The Voice of Firestone (music)
.... narrator (1958–59)

Emmy Award: Best News Reporter or Commentator (1954)

Witty, urbane John Charles Daly had the distinction of being a popular entertainment personality on one network while simultaneously serving as the evening news anchorman—and a top executive—at another. That was in the 1950s, when TV news was taken perhaps a bit less seriously than it is now and when newsmen could double on all manner of entertainment shows. (For example, Walter Cronkite was once a game-show host, and Mike Wallace both an quiz show host and a dramatic actor.)

Despite his versatility, Daly was primarily a newsman. He worked for NBC in the 1930s and then, from 1937–50, was a correspondent for CBS. In 1941, he announced the bombing of Pearl Harbor. In the late '40s Daly became a panelist on a news-oriented game show called *Celebrity Time* (originally hosted by Douglas Edwards) and for a short time was an actor playing the role of a newspaper editor on the dramatic series *The Front Page*. CBS felt his real-life journalistic experience would lend the series "authenticity." Then, starting in the early '50s, Daly began appearing on both CBS and ABC on news and game shows; one of the latter, CBS's *What's My Line,* was to become his most famous and longest-running vehicle. Unfailingly charming and well-mannered ("That's three down and seven to go. Mr. Cerf?"), Daly was perfect for this sort of polite parlor game. The show was a Sunday night fixture for 17 years.

Daly became ABC's evening news anchorman in 1953 and immediately brought a bit of much-needed class to the struggling network. He was seen for the next seven years in that role, the longest solo run for any ABC anchorman to date. (In the 1970s, Harry Reasoner, and later Peter Jennings, equaled that record as part of various anchor *teams*.) Simultaneously, from 1953–60, Daly was ABC's vice president in charge of news. Apparently, neither ABC, CBS, nor Daly's viewers saw any conflict in this bizarre arrangement in which he served both networks. In 1955 he was nominated for Emmy Awards in both the news and entertainment categories; he lost to Edward R. Murrow in the former and Perry Como in the latter.

In 1960 Daly resigned his ABC positions in a clash with management over policy matters. After *What's My Line* finally reached the end of its run in 1967 he served the government for a year as director of the Voice of America (1967–68), resigning there in another internal dispute. He was later seen for a time on PBS.

DALY, JONATHAN—actor
b: Jan 14, Chicago, Ill.

Petticoat Junction (com)
.... Orrin Pike (1969–70)
The Jimmy Stewart Show (com)
.... Peter Howard (1971–72)
C.P.O. Sharkey (com)
.... Lt. Whipple (1976–78)

DALY, RAD—juvenile actor

The Bad News Bears (com)
.... Josh Matthews (1979–80)
Walking Tall (police)
.... Michael Pusser (1981)

DALY, TIMOTHY—actor

Ryan's Four (drama)
.... Dr. Edward Gillian (1983)

DALY, TYNE—actress
b: Feb 21, 1947, Madison, Wis.

Cagney & Lacey (police)
.... Det. Mary Beth Lacey (1982–)

Emmy Award: Best Actress in a Drama, for *Cagney & Lacey* (1983, 1984, 1985)

Tyne Daly is one of Hollywood's "modern women." Where there is a Tyne Daly movie these days, there is probably a message—often one having something to do with feminism or other volatile issues. Her career began with more traditional roles, however. She was born to actor parents James Daly *(Medical Center)* and Hope Newell, and drifted into acting despite their objections. After some stage experience she made her television debut in an episode of *The Virginian,* followed by three months in the daytime soap opera *General Hospital.*

During the early 1970s Tyne appeared in episodes of numerous series (including her dad's), as well as in a succession of low-budget TV and theatrical movies. These were run-of-the-mill fare such as *Angel Unchained* (hippies fighting off the local thugs) and *A Howling in the Woods* (terror at Lake Tahoe). By 1976–77 she seemed to be favored as the wisecracking partner of some of the screen's leading tough guys—Clint Eastwood's in *The Enforcer,* Charles Bronson's in *Telefon,* Joe Don Baker's in *Speedtrap.*

Then, in 1977, she made the TV movie that set her future pattern. *Intimate Strangers,* the story of a battered wife, won her an Emmy nomination as best supporting actress. It was followed by *The Women's Room* (about feminism), *Zoot Suit* (wrongfully imprisoned Chicanos), *A Matter of Life or Death* (caring for the terminally ill) and the pilot for *Cagney & Lacey,* the latter about two lady police officers dealing with the problems of being women as well as those of being cops. Tyne played the married partner, who had to juggle husband and family as well as her demanding career. Her partner, Chris Lacey, was first played by

Loretta Swit, then by Meg Foster, and finally by Sharon Gless. Canceled twice due to anemic audiences, and brought back each time by insistent letter-writing campaigns and critical acclaim, *Cagney & Lacey* eventually became one of the most honored series on television.

Tyne is married to actor/director Georg Stanford Brown.

DAMON, ANDREW—actor

Once an Eagle (drama)
.... Donny Damon (1976–77)

DAMON, CATHRYN—actress

b: Sep 11, 1930, Seattle, Wash. d: May 4, 1987

Soap (com)
.... Mary Dallas Campbell (1977–81)
Webster (com) ..... Cassie Parker (1984–86)

Emmy Award: Best Actress in a Comedy Series, for *Soap* (1980)

DAMON, GABRIEL—juvenile actor

Call to Glory (drama)
.... RH Sarnac (1984–85)

DAMON, JERRY—comedian

b: 1927 d: Jan 24, 1979

That Was the Week That Was (com)
.... regular (1964–65)

DAMON, STUART—actor

b: Feb 5, 1937, Brooklyn, N.Y.

The Champions (adv).. Craig Stirling (1968)

After a career on Broadway in the early 1960s, Stuart traveled to England to star in the adventure series *The Champions,* which was seen in the U.S. in the summer of '68. He liked England so much he stayed there with his English wife for the next 12 years, acting on English TV and in the theater. In 1977 the couple returned to the U.S., where the actor became a star of American daytime TV as Dr. Alan Quartermaine on *General Hospital.* That role has subsequently won him several Emmy nominations.

DAMONE, VIC—singer

b: Jun 12, 1928, Brooklyn, N.Y.

The Vic Damone Show (var)
.... host (1956–57)
The Lively Ones (var) .... host (1962–63)
The Dean Martin Summer Show (var)
.... host (1967)

Handsome crooner Vic Damone got his first big break as a teenager when he won first place on *Arthur Godfrey's Talent Scouts* radio program in the mid-1940s. With the help of Milton Berle he landed some nightclub work and then a recording contract. Vic soon became a youthful singing sensation with such hits as "Again" and "You're Breaking My Heart" in 1949.

His career was interrupted for military service in the early '50s, after which he returned a more mature entertainer. During the '50s and '60s he was seen frequently on television, mostly as a singer but occasionally as an actor, on both dramas and comedies. On *The Dick Van Dyke Show* in 1962 he played handsome singer Ric Vallone, with whom Rose Marie fell madly in love. Vic's career began to fade in the late '60s, and in 1971 he filed for bankruptcy due to government demands for back taxes. In later years he performed mostly in Las Vegas.

DANA, BILL—comedian, writer

b: Oct 5, 1924, Quincy, Mass.

The Steve Allen Show (var)
.... regular (1959–60)
The Spike Jones Show (var).. regular (1960)
The Bill Dana Show (com)
.... Jose Jimenez (1963–65)
No Soap, Radio (com) ... Mr. Plitzky (1982)
Zorro and Son (com) ...... Bernardo (1983)

Despite the fact that he officially "buried" the character in 1970, due to growing ethnic protests, Bill Dana will always be remembered by viewers of the '60s as the ever-resourceful Hispanic whose trademark was his fractured English. "My name ...," he would announce in a loud but halting voice, "Jose Jiminez!"

Dana began his show business career as a page at NBC shortly after he graduated from college in 1950. He did some nightclub work in the early '50s and had small parts in TV shows featuring such stars as Imogene Coca and Martha Raye, but he soon moved into steadier employment as a comedy writer for *The Steve Allen Show* in

1956. He eventually became Steve's head writer and was nominated for an Emmy Award for his work. However, Allen found him so funny reading his own material that in 1959 Bill was performing again—on the show. One of his characters, based on no one in particular, was the inimitable Jose Jiminez. The humor was based largely on Jose's broken English, but the little fellow was no fool—his clever solutions to all sorts of problems made him more than a racial put-down, and he was liked by Hispanics and non-Hispanics alike.

After leaving the Allen show in 1960 Bill parlayed the character into several best-selling LP's, a recurring role on *The Danny Thomas Show,* and finally his own series, in which Jose was a bellhop. Following a period of relative inactivity in the '70s, Bill returned to television late in the decade as a supporting actor on series and in TV movies, and he has been seen fairly often since then.

DANA, DICK—comedian

Doodles Weaver (var) ...... regular (1951)

DANA, JUSTIN—juvenile actor

Knots Landing (drama)
.... Jason Avery (1979–80)
United States (com) ... Nicky Chapin (1980)

DANCING BLADES, THE—

Music on Ice (var).......... regulars (1960)

DANCY, JOHN—newscaster
b: Aug 5, 1936, Jackson, Tenn.

Prime Time Sunday (pub aff)
.... correspondent (1980)

Emmy Award: For the special report "Ure-thane," on *Prime Time Saturday* (1980)

D'ANDREA, TOM—actor
b: May 15, 1909, Chicago, Ill.

The Life of Riley (com)
.... Jim Gillis (1953–58)
The Soldiers (com) .... Tom (1955)
Dante (adv)................. Biff (1960–61)

DANDRIDGE, RUBY—black actress
b: Mar 3, 1902, Memphis, Tenn.

Father of the Bride (com)
.... Delilah (1961–62)

DANE, FRANK—actor

Hawkins Falls, Population 6,200 (com)
.... Clate Weathers (1950)

DANEHE, DICK—sportscaster

Top Pro Golf (sport)... commentator (1959)

DANESE, SHERA—actress

Ace Crawford, Private Eye (com)
.... Luana (1983)
Suzanne Pleshette is Maggie Briggs (com)
.... Connie Piscipoli (1984)

The wife of actor Peter Falk.

DANGCIL, LINDA—actress

The Flying Nun (com)
.... Sister Ana (1967–70)

D'ANGELO, BEVERLY—actress
b: 1954, Columbus, Ohio

Captains and the Kings (drama)
.... Miss Emmy (1976)

DANGERFIELD, RODNEY—comedian
b: Nov 22, 1921, Babylon, N.Y.

The Dean Martin Show (var)
.... regular (1972–73)

Rodney Dangerfield is exactly what he appears to be—a middle class *schlepp* who had to work seemingly forever to get anywhere. "I started at 19," he says, "and at 40 I was still just a businessman going to the office during the week to support my weekend 'career' as an entertainer." The story, which is true, always ends with his most famous line: "I don't get no respect!"

By the late '60s, Rodney was finally able to chuck the nine-to-five job and make it in comedy as a writer and a stand-up comic in clubs, on records, and on TV. In the '80s he was more popular than ever, doing hilarious bits on TV and in movies such as *Caddyshack.* He even owned his own club in Manhattan, where he was the featured performer. But the put-downs—of himself—will never end. The title of one of his albums sums up his routine: "Rodney Dangerfield—Loser."

DANIELS, BILLY—black singer, actor
b: Sep 12, 1915, Jacksonville, Fla.

The Billy Daniels Show (music)
.... regular (1952)

DANIELS, CAROLYN—actress

That Girl (com) .... Ruth Bauman (1967–69)

DANIELS, DANNY, DANCERS—

The Martha Raye Show (var)
.... regulars (1955–56)

DANIELS, WILLIAM—actor
b: Mar 31, 1927, Brooklyn, N.Y.

Captain Nice (com)
.... Carter Nash (Capt. Nice) (1967)
The Nancy Walker Show (com)
...... Lt. Cmdr. Kenneth Kitteridge (1976)
Freebie and the Bean (police)
.... D.A. Walter W. Cruikshank (1980–81)
St. Elsewhere (drama)
.... Dr. Mark Craig (1982–)
Knight Rider (adv)
.... voice of KITT (1982–86)

Emmy Awards: Best Actor in a Drama Series, for *St. Elsewhere* (1985, 1986)

William Daniels was known in the 1980s as the demanding heart surgeon Dr. Craig on *St. Elsewhere* and as the equally sarcastic voice of KITT (the car) on *Knight Rider*—he played both roles simultaneously. However, he had a long career in show business before that—one he didn't always want. At the tender age of four he was pushed onto the stage (his description) by his mother and "told to sing and dance." "When you are four years old, you do what you are told," he observes. Most of his youth, in the '30s, was spent traveling around the New York area as part of "The Daniels Family" song and dance troupe. While this may have cost him a normal childhood, it certainly gave him a great deal of experience. As early as 1941 he appeared with his family on experimental TV, and in 1943 he had a juvenile role in *Life with Father* on Broadway.

After military service from 1945–47, the young actor found the transition from child to adult performer difficult. Supported at times by his wife, actress Bonnie Bartlett (who had a starring role on TV's *Love of Life*), he worked off-Broadway for most of the '50s, finally making it to the big time in Edward Albee's hit play *The Zoo Story* in 1960. He did more stage work in the '60s, as well as TV and movies. He played John Adams in both the stage and film versions of *1776* and Dustin Hoffman's father in *The Graduate* (1967). On television since the mid-1950s, he won increasingly better roles and in 1967 landed his own situation comedy, *Captain Nice*. It was a flop, though it is fondly remembered by trivia buffs for its rather preposterous premise—Daniels played a shy, mother-dominated young man (shades of his childhood!) who accidentally gained superhuman powers and became a flying crime fighter.

Daniels continued to play many roles in TV movies and series during the '70s and '80s, among them John Quincy Adams in *The Adams Chronicles* (1976) and G. Gordon Liddy in *Blind Ambition* (1979). His wife, Bonnie, occasionally appeared on *St. Elsewhere* as Dr. Craig's wife.

DANIELY, LISA—actress
b: 1930, England

The Invisible Man (drama)
.... Diane Brady (1958–60)

DANNER, BLYTHE—actress
b: Feb 3, 1943, Philadelphia, Pa.

Adam's Rib (com)
.... Amanda Bonner (1973)

DANO, LINDA—actress
b: c. 1943

The Montefuscos (com)
.... Angela Montefusco Cooney (1975)

DANO, ROYAL—actor
b: Nov 16, 1922, New York City, N.Y.

How the West Was Won (miniseries) (drama)
.... Elam Hanks (1977)

DANOVA, CESARE—actor
b: Mar 1, 1926, Rome, Italy

Garrison's Gorillas (drama)
.... actor (1967–68)

DANSON, TED—actor

b: Dec 29, 1947*, San Diego, Calif. r: Flagstaff, Ariz.

Cheers (com)......... Sam Malone (1982–)

Ted Danson, son of an archeologist, spent much of his youth in the wide-open country of Arizona. He became interested in acting when he was sent East to boarding school and had his first job as an understudy on Broadway in the late '60s. Ted followed the familiar course of a struggling actor in the '70s, mostly in New York, with stage roles including outdoor performances of Shakespeare in the Park. From 1974–76 he played Tom Conway on the daytime soap opera *Somerset*. By 1978 he had returned to Los Angeles, where he began getting movie and TV roles, among them those of Lee Remick's insensitive husband in *The Women's Room* (1980) and the zombie in Stephen King's *Creepshow* (1982). Though his imposing stature (6'2") and suspicious eyes make him a marvelous villain, his greatest success came in comedy, as the womanizing bartender on *Cheers*.

DANTE, MICHAEL—actor

b: 1935**, Stamford, Conn.

Custer (wes).......... Crazy Horse (1967)

DANTINE, HELMUT—actor

b: Oct 7, 1917, Vienna, Austria d: May 3, 1982

Shadow of the Cloak (drama)
.... Peter House (1951–52)

DANTON, RAY—actor, director

b: Sep 19, 1931, New York City, N.Y.

The Alaskans (adv) . Nifty Cronin (1959–60)

The husband of actress Julie Adams.

DANZA, TONY—actor

b: Apr 21, 1951, Brooklyn, N.Y.

Taxi (com).......... Tony Banta (1978–83)
Who's the Boss? (com)
.... Tony Micelli (1984–)

Tony Danza was a Brooklyn kid who was determined to become a professional

*Some sources give 1949 or 1952.
**Some sources give 1931.

228

boxer, until a persistent agent shanghaied him into show business—so the story goes. After graduating from college in the early '70s, Tony entered the New York Golden Gloves competition, made it all the way to the semifinals in the light heavyweight category, and then switched to middleweight in his second year. His record was good enough for him to turn pro. He was 8–3 when a talent scout approached him in Gleason's Gym and asked if he would screen-test for a film about boxing. He did. The movie never was made, but his test found its way to Hollywood, where ABC executives saw it and called him to appear in the TV film *Fast Lane Blues*. Tony played his role and then returned to boxing. He was called back for another part, this time as a boxer-turned-cabbie in the pilot for a series called *Taxi*.

Even after *Taxi* went on the air Tony did not give up boxing, fighting two additional bouts (which he won) before he finally accepted the obvious and retired from the ring. He has since appeared in several films and in the mid-1980s scored with a hit comedy of his own called *Who's the Boss?* If you ask him, however, he may still spar with you.

DAPO, RONNIE—actor

Room for One More (com)
.... Flip Rose (1962)
The New Phil Silvers Show (com)
.... Andy (1964)

DAPPER DANS, THE—

Mickie Finn's (var)......... regulars (1966)

DA PRON, LOUIS, DANCERS—

The Perry Como Show (var)
.... regulars (1955–60)
The Julius La Rosa Show (var)
.... regulars (1957)
Perry Presents (var)........ regulars (1959)
The Smothers Brothers Comedy Hour (var)
.... regulars (1967–68)

DARBY, KIM—actress

b: Jul 8, 1947*, Los Angeles, Calif.

Rich Man, Poor Man—Book I (drama)
.... Virginia Calderwood (1976)

*Some sources give 1948.

The Last Convertible (drama)
.... Ann Rowan (1979)

DARCEL, DENISE—actress
b: Sep 8, 1925, Paris, France

Gamble on Love (quiz)....... hostess (1954)

DARCY, GEORGINE—actress
Harrigan and Son (com) ... Gypsy (1960–61)

DARDEN, SEVERN—actor
b: Nov 9, 1929

Mary Hartman, Mary Hartman (com)
.... Popesco (1977–78)
Beyond Westworld (sci fi) .... Foley (1980)

DARIN, BOBBY—singer, actor
b: May 14, 1936, The Bronx, N.Y. d: Dec 20, 1973

Dean Martin Presents Bobby Darin (var)
.... host (1972)
The Bobby Darin Show (var).... host (1973)

Darin, a very popular pop-rock singer of the '50s and '60s ("Mack the Knife," etc.) was just launching a new career as a host of TV variety shows when he died rather suddenly following heart surgery in 1973. He had previously been a guest on most of the medium's top variety shows, including several appearances in the early '70s with his friend Flip Wilson. Darin was married during the 1960s to actress Sandra Dee.

DARK, JOHNNY—
The Jacksons (var) .... regular (1977)
Donny and Marie (var) ... regular (1978–79)

DARLING, JENNIFER—actress
Temperatures Rising (com)
.... Nurse "Windy" Winchester (1973–74)
Eight Is Enough (com) .... Donna (1978–81)

DARLING, JOAN—actress, director
b: Apr 14, 1935, Boston, Mass.

Owen Marshall, Counselor at Law (drama)
.... Frieda Krause (1971–74)

DARREN, JAMES—actor
b: Jun 8, 1936, Philadelphia, Pa.

The Time Tunnel (sci fi)
.... Dr. Tony Newman (1966–67)
T. J. Hooker (police)
.... Off. Jim Corrigan (1983–86)

Although he has been quite active as a television supporting actor since the late 1970s, James Darren is still remembered as a teen idol of the '50s and '60s. He had just begun to study acting in New York when he was spotted in 1956 by influential talent agent Joyce Selznick and then signed by Columbia Pictures. Columbia put him in a number of its teen films of the late '50s and early '60s, but none were more successful than the *Gidget* movies, in which he played Gidget's surfing boyfriend. When the studio started its own record label it used his singing talents, too. He scored first with a song called "Gidget" and later in 1961 had two top-ten hits with "Goodbye Cruel World" and "Her Royal Majesty."

By age 28 James was becoming hard to pass off as a frolicsome teenager. He starred in the science fiction series *The Time Tunnel* but was seen only rarely for the next ten years. In the late '70s he began to work regularly again, on series such as *Fantasy Island* and *Vega$*. In 1983 he donned a uniform as William Shatner's young (though he was nearing 50) partner in the popular police show *T. J. Hooker*.

DARROW, BARBARA—actress
Doctors' Hospital (drama)
.... Nurse Forester (1975–76)

DARROW, HENRY—actor
b: Sep 15, 1933, New York City, N.Y.

The High Chaparral (wes)
.... Manolito Montoya (1967–71)
The New Dick Van Dyke Show (com)
.... Alex Montenez (1973–74)
Harry-O (drama)
.... Det. Lt. Manny Quinlan (1974–75)
Zorro and Son (com)
..Don Diego de la Vega (Zorro Sr.) (1983)
Me and Mom (drama) ..... Lt. Rojas (1985)

DARROW, MIKE—host
Dream House (quiz) .... emcee (1968)
The $128,000 Question (quiz)
.... host (1976–77)

DA SILVA, HOWARD—actor
b: May 4, 1909, Cleveland, Ohio d: Feb 16, 1986

For the People (police)
.... Anthony Celese (1965)

Emmy Award: Best Supporting Actor in a Special, for the PBS *Great Performances* production "Verna: U.S.O. Girl" (1978)

DAUPHIN, CLAUDE—actor
b: Aug 19, 1903, Corbeil, France d: Nov 17, 1978

Paris Precinct (police)
.... Inspector Bolbec (1954–55)

A dapper little French film actor, often seen as an inspector or other official in TV dramas of the '50s and '60s.

D'AVALOS—dance instructor
Let's Rhumba (info) .... host (1946–47)

DAVALOS, DICK—actor
b: Nov 5, 1935, The Bronx, N.Y.

The Americans (drama)
.... Jeff Canfield (1961)

DAVENPORT, BASIL—panelist
Who's Whose (quiz)........ panelist (1951)
Down You Go (quiz)
.... regular panelist (1955)

DAVENPORT, NIGEL—actor
b: May 23, 1928, Cambridge, England

Masada (drama) .... Mucianus (1981)

DAVI, ROBERT—actor
The Gangster Chronicles (drama)
.... Vito Genovese (1981)

DAVID, BRAD—actor
Firehouse (adv) .... Billy Dalzell (1974)

DAVID, JEFF—actor
Buck Rogers in the 25th Century (sci fi)
.... Crichton the robot (voice) (1981)

DAVID, LARRY—comedian
b: Jul 2, Brooklyn, N.Y.

Fridays (var)........... regular (1980–82)

DAVIDSON, BEN—actor
b: June 14, 1940, Los Angeles, Calif.

Ball Four (com)
.... "Rhino" Rhinelander (1976)
Code R (adv) .... Ted Milbank (1977)

A 6' 8", 250-pound former defensive end for the Oakland Raiders and other professional football teams. He says he was introduced to acting by football buddy Fred Williamson; "Up to that point I'd never given show business a thought."

DAVIDSON, JAMES—actor
b: 1942

Window on Main Street (com)
.... Wally Evans (1961–62)

DAVIDSON, JOHN—singer, host
b: Dec 13, 1941, Pittsburgh, Pa.

The Entertainers (var) .... regular (1964–65)
The Kraft Summer Music Hall (var)
.... host (1966)
The John Davidson Show (var) .. host (1969)
The Girl with Something Extra (com)
.... John Burton (1973–74)
The John Davidson Show (var) .. host (1976)
That's Incredible (aud par)... host (1980–84)

A popular singer and sometime actor who originally planned to go into the ministry. He also hosted a syndicated daytime talk show from 1980–82.

DAVIES, ALLAN, SINGERS—
The Pearl Bailey Show (var)
.... regulars (1971)

DAVIES, GEOFFREY—actor
b: 1941

Doctor in the House (com)
.... Dr. Dick Stuart-Clark (1970–73)

DAVIES, IRVING, DANCERS—
The Engelbert Humperdinck Show (var)
.... regulars (1970)

DAVIES, JOHN RHYS—actor
b: May 5, 1944, Salisbury, England

The Quest (adv)........ Sir Edward (1982)

DAVION, ALEX—actor
b: 1929

The Man Who Never Was (drama)
.... Roger Barry (1966–67)

DAVIS, ANN B.—actress
b: May 5, 1926, Schenectady, N.Y.

The Bob Cummings Show (com)
.. Charmaine "Shultzy" Schultz (1955–59)
The Keefe Brasselle Show (var)
.... regular (1963)
The John Forsythe Show (com)
.... Miss Wilson (1965–66)
The Brady Bunch (com)
.... Alice Nelson (1969–74)
The Brady Bunch Hour (var)
.... Alice (1977)
The Brady Brides (com)
.... Alice Nelson (1981)

Emmy Awards: Best Supporting Actress in a Comedy, for *The Bob Cummings Show* (1957, 1959)

Ann B. Davis parlayed a homely face and a talent for wisecracks into two well-remembered supporting roles, as Bob Cummings' lovelorn assistant Shultzy in the 1950s and as *The Brady Bunch*'s nutty housekeeper Alice in the '70s. Ann had not originally intended to go into acting, having enrolled in college as a premed student. However, campus theater productions got the best of her and, upon graduation in the late '40s, she began a long apprenticeship in local theater on the West Coast. The role of Shultzy was her first big break, and it led to more steady work. She appeared in stage productions, in a few films, and in a couple of unsuccessful series during the 1960s, and then landed her second famous role, on *The Brady Bunch,* in 1969. It kept her busy, off and on, until the '80s.

DAVIS, BILLY, JR.—singer
b: Jun 26, 1940, St. Louis, Mo.

The Marilyn McCoo and Billy Davis, Jr. Show (var)...................... cohost (1977)

The husband and performing partner of singer Marilyn McCoo.

DAVIS, BRAD—actor
b: Nov 6, 1949, Tallahassee, Fla.

Roots (drama)... Ol' George Johnson (1977)
Chiefs (drama).... Chief Sonny Butts (1983)

DAVIS, BUSTER—choral director
b: Jul 4, 1918, Johnstown, Pa.

The Garry Moore Show (var)
.... regular (1958–59)

DAVIS, BUZZ—singer

Campus Corner (music)...... regular (1949)

DAVIS, CLIFTON—black actor, singer
b: Oct 4, 1945, Chicago, Ill.

Love, American Style (com)
.... repertory player (1971)
The Melba Moore-Clifton Davis Show (var)
.... cohost (1972)
That's My Mama (com)
.... Clifton Curtis (1974–75)
Amen (com).. Rev. Reuben Gregory (1986–)

Davis is the son of an evangelist, but he pursued an acting career in the '60s and '70s before turning to the ministry. He was serving as associate pastor at a California church (Seventh Day Adventist) while he appeared as a minister on *Amen*. Clifton is also a successful songwriter, his best-known number being the Jackson 5 hit "Never Can Say Goodbye."

DAVIS, DAVE—

The Wendy Barrie Show (talk)
.... regular (1949)

DAVIS, FRED—host

Brains & Brawn (quiz)........ emcee (1958)

DAVIS, GAIL—actress
b: Oct 5, 1925, Little Rock, Ark.

Annie Oakley (wes)
.... Annie Oakley (1953–56)

This petite (5' 2"), pigtailed actress was an unlikely choice to become the first woman to star in a television action series. However, her Annie Oakley was a hard-ridin' crack shot who was able to keep the peace around the territory as well as any man, while still maintaining a certain softness and femininity. She was a favorite of kids in the '50s.

Gail was as wholesome and pretty as her character. She won several beauty titles during her school years in Texas and Pennsylvania, and, upon graduation from college in 1945, she married an aspiring actor and moved to California. *She* was the one who was spotted by an agent, however, leading to roles in a number of westerns and other B films of the late 1940s—including one opposite Roy Rogers when Dale Evans was unable to appear.

In 1950 Gail began a long and fruitful association with Gene Autry. She was featured in 15 of his films and some 30 episodes of his TV show, until canny businessman Gene figured that the kids were ready for a series starring a western heroine. *Annie Oakley* was produced by Autry's production company and was a considerable success in syndication throughout the '50s and into the '60s. The formula was always the same—simple plots, plenty of action, but no real violence (Annie never killed anyone, she just shot the guns out of their hands).

In later years, Gail toured with Gene's rodeo (she was an excellent horsewoman and trick shot), but did little additional TV or movie work. She once said, "So far as I'm concerned I'm going to be Annie Oakley for the rest of my born days," and apparently she was right. Today she is a partner in a firm that manages other celebrities.

DAVIS, GEENA—actress
b: Jan 21, 1957, Wareham, Mass.

Buffalo Bill (com) . Wendy Killian (1983–84)
Sara (com).......... Sara McKenna (1985)

DAVIS, HUMPHREY—actor

Operation Neptune (sci fi)... Trychus (1953)

DAVIS, JANETTE—singer
b: c. 1924, Pine Bluff, Tenn. r: Memphis, Tenn.

Arthur Godfrey and His Friends (var)
.... singer (1949–57)

DAVIS, JENNIFER—actress

M*A*S*H (com)... various nurses (1979–80)

DAVIS, JIM—actor
b: Aug 26, 1915, Edgerton, Mo. d: Apr 26, 1981

Stories of the Century (wes)
.... Matt Clark (1954)
Rescue 8 (adv).... Wes Cameron (1958–59)
The Cowboys (wes)
.... U.S. Marshal Bill Winter (1974)
Dallas (drama)....... Jock Ewing (1978–81)

Tall, silver-haired Jim Davis was a star of many Hollywood action films of the '40s and '50s who found his greatest fame shortly before his death as the patriarch of *Dallas*'s scheming, oil-rich Ewing family.

He started out, ironically, as a salesman for an oil company in the 1930s. The job brought him to Los Angeles around 1940, where he gradually schemed his way into acting. Most of his films (beginning with *Safari* in 1940 and *King of the Zombies* in '41) were routine action melodramas, but occasionally there was a meatier role—as when he costarred opposite Bette Davis in *Winter Meeting* in 1948.

Jim did a fair amount of television in the '50s and starred in two syndicated action series. However, as with his film roles, they did not generate much lasting interest. He was seen less often through most of the '60s. He then returned as a character actor in the late '60s and '70s, playing supporting roles in many dramas (*Gunsmoke, The F.B.I., Kung Fu,* etc.) and for a brief time had a leading role in a forgettable western called *The Cowboys*. He ended his days on *Dallas*—the best role of his career.

DAVIS, JO—

The Jimmy Dean Show (var) . regular (1957)

DAVIS, JOAN—actress
b: Jun 29, 1907, St. Paul, Minn. d: May 23, 1961

I Married Joan (com)
.... Joan Stevens (1952–55)

Joan Davis was a rubber-faced, knockabout comedienne in the Lucille Ball tradition, whose series *I Married Joan* (costarring Jim Backus, as the hubby) was a popular variation on *I Love Lucy* in the 1950s. Joan had been a trooper since she was a tot, marrying a vaudevillian and performing with him in the early '30s. She made it to Hollywood in 1934 and over the following 18 years turned out a long series of comedy B films. She was also quite popular on radio in the '40s.

I Married Joan was her pièce de résistance, however, and the vehicle by which she is best remembered. She did little TV work afterward and died of a heart attack in 1961. Joan's daughter, comedienne Beverly Wills (who appeared as a younger sister in *I Married Joan*), had begun to follow in her mother's footsteps but survived her by only two years, perishing in a fire in 1963.

DAVIS, KENNY—

The Vaughn Monroe Show (var)
.... regular (1950–51)

DAVIS, LISA—actress

The George Burns Show (com)
.... Miss Jenkins (1958–59)

DAVIS, MAC—singer, songwriter
b: Jan 21, 1942, Lubbock, Texas

The Mac Davis Show (var)... host (1974–76)

DAVIS, MICHAEL—comedian, juggler
b: Aug 23, San Francisco, Calif.

The News Is the News (var) . regular (1983)

DAVIS, PATSY—model

The Fashion Story (misc) . regular (1948–49)

DAVIS, PHYLLIS—actress
b: Jul 17, 1940, Port Arthur, Texas r: Nederland, Texas

Love, American Style (com)
.... repertory player (1970–74)
Vega$ (drama) ... Beatrice Travis (1978–81)

DAVIS, ROGER—actor

The Gallant Men (drama)
.... Pvt. Roger Gibson (1962–63)
Redigo (wes).................. Mike (1963)
Alias Smith and Jones (wes)
.... narrator (1971–72)
Alias Smith and Jones (wes)
. Joshua Smith/Hannibal Heyes (1972–73)
Aspen (drama) .... Max Kendrick (1977)

DAVIS, RUFE—actor
b: 1908, Dinson, Okla. d: Dec 13, 1974

Petticoat Junction (com)
.... Floyd Smoot (1963–68)

DAVIS, SAMMY, JR.—black singer, actor
b: Dec 8, 1925, New York City, N.Y.

The Sammy Davis Jr. Show (var)
.... host (1966)
NBC Follies (var) .... regular (1973)
Sammy and Company (talk).. host (1975–77)
Baretta (police) ...... sang theme (1975–78)

This boundlessly energetic performer has had a very long career in show business, beginning as a child in a family act and later with his uncle's Will Mastin Trio in the 1930s and '40s. A star of the lounge circuit in the early 1950s, he then branched into records, films, theater and television—seemingly all at once. Since the mid-1950s he has made many TV appearances in both singing and acting roles. Among the latter have been guest shots on *The Rifleman, The Mod Squad, One Life to Live*, and other programs.

Sammy's personal life has certainly lived up to his "do it" credo as well. He attracted much notoriety for his marriage to Swedish actress May Britt, his conversion to Judiasm, and his abrupt switch from Kennedy Democrat to prominent supporter of Richard Nixon (the sight of the ebullient Sammy hugging a startled Nixon on national TV will not soon be forgotten!). He has described himself as a "one-eyed Jewish Negro" (he lost an eye in a 1954 auto accident), but nothing seems to slow him down. The title of his best-selling 1965 autobiography says it all: *Yes I Can!*

DAVIS, SUSAN—actress

The New Andy Griffith Show (com)
.... Verline MacKnight (1971)

DAVIS, TOM—comedian, writer

NBC's Saturday Night Live (com)
.... regular (1979–80)

Emmy Awards: Best Writing for a Comedy-Variety Series, for *NBC's Saturday Night Live* (1976, 1977); Best Writing for a Comedy or Music Special, for *The Paul Simon Special* (1978)

DAVISON, BRUCE—actor
b: 1948, Philadelphia, Pa.

Hunter (police) ...... Capt. Wyler (1985–86)

DAVISON, JOEL—actor

O. K. Crackerby (com)
.... Hobart Crackerby (1965–66)

DAWBER, PAM—actress
b: Oct 18, 1951, Farmington Hills, Mich.

Mork & Mindy (com)
.... Mindy Beth McConnell (1978–82)
My Sister Sam (com)
.... Samantha "Sam" Russell (1986–)

DAWSON, GREG—actor

The Adventures of Ozzie & Harriet (com)
.... Greg (1965–66)

DAWSON, RICHARD—host, actor
b: Nov 20, 1932, Gosport, Hampshire, England

Hogan's Heroes (com)
.... Peter Newkirk (1965–71)
Can You Top This? (com)
.... assistant (1969–70)
Rowan & Martin's Laugh-In (var)
.... regular (1971–73)
The New Dick Van Dyke Show (com)
.... Richard Richardson (1973–74)
Masquerade Party (quiz) ... emcee (1974–75)
Match Game P.M. (quiz) . panelist (1975–78)
I've Got a Secret (quiz) ..... panelist (1976)
Family Feud (quiz) .... host (1977–85)

Emmy Award: Best Host of a Game Show, for *Family Feud* (1978)

Bouncy, boutonniered Richard Dawson, who smooches the ladies on *Family Feud,* is a product of the English music hall tradition. He began there as an actor in the 1940s, after a stint as a merchant seaman, and during the '50s evolved into a popular British stage comedian. In 1962 he came to the U.S. to do some nightclub work in Beverly Hills and was seen by Carl Reiner, creator of *The Dick Van Dyke Show.* Reiner wrote a part especially for him in a 1963 episode of the series. Dawson guest-starred as "Tracy Rattigan," a visiting English comic with an eye for the ladies—including Mary Tyler Moore. Dickie Daw-

son, as he was then billing himself, was a hit.

Word began to get around about the effervescent Englishman (England was very much in vogue at the time) and more offers came his way. In 1965 he was cast as the sticky-fingered British safecracker Newkirk in *Hogan's Heroes,* a role that lasted for six years. He then became a regular on *Laugh In.* Simultaneously, in the late 1960s, Richard began to branch into quiz and game shows which, after a number of false starts, led to his great success in *Family Feud.* The show began in daytime in 1976 and went into nighttime syndication the following year. It was one of the biggest game show hits of the period, and its popularity was almost universally attributed to Dawson himself.

DAY, DENNIS—singer, actor
b: May 21, 1917, New York City, N.Y.

The Jack Benny Show (com)
.... as himself (1950–65)
The RCA Victor Show (com)
.... as himself (1952–54)

Fresh-faced Dennis Day played the naive "boy singer" on Jack Benny's series for more than 25 years—despite the fact he was pushing 50 by the time the program left the air. Born with the distinctively Irish name of McNulty, Dennis was fresh out of college and had little experience when Benny hired him in 1939 to replace his departing tenor, Kenny Baker. Dennis soon became one of the most popular characters on the show. Ever the simpleton, he nevertheless got the laughs in his exchanges with the boss, Mr. Benny. Then he would do a number, usually something Irish, like his perennial "Clancy Lowered the Boom" (has anyone else ever sung that song?).

Benny was very supportive of his cast and allowed Dennis to pursue a successful solo career on records and radio in the late 1940s. Dennis also had his own TV situation comedy from 1952–54—playing a naive young bachelor—while still appearing with Benny. After *The Jack Benny Show* finally left the air in 1965, Dennis was seen only occasionally, spending most of his time in clubs and dinner theater engagements. "I still mix in some of the old Irish songs ... tell some of my favorite Irish stories . . . and generally have a grand time," he said in 1978. He also did voice work for some animated specials, including Christmas specials in 1976 and 1978. The father of ten children, he now lives in mellow retirement in Southern California in a house filled with antiques and fond memories—especially of his old boss, Jack Benny. "He was like a father to me, so kind and gentle . . . God rest the immortal soul of my dear friend."

DAY, DIANNE—dancer

Dance Fever (dance) . . . . . . dancer (1979–)

DAY, DORIS—singer, actress
b: Apr 3, 1924, Cincinnati, Ohio

The Doris Day Show (com)
. . . . Doris Martin (1968–73)

Doris Day had been a superstar of music and movies for 20 years when she came to television in 1968. Her series was one of the earliest "independent woman" shows; Doris was cast initially as a single mom living out in the country with two young sons, but she soon evolved into a career woman struggling to make it on her own in the big city, a la Mary Tyler Moore.

The series was the outgrowth of one of the unhappiest episodes in Doris Day's life, and came on the heels of a series of devastating personal tragedies. First was the sudden death of her beloved husband and manager for 17 years, Marty Melcher, in early 1968. It was only after his death that Doris learned that he had committed her to do a television series. Doris hated the idea of series TV and had no plans to enter the medium, and she had known nothing of this arrangement. At the same time, she learned something far worse. Her husband and a lawyer associate had been systematically bilking her of everything she owned, and the millions she had earned over the previous 20 years were totally gone. She was, in fact, ruined and deeply in debt.

Doris was, by her own admission, a physical and emotional wreck during the first year of the series, but she had to do it —she had no choice—and she gave it the best she could muster. In an unexpected way, *The Doris Day Show* proved to be a blessing in disguise. Both in terms of the regular work schedule it gave her and the income it provided, it gradually helped her get back on her feet. The series ran for a full five years and was a considerable ratings success. Nevertheless, when it ended she showed little interest in any further TV work.

Doris told all concerning her roller coaster career in the best-selling biography *Doris Day: Her Own Story,* which was published in 1975.

DAY, DOROTHY—author
b: Nov 8, 1897 d: Nov 29, 1980

Stump the Authors (talk). . . . . author (1949)

DAY, JACK—

Hayloft Hoedown (music). . . . regular (1948)

DAY, LARAINE—actress
b: Oct 13, 1917, Roosevelt, Utah

Day Dreaming with Laraine Day (int)
. . . . hostess (1951)
I've Got a Secret (quiz) . . . . . panelist (1952)

DAY, LYNDA—

See George, Lynda Day

DAY, MARILYN—actress

The Fashion Story (misc)
. . . . Lucky Marshall (1948–49)
Fifty-Fourth Street Revue (var)
. . . . regular (1949–50)

DAYDREAMERS, THE—

Garroway at Large (var). . . . regulars (1950)

DAYTON, DANNY—actor, comedian

Joey Faye's Frolics (var) . . . . . regular (1950)
Keep Talking (quiz) . . . . . . regular (1958–60)
All in the Family (com)
. . . . Hank Pivnik (1977–81)

Husband (in the 1950s) of TV sex symbol Dagmar.

DAYTON, JUNE—actress

The Aldrich Family (com)
. . . . Mary Aldrich (1952–53)

235

DEACON, RICHARD—actor
b: 1922, Philadelphia, Pa. d: Aug 8, 1984

The Charlie Farrell Show (com)
.... Sherman Hull (1956)
Date with the Angels (com)
.... Roger Finley (1957–58)
Leave It to Beaver (com)
.... Mr. Fred Rutherford (1957–63)
The Dick Van Dyke Show (com)
.... Melvin Cooley (1961–66)
The Pruitts of Southampton (com)
.... Mr. Baldwin (1967)
The Mothers-in-Law (com)
.... Roger Buell (1968–69)
B.J. and The Bear (adv)
.... Sheriff Masters (1979)

If you were a TV producer in the 1950s or '60s and you needed someone to play the stock role of the pompous, overbearing boss—and Gale Gordon was not available —you would probably have turned to Richard Deacon. Deacon made quite a career of playing humorous stuffed shirts. Tall, balding and usually wearing horn-rimmed glasses, he was a guest or regular on many situation comedies. He was the resort manager on *The Charlie Farrell Show,* Ward Cleaver's boss (and Lumpy Rutherford's father) on *Leave It to Beaver,* Dick Van Dyke's boss on *The Dick Van Dyke Show,* and Phyllis Diller's nemesis from the IRS on *The Pruitts of Southampton,* among others. On a clever *Twilight Zone* episode in 1964 he played a callous factory owner who goes a bit too far when he automates his plant and fires all the workers. The board of directors then replaces *him* with a machine.

Deacon had a background in regional theater, and he costarred with Phyllis Diller in the Broadway version of *Hello, Dolly* in the early 1970s. He also played comic roles in quite a few movies from the mid-1950s on. Among his favorites: *The Solid Gold Cadillac* (1956). In private life, he took pride in his extensive collection of rocks.

DEAN, ABNER—cartoonist
Draw to Win (quiz)........ panelist (1952)

DEAN, EDDIE—cowboy actor, singer
b: c. 1910, Posey, Texas

The Marshal of Gunsight Pass (wes)
.... Marshal Eddie Dean (1950)

DEAN, FABIAN—actor
b: c. 1931 d: 1971

The Tim Conway Show (com)
.... Harry Wetzel (1970)

DEAN, HANNAH—actress
Out of the Blue (com)........ Gladys (1979)

DEAN, IVOR—actor
b: c. 1907, England

The Saint (adv)
.... Inspector Claude Teal (1967–69)
My Partner the Ghost (drama)
.... Inspector Large (1973–74)

DEAN, JIMMY—singer
b: Aug 10, 1928, near Plainview, Texas

The Jimmy Dean Show (var) .... host (1957)
The Jimmy Dean Show (var)
.... host (1963–66)
Daniel Boone (wes)
.... Josh Clements (1968–70)
The Jimmy Dean Show (var)
.... host (1973–75)

This drawling Texas singer was one of the leading exponents of the country-pop sound of the early 1960s—basically country music watered down enough to be palatable to the mass audience, as exemplified by his own biggest hit, "Big Bad John."

Jimmy certainly came from an authentic country background. He told *TV Guide* in 1964, "Oh, I was a hard-workin' little boy. Pullin' cotton, shockin' grain, cuttin' wheat, loadin' wheat, choppin' cotton, cleanin' chicken houses, milkin' cows, plowin'. They used to laugh at my clothes, my bib overalls and galluses, because we were dirt poor. And I'd go home and tell Mom how miserable I felt being laughed at. I dreamt of havin' a beautiful home, a nice car, an' nice clothes. I wanted to be somebody."

It took a while to get there. After military service in the mid-1940s he formed a local band in the Washington, D.C., area called The Texas Wildcats, and by the mid-1950s he had a show on local station WMAL-TV. City slicker sponsors didn't want to advertise on it, despite its popularity, and it folded. Nevertheless, Jimmy managed to get another chance on the CBS network with a show that ran intermittently in daytime and nighttime from 1957–59. It also had sponsor problems. Finally, in the early 1960s, his enormous record hits ("Big Bad John" was the number-one song for much of the winter of 1961–62) won him guest spots on all the top shows as well as his own cornpone variety hour from 1963–66. Jimmy toured widely in later years, and he also had some acting roles in various series and movies, including *Daniel Boone, Vega$,* and *The Ballad of Andy Crocker* (1969), the latter being the first TV movie to deal with a returning veteran of the Vietnam War.

DEAN, LARRY—singer
b: c. 1936

The Lawrence Welk Show (music)
.... regular (1956–60)

DEAN, MORTON—newscaster
b: Aug 22, 1935, Fall River, Mass.

CBS Weekend News (news)
.... anchorman (1975–84)
The American Parade (pub aff)
.... correspondent (1984)

Emmy Award: Best News Program Segment, for "Louis Is 13" report on *CBS News Sunday Morning* (1981)

DEAN, RON—actress

Lady Blue (police)
.... Sgt. Gina Ginelli (1985–86)

DEAN, SUZI—actress

Harper Valley P.T.A. (com)
.... Scarlett Taylor (1981–82)

DE AZEVEDO, LEX—orchestra leader

The Sonny Comedy Revue (var)
.... orch. leader (1974)
Joey & Dad (var) .... orch. leader (1975)

DE BROUX, LEE—actor

Salvage 1 (adv) ...... Hank Beddoes (1979)
MacGruder & Loud (police)
.... Sgt. Hanson (1985)

DEBUTONES, THE—singers

The Julius La Rosa Show (music)
.... regular (1955)

DECAMP, ROSEMARY—actress
b: Nov 14, 1914*, Prescott, Ariz.

The Life of Riley (com)
.... Peg Riley (1949–50)
Bob Cummings Show (com)
.... Margaret MacDonald (1955–59)
That Girl (com) ..... Helen Marie (1966–70)

DECARLO, YVONNE—actress
b: Sep 1, 1922, Vancouver, British Columbia, Canada

The Munsters (com)
.... Lily Munster (1964–66)

This actress was one of Hollywood's starlets of the 1940s, noted for her exotic and sensual roles in such films as *Salome, Where She Danced.* She did not do much television but is well remembered for her one series role—as the bizarre wife in the mock-horror comedy *The Munsters.*

DECKER, DIANA—actress
b: 1926

The Vise (Mark Saber) (drama)
.... Stephanie Ames (1956–57)

DECORSIA, TED—actor
b: Sep 29, 1904**, Brooklyn, N.Y. d: Apr 11, 1973

Steve Canyon (adv)
.... Police Chief Hagedorn (1959)

DE COSTA, TONY—actor

Search (adv)............ Ramos (1972–73)

DE CRAFT, JOSEPH—actor

Born Free (adv) .... Joe Kanini (1974)

DEE, RUBY—black actress
b: Oct 27, 1923†, Cleveland, Ohio, r: Harlem, New York

Peyton Place (drama)
.... Alma Miles (1968–69)

*Some sources give 1913.
**Some sources give 1903 or 1905.
†Some sources give 1924.

Roots: The Next Generations (drama)
.... Queen Haley (1979)

Married to actor Ossie Davis.

DEEB, GARY—Chicago television critic

Television: Inside and Out (mag)
.... regular (1981–82)

DEEL, SANDRA—singer, actress

Caesar Presents (var)
.... Sandy Williams (1955)
Caesar's Hour (var)
.... Betty Hansen (1955–56)
Needles and Pins (com)
.... Sonia Baker (1973)

DEEMS, MICKEY—actor

The Don Knotts Show (var)
.... regular (1970–71)
Hizzonner (com) .... Nails (1979)

DEER, GARY MULE—actor

Dinah and Her New Best Friends (var)
.... regular (1976)

DEES, JULIE—assistant

TV's Bloopers & Practical Jokes (com)
.... regular (1984)

DEES, RICK—host, disc jockey
b: 1950, Memphis, Tenn.

Solid Gold (music) .... host (1984–85)

A disc jockey best known for one of the most popular (among teenyboppers) and most widely despised (by everybody else) novelty records of the mid-1970s: "Disco Duck."

DEEZEN, EDDIE—actor

Punky Brewster (com)
.... Eddie Malvin (1984)

DEFORE, DON—actor
b: Aug 25, 1917, Cedar Rapids, Iowa

The Adventures of Ozzie & Harriet (com)
.... Thorney Thornberry (1952–58)
Hazel (com) ...... George Baxter (1961–65)

DEFOREST, CALVERT—actor
b: Jul 23, Brooklyn, N.Y.

Late Night with David Letterman (talk)
.... Larry "Bud" Melman (1982–)

The very first face seen at the opening of the first telecast of *Late Night With David Letterman*, on February 1, 1982, was that of a small middle-aged man with a bullet-shaped head, thick horn-rimmed glasses, and a very deliberate manner of speech. Larry "Bud" Melman—aka Calvert DeForest—has since then become a cult star by doing almost nothing unusual at all. He simply looks and sounds hilarious, whether he is conducting an interview, dispensing advice (on "Ask Mr. Melman"), or asking passersby on the street to welcome spring.

Before his national exposure on the Letterman show, DeForest had hardly any professional career at all, only a few small parts in local theater and nonprofessional films. Since February, 1982, he has done cameos in several motion pictures, become a regular on the personal appearance circuit, and even appeared in two music videos seen on MTV. He was eventually forced to give up his job as a receptionist at a New York City drug rehabilitation center when city authorities found out about this "other life." They were not amused.

It's hard to know what comes next, a career as a romantic leading man in big-screen epics, or a permanent job handing out warm towels to arrivals at the city's seedy bus terminal. Whichever it is, "Bud" Melman is tomorrow's TV trivia in the making.

DEFREITAS, DICK—

Your Show of Shows (var)
.... regular (1950–53)

DE GORE, JANET—actress
b: c. 1934 r: Philadelphia, Pa.

The Law and Mr. Jones (drama)
.... Marsha Spear (1960–62)
The Real McCoys (com)
.... Louise Howard (1963)

DE GROSA, JOHN—Pennsylvania Athletic Commissioner

Kid Gloves (sport)....... interviewer (1951)

DEGRUY, OSCAR—

The New Bill Cosby Show (var)
.... regular (1972–73)

DEHAVEN, GLORIA—actress
b: Jul 23, 1925*, Los Angeles, Calif.

Make the Connection (quiz) . panelist (1955)
Nakia (police)........... Irene James (1974)

DE HAVILLAND, OLIVIA—actress
b: Jul 1, 1916, Tokyo, Japan

Roots: The Next Generations (drama)
.... Mrs. Warner (1979)

This movie queen of the 1930s and '40s *(Gone with the Wind, etc.)* has made very few appearances on television, certainly fewer than her equally famous sister Joan Fontaine. She did, however, take a trip on *The Love Boat* in 1981.

DEHNER, JOHN—actor
b: Nov 23, 1915, Staten Island, N.Y.

The Westerner (wes)
.... Burgundy Smith (1960)
The Roaring Twenties (drama)
.... Jim Duke Williams (1960–62)
The Baileys of Balboa (com)
.... Commodore Cecil Wyntoon (1964–65)
The Don Knotts Show (var)
.... regular (1970–71)
The Doris Day Show (com)
.... Cy Bennett (1971–73)
Temperatures Rising (com)
.. Dr. Charles Cleveland Claver (1973–74)
Big Hawaii (drama) ... Barrett Fears (1977)
How the West Was Won (miniseries) (drama)
.... Bishop Benjamin (1977)
Young Maverick (wes)
.... Marshal Edge Troy (1979–80)
Enos (com) ...... Lt. Jacob Broggi (1980–81)
Bare Essence (drama)
.... Hadden Marshall (1983)
The Winds of War (drama)
.... Adm. King (1983)

If you have watched television, gone to the movies, or listened to radio during the past half-century or so you have probably heard or seen John Dehner hundreds of times. Unfortunately for him, none of his many roles, including regular parts in 11 TV series, have been distinctive enough to

*Some sources give 1923 or 1924.

make him a major star.

The tall, distinguished actor has certainly been around. The son of an artist, he lived in Europe for much of his youth, returning to the U.S. in the 1930s to try his hand as a stage actor. After a short stint as an animator for Walt Disney and as a publicist for the army during World War II (following General Patton around), he went into radio, where he worked for a number of years as a newsman. In the 1950s he was quite busy as a radio actor, starring in several series, including *Frontier Gentleman* and *Have Gun Will Travel* (in the role Richard Boone made famous on television). He was also in dozens of B-grade action films, usually as the steely-eyed villain.

By the 1960s, with radio drama dead, Dehner turned to television, where he was generally the humorless authority figure—either straight (e.g., *Big Hawaii, Bare Essence*) or as a buffoon (e.g., *The Baileys of Balboa, Enos*). An imposing figure, with his trim mustache and calculated glare, he was also a favorite in TV movies and miniseries such as *The Missiles of October* (as Secretary of State Dean Acheson) and *The Winds of War* (as Admiral King).

DEIGNAN, MARTINA—actress

Code Red (adv) ..... Haley Green (1981–82)

DEKOVA, FRANK—actor
b: 1910 d: Oct 15, 1981

F Troop (com)
.... Chief Wild Eagle (1965–67)

DELANEY, STEVE—newscaster
b: Aug 30, 1938, Dobbs Ferry, N.Y.

Monitor (pub aff)
.... correspondent (1983–84)

DELANO, MICHAEL—actor

Firehouse (adv) ...... Sonny Caputo (1974)
Rhoda (com)..... Johnny Venture (1977–78)
Supertrain (drama)
.... Bartender Lou Atkins (1979)

DELANY, PAT—actress

Swiss Family Robinson (adv)
.... Lotte Robinson (1975–76)

DELEVANTI, CYRIL—actor
b: 1887, England d: Dec 13, 1975

Jefferson Drum (wes)
.... Lucius Coin (1958–59)

DELFINO, FRANK—actor

The Feather and Father Gang (drama)
.... Enzo (1977)

DELGADO, EMILIO—actor

Lou Grant (drama)
.... national editor (1979–82)
Born to the Wind (adv)... White Bull (1982)

Delgado was a regular on *Sesame Street* during the 1970s, as Luis.

DELGADO, LUIS—actor

Bret Maverick (wes)
.... Shifty Delgrado (1981–82)

DELGADO, ROGER—actor
b: 1920 d: Jun 19, 1973

The Adventures of Sir Francis Drake (adv)
.... Mendoza, Spanish Amb. (1962)

DELGARDE, DOMINICK—actor

Combat Sergeant (drama)... Abdulla (1956)

DELL AND ABBOTT—

Broadway Open House (talk)
.... regulars (1951)

DELL, CHARLIE—actor

The Dukes of Hazzard (com)
.... Emery Potter (1981–85)

DELL, GABRIEL—actor
b: Oct 7, 1919*, Barbados, British West Indies

The Steve Allen Show 'var)
.... regular (1956–61)
The Corner Bar (com) .. Harry Grant (1972)
A Year at the Top (com)
.... Frederick J. Hanover (1977)

Gabe was one of the original Dead End Kids (also known as The Bowery Boys), appearing with them in films from 1937–

*Some sources give 1920, 1921, or 1923.

240

1950. He became a character actor in the 1960s.

DELL, MYRNA—actress

China Smith (adv)
.... Shira ("Empress") (1952–55)

DELMAR, KENNY—comedian
b: 1910, Boston, Mass. d: Jul 14, 1984

School House (var)....... "Teacher" (1949)

Delmar is fondly remembered by radio listeners of the late 1940s as Senator Claghorn on *The Fred Allen Show,* a booming, blustering Southern stereotype so outrageous he became a national sensation ("That's a joke, son!"). Delmar continued to do variations on the character for many years thereafter, including various cartoon characters on Saturday morning throughout the 1960s. He also appeared in episodes of several playhouse series during the 1950s and was "Colonel Culpepper" in an episode of *Car 54, Where Are You?* in 1962. His sole regular series role was as the harried "teacher" of a group of precocious kids (including some future TV stars) on *School House* in 1949.

DELOY, GEORGE—actor
b: Nov 23, Canelones, Uruguay r: Salt Lake City

Star of the Family (com)
.... Frank Rosetti (1982)
9 to 5 (com)..... Michael Henderson (1983)
St. Elsewhere (drama)
.... Ken Valerie (1985–)

DEL REGNO, JOHN—actor

Baker's Dozen (com)..... Jeff Diggins (1982)

DELUGG, MILTON—orchestra leader
b: Dec 2, 1918, Los Angeles, Calif.

Abe Burrows' Almanac (var)
.... orch. leader (1950)
Broadway Open House (talk)
.... orch. leader (1950–51)
Doodles Weaver (var) .. orch. leader (1951)
Seven at Eleven (var).. sextet leader (1951)
Dagmar's Canteen (var). orch. leader (1952)
Judge for Yourself (quiz)
.... orch. leader (1953–54)

The Tonight Show Starring Johnny Carson
(talk) .... orch. leader (1966–67)
Your Hit Parade (music)
.... orch. leader (1974)
The Gong Show (com)
.... orch. leader (1976–80)
The Chuck Barris Rah Rah Show (var)
.... orch. leader (1978)

DELUISE, DOM—comedian
b: Aug 1, 1933, Brooklyn, N.Y.

The Entertainers (var) .... regular (1964–65)
The Dean Martin Summer Show (var)
.... regular (1966)
The Dom DeLuise Show (var) ... host (1968)
The Glen Campbell Goodtime Hour (var)
.... regular (1971–72)
The Dean Martin Show (var)
.... regular (1972–73)
Lotsa Luck (com)
.... Stanley Belmont (1973–74)

Chubby, bubbly Dom DeLuise is one of those nutty comics who turns up frequently in other people's movies and TV shows but who has never managed to find a successful starring vehicle of his own. He first attracted attention in the early '60s as "Dominick the Great," the ham-handed magician on *The Garry Moore Show*. That lead to regular supporting roles on two other variety shows and finally to his own CBS summer show in 1968—which was not, however, invited back for the regular fall season.

So Dom went back to supporting roles, for Glen Campbell, Dean Martin and others. He then landed the starring role of a harried family man in the situation comedy *Lotsa Luck,* but it lasted only half a season in 1973–74. Since then, he has concentrated mostly on guest appearances on variety shows and in movies, especially those involving his friends Mel Brooks and Burt Reynolds, who find him hysterical.

In 1983 Dom played an unusual dramatic role in the TV movie *Happy,* as a down-on-his-luck TV comic who puts his family in jeopardy as he tries to find his partner's killer.

DELYON, LEO—actor
It's a Business (com) .... regular (1952)
Top Cat (cartn)
...... Spook/The Brain (voices) (1961–62)

This name was evidently a pseudonym. Get it?

DE MAR, JAKI—actress
Love, American Style (com)
.... repertory player (1970–72)

DEMAREST, WILLIAM—actor
b: Feb 27, 1892*, St. Paul, Minn. d: Dec 28, 1983

Love & Marriage (com)
.... William Harris (1959–60)
Tales of Wells Fargo (wes)
.... Jeb Gaine (1961–62)
My Three Sons (com)
.... Uncle Charley O'Casey (1965–72)

This old-timer was beloved as crusty Uncle Charley on *My Three Sons* in the late 1960s. Forty years earlier he had appeared in his first notable film role in *The Jazz Singer* (1927), the Al Jolson classic that launched talking pictures. For 20 years before *that* he was in vaudeville, where he was a headliner in the years after World War I. He made scores of movies over the years and was seen as late as 1978 in the TV revival of *The Millionaire*—capping a 73-year career in show business.

DE MARNEY, TERENCE—actor
b: Mar 1, 1909, England d: May 25, 1971
Johnny Ringo (wes)
.... Case Thomas (1959–60)

DE MAVE, JACK—actor
Lassie (adv) .... Bob Erickson (1968–70)

DEMAY, JANET—actress
Remington Steele (drama)
.... Bernice Foxe (1982–83)

DEMETRIO, ANNA—actress
Mama Rosa (com)...... Mama Rosa (1950)

DEMPSEY, PATRICK—actor
Fast Times (com)..... Mike Damone (1986)

DENISON, ANTHONY—actor
b: The Bronx, N.Y.
Crime Story (police)..... Ray Luca (1986–)

*Some sources give 1894.

241

DENNEHY, BRIAN—actor

b: Jul 9, 1940, Bridgeport, Conn. r: Long Island, N.Y.

Pearl (drama) .... Sgt. Chain (1978)
Big Shamus, Little Shamus (drama)
.... Arnie Sutter (1979)
Star of the Family (com)
.... Buddy Krebs (1982)

DENNING, RICHARD—actor

b: Mar 27, 1914, Poughkeepsie, N.Y.

Mr. & Mrs. North (drama)
.... Jerry North (1952–54)
The Flying Doctor (drama)
.... Greg, the Doctor (1959)
Michael Shayne (drama)
.... Michael Shane (1960–61)
Karen (com) .... Steve Scott (1964–65)
Hawaii Five-O (police)
.... Gov. Philip Grey (1968–80)

Richard Denning is a tall, athletic, and very handsome actor who, thanks to those attributes, has had no trouble finding work since he entered show business in the late 1930s. He was born the son of a clothing manufacturer and originally went into that business, but, after winning first place on the radio show *Do You Want to Be an Actor?* in 1936, he decided he did.

Denning appeared in B films in the late 1930s and '40s, as well as on radio. He was Lucille Ball's hubby on the radio version of *My Favorite Husband* and Jerry North on *Mr. & Mrs. North,* a role he carried over to television in 1952. His handsome face was also seen on live playhouse series of the '50s, most notably *Ford Theatre,* and he starred in *The Flying Doctor* (as an American M.D. in Australia) and in *Michael Shayne* (as the suave detective).

By the '60s he was less active. Eventually he and his wife, English-born actress Evelyn Ankers, moved to Hawaii to enjoy a well-earned retirement. "It's about as close to paradise as we could find on earth," he once commented, "and we love it more each day." However, even there producers came looking for him; he was persuaded to play the recurring role of the distinguished-looking governor on *Hawaii Five-O,* which was filmed on the islands.

DENNIS, BEVERLY—actress

The Red Buttons Show (var)
.... regular (1952–53)

DENNIS, MATT—singer, songwriter

b: Feb 11, 1914, Seattle, Wash.

The Matt Dennis Show (music)
.... host (1955)

DENNIS, NICK—actor

b: Thessaly, Greece r: Lowell, Mass. deceased

Ben Casey (drama)
.... Nick Kanavaras (1961–68)

DENNISON, RACHEL—actress

b: Aug 31, 1959, Knoxville, Tenn.

9 to 5 (com) ...... Doralee Rhodes (1982–83)
9 to 5 (com) .... Doralee Rhodes (1986–)

Dolly Parton's look-alike kid sister; she played on television the role that Dolly had in the movie version of *9 to 5.*

DENNY, GEORGE V., JR.—lecturer, host

America's Town Meeting (pub aff)
.... moderator (1948–52)

DENVER, BOB—actor

b: Jan 9, 1935, New Rochelle, N.Y.

The Many Loves of Dobie Gillis (com)
.... Maynard G. Krebs (1959–63)
Gilligan's Island (com)... Gilligan (1964–67)
The Good Guys (com)
.... Rufus Butterworth (1968–70)
Dusty's Trail (com).......... Dusty (1973)

It looks as if Bob Denver will always be Gilligan in one form or another. The slapstick children's favorite of the 1960s comes back every few years in another cartoon or revival, and despite several attempts to launch another series, he is always—even in his 50s—associated with that role.

Bob began playing comedy supporting roles as soon as he graduated from college in 1957. His first great success was as Dobie Gillis' "beatnik" buddy in *The Many Loves of Dobie Gillis,* a role that lasted for four years. Then came *Gilligan.* He also did guest shots on other shows, including *The Farmer's Daughter, I Dream of Jeannie,* and *Love, American Style* among others, and provided voices for two Saturday morning kiddie shows in the '70s—*The Far Out Space Nuts* and the cartoon version of *Gilligan.* Then he started turning up in reunion specials, one of *Dobie Gillis* and three of *Gilligan.* He is also seen once in a while in a TV movie; e.g., *High School U.S.A.* and *The Invisible Woman* (both in '83). Even there, however, most viewers' reaction is, "There's Gilligan!"

DER, RICKY—juvenile actor
b: c. 1953 r: San Francisco (Chinatown)

Kentucky Jones (drama)
.... Ike Wong (1964–65)

DEREK, JOHN—actor
b: Aug 12, 1926, Los Angeles, Calif.

Frontier Circus (drama)
.... Ben Travis (1961–62)

Although this dashing leading man appeared in quite a few films in the 1940s and '50s, he is probably better known for his many marriages to exceptionally glamorous women: Ursula Andress, Linda Evans, and, most recently, Bo Derek. He is now a director.

DERN, BRUCE—actor
b: Jun 4, 1936, Winnetka, Ill.

Stoney Burke (wes).. E. J. Stocker (1962–63)

DE ROSE, CHRIS—actor

The San Pedro Beach Bums (com)
.... Boychick (1977)

DERR, RICHARD—actor
b: 1917

Fanfare (drama)............... host (1959)

DERRICKS-CARROLL, CLINTON—black actor

Sanford (com)..... Cliff Anderson (1980–81)

DE SALES, FRANCIS—actor

Mr. & Mrs. North (drama)
.... Lt. Bill Weigand (1952–54)

DESANTIS, JOE—actor
b: 1909, New York City, N.Y.

Photocrime (drama) .... regular (1949)
The Trap (drama) .... narrator (1950)

DE SANTIS, STANLEY—actor

The Paper Chase (drama)
.... Gagarian (1978–79)

DESCHER, SANDY—actress
b: c. 1945

The New Loretta Young Show (drama)
.... Judy Massey (1962–63)
The New Phil Silvers Show (com)
.... Susan (1964)

DESIDERIO, ROBERT—actor
b: Sep 9, c. 1951, The Bronx, N.Y.

Heart of the City (drama)
.... Det. Wes Kennedy (1986–)

A former disc jockey, daytime soap opera actor, and the husband of actress Judith Light.

DESIMONE, TONY—combo leader
b: c. 1920 d: Jun 12, 1986

Melody, Harmony & Rhythm (music)
.... regular (1949–50)
Rendezvous with Music (music)
.... regular (1950)
Ernie in Kovacsland (var).... regular (1951)

DESMOND, JOHNNY—singer
b: Nov 14, 1920, Detroit, Mich. d: Sep 6, 1985

Face the Music (music) ...... regular (1948)
Tin Pan Alley TV (var) ...... regular (1950)
Don McNeill TV Club (var)
.... vocalist (1950–51)
The Jack Paar Program (var)
.... regular (1954)
Sally (com) .... Jim Kendall (1958)
Your Hit Parade (music) . vocalist (1958–59)
Music on Ice (var)............. host (1960)
Glenn Miller Time (music) ... cohost (1961)
Blansky's Beauties (com) ..... Emilio (1977)

"Desmo" was a bobbysoxers' dreamboat delight in the early 1940s when he sang with Bob Crosby, Gene Krupa, and the Glenn Miller Army Air Force Band. Later, the handsome young crooner was a regular on Don McNeill's *Breakfast Club* on radio from 1948–54 and was seen quite a bit on early television as well. Most of his appearances were as a singer, but in 1953 he made his acting debut in an episode of *Danger* (entitled "Sing for Your Life") and he was subsequently seen from time to time in acting roles, including the 1977 sitcom *Blansky's Beauties*. After the '60s, he concentrated mostly on clubs and stock theater, with only occasional television appearances.

DESOTO, ROSANA—actress
b: Sep 2, San Jose, Calif.

The Redd Foxx Show (com)
.... Diana Olmos (1986)

DESPIRITO, ROMOLO—singer

Village Barn (var)
...... The Road Agent (aka The Masked
.... Singer) (1949)

Who was that masked man?

DESPO—actress, singer

Ivan the Terrible (com) ..... Tatiana (1976)

DE TOLEDANO, RALPH—commentator

Our Secret Weapon—The Truth (info)
.... panelist (1951)

DEUEL, PETER—actor
b: 1940, Rochester, N.Y. d: Dec 31, 1971

Gidget (com) .... John Cooper (1965–66)
Love on a Rooftop (com)
.... David Willis (1966–67)
Alias Smith and Jones (wes)
. Joshua Smith/Hannibal Heyes (1971–72)

Peter Deuel is one of Hollywood's saddest stories. He was a handsome young actor, much in demand, and in the midst of a successful series; yet one night he raised a .38-caliber pistol to his head and put a bullet through his temple. Why?

Deuel had begun getting roles almost as soon as he launched his career, appearing in such mid-1960s series as *Combat*, *Twelve O'Clock High*, *The Fugitive*, *The Big Valley*, and *Gidget* (a regular, as Sally Field's young brother-in-law). A major break came in 1966 with his own well-

received, though short-lived, situation comedy, *Love on a Rooftop*. Then came his first feature-film roles and the popular ABC series *Alias Smith and Jones*.

Deuel (he later changed it to Duel for simplicity) had high expectations—perhaps too high for the TV career in which he found himself. He thought the scripts were garbage, had a reputation for fighting with directors, and was angered when his efforts to change the system by running for office in the Screen Actors Guild were rebuffed (he lost). Usually clad in jeans, he was a political activist working for McCarthy in '68 and cared about ecology—he was a true child of the '60s. Thousands of young hopefuls would have given their eyeteeth for his success, but Deuel always wanted more, both as an actor and as a person.

Still, he did not appear suicidal and was deeply involved with *Alias Smith and Jones*. He had just finished filming an episode, and on the fatal night had read the script for the next and watched an episode of his show. He was with a girlfriend who later said nothing seemed wrong, although he had been drinking and hated the show he saw. Late at night she heard a gunshot from the next room, and ran in to find him sprawled on the floor. Despite all evidence to the contrary, many feel to this day that it must have been a terrible accident—or murder.

DEUTSCH, PATTI—actress
b: Dec 16, Pittsburgh, Pa.

The John Byner Comedy Hour (var)
.... regular (1972)
Rowan & Martin's Laugh-In (var)
.... regular (1972–73)

DEVANE, WILLIAM—actor
b: Sep 5, 1939, Albany, N.Y.

From Here to Eternity (drama)
...... Master Sgt. Milt Warden (1979–80)
Knots Landing (drama)
.... Gregory Sumner (1983–)

DEVARONA, DONNA—hostess, Olympic swimmer
b: c. 1947, San Diego, Calif. r: Lafayette, Calif.

Games People Play (sport)
.... field reporter (1980–81)

DEVINE, ANDY—actor

b: Oct 7, 1905, Flagstaff, Ariz. d: Feb 18, 1977

The Adventures of Wild Bill Hickok (wes)
.... Jingles (1951–58)
Flipper (adv)....... Hap Gorman (1964–65)

Thanks to his incredibly raspy voice, Andy Devine's acting career was almost over before it began. He entered movies fresh out of college, where he had been a husky football star, during the last days of silent films (1926). Almost immediately, talking pictures took over the business, and Andy, like many others, seemed to have little chance of making the transition. However, he soon discovered that by forsaking leading-man parts for comic supporting roles, his gravelly voice (the result of a childhood accident) could become a distinctive advantage. It made him a busy actor during the 1930s and '40s, especially in westerns. He was also heard frequently on the radio, including a recurring spot on the top-rated *Jack Benny Show* ("Hi-ya, Buck!").

With his movie career winding down in the 1950s, Andy took on the role of Guy Madison's roly-poly partner on *Wild Bill Hickok* in 1951. The show was a low-budget, syndicated affair, but Andy wisely agreed to work without a salary in return for a 10% share of the show's income. It was the most profitable role he ever played. In the late 1950s, he was also seen on Saturday mornings as the host of *Andy's Gang,* which he took over upon the death of Smilin' Ed McConnell.

Andy continued to appear periodically in the 1960s, including a recurring part on *Flipper.* One of his last principal roles was as the drunken judge in the TV movie *The Over the Hill Gang* and its sequel, in 1969–70.

DEVITO, DANNY—actor

b: Nov 17, 1944, Neptune, N.J. r: Asbury Park, N.J.

Taxi (com)....... Louie De Palma (1978–83)

Emmy Award: Best Supporting Actor in a Comedy, for *Taxi* (1981)

"In my heart I knew we'd be back ... It's too good a show not to have found a place on television," said Danny DeVito of *Taxi,* after it was rescued from ABC's cancellation by NBC, which picked it up for another year in 1982. The show was a classic, as was DeVito's portrayal of the diminutive, tyrannical dispatcher who made life miserable for the cheerful cabbies from inside his wire dispatcher's cage.

DeVito was a relatively unknown character actor when he was picked for the part. His small stature (5') limited his roles, and he appeared mostly in off-Broadway plays in the late 1960s and early '70s. His movie debut was in *One Flew Over the Cuckoo's Nest* (1975), as the mental patient Martini—a role he had also played in the stage version. He has since appeared in a number of comedy movies, including *Goin' South* and *Going Ape.*

DeVito is married to actress Rhea Perlman of *Cheers.*

DEVLIN, DONALD—juvenile actor

Wesley (com)..... Wesley Eggleston (1949)

DEVLIN, JOE—actor

b: 1899 d: Oct 1, 1973

Dick Tracy (police)
.... Sam Catchem (1950–51)

DEVOL, FRANK—orchestra leader, actor

b: Sep 20, 1911, Moundsville, W. Va.

College of Musical Knowledge (quiz)
.... orch. leader (1954)
The Lux Show Starring Rosemary Clooney (var)................ orch. leader (1957–58)
The Betty White Show (var)
.... orch. leader/skits (1958)
The George Gobel Show (var)
.... orch. leader (1958–59)
The Dinah Shore Chevy Show (var)
.... orch. leader (1961–62)
I'm Dickens—He's Fenster (com)
.... Myron Bannister (1962–63)
Fernwood 2-Night (com)
.... Happy Kyne (1977–78)

DEVON, LAURA—actress

b: 1940, Chicago, Ill.

The Richard Boone Show (drama)
.... regular (1963–64)

DEVORE, CAIN—actor
b: Kansas City, Mo.

Dreams (com).......... Phil Taylor (1984)

DEWHURST, COLLEEN—actress
b: Jun 3, 1926, Montreal, Canada

Studs Lonigan (drama)
.... Mrs. Lonigan (1979)
The Blue and the Gray (drama)
.... Maggie Geyser (1982)

Emmy Award: Best Supporting Actress in a Special, for "Between Two Women" (1986)
Twice married to and twice divorced from actor George C. Scott.

DE WILDE, BRANDON—actor
b: Apr 9, 1942, Brooklyn, N.Y. d: Jul 6, 1972

Jamie (com).... Jamie McHummer (1953–54)

The son of actor Frederic De Wilde and a major child star of stage and screen in the 1950s (*The Member of the Wedding, Shane,* etc.). Young Brandon was seen fairly often on television in those days, mostly in dramatic productions, and he also starred in his own well-received series. During the '60s he turned up in lesser roles on *The Virginian, The Defenders, ABC Stage '67,* etc. One notable appearance that was *not* seen was in an episode of *Alfred Hitchcock Presents.* He played a retarded boy who, taking a magic act too literally, mistakenly saws a woman in half—a premise so frightening that the network refused to air the episode, the only such instance in the series' ten-year run. (It was later seen in syndication.)
In his later years Brandon was never able to recapture the spectacular success of his youth. He died in an auto accident in 1972.

DE WILDE, FREDERIC (FRITZ)—actor
d: 1980

Musical Merry-Go-Round (music)
.... regular (1947–49)

Stage actor/manager and father of juvenile star Brandon De Wilde.

DEWINDT, SHEILA—actress

B.J. and the Bear (adv)
.... Angie Cartwright (1981)

DE WINTER, JO—actress
b: Mar 5, Sacramento, Calif. r: New Orleans, La.

Gloria (com)
.... Dr. Maggie Lawrence (1982–83)

DEWITT, ALAN—actor
b: c. 1924 d: Jun 2, 1976

It's About Time (com) .. Mr. Tyler (1966–67)

DEWITT, FAY—actress

Harris Against the World (com)
.... Helen Miller (1964–65)

DE WITT, GEORGE—host
b: c. 1923, Atlantic City, N.J. d: Jul 14, 1979

Seven at Eleven (var)........ regular (1951)
All in One (var)............. host (1952–53)
Name That Tune (quiz).... emcee (1955–59)
Be Our Guest (var)............. host (1960)

DEWITT, JOYCE—actress
b: Apr 23, 1949, Wheeling, W. Va. r: Speedway, Ind.

Three's Company (com)
.... Janet Wood (1977–84)

DEWOLFE, BILLY—actor
b: Feb 18, 1907, Wollaston, Mass. d: Mar 5, 1974

The Pruitts of Southampton (com)
.... Vernon Bradley (1967)
Good Morning, World (com)
.... Roland B. Hutton, Jr. (1967–68)
The Queen and I (com)
.... Oliver Nelson (1969)

DEXTER, JERRY—comedian

Happy Days (var) .... regular (1970)

A Saturday morning "voice man" from the late 1960s to the '80s.

DEY, SUSAN—actress
b: Dec 10, 1952, Pekin, Ill. r: Mt. Kisco, N.Y.

The Partridge Family (com)
.... Laurie Partridge (1970–74)
Loves Me, Loves Me Not (com)
.... Jane (1977)
Emerald Point N.A.S. (drama)
.... Celia Mallory Warren (1983–84)
L.A. Law (drama)
..... Dep. D.A. Grace Van Owen (1986–)

DEYOUNG, CLIFF—actor
b: Feb 12, 1945*, Inglewood, Calif.

Sunshine (com)....... Sam Hayden (1975)
Centennial (drama)
.... John Skimmerhorn (1978–79)
Master of the Game (drama)
.... Brad Rogers (1984)

DEZINA, KATE—actress
The Hamptons (drama)
.... Cheryl Ashcroft (1983)

DEZURIK, CAROLYN—
Polka Time (music)....... regular (1956–57)
Polka-Go-Round (music) .. regular (1958–59)

DHIEGH, KHIGH—actor
b: 1910, New Jersey

Hawaii Five-O (police) .. Wo Fat (1968–75)
Khan (drama)................. Khan (1975)

Pronounced "ki-dee." Though of Anglo-Egyptian-Sudanese extraction, he is a leading proponent of the ancient Chinese philosophy *I Ching*.

DIAMOND, BARRY—actor
The Half Hour Comedy Hour (var)
.... regular (1983)

DIAMOND, BOBBY—juvenile actor
b: Aug 23, 1943, Los Angeles, Calif.

Westinghouse Playhouse (com)
.... Buddy (1961)
The Many Loves of Dobie Gillis (com)
.... Duncan Gillis (1962–63)

If you get into a traffic accident in Los Angeles and you need a lawyer, you may find yourself in court with Bobby Diamond, the onetime child star of *Fury*. Bobby has been a practicing attorney since the early 1970s,

*Some sources give 1946.

and he doesn't miss acting—too much.

Bobby was in show business for 26 years before beginning his present career at age 28. He started out as a toddler gracing the covers of such national magazines as *Collier's* and *Parade* and appeared in his first film *(The Mating of Millie)* at age four. He was in a number of TV dramas in the early 1950s *(The Loretta Young Show, Cavalcade of Stars)* before beginning—at age 12—the role that would make him famous, that of the young waif in love with his horse on *Fury*. The series ran for five years on Saturday morning and was rerun long afterward. After it ended production in 1960 Bobby moved on to other roles for a time, but he missed a big one. He turned down the chance to become one of Fred MacMurray's sons on *My Three Sons* in favor of a Nanette Fabray situation comedy called *Westinghouse Playhouse*. That lasted for six months, while *My Three Sons* ran for 12 years. You never can tell.

DIAMOND, DON—actor
b: Brooklyn, N.Y.

The Adventures of Kit Carson (wes)
.... El Toro (1951–55)
Zorro (wes)........... Cpl. Reyes (1958–59)
F Troop (com)........ Crazy Cat (1965–67)

DIAMOND, PETER—actor
The Adventures of Sir Francis Drake (adv)
.... Bosun (1962)

DIAMOND, SELMA—actress, writer
b: Aug 5, 1920, London, Ont., Canada d: May 14, 1985

Too Close for Comfort (com)
.... Mildred Rafkin (occasional) (1980–81)
Night Court (com) . Selma Hacker (1984–85)

DIAQUINTO, JOHN—actor
b: Apr 14, Brooklyn, N.Y. r: Fort Lauderdale, Fla.

Wildside (wes).. Varges De La Cosa (1985)

DIAZ, EDITH—actress
Popi (com)................... Lupe (1976)

DIBBS, KEM—actor
Buck Rogers (sci fi)..... Buck Rogers (1950)

DICENZO, GEORGE—actor

Aspen (drama) .... Abe Singer (1977)
McClain's Law (police)
.... Lt. Edward DeNisco (1981–82)
Dynasty (drama) .... Charles (1984–85)

DICK, DOUGLAS—actor

b: Nov 20, 1920, Charles Town, W. Va. r: Versailles, Ky

Waterfront (adv) .... Carl Herrick (1953–56)

DICKENS SISTERS, THE—

The Eddy Arnold Show (var)
.... regulars (1953)

DICKENS, JIMMY—country singer

b: Dec 19, 1925, Bolt, W. Va.

Grand Ole Opry (music) .. regular (1955–56)

DICKINSON, ANGIE—actress

b: Sep 30, 1931*, Kulm, N.D. r: Edgelev, N.D.

Police Woman (police)
  Sgt. Suzanne "Pepper" Anderson (1974–78)
Pearl (drama) .... Midge (1978)
Cassie & Company (drama)
.... Cassie Holland (1982)

A veteran police chief, upon being introduced to *Police Woman* star Angie Dickenson, remarked, "I was born 30 years too early. Can you imagine riding in a patrol car with *her*?"

Angie is one of those Hollywood beauties who has managed to carry glamour well into middle age—certainly to age 50, as the sexy detective on *Cassie & Company*. She started out on the right foot, getting into show business after unexpectedly winning a school beauty contest in the early 1950s. That led to an appearance on *The Jimmy Durante Show* (where he no doubt noticed those legs), a job in a commercial wearing a giant cigarette pack for a costume (legs, again), and small parts in a number of movies, beginning in 1954. She also appeared in quite a few dramatic shows of the mid and late 1950s, including *The Lineup, Meet McGraw,* and *Perry Mason.* However, it was not until her featured role as the sexy dance hall girl with a past in the John Wayne film *Rio Bravo* (1959) that

*Some sources give 1932.

she really began to attract attention.

More films and TV roles followed, including episodes of *Dr. Kildare, The Fugitive,* and *Alfred Hitchcock Presents* (where she tried to get James Mason to bump off her husband, with unexpected results). Finally, in the mid-1970s—in her midforties—she became a TV superstar via her hit series *Police Woman.*

Angie was married from 1965–80 to composer Burt Bacharach.

DIEHL, JOHN—actor

b: May 1, Cincinnati, Ohio

Miami Vice (police)
.... Det. Larry Zito (1984–)

DIENER, JOAN—actress

b: Feb 24, Cleveland, Ohio

Fifty-Fourth Street Revue (var)
.... regular (1949–50)

DIERKOP, CHARLES—actor

b: Sep 11, 1936, LaCrosse, Wis.

Police Woman (police)
.... Det. Pete Royster (1974–78)

DIETRICH, DENA—actress

b: Dec 4, Pittsburgh, Pa.

Adam's Rib (com) .... Gracie (1973)
Karen (com) .... Dena Madison (1975)
The Practice (com)
.... Molly Gibbons (1976–77)
The Ropers (com) .... Ethel (1979–80)

Dena Dietrich had been around since the 1950s, without making much of a splash, when a rather distinctive and long-running margarine commercial suddenly thrust her into the limelight. "It's not nice to fool Mother Nature!" she would exclaim, as lightning crashed.

Did that single commercial help her acting career? "Are you kidding—I'm here, aren't I?" she responded, referring to one of her series roles. "Every now and then a good commercial will thrust an actor into the public eye ... and that sure helps when the acting parts are being passed out."

Besides her television roles in the 1970s, she has done stage work and appeared in a number of films, none of them as memorable as those commercials.

DIFFRING, ANTON—actor
b: Oct 20, 1918, Koblenz, Germany

Assignment Vienna (drama)
.... Inspector Hoffman (1972–73)
The Winds of War (drama)
.... Foreign Minister Joachim von
.... Ribbentrop (1983)

DILLARD, MIMI—actress

Valentine's Day (com)..... Molly (1964–65)

DILLER, PHYLLIS—comedienne, actress
b: Jul 17, 1917, Lima, Ohio

The Pruitts of Southampton (com)
. Phyllis (Mrs. Poindexter) Pruitt (1966–67)
The Beautiful Phyllis Diller Show (var)
.... star (1968)
The Gong Show (com) ... panelist (1976–80)

Her ribald cackle and fright wig are by now virtually patented, but when Phyllis Diller first stepped on a stage in the mid-1950s, audiences were taken aback, to say the least. She certainly broke the show business mold. Nearly 40 and with five kids, she was a copywriter for a California radio station before her debut at San Francisco's Purple Onion in 1955. She quickly caught the public's fancy and became one of comedy's most outrageous stars during the 1960s. Most of her routines dealt with the frustrations of being a middle-aged housewife ("I bury a lot of my ironing in the backyard"), none too beautiful ("When I go to the beach wearing a bikini even the tide won't come in!"), and married to a husband she called "Fang."

Though she was a big hit on most of the major variety shows, two attempts to launch her own series were unsuccessful. She has since concentrated on guest appearances on such shows as *Love, American Style; The Love Boat;* and numerous specials, including those of her idol, Bob Hope.

DILLMAN, BRADFORD—actor
b: Apr 14, 1930, San Francisco, Calif.

Court-Martial (drama)
.... Capt. David Young (1966)
King's Crossing (drama)
.... Paul Hollister (1982)

Falcon Crest (drama)
.... Darryl Clayton (1982–83)

Emmy Award: Best Actor in a Daytime Drama Special, for the *ABC Afternoon Playbreak* production, "The Last Bride of Salem" (1975)

DILLON, BRENDON—actor

All in the Family (com)
.... Tommy Kelsey (1972–73)

DILLON, DENNY—actress

NBC's Saturday Night Live (com)
.... regular (1980–81)

DILWORTH, GORDON—singer

Spin the Picture (quiz).... regular (1949–50)
Country Style (var).......... regular (1950)
Starlit Time (var) .... regular (1950)

DIMITRI, RICHARD—actor

When Things Were Rotten (com)
.... Bertram/Renaldo (1975)
Seventh Avenue (drama)
.... Frank Topo (1977)

DINEHART, MASON ALAN, III—actor

The Life and Legend of Wyatt Earp (wes)
.... Bat Masterson (1955–57)

DING-A-LING SISTERS, THE—dancers

The Dean Martin Show (var)
.... regulars (1970–73)

Two of the members of this comedy quartet were drawn from Dean Martin's Golddiggers troupe, and two were new. They were (in 1972): Michelle Della Fave, 21; Tara Leigh, 21; Lynne Latham, 23; and Taffy Jones, 20.

DINSDALE, SHIRLEY—ventriloquist
b: Oct 31, 1926, San Francisco, Calif.

Judy Splinters (child) .... host (1949)

Emmy Award: Outstanding Personality (1948)

Shirley was the first performer to win an Emmy Award.

DISCO DOZEN, THE—

Donny and Marie (var) .. regulars (1978–79)

DISHY, BOB—actor
b: Brooklyn, N.Y.

That Was the Week That Was (com)
.... regular (1964–65)

DISNEY, WALT—producer, host
b: Dec 5, 1901, Chicago, Ill. d: Dec 15, 1966

Disneyland/Walt Disney Presents (misc)
.... host (1954–66)

Emmy Award: Best Producer of a Filmed Series, for *Disneyland* (1955)

The man who created Mickey Mouse, Donald Duck, and one of the largest entertainment empires in the world became a friendly and familiar face to home viewers as host of this pioneering series in the '50s and '60s. The series was historic in several ways; it significantly raised the standards of children's entertainment on television, it was the first major hit series on the struggling ABC network, and—most important —it marked the first significant involvement by a major Hollywood studio in the new medium of television. It thus opened the way for both the eventual movement to Hollywood of virtually all TV production and the massive changeover from live to filmed series.

Walt had previously produced TV Christmas specials in 1950 and 1951, and appeared in person on *The Ed Sullivan Show* in 1953, before launching *Disneyland*. In addition to hosting the series, he provided the voice for his most famous character, Mickey Mouse.

DIX, TOMMY—actor

School House (var) .... regular (1949)

DIXIE DOZEN DANCERS, THE—

The Nashville Palace (var)
.... regulars (1981–82)

DIXON, BOB—announcer

The Singing Lady (child).. announcer (1949)

DIXON, DONNA—actress
b: Jul 20, 1957, Alexandria, Va. r: Europe

Bosom Buddies (com)
.... Sonny Lumet (1980–82)
Berrengers (drama)... Allison Harris (1985)

DIXON, IVAN—black actor, director
b: Apr 6, 1931, New York City, N.Y.

Hogan's Heroes (com)
.... Corp. James Kinchloe (1965–70)

DIXON, MACINTYRE—actor

Comedy Tonight (var) .... regular (1970)

DIXON, PAUL—Ohio talk show host
b: Oct 27, 1918, Earling, Iowa d: 1975

The Paul Dixon Show (var) .. host (1951–52)
Midwestern Hayride (var) . emcee (1957–58)

DIZON, JESSE—actor
b: Jun 16, 1950, Oceanside, Calif.

Operation Petticoat (com)
.... Ramon Gallardo (1977–78)

DOBB, GILLIAN—actress

Magnum, P.I. (drama)
.... Agatha Chumley (1982–)

DOBSON, CHARLIE—singer

Melody, Harmony & Rhythm (music)
.... regular (1949–50)

DOBSON, KEVIN—actor
b: Mar 18, 1943, Jackson Heights, N.Y.

Kojak (police).. Lt. Bobby Crocker (1973–78)
Shannon (police)
.... Det. Jack Shannon (1981–82)
Knots Landing (drama)
... M. (Mack) Patrick MacKenzie (1982–)

DOBTCHEFF, VERNON—actor

Ike (drama).. Gen. Charles DeGaulle (1979)
Masada (drama) .... Chief Priest (1981)

DOBYNS, LLOYD—newscaster
b: Mar 12, 1936, Newport News, Va.

Weekend (pub aff) .... host (1974–79)
NBC News Overnight (news)
.... anchorman (1982)
Monitor (pub aff)..... anchorman (1983–84)

DODSON, JACK—actor

b: May 16, c. 1931, Pittsburgh, Pa.

The Andy Griffith Show (com)
.... Howard Sprague (1966–68)
Mayberry R.F.D. (com)
.... Howard Sprague (1968–71)
All's Fair (com)
.... Sen. Wayne Joplin (1976–77)
In the Beginning (com)
.... Msgr. Francis X. Barlow (1978)
Phyl & Mikhy (com)
.... Edgar "Truck" Morley (1980)

DODSON, RHONDA—actress

Hell Town (drama)..... Sister Daisy (1985)

DOERR-HUTCHINSON DANCERS—

The Jimmy Dean Show (var)
.... regulars (1964–65)

DOHERTY, SHANNEN—juvenile actress

b: Apr 12, 1971, Memphis, Tenn.

Little House on the Prairie (adv)
.... Jenny Wilder (1982–83)
Our House (drama)
.... Kris Witherspoon (1986–)

DOIG, BARRY—actor

Faraway Hill (drama) .... regular (1946)

DOLENZ, GEORGE—actor

b: Jan 5, 1908, Trieste, Italy d: Feb 8, 1963

The Count of Monte Cristo (drama)
.... Edmond Dantes (1955–56)

The father of Mickey Dolenz.

DOLENZ, MICKEY—actor

b: Mar 8, 1945, Los Angeles, Calif.

Circus Boy (adv).......... Corky (1956–58)
The Monkees (com) .... Micky (1966–68)

Any true child of the 1960s remembers The Monkees—and doesn't care *what* any egghead music critics say about them. Sure they were "manufactured," sure they turned out "pablum rock"; but they belonged to the kids of America.

Mickey Dolenz was one of the two young members of the group who had some prior acting experience (Davy Jones was the other; Peter Tork and Mike Nesmith were musicians). He had no musical experience, however. Mickey was the son of George Dolenz, a Hollywood restaurant owner and character actor of the 1940s and '50s who is best remembered for his linguini—and perhaps for his starring role in the obscure 1955 TV series *The Count of Monte Cristo.* Young Mickey had little prior exposure when, at age 11, he was cast as the orphan boy adopted by a circus in *Circus Boy.* He used the stage name Mickey Braddock at the time. *Circus Boy* ran for two years (and in reruns for many more) and it opened the way for guest roles on other shows, including *Playhouse 90, Zane Grey Theater, Mr. Novak,* and *Peyton Place.* Mickey also made sure he continued his education. Though he wanted to be an actor, he knew how fickle show business could be; "If you're smart you don't put all your eggs in one basket," he was quoted as saying.

However, his career was not quite over. In the fall of 1965 he and about 500 other young hopefuls attended a mass audition for a new TV series intended to ape the success of the Beatles' first film, *A Hard Day's Night.* Mickey was picked and for the next few years rode a roller coaster of sensational success on TV and on records. Since he was supposed to be a musician, the producers gave him a crash course as a drummer, and he also (with the others) sang vocals.

The Monkees broke up almost as soon as the series left the air. In the mid-1970s Dolenz and Jones, along with Tommy Boyce and Bobby Hart (who had written many of the Monkees' songs), attempted to reform the group, but without much success. Mickey had occasional guest roles on prime time series in the early '70s and did voices for Hanna-Barbera cartoons on Saturday morning throughout most of the decade (*Funky Phantom, Skatebirds,* etc.). He also auditioned for, but did not get, the role of Fonzie on *Happy Days.* Then he faded from sight, until a highly publicized Monkees revival tour in 1986.

DOLLAR, LYNN—hostess

b: c. 1930 r: North Dakota

The $64,000 Question (quiz)
.... assistant (1955–58)

DONAHUE, ELINOR—actress

b: Apr 19, 1937, Tacoma, Wash.

Father Knows Best (com)
.... Betty (Princess) Anderson (1954–60)
The Andy Griffith Show (com)
.... Ellie Walker (1960–61)
Many Happy Returns (com)
.... Joan Randall (1964–65)
The Odd Couple (com)
.... Miriam Welby (1972–74)
Mulligan's Stew (drama)
.... Jane Mulligan (1977)
Please Stand By (com)
.... Carol Lambert (1978–79)

Of the three children in Robert Young's idealized *Father Knows Best* TV family of the 1950s, Elinor Donahue seems to have had the most successful subsequent career. (For what happened to the others, see the entries for Lauren Chapin and Billy Gray.) Elinor was a show business veteran before she got the role. Her mother had pushed her into tap dancing lessons at 16 months, she began singing on the radio at two, and she had her first movie role at age five—in *Mr. Big,* starring Donald O'Connor. Elinor then appeared as a juvenile in several more films of the 1940s and on television in the early '50s. Among her TV appearances was a role in the 1952 *Schlitz Playhouse* production, "I Want to Be a Star."

Father Knows Best made her one of America's most familiar teens, though she was never a "teenage idol," perhaps because she was already too grown-up looking. She continued to appear on TV in the 1960s and '70s, in guest roles on series ranging from *Star Trek* to *The Flying Nun.* She also had regular parts, including that of Andy Griffith's original girlfriend on *The Andy Griffith Show,* Tony Randall's girlfriend on *The Odd Couple,* and John McGyver's daughter on *Many Happy Returns.*

In later years, Elinor dutifully showed up for the *Father Knows Best* reunion shows and continued to accept roles on *Police Story, The Love Boat,* and other series. For a time in 1984–85 she played a rather evil nurse on the daytime soap *Days of Our Lives.* It was quite a departure from her usual sunny image. "If I start getting hate mail I'm not sure what I'll do," she said. Maybe ask dad for advice?

DONAHUE, PATRICIA—actress

The Thin Man (drama) .... Hazel (1958–59)
Michael Shayne (drama)
.... Lucy Hamilton (1960–61)

DONAHUE, PHIL—host

b: Dec 21, 1935, Cleveland, Ohio

The Last Word (news).... regular (1982–83)

Emmy Awards: Best Host of a Talk Show, for *Donahue* (1977, 1978, 1979, 1980, 1982, 1983, 1985, 1986)

Although Phil Donahue has had infrequent exposure in prime time, he is a fixture in daytime television with his long-running and extremely popular talk show, *Donahue.* His style is distinctive: one topic per show—usually something relevant or outrageous, like disabled children or lesbian nuns. White-haired and earnest, he prowls his audience, pulling opinions from the onlookers and frequently interjecting his own.

Phil began as an announcer at local station KYW in Cleveland the day after he graduated from college in 1957. (He had worked on radio during the summers before that.) He later moved on to a TV/radio news career, in which he remained until the mid-1960s. The talk show that would make him famous premiered on a TV station in Dayton on November 6, 1967. It was soon fed to a few other stations in the area, then went into national syndication in 1969. It was not a hit at first, but by the mid-1970s it was dominating its time period (usually in the morning) wherever it ran. Phil was by then being courted by the networks. He contributed segments to *The Today Show* for a time beginning in 1979 and to ABC's late-night series *The Last Word* in 1982–83. Daytime, however, has remained his home base.

Phil's best-selling autobiography is titled *Donahue: My Own Story* (1980). He is married to actress Marlo Thomas.

DONAHUE, TROY—actor

b: Jan 27, 1936*, New York City, N.Y.

Surfside Six (drama)
.... Sandy Winfield II (1960–62)

*Some sources give 1937.

Hawaiian Eye (drama)
.... Philip Barton (1962–63)

This blonde, wavy-haired hunk was the heartthrob of a million girls in the 1960s, but he seems to have been reduced to minor roles since then. He did a good deal of guest work around the time of his two series, including *Wagon Train, 77 Sunset Strip,* and *Colt 45.* In more recent years you've really had to watch for him. He spent a few months on *The Secret Storm* in 1970, washed up on *Fantasy Island* in 1978 and 1981, and was spotted living by the beach as a "mysterious recluse" in the 1983 TV movie *Malibu.*

DONALD, PETER—host, panelist, producer
b: 1918, Bristol, England d: Apr 20, 1979

Prize Performance (var)..... panelist (1950)
Can You Top This? (com)
.... panelist (1950–51)
Ad Libbers (var) .... host (1951)
Masquerade Party (quiz)
.... panelist (1952–53)
Where Was I? (quiz) .... panelist (1952–53)
Pantomime Quiz (quiz) ... regular (1953–55)
Masquerade Party (quiz)... emcee (1954–56)
Pantomime Quiz (quiz) ...... regular (1957)

DONALDSON, SAM—newscaster
b: Mar 11, 1934, El Paso, Texas

ABC Weekend News (news)
.... anchorman (1979—)

DONAT, PETER—actor
b: Jan 20, 1928, Kentville, Nova Scotia, Canada

Rich Man, Poor Man—Book II (drama)
.... Arthur Raymond (1976–77)
Flamingo Road (drama)
.... Elmo Tyson (1981–82)

DONELLY, CAROL—actress

The Steve Allen Comedy Hour (var)
.... regular (1980–81)

DONHOWE, GWYDA—actress
b: Oct 20, Oak Park, Ill.

Executive Suite (drama)
.... Astrid Rutledge (1976–77)

DONLEVY, BRIAN—actor
b: Feb 9, 1899, Portadown County, Armagh, Ireland r: Wisconsin d: Apr 5, 1972

Dangerous Assignment (drama)
.... Steve Mitchell (1952)

DONNELL, JEFF—actress
b: Jul 10, 1921, South Windham, Me.

The George Gobel Show (var)
.... Alice (1954–58)
Matt Helm (drama)........ Ethel (1975–76)

DONNELLY, TIM—actor

Emergency (drama)
.... fireman Chet Kelly (1973–77)

DONNER, ROBERT—actor
b: Apr 27, New York City, N.Y.

The Waltons (drama)
.... Yancy Tucker (1972–79)
Mork & Mindy (com) ..... Exidor (1978–82)

Donner's most striking role was no doubt that of the flaky prophet Exidor on *Mork & Mindy,* but he is a versatile actor who has had roles in about three dozen movies (including *Cool Hand Luke, Damnation Alley, Chisum,* etc.) and many TV series. He estimates that he has appeared on approximately 150 series altogether.

Donner did not originally intend to go into show business, but he became friendly with a young actor who had an apartment in his building. "He kept telling me I was a funny guy and had a good face. He thought I could make a good living as an actor. He got a television series and kept after me to study with his coach, and my first acting job was a direct result of his help and advice. His name, by the way," says Donner, "is Clint Eastwood."

DONOVAN, KING—actor
b: c. 1919

Bob Cummings Show (com)
.... Harvey Helm (1955–58)
Please Don't Eat the Daisies (com)
.... Herb Thornton (1966–67)

DOODLES AND SPICER—pantomime team

Party Time at Club Roma (var)
.... regular (1950–51)

DOODLETOWN PIPERS, THE—singers

Our Place (var) . . . . regulars (1967)

DOOHAN, JAMES—actor
b: Mar 3, 1920, Vancouver, B.C., Canada

Star Trek (sci fi)
. . . . engineer Montgomery Scott
. . . . (Scotty) (1966–69)

When William Shatner barked "Beam us up, Scotty" on *Star Trek,* he was talking to the trusted chief engineer of the Starship Enterprise. It is a character trivia buffs of the '60s love to remember. It is one Canadian actor James Doohan likes, too; but for this role, he would probably have remained in obscurity for his entire career.

Doohan was a military pilot during World War II and a rather rambunctious one at that; he was known as the "bad boy" of his unit due to his penchant for flying a slalom course though the telephone poles. He worked as a radio actor for a time, then came to the U.S. in 1946. He found work in the theater, on television, and in movies, but it was in small, often unbilled, roles. You can see him in the background in the mid-1960s films *The Wheeler Dealers* and *The Satan Bug* and in the TV movie *Scalplock,* the pilot for the *Iron Horse* series.

Star Trek beamed him up to a role he could be identified with, and he has been a dependable player in revivals of the series ever since—the Saturday morning cartoon version from 1973–75 and the various movie versions beginning in 1979. In addition, he got to command his own team of space heroes on the Saturday morning live action series *Jason of Star Command* from 1978–79.

DOOLEY, PAUL—actor
b: Feb 22, 1928, Parkersburg, W. Va.

The Dom DeLuise Show (var)
. . . . regular (1968)

DOONICAN, VAL—British pop singer
b: 1932, Ireland

The Val Doonican Show (var) . . . host (1971)

DOQUI, ROBERT—black actor

Felony Squad (police)
. . . . Det. Cliff Sims (1968–69)

DORAN, ANN—actress
b: Jul 28, 1911*, Amarillo, Texas

National Velvet (adv)
. . . . Martha Brown (1960–62)
The Legend of Jesse James (wes)
. . . . Mrs. James (1965–66)
Longstreet (drama)
. . . . Mrs. Kingston (1971–72)
Shirley (com)
. . . . Charlotte McHenry (1979–80)

DORAN, JOHNNY—juvenile actor

Salty (adv) . . . . Tim Reed (1974–75)
Mulligan's Stew (drama)
. . . . Mark Mulligan (1977)

DORAN, NANCY AND DICK FRANCE—dancers

The Little Revue (music). dancers (1949–50)

DOREMUS, DAVID—actor

Nanny and the Professor (com)
. . . . Hal Everett (1970–71)

DORIN, PHOEBE—actress

The Montefuscos (com)
. . . . Theresa Montefusco (1975)

DORN, MICHAEL—actor

CHiPs (police) . . . . Off. Turner (1980–82)

DORSEY, JIMMY—orchestra leader
b: Feb 29, 1904, Shenandoah, Pa. d: Jun 12, 1957

Stage Show (var) . . . . cohost (1954–56)

DORSEY, TOMMY—orchestra leader
b: Nov 19, 1905, Mahanoy Plane, Pa. d: Nov 26, 1956

Stage Show (var) . . . . cohost (1954–56)

Fractious brothers Tommy and Jimmy Dorsey were two of the most famous bandleaders of the big band era, each responsible for many classic recordings that are still heard today. After years of alternately fighting and working together (notably on the 1947 movie biography *The Fabulous Dorseys*), they joined forces in a single orchestra in 1953. The following year, big band enthusiast Jackie Gleason got them

*Some sources give 1913 or 1914.

their own prime time variety show. *Stage Show* first ran as a summer show in 1954, then as a series of specials in 1954–55, then as a regular series in 1955–56. Gleason himself booked the show, and it was he who was responsible for agreeing to let an unknown young rockabilly singer make his national TV debut there in January 1956—Elvis Presley.

A few days after Tommy's tragic death in November 1956 (he choked to death in his sleep), Gleason presented a TV tribute to the great bandleader—even as Elvis and his fellow rockers were rapidly relegating his kind of music to the misty past.

D'ORSO, WISA—dancer
b: Lihue, Kauai, Hawaii

The Dean Martin Summer Show (var)
. . . . regular (1966)
The Jonathan Winters Show (var)
. . . . dancers (1968–69)
Happy Days (var) . . . . dancers (1970)

DOTRICE, ROY—actor
b: May 26, 1923, Guernsey, Channel Islands, England

The Wizard (adv)
. . . . Troyan (recurring) (1986–)

DOTSON, BOB—newscaster
b: Oct 3, 1946, St. Louis, Mo.

Prime Time Sunday (pub aff)
. . . . correspondent (1979–80)

DOUBLE DATERS, THE—singers
And Here's the Show (var)
. . . . regular (1955)

DOUCETTE, JEFF—actor
Newhart (com) . . . . Harley Estin (1984–)
E/R (com)
. . . . Bert, the paramedic (1984–85)

DOUCETTE, JOHN—actor
b: Jan 21, 1921, Brockton, Mass.

Big Town (drama)
. . . . Lt. Tom Greggory (1954–55)
Lock Up (drama) . . . . . Jim Weston (1959–61)
The Partners (com)
. . . . Capt. Andrews (1971–72)

DOUGLAS, DIANA—actress
b: Jan 22, 1923, Devonshire, Bermuda

Photocrime (drama) . . . . regular (1949)
The Cowboys (wes)
. . . . Mrs. Annie Andersen (1974)

DOUGLAS, DONNA—actress
b: 1933, Baywood, La.

The Beverly Hillbillies (com)
. . . . Elly May Clampett (1962–71)

DOUGLAS, JACK—producer, host
Bold Journey (doc) . . . . host (1957–59)

DOUGLAS, JACK D.—British comedian
b: 1927

Kraft Music Hall Presents The Des O'Connor Show (var) . . . . regular (1970–71)

DOUGLAS, JAMES—actor
b: 1933, Los Angeles, Calif.

Peyton Place (drama)
. . . . Steven Cord (1964–69)

James Douglas worked primarily in daytime soap operas in the '70s and '80s, including seven years as Grant Colman on *As the World Turns* (1974–81).

DOUGLAS, MELVYN—actor
b: Apr 5, 1901, Macon, Ga. d: Aug 4, 1981

Steve Randall (drama)
. . . . Steve Randall (1952–53)
Blind Date (aud par) . . . . emcee (1953)
Frontier Justice (wes) . . . . host (1959)

Emmy Award: Best Actor in a Single Performance in a Drama, for the *CBS Playhouse* production, "Do Not Go Gentle into That Good Night" (1968)

This famous actor had a 60-year career in film and theater, winning two Oscars and a Tony along the way. He was also quite active on television, especially on playhouse series such as *Ford Theatre* and *Playhouse 90*.

DOUGLAS, MICHAEL—actor, producer
b: Sep 25, 1944*, New Brunswick, N.J.

*Some sources give 1945.

The Streets of San Francisco (police)
.... Inspector Steve Keller (1972–76)

The son of film star Kirk Douglas. In addition to having a busy acting career in movies and on television, he has become an important Hollywood producer, responsible for the Oscar-winning *One Flew Over the Cuckoo's Nest, The China Syndrome,* and other films. He maintains a sense of humor about his considerable success, however. As guest host of *NBC's, Saturday Night Live* in 1984 he impersonated his famous father in a mock "bloopers" segment, "accidently" plugged his latest film *(Romancing the Stone)* at every turn, and threw movie critic Gary Kroeger off the set when Kroeger blasted the film and called its star a wimp.

DOUGLAS, MIKE—host, singer
b: Aug 11, 1925, Chicago, Ill.

Kay Kyser's Kollege of Musical Knowledge (quiz).................. vocalist (1949–50)
The Music Show (music).. regular (1953–54)

Emmy Award: Outstanding Daytime Performance, for *The Mike Douglas Show* (1967)

For some reason, the Midwest seems to have been the breeding ground for most of America's top talk-show hosts—Johnny Carson, Dick Cavett, and Phil Donahue to name a few. Mike Douglas, who is most famous for his syndicated daytime chatter show, got his start there as well.

Mike began his career as a singer, and a very successful one at that. In 1945, after wartime service with the navy, he turned down a Hollywood contract to join the Kay Kyser band as its "boy singer." He appeared with the band on radio, television, and on some of its biggest-selling records, often as part of an ensemble billed as "Michael Douglas and the Campus Kids." In 1950 he dubbed the singing voice of Prince Charming in the Disney film *Cinderella.*

When Kyser abruptly quit show business in 1950, Mike was suddenly on his own. He hosted a local Chicago variety show called *Hi Ladies* from 1953–55 and became a regular singer on several Chicago-originated network shows, including the nighttime *Music Show* and the daytime *Club 60* (1957–58). Then, in 1961, he moved to Cleveland to begin his own local talk show. Two years later it was syndicated nationally and became a popular daytime entry in many markets. It was the first daytime talk show to win an Emmy, but in later years it was overshadowed by more distinctive shows such as *Donahue.* In 1980 the production company dropped Mike in favor of a younger host, John Davidson. Mike continued to produce the show himself for another two years, but it finally ceased production in 1982.

DOUGLAS, PAUL—actor
b: Apr 11, 1907, Philadelphia, Pa. d: Sep 11, 1959

Adventure Theater (adv)........ host (1956)

DOUGLAS, RONALDA—actress, singer
b: Oct 12, Opelousas, La.

The New Odd Couple (com)
.... Gwendolyn Pigeon (1982–83)

DOUGLAS, SARAH—actress
b: Dec 12, 1952, Stratford-on-Avon, England

Falcon Crest (drama)
.... Pamela Lynch (1983–85)
V: The Final Battle (miniseries) (sci fi)
.... Pamela (1984)

DOUGLASS, ROBYN—actress
b: Jun 21, 1953, Sendai, Japan

Battlestar Galactica (sci fi)
.... Jamie Hamilton (1980)

DOURIF, BRAD—actor
b: Mar 18, 1950, Huntington, W. Va.

Studs Lonigan (drama)
.... Danny O'Neill (1979)

DOVA, BEN—
Music on Ice (var).......... regular (1960)

Could this name be a pun?

DOW, HAROLD—black newscaster
b: Hackensack, N.J.

CBS News Nightwatch (news)
.... anchorman (1982–84)

DOW, TONY—actor
b: Apr 13, 1945, Hollywood, Calif.

Leave It to Beaver (com)
.... Wally Cleaver (1957–63)

Tony Dow, the good-looking if somewhat bland teenager on *Leave It to Beaver,* came to his famous role with almost no prior experience. He was, however, a star athlete—a Junior Olympics Diving Champion—and he became a favorite among kids as Beaver's understanding older brother.

After the classic series left the air, Tony continued his acting career, with mixed results. He had guest shots on *The Eleventh Hour* and *Dr. Kildare* and a recurring part as a student (George Scheros) on *Mr. Novak.* From 1965–66 he starred in *Never Too Young,* ABC's unsuccessful attempt to launch a youth-oriented daytime soap opera. He was quoted in the mid-1960s as saying he had been urged to become a teenage singing idol. "I tell them I can't sing, but they say that doesn't matter. I wouldn't do anything like that, though. If you can sing, fine. I can't. And I'd feel wrong being screamed over just for doing nothing."

Tony eventually finished his education and entered the construction business, but show business remained closest to his heart. In the 1970s he made personal appearances with *Beaver* costar Jerry Mathers—in a kind of living nostalgia show—and he had small roles in occasional TV movies. Then, in the early 1980s, there was something of a *Leave It to Beaver* boom, bringing Tony work in the TV reunion movie *Still The Beaver* and a spin-off series that ran on cable television.

DOWDELL, ROBERT—actor

Stoney Burke (wes)
.... Cody Bristol (1962–63)
Voyage to the Bottom of the Sea (sci fi)
.... Lt. Cmdr. Chip Morton (1964–68)

DOWLING, DORIS—actress
b: 1921

My Living Doll (com)
.... Irene Adams (1964–65)

DOWLING, EDDIE—actor, producer, composer
b: Dec 11, 1894*, Woonsocket, R.I. d: Feb 18, 1976

Anywhere, U.S.A. (doc)... the doctor (1952)

DOWN, LESLEY-ANNE—actress
b: Mar 17, 1954, London, England

North and South (drama)
.... Madeline Fabray (1985)

A leading lady of the '80s, in show business since her youth (she was once voted Great Britain's "Most Beautiful Teenager"). American viewers came to know her from her role as Lady Georgina in "Upstairs, Downstairs" on PBS's *Masterpiece Theatre* in the early '70s; she has since appeared mostly in TV movies and big, flashy miniseries such as *The Last Days of Pompeii* and *North and South.* One critic, noting her rather cool, aloof beauty, predicted she would become the Joan Collins of the 1990s.

DOWNES, ANSON—actor

Man from Atlantis (adv)... Allen (1977–78)

DOWNEY, MORTON—singer
b: Nov 14, 1901, Wallingford, Conn. d: Oct 25, 1985

Mohawk Showroom (music)..... host (1949)
Star of the Family (var)...... host (1950–51)

DOWNEY, ROBERT—comedian
b: Apr 4, 1965, New York City, N.Y.

NBC's Saturday Night Live (var)
.... regular (1985–86)

DOWNING, DAVID—black actor
b: Jul 21, 1943, New York City, N.Y.

Backstairs at the White House (drama)
.... Dixon (1979)

DOWNING, WILFRID—actor

The Buccaneers (adv)
.... Crewman Dickon (1956–57)

DOWNS, HUGH—announcer, host
b: Feb 14, 1921, Akron, Ohio

*Some sources give 1895.

257

Caesar's Hour (var) ... announcer (1956–57)
The Jack Paar Show (talk)
.... announcer (1957–62)
Concentration (quiz).......... emcee (1961)
The Tonight Show (talk) .. announcer (1962)
20/20 (mag)................. host (1978–)

Emmy Award: Best Host of a Talk Show,
for *Over Easy* (1981)

Friendly, low-keyed Hugh Downs has
been a television standby in various roles
since the early days of the medium. While
he is not the sort to galvanize viewers, he
has a considerable talent for making them
comfortable, even while slipping them useful information.

Downs began his career on radio in the
early 1940s and after World War II service
joined NBC in Chicago as a staff announcer. Among other things he was the
announcer on the Chicago-originated children's show *Kukla, Fran & Ollie*. In 1954,
NBC brought him to New York to become
announcer and sidekick to hostess Arlene
Francis on its new daytime service show
Home (envisioned as the daytime counterpart to the *Today* show and *The Tonight
Show.*) He was soon one of the network's
busiest host/announcers—for Sid Caesar,
for Jack Paar, and as host of his own rather
intelligent daytime quiz program, *Concentration* (from 1958–65, including a prime
time run in 1961).

In 1962, while still helming *Concentration,* he became host of the early morning
Today show. His unhurried style was perfect for that blurry-eyed time of the morning, and he stayed with the show for nine
years. NBC also had him narrate a number
of important nature documentaries during
1969–71.

Downs left *Today* in 1971 "to move on to
other things" (and maybe to sleep late for
a change). He was host or cohost of some
public service shows, including PBS's *Over
Easy* (for the aging), but generally he
seemed to be easing himself out of the
limelight. In 1978 ABC, desperately looking
for a quick replacement for the hosts of its
new newsmagazine *20/20*, which had had
a disastrous premiere, rushed him back
into nighttime TV. He was just what the
show needed—fatherly, intelligent, and a
calm counterweight to such "hotshot" reporters as Geraldo Rivera.

Downs is a man of many interests and
has authored six books, including *Thirty
Dirty Lies About Old,* which debunks
myths about aging; *Rings Around Tomorrow,* a collection of science articles; and *A
Shoal of Stars,* an account of his true-life
voyage across the Pacific in a 65-foot
ketch. His autobiographies are titled *Yours
Truly, Hugh Downs,* and *On Camera: My
Ten Thousand Hours on Television (1986).*

DOWNS, JOHNNY—actor
b: Oct 10, 1913, Brooklyn, N.Y.

Captain Billy's Mississippi Music Hall (var)
.... regular (1948)
Girl About Town (music) .... cohost (1948)
Manhattan Showcase (var)...... host (1949)

DOXEE, DIANE—singer

Diane Doxee Show (music)
.... featured vocalist (1950)

DOYLE, DAVID—actor
b: Dec 1, 1925, Omaha, Neb.

Bridget Loves Bernie (com)
.... Walt Fitzgerald (1972–73)
The New Dick Van Dyke Show (com)
.... Ted Atwater (1972–73)
Charlie's Angels (drama)
.... John Bosley (1976–81)
The Blue and the Gray (drama)
.... Phineas Wade (1982)

David Doyle, the avuncular helper and
go-between to the unseen boss on
Charlie's Angels, was an actor with much
experience when he landed his most famous role. He originally trained to be a
lawyer, and, though he passed his bar
exams detoured into acting instead. He
spent the 1950s and '60s on the Broadway
stage and also had parts in a few films.
David did not begin to concentrate on television until the '70s, but he soon landed
recurring roles on several series and guest
appearances on many others. He was
Meredith Baxter-Birney's wealthy father
on *Bridget Loves Bernie* and Dick Van
Dyke's boss on *The New Dick Van Dyke
Show;* other credits include multiple episodes of *Ozzie's Girls, Police Story,* and
Fantasy Island. In 1977 he surprised
viewers by playing a rather serious role
opposite Jessica Walter in the TV movie

Black Market Baby, but he subsequently returned to lighter fare.

DOYLE, LEN—actor
b: c. 1893 d: Dec 6, 1959

Mr. District Attorney (police)
.... Harrington (1951–52)

DOYLE, ROBERT—actor

Lanigan's Rabbi (police) . Lt. Osgood (1977)

DOYLE-MURRAY, BRIAN—comedian, writer

NBC's Saturday Night Live (com)
.... regular (1981–82)

DRAGON, DARYL—musician (keyboards)
b: Aug 27, 1942, Pasadena, Calif.

The Captain and Tennille (music)
.... cohost (1976–77)

The silent "Captain" of the Captain and Tennille, and also Toni Tennille's husband. Daryl spent seven years as an arranger for the Beach Boys before he and Toni formed an independent act of their own, which became very popular in the mid-1970s. Daryl is the son of famed classical composer/conductor Carmen Dragon.

DRAKE, CHARLES—actor
b: Oct 2, 1914, Bayside, New York City r: New London, Conn.

Robert Montgomery Presents (summer) (drama)......... repertory player (1955–56)

DRAKE, CHRISTIAN—actor

Sheena, Queen of the Jungle (adv)
.... Bob (1955–56)

DRAKE, GABE—country musician (bass)

Saturday Night Jamboree (music)
.... regular (1948–49)

DRAKE, GABRIELLE—actress

UFO (sci fi)........... Lt. Gay Ellis (1970)

DRAKE, GALEN—host

The Galen Drake Show (child) .. host (1957)

DRAKE, GEORGIA—

Polka-Go-Round (music) .. regular (1958–59)

DRAKE-HOOKS, BEBE—actress

The Sanford Arms (com)..... Jeannie (1977)

DREES, JACK—sportscaster

Wednesday Night Fights (sport)
.... sportscaster (1954–60)
The Jack Drees Sports Show (sports)
.... reporter (1956)
Saturday Sports Mirror (sport)
.... sportscaster (1956)

DREIER, ALEX—newscaster, actor
b: Jun 26, 1916, Honolulu, Hawaii

What's It All About, World? (var)
.... regular (1969)

DREW, PAULA—actress

Front Page Detective (drama)
.... the girlfriend (1951–53)

DREW, WENDY—actress

School House (var)......... regular (1949)
Jimmy Hughes, Rookie Cop (police)
.... Betty Hughes (1953)

DREYFUSS, RANDY—actor

It Takes Two (com) ...... Decker (1982–83)

DREYFUSS, RICHARD—actor
b: Oct 19, 1947*, Brooklyn, N.Y.

Karen (com) ..... David Rowe III (1964–65)

DRIER, MOOSIE—juvenile actor
b: Aug 6, 1964, Chicago, Ill.

Rowan & Martin's Laugh-In (var)
.... regular (1971–73)

DRISCOLL, PATRICIA—actress
b: c. 1930, Cork, Ireland

Adventures of Robin Hood (adv)
.... Maid Marian (1957–58)

DRIVAS, ROBERT—actor
b: Nov 21, 1938, Chicago, Ill. d: Jun 29, 1986

*Some sources give 1948 or 1949.

Our Private World (drama)
.... Brad Robinson (1965)

DRU, JOANNE—actress
b: Jan 31, 1923, Logan, W. Va.

Guestward Ho! (com)
.... Babs Hooten (1960–61)

This film star of the 1940s and '50s is the sister of TV game-show host Peter Marshall. She was married to actors Dick Haymes in the '40s and John Ireland in the '50s. She did a good deal of television "theater" work in the 1950s but has been seen much less often since then.

DRUMMOND, ALICE—actress
Park Place (com)..... Frances Heine (1981)

DRURY, JAMES—actor
b: Apr 18, 1934, New York City, N.Y.

The Virginian (wes)
.... The Virginian (1962–71)
Firehouse (adv)
.... Capt. Spike Ryerson (1974)

James Drury was the embodiment of Owen Wister's famous western hero, the Virginian, on television in the '60s. Tall and taciturn, he was a tower of quiet, masculine strength. Interestingly, the actor had played the same role quite differently in an earlier pilot for the series—as a western dandy with shiny hunting boots, skin-tight pants, lace cuffs, and tiny pistols. Fortunately, this version didn't sell (it was telecast once as part of the summer 1958 *Decision* anthology series). When the Virginian returned to the screen four years later he was a *real* man, pardner.

Drury, the son of a New York University professor, grew up under western skies on the family ranch in Oregon. He did some theater work as a juvenile and in the early '50s made his way to Hollywood. His big break came in 1954 when he signed a contract with MGM, and he subsequently had supporting roles in a dozen or so features, several of them "teen" appeal films such as *Bernadine* (with Pat Boone), *Love Me Tender* (with Elvis Presley), and *Polyanna* (with Hayley Mills). On television his roles were usually in westerns—*Gunsmoke*, *The Rebel*, *The Rifleman*, etc.

After the long run of *The Virginian* and

the short one of his follow-up series, *Firehouse*, Drury virtually dropped from sight.

DRYER, FRED—actor
b: Jul 6, 1946, Hawthorne, Calif.

Hunter (police)
.... Det. Sgt. Rick Hunter (1984–)

Rick Hunter, television's version of Dirty Harry, may be somewhat less violent than his big screen counterpart, but the actor who plays him—a 6'6" 220-pound former football pro—is certainly formidable. Fred Dryer joined the New York Giants in 1969 and was traded to the Los Angeles Rams in 1971, where he compiled an impressive record in ten years of play. In 1981, however, the Rams announced they were dropping him from the roster. Dryer turned briefly to sports commentary for CBS, and then to acting, studying under famed acting coach Nina Foch. A natural actor with a rather forceful personality, he quickly landed roles in a number of series episodes and TV movies *(The Kid from Nowhere, The Fantastic World of D.C. Collins)*. By 1984 he had his first starring role as the maverick cop *Hunter*.

DRYSDALE, DON—sportscaster
b: Jul 23, 1936, Van Nuys, Calif.

Monday Night Baseball (sport)
.... sportscaster (1978–85)

Don Drysdale was a true baseball superstar before he turned to sportscasting. During 14 years as a pitcher with the Brooklyn and Los Angeles Dodgers, he set several league records. He compiled a 209–169 record of wins, participated in five World Series, and was named to nine National League All-Star Teams. He also won the Cy Young award as outstanding pitcher in 1962, but the peak of his baseball career came in 1984, long after his playing days were over, when he was named to the Baseball Hall of Fame.

Don was forced to retire in 1969, due to injury. He immediately turned to sportscasting, first in Canada and later as the voice of the California Angels and the Chicago White Socks. ABC made him its Monday Night Baseball expert commentator in 1978.

DUBARRY, DENISE—actress

Baa Baa Black Sheep (drama)
.... Nurse Samantha Green (1978)

DU BIEF, JACQUELINE—professional skater
b: France

Music on Ice (var).......... regular (1960)

The winner of the World Figure Skating Championship in 1952; she later turned professional and toured with the Ice Capades and other shows.

DUBIN, GARY—actor

Bracken's World (drama)
.... Mark Grant (1970)

DUBOIS, JA'NET—black actress
b: Aug 5, 1938*, Philadelphia, Pa. r: Brooklyn, N.Y.

Good Times (com)
.... Willona Woods (1974–79)

DUBOIS, MARTA—actress
b: Dec 15, David, Panama

Tales of the Gold Monkey (adv)
.... Princess Koji (1982–83)

DUCOMMUN, RICK—comedian

Thicke of the Night (talk)
.... recurring player (1983–84)
The Last Precinct (com)
.... Off. William "Raid" Raider (1986)

DUDDY, LYNN—choral director
b: New York City, N.Y.

Frankie Laine Time (var) .... singers (1955)

DUDIKOFF, MICHAEL—actor
b: Oct 8, Redondo Beach, Calif.

Star of the Family (com)
.... Douggie Krebs (1982)

DUDLEY, BERNARD—host
b: c. 1878 d: Oct 1964

Sportsman's Quiz (sport).. regular (1948–49)

*Some sources give 1944.

DUDLEY, DICK—announcer, host
b: Apr 22, 1915 r: Tennessee

Village Barn (var)........ emcee (1948–49)

DUEL, PETER—
See Deuel, Peter

DUELL, WILLIAM—actor

Police Squad (com)
.... Johnny the Snitch (1982)

DUFF, HOWARD—actor
b: Nov 24, 1917, Bremerton, Wash.

Mr. Adams and Eve (com)
.... Howard Adams (1957–58)
Dante (adv)........ Willie Dante (1960–61)
Felony Squad (police)
.... Det. Sgt. Sam Stone (1966–69)
East of Eden (drama).. Mr. Edwards (1981)
Flamingo Road (drama)
.... Sheriff Titus Semple (1981–82)
Knots Landing (drama)
.... Paul Galveston (1984–85)

Howard Duff is an actor who first achieved fame as a result of his voice. He became infatuated with acting while in high school in Seattle and after graduation in 1934 financed his drama studies by working at a local radio station. Within a few years he was playing the lead in a children's serial called *Phantom Pilot*.

Following service in World War II (as a correspondent for Armed Forces Radio), he returned to radio acting and landed the role that ignited his career, that of Dashiell Hammett's hard-boiled detective Sam Spade. The series was a major hit, and Duff's tough, cynical voice attracted widespread attention in Hollywood—from producers (who gave him his first film contract) and from actress Ida Lupino, who later became his wife. ("I fell in love with his voice on the radio before I even met him," she said later.) Duff played Sam Spade from 1946–49; meanwhile, he began a successful movie career as costar of the 1947 prison film *Brute Force*.

While turning out many films—generally supporting roles in major features and leads in B films—Duff became quite active on television. He appeared in many of the dramatic anthologies of the 1950s, among them *Ford Theatre, Rheingold Theatre* and *Science Fiction Theater.* He costarred with his wife Ida Lupino (they were married in '51) in the comedy *Mr. Adams and Eve,* which was supposedly based on their real life in Hollywood; she also directed the pilot for his next series, *Dante.*

During the '60s and '70s Duff was seen frequently as the veteran cop on *Felony Squad* and in guest roles on many other series, particularly crime shows (e.g., *Police Story*). On one of the last *Batman* episodes he got to ham it up as the helper of a loony alchemist (Lupino). The two of them turned Batman and Robin into cardboard slabs, freed all of Gotham's criminals and made them invisible!

In recent years Duff has favored TV movies and miniseries, as well as roles as ruthless wheeler-dealers on prime time soap operas *(Flamingo Road, Knots Landing).* His goal, he says, has always been to play the most evil villain of all, Shakespeare's Richard III. However, in 1981, upon receiving a large check from NBC, he was quoted as saying, "I am happy to settle for Sheriff Semple."

DUFFY, JACK—actor, sketch comedian

The Kraft Music Hall (var)
.... regular (1961–63)
The Bobby Vinton Show (var)
.... regular (1975–76)

DUFFY, JULIA—actress
b: Jun 27, 1950, Minneapolis, Minn.

The Blue and the Gray (drama)
.... Mary Hale (1982)
Wizards and Warriors (adv)
.... Princess Ariel (1983)
Newhart (com)
.... Stephanie Vanderkellen (1983–)

DUFFY, PATRICK—actor
b: Mar 17, 1949, Townsend, Mont.

Man from Atlantis (adv)
.... Mark Harris (1977–78)
Dallas (drama)...... Bobby Ewing (1978–)

Patrick Duffy, the "good brother" on *Dallas,* decided on an acting career while still in high school in Everett, Washington. He then spent four years in a special program at the University of Washington studying all aspects of the theater; practically all other academic requirements were waived.

The training paid off. After a brief period of theater work, Patrick moved to Los Angeles and began getting roles in series episodes and TV movies, beginning with *The Stranger Who Looks Like Me* (as one of the adopted kids) in 1974. He was seen as an attractive young talent by producers, and he landed the starring role of the underwater hero in the adventure series *The Man from Atlantis* in 1977. That series was short-lived, but the following year *Dallas* premiered and Patrick became a key character on what was soon television's number-one program.

DUGAN, DENNIS—actor
b: 1948, Wheaton, Ill.

Rich Man, Poor Man—Book I (drama)
.... Claude Tinker (1976)
Richie Brockelman, Private Eye (drama)
.... Richie Brockelman (1978)
Empire (com) .... Ben Christian (1984)
Shadow Chasers (drama)
.... Edgar (Benny) Benedek (1985–86)

Although baby-faced Dennis Dugan played a wet-behind-the-ears "23 year old" detective in *Richie Brockelman,* he was hardly a newcomer to acting at the time. Dugan began in summer stock while still in school and was in a number of off-Broadway productions in the late '60s and early '70s. It took him a while to crash Hollywood, but after he played a few small parts in TV movies the producers of *The Rockford Files* decided to try him out as a potential younger partner for James Garner. Instead, his character was spun off into the *Brockelman* series, which was unsuccessful. It did get Dugan bigger roles in later years, however. One of these days he may land a hit series.

Dugan was married in the late 1970s to actress Joyce Van Patten.

DUGGAN, ANDREW—actor
b: Dec 28, 1923

Bourbon Street Beat (drama)
.... Cal Calhoun (1959–60)
Room for One More (com)
.... George Rose (1962)
Twelve O'Clock High (drama)
..... Brigadier General Ed Britt (1965–67)

Lancer (wes).... Murdoch Lancer (1968–70)
Rich Man, Poor Man—Book I (drama)
.... Col. Deiner (1976)
Backstairs at the White House (drama)
.... Pres. Dwight D. Eisenhower (1979)
The Winds of War (drama)
.... Adm. Kimmel (1983)

Craggy Andrew Duggan was seen a great deal as a leading man in the '50s and '60s, with producers seemingly intent on finding the right vehicle for him—somewhere. His first major TV exposure (he had been in the theater earlier) was as one of the sidekicks in Disney's "Saga of Andy Burnett" in 1957–58. He then was given leading roles in a detective series *(Bourbon Street Beat)*, a situation comedy *(Room for One More)*, a war adventure *(Twelve O'Clock High)*, and a western *(Lancer)*, all with only middling success.

In the '70s he accepted the obvious and settled down to an extremely busy career doing guest roles on other people's series, especially crime shows such as *Cannon*, *McMillan & Wife*, and *Hawaii Five-O*. He has also appeared in quite a few TV movies and miniseries.

DUGGAN, BOB—actor

The Red Skelton Show (var)
.... regular (1970–71)

DUGGAN, TOM—sports commentator
b: c. 1916 d: 1969

Ask Me Another (quiz) ..... panelist (1952)

DUKE, BILL—black actor

Palmerstown, U.S.A. (drama)
.... Luther Freeman (1980–81)

DUKE, PATTY—

See Astin, Patty Duke

DUKE, ROBIN—comedienne
b: Mar 13, 1954, Toronto, Canada

Second City TV (com)
.... Molly Earl (1980–81)
NBC's Saturday Night Live (com)
.... regular (1981–84)

DUKES, DAVID—actor
b: June 6, San Francisco, Calif.

Beacon Hill (drama). Robert Lassiter (1975)
79 Park Avenue (drama)
.... Mike Koshko (1977)
The Winds of War (drama)
.... Leslie Slote (1983)

David Dukes once told *The New York Times*, "I have no ambition to be a star, as long as I get interesting roles and work with good folk." Those who remember notable roles will certainly recall him as: the man who attempted to rape Edith Bunker on one of the most famous episodes of *All in the Family;* the writer in love with transsexual model Linda Gray in the soap spoof *All That Glitters;* the embittered son who had lost an arm in World War I, in *Beacon Hill;* and the earnest young diplomat spurned by Ali McGraw in *The Winds of War*. He seems to have gotten his wish.

DULO, JANE—actress

Hey Jeannie (com).... Liz Murray (1956–57)
McHale's Navy (com)
.... Nurse Molly Turner (1962–64)
Get Smart (com) ..... 99's Mother (1968–69)
Medical Center (drama)
.... Nurse Murphy (1971–72)
Sha Na Na (var) .... regular (1977–81)
Gimme a Break (com)
.... Grandma Kanisky (1982–83)

Let Jane Dulo tell her own story: "If you want to know the truth, I've been around forever. At three, I was one of those terrible children that sang and danced at weddings and bar mitzvahs. By 10, I was in vaudeville. By 19, I had been 'discovered' 19 different times by 19 different people. All were going to make me a big star. I finally got tired of being annually discovered, so at 19, I decided to quit the business.

"My farewell engagement was at one of those summer adult camps in the Catskills. And I was great, giving it my all for my last appearance. So what happened? Just that night some nut reviewer from *Billboard* was in the audience and he goes back to New York and writes a rave review about me, saying how some smart producer should latch onto me. After 100 different calls from producers and 100 auditions, I was discovered again ... at the unemployment office. That year was the worst of my life."

Finally, Jane was booked into a night-club noted for giving stars their start. "They weren't noted for anything after I got through with them ... I'm not a star and I never will be one. And, thankfully, I'm long past the point of 'wanting-to-be-ultimately.' I am now what I will always be and for that I am grateful. If I could have anything more, it would only be additional work with more lines. I love this business, and, who knows, if I hang around long enough, I just might be discovered some-day."*

Truth be told, Jane had a very successful career as a supporting actress in comedies, from *The Phil Silvers Show* in the '50s to *Gimme a Break* in the '80s. She is a very funny lady.

DUMBRILLE, DOUGLAS—actor
b: Oct 13, 1889**, Hamilton, Ont., Canada d: Apr 2, 1974

China Smith (adv)
.... Inspector Hobson (1952–55)
The Life of Riley (com)
.... Cunningham (1953–58)
The Grand Jury (drama)
.... Grand Jury investigator (1958–59)
The New Phil Silvers Show (com)
.... Mr. Osborne (1963–64)

DUMKE, RALPH—actor
b: Jul 25, 1899, Indiana d: Jan 4, 1964

Captain Billy's Mississippi Music Hall (var)
.... host (Captain Billy) (1948)
Movieland Quiz (quiz)........ emcee (1948)

DUMONT, MARGARET—actress
b: Oct 20, 1889 d: Mar 6, 1965

My Friend Irma (com)
.... Mrs. Rhinelander (1952–53)

The wonderful, stately dowager who was the Marx Brothers' foil in so many of their films of the 1930s. She was seen occasionally in supporting roles on early television, including sketches with Groucho. Groucho claimed that she stayed so serene amid the brothers' lunatic antics because she didn't understand the jokes.

*Quoted in a 1965 NBC press release.
**Some sources give 1888 or 1890.

264

DUNBAR, OLIVE—actress
My Three Sons (com)
.... Mrs. Pfeiffer (1961–63)

DUNCAN, ANGUS—actor
Aspen (drama)........ Len Ralston (1977)

DUNCAN, ARCHIE—actor
b: May 26, 1914, Glasgow, Scotland d: Jul 24, 1979

Sherlock Holmes (drama)
.... Inspector Lestrade (1954–55)
The Adventures of Robin Hood (adv)
.... Little John (1955–58)

DUNCAN, ART—black dancer
The Lawrence Welk Show (music)
.... regular (1964–82)

DUNCAN, SANDY—actress
b: Feb 20, 1946, Henderson, Texas

Funny Face (com) ... Sandy Stockton (1971)
The Sandy Duncan Show (com)
.... Sandy Stockton (1972)
Roots (drama)......... Missy Anne (1977)

This pert, tomboyish ingenue seemed a natural for television when she arrived on the small screen, amid much publicity, in 1971. However, none of her shows was successful and she has since been seen mostly on specials. Her principal career has been on Broadway, where she has often appeared in revivals of classic musical comedies (*The Music Man, The Sound of Music, The Boy Friend, Peter Pan*, etc.).

DUNIGAN, TIM—actor
b: Aug 2, St. Louis, Mo.

The A-Team (adv)
.... Lt. Templeton Peck (pilot only) (1983)
Mr. Smith (com).... Tommy Atwood (1983)
Wizards and Warriors (adv)
.... Geoffrey Blackpool (1983)

DUNLOP, VIC—comedian
The Richard Pryor Show (var)
.... regular (1977)
Harper Valley P.T.A. (com)
.... George Kelly (1981)
The Half Hour Comedy Hour (var)
.... regular (1983)

DUNN, BILL—cartoonist

Face to Face (quiz)........ artist (1946–47)

DUNN, BOB—cartoonist

Spin the Picture (quiz).... regular (1949–50)
Quick on the Draw (quiz). cartoonist (1952)

DUNN, EDDIE—comedian, host
b: 1896 d: May 5, 1951

Face to Face (quiz).... interviews (1946–47)
Spin the Picture (quiz)....... emcee (1949)

DUNN, ELAINE—singer, dancer
b: c. 1935, Cleveland, Ohio

Broadway Open House (talk)
.... regular (1951)

DUNN, GEORGE—actor

Cimarron City (wes)
.... Jesse Williams (1958–59)
Camp Runamuck (com)
.... the Sheriff (1965–66)

DUNN, JAMES—actor
b: Nov 2, 1901*, New York City, N.Y. d: Sep 1, 1967

It's a Great Life (com)
.... Uncle Earl (1954–56)

DUNN, KATHY—actress
b: Oct 1946

Our Private World (drama) ..... Pat (1965)

DUNN, KEVIN—actor

Jack and Mike (drama)
.... Anthony Kubacek (1986–)

DUNN, LIAM—actor
b: c. 1916 d: Apr 11, 1976

Captain Nice (com)... Mayor Finney (1967)
The Queen and I (com)
.... Capt. Washburn (1969)
Diana (com) .. Smitty, the bellboy (1973–74)

DUNN, NORA—comedienne
b: Apr 29, 1952, Chicago, Ill.

NBC's Saturday Night Live (var)
.... regular (1985–)

*Some sources give 1905.

Kevin and Nora Dunn are brother and sister.

DUNN, PETE—actor

Cimarron City (wes)
.... Dody Hamer (1958–59)

DUNN, RALPH—actor
b: 1902, Titusville, Pa. d: Feb 19, 1968

Norby (com) .... Mr. Rudge (1955)

DUNNAM, STEPHANIE—actress
b: Mar 28, Oak Harbor, Wash. r: Dallas, Texas

Emerald Point N.A.S. (drama)
.... Kay Mallory Matthews (1983–84)

DUNNE, IRENE—actress
b: Dec 20, 1901*, Louisville, Ky.

Schlitz Playhouse of Stars (drama)
.... hostess (1952)

DUNNE, STEVE—actor, host
b: Jan 13, 1918, Northampton, Mass. d: Aug 27, 1977

Professional Father (com)
.... Thomas Wilson, M.D. (1955)
You're on Your Own (quiz)
.... emcee (1956–57)
Truth or Consequences (quiz)
.... emcee (1957–58)

DUNNINGER, JOSEPH—mentalist
b: Apr 28, 1892, New York City d: Mar 9, 1975

The Bigelow Show (var) .. regular (1948–49)
The Amazing Dunninger (audpar)
.... host (1955–56)

Dunninger, a somewhat creepy-looking man who was billed as "the master mentalist," had been a well-known figure in show business for many years before television came along. His ability to read minds and foretell events developed as a child, it was said, and he was quite a sensation as a young man, being asked to perform for presidents Theodore Roosevelt, Calvin Coolidge, and Franklin D. Roosevelt. He was a great friend of magician Harry Houdini in the 1920s. During the '30s

*Some sources give 1898 or 1904.

and '40s he made radio appearances, and in the '50s he was seen on television, amazing audiences by telling them their birthdays or what was in their right coat pockets. Throughout his long career he had a standing offer of $10,000 to anyone who could prove he used an accomplice. No one ever collected.

DUNPHY, DON—sportscaster
b: New York City, N.Y.

Cavalcade of Sports (sport)
.... commentator (1950)
Prime Time Baseball (sport)
.... sportscaster (1952)
Fight Talk (sport) .. commentator (1953–55)
Saturday/Friday Night Fights (sport)
.... sportscaster (1960–64)

DURANT, DON—actor
The Ray Anthony Show (var)
.... regular (1956–57)
Johnny Ringo (wes)
.... Johnny Ringo (1959–60)

DURANTE, JIMMY—comedian
b: Feb 10, 1893, New York City, N.Y. d: Jan 28, 1980

All Star Revue (var)
.... alternating host (1950–53)
Colgate Comedy Hour (var)
.... rotating host (1953–54)
The Jimmy Durante Show (var)
.... host (1954–56)
Jimmy Durante Presents The Lennon Sisters (var)...................... host (1969–70)

Emmy Award: Best Comedian (1952)

Of all the old-time show-business troopers who attempted to make the transition into television, Jimmy Durante was one of the most successful. To a kid watching TV in the '50s, he seemed ancient; in fact, he had made his debut as a piano player at Coney Island around 1910 and had a very successful career in vaudeville, clubs, and radio in the '20s, '30s, and '40s. His time-worn act changed little for TV. There were patter songs such as "Inka Dinka Do" and "Can Broadway Do Without Me?", frequently interrupted by jokes ("I got a million of 'em!"), and all delivered in his inimitable raspy voice and heavy Bronx accent.

Always, of course, there were jokes about his enormous nose, whence his nickname "Schnozzola." At the end of the act would come a sentimental number like "September Song." Then, just when the audience was getting mellow, he would walk slowly off the stage holding high his battered fedora and uttering his famous farewell, "Goodnight, Mrs. Calabash, wherever you are."

Jimmy was seen regularly during the early and mid 1950s and fairly often on variety shows and specials after that. Once in a while he would turn up in a guest spot on somebody's comedy series, such as *The Danny Thomas Show* in '61 and *The Lucy Show* in '66. In 1969, ABC announced a peculiar series which paired him with the Lennon Sisters (the Young and the Old, presumably), but it didn't work. Nevertheless, Jimmy stayed active until the early '70s, when he was felled by a series of strokes. He spent his last few years in a wheelchair.

But who, you ask, was Mrs. Calabash? Jimmy never said—until one night, in 1966, at the end of a speech, he finally identified the term as an affectionate nickname for his beloved wife, who had died in 1943. The original Mrs. Calabash, he said, was the kindly owner of a Chicago rooming house where Jimmy and his bride had lived shortly after their marriage in 1916.

Two Durante biographies are titled *Goodnight, Mrs. Calabash,* by William Cahn (1963), and *Schnozzola* by Gene Fowler (1951).

DURNING, CHARLES—actor
b: Feb 28, 1923, Highland Falls, N.Y.

The Cop and the Kid (com)
.... Officer Frank Murphy (1975–76)
Captains and the Kings (drama)
.... Big Ed Healey (1976)
Studs Lonigan (drama).. Mr. Lonigan (1979)
Eye to Eye (drama)..... Oscar Poole (1985)

Charles Durning is short and chunky, but he has a twinkle in his eye these days. And well he should. From rather dismal beginnings, his career seems to have gotten better and better as years have passed. Born to an army family, he left home at 15 and worked at menial jobs, with occasional low-paying gigs in burlesque. He returned from military service in Korea all fired up to study acting on the GI Bill, but was told he had no talent, was too short for acting, and had no future in the business. Faced with such rejection, he got out of show business for a while, but later returned to the stage to try again. He eventually got some roles off-Broadway and with touring companies; he credits New York producer Joseph Papp with putting his career into high gear by using him in a series of Shakespearean productions in the '60s.

Durning finally began to make a dent in television in the '70s, mostly in TV movies and specials. He attracted much notice, and an Emmy nomination, for his role opposite Maureen Stapleton in the 1975 special "Queen of the Stardust Ballroom," and more kudos for *Studs Lonigan* and *Captains and the Kings* (an abortive 1975 sitcom called *The Cop and the Kid* was mercifully overlooked). In the '80s things got even better, with Oscar-nominated comedy performances in the movies *The Best Little Whorehouse in Texas* and *To Be or Not to Be*. There is one movie actor he particularly admires. Says Durning, "I think I learned much of what I know about acting from watching James Cagney movies. When people ask me I tell them I didn't go to school . . . I learned directly from Cagney."

DUROCHER, LEO—baseball manager, host
b: Jul 27, 1906, West Springfield, Mass.

Jackpot Bowling Starring Milton Berle (sports) .... host (1959)

Leo "the Lip" Durocher was one of the most colorful figures in baseball history. For a time after he quit as the New York Giants manager in 1955, he was a play-by-play commentator and occasional host of other programs. It was Leo who coined the enduring phrase, "Nice guys finish last."

He was married from 1947–60 to actress Laraine Day.

DURRELL, MICHAEL—actor
b: Oct 6, 1943, Brooklyn, N.Y.

Nobody's Perfect (com)
.... Lt. Vince de Gennaro (1980)
I'm a Big Girl Now (com)
.... Walter Douglass (1980–81)
Shannon (police) ..... Lt. Moraga (1981–82)

V (movie) (sci fi) ... Robert Maxwell (1983)
Chiefs (drama) .... John Howell (1983)
V: The Final Battle (miniseries) (sci fi)
.... Robert Maxwell (1984)
Alice (com) ...... Nicholas Stone (1984–85)

DURSTON, GIGI—singer
b: Oct 8, 1927, Baltimore, Md.

The Sonny Kendis Show (music)
.... regular (1949–50)

DURYEA, DAN—actor
b: Jan 23, 1907, White Plains, N.Y. d: Jun 7, 1968

China Smith (adv)... China Smith (1952–55)
Peyton Place (drama)
.... Eddie Jacks (1967–68)

DUSAY, MARJ—actress
b: Feb 20, 1936, Russell, Kansas

Stop Susan Williams (drama)
.... Jennifer Selden (1979)
Bret Maverick (wes)
.... Kate Hanrahan (1981–82)

DUSENBERRY, ANN—actress
b: Sep 13, Tucson, Ariz.

Little Women (drama)
.... Amy March Laurence (1979)
The Family Tree (drama)
.... Molly Nichols Tanner (1983)
Life with Lucy (com)
.... Margo McGibbon (1986–)

DUSKIN, RUTHIE—panelist
It's About Time (quiz) .... panel (1954)

DUSSAULT, NANCY—actress
b: Jun 30, 1936, Pensacola, Fla.

The New Dick Van Dyke Show (com)
.... Carol Davis (1971–73)
Too Close for Comfort (com)
.... Muriel Rush (1980–85)
The Ted Knight Show (com)
.... Muriel Rush (1986)

DUVALL, ROBERT—actor
b: Jan 5, 1931, San Diego, Calif.

Ike (drama)
.... Gen. Dwight D. Eisenhower (1979)

The noted actor was seen frequently in television dramas in the 1960s, until movies got the best of him. Among his credits were multiple appearances on *Naked City, The Defenders, The F.B.I.,* and *Route 66.*

DUVALL, SUSAN—actress

Angie (com)........ Mary Grace (1979–80)

DWIGHT-SMITH, MICHAEL—actor

Lucas Tanner (drama)
.... Wally Moore (1974–75)

DWYER, VIRGINIA—actress

The Wonderful John Acton (drama)
.... Julia Acton (1953)

Dwyer is best known as a soap opera actress on radio in the '40s and on television since the '50s. Perhaps her most famous role was that of Mary Matthews on *Another World* (1964–75).

DYER, JEANNE—actress

Mayor of Hollywood (var) . secretary (1952)

DYKERS, REAR ADM. THOMAS—

The Silent Service (drama)
.... host/narrator (1956–58)

The Admiral had retired from the Navy in 1949 and become a producer and technical adviser for Hollywood films.

DYSART, RICHARD—actor
b: Mar 30, Brighton, Mass. r: Augusta, Me.

L.A. Law (drama)
.... Leland McKenzie (1986–)

DZIUBINSKA, ANULKA—actress

Bare Essence (drama) ...... Natasha (1983)

DZUNDZA, GEORGE—actor
b: Rosenheim, Germany

Open All Night (com)
.... Gordon Feester (1981–82)

E

EADIE AND RACK—duo pianists

Club Seven (music)...... pianists (1950–51)

EARL, JOHN—black juvenile actor

The Sanford Arms (com)
.... Nat Wheeler (1977)

EARLE, MERIE—actress
b: c. 1889, Ohio d: Nov 4, 1984

*The Jerry Reed When You're Hot You're Hot
Hour* (var).................. regular (1972)
The Waltons (drama)
.... Maude Gormsley (1973–79)

EARLE, ROBERT—host, executive
b: Jan 5, 1926, Baldwin, N.Y.

The G.E. College Bowl (quiz)
.·............. host/moderator (1962–70)

EASTERBROOK, LESLIE—actress
b: Jul 29, Los Angeles, Calif. r: Kearney,
Nebr.

Laverne & Shirley (com)
.... Rhonda Lee (1980–83)

EASTHAM, RICHARD—actor
b: Jun 22, 1918, Opelousas, La.

Tombstone Territory (wes)
.... Harris Claibourne (1957–60)
Wonder Woman (adv)
.... Gen. Blankenship (1976–77)
Falcon Crest (drama). Dr. Howell (1982–83)

EASTWOOD, CLINT—actor, director
b: May 31, 1930, San Francisco, Calif.

Rawhide (wes)..... Rowdy Yates (1959–66)

Many well-known movie actors have enjoyed a "second stardom" on television, after their days of cinema glory were over. Clint Eastwood went the other way—from stardom on television (seven years in a top-rated series) to superstardom in films. Apparently, the public just can't get enough of him.

Clint came from a hardscrabble background, working as a laborer before he settled down to a small-time acting career in Hollywood in the mid-1950s. His first movie roles were in B films such as *Revenge of the Creature* and *Frances in the Navy*. His TV work was hardly even noticed, although he is known to have appeared in episodes of *Navy Log* and *West Point* in 1958. When *Rawhide* premiered in January 1959 he was a virtual unknown. All that changed as the series soared into the top ten.

Even during *Rawhide*'s run Clint continued to make films, mostly in the same tough, macho mold as his TV role. A trio of "spaghetti westerns" made in Italy in 1964–66—*A Fistful of Dollars, For a Few Dollars More,* and *The Good, the Bad, and the Ugly*—suddenly sent his career skyrocketing. Once *Rawhide* ended its run he went on to such megahits as *Coogan's Bluff* (1968) and *Dirty Harry* (1971) and was lost to the small screen for good.

A 1977 biography is titled *Clint Eastwood, The Man Behind the Myth,* by Patrick Agan.

EBEN, AL—actor
b: March 11, Philadelphia, Pa.

Hawaii Five-O (police)
.... Doc Bergman (1970–76)

EBERLY, BOB—singer
b: Jul 24, 1916*, Mechanicsville, N.Y. d: Nov
17, 1981

TV's Top Tunes (music) .... host (1953)

This famous vocalist was a major star with Jimmy Dorsey's band in the early 1940s; later, his career went into decline. He was the brother of Glenn Miller's vocalist, Ray Eberle.

**EBERSOLE, CHRISTINE—actress,
comedienne**
b: Feb 21, Park Forest, Ill.

NBC's Saturday Night Live (com)
.... regular (1981–82)
Valerie (com) ... Barbara Goodwin (1986–)

EBERT, ROGER—film critic
b: Jun 18, 1942, Urbana, Ill.

Sneak Previews (misc).... cohost (1977–82)
At the Movies (misc) ..... cohost (1982–86)

*Some sources give 1918.

Siskel & Ebert & The Movies (misc)
.... cohost (1986–)

Winner of the Pulitzer Prize for criticism in 1975 for his *Chicago Sun-Times* column.

EBSEN, BONNIE—actress
b: c. 1952

The Kallikaks (com)
.... Bobbi Lou Kallikak (1977)

The daughter of Buddy Ebsen.

EBSEN, BUDDY—actor
b: Apr 2, 1908, Belleville, Ill.

Disneyland (misc) . George Russel (1954–55)
Northwest Passage (adv)
.... Sgt. Hunk Marriner (1958–59)
The Beverly Hillbillies (com)
.... Jed Clampett (1962–71)
Barnaby Jones (drama)
.... Barnaby Jones (1973–80)
Matt Houston (drama)
.... Roy Houston (1984–85)

Buddy Ebsen is one of an elite group of actors who has starred in *two* major hit series, and rather different ones at that— *The Beverly Hillbillies* and *Barnaby Jones.*

Buddy started out as a dancer. His father owned a dance studio and insisted that his son take lessons. They proved handy when the young lad made his way to New York in the late 1920s and found himself broke. He auditioned as a dancer for the new Broadway show *Whoopee*, starring Eddie Cantor, won the job, and saw the show become a major hit. Later, Buddy and his sister Vilma had a successful dancing act together. Hollywood used him as a dancer at first as well, in a film career that began in 1935.

By the 1950s Buddy had switched to acting and was well established, though hardly famous. He did television work early in the decade on several playhouse series, before his friend Walt Disney tapped him to play Davy Crockett's weather-beaten partner in the *Davy Crockett* episodes which aired as part of the Disney series in 1954–55. This exposure led to more parts, including a costarring role in the 1958 adventure series *Northwest Passage.* Following that, he was seen mostly

in westerns, including *Rawhide, Have Gun Will Travel,* and *Gunsmoke.* However, it was a rural comedy that made him famous —*The Beverly Hillbillies* was the number-one rated series of the early 1960s.

Such a distinctive and long-running role as that of Jed Clampett might have typecast him, but a year and a half after the comedy ended, Buddy was back as an affable, older detective in *Barnaby Jones,* which was a hit for the rest of the 1970s. He also appeared in a number of TV movies and miniseries during and after *Barnaby's* run.

Despite all of this success, he is still asked, from time to time, "Do you still dance?"

ECHEVARRIA, ROCKY—actor

From Here to Eternity (drama)
.... Pfc. Ignacio Carmona (1980)

ECHOES, THE—singers

Coke Time with Eddie Fisher (music)
.... vocal group (1956–57)

EDELMAN, BARBARA JANE—actress

Lou Grant (drama) .... Linda (1981–82)

EDELMAN, HERB—actor
b: Nov 5, 1930, Brooklyn, N.Y.

The Good Guys (com)
.... Bert Gramus (1968–70)
Ladies' Man (com) .... Reggie (1980–81)
Strike Force (police)
.. Deputy Comm. Herbert Klein (1981–82)
9 to 5 (com)..... Harry Nussbaum (1982–83)

EDEN, BARBARA—actress
b: Aug 23, 1934, Tucson, Ariz. r: San Francisco, Calif.

How to Marry a Millionaire (com)
.... Loco Jones (1957–59)
I Dream of Jeannie (com)
.... Jeannie (1965–70)
Harper Valley P.T.A. (com)
.... Stella Johnson (1981–82)

NBC in 1965 could hardly have found a better actress to play the title role in *I Dream of Jeannie* than Barbara Eden. Pert, shapely, and with a sexy twinkle in her eye, she was made for the role. Barbara had been a cheerleader in high school (of course) and upon graduation would have headed straight for Hollywood had not her parents insisted that she spend a year studying voice and drama in her hometown of San Francisco. When she did move to Los Angeles, she quickly found jobs in little theaters and eventually minor roles on television and in films (one of her first was *The Wayward Girl*). At first she seemed to be typed as a dumb blonde. On a 1957 *I Love Lucy* episode she played a sexy young thing who temporarily led Ricky and Fred to forget their wives, until Lucy and Ethel fought back with their own burlesque version of "alluring" charms. Barbara's first major break was in the TV version of *How to Marry a Millionaire,* playing the Marilyn Monroe film role of the dim-witted, nearsighted blonde who kept walking into walls. More guest appearance roles followed, including several on *Burke's Law* and *Rawhide* (on which she was aptly cast as a dance-hall queen).

Barbara has made attempts to broaden her horizons. While *I Dream of Jeannie* was riding high she tried for a time to launch a singing career, appearing on the Dean Martin, Ed Sullivan and *Kraft* variety shows, among others. In 1971 she and her *Jeannie* costar, Larry Hagman, tried an unusual change of pace playing an unhappily married couple in the horror film *A Howling in the Woods;* and in 1977 she starred as a female private eye in the TV film *Stonestreet,* the pilot for a series that never came about. Nevertheless, comedy remained her forte. During the '70s she appeared mostly in lightweight TV films such as *The Feminist and the Fuzz* (with David Hartman as the cop). She also starred in a 1981 TV spin-off from her hit film *Harper Valley P.T.A.;* and in 1985 she reprised her most famous role in the TV movie *I Dream of Jeannie, 15 Years Later.* The public knows what it wants from Barbara Eden; once a Jeannie, always a Jeannie.

Barbara was married from 1958–73 to actor Michael Ansara.

EDMISTON, WALKER—actor

The Rounders (com) . . . . Regan (1966–67)

EDMONDS, DON—actor

Broadside (com) . . . . . Nicky D'Angelo (1964)

EDMUNDS, NOEL—comedian

Foul-Ups, Bleeps & Blunders (com)
. . . . foreign correspondent (1984–85)

EDWARDS, ALLYN—host
b: c. 1915 d: Jul 9, 1968

A Couple of Joes (var) . . . . regular (1950)
One Minute Please (quiz)
. . . . moderator (1954–55)
Mr. Citizen (drama) . . . . host (1955)

EDWARDS, ANTHONY—actor
b: Jul 19, Santa Barbara, Calif.

It Takes Two (com) . Andy Quinn (1982–83)

EDWARDS, CLIFF "UKULELE IKE"—singer
b: Jun 14, 1895, Hannibal, Mo. d: Jul 17, 1971

The Cliff Edwards Show (music)
. . . . host (1949)
The Fifty-Fourth Street Revue (var)
. . . . regular (1949)

This old trooper was a very popular recording artist and Broadway musical star in the 1920s and a supporting actor in movie musicals of the '30s. His high-pitched voice and ever-present ukulele certainly made him distinctive; it was he who chirped "Singin' in the Rain" for the first time in the movie *The Hollywood Revue of 1929;* he introduced scores of other famous songs as well, including "When You Wish Upon a Star" in Disney's *Pinocchio* (1940), for which he supplied the voice of Jiminy Cricket.

Cliff entered television near the end of his career, plunking his uke, singing the old songs, and telling a few stories. He later guested on various shows, including *The Mickey Mouse Club* (where Jiminy Cricket was always welcome), before he faded into the mists of memory.

EDWARDS, DOUGLAS—newscaster
b: Jul 14, 1917, Ada, Okla.

CBS Evening News (news)
. . . . anchorman (1948–62)
Masquerade Party (quiz) . . . . . . emcee (1953)
Armstrong Circle Theatre (drama)
. . . . host/narrator (1957–61)
F.Y.I. (pub aff) . . . . host (1960)

Douglas Edwards holds a unique distinction; he has anchored a daily network newscast for longer than anyone in TV history, from the virtual inception of the medium in 1948 continuously into the '80s. For 14 of those years he was CBS's principal evening anchorman on the *CBS Evening News* (then called *Douglas Edwards and the News*). His sober, authoritative style lacked the flamboyance or catchphrases of his competition, however, and, during his tenure, CBS was perennially second to NBC's John Cameron Swayze and Huntley-Brinkley. In 1962 Edwards was finally replaced by Walter Cronkite. He has since anchored daytime newsbreaks and other peripheral telecasts.

Edwards joined CBS in 1942 as a radio reporter, and he continues to be a principal newscaster on the CBS radio network even today.

EDWARDS, GAIL—actress
b: Sep 27, Coral Gables, Fla.

It's a Living (com).... Dot Higgins (1980–82)
It's a Living (com)..... Dot Higgins (1985–)

EDWARDS, GEOFF—host, actor
b: Feb 15, Westfield, N.J.

Petticoat Junction (com) . Jeff Powers (1968)
The Bobby Darin Show (var)
.... regular (1973)
The New Treasure Hunt (quiz)
.... emcee (1973–76)

Geoff now hosts a morning TV talk show in Los Angeles.

EDWARDS, GERALD—actor

Cowboy in Africa (adv).. Samson (1967–68)

EDWARDS, JOAN—singer
b: Feb 13, 1919*, New York City, N.Y. d: Aug 27, 1981

The Joan Edwards Show (music)
.... hostess (1950)

The niece of old-time songwriter-showman Gus Edwards ("School Days," "By the Light of the Silvery Moon," etc.). Joan was quite popular on radio in the '40s, with Paul Whiteman and on *Your Hit Parade*. She

*Some sources give 1920.

272

later turned to writing songs, one of which was a number called "Television's Tough on Love." It was tough on her, too. She had only a minor career in the medium before fading from sight.

EDWARDS, RALPH—host, producer
b: Jun 13, 1913, Merino, Colo.

Truth or Consequences (quiz)
.... emcee (1950–51)
This Is Your Life (misc)...... host (1952–61)
This Is Your Life (misc)...... host (1971–72)

Ralph Edwards, like Dick Clark, is one of those businessmen-entertainers who made far more money behind the cameras than in front of them. He started out in the 1930s making an uneven living as a radio announcer, until one day he decided he could cook up a show as good as the ones that were making fortunes for others. That first show was *Truth or Consequences,* a simple game based on "penalty" stunts which premiered in 1940 and was a smash hit for the rest of the decade. Ralph both produced and emceed it. He brought it to television in 1950 and it continued to have periodical revivals in the '50s, '60s, and '70s with other hosts. Ralph's second great hit was the syrupy *This Is Your Life,* which he created for radio in 1948. That, too, has been revived several times since. Other game shows which he produced have included *It Could Be You, Name That Tune* (in the '70s), *The Cross-Wits,* and *The People's Court.* Not surprisingly, Ralph lives today in a very comfortable retirement.

EDWARDS, RICK—actor
b: Northfield, Mass.

High Performance (adv)
.... Shane Adams (1983)

EDWARDS, RONNIE CLAIRE—actress
b: Feb 9, Oklahoma City, Okla.

The Waltons (drama)
.... Corabeth Godsey (1974–81)
Boone (drama) .... Aunt Dolly (1983–84)
Sara (com)........ Helen Newcombe (1985)

EDWARDS, STEPHANIE—actress

Girl with Something Extra (com)
.... Angela (1973–74)

The Hudson Brothers Show (var)
.... regular (1974)

EDWARDS, STEVE—host

Entertainment Tonight (news)
.... host (1982–83)

EDWARDS, VINCE—actor
b: Jul 9, 1928, Brooklyn, N.Y.

Ben Casey (drama)
.... Dr. Ben Casey (1961–66)
Matt Lincoln (drama)
.... Dr. Matt Lincoln (1970–71)
The Rhinemann Exchange (drama)
.... Gen. Swanson (1977)

This handsome, intense actor is best remembered for his role as Ben Casey in the '60s, though he has a scattering of credits in other media as well. He began on stage in the late 1940s and appeared both in films and in television productions during the '50s. Among the latter were episodes of *Fireside Theatre, The Untouchables,* and *Alfred Hitchcock Presents.* Though *Ben Casey* represented his big break, he did not really capitalize on it in later years, making only occasional guest appearances and one more series *(Matt Lincoln)*. He was seen most often in TV movies, including some intended to become series which didn't *(Cover Girls, The Courage and the Passion)* and others which did, but without him *(Firehouse, Knight Rider)*. Vince also pursued a musical career during the early '60s, with one best-selling album called *Vince Edwards Sings;* used copies can now be found for rather reasonable prices in flea markets.

EFRON, MARSHALL—comedian
b: c. 1938

The Dick Cavett Show (var). . regular (1975)

EGAN, EDDIE—actor
b: Jan 3, 1930, The Bronx, N.Y.

Joe Forrester (police)
.... Sgt. Bernie Vincent (1975–76)
Eischied (police)
...... Chief Inspector Ed Parks (1979–80)
Mickey Spillane's Mike Hammer (drama)
.... Hennessey (1984–)

Egan was a real-life New York City cop for 20 years prior to becoming an actor. He was one of the city's top narcotics detectives and was responsible for a series of major drug busts which became the basis for the hit movie *The French Connection,* in which he had a small role. On television he usually plays cops.

EGAN, JENNY—actress

Mr. Peepers (com)
.... Agnes Peepers (1953–55)

EGAN, RICHARD—actor
b: Jul 29, 1921, San Francisco, Calif.

Empire (wes) .... Jim Redigo (1962–63)
Redigo (wes)............ Jim Redigo (1963)

EGGAR, SAMANTHA—actress
b: Mar 5, 1938*, London, England

Anna and the King (com)
.... Anna Owens (1972)

This British film star (since the early '60s) was seen rather infrequently on television until the mid-1970s, when she began appearing in TV movies and episodes of selected series, notably *The Love Boat* and *Fantasy Island.*

EGO, SANDRA—actress
b: c. 1951, New Mexico

Cade's County (police)
.... Joannie Little Bird (1971–72)

A young actress of American Indian heritage. She is a member of the Apache-Mescalero tribe.

EHLERS, BETH—actress

The Best Times (drama)
.... Mia Braithwaite (1985)

EICHEN, CHERI—actress

Pink Lady (var) .... regular (1980)

EIKENBERRY, JILL—actress
b: Jan 21, 1947, New Haven, Conn.

L.A. Law (drama) ..... Ann Kelsey (1986–)

EILBACHER, CINDY—actress
b: Jul 7, Saudi Arabia

*Some sources give 1939.

273

My Mother the Car (com)
.... Cindy Crabtree (1965–66)
The Senator (drama)
.... Norma Stowe (1970–71)
Shirley (com) .... Tracey McCord (1979–80)

The younger sister of Lisa Eilbacher. Both sisters had active TV careers playing juveniles in the '60s and '70s. In the late '70s and early '80s Cindy was a regular on daytime's *The Young and the Restless*.

EILBACHER, LISA—actress
b: May 5, Dharan, Saudi Arabia

The Texas Wheelers (com) . Sally (1974–75)
The Hardy Boys Mysteries (adv)
.... Callie Shaw (1977)
Wheels (drama)........ Jody Horton (1978)
The Winds of War (drama)
.... Madeline Henry (1983)
Ryan's Four (drama)
.... Dr. Ingrid Sorenson (1983)
Me and Mom (drama) . Kate Morgan (1985)

Sister of Cindy. After following the TV juvenile route for a number of years, Lisa blossomed into a promising film star with the 1979 TV movie *The Ordeal of Patty Hearst* (as Patty); this was followed by featured roles in such box-office hits as *An Officer and a Gentleman* and *Beverly Hills Cop*.

EILBER, JANET—actress
b: Jul 27, 1951, Detroit, Mich.

Two Marriages (drama)
.... Nancy Armstrong (1983–84)
The Best Times (drama)
.... Joanne Braithwaite (1985)

EIMEN, JOHNNY—juvenile actor

McKeever & the Colonel (com)
.... Monk (1962–63)

EINSTEIN, BOB—writer, producer, comedian
b: Nov 20, 1940, Los Angeles, Calif.

The Smothers Brothers Comedy Hour (var)
.... Off. Judy (1967–69)
Pat Paulsen's Half a Comedy Hour (var)
.... regular (1970)
The Sonny and Cher Comedy Hour (var)
.... regular (1973–74)

The Smothers Brothers Show (var)
.... regular (1975)
Joey & Dad (var) .... regular (1975)
Van Dyke and Company (var)
.... regular (1976)

Emmy Awards: Best Comedy Writing, for *The Smothers Brothers Comedy Hour* (1969); Producer, Best Comedy-Variety Series, for *Van Dyke and Company* (1977)

The son of the late radio comedian Parkyakarkus and brother of comedian Albert Brooks.

EISELEY, DR. LOREN—Professor of Anthropology
b: Sep 3, 1907 d: Jul 9, 1977

Animal Secrets (doc) .... host (1967)

EISENMANN, AL—juvenile actor
b: c. 1965

Another Day (com)... Mark Gardner (1978)

EISENMANN, IKE—juvenile actor
b: Jul 21, 1962, Houston, Texas

Fantastic Journey (sci fi)
.... Scott Jordan (1977)

Al and Ike are brothers.

EISLEY, ANTHONY (FRED)—actor
b: c. 1925, Philadelphia, Pa.

Bonino (com) .... John Clinton (1953)
Pete Kelly's Blues (drama)
.... Johnny Cassiano (1959)
Hawaiian Eye (drama)
.... Tracy Stele (1959–62)

EISNER, MICHAEL—executive
b: Mar 7, 1942, New York City, N.Y.

Disney Sunday Movie (film)... host (1986–)

The chairman of Walt Disney Productions.

ELAM, JACK—actor
b: Nov 13, 1916, Miami, Ariz. r: Phoenix and Los Angeles

The Dakotas (wes) .. Dep. J. D. Smith (1963)
Temple Houston (wes)
.... George Taggart (1963–64)

The Texas Wheelers (com)
.... Zack Wheeler (1974–75)
How the West Was Won (miniseries) (drama)
.... Cully (1977)
Struck by Lightning (com)..... Frank (1979)
Detective in the House (drama)
.... Nick Turner (1985)
Easy Street (com)
.. Uncle Alvin "Bully" Stevenson (1986–)

Jack Elam, who was described by one movie critic as "the roughest, meanest, dirtiest heavy ever to cast a shadow across a movie-lot cowtown," was a successful show-business bookkeeper and accountant in the 1940s. Among other things he worked for Sam Goldwyn and handled the finances for the *Hopalong Cassidy* movies. Late in the '40s he made a deal with a producer, promising to find financing for a proposed western in return for a role as a heavy in the film. The result was *The Sundowners* (1950), starring Robert Preston, which launched a long and villainous on-screen career for the tall, strapping Elam.

Jack later played similar roles on television, including some 24 episodes of *Gunsmoke*. By the '60s he was also playing some heroic roles, and occasionally he even showed up in a comedy. In *Struck by Lightning* he portrayed a comic version of the Frankenstein monster!

ELCAR, DANA—actor
b: Oct 10, Ferndale, Mich.

Baretta (police) .... Inspector Shiller (1975)
Baa Baa Black Sheep (drama)
.... Col. Lard (1976–78)
MacGyver (drama)
.... Peter Thornton (1986–)

ELDER, ANN—writer, comedienne
b: Sep 21, 1942, Cleveland, Ohio

The Smothers Brothers Show (com)
.... Janet (1965–66)
Rowan & Martin's Laugh-In (var)
.... regular (1970–72)

Emmy Awards: Best Comedy Writing for a Special, for *Lily* (1974) and for *Lily Tomlin* (1976)

ELHARDT, KAY—actress
b: c. 1935, Los Angeles, Calif.

Love That Jill (com) .... Peaches (1958)

ELIAS, ALIX—actress

Karen (com) .... Cheryl Siegel (1975)
Grady (com) ...... Rose Kosinski (1975–76)

ELIAS, MIKE—

The New Bill Cosby Show (var)
.... regular (1972–73)

ELIZONDO, HECTOR—actor
b: Dec 22, 1936, New York City, N.Y.

Popi (com)...... Abraham Rodriguez (1976)
Freebie and the Bean (police)
.. Det. Sgt. Don Delgado (Bean) (1980–81)
Casablanca (drama)
.... Capt. Louis Renault (1983)
a.k.a. Pablo (com)
.... Jose Sanchez/Shapiro (1984)
Foley Square (com)
.... D.A. Jesse Steinberg (1985–86)

A small, worried-looking Hispanic actor with wide experience on stage, in films, and on television.

ELLERBEE, BOBBY—actor
b: Oct 31, Upson County, Ga.

In the Beginning (com)
.... Jerome Rockefeller (1978)

ELLERBEE, LINDA—newscaster
b: Aug 15, 1944, Bryan, Texas

Weekend (pub aff) .... cohost (1978–79)
NBC News Overnight (news)
.... anchor (1982–83)
Summer Sunday U.S.A. (pub aff)
.... anchor (1984)
Our World (pub aff) .... cohost (1986–)

ELLIOT, "MAMA" CASS—singer
b: Sep 19, 1943, Baltimore, Md. d: Jul 29, 1974

Andy Williams Presents Ray Stevens (var)
.... regular (1970)

Big, booming "Mama" Cass was a member of one of the most popular rock groups of the late '60s, the Mamas and the Papas, before striking out on her own very successful singing career in 1968. She also showed signs of developing into a popular TV actress/personality in the early '70s. During 1970 alone she cohosted an ABC

Saturday morning music show called *Get It Together,* was a regular on Ray Stevens' prime time variety series, and costarred in the fantasy movie *Puf'n'Stuff* (as the flamboyant Witch Hazel), the latter being well-received by critics. She also had parts in *Love, American Style; Young Doctor Malone;* and the Saturday morning *Scooby Doo* special "The Haunted Candy Factory." A 1973 CBS special titled *Don't Call Me Mama Anymore* seemed to sum up the direction her career was taking. Then in 1974 came the news of her sudden death, at the age of 30. How she died so young has been the subject of some controversy; although the most widely repeated story is that she accidentally choked to death on a ham sandwich, an autopsy report indicated a heart attack. It was an untimely end to a promising career.

ELLIOT, JANE—actress
b: Jan 17, New York, N.Y.

Rosetti and Ryan (drama)
.... Jessica Hornesby (1977)
Knots Landing (drama)
.... Judy Trent (1980–81)

Emmy Award: Best Supporting Actress in a Daytime Drama Series, for *General Hospital* (1981).

Though active in prime time supporting roles since the '60s, Jane became better-known in the late '70s and '80s in a succession of vivid roles in daytime soap operas, notably that of Tracy Quartermaine on *General Hospital.*

ELLIOT, SUSAN—actress

13 Queens Boulevard (com)
.... Annie Capestro (1979)

ELLIOT, WIN—host, sportscaster
r: Everett, Mass.

Fireside Theatre (drama) . announcer (1949)
Tic Tac Dough (quiz) ...... emcee (1957–58)
Win with a Winner (quiz)..... emcee (1958)
Make That Spare (sport)
.... commentator (1961–62)

ELLIOTT, BOB—comedian
See Bob & Ray

ELLIOTT, DAVID—juvenile actor
b: c. 1959, New York City r: Spring Valley, N.Y.

Joe & Valerie (com)
.... Paulie Barone (1978–79)

ELLIOTT, EVAN—juvenile actor
Norby (com) .... Hank Norby (1955)
Harbourmaster (adv) ..... Danny (1957–58)

ELLIOTT, GEOFFREY—actor
The Last Precinct (com) .. Justin Dial (1986)

ELLIOTT, JACK—orchestra leader
The Beautiful Phyllis Diller Show (var)
.... orch. leader (1968)
Happy Days (var) .... orch. co-leader (1970)
Make Your Own Kind of Music (var)
.... orch. co-leader (1971)
Burns and Schreiber Comedy Hour (var)
.... orch. co-leader (1973)
Ben Vereen . . . Comin' at Ya (var)
.... orch. co-leader (1975)

ELLIOTT, PATRICIA—actress
b: Jul 21, 1942, Gunnison, Colo.

Empire (com) .... Renee (1984)

ELLIOTT, ROSS—actor
The Virginian (wes)
.... Sheriff Abbott (1967–70)

ELLIOTT, SAM—actor
b: Aug 9, 1944, California r: Oregon

Mission: Impossible (drama)
.... Doug (1970–71)
Once an Eagle (drama)
.... Sam Damon (1976–77)
Aspen (drama) .... Tom Keating (1977)
The Yellow Rose (drama)
.... Chance McKenzie (1983–84)

ELLIOTT, STEPHEN—actor
b: Nov 27, New York City, N.Y.

Beacon Hill (drama)
.... Benjamin Lassiter (1975)
Executive Suite (drama)
.... Howell Rutledge (1976–77)
Falcon Crest (drama)
.... Douglas Channing (1981–82)
Dallas (drama)..... Scotty Demarest (1985)

ELLIOTT, WILLIAM—black actor
b: c. 1934 d: Sep 30, 1983

Bridget Loves Bernie (com)
.... Otis Foster (1972–73)
Adam 12 (police)...... Off. Grant (1974–75)

ELLIS, BOBBY—juvenile actor
b: 1933, Chicago, Ill.

Meet Corliss Archer (com)
.... Dexter Franklin (1951–52)
The Aldrich Family (com)
.... Henry Aldrich (1952–53)
Meet Corliss Archer (com)
.... Dexter (1954–55)

ELLIS, HERB—actor
Dragnet (police).... Off. Frank Smith (1952)
The D.A.'s Man (police)
.... Frank LaValle (1959)
Not for Hire (drama) ..... regular (1959–60)
Hennesey (com)
.... Dr. Dan Wagner (1960–62)

ELLIS, KATHLEEN—actress
Mr. Novak (drama)
.... Mrs. Ann Floyd (1963–65)

ELLIS, LARRY—singer
The Sammy Kaye Show (var)
.... regular (1958–59)

ELLIS, PEGGY ANN—hostess
Country Style (var)......... regular (1950)

ELLIS, RITA—singer
The Galen Drake Show (child)
.... singer (1957)

ELLISON, CASEY—actor
Punky Brewster (com)
.... Allen Anderson (1984–86)

ELLSWORTH & FAIRCHILD—dancers
Song and Dance (music)
.... dancers (1948–49)

ELSON, ANDREA—juvenile actress
b: Mar 6, 1969, New York City, N.Y.

Whiz Kids (drama)... Alice Tyler (1983–84)
Alf (com) .... Lynn Tanner (1986–)

ELSON, BOB—host, sportscaster
Identify (quiz)................. host (1949)
Tuesday Night Fights (sport)
.... sportscaster (1949–50)

ELY, RICK—actor
The Young Rebels (adv)
.... Jeremy Larkin (1970–71)

ELY, RON—actor
b: Jun 21, 1938, Hereford, Texas

The Aquanauts (Malibu Run) (adv)
.... Mike Madison (1961)
Tarzan (adv)............ Tarzan (1966–68)

Ron Ely made his mark in television the hard way, with scars, bruises and fractures —and practically naked in front of the cameras the whole time. He was, of course, Tarzan, the fifteenth actor to play the role in a lineage going back to 1918. The trim, athletic, 6'4" actor had his first break in Hollywood with a small role in the movie version of *South Pacific* in 1958. Later, he landed parts in such series as *Wyatt Earp* and *Father Knows Best* and a brief costarring role as a diver in *The Aquanauts* in early 1961.

However, his career was not really going anywhere until he was cast as Tarzan in 1966. Clad in nothing but a skimpy loincloth, Ely did most of the difficult vine-swinging and other rough stunts himself. Early in the series' run he was said to have been hurt in every episode filmed thus far, including four stitches from a lion bite in the head, a claw-ripped leg, and multiple scratches and bruises from swings and falls. The bottoms of his feet were like leather from running barefoot through the jungle and burning villages. Of the "big cats" with whom he worked, he said, "They can kill me and I know it." At least he fared better than the show's animal trainer, who was killed when a startled elephant picked him up and flung him against a wall.

In later years Ely understandably opted for less dangerous roles, including occasional appearances on *Marcus Welby, Fantasy Island*, and other series. From 1979–81 he was host of the *Miss America* pageant, replacing Bert Parks.

ELYEA, BOB—actor

Buck Rogers in the 25th Century (sci fi)
.... Twiki (voice) (1981)

EMBASSY QUARTET—instrumental quartet

Club Embassy (var) ...... regular (1952–53)

EMBREY, JOAN—animal expert
b: c. 1951, San Diego, Calif.

Those Amazing Animals (doc)
.... regular (1980–81)

EMERSON, DOUGLAS—juvenile actor

Herbie, The Love Bug (com)
.... Robbie MacLane (1982)

EMERSON, FAYE—actress, hostess
b: Jul 8, 1917, Elizabeth, La. d: Mar 9, 1983

Paris Cavalcade of Fashions (misc)
.... narrator (1948)
Faye Emerson Show (talk) ... hostess (1950)
Faye Emerson's Wonderful Town (var)
.... hostess (1951–52)
Author Meets the Critics (int)
.... moderator (1952)
I've Got a Secret (quiz) .. panelist (1952–58)
Quick As a Flash (quiz).. panelist (1953–54)
What's in a Word? (quiz) ... panelist (1954)
Masquerade Party (quiz)
.... panelist (1958–60)

Faye Emerson was one of the leading personalities on early, New York–originated television. The story of "whatever happened to her" in later years is one of the more interesting in TV annals.

Faye's first, and lesser, career was in films. The daughter of divorced parents, she grew up in various parts of the South and Midwest until, as a teenager, she settled with her mother in San Diego. While in college she began appearing in plays and in 1941 she became a contract player for Warner Brothers, appearing in several dozen B movies. She made bigger headlines in 1944 when she married Elliot Roosevelt, the son of the President. Thereafter, she was a leading figure in high society, living part of the time in the White House.

Her first television appearance came in May 1948 on *Tonight on Broadway* (she was making her Broadway debut at the time in a revival of *The Play's the Thing*). During the next dozen years she became a very familiar figure on TV, appearing as a glamorous host or panelist on a long succession of talk and game shows. She was known for her wit, her obvious intelligence, and perhaps most of all for the plunging necklines of her revealing, off-the-shoulder gowns, which were considered the most daring on TV.

Divorced from Roosevelt in 1950, she married bandleader Skitch Henderson and had a local show with him called *Faye and Skitch*. She appeared from time to time in dramatic productions, particularly on *The U.S. Steel Hour,* and also wrote a syndicated TV column for United Press.

As TV moved west to Hollywood in the late '50s, it gradually left Faye and "New York glamour" behind. In 1963, rich and weary of show business demands, she sailed away for a "year in Europe"—and never came back. Though she received many more offers of roles in films and plays, she declined them all and settled in a remote section of the island of Majorca, where she led a life of leisure, quite alone (Faye and Skitch had divorced in '57) in a beautiful, whitewashed house on a hillside. Friendly townspeople ensured that she was not bothered by the occasional reporters and photographers who tried to seek her out. Reportedly, she also wrote an autobiography there, but nothing has ever been published.

EMERSON, HOPE—actress
b: Oct 29, 1897, Hawarden, Iowa d: Apr 25, 1960

Kobb's Korner (var)
.... Maw Shufflebottom (1948–49)
Doc Corkle (com) ..... Nellie Corkle (1952)
I Married Joan (com)
.... Minerva Parker (1952–53)
Peter Gunn (drama) .... "Mother" (1958–59)
The Dennis O'Keefe Show (com)
.... Sarge (1959–60)

A towering, 6'2", 230-pound actress who often played murderous roles in films but who turned to comedy on television.

EMERY, BOB—host
b: c. 1897

Small Fry Club (child)...... host (1947–51)

The pioneer kid's show host, whose *Small Fry Club* stressed good habits, milk, and kindness toward others. Bob started his children's show on radio in Massachussets in the early 1920s, and later became a local and network announcer. By the time he reached television he was a middle-aged man with horn-rimmed glasses, known to his little friends as "Big Brother." *The Small Fry Club* was quite a hit on Dumont in the late '40s, but it faded with the arrival of more original—and more widely distributed—children's programs on the major networks, such as *Howdy Doody* and *Kukla, Fran & Ollie*. After its run Bob returned quietly to Boston, where he continued his gentle program on local television well into the '60s.

EMERY, CHRIS—assistant

Party Time at Club Roma (var)
.... regular (1950–51)

EMERY, PAT—assistant

Party Time at Club Roma (var)
.... regular (1950–51)

Chris and Pat were two young ladies who were identical twins.

EMERY, RALPH—host

Pop! Goes the Country (music)
.... host (1974–80)

ENBERG, DICK—sportscaster, host
b: Jan 9, 1935, Mt. Clemens, Mich.*

Where's Huddles? (cartn)
.... sports announcer (voice) (1970)

Emmy Awards: Producer, Best Sports Series, for *The Way It Was* (1978); Best Play-by-Play Sports Personality (1981, 1983)

Enberg is a former college professor and baseball coach with a Ph.D. from Indiana University. He began sports announcing during his teaching days in 1965 and joined NBC ten years later as one of its principal

*Some sources give Bridgeport, Conn.

play-by-play men. He has also tried his hand at daytime game shows, hosting *Baffle, Three for the Money,* and others, and co-produced the PBS sports series *The Way It Was.*

ENCHANTERS, THE—vocal group

The Ken Murray Show (var)
.... regular (1950–51)

ENDERS, RUTH—actress

Mr. I Magination (child) .. regular (1949–52)

The wife of Paul Tripp, star of *Mr. I Magination.*

ENDO, HARRY—actor

Hawaii Five-O (police)
.... Coroner Che Fong (1970–77)

ENGEL, GEORGIA—actress
b: Jul 28, 1948, Washington, D.C.

The Mary Tyler Moore Show (com)
..... Georgette Franklin Baxter (1973–77)
The Betty White Show (com)
.... Mitzi Maloney (1977–78)
Goodtime Girls (com)
.... Loretta Smoot (1980)
Jennifer Slept Here (com)
.... Susan Elliot (1983–84)

ENGLE, ROY—actor
b: Sep 13, 1913, Mo. d: Dec 29, 1980

Date with the Angels (com)
.... George Clemson (1957–58)
My Favorite Martian (com)
.... the police chief (1965–66)

ENGLUND, PAT—actress
b: Philadelphia, Pa.

That Was the Week That Was (com)
.... regular (1964–65)

The daughter of actress Mabel Albertson, and niece of actor Jack Albertson.

ENGLUND, ROBERT—actor
b: Jun 6, Glendale, Calif.

V: The Final Battle (miniseries) (sci fi)
.... Willie (1984)
V (sci fi)................. Willie (1984–85)

Downtown (police)
.... Dennis Shothaffer (1986–)

ENRIQUEZ, RENE—actor
b: Nov 25, 1933, San Francisco, Calif.

Hill Street Blues (police)
.... Lt. Ray Calletano (1981–86)

Rene Enriquez, the perpetually worried second-in-command on *Hill Street Blues,* was one of the more visible Hispanic actors on television in the 1980s. He was born to a family active in Central American politics; his uncle, Emiliano Chamorro, was president of Nicaragua before the Somozas. Rene chose acting as a career instead ("My father didn't like the idea") and spent the '50s and '60s playing minor roles, mostly on the New York stage. In 1974 he moved to Los Angeles and landed supporting roles in films *(Harry and Tonto, Bananas)* and TV episodes, the latter consisting mostly of crime dramas such as *Police Story* and *Quincy.*
On *Hill Street Blues* Rene became something of a symbol to Hispanics, particularly after a dramatic 1982 episode in which his character lashed out at the establishment's insensitivity toward his people. In real life, the actor is quite dedicated to rectifying that situation, heading a foundation called The National Hispanic Arts Endowment, which helps train young Hispanic actors.

ENTEN, BONI—actress
Comedy Tonight (var)
.... regular (1970)

EPP, GARY—actor
Married: The First Year (drama)
.... Tom Liberatore (1979)

ERDMAN, RICHARD—actor, director
b: Jun 1, 1925, Enid, Okla.

The Ray Bolger Show (com)
.... Pete Morrisey (1953–55)
The Tab Hunter Show (com)
.... Peter Fairfield III (1960–61)
Saints and Sinners (drama)
.... Klugie (1962–63)
From Here to Eternity (drama)
.... Kurt Von Nordlund (1980)

ERICKSON, LEIF—actor
b: Oct 27, 1911, Alameda, Calif. d: Jan 29, 1986

The High Chaparral (wes)
.... Big John Cannon (1967–71)

This big, brawny actor, an authentic World War II hero, appeared frequently in supporting roles in films (from 1935 on) as well as in television dramas. In the '50s and '60s he was seen mostly in westerns, including *Zane Grey Theater, The Virginian, Bonanza, Rawhide,* and in the continuing role of the unsmiling patriarch on *The High Chaparral.* He also had a certain talent for macabre tales. On *The Alfred Hitchcock Hour* he played a man with a magical monkey's paw whose three wishes go awry (wishing for a large sum of money, he gets it—in an insurance settlement when his son is killed); on *Night Gallery* he stalked an alcoholic woman who was convinced that a convict who had been killed in her house still lived; and on *The Sixth Sense* he guest-starred in a story called "The Heart That Wouldn't Stay Buried."

ERICSON, DEVON—actress
b: Dec 21, Salt Lake City, Utah

Young Dan'l Boone (adv)
.... Rebecca Bryan (1977)
Studs Lonigan (drama)......... Fran (1979)
The Chisholms (wes) .. Betsy O'Neal (1980)

ERICSON, JOHN—actor
b: Sep 25, 1926*, Dusseldorf, Germany

Honey West (drama) ... Sam Bolt (1965–66)

ERLENBORN, RAY—actor
Life with Elizabeth (com)
.... Mr. Fuddy (1953–55)

ERRICKSON, KRISTA—juvenile actress
b: c. 1963, Abington, Pa.

Hello, Larry (com)... Diane Adler (1979–80)

ERSKINE, MARILYN—actress
b: Apr 24, 1924, Rochester, N.Y.

The Tom Ewell Show (com)
.... Fran Potter (1960–61)

*Some sources give 1927.

ERWIN, BILL—actor

b: Dec 2, Honey Grove, Texas

Struck by Lightning (com)..... Glenn (1979)

ERWIN, STU—actor

b: Feb 14, 1902, Squaw Valley, Calif. d: Dec 21, 1967

The Stu Erwin Show (com)
.... as himself (1950–55)
The Greatest Show on Earth (drama)
.... Otto King (1963–64)

Stu Erwin made a career out of one distinctive character type, the amiable, well-meaning, but completely inept bumbler. In movies in the late '20s and '30s he was often a bumbling college student or young friend of the star; by the time television came along in the '50s he was a bumbling middle-aged father, still with the same pleasant, friendly look of disbelief on his face.

The Stu Erwin Show (also known as *The Trouble with Father*) was quite a hit in the early '50s, but even Stu began to tire of constantly burning steaks and dropping lightbulbs. Toward the end of its run the producers made him a little less blundering (he was, after all, supposed to be a high school principal), although the change didn't prolong the show's run. In later years Stu tried to seek out a greater variety of roles, including several guest appearances on *Perry Mason* (once as a meek accountant who was stealing his company blind, another time as a powerful publisher involved in murder). On *The Greatest Show on Earth* he played a circus business manager, co-starring opposite Jack Palance as the hard-driving straw boss. Stu's last role was in a TV murder mystery called *Shadow over Elveron,* which was aired in early 1968.

ESKEW, JACK—orchestra leader

The Hudson Brothers Show (var)
.... orch. leader (1974)
Cher (var) .... orch. leader (1975–76)

ESTABLISHMENT, THE—

The Jonathan Winters Show (var)
.... regulars (1968–69)

ESTABROOK, CHRISTINE—actress

b: Sep 13, Erie, Pa. r: East Aurora, N.Y.

Hometown (drama)..... Jane Parnell (1985)

ESTRADA, ERIK—actor

b: Mar 16, 1949, New York City, N.Y.

CHiPs (police)
 Off. Frank "Ponch" Poncherello (1977–83)

This grinning, energetic young actor was a favorite with younger viewers in the late '70s as motorcycle cop "Ponch" on the police series *CHiPs.* Though he was considered a discovery when the series began, he had been appearing in guest roles on television for half a dozen years before that.

Estrada was born in New York's Spanish Harlem and first began performing with a group called The Kids from San Juan in ethnic shows in city parks, as part of a cultural program sponsored by then–Mayor John Lindsay. His first film role was in a 1972 Pat Boone movie called *The Cross and the Switchblade* (guess which one Estrada carried!). This was followed by Hispanic youth roles in series including *Hawaii Five-O, Kojak, Mannix,* and *The Night Stalker,* among others.

CHiPs was his big break, but it was almost his epitaph as well. On August 6, 1979, while filming the season's premiere episode, Estrada was supposed to chase a car down an alleyway on his Kowasaki, forcing it to stop. Either the car stopped too soon or Estrada was hot-rodding (depending on whose version you believe); the 1200-pound motorcycle slammed into the car, was upended, and fell directly on top of him. The young actor came within inches of being killed. His excellent physical condition probably helped save his life, though as it was he suffered multiple broken bones and deep cuts on his face, limbs, and body. The footage was never used on the series, though an "accident" was written into the script to explain why Ponch had to hobble through much of the rest of the season.

Estrada eventually recovered completely. Toward the end of the series' run he appeared in his first starring role in a film, as the disillusioned boxer in the somewhat controversial (due to his skimpy bedroom attire) 1982 TV movie *Honey Boy.* He also spoke out often on the subject of motorcycle safety.

EUBANKS, BOB—host, manager

b: Jan 8, Flint, Mich. r: Los Angeles, Calif.

The Newlywed Game (quiz)
.... emcee (1967–71)
The Newlywed Game (quiz)
.... emcee (1977–80)
Dream House (quiz) .... emcee (1983–84)
The Newlywed Game (quiz)
.... emcee (1985)

In addition to being seen as host of *The Newlywed Game* and other quiz shows, Bob has been quite active as a concert promoter and personal manager of music celebrities. Among his clients: The Lennon Sisters, Merle Haggard, Dolly Parton, and Barbara Mandrell. He is also something of an entrepreneur; during the '60s he began a chain of young adult nightclubs called The Cinnamon Cinder, and in 1964 he borrowed money to stage the first West Coast concert of the Beatles.

Before entering the game show world, Bob was a West Coast disc jockey for many years.

EVANS, BARRY—actor

b: 1945

Doctor in the House (com)
.... Dr. Michael Upton (1970–72)

EVANS, DALE—actress

b: Oct 31, 1912, Uvalde, Texas

The Roy Rogers Show (wes)
.... as herself (1951–57)
The Roy Rogers and Dale Evans Show (var)
.... cohost (1962)

The wife, since 1947, of cowboy star Roy Rogers, and "The Queen of the West." Before meeting Roy she was a singer on radio and with some top bands (including Abe Lyman's and Anson Weeks'). Dale has also written quite a few books, articles, and songs, many in an inspirational vein, including a book about her retarded child called *Angel Unaware.* Perhaps her most famous song is Dale and Roy's theme, "Happy Trails to You."

EVANS, DAMON—black actor

b: Nov 24, 1950, Baltimore, Md.

The Jeffersons (com)
.... Lionel Jefferson (1975–78)

Roots: The Next Generations (drama)
.... Alex Haley (as young man) (1979)

EVANS, DENNY—actor

The Peter Marshall Variety Show (var)
.... regular (1976)
Me and Maxx (com).......... Gary (1980)
Our Time (var)............. regular (1985)

EVANS, DR. BERGEN—professor of English

b: Sep 19, 1904, Ohio d: Feb 4, 1978

Down You Go (quiz)....... emcee (1951–56)
Super Ghost (quiz) .... emcee (1952–53)
Of Many Things (pub aff).... host (1953–54)
It's About Time (quiz) .... emcee (1954)
The $64,000 Question (quiz)
.... question authority (1955–58)
The Last Word (info)........ host (1957–58)

EVANS, GENE—actor

b: Jul 11, 1922, Holbrook, Ariz.

My Friend Flicka (adv)
.... Rob McLaughlin (1956–57)
Matt Helm (drama)
.... Sgt. Hanrahan (1975–76)
Spencer's Pilots (adv)
.... Spencer Parish (1976)

EVANS, LINDA—actress

b: Nov 18, 1942, Hartford, Conn.

Big Valley (wes) .. Audra Barkley (1965–69)
Hunter (drama) .... Marty Shaw (1977)
Dynasty (drama)
..... Krystle Jennings Carrington (1981–)

Linda Evans began her acting career appearing in commercials while she was still a coed at Hollywood High School in Los Angeles. She was also seen as a teenager in several prime time series; one of these was an October 1960 episode of *Bachelor Father* called "A Crush on Bentley." In a bit of irony, Bentley was played by middle-aged series star John Forsythe, who years later would become Blake Carrington, Linda's distinguished (and much older) husband on *Dynasty.*

For the next few years Linda continued to play supporting roles on TV series such as *Ozzie and Harriet* and *My Favorite Martian.* Her movie career began with *Twilight of Honor,* starring Richard Chamberlain, in 1963. Her big break, however, came in 1965 with the role of Barbara Stanwyck's beautiful daughter Audra on *The Big Valley*.

Following that series' long run, Linda moved to Europe for a time, but she later returned to the U.S. and began appearing in movies and series episodes of the mid-1970s. She had a short run in early 1977 as James Franciscus's partner in the espionage series *Hunter* and was Steve McQueen's love interest in the 1980 film *Tom Horn* before she and John Forsythe got together again on *Dynasty*.

EVANS, MADGE—actress
b: Jul 1, 1909, Manhattan, N.Y. d: Apr 26, 1981

Masquerade Party (quiz).... panelist (1952)

EVANS, MAURICE—actor
b: Jun 3, 1901, Dorchester, England

Bewitched (com) .... Maurice (1964–72)

Emmy Award: best actor in a single performance, for the *Hallmark Hall of Fame* production of *Macbeth* (1961)

This distinguished Shakespearean actor appeared in numerous *Hallmark* and other dramatic productions (including at least two TV stagings of *Macbeth*), as well as in such unlikely vehicles as *Batman* (as the Puzzler), *Tarzan* ("Basil of the Jungle") and *The Six Million Dollar Man*. On *Bewitched* he had a grand old time playing the recurring role of Elizabeth Montgomery's warlock father, Maurice.

EVANS, MIKE—black actor
b: Nov 3, 1949, Salisbury, N.C.

All in the Family (com)
 .... Lionel Jefferson (1971–75)
The Jeffersons (com)
 .... Lionel Jefferson (1975)
Rich Man, Poor Man—Book I (drama)
 .... Arnold Simms (1976)
The Practice (com) .... Lenny (1976–77)
The Jeffersons (com)
 .... Lionel Jefferson (1979–81)

Mike Evans landed his first and most famous role—that of Lionel Jefferson—while he was still a student in acting school. He has since starred in a number of TV movies, and was co-creator of the spin-off series *Good Times*. He says his ambition is to make a fortune.

EVANS, MONICA—actress

The Odd Couple (com)
 .... Cecily Pigeon (1970–71)

EVANS, NANCY—singer

The Little Revue (music).. regular (1949–50)
Wayne King (music)...... regular (1949–51)

EVANS, RICHARD—actor

Peyton Place (drama)... Paul Hanley (1965)

EVE, TREVOR—actor
b: Jul 1, 1951, Wales r: Birmingham, England

Shadow Chasers (drama)
 ..... Prof. Jonathan MacKenzie (1985–86)

EVEN DOZEN, THE—

The Dinah Shore Chevy Show (var)
 .... regulars (1961–62)

EVERETT, CHAD—actor
b: Jun 11, 1936, South Bend, Ind.

The Dakotas (wes) ... Dep. Del Stark (1963)
Medical Center (drama)
 .... Dr. Joe Gannon (1969–76)
Centennial (drama)
 .... Maxwell Mercy (1978–79)
Hagen (drama)......... Paul Hagen (1980)
The Rousters (adv)
 .... Wyatt Earp III (1983–84)

This handsome, athletic, but somewhat bland leading man got his first break when he met the head of Warner Brothers Television around 1960 and secured a three-year contract as one of the studio's stock players. Warner Brothers had quite a few series on the air at the time, and Chad was given guest roles in many of them, including *Hawaiian Eye*, *77 Sunset Strip*, *Surfside Six*, and *Cheyenne;* finally he was given a costarring role in *The Dakotas*. When his contract expired he moved to MGM for a time and then went out on his own, appearing through the 1960s in scattered episodes of various series. The role of the heroic young surgeon on *Medical*

Center was by far his most successful. In later years, Chad was seen mostly in TV movies and miniseries, plus two additional unsuccessful series, *Hagen* and *The Rousters* (as the much put-upon grandson of Wyatt Earp).

EVERLY BROTHERS, THE—singers
Don Everly, b: Feb. 1, 1937, Brownie, Ky.
Phil Everly, b: Jan. 19, 1939, Brownie, Ky.

Shindig (music) .. frequent guests (1964–66)
Johnny Cash Presents The Everly Brothers (var)...................... cohosts (1970)

EVERS, JASON—actor
b: Jan 2, 1922, New York City, N.Y.

Wrangler (wes)
.... Pitcairn, the Wrangler (1960)
Channing (drama)
.... Prof. Joseph Howe (1963–64)

EVIGAN, GREG—actor
b: Oct 14, 1953, South Amboy, N.J.

A Year at the Top (com)....... Greg (1977)
B.J. and the Bear (adv)
.... B. J. McCoy (1979–81)
Masquerade (drama)
.... Danny Doyle (1983–84)

Boyish Greg Evigan got his start in the stage hit *Jesus Christ, Superstar* and later played the lead in the stage version of *Grease.* He began appearing in TV episodes in the mid-1970s. Greg also aspires to a career in rock music; he has released two albums and at one time had his own rock group, called GhettoWay City.

EWELL, TOM—actor
b: Apr 29, 1909, Owensboro, Ky.

The Tom Ewell Show (com)
.... Tom Potter (1960–61)
Baretta (police) .... Billy Truman (1975–78)
Best of the West (com)
.... Doc Jerome Kullens (1981–82)

EWING, OSCAR—U.S. government official
b: Mar 8, 1889 d: Jan 8, 1980

Everybody's Business (doc) ..... host (1951)

EWING, ROGER—actor

Gunsmoke (wes) . Clayton Thaddeus (Thad)
.... Greenwood (1965–67)

EWINS, BONNIE LOU—

Midwestern Hayride (var)
.... regular (1952–59)

EYER, RICHARD—juvenile actor
b: May 6, 1945, Los Angeles, Calif.

My Friend Irma (com)
.... Bobby Peterson (1953–54)
Stagecoach West (wes)
.... David Kane (1960–61)

This child actor appeared in numerous TV anthologies and other series of the 1950s and early '60s, including episodes of *The Loretta Young Show, General Electric Theater* and *Stoney Burke.* He left acting in the mid-1960s (after a performance in *Combat* that he particularly disliked) and is now an elementary school teacher.

F

FABARES, SHELLEY—actress
b: Jan 19, 1944*, Santa Monica, Calif.

The Donna Reed Show (com)
.... Mary Stone (1958–63)
The Brian Keith Show (com)
.... Dr. Anne Jamison (1972–74)
The Practice (com)
.... Jenny Bedford (1976–77)
Mary Hartman, Mary Hartman (com)
.... Eleanor Major (1977–78)
Highcliffe Manor (com)
.... Helen Blacke (1979)
One Day at a Time (com)
.... Francine Webster (1981–84)

Shelley Fabares is one of those "TV kids" who practically grew up on-screen. As the niece of 1950s star Nanette Fabray, Shelley was exposed to show business at an early age. At age 7 she was an extra in a movie, and at 9 she appeared in a TV special with Frank Sinatra. By the late '50s she had played juvenile roles in a variety of shows, including *Captain Midnight* and *The Mickey Mouse Club,* but her major break came as Donna Reed's daughter in *The Donna Reed Show.* The series was so popular in the early '60s that her astute managers were able to parlay her fame into a teen recording career, yielding a million-selling hit called "Johnny Angel" (even though she neither was nor is known as a singer). Shelley also appeared in several teen-oriented movies of the period, starring opposite Fabian in *Ride the Wild Surf* and with Elvis Presley in *Girl Happy, Spinout,* and *Clambake.*

After all this sun and fun, Shelley's career slowed down noticeably in the late '60s. As she remarked later, "There just weren't roles that fit my image. It was a period of girls being involved in dope and other seedier problems. Producers just didn't think of me at casting time." She did do a few series episodes (including several for *Love, American Style*), but it was a 1971 TV movie that rekindled her career and made her, in the eyes of many, an adult star. *Brian's Song* was an enormous hit, and Shelley, as the dying athlete's wife, was back in the spotlight.

*Some sources give 1942.

Since then she has appeared fairly regularly in TV movies and series episodes, including a three-year run in the '80s on the comedy *One Day at a Time* as Bonnie Franklin's ad agency partner. Ironically, Shelley's famous aunt, Nanette Fabray, appeared in the series at the same time, as Grandma Romano.

FABIAN, OLGA—actress

The Goldbergs (com) .... Mrs. Bloom (1953)

FABIANI, JOEL—actor

Department S (police)
.... Stewart Sullivan (1971)
Dallas (drama)....... Alex Ward (1980–81)
Dynasty (drama) ..... King Galen (1985–   )

FABRAY, NANETTE—actress
b: Oct 27, 1920, San Diego, Calif.

Caesar's Hour (var) .. Ann Victor (1954–56)
Westinghouse Playhouse (com)
.... Nan McGovern (1961)
One Day at a Time (com)
... Grandma Katherine Romano (1979–84)

Emmy Awards: Best Supporting Actress, for *Caesar's Hour* (1955), Best Comedienne (1955, 1956)

Nanette Fabray was a bright, vivacious Broadway musical star of the '40s and '50s who was chosen by Sid Caesar to play his female lead after he split up with Imogene Coca in 1954. Nanette was no slouch at comedy herself and made a strong initial impression. Ultimately, she failed to recreate the special magic that Caesar and Coca had together, and she left the show. Perhaps the assignment was too much to expect of any actress. Caesar subsequently tried Janet Blair and then Gisele MacKenzie as his partner, with even less success.

Nanette had been in show business since childhood, making her stage debut at 4 and appearing as "Baby Nan" in *Our Gang (Little Rascals)* comedy shorts in the late 1920s. She had some supporting roles in films in 1939–40, but real fame came on Broadway in the '40s, especially with her starring role in the 1947 musical *High Button Shoes.* She appeared in occasional TV specials in the '50s and '60s, including a 1956 TV version of *High Button Shoes* costarring Hal March and Don Ameche, but never recaptured the success of her early video days with Caesar. A 1961 situation comedy with Nanette as a mom who was also a Broadway star was a flop; later she made only infrequent appearances on specials, TV movies and a few series, including *Love, American Style* and *One Day at a Time.*

Nanette is the aunt of young actress Shelley Fabares.

FACENDA, JOHN—sportscaster
b: c. 1912 d: Sep 27, 1984

NFL Action (sport) . . . . narrator (1971)

FADDEN, TOM—actor
b: 1895 d: Apr 14, 1980

Broken Arrow (wes) . . . . . Duffield (1956–58)
Cimarron City (wes) . . Silas Perry (1958–59)

FADIMAN, CLIFTON—host, literary editor
b: May 15, 1904, Brooklyn, N.Y.

This Is Show Business (var)
. . . . emcee (1949–54)
Information Please (quiz) . . . . . emcee (1952)
What's in a Word? (quiz)
. . . . moderator (1954)
The Name's the Same (quiz) . . emcee (1955)
Quiz Kids (quiz) . . . . emcee (1956)
This Is Show Business (var) . . . emcee (1956)

The creator and longtime host of radio's *Information Please,* which he brought to television in 1952. Fadiman was perhaps the leading example of the "witty intellectual" type popular on TV in the 1950s; apart from his TV appearances, he was known primarily as an editor and columnist.

FAFARA, STANLEY—juvenile actor
Leave It to Beaver (com)
. . . . Whitey Whitney (1957–63)

FAHEY, MYRNA—actress
b: c. 1936, Maine d: 1973

Father of the Bride (com)
. . . . Kay Banks Dunston (1961–62)

FAHIR, RHILO—comedian
Keep On Truckin' (var) . . . . . . regular (1975)

FAIRBAIRN, BRUCE—actor
The Rookies (police)
. . . . Off. Chris Owens (1974–76)
Behind the Screen (drama)
. . . . Bobby Danzig (1981–82)
Knots Landing (drama) . . Ray Geary (1984)

FAIRBANKS, DOUGLAS, JR.—actor
b: Dec 9, 1909, New York City, N.Y.

Douglas Fairbanks, Jr., Presents (misc)
. . . . host (1953–57)

The famous movie star hosted and often acted in this syndicated anthology series, which was filmed in England, where he lived for many years. Fairbanks has done relatively little television since then, although he was seen happily sailing away on *The Love Boat* in the early 1980s. He also appeared in a rather ridiculous 1980 TV movie about a terrorist who tries to hijack the Eiffel Tower—*The Hostage Tower.* Fairbanks' biography is titled *Knight Errant,* by Brian Connell (1955).

FAIRCHILD, EDGAR "COOKIE"—orchestra leader
b: Jun 1, 1898, New York City, N.Y. d: Feb 20, 1975

The Jerry Colonna Show (var)
. . . . bandleader (1951)

FAIRCHILD, MARGARET—actress
79 Park Avenue (drama)
. . . . Myrna Savitch (1977)

FAIRCHILD, MORGAN—actress
b: Feb 3, 1950, Dallas, Texas

Flamingo Road (drama)
. . . . Constance Weldon Carlyle (1981–82)
Paper Dolls (drama) . . . . Racine (1984)
North and South (drama)
. . . . Burdetta Halloran (1985)
Falcon Crest (drama)
. . . . Jordan Roberts (1985–86)

This actress seemed to be on the verge of becoming a major television sex symbol on several occasions, without landing the role that would have clinched her place in TV history. She first came to notice as the murderous Jennifer Pace on daytime's *Search for Tomorrow* from 1973–77; unfortunately the show was already past its heyday by that time. In the mid and late '70s she appeared in episodes of many series, including once as the original Jenna Wade on *Dallas.* However, by the time Jenna became a major character on the show, the part was played by another actress. Morgan then landed the leading role of sultry Constance Carlyle on NBC's *Flamingo Road;* but that series failed to survive the prime time soap opera competition. Neither did her next series, ABC's *Paper Dolls.*

Morgan was not dismayed by all these "almosts." "I've worked hard for many years, but because of the way I look, people just assume I'm just another blonde who's where I am because I have the right look at the right moment," she said in 1981. "But I'll tell you this, I'm here to stay."

Morgan is said to be a collector of movie memorabilia, particularly momentos of Marilyn Monroe.

FAIRCHILDS, THE—

Nashville on the Road (music)
.... regulars (1976–77)

FAIRFAX, JAMES—actor
b: c. 1897 d: May 8, 1961

Ramar of the Jungle (adv)
.... regular (1952–54)
The Gale Storm Show (com)
.... Cedric (1956–59)

FAIRMAN, MICHAEL—actor

Cagney & Lacey (police)
.... Inspector Knelman (1984–)

FALANA, AVELIO—actress

Dinah and Her New Best Friends (var)
.... regular (1976)

FALANA, LOLA—black actress, singer
b: Sep 11, 1943*, Camden, N.J.

The New Bill Cosby Show (var)
.... regular (1972–73)
Ben Vereen . . . Comin' At Ya (var)
.... regular (1975)

FALK, PETER—actor
b: Sep 16, 1927, New York City, N.Y.
*Some sources give 1939.

The Trials of O'Brien (drama)
.... Daniel J. O'Brien (1965–66)
Columbo (police) .... Lt. Columbo (1971–77)

Emmy Awards: Best Actor in a Single Performance, for "The Price of Tomatoes" on *The Dick Powell Show* (1962); Best Actor in a Drama or Limited Series, for *Columbo* (1972, 1975, 1976)

For short, squinty Peter Falk, sudden success in the 1970s must have seemed rather ironic. Both he and the character that made him famous had been around for a while, in one form or another.

Falk's squint resulted from the loss of an eye during childhood. He did not originally intend to become an actor, graduating from college with a master's degree in public administration and working for several years as an efficiency expert for the budget bureau of the state of Connecticut. All those figures proved rather boring, however. In 1955, with the encouragement of actress Eva LaGallienne, he turned to acting. He appeared in off-Broadway plays and also in some live TV productions of the late 1950s, including *Studio One* in 1957. By the early '60s he was quite busy on television, often playing gangster roles (on *The Untouchables*, *Naked City*, etc.). He was nominated for an Emmy for a performance on *The Law and Mr. Jones* and won for his role as the truck driver on a memorable episode of *The Dick Powell Show.*

In 1965 Falk starred in his first series, as the raffish small-time lawyer in *The Trials of O'Brien.* The series was not successful, but two years later, in early 1968, he created a similar character, the rumpled but wily Lieutenant Columbo, who outwitted murderous psychiatrist Gene Barry in the TV movie *Prescription: Murder.* Another *Columbo* movie followed in 1971 (in which he tripped up Lee Grant), and the following fall the semiregular *Columbo* series began, making Falk a major star.

He does not seem to have been very interested in TV work since that time, appearing instead in occasional movies such as *The In-Laws* and *All the Marbles.*

FALKENBURG, JINX—actress
b: Jan 21, 1919, Barcelona, Spain

At Home with Tex and Jinx (talk)
.... cohost (1947)

Preview with Tex and Jinx (talk)
.... cohost (1949)
Masquerade Party (quiz).... panelist (1958)

Biography: *Jinx* (1951).

FANN, AL—black actor
b: Feb 21, 1925, Cleveland, Ohio

He's the Mayor (com)
.... Alvin Burke (1986)

FANNING, BILL—

The Jimmie Rodgers Show (var)
.... regular (1969)

FANT, LOU—actor

Thicker Than Water (com)
.... Walter (1973)

FARACY, STEPHANIE—actress
b: Jan 1, Brooklyn, N.Y.

The Last Resort (com)
.... Gail Collins (1979–80)
The Thorn Birds (drama) ...... Judy (1983)
Goodnight, Beantown (com)
.... Valerie Wood (1983–84)
Eye to Eye (drama)..... Tracy Doyle (1985)

FARBER, BERT—orchestra leader
b: June 2, 1913, Brooklyn, N.Y.

Arthur Godfrey's Talent Scouts (talent)
.... orch. leader (1955–58)
Arthur Godfrey and His Friends (var)
.... orch. leader (1955–58)
The Vic Damone Show (var)
.... orch. leader (1957)

FARENTINO, JAMES—actor
b: Feb 24, 1938, Brooklyn, N.Y.

The Lawyers (drama)
.... Neil Darrell (1969–72)
Cool Million (drama)
.... Jefferson Keyes (1972–73)
Dynasty (drama)
.... Dr. Nick Toscanni (1981–82)
Blue Thunder (police)
.... Frank Chaney (1984)
Mary (com)...... Frank DeMarco (1985–86)

This forceful actor began his career on the New York stage shortly after graduation from the American Academy of Dramatic Arts in 1958. His first big break was in the Tennessee Williams play *Night of the Iguana* on Broadway in 1961; at about the same time he was appearing in minor roles in New York–originated TV series, including *Naked City* and *The Defenders*. By the end of 1963 he had decided to move west, to lusher climes and to the likes of *77 Sunset Strip* and *Laredo*. Farentino's specialty was the self-assured, determined, often somewhat cocky young man, and he carried this persona into his first two series, *The Lawyers* (part of *The Bold Ones* anthology), as an idealistic young attorney, and *Cool Million*, as a high-priced detective. More guest roles and some routine TV movies followed; in the '80s he was playing more mature, but still quite assertive, parts in *Dynasty* (as one of Fallon's parade of lovers) and *Blue Thunder*.

Farentino's one Emmy nomination was in 1978 for a rather different role, however —that of the disciple Peter in *Jesus of Nazareth*.

FARGAS, ANTONIO—black actor
b: Aug 14, 1946, The Bronx, N.Y.

Starsky and Hutch (police)
.... Huggy Bear (1975–79)

FARGE, ANNIE—actress
b: c. 1935, France

Angel (com).............. Angel (1960–61)

FARINA, DENNIS—actor
b: c. 1944, Chicago, Ill.

Crime Story (police)
.... Lt. Mike Torello (1986–)

This tough-looking TV cop was authentic —a veteran of 18 years with the Chicago P.D. Detective Farina began acting professionally in the early '80s, appearing in such series as *Chicago Story* and *Hardcastle & McCormick* and did not quit the force for good until *Crime Story* went into production in 1986. Asked how playing a cop on TV compared with the real thing, he replied, "Police work, for the most part, is pretty boring. You don't get up every day, walk out of the house and get in a car chase, shoot five people, and make twenty arrests ... Sometimes I gotta remember, 'This is TV, not the street!' "

FARLEY, DUKE—actor

Car 54, Where Are You? (com)
.... Officer Riley (1961–62)

FARMER, LILLIAN—

The Ken Murray Show (var)
.... regular (1951–52)

FARR, JAMIE—actor
b: Jul 1, 1934, Toledo, Ohio

Chicago Teddy Bears (com).... Lefty (1971)
M*A*S*H (com)
.... Cpl. Maxwell Klinger (1973–83)
The Gong Show (com)
.... panelist (1976–80)
The $1.98 Beauty Show (com)
.... frequent panelist (1978–80)
AfterMASH (com)... Max Klinger (1983–84)

Jamie Farr, a happy guy with a big nose, bummed around TV for 20 years making little impression until a single guest appearance on *M*A*S*H* brought him the role that set his career in motion. Jamie's first TV appearance was in an episode of a situation comedy called *Dear Phoebe,* starring Peter Lawford, during the 1954–55 season. Subsequently, he had small parts in such series as *The Red Skelton Show, The Rebel, The Danny Kaye Show,* and *The Dick Van Dyke Show.* He also turned up in such diverse movies as the 1955 classic *Blackboard Jungle* (as Santini) and the 1965 biblical epic *The Greatest Story Ever Told* (as Thaddaeus).

The continuing part of an inept bodyguard in *The Chicago Teddy Bears* in 1971 didn't attract much attention, but a guest appearance on *M*A*S*H* the following year—as a nutty soldier who dressed like a woman so he would be discharged as mentally unfit—did. Jamie was invited back and Maxwell Klinger became a favorite character on the series. Jamie parlayed his newfound fame into guest appearances on many game shows, as well as roles in an assortment of TV movies and specials. He seems content, however, to be remembered as Maxwell Klinger for the rest of his days.

FARR, LEE—actor

The Detectives, Starring Robert Taylor (police) .... Lt. James Conway (1959–60)

FARRELL, AMY—actress

Search (adv) .... Murdock (1972–73)

FARRELL, CHARLES—actor
b: Aug 9, 1901, Onset Bay, Cape Cod, Mass.

My Little Margie (com)
.... Vernon Albright (1952–55)
The Charlie Farrell Show (com)
.... as himself (1956)

Charlie Farrell is known to television viewers as Gale Storm's smiling, handsome, silver-haired dad on *My Little Margie,* but he had a long and equally sunny career in movies before that. He started as a bit player in silents in the early 1920s and gained great fame playing opposite Janet Gaynor in a series of romantic films of the late '20s and early '30s, including the Academy Award–winning *Seventh Heaven.* His career declined as fast as it had risen, however, and by 1941 his movie-making days were essentially over. He was well off, so he retired to Palm Springs, where he founded and operated the very fashionable Palm Springs Racquet Club for the rest of his days. He became such a fixture of that chic resort town that he was elected mayor for several terms.

Charlie was lured out of this pleasant retirement only briefly to do the *Margie* series and a summer replacement series called *The Charlie Farrell Show* in 1956, the latter set at his beloved racquet club. Otherwise, he did little television.

FARRELL, GWEN—actress

M*A*S*H (com)... various nurses (1979–83)

FARRELL, JUDY—actress

M*A*S*H (com)... various nurses (1976–83)
Fame (drama)
.... Mrs. Charlotte Miller (1982–83)

The wife of actor Mike Farrell.

FARRELL, MIKE—actor
b: Feb 6, 1939, St. Paul, Minn. r: Los Angeles

The Interns (drama)
.... Dr. Sam Marsh (1970–71)
The Man and the City (drama)
.... Andy Hays (1971–72)

M*A*S*H (com)
.... Capt. B. J. Hunnicut (1975–83)

Before lanky Mike Farrell became Alan Alda's tentmate and coconspirator on M*A*S*H (replacing Wayne Rogers), he was an actor with solid if unspectacular credits. As many others have proven, it takes only one good role to make an actor famous.

The son of a movie-studio carpenter, Mike went directly into acting but was scarcely noticed at all during the '60s as he appeared in small roles in a number of films and occasional TV series, including Lassie and Combat. His first real break came in 1968 with the role of Scott Banning in the daytime soap opera Days of our Lives, which he played for two years. Then things started to click, with regular roles as an intern on The Interns and as a mayor's political aide on The Man and the City. A lot of guest appearances on dramas of the early '70s followed, but it was not until he combined medicine and political opinion on M*A*S*H that he hit it big.

During and since his days on that famous series, Mike has appeared in quite a few TV movies, many of which seem to be "message" oriented. Among them: Battered (1978), about wife beating; Damien, The Leper Priest (1980); Prime Suspect (1982), about excesses of the press; and Choices of the Heart (1983), about murdered religious workers in El Salvador. He has also appeared in a number of unsuccessful movie pilots for proposed series, one of the more recent being 1985's Private Sessions, which cast him as a caring psychologist.

FARRELL, SHARON—actress
b: Dec 24, 1946, Sioux City, Iowa

Saints and Sinners (drama) . Polly (1962–63)
Hawaii Five-O (police)
.... Lori Wilson (1979–80)
Rituals (drama) ..... Cherry Lane (1984–85)

FARRELL, SHEA—actor
b: Oct 21, 1957, Cornwall, N.Y.

Hotel (drama)..... Mark Danning (1983–86)

FARRELL, SKIP—singer
b: c. 1920 d: 1962

The Skip Farrell Show (music) .. host (1949)

FARRELL, TERRY—actress
b: Nov 19, 1963, Cedar Rapids, Iowa

Paper Dolls (drama).. Laurie Caswell (1984)

FARRELL, TIM—actor

Accused (drama)......... bailiff (1958–59)

FARRELL, TOMMY—actor

The Many Loves of Dobie Gillis (com)
.... Riff Ryan (1959–60)

FARRINGER, LISA—comedienne

Rowan & Martin's Laugh-In (var)
.... regular (1972–73)

FARROW, MIA—actress
b: Feb 9, 1945, Los Angeles, Calif.

Peyton Place (drama)
.... Allison MacKenzie/Harrington
(1964–66)

The willowy star of such films as Rosemary's Baby and Death on the Nile is very well remembered by TV viewers for her two seasons on Peyton Place in the '60s. She was fondly remembered by the writers of that show, too; her character continued to be the subject of storylines for several years after Allison "disappeared." Mia did not appear in any of the various revivals of Peyton Place, but she certainly wasn't forgotten; the "lost" Allison was always much-talked about, and Mia herself was even seen via film clips in the 1977 TV movie Murder in Peyton Place.

Otherwise, Mia has done little television. She starred in Johnny Belinda in 1967, in Goodbye Raggedy Ann in 1971, and in Peter Pan in 1975. The actress was married to Frank Sinatra briefly in the '60s and to composer Andre Previn in the '70s. She is the daughter of actress Maureen O'Sullivan. Her wispy, vulnerable appearance is genuine; she was the victim of polio as a child.

FASCINATO, JACK—orchestra leader, pianist
b: Sep 11, 1915, Bevier, Mo.

Kukla, Fran & Ollie (child)
.... musical director (1948–57)
Sing-co-pation (music) .... trio (1949)

FATES, GIL—host, producer

What's It Worth? (misc) ... emcee (1948–49)
Hold It Please (quiz)......... emcee (1949)

FAULK, JOHN HENRY—humorist
b: c. 1918

It's News to Me (quiz) ... panelist (1951–54)
Leave It to the Girls (talk) .. panelist (1954)
Hee Haw (var).......... regular (1975–82)

John Henry Faulk would scarcely be a foot-note in TV history were it not for the celebrated court case he initiated that broke the back of political blacklisting in television. Though he was ultimately successful, it was a long and painful experience for the folksy humorist and raconteur.

Faulk was a local New York radio personality who was seen from time to time on TV panel shows of the early 1950s. In 1955 CBS used him briefly as the host of its *Morning Show,* the network's first attempt to compete with NBC's very successful *Today* show. He also had a regular show on radio station WCBS.

Blacklisting was at that time rampant in the industry. A small group of right-wing activists had been able to capitalize on the public's fear of Communist infiltration to pressure sponsors and networks into refusing to employ anyone with left-wing—sometimes even liberal—political beliefs. What was worse, virtually all of the blacklisting was carried out behind closed doors; it was a time of secret lists and whispered allegations. Performers never knew what was said about them or by whom; some simply found they couldn't get work anymore. Few executives were willing to speak out against the practice for fear of being themselves labeled as "Communist sympathizers." In 1955 a group of New York performers, headed by the highly respected CBS newsman Charles Collingwood, ran for office in the New York performer's union on a platform openly condemning such practices, and they were elected. The right-wing political action group Aware, Inc., fought back. Collingwood himself was too well-established to be discredited, but Orson Bean and John Henry Faulk, who were also on the ticket, were subjected to a tremendous vilification campaign, and both saw their employment reduced—because they had become "too controversial." Bean ultimately survived the hate campaign, but Faulk was virtually run out of the business. His annual income dropped from $35,000 to $2,000.

With the help of Edward R. Murrow and famed lawyer Louis Nizer, Faulk filed suit against Aware and its founders for destroying his career. It was a very difficult case to prove, since employment in show business is by its nature uncertain. There was much legal wrangling, but finally, in 1962, the case came to trial—and, in a landmark decision, Faulk was awarded $3.5 million in damages (later reduced). Lawrence Johnson, the head of Aware, suffered a heart attack and died.

While Faulk was vindicated, his show business career never really recovered. His main claim to fame seems to have been the case itself, and his resulting book, *Fear on Trial,* was dramatized in a 1975 TV movie starring George C. Scott (as Nizer) and William Devane (as Faulk). Faulk was later a regular on *Hee Haw* for a while, and in 1983 he could be glimpsed playing—of all people—right-wing Senator Strom Thurmond in the TV movie *Adam.*

FAULKONBRIDGE, CLAIRE— comedienne

Laugh-In (revival) (var) ... regular (1977–78)

FAUSTINO, DAVID—actor

I Had Three Wives (drama)
.... Andrew Beaudine (1985)

FAWCETT, FARRAH—actress
b: Feb 2, 1946*, Corpus Christi, Texas

Harry-O (drama)
.... next door neighbor (1974–76)
Charlie's Angels (drama)
.... Jill Munroe (1976–77)

Farrah Fawcett is one overnight sex symbol who went on to prove herself as an accomplished actress. Her rise to stardom was certainly sudden. The daughter of a Texas oil contractor, she began her career doing commercials (for Wella Balsam, Mercury Cougar, etc.) and playing bit parts in movies, beginning with a forgettable 1969 French/Italian opus called *The Best*

*Some sources give 1942 or 1947.

Man. Later films weren't much better *(The Great American Beauty Contest, The Girl Who Came Gift-Wrapped)*, while her TV series appearances consisted of small parts in *The Flying Nun, Marcus Welby*, etc. As the girlfriend of Lee Majors, she got roles in his series *Owen Marshall* and *The Six Million Dollar Man.* She also had a running part as the sexy girl-next-door on *Harry-O.*

At the start of 1976 she was just one of a million sexy young hopefuls in Hollywood; then she appeared in the TV movie pilot for *Charlie's Angels.* When the movie became a series the following fall, Farrah (by then married to Majors, and calling herself Farrah Fawcett-Majors) was an overnight sensation. A cheesecake swimsuit poster of her sold more than two million copies, while Farrah dolls, T-shirts and wigs flooded the market (she turned down a deal for Farrah sheets bearing her lifesize likeness). No one knew why she, and the series, was such an enormous hit. "When the show was number three I figured it was our acting," she told *TV Guide* in 1977. "When we got to be number one I decided it could only be because none of us wears a bra."

Her publicist added, "The only thing she still has to prove is that she can act." Farrah left *Charlie's Angels* after a single season to do just that (in order to get out of her contract she had to make periodic guest appearances for the next three years). At first it seemed that her career was collapsing as quickly as it had boomed, as her first few films were flops. Her image as "yesterday's bimbo" was just too strong. She decided to make a dramatic change. In 1983 Farrah surprised New York critics with her performance as an enraged woman who turns the tables on her would-be rapist in the off-Broadway play *Extremities.* Then in 1984 she won national acclaim as the battered wife in one of the highest-rated TV movies of all time, *The Burning Bed.* Farrah seems to have overcome her early image.

FAX, JESSLYN—actress

Our Miss Brooks (com)
.... Angela (1954–56)
Many Happy Returns (com)
.... Wilma Fritter (1964–65)

FAYE, HERBIE—actor, comedian
b: c. 1899 d: June 28, 1980

Seven at Eleven (var)....... regular (1951)
The Phil Silvers Show (com)
.... Pvt. Sam Fender (1955–59)
The New Phil Silvers Show (com)
.... Waluska (1963–64)
Love Thy Neighbor (com)
.... Harry Mulligan (1973)
Doc (com) .... Ben Goldman (1975–76)

FAYE, JOEY—comedian
b: Jul 12, 1909, New York City, N.Y.

Broadway Spotlight (var) .... regular (1949)
Fifty-Fourth Street Revue (var) .. host (1950)
Joey Faye's Frolics (var) .... host (1950)
Guess Again (quiz) .... regular (1951)

FAYLEN, CAROL—actress
b: c. 1949

The Bing Crosby Show (com)
.... Janice Collins (1964–65)

The daughter of Frank Faylen.

FAYLEN, FRANK—actor
b: Dec 8, 1907*, St. Louis, Mo. d: Aug 2, 1985

The Many Loves of Dobie Gillis (com)
.... Herbert T. Gillis (1959–63)

FEE, MELINDA—actress
b: Oct 7, Los Angeles, Calif.

The Invisible Man (adv)
.... Dr. Kate Westin (1975–76)

FEENEY, JOE—Irish tenor

The Lawrence Welk Show (music)
.... regular (1957–82)

FEINSTEIN, ALAN—actor
b: Sep 8, 1941, New York City, N.Y.

Jigsaw John (police) .... Sam Donner (1976)
The Runaways (drama)
.... Steve Arizzio (1979)
Masada (drama) .... Aaron (1981)
The Family Tree (drama)
.... Dr. David Benjamin (1983)
Berrengers (drama)... Max Kaufman (1985)

*Some sources give 1905 or 1909.

FELDMAN, COREY—juvenile actor
b: Jul 16, 1971, Reseda, Calif.

The Bad News Bears (com)
.... Regi Tower (1979–80)
Madame's Place (com)....... Buzzy (1982)

FELDMAN, MARTY—comedian
b: Jul 8, 1933, London, England d: Dec 2, 1982

Dean Martin Presents the Golddiggers (var)
.... regular (1970)
The Marty Feldman Comedy Machine (var)
.... host (1972)

An English comic with a striking appearance: bulging eyes, shaggy hair, and a hooked nose. He began as a scriptwriter and was a popular TV personality in England before coming to the U.S. in the 1970s.

FELDON, BARBARA—actress
b: Mar 12, 1939, Pittsburgh, Pa.

Get Smart (com) .... Agent 99 (1965–70)
The Marty Feldman Comedy Machine (var)
.... regular (1972)
The Dean Martin Comedy World (var)
.... host (1974)

Barbara started out as a dancer in the chorus line at the Copacabana nightclub in New York and later (in 1957) danced in a Broadway revival of *The Ziegfeld Follies*. As a publicity stunt during the run of the *Follies*, the entire chorus line was given I.Q. tests, with surprising results, at least for Barbara. She did so well she was chosen as a contestant on *The $64,000 Question*, where she won the top prize for her extensive knowledge of Shakespeare.

Though her brains had gotten her out of the chorus line, they did not automatically bring better roles. She worked for a time as a fashion model, as well as in some rather sexy TV commercials (in one of them she was the Tiger Girl, purring "Sic 'em, tiger"). By the early 1960s she was gradually gaining roles on prime time series such as *East Side/West Side*, *Slattery's People*, and *Flipper*. A role as an industrial spy on *Mr. Broadway* led to the part of Agent 99 on *Get Smart*, which secured her fame, at least among fans of that classic comedy series.

Since *Get Smart* ended its run Barbara

has been seen mostly in TV movies and specials. She has also appeared in a number of pilots for proposed series that did not make it to the regular schedule and in a syndicated magazine series called *Special Edition* (1977), which was not successful.

FELDSHUH, TOVAH—actress
b: Dec 27, 1953, New York City, N.Y.

Holocaust (drama) . Helena Slomova (1978)

FELICIANO, JOSE—singer
b: Sep 10, 1945, Lares, Puerto Rico

Chico and the Man (com)
.... sang theme (1974–78)

FELIX, OTTO—actor

B.J. and the Bear (adv)
.... Dep. Higgins (1979–80)

FELL, NORMAN—actor
b: Mar 24, 1924, Philadelphia, Pa.

Joe & Mabel (com) . Mike the Cabbie (1956)
87th Precinct (police)
.... Det. Meyer Meyer (1961–62)
Dan August (police)
.... Sgt. Charles Wilentz (1970–71)
Needles and Pins (com)
.... Nathan Davidson (1973)
Rich Man, Poor Man—Book I (drama)
.... Smitty (1976)
Three's Company (com)
.... Stanley Roper (1977–79)
The Ropers (com) . Stanley Roper (1979–80)
Teachers Only (com)
.... Ben Cooper (1982–83)

Despite a face that looks something like a prune, and a perpetually worried expression, Norman Fell has worked steadily in television for more than 30 years, in a wide variety of roles. His father was in the restaurant business, but young Norman had other plans; while serving as a tail gunner in the Pacific during World War II, he decided he would become an actor—if he got out alive.

An acting career proved scarcely less difficult than his wartime service. After years of acting school and a great deal of rejection, he began to get small parts in New York stage and television productions of the 1950s and on such series as *Goodyear Theater, Philco Theatre,* and *Studio One.* By the time he moved to Hollywood in 1958 he had appeared in perhaps 150 live TV plays, but gained little notice; probably the most notable was the 1954 *Studio One* production of "Twelve Angry Men," in which he was one of the unnoticed jurors. He also had his first regular role during his New York years, in the short-lived 1956 comedy *Joe & Mabel,* as the star's best friend.

In the 1960s the roles slowly got better. Norman played an older (already!), seen-it-all detective in *87th Precinct* and later one of Burt Reynolds' fellow cops in *Dan August.* His film credits included *Pork Chop Hill* and *The Graduate.* In the mid-1970s Norman began shifting toward comedy, and in 1977 he joined the cast of *Three's Company* as the irritable landlord, Mr. Roper—probably his most famous role. It was later spun off into a series of his own, *The Ropers.*

FELTON, VERNA—actress
b: Jul 20, 1890, Salinas, Calif. d: Dec 14, 1966

The RCA Victor Show (com)
.... Mrs. Day (1952)
December Bride (com)
.... Hilda Crocker (1954–59)
Pete and Gladys (com)
.... Hilda Crocker (1960–61)

FEMIA, JOHN—juvenile actor
b: Aug 3, c. 1967, Brooklyn, N.Y.

Hello, Larry (com)
.... Tommy Roscini (1979–80)
Square Pegs (com)
.... Marshall Blechtman (1982–83)

FENNELLY, PARKER—actor
b: Northeast Harbor, Me.

The Headmaster (drama)
.... Mr. Purdy (1970–71)

FENNEMAN, GEORGE—announcer, host
b: Nov 19, 1919, Peking, China

You Bet Your Life (quiz)
.... announcer (1950–61)
Anybody Can Play (quiz) ..... emcee (1958)
Tell It to Groucho (quiz) .. announcer (1962)

Your Funny, Funny Films (com)
.... host (1963)

George Fenneman—the dark, handsome, and apparently unflappable announcer on *You Bet Your Life*—was a radio actor and announcer in the 1940s before he became Groucho Marx's straight man and major domo in 1947. He also served as announcer for other programs over the years, from *Dragnet* in the '50s to *Donny and Marie* in the '70s.

FENWICK, ELLEN—actress

Charade Quiz (quiz)
.... repertory player (1947–49)

FENWICK, MILLICENT—writer
b: Feb 25, 1910, New York City, N.Y.

Television Screen Magazine (mag)
.... emcee/"editor" (1948)

An editor of *Vogue* magazine; later a U.S. congresswoman from New Jersey.

FERDIN, PAMELYN—juvenile actress
b: Feb 4, 1959

The John Forsythe Show (com)
.... Pamela (1965–66)
Blondie (com).. Cookie Bumstead (1968–69)
The Paul Lynde Show (com)
.... Sally Simms (1972–73)
Lassie (adv) .... Lucy Baker (1973–74)

Young Pamelyn was quite active on Saturday morning series of the 1970s, both providing cartoon voices and appearing in live-action shows.

FERGUSON, ALLYN—orchestra leader
b: Oct 18, 1924, San Jose, Calif.

The Andy Williams Show (var)
.... orch. leader (1966–67)
Away We Go (var)..... orch. leader (1967)
Happy Days (var)....... bandleader (1970)
Make Your Own Kind of Music (var)
.... orch. co-leader (1971)
Burns and Schreiber Comedy Hour (var)
.... orch. co-leader (1973)
Ben Vereen . . . Comin' At Ya (var)
.... orch. leader (1975)

Emmy Award: Best Music Composition for a Special, for *The Hallmark Hall of Fame* Production "Camille" (1985)

FERGUSON, FRANK—actor
b: Dec 25, 1899 d: Sep 12, 1978

My Friend Flicka (adv)
.... Gus Broeberg (1956–57)
Peyton Place (drama).. Eli Carson (1964–69)

FERNANDEZ, ABEL—actor

Steve Canyon (adv)
.... Airman Abel Featherstone (1959)
The Untouchables (police)
.... Agent William Youngfellow (1959–63)

FERRADAY, LISA—actress
b: Hungary

Leave It to the Girls (talk)
.... panelist (1949–54)
What Happened? (quiz)..... panelist (1952)
Personality Puzzle (quiz).... panelist (1953)
What's It For? (quiz) .... panelist (1957–58)

FERRAR, CATHERINE—actress

The Sixth Sense (drama)
.... Nancy Murphy (1972)

FERRELL, CONCHATA—actress
b: Mar 28, 1943, Charleston, W. Va. r: Cane
Fork, W. Va.

Hot L Baltimore (com).. April Green (1975)
B.J. and the Bear (adv)
. Wilhelmina "the Fox" Johnson (1979–80)
McClain's Law (police)
.... Vangie Cruise (1981–82)
E/R (com) ...... Nurse Joan Thor (1984–85)

FERRELL, RAY—juvenile actor

Peck's Bad Girl (com) ... Roger Peck (1959)

FERRELL, TODD—actor

Lassie (adv) .... Boomer Bates (1958–59)

FERRER, JOSE—actor
b: Jan 8, 1909*, Santurce, Puerto Rico

The Rhinemann Exchange (drama)
.... Erich Rhinemann (1977)
Bridges to Cross (drama)
.... Morris Kane (1986)

This distinguished, somewhat forbidding
stage and film actor used to appear in some
*Some sources give 1912.

of television's more prestigious productions, although lately he seems to turn up
in routine fare like *The French-Atlantic
Affair* and *The Dream Merchants*. One of
his greatest roles was the lead in *Cyrano
de Bergerac,* which he played to acclaim
on Broadway (1947), in a movie (1950), and
in a television special (1955).

He was married at one time to singer
Rosemary Clooney, who barely survived
the experience.

FERRER, MEL—actor, director
b: Aug 25, 1917, Elberon, N.J.

Behind the Screen (drama)
.... Evan Hammer (1981–82)
Falcon Crest (drama)
.... Phillip Erikson (1981–84)

FERRIGNO, LOU—actor
b: Nov 9, 1952, Brooklyn, N.Y.

The Incredible Hulk (drama)
.... The Incredible Hulk (1978–82)
Trauma Center (drama)..... John Six (1983)

What is big, has bulging muscles, and is
green all over? *The Incredible Hulk,* of
course, as well as muscleman Lou Ferrigno, who portrayed him. Ferrigno's dimensions are, well, awesome: 6′5″, 275
pounds, 59-inch chest, 19-inch neck, 22-
inch biceps. The son of a New York City
police lieutenant, Lou has had a lifelong
interest in bodybuilding and has won
every major title in the field, including
Teenage Mr. America (1971), Mr. America
(1973), Mr. Universe (1973), Mr. International (1974), and Mr. Universe again
(1974).

Fresh from these triumphs he decided to
become a football player, signing with the
Toronto Argonauts. The team was delighted to have a human bulldozer on its
line, but during a scrimmage Lou blocked
another player and broke the man's legs.
Lou, a sensitive man, was so upset by the
incident he quit football and moved to
Los Angeles to pursue bodybuilding instead. Several months later he won a part
in the movie *Pumping Iron,* as Arnold
Schwarzenegger's rival, and this led to
an interest in acting. Next came the role
of Bill Bixby's snarling alter ego in
The Incredible Hulk, which was first seen as
a TV movie in November 1977 and be-

came a hit series the following spring.

It was during the run of *Hulk* that Lou decided to do something about a handicap that had dogged him from youth. As the result of an inner-ear infection as a child, Lou was 60% deaf and he had a halting speech pattern characteristic of children who grow up unable to hear the sound of their own voice. He worked diligently to overcome his speech impediment, accepting dozens of speaking engagements and appearances on talk shows—any public event where he would be required to talk. He became a spokesman for hearing-and-speech-impairment associations and during episodes of *Trauma Center* was seen in stories urging understanding of the problem, especially as it affects children. "We are all handicapped," he points out. "Some more noticeably than others."

FERRIS, BARBARA—actress
b: 1940, London, England

The Strauss Family (drama)
.... Emilie Trampusch (1973)

FERRIS, IRENE—actress

Cover Up (drama) .... Billie (1984–85)

FERRIS, PAUL—actor

The Baron (drama) .. David Marlowe (1966)

FERRUGIA, JOHN—newscaster
b: Fulton, Mo.

West 57th (pub aff)
.... correspondent (1985–)

FIDLER, JIMMY—gossip columnist
b: 1900, Memphis, Tenn.

Hollywood Opening Night (drama)
.... host (1952–53)

FIEDLER, ARTHUR—orchestra leader
b: Dec 17, 1894, Boston, Mass. d: Jul 10, 1979

The Voice of Firestone (music)
.... conductor (occasional) (1962–63)

FIEDLER, JOHN—actor
b: Feb 3, 1925, Platville, Wis.

The Bob Newhart Show (com)
.... Mr. Peterson (1973–78)

Kolchak: The Night Stalker (drama)
.... Gordy Spangler (1974–75)
Buffalo Bill (com) .... Woody (1983–84)

FIELD, BYRON—sportscaster

They're Off (quiz) .... race caller (1949)

FIELD, SALLY—actress
b: Nov 6, 1946, Pasadena, Calif.

Gidget (com)
... Francine "Gidget" Lawrence (1965–66)
The Flying Nun (com)
.... Sister Bertrille (1967–70)
Alias Smith and Jones (wes)
.... Clementine Hale (1971–73)
Girl with Something Extra (com)
.... Sally Burton (1973–74)

Emmy Award: Best Actress in a Drama Special, for *Sybil* (1977)

Diminutive Sally Field might be considered cute as a button—unless you happened to get in her way in *Norma Rae*. The onetime beach bunny of the '60s has turned to playing very determined little ladies in the '70s and '80s.

Sally was raised in show business. Her mother was actress Margaret Field and her stepfather, actor Jock Mahoney. Fresh out of high school, she enrolled in the Columbia Pictures actors' workshop and was promptly chosen for the lead role in *Gidget*, a frolicsome teen comedy full of sun, surf, and bikinis. She scored an even bigger success in 1967 as *The Flying Nun*, whose tiny size (Sally is 5′2″, 97 pounds) as well as her large, starched cornette no doubt helped her become airborne. Later she was a young bride with an embarrassing penchant for reading hubby John Davidson's mind on *The Girl with Something Extra*.

All this fluff hardly established Sally as a serious adult actress. By the mid-1970s, just as she began to turn from TV to movies, her career seemed to be fading. A turning point came with the role of the mentally disturbed young woman with multiple personalities in the acclaimed 1976 TV movie *Sybil*. Three years later she again surprised Hollywood and won an Academy Award for her portrayal of the spunky union organizer in *Norma Rae*; this was followed by further acclaim for her role opposite Paul Newman in *Ab-*

sence of Malice. "I try to take roles that are different each time," she says. "I don't like to repeat myself. I like to be challenged."

FIELD, SYLVIA—actress

Mr. Peepers (com)
.... Mrs. Remington (1953–55)
Dennis the Menace (com)
.... Martha Wilson (1961–62)

FIELDING, DOROTHY—actress

One in a Million (com)
.... Nancy Boyer (1980)

FIELDING, JERRY—orchestra leader, composer
b: June 17, 1922, Pittsburgh, Pa. d: Feb 17, 1980

The Lively Ones (var)
.... orch. leader (1962–63)

Fielding scored many films and television series, including *Bewitched, Hogan's Heroes, McMillan and Wife, The Bionic Woman,* etc.

FIELDS, CHARLIE—actor
b: Sep 16, c. 1971, Brooklyn, N.Y.

Shannon (police)
.... Johnny Shannon (1981–82)

FIELDS, CHIP—black actress
b: New York City, N.Y.

The Amazing Spider-Man (adv)
.... Rita Conway (1978–79)

FIELDS, IRVING—pianist, combo leader
b: Aug 4, 1915, New York City, N.Y.

The Ilona Massey Show (music)
.... trio (1954–55)

FIELDS, JOAN—

Front Row Center (var)
.... regular (1949–50)

FIELDS, KIM—black actress
b: May 12, 1969, Los Angeles, Calif.

Baby, I'm Back (com).... Angie Ellis (1978)
The Facts of Life (com)
.... Tootie Ramsey (1979–)

The daughter of actress Chip Fields. Kim blossomed on television from a cute little kid (she was Alex Haley's daughter on *Roots*) to a rapidly expanding young woman during the later years of *The Facts of Life.*

FIELDS, SID—comedian
b: c. 1898 d: Sep 28, 1975

The Frank Sinatra Show (var)
.... regular (1950–51)
The Abbott and Costello Show (com)
.... as himself (1951–53)
The Jackie Gleason Show (var)
.... regular (1964–66)

FINGER, DAVID AND MICHAEL—infant actors

Miss Winslow and Son (com)
.... Edmund Hillary Warren Winslow (1979)

FINK, JOHN—actor
b: Feb 11, Detroit, Mich.

Nancy (com)... Dr. Adam Hudson (1970–71)

FINLEY, PAT—actress
b: Oct 14, c. 1940, Asheville, N.C. r: Washington State

From a Bird's Eye View (com)
.... Maggie Ralston (1971)
The Funny Side (var)........ regular (1971)
The Bob Newhart Show (com)
.... Ellen Hartley (1974–76)

FINN, FRED E.—host, pianist
b: Oct 24, 1938, San Francisco, Calif.

Mickie Finn's (var)......... regular (1966)

FINN, MICKIE—hostess, banjo player
b: Jun 16, 1938, Hugo, Okla.

Mickie Finn's (var)......... regular (1966)

Fred and Mickie were a husband and wife team who founded a popular Gay 90s–style club in San Diego, which served as the setting for this 1966 NBC summer series.

FINNEGAN, BOB—sportscaster

Prime Time Baseball (sport)
.... sportscaster (1952)

Tuesday/Monday Night Fights (sport)
.... sportscaster (1953–55)

FINNEY, MARY—actress
b: c. 1904 d: Feb 26, 1973

Honestly Celeste (com)
.... the secretary (1954)

FIORE, BILL—actor
b: c. 1940, Williston Park, N.Y.

The Corner Bar (com)
.... Phil Bracken (1972–73)

FIORE & ELDRIDGE—

Dean Martin Presents the Golddiggers (var)
.... regulars (1969)

FIRESTONE, EDDY—actor
b: Dec 11, 1920, San Francisco, Calif.

Mixed Doubles (drama)
.... Eddy Coleman (1949)

FISCH, FRANK—sports commentator

Are You Positive? (quiz) .... panelist (1952)

FISCHER, COREY—actor

Sunshine (com)............... Givits (1975)

FISHBEIN, BEN—actor

The O'Neills (drama)
.... Morris Levy (1949–50)

FISHER, BILL—sportscaster

Prime Time Football (sport)
.... announcer (1950–51)

FISHER, EDDIE—singer
b: Aug 10, 1928, Philadelphia, Pa.

Coke Time with Eddie Fisher (music)
.... star (1953–57)
The George Gobel Show (var)
.... regular (1957–58)
The Eddie Fisher Show (var)
.... host (1957–59)

This handsome young crooner with a big, booming voice was extremely popular in the early and mid-1950s, both on records and TV. He had started in clubs as a teenager and was discovered in 1949 by Eddie Cantor, who featured him on his radio show. A string of enormous hits followed, including "Thinking of You," "Any Time," "Wish You Were Here," etc. Eddie was widely seen on TV variety shows to the squeals of delighted teenagers who had not yet discovered rock 'n' roll.

Drafted into the army in 1952, he appeared on TV (while on leave) as PFC Eddie Fisher, then got his own early-evening 15-minute series upon his discharge in 1953. In the late 1950s he hosted a prime time variety hour, which alternated for a time with George Gobel's show. By then a different kind of music was taking over, however, but Eddie remained in the news mostly for his marital adventures: he was first married to Debbie Reynolds, whom he dumped in 1959 for screen star Elizabeth Taylor, who dumped *him* in 1964 for Richard Burton. He was later wed to Connie Stevens, then went through a very trying, self-destructive period that was described in agonizing detail in his biography *Eddie: My Life, My Loves* published in 1981.

Eddie is the father of actress Carrie Fisher, by Miss Reynolds.

FISHER, GAIL—black actress
b: Aug 18, 1935, Orange, N.J.

Mannix (drama)....... Peggy Fair (1968–75)

Emmy Award: best supporting actress, for *Mannix* (1970)

FISHER, GEORGE "SHUG"—actor

Ozark Jubilee (music)........ regular (1960)
Ripcord (adv)....... Charlie Kern (1962–63)
The Beverly Hillbillies (com)
.... Shorty Kellems (1969–71)

FISHER, NELLIE—dancer

American Song (music)
.... dancer (1948–49)
Your Show of Shows (var)
.... regular (1950–52)
Melody Tour (var).......... regular (1954)

FITCH, LOUISE—actress

Medical Center (drama)
.... Nurse Bascomb (1971–73)

FITE, BEVERLY—singer

Campus Corner (music)...... hostess (1949)
School House (var)......... regular (1949)
Alkali Ike (com)............. singer (1950)

FITE, BOBBY—actor

Silver Spoons (com) .. J. T. Martin (1983–84)

FITHIAN, JEFF—juvenile actor
b: Feb 26, 1958

Please Don't Eat the Daisies (com)
.... Trevor Nash (1965–67)

FITHIAN, JOE—juvenile actor
b: Feb 26, 1958

Please Don't Eat the Daisies (com)
.·.·.............. Tracey Nash (1965–67)

Jeff and Joe are identical twins.

FITZGERALD, FERN—actress

Dallas (drama).... Marilee Stone (1980–)

FITZGERALD, GERALDINE—actress
b: Nov 24, 1912, Dublin, Ireland

Our Private World (drama)
.... Helen Eldredge (1965)

This celebrated dramatic actress made quite a few appearances on television in the 1950s, particularly on *Robert Montgomery Presents.* In the '60s she had a fling at soap opera, but neither *Our Private World* (in prime time) nor 1970's *The Best of Everything* (in daytime) was successful. Otherwise, she has been seen infrequently in the '70s and '80s playing an occasional mature woman role such as that of Rose Kennedy in the 1983 miniseries *Kennedy.*

FITZGERALD, NUALA—actress

Dr. Simon Locke (drama)
.... Nurse Wynn (1971–72)

FITZSIMMONS, TOM—actor
b: Oct 28, 1947, San Francisco, Calif.

The Paper Chase (drama)
.... Franklin Ford III (1978–79)
The Paper Chase (drama)
.... Franklin Ford III (1983–84)

FIX, PAUL—actor
b: Mar 13, 1901*, Dobbs Ferry, N.Y. d: Oct 14, 1983

The Rifleman (wes)
...... Marshal Micah Torrance (1958–63)

FLAGG, FANNIE—actress, comedienne
b: Sep 21, Birmingham, Ala.

The New Dick Van Dyke Show (com)
.... "Mike" Preston (1971–73)
Match Game P.M. (quiz) . panelist (1975–82)
Liar's Club (quiz)........ panelist (1976–78)
Harper Valley P.T.A. (com)
.... Cassie Bowman (1981–82)

FLAHERTY, JOE—comedian
b: Jun 21, 1940, Pittsburgh, Pa.

Second City TV (com)
.... Guy Caballero (1977–81)
SCTV Network 90 (com) .. regular (1981–83)

Emmy Awards: Best Writing for a Comedy Series, for *SCTV Network* (1982, 1983)

FLANAGAN, FIONNULA—actress
b: Dec 10, 1941, Dublin, Ireland

Rich Man, Poor Man—Book I (drama)
.... Clothilde (1976)
How the West Was Won (wes)
.... Aunt Molly Culhane (1978–79)

Emmy Award: Best Supporting Actress in a Single Appearance, for *Rich Man, Poor Man* (1976)

FLANAGAN, KELLIE—juvenile actress
b: c. 1960

The Ghost and Mrs. Muir (com)
.... Candice Muir (1968–70)

FLANAGAN, PAT—sportscaster

Prime Time Baseball (sport)
.... sportscaster (1951)

FLANAGAN, RALPH—orchestra leader
b: Apr 7, 1919, Loraine, Ohio

Let's Dance (music) .... orch. leader (1954)

FLANDERS, ED—actor
b: Dec 29, 1934, Minneapolis, Minn.

*Some sources give 1902.

Backstairs at the White House (drama)
.... Pres. Calvin Coolidge (1979)
St. Elsewhere (drama)
.... Dr. Donald Westphall (1982–)

Emmy Awards: Best Supporting Actor in a Special, for the *ABC Theatre* presentation *A Moon for the Misbegotten* (1976); Best Actor in a Special, for the PBS production *Harry S Truman: Plain Speaking* (1977); Best Actor in a Drama Series, for *St. Elsewhere* (1983)

Ed Flanders, the calm, sagacious senior physician at *St. Elsewhere,* began as a stage actor in Minneapolis in the 1950s and slowly but surely worked his way up to Broadway roles in the '60s and '70s. His greatest stage triumph was in *A Moon for the Misbegotten,* for which he received a Tony Award in 1974; he later brought the role to television and won an Emmy for it as well.

He has been active in television primarily since the early 1970s, mostly in TV movies and dramatic specials. Many of them have been political or otherwise reality-based docudramas—he seems to be quite believable in "real" situations. Among these have been *Eleanor and Franklin* in 1976, *Backstairs at the White House* (as President Coolidge) in 1979, *Blind Ambition* in 1979, *Skokie* (as the Mayor) in 1981, and *Special Bulletin* (as the all-too-believable newscaster reporting imminent nuclear destruction) in 1983. His impersonation of President Truman won him an Emmy. Though he has been associated with quality productions throughout his career, he does not feel he has accomplished all he can. "I'm too young to say that I've done the ones I want to be remembered for," he commented in 1982.

FLANNERY, SUSAN—actress
b: Jul 31, 1943, New York City, N.Y.

Dallas (drama)
.... Leslie Stewart (1981)

Emmy Award: Best Actress in a Daytime Drama, for *Days of Our Lives* (1975)

Susan is best known for her long run (from 1966–75) as psychiatrist Dr. Laura Spencer in *Days of Our Lives.* She has since appeared in a number of TV movies,

including *The Moneychangers* (1976) and *Women in White* (1979).

FLANNIGAN, DENNIS—actor

The John Byner Comedy Hour (var)
.... regular (1972)

FLASH & WHISTLER—

Ozark Jubilee (music).... regulars (1956–57)

FLATT, ERNEST—choreographer
b: Oct 30, 1928

The Garry Moore Show (var)
.... dancers (1959–63)
The Judy Garland Show (var)
.... dancers (1963)
The Entertainers (var) ...... dancers (1964)
The Steve Lawrence Show (var)
.... dancers (1965)
The Carol Burnett Show (var)
.... dancers (1967–79)

Emmy Award: Best Choreography, for *The Carol Burnett Show* (1971)

FLAVIN, JAMES—actor
b: May 14, 1906, Portland, Me. d: Apr 23, 1976

Man with a Camera (drama)
.... Lt. Donovan (1959–60)
The Roaring Twenties (drama)
.... Robert Howard (1960–62)

FLEER, ALICIA—juvenile actress

Friends (com) ..... Cynthia Richards (1979)

FLEICHER, WALTER, TRIO—

The Fashion Story (misc)
.... regulars (1948–49)

FLEISCHER, CHARLES—comedian
b: Aug 27, 1950, Washington D.C.

Keep On Truckin' (var)
.... regular (1975)
Welcome Back, Kotter (com)
.... Carvelli (1978–79)
Thicke of the Night (talk)
.... regular (1983–84)

FLEMING, ART—actor, host
b: May 1, The Bronx, N.Y.

The Californians (wes)
.... Jeremy Pitt (1958–59)
International Detective (drama)
.... Ken Franklin (1959)
NBC Adventure Theatre (drama)
.... host (1971)

Art is probably best remembered as the host of the popular daytime game show *Jeopardy* in the '60s and '70s.

FLEMING, ERIC—actor
b: 1925*, Santa Paula, Calif. d: Sep 28, 1966

Major Dell Conway of the Flying Tigers (adv)
.... Maj. Dell Conway (1951)
Rawhide (wes)......... Gil Favor (1959–65)

Fleming—the rugged, taciturn trail boss on *Rawhide*—drowned while filming a movie at a jungle river in Peru the summer after he left the series.

FLETCHER, AARON—actor
Lewis & Clark (com)...... Lester (1981–82)

FLETCHER, JACK—actor
b: April 21, Forest Hills, N.Y., r: Calif., Ill.

Calucci's Department (com)
.... Cosgrove (1973)
The Bob Crane Show (com)
.... Dean Lyle Ingersoll (1975)
Grady (com).......... Mr. Pratt (1975–76)
Presenting Susan Anton (var)
.... Robert Tibidas (1979)

FLINDERS, KATHE—actress
Marie (var)............. regular (1980–81)

FLIPPEN, JAY C.—actor
b: Mar 6, 1898**, Little Rock, Ark. d: Feb 3, 1971

Ensign O'Toole (com)
.... C.P.O. Homer Nelson (1962–63)

FLIPPIN, LUCY LEE—actress
b: Jul 23, Philadelphia, Pa.

Little House on the Prairie (adv)
.... Eliza Jane Wilder (1979–82)
Flo (com)...... Fran Castleberry (1980–81)
The Last Precinct (com)
.... Off. Rina Starland (1986)

*Some sources give 1924 or 1926.
**Some sources give 1899 or 1900.

FLORADORA GIRLS, THE—singers
Gay Nineties Revue (var)
.... regulars (1948–49)

FLOREN, MYRON—accordionist
b: Nov 5, 1919, Webster, S.D.

The Lawrence Welk Show (music)
.... regular (1955–82)

Autobiography: *Accordion Man* (Greene, 1981).

FLORY, MED—actor
The Ray Anthony Show (var)
.... regular (1956–57)

FLOWERS, WAYLAND—comedian, puppeteer
Keep On Truckin' (var)...... regular (1975)
The Andy Williams Show (var)
.... regular (1976–77)
Laugh-In (revival) (var)... regular (1977–78)
Solid Gold (music) .... regular (1980–84)
Madame's Place (com).... puppeteer (1982)

Flowers is usually seen with his puppet "Madame," a cackling, foul-mouthed old movie queen who considers herself still quite glamorous.

FLUEGEL, DARLANNE—actress
b: Wilkes-Barre, Pa.

Crime Story (police). Julie Torello (1986–)

FLYNN, JOE—actor
b: Nov 8, 1924, Youngstown, Ohio d: July 19, 1974

The George Gobel Show (var)
.... regular (1958–59)
The Adventures of Ozzie & Harriet (com)
.... Mr. Kelley (1960–62)
The Bob Newhart Show (var)
.... regular (1961–62)
The Joey Bishop Show (com)
.... Frank (1961–62)
McHale's Navy (com)
.. Capt. Wallace B. Binghamton (1962–66)
The Tim Conway Show (com)
.... Herbert T. Kenworth (1970)

The blustery, bespectacled, long-suffering captain on *McHale's Navy* was a favorite comic figure in the 1960s. The actor who played him was long suffering, too. Joe Flynn had tried to break into show business after World War II, but failed, and then tried again in the early '50s and met nothing but frustration. Shows he appeared in closed quickly; he managed to land a role in a traveling tent show, only to have a windstorm blow the tent away; then he got a small role in the Hitchcock film *Rear Window,* but his scene was cut out of the final release print.

At first Flynn was cast (if at all) in dramatic roles, but eventually he began to get small parts in TV comedies, and there he found his mark. He had a recurring part in *The Life of Riley* and was David Nelson's boss in *Ozzie & Harriet* and Joey Bishop's brother-in-law, an unsuccessful salesman, in *The Joey Bishop Show.* Flynn attracted a lot of attention in a sketch on the 1960 Emmy Awards show as "The Keeper of the Emmies" (he refused to give them up). He was also a favorite in Disney comedy movies, but *McHale's Navy* clinched his career. "I have no frustrations," he said in 1972. "I've found my character and will go on playing him as long as someone wants me."

FLYNN, MIRIAM—actress
b: Jun 18, Cleveland, Ohio

The Tim Conway Show (var)
.... regular (1980–81)
Maggie (com) .... Maggie Weston (1981–82)

FLYNN, SALLI—singer

The Lawrence Welk Show (music)
.... regular (1968–72)

FOCH, NINA—actress
b: Apr 20, 1924, Leiden, Holland

Q.E.D. (quiz) .... panelist (1951)
It's News to Me (quiz) ...... panelist (1954)
Shadow Chasers (drama)
.... Dr. Julianne Moorhouse (1985–86)

This cool, aristocratic blonde movie starlet of the '40s and early '50s was all over television in the '50s and '60s, appearing in practically every dramatic series on the air (or so it seemed). Oddly, her only regular acting role was in a short-lived 1951 daytime comedy called *Two Girls Named Smith.* She continued to appear in the '70s

and '80s, but on a reduced scale, winning an Emmy nomination for a guest appearance on *Lou Grant* in 1979.

FOGEL, JERRY—actor
b: Jan 17, 1936, Rochester, N.Y.

The Mothers-in-Law (com)
.... Jerry Buell (1967–69)
The White Shadow (drama)
.... Bill Donahue (1978–79)

FOGEL, LEE—singer

This Is Music (music)..... regular (1958–59)

FOGGY RIVER BOYS/MARKSMEN— vocal quartet

Ozark Jubilee (music).... regulars (1955–59)

FOLEY, ELLEN—actress
b: c. 1951 r: St. Louis, Mo.

3 Girls 3 (var)............. regular (1977)
Night Court (com) ... Billie Young (1984–85)

FOLEY, JOSEPH—actor
b: c. 1910 d: Jul 22, 1955

The Aldrich Family (com)
.... Mr. Bradley (1950–53)
Mr. Peepers (com)
.... Mr. Gabriel Gurney (1952–53)

FOLEY, RED—country singer
b: Jun 17, 1910, Blue Lick (or Berea), Ky. d: Sep 19, 1968

Ozark Jubilee (music)....... host (1955–60)
Mr. Smith Goes to Washington (com)
.... Uncle Cooter (1962–63)

This country music superstar of the 1940s and early '50s was seen quite a bit on television in later years as an elder statesman of the country music field. He was always a booster of new young talent and lived to see some of it—including Charley Pride and Brenda Lee (who got her start on *Ozark Jubilee*)—replace him on the best-seller charts. Though not known primarily as an actor, Red did appear as Fess Parker's philosophical, guitar-strumming uncle on *Mr. Smith Goes to Washington.*

Red was the father-in-law of singer Pat Boone.

FOLLETT, CHARON—juvenile actress

Those Endearing Young Charms (com)
.... Connie Charm (1952)

FOLLOWS, MEGAN—juvenile actress

The Baxters (com)... Lucy Baxter (1980–81)
Domestic Life (com)..... Didi Crane (1984)

FONDA, HENRY—actor

b: May 16, 1905, Grand Island, Neb. d: Aug 12, 1982

The Star and the Story (drama)
.... host (1955)
The Deputy (wes)
... Marshal Simon Fry/Narrator (1959–61)
The Smith Family (drama)
.... Det. Sgt. Chad Smith (1971–72)
Roots: The Next Generations (drama)
.... Col. Warner (1979)

Screen legend Henry Fonda seemed genuinely to like television. Though he did not need TV to assure his fame, and in fact the small screen was not overly kind to him, he dabbled in the medium for 30 years in both dramas and comedies as well as in specials and regular series.

Fonda was a major star and one of Hollywood's most beloved citizens when he first began to appear in occasional television dramatic programs of the 1950s, including the famous *Producer's Showcase* production of *The Petrified Forest* (costarring Humphrey Bogart) in 1955. He also hosted a syndicated drama anthology series called *The Star and the Story*. A few years later, with a wry grin on his face, he hosted a 1960 special that took a nostalgic look back at *The Fabulous '50s*, and soon afterwards another which took a satirical look at the American Family *(Henry Fonda and the Family)*. Westerns had been among his most successful movies, so from 1959–61 he starred in his own regular western series, *The Deputy*. Despite his presence in the cast, the show got lost in the welter of westerns then on the air and was not successful.

Ten years and several specials later, Fonda surprised viewers by returning in another series, *The Smith Family*, this one about the homelife of a big-city cop. It did no better than *The Deputy*. He continued to make occasional appearances during the following years, however, sometimes in comedies such as *The Doris Day Show* and *Maude*, more often in high-class dramatic specials such as *Collision Course*, *Roots*, and *The Oldest Living Graduate* (a live TV play in 1980!). One of the last times viewers saw him was in a December 1981 ABC special reminiscent of his hit film *On Golden Pond*, called *Summer Solstice;* Fonda and Myrna Loy played an aging couple visiting Cape Cod to reminisce about their half century together. It was a touching farewell for the lanky midwesterner some critics had called "the true face of America."

Fonda's 1981 biography was titled *Fonda: My Life,* by Howard Teichmann.

FONG, BRIAN—actor

b: Jul 3, Oahu, Hawaii

Chase (police) .... Off. Fred Sing (1973–74)

FONG, HAROLD—actor

Hong Kong (adv)............. Fong (1960)

FONG, JON—actor

Wildside (wes).......... Keye Ahn (1985)

FONG, KAM—actor

b: May 27, Honolulu, Hawaii

Hawaii Five-O (police)
.... Det. Chin Ho Kelly (1968–78)

FONTAINE, EDDIE—actor, singer

The Gallant Men (drama)
.... PFC Pete D'Angelo (1962–63)

FONTAINE, FRANK—comedian, singer

b: Apr 19, 1920, Cambridge, Mass. d: Aug 4, 1978

The Swift Show (var)........ regular (1949)
Scott Music Hall (var)
.... regular (1952–53)
The Jackie Gleason Show (var)
.... Crazy Guggenheim (1962–66)

A minor-league comic who bounced around radio and television for more than 20 years before he suddenly shot to fame as "Crazy Guggenheim," the tipsy barfly who sang in a startlingly big, booming voice on *The Jackie Gleason Show.*

FONTAINE, MICHAEL—actor

Shaping Up (com) ...... Ben Zachary (1984)

FONTANE, CHAR—actress
b: Los Angeles, Calif.

Pearl (drama) .... Shirley (1978)
Joe & Valerie (com)
.... Valerie Sweetzer (1978–79)

FONTANE SISTERS, THE (MARGE, BEA, AND GERI)—vocal trio
r: New Milford, N.J.

The Chesterfield Supper Club (var)
.... regulars (1948–50)
The Perry Como Show (var)
.... regulars (1950–54)
TV's Top Tunes (music) .... regulars (1951)

A popular female vocal group of the 1950s that hung around Perry Como a lot. Among their big record hits were "Hearts of Stone" and "Seventeen."

FOOTE, BRUCE—singer

This Is Music (music)..... regular (1951–52)

FORAKER, LOIS—actress

AfterMASH (com)
.... Nurse Coleman (1983–84)

FORAN, DICK—actor
b: Jun 18, 1910, Flemington, N.J. d: Aug 10, 1979

O. K. Crackerby (com) ...... Slim (1965–66)

FORAY, JUNE—voice specialist
b: Springfield, Mass.

The Bullwinkle Show (cartn)
...... Rocket J. Squirrel (voice) (1961–62)
The Bullwinkle Show (cartn)
.... Natasha Fatale (voice) (1961–62)

Who was: (1) Midnight the Cat and Old Grandie the talking piano on *Andy's Gang;* (2) Alvin's girlfriend on *The Alvin Show;* (3) Dudley Do-Right's girlfriend Nell; (4) Broom Hilda and Sluggo on *The Fabulous Funnies;* (5) Mother Wolf on *The Jungle Book;* (6) Jerry of *Tom and Jerry;* (7) Pogo the Possum; (8) Granny on *Tweety and Sylvester* and (9) Miss Mam'selle Hepzibah, a Parisian skunk? A tiny lady named

June Foray, of course. June was the voice of countless characters in hundreds of children's cartoons, records, and TV shows, from *Bugs Bunny* to *The Smurfs.* Her voice was even squeezed into those little talking dolls. "Luckily for me I've always had terrific control of my voice muscles," she once said. "I can make them do just about anything."

FORBES, KENNETH—actor

The Girls (com) .. Todhunter Smith II (1950)

FORBES, SCOTT—actor
b: 1921, Cape Town, South Africa r: Easton, Pa.

The Adventures of Jim Bowie (wes)
.... Jim Bowie (1956–58)

FORD, ART—host, disc jockey
b: Apr 15, New York City, N.Y.

Art Ford on Broadway (int) ..... host (1950)
The Art Ford Show (quiz)....... host (1951)
Who's Whose (quiz)........ panelist (1951)

FORD, CHARLIE—organist

The Benny Rubin Show (com)
.... organist (1949)

FORD, ED ("SENATOR" ED)—comedian
b: 1887, Brooklyn, N.Y. d: Jan 27, 1970

Can You Top This? (com)
.... panelist (1950–51)

FORD, GLENN—actor
b: May 1, 1916, Quebec, Canada

Cade's County (police)
.... Sheriff Sam Cade (1971–72)
Friends of Man (doc) .... narrator (1973–74)
The Family Holvak (drama)
.... Rev. Tom Holvak (1975)
Once an Eagle (drama)
.... George Caldwell (1976–77)
When Havoc Struck (doc) .. narrator (1978)

After a long and highly successful career in Hollywood, movie star Glenn Ford abruptly turned to television in the early 1970s (he had done little TV before that), starring in two series and in numerous TV movies, miniseries, and specials. Despite his stature, neither of his series was successful. Both reflected the amiable yet determined persona he had developed on the big screen, however: in *Cade's County* he was a contemporary western sheriff and in *The Family Holvak* a God-fearin' southern minister caring for his family as best he could during the Depression. Glenn's other appearances included the miniseries *Once an Eagle, The Sacketts,* and *Evening in Byzantium;* a rather cheap syndicated documentary series about famous disasters called *When Havoc Struck;* and the lighthearted special *When the West Was Fun.*

FORD, JANIE—singer

The Alan Dale Show (music)
.... regular (1948)

FORD, PAUL—actor

b: Nov 2, 1901, Baltimore, Md. d: Apr 12, 1976

The Phil Silvers Show (com)
.... Col. John Hall (1955–59)
The Baileys of Balboa (com)
.... Sam Bailey (1964–65)

FORD, PETER—actor

Cade's County (police)....... Pete (1971–72)

The son of actor Glenn Ford, star of *Cade's County.*

FORD, ROSS—actor

b: 1923

Meet Millie (com)
.... Johnny Boone, Jr. (1952–55)

FORD, TENNESSEE ERNIE—singer

b: Feb 13, 1919, Bristol, Tenn.

The College of Musical Knowledge (quiz)
.... emcee (1954)
The Ford Show (var) .... host (1956–61)

Tennessee Ernie Ford really was born in Tennessee, but just barely. Bristol is half in Tennessee and half in Virginia, and Ernie was born on Anderson Street, just a few blocks from the border on the Tennessee side. Otherwise, he might have become Virginia Ernie Ford.

Ernie was no pea picker when he was young, studying music (briefly) at Intermont College and the Cincinnati Conserva-

tory of Music. After service in World War II, his rich, deep voice won him a job as a country-music disc jockey on the West Coast and later a contract with Los Angeles–based Capitol records, for whom he recorded several fairly popular country-flavored records circa 1950. (One of these, "Shotgun Boogie," was allegedly a favorite of Queen Elizabeth.)

Ernie's friendly manner and sincerity was perfect for a radio-TV host, and his career began to move quickly in the early 1950s. He made nightclub appearances in such non-hick venues as the Copacabana in New York and the Thunderbird in Las Vegas in 1950; had his own ABC network radio show in 1952; and was a regular on TV's *Old American Barn Dance* in 1953. In May 1954 he appeared in a two-part story on TV's top-rated sitcom, *I Love Lucy,* as a country cousin from Bent Fork, Tennessee, who descended on the Ricardos and eventually got Lucy, Ricky, Fred, and Ethel to dress up as bumpkins and sing "Ya' all Come to Meet Us When You Can" on a talent show—to win enough money to send him home! A few months later Ernie hosted a summer revival of *The College of Musical Knowledge* on NBC-TV, and a few months after that he had his own daytime show on the same network, which ran from 1955–57.

In late 1955 Ernie recorded a song whose sales dwarfed anything he did before or after, and which became permanently identified with him—"Sixteen Tons." On the heels of the song's enormous success he began a nighttime variety show, which was a major hit as well. He frequently sang "Sixteen Tons" and other pop-country songs, but he closed every show with a hymn, and he probably sold more religious albums than anyone within a country mile.

Five years of the weekly grind took its toll, and Ernie finally elected to quit show business for a year or so to spend time with his wife and young sons on his newly bought farm in northern California. He returned to ABC-TV for another daytime series from 1962-65, but his activities after that were basically low-key, with only occasional appearances on specials such as *The Country Music Awards.* In recent years Ernie has spent a whole lot of easygoin' time down on the farm. To paraphrase his most famous song, he may be getting another day older, but he sure isn't deeper in debt.

Ernie's biography, *This Is My Song, This Is My Story,* was published in 1963.

FORD, WALLACE—actor
b: Feb 12, 1898, Batton, England d: June 11, 1966

The Deputy (wes)
.... Marshal Herk Lamson (1959–60)

FOREE, KEN—black actor

Report to Murphy (com) . Big Walter (1982)

FORMAN, JOEY—actor
b: c. 1929 d: Dec 9, 1982

The Mickey Rooney Show (com)
.... Freddie (1954–55)
The Steve Allen Show (var).. regular (1961)
The Sid Caesar Show (var)
.... regular (1963–64)
The Joey Bishop Show (com)
.... Dr. Sam Nolan (1964–65)
The Steve Allen Comedy Hour (var)
.... regular (1980–81)

FORQUET, PHILIPPE—actor

The Young Rebels (adv)
General the Marquis de Lafayette (1970–71)

FORREST, GREGG—actor

The Bad News Bears (com)
.... Kelly Leek (1979–80)

FORREST, RAY—newscaster

The War As It Happens (news)
.... anchorman (1944–45)
Gillette Cavalcade of Sports (Friday Night Fights) (sport) .... sportscaster (1948–49)
Television Screen Magazine (mag)
.... emcee/"editor" (1948–49)
The Village Barn (var)........ emcee (1949)

Though he is practically forgotten today, announcer/host Ray Forrest was seen a great deal on NBC's fledgling East Coast network in the 1940s, at least by those few people who had sets then. He also holds the honor of having been the very first network "anchorman" (news reader, actually). He anchored the first regular network newscast, which began on NBC in 1944.

FORREST, STEVE—actor
b: Sep 29, 1924, Huntsville, Texas

The Baron (drama)
.... John ("The Baron") Mannering (1966)
S.W.A.T. (police)
.... Lt. Dan "Hondo" Harrelson (1975–76)
Dallas (drama)....... Ben Stivers (1986–)

The brother of actor Dana Andrews. Steve was quite active on television from the mid-1950s onward.

FORSTER, BRIAN—juvenile actor

The Partridge Family (com)
.... Christopher Partridge (1971–74)

FORSTER, ROBERT—actor
b: Jul 13, 1941, Rochester, N.Y.

Banyon (drama)
.... Miles C. Banyon (1972–73)
Nakia (police).... Dep. Nakia Parker (1974)

FORSYTHE, BROOKE—juvenile actress
b: c. 1954

The John Forsythe Show (com)
.... Norma Jean (1965–66)

The daughter of John Forsythe.

FORSYTHE, JOHN—actor
b: Jan 29, 1918, Penn's Grove, N.J.

Bachelor Father (com)
.... Bentley Gregg (1957–62)
The John Forsythe Show (com)
.... Major John Foster (1965–66)
To Rome with Love (com)
.... Michael Endicott (1969–71)
The World of Survival (doc)
.... narrator (1971–77)
Charlie's Angels (drama)
. Charlie Townsend (voice only) (1976–81)
Dynasty (drama)
.... Blake Carrington (1981–)

John Forsythe has certainly been one of television's more popular father figures over the years, though the type has changed. In the '50s he was a playboy uncle raising a teenage niece in a frothy comedy; by the '80s he was a ruthless tycoon with a whole houseful of unhappy offspring in an anxiety-ridden soap opera. In between, he played the harried head of a girls' school, a widowed professor with three daughters, and the employer of a trio of lovelies. Two pleasant characteristics have remained constant throughout most of his series; he has usually been wealthy and surrounded by beautiful women (although on *Charlie's Angels* he never got to see them).

John was equally devoted to drama and sports while he was in school in the '30s. For a time after graduation he worked as a baseball commentator for the Brooklyn Dodgers at Ebbets Field in New York City. From there he moved on to stage work and daytime radio serials. He reached Broadway in the early '40s and made his first movie in 1944 (*Destination Tokyo,* starring Cary Grant). Television, which would occupy the largest part of his career, came on the scene in the late '40s, and soon John was appearing in most of the New York–based live drama series, including *Studio One, Lights Out, Schlitz Playhouse of Stars,* and *Climax.* Alfred Hitchcock, who had used him in his 1955 film *The Trouble with Harry,* cast him in a couple episodes of *Alfred Hitchcock Presents.* The famous director, for whom *The Trouble with Harry* had been a less than successful film, reportedly told Forsythe that he was best suited to TV. John took the advice to heart, keeping quite busy with TV series work throughout the '60s, as well as appearing on *The Hallmark Hall of Fame* and other dramatic shows.

After *To Rome with Love* he concentrated mostly on TV movies and relatively undemanding voice work on *Charlie's Angels* and the nature documentary *World of Survival.* Not until *Dynasty* was he lured back, by this time distinguished and graying, into series TV. It proved to be his most successful role of all.

FORSYTHE, PAGE—juvenile actress
b: c. 1951

The John Forsythe Show (com)
.... Marcia (1965–66)

Daughter of John Forsythe.

FORTE, JOE—actor
b: 1896 d: Feb 22, 1967

Life with Luigi (com) .... Horwitz (1952)

FORTIER, BOB—actor

The Troubleshooters (adv)
.... Scotty (1959–60)

FOSSE, BOB—choreographer, director, actor
b: June 23, 1927, Chicago, Ill.

The Fifty-Fourth Street Revue (var)
.... dancer (1949–50)

Emmy Awards: Producer, Director and Choreographer, Outstanding Variety Special, for "Liza With a 'Z' " (1973)

Though he has been active in several areas of show business, Fosse is best known as one of the leading dancers and choreographers for movies and Broadway. In the '50s he was seen as a dancer on such TV variety shows as *Your Hit Parade* and *The Fifty-Fourth Street Revue,* often teamed with his then-wife Mary Ann Niles (as Fosse and Niles).

FOSTER, AMI—juvenile actress

Punky Brewster (com)
.... Margaux Kramer (1984–86)

FOSTER, BILL—choreographer
b: c. 1932, Dickeyville, Ky.

Kraft Music Hall Presents The Dave King Show (var)................. dancers (1959)
The Keefe Brasselle Show (var)
.... dancers (1963)

FOSTER, BUDDY—juvenile actor
b: Jul 12, 1957

Hondo (wes)........... Johnny Dow (1967)
Mayberry R.F.D. (com)
.... Mike Jones (1968–71)

FOSTER, CONNIE—actress

Chicago Story (drama)
.... Annie Gilland (1982)

FOSTER, DONALD—actor
b: c. 1889 d: Dec 22, 1969

Hazel (com)
.... Herbert Johnson (1961–65)

FOSTER, JODIE—actress
b: Nov 19, 1962, The Bronx, N.Y.

Bob & Carol & Ted & Alice (com)
.... Elizabeth Henderson (1973)
Paper Moon (com).... Addie Pray (1974–75)

Jodie Foster was a precocious young actress who startled moviegoers with some of her early big-screen roles: a teenage prostitute at age 12 (in *Taxi Driver*), a gangster's moll at 13 *(Bugsy Malone),* and a murderess at 14 *(The Little Girl Who Lived Down the Lane).* Her career before that, on television, was a little less shocking, though certainly busy. She began working in commercials at age three and made her first series appearance at five in a 1969 episode of *Mayberry R.F.D.* For the next eight years she appeared on television a great deal, in both comedies (including multiple episodes of *The Courtship of Eddie's Father*) and dramas (*Gunsmoke, Ghost Story,* etc.). She was also seen in several Disney TV productions, provided voices for Saturday morning cartoons, and was one of the youngest hosts ever on *NBC's Saturday Night Live* (in 1976).

Neither of Jodie's two regular series was successful, however; otherwise she might have stayed in the medium longer. As it was, the young actress left TV in the late '70s and has since been seen mostly in movies, including the 1983 TV film *Svengali.*

FOSTER, LINDA—actress
b: June 12, 1944, Lancaster, England

Hank (com)........ Doris Royal (1965–66)

FOSTER, MEG—actress
b: May 14, r: Connecticut

Sunshine (com)............... Nora (1975)
Cagney & Lacey (police)
.... Det. Chris Cagney (1982)

FOSTER, PHIL—comedian
b: Mar 29, 1913*, Brooklyn, N.Y. d: Jul 8, 1985

Caesar Presents (var)
.... Charles Williams (1955)
Laverne & Shirley (com)
.... Frank De Fazio (1976–83)

Phil Foster was a minor-league comic who was active in show business from the

*Some sources give 1914.

308

1930s. He was once billed as "Brooklyn's Ambassador to the U.S.A.," and is known to Ph.D.'s in Trivia as the man who in 1957 recorded the song, "Let's Keep the Dodgers in Brooklyn."

FOSTER, PRESTON—actor
b: Aug 24, 1900, Ocean City, N.J. d: Jul 14, 1970

Waterfront (adv)
.... Capt. John Herrick (1953–56)
Gunslinger (wes)
.... Capt. Zachary Wingate (1961)

FOSTER, STUART—singer
b: June 30, 1918, Binghamton, N.Y. d: Feb 7, 1968

The Galen Drake Show (child)
.... singer (1957)

FOSTER, SUSAN—actress
b: May 27, Torrance, Calif.

Sierra (adv)....... Ranger Julie Beck (1974)

FOULGER, BYRON—actor
b: 1899* d: Apr 4, 1970

Captain Nice (com)........ Mr. Nash (1967)
Petticoat Junction (com)
.... Wendell Gibbs (1968–70)

FOULK, ROBERT—actor

Father Knows Best (com)
.... Ed Davis (1955–59)
Wichita Town (wes)
.... Joe Kingston (1959–60)

FOUNTAIN, PETE—dixieland clarinetist
b: Jul 3, 1930, New Orleans, La.

The Lawrence Welk Show (music)
.... regular (1957–59)

FOUR FRESHMAN, THE—vocal quartet
Ross Barbour, b: Dec 31, 1928, Columbus, Ind.
Don Barbour, b: Apr 19, 1927, Greencastle, Ind.
Bob Flanigan, b: Aug 22, 1926, Greencastle, Ind.
Ken Albers, b: Pittman, N.J.

The Ray Anthony Show (var)
.... regulars (1956–57)

*Some sources give 1900.

FOUR LADS, THE—vocal quartet
(Frank Busseri, Bernard Toorish, James Arnold, Connie Codarini)

Perry Presents (var) . . . . regulars (1959)

A very popular male quartet of the mid-1950s, with hits such as "Moments to Remember," "No, Not Much," etc. The boys hailed from Toronto, Canada.

FOUTS, TOM "STUBBY"—
b: Nov 24, 1918, Carroll County, Ind.

Polka-Go-Round (music) . . regular (1958–59)

FOWLER, JIM—naturalist
b: Apr 9, 1932, near Albany, Ga.

Wild Kingdom (doc) . . . . assistant (1968–)

FOWLEY, DOUGLAS—actor
b: May 30, 1911, New York City, N.Y.

The Life and Legend of Wyatt Earp (wes)
. . . . Doc Fabrique (1955–56)
The Life and Legend of Wyatt Earp (wes)
. . . . Doc Holliday (1957–61)
Pistols 'n' Petticoats (com)
. . . . Grandpa (1966–67)
Detective School (com)
. . . . Robert Redford (1979)

FOX, BERNARD—actor

Bewitched (com) . . . . . Dr. Bombay (1967–72)

FOX, MICHAEL—actor

Casablanca (drama) . . . . Sasha (1955–56)

FOX, MICHAEL J.—actor
b: Jun 9, 1961, Edmonton, Canada

Palmerstown, U.S.A. (drama)
. . . . Willy-Joe Hall (1980–81)
Family Ties (com)
. . . . Alex P. Keaton (1982–)

Emmy Award: Best Actor in a Comedy Series, for *Family Ties* (1986)

Michael J. Fox became a major teen star of the mid-1980s and a favorite among adults as well for his winning portrayal of the likable, jittery teenager on *Family Ties.* An intelligent, hardworking lad ("I was always kind of a hyper kid," he says), Michael was born the son of an army officer. He began his acting career on Canadian television at the age of 15 in a series called *Leo and Me;* this attracted the attention of American producers and led to a part in a 1979 Art Carney movie called *Letters from Frank.* Michael moved to Los Angeles and in 1980 was cast as the older brother in *Palmerstown, U.S.A.* He also began making appearances in other series *(Trapper John, M.D., Lou Grant)* and in some rather frothy TV teen films such as *Poison Ivy* and *High School U.S.A.*

In 1985 his career soared when he starred in the Steven Spielberg movie *Back to the Future.* Loyal to the TV series that had brought him to prominence, he continued to tape *Family Ties* during the day while working on the movie at night. The kid has a lot of energy.

FOX, NANCY—actress

Temperatures Rising (com)
. . . . . student nurse Ellen Turner (1972–74)

FOX, PETER—actor

The Waltons (drama)
. . . . Rev. Hank Buchanan (1977–78)
Delta House (com)
. . . . Eric ("Otter") Stratton (1979)
Knots Landing (drama)
. . . . Tom Jezik (1984–85)

FOX, SONNY—host, producer
b: Jun 17, Brooklyn, N.Y.

The $64,000 Challenge (quiz) . . emcee (1956)

Sonny is best known as the host of some rather intelligent children's shows of the '50s and '60s, including *Let's Take a Trip* (1955–58), *On Your Mark* (1961), and the long-running local New York series *Wonderama* (1959–67).

FOX, STEVE—newscaster

20/20 (mag) . . . . correspondent (1980–83)

FOXWORTH, ROBERT—actor
b: Nov 1, 1941, Houston, Texas

Storefront Lawyers (drama)
. . . . David Hansen (1970–71)
Falcon Crest (drama)
. . . . Chase Gioberti (1981–)

FOXX, REDD—black actor, comedian
b: Dec 9, 1922, St. Louis, Mo.

Sanford and Son (com)
.... Fred Sanford (1972–77)
Redd Foxx (var)............ host (1977–78)
Sanford (com)...... Fred Sanford (1980–81)
The Redd Foxx Show (com)
.... Al Hughes (1986)

Redd Foxx is living proof that practically any entertainer, from any corner of show business (no matter how seedy), can become a TV star—given the right role. In Redd's case, the role was that of the lovable old scoundrel Fred Sanford, whose raspy voice and cantankerous attitude made *Sanford and Son* one of the biggest hits of the mid-1970s.

The series' success was certainly a surprise to all concerned. Redd had been a nightclub comic for virtually his entire career and only rarely appeared on television—primarily because of his reputation for off-color material. A hustler from childhood (when he ran away from home and joined a street-corner band), he bummed around show business in the '40s as a single and in the '50s as part of a two-man act with Slappy White. Redd was best known for his raunchy "party" records, which were available under the counter (or in the back) at record stores across America.

His first network TV appearance was in 1964 on the *Today* show, hosted by an apprehensive Hugh Downs; later he guested on *The Lucy Show, The Addams Family, Mr. Ed, Green Acres,* and *The Name of the Game,* among others, all in the late '60s. *Sanford and Son* made him a star—and rich. However, he did not forget his friends from the scruffling days on the chitlin circuit, giving many of them their first national exposure on his series, especially his 1977–78 variety show. White middle-class viewers in the suburbs watched in bewilderment such acts as "Iron Jaw" Wilson and various wheezy old-timers who otherwise, and deservedly, might never have been seen on network TV.

Redd, like Fred, is quite a character.

FOXX, RHONDA—actress
Stockard Channing in Just Friends (com)
.... Mrs. Blanchard (1979)

FOY, EDDIE, JR.—actor, dancer
b: Feb 4, 1905, New Rochelle, N.Y. d: Jul 15, 1983

Fair Exchange (com)
.... Eddie Walker (1962–63)

FOY, FRED—announcer
b: c. 1921, Detroit, Mich.

The Lone Ranger (wes)
.... announcer (1949–57)
The Dick Cavett Show (talk)
.... announcer (1969–72)

If there was an announcers' Hall of Fame, Fred Foy should be in it, for just one assignment, which he fulfilled memorably on both radio and TV. In fact, he was so identified with it that he could scarcely get other work. It was Foy whose stirring voice was heard over the strains of *The William Tell Overture,* booming "Return with us now to those thrilling days of yesteryear . . . the Lone Ranger rides again!"

FRAKES, JONATHAN—actor
r: Bethlehem, Pa.

Bare Essence (drama)
.... Marcus Marshall (1983)
Paper Dolls (drama).... Sandy Parris (1984)
North and South (drama)
.... Stanley Hazard (1985)

FRANCE, DICK—
See Doran, Nancy, and Dick France

FRANCINE, ANNE—actress
b: Aug 8, Philadelphia, Pa.

Harper Valley P.T.A. (com)
.... Flora Simpson Reilly (1981–82)

FRANCIOSA, ANTHONY—actor
b: Oct 25, 1928, New York City, N.Y.

Valentine's Day (com)
.... Valentine Farrow (1964–65)
The Name of the Game (adv)
.... Jeff Dillon (1968–71)
Search (adv)....... Nick Bianco (1972–73)
Matt Helm (drama)
.... Matt Helm (1975–76)
Aspen (drama)......... Alex Budde (1977)
Wheels (drama)
.... Smokey Stephenson (1978)

Finder of Lost Loves (drama)
.... Cary Maxwell (1984–85)

Tony Franciosa is the pride of New York City's P.S. 52. The lean, smiling young Italian-American found his calling in local stage productions in that city as soon as he graduated from high school, and he worked his way up to a Broadway debut in the early 1950s. His greatest stage triumph came with the supporting role of Polo in *A Hatful of Rain* in 1955, which he repeated for the movie version in 1957.

Tony also appeared in scattered TV plays of the '50s and early '60s on *Goodyear Playhouse, DuPont Show of the Month*, etc. It was not until the mid-1960s that he began to make a strong impression on the medium, however, in a series of glamorous roles on regular series. He was the suave playboy publisher on *Valentine's Day*, a flip, fast-talking reporter on *The Name of the Game*, and a hip detective on *Search* and *Matt Helm*. Since the mid-1970s he has been seen mostly in TV movies and miniseries (including *Aspen* and *Wheels*); another debonair role on the series *Finder of Lost Loves* was short-lived. At least, as in all of his previous series, there were plenty of beautiful women around.

FRANCIS, ANNE—actress
b: Sep 16, 1930, Ossining, N.Y.

Versatile Varieties (var)
.... Bonny Maid (1949–50)
Honey West (drama)
.... Honey West (1965–66)
My Three Sons (com)
.... Terri Dowling (1971–72)
Dallas (drama)........ Arliss Cooper (1981)
Riptide (drama)
.... Mama Jo (occasional) (1984)

Anne Francis is an actress who has had a long and busy career in films and television without ever quite becoming a star of the first rank. She has been in show business since childhood, on radio (where she was billed as "The Little Queen of Soap Operas"), on experimental TV shows of the '40s, and in films since the age of 14 (in *Summer Holiday*, which was not released until 1948).

Anne's early TV work included a stint as one of the singing commercial girls, The Bonny Maids, on *Versatile Varieties* (sponsored by a floor-covering manufacturer) while she was still in her teens. She appeared in TV plays of the '50s and was extremely active in the '60s, with multiple appearances on such shows as *The Twilight Zone, Alfred Hitchcock Presents, Route 66, Burke's Law*, and *The Name of the Game*. In her first regular series, *Honey West*, she played a lithe and sexy female James Bond; on *My Three Sons* she was a cocktail waitress who fell in love with Steve Douglas's Scottish cousin Fergus (both roles were played by Fred MacMurray). Gradually, her days as a sexy young thing ended; on *Riptide* in 1984 she was a mature and cantankerous housemother to a boatful of young lovelies. Perhaps Anne's "perfect" role is still to come.

FRANCIS, ARLENE—hostess, actress
b: Oct 20, 1908, Boston, Mass.

Blind Date (aud par)....... emcee (1949–52)
Answer Yes or No (quiz).... panelist (1950)
By Popular Demand (talent)... emcee (1950)
Prize Performance (talent) .. panelist (1950)
What's My Line (quiz)... panelist (1950–67)
Who's There? (quiz).......... emcee (1952)
Talent Patrol (talent) ...... emcee (1953–55)
The Comeback Story (drama)
.... emcee (1954)
What's My Line (quiz)... panelist (1968–75)

Though she had only minor success on the stage (from the late 1920s) and in films (since 1943), Arlene Francis carved out a major career as a glamorous "personality" on radio and TV in the '40s and '50s. She was seen on many live, New York–originated game and talk shows in the 1950s and hosted two talent shows, *By Popular Demand* and *Talent Patrol* (the latter eventually turned into a straight variety show). NBC had great hopes for her as the hostess of its *Home* show (1954–57), which was envisioned as the daytime counterpart to *Today* and *Tonight*. This might have assured Arlene a place in TV history comparable to that of Dave Garroway and Steve Allen; however, *Home* was not successful. Arlene's most familiar role was as one of the witty panelists on *What's My Line*, with which she remained for 25 years, long after viewers had forgotten that she had ever done anything else.

Her acting appearances were rare; a couple of times on *The U.S. Steel Hour* in 1960–61, once on *The Hallmark Hall of Fame* in 1972, etc.

In the 1980s Arlene was hosting a local New York public service show for older citizens called *The Prime of Your Life.* Her autobiography, *Arlene Francis, A Memoir,* was published in 1978.

FRANCIS, CLIVE—actor
b: June 26, 1946, London, England

Masada (drama) .... Attius (1981)

FRANCIS, CONNIE—singer
b: Dec 12, 1938, Newark, N.J.

The Jimmie Rodgers Show (var)
.... regular (1959)

Connie, a top popular singer of the late 1950s and early '60s, got her start playing the accordion on *Arthur Godfrey's Talents Scouts* at the age of 12, in 1950. She was later seen mostly as a guest on many TV variety shows, including two dozen appearances on *The Ed Sullivan Show.*

Her best-selling 1984 autobiography, *Who's Sorry Now,* recounted the sharp ups and downs of her career, including the influence of her domineering father, the gangland murder of her brother, the death of her sweetheart Bobby Darin, and the brutal rape in a Long Island motel room in 1974 that almost ended her career. "My life always reads like a Greek tragedy," she once said. "It's true that I have been to the depths of depression, [but] I guess if I hadn't had the same kind of life that exposed me to the pitfalls, I wouldn't have been exposed to the happy and exhilarating heights that I've also enjoyed. It's been an eventful life."

FRANCIS, GENIE—actress
b: May 26, 1962, Englewood, N.J. r: Los Angeles, Calif.

Bare Essence (drama) .. Tyger Hayes (1983)
North and South (drama)
.... Brett Main (1985)

Though Genie has lately been trying to break into prime time, she is best known as one of the most popular romantic leads in daytime soap opera history—as the teen-age Laura (as in Luke and Laura) on *General Hospital.* She appeared on the serial, off and on, from 1976 to 1984. She is the daughter of character actor Ivor Francis.

FRANCIS, IVOR—actor
b: c. 1918, Toronto, Canada d: Oct 22, 1986

Dusty's Trail (com).. Mr. Brookhaven (1973)

FRANCIS, MISSY—juvenile actress
b: Dec 12, 1972, Los Angeles, Calif.

Joe's World (com)
.... Linda Wabash (1979–80)
Little House on the Prairie (adv)
.... Cassandra Cooper (1981–82)
Morningstar/Eveningstar (drama)
.... Sarah Bishop (1986)

FRANCISCUS, JAMES—actor
b: Jan 31, 1934, Clayton, Mo.

Naked City (police)
.... Det. Jim Halloran (1958–59)
The Investigators (drama)
.... Russ Andrews (1961)
Mr. Novak (drama)... John Novak (1963–65)
Longstreet (drama)
.... Mike Longstreet (1971–72)
Doc Elliot (drama)
.... Dr. Benjamin Elliot (1974)
Hunter (drama) .... James Hunter (1977)

This handsome, fair-haired actor, who looks a lot like Richard Chamberlain, had a very promising career in the '60s, which does not seem to have developed into major stardom. Born in Missouri and educated on the East Coast, he began getting professional acting offers while he was still a student at Yale. Spotted by a Disney scout, he won his first film role in *Four Boys and a Gun* in 1957. He also worked in television in the late 1950s in such series as *Studio One, Have Gun Will Travel, Father Knows Best,* and *The Twilight Zone* (as a nervous U-boat lieutenant with a dreadful German accent!).

A major break came in 1958 with the role of the young policeman in *Naked City,* but after a year Franciscus left the New York–based series, saying he preferred to work in Los Angeles. This was followed by a short run as an insurance investigator on *The Investigators* and then his most famous role, that of the dedicated English teacher on *Mr. Novak*. Thereafter he worked fairly regularly in TV, including multiple appearances on *The F.B.I.* and even a guest role on the series that had driven *Mr. Novak* off the air, *Combat*. However, none of his subsequent series roles lasted more than a season: *Longstreet* (again an insurance investigator, this one blind); *Doc Elliot* (an M.D. out west); and *Hunter* (a spy). His film career was uneven as well after the failure of his much-touted starring vehicle, *Youngblood Hawke*, in 1964.

Since the early 1970s Franciscus has appeared mostly in TV movies, including *The Pirate* in 1978 and *Jacqueline Bouvier Kennedy* (as J.F.K.) in 1981.

FRANCKS, DON—actor

b: Feb 28, 1932, Vancouver, B.C., Canada

Royal Canadian Mounted Police (police)
.... Constable Bill Mitchell (1960)
Jericho (drama)
.... Franklin Sheppard (1966–67)

FRANK, ALLAN—actor

b: c. 1915, New York City, N.Y. d: Aug 9, 1979

Charade Quiz (quiz)
.... repertory player (1947–49)

FRANK, CARL—actor

b: c. 1909 d: Sep 23, 1972

Mama (com)
...... Uncle Gunnar Gunnerson (1949–57)

FRANK, CHARLES—actor

b: Apr 17, Olympia, Wash.

The Chisholms (wes)
.... Lester Hackett (1979)
Young Maverick (wes)
.... Ben Maverick (1979–80)
Filthy Rich (com)... Stanley Beck (1982–83)
Emerald Point N.A.S. (drama)
.... Lt. Cmdr. Jack Warren (1983–84)

FRANK, GARY—actor

b: Oct 9, 1950, Spokane, Wash. r: Los Angeles

Sons and Daughters (drama)
.... Jeff Reed (1974)
Family (drama) . Willie Lawrence (1976–80)

Emmy Award: Best Supporting Actor in a Drama Series, for *Family* (1977)

FRANKEN, AL—writer, comedian

NBC's Saturday Night Live (com)
.... regular (1979–80)

Emmy Award: Best Writing for a Comedy Series, for *NBC's Saturday Night Live* (1976, 1977); Best Writing for a Music Special, for *The Paul Simon Special* (1978)

FRANKEN, STEVE—actor

b: c. 1933, Brooklyn, N.Y.

The Many Loves of Dobie Gillis (com)
.... Chatsworth Osborne, Jr. (1960–63)
The Lieutenant (drama)
... Lt. Samwell (Sanpan) Panosian (1963)
Mr. Novak (drama)
.... Mr. Jerry Allen (1963–64)
Tom, Dick and Mary (com)
.... Dr. Dick Moran (1964–65)

FRANKLIN, BONNIE—actress

b: Jan 6, 1944, Santa Monica, Calif.

One Day at a Time (com)
.... Ann Romano Royer (1975–84)

Bonnie Franklin, familiar as the mom in *One Day at a Time*, has been performing since her youth—when she was a child actor and a tap-dancing protégé of Donald O'Connor. While still a student at U.C.L.A., in 1965–66, she appeared in several episodes of *Gidget* and *Please Don't Eat the Daisies*, but her career did not really begin to blossom until 1970, when she won a slew of awards for her performance in the Broadway musical *Applause*. Still, her pleasant but not too distinctive personality limited her TV roles until she won the part of the problem-ridden but still sunny divorced mother on *One Day at a Time*, which proved perfect for her "everywoman" style. The series remained on the CBS schedule for nine years.

Bonnie tried a somewhat meatier role in 1980 in the TV movie *Portrait of a Rebel: Margaret Sanger*, in which she played the turn-of-the-century birth control crusader, but it did not lead to any major change in her career direction.

FRANKLIN, CARL—black actor

b: Apr 11, 1930, Richmond, Calif.

Caribe (police)... Sgt. Mark Walters (1975)
Fantastic Journey (sci fi)
.... Dr. Fred Walters (1977)
McClain's Law (police)
.... Det. Jerry Cross (1981–82)

"When Marlon Brando said to Rod Steiger, 'I could have been somebody' in *On The Waterfront,* it had such a staggering effect on me that I knew I wanted to be like Brando," young actor Carl Franklin told a reporter in 1977. He still has a way to go.

FRANKLIN, CASS—

Front Row Center (var)... regular (1949–50)

FRANKLIN, NANCY—actress, writer

One Man's Family (drama)
.... Claudia Barbour (1949–50)
One Man's Family (drama)
.... Ann Waite (1951–52)

Emmy Awards: Best Writing for a Daytime Drama Series, for *The Guiding Light* (1981, 1982)

FRANKLIN, SUSAN—actress

Doctors' Hospital (drama)
.... Nurse Franklin (1975–76)

FRANN, MARY—actress
b: Feb 27, 1943, St. Louis, Mo.

King's Crossing (drama)
.... Nan Hollister (1982)
Newhart (com)... Joanna Loudon (1982–   )

FRANZ, DENNIS—actor
b: Oct 28, 1944, Maywood, Ill.

Chicago Story (drama)
.... Officer Joe Gilland (1982)
Bay City Blues (drama)
.... Angelo Carbone (1983)
Hill Street Blues (drama)
.... Lt. Norman Buntz (1985–   )

TV Guide called him "The Best TV Villain of the Year" for his role as "Bad Sal" Benedetto, the vicious narcotics cop on several episodes of *Hill Street Blues* during the 1982–83 season. Bad Sal eventually committed suicide, but Franz—a beefy Chicago native who *looks* like a tough character—returned to the series in 1985 as rule-bend-

ing Lieutenant Buntz. Franz is also a favorite of film directors Robert Altman and Brian DePalma and has been seen in a number of their violent films. His background is in Chicago stage productions of the 1970s.

FRANZ, EDUARD—actor
b: Oct 31, 1902, Milwaukee, Wis. d: Feb 10, 1983

Zorro (wes)
.... Senor Gregorio Verdugo (1958–59)
Breaking Point (drama)
.... Dr. Edward Raymer (1963–64)

FRASER, ELISABETH—actress
b: Brooklyn, N.Y. r: Haiti

The Phil Silvers Show (com)
.... Sgt. Joan Hogan (1955–58)
Fibber McGee and Molly (com)
.... Hazel Norris (1959–60)
One Happy Family (com)
.... Mildred Hogan (1961)
McKeever & the Colonel (com)
.... Mrs. Warner (1962–63)

FRASER, GORDON—newscaster
b: Feb 4, 1908, Lawrence, Mass.

All Star News (news)
.... correspondent (1952–53)

FRAWLEY, WILLIAM—actor
b: Feb 26, 1887, Burlington, Iowa d: Mar 3, 1966

I Love Lucy (com).... Fred Mertz (1951–57)
The Lucy-Desi Comedy Hour (specials) (com)
.... Fred Mertz (1957–60)
My Three Sons (com)
Michael Francis "Bub" O'Casey (1960–64)

William Frawley was actually the second choice to play the role that brought him TV immortality, that of next-door-neighbor Fred Mertz on *I Love Lucy.* An old show business trooper from *way* back, he had a reputation for hitting the sauce a little too heavily and was vetoed for the part by network officials. However, Lucy and Desi finally signed him when their first choice, blustery Gale Gordon (who had been with Lucy on radio), was unavailable.

Frawley had broken into acting before 1910, over the objections of his strong-willed mother, and spent much of the 1910s

314

and 1920s touring in vaudeville with his then-wife, Louise. In the '30s he moved into films as a character actor and had 20 very successful years playing bluff and hearty Irish cops, cigar-chomping politicians, and the like. In all, he was in more than 100 films. As the movie roles began to thin out around 1950, he tried to get into television —at first with limited success. He was in a few live dramas in 1950–51, including a production on *The Silver Theater* and for 13 weeks had a role on the early daytime soap opera *The First Hundred Years* (1950–51). He pitched hard for the role on *Lucy* and was glad to get it. He should have been; it gave him ten years of work and greatly enhanced his visibility in the business (the series was Number One for four years).

Bill continued to make occasional guest appearances on other shows, as the filming of *Lucy* permitted. Among them were *The Loretta Young Show, Shower of Stars,* and *The Gale Storm Show.* He was just as cantankerous offscreen as on and was sometimes rather blunt in his opinions. On *I Love Lucy,* later in its run: "It's like eating stew every night—stale and not a bit funny." On his loving TV wife Vivian Vance: "She's one of the finest gals to come out of Kansas, but I often wish she'd go back there."

When *Lucy* finally ended its run, Bill went straight into another long-running role, as Uncle Bub on *My Three Sons.* But it is as balding, chuckling, irascible Fred Mertz that he will always be remembered. His last major appearance, appropriately, was in a *Lucy Show* episode in late 1965.

FRAY, JACQUES—pianist

The Jacques Fray Music Room (music)
.... regular (1949)

FRAZEE, JANE—actress, singer ❦
b: Jul 18, 1918, Duluth, Minn. d: Sep 6, 1985

Beulah (com) ... Alice Henderson (1952–53)

FRAZER, DAN—actor
b: Nov 20, New York City, N.Y.

Kojak (police)...... Frank McNeil (1973–78)

FRAZIER, SHEILA—black actress
b: Nov 13, 1948, New York City, N.Y.

The Lazarus Syndrome (drama)
.... Gloria St. Clair (1979)

FREBERG, STAN—satirist
b: Aug 7, 1926, Los Angeles, Calif.

The Chevy Show (music) .... regular (1958)

Though Freberg is best known as an extremely creative satirist on radio and records, he got his start in the late 1940s and early '50s doing voices for cartoons and TV children's shows. He was, in fact, nominated for an Emmy Award in 1950 for his character Cecil the Seasick Sea Serpent on the puppet show *Time for Beany.* Stan then produced some of the funniest recorded parodies on TV shows ever made, including *John and Marsha* (two lovers panting, as on a soap opera) and the million-selling hit *St. George and the Dragonet* ("How are you going to catch the dragon, St. George?" "I thought you'd never ask. A dragon net." *Dum-de-dum-dum!*).

TV executives laughed so hard they later paid him a ton of money to produce commercials satirizing their own products.

FREDERICK, HAL—black actor

The Interns (drama)
.... Dr. Cal Barrin (1970–71)
Born Free (adv) .... Makedde (1974)

FREDERICK, PAULINE—newscaster
b: Gallitzin, Pa. r: Harrisburg, Pa.

Pauline Frederick's Guestbook (int)
.... hostess (1949)
All Star News (news)
.... correspondent (1952–53)

Miss Frederick was one of the few women reporters on television in the 1950s and '60s. She got her start interviewing wives of diplomats for the *Washington Star* and later worked as a foreign correspondent for various newspaper services and in radio. After several years with ABC-TV she joined NBC in 1953 and became best known as that network's United Nations correspondent. She retired in 1975.

FREDERICKS, DEAN—actor

Jungle Jim (adv)............ Kassim (1955)
Steve Canyon (adv)
.... Lt. Col. Steve Canyon (1958–59)

FREED, ALAN—disc jockey

b: Dec 15, 1922, Johnstown, Pa. d: Jan 20, 1965

The Big Beat (music) .... host (1957)

Freed was the man who allegedly coined the term "rock 'n' roll" —though there is some controversy on that point. He was certainly a central figure and kingmaker in rock 'n' roll in the late 1950s, as well a champion of the real thing (read "Black music"). His career was destroyed in the payola scandals.

FREED, BERT—actor

b: Nov 3, 1919, New York City, N.Y.

Shane (wes) .... Rufe Ryker (1966)

FREEDLEY, VINTON—Broadway producer, host

Talent Jackpot (talent)........ emcee (1949)
Showtime, U.S.A. (var)..... emcee (1950–51)

FREEDMAN, WINIFRED—actress

b: Jul 23, Granite City, Ill.

Joanie Loves Chachi (com)
.... Annette (1982–83)
Rituals (drama)
.... Patty Dupunt (1984–85)

FREEMAN, AL, JR.—black actor

b: Mar 21, 1934, San Antonio, Texas

Hot L Baltimore (com)
.... Charles Bingham (1975)
Roots: The Next Generations (drama)
.... Malcolm X (1979)

Emmy Award: Best Actor in a Daytime Drama Series, for *One Life to Live* (1979)

Freeman is best known for his role as police officer Ed Hall on the daytime soap *One Life to Live,* which he has played more or less continuously since 1972. He was the first black actor to win a daytime Emmy. He also does occasional prime time work and was nominated for another Emmy for his role in the 1970 TV movie *My Sweet Charlie.*

FREEMAN, DAMITA JO—black actress, choreographer

b: Feb 26, Palestine, Texas

Private Benjamin (com)
.... Pvt. Jackie Sims (1981–83)

The niece of 1950s–60s pop singer Damita Jo.

FREEMAN, DEENA—actress

b: Feb 11, Palo Alto, Calif.

Too Close for Comfort (com)
.... April Rush (1981–82)

FREEMAN, J. PAUL—actor

b: London, England

Falcon Crest (drama)
.... Gustav Riebmann (1984–85)

FREEMAN, JOAN—actress

b: 1942, Council Bluffs, Iowa r: Burbank, Calif.

Bus Stop (drama)
.... Elma Gahringer (1961–62)

FREEMAN, KATHLEEN—actress

b: Feb 17, 1919*, Chicago, Ill.

Topper (com) .... Katie, the maid (1953–54)
Mayor of the Town (com)
...... Marilly, the housekeeper (1954–55)
It's About Time (com) . Mrs. Boss (1966–67)
The Beverly Hillbillies (com)
.... Flo Shafer (1969–71)
Funny Face (com) ..... Kate Harwell (1971)
Lotsa Luck (com)... Mrs. Belmont (1973–74)

FREEMAN, MICKEY—actor

The Phil Silvers Show (com)
.... Pvt. Zimmerman (1955–59)

FREEMAN, PAM—actress

The Pruitts of Southampton (com)
.... Stephanie Pruitt (1966–67)

FREEMAN, SANDY—actress

b: Jacksonville, Fla.

Dreams (com)....... Louise Franconi (1984)

FREEMAN, STAN—pianist

b: Apr 3, 1920, Waterbury, Conn.

Three's Company (music).... pianist (1950)
Melody Tour (var).......... regular (1954)

*Some sources give 1922.

Emmy Award: Best Special Musical Material, for the mini-musical "Hi-Hat" on *The Carol Burnett Show* (1978)

FREEMAN, TICKER—pianist
b: Oct 13, 1911, Paterson, N.J. d: Jan 30, 1986

The Dinah Shore Show (music)
.... pianist (1951–57)

FREEMS, GEORGE—
Seven at Eleven (var)....... regular (1951)

FREES, PAUL—voice specialist, actor
b: Jun 22, 1920, Chicago, Ill. d: Nov 1, 1986

The Millionaire (drama)
.. John Beresford Tipton (voice) (1955–60)
The Bullwinkle Show (cartn)
.... Boris Badenov (voice) (1961–62)
Calvin and the Colonel (cartn)
.. Oliver Wendell Clutch (voice) (1961–62)
The Famous Adventures of Mr. Magoo (cartn)
.... voices (1964–65)

Paul Frees was one of those people who, like Mel Blanc, worked steadily in TV without ever being seen. A child performer in vaudeville at the age of 13, he worked in radio in the '40s and '50s and was familiar to listeners as the "voice of doom" announcer on such eerie shows as *Escape* and *Suspense.* He appeared on-screen in a dozen or so films of the '50s and '60s (*Riot in Cell Block 11,* etc.), but his fortune was in his voice. A generation of TV viewers will remember him for the deep-rolling tones of the never-seen millionaire on *The Millionaire* in the '50s.

Another generation probably knows him better for his work on Saturday morning children's shows, where he was extremely active during the 1960s. Among his many characters were the speaking voices of John Lennon and George Harrison on *The Beatles* cartoon; he was also Professor Ludwig Von Drake on the *Disney* show in prime time. He was mostly inactive after 1970.

Like others pursuing his particular specialty, Frees learned to live with anonymous success. "Sometimes it creates an ego problem," he commented in 1961, "but nothing so serious I can't overcome it when I look at the bank balance."

FREMIN, JOURDAN—actress
b: Dec 19, New Orleans, La.

At Ease (com)....... Cpl. Lola Grey (1983)

FRENCH, LEIGH—comedienne, actress
The Smothers Brothers Comedy Hour (var)
.... regular (1967–69)
The Summer Smothers Brothers Show (var)
.... regular (1968)
The Dick Cavett Show (var).. regular (1975)
The Smothers Brothers Show (var)
.... regular (1975)

FRENCH, SUSAN—actress
Bare Essence (drama)
.... Margaret Marshall (1983)

FRENCH, VICTOR—actor, director
b: Dec 4, 1934, Santa Barbara, Calif.

Get Smart (com) ....'. Agent 44 (1965–70)
The Hero (com) ..... Fred Gilman (1966–67)
Little House on the Prairie (adv)
.... Mr. Isaiah Edwards (1974–77)
Carter Country (com)
.... Chief Roy Mobey (1977–79)
Little House on the Prairie (adv)
.... Mr. Isaiah Edwards (1982–83)
Highway to Heaven (drama)
.... Mark Gordon (1984–)

Beefy, bearded Victor French seems to be Michael Landon's one-man stock company. The two actors first appeared together when French had a role in an episode of *Bonanza;* later he was signed for a guest shot on *Little House on the Prairie,* then for two, then for a regular role. When Landon launched his new series *Highway to Heaven* in 1984, French joined him there too, this time as costar.

The role of a sidekick to an angel was quite a change for an actor who spent 20 years playing killers, rapists, and robbers prior to his *Little House* days. The son of a Hollywood stuntman, Victor played small parts in movies and TV for many years, though he did have a supporting role as the neighbor in the short-lived 1966 comedy *The Hero.* The 1970s were his breakthrough years. Besides *Little House,* he appeared in more than 20 episodes of *Gunsmoke* and launched his directing career during that series' final season. In 1977 he left *Little House* to star in his own series, *Carter Country,* which ran for two years on ABC.

Victor has continued to work as a director as well as an actor and has directed many episodes of *Little House* and *Highway to Heaven.* His second love is boxing; he is part owner of a boxing club in North Hollywood and holds a boxing manager's license. He was married in the '70s to actress Julie Cobb.

FRENETTE, CECILLE—actress

Thicke of the Night (talk)
. . . . recurring player (1983–84)

FREY, LEONARD—actor
b: Sep 4, 1938, Brooklyn, N.Y.

Best of the West (com)
. . . . Parker Tillman (1981–82)
Mr. Smith (com). . Raymond Holyoke (1983)
Mr. Sunshine (com)
. . . . Prof. Leon Walters (1986)

FRIDAY, NANCY—author, commentator

The Tomorrow Show (talk)
. . . . regular (1980–81)

The best-selling author of *Men in Love* and *My Mother/My Self* commented on "human relationships" for NBC's late-night series.

FRIDELL, SQUIRE—actor
b: Feb 9, 1943, Oakland, Calif.

Rosetti and Ryan (drama)
. . . . Frank Ryan (1977)

FRIEBUS, FLORIDA—actress

The Many Loves of Dobie Gillis (com)
. . . . Winifred (Winnie) Gillis (1959–63)
The Bob Newhart Show (com)
. . . . Mrs. Bakerman (1972–78)

FRIED, IAN—juvenile actor

Two Marriages (drama)
. . . . Willie Daley (1983–84)
Fathers and Sons (com)
. . . . Matty Bolen (1986)

FRIEDMAN, ADA—actress

Mixed Doubles (drama). Ada Abbott (1949)

FRIEDMAN, DAVID—juvenile actor
b: Jun 10, 1973, Los Angeles, Calif.

Little House on the Prairie (adv)
. . . . Jason Carter (1982–83)

FRIEDRICH, JOHN—actor

Studs Lonigan (drama). . . . . . Martin (1979)
The Thorn Birds (drama)
. . . . Frank Cleary (1983)

FRIMPLE, DENNIS—actor

Matt Houston (drama) . . . . Bo (1982–83)

FRISCHMAN, DAN—actor
b: Apr 23, Whippany, N.J.

Head of the Class (com)
. . . . Arvid Engen (1986–)

FRITTS, STAN & HIS KORN KOBBLERS —band

Kobb's Korner (var) . . . . . . regular (1948–49)

FRIZZEL, LOU—actor
b: c. 1920 d: Jun 17, 1979

Bonanza (wes) . . . Dusty Rhoades (1970–72)
Chopper One (police) . . . . Mitch (1974)
The New Land (adv) . . . . . . Murdock (1974)

FROMAN, JANE—singer
b: Nov 10, 1907, St. Louis, Mo. d: Apr 22, 1980

Jane Froman's U.S.A. Canteen (var)
. . . . hostess (1952–55)

Younger viewers who were confronted by the Jane Froman revival of the early 1950s might have been excused if they had asked, "Jane who?" She made just two films in the 1930s and appeared in a few Broadway shows of the early '40s. She had no hit records, though she had been heard a good deal on radio.

The event that changed her life, for better and worse, occurred on February 22, 1943, when a plane carrying Jane and a troupe of U.S.O. performers crashed off the coast of Lisbon, Portugal. Jane's legs were crushed, and the injuries would keep her undergoing constant operations for the rest of her life. Her reaction to this misfortune captured the public's imagination. Driven by an indomitable spirit, she returned to entertaining World War II servicemen in a wheelchair, and later with a giant cast (concealed under her flowing gown) and braces. In 1952 Hollywood made a movie about her struggle, called *With a Song in My Heart,* starring Susan Hayward and with Jane herself providing the singing voice. The Froman boom was on. Her records began to sell as never before, and she was starred in a CBS variety show that ran for three years, mostly in the early evening.

Jane retired to her native Missouri in 1959 and later married a college administrator there.

FROME, MILTON—actor

The Milton Berle Show (var)
.... regular (1953–55)
The Beverly Hillbillies (com)
.... Lawrence Chapman (1964–67)

FROST, ALICE—actress

Mama (com)
.... Aunt Trina Gunnerson (1949–57)

FROST, DAVID—host

b: Apr 7, 1939, Tenterden, England

That Was the Week That Was (com)
.... host (1964–65)
The David Frost Show (talk)
.... host (1969–72)
The David Frost Revue (com)
.... host (1971–73)
Headliners with David Frost (talk)
.... host (1978)

Emmy Awards: Star, Best Variety Series, for *The David Frost Show* (1970, 1971).

"Haven't I met you in Johannesburg?", nine-year-old would stop and ask a total stranger. "Why, no, I've never been to Johannesburg," would be the usual reply. "Neither have I," the boy shot back, "it must have been two other people." Then young David Frost would run off, giggling at the joke, while the stranger stood there nonplussed. On the way home the lad might stop off at a grocery and ask the proprietor, "Have you any broken biscuits?" If the man answered "Yes, I do," back would come, "Why don't you mend them, then!" as David ran out the door.

Even as a child David Frost delighted in practical jokes—good and bad—and his ir-reverence has continued throughout his adult career. While attending Cambridge University he edited the university's student magazine and was a prime mover in the drama club. When he graduated he went to work as a trainee for a TV company. Given the choice in 1962 of a "safe" job with the company or a risky position elsewhere working on the pilot for a program that might never get on the air, he immediately chose the latter. The show, *That Was the Week That Was,* proved to be a hit on British television in 1963 and was exported to the U.S. that fall as a one-time special. The special caused a sensation here, and *TW3* became a regular series on NBC as well, exposing David Frost and his satirical barbs to a mass audience in America.

Things English were big in the U.S. at the time (e.g., the Beatles) and David made quite an initial splash. In 1969 he was signed to host a syndicated daily talk show, and in 1971 a syndicated weekly satirical series. His style could be a bit overpowering ("Marvelous! Smashing! Terrific! It's been a joy having you here!"), but the shows were star-laden and reasonably popular. The irrepressible Englishman also popped up in other places, including a guest shot on *Here's Lucy* in 1971.

In the mid-1970s, just when David's star seemed to be fading, he bounced back with a journalistic coup that staggered the TV industry. Former President Richard Nixon was negotiating with the networks over the rights to a series of exclusive interviews, his first since he left office in disgrace three years earlier. CBS and ABC refused to pay, and NBC haggled over the price, whereupon Frost stepped in and put together a deal that would guarantee Nixon a minimum of $600,000 for the rights. He then taped 28 hours worth of intensive conversations with the former president at San Clemente, California, subjecting him to a probing, prosecutorial interview that surprised those who expected a whitewash. The historic interviews, edited down to four 90-minute telecasts, were aired on an ad-hoc lineup of 155 U.S. stations and in many foreign countries. They made headlines, made everybody concerned lots of money (from advertising revenues), and put Frost back in the limelight.

David subsequently hosted a live summer talk series on NBC, but he has since been seen mostly in specials such as UNICEF's *A Gift of Song* in 1979 and the *This Is Your Life* thirtieth anniversary show in 1981.

FRYE, CHIP—actor

The Powers of Matthew Star (sci fi)
.... Bob Alexander (1982)

FRYE, SOLEIL MOON—juvenile actress
b: Aug 6, 1976, Glendora, Calif.

Punky Brewster (com)
.... Penelope "Punky" Brewster (1984–86)

The kid sister of young actor Meeno Peluce.

FUCCELLO, TOM—actor
b: Dec 11, Newark, N.J.

Dallas (drama)...... Dave Culver (1979–82)

FUDGE, ALAN—actor
b: Feb 27, 1944, Wichita, Kan.

Man from Atlantis (adv)
.... C. W. Crawford (1977–78)
Eischied (police)
. Dep. Commissioner Kimbrough (1979–80)
Paper Dolls (drama)
.... Dr. Van Adams (1984)

FUJIKAWA, "JERRY" HATSUO—actor
b: c. 1911 d: Apr 30, 1983

Mr. T and Tina (com) .. Uncle Matsu (1976)

FUJIOKA, JOHN—actor
b: Jun 29, Olaa, Hawaii

The Last Resort (com)..... Kevin (1979–80)
Tales of the Gold Monkey (adv)
.... Todo (1982–83)

FULGER, HOLLY—actress

Jack and Mike (drama) .... Carol (1986–)

FULLER, KURT—actor

Wildside (wes).... Elliot Thogmorton (1985)

FULLER, PENNY—actress
b: 1940, Durham, N.C.

Bare Essence (drama) . Laura Parker (1983)

Fortune Dane (police)
.... Mayor Amanda Harding (1986)

Emmy Award: Best Supporting Actress in a Special, for *The Elephant Man* (1982)

FULLER, ROBERT—actor
b: Jul 29, 1933, Troy, N.Y.

Laramie (wes) .... Jess Harper (1959–63)
Wagon Train (wes)
.... Cooper Smith (1963–65)
Emergency (drama)
.... Dr. Kelly Brackett (1972–77)

FULLERTON, MELANIE—actress

To Rome with Love (com)
.... Mary Jane (Pokey) Endicott (1969–71)

FULMER, RAY—actor

Hazel (com) .... Steve Baxter (1965–66)

FULTON, EILEEN—actress
b: Sep 13, 1933, Asheville, N.C.

Our Private World (drama)
.... Lisa Hughes (1965)

Eileen is a superstar of daytime television, having starred as the conniving Lisa on *As the World Turns* since 1960. *Our Private World* was a short-lived attempt to launch a prime time spin-off from the hit daytime soap.

FULTON, JULIE—actress
b: Apr 10, c. 1960, Evanston, Ill.

Lime Street (drama) .. Celia Wesphal (1985)

FULTON, WENDY—actress
b: Stewartstown, Pa.

Bare Essence (drama)
.... Muffin Marshall (1983)

The wife of actor Dwight Schultz of *The A-Team*.

FUNICELLO, ANNETTE—actress
b: Oct 22, 1942, Utica, N.Y. r: Los Angeles, Calif.

The Danny Thomas Show (com)
.... Gina (1959)
Easy Does It ... Starring Frankie Avalon (var)
.... regular (1976)

The most famous of the *Mickey Mouse Club* Mouseketeers of the late '50s, Annette appeared in numerous Disney films and in guest appearances on the studio's *Zorro* TV series. In the '60s she was paired with Frankie Avalon in a string of teenage "beach" movies. Following about ten years of obscurity, she reemerged in the late '70s as a living piece of '50s and '60s nostalgia.

FUNK, TERRY—actor
b: June 30, Hammond, Ind. r: Amarillo, Texas

Wildside (wes).... Prometheus Jones (1985)

A former professional wrestler and onetime (1977–78) world's champion in that sport, his acting debut was in Sylvester Stallone's 1978 wrestling film, *Paradise Alley.*

FUNT, ALLEN—host
b: Sep 16, 1914, Brooklyn, N.Y.

Candid Camera (aud par).... host (1948–67)
The Garry Moore Show (var)
.... regular (1959–60)
Candid Camera (aud par).... host (1974–78)

Some folks say that you need to have only one good idea in life to be successful, and Allen Funt seems to prove it's true. The idea came to him while he was serving in the army during World War II, stationed at a base in Oklahoma. He was working on a radio show consisting of servicemen's gripes, and he noticed how nervous his subjects became when confronted with a microphone. So he hid the mike and didn't tell them they were being recorded. Voila! *Candid Microphone* was born!

Funt was no stranger to show business, having been an independent producer before the war, as well as a onetime gag writer for radio's *Truth or Consequences.* After his discharge he set about packaging his Big Idea, first as a radio show and then, with cameras, for early television under the title *Candid Camera.* Funt himself was the perfect host—deadpan, ordinary-looking, and just pushy enough to get the reaction he wanted from unsuspecting strangers who had walked into one of his carefully contrived setups. It was one of the most original ideas on TV, and it was seen, off and on, for more

than 30 years. It is still revived from time to time.

FURLONG, KIRBY—juvenile actor
b: c. 1963 r: Canoga Park, Calif.

The Jimmy Stewart Show (com)
.... Jake Howard (1971–72)

FURNESS, BETTY—actress, consumer advocate
b: Jan 3, 1916, New York City, N.Y.

Studio One (drama)
.... commercial announcer (1949–58)
Penthouse Party (var)..... hostess (1950–51)
Byline (drama)......... the reporter (1951)
The Best of Broadway (drama)
.... commercials (1954–55)
Westinghouse Desilu Playhouse (drama)
...... commercial spokesperson (1958–60)

Betty Furness spent the first part of her television career pitching products on behalf of advertisers, and the rest of it defending consumers against some of those advertisers.

Before television came along, however, she had another career, as an actress. The daughter of a corporate executive, she was raised on Manhattan's Park Avenue and became a child model at age 14. At 16 she moved west and began a movie career that included more than 30 films, mostly Bs, all made during the 1930s. A short stage career and some radio work followed in the '40s, but by the time TV came along her career was in low gear and she decided to take on commercial spokesperson assignments. For the next dozen years she was one of the most famous pitchwomen on TV, primarily for Westinghouse appliances ("You can be sure ... if it's Westinghouse"). She also acted occasionally, on *Studio One, Climax,* and her own short-lived drama series, *Byline,* and hosted some daytime and nighttime chatter shows.

In 1960 she left the commercial field and gradually shifted into consumer advocacy. In 1967 she was appointed by President Lyndon B. Johnson to become his special assistant for consumer affairs, and three years later she became a consumer affairs official for New York State and then for New York City. She also was elected (in 1969) to the board of *Consumer Reports,* a position she has held to the present day.

In the 1970s Betty returned to television in a new role, as a consumer reporter for WNBC-TV in New York and occasional contributor to the *Today* show. She was also given an on-air tryout as cohost of *Today* after the departure of Barbara Walters in 1976, but the spot went to Jane Pauley instead.

FURST, STEPHEN—actor
b: May 8, Norfolk, Va.

Delta House (com)
.... Kent "Flounder" Dorfman (1979)
St. Elsewhere (drama)
.... Dr. Elliot Axelrod (1983–   )

FURTH, GEORGE—actor
b: Dec 14, 1932, Chicago, Ill.

Broadside (com).. Ensign Beasley (1964–65)
Tammy (com)..... Dwayne Whitt (1965–66)
The Good Guys (com)
.... Hal Dawson (1968–69)
The Dumplings (com)
.... Frederic Steele (1976)

G

GABEL, MARTIN—actor, director
b: Jun 19, 1912, Philadelphia, Pa. d: May 22, 1986

With This Ring (quiz) .... host (1951)

Onetime husband of TV personality Arlene Francis, and a frequent guest panelist on *What's My Line?*

GABLE, JUNE—actress
Barney Miller (com)
.... Det. Baptista (1976–77)
Laugh-In (revival) (var) ... regular (1977–78)
Sha Na Na (var) .... regular (1978–81)

GABLE, SANDRA—model
The Swift Show (var)........ model (1948)

GABLER, MUNROE—actor
Faraway Hill (drama) .... regular (1946)

GABOR, EVA—actress
b: Feb 11, 1921, Budapest, Hungary

Green Acres (com) .. Lisa Douglas (1965–71)
Bridges to Cross (drama)
.... Maria Talbot (1986)

The glamorous Gabor sisters Eva and Zsa Zsa have been exotic fixtures in show business for many years. (A third beautiful sister, Magda, is a society figure in New York.) Eva was the first to come to the U.S. from the family's native Hungary, in the '30s, and she quickly launched a minor career in films and later on Broadway. She was a familiar (and shapely) figure on early television as well, especially on New York–based live drama series such as *Philco Playhouse, Climax, Ellery Queen,* and *General Electric Theater.* She continued to make guest appearances in the '60s (*Burke's Law,* etc.), but she is best remembered for her long-running role as the socialite wife who finds herself down on the farm on *Green Acres.*

Eva in real life is true to the chic, continental image she conveyed in her most famous role. She speaks English, French,

German, and Hungarian, plays the piano well, and wrote her own autobiography, in 1951 (before the best part of her career), calling it *Orchids and Salamis.* Why *Orchids and Salamis?* Because, she says, friends once found nothing but those two items in her refrigerator. *That's* chic!

Since *Green Acres* left the air she has been seen infrequently, including a couple of appearances on *The Love Boat* and *Fantasy Island.*

GABRIELLE—singer
Gabrielle (music)........... hostess (1948)

GAFFIN, MELANIE—juvenile actress
b: Nov 12, 1973, Santa Monica, Calif.

Whiz Kids (drama)
.... Cheryl Adler (1983–84)

GAIL, MAX—actor
b: Apr 5, 1943, Grosse Pointe, Mich.

Barney Miller (com)
Det. Stanley ("Wojo") Wojohowicz (1975–82)
Pearl (drama).......... Sgt. Walder (1978)
Whiz Kids (drama)
.... Llewellen Farley, Jr. (1983–84)

Max Gail, the dim-witted detective Wojo on *Barney Miller,* is anything but dim-witted off screen. He holds a master's degree in international finance from the University of Michigan, fronts his own rock band (handling keyboards and vocals), and during his last two years on *Barney Miller* founded a production company that has produced several documentaries on social issues such as nuclear power and agent orange. Gail is very committed to social causes, particularly those dealing with American Indians.

He was born to a family of seven children, including three sets of twins. His twin, Mary, is a singer and songwriter. Max began attracting attention as an actor in the early '70s, with roles in *Cannon, Shaft,* etc., and has since appeared in an assortment of TV movies and miniseries, including *Pearl* in 1978.

GAINER, RICHARD—actor
Boss Lady (com) .... Roger (1952)

GAINES, BOYD—actor
b: May 11, 1953, Atlanta, Ga.

One Day at a Time (com)
.... Mark Royer (1981–84)

GAINES, JIMMY—

The Andy Williams Show (var)
.... regular (1962–63)

GALE, BILL—actor

Faraway Hill (drama) .... regular (1946)

GALE, BOBBY—

Kraft Music Hall Presents The Dave King Show (var)................. regular (1959)

GALIK, DENISE—actress

79 Park Avenue (drama)
.... Candy Berkowski (1977)
Knots Landing (drama)
.... Linda Striker (1980–81)
Flamingo Road (drama)
.... Christie Kovacs (1981–82)

GALLAGHER, DON—actor

ABC Television Players (drama)
.... narrator (1949)
Rendezvous with Music (music)
.... regular (1950)

GALLAGHER, HELEN—actress
b: Jul 19, 1926, Brooklyn, N.Y.

Manhattan Showcase (var)... regular (1949)

Emmy Awards: Best Actress in a Daytime Drama Series, for *Ryan's Hope* (1976, 1977)

A successful Broadway musical actress of the 1950s and '60s, Helen has played Maeve Ryan on *Ryan's Hope* since the show premiered in 1975.

GALLAGHER, MEG—actress

Dallas (drama)........... Louella (1979–81)
Hill Street Blues (drama)
.... Tina Russo (1986–)

GALLAGHER, PETER—actor
b: 1956, Armonk, N.Y.

Skag (drama) .... John Skagska (1980)

GALLEGO, GINA—actress

Flamingo Road (drama)
.... Alicia Sanchez (1981–82)
Rituals (drama)
.... Diandra Santiago (1984–85)

GALLERY, JAMES—actor

Billy (com)........... George Fisher (1979)

GALLIART, MELVILLE—actor

Faraway Hill (drama) .... regular (1946)

GALLICHIO, JOSEPH—orchestra leader

Garroway at Large (var)
.... orch. leader (1949–51)

GALLICO, ROBERT—actor

O.S.S. (drama) ...... Sgt. O'Brien (1957–58)

GALLO, LEW—actor, producer
b: Jun 12, 1928, Mt. Kisco, N.Y.

Twelve O'Clock High (drama)
.... Major Joe Cobb (1964–65)

GALLO, MARIO—actor
b: c. 1923 Brooklyn, N.Y. d: Oct 30, 1984

Delvecchio (police)
.... Tomaso Delvecchio (1976–77)

GALLOP, FRANK—announcer, actor

Lights Out (drama) ...... narrator (1950–52)
Broadway Open House (talk)
.... regular (1951)
What Happened? (quiz)..... panelist (1952)
The Buick Circus Hour (drama)
.... the ringmaster (1952–53)
The Perry Como Show (var)
.... announcer (1955–61)
Kraft Mystery Theater (drama)
.... host (1961)
The Kraft Music Hall (var)
.... announcer (1961–63)

This deep-voiced veteran announcer served as Perry Como's scornful, slightly sarcastic offscreen foil for years on Como's shows. The idea of using the announcer to add to a show's humor in this way was not exactly new; Gallop had filled the same role vis a vis Milton Berle on Berle's radio series in the late 1940s.

GALLOWAY, DON—actor
b: Jul 27, 1937, Brooksville, Ky.

Arrest and Trial (drama)
.... Mitchell Harris (1963–64)
Tom, Dick and Mary (com)
.... Dr. Tom Gentry (1964–65)
Ironside (police)
.... Det. Sgt. Ed Brown (1967–75)
The Guinness Game (quiz)..... host (1979)
Hizzonner (com) .... Timmons (1979)

GALLOWAY, MICHAEL—actor

The Blue Angels (adv)
.... Lt. Russ MacDonald (1960)

GALLUP, DR. GEORGE—public opinion expert
b: Nov 18, 1901, Jefferson, Iowa d: Jul 26, 1984

America Speaks (pub aff) .... host (1948)

The founder of the Gallup Poll, and the man who frequently told us what we were thinking (as a nation) over the years. He founded his American Institute of Public Opinion in 1935. In the next ten national elections he claimed to have been wrong only once, in 1948. Gallup appeared on television as an expert commentator in the '40s and '50s, especially around election time.

GANAS, MONICA—actress

The Billy Crystal Comedy Hour (var)
.... regular (1982)

GANDOLF, RAY—newscaster
b: Norwalk, Ohio

Our World (pub aff) ...... cohost (1986–)

GANZEL, TERESA—actress
b: Mar 23, 1957, Toledo, Ohio

Teachers Only (com)
.... Samantha "Sam" Keating (1983)
The Duck Factory (com)
.... Mrs. Sheree Winkler (1984)

GARAGIOLA, JOE—sportscaster, host
b: Feb 12, 1926, St. Louis, Mo.

The Baseball World of Joe Garagiola (sport)
.... host (1972–75)

Monday Night Baseball (sport)
.... sportscaster (1975)
To Tell the Truth (quiz).... emcee (1976–77)

"Your honest shiny head is one of the few real things on TV," wrote a woman from New Jersey, after Joe Garagiola asked viewers of the *Today* show whether he should start wearing a toupee. Even though the vote was 1,500 to 250 in favor of a rug, Joe decided to stay honest—and bald.

The smiling, affable sportscaster has been a fixture on NBC for more than 25 years. Before that he was a major-league baseball catcher for nine years (1946–55), including five and a half with the St. Louis Cardinals. The high point of his playing days came in his rookie season, with a .316 batting average that helped the Cardinals reach and win the World Series. On his retirement in 1955 he became a television sportscaster, covering the Cardinals, and later the New York Yankees. In 1961 he joined NBC as part of the game of the week play-by-play team, and he has been with the network ever since.

Beginning in the late '60s Joe attempted to broaden his activities by becoming a regular on the *Today* show (1969–73) and emcee of a succession of game shows, including *Sale of the Century* and *To Tell the Truth*. He remains best known for sports commentary and coverage, however, his quick wit and good nature serving him well in that capacity, too.

GARAS, KAS—actor
b: Mar 4, 1940, Kaunas, Lithuania

Strange Report (drama)
.... Hamlyn Gynt (1971)

GARBER, TERRI—actress
b: Miami, Fla.

Mr. Smith (com)
.... Dr. Judy Tyson (1983)
North and South (drama)
.... Ashton Main (1985)

GARBER, VICTOR—actor

I Had Three Wives (drama)
.... Jackson Beaudine (1985)

GARDE, BETTY—actress
b: Sep 19, 1905, Philadelphia, Pa.

Kobb's Korner (var) . . . . regular (1949)
Easy Aces (talk) . . . . regular (1949–50)
The Real McCoys (com)
. . . . Aggie Larkin (1959–60)

GARDENIA, VINCENT—actor
b: Jan 7, 1922, Naples, Italy r: New York City, N.Y.

All in the Family (com)
. . . . Frank Lorenzo (1973–74)
Breaking Away (com)
. . . . Ray Stohler (1980–81)

GARDINER, REGINALD—actor
b: Feb 27, 1903, Wimbledon, Surrey, England
d: Jul 7, 1980

The Pruitts of Southampton (com)
. . . . Uncle Ned Pruitt (1966–67)

GARDNER, AVA—actress
b: Dec 24, 1922, Grabtown, N.C. r: Smithfield, N.C.

Knots Landing (drama)
. . . . Ruth Galveston (1985)

The smoldering film beauty of the '40s and '50s was long a holdout from television; not until the '80s did she join the parade of Hollywood legends making brief but regal appearances on the small screen—in *Knots Landing* and the miniseries *A.D.* In the latter she played Agrippina, scheming mother of the mad Emperor Nero, who eventually had her killed.

GARDNER, CRAIG—actor
b: c. 1951, Santa Monica, Calif.

Chase (police)
. . . . Officer Tom Wilson (1973–74)

GARDNER, HY—columnist
b: 1904, New York City, N.Y.

What's Going On? (quiz) . . . . panelist (1954)
To Tell the Truth (quiz)
. . . . panelist (1956–59)
Tonight! America After Dark (talk)
. . . . regular (1957)

GARDNER, TERRI—
The Nashville Palace (var)
. . . . regular (1981–82)

GAREN, SOPHRONY—singer
Saturday Night Jamboree (music)
. . . . regular (1948–49)

GARGAN, WILLIAM—actor
b: Jul 17, 1905, Brooklyn, N.Y. d: Feb 16, 1979

Martin Kane, Private Eye (drama)
. . . . Martin Kane (1949–51)
The New Adventures of Martin Kane (drama)
. . . . Martin Kane (1957)

William Gargan, a veteran B movie actor who had played Ellery Queen in films of the 1940s, created a new detective for radio and television in 1949 called Martin Kane. The show became one of the first popular detective series on TV and provided the actor with a significant career boost. Nevertheless, he left after two seasons to try his hand at producing.

The switch proved unsuccessful. Gargan later appeared in a few live dramatic productions and in a syndicated revival of the *Kane* series filmed in Europe in 1957, but his TV career never regained its early momentum. In 1960 the actor, a heavy smoker, was diagnosed as having throat cancer and underwent surgery for the removal of his larynx. That effectively ended his career; he lived for another 19 years but could speak only with the aid of an artificial voice box. He devoted the rest of his life to the fight against cancer and to warning others of the dangers of smoking.

His ordeal and subsequent activities were described in his 1969 autobiography, *Why Me?*

GARLAND, BEVERLY—actress
b: Oct 17, 1926, Santa Cruz, Calif.

Decoy (police) . . . . Casey Jones (1957)
Coronado 9 (drama) . . . . regular (1959)
The Bing Crosby Show (com)
. . . . Ellie Collins (1964–65)
My Three Sons (com)
. . . . Barbara Harper Douglas (1969–72)
Scarecrow and Mrs. King (adv)
. . . . Dotty West (1983–   )

GARLAND, JUDY—actress, singer
b: Jun 10, 1922, Grand Rapids, Minn. d: Jun 22, 1969

The Judy Garland Show (var)
.... hostess (1963–64)

The bittersweet legend of Judy Garland is too familiar to need repeating here. It is, in any event, a legend of the silver screen, from the radiant innocence of *The Wizard of Oz* in the 1930s to the self-destruction of the '50s and '60s.

Judy's career on television came during her troubled later years, yet it was filled with the same flashes of magic that characterized so much of her movie career. Her TV debut in 1955 was spectacular, a 90-minute tour de force presented as the first of CBS's *Ford Star Jubilee* big-budget specials. It had one of the largest audiences of any TV special up to that time. Judy was booked for another special in 1957, which was to serve as the pilot for a possible series, but squabbles with the network prevented it from ever reaching the air. It took five more years for the singer and the network to patch up their differences, but in 1962 and 1963 Judy was back in two more highly acclaimed specials which did lead to a weekly series in 1963–64.

The series, unfortunately, was an unmitigated disaster. Dogged by indecision as to its format, revolving-door producers, and the overwhelming competition of the number-two program on television, *Bonanza*, *The Judy Garland Show* never got off the ground. It averaged only 19% of the audience to *Bonanza*'s 56%. Even the third show in the time period, ABC's *Arrest and Trial*, did better, with 22%. The last few episodes, after all was lost, were perhaps the best; no guest stars, no gimmicks, just Judy by herself, singing her heart out.

After this debacle Judy continued to be seen from time to time on variety shows such as *The Hollywood Palace* and even as a mystery guest on *What's My Line?* But television audiences will remember her as moviegoers do, for those magical early films, particularly *The Wizard of Oz*, whose showing has become an annual TV event.

A fascinating behind-the-scenes account of the 1963 series, from its creation to its demise, is contained in the 1970 book *The Other Side of the Rainbow*, by Judy's friend, fellow artist, and "musical adviser," Mel Torme.

GARLAND, MARGARET—actress

Tom Corbett, Space Cadet (child)
.... Dr. Joan Dale (1950–55)

GARNER, JACK—actor

Bret Maverick (wes)
.... Jack, the bartender (1981–82)

The brother of actor James Garner, star of *Bret Maverick*.

GARNER, JAMES—actor
b: Apr 7, 1928, Norman, Okla.

Maverick (wes) ... Bret Maverick (1957–60)
Nichols (wes) .... Nichols (1971–72)
The Rockford Files (drama)
.... Jim Rockford (1974–80)
Bret Maverick (wes)
.... Bret Maverick (1981–82)

Emmy Award: Best Actor in a Drama Series, for *The Rockford Files* (1977)

James Garner has one of television's most engaging personalities: good-natured, often a bit put-upon, always anxious to use his wits rather than his muscles to get out of a scrape—if he can get away with it. Rugged and handsome, he has usually appeared in action series, bringing to them an understated sense of humor that set them apart from ordinary shoot-'em-up TV fare.

As a young man Garner took a while to find his calling. He dropped out of high school at 16 and joined the merchant marine, worked at odd jobs (including one in his father's carpet business and another modeling swim trunks), and saw combat during the Korean War.

After his discharge a friend got him a nonspeaking role in the stage play *The Caine Mutiny Court Martial*, which led to small parts on television and a contract with Warner Brothers. The studio was just getting into TV production, and in addition to casting him in some of its minor films *(Toward the Unknown, Shoot-out at Medicine Bend)*, it used him in episodes of such TV series as *Cheyenne* and *Conflict* during 1956–57. By 1957 Warner was ready to give him the costarring role in a new western called *Maverick*. The series started out relatively straight but soon took on an unusual, humorous tone reflecting Garner's own personality. Some episodes, in fact, were outright parodies of other famous series, like *Bonanza* and *Dragnet*. *Maverick* was a top-ten hit and Garner became a major star. However, the studio held him to a rather oppressive contract signed years before, and Jim, like some of Warner's other stars, rebelled. After considerable behind-the-scenes bickering, he finally walked off the series in 1960.

For the next 11 years Jim was out of television, trying to parlay his TV success into movie stardom. Though he made some fine films *(The Great Escape, The Americanization of Emily)*, his close-up style never really translated into the larger-than-life requirements of the big screen. In 1971 he returned to television in a role close to the one he had on *Maverick*, on a western called *Nichols*. It was a flop, but three years later he tried again with *The Rockford Files* (Maverick-as-a-detective), scoring his second major hit series.

Obviously enamored of the *Maverick* character, Jim later appeared in a *Maverick* reunion movie in 1978, helped kick off a spin-off series called *Young Maverick* (starring Charles Frank) in 1979, and starred in his own sequel series, *Bret Maverick*, in 1981. He has since appeared mostly in films, some produced by his own company, Cherokee Productions.

GARNER, JAY—actor

Buck Rogers in the 25th Century (sci fi)
.... Admiral Asimov (1981)

GARNER, MOUSIE—actor, comedian
b: 1909, Washington, D.C.

Surfside Six (drama)...... Mousie (1960–62)

GARR, TERI—actress
b: Dec 11, 1949, Lakewood, Ohio, r: Hollywood, Calif.

The Ken Berry "Wow" Show (var)
.... regular (1972)
Burns and Schreiber Comedy Hour (var)
.... regular (1973)
Girl with Something Extra (com)
.... Amber (1973–74)
The Sonny and Cher Comedy Hour (var)
.... regular (1973–74)
The Sonny Comedy Revue (var)
.... regular (1974)

GARRETT, BETTY—actress
b: May 23, 1919, St. Joseph, Mo. r: Seattle, Wash.

All in the Family (com)
.... Irene Lorenzo (1973–75)
Laverne & Shirley (com)
.... Mrs. Edna Babish De Fazio (1976–81)

GARRETT, ED—actor

Quincy, M.E. (police) ...... Eddie (1976–83)

GARRETT, HANK—actor
b: Oct 26, 1931, Monticello, N.Y.

Car 54, Where Are You? (com)
.... Off. Ed Nicholson (1961–63)
Paris (police)
...... Dep. Chief Jerome Bench (1979–80)

GARRETT, JIMMY—actor

The Lucy Show (com)
.... Jerry Carmichael (1962–66)

GARRETT, KELLY—singer

Your Hit Parade (music).... vocalist (1974)
Headliners with David Frost (talk)
.... regular (1978)

GARRETT, LEIF—actor
b: Nov 8, 1961, Hollywood, Calif.

Three for the Road (adv)
.... Endy Karras (1975)

A former teenage heartthrob, who appeared in juvenile roles throughout the 1970s (*Cade's County, Gunsmoke, The Odd Couple, Family*, etc.). He also had a fleeting recording career in 1977–79, but he never really ascended to the Shaun Cassidy "Young Hunk" throne. His only regular series, *Three for the Road*, lasted a scant two months.

GARRETT, PATSY—actress
b: May 4, 1921, Atlantic City, N.J.

Nanny and the Professor (com)
.... Mrs. Florence Fowler (1970–71)

GARRETT, SUSIE—black actress
b: Dec 29, Detroit, Mich.

Punky Brewster (com)
.... Mrs. Betty Johnson (1984–86)

The sister of actress Marla Gibbs, who got her into show business.

GARRICK, RIAN—actor

Manhunt (police)
.... Det. Bruce Hanna (1959–60)

GARRISON, DAVID—actor

It's Your Move (com)
.... Norman Lamb (1984–85)

GARRISON, SEAN—actor
b: Oct 19, 1937, New York City, N.Y.

Dundee and the Culhane (wes)
.... Culhane (1967)
The Secret Empire (drama)
.... Yannuck (1979)

GARRITY, DEVIN—publisher

Answers for Americans (pub aff)
.... panelist (1953–54)

GARRITY, VINCE—sportscaster

Saturday Night Basketball (sport)
.... sportscaster (1951–52)

GARROWAY, DAVE—host
b: Jul 13, 1913, Schenectady, N.Y. d: Jul 21, 1982

Garroway at Large (var) ..... host (1949–51)
The Dave Garroway Show (var)
.... host (1953–54)
CBS Newcomers (var) .... host (1971)

Dave Garroway was one of the pioneers of television whose later years were unfortunately rather tragic. His casual, intimate approach was a welcome counterbalance to the frantic vaudeville of early TV, but his resistance to the behind-the-scenes pressures of the business proved to be his undoing.

The son of an electrical engineer, Dave had a fragmented childhood, always on the move and never really settled on a hometown or an intended career. In 1937 a friend talked him into becoming an NBC page, and broadcasting got into his blood. Thereafter he was an announcer, first in Pittsburgh and then in Chicago, where he became a local fixture (as a dj) in the 1940s. Chicago was an important TV production center in those days, and Dave had his first national exposure as the host of an unusually witty, improvised variety show called *Garroway at Large,* which originated from that city from 1949–51. That led NBC to make him the first host of its new *Today* show in 1952. It is for his nine years on *Today* that he is fondly remembered. His intelligent, low-energy approach fit the morning hours perfectly (can you imagine Milton Berle in the morning?). Dave's career boomed as a result, as he added a prime time variety series in 1953–54 and hosted the acclaimed *Wide Wide World* on Sunday afternoons from 1955–58.

Unlike some of TV's seemingly low-key stars who are actually hard-driving underneath, Dave really was as easygoing as he seemed on the air, and the pressures of show business eventually became too great for him. After his wife's suicide in 1961 he simply left the medium, to take stock and "be the best father I can to my children." In time he began to itch to get back into the mainstream, on his own low-pressure terms, but he found the door he had closed behind him was now locked tight. He tried a number of projects, including a public broadcasting series called *Exploring the Universe* from 1962–63, an abortive syndicated talk show called *Tempo* in 1969, and a little-watched summer variety series, *The CBS Newcomers,* in 1971. The public seemed to accept him only as a figure of nostalgia, on periodic *Today* show anniversary telecasts.

Dave's last major appearance, in fact, was on *Today*'s thirtieth anniversary show in early 1982. He ended that telecast with his traditional farewell, an upraised palm and the word "peace." Embittered at the way his career had turned out and despondent about his declining health (he had undergone open-heart surgery in 1981), he finally decided there was only one way out. One morning in July 1982, after seeing his wife off to work, he quietly went back into his house, raised a gun to his head, and killed himself.

GART, JOHN—orchestra leader
b: Jun 6, 1905, Russia

The Jacques Fray Music Room (music)
.... organist (1949)
The Paul Winchell-Jerry Mahoney Show (var)................ orch. leader (1953–54)

GARTON, DICK—actor

Life with Elizabeth (com)
.... Richard (1953–55)

GARVER, KATHY—actress
b: 1948, Long Beach, Calif.

Family Affair (com) .... Cissy (1966–71)

GARVEY, CYNDY—hostess
b: Detroit, Mich.

Games People Play (sport)
.... cohost (1980–81)

A local talk-show hostess in Los Angeles, and the wife of baseball star and sometime TV personality Steve Garvey.

GARVEY, GERALD—actor

Those Endearing Young Charms (com)
.... Clem Charm (1952)

GARVEY, STEVE—panelist
b: Dec 22, 1948

The Gong Show (com)
.... panelist (1976–80)

Los Angeles Dodgers All-Star baseball player; husband of Cyndy.

GARY, JOHN—singer
b: Nov 29, 1932, Watertown, N.Y.

The John Gary Show (var) ...... host (1966)
The John Gary Show (var) ...... host (1968)

GARZA, JOEY—comedian

CBS Newcomers (var) .... regular (1971)

GATES, LARRY—actor
b: Sep 24, 1915, St. Paul, Minn.

Backstairs at the White House (drama)
.... Pres. Herbert Hoover (1979)

Emmy Award: Best Supporting Actor in a Daytime Drama, for *The Guiding Light* (1985)

GATES, RUTH—actress
b: c. 1886 d: May 23, 1966

Mama (com) .... Aunt Jenny (1949–57)

GATESON, MARJORIE—actress
b: Jan 17, 1891, Brooklyn, N.Y. d: Apr 17, 1977

One Man's Family (drama)
.... Fanny Barbour (1949–52)

This veteran of vaudeville, Broadway, and scores of minor films of the '30s and '40s had a very long run on television as Grace Tyrell on *The Secret Storm* (1954–69).

GAUGE, ALEXANDER—British actor
b: 1914, Wenchow, China d: Aug 29, 1960

The Adventures of Robin Hood (adv)
.... Friar Tuck (1955–58)

GAUNT, WILLIAM—actor
b: Apr 3, 1937, Leeds, England

The Champions (adv)
.... Richard Barrett (1968)

GAUTIER, DICK—actor
b: Oct 30, 1939*, Los Angeles, Calif.

Get Smart (com)
..... The C.O.N.T.R.O.L. Robot (1966–69)
Mr. Terrific (com) ...... Hal Walters (1967)
Here We Go Again (com)
.... Jerry Standish (1973)
When Things Were Rotten (com)
.... Robin Hood (1975)
Liar's Club (quiz)........ panelist (1976–78)

This darkly handsome comic actor has played quite a few nutty roles during his career, but none made him a major star. He first came to notice in the early 1960s on Broadway, as rock star "Conrad Birdie" (a sendup of Elvis Presley) in the hit musical *Bye, Bye Birdie*. Later, on television, he was Hymie, the C.O.N.T.R.O.L. robot on *Get Smart*, the hero's best friend on the short-lived but notorious comedy series *Mr. Terrific*, Jerry the swinging owner of Jerry's Polynesian Paradise restaurant on the even shorter-lived *Here We Go Again*, and the star of Mel Brooks' slapstick version of the Robin Hood legend, *When Things Were Rotten*. In between these mostly short engagements, Dick played guest roles on many other comedies, especially *Love, American Style* and *The Love Boat*.

*Some sources give 1931.

330

GAVIN, JOHN—actor
b: Apr 8, 1928, Los Angeles, Calif.

Destry (wes) . . . . Harrison Destry (1964)
Convoy (drama) . . Comdr. Dan Talbot (1965)
Doctors' Private Lives (drama)
. . . . Dr. Jeffrey Latimer (1979)

GAXTON, WILLIAM—actor
b: Dec 2, 1893, San Francisco, Calif. d: 1963

Nash Airflyte Theater (drama)
. . . . host (1950–51)

GAYE, LISA—actress
b: c. 1935, Denver, Colo.

The Bob Cummings Show (com)
. . . . Collette DuBois (1955–59)
How to Marry a Millionaire (com)
. . . . Gwen Kirby (1958–59)

The younger sister of screen actress Debra
Paget.

GAYE, PAT—

The Frank Sinatra Show (var)
. . . . regular (1950–51)

GAYLE, CRYSTAL—singer
b: Jan 9, 1951, Paintsville, Ky.

Masquerade (drama) . sang theme (1983–84)

The sister of country songstress Loretta
Lynn. Crystal has appeared on many TV
music specials and is readily recognizable
for her Rapunzel-like floor-length hair; her
most famous hit is "Don't It Make My
Brown Eyes Blue."

GAYLE, TINA—actress
b: Dec 11, c. 1959, Frankfurt, Germany

CHiPs (police)
. . . . Off Kathy Linahan (1982–83)

A former Dallas Cowboys cheerleader
(1977–78).

GAYNES, GEORGE—actor
b: May 16, 1917, Helsinki, Finland

Rich Man, Poor Man—Book II (drama)
. . . . Max Vincent (1976–77)
Scruples (drama) . . . . John Prince (1980)
Punky Brewster (com)
. . . . Henry Warnimont (1984–86)

George Gaynes, an imposing actor with a
booming operatic voice, was in fact an
opera singer in the 1940s, appearing with
opera companies in Europe and later with
the New York City Opera. In the '50s and
'60s he moved on to the Broadway stage,
and also appeared in occasional TV productions such as *One Touch of Venus* in
1955. He also turned up occasionally on TV
soap operas. His greatest fame, however,
has come in recent years as a character
actor playing distinctive roles in such hit
films as *Tootsie* (as the aging soap-opera
star) and *Police Academy* (as the out-to-
lunch commandant).

GAYNOR, JOCK—actor
b: New York City, N.Y.

The Outlaws (wes)
. . . . . Dep Marshal Heck Martin (1960–61)

GAZZARA, BEN—actor
b: Aug 28, 1930, New York City, N.Y.

Arrest and Trial (drama)
. . . . Det. Sgt. Nick Anderson (1963–64)
Run for Your Life (adv)
. . . . Paul Bryan (1965–68)

This intense, Italian-American actor (born
and raised in New York's tough Lower East
Side) seemed to have a promising career in
the 1960s. Following ten years on the New
York stage, and two critically acclaimed
movies, *The Strange One* in 1957 and
Anatomy of a Murder in 1959, he starred in
two critically well-received TV series, *Arrest and Trial* and *Run for Your Life*. Although the latter was a substantial hit, it
did not lead to much else for Gazzara. He
has since been seen primarily in routine
TV movies and miniseries, the most notable being *QB VII* (1974) and *The Trial of
Lee Harvey Oswald* (1977). The actor often
works with his close friends John Cas-
savettes and Peter Falk on film projects.
He has also done some TV directing, including episodes of *Run for Your Life* and
Columbo. Perhaps his failure to achieve
greater stardom is explained by his rather
combative credo. "You make your own
rules if you've got the guts," he said in 1966.
"You work hard and don't stand still for
rules set up by narrow-minded, all too clin-
ical, noncreative businessmen."

GEAR, LUELLA—actress
b: Sep 5, 1897, New York City, N.Y. d: Apr 3, 1980

Joe & Mabel (com) .... Mrs. Spooner (1956)

GEARY, PAUL—actor

Slattery's People (drama)
.... Johnny Ramos (1964–65)
The Long Hot Summer (drama)
.... Jody Varner (1965–66)

GEER, ELLEN—actress
b: Aug 29, West Nyack, N.Y.

The Jimmy Stewart Show (com)
.... Wendy Howard (1971–72)

The daughter of veteran actor Will Geer.

GEER, WILL—actor
b: Mar 9, 1902, Frankfort, Ind. d: Apr 22, 1978

The Waltons (drama)
.... Zeb (Grandpa) Walton (1972–78)

Emmy Award: Best Supporting Actor in a Drama Series, for *The Waltons* (1975)

This lovable old coot was not considered so lovable in the 1950s, at least by some. A stage actor in the '20s and in films since the '30s, in supporting roles, Will saw his career come to a screeching halt in the early '50s when he was blacklisted for refusing to cooperate with the House Un-American Activities Committee in its political investigations.

Not until the 1960s was he able to resume his screen and television career on anything like its former scale. Thereafter he did quite a bit of supporting work on TV, in "old man" roles, sometimes sinister, sometimes kindly. Series on which he appeared ranged from *The Trials of O'-Brien*, *The Bold Ones*, and *Bonanza* to comedies such as *Mayberry R.F.D.* and *Bewitched*. By far his most famous role was his last, that of grandpa on *The Waltons*.

GEHRING, TED—actor

The Family Holvak (drama)
.... Chester Purdle (1975)
Little House on the Prairie (adv)
.... Ebenezer Sprague (1975–76)

Alice (com) .... Charlie (1979–81)
Dallas (drama) .... Brady York (1980–81)

GELBWAKS, JEREMY—juvenile actor

The Partridge Family (com)
.... Christopher Partridge (1970–71)

GELLER, HARRY—orchestra leader

The Ford Show (var)
.... orch. leader (1956–61)

GELLIS, DANNY—actor

Knots Landing (drama)
.... Jason Avery (1980–82)

GELMAN, LARRY—actor

The Odd Couple (com).... Vinnie (1970–75)
The Bob Newhart Show (com)
.... Dr. Bernie Tupperman (1972–76)
Needles and Pins (com)....... Max (1973)
Free Country (com)....... Leo Gold (1978)

GENEVIEVE—singer
b: Apr 17, 1930, Paris, France

The Jack Paar Show (talk)
.... semiregular (1958–62)
Scruples (drama)
.... Lilianne de Vertdulac (1980)

GENNARO, PETER—choreographer
b: 1924, Metairie, La.

The Polly Bergen Show (var)
.... dancers (1957–58)
The Bob Crosby Show (var)
.... dancers (1958)
Your Hit Parade (music)
.... dancers (1958–59)
The Andy Williams Show (var)
.... dancers (1959)
The Perry Como Show (var)
.... dancers (1960–61)
The Kraft Music Hall (var)
.... dancers (1961–63)
The Judy Garland Show (var)
.... dancers (1963–64)
The Entertainers (var) ...... dancers (1965)

This famous Broadway dancer and choreographer has done much work for television over the years, including *Miss American* pageants and various specials in the 1970s and '80s.

GENOVESE, MIKE—actor

Falcon Crest (drama) ..... Al Hurley (1985)

GENTRY, BOBBIE—singer
b: Jul 27, 1944, Chickasaw County, Miss.

The Bobbie Gentry Show (var)
.... hostess (1974)

This sensuous country singer is most famous, by far, for her moody 1967 hit "Ode to Billy Joe." It won her network TV series in the U.S. and England and years of appearances on TV variety shows. The story-song eventually began to take on a life of its own, being expanded into a book and then made into a movie in 1976. Miss Gentry has had no other hits remotely as successful and consequently has been seen less often in recent years.

GENTRY, MIKE AND JOE—actors

The Dom DeLuise Show (var)
.... regulars (1968)

GEORGE, ANTHONY—actor
b: Jan 29, 1925, Endicott, N.Y.

The Untouchables (police)
.... Agent Cam Allison (1960)
Checkmate (drama)... Don Corey (1960–62)

Tony first appeared on television in the early 1950s in minor roles on such series as *Studio One* and the Pinky Lee variety show *Those Two*. Since his moment in the prime time spotlight as the handsome detective on *Checkmate* in the '60s, he has worked on stage and, rather continuously, as a daytime soap opera actor. His two longest-running roles have been those of Dr. Tony Vincente on *Search for Tomorrow* from 1970–75 and Dr. Will Vernon on *One Life to Live* from 1977–84.

GEORGE, CHRISTOPHER—actor
b: Feb 25, 1929, Royal Oak, Minn. d: Nov 29, 1983

The Rat Patrol (adv)
.... Sgt. Sam Troy (1966–68)
The Immortal (adv)
.... Ben Richards (1970–71)

GEORGE, JOHN—actor
b: Jan 21, 1898, Syria d: Aug 25, 1968

The Adventures of Fu Manchu (drama)
.... Kolb (1955–56)

GEORGE, LYNDA DAY—actress
b: Dec 11, 1944, San Marcos, Texas

The Silent Force (police)
.... Amelia Cole (1970–71)
Mission: Impossible (drama)
.... Casey (1971–73)
Rich Man, Poor Man—Book I (drama)
.... Linda Quales (1976)
Roots (drama)........ Mrs. Reynolds (1977)

The wife of actor Christopher George. She has been active on television since the early 1960s (as Lynda Day) and was nominated for Emmy Awards for *Mission: Impossible* and a 1981 episode of *Archie Bunker's Place* called "Tough Love."

GEORGE, PHYLLIS—host, sportscaster
b: Jun 25, 1949, Denton, Texas

Candid Camera (aud par). cohost (1974–78)
People (mag)............... hostess (1978)

This glamorous Miss America of 1971 was most successful on television as, of all things, a sports personality. She joined CBS in 1972 and for eight seasons was cohost of *The NFL Today*. She also hosted or cohosted *The Challenge of the Sexes* sports specials, Rose Bowl parades, *The Miss America Pageant* (from 1972–79, with Bert Parks), and the short-lived prime time series *People*. In 1985 CBS tried her out as cohost of its faltering *CBS Morning News*, but her gushy style seemed quite incongruous on a "news" program and she was soon replaced.

During the late 1970s Phyllis married John Y. Brown, head of the Kentucky Fried Chicken empire; he became governor of Kentucky from 1979–83, making her the first lady of that state.

GEORGE, SUE—juvenile actress
b: c. 1938

Father Knows Best (com)
.... April Adams (1957–58)

GEORGIADE, NICK—actor
b: Feb 5, 1933, New York City, N.Y.

The Untouchables (police)
.... agent Enrico Rossi (1959–63)
Run Buddy Run (com) ... Wendell (1966–67)

GERARD, GIL—actor

b: Jan 23, 1943, Little Rock, Ark.

Buck Rogers in the 25th Century (sci fi)
.. Capt. William "Buck" Rogers (1979–81)
Sidekicks (adv) . Sgt. Jacob Rizzo (1986–)

GERARD, PENNY—singer

Musical Merry-Go-Round (music)
.... regular (1948–49)

GERBER, BILL—actor

Fay (com) .... Danny Messina (1975–76)

GERBER, JOAN—actress

Pat Paulsen's Half a Comedy Hour (var)
.... regular (1970)
Wait Till Your Father Gets Home (cartn)
.... Irma Boyle (voice) (1972–74)

GERING, RICHARD—actor

Margie (com) ...... Johnny Green (1961–62)

GERRITSEN, LISA—actress

b: Dec 21, 1957, Los Angeles, Calif.

My World and Welcome to It (com)
.... Lydia Monroe (1969–70)
The Mary Tyler Moore Show (com)
.... Bess Lindstrom (1970–75)
Phyllis (com)..... Bess Lindstrom (1975–77)

GERTZ, JAMI—actress

b: Oct 28, 1965, Chicago, Ill. r: Glenview, Ill.

Square Pegs (com)
.... Muffy Tepperman (1982–83)
Dreams (com)........ Martha Spino (1984)

GETTY, ESTELLE—actress

b: Jul 25, 1924, New York City, N.Y.

Golden Girls (com)
.... Sophia Petrillo (1985–)

One of the curiosities of the "graying" of TV in the mid-1980s was the boom in work for actors who could play *older* than their real age. On *Our House*, 51-year-old Wilford Brimley played an elderly grandpa; on *The Golden Girls*, sixtyish stage actress Estelle Getty donned a gray wig and became the semi-senile mother of Bea Arthur (who was herself about 60 in real life).

Before this bit of video serendipity befell Estelle, the petite actress had toiled in obscurity for many years on and off Broadway. Her breakthrough finally came via the early '80s stage hit *Torch Song Trilogy*, in which she appeared for five years in New York and on tour (she played the lead character's mother). After appearing in the theatrical film *Mask* (as Cher's mother), Estelle turned to TV and almost immediately landed her most famous role, that of the outrageous, wisecracking oldster on *The Golden Girls*. Her other appearances in the mid-1980s included the TV films *Victims for Victims* and *Copacabana*. You might not recognize her without that wig, however.

GETZ, JOHN—actor

b: Oct 15, Davenport, Iowa

Rafferty (drama)
.... Daniel Gentry, M.D. (1977)
Suzanne Pleshette Is Maggie Briggs (com)
.... Geoff Bennett (1984)
MacGruder & Loud (police)
.... Det. Malcolm MacGruder (1985)

GETZOFF, JIMMY—violinist

The Lawrence Welk Show (music)
.... regular (1960–62)

GHOSTLEY, ALICE—actress

b: Aug 14, 1926, Eve, Mo. r: Henryetta, Okla.

The Jackie Gleason Show (var)
.... Agnes (1962–64)
Captain Nice (com)....... Mrs. Nash (1967)
The Jonathan Winters Show (var)
.... regular (1968–69)
Bewitched (com) ...... Esmerelda (1969–72)
Mayberry R.F.D. (com) ..... Alice (1970–71)
Nichols (wes)........... Bertha (1971–72)
The Julie Andrews Hour (var)
.... regular (1972–73)
Temperatures Rising (com)
.... Edwina Moffitt (1974)

Comic actress Alice Ghostley was born in a whistle-stop railroad station in tiny Eve, Missouri (her father was a telegrapher), and raised in small towns in the Midwest. Hooked on the theater while attending the University of Oklahoma, she made her way to New York and, after some lean times, made her first big splash singing

"The Boston Beguine" in the Broadway revue *New Faces of 1952*. Thereafter, Alice was active on Broadway and on television, where she was most often seen as a sketch comedienne. Not always, though. In 1957 she appeared in a *Hallmark Hall of Fame* production of *Twelfth Night,* starring the distinguished Shakespearean actor Maurice Evans. Years later she and Evans, who obviously had a sense of humor, both had occasional roles in the hit comedy *Bewitched,* as a witch and a warlock.

Alice's other roles over the years included a kind of latter-day Alice Kramden ("Agnes" to Jackie Gleason's "Arthur") on *The Jackie Gleason Show, Captain Nice*'s mother, Aunt Alice on *Mayberry R.F.D.,* and the saloon keeper on James Garner's *Nichols.*

When asked whether Ghostley is her real name, the actress replies, "Of course. Who would change her name to Ghostley?" In fact, she points out, she and her sister once had an act in which they were billed, in rather eerie fashion, as "The Ghostley Sisters."

GIAMBALVO, LOUIS—actor
b: Feb 8, Brooklyn, N.Y.

The Gangster Chronicles (drama)
.... Al Capone (1981)
The Devlin Connection (drama)
.... Lt. Earl Borden (1982)
Oh Madeline (com)
.... Robert Leone (1983–84)

GIBB, ANDY—singer
b: Mar 5, 1958, Manchester, England r: Bisbane, Australia

Solid Gold (music) .... host (1981–82)

Andy Gibb, the runt of the Gibb family's musical litter, blossomed into a top-selling recording artist in 1977, with the help of his three famous older brothers (who comprised the Bee Gees rock group). With flowing locks, a toothy smile—and usually an open shirt—he was an idol of the younger set. That fact helped him land the host position on the syndicated rock show *Solid Gold* in 1981. Unfortunately, superstar Andy proved to be a somewhat unreliable performer and was soon replaced.

GIBB, CYNTHIA—actress
b: Dec 14, 1963, Bennington, Vt.

Fame (drama)....... Holly Laird (1983–86)

GIBBON, TIM—actor

The Steve Allen Comedy Hour (var)
.... regular (1980–81)

GIBBONS, JIM—newscaster

News and Views (news)
.... anchorman (1948–52)

GIBBONS, LEEZA—hostess

Entertainment Tonight (news) .. host (1984–)

GIBBS, GEORGIA—singer
b: Aug 17, 1920, Worcester, Mass.

Georgia Gibbs and Her Million Record Show (music) .... hostess (1957)

In the early 1940s, Georgia changed her stage billing from Fredda Gibson (her real name) to Gibbs, which was fortunate, for otherwise she couldn't have become known as "Her Nibs, Miss Georgia Gibbs!"

GIBBS, JORDAN—black actor

Checking In (com)
.... Dennis, the bellboy (1981)

The son of actress Marla Gibbs.

GIBBS, LYN—singer

Melody Street (music) .... regular (1953–54)

GIBBS, MARLA—black actress
b: Jun 14, 1946,*, Chicago, Ill.

The Jeffersons (com)
.... Florence Johnston (1975–85)
Checking In (com)
.... Florence Johnston (1981)
227 (com)............ Mary Jenkins (1985–)

If comic actress Marla Gibbs looks a bit worldly-wise, it's not without reason. She was born in a black neighborhood in Chicago (not unlike the one depicted on *227),* married at 13, and had three children while still in her teens. Her mother was Ophelia Kemp, an opera singer and later pastor of

*Some sources give 1931 or 1941.

Detroit's Universal Guiding Light Church, known from her radio broadcasts as "Princess Kemp."

Marla was divorced after 12 years of marriage and made her way to Hollywood, determined to try to become an actress. Some minor stage and television work followed, but her big break was a guest appearance on *The Jeffersons,* which led to a regular role on that series as the sarcastic maid. After *The Jeffersons* (and a short-lived spin-off called *Checking In),* Marla appeared in a stage play called *227,* which was developed into another series for her.

Marla compares *227* to *I Love Lucy;* critics don't, but it nevertheless became a popular entry on the NBC schedule.

GIBBS, TERRY—orchestra leader, jazz vibraphone
b: Oct 13, 1924, Brooklyn, N.Y.

The Steve Allen Comedy Hour (var)
.... orch. leader (1967)
Operation: Entertainment (var)
.... orch. leader (1968–69)
The Steve Allen Comedy Hour (var)
.... orch. leader (1980–81)

GIBBS, TIMOTHY—juvenile actor
b: Apr 17, 1967, Burbank, Calif.

Father Murphy (drama)
.... Will Adams (1981–82)
The Rousters (adv). Michael Earp (1983–84)

GIBSON, BOB—sportscaster

Monday Night Baseball (sport)
.... sportscaster (1976–77)

GIBSON, CAL—black actor

Park Place (com)........ Ernie Rice (1981)

GIBSON, HENRY—actor, comedian
b: Sep 21, 1935, Germantown, Pa.

Rowan & Martin's Laugh-In (var)
.... regular (1968–71)

The mousy Poet-in-Residence on *Laugh-In* was a relatively minor comic character actor before his sensational success on that hit series, and he has apparently reverted back to that status since it left the air.

Henry worked fairly regularly on television in the early and mid-1960s, with small but recurring roles on *The Joey Bishop Show* and *Mr. Roberts.* One of his funnier guest appearances was on *F Troop* in 1966 as Wrongo Starr, a jinxed cavalry trooper. However, it was a guest shot on a Mike Wallace show, reading poetry, that paved the way for his being signed as a regular on *Laugh-In.*

Since 1971 Henry has appeared in a variety of series episodes *(Love, American Style, Wonder Woman, The Dukes of Hazzard)* as well as in mostly run-of-the-mill TV and theatrical movies. One of his more distinctive roles was that of the old-fashioned country music star in the 1975 film *Nashville.*

GIBSON, JOHN—actor
r: Oakland, Calif.

Crime Photographer (drama)
.... Ethelbert (1951)
A Date with Judy (com)
.... Melvyn Foster (1952–53)
Robert Montgomery Presents (summer) (drama)............... repertory player (1956)

GIBSON, JULIE—narrator

Paris Cavalcade of Fashions (misc)
.... narrator (1948–49)

GIBSON, VIRGINIA—actress, singer

So This Is Hollywood (com)
.... Kim Tracy (1955)
The Johnny Carson Show (var)
.... regular (1955–56)
Your Hit Parade (music)
.... vocalist (1957–58)

GIDDINGS, AL—cinematographer

OceanQuest (adv).......... regular (1985)

Emmy Award: Best Individual Achievement, as Cinematographer of the Documentary Special *Mysteries of the Sea* (1980)

An award-winning producer of nature films, who appeared on-screen (with Miss Universe!) in his own seafaring travelogue, *OceanQuest.*

GIDEON, BOND—actress

Blansky's Beauties (com)
.... Lovely Carson (1977)
Operation Petticoat (com)
.... Lt. Claire Reid (1977–78)

GIERASCH, STEFAN—actor

A.E.S Hudson Street (com)
.... J. Powell Karbo (1978)

GIFFORD, FRANK—sportscaster
b: Aug 16, 1930, Santa Monica, Calif.

Monday Night Football (sport)
.... announcer (1971–   )

Emmy Award: Best Sports Personality
(1977)

This handsome, personable star has
gone from one success to another in his
sports and television careers. An All-
American at the University of Southern
California, he was the number-one draft
pick of the New York Giants in 1952. During the next 12 years he had a stellar career in pro football: All-Pro halfback (six
times), Most Valuable Player (twice), and
Pro Bowl pick. He set several NFL records, including most touchdowns (78) and
most yards gained pass-receiving (5,434).
An injury forced his temporary retirement
in 1961, but he returned the following season and was named Comeback Player
of the Year by UPI. Frank was inducted
into the Pro Football Hall of Fame in
1977.

Gifford began sportscasting in the late
1950s, while still an active player. For a
time it seemed that he might become an
actor; he made his film debut in the 1959
war movie *Up Periscope.* However, upon
his retirement from football in 1964 he
joined CBS as a full-time commentator.
Seven years later ABC stole him away, and
he has been a fixture on their broadcast
team ever since. In addition to *Monday
Night Football,* he is a contributor to
ABC's *Wide World of Sports,* a member of
the network's Olympics coverage team,
and a frequent substitute host on *Good
Morning, America.*

Gifford is quite active in charitable
work, principally on behalf of the Multiple
Sclerosis Society and the Special Olympics.

GIFTOS, ELAINE—actress
b: Pittsfield, Mass.

The Interns (drama)
.... Bobbe Marsh (1970–71)

GILBERT, CAROLYN—singer, pianist

Garroway at Large (var)..... regular (1949)
The Carolyn Gilbert Show (music)
.... hostess (1950)

GILBERT, EDMUND—actor

The Hardy Boys Mysteries (adv)
.... Fenton Hardy (1977–79)

GILBERT, JANICE—actress

The O'Neills (drama)
.... Janice O'Neill (1949–50)
Break the Bank (quiz)
.... paying teller (1953–57)

GILBERT, JODY—actress
b: 1916, Fort Worth, Texas d: Feb 3, 1979

Life with Luigi (com) .... Rosa (1952)

GILBERT, JOHNNY—host

Music Bingo (quiz) .... emcee (1958)

GILBERT, JONATHAN—juvenile actor

Little House on the Prairie (adv)
.... Willie Oleson (1975–83)

The younger brother of Melissa Gilbert.

GILBERT, MELISSA—actress
b: May 8, 1964, Los Angeles, Calif.

Little House on the Prairie (adv)
.... Laura Ingalls Wilder (1974–83)

Melissa is one of those young actresses
who has virtually grown up in front of the
cameras, principally on *Little House on the
Prairie.* The daughter of comedian Paul
Gilbert, she appeared in a commercial for
baby clothing at age three; later, she did
more commercials and appeared in episodes of *Gunsmoke, Emergency,* and
Tenafly in the early 1970s. She was a winsome nine-year-old when she won the part
of Laura in the TV movie that launched the
Little House series in 1974. She outlasted
the series' star, Michael Landon; by the

1982–83 season her character had grown up, married, and had a baby, and the series had been renamed *Little House: A New Beginning,* with Melissa and her TV husband Dean Butler as its principal stars.

Melissa has sought to broaden her acting horizons beyond the *Little House* role for which she is known so well. In 1979 she received an Emmy nomination for her performance opposite Patty Duke Astin in the TV movie *The Miracle Worker.* In the 1980s she has become one of TV's most promising young actresses, starring in the TV movies *The Diary of Anne Frank, Splendor in the Grass,* and *Choices of the Heart,* among others.

GILBERT, PAUL—comedian, dancer
b: 1917

The Duke (com)
.... "The Duke" London (1954)

GILBERT, RUTH—comedienne

Ruthie on the Telephone (com)
.... Ruthie (1949)
The Milton Berle Show (var)
.... regular (1952–55)

GILFORD, GWYNNE—actress
b: Jul 27, Los Angeles, Calif.

The Waverly Wonders (com)
.... Linda Harris (1978)
A New Kind of Family (com)
.... Abby Stone (1979)

The wife of actor Robert Pine, whose spouse she sometimes portrayed on his series *CHiPs.*

GILFORD, JACK—actor
b: Jul 25, 1907, New York City, N.Y.

The Arrow Show (var).... regular (1948–49)
The David Frost Revue (com)
.... regular (1971–73)
Paul Sand in Friends and Lovers (com)
.... Ben Dreyfuss (1974–75)
Apple Pie (com). Grandpa Hollyhock (1978)
The Duck Factory (com)
.... Brooks Carmichael (1984)

An older actor of the "kindly" school, Jack has played supporting roles on television since the early 1950s. He also had a long career on Broadway (since 1940) and in films (since 1944). Despite his many roles over the years, he is perhaps best known for his commercials for Cracker Jacks, which ran incessantly from 1962–1972. A dozen years later he commented, "Policemen, clerks, people in restaurants—all of them stop me and say they grew up on my commercials . . . Not a day passes that someone doesn't point a finger at me and yell, 'Cracker Jacks!' "

Disconcerting as that may be, Gilford can point to other talents as well. He was a stand-up comic for 20 years, doing impressions of famous people of the '30s and '40s. He can also mimic a goldfish, a camel, an elephant, an owl, an eagle, a chicken, and—best of all—thick pea soup with ham and croutons coming to a ferocious boil.

GILL, RUSTY—singer
b: Jun 10, 1919, St. Louis, Mo.

Polka Time (music)....... regular (1956–57)

GILLAM, LORNA—juvenile actress

Too Young to Go Steady (com)
.... Timmy (1959)

GILLESPIE, GINA—juvenile actress
b: c. 1951, Los Angeles, Calif.

Law of the Plainsman (wes)
.... Tess Logan (1959–60)
Karen (com) .... Mimi Scott (1964–65)

The younger sister of *Mickey Mouse Club* mouseketeer Darlene Gillespie.

GILLETTE, ANITA—actress
b: Aug 16, 1936, r: Baltimore, Md.

Me and the Chimp (com)
.... Liz Reynolds (1972)
Bob & Carol & Ted & Alice (com)
.... Alice Henderson (1973)
All That Glitters (com)
.... Nancy Bankston (1977)
The Baxters (com).. Nancy Baxter (1979–80)
Quincy, M. E. (police)
.... Dr. Emily Hanover (1982–83)

GILLETTE, HELEN—actress

The Plainclothesman (police)
.... Annie, the waitress (1952)

GILLIAM, BYRON—comedian

Rowan & Martin's Laugh-In (var)
.... regular (1969–70)

GILLIAM, STU—black actor, comedian
b: Jul 27, 1943, Detroit, Mich.

Dean Martin Presents the Golddiggers (var)
.... regular (1968)
Roll Out (com)
.... Cpl. "Sweet" Williams (1973–74)
Harris and Company (drama)
.... Charlie Adams (1979)

As a comic in the 1950s, Stu worked with a dapper dummy named Oscar.

GILLILAND, RICHARD—actor
b: Jan 23, Fort Worth, Texas

McMillan and Wife (police)
.... Sgt. Steve DiMaggio (1976–77)
Operation Petticoat (com)
.... Lt. Nick Holden (1977–78)
Little Women (drama)
.... Theodore Laurie Lawrence (1979)
The Waltons (drama)
.... Jonesy Formula (1981)
Just Our Luck (com)... Keith Barrow (1983)

GILLIN, HUGH—actor

Semi-Tough (com)
.... Big Ed Bookman (1980)
The Facts of Life (com)
.... Howard (1980–81)

GILMAN, KENNETH—actor

Loves Me, Loves Me Not (com)
.... Dick (1977)
Dorothy (com) .... Jack Landis (1979)
Jessica Novak (drama)
.... Vince Halloran (1981)
Foot in the Door (com)...... Jim Foot (1983)

GILMAN, SAM—actor
b: 1915, Lynn, Mass. d: Dec 3, 1985

Shane (wes) .... Sam Grafton (1966)

GILMAN, TONI—actress

Down You Go (quiz)..... panelist (1951–54)
What's It For? (quiz) .... panelist (1957)
The Good Guys (com) .... Gertie (1969)

GILMORE, ART—announcer, host

Highway Patrol (police).. narrator (1955–59)
The Comedy Spot (com) .... host (1960)

GILMORE, VIOLET—actress

Accused (drama)... court reporter (1958–59)

GILMOUR, SANDY—newscaster
b: Aug 14, 1942, Montclair, N.J.

Prime Time Sunday (pub aff)
.... correspondent (1980)

GILYARD, CLARENCE, JR.—black actor
b: Dec 24, 1957, Moses Lake, Wash.

CHiPs (police) ..... Off. Webster (1982–83)
The Duck Factory (com)
.... Roland Culp (1984)

GIMPEL, ERICA—actress
b: New York City, N.Y.

Fame (drama)... Coco Hernandez (1982–83)

A real life graduate of New York's High School for the Performing Arts, the setting for *Fame*.

GING, JACK—actor
b: Nov 30, 1931, near Alva, Okla.

Tales of Wells Fargo (wes)
.... Beau McCloud (1961–62)
The Eleventh Hour (drama)
.... Dr. Paul Graham (1962–64)
Dear Detective (police)
.... Det. Chuck Morris (1979)
The Winds of War (drama)
.... Cmdr. Baldwin (1983)
Riptide (drama).. Lt. Ted Quinlan (1984–85)

"To tell Ging he can't do what he wants is a mistake because he'll turn right around and do it," commented actor-director Richard Carlson during the run of *The Eleventh Hour*. "They told him he was too small to play football, so he made All-America. They told him he couldn't get into the marines, but he did, and came out as a commander of a prize outfit. Now they're telling him how tough it is to become a star."

Apparently thinking he was still leading his marines in a charge, the feisty Ging stormed Hollywood shortly after his discharge in 1957, and within a year was landing roles in action B films and TV series. He appeared several times in 1958–59 in Carlson's *MacKenzie's Raiders* and in 1959–60 in *The Man and the Challenge* (in which athletes, explorers, and others were constantly being tested for endurance). Later he was seen in *Perry Mason, Sea Hunt, Men into Space, Alfred Hitchcock Presents,* and many other series. In the late 1960s and early '70s he was a rather frequent supporting player on *Mannix.*

Although none of his regular roles has brought him major stardom, Ging continues to be a familiar face on TV in the 1980s, in roles such as that of a destroyer commander in *The Winds of War* and the irritable police lieutenant on *Riptide.*

GINGOLD, HERMIONE—actress
b: Dec 9, 1897, London, England d: May 24, 1987

One Minute Please (quiz)
.... panelist (1954–55)
The Jack Paar Show (talk)
.... semiregular (1958–62)

This outrageous and veddy British movie and music hall comedienne has made occasional TV acting appearances over the years but is more familiar for films such as *Gigi* and *The Music Man.* Few, however, remember that she was also in a 1966 movie spin-off of *The Munsters,* called *Munster Go Home!.* Her 1958 autobiography was titled *The World Is Square.*

GINSBURG, ROBIN—actress
Knots Landing (drama)
.... Sheila Fisher (1985)

GINTY, ROBERT—actor
b: Nov 14, 1948, Brooklyn, N.Y.

Baa Baa Black Sheep (drama)
.... Lt. T. J. Wiley (1976–78)
The Paper Chase (drama)
.... Thomas Craig Anderson (1978–79)
Hawaiian Heat (police)... Mac Riley (1984)

The husband of actress Lorna Patterson.

GIOVANNI, JIM—comedian
Laugh-In (revival) (var)... regular (1977–78)

GIRARD, HENRY—actor
The Aldrich Family (com)
.... Henry Aldrich (1951–52)

GIRARD, WENDY—actress
AfterMASH (com)... Lenore Dudziak (1984)

GIRARDIN, RAY—actor
b: Jan 23, Wakefield, Mass.

Charlie & Company (com)
.... Walter Simpson (1985–86)

GIROUX, LEE—correspondent
Tonight! America After Dark (talk)
.... regular (1957)

GIST, ROBERT—actor, director
b: 1924

Hennesey (com)...... Dr. Owen King (1960)

GIST, ROD—black actor
Roll Out (com)...... Phone Booth (1973–74)
The Peter Marshall Variety Show (var)
.... regular (1976)

GITTLIN, JOYCE—actress
Paper Dolls (drama)....... Gabrielle (1984)

GIVENS, ROBIN—black actress
b: Nov 27, 1964, New York, N.Y.

Head of the Class (com). Darlene (1986–   )

A medical student who became a protégé of Bill Cosby. She originally auditioned for a role on *The Cosby Show* to help pay her college bills, but Cosby urged her to pursue an acting career instead. He reportedly made her a unique offer: if she did not become a successful actress within two years he would pay for the remainder of her medical education himself. Within the next year Robin had won roles in a made-for-cable TV series, a TV movie *(Beverly Hills Madam),* and *Head of the Class.*

GIVOT, GEORGE—actor, host
b: 1903, Omaha, Neb. d: Jun 7, 1984

Stop Me If You've Heard This One (quiz)
.... panelist (1949)
Versatile Varieties (var)...... emcee (1949)

A comedian known on radio as "The Greek Ambassador of Good Will."

GLADKE, PETER—

Melody Tour (var).......... regular (1954)

GLASER, PAUL MICHAEL—actor, director
b: Mar 25, 1943, Cambridge, Mass.

Starsky and Hutch (police)
.... Det. Dave Starsky (1975–79)

Paul Michael Glaser is one of Hollywood's angry young men, an intense actor who (like Peter Duel and others) was caught in the dilemma of wanting to be an "artist" while starring in a popular but thoroughly clichéd action show.

Before he gained some clout via the hit series *Starsky and Hutch*, Glaser was just another Hollywood hopeful and no one paid much attention to his tantrums. He made his stage debut in 1968, after much schooling (he has master's degrees in theater from Tulane and from Boston University). His first role was in Joseph Papp's rock version of *Hamlet;* he then went on to appear in a number of Broadway and off-Broadway plays, the most notable being *The Man in the Glass Booth.* Glaser's early television work was mostly in soap operas; he was Dr. Peter Chernak on *Love Is a Many Splendored Thing* from 1969–70, and Dr. Joe Corelli on *Love of Life* from 1971–72.

In the early '70s, Paul played guest roles on a variety of series, including *The Sixth Sense, The Waltons,* and *Toma,* and he also began a movie career in such films as *Butterflies Are Free* and *Fiddler on the Roof.* However, it was *Starsky and Hutch* that made him a star—and virtually intractable, according to many people who had to work with him. Depending on your point of view, he was either a compulsive perfectionist, striving to make the screeching-tires cop show better than anyone expected it to be, or an insufferable egomaniac. Glaser particularly disdained the producers who had hired him. "Let's correct the impression that they made me a star," he said in 1977. "It wasn't that way at all. You see, I'm an artist . . . so they called me in. The public applauded and gave me fame. All of the above has nothing

to do with the producers. It was *me* who made it a success."

Glaser has restlessly searched for other TV vehicles to express himself, although—perhaps understandably—producers have not exactly fallen over themselves to bring him choice assignments. He starred in the 1976 TV movie *The Great Houdinis* (as Harry Houdini) and in 1983's *Princess Daisy.* He has also pursued a career as a director, beginning with episodes of *Starsky and Hutch* and more recently in TV movies.

GLASS, NED—actor
b: Apr 1, 1906, Poland d: Jun 15, 1984

Julia (com)........... Sol Cooper (1968–71)
Bridget Loves Bernie (com)
.... Uncle Moe Plotnick (1972–73)

GLASS, RON—black actor
b: Jul 10, 1945, Evansville, Ind.

Barney Miller (com)
.... Det. Ron Harris (1975–82)
The New Odd Couple (com)
.... Felix Unger (1982–83)

GLAZER, VIC—orchestra leader

Easy Does It . . . Starring Frankie Avalon (var)
.... orch. leader (1976)

GLEASON, JACKIE—actor, comedian
b: Feb 26, 1916, Brooklyn, N.Y. d: Jun 24, 1987

The Life of Riley (com)
.... Chester A. Riley (1949–50)
Cavalcade of Stars (var)... emcee (1950–52)
The Jackie Gleason Show (var)
.... host (1952–55)
The Honeymooners (series) (com)
.... Ralph Kramden (1955–56)
The Jackie Gleason Show (var)
.... host (1956–59)
You're in the Picture (quiz)...... host (1961)
The Jackie Gleason Show (talk)
.... host (1961)
The Jackie Gleason Show (var)
.... host (1962–70)

Jackie Gleason is one of the great originals of American television. Although he has had considerable success in other media—theater, film, even music—he is essentially TV's own. A portly, brash, Rabelasian character, he is nevertheless quite thoughtful about art and about life, including his own spectacular career. He once told a reporter—without a hint of the braggadocio viewers have come to know and love him for—"I have no use for humility. I am a fellow with an exceptional talent. In my work, I stand or fall by my own judgment."

He has certainly seen both success and failure. Jackie was born in a grungy *Honeymooners*-like neighborhood in Brooklyn. His father deserted the family when he was eight, and his mother had to earn a modest living as a subway change clerk. Jackie was "educated" in the local pool halls. Never a shy kid, he was a hustler from the beginning. He had a fling as a boxer and as a stunt diver in Atlantic City before he found his calling in show business—after winning a talent contest at age 15. During the 1930s Jackie performed as a comic in carnivals, nightclubs and roadhouses.

The young comedian landed a contract with Warner Brothers in 1940, but this did not turn out to be the break he expected. After supporting roles in a few films in 1941–42 (he can be seen "sitting in" with the Glenn Miller Orchestra in *Orchestra Wives*), he turned mostly to nightclub and stage work. Like many others in the backwaters of show business, he tried to crash early television, but his first series, *The Life of Riley,* was a flop. (William Bendix, the screen Riley, revived it with much greater success a few years later.) Gleason reverted to doing what he knew best, essentially a nightclub act, on *Cavalcade of Stars*. The show was carried by the poorhouse of the networks, DuMont.

Despite DuMont's limited coverage, Gleason began to catch on. He introduced on *Cavalcade* a wide range of characters for which he would later become famous, notably Ralph Kramden of *The Honeymooners*. Others included Reggie Van Gleason; The Poor Soul; garrulous Joe the Bartender; and Charlie Bratton, "The Loudmouth." Jackie soon grew too popular for the paltry DuMont network. CBS stole him away in 1952 at a huge salary increase, and for the next several years he was one of TV's top stars; his variety show ranked number two, just behind *I Love Lucy,* in the 1954–55 season.

Jackie had found his milieu and was by this time bursting with creativity. He branched into music, writing his own famous theme song, "Melancholy Serenade," and recording a series of top-selling mood music LPs (billed as by "Jackie Gleason and his Orchestra"). These included such titles as *Music for Lovers Only* and *Music, Martinis and Memories*. He also produced a Tommy and Jimmy Dorsey summer music show in 1954, which became a series of specials in 1954–55 and a regular series *(Stage Show)* in 1955–56. *Stage Show* was historic as the series that provided the first network exposure for a little-known Memphis rock 'n' roller named Elvis Presley. Gleason himself booked Elvis; when asked why, he replied that if he only booked what *he* liked, he would have had nothing but bigband saxophone players on the show.

Jackie abandoned his successful variety show format in 1955 to concentrate on a filmed situation-comedy version of his most famous sketch, *The Honeymooners*. Surprisingly, it was not successful at the time (although its 39 episodes have since become some of the most popular reruns in TV history). Tasting what seemed like a setback, Jackie reverted to a variety-show format in the late 1950s, but that too declined in popularity during the era of the westerns.

The nadir came in 1961. Jackie decided to try a quiz show, but *You're in the Picture* was one of the most famous debacles in TV history, lasting exactly one telecast. Jackie himself was so embarrassed by it that he returned the following week, in the same time period, and apologized to a live nationwide audience (a precedent other guilty producers might heed!). For the rest of the season he turned his half hour into a celebrity interview show.

It appeared that "The Great One" 's TV career might well be over. He had no series at all in 1961–62. Having scored a triumph on Broadway in 1959 with the musical *Take Me Along,* he now returned to movies after a ten year absence and won an Academy Award nomination for his role as Minnesota Fats in *The Hustler*. Then, in 1962, Jackie made a major television comeback with a big, splashy CBS variety show that ran for the rest of the decade. Resplendent with his red boutonniere, slyly fondling a teacup of—?—("How sweet it is!"), Gleason once again had audiences, and CBS, in the palm of his hand. They howled at his ribbing of orchestra leader Sammy Spear and at catch lines such as "Away we go!" In 1964 the show moved to Miami, so Jackie could indulge his passion for golf year round, lending an even more glamorous setting.

Jackie's career began to slow down again in the 1970s, only to be revived once more via character roles in hit films such as *Smokey and the Bandit* and *The Toy*. His appearances on television were limited to occasional specials, including a series of *Honeymooners* reunions on ABC from 1976–78. Gleason has given a great deal to TV, and it in return has made him a rich and happy man. "I knew I had a lot of hard work ahead of me before I achieved my goals," he said in 1973. "I didn't mind very much. I knew I would eventually get them. And it turned out right. It has been a happy story."

A recent biography of Jackie is titled *How Sweet It Is,* by James Bacon (1985).

GLEASON, JOANNA—actress
b: Jun 2, Toronto, Canada

Hello, Larry (com)
.... Morgan Winslow (1979–80)

The daughter of game show host Monty Hall.

GLEASON, PAUL—actor
Ike (drama)......... Capt. Tex Lee (1979)

GLENN, CHRISTOPHER—newscaster
b: Mar 23, 1938, New York, N.Y.

CBS News Nightwatch (news)
.... anchorman (1982–84)

GLENN, LOUISE—actress
Don't Call Me Charlie (com)
.... Selma Yossarian (1962–63)

GLESS, SHARON—actress
b: May 31, 1943, Los Angeles, Calif.

Faraday and Company (drama)
.... Holly Barrett (1973–74)
Marcus Welby, M.D. (drama)
.... Kathleen Faverty (1974–76)
Switch (drama).......... Maggie (1975–78)
Centennial (drama)
.... Sidney Enderman (1978–79)

The Last Convertible (drama)
.... Kay Haddon (1979)
Turnabout (com) ...... Penny Alston (1979)
House Calls (com)...... Jane Jeffries (1982)
Cagney & Lacey (police)
.... Det. Chris Cagney (1982–)

Emmy Award: Best Actress in a Drama Series, for *Cagney & Lacey* (1986)

This popular actress started out as a secretary for an advertising agency in the mid-1960s, but, after working as a production assistant on an independent film, decided to try acting as a career. At first she played small roles in episodes of series such as *McCloud* and *Cool Million*. Robert Young liked her well enough to use her in two of his TV movies, *All My Darling Daughters* (1972) and *My Darling Daughters Anniversary* (1973), and then in his series *Marcus Welby*.

Sharon's roles at the time were mostly as a helper to the male leads: she was a nurse on *Welby* and a gal Friday on *Faraday and Company* and *Switch*. It must have given her some satisfaction to advance to playing less dependent characters in the late '70s and early '80s, including movie star Carol Lombard in *Moviola* (1980) and the hospital administrator in *House Calls*. Sharon's greatest role came amid some controversy, however. Feminist and gay groups were angered over the firing of Meg Foster as the original Chris Cagney on the *Cagney & Lacey* series—reportedly because the network thought she and costar Tyne Daly came across as "too tough, too hard, not feminine . . . as dykes." The protest groups vented some of their spleen on Gless because she was Foster's replacement. "She's from the Copacabana school of acting," complained the Gay Media Task Force, "very kittenish and feminine . . ."

Nevertheless, after a rocky start, the series became one of the most popular and acclaimed series on television, lauded for its hard-hitting stories. No one is calling Sharon "kittenish" anymore.

GLICK, PHYLLIS—actress
Loves Me, Loves Me Not (com).. Sue (1977)

GLICKMAN, MARTY—sportscaster
b: c. 1917, Brooklyn, N.Y.

Madison Square Garden Highlights (sport)
.... host (1953–54)
Greatest Sport Thrills (sport)
.... host (1954–56)
Cowtown Rodeo (sport)
.... commentator (1957–58)

GLOVER, BRUCE—actor

Hawk (police)
.... Asst. D.A. Murray Slaken (1966)

GLOVER, DANNY—black actor

Chiefs (drama) ..... Marshall Peters (1983)

GLOVER, JULIAN—actor

b: Mar 27, 1935, London, England

Q.E.D. (adv) ...... Dr. Stefan Kilkiss (1982)

GLUSKIN, LUD—orchestra leader

b: 1901, New York City, N.Y.

The Ed Wynn Show (var)
.... orch. leader (1949–50)
The Johnny Carson Show (var)
.... orch. leader (1955–56)

GNAGY, JOHN—art instructor

b: 1907, Varner's Forge, Kan d: Mar 7, 1981

You Are an Artist (info)
.... host (1946–50)

GOBEL, GEORGE—actor

b: May 20, 1919, Chicago, Ill.

The George Gobel Show (var)
.... host (1954–60)
The Eddie Fisher Show (var)
.... regular guest (1957–59)
Harper Valley P.T.A. (com)
.... Mayor Otis Harper, Jr. (1981–82)

Emmy Award: Outstanding New Personality (1954)

George Gobel was one of those overnight sensations who had been in show business much longer than most people realized—15 years, to be exact—at the time he won his Emmy as "outstanding new personality." Radio listeners throughout the Midwest knew him well for his years as "Little Georgie Gobel," the boy soprano, on the popular *National Barn Dance* broadcasts from Chicago during the 1930s. He also toured with country music

bands, billed as "The Littlest Cowboy."

During World War II he served as a pilot instructor in Frederick, Oklahoma. "You might laugh at that," he said later, "but we must have done a good job down there because not one enemy plane got past Tulsa." He was soon doing stand-up routines for his fellow servicemen, and after the war he began to work the nightclub, hotel, and fair circuit as an easygoin' country comic. His specialty was life as seen from the point of view of the little guy, a little henpecked, a little bewildered, but gamely coping with life all the same. His favorite exclamation: "Well, I'll be a dirty bird!"

"Lonesome George" did not bring his act to television until 1952, but when he did he was seen on practically every major variety show. Following seven consecutive appearances on NBC's *Saturday Night Revue* in 1953–54, plus others on Garry Moore's daytime show and on the panel show *Who Said That?*, he debuted as host of his own variety series in 1954. It was a substantial hit. The most popular sketch revolved around George and his wife Alice, played by Jeff Donnell.

George continued to be seen after the 1950s, but on a much reduced scale. Among other things, he earned a nice income from the series *Leave It to Beaver*, which was produced by his production company. He made occasional appearances in specials and series episodes (*My Three Sons, Daniel Boone, Love, American Style,* etc.) and he was a regular in the 1970s on the hit daytime game show *Hollywood Squares.* Often he played short cameo roles; for example, the drunk in the 1977 TV movie *Benny and Barney: Las Vegas Undercover* and the old sea dog in 1979's *Never Late Than Better.* In 1982, viewers were surprised to see him in his first regular prime time series role in 22 years, as the drunken mayor on *Harper Valley P.T.A.*

GODDARD, DON—host, newscaster

b: Jul 5, 1904, Binghamton, N.Y.

Watch the World (doc)
.... commentator (1950)
Medical Horizons (pub aff)... host (1955–56)
ABC Evening News (news)
.... anchorman (1958–59)
Focus on America (doc)........ host (1963)

GODDARD, MARK—actor

b: Jul 24, 1936, Lowell, Mass. r: Scituate, Mass.

Johnny Ringo (wes)........ Cully (1959–60)
The Detectives, Starring Robert Taylor (police) .... Sgt. Chris Ballard (1960–62)
Many Happy Returns (com)
.... Bob Randall (1964–65)
Lost in Space (sci fi)... Don West (1965–68)

After his prime time career wound down in the 1970s, Mark left show business for a time to work with volunteer child-rearing programs, including Headstart and Parents Anonymous. He returned to television in the 1980s as an actor on daytime soap operas.

GODFREY, ARTHUR—host

b: Aug 31, 1903, New York City, N.Y. d: Mar 16, 1983

Arthur Godfrey's Talent Scouts (talent)
.... host (1948–58)
Arthur Godfrey and His Friends (var)
.... host (1949–59)
Arthur Godfrey and His Ukulele (misc)
.... host (1950)
Candid Camera (aud par). cohost (1960–61)

Arthur Godfrey, like Jackie Gleason and Lucille Ball, was one of the giants of television in the 1950s. At his peak, he was arguably the most popular performer in the history of the medium; no one else has ever been the star of two of the top three series on TV *simultaneously* (his *Talent Scouts* ranked number two and *Friends* number three for the 1952–53 season; the previous year, *Talent Scouts* had been number one). As if that weren't enough, he simultaneously hosted a top-rated show in the daytime, too, called *Arthur Godfrey Time*. In one year he was said to have been personally responsible for 12% of the income of the entire CBS network. Yet, ten years later, "The Old Redhead" was a has-been. Unlike Ball and Gleason, he was not able to continue his success into later years. Partly that was his own doing, and partly it was the result of a changing medium.

Despite his folksy, down-home on-air personality, Arthur was a hard-driving boss behind the scenes. He left home at 14 and spent the 1920s bumming around from job to job, uncertain what he wanted to do. He served two stints as a seaman (once in the navy, once in the coast guard) and made an abortive attempt to get into show business with a traveling vaudeville act, which went broke.

He found his calling on radio in 1929 and spent the next decade as a local personality, mostly in the Washington area. After years of trying to land a network slot, he began to get national assignments from CBS in the 1940s. Probably the most famous was in April 1945, when he was a special reporter at the funeral of President Franklin D. Roosevelt. Godfrey broke down and cried on the air, a touch of humanity which was much in character for him. After the war he became a top name on radio, and when CBS opened its TV network in 1948 he was a natural to transfer to the new medium. His debut was widely heralded and fully lived up to its advance billing. Both *Arthur Godfrey's Talent Scouts* and *Arthur Godfrey and His Friends* were consistently among the biggest hits on television during the early 1950s.

Arthur did not follow the usual practice of using guest stars on his variety show, but relied on a small, close-knit family of regulars who stayed with him for years. The centerpiece was always Arthur himself, chatting amiably and pitching products such as Lipton Tea as if he really, truly believed in them (and ribbing them when he saw fit). He treated his "little Godfreys" (the regulars) as if they were his kids. The first crack in this "one big happy family" facade came in 1953. Suddenly, and very publicly, Arthur fired Julius LaRosa on the air, citing what he said was the young singer's "lack of humility." Soon after, he cleaned out much of the rest of the cast as well for what often seemed petty reasons. The press, which had previously lionized Godfrey, had a field day serving up an enormous amount of adverse publicity. Arthur made things worse by responding with thin-skinned vituperation, labeling his detractors as "Dope!" (Ed Sullivan), "Liar!" (or words to that effect, for Dorothy Kilgallen), "Fatuous Ass!" (John Crosby), "These jerk newspapermen!" and "Muckrakers!" for all and sundry.

By the mid-1950s Godfrey's honeymoon with press and public was over. His ratings began to drop, although all three of his network series remained popular enough to stay on the air until the end of the decade.

He gave up the last of them in 1959 when he learned he had lung cancer. After a successful operation, he overcame the disease and attempted to make a comeback, but aside from one uncomfortable year as cohost of *Candid Camera,* with Allen Funt, it was to no avail. (Ironically, another legend of the 1950s, Milton Berle, tried to make his own comeback that same season as cohost of *Jackpot Bowling,* with a similar lack of success.)

Arthur continued his radio show until 1972, but his appearances on television in the '60s and '70s were rare; an episode of *The Lucy Show* in 1965, an appearance on *The Bob Hope Chrysler Theatre* in 1967. Around 1970 he briefly hosted a syndicated talent show for college-age acts called *Your All-American College Show.* Nobody watched. He appeared in some commercials in the '70s and turned up on *The Love Boat* as late as 1979. His last years were spent as a spokesman for a new cause, that of ecology and conservation. Arthur Godfrey ended his life as an icon from TV history, rather like a faded kinescope from a much earlier day.

GODFREY, KATHY—hostess
b: c. 1910, Hasbrouck Heights, N.J.

On Your Way (quiz).........emcee (1954)

The younger sister of Arthur Godfrey.

GODKIN, PAUL—choreographer
b: c. 1914, Beaumont, Texas d: Jun 7, 1985

The Garry Moore Show (var)
.... dancers (1958–59)
The Edie Adams Show (var)
.... dancers (1963–64)

GODWIN, EARL—newscaster
b: c. 1881 d: Sep 23, 1956

Meet the Veep (info) .... regular (1953)

GOELZ, DAVE—puppeteer
The Muppet Show (var)
.........Dr. Bunsen Honeydew (1976–81)
The Muppet Show (var)
.... Gonzo (1976–81)
The Muppet Show (var)..... Zoot (1976–81)
The Muppet Show (var)
.... Beauregard (1980–81)

Emmy Award: Star, Best Comedy Variety Show, for *The Muppet Show* (1978)

GOETZ, PETER MICHAEL—actor
AfterMASH (com)
.... Wally Wainwright (1984)

GOINS, JESSE D.—black actor
The Greatest American Hero (adv)
.... Cyler Johnson (1981–83)

GOLD, BRANDY—juvenile actress
b: Jul 11, 1977, Northridge, Calif.

Baby Makes Five (com)
.... Annie Riddle (1983)

GOLD, MISSY—juvenile actress
b: Jul 14, 1970, Great Falls, Mont. r: California

Benson (com) ...... Katie Gatling (1979–86)

GOLD, TRACEY—juvenile actress
b: May 16, 1969, New York City, N.Y. r: California

Shirley (com) .... Michelle Miller (1979–80)
Goodnight, Beantown (com)
.... Susan Barnes (1983–84)
Growing Pains (com)
.... Carol Seaver (1985–   )

Brandy, Missy, and Tracey are sisters.

GOLDBERG, JASON—actor
Falcon Crest (drama)
.... Joseph Gioberti (1983–   )

GOLDBLUM, JEFF—actor
b: Oct 22, 1952, Pittsburgh, Pa.

Tenspeed and Brown Shoe (drama)
.... Lionel "Brown Shoe" Whitney (1980)

GOLDDIGGERS, THE—chorus line
The Dean Martin Show (var)
.... regulars (1967–71)
Dean Martin Presents the Golddiggers (var)
.... regulars (1968–70)
The Golddiggers (var) .... stars (1971)
The Wacky World of Jonathan Winters (var)
.... regular (1973–74)

This was a 10-12 member chorus line of shapely beauties put together in 1967 to decorate *The Dean Martin Show.* The membership changed constantly. It was probably the only chorus line ever to headline its own show—as a summer replacement for Martin from 1968–70 and then in its own syndicated series in 1971, all with varying hosts.

A 1971 press release spelled out the qualifications for becoming a Golddigger: "A girl has to be between 18 and 22, unmarried, and with a sort of special look and quality which producer Greg Garrison seeks for the group." Seldom has a producer crafted for himself such a delicious assignment!

GOLDEN, GINNY—actress

Search (adv) . . . . Miss Keach (1972)

GOLDIN, RICKY PAULL—actor
b: Jan 5, San Francisco, Calif.

Hail to the Chief (com) . . . . Doug (1985)

GOLDMAN, CAROLE—actress

The Paper Chase (drama)
. . . . Carol (1978–79)

GOLDMAN, DANNY—actor
b: Oct 30, New York City, N.Y.

The Good Life (com)
. . . . Nick Dutton (1971–72)
Busting Loose (com) . . Lester Bellman (1977)
Mickey Spillane's Mike Hammer (drama)
. . . . Ozzie the Answer (1984–   )

GOLDMAN, ROY—actor

M*A*S*H (com) . . . . Roy (1981–83)

GOLDMAN, WENDY—actress

Delta House (com) . . . . Muffy (1979)

GOLDNONI, LELIA—actress
b: New York City, N.Y.

Scruples (drama) . . . . Joanne Hillman (1980)

GOLDSBORO, BOBBY—singer, songwriter
b: Jan 18, 1941, Marianna, Fla.

The Bobby Goldsboro Show (music)
. . . . host (1973–75)

GOLDSMITH, DAVID—actor

Morningstar/Eveningstar (drama)
. . . . Martin Palmer (1986)

GOLDSMITH, JONATHAN—actor

Knots Landing (drama) . . Frank Elliot (1985)

GOLDSMITH, MERWIN—actor

Goodtime Girls (com)
. . . . George Coolidge (1980)

GOLDSMITH, SYDNEY—black actress

Stockard Channing in Just Friends (com)
. . . . Coral (1979)
The Stockard Channing Show (com)
. . . . Earline Cunningham (1980)

GOLONKA, ARLENE—actress
b: Jan 23, 1939, Chicago, Ill.

Mayberry R.F.D. (com)
. . . . Millie Swanson (1968–71)
Joe & Valerie (com) . . Stella Sweetzer (1979)

GONZALES, CLAUDIA—actress

a.k.a. Pablo (com)
. . . . Anna Maria Del Gato (1984)

GONZALES, MARTHA—actress

a.k.a. Pablo (com) . . Susana Del Gato (1984)

GOOD HUMOR COMPANY, THE—

CBS Newcomers (var) . . . . . . regulars (1971)

GOOD TIME SINGERS, THE—

The Andy Williams Show (var)
. . . . regulars (1963–66)

GOODE, RICHARD—actor

Dress Rehearsal (misc)
. . . . "Director" (on-camera) (1948)

GOODEVE, GRANT—actor
b: Jul 6, 1952, New Haven, Conn. r: Middlebury, Conn.

Eight Is Enough (com)
. . . . David Bradford (1977–81)
Dynasty (drama) . . . . . . Chris Deegan (1983)

The eldest son on *Eight Is Enough* has made guest appearances on a number of prime time series since 1981, including *Murder, She Wrote, T. J. Hooker,* and *Finder of Lost Loves.* Soap opera may become his forte: he has appeared on *Dynasty,* the daytime serial *One Life to Live,* and the syndicated soap *Rituals,* among others. He has also done a good deal of work in the theater, and is trying to start a career as a rock singer.

GOODFRIEND, LYNDA—actress
b: Oct 31, Miami, Fla.

Blansky's Beauties (com)
.... Ethel "Sunshine" Akalino (1977)
Happy Days (com)
... Lori Beth Allen Cunningham (1977–82)
Who's Watching the Kids? (com)
.... Angie Vitola (1978)

Lynda, a high school cheerleader from Florida, headed for New York after graduation from college to become a dancer on Broadway. That didn't work out too well, but she did get a job as a hoofer in a revival of *Good News,* and there met scriptwriter Garry Marshall. Marshall went on to create *Happy Days,* remembered the young dancer, and arranged an audition that resulted in three separate guest appearances for her on the show—as girlfriend to Ron Howard, Donny Most, and Anson Williams. Having played the field among the show's male leads, she settled down to become Howard's steady girlfriend in 1977, after Marshall had first tried her out in another sitcom that same spring called *Blansky's Beauties.*

Marshall placed Lynda in another comedy in 1978, but *Who's Watching the Kids?* was no more successful than *Blansky's* had been. She returned to *Happy Days,* where her character Lori Beth eventually married Richie and bore him a child.

GOODMAN, AL—orchestra leader
b: Aug 12, 1890, Nikopol, Russia d: Jan 10, 1972

Fireball Fun-for-All (var)
.... orch. leader (1949)
NBC Comedy Hour (var)
.... orch. leader (1956)

GOODMAN, BENNY—orchestra leader
b: May 30, 1909, Chicago, Ill. d: Jun 13, 1986

Star Time (var) .... sextet (1950–51)

The famous bandleader brought his jazz-flavored sextet to this obscure DuMont musical series for a few months in the winter of 1950–51. He was doubtless the best thing about the show.

GOODMAN, DIANA—
Hee Haw (var).......... regular (1981–85)

GOODMAN, DODY—comedienne
b: Oct 28, 1929*, Columbus, Ohio

The Jack Paar Show (talk)
.... regular (1957–58)
Liar's Club (quiz)....... panelist (1976–78)
Mary Hartman, Mary Hartman (com)
.... Martha Shumway (1976–78)
The Mary Tyler Moore Hour (var)
.... Ruby Bell (1979)
Diff'rent Strokes (com)
.... Aunt Sophia (1981–82)

Dody began her career as a dancer at New York's Radio City Music Hall and appeared for a number of years as a dancer in Broadway and off-Broadway musicals of the late '40s and '50s, including *High Button Shoes* and *Call Me Madam.* She was such a cut-up backstage that friends eventually persuaded her to try comedy, and she first attracted national attention as the spacey innocent who was a regular guest on Jack Paar's version of *The Tonight Show.*

In later years, Dody appeared occasionally as a TV guest but was active mostly on the stage. Then, in the late '70s, as flaky as ever, she started turning up in regular series and TV movies. "I like humor and I like laughter," she told a reporter in 1982. "Sometimes I meet people who don't seem to have much sense of humor at all and I wonder how they manage in life without one. Of course, maybe they manage better!"

GOODMAN, FRANK—referee
Kid Gloves (sport).......... referee (1951)

GOODROW, MICHAEL—actor
Eight Is Enough (com)
.... Ernie Fields (1979–81)

*Some sources give 1915.

GOODWIN, BILL—actor, announcer

b: Jul 28, 1910, San Francisco, Calif. d: May 9, 1958

The George Burns and Gracie Allen Show (com).............. .. as himself (1950–51)
Penny to a Million (quiz) ..... emcee (1955)
The Boing Boing Show (cartn)
.... narrator (1958)

The longtime, genial announcer for *The Burns and Allen Show* and other hits on radio.

GOODWIN, JOSHUA—juvenile actor

Too Close for Comfort (com)
.... Andrew Rush (1984–85)

GOODWIN, KIA—black juvenile actress

b: Aug 2, 1973, Livingston, N.J.

227 (com)...... Tiffany Holloway (1985–)

GOODWIN, MICHAEL—actor

b: Aug 19, Virginia, Minn. r: Washington state

Strike Force (police)
.... Det. Mark Osborn (1981–82)
The Hamptons (drama)
.... Peter Chadway (1983)

GOORIAN, LEN—

The Paul Dixon Show (var)
.... regular (1951–52)

GORDEN, HAYES—

The Fashion Story (misc) . regular (1948–49)

GORDENO, PETER—actor

UFO (sci fi) .... Capt. Peter Karlin (1970)

GORDON, ANITA—singer

The Ken Murray Show (var)
.... regular (1951–53)

GORDON, BARRY—actor

b: Dec 21, 1948, Brookline, Mass.

The Don Rickles Show (com)
.... Conrad Musk (1972)
The New Dick Van Dyke Show (com)
.... Dennis Whitehead (1973–74)
Fish (com) ...... Charlie Harrison (1977–78)
Good Time Harry (com) .... Stan (1980)

Archie Bunker's Place (com)
.... Gary Rabinowitz (1981–83)

Barry Gordon is a mild-mannered, rather small (5'6") character actor who had a very successful—if not well-remembered—childhood in show business. At age six he made a recording that sold more than two million copies; at ten he was appearing in many prime time series; and at 14 he won a Tony Award nomination for his role in a hit play.

The son of a disc jockey, young Barry won a talent contest at age three-and-a-half, which led to his television debut on Ted Mack's *Original Amateur Hour* (Ted liked that sort of act). During the early '50s the precocious child appeared on a number of early variety shows, including *Star Time* and *The Jackie Gleason Show*. Then, in 1955, he recorded, in his piping juvenile soprano voice, a song called "Nuttin' for Christmas" ("I'm gettin' nuttin' for Christmas/'Cause I ain't been nuttin' but bad"). It was a huge hit at Christmas 1955.

"Nuttin' for Christmas" was Barry's only hit record, but it opened the door to quite a lot of TV work, including roles on *The Danny Thomas Show* and later *Alfred Hitchcock Presents, The Jack Benny Show,* and dozens of other series of the '50s and '60s. He also had juvenile roles in films and onstage, winning his Tony nomination in 1963 for *A Thousand Clowns,* with Jason Robards and Sandy Dennis. He finally took time out to study acting at U.C.L.A., but, like many another child star, his adult years proved less productive. Grown-up Barry has usually been seen in the background—as the young ad-agency salesman on *The Don Rickles Show,* the soap opera writer on *The New Dick Van Dyke Show,* the social worker on *Fish,* and Archie Bunker's last accountant (before the bar closed) on *Archie Bunker's Place.* He has also done voices for Saturday morning cartoons. Once in a while someone will still ask, "Were *you* the little kid who . . .?"

GORDON, BRUCE—actor

b: Jun 20, 1919, London England

Behind Closed Doors (drama)
.... Commander Matson (1958–59)
The Untouchables (police)
.... Frank Nitti (1959–63)

Peyton Place (drama)
.... Gus Chernak (1965–66)
Run Buddy Run (com)
.... Devere (Mr. D.) (1966–67)

GORDON, COLIN—actor
b: Apr 27, 1911, Ceylon d: Oct 4, 1972

The Baron (drama)
.... John Alexander Templeton-Green
(1966)

GORDON, DON—actor
b: Nov 23, 1926, Los Angeles, Calif.

The Blue Angels (adv)
.... Lt. Hank Bertelli (1960)
Lucan (adv)............. Prentiss (1977–78)
The Contender (drama) .... Harry (1980)

GORDON, GALE—actor
b: Feb 22, 1906*, New York City, N.Y.

Our Miss Brooks (com)
.... Osgood Conklin (1952–56)
The Brothers (com).. Harvey Box (1956–57)
Sally (com) ...... Bascomb Bleacher (1958)
Pete and Gladys (com)
.... Uncle Paul (1960–62)
Dennis the Menace (com)
.... John Wilson (1962–63)
The Lucy Show (com)
.... Theodore J. Mooney (1963–68)
Here's Lucy (com)
.... Harrison Otis Carter (1968–74)
Life With Lucy (com)
.... Curtis McGibbon (1986–)

This tall, dapper actor with a trim mustache was everybody's idea of the perfect stuffed shirt in the '40s, '50s, and '60s—and the master of the slow burn. He seldom played anything else, but what he did he did so well that he never lacked for work. TV's top stars sought his services; for example, Lucille Ball wanted him to play Fred Mertz on *I Love Lucy*. Unfortunately Gordon was already committed to another hit show, as Eve Arden's blustery principal on *Our Miss Brooks*.

Interestingly, Gordon was born with a cleft palate, and it was during rehabilitation from boyhood surgery that he developed the marvelous, deliberate voice that became his trademark. He always wanted to be an actor (both his parents

*Some sources give 1905.

350

were in the theater) and he made his debut on the New York stage while still a teenager—though it is hard to imagine "Old Marblehead" (of *Our Miss Brooks)* ever being that young. During the 1930s Gale got into radio, where he was soon much in demand for all sorts of roles, especially those of a comic foil. Among his long-running radio roles were those of Mayor La Trivia on *Fibber McGee and Molly,* the harried sponsor on *The Phil Harris-Alice Faye Show,* and the apoplectic banker Atterbury on Lucille Ball's *My Favorite Husband.*

Gale did appear a couple of times as a guest on *I Love Lucy* in the early 1950s as Ricky's stuffy boss at the Tropicana Night Club, Mr. Littlefield. However, for most of the period from 1952 to 1974 he was steadily engaged as a featured regular on one series or another. His most famous roles were those of Mr. Conklin on *Our Miss Brooks* and Lucy's nemesis, the banker, on *The Lucy Show/Here's Lucy*. After the latter series left the air in 1974, Gale was seen only rarely on television, once in an appearance with "my dear friend" Lucille Ball on the *Lucy Moves to NBC* special in 1980. He has turned down many other offers, including a *Love Boat* appearance, preferring instead to appear in local stage productions in the U.S. and Canada. Of his long and successful career, he recently commented, "I have been very, very lucky. But I also have no illusions about my capabilities. A 'Hamlet' I never was. From time to time someone needs a character actor who can yell. That's my specialty, yelling . . . at stars, mostly."*

GORDON, GERALD—actor
b: Jul 12, Chicago, Ill.

Highcliffe Manor (com)
.... Dr. Felix Morger (1979)

Emmy Award: Best Actor in a Daytime Drama Special, for *First Ladies Diaries: Rachel Jackson* (1976)

This actor is best known for his work in daytime, particularly his long runs on *The Doctors* (1966–76) and on *General Hospital* (1976–78, 1982–83).

*Quoted in *Whatever Became Of . . .*, Volume Nine, by Richard Lamparski (Crown, 1985).

GORDON, GLEN—actor

Adventures of Fu Manchu (drama)
.... Dr. Fu Manchu (1955–56)

GORDON, GLORIA—actress
b: c. 1881 d: Nov 23, 1962

My Friend Irma (com)
.... Mrs. O'Reilly (1952–54)

GORDON, JOANN—actress

From Here to Eternity (drama)
.... Aimee (1980)

GORDON, LEO V.—actor, writer
b: Dec 2, 1922, New York City, N.Y.

Circus Boy (adv) .... Hank Miller (1956–58)
Enos (com) ... Sgt. Theodore Kick (1980–81)
The Winds of War (drama)
.... Gen. Benton (1983)

GORDON, PHIL—jazz pianist, singer, actor
b: May 5, 1922, Meridian, Miss.

Pete Kelly's Blues (drama) ..... Fred (1959)
The Beverly Hillbillies (com)
.... Jasper DePew (1962–63)

GORDON, VIRGINIA—actress

Our Miss Brooks (com)
.... Mrs. Martha Conklin (1952–53)

The real-life wife of actor Gale Gordon, who played Mr. Conklin.

GORDON, WILLIAM D.—actor

Riverboat (adv) .... Travis (1959–60)

GORING, MARIUS—actor
b: May 23, 1912, Newport, Isle of Wight, England

The Scarlet Pimpernell (adv)
.... the Scarlet Pimpernell (1958)
Holocaust (drama) ...... Herr Palitz (1978)

GORMAN, MARI—actress
b: Sep 1, New York City, N.Y.

Harper Valley P.T.A. (com)
.... Vivian Washburn (1981)
He's the Mayor (com)
.... Paula Hendricks (1986)

GORME, EYDIE—singer
b: Aug 16, 1931, The Bronx, N.Y.

Tonight (talk) .... regular (1954–57)
The Steve Lawrence-Eydie Gorme Show (var)
.... cohost (1958)

Emmy Award: Costar, Best Music Program, for *Steve and Eydie Celebrate Irving Berlin* (1979)

Wife of singer Steve Lawrence, with whom she often appeared in classy musical specials.

GORMLEY, JIM—actor

Car 54, Where Are You? (com)
.... Off. Nelson (1961–63)

GORSHIN, FRANK—comedian, impressionist
b: Apr 5, 1935, Pittsburgh, Pa.

ABC Comedy Hour (com)
.... regular (1972)

Gorshin is perhaps best remembered as the hilariously maniacal Riddler on *Batman*. On the *ABC Comedy Hour* he was a member of a repertory company made up entirely of impressionists, called The Kopycats.

GORSKI, VIRGINIA—hostess

Manhattan Showcase (var)... regular (1949)
The Fifty-Fourth Street Revue (var)
.... regular (1949–50)

GORTNER, MARJOE—actor
b: Jan 14, 1941*, Long Beach, Calif.

Speak Up, America (aud par)
.... regular (1980)

A former child evangelist who now plays wild-eyed maniacs, as well as other rather bizarre roles (e.g., in *The Gun and the Pulpit*). He turned to acting after the release in 1972 of a none-too-complimentary documentary about his life as a hustler on the evangelism circuit, called *Marjoe*.

GOSDEN, FREEMAN—actor
b: May 5, 1899, Richmond, Va. d: Dec 10, 1982

*Some sources give 1944.

Calvin and the Colonel (cartn)
.... the Colonel (voice) (1961–62)

White actor and co-creator, with Charles Correll, of the famous black comedy series *Amos 'n' Andy,* on which *Calvin and the Colonel* was based.

GOSFIELD, MAURICE—actor
b: c. 1913 d: Oct 19, 1964

The Phil Silvers Show (com)
.... Pvt. Duane Doberman (1955–59)
Top Cat (cartn)
.... Benny the Ball (voice) (1961–62)

The wonderfully short (5'6"), dumpy mascot of Sgt. Bilko's platoon on *The Phil Silvers Show.* "Doberman," barked Bilko, "you look like an unmade bed!"

GOSSETT, LOUIS, JR.—black actor
b: May 27, 1936*, Brooklyn, N.Y.

The Young Rebels (adv)
.... Isak Poole (1970–71)
Roots (drama)............. Fiddler (1977)
Backstairs at the White House (drama)
.... Levi Mercer (1979)
The Lazarus Syndrome (drama)
.... Dr. MacArthur St. Clair (1979)
The Powers of Matthew Star (sci fi)
.... Walt Shephard (1982–83)

Emmy Award: Best Actor in a Drama Series, for *Roots* (1977)

This tall (6'4") actor with a commanding presence traveled a long road to stardom, from bit parts in the 1950s to an Academy Award in the 1980s. He has done a great deal of television along the way.

Gossett was born the son of a porter and a maid, who worked hard to save enough to send their beloved son to college. While still in high school he was persuaded to answer an acting call for young black actors needed for a Broadway play, and to his surprise he won a part, making his debut in *Take a Giant Step* in 1953. However, his sights were on a basketball career and he entered New York University on an athletic scholarship. Soon the strapping young man received an offer to join the New York Knicks and turn professional; however, by that time he was showing ever greater

*Some sources give 1937.

promise as an actor and he decided to concentrate on acting instead.

Throughout the '50s and '60s Gossett played many supporting roles on television on such series as *Goodyear Theatre, Kraft Theatre, The Big Story,* and *You Are There.* Usually his roles were distinctively, even stereotypically, black—for example on *East Side/West Side* (set in a ghetto), *Cowboy in Africa,* and *Daktari.* Only occasionally was he seen in a comedy; in 1970 he appeared in an episode of *The Bill Cosby Show* called "The Return of Big Bad Bubber Johnson." A costarring role as the ex-slave Isak in the short-lived *Young Rebels* failed to lift him out of the supporting ranks, but he did continue to be seen frequently through the '70s, mostly in crime shows such as *The Mod Squad* and *Police Story.*

Gossett's major breakthrough came in 1977, in another role that might be called a stereotype. However, his powerful performance as the older slave who became LeVar Burton's friend and companion on *Roots* won him an Emmy Award and new stature in the industry. He subsequently played a leading role in the miniseries *Backstairs at the White House,* starred in the doctor series *The Lazarus Syndrome* (a rare achievement for a black on television), and was young Matthew Star's wise mentor on *The Powers of Matthew Star*— none of these being necessarily "black" roles. Neither was his Oscar-winning performance as the drill instructor in *An Officer and a Gentleman* or his Emmy-nominated starring role as Egyptian President Anwar Sadat in the 1983 miniseries *Sadat.* Gossett appears to have a bright future as an actor of the first rank in roles that no longer need be tied to his color.

GOTHIE, ROBERT—actor
The Gallant Men (drama)
.... Private Sam Hanson (1962–63)

GOTTFRIED, GILBERT—comedian
NBC's Saturday Night Live (com)
.... regular (1980–81)
Thicke of the Night (talk).... regular (1983)

GOTTLIEB, BROTHER THEODORE—comedian
The Billy Crystal Comedy Hour (var)
.... regular (1982)

An off-the-wall comic known for his appearances on *The David Letterman Show.*

GOTTLIEB, CARL—comedian, writer
b: Mar 18, 1938

The Ken Berry "Wow" Show (var)
.... regular (1972)

Emmy Award: Best Writing for a Comedy Variety Show, for *The Smothers Brothers Comedy Hour* (1969)

GOTTLIEB, STAN—actor

Hot L Baltimore (com).... Mr. Morse (1975)

GOTTSCHALK, VIM—panelist

It's About Time (quiz) .... panel (1954)

GOUDE, INGRID—actress
b: c. 1937, Sandviken, Sweden

The Bob Cummings Show (com)
.... as herself (1957–58)
Steve Canyon (adv) .... Ingrid (1959)

Miss Sweden of 1956.

GOUGH, LLOYD—actor
b: Sep 21, 1907 d: Jul 23, 1984

The Green Hornet (drama)
.... Mike Axford (1966–67)

GOUGH, MICHAEL—actor
b: Nov 23, 1917, Malaya

The Search for the Nile (drama)
.... Dr. David Livingstone (1972)

GOULD, ELLIOTT—actor
b: Aug 29, 1938, Far Rockaway, Queens, N.Y.

E/R (com) . Dr. Howard Sheinfeld (1984–85)
Together We Stand (com)
.... David Randall (1986–)

This Hollywood star has been active mostly on stage and in movies—including the role of the original Trapper John in the film version of *M*A*S*H*. His first professional appearance, however, was as one of 50 child tap-dancers performing "Lullabye of Broadway" on *The Ernie Kovacs Show!*
He was married to singer Barbra Streisand in the 1960s.

GOULD, HAROLD—actor
b: Dec 10, 1923, Schenectady, N.Y.

He & She (com) .. Norman Nugent (1967–68)
Rhoda (com)
.... Martin Morgenstern (1974–78)
The Feather and Father Gang (drama)
.... Harry Danton (1977)
Park Place (com)....... David Ross (1981)
Foot in the Door (com)... Jonah Foot (1983)
Under One Roof (com).. Ben Sprague (1985)

Harold Gould is one of television's best-educated character actors. The likable, often caustic older performer holds a Ph.D. in theater; he taught drama and speech at Cornell and the University of California for ten years before he decided to practice what he was preaching and become a full-time actor himself. That was in 1960. In the years since, Gould has appeared in more than 300 TV shows, 25 films, and 50 stage plays, usually as a grumpy grandpa or other authority figure (one of them being Rhoda's father on *Rhoda*). He is quite candid about the difference between teaching and doing. "After I stopped teaching and became a professional actor," he said in 1981, "I saw other actors successfully violating every principle I held and had taught. So much for the voice of authority."

GOULD, SANDRA—actress
b: Brooklyn, N.Y.

Bewitched (com) . Gladys Kravitz (1966–72)

GOULD, SID—actor

Seven at Eleven (var)....... regular (1951)
Caesar Presents (var).. various roles (1955)

GOULDING, RAY—

see Bob & Ray

GOULET, ROBERT—singer
b: Nov 26, 1933, Lawrence, Mass.

Blue Light (drama) .... David March (1966)

A darkly handsome singer with a deep, rich voice but a rather saccharine style (hence, "Gooey Goulet"). On television, he has appeared mostly on variety shows and in musical productions such as *Brigadoon, Carousel,* and *Kiss Me Kate;* however, he has also tried his hand at acting from time to time, including his own 1966 spy series, *Blue Light.*

Goulet began his career in Canada and is generally thought to be Canadian. Actually, he was born in the U.S. with the rather unromantic name of Stanley Applebaum.

GOWDY, CURT—sportscaster
b: Jul 31, 1919, Green River, Wyo

Saturday Night Basketball (sport)
.... sportscaster (1951–52)
Monday Night Baseball (sport)
.... sportscaster (1972–75)

Emmy Award: Best Edited Sports Series, for *American Sportsman* (1981, 1983, 1986)

Curt is one of the grand old men of sportscasting. His talent and versatility is attested to by the fact that he seems to have been inducted into practically every hall of fame around: the Baseball Hall of Fame, the Sportswriters and Broadcasters Hall of Fame, and even the International Fishing Hall of Fame. He is president of the Basketball Hall of Fame and has received a Hall of Fame Gold Medal Award from the National Academy of Television Arts and Sciences. As if all those halls weren't tribute enough, there is also a "Curt Gowdy State Park" in his native Wyoming. Curt began his career as a local sportscaster in the Midwest in the 1940s and moved to New York in 1949 after winning a national audition to replace Russ Hodges doing play-by-play for the New York Yankees. Two years later he switched to covering the Boston Red Sox and stayed with that team for 15 years. He has also done a great deal of network play-by-play since the 1950s on all three networks. In addition, he is well known as host and producer of the long-running (since 1965) ABC weekend outdoor series, *American Sportsman,* on which celebrities and athletes go hunting and fishing.

In recent years Curt has competed for Emmy Awards with his son, ABC sports producer Curt Gowdy, Jr.

GOWER, ANDRE—juvenile actor
b: Apr 27, 1973, Culver City, Calif.

Baby Makes Five (com)
.... Michael Riddle (1983)

Fathers and Sons (com)
.... Sean Flynn (1986)

GOZIER, BERNIE—actor

Bold Venture (adv) ...... King Moses (1959)

GRABOWSKI, NORM—actor

The New Phil Silvers Show (com)
.... Grabowski (1963–64)

GRACE, MARY—juvenile actor

It's About Time (com) ...... Mlor (1966–67)

GRADY, DON—actor
b: c. 1944

My Three Sons (com)
.... Robbie Douglas (1960–72)

Don was a *Mickey Mouse Club* Mouseketeer in the late 1950s, under his real name Don Agrati, before his long run as middle son Robbie on *My Three Sons* (on which he grew from a 14-year-old to a young man). In 1967, dissatisfied with acting, he tried to launch a career in rock music by posing as a mystery vocalist ("Luke R. Yoo") with a band called The Yellow Balloon; Don appeared on the cover of the group's first album wearing a fake mustache and a wig. Despite a contest to guess the singer's real identity, the gimmick, the record, and his career never got off the ground.

GRAFF, DAVID—actor
b: Apr 16, Lancaster, Ohio

He's the Mayor (com)
.... Councilman Nash (1986)

GRAFF, ILENE—actress
b: Feb 28, Brooklyn, N.Y.

Supertrain (drama)
... social director Penny Whitaker (1979)
Lewis & Clark (com)
.... Alicia Lewis (1981–82)
Mr. Belvedere (com)
.... Marsha Owens (1985–)

GRAFF, JERRY, SINGERS—

The Nat "King" Cole Show (var)
.... regulars (1957)

GRAFTON, SAMUEL—panelist

Where Was I? (quiz) .... panelist (1953)

GRAHAM, GARY—actor

Scruples (drama)...... Jake Cassidy (1980)

GRAHAM, GERRIT—actor

Stockard Channing in Just Friends (com)
.... Leonard Scribner (1979)

GRAHAM, JOE—actor

Major Dell Conway of the Flying Tigers (adv)
.... regular (1951)

GRAHAM, JOHN—actor

Show Business, Inc. (var)
.... regular (1947)

GRAHAM, THE JUNE, DANCERS—

Holiday Hotel (var)
.... regulars (1950–51)

GRAHAM, REV. BILLY—evangelist
b: Nov 7, 1918, Charlotte, N.C.

Hour of Decision (misc)...... host (1951–54)
The Billy Graham Crusade (misc)
.... host (1957–59)

Rev. Graham has been seen frequently over the years, usually in specials telecast two or three times per year. The above two programs were regular nighttime series.

GRAHAM, RONNY—actor, writer
b: Aug 26, 1919, Philadelphia, Pa.

The New Bill Cosby Show (var)
.... regular (1972–73)
The Hudson Brothers Show (var)
.... regular (1974)
The Bob Crane Show (com)
.... Mr. Ernest Busso (1975)
Chico and the Man (com)
.... Rev. Bemis (1975–76)

GRAHAM, SHEILAH—Hollywood columnist
b: 1912*, England

Sheilah Graham in Hollywood (talk)
.... hostess (1951)

*Some sources give 1908.

GRAHAM, SONNY—

Paul Whiteman's TV Teen Club (talent)
.... regular (1950)

GRAHAM, VIRGINIA—actress, talk show host
b: Jul 4, 1913, Chicago, Ill.

Where Was I? (quiz) .... panelist (1952)
Summer in the Park (var)..... emcee (1954)

A victim of cancer at age 37, Graham overcame the disease and went on to a long career as a syndicated TV talk show host and sometime actress. Among her notable daytime chatter shows: *Food for Thought* (1956–61), *Girl Talk* (1963–69) and *The Virginia Graham Show* (1970–72). She has contributed a great deal of her time to charitable activities, including the American Cancer Society. Her autobiography is titled *There Goes What's Her Name.*

GRAHAME, GLORIA—actress
b: Nov 28, 1925, Los Angeles, Calif. d: Oct 5, 1981

Rich Man, Poor Man—Book I (drama)
.... Sue Prescott (1976)

GRAMMER, KELSEY—actor
b: St. Thomas, Virgin Islands

Cheers (com)... Dr. Frasier Crane (1984–)

GRANDIN, ISABEL—actress

Thicke of the Night (talk)
.... regular (1983–84)
Hell Town (drama)
.... Sister Angel Cake (1985)

GRANDY, FRED—actor
b: Jun 29, 1948, Sioux City, Iowa

Maude (com).............. Chris (1973–74)
The Love Boat (com)
  Yeoman-Purser Burl Smith ("Gopher")
  (1977–86)

The cheerful little "Go-fer" on *The Love Boat* returned to Iowa and was elected to the U.S. House of Representatives in 1986.

GRANGER, GERRI—singer

What's It All About World? (var)
.... regular (1969)

GRANGER, STEWART—actor

b: May 6, 1913, London, England

The Men From Shiloh (wes)
.... Col. Alan MacKenzie (1970–71)

This rugged Hollywood leading man did no television at all until his film career was in severe decline in the late 1960s. He was then lured to the small screen for a single season as the owner of the Shiloh Ranch on *The Men From Shiloh,* successor to *The Virginian.* His TV movie appearances have also been quite rare; he was in *Any Second Now* in '69, played Sherlock Holmes in *The Hound of the Baskervilles* in '72, and was, Prince Phillip in *The Royal Romance of Charles and Diana* in '82. That's all.

Granger's autobiography is titled *Sparks Fly Upward* (1981).

GRANIK, THEODORE—lawyer, host

b: c. 1907 d: 1970

American Forum of the Air (pub aff)
.... moderator (1950–52)
Youth Wants to Know (pub aff)
.... moderator (1951–52)
Youth Wants to Know (pub aff)
.... moderator (1954)

GRANT, ALBERTA—actress

The Patty Duke Show (com)
.... Maggie (1963–65)

GRANT, FAYE—actress

b: Jul 16, Detroit, Mich.

Greatest American Hero (adv)
.... Rhonda Blake (1981–83)
V (movie) (sci fi) .... Dr. Julie Parrish (1983)
V: The Final Battle (miniseries) (sci fi)
.... Dr. Julie Parrish (1984)
V (sci fi)......... Dr. Julie Parrish (1984–85)

GRANT, HARVEY—actor

Life with Father (com)
.... Harlan Day (1953–55)

GRANT, KIRBY—actor

b: Nov 24, 1911*, Butte, Montana d: Oct 30, 1985

Sky King (wes)........ Sky King (1953–54)

*Some sources give 1914.

The stolid, up-to-date hero of *Sky King* (he chased bad guys in a small plane) had starred in many standard film westerns in the '40s and early '50s. He also had other, rather diverse occupations before his movie days, including those of a child violinist, singer, and sculptor. After his Hollywood career he became a public relations director in Texas and Florida (for Sea World) and, still later, a Florida real estate developer. Grand plans in the '70s to revive *Sky King* and open a Sky King Theme Park did not come to fruition, however.

GRANT, LEE—actress

b: Oct 31, 1927*, New York City, N.Y.

Peyton Place (drama)
.... Stella Chernak (1965–66)
Fay (com) .... Fay Stewart (1975–76)
Backstairs at the White House (drama)
.... Grace Coolidge (1979)

Emmy Awards: Best Supporting Actress in a Drama, for *Peyton Place* (1966); Best Actress in a Single Performance, for the TV movie *The Neon Ceiling* (1971)

This Oscar, Emmy, and Tony award winning actress has been active in show business since age four (as a child, she danced in the Metropolitan Opera Company Ballet) and in television since the early 1950s. An outspoken woman, she has been at the center of controversy more than once. In the 1950s she got into trouble with the political blacklisters by staunchly defending her director-husband, who had been accused of left-wing leanings. That hobbled her film career quite a bit, but she did continue to appear in TV drama series such as *Philco TV Playhouse* and *Kraft Theatre.* In the '60s and '70s she won much acclaim for her guest roles on series such as *The Defenders, The Nurses, Ben Casey,* and (as a regular) on *Peyton Place.*

Her only starring role in a series was as the liberated divorcé in *Fay,* a program that attracted more headlines than viewers. NBC canceled the show after only four episodes, whereupon Miss Grant, on *The Tonight Show,* publicly blasted the network for meddling with the scripts and for its irrational scheduling of the adult-theme show so early in the evening. In one of the

*Some sources give 1929.

356

evening's more memorable quotes, she labeled NBC program chief Marvin Antonowsky as "The Mad Programmer."

The uproar didn't hurt anyone's career, however. Lee won her Oscar for *Shampoo* the same year, and the producer of *Fay* went on to create such breakthrough hits as *Soap* and *Golden Girls.* As for "The Mad Programmer," he became a top Hollywood movie executive.

GRANT, TED—violinist

Saturday Night Jamboree (music)
.... regular (1948–49)

GRASSLE, KAREN—actress
b: Feb 25, 1944, Berkeley, Calif.

Little House on the Prairie (adv)
.... Caroline Ingalls (1974–82)

GRATE, GAIL—actress

MacGruder & Loud (police) .. Naomi (1985)

GRAUBART, JUDY—actress

Comedy Tonight (var) ...... regular (1970)

GRAUER, BEN—newscaster, commentator, host
b: Jun 2, 1908, New York City, N.Y. d: May 31, 1977

Eye Witness (doc).......... host (1947–48)
Americana (quiz)...... moderator (1948–49)
Kay Kyser's Kollege of Musical Knowledge (quiz)................ announcer (1949–50)
The Ben Grauer Show (talk) .... host (1950)
What Happened? (quiz)... moderator (1952)
The Big Story (drama)... narrator (1955–57)
The March of Medicine (doc)
.... narrator (1958)

Older viewers will recall Grauer as one of the pioneer news personalities on radio and television. A onetime child actor (he appeared in silent films made in Fort Lee, N.J.), he joined NBC in 1930 as a special-events reporter and during the following years provided colorful commentary for many famous events. His ability to ad lib for long periods of time, as he did during parades and interminable political conventions, was legendary.

Grauer was on television from the start,

covering the opening of the World's Fair (and the initiation of regular TV service) in 1939. He also broadcast the first airplane-to-ground TV show in 1949. His early TV series were mostly informational. *Eye Witness* was a behind-the-scenes look at how the new medium worked; *Americana* gave away encyclopedias for smart questions; *The Ben Grauer Show* featured interviews with authors. Ben was perhaps best known for his coverage of New Year's Eve at Times Square, which he continued over a period spanning 20 years. Like Guy Lombardo, he was a fixture on that special night. He retired from NBC in 1973.

GRAVES, LESLIE—juvenile actress
b: c. 1960, Silver City, N.M. r: New York City, N.Y.

Here We Go Again (com)..... Cindy (1973)

GRAVES, PETER—actor
b: Mar 18, 1925, Minneapolis, Minn.

Whiplash (wes)
.... Christopher Cobb (1960–61)
Court-Martial (drama)
.... Maj. Frank Whittaker (1966)
Mission: Impossible (drama)
.... James Phelps (1967–73)
The Winds of War (drama)
.... Fred "Palmer" Kirby (1983)

This tall, handsome actor changed his name to avoid confusion with his more famous brother James Arness, but he later became equally well-known. Like Jim, Peter grew up in Minneapolis, served in World War II, and drifted to Hollywood after the war. A bit part in a live TV play won him his first movie role in 1950 (three years after Jim's first), in a western called *Rogue River.* Thereafter, he appeared in a number of action films, scoring as the serpentine German spy in *Stalag 17* in 1953.

Peter also had roles in an assortment of TV theater productions, but his big break came the same year as brother Jim's, in 1955. At the same time Jim was beginning work on *Gunsmoke,* Peter began appearing as the father figure on the Saturday morning adventure series *Fury,* which was a huge hit among kids. It continued in production for five years and was rerun for years after. When *Fury* finally ceased production, Peter went on to a couple of less successful series, the syndicated *Whip-lash* (filmed in Australia) and *Court-Martial* (filmed in Europe), and also made guest appearances on series such as *Climax, Route 66,* and *Alfred Hitchcock Presents.* Then came the big one: the role of I.M.F. leader Jim Phelps (replacing the original lead, Steven Hill), in the high-tech adventure series *Mission: Impossible.*

After that series' long run, Graves was seen mostly in TV movies and miniseries playing a prematurely silver-haired but still quite handsome hero and, sometimes, lover.

GRAVES, TERESA—black actress, singer
b: Jan 10, 1949, Houston, Texas, r: Los Angeles, Calif.

Turn-On (var).............. regular (1969)
Rowan & Martin's Laugh-In (var)
.... regular (1969–70)
The Funny Side (var)....... regular (1971)
Get Christie Love (police)
.... Det. Christie Love (1974–75)

A former member of The Doodletown Pipers singing group, with whom she appeared on the 1967 summer series *Our Place* and in other network appearances.

GRAVITTE, BEAU—actor
Trapper John, M.D. (drama)
.... Dr. Andy Pagano (1985–86)

GRAY, ALEXANDER—singer, actor
b: Jan 8, 1902, Wrightsville, Pa. d: Oct 4, 1976

This Is Music (music)....... host (1951–52)

GRAY, BARRY—host, announcer
Songs for Sale (music)...... panelist (1952)

GRAY, BILLY—actor
b: Jan 13, 1938, Los Angeles, Calif.

Father Knows Best (com)
..... James (Bud) Anderson, Jr. (1954–60)

Billy Gray is one child actor for whom adulthood proved a bitter pill. Born into show business (his mother Beatrice was a minor film actress in the '30s), Billy began playing bit parts at the age of six and was in several movies during the late '40s and early '50s. He also did some early television dramas. The role for which he will always be known—the idealized teenager "Bud" on *Father Knows Best*—came in 1954.

Billy looks back on those days with undisguised resentment. Despite the warmth projected by the show's "perfect American family," he feels that he was shortchanged in his education by the studio schools, ignored by the producers when he protested the "golly-gee-whiz" nature of his character, and denied the opportunity to try meatier outside roles. (He could, he says, have had a part in *Rebel Without a Cause* if they had given him a few weeks off from the TV filming.)

Things got worse after *Father Knows Best* left the air. For about a year (1960–61) Billy made guest appearances on series such as *General Electric Theater* and *The Deputy.* Then, in early 1962, he was stopped for drunken driving, and the officers found a quantity of marijuana in his car. Billy was sentenced to three months in jail and three years probation, amid a great deal of publicity. His "wholesome" image shot, the young actor could find practically no work at all. He settled down on the outskirts of L.A. (literally and figuratively), living with a woman for a time, and married twice. For several years he traveled the West Coast racing circuit as a motorcycle racer. Occasional attempts to get back into acting were to no avail, though he did appear, ironically, on the 1979 *Father Knows Best* reunion special.

Mention of his famous role still makes Billy wince. "I'm so ashamed that I had any part in all that," he said in the '70s. "I wish there was some way I could tell kids not to believe it—the dialogue, the situations, the characters; they were all totally false."

GRAY, CHARLES—actor
b: Aug 29, 1928, Bournemouth, England

Gunslinger (wes)...... Pico McGuire (1961)
Rawhide (wes).... Clay Forrester (1962–63)

GRAY, CHARLIE—
Marie (var).............. regular (1980–81)

GRAY, COLEEN—actress
b: Oct 23, 1922, Staplehurst, Neb.

Window on Main Street (com)
.... Miss Wycliffe (1961–62)

GRAY, DOLORES—singer, actress
b: Jun 7, 1924, Chicago, Ill. r: Los Angeles, Calif.

Buick Circus Hour (drama)
.... Kim O'Neill (1952–53)

GRAY, DONALD—actor
b: 1914, Cape Province, South Africa d: 1978

The Vise/Saber of London (drama)
.... Mark Saber (1955–60)

English actor who lost an arm in World War II but who nevertheless pursued an acting career and an active, athletic life. He was one of the few one-armed actors to star in a TV series and probably the only one to play a hero. Another famous one-armed actor, Bill Raisch of *The Fugitive*, played a killer.

GRAY, ERIN—actress
b: Jan 7, 1952, Honolulu, Hawaii

Buck Rogers in the 25th Century (sci fi)
.... Col. Wilma Deering (1979–81)
Silver Spoons (com)
.... Kate Summers Stratton (1982–86)

GRAY, LINDA—actress
b: Sep 12, 1940, Santa Monica, Calif.

All That Glitters (com)
.... Linda Murkland (1977)
Dallas (drama).. Sue Ellen Ewing (1978–)

GRAY, MICHAEL—juvenile actor
b: Sept 2 ,1951, Chicago, Ill. r: Miami Fla.

The Brian Keith Show (com)
.... Ronnie (1972–73)

GRAY, ROBERT—actor

Harper Valley P.T.A. (com)
.... Cliff Willoughby (1981)

GRAYCO, HELEN—singer
b: c. 1924, Tacoma, Wash.

The Spike Jones Show (var).. regular (1954)
The Spike Jones Show (var).. regular (1957)
Club Oasis (var) .... regular (1958)
The Spike Jones Show (var)
.... regular (1960–61)

This pleasant singer, said a press release, "survived years of practically living amidst sirens, gunshots, steam whistles and pneumatic drills." That's what you get, Helen, for having married lunatic bandleader Spike Jones.

GRAZIANO, ROCKY—boxer, actor
b: Dec 31, 1921, New York City, N.Y.

Pantomime Quiz (quiz)
.... regular (1954–56)
The Henny and Rocky Show (var)
.... cohost (1955)
The Martha Raye Show (var)
.... regular (1955–56)
Miami Undercover (drama)
.... Rocky (1961)
The Keefe Brasselle Show (var)
.... regular (1963)

Rocky, the tough-talking World Middleweight Champion in the late 1940s, became something of a novelty attraction on television in the '50s. "I get a real belt out of this racket," he said in 1955, "where I get paid because people laugh instead of stand up and scream for me to belt somebody." The Rock had a great sense of humor and was a natural on camera. "They won't let me take acting lessons," he said. "One day I walked into a rehearsal and told Martha (Raye) I was going to take lessons. You know what she told me? She said, 'You take one acting lesson and you're out of a job!' "

Rocky's life story, from tough inner-city kid to the World Boxing Champ, was dramatized in the 1956 film *Somebody Up There Likes Me,* which was based on his best-selling 1955 autobiography. He later wrote *Somebody Down Here Likes Me Too* (1981).

GREAZA, WALTER—actor
b: Jan 1, 1897, St. Paul, Minn. d: 1973

Treasury Men in Action (drama)
.... the chief (1950–55)
Martin Kane, Private Eye (drama)
.... Capt. Leonard (1951)

Pronounced "Grizz-ay." After a long career as a crimefighter on radio and television, Greaza had an almost equally long run as Grandfather Grimsley on daytime's *The Edge of Night* (1956–73).

GRECCO, CYNDI—singer

Laverne & Shirley (com)
.... sang theme (1976–83)

GRECO, BUDDY—singer, pianist
b: Aug 14, 1926, Philadelphia, Pa.

Broadway Open House (talk)
.... regular (1951)
Songs at Twilight (music) .... host (1951)
Away We Go (var) .... regular (1967)

GREEN, BERNIE—orchestra leader
b: Sep 14, 1908, New York City, N.Y. d: Aug 8, 1975

Holiday Hotel (var)
.... orch. leader (1950–51)
Henry Morgan's Great Talent Hunt (var)
.... orch. leader (1951)
Sid Caesar Invites You (var)
.... orch. leader (1958)
Arthur Godfrey and His Friends (var)
.... orch. leader (1958–59)
The Garry Moore Show (var)
.... orch. leader (1966–67)

GREEN, DOROTHY—actress
b: Jan 12, Los Angeles, Calif.

Tammy (com) .... Lavinia Tate (1965–66)

GREEN, JOHN—actor

The Black Robe (aud par)
.... police officer (1949–50)

GREEN, LYNDA MASON—actress

Night Heat (police)
.... Det. Fleece Toland (1985)

GREEN, MILT, TRIO—

The Alan Dale Show (music)
.... regulars (1950–51)

GREEN, MITZI—actress
b: Oct 22, 1920, New York City, N.Y. d: May 24, 1969

So This Is Hollywood (com)
.... Queenie Dugan (1955)

Hollywood child star of the 1930s (*Little Orphan Annie,* etc.) who here played a movie stuntwoman who knew her way around Tinsel Town.

GREENBUSH, LINDSAY AND SIDNEY— twins
b: May 25, 1970, Los Angeles, Calif.

Little House on the Prairie (adv)
.... Carrie Ingalls (1974–82)

Lindsay and Sidney are twins who alternated in the role of little Carrie on *Little House.*

GREENE, BILLY—actor
b: Jan 6, 1897 d: Aug 24, 1973

One Man's Family (drama)
.... Burton (1951–52)

GREENE, DANIEL—actor

Falcon Crest (drama)
.... Dwayne Cooley (1985–)

GREENE, KAREN—actress

The Eve Arden Show (com)
.... Mary (1957–58)

GREENE, KIM MORGAN—actress

Dynasty II: The Colbys (drama)
.... Channing Carter (1986–)

GREENE, LAURA—actress
b: Cleveland, Ohio

Comedy Tonight (var) .... regular (1970)

GREENE, LORNE—actor
b: Feb 12, 1915, Ottawa, Canada

Sailor of Fortune (adv)
..... Capt. Grant "Mitch" Mitchell (1957)
Bonanza (wes) ... Ben Cartwright (1959–73)
Griff (drama) .... Wade Griffin (1973–74)
Lorne Greene's Last of the Wild (doc)
.... host/narrator (1974–79)
Roots (drama) .... John Reynolds (1977)
Battlestar Galactica (sci fi)
.... Cmdr. Adama (1978–80)
Code Red (adv)
.... Battalion Chief Joe Rorchek (1981–82)

To kids in the '80s he was the stoic, firm-handed commander of an intergalactic starship; to young viewers in the '60s he was the father figure on the long-running, enormously popular western *Bonanza;* and 20 years before *that* he was the radio "Voice of Canada," reassuring his countrymen during the dark days of World War II. Lorne Greene, a solidly built actor with a deep, commanding voice, has spent most of his career as the "man in charge."

As a young man, Lorne studied chemical engineering, with acting only a sideline, but soon the theater began to dominate his interests. Upon graduation from college he came to the U.S. to seek his fortune. He didn't find it that trip and so returned to Canada where, acting jobs being scarce, he decided to use his authoritative voice on radio. Within a short time he rose to become the chief announcer for the Canadian Broadcasting Corporation and was known across that land.

Acting was never out of his mind, however. He established the Academy of Radio Arts and the Jupiter Theatre in 1946, each to serve as a training ground for young Canadian talent. Then, on a trip to New York in the early '50s to demonstrate a special stopwatch he had invented (it ran backward, so a radio director would know how much time was left), he had a chance encounter with a producer-friend. That led to a role on *Studio One*. More TV work in the U.S. followed, along with films and stage plays. In the mid and late 1950s Lorne was seen on such series as *Climax, Star Stage, You Are There* ("The Torment of Beethoven") and *Alfred Hitchcock Presents* (as the murderous "Mr. X"). He also starred as a freighter captain in the Canadian-produced adventure series *Sailor of Fortune*. Then a guest role on *Wagon Train* in early 1959 caught the eye of producer David Dortort, who was casting *Bonanza* for NBC. The rest, as they say, is history.

Bonanza occupied Lorne for the next 14 years to the exclusion of almost everything else. When it finally left the air in 1973 he tried his hand at a police show, *Griff*, which was not successful, and then settled down to a more leisurely schedule of TV movies and miniseries (e.g., *The Moneychangers, Roots*). His *Last of the Wild* nature documentary allowed him to use that famous voice with a minimum of on-screen work. In the late '70s and early '80s he was back in series TV, with *Battlestar Galactica* (a *Star Wars* clone) and *Code Red* ("Lorne Green with fire trucks"), but neither did very well. After that, as he entered his 70s, his appearances became less frequent.

GREENE, LYNNIE—actress
b: May 21, Boston, Mass. r: Newton, Mass.

On Our Own (com)
.... Maria Teresa Bonino (1977–78)

GREENE, MARGE—actress
b: Scotland r: U.S.A.

Marge and Jeff (com) ...... Marge (1953–54)

GREENE, MAXINE—
Turn-On (var).............. regular (1969)

GREENE, MICHELE—actress
b: Feb 3, Las Vegas, Nev.

Dorothy (com) .... Margo (1979)
Bay City Blues (drama)
.... Judy Nuckles (1983)
L.A. Law (drama) .. Abby Perkins (1986–)

GREENE, MIKE—actor
The Dakotas (wes)
.... Dep. Vance Porter (1963)

GREENE, MORT—panelist
Where Was I? (quiz) .... panelist (1953)

GREENE, RICHARD—actor
b: Aug 25, 1918, Plymouth, England d: Jun 1, 1985

The Adventures of Robin Hood (adv)
.... Robin Hood (1955–58)

This boyishly handsome romantic star of the late '30s and '40s appeared in a few TV playhouse productions in the early '50s, then returned to his native England to film *The Adventures of Robin Hood*, which was quite successful on CBS. It revived his fortunes, in fact, allowing him to retire to a large estate in Ireland, where he bred thoroughbreds. He did little TV or movie work afterward.

GREENE, SHECKY—comedian, actor
b: Apr 8, 1925, Chicago, Ill.

Combat (drama)... Pvt. Braddock (1962–63)

GREENE, SID—writer, comedian
Kraft Music Hall Presents The Dave King Show (var)................. regular (1959)

GREENER, DOROTHY—

Holiday Hotel (var) .... regular (1951)

GREENLEE, DAVID—actor

Fame (drama)........... Dwight (1982–85)

GREENWALD, KEN—actor

Turn-On (var).............. regular (1969)

GREENWOOD, BRUCE—actor
b: Vancouver, B.C., Canada

Legmen (drama).......... Jack Gage (1984)
St. Elsewhere (drama)
.... Dr. Seth Griffin (1986–)

GREER, BRODIE—actor

CHiPs (police) ...... Off. Baricza (1977–82)

GREER, DABBS—actor
b: Apr 2, 1917, Fairview, Mo. r: Anderson, Mo.

Gunsmoke (wes) .... Mr. Jones (1955–60)
Hank (com)......... Ossie Weiss (1965–66)
Little House on the Prairie (adv)
.... Rev. Robert Alden (1974–83)

GREER, MICHAEL—actor
b: Dec 16, 1938, Durham, N.C.

The Bobbie Gentry Show (var)
.... regular (1974)

GREGG, JULIE—actress

Banyon (drama)... Abby Graham (1972–73)
Mobile One (adv) ... Maggie Spencer (1975)

GREGG, VIRGINIA—actress
b: c. 1917 d: Sep 15, 1986

Calvin and the Colonel (cartn)
.... Maggie Belle (voice) (1961–62)
Little Women (drama) ...... Hannah (1979)

GREGORY, BENJI—juvenile actor
b: May 26, 1978, Encino, Calif.

Alf (com) .... Brian Tanner (1986–)

GREGORY, FRAN—actress

The Robbins Nest (var) ...... regular (1950)

GREGORY, JAMES—actor
b: Dec 23, 1911, The Bronx, N.Y. r: New Rochelle, N.Y.

The Lawless Years (police)
.... Barney Ruditsky (1959–61)
The Paul Lynde Show (com)
.... T. R. Scott (1972–73)
Barney Miller (com)
.... Inspector Luger (1975–82)
Detective School (com)
.... Nick Hannigan (1979)

Gregory, the irritable Inspector Luger on *Barney Miller,* is a veteran character actor, having appeared on the New York stage since the late '30s and in films since 1948. He was a frequent, if minor, player in live TV dramas of the '50s (*Studio One,* etc.) and was seen as a tough old bird in many action series of the '60s (*Bonanza, The Big Valley, Ironside*). He turned to comedy—playing a lovable old bird—in the '70s.

GREGORY, MARY—

The Wacky World of Jonathan Winters (var)
.... regular (1972–74)

GREGSON, JACK—host, sportscaster

Auction-Aire (aud par)..... emcee (1949–50)
Saturday Night Fights (sport)
.... sportscaster (1953–55)

GREGSON, JOHN—actor
b: Mar 15, 1919, Liverpool, England d: Jan 8, 1975

Gideon, C.I.D. (police)
.... Cmdr. George Gideon (1966)
Shirley's World (com)
.... Dennis Croft (1971–72)

GRENROCK, JOSHUA—actor

The Waverly Wonders (com)
.... Tony Faguzzi (1978)

GRICE, WAYNE—black actor

Hawk (police)....... Det. Dan Carter (1966)

GRIER, DAVID ALAN—actor

All Is Forgiven (com)
.... Oliver Royce (1986)

GRIER, ROOSEVELT—black actor

b: Jul 14, 1932, Cuthbert, Ga.

Daniel Boone (wes)
.... Gabe Cooper (1969–70)
Make Room for Granddaddy (com)
.... Rosey Robbins (1970–71)
Movin' On (adv) .... Moose (1975–76)
Roots: The Next Generations (drama)
.... Big Slew Johnson (1979)

Rosy Grier was one of many professional athletes to make the transition into acting, but, given his ox-like build (300 pounds), perhaps one of the less likely. From 1955 until the late '60s he was a fearsome bulldozer on the gridiron for the New York Giants and later the Los Angeles Rams. Always interested in music (during his rookie days he woke the team in the morning with a song on his electric guitar), he began his own show in Los Angeles in 1968, which showcased his musical talents. The following year he was signed to play the runaway-slave-turned-Indian-chief on *Daniel Boone*. During the rest of the '70s he had roles on numerous crime and comedy series, including appearances on *Quincy, M.E. CHiPs,* and *The Love Boat*. In 1981 Rosy was one of the leads in the miniseries *Sophisticated Gents,* about a black athletic/social club whose twenty-fifth anniversary reunion is marred by murder.

GRIFFETH, SIMONE—actress

b: Apr 14, Savannah, Ga.

Ladies' Man (com) ..... Gretchen (1980–81)
Bret Maverick (wes)
.... Jasmine DuBois (1982)
Amanda's (com)... Arlene Cartwright (1983)

GRIFFIN, MERV—host

b: Jul 6, 1925, San Mateo, Calif.

The Freddy Martin Show (var)
.... vocalist (1951)
Summer Holiday (music)..... regular (1954)
Keep Talking (quiz) .... emcee (1959–60)
Play Your Hunch (quiz)....... emcee (1960)
Play Your Hunch (quiz)....... emcee (1962)
Talent Scouts (talent).......... host (1963)
The Merv Griffin Show (talk)
.... host (1965–86)

Emmy Awards: Best Writing for a Daytime Talk Show, for *The Merv Griffin Show* (1974); Best Host on a Variety Series, for *The Merv Griffin Show* (1982, 1984)

Merv Griffin is one of those performer/tycoons who, like Dick Clark, seems to be happier swinging deals behind the camera than performing in front of it. On-camera he is easygoing to the point of being bland —in fact, he *looks* like a businessman. Even his wife once described him as "the staff of life, sort of like whole-wheat toast." Nevertheless, he has had remarkable success as a performer.

Merv's first career, like that of fellow talk-show host Mike Douglas, was in music. He sang on radio in his native San Francisco in the late '40s and in 1948 landed a job as a vocalist with Freddy Martin, then one of the top bandleaders in the country. The following year Martin had Merv record, in a fake Cockney accent, a bouncy novelty tune called "I've Got a Lovely Bunch of Coconuts," which became a major hit. (Merv later said of this record, "That thing embarrasses me. What talent did *that* take? I was all gimmicked up, phony, fake.") The young singer appeared with Martin on the latter's network series in 1951 and then went out on his own on an assortment of daytime and nighttime series, including CBS's *Summer Holiday, Morning Show,* and *The Robert Q. Lewis Show*. He also tried his hand at acting, making four films between 1952–54, the most successful being *So This Is Love* with Kathryn Grayson. However, for Merv, acting did not hold much promise.

Merv's last musical show was in 1960, an abortive copy of *American Bandstand* called *Saturday Prom*. Rock-era teenagers were not interested in dancing to businessman Merv and the Si Zentner big band, so the amiable host, taking a hint, decided to give game shows a try. He appeared in several and then began to develop them for others. In the years since, Merv has made an enormous amount of money in this field; among other things, he created *Jeopardy* and *Wheel of Fortune* and continues to reap the financial rewards as these two giant hits continue into the '80s.

Merv next got into the talk-show field, which was booming in the '60s, as a substitute host on *The Tonight Show*. He had a daytime chatter show on NBC in 1962–63, which was not successful, then began a syndicated talk show in 1965 which did so well that CBS picked it up in 1969 to compete with Johnny Carson. Running opposite the King of Late Night had proven too much for several other pretenders to the throne, and so it was for Merv. He returned to syndication in 1972 and his show, run mostly in the afternoon and early evening, remained quite successful in that form.

TV Guide once asked Merv how he would explain his success. "I don't know and I don't care what makes me tick," he blandly replied. "I'm not self-analytical. I'm emotionally secure and happy." A longtime associate shed a little more light on the subject: "Merv's always been a promoter, a con man. But not offensively so. He's just a nice, happy guy getting what he wants."

Next guest!

GRIFFIN, TODD—actor

Operation Neptune (sci fi)
.... Cmdr. Bill Hollister (1953)

GRIFFIS, WILLIAM—actor

The Witness (drama)
.... Court Clerk (1960–61)

GRIFFITH, ANDY—actor

b: Jun 1, 1926, Mount Airy, N.C.

The Andy Griffith Show (com)
.... Andy Taylor (1960–68)
The Headmaster (drama)
.... Andy Thompson (1970–71)
The New Andy Griffith Show (com)
.... Andy Sawyer (1971)
Centennial (drama).. Lew Vernor (1978–79)
Salvage 1 (adv) .... Harry Broderick (1979)
Matlock (drama)
.... Benjamin Matlock (1986–)

Andy Griffith's image was well established in the '50s and '60s as that of an easygoing, folksy Southerner who, despite his slow drawl, was pretty cagey. It is an image that has followed him through practically every role he has ever played.

Andy originally studied to be a preacher, then taught for a time before becoming an actor/monologuist on the East Coast theater circuit in the late '40s. For several years he played Sir Walter Raleigh in the annual Virginia pageant *The Lost Colony*. He first attracted national attention in 1954 with a comedy record called "What It Was—Was Football," a rustic's wide-eyed description of his first game. A year later Andy made his TV acting debut in another rural characterization, that of the bucolic recruit in *The U.S. Steel Hour* production *No Time for Sergeants*. This play proved to be his first major vehicle—it later became a hit on Broadway (1955) and then a movie (1958), both starring Griffith. Still later, without him, it became a TV series (1964).

After several more TV playhouse appearances and another Broadway play, *Destry Rides Again* in 1959, Andy began the role that would make him a superstar. *The Andy Griffith Show,* set in rural Mayberry, North Carolina, was about as comfortable and down-home a series TV has ever seen, and it was an enormous hit. It was, in fact, one of only two series in TV history to end its run while still ranking number-one in the ratings (the other was *I Love Lucy*); by 1968, Andy had decided to move on to meatier stuff.

Andy attempted another series in 1970, as the head of a private school, but the public did not take to him in this more dramatic setting and he reverted to a Mayberry clone *(The New Andy Griffith Show)* for the balance of the season. For the rest of the '70s he was seen mostly in TV movies and miniseries, where he could essay harder-edged roles (e.g., *Washington Behind Closed Doors, Centennial, Roots: The Next Generations)*. For some reason he agreed to star in a flimsy adventure series in 1979 *(Salvage I,* about a junk dealer who built outer-space rockets), but this was short-lived.

In the '80s Andy turned increasingly to murder mysteries *(Murder in Texas, Fatal Vision),* where his Southern drawl could signify either a slippery villian or, more often, the dogged, homespun hero (as in *Matlock*). Perhaps he will one day find the series he is really looking for. Could it be called *Escape from Mayberry?*

GRIFFITH, JAMES—actor

b: Feb 13, 1916*, Los Angeles, Calif.

The Sheriff of Cochise (police)
.... Dep. Tom Ferguson (1959–60)

*Some sources give 1919.

GRIFFITH, MELANIE—actress
b: Aug 9, 1957, New York City, N.Y.

Once an Eagle (drama)
.... Jinny Massengale (1976–77)
Carter Country (com)
.... Tracy Quinn (1978–79)

The daughter of film actress Tippi Hedren.

GRIGGS, JOHN—actor
b: c. 1909 d: Feb 25, 1967

The Singing Lady (child).. announcer (1950)
The Joey Bishop Show (com)
.... J. P. Willoughby (1961–62)

GRIMES, JACK—actor

The Aldrich Family (com)
.... Homer Brown (1952–53)
On the Rocks (com) ...... Baxter (1975–76)

GRIMES, SCOTT—juvenile actor
b: Jul 9, 1971, Lowell, Mass r: Dracut, Mass.

Together We Stand (com)
.... Jack Randall (1986–)

GRIMES, TAMMY—actress
b: Jan 30, 1934, Lynn, Mass.

The Tammy Grimes Show (com)
.... Tammy Ward (1966)

GRIMM, PAUL—

The Big Show (var)......... regular (1980)

GRINNAGE, JACK—actor

The Bob Newhart Show (var)
.... regular (1961)
Kolchak: The Night Stalker (drama)
.... Ron Updyke (1974–75)

GROH, DAVID—actor
b: May 21, 1939, Brooklyn, N.Y.

Rhoda (com)........ Joe Gerard (1974–77)
Another Day (com).... Don Gardner (1978)

GROOM, SAM—actor

Our Private World (drama)
.... Tom Eldredge (1965)
Dr. Simon Locke (drama)
.... Dr. Simon Locke (1971–74)
Otherworld (sci fi)...... Hal Sterling (1985)

GROSS, DR. MASON—professor
b: Jun 3, 1911 d: Oct 11, 1977

Think Fast (quiz)...... moderator (1949–50)
Two for the Money (quiz)
.... question authority (1952–57)

Provost and professor of philosophy at
Rutgers University.

GROSS, MARY—comedienne
b: Mar 25, 1953, Chicago, Ill.

NBC's Saturday Night Live (com)
.... regular (1981–85)

GROSS, MICHAEL—actor
b: Jun 21, 1947, Chicago, Ill.

Family Ties (com)... Steve Keaton (1982–)

Michael and Mary are brother and sister.

GROUP, MITCHELL—actor

Mama Malone (com) .... Harry (1984)

GROVE, BETTY ANN—singer
b: c. 1928, Boston, Mass.

Stop the Music (quiz).... vocalist (1949–52)
The Red Buttons Show (var)
.... regular (1953–54)
Summer Holiday (music)..... regular (1954)
Stop the Music (quiz).... vocalist (1954–55)
Circus Time (var) .... regular (1957)

GROVER, CINDY—actress

Married: The First Year (drama)
.... Joanna Huffman Baker (1979)

GROVER, DEBORAH—actress

Night Heat (police)
.... D.A. Elaine Jeffers (1985–)

GROVER, EDWARD—actor

Baretta (police) . Lt. Hal Brubaker (1975–78)

GROVER, MARY—actress

Love, American Style (com)
.... repertory player (1969–70)

GROVER, STANLEY—actor

That Was the Week That Was (com)
.... regular (1964)

Married: The First Year (drama)
.... Bert Baker (1979)

GROVES, REGINA—actress
b: c. 1944, Boston, Mass.

Our Man Higgins (com)
.... Joanie MacRoberts (1962–63)

GRUBBS, GARY—actor
b: Nov 14, 1949, Amory, Miss.

For Love and Honor (drama)
.... Capt. Stephen Wiecek (1983)
Half Nelson (drama)..... Det. Hamill (1985)

GRULIOW, LEO—journalist
Through the Curtain (pub aff)
.... regular (1953–54)

The editor of *The Current Digest of the Soviet Press.*

GRUSIN, DAVE—orchestra leader, composer
The Andy Williams Show (var)
.... orch. leader (1963–66)

GUARDINO, HARRY—actor
b: Dec 23, 1925*, New York City, N.Y.

The Reporter (drama)
.... Danny Taylor (1964)
Monty Nash (adv)...... Monty Nash (1971)
Perry Mason (revival) (drama)
.... Hamilton Burger (1973–74)

Guardino is one of those very familiar TV faces who has managed to remain virtually unknown by name, despite years of exposure. A tough-talking, worried-looking big city type, he has appeared in hundreds of dramas, from *Kraft Theatre* and *Naked City* in the '50s to *Police Story* (often), *Kojak*, and *Barnaby Jones* in the '70s and '80s. The two series in which he starred are among the most obscure in television history: *The Reporter*, which ran for a few months in 1964, and the syndicated *Monty Nash* (about a government investigator), which was hardly seen at all. As for the 1973 revival of *Perry Mason*, did you remember that it *had* been revived?

At least he works steadily.

*Some sources give Dec. 22.

GUARDINO, JEROME—actor
Car 54, Where Are You? (com)
.... Off. Antonnucci (1961–62)

GUARNIERI, JOHNNY—jazz pianist, orchestra leader
b: Mar 23, 1917, New York City, N.Y. d: Jan 7, 1985

The Gulf Road Show Starring Bob Smith (var)
.... orch. leader (1948–49)
The Morey Amsterdam Show (var)
.... orch. leader (1948–50)
Tonight! America After Dark (talk)
.... quartet (1957)

GUDEGAST, HANS—actor
b: Kiel, Germany

The Rat Patrol (adv)
. Capt. Hauptman Hans Dietrich (1966–68)

Hans later changed his name to Eric Braeden, under which he now appears. He was a regular on the daytime soap opera *The Young and The Restless* in the 1980s.

GUERCIO, JOE—orchestra leader
The Steve Lawrence Show (var)
.... orch. leader (1965)

GUEST, CHRISTOPHER—writer, comedian
b: Feb 5, 1948, New York City, N.Y.

NBC's Saturday Night Live (com)
.... regular (1984–85)

Emmy Award: Best Writing for a Comedy Special, for *Lily Tomlin* (1976)

GUEST, LANCE—actor
b: Jul 21, 1960, Saratoga, Calif.

Lou Grant (drama) .... Lance (1981–82)

GUEST, NICHOLAS—actor
Fathers and Sons (com)
.... Dr. Richard Bolen (1986)

GUEST, WILLIAM—black singer
b: Jun 2, 1941 r: Atlanta, Ga.

The Gladys Knight & The Pips Show (var)
.... regular (1975)

A member of The Pips.

GUFFEY, CARY—juvenile actor

Chiefs (drama)
.... Billy Lee (as a child) (1983)

GUILBERT, ANN MORGAN—actress
b: c. 1928, Minneapolis, Minn.

The Dick Van Dyke Show (com)
.... Millie Helper (1961–66)
The New Andy Griffith Show (com)
.... Nora (1971)

GUILD, NANCY—actress
b: Oct 11, 1925, Los Angeles, Calif.

Where Was I? (quiz) .... panelist (1952–53)

GUILLAUME, ROBERT—black actor
b: Nov 30, 1927, St. Louis, Mo.

Soap (com) .... Benson (1977–79)
Benson (com) ..... Benson DuBois (1979–86)
North and South (drama)
.... Frederick Douglass (1985)

Emmy Award: Best Supporting Actor in a Comedy Series, for *Soap* (1979); Best Actor in a Comedy Series, for *Benson* (1985)

Though it might not be apparent from his rather whiny comic delivery, Robert Guillaume has a fine singing voice and in fact began his career on the musical stage. While in college he won a scholarship to a musical festival in Aspen, Colorado, then studied opera and musical theater in Cleveland. His debut as Billy Bigelow in *Carousel* was a rousing success (applauded by none other than Oscar Hammerstein), and the young singer made his way to New York, where he served a long apprenticeship in the '60s and '70s in musicals including *Porgy and Bess, Purlie* and *Guys and Dolls* (as Nathan Detroit).

Guillaume's TV appearances, in the '70s, did not attract much notice. Then, in 1977, he began the regular role of the insolent butler on *Soap,* which catapulted him to fame. The character was later spun off into a series of its own, in which he became a governor's aide and later the Lieutenant Governor. *Benson* ran longer than *Soap* had. Meanwhile, Guillaume branched into TV movies, appearing in three with youthful star Gary Coleman, one of which he also co-produced.

GULAGER, CLU—actor
b: Nov 16, 1928, Holdenville, Okla. r: Muskogee, Okla.

The Tall Man (wes)
.... Billy the Kid (1960–62)
The Virginian (wes)
.... Emmett Ryker (1964–68)
The Survivors (drama)
.... Sen. Mark Jennings (1969–70)
San Francisco International Airport (drama)
.... Bob Hatten (1970–71)
Once an Eagle (drama)
.... Lt. Merrick (1976–77)
The Mackenzies of Paradise Cove (adv)
.... Cuda Weber (1979)

Tough, baby-faced, former marine, on television since the '50s in numerous roles. Gulager made an early impression as "Mad Dog" Coll on *The Untouchables* in 1959, then starred in *The Tall Man* (as Billy the Kid) and *The Virginian* (as Sheriff Ryker) in the '60s. He has since appeared as a guest star in many crime dramas. He also teaches acting.

GUMBEL, BRYANT—black host, sportscaster
b: Sep 29, 1948, New Orleans, La. r: Chicago, Ill.

Games People Play (sport)
.... cohost (1980–81)

A former NBC sportscaster, Bryant made history in January 1982 when he became the first black host of a major network talk/service program, the *Today* show. The secret of his success, perhaps, is that hardly anyone talks about, or even notices, that fact.

Bryant's meteoric rise began immediately after his graduation from college in 1970. At first intending to become a sportswriter, he submitted some articles to a magazine, was promptly hired as a staff writer, and within months was made editor in chief. He moved to Los Angeles' KNBC-TV in 1972 as a sportscaster, rising there to become the station's sports director. The NBC network recognized his talent for glib commentary and quick thinking and began featuring him on its NFL pregame show in 1975. Later, he covered baseball and basketball for the network and cohosted a bit of prime time fluff called *Games People Play* (in which participants competed in such "sports" as bellyflopping, backward motor racing and a "Disc Jockey Invitational Talk-Off"). Beginning in 1985 he also hosted a series of afternoon newsmagazine specials for young people called *Main Street*.

Bryant has not covered sports since beginning his *Today* assignment. Instead, NBC has concentrated on establishing his credibility as an interviewer of national and international political figures. By most accounts, he is doing extremely well in his new role.

GUNN, MOSES—black actor
b: Oct 2, 1929, St. Louis, Mo.

The Cowboys (wes)
. . . . Jebediah Nightlinger (1974)
Roots (drama). . . . . Kintango (1977)
Good Times (com). . . . . . . Carl Dixon (1977)
The Contender (drama)
. . . . George Beifus (1980)
Father Murphy (drama)
. . . . Moses Gage (1981–82)

GUNTHER, JOHN—author, host
b: Aug 30, 1901, Chicago, Ill. d: May 29, 1970

John Gunther's High Road (doc)
. . . . host (1959–60)

GUNTON, BOB—actor

Comedy Zone (com) . . . . regular (1984)

GUTTENBERG, STEVE—actor
b: Aug 24, 1958, Brooklyn, N.Y.

Billy (com). . . . . Billy Fisher (1979)
No Soap, Radio (com) . . . . Roger (1982)

GUZALDO, JOSEPH—actor
b: Apr 29, c. 1960, Chicago, Ill.

Stir Crazy (adv). . Skip Harrington (1985–86)

GWINN, BILL—host

The Bill Gwinn Show (quiz)
. . . . emcee (1951–52)

GWINN, WILLIAM—actor

Accused (drama)
. . presiding judge (occasionally) (1958–59)

A former law professor who decided to ply his trade on television; he later appeared as the judge on ABC's daytime series *Morning Court.*

GWYNNE, FRED—actor
b: Jul 10, 1926, New York City, N.Y.

Car 54, Where Are You? (com)
. . . . Off. Francis Muldoon (1961–63)
The Munsters (com)
. . . . Herman Munster (1964–66)

Most kids of the '60s know Fred Gwynne as the "funny monster" on *The Munsters,* or as half of the slapstick cop team of Toody (short) and Muldoon (tall) on *Car 54, Where Are You?* They might not recognize him as the author and/or illustrator of several gentle children's books, including *The King Who Rained* and *Chocolate Moose For Dinner.*

The lanky (6′5″) actor began his career on Broadway shortly after graduation from Harvard in 1951. Acting was not all that remunerative, however, and Gwynne had a talent for writing, so he combined the two and worked as a copywriter for a New York advertising agency from 1954–60—while moonlighting in TV series episodes in his spare time ("I had a good boss," he says). Among these were several episodes of *The Phil Silvers Show.* Its producer, Nat Hiken, remembered Gwynne and signed him for the costarring role in his new comedy, *Car 54,* in 1961.

After his two big roles (including two years wearing a square head, plugs in his neck, and enormous elevator shoes to make him seem even bigger on *The Munsters),* Gwynne settled down to a more leisurely career of writing and doing occasional TV and film work in the late '60s and '70s. He was seen in his familiar garb in the Munsters' reunion special, *The Munsters' Revenge,* in 1981.

HACK, SHELLEY—actress
b: Jul 6, Greenwich, Conn.

Charlie's Angels (drama)
.... Tiffany Welles (1979–80)
Cutter to Houston (drama)
.... Dr. Beth Gilbert (1983)
Jack and Mike (drama)
.... Jackie Shea (1986–)

A blonde former model (she was on the cover of *Glamour* magazine at age 14), Shelly's first acting role was a small part in the 1977 Woody Allen movie *Annie Hall,* followed by her big break as one of the sexy "Angels" on *Charlie's Angels.* She has also decorated a number of routine TV movies, including *Death Car on the Freeway, Trackdown—Finding the Goodbar Killer* and *Singles Bars, Single Women.*

HACKER, JOSEPH—actor

Knots Landing (drama)
.... Jim Westmont (1983)
The Winds of War (drama)
.... Lt. Aster (1983)

HACKETT, BOBBY—trumpet player, orchestra leader
b: Jan 31, 1915, Providence, R.I.

The Martha Wright Show (music)
.... orch. leader (1954)
The Henny and Rocky Show (var)
.... regular (1955)
Air Time '57 (var) .... regular (1956–57)

HACKETT, BUDDY—comedian
b: Aug 31, 1924, Brooklyn, N.Y.

School House (var) .... regular (1949)
Stanley (com) ...... Stanley Peck (1956–57)
The Jackie Gleason Show (var)
.... regular (1958–59)
The Jack Paar Show (talk)
.... semiregular (1958–62)
You Bet Your Life (quiz) .... host (1980)

This chubby little guy with a sad sack face has been a popular and familiar chatterbox on talk shows and comedies since the '40s. "I'm not really a human being, I'm a cartoon," he says. "And when I say something serious, it still comes out funny." The son of a Brooklyn upholsterer, Buddy was introduced to the entertainment world as he followed his father servicing the furniture in clubs and hotels in upstate New York. He became a stand-up comic in the 1940s and served a long apprenticeship, including many appearances on early, live television (starting in 1945). His first regular series was an interesting DuMont variety show called *School House,* which featured a number of soon-to-be-famous comics as "kids." From then on he appeared mostly on variety and talk shows, though he did star for one season as a gossipy newsstand operator in his own live situation comedy, *Stanley*—which had the misfortune to be scheduled opposite *Arthur Godfrey's Talent Scouts* and was seen by hardly anyone except Buddy's immediate relatives.

In the '60s and '70s Buddy appeared occasionally in comic roles in westerns and cop shows *(Big Valley, Quincy, M.E.),* as well as in a few comedies, such as *Get Smart* and *The Lucy Show.* In 1978 he tried an unusual change of pace, portraying a famous comedian of another era, Lou Costello, in the dramatic TV movie *Bud and Lou* (with Harvey Korman as Bud Abbott).

HACKETT, JOAN—actress
b: May 1, 1942*, New York City, N.Y. d: Oct 8, 1983

The Defenders (drama)
.... Joan Miller (1961–62)
Another Day (com) .. Ginny Gardner (1978)

HADDOCK, JULIE ANNE—actress

Mulligan's Stew (drama)
.... Melinda Mulligan (1977)
The Facts of Life (com)
.... Cindy Webster (1980–82)
Boone (drama) .... Banjo (1983–84)

HADDON, LAURENCE—actor

Lou Grant (drama)
.... foreign editor (1977–80)

HADDON, RAYMOND—actor

Waterfront (adv) ..... Tom Bailey (1953–56)
*Some sources give 1933, 1934, or 1939.

369

HADLEY, NANCY—actress
b: Aug 21, 1931, Los Angeles, Calif.

The Brothers (com)..Marilee Dorf (1956–57)
Love That Jill (com) .... Melody (1958)
The Joey Bishop Show (com)
.... Barbara Simpson (1961–62)

HADLEY, REED—actor
b: 1911, Petrolia, Texas d: Dec 11, 1974

Racket Squad (police)
.... Capt. John Braddock (1950–53)
The Public Defender (drama)
.... Bart Matthews (1954–55)

A grim-faced, businesslike former B-movie actor who found fleeting fame on television in the '50s in two rather routine crime shows. Later, in the '60s, he was reduced to supporting roles in such embarrassing films as *Moro Witch Doctor* and *Brain of Blood*.

HAGEN, JEAN—actress
b: Aug 3, 1923*, Chicago, Ill. d: Aug 29, 1977

The Danny Thomas Show (com)
...... Mrs. Margaret Williams (1953–56)

Danny Thomas's first TV wife (before Marjorie Lord) was a pert young movie actress whose career never quite jelled, despite some fine performances in films like *The Asphalt Jungle* and *Singing in the Rain* (in which she played the screechy-voiced silent movie star). She was twice nominated for an Emmy Award for her role in *The Danny Thomas Show* but made little further impact after she left the series in 1956. She appeared in a scattering of TV dramas until the early '60s, when prolonged illness confined her to a nursing home for the rest of her life. Her fondest wish was to act once more, and that wish was granted. She made one final isolated appearance in the TV movie *Alexander: The Other Side of Dawn* (as the landlady) a few months before her death in 1977.

HAGEN, KEVIN—actor

Yancy Derringer (adv)
.... John Colton (1958–59)
Land of the Giants (sci fi)
.... Insp. Kobrick (1968–70)
Little House on the Prairie (adv)
.... Dr. Baker (1974–83)

*Some sources give 1924 or 1925.

HAGEN, ROSS—actor

Daktari (adv) .... Bart Jason (1968–69)

HAGER, JIM AND JON—country singers
b: Chicago, Ill.

Hee Haw (var) .... regulars (1969–)

Jim and Jon are identical twins.

HAGERTHY, RON—actor
b: 1932

Sky King (wes) .... Clipper (1953–54)

HAGGARD, MERLE—country singer
b: Apr 6, 1937, Bakersfield, Calif.

Movin' On (adv) ..... sang theme (1974–76)
Death Valley Days (wes) .... host (1975)

HAGGERTY, DAN—actor
b: Nov 19, 1941, Hollywood, Calif.

The Life and Times of Grizzly Adams (adv)
.... James "Grizzly" Adams (1977–78)

A bearded former animal trainer who won the role of "Grizzly" Adams in part because of his rapport with Ben, the huge bear who costarred in the series. He has not been seen much since, but is presumably available for further series costarring bears.

HAGGERTY, DON—actor

The Cases of Eddie Drake (drama)
.... Eddie Drake (1952)
The Files of Jeffrey Jones (drama)
.... Jeffrey Jones (1952)
The Life and Legend of Wyatt Earp (wes)
.... Marsh Murdock (1955–56)

HAGMAN, HEIDI—actress
b: Feb 17, 1958

Archie Bunker's Place (com)
.... Linda (1980–81)

The daughter of Larry Hagman.

HAGMAN, LARRY—actor
b: Sep 21, 1931, Fort Worth, Texas r: Weatherford, Texas

I Dream of Jeannie (com)
.... Capt. Tony Nelson (1965–70)

The Good Life (com)
.... Albert Miller (1971–72)
Here We Go Again (com)
.... Richard Evans (1973)
Dallas (drama)...... J. R. Ewing, Jr. (1978–)

Larry Hagman is one of those lucky actors who was rescued from becoming a TV has-been by a second big series role that was even juicier than his first. His first, of course, was that of Barbara Eden's frustrated "master" on the fondly remembered '60s comedy *I Dream of Jeannie;* the second was the quite different role of the amoral, scheming J.R. on the number-one hit of the early '80s, *Dallas.*

Larry grew up in circumstances that were somewhat similar to those of J.R.—rich, but not happy. Born the son of teen-aged Mary Martin (then only 17) and Texas lawyer Ben Hagman, he was reared by his father and later by his grandmother in California. During the period in which his mother was becoming a world-famous musical star, young Larry was shunted through 16 private schools, raising cain in many of them; he finally launched a rather shaky acting career in the New York theater in the early '50s. Among other things, he was a chorus boy in a road-company staging of his mother's hit musical *South Pacific.* Larry then enlisted in the air force for four years (1952–56), emerging in the late '50s to do more plays and appear in such TV series as *The U.S. Steel Hour, The Defenders,* and *Sea Hunt.* His first continuing role was as lawyer Ed Gibson on the daytime serial *The Edge of Night* from 1961–63; two years later he landed the leading role on a seemingly innocuous sitcom and found stardom.

I Dream of Jeannie finally established Larry as someone other than "Mary Martin's son." From 1970–78 he appeared in two more lightweight comedies, quite a few TV movies and series episodes, a failed pilot called *Detective: Bull in a China Shop* (1975), and the 1976 film *The Return of the World's Greatest Detective* (in which he played a bumbling motorcycle cop who fell off his motorcycle and thought he had become Sherlock Holmes). After such silliness it must have been a relief to land the role of the slimy J.R. He played it with such campy enthusiasm that he—and the series—became a major sensation, peaking in the phenomenal "Who shot J.R.?" story in 1980.

Larry once said of his early comedies, "They're fun roles and nobody gets hurt. How can you beat that?" Obviously, he has answered his own question.

HAGUE, ALBERT—actor, composer
b: Oct 13, 1920, Berlin, Germany

Fame (drama)
.... Mr. Benjamin Shorofsky (1982–)

A longtime Broadway composer who won a Tony Award in 1959 for the score to the musical *Redhead.*

HAGUE, STEVEN—juvenile actor

The Brian Keith Show (com)
.... Alfred Landis (1972–73)

HAGY, RUTH GERI—moderator

Junior Press Conference (int)
.... moderator (1953–54)

HAHN, ARCHIE—actor

The Odd Couple (com)..... Roger (1973–74)
Manhattan Transfer (var)
.... Doughie Duck (1975)

HAID, CHARLES—actor, producer
b: Jun 2, 1943, San Francisco r: Palo Alto, Calif.

Kate McShane (drama)
.... Ed McShane (1975)
Delvecchio (police)
.... Sgt. Paul Shonski (1976–77)
Hill Street Blues (police)
.... Off. Andy Renko (1981–)

The somewhat grumpy Officer Renko of *Hill Street Blues* has had a divided career, sometimes as a producer/director, sometimes as an actor. In the former field he was associate producer of the hit musical *Godspell* on Broadway and of the Emmy Award–winning TV documentary *Who Are the De Bolts and Where Did They Get 19 Kids?* As an actor, he has been seen on television since the early '70s. He had a role on the pilot for *Barney Miller* but turned down a chance to appear in the series, opting instead for the rather less successful *Kate McShane* (as a priest) and

Delvecchio (as Judd Hirsch's partner). His next big break almost ended prematurely, too: his character on *Hill Street Blues* was supposed to be shot and killed in the premiere episode. At the last minute the producers changed their minds and let him live.

Haid was born to a prominent Irish Catholic family in San Francisco and is a cousin of talk show host Merv Griffin.

HAIGH, KENNETH—actor
b: Mar 25, 1929, Yorkshire, England

The Search for the Nile (drama)
.... Sir Richard Burton (1972)

HAINES, LARRY—actor
b: Aug 3, Mount Vernon, N.Y.

Phyl & Mikhy (com)
.... Max Wilson (1980)

Emmy Awards: Best Actor in a Daytime Drama, for *Search for Tomorrow* (1976); Best Supporting Actor in a Daytime Drama, for *Search for Tomorrow* (1981)

Larry Haines played Stu Bergman on daytime's *Search for Tomorrow* from 1951 to 1986, one of the longest single-character runs in television history. Before that he was a prolific radio actor, appearing in a reported 15,000 live radio broadcasts, including *Gangbusters* and *Mike Hammer* (in the title role).

HAIRSTON, JESTER—black actor, composer
b: Jul 9, 1901, North Carolina

That's My Mama (com).. Wildcat (1974–75)
Amen (com)......... Rolly Forbes (1986–)

HAJE, KHRYSTYNE—actress
b: Dec 21, 1968, Santa Clara, Calif.

Head of the Class (com)
.... Simone Foster (1986–)

HAKEEM—actor

Fathers and Sons (com)
.... Brandon Russo (1986)

HALE, ALAN, JR.—actor
b: Mar 8, 1918, Los Angeles, Calif.

Biff Baker U.S.A. (adv)
.... Biff Baker (1952–53)
Casey Jones (adv)...... Casey Jones (1958)
Gilligan's Island (com)
.... Jonas Grumby (the Skipper) (1964–67)
The Good Guys (com)
.... Big Tom (1969)

This cheerful, hefty actor was the spittin' image of his father, a successful character actor from silent movie days until his death in 1950. Alan Jr. followed in his father's footsteps, playing bluff and hearty supporting roles in movies of the '40s and '50s and on television from the '50s on. He had two series starring roles in the '50s, as a globe trotting spy in *Biff Baker U.S.A.* and as the famous engineer of legend in the syndicated *Casey Jones*, but neither was successful. Of the latter he once said, "We were betwixt and between whether we should make *Casey* for adults or for kids. Apparently it showed." It attracted few viewers; even Hale admits he never saw any of the episodes.

In the mid-1960s, still toiling in obscurity, Alan finally landed the supporting role that brought him enduring fame, that of the skipper on *Gilligan's Island*. The show was idiotic, and Hale's performance a cartoon, but the series obviously struck a chord with young viewers and is still rerun today. Alan was never able to top it; he was later seen in a few more films, and, of course, in the *Gilligan* reunion specials of 1978–81. He has also run a restaurant in West Hollywood.

HALE, BARBARA—actress
b: Apr 18, 1921, DeKalb, Ill.

Perry Mason (drama)
.... Della Street (1957–66)

Emmy Award: Best Supporting Actress in a Drama, for *Perry Mason* (1959)

Barbara Hale was the very picture of the pleasant, businesslike, important man's secretary in the '50s and '60s. In this case the important man was famous sleuth Perry Mason; his series was so popular that Barbara will always be remembered as his loyal helper. Prior to *Mason*, she had appeared in movies of the '40s and '50s and on early television dramas but attracted little notice. Her career after the series ended was similarly low-key; she appeared in a few films (including *Airport* in 1970) and for 12 years was the Amana TV spokeswoman.

Barbara went into semiretirement in the mid-1970s but was seen in the '80s in a few interesting roles: on *The Greatest American Hero,* she was the mother of the hero (played by her real-life son William Katt), and in 1985's *Return of Perry Mason,* she was once again Della Street, this time in need of a lawyer herself (Perry had to defend her against a murder rap). Still, Barbara looks back on the *Perry Mason* days with fondness and occasionally sees an old episode. "I get the biggest kick out of them," she admits. "I can always tell what year they were made by how much we weighed."

Barbara has been married for many years to actor Bill Williams, TV's *Kit Carson.*

HALE, CHANIN—actress

The Red Skelton Show (var)
.... regular (1970–71)

HALE, ELVI—actress

The Six Wives of Henry VIII (drama)
.... Anne of Cleves (1971)

HALE, LEE—choral director
b: Mar 25, 1923, Tacoma, Wash.

The Entertainers (var) .... singers (1964–65)

HALE, NANCY—actress

The Whirlybirds (adv)
.... Helen Carter (1957–59)

HALELOKE—Hawaiian singer, dancer
b: Hawaii

Arthur Godfrey and His Friends (var)
.... singer (1950–55)

This shy and pretty young singer and hula dancer was spotted by Arthur Godfrey on a trip to Hawaii in 1950 and added to his show to provide a bit of exotic charm. She was so quiet and timorous that she seemed to be embarrassed if he so much as asked her a question on the air. Eventually, Arthur replaced her with Miyoshi Umeki, whereupon shy little Haleloke quietly dis-

appeared. In later years she was associated with a New York importing firm called Orchids of Hawaii. Her last name is Kahauolopua.

HALEY, JACK—actor
b: Aug 10, 1899, Boston, Mass. d: Jun 6, 1979

Ford Star Revue (var) .... host (1950–51)

HALEY, JACKIE—actor

Wait Till Your Father Gets Home (cartn)
.... Jamie Boyle (voice) (1972–74)

HALEY, JACKIE EARLE—actor
b: Jul 14, 1961, Northridge, Calif.

Breaking Away (com)... Moocher (1980–81)

HALL, ALBERT—black actor
b: Nov 10, 1937, Boothton, Ala.

Ryan's Four (drama)
.... Dr. Terry Wilson (1983)

HALL, ANTHONY MICHAEL—comedian
b: Apr 14, 1968, Boston, Mass.

NBC's Saturday Night Live (var)
.... regular (1985–86)

HALL, ARSENIO—black comic
b: Feb 12, Cleveland, Ohio

The Half Hour Comedy Hour (var)
.... host (1983)
Thicke of the Night (talk) .... regular (1984)
Motown Revue (var)........ regular (1985)

HALL, BRAD—comedian
b: Mar 21, 1958, Santa Barbara, Calif.

NBC's Saturday Night Live (com)
.... regular (1982–84)

HALL, CLIFF—actor
b: Oct 4, 1894, Brooklyn, N.Y. d: Oct 6, 1972

Crime Photographer (drama)
.... Ethelbert (1951–52)

HALL, DEIDRE—actress
b: Oct 31, 1948, Lake Worth, Fla.

Our House (drama)
.... Jesse Witherspoon (1986–)

One of the most popular actresses in daytime television during the 1980s was

373

Deidre Hall, the beautiful, understanding psychologist Dr. Marlena Evans of *Days of Our Lives*. Deidre originally began acting to pay for her education as a real-life psychologist, but her success on *The Young and the Restless* (1973–75) and then *Days of Our Lives* (beginning in 1976) convinced her to make her sideline her career.

She has worked only occasionally in other areas of television. For a year in the late '70s she was the voice of Electra-Woman on Saturday mornings and she has appeared in a few TV movies, including *The Million Dollar Face* and *A Reason to Live*. In 1986 she launched her prime time career in earnest with the costarring role in the series *Our House*.

Deidre has a twin sister, Andrea, who appeared with her for a time on *Days*.

HALL, ED—black actor
b: Jan 11, 1931, Roxbury, Mass.

Medical Center (drama)
.... Dr. Bricker (1970–74)
Baby, I'm Back (com)
.... Col. Wallace Dickey (1978)

HALL, HARRY—
Wayne King (music)...... regular (1949–52)

HALL, HUNTZ—actor
b: 1920, New York City, N.Y.

The Chicago Teddy Bears (com)
.... Dutch (1971)

Famous as the dumbest of the movie's Dead End Kids (aka Bowery Boys) from the 1930s to the '50s.

HALL, JON—actor
b: Feb 26, 1913, Fresno, Calif. d: Dec 13, 1979

Ramar of the Jungle (adv)
.... Dr. Tom Reynolds (Ramar) (1952–54)

Jon Hall made his name in the late 1930s and '40s as a handsome, often bare-chested native lover in some of Hollywood's more exotic B films, usually set either in the jungle or in Arabia. His career was declining, and his waistline expanding, by the time he latched on to the *Ramar* TV role in the early '50s. Despite wooden acting and extremely cheap production

(bits of stock footage were spliced in to simulate "location" shots), it was a hit with kids and made Hall a great deal of money. An astute businessman, he had insisted on owning a percentage of the show.

Jon's business sense served him well when his acting days were over. He owned companies that developed and leased special underwater camera equipment to moviemakers, and he ran a fleet of airplanes and a flying school. His last public appearance was in April 1979, at the premiere of the remake of his most famous movie, *Hurricane*. He had already been diagnosed as having cancer. Eight months later, in deteriorating health, he shot himself to death.

HALL, JUANITA—black actress
b: Nov 6, 1901, Keyport, N.J. d: Feb 28, 1968

Captain Billy's Mississippi Music Hall (var)
.... regular (1948)

Actress best known as Bloody Mary in the stage and screen versions of *South Pacific*. Her stint on this obscure early variety show came a few months before *South Pacific* opened on Broadway in early 1949.

HALL, KEVIN PETER—black actor
b: May 9, c. 1955, Pittsburgh, Pa.

Misfits of Science (adv)
.... Dr. Elvin "El" Lincoln (1985–86)

One of the tallest actors in prime time TV —he's 7'2". The gimmick on *Misfits of Science* was that by touching the back of his neck he could shrink to a mere six inches high. Kevin tried a career in professional sports at first, but acting and stand-up comedy (with a very short partner, of course) are his main interest. "Everyone expects me to be a basketball player," he says. "I want to prove that big guys can do *more* than play basketball."

HALL, LASAUNDRA—actress
The Best Times (drama)
.... Dionne MacAllister (1985)

HALL, MICHAEL—juvenile actor
This Is the Life (drama)
.... Pete Fisher (1952–56)

HALL, MONTY—host

b: Aug 25, 1923, Winnipeg, Canada

Cowboy Theatre (wes).......... host (1957)
Keep Talking (quiz) .... emcee (1958)
Let's Make a Deal (quiz)... emcee (1967–71)
NBC Comedy Playhouse (com) .. host (1968)

Monty is best known by far as the host of Let's Make a Deal, which he created, produced, and hosted in daytime, nighttime, and syndicated versions from 1963 to the '80s. His earlier career almost took him into children's TV, however.

Born in Canada, Monty began as a radio actor there in 1940. He produced and sometimes hosted one of Canada's more popular radio game shows, Who Am I?, for ten years before he migrated to the U.S. in 1955 in search of wider fame. He first exposure to American audiences was as substitute host for Warren Hull on daytime's Strike It Rich and briefly on another daytime quiz called The Sky's the Limit. Then, in late 1956, he was signed as host of the Saturday morning series Cowboy Theatre, a collection of edited reruns of old Charles Starrett westerns. NBC promoted Monty as an authentic cowpoke descended from Canadian ranchers and even wanted him to lead the Macy's Thanksgiving Day parade on horseback, which he refused to do (he had never ridden a horse). After a few months on Cowboy Theatre (including a run in early evening) Monty hosted the prime time comedy game show Keep Talking in 1958 and the daytime and Saturday morning children's versions of Video Village in the early '60s. Then he landed his own big deal, in 1963, as "TV's Big Dealer" on the garish Let's Make a Deal.

Deal has been Monty's main livelihood since then, although he has had short hosting stints on other quiz shows (It's Anybody's Guess, Beat the Clock) and has also produced several with his longtime partner Stefen Hajos. In 1978 Monty surprised viewers by playing a straight dramatic role in the TV movie The Courage and the Passion, a pilot for a series that never made it to the schedule. Monty's autobiography is titled Emcee: Monty Hall (1973).

HALL, RADCLIFF—sportscaster

Sportsreel (sport)...... commentator (1955)

HALL, RICH—comedian, writer

NBC's Saturday Night Live (com)
.... regular (1984–85)

Emmy Award: Best Writing, for The David Letterman Show (daytime) (1981)

HALL, SEAN TYLER—juvenile actor

The Brian Keith Show (com)
.... Stewart (1972–74)
The Mackenzies of Paradise Cove (adv)
.... Little Ben Kalikini (1979)

HALL, THURSTON—actor

b: 1882, Boston, Mass. d: Feb 20, 1958

Topper (com) .... Mr. Schuyler (1953–55)

HALL, TOM T.—country singer, songwriter

b: May 25, 1936, Olive Hill, Ky.

Pop! Goes the Country (music)
.... host (1980–82)

The writer of "Harper Valley P.T.A." and other country hits.

HALL, TONY—English TV host

Oh, Boy (music)............... host (1959)

HALL, ZOOEY—actor

The New People (drama)
.... Bob Lee (1969–70)

HALLAHAN, CHARLES—actor

The Paper Chase (drama)... Ernie (1978–79)
Hunter (police)...... Capt. Devane (1986–)

HALLARAN, SUSAN—actress

Norby (com) .... Diane Norby (1955)

HALLER, MELONIE—actress

Welcome Back, Kotter (com)
.... Angie Globagoski (1978)

HALLEY, RUDOLPH—announcer

Crime Syndicated (police)
.... narrator (1951–53)

HALLICK, TOM—actor, host

b: June 13, 1941, Buffalo, N.Y.

Search (adv) .... Harris (1973)
Entertainment Tonight (news) ... host (1981)

Daytime soap opera actor, best known as Brad Eliot on *The Young and the Restless* (1973–78).

HALLMAN, VICTORIA—

Hee Haw (var) .... regular (1980–)

HALLORAN, JACK—actor

Faraway Hill (drama) .... regular (1946)

HALOP, BILLY—actor
b: Feb 11, 1920*, New York City, N.Y. d: Nov 9, 1976

All in the Family (com)
.... Bert Munson (1972–77)

The brother of actress Florence Halop and a member of the original Dead End Kids in movies. His life was beset with trouble—alcoholism, failed marriages, illness—but he managed to overcome most of it and work sporatically in films and television, including a long-running role during his last years on *All in the Family*. When not acting, he supported himself as a male nurse. His upbeat autobiography is titled *There's No Dead End.*

HALOP, FLORENCE—actress
b: Jan 23, 1923, Queens, N.Y. d: Jul 15, 1986

Holiday Hotel (var) .... regular (1951)
Meet Millie (com)
.... "Mama" Bronson (1952–56)
St. Elsewhere (drama)
.... Mrs. Hufnagel (1984–85)
Night Court (com)
.... Florence Kleiner (1985–86)

HALPIN, LUKE—juvenile actor
b: Apr 4, Astoria, N.Y.

Flipper (adv) .... Sandy Ricks (1964–68)

HALPIN, MILES—actor

Waterfront (adv) ... Capt. Winant (1953–56)

HALSEY, BRETT—actor
b: Jun 20, 1933, Santa Ana, Calif. 1933

*Some sources give 1921 or 1922.

Follow the Sun (adv)
.... Paul Templin (1961–62)

HAMEL, VERONICA—actress
b: Nov 20, 1943, Philadelphia, Pa.

79 Park Avenue (drama)
.... Laura DeWitt Koshko (1977)
Hill Street Blues (police)
.... Joyce Davenport (1981–)

Victoria Hamel is constantly surprised by the classy image she has gained from her role as the public defender on *Hill Street Blues.* "When you're good-looking," she says of her earlier career, "not only do they think you can't act, but that you're brainless." Now fans think that since she plays a lady lawyer so convincingly, she must be one.

Hamel is in fact an intelligent and determined young woman. The daughter of a carpenter, she worked her way through college and, while still a student, started a sideline career as a model to help pay the bills. Commercial modeling lasted for ten years (you might see her smiling at you from the wrapper on a new ironing board, for example); then, after some minor stage work, she made her way to Hollywood in 1975 and began playing supporting roles in various series, including *The Bob Newhart Show, City of Angels, Starsky and Hutch,* and the miniseries *79 Park Avenue.* She turned down the chance to become one of the original angels on *Charlie's Angels,* but when given the opportunity to read for *Hill Street Blues,* she jumped at it. It has certainly given her a different image than *Charlie's Angels* would have!

HAMER, RUSTY—juvenile actor
b: Feb 15, 1947, Tenafly, N.J.

The Danny Thomas Show (com)
.... Rusty Williams (1953–64)
Make Room for Granddaddy (com)
.... Rusty Williams (1970–71)

Danny Thomas's cute young TV son of the '50s and '60s has left acting entirely. The real-life son of a shirt salesman who died when he was six, Rusty had only a little acting experience when he was picked by Thomas at open auditions in 1952. The original *Danny Thomas Show* then ran for 11 years, so Rusty was brought up on a soundstage and tutored in studio schools, a fact he regrets today as having given him an inferior education and little contact with the "real" world.

Since the show left the air in 1964, Rusty has been seen only in a short-lived 1970 revival and a later nostalgia special or two. Without much income from any of these, he worked for a time as a house painter and a messenger and at last report had settled in Louisiana, where he never mentions his background and is hardly ever recognized.

HAMILL, MARK—actor
b: Sep 25, 1951*, Oakland, Calif.

The Texas Wheelers (com)
.... Doobie Wheeler (1974–75)

Baby-faced Mark Hamill did a great deal of television work in the years before he shot to fame as Luke Skywalker in the box-office smash *Star Wars* (1977). His TV debut was on an episode of *The Bill Cosby Show* in 1970. Subsequently, he played guest roles on various prime time series, including several appearances on *Owen Marshall;* appeared in five TV movies; was a regular on the daytime soap *General Hospital* (1972–73) and the nighttime comedy *The Texas Wheelers;* and provided voices for Saturday morning cartoons. Since 1977, however, he has not looked back toward the small screen.

HAMILTON, ALEXA—actress
Hail to the Chief (com)
.... Darlene the spy (1985)

HAMILTON, ANTONY—actor
b: c. 1954, Liverpool, England r: Australia

Cover Up (drama) .... Jack Striker (1984–85)

HAMILTON, ARGUS—actor
The Richard Pryor Show (var)
.... regular (1977)

HAMILTON, BERNIE—black actor
b: Jun 12, Los Angeles, Calif.

Starsky and Hutch (police)
.... Capt. Harold Dobey (1975–79)

*Some sources give 1952 or 1953.

HAMILTON, BOB—dancer, musician
b: c. 1925, San Fransicsco, Calif.

Your Show of Shows (var)
.... dancers (1950–54)
The Chevy Showroom starring Andy Williams (var)..................... trio (1958)
The Garry Moore Show (var)
.... dancers (1966–67)

The dancing "Hamilton Trio" of the '50s consisted of Bob, Pat Horn, and Gloria Stevens.

HAMILTON, CARRIE—actress
Fame (drama)
.... Reggie Higgins (1986–)

Carrie is the daughter of Carol Burnette.

HAMILTON, GEORGE—actor
b: Aug 12, 1939, Memphis, Tenn.

The Survivors (drama)
.... Duncan Carlyle (1969–70)
Paris 7000 (adv)....... Jack Brennan (1970)
Roots (drama)...... Stephen Bennett (1977)
Dynasty (drama)
.... Joel Abrigore (1985–86)

This darkly handsome Hollywood leading man has done occasional television since he began his acting career in the late '50s, but nothing, one suspects, that is quite equal to his talents. His first two series, both in the same season, were flops: *The Survivors* was an overblown soap opera headlining Lana Turner, and *Paris 7000* a routine international intrigue series. Otherwise, George has been seen mostly in forgettable TV movies, many of them crime stories, and in occasional episodes of drama series such as *Burke's Law* and *Columbo*. Normally, he plays a suave, elegant type (villain or hero), though as his hit movie *Love at First Bite* showed, he clearly has a sense of humor about his image. One of his more unusual recent roles was in the 1985 TV movie *Two Fathers' Justice,* in which dapper George and macho Robert Conrad both got down and dirty on a mission into the jungles of South America.

HAMILTON, HENRY—host
Armstrong Circle Theatre (drama)
.... host/narrator (1962–63)

HAMILTON, JOHN—actor
b: 1887 d: Oct 15, 1958

The Adventures of Superman (adv)
.... Perry White (1951–57)

HAMILTON, LINDA—actress
b: Sep 26, Salisbury, Md.

Secrets of Midland Heights (drama)
.... Lisa Rogers (1980–81)
King's Crossing (drama)
.... Lauren Hollister (1982)

HAMILTON, LYNN—black actress
b: Apr 25, Yazoo City, Miss.

Sanford and Son (com)
.... Donna Harris (1972–77)
The Waltons (drama)
.... Verdie Foster (1972–81)
Roots: The Next Generations (drama)
.... Cousin Georgia (1979)

HAMILTON, MARGARET—actress
b: Dec 9, 1902, Cleveland, Ohio d: May 16, 1985

The Paul Winchell-Jerry Mahoney Show
(var).................... regular (1953–54)

This beak-nosed, prissy character actress
will always be remembered as the Wicked
Witch of the West in the film classic *The
Wizard of Oz* (a role she steadfastly
refused to repeat in later years for fear of
frightening children who thought the witch
was dead). She appeared fairly often on
television in the '50s in dramatic productions (*Studio One, Omnibus,* etc.) and then
did occasional comedy roles in the '60s
and '70s—on *Car 54, Where Are You?, The
Partridge Family, The Addams Family* (as
Morticia's cranky mother), etc. She was
also seen in many commercials, including
a long run as Cora the Maxwell House
Coffee lady.

HAMILTON, MURRAY—actor
b: Mar 24, 1923, Washington, N.C. d: Sep 1, 1986

Love and Marriage (com)
.... Steve Baker (1959–60)
The Man Who Never Was (drama)
.... Col. Jack Forbes (1966–67)
Rich Man, Poor Man—Book I (drama)
.... Sid Gossett (1976)
B.J. and the Bear (adv)
.... Rutherford T. Grant (1981)

Hail to the Chief (com)
.... Sen. Sam Cotton (1985)

HAMILTON, NEIL—actor
b: Sep 9, 1899, Lynn, Mass. d: Sep 24, 1984

Hollywood Screen Test (talent)
.... host (1948–53)
That Wonderful Guy (com)
.... Franklin Westbrook (1949–50)
Batman (adv)
.... Police Com. Gordon (1966–68)

HAMILTON, RAY—actor
b: Santa Fe, N.M. r: Seattle, Wash.

King of Diamonds (drama)
.... Al Casey (1961–62)

HAMILTON, RICHARD—actor

Bret Maverick (wes)
.... Cy Whittaker (1981–82)

HAMILTON, RICKI—

The Swift Show (var)........ regular (1949)

HAMLIN, HARRY—actor
b: Oct 30, 1951, Pasadena, Calif.

Studs Lonigan (drama)
.... Studs Lonigan (1979)
Master of the Game (drama)
.... Tony Blackwell (1984)
L.A. Law (drama) .. Michael Kuzak (1986–)

HAMMER, JAY—actor
b: San Francisco, Calif.

The Jeffersons (com)
.... Allan Willis (1978–79)

Also known as Charles Jay Hammer. In the
'80s he was seen in the daytime serials
Texas and *The Guiding Light.*

HAMMOND, EARL—actor

Rocky King, Inside Detective (police)
.... Sgt. Lane (1950–53)
Ad Libbers (var) .... regular (1951)

HAMMOND, JOHN—actor

The Blue and the Gray (drama)
.... John Geyser (1982)

HAMMOND, NICHOLAS—actor

The Amazing Spider-Man (adv)
...... Spider-Man/Peter Parker (1978–79)

HAMMOND, PETER—actor, director
b: Nov 15, 1923, London, England

The Buccaneers (adv)
.... Lt. Beamish (1956–57)

HAMNER, EARL, JR.—producer, writer
b: Jul 10, 1923, Schuyler, Va.

The Waltons (drama).... narrator (1972–81)

The creator and producer of *The Waltons*, which was based on his own boyhood experiences. Hamner was one of eight children, grew up in rural Virginia in the 1930s, and, like John Boy, left home to seek his fortune as a writer. Hamner, at least, found it: in addition to *The Waltons*, he created and produced the hit serial *Falcon Crest*.

HAMPTON, JAMES—actor
b: Jul 9, 1939, Oklahoma City, Okla. r: Dallas, Texas

F Troop (com)
.... bugler Hannibal Dobbs (1965–67)
The Doris Day Show (com)
.... Leroy B. Simpson (1968–69)
Love, American Style (com)
.... repertory player (1971–74)
Mary (var).................. regular (1978)
Maggie (com) .... Len Weston (1981–82)

HANCOCK, JOHN—black actor

Stop Susan Williams (drama)
.... Gold Tooth (1979)
Scruples (drama)..... Lt. Bakersmith (1980)
Hardcastle & McCormick (drama)
.... Lt. Michael Delaney (1984–85)

HANCOCK, LYNN—actress

The Nashville Palace (var)
.... regular (1981–82)

HANCOCK, PRENTIS—actor

Space 1999 (sci fi).. Paul Morrow (1975–77)

HANDLEMAN, STANLEY MYRON—comedian
b: Brooklyn, N.Y.

Dean Martin Presents the Golddiggers (var)
.... regular (1968–69)
Make Room for Granddaddy (com)
.... Henry (1970–71)

HANEY, ANNE—actress
b: Mar 4, Memphis, Tenn.

Lime Street (drama) ... Evelyn Camp (1985)

HANEY, CAROL—actress, dancer
b: 1928, New Bedford, Mass. d: May 10, 1964

Pantomime Quiz (quiz) ... regular (1955–56)

HANKBONER, SARA—

Dean Martin Presents Bobby Darin (var)
.... regular (1972)

HANKIN, LARRY—host

The Music Scene (music)
.... rotating host (1969)

HANKS, STEVE—actor
b: Aug 24, Wadsworth, Ohio

B.A.D. Cats (police)
.... Off. Ocee James (1980)

HANKS, TOM—actor
b: Jul 9, 1956, Concord, Calif.

Bosom Buddies (com)
.... Kip Wilson (Buffy) (1980–82)

HANLEY, BRIDGET—actress
b: Feb 3, 1941, Minneapolis, Minn. r: Edmonds, Wash.

The Second Hundred Years (com)
.... Nurse Lucille Anderson (1967–68)
Here Come the Brides (adv)
.... Candy Pruitt (1968–70)
How the West Was Won (miniseries) (drama)
.... Sheila (1977)
Harper Valley P.T.A. (com)
.... Wanda Reilly Taylor (1981–82)

HANLEY, PETER—actor

The Ernie Kovacs Show (var)
.... regular (1956)
Tonight (talk) .... regular (1956–57)
The Edie Adams Show (var)
.... regular (1963–64)

HANLEY, ROBERT—actor

Crazy Like a Fox (drama)
.... Lt. Walker (1985–86)

HANNA, MARK—

Guess What (quiz) .... panelist (1952)

HANNA, PHIL—singer
b: Oct 9, 1910, River Forest, Ill. d: Jul 20, 1957

Starlit Time (var) .... host (1950)
Once Upon a Tune (music)... regular (1951)

HANNAH, PAGE—actress
b: Apr 13, 1964, Chicago, Ill.

Fame (drama)......... Kate Riley (1986–)

The younger sister of film actress Daryl Hannah.

HANOLD, MARILYN—actress

The Sid Caesar Show (var)
.... regular (1963–64)

HANSARD, PAUL—actor

The Buccaneers (adv)
.... Crewman Taffy (1956–57)

HANSEN, JANIS—actress

The Rounders (com)........ Sally (1966–67)
The Odd Couple (com)
.... Gloria Unger (1971–75)

HANSEN, JUDITH—actress

St. Elsewhere (drama)
.... Dr. Emily Humes (1984–85)
Hill Street Blues (drama)
.... Celeste Patterson (1985–)

HANSEN, PETER—actor
b: Dec 5, 1921, Oakland, Calif.

Mr. Novak (drama)
.... Mr. Parkson (1964–65)

Emmy Award: Best Supporting Actor in a Daytime Drama, for *General Hospital* (1979)

Following his role in *Mr. Novak,* Hansen retired to daytime TV, where he has played Lee Baldwin on *General Hospital* since 1965.

HANSEN, TOM, DANCERS—

The Tim Conway Comedy Hour (var)
.... regulars (1970)
Your Hit Parade (music).... regulars (1974)

HANSON, MARCY—actress
b: Galveston, Texas

The Roller Girls (com)
.... Honey Bee Novak (1978)

HANSON, PETER—actor

The Adventures of Jim Bowie (wes)
.... Rezin Bowie (1956–58)

HARCUM, BOB—actor

Welcome Back, Kotter (com)
.... Murray (1978–79)

HARDEN, ERNEST, JR.—black actor
b: Nov 25, 1952, Detroit, Mich.

The Jeffersons (com)
.... Marcus Garvey (1977–79)

HARDIMAN, HILARY—actress

The Strauss Family (drama).. Annele (1973)

HARDIN, JERRY—actor

Filthy Rich (com)
.... Wild Bill Weschester (1982–83)

HARDIN, MELORA—juvenile actress
b: Jun 29, 1967, Houston, Texas r: Los Angeles

Secrets of Midland Heights (drama)
.... Micki Carroll (1980–81)
The Family Tree (drama)
.... Tess Benjamin (1983)
The Best Times (drama)
.... Joy Villafranco (1985)

The daughter of actor Jerry Hardin.

HARDIN, TY—actor
b: Jan 1, 1930, New York City, N.Y. r: Texas

Bronco (wes)...... Bronco Layne (1958–62)
Riptide (adv)........ Moss Andrews (1965)

"Try Harder," Veronica Lake once called him, when they appeared in a play together. Ty Hardin has certainly tried a lot of things in his life, not all of which kept him in show business, or even on the right side of the law.

Raised in an impoverished and broken home, Ty moved to California in the mid-1950s to take a job in engineering. His rugged good looks and charm with the ladies soon won him a contract with Paramount, which used him under his real name of Ty Hungerford in bit parts in such potboilers as *The Buccaneer* and *I Married a Monster from Outer Space* (both in 1958). Meanwhile, across town, Warner Brothers was facing a crisis; Clint Walker, the macho star of its hit series *Cheyenne,* had suddenly quit. Seeing a younger, more pliable, and equally macho actor in Hardin, Warners quickly bought his contract and put him in the *Cheyenne* series as "Bronco Layne."

Walker reconciled his differences with the studio and returned in 1959, but *Bronco* was continued as a separate series, alternating with *Sugarfoot* (and later with Walker's series) until 1962. Ty did very little television after that, though he did appear in several action B films in the early '60s and in an obscure syndicated TV series called *Riptide* (in which he played a charter boat captain). As roles became fewer he moved to Spain and began turning out cheap action films there, but even those petered out in the early '70s. Ty— then in his forties—supported himself by operating a chain of laundromats and a wild west restaurant and bar on the Costa Brava. Apparently he had other businesses going as well; in 1974 he was jailed by Spanish authorities for dealing in hashish. He was eventually fined and left the country.

Back in the America, Ty took a look at his life, got religion, and became a TV evangelist, thumping Bibles across the western U.S. By the early 1980s he had gotten out of that field, moved to Arizona, and become involved in right-wing political activities. He announced in 1984 that he was running for president on the Populist Party ticket.

Still handsome and now graying, Ty has made only rare television appearances in recent years, including one on a 1981 episode of *The Love Boat* called "First Voyage, Last Voyage." One wonders where he's headed next.

HARDING, HARVEY—pianist, singer

Musical Almanac (music).. emcee (1948–49)

HARDING, JUNE—actress
b: c. 1938, Emporia, Va.

The Richard Boone Show (drama)
.... regular (1963–64)
Matt Lincoln (drama)........ Ann (1970–71)

HARDT, ELOISE—actress

The Dennis O'Keefe Show (com)
.... Karen Hadley (1959–60)
The Winds of War (drama)
.... Mrs. LaCouture (1983)

HARDWICKE, SIR CEDRIC—actor
b: Feb 19, 1893, Stourbridge, England* d: Aug 6, 1964

Who Pays? (quiz) .... panelist (1959)
The Gertrude Berg Show (com)
.... Prof. Crayton (1961–62)

This distinguished, scholarly looking British actor appeared quite frequently on television playhouse productions of the '50s, including those of *Schlitz Playhouse of Stars, Climax, The U.S. Steel Hour,* and *Alfred Hitchcock Presents*. His 1961 autobiography is titled *A Victorian in Orbit.*

HAREWOOD, DORIAN—black actor
b: Aug 6, c. 1950, Dayton, Ohio

Roots: The Next Generations (drama)
.... Simon Haley (1979)
Strike Force (police)
.... Det. Paul Strobber (1981–82)
Trauma Center (drama)
.... Dr. Nate "Skate" Baylor (1983)
Glitter (drama)........ Earl Tobin (1984–85)

HARFORD, BETTY—actress

The Paper Chase (drama)
.... Mrs. Nottingham (1978–79)

HARGITAY, MARISKA—actress
b: Jan 23, 1964, Los Angeles, Calif.

Downtown (police) .... Jesse Smith (1986–)

The daughter of the late Jayne Mansfield and onetime Mr. Universe Mickey Hargitay.

*Some sources give Lye, England.

HARKINS, "UNCLE JIM"—comedian

That Reminds Me (talk) ..... regular (1948)

HARKINS, JOHN—actor

Doc (com) .... Fred Fenner (1975–76)

HARKNESS, RICHARD—newscaster
b: Sep 29, 1907, Artesian, S.D.

Story of the Week (int) ..... host (1948–49)

HARLAND, MICHAEL—actor

S.W.A.T. (police) . Matt Harrelson (1975–76)

HARLAND, ROBERT—actor

Target: The Corruptors (drama)
.... Jack Flood (1961–62)

HARMER, SHIRLEY—singer
b: c. 1934, Oshawa, Ont., Canada

Garroway at Large (var).. regular (1953–54)
The George Gobel Show (var)
.... regular (1957–58)

HARMON, DEBORAH—actress

The Ted Knight Show (com) .... Joy (1978)
M*A*S*H (com)... various nurses (1982–83)
Leo & Liz in Beverly Hills (com)
.... Diane Fedderson (1986)

HARMON, KELLY—actress

Bay City Blues (drama)
.... Sunny Hayward (1983)

Good-looking daughter of football great Tom Harmon. She was formerly a model.

HARMON, KRISTIN—actress

The Adventures of Ozzie & Harriet (com)
.... Kris (Mrs. Rick) Nelson (1964–66)

Kristin was at the time of her *Ozzie & Harriet* appearances the real-life wife of Rick Nelson. She later became an artist. She is the oldest daughter of Tom Harmon.

HARMON, MARK—actor
b: Sep 2, 1951, Burbank, Calif.

Sam (police) .... Off. Mike Breen (1978)
Centennial (drama)
.... John McIntosh (1978–79)

240-Robert (adv)
...... Dep. Dwayne Thibideaux (1979–80)
Flamingo Road (drama)
.... Fielding Carlyle (1981–82)
St. Elsewhere (drama)
.... Dr. Robert Caldwell (1983–86)

The younger brother of Kris and Kelly Harmon, and son of All-American football legend Tom Harmon (now a sportscaster). Mark followed in his father's footsteps and was a star quarterback on UCLA's winning teams in 1972 and '73. He then turned to acting, where his athletic good looks and charm immediately won him guest roles on such series as *Ozzie's Girls, Adam 12* and *Police Story*.

Though he is better known as a handsome hunk than as a particularly intense actor, Mark did receive an Emmy Award nomination for his role in *Eleanor and Franklin: The White House Years* in 1977. He has also appeared in several other TV movies and miniseries, including *Centennial*, and had leading roles in *The Dream Merchants* and *Goliath Awaits*. His regular series have been less successful, however. *Sam* (in which he costarred with a dog) and *240-Robert* were routine action shows and *Flamingo Road* (in which he played an ambitious young politician), a short-lived soap opera. Mark made a stronger impression on *St. Elsewhere* as the young doctor who charmed the ladies but who eventually contracted AIDS.

HARMON, MERLE—sportscaster
b: c. 1927

The Saturday Sports Final (sport)
.... sportscaster (1962)

HARMON, PATTY—juvenile hostess

Tell It to Groucho (com)
.... regular (1962)

HARMON, STEVE—actor
b: Dec 13, 1940, Brooklyn, N.Y.

Mr. Roberts (com)
.... Ens. Frank Pulver (1965–66)

Steve was originally a singer and dancer on late '50s and early '60s variety shows, using the name Johnny Harmon.

HARPER, CONSTANCE—actress

Adventures of Ozzie & Harriet (com)
.... Connie Edwards (1960–66)

HARPER, DAVID W.—actor
b: Oct 4, 1961, Abilene, Texas

The Waltons (drama)
.... Jim-Bob Walton (1972–81)
The Blue and the Gray (drama)
.... James Hale (1982)

HARPER, JESSICA—actress
b: 1949, Chicago, Ill.

Aspen (drama) .... Kit Pepe (1977)
Little Women (drama) ..... Jo March (1979)
Studs Lonigan (drama) ...... Loretta (1979)

HARPER, JOHN—actor
b: c. 1928, Columbus, Ohio

Gunsmoke (wes) ... Percy Crump (1955–75)

HARPER, RON—actor
b: Jan 12, 1935, Turtle Creek, Pa.

87th Precinct (police)
.... Det. Bert Kling (1961–62)
Wendy and Me (com)
.... Jeff Conway (1964–65)
The Jean Arthur Show (com)
.... Paul Marshall (1966)
Garrison's Gorillas (drama)
.... Lt. Craig Garrison (1967–68)
The Planet of the Apes (sci fi)
.... Alan Virdon (1974)

HARPER, TESS—actress

Chiefs (drama) .... Carrie Lee (1983)

HARPER, VALERIE—actress
b: Aug 22, 1940, Suffern, N.Y.

The Mary Tyler Moore Show (com)
.... Rhoda Morgenstern (1970–74)
Rhoda (com)
.... Rhoda Morgenstern Gerard (1974–78)
Valerie (com) ...... Valerie Hogan (1986–)

Emmy Awards: Best Supporting Actress in a Comedy Series, for *The Mary Tyler Moore Show* (1971, 1972, 1973); Best Actress in a Comedy Series, for *Rhoda* (1975)

Mary Tyler Moore's worrywart friend on *The Mary Tyler Moore Show* is as much a dyed-in-the-wool New Yorker as the character she played. Valerie got her start as a dancer at New York's Radio City Music Hall, and, after experience in stock, appeared in such Broadway musicals as *Story Theater, Take Me Along,* and *Subways Are for Sleeping.*

The Mary Tyler Moore Show was her first major break on television, and it was a big one. For the next eight years Valerie played the same man-hungry character, first in the original series and then in her own spin-off, in which Rhoda returned to New York (where else?) and married a nice Jewish boy named Joe. Since *Rhoda* left the air, Valerie has apparently been intent on changing her comedy image and has concentrated on dramatic TV movies. Among them have been *The Day the Loving Stopped* (about divorce), *Don't Go to Sleep* (a horror flick), *An Invasion of Privacy* (rape), and *The Execution* (revenge against a Nazi concentration-camp doctor). She also made a pilot for a proposed new series, *Farrell for the People* (1982), in which she was cast as a spunky assistant district attorney, but this did not make it to the regular schedule. The family sitcom *Valerie,* in 1986, was more successful; sometimes old images are the best.

HARRELL, JACK—

The Sonny and Cher Show (var)
.... regular (1976)

HARRELSON, WOODY—actor
b: Jul 23, Midland, Texas

Cheers (com) .... Woody Boyd (1985–)

HARRIMAN, FAWNE—actress
r: Chico, Calif.

The Ted Knight Show (com)
.... Honey (1978)

HARRINGTON, AL—actor
b: Dec 12, American Somoa r: Hawaii

Hawaii Five-O (police)
.... Det. Ben Kokua (1972–74)

HARRINGTON, BILL—singer

Holiday Hotel (var) .... regular (1950)

HARRINGTON, PAT, JR.—actor, comedian
b: Aug 13, 1929, New York City, N.Y.

The Steve Allen Show (var)
.... regular (1958–61)
The Danny Thomas Show (com)
.... Pat Hannigan (1959–60)
The Jack Paar Show (talk)
.... Guido Panzini (1959–62)
Pantomime Quiz (quiz) .... host (1962)
Mr. Deeds Goes to Town (com)
.... Tony Lawrence (1969–70)
One Day at a Time (com)
.... Dwayne Schneider (1975–84)

Emmy Award: Best Supporting Actor in a Comedy, for *One Day at a Time* (1984)

Pat Harrington, Jr., is possibly the only network salesman who proved so glib that he switched from selling programs to performing on them. Although he was born the son of an old-time Irish singer-dancer-actor, Pat, Jr. prepared himself for a business career, earning a master's degree from Fordham University in 1952. He joined NBC a couple of years later, rising from the mailroom to the position of salesman in the national TV sales department.

In 1957 he met comedian Jonathan Winters, who was guest-hosting *The Jack Paar Show.* Even then Pat was known for his dialects and mimicry, and Winters invited him to appear on one telecast and do his burlesque Guido Panzini routine. It was such a hit that Pat stopped taking sales orders and began appearing regularly, on both the Steve Allen and Jack Paar series. He also landed a role for a season on *The Danny Thomas Show* as Danny's son-in-law.

After his first blush of exposure in 1958–62, Pat settled down to a life of touring with his nightclub act and appearing on TV talk and game shows. He also made some TV movies and appeared in such series as *Mr. Deeds Goes to Town* (as a regular), *The Man from U.N.C.L.E., McMillan and Wife,* and, numerous times, *Owen Marshall.* In 1975 he began the role as the wisecracking, T-shirted building super on *One Day at a Time,* which made him familiar to a whole new generation of viewers. Young viewers may also recognize his voice as that of the inspector on the Saturday morning *Pink Panther Show* for most of the '70s.

384

HARRINGTON, PAT, SR.—actor
b: c. 1901 d: 1965

A Couple of Joes (var) .... regular (1950)
The Wonderful John Acton (drama)
.... Peter Bodkin, Sr. (1953)

Father of Pat, Jr., and an old-time show biz trooper.

HARRIS, ARLENE—comedienne
b: Jul 7, Toronto, Canada

Stage Two Revue (var) ...... regular (1950)

"The Human Chatterbox," who was once clocked at 240 words per minute during a radio monologue.

HARRIS, BILL—movie critic

At the Movies (misc) .... cohost (1986–)

HARRIS, BOB—actor
b: Nov 8, 1930, Long Beach, Calif.

Troubleshooters (adv) .... Jim (1959–60)

HARRIS, CYNTHIA—actress

Sirota's Court (com)
.... Maureen O'Connor (1976–77)
Husbands, Wives & Lovers (com)
.... Paula Zuckerman (1978)

HARRIS, DAVID—actor

North and South (drama) ..... Priam (1985)

HARRIS, DONALD—juvenile actor

Bonino (com) .... Jerry (1953)

HARRIS, HOLLY—

Starlit Time (var) .... regular (1950)
Once Upon a Tune (music)... regular (1951)

HARRIS, HOWARD "STONY"—rodeo commentator

Cowtown Rodeo (sport)
.... commentator (1957–58)

HARRIS, JO ANN—actress

Rich Man, Poor Man—Book I (drama)
.... Gloria Bartley (1976)
Most Wanted (police)
.... Off. Kate Manners (1976–77)

Detective School (com)
.... Teresa Cleary (1979)

HARRIS, JONATHAN—actor
b: 1914, New York City, N.Y.

The Third Man (drama)
.... Bradford Webster (1959–62)
The Bill Dana Show (com)
.... Mr. Phillips (1963–65)
Lost in Space (sci fi)
.... Dr. Zachary Smith (1965–68)

Harris specialized in the sort of fussy, overbearing characters who are always in demand on television. He gave Michael Rennie grief in *The Third Man* and (as the hotel manager) berated Jose Jiminez on *The Bill Dana Show.* However, his most memorable role was as the self-centered and thoroughly incompetent Dr. Smith on the popular kids' sci-fi series *Lost in Space.*

Harris's background was in the theater, where he had appeared, primarily in the East, during the '30s, '40s, and '50s. His favorite TV role was a guest appearance on *The Outlaws,* in which he played a meek railroad conductor who robbed the train of a million dollars.

HARRIS, JOSHUA—juvenile actor

Dallas (drama).. Christopher Ewing (1984–)

HARRIS, JULIE—actress
b: Dec 2, 1925, Grosse Pointe Park, Mich.

Thicker Than Water (com)
.... Nellie Paine (1973)
The Family Holvak (drama)
.... Elizabeth Holvak (1975)
Backstairs at the White House (drama)
.... Helen "Nellie" Taft (1979)
Knots Landing (drama)
.... Lilimae Clements (1981–)

Emmy Awards: Best Single Performance by an Actress, for the *Hallmark Hall of Fame* productions *Little Moon of Alban* (1959) and *Victoria Regina* (1962)

This multi–award winning actress is known for her sensitive, emotional performances in all media. Raised in an upper-class suburb of Detroit and educated at finishing schools, Julie won her first

Broadway role while still studying drama at Yale, in 1945. Five years later she gained fame as the lonely, motherless tomboy in *The Member of the Wedding,* a role which she repeated for the movie version in 1952.

Julie has appeared in many stage productions since then, winning five Tony Awards along the way. She has also done a great deal of television work, including dozens of appearances on *The Hallmark Hall of Fame* from the '50s to the '80s. Other series on which she has made multiple appearances include *Goodyear Playhouse, DuPont Show of the Month, The Name of the Game,* and *Tarzan.* Although she has won much acclaim for her dramatic specials, her first two regular series —a comedy and a drama—were both short-lived. At least her supporting role as Gary Ewing's mother on *Knots Landing,* while not central to the series plot, has lasted longer.

HARRIS, LEE—actor

The Streets of San Francisco (police)
.... Lt. Lessing (1972–77)

HARRIS, PERCY (BUD)—black actor

Beulah (com) .... Bill Jackson (1950–51)

HARRIS, ROBERT H.—actor
b: 1909* d: Nov 30, 1981

The Goldbergs (com)
.... Jake Goldberg (1953–55)
Court of Last Resort (drama)
.... Raymond Schindler (1957–58)

A frequent player on *Alfred Hitchcock Presents* in the '50s and '60s.

HARRIS, ROSEMARY—actress
b: Sep 19, 1930, Ashby, Suffolk, England

Holocaust (drama)
.... Berta Weiss (1978)
The Chisholms (wes)
.... Minerva Chisholm (1979–80)

Emmy Award: Best Actress in a Limited Series, for the *Masterpiece Theatre* production *Notorious Woman* (1976)

*Some sources give 1911.

385

HARRIS, ROSS—juvenile actor

United States (com)
.... Dylan Chapin (1980)
Under One Roof (com)
.... Spencer Winger (1985)

HARRIS, STACY—actor

b: 1918, Big Timber, Quebec, Canada d: Mar 13, 1973

Doorway to Danger (drama)
.... Doug Carter (1953)
N.O.P.D. (police) .... Det. Beaujac (1956–57)
The Life and Legend of Wyatt Earp (wes)
.... Mayor Clum (1960–61)

HARRISON, DICKIE—juvenile panelist

Twenty Questions (quiz). panelist (1953–54)

HARRISON, GRACIE—actress

b: Kansas City, Mo.

Melba (com) .... Susan Slater (1986)

HARRISON, GREGORY—actor

b: May 31, 1950, Avalon, Catalina Island, Calif.

Logan's Run (sci fi) .... Logan (1977–78)
Centennial (drama) ... Levi Zandt (1978–79)
Trapper John, M.D. (drama)
.... Dr. George Alonzo Gates (Gonzo) (1979–86)

HARRISON, JENILEE—actress

b: Jun 12, 1959, Glendale, Calif. r: Northridge, Calif.

Three's Company (com)
.... Cindy Snow (1980–82)
Dallas (drama) ...... Jamie Ewing (1984–)

HARRISON, LINDA—actress

b: Jul 26, 1945, Berlin, Md.

Bracken's World (drama)
.... Paulette Douglas (1969–70)

HARRISON, LISA—actress

The Waltons (drama)
.... Toni Hazleton (1981)

HARRISON, NOEL—actor, singer

b: Jan 29, 1936, London, England

The Girl from U.N.C.L.E. (drama)
.... Mark Slate (1966–67)

The son of stage and screen star Rex Harrison.

HARRISON, RAY—dancer

b: c. 1917, St. Louis, Mo. d: Jul 27, 1981

America Song (music) .... dancer (1948–49)

HARROLD, KATHRYN—actress

b: Aug 2, 1950, Tazewell, Va.

MacGruder & Loud (police)
...... Det. Jenny Loud MacGruder (1985)

HARRON, DON—comedian

Hee Haw (var)
.... Charlie Farquharson (1969–)

HARRY, JACKEE—black actress

b: Aug 14, Winston-Salem, N.C.

227 (com) .... Sandra Clark (1985–)

One of the more outrageous characters in TV comedy in the mid-1980s was Jackee (pronounced Jack-kay) Harry's hilarious vamp Sandra on *227*. She developed the sexy, sauntering, wisecracking characterization—a sort of updated Mae West—during her long tenure on the daytime soap opera *Another World,* on which she played hooker-with-a-heart-of-gold Lily Mason. "She just hasn't found the right man yet," drawls Jackee of Sandra/Lily, "and in the meantime she's going to keep on havin' fun."

In the late '70s, prior to her TV success, Jackee was a New York stage actress.

HARSCH, JOSEPH C.—newscaster

b: May 25, 1905, Toledo, Ohio

Background (news) .... commentator (1954)

HART, BILL—actor

Stoney Burke (wes) .... Red (1962–63)

HART, CECILIA—actress

Paris (police) .... Stacey Erickson (1979–80)
Mr. Sunshine (com) ...... Janice Hall (1986)

HART, CLAY—singer

The Lawrence Welk Show (music)
.... regular (1969–75)

HART, DOROTHY—actress
b: 1923, Cleveland, Ohio

Take a Guess (quiz) .... panelist (1953)
Pantomime Quiz (quiz)
.... regular (1953–58)

HART, JOHN—actor
b: c. 1921, Los Angeles, Calif.

The Lone Ranger (wes)
.... the Lone Ranger (1952–54)
Hawkeye (wes) .... Hawkeye (1957)

HART, JOHN—newsman
b: Feb 1, 1932, Denver, Colo.

CBS News Retrospective (doc)
.... host (1973–74)
NBC Weekend News (news)
.... anchorman (1976–77)

Emmy Awards: Outstanding Achievement
Within a Regularly Scheduled News Pro-
gram, for *CBS Evening News* report "The
Agnew Resignation" (1974); for *NBC
Nightly News* segment "Erasing Vietnam"
(1979)

HART, MARY—hostess
b: c. 1950, Sioux Falls, S.D.

Entertainment Tonight (news)
.... host (1982–)

HART, MOSS—playwright
b: Oct 24, 1904, The Bronx, N.Y. d: Dec 20,
1961

Answer Yes or No (quiz)
.... emcee (1950)

The most unlikely people turned up on
early television! The famous playwright
was married to TV personality Kitty Carlisle, which may have had something to do
with it. His autobiography is titled *Act One*
(1959).

HART, RALPH—actor

The Lucy Show (com)
.... Sherman Bagley (1962–65)

HART, RICHARD—actor
b: c. 1915 d: Jan 1951

The Adventures of Ellery Queen (drama)
.... Ellery Queen (1950–51)

HART, SUZANNE—actress

House Calls (com)
.... Nurse Shirley Bryan (1980–82)

HART, TRISHA—
see Harty, Patricia

HARTFORD, JOHN—singer, songwriter
b: Dec 30, 1937, New York City, N.Y., r: St.
Louis, Mo.

The Summer Smothers Brothers Show (var)
.... regular (1968)
The Smothers Brothers Comedy Hour (var)
.... regular (1968–69)
Something Else (var) .... cohost (1970)

HARTLEY, MARIETTE—actress
b: Jun 21, 1940, New York City, N.Y. r: Weston,
Conn.

Peyton Place (drama)
.... Dr. Claire Morton (1965)
The Hero (com)
.... Ruth Garret (1966–67)
Goodnight, Beantown (com)
.... Jennifer Barnes (1983–84)

Emmy Award: Best Actress in a Single Performance in a Drama Series, for *The Incredible Hulk* (1979)

"I'm *not* Mrs. James Garner," read the
title of the story in *TV Guide.* Protest as
she would, Mariette Hartley's banter with
Garner in those famous Polaroid commercials was so natural than many thought she
was his heretofore unseen real-life wife.
The sudden attention was no doubt welcome to the actress, but it must have
seemed ironic. After 15 years on television,
including costarring roles in two series and
scores of guest appearances, she was suddenly "discovered"—all because of a commercial.
In fact, Mariette began acting onstage as
a teenager, appearing with New York's
Shakespeare in the Park and on tour with
the Stratford Shakespeare Festival. She
made her film debut in 1962 in Sam Peckin-
pah's *Ride the High Country* and two
years later had a role in Hitchcock's *Marnie.* Simultaneously, she began appearing
in episodes of TV series, including *The
Twilight Zone, Daniel Boone,* and *Bonanza.* She was a regular on *Peyton Place*

as a doctor and on *The Hero* as Richard Mulligan's wife.

Mariette guested on many series in the '70s, from *The Bob Newhart Show* to *Ghost Story.* She was nominated for an Emmy for a 1977 performance on *The Hallmark Hall of Fame* and won one for an episode of *The Incredible Hulk.* Nevertheless, it took those crazy camera commercials to make her a star. In their wake she guest-starred on *The Rockford Files* (of course), won awards as "best new star," and even substituted for Jane Pauley on the *Today* show. A fine actress, she has also been nominated for several more Emmys. In 1983 she costarred with Bill Bixby in the comedy *Goodnight, Beantown,* but it was not successful. Perhaps she should try a series with James Garner and a camera.

HARTLEY, TED—actor

Chopper One (police)
.... Capt. McKeegan (1974)

HARTMAN, DAVID—actor, host
b: May 19, 1935, Pawtucket, R.I.

The Virginian (wes)
.... David Sutton (1968–69)
The New Doctors (drama)
.... Dr. Paul Hunter (1969–73)
Lucas Tanner (drama)
.... Lucas Tanner (1974–75)

Emmy Award: Best Informational Segment, for the *Good Morning, America* report "B-1 Bomber"

David Hartman is probably the best recent example of the fine line that separates TV news and entertainment. Not since the '50s—when even Walter Cronkite was obliged to host a game show—has someone so identified with one field become so prominent in the other.

Hartman has quite a varied background. However, despite the efforts of ABC to portray his entire previous career as dedicated to "entertaining and informative" TV, none of it was associated with news—unless one considers comedies like *The Feminist and the Fuzz* and murder mysteries like *You'll Never See Me Again* to be "informational." A star student athlete, David was offered baseball contracts by both the Boston Braves and the Philadelphia Phillies upon graduation from high school but turned them down to get a college education instead. That was followed by three years in the air force and then by drama study. He had always excelled in music, and his earliest roles were singing and dancing in off-Broadway and Broadway musicals; perhaps his best role was that of Rudolph the singing waiter in the original Broadway production of *Hello Dolly* in 1964. He also toured with the Harry Belafonte Singers and with the road company of *My Fair Lady* in the '60s.

David then turned to straight acting, signing with Universal Studios in 1966 and subsequently appearing in both TV movies and series episodes. A guest appearance on *The Virginian* in 1967 led to a regular role the following season; he then became one of the young physicians on "The New Doctors" segment of *The Bold Ones* anthology for four years. No doubt his best-known role was as the dedicated English teacher in *Lucas Tanner.*

No sooner was *Lucas Tanner* off the air than David surprised viewers by agreeing to host, of all things, a new morning news and information series on ABC, *Good Morning, America.* It proved to be an astute change of direction. David's low-key manner, inquisitive intellect, and air of authority (he had just been playing an English teacher, after all) combined with the show's friendly living-room setting to make *GMA* a hit; within five years it had overtaken the venerable *Today* show in audience, and most observers gave Hartman much of the credit for the rise.

Despite the demands of a five-day-a-week, two-hour show, Hartman has also been active in documentary production. In 1974, before *GMA,* he produced an acclaimed special on *Birth and Babies.* More recent productions have looked at gambling, at the work of leading photojournalists, and at the microchip revolution. He left the anchor position on *GMA* in 1987.

HARTMAN, GRACE—actress, dancer
b: c. 1907 d: 1955

The Hartmans (com) ..... as herself (1949)

The wife of Paul Hartman.

HARTMAN, KAREN—comedienne

Sha Na Na (var) .... regular (1980–81)

HARTMAN, LISA—actress
b: Jun 1, 1956, Houston, Texas

Tabitha (com).. Tabitha Stephens (1977–78)
Knots Landing (drama)
.... Ciji Dunne (1982–83)
High Performance (adv)
.... Kate Flannery (1983)
Knots Landing (drama)
.... Cathy Geary (1983–86)

HARTMAN, PAUL—actor, dancer
b: Mar 1, 1904, San Francisco, Calif. d: Oct 2, 1973

The Hartmans (com) ..... as himself (1949)
The Pride of the Family (com)
.... Albie Morrison (1953–55)
The Andy Griffith Show (com)
.... Emmett Clark (1967–68)
Petticoat Junction (com)
.... Bert Smedley (1968–69)
Mayberry R.F.D. (com)
.... Emmett Clark (1968–71)

Paul Hartman was a rubber-faced, rubber-legged comic dancer who, with various partners (including his wife Grace), delighted audiences with his "dance satires." He was seen on television frequently in the 1950s, both on variety shows and in occasional straight acting roles—most frequently on *Kraft Television Theatre.* In the '60s he switched to playing character roles on numerous series, ending his career as a rustic on three rural situation comedies.

HARTMAN, PHIL—writer, comedian
b: Ontario, Canada r: Conn., Calif.

Our Time (var)............. regular (1985)
NBC's Saturday Night Live (var)
.... regular (1986–)

HARTMANN, ENA—actress

Dan August (police)
.... Katy Grant (1970–71)

HARTY, PATRICIA—actress
b: Nov 5, 1941, Washington, D.C.

Occasional Wife (com)
.... Greta Patterson (1966–67)
Blondie (com).. Blondie Bumstead (1968–69)
The Bob Crane Show (com)
.... Ellie Wilcox (1975)

Herbie, The Love Bug (com)
.... Susan MacLane (1982)

Many frustrated people have probably considered doing what Patricia Harty did in the early '70s, but few have had the nerve to go through with it. This spunky little lady literally dumped her entire previous career—name, credits, appearance and all—and started out fresh.

Not that her previous career had been particularly unsuccessful. Pat started out as a dancer in the '50s and appeared on the Perry Como, Pat Boone, and Garry Moore variety shows. Later she appeared in such Broadway musicals as *Fiorello* and *Sail Away.* In the early '60s she began to shift into acting, with guest roles in prime time series, including *Route 66* and a running part (during 1965) in the daytime soap opera *Search for Tomorrow.* With a growing reputation, she then won costarring roles in two situation comedies, *Occasional Wife* and *Blondie.*

Her personal life, however, was falling apart. "I decided to walk away from everything and take a look at my life and where it was going," she later said. "I was newly divorced and, for many reasons, my life had become unsatisfactory. So I decided to make myself over. I wanted to follow some of the things which had made me happier in the past, things I had dropped along the way." She straightened out her living and eating habits, let her hair turn from 20 years of Hollywood blonde to its natural brunette, and returned to college to finish work on her long-postponed degree. Then, as if to cap it all off, she changed her name to Trisha Hart.

It was as Trisha Hart that she landed her next regular role, on *The Bob Crane Show* in 1975. Later she returned to using her original (and real) name, but it was as a new person. "When I went back to work as an actress I felt renewed. Since I didn't spend every waking moment thinking about show business, I had a lot more to bring to every role. The creative juices were flowing again. I felt and still feel that I've made a whole new start in life. It takes a lot of doing, but it's well worth it."

HARTZELL, CLARENCE—actor
b: Huntington, W. Va.

Cactus Jim (child) .... Cactus Jim (1949–51)

Those Endearing Young Charms (com)
.... Uncle Duff (1952)

HARVEY, HARRY, SR.—actor
b: 1901, Indian Territory, Okla. d: Nov 27, 1985

Man Without a Gun (wes)
.... Mayor George Dixon (1957–59)
It's a Man's World (com)
.... Houghton Stott (1962–63)

HARVEY, JANE—singer
Broadway Open House (talk)
.... regular (1950)

HARVEY, JOHN—actor
b: c. 1917 d: 1970

The Growing Paynes (com)
.... Mr. Payne (1948–49)

HARVEY, MICHAEL—actor
Tom Corbett, Space Cadet (child)
.... Capt. Steve Strong (1950)

HARVEY, NED—orchestra leader
Doorway to Fame (talent)
.... orch. leader (1947–49)

HARVEY, PAUL—commentator
b: Sep 4, 1918, Tulsa, Okla.

Paul Harvey News (news)
.... commentator (1952–53)

A contentious conservative commentator, renowned for his theatrical delivery ("Paul Harvey . . . good . . . *Day!*"). *TV Guide* described him as "a combination of Billy Graham, Bishop Sheen, and Charlton Heston as Moses." Harvey's political stands sometimes surprised those who tried to pigeonhole him; for example he was an early opponent of the U.S. involvement in Vietnam. He was best known as a radio personality, although he had a TV commentary show on ABC in 1952 and in syndication in later years.

HASEL, JOE—sportscaster
Sports with Joe Hasel (sport)
.... commentator (1948–49)
Bowling Headliners (sport)
.... announcer (1949)

Roller Derby (sport) ... announcer (1949–50)
New York Giants Quarterback Huddle (sport)
.... host (1950)

HASKELL, JACK—singer, announcer
Garroway at Large (var) .. regular (1949–51)
The Dave Garroway Show (var)
.... vocalist (1953–54)
The Tonight Show (talk) .. announcer (1962)

HASKELL, JIMMIE—orchestra leader, composer
b: Brooklyn, N.Y.

The Kraft Summer Music Hall (var)
.... orch. leader (1966)

Emmy Award: Best Score for a Dramatic Special, for the *General Electric Theater* production *See How She Runs* (1978)

HASKELL, PETER—actor
b: Oct 15, 1934, Boston, Mass.

Bracken's World (drama)
.... Kevin Grant (1969–70)
Rich Man, Poor Man—Book II (drama)
.... Charles Estep (1976–77)
Rituals (drama) .... C. J. Fields (1984–85)

HASLAM, LU ANN—juvenile actress
The New Adventures of Huck Finn (adv)
.... Becky Thatcher (1968–69)

HASSELHOFF, DAVID—actor
b: Jul 17, 1952, Baltimore, Md.

Semi-Tough (com) ...... Shake Tiller (1980)
Knight Rider (adv)
.... Michael Knight (1982–86)

The "hunk of the hour" in 1982 was tall (6'4"), grinning David Hasselhoff, a handsome, macho type who emerged from a long apprenticeship in daytime to star in one of the most popular kids' shows of the '80s. His acting experience prior to his first network exposure was relatively brief (it *can* be when you look like he does); David was a student in a Los Angeles acting school when he was spotted waiting on tables by casting director Joyce Selznick ("Look at *him!*"). She got him roles in *Police Story* and *The Love Boat* and the continuing part of Snapper Foster on the daytime soap opera *The Young and the*

Restless, which won him legions of admiring female fans. He played Snapper for seven years altogether (1975–82), taking time out to appear in an obscure and raunchy sex farce called *Revenge of the Cheerleaders* (1976), a TV movie (*Pleasure Cove,* 1979), and the short-lived sitcom *Semi-Tough* (1980).

David's big break, however, was to co-star with a car—the talking, thinking, crime-fighting K.I.T.T. of *Knight Rider.* Reportedly, network executives were so fed up with handsome leading men who couldn't act that they designed a show in which the hero wouldn't have to say anything at all—the car would do all the talking. That probably sold Hasselhoff short, since his laid-back good humor and banter with his mechanical friend provided much of the show's charm. However, even he could see the role's limitations. Taking a break to film a lightweight TV movie called *The Cartier Affair,* he commented "I'm certainly not putting down *Knight Rider,* but it doesn't show everything I can do as an actor. This (movie) was really a big stretch for me as an actor . . ." Do we detect a twinkle in your eye, David?

HASTINGS, BOB—actor
b: Apr 18, 1925, Brooklyn, N.Y.

McHale's Navy (com)
.... Lt. Elroy Carpenter (1962–66)
All in the Family (com)
.... Tommy Kelsey (1973–77)
Dealer's Choice (quiz) .... host (1974–75)

The brother of actor Don Hastings, and, like him, a longtime performer on radio (in the '30s and '40s) and on daytime, nighttime, and Saturday morning television. Bob's first TV exposure was on an experimental telecast in 1939; in the '80s he was playing the long-running role of Capt. Burt Ramsey on *General Hospital.*

HASTINGS, DON—actor
b: Apr 1, 1934, Brooklyn, N.Y.

Captain Video and His Video Rangers (child)
.... the Ranger (1949–55)

This veteran actor is a bit of walking TV history in two respects. He was television's first teenage idol, as the "Video Ranger" on *Captain Video* in the 1950s,

and he is the longest-running romantic lead on a daytime soap opera, with more than 25 years on *As the World Turns.*

Don was introduced to show business by his older brother Bob, whom he joined on radio in 1940. After some stage work as a juvenile in the '40s (*Life with Father, I Remember Mama*), he won the role of Captain Video's enthusiastic young helper in 1949 and continued it for six years. When the series ended in 1955 he quickly moved through a couple of daytime flops (*A Date with Life, Modern Romances*) and then joined *The Edge of Night* on its 1956 premiere telecast, staying with it for four years. In 1960 he switched to *As the World Turns* as Dr. Bob Hughes, a role he has continued ever since. *A WT* now seems to be his world—he has contributed scripts to it, played nightclub and off-Broadway theater with fellow cast member Kathryn Hays, and married former cast member Leslie Denniston.

HASTINGS, HAL—orchestra leader
b: Dec 19, 1916, New York City, N.Y. d: May 30, 1973

Chevrolet on Broadway (music)
.... orch. leader (1956)

HATCH, RICHARD—actor
b: May 21, 1947, Santa Monica, Calif.

The Streets of San Francisco (police)
.... Insp. Dan Robbins (1976–77)
Mary Hartman, Mary Hartman (com)
.... Harmon Farinella (1977–78)
Battlestar Galactica (sci fi)
.... Capt. Apollo (1978–79)

HATHAWAY, NOAH—actor

Battlestar Galactica (sci fi)
.... Boxey (1978–79)

HATRAK, ERNIE—pianist

The Ernie Kovacs Show (var)
.... regular (1952–53)

HAUFRECT, ALAN—actor

Alice (com) .... Brian (1979–80)

HAUSER, FAYETTE—

Manhattan Transfer (var) .... regular (1975)

HAUSER, WINGS—actor

The Last Precinct (com)
.... Lt. Ronald Hobbs (1986)

A soap opera actor of the late '70s and early '80s *(The Young and the Restless)*; also known as J. D. Hauser.

HAUSNER, JERRY—actor

Valentine's Day (com)
.... O. D. Dunstall (1964–65)

HAVEL BROTHERS—

Ford Star Revue (var) ...... regulars (1950)

HAVENS, JOHN—guitarist

Saturday Night Jamboree (music)
.... regular (1948–49)

HAVOC, JUNE—actress
b: Nov 8, 1916, Seattle, Wash.

Willy (drama)...... Willa Dodger (1954–55)

Autobiography: *Early Havoc* (1960).

HAWKINS, DOLORES—singer
b: 1928, Brooklyn, N.Y. d: Jan 15, 1987

The Guy Mitchell Show (var)
.... regular (1957–58)

HAWKINS, HAWKSHAW—country singer
b: Dec 22, 1921, Huntington, W. Va. d: Mar 5, 1963

Ozark Jubilee (music)........ regular (1955)

HAWKINS, JACK—actor
b: Sep 1, 1910, London, England d: Jul 18, 1973

Four Just Men (adv) ... Ben Manfred (1959)

HAWKINS, JIMMY—actor

The Ruggles (com)
.... Donald Ruggles (1949–52)
Annie Oakley (wes)
.... Tagg Oakley (1953–56)
Ichabod and Me (com)
.... Jonathan Baylor (1961–62)

HAWKINS, VIRGINIA—actress

Medical Center (drama)
.... Nurse Canford (1969–76)

HAWLEY, ADELAIDE—hostess

Fashions on Parade (misc)
.... narrator (1948–49)

HAWN, GOLDIE—actress
b: Nov 21, 1945, Washington, D.C.

Good Morning, World (com)
.... Sandy Kramer (1967–68)
Rowan & Martin's Laugh-In (var)
.... regular (1968–70)

This top Hollywood star had a short but well-remembered television career before the movies stole her away. She is perhaps the biggest of the many stars created by that famous launching pad for new talent, *Rowan & Martin's Laugh-In*.

Goldie's rise was meteoric. She made her professional debut as a dancer in the 1964 New York World's Fair production of *Can Can* and was a go-go dancer after that. In 1967 she was spotted in the chorus line of an Andy Griffith TV special and promptly signed for her first series, *Good Morning, World*, as the gossipy neighbor. From that she went straight into *Laugh-In* and fame as America's favorite, squeaky, giggly, sexy, dumb blonde.

The following year Goldie played her first major film role, in *Cactus Flower* (1969), and won an Academy Award. She never looked back.

HAYDEN, DON—actor

My Little Margie (com)
.... Freddie Wilson (1952–55)

HAYDEN, HARRY—actor
b: 1882* d: Jul 23, 1955

The Stu Erwin Show (com)
.... Harry (1954–55)

HAYDEN, RUSSELL "LUCKY"—actor
b: Jun 12, 1912, Chico, Calif. d: Jun 10, 1981

The Marshal of Gunsight Pass (wes)
.... the Marshal (1950)
Cowboy G-Men (wes) . Pat Gallagher (1952)
Judge Roy Bean (wes) .... Steve (1956)

HAYDEN, STERLING—actor
b: Mar 26, 1916, Montclair, N.J. d: May 23, 1986

*Some sources give 1884.

The Blue and the Gray (drama)
.... John Brown (1982)

HAYDN, LILI—juvenile actress

Kate Loves a Mystery (drama)
.... Jenny Columbo/Callahan (1979)

HAYDON, CHARLES—actor

The Witness (drama)
.... committee member (1960–61)

HAYES, ALLISON—actress
b: Mar 6, 1930, Charleston, W. Va. d: Feb 27, 1977

Acapulco (adv).............. Chloe (1961)

HAYES, BILL—actor, singer
b: Jun 5, 1925, Harvey, Ill.

Fireball Fun-for-All (var)..... regular (1949)
Your Show of Shows (var)
.... regular (1950–53)
Caesar Presents (var)....... vocalist (1955)
Oldsmobile Music Theatre (music)
.... host (1959)

Often, as the suave, boutonniered night-club owner on *Days of Our Lives*, Bill Hayes would step into the spotlight and begin to croon a beautiful love song to the admiring ladies in the audience. I always imagined myself in that club, shouting from the rear, "Sing your big hit, Bill . . . sing *Davy Crockett!*"

While Bill's corn-pone novelty hit of the 1950s hardly fit in with his matinee idol image of the '70s, he did have an extensive career as a singer in his younger days. He had pursued both acting and singing during his school days (and even during World War II service) and made his professional stage debut in a small role in *Carousel* in the late '40s. He then landed a spot with zany comics Olsen and Johnson in their touring show *Funzapoppin'*. When the revue opened at New York's Madison Square Garden in 1949, Bill sang an aria from *Pagliacci* amid sheer bedlam—guns and cannons firing, hysterical shrieking, animals chasing each other around him. The lunatic comedians brought their show to television in June 1949, as *Fireball Fun-for-All*, and Bill went with them.

He was spotted in those telecasts by producer Max Liebman, who hired him

for a three-year run on Sid Caesar's *Your Show of Shows*, a series that was only slightly less manic. After that, Bill continued to appear on other '50s variety shows, as a "bright young singer." He was said in the early '50s to have 150 fan clubs across the U.S. His one major hit-record was a pure fluke, however, and quite different from his middle-of-the-road image. Walt Disney's *Davy Crockett* had become a national sensation during the winter of 1954–55, and kids were clamoring for its folksy theme song ("Born on a mountain top 'n Tennessee . . ."). Disney was a little slow in releasing a version, so a small record label called Cadence rushed Bill into the studio, got his version into the stores before Fess Parker's original was out, and proceeded to sell more than two million copies almost overnight. Bill never had another hit record (he was hardly a charter member of the rock generation), but he did continue his career as a TV singer for the rest of the decade, including a short run with Florence Henderson in 1959 on *Oldsmobile Music Theatre,* an unusual interweaving of story and song.

The '60s began well enough, with a starring role in the Broadway musical *Bye Bye Birdie,* club work, and an acting role in the 1963 movie *The Cardinal.* But after that things slowed down considerably and by 1970 Bill was happy to land the part of Doug Williams on the soap opera *Days of Our Lives.* The show proved to be his comeback vehicle, and for the next 14 years Bill and his new wife, Susan Seaforth Hayes (whom he met on the show), reigned as one of the most popular couples in daytime television.

HAYES, HAROLD—editor
b: Winston-Salem, N.C.

20/20 (mag)........ host (premiere) (1978)

The former editor of *Esquire* magazine.

HAYES, HELEN—actress
b: Oct 10, 1900, Washington, D.C.

The Snoop Sisters (drama)
.... Ernesta Snoop (1973–74)

Emmy Award: Best Actress (1952)

The mother of actor James MacArthur, and "The First Lady of the American Theater." Miss Hayes starred in many dramatic productions during the '50s (on *Omnibus, Schlitz Playhouse of Stars,* etc.), but has been seen only occasionally since then. Her 1971 autobiography was titled *Twice Over Lightly.*

HAYES, MARGARET—actress
b: Dec 5, 1915*, Baltimore, Md. d: Jan 26, 1977

Robert Montgomery Presents (summer) (drama). . . . . repertory player (1952–53)

HAYES, PETER LIND—comedian, singer
b: Jun 25, 1915, San Francisco, Calif.

Inside U.S.A. with Chevrolet (var)
. . . . host (1949–50)
The Stork Club (talk) . . . . cohost (1950)
The Peter Lind Hayes Show (com)
. . . . as himself (1950–51)
Star of the Family (var). . . . . . host (1951–52)
Peter Loves Mary (com)
. . . . Peter Lindsey (1960–61)

HAYES, RICHARD—singer
b: Jan 5, 1930, Passaic, N.J.

Songs for Sale (music) . . . . regular (1950–51)
Broadway Open House (talk)
. . . . regular (1951)
Talent Patrol (talent) . . . . emcee (1955)
Name That Tune (quiz) . . . . emcee (1970–71)

HAYES, RITA—assistant
Win with a Winner (quiz)
. . . . "Postcard Girl" (1958)

HAYES, RON—actor
The Everglades (police)
. . . . Lincoln Vail (1961–62)
The Rounders (com) . . . Ben Jones (1966–67)
Lassie (adv) . . . . Garth Holden (1972–73)

HAYGARTH, ANTHONY—actor
Holocaust (drama) . . . . Muller (1978)

HAYMAN, LILLIAN—black actress
b: Jul 17, 1922, Baltimore, Md.

The Leslie Uggams Show (var)
. . . . regular (1969)

*Some sources give 1916 or even 1924.

394

HAYMAN, RICHARD—orchestra leader, harmonica player
b: Mar 27, 1920, Cambridge, Mass.

The Vaughn Monroe Show (var)
. . . . orch. leader (1954)

HAYMER, JOHNNY—actor
M*A*S*H (com). . . . . Sgt. Zale (1977–79)
Madame's Place (com). . . . . Pinkerton (1982)

HAYMES, BOB—singer
b: c. 1922

It's a Business (com) . . . . regular (1952)

The younger, less famous brother of big-band singer Dick Haymes. Also known as Bob Stanton (but not to be confused with the early NBC sportscaster of that name).

HAYNES, GARY—actor
Peyton Place (drama)
. . . . Chris Webber (1966–67)

HAYNES, LLOYD—black actor
b: Oct 19, 1934*, South Bend, Ind. d: Dec 31, 1986

Room 222 (drama) . . . . Pete Dixon (1969–74)
79 Park Avenue (drama)
. . . . Martin Stevens (1977)

This promising young actor did little on television after his starring days on *Room 222.* Originally a production assistant for TV game shows, he broke into acting with supporting roles on episodes of such mid-1960s series as *Batman, Julia,* and *Tarzan* (as a native). After 1974 he slipped back into supporting roles, and infrequent ones at that, in a few TV movies and series. Among these was a brief stint on *Dynasty* in 1981.

HAYS, KATHRYN—actress
b: Princeton, Ill.

The Road West (wes)
. . . . Elizabeth Reynolds (1966–67)

A veteran stage and television actress, seen often as a prime time guest star during the '60s; since 1972 she has played Kim Hughes on *As the World Turns.*

*Some sources give 1932.

HAYS, ROBERT—actor
b: Jul 24, 1947, Bethesda, Md.

Angie (com)........ Brad Benson (1979–80)
Starman (adv)
...... Starman ("Paul Forrester") (1986–)

HAYSBERT, DENNIS—black actor
b: Jun 2, San Mateo, Calif.

Code Red (adv) .... "Stuff" Wade (1981–82)
Off the Rack (com) .. Cletus Maxwell (1985)

HAYWARD, DAVID—actor

Wait Till Your Father Gets Home (cartn)
.... Chet Boyle (voice) (1972–74)

HAYWARD, LOUIS—actor
b: Mar 19, 1909, Johannesburg, South Africa d:
Feb 21, 1985

The Lone Wolf (drama)
.... Mike Lanyard (1954)
The Survivors (drama) .. Jonathan (1969–70)

HAYWORTH, VINTON—actor
b: 1906 d: May 21, 1970

Zorro (wes) ... magistrate Galindo (1957–59)
I Dream of Jeannie (com)
.... Gen. Winfield Schaeffer (1969–70)

HEALEY, MYRON—actor
b: Jun 8, 1922, Petaluma, Calif.

The Life and Legend of Wyatt Earp (wes)
.... Doc Holliday (temporary) (1959)

HEALY, MARY—actress
b: Apr 14, 1918, New Orleans, La.

Inside U.S.A. with Chevrolet (var)
.... regular (1949–50)
The Stork Club (talk)........ cohost (1950)
The Peter Lind Hayes Show (com)
.... as herself (1950–51)
Star of the Family (var)...... host (1951–52)
Masquerade Party (quiz)
.... panelist (1955–56)
Peter Loves Mary (com)
.... Mary Lindsey (1960–61)

The wife (since 1940) of comedian Peter
Lind Hayes, with whom she was invariably seen on television.

HEAPS, PORTER—orchestra leader

Sit or Miss (quiz)....... orch. leader (1950)

HEARN, CHICK—announcer

Stock Car Races (sport)... announcer (1952)
Prime Time Football (sport)
.... announcer (1957)

HEARN, CONNIE ANN—juvenile actress
b: Oct 17, c.1965, Anchorage, Alaska, r: California

A New Kind of Family..... Jill Stone (1979)

HEASLEY, MARLA—actress
b: Hollywood, Calif.

The A-Team (adv).... Tawnia Baker (1984)

HEATH, BOYD—host

Saturday Night Jamboree (music)
.... Emcee (1949)

HEATHERTON, JOEY—actress, dancer
b: Sep 14, 1944, Rockville Centre, N.Y.

Dean Martin Presents the Golddiggers (var)
.... regular (1968)
Joey & Dad (var) .... cohost (1975)

This sexy young thing was seen quite a bit
on television in the 1960s; she was the
teenager with a perpetual crush on Perry
Como on *The Perry Como Show*, the
youthful guest who taught Johnny Carson
to do the frug on *The Tonight Show*, and
the pin-up girl who wowed the troops in
Vietnam during Bob Hope's Christmas
tours. The daughter of veteran song-and-
dance man Ray Heatherton, Joey was introduced to show business at an early age.
She guested on episodes of various series
from 1960 until the early '70s, and in 1975
appeared with her dad in a summer variety
show called, appropriately enough, *Joey &
Dad*. She was not seen very much after
that.

**HEATHERTON, RAY—actor, dancer,
singer**
b: c. 1910

Joey & Dad (var) .... cohost (1975)

Joey's dad, and New York TV's "Merry
Mailman" during the 1950s. Later he was
best known to viewers as the commercial spokesperson for Tropicana orange
juice.

HEATHERTONES—singers

The Gulf Road Show Starring Bob Smith (var)
.... regulars (1949)

HEBERT, CHRIS—actor

Boone (drama) .... Norman (1983–84)

HECHT, BEN—writer, playwright
b: Feb 28, 1893, New York City, N.Y. d: Apr 18, 1964

Willys Theatre Presenting Ben Hecht's Tales of the City (drama) .. narrator (1953)

Famous as one of Hollywood's leading screenwriters and leading characters. His 1954 autobiography was *A Child of the Century;* a more recent biography is *The Five Lives of Ben Hecht,* by Doug Fetherling (1978).

HECHT, GINA—actress
b: Dec 6, Houston, Texas

Hizzonner (com) .... Melanie (1979)
Mork & Mindy (com)
.... Jean DaVinci (1979–81)

HECHT, PAUL—actor

Kate & Allie (com) . Charles Lowell (1984–)

HECKART, EILEEN—actress
b: Mar 29, 1919, Columbus, Ohio

Backstairs at the White House (drama)
.... Eleanor Roosevelt (1979)
Out of the Blue (com).... Boss Angel (1979)
Trauma Center (drama)
.... Amy Decker (1983)
Partners in Crime (drama) ... Jeanine (1984)

HEDISON, DAVID—actor
b: May 20, 1929*, Providence, R.I.

Five Fingers (drama)
............,....... Victor Sebastian (1959–60)
Voyage to the Bottom of the Sea (sci fi)
.... Cmdr./Capt. Lee Crane (1964–68)
Dynasty II: The Colbys (drama)
.... Roger Langdon (1985–)

A handsome, stalwart actor who overcame a serious stuttering problem as a child to pursue his chosen career in the theater. He

*Some sources give 1926.

396

began onstage in New York in the mid-1950s, but despite two good breaks early in his career—the lead in the spy series *Five Fingers* and a costarring role in the popular *Voyage to the Bottom of the Sea*—his work in later years was undistinguished. He has worked irly steadily in TV movies and series episodes (*Cannon, The Love Boat,* etc.) right up to the 1980s.

HEFLIN, VAN—actor
b: Dec 13, 1910, Walters, Okla. d: Jul 23, 1971

The Great Adventure (drama)
.... narrator (1963–65)

This highly regarded Hollywood leading man—an "actor's actor"—apparently didn't like television very much and made only rare appearances in dramatic productions such as those of *Playhouse 90.* Perhaps it had something to do with the time he was tricked into appearing on Ralph Edwards' *This Is Your Life* and made to stand by while his life was paraded before viewers; visibly angry, he was icy and uncommunicative throughout the uncomfortable telecast.

HEFTI, NEAL—orchestra leader
b: Oct 29, 1922, Hastings, Neb.

The Kate Smith Show (var)
.................../....... orch. leader (1960)

HEGER, KATHERINE—actress, dancer

Once Upon a Fence (child)
... Princess Katherine of Storyland (1952)

HEGYES, ROBERT—actor
b: May 7, 1951, New Jersey

Welcome Back, Kotter (com)
.... Juan Luis Pedro Phillipo Epstein de Huevos (1975–79)

HEIDT, HORACE—orchestra leader
b: May 21, 1901, Alameda, Calif. d: Dec 1, 1986

The Horace Heidt Show (talent)
.... host (1950–51)
The Swift Show Wagon (var).... host (1955)

Horace Heidt's thoroughly commercial dance band of the '30s and '40s was a breeding ground for ideas and performers later familiar to TV viewers. It was, in the late '30s, one of the first to feature an electric guitar (played by Alvino Rey); among Heidt's band members were the King Sisters, Frankie Carle, Gordon MacRae, Art Carney (then a singer), and Frank DeVol (who wrote the band's arrangements). Heidt himself was seen on television in the 1950s, often with his "Youth Opportunity Program," a traveling talent show. He retired from show business in the mid-1950s to pursue business interests.

HEILVEIL, ELAYNE—actress

Family (drama)
.... Nancy Lawrence Maitland (1976)

HEINE, LEINAALA—actress

The Mackenzies of Paradise Cove (adv)
.... Mrs. Kalikini (1979)

HEINEMAN, LAURIE—actress

Studs Lonigan (drama)....... Eileen (1979)

Emmy Award: Best Actress in a Daytime Drama, for Another World (1978)

HELBERG, SANDY—actor
b: May 29, Frankfurt, Germany r: Toledo, Ohio

79 Park Avenue (drama) .... Joey (1977)
Flatbush (com) .... Figgy Figueroa (1979)

HELD, KARL—actor

Perry Mason (drama)
.... David Gideon (1960–62)

HELLER, BARBARA—actress

The Jackie Gleason Show (var)
.... Christine Clam (1963–65)
Dean Martin Presents the Golddiggers (var)
.... regular (1968)

HELLER, RANDEE—actress
b: Jun 10, Brooklyn, N.Y. r: West Hempstead, Long Island, N.Y.

Husbands, Wives & Lovers (com)
.... Rita DeLatorre (1978)
Soap (com) .... Alice (1979)
Number 96 (drama)
.... Marion Quintzel (1980–81)

Mama Malone (com)
.... Connie Karamakopoulos (1984)
Better Days (com)
.... Harriet Winners (1986–)

HELLMAN, BONNIE—actress
b: Jan 10, San Francisco r: Palo Alto, Calif.

Nurse (drama)
.... Nurse Penny Brooks (1981–82)

HELMOND, KATHERINE—actress
b: Jul 5, 1934*, Galveston, Texas

Soap (com) .... Jessica Tate (1977–81)
Pearl (drama) .... Sally (1978)
Who's the Boss? (com)
.... Mona Robinson (1984–)

If you're past forty and you still have not made your mark in life, don't be discouraged. Katherine Helmond toiled for years in obscurity in the theater until, in her midforties, she suddenly made a very big mark indeed, winning fame and a string of Emmy nominations for her role as the eccentric Jessica on Soap.

Katherine worked long and hard to gain her eventual success. She began acting in high school in Texas and spent years in stock and repertory theater up and down the East Coast. Nobody noticed. She finally began to attract attention in the early '70s when she won a number of stage awards; about the same time, she started to turn up rather frequently in TV movies and in episodes of series (Gunsmoke, Mannix, etc.), often as someone's older friend or mother. Then came Soap. Even after this hit, she has generally played supporting roles, but today it is accompanied by a much larger billing and much larger checks.

HELTON, PERCY—actor
b: 1894, New York City, N.Y. d: Sep 11, 1971

The Beverly Hillbillies (com)
.... Homer Cratchit (1968–71)

HEMPHILL, SHIRLEY—black actress
b: Jul 1, Asheville, N.C.

What's Happening!! (com)
.... Shirley (1976–79)
One in a Million (com)
.... Shirley Simmons (1980)

*Some sources give 1929 or 1930.

What's Happening Now!! (com)
.... Shirley Wilson (1985–)

HEMSLEY, SHERMAN—black actor
b: Feb 1, 1938, Philadelphia, Pa.

All in the Family (com)
.... George Jefferson (1973–75)
The Jeffersons (com)
.... George Jefferson (1975–85)
Amen (com)... Deacon Ernest Frye (1986–)

Sherman Hemsley, the strutting, outrageous star of *The Jeffersons* very nearly spent his adult life as a mailman. He showed little interest in acting until after he had completed his military service in the late 1950s. He then attended acting school, but his appearances were limited to local Philadelphia theater groups; he worked by day for the postal service. Sherman had been with the post office for five years when actor-director Robert Hooks persuaded him to move to New York and try to crash the big time, but even then Sherman was so cautious that he arranged a transfer to the New York postal service so that he would still have steady employment. He needn't have worried. Within a year he had become a working actor. In 1968 he made his off-Broadway debut, followed by his Broadway debut in 1970 as the conman Gitlow in *Purlie*. After a couple more years of stage work, Sherman moved to Hollywood to begin his very first network TV role, and it proved to be his ticket to stardom.

HENDERSON, ALBERT—actor

Car 54, Where Are You? (com)
.... Off. O'Hara (1961–63)

HENDERSON, BILL—jazz singer
b: Mar 19, 1930, Chicago, Ill.

Ace Crawford, Private Eye (com)
.... Mello (1983)
Dreams (com)............. Torpedo (1984)

HENDERSON, CHUCK—actor

Manhunt (police)
.... Det. Dan Kramer (1959–60)

HENDERSON, FLORENCE—actress, singer
b: Feb 14, 1934, Dale, Ind.

Sing Along (music) .... regular (1958)
The Jack Paar Show (talk)
.... semiregular (1958–62)
Oldsmobile Music Theatre (music)
.... host (1959)
The Brady Bunch (com)
.... Carol Brady (1969–74)
The Brady Bunch Hour (var)
.... Carol Brady (1977)
The Brady Brides (com)
.... Carol Brady (1981)

Florence Henderson began her career in musical comedy. She landed her first Broadway role while still a student in acting school, in the 1952 musical *Wish You Were Here;* this led to more stage work, including a starring role opposite Ezio Pinza in *Fanny*. Her early television exposure was mostly as a singer, including a four-year stint on Jack Paar's version of *The Tonight Show* from 1958–62.

Florence also found some roles as an actress, including one in the well-received 1958 TV production of *Little Women*. In the 1960s her musical career began to fade, and, by 1969, when she began her role as the mom on *The Brady Bunch,* it had all but been forgotten. "Carol Brady" has provided her with a good living ever since in assorted reunions and revivals. She has also brought her sunny disposition to *The Love Boat* a number of times.

HENDERSON, KELO—actor

26 Men (wes)
.... Ranger Clint Travis (1957–59)

HENDERSON, LUTHER, JR.—orchestra leader
b: Mar 14, 1919, Kansas City, Mo.

The Polly Bergen Show (var)
.... orch. leader (1957–58)

HENDERSON, MARCIA—actress
b: Jul 22, 1930*, Andover, Mass.

The Aldrich Family (com)
.... Kathleen (1949–53)
Dear Phoebe (com). Mickey Riley (1954–55)

HENDERSON, SKITCH—orchestra leader
b: Jan 27, 1918, Birmingham, England r: Halstad, Minn.

*Some sources give 1932.

Nothing But the Best (var)
.... orch. leader (1953)
Where Was I? (quiz) .... panelist (1953)
Garroway at Large (var)
.... orch. leader (1953–54)
Tonight (talk) .... orch. leader (1954–57)
The Steve Allen Show (var)
.... regular (1956–59)
The Tonight Show (talk)
.... orch. leader (1962)
The Tonight Show Starring Johnny Carson
(talk) .... orch. leader (1962–66)

The famous, goateed bandleader and one-time sidekick on *The Tonight Show* (where he would masquerade in skits as "Sydney Ferguson"). He was married during the 1950s to actress Faye Emerson.

HENDERSON, TY—black actor

Big Shamus, Little Shamus (drama)
.... Jerry Wilson (1979)

HENDLER, LAURI—actress
b: Apr 22, 1965, Ft. Belvoir, Va.

A New Kind of Family (com)
.... Hillary Flanagan (1979–80)
Gimme a Break (com)
.... Julie Kanisky (1981–86)

HENDREN, RON—host
b: Aug 3, 1945, Pinehurst, N.C.

Entertainment Tonight (news)
.... host (1981–84)

HENDRIKS, JIM—actor

Mr. Novak (drama)... Larry Thor (1963–65)

HENNER, MARILU—actress
b: Apr 6, 1952, Chicago, Ill.

Taxi (com)........ Elaine Nardo (1978–83)

HENNIGER, GEORGE—organist

Starring Boris Karloff (drama)
.... organist (1950)

HENNING, CAROL—actress

The Bob Cummings Show (com)
.... Olive Sturgess (1956–57)

HENNING, LINDA KAYE—

see Kaye, Linda

HENRY, BILL—newscaster
b: Aug 21, 1890, San Francisco, Calif.

Who Said That? (quiz)
.... panelist (1952–53)

HENRY, BUCK—writer, actor
b: 1930, New York City, N.Y.

The Steve Allen Show (var)
.... regular (1961)
That Was the Week That Was (com)
.... regular (1964–65)
The New Show (var) .... regular (1984)

Emmy Award: Best Writing for a Comedy, for *Get Smart* (1967)

Mild-looking Buck Henry is one of those offbeat characters who has brought some very funny comedy to television over the years. The son of a former Mack Sennett bathing beauty, he played his first stage roles on Broadway as a teenager in the late 1940s, but in the '50s, after military service, he returned to find jobs scarce. So, with a friend, he masqueraded as the co-founder of SINA—The Society for Indecency to Naked Animals—and gained notoriety by appearing on talk shows to propound, with a perfectly straight face, the idea that there was a link between animal nudity and the moral decline of Western civilization. In the early '60s Buck, nutty as ever, began contributing material to the Garry Moore and Steve Allen shows, as well as appearing on the latter. In 1964 he co-wrote and appeared in a hilarious little film called *The Troublemaker,* about a country boy who tries to open a coffeehouse in Greenwich Village (catch it on the late show if you can). That same year, 1964, he helped make television history as one of the original writers and cast members of the outrageous news satire, *That Was the Week That Was.*

Comedy fans are most in his debt, however, for the show he co-created (with Mel Brooks) two years later—*Get Smart.* Bumbling secret agent Maxwell Smart and his catch phrases ("Sorry about that, Chief!") were mimicked by an entire generation. Though in later years he went on to great success as a movie screenwriter (*The Graduate,* etc.), it is for *Get Smart* that Buck Henry will be most fondly remembered.

HENRY, CAROL—choreographer
b: Jul 8, 1928, Newark, N.J.

The Garry Moore Show (var)
.... dancers (1963–64)

HENRY, CHUCK—host
b: Los Angeles, Calif.

Eye on Hollywood (mag)..... host (1983–86)

HENRY, EMMALINE—actress
b: c. 1930, Philadelphia, Pa.

I'm Dickens—He's Fenster (com)
.... Kate Dickens (1962–63)
Mickey (com)....... Nora Grady (1964–65)
I Dream of Jeannie (com)
.... Amanda Bellows (1966–70)

HENRY, GLORIA—actress
b: 1923

The Files of Jeffrey Jones (drama)
.... Michele "Mike" Malone (1952)
Dennis the Menace (com)
.... Alice Mitchell (1959–63)

HENRY, GREGG—actor

Rich Man, Poor Man—Book II (drama)
.... Wesley Jordache (1976–77)
Pearl (drama)........... Doug North (1978)
The Blue and the Gray (drama)
.... Lester Bedell (1982)

HENRY, JOHN—

see Harvey, John

HENSLEY, PAMELA—actress
b: Oct 3, 1950, Los Angeles, Calif.

Marcus Welby, M. D. (drama)
.... Janet Blake (1975–76)
Kingston: Confidential (drama)
.... Beth Kelly (1977)
Buck Rogers in the 25th Century (sci fi)
.... Princess Ardala (1979–80)
240-Robert (adv)
.... Deputy Sandy Harper (1981)
Matt Houston (drama)
.... C. J. Parsons (1982–85)

HENSON, JIM—puppeteer
b: Sep 24, 1936, Greenville, Miss.

NBC's Saturday Night Live (com)
.... regular (1975–76)

The Muppet Show (var)
.... Kermit The Frog (1976–81)
The Muppet Show (var)
.... The Swedish Chef (1976–81)
The Muppet Show (var)
.... Capt. Link Heartthrob (1976–81)
The Muppet Show (var).... Rowlf (1976–81)
The Muppet Show (var)
.... Dr. Teeth (1976–81)

Emmy Awards: Outstanding Individual Achievement in a Children's Program, for *Sesame Street* (1974, 1976); Producer and Star, Best Comedy-Variety Series, for *The Muppet Show* (1978); Best Writing for a Comedy, for *The Muppet Show* (1981); Producer, Best Animated Series, for *Jim Henson's Muppet Babies* (1986)

"A puppet show in prime time? In 1976? Try Saturday morning, or better yet, get lost!" That, or words to that effect, is what Jim Henson heard from one network executive after another when he pitched his latest brainchild to them in the mid-1970s. No one was interested in a nighttime puppet show. They knew what worked on television and what didn't. And they learned, within a fairly short time, how to eat crow.

Jim had been fascinated with puppets from childhood and followed *Kukla, Fran & Ollie* and the Baird puppets from the first time he saw a TV set. He had his first short-lived TV puppet show as a senior in high school, on a local station in Maryland. In 1955, as a freshman at the University of Maryland, he and his then future wife, Jane Nebel, teamed to present a regular series on WRC-TV, Washington, called *Sam and Friends*. Henson coined the term "Muppet" at about this time, to indicate the combination of marionette and puppet. Soon he was doing commercials and then making appearances on such network shows as *Tonight, Today, The Ed Sullivan Show, The Jimmy Dean Show* (where Rowlf was a regular) and *Perry Como*. On his very first network appearance (Steve Allen's *Tonight Show* in 1957) a one-year-old Kermit (Henson) sang "I've Grown Accustomed to Your Face" to a purple monster (Nebel), which was so enchanted that it proceeded to eat its own face, and then attempted to devour Kermit, too.

The Muppets gained even greater fame with their debut on *Sesame Street* in 1969, but a prime time network show of their own eluded them. NBC tried out some of Jim's more grotesque creations (including "The Mighty Fafag") on its hip *Saturday Night Live*, but they didn't go over well, and that only confirmed the networks' opinion that hand puppets—no matter how clever—were basically for kids. Finally, Jim managed to persuade English showman Sir Lew Grade to back him in a syndicated series, produced in England, which was offered to stations for airing mostly in the early evening. Despite the skeptics, *The Muppets* became a major hit, with a larger audience than many network shows.

HENTELOFF, ALEX—actor

Pistols 'N' Petticoats (com)
.... Little Bear (1966–67)
The Young Rebels (adv)
.... Henry Abington (1970–71)
Needles and Pins (com)
.... Myron Russo (1973)
The Betty White Show (com)
.... Doug Porterfield (1977–78)

HEPTON, BERNARD—actor
b: Oct 19, 1925, Bradford, England

The Six Wives of Henry VIII (drama)
.... Archbishop Cranmer (1971)

HERBERT, DON—host
b: Jul 10, 1917, Waconia, Minn.

Watch Mr. Wizard (info)
.... Mr. Wizard (1951–55)

TV's "Mr. Wizard" was a former freelance writer and radio actor whose interest in science and teaching led him to devise a clever instructional program for kids on NBC's Chicago station in early 1951. Through bits of apparent "magic" he would demonstrate sound scientific principles to his youthful helper. The low-key but engaging show proved successful enough to be picked up by the NBC-TV network a few months after its local premiere, and it remained on the network for the next 14 years—first in the early evening and then, from 1955–65, on Saturday or Sunday during the day.

Kindly "Mr. Wizard" continued to be active with similar projects in later years as well. He hosted eight *Experiment* specials

for public broadcasting in 1962, a series of classroom films in the late '60s, a revival of *Watch Mr. Wizard* in 1971–72, and a series of short, syndicated *Mr. Wizard Close-Ups* in the late 1970s. He was also a regular on the children's magazine show *Razzmatazz* in the late '70s. Not to ignore adults, Herbert was seen during the '50s as the "G.E. Progress Reporter" in commercials on *General Electric Theater* for eight years.

HERBERT, PERCY—actor
b: 1925

Cimarron Strip (wes)
.... Mac Gregor (1967–68)

HERBERT, TIM—comedian
b: c. 1915 d: Jun 20, 1986

Dagmar's Canteen (var)...... regular (1952)

HERD, RICHARD—actor
b: Sep 26, Brighton, Mass.

Ike (drama)..... Gen. Omar Bradley (1979)
T. J. Hooker (police)
...... Capt. Dennis Sheridan (occasional)
(1982–84)
V (movie) (sci fi) .... John (1983)
V: The Final Battle (miniseries) (sci fi)
.... John (1984)

HERLIHY, ED—announcer
b: Dorchester, Mass.

Kraft Television Theatre (drama)
.... announcer (1947–55)
The Perry Como Show (var)
.... announcer (1959–61)
The Kraft Music Hall (var)
.... announcer (1961–63)
The Tonight Show (talk) .. announcer (1962)
The Kraft Music Hall (var)
.... announcer (1967–71)

HERLIHY, WALTER—announcer
b: c. 1914 d: Oct 6, 1956

Music at the Meadowbrook (var)
..........................host (1953)
Music at the Meadowbrook (var)
..........................host (1956)

HERMAN, RALPH—orchestra leader
b: Feb 9, 1914, Milwaukee, Wis.

Circus Time (var) ... orch. leader (1956–57)

HERMANN, EDWARD—actor
b: Jul 21, 1943, Washington, D.C. r: Detroit, Mich.

Beacon Hill (drama)
.... Richard Palmer (1975)

HERRON, JOEL—orchestra leader
b: Jan 17, 1916, Chicago, Ill.

The Jaye P. Morgan Show (music)
.... orch. leader (1956)

HERSHEWE, MICHAEL—juvenile actor

American Dream (drama)
.... Todd Novak (1981)

HERSHEY, BARBARA—actress
b: Feb 5, 1948*, Hollywood, Calif.

The Monroes (wes)
.... Kathy Monroe (1966–67)
From Here to Eternity (drama)
.... Karen Holmes (1980)

A handsome, dark-haired actress, onetime companion of David Carradine, active in television since the mid-1960s. For a time in the mid-1970s she appeared under the name Barbara Seagull.

HERSHFIELD, HARRY—cartoonist, humorist
b: Oct 13, 1885, Cedar Rapids, Iowa d: Dec 15, 1974

Can You Top This? (com).. panel (1950–51)

HERVEY, IRENE—actress
b: Jul 11, 1910, Los Angeles, Calif.

Honey West (drama) .. Aunt Meg (1965–66)

The wife of actor-singer Allan Jones, and mother of Jack Jones. She was quite active playing guest roles on TV during the '50s and '60s.

HERVEY, JASON—actor

Wildside (wes)................ Zeke (1985)
Diff'rent Strokes (com).... Charlie (1985–86)
Fast Times (com)...... Curtis Spicoli (1986)

HESHIMU—actor

Room 222 (drama).... Jason Allen (1969–74)

*Some sources give 1947.

402

HESLOV, GRANT—actor
b: May 15, 1963, Los Angeles, Calif.

Spencer (com)........... Wayne (1984–85)
Under One Roof (com)....... Wayne (1985)

HESS, DORIS—actress

Marie (var) .... regular (1980–81)
The Steve Allen Comedy Hour (var)
.... regular (1980–81)

HESSEMAN, HOWARD—actor
b: Feb 27, 1940, Salem, Ore.

WKRP in Cincinnati (com)
..... Johnny Caravella (Dr. Johnny Fever)
(1978–82)
One Day at a Time (com)
.... Sam Royer (1982–84)
Head of the Class (com)
.... Charlie Moore (1986–)

A tall, rough-hewn comic actor—he looks something like a spaced-out truck driver—who is best known as the growling bossman disc jockey Dr. Johnny Fever on *WKRP in Cincinnati.* Hesseman *was* in fact a DJ for a time, on an "underground" rock station in San Francisco during that city's acid rock days in the late 1960s. Primarily, though, he was a wandering hand-to-mouth comedian, appearing with the San Francisco improvisational troupe The Committee from 1965 to 1974, as well as with other West Coast groups. In the early 1970s he decided to get serious (a little) and make some money in the "straight" entertainment world; he began showing up in episodes of various prime time situation comedies, including *The Bob Newhart Show, Rhoda, Laverne and Shirley,* and *Mary Hartman, Mary Hartman.*

In addition to his series roles, Howard has played supporting parts in a number of TV and theatrical movies and has hosted such specials as 1984's *Super Night of Rock 'n' Roll*—as the "guest veejay," natch.

HESTON, CHARLTON—actor
b: Oct 4, 1923*, Evanston, Ill.

F.D.R. (doc)............... narrator (1965)
Chiefs (drama)... Sen. Hugh Holmes (1983)
Dynasty II: The Colbys (drama)
.... Jason Colby (1985–)

*Some sources give 1924.

This famous movie actor made many appearances on television in the 1950s, primarily in dramatic productions on *Studio One, Robert Montgomery Presents,* etc. Since the early '60s his small-screen visits have been few. Autobiography: *The Actor's Life* (1978).

HEWETT, CHRISTOPHER—actor
b: Apr 5, Worthing, Sussex, England

Ivan the Terrible (com) . . . . . Federov (1976)
Fantasy Island (drama)
. . . . Lawrence (1983–84)
Mr. Belvedere (com)
. . . . Mr. Lynn Belvedere (1985–)

HEWITT, ALAN—actor
b: Jan 21, 1915, New York City, N.Y. d: Nov 7, 1986

My Favorite Martian (com)
. . . . Det. Bill Brennan (1964–66)

HEWITT, MARTIN—actor
b: 1960, Claremont, Calif.

The Family Tree (drama)
. . . . Sam Benjamin (1983)

HEWITT, VIRGINIA—actress
b: Nov 28, 1925, 1928, Shreveport, La. r: Kansas City, Mo. d: Jul 21, 1986

Space Patrol (child)
. . . . Carol Karlyle (1951–52)

HEXUM, JON-ERIK—actor
b: Nov 5, 1957, Tenafly, N.J. d: Oct 18, 1984

Voyagers (sci fi) . . . . Phineas Bogg (1982–83)
Cover Up (drama) . . . . . . Mac Harper (1984)

Hexum was a handsome young actor with an apparently bright future in television when his life was snuffed out by a needless accident on the set of his series *Cover Up.*

Jon first tried to launch his acting career onstage in New York in 1980, but made little headway until he posed for two best-selling beefcake calendars. Realizing that for the time being at least, his looks would get him more work than his acting ability, he headed for Los Angeles where, within four months of arrival, he won the part of the macho time-traveler in NBC's *Voyagers.* The following year Jon starred in his first TV movie, in a role even more appro-

priate to his growing reputation as a "hunk": *The Making of a Male Model* (in which he was manipulated by no less than Joan Collins). That was followed by a second adventure series, *Cover Up,* in which his physique was once again on display via his role as a combination male model and secret agent.

Only a few weeks after filming of *Cover Up* began, while on the set, Jon carelessly put a gun loaded with "blanks" (actually a small charge and a wad of cotton) to his head and pulled the trigger, apparently to show off. Even blanks can at that range be deadly. The proximity of the explosion shattered his skull; he went into a coma, and soon after died.

HEYDT, LOUIS JEAN—actor
b: Apr 17, 1905, Montclair, N.J. d: Jan 29, 1960

Waterfront (adv) . . . . . Joe Johnson (1953–56)

HEYES, DOUGLAS, JR.—actor
b: May 22, 1956, Los Angeles, Calif.

Captains and the Kings (drama)
. . . . Kevin Armagh (1976)
Aspen (drama) . . . . Jon Osborne (1977)

The son of one of television's most prolific directors. Perhaps not coincidentally, dad just happened to be the writer and director of both *Captains and the Kings* and *Aspen.*

HICKEY, BILL—sportscaster

Saturday Sports Mirror (sport)
. . . . sportscaster (1956)

HICKMAN, DARRYL—actor, producer
b: Jul 28, 1931, Hollywood, Calif.

The Many Loves of Dobie Gillis (com)
. . . . Davey Gillis (1959–60)
The Americans (drama)
. . . . Ben Canfield (1961)

Dwayne Hickman's older brother was the sibling that their stage mother wanted to see a star. Pushed into movies at the age of four, he soon became one of Hollywood's busiest child performers in the late '30s and '40s, appearing in such films as *The Grapes of Wrath, The Star Maker,* and *Rhapsody in Blue* (as young Ira Gershwin). He later estimated that he had been in almost 200 films, in big parts and small. By the 1950s, Darryl's career was fading, however, just as that of his younger brother began to boom. Darryl appeared in dramatic TV shows and played Dwayne's brother on *Dobie Gillis* for a season, but his own starring vehicle, a Civil War adventure called *The Americans,* was a flop.

Darryl then moved into the production end of the business and in the late 1960s became a daytime program executive at CBS. A few years later he was made executive producer of the daytime soap *Love of Life,* and he has also produced occasional prime time series *(The Keane Brothers, A Year at the Top).* He still acts occasionally and made a particularly appropriate appearance in the 1976 movie put-down of TV, *Network.*

HICKMAN, DWAYNE—actor
b: May 18, 1934, Los Angeles, Calif.

The Bob Cummings Show (com)
.... Chuck MacDonald (1955–59)
The Many Loves of Dobie Gillis (com)
.... Dobie Gillis (1959–63)

Dwayne followed his brother Darryl into movies in the mid-1940s, but, not pushed as hard by their mother, he had a lesser film career. He began appearing on television in the early '50s, on *The Lone Ranger, Lux Video Theatre* and *Public Defender* among others. His big break came with the role of Bob Cummings' nephew on *The Bob Cummings Show* in 1955, followed by four memorable years as America's most famous teenager, *Dobie Gillis.* Dwayne's boyish looks allowed him to get away with juvenile roles for a long time, but then they boomeranged. After *Dobie Gillis* left the air he played guest roles in episodes of various series for a while and appeared in some teen "beach" movies (e.g., *How to Stuff a Wild Bikini*), but the offers gradually became less and less frequent as the '60s wore on.

In 1976, as he prepared for a part in an episode of *Ellery Queen*—looking maybe three months older than when he last played Dobie Gillis—Dwayne told a reporter, "Look at me. I'll be 42 in May and I still look like—what? 32? 27? 24? When it comes to aging I'm not doing so well. Producers and casting directors still want me as a juvenile. With those roles, I've had it.

I started at MGM when I was seven. And when I stopped playing Dobie Gillis I was 30. That's 23 years in the same mold. I was so sick of that rut that when I got out of it, I went all the way out."

Dwayne did abandon acting for a time to become a public relations man in Las Vegas. Later, he tried to make a comeback, but after the 1977 reunion special *Whatever Happened to Dobie Gillis?* failed to attract much interest he joined his brother in the executive ranks at CBS, in 1979, as a supervisor of comedy series. He still makes an appearance now and then, when he can find a role (for example, in 1983's *High School U.S.A.*). As he said in 1976, "once an actor, always an actor, I suppose."

HICKMAN, HERMAN—football coach, host
b: 1911, Johnson City, Tenn.

Celebrity Time (quiz).... panelist (1950–52)
The Herman Hickman Show (sports)
.... host (1952–53)

The former college football coach at West Point and Yale. His humor and versatility, including an extensive knowledge of literature and poetry, made him a popular TV personality in the 1950s.

HICKOX, HARRY—actor
b: Oct 22, 1915, Big Spring, Texas

No Time for Sergeants (com)
.... Sgt. King (1964–65)
Please Don't Eat the Daisies (com)
.... Herb Thornton (1965–66)

HICKS, CATHERINE—actress
b: Aug 6, 1951, Scottsdale, Ariz.

The Bad News Bears (com)
.... Dr. Emily Rappant (1979–80)
Tucker's Witch (drama)
.... Amanda Tucker (1982–83)

HICKS, HILLY—black actor
b: May 4, 1950, Los Angeles, Calif.

Roll Out (com)... Pfc. Jed Brooks (1973–74)
Roots (drama)............... Lewis (1977)

HIGGINS, JOE—actor

Arrest and Trial (drama)
.... Jake Shakespeare (1963–64)

Johnny Cash Presents The Everly Brothers Show (var)................. regular (1970)

HIGGINS, JOEL—actor
b: Sep 28, 1943, Bloomington, Ill.

Salvage 1 (adv) .... Skip Carmichael (1979)
Best of the West (com)
.... Marshal Sam Best (1981–82)
Silver Spoons (com)
.... Edward Stratton III (1982–86)

HIGGINS, MICHAEL—actor

One Man's Family (drama)
.... Johnny Roberts (1949–51)

HILBER, BURT—host

The Adventures of Oky Doky (child)
.... host (1948–49)

HILL, ARTHUR—actor
b: Aug 1, 1922, Melfort, Saskatchewan, Canada

Owen Marshall, Counselor at Law (drama)
.... Owen Marshall (1971–74)
Hagen (drama)........ Carl Palmer (1980)
Glitter (drama)
.... Charles Hardwick (1984–85)

When producer David Victor decided to use the elements that had made his *Marcus Welby, M.D.* a hit in a new series built around a lawyer, he looked for a leading man with the same qualities as *Welby*'s Robert Young: mature, soft-spoken, thoughtful and concerned. Canadian actor Arthur Hill, a veteran of stage, television, and movies, fit the bill. He was the perfect *Welby* clone, even though he was not as familiar to viewers as Young.

Hill had begun his acting career in Canada and England after he mustered out of the Canadian Air Force in 1945. In 1954 he made a strong impression on Broadway in *The Matchmaker,* which led to more stage work in the late '50s and '60s—most notably in the controversial play *Who's Afraid of Virginia Woolf?* in 1962. Hill's television debut was in a 1956 *Hallmark Hall of Fame* drama, "Born Yesterday"; thereafter, he worked steadily in TV dramas, especially during the '60s, specializing in noble, mature types. Since his years as *Owen Marshall* he has played supporting roles in many TV movies and was perhaps at his noblest as the southern judge who endured community outrage when he freed a group of black youths falsely accused of rape, in *Judge Horton and the Scottsboro Boys* (1976).

HILL, BENNY—comedian
b: Jan 21, 1925, Southampton, England

The Benny Hill Show (com).. star (1979–82)

This pudgy, slapstick comedian, who had been convulsing British television viewers since 1969, became a surprise hit on American TV ten years later, when syndicated (and edited) reruns of his British specials were released here. Due to the rather bawdy nature of his humor (lots of bosomy girls, there), they were run after 11 P.M. on most stations.

Benny had been seen in the U.S. before this, but was not particularly noticed, in such films as *Those Magnificent Men in Their Flying Machines* (1965) and *Chitty Chitty Bang Bang* (1968).

HILL, CHARLIE—actor

The Big Show (var)......... regular (1980)

HILL, CRAIG—actor
b: 1926, Los Angeles, Calif.

The Whirlybirds (adv)
.... Pete ("P.T.") Moore (1956–59)

HILL, DANA—actress
b: May 6, 1964, Van Nuys, Calif.

The Two of Us (com)
.. Gabrielle "Gabby" Gallagher (1981–82)

HILL, GOLDIE—country singer
b: Jan 11, 1933, Karnes County, Texas

The Grand Ole Opry (music)
.... regular (1955–56)

The year after her network appearance on *The Grand Ole Opry,* Goldie married country star Carl Smith and retired. "I'm just plain Mrs. Smith," she says now.

HILL, JOHNNY—singer

Music in Velvet (music) ..... regular (1949)

HILL, RICHARD—actor
b: Jan 26, Harlan, Ky. r: Toledo, Ohio

Today's F.B.I. (police)
.... Al Gordean (1981–82)

HILL, STEVEN—actor
b: Feb 24, 1922, Seattle, Wash.

Mission: Impossible (drama)
.... Daniel Briggs (1966–67)

HILL, TOM—actor
b: Jun 2, Mussoorie, India

Wizards and Warriors (adv)
.... King Baaldorf (1983)

HILLAIRE, MARCEL—actor
b: Apr 23, 1908, Cologne, Germany

Adventures in Paradise (adv)
.... Inspector Bouchard (1961–62)

HILLEBRAND, FRED—actor
b: Dec 25, 1893, Brooklyn, N.Y. d: Sep 15, 1963

Martin Kane, Private Eye (drama)
.... Lt. Bender (1949–50)

HILLERMAN, JOHN—actor
b: Dec 20, 1932*, Denison, Texas

The Adventures of Ellery Queen (drama)
.... Simon Brimmer (1975–76)
The Betty White Show (com)
.... John Elliot (1977–78)
Magnum, P.I. (drama)
...... Jonathan Quale Higgins III (1980–)

John Hillerman is a former stage actor who spent most of the 1950s and '60s in the New York theater, fulfilling himself artistically but not making much financial progress. In 1969 he decided to go West, enjoy the sun, and perhaps make some money. There, among many other theatrical refugees, he began to work rather steadily in supporting roles in series episodes. He also had parts in several films directed by his friend from New York days, Peter Bogdanovich, including *What's Up Doc?* (1972), in which he first developed the dapper, slightly prissy character that would later become his trademark.

By the mid-1970s John was well enough established to win the role of Ellery Queen's arrogant rival on *Ellery Queen* and then of Betty White's suave, sarcastic

*Some sources give Dec. 30.

ex-husband on *The Betty White Show*. The character was perfected with the stuffy British major domo on *Magnum, P.I.*, a role that has made him wealthy and secure. Was he being typecast? "I am not one of those who yearn to play Hamlet," he told *TV Guide* in 1982. "Higgins will do."

HILLIARD, HARRIET—
see Nelson, Harriet

HILLS, DICK—writer, comedian
Kraft Music Hall Presents The Dave King Show (var)................. regular (1959)

HINDLE, ART—actor
b: Jul 21, 1948, Halifax, Nova Scotia, Canada

Kingston: Confidential (drama)
.... Tony Marino (1977)
Dallas (drama)..... Jeff Farraday (1981–82)
Berrengers (drama)... Todd Hughes (1985)

HINES, CONNIE—actress
b: c. 1936, Dedham, Mass.

Mr. Ed (com)......... Carol Post (1961–66)

HINES, JANEAR—actress
b: c. 1950 d: Mar 2, 1981

Julia (com)............. Roberta (1970–71)

HINGLE, PAT—actor
b: Jul 19, 1923, Denver, Colo.

Stone (police)........ Chief Paulton (1980)

HINNANT, SKIP—actor
The Patty Duke Show (com) . Ted (1963–65)

HINTON, DARBY—juvenile actor
b: Aug 19, 1957, Santa Monica, Calif.

Daniel Boone (wes) . Israel Boone (1964–70)

The son of actor Ed Hinton, and, the press releases claimed, an indirect descendant of the real-life Daniel Boone. The young lad made his acting debut at the age of six months in a *Playhouse 90* production and appeared in an assortment of juvenile guest roles during the early 1960s.

HINTON, ED—actor
b: 1928 d: Oct 12, 1958

I Led Three Lives (drama)
.... special agent Henderson (1953–56)

HINTON, JAMES DAVID—actor
Jessie (police).................. Phil (1984)

HIRSCH, JUDD—actor
b: Mar 15, 1935, New York City, N.Y.

Delvecchio (police)
...... Sgt. Dominick Delvecchio (1976–77)
Taxi (com)......... Alex Rieger (1978–83)
Detective in the House (drama)
.... Press Wyman (1985)

Emmy Awards: Best Actor in a Comedy Series, for *Taxi* (1981, 1983)

Despite his considerable success on television in the 1970s and '80s, Judd Hirsch's first love seems to be the New York stage. It took him quite a while to become established there, however. Judd did not win his first professional acting role until age 27, with a stock company in Colorado, and he spent the next dozen years mostly in minor roles, gradually working his way up.

His television debut came in 1974, when he was almost 40, as the dedicated public defender in the Emmy Award winning TV movie *The Law*. Two years later he starred as a similarly noble upholder of the law in *Delvecchio* (where his superior officer, interestingly enough, was played by Michael Conrad, later the head sergeant on *Hill Street Blues;* Judd's partner was *Hill Street's* Charles Haid). By this time Judd's Broadway career was finally in high gear as well, and he alternated between the two media as few others have. In 1978 he left the cast of Neil Simon's hit play *Chapter Two* to begin the role of Alex Rieger on *Taxi*. The following year he split his time between *Taxi* filming and the stage hit *Talley's Folly*, which was written by his friend Lanford Wilson. In 1980, Judd found time to appear in that play as well as in the Academy Award–winning film *Ordinary People*—and, of course, to continue in *Taxi*.

HIRSCH, STEVEN—actor
Knots Landing (drama)
.... Roy Lance (1980–82)

HIRSCHFIELD, ROBERT—actor
b: Jun 8, New York City, N.Y.

Hill Street Blues (police)
.... Off. Leo Schnitz (1981–85)

HIRSON, ALICE—actress
When the Whistle Blows (com)
.... Dottie Jenkins (1980)
Dallas (drama).. Mavis Anderson (1982–84)

HIRT, AL—trumpet player, host
b: Nov 7, 1922, New Orleans, La.

Fanfare (var).................. host (1965)
The Green Hornet (drama)
.... played theme (1966–67)
Make Your Own Kind of Music (var)
.... regular (1971)

HITCHCOCK, ALFRED—director, host
b: Aug 13, 1899, London, England d: Apr 29, 1980

Alfred Hitchcock Presents (drama)
.... host (1955–65)
Alfred Hitchcock Presents (drama)
.... host (1985–86)

The legendary director of some of Hollywood's most enduring film classics put his unique stamp on television as well with this long-running (and oft rerun) anthology series. As host, his pudgy countenance and droll wit provided a nice counterpoint to the black humor of the little tales that followed. Though Hitch personally directed only a handful of the episodes, he oversaw them all, and all reflected the special style of the "Master of Suspense."

So great was Hitchcock's appeal, and so sorely was he missed in later years, that TV executives finally decided that, dead or not, they simply had to have him back. He thereby became the first TV personality in history to return after death to host an entirely new series; films of his original black & white appearances were electronically processed into color and spliced into the new 1985 shows, as if he had never left us. It was just the sort of macabre touch the master would have enjoyed.

HOAG, MITZI—actress

Here Come the Brides (adv)
.... Miss Essie Gillis (1968–70)
We'll Get By (com)........ Liz Platt (1975)

HOBBS, JOHN—actor

Michael Nesmith in Television Parts (var)
.... regular (1985)

HOBSON, LAURA—writer

b: Jun 19, 1900, New York City r: Long Island, N.Y. d: Feb 28, 1986

I've Got a Secret (quiz) ..... panelist (1952)

HOCTOR, DANNY—dancer

Club Embassy (var) ...... dancer (1952–53)

HODGE, AL—actor

b: Apr 18, 1913 d: Mar 19, 1979

Captain Video and His Video Rangers (child)
.... Captain Video (1951–55)

Al Hodge typified both the bright and dark sides of television, the former for the magic it could weave for young viewers, and the latter for the way in which it could discard and destroy performers it no longer needed.

Hodge was just another journeyman actor when he was called upon to play the role of Captain Video, after the dismissal of the original star, Richard Coogan. Hodge had previously worked in radio and in fact had a seven-year run as the voice of the *Green Hornet* in the late 1930s and early '40s; later, he had directed such radio adventure series as *The Lone Ranger* and *Challenge of the Yukon.* However, radio actors labor in relative anonymity. With *Captain Video,* Hodge became a familiar and trusted hero to kids across America as they followed his incredibly (for the time) futuristic-looking adventures. So closely was the actor associated with the role, that when he testified before Congress in 1954 on the subject of violence on television, the senators routinely addressed him as "Captain."

That close identification, he later claimed, became his downfall. After *Captain Video,* Hodge said he couldn't get a job doing even cigarette commercials—because no one wanted to see the righteous upholder of truth and decency smoking a cigarette. Much has been written about Hodge as the ultimate victim of typecasting, but, truth be told, he was hardly a charismatic actor and it is unlikely that most viewers would have ever heard of him had it not been for his one famous role.

Whatever the reasons, Hodge spent the late 1950s hosting cartoon shows on local New York television and playing a few bit parts in network dramatic series. After that he worked at odd jobs such as bank guard and store clerk, always hoping to make his comeback. He died of emphysema in his cheap Manhattan hotel room in 1979, surrounded by mementos of his glory days.

HODGES, CHARLES—newscaster

Report On . . . (doc) .... narrator (1949)

HODGES, DR. CHARLES—New York University professor

b: Oct 12, 1894, Palo Alto, Calif. d: Oct 8, 1964

Answers for Americans (pub aff)
.... panelist (1953–54)

HODGES, RUSS—sportscaster

b: Jun 11, 1911, Dayton, Tenn. r: Danville, Ky.

Russ Hodges' Scoreboard (sport)
.... reporter (1948–49)
Wednesday Night Fights (sport)
.... sportscaster (1948–55)

HODGINS, EARLE—actor

b: 1899 d: Apr 14, 1964

Guestward Ho! (com).. Lonesome (1960–61)

HODSON, JIM—actor

Accused (drama) ..... court clerk (1958–59)

HOFF, CARL—orchestra leader

b: c. 1905, Oxnard, Calif. d: Oct 15, 1965

Kay Kyser's Kollege of Musical Knowledge (quiz).............. orch. leader (1949–50)
Star of the Family (var)
.... orch. leader (1950–52)
Ford Star Revue (var)
.... orch. leader (1951)
Music Hall (music)..... orch. leader (1952)
The Scott Music Hall (var)
.... orch. leader (1952–53)

The Imogene Coca Show (var)
.... orch. leader (1954–55)
The Martha Raye Show (var)
.... orch. leader (1955–56)
The Julius La Rosa Show (var)
.... orch. leader (1956)
The Patti Page Show (var)
.... orch. leader (1956)
The Tony Bennett Show (var)
.... orch. leader (1956)
Bob Crosby Show (var) . orch. leader (1958)

HOFF, ROBIN—actress

Wildside (wes)........ Alice Freeze (1985)

HOFFMAN, BASIL—actor
b: 1941

Square Pegs (com)
.... Principal Dingleman (1982–83)

HOFFMAN, BERN—actor
b: 1913 d: Dec 15, 1979

Major Dell Conway of the Flying Tigers (adv)
.... regular (1951)

HOFFMAN, ELIZABETH—actress

The Winds of War (drama)
.... Eleanor Roosevelt (1983)

HOFFMAN, GERTRUDE—actress
b: 1871* d: Oct 21, 1966

My Little Margie (com)
.... Mrs. Odetts (1952–55)

HOFFMAN, HAROLD—politician, humorist
b: Feb 7, 1896, South Amboy, N.J. d: Jun 4, 1954

That Reminds Me (talk) ..... regular (1948)
Q.E.D. (quiz).............. panelist (1951)

A former governor of New Jersey.

HOFFMAN, WENDY—actress

Makin' It (adv)............ Suzanne (1979)

HOGAN, JACK—actor
b: Nov 24, Chapel Hill, N.C.

Combat (drama).......... Kirby (1963–67)

*Some sources give c.1886.

Adam 12 (police)
.... Sgt. Jerry Miller (1969)
Sierra (adv)
.... Chief Ranger Jack Moore (1974)

HOGAN, ROBERT—actor
b: Sep 28, New York City, N.Y.

Peyton Place (drama)
.... Rev. Tom Winter (1968–69)
The Don Rickles Show (com)
.... Tyler Benedict (1972)
The Manhunter (drama)
.... Sheriff Paul Tate (1974–75)
Richie Brockelman, Private Eye (drama)
.... Sgt. Ted Coopersmith (1978)
Operation Petticoat (com)
.... Lt. Comdr. Haller (1978–79)
Secrets of Midland Heights (drama)
.... Nathan Welsh (1980–81)

HOGAN, SUSAN—actress

Night Heat (police)
.... Nicole "Nickie" Rimbaud (1985–)

HOGESTYN, DRAKE—actor
b: Sep 29, Fort Wayne, Ind.

Seven Brides for Seven Brothers (adv)
.... Brian McFadden (1982–83)

HOLBROOK, HAL—actor
b: Feb 17, 1925, Cleveland, Ohio, r: South Weymouth, Mass

The Senator (drama)
.... Sen. Hayes Stowe (1970–71)
North and South (drama)
.... Pres. Abraham Lincoln (1985)

Emmy Awards: Best Actor in a Drama Series, for *The Senator* (1971); Best Actor in a Dramatic Special and Actor of the Year in a Special, both for the *ABC Theatre* production "Pueblo" (1974); Best Actor in a Limited Series, for *Sandburg's Lincoln* (1976)

Abandoned by his parents at the age of two, Hal Holbrook was raised by relatives and educated at Culver Military Academy. His theatrical career was slow in getting started. For most of the 1950s he appeared in clubs and as a daytime soap opera actor; from 1954–59 he played the drunken Grayling Dennis on the then-popular soap *The Brighter Day*.

Holbook's reputation began to grow

with his impersonation of Mark Twain, which he began off-Broadway in 1959 and brought to Broadway and to television in the 1960s; he estimates that he has played the American humorist more than 2,000 times in one-man shows in the U.S. and overseas. He also began another historical characterization in the early 1960s, that of Abraham Lincoln, which he has repeated many times since, including his performance in the 1985 miniseries *North and South*.

Hal was quite active in the New York theater beginning in the early 1960s. Since the mid-1960s he has been seen fairly often in prime time television as well, in prestigious (and often Emmy-winning) dramatic productions. Among these have been *A Clear and Present Danger* (1970), which led to *The Senator* segment of the *Bold Ones* anthology; *That Certain Summer* (1972), one of TV's first major attempts to deal with the subject of homosexuality; and the docudrama *Pueblo* (1973), in which Holbook played Commander Boucher.

A consummate actor who is particularly believable in fact-based dramas, Holbook has come to specialize in sensitive, caring authority figures—whether fathers or presidents. Some of his recent notable roles have been those of the heroic navy commander who became a prisoner of war, in *When Hell Was in Session* (1979); future president John Adams in the miniseries *George Washington* (1984); and an embattled president in *Under Siege* (1986). Of course, he is not always on the side of the system. In the movie *All the President's Men,* that was Holbrook in the shadows as "Deep Throat."

HOLCOMB, KATHRYN—actress

How the West Was Won (miniseries) (drama)
.... Laura (1977)
How the West Was Won (wes)
.... Laura Macahan (1978–79)
Skag (drama)
.... Patricia Skagska (1980)

HOLCOMBE, HARRY—actor

The Wonderful John Acton (drama)
.... John Acton (1953)
Barefoot in the Park (com)
.... Mr. Kendricks (1970–71)

HOLCOMBE, WENDY—singer, actress
b: c. 1963, Alabaster, Ala.

Nashville on the Road (music)
.... regular (1975–81)
Lewis & Clark (com)
.... Wendy, the waitress (1981–82)

HOLDEN, JAMES—actor

Adventures in Paradise (adv)
.... Clay Baker (1960–62)

HOLDEN, REBECCA—actress
b: Jun 12, 1953, Austin, Texas

Knight Rider (adv) .. April Curtis (1983–84)

HOLE, JONATHAN—actor

Stud's Place (var) .... Mr. Denby (1950)

HOLLAND, GINA—actress

One Man's Family (drama)
.... Jo Collier (1952)

HOLLAND, KRISTINA—actress
b: Feb 25, 1944, Fayetteville, N.C.

The Courtship of Eddie's Father (com)
.... Tina Rickles (1969–72)
Wait Till Your Father Gets Home (cartn)
.... Alice Boyle (voice) (1972–74)

HOLLAND, RICHARD—actor, writer

Operation Neptune (sci fi)
.... Dink Saunders (1953)

HOLLAND, STEVE—actor
b: Germany

Flash Gordon (sci fi)
.... Flash Gordon (1953–54)

HOLLANDER, DAVID—juvenile actor
b: Aug 7, c. 1969, Los Angeles, Calif.

The McLean Stevenson Show (com)
.... David (1976–77)
What's Happening!! (com)
.... Little Earl (1978–79)
A New Kind of Family (com)
.... Andy Flanagan (1979–80)
Lewis & Clark (com). Keith Lewis (1981–82)
Call to Glory (drama)
.... Wesley Sarnac (1984–85)

HOLLENBECK, DON—newscaster
b: c. 1905 d: Jun 22, 1954

CBS Weekend News (news)
.... anchorman (1950)

A CBS newsman active on radio and television in the 1940s and '50s; he served as a reporter on *You Are There* and was associated with Edward R. Murrow on *See It Now,* among other programs. Hollenbeck came under heavy attack by right-wing columnists in the early 1950s due to his alleged leftist leanings in his broadcast commentaries. Depressed at the vituperation leveled against him, and ill, he committed suicide in 1954.

HOLLIDAY, ART—actor
b: Jul 18, Hartford, Conn.

The White Shadow (drama)
.... Eddie Franklin (1980–81)

HOLLIDAY, FRED—actor, host

Medical Center (drama)
.... Dr. Barnes (1970–71)

HOLLIDAY, KENE—black actor
b: Jun 25, New York City, N.Y.

Carter Country (com)
.... Sgt. Curtis Baker (1977–79)
Matlock (drama)
.... Tyler Hudson (1986–)

HOLLIDAY, POLLY—actress
b: Jul 2, 1937, Jasper, Ala.

Alice (com) ...... Flo Castleberry (1976–80)
Flo (com)
     Florence Jean (Flo) Castleberry (1980–81)

When Polly Holliday hollered "Kiss ma grits!" she knew what she was talking about. The actress who played the colorful, drawling waitress on *Alice* was born and raised a southerner. As the daughter of a truck driver, she knew all about truck stops and diners too. Polly started out as a music teacher in public schools, then switched to acting and spent seven years with a regional theater company in Florida. She made her Broadway debut in 1974, but her real break, and her first major television role, was in *Alice,* followed by her own spin-off series, *Flo.* Since that left the air she has been seen in specials and TV movies.

HOLLIMAN, EARL—actor
b: Sep 11, 1928, Tensas Swamp, Delhi, La.

Hotel de Paree (wes) .. Sundance (1959–60)
The Wide Country (wes)
.... Mitch Guthrie (1962–63)
Police Woman (police)
.... Lt. Bill Crowley (1974–78)
The Thorn Birds (drama)
.... Luddie Mueller (1983)

Earl Holliman is a rugged, slightly surly hunk of masculinity who has been active in television since the 1950s. A bit of a hustler in his youth, he hitchhiked to Hollywood at 14 and tried to break into films; that failed, he joined the navy and was sent to radio school before officials discovered that he was underage and sent him packing.

He finally did get into both the navy and acting, in that order. His first small movie roles were in the early 1950s (he had one line in the Martin and Lewis film *Scared Stiff*). By the late '50s he was appearing in TV dramas, including a notable two-man tour de force with Sessue Hayakawa on *Kraft Theatre* in 1958 called "The Sea is Boiling Hot." A well-remembered, if slightly offbeat, role was in the very first episode of *The Twilight Zone,* called "Where Is Everybody?", in which he played a hallucinating astronaut who has been alone in space for too long. Westerns proved best-suited to his rugged build, however, and he starred in two of them, *Hotel de Paree* and *The Wide Country* (as a modern-day bronco rider).

Later, "Big Earl" shifted with the prime time tides and went into crime shows, guesting in *The F.B.I., Ironside, The Rookies,* and others. His most famous role was as Angie Dickinson's boss (lucky him!) in *Police Woman.* He has since worked mostly in TV movies and miniseries, including *The Thorn Birds.*

HOLLIS, JEFF—actor

C.P.O. Sharkey (com).... Daniels (1976–78)

HOLLOWAY, JOAN—actress

The College Bowl (com)
.... regular (1950–51)

HOLLOWAY, STANLEY—actor
b: Oct 1, 1890, London, England d: Jan 30, 1982

Our Man Higgins (com)... Higgins (1962–63)

Booming English character actor who was most famous in America as Liza Doolittle's father in *My Fair Lady*. Autobiography: *Wiv a Little Bit of Luck* (1969).

HOLLOWAY, STERLING—actor
b: Jan 4, 1905, Cedartown, Ga.

The Life of Riley (com)
.... Waldo Binney (1953–58)
Willy (drama)....... Harvey Evelyn (1955)
Baileys of Balboa (com)
.... Buck Singleton (1964–65)

Soft-voiced, American-born comic actor, who usually played yokels; in no way to be confused with Stanley Holloway. Sterling provided the voices of many Disney and other animated characters, including TV's *Winnie the Pooh*.

HOLM, CELESTE—actress
b: Apr 29, 1919, New York City, N.Y.

Honestly Celeste (com)
.... Celeste Anders (1954)
Who Pays? (quiz) .... panelist (1959)
Nancy (com).. Abigail Townsend (1970–71)
Backstairs at the White House (drama)
.... Florence Harding (1979)
Jessie (police)........ Molly Hayden (1984)
Falcon Crest (drama).. Anna Rossini (1985)

Celeste Holm made her first big splash in the original Broadway production of *Oklahoma!* in 1943, singing "I'm Just a Gal That Cain't Say No." She has been most famous for her comedy roles ever since, though she is a versatile actress who has given strong performances in many dramas. She was already well-established as a stage and screen star when she began appearing on television in the early 1950s in such showcases as *Lux Video Theatre* and *Schlitz Playhouse of Stars*. She continued to appear in dramas in the '60s and '70s (*The Fugitive, Medical Center*, etc.), but on television, as elsewhere, her comic vehicles are best remembered. She was a sprightly young reporter on *Honestly Celeste* and a more mature but still cheerful chaperone to the president's daughter on *Nancy*. Later, she had a recurring role on *Archie's Place*.

By the 1980s Celeste's series television work was leaning more toward the dramatic, with supporting roles in the police series *Jessie* (as Lindsay Wagner's mother) and in the soap opera *Falcon Crest*. She is quite active in both New York and national cultural affairs; in 1982 President Reagan named her to a six-year term on the National Arts Council.

HOLM, IAN—actor
b: Sep 12, 1931*, Ilford, Essex, England

Holocaust (drama)
.... Heinrich Himmler (1978)

HOLMAN, BILL—

Draw to Win (quiz)........ panelist (1952)

HOLMES, DENNIS—juvenile actor
b: Oct 10, 1950

Laramie (wes) .... Mike Williams (1961–63)

HOLMES, ED—actor
b: c. 1911, Canada d: Jul 12, 1977

The Growing Paynes (com)
.... Mr. Payne (1949)
Starlit Time (var) .... regular (1950)
Once Upon a Tune (music)... regular (1951)

HOLMES, JENNIFER—actress
b: Aug 23, Fall River, Mass. r: Seekonk, Mass.

Newhart (com)
.... Leslie Vanderkellen (1982–83)
Misfits of Science (adv)
.... Jane Miller (1985–86)

HOLMES, LEROY—orchestra leader
b: Sep 22, 1913, Pittsburgh, Pa. d: Jul 27, 1986

Tonight (talk) .... orch. leader (1956–57)

HOLMES, TONY—black juvenile actor

Baby, I'm Back (com).... Jordan Ellis (1978)

HOLT, BOB—actor, voice specialist

Tony Orlando and Dawn (var)
.... regular (1976)

*Some sources give 1932.

412

HOLT, JOHNNY—

see Hill, Johnny

HOMEIER, SKIP—actor
b: Oct 5, 1929*, Chicago, Ill.

Dan Raven (police)
.... Lt. Dan Raven (1960–61)
The Interns (drama)
.... Dr. Hugh Jacoby (1970–71)

HOMETOWNERS, THE—

Midwestern Hayride (var)
.... regulars (1957–59)

HON, JEAN MARIE—actress
b: Mar 21, 1955, San Francisco, Calif. r: Los Angeles, Calif.

Man from Atlantis (adv).... Jane (1977–78)

HONEYDREAMERS, THE—singing group

The Skip Farrell Show (music)
.... regulars (1949)
Kay Kyser's Kollege of Musical Knowledge (quiz).................. regulars (1949–50)
Broadway Open House (talk)
.... regulars (1950–51)
Summertime U.S.A. (music) . regulars (1953)
Upbeat (music)............ regulars (1955)

HONG, JAMES—actor
b: c. 1929, Minneapolis, Minn.

The Adventures of Charlie Chan (drama)
.... Barry Chan (1956–57)
Jigsaw John (police) ..... Frank Chen (1976)
Switch (drama)........... Wang (1977–78)

HOOD, DARLA—actress, singer
b: Nov 4, 1931, Leedey, Okla. d: Jun 13, 1979

The Ken Murray Show (var)
.... regular (1950–51)

Perky former member of *Our Gang (The Little Rascals)*, from 1935–45. She later did voices for cartoons and commercials.

HOOD, NOEL—actress

From a Bird's Eye View (com)
.... Miss Fosdyke (1971)

*Some sources give 1930.

HOOKS, JAN—actress
b: Atlanta, Ga.

The Half Hour Comedy Hour (var)
.... regular (1983)
NBC's Saturday Night Live (var)
.... regular (1986–)

HOOKS, KEVIN—black actor, director
b: Sep 19, 1958, Philadelphia, Pa.

The White Shadow (drama)
.... Morris Thorpe (1978–81)
He's the Mayor (com)
.... Mayor Carl Burke (1986)

The son of Robert Hooks.

HOOKS, ROBERT—black actor
b: Apr 18, 1937, Washington, D.C.

N.Y.P.D. (police)
.... Det. Jeff Ward (1967–69)
Backstairs at the White House (drama)
.... Mays (1979)

HOOPER, LARRY—singer, pianist

The Lawrence Welk Show (music)
.... regular (1955–82)

HOPE, BOB—comedian
b: May 29, 1903, Eltham, Kent, England r: Cleveland, Ohio

Chesterfield Sound Off Time (var)
.... star (1951–52)
Colgate Comedy Hour (var)
.... rotating host (1952–53)
Bob Hope Presents the Chrysler Theatre (misc) .... host (1963–67)

Emmy Awards: Trustees Award for "The Consistently High Quality of His Television Programs Through the Years" (1959); Executive Producer and Star, Best Variety Special, for *The Bob Hope Christmas Special* (1966)

Leslie Townes Hope is such a thoroughly American institution that people are often surprised to learn he was born in England. His father, a stonemason, moved his large family to Cleveland when Bob was four, and, eventually, through his father's naturalization in 1920, Bob became a U.S. citizen. Long before that, however, the young comic had hit the boards in vaudeville with an act of "song, patter, and eccentric danc-

413

ing" (he was still doing the first two in the 1980s). He reached Broadway in the late 1920s and scored his first great success there in *Roberta* in 1933. In the late '30s he achieved national stardom on radio and in films.

Bob was one of the very biggest names in show business when television came on the scene. Unlike some major stars, he immediately jumped into the new medium, making his debut on Easter Sunday, 1950. For the next several years he was seen on a regular basis on two big budget variety shows, *Chesterfield Sound Off Time* and *The Colgate Comedy Hour*. After that, he settled down to his familiar pattern of several specials a year, all of them major TV events drawing huge audiences. One which became an annual tradition was his Christmas special, filmed each year during his regular tour to entertain American troops overseas (these continued until 1972). He was also seen frequently as host of the Academy Awards telecast. During the '60s, Bob returned to series TV for a time to host, and sometimes star in, a comedy/drama anthology sponsored by Chrysler.

Aside from his specials, Bob's television appearances were few—but unusual. He appeared several times on Lucille Ball's various series, the first time in a 1956 episode of *I Love Lucy,* in which Lucy donned preposterous disguises so that she could get to Hope and convince him to appear at Ricky's nightclub. Bob did, of course, and sang them a special version of "Thanks for the Memories."

Later, Bob made a few appearances on *The Danny Thomas Show* and in TV productions of his first stage hit, *Roberta,* in 1958 and again in 1969. He is best known, however, for his specials—always packed with mile-a-minute wisecracks (many of them corny, but, well, he's Bob Hope)—lots of pretty girls, some contemporary popular guest stars, and maybe a football team or two. He's made enough money to practically buy NBC, with which he's long been associated, but he says he'll never retire, and audiences show no sign of retiring him.

Someone once asked Bob how he would like to be remembered. "I don't care," he replied, "just so they don't say 'Who was he?' "

A recent autobiography is titled *The Road to Hollywood* (1977).

HOPE, LESLIE—actress
Berrengers (drama)
.... Cammie Springer (1985)
Knots Landing (drama)
.... Linda Martin (1985–86)

HOPKINS, BO—actor
b: Feb 2, 1942, Greenville, S.C.

Doc Elliot (drama) ... Eldred McCoy (1974)
Aspen (drama) ..... Budd Townsend (1977)
The Rockford Files (drama)
.... John Cooper (1978–79)
Dynasty (drama) .. Matthew Blaisdel (1981)

HOPKINS, TELMA—black singer, actress
b: Oct 28, 1948, Louisville, Ky. r: Detroit, Mich.

Tony Orlando and Dawn (var)
.... member of Dawn (1974–76)
A New Kind of Family (com)
.... Jess Ashton (1979–80)
Bosom Buddies (com).... Isabelle (1980–82)
Gimme a Break (com)
.... Addy Wilson (1984–)

HOPPER, WILLIAM—actor
b: Jan 26, 1915, New York City, N.Y. d: Mar 6, 1970

Perry Mason (drama)
.... Paul Drake (1957–66)

The son of actress/columnist Hedda Hopper and vaudeville superstar De Wolf Hopper. Viewers are often surprised to learn that Hopper was supposed to play the lead in *Perry Mason* but switched roles with Raymond Burr at the last minute.

HORAN, BARBRA—actress
B.J. and the Bear (adv) ... Samantha (1981)

HORAN, BOBBY—juvenile actor
The Hero (com) ...... Paul Garret (1966–67)

HORDERN, MICHAEL—actor
b: Oct 3, 1911, Berkhampstead, England

Shogun (drama) ...... Friar Domingo (1980)

414

HORGAN, PATRICK—actor

Casablanca (drama)
.... Maj. Heinrik Strasser (1983)

HORSFORD, ANNA MARIA—black actress
b: Mar 6, 1945, New York City, N.Y.

Amen (com)......... Thelma Frye (1986–)

HORSLEY, LEE—actor
b: May 15, 1955, Muleshoe, Texas

Nero Wolfe (drama)
.... Archie Goodwin (1981)
Matt Houston (drama)
.... Matt Houston (1982–85)

Probably the unkindest cut was the headline over the *TV Guide* feature story: "Presenting Tom Selleck . . . Oops, Lee Horsley." Lee certainly did look a lot like the *Magnum, P.I.* star—macho build, mustache, and all—and that is frankly what the network had in mind when it cast him.

Lee was born in Texas and grew up in the wide open spaces of Colorado. He loved acting and singing and upon graduation from college headed straight for New York to get a start in the theater, which the city seemed noticeably reluctant to provide. After a period of struggle, he flew to Los Angeles to test for *The Gangster Chronicles* series, lost out, but instead won the role of William Conrad's flunky in *Nero Wolfe*.

This was hardly the sort of role to make him a star, however, and the series' early demise was probably a blessing. He then landed a starring role in the 1982 adventure movie *The Sword and the Sorcerer,* was seen there by the right folks, and moved into his own series as the fast-driving, womanizing, super-rich private eye *Matt Houston*. Was it an imitation *Magnum?* Well, no, Lee would insist, "but I'm flattered you see a resemblance."

HORTON, EDWARD EVERETT—actor
b: Mar 18, 1886, Brooklyn, N.Y. d: Sep 29, 1970

Holiday Hotel (var) .. hotel manager (1950)
The Bullwinkle Show (cartn)
...... narrator of "Fractured Fairy Tales"
1961–62)

HORTON, MICHAEL—actor

Eddie Capra Mysteries (drama)
.... Harvey Winchell (1978–79)
The Blue and the Gray (drama)
.... Mark Geyser (1982)

HORTON, PETER—actor
b: Aug 20, Bellevue, Wash.

Seven Brides for Seven Brothers (adv)
.... Crane McFadden (1982–83)

HORTON, ROBERT—actor
b: Jul 29, 1924, Los Angeles, Calif.

Kings Row (drama)
.... Drake McHugh (1955–56)
Wagon Train (wes)
.... Flint McCullough (1957–62)
A Man Called Shenandoah (wes)
.... Shenandoah (1965–66)

Robert Horton was one of those rugged, masculine types who looked good in buckskin and who became quite popular during television's western era. He followed a traditional route to get there, studying acting in the late 1940s (after World War II service in the coast guard) and launching his career in stock theater in 1950. He played small roles on New York–based live TV, but his first real break was in the filmed romantic drama *King's Row* in 1955. Two years later he began his most famous role, as the trail scout on the very popular *Wagon Train.*

After five years on horseback Horton quit the number-one rated series, claiming that he was "fed up" with westerns. This did not stop him from returning in another one, *A Man Called Shenandoah,* in 1965, or starring in a western feature film *(The Dangerous Days of Kiowa Jones)* in 1966. He did try other types of roles as well, including quite a few appearances on *Alfred Hitchcock Presents;* one of these was in a most unusual episode which parodied Hithcock's own film classic *Rear Window* (this time the neighbor hadn't murdered his wife at all, he was merely lugging out a sack of old clothes). Horton also tried his hand at musical comedy, starring on Broadway in *110 in the Shade* in 1963.

After he left *Shenandoah,* though, Horton's TV appearances were few. He was in a few B-grade movies (the last being *The Green Slime* in 1969), but his main activity in later years was appearing in stock productions with his wife, Marilynn. He was seen for a couple of years in the 1980s in the daytime soap opera *As the World Turns.*

HOSLEY, PATRICIA—actress

Ad Libbers (var) .... regular (1951)
Young Mr. Bobbin (com).. Nancy (1951–52)

HOTCHKIS, JOAN—actress
b: Pasadena, Calif.

My World and Welcome to It (com)
.... Ellen Monroe (1969–70)
The Odd Couple (com)
.... Dr. Nancy Cunningham (1970–72)
The Life and Times of Eddie Roberts (com)
.... Lydia Knitzer (1980)

HOTSY TOTSY BOYS—

The Lawrence Welk Show (music)
.... regulars (1969–80)

HOUGHTON, JAMES—actor
b: Nov 7, Los Angeles, Calif.

Code R (adv) .... Rick Wilson (1977)
Knots Landing (drama)
.... Kenny Ward (1979–83)

HOULIHAN, KERI—juvenile actress
b: Jul 3, 1975, Pennsylvania

Our House (drama)
.... Molly Witherspoon (1986–)

HOUSEMAN, JOHN—producer, director, actor
b: Sep 22, 1902, Bucharest, Rumania

Aspen (drama) ... Joseph Drummond (1977)
The Paper Chase (drama)
. Prof. Charles W. Kingsfield, Jr. (1978–79)
Silver Spoons (com)
.... Grandfather Edward Stratton II
(occasional) (1982–86)
The Winds of War (drama)
.... Aaron Jastrow (1983)
The Paper Chase (drama)
. Prof. Charles W. Kingsfield, Jr. (1983–84)

Fame as an actor came to John Houseman rather late in life—in his seventies to be exact—as the imperious, demanding, but fair law professor in *The Paper Chase.* For

nearly 50 years before that he had been one of the most respected producers, directors, and writers in show business.

Born in Rumania, Houseman came to the U.S. in 1925 on assignment with his father's grain company. By the early 1930s he had become active as a writer-director for the New York stage, and in 1937 he and Orson Welles co-founded radio's famed *Mercury Theatre.* Among other things, he worked on the infamous *War of the Worlds* broadcast and helped develop the script for the film classic *Citizen Kane*—before angrily parting company with Welles in 1941.

During World War II Houseman headed the Voice of America. He then returned to production, producing plays, films, and some of television's classiest programs: *The Seven Lively Arts* in the '50s, *The Great Adventure* in the '60s, and seven dramatic presentations on *Playhouse 90.* He acted only rarely and did not enter that field full-time until he was in his seventies, whereupon he won an Academy Award for his first major role—in the film version of *The Paper Chase* (1973). His television roles were not quite as high-class at first; he appeared in a three-part story on *The Six Million Dollar Man/Bionic Woman* in 1976, and was later in the miniseries *Aspen* and *Washington: Behind Closed Doors.* However, with the TV version of *The Paper Chase* in 1978, his fame—and prestige—were assured. Incidentally, he was not the first choice for the role of Professor Kingsfield when the movie was being cast; the producers wanted James Mason. But Mason was not available, and Houseman made it his own.

The veteran Houseman has taught drama to real-life (and presumably awed) students at several universities. He has written several books of memoirs, including *Run-Through* in 1972 and *Front and Center* in 1979.

HOUSER, JERRY—actor
b: Jul 14, 1952, Los Angeles, Calif.

We'll Get By (com)....... Muff Platt (1975)
The Brady Brides (com)
.... Wally Logan (1981)

HOUSTON, THELMA—singer
b: Long Beach, Calif.

The Marty Feldman Comedy Machine (var)
.... regular (1972)

HOVEN, LOUISE—actress

The San Pedro Beach Bums (com)
.... Louise (1977)

HOVING, THOMAS—correspondent
b: Jan 15, 1931, New York City, N.Y

20/20 (mag)....... correspondent (1978–84)

A longtime museum and cultural affairs administrator, and from 1967–77 the director of New York's Metropolitan Museum of Art. Though his television work veered sharply toward pop culture (e.g., profiles of rock stars), Hoving continued active in more erudite fields, as a museum consultant and as editor in chief of *Connoisseur* magazine.

HOVIS, GUY—singer

The Lawrence Welk Show (music)
.... regular (1970–82)

HOVIS, LARRY—comedian, writer
b: Feb 20, 1936, Wapito, Wash., r: Houston, Texas

Gomer Pyle, U.S.M.C. (com)
.... Larry (1964–65)
Hogan's Heroes (com) .. Lt. Carter (1965–71)
Rowan & Martin's Laugh-In (var)
.... regular (1968)
Rowan & Martin's Laugh-In (var)
.... regular (1971–72)
Liar's Club (quiz)....... panelist (1976–78)

HOVIS, RALNA ENGLISH—singer

The Lawrence Welk Show (music)
.... regular (1969–82)

HOWAR, BARBARA—hostess, writer
b: Sep 27, 1934, Nashville, Tenn.

Who's Who? (pub aff) ...... reporter (1977)

HOWARD, ANDREA—actress

Holmes and Yoyo (com)
.... Off. Maxine Moon (1976)

HOWARD, BARBARA—actress
b: Nov 4, Chicago, Ill.

Falcon Crest (drama)
.... Robin Agretti (1985–)

HOWARD, BOB—black singer, pianist
b: Jun 20, 1906, Newton, Mass.

Sing It Again (quiz)....... regular (1950–51)

A swinging, humorous pianist-vocalist who was quite reminiscent of the late Fats Waller, in both style and appearance.

HOWARD, CAL—

The Steve Allen Show (var)
.... regular (1959–60)

HOWARD, CLINT—juvenile actor
b: Apr 20, 1959, Burbank, Calif.

The Baileys of Balboa (com)
.... Stanley (1964–65)
Gentle Ben (adv)... Mark Wedloe (1967–69)
The Cowboys (wes) .... Steve (1974)

The younger brother of Ron Howard, and son of Rance (who also appeared in *Gentle Ben*). Clint made his television debut in brother Ron's series *The Andy Griffith Show*.

HOWARD, CYNTHIA—actress

The Family Holvak (drama)..... Ida (1975)

HOWARD, DENNIS—actor

Having Babies (drama)
.... Dr. Ron Danvers (1978–79)

HOWARD, EDDIE—banjo player

Saturday Night Jamboree (music)
.... regular (1948–49)

Not to be confused with the popular 1940s singer and bandleader Eddy Howard.

HOWARD, JOE—host, singer
b: Feb 12, 1867, New York City, N.Y. d: May 19, 1961

The Gay Nineties Revue (var)
.... host (1948–49)

One of the oldest of the old-timers seen on television in its early days was this authentic relic of the Gay '90s. Howard had been a popular songwriter and vaudevillian well before the turn of the century and was responsible for such songs of that day as "Hello Ma Baby" and "Goodbye My Lady Love"—but not for his famous theme song, "I Wonder Who's Kissing Her Now," as he so often claimed.

The latter tune represents one of the most famous cases of song misappropriation in show business history. For nearly 50 years Joe regaled listeners with stories of how he had composed it; he sang it onstage and on radio, he wrote about it, and it even became the title of a 1947 Hollywood movie in which the song's creation (by Joe) was dramatized. All of this turned out to be a massive fraud. An obscure composer named Harold Orlob finally came forward, after the movie was released, and proved that he had actually written the song and sold it to Howard, who then proceeded to claim it as his own. Orlob said he didn't want any money, he just wanted recognition for his work.

The revelations didn't faze Joe at all. The old trooper kept on singing the song as part of his Gay '90s act on television and on stage. He died while in the midst of a chorus of "Let Me Call You Sweetheart" on the stage of a Chicago theater in 1961. Most obituaries automatically credited him as the composer of his famous theme song, as if Orlob had never existed.

Joe also did his best, in later years, to obscure his true date of birth. As his *New York Times* obituary tactfully observed, "Mr. Howard's memories of his beginnings altered as he aged." However, if he was performing onstage with his first wife in 1885, he was obviously born before 1878, the date that is often reported; the most widely accepted date is 1867. That would make him, at 81 (in 1948), the oldest performer ever to to host a TV variety show, edging out Lawrence Welk (who retired at 79). He was not the oldest TV host of any kind, however; George Burns was still hosting a weekly comedy series at 89.

Joe's autobiography is titled *Gay Nineties Troubadour.*

HOWARD, JOHN—actor
b: Apr 14, 1913, Cleveland, Ohio

Crawford Mystery Theatre (drama)
.... host/moderator (1951)

Dr. Hudson's Secret Journal (drama)
.... Dr. Wayne Hudson (1955–57)
The Adventures of the Sea Hawk (adv)
.... John Hawk (1958–59)
My Three Sons (com)
.... Dave Welch (1965–67)

HOWARD, KEN—actor
b: Mar 28, 1944, El Centro, Calif. r: Manhasset, N.Y.

Adam's Rib (com) ..... Adam Bonner (1973)
The Manhunter (drama)
.... Dave Barrett (1974–75)
The White Shadow (drama)
.... Ken Reeves (1978–81)
It's Not Easy (com) .... Jack Long (1983)
The Thorn Birds (drama)
.... Ranier Hartheim (1983)
Dynasty (drama)
.... Garrett Boydston (1985–86)
Dynasty II: The Colbys (drama)
.... Garrett Boydston (1985–)

Emmy Award: Outstanding Performer in a Daytime Children's Program, for *The Body Human: Facts For Boys* (1981)

Ken Howard is most famous as the inner-city high school basketball coach on *The White Shadow,* a role in which he was extremely believable. "Some people really think I'm an ex-pro player," he once told a reporter, "but I'm not." Did he at least think of turning pro? "Not really . . . in terms of sports, even back in high school, I knew people who could 'put me in jail.'"

Despite his modesty, Ken did play basketball throughout his high school and college days and insisted on doing his own playing on the court in *White Shadow* (his only compromise was that they lower the basket a bit for him). His early professional career was directed more toward the stage, however, on which he enjoyed a meteoric rise. He began appearing in New York productions while a student at Yale drama school (his first being *We Bombed in New Haven* in 1967). While still a student he made his Broadway debut in *Promises, Promises* (1968). He left that show the following year to star as Thomas Jefferson in *1776* and a year after that won a Tony Award for his role in *Child's Play.*

This bright young stage star began doing television episode work in the early 1970s and landed his first series, the situation comedy *Adam's Rib,* in 1973. That flopped, as did the period detective series *Man-hunter* in 1974. The amiable, athletic actor finally hit his stride a few years later in *The White Shadow,* which he co-created and based on his own high school experiences in New York. During and after that series, Ken appeared in a variety of TV movies and miniseries *(Rage of Angels, The Thorn Birds)* and won an Emmy for a 1980 documentary special.

HOWARD, PAPPY, & HIS TUMBLEWEED GANG—

Village Barn (var) . . . . . . regulars (1948–50)

HOWARD, RANCE—actor

Gentle Ben (adv)
. . . . Henry Boomhauer (1967–69)
The Thorn Birds (drama)
. . . . Doc Wilson (1983)

The father of Ron and Clint Howard.

HOWARD, RON—actor, producer, director

b: Mar 1, 1954, Duncan, Okla.

The Andy Griffith Show (com)
. . . . Opie Taylor (1960–68)
The Smith Family (drama)
. . . . Bob Smith (1971–72)
Happy Days (com)
. . . . Richie Cunningham (1974–80)

"I'm kind of dull," he has said of himself, and some critics would probably agree. Despite predictions that he would fade into the realm of TV nostalgia, however, "Ronny" Howard has remained a popular and interesting actor as he enters his thirties. His fresh-faced, all American–boy appeal may have something to do with it. There's also the fact that viewers consider him an old friend; he has been on their TV screens more or less continuously since he was a tot.

Little Ronny began appearing in the late 1950s on series such as *The Red Skelton Show* and *Playhouse 90* and played one of his earliest dramatic roles in a particularly touching episode of *The Twilight Zone*—about a man (Gig Young) who literally walked back into his youth. After appearances on *The Danny Thomas Show* and *Dennis the Menace,* among others, he

landed his first regular role in 1960, as Andy Griffith's winsome son Opie on *The Andy Griffith Show.* The series was an enormous hit, and Ronny became a star.

Even during the *Andy Griffith* years Ron continued to appear in guest roles in other series, including dramas such as *The Eleventh Hour* and *The Fugitive.* He remained quite busy in the late '60s and early '70s as well, including a run as Henry Fonda's teenage son on *The Smith Family.* A sketch Ron played with Anson Williams on *Love, American Style* in 1972, called "Love and the Happy Day," led to his greatest role: all-American teenager Richie in the number-one hit *Happy Days.* Ron was by this time in his twenties.

In recent years Ron has downplayed his acting in favor of a very successful producing and directing career, which has included the movies *Skyward, Cocoon,* and *Splash.* He is still willing to emulate that *Twilight Zone* episode of many years ago, however, and look back to his roots. In a 1986 reunion of *The Andy Griffith Show* cast, Opie—who was such a little kid when we last saw him—was all grown-up, married, and about to have a child of his own.

HOWARD, RONALD—actor

b: Apr 7, 1918, Anerley, England

Sherlock Holmes (drama)
. . . . Sherlock Holmes (1954–55)
Cowboy in Africa (adv)
. . Wing Comdr. Howard Hayes (1967–68)

The son of film star Leslie Howard, to whom he bears a remarkable resemblance.

HOWARD, SUSAN—actress

b: Jan 28, 1946, Marshall, Texas

Petrocelli (drama)
. . . . Maggie Petrocelli (1974–76)
Dallas (drama)
. . . . Donna Culver Krebbs (1979–)

HOWARD, TOM—comedian

b: 1886 d: Feb 27, 1955

It Pays to Be Ignorant (quiz)
. . . . emcee (1949–51)

HOWARD, VINCE—black actor

Mr. Novak (drama)
. . . . Mr. Pete Butler (1963–65)

Barnaby Jones (drama)
.... Lt. Joe Taylor (1973)
Emergency (drama).... Off. Vince (1976–77)

HOWAT, CLARK—actor

The Adventures of Fu Manchu (drama)
.... Dr. John Petrie (1955–56)

HOWE, QUINCY—newscaster, writer, editor
b: Aug 17, 1900, Boston, Mass. d: Feb 17, 1977

U.N. Casebook (doc)... moderator (1948–49)
People's Platform (pub aff)
.... moderator (1948–50)
In the First Person (int)...... host (1949–50)
CBS Weekend News (news)
.... anchorman (1949–50)
It's News to Me (quiz)... panelist (1951–52)
Both Sides (pub aff) ...... moderator (1953)
Medical Horizons (pub aff)...... host (1955)
Outside U.S.A. (doc)
.... narrator/commentator (1955–56)
Campaign Roundup (news)
.... moderator (1958)

HOWELL, ARLENE—actress
b: c. 1940, Louisiana

Bourbon Street Beat (drama)
.... Melody Lee Mercer (1959–60)

Miss America of 1958.

HOWELL, C. THOMAS—juvenile actor
b: Dec 7, 1966, Los Angeles, Calif.

Two Marriages (drama)
.... Scott Morgan (1983–84)

HOWELL, HOKE—actor

Here Come the Brides (adv)
.... Ben Jenkins (1968–70)

HOWELL, WAYNE—announcer, host

Broadway Open House (talk)
.... regular (1950–51)
The Jonathan Winters Show (var)
.... announcer (1957)

HOWLAND, BETH—actress
b: May 28, 1947, Boston, Mass.

Alice (com). Vera Louise Gorman (1976–85)

HOWLEY, BRIGADIER GENERAL FRANK—educator
b: Feb 4, 1903, Hampton, N.J.

Answers for Americans (pub aff)
.... panelist (1953–54)

The general was at this time vice chancellor of New York University.

HOWLIN, OLIN—actor
b: Feb 10, 1896, Denver, Colo. d: Sep 20, 1959

Circus Boy (adv) .... Swifty (1956–58)

HOY, ROBERT—actor

Steve Canyon (adv)
.... Sgt. Charley Berger (1959)
The High Chaparral (wes)
.... Joe (1967–71)

HOYOS, RODOLFO—actor
b: c. 1914 d: Apr 15, 1983

Viva Valdez (com)
.... Luis Valdez (1976)

HOYT, JOHN—actor
b: Oct 5, 1904, Bronxville, N.Y.

Tom, Dick and Mary (com)
.... Dr. Krevoy (1964–65)
Gimme a Break (com)
.... Grandpa Stanley Kanisky (1982–)

HUBBARD, DAVID—black juvenile actor

James at 15 (drama)
.... Sly Hazeltine (1977–78)
Harris and Company (drama)
.... David Harris (1979)

HUBBARD, EDDIE—host

Vaudeo Varieties (var) .... emcee (1949)

HUBBARD, JOHN—actor
b: Apr 23, 1914, Indiana Harbor, Ind.

The Mickey Rooney Show (com)
.... Mr. Brown (1954–55)
Don't Call Me Charlie (com)
.... Col. U. Charles Barker (1962–63)

HUBBELL, ELNA—actress

Petticoat Junction (com)
.... Kathy Jo Elliott (1968–70)

HUBER, HAROLD—actor
b: 1910*, New York City, N.Y. d: Sep 29, 1959

I Cover Times Square (drama)
.... Johnny Warren (1950–51)

This scowling, beady-eyed little man had a long career playing evil henchmen in the movies (e.g., *20,000 Years in Sing Sing*) and seemed a bit miscast as a crusading reporter covering the New York show business beat. Then again, the real-life reporter on whom the role was supposedly based—Walter Winchell—looked pretty suspicious too.

HUBLEY, SEASON—actress
b: May 14, 1951, New York City, N.Y.

Kung Fu (wes)
... Margit McLean (occasional) (1974–75)
Family (drama) .... Salina Magee (1976–77)

The former wife of actor Kurt Russell.

HUCKO, PEANUTS—Dixieland clarinetist
b: Apr 7, 1918, Syracuse, N.Y.

The Lawrence Welk Show (music)
.... regular (1970–72)

HUDDLE, ELIZABETH—actress

Boone (drama) ..... Faye Sawyer (1983–84)

HUDDLESTON, DAVID—actor
b: Sep 17, 1930, Vinton, Va.

Tenafly (drama).. Lt. Sam Church (1973–74)
Petrocelli (drama). Lt. John Ponce (1974–76)
The Kallikaks (com)
.... Jasper T. Kallikak (1977)
How the West Was Won (miniseries) (drama)
.... Christy Judson (1977)
Hizzonner (com) ..... Mayor Cooper (1979)

This paunchy, happy character actor cut his eyeteeth in Broadway musicals, but in films and on television in the '60s and '70s he was seen mostly in westerns, cop shows (often as the hero's friendly police contact), and straight situation comedies. Both of his own TV starring vehicles were short-lived—in *The Kallikaks* he was a conniving garage owner and in *Hizzonner* a con-

*Some sources give 1904.

niving mayor. At least in the latter series he got to periodically burst out in song.

HUDNUT, BILL—comedian

Thicke of the Night (talk)
.... recurring player (1983–84)

HUDSON BROTHERS, THE—comedians
Bill Hudson, b: Oct 17, 1949
Mark Hudson, b: Aug 23, 1951
Brett Hudson, b: Jan 18, 1953; all b: Portland, Ore.

The Hudson Brothers Show (var)
.... regulars (1974)
Bonkers (com) .... as themselves (1978–79)

"But *who* are the Hudson Brothers?" asked the *TV Guide* reporter, reflecting the lack of recognition that bedeviled this trio throughout their career. Despite some excellent exposure in the mid-1970s—including a prime time summer replacement show, the Saturday morning *Hudson Brothers Razzle Dazzle Comedy Show* (1974–75), and the syndicated *Bonkers,* plus many guest spots and several popular records—these youthful, knockabout comics (a sort of updated version of the Marx Brothers or the Three Stooges) never really caught on with young viewers. For some reason, kids seemed to prefer black-and-white footage of the *old* Marx Brothers and Three Stooges.

See also separate entry for Mark Hudson.

HUDSON, ERNIE—black actor

Highcliffe Manor (com) ...... Smythe (1979)
The Last Precinct (com)
. Det. Sgt. Tremaine Lane ("Night Train")
(1986)

HUDSON, JIM—

Marie (var) .... regular (1980–81)

HUDSON, MARK—actor, comedian
b: Aug 23, 1951, Portland, Ore.

Sara (com)........... Stuart Webber (1985)

One of the Hudson Brothers comedy trio of the 1970s. The brothers decided to try separate careers in the mid-1980s, leading to this sitcom role for Mark. "It's a little scary," he admitted. "I'm used to having my two brothers on either side of me and if anything went wrong they could help me out."

Mark is also a songwriter and contributed to the score of the Steven Spielberg film *Gremlins.*

HUDSON, ROCHELLE—actress
b: Mar 6, 1916*, Oklahoma City, Okla. d: Jan 17, 1972

That's My Boy (com)
.... Alice Jackson (1954–55)

HUDSON, ROCK—actor
b: Nov 17, 1925, Winnetka, Ill. d: Oct 2, 1985

McMillan and Wife (police)
...... Comm. Stewart McMillan (1971–77)
Wheels (drama)...... Adam Trenton (1978)
The Devlin Connection (drama)
.... Brian Devlin (1982)
Dynasty (drama) ... Daniel Reece (1984–85)

One of the most likable and engaging of Hollywood's major stars, handsome Rock Hudson was rarely seen on television during his movie heyday of the '50s and '60s. He did turn up in an episode of *I Love Lucy* in 1955, meeting Lucy and Ethel at poolside (they almost fell in!), and he hosted the premiere of CBS's ill-fated *Big Party* series in 1959.

Rock's real TV debut was in 1971, and it made a very big splash indeed. On September 17th he starred in his first TV movie, *Once Upon a Dead Man;* this served to launch the very successful series *McMillan and Wife,* in which he starred as the charming and witty San Francisco police commissioner. The series fit his image perfectly. Patterned after the Nick and Nora Charles *Thin Man* romantic mysteries, it had Rock and his meddlesome wife (played by Susan St. James) solving glamorous murders with the "help" of his dim-witted police assistant (John Schuck) and the wisecracks of their sarcastic housekeeper (Nancy Walker). After *McMillan,* Rock continued to be quite active in television, bringing his manly good

*Many sources give 1914, but 1916 is apparently correct. Many sources also perpetuate the fiction that she was born in Claremont, Okla. (Will Rogers' hometown); this was invented by movie publicists in the 1940s.

looks to such dramatic TV movies and miniseries as *Wheels, The Martian Chronicles,* and *World War III.* In 1984–85 he was a mature heartthrob in *Dynasty.*

A proposed 1981 detective series called *The Devlin Connection* had to be postponed a year when Rock underwent quintuple-bypass heart surgery. Four years later he learned that he was suffering from something far worse. As a result of a lifetime of homosexuality, he had contracted AIDS. Playing perhaps the bravest role of his life, the dying actor went public with this previously well-kept secret in the hope that the public might better understand and fight the dreaded disease.

HUDSON, WILLIAM—actor
b: Jan 24, 1925, California d: Apr 5, 1974

I Led Three Lives (drama)
.... special agent Mike Andrews (occasional) (1953–56)

HUFFMAN, ROSANNA—actress
Tenafly (drama).......... Lorrie (1973–74)

HUFSEY, BILLY—actor
Fame (drama).. Christopher Donlon (1983–)

HUGH-KELLY, DANIEL—actor
b: Aug 10, Hoboken, N.J. r: Elizabeth, N.J.

Chicago Story (drama)
.... Det. Frank Wajorski (1982)
Hardcastle & McCormick (drama)
...... Mark "Skid" McCormick (1983–86)

The son of a New Jersey policeman, Dan got his start on the stages of Washington and New York in the mid-1970s. He became known to TV viewers as handsome young lawyer-politician Frank Ryan in the daytime soap opera *Ryan's Hope,* from 1977–81.

HUGHES, BARNARD—actor
b: Jul 16, 1915, Bedford Hills, N.Y.

Doc (com) ...... "Doc" Joe Bogert (1975–76)
Mr. Merlin (com)..... Max Merlin (1981–82)

Emmy Award: Best Actor in a Single Performance in a Drama Series, for *Lou Grant* (1978)

HUGHES, MICHAEL—juvenile actor

Make Room for Granddaddy (com)
.... Michael (1970–71)

HUGHES, ROBERT—critic, producer

20/20 (mag) .. host (premiere telecast) (1978)

Emmy Award: Producer, Best Cultural Documentary Program, for *Arthur Penn, 1922: Themes and Variants* (1971)

HUGHES, ROBERT E.—orchestra leader
b: Oct 29, 1934, New York City, N.Y.

The Rich Little Show (var)
.... orch. leader (1976)

HUGHES, ROBIN—actor

The Brothers (com)
.... Barrington Steel (1956–57)

HUIE, WILLIAM BRADFORD—host

Chronoscope (int) ..... moderator (1951–53)

HULL, RON—comedian

The Hudson Brothers Show (var)
.... regular (1974)

HULL, WARREN—host, actor
b: Jan 17, 1903, Gasport, N.Y. d: Sep 14, 1974

A Couple of Joes (var) .... regular (1949–50)
The Warren Hull Show (talk) ... host (1950)
Cavalcade of Bands (music)... emcee (1950)
Crawford Mystery Theatre (drama)
.... host/moderator (1951)
Strike It Rich (quiz) .... emcee (1951–55)
Who in the World? (int) .... host (1962)

For one of show business's minor players, this TV personality of the 1950s certainly had a varied career. He dropped out of college to study voice and made his professional debut singing in stage musicals such as *The Student Prince.* Later he used his mellifluous tones as a radio announcer and host while he simultaneously began an acting career in a long series of campy B-films and movie serials of the late '30s and early '40s. Among other things, he played such comic strip heroes as the Spider, Mandrake the Magician and the Green Hornet.
Retreating to radio in the late '40s, War-

ren struck gold as host of the bizarre quiz show *Strike It Rich,* in which cripples and other unfortunates were paraded before the audience; after they played a simple game, listeners could call in on "The Heart Line" with appropriate contributions (e.g., an iron lung for someone who needed one). Though he did appear in a number of other series, it was for the TV version of *Strike It Rich* that Warren became famous.

HUMBLE, GWEN—actress

Doctors' Private Lives (drama)
.... Sheila Castle (1979)

HUME, BENITA—actress
b: Oct 14, 1906, London, England d: Nov 1, 1967

The Halls of Ivy (com)
.... Vicky Hall (1954–55)

The lovely wife of actor Ronald Colman (from 1938–58), with whom she starred in *The Halls of Ivy.* After his death she married the equally debonair British actor George Sanders.

HUMPERDINCK, ENGELBERT—singer
b: May 3, 1936, Madras, India r: Leicester, England

The Engelbert Humperdinck Show (var)
.... host (1970)

Real name: Arnold George Dorsey. A clone of singer Tom Jones, whom he resembles and sounds like, and with whom he shares the same personal manager.

HUNLEY, LEANN—actress
b: Forks, Wash.

Lobo (com) ... Sarah Cumberland (1979–80)

Emmy Award: Best Supporting Actress in a Daytime Drama, for *Days of Our Lives* (1986)

HUNT, ALLAN—actor

Voyage to the Bottom of the Sea (sci fi)
.... Stu Riley (1965–67)

HUNT, GARETH—actor
b: 1943

The New Avengers (drama)
.... Mike Gambit (1978–80)

HUNT, HELEN—juvenile actress
b: Jun 15, 1963, Los Angeles, Calif.

Amy Prentiss (police)
.... Jill Prentiss (1974–75)
Swiss Family Robinson (adv)
.... Helga Wagner (1975–76)
The Fitzpatricks (drama)
.... Kerry Gerardi (1977–78)
It Takes Two (com) .. Lisa Quinn (1982–83)

HUNT, MARSHA—actress
b: Oct 17, 1917, Chicago, Ill.

Peck's Bad Girl (com) . Jennifer Peck (1959)

HUNT, MIE—actress

Domestic Life (com) .. Jane Funakubo (1984)

HUNT, RICHARD—puppeteer

The Muppet Show (var)
.... Sweetums (1976–81)
The Muppet Show (var).. Scooter (1976–81)
The Muppet Show (var).... Janice (1976–81)

Emmy Awards: Outstanding Individual Achievement in a Children's Program, for *Sesame Street* (1974, 1976); Star, Best Comedy-Variety Series, for *The Muppet Show* (1978)

HUNT, SUZANNE—actress

House Calls (com)
.... Nurse Shirley Bryan (1981–82)

HUNTER, IAN—actor
b: Jun 13, 1900, Kenilworth, South Africa d: Sep 24, 1975

The Adventures of Robin Hood (adv)
.... Sir Richard (1955–58)

HUNTER, JEFFREY—actor
b: Nov 25, 1925*, Orleans, La. d: May 27, 1969

Temple Houston (wes)
.... Temple Houston (1963–64)

HUNTER, KIM—actress
b: Nov 12, 1922, Detroit, Mich.

*Some sources give 1926.

424

Backstairs at the White House (drama)
.... Ellen Wilson (1979)

This spunky lady was the real-life heroine of the celebrated court case that broke the back of the political blacklisting movement of the 1950s. It was her testimony in support of TV personality John Henry Faulk, who had sued the blacklisters, that helped win the case.

Miss Hunter knew whereof she spoke. She had begun her acting career onstage and in films during the '40s, scoring her greatest triumph with her Academy Award–winning portrayal of Stella in the 1951 movie version of *A Streetcar Named Desire.* Her television debut was in 1948 on *Actor's Studio,* and she worked steadily in all three media until the early 1950s. Then her name appeared in *Red Channels,* a small booklet that purported to list performers with left-wing affiliations. Despite her stature, she suddenly found that few roles were being offered to her. However, unlike some others who were similarly accused, her career began to revive around 1955–56, and thereafter she worked frequently in television (less so in films) in all manner of dramatic productions and series. Among the many series on which she appeared over the years were *Playhouse 90, Hallmark Hall of Fame, Mannix, Ironside, Marcus Welby, M.D.,* and *The Rockford Files.* She was also a regular on daytime's *The Edge of Night* from 1979–80.

Asked in 1966 about her career, Kim commented, "I used to think talent will win out. That's a naive point of view. It doesn't win out at all. It gets trampled on the ladder to success, unless that talent is matched by drive. I sometimes think of myself as one who has been wounded on that crowded and shaky ladder."

Kim wrote a rather unusual autobiography, combined with a cookbook, called *Loose in the Kitchen* (1975).

HUNTER, RONALD—actor
b: Jun 14, 1943, Boston, Mass.

The Lazarus Syndrome (drama)
.... Joe Hamill (1979)

HUNTER, TAB—actor
b: Jul 11, 1931, New York City, N.Y.

The Tab Hunter Show (com)
.... Paul Morgan (1960–61)

Mary Hartman, Mary Hartman (com)
.... George Shumway (1977–78)

This blond dreamboat hunk of the '50s (*sigh*) was seen fairly often on television from 1955 to 1965, but his appearances have been intermittent since then. His only starring vehicle on TV was a lightweight, swinging-bachelor situation comedy that lasted only a year.

In 1971 Tab was quoted as saying, "The star thing is over. I've knocked around quite a bit in the past few years and now I'm just another actor looking for work. Acting is what I know and what I do best." He added, "I'm trying to find a new niche . . . something to help erase that bland image the studios gave me in the Fifties. I'm looking for roles that will establish me as a more mature actor." Since that time he has played mostly guest roles which, while they may not have been "artistically satisfying," have certainly been varied, ranging from *Hawaii Five-O* and *Circle of Fear* to *Mary Hartman, Mary Hartman,* and, of course, the inevitable *Love Boat.*

HUNTLEY, CHET—newscaster
b: Dec 10, 1911, Cardwell, Mont. d: Mar 20, 1974

The Huntley-Brinkley Report (news)
.... anchorman (1956–70)
Chet Huntley Reporting (news)
.... host/reporter (1957–63)

Chet Huntley was the solid, sober half of the most famous news reporting team in television history—Huntley and Brinkley. At the height of their popularity in the early '60s, they were recognized by more people (according to one poll) than Cary Grant, James Stewart, or The Beatles.

This unlikely superstar of news began his career on radio in the Northwest in 1934, moving to Los Angeles in 1939 to join CBS as a West Coast reporter. Twelve years later he switched to ABC in Los Angeles. However, his major break came in 1955 when he was hired away by NBC and given the plum assignment of coanchoring, with David Brinkley, the network's coverage of the 1956 political conventions. The two of them clicked at once and within a few months were made co-anchors of the evening news, replacing John Cameron Swayze.

The show was telecast from New York (Huntley) and Washington (Brinkley), and their closing sign-off—"Goodnight, Chet . . . Goodnight, David"—became a national catchphrase.

Despite his stolid demeanor, Huntley was at times a controversial figure, particularly for his off-camera habit of speaking out on public issues. His one public disagreement with Brinkley came during a 1968 technicians' strike, when Huntley crossed the picket line while Brinkley refused to do so. In 1979, at the age of 58, Huntley retired to his beloved Montana to tend his cattle ranch and work on the development of the Big Sky Resort (which did not open until after his death). He was not out of the limelight for long, however, engendering more controversy by appearing in airline commercials. His retirement, unfortunately, was short, as he died at the age of 62.

Huntley was the author of *The Generous Years* (1968), a book about his boyhood in Montana.

HURLEY, WALTER—host
Draw Me a Laugh! (quiz) ..... emcee (1949)

HURSEY, SHERRY—actress
Number 96 (drama).... Jill Keaton (1980–81)
Morningstar/Eveningstar (drama)
.... Debbie Flynn (1986)

HURST, RICK—actor
b: Jan 1, Houston, Texas

On the Rocks (com) ..... Cleaver (1975–76)
The Dukes of Hazzard (com)
.... Deputy Cletus (1980–83)
Amanda's (com).......... Earl Nash (1983)

HURT, CHICK—banjo player
Polka Time (music)....... regular (1956–57)

HURT, JO—actress
Kobb's Korner (var)
.... Josiebelle Shufflebottom (1948–49)

HUSAIN, JORY—actor
b: Nov 25, Milwaukee, Wis.

Head of the Class (com)
.... Jawaharlal (1986–)

HUSING, TED—sportscaster
b: Nov 27, 1901, New York City, N.Y. d: Aug 10 1962

Wednesday/Monday Night Fights (sport)
.... sportscaster (1950–53)

Autobiography: *My Eyes Are In My Heart.* (1959)

HUSTON, GAYE—actress

Bonino (com) .... Francesco (1953)

HUSTON, JOHN—actor, director
b: Aug 5, 1906, Nevada, Mo.

The Rhinemann Exchange (drama)
.... Ambass. Granville (1977)

Autobiography: *An Open Book* (1981).

HUSTON, MARTIN—juvenile actor
b: c. 1943

My Son Jeep (com) ..... Jeep Allison (1953)
Jungle Jim (adv)............ Skipper (1955)
Too Young to Go Steady (com)
.... Johnny Blake (1959)
Diagnosis: Unknown (drama)... Link (1960)

HUSTON, PAULA—actress

The College Bowl (com) .. regular (1950–51)

HUTCHINS, WILL—actor
b: May 5, 1932, Atwater, Calif.

Sugarfoot (wes)
..... Tom "Sugarfoot" Brewster (1957–61)
Hey Landlord (com)
.... Woody Banner (1966–67)
Blondie (com)
.... Dagwood Bumstead (1968–69)

Will Hutchins, the amiable, shy cowpoke of *Sugarfoot,* has followed a rather unusual trail since his starring days in prime time. He entered show business in the mid-1950s after his military service, and almost immediately his career took off. Beginning in 1956 he made appearances on *Matinee Theatre* and *Conflict,* and the following year he found fame via his starring role in *Sugarfoot.* The role was a pleasant variation on the macho cowboys who were then thundering across the screen; "Sugarfoot" was so named be-cause he was so inept and green he even ranked below a "Tenderfoot."

After the series ended Will guested a few times in series such as *Gunsmoke* and *Alfred Hitchcock,* then had two more star-ring roles, in situation comedies of the late '60s. Neither was successful. He then de-cided to try a different tack, something the little boy in him had always wanted to do. He joined a circus as a ringmaster and clown, traveling far and wide. Though he still guests on TV series occasionally, Will's main activity since the '70s has been with various circuses. He has developed a clown character called "Patches," is enjoy-ing himself immensely, and says "I hope I can be 'Patches' forever."

HUTCHINSON, KEN—actor

Masada (drama) .... Fronto (1981)

HUTSON, CHRIS—actress

Medical Center (drama)
.... Nurse Courtland (1969–76)
Trapper John, M.D. (drama)
.... nurse (1981–85)

HUTTON, BETTY—actress
b: Feb 26, 1921, Battle Creek, Mich.

The Betty Hutton Show (com)
.... Goldie Appleby (1959–60)

This blonde bombshell of the '40s was known for her slam-bang, rip-roaring per-formances in some of Hollywood's most enjoyable musicals. She was as tempestu-ous offscreen as on, and in 1952 she virtu-ally wrecked her movie career when she walked out on her studio—because it would not hire her choreographer-husband to direct her next picture. In the years that followed Betty was in and out of stage, cabaret, and television work. On TV she starred in the 1954 special *Satins and Spurs* and in her own 1959 comedy series, in which she played a dippy manicurist who suddenly inherited a fortune (and a family). She also guested in a few episodes of *Burke's Law* and other series in the mid-1960s, but other than that, her TV appear-ances have been quite infrequent.

Betty has received some publicity in re-cent years for her numerous brash, but un-successful, attempts at a comeback. These reports have been interspersed with stories of walkouts from shows, filings for bankruptcy, and retreats to a Catholic rectory in Rhode Island, where she has lived and worked for various periods as a simple housekeeper.

HUTTON, GUNILLA—actress
b: May 15, 1944, Goteborg, Sweden

Petticoat Junction (com)
.... Billie Jo Bradley (1965–66)
Hee Haw (var)............ regular (1969–)

HUTTON, INA RAY—orchestra leader
b: Mar 13, 1917, Chicago, Ill. d: Feb 19, 1984

The Ina Ray Hutton Show (var)
.... hostess/orch. leader (1956)

The sexy, blonde leader of an all-girl band.

HUTTON, JIM—actor
b: May 31, 1934, Binghamton, N.Y. r: Albany, N.Y. d: Jun 2, 1979

The Adventures of Ellery Queen (drama)
.... Ellery Queen (1975–76)

HUTTON, LAUREN—actress
b: Nov 17, 1943, Charleston, S.C.

The Rhinemann Exchange (drama)
.... Leslie Hawkewood (1977)
Paper Dolls (drama).. Colette Ferrier (1984)

One of America's most famous fashion models during the 1960s and '70s.

HYATT, BOBBY—juvenile actor
The Pride of the Family (com)
.... Junior Morrison (1953–55)

HYDE-WHITE, WILFRED—actor
b: May 12, 1903, Bourton-on-the-Water, Gloucester, England

Peyton Place (drama)
.... Martin Peyton (1967)
The Associates (com)
.... Emerson Marshall (1979–80)
Buck Rogers in the 25th Century (sci fi)
.... Dr. Goodfellow (1981)

HYLAND, DIANA—actress
b: 1936, Cleveland Heights, Ohio d: Mar 27, 1977

Peyton Place (drama)
.... Susan Winter (1968–69)
Eight Is Enough (com)
.... Joan Bradford (1977)

Emmy Award: Best Supporting Actress in a Drama, for the TV Movie *The Boy in the Plastic Bubble* (1977)

HYLANDS, SCOTT—actor
b: c. 1943, Vancouver, B.C., Canada

Night Heat (police)
.... Det. Kevin O'Brien (1985–)

HYLTON, JANE—actress
b: Jul 16, 1926*, London, England d: Feb 28, 1979

The Adventures of Sir Lancelot (adv)
.... Queen Guinevere (1956–57)
*Some sources give 1927.

I

ICE ANGELS, THE—skaters

Donny and Marie (var) .. regulars (1977–78)

ICE VANITIES, THE—skaters

Donny and Marie (var) .. regulars (1976–77)

ICHINO, LAURIE—juvenile actress

The Danny Kaye Show (var)
.... regular (1964–65)

IDELSON, BILLY—actor, producer

Mixed Doubles (drama).. Bill Abbott (1949)
One Man's Family (drama)
.... Cliff Barbour (1949)

A juvenile radio star of the '30s and '40s *(Vic and Sade)* who later became a TV producer responsible for such series as *Love, American Style* and *The Bob Newhart Show.*

IGNICO, ROBIN—actress

Trapper John, M.D. (drama)
.... Andrea Brancusi (1983–85)

IGUS, DARROW—black comedian
b: May 11, Newark, N.J.

Roll Out (com) .... Jersey (1973–74)
Fridays (var)............ regular (1980–82)

IMEL, JACK—tap dancer
b: c. 1932

The Lawrence Welk Show (music)
.... regular (1957–82)

IMPERATO, CARLO—actor

Fame (drama).... Danny Amatullo (1982–)

IMPERT, MARGARET—actress
b: Jun 4, 1945, Horseheads, N.Y.

Spencer's Pilots (adv).... Linda Dann (1976)
Maggie (com) .... Chris (1981–82)

INDRISANO, JOHN—actor
b: 1906, Boston, Mass. d: Jul 9, 1968

O. K. Crackerby (com)
.... the chauffeur (1965–66)

INESCORT, FRIEDA—actress
b: Jun 29, 1901, Edinburgh, Scotland d: Feb 21, 1976

Meet Corliss Archer (com)
.... Mrs. Janet Archer (1951)

ING, DEBI—

Marie (var) .... regular (1980–81)

INGALLS, PHIL—orchestra leader

The Victor Borge Show (var)
.... orch. leader (1951)

INGBER, MANDY—actress

Detective in the House (drama)
.... Deborah Wyman (1985)

INGELS, MARTY—actor, comedian
b: Mar 9, 1936, Brooklyn, N.Y.

I'm Dickens—He's Fenster (com)
.... Arch Fenster (1962–63)
The Pruitts of Southampton (com)
.... Norman Krump (1967)

The curly-haired actor has in recent years become a talent broker, arranging star appearances in commercials. He is married to actress Shirley Jones.

INNES, GEORGE—actor

Shogun (drama) .... Vinck (1980)
Q.E.D. (adv) .... Phipps (1982)

INSANA, TINO—actor

The Billy Crystal Comedy Hour (var)
.... regular (1982)

INTERLUDES, THE—vocal group

The Tony Martin Show (music)
.... regular (1954–56)

IRELAND, JILL—actress
b: Apr 24, 1936, London, England

Shane (wes) .... Marian Starett (1966)

This perky, blonde dancer-actress was married from 1957–67 to David McCallum and made several appearances in his series *The Man from U.N.C.L.E.;* she then wed Charles Bronson and began turning up in his movies.

IRELAND, JOHN—actor
b: Jan 30, 1914, Vancouver, B.C., Canada r: New York City

The Cheaters (drama) .. John Hunter (1961)
Rawhide (wes)........ Jed Colby (1965–66)
Cassie & Company (drama)
...... Lyman "Shack" Shackelford (1982)

IRONSIDE, MICHAEL—actor
V: The Final Battle (miniseries) (sci fi)
.... Ham Tyler (1984)
V (sci fi)............. Ham Tyler (1984–85)

IRVING, AMY—actress
b: Sep 10, 1953, Palo Alto, Calif.

Once an Eagle (drama)
.... Emily Massengale (1976–77)

IRVING, CHARLES—actor
The Wackiest Ship in the Army (adv)
.... Adm. Vincent Beckett (1965–66)

IRVING, GEORGE S.—actor, singer
b: Nov 1, 1922, Springfield, Mass.

The David Frost Revue (com)
.... regular (1971–73)
The Dumplings (com)
.... Charles Sweetzer (1976)

Long a supporting player in Broadway musicals (beginning with *Oklahoma!* in 1943), Irving has from time to time delighted television audiences with his comic characterizations. Perhaps his most memorable stage role was one that TV would not touch, however—he portrayed the title role in Gore Vidal's biting 1972 satire *An Evening with Richard Nixon.*

IRVING, HOLLIS—actress
Margie (com) ...... Aunt Phoebe (1961–62)

IRVING, JAY—cartoonist
b: Oct 3, 1900, New York City, N.Y. d: Jun 5, 1970

Draw Me a Laugh! (quiz) .... regular (1949)

IRVING, MARGARET—actress
The People's Choice (com)
.... Aunt Gus (1955–58)

IRWIN, STAN—actor, producer
Mr. Smith Goes to Washington (com)
.... Arnie (1962–63)

Irwin later became producer of *The Tonight Show Starring Johnny Carson.* He also provided the voice of the Lou Costello in the Saturday morning *Abbott and Costello* cartoon series in the late 1960s.

IRWIN, WYNN—actor
b: Dec 11, 1932, New York City, N.Y.

Lotsa Luck (com).. Arthur Swann (1973–74)
Sugar Time! (com)...... Al Marks (1977–78)

ISAAC, BUD—
Ozark Jubilee (music)........ regular (1955)

ISACKSEN, PETER—actor
b: Dec 11, c. 1953, Dover, N.H. r: California

C.P.O. Sharkey (com)
.... Seaman Pruitt (1976–78)
The Half Hour Comedy Hour (var)
.... regular (1983)
Jessie (police).. Off. Floyd Comstock (1984)

A blond, skinny, and very tall (6'6") character actor who is particularly adept at comic roles—where his height can be used to advantage. In addition to having been Don Rickles' verbal punching bag on *C.P.O. Sharkey,* he has guested on such series as *Three's Company, Fantasy Island,* and *B.J. and the Bear.*

ITO, ROBERT—actor
b: Jul 2, 1931, Vancouver, B.C., Canada

Quincy, M.E. (police)
.... Sam Fujiyama (1976–83)

A former dancer, Ito spent ten years as a member of the National Ballet of Canada and later (in the '60s) appeared on Broadway in *The Flower Drum Song* and *Our Town.*

ITZKOWITZ, HOWARD—
Marie (var)............. regular (1980–81)

IVAR, STAN—actor

b: Jan 11, Brooklyn, N.Y.

Little House on the Prairie (adv)
.... John Carter (1982–83)

IVES, BURL—actor, folk singer

b: Jun 14, 1909, Hunt Township, Ill.

High-Low (quiz)........... panelist (1957)
O. K. Crackerby (com)
.... O. K. Crackerby (1965–66)
The Lawyers (drama)
.... Walter Nichols (1969–72)
Roots (drama)............... Justin (1977)

This burly, bearded actor first made his name as a singer and scholar of traditional folk songs ("Bluetail Fly," "Big Rock Candy Mountain," etc.) on records and radio in the '30s and '40s. He was known then as "the Wayfaring Stranger." In the late 1940s he began to appear in movies and soon surprised everyone with superb portrayals of dominant older men in some of Hollywood's finest dramas. He was excellent as "Big Daddy" in *Cat on a Hot Tin Roof* and won an Academy Award for his role as another family patriarch, in *The Big Country.*

Ives appeared occasionally on TV playhouse series of the "Golden Age" *(U.S. Steel Hour, Playhouse 90),* but he was more frequently seen in the late '60s and early '70s—in his own two series, as well as in episodes of such series as *Daniel Boone* and *Alias Smith and Jones.* He was active in the '70s in the conservationist movement.

IVES, GEORGE—actor

Mr. Roberts (com).......... Doc (1965–66)

IVEY, DANA—actress

b: Aug 12, Atlanta, Ga.

Easy Street (com)
.... Eleanor Standard (1986–)

IVO, TOMMY—juvenile actor

Margie (com) .... Heywood Botts (1961–62)

IZAY, CONNIE—actress

*M*A*S*H* (com)... various nurses (1979–81)

J

JABLONS-ALEXANDER, KAREN—actress

The Lucie Arnaz Show (com)
..........................Loretta (1985)

JABLONSKI, CARL, DANCERS—

NBC Follies (var) ....regulars (1973)
The Diahann Carroll Show (var)
..........................dancers (1976)

JACK AND JILL—dance team

For Your Pleasure (music)
..........................dancers (1948)

JACKIE AND GAYLE—

The Kraft Summer Music Hall (var)
..........................regular (1966)

JACKSON, ALLAN—newscaster

b: Dec 4, 1915, Hot Springs, Ark. d: Apr 26, 1976

Youth Takes a Stand (info)
..........................moderator (1953)

JACKSON, EDDIE—comedian

b: 1896, Brooklyn, N.Y. d: Jul 15, 1980

The Jimmy Durante Show (var)
..........................regular (1954–56)

Jimmy Durante's longtime song-and-dance partner.

JACKSON, GREG—newscaster

The Last Word (news)......host (1982–83)
One on One (int).......interviewer (1983)

JACKSON, JACKIE—black singer

b: May 4, 1951 r: Gary, Ind.

The Jacksons (var) ....regular (1976–77)

A member of the musical Jackson family.

JACKSON, JANET—black actress, singer

b: May 16, 1966 r: Gary, Ind.

The Jacksons (var) ....regular (1976–77)

Good Times (com)
........Penny Gordon Woods (1977–79)
A New Kind of Family (com)
...................Jojo Ashton (1979–80)
Diff'rent Strokes (com)
.............Charlene DuPrey (1981–82)
Fame (drama)...... Cleo Hewitt (1984–85)

The "little sister" of the famous musical Jacksons started out by touring with her family—singing, dancing, and doing a child's cute impersonations of such stars as Cher, Diana Ross, and even Mae West (!). She soon set out in a different direction from her musically oriented brothers, however, by becoming an actress as well as a singer. Her career has flourished, with numerous juvenile roles in the late '70s and '80s.

JACKSON, JAY—host

Twenty Questions (quiz).....host (1953–55)
Tic Tac Dough (quiz)........emcee (1957)

JACKSON, JERRY, SINGERS—

Tony Orlando and Dawn (var)
.....................regulars (1974–76)

JACKSON, KATE—actress

b: Oct 29, 1948, Birmingham, Ala.

The Rookies (police)... Jill Danko (1972–76)
Charlie's Angels (drama)
...............Sabrina Duncan (1976–79)
Scarecrow and Mrs. King (adv)
.... Amanda King (1983–)

This beautiful, intelligent-looking actress has worked steadily in television since the early '70s, when she was fresh out of acting school. Her first major exposure was as a gorgeous ghost during the waning days of the Gothic soap opera *Dark Shadows.* When the serial ended in 1971 she appeared in episodes of prime time series *(Movin' On, The Jimmy Stewart Show, Bonanza)* for about a year before she began the regular role of Jill, wife of one of the rookie policemen on *The Rookies.*

The Rookies lasted for four years. When it ended, its producers—Aaron Spelling and Leonard Goldberg—promptly cast Kate in their new female detective show, *Charlie's Angels,* as the leader of the Angels. She was the most experienced of the three actresses cast and was supposed to be the star of the series, but she soon found herself overshadowed by the sudden and enormous popularity of newcomer Farrah Fawcett-Majors. Even after Farrah left, Kate remained merely "one of the girls"— the show had become bigger than its stars. In 1979 she quit to pursue a more individual career in TV movies; these have included *Topper* (1979), *Thin Ice* (1981), and *Listen to Your Heart* (1983). Kate returned to series TV in 1983, as the costar of the popular and light spy adventure, *Scarecrow and Mrs. King*.

JACKSON, KEITH—sportscaster
b: Oct 18, 1928, Carrollton, Ga.

Monday Night Football (sport)
.... announcer (1970)
Monday Night Baseball (sport)
.... sportscaster (1978–82)
Monday Night Baseball (sport)
.... sportscaster (1986–)

JACKSON, LATOYA—black singer
b: Mar 29, 1956

The Jacksons (var) .... regular (1976–77)

One of the musical Jackson family; she joined the act in 1975.

JACKSON, LIA—black actress

Harris and Company (drama)
...... Juanita Priscilla (J.P.) Harris (1979)

JACKSON, MARLON—black singer
b: Mar 12, 1957 r: Gary, Ind.

The Jacksons (var)
.... regular (1976–77)

One of the musical Jackson family.

JACKSON, MARY—actress
b: Nov 22, Milford, Mich.

The Waltons (drama)
.... Emily Baldwin (1972–81)
Hardcastle & McCormick (drama)
.... Sarah Wicks (1983)

JACKSON, MICHAEL—black singer
b: Aug 29, 1958, Gary, Ind.

The Jacksons (var) .... regular (1976–77)

The androgynous rock star of the '70s and '80s was first heard, but not seen, on television. He and his brothers supplied the voices for (and were depicted in) a Saturday morning cartoon series called *The Jackson 5ive*, which ran from 1971–73. Three years later, Michael, four of his brothers, and three of his sisters were all featured in a 1976 summer variety show on CBS, which did well enough to be brought back the following spring for an additional two month run.

Michael's other appearances on TV have been infrequent and limited mostly to music shows (of the entire family only sister Janet has seriously pursued an acting career). Some of his appearances have been spectacularly well-received, however; he brought down the house when, at the height of his solo fame, he "reunited" with his brothers on NBC's *Motown 25th Anniversary Special* in May 1983.

JACKSON, PAUL—black actor

Tenafly (drama).... Herb Tenafly (1973–74)

JACKSON, RANDY—black singer
b: Oct 29, 1961 r: Gary, Ind.

The Jacksons (var) .... regular (1976–77)

A member of the musical Jacksons; he joined the act in 1975.

JACKSON, REBIE (MAUREEN)—black singer
b: May 29, 1950 r: Gary, Ind.

The Jacksons (var) .... regular (1976–77)

Still another member of the musical Jacksons; she also joined in 1975.

JACKSON, SAMMY—actor
b: c. 1937, Henderson, N.C.

No Time for Sergeants (com)
.... Airman Will Stockdale (1964–65)

JACKSON, SELMER—actor
b: May 7, 1888, Iowa d: Mar 30, 1971

The Life and Legend of Wyatt Earp (wes)
.... Mayor Hoover (1956–57)

JACKSON, SHERRY—actress
b: 1942, Wendell, Idaho r: Hollywood, Calif.

The Danny Thomas Show (com)
.... Terry Williams (1953–58)

Danny Thomas's 11-year-old TV daughter (in 1953) has worked steadily in television and movies since leaving that series, including a guest role in the sequel *Make Room for Granddaddy* in 1970. By that time, she was all grown up and married; it was her "son," left in Danny's care, that made him the "granddaddy." During the '70s and '80s Sherry appeared in a number of pilots for prospective series that did not make it to the regular schedule; these have included *Enigma, Brenda Starr, Reporter* and an updated version of *Mr. Lucky* called *Casino*.

JACKSON, SLIM, QUARTET—

Alkali Ike (com)......... musicians (1950)

JACKSON, STONEY—black actor
b: Feb 27, c. 1960, Richmond, Va.

The White Shadow (drama)
.... Jesse B. Mitchell (1980–81)
The Insiders (drama)
.... James Mackey (1985–86)

JACKSON, TITO—black singer
b: Oct 15, 1953 r: Gary, Ind.

The Jacksons (var) .... regular (1976–77)

Another member of the musical Jacksons.

JACKSON, VICTORIA—actress
b: Miami, Fla.

The Half Hour Comedy Hour (var)
.... regular (1983)
Half Nelson (drama).. Annie O'Hara (1985)
NBC's Saturday Night Live (var)
.... regular (1986–)

This pretty young actress first attracted attention when she appeared for the first time on *The Tonight Show*—and proceeded to startle Johnny Carson, and viewers, by standing on her head and reciting poetry she had written. (She is, in fact, a trained gymnast.) After that, she reports, "my career began to take shape." Victoria is married to Nisan Eventoff, a Gypsy musician and fire eater whom she met when both were hired to entertain at a picnic.

JACKSON, WANDA—country singer
b: Oct 20, 1937, Maud, Okla.

Ozark Jubilee (music)..... regular (1957–60)

JACOBI, DEREK—actor
b: Oct 22, 1938, London, England

The Strauss Family (drama).. Lanner (1973)

Perhaps best known to TV viewers as the title character in the PBS miniseries *I, Claudius*.

JACOBI, LOU—actor
b: Dec 28, 1913, Toronto, Ont., Canada

The Dean Martin Show (var)
.... regular (1971–73)
Ivan the Terrible (com)....... Ivan (1976)
Melba (com).................. Jack (1986)

JACOBS, BETH—actress

House Calls (com).. Nurse Nancy (1980–82)

JACOBS, CHRISTIAN—juvenile actor
b: Jan 11, Rexburg, Idaho

Maggie (com) ..... Bruce Weston (1981–82)
Gloria (com) .... Joey Stivic (1982–83)

The younger brother of Rachael Jacobs.

JACOBS, JOHNNY—actor

The Betty White Show (var)
.... regular (1958)

JACOBS, LAWRENCE-HILTON—black actor
b: Sep 4, 1953, New York City, N.Y.

Welcome Back, Kotter (com)
Freddie "Boom Boom" Washington (1975–79)
Roots (drama)................ Noah (1977)

JACOBS, MARILYN—

The Steve Allen Show (var)
.... regular (1956–57)

JACOBS, RACHAEL—juvenile actress
b: Sep 26, Ririe, Idaho

It's Not Easy (com)...... Carol Long (1983)

Sister of juvenile actor Christian Jacobs.

JACOBSON, JILL—actress

Falcon Crest (drama) ... Erin Jones (1986–)

JACOBY, BILLY—juvenile actor

b: Apr 10, 1969, Flushing, N.Y.

The Bad News Bears (com)
.... Rudi Stein (1979–80)
Maggie (com) ..... Mark Weston (1981–82)
It's Not Easy (com)
.... Matthew Townsend (1983)
Silver Spoons (com) .... Brad Hill (1985–86)

JACOBY, BOBBY—juvenile actor

Knots Landing (drama)
.... Brian Cunningham (1980–85)

JACOBY, LAURA—juvenile actress

Mr. Smith (com)....... Ellie Atwood (1983)

JACOBY, SCOTT—juvenile actor

b: Nov 19, 1956, Chicago, Ill.

79 Park Avenue (drama)
.... Paulie (as teenager) (1977)

Emmy Award: Best Supporting Actor in a Drama, for the TV movie *That Certain Summer* (1973)

Billy, Bobby, Laura, and Scott are brothers and sister. Scott is the oldest.

JACQUET, JEFFREY—black juvenile actor

b: Oct 15, 1966, Bay City, Texas

Mork & Mindy (com) ..... Eugene (1978–79)
Whiz Kids (drama)
.... Jeremy Saldino (1983–84)

JAECKEL, RICHARD—actor

b: Oct 10, 1926, Long Beach, N.Y.

Frontier Circus (drama)
.... Tony Gentry (1961–62)
Banyon (drama).. Lt. Pete McNeil (1972–73)
Firehouse (adv) .... Hank Myers (1974)
Salvage 1 (adv) .... Klinger (1979)
At Ease (com)....... Maj. Hawkins (1983)
Spenser: For Hire (drama)
.... Lt. Martin Quirk (1985–)

This youthful-looking actor has worked steadily in television since the early 1950s in every conceivable drama and western series, from *Bigelow Theatre* (1951) to *Spenser: For Hire* (1986). He almost always plays supporting roles.

JAENICKE, KATE—actress

Holocaust (drama) ...... Frau Lowy (1978)

JAFFE, SAM—actor

b: Mar 10, 1891*, New York City, N.Y. d: Mar 24, 1984

Ben Casey (drama)
.... Dr. David Zorba (1961–65)

This small and wiry character actor was frail of appearance, but he brought a commanding presence to his roles. He had an extraordinarily long career—he began onstage in 1915, made his film debut in 1934, and was still active on television in the early 1980s. During his years on TV he appeared in many dramatic series, ranging from *Playhouse 90* to *Alfred Hitchcock Presents, Alias Smith and Jones,* and *Buck Rogers in the 25th Century*. He is best remembered, though, as the experienced Dr. Zorba, mentor to Ben Casey.

JAFFE, TALIESIN—juvenile actor

b: Jan 19, 1977, Venice, Calif.

Hail to the Chief (com)
.... Willy Mansfield (1985)

JAGGER, DEAN—actor

b: Nov 7, 1903, Lima, Ohio

Mr. Novak (drama)
.... Albert Vane (1963–65)

Emmy Award: Best Performance in a Religious Program, for "Independence and 76" on *This Is the Life* (1980)

JAKOBSON, MAGGIE—actress

The New Show (var) .... regular (1984)

JALBERT, PIERRE—actor

Combat (drama)
.... Caddy Cadron ("Caje") (1962–67)

JAMES, CLIFTON—actor

b: May 29, 1921, New York City, N.Y.

*Some sources give 1893.

434

City of Angels (drama)
.... Lt. Murray Quint (1976)
Lewis & Clark (com).. Silas Jones (1981–82)

JAMES, DENNIS—host, announcer
b: Aug 24, 1917, Jersey City, N.J.

Cash and Carry (quiz)..... emcee (1946–47)
Prime Time Boxing (DuMont) (sport)
.... sportscaster (1948–50)
The Original Amateur Hour (talent)
.... announcer (1948–60)
Chance of a Lifetime (talent)
.... emcee (1952–56)
Judge for Yourself (quiz)
.... announcer (1953–54)
The Name's the Same (quiz)
.... emcee (1954–55)
High Finance (quiz) .... emcee (1956)
Can You Top This? (com)..... emcee (1970)
The Price Is Right (quiz)..... host (1972–79)

When the first TV set was turned on by the first home viewer, the pitchman on the screen was probably Dennis James. The smiling, businesslike host was present practically at the birth of home TV, long before the networks even existed. What is more remarkable, he remained prominently on view for more than 40 years.

Dennis's firsts, according to an NBC press release, read like a history of the medium: first emcee of a daytime game show (later his forte), first host of a TV variety show, first host of a TV sports show, first emcee of the Easter Parade telecast, first on-the-spot live TV newsreel commentator, first TV wrestling announcer, and first to appear on videotape for commercial use.

Dennis began his career in the early '30s as an announcer on radio—probably because no one had built a regular TV studio yet. As soon as they did, he found it and began appearing twice weekly on DuMont's experimental station in New York in 1938. He continued to be associated with DuMont in the 1940s, and when that company inaugurated its TV network in 1946, he hosted some of its earliest and most primitive game shows, including *Cash and Carry* (set in a mock grocery store lined with shelves of the sponsor's canned goods). However, Dennis's reputation began to really grow as a result of his coverage of DuMont's wrestling matches, of all things. His comical asides, sound effects (bones crushing, etc.), and catchphrases such as "Okay, Mother!" added just the right note of comic relief to that rather ridiculous sport. He became so popular that he was given his own daytime variety show, called, appropriately, *Okay, Mother* (1948–51).

From then on, through the '50s, '60s, and '70s, Dennis hosted a long string of daytime and nighttime of game shows—perhaps a dozen in all—with *The Price Is Right* and *Name That Tune* being the most famous. He also handled announcing chores for some shows (including *The Original Amateur Hour* for many years) and occasionally acted on such series as *Dick Powell Theatre, 77 Sunset Strip, The Farmer's Daughter,* and *Batman.*

JAMES, JACQUELINE—singer

This Is Music (music)........ regular (1952)

JAMES, JERI LOU—actress
b: c. 1945

The RCA Victor Show (com)
.... Susan Sterling (1952–54)
It's Always Jan (com)
.... Josie Stewart (1955–56)

JAMES, JOANELLE—singer, hostess

The Skip Farrell Show (music)
.... regular (1949)

JAMES, JOHN—actor
b: Apr 18, 1956, Minneapolis, Minn. r: New Canaan, Conn.

Dynasty (drama) ...... Jeff Colby (1981–85)
Dynasty II: The Colbys (drama)
.... Jeff Colby (1985–)

John James was a discovery of ABC's National Talent Search; he was "discovered" after appearing on CBS's daytime soap opera *Search for Tomorrow* for two and a half years in the late 1970s. John is the son of veteran New York area radio personality Herb Oscar Anderson.

JAMES, OLGA—black actress, singer

The Bill Cosby Show (com)
.... Verna Kincaid (1969–71)

JAMES, RALPH—actor

Mork & Mindy (com)
.... Orson (voice) (1978–82)

According to press reports in 1980, the booming voice of the unseen Orson on *Mork & Mindy* was supplied by a former stevedore named Ralph James. Oddly enough, he sounded, and even looked a little like, Orson Welles.

JAMES, SHEILA—actress

b: c. 1940, Tulsa, Okla. r: Los Angeles, Calif.

The Stu Erwin Show (com)
.... Jackie Erwin (1950–55)
The Many Loves of Dobie Gillis (com)
.... Zelda Gilroy (1959–63)
Broadside (com)
Machinist's Mate Selma Kowalski (1964–65)

JAMES, STEPHANIE—black juvenile actress

Julia (com)............ Kim Bruce (1970–71)

JAMESON, HOUSE—actor

b: c. 1903, Texas d: 1971

The Aldrich Family (com)
.... Mr. Sam Aldrich (1949–53)
Robert Montgomery Presents (summer) (drama)............... repertory player (1955)

This actor was most famous as "Father" Aldrich for many years on radio.

JAMESON, JOYCE—comedienne

b: Sep 26, 1932, Chicago, Ill. d: Jan 16, 1987

Club Oasis (var) .... regular (1958)
The Spike Jones Show (var).. regular (1960)

JAMISON, MIKKI—actress

b: c. 1944, Spokane, Wash.

Adam 12 (police)......... Jean Reed (1969)

JANE, PAULA—

This Is Music (music)..... regular (1958–59)

JANES, SALLIE—

The Late Summer Early Fall Bert Convy Show (var)...................... regular (1976)

436

JANIS, CONRAD—actor, musician

b: Feb 11, 1928*, New York City, N.Y.

Bonino (com) .... Edward (1953)
Jimmy Hughes, Rookie Cop (police)
.... Off. Jimmy Hughes (1953)
Quark (com) .... Otto Palindrome (1978)
Mork & Mindy (com)
.... Frederick McConnell (1978–82)

Conrad Janis has for many years led a double life as a jazz trombonist and a character actor. His musical career has been mostly in the Dixieland vein, as leader of such combos as Conrad Janis's Tailgate Jazz Band and more recently the Beverly Hills Unlisted Jazz Band (which sometimes includes actor George Segal on banjo). Janis and his band have performed everywhere from clubs to Carnegie Hall, recorded widely, won several national polls, and appeared on numerous TV shows, including those of Johnny Carson and Dinah Shore.

As an actor, Conrad began by playing teenage roles onstage and in films of the mid-1940s. He was seen often on television in the early '50s in more than 300 dramatic productions (sometimes with his band) and in the starring role on the short-lived cop series *Jimmy Hughes*. He was less active as an actor in the 1960s, but younger viewers know him well as Mindy's dad— the owner of a music store, natch—on *Mork & Mindy*.

JANN, GERALD—actor

Hong Kong (adv)........... Ling (1960–61)

JANNEY, LEON—actor

b: Apr 1, 1917, Ogden, Utah d: Oct 28, 1980

Stop Me If You've Heard This One (quiz)
.... emcee (1948–49)
Think Fast (quiz)........ panelist (1949–50)
Hawk (police)
.... Asst. D.A. Ed Gorton (1966)

JANNIS, VIVI—actress

Father Knows Best (com)
.... Myrtle Davis (1955–59)

JANSSEN, DAVID—actor

b: Mar 27, 1930, Naponee, Neb. d: Feb 13, 1980

*Some sources give 1926.

Richard Diamond, Private Detective (drama)
.... Richard Diamond (1957–60)
The Fugitive (drama)
.... Dr. Richard Kimble (1963–67)
O'Hara, U.S. Treasury (police)
.... Jim O'Hara (1971–72)
Harry-O (drama) ... Harry Orwell (1974–76)
Centennial (drama).. Paul Garrett (1978–79)
Biography (doc)............ narrator (1979)

David Janssen was one of television's most memorable actors, almost always cynical and unsmiling, yet magnetic on-screen. He usually played a man of action, but one who was somehow aware of the uncertainties of life. Oddly, this unexpected dramatic depth never translated well into motion pictures. On television, however, he was a major star.

David was brought up in the theater, the son of an actress who was a former Miss America runner-up (she was touring in the musical *Rio Rita* at the time of his birth). He made his film debut in the mid-1940s while still a teenager, playing (among other things) Johnny Weismuller's kid brother in *Swamp Fire* (1946). Then he worked on-stage for a few years, returning to films in the early '50s. His television roles were minor until Dick Powell cast him in a new detective series he was producing—after he had tried 25 other actors first. As the smooth, charismatic private-eye Richard Diamond, Janssen caught on immediately; the show had a healthy three-year run.

During and after the run of *Richard Diamond*, David appeared in other shows as well, including several times on *The Millionaire* and on Powell's *Zane Grey Theatre*. In 1963 he was cast in one of the most famous of all TV series, *The Fugitive*, as the hunted doctor trying to clear his name. Both viewers and critics embraced the show; its moody existentialism was unusual for TV, and it fit Janssen's growing image perfectly. After its climactic episode —one of the most widely viewed in TV history—in which the doctor found his man, David turned to making films for a few years. None of them (including John Wayne's *The Green Berets*) brought him any great success, and in 1970 he returned to TV to star in *O'Hara, U.S. Treasury*. *Harry-O*, about a bohemian private eye, fit him better and had a respectable run in the mid-1970s. After that, David appeared exclusively in TV movies, starring in *A Sensi-*

tive, Passionate Man in 1977 and later in *The Word, High Ice,* and his last, *City In Fear*. Even the potboilers among these were made more interesting by his presence, though one gets the feeling he never fully realized his potential in TV films either. He died unexpectedly of a heart attack at the age of 49.

Of his craft, Janssen once said, "I put myself completely into the character, to make him believable. I close out whatever is beyond the lines of the set. The part I'm playing and the situation I'm in are real." He was a rare and thoughtful talent, and he will be missed.

JARESS, JILL—actress

The New People (drama)
.... Ginny Loomis (1969–70)

JARNAC, DOROTHY—dancer

Henry Morgan's Great Talent Hunt (var)
.... regular (1951)

JARRETT, ART—singer, actor
b: 1909, New York City, N.Y.

Rhythm Rodeo (music)....... host (1950–51)

JARRETT, RENNE—actress
b: Jan 28, 1946, Brooklyn, N.Y.

Nancy (com)....... Nancy Smith (1970–71)

Renne (pronounced "Renny") appeared as a child performer in the daytime soap opera *Portia Faces Life* in the mid-1950s and so enjoyed the experience that she decided that when she grew up she would become an actress. She did, but with only marginal success. After some stage work and additional TV roles in the late '60s, Renne got her big break in 1970 playing the daughter of the president in the NBC comedy *Nancy*. Unfortunately, the series flopped, and Renne has since been seen in TV supporting roles in daytime *(Somerset)* and nighttime *(Barnaby Jones*, etc.).

JARRIEL, TOM—newscaster
b: Dec 29, 1934, LaGrange, Ga.

ABC Weekend News (news)
.... anchorman (1975–)
20/20 (mag)........ correspondent (1979–)

Emmy Award: Correspondent, Best News Segments, for the "Moment of Crisis" series: "The Hyatt Disaster," "The Berlin Wall," and "Vietnam Withdrawal" (1981); and for "What Happened to the Children" (1985).

JARRIN, MAURICIO—juvenile actor

Cos (var) .... regular (1976)

JARVIS, GRAHAM—actor
b: Aug 25, 1930, Toronto, Ont., Canada

Mary Hartman, Mary Hartman (com)
.... Charlie Haggers (1976–78)
Making the Grade (com)
.... Jack Felspar (1982)
Fame (drama)..... Bob Dyrenforth (1986–)

JASON, GEORGE—

Captain Billy's Mississippi Music Hall (var)
.... regular (1948)

JASON, HARVEY—actor
b: London, England

Rowan & Martin's Laugh-In (var)
.... regular (1970–71)
Captains and the Kings (drama)
.... Harry Zieff (1976)
Rich Man, Poor Man—Book I (drama)
.... Pinky (1976)
Bring 'Em Back Alive (adv)
.... Bhundi (1982–83)

JASON, RICK—actor
b: May 21, 1926, New York City, N.Y.

The Case of the Dangerous Robin (drama)
.... Robin Scott (1960–61)
Combat (drama)... Lt. Gil Hanley (1962–67)

JEAN, NORMA—country singer
b: Jan 30, 1938, Wellston, Okla.

Ozark Jubilee (music)........ regular (1958)

JEFFERSON, HERBERT, JR.—black
actor
b: Sep 28, 1946, Jersey City, N.J.*

Rich Man, Poor Man—Book I (drama)
.... Ray Dwyer (1976)
Battlestar Galactica (sci fi)
.... Lt. Boomer (1978–79)

*Some sources give Sandersville, Ga.

438

The Devlin Connection (drama)
.... Otis Barnes (1982)

JEFFREYS, ANNE—actress
b: Jan 26, 1923, Goldsboro, N.C.

Topper (com) ...... Marion Kerby (1953–55)
Love That Jill (com)
.... Jill Johnson (1958)
The Delphi Bureau (drama)
.... Sybil Van Loween (1972–73)
Finder of Lost Loves (drama)
.... Rita Hargrove (1984–85)

Vivacious Anne Jeffreys, who was once named by *Theatre Arts* magazine as "one of the ten outstanding beauties of the stage," has been successful as both a singer and an actress. Her first career was in opera, for which she began training as a teenager. Following a period around 1940 singing with New York's Municipal Opera Company (while supplementing her income as a Powers model), Anne left for Hollywood, where she appeared in a string of B films from 1942–48. Among other things, she was Tess Trueheart in some Dick Tracy features.

Her movie career failed to rise above the B level, however, so Anne returned to New York in the late '40s and sought additional opera engagements. Then she began to concentrate on the stage—especially musical comedy—and scored her greatest triumph in *Kiss Me Kate*. She also appeared on television, where her most famous role was that of the ghostly Marion on *Topper*. Her costar on *Topper* was her new husband, Robert Sterling, whom she had married in 1951. Anne and Robert starred together in other TV productions as well, including the musical special *Dearest Enemy* in 1955 and the short-lived series *Love That Jill* in 1958. By the early '60s, with her husband mostly retired from acting (to become a businessman), Anne continued alone, in occasional appearances on episodes of various series. In 1971 she was a regular on the daytime soap *Bright Promise*, and a year later she appeared as a glamorous Washington hostess-cum-spy on *The Delphi Bureau*. Neither lasted long. In the late '70s and '80s she was seen periodically, in both daytime *(General Hospital)* and nighttime TV, a lovely and mature supporting actress.

JEFFRIES, HERB—black actor, singer
b: Sep 24, 1914, Detroit, Mich.

Where's Huddles? (cartn)
.... Freight Train (voice) (1970)

JEFFRIES, LANG—actor
b: Jun 7, 1931, Ontario, Canada d: Feb 12, 1987

Rescue 8 (adv) ..... Skip Johnson (1958–59)

JELLISON, BOB—

The Beautiful Phyllis Diller Show (var)
.... regular (1968)

JENKINS, ALLEN—actor
b: Apr 9, 1900*, New York City, N.Y. d: Jul 20, 1974

Waterfront (adv) .... Sid (1953–56)
The Duke (com) .... Johnny (1954)
Hey Jeannie (com)..... Al Murray (1956–57)
Top Cat (cartn)
.... Officer Dibble (voice) (1961–62)

JENKINS, CAROL MAYO—actress
b: Nov 24, Knoxville, Tenn.

Fame (drama)
.... Elizabeth Sherwood (1982–)

JENKINS, GORDON—orchestra leader
b: May 12, 1910, Webster Groves, Mo. d: May 1, 1984

NBC Comedy Hour (var)
.... orch. leader (1956)

A famous composer and conductor of the '30s through the '60s, who was more active on records and radio than on television. He was also the conductor for several of Frank Sinatra's TV specials in the late '60s.

JENKINS, LARRY FLASH—black actor
b: May 10, Long Island, N.Y. r: Chicago

The White Shadow (drama)
.... Wardell Stone (1980–81)
Bay City Blues (drama)
.... Lynwood Scott (1983)
Finder of Lost Loves (drama)
.... Lyman Whittaker (1985)

So named for his speed in karate and other sports.

*Some sources give 1890.

JENKINS, MARK—actor

Young Dr. Kildare (drama)
.... Dr. James Kildare (1972)

JENKS, FRANK—actor
b: 1902, Des Moines, Iowa d: May 13, 1962

Colonel Humphrey Flack (com)
.... Uthas P. Garvey (1953–54)
Colonel Flack (com)
.... Uthas P. Garvey (1958)

JENNER, BARRY—actor
b: Philadelphia, Pa.

Dallas (drama)
.... Dr. Jerry Kenderson (1985–)

JENNER, LINDA THOMPSON—

Hee Haw (var) .... regular (1977–)

JENNINGS, PETER—newscaster
b: Jul 29, 1938, Toronto, Canada

ABC Evening News (news)
.... anchorman (1965–68)
ABC Evening News (news)
.... anchorman (1978–)

Emmy Award: Best Coverage of a Single Breaking News Story, for "Personal Note/ Beirut" (1982)

Early in his career Peter Jennings was looked down upon by many in the TV industry as the "James Bond" of TV news. His boyish looks, his natty Saville Row suits and his on-the-move reports from exotic overseas locations left him with an image as a shallow, globetrotting pretty-boy. It is an image that he has worked long and hard to overcome.

Peter's rise in the news business was certainly meteoric. A high school dropout, he began his career at a local radio station in Canada in 1959 and within a few years had become co-anchor of Canada's first national newscast on a commercial network, the CTV. ABC, which was then looking for a bright young face to lure the youth market, brought him to New York in 1964 and in February 1965 named him anchor of its evening news—making him, at 26, probably the youngest (and certainly the youngest looking) newsman ever to anchor a major network newscast. He was also the least experienced, with a scant half-dozen years in the business (most anchors have at least 20), nearly all of that in Canada.

The result was predictable. When there were crises, viewers, even young ones, instinctively turned to "Uncle Walter" Cronkite on CBS, or to Huntley and Brinkley on NBC, but not to "the kid" on ABC. "Everybody was calling me 'pretty-boy,'" Peter later recalled. "I hated it . . . it was a personal disaster."

After three years, Peter was replaced by veteran newsman Frank Reynolds, and shortly thereafter he was sent overseas as an international correspondent. He spent most of the next decade learning the international beat, especially the Middle East (he was Beirut bureau chief for six years). He worked hard at it and finally, in the late '70s, ABC brought him in from the cold to become "foreign anchor" of its new, three-anchor *World News Tonight*. He was still based in London, and he still globe-trotted to hot spots to file his reports, but now he sounded like he knew what he was talking about. He was especially good during the Mideast fighting, when his reports from Beirut were widely praised. He wrangled an exclusive interview with Yasir Arafat and was on the scene in Cairo after the assassination of President Sadat before Walter Cronkite could even get out of New York.

In 1983, upon the death of Frank Reynolds, Peter returned to New York to resume the position he had vacated more than 15 years before—sole, New York–based anchor of ABC's evening news. He is no longer compared to James Bond . . . even though he does still look a bit like Roger Moore.

JENNINGS, WAYLON—country singer
b: Jun 15, 1937, Littlefield, Texas

The Dukes of Hazzard (com)
.... the balladeer (1979–85)

JENS, SALOME—actress
b: May 8, 1935, Milwaukee, Wisc.

From Here to Eternity (drama)
.... Mrs. Kipfer (1979)

JENSEN, KAREN—actress
b: Aug 18, San Francisco, Calif.

Bracken's World (drama)
.... Rachel Holt (1969–70)

JENSEN, MAREN—actress
b: Sep 23, 1956, Arcadia, Calif.

Battlestar Galactica (sci fi)
.... Athena (1978–79)

JENSEN, SANDI—singer

The Lawrence Welk Show (music)
.... regular (1968–80)

JENSEN, SANFORD—actor
b: Aug 11, 1953, South Haven, Mich.

Foley Square (com)
..... Asst. D.A. Carter DeVries (1985–86)

JENSON, ROY—actor
b: Feb 1935, Calgary, Alta. Canada

Rich Man, Poor Man—Book I (drama)
.... Pete Tierney (1976)

JERGENS, ADELE—actress
b: Nov 26, 1917*, Brooklyn, N.Y.

Pantomime Quiz (quiz) ... regular (1950–52)

Platinum blonde of Broadway and Hollywood B-film fame who was dubbed "Miss World's Fairest" at the 1939 New York World's Fair. A favorite pin-up in the '40s, she appeared occasionally on television during the '50s, in both dramas *(Damon Runyon Theatre)* and comedies *(Abbott & Costello)*. She retired in the late '50s as youth began to fade.

JERGENS, DIANE—actress

The Bob Cummings Show (com)
.... Francine Williams (1955–56)
Counterthrust (drama) .... agent (1959)

JEROME, JERRY—orchestra leader, saxophone
b: Jun 19, 1912, Brooklyn, N.Y.

Words and Music (music) .... trio (1949)
Versatile Varieties (var)
.... orch. leader (1949–50)

JESSEL, GEORGE—humorist, host, producer
b: Apr 3, 1898, New York City, N.Y. d: May 23, 1981

All Star Revue (var)
.... alternating host (1952–53)

*Some sources give 1922.

The Comeback Story (drama)
.... emcee (1953–54)
The George Jessel Show (var)
.... host (1953–54)
The Jackie Gleason Show (var)
.... regular (1965–66)

One of the grand old men of show business, for whom vaudeville never died. Jessel had been onstage since 1907 and in movies since 1911, and when television came on the scene he brought his act there virtually unchanged. He was best known as an effusive storyteller, and a highlight of his shows was his mock after-dinner testimonial speech, directed at a guest celebrity—the original "TV roast." It was from these comic orations that he became known as "America's Toastmaster General."

Georgie was also pretty smooth with the ladies, it seems, having gone through four marriages and many affairs during his years in Hollywood. In 1975 he published a tell-all autobiography titled *The World I Lived In,* which *Variety* said "might as easily have been called *The Beds I Slept In.*"

JESSEL, RAY—comedian

The New Bill Cosby Show (var)
.... regular (1972–73)

JETER, FELICIA—black newscaster
b: Atlanta, Ga.

CBS News Nightwatch (news)
.... anchor (1982–84)

JEWELL, GERI—actress
b: c. 1956, Buffalo, N.Y.

The Facts of Life (com)
.... Cousin Geri Warner (occasional)
(1981–84)

"I'm one of the few people who drive better than they walk," cracked the young comedienne with jerky movements, slightly slurred speech, and listing head. "I've been pulled over once for speeding and four times for walking ... Ever notice there are no handicapped people on TV? *Name That Handicap? Bowling for Crutches?* I've had some really high scores bowling . . . only never in my lane."

Geri Jewell was certainly one of the

most unusual, and plucky, comics on television in the '80s. She has cerebral palsy. She jokes about it, capitalizes on it, and ultimately thumbs her nose at it. She always wanted to be a stand-up comedian. Everyone told her that it was impossible for someone in her condition, but she did it anyway.

Geri was born with the affliction; it impairs her hearing, speech, and ability to walk (but not much else). In fact, she was declared dead at birth, and doctors worked on her for hours to revive her. An uncommonly bright and determined young girl, she decided she wanted to become a comic. She wrote of her impossible dream to her idol, Carol Burnett, who answered immediately and corresponded with her for several years. "Success comes from within," Burnett wrote. "Try hard and you'll make it."

Geri made her debut in 1978 at the Comedy Store in Los Angeles. Audiences were at first taken aback, but she soon won converts with her disarming charm and lopsided smile. One was Norman Lear, producer of *The Facts of Life,* who gave her a recurring part in the series as Blair's "Cousin Geri." The first taping was the high point of Geri's life. She has since appeared on other shows and in movies, including the 1982 TV film *Two of a Kind.*

"I owe a lot to my mother," Geri says. "She and my father made me help myself as much as I could before they allowed anyone to give me a hand. I thank her now for it, even though at times it was very painful for me. I was always a fighter. But everyone in life has one handicap or another to overcome."

JILLIAN, ANN—actress
b: Jan 29, 1951, Cambridge, Mass.

Hazel (com) .... Millie Ballard (1965–66)
It's a Living (com)
.... Cassie Cranston (1980–82)
Jennifer Slept Here (com)
.... Jennifer Farrell (1983–84)
It's a Living (com)
.... Cassie Cranston (1985–86)

JILLSON, JOYCE—actress
b: c. 1947, Cranston, R.I.

Peyton Place (drama)
.... Jill Smith/Rossi (1968)

JOEL, DENNIS—actor

The Betty Hutton Show (com)
.... Roy Strickland (1959–60)

JOHANSEN, DAVID—musician

NBC's Saturday Night Live (var)
.... Buster Poindexter (1986–)

JOHNS, BIBI—

Continental Showcase (var).. regular (1966)

JOHNS, GLYNIS—actress
b: Oct 5, 1923, Pretoria, South Africa

Glynis (com)....... Glynis Granville (1963)

JOHNSON, ALAN—choreographer

3 Girls 3 (var)............. dancers (1977)

Emmy Awards: Best Choreography, for the specials *Jack Lemmon in 'S Wonderful, 'S Marvelous, 'S Gershwin* (1972) and *Shirley MacLaine . . . Every Little Movement* (1980)

JOHNSON, ANNE-MARIE—actress

Double Trouble (com)
.... Aileen Lewis (1984–85)
What's Happening Now!! (com)
.... Nadine Thomas (1985–)

JOHNSON, ARCH—actor
b: 1923, Minneapolis, Minn.

Peter Loves Mary (com) .. Charlie (1960–61)
The Asphalt Jungle (police)
.... Capt. Gus Honochek (1961)
Camp Runamuck (com)
.... Cmdr. Wivenhoe (1965–66)

JOHNSON, ARTE—actor
b: Jan 20, 1934*, Chicago, Ill.

It's Always Jan (com)
.... Stanley Schreiber (1955–56)
Sally (com) ... Bascomb Bleacher, Jr. (1958)
Hennesey (com)... Seaman Shatz (1959–62)
Don't Call Me Charlie (com)
.... Cpl. Lefkowitz (1962–63)
Rowan & Martin's Laugh-In (var)
.... regular (1968–71)
Ben Vereen . . . Comin' At Ya (var)
.... regular (1975)

*Some sources give 1929.

The Gong Show (com) ... panelist (1976–80)
Games People Play (sport)
.... field reporter (1980–81)
Glitter (drama)..... Clive Richlin (1984–85)

Emmy Award: Best Performance in a Variety Show, for *Rowan & Martin's Laugh-In* (1969)

Diminutive Arte Johnson had been a regular on no fewer than four prime time series, and a guest on many others, during the 15 years before his phenomenal success as one of the "newcomers" on *Laugh-In*. His kooky characterizations took *Laugh-In*'s hip young audience by storm—Tyrone, the little old man on a park bench; Rosmenko, the incredulous Russian; the professor who was so boring he put himself to sleep; and of course Wolfgang, the German soldier lurking behind a potted palm ("Verrry interesting"). Once while Bob Hope was onstage delivering one-liners, Wolfgang trotted out in full German uniform, looked up at the startled comedian, and purred, "Mr. Hope, I vaited for you every Christmas."

Arte has always been good at doing old people and dialects. He came to New York in the early '50s after graduation from the University of Illinois and promptly won a bit part as a 65-year-old Frenchman in the Broadway musical *Gentlemen Prefer Blondes*. That led to summer stock, nightclubs, TV commercials, and a regular role as the delivery boy on the 1955 Janis Paige situation comedy, *It's Always Jan*. Later, he was Gale Gordon's incompetent son on *Sally* and one of the seamen on Jackie Cooper's navy comedy *Hennesey*.

Arte had a few more roles in comedies of the early '60s, but as he got a little too old to play "young" parts his career began to slow down. *Laugh-In* was something of a second chance for him. By the end of the '60s he had gone from "that second banana a few years back" to a bright new comedy star. He played frequent guest roles in the '70s and '80s (several on *Fantasy Island*) and also developed a busy career doing voices for children's specials and Saturday morning cartoons. Among the latter was a spin-off from one of his most famous characters—Tyrone, the little old man—on the cartoon series *Baggy Pants and the Nitwits* (costarring Ruth Buzzi).

JOHNSON, BAYN—juvenile actor
b: c. 1959

What's It All About, World? (var)
.... regular (1969)

JOHNSON, BEN—actor
b: Jun 13, 1918*, Foraker, Okla.

The Monroes (wes)....... Sleeve (1966–67)

A rugged former world's champion rodeo steer-roper and a movie stunt man, who became known to a wider public through his roles in TV and movie westerns.

JOHNSON, BETTY—singer
b: Mar 16, 1931, Guilford County, N.C.

The Jack Paar Show (talk)
.... semiregular (1957–58)

JOHNSON, BILLY—
The Little Revue (music).. regular (1949–50)

JOHNSON, BOB—actor
Mission: Impossible (drama)
.... voice on tape (1966–73)

JOHNSON, BRAD—actor
b: c. 1924 d: Apr 4, 1981

Annie Oakley (wes)
.... Dep. Sheriff Lofty Craig (1953–56)

JOHNSON, CHERIE—black juvenile actress
b: Nov 21, 1975, Pittsburgh, Pa.

Punky Brewster (com)
.... Cherie Johnson (1984–86)

The niece of *Punky Brewster* producer David Duclon. Duclon says he originally intended to simply name a little girl in the series after his niece, to surprise her. However, when he told Cherie about it, she shot back, "Uncle David, if my name is in it why can't I do the part?"

The girl has the makings of a first-class agent.

JOHNSON, CHIC—
see Olsen & Johnson

*Some sources give 1919 or 1920; some also list the larger nearby town of Pawhuska as his birthplace (Foraker has a population of 74).

JOHNSON, CLARK—actor
Hot Shots (drama)....... Pendleton (1986–)

JOHNSON, CLAUDE—actor
Adam 12 (police)
.... Off. Norm Green (1970–71)

JOHNSON, DON—actor
b: Dec 15, 1949, Flatt Creek, Mo.

From Here to Eternity (drama)
.... Jefferson Davis Prewitt (1980)
Miami Vice (police)
.... Det. James "Sonny" Crockett (1984–)

Don Johnson was part of the wave of macho actors who swept on to television in the mid-1980s. This was no sensitive, thoughtful Alan Alda type; with his cut-off T-shirt revealing bulging muscles, his shades, and his perpetual scowl, he exuded a kind of growling "Get the hell out of my way" masculinity that fit his hard-driving series *Miami Vice* perfectly.

Don spent 15 sometimes frustrating years as an actor before he landed his hit show. He got into acting after two years at the University of Kansas, and at first his career seemed to be poised for a rapid takeoff. He was only 20 when he starred in his first film, *The Magic Garden of Stanley Sweetheart* (1970), a contemporary tale of drugs and the '60s generation. Three years later he appeared in the cult film *A Boy and His Dog,* an allegory about the postnuclear age. Don continued to work frequently in the late '70s, but increasingly in more routine TV movies. Between 1976 and 1981 he made no fewer than five pilots for prospective series, several of them cop shows; none made it to the schedule. Among his TV films were *Beulah Land, The Rebels, Amateur Night at the Dixie Bar and Grill* (his personal favorite) and *Elvis and the Beauty Queen* (as Elvis). As his once-promising career began to slow down, he developed a serious drinking problem, which made things even worse.

Miami Vice was a chance to get his career back on track, and it certainly accomplished that. After 15 years, Don was suddenly one of TV's top stars.

JOHNSON, GAIL—singer
This Is Music (music)..... regular (1958–59)

443

JOHNSON, GEORGIANN—actress
b: Aug 15, 1926, Decorah, Iowa

Mr. Peepers (com). Marge Weskit (1952–55)
Our Family Honor (drama)
.... Katherine McKay (1985–86)

JOHNSON, GERRY—actress

The Flintstones (cartn)
.... Betty Rubble (voice) (1964–66)

JOHNSON, JANET LOUISE—actress

The Hardy Boys Mysteries (adv)
.... Nancy Drew (1978)
B.J. and the Bear (adv) ... Tommy (1979–80)

JOHNSON, JARROD—juvenile actor

Szysznyk (com) .... Ralph (1977–78)
Friends (com) ... Randy Summerfield (1979)

JOHNSON, JAY—actor, ventriloquist
b: Jul 11, Abernathy, Texas

Soap (com)
.... Chuck/Bob Campbell (1977–81)

Jay and his puppets have been seen on numerous TV talk shows, as well as on *Soap*.

JOHNSON, JERMAIN HODGE—black juvenile actor

Palmerstown, U.S.A. (drama)
.... Booker T. Freeman (1980–81)

JOHNSON, JUDY—singer
b: Mar 8, 1928, Norfolk, Va.

The Sammy Kaye Show (var)
.... regular (1950)
Your Show of Shows (var)
.... regular (1950–53)
Judge for Yourself (quiz) .... vocalist (1954)
Tonight! America After Dark (talk)
.... regular (1957)

JOHNSON, JUNE—

Fireball Fun-for-All (var)..... regular (1949)

The daughter of comedian Chic Johnson (of Olsen & Johnson).

JOHNSON, KATHIE LEE—actress, singer
b: Paris, France r: Annapolis, Md.

Hee Haw Honeys (com)
.... Kathie Honey (1978–79)

Kathie later became a talk show hostess and then a correspondent on *Good Morning, America.*

JOHNSON, LAURA—actress
b: Aug 1, Burbank, Calif.

Falcon Crest (drama)
.... Terry Hartford (1983–)

JOHNSON, ROBIN—actor

Codename: Foxfire (drama)
.... Danny O'Toole (1985)

JOHNSON, RUSSELL—actor
b: 1924, Ashley, Pa.

Black Saddle (wes)
.... Marshal Gib Scott (1959–60)
Gilligan's Island (com)
.... Roy Hinkley (the professor) (1964–67)

JOHNSON, STEPHEN—actor

Curse of Dracula (adv)
.... Kurt von Helsing (1979)

JOHNSON, TANIA—black juvenile actress

Backstairs at the White House (drama)
.... Lillian Rogers (1979)

JOHNSON, VAN—actor
b: Aug 25, 1916, Newport, R.I.

Rich Man, Poor Man—Book I (drama)
.... Marsh Goodwin (1976)

The freckled-faced, sandy-haired movie star of the '40s has appeared intermittently on television over the years, in shows ranging from *I Love Lucy* in the '50s to *Aloha Paradise* in the '80s. On *Batman* he was the bizarre, singing "Minstrel." Van has been active in recent years mostly in dinner theater productions.

JOHNSTON, AMY—actress

Brothers and Sisters (com)
.... Mary Lee (1979)

JOHNSTON, ERIC—actor

V: The Final Battle (miniseries) (sci fi)
.... Sean Donovan (1984)

JOHNSTON, JANE A.—actress

When Things Were Rotten (com)
.... Princess Isabelle (1975)

JOHNSTON, JOHN DENNIS—actor

Dear Detective (police) .... Det. Clay (1979)

JOHNSTON, JOHNNY—singer, host
b: Dec 1, 1914*, St. Louis, Mo.

The Stork Club (talk)..... cohost (1950–51)
The Ken Murray Show (var) . regular (1953)
Masquerade Party (quiz)
.... panelist (1957–58)
Make That Spare (sport)
.... commentator (1960–64)

The popular singer and sometimes actor of the '40s was seen on television in the '50s and early '60s. Later, he retired to Arizona, where he managed a sporting goods company.

JOHNSTON, LIONEL—actor
b: Apr 23, 1952, Augusta, Ga.

Sons and Daughters (drama)
.... Charlie (1974)

JOLLEY, NORMAN—actor

Space Patrol (child) .... Sec. Gen. of the United Planets (1951–52)

JOLLIFFE, DAVID—actor

Room 222 (drama)........ Bernie (1970–74)

JOLLIFFE, DOROTHY—actress

The Red Buttons Show (var) . regular (1952)

JONES BOYS, THE—singers

The Lux Show Starring Rosemary Clooney (var)..................... regulars (1958)

JONES, ANISSA—juvenile actress
b: 1958 d: Aug 29, 1976

Family Affair (com) .... Buffy (1966–71)

*Some sources give 1915.

Cuddly, pigtailed Anissa Jones was a little girl who came to a sad end. Barely five years after *Family Affair* left the air, she was already immersed in the Southern California drug culture; she died of an overdose of Quaaludes and liquor at the age of 18.

JONES, ARCHDALE J.—host

Key to the Missing (int)...... host (1948–49)

JONES, BEN—actor
b: Aug 30, Edgecombe County, N.C.

The Dukes of Hazzard (com)
.... Cooter Davenport (1979–85)

JONES, CAROLYN—actress
b: Apr 28, 1929, Amarillo, Texas d: Aug 3, 1983

The Addams Family (com)
.... Morticia Addams (1964–66)
Roots (drama).......... Mrs. Moore (1977)

Carolyn Jones was a leading lady with a vague air of mystery about her. Her sharp features, inquiring eyes and (at least during the filming of *The Addams Family*) long black tresses made her interestingly cast in her most famous TV role; she was quite unlike the more ghoulish Yvonne DeCarlo on the similar series, *The Munsters.*

Carolyn's distinctive appearance had often won her offbeat roles. She had wanted to become an actress from the time she was in high school in Texas, and she made her stage debut in the late 1940s while still in her teens. She was soon recruited for films, playing roles in such hard-knuckles crime dramas as *The Big Heat* and *Shield for Murder,* as well as in a couple of Bob Hope comedies. Perhaps her most memorable role of the early '50s was in the terrifying 3-D chiller, *The House of Wax.*

Carolyn also began doing television in the early '50s, with multiple appearances on *Dragnet, Treasury Men in Action,* and *Pepsi Cola Playhouse,* among others. Though she worked steadily she remained a second-rank supporting player until her perfect casting in *The Addams Family* secured her place in TV history. Another colorful role in the mid-1960s was that of

Marsha, the Queen of Diamonds on *Batman*. She continued to appear in series episodes, TV movies, and miniseries during the '70s and into the '80s. At the time of her death of cancer she was a regular on the daytime soap opera *Capitol*, as manipulative power broker Myrna Clegg.

Carolyn was married in the '50s to producer Aaron Spelling.

JONES, CHARLIE—sportscaster, actor
b: Nov 9, 1930, Fort Smith, Ark.

Almost Anything Goes (aud par)
.... play-by-play (1975–76)

JONES, CHRISTINE—actress

Number 96 (drama)
.... Lisa Brendon (1980–81)
Rituals (drama)
.... Christina Robinson (1984–85)

JONES, CHRISTOPHER—actor
b: Aug 18, 1941, Jackson, Tenn.

The Legend of Jesse James (wes)
.... Jesse James (1965–66)

JONES, CLAUDE EARL—actor

Buffalo Bill (com) .... Stan Fluger (1983–84)

JONES, CLIFTON—actor

Space 1999 (sci fi) .... David (1975–77)

JONES, DAVID—actor, singer
b: Dec 30, 1946, Manchester, England

The Monkees (com) .... Davy (1966–68)

Davy Jones was the youngest and smallest (at 5' 3") of the Monkees and also an experienced actor when he joined the famous foursome. He had appeared on English television in the early '60s and in 1963 began a two-year run on Broadway in the musical *Oliver*, as the Artful Dodger. He was nominated for a Tony Award for this role. He also starred in the Broadway musical *Pickwick* and guested on a number of TV shows, including *Ben Casey*.

Like the other members of the Monkees Davy has had only a minor career in show business since the group broke up in 1969. He played guest roles on such series as *The Brady Bunch* and *Love American*

Style, and had a minor role in a 1971 TV movie called *Hunter*. Later he cut some unsuccessful solo records, and performed in off-and-on reunions with Mickey Dolenz and two of the Monkees' songwriters in a new group in the mid and late '70s.

JONES, DEAN—actor
b: Jan 25, 1931*, Decatur, Ala.

Ensign O'Toole (com)
.... Ens. O'Toole (1962–63)
What's It All About, World? (var)
.... host (1969)
Chicago Teddy Bears (com)
.... Linc McCray (1971)
Herbie, The Love Bug (com)
.... Jim Douglas (1982)

The squeaky-clean star of more than a few Disney movies. Oddly enough, Dean's first professional work in show business was as a teenage blues singer in the French Quarter of New Orleans. After four years in the navy he returned in the late '50s as an actor, making his movie debut in 1956 in *Tea and Sympathy*. Soon after, he began to do television work as well. Although he has appeared as a regular in four short-lived series—including one based on his Disney movie *The Love Bug*— his TV appearances have been infrequent since mid-1960s.

JONES, DICK—actor
b: Feb 25, 1927, Snyder, Texas

The Range Rider (wes)
.... Dick West (1951–52)
Buffalo Bill, Jr. (wes) . Buffalo Bill, Jr. (1955)

JONES, EDGAR ALLAN, JR.—Law Professor
b: c. 1920, Brooklyn, N.Y.

Accused (drama) . presiding judge (1958–59)
Traffic Court (drama)... the judge (1958–59)

The assistant dean of the U.C.L.A. law school. In Hollywood, everybody gets into show business!

JONES, GINGER—actress

Beulah (com) ... Alice Henderson (1950–52)

*Some sources give 1935 or 1936.

JONES, GORDON—actor
b: Apr 5, 1911, Alden, Iowa d: Jun 20, 1963

The Abbott and Costello Show (com)
.... Mike the cop (1951–53)
The Ray Milland Show (com)
.... Pete Thompson (1953–54)
So This Is Hollywood (com)
.... Hubie Dodd (1955)
The Adventures of Ozzie & Harriet (com)
.... Butch Barton (1958–60)

JONES, HENRY—actor
b: Aug 1, 1912, Philadelphia, Pa.

Channing (drama)
.... Dean Fred Baker (1963–64)
The Girl with Something Extra (com)
.... Owen Metcalf (1973–74)
Phyllis (com)
.... Judge Jonathan Dexter (1975–77)
Kate Loves a Mystery (drama)
.... Josh Alden (1979)
Gun Shy (com)....... Homer McCoy (1983)
Codename: Foxfire (drama) .. Phillips (1985)
Falcon Crest (drama)
.... R. Riley Wicker (1985–)

This little character-actor with a bulldog face is said to have appeared in more than 400 TV dramas over the years. He was a standby on *Kraft Theatre* and *Alfred Hitchcock Presents* in the '50s and a frequent player on *Bonanza, Gunsmoke, The Name of the Game*, and many other shows in later years. He has said that he wants to act as long as he can remember his lines. He seemed to be having no trouble as he entered his seventies.

JONES, JACK—singer
b: Jan 14, 1938*, Los Angeles, Calif.

The Love Boat (com) . sang theme (1977–85)

JONES, JAMES EARL—black actor
b: Jan 17, 1931, Arkabutla, Miss. r: Maniste, Mich.

Roots: The Next Generations (drama)
.... Alex Haley (as adult) (1979)
Paris (police) ...... Woody Paris (1979–80)
Me and Mom (drama) .. Lou Garfield (1985)

This imposing actor, with a deep, rumbling voice, has appeared in many quality dramas over the years. Born in Mississippi

*Some sources give 1942.

and raised on a farm in Michigan, he made his way to New York in the late '50s with his father, who also had theatrical ambitions. The two of them waxed floors while working for their break; James got his in a 1957 off-Broadway production, *Wedding in Japan*. He was soon in demand for black stage roles, and in 1960 he joined the New York Shakespeare Festival, where he essayed such classics as *Othello, Macbeth*, and *The Emperor Jones*. He began to accumulate awards for his work in the early '60s; however, it was his role in the Broadway hit *The Great White Hope* in '67 that catapulted him to fame and brought him a Tony Award. He also starred in the movie version (1970), for which he was nominated for an Academy Award.

Jones began appearing on television in the early '60s at the same time he was building his stage career. He was nominated for an Emmy for a 1963 episode of *East Side/West Side* and later played such varied roles as an African chieftain on *Tarzan*, doctors on *As the World Turns* and *The Guiding Light*, Balthazar in the miniseries *Jesus of Nazareth*, and King Lear in a 1974 special. In 1973 he hosted the syndicated black talent show *Black Omnibus* and in 1975 the children's series *Vegetable Soup*.

His fame grew still further in the late '70s, with two major roles in 1979: as Alex Haley in *Roots: The Next Generations* and as the star of his own police series, which was not successful (no drama series starring a black ever has been). Jones is also known for his magnificent, Shakespearean voice, which was used to greatest advantage as the voice of Darth Vader in the box-office smash *Star Wars*.

JONES, JANET MARIE—dancer

Dance Fever (dance) ...... dancer (1980–)

JONES, JOHN CHRISTOPHER—actor

On Our Own (com)
.... Eddie Barnes (1977–78)

JONES, L.Q.—actor
b: 1936*, Beaumont, Texas

Cheyenne (wes).......... Smitty (1955–56)
The Virginian (wes) ...... Belden (1964–67)

*Some sources give 1927.

JONES, LOUIS M. "GRANDPA"— country singer, banjoist

b: Oct 20, 1913, Niagra, Ky.

Hee Haw (var) . . . . regular (1969–)

This old-timey country favorite adopted his "Grandpa" persona while he was still in his twenties, using false gray hair and makeup. He has long been a regular on the *Grand Ole Opry*, where he is known for his enthusiastic banjo playing and cornball jokes. His autobiography: *Everybody's Grandpa: Fifty Years Behind the Mike*, with Charles Wolfe (1984).

JONES, MARILYN—actress

b: Jun 6, c. 1956, Pittsburgh, Pa. r: Grosse Pointe, Mich.

Secrets of Midland Heights (drama)
. . . . Holly Wheeler (1980–81)
King's Crossing (drama)
. . . . Carey Hollister (1982)

JONES, MICKEY—actor

Flo (com) . . . . Chester (1980–81)
V: The Final Battle (miniseries) (sci fi)
. . . . Chris (1984)

JONES, MORGAN—actor

The Blue Angels (adv)
. . . . Cmdr. Donovan (1960)

JONES, PAMELA—actress

Search (adv) . . . . Miss James (1973)

JONES, PETER—actor

b: Jun 12, 1920, Wem, Shropshire, England

From a Bird's Eye View (com)
. . . . Mr. Clive Beauchamp (1971)

JONES, QUINCY—black orchestra leader, arranger

b: Mar 14, 1933, Chicago, Ill. r: Seattle, Wash.

The New Bill Cosby Show (var)
. . . . orch. leader (1972–73)

Emmy Award: Best Music Composition, for *Roots* (1977)

One of the leading composers and arrangers for movies and for pop records. On television he has provided the music for *Ironside* and *Sanford and Son*, among other programs.

JONES, RENEE—actress

Jessie (police) . . . . Ellie (1984)

JONES, SAM J.—actor

b: Aug 12, 1954, Chicago, Ill. r: West Palm Beach, Fla.

Code Red (adv) . . . Chris Rorchek (1981–82)

Better known perhaps as Flash Gordon, in the 1980 film of that name.

JONES, SHIRLEY—actress

b: Mar 31, 1934*, Smithton, Pa.

The Partridge Family (com)
. . . . Shirley Partridge (1970–74)
Shirley (com) . . . . . . Shirley Miller (1979–80)

Despite her image as "Miss Wholesomeness"—gained from her film musicals of the '50s *(Oklahoma!, Carousel)*, as well as from *The Partridge Family*—Shirley Jones is an actress with considerable range. She won an Academy Award in 1960 for her role as the prostitute in *Elmer Gantry* and was nominated for an Emmy for her portrayal of a lonely wife whose husband has been unfaithful in the 1969 TV film *Silent Night, Lonely Night*. She was a compulsive gambler in the TV film *Winner Take All* and a prison superintendent in *Inmates: A Love Story*.

Nevertheless, Shirley usually plays the all-American girl—or mom. She studied singing as a child and came to New York while still in her teens to launch her career in the theater. Her first Broadway role was as one of the nurses in the chorus of *South Pacific*. While working on stage she also did some television, including *Fireside Theatre* (in 1951) and other playhouse series. Her TV appearances were fairly infrequent, however, until she signed for *The Partridge Family*. Since then she has appeared mostly in TV movies, often of the three-hanky variety (e.g., a mother coping with teenage suicide, a woman trying to rescue Vietnamese orphans, etc.).

Shirley was married to actor Jack Cassidy and later (in 1977) to comedian/agent

*Some sources give 1933.

Marty Ingels. Her son Shaun and stepson David Cassidy have both had successful show business careers.

JONES, SIMON—comedian
b: Jul 27, Wiltshire, England

The News Is the News (var) . regular (1983)

JONES, SPIKE—host, orchestra leader
b: Dec 14, 1911, Long Beach, Calif. d: May 1, 1965

The Spike Jones Show (var)..... host (1954)
The Spike Jones Show (var)..... host (1957)
Club Oasis (var) .... star (1958)
The Spike Jones Show (var).. host (1960–61)

The zany bandleader of the '40s was a frequent novelty act on television in the '50s, with his wild burlesques of current popular songs and his familiar comedy troupe (Dr. Horatio Q. Birdbath, midget Billy Barty, etc.). Spike himself always appeared in a loud, checkered suit, chewing gum. There was nothing subtle about this gang!

A recent and revealing biography is titled *Spike Jones and His City Slickers,* by Jordan R. Young (Disharmony Books, 1984).

JONES, STAN—actor, songwriter
b: Jun 5, 1914, Douglas, Ariz. d: Dec 13, 1963

The Sheriff of Cochise (police)
.... Dep. Olson (1956–58)

Stan was the composer of "Ghost Riders in the Sky" and many other songs, including the themes for *Cheyenne,* Disney's *Texas John Slaughter,* and other TV westerns. He also appeared frequently as a supporting actor and was the creator of *Sheriff of Cochise.*

Before getting into show business, Stan had been a U.S. national park ranger for 15 years.

JONES, THOMAS LEANDER—orchestra leader

Try and Do It (var)...... bandleader (1948)

JONES, TOM—singer
b: Jun 7, 1940, Pontypridd, Wales, U.K.

This Is Tom Jones (var)...... host (1969–71)

Booming, sexy baritone Tom Jones was seen on television mostly in guest appearances, although he did have his own popular series from 1969–71. He now works primarily onstage in Las Vegas and on the road.

JONES, WARNER—actor

The Blue Angels (adv)
.... Capt. Wilbur Scott (1960)
Window on Main Street (com)
.... Harry McGill (1961–62)

JONES-DEBROUX, LEE—actor

Aspen (drama) ...... Sheriff Dinehart (1977)

JONSON, KEVIN, DANCERS—

Musical Comedy Time (com)
.... regular (1950–51)

JORDAN, BOBBI—actress
b: Jul 11, Hardensburg, Ky.

The Rounders (com)......... Ada (1966–67)
Blondie (com)... Tootsie Woodley (1968–69)
Joe and Sons (com)....... Estelle (1975–76)
Turnabout (com) ... Judy Overmeyer (1979)

JORDAN, DULCY—

The Swift Show (var)........ regular (1949)

JORDAN, JAMES CARROLL—actor
b: c. 1950

Rich Man, Poor Man—Book II (drama)
.... Billy Abbott (1976–77)
Wheels (drama)........ Kirk Trenton (1978)
The Blue and the Gray (drama)
.... Prof. Lowe (1982)

JORDAN, JAN—actress

M*A*S*H (com)... various nurses (1978–83)

JORDAN, JUDY—actress

The Beverly Hillbillies (com)
.... Miss Switzer (1969–70)

JORDAN, RICHARD—actor
b: Jul 19, 1938, New York City, N.Y.

Captains and the Kings (drama)
.... Joseph Armagh (1976)

JORDAN, TED—actor
b: 1925, Circleville, Ohio

Gunsmoke (wes) . . . Nathan Burke (1964–75)

JORDAN, WILLIAM—actor
b: Oct 13, Milan, Ind.

Project U.F.O. (drama)
. . . . Maj. Jake Gatlin (1978)
Beyond Westworld (sci fi)
. . . . Joseph Oppenheimer (1980)

JORY, VICTOR—actor
b: Nov 28, 1902, Dawson City, Canada d: Feb 11, 1982

Kings Row (drama) . . . . Dr. Tower (1955–56)
Manhunt (police)
. . . . . Det. Lt. Howard Finucane (1959–61)

This grim-faced character actor, a former coast-guard boxing and wrestling champion, played unforgiving villains in movies for 50 years (1930–80). He was also extremely active on television, appearing in hundreds of telecasts, including all of the major playhouse series of the '50s and many of the westerns and dramas of the '60s and '70s. After a lifetime of almost unremitting villainy, he ended his career as narrator of *The Greatest Heroes of the Bible* specials (1978–81).

JOSEPH, JACKIE—comedienne

The Bob Newhart Show (var)
. . . . regular (1961–62)
The Doris Day Show (com)
. . . . Jackie Parker (1971–73)

JOSLYN, ALLYN—actor
b: Jul 21, 1901*, Milford, Pa. r: New York City, N.Y. d: Jan 21, 1981

The Ray Bolger Show (com)
. . . . Jonathan (1953–54)
The Eve Arden Show (com)
. . . . George Howell (1957–58)
McKeever & the Colonel (com)
. . . . Col. Harvey Blackwell (1962–63)

JOSTYN, JAY—actor

Mr. District Attorney (police)
. . . . D. A. Paul Garrett (1951–52)
*Some sources give 1905.

450

JOURDAN, LOUIS—actor
b: Jun 19, 1919, Marseilles, France

Paris Precinct (police)
. . . . Insp. Beaumont (1954–55)

This darkly handsome continental charmer, a sort of younger version of Maurice Chevalier or Charles Boyer, has been a movie star since the early '40s; he reached the pinnacle of his career in the frothy 1958 musical *Gigi*. His television appearances have been intermittent. Besides the syndicated '50s crime show *Paris Precinct*, Louis was seen in some TV playhouse productions in the '50s and '60s and in occasional TV movies after that—along with a rare guest role or two in series as diverse as *The F.B.I.* and *Charlie's Angels*. In 1978 he tried a change of pace as the title character in a PBS production of *Dracula*, but then returned to more familiar ground as host of the obscure syndicated anthology *Romance Theatre* in the early '80s. He would seem to be ripe for a guest turn on *Dallas* or *Dynasty*.

JOY, CHRISTOPHER—actor

The New Odd Couple (com)
. . . . Speed (1982–83)

JOY, MERRYL—

The Beautiful Phyllis Diller Show (var)
. . . . regular (1968)

JOY, NICHOLAS—actor
b: Jan 31, 1884, Paris, France d: Mar 16, 1964

Boss Lady (com) . . . . . Gwen's father (1952)

JOYCE, BARBARA—actor

The Ken Berry "Wow" Show (var)
. . . . regular (1972)

JOYCE, ELAINE—actress
b: Dec 19, 1945, Cleveland, Ohio r: Beverly Hills, Calif

The Don Knotts Show (var)
. . . . regular (1970–71)
I've Got a Secret (quiz) . . . . . panelist (1976)
City of Angels (drama) . . . . . Marsha (1976)
Mr. Merlin (com) . . . . . Alexandria (1981–82)

The wife of Bobby Van, with whom she occasionally appeared (once in a 1976 TV special). Elaine began her career as a teen-ager in the early '60s, appearing in films and later on television (*The Danny Kaye Show, The Carol Burnett Show,* etc.). She is apparently not the same Elaine Joyce who appeared in the 1948 series *The Fashion Story.*

JOYCE, ELAINE (1948)—

    The Fashion Story (misc) . regular (1948–49)

JOYCE, JIMMY, SINGERS—

    The John Gary Show (var) .. regulars (1966)
    The Smothers Brothers Comedy Hour (var)
    .... regulars (1967–69)
    The Summer Smothers Brothers Show (var)
    .... regulars (1968)
    The Tim Conway Comedy Hour (var)
    .... regulars (1970)

JOYCE, MAURICE—narrator

    Crusade in Europe (doc) .... narrator (1949)

JUARBE, ISRAEL—actor

    Foley Square (com)
    .... Angel Gomez (1985–86)

JUBILAIRES, THE—singers

    Five Star Jubilee (var) .... regular (1961)

JUBILEERS, THE—singers

    Sugar Hill Times (var)....... regular (1949)

JUMP, GORDON—actor
    b: Apr 1, 1932, Dayton, Ohio

    WKRP in Cincinnati (com)
    .... Arthur Carlson (1978–82)

Gordon Jump, who played the plump, pompous station manager on *WKRP*, did in fact begin his career working behind the scenes at local radio and TV stations in the Midwest—as a producer for stations in Kansas and Ohio. He moved to Hollywood in 1963, when he was 31, and began looking for work as an actor. His first role was a bit part in *Daniel Boone,* followed by some commercials and then guest roles on a succession of comedies including *Get Smart, Bewitched, The Mary Tyler Moore Show,* and *The Partridge Family* (multiple appearances). Though he is best known as a comic actor, he has played other kinds of parts as well; for example, a supporting role in the TV movie *Ruby and Oswald* and a child molester in an episode of *Diff'rent Strokes.*

JUPITER, JOEY—actor

    Mama Malone (com) .... Jackie (1984)

JURADO, KATY—actress
    b: Jan 16, 1927*, Guadalajara, Mexico

    a.k.a. Pablo (com)
    .... Rosa Maria Rivera (1984)

A smoldering Mexican movie starlet of the '40s who came to Hollywood in 1951 and subsequently appeared in many U.S. films as a beautiful, fiery senorita. She appeared occasionally on television from the '50s onward (*Playhouse 90, The Rifleman, Death Valley Days,* etc.), but spent most of her time making films, both north and south of the border.

By the 1980s, when she appeared briefly as Pablo's mama in *a.k.a. Pablo,* Katy was no longer smoldering but had become a mature senora who was a much-honored actress in both Hollywood and Mexico.

She was once married to Ernest Borgnine.

JURASIK, PETER—actor

    Bay City Blues (drama).. Mitch Klein (1983)
    Hill Street Blues (drama)
        Sidney (Sid the Snitch) Thurston (1985–)

*Some sources give 1924.

K

KABBIBLE, ISH—comedian
b: Jan 19, 1908, Pennsylvania r: Erie, Pa.

Kay Kyser's Kollege of Musical Knowledge
(quiz).................... regular (1949–50)

This longtime member of the Kay Kyser troupe was known for his pre-Beatles Beatles haircut (with bangs) and his nonsense songs, such as "Three Little Fishies" and "Foodley Racky-Sacky." In later years he retired to sell real estate in Arizona and Hawaii. His real name: Merwyn Bogue.

KACZMAREK, JANE—actress
b: Dec 21, Milwaukee, Wis. r: Greendale, Wis.

Hometown (drama)
.... Mary Newell Abbott (1985)

KAHAN, JUDY—actress
b: May 24, Roslyn Heights, N.Y.

Doc (com) .. Laurie Bogert Fenner (1975–76)
All's Fair (com)
.... Ginger Livingston (1976–77)
Mary Hartman, Mary Hartman (com)
.... Penny Major (1977–78)
Free Country (com).... Anna Bresner (1978)
Mary (var)................. regular (1978)

KAHAN, STEVE—actor
Knots Landing (drama)
.... Nick Morrison (1983–84)
Berrengers (drama)... Nick Morrison (1985)

KAHN, MADELINE—actress
b: Sep 29, 1942, Boston, Mass.

Comedy Tonight (var) .... regular (1970)
Oh Madeline (com)
.... Madeline Wayne (1983–84)

KAI, LANI—actress
Adventures in Paradise (adv)
.... Kelly (1960–62)

KAIGLER, DAVE—singer, guitarist
Once Upon a Fence (child)... regular (1952)

KAJUNA, NELSON—actor
Born Free (adv)............. Awaru (1974)

KALBER, FLOYD—newscaster
b: Dec 23, 1924, Omaha, Neb.

NBC Weekend News (news)
.... anchorman (1973–75)

Kalber was a leading local TV anchorman in Chicago from 1960 until the mid-1970s, when he became the newsreader on the *Today Show* (from 1976–79). He has since returned to Chicago.

KALEMBER, PATRICIA—actress
b: Dec 30, Schenectady, N.Y. r: Louisville, Ky.

Kay O'Brien (drama)
.... Dr. Kay "Kayo" O'Brien (1986–)

KALLEN, KITTY—singer
b: May 25, 1922, Philadelphia, Pa.

Judge for Yourself (quiz) .... vocalist (1954)

KALLMAN, DICK—actor
b: c. 1933, b: Dixville Notch, N.H. d: Feb 22, 1980 (murdered)

Hank (com)...... Hank Dearborn (1965–66)

KALTENBORN, H.V.—newscaster
b: Jul 9, 1878, Milwaukee, Wis. d: Jun 14, 1965

Who Said That? (quiz)...... panelist (1954)

One of the most famous and prestigious radio commentators of the '30s and '40s, whose precise, clipped speech was so renowned it was even parodied by President Truman—after Kaltenborn (and everybody else) inaccurately reported that Dewey had won the 1948 election. An elder statesman with a sense of humor, Kaltenborn appeared as himself in a couple of movies and was seen occasionally on early television—including a stint on the news quiz show *Who Said That?* He lived to be 86.

His autobiography, *Fifty Fabulous Years*, was published in 1950.

KALTENBORN, MRS. H.V.—panelist
b: c. 1888

Wisdom of the Ages (info)
.... panelist (1952–53)

The wife of "The Dean of Radio Commentators," and the former German Baroness Olga von Nordenflycht.

KAMEN, MILT—actor, comedian
b: 1922, Hurleyville, N.Y. d: Feb 25, 1977

Caesar's Hour (var) ...... regular (1956–57)
Pantomime Quiz (quiz) ... regular (1957–59)
Sid Caesar Invites You (var) . regular (1958)
Love Thy Neighbor (com)
.... Murray Bronson (1973)

Milt's comic specialty was mock movie reviews.

KAMPMANN, STEVEN—actor
b: May 31, 1949, Philadelphia, Pa.

Newhart (com)...... Kirk Devane (1982–84)

KANALY, STEVE—actor
b: Mar 14, 1946, Burbank, Calif.

Dallas (drama)........ Ray Krebbs (1978–)

KANE, CAROL—actress
b: Jun 18, 1952, Cleveland, Ohio

Taxi (com)....... Simka Gravas (1981–83)
All Is Forgiven (com)
.... Nicolette Bingham (1986)

Emmy Award: Best Supporting Actress in a Comedy, for Taxi (1983)

KANE, JACK—orchestra leader
b: c. 1923 d: Mar 27, 1961

The Steve Lawrence-Eydie Gorme Show (var)
.... orch. leader (1958)
The Andy Williams Show (var)
.... orch. leader (1959)

KANEDO, NOBUO—actor
Shogun (drama) .... Lord Ishido (1980)

KANTOR, RICHARD—actor
b: Aug 26, Brooklyn, N.Y.

Finder of Lost Loves (drama)
.... Brian Fletcher (1984–85)

KANUI, HANK—singer
The Sammy Kaye Show (var)
.... regular (1958–59)

KAPLAN, GABE—actor
b: Mar 31, 1946, Brooklyn, N.Y.

Welcome Back, Kotter (com)
.... Gabe Kotter (1975–79)

Lewis & Clark (com)
.... Stewart Lewis (1981–82)

A show with a slogan like "Up your nose with a rubber hose" was bound to catch the attention of hip teenagers in the late '70s. Nightclub comic Gabe Kaplan had more in mind for Welcome Back, Kotter, than gross-you-out jokes, however. The series, which he created, was based on his own experiences in a blue-collar Brooklyn high school, particularly on the way the school handled remedial education for tough street kids who might otherwise have come to no good—the "sweathogs."

Gabe was a small-time stand-up comic before his program idea brought him fame. He originally aspired to a career in baseball, but made it only as far as the minor leagues (his press release says he was sidelined by an injury; Gabe says, "I just didn't have it"). He then turned to bellhopping and finally to coffeehouse comedy, one of his favorite routines being his imitation of a drunken Ed Sullivan. Gabe worked his way up to larger clubs and TV talk shows, but Kotter was his ticket to stardom. Even there, he was true to his stand-up comedy roots, often doing a few solo jokes at the end of an episode. Likewise, his subsequent series, Lewis & Clark, was built around his somewhat corny gags, but without the appealing premise and supporting cast of Kotter, it failed to last.

KAPLAN, MARVIN—actor
b: Jan 24, 1927*, New York City, N.Y.

Meet Millie (com)
.... Alfred Prinzmetal (1952–56)
Top Cat (cartn)
.... Choo Choo (voice) (1961–62)
Chicago Teddy Bears (com).. Marvin (1971)
Alice (com) .... Henry (1977–85)

Owlish little character actor with horn-rimmed glasses, who has been active in television and movies since about 1950.

KARABATSOS, RON—actor
b: Hackensack, N.J. r: Union City, N.J.

Dreams (com)....... Frank Franconi (1984)
Our Family Honor (drama)
.... George Bennett (1985–86)

*Some sources give 1924.

An actor with an unlikely background. In the '50s he was a professional wrestler ("The Golden Greek"), then a foreman at a General Motors plant, and then, for 24 years, a police officer with the Union City police department. He also moonlighted for 20 years as a bouncer at Brooklyn discos before turning to acting in the early '80s. He is 6' 2" and weighs 350 pounds.

You can imagine the kind of role he plays.

KARAM, EDDIE—orchestra leader

The Roger Miller Show (var)
.... orch. leader (1966)
Dean Martin Presents Bobby Darin (var)
.... orch. leader (1972)
The Jim Stafford Show (var)
.... orch. leader (1975)

KAREMAN, FRED—actor

Operation Petticoat (com)
.... Doplos (1978–79)

KAREN, JAMES—actor
b: c. 1923, Wilkes Barre, Pa.

The Powers of Matthew Star (sci fi)
.... Major Wymore (1983)

KARLEN, JOHN—actor
b: May 28, Brooklyn, N.Y.

Cagney & Lacey (police)
.... Harvey Lacey (1982–)
The Winds of War (drama)
.... Capt. Connelly (1983)

Emmy Award: Best Supporting Actor in a Drama, for *Cagney & Lacey* (1986)

KARLOFF, BORIS—actor
b: Nov 23, 1887, Dulwich, England d: Feb 2, 1969

Starring Boris Karloff (drama)... host (1949)
Colonel March of Scotland Yard (police)
.... Col. March (1953–54)
Down You Go (quiz)
.... regular panelist (1954–55)
Thriller (drama)............ host (1960–62)

The famous horror movie actor, who, after his great success in *Frankenstein,* in 1931, was forever typecast as a gaunt, cadaverous monster. He brought his se-

pulchral tones to television many times in the '50s and '60s, usually in similarly ominous roles on *Starring Boris Karloff, Climax, Suspense, Thriller,* etc. Although he was an actor of wider range than his usual threatening parts would suggest (the sadness in those eyes . . .), he didn't really mind the typecasting. "The monster is the best friend I ever had," he once said.

His biographies include *Karloff: The Man, The Monster, The Movies,* by Denis Gifford (1973).

KARNES, ROBERT—actor
b: 1917, Kentucky d: Dec 4, 1979

The Lawless Years (police)
.... Max (1959–61)

KARNILOVA, MARIA—actress, ballerina
b: Aug 3, 1920, Hartford, Conn.

Ivan the Terrible (com)........ Olga (1976)

KARNS, ROSCOE—actor
b: Sep 7, 1893*, San Bernadino, Calif. d: Feb 6, 1970

Rocky King, Inside Detective (police)
.... Det. Rocky King (1950–54)
Hennesey (com)
.... Capt. Walter Shafer (1959–62)

A second-string Hollywood character actor who was active in the '30s and '40s, usually playing rough-edged, happy-go-lucky supporting roles (often as a newspaper reporter). After 30 years of steady work but relentless obscurity, he suddenly became a minor celebrity in the early '50s thanks to his starring role in TV's first popular police series, *Rocky King.* What made this show so appealing was the combination of Rocky's careful, realistic crime-solving and his sense of humor, especially about his homelife and his somewhat overbearing wife, Mabel.

Karns was greatly appreciative of television for extending his declining career and finally bringing him recognition. He later had occasional guest roles on *December Bride, Richard Diamond,* and *The Lucy Show,* and a starring role as Jackie Cooper's boss on *Hennesey.*

*Some sources give 1891.

KARNS, TODD—actor

Rocky King, Inside Detective (police)
.... Det. Hart (1953–54)

The son of Roscoe Karns.

KARRAS, ALEX—actor
b: Jul 15, 1935, Gary, Ind.

Monday Night Football (sport)
.... announcer (1974–76)
Centennial (drama)
.... Hans Brumbaugh (1978–79)
Webster (com)
.... George Papadapolis (1983–)

Big, beefy Alex Karras has made one of the most successful transitions from football to acting—despite the fact that he still looks very much like a gridiron behemoth.

The first 35 years of Alex's life was spent in sports. Two of his brothers were in pro football (Lou with the Redskins, Teddy with the Steelers), and Alex himself was a high school All-American in 1953. He then was an All-American for four years at the University of Iowa and then a first-round draft choice of the Detroit Lions when he graduated in 1958. For the next 12 years he was a 250-pound terror on the field as a starting defensive tackle.

Alex was always something of a cut-up in the clubhouse; he began making show business appearances in the mid-1960s on *The Tonight Show* and elsewhere. He made a hilarious movie debut in *Paper Lion* in 1968 (playing himself), and, since retiring from football in 1971, has played similar parodies on the dumb jock in such movies as *Blazing Saddles* (where he punched a stubborn horse to the ground) and *Victor/Victoria* (as James Garner's gay bodyguard). He also parlayed his football fame into a three year stint on ABC's *Monday Night Football.*

But Alex didn't want to be typed forever as the hulking jock. In 1975 he co-starred with stylish Canadian actress Susan Clark in the dramatic TV movie *Babe.* The two of them hit it off so well they were married in real life. They have since costarred with each other in several other productions, including the 1983 comedy *Webster,* and have also founded their own production company. "We make small films . . . real-life situations (seen) in a mature manner," Alex says.

Though he still makes use of his "big guy" image, he now seeks gentler roles. "Dammit," he told a reporter in 1982, "I'm 47 years old and I know things are complex . . . funny, sad, warm, silly. I want these things in my films."

Alex has written two autobiographical books, *Even Big Guys Cry* (with Herb Gluck, 1977) and *Alex Karras by Alex Karras.*

KARRON, RICHARD—actor
b: Apr 13, New York City, N.Y.

Good Time Harry (com)
.... Lenny the bartender (1980)
Teachers Only (com) ..... Mr. Pafko (1982)
Charlie & Company (com)
.... Milton Bieberman (1985–86)

This television and movie character-actor barged into the business in the early 1970s, at which time he weighed approximately 400 pounds. After appearing in the movie *Fatso* (1979), and, in the interests of longevity, he cut his bulk to about 200.

KARVELAS, ROBERT—actor

Get Smart (com) .... Larrabee (1967–70)
The Partners (com)
.... Freddie Butler (1971–72)

KASDAY, DAVID—juvenile actor

This Is the Life (drama)
.... Freddie Fisher (1952–56)

KASTNER, PETER—actor
b: 1944

The Ugliest Girl in Town (com)
...... Timothy Blair ("Timmie") (1968–69)
Delta House (com)
.... Prof. Dave Jennings (1979)

KASZNAR, KURT—actor
b: Aug 12, 1913, Vienna, Austria d: Aug 6, 1979

Land of the Giants (sci fi)
..... Cmdr. Alexander Fitzhugh (1968–70)

KATAN, ROSEANNE—black juvenile actress

Grady (com) ..... Laurie Marshall (1975–76)

455

KATT, NICKY—juvenile actor

Herbie, The Love Bug (com)
.... Matthew MacLane (1982)

KATT, WILLIAM—actor

b: Feb 16, 1950, Los Angeles, Calif.

The Greatest American Hero (adv)
.... Ralph Hinkley (Hanley) (1981–83)

Blonde, curly-haired William Katt claimed he was unhappy with the mock superhero role that made him famous. "I'm more into human drama than this sort of thing," he complained to a reporter as he pulled on his flying suit (which looked like red jammies) and prepared to leap into the air once again. "Believe it or not, I used to be a serious actor."

Complaints or not, it was the gimmicky *Greatest American Hero* that made Katt familiar to a generation of young TV viewers. He is a second-generation TV star, the son of actors Bill Williams *(Kit Carson)* and Barbara Hale (Della Street on *Perry Mason*). He began his career in local and touring stage productions in 1969 and made his screen debut as the well-scrubbed football hero in *Carrie* (1976). Later, he drew some criticism by presuming to play the Robert Redford role in the 1979 movie sequel to *Butch Cassidy and the Sundance Kid (Butch and Sundance: The Early Years)*. However, TV success in the '80s has given him his own image, even if it is not quite the one he intended. Perhaps artistic frustration runs in the family; his dad once said he hated playing *Kit Carson*, too.

KATZ, OMRI—juvenile actor

Dallas (drama)
.... John Ross Ewing III (1983–)

KATZ, PHYLLIS—actress

The Billy Crystal Comedy Hour (var)
.... regular (1982)
Wizards and Warriors (adv)
.... Cassandra (1983)

KAUFMAN, ANDY—comedian, actor

b: Jan 17, 1949, New York City r: Great Neck, N.Y. d: May 16, 1984

Van Dyke and Company (var)
.... regular (1976)
Taxi (com)........ Latka Gravas (1978–83)

What do you make of a comedian who makes his entrance on a TV talk show, starts to talk about his impending divorce, hushes the audience when they start to giggle ("I'm not being funny right now"), and winds up suggesting that they send him money? Or one who challenges young ladies to come up onstage and wrestle him, and when they do (thinking it's an act), quite straightforwardly pins them to the mat?

Andy Kaufman was certainly one of the more unconventional comics of recent times, leaving audiences either in hysterics or totally bewildered. He once said, in one of his more lucid moments, "I like the kind of humor where nobody knows what's going on. I'm not into comedy." One of his familiar routines was as the lounge performer Tony Clifton, who could be a wild burlesque or genuinely obnoxious. Another was "The Foreign Man," a heavily accented, apparently somewhat dense character who announces that he is going to do celebrity imitations, does a couple that are horrendously bad, and then says for his last one he will imitate Elvis Presley. As the audience girds itself for a truly terrible impression of the singer, Kaufman spins around and delivers perhaps the most stunning, intense version of "The King" ever seen; then he lapses into the glassy eyed, inept foreigner and shuffles away. Hey, did you see *that*?

Andy led what was by most accounts a rich fantasy life while he was growing up in the middle-class suburbs of New York. He began appearing in improvisational comedy clubs in the late '60s and early '70s but did not make his first major-network appearance until 1975, when he was booked on *NBC's Saturday Night Live*—where he became a favorite guest host. More guest spots followed, then a regular part on Dick Van Dyke's ill-fated fall 1976 series; then came major fame with the role of the unpredictable immigrant mechanic Latka (i.e., The Foreign Man) on *Taxi*.

Andy was at the time of his premature death one of the most promising if least conventional young comic talents on television, headed either for lasting fame or an asylum. Part of his appeal, especially with younger viewers, was exactly that dichotomy—you could never quite be sure which it would be. As David Letterman once said, "Sometimes, when you look Andy in the eyes, you get a feeling somebody else is driving."

KAUFMAN, GEORGE S.—playwright
b: Nov 16, 1889, Pittsburgh, Pa. d: Jun 2, 1961

This Is Show Business (var)
.... panelist (1949–54)
This Is Show Business (var)
.... panelist (1956)

Biography: *George S. Kaufman* by Howard Teichman (1972).

KAVA, CAROLINE—actress

Ivan the Terrible (com) .... Sonya (1976)

KAVNER, JULIE—actress
b: Sep 7, 1951, Los Angeles, Calif.

Rhoda (com)
.... Brenda Morgenstern (1974–78)

Emmy Award: Best Supporting Actress in a Comedy Series, for *Rhoda* (1978)

KAY, BEATRICE—singer, actress
b: Apr 21, 1907, New York City, N.Y. d: Nov 8, 1986

Calvin and the Colonel (cartn)
.... Sister Sue (voice) (1961–62)

Best known as a raucous, husky belter of old time Gay 90's songs on radio and in movies of the 1940s. She did little television work.

KAY, DIANNE—actress
b: Mar 29, 1955, Phoenix, Ariz.

Eight Is Enough (com)
.... Nancy Bradford (1977–81)
Reggie (com).... Linda Potter Lockett (1983)
Glitter (drama).. Jennifer Douglas (1984–85)

KAYE, CAREN—actress
b: Mar 12, New York City, N.Y.

Blansky's Beauties (com)
.... Bambi Benton (1977)
The Betty White Show (com)
.... Tracy Garrett (1977–78)
Who's Watching The Kids? (com)
.... Stacy Turner (1978)

Empire (com) .... Meredith (1984)
It's Your Move (com)
.... Eileen Burton (1984–85)

KAYE, CELIA—actress
b: c. 1941, Carthage, Mo. r: Wilmington, Del.

The New Loretta Young Show (drama)
.... Marnie Massey (1962–63)

KAYE, DANNY—actor, comedian
b: Jan 18, 1913, Brooklyn, N.Y. d: Mar 3, 1987

The Danny Kaye Show (var)
.... host (1963–67)

Emmy Award: Best Performance in a Variety Series, for *The Danny Kaye Show* (1964)

The beloved star of stage and film has appeared only rarely on television, aside from the run of his own variety series in the mid-1960s. One of his earliest appearances was on a 1957 segment of *See It Now,* which traced his work on behalf of UNICEF, entertaining children around the world. In 1960 he starred in his first prime time special, followed by another in 1962 and then his own series in 1963. For some reason this was scheduled at 10 P.M., despite Danny's great appeal to children, several of whom were regulars on the show. Among his delightful routines were his famous tongue-twisting songs, notably "Tchaikovsky"—in which he rattled off the names of 54 Russian composers (real or imagined) in 38 seconds. Much of his special material was written by his wife of many years (since 1940), Sylvia Fine Kaye.

Danny's TV appearances were once again infrequent after his series left the air; he also stopped making movies in 1969. He was seen, or heard, in a few children's specials in the '70s, including *Pinocchio* and *Peter Pan* in 1976. A later and most unusual role was as the Nazi concentration camp survivor in the TV film *Skokie,* in 1981.

Danny's life for his last 30 years was devoted to children, especially through his work for UNICEF. "I believe the world's children are the most important part of the world's future," he said in 1962. "Unless we adults face up to that, we might as well all pack up and go home. If we want we can give these kids a better world than we've known."

KAYE, LILA—actress
b: Nov 7, London, England

Mama Malone (com)
.... Mama Renate Malone (1984)

Miss Kaye, a member of England's Royal Shakespeare Company, won the part of Mama Malone as a result of her virtuoso comedy performance (in two roles) during the American stage and TV run of *Nicholas Nickleby.*

KAYE, LINDA—actress
b: 1944, Toluca Lake, Calif.

Petticoat Junction (com)
.... Betty Jo Bradley Elliott (1963–70)

The pretty daughter of *Petticoat Junction* producer Paul Henning.

KAYE, MANDY—

Joey Faye's Frolics (var)..... regular (1950)
Guess Again (quiz) .... regular (1951)

KAYE, SAMMY—orchestra leader
b: Mar 13, 1910, Rocky River, Ohio d: Jun 2, 1987

The Sammy Kaye Show (var)
.... host (1950–55)
Sammy Kaye's Music from Manhattan (var)
.... host (1958–59)
The Keefe Brasselle Show (var)
.... regular (1963)

The bow-tied, "sweet" bandleader of the 1940s, famous on television for his "So You Want to Lead a Band" audience participation routine. His well-known slogan: "Swing and Sway with Sammy Kaye."

KAYE, STUBBY—actor
b: Nov 11, 1918, New York City, N.Y.

Pantomime Quiz (quiz) ... regular (1958–59)
Love & Marriage (com)
.... Stubby Wilson (1959–60)
My Sister Eileen (com)
.... Marty Scott (1960–61)
Pantomime Quiz (quiz)
.... regular (1962–63)

KAZAN, LAINIE—actress
b: May 15, 1943, Brooklyn, N.Y.

The Dean Martin Summer Show (var)
.... regular (1966)
Tough Cookies (com) .... Rita (1986)

KAZANN, ZITTO—actor

Hell Town (drama)..... Crazy Horse (1985)

KAZURINSKY, TIM—comedian, writer
b: Mar 3, 1950, Johnstown, Pa. r: Australia

NBC's Saturday Night Live (com)
.... regular (1981–84)

KEACH, STACY—actor
b: Jun 2, 1941, Savannah, Ga.

Caribe (police)........ Lt. Ben Logan (1975)
The Blue and the Gray (drama)
.... Jonas Steele (1982)
Mickey Spillane's Mike Hammer (drama)
.... Mike Hammer (1984–)

What do Hamlet and Mike Hammer have in common? Stacy Keach, for one thing. The actor was well-known for his Shakespearean roles in the 1960s, before turning to playing TV tough guys in more recent years.

One of Stacy's earliest professional roles, shortly after graduation from college, was Hamlet, which he played both on the New York stage and in a CBS-TV special in 1964. Over the next few years he appeared in many other classics, including TV productions of *Twelfth Night, Macbeth,* and *Antigone.* However, his first major breakthrough was in the off-Broadway play *MacBird* in 1967; he has since appeared in many more stage productions, including *Long Day's Journey into Night* and *Deathtrap.*

Stacy's TV career began to broaden in the 1970s, with roles on series episodes and in TV movies. He costarred with his brother James Keach in *Orville and Wilbur* in 1971 (as Orville and Wilbur Wright), then had his first series in 1975, the short-lived cop show *Caribe.* Stacy appeared mostly in TV movies and miniseries after that, including the role of Babarras in *Jesus of Nazareth* in 1977. In 1983 he played the famous hard-boiled detective Mike Hammer in a TV movie, and this led to a *Hammer* series which premiered in early 1984.

The series ended rather abruptly, however, for quite unexpected reasons. No sooner had it begun than the actor was arrested in April 1984, at London's Heathrow Airport, after 30 grams of cocaine were found in his luggage (he had come to England to film an episode). He was released on bail, but when he returned to face the charges he was convicted and given a stiff jail sentence by an angry judge—effectively ending the *Hammer* series for a time. "Hammer in the slammer" crowed the headlines.

KEACH, STACY, SR.—actor

Get Smart (com) ... Prof. Carlson (1966–67)

Stacy Keach's father, a drama coach.

KEALE, MOE—actor
b: Dec 3, Honolulu, Hawaii

Big Hawaii (drama)
.... Garfield Kalahani (1977)
The Mackenzies of Paradise Cove (adv)
.... Big Ben Kalikini (1979)
Hawaii Five-O (police)
.... Truck Kealoha (1979–80)

Heavyweight Hawaiian, formerly a crew member working behind the scenes on the *Hawaii Five-O* series; later, he began playing guest and regular roles on that and other Hawaii-based series.

KEAN, BETTY—actress
b: c. 1917, Hartford, Conn. d: Sep 29, 1986

Leave It to Larry (com)
.... Amy Tucker (1952)

KEAN, JANE—actress
b: Hartford, Conn.

The Jackie Gleason Show (var)
.... Trixie Norton (1966–70)

Betty and Jane are sisters and had a song-and-dance act together on television in the early 1950s.

KEANE, JAMES—actor
b: Sep 26, 1952, Buffalo, N.Y.

The Paper Chase (drama)
.... Willis Bell (1978–79)
The Paper Chase (drama)
.... Willis Bell (1983–84)

KEANE, JOHN—juvenile host
b: c. 1965

The Keane Brothers Show (var)
.... cohost (1977)

Mop-topped Tom and John Keane were probably the youngest performers ever to host their own prime time variety series. The sons of jazz clarinetist John Keane, John (age 12) played drums and Tom (age 13) played piano, supported by a troupe of adult comics and musicians. *The Keane Brothers Show* was supposed to be the ultimate in "youth appeal," but it lasted only four weeks.

KEANE, KERRIE—actress

The Yellow Rose (drama)
.... Caryn Cabrera (1983–84)
Hot Pursuit (drama) ..... Kate Wyler (1984)
Hot Pursuit (drama) ..... Cathy Ladd (1984)

KEANE, TOM—juvenile host
b: c. 1964

The Keane Brothers Show (var)
.... cohost (1977)

The brother of John Keane.

KEARNS, JOSEPH—actor
b: 1907, Salt Lake City, Utah d: Feb 17, 1962

Our Miss Brooks (com)
.... Supt. Stone (1953–55)
Dennis the Menace (com)
.... George Wilson (1959–62)

KEARNS, SANDRA—actress

Flamingo Road (drama)
.... Beth MacDonald (1981–82)

KEATING, LARRY—actor
b: 1896*, St. Paul, Minn. d: Aug 26, 1963

The Hank McCune Show (com)
.... regular (1950)
The George Burns and Gracie Allen Show (com)............. Harry Morton (1953–58)
The George Burns Show (com)
.... Harry Morton (1958–59)
Mr. Ed (com)...... Roger Addison (1961–63)

KEATON, MICHAEL—actor
b: Sep 9, 1951, Pittsburgh, Pa.

*Some sources give 1897 or 1899.

All's Fair (com) . . . . Lanny Wolf (1977)
Mary (var). . . . . regular (1978)
The Mary Tyler Moore Hour (var)
. . . . Kenneth Christy (1979)
Working Stiffs (com)
. . . . Mike O'Rourke (1979)
Report to Murphy (com) . . . . Murphy (1982)

A young comic actor who started out in improvisational comedy clubs on the East and West coasts, then got not one but several shots at TV stardom in the late '70s and early '80s. None of his series seemed to click. He has lately been trying his hand in feature films.

KEATS, STEVEN—actor
b: 1945, The Bronx, N.Y.

Seventh Avenue (drama)
. . . . Jay Blackman (1977)

KEEFER, DON—actor
b: High Spire, Pa.

Angel (com). . . . . George (1960–61)

KEEGAN, CHRIS—actor

Big Top (var) . . . . clown (1950–51)

KEEGAN, JUNIE—juvenile singer
b: c. 1936

Paul Whiteman's TV Teen Club (talent)
. . . . regular (1949–53)

KEEL, HOWARD—actor, singer
b: Apr 13, 1917, Gillespie, Ill.

Dallas (drama)
. . . . Clayton Farlow (1981–)

The bright, booming musical comedy star of stage and screen made only rare appearances on television—an episode of *Zane Grey Theatre* in the '50s, *Here's Lucy* in the '60s, *The Quest* in the '70s, and a few others. In the '80s he played wealthy Clayton Farlow, who wooed and won Miss Ellie on *Dallas,* thereby making him scoundrel J.R.'s father-in-law.

KEELER, DONALD—juvenile actor
b: Apr 8, 1944, Los Angeles, Calif.

Lassie (adv)
. . . Sylvester "Porky" Brockway (1954–57)

The brother of another chubby child actor, Ken Weatherwax ("Pugsley" on *The Addams Family*), and the nephew of actress Ruby Keeler—from whom he took his professional name. Donald played chubby-kid roles on episodes of a number of other series in the '50s and early '60s, then dropped out of acting to become a businessman. He has acted only rarely since then, generally under his real name, Joey Vieira.

KEEN, MALCOLM—actor
b: Aug 8, 1887, Bristol, England d: Jan 30, 1970

Mama (com) . . . . Uncle Chris (1949–51)

KEEN, NOAH—actor
b: Oct 10, Cincinnati, Ohio

Arrest and Trial (drama)
. . . . Det. Lt. Bone (1963–64)

KEENS, MICHAEL—actor

Harbourmaster (adv) . . Cap'n Dan (1957–58)

KEEP, STEPHEN—actor
b: Aug 24, Camden, S.C.

Flo (com) . . . . Les Kincaid (1980–81)

KEIM, BETTY LOU—actress
b: 1938, Malden, Mass.

My Son Jeep (com) . . . . Peggy Allison (1953)
The Deputy (wes) . . Fran McCord (1959–60)

KEITH, BRIAN—actor
b: Nov 14, 1921, Bayonne, N.J.

Crusader (drama) . . . Matt Anders (1955–56)
The Westerner (wes)
. . . . Dave Blassingame (1960)
Family Affair (com) . . . Bill Davis (1966–71)
The Brian Keith Show (com)
. . . . Dr. Sean Jamison (1972–74)
Archer (drama) . . . . Lew Archer (1975)
Centennial (drama) . . Axel Dumire (1978–79)
Hardcastle & McCormick (drama)
. . . . Judge Milton G. Hardcastle (1983–86)

Brian Keith has had a long but somewhat uneven career in show business—which is perhaps why he gets progressively more irascible as the years go by. His specialty, the gruff guy with a heart of gold, has worked particularly well in shows costarring kids or young adults.

Brian was practically born backstage, to actor-parents who brought him onstage at the age of one month and who got him his first film role at three, in 1924. He did not make another movie for nearly 30 years, however (apparently he was irascible even as a kid). After World War II service as a tail gunner in the Pacific, he tried to get his start on stage in the late '40s, but without much success—until his father got him a bit part in *Mr. Roberts,* in which Keith Sr. was starring as "Doc."

Television seemed to offer more potential for the struggling actor, and Brian made his debut there in 1952 on *The Campbell Sound Stage,* followed by parts in many of the live playhouse series of the '50s—*Studio 57, Ford Theatre, Lux Video Theatre,* etc. In 1955 he had his first chance at series stardom, playing a lone hero who rescued victims of Communist oppression in the Cold War drama *Crusader.* Neither that nor a subsequent western, *The Westerner* (costarring a large mongrel dog), were particularly successful.

Brian seemed to be slipping into a career of guest roles in dramas (including quite a few episodes of *Alfred Hitchcock Presents*), westerns, and Disney movies. Then along came the opportunity to star in a Disney-esque comedy opposite a stuffy English butler and three supercute kids. Many actors would have recoiled in horror at such a role, but Brian more than held his own against such odds, and *Family Affair* became his first major hit. What did he think of this syrupy fare? "I thought of it as a tugboat with dollar signs attached," he harrumphed.

When *Family Affair* finally ended, Brian grumbled his way through another show with kids, *The Brian Keith Show* (also known as *The Little People*), which was set in his adopted home state of Hawaii. He then tried a detective series *(Archer)* and a short-run European adventure series *(The Zoo Gang),* both in 1975, before settling down to TV movies and miniseries in the late '70s. Soft roles and semiretirement apparently made him uneasy, however. Despite his avowed intention to retire with his millions to Diamond Head, Hawaii, he was lured back to series TV in 1983 with the role of the grouchy but remarkably muscular (for a man in his 60's) Judge Hardcastle on *Hardcastle & McCormick.*

Brian is married to Hawaiian actress Victoria Young, who costarred as Nurse Puni in *The Brian Keith Show.*

KEITH, BYRON—actor

77 Sunset Strip (drama)
.... Lt. Gilmore (1958–63)

KEITH, DAVID—actor
b: May 8, 1954, Knoxville, Tenn.

Co-ed Fever (com)............ Tuck (1979)

KEITH, LARRY—actor

The Baxters (com).... Fred Baxter (1979–80)

KEITH, RICHARD—juvenile actor
b: Dec 1, 1950, Lafayette, La.

I Love Lucy (com)
.... Little Ricky Ricardo (1956–57)
The Lucy-Desi Comedy Hour (specials) (com)
.... Little Ricky (1957–60)

The child actor who played Lucy and Desi's TV son was discovered by bandleader Horace Heidt and came to Los Angeles as part of Heidt's traveling "Youth Opportunity Show" in the mid-1950s. After the Lucy-Desi show left the air, he played guest roles on other series for a few years, then returned to his native Louisiana in 1965, where he has been an oil worker and a drummer in a rock band. He now goes under his real name, Keith Thibodeaux.

KEITH, RONALD—juvenile actor
b: c. 194'

Life with Father (com)
.... Whitney Day (1953–54)
The Great Gildersleeve (com)
.... Leroy Forrester (1955–56)

KELK, JACKIE—actor
b: Aug 6, 1923, Brooklyn, N.Y.

The Aldrich Family (com)
.... Homer Brown (1949–51)
Young Mr. Bobbin (com)
. Alexander Hawthorne Bobbin (1951–52)

One of radio's perennial teenagers, most famous as crackly voiced Homer on the long-running *Aldrich Family.* Unfortunately, when the show reached TV, viewers could see that he was no teenager, and his career gradually petered out.

KELLEMS, VIVIEN—hostess
b: Jun 7, 1896 d: Jan 25, 1975

The Power of Women (pub aff)
.... hostess (1952)

Social activist and president of an organization called The Liberty Belles.

KELLER, DOROTHY—
Seven at Eleven (var)....... regular (1951)

KELLER, JASON—juvenile actor
b: Feb 23, 1971, Scarsdale, N.Y.

Out of the Blue (com)
.... Jason Richards (1979)

KELLER, SHANE—juvenile actor
b: Feb 23, 1971, Scarsdale, N.Y.

Out of the Blue (com)
.... Shane Richards (1979)

Jason and Shane are twins.

KELLERMAN, SALLY—actress
b: Jun 2, 1936*, Long Beach, Calif.

Centennial (drama)
.... Lise Bockweiss (1978–79)

KELLEY, BARRY—actor
b: 1908, Chicago, Ill.

Big Town (drama)
.... Charlie Anderson (1954–56)

KELLEY, DEFOREST—actor
b: Jan 20, 1920, Atlanta, Ga.

Star Trek (sci fi)
.... Dr. Leonard McCoy (1966–69)

Although he appeared in dozens of movies, including such classics as *Gunfight at the O.K. Corral* and *Raintree County,* and in scores of television shows, DeForest Kelley will surely be remembered for just one role—that of Dr. "Bones" McCoy on *Star Trek.* He began his acting career in the late

*Some sources give 1938.

462

1940s playing supporting roles in movies and moved into television in the early '50s with frequent (but largely unnoticed) appearances on *You Are There, Navy Log, Matinee Theatre,* and *Silent Service,* among others. Usually he played a villain; on *Bonanza* in the early '60s he once portrayed a frontier doctor accused of murder. Then the starship Enterprise blasted him off to good-guy immortality in 1966. Since that classic series ended, Kelley has practically disappeared from sight, emerging only for the *Star Trek* revival movies in 1979 and the early '80s.

KELLIN, MIKE—actor
b: Apr 26, 1922, Hartford, Conn. d: Aug 26, 1983

Bonino (com) .... Rusty (1953)
Honestly Celeste (com)
.... Marty Gordon (1954)
The Wackiest Ship in the Army (adv)
.... C.P. Off. Willie Miller (1965–66)
Seventh Avenue (drama)
.... Morris Blackman (1977)
Fitz and Bones (com)
.... Robert Whitmore (1981)

KELLOGG, JOHN—actor
b: 1916

Peyton Place (drama)
.... Jack Chandler (1966–67)

KELLOGG, RAY—actor
The Beverly Hillbillies (com)
.... studio guard (1964–66)

KELLY, AL—comedian
b: c. 1899 d: Sep 7, 1966

Back That Fact (aud par) .. assistant (1953)
The Ernie Kovacs Show (var)
.... regular (1956)

A specialist in comedy double-talk routines. What *did* he say?

KELLY, BEBE—actress
Trapper John, M.D. (drama)
.... Nurse Clover (1981–84)

KELLY, BRIAN—actor
b: Feb 14, Detroit, Mich.

21 Beacon Street (drama) . . . . . . Brian (1959)
Straightaway (adv) . . . . Scott Ross (1961–62)
Flipper (adv) . . . . Porter Ricks (1964–68)

KELLY, GENE—actor, dancer
b: Aug 23, 1912, Pittsburgh, Pa.

Going My Way (com)
. . . . Father Chuck O'Malley (1962–63)
The Funny Side (var) . . . . host (1971)
North and South (drama)
. . . . Sen. Charles Edwards (1985)

Emmy Award: Producer, Best Children's Program, for *Jack and the Beanstalk* (1967)

Hollywood's favorite song-and-dance man of the '40s and '50s has made occasional visits to television over the years. His TV acting debut was in 1957, on *Schlitz Playhouse of Stars*, but in the '50s he was known to small-screen viewers primarily for his big, glossy musical specials (1957, 1959) and for a notable segment of *Omnibus* titled "Dancing: A Man's Game."

In 1962, Gene surprised almost everyone by agreeing to star in his own one-hour comedy, an adaptation of the famous Bing Crosby movie *Going My Way*, about a cheerful young priest in a lower-class neighborhood. It was not successful, scheduled as it was opposite the red-hot hit *The Beverly Hillbillies*, and Gene returned to making special guest appearances on other shows. One of the most notable (Emmy-nominated) was on *The Julie Andrews Show;* another (Emmy-winning) was on the special *Jack and the Beanstalk.* In 1971 he briefly hosted the comedy anthology *The Funny Side.* Later, he was seen in a dramatized tribute to Rodgers and Hart (Gene played Rodgers to Henry Winkler's Lorenz Hart), in periodic music specials, and in the 1985 miniseries *North and South.*

Gene's style of dancing was quite athletic, and distinct from the more elegant choreography of Fred Astaire. "I searched for a form of my own," he once said. "I tried to base it on male movements, athletic movements. I wanted to get rid of the idea that dancing was not manly and get it across that it is just as manly as any other form of athletics. Being a dancer is closely allied to being an athlete, and that is the premise on which my whole style is based. I was always a pretty good athlete." He no

longer dances, having turned to choreography, straight acting, and production. "There's a time when you have to quit being a shortstop and start managing," he said in 1982. "I'm seventy years old. When you get to that age, you can dance, but it's not very exciting. I can't swing from lampposts anymore. Once you've swum a strong river, you don't get much of a kick out of walking through a puddle."

A principal biography: *Gene Kelly* by Clive Hirschhorn (1974).

KELLY, GENE—sportscaster
b: c. 1919 d: Sep 18, 1979

Sportsreel (sport) . . . . . . commentator (1954)

KELLY, JACK—actor
b: Sep 16, 1927, Astoria, N.Y.

Kings Row (drama)
. . . . Dr. Parris Mitchell (1955–56)
Dr. Hudson's Secret Journal (drama)
. . . . Dr. Bennett (1955–57)
Maverick (wes) . . . Bart Maverick (1957–62)
NBC Comedy Playhouse (com) . . host (1970)
NBC Comedy Theater (com)
. . . . host (1971–72)
Get Christie Love (police)
. . . . Capt. Arthur P. Ryan (1975)
The Hardy Boys Mysteries (adv)
. . . . Harry Hammond (1978–79)

If it had not been for his costar, it would probably be Jack Kelly who was remembered today as the wry, laid-back frontier hustler made famous by that most unusual of westerns, *Maverick.* Kelly affected the same sort of slippery charm and sense of humor as the "other" Maverick, but he did not carry it quite so far, and so it was James Garner who became most identified with the series.

Jack had certainly been in show business longer than Garner. Born of actor parents, and the brother of actress Nancy Kelly, he had stage and radio experience as a child in the '30s and made his film debut in second features of the late '40s. During the early '50s, Jack appeared in quite a few TV playhouse series, including *Kraft Theatre, Philco Playhouse,* and *Pepsi-Cola Playhouse,* and in 1955 he landed the romantic lead in the prime time soap opera *King's Row.* At about the same time, he played another physician on the syndicated *Dr. Hudson's Secret Journal,* but neither of these roles brought him the recognition *Maverick* did in 1957.

Jack continued to guest-star on dramas and westerns during the '60s (several times on *Bob Hope's Chrysler Theatre*), as well as drop in on *The Lucy Show* in 1964 and *Batman* in 1966. During the '70s he served a short stint as host of the daytime game show *Sale of the Century* while continuing to appear in a few prime time series episodes each year. In 1978 he costarred with Garner in the TV movie that kicked off *The Young Maverick* series, but that series was short-lived.

KELLY, JOE—host

b: c. 1901 d: May 26, 1959

Quiz Kids (quiz).......... emcee (1949–53)

KELLY, PATSY—actress

b: Jan 12, 1910, Brooklyn, N.Y. d: Sep 24, 1981

The Cop and the Kid (com)
.... Mrs. Brigid Murphy (1975–76)

KELLY, PAULA—black actress, dancer

b: Oct 21, 1943, Jacksonville, Fla.

Chiefs (drama)........... Liz Watts (1983)
Night Court (com)...... Liz Williams (1984)

KELLY, PAULA—singer

see Modernaires, The

KELLY, SEAN—actor

The Cowboys (wes) .... Jimmy (1974)

KELLY, TOM—host

Strike It Rich (quiz) .... host (1978)

KELMAN, RICKEY—juvenile actor

The Dennis O'Keefe Show (com)
.... Randy Towne (1959–60)
National Velvet (adv)
.... John Hadley (1961–62)
Our Man Higgins (com)
.... Tommy MacRoberts (1962–63)

KELSEY, LINDA—actress

b: Jul 28, 1946, Minneapolis, Minn.

Lou Grant (drama)
...... Billie Newman McCovey (1977–82)

KELTON, PERT—actress

b: Oct 14, 1907, Great Falls, Mont. d: Oct 30, 1968

Cavalcade of Stars (var).. regular (1950–52)
Henry Morgan's Great Talent Hunt (var)
.... regular (1951)

Not very many TV viewers now remember the actress who played Jackie Gleason's wife Alice in the very first *Honeymooners* sketches, on *The Cavalcade of Stars.* Only a few faint kinescopes survive to remind us that there even was another Alice before Audrey Meadows, and quite a different one at that—much older, harder-looking, and a good deal more shrewish than the sarcastic but still vaguely sexy Miss Meadows.

Pert was born the daughter of vaudevillians and had been in show business since 1910, when she was a child. She made her Broadway stage debut in 1925 in the musical *Sunny,* and her film debut in 1929; during the '30s she was one of Hollywood's more familiar wisecracking dames, often the friend of the star, in numerous B films. Never a major star in her own right, she was readily available for television work in the early, live days. However, she failed to follow Gleason when he moved from DuMont to CBS—and fame—in 1952. The reason was never publicly stated but may have been due to that scourge of the times, political blacklisting. Pert was listed in *Red Channels,* the little booklet that ruined many careers by purporting to identify performers with left-wing associations. CBS was notoriously reluctant to hire such performers.

Pert did do some stage work in the late 1950s (including *The Music Man* in 1957) and appeared in a few films in the '60s. She was still active, in a minor way, at the time of her death in 1968. Ironically, by that time *The Honeymooners* was back in production in the form of big, glossy one-hour specials on CBS, starring still another actress, Sheila MacRae, as Alice.

KELTON, RICHARD—actor

Quark (com) .... Ficus (1978)

KEMMER, ED—actor
b: Oct 29, 1921, Reading, Pa.

Space Patrol (child)
.... Cmdr. Buzz Corey (1951–52)

Ed Kemmer was an authentic World War II fighter pilot who was imprisoned in Germany after he crash-landed on his forty-eighth combat mission. Following his years on *Space Patrol* (which continued in daytime until 1955), he went into soap operas, including *Clear Horizon* (1960–62), on which he played an astronaut stationed at Cape Canaveral.

KEMP, BRANDIS—actress
b: Feb 1, Palo Alto, Calif.

Fridays (var)............ regular (1980–82)
AfterMASH (com)..... Alma Cox (1983–84)

The wife of comedian Mark Blankfield.

KEMP, JEREMY—actor
b: Feb 3, 1934*, Chesterfield, England

The Rhinemann Exchange (drama)
.... Geoffrey Moore (1977)
The Winds of War (drama)
.... Brig. Gen. Armin von Roon (1983)

KEMPER, DORIS—actress

Westinghouse Playhouse (com)
.... Mrs. Harper (1961)

KENDALL, CY—actor
b: Mar 10, 1898, St. Louis, Mo. d: Jul 22, 1953

Mysteries of Chinatown (drama)
.... regular (1949–50)

Heavyweight villain in scores of films.

KENDIS, SONNY—pianist, host

The Sonny Kendis Show (music)
.... host (1949–50)

KENDRICK, MERLE—orchestra leader
b: c. 1896 d: May 23, 1968

Window on the World (var)
.... orch. leader (1949)

*Some sources give 1935.

KENIN, ALEXA—juvenile actress
b: Feb 16, 1962, New York City, N.Y. d: Sep 10, 1985

Co-ed Fever (com).......... Mousie (1979)

KENNEDY, ADAM—actor
b: Mar 10, 1922, near Lafayette, Ind.

The Californians (wes)
.... Dion Patrick (1957–58)

KENNEDY, ARTHUR—actor
b: Feb 17, 1914, Worcester, Mass.

F.D.R. (doc)............... narrator (1965)
Nakia (police).... Sheriff Sam Jericho (1974)

KENNEDY, BETTY—actress
b: Oct 2, Roswell, N.M.

Ladies' Man (com)
.... Andrea Gibbons (1980–81)

KENNEDY, BOB—host
b: c. 1937

Wingo (quiz)................ emcee (1958)

A minor daytime personality, on several game shows during the '50s and early '60s.

KENNEDY, GEORGE—actor
b: Feb 18, 1925, New York City, N.Y.

Sarge (drama)
..... Father Samuel Cavanaugh (1971–72)
The Blue Knight (police)
.... Bumper Morgan (1975–76)
Backstairs at the White House (drama)
.... Pres. Warren Harding (1979)
Counterattack: Crime in America (pub aff)
.... host (1982)

"I'm an older man to whom success was a long time in coming," said George Kennedy as he began work on his first series, in 1971. The "long time" was due at least in part to George's own decision to spend 16 years, from age 17 to his early thirties, in the army. In an odd way, however, his long military career led him into acting. He was eventually commissioned as an officer and put in charge of the army's information office in New York, where he became involved in advising the producers of service-oriented films and TV shows produced in the New York area. One of these was *The Phil Silvers Show,* for which he served as technical advisor and on which he even made occasional brief appearances.

Discharged from the army in 1959 due to a spinal injury, with a disability pension, George decided to pursue acting full time. (He was the son of actor parents and had done some acting as a child on stage and radio.) Almost immediately he began landing supporting roles in films and TV episodes, the latter including *Sugarfoot, Colt .45, Gunsmoke,* and *Have Gun Will Travel* (on which he made numerous appearances). At first he was used as a lumbering villain—he is 6′ 4″ and weighs 230 pounds —but soon he became known for more multidimensional roles.

Major stardom came in 1967 with his Academy Award–winning performance in the hit movie *Cool Hand Luke;* subsequently, he starred in two TV crime dramas, the first *(Sarge)* about a cop-turned-priest and the second *(The Blue Knight)* about a veteran cop on the beat. He has also appeared in quite a few TV movies and miniseries and hosted—rather uneasily—a bizarre crime call-in show called *Counterattack: Crime in America.*

KENNEDY, JAYNE—actress
b: Oct 27, 1951, Washington, D.C.

Speak Up, America (aud par)
.... regular (1980)
You Asked for It (aud par)
.... assistant (1981–83)

KENNEDY, JOHN MILTON—actor, announcer

Armchair Detective (drama)
.... Mr. Crime Interrogator (1949)

KENNEDY, LINDSAY—juvenile actor
b: Jan 4, 1969, Atlanta, Ga.

Little House on the Prairie (adv)
.... Jeb Carter (1982–83)

KENNEDY, MIMI—actress
b: Sep 25, 1949, Rochester, N.Y.

3 Girls 3 (var).............. regular (1977)
Stockard Channing in Just Friends (com)
.... Victoria (1979)
The Big Show (var)......... regular (1980)

The Two of Us (com)
.... Nan Gallagher (1981–82)
Spencer (com)...... Doris Winger (1984–85)
Under One Roof (com)
.... Doris Winger (1985)

KENNEDY, SARAH—comedienne
b: Jan 27, Coquille, Ore.

Rowan & Martin's Laugh-In (var)
.... regular (1972–73)

A five-foot-two, eyes-of-blue blonde with a little-girl voice rather like that of Goldie Hawn—which may have been what won Sarah her spot on *Laugh-In* after Goldie left. Sarah also did some Saturday morning voice work on cartoons during the early 1970s.

KENNEDY, TOM—host
b: Feb 26, 1927, Louisville, Ky.

The Big Game (quiz) .... emcee (1958)
The Gisele MacKenzie Show (var)
.... announcer (1958)
Doctor I.Q. (quiz)......... emcee (1958–59)
You Don't Say (quiz) .... emcee (1964)
Name That Tune (quiz) .... emcee (1974–81)

Tom Kennedy is one of that small group of smiling, quick-witted men who have made a career out of hosting game shows in both daytime and nighttime television. It's no easy calling. As one of Tom's press releases put it, "the job calls for friendliness, humor, grace under pressure, thorough professionalism and above all—an engaging personality that registers immediately, and wears well."

Tom rattled into Los Angeles in 1952 in an old jalopy with a new bride and $150 in his pocket and found work as an announcer in local radio and TV. His first major-network TV break came with the peculiar 1958 summer series *Big Game,* a board game based on big-game hunting which had host Kennedy wearing a pith helmet. Later assignments were more traditional quiz shows. Tom also appeared occasionally as an actor (*The Ghost and Mrs. Muir, That Girl,* etc.) and briefly hosted a syndicated talk show called *The Real Tom Kennedy Show,* in 1970.

Tom's real name is Jim Narz. He is the younger brother of game show host Jack Narz.

KENNY, NICK—columnist, songwriter
b: Feb 3, 1895, Astoria, N.Y. d: Dec 1, 1975

The Nick Kenny Show (talk)
.... host (1951–52)

Nick Kenny was a newspaper columnist long with the *New York Daily Mirror,* as well as a poet and a very successful songwriter. A Runyonesque character with a gravelly voice, he read his syrupy, inspirational verse ("dipping your pen in sunshine," he called it) to great effect on radio in the '40s and later had his own live show on early television. Among his song hits, most of which were coauthored with his brother Charles, was "Love Letters in the Sand."

KENNY, TOM—

The Ken Berry "Wow" Show (var)
.... regular (1972)

KENT, ENID—actress

*M*A*S*H* (com)... Nurse Bigelow (1977–79)

KENT, JANICE—actress

The Ted Knight Show (com) . Cheryl (1978)

KENT, JEAN—actress
b: Jun 21, 1921, London, England

The Adventures of Sir Francis Drake (adv)
.... Queen Elizabeth I (1962)

KENT, LILA—actress

The Dukes of Hazzard (com)
.... Laverne (1981–85)

KENTON, STAN—orchestra leader
b: Feb 19, 1912, Wichita, Kans. r: Los Angeles, Calif. d: Aug 25, 1979

Music 55 (music) .... host (1955)

KENYON, NANCY—singer

Opera vs. Jazz (music) .... hostess (1953)
Melody Tour (var) .... regular (1954)

KENYON, SANDY—actor

Crunch and Des (adv) . Des Smith (1955–56)
The Travels of Jaimie McPheeters (wes)
.... Shep Baggott (1963–64)

Love on a Rooftop (com)
.... Jim Lucas (1966–67)
Knots Landing (drama)
.... Rev. Kathrun (1984–85)

KERCHEVAL, KEN—actor
b: Jul 15, 1935, Wolcottville, Ind. r: Clinton, Ind.

Dallas (drama)........ Cliff Barnes (1978–)

A Broadway actor who originally specialized in musical comedies but later branched into drama. Active on stage since the 1950s, Ken appeared on the daytime soap *Search for Tomorrow* from 1965–67, and again from 1972–73, as the fun-loving Dr. Nick Hunter. Later in the '70s he appeared for a time on *The Secret Storm.* Ken began to do TV movies and prime time series episodes toward the end of the '70s, including segments of *Kojak* and *Family.* For $12,000 per episode he consented to become a regular on the prime time soap opera *Dallas,* but through all of this his heart remained with the stage. *TV Guide* called him "the epitome of the New York actor who comes to Hollywood and never unpacks."

KERNS, JOANNA—actress
b: Feb 12, 1953, San Francisco, Calif.

The Four Seasons (com) .. Pat Devon (1984)
Growing Pains (com)
.... Maggie Seaver (1985–)

A former national caliber gymnast, and the sister of Olympic swimming champion (and ABC commentator) Donna de Varonna. Joanna has been an actress and dancer since the early 1970s.

KERR, ANITA—singer
b: Oct 13, 1927, Memphis, Tenn.

The Smothers Brothers Comedy Hour (var)
.... singers (1967)

Leader of the Anita Kerr Singers, one of the most widely recorded backup vocal groups in country music.

KERR, ELIZABETH—actress
b: Aug 12, Kansas City, Mo.

Mork & Mindy (com)
.... Cora Hudson (1978–79)

Mork & Mindy (com)
.... Cora Hudson (1981–82)

This white-haired late bloomer had no thought of becoming a professional actress until 1944, after her sons were grown. For the next 30 years she was active mostly onstage. Beginning in the '70s she also took on television assignments, whenever a little old lady was called for; she is most famous as Mindy's grandmother on *Mork & Mindy*.

KERR, JAY—actor
b: Nov 16, Del Rio, Texas

Wizards and Warriors (adv)
.... Justin Greystone (1983)

KERR, JEAN—author
b: Jul 10, 1923, Scranton, Pa.

Down You Go (quiz)
.... regular panelist (1955)

Jean's humorous book, *Please Don't Eat the Daisies,* was adapted into a movie and later a television series (1965–67).

KERR, JOHN—actor
b: Nov 15, 1931, New York City, N.Y.

Arrest and Trial (drama)
..... Asst. Dep. D.A. Barry Pine (1963–64)
Peyton Place (drama)
.... D.A. John Fowler (1965–66)

Kerr was fairly active on television from the early 1950s through the '70s on series episodes (including a recurring role on *The Streets of San Francisco*) and TV movies (including *Washington: Behind Closed Doors*). He is now a practicing attorney.

KERRY, MARGARET—juvenile actress
The Ruggles (com)
.... Sharon Ruggles (1949–52)

KERSHAW, WHITNEY—actress
Knots Landing (drama)
.... Mary Kathrun (1984)

KERWIN, BRIAN—actor
b: Oct 25, 1949, Chicago, Ill.

The Chisholms (wes)
.... Gideon Chisholm (1979)

Lobo (com)
Dep. Birdwell "Birdie" Hawkins (1979–81)
The Blue and the Gray (drama)
.... Malachi Hale (1982)

KERWIN, LANCE—juvenile actor
b: Nov 6, 1960, Newport Beach, Calif.

The Family Holvak (drama)
.... Ramey Holvak (1975)
James at 15 (drama)
.... James Hunter (1977–78)

As a struggling child actor in Hollywood in the early 1970s, Lance supposedly wrote Clint Eastwood a letter describing his talents and ended with the pitch, ". . . if you ever need a kid like me, just give me a call." Clint didn't, but evidently somebody else did; Lance went on to become one of the busiest kids in town for the balance of the '70s, appearing in numerous series episodes, *Afterschool Special*s, and TV movies. Among his roles was the lead in his own series, *James at 15.*

KESNER, DICK—violinist
The Lawrence Welk Show (music)
.... regular (1955–59)

KESNER, JILLIAN—actress
Co-ed Fever (com)........... Melba (1979)

KESSLER TWINS, THE—
Continental Showcase (var) . regulars (1966)

KETCHUM, DAVE—actor
b: c. 1928, Quincy, Ill.*

I'm Dickens—He's Fenster (com)
.... Mel Warshaw (1962–63)
Camp Runamuck (com)
.... senior counselor Spiffy (1965–66)
Get Smart (com) .... Agent 13 (1966–67)

Did you ever wonder what would lead a young man to choose a career as a fall-down, slapstick comedian? Dave Ketchum says that for him it was an incident in high school. One day in 1941 Red Skelton came to the school for a war bond rally, stepped out of his jeep and promptly broke everyone up by falling flat on his face. Dave and some of his young buddies thought that

*Some sources give Milwaukee, Wis.

looked like a lot of fun, so they formed an act and practiced their pratfalls at servicemen's shows. Most members of the group eventually drifted off into more respectable occupations, but Dave had such a good time he just kept falling down for the rest of his professional career.

KEYES, JOE—actor

The Corner Bar (com) .... Joe (1972)

KHAN, SAJID—juvenile actor
b: India

Maya (adv) .... Raji (1967–68)

A youthful Indian actor who gained recognition in his own country in the film *Son of India* and in the U.S. in the 1966 film *Maya,* on which this series was based. His costar in both the movie and series was Jay North.

KIDDER, MARGOT—actress
b: Oct 17, 1948, Yellowknife, Canada

Nichols (wes) .... Ruth (1971–72)

KIDS NEXT DOOR, THE—

The George Gobel Show (var)
.... regulars (1958–59)

KIEL, RICHARD—actor
b: Sep 13, 1939, Detroit, Mich.

The Barbary Coast (wes)
.... Moose Moran (1975–76)
Van Dyke and Company (var)
.... regular (1976)

A towering (7'2") actor, best known as James Bond's adversary in films.

KIERAN, JOHN—columnist, host
b: Aug 2, 1892, New York City, N.Y. d: Dec 10, 1981

Kieran's Kaleidoscope (doc).. host (1949–52)
Information Please (quiz) ... panelist (1952)

One of the most popular intellectuals of radio days, who awed the listening public with his air of unassuming modesty combined with an encyclopedic knowledge about almost everything. He was long a panelist on radio's *Information Please* series. John was also a longtime sports columnist for various New York newspapers and host of one of the first widely distributed syndicated television shows, *Kieran's Kaleidoscope,* on which he dispensed engaging chatter on diverse subjects.

KIERAN, JOHN, JR.—panelist

Down You Go (quiz)
.... regular panelist (1955)

The son of John Kieran, of *Kieran's Kaleidoscope.*

KIERNAN, WALTER—radio commentator, newscaster
b: Jan 24, 1902, New Haven, Conn. d: Jan 8, 1978

That Reminds Me (talk) ...... emcee (1948)
Kiernan's Corner (int) .... host (1948–49)
Sparring Partners with Walter Kiernan (quiz)
.... emcee (1949)
What's the Story? (quiz)
.... moderator (1951–53)
Who Said That? (quiz)..... emcee (1951–54)
I've Got a Secret (quiz) ..... panelist (1952)
Who's the Boss? (quiz)....... emcee (1954)
Greatest Moments in Sports (sport)
.... host (1954–55)

Radio commentator Walter Kiernan entered television in the mid-1940s, in prenetwork days, and became a familiar face on TV talk and panel shows over the next dozen years. He was best known for his interviews of famous people, for which he employed his own special technique. "I interview big shots the same way I talk to the cop on the corner," he said. "I give them the red flannel test that one of my early editors taught me. Whenever I come face-to-face with famous people, I forget their names and think of them dressed in the long-handles.* It works. First time I tried it was when I met President William Howard Taft. Meeting VIPs has been easy ever since."

KIFF, KALEENA—juvenile actress
b: Oct 23, 1974, Santa Monica, Calif.

Love, Sidney (com) . Patti Morgan (1981–83)

*Long underwear.

KIGER, RANDI—juvenile actress
b: c. 1968

The Mackenzies of Paradise Cove (adv)
.... Celia Mackenzie (1979)

KIGER, ROBBY—juvenile actor
b: Jun 11, 1973, Encino, Calif.

Crazy Like a Fox (drama)
.... Josh Fox (1984–86)

KIKER, DOUGLAS—newscaster
b: Griffin, Ga.

NBC Magazine with David Brinkley (pub aff)
.... correspondent (1980–82)

KILBOURNE, WENDY—actress

North and South (drama)
.... Constance Flynn Hazard (1985)

KILEY, RICHARD—actor
b: Mar 31, 1922, Chicago, Ill.

The Thorn Birds (drama)
.... Paddy Cleary (1983)

Emmy Award: Best Supporting Actor in a Limited Series, for *The Thorn Birds* (1983)

Film and Broadway actor *(The Man of La Mancha)* who made a great many appearances in TV playhouse productions of the 1950s and in drama series episodes in later years.

KILGALLEN, DOROTHY—columnist
b: Jul 3, 1913, Chicago, Ill. r: Brooklyn, N.Y. d: Nov 8, 1965

What's My Line? (quiz).. panelist (1950–65)

Dorothy Kilgallen was to television viewers perhaps the ultimate panel show habituée. A bright, literate woman, she belonged in one place and one place only: the end seat on the long-running Sunday night parlor game *What's My Line?*, joining witty Arlene Francis, Bennett Cerf, and debonair host John Daly. Her small, pinched features seemed to reflect the intensity with which she played the game— with humor, with decorum, but always with a great determination to win. As producer Gil Fates later wrote, "She cared about our silly game."

Dorothy was a driven woman in other ways as well. The daughter of a newspaper reporter who moved to New York when she was young, she enrolled in college (unusual for a woman then) but couldn't wait to finish it; she dropped out after her freshman year when she won a job with the *New York Evening Journal* (later the *New York Journal-American*). By age 20 she had her own byline, and by the 1940s she had become one of the most famous show business gossip columnists in New York, and America. She was a regular on several radio chatter programs in the '40s, including one with her husband, actor-producer Dick Kollmar, and in 1950 she signed on as one of the original panelists on the new TV series *What's My Line?* She remained with it for the rest of her life.

A very opinionated woman, Dorothy certainly added spice to the show—viewers either loved her or couldn't stand her— and when she died unexpectedly, of an overdose of medication during the night following a *What's My Line?* appearance, she left a void that could not be filled. The program survived her on the network by only two years.

KILIAN, VICTOR—actor
b: Mar 6, 1891, Jersey City, N.J. d: Mar 11, 1979

Mary Hartman, Mary Hartman (com)
.... Raymond Larkin (1976–78)

This tall, heavyset character actor was known to filmgoers of the '30s and '40s as a menacing villain and to television viewers of the '70s as Mary Hartman's eccentric grandfather, the infamous "Fernwood Flasher." In between he made both friends and enemies for his frank opinions of Hollywood's "snobs" and for his outspoken political beliefs (during the '50s he was a victim of McCarthy-era political blacklisting and worked little). He lived into his eighties, just long enough to see his career revived by the *Mary Hartman* role; a year later he was murdered by an intruder into his Hollywood apartment. The crime remains unsolved.

KILLUM, GUY—black actor
b: Aug 17, Los Angeles, Calif.

Better Days (com)
.. Anthony "The Snake" Johnson (1986–)

KILPATRICK, ERIC—black actor
b: Oct 4, St. Louis, Mo.

The White Shadow (drama)
.... Curtis Jackson (1978–80)
Jessica Novak (drama).. Ricky Duran (1981)

The son of Lincoln Kilpatrick.

KILPATRICK, JAMES J.—columnist
b: Nov 1, 1920, Oklahoma City, Okla.

60 Minutes (pub aff)..... debater (1971–79)

The conservative side of *60 Minutes'* "Point-Counterpoint" political debates.

KILPATRICK, LINCOLN—black actor
b: Feb 12, 1932, St. Louis, Mo.

The Leslie Uggams Show (var).. B.J. (1969)
Matt Houston (drama)
.... Det. Lt. Michael Hoyt (1983–85)

KILTY, JACK—disc jockey

Musical Merry-Go-Round (music)
.... host (1947–49)

KIM, EVAN—actor

Khan (drama)........... Kim Khan (1975)
V (movie) (sci fi)............. Tony (1983)

KIMBALL, BRUCE—actor

The Texas Wheelers (com) .. Lyle (1974–75)

KIMBROUGH, EMILY—author

Who's Whose (quiz)........ panelist (1951)

KIMMEL, BRUCE—actor

Dinah and Her New Best Friends (var)
.... regular (1976)

KIMMINS, KENNETH—actor

Dallas (drama)
.... Thornton McLeish (1982–83)
Leo & Liz in Beverly Hills (com)
.... Jerry Fedderson (1986)

KINCAID, ARON—actor
b: Jun 15, 1943, Los Angeles, Calif.

Bachelor Father (com)
.... Warren Dawson (1962)

KING, ALAN—actor, comedian
b: Dec 26, 1927, Brooklyn, N.Y.

Seventh Avenue (drama)
.... Harry Lee (1977)

Cigar-puffing Alan King is a comedian who aims most of his barbs at the middle class; he is most familiar for his many TV comedy specials and for his appearances on variety shows such as *The Kraft Music Hall* and *The Tonight Show*. A high school dropout, he got his start as a teenager in upstate New York resorts and by 17 was a regular nightclub performer. He began appearing in films in the mid-1950s and was a familiar television face by the 1960s.

Alan is the author of two books: *Help! I'm a Prisoner in a Chinese Bakery* and *Anyone Who Owns His Own House Deserves It.*

KING, ALDINE—black actress

Karen (com) .... Cissy Peterson (1975)
Project U.F.O. (drama)
.... Libby Virdon (1978–79)
Hagen (drama)............... Jody (1980)

KING, ALEXANDER—writer, editor
b: c. 1899 d: Nov 16, 1965

The Jack Paar Show (talk)
.... semiregular (1958–62)

Autobiography: *Mine Enemy Grows Older* (1958).

KING, B.B.—blues singer
b: Sep 16, 1925, Itta Bena (near Indianola), Miss.

The Associates (com)
.... sang theme (1979–80)

The initials stand for "Blues Boy."

KING, CISSY—dancer

The Lawrence Welk Show (music)
.... regular (1967–78)

KING, DAVE—comedian, singer
b: Jun 23, 1929, Twickenham, England

Kraft Music Hall Presents The Dave King Show (var).................... host (1959)

KING, FREEMAN—black actor

The Sonny and Cher Comedy Hour (var)
.... regular (1971–74)
The Sonny Comedy Revue (var)
.... regular (1974)
The Bobby Vinton Show (var)
.... regular (1975–76)
Dance Fever (dance)
.... video disc jockey (1979–80)
Semi-Tough (com)....... Story Time (1980)

KING, JOHN REED—host

b: Oct 25, 1914, Atlantic City, N.J. d: Jul 8, 1979

Chance of a Lifetime (quiz)
.... emcee (1950–51)
Battle of the Ages (talent)..... emcee (1952)
Where Was I? (quiz) ...... emcee (1952–53)
What's Your Bid? (aud par)
.... announcer (1953)
Why? (quiz)................. emcee (1953)
On Your Way (quiz)......... emcee (1954)
Let's See (quiz).............. emcee (1955)

A radio game-show announcer and actor of the 1940s—he was once the radio voice of *Sky King*. He hosted many early television quiz shows, both in daytime and nighttime, from the late 1940s to the mid-1950s. Then, abruptly, he disappeared from the screen. In later years he was a news caster for radio stations in Pittsburgh and Fresno, California.

KING, KIP—actor

b: Aug 11, c. 1940, Chicago, Ill.

Charlie & Company (com)
.... Ronald Sandler (1985–86)

KING, MABEL—black actress

b: Dec 25, Charleston, S.C.

What's Happening!! (com)
.... Mrs. Thomas (Mama) (1976–79)

KING, PEE WEE—country bandleader, singer

b: Feb 18, 1914, Milwaukee, Wis.

The Pee Wee King Show (var) .. host (1955)

A very popular country performer from the 1930s to the '50s, and the composer of such country/popular hits as "The Tennessee Waltz," "Bonaparte's Retreat," "Slow Poke," and "You Belong to Me." He is said to have been the first to use an electric guitar on the stage of that bastion of musical conservatism, the Grand Ole Opry, in 1940.

KING, PEGGY—singer, actress

b: Feb 16, 1930, Greensburg, Pa.*

The George Gobel Show (var)
.... regular (1954–56)

Petite (5') red-haired Peggy King enlivened *The George Gobel Show* and no doubt made Lonesome George feel mighty comfortable, since she was even shorter than he was. She had started out as a band singer around 1950, then received a big build-up by MGM as "The New Judy Garland." Fans of the *old* Judy Garland didn't take too kindly to that, and Peggy's screen career fizzled. She then toured a bit but failed to attract much notice until a bouncy Hunt's Tomato Sauce commercial she had recorded became a national sensation. The Gobel show made her familiar to television viewers (producer Hal Kantor said she did the impossible by making George seem sexy), after which she appeared as a guest on other shows for several years. She retired in the 1960s and married a manufacturer of men's clothing.

KING, PERRY—actor

b: Apr 30, 1948, Alliance, Ohio

Captains and the Kings (drama)
.... Rory Armagh (1976)
Aspen (drama) .... Lee Bishop (1977)
The Last Convertible (drama)
.... Russ Currier (1979)
The Quest (adv) ..... Dan Underwood (1982)
Riptide (drama)........ Cody Allen (1984–86)

Following an Ivy League education (St. Paul's Prep School, Yale), Perry studied acting at Juilliard under John Houseman. He broke into films in the early 1970s, making his first major impression in *The Lords of Flatbush* (1974)—which was also the jumping off point for Sylvester Stallone and Henry Winkler. Perry went in a slightly different direction from his two *Lords* costars, however; for the next eight years he was seen mostly as a virile, romantic lead in TV movies and miniseries. His first two regular series roles were in

*Some sources give Ravenna, Ohio.

lightweight adventure shows of the early '80s, *The Quest* and *Riptide*.

KING, REGINA—black juvenile actress
b: Jan 15, 1971, Los Angeles, Calif.

227 (com) .... Brenda Jenkins (1985–)

KING, REINA—black juvenile actress
b: c. 1976

What's Happening Now!! (com)
.... Carolyn (1985–86)

Regina and Reina King are sisters.

KING, RORI—juvenile actress
b: Oct 14, Los Angeles, Calif.

I'm a Big Girl Now (com)
.... Rebecca "Becky" Cassidy (1980–81)

KING, SLIM & HIS PINE MT. BOYS—

Midwestern Hayride (var)
.... regulars (1951–59)

KING, TONY—black actor
b: May 6, Canton, Ohio

Bronk (police) ... Sgt. John Webber (1975–76)

KING, VIVIAN—actress

Faraway Hill (drama) .... regular (1946)

KING, WALTER WOOLF—actor, host
b: 1899, San Francisco, Calif. d: Oct 24, 1984

Lights, Camera, Action (talent)
.... emcee (1950)

KING, WAYNE—orchestra leader
b: Feb 16, 1901, Savannah, Ill. d: Jul 16, 1985

Wayne King (music)......... host (1949–52)

This famous maestro, known as "The Waltz King," was a precursor of Lawrence Welk in the realm of sedate, melodious music that appealed to the older folks. His theme song: "The Waltz You Saved for Me."

KING, WRIGHT—actor

Wanted: Dead or Alive (wes)
.... Jason Nichols (1960)

KING, ZALMAN—actor
b: New Jersey

The Young Lawyers (drama)
.... Aaron Silverman (1970–71)

KING COUSINS, THE FIVE—singers

The Kraft Summer Music Hall (var)
.... regulars (1966)

A younger subgroup of the sprawling King Family singers.

KING SISTERS, THE—singers
(Yvonne, Luise, Marilyn, Alyce, Maxine, Donna).

The King Family Show (var)
.... regulars (1965–66)
The King Family Show (var)
.... regulars (1969)

The singing King Sisters began performing together in the 1930s on radio, records, and even in a few movies. The sisters, then consisting of just four—Yvonne, Luise, Alyce and Donna—were a popular act with Horace Heidt's Orchestra, and later with Alvino Rey (who married Luise). That was in the late '30s and '40s; by the 1960s their day was pretty far past and their music was considered distinctly old fashioned. Nevertheless, an appearance in August 1964 on *The Hollywood Palace* brought a tremendous response—"old fashioned" was back in, at least with some viewers—and in early 1965 they began their own, homey ABC series, augmented by platoons of sisters, brothers, husbands, nephews, cousins, and miscellaneous kids. The show lasted for a year and was revived as a summer series in 1969.

KINGSTON, HARRY—actor

Buck Rogers (sci fi)
.... Black Barney (1950–51)
Major Dell Conway of the Flying Tigers (adv)
.... regular (1951)

KINSELLA, WALTER—actor
b: c. 1901 d: May 11, 1975

Martin Kane, Private Eye (drama)
.... Happy McMann (1949–54)

KINSKEY, LEONID—actor
b: Apr 18, 1903, St. Petersburg, Russia

The People's Choice (com)
.... Pierre (1955–56)

473

Lanky Russian comic actor with a huge grin and a bulbous nose, who played foreign types frequently in films of the '30s and '40s, and occasionally on television. In addition to his regular role on *The People's Choice,* he was Aunt Alice's harp teacher and suitor, Professor Wolfgang Radetsky, a number of times on *Mayberry R.F.D.,* and he also appeared in the pilot for *Hogan's Heroes.* He refused to become a regular on the latter series because, he said, he didn't think Nazis were either dumb or funny.

KIPER, TAMMY—actress

The Hank McCune Show (com)
.... regular (1950)

KIRBY, BRUCE—actor

Car 54, Where Are You? (com)
.... Officer Kissel (1961–63)
Holmes and Yoyo (com)
.... Capt. Harry Sedford (1976)
Turnabout (com) .... Al Brennan (1979)
Shannon (police)
.... Insp. Schmidt (1981–82)

KIRBY, BRUCE, JR.—juvenile actor

The Super (com) .... Anthony Girelli (1972)

KIRBY, DURWARD—announcer, host

b: Aug 24, 1912, Indianapolis, Ind. r: Covington, Ky.

Glamour-Go-Round (int) .... host (1950)
The Garry Moore Show (var)
.... regular (1950–51)
The Perry Como Show (var)
.... announcer (1950–51)
G.E. Guest House (quiz) ...... emcee (1951)
The Garry Moore Show (var)
.... regular (1958–64)
Candid Camera (aud par). cohost (1961–66)
The Garry Moore Show (var)
.... regular (1966–67)

Kirby is best known as Garry Moore's lanky sidekick on radio in the 1940s and on television in the '50s and '60s.

KIRBY, GEORGE—black comedian

b: Jun 8, 1924, Chicago, Ill.

ABC Comedy Hour (com) .... regular (1972)

Portly comic impressionist whose most requested routine is his impression of Pearl Bailey.

KIRBY, PAT—

Tonight (talk) .... regular (1955–57)

KIRBY, RANDY—actor

b: Dec 5, 1942, Chicago, Ill.

The Girl from U.N.C.L.E. (drama)
.... Randy Kovacs (1966–67)

This aspiring actor was the son of Durward Kirby. On the eve of his big break, as a regular on *The Girl from U.N.C.L.E.,* Randy was quoted as saying, "Pop told me show business is just that—a business—and that if I didn't treat it that way, I might as well forget it. But I must admit I can't think of another profession or business in which a guy can have so much fun."

KIRCHENBAUER, BILL—actor

Fernwood 2-Night (com)
.... Tony Roletti (1977–78)

KIRK, JOE—actor

b: c. 1904 d: 1975

The Abbott and Costello Show (com)
.... Mr. Bacciagalupe (1951–52)

KIRK, PHYLLIS—actress

b: Sep 18, 1926, Syracuse, N.Y.

The Red Buttons Show (var) . regular (1955)
The Thin Man (drama)
.... Nora Charles (1957–59)

This beautiful actress, a former model, was quite active during the 1950s in television playhouse productions and as a regular on two series. She has seldom acted since then, however. A hip injury severely restricted her mobility in later years.

KIRKES, SHIRLEY—actress

Blansky's Beauties (com)
.... Gladys "Cochise" Littlefeather (1977)
Who's Watching the Kids (com)
.... Venus (1978)

KIRKWOOD, JACK—actor

b: c. 1895 d: Aug 2, 1964

Fibber McGee and Molly (com)
.... Fred Nitney (1959–60)
One Happy Family (com)
.... Charlie Hackett (1961)

KIRSHNER, DON—producer
b: Apr 17, 1934

Don Kirshner's Rock Concert (music)
.... host (1973–81)

This powerful rock-music producer and promoter was, among other things, the music supervisor of *The Monkees* TV series. Later, he was responsible for ABC's late night *In Concert* specials as well as his own syndicated *Rock Concert.* Why did he leave the networks to produce his own music series? Because, he later remarked, some of the executives at ABC didn't seem to know the difference between the Allman Brothers and the Osmond Brothers.

KIRSTEN, DOROTHY—opera singer
b: Jul 6, 1917, Montclair, N.J.

The Chevy Show (music) . regular (1958–59)

KISER, TERRY—actor

The Roller Girls (com). Don Mitchell (1978)
Night Court (com)........ Al Craven (1984)

KITCHELL, ALMA—woman's show hostess

In the Kelvinator Kitchen (info)
.... hostess (1947–48)

KJAR, JOAN—actress

Seven Brides for Seven Brothers (adv)
.... Marie (1982–83)

KLAVAN, GENE—disc jockey

Make the Connection (quiz). panelist (1955)
Who Pays? (quiz) .... panelist (1959)

KLEEB, HELEN—actress
b: 1907

Harrigan and Son (com)
.... Miss Claridge (1960–61)
The Waltons (drama)
.... Mamie Baldwin (1972–81)

KLEIN, ROBERT—comedian
b: Feb 8, 1942, The Bronx, N.Y.

Comedy Tonight (var) .... host (1970)
TV's Bloopers & Practical Jokes (com)
.... regular (1984–85)

One of the many bright young stand-up comics who emerged during the 1960s but who never seemed to quite make it to major show business stardom—despite, in Klein's case, a well-received summer show in 1970. Klein made his network TV debut on *The Tonight Show* in January 1968 and was a frequent guest, and guest host, on that show. He later hosted *Saturday Night Live.* He is a regular on the college concert circuit.

KLEMPERER, WERNER—actor
b: Mar 20, 1920*, Cologne, Germany

Hogan's Heroes (com)
.... Col. Wilhelm Klink (1965–71)

Emmy Awards: Best Supporting Actor in a Comedy, for *Hogan's Heroes* (1968, 1969)

Tall, balding Werner Klemperer has spent a lifetime playing Nazis, both comic and sinister, despite an unlikely background for such a vocation. An urbane, sophisticated man, he is the son of famed symphony conductor Otto Klemperer; father and son were forced to flee to America when the Nazis came to power in their homeland in 1933. Werner's most famous role is undoubtedly that of the incompetent camp commandant in *Hogan's Heroes.* He continued to appear on television in the '70s and '80s on such programming as *The Rhinemann Exchange* (1977) and *The Return of the Beverly Hillbillies* (1981), among others.

KLET, STANLEY—singer
b: c. 1936

Paul Whiteman's TV Teen Club (talent)
.... regular (1950–53)

KLICK, MARY—

The Jimmy Dean Show (var) . regular (1957)

KLINE, RICHARD—actor
b: Apr 29, New York City, N.Y.

Three's Company (com)
.... Larry Dallas (1978–84)
It's a Living (com)..... Richie Gray (1985–)

*Some sources give March 22.

475

KLOUS, PAT—actress

b: Oct 19, 1955, Hutchinson, Kan. r: Texas

Flying High (adv) . Marcy Bowers (1978–79)
Aloha Paradise (com)... Fran Linhart (1981)
The Love Boat (com)
..... cruise director Judy McCoy (1984–86)

KLUGMAN, JACK—actor

b: Apr 27, 1922, South Philadelphia, Pa.

Harris Against the World (com)
.... Alan Harris (1964–65)
The Odd Couple (com)
.... Oscar Madison (1970–75)
Quincy, M. E. (police)
.... Quincy, M.E. (1976–83)
You Again? (com) .. Henry Willows (1986–)

Emmy Awards: Best Actor in a Single Performance, for *The Defenders* (1964); Best Actor in a Comedy Series, for *The Odd Couple* (1971, 1973)

"There is not enough anger in television. I planned to supply some." Jack Klugman did indeed do that on the set of *Quincy,* yelling a lot both on-screen and off, keeping writers, producers, and studio in constant turmoil. However, the yelling was not for the usual star reasons—money or ego gratification—but for better scripts, better character motivation, and a show that had something worthwhile to say. By and large, he got it.

It was a long way from bit parts in *Captain Video* (perhaps the most cheaply made hit series in TV history) to the starring role in *Quincy, M.E.,* where he finally had enough clout to get what he wanted. Nor was Jack the most likely actor to make the grade. Besides being a chronic complainer (a "kvetch," as Tony Randall called him), Jack's rutted face was hardly that of a matinee idol; it might better be likened to that of a dyspeptic gargoyle.

Nevertheless, as a young man Jack worked hard at his craft, struggling through lean years as a stage actor in New York after World War II (in which he had served). For a time he shared a $14 per week apartment with another struggling unknown, Charles Bronson. Jack's first notable stage role was opposite Kim Stanley in *St. Joan;* the second, in 1949, was with a young Rod Steiger in *Stevedore.* Jack also did a lot of live television work in New York in the early 1950s, both in potboilers like *Captain Video* and *Tom Corbett—Space Cadet* and in more prestigious showcases like *The U.S. Steel Hour* and *Kraft Television Theatre.* For several months in 1954–55 he was a regular in a now-forgotten daytime soap opera called *The Greatest Gift.* One of his best remembered roles of the period was in "The Velvet Alley" on *Playhouse 90* in 1959.

Jack made many appearances in dramas of the '60s, especially *Naked City* and *The Twilight Zone.* His first prime time series, however, was a short-lived comedy called *Harris Against the World* in 1964. In it he played classic Klugman: a complainer with a heart of gold.

Jack sought quality roles when he could get them, and he won his first Emmy for a particularly stunning performance as a blacklisted small-time actor who stands up and fights, on *The Defenders.* In 1970 he was back in series work in what many consider to be one of the classic TV comedies of all time, *The Odd Couple,* playing grouchy, slovenly Oscar Madison to Tony Randall's fastidious Felix Unger. After that series' five-year run, Jack wanted something meaty, something he could get his famous teeth into. Producer Glen Larson envisioned *Quincy, M.E.* as a light, funny, cop show, with a maximum of car chases (his trademark) and a minimum of medicine. Klugman agreed to do the show but immediately started yelling about the scripts. Within a year *Quincy* was a hit and Larson was out. Later, Jack complained so publicly about the show's writers (even going to college campuses to try to recruit replacements) that he could hardly find anyone to write for him at all. Eventually he had to back down—a little.

All in all, Jack figures he has been in more than 400 television shows over the years, as well as 15 movies and scores of stage plays. "I'm compulsive about my work," he growls, "and not beyond rewriting a scene when I know it is not playing right." Not all of his roles have been of Emmy caliber, perhaps, but it is not for lack of loudly demanding better. Ask Glen Larson. As that highly successful producer diplomatically remarked, "Jack . . . is not very forgiving."

KNELL, DAVID—actor

Bret Maverick (wes)
.... Rodney Catlow (1981–82)
Mr. Sunshine (com)
.... Warren Leftwich (1986)

KNIGHT, CHRISTOPHER—actor
b: c. 1958, New York City r: Los Angeles, Calif.

The Brady Bunch (com)
.... Peter Brady (1969–74)
The Brady Bunch Hour (var)
.... Peter Brady (1977)
Joe's World (com)
.... Steve Wabash (1979–80)

KNIGHT, DON—actor

The Immortal (adv)...... Fletcher (1970–71)

KNIGHT, FRANK—announcer, host
b: c. 1894 d: Oct 18, 1973

Chronoscope (int) .... moderator (1951)

KNIGHT, GLADYS—black singer, actress
b: May 28, 1944, Atlanta, Ga.

The Gladys Knight & the Pips Show (var)
.... hostess (1975)
Charlie & Company (com)
.... Diana Richmond (1985–86)

The lead singer of a very popular rhythm and blues vocal group, which has been turning out hits since the early 1960s ("Every Beat of My Heart," "I Heard It Through the Grapevine," "Midnight Train to Georgia"). Gladys got her first big break at age seven as a grand prize–winner on Ted Mack's *Original Amateur Hour*. In recent years she has branched into acting, with the starring role in the dramatic movie *Pipe Dreams* (1976) and occasional roles in TV series.

KNIGHT, JACK—actor
b: Feb 26, 1938, Somerville, Mass.

Lotsa Luck (com)........ Bummy (1973–74)
James at 15 (drama)
.... Mr. Shamley (1977–78)
Presenting Susan Anton (var)
.... regular (1979)

KNIGHT, MERALD—black singer
b: Sep 4, 1942, Atlanta, Ga.

The Gladys Knight & the Pips Show (var)
.... regular (1975)

The brother of Gladys Knight, and a member of the Pips.

KNIGHT, TED—actor
b: Dec 7, 1923, Terryville, Conn. d: Aug 26, 1986

The Mary Tyler Moore Show (com)
.... Ted Baxter (1970–77)
The Ted Knight Show (com)
.... Roger Dennis (1978)
Too Close for Comfort (com)
.... Henry Rush (1980–85)
The Ted Knight Show (com)
.... Henry Rush (1986)

Emmy Awards: Best Supporting Actor in a Comedy, for *The Mary Tyler Moore Show* (1973, 1976)

Ted Knight is one of those actors who labored for many years in obscurity before one perfect role suddenly thrust him to fame. His early career, after graduating from acting school, took him up and down the East Coast as a disc jockey, announcer, singer, ventriloquist, puppeteer, and pantomimist. In the 1950s he appeared in small roles on such shows as *Lux Video Theatre* and *Big Town* and in the '60s on *The Lieutenant, The Outer Limits, The Wild Wild West,* and other series. A master of voices, he did voice work for many Saturday morning cartoons, talking to the kiddies as Aquaman, Cosby Birdwell (on *Fantastic Voyage*), Professor Lindenbrook (on *Journey to the Center of the Earth*), and, later, as the narrator of *Superfriends*.

The role that made him famous was, of course, that of white-haired, addle-brained newscaster Ted Baxter on *The Mary Tyler Moore Show*. Knowing a good thing when he finally found it, he later played practically identical comic roles on two other series, as well as in movies such as *Caddyshack* (1980).

Ted's real name: Tadewurz Wladzui Konopka.

KNOTTS, DON—actor
b: Jul 21, 1924, Morgantown, W. Va.

The Steve Allen Show (var)
.... regular (1956–60)
The Andy Griffith Show (com)
.... Barney Fife (1960–65)
The Don Knotts Show (var) .. host (1970–71)
Three's Company (com)
.... Ralph Furley (1979–84)

Emmy Awards: Best Supporting Actor in a Comedy Series, for *The Andy Griffith Show* (1961, 1962, 1963, 1966, 1967)

"Why shouldn't I be nervous?" says Don Knotts, fidgeting. "You'd be nervous too if you spent your first five years as a radio performer under the name of Windy Wails. I was supposed to be a cowboy. My next job was in a serial. I was Wilbur Peterson, a neurotic. Not only neurotic, but nervous."

Don plays only one role, but he plays it so well he has become something of a television institution. It all began not as the radio cowboy ("Windy Wails, Teller of Tall Tales" on *Bobby Benson's B-Bar-B Ranch*) nor as the neurotic soap opera character (on *Search for Tomorrow* in the mid-1950s), but as a gag on *The Garry Moore Show*. The small, wiry Knotts was hilarious as the fidgety, tense little man whose speech was peppered with garbled malapropisms. Steve Allen quickly added him to his regular company of schtick comedians. Then, in 1960, Andy Griffith—with whom Don had appeared in both the stage and screen versions of *No Time for Sergeants*—cast him in his most unforgettable role, as Deputy Barney Fife on *The Andy Griffith Show*. Don was nominated five times for an Emmy Award for his portrayal and won every time.

Don has brought his jumpy character to a variety of series, specials, and movies in the years since then. In *Three's Company* he was only slightly toned down as the sarcastic landlord. He was most at home, perhaps, in the 1986 reunion special *Return to Mayberry*, in which Andy returned to town once more to bail Barney Fife out of another self-made dilemma.

KNOWLES, AARIANA—

Your Show of Shows (var)
.... regular (1951–52)

KNOX, TERENCE—actor
b: Dec 16, Richland, Wash.

St. Elsewhere (drama)
.... Dr. Peter White (1982–85)
All Is Forgiven (com) ... Matt Russell (1986)

KNUDSEN, PEGGY—actress
b: 1923, Duluth, Minn. d: Jul 11, 1980

So This Is Hollywood (com)
.... April Adams (1955)

KOBE, GAIL—actress, producer

Peyton Place (drama)
.... Doris Schuster (1965)

This onetime soap opera actress (in *Peyton Place, Bright Promise*) later became a producer of daytime serials, including the 1972 revival of the show she had once starred in, *Peyton Place*. In the mid-1980s she was producer of CBS's *Guiding Light*. How did behind-the-scenes work compare with her former life in front of the cameras? "I can't imagine doing anything that would be more satisfying than what I'm doing now," she said. "This is more an expression of my real self than acting ever was."

KOCHHEIM, LORY—actress

Mulligan's Stew (drama)
.... Polly Friedman (1977)

KOEHLER, FREDERICK—juvenile actor
b: Jun 17, Queens, N.Y.

Kate & Allie (com) .... Chip Lowell (1984–)

KOENIG, WALTER—actor
b: Sep 14, Chicago, Ill.

Star Trek (sci fi)
.... Ensign Pavel Chekov (1967–69)

KOLB, CLARENCE—actor
b: 1974, Cleveland, Ohio d: Nov 25, 1964

My Little Margie (com)
.... Mr. George Honeywell (1952–55)

KOLB, MINA—actress

Pete and Gladys (com)
.... Peggy Briggs (1961–62)

KOLDEN, SCOTT—juvenile actor
b: Feb 11, 1962, Torrance, Calif.

Me and The Chimp (com)
.... Scott Reynolds (1972)

KOLLDEHOFF, RENE—actor

The Winds of War (drama)
.... Hermann Goering (1983)

KOLLMAR, DICK—host, actor

b: Dec 31, 1910, Ridgewood, N.J. d: Jan 7, 1971

Broadway Spotlight (var) .... host (1949)
Guess What (quiz) .... emcee (1952)
Who's the Boss? (quiz). ..... panelist (1954)

This young actor married columnist Dorothy Kilgallen shortly after she gave him a plug in her syndicated column. They later appeared on radio together. Dick was also a theatrical producer.

KOMACK, JAMES—writer, director, actor

b: Aug 3, 1930, New York City, N.Y.

Hennesey (com)
.... Harvey Spencer Blair III (1959–62)
The Courtship of Eddie's Father (com)
.... Norman Tinker (1969–72)

James "Jimmie" Komack has made one of the most successful transitions from acting to writing and directing of anyone in Hollywood. A onetime stand-up comedian and Broadway actor(he was in *Damn Yankees*), he began writing scripts for *Hennesey* while appearing on that series as the millionaire dentist, Harvey Spencer Blair III. He later created or co-created three of television's all-time hit comedies: *The Courtship of Eddie's Father* (in which he also acted), *Chico and the Man,* and *Welcome Back, Kotter.*

KONDAZIAN, KAREN—actress

b: Jan 27, Boston, Mass. r: California

Shannon (police)
.... Irene Locatelli (1981–82)

KONRAD, DOROTHY—actress

The Last Resort (com)
.... Mrs. Trilling (1979–80)

KOOCK, GUICH—actor

b: Jul 22, 1944, Austin, Texas

Carter Country (com)
.... Dep. Harley Puckett (1977–79)

The Chisholms (wes) .. Frank O'Neal (1980)
Lewis & Clark (com)
.... Roscoe Clark (1981–82)

KOPELL, BERNIE—actor

b: Jun 21, 1933, New York City, N.Y.

Get Smart (com)
.... Conrad Siegfried (1966–69)
That Girl (com) .... Jerry Bauman (1966–71)
The Doris Day Show (com)
.... Louie Palucci (1970–71)
Needles and Pins (com)
.... Charlie Miller (1973)
When Things Were Rotten (com)
.... Alan-a-Dale (1975)
The Love Boat (com)
.... ship's doctor Adam Bricker (1977–86)

Bernie Kopell, the *Love Boat*'s version of Marcus Welby, M.D., was a busy actor indeed during the 1960s, playing a succession of rather nutty roles. His knack for dialects won him his first regular TV part, as a Cuban heavy on the daytime serial *The Brighter Day.* Later, he made guest appearances in several situation comedies and was then signed as Siegfried the leather-jacketed K.A.O.S. agent on *Get Smart,* as Jerry the neighbor on *That Girl,* and as Louie the Italian restaurateur on *The Doris Day Show.* As a frequent guest on *Bewitched,* he alternated as a 100-year-old apothecary, a Viennese psychiatrist, a German U-boat captain, and a blond hippie. As if all that wasn't enough, Mel Brooks had him portray Robin Hood's friend Alan-a-Dale as a Las Vegas lounge comic in the bizarre comedy *When Things Were Rotten.* In comparison, the role of Doc Bricker on *The Love Boat* was positively sedate.

KOPPEL, TED—newscaster

b: 1940, Lancashire, England

ABC Weekend News (news)
.... anchorman (1975–77)
Nightline (news) ...... anchorman (1979–)

Emmy Awards: correspondent, ABC post election special (1980); interviewer for "The Palestinian's Viewpoint" (1982); anchorman for "Disaster on the Potomac" (1982), "Massacre in San Ysidro" (1985), "The Hostage Crisis Five Years Later" (1985), "Crash of Delta" (1986) and "Colombian Volcano" (1986)

A native of England, Ted Koppel moved to the U.S. when he was 13 years old and received his college education in this country, at Syracuse and Stanford Universities. He joined ABC as a national reporter at the remarkably young age of 23 (ABC was on a youth kick then) and has been with that network ever since. After being posted to Latin America, Vietnam, and Hong Kong, he returned to the U.S. as ABC's chief diplomatic correspondent in 1971. His major breakthrough, however, came when he was made interim anchor of the nightly Iran hostage updates in the fall of 1979; these became a regular newscast called *Nightline* the following spring, and Koppel, as its regular anchorman, became one of the most visible newscasters in television.

KORMAN, HARVEY—actor
b: Feb 15, 1927, Chicago, Ill.

The Danny Kaye Show (var)
.... regular (1964–67)
The Carol Burnett Show (var)
.... regular (1967–77)
The Tim Conway Show (var)
.... regular (1980–81)
Mama's Family (com)
.... Alistair Quince (1983–84)
Mama's Family (com)
.... Ed Higgins (1983–84)
Leo & Liz in Beverly Hills (com)
.... Leo Green (1986)

Emmy Awards: best individual performance in a variety series, for *The Carol Burnett Show* (1969, 1971, 1972); Best Supporting Actor in a Variety Series, for *The Carol Burnett Show* (1974)

KORN, IRIS—actress
b: c. 1921 d: Jan 27, 1982

Palmerstown, U.S.A. (drama)
.... Widder Brown (1981)

KOSLO, PAUL—actor

Roots: The Next Generations (drama)
.... Earl Crowther (1979)

KOSTAL, IRWIN—orchestra leader
b: Oct 1, 1911, Chicago, Ill.

The Garry Moore Show (var)
.... orch. leader (1959–64)

KOSUGI, SHO—actor

The Master (adv)........... Okasa (1984)

KOTERO, PATRICIA "APOLLONIA"— singer, actress
b: Aug 2, Santa Monica, Calif.

Falcon Crest (drama)
.... Apollonia (1985–86)

A singer and actress who appeared in Spanish-language films and TV productions in South America before making a splash in the U.S.—in the 1984 movie *Purple Rain* (with Prince); the songs from the film also launched her recording career. She was also seen in the 1984 miniseries *Mystic Warrior,* but it was a year on *Falcon Crest* that brought her her greatest notoriety to date. She is of German, Hispanic, and Italian descent.

KOTTO, YAPHET—black actor
b: Nov 15, 1937, New York City, N.Y.

For Love and Honor (drama)
... Platoon Sgt. James "China" Bell (1983)

KOUFAX, SANDY—sportscaster
b: Dec 30, 1936, Brooklyn, N.Y.

Monday Night Baseball (sport)
.... sportscaster (1972)

A former major-league baseball pitcher, with the Dodgers in the '50s and '60s.

KOVACS, BELLA—actor, producer

Space Patrol (child)
Prince Baccarratti (the Black Falcon) (1951–52)

KOVACS, ERNIE—comedian
b: Jan 23, 1919, Trenton, N.J. d: Jan 13, 1962

Ernie in Kovacsland (var)...... host (1951)
The Ernie Kovacs Show (var)
..........................host (1952–53)
Take a Guess (quiz)........ panelist (1953)
Time Will Tell (quiz)........ emcee (1954)
One Minute Please (quiz)
.... panelist (1954–55)
The Ernie Kovacs Show (var) ... host (1956)
Tonight (talk) .... host (1956–57)
Take a Good Look (quiz) .... host (1959–61)
Silents Please (misc) .... host (1961)

Emmy Award: Best Electronic Camera Work, for *The Ernie Kovacs Shows* (1962)

Burly, mustachioed Ernie Kovacs was quite possibly one of the most creative individuals who ever inhabited the television medium. Unfortunately, his career was short and harried, and he was never appreciated as much in life as he has been since his early death.

Ernie started out as a disc jockey and sportscaster on a local radio station in the early '40s, but he knew as soon as television began to spread that his future lay in the visual medium. Eventually he wrangled a 15-minute spot on a Philadelphia station to try out his comedy, and the results were, well, unconventional. What do you make of a cigar-puffing host who has his guests freeze in midsentence when a commercial comes on and then resume when it ends as if time had stood still? Or one who roams out into the streets of Philadelphia, accosts an Oriental man and interviews him on the assumption that he had just dug his way through the earth from China? Or one who simply interrupts his program in midstream to sing "Mona Lisa" in Polish? Some critics, who liked their comedy predictable, thought it was all quite juvenile, but Ernie began to build up a cult following of fans who recognized that here was something really different.

Within a few months Ernie had his first network show, a daytime series on NBC called *It's Time for Ernie* in May 1951. He then moved into prime time with *Ernie in Kovacsland*, a summer replacement for (of all things) *Kukla, Fran & Ollie*, followed by another daytime series *(Kovacs on the Korner)* on NBC in early 1952. Ernie was never very practical with money, and network budgets just seemed an opportunity to stretch his imagination even farther. He would think nothing of spending thousands on a sequence only a few seconds long. Once he built an entire room on an angle and mounted the camera on the same angle, so that everything would look normal—except that liquids, loose objects, and people cascaded crazily from one side to the other, for no apparent reason.

NBC's accountants did not see the humor in this budget busting, and by late 1952 Ernie found himself across the street at CBS with *The Ernie Kovacs Show*, which, like its predecessors, lasted only a few months. He then appeared on a succession of quiz and local shows, until NBC decided to take him back in late '55 for another daytime and then a summer prime time show (1956). One of his best-known routines of this period was the Nairobi Trio, three musicians dressed in ape suits who mechanically played a clockwork tune in which the drummer periodically pummeled the ape in front of him instead of his drums. There were also such characters as lisping poet Percy Dovetonsils, disc jockey Wolfgang Sauerbraten, and Clowdy Faire, Your Weather Girl. Ernie was joined on nearly all of his shows by Edie Adams, whom he had originally hired as an extra on one of his first programs. In their first scene together he hit her in the face with a pie. Apparently she could take a joke; in 1955 they were married.

Ernie's last years were painful. There were fights with the network, shaky ratings (none of his shows lasted long—it is a wonder he was given so many chances), and a bitter divorce from his first wife which led to her abducting their two young daughters (who had been put in his custody) and disappearing. Ernie spent three years and many thousands of dollars trying to find them, which he finally did, living in poverty in Florida. Then, in 1959, the IRS landed on him like a ton of bricks, demanding half a million dollars in back taxes. Ernie had always spent money freely and even put his own money into the production of his shows when the network wouldn't cover the cost. However, he had simply ignored the IRS. The government was unamused and attempted to confiscate his furniture and attach nearly all of his income. Ernie had to scramble for any paying work he could find, including a string of grind-'em-out movies on which he worked until the day of his death. His last major TV project was a series of specials which aired on ABC in 1961–62.

One night in early 1962, after a Hollywood party (he despised them), slightly drunk, Ernie stepped into his car and drove off alone. A few minutes later the car skidded on a rain-slicked street and slammed into a telephone pole; Ernie was killed instantly. His widow Edie fought off claims by his first wife and by Ernie's mother for what was left of his estate and then went to work to pay off the IRS debts herself.

Ernie's biography is titled *Nothing in Moderation,* by David G. Walley (1976).

KOVACS, JONATHAN HALL—juvenile actor

The Family Tree (drama)
.... Toby Benjamin (1983)

KOVE, MARTIN—actor
b: Mar 6, Brooklyn, N.Y.

Code R (adv) .... George Baker (1977)
We've Got Each Other (com)
.... Ken Redford (1977–78)
Cagney & Lacey (police)
.... Det. Victor Isbecki (1982–)

KOWANKO, PETE—actor

For Love and Honor (drama)
.... Pvt. Chris Dolan (1983)

KRAMER, BERT—actor
b: Oct 10, San Diego, Calif.

Sara (wes)........ Emmet Ferguson (1976)
The Fitzpatricks (drama)
.... Mike Fitzpatrick (1977–78)

KRAMER, JEFFREY—actor
b: Jul 15, c. 1945, New York City, N.Y.

Struck by Lightning (com). Ted Stein (1979)

KRAMER, STEPFANIE—actress
b: Aug 6, 1956, Los Angeles, Calif.

Married: The First Year (drama)
.... Sharon Kelly (1979)
The Secret Empire (drama)
.... Princess Tara (1979)
We Got It Made (com)... Claudia (1983–84)
Hunter (police)
.... Det. Sgt. Dee Dee McCall (1984–)

KRATOCHZIL, TOM—actor

Wonder Woman (adv)
.... voice of I.R.A. (1977–78)

KREPPEL, PAUL—actor
b: Jun 20, Kingston, N.Y.

It's a Living (com)... Sonny Mann (1980–82)
It's a Living (com).... Sonny Mann (1985–)

KRESKIN—mentalist
b: Jan 12, 1935, Montclair, N.J.

The Amazing World of Kreskin (aud par)
.... regular (1971–75)

KRISTEN, MARTA—actress
b: c. 1945, Norway

Lost in Space (sci fi)
.... Judy Robinson (1965–68)

KROEGER, GARY—comedian
b: Apr 13, 1957, Cedar Falls, Iowa

NBC's Saturday Night Live (com)
.... regular (1982–85)

KROFFT PUPPETS, THE—
Marty Krofft, b: Montreal, Canada
Sid Krofft, b: Jul 30, 1929, Athens, Greece

Barbara Mandrell & The Mandrell Sisters (var).................. regulars (1980–82)

This brother team of puppeteers is descended from a European family of puppeteers that dates back to the 1700s. Sid and Marty have been responsible for many Saturday morning shows of the '70s and '80s and have produced such prime time series as *Barbara Mandrell* and *Donny and Marie.*

KRUGER, OTTO—actor
b: Sep 6, 1885, Toledo, Ohio d: Sep 6, 1974

Lux Video Theatre (drama) .. host (1955–56)

KRUSCHEN, JACK—actor
b: Mar 20, 1922, Winnipeg, Canada

Hong Kong (adv).......... Tully (1960–61)
Busting Loose (com)
.... Sam Markowitz (1977)
Webster (com)............. Papa (1986–)

KUBEK, TONY—sportscaster
b: c. 1936, Milwaukee, Wis.

Monday Night Baseball (sport)
.... sportscaster (1972–75)

A former major-league shortstop with the New York Yankees (1957–65).

KUBELIK, RAFAEL—conductor
b: Jun 29, 1914, Batchory, Czechoslovakia

Chicago Symphony Chamber Orchestra (music) .... conductor (1951–52)

KUHLMAN, RON—actor

The Brady Brides (com)
.... Philip Covington III (1981)

KULKY, HENRY—actor
b: Aug 11, 1911, Hastings-on-the-Hudson, N.Y.
d: Feb 12, 1965

The Life of Riley (com)
.... Otto Schmidlap (1953–58)
Hennesey (com)..... Max Bronski (1959–62)
Voyage to the Bottom of the Sea (sci fi)
.... C.P. Off. Curley Jones (1964–65)

A former champion wrestler of the 1940s ("Bomber Kulkavich") who was proud of the fact that he had never taken an acting lesson. He said he learned all he needed about emoting during his 7,000 wrestling matches.

KULP, NANCY—actress
b: Aug 28, 1921, Harrisburg, Pa.

The Bob Cummings Show (com)
.... Pamela Livingston (1955–59)
The Beverly Hillbillies (com)
.... Jane Hathaway (1962–71)
The Brian Keith Show (com)
.... Mrs. Gruber (1973–74)

KULUVA, WILL—actor

Primus (adv)....... Charlie Kingman (1971)

KUMAGAI, DENICE—actress

Night Court (com)
.... Quon Le Robinson (1985–)

KUPCINET, IRV—host, columnist
b: Jul 31, 1912, Chicago, Ill.

Tonight! America After Dark (talk)
.... regular (1957)

A loyal son of Chicago, born and raised there, and long a leading personality in the Windy City. "Kup" has for many years been a columnist for *The Chicago Sun-Times* and—since 1962—host of the syndicated *Kup's Show* talk program.

KUPCINET, KARYN—actress
b: Mar 6, 1941 d: Nov 28, 1963

The Gertrude Berg Show (com)
.... Carol (1961–62)

The daughter of Chicago newspaperman Irv Kupcinet, and the victim in one of Hollywood's celebrated unsolved murders. The pretty Karyn had come to the film capital around 1961 and quickly found both an active social life and roles on episodes of a number of series, including *The Red Skelton Show, Hawaiian Eye,* and *Surfside Six;* she also had a continuing part on the Gertrude Berg series. Her future seemed bright. Then one day in late 1963 a friend, actor Mark Goddard, unable to reach her, came to her bachelor apartment and found her strangled to death on the couch. She had been dead for several days. There were few clues, and, despite a reward posted by her grieving father, no suspects.

Once every year since that time, in late November, a small memorial notice has appeared in the obituary pages of *Variety.* It contains a photo of a young and extraordinarily pretty girl, and a simple caption: "The passing of years can never fill the void in our hearts and lives."

KURALT, CHARLES—newscaster
b: Sep 10, 1934, Wilmington, N.C.

Eyewitness to History (news)
.... anchorman (1960–61)
CBS News Adventure (doc) . narrator (1970)
Who's Who? (pub aff) ...... reporter (1977)
On the Road with Charles Kuralt (pub aff)
.... host/correspondent (1983)
The American Parade (pub aff)
.... anchorman (1984)

Emmy Awards: Best News Program Segments, for "On the Road" segment on *The CBS Evening News* (1969, 1980); Achievement in Broadcast Journalism, for "On the Road" Segments (1978); Best Newswriting, for "Cicada Invasion" on *The CBS Evening News* (1982); Best Informational Segments, for "Steeplejacks" (1985) and "Bicycle Messengers" (1986)

"From the Interstate, America is all steel guardrails and plastic signs. And every place looks and feels and sounds and smells like every other place. We stick to the backroads, where Kansas still looks like Kansas and Georgia still looks like Georgia, where there is room for diversity and for the occurrence of small miracles." So wrote Charles Kuralt of his first dozen years "On the Road," exploring the back roads, the small towns, the odd and interesting "ordinary" people who were seldom seen on network newscasts until he began his periodic features on *The CBS Evening News* in October 1967. Before Charles stumbled on his unique format he was pretty much indistinguishable from dozens of other network reporters. A chubby, balding man with a rather wistful manner (and writing style), he hardly seemed the type to become a superstar in the highly competitive news business. He had joined CBS in 1956 as a writer only a year after graduating from the University of North Carolina and was soon being posted to domestic and foreign trouble spots. A short stint as anchor of the news analysis program *Eyewitness to History* went virtually unnoticed; he had to wait until the late '60s for his break, when CBS issued him a 25-foot van and a camera crew and sent him out to think, write, and meet folks and hopefully to bring mighty CBS a little closer to the fabric of America. Such an assignment might have driven a more ambitious newshound up the wall, but for Kuralt it was perfect. Intended as a three-month experiment, "On the Road" has lasted 20 years.

Charles brought his road show to a number of prime time news specials and series during the 1970s. He left the road for a period in the early '80s to anchor CBS's *Morning*, as well as its *Sunday Morning* magazine show. But he couldn't stay for long, as he once again heard the call of the open road.

KURTIS, BILL—newscaster
b: Sep 21, 1940, Pensacola, Fla. r: Kansas

The American Parade (pub aff)
.... correspondent (1984)

KURTY, LEE—actress
b: c. 1937, Pittsburgh, Pa.

Dr. Kildare (drama)
.... Nurse Zoe Lawton (1965–66)

KURTZ, SWOOSIE—actress
b: Sep 6, 1944, Omaha, Neb.

Mary (var)................. regular (1978)
Love, Sidney (com)
.... Laurie Morgan (1981–83)

All right, the first thing you want to know is whether her name is really "Swoosie" and if so, how would someone get a name like that? Yes it is, and I'll tell you how. She was born the daughter of a much-decorated army air force pilot during World War II. Her parents had intended to name her Margo, after her mother, but during the war there was a popular song about her father's B-17D bomber called "Alexander the Swoose" ("Half swan, half goose, Alexander is a Swoose"). This particular aircraft, it seems, had become something of a legend, apparently possessing nine lives. "The newspapers called me the little Swoosie," she recalls, "and (my parents) went for it. I've never thought of changing my name."

Red-haired Swoosie went on to become a successful New York stage actress in the '60s and '70s, doing only occasionally television work (including a stint on *As the World Turns* in 1971). Her stay on *Mary* was brief—the series lasted only three weeks—but in 1981 she was lured away from the hit Broadway show *Fifth of July* to costar with Tony Randall in the much-acclaimed *Love, Sidney*.

Meanwhile, in case you're still interested, that famous B-17D bomber—the original "Swoosie"—can still be seen, enshrined in the Smithsonian Institution in Washington.

KURTZMAN, KATY—juvenile actress
b: Sep 16, 1965, Washington, D.C.

Dynasty (drama) ... Lindsay Blaisdel (1981)

KUSATSU, CLYDE—actor
b: Sep 13, c. 1948, Honolulu, Hawaii

Bring 'Em Back Alive (adv) ... Ali (1982–83)

KUTASH, JEFF, DANCERS—

Dick Clark Presents the Rock and Roll Years (music) .... dancers (1973–74)

KUTER, KAY E.—actor

Petticoat Junction (com)
.... Newt Kiley (1964–70)
Green Acres (com) ... Newt Kiley (1965–70)

KUYPER, GEORGE—announcer

Chicago Symphony (music)
.... commentator (1954–55)

KUZYK, MIMI—actress
b: Winnipeg, Canada

Hill Street Blues (police)
.... Det. Patricia Mayo (1984–85)

KYSER, KAY—orchestra leader, host
b: Jun 18, 1906, Rocky Mount, N.C. d: Jul 23, 1985

Kay Kyser's Kollege of Musical Knowledge (quiz).................... emcee (1949–50)

Kay was a highly successful novelty bandleader of the '40s who brought his "Kollege of Musical Knowledge" quiz show routine to television in the early days. When his show was canceled in 1950, "the Old Professor" decided he'd had enough of both the vicissitudes of show business and of 20 years on the road and so quit the entertainment world for good. Many subsequent offers failed to lure him back, even when the popular *Kollege* was revived in 1954. In later years he was reluctant to even talk about his years on radio, in movies, and in music (he had several million-selling records). He spent the rest of his days as a Christian Science religious leader.

L

L.A. MIME COMPANY, THE—

Van Dyke and Company (var)
.... regulars (1976)

LABORTEAUX, MATTHEW—juvenile actor
b: Dec 8, 1966, Los Angeles, Calif.

79 Park Avenue (drama)
.... Paulie (as a child) (1977)
Little House on the Prairie (adv)
.... Albert Ingalls (1978–82)
Whiz Kids (drama).. Richie Adler (1983–84)

Matthew was an autistic child who was adopted as an infant by a Los Angeles couple named Laborteaux. Through years of love, attention, and hard work, his foster parents helped bring him out of his shell. He did not speak until the age of five; by age 8 he was a child actor, appearing in the critically acclaimed special *Poppa and Me.* More roles followed and in 1978 he became a regular on *Little House on the Prairie,* playing the role of adopted son Albert.

LABORTEAUX, PATRICK—juvenile actor
b: Jul 22, 1965, Los Angeles, Calif.

Little House on the Prairie (adv)
.... Andy Garvey (1977–81)

The adoptive brother of Matthew. Patrick was also emotionally disturbed as a child but was helped to normalcy by his loving foster parents, the Laborteauxs.

LABRIOLA, TONY—

The Ken Murray Show (var)
.... regular (1950–51)

LA CENTRA, PEG—singer, actress
b: c. 1917, Boston, Mass.

The Marge and Gower Champion Show (com)
.... Amanda (1957)

LACEY, LAARA—

Happy Days (var) .... regular (1970)
The Ken Berry "Wow" Show (var)
.... regular (1972)

LACHER, TAYLOR—actor

Cade's County (police)
.... Arlo Pritchard (1971–72)
Nakia (police)... Dep. Hubbel Martin (1974)
Joe Forrester (police)
.... Det. Will Carson (1975–76)

LACK, ANDREW—news producer, correspondent

The American Parade (pub aff)
.... correspondent (1984)

Emmy Awards: Best News Producer and Director, for *CBS Reports: The Boat People* (1979); Best News Producer, for *CBS Reports: Teddy* (1980); Best News Writer, for *CBS Reports: The Defense of the United States* (1981)

LADD, CHERYL—actress
b: Jul 2, 1951, Huron, S.D.

The Ken Berry "Wow" Show (var)
.... regular (1972)
Charlie's Angels (drama)
.... Kris Munroe (1977–81)

After high school, Cheryl Ladd made her way to Los Angeles with a small time band and almost immediately began landing television assignments. Her first was to provide a singing voice for the Saturday morning cartoon show *Josie and the Pussycats.* That seemed a waste of a very pretty face, and soon she was getting on-camera work as well.

For the cartoon work she used the name Cherie Moore; when she appeared on Ken Berry's 1972 summer show, it was Cheryl Stoppelmoor, her real name; later, when she married David Ladd (son of Alan Ladd), it became Cheryl Ladd. Cheryl appeared in an assortment of TV series episodes during the mid-1970s, as well as in a widely seen Max Factor commercial. However, it was her casting in *Charlie's Angels,* as the replacement for Farrah Fawcett-Majors, that made her a star. Later, she appeared in her own specials and in TV movies, including a 1983 film in which she portrayed Grace Kelly.

LADD, DIANE—actress
b: Nov 29, 1932, Meridian, Miss.

Alice (com) .... Belle Dupree (1980–81)

The original "Flo" in the movie version of *Alice Doesn't Live Here Anymore* (1975).

LADD, HANK—host
b: c. 1908, Chicago, Ill. d: Jun 9, 1982

The Arrow Show (var).........host (1949)
Waiting for the Break (var).....host (1950)

LADD, MARGARET—actress
b: Nov 8, Rhode Island

Falcon Crest (drama)
...............Emma Channing (1981–)

LAINE, FRANKIE—singer, actor
b: Mar 30, 1913, Chicago, Ill.

Frankie Laine Time (var) .... host (1955–56)
The Frankie Laine Show (var)... host (1957)
Rawhide (wes)....... sang theme (1959–66)
Rango (com) .... sang theme (1967)

LAIRD, MARVIN—orchestra leader

3 Girls 3 (var)......... orch. leader (1977)

LAIRE, JUDSON—actor, singer
b: Aug 3, 1902, New York City, r: Pleasantville, N.Y. d: Jul 5, 1979

Admiral Broadway Revue (var)
.... singer (1949)
Mama (com)
.... "Papa" Lars Hansen (1949–57)

LAKE, ARTHUR—actor
b: Apr 17, 1905, Corbin, Ky. d: Jan 9, 1987

Blondie (com)... Dagwood Bumstead (1957)

The star (with Penny Singleton) of the *Blondie* movies and radio series during the 1940s.

LAKE, JANET—actress
b: c. 1935, Norristown, Pa.

The Tycoon (com). Betty Franklin (1964–65)

LALLY, MICHAEL DAVID—actor

Berrengers (drama)....... Mr. Allen (1985)

LALLY, WILLIAM—actor

My Son Jeep (com) .. Tommy Clifford (1953)

LAMAS, LORENZO—actor
b: Jan 20, 1958, Los Angeles, Calif.

California Fever (adv)......... Rick (1979)
Secrets of Midland Heights (drama)
.... Burt Carroll (1980–81)
Falcon Crest (drama)
.... Lance Cumson (1981–)

The darkly handsome son of actors Fernando Lamas and Arlene Dahl has lived one of Hollywood's charmed lives—thus far. Raised in the lap of luxury by famous parents (his father remarried, to Esther Williams), Lorenzo began getting roles almost as soon as he said "Mother, I want to be a star...I mean an actor." "I heard you the first time," she replied.

Lorenzo appeared in a number of series episodes and pilots in the late '70s, some while still in his teens. Among them were *Switch, The Hardy Boys,* and *Whatever Happened to Dobie Gillis?* He then landed the regular role of the malt-shop operator in the lightweight teen series *California Fever.* His "Valentino look" seemed to fit soap operas better, however, and he was soon in *Secrets of Midland Heights,* followed by a starring role as Jane Wyman's playboy grandson in *Falcon Crest.* Meanwhile, it is said, he learned to act while on the job.

Nice work if you can get it.

LAMB, CLAUDIA—actress

Mary Hartman, Mary Hartman (com)
.... Heather Hartman (1976–78)

LAMBERT, GLORIA—singer
b: Jul 14, 1936, Worcester, Mass.

Sing Along with Mitch (var)
.... regular (1961–64)

LAMBERT, JACK—actor
b: 1920, Yonkers, N.Y.

Riverboat (adv) .... Joshua (1959–61)

LAMBERT, PAUL—actor
b: Aug 1, El Paso, Texas r: Kansas City.

Executive Suite (drama)
.... Tom Dalessio (1976–77)

LAMBIE, JOE—actor

Falcon Crest (drama)
.... Sheriff Robbins (1982–85)

LAMPERT, ZOHRA—actress

b: May 13, 1937, New York City, N.Y.

Girl with Something Extra (com)
.... Anne (1973–74)
Doctor's Hospital (drama)
.... Dr. Norah Purcell (1975–76)

Emmy Award: Best Supporting Actress in a Single Performance, for an episode of *Kojak* (1975)

LAMPLEY, JIM—sportscaster

b: Apr 8, 1949, Hendersonville, N.C.

Monday Night Baseball (sport)
.... sportscaster (1978–79)

LANCASTER, BURT—actor

b: Nov 2, 1913, New York City, N.Y.

Moses—The Lawgiver (drama)
.... Moses (1975)

This rugged Hollywood movie star has basically ignored television throughout most of his career. He has appeared in only a few TV movies and miniseries in his later years, including *Victory at Entebbe* (as Shimon Peres), *Marco Polo* (as Pope Gregory X), and *Moses—The Lawgiver* (as guess who).

LANCHESTER, ELSA—actress

b: Oct 28, 1902, Lewisham, London, England d: Dec 26, 1986

The John Forsythe Show (com)
.... Miss Margaret Culver (1965–66)
Nanny and the Professor (com)
.... Aunt Henrietta (1971)

LANDAU, MARTIN—actor

b: Jun 20, 1928*, Brooklyn, N.Y.

Mission: Impossible (drama)
.... Rollin Hand (1966–69)
Space 1999 (sci fi)
...... Commander John Koenig (1975–77)

As Rollin Hand on *Mission: Impossible*, Martin Landau seemed always to have a worried look on his face, as if he had just

*Some sources give 1931 or 1933.

made a mistake. Indeed, he seems to have made one: since he and his wife Barbara Bain quit that hit series in a huff over contract demands, further big roles have eluded him.

A onetime cartoonist for the New York *Daily News,* Landau broke into acting in the 1950s playing supporting roles in films *(North by Northwest, Pork Chop Hill)* and in quite a few television series episodes. His characters were often foreign and/or bizarre. On *The Twilight Zone* he played a Russian defector who was too clever for his intended assassin; on *I Spy* a not-so-clever mobster in Hong Kong, whom the mob wanted dead; on *Bonanza* a Spanish vaquero trapped in the desert with Little Joe; and on *The Wild Wild West* a mad general organizing a private army in order to overthrow society.

Mission: Impossible provided his first regular series role and made him a star as the team's slippery master of disguise. Unfortunately, he was never able to top that performance. Aside from the syndicated *Space 1999,* which despite two years on the air was essentially a flop, he has been seen mostly in occasional films of dubious quality, such as *The Harlem Globetrotters on Gilligan's Island* (as, of course, a mad scientist). A more recent effort, also in character, was *The Fall of the House of Usher* (1982) with Landau as the ill-fated Roderick Usher.

LANDER, DAVID L.—actor

b: Jun 22, 1947, Brooklyn, N.Y.

Laverne & Shirley (com)
Andrew "Squiggy" Squiggman (1976–83)

LANDER, DIANE—actress

House Calls (com)
.... Nurse Sally Bowman (1979–80)

LANDERS, AUDREY—actress

b: Jul 18, 1959, Philadelphia, Pa. r: Valley Cottage, N.Y.

Highcliffe Manor (com)
.... Wendy Sparkes (1979)
Dallas (drama)..... Afton Cooper (1981–84)

LANDERS, HARRY—actor

b: Apr 3, 1921, New York City, N.Y.

Ben Casey (drama)
.... Dr. Ted Hoffman (1961–68)

LANDERS, JUDY—actress

b: Oct 7, 1961, Philadelphia, Pa. r: Valley Cottage, N.Y.

Vega$ (drama) ..... Angie Turner (1978–79)
B.J. and the Bear (adv) ...... Stacks (1981)
Madame's Place (com)...... Sara Joy (1982)

Judy and Audrey Landers are the Sex Symbol Sisters, both blonde, petite, and renown for their pneumatic bosoms. Judy's first major TV break was the role of Wanda "The Bod" on an episode of What Really Happened to the Class of '65?

LANDESBERG, STEVE—actor

b: Nov 3, 1945, The Bronx, N.Y.

Dean Martin Presents Bobby Darin (var)
.... regular (1972)
Paul Sand in Friends and Lovers (com)
.... Fred Meyerbach (1974–75)
Barney Miller (com)
.... Det. Arthur Dietrich (1976–82)

Steve is a former stand-up comic, who specializes in rather offbeat characters, such as the crazed German psychiatrist he portrayed on the Bobby Darin summer show. He was a frequent guest on The Tonight Show (Johnny Carson liked his "slightly wacko" humor) before becoming famous as the amiable, droll Detective Dietrich on Barney Miller. It was a role, he says, in which he could simply play himself.

LANDIS, MONTE—actor

The Feather and Father Gang (drama)
.... Michael (1977)

LANDON, LESLIE—actress

b: Oct 11, 1962, Los Angeles, Calif.

Little House on the Prairie (adv)
.... Etta Plum (1982–83)

The daughter of Michael Landon, which might have had something to do with her getting this role.

LANDON, MICHAEL—actor

b: Oct 31, 1937, Forest Hills, N.Y. r: Collingswood, N.J.

Bonanza (wes)
.... Little Joe Cartwright (1959–73)

Little House on the Prairie (adv)
.... Charles Ingalls (1974–82)
Highway to Heaven (drama)
.... Jonathan Smith (1984–)

Emmy Award: Academy Founders Award (1982)

"I want people to laugh and cry, not just sit and stare at the TV," says Michael Landon. "Maybe I'm old-fashioned, but I think viewers are hungry for shows in which people say something meaningful."

The "something meaningful" Landon is referring to is good old-fashioned simple moral values—hearth, home, family, and hard work. Michael is perhaps the straightest straight arrow in Hollywood, both on-screen and off (the shows he produces run like clockwork, are never over budget, and are always delivered on time). His sentimental vision of a better world comes, in part, from his own background. He was born Eugene Orowitz, the son of an East Coast movie studio publicist, and raised in a tension-filled home in a white Protestant suburb that, he says, wasn't very friendly to a skinny little Jewish kid. He finally found something he could excel at—javelin throwing—and moved to Los Angeles when he got an athletic scholarship from the University of Southern California. A torn ligament ended his sports career, but, beginning around 1956, he soon found himself picking up small roles in movies and television shows.

The movies were strictly B-grade—he will never live down his starring role in the camp classic I Was a Teenage Werewolf—but the television work was more varied, ranging from Wire Service and DuPont Theater to a spate of westerns, including The Texan, Wanted Dead or Alive, and several appearances on Tales of Wells Fargo. A part in the pilot telecast of The Restless Gun in early 1957 caught the eye of producer David Dortort, who later began casting a new series called Bonanza. Michael, 21, long-haired and baby-faced, was signed as Little Joe and went on to an incredible 14-year run on one of the most popular series in television history.

By the time it finally ended, Michael was in his midthirties, still long-haired and baby-faced, but with rapidly expanding credentials. He had written and directed episodes during Bonanza's final years, and in

1974 he created a new series of his own, *Little House on the Prairie,* which became one of the major hits of the 1970s. Even more clearly than *Bonanza,* it espoused Michael's traditional American values. He followed this remarkable run with yet another hit, *Highway to Heaven,* giving him a record of more than 25 years in which he was almost continuously on view in three hit series. He also produced, wrote and/or directed TV movies and the series *Father Murphy.* Two of his movies have been based on incidents in his own life: *The Loneliest Runner* and *Sam's Son.*

LANDSBERG, DAVID—actor

C.P.O. Sharkey (com).... Skolnick (1976–78)

LANDSBURG, VALERIE—actress
b: Aug 12, New York City, N.Y.

Fame (drama).... Doris Schwartz (1982–85)
All Is Forgiven (com). Lorraine Elder (1986)

The daughter of television producer Alan Landsburg (*That's Incredible, Gimme A Break,* etc.), who, she says, "did everything he could to dissuade me from an entertainment career."

LANE, ABBE—singer
b: Dec 14, 1932, Brooklyn, N.Y.

The Xavier Cugat Show (music)
.... regular (1957)

The wife of Latin bandleader Xavier Cugat, and seen almost exclusively in appearances with him.

LANE, ALLAN "ROCKY"—actor
b: Sep 22, 1901*, Mishawaka, Ind. d: Oct 24, 1973

Red Ryder (wes) .... Red Ryder (1956)
Mr. Ed (com)..... voice of Mr. Ed (1961–66)

LANE, CHARLES—actor
b: 1899, San Francisco, Calif.

Dear Phoebe (com).. Mr. Fosdick (1954–55)
The Lucy Show (com)
.... Mr. Barnsdahl (1962–63)
Petticoat Junction (com)
.... Homer Bedloe (1963–68)

*Some sources give 1904.

490

The Pruitts of Southampton (com)
.... Maxwell (1966–67)
Karen (com) .... Dale Busch (1975)

LANE, DON—actor, host
r: New York City, N.Y.

The Ken Berry "Wow" Show (var)
.... regular (1972)

LANE, DORIS—

The Fashion Story (misc)
.... regular (1948–49)

LANE, KEN—pianist, choral director
b: Brooklyn, N.Y.

The Dean Martin Show (var)
.... pianist (1965–74)

Dean's longtime accompanist (beginning in 1956), and also the composer of one of his biggest hits, "Everybody Loves Somebody."

LANE, NANCY—actress
b: Jun 16, Passaic, N.J. r: Clifton, N.J.

Rhoda (com).......... Tina Molinari (1978)
Angie (com)...... Mary Katherine (1979–80)
The Duck Factory (com)
.... Andrea Lewin (1984)

LANE, NATHAN—actor
b: Feb 3, Jersey City, N.J.

One of the Boys (com)
.... Jonathan Burns (1982)

LANE, RUSTY—actor

Crime with Father (police)
.... Capt. Jim Riland (1951–52)
Jimmy Hughes, Rookie Cop (police)
.... Insp. Ferguson (1953)
Operation Neptune (sci fi)
.... Admiral Bigelow (1953)

LANE, SARA—actress
b: Mar 12, 1949, New York City, N.Y.

The Virginian (wes)
.... Elizabeth Grainger (1966–67)

LANE, SCOTT—juvenile actor
b: Jan 27, 1951, New York City, N.Y.

McKeever & the Colonel (com)
.... cadet Gary McKeever (1962–63)

LANEUVILLE, ERIC—black actor, director
b: Jul 14, 1952, New Orleans, La.

Room 222 (drama)......... Larry (1971–73)
The Cop and the Kid (com)
.... Mouse (1975–76)
St. Elsewhere (drama)
.... orderly Luther Hawkins (1982–)

LANG, HOWARD—actor

The Adventures of Sir Francis Drake (adv)
.... Grenville (1962)
The Winds of War (drama)
.... Winston Churchill (1983)

LANG, PERRY—actor

Bay City Blues (drama)
.... Frenchy Nuckles (1983)

LANG, SHIRLEY—actress

AfterMASH (com).. Nurse Crown (1983–84)

LANG, STEPHEN—actor
b: New York City, N.Y.

Crime Story (police)
.... atty. David Abrams (1986–)

LANGAN, GLENN—actor
b: Jul 8, 1917, Denver, Colo.

Boss Lady (com) ...... Jeff Standish (1952)

LANGARD, JANET—actress

The Donna Reed Show (com)
.... Karen Holmby (1964–65)

LANGDON, SUE ANE—actress
b: Mar 8, 1936, Paterson, N.J., r: Kingsville, Texas

Bachelor Father (com)
.... Kitty Marsh (1959–61)
The Jackie Gleason Show (var)
.... regular (1962–63)
Arnie (com)......... Lillian Nuvo (1970–72)
Grandpa Goes to Washington (com)
.... Rosie Kelley (1978–79)
When the Whistle Blows (com)
.... Darlene Ridgeway (1980)

LANGE, ANN—actress

Comedy Zone (com)........ regular (1984)

LANGE, HOPE—actress
b: Nov 28, 1931, Redding Ridge, Conn.

Back That Fact (aud par) .. assistant (1953)
The Ghost and Mrs. Muir (com)
.... Mrs. Carolyn Muir (1968–70)
The New Dick Van Dyke Show (com)
.... Jenny Preston (1971–74)

Emmy Awards: Best Actress in a Comedy Series, for The Ghost and Mrs. Muir (1969, 1970)

This attractive middle-aged blonde is best known to television viewers for two light situation comedies of the late '60s and early '70s, The Ghost and Mrs. Muir (as Mrs. Muir) and The New Dick Van Dyke Show (as Dick's wife). She had a considerable career in TV and movies before that, however.

Hope was the daughter of a musician and an actress and made her stage debut at the age of 12 in the Pulitzer Prize–winning play The Patriots (1943). Her parents felt she should finish her education before continuing with an acting career, so she then left show business until 1950 when, as a college student in New York, she began to do commercials and small parts on live TV. Among other things, she was a dancer on The Jackie Gleason Show and an assistant on the short-lived quiz program Back That Fact.

Better television roles followed in the late 1950s, including several on Playhouse 90 dramas. An appearance in the acclaimed play "Snap Finger Creek" on Kraft Television Theatre in 1956 attracted the attention of producer Buddy Adler, who was then casting the film Bus Stop; this led to a most auspicious movie debut for Hope as the waitress Emma. Thereafter she appeared mostly in movies (The Young Lovers, Peyton Place, etc.), until returning to TV for her two sitcoms. She has since made quite a few TV movies, running the gamut from classy (That Certain Summer) to pretentious (Beulah Land) to lightweight entertainment (a Love Boat film).

LANGE, JIM—host
b: Aug 15, St. Paul, Minn.

The Dating Game (quiz) ..... host (1966–70)
The Dating Game (quiz) ..... host (1973–74)
The Dating Game (quiz) ..... host (1977–80)

$100,000 Name That Tune (quiz)
.... emcee (1984–85)

LANGE, TED—black actor, director
b: Jan 5, 1947, Oakland, Calif.

That's My Mama (com).... Junior (1974–75)
Mr. T and Tina (com) ...... Harvard (1976)
The Love Boat (com)
... bartender Isaac Washington (1977–86)

LANGFORD, FRANCES—singer
b: Apr 4, 1914, Lakeland, Fla.

Star Time (var) .... regular (1950–51)

A beautiful and popular singer of the '30s and '40s who often appeared on radio and on tour with Bob Hope. She was also known on radio and early television for her comedy sketches with Don Ameche, called "The Bickersons"; she appeared with Ameche in a prime time series in 1950–51 and a daytime show in 1951–52. Her last major TV work was in a pair of prime time specials in 1959 and 1960.

Frances was married from 1938–55 to actor Jon Hall *(Ramar of the Jungle)*. In 1955 she wed millionaire outboard-motor tycoon Ralph Evinrude and by the '60s she had retired to a very plush life indeed, singing only occasionally for wealthy guests at their large resort/estate in Jensen Beach, Florida.

LANGLAND, LIANE—actress
b: Colorado

Master of the Game (drama)
..... Eve and Alexandra Blackwell (1984)

LANGRISHE, CAROLINE—actress

Q.E.D. (adv) .... Jenny Martin (1982)

LANGSTON, MURRAY—comedian

The Sonny and Cher Comedy Hour (var)
.... regular (1971–74)
The Sonny Comedy Revue (var)
.... regular (1974)
The $1.98 Beauty Show (com)
.... the Unknown Comic (1978–80)

LANGTON, PAUL—actor
b: Apr 17, 1913, Salt Lake City, Utah d: Apr 15, 1980

Peyton Place (drama)
.... Leslie Harrington (1964–68)

LANIER, SUSAN—actress

Tony Orlando and Dawn (var)
.... regular (1976)
Szysznyk (com) ..... Sandi Chandler (1977)

LANIN, JAY—actor

Follow the Sun (adv)
.... Lt. Frank Roper (1961–62)

LANKFORD, KIM—actress
b: Jun 14, Montebello, Calif. r: Orange County, Calif.

The Waverly Wonders (com)
.... Connie Rafkin (1978)
Knots Landing (drama)
.... Ginger Ward (1979–83)

LANNOM, LES—actor

Harry-O (drama) .. Lester Hodges (1975–76)
Centennial (drama)... Bufe Coker (1978–79)
The Chisholms (wes) . Jeremy O'Neal (1980)

LANSBURY, ANGELA—actress
b: Oct 16, 1925, London, England

Murder, She Wrote (drama)
.... Jessica Beatrice Fletcher (1984–)

Angela Lansbury seems to have played her career backward. In her 20's and 30's, looking much more mature than her years, she was a Hollywood character actress, almost always cast in bitchy, domineering, "older" roles. In her forties, at a time when many formerly youthful stars begin to turn to character parts, she suddenly burst forth as an energetic musical-comedy star on Broadway. In her sixties she was starring in a top-rated detective show on television, a medium that generally prefers young people in such roles.

Angela was born in England, the daughter of an actress, and came to the U.S. in 1940 to escape the German blitz. She broke into movies in 1943 and immediately attracted attention as the disagreeable little housemaid in *Gaslight* (1943). Many similar roles followed. She appeared frequently on television in the '50s, mostly in dramatic productions on playhouse series such as *Robert Montgomery Presents,*

Stage 7, and *Playhouse 90.* Her TV work tapered off in the '60s, however, as she began to concentrate on Broadway. She scored a tremendous personal triumph there—and finally altered the kind of roles she could get—playing the title role in the hit musical *Mame* in 1966. She won a Tony Award for this lively portrayal, and then three more in later years for *Dear World, Gypsy,* and *Sweeney Todd.*

Since Angela was so well-established on Broadway, it came as a surprise to many when, in the early '80s, she began to work in television again. First she was in the TV movie *Little Gloria, Happy at Last* (1982); this was followed by additional TV films and then the series *Murder, She Wrote.* Does she regret not having started her career in more traditional leading lady roles? "Well, I suppose if I had gotten the guy I might have been one of those actresses whose careers came and went so fast, poor dears. I was never the sex symbol or the glamour queen . . . I always felt 29. I felt 29 for years and years. Now I feel 40."

LANSING, JOI—actress

b: Apr 6, 1928, Salt Lake City, Utah d: Aug 7, 1972

The Bob Cummings Show (com)
. . . . Shirley Swanson (1956–59)
Klondike (adv) . . . . Goldie (1960–61)

Sexy, busty blonde who died relatively young, of cancer.

LANSING, ROBERT—actor

b: Jun 5, 1928, San Diego, Calif.

87th Precinct (police)
. . . . Det. Steve Carella (1961–62)
Twelve O'Clock High (drama)
. . . . . . Brig. Gen. Frank Savage (1964–65)
The Man Who Never Was (drama)
. . . . Peter Murphy (1966–67)
The Man Who Never Was (drama)
. . . . Mark Wainwright (1966–67)
Automan (police) . . Lt. Jack Curtis (1983–84)
The Equalizer (drama) . . . . . Control (1985–)

This tough, rather suspicious-looking leading man appeared a great deal on television from the mid-1950s to the mid-1970s and occasionally thereafter. He began on Broadway in the early '50s (in *Stalag 17*) and received rave notices a few years later

as the psychiatrist in Tennessee Williams' *Suddenly Last Summer* (1958). However, he didn't get the role in the movie—Montgomery Clift did.

Lansing's salad days were on TV in the '60s. After frequent appearances on *The U.S. Steel Hour* and other dramatic playhouses, he was cast as one of the hardnosed detectives on *87th Precinct;* then as the lead in the war drama *Twelve O'Clock High* (he got shot down at the beginning of the second season); and then in his own espionage series, *The Man Who Never Was.* In later years he appeared mostly in episodes of various other series and in a few TV movies. In 1983 he turned up as the cynical older detective on *Automan.*

LANSON, SNOOKY—singer

b: Mar 27, 1914*, Memphis, Tenn.

Your Hit Parade (music) . vocalist (1950–57)
Chevrolet on Broadway (music)
. . . . host (1956)
Five Star Jubilee (var) . . . . host (1961)

It is possible that if Snooky Lanson had used his real first name—Roy—during his years in the limelight, he wouldn't be as well-remembered today. Certainly, a lot of other pleasant, undistinguished TV singers of the 1950s came and went without leaving a trace.

However, he didn't, and he is. He is remembered even though he has had very little national exposure in the years since he sang the top tunes every week for a nationwide audience. Snooky made TV guest appearances and played club dates in the late '50s and '60s and had a short run on the summer country-music show *Five Star Jubilee* in 1961. In 1962 he moved to Atlanta and he has lived in the Southeast ever since, doing occasional club dates and local television shows. As of the mid-1970s his regular employment was selling automobiles for a Ford dealership in Nashville.

The nickname that brought him fame, incidentally, was taken by his mother from a 1913 baby-talk song written by Irving Berlin—"Snooky Ookums."

LAPLACA, ALISON—actress

Suzanne Pleshette Is Maggie Briggs (com)
. . . . Melanie Bitterman (1984)

*Some sources give 1919.

LARCH, JOHN—actor
b: 1924, Salem, Mass. r: Brooklyn, N.Y.

Arrest and Trial (drama)
.... Dep. D.A. Jerry Miller (1963–64)
Convoy (drama)
.... merchant capt. Ben Foster (1965)

LARGE, DON—choral director
b: Nov 15, 1909, Canada

Wayne King (music)...... chorus (1949–52)

LARKIN, DICK—

The Little Revue (music).. regular (1949–50)

LARKIN, JOHN—actor
b: Apr 11, 1912, Oakland, Calif. d: Jan 29, 1965

Saints and Sinners (drama)
.... Mark Grainger (1962–63)
Twelve O'Clock High (drama)
.... Maj. Gen. Wiley Crowe (1964–65)

Larkin played Perry Mason on radio in the late '40s and '50s and from 1955–62 originated the counterpart role of detective Mike Karr on the daytime soap opera *The Edge of Night* (this was one of two series spun off to television from the radio *Perry Mason;* the other, of course, was the nighttime series called *Perry Mason*). Larkin died suddenly during the run of his second prime time series, *Twelve O'Clock High.*

LARKIN, SHEILA—actress
b: 1944, Brooklyn, N.Y.

Storefront Lawyers (drama)
.... Deborah Sullivan (1970–71)

LAROCHE, MARY—actress
b: Rochester, N.Y.

Karen (com) .... Barbara Scott (1964–65)

LAROSA, JULIUS—singer, actor
b: Jan 2, 1930, Brooklyn, N.Y.

Arthur Godfrey and His Friends (var)
.... singer (1952–53)
Let's Dance (music) .... regular (1954)
TV's Top Tunes (music) .... host (1955)
The Julius La Rosa Show (music)
.... host (1955)
The Julius La Rosa Show (var)
.... host (1956–57)

Julius LaRosa is probably best-remembered today as the victim of the most famous firing in television history—on the air, by superstar Arthur Godfrey, who later commented that Julie's sin had been that he "lacked humility" (Godfrey never lived that one down).

Godfrey had certainly made Julie a star. The young singer was an enlisted man in the navy when Godfrey heard him perform in a service show in Florida. Upon his discharge in 1951, Julie was given a spot on Godfrey's daytime and nighttime shows, which were then the hottest thing in television. A fresh-scrubbed young lad with a clear, strong voice, he became famous overnight, and when Godfrey dumped him two years later, he took on the air of a folk hero as well. In public, at least, he was all humility, and he would never say an unkind word about his former boss. For a few years Julie was all over television, commanded top money in personal appearances, and sold millions of records. Gradually, the novelty wore off and the public turned its attention elsewhere (and to other, more raucous kinds of music). By the '60s Julie was working as a disc jockey in New York. He occasionally acted and in 1980 played a short but well-received role on the daytime serial *Another World,* for which he received an Emmy Award nomination.

LARRAIN, MICHAEL—actor

Matt Lincoln (drama)...... Kevin (1970–71)

LARROQUETTE, JOHN—actor
b: Nov 25, 1947, New Orleans, La.

Doctors' Hospital (drama)
.... Dr. Paul Herman (1975–76)
Baa Baa Black Sheep (drama)
.... Lt. Bob Anderson (1976–78)
Night Court (com)
.... Asst. D.A. Dan Fielding (1984–)

Emmy Award: Best Supporting Actor in a Comedy Series, for *Night Court* (1985, 1986)

LARSEN, KEITH—actor
b: Jun 17, 1925, Salt Lake City, Utah

The Hunter (drama) .... Bart Adams (1954)
Brave Eagle (wes)... Brave Eagle (1955–56)

Northwest Passage (adv)
.... Maj. Robert Rogers (1958–59)
The Aquanauts (Malibu Run) (adv)
.... Drake Andrews (1960–61)

LARSEN, LARRY—actor
b: c. 1940

Donny and Marie (var) ... regular (1976–79)

LARSON, DARRELL—actor

Morningstar/Eveningstar (drama)
.... Bob Lane (1986)

LARSON, DENNIS—juvenile actor
b: c. 1963, Sacramento, Calif.

The Jimmy Stewart Show (com)
.... Teddy Howard (1971–72)

LARSON, JACK—actor
b: Feb 8, 1933, Los Angeles, Calif.

The Adventures of Superman (adv)
.... Jimmy Olsen (1951–57)

LA RUE, JACK—actor
b: May 3, 1900*, New York City, N.Y. d: Jan 11, 1984

Lights Out (drama) ...... narrator (1949–50)

LA RUE, LASH—cowboy actor
b: Jun 14, 1917, Gretna, La.

Lash of the West (wes)
.... Marshal Lash La Rue (1952–53)
The Life and Legend of Wyatt Earp (wes)
.... Sheriff Johnny Behan (1959)

This was surely one of the most unusual B-movie cowboy stars of the late '40s, and also one who has followed a strange odyssey in his later years.

The first thing moviegoers noticed was that he bore a striking resemblance to Humphrey Bogart, both in appearance and in his somewhat gruff manner. Then too, he didn't act much like the clean-cut western heroes of the day—he dressed all in black (the villain's garb) and nailed the bad guys with a long bullwhip, which he wielded with a fearsome crack. As with Bogart, there was something fascinating about this man.

Lash's day in the western sun was brief,

*Some sources give 1902.

lasting only from 1945 until the early '50s. *Lash of the West* was a syndicated series consisting of edited versions of his feature films, introduced by Lash himself. A short stint on *Wyatt Earp* was his only other major television exposure. For a time in the early '50s he hit the rodeo and carnival circuit, but his life soon entered rough times with numerous failed marriages (he says 10), the government after him for back taxes, and several well-publicized arrests —one for receiving stolen property, another for drugs, another for vagrancy. At one point he was reported to be selling furniture in Atlanta. In the mid-1960s he declared he had seen the error of his ways and became a Bible-thumping evangelist. However, after a few years he was once again in trouble with the law and embittered about the life that fate had dealt him. His only movie in later years—and a notorious one at that—was *Hard on the Trail*, a porno film in which Lash, however, kept his clothes on. He could still be seen in the '80s, driving around Hollywood in an old black hearse.

LARUSSA, ADRIENNE—actress

Centennial (drama)...... Clemma (1978–79)

LASCOE, HENRY—actor
b: c. 1914 d: 1964

The Ernie Kovacs Show (var)
.... regular (1956)

LASKEY, KATHLEEN—actress

Check It Out (com)....... Marlene (1985–)

LASKY, ZANE—actor

The Tony Randall Show (com)
.... Mario Lanza (1976–78)
The Last Resort (com)
.... Duane Kaminsky (1979–80)
Making the Grade (com)
.... Anton Zemeckis (1982)

LASSER, LOUISE—actress
b: Apr 11, 1939, New York City, N.Y.

Mary Hartman, Mary Hartman (com)
.... Mary Hartman (1976–77)
It's a Living (com)
.... Maggie McBurney (1981–82)

Even television's flops can sometimes make an actor famous. The syndicated *Mary Hartman, Mary Hartman* was not even seen in much of the country and was certainly not a ratings hit where it was; compared to the five-to-20 year runs of the networks' top series, it was barely a flash in the TV firmament. Yet it will long be remembered as a truly nutty parody of soap operas, while Louise Lasser, as its pigtailed, spaced-out heroine, will always be identified as Mary.

Louise had, shall we say, a history of this sort of role. The daughter of famed tax expert S. Jay Lasser, she had started life conventionally enough, entering college as a political science major. However, acting got the best of her, and in the early '60s she won a part in Elaine May's improvisational revue *The Third Ear* in New York. More stage roles followed, as well as TV commercials and movies—particularly the early and offbeat films of Woody Allen. Louise was in *What's New Pussycat, What's Up Tiger Lily, Bananas* and others; her later films have included *Everything You Always Wanted to Know About Sex (but Were Afraid to Ask)* and *In God We Trust (or, Gimme That Prime Time Religion)*. She was married to Woody Allen from 1966–70.

Louise had been making sporadic appearances on television for about ten years in both series episodes *(Love, American Style, The Bob Newhart Show)* and TV movies *(Coffee, Tea or Me?)* when Norman Lear asked her to star in his projected soap-opera spoof, *Mary Hartman*. Though she was on the show for only a little over a year, Louise found the pace exhausting—five episodes a week, 325 in all. In 1977 she quit to recuperate (rumors were that she was becoming so identified with the role she thought she really *was* Mary Hartman); she also had to deal with an arrest for cocaine possession. She subsequently wrote and starred in the TV movie *Just Me and You*, about a dippy, talkative New Yorker on a cross-country trip, and in several stage plays, including the offbeat *A Coupla White Chicks Sitting Around Talking*. A more conventional role was that of a waitress in the 1981 comedy *Making a Living*. She was presented there as the "new" Louise Lasser, but audiences immediately recognized who it was—Mary Hartman!

LASTARZA, ROLAND—actor, prizefighter

The Gallant Men (drama)
.... Pvt. Ernie Lucavich (1962–63)

LATE, JASON—actor

Fathers and Sons (com)
.... Lanny Landau (1986)

LATHAM, LOUISE—actress

Sara (wes).......... Martha Higgins (1976)
The Contender (drama)
.... Alma Captor (1980)
Scruples (drama)
................,.... Mary Ann Evans (1980)

LATORRA, TONY—juvenile actor

9 to 5 (com)................. Tommy (1983)

LA TORRE, TONY—juvenile actor

Cagney & Lacey (police)
.... Harvey Lacey, Jr. (1982–)

LAU, WESLEY—actor

b: c. 1921, Sheboygan, Wis. d: Aug 30, 1984

Perry Mason (drama)
.... Lt. Anderson (1961–65)

LAUGHLIN, JOHN—actor

b: Apr 3, Memphis, Tenn.

The White Shadow (drama)
.... Paddy Falahey (1980–81)

LAUHER, BOBBY—actor

Take a Good Look (quiz) . regular (1959–61)

LAUNER, JOHN—actor

Court of Last Resort (drama)
.... Marshall Houts (1957–58)

LAUREN, TAMMY—juvenile actress

b: Nov 16, 1969, San Diego, Calif.

Who's Watching the Kids? (com)
.... Melissa Turner (1978)
Angie (com)................. Hillary (1979)
Out of the Blue (com)
.... Stacey Richards (1979)
The Best Times (drama)
.... Giselle Kraft (1985)

Morningstar/Eveningstar (drama)
.... Lisa Thurston (1986)

LAURIE, JOE, JR.—comedian
b: 1892 d: Apr 19, 1954

Can You Top This? (com)
.... panelist (1950–51)

LAURIE, PIPER—actress
b: Jan 22, 1932, Detroit, Mich.

Skag (drama) .... Jo Skagska (1980)
The Thorn Birds (drama)
.... Anne Mueller (1983)

LAUTER, ED—actor
b: Oct 30, 1940, Long Beach, N.Y.

B.J. and the Bear (adv)
.... Sheriff Cain (1979–80)

LAUTER, HARRY—actor
b: Jun 19, 1914*, White Plains, N.Y. r: Colorado

Waterfront (adv) ..... Jim Herrick (1953–56)
Tales of the Texas Rangers (wes)
.... Ranger Clay Morgan (1958–59)

LAVALLE, PAUL—band leader
b: Sep 6, 1908, Beacon, N.Y.

Cities Service Band of America (music)
.... conductor (1949–50)

LAVIN, LINDA—actress
b: Oct 15, 1937, Portland, Me.

Barney Miller (com)
.... Det. Janice Wentworth (1975–76)
Alice (com) .... Alice Hyatt (1976–85)

Linda Lavin was primarily a New York stage actress during the 1960s, appearing in such productions as Jules Feiffer's *Little Murders* and the musical *It's a Bird—It's a Plane—It's Superman*. She did relatively little television work until she took the role of the female detective in the first season of *Barney Miller*. She is best known as the resourceful waitress Alice, on *Alice*.

LAWFORD, PETER—actor
b: Sep 7, 1923, London, England d: Dec 24, 1984

*Some sources give 1920.

Dear Phoebe (com) .. Bill Hastings (1954–55)
The Thin Man (drama)
.... Nick Charles (1957–59)

This witty and well-connected English film star (he was married to President Kennedy's sister Pat from 1954–66) starred in two series and dozens of dramatic productions on television in the '50s and '60s. He was also seen as Doris Day's romantic interest in occasional appearances on *The Doris Day Show* from 1971–73.

LAWLOR, JOHN—actor

Phyllis (com)..... Leonard Marsh (1976–77)
The Facts of Life (com)
.... Steven Bradley (1979–80)

LAWRENCE, BILL—newsman
b: c. 1915, Lincoln, Neb. d: Mar 2, 1972

ABC Evening News (news)
.... anchorman (1960)

Emmy Award: Trustee's Award (1972)

LAWRENCE, BILL—singer
b: 1926, East St. Louis, Ill.

Arthur Godfrey and His Friends (var)
.... singer (1949–50)

LAWRENCE, CAROL—actress, singer
b: Sep 5, 1934, Melrose Park, Ill.

The Dean Martin Summer Show (var)
.... regular (1967)

This Broadway star *(West Side Story)* was married to singer Robert Goulet. She has appeared on television periodically since the late 1950s, on series ranging from *Run for Your Life* to *The Love Boat*.

LAWRENCE, DAVID AND GREG—juvenile actors

Bewitched (com) . Adam Stephens (1971–72)

LAWRENCE, ELLIOT—orchestra leader
b: Feb 14, 1925, Philadelphia, Pa.

Guide Right (var).... orch. leader (1952–53)
The Red Buttons Show (var)
.... orch. leader (1952–55)
Melody Street (music) .... host (1953)
Stars on Parade (var)
.... orch. leader (1953–54)

Air Time '57 (var)... orch. leader (1956–57)
ABC's Nightlife (talk)... orch. leader (1965)
Saturday Night Live with Howard Cosell (var)............... orch. leader (1975–76)

Emmy Awards: Best Musical Direction for a Variety Show, for *'S Wonderful, 'S Marvelous, 'S Gershwin* (1972); and for *Night of 100 Stars* (1982); Best Composer/Director for a Children's Program, for the *ABC Afterschool Special*'s "The Unforgiveable Secret" (1982) and "Sometimes I Don't Love My Mother" (1983); Best Composition for a Daytime Program, for *The Edge of Night* (1985).

LAWRENCE, JOEY—juvenile actor
b: Apr 20, 1976, Montgomery, Pa.

Gimme a Break (com)
.... Joey Donovan (1983–)

LAWRENCE, MARK—pianist
b: Jan 14, 1921, Washington, D.C.

Alice Pearce (var).......... pianist (1949)

LAWRENCE, MARY—actress

The Bob Cummings Show (com)
.... Ruth Helm (1956–58)
Casey Jones (adv).... Alice Jones (1957–58)

LAWRENCE, MATTHEW—juvenile actor
b: Feb 11, 1980, Montgomery, Pa.

Sara (com)........... Jesse Webber (1985)
Gimme a Break (com)
.... Matthew Donovan (1986–)

The mop-topped younger brother of Joey Lawrence, with whom he appeared on *Gimme a Break.* He began by doing pudding commercials with Bill Cosby.

LAWRENCE, STEVE—singer
b: Jul 8, 1935, Brooklyn, N.Y.

Tonight (talk) .... regular (1954–57)
The Steve Lawrence-Eydie Gorme Show (var)
.... cohost (1958)
The Steve Lawrence Show (var)
.... host (1965)
Foul-Ups, Bleeps & Blunders (com)
.... host (1984–85)

Emmy Award: costar and Producer, Best Music Program, for *Steve and Eydie Celebrate Irving Berlin* (1979)

Steve got his start as a winner on *Arthur Godfrey's Talent Scouts* in 1952. He has been married since 1957 to singer Eydie Gorme.

LAWRENCE, VICKI—actress, singer
b: Mar 26, 1949, Inglewood, Calif.

The Carol Burnett Show (var)
.... regular (1967–79)
The Jimmie Rodgers Show (var)
.... regular (1969)
Mama's Family (com)
.... Mama (Thelma) Harper (1983–)

Emmy Award: Best Supporting Actress in a Variety Show, for *The Carol Burnett Show* (1976)

Carol Burnett's young look-alike sidekick differentiated herself from her mentor by donning a gray wig and outrageous padding and playing feisty old "Mama"— about as far from her natural kid-sister look as she could get.

Vicki was a show business veteran by the time she was 20. She joined the Young Americans singing group at 15 and appeared with them on television and on tour for several years in the mid-1960s. One day a reporter wrote an article pointing out Vicki's striking resemblance to comedy star Carol Burnett; Vicki sent the piece to Burnett, along with a fan letter. To her surprise, she received a phone call from the star, who—unknown to Vicki—was looking for an actress to play her younger sister on television. Vicki got the part and, at age 18, with no acting training, was thrust into the high-powered world of series TV.

The adjustment was not easy, but Carol and the rest of the cast helped her along, and in time "the kid" blossomed into a first-class comedy talent—particularly in the "Eunice" sketches, in which she played Carol's Mama. A further boost to Vicki's career came in 1973 when she recorded a story-song written by her husband, Bobby Russell. "The Night the Lights Went Out in Georgia" was a freak number-one hit, though it led to no further musical success —and it cost Vicki her marriage. She subsequently remarried, to a makeup man on the Burnett show staff.

Vicki appeared on other series, did some stage work, and after the *Burnett* series ended went on to star in her own series based on the Eunice sketches, called *Mama's Family*. Carol Burnett was a frequent and approving guest star. "We started out as mother-daughter," Carol told *TV Guide;* "we soon matured to big sis–little sis. Now we're peers, because Vicki's a grown-up woman. Besides, I don't think anybody owes their career to anyone. People can open doors for you, but unless you can walk through, you're not going to last. Vicki might owe me her break, just as I feel I owe my break to Garry Moore. But Vicki owes her career to Vicki."

LAWS, SAM—black actor

The Practice (com) . . . . Nate (1976–77)

LAWSON, LINDA—actress
b: Jan 11, 1936, Ann Arbor, Mich.

Adventures in Paradise (adv)
. . . . Renee (1960–61)
Don't Call Me Charlie (com)
. . . . Pat Perry (1962–63)

LAWSON, MICHAEL—actor

The O'Neills (drama)
. . . . Eddie O'Neill (1949–50)

LAWSON, RICHARD—black actor
b: Mar 7, Loma Linda, Calif.

Chicago Story (drama)
. . . . Det. O. Z. Tate (1982)

LAY, RODNEY—

Hee Haw (var) . . . . regular (1980–)

LAYTON, GEORGE—actor
b: 1943

Doctor in the House (com)
. . . . Paul Collier (1970–73)

LAZARUS, BILL—actor
b: Apr 18, Washington, D.C.

Calucci's Department (com)
. . . . Woods (1973)
The Bad News Bears (com)
. . . . Frosty (1979–80)

LEACH, BRITT—actor
b: Jul 18, 1938, Gadsen, Ala.

Spencer's Pilots (adv)
. . . . Mickey Wiggins (1976)

LEACH, ROBIN—host, producer
b: c.1941 London, England

Lifestyles of the Rich and Famous (mag)
. . . . host (1984–)

LEACHMAN, CLORIS—actress
b: Apr 30, 1926, Des Moines, Iowa

Hold It Please (quiz) . . . . regular (1949)
Charlie Wild, Private Detective (drama)
. . . . Effie Perrine (1950–52)
Bob and Ray (var) . . . . regular (1952)
Lassie (adv) . . . . Ruth Martin (1957–58)
The Mary Tyler Moore Show (com)
. . . . Phyllis Lindstrom (1970–75)
Phyllis (com) . . . Phyllis Lindstrom (1975–77)
Backstairs at the White House (drama)
. . . . Mrs. Jaffray (1979)
The Facts of Life (com)
. . . . Beverly Ann Stickle (1986–)

Emmy Awards: Best Actress in a Single Performance, for the TV movie *A Brand New Life* (1973); Best Supporting Actress in a Comedy, for *The Mary Tyler Moore Show* (1974, 1975); Best Supporting Actress in a Variety Show, for an appearance on *Cher* (1975); Best Performer on a Children's Program, for the *ABC Afterschool Special* "The Woman Who Willed a Miracle" (1983); Best Performance in a Variety Show for "The Screen Actors' Guild 50th Anniversary Celebration" (1984)

Cloris Leachman has long been one of television's busiest actresses, active since the early days of the medium. She is now known for her gaunt, rather worried look (either comic or serious); it may come as a surprise to learn that she was once a national beauty queen.

Cloris was on local radio as a teenager in the 1940s and studied drama at Northwestern University on an Edgar Bergen scholarship. Along the way she won the Miss Chicago beauty title, bringing her to Atlantic City, where she was a runner-up in the 1946 Miss America Pageant. The exposure brought her stage work in New York and the chance to break into the new medium of live television; New York was then America's TV capital. Cloris did anything and everything. Her earliest regular role (for three weeks) was on a 1949 quiz

499

show, *Hold It Please,* acting out the questions for the contestants. She was the gal Friday on the early detective series *Charlie Wild,* a repertory player on *The Bob and Ray Show,* and—perhaps best remembered because of its many reruns—a hayseed housewife for a season on *Lassie* (a role she disliked). In addition, she appeared on a wide range of dramatic showcases, including *Philco Playhouse, Zane Grey Theatre,* and *Alfred Hitchcock Presents.* In the 1960s she was seen on scores of leading dramatic shows and some comedies, among them *The Untouchables, The Virginian, The Donna Reed Show,* and *Dr. Kildare.*

It seemed that Cloris was becoming, in her forties, the archetypal TV guest player—a recognizable face but an unknown name. Then, in the 1970s, her career suddenly began to ignite. In 1970 she became a regular on *The Mary Tyler Moore Show* as busybody Phyllis, the apartment-building manager and resident flake. A year later, after a long but indifferent movie career, she electrified filmgoers and won an Academy Award for her portrayal of the desperate small-town housewife in *The Last Picture Show.* Suddenly very much in demand, Cloris turned increasingly to filmmaking, even while continuing to appear on *Mary Tyler Moore* and then on her own spin-off series, *Phyllis.* She has since played a wide range of TV-movie roles, in films that run the gamut from the superb to the ridiculous. Among them: Ernie Kovak's self-centered mother in *Between the Laughter,* a hard-edged beauty pageant trainer in *Miss All American Beauty,* Queen Hippolyte in *The New Original Wonder Woman,* and "the unsinkable" Molly Brown in *S.O.S. Titanic*—that last one a role she had played 22 years before on live TV, on *Telephone Time.* She had been in the business so long, the same roles were starting to come around a second time.

LEAHY, FRANK—football coach
b: Aug 27, 1908, O'Neill, Neb. d: Jun 21, 1973

The Frank Leahy Show (sport) .. host (1953)
The Ray Anthony Show (var)
.... sports features (1956–57)

The famous Notre Dame football coach.

LEAL, PETE—actor
Zorro and Son (com) .... Peasant (1983)

LEAMING, JIM—sportscaster
Sportsreel (sport)...... commentator (1954)

LEARNED, MICHAEL—actress
b: Apr 9, 1939, Washington, D.C.

The Waltons (drama)
.... Olivia Walton (1972–80)
Nurse (drama)
.... Nurse Mary Benjamin (1981–82)

Emmy Awards: Best Actress in a Drama Series, for *The Waltons* (1973, 1974, 1976); and for *Nurse* (1982)

A motherly actress with a stage background, who became active in television in the late 1960s and promptly went into the long-running role of Mother Walton on *The Waltons.* Even while appearing on that series she played frequent guest roles on episodes of other shows and appeared in TV movies, including *The Missiles of October* and *Little Mo.* She often seems to specialize in brave widows, as in the TV movie *Widow* and in her own series *Nurse.*

Her first name? She doesn't know why her parents named her that, she says. "Maybe they thought it was a good joke."

LEARY, BRIANNE—actress
b: Jul 28, Providence, R.I. r: Tucson, Ariz.

Baa Baa Black Sheep (drama)
.... Nurse Susan (1977–78)
CHiPs (police) .. Off. Sindy Cahill (1978–79)

LEBEAUF, SABRINA—black actress
b: Mar 21, New Orleans, La.

The Cosby Show (com)
.... Sondra Huxtable (1984–)

LEBOR, STANLEY—actor
Holocaust (drama) .... Zalman (1978)

LEDERER, SUZANNE—actress
b: Sep 29, Great Neck, N.Y.

Eischied (police) ... Carol Wright (1979–80)

LEDFORD, JUDY—actress
The A-Team (adv).......... Carla (1986–)

LEE, ANNA—actress
b: Jan 2, 1913*, Ightham, Kent, England

It's News to Me (quiz)... panelist (1951–54)
Scruples (drama).. Aunt Wilhelmina (1980)

LEE, BRUCE—actor
b: Nov 27, 1940, San Francisco, Calif. d: Jul 20, 1973

The Green Hornet (drama).. Kato (1966–67)
Longstreet (drama)
.... Longstreet's instructor (1971–72)

This small, intense master of the martial arts was a cult sensation in the early 1970s in a series of violent "chop sockey" movies made in Hong Kong. His first show-business break had been on television, however. Lee was born in San Francisco to a touring vaudeville family from Hong Kong, and he appeared in numerous low-budget films as a child. A hotheaded youth, he began studying kung fu as a teenager and eventually opened his own martial arts school in the U.S.

Most Americans first heard of him as Van Williams' faithful but fearsome manservant Kato on *The Green Hornet*. Later, Lee played the same role on episodes of *Batman* and had guest roles on *Ironside, Blondie,* and *Here Come the Brides;* he then won the recurring role of James Franciscus' self-defense instructor on *Longstreet*.

Then came the Hong Kong kick-'em-down movies, and worldwide fame. A hero of Asian youths—he almost always played the underdog fighting the system with violence—he seemed to be on his way to becoming a kind of Asian James Dean. Then, mysteriously, he died during the filming of a new picture in Hong Kong. The coroner said it was a cerebral hemorrhage probably caused by a freak reaction to a painkiller and, aggravated by his use of marijuana. Others, pointing to the kind of violent rebellion against authority his films seemed to promote, hinted at darker causes. No one will ever know for sure.

A biography: *The Legend of Bruce Lee* by Alex Ben Block.

LEE, CHERYLENE—actress
Kentucky Jones (drama)
.... Annie Ng (1964–65)
*Some sources give 1914.

LEE, FRAN—actress
b: Sep 28, 1910, New York City, N.Y.

Major Dell Conway of the Flying Tigers (adv)
.... Ma Wong (1951)

A book—or a musical, or a sitcom—could be written about this busy bit player of the '40s, '50s and '60s. A rather forceful woman, she usually played matronly ladies, either indignant or alarmed, in live TV dramas, plays and many feature films (in *Miracle on 34th Street* she was the lady Macy's sent to Gimbels). In *Flying Tigers* she was the Chinese heroine; "I was always tied to a chair and they ran in to rescue me," she laughs. Fran's major career, however, was as television's first and loudest consumer activist. Initially she was billed as "Mrs. Fixit," dispensing household hints on daytime TV in the '40s and '50s, including a long stint on the *Frances Langford-Don Ameche Show.* She then launched into a series of crusades, fighting government and large corporations over the health dangers of cyclamates, microwave ovens, and oral sex. A veritable tornado of energy, she gained great notoriety in New York in the '70s as the foul-mouthed "dog poop lady," battling loudly to rid the city streets of dog feces.

In her seventies, Fran is still crusading. While there is as yet no biography of her, she is prominently (and appropriately) featured in the 1973 book *Disturbers of the Peace* by Colman McCarthy. Fran is the sister of actress Madeline Lee (the wife of actor Jack Gilford), and the mother of one-time child actor Gene Lee.

LEE, GEORGIA—singer
Stage Two Revue (var) ...... regular (1950)

LEE, GYPSY ROSE—actress
b: Feb 9, 1914, Seattle, Wash. d: Apr 26, 1970

Think Fast (quiz)........ moderator (1950)
The Pruitts of Southampton (com)
.... Regina Wentworth (1966–67)

The famous ecdysiast, and sister of June Havoc. Her autobiography, which was made into a play and movie, was titled *Gypsy* (1957).

LEE, JAMES—actor

One Man's Family (drama)
.... Cliff Barbour (1949–52)

LEE, JOHNNY—black actor
b: Jul 4, 1898, Missouri r: Pueblo, Colo. d: Dec 12, 1965

Amos 'n' Andy (com)
.... Algonquin J. Calhoun (1951–53)

LEE, JONNA—actress

Otherworld (sci fi)..... Gina Sterling (1985)

LEE, KATHRYN—

Star Time (var) .... regular (1950–51)

LEE, MICHELE—actress, singer
b: Jun 24, 1942, Los Angeles, Calif.

Knots Landing (drama)
...... Karen Fairgate MacKenzie (1979–)

LEE, MRS. JOHN G.—hostess

The Power of Women (pub aff)
.... hostess (1952)

The president of the League of Women Voters.

LEE, PATSY—comedienne

Don McNeill TV Club (var)
.... regular (1950–51)

LEE, PATTI—

Our Time (var)............. regular (1985)

LEE, PEGGY—singer, songwriter
b: May 26, 1920, Jamestown, N.D.

TV's Top Tunes (music) ..... hostess (1951)
Songs for Sale (music).... regular (1951–52)

LEE, PINKY—comedian, actor
b: 1916, St. Paul, Minn.

The Pinky Lee Show (com)
.... the Stagehand (1950)
Those Two (com)........ regular (1951–53)

This bouncy, animated little comic got his start in burlesque in the 1930s and never rose above it; he specialized in noisy, bag-502

gy-pants routines for the rest of his career. His funny checkered hat and comic lisp (which was real) wore quickly on adult viewers of early TV, but he continued to be popular on daytime childrens' shows from 1954–1957.

Pinky suffered from a severe sinus condition, and it was that—not a heart attack, as was widely reported—that caused his collapse, on-camera, during one of his frantic routines in September 1955. After a few days in the hospital he continued with his daytime series, which was, however, toned down during the 1955–56 season (more because of educators' criticism than his condition). After a year's recuperation in Arizona, he briefly hosted the puppet show *Gumby* in 1957, then left network television to play clubs and local TV in the late '50s and '60s. He often said he would like to make a comeback, but the day of his mindless, screaming-kids humor seemed to have ended.

LEE, ROBERTA—

The Frank Sinatra Show (var)
.... regular (1950–51)

LEE, SONDRA & SAM STEEN—dancers

Starlit Time (var) .... regulars (1950)

LEE, STEPHEN—actor

Suzanne Pleshette Is Maggie Briggs (com)
.... Sherman Milslagle (1984)

LEE, SUNSHINE—juvenile actress

Mulligan's Stew (drama)
.... Kimmy Friedman (1977)

LEEDS, ELISSA—actress
b: Apr 12, c. 1959, New York City, N.Y.

Dorothy (com) .... Cissy (1979)

LEEDS, PETER—actor

Pete and Gladys (com)
.... George Colton (1960–62)

LEEDS, PHIL—actor

Front Row Center (var) ... regular (1949–50)
Ivan the Terrible (com).... Vladimir (1976)

LEEK, TIIU—reporter

That's My Line (com).... reporter (1980–81)

LEGAULT, LANCE—actor

The A-Team (adv)
.... Col. Roderick Decker (1983–)

LEHMAN, LILLIAN—black actress

b: Feb 12, Selma, Ala. r: Buffalo, N.Y.

Tenafly (drama).... Ruth Tenafly (1973–74)
Fay (com) .... Letty Gilmore (1975–76)

LEHMAN, TRENT—juvenile actor

b: 1961 d: Jan 18, 1982

Nanny and the Professor (com)
.... Butch Everett (1970–71)

LEHNE, FREDRIC—actor

Dallas (drama)..... Eddie Cronin (1984–85)

LEHR, LEW—comedian

b: May 14, 1895, Philadelphia, Pa. d: Mar 6, 1950

Stop Me If You've Heard This One (quiz)
.... panelist (1948)

LEI, LYDIA—actress

Crazy Like a Fox (drama)
.... Allison Ling (1984–85)

LEIBMAN, RON—actor

b: Oct 11, 1937, New York City, N.Y.

Kaz (drama)
.... Martin "Kaz" Kazinsky (1978–79)

Emmy Award: Best Actor in a Drama Series, for *Kaz* (1979)

Ron was married to actress Linda Lavin.

LEIGH, NELSON—actor

b: c. 1914 d: 1967

This Is the Life (drama)
.... Pastor Martin (1952–56)

LEIGH-HUNT, BARBARA—actress

b: Dec 14, 1935, Bath, Somerset, England

The Search for the Nile (drama)
.... Isabel Arundell Burton (1972)

LEIGH-HUNT, RONALD—actor

b: 1916

The Adventures of Sir Lancelot (adv)
.... King Arthur (1956–57)

LEIGHTON, BERNIE—orchestra leader

b: Jan 30, 1921, West Haven, Conn.

Chance of a Lifetime (talent)
.... orch. leader (1952–56)

LEIGHTON, ISABELLE—moderator

How Did They Get That Way? (info)
.... moderator (1951–52)

LEISTON, FREDDIE—actor

Life with Father (com).. John Day (1953–54)

LEMBECK, HARVEY—actor

b: 1925, Brooklyn, N.Y. d: Jan 5, 1982

The Phil Silvers Show (com)
.... Cpl. Rocco Barbella (1955–59)
The Hathaways (com)
.... Jerry Roper (1961–62)
Ensign O'Toole (com)
.... seaman Gabby Di Julio (1962–63)

LEMBECK, HELAINE—actress

Welcome Back, Kotter (com)
.... Judy Borden (1975–77)

LEMBECK, MICHAEL—actor

b: Jun 25, 1948, Brooklyn, N.Y.

The Funny Side (var)........ regular (1971)
One Day at a Time (com)
.... Max Horvath (1979–84)
Foley Square (com)
.... Peter Newman (1985–86)

The son of comic actor Harvey Lembeck.

LEMMON, CHRIS—actor

b: Jan 22, 1954, Los Angeles, Calif.

Brothers and Sisters (com)
.... Milos "Checko" Sabolcik (1979)

The son of Jack Lemmon.

LEMMON, JACK—actor

b: Feb 8, 1925, Boston, Mass.

That Wonderful Guy (com)
.... Harold (1949–50)

Toni Twin Time (var)........... host (1950)
Ad Libbers (var) .... regular (1951)
Heaven for Betsy (com).... Pete Bell (1952)
Alcoa Theatre (drama)
.... recurring star (1957–58)

Emmy Award: Star, Outstanding Musical Special, for "'S Wonderful, 'S Marvelous, 'S Gershwin" (1972)

Before he became a major movie star, Jack Lemmon spent five busy years on live, network TV in New York, in both series and guest appearances. Jack had come to New York—after serving in the navy during World War II—to try his luck in the theater. Radio and the emerging medium of television offered employment for struggling young actors, and Jack worked steadily in both while trying to get his break on Broadway. His earliest TV series—which hardly anyone remembers today—was *That Wonderful Guy,* in which Jack played the bumbling valet to a pompous Broadway critic. Jack's girlfriend on the show was played by actress Cynthia Stone. She and Jack were married in real life in 1950, and they appeared together in several other programs, including the improvisational comedy show *Ad Libbers* in 1951 and the domestic sitcom *Heaven for Betsy* (playing newlyweds) in 1952. Jack was also seen on several of the dramatic showcases of the day, such as *Danger* and *Kraft Theatre,* as well as in two obscure daytime soap operas *(The Brighter Day, Road of Life).* However, comedy was his strong suit—even then the amiable, frustrated, somewhat neurotic character moviegoers came to love was evident—and it was in the Broadway farce *Room Service* in 1953 that he got the break he was looking for.

It proved to be only a prelude. Spotted by movie scouts, Jack landed his first film role opposite Judy Holliday in *It Should Happen To You* (1954); a year later he won an Academy Award for his portrayal of Ensign Pulver in *Mr. Roberts,* and his big screen career was off and running.

Jack did no more series TV after that, although he did continue to appear in occasional playhouse productions until the end of the 1950s (*Goodyear Theatre, Alcoa Theatre,* etc.). After 1959 he did not act on television for 17 years—returning in 1976, to play the aging vaudevillian in the dramatic special *The Entertainer.*

LEMON, MEADOWLARK—black athlete
b: Apr 25, 1932, Lexington County, S.C. r: Wilmington, N.C.

Hello, Larry (com)..... as himself (1979–80)

The famous trick-shot basketball player with the Harlem Globetrotters.

LEMOND, BOB—announcer
And Here's the Show (var)
.... announcer (1955)

LENARD, MARK—actor
b: Oct 15 Chicago, Ill. r: South Haren, Mich.

Here Come the Brides (adv)
.... Aaron Stempel (1968–70)
The Planet of the Apes (sci fi).. Urko (1974)
The Secret Empire (drama)
.... Emperor Thorval (1979)

LENIHAN, DEIRDRE—actress
b: May 19, 1946, Atlanta, Ga. r: New York City, N.Y.

Needles and Pins (com)
.... Wendy Nelson (1973)

LENNON SISTERS, THE—vocal quartet
Dianne, b: Dec 1, 1939, Los Angeles
Peggy, b: Apr 8, 1941, Los Angeles
Kathy, b: Aug 22, 1942, Santa Monica, Calif.
Janet, b: Nov 15, 1946, Culver City, Calif.

The Lawrence Welk Show (music)
.... regulars (1955–68)
Jimmy Durante Presents the Lennon Sisters (var).................... regulars (1969–70)
The Andy Williams Show (var)
.... regulars (1970–71)

The sweetly harmonizing Lennon Sisters were what older Americans thought younger Americans *should* be listening to during the rock 'n' roll era. Obviously, younger Americans did not agree, as the girls did not have much of an independent musical career after they were out from under the protective wing of Lawrence Welk.

Their autobiography: *Same Song, Separate Voices* (1985), written by all four.

LENO, JAY—comedian
b: Apr 29, 1951

The Marilyn McCoo & Billy Davis, Jr. Show (var)....................... regular (1977)

LENOIR, ROSETTA—actress

Calucci's Department (com)
.... Mitzi Gordon (1973)

LENZ, KAY—actress
b: Mar 4, 1953, Los Angeles, Calif.

Rich Man, Poor Man—Book I (drama)
.... Kate Jordache (1976)
Rich Man, Poor Man—Book II (drama)
.... Kate Jordache (1976–77)

Emmy Award: Best Actress in a Daytime Drama Special, for the *ABC Afternoon Playbreak* "Heart in Hiding" (1975)

Married to actor-singer David Cassidy.

LENZ, RICHARD—actor
b: Nov 21, 1939, Springfield, Ill. r: Jackson, Mich.

Hec Ramsey (wes)
.... Sheriff Oliver B. Stamp (1972–74)

LEONARD, JACK—singer

Jack Leonard (music) .... host (1949)
Broadway Open House (talk).... host (1951)

The former big-band singer, with Tommy Dorsey in the '30s.

LEONARD, JACK E.—comedian
b: Apr 24, 1911, Chicago, Ill. d: May 10, 1973

Dick Clark's World of Talent (var)
.... regular (1959)

The portly (300 pound) bald comic, who specialized in insult jokes. Of his pal Ed Sullivan, he said "There's absolutely nothing wrong with you that reincarnation won't cure."

LEONARD, SHELDON—actor, director, producer
b: Feb 22, 1907, New York City, N.Y.

The Duke (com) .... Sam Marco (1954)
The Danny Thomas Show (com)
.... Phil Brokaw (1959–61)
Big Eddie (com) .... Eddie Smith (1975)

Emmy Awards: Best Direction of a Half Hour Program, for *The Danny Thomas Show* (1956); Best Direction of a Comedy Program, for *The Danny Thomas Show* (1961); Executive Producer, Best Comedy Series, for *My World and Welcome To It* (1970)

This balding, Damon Runyon–esque producer has been responsible for some of television's all-time top hits—*The Danny Thomas Show, The Andy Griffith Show, The Dick Van Dyke Show, Gomer Pyle,* and *I Spy* among others. He has been seen on-camera in several series and starred in his own series, *Big Eddie,* in the '70s. Sheldon started out as a stage actor in New York and then moved to Hollywood to become a movie character-actor in the late '30s and '40s. He was almost always cast as a gangster, either comic or dramatic, and appeared in a great many films—he estimates more than 140. It is television production, however, that has made him a very rich man.

LEONETTI, TOMMY—singer, actor
b: 1929 d: Sep 15, 1979

Your Hit Parade (music) . vocalist (1957–58)
Gomer Pyle, U.S.M.C. (com)
.... Cpl. Nick Guccinello (1964–65)

LEONG, CAMILLE—assistant

Party Time at Club Roma (var)
.... regular (1950–51)

LEOPOLD, THOMAS—actor
b: Oct 14, Miami, Fla.

The Ted Knight Show (com)
.... Winston Dennis (1978)
The Steve Allen Comedy Hour (var)
.... regular (1980–81)

LERMAN, APRIL—juvenile actress
b: Feb 6, 1969, Chicago, Ill r: New York City, N.Y.

Charles in Charge (com)
.... Lila Pembroke (1984–85)

LE ROY, GLORIA—actress
b: Nov 7, Bucyrus, Ohio r: The Bronx, N.Y.

Hot L Baltimore (com)........ Millie (1975)
Kaz (drama) .... Mary Parnell (1978–79)

LEROY, PHILIPPE—actor
b: Oct 15, 1930, Paris, France

The Life of Leonardo da Vinci (drama)
.... Leonardo da Vinci (1972)

LESCOULIE, JACK—announcer, host
b: Nov 17, 1917, Sacramento, Calif.

The Jackie Gleason Show (var)
.... announcer (1952–55)
The Milton Berle Show (var)
.... commercial announcer (1954–55)
Meet the Champions (sport).. host (1956–57)
The Jackie Gleason Show (var)
.... announcer (1956–59)
Tonight! America After Dark (talk)
.... host (1957)
Brains & Brawn (quiz) .... emcee (1958)
1,2,3, Go (child) .... regular (1961–62)

Viewers who woke up to the Today show in the '50s and '60s remember Jack Lescoulie as the announcer/sidekick with the boyish grin who helped make the early mornings a little more bearable. Though he is best known for his long stint on Today (1952–67), he had a varied career elsewhere in show business.

Jack started out intending to become an actor and came to New York in the mid-1930s with a touring play; his role was to provide offstage elephant noises (everybody has to start somewhere!). He landed a few small roles in the general vicinity of Broadway, including one in Tapestry in Grey with Melvyn Douglas (1935), but not enough to keep him fed. So the young actor returned to California, where he worked in radio and played small parts in movie westerns. After the war Jack drifted mostly into announcing, and it was in that capacity that television viewers came to know him—not only on Today but on the prime time shows of Jackie Gleason, Milton Berle, and others. He also hosted the Tonight! America After Dark show for six months in 1957, after the departure of Steve Allen and before the arrival of Jack Paar.

Since leaving Today in 1967, Jack has been semiactive doing commercials, working for a time on local TV in Cincinnati, and reportedly writing a novel to be called Born with Teeth. Referring, perhaps, to that boyish grin?

LESLIE, BETHEL—actress
b: Aug 3, 1929, New York City, N.Y.

The Girls (com)
.... Cornelia Otis Skinner (1950)
The Richard Boone Show (drama)
.... regular (1963–64)

A frequent supporting player in dramatic presentations of the 1950s and in westerns and crime dramas of the '60s. Bethel was a regular on the daytime serial The Doctors in the late '60s (as Dr. Maggie Powers) and later was headwriter of The Secret Storm. A more recent appearance was in the Marie Osmond TV movie The Gift of Love (1978).

LESLIE, NAN—actress
b: Jun 4, 1926, Los Angeles, Calif.

Kings Row (drama)
.... Randy Monaghan (1955–56)
The Californians (wes)
.... Martha McGivern (1957–58)

LESLIE, WILLIAM—actor

The Lineup (police)
.... Insp. Dan Delaney (1959–60)

LESSY, BEN—actor

The Danny Thomas Show (com)
.... Benny (1953–57)

LESTER, BUDDY—actor
b: Jan 16, 1917, Chicago, Ill.

The New Phil Silvers Show (com)
.... Nick (1963–64)

LESTER, JEFF—actor

Walking Tall (police)
.... Dep. Grady Spooner (1981)

LESTER, JERRY—comedian
b: 1911, Chicago, Ill.

Cavalcade of Stars (var) ...... emcee (1950)
Broadway Open House (talk)
.... host (1950–51)
Chesterfield Sound Off Time (var)
.... star (1951–52)
Saturday Night Dance Party (var)
.... host (1952)
Pantomime Quiz (quiz) ... regular (1953–55)

Jerry Lester was one of those noisy, gag-a-minute vaudeville comics who invaded television during its early, live years, but who faded from the scene when more polished filmed series began to take over in the mid-1950s. A feisty little guy who made a lot of "beanbag" jokes, he got his start in vaudeville (natch) and clubs in the 1930s and had a minor radio career in the '40s, before wisecracking his way into early TV. His most notable series was *Broadway Open House,* a frantic revue that was the late-night precursor of *The Tonight Show*—but as different in content from that long-running, low-energy talk show as possible. Jerry was mostly inactive in later years, turning up occasionally in cameo appearances in such diverse series as *The Girl from U.N.C.L.E.* (1967), *The Monkees,* (1967) and *Barnaby Jones* (1973).

LESTER, KETTY—black actress
b: Aug 16, 1938 r: Hope, Ark.

Little House on the Prairie (adv)
.... Hester Sue Terhune (1978–83)
Morningstar/Eveningstar (drama)
.... Nora Blake (1986)

LESTER, TOM—actor
b: 1938, Jackson, Miss.

Green Acres (com) ... Eb Dawson (1965–71)
Petticoat Junction (com)
.... Eb Dawson (1966–70)

LE SUEUR, LARRY—newscaster
Chronoscope (int) ..... moderator (1953–55)

LETNER, KEN—actor
Falcon Crest (drama) .... Spheeris (1983–85)

LETTERMAN, DAVID—comedian, writer
b: Apr 12, 1947, Indianapolis, Ind.

The Starland Vocal Band Show (var)
.... regular (1977)
Mary (var)................. regular (1978)
Late Night with David Letterman (talk)
.... host (1982–)

Emmy Awards: Best Host of and Best Writing for a Daytime Variety Series, for *The David Letterman Show* (1981); Best Writing for a Variety Show, for *Late Night With David Letterman* (1984, 1985, 1986)

This contemporary humorist is widely recognized as a potential successor to Johnny Carson—even by Johnny, it seems (his company produces David's late-night show). David's rise has been rapid, thanks in no small part to Carson. David started out in local radio and TV while a college student in Indiana in the late '60s and landed a full-time job at the same station upon graduation. One can only guess what he must have been like as a local children's show host, late-night movie announcer, or weatherman, but his superiors are said not to have been amused when in the middle of a forecast he congratulated a tropical storm upon being promoted to hurricane.

In 1975 David moved to Los Angeles to do stand-up comedy in clubs and write—activities that proved to be his entrée into the big time. He sold material to *Good Times, The Paul Lynde Comedy Hour,* and a Bob Hope special, and then began getting on-camera shots as a lanky, somewhat off-beat repertory player. He was on *The Starland Vocal Band Show* in the summer of 1977 and on Mary Tyler Moore's short-lived *Mary* in 1978; she had no idea what to make of him, nor he of her. His big break was on *The Tonight Show,* where a more appreciative Johnny Carson gave the young comic multiple guest shots and then guest host duties—more than 50 times in all—starting in November 1978.

NBC signed David for his first network talk show in June 1980, but inexplicably scheduled it at 10 A.M.—a time when waking housewives had roughly the same reaction to his smart-alecky, camp humor as Mary Tyler Moore had. NBC canceled the series and went back to mindless game shows. The network did not give up on David, however, and in February 1982 he began a late-night show that has become something of a cult favorite among younger viewers. It looks like a normal talk show at first glance, but on closer inspection is a sly put-down of just about everything middle class (including, by extension, Johnny Carson). Could it really become the replacement for Carson's venerable, middle-of-the-road *Tonight Show?* Only if America becomes a very hip land.

LEVANT, OSCAR—pianist, humorist
b: Dec 27, 1906, Pittsburgh, Pa. d: Aug 14, 1972

G.E. Guest House (quiz) ...... emcee (1951)

The famous comedy curmudgeon, known for his cigar, his neuroses, and his dry wit. His own self description: "a verbal vampire." Oscar was a frequent, if grouchy, guest on Jack Paar's *Tonight Show.*

His autobiography: *The Unimportance of Being Oscar* (1968).

LEVENSON, SAM—humorist
b: Dec 28, 1911, New York City, N.Y. d: Aug 27, 1980

The Sam Levenson Show (com)
.... host (1951–52)
This Is Show Business (var)
.... panelist (1951–54)
Two for the Money (quiz)
.... emcee (1955–57)
Masquerade Party (quiz)
.... panelist (1958–60)
Celebrity Talent Scouts (var).... host (1960)

A gentle, folksy raconteur, and commentator on changing social mores. Among his books: *In One Era and Out the Other* and *You Don't Have To Be in Who's Who To Know What's What*

LEVERSEE, LORETTA—actress
The Aldrich Family (com)
.... Eleanor (1952–53)

LEVIEN, PHIL—actor
Doctors' Private Lives (drama)
.... Kenny Wise (1979)

LEVIN, CHARLES—actor
Goodnight, Beantown (com)
.... Sam Holliday (1983)
Alice (com)......... Eliot Novak (1983–85)

LEVIN, JEREMY—actor
Holocaust (drama) .... Aaron (1978)

LEVITAN, DAVID—host
On Trial (pub aff) ..... moderator (1948–52)

LEVY, EUGENE—comedian, writer
b: Dec 17, 1946, Hamilton, Canada

Second City TV (com)
.... Earl Camembert (1977–81)
SCTV Network 90 (com).. regular (1981–83)

Emmy Awards: Best Writing for a Comedy Program, for *SCTV Network 90* (1982, 1983)

LEVY, WEAVER—actor
Adventures in Paradise (adv)
.... Oliver Lee (1959–61)

LEWANDOWSKI, BOB—host
Polka-Go-Round (music) .. regular (1958–59)

LEWIS, AL—actor
Car 54, Where Are You? (com)
.... Off. Leo Schnauser (1961–63)
The Munsters (com)
.... Grandpa Munster (1964–66)

LEWIS, CATHY—actress
b: 1918, Spokane, Wash. d: Nov 20, 1968

My Friend Irma (com)
.... Jane Stacy (1952–53)
Fibber McGee and Molly (com)
.... Molly McGee (1959–60)
Hazel (com) ... Deidre Thompson (1961–65)

LEWIS, EMMANUEL—black juvenile actor
b: Mar 9, 1971, Brooklyn, N.Y.

Webster (com) ...... Webster Long (1983–)

"The tallest 40 inches in Hollywood," *TV Guide* called him, and little Emmanuel Lewis did indeed seem to be a producer's dream. An intelligent lad with an infectious giggle, he looks, and can act, much younger than his real age—a situation that may not last. His brother Roscoe was similarly small until his midteens, then shot up so fast he had to be hospitalized for "growing pains."

The son of a former computer programmer, Emmanuel began doing commercials in 1980 for cereals and other products. It was a Burger King commercial (and that giggle) that made him a star; the spot was seen by an ABC executive who signed him immediately, then convened a roomful of producers and writers to create a show for him. Despite invidious comparisons with *Diff'rent Strokes*, *Webster* was quite popular, and Emmanuel has become something of a pint-sized media celebrity.

He is also a star in Japan, where, it is

said, they consider him to be some sort of magic doll.

LEWIS, FORREST—actor
b: 1900 d: Jun 2, 1977

Sandy Strong (child)... Mr. Mack (1950–51)
The Great Gildersleeve (com)
.... Mr. Peavey (1955–56)
Ichabod and Me (com)..... Colby (1961–62)

LEWIS, FRANK—choreographer

The Julius La Rosa Show (var)
.... dancers (1956)
The Patti Page Show (var) .. dancers (1956)
The Tony Bennett Show (var)
.... dancers (1956)

LEWIS, GEOFFREY—actor
b: Jul 31, 1935*, Plainfield, N.J.

Flo (com)............ Earl Tucker (1980–81)
Gun Shy (com)........ Amos Tucker (1983)

LEWIS, GEORGE J.—actor
b: Dec 10, 1903, Guadalajara, Mexico

Zorro (wes)....... Don Alejandro (1957–59)

LEWIS, JEANNE—actress
b: c. 1929

Dagmar's Canteen (var)...... regular (1952)

Dagmar's sister.

LEWIS, JENNY—juvenile actress
b: Jan 8, 1977, Las Vegas, Nev.

Life with Lucy (com)
.... Becky McGibbon (1986)

LEWIS, JERRY—comedian
b: Mar 16, 1926, Newark, N.J.

The Colgate Comedy Hour (var)
.... cohost (with Dean Martin)
(1950–55)
The Jerry Lewis Show (talk) .... host (1963)
The Jerry Lewis Show (var) .. host (1967–69)

The full saga of this squalky, goofy, constantly mugging comedian can be found elsewhere. He is perhaps the most controversial performer in show business; depending on whom you read, he is either the greatest comic genius of the Western

*Some sources give Jan. 1, in San Diego, Calif.

world, or the most idiotic no-talent ever to foul the screen. This author takes no sides. Suffice it to say that Jerry Lewis was a very big star on television in the '50s and has had a rather unique career since then.

Jerry met Dean Martin in Atlantic City in 1946, when both were struggling nightclub performers. As a team—Martin the suave, romantic crooner and Lewis the kibitzing, antic clown—they were a very big hit. Their TV debut was on the first telecast of *The Ed Sullivan Show* on the night of June 20, 1948 (proving from the start that Ed knew what was hot in show business, and how to book it). For the next eight years the pair appeared on the biggest, splashiest TV variety shows, including a five-year run as rotating hosts of NBC's big budget *Colgate Comedy Hour.* It was the only show on TV able to beat Ed Sullivan at his own game.

In 1956, Martin and Lewis split, and Jerry went on to a very successful solo career. In addition to appearing in TV specials, he acted occasionally, as in a TV production of "The Jazz Singer" in 1959 and an episode of *Ben Casey* in 1965. He was also a guest host on *The Tonight Show.* In 1963, amid a blaze of publicity, Jerry signed with ABC to do his first series. The result was a program unprecedented in its scope—a two-hour prime time talk show packed with guest stars and originating live from Hollywood. It was possibly the most spectacular attempt at big-name variety programming in television history—and also the most colossal flop. It was canceled after three months.

Jerry licked his wounds but showed that he hadn't lost his sense of humor about TV by making a cameo appearance on an episode of *Batman* in 1966. The following year, he returned in a more traditional variety hour on NBC, which ran for two seasons and featured some of his familiar characters from movies—the nutty professor, the poor soul, the shoeshine boy, etc. The series was scheduled in the early evening and included many youth-oriented acts (e.g., the Osmond Brothers), which made it popular with younger viewers. The controversial star was not above making fun of himself, either. In the early '70s he lent his name (though not his voice) to a Saturday morning cartoon series called *Will the Real Jerry Lewis Please Sit Down?* (1970–72), a kind of self-lampoon.

Jerry has been much less active since

then, either in television or films, concentrating mostly on live Las Vegas performances. An experimental Las Vegas talk-show project in the early '80s failed to become a series. He is best known to viewers now for his annual Labor Day Muscular Dystrophy telethons, a cause to which he has dedicated his talents and much of his own money for more than 20 years.

LEWIS, JUDY—actress

The Outlaws (wes)
.... Connie Masters (1961–62)

LEWIS, MARCIA—actress
b: Boston, Mass. r: Cincinnati, Ohio

Who's Watching The Kids? (com)
.... Mitzi Logan (1978)
Goodtime Girls (com)
.... Irma Coolidge (1980)

LEWIS, MINNABESS—panelist

Charade Quiz (quiz)..... panelist (1947–49)

LEWIS, NANCY—juvenile hostess
b: c. 1936

Paul Whiteman's TV Teen Club (talent)
.... cohost (1950–53)

LEWIS, ROBERT Q.—host
b: Apr 5, 1921, New York City, N.Y.

The Robert Q. Lewis Show (com)
.... host (1950–51)
The Show Goes On (var)..... host (1950–52)
The Name's the Same (quiz)
.... emcee (1951–54)
Make Me Laugh (quiz)........ emcee (1958)
Masquerade party (quiz)...... emcee (1958)

This amiable host had a rather studious look, accentuated by his quiet air and horn-rimmed glasses, but his quick wit—especially in conversation—made him a popular emcee during the 1950s. Before coming to television he had been a radio announcer and disc jockey for about ten years. He hosted an assortment of prime time variety and quiz programs on TV and also had a popular daytime show that ran off and on from 1950 to 1956. In addition, he was a frequent substitute host for Arthur Godfrey on the latter's top-rated shows. Lewis's most recent network assignment

was the daytime quiz show *Play Your Hunch* in the early '60s. He has not been seen much since then, although he has had small roles in a few films, including *How to Succeed in Business Without Really Trying* (1967) and the Judd Hirsch TV movie *The Law* (1974)—in the latter playing a dinner speaker at a convention of lawyers.

LEWIS, SAGAN—actress

St. Elsewhere (drama)
.... Dr. Jacqueline Wade (1983–)

LEWIS, SYLVIA—dancer

The Ray Bolger Show (com)
.... Ray's dancing partner (1953–55)

LEWIS, WANDA—actress
b: Feb 2, 1926, Struthers, Ohio

The Paul Dixon Show (var)
.... regular (1951–52)
This Is Music (music)..... regular (1958–59)

LEWIS, WILLIAM—

Caesar's Hour (var) ...... regular (1955–57)

LEYDEN, BILL—host
b: Feb 1, Chicago, Ill.

Musical Chairs (quiz)..... moderator (1955)
It Could Be You (quiz)..... emcee (1958–61)

LEYTON, JOHN—actor
b: 1939

Jericho (drama) ... Nicholas Gage (1966–67)

LIBERACE—pianist, host
b: May 16, 1919, Milwaukee, Wis. d: Feb 4, 1987

The Liberace Show (var)........ host (1952)
The Liberace Show (music) .. host (1953–55)
The Liberace Show (var)....... host (1969)

Classically trained pianist "Lee" Liberace was certainly one of the most flamboyant figures in television history. His trademarks were familiar and the butt of innumerable jokes: the outlandish and very expensive sequined wardrobe, the curly hair and pearly-toothed smile, and a florid piano style. Atop his Steinway was perched an ornate candelabra (imitation

Louis XIV). As if that weren't enough, he talked constantly about his beloved mother. Women, especially older ones, loved it. The critics were not kind, but Liberace did not mind. As he remarked, in one of show business's most memorable quotes, "I cried all the way to the bank."

Liberace's first television exposure was on a local program in Los Angeles in 1951, followed by a 15-minute network summer series in 1952. The following year he began filming a syndicated series that received extremely wide circulation and made him a great deal of money. These films were rerun for years and are said to have aired on more stations than any network or syndicated program up to that time. Later programs included an ABC daytime series in 1958–59 and a prime time summer show in 1969, the latter a full hour in length. With Lee in the early years was violinist brother George, who also led the orchestra.

Liberace made periodic guest appearances on other shows and was not above spoofing his own outrageous image. Perhaps most memorable was an appearance on *Batman* in 1966, in which Lee played Chandell, "The Devil's Fingers," as well as Chandell's evil twin, Harry, who attempted to perforate the Dynamic Duo into music rolls and put them in a player piano.

In later years, Liberace concentrated on personal appearances, especially in Las Vegas, where he had a loyal, if aging, following. His autobiographies: *Liberace* (1973) and *The Things I Love* (1977).

LIBERACE, GEORGE—violinist, orchestra leader
b: Jul 31, 1911, Menasha, Wis. d: Oct 16, 1983

The Liberace Show (var)
.... orch. leader (1952)

Liberace's mustachoied, silent brother. Jealous at Lee's success, George split with his famous brother in 1957 and pursued a variety of solo endeavors, some musical and some not (among the latter were two fast-food franchises in California).

LIBERTINI, RICHARD—actor
b: May 21, Cambridge, Mass.

The Melba Moore-Clifton Davis Show (var)
.... regular (1972)
Soap (com) .... The Godfather (1977–78)

LICHT, JEREMY—juvenile actor
b: Jan 4, 1971, Los Angeles, Calif.

Valerie (com) .... Mark Hogan (1986–)

LIDO, BOB—violinist

The Lawrence Welk Show (music)
.... regular (1955–82)

LIEB, ROBERT P.—actor

My Three Sons (com)
.... Mr. Henry Pearson (1960–61)
Hazel (com) .... Harry Thompson (1961–65)

LIGHT, ENOCH—orchestra leader
b: Aug 18, 1907, Canton, Ohio d: Jul 31, 1978

The Gulf Road Show Starring Bob Smith (var)
.... orch. leader (1948)

LIGHT, JUDITH—actress
b: Feb 9, 1949, Trenton, N.J.

Who's the Boss? (com)
.... Angela Bower (1984–)

Emmy Awards: Best Actress in a Daytime Drama Series, for *One Life to Live* (1980, 1981)

Judith played the role of Karen Wolek for more than five years (1977–83) on daytime's *One Life to Live*.

LIGHTFOOT, LEONARD—black actor

Silver Spoons (com)
.... Leonard Rollins (1982–83)

LIM, KWAN HI—actor

Magnum, P.I. (drama)
.... Lt. Tanaka (1982–)

LIME, YVONNE—actress
b: Apr 7, 1938, Glendale, Calif.

Father Knows Best (com)
................,..... Dotty Snow (1954–57)
The Many Loves of Dobie Gillis (com)
.... Melissa Frome (1959–60)
Happy (com).......... Sally Day (1960–61)

LIND, BRIT—actress

How the West Was Won (miniseries) (drama)
.... Erika (1977)

LINDEN, HAL—actor
b: Mar 20, 1931, The Bronx, N.Y.

Barney Miller (com)
.... Capt. Barney Miller (1975–82)
Blacke's Magic (drama)
.... Alexander Blacke (1986)

Emmy Award: Outstanding Individual Achievement as a Daytime Performer, for *F.Y.I.* (1983, 1984)

Hal Linden is one of the many Broadway denizens who has found national fame on TV. A New Yorker through and through (born in the Bronx, studied at the city's High School of Music and Art, graduated from City College), he began his career as a saxophonist and singer in the bands of Sammy Kaye, Bobby Sherwood and Boyd Raeburn. After acting study, he got his first major break on stage in the late '50s, replacing the original lead in *The Bells Are Ringing.* Roles in other musicals followed in the '60s, including *Wildcat, Subways Are for Sleeping,* and *On a Clear Day You Can See Forever.* Perhaps his greatest stage triumph was in *The Rothschilds* in 1971, for which he received a Tony Award.

Hal did little television in the '60s (a guest appearance on *Car 54, Where Are You?* in 1963, a stint on *Search for Tomorrow* in 1969); in the early '70s, however, his TV work began to increase, leading in 1975 to his hit series *Barney Miller*—which was set, of course, in New York. He has also hosted two daytime programs for youngsters, *Animals, Animals, Animals* (beginning in 1976) and the short, informational series *F.Y.I.* (1979). In 1986 he began a new series with Harry Morgan, *Blacke's Magic,* which was set in Southern California. His co-opting by Hollywood was complete; a 1980 special called *Hal Linden's Big Apple,* in which he danced and sang his way around the streets of his native city, was perhaps his nostalgic farewell to his former life.

LINDGREN, LISA—actress

Another Day (com)
.... Kelly Gardner (1978)

LINDINE, JACK—actor

Code Red (adv) ...... Al Martelli (1981–82)

LINDLEY, AUDRA—actress
b: Sep 24, Los Angeles, Calif.

Bridget Loves Bernie (com)
.... Amy Fitzgerald (1972–73)
Fay (com) .... Lillian (1975–76)
Doc (com) .... Janet Scott (1976)
Three's Company (com)
.... Helen Roper (1977–79)
The Ropers (com) ... Helen Roper (1979–80)

LINDLEY, DON—orchestra leader

Music in Velvet (music)
.... orch. leader (1949)

LINDLEY, ERNEST K.—newscaster

Newsweek Analysis (news)
.... moderator (1948–50)

LINDSAY, MARGARET—actress
b: Sep 19, 1910, Dubuque, Iowa d: May 8, 1981

Take a Guess (quiz) .... panelist (1953)

LINDSAY, MARK—singer
b: Mar 9, 1944, Eugene, Oregon

Make Your Own Kind of Music (var)
.... regular (1971)

Sometime lead singer of the rock group Paul Revere and the Raiders.

LINDSEY, GEORGE—actor
b: Jasper, Ala.

The Andy Griffith Show (com)
.... Goober Pyle (1965–68)
Mayberry R.F.D. (com)
.... Goober Pyle (1968–71)
Hee Haw (var)............ regular (1972–)

LINDSEY, LEE—

The College Bowl (com) .. regular (1950–51)

LINDSEY, MORT—orchestra leader
b: Mar 21, 1923, Newark, N.J.

Tonight! America After Dark (talk)
.... quartet (1957)
The Pat Boone-Chevy Showroom (var)
.... orch. leader (1957–60)
Chevy Showroom (var) . orch. leader (1958)
The Judy Garland Show (var)
.... orch. leader (1963–64)

Fanfare (var)........... orch. leader (1965)
The Merv Griffin Show (talk)
.... orch. leader (1969–72)

Emmy Award: Outstanding Achievement as Musical Director, for *Barbra Streisand: A Happening in Central Park* (1969)

LINERO, JEANNIE—actress

Hot L Baltimore (com)
.... Suzy Marta Rocket (1975)
Berrengers (drama).... Ana Morales (1985)

LINHART, BUZZY—actor

Cos (var) .... regular (1976)

LINK, FRANK—

b: 1937, Louisville, Ky. d: Dec 31, 1983

The Burns and Schreiber Comedy Hour (var)
.... regular (1973)

LINK, MICHAEL—juvenile actor

b: Jun 12, 1962, Provo, Utah r: Los Angeles, Calif.

Julia (com).... Earl J. Waggedorn (1968–71)

LINKE, PAUL—actor

CHiPs (police) .... Off. Grossman (1977–83)

LINKER, AMY—juvenile actress

b: Oct 19, 1966, Brooklyn, N.Y.

Lewis & Clark (com)
.... Kelly Lewis (1981–82)
Square Pegs (com)
.... Lauren Hutchinson (1982–83)

LINKLETTER, ART—host

b: Jul 17, 1912, Moose Jaw, Sask., Canada r: San Diego

Life with Linkletter (var)... emcee (1950–52)
People Are Funny (quiz) ... emcee (1954–61)
The Art Linkletter Show (quiz)
.... host (1963)
Hollywood Talent Scouts (var)
.... host (1965–66)

Art Linkletter, one of television's friendliest and most engaging hosts, is closely identified with two programs: the daytime *Art Linkletter's House Party*, which ran on radio and later TV for a total of 24 years (1945–69); and *People Are Funny*, with a 19-year radio-TV run (1942–61). Art was basically a "people person," glib, full of pranks, at home with an audience, and especially warm with children. One of the highlights of his *House Party* (which ran in prime time for a while as *Life with Linkletter*) was his interviews with kids, about life and family, always with unpredictable results. ("What does Mommy do?" "Nothing," squealed a pigtailed youngster, "she's too busy having babies.") From these bits came a series of best-selling books, the first called *Kids Say the Darndest Things*.

Art's involvement with children was a result of his own unhappy childhood. Unwanted by his natural parents, he was adopted by an intinerant Canadian preacher and his wife, who moved often when he was young. Art broke into radio as a young man, at first as announcer for fairs and expositions in the '30s, and later as cohost and then host of the popular stunt show *People Are Funny. House Party* followed in 1945.

Both shows were brought to television in the early '50s and were major hits. Art also made a few acting appearances, including several on *General Electric Theater*, but hosting was his forte. He continued in the '60s with his enormously popular daytime show and a couple of less successful nighttime efforts. After *House Party* left the air in 1969 he had another daytime show for a year, but then was seen only occasionally. He was heard from mostly on matters regarding drug abuse among young people, a concern made more poignant by the suicide death of his own daughter, Diane, after an overdose of LSD in 1969.

LINKLETTER, JACK—host

b: Nov 20, 1937, San Francisco, Calif.

Haggis Baggis (quiz)......... emcee (1958)
Hootenanny (music) .... host (1963–64)

The eldest son of Art Linkletter. Jack hosted a succession of daytime game and variety shows, undertaking his first, *Haggis Baggis* (in prime time), while still a student at the University of Southern California. "One of the reasons I get these jobs," he said, "is because my price is less than dad's."

LINN, BAMBI, & ROD ALEXANDER—dancers
b: Bambi Linn, b: 1926, Brooklyn, N.Y.
Rod Alexander, b: Los Angeles, Calif.

Your Show of Shows (var)
.... dancers (1952–54)
Max Liebman Presents (var)
.... dancers (1954–56)

Husband and wife dance team, from Broadway.

LINN-BAKER, MARK—actor
b: Jun 17, 1953, St. Louis, Mo. r: Wethersfield, Conn.

Comedy Zone (com) .... regular (1984)
Perfect Strangers (com)
.... Larry Appleton (1986–)

LINVILLE, JOANNE—actress
b: c. 1926 r: Long Beach, Calif.

Behind the Screen (drama)
.... Zina Willow (1981–82)

LINVILLE, LARRY—actor
b: Sep 29, 1939, Ojai, Calif.

*M*A*S*H* (com)
.... Maj. Frank Burns (1972–77)
Grandpa Goes to Washington (com)
.... Maj. Gen. Kevin Kelley (1978–79)
Checking In (com)........ Lyle Block (1981)
Herbie, The Love Bug (com)
.... Randy Bigelow (1981)
Paper Dolls (drama)... Grayson Carr (1984)

LIOTTA, RAY—actor
b: Dec 18, Newark, N.J.

Casablanca (drama).......... Sacha (1983)
Our Family Honor (drama)
.... Off. Ed Santini (1985–86)

LIPPIN, RENEE—actress

The Bob Newhart Show (com)
.... Michelle Nardo (1973–76)
Free Country (com)
.... Ida Gewertzman (1978)

LIPPMAN, DAVID—musician

Champagne and Orchids (music)
.... playing the theremin (1948–49)

LIPPMAN, MORT—pianist

Andy and Della Russell (music)
.... pianist (1950–51)

LIPTON, LYNN—actress

Comedy Tonight (var) .... regular (1970)
David Frost Revue (com) . regular (1971–73)

LIPTON, MICHAEL—actor

Buckskin (wes)....... Ben Newcomb (1959)

LIPTON, PEGGY—actress
b: 1948, Lawrence, N.Y.

The John Forsythe Show (com)
.... Joanna (1965–66)
The Mod Squad (police)
.... Julie Barnes (1968–73)

LIPTON, ROBERT—actor
b: Nov 20, New York City, N.Y.

The Survivors (drama)...... Tom (1969–70)

LISA, ANNA—actress
b: Oslo, Norway

Black Saddle (wes)
.... Nora Travers (1959–60)

LISSEK, LEON—actor

Shogun (drama) ..... Father Sebastio (1980)

LISTER, CHEZ—black juvenile actor

Father Murphy (drama)......... Eli (1982)

LITEL, JOHN—actor
b: Dec 30, 1894*, Albany, Wis. d: Feb 3, 1972

My Hero (com)... Willis Thackery (1952–53)

LITONDE, OLIVER—actor

The Search for the Nile (drama)
.... King Mutesa (1972)

LITTLE, CLEAVON—black actor
b: Jun 1, 1939, Chickasha, Okla.

The David Frost Revue (com)
.... regular (1971–73)
Temperatures Rising (com)
.... Dr. Jerry Noland (1972–74)

*Some sources give 1892 or 1895.

This upbeat actor made a splash on Broadway in the late '60s and early '70s in black-consciousness plays *(The Ofay Watcher, Purlie)*; however, he is best known on television for his comedy roles, both in guest shots *(All in the Family)* and series. He was supposed to star in a situation comedy called *Mr. Dugan*—about a comical black congressman—in 1979, but the show was pulled just before its premiere, in one of the medium's more egregious cases of self-censorship due to outside pressure (some black politicians complained).

Little is also well remembered for his role as the effete black sheriff in the riotous Mel Brooks movie *Blazing Saddles* (1974).

LITTLE, JIMMY—actor

The Phil Silvers Show (com)
.... Sgt. Grover (1955–59)

LITTLE, JOYCE—actress

Private Benjamin (com)
.... Pvt. Rayleen White (1981)

LITTLE, RICH—comedian
b: Nov 26, 1938, Ottawa, Canada

Love on a Rooftop (com)
.... Stan Parker (1966–67)
The John Davidson Show (var)
.... regular (1969)
ABC Comedy Hour (com) .... regular (1972)
The Julie Andrews Hour (var)
.... regular (1972–73)
The Rich Little Show (var)...... host (1976)
You Asked for It (aud par)
.... host (1981–83)

Television's master impressionist has been a familiar and popular guest star on many programs over the years, although none of his own series have lasted long. Unlike some mimics, who are known primarily for one subject (Will Jordan's Ed Sullivan, David Frye's Richard Nixon, etc.), Rich seems to be able to do almost anyone well. He is said to have a repertoire of more than 160 characterizations.

Rich's early experience was in Canada (where mimicking Americans goes over well); he was a disc jockey, actor, and talk show host in Ottawa. His career was launched in the U.S. with a 1964 appearance on *The Judy Garland Show,* and

thereafter he was seen regularly on American shows, including numerous appearances on *The Tonight Show.*

Rich's humor is gentle, not biting, and his subjects generally do not object; in fact, some are quite appreciative. Jack Benny once wrote him, "With Bob Hope doing my walk and you doing my voice, I can be a star and do nothing."

LITTLE, TINY, JR.—pianist
b: Aug 31, 1930, Worthington, Minn.

The Lawrence Welk Show (music)
.... regular (1955–59)

LITTLEFIELD, LUCIEN—actor
b: Aug 16, 1895, San Antonio, Texas d: Jun 4, 1960

Blondie (com).......... Mr. Beasley (1957)

LIVELY SET, THE—

The Kraft Summer Music Hall (var)
.... regulars (1966)

LIVELY, ROBYN—actress

Boone (drama) .... Amanda (1983–84)

LIVINGSTON, BARRY—actor
b: Dec 17, 1953, Los Angeles, Calif.

My Three Sons (com)
.... Ernie Douglas (1963–72)
Sons and Daughters (drama)
.... Murray "Moose" Kerner (1974)

LIVINGSTON, MICHELLE—actress

Toma (police) ...... Donna Toma (1973–74)

LIVINGSTON, STANLEY—actor
b: 1950, Los Angeles, Calif.

My Three Sons (com)
.... Chip Douglas (1960–72)

Barry, Michelle, and Stanley are brothers and sisters.

LIVINGSTONE, MARY—actress
b: 1908, Seattle, Wash. d: Jun 30, 1983

The Jack Benny Show (com)
.... as herself (1950–65)

The wife of Jack Benny, whom she met at age 13 and married when she was 18. She appeared with him professionally for the rest of his life. A standing joke on their shows was that he had met her when she was selling hosiery at Mays Department Store.

LIVOTI, JOE—violinist

The Lawrence Welk Show (music)
.... regular (1962–82)

LLEWELYN, DOUG—host

The People's Court (misc). reporter (1981–)

LLOYD, CHRISTOPHER—actor
b: Oct 22, 1938, Stamford, Conn.

Taxi (com)
.... "Reverend Jim" Ignatowski (1979–83)

Emmy Award: Best Supporting Actor in a Comedy, for *Taxi* (1982)

TV Guide called him a "One Minute Superstar," one of those second or third-line character actors who happen to land a brief but juicy supporting role and make it their own—gaining instant (if minor) fame. In Chris's case the role was that of the spaced-out "Reverend Jim" on *Taxi*, a burned-out flower child of the '60s whom he portrayed so vividly that few who ever saw the show will forget it. Before that serendipitous role, Chris had a long and mostly obscure career onstage in the '60s and '70s and had also played small parts in movies, including *One Flew over the Cuckoo's Nest* in 1975. He had also been in episodes of TV series. After his success on *Taxi*, which blossomed from a single guest appearance into a regular role, he was seen a lot more often, in series including *Barney Miller* and *Best of the West* (as the Calico Kid) and in TV movies.

LLOYD, JEREMY—comedian, writer

Rowan & Martin's Laugh-In (var)
.... regular (1969–70)

LLOYD, KATHLEEN—actress

Gangster Chronicles (drama)
.... Stella Siegel (1981)
Magnum, P.I. (drama)
.... Asst. D.A. Carol Baldwin (1983–)

LLOYD, NORMAN—actor, producer
b: Nov 8, 1914, Jersey City, N.J.

St. Elsewhere (drama)
.... Dr. Daniel Auschlander (1982–)

The kindly Dr. Auschlander of *St. Elsewhere* played some memorable villains in movies of the '40s and '50s, notably the evil character who fell from the Statue of Liberty at the climax of Alfred Hitchcock's *Saboteur* in 1942. A longtime associate of Hitchcock, Lloyd later turned to producing and was executive producer and sometimes director of *Alfred Hitchcock Presents*, as well as of such other series as *The Name of the Game* and *Omnibus*.

Lloyd got his start onstage in the early 1930s and was a co-founder, with Orson Welles and John Houseman, of the Mercury Theatre late in that decade.

LLOYD, SUE—actress
b: 1939

The Baron (drama)
.... Cordelia Winfield (1966)

LOBBIN, PEGGY—actress

Crime with Father (police)
.... Chris Riland (1951–52)

LO BIANCO, TONY—actor
b: Oct 19, Brooklyn, N.Y.

Jessie (police)....... Lt. Alex Ascoli (1984)

LOCANE, AMY—juvenile actress
b: Dec 19, 1971, Trenton, N.J.

Spencer (com)... Andrea Winger (1984–85)

LOCKE, RALPH—actor

One Man's Family (drama)
.... Mr. Roberts (1950–52)

LOCKE, TAMMY—juvenile actress

The Monroes (wes)
.... Amy Monroe (1966–67)

LOCKHART, ANNE—actress

Battlestar Galactica (sci fi) ... Sheba (1979)

The daughter of June Lockhart, with whom she occasionally appeared on *Lassie*.

Later, somewhat older and more shapely, she was "Pogo Lil" on several episodes of *B.J. and the Bear.*

LOCKHART, JUNE—actress
b: Jun 25, 1925, New York City, N.Y.

Who Said That? (quiz)... panelist (1952–55)
Lassie (adv) .... Ruth Martin (1958–64)
Lost in Space (sci fi)
.... Maureen Robinson (1965–68)
Petticoat Junction (com)
.... Dr. Janet Craig (1968–70)

It's hard to believe that the pleasant mom of *Lassie* and *Lost in Space* once played the title character in the B film *The She-Wolf of London* (1946). However, when you come from a family of character actors and practically grow up onstage (from age eight in June's case), you get used to all sorts of roles.

June's parents, Gene and Kathleen Lockhart, were two of Hollywood's leading character players; her grandfather was a performer as well. June's credits include quite a few films in the '40s (including, ironically, *Son of Lassie*) and many television appearances in the '50s, including frequent roles on *Robert Montgomery Presents.* She has continued to appear periodically since her series of the '60s, in guest roles and TV movies, most often in pleasant but undistinguished parts. In the mid-1980s she was portraying a Spanish princess on daytime's *General Hospital.* Her fondest memories, though, are of *Lassie:* "It was a sweet, fairy tale–like show. And, well, you can't beat the combination of a small boy and his dog. Never."

June's daughter Anne is a fourth-generation actress.

LOCKIN, DANNY—
Dean Martin Presents the Golddiggers (var)
.... regular (1969)

LOCKLEAR, HEATHER—actress
b: Sep 25, 1961, Los Angeles, Calif.

Dynasty (drama) .. Sammy Jo Dean (1981–)
T. J. Hooker (police)
.... Off. Stacy Sheridan (1982–86)

This perky, sexy blonde with a Farrah Fawcett hairdo made it big very quickly on television. She began doing commercials during her freshman year at U.C.L.A.; within a couple of years she had quit college and was appearing on two popular prime time series simultaneously, *T. J. Hooker* (as sweet Stacy) and *Dynasty* (as nasty Sammy Jo). "Who says you have to pay dues?" she says, with a pixieish grin you can't get mad at.

LOCKWOOD, GARY—actor
b: Feb 21, 1937, Van Nuys, Calif.

Follow the Sun (adv) .. Eric Jason (1961–62)
The Lieutenant (drama)
.... Lt. William (Bill) Rice (1963–64)

This rugged he-man actor of the '60s was a former movie stuntman and stand-in for Anthony Perkins. He has guest-starred in many series over the years, especially crime shows such as *Barnaby Jones* and *Police Story.*

LODEN, BARBARA—actress, director
b: 1932, Marion, N.C. d: Sep 5, 1980

The Ernie Kovacs Show (var)
.... regular (1956)
Tonight (talk) .... regular (1956–57)

LOEB, PHILIP—actor
b: 1894 Philadelphia, Pa. d: Sep 1, 1955

The Goldbergs (com)
.... Jake Goldberg (1949–51)

This unfortunate actor was driven from television by political blacklisting in the 1950s, after a long career (since the '20s) onstage and in a few movies. Despondent and embittered, he committed suicide in 1955.

LOFTIN, CAREY—actor
b: Jan 31, 1914, Blountstown, Fla.

Troubleshooters (adv) ... Skinner (1959–60)

LOGAN, ALAN—pianist
Teen Time Tunes (music) .... trio (1949)

LOGAN, BRAD—actor
The Red Skelton Show (var)
.... regular (1970–71)

LOGAN, MARTHA—actress

The Swift Show (var)
...... commercial spokesperson (1948–49)

LOGAN, MICHAEL—actor

The Winds of War (drama)
.... Alistair Tudsbury (1983)

LOGAN, ROBERT—actor
b: Brooklyn, N.Y.

77 Sunset Strip (drama)
.... J. R. Hale (1961–63)
Daniel Boone (wes)
.... Jericho Jones (1965–66)

LOGGIA, ROBERT—actor
b: Jan 3, 1930, Staten Island, New York City, N.Y.

T.H.E. Cat (adv)
... Thomas Hewitt Edward Cat (1966–67)
Emerald Point N.A.S. (drama)
.... Adm. Yuri Bukharin (1983–84)

Loggia, an agile "ethnic" actor of Sicilian descent, played El Gato ("the cat") on Disney's *The Nine Lives of Elfego Baca* in 1958, as well as many other television roles, before starring as cat burglar T.H.E. Cat in the '60s. He has also appeared in movies, ranging from *Somebody up There Likes Me* in the '50s to *An Officer and a Gentleman* in the '80s.

He was raised in the Little Italy section of New York City.

LOGRAN, TOMMY—sportscaster

Monday Night Fights (sport)
.... sportscaster (1954–55)

LOHMAN, RICK—actor
b: Feb 28, Cleveland, Ohio

Phyl & Mikhy (com) .. Mikhail Orlov (1980)

LOLLOBRIGIDA, GINA—actress
b: Jul 4, 1927, Subiaco, Italy

Falcon Crest (drama)
.... Francesca Gioberti (1984)

The famous Italian sexpot is not known for her television work, although she was often referred to by leering stand-up comedians on variety shows. *The Flint-*

stones portrayed her, in animated form, as a sexy cook (Lollobrickida). In the mid-1980s she was lured onto the small screen in person for a celebrity role on *Falcon Crest*.

Gina has acted less frequently since the early 1970s, when she began pursuing a career as a photographer and journalist. She managed to arrange interviews with some pretty elusive people (wonder how?), including a widely publicized session with Cuban dictator Fidel Castro.

LOMAN, HAL—

Front Row Center (var) ... regular (1949–50)

LOMAX, STAN—sportscaster

Madison Square Garden Highlights (sport)
.... host (1953–54)
Greatest Sport Thrills (sport)
.... host (1954–56)

LOMBARD, MICHAEL—actor

The Mary Tyler Moore Hour (var)
.... Harry Sinclair (1979)
Filthy Rich (com).. Marshall Beck (1982–83)

LOMBARDO, GUY—orchestra leader
b: Jun 19, 1902, London, Ont., Canada d: Nov 5, 1977

Guy Lombardo & His Royal Canadians (music) .... host (1954–55)
Guy Lombardo's Diamond Jubilee (var)
.... host (1956)

The genial maestro of "The Sweetest Music This Side of Heaven"—or, to the more scornful, a sort of cornball "Businessman's Bounce." Guy was better known to TV audiences for his annual New Year's Eve telecasts than for his syndicated and network series in the 1950s. His brothers Carmen (the band's musical director), Victor, and Lebert were all members of the orchestra. Guy, as the eldest, was designated the leader.

For most of his years in television, Guy represented nostalgia for the '30s and '40s. One of his last appearances was in the period detective series *Ellery Queen;* no one could better evoke the flavor of New York in the '40s. His autobiography was titled *Auld Acquaintance* (1975).

518

LOMOND, BRITT—actor, producer

Zorro (wes).... Capt. Monastario (1957–59)
The Life and Legend of Wyatt Earp (wes)
.... Johnny Ringo (1960–61)

LON, ALICE—singer, hostess
b: c. 1926, Kilgore, Texas d: Apr 24, 1981

The Lawrence Welk Show (music)
.... Champagne Lady (1955–59)

Lawrence Welk's original Champagne Lady, fired by the straitlaced maestro, it is said, because she showed "too much knee" on camera. "Cheesecake does not fit our show," he fumed. "All I did was sit on a desk and cross my legs," Miss Lon primly replied. "That is the way a lady sits down."

Lawrence later apologized, but Alice would not come back.

LONDON LINE DANCERS—

Showtime (var)............ regulars (1968)

LONDON, DIRK—actor

The Life and Legend of Wyatt Earp (wes)
.... Morgan Earp (1959–61)

LONDON, JULIE—singer, actress
b: Sep 26, 1926, Santa Rosa, Calif.

Emergency (drama)
.... Nurse Dixie McCall (1972–77)

Although she had been appearing in minor films since 1944's *Jungle Woman*, Julie London first attracted national attention as a singer, with an extremely sultry, sexy torch song called "Cry Me a River" in 1955. The record—and an album jacket that showed a striking decolletage—gave her career a major boost and led not only to variety show appearances (with Ed Sullivan, Perry Como, etc.) but also to TV acting roles. During the late '50s and early '60s Julie was featured in such series as *Zane Grey Theatre*, *Adventures in Paradise*, and *Laramie* (as a blackjack queen with whom it was dangerous to flirt!). After a period of less activity she returned in 1972 as a regular on the popular Saturday night series *Emergency*, which ran for five years. The show represented a rather interesting marital ménage à trois; it was produced by her former husband (from 1945–

53), Jack Webb, and costarred her current husband, Bobby Troup. Apparently no one had any hard feelings.

LONDON, MARC—actor, writer

The Hero (com) .... Dewey (1966–67)

Emmy Award: Best Writing for a Comedy Show, for *Rowan & Martin's Laugh-In* (1968)

LONDON, STEVE—actor

The Untouchables (police)
.... Agent Rossman (1960–63)

LONERGAN, LEONORE—comedienne

Holiday Hotel (var)
.... switchboard operator (1950)

LONERGAN, LESTER, JR.—actor
b: c. 1894 d: Dec 23, 1959

The Growing Paynes (com)
.... regular (1948–49)

LONG, AVON—black actor
b: Jun 18, 1910, Baltimore, Md. d: Feb 15, 1984

Roots: The Next Generations (drama)
.... Chicken George Moore (1979)

LONG, BILL, & HIS RANCH GIRLS—band

Village Barn (var)....... regulars (1948–50)

LONG, LITTLE ELLER—comedienne

The Pee Wee King Show (var)
.... regular (1955)

They called 'er "Little Eller" 'cause she was six-foot-five. Yuk!

LONG, MARY—actress

The Comedy Factory (var) ... regular (1985)

LONG, RICHARD—actor
b: Dec 17, 1927, Chicago, Ill. d: Dec 22, 1974

Bourbon Street Beat (drama)
.... Rex Randolph (1959–60)
77 Sunset Strip (drama)
.... Rex Randolph (1960–61)

Big Valley (wes) .. Jarrod Barkley (1965–69)
Nanny and the Professor (com)
.... Prof. Howard Everett (1970–71)
Thicker Than Water (com)
.... Ernie Paine (1973)

LONG, SHELLEY—actress
b: Aug 23, 1949, Fort Wayne, Ind.

Cheers (com)..... Diane Chambers (1982–)

Emmy Award: Best Actress in a Comedy Series, for *Cheers* (1983)

This sharp-featured, quizzical-looking actress got her professional start as cohost of a local TV magazine show called *Sorting It Out* in Chicago in the early '70s. Comedy proved a more productive path, however, as she moved on to the city's famous Second City improvisational theater and then to Hollywood for guest roles on TV series. Her first major break was on a special called *That Thing on ABC*. She is most famous as the intellectual waitress—and Ted Danson's love interest—on *Cheers*.

LONG, WAYNE—actor
Operation Petticoat (com)
.... Chief Herbert Molumphrey (1977–78)

LONGDEN, JOHN—actor
b: Nov 11, 1900, West Indies d: May 26, 1971

Man from Interpol (police)
.... Supt. Mercer (1960)

LONGO, TONY—actor
Alice (com) .... Artie (1982–85)
Hell Town (drama) .... Stump (1985)

LONOW, CLAUDIA—actress
b: Jan 26, New York City, N.Y.

Knots Landing (drama)
.... Diana Fairgate (1979–84)

The stepdaughter of actor Mark Lonow. She joined the cast of *Knots Landing* while still a high school student.

LONOW, MARK—actor
b: Brooklyn, N.Y.

Husbands, Wives & Lovers (com)
.... Lennie Bellini (1978)

LONTOC, LEON—actor
b: 1909 d: Jan 22, 1974

Burke's Law (police)....... Henry (1963–65)

Gene Barry's chauffeur on *Burke's Law*.

LOOKINLAND, MIKE—juvenile actor
b: c. 1960, Mount Pleasant, Utah

The Brady Bunch (com)
.... Bobby Brady (1969–74)
The Brady Bunch Hour (var)
.... Bobby Brady (1977)

LOOKINLAND, TODD—juvenile actor
The New Land (adv) ... Tuliff Larsen (1974)

LOPEZ, J. VICTOR—actor
b: c. 1946 d: Mar 28, 1986

Man from Atlantis (adv)... Chuey (1977–78)

LOPEZ, MARCO—actor
Emergency (drama)
.... Fireman Lopez (1973–77)

LOPEZ, MARIO—actor
a.k.a. Pablo (com)
.... Tomas Del Gato (1984)

LOPEZ, PRISCILLA—actress
b: Feb 26, 1948, The Bronx, N.Y. r: Brooklyn, N.Y.

In the Beginning (com)
.... Sister Agnes (1978)
Kay O'Brien (drama)
.... Nurse Rosa Villanueva (1986–)

LOPEZ, VINCENT—orchestra leader
b: Dec 30, 1898, Brooklyn, N.Y. d: Sep 20, 1975

Welcome Aboard (var)
.... host/orch. leader (1948–49)
Vincent Lopez (var) .... host (1949–50)
The Vincent Lopez Show (music)
.... host (1957)

Pianist and popular bandleader on radio and records from the 1920s onward. His theme song, performed with flying fingers, was "Nola." Lopez was seen occasionally on television in the early days.

LOR, DENISE—singer
b: California

The Garry Moore Show (var)
.... regular (1950–51)
Seven at Eleven (var)........ regular (1951)
Droodles (quiz)............. panelist (1954)

LORD, BOBBY—country singer
b: Jan 6, 1934, Sanford, Fla.

Ozark Jubilee (music)..... regular (1957–60)

LORD, JACK—actor
b: Dec 30, 1930*, New York City, N.Y.

Stoney Burke (wes)
.... Stoney Burke (1962–63)
Hawaii Five-O (police)
.... Det. Steve McGarrett (1968–80)

Jack Lord presents an interesting mix of images. His hard, craggy features suggest a TV tough guy, and indeed he played a role not far from that for many years, as the hard-driving chief detective on *Hawaii Five-O*. His professional rodeo rider, *Stoney Burke*, was a pretty tough customer, too, and Jack played many similar characters—often villains—on westerns and crime shows of the '50s and '60s.

On the other hand, there is Jack Lord the artist, a prolific and sensitive talent whose paintings and sketches are widely acclaimed. His works are in the permanent collections of some 40 museums and universities in six countries, including the Metropolitan Museum of Art, the Library of Congress, and the British Museum.

Jack, the son of a steamship executive, developed a love of art, and exotic locales, as a young seaman watching the world from the decks of freighters in the Mediterranean and off the coasts of China, Persia, and Africa. He graduated from a maritime academy as a merchant marine officer (he still holds a second-mate's license) and first became interested in acting while making maritime training films. After study in New York he broke into the theater in the early 1950s and landed his first TV role in a episode of *Man Against Crime*. This was followed by many more, on series ranging from *Studio One* to *Stagecoach West*. The chance to move to sunny Hawaiian climes, surrounded by

*Some sources give 1922 or 1928.

ocean, for the series *Hawaii Five-O* was more than he could resist. He has made Hawaii his home ever since and has been quite active in local civic affairs there.

LORD, MARJORIE—actress
b: Jul 26, 1922, San Francisco, Calif.

The Danny Thomas Show (com)
.... Mrs. Kathy ("Clancey") Williams
(1957–64)
Make Room for Granddaddy (com)
... Kathy Williams ("Clancey") (1970–71)

Though she is best known as Danny Thomas's TV wife "Clancey," Marjorie Lord has had a long and varied career. She began in movies at the age of 15 (in *Border Cafe* and *Forty Naughty Girls*) and appeared in many B films during the late '30s and '40s. She was also active onstage and began doing TV work in the early days of the medium, in *Fireside Theatre, Cavalcade of America, The Lone Ranger*, and *Ramar of the Jungle*—shows that were, roughly, TV's equivalent of the B movie. *The Danny Thomas Show* secured her place in TV history, and she has done relatively little in the medium since then, aside from an occasional TV movie or visit to *Fantasy Island*. She has been more active in dinner theater productions.

Marjorie is the mother of actress Anne Archer, by her first husband actor John Archer.

LORD, PHIL—actor
b: c. 1879 d: Nov 25, 1968

Hawkins Falls, Population 6,200 (com)
.... the judge (1950)
Stud's Place (var) .... Mr. Lord (1950)

LORDE, ATHENA—actress
b: 1915 d: May 23, 1973

One Man's Family (drama)
.... Judith Richardson (1950)

Married to actor Jim Boles.

LOREN, DONNA—singer
b: Mar 7, 1947, Boston, Mass.

Shindig (music) ... frequent guest (1964–66)
The Milton Berle Show (var)
.... regular (1966)

The pretty teenage singer of the 1960s, famous as the "Dr. Pepper Girl" in commercials and for her many appearances in beach-party movies and on TV contemporary music shows. Although she was the marketing man's idea of the "youth generation" (at least, Dr. Pepper thought so), she never had a hit record or starring vehicle of her own. She married and retired at the age of 21.

LORING, ESTELLE—singer

Admiral Broadway Revue (var)
.... regular (1949)
Stop the Music (quiz).... vocalist (1949–50)

LORING, LISA—actress
b: Feb 16, 1958, in the South Pacific

The Addams Family (com)
Wednesday Thursday Addams (1964–66)

Lisa Loring, the little pigtailed girl in the macabre *Addams Family* comedy, has had a rather tumultuous life. She was born on a remote South Pacific island to navy parents, who divorced a short time later, and grew up in Hawaii and later Los Angeles. At six she was cast in *The Addams Family,* bringing both show-business pressures and a lot of money (which she squandered quickly when she got control of it in her teens). Her mother, an alcoholic, died while she was still young and Lisa married and became pregnant at 15, then was divorced at 16. She tried to get back into acting but found only commercial work until she landed the role of the "troubled teen," Cricket Montgomery, on *As the World Turns* in 1980.

"Sure, life's a soap opera," she told a reporter in 1982. "Disasters, extreme happiness. It's *everybody's* life, not just mine."

LORING, LYNN—actress
b: c. 1945

Take It from Me (com) . daughter (1953–54)
Fair Exchange (com)
.... Patty Walker (1962–63)
The F.B.I. (police)
.... Barbara Erskine (1965–66)

Dark-haired Lynn Loring grew up on television as the trouble-prone Patti Barron, daughter of soap opera queen Mary Stuart

on daytime's *Search for Tomorrow* (from 1951–61). She moved into prime time during the 1960s with two regular series roles and numerous guest appearances and was seen in scattered TV movies after that—some costarring her husband Roy Thinnes (e.g., *The Horror at 37,000 Feet*). In more recent years Lynn has become a movie executive, producing such films as *The Making of a Male Model* (for Joan Collins), *Sizzle* (for Loni Anderson), and *Mr. Mom.*

LORNE, MARION—actress
b: 1886, Wilkes Barre, Pa. d: May 9, 1968

Mr. Peepers (com)... Mrs. Gurney (1952–55)
Sally (com) .. Mrs. Myrtle Banford (1957–58)
The Garry Moore Show (var)
.... regular (1958–62)
Bewitched (com) ..... Aunt Clara (1964–68)

Emmy Award: Best Supporting Actress in a Comedy, for *Bewitched* (1968)

This character actress had long stage experience, much of it in England, extending back to the early years of the century. Television viewers knew her as a delightfully dithery old lady, especially on *Bewitched* in the 1960s. She died in her eighties, still performing, and never lost her love for pleasing audiences. She said, toward the end of her years, "show business is still the most exciting thing I know."

LORRING, JOAN—actress
b: 1926*, Hong Kong, r: Shanghai, China

Norby (com) .... Helen Norby (1955)

LOUANNE—actress

Two Marriages (drama)
............., Shelby Armstrong (1983–84)

LOUDON, DOROTHY—actress, singer
b: Sep 17, 1930, Cambridge, Mass.

It's a Business (com) .... regular (1952)
Laugh Line (quiz).......... panelist (1959)
The Garry Moore Show (var)
.... regular (1962–64)
Dorothy (com) .... Dorothy Banks (1979)

This actress-singer specializes in belting out tunes from the Roaring Twenties. She

*Some sources give 1931.

has been most successful on Broadway, where she won a Tony Award in 1977 for her role in the musical *Annie.*

LOUGHERY, JACKIE—actress
b: 1930

Seven at Eleven (var)........ regular (1951)
Mr. District Attorney (police)
.... Miss Miller (1954)
The Adventures of Judge Roy Bean (wes)
.... Letty Bean (1955–56)

Miss U.S.A. of 1952, and one of Jack Webb's former wives.

LOUIS-DREYFUS, JULIA—comedienne
b: Jan 13, 1961, New York City, N.Y.

NBC's Saturday Night Live (com)
.... regular (1982–85)

LOUISE, ANITA—actress
b: Jan 9, 1915, New York City, N.Y. d: Apr 25, 1970

My Friend Flicka (adv)
.... Nell McLaughlin (1956–57)
Theater Time (drama) .... hostess (1957)
Spotlight Playhouse (drama) . hostess (1958)

LOUISE, TINA—actress
b: Feb 11, 1934, New York City, N.Y.

Jan Murray Time (var)...... vocalist (1955)
Gilligan's Island (com)
.... Ginger Grant (1964–67)
Dallas (drama)........... Julie Grey (1978)
Rituals (drama) ...... Taylor Chapin (1985)

This statuesque beauty began appearing on television in the mid-1950s in both dramas and comedies (such as *The Phil Silvers Show*) at about the same time she was attracting wolf whistles on Broadway in *Li'l Abner.* She worked steadily in TV and somehow, in the mid-1960s, managed to get involved with a particularly silly situation comedy, probably thinking that it would not last very long. The program, of course, was *Gilligan's Island,* and it has become one of TV's cult classics. Tina, the "movie star" on the show, has had a hard time living it down, although she has tried. She appeared in the '70s and '80s in a succession of dramatic roles on *Mannix, Police Story, CHiPs,* and other series and

was briefly seen on *Dallas* during its first season. She appeared in several TV movies, including the aptly named *The Day the Women Got Even* (1980). She was also the only member of the original *Gilligan* cast who refused to take part in the show's reunion specials between 1978–81. It made no difference. No matter what else she has done, to millions of viewers she will always be "the movie star" on that infernal island.

Tina was married to talk show host Les Crane.

LOUVIN BROTHERS—country singers
Charlie, b: Jul 7, 1927, Rainsville, Ala.
Ira, b: Apr 21, 1924, Rainsville, Ala. d: Jun 20, 1965

Grand Ole Opry (music) .. regular (1955–56)

LOVATO, BETO—actress
a.k.a. Pablo (com) ... Mario Del Gato (1984)

LOVE, KELAND—actor
The Brady Brides (com) ...... Harry (1981)

LOVEJOY, FRANK—actor
b: Mar 28, 1914*, The Bronx, N.Y. d: Oct 2, 1962

Man Against Crime (drama)
.... Mike Barnett (1956)
Meet McGraw (drama) . McGraw (1957–59)

The radio and movie tough guy, who plied his hard-knuckles trade on many television dramas from the early 1950s until his death in 1962.

LOVITZ, JON—comedian
b: Jul 21, 1957, Tarzana, Calif.

NBC's Saturday Night Live (var)
.... regular (1985–)
Foley Square (com)........ Mole (1985–86)

Lovitz is best known as the pathological liar Tommy Flanagan on *Saturday Night Live,* who ended every preposterous excuse with "Yeah, that's the ticket."

LOW, BEN—actor
Faraway Hill (drama) .... regular (1946)

*Some sources give 1912.

LOW, DR. THEODORE—host

Key to the Ages (info) . . . . host (1955)

LOWE, CHAD—actor
b: Jan 15, 1968, Dayton, Ohio

Spencer (com). . . . Spencer Winger (1984–85)

The handsome younger brother of teen movie heartthrob Rob Lowe. Chad had a major break when he was offered the starring role in his own series, *Spencer*, only a few months after he decided that he would try acting too; however, he quit TV after only a few episodes, after a contract dispute with NBC.

LOWE, EDMUND—actor
b: Mar 3, 1890, San Jose, Calif. d: Apr 21, 1971

Your Witness (drama) . . . . regular (1949–50)
Front Page Detective (drama)
. . . . David Chase (1951–53)

LOWE, JIM—disc jockey, host
b: May 7, 1927, Springfield, Mo.

Jim has been a leading New York disc jockey since the mid-1950s and is presently on station WNEW, where he is billed as "The King of Trivia." His own music and television successes are so obscure they might well provide questions for his "Trivia Hall of Fame." In case he asks you, here are some clues about his own career: (1) Jim wrote a very popular song in the early '50s, which was recorded by others but is hardly ever heard today; (2) his own big-hit record sold several million copies in 1956 and is better remembered; (3) he hosted one network TV series, a 1958 CBS summer show, which is almost totally forgotten; (4) Jim's TV series was evidently ahead of its time—a few years later a rather stiff and awkward record company executive hosted a virtually identical show, and *he* scored a major hit with it. Can you name each of these songs and shows? (Answers below).*

LOWE, ROB—actor
b: Mar 17, 1964, Charlottesville, Va.

*(1) "Gambler's Guitar"; (2) "The Green Door"; (4) *Sing Along;* (4) Mitch Miller's *Sing Along with Mitch,* in 1961.

A New Kind of Family (com)
. . . . Tony Flanagan (1979–80)

LOWELL, TOM—actor
b: 1941

Combat (drama) . . . . Nelson (1963–64)

LOWERY, ROBERT—actor
b: 1914, Kansas City, Mo. d: Dec 26, 1971

Circus Boy (adv)
. . . . Big Tim Champion (1956–58)
Pistols 'n' Petticoats (com)
. . . . Buss Courtney (1966–67)

LOWRY, JUDITH—actress
b: Jul 27, 1890, Ft. Sill, Okla.** d: Nov 29, 1976

Phyllis (com)
. . . . Sally "Mother" Dexter (1975–77)

LU, LISA—actress
Have Gun Will Travel (wes)
. . . . Hey Girl (1960–61)
Anna and the King (com)
. . . . Lady Thiang (1972)

LUCAS, DIONE—cooking expert
To the Queen's Taste (info) . . chef (1948–49)

LUCAS, JONATHAN—
Melody Tour (var) . . . . regular (1954)

LUCHSINGER, CHUCK—actor
r: Moline, Ill.

Cartoon Teletales (child) . . cohost (1948–50)

LUCHSINGER, JACK—artist
r: Moline, Ill.

Cartoon Teletales (child) . . cohost (1948–50)

LUCK, SUSAN—actress
AfterMASH (com) . . . . . Nurse Weber (1984)

LUCKINBILL, LAURENCE—actor
b: Nov 21, 1934, Fort Smith, Ark.

The Delphi Bureau (drama)
. . . . Glenn Garth Gregory (1972–73)
Ike (drama) . . . . Maj. Richard Arnold (1979)

**Some sources give Morristown, N.J.

LUCKING, WILLIAM—actor

b: Jun 17, Vicksburg, Mich.

Big Hawaii (drama) . Oscar Kalahani (1977)
Shannon (police)
.... Det. Norm White (1981–82)
The Blue and the Gray (drama)
.... Capt. Potts (1982)
The A-Team (adv)..... Col. Lynch (1983–84)
Jessie (police)... Sgt. Mac McClellan (1984)

LUDDEN, ALLEN—host

b: Oct 5, 1919*, Mineral Point, Wis. d: Jun 9, 1981

Password (quiz).......... emcee (1962–67)
Liar's Club (quiz)........... host (1977–78)

Emmy Award: Best Host of a Daytime Game Show, for *Password* (1976)

Who says television executives are a bunch of coldhearted businessmen with no on-camera talent? Maybe some are, but Allen Ludden is one executive who stepped out from behind his desk to become a very popular and beloved TV personality.

Allen entered the industry in 1948 as continuity director for a radio station in Hartford, Connecticut. While there, he created his first program, *Mind Your Manners,* a talk show for teenagers that he wrote and hosted; it was eventually picked up for a daytime run on the NBC–TV network in 1951–52. Allen continued to work as a program executive during the 1950s, eventually moving to CBS as program director for its owned stations. At the same time, he produced another daytime show, *College Bowl,* which began on radio in 1953 and moved to television in 1958 (as *G.E. College Bowl*) with himself as host. In 1961 he finally gave up his executive responsibilities to concentrate on a career in front of the camera. That same year he debuted in his most famous show, *Password,* which has run, on and off, ever since—in daytime, nighttime, and syndicated versions. Allen himself was the gentle, silver-haired emcee of all versions until 1980, when illness forced his retirement. He also hosted several other daytime and nighttime game shows over the years, including *Liar's Club* and *Stumpers.*

*Some sources give 1918 or (less likely) 1929.

Allen was married for many years to actress Betty White.

LUEZ, LAURETTE—actress

The Adventures of Fu Manchu (drama)
.... Karamanch (1955–56)

LUFT, LORNA—actress

b: Nov 21, 1952, Los Angeles, Calif.

Trapper John, M.D. (drama)
.... Nurse Libby Kegler (1985–86)

The daughter of legendary Hollywood star Judy Garland. Lorna made her first appearances as a child with her mother and by the 1980s had carved out a minor career in guest roles on such series as *Murder, She Wrote* and *Tales from the Dark Side.* Her more successful sister is singer Liza Minelli.

LUISI, JAMES—actor

The Rockford Files (drama)
.... Lt. Doug Chapman (1976–80)
Harris and Company (drama)
.... Harry Foreman (1979)
Renegades (police) ..... Lt. Marciano (1983)

Emmy Award: Best Actor in a Daytime Drama Special, for *First Ladies' Diaries: Martha Washington* (1976)

LUJACK, JOHNNY—football player

Ask Me Another (quiz) ..... panelist (1952)

LUKE, KEYE—actor

b: Jun 18, 1904, Canton, China r: Seattle, Wash.

Kentucky Jones (drama)
.... Thomas Wong (1964–65)
Anna and the King (com)
.... Kralahome (1972)
Kung Fu (wes) .... Master Po (1972–75)
Harry-O (drama) .... Dr. Fong (1976)

One of Hollywood's leading Chinese-American actors, famous as Charlie Chan's "Number One Son" in movies of the 1930s. He finally got to play Chan himself —at least his voice—in the Saturday morning cartoon *Amazing Chan and the Chan Clan* from 1972–74.

Luke made many other television appearances over the years as well, from

Fireside Theatre in the '50s to *Star Trek* in the '60s and *Charlie's Angels* in the '80s. He is perhaps best remembered, under heavy makeup (to age his still rather youthful face), as the ancient Master Po on *Kung Fu*.

LUKOYE, PETER—actor

Born Free (adv) .... Nuru (1974)

LULU—singer
b: Nov 3, 1948, Lennoxtown, Scotland

Andy Williams Presents Ray Stevens (var)
.... regular (1970)

Pop singer ("To Sir with Love") much seen on TV variety shows of the late '60s and early '70s, but not much seen since then.

LUMB, GEOFFREY—actor

Honestly Celeste (com) . Mr. Wallace (1954)

LUMBLY, CARL—black actor
b: Jamaica r: Minneapolis, Minn.

Cagney & Lacey (police)
.... Det. Marcus Petrie (1982–)

LUMLEY, JOANNA—actress
b: 1946

The New Avengers (drama)
.... Purdey (1978–80)

LUMMIS, DAYTON—actor
b: 1903

Law of the Plainsman (wes)
.... Marshal Andy Morrison (1959–60)

LUND, ART—singer
b: Apr 1, 1915*, Salt Lake City, Utah

The Ken Murray Show (var)
.... regular (1951–52)

LUND, DEANNA—actress
b: Oak Park, Ill.

Land of the Giants (sci fi)
.... Valerie Scott (1968–70)

LUND, LEE—

Ben Vereen . . . Comin' at Ya (var)
.... regular (1975)

*Some sources give 1920.

LUND, TIM—

The Steve Allen Comedy Hour (var)
.... regular (1980–81)

LUND, TRIGGER—

The Ernie Kovacs Show (var)
.... regular (1952–53)

LUNDIGAN, WILLIAM—actor
b: Jun 12, 1914, Syracuse, N.Y. d: Dec 20, 1975

Climax (drama) .... host (1954–58)
Shower of Stars (var)........ host (1954–58)
Men into Space (sci fi)
.... Col. Edward McCauley (1959–60)

LUNGHI, CHERIE—actress
b: 1953, London, England

Master of the Game (drama)
.... Margaret Van der Merwe (1984)

LUPINO, IDA—actress
b: Feb 4, 1914**, London, England

Four Star Playhouse (drama)
.... costar (1952–56)
Mr. Adams and Eve (com)
.... Eve Drake (1957–58)

This Hollywood star was famous for her movie "tough" roles (she once called herself "the poor man's Bette Davis"). From the 1950s to the early '70s she was quite active in television, both in acting and production. On-camera she played many roles, on *Four Star Playhouse* in the '50s and in guest appearances in later series ranging from *The Twilight Zone* to *Batman* (as Dr. Cassandra, an alchemist who gleefully turned Batman and Robin into cardboard slabs). Many of her appearances were dramatic, but the nutty ones were more fun—for example, in *The Wild Wild West* she was Dr. Faustina, a mad scientist who created a robot that looked exactly like Robert Conrad so that she could blow him up.

Although Ida projected much grief and anguish on the movie screen, she and her husband Howard Duff evidently found quite a bit of humor in real-life Hollywood. Their comedy series *Mr. Adams and Eve* was based on their own experiences in the film capital.

**Some sources give 1918.

Ida's other career, that of a producer-director, also flourished on TV. She directed many episodes of *Four Star Playhouse, Dick Powell Theatre,* and *The Big Valley,* as well as segments of numerous other series, among them *Alfred Hitchcock Presents, The Fugitive,* and *Bewitched.*

LUPTON, JOHN—actor
b: Aug 22, 1928, Highland Park, Ill. r: Milwaukee, Wisc.

Broken Arrow (wes)
.... Tom Jeffords (1956–58)

This boyish-looking actor interrupted a busy career playing guest roles on prime time series for two long stretches in the '60s and '70s on the daytime soap opera *Days of Our Lives*—where he was Dr. Tommy Horton (1965–72, 1975–79). He has been seen in the '80s mainly in secondary roles in such TV movies as *Sidney Shorr* and *Bare Essence.*

LUPUS, PETER—actor
b: 1937

Mission: Impossible (drama)
.... Willie Armitage (1966–73)

The muscle man of the Impossible Missions Force.

LURIE, DAN—actor
Big Top (var) ..... the strongman (1950–51)

LUSSIER, ROBERT—actor
b: Dec 14, West Warwick R.I.

Man from Atlantis (adv) .... Brent (1977–78)

LUSTER, BETTY—singer
Sing It Again (quiz)....... regular (1950–51)
Seven at Eleven (var)....... regular (1951)

LUSTGARTEN, EDGAR—journalist, author
b: 1907 d: 1979

Scotland Yard (police)....... host (1957–58)

LUXTON, BILL—host
The Amazing World of Kreskin (aud par)
.... host (1971–75)

LUZ, FRANC—actor
b: Dec 22, Cambridge, Mass.

Hometown (drama)...... Ben Abbott (1985)

LYDON, JIMMY—actor, director
b: May 30, 1923, Harrington Park, N.J.

So This Is Hollywood (com)
.... Andy Boone (1955)
Love That Jill (com) .... Richard (1958)

The juvenile actor of the 1940s Henry Aldrich movies is now active mainly as a producer-director. He has worked behind the scenes on such TV series as *McHale's Navy, Wagon Train, Temple Houston,* and *M*A*S*H.* He also acts occasionally.

LYMAN, DOROTHY—actress
b: Apr 18, 1947, Minneapolis, Minn.

Mama's Family (com)
.... Naomi Oates Harper (1983–)

Emmy Awards: Best Supporting Actress in a Daytime Drama Series, for *All My Children* (1982); Best Actress in a Daytime Drama Series, for *All My Children* (1983)

Dorothy played colorful characters on several daytime soap operas during the '70s and '80s, notably on *The Edge of Night* (1972–73), *Another World* (1976–80), and *All My Children* (1981–83; as the delightful Opal Gardner), before scoring a prime time success in the comedy *Mama's Family.*

LYN, DAWN—juvenile actress
b: 1963

My Three Sons (com)
.... Dodie Harper Douglas (1969–72)

LYNCH, KEN—actor
The Plainclothesman (police)
.... the lieutenant (1949–54)
McCloud (police)..... Sgt. Grover (1970–77)

LYNCH, PEG—actress
b: Lincoln, Neb. r: Minnesota

Ethel and Albert (com)
.... Ethel Arbuckle (1953–56)

LYNCH, RICHARD—actor
b: Apr 29, 1936

Battlestar Galactica (sci fi) .. Xavier (1980)
The Phoenix (sci fi)...... Preminger (1982)

LYNDE, PAUL—comedian
b: Jun 13, 1926, Mt. Vernon, Ohio d: Jan 10, 1982

The Red Buttons Show (var)
.... Mr. Standish (1955)
Stanley (com)..... Horace Fenton (1956–57)
The Kraft Music Hall (var)
.... regular (1961–62)
Bewitched (com)
.... Uncle Arthur (occasional) (1965–72)
The Pruitts of Southampton (com)
.... Harvey (1967)
The Jonathan Winters Show (var)
.... regular (1968–69)
Dean Martin Presents the Golddiggers (var)
.... regular (1968–69)
Where's Huddles? (cartn)
.... Claude Pertwee (voice) (1970)
The Paul Lynde Show (com)
.... Paul Simms (1972–73)
Temperatures Rising (com)
.... Dr. Paul Mercy (1973–74)
Donny and Marie (var)
.... frequent guest (1976–79)

"When my classmates started to laugh before I even opened my mouth I had an inkling that maybe dramatic acting wasn't for me, so I did the logical thing and set out to study comedy." Paul Lynde's description of how, as a high school student, he got into comedy is a good example of the combination of bewilderment and sarcasm that made him so popular with television audiences for many years. He could be a very funny man and was much in demand for guest appearances on variety and comedy shows. However, his best roles were in support of others. Too much of him, it seems, could wear a little thin, as evidenced by the relative lack of success of his own shows (*The Paul Lynde Show, Temperatures Rising*) in the early 1970s.

Paul came to New York in the late '40s and "did the starving actor bit" (as he put it) for a few years before landing his big break in the Broadway revue *New Faces of 1952*. Television work followed and by the end of the 1950s he was rapidly becoming very popular on the small screen. His starring role in the Broadway (1960) and film (1963) versions of *Bye Bye Birdie*—a rousing parody of rock 'n' roll, Ed Sullivan, and

show biz in general—brought his career to new heights. He was especially good in sketches (on *That's Life, Love, American Style*, etc.) and tossing off quips on daytime's *Hollywood Squares*, where he was a regular for many years. A couple examples from *Squares'* center square:

Q: "Your elephant is purring. Does that mean he's contented?"
Paul: "He should be, he just ate my cat."

Q: "According to the World Book, what is the average person in Spain doing between 10 P.M. and midnight?"
Paul: "Killing flies."

By the late 1970s, Paul was being seen less often and made his last semiregular appearances as a kind of comic father-figure on the youthful *Donny and Marie* variety series. Though never a superstar, he was a unique talent and one who will not soon be replaced.

LYNLEY, CAROL—actress
b: Feb 13, 1942, New York City, N.Y.

The Immortal (adv)........ Sylvia (1970–71)

LYNN, BETTY—actress
The Ray Bolger Show (com)
.... June (1953–54)
Love That Jill (com) .... Pearl (1958)
The Andy Griffith Show (com)
.... Thelma Lou (1960–65)

LYNN, CYNTHIA—actress
Hogan's Heroes (com) ..... Helga (1965–66)

LYNN, DICK—
The Dom DeLuise Show (var)
.... regular (1968)

LYNN, JEFFREY—actor
b: Feb 16, 1909, Auburn, Mass.

My Son Jeep (com)
.... Dr. Robert Allison (1953)
Star Stage (drama) .... host (1955–56)

LYNN, JENNIE—juvenile actress
b: Feb 28, 1952, San Diego, Calif.

Love & Marriage (com)
.... Jennie Baker (1959–60)

LYNN, JONATHAN—actor
b: Apr 3, 1943, Bath, England

Doctor in the House (com)
.... Danny Hooley (1970–73)

LYNN, JUDY—singer

Three's Company (music) .... regular (1950)
Sing It Again (quiz)....... regular (1950–51)

LYNN, LORETTA—country singer
b: Apr 14, 1935, Butchers Hollow, Ky.

Dean Martin Presents Music Country (var)
.... regular (1973)

The "Coal Miner's Daughter," whose life story of struggle and success has been delineated in song and in a very popular movie of that name. Her younger sister, Crystal Gayle, is also a country singer. Autobiography: *Coal Miner's Daughter* (with George Vecsey, 1976).

LYNN, RITA—actress

Mr. Smith Goes to Washington (com)
.... Miss Kelly (1962–63)

LYONS, GENE—actor
b: 1923, Pittsburgh, Pa. d: 1974

Ironside (police)
.... Comm. Dennis Randall (1967–75)

LYONS, SYLVIA—panelist

Who's the Boss? (quiz)...... panelist (1954)

LYTELL, BERT—actor
b: Feb 24, 1885, New York City, N.Y. d: Sep 28, 1954

Hollywood Screen Test (talent).. host (1948)
Philco TV Playhouse (drama)
.... host (1948–49)
One Man's Family (drama)
.... Henry Barbour (1949–52)
The Orchid Award (var) ...... emcee (1953)

A silent-movie matinee idol of the 1920s who had a brief but rather active career playing distinguished roles on television until his death following surgery in 1954.

LYTTON, DEBBIE—juvenile actress

The New Land (adv)
.... Anneliese Larsen (1974)
Sara (wes)......... Debbie Higgins (1976)

Debbie played the teenager Melissa on daytime's *Days of Our Lives* during the late '70s and early '80s.

M

MACARTHUR, JAMES—actor

b: Dec 8, 1937, Los Angeles, Calif. r: Nyack, N.Y.

Hawaii Five-O (police)
.... Det. Danny Williams (1968–79)

The adopted son of actress Helen Hayes and playwright Charles MacArthur. Raised in theatrical surroundings, James made his debut at the age of eight in a summer stock production and began appearing on television in his teens. His first major exposure was on *Climax* in 1955 in the story of a young boy's brush with delinquency; he repeated the role a year later, to excellent notices, in his first film, *The Young Stranger*. James's extremely youthful looks got him many more semijuvenile TV roles over the next decade (*Alfred Hitchcock Presents, Wagon Train, Tarzan,* etc.) but were beginning to become something of a liability by the time he landed the role of Jack Lord's young assistant "Danno" on *Hawaii Five-O*. That series turned into an eleven-year career for him, ending only when he quit in 1979 to pursue "bigger things." Still looking young, he has since been seen in infrequent guest appearances and in some rather second-rate TV movies (e.g., *The Night the Bridge Fell Down,* which was made in 1979 but was so bad it was withheld by an embarrassed network until 1983).

MACATEER, ALAN—actor

Kraft Music Hall Presents The Dave King Show (var)................. regular (1959)

MACCHIO, RALPH—juvenile actor

b: Nov 4, 1962, Huntington, N.Y.

Eight Is Enough (com)
.... Jeremy Andretti (1980–81)

MACCORKINDALE, SIMON—actor

b: Feb 12, 1953, Ely, Cambridge, England

Manimal (police).... Jonathan Chase (1983)
Falcon Crest (drama)
.... Greg Reardon (1984–86)

Handsome English actor Simon MacCorkindale first became known to U.S. view-ers through his appearances on such classy British productions as *I. Claudius* and *The Manions of America*. American producers preferred to cast him as a detective with the bizarre ability to turn himself into various animals—on the gimmicky *Manimal*. Was this a comedown for an actor who had once specialized in Shakespeare and Shaw? Simon took it like a trooper, remarking "I have been shot and killed, had my hand smashed, been shot in the shoulder, hanged, beheaded, drowned, hung in chains and tortured, shot in a duel, beaten, chased, and, in *Jaws 3-D,* I am devoured by a 35-foot shark. After all this I can certainly deal with (*Manimal*)."

MACDONALD, AIMI—

The John Davidson Show (var)
.... regular (1969)

MACDONALD, ED—actor

b: May 7, 1908 d: Sep 1951

Mysteries of Chinatown (drama)
.... regular (1949–50)

MACDONNELL, KYLE—singer, hostess

b: Austin, Texas r: Lancard, Kansas

For Your Pleasure (music)
.... regular (1948–49)
Girl About Town (music)
.... hostess (1948–49)
Hold That Camera (var) ...... emcee (1950)
Celebrity Time (quiz).... panelist (1950–51)

MACGIBBON, HARRIET—actress

b: c. 1905, Chicago, Ill. d: Feb 8, 1987

The Beverly Hillbillies (com)
.... Mrs. Margaret Drysdale (1962–69)
The Smothers Brothers Show (com)
.... Mrs. Costello (1965–66)

MACGRAW, ALI—actress

b: Apr 1, 1938, Pound Ridge, N.Y.

The Winds of War (drama)
.... Natalie Jastrow (1983)
Dynasty (drama)
.... Lady Ashley Montague (1985)

Married to actor Steve McQueen in the 1970s.

MACGREGOR BROTHERS, THE—

Kraft Music Hall Presents The Des O'Connor Show (var) .... regulars (1970)

MACGREGOR, KATHERINE—actress
b: Glendale, Calif., r: Wyoming, Colorado

Little House on the Prairie (adv)
.... Harriet Oleson (1974–83)

MACGREGOR, SCOTTY—host

Scrapbook Junior Edition (child)
.... host (1948)

MACHON, KAREN—actress

The Runaways (drama)
.... Karen Wingate (1978–79)

MACHT, STEPHEN—actor
b: May 1, 1942, Philadelphia, Pa.

American Dream (drama)
.... Mr. Danny Novak (1981)
Knots Landing (drama)
.... Joe Cooper (1982–83)
Cagney & Lacey (police)
.... David Keeler (1985–)

MACIAS, ERNESTO—actor

Nancy (com) .... Rodriguez (1970–71)

MACINTOSH, JAY W.—actress
b: Mar 30, 1937, Gainesville, Ga.

Sons and Daughters (drama)
.... Lucille Reed (1974)

MACK & JAMIE—comedy team

Solid Gold (music) .... regulars (1982)

MACK, DOTTY—actress
b: Apr 25, 1930, Cincinnati, Ohio

The Paul Dixon Show (var)
.... regular (1951–52)
Dotty Mack Show (aka Girl Alone) (music)
.... hostess (1952–56)

MACK, GILBERT—actor

Johnny Jupiter (child) .... regular (1953)

MACK, TED—host
b: Feb 12, 1904, Denver, Colo. d: Jul 12, 1976

The Original Amateur Hour (talent)
.... emcee (1948–70)
The Ted Mack Family Hour (var)
.... host (1951)

"Round and round she goes, where she stops, nobody knows." With those words, solid, fatherly Ted Mack spun the Wheel of Fortune each week for 22 years to open *The Original Amateur Hour,* the TV talent show that was supposed to allow anybody —absolutely anybody—a chance at stardom. Few ever made it, even from among those who were grand prize winners, but the competition among all those eager unknowns held a special fascination for viewers.

Its host, Ted Mack, was so completely identified with the show that he is scarcely remembered for anything else. He did not originate it, however. Ted was a former musician, a saxophonist, who had played with the Ben Pollack band in the late '20s, then formed his own band, and then directed the orchestra for some MGM movie musicals during the early 1930s. In 1935 he joined Major Edward Bowes as talent coordinator for the Major's new radio show, *The Original Amateur Hour.* He remained the Major's lieutenant until Bowes' death in 1946 and then took the series to television himself. The *Amateur Hour* nearly constituted Mack's entire career from 1935–70 (a prime time variety hour in 1951 and a daytime show in 1955 starring him were both short-lived).

MACKAY, HARPER—orchestra leader
b: Oct 13, 1921, Boston, Mass.

NBC Follies (var) ...... orch. leader (1973)

MACKAY, JEFF—actor
b: Oct 20, Dallas, Texas

Baa Baa Black Sheep (drama)
.... Lt. Don French (1976–78)
Magnum, P.I. (drama)
.... Lt. Mac Reynolds (1981–82)
Tales of the Gold Monkey (adv)
.... Corky (1982–83)
Magnum, P.I. (drama)
.... Mac Reynolds (1984–85)

MACKENZIE, GISELE—singer, actress
b: Jan 10, 1927, Winnipeg, Canada

Your Hit Parade (music) . vocalist (1953–57)
The Gisele MacKenzie Show (var)
.... hostess (1957–58)
The Sid Caesar Show (var)
.... regular (1963–64)

The popular songstress of *Your Hit Parade* was also seen as an actress and comedienne from time to time during the '50s and '60s. She often played opposite Jack Benny and was Sid Caesar's TV wife for a season in 1963–64. She now appears mostly in stock productions, but she might sing her sole record hit, "Hard To Get," (remember that?) for you if you give her a call.

Gisele began on radio in Canada in the late 1940s and came to the U.S. in 1951.

MACKENZIE, PHIL—actor

The Jim Stafford Show (var)... Adam (1975)

MACKENZIE, PHILIP CHARLES—actor

Making the Grade (com)
.... David Wasserman (1982)

MACKENZIE, WILL—actor

The Bob Newhart Show (com)
.... Larry Bondurant (1975–77)

MACKIN, CATHERINE—newscaster
b: Baltimore, Md.

NBC Weekend News (news) . anchor (1977)

Emmy Award: Best Documentary Segment, for the *20/20* Report "Death in the Fast Lane" (1981)

The blond, blue-eyed Miss Mackin—who looks a bit like Angie Dickinson—was the first woman to be named sole anchor of a major network newscast, on NBC in early 1977. Despite this honor, she left NBC (where she had been since 1969) later that year for ABC.

MACKLIN, ALBERT—actor
b: c. 1957, Los Angeles, Calif.

Dreams (com)........ Morris Weiner (1984)

MACKLIN, DAVID—juvenile actor

Harris Against the World (com)
.... Billy Harris (1964–65)

Tammy (com)........ Peter Tate (1965–66)

MACLACHLAN, JANET—black actress

Love Thy Neighbor (com)
.... Jackie Bruce (1973)
Friends (com)
.... Mrs. Jane Summerfield (1979)
Archie Bunker's Place (com)
.... Polly Swanson (1980–81)

MACLAINE, SHIRLEY—actress
b: Apr 24, 1934, Richmond, Va.

Shirley's World (com)
.... Shirley Logan (1971–72)

Emmy Award: Star, Best Variety Special, for *Gypsy in My Soul* (1976)

This impish Hollywood star was seen on television primarily in big, splashy musical specials during the 1970s—and in one short-lived comedy series. The latter at least gave her a chance to indulge her love for travel; in it she played a globe-trotting photographer and journalist.

Shirley is the sister of actor Warren Beatty and is an active crusader for liberal causes. Her autobiography is titled *Don't Fall Off the Mountain* (1970); another, more mystical book by Shirley is *Out on a Limb* (1983).

MACLANE, BARTON—actor
b: Dec 25, 1900*, Columbia, S.C. d: Jan 1, 1969

The Outlaws (wes)
..... U.S. Marshal Frank Caine (1960–61)
I Dream of Jeannie (com)
.... Gen. Martin Peterson (1965–69)

MACLANE, KERRY—juvenile actor

The Cowboys (wes) .... Homer (1974)

MACLEAN, BARBARA BARONDESS—panelist

Where Was I? (quiz) .... panelist (1953)

MACLEOD, GAVIN—actor
b: Feb 28, 1931, Mt. Kisco, N.Y.

McHale's Navy (com)
.... Happy Haines (1962–64)

*Some sources give 1902.

The Mary Tyler Moore Show (com)
.... Murray Slaughter (1970–77)
The Love Boat (com)
.... Capt. Merrill Stubing (1977–86)
Scruples (drama) .... Curt Arvey (1980)

Gavin MacLeod, a tall, bald, happy guy with a big smile, has carved out a lasting career for himself in ensemble comedy. His parents thought he looked like he would become an accountant, but instead he pursued an acting career, starting with minor stage work in New York in the 1950s. Television guest roles followed, including a couple aboard Mr. Lucky's floating gambling casino in 1959–60 (shades of things to come!). His big break was as seaman Happy (natch) on McHale's Navy.

In the late 1960s, Gavin played many more guest roles, including several on Big Valley, and for a time it looked as if he might become typecast as a villain; for example, he was "Big Chicken" on Hawaii Five-O. Then along came the role of a lifetime, that of sardonic newswriter Murray Slaughter on the classic Mary Tyler Moore Show, and his place in TV annals was secure. By comparison, his many years as the sunny skipper of The Love Boat have been like an extended vacation—pleasant and diverting, but hardly the stuff of which great TV is made.

MACLEOD, MURRAY—actor

Karen (com) ...... Spider Gibson (1964–65)

MACMAHON, HORACE—

see McMahon, Horace

MACMICHAEL, FLORENCE—actress

My Three Sons (com)
.... Mrs. Florence Pearson (1960–61)
Mr. Ed (com)
.... Winnie Kirkwood (1963–65)

MACMURRAY, FRED—actor

b: Aug 30, 1907*, Kankakee, Ill. r: Beaver Dam, Wis.

My Three Sons (com)
.... Steve Douglas (1960–72)
My Three Sons (com)
.... Fergus McBain Douglas (1971–72)

*Some sources give 1908.

"Bland and agreeable" is what one critic called him, but Fred MacMurray was certainly Walt Disney's most popular dad in films of the '50s and '60s (The Shaggy Dog, Son of Flubber, etc.). Disney did not produce My Three Sons, but he might as well have. It was exactly the sort of all-around family entertainment, sprinkled with plenty of kids, for which Walt was famous. Before Fred appeared in that long-running hit, he had had a 35-year career in show business. He started out as a saxophonist and singer in the late 1920s with such top bands of the day as those of George Olsen and Gus Arnheim. His movie career was launched in the '30s with a seemingly endless stream of B films (mostly, but not all, comedies), and when television came upon the scene he appeared there, too, in TV plays and comedies such as December Bride and The Lucy-Desi Hour.

Since My Three Sons left the air, Fred has appeared very infrequently. He does not have to. All those years of large, steady earnings and wise investments have made him one of Hollywood's wealthiest citizens. "Bland and agreeable" pays.

MACNEE, PATRICK—actor

b: Feb 6, 1922, London, England

The Avengers (drama)
.... Jonathan Steed (1966–69)
The New Avengers (drama)
.... Jonathan Steed (1978–80)
Gavilan (adv) .... Milo Bentley (1982–83)
Empire (com) ...... Calvin Cromwell (1984)

This cherubic Englishman with a bowler and cane played Mr. Steed opposite a succession of beautiful female agents on British TV from 1960–68. To his surprise, he found that The Avengers made him a star in America as well, via reruns on ABC. Macnee has been turning up on American series ever since, usually cast as the archetypal eccentric Briton.

MACNEIL, ROBERT—newscaster

b: Jan 19, 1931, Montreal, Canada

NBC Weekend News (news)
.... anchorman (1965–67)

Emmy Award: Outstanding Achievement in Coverage of Special Events, for PBS's Watergate coverage (1974)

A true internationalist. Robert MacNeil entered radio in 1951 in Canada and has since been with the CBC, the Reuters wire service in Europe, NBC in America, and the BBC in Britain. He moved to public television in 1971 and since 1976 has co-anchored, along with Jim Lehrer, the *Mac-Neil-Lehrer Report.* His autobiography is titled *The Right Place at the Right Time* (1982).

MACRAE, GORDON—singer
b: Mar 12, 1921, East Orange, N.J. r: Syracuse, N.Y. d: Jan 24, 1986

The Colgate Comedy Hour (var)
.... rotating host (1954–55)
The Gordon MacRae Show (music)
.... host (1956)
Lux Video Theatre (drama) .. host (1956–57)

This handsome, curly-haired, golden-voiced baritone had a short but spectacular career in movie musicals between 1948–56 (*Oklahoma!, Carousel,* etc.) and a similarly short but prominent run on television at about the same time. During the mid-1950s he was all over TV, booming out show tunes and other "good" music for the adult audience. By the hipper early '60s he had already slipped from view; he spent the rest of his days appearing in summer stock and nightclubs.

Gordon was the husband of Sheila MacRae (with whom he sometimes appeared) and the father of Meredith Mac-Rae.

MACRAE, MEREDITH—actress
b: 1945, Houston, Texas

My Three Sons (com)
... Sally Ann Morrison Douglas (1963–65)
Petticoat Junction (com)
.... Billie Jo Bradley (1966–70)

The daughter of Gordon MacRae. In the 1980s she was cohosting a local Los Angeles TV talk show.

MACRAE, SHEILA—actress
b: Sep 24, 1924, London, England

The Jackie Gleason Show (var)
.... Alice Kramden (1966–70)

Wife of Gordon MacRae.

MACREADY, GEORGE—actor
b: Aug 29, 1899*, Providence, R.I. d: Jul 2, 1973

Peyton Place (drama)
.... Martin Peyton (1965–68)

One of Hollywood's most cold-blooded, aristocratic villains, perfect as the ruthless millionaire Martin Peyton on *Peyton Place* and in many similar TV roles in the '50s and '60s. *Perry Mason* used him a lot, and *Alfred Hitchcock Presents* found him a fine evil-doer as well.

MACVANE, JOHN—newscaster
b: 1912, Portland, Me. d: Jan 28, 1984

United or Not (int) .... moderator (1951–52)

A longtime correspondent for ABC, specializing in the United Nations. He began as a newspaper reporter in the mid-1930s and was still active in the '70s.

MACY, BILL—actor
b: May 18, 1922, Revere, Mass. r: Brooklyn, N.Y.

Maude (com)..... Walter Findlay (1972–78)
Hanging In (com)...... Louis Harper (1979)

MADDEN, DAVE—actor, comedian
b: c. 1933, Sarnia, Ont., Canada r: Terre Haute Ind.

Camp Runamuck (com) .... Pruett (1965–66)
Rowan & Martin's Laugh-In (var)
.... regular (1968–69)
The Partridge Family (com)
.... Reuben Kinkaid (1970–74)
Alice (com) .... Earl Hicks (1978–85)

MADDERN, VICTOR—British actor
b: 1926

Fair Exchange (com)
.... Tommy Finch (1962–63)

MADISON, GUY—actor
b: Jan 19, 1922, Bakersfield, Calif.

The Adventures of Wild Bill Hickok (wes)
...... Marshal Wild Bill Hickok (1951–58)

During the 1950s Guy Madison could surely have given Roy Rogers a run for his

*Some sources give 1908 or 1909.

534

money as the handsomest cowboy on the TV range—even if he hadn't had his sidekick Jingles (Andy Devine) puffing along behind him and constantly announcing to one and all how great he was ("That's Wild Bill Hickok, Mister, the bravest, strongest, fightingest U.S. Marshal in the whole West!"). Guy had made his movie debut in the mid-1940s following service in World War II and had appeared in many films, but, to TV kids, he will always be Wild Bill. The typecasting almost ruined his career. After a few guest guest roles in the late 1950s on other dramas and westerns, he virtually disappeared from television. He spent the 1960s in Europe making "spaghetti westerns" (including one as Wyatt Earp) and has only occasionally acted since then. In 1979 he could be glimpsed, like a shadow from the past, passing through an episode of *Fantasy Island*—without Jingles to announce his presence.

MADSEN, MICHAEL—actor
b: Sep 25, Chicago, Ill.

Our Family Honor (drama)
.... Augie Danzig (1985–86)

MAEN, NORMAN—choreographer

This Is Tom Jones (var)
.... dancers (1969–71)
The Val Doonican Show (var)
.... dancers (1971)

Emmy Award: Best Choreography, for *This Is Tom Jones* (1970)

MAGGART, BRANDON—actor
b: Dec 12, Carthage, Tenn.

Jennifer Slept Here (com)
.... George Elliot (1983–84)

MAGUIRE, MADY—actress

The Beverly Hillbillies (com)
.... Susan Graham (1969–71)

MAHAFFEY, LORRIE—actress

Who's Watching the Kids? (com)
.... Memphis O'Hara (1978)

The gorgeous wife of Anson Williams.

MAHARIS, GEORGE—actor
b: Sep 1, 1938*, Astoria, N.Y.

Route 66 (adv) ..... Buz Murdock (1960–63)
The Most Deadly Game (drama)
.... Jonathan Croft (1970–71)
Rich Man, Poor Man—Book I (drama)
.... Joey Quales (1976)

MAHER, BILL—actor, comedian
r: New Jersey

Sara (com)............. Marty Lang (1985)

MAHER, JOE—actor

Double Dare (police) ...... Sylvester (1985)

MAHLER, BRUCE—comedian, writer
b: Sep 12, New York City, N.Y.

Fridays (var)............ regular (1980–82)

MAHONEY, JOCK—actor
b: Feb 7, 1919, Chicago, Ill.

The Range Rider (wes)
.... the Range Rider (1951–52)
Yancy Derringer (adv)
.... Yancy Derringer (1958–59)

Jock Mahoney is probably Hollywood's most famous stuntman-turned-actor, and his rough and tumble series reflect that background. Born Jacques O'Mahoney, he was a tall, rugged youth and a standout gymnast and diving champion at the University of Iowa. After serving as a fighter pilot in World War II, he entered films in 1945 doing stunt work for Errol Flynn, Gregory Peck, Gene Autry, and others. Autry put him under contract and cast him in *The Range Rider* syndicated TV series, one of the more action-packed oaters of the '50s. Jock punched and tumbled his way through other westerns and dramas as well (most frequently *The Loretta Young Show*, but also *Rawhide*, *Laramie*, and others) until his star began to fade in the '60s. He then appeared in a low-budget *Tarzan* movie, which led to his assuming the title role of the loin-clothed jungle hero in three of those features during the '60s.

Unfortunately, *Tarzan* resulted in his first major bout with illness. While filming in India he came down with dengue fever, dysentery, and pneumonia. It took him

*Some sources give 1928.

two-and-a-half years to regain his health—"because I refused to take my own advice; know your limitations and fight the urge to do the stunt just one more time," he later said.

By the late 1960s Jock, nearly 50, was back in full swing, appearing in numerous TV episodes (including several on the TV *Tarzan*), but then advancing years slowed him down for good. On the set of *Kung Fu* in 1973 he suffered a severe stroke. He made only occasional appearances thereafter, sometimes in a wheelchair (from which he would still do a stunt fall). He was seen in several episodes of *B.J. and the Bear* in 1981.

Jock is the stepfather of actress Sally Field.

MAHONEY, JOHN—actor

Chicago Story (drama).... Lt. Roselli (1982)

MAISNIK, KATHY—actress

b: Aug 12, c. 1962, Burbank, Calif.

Star of the Family (com)
.... Jennie Lee Krebs (1982)

MAJORS, LEE—actor

b: Aug 23, 1942*, Wyandotte, Mich.

Big Valley (wes) .. Heath Barkley (1965–69)
The Men from Shiloh (wes)
.... Roy Tate (1970–71)
Owen Marshall, Counselor at Law (drama)
.... Jess Brandon (1971–74)
The Six Million Dollar Man (adv)
.... Col. Steve Austin (1974–78)
The Fall Guy (adv).. Colt Seavers (1981–86)

Lee Majors has had the kind of career that acting students dream about—straight from college into a top-rated series, followed by starring roles in one hit series after another. Plus, of course, good looks, adoring fans, a beautiful wife (at least for a while), and piles of money.

It happened almost that way for Lee; however, his childhood was less than ideal. Orphaned at an early age (his father died before he was born, and his mother when he was two), he was brought up by relatives in Kentucky and attended college on an athletic scholarship. Turning down an offer to try out for the St. Louis Cardi-

*Some sources give 1939 or 1940.

nals, he headed for Hollywood upon graduation. His first job was as an assistant playground director for the parks department. "I met quite a few actors in the park," he says laconically, "and they encouraged me to give acting a try." So he enrolled in the MGM acting school and in early 1965, only a year or so after arriving in town, was signed for his first major TV appearances, in episodes of *Gunsmoke* and *The Alfred Hitchcock Hour* (on which he played a doomed race car driver). In the fall of 1965 he began his role as one of Barbara Stanwyck's sons on *The Big Valley,* and he has been almost continuously seen in hit series since then—achieving superstar status in the '70s as *The Six Million Dollar Man*.

Of course, not everything has come his way. Movie stardom has eluded him so far, and his TV vehicles tend to be in the "lightweight entertainment" category (no Emmys line his shelves). But if it was stardom and steady employment he was seeking when he drove west, he certainly found it.

Lee was married in the '70s to actress Farrah Fawcett.

MAKO—actor

b: Dec 10, Kobe, Japan

Hawaiian Heat (police)
.... Maj. Taro Oshira (1984)

Full name: Mako Iwamatsu.

MALDEN, KARL—actor

b: Mar 22, 1913, Chicago, Ill. r: Gary, Ind.

The Streets of San Francisco (police)
.... Det. Lt. Mike Stone (1972–77)
Skag (drama) .. Pete "Skag" Skagska (1980)

Emmy Award: Best Supporting Actor in a Special, for *Fatal Vision* (1985)

"Now, you look at this face," says bulbnosed, weather-beaten Karl Malden. "Does this look like the face of a leading man? I came out of the steel mills of Indiana and had to work like crazy to be successful as an actor." The face is surely not matinee material, but Malden has made up for it with complex and interesting characterizations that have made him a popular figure on stage, screen, and television for 50 years.

Born of Yugoslav ancestry, Karl took to the stage in Chicago in his early twenties, after dropping out of college for lack of funds. He was soon in New York, appearing on Broadway as early as 1937. His movie debut came three years later, but he made little headway at first. It was a Broadway role in 1947—that of Mitch in the original production of *A Streetcar Named Desire*—that led to his greatest screen success, as he played the same role in the movie version (1951) and won an Academy Award.

Karl worked primarily in movies during the '50s and '60s. He did virtually no television until the 1972 TV movie *Streets of San Francisco,* which led to the highly successful series of the same name. Since then, he has been more active in the medium, most often seen in high-quality TV movies such as *Captains Courageous* (1977), *Word of Honor* (1981), and *Fatal Vision* (1985). His second series, *Skag,* was a gritty drama about the family life of an aging steelworker; though much-acclaimed, it was short-lived.

MALE, COLIN—host, singer

The Dotty Mack Show (music)
.... regular (1952–56)
This Is Music (music)...... emcee (1958–59)

MALET, ARTHUR—actor
b: Lee-on-Solvent, England r: Wales

Casablanca (drama) .... Carl (1983)
Easy Street (com)
.... Bobby the butler (1986–)

MALICK, WENDIE—actress
b: Dec 13, Buffalo, N.Y.

Trauma Center (drama)
.... Dr. Brigitte Blaine (1983)

MALIS, CLAIRE—actress

From Here to Eternity (drama)
.... Dr. Anne Brewster (1980)

MALONE, DOROTHY—actress
b: Jan 30, 1925, Chicago, Ill. r: Dallas, Texas

Peyton Place (drama)
      Constance MacKenzie/Carson (1964–68)
Rich Man, Poor Man—Book I (drama)
.... Irene Goodwin (1976)

The tormented heroine of *Peyton Place* has had a similarly unsatisfactory career in real life, although it began auspiciously enough. Spotted by a talent agent in an amateur play during her freshman year in college, she was whisked away to Hollywood at age 18 and immediately began playing small, pleasant roles in RKO and Warner Brothers B films. That went on for 14 years until, in 1957, she finally switched from nice girl to neurotic nymphomaniac and won an Academy Award for her performance in *Written on the Wind.*

Dorothy had been appearing on television dramas since the early '50s (*Fireside Theatre,* etc.), but after winning the Oscar she concentrated mostly on films, hoping for a major career breakthrough. Unfortunately, the award did not bring her notably better roles, and by the '60s she had slid back into TV again, appearing in episodes of drama series such as *Route 66* and *Dr. Kildare.* In 1964 she assumed the leading role of Constance MacKenzie in the prime time soap opera *Peyton Place,* which was certainly profitable ($250,000 per year), if not prestigious.

Illness and frustration at the failure of her movie career to take off eventually took their toll. When *Peyton Place* ended in 1968, Dorothy moved back to Texas and, since then, has been only intermittently active in films and TV, commuting to Hollywood as necessary. She hopes her daughters do not become actresses.

MALONE, MARY—actress

The Girls (com) ... Emily Kimbrough (1950)
The Aldrich Family (com)
.... Mary Aldrich (1950–52)

MALONE, NANCY—actress, producer
b: 1935, New York City, N.Y.

Naked City (police)........ Libby (1960–63)
The Long Hot Summer (drama)
.... Clara Varner (1965–66)

MALONE, RAY—dancer

Broadway Open House (talk)
.... regular (1950–51)
Dagmar's Canteen (var)...... regular (1952)

MALONEY, JAMES—actor
b: 1915 d: Aug 19, 1978

21 Beacon Street (drama)
.... Jim (1959)

MALONEY, LAUREN AND PAIGE— juvenile actresses

One Day at a Time (com)
.... Annie Horvath (1983–84)

MALOOLY, MAGGIE—actress

Little Women (drama) ...... Amanda (1979)

MALTBY, RICHARD—orchestra leader
b: Jun 26, 1914, Chicago, Ill.

The Vaughn Monroe Show (var)
.... orch. leader (1955)

MALTIN, LEONARD—movie critic, historian
b: Dec 18, 1950, New York City, N.Y.

Entertainment Tonight (news)
.... movie critic (1981–)

MALVIN, ARTIE—music director
b: Jul 7, 1922, New York City, N.Y.

The Julius La Rosa Show (var)
.... singers (1957)
The Steve Lawrence-Eydie Gorme Show (var)
.... singers (1958)
The Pat Boone-Chevy Showroom (var)
.... chorus (1958–60)
The Tim Conway Show (var)
.... singers (1980–81)

Emmy Awards: Best Special Musical Material, for *The Carol Burnett Show* (1976, 1978).

MANARD, BIFF—actor

The Jacksons (var) .... regular (1977)

MANCUSO, NICK—actor
b: c. 1956, Italy r: Toronto, Canada

Scruples (drama) .... Vito Orsini (1980)
Stingray (drama) .... Stingray (1986–)

MANDAN, ROBERT—actor
b: Feb 2, 1932, Clever, Mo.

Caribe (police)
.... Dep. Comm. Ed Rawlings (1975)
Soap (com) .... Chester Tate (1977–81)
Private Benjamin (com)
.... Col. Lawrence Fielding (1982–83)

Three's a Crowd (com)
.... James Bradford (1984–85)

"Beneath that noble exterior," said costar John Ritter, "is a simple, everyday maniac." *TV Guide* observed, "he looks like a bank president and thinks like a baggy-pants comic." Graying and distinguished Robert Mandan ached for years to escape the "straight," often unsympathetic, dramatic roles that his looks got him and try a little lunacy. He finally got his chance, in *Soap*.

Robert spent a lot of years being serious before that. He broke into acting in New York in the early '50s and, like many other stage folk of that period, also played small TV roles in prime time dramas and daytime soap operas. Gradually, soaps became his principal employment; from the mid-1950s to 1970 he was seen regularly in such serials as *From These Roots, The Edge of Night,* and *Search for Tomorrow* (a long run in the late '60s as tycoon Sam Reynolds). He then spent three years in the Broadway musical *Applause* before moving to Los Angeles, where he found much work—but little satisfaction—as a stock "older" actor in 1970s crime dramas such as *Cannon* and *Barnaby Jones*. On the short-lived Stacy Keach series *Caribe*, he was a Miami police official. Occasionally he got to do a comedy (*Maude, All in the Family*), but it was not until 1977 that he found the role he was looking for, as the pompous businessman Chester Tate on the rowdy soap spoof *Soap*. Competition for the part was heavy (there are a lot of older actors looking for work in Hollywood), but ultimately he won it, and it made him a star —and a happy man.

MANDEL, HOWIE—actor, comedian
b: Nov 29, Toronto, Canada

St. Elsewhere (drama)
.... Dr. Wayne Fiscus (1982–)

Howie, a happy guy with a lot of curly hair, has frequently appeared as a stand-up comic on such syndicated series as *Make Me Laugh* and *Laugh Trax*.

MANDRELL, BARBARA—country singer
b: Dec 25, 1948, Houston, Texas

Barbara Mandrell & The Mandrell Sisters (var)..................... regular (1980–82)

Barbara, a petite (5'2") blonde, came from a musical family and has been a very popular country recording artist since the early 1970s. She has been seen on many television specials; however, her own network series left the air after only a year and a half—not became of its ratings (which were good) but because she did not feel she could keep up the heavy workload of a weekly show.

Barbara made her network TV debut at the age of 12 on NBC's *Five Star Jubilee.*

MANDRELL, IRLENE—country singer
b: Jan 29, 1957, Corpus Christi, Texas

Barbara Mandrell & The Mandrell Sisters (var).................... regular (1980–82)
Hee Haw (var)........... regular (1984–)

Sister of Barbara, the youngest of the sisters, and the kittenish "sex symbol" of the three.

MANDRELL, LOUISE—country singer
b: Jul 13, 1954, Corpus Christi, Texas

Barbara Mandrell & The Mandrell Sisters (var).................... regular (1980–82)

Sister of Barbara.

MANETTI, LARRY—actor
b: Jul 23, Pendleton, Ore. r: Chicago, Ill.

Baa Baa Black Sheep (drama)
.... Lt. Bob Boyle (1976–78)
The Duke (drama)...... Joe Cadillac (1979)
Magnum, P.I. (drama)
.... Orville Wright (Rick) (1980–)

MANEY, NORMAN—orchestra leader
Shields and Yarnell (var)
.... orch. leader (1977–78)

MANGO, ALEX—actor
The Buccaneers (adv)
.... crewman Van Bruch (1956–57)

MANHATTAN TRANSFER, THE—singers
Tim Hauser, b: Dec 12, 1941
Laurel Masse, b: Dec 29, 1951, Holland, Mich.
Alan Paul, b: Nov 1949
Janis Siegel, b: Jul 23, 1952 r: New York City, N.Y.

Manhattan Transfer (var)... regulars (1975)

A stylish pop singing group formed by Tim Hauser in 1973, and specializing in nostalgic tunes. One of their hits (in 1980) was an imaginative adaptation of the theme from *The Twilight Zone.*

MANLEY, STEPHEN—juvenile actor
b: Feb 13, 1965, Los Angeles, Calif.

Married: The First Year (drama)
.... Donny Baker (1979)
Secrets of Midland Heights (drama)
.... Danny Welsh (1980–81)

MANN, AL—newscaster
ABC Evening News (news)
.... anchorman (1960)

MANN, ANITA, DANCERS—
Cher (var) .... regular (1975–76)
The Keane Brothers Show (var)
.... regular (1977)

MANN, HOWARD—actor
The Johnny Cash Show (var)
.... regular (1976)

MANN, IRIS—actress
b: 1939, Brooklyn, N.Y.

Mama (com).............. Dagmar (1949)

MANN, JOHNNY—musical director, host
b: Aug 30, 1928, Baltimore, Md.

The George Gobel Show (var)
.... singers (1957–58)
The Eddie Fisher Show (var)
.... singers (1959)
The Danny Kaye Show (var)
.... singers (1963–64)
The Joey Bishop Show (talk)
.... musical director (1967–69)
Johnny Mann's Stand Up and Cheer (music)
.... host (1971–73)

MANN, LARRY D.—actor
b: Dec 18, 1922, Toronto, Canada

Accidental Family (com)
.... Marty Warren (1967–68)
Dr. Simon Locke (drama)
.... Lt. Jack Gordon (1973–74)

Canadian actor-announcer who has done much work on Canadian radio and television as well as on American TV. He won the Canadian "Best Character Actor" award several times in the early 1960s.

MANN, MICHAEL—actor

Joe & Mabel (com)
.... Sherman Spooner (1956)

MANN, PEANUTS—comedian

Doodles Weaver (var) .... regular (1951)

MANNERS, MICKEY—actor

The Bob Newhart Show (var)
.... regular (1961)
Many Happy Returns (com)
.... Joe Foley (1964–65)
Mickie Finn's (var) .... regular (1966)

MANNING, JACK—actor

The Paper Chase (drama)
.... Dean Rutherford (1978–79)

MANNING, RUTH—actress

Good Time Harry (com) .... Sally (1980)

MANNING, SEAN—juvenile actor

Toma (police) .... Jimmy Toma (1973–74)

MANOFF, DINAH—actress
b: Jan 25, 1958, New York City, N.Y.

Soap (com) ..... Elaine Lefkowitz (1978–79)

The daughter of actress Lee Grant.

MANSFIELD, JAYNE—actress
b: Apr 19, 1933*, Bryn Mawr, Pa. d: Jun 29, 1967

Down You Go (quiz)
.... regular panelist (1956)

Hollywood's most bosomy blonde, once touted as the successor to Marilyn Monroe in the sexpot sweepstakes—but she never was. Jayne was seen only occasionally on television between her sudden rise to fame in the mid-1950s and her death in an auto accident in 1967—here, in a 1956 special

*Some sources give 1932.

called "The Bachelors"; there, on a 1962 episode of *Alfred Hitchcock Presents*. She was, however, the butt of a great many bosom jokes. On *Hitchcock*, for example, she did a walk-on opposite Tony Randall, who played an alcoholic so drunk he couldn't even remember *her* the next day. For a couple of months in 1956 she was a giggly panelist on the game show *Down You Go*.

Loni Anderson portrayed Jayne in the 1980 TV movie *The Jayne Mansfield Story*, which costarred Arnold Schwarzenegger as Jayne's muscle-man husband, Mickey Hargitay. A biography by May Mann, titled *Jayne Mansfield*, was published in 1973.

Those legendary dimensions, incidentally, were reputed to be 40-18-36.

MANSFIELD, SALLY—actress

Bachelor Father (com) .... Connie (1961–62)

MANSON, MAURICE—actor

One Man's Family (drama)
.... Sir Guy Vane (1952)

MANTECA, CARLOS—comedian

Turn-On (var) .... regular (1969)

MANTEGNA, JOE—actor
b: Nov 13, 1947, Chicago, Ill.

Comedy Zone (com) .... regular (1984)

MANTELL, JOE—actor

Pete and Gladys (com)
.... Ernie Briggs (1961–62)

MANTOOTH, RANDOLPH—actor
b: Sep 19, 1945, Sacramento, Calif.

Emergency (drama)
.... paramedic John Gage (1972–77)
Operation Petticoat (com)
.... Lt. Mike Bender (1978–79)
Detective School (com)
.... Eddie Dawkins (1979)

Randy is the son of a full-blooded Seminole Indian who roamed the country as a pipeline worker. Randy came to Hollywood around 1970 after brief stage exposure, won a contract with Universal, and played guest roles in a number of routine dramas and westerns. His main claim to fame is *Emergency,* a formulaic Jack Webb–directed series in which he and co-star Kevin Tighe played paramedics rushing from one disaster to another. Randy's regular-guy looks and Indian agility served him well.

Randy has generally been relegated to supporting roles in the years since then. He got his chance to head the cast in a 1979 TV movie called *The Seekers*—but, unfortunately, nobody noticed.

MANTOVANI—orchestra leader
b: Nov 15, 1905, Venice, Italy, r: England d: Mar 29, 1980

Mantovani (music)
.... orch. leader (1958–59)

This English orchestra leader was famous for his lush, cascading arrangements and huge string section. If you wanted music to go with your potted palms, you would probably have turned to him. This popular syndicated series was filmed in England. The maestro's full name: Annunzio Paolo Mantovani.

MANZ, LINDA—actress
b: Aug 20, 1961, New York City, N.Y.

Dorothy (com) .... Frankie (1979)

MANZA, RALPH—actor
b: Dec 1, 1921, San Francisco, Calif.

The D.A.'s Man (police)
.... Asst. D.A. Al Bonacorsi (1959)
Banacek (drama)...... Jay Drury (1972–74)
A.E.S. Hudson Street (com)
.... ambulance driver Stanke (1978)
Mama Malone (com)
.... Padre Guardiano (1984)
Newhart (com).............. Bud (1985–)

MARA, ADELE—actress, singer
b: Apr 28, 1923, Dearborn, Mich.

Cool Million (drama) ...... Elena (1972–73)
Wheels (drama).... Teresa Chapman (1978)

One way to get into television is to marry in. This Latin B movie actress of the '40s was later married to TV producer Roy Huggins and occasionally appeared in his productions, such as the series *Cool Million* and the miniseries *Wheels.*

MARASH, DAVE—newscaster
b: 1942, Atlanta, Ga. r: Richmond, Va.

20/20 (mag)...... correspondent (1978–81)

Emmy Award: Best News Program Segment, for the *20/20* report "Nicaragua" (1980)

MARC, TED—juvenile actor

Professional Father (com)
.... Thomas (Twig) Wilson, Jr. (1955)

MARCANTEL, CHRISTOPHER—actor
b: Jun 7, 1958, Smithtown, N.Y.

Nurse (drama) .... Chip Benjamin (1981–82)

A young daytime soap-opera heartthrob of the 1980s (*Another World, Loving,* etc.).

MARCELINO, MARIO—actor

Falcon Crest (drama)...... Mario (1981–82)

MARCELLINO, MUZZY—orchestra leader

Life with Linkletter (var)
.... orch. leader (1950–52)

Muzzy, who was associated with Linkletter on both his daytime and nighttime TV shows, was also a singer and whistler. It was he who whistled the haunting theme on the soundtrack of the 1954 John Wayne movie *The High and the Mighty.*

MARCH, HAL—actor, host
b: Apr 22, 1920, San Francisco, Calif. d: Jan 19, 1970

The George Burns and Gracie Allen Show (com).............. Harry Morton (1950–51)
The RCA Victor Show (com)
.... as himself (1952–53)
My Friend Irma (com) . Joe Vance (1953–54)
The Imogene Coca Show (var)
.... Jerry Crane (1955)
The Soldiers (com) .... Hal (1955)
The $64,000 Question (quiz)
.... emcee (1955–58)
What's It For? (quiz) ...... emcee (1957–58)
Laughs for Sale (com) .... emcee (1963)

Hal March was one of television's—and radio's, and movies'—"almosts." He almost, but never quite, became a major star. Hal first attracted attention on radio in the late 1940s, where he was often heard as half of a comedy team with Bob Sweeney; however, the medium died before they could really catch on. Hal began appearing in films in 1950 in such classics as *Ma and Pa Kettle Go to Town,* but stardom eluded him there as well. His early television work, also mostly in comedy, was a little more promising. He appeared both in guest roles *(I Love Lucy)* and in regular series roles on several shows. Finally he got the chance to star in his own live comedy series, *The Soldiers,* but it flopped.

During the summer of 1955, while appearing live in *The Soldiers* on Saturday nights, Hal doubled as the host of a new quiz show (also live) called *The $64,000 Question* on Sunday nights. It was this latter program that provided his greatest success. *The $64,000 Question* shot virtually overnight to number one in the ratings, and Hal became famous as the darkly handsome and considerate host who guided nervous contestants through ever-more complex questions as they sought the biggest prize ever offered on TV up to that time.

The quiz-show scandals of the late '50s seemed to taint Hal's reputation, even though he was not implicated, and during the late '50s and early '60s he was little seen. Later in the '60s, he made periodic appearances on *Burke's Law, The Lucy Show,* and even *The Monkees,* but by the time he died, in 1970, his heyday was past.

MARCHAND, NANCY—actress
b: Jun 19, 1928, Buffalo, N.Y.

Beacon Hill (drama)... Mary Lassiter (1975)
Lou Grant (drama)
.... Margaret Pynchon (1977–82)

Emmy Awards: Best Supporting Actress in a Drama Series, for *Lou Grant* (1978, 1980, 1981, 1982)

Though she is known to younger viewers as the aristocratic Mrs. Pynchon, Lou Grant's boss on *Lou Grant,* Nancy Marchand is familiar to those with longer memories for many roles over practically the entire history of TV. Her first major break came in 1950 when she was fresh out of acting school—a part in a live *Studio One* production of "Little Women." She appeared in many more playhouse dramas during the '50s, most frequently on *Kraft Television Theatre.* Perhaps her best known role was in one of TV's all-time classics, the original 1953 production of "Marty," in which she played the plain girl who brought love into Rod Steiger's drab life.

During the 1960s, Nancy was active mostly on the stage, but in the '70s she returned to television in a succession of daytime soap opera roles, including four years on *Love of Life.* She also had a short stint as the *grand dame* on the nighttime serial *Beacon Hill.* Finally, in 1977, *Lou Grant* did for her what soaps and live TV plays had not—won her multiple Emmys and made her a star.

MARCO, FATSO—comedian
b: c. 1909 d: Oct 27, 1962

The Milton Berle Show (var)
.... regular (1948–52)

Real name: Marco Marcella.

MARCOVICCI, ANDREA—actress
b: Nov 18, 1948, New York City, N.Y.

Berrengers (drama)
.... Gloria Berrenger (1985)
Trapper John, M.D. (drama)
.... Fran Brennan (1985–86)

This actress got her start in soap operas, spending three years on *Love Is a Many Splendored Thing* before making a major impact in the lead role in the TV movie *Cry Rape* in 1973. She has since appeared in a variety of series episodes and TV films, the latter including *Smile Jenny, You're Dead; Some Kind of Miracle,* and *Vacation in Hell.*

MARCUS, SPARKY—juvenile actor
b: Dec 6, 1967, Hollywood, Calif.

The Nancy Walker Show (com)
.... Michael Futterman (1976)
Mary Hartman, Mary Hartman (com)
.... Jimmy Joe Jeeter (1976–77)
Grandpa Goes to Washington (com)
.... Kevin Kelley, Jr. (1978–79)

The Bad News Bears (com)
.... Leslie Ogilvie (1979–80)
Goodtime Girls (com)....... Skeeter (1980)

Little Sparky was also the voice of Richie Rich on the Saturday morning *Richie Rich/Scooby Doo* hour in the early 1980s. Even earlier, at age six, he was doing voices for the *Sigmund and the Sea Monsters* cartoon series.

MARDI, DANIELLE—actress

The Beverly Hillbillies (com)
.... Helen Thompson (1969–71)

MAREN, JERRY—midget actor

No Soap, Radio (com) .... Morris (1982)

MARGETTS, MONTY—actress

The Tycoon (com).... Una Fields (1964–65)

MARGOLIN, JANET—actress
b: Jul 25, 1943, New York City, N.Y.

Lanigan's Rabbi (police)
.... Miriam Small (1977)

MARGOLIN, STUART—actor
b: Jan 31, c. 1940, Davenport, Iowa

Occasional Wife (com)
.... Bernie (1966–67)
Love, American Style (com)
.... repertory player (1969–73)
Nichols (wes)............ Mitch (1971–72)
The Rockford Files (drama)
.... Evelyn "Angel" Martin (1974–80)
Bret Maverick (wes)
.... Philo Sandine (1981–82)
Mr. Smith (com).......... Dr. Klein (1983)

Emmy Awards: Best Supporting Actor in a Drama Series, for *The Rockford Files* (1979, 1980)

Stuart Margolin, the shifty fellow in several of James Garner's series, seems to have become Garner's one-man stock company in recent years—rather like Victor French was for Michael Landon. Margolin usually plays a scruffy small-time con man who serves to make the merely cowardly Garner seem almost honorable by comparison.

Stuart was born on the Mississippi River near Davenport, Iowa, and moved around a bit as a youth. Originally intending to become a writer, he made it to New York by 1960, where, at the age of 20, he became one of the youngest playwrights ever to have his own play produced off-Broadway (the play, *Sad Choices,* seems to have disappeared from the literature, however). In the mid-1960s he played guest roles on series such as *Blue Light* and *Hey, Landlord,* and in 1966–67 he was a regular on *Occasional Wife* as the shy boyfriend Bernie.

Stuart linked up with Garner on *Nichols* in 1971, playing the disreputable deputy, and he has remained with him, more or less, ever since. He has also played offbeat characters in a number of TV movies, from the crime-solving rabbi in *Lanigan's Rabbi* (1976) to the vicious hood in *A Killer in the Family* (1983). A talented behind-the-scenes man, he has also written and directed a number of TV movies, including *The Ballad of Andy Crocker* (1969), which was one of the first TV films to deal with the Vietnam War.

MARIE, JULIENNE—actress

Our Private World (drama)
.... Eve Eldredge (1965)

MARIE, ROSE—
see Rose Marie (under "R")

MARIHUGH, TAMMY LEA—juvenile actress

The Bob Cummings Show (com)
.... Tammy Johnson (1959)

MARINARO, ED—actor
b: Mar 31, 1951, New York City r: New Milford, N.J.

Laverne & Shirley (com)
.... Sonny St. Jacques (1980–81)
Hill Street Blues (police)
.... Off. Joe Coffey (1981–)

A former pro-football running back in the 1970s with the Minnesota Vikings, the New York Jets, and the Seattle Seahawks. He turned to acting in the late '70s when a foot injury ended his playing days.

MARINERS, THE—singers

Tom Lockard, b: Pasadena, Calif.
James O. Lewis, b: Birmingham, Ala.
Martin Karl, b: Stanberry, Mo.
Nathaniel Dickerson, b: Waycross, Ga.

Arthur Godfrey and His Friends (var)
.... singers (1949–55)

A racially mixed quartet of former coast-guardsmen who first joined Godfrey on radio in 1946.

MARION, RICHARD—actor

Operation Petticoat (com)
.... pharmacist's mate Williams (1977–78)

MARK, FLIP—juvenile actor

Guestward Ho! (com)
.... Brook Hooten (1960–61)
Fair Exchange (com)
.... Larry Walker (1962–63)

MARKEY, ENID—actress

b: Feb 22, 1896, Dillon, Colo. d: Nov 16, 1981

Bringing Up Buddy (com)
.... Aunt Violet Flower (1960–61)

A character actress whose career stretched from silent movie days in the 1910s (she was Tarzan's first Jane, in 1918) to TV situation comedies of the mid and late 1960s *(Ozzie and Harriet, Please Don't Eat the Daisies).*

MARKHAM, MONTE—actor

b: Jun 21, 1935*, Manatee, Fla.

The Second Hundred Years (com)
.... Luke/Ken Carpenter (1967–68)
Mr. Deeds Goes to Town (com)
.... Longfellow Deeds (1969–70)
Perry Mason (revival) (drama)
.... Perry Mason (1973–74)
Dallas (drama)......... Clint Ogden (1981)
Rituals (drama) . Carter Robinson (1984–85)

Despite three major chances at stardom by headlining series of his own between 1967 and 1973, plus scores of guest appearances in both dramatic and comedy roles, Monte Markham failed to catch on with the viewing public. He continues to been seen in supporting roles, including a short stint on

*Some sources give 1938.

Dallas in 1981 and briefly as cohost of the syndicated talk show *Breakaway* in 1983.

MARKHAM, PIGMEAT—black comedian

b: Apr 18, 1906, Durham, N.C. d: Dec 13, 1981

Rowan & Martin's Laugh-In (var)
.... regular (1968–69)

The "Here come de judge" man.

MARKIM, AL—actor

Tom Corbett, Space Cadet (child)
.... Astro the Venusian (1950–55)

MARKLAND, TEX—actor

The High Chaparral (wes) .. Reno (1967–70)

MARKOFF, DIANE—actress

The Secret Empire (drama)
.... Princess Tara (1979)
Quincy, M. E. (police)
.... Diane, the waitress (1980–83)

MARKS, GUY—comedian, actor

b: Philadelphia, Pa.

The Joey Bishop Show (com)
.... Freddie (1962)
The John Forsythe Show (com)
.... Ed Robbins (1965–66)
Rango (com) .... Pink Cloud (1967)

MARLOWE, CHRISTIAN—actor

b: Sep 28, 1951, Los Angeles, Calif.

Highcliffe Manor (com)
.... Bram Shelley (1979)

The son of actor Hugh Marlowe and actress K.T. Stevens.

MARLOWE, HUGH—actor

b: Jan 30, 1911, Philadelphia, Pa. d: May 2, 1982

The Adventures of Ellery Queen (drama)
.... Ellery Queen (1954)

This solid if unexceptional actor began in films in the 1930s and later played Ellery Queen on both radio and television. He was a guest star on many TV drama series of the '50s and '60s, being seen especially often on *Alfred Hitchcock Presents* and *Perry Mason*. In 1969 he forsook both movies and prime time for daytime TV, becoming family patriarch Jim Matthews on the soap opera *Another World;* he must have liked the role, as he continued to play it until the day he died 13 years later.

MARLOWE, MARION—singer
b: Mar 7, 1929, St. Louis

Arthur Godfrey and His Friends (var)
.... singer (1950–55)

Marion was the surprisingly young singer (she looked rather mature) who sang romantic duets with Frank Parker on the *Godfrey* show, until Godfrey fired her in one of his purges. Like many other Godfrey fire-ees, she then enjoyed a flurry of bookings in nightclubs and on *The Ed Sullivan Show*, after which she receded into obscurity. In later years she lived in New Jersey and did occasional dinner theater work.

MARLOWE, NORA—actress
d: Dec 31, 1977

Law of the Plainsman (wes)
.... Martha Commager (1959–60)
The Governor & J.J. (com)
.... Sara Andrews (1969–70)
The Waltons (drama)
.... Flossie Brimmer (1972–77)

MARLOWE, NORMA JEAN—actress

One Man's Family (drama)
.... Betty Carter (1950)

MAROSS, JOE—actor

Peyton Place (drama)
.... Fred Russell (1968–69)
Code Red (adv)
.... Capt. Mike Benton (1981–82)

MARR, EDDIE—actor

Circus Boy (adv) .... barker (1956–58)

MARS, JANICE—actress

Norby (com) ...... Wahleen Johnson (1955)

MARS, KENNETH—comedian, actor
b: 1936, Chicago, Ill.

He & She (com)
.... Harry Zarakardos (1967–68)
The Don Knotts Show (var)
.... regular (1970–71)
Sha Na Na (var) .... regular (1977–78)
The Carol Burnett Show (var)
.... regular (1979)

MARSH, JEAN—actress
b: Jul 1, 1934, Stoke Newington, London, England

9 to 5 (com).......... Roz Keith (1982–83)
Master of the Game (drama)
.... Mrs. Talley (1984)

Emmy Award: Best Actress in a Drama Series, for the *Masterpiece Theatre* Production *Upstairs, Downstairs* (1975)

This British actress became became internationally known as Rose the parlor maid in *Upstairs, Downstairs* (1974–77), a series that she also helped create.

MARSHALL, ANN—juvenile actress

My Favorite Martian (com)
.... Angela Brown (1963–64)

MARSHALL, BARBARA—singer, pianist

Song and Dance (music) ...... emcee (1949)
Words and Music (music)
.... hostess (1949)

MARSHALL, CONNIE—juvenile actress
b: 1938

Doc Corkle (com) ..... Laurie Corkle (1952)

MARSHALL, DOLORES—singer

Sing-co-pation (music) .... regular (1949)

MARSHALL, DON—black actor

Land of the Giants (sci fi)
.... Dan Erikson (1968–70)

MARSHALL, E.G.—actor
b: Jun 18, 1910, Owatonna, Minn.

The Defenders (drama)
.... Lawrence Preston (1961–65)
The New Doctors (drama)
.... Dr. David Craig (1969–73)
The Gangster Chronicles (drama)
.... narrator (1981)

545

Emmy Awards: Best Actor in a Series, for *The Defenders* (1962, 1963)

After 50 years of acting and scores of famous roles, the first question E. G. Marshall is usually asked is "What do your initials stand for?" "To which," he says with his down-home grin, "I have a catalog of answers. Among them is 'It's *E*verybody's *G*uess.' Or, 'gosh, I don't know, I wish I did. It's an interesting question.' "

While few may know his first name, everyone knows his face—studious, balding, the picture of a highly moral authority figure (one critic commented, "He looks like a serious Bob Hope"). Born of Norwegian parents, Marshall had a long career in the theater in the '30s and '40s before coming to television in the early '50s. He was one of the most familiar actors in playhouse productions on early, live TV, playing prominent roles in hundreds of dramas on *Kraft, Philco, Goodyear, Playhouse 90,* and all the rest. In the early '60s he gained even greater renown, and two Emmys, as the star of *The Defenders,* one of the few socially conscious dramas of that comedy-oriented period. His pace slowed down a bit after that, but he continued to appear in TV movies and specials and had a four year stint in *The New Doctors* segment of *The Bold Ones.* He also did quite a bit of narration work for *The National Geographic Special*s and other documentaries.

The first initial, incidentally, stands for Everett—but "Everett Marshall" just doesn't have the same ring, does it?

MARSHALL, GARRY—actor

The Ugliest Girl in Town (com)
.... Gene Blair (1968–69)

MARSHALL, GLORIA—actress

The Bob Cummings Show (com)
.... Mary Beth Hall (1956–57)

MARSHALL, GREGORY—juvenile actor

The Life of Riley (com)
.... Egbert Gillis (1953–55)

MARSHALL, JOAN—actress
b: c. 1934, Evanston, Ill.

Bold Venture (adv)..... Sailor Duval (1959)

MARSHALL, LINDA—actress

Tammy (com)....... Gloria Tate (1965–66)

MARSHALL, MORT—actor
b: Aug 17, 1918, New York City, N.Y. d: Feb 1, 1979

Hold It Please (quiz)........ regular (1949)
The Fifty-Fourth Street Revue (var)
.... regular (1949–50)
The Dumplings (com)......... Cully (1976)

MARSHALL, PAT—singer

Tonight (talk)............ regular (1954–55)

Singer-actress, long married to television writer Larry Gelbart of *M*A*S*H* fame.

MARSHALL, PENNY—actress
b: Oct 15, 1942, The Bronx, N.Y.

The Odd Couple (com)
.... Myrna Turner (1971–75)
The Bob Newhart Show (com)
.... Miss Larson (1972–73)
Paul Sand in Friends and Lovers (com)
.... Janice Dreyfuss (1974–75)
Laverne & Shirley (com)
.... Laverne De Fazio (1976–83)

Raised in a show-business family (her father was an industrial filmmaker and her mother a dance instructor), Penny Marshall ventured into acting in the '60s, several years before her producer-brother Garry became a Hollywood mogul. She was in stock productions in the mid-1960s, competed on *The Original Amateur Hour,* and made her network acting debut on *The Danny Thomas Hour* anthology series during the 1967–68 season.

Nevertheless, having a relative in important places certainly didn't hurt her career. In 1971 she got her first big break as Jack Klugman's secretary Myrna on *The Odd Couple,* which coincidentally was brother Garry's first hit series. She then had regular roles on *The Bob Newhart Show* and *Friends and Lovers* (not Garry's) and guest roles on other comedies such as *The Mary Tyler Moore Show.* However, it was another of her brother's megahits—*Laverne & Shirley*—that made her a superstar. The behind-the-scenes turmoil on the *L&S* set was well publicized at the time as Penny fought with costar Cindy Williams, Williams claiming that Penny was shown favoritism by her family (not only was Garry executive producer of the series, but father Tony was producer and sister Ronny casting coordinator). Finally, Williams left the series, which ended its run shortly thereafter.

Penny has since been seen in TV specials and movies, including 1984's *Love Thy Neighbor* opposite John Ritter. She was married in the '70s to actor Rob Reiner.

MARSHALL, PETER—host
b: Mar 30, 1927, Huntington, W. Va.

Hollywood Squares (quiz)..... emcee (1968)
NBC Action Playhouse (drama) . host (1971)
Hollywood Squares (quiz).. emcee (1971–82)
The Peter Marshall Variety Show (var)
.... host (1976)
79 Park Avenue (drama)
.... Brian Whitfield (1977)

Emmy Awards: Best Game Show Host, for *The Hollywood Squares* (1974, 1975, 1980, 1981); Daytime Host of the Year (1974)

Peter Marshall has been a stand-up comic, a singer, a legitimate actor and a variety show host, but he is known for one thing and one thing only—straight man/host of one of TV's most popular comedy game shows ever, *The Hollywood Squares*. The series was on the air for 16 consecutive years in daytime, nighttime, and syndicated versions (1966–82), and Peter was the host of all of them.

Peter started out as a page at the NBC studios in New York, then joined with the late Tommy Noonan to form a comedy team that played clubs around the country and made several appearances on *The Ed Sullivan Show*. In the '60s he had acting roles on and off Broadway and was also seen in a few films. However, it was while doing a cereal commercial that he was spotted and asked to audition for *Squares*. At the time, he was delighted with the break. "I've been trying to get a show for years," he said in 1967. "I saw what happened to people like Jan Murray and Bert Parks when they had a game show. Their popularity went up. So did their stock."

Despite his efforts to diversify during later years, including hosting an abortive *Tonight Show*–like variety show in 1976, Peter is inextricably linked with *Squares*.

And vice versa. An attempt to revive it in 1983 without him (as *The Hollywood Squares/Match Game Hour*) was a flop. Meanwhile, Peter stayed busy with stage work *(La Cage aux Folles)*, miscellaneous hosting assignments, and another daytime game show, this one called *All Star Blitz*.

Peter's sister is actress Joanne Dru. His real name is Pierre La Cock.

MARSHALL, RED—comedian
Doodles Weaver (var) .... regular (1951)

MARSHALL, REX—announcer
b: c. 1918 d: Mar 9, 1983

Kuda Bux, Hindu Mystic (misc)
.... announcer (1950)
Circuit Rider (misc) .... narrator (1951)
The Herman Hickman Show (sports)
.... regular (1952–53)

MARSHALL, DR. ROY K.—scientist
Aug 21, 1907, Glen Carbon, Ill.

The Nature of Things (info) .. host (1948–52)
Kay Kyser's Kollege of Musical Knowledge
(quiz)................. announcer (1949–50)
Ford Star Revue (var) .... regular (1950–51)

Dr. Marshall, an astronomer with Philadelphia's Fels Planetarium, was one of early television's favorite scientists.

MARSHALL, SARAH—actress
b: 1933, London, England

Miss Winslow and Son (com)
.... Evelyn Winslow (1979)
Scruples (drama) .... Susan Arvey (1980)

The daughter of movie star Herbert Marshall.

MARSHALL, SEAN—juvenile actor
b: Jun 19, 1965, Canoga Park, Calif.

The Fitzpatricks (drama)
.... Max Fitzpatrick (1977–78)
The Mackenzies of Paradise Cove (adv)
.... Michael Mackenzie (1979)

MARSHALL, WILLIAM—black actor, singer
b: Aug 19, 1924, Gary, Ind.

Rosetti and Ryan (drama)
.... Judge Black (1977)

MARTA, LYNNE—actress

b: Oct 30, 1946, Philadelphia, Pa.

Love, American Style (com)
.... repertory player (1969–70)

MARTEL, K.C.—juvenile actor

Mulligan's Stew (drama)
.... Jimmy Mulligan (1977)
The Best Times (drama)
.... Dale Troutman (1985)

MARTELL, ANITA—panelist

How To (info)............. panelist (1951)

MARTIN MEN, THE—singers

The Freddy Martin Show (var)
.... regular (1951)

MARTIN, ANDREA—comedienne, writer

b: Jan 15, Portland, Maine

Second City TV (com)
.... Edith Prickly (1977–81)
SCTV Network 90 (com).. regular (1981–83)

Emmy Awards: Best Writing for a Comedy
Program, for *SCTV Network* (1982, 1983)

MARTIN, ANNE-MARIE—actress

b: Nov 11, Toronto, Canada

Sledge Hammer! (com)
.... Off. Dori Doreau (1986–)

MARTIN, BARNEY—actor

*Kraft Music Hall Presents The Dave King
Show* (var)................. regular (1959)
The Tony Randall Show (com)
.... Jack Terwilliger (1976–78)
Number 96 (drama)
.... Horace Batterson (1980–81)
Zorro and Son (com)
.... Brothers Napa and Sonoma (1983)

MARTIN, BOBBY—panelist

Guess Again (quiz)......... regular (1951)

MARTIN, DEAN—singer, actor

b: Jun 17, 1917, Steubenville, Ohio

The Colgate Comedy Hour (var)
.... cohost (with Jerry Lewis)
(1950–55)

The Dean Martin Show (var)
.... host (1965–74)
Half Nelson (drama)...... as himself (1985)

Q: What's the worst part about being a
teetotaler?

A: Waking up in the morning and knowing that that's the best you're going to feel
all day.

Dean Martin's suspiciously flush complexion, his swaggering manner, and constant
references to booze (Dean, singing: "Every
time it rains, it rains bourbon from
heaven") all identify him as American's favorite drunk. It's an act, of course. No real
alcoholic could have achieved the tremendous success he has in the fiercely competitive world of show business. At the same
time, few could have guessed in 1956,
when he broke up the very popular Martin
and Lewis team, that he would go so far on
his own.

Dean was born Dino Crocetti in industrial Ohio and began performing locally in
the late '30s, along with odd jobs as a
boxer and a croupier in a gambling establishment. He followed his star to the West
Coast and then back East, where he met
Jerry Lewis on an Atlantic City bill in 1946.
They formed a team—handsome Italian
crooner/straight man (Martin) versus antic
young comic who always breaks up the act
(Lewis). Within a few years they were the
hottest team in comedy, appearing regularly on NBC's big budget *Colgate Comedy
Hour* in the early '50s.

When each went his separate way in
1956, most of the smart money was on
Lewis. Sure enough, Dean's first solo film,
10,000 Bedrooms, was a bomb. However,
Dean was astute enough to then try a real
change of pace, taking a much lower salary
to play a difficult dramatic role in *The
Young Lions.* Public and critics alike loved
it, and his acting career began to take off.
Meanwhile, Dean's singing career was
booming with million-selling hits like
"Memories Are Made of This" and "Return
to Me." He maintained his visibility on television chiefly via specials, signing to do
eight during 1957 alone. He also made a
few appearances on other shows, such as
The Danny Thomas Show in 1958 and
Rawhide in 1964—on the latter playing an
aging gunfighter on his way to his last
shoot-out.

It was in the variety format that Dean

excelled, though, and in 1965 he finally agreed to do his own weekly series—after NBC met every one of his terms (minimal rehearsals, freeform "improvised" format, a great deal of money). *The Dean Martin Show* resembled a friendly cocktail party with Dino, and it worked, running for nine years and spawning specials, summer shows, and supporting talent such as the Golddiggers, Foster Brooks (even drunker than Dean), and others. A popular feature in its later years were Dean's comic celebrity roasts, which continued as specials for years after the original weekly series left the air.

Still loose and insouciant, Dean has continued on view in specials during the late '70s and '80s. Among these have been his annual Christmas programs. Perhaps his most unusual appearance was a reunion with Jerry Lewis (engineered by mutual friend Frank Sinatra) on a Muscular Dystrophy Telethon from Las Vegas in 1976. Dean also likes to turn up once in a while in unlikely guest shots, such as on *Vega$* in 1979 and in *Half Nelson* in 1985, playing a celebrity "friend" of the half-pint hero.

MARTIN, DEAN PAUL—actor

b: Nov 17, 1951, Santa Monica, Calif. d: Mar 21, 1987

Misfits of Science (adv)
.... Dr. Billy Hayes (1985–86)

Although he "lived in a fishbowl" all his life as the son of superstar Dean Martin, tall, blond Dean Paul Martin packed a lot into his 30-plus years. At 13 he formed the rock group Dino, Desi and Billy with friends Desi Arnaz, Jr., and Billy Hinsche and had several juvenile record hits. He then went into professional sports, playing in the World Football League and then becoming a tennis pro on the Grand Prix circuit. He left that to fly F-4 Phantom jets for the Air National Guard.

Little wonder that when Dean Paul turned to acting, people wondered if he were serious about it. His debut was in the 1978 film *Players* (which one critic summarized thusly: "Aspiring tennis pro has to choose between forehand and foreplay"). Later, he starred in the rather silly and short-lived adventure series *Misfits of Science*. He died at age 35 in the crash of his Air National Guard Jet.

MARTIN, DICK—comedian

b: Jan 30, 1922*, Detroit, Mich.

The Chevy Show (var)...... regular (1958)
The Lucy Show (com)
.... Harry Conners (1962–64)
The Dean Martin Summer Show (var)
.... cohost (1966)
Rowan & Martin's Laugh-In (var)
.... cohost (1968–73)
Match Game P.M. (quiz). panelist (1975–82)

Emmy Award: Costar, Best Variety Show, for *Rowan & Martin's Laugh-In* (1969)

The "dumb" half of the Rowan and Martin comedy team. Rowan and Martin were among the also-rans of show business, seen from time to time during the '50s and '60s but hardly major stars, until dumb luck landed them in the middle of one of the most phenomenally popular comedy shows of all time, *Laugh-In*. Nobody tuned in just to see them; the entire lunatic cast and the bizarre and innovative lightning-fast pace were the attractions. The sight of a pair of traditional nightclub comics in the midst of such hip lunacy only added to the comedy.

Dick was a former show-business publicist who moved to California in 1949 to write for such radio programs and *Lux Radio Theatre, The Bing Crosby Show*, and *Duffy's Tavern*. He met Dan Rowan at a party in 1952 and together they wrote material for others and finally for themselves. They appeared on variety shows and had regular stints on summer series in 1958 and 1966, without really standing out from the pack. In addition, Dick had a solo role as Lucille Ball's friend on *The Lucy Show* for a couple of seasons in the early '60s.

Then came *Laugh-In*. After those heady days were over, Rowan and Martin pretty much reverted to their former status. Dick has since been seen, occasionally, in light acting roles on series including *The Love Boat;* he has also turned up on specials such as *Ultra Quiz*. It seems unlikely, however, that lightning will strike him twice.

MARTIN, EUGENE—juvenile actor

Jefferson Drum (wes)
.... Joey Drum (1958–59)
*Some sources give 1923 or 1928.

MARTIN, FREDDY—orchestra leader
b: Dec 9, 1906, Cleveland, Ohio d: Sep 30, 1983

The Freddy Martin Show (var)
.... host/orch. leader (1951)

The famous bandleader of the 1940s who gave Merv Griffin his start—singing "I've Got a Lovely Bunch of Cocoanuts."

MARTIN, GAIL—actress
b: Steubenville, Ohio

The Dean Martin Summer Show (var)
.... regular (1967)
Dean Martin Presents the Golddiggers (var)
.... regular (1969)

The daughter of Dean Martin.

MARTIN, HELEN—black actress
b: Jul 23, St. Louis, Mo.

Baby, I'm Back (com). Luzelle Carter (1978)
227 (com)............. Pearl Shay (1985–)

MARTIN, IAN—actor
b: c. 1912, Glasgow, Scotland d: Jul 25, 1981

The O'Neills (drama).. Uncle Bill (1949–50)
The Wonderful John Acton (drama)
.... Uncle Terrence (1953)

MARTIN, JARED—actor
b: Dec 21, 1944*, New York City, N.Y.

Fantastic Journey (sci fi)..... Varian (1977)
Dallas (drama)..... Dusty Farlow (1979–82)
Dallas (drama)....... Dusty Farlow (1985)

MARTIN, JOHN—actor

Lash of the West (wes).. Stratton (1952–53)

MARTIN, KIEL—actor
b: Jul 26, Pittsburgh, Pa. r: Miami, Fla.

Hill Street Blues (police)
.... Det. Johnny (J.D.) LaRue (1981–)

MARTIN, LORI—juvenile actress
b: Apr 18, 1947, Glendale, Calif.

National Velvet (adv)
.... Velvet Brown (1960–62)

Lori was the young teenager who in 1960 was chosen to recreate the role originally

*Some sources give 1941.

550

played by Elizabeth Taylor in the classic 1944 film *National Velvet*—because, it is said, she looked so much like the young Taylor. Lori gave up acting in her late teens to go to college. She has since married and is pursuing the life of a middle-class mom, in lieu of a show business career.

MARTIN, MERRY—juvenile actress
b: Oct 18, 1950, Camden, Mich.

Peter Loves Mary (com)
.... Leslie Lindsey (1960–61)

MARTIN, MILLICENT—actress
b: Jun 8, 1934, Romford, England

The Piccadilly Palace (var) .. cohost (1967)
From a Bird's Eye View (com)
.... Millie Grover (1971)
Downtown (police)
.... Harriet Conover (1986–)

MARTIN, MURPHY—newscaster
b: Lufkin, Texas

ABC Late News (news)
.... anchorman (1963–64)

MARTIN, NAN—actress

Mr. Sunshine (com).. Grace D'Angelo (1986)

MARTIN, PAMELA SUE—actress
b: Jan 5, 1953, Westport, Conn.

The Hardy Boys Mysteries (adv)
.... Nancy Drew (1977–78)
The Nancy Drew Mysteries (adv)
.... Nancy Drew (1977–78)
Dynasty (drama)
.... Fallon Carrington Colby (1981–84)

This sexy actress started out as a model in New York—while she was still in high school—and moved into television in the early 1970s. One of her earliest TV movies was *The Girls of Huntington House* (1973), in which she played a victimized teenager in a home for unwed mothers. Later (at age 24) she starred as teenage sleuth Nancy Drew, but her most famous role without doubt was that of fickle Fallon on *Dynasty*.

MARTIN, ROSS—actor
b: Mar 22, 1920, Grodek, Poland r: New York City, N.Y. d: Jul 3, 1981

Mr. Lucky (adv)......... Andamo (1959–60)
The Wild Wild West (wes)
.... Artemus Gordon (1965–69)

Ross Martin, the heavyset man of many faces and dialects on *The Wild Wild West,* had a long, chameleonlike career in acting before his hit series. He had started out as a college student prior to World War II, teaming up with Bernie West (later a very successful TV comedy producer) in a stand-up comedy act called Ross & West. The two of them did send-ups of the popular stars of the day; for example, Nelson Eddy bellowing a love song into the ear of a bravely smiling Jeanette MacDonald.

After earning his master's degree in psychometrics (the science of measuring intelligence and aptitudes), Ross plunged full-time into acting. During the late '40s he played three parts on the radio soap opera *Janice Grey* and had guest roles on such early TV drama series as *Philco TV Playhouse* and *Studio One* (in 1948). Later, he turned up rather often on the creepy suspense anthology *Lights Out* (1949–52) and was also seen in other drama shows, including *Treasury Men in Action, Court of Last Resort,* and *Alcoa Presents.* His first regular series role was as John Vivyan's helper in the short-lived *Mr. Lucky* in 1959.

Mostly, Ross played villains, often those marked by unusual traits or appearance. On a famous *Twilight Zone* episode, "The Four of Us Are Dying," he was one of the four personalities of a small, mean man. His most acclaimed movie role was that of the asthmatic killer in *Experiment in Terror* in 1962. Finally, with *The Wild Wild West,* he got the chance to play multiple characters every week, everything from a drunken Portugese fisherman to a haughty German baron. He continued active throughout the '70s, both in prime time guest roles and providing voices for the Saturday morning cartoons *Sealab 2000* (as a Chinook Indian) and *The Three Robonic Stooges* (as the Three Stooges' boss). He was Charlie Chan in the TV movie *Happiness Is a Warm Clue.* Ross participated in two *Wild Wild West* reunion films in 1979–80 and remained a busy actor until his death of a heart attack in 1981.

MARTIN, RUSS—actor

Doctors' Hospital (drama)
.... Dr. Chaffey (1975–76)

MARTIN, STEVE—comedian
b: Aug 1945, Waco, Texas r: California

Andy Williams Presents Ray Stevens (var)
.... regular (1970)
The Ken Berry "Wow" Show (var)
.... regular (1972)
The Sonny and Cher Comedy Hour (var)
.... regular (1972–73)
The Smothers Brothers Show (var)
.... regular (1975)
The Johnny Cash Show (var)
.... regular (1976)

Emmy Award: Best Comedy Writing, for *The Smothers Brothers Comedy Hour* (1969)

Many viewers were amazed when this prematurely graying, seemingly cornball comedian became a sensation with young viewers in the mid-1970s. His jokes were silly, his props embarrassing (for example, the famous arrow-through-the-head), and his patter totally unstructured as he constantly interrupted himself and digressed into nonsensical babble ("well, excu-u-use me!"). The key seems to be that Steve was, in fact, a kind of parody of middle age. He played a character who in his own eyes was "just a wild and crazy guy," but who in reality was "the jerk" (the title of his first hit movie). Is that, perhaps, how teens regarded their pseudo-hip elders?

Steve started out as the very thing he later parodied—an authentic, un-hip nightclub comic who bombed in Las Vegas and was an opening act for touring rock shows ("Chaos in the midst of chaos is not funny," he later said. "As a comedian you can only succeed if you create chaos in the midst of *order*"). His first success was as a writer for the Smothers Brothers in the late '60s, after which he went on to perform similar chores for Sonny and Cher, Pat Paulsen, John Denver, and others. He was a cast member on several comedy-variety series in the early and mid 1970s, but none brought him much renown until he started mocking himself on such youth-oriented shows as *NBC's Saturday Night Live.* Numerous appearances on *The Tonight Show,* as both a guest and guest host, also helped establish him, and by the time *The Jerk* came out in 1979 he was one of the hottest names in show business. He has continued to make films and occasional television specials in the '80s and has also worked behind the scenes on such TV projects as the late-night *Twilight Theater* and the Martin Mull comedy *Domestic Life;* these have not been particularly successful, however. It may be that, as *Rolling Stone* commented, "Basically Steve Martin has one joke—and he's it."

MARTIN, STROTHER—actor
b: Mar 26, 1919, Kokomo, Ind. d: Aug 1, 1980

Hotel De Paree (wes)
.... Aaron Donager (1959–60)
Hawkins (drama)... R. J. Hawkins (1973–74)

A familiar, grizzled character actor, most often seen as a worried villain in westerns and crime shows. He also appeared in many films from the 1950s on and was especially good as the camp captain in *Cool Hand Luke.* In series television (which tends to make movie villains into heroes) he played James Stewart's cousin on *Hawkins.*

MARTIN, TONY—singer
b: Dec 25, 1912, Oakland, Calif.

The Tony Martin Show (music)
.... host (1954–56)

The handsome, big-voiced crooner, popular since the 1930s and seen on television mostly in guest appearances during the '50s and '60s. He was married in 1948 to dancer Cyd Charisse. Their joint memoirs are titled *The Two of Us* (1976).

MARTINDALE, WINK—host
b: Dec 4, 1934, Jackson, Tenn.

Can You Top This? (com) ..... emcee (1969)
Tic Tac Dough (quiz) ...... emcee (1978–85)

For some reason, comics who want to lampoon a game-show host often pick on Wink Martindale. Perhaps it's his name (which is certainly funnier than his real moniker, Winston Conrad), perhaps his image as the distillation of all those smiling, plastic quiz-show hosts—sort of handsome, sort of glib, familiar from lots of quiz shows but not famous for any one in particular. In other words, your basic generic game-show host.

Wink started out as a disc jockey in the '50s and moved into the record industry as a promotion man in the early '60s (he even had a hit record of his own, the narrative *Deck of Cards,* in 1959). He got into game shows in 1965.

MARTINELLI, GIOVANNI—opera singer
b: Oct 22, 1885, Montagnana, Italy d: Feb 2, 1969

Opera Cameos (music)
.... commentator (1954)

A leading tenor of New York's Metropolitan Opera from 1913 until 1946, and a charming host on early television.

MARTINEZ, A—actor
b: Sep 27, Glendale, Calif.

Storefront Lawyers, (drama)
.... Roberto Alvarez (1970–71)
The Cowboys (wes) .... Cimarron (1974)
Centennial (drama)... Tranquilino (1978–79)
Born to the Wind (adv)... Low Wolf (1982)
Cassie & Company (drama)
.... Benny Silva (1982)
Whiz Kids (drama)
.... Lt. Neal Quinn (1983–84)

An accomplished actor who has filled the "Hispanic role" on quite a few series and series episodes since 1968. He found a new career as a daytime soap-opera heartthrob in the mid-1980s, on *Santa Barbara.* In the mid-1970s he was a semipro baseball player for a time. Real name: Adolf Martinez III.

MARTINEZ, CLAUDIO—juvenile actor
Viva Valdez (com) ..... Pepe Valdez (1976)

MARTINEZ, JIMMY—comedian
Tony Orlando and Dawn (var)
.... regular (1976)
The Richard Pryor Show (var)
.... regular (1977)
Presenting Susan Anton (var)
.... regular (1979)

MARTINEZ, MANUEL—actor
Ivan the Terrible (com) .... Raoul (1976)

MARTINEZ, MINA—actress
Redigo (wes)....... Linda Martinez (1963)

MARTINEZ, TONY—actor

The Real McCoys (com)
.... Pepino Garcia (1957–63)

MARTINS QUARTET, THE—

The Patrice Munsel Show (var)
.... regulars (1957–58)

MARVIN, LEE—actor
b: Feb 19, 1924, New York City, N.Y.

M Squad (police)
.... Lt. Frank Ballinger (1957–60)
Lawbreaker (doc) .... narrator (1963)

Tough guy Lee Marvin was seen frequently in the '50s and '60s on television playhouse series such as *Pepsi Cola Playhouse* and *Kraft Suspense Theatre,* as well as appearing in Hollywood films from 1951 on. He has not done much television work since he became a major movie star in the '60s with westerns such as *The Man Who Shot Liberty Valance* and *Cat Ballou.* In addition to his one network series role on *M Squad,* he narrated a 1963 syndicated series about real-life criminals called *Lawbreaker.*

MARVIN, TONY—announcer
b: Oct 5, 1912, Brooklyn, N.Y.

Arthur Godfrey's Talent Scouts (talent)
.... announcer (1948–58)
Arthur Godfrey and His Friends (var)
.... announcer (1949–59)

MARX, CHICO—comedian
b: Mar 22, 1887*, New York City, N.Y. d: Oct 11, 1961

The College Bowl (com) ..... host (1950–51)

Eldest of the famed Marx Brothers comedy team. He hosted (as the proprietor of a campus soda fountain) a live, youth-oriented variety show in 1950–51.

MARX, GROUCHO—comedian
b: Oct 2, 1890**, New York City, N.Y. d: Aug 19, 1977

You Bet Your Life (quiz) ... emcee (1950–61)
Tell It to Groucho (com) ..... regular (1962)

*Some sources give 1886 or 1891.
**Some sources give 1895, but this seems unlikely.

Emmy Award: Outstanding Personality (1950)

One of the treasures of twentieth-century American show business. Groucho and his nutty brothers were responsible for some of the most timeless slapstick movies ever made (mostly in the 1930s). By the '40s their career was in decline; nevertheless, Groucho surprised everyone by agreeing to host a radio quiz show, seemingly quite a comedown for a major movie star. It proved to be a brilliant choice, as the 1947 radio quiz became a hit 1950 TV series that ran for a total of eleven years. The "quiz" was merely a device to showcase Groucho's sarcastic wit and the barbs he directed toward his hapless contestants—and himself. His cartoonlike appearance (thick square mustache, horn-rimmed glasses) completed the picture of what was actually a comedy show. It was one of the few "quiz shows" to be successfully rerun years later.

Groucho made only a few other appearances on television, the most notable being the 1959 *General Electric Theater* production "The Incredible Jewel Robbery," in which Groucho, Harpo, and Chico were reunited for the last time. Groucho was seen solo on a few other occasions, including a *Bell Telephone Hour* production of *The Mikado* (which must have been hilarious) and episodes of *I Dream of Jeannie* in 1967 and *Julia* in 1968. Many books have been written about him, and he himself penned three funny memoirs: *Groucho and Me* (1959), *Memoirs of a Mangy Lover* (1964) and *The Groucho Letters* (1967).

MASAK, RON—actor

The Good Guys (com)
.... Andy Gardna (1968)
Love Thy Neighbor (com)
.... Charlie Wilson (1973)

MASCOLO, JOSEPH—actor
b: West Hartford, Conn.

Bronk (police)
.... Mayor Pete Santori (1975–76)
The Gangster Chronicles (drama)
.... Salvatore Maranzano (1981)

Later well-known to daytime viewers as one of soap operas' great villains, the sinister Stefano DiMera on *Days of Our Lives.*

MASE, MARINO—actor

Jericho (drama)
.... Jean-Gaston Andre (1966–67)

MASON, JAMES—actor
b: May 15, 1909, Huddersfield, England d: Jul 27, 1984

Lux Video Theatre (drama) .. host (1954–55)
The Search for the Nile (drama)
.... narrator (1972)

The eminent screen actor appeared only occasionally on television over the years, mostly in dramatic productions (several on *Playhouse 90*), specials, and large-canvas miniseries. Among the latter were *Jesus of Nazareth* (1977), *Salem's Lot* (1979), and *George Washington* (1984). His rich British tones were also used for narration of a number of documentaries. His last appearance was as the aging, melancholy Roman emperor Tiberius in the miniseres *A.D.,* aired postumously in April 1985.

His autobiography was titled *Before I Forget* (1982).

MASON, MADISON—actor

Knots Landing (drama)
.... John Coblenz (1985)

MASON, MARLYN—actress
b: Aug 7, 1940, San Fernando, Calif.

Ben Casey (drama)
.... Sally Welden (1965–66)
Longstreet (drama) .... Nikki Bell (1971–72)

MASON, TOM—actor
b: Mar 1, Brooklyn, N.Y.

Grandpa Goes to Washignton (com)
.... Tony DeLuca (1978–79)
Freebie and the Bean (police)
. Det. Sgt. Tim Walker (Freebie) (1980–81)
Two Marriages (drama)
.... Jim Daley (1983–84)
Our Family Honor (drama)
.... Det. Sgt. Frank McKay (1985–86)
Jack and Mike (drama)
.... Mike Brennan (1986–)

MASSEY, DARIA—actress

The Islanders (adv) .... Naja (1960–61)

MASSEY, ILONA—actress, singer
b: Jun 16, 1910, Budapest, Hungary d: Aug 10, 1974

Rendezvous (drama).... Nikki Angell (1952)
The Ilona Massey Show (music)
.... hostess (1954–55)

Glamorous continental star, seen briefly on television in the '50s both as a hostess (on *The Ilona Massey Show*) and an actress (on *Rendezvous, Studio One,* etc.). She retired in 1960 to devote her final years to charitable and political causes, including speaking out on behalf of her oppressed homeland.

MASSEY, RAYMOND—actor
b: Aug 30, 1896, Toronto, Canada d: Jul 29, 1983

I Spy (drama)
.... Anton, the spymaster (1955–56)
Dr. Kildare (drama)
.... Dr. Leonard Gillespie (1961–66)

The distinguished, thick-browed actor, who had been in films since 1931, played many roles in television dramatic productions of the '50s. One which he essayed several times was his well-known characterization of Abe Lincoln. In *Dr. Kildare* he played the part, originated in movies by Lionel Barrymore, of the crochety but caring senior physician to the young Kildare (Richard Chamberlain). Massey was seen only occasionally after that in a few dramatic episodes and TV movies of the late '60s and early '70s; he then retired.

Autobiographies: *When I Was Young* (1976), *A Hundred Lives* (1979).

MASTERS, NATALIE—actress

Date with the Angels (com)
.... Wilma Clemson (1957–58)

MASUR, RICHARD—actor
b: Nov 20, New York City, N.Y.

Hot L Baltimore (com)
.... Clifford Ainsley (1975)
One Day at a Time (com)
.... David Kane (1975–76)
East of Eden (drama)
.... Will Hamilton (1981)
Empire (com) .... Jack Willow (1984)

MATA & HARI—dancers

Your Show of Shows (var)
.... regular (1950–53)

MATCHETT, CHRISTINE—juvenile actress

Owen Marshall, Counselor at Law (drama)
.... Melissa Marshall (1971–74)

MATHERS, JERRY—actor
b: Jun 2, 1948, Sioux City, Iowa r: Tarzana, Calif.

Leave It to Beaver (com)
.... Beaver (Theodore) Cleaver (1957–63)

Arguably America's most famous "TV kid" of the '50s and '60s. He had an active show business career in the half dozen years before his famous role, but practically none afterward, until he became the center of a major nostalgia craze in the 1980s.

Jerry made his TV debut in 1950 at the age of two on *The Ed Wynn Show* and had small roles in dramatic series such as *Lux Video Theatre* after that. He had parts in five movies between 1954–57, including Hitchcock's *The Trouble with Harry,* and was an acting "pro" by the time he auditioned for the role of Beaver. It was his little-boy innocence that won him the part, however. Reportedly, he told the producers that he hoped the audition wouldn't run too long, so he wouldn't miss his cub scout meeting.

After six happy years on *Beaver,* Jerry (by then in his awkward teens) found the acting pickings slim. He played a few roles on *Batman, Lassie,* and *My Three Sons,* but spent the majority of his time completing his college education and trying to establish himself as a businessman. During the mid and late 1970s, Jerry and his TV brother Tony Dow made personal appearances around the country; then, in the early '80s, they were suddenly thrust back into the spotlight via books *(The Beaver Papers),* articles, and the 1983 reunion special *Still the Beaver,* which later became a cable TV series. Beaver and Wally even found themselves staring out from the front panels of cornflakes boxes. Jerry's adult acting left something to be desired, however, and the revival of interest seemed unlikely to lead to anything more than nostalgia appearances. But

then, nostalgia jobs were better than none at all.

MATHERS, JIMMY—juvenile actor

Ichabod and Me (com)
.... Benjie Major (1961–62)

MATHESON, DON—actor
b: Aug 5, Dearborn, Mich.

Land of the Giants (sci fi)
.... Mark Wilson (1968–70)
Falcon Crest (drama) .... Padgett (1984)

MATHESON, MURRAY—actor
b: 1912, Australia d: Apr 25, 1985

Banacek (drama)
.... Felix Mulholland (1972–74)

MATHESON, TIM—actor
b: Dec 31, 1947, Glendale, Calif.

Window on Main Street (com)
.... Roddy Miller (1961–62)
Jonny Quest (cartn)
.... Jonny Quest (voice) (1964–65)
The Virginian (wes) .... Jim Horn (1969–70)
Bonanza (wes) .... Griff King (1972–73)
The Quest (wes) .. Quentin Beaudine (1976)
Tucker's Witch (drama)
.... Rick Tucker (1982–83)

Tim Matheson got his start in acting while in grade school, when one of his chums introduced him to his producer-father, Mike Stokey. Young Tim was soon hooked on show business and landed his first regular role within a year on the Robert Young series *Window on Main Street.* He then worked fairly steadily in episodes of series such as *The Twilight Zone, My Three Sons, The Farmer's Daughter,* and *Leave It to Beaver.* In addition, he provided voices for numerous Hanna-Barbera cartoons, playing Jonny Quest, Young Sampson, Sinbad, Jr., and others.

During the '70s Tim successfully graduated to adult roles in prime time series, series episodes, and TV movies. He has been the co-lead in two series *(The Quest* and *Tucker's Witch),* though he has yet to star in a genuine hit of his own.

MATHEWS, CAROLE—actress
b: Sep 13, 1920, Montgomery, Ill.

The Californians (wes)
.... Wilma Fansler (1958–59)

MATHEWS, GEORGE—actor
b: c. 1911, Brooklyn, N.Y. d: Nov 14, 1984

Glynis (com).......... Chick Rogers (1963)

MATHEWS, LARRY—juvenile actor
b: Aug 15, 1955, Burbank, Calif.

The Dick Van Dyke Show (com)
.... Ritchie Petrie (1961–66)

Dick Van Dyke's TV son was able to find few roles after the run of that classic series and so went to work behind the scenes in the production end of television. He now goes under his real name, Larry Mazzeo.

MATHEWS, THOM—actor

Paper Dolls (drama)... Lewis Crosby (1984)

MATHIAS, ANNA—actress

Pink Lady (var) .... regular (1980)

MATHIAS, BOB—actor, athlete
b: Nov 17, 1930, Tulare, Calif.

The Troubleshooters (adv)
.... Frank Dugan (1959–60)

The former Olympic decathlon champion (in '48 and '52) made his acting debut as himself in the 1954 film *The Bob Mathias Story*. He later played roles in both films and television. On *The Troubleshooters* he costarred with Keenan Wynn as an athletic, globe-trotting problem solver for a construction firm. Bob then entered politics and was elected a U.S. congressman from California.

MATHIAS, DARIAN—actress

Please Stand By (com)
.... Susan Lambert (1978–79)
Hanging In (com)...... Rita Zefferelli (1979)

MATHIEU, MIREILLE—
b: 1946, Avignon, France

The John Davidson Show (var)
.... regular (1969)

MATLOCK, NORMAN—actor

Chiefs (drama).......... Jesse Cole (1983)

MATTHAU, WALTER—actor
b: Oct 1, 1920, New York City, N.Y.

Tallahassee 7000 (police)
.... Lex Rogers (1961)

With a jowly, crumpled face one critic likened to a "bloodhound with a head cold," Walter Matthau has had a corner on comic grouch roles in movies of the '60s, '70s, and '80s. Before that, however, directors didn't know what to do with him. He was most often cast as a villain, stalking stars such as Burt Lancaster and Audrey Hepburn on screen and TV.

Matthau did quite a bit of television work early in his career, mostly in playhouse dramas of the '50s and early '60s. He was a frequent player on the alternating *Goodyear/Philco Playhouse* and appeared a number of times on *Alfred Hitchcock Presents*—always as a criminal or crooked official. On the syndicated *Tallahassee 7000*, at least, he got to play the right side of the law tracking down criminals for the Florida sheriff's bureau.

Playwright Neil Simon was the first to really capitalize on the comic possibilities of Matthau's slouch and grouch, specifically writing for him the role of Oscar in his 1965 play *The Odd Couple*. The play was a smash hit, and thereafter Matthau was lost to TV as he shifted full-time into comic movies, with great success. Even the TV role of Oscar (which Matthau played on stage and screen) went to someone else—television's own veteran grouch, Jack Klugman.

MATTHEWS, LESTER—actor
b: Dec 3, 1900, Nottingham, England d: Jun 6, 1975

The Adventures of Fu Manchu (drama)
..... Sir Dennis Nayland-Smith (1955–56)

MATTHIUS, GAIL—comedienne

NBC's Saturday Night Live (com)
.... regular (1980–81)

MATTINGLY, HEDLEY—actor
b: England

The Travels of Jaimie McPheeters (wes)
.... Henry T. Coe (1963–64)
Daktari (adv) .... Hedley (1966–69)

MATTOX, MATT—choreographer
b: 1921

The Patti Page Olds Show (var)
.... dancers (1958–59)

MATUSZAK, JOHN—actor
b: Oct 25, Milwaukee, Wisc.

Hollywood Beat (police)
.... George Grinsky (1985)

A former football pro, with the Oakland Raiders in the '70s and early '80s. At 6' 8" and 288 pounds, he is surely one of the more imposing sports converts to acting. On *Hollywood Beat* he played a police informant who was openly gay but too big for anyone to say anything about it.

MATZ, PETER—orchestra leader
b: Nov 6, 1928, Pittsburgh, Pa.

The Edie Adams Show (var)
.... orch. leader (1963–64)
The Jimmy Dean Show (var)
.... orch. leader (1963–65)
Hullabaloo (music) .. orch. leader (1965–66)
The Kraft Music Hall (var)
.... orch. leader (1967–71)
The Carol Burnett Show (var)
.... orch. leader (1971–78)
The Tim Conway Show (var)
.... orch. leader (1980–81)

Emmy Awards: Best Music Direction, for the special *My Name Is Barbra* (1965); for *The Kraft Music Hall* production *The Sound of Burt Bacharach* (1970); for *The Carol Burnett Show* (1973)

MAUGHAM, W. SOMERSET—author
b: Jan 25, 1874, Paris, France d: Dec 16, 1965

Somerset Maugham TV Theatre (drama)
.... host (1950–51)

MAUNDER, WAYNE—actor
b: c. 1938, Canada, r: Bangor, Me.

Custer (wes)
.... Lt. Col. George A. Custer (1967)
Lancer (wes)........ Scott Lancer (1968–70)
Chase (police)
.... Sgt. Sam MacCray (1973–74)

After three unsuccessful shots at series stardom in the late '60s and early '70s,

Wayne more or less gave up. He has virtually disappeared from view in the years since.

MAUPIN, REX—orchestra leader
b: Nov 25, 1886, St. Joseph, Mo. d: Jul 28, 1966

The Benny Rubin Show (com)
.... orch. leader (1949)
The Little Revue (music)
.... orch. leader (1949–50)
Tin Pan Alley TV (var) . orch. leader (1950)
Music in Velvet (music) ..... regular (1951)

MAURY, DERREL—actor
b: Apr 15, Los Angeles, Calif.

Apple Pie (com).... Junior Hollyhock (1978)
Joanie Loves Chachi (com)
.... Mario (1982–83)

MAXEY, PAUL—actor
b: Mar 15, 1907, Wheaton, Ill. d: Jun 3, 1963

Lassie (adv) ..... Matt Brockway (1954–57)
The People's Choice (com)
.... Mayor John Peoples (1955–58)

MAXTED, ELLEN—actress
b: Jun 8, Birmingham, Mich.

Just Our Luck (com)
.... Meagan Huxley (1983)

MAXWELL, CHARLES—actor

I Led Three Lives (drama)
..... special agent Joe Carey (occasional)
(1953–56)

MAXWELL, ELSA—writer
b: May 24, 1883, Keokuk, Iowa d: Nov 1, 1963

The Jack Paar Show (talk)
.... semiregular (1957–58)

The famous, corpulent Hollywood party giver of the '30s, '40s, and '50s. Elsa was a cheerful and bubbly guest on talk shows during television's early days. Two of her autobiographical books: *I Married the World* (1955) and *Celebrity Circus* (1961).

MAXWELL, FRANK—actor
b: Nov 17, The Bronx, N.Y.

Our Man Higgins (com)
.... Duncan MacRoberts (1962–63)
Felony Squad (police).. Capt. Nye (1966–69)
The Second Hundred Years (com)
.... Col. Garroway (1967–68)

MAXWELL, JEFF—actor

M*A*S*H (com)............ Igor (1976–83)

MAXWELL, JOHN—actor

Court of Last Resort (drama)
.... Alex Gregory (1957–58)

MAXWELL, MARILYN—actress
b: Aug 3, 1921, Clarinda, Iowa d: Mar 20, 1972

Bus Stop (drama)
.... Grace Sherwood (1961–62)

A vivacious blonde actress, singer, and
dancer of the 1940s who appeared in scattered television series episodes of the '50s
and '60s and was a regular on *Bus Stop,* as
the owner of the diner. Her TV work was
beginning to increase in 1970–71 (*Here's
Lucy, Men at Law,* etc.), just before her
death of high blood pressure and other
causes in 1972.

MAY, BILLY—orchestra leader
b: Nov 10, 1916, Pittsburgh, Pa.

The Milton Berle Show (var)
.... orch. leader (1958–59)

The well-known bandleader has composed a good deal of TV music, including
the *Naked City* theme; he has also composed and conducted the musical background for *Batman, The Green Hornet,
The Mod Squad, Emergency, CHiPs,* and
many other shows. He has recorded
widely, with some of his most famous work
being his backing of Frank Sinatra on LPs
during the '50s.

MAY, BOB—actor

Lost in Space (sci fi).... the robot (1965–68)

MAY, DEBORAH—actress

St. Elsewhere (drama)
.... Terri Valerie (1985–)

MAY, DONALD—actor
b: Feb 22, c. 1927, Chicago, Ill.

The West Point Story (drama)
.... cadet Charles C. Thompson (1956)
Colt .45 (wes)...... Sam Colt, Jr. (1959–60)
The Roaring Twenties (drama)
.... Pat Garrison (1960–62)

After 15 years as a prime time actor in the
'50s and '60s, starring in three series and
playing guest roles on many others, Donald
May abruptly shifted into daytime soap
operas in 1967 and had a marathon ten-
year run as attorney Adam Drake on *The
Edge of Night* (1967–77). He still makes occasional guest appearances but is now
known primarily as a mature leading man
on soap operas, with continuing roles in
the '80s on *Texas, As the World Turns,*
and *Falcon Crest.*

MAY, ELAINE—comedienne, writer
b: Apr 21, 1932, Philadelphia, Pa.

Keep Talking (quiz) ...... regular (1958–59)

The onetime partner of Mike Nichols in a
stand-up comedy act (in the '50s), Elaine is
now a successful screenwriter and director. She still acts, but her television appearances have been few.

MAY, MARTY—
b: c. 1898 d: Nov 11, 1975

Fireball Fun-for-All (var)..... regular (1949)

MAYAMA, MIKO—actress

Hey Landlord (com)
.... Kyoko Mitsui (1966–67)

MAYEHOFF, EDDIE—actor
b: Jul 7, 1911, Baltimore, Md.

Hour Glass (var).......... emcee (1946–47)
Doc Corkle (com) .... Doc Corkle (1952)
That's My Boy (com)
.... "Jarring" Jack Jackson (1954–55)

MAYER, CHRISTOPHER—actor
b: Apr 21, New York City r: Ridgewood,
N.J.

The Dukes of Hazzard (com)
.... Vance Duke (1982–83)
Glitter (drama)....... Pete Bozak (1984–85)

Married to actress Teri Copley, who is even prettier than he is.

MAYER, KEN—actor
b: Jun 25, 1918 d: Jan 30, 1985

Space Patrol (child)
.... Maj. Robbie Robertson (1951–52)

MAYNARD, KERMIT—cowboy actor
b: Sep 20, 1902*, Vevey, Ind. d: Jan 16, 1971

Saturday Roundup (wes)..... regular (1951)

The younger brother of cowboy star Ken Maynard.

MAYO, WHITMAN—black actor
b: Nov 15, 1930, New York

Sanford and Son (com)
.... Grady Wilson (1973–77)
Grady (com)...... Grady Wilson (1975–76)
The Sanford Arms (com)
.... Grady Wilson (1977)
Hell Town (drama)........ One Ball (1985)

MAZES, MICHAEL—actor

Operation Petticoat (com)
.... Radioman Gossett (1977–78)

MAZURKI, MIKE—actor
b: Dec 25, 1909, Tarnopal, Austria** r: Cohoes, N.Y.

It's About Time (com) ...... Clon (1966–67)
Chicago Teddy Bears (com)... Julius (1971)

A towering former wrestler of Ukrainian descent who looked extremely dim-witted (and played roles to match) but who was in fact one of Hollywood's most erudite gentlemen.

MCADAMS, HEATHER—juvenile actress

Walking Tall (police)
.... Dwana Pusser (1981)

MCAFEE, JOHNNY—singer
b: Jul 24, 1913, Dallas, Texas

The Sammy Kaye Show (var)
.... regular (1958–59)

*Some sources give 1898.
**Some sources give Lwow, Ukraine.

MCALLISTER, CHIP—black actor
b: Oct 2, St. Louis, Mo. r: Los Angeles, Calif.

Better Days (com)..... Luther Cain (1986–)

MCALLISTER, JENNIFER—juvenile actress

Married: The First Year (drama)
.... Millie Baker (1979)

MCALONEY, MICHAEL—actor

One Man's Family (drama)
.... Sgt. Tony Adams (1952)

MCBAIN, DIANE—actress
b: 1941

Surfside Six (drama)
.... Daphne Dutton (1960–62)

When her acting career waned in the late 1960s, Diane switched careers and became an executive secretary. She has acted occasionally since then, including a brief stint as "Foxy Humdinger" on daytime's *Days of Our Lives* in the early '80s. On *Surfside Six* she played a sexy socialite.

MCBRIDE, DON—actor
b: 1889*, Brooklyn, N.Y. d: Jun 21, 1957

My Friend Irma (com) . Mr. Clyde (1952–54)

MCBRIDE, MARY MARGARET—hostess
b: Nov 16, 1899, Paris, Mo. d: Apr 7, 1976

Mary Margaret McBride (int)
.... hostess (1948)

The famous, folksy radio interviewer of the '30s and '40s. One writer called her "the woman's answer to Arthur Godfrey." Her memoirs: *A Long Way From Missouri* (1959) and *Out of the Air* (1960).

MCCAFFERY, JOHN K.M.—host
b: Nov 30, 1913, Moscow, Idaho d: Oct 3, 1983

Television Screen Magazine (mag)
.... emcee/"editor" (1948)
Author Meets the Critics (int)
.... moderator (1948–51)
We Take Your Word (quiz)
.... word master (1950–51)

*Some sources give 1894.

Take a Guess (quiz) ...... moderator (1953)
What's the Story? (quiz)
.... moderator (1953–55)
One Minute Please (quiz)
.... moderator (1954)
The Nation's Future (pub aff)
.... moderator (1960–61)

The editor of *American Mercury* magazine and a frequent host on early television.

MCCAIN, FRANCES LEE—actress
b: Jul 28, York, Pa.

Apple's Way (drama)
.... Barbara Apple (1974–75)
13 Queens Boulevard (com) ..... Lois (1979)

MCCALL, MARTY—juvenile actor
The New Andy Griffith Show (com)
.... T. J. Sawyer (1971)

MCCALL, MITZI—comedienne, actress
Rowan & Martin's Laugh-In (var)
.... regular (1968–69)

Mitzi was also the voice of Penny on *The Flintstones* cartoon spin-offs in the '70s and '80s.

MCCALL, SHALANE—actor
b: Sep 16, 1972

Dallas (drama)...... Charlie Wade (1983–)

MCCALLA, IRISH—actress
b: Dec 25, 1929, Pawnee City, Neb.

Sheena, Queen of the Jungle (adv)
.... Sheena (1955–56)

Sheena, Queen of the Jungle is one of those shows that is well-remembered even though it was not really much of a hit when it originally aired (only 26 episodes were made). Sheena was a kind of female Tarzan, swinging from vine to vine, leotard clinging to her voluptuous figure as she went about helping the innocent natives and foiling the evil jungle interlopers. She was a true liberated woman, very much in charge and often called upon to rescue her inept male companion, Trader Bob. The dialogue was cliché ridden and the acting

wooden, but with a figure like *that* who cared?

Irish was an obscure Hollywood model when she got her big break (Anita Ekberg had been signed for the role but failed to show up). She later landed a few small roles on the strength of her *Sheena* notoriety—for example, on *77 Sunset Strip* and in a few B movies—but her acting career soon petered out. She then changed careers and became quite successful as a painter specializing in Old West subjects. She is still recognized as Sheena and loves it.

MCCALLION, JAMES—actor
b: Sep 27, 1918, Glasgow, Scotland

National Velvet (adv)
.... Mi Taylor (1960–62)

MCCALLUM, DAVID—actor
b: Sep 19, 1933, Glasgow, Scotland

The Man from U.N.C.L.E. (drama)
.... Illya Kuryakin (1964–68)
The Invisible Man (adv)
.... Dr. Daniel Westin (1975–76)

This blond, slightly built actor was one of the more exotic figures on television during the '60s, as the soft-spoken Russian who was teamed with Robert Vaughn to fight international crime on *The Man from U.N.C.L.E.* McCallum was born and raised in Great Britain, the son of a concert violinist, and he got his start there as a stage and screen actor during the 1950s. He came to the U.S. in the early '60s and played guest roles in series including *The Outer Limits*, *Perry Mason*, and *The Travels of Jamie McPheeters* before he won the role that made him famous. After the run of *U.N.C.L.E.*, David was seen in a number of TV movies and series episodes, often as a quiet, intellectual foreigner, and he starred in a short-lived series of his own called *The Invisible Man*. He was less active after that, although he continued to play some roles on both American and British TV (he has had several series on the latter).

David appeared in the 1983 reunion special *Return of the Man from U.N.C.L.E.*, in which Illya Kuryakin was said (in the story) to have become the owner of a trendy Park Avenue fashion salon.

MCCALLUM, NEIL—actor

b: 1930*, Saskatchewan, Canada d: Apr 26, 1976

Saber of London (drama)
.... Pete Paulson (1957-58)

MCCALMAN, MACON—actor

Best of the West (com)
.... Mayor Fletcher (1981-82)

MCCAMBRIDGE, MERCEDES—actress

b: Mar 17, 1918, Joliet, Ill.

One Man's Family (drama)
.... Beth Holly (1949-50)
Wire Service (drama)
.... Katherine Wells (1956-57)

An actress known for her hard-bitten, even menacing roles—although she is actually a rather warm and gracious person in real life. She had an active career on radio in the '40s but has been seen only intermittently since the early '50s, in films and on television. She was the unseen voice of Satan in the 1973 movie *The Exorcist*. Roles appropriate to her intensity have not been easy to find, and she is sometimes embittered by the failure of Hollywood to make better use of her talents. She has said, "In my next life maybe I can come back looking like Doris Day or Julie Andrews, but right now I am what I am and if that's not what they want then I won't work here much."

Her autobiography is titled *The Two of Us* (1960).

MCCANN, CHUCK—comedian, actor

b: Sep 2, Brooklyn, N.Y.

The Garry Moore Show (var)
.... regular (1966-67)
Turn-On (var)............... regular (1969)
Happy Days (var)........... regular (1970)
Van Dyke and Company (var)
.... regular (1976)
All That Glitters (com)
.... Bert Stockwood (1977)
A New Kind of Family (com)
.... Harold Zimmerman (1979-80)

Roly-poly actor, who sometimes impersonates the late Oliver Hardy (of Laurel and Hardy).

*Some sources give 1929 or 1931.

MCCANN, SEAN—actor

The Baxters (com)..... Jim Baxter (1980-81)
Night Heat (police)
.... Lt. Jim Hogan (1985-)

MCCARREN, FRED—actor

b: Apr 12, Butler, Pa.

Free Country (com)
.... Sidney Gewertzman (1978)
The Last Convertible (drama)
.... Paul McCreed (1979)
Amanda's (com)
.... Marty Cartwright (1983)

MCCARTHY, CLEM—sportscaster

Harness Racing (sport)
.... announcer (1949-50)
Gillette Summer Sports Reel (sport)
.... commentator (1953)

MCCARTHY, FRANK—actor

MacGruder & Loud (police)
.... Sgt. Myhrum (1985)

MCCARTHY, KEVIN—actor

b: Feb 15, 1914, Seattle, Wash.

The Survivors (drama)
.... Philip Hastings (1969-70)
Flamingo Road (drama)
............'.... Claude Weldon (1981-82)
Amanda's (com)
.... Zack Cartwright (1983)

A veteran, all-purpose actor (onstage since 1938, in films since 1951) who in recent years has specialized in steely-eyed, rather untrustworthy authority figures—for example, the ruthless small-town despot on *Flamingo Road*. Kevin has been active on television since 1949, playing many hundreds of roles on everything from live dramas of the '50s such as *Prudential Playhouse* and *Ford Theatre* to B-grade movies of the '80s, including *Invitation to Hell* and *The Making of a Male Model*. One of his best roles was in a 1960 episode of *The Twilight Zone*, as a man who had been given the gift—or curse?—of immortality; at the end of the story the character was shot and turned to dust before the viewer's eyes.

Kevin is the brother of author Mary McCarthy.

MCCARTHY, LARK—newscaster

CBS News Nightwatch (news)
.... co-anchor (1984)

MCCARTHY, LINWOOD—actor

The Blue Knight (police) .. Lt. Hauser (1976)
The Winds of War (drama)
.... Blinker Vance (1983)

MCCARTY, MARY—actress, singer
b: Sep 27, 1923, Winfield, Kansas, r: Los Angeles d: Apr 3, 1980

Admiral Broadway Revue (var)
.... regular (1949)
Celebrity Time (quiz).... panelist (1951–52)
Trapper John, M.D. (drama)
Nurse Clara Willoughly (Starch) (1979–80)

MCCARVER, TIM—sportscaster
b: Oct 16, 1941, Memphis, Tenn.

Monday Night Baseball (sport)
.... sportscaster (1984–   )

A former baseball catcher who spent 21 years in the major leagues (1959–1980), mostly with the St. Louis Cardinals and the Philadelphia Phillies.

MCCARY, ROD—actor
b: Apr 15, St. Cloud, Minn.

Harper Valley P.T.A. (com)
.... Bobby Taylor (1981–82)
Just Our Luck (com)
.... Nelson Marriott (1983)

MCCASHIN, CONSTANCE—actress
b: Jun 18, Chicago, Ill. r: Greenwich, Conn.

Knots Landing (drama)
.... Laura Avery (1979–   )

This alluring soap opera actress made her professional debut at age five doing live commercials on *The Howdy Doody Show.* Later, in her teens, she pursued a marginally successful stage career, then taught retarded children for a time. Finding herself short of cash, she became a contestant on *The $25,000 Pyramid,* where she won $2,000, which she used to help pay for her move to Hollywood. Seldom have quiz-show winnings been better spent; she soon began to make a name for herself in TV movies and then won a starring role in the prime time serial *Knots Landing.*

MCCAY, PEGGY—actress
b: c. 1930, New York City, N.Y.

Room for One More (com)
.... Anna Rose (1962)
Gibbsville (drama) ..... Mrs. Malloy (1976)

Primarily a daytime soap opera actress, on *Love of Life* in the '50s, *General Hospital* in the '60s, and *Days of Our Lives* in the '80s, among others.

MCCLAIN, JAMES—host

Doctor I.Q. (quiz)............. emcee (1954)

MCCLANAHAN, RUE—actress
b: Feb 21, 1934, Healdton, Okla.

Maude (com)
...... Vivian Cavender Harmon (1972–78)
Apple Pie (com)
.... Ginger-Nell Hollyhock (1978)
Mama's Family (com)
.... Aunt Fran Crowley (1983–84)
Golden Girls (com)
.... Blanche Devereaux (1985–   )

The tart-tongued, mature Southern belle of *Mama's Family* and *The Golden Girls,* and Maude's best friend on *Maude.* Rue began her television career playing dramatic roles in the '60s while simultaneously appearing in stage productions in New York. In the early '70s she projected more anguish on daytime soap operas for a few years *(Another World, Where the Heart Is)* but then hit her stride when she switched to comedy on *Maude.* She has been a delightful and distinctive supporting player on numerous TV comedies since then, including a smash hit of the mid-1980s, *Golden Girls.*

MCCLELLAND, DONALD—actor

Crime Photographer (drama)
.... Capt. Logan (1951–52)

MCCLINTOCK, DR. GUTHRIE—host

Serving Through Science (info)
.........................host (1946–47)

MCCLORY, SEAN—actor
b: Mar 8, 1924, Dublin, Ireland

The Californians (wes)
.... Jack McGivern (1957–58)

Kate McShane (drama)
.... Pat McShane (1975)
Bring 'Em Back Alive (adv)
.... Myles Delany (1982–83)

MCCLOSKEY, LEIGH—actor
b: Jun 21, Los Angeles, Calif.

Rich Man, Poor Man—Book I (drama)
.... Billy (1976)
Executive Suite (drama)
.... Brian Walling (1976–77)
Married: The First Year (drama)
.... Billy Baker (1979)
Dallas (drama)..... Mitch Cooper (1979–82)

MCCLOUD, MERCER—actor

Claudia, The Story of a Marriage (drama)
.... Roger (1952)

MCCLURE, DOUG—actor
b: May 11, 1935, Glendale, Calif.

The Overland Trail (wes)
.... Frank "Flip" Flippen (1960)
Checkmate (drama)...... Jed Sills (1960–62)
The Virginian (wes) .... Trampas (1962–71)
Search (adv)........ C. R. Grover (1972–73)
The Barbary Coast (wes)
.... Cash Conover (1975–76)
Roots (drama)......... Jemmy Brent (1977)

"I'm 37 years old," said Doug McClure as he began work on *Search* in the early '70s. "I don't want to hide that! It's neat! I dig every gray hair." He added, "When another actor was described as a 'young Doug McClure' I knew I was (finally) over the hump."

Doug was referring to the persistent "young sidekick" image that gave him his start in television in the 1950s but then dogged him throughout the '60s to an age when other actors would have moved into more mature roles. Rugged and undeniably boyish-looking, he got into acting in his early twenties with roles in a few forgettable movies (*The Enemy Below*, 1957; *Because They're Young*, 1959) and on such TV series as the syndicated *Men of Annapolis* (1957) and, a little later, *Jim Bowie, Court of Last Resort*, and *The Gale Storm Show*, among others.

Doug's first real break was as William Bendix's enthusiastic young partner in the short-lived western *The Overland Trail. Checkmate*, on which he was the youngest member of a smooth crime-fighting team, did better, but it was the role of the wild young cowhand Trampas on *The Virginian* that made him a star. By the time he began work on the high-tech adventure series *Search*, the "young sidekick" bit was becoming something of a liability. The new, more mature Doug McClure of the '70s and '80s has not had another hit series to match *The Virginian*, but he does work fairly regularly in TV movies and miniseries. One of his films, *Nightside* (1980), was the pilot for a series that would have starred him as a seasoned, streetwise cop working the night shift in L.A. with his *own* young sidekick.

MCCLURE, FRANK CHANDLER—actor
b: c. 1895 d: 1960

Traffic Court (drama)...... bailiff (1958–59)

MCCLURE, KATEE—comedienne

The Hudson Brothers Show (var)
.... regular (1974)

MCCLURE, M'LISS—juvenile actor

Ramar of the Jungle (adv)
.... regular (1952–54)

MCCLURE, MARC—actor
b: Mar 31, 1957, San Mateo, Calif. r: Glendale, Calif.

California Fever (adv)
.... Ross Whitman (1979)

Marc played eager young reporter Jimmy Olsen in the movie *Superman*.

MCCLURG, BOB—actor

Alice (com) .... Cecil (1978–79)

MCCLURG, EDIE—actress, comedienne
b: Kansas City, Mo.

Tony Orlando and Dawn (var)
.... regular (1976)
The Kallikaks (com)
.... Venus Kallikak (1977)
The Big Show (var)......... regular (1980)
Harper Valley P.T.A. (com)
.... Willamae Jones (1981)

563

No Soap, Radio (com) ...... Marion (1982)
Valerie (com) .... Mrs. Poole (1986–)

MCCONNELL, ED—host
b: 1892 d: 1954

Smilin' Ed McConnell and His Buster Brown Gang (child) .... host (1950–51)

The jovial host of the *Buster Brown Gang* children's variety show, on radio in the '40s and television (daytime and early evening) from 1950–54. He was a former vaudevillian who plunked the banjo and had a fine old time with the various props and regular characters on the show (e.g., Froggy the Gremlin, Grandie the Piano). After Smilin' Ed smiled his last in 1954 the series was taken over by Andy Devine, who continued it until 1960.

MCCONNELL, JUDY—actress

The Beverly Hillbillies (com)
.... Miss Leeds (1969)
Green Acres (com)
.... Darlene Wheeler (1970–71)

MCCONNELL, LULU—comedienne
b: 1882, Kansas City, Mo. d: Oct 9, 1962

It Pays to Be Ignorant (quiz)
.... panelist (1949–51)

MCCOO, MARILYN—black singer, hostess
b: Sep 30, 1943, Jersey City, N.J.

The Marilyn McCoo and Billy Davis, Jr. Show (var)....................... cohost (1977)
Solid Gold (music) .... host (1981–84)
Solid Gold (music) .... host (1986–)

A former member of the Fifth Dimension singing group (from 1966–75), and later the partner with her husband, singer Billy Davis, Jr., as a popular duo.

MCCOOK, JOHN—actor
b: Jun 20, 1945, Ventura, Calif.

Codename: Foxfire (drama)
.... Larry Hutchins (1985)

MCCORD, KENT—actor
b: Sep 26, 1942, Los Angeles, Calif.

Adam 12 (police)... Off. Jim Reed (1968–75)

Battlestar Galactica (sci fi)
.... Capt. Troy (1980)

Producer Jack Webb seemed to like clean-cut, somewhat colorless young actors in his series (whatever became of Randolph Mantooth and Kevin Tighe?) and Kent McCord certainly filled that bill. He began his television career as an extra on *Ozzie and Harriet*, then landed a contract with Universal Studios in 1965, which led to roles in such series as *The Virginian* and *Run for Your Life*. Webb used him several times on *Dragnet '67*, then had him costar as the green young officer partnered with experienced Martin Milner on the popular *Adam 12*.

Since then, Kent has appeared periodically in series episodes and TV movies, including an unsuccessful 1977 pilot produced by Webb that cast him as a small-town fireman *(Pine Canyon Is Burning)*.

MCCORMACK, PATTY—actress
b: Aug 21, 1945, Brooklyn, N.Y.

Mama (com).......... Ingeborg (1953–57)
Peck's Bad Girl (com) ... Torey Peck (1959)
The Ropers (com) . Anne Brookes (1979–80)

Patty McCormack got quite a start in show business, rocketing to fame as the pig-tailed, murderous little girl in the Broadway (1954) and movie (1956) versions of *The Bad Seed*. She was a "professional child" even before that, however, appearing as a model at age four and on *Kraft Television Theatre* at seven. Throughout the '50s she appeared frequently on TV, in roles ranging from the sympathetic *(The Miracle Worker* on *Playhouse 90)* to the obnoxious ("Dan Marshall's Brat" on *DuPont Theater*). She was also a regular on *(I Remember) Mama* and had her own summer comedy series, *Peck's Bad Girl*—as a trouble-prone, but fortunately not homicidal, teenager.

The "bad girl" image followed Patty into the '60s, as she played roles on TV and in youth movies such as *The Explosive Generation, The Miniskirt Mob,* and *Born Wild*. She also had recurring parts as a troubled teen on some daytime soap operas. From time to time she dropped out of acting, including a few years in the mid-1960s when she worked at other jobs, got fat, and sang with a rock band.

By the mid-1970s Patty was back, determined to become a more adult actress and playing guest roles on crime shows and light comedies (e.g., *The Love Boat*). Now billed as Patricia McCormack, the former enfant terrible played everything from a comic wife on *The Ropers* to a terrorized kidnap victim on the TV movie *Night Partners*. Still, it's hard to shake an image as striking as that won from *The Bad Seed*.

MCCORMICK, CAROLYN—actress
b: Sep 19, Midland, Texas r: Houston, Texas

Spenser: For Hire (drama)
.... Rita Fiori (1986–   )

MCCORMICK, MAUREEN—actress
b: c. 1956, California

The Brady Bunch (com)
.... Marcia Brady (1969–74)
Brady Bunch Hour (var)
.... Marcia Brady (1977)
The Brady Brides (com)
.... Marcia Brady Logan (1981)

MCCORMICK, PAT—comedian, writer
b: Jul 17, 1934

The Don Rickles Show (var)
.... regular (1968–69)
The New Bill Cosby Show (var)
.... regular (1972–73)
Gun Shy (com)......... Col. Mound (1983)

MCCORMICK, ROBERT—newscaster
b: Aug 9, 1911, Danville, Ky. d: Sep 4, 1985

Current Opinion (news)........ host (1947)
Battle Report (doc).......... host (1950–51)

NBC newsman Robert McCormick once reminisced that he had been shot at by Japanese snipers on Iwo Jima, by Communist rioters in Berlin, and by Angolan rebels in Africa—but the closest he came to being "wounded in action" was at the Republican National Convention in 1948. McCormick was a floor reporter for NBC at the convention, when he was caught in the middle of a wild demonstration for General MacArthur by a thundering herd of delegates. His one thought was to protect his walkie-talkie. He managed to save the radio as he was smashed up against a wall, but he suffered two dislocated ribs.

Eight years later, at the 1956 Democratic Convention, he was bruised and bitten when a donkey and a huge St. Bernard, each festooned with signs promoting a different candidate, suddenly set upon each other—with McCormick caught in the middle.

They don't treat political reporters like that anymore!

MCCOY, CHARLIE—harmonica player, singer
b: Mar 28, 1941, Oak Hill, W. Va.

Hee Haw (var)........... regular (1976–   )
The Nashville Palace (var)
.... bandleader (1981–82)

The musical director of *Hee Haw* (yeah, he's responsible) as well as a featured performer on that and other country music shows.

MCCOY, HERMAN, SINGERS—
The Nat "King" Cole Show (var)
.... regulars (1956–57)

MCCOY, JACK—host
b: Nov 10, 1918, Akron, Ohio

Live Like a Millionaire (talent)
.... emcee (1951)

MCCOY, MATT—actor
We Got It Made (com)
.... David Tucker (1983–84)

MCCOY, SID—black actor
b: Chicago, Ill.

The Bill Cosby Show (com)
.... Mr. Langford (1969–71)

A longtime Chicago disc jockey, known as "the coolest DJ in the Windy City." He broke into television in the late '60s with roles on *Tarzan, The Wild Wild West*, and other series.

MCCRACKEN, JEFF—actor
b: Sep 12, Chicago, Ill.

Bay City Blues (drama).. Vic Kresky (1983)
Hawaiian Heat (police)
.... Andy Senkowski (1984)

MCCRACKEN, JOAN—actress
b: Dec 31, 1922, Philadelphia, Pa. d: Nov 1, 1961

Claudia, The Story of a Marriage (drama)
.... Claudia Naughton (1952)

MCCRARY, TEX—host, writer
b: 1910, Calvert, Texas

At Home with Tex and Jinx (talk)
.... cohost (1947)
Preview with Tex and Jinx (talk)
.... host (1949)

Husband and on-air talk show partner of Jinx Falkenburg.

MCCREA, ANN—actress

The Donna Reed Show (com)
.... Midge Kelsey (1963–66)

MCCREA, JODY—actor
b: Sep 6, 1934, Los Angeles, Calif. r: Camarillo, Calif.

Wichita Town (wes)
.... Ben Matheson (1959–60)

The lanky son of actor Joel McCrea. He was raised on his father's ranch in Camarillo and seldom saw Hollywood as a youth. After a brief acting career in the '50s and '60s he retired to become a rancher and rodeo rider.

MCCREA, JOEL—actor
b: Nov 5, 1905, South Pasadena, Calif.

Wichita Town (wes)
.... Marshal Mike Dunbar (1959–60)

This amiable cowboy star of the '30s, '40s, and '50s pursued his very successful movie career mainly to earn money to do what he loved most—own and operate a large ranch west of Los Angeles. So fond was he of life in the saddle, in fact, that he eventually turned down all roles except those in westerns. His television work was limited, and there, too, he was best known for work in the western genre, starring in *Wichita Town*, based on one of his films. He had portrayed Wyatt Earp in the film version; however, that character was already spoken for on TV by Hugh O'Brian. Joel was also one of the actor-founders of the highly profitable Four Star Television production company.

566

In earlier days, Joel was a close friend of humorist Will Rogers, who had helped guide his career and advised him to always save half of everything he earned and invest it in real estate. That was good advice. By the time Joel retired he was said to be worth more than $50 million.

MCCULLEN, KATHY—actress
b: Los Angeles, Calif.

Baa Baa Black Sheep (drama)
.... Nurse Ellie (1977–78)

MCCULLOCH, IAN—actor

The Search for the Nile (drama)
.... Capt. James Grant (1972)

MCCULLOUGH, DARRYL—actor

The San Pedro Beach Bums (com)
.... Moose (1977)

MCCULLOUGH, LINDA—actress

B.J. and the Bear (adv) .... Callie (1981)

MCCUNE, HANK—actor

The Hank McCune Show (com) . star (1950)

MCCURRY, ANN—actress

Beyond Westworld (sci fi) .. Roberta (1980)

MCCUTCHEON, BILL—actor
b: May 23, Russell Ky.

The Dom DeLuise Show (var)
.... regular (1968)
Ball Four (com)
.... coach Pinky Pinkney (1976)

MCDANIEL, GEORGE—actor

Falcon Crest (drama)
.... Alan Caldwell (1984)

MCDEVITT, RUTH—actress
b: Sep 13, 1895, Coldwater, Mich. d: May 27, 1976

A Woman to Remember (drama)
.... Bessie Thatcher (1949)
Mr. Peepers (com).. Mom Peepers (1953–55)
Pistols 'n' Petticoats (com)
.... Grandma (1966–67)
Johnny Cash Presents the Everly Brothers Show (var)............... regular (1970)

All in the Family (com)
.... Jo Nelson (1973–75)
Kolchak: The Night Stalker (drama)
.... Emily Cowles (1974–75)

MCDONALD, FRANCIS—actor
b: Aug 22, 1891, Bowling Green, Ky. d: Sep 18, 1968

The Adventures of Champion (adv)
.... Will Calhoun (1955–56)

MCDONALD, MARY ANN—comedienne

The Comedy Factory (var) ... regular (1985)

MCDONALD, MICHAEL—actor

No Time for Sergeants (com)
.... Pvt. Jack Langdon (1964–65)

MCDONALD, ROBERTA—singer

Melody Street (music) .... regular (1953–54)

MCDONALD, RYAN—actor

The Odd Couple (com)....... Roy (1970–71)

MCDONALD, SEVEN ANN—juvenile actress

Eddie Capra Mysteries (drama)
.... Jennie Brown (1978–79)

MCDONNELL, MARY—actress
b: Wilkes Barre, Pa. r: Ithaca, N.Y.

E/R (com) ...... Dr. Eve Sheridan (1984–85)

MCDONOUGH, KIT—actress

Teachers Only (com) . Lois McCardle (1982)
Fast Times (com)... Ms. Leslie Melon (1986)

MCDONOUGH, MARY ELIZABETH—juvenile actress
b: May 4, 1961, Van Nuys, Calif.

The Waltons (drama)
.... Erin Walton (1972–81)

MCDOWALL, RODDY—actor
b: Sep 17, 1928, London, England

The Planet of the Apes (sci fi)
.... Galen (1974)
The Rhinemann Exchange (drama)
.... Bobby Ballard (1977)

Fantastic Journey (sci fi)
.... Dr. Jonathan Willaway (1977)
Tales of the Gold Monkey (adv)
.... Bon Chance Louis (1982–83)
Bridges to Cross (drama)
.... Norman Parks (1986)

Emmy Award: Best Supporting Actor in a Dramatic Special, for "Not Without Honor" (1961)

This sharp-featured actor, a famous child star of the '40s, has become known for some rather offbeat adult roles. The son of a merchant seaman, he began making films in his native England at the age of eight and appeared in 22 before he was brought to the U.S. during the Blitz. He then played many juvenile roles in Hollywood, especially in the "boy-and-his-animal" type of film. Among these were the movie precursors of two popular TV series, *Lassie* and *My Friend Flicka*. His youthful appearance kept him in juvenile roles to age 20, but then work began to dry up—as it does for many former child stars. Roddy moved to New York and for the next 20 years combined a stage career with a great many appearances on TV, including practically all the major live drama series of the '50s. Among the productions in which he appeared were "Ah, Wilderness" in 1951 (the first coast-to-coast live play), "Heart of Darkness" on *Playhouse 90*, and "Billy Budd" on *The DuPont Show of the Month*. No snob, Roddy also did the Charleston and the Cha Cha on *The Arthur Murray Dance Party*, then parodied that show with a burlesque "Arthur Murray Sword Dance" on a 1960 Art Carney special.

In the '60s Roddy continued to play dramatic roles (on *Alfred Hitchcock, Naked City, Arrest and Trial*, etc.) and also some with a twinkle in his eye. On *Batman* he was "The Bookworm," bent on tying Robin to a giant library bell and ringing it. He finally began to star in series of his own in the 1970s, the first being a spin-off from his popular *Planet of the Apes* movies, both of which required him to be made up as an intellectual chimpanzee. Later, he was a scientist caught in a time warp on *Fantastic Journey* and the dapper French proprietor of a South Seas bistro on *Tales of the Gold Monkey*.

Roddy has had two other rather interesting careers besides acting. He is a highly regarded still photographer whose celebrity photo essays have appeared in several major magazines and been collected in the book *Double Exposure* (1966); and he is one of Hollywood's leading collectors of cinematic memorabilia and experts on movie history, as well as the knowledgeable host of several documentaries on the subject.

MCEACHIN, JAMES—black actor

b: May 20, 1930, Pennert, N.C. r: Hackensack, N.J.

Tenafly (drama)... Harry Tenafly (1973–74)

MCELHONE, ELOISE—panelist

Think Fast (quiz)........ panelist (1949–50)
Leave It to the Girls (talk)
.... panelist (1949–54)

Eloise was known as "The Mouth" for her chatterbox tendencies.

MCFADDEN, TOM—actor

The Winds of War (drama)
.... Hugh Cleveland (1983)

MCGAVIN, DARREN—actor

b: May 7, 1922, Spokane, Wash. r: Galt, Calif.

Crime Photographer (drama)
.... Casey (1951–52)
Mickey Spillane's Mike Hammer (drama)
.... Mike Hammer (1957–59)
Riverboat (adv) ..... Grey Holden (1959–61)
The Outsider (drama)
.... David Ross (1968–69)
Kolchak: The Night Stalker (drama)
.... Carl Kolchak (1974–75)
Ike (drama)..... Gen. George Patton (1979)
Small & Frye (com)...... Nick Small (1983)

A hard-knuckles hero who starred in no fewer than six series from 1951 to 1983; none were big hits, though several of them are well remembered. Nearly all were of the "rough 'em up" type, leading one critic to call McGavin the "Gene Hackman of TV." (Word around Hollywood: if you want to get punched out, guest-star on a McGavin series). Darren had no apologies for the rough stuff, even when it involved women. Of his Mike Hammer character,

the actor growled that he was merely "an emotional nonconformist—and aggressively so."

Darren began in Hollywood shortly after college but was strictly out of camera range. "I was working as a scene painter at Paramount," he later said. "When I saw all the activity, the costumes, and most especially the warm lights—it was cold where I was—I knew I wanted to be not only in the scene but in the center of it." Easier said than done. He got a few small roles in the late '40s but did not make much of a splash in films until his roles as the young painter in *Summertime* and the cold-blooded drug pusher in *The Man with the Golden Arm,* both in 1955.

Meanwhile, Darren's television career had begun with the live *Crime Photographer* series and guest roles in numerous dramatic productions. He later became the original TV Mike Hammer, Burt Reynolds' partner on *Riverboat,* and a seedy reporter beset by poltergeists on *Kolchak.* He continued to be very active as a guest star on action and crime shows of the '60s and '70s and even spoofed himself—a bit—on the detective comedy *Small & Frye.* He has also been active as a director for series including *Buckskin, Riverboat,* and *Kolchak.*

MCGEE, FRANK—newscaster

b: Sep 12, 1921, Monroe, La. d: Apr 17, 1974

Campaign and the Candidates (news)
.... anchorman (1960)
World Wide 60 (doc).......... host (1960)
Here and Now (doc)........... host (1961)
NBC Weekend News (news)
.... anchorman (1965–71)
NBC Evening News (news)
.... anchorman (1970–71)

Emmy Award: Outstanding Achievement in Special Events Reporting, for coverage of the Adenauer funeral (1968)

This bespectacled, scholarly looking newsman was one of NBC's most familiar reporters during the 1960s. He began on local radio and TV in Oklahoma and Alabama during the '50s and joined NBC in 1957 as a Washington correspondent. His careful, serious reporting brought him many assignments, particularly in the areas of politics and civil rights, and he was eventually made standby reporter for the network's "instant news specials" on breaking world events; he did more than 450 of these between 1960 and 1964.

In 1970 McGee became co-anchor of NBC's evening newscast (with David Brinkley and John Chancellor) and in 1971 he was given the important post of host of the early morning *Today* show. This latter assignment was none too successful, as he remade the light, early-morning features show into a much more serious affair (paving the way for the rise of ABC's lighter, and competing, *Good Morning, America* a few years later). However, McGee remained on the job until the week before his untimely death in 1974.

MCGEE, HENRY—comedian

The Benny Hill Show (com)
.... regular (1969–82)

MCGEE, VONETTA—black actress
b: San Francisco, Calif.

Hell Town (drama)
.... Sister Indigo (1985)

MCGEEHAN, MARY KATE—actress

Falcon Crest (drama)
.... Linda Caproni (1982–84)

MCGEORGE, JIM—actor

Happy Days (var) .... regular (1970)

Comedian and cartoon voice specialist who often impersonated Stan Laurel opposite Chuck McCann's Oliver Hardy. He was active on TV from the '50s to the '70s.

MCGILL, BRUCE—actor

Delta House (com)
... Daniel Simpson Day ("D-Day") (1979)
Semi-Tough (com)
.... Billy Clyde Pucket (1980)

MCGILLIN, HOWARD—actor

Wheels (drama)........ Greg Trenton (1978)
Number 96 (drama)
.... Mark Keaton (1980–81)

MCGINLEY, TED—actor
b: May 30, Newport Beach, Calif.

Happy Days (com)
.... Roger Phillips (1980–84)
The Love Boat (com)
photographer Ashley Covington Evans ("Ace") (1984–86)
Dynasty (drama) ... Clay Falmont (1986–   )

MCGINNIS, SCOTT—actor

Operation Petticoat (com)
.... Seaman Dixon (1978–79)

MCGIVENEY, MAURA—

Turn-On (var).............. regular (1969)

MCGIVER, JOHN—actor
b: Nov 5, 1913, New York City, N.Y. d: Sep 9, 1975

The Patty Duke Show (com)
.... J. R. Castle (1963–64)
Many Happy Returns (com)
.... Walter Burnley (1964–65)
Mr. Terrific (com) .... Barton J. Reed (1967)
The Jimmy Stewart Show (com)
.... Dr. Luther Quince (1971–72)

Pudgy, round-faced comic actor who looked a bit like Dick Van Patten and who appeared often in TV comedies of the '60s. He stole many a scene with his pursed lips and what's-going-to-happen-next expression but he never became a major star in his own right.

MCGOOHAN, PATRICK—actor, director
b: Mar 19, 1928, Astoria, N.Y. r: England

Danger Man (drama) .... John Drake (1961)
Secret Agent (drama)
.... John Drake (1965–66)
The Prisoner (adv) ..... The Prisoner (1968)
Rafferty (drama) .. Sid Rafferty, M.D. (1977)

Emmy Award: Best Supporting Actor in a Single Performance, for *Columbo* (1975)

A wiry actor in the David Janssen, thinking-man-in-danger mold, who became quite popular during the '60s via a trilogy of British spy series imported to the U.S.: *Danger Man, Secret Agent,* and the cult classic *The Prisoner* (which was so obscure *nobody* knew what it meant). McGoohan was also creator and producer of the latter series.

Although he was born in New York,

McGoohan made his name in British films in the late 1950s and spent most of his career there. He was seen on American TV mostly in occasional British imports (e.g., the '50s series *The Vise,* the 1977 TV movie *The Man in the Iron Mask*). Occasionally he flew to Hollywood to appear in, or direct, an odd episode of *Columbo.* In 1977, looking much less trim and athletic than he had ten years before, he appeared briefly in a medical series called *Rafferty.*

MCGOVERN, TERRY—actor
b: May 11, Berkeley, Calif. r: Pittsburgh, Pa.

Presenting Susan Anton (var)
.... Bruce Larson (1979)
Charlie & Company (com)
.... Jim Coyle (1985–86)

MCGRATH, DEREK—actor
The Comedy Factory (var) ... regular (1985)
Mary (com)....... Ronnie Dicker (1985–86)

MCGRATH, FRANK—actor
b: Feb 2, 1903, Mound City, Mo. d: May 13, 1967

Wagon Train (wes)
.... Charlie Wooster (1957–65)
Tammy (com)...... Uncle Lucius (1965–66)

The grizzled, cantankerous trail cook on *Wagon Train.*

MCGRATH, PAUL—actor
b: 1904, Chicago, Ill. d: Apr 13, 1978

The Witness (drama)
.... committee member (1960–61)

MCGRAW, BILL—actor
Hold It Please (quiz)........ regular (1949)

MCGRAW, CHARLES—actor
b: May 10, 1914, New York City r: Akron, Ohio* d: Jul 30, 1980

The Falcon (drama)
.... Michael Waring (1954–55)
Casablanca (drama)... Rick Jason (1955–56)
The Smith Family (drama)
.... Capt. Hughes (1971–72)

*Some sources indicate that he was born in the Orient.

Hollywood tough-guy actor, quite active on television from the mid-1950s to the mid-1970s in espionage series, crime shows, and westerns. Oddly, despite the right name and image, he did *not* star as the tough private eye on *Meet McGraw* in 1957; Frank Lovejoy got that role.

MCGRAW, WALTER—producer, narrator
Wanted (doc) .... narrator (1955–56)

MCGREEVEY, MIKE—actor
Riverboat (adv) .... Chip (1959–60)

MCGUIRE SISTERS, THE—singing group
Chris, b: Jul 30, 1928, Middletown, Ohio
Dotty, b: Feb 13, 1930, Middletown, Ohio
Phyllis, b: Feb 14, 1931, Middletown, Ohio

Arthur Godfrey and His Friends (var)
.... singers (1952–57)

"Discovered" when they won the competition on *Arthur Godfrey's Talent Scouts,* the McGuire Sisters became nationally famous on Godfrey's variety series—where they succeeded the Chordettes, who had been fired because of their recording activities. Arthur apparently didn't object to the fact that the McGuires became major recording stars while on his show; the girls scored top-ten hits such as "Sincerely" and "Sugartime" in the mid-1950s. The three were daughters of a lady minister, who was not appreciative of their show-biz career. "Mother thinks we should be using our talents for the church," said Phyllis. They disbanded in the '60s, after which Phyllis continued as a single in nightclubs and Las Vegas.

MCGUIRE, BIFF—actor
b: Oct 25, 1926, New Haven, Conn.

Gibbsville (drama) .... Dr. Malloy (1976)

MCGUIRE, BOBBY—panelist
Twenty Questions (quiz) . panelist (1954–55)

MCGUIRE, DOROTHY—actress
b: Jun 14, 1918, Omaha, Nebr.

Rich Man, Poor Man—Book I (drama)
.... Mary Jordache (1976)

Little Women (drama)
.... Marmee March (1979)

Gentle stage and screen actress who was active on television in the early and mid-1950s but then was not seen for more than 15 years, until her return in the 1972 TV movie *She Waits,* a macabre ghost story. Dorothy has since appeared only occasionally, mostly in TV movies such as *Little Women* (which led to a short-run series) and *Ghost Dancing.*

MCGUIRE, MAEVE—actress
b: Jul 24, Cleveland, Ohio

Beacon Hill (drama)
.... Maude Palmer (1975)

Better known, perhaps, as Nicole Travis on the daytime soap opera *The Edge of Night,* a role she played off and on for ten years (1968–77).

MCGUIRE, MICHAEL—actor

The Winds of War (drama)
.... Fred Fearing (1983)
Empire (com) .... Edward Roland (1984)

MCHATTIE, STEPHEN—actor
b: Feb 3, Antigonish, Nova Scotia, Canada

Centennial (drama)
.... Jake Pasquinel (1978–79)
Highcliffe Manor (com)
.... Rev. Ian Glenville (1979)

MCHUGH, FRANK—actor
b: May 23, 1898, Homestead, Pa. d: Sep 11, 1981

The Bing Crosby Show (com)
.... Willie Walter (1964–65)

MCINTIRE, JOHN—actor
b: Jun 27, 1907, Spokane, Wash.

Naked City (police)
.... Det. Lt. Dan Muldoon (1958–59)
Wagon Train (wes)
.... Christopher Hale (1961–65)
The Virginian (wes)
.... Clay Grainger (1967–68)
Aspen (drama) .... Owen Keating (1977)
Shirley (com) .... Dutch McHenry (1979–80)
American Dream (drama)
.... Sam Whittier (1981)

To movie and television audiences, John McIntire never seemed to have been young; he always played a craggy, mature authority figure. This was because McIntire did not enter films until he was in his forties (in 1948), or television until he was nearly 50. Once he did, he worked steadily in a long series of hard-edged dramas. His TV debut was on *General Electric Theater* in 1955, and a few years later he found his true calling in series roles. His first, that of the veteran cop in *Naked City* (a show full of veteran cops), ended spectacularly when his character was killed in a fiery car crash—one of the earliest uses of such special effects in series TV. He then got into westerns, where his leathery appearance complemented the rugged surroundings perfectly. After a couple of seasons of guest roles he replaced the late Ward Bond as the trail boss on *Wagon Train,* and then Lee J. Cobb as the owner of the Shiloh Ranch on *The Virginian.*

In the 1970s McIntire turned to somewhat softer roles, on *Love, American Style, The Love Boat, Shirley* (a regular, as the neighborly boat builder), and even comedies such as *Dirty Sally.*

Before he began his screen career, McIntire had been a general-purpose radio actor for many years, often appearing with his wife (since 1935), Jeanette Nolan. She later costarred with him in *The Virginian.*

MCINTIRE, TIM—actor
b: c. 1943 d: Apr 15, 1986

The Legend of Jesse James (wes)
.... Bob Younger (1965–66)
Rich Man, Poor Man—Book I (drama)
.... Brad Knight (1976)

The son of actor John McIntire and actress Jeanette Nolan.

MCISAAC, MARIANNE—actress

The Baxters (com)
.... Allison Baxter (1980–81)

MCK, MISHA—black actress
b: Jan 23, c. 1960, East Orange, N.J.

Me & Mrs. C. (com)
.... Gerri Kilgore (1986–)

MCKAY, ALLISON—actress

Dean Martin Presents the Golddiggers (var)
.... regular (1969)
The Paul Lynde Show (com)
.... Alice (1972–73)

MCKAY, ANDY—comedian

The Ernie Kovacs Show (var)
.... regular (1952–53)

MCKAY, DAVID—actor

Rendezvous (drama)........ regular (1952)

MCKAY, GARDNER—actor
b: Jun 10, 1932, New York City, N.Y.

Boots and Saddles—The Story of the 5th Cavalry (wes) .... Lt. Kelly (1957–58)
Adventures in Paradise (adv)
.... Capt. Adam Troy (1959–62)

The "hunk of the month" in 1959 was handsome, square-jawed Gardner McKay, a pipe-smoking heartthrob cast in the romantic role of a free-lance skipper plying the South Seas and seeking *Adventures in Paradise*. Prior to this hit series, Gardner had been a minor supporting player, with a secondary role on the briefly syndicated *Boots and Saddles* and guest appearances on series including *The Thin Man* and *Death Valley Days* (as a knife-wielding rapist). After it, he became thoroughly stereotyped and could find hardly any work at all. He later became a moderately successful TV writer.

MCKAY, JIM—sportscaster
b: Sep 24, 1921, Philadelphia, Pa.

Sports Spot (sport) .... host (1951)
Make the Connection (quiz)
.... moderator (1955)
The Verdict Is Yours (drama)
.... court reporter (1958)

Emmy Awards: Best Sports Commentator, for *ABC's Wide World of Sports* (1968, 1971, 1974, 1975, 1976, 1979, 1980, 1982); Best Special Events Reporting, for coverage of the Munich Olympic tragedy (1973)

Compact, diligent Jim McKay, probably the most honored sportscaster in television, is the "Iron Man" of *ABC's* long-running *Wide World of Sports*. He began as a

newspaper reporter for *The Baltimore Sun* in the '40s but switched to the paper's new television station as soon as it opened in 1947. In 1950 CBS brought him to New York to host a variety show, and he spent most of the '50s as a general-purpose host/moderator on quiz, panel, and even dramatic shows. His career was taking no clear-cut direction until 1960, when CBS assigned him to cover the Olympic Games, then a rather minor TV sports event. Now there was something he could do really well!

The following year, Jim appeared on the very first telecast of *The Wide World of Sports* and he has been with the show ever since. He has covered all subsequent Olympics for ABC, his star rising as viewer interest in the games increased. His greatest acclaim came in one of the classic cases of being in the right place at the right time and rising to the occasion: namely, his marathon reporting of the terrorist massacre of Israeli athletes at the 1972 Munich games. He happened to be on the spot when the networks' heavyweight news reporters were not, and his thorough and sensitive coverage won him several prestigious news awards.

MCKAY, PEGGY—actress

Who's The Boss? (quiz)..... panelist (1954)
The Lazarus Syndrome (drama)
.... Stacy (1979)

MCKAY, SCOTT—actor
b: May 28, 1915, Pleasantville, Iowa d: 1987

The Stage Door (drama)
.... Hank Merlin (1950)
Honestly Celeste (com)
.... Bob Wallace (1954)

The husband of the late Ann Sheridan; he was primarily a stage actor, seen on television mostly in live dramas of the 1950s.

MCKAYLE, DON—black choreographer
b: Jul 6, 1930, New York City, N.Y.

Fanfare (var).............. dancers (1965)
The Leslie Uggams Show (var)
.... dancers (1969)

MCKEAN, MICHAEL—actor
b: Oct 17, 1947, New York City r: Sea Cliff, N.Y.

Laverne & Shirley (com)
  Lenny Kosnowski (aka Kolowski) (1976–83)

MCKENNA, T.P.—actor
b: Sep 7, 1929, County Cavan, Ireland

Holocaust (drama) .... Blobel (1978)

Thomas Patrick McKenna, if you must be formal. He appears mostly in TV movies and miniseries (*The Manions of America, The Rivals,* etc.).

MCKENNON, DAL—actor

Daniel Boone (wes) . Cincinnatus (1964–70)

MCKENZIE, RICHARD—actor
b: Jun 2, Chattanooga, Tenn.

It Takes Two (com)
  .... Walter Chaiken (1982–83)

MCKEON, DOUG—juvenile actor
b: Jun 10, 1966, Pompton Plains, N.J. r: Oakland, N.J.

Centennial (drama)
  .... Philip Wendell (1978–79)
Big Shamus, Little Shamus (drama)
  .... Max Sutter (1979)

MCKEON, NANCY—actress
b: Apr 4, 1966, Westbury, N.Y.

The Facts of Life (com)
  .... Jo Polniazek (1980–)

Nancy was originally added to the cast of *The Facts of Life* in the role of a tough-talking teenager in order to spice up a rather sedate show. She certainly gave the producers what they wanted and in the process became one of TV's favorite tough kids with a heart of gold. She can also be vulnerable when required; "they call me faucet-face," she laughs, after her ability to call up tears on cue.
  Nancy is the daughter of a New York travel agent who got both of his kids (Nancy and brother Philip) into modeling, commercials, and even soap operas while they were still tots. When Philip landed the role of Tommy on *Alice* in 1976, the whole family moved to Los Angeles, and soon Nancy was also getting small roles—on *Fantasy Island, Stone,* and ABC's Saturday morning *Weekend Special*s (doing

voices), among others. Her performance as a kind of female Fonzie in an unsuccessful pilot film caught the eye of NBC executives and got her the role of Jo.

MCKEON, PHILIP—actor
b: Nov 11, 1964, Westbury, N.Y.

Alice (com) .... Tommy Hyatt (1976–85)

The older brother of Nancy McKeon. Like her, Philip was modeling and appearing in commercials while still a youngster in New York. He has appeared in several films (the first being *Up the Sandbox* with Barbra Streisand, in 1972), plays, and an assortment of TV shows, including *Hollywood Squares. Alice* encompassed his growing-up years; he started on the show as a little boy of 11 and by the time it ended he was 20 years old and 6'2".

MCKINLEY, J. EDWARD—actor

Tom, Dick and Mary (com)
  .... Horace Moran (1964–65)

MCKINLEY, RAY—orchestra leader, host
b: Jun 18, 1910, Fort Worth, Texas

Be Our Guest (var) ..... orch. leader (1960)
Glenn Miller Time (music) ... cohost (1961)

Former drummer with Glenn Miller's World War II Army Air Force Band, who eventually fronted the Miller band on television years after Glenn's death.

MCKINNEY, WILLIAM—actor

The Family Holvak (drama)
  .... Dep. Jim Shanks (1975)

MCKINNON, PATRICIA—

Hee Haw (var) .... regular (1985–)

MCKRELL, JIM—actor, host
b: Oct 12, Little Rock, Ark.

Semi-Tough (com) .... Burt Danby (1980)

A former game-show host *(Celebrity Sweepstakes),* sometime soap opera actor *(General Hospital, Capitol),* and frequent prime time supporting player of the '70s and '80s.

MCLARTY, RON—actor
b: Apr 26, Providence, R.I.

Spenser: For Hire (drama)
.... Sgt. Frank Belson (1985–)

MCLAUGHLIN, ANDREA—juvenile performer
b: c. 1946

Paul Whiteman's TV Teen Club (talent)
.... regular (1949–54)

One of the much-touted juvenile discoveries on Paul Whiteman's teen club, at age four—though she does not seem to have had much of a show business career afterward.

MCLEAN, DAVID—actor
b: May 19, 1922, Akron, Ohio

Tate (wes).................... Tate (1960)

MCLERIE, ALLYN ANN—actress
b: Dec 1, 1926, Grand'Mere, Quebec, Canada
r: Brooklyn, N.Y.

The Tony Randall Show (com)
.... Miss Janet Reubner (1976–78)
The Thorn Birds (drama)
.... Mrs. Smith (1983)

MCLIAM, JOHN—actor
b: Jan 24, 1918, Alberta, Canada

The Men from Shiloh (wes)
.... Parker (1970–71)
Two Marriages (drama)
.... Woody Daley (1983–84)

MCLOUGHLIN, PATRICK—actor

The Adventures of Sir Francis Drake (adv)
.... Richard Trevelyan (1962)

MCMAHON, ED—host
b: Mar 6, 1923, Detroit, Mich. r: Lowell, Mass.

Big Top (var) .... clown (1950–51)
The Tonight Show Starring Johnny Carson (talk) .... regular (1962–)
The Kraft Music Hall (var)
.... host (1968)
NBC Adventure Theatre (drama)
.... host (1972)
Whodunnit? (quiz)........... emcee (1979)
Star Search (talent)......... host (1983–)

TV's Bloopers & Practical Jokes (com)
.... host (1984–86)

Big, jovial Ed McMahon got his start on television playing a jolly circus clown on *Big Top;* he was supposed to have been the ringmaster, but a better-known performer named Jack Sterling got the job instead. Each show opened with a close-up top shot of Ed's apparently bald head, on which was written the words "Big Top," surrounded by a fringe of gaudy red hair. He then lifted his head and into view came his large, bulbous nose, on which was painted "Hello!"

Ed's later assignments were not quite as garish, but he does seem to have spent his entire career introducing other people. Following an interruption for service as a fighter pilot in Korea (he had also served in World War II), he resumed his TV career in the mid-1950s and in 1958 made a fateful acquaintance. It was then that he became Johnny Carson's sidekick for the first time, on the daytime quiz show *Who Do You Trust?* Johnny brought Ed with him when he took over *The Tonight Show,* and the rest, as they say, is late-night history.

Though Ed is mostly associated with Carson, he has also had his own career, on the side, as it were. He hosted three daytime game shows in the '60s and '70s (can you name them? See below for answers), provided coverage of the Macy's Thanksgiving Day Parade and other events, and even played supporting roles in a number of TV movies. Among the latter were such typical TV fare as *Star Maker, The Great American Traffic Jam,* and *The Kid from Left Field.* Ed's "other" career really began to blossom in the 1980s, as he hosted two very popular variety shows—*Star Search* and *TV's Bloopers*—while continuing on *Tonight.* "It seems the busier I am, the more I can do," he says.

(Ed's daytime game shows: *Missing Links, Concentration, Snap Judgment.* The bizarre crime-quiz *Whodunnit?* was, of course, a prime time entry.)

MCMAHON, HORACE—actor
b: May 17, 1907, South Norwalk, Conn. d: Aug 17, 1971

Martin Kane, Private Eye (drama)
.... Capt. Willis (1950–51)

The Danny Thomas Show (com)
.... Horace (1953–54)
Naked City (police)
.... Lt. Mike Parker (1959–63)
The Jackie Gleason Show (var)
.... regular (1963–64)
Mr. Broadway (drama)
.... Hank McClure (1964)

Gruff, gravel-voiced character actor who played both sides of the law in films of the '30s and '40s, but became best-known on TV as the tough police lieutenant on *Naked City*. He could also play comedy; besides a regular role as Danny Thomas's agent on *The Danny Thomas Show,* he made guest appearances on *Father Knows Best, Family Affair, My Three Sons,* and other comedies.

Early in his career he spelled his last name MacMahon, and thus it is found in some reference books.

MCMAHON, JENNA—writer, comedienne

What's It All About, World? (var)
.... regular (1969)
The Funny Side (var)........ regular (1971)

Emmy Awards: Best Writing for a Comedy, for *The Carol Burnett Show* (1974, 1975, 1978)

Partnered with Dick Clair, both as a writer and as a comedian.

MCMAIN, BILL—

Ozark Jubilee (music)........ regular (1957)

MCMANUS, MICHAEL—actor

Lewis & Clark (com)
.... John the bartender (1981–82)
Thicke of the Night (talk)
.... regular (1983–84)

MCMARTIN, JOHN—actor
b: Warsaw, Ind.

Falcon Crest (drama)
.... Julian J. Roberts (1985–   )

MCMILLAN, GLORIA—actress
b: c. 1934, Portland, Ore.

Our Miss Brooks (com)
.... Harriet Conklin (1952–55)

MCMILLAN, KENNETH—actor
b: Jul 2, Brooklyn, N.Y.

Rhoda (com)........ Jack Doyle (1977–78)
Suzanne Pleshette Is Maggie Briggs (com)
.... Walter Holden (1984)
Our Family Honor (drama)
.... Comm. Patrick McKay (1985–86)

MCMULLAN, JIM—actor
b: Oct 13, 1938, Long Beach, N.Y.

Ben Casey (drama)
.... Dr. Terry McDaniel (1965–66)
Chopper One (police)
.... Off. Don Burdick (1974)
Beyond Westworld (sci fi)
.... John Moore (1980)

MCMURRAY, SAM—actor

Baker's Dozen (com)
.... Harve Schoendorf (1982)

MCNAIR, BARBARA—black singer, actress
b: Mar 4, 1934*, Racine, Wis.

The Barbara McNair Show (var)
.... hostess (1969)

In addition to hosting her own syndicated music show, Barbara acted occasionally in episodes of comedy and action series from the mid-1960s onward.

MCNAIR, HEATHER—actress

Automan (police)....... Roxanne (1983–84)
Cover Up (drama)............ Cindy (1984)

MCNAIR, RALPH—host

The Eyes Have It (quiz)
.... moderator (1948–49)

MCNALLY, STEPHEN—actor
b: Jul 29, 1913, New York City, N.Y.

Target: The Corruptors (drama)
.... Paul Marino (1961–62)

A former practicing attorney who turned to acting in the late '30s and appeared in many second-rate B films. From the early 1950s onward he was seen a great deal on television, mostly as a routine authority figure—indistinguishable from so many

*Some sources give 1939.

others—on drama series such as *Zane Grey Theatre, Run for Your Life, The Bold Ones,* etc. His one starring series, *Target: The Corruptors,* was a newspaper drama.

MCNAMARA, J. PATRICK—actor

Dallas (drama)... Jarrett McLeish (1982–83)

MCNAUGHTON, FRANK—host

Washington Exclusive (info)
.... moderator (1953)

MCNAUGHTON, HARRY—comedian
b: 1896, Surbiton, England d: Feb 26, 1967

It Pays to Be Ignorant (quiz)
.... panelist (1949–51)

MCNEAR, HOWARD—actor
b: 1905, Los Angeles, Calif. d: 1969

The Brothers (com)
.... Capt. Sam Box (1956–57)
The Andy Griffith Show (com)
.... Floyd Lawson (1960–68)
The Jetsons (cartn)
.... various voices (1962–63)

A comic character actor with a pencil-thin mustache, who looked a bit like Gale Gordon. He was best known as the jittery Floyd the Barber on *The Andy Griffith Show.* He also played the recurring character of the bumbling Mr. Hamish on *The George Gobel Show* in the '50s and before that was Doc Adams on the radio version of *Gunsmoke.*

MCNEELEY, LARRY—banjo player
b: Jan 3, 1948, Lafayette, Ind.

The Glen Campbell Goodtime Hour (var)
.... regular (1970–72)

MCNEILL, DON—host
b: Dec 23, 1907, Galena, Ill.

Don McNeill TV Club (var) .. host (1950–51)

Due to his folksy style, Don was often referred to as the Midwest's answer to Arthur Godfrey; he was best known as host of *The Breakfast Club,* which had an extraordinary run on radio from 1933 to 1968. This popular show was tried on television twice in the 1950s, in nighttime (1950) and daytime (1954) versions, but despite Don's similarities to Godfrey—or perhaps because of them—it was not successful.

MCNELLIS, MAGGI—hostess
b: Chicago, Ill.

Crystal Room (var) .... hostess (1948)
Maggi's Private Wire (talk) .. hostess (1949)
Leave It to the Girls (talk)
.... moderator (1949–54)
Say It with Acting (quiz)
.... team captain (1951)

MCNICHOL, JIMMY—actor
b: Jul 2, 1961, Los Angeles, Calif.

The Fitzpatricks (drama)
.... Jack Fitzpatrick (1977–78)
California Fever (adv) .. Vince Butler (1979)

The brother of Kristy McNichol. He began making commercials at the age of seven and made his acting debut at 12 (in 1973) with a small part in the TV movie *Sunshine.* Promoted as a teen heartthrob, he appeared in the late '70s in both series roles and as host of a syndicated talk-variety show called *Hollywood Teen.*

MCNICHOL, KRISTY—actress
b: Sep 11, 1962, Los Angeles, Calif.

Apple's Way (drama)
.... Patricia Apple (1974–75)
Family (drama)
..... Letitia "Buddy" Lawrence (1976–80)

Emmy Awards: Best Supporting Actress in a Drama Series, for *Family* (1977, 1979)

Jimmy's sister, and a gifted young actress who began winning Emmy Awards while still in her midteens. The daughter of a divorced former actress (and latter-day stage mother), Kristy, like her brother, began early; she was appearing in commercials at six and in prime time series *(Love, American Style)* at nine. After a series of guest appearances on various series in the mid-1970s, and the regular role of one of the daughters in *Apple's Way,* she hit the big time in 1976 as the troubled teenager in *Family,* a performance that brought her great acclaim.

So much so soon created personal problems for young Kristy ("She had become an actress before she ever became a person," opined *TV Guide*, reporting on her burgeoning ego). However, she continued to expand her acting horizons, in dramatic TV movies such as *Like Mom, Like Me* and *Summer of My German Soldier,* and in a daring theatrical film called *White Dog*—which was so controversial (some mistook its antiracist message for racism) that it was withheld from general release in the U.S.

MCNULTY, PAT—actress

The Tycoon (com). Martha Keane (1964–65)

MCPEAK, SANDY—actor

Blue Thunder (police)
.... Capt. Braddock (1984)
Wildside (wes)
.... Gov. J. Wendell Summerhayes (1985)

MCPHEE, JOHNNIE—juvenile panelist

Twenty Questions (quiz). panelist (1949–53)

MCPHERSON, PATRICIA—actress

b: Nov 27, 1954, Oak Harbor, Wash.

Knight Rider (adv)
.... Bonnie Barstow (1982–86)

MCQUADE, ARLENE—actress

b: May 29, 1936, New York City, N.Y.

The Goldbergs (com)
.... Rosalie Goldberg (1949–55)

MCQUADE, JOHN—actor

b: c. 1916, Pittsburgh, Pa. d: Sep 21, 1979

Charlie Wild, Private Detective (drama)
.... Charlie Wild (1951–52)

MCQUEEN, BUTTERFLY—black actress

b: Jan 8, 1911, Tampa, Fla.

Beulah (com) .... Oriole (1950–53)

Emmy Award: Best Performance in a Children's Program, for the *ABC Afterschool Special* "The Seven Wishes of a Rich Kid" (1980)

Veteran black actress of the '30s and '40s, often in stereotyped roles (*Gone with the Wind,* her first; *Cabin In the Sky;* etc.). On television she was best-known as Beulah's scatterbrained friend Oriole; she did relatively little other TV. In later years she was active in community-relations work in Harlem.

MCQUEEN, STEVE—actor

b: Mar 24, 1930, Slater, Mo.* d: Nov 7, 1980

Wanted: Dead or Alive (wes)
.... Josh Randall (1958–61)

Steve McQueen is one of those Hollywood stars who got his first big break on television but then abandoned the small screen in favor of cinema glory (another: Clint Eastwood). As a struggling young actor in New York in the mid-1950s he played small parts on a number of TV dramatic shows, gradually working his way up to more substantial roles on *Studio One, Climax,* and *Trackdown,* among others. His performance on the last-named series won him the lead in *Wanted: Dead or Alive,* which shot into the top-ten during its three-year run on CBS. Steve had no trouble finding TV work after that, but he didn't want it. After his success in the movie *The Great Escape* in 1963, he left TV.

A biography: *Steve McQueen* by Malachy McCoy (1974).

MCQUEENEY, ROBERT—actor

The Gallant Men (drama)
.... Conley Wright (1962–63)

MCRAE, ELLEN—

see Burstyn, Ellen

MCRAE, MICHAEL—actor

Dear Detective (police) ... Det. Brock (1979)

MCRANEY, GERALD—actor

b: Aug 19, 1947, Collins, Miss.

Simon & Simon (drama)
.... Rick Simon (1981–)

The funky older brother on *Simon & Simon.* He has been active on television since his debut on an episode of *Night Gallery* in the early '70s, but until his laid-back hit series arrived he was usually cast as a villain, often a vicious one. Among other things, he holds the distinction of having

*Some sources give Indianapolis or Beach Grove, Indiana.

been the last guest star on *Gunsmoke* to have a face to face shoot-out with Matt Dillon.

MCSHANE, IAN—actor
b: Sep 29, 1942, Blackburn, England

Roots (drama) . . . . . . Sir Eric Russell (1977)
Bare Essence (drama)
. . . . Niko Theophilus (1983)

MCVEAGH, EVE—actress

Faraway Hill (drama) . . . . regular (1946)

MCVEY, PATRICK—actor
b: 1910 d: Jul 6, 1973

Big Town (drama) . . Steve Wilson (1950–54)
Boots and Saddles—The Story of the 5th Cavalry (wes) . . . . Lt. Col. Hayes (1957–58)
Manhunt (police) . . . Ben Andrews (1959–61)

MCWHIRTER, JULIE—comedienne
b: Oct 12, Indianapolis, Ind.

Happy Days (var) . . . . regular (1970)
The Rich Little Show (var) . . . regular (1976)

A comic actress who has provided voices for many Saturday morning cartoon characters of the '70s and '80s, including Casper the Friendly Ghost, Vampira (on *The Drak Pack*), and Jeannie (on the cartoon version of *I Dream of Jeannie*).

MCWILLIAMS, CAROLINE—actress
b: Apr 4, 1945, Seattle, Wash. r: Barrington, R.I.

Soap (com) . . . . Sally (1978–79)
Benson (com) . . . . Marcy Hill (1979–81)

A former soap opera actress, on *The Guiding Light* for six years (1969–75) before she moved into prime time.

MEADE, JULIA—actress
b: 1928

Club Embassy (var) . . . . cigarette girl (1952)
Spotlight Playhouse (drama) . . . . host (1959)
Gas Company Playhouse (drama)
. . . . hostess (1960)

MEADOWS, AUDREY—actress
b: Feb 8, 1924, Wu Chang, China

Bob and Ray (var) . . . . regular (1951–53)
Club Embassy (var) . . . . regular (1952)
The Jackie Gleason Show (var)
. . . . regular (1952–55)
What's in a Word? (quiz) . . . panelist (1954)
What's Going On? (quiz) . . . . panelist (1954)
The Name's the Same (quiz)
. . . . panelist (1955)
The Honeymooners (series) (com)
. . . . Alice Kramden (1955–56)
The Jackie Gleason Show (var)
. . . . regular (1956–57)
Keep Talking (quiz) . . . . . . regular (1958–59)
Masquerade Party (quiz)
. . . . panelist (1958–60)
Too Close for Comfort (com)
. . . . Iris Martin (1982–83)

Emmy Award: Best Supporting Actress in a Series, for *The Jackie Gleason Show* (1954)

Audrey Meadows was born to Episcopal missionary parents in China and spoke only Chinese when she first came to the U.S. in the 1930s. She had not intended to pursue an acting career, but sister Jayne persuaded her to join her in a "fling on Broadway" when both were in their teens. This led eventually to Audrey's debut at Carnegie Hall as a coloratura soprano, some light opera, and a role on Broadway with Phil Silvers in *Top Banana* (1951). Audrey appeared as a singer and sketch comedienne on two early Bob and Ray TV series *(Bob and Ray* and *Club Embassy)* before she found fame, and TV immortality, as Alice Kramden in the "Honeymooners" sketches on *The Jackie Gleason Show.* When Jackie roared, "To the moon, Alice!" he was talking about Audrey; she was not the least bit intimidated by his bluster.

Audrey stayed with Gleason from 1952–57, and though she was not the only actress to play Alice (Pert Kelton preceded her, and Sheila MacRae followed in the '60s), she was the best known. She also played occasional guest roles in dramas and appeared on panel shows throughout the '50s and early '60s. Then she married Robert Six, the president and chairman of Continental Airlines, and virtually retired from acting. For the next 15 years Audrey devoted herself to business activities, including Continental's affairs, and to raising a family. She finally returned to television in 1977 for the first of a series of "Honeymooners" reunions and liked it so much that she began to play other roles as well, including several appearances on *The Love Boat* and a recurring part on *Too Close for Comfort*—her first regular series in 22 years.

MEADOWS, JAYNE—actress
b: Sep 27, 1926, Wu Chang, China

I've Got a Secret (quiz) .. panelist (1952–59)
The Steve Allen Show (var).. regular (1961)
The Art Linkletter Show (quiz)
.... regular (1963)
The Steve Allen Comedy Hour (var)
.... regular (1967)
Medical Center (drama)
.... Nurse Chambers (1969–72)
Steve Allen's Laugh Back (com)
.... regular (1976)
It's Not Easy (com) .... Ruth Long (1983)

Like her sister Audrey, Jayne Meadows was born in China, coming to the U.S. at the age of seven. While she has not had a role as famous as that of Audrey's Alice Kramden, she has been the most consistently active of the two sisters over the years. Jayne made her Broadway debut in 1941 and four years later launched her movie career with a fine performance in the melodrama *Undercurrent*. She appeared in TV dramas of the '50s but became best known to viewers as a witty panelist on the popular game show *I've Got a Secret*. It was there that she met Steve Allen, whom she married in 1954, and with whom she has since appeared on TV and in nightclubs. Perhaps their most fruitful collaboration was the PBS series *Meeting of Minds*, for which Jayne wrote and on which she played such diverse historical figures as Florence Nightingale, Marie Antionette, and Cleopatra.

Jayne has also continued her solo career over the years, appearing in TV movies and series (*Fantasy Island, Trapper John, M.D.*, etc.).

MEARA, ANNE—actress
b: Sep 20, 1929, Brooklyn, N.Y.

The Paul Lynde Show (com)
.... Grace Dickerson (1972–73)
The Corner Bar (com) .... Mae (1973)
Kate McShane (drama)
.... Kate McShane (1975)

Rhoda (com) ..... Sally Gallagher (1976–77)
Archie Bunker's Place (com)
.... Veronica Rooney (1979–82)

Jerry Stiller and Anne Meara, the ultimate wisecracking New York couple, have had a popular husband-and-wife comedy act since 1962. She is the redheaded Irish lass, and he the short, frumpy Jewish husband. They met and married in 1954, when both were struggling actors in New York. Throughout the '50s Anne worked mostly onstage, primarily in dramas, doing only occasional television—including a short stint on an obscure NBC soap opera, *The Greatest Gift*, in 1954. She spent the '60s mostly as part of a comedy act with her husband, appearing on the top variety shows of the day (34 times on *The Ed Sullivan Show*). In the '70s Jerry and Anne each began to do more solo work on TV. Anne was a regular on five different series, including her first drama, *Kate McShane*, in which she played a feisty lady lawyer. She added a certain impulsive sparkle to all her roles, hitting it off especially well with Carroll O'Connor on *Archie Bunker's Place*. Of him she said, "Carroll is shanty Irish, and so am I. We understand each other."

Jerry and Anne still worked together on occasion, on *Rhoda* and in a hilarious series of radio commercials for Blue Nun Wine (among other products). They also formed their own production company, for which they wrote and produced commercials and programs.

MEARS, DEANN—actress
b: Jun 13, Fort Fairfield, Me.

Beacon Hill (drama)... Emily Bullock (1975)

MEDFORD, KAY—actress
b: Sep 14, 1914*, New York City, N.Y. d: Apr 10, 1980

To Rome with Love (com)
.... Aunt Harriet Endicott (1969–70)
The Dean Martin Show (var)
.... regular (1970–73)

MEDINA, PATRICIA—actress
b: Jul 19, 1919**, Liverpool, England

High-Low (quiz) .... panelist (1957)

*Some sources give 1920.
**Some sources give 1920 or 1921.

Screen actress, on television in the '50s and '60s. Formerly married to Richard Greene (1941–51), later to Joseph Cotten (from 1960).

MEEK, BARBARA—black actress
b: Feb 26, Detroit, Mich.

Archie Bunker's Place (com)
.... Ellen Canby (1980–82)
Melba (com) .... Mama Rose (1986)

MEGURO, YUKI—
Shogun (drama) .... Omi (1980)

MEIKLE, PAT—hostess
Magic Cottage (child)
.... hostess (1949–51)

A longtime New York TV personality, who was the gentle hostess of *Your TV Baby Sitter* in 1948 and *Magic Cottage* from 1949–51. For many years thereafter she was seen on local TV in New York.

MEIKLEJOHN, LINDA—actress
*M*A*S*H* (com)
.... Lt. Leslie Scorch (1972–73)

MEISNER, GUNTER—actor
b: Rhineland, Germany

The Winds of War (drama)
.... Adolf Hitler (1983)

MEKKA, EDDIE—actor
b: Jun 14, 1952, Worcester, Mass.

Laverne & Shirley (com)
.... Carmine Ragusa (1976–83)
Blansky's Beauties (com)
.... Joey DeLuca (1977)

Amorous Carmine, "The Big Ragu" (though he was only 5'6") on *Laverne & Shirley*. He swears that he was trained as an opera singer—"but," he says, "I could never limit myself to that style."

MELBA, STANLEY—orchestra leader
The Arthur Murray Party (var)
.... orch. leader (1950)

MELDRUM, WENDEL—actor
Knots Landing (drama)
.... P. K. Kelly (1984–85)

MELGAR, GABRIEL—juvenile actor
Chico and the Man (com)
.... Raul Garcia (1977–78)

MELIS, JOSE—orchestra leader
b: Feb 27, 1920, Havana, Cuba

The Jack Paar Program (var)
.... regular (1954)
The Jack Paar Show (talk)
.... orch. leader (1957–62)
The Jack Paar Program (var)
.... orch. leader (1962–65)

MELLINI, SCOTT—juvenile actor
Father Murphy (drama)
.... Ephram Winkler (1981–82)

MELLODAIRES, THE—vocal group
Adventures of Oky Doky (child)
.... regulars (1948–49)

MELLOLARKS, THE—vocal group
Broadway Open House (talk)
.... regulars (1950–51)
Chevrolet on Broadway (music)
.... vocals (1956)
Frankie Laine Time (var) ... regulars (1956)

MELTON, JAMES—singer
b: Jan 1904, Moultrie, Ga. d: Apr 21, 1961

Ford Festival (var) .... regular (1951–52)

A robust popular tenor, on radio, records, and in movies during the late '20s and '30s. In the '40s he switched to opera (singing at the Metropolitan Opera) but then went back to lighter fare for his television appearances in the '50s.

MELTON, SID—actor
b: May 23, 1920, Brooklyn, N.Y.

It's Always Jan (com)
.... Harry Cooper (1955–56)
The Danny Thomas Show (com)
.... "Uncle Charley" Halper (1959–64)
Green Acres (com) ... Alf Monroe (1966–69)
Make Room for Granddaddy (com)
.... "Uncle Charley" Halper (1970–71)

Danny Thomas' fretful manager on *The Danny Thomas Show*.

MELVILLE, SAM—actor
b: Aug 20, 1940, Utah

The Rookies (police)
.... Off. Mike Danko (1972–76)

MELVIN, ALLAN—actor
b: Feb 18, Kansas City, Mo. r: New York City, N.Y.

The Phil Silvers Show (com)
.... Cpl. Henshaw (1955–59)
Gomer Pyle, U.S.M.C. (com)
.... Sgt. Hacker (1965–69)
All in the Family (com)
.... Barney Hefner (1973–83)

MELVIN, SUSAN—actress

The Patty Duke Show (com)
.... Nicki Lee (1963–64)

MEMMOLI, GEORGE—actor
b: Aug 3, 1938, New York City, N.Y. d: May 20, 1985

Hello, Larry (com).......... Earl (1979–80)

A corpulent actor who was the butt of many "fat jokes" on *Hello, Larry*. He was a former member of the Ace Trucking Company comedy troupe.

MENARD, GEORGE—host

Pet Shop (misc) .... host (1953)

MENDEL, STEPHEN—actor

Night Heat (police)
.... Det. Freddie Carson (1985–   )

MENDICK, CHARLES—comedian

Ad Libbers (var) .... regular (1951)

MENGATTI, JOHN—actor
b: Sep 21, c. 1953, New York City, N.Y.

The White Shadow (drama)
.... Nick Vitaglia (1979–81)
For Love and Honor (drama)
.... Pvt. Dominick Petrizzo (1983)

A former juvenile street gang member from New York's West Harlem who, ac-

cording to his bio, saw the light when his gang's leader was killed; at that point, John decided to get a college education and try to find a more productive career. He has since produced short films as well as acted, usually in "street tough" roles.

MENGES, JOYCE—actress

To Rome with Love (com)
.... Alison Endicott (1969–71)

MENJOU, ADOLPHE—actor
b: Feb 18, 1890, Pittsburgh, Pa. d: Oct 29, 1963

Favorite Story (drama)
.... host/occasional star (1952–54)
Target (drama)............. host (1957–58)

A onetime Hollywood matinee idol (onscreen since 1916), Menjou was the picture of debonair elegance and sartorial splendor, and often on Hollywood's "Ten Best-Dressed" list. His neatly trimmed handlebar mustache was perhaps his most distinctive characteristic. He was seen occasionally on television in the '50s, by which time he was already getting on in years.

His autobiography: *It Took Nine Tailors* (1952).

MENKEN, SHEPARD—actor

The Alvin Show (cartn)
.... voice of Clyde Crashcup (1961–62)

MENZIES, HEATHER—actress
b: Dec 3, 1949, Toronto, Canada

Logan's Run (sci fi) .... Jessica (1977–78)

MERANDE, DORO—actress
b: c. 1898 d: Nov 1, 1975

Bringing Up Buddy (com)
.... Aunt Iris Flower (1960–61)
That Was the Week That Was (com)
.... regular (1964)

MERCER, FRANCES—actress
b: New Rochelle, N.Y.

Dr. Hudson's Secret Journal (drama)
.... Nurse Ann Talbot (1955–57)

MERCER, JOHNNY—lyricist

b: Nov 18, 1909, Savannah, Ga. d: Jun 25, 1976

Musical Chairs (quiz)...... panelist (1955)

One of the giants of American popular songwriting ("In the Cool, Cool, Cool of the Evening," "Moon River," "That Old Black Magic," and hundreds of others). He was also a popular host and singer, and his friendly southern drawl was heard periodically in TV guest shots during the '50s and '60s. His original ambition, he said, was to be an actor.

MERCER, MARIAN—actress, singer

b: Nov 26, 1935, Akron, Ohio

The Andy Williams Show (var)
.... regular (1962–63)
The Dom DeLuise Show (var)
.... regular (1968)
The Dean Martin Show (var)
.... regular (1971–72)
The Sandy Duncan Show (com)
.... Kay Fox (1972)
The Wacky World of Jonathan Winters (var)
.... regular (1972–74)
A Touch of Grace (com)
.... Myra Bradley (1973)
Mary Hartman, Mary Hartman (com)
.... Wanda Jeeter (1976–78)
It's a Living (com).. Nancy Beebe (1980–82)
Foot in the Door (com)... Mrs. Griffin (1983)
It's a Living (com).. Nancy Beebe (1985–)

Marian began as a musical comedy star on Broadway, getting her first big break there in *Little Mary Sunshine* in 1960 (she took over the lead after the departure of Eileen Brennan). She later played many comedy roles on television, including that of the stuffy restaurant boss on *It's a Living*. Of this role she said, "I had turned down four other pilots before (this one), because I had gotten typed as a sort of young Eve Arden, like the saucy neighbor I played on Sandy Duncan's series. But Nancy Beebe is a lot classier than some characters I've played, and she's the first villain I've done on television. She appealed to me as a kind of female George Sanders, but with a vulnerable side—a velvet snake."

MERCER, TOMMY—singer

b: c. 1925, Ossining, N.Y.

TV's Top Tunes (music) .... host (1954)

MEREDITH, BURGESS—actor

b: Nov 16, 1908, Cleveland, Ohio

The Big Story (drama)... narrator (1957–58)
Mr. Novak (drama)
.... Martin Woodridge (1964–65)
Search (adv).......... Cameron (1972–73)
Those Amazing Animals (doc)
.... host (1980–81)
Gloria (com).. Dr. Willard Adams (1982–83)

Emmy Award: Best Supporting Actor in a Drama Special, for *Tail Gunner Joe* (1977)

Burgess Meredith began his career as a stage actor in the '30s, playing roles including that of the door mouse in Eva Le Gallienne's production of *Alice in Wonderland*. His first great triumph on Broadway was in *Winterset* in 1935, in a role written especially for him by playwright Maxwell Anderson.

Burgess was a busy character actor on stage and in films from then on. He entered television during the early, live period of the '50s on drama showcases such as *Robert Montgomery Presents, Lights Out,* and *General Electric Theater.* Although he usually appeared in dramas, his impish twinkle and feisty good humor lent itself well to comedy, and he scored quite a hit in the '60s as the most frequently seen of the bizarre villains on *Batman*—the Penguin. On the other side of the coin, Burgess was featured several times on *The Twilight Zone.* Perhaps the best-remembered episode of this classic series was his "Time Enough at Last" (1959), about a meek bookworm who is the only survivor of a nuclear holocaust; the little man realizes that now at last, free of wives and employers, he can read to his heart's content—and then accidentally breaks his glasses. Says Burgess of this simple but enormously affecting little piece, "I've heard more about it than (almost) anything else I've done on TV. I think it must have had a great impact on people. I don't suppose there's a single month goes by, even to this day, that people don't come up and remind me of that episode."

Burgess played many other roles in the years that followed, including regular parts as kindly, avuncular older men on several series. He finally won an Emmy in 1977 for his portrayal of lawyer Joseph Welch in the docudrama *Tail Gunner Joe* (about the life and times of Senator Joseph

McCarthy). He also provided narration for various specials.

MEREDITH, CHARLES—actor
b: Aug 27, 1894, Knoxville, Pa. d: Nov 28, 1964

Court of Last Resort (drama)
.... Dr. LeMoyne Snyder (1957–58)

MEREDITH, CHEERIO—actress
b: 1890 d: Dec 25, 1964

One Happy Family (com)
.... Lovey Hackett (1961)

MEREDITH, DON—sportscaster, actor
b: Apr 10, 1938, Mount Vernon, Texas

Monday Night Football (sport)
.... announcer (1970–73)
Monday Night Football (sport)
.... announcer (1977–84)

Emmy Award: Outstanding Achievement in Sportscasting, as commentator for ABC's *Monday Night Football* (1971)

"I do not understand Don Meredith and I never will," remarked Howard Cosell, which is a remarkable statement from a man who is quite *certain* about practically everything else. Howard was reflecting on who the real Don Meredith might be: (a) a sportscaster, (b) an entertainer, or (c) an unprepared ex-jock who was simply winging it as he provided "color" for Monday night NFL contests.

As to (c), Don certainly did have professional sports credentials, having been an All-American in college and a star quarterback for the Dallas Cowboys from the 1960 to 1968 seasons, two of which led to the Superbowl. Concerning (b), he did make a serious stab at acting in the mid-1970s, when he left ABC to sign a three-year contract with NBC (1974–77) which guaranteed him both series and TV movie exposure. During this period he played the recurring role of Officer Bert Jameson on *Police Story*, guest-hosted *The Tonight Show* and appeared in such TV B films as *Terror on the 40th Floor* and *Sky Heist*, among others.

However, "Dandy Don's" real talents were in category (a), and viewers welcomed him back to *Monday Night Football* in 1977, where he once again held forth with commentary, an occasional song, and his unique brand of homespun wit. Not a little of the latter was aimed squarely at—guess who?—Howard Cosell.

MEREDITH, JUDI—actress
b: c. 1937, r: Portland, Ore.

The George Burns and Gracie Allen Show (com)....... Bonnie Sue McAfee (1957–58)
The George Burns Show (com)
.... as herself (1958–59)
Hotel De Paree (wes)
.... Monique (1959–60)

Ronnie Burns's girlfriend on the *Burns and Allen* show.

MERIWETHER, LEE—actress
b: May 27, 1935, Los Angeles, Calif.

The Time Tunnel (sci fi)
.... Dr. Ann MacGregor (1966–67)
The New Andy Griffith Show (com)
.... Lee Sawyer (1971)
Barnaby Jones (drama)
.... Betty Jones (1973–80)
Masquerade Party (quiz)
.... regular panelist (1974–75)

Miss America of 1955, who rocketed from obscure San Francisco schoolgirl in 1954 (whose name was entered in her first beauty contest without her knowledge) to a national celebrity the following year. She used her pageant winnings to enroll in acting school, and found a good deal of television work over the following decades. Lee's TV debut was on *Philco Television Playhouse* in December 1954; she was also fashion editor on the *Today* show in 1955–56 and a regular on two soap operas *(Clear Horizon* and *The Young Marrieds)* and several prime time series in the '60s and '70s, most notably as Buddy Ebsen's daughter-in-law for eight years on *Barnaby Jones*.

MERLIN, JAN—actor, writer

Tom Corbett, Space Cadet (child)
.... Roger Manning (1950–52)
The Rough Riders (wes)
.... Lt. Kirby (1958–59)

Emmy Award: Best Writing for a Daytime Drama Series, for *Another World* (1975)

MERLIN, VING—orchestra leader

Broadway Spotlight (var)
.... orch. leader (1949)
Hold That Camera (var)
.... orch. leader (1950)

MERLINO, GENE—

The Ray Anthony Show (var)
.... regular (1956–57)
The Ken Berry "Wow' Show (var)
.... regular (1972)

MERRILL, BUDDY—guitarist
b: Jul 16, 1936, Torrey, Utah

The Lawrence Welk Show (music)
.... regular (1955–74)

MERRILL, DINA—actress
b: Dec 9, 1925, New York City, N.Y.

Hot Pursuit (drama)
.... Estelle Modrian (1984)

Socialite actress, the daughter of millionairess Marjorie Merriweather Post. Dina has been active on television since the mid-1950s, often in roles befitting her elegance.

MERRILL, GARY—actor
b: Aug 2, 1914, Hartford, Conn.

The Mask (drama) . Walter Guilfoyle (1954)
Justice (drama)....... Jason Tyler (1954–55)
Winston Churchill—The Valiant Years (doc)
.... narrator (1960–61)
The Reporter (drama)... Lou Sheldon (1964)
Young Dr. Kildare (drama)
.... Dr. Leonard Gillespie (1972)

This determined, somewhat colorless leading man was frequently seen on television from the '50s to the '70s. In addition to his regular series roles, he was a frequent player on *Alfred Hitchcock Presents*. He is perhaps equally well-known for his ten-year marriage to actress Bette Davis (1950–60).

MERRILL, ROBERT—singer
b: Jun 4, 1917*, Brooklyn, N.Y.

Your Show of Shows (var)
.... regular (1950–51)

*Some sources give 1919.

A well-known concert baritone with the Metropolitan Opera, beginning in 1945. He also appeared on television singing lighter fare, such as his best-selling version of "The Whiffenpoof Song."

MERRIMAN, RANDY—host

The Big Payoff (quiz)...... emcee (1952–53)

MERRITT, THERESA—black actress
b: Sep 24, 1922, Newport News, Va.

That's My Mama (com)
.... "Mama" Eloise Curtis (1974–75)

MERTON, ZIENIA—actress

Space 1999 (sci fi)......... Sandra (1975–77)

MESSICK, DON—voice specialist, actor
b: Sep 7, Buffalo, N.Y.

The Jetsons (cartn)
.... Astro (voice) (1962–63)
The Flintstones (cartn)
.... Bamm Bamm (voice) (1963–66)
Jonny Quest (cartn)
...... Dr. Benton Quest (voice) (1964–65)
Where's Huddles? (cartn)
.... Fumbles (voice) (1970)
The Duck Factory (com)
.... Wally Wooster (1984)

This pint-sized actor was, along with Mel Blanc and Daws Butler, one of the busiest "voice men" in the history of Saturday morning cartoons. He provided voices for approximately 90 different cartoon series, as well as for dozens of television and radio commercials. Among his personae were Mr. Rogers and Boo-Boo Bear on *Yogi Bear*, Scooby Doo on *Scooby Doo, Where Are You?*, the family dog on *The Jetsons*, little Bamm Bamm on *The Flintstones*, Papa Smurf and Azrael the cat on *The Smurfs*, and the "Snap" in the "Snap, Crackle, and Pop" of Rice Crispies cereal commercials.

Don had a rare opportunity (for one in his profession) to be seen on-camera in the situation comedy *The Duck Factory*, playing—what else?—a man who did voices for cartoons. He began his career in the early '40s as a ventriloquist, then was heard on radio before moving to TV in the late '50s. He was heard on some of the earliest cartoons made especially for television (e.g., *Ruff and Ready,* as Ruff, in 1957).

METCALFE, BURT—actor, producer, director
b: Mar 19, 1935, Saskatchewan, Canada

Father of the Bride (com)
.... Buckley Dunston (1961–62)

Burt later became the producer of *M*A*S*H.*

METRANO, ART—actor
b: Sep 22, 1936, Brooklyn, N.Y.

The Tim Conway Comedy Hour (var)
.... regular (1970)
The Chicago Teddy Bears (com)
.... Big Nick Marr (1971)
Amy Prentiss (police)
.... Det. Rod Pena (1974–75)
Movin' On (adv) .... Benjy (1975–76)
Loves Me, Loves Me Not (com)
.... Tom (1977)
Joanie Loves Chachi (com)
.... Uncle Rico (1982–83)
Tough Cookies (com) ..... Lt. Iverson (1986)

A chubby character actor who has played support in numerous series and TV movies. He got his start in the '60s on *The Tonight Show,* as a nutty magician who performed absurd tricks to his own rendition of "Fine and Dandy." He also made multiple appearances on *Laugh-In.*

METTEY, LYNETTE—actress
M*A*S*H (com).... Lt. Nancy Griffin (1973)
Quincy, M. E. (police) . Lee Potter (1976–77)
Fitz and Bones (com)
.... Lt. Rosie Cochran (1981)

METZINGER, KRAIG—juvenile actor
Sara (wes).......... Georgie Bailey (1976)
Maude (com)............. Phillip (1977–78)

METZLER, JIM—actor
b: Jun 23, Newburgh, N.Y.

Cutter to Houston (drama)
.... Dr. Andy Fenton (1983)
North and South (drama)
.... James Huntoon (1985)
The Best Times (drama)
.... Dan Bragen (1985)

MEYER, DOROTHY—black actress
b: Nov 6, Indianapolis, Ind.

King's Crossing (drama)
.... Willa Bristol (1982)

MEYER, FREDERIC—actor
b: c. 1910 d: Sep 16, 1973

Faraway Hill (drama) .... regular (1946)

MEYER, HANS—actor
Holocaust (drama)
.... Kaltenbrunner (1978)

MEYERINK, VICTORIA—juvenile actress
b: c. 1960

The Danny Kaye Show (var)
.... regular (1964–67)

MEYERS, ARI—juvenile actress
b: Apr 6, 1969, San Juan, Puerto Rico

Kate & Allie (com)
.... Emma McArdle (1984–   )

MEYERS, MARSHA—
Easy Does It ... Starring Frankie Avalon (var)
.... regular (1976)

MICHAEL, GEORGE—sportscaster
The George Michael Sports Machine (sport)
.... host (1984–   )

Emmy Award: Outstanding Sports Personality (1986)

MICHAEL, MARY—actress
b: c. 1903, Colorado d: Nov 6, 1980

The Wonderful John Acton (drama)
.... Birdie Bodkin (1953)

MICHAEL, RALPH—actor
b: Sep 26, 1907, London, England

Doctor in the House (com)
.... The Dean (1970–73)
The Quest (adv)....... King Charles (1982)

MICHAELS, AL—sportscaster
b: 1945, Brooklyn, N.Y.

Monday Night Baseball (sport)
.... sportscaster (1976–   )

Monday Night Football (sport)
.... sportscaster (1986–)

A former local sportscaster (in the late '60s) and part-timer for NBC (in the early '70s). Michaels joined ABC in 1977 as one of its principal baseball play-by-play men.

MICHAELS, JEANNA—actress
b: May 9, New London, Conn.

Dallas (drama).......... Connie (1979–81)

MICHAELS, MARILYN—comedienne, singer

ABC Comedy Hour (com).... regular (1972)

One of The Kopykats impressionists troupe on the *ABC Comedy Hour.*

MICHAELS, NICK—announcer

Friday Night Videos (music)
.... announcer (offscreen) (1983–85)

MICHAELS, RAY—singer

The Sammy Kaye Show (var)
.... regular (1958–59)

MICHAELSEN, KARI—actress
b: Nov 3, 1961, New York City, N.Y.

Gimme a Break (com)
.... Katie Kanisky (1981–86)

MICHAELSEN, MELISSA—juvenile actress

Me and Maxx (com).... Maxx Davis (1980)

MICHAUX, ELDER LIGHTFOOT SOLOMON—black preacher
b: Nov 7, 1883, Newport News, Va. d: Oct 20, 1968

Elder Michaux (misc)... preacher (1948–49)

MICHEL, FRANNY—juvenile actress
b: Sep 8, 1961, Brooklyn, N.Y.

Apple's Way (drama)
.... Patricia Apple (1974)

MICHELL, KEITH—actor
b: Dec 1, 1926, Adelaide, Australia

The Six Wives of Henry VIII (drama)
.... Henry VIII (1971)

Emmy Award: Best Actor in a Single Performance, for *The Six Wives of Henry VIII* (1972)

MICHELMAN, KEN—actor
b: May 23, New York City, N.Y.

The White Shadow (drama)
.... Abner Goldstein (1978–80)

MICHENAUD, GERALD—actor

To Rome with Love (com)... Nico (1969–71)

MIDDLETON, ROBERT—actor
b: May 13, 1911, Cincinnati, Ohio d: Jun 14, 1977

The Monroes (wes)
.... Barney Wales (1966–67)

MIDDLETON, TOM—juvenile actor

Robert Montgomery Presents (summer) (drama)........... repertory player (1956)

MIDGLEY, RICHARD—actor
b: c. 1910 d: 1956

The Aldrich Family (com)
.... Mr. Bradley (1949)

MIDWESTERNERS, THE—dancers

Midwestern Hayride (var)
.... regulars (1954–59)

MIFUNE, TOSHIRO—actor
b: Apr 1, 1920, Tsing-tao, China

Shogun (drama)...... Lord Toranaga (1980)

A powerful, glowering Japanese film and television star, who appeared there in numerous TV series, including one (in the '70s) as a Samurai detective. He is Japan's biggest international star and has been described as that country's equivalent of John Wayne.

MILAN, FRANK—actor
b: c. 1905 d: Apr 8, 1977

The Witness (drama)
.... committee member (1960–61)

MILANO, ALYSSA—juvenile actress
b: Dec 19, 1972, Brooklyn, N.Y.

Who's the Boss? (com)
.... Samantha Micelli (1984–)

MILES, RICHARD—actor

The Betty Hutton Show (com)
.... Nicky Strickland (1959–60)

MILES, SHERRY—actress
b: c. 1952, Honolulu, Hawaii

Pat Paulsen's Half a Comedy Hour (var)
.... regular (1970)
Hee Haw (var).......... regular (1971–72)

MILFORD, JOHN—actor
b: Sep 7, 1929, Johnstown, N.Y.

The Lieutenant (drama)
.... Sgt. Kagey (1963–64)
The Legend of Jesse James (wes)
.... Cole Younger (1965–66)
Enos (com) ...... Capt. Dempsey (1980–81)

MILLAND, RAY—actor
b: Jan 3, 1905*, Neath, Wales d: Mar 10, 1986

The Ray Milland Show (com)
.. Prof. Ray McNutley/McNulty (1953–55)
Markham (drama). Roy Markham (1959–60)
Rich Man, Poor Man—Book I (drama)
.... Duncan Calderwood (1976)

This pleasant, rather ordinary-looking film star was known mostly as an amiable leading man in romantic comedies until he made Hollywood sit up and take notice with his gripping portrayal of an alcoholic writer in *The Lost Weekend* (1945)—for which he won an Academy Award. Unfortunately, this dramatic triumph was an exception in a career filled largely with second-rate properties, both on film and TV. In films since 1929, he made two stabs at series TV in the '50s, first as a teacher in a 1953 comedy, and later as a wealthy, globe-trotting detective in the 1959 drama *Markham.* Neither was successful. Ray also appeared occasionally as a guest star in live and filmed dramas from the '50s to the '80s and was nominated for an Emmy for his role in *Rich Man, Poor Man.* As with his movies, however, most of his television vehicles (especially the later ones) tended to be undistinguished for an actor of his stature. One of his last appearances

*Some sources give 1908.

was in Irwin Allen's TV disaster film *Cave In* in 1983.

His autobiography: *Wide-Eyed in Babylon* (1954).

MILLAR, MARJIE—actress, dancer
b: 1930, Tacoma, Wash. d: 1970

The Ray Bolger Show (com)
.... Susan (1954–55)

Ray Bolger's fresh-faced young girlfriend in his mid-1950s comedy series (in fact, she was 30 years younger than he). She was later crippled in an auto accident and died of its lingering aftereffects.

MILLER, ALLAN—actor

A.E.S. Hudson Street (com)
.... Dr. Glick (1978)
Battlestar Galactica (sci fi)
.... Col. Sydell (1980)
Soap (com) ......Dr. Alan Posner (1980–81)
Nero Wolfe (drama)... Insp. Cramer (1981)
Knots Landing (drama)
.... Scooter Warren (1981–82)

A supporting actor who was active in soap operas in the late '60s and '70s *(One Life to Live, How to Survive a Marriage)* before crashing prime time in the late '70s. He usually plays a background authority figure such as a doctor or police official.

MILLER, BARRY—actor
b: Feb 8, 1958, New York City, N.Y.

Joe and Sons (com).. Mark Vitale (1975–76)
Szysznyk (com) ..... Fortwengler (1977–78)

MILLER, CHERYL—actress
b: Feb 4, 1943, Sherman Oaks, Calif.

Daktari (adv) .... Paula Tracy (1966–69)

MILLER, DEAN—actor

December Bride (com)
.... Matt Henshaw (1954–59)

MILLER, DENISE—juvenile actress
b: Jul 17, 1963, Brooklyn, N.Y.

Fish (com)........ Jilly Papalardo (1977–78)
Makin' It (adv)........ Tina Manucci (1979)
Archie Bunker's Place (com)
.... Billie Bunker (1981–83)

MILLER, DENNIS—comedian
b: Nov 3, 1953, Pittsburgh, Pa.

NBC's Saturday Night Live (var)
.... regular (1985–)

MILLER, DENNY (SCOTT)—actor
b: Apr 25, 1934, Bloomington, Ind.

Wagon Train (wes)
.... Duke Shannon (1961–64)
Mona McCluskey (com)
.... Mike McCluskey (1965–66)

An athletic, blond-haired Adonis who got his first break in 1959 as a movie Tarzan and then went on to play the recurring role of a trail scout on *Wagon Train* and Juliet Prowse's TV hubby on *Mona McCluskey.* He later became a real-life advertising executive while continuing to play small supporting roles in TV movies (e.g., the 1983 film *V*) and series episodes. He used the first name Scott early in his career, then switched to Denny.

MILLER, GARY—

The John Byner Comedy Hour (var)
.... regular (1972)

MILLER, JACK—orchestra leader
b: c. 1895 d: Mar 18, 1985

The Kate Smith Evening Hour (var)
.... orch. leader (1951–52)

MILLER, JEREMY—juvenile actor
b: Oct 21, 1976, West Covina, Calif.

Growing Pains (com) . Ben Seaver (1985–)

MILLER, KATHLEEN—actress

Sirota's Court (com)
.... Gail Goodman (1976–77)

MILLER, LARA JILL—juvenile actress
b: Apr 20, 1967, Allentown, Pa.

Gimme a Break (com)
..... Samantha "Sam" Kanisky (1981–86)

MILLER, LEE—actor

Perry Mason (drama)... Sgt. Brice (1965–66)

Raymond Burr's longtime stand-in and double, in both television and movies

(since the '40s). He looks remarkably similar to the star, although he did have to pad his costumes when Burr gained weight and slim down his own portly frame whenever Burr went on a diet.

In appreciation of such devoted service, Burr gave him a role of his own during the final season of *Perry Mason.*

MILLER, LINDA G.—actress
b: Sep 16, 1942, New York City, N.Y.

The Mississippi (drama)
.... Stella McMullen (1983–84)

The actress daughter of superstar Jackie Gleason.

MILLER, MARK—actor
b: Nov 20, Houston, Texas

Guestward Ho! (com)
.... Bill Hooten (1960–61)
Please Don't Eat the Daisies (com)
.... James (Jim) Nash (1965–67)
The Name of the Game (adv)
.... Ross Craig (1968–71)

MILLER, MARK THOMAS—actor
b: May 3, Louisville, Ky.

Misfits of Science (adv)
Johnny ("Johnny B") Bukowski (1985–86)

MILLER, MARVIN—actor
b: Jul 18, 1913, St. Louis, Mo. d: Feb 8, 1985

Mysteries of Chinatown (drama)
.... Dr. Yat Fu (1949–50)
Space Patrol (child) .. Mr. Proteus (1951–52)
The Millionaire (drama)
.... Michael Anthony (1955–60)
The Famous Adventures of Mr. Magoo (cartn)
.... voices (1964–65)

Marvin Miller was known in the '40s and early '50s as an actor able to portray a wide range of nationalities, including Orientals; on *Space Patrol,* in fact, he was a master of disguises. Then he became famous as the discreet, businesslike personal secretary who delivered a million dollars to some lucky person each week on the hit series *The Millionaire.* That seemingly innocuous role left him so typecast that afterward he found on-screen parts rather hard to come by. He turned instead to voice work, doing Saturday morning cartoons *(Fantastic Voyage)* and narration for TV movies and series (including *The F.B.I.*). He had a small role, as a radio actor, in the 1981 TV film *Evita Peron.*

MILLER, MINDI—actress

Switch (drama)........... Revel (1975–78)

MILLER, MITCH—orchestra leader
b: Jul 4, 1911, Rochester, N.Y.

Songs for Sale (music)...... panelist (1951)
Sing Along with Mitch (var).. host (1961–64)

The bearded, taciturn maestro was one of the most powerful men in the record business in the 1950s, as head of recording for mighty Columbia records. He hated rock 'n' roll, which proved to be his downfall, but before he fell he spearheaded a notable last hurrah for "his" kind of old-fashioned melodious music on television on the popular *Sing Along with Mitch* series.

Mitch started out as a classical oboe player in the '30s but switched to producing popular records in the mid-1940s, using many novel effects such as French horns, harpsichords, and bullwhips to make ordinary pop songs sound distinctive. He was spectacularly successful at this, and much of what America whistled and listened to on the radio in the early '50s (by artists from Frankie Laine to Johnnie Ray) was the product of his imaginative production. He himself was virtually unknown to the public, however, until TV made him—briefly—the most famous music mogul in the land.

MILLER, NORMA—black actress

The Sanford Arms (com)
.... Dolly Wilson (1977)

MILLER, ROBYN—actress

The Patty Duke Show (com) . Roz (1965–66)

MILLER, ROGER—country singer, songwriter
b: Jan 2, 1936, Fort Worth, Texas r: Erick, Okla.

The Roger Miller Show (var).... host (1966)

An ingratiating country singer whose eccentric songs ("Dang Me," "King of the Road," etc.) took America by storm in the mid-1960s. He says he doesn't follow trends; "I prefer to go in my own direction and let someone follow me."

MILLER, SCOTT—actor

See Miller, Denny

MILLER, SID—actor, director, songwriter
b: Oct 22, 1916, Shenandoah, Pa.

The Donald O'Connor Texaco Show (com)
.... as himself (1954–55)

A very successful TV director of the '60s and '70s (*Get Smart, Bewitched, What's Happening*, etc.). He still acts occasionally.

MILLERICK, KERRY—host, producer
b: New York City, N.Y.

That's My Line (com)....... reporter (1981)
Real People (aud par)
.... regular (1982–83)

MILLHOLLIN, JAMES—actor
b: 1920

Grindl (com)....... Anson Foster (1963–64)

MILLIGAN, PATTI—juvenile actress

Billy Boone and Cousin Kib (child)
.... regular (1950)

MILLIGAN, SPIKE—comedian, writer
b: Apr 16, 1918, India

The Marty Feldman Comedy Machine (var)
.... regular (1972)

An off-the-wall British comedian, quite popular in films and television in that country. He was one of the creators of the infamous *Goon Show* on British radio.

MILLS, ALLEY—actress
b: May 9, Chicago, Ill., r: N.Y.

The Associates (com)
.... Leslie Dunn (1979–80)
Making the Grade (com)
.... Sara Conover (1982)

MILLS, ALLISON—actress

Julia (com)........ Carol Deering (1968–69)
The Leslie Uggams Show (var)
.... Oletha (1969)

MILLS, DONNA—actress

b: Dec 11, 1943, Chicago, Ill.

The Good Life (com) . Jane Miller (1971–72)
Knots Landing (drama)
...... Abby Cunningham Ewing (1980–)

Donna Mills, the sexy, devious vixen Abby on *Knots Landing,* was a 15-year veteran of television when she landed her most famous role. She took part in Chicago stage productions as a child; arrived in New York in 1964, where she had a few small roles in prime time; and then went into daytime soap operas: seven months on *The Secret Storm* and three years (1967–70) as ex-nun Laura Donnelly on *Love Is a Many Splendored Thing.*

Donna returned to prime time in the '70s, with roles in series episodes and TV films (she is one of the "queens of the TV movies," having done nearly 20 to date). She appeared as a woman in danger in many action dramas, such as *Gunsmoke, Police Story,* and *S.W.A.T.*. "No girl on TV has ever been raped, strangled, assaulted, kidnapped, beaten, or killed more than I," she later said. "You can see why I wanted Abby so badly."

Her first regular role was as Larry Hagman's wife on the comedy *The Good Life,* in which they played servants to the wealthy. Hagman later found fame as a rotten-to-the-core schemer on *Dallas,* while Donna did the same on the *Dallas* spin-off, *Knots Landing.* These two rich troublemakers even got to sleep together on the latter show, something they could never do (on-screen, at least) when they had played a married couple ten years before.

MILLS, JOHN—actor

b: Feb 22, 1908, Felixstowe, Suffolk, England

Dundee and the Culhane (wes)
.... Dundee (1967)

Eminent British actor, the father of Juliet and Hayley Mills. He appeared only occasionally on U.S. television, his debut being on *Producers' Showcase* in 1956.

MILLS, JULIET—actress

b: Nov 21, 1941, London, England

Nanny and the Professor (com)
.... Phoebe Figalilly (1970–71)

Emmy Award: Best Supporting Actress in a Drama Special, for *QB VII* (1975)

The daughter of Sir John. She has been seen on television since the mid-1960s.

MILLS, MARCIE—singer

TV's Top Tunes (music) ..... regular (1954)

MILLS, MORT—actor

Man Without a Gun (wes)
.... Marshal Frank Tallman (1957–59)

MILNER, MARTIN—actor

b: Dec 28, 1927*, Detroit, Mich. r: Wash., Calif.

The Stu Erwin Show (com)
.... Jimmy Clark (1954–55)
The Life of Riley (com)
.... Don Marshall (1957–58)
Route 66 (adv) .... Tod Stiles (1960–64)
Adam 12 (police)
.... Off. Pete Malloy (1968–75)
Swiss Family Robinson (adv)
.... Karl Robinson (1975–76)

Youthful-looking Martin Milner has had a long career in family comedies and light action series, including leading roles on two major hits. An acting buff since his grade school days, Marty won his first major role at the age of 19 in the 1947 film *Life with Father,* as one of the sons. His career then suffered a setback when he was stricken with polio. He was bedridden for a year but eventually recovered and picked up where he had left off, playing youthful roles in B films and on television; one of the earliest was in an episode of *The Lone Ranger.* He soon became known as the clean-cut "boy next door" in family comedies, courting and marrying Stu Erwin's TV daughter on *The Stu Erwin Show* and then William Bendix's on *The Life of Riley.* But domesticity was not what made him a star; in 1960 he captured the imagination of young viewers as a footloose wanderer cruising the open road in

*Some sources give 1931 or 1932.

590

a sleek Corvette, in the hit series *Route 66*.

Martin continued to work steadily in guest roles during the mid-1960s and then scored his second major youth-oriented hit, the Jack Webb–produced police show *Adam 12*—this time portraying the *senior* of the two street cops. Since that time he has been seen mostly in TV movies and miniseries, in progressively more mature (and interesting) roles. In *The Seekers* (1979), he played the aging Philip Kent; a more recent Jack Webb discovery, Randolph Mantooth, was cast in the role of his son.

MIMIEUX, YVETTE—actress
b: Jan 8, 1939, Los Angeles, Calif.

The Most Deadly Game (drama)
.... Vanessa Smith (1970–71)
Berrengers (drama)
.... Shane Bradley (1985)

Sexy, but tough, blonde leading lady. On *The Most Deadly Game* she played a college-educated criminologist. Offscreen she is a successful businesswoman.

MINER, JAN—actress
b: Oct 15, 1917, Boston, Mass.

Crime Photographer (drama)
.... Ann Williams (1951–52)
Robert Montgomery Presents (summer) (drama)........ repertory player (1954–56)

MINKUS, BARBARA—actress

Love, American Style (com)
.... repertory player (1969–74)

MINOR, MIKE—actor
b: Dec 7, San Francisco, Calif.

Petticoat Junction (com)
.... Steve Elliott (1966–70)
The Smith Family (drama)
.... sang theme (1971–72)

The son of Don Fedderson, producer of such popular series as *My Three Sons* and *Family Affair*—and also of *The Smith Family*. Mike later retreated into daytime television, where he played continuing roles on *All My Children* and *Another World* in the '80s.

MINTZ, ELI—actor
b: c. 1904, Lemberg, Austria

The Goldbergs (com)
.... Uncle David (1949–55)

MIRAND, EVAN—actor

Melba (com).................... Gil (1986)

MIRATTI, TI—actor

Stop Susan Williams (drama) ..... Ti (1979)

MISHKIN, PHIL—actor

The Super (com) ..... Frankie Girelli (1972)

MITCHELL, ANDREA—newscaster
b: Oct 30, 1946, New York City r: New Rochelle, N.Y.

Summer Sunday U.S.A. (pub aff)
.... anchor (1984)

MITCHELL, BOBBIE—actress

M*A*S*H (com)... various nurses (1973–77)

MITCHELL, BRIAN—black actor
b: Oct 31, Seattle, Wash.

Trapper John, M.D. (drama)
.... Dr. Justin Jackson (Jackpot) (1979–86)

MITCHELL, CAMERON—actor
b: Nov 4, 1918, Dallastown, Pa.

The Beachcomber (adv)
.... John Lackland (1960–61)
The High Chaparral (wes)
.... Buck Cannon (1967–71)
Swiss Family Robinson (adv)
.... Jeremiah Worth (1975–76)

Gruff, tough second lead in many films of the mid-1940s onward. He appeared on television beginning in the early days, in numerous dramatic productions, especially westerns and cop shows.

MITCHELL, DON—black actor
b: Mar 17, 1943, Houston, Texas

Ironside (police)..... Mark Sanger (1967–75)

Don Mitchell began as a stage actor in the '60s, playing predominantly "angry black" roles, and eventually landed a similar part in the 1967 TV movie *Ironside*. When the movie became a series, his character underwent a gradual but dramatic evolution: from alienated street tough, to Chief Ironside's assistant, to police officer, to law student. By the end of the series' run he was a practicing attorney, proving that when the scriptwriters are on your side, you can do almost anything.

When they are not, the going can get a little tough, however; Don was not seen much after his *Ironside* days.

MITCHELL, EWING—actor

The Adventures of Champion (adv)
.... Sheriff Powers (1955–56)

MITCHELL, GUY—singer, actor
b: Feb 27, 1925*, Detroit, Mich. r: Calif.

The Guy Mitchell Show (var)
.... host (1957–58)
Whispering Smith (wes)
.... Det. George Romack (1961)

This robust-voiced, boyishly handsome singer was a major recording star in the early and mid 1950s, with hits including "My Truly, Truly Fair" and "Singing the Blues." His first big break was as a winner on *Arthur Godfrey's Talent Scouts* in 1949; he subsequently made many guest appearances, had his own ABC variety show (briefly), and even tried his hand at acting in the 1961 western *Whispering Smith*.

Plagued by illness and injury throughout his career (*Whispering Smith* was postponed a year and a half when Guy broke his shoulder), the singer was incapacitated for long periods during the '60s and '70s.

MITCHELL, GWENN—black actress
b: Jul 6, Morristown, N.J.

Amy Prentiss (police)
.... Joan Carter (1974–75)

MITCHELL, JAKE—actor

Paris (police) ..... Charlie Bogart (1979–80)

MITCHELL, KEITH—juvenile actor
b: Jan 13, 1970, Palm Springs, Calif.

The Mackenzies of Paradise Cove (adv)
.... Timothy Mackenzie (1979)

*Some sources give 1927.

The Waltons (drama)
.... Jeffrey Burton (1979–81)
Gun Shy (com).............. Clovis (1983)

The grandson of actor Jackie Coogan, a famous child star of the '20s.

MITCHELL, PAUL, QUINTET— instrumental

The Eddy Arnold Show (var)
.... regular (1956)

MITCHELL, ROBERT, BOYS CHOIR—

Men of Tomorrow (doc)..... regulars (1954)

MITCHELL, SHIRLEY—actress

The Great Gildersleeve (com)
.... Leila Ransom (1955–56)
Bachelor Father (com)
.... Kitty Deveraux (1958–59)
Pete and Gladys (com)
.... Janet Colton (1960–62)
Please Don't Eat the Daisies (com)
.... Marge Thornton (1965–67)

MITCHELL, STEVE—actor

The New Phil Silvers Show (com)
.... Fred Starkey (1963–64)

MITCHELL, THOMAS—actor, writer
b: Jul 11, 1892, Elizabeth, N.J. d: Dec 17, 1962

Mayor of the Town (com)
.... Mayor Thomas Russell (1954–55)
O. Henry Playhouse (drama)
.... host (as O. Henry) (1957)
Glencannon (adv)
.... Capt. Colin Gl·ncannon (1958–59)

Emmy Award: Best Actor (1952)

A veteran Irish-American character actor, one of Hollywood's very best; he had a cherubic face and often a twinkle in his eye, but he was capable of an extraordinary range of comic and dramatic roles. Mitchell began on stage in the 1910s, entered movies in the '30s (at age 42), and by the '50s was in decline. So in his sixties he turned to television and became one of the busiest actors on all the major playhouse series of that day, from *Studio One* to *Lights Out*. He also starred in three minor syndicated series, a comedy, a dramatic anthology, and an adventure. Most of his best TV work was in live productions, however, and is now fondly but only faintly remembered.

MITCHLLL, SCOEY—black actor, producer
b: Mar 12, 1930, Newburgh, N.Y.

What's It All About, World? (var)
.... regular (1969)
Barefoot in the Park (com)
.... Paul Bratter (1970–71)
Rhoda (com)......... Justin Culp (1975–76)

No, that's not a typographical error—he spells it with three "l's" (Mitchlll).

MITCHUM, JACK—actor
Riverboat (adv) .... Pickalong (1959–60)

MITCHUM, ROBERT—actor
b: Aug 6, 1917, Bridgeport, Conn.

The Winds of War (drama)
.... Victor "Pug" Henry (1983)
North and South (drama)
.... Col. Patrick Flynn, M.D. (1985)

One of Hollywood's longest major hold-outs from TV. This sleepy-looking yet commanding actor, a star of the big screen since the early '40s, did not make his television acting debut until the early '80s, in the 18-hour epic *The Winds of War* (although a second TV film called *One Shoe Makes It Murder,* made shortly afterward, actually aired first). The miniseries took 13 months to complete, in locations around the world. When asked why he had agreed to such a monumental undertaking, the 65-year-old actor replied in his usual laconic fashion, "It promised a year of free lunches."

Apparently he liked the food, as he agreed to appear in several more TV productions during the years that followed, including another mega-epic, *North and South.*

His autobiography: *It Sure Beats Working* (1975).

MIXON, ALAN—actor
Andros Targets (drama)
.... Norman Kale (1977)

MIYA, JO ANNE—actress
Arrest and Trial (drama)
.... Janet Okada (1963–64)

MIYAZAKI, LANI—actress
Mr. Broadway (drama) .... Toki (1964)

MIYORI, KIM—actress
b: Santa Maria, Calif.

St. Elsewhere (drama)
.... Dr. Wendy Armstrong (1982–84)

MIZADA, JAMIE—
Marie (var)............. regular (1980–81)

MIZZY, VIC—orchestra leader
b: Jan 9, 1916*, Brooklyn, N.Y.

The Don Rickles Show (var)
.... orch. leader (1968–69)

MOBLEY, MARY ANN—actress
b: Feb 17, 1939, Biloxi, Miss.

Be Our Guest (var)......... regular (1960)
Diff'rent Strokes (com)
.... Maggie McKinney (1985–86)

Miss America of 1959. She has decorated a variety of TV movies and series episodes since the 1960s (watch for her on reruns of *The Love Boat* and *Fantasy Island*) and has cohosted TV events including the Miss America Pageant. She and her husband, Gary Collins, are also quite active in charitable endeavors.

MODEAN, JAYNE—actress
b: Oct 15, c. 1958, Hartford, Conn.

Trauma Center (drama)
.... Nurse Hooter (1983)

MODERNAIRES, THE—singers
Including: Paula Kelly
        Hal Dickinson, b: Dec 12, 1913, Buffalo, N.Y. d: Nov 18, 1970

The Lux Show Starring Rosemary Clooney (var).................... regulars (1957–58)
Perry Presents (var) .... regulars (1959)
The George Gobel Show (var)
.... regulars (1959–60)

*Some sources give 1922.

This venerable vocal group was formed in the mid-1930s by Hal Dickinson and achieved its greatest fame with the Glenn Miller Orchestra in the early '40s. Personnel changed over the years, but Dickinson and his wife, Paula Kelly, were with the group throughout, including its years on television. The Modernaires continued to perform after Dickinson's death in 1970.

MOFFAT, DONALD—actor
b: Dec 26, 1930, Plymouth, England

The New Land (adv)
.... Rev. Lundstrom (1974)
Logan's Run (sci fi)........ Rem (1977–78)

MOFFAT, KITTY—actress

Boone (drama)
.... Susannah Sawyer (1983–84)

MOHR, GERALD—actor
b: Jun 11, 1914, New York City, N.Y. d: Nov 10, 1968

Foreign Intrigue (drama)
.... Christopher Storm (1954–55)

MOKIHANA—actress

Aloha Paradise (com)
.... Evelyn Pahinui (1981)

MOLINARO, AL—actor
b: Jun 24, 1919, Kenosha, Wis.

The Odd Couple (com)
.... Murray Greshner (1970–75)
Happy Days (com)
.... Alfred Delvecchio (1976–82)
Joanie Loves Chachi (com)
.... Alfred Delvecchio (1982–83)

Al Molinaro's face is his fortune; he bears a striking resemblance to a basset hound, a fact which has kept him steadily employed in television comedies since the mid-1960s. Formerly a musician, Al entered TV as a local producer in Los Angeles around 1960, but soon began doing comic commercials (wouldn't you buy a car from that incredibly sad-looking man?). He landed his first acting job on *Green Acres* when the casting director mistook him for someone else.

Al's big break came as Murray the dense cop, one of Jack Klugman's poker partners on *The Odd Couple*. Al played one memorable scene with only his huge nose sticking through a peephole in the door. "I can't play to that," a convulsed Tony Randall exclaimed off-camera. "I can't even look at it!" "Believe it or not," Al later said, "I was thought of by (producer) Garry Marshall as comedy relief— on a *comedy*." Marshall was so happy with him, in fact, that he cast him in his next series as well, and *Happy Days* lasted even longer than *The Odd Couple*. Although *TV Guide* once labeled Al as one of TV's "one-minute superstars" (a momentary but striking success in a brief supporting role), 13 years of steady series work does not seem bad for a guy with a big nose.

MOLL, RICHARD—actor
b: Jan 13, Pasadena, Calif.

Night Court (com)
.... bailiff Bull Shannon (1984–)

The towering (6'8"), bald bailiff on *Night Court*. The actor's previous roles invariably had him as a menace: he played an evil sorcerer in the movie *The Sword and the Sorcerer*, an abominable snowman in *Caveman*, an ox-man in *The Archer*, a snake-man in the PBS special *Reach for the Sun*, a demonic wizard in *Ragewar*, and a murdered Vietnam veteran who returned as a zombie to haunt his former platoon leader in *House*. In a complete turnabout, the *Night Court* writers made his character quite sensitive about frightening people.

MOND, STEVEN—actor

Diff'rent Strokes (com)
.... Robbie Jason (1982–83)

MONDO, PEGGY—actress

McHale's Navy (com)
.... Rosa Giovanni (1965–66)
To Rome with Love (com)
.... Mama Vitale (1969–71)

MONES, PAUL—actor
b: Mar 2, Newark, N.J. r: West Orange, N.J.

Renegades (police) .... J.T. (1983)

594

MONICA, CORBETT—comedian
b: St. Louis, Mo.

The Joey Bishop Show (com)
.... Larry Corbett (1963–65)

Corbett's moniker was derived from "Gentleman Jim" Corbett, the onetime heavyweight boxing champ. The comedian got his first major break on *The Tonight Show* in 1961.

MONKHOUSE, BOB—comedian
b: Jun 1, 1928, Beckenham, Kent, England

Bonkers (com) .... as himself (1978–79)

A popular comedian on British television, including that country's versions of *What's My Line?* and *Candid Camera.*

MONROE, BILL—newscaster
b: Jul 17, 1920, New Orleans, La.

Congressional Report (pub aff)
.... moderator (1969)

Monroe was a Washington correspondent for NBC from 1961 until his retirement in 1986. During the late '70s and early '80s he was moderator of the influential Sunday afternoon public affairs show *Meet the Press.* Prior to joining the network, Monroe had been a local newsman in New Orleans in the '40s and '50s.

MONROE, DEL—actor

Voyage to the Bottom of the Sea (sci fi)
.... Kowalsky (1964–68)

MONROE, VAUGHN—singer, orchestra leader
b: Oct 7, 1911, Akron, Ohio d: May 21, 1973

The Vaughn Monroe Show (var)
.... host (1950–51)
The Vaughn Monroe Show (music)
.... host (1954–55)
Air Time '57 (var) .... host (1956–57)

MONTAGUE, LEE—actor
b: Oct 16, 1927, Bow, London, England

Holocaust (drama) ..... Uncle Sasha (1978)

MONTALBAN, RICARDO—actor
b: Nov 25, 1920, Mexico City, Mexico

Fantasy Island (drama)
.... Mr. Roarke (1978–84)
Dynasty II: The Colbys (drama)
.... Zachary Powers (1985–   )

Emmy Award: Best Supporting Actor in a Single Performance, for *How the West Was Won Part II* (1978)

One of Hollywood's all-time favorite Latin actors, and TV's too. Born in Mexico, Ricardo was educated in California and got his start onstage around 1940, appearing on Broadway with Tallulah Bankhead in *Her Cardboard Lover.* He made only one short film in the U.S. (*He's a Latin from Staten Island,* 1941) before returning to Mexico to begin an active screen career there that lasted for the next half dozen years. Once established in his native land, he moved to Hollywood and embarked on a long American career, beginning with the 1947 film *Fiesta.*

Ricardo began appearing on television in the mid-1950s and was seen most frequently on *The Loretta Young Show* (Miss Young was his sister-in-law). Determined to break the rut of stereotyped Latin roles into which movies had put him, he played a wide range of characters and nationalities on TV, on series ranging from *Wagon Train* to *Wonder Woman.* One of his most famous roles was on *Star Trek* in 1967, in an episode called "Space Seed." Fifteen years later, this became the basis for the movie *Star Trek: The Wrath of Khan* (1982), in which he also appeared.

In the late '70s Ricardo became the commercial spokesman for Ford automobiles; the commercials, in turn, caught the eye of the producers of a forthcoming TV movie called *Fantasy Island,* and he was cast in the leading role of the mysterious Mr. Roarke. The movie became a series and gave the actor his most prominent role yet. *Fantasy Island* went on to become TV's longest-running series (six and a half seasons) starring a Latin actor.

His autobiography (with Bob Thomas): *Reflections: A Life in Two Worlds* (1980).

MONTE, VINNIE—actor

The Benny Rubin Show (com)
.... office boy (1949)

MONTEITH, KELLY—host, comedian

The Kelly Monteith Show (var).. host (1976)
No Holds Barred (com).........host (1980)

MONTENARO, TONY, JR.—actor

Guestward Ho! (com)......Rocky (1960–61)

MONTGOMERY, BARBARA—black actress
b: Jun 25, 1939, East Orange, N.J.

Amen (com)...Casietta Hetebrink (1986–)

MONTGOMERY, BELINDA—actress
b: Jul 23, 1950, Winnipeg, Manitoba, Canada

Man from Atlantis (adv)
.........Dr. Elizabeth Merrill (1977–78)

MONTGOMERY, ELIZABETH—actress
b: Apr 15, 1933, Los Angeles, Calif.

Robert Montgomery Presents (summer) (drama)........ repertory player (1953–54)
Robert Montgomery Presents (summer) (drama)........... repertory player (1956)
Bewitched (com)
..........Samantha Stephens (1964–72)
Bewitched (com) ....Serena (1964–72)

"It wasn't that he never gave me any encouragement," says Elizabeth Montgomery of her famous father, actor Robert Montgomery. "It's that he was entirely unsuccessful in trying to discourage me." Faced with his daughter's determination, Robert gave Elizabeth her first television exposure on his live dramatic anthology series, *Robert Montgomery Presents,* in December 1951. The play was called "Top Secret," and in it she played Robert's daughter. "I remember that the critics were good to me and thought I had done well," she recalls. "My father clipped a few reviews and sent them to me with a note: 'Don't believe a word of it. Love, Dad.' He was my most severe critic, but also a true friend."

Following her debut, Elizabeth appeared in some 250 live TV programs over the next 12 years, including three years in the summer repertory company of her father's series. Then, in 1964, she began her first continuing role, in a comedy produced by her husband William Asher. *Bewitched* became one of the biggest hits of the '60s, and

indelibly identified with her. Since that time she has concentrated on TV movies, making approximately one per year; these have included acclaimed performances in *A Case of Rape* (1974), *The Legend of Lizzie Borden* (1975), and *The Awakening Land* (1978).

MONTGOMERY, GEORGE—actor, director
b: Aug 29, 1916, Brady, Mont.

Cimarron City (wes)
...........Matthew Rockford (1958–59)

Solid actor of Hollywood action films, including many westerns. His television appearances were fairly infrequent. Married to Dinah Shore from 1943–1960.

MONTGOMERY, MARK—actor

Curse of Dracula (adv) ......Darryl (1979)

MONTGOMERY, RAY—actor

Ramar of the Jungle (adv)
.........Prof. Howard Ogden (1952–54)

MONTGOMERY, ROBERT—actor, director
b: May 21, 1904, Beacon, N.Y. d: Sep 27, 1981

Robert Montgomery Presents (drama)
........................host (1950–57)

Robert Montgomery had one of the strangest love-hate relationships with television of any of the medium's major stars. A well-known film actor of the '30s and '40s, usually cast in light, dapper roles, he came to TV in January 1950 as producer, host, and sometimes star of the live anthology *Robert Montgomery Presents.* His Monday-night hour became one of TV's favorite playhouse series and a showcase for many current and future stars (including his own daughter Elizabeth). Montgomery himself was a smooth and ingratiating host, often interviewing the night's stars.

Once the series ended, Robert had virtually nothing further to do with TV except to violently denounce it, particularly what he saw as the corrupting power of the networks. His campaign, which included a critical book called *An Open Letter from a Television Viewer* (1968), had little impact, however. Parallel with his TV and post-TV activities, he became quite active in conservative politics, testifying before the House Un-American Activities Committee of Congress about Communist infiltration into Hollywood and promoting Dewey for president. From 1952–60 he was special TV consultant to President Eisenhower, helping polish Ike's on-camera presence and thus helping his election campaign. Later, in the '60s, he was involved with public television and various arts groups. His biography in *Who's Who in America* never even mentioned *Robert Montgomery Presents.*

MONTI, MARY ELAINE—actress

Park Place (com).... Joel "Jo" Keene (1981)

MONTROSE, BELLE—actress
b: c. 1886 d: Oct 25, 1964

The Hathaways (com)
.... Mrs. Harrison (1961–62)

Steve Allen's mother, an actress and former vaudevillian.

MOODY, SENATOR BLAIR—host
b: Feb 13, 1902, New Haven, Conn. d: Jul 20, 1954

Meet Your Congress (pub aff)
.... moderator (1949)
Meet Your Congress (pub aff)
.... moderator (1953–54)

A former U.S. senator from Michigan.

MOODY, KING—actor

Get Smart (com) .... Starker (1966–69)

MOODY, LYNNE—black actress
b: Detroit, Mich. r: Evanston, Ill.

That's My Mama (com)
.... Tracy Curtis Taylor (1974–75)
Roots (drama)................ Irene (1977)
Roots: The Next Generations (drama)
.... Irene Harvey (1979)
Soap (com) .... Polly Dawson (1979–81)
E/R (com) .. Nurse Julie Williams (1984–85)

MOODY, RON—actor
b: Jan 8, 1924, London, England

Nobody's Perfect (com)
.... Det. Insp. Roger Hart (1980)

A mournful-looking British comic actor; he played Fagin in both the stage and screen versions of *Oliver!* in the '60s.

MOON, GEORGINA—actress

The Liberace Show (var)..... regular (1969)

MOONEY, ART—orchestra leader
b: Lowell, Mass.

Let's Dance (music) .... orch. leader (1954)

MOONEY, PAUL—actor

The Richard Pryor Show (var)
.... regular (1977)

MOORE, ALVY—actor, producer
b: 1925

Green Acres (com)
.... Hank Kimball (1965–71)

MOORE, BARBARA—actress
b: Jan 29, Wardell, Mo.

The Man from U.N.C.L.E. (drama)
.... Lisa Rogers (1967–68)

MOORE, CANDY—juvenile actress

The Lucy Show (com)
.... Chris Carmichael (1962–65)

MOORE, CHARLOTTE—actress
b: Jul 7, Herin, Ill.

The News Is the News (var) . regular (1983)

MOORE, CLAYTON—actor
b: Sep 14, 1908*, Chicago, Ill.

The Lone Ranger (wes)
.... the Lone Ranger (1949–52)
The Lone Ranger (wes)
.... the Lone Ranger (1954–57)

Seldom has any actor been so thoroughly, or willingly, identified with a single role as has Clayton Moore. Could he ever have played anyone other than the masked rider of the plains, the Lone Ranger? He did, in fact, in a long string of westerns during the 1940s and early '50s, two of them costar-

*Some sources give 1914.

ring his TV Tonto, Jay Silverheels, in another role (*The Cowboy and the Indians,* 1949, *Black Dakota,* 1954). In some of them he was even a villain. On television, however, Moore was always the Lone Ranger; he rarely appeared as anyone else. For years after the famous series ended, he appeared in costume and mask, in commercials and personal appearances, always preaching the Ranger's code of good behavior to his young fans.

Then, in 1980, the mean and nasty owners of the Lone Ranger copyrights did what none of his screen villains could do: they stripped him of the mask—by court order (they wanted another, younger actor to play the Ranger in an upcoming movie). The Ranger fought back, fair and square, as only he could, by donning wraparound sunglasses that *looked* like a mask and gaining a great deal of sympathetic publicity. Finally, the lawyers relented. The Lone Ranger rides again!

A former circus performer and male model, Moore originally entered films in 1938 as a stuntman and bit player. By the early '40s he was playing leads in B films and serials. His last original film (aside from reissues of earlier material) was *The Lone Ranger and the Lost City of Gold* in 1958.

MOORE, CONSTANCE—actress
b: Jan 18, 1920*, Sioux City, Iowa

Window on Main Street (com)
.... Chris Logan (1961–62)

MOORE, DEL—actor, announcer
b: 1917 d: Aug 30, 1970

Life with Elizabeth (com) .. Alvin (1953–55)
The Betty White Show (var) . regular (1958)
Bachelor Father (com)
.... Cal Mitchell (1960–62)
The Jerry Lewis Show (talk)
.... announcer (1963)

MOORE, GARRY—host
b: Jan 31, 1915, Baltimore, Md.

The Garry Moore Show (var)
.... host (1950–51)
I've Got a Secret (quiz)
.... moderator (1952–64)
The Garry Moore Show (var)
.... host (1958–64)

*Some sources give 1919 or 1922.

The Garry Moore Show (var)
.... host (1966–67)
To Tell the Truth (quiz).... emcee (1969–76)

One of the friendliest television emcees of the '50s and early '60s was surely Garry Moore, an amiable little fellow with a bow tie and trademark crew cut (they were popular then). Born Thomas Garrison Morfit, he had been in network radio since 1939 on a succession of shows. One of his early stunts was an on-air contest to find a new name for himself. "Clapbridge Kelly" and "John Sebastian Potts" were among the entries, but he finally decided to adopt the more conservative suggestion of a Pittsburgh woman—Garry Moore.

Garry entered television in 1950 with a popular daytime show that lasted for eight years. He also tried prime time in 1950, but found a better niche as host of the long-running panel show *I've Got a Secret.* In 1958 he dropped his daytime show and tried another variety series in the evening, and this time he struck gold. His Tuesday-night hour, featuring such regulars as Carol Burnett, "Candid Camera" man Allen Funt and sidekick Durward Kirby, became an anchor of the CBS schedule.

In 1964, exhausted after 14 continuous years on-camera (sometimes with two shows), Garry temporarily retired. A "comeback" variety series in 1966 was not successful, but he did have another long run as host of the syndicated version of *To Tell the Truth* in the '70s. Amiability, it seems, wears well.

MOORE, IDA—actress
b: 1883, Altoona, Kan. d: 1964

The RCA Victor Show (com)
.... Lavinia (1953–54)

MOORE, MARY TYLER—actress
b: Dec 29, 1936, Brooklyn, N.Y.

Richard Diamond, Private Detective (drama)
.... "Sam" (1959)
The Dick Van Dyke Show (com)
.... Laura Petrie (1961–66)
The Mary Tyler Moore Show (com)
.... Mary Richards (1970–77)
Mary (var)................. hostess (1978)
The Mary Tyler Moore Hour (var)
.... Mary McKinnon (1979)
Mary (com)....... Mary Brenner (1985–86)

598

Emmy Awards: Best Actress in a Series, for *The Dick Van Dyke Show* (1964, 1966); Best Actress in a Comedy Series, for *The Mary Tyler Moore Show* (1973, 1974, 1976); Series Actress of the Year (1974)

Mary Tyler Moore must be counted, along with Lucille Ball and Carol Burnett, as one of the great comediennes of American television. She is quite different from those other two raucous clowns, however; doll-like and a little distant, projecting a kind of determined innocence that was captured most perfectly in her famous role as a single career woman on *The Mary Tyler Moore Show*.

Mary's career needed determination; it has had its ups and downs. She began as a dancer and got her first TV break as a teenager in commercials, notably as the elf in Happy Hotpoint dancing on Hotpoint appliances. That was in the mid-1950s. She began to get small roles in series, including *Bachelor Father* and *Steve Canyon* in 1958, and in early 1959 landed her first continuing role on the David Janssen detective series, *Richard Diamond*. Unfortunately, the part called for only her legs to be seen, as she played the sexy switchboard operator for Diamond's answering service. Mary was so disappointed that she quit the series after only three months.

More guest roles followed, including several on *Hawaiian Eye,* before Mary began the role that made her famous, that of Dick Van Dyke's TV wife. The series was a traditional family sitcom in format (mom, dad, cute kid, kooky friends) but so well-written and cast that it has become one of TV's all-time classics. Following such a stunning success, Mary, it seemed, could go nowhere but down. First she set out to conquer Broadway as Holly Golightly in *Breakfast at Tiffany's;* it was a dreadful flop. A few months later her first major motion picture, *Thoroughly Modern Millie* (with Julie Andrews), was released and it, too, was a disappointment. She appeared in a few more films, including *Change of Habit* with Elvis Presley (an embarrassment even to him), but by 1969 she seemed to be rapidly becoming a show biz has-been.

In early 1969 Mary was reunited with Dick Van Dyke in a prime time special which did quite well, renewing interest in her. CBS gave her free rein to do a new series, and the result was one of the most superbly written and excellently cast series in television history, *The Mary Tyler Moore Show*. It had a theme whose time had come—the distinctly nontraditional (at least for TV) premise of a single career woman making it on her own. Seven glorious years and multiple Emmys followed, after which Mary could once again write her own ticket. She did, but this time the results—two ill-conceived song-and-dance shows during a single season—were critical and audience disasters.

Mary salvaged some esteem by turning to drama in two acclaimed films, the 1978 TV movie *First You Cry* (as newswoman Betty Rollin fighting cancer) and the 1980 theatrical blockbuster *Ordinary People.* She finally scored a triumph on Broadway as well, winning a Special Tony Award for *Whose Life Is It Anyway* in 1980. Ironically, her attempts to make a television comeback proved less successful. A new series in 1985, which looked suspiciously like the old *Mary Tyler Moore Show* in a new setting, was a bust.

MOORE, MELBA—black singer, actress
b: Oct 27, 1945, New York City, N.Y.

The Melba Moore-Clifton Davis Show (var)
.... cohost (1972)
Melba (com) .... Melba Patterson (1986)

MOORE, MONICA—

Front Row Center (var) ... regular (1949–50)

MOORE, ROBERT—actor, director
b: Aug 17, 1927, Detroit, Mich. d: May 10, 1984

Diana (com) ...... Marshall Tyler (1973–74)

One of Broadway's most successful directors in the '70s and '80s *(Promises, Promises; Deathtrap; Woman of the Year).* Earlier, he was primarily a stage actor.

MOORE, ROGER—actor
b: Oct 14, 1927*, London, England

Ivanhoe (adv) .... Ivanhoe (1957–58)
The Alaskans (adv) . Silky Harris (1959–60)
Maverick (wes)
... Cousin Beauregard Maverick (1960–61)

*Some sources give 1928.

The Saint (adv) .. Simon Templar (1967–69)
The Persuaders (adv)
.... Lord Brett Sinclair (1971–72)

"He likes good food, good drink, good clothes. He gambles. He likes women who are essentially feminine. His athletic prowess goes without saying . . ." That description, from a press release, sums up one of Roger Moore's suave, manly heroes. But which one? It could be any of them, from *Ivanhoe* in the '50s to James Bond in movies of the '80s. Moore consistently seems to play the same character, in various guises and historical periods, on both film and TV.

Roger began acting in films in England as a teenager, then immigrated to the U.S. when he was in his midtwenties. From the mid-1950s on he was seen in TV series produced on both sides of the Atlantic, including the British produced *Ivanhoe*, *The Saint*, and *The Persuaders* and the U.S. originated *Maverick* and *Alaskans*. He was elegant in all of these, and also in the famous movie role that he assumed in 1972 —James Bond. He has not been seen much on television since then, though he did appear in the 1976 TV spoof *Sherlock Holmes in New York* with Patrick Macnee, another ex–TV secret agent, as his Dr. Watson.

By the way, it was *The Saint* that was being described above, although it could just as easily have been Silky, Beauregard, Lord Brett, or Mr. Bond.

MOORE, TERRY—actress
b: Jan 7, 1929, Los Angeles, Calif.

Empire (wes) .. Constance Garret (1962–63)

MOORE, TIM—black actor
b: 1888, Rock Island, Ill. d: Dec 13, 1958

Amos 'n' Andy (com)
..... George "Kingfish" Stevens (1951–53)

The large, blustering black comic who was the centerpiece of the TV *Amos 'n' Andy* series, as the conniving Kingfish. More than any of the other characters, he gave the series its reputation for racial stereotyping with his portrayal of a lazy, untrustworthy, none-too-bright schemer ("Holy mack'rel, Andy, we is in big trouble now!"). Tim's background was in black vaudeville, where his specialty had

been—of all things—a comic black Scotsman in kilts.

MOORE, TOM—host, actor
b: 1883, County Meath, Ireland d: Feb 12, 1955

Ladies Be Seated (quiz)....... emcee (1949)
Majority Rules (quiz) ...... emcee (1949–50)

MOORE, WALLY—banjo player
Polka Time (music)....... regular (1956–57)

MOOREHEAD, AGNES—actress
b: Dec 6, 1906, Clinton, Mass. d: Apr 30, 1974

Bewitched (com) .... Endora (1964–72)

Emmy Award: Best Supporting Actress in an Episode of a Dramatic Series, for *The Wild Wild West* (1967)

A famous character actress who appeared often in television dramas, from the '50s until the year of her death. She generally played an old and rather acerbic woman; she was delightful, though, as Elizabeth Montgomery's batty mother, a witch, on *Bewitched*.

MORA, DANNY—actor
Please Stand By (com)
.... Dennis "Crash" Lopez (1978–79)
Star of the Family (com)....... Max (1982)

MORAN, ERIN—actress
b: Oct 18, 1961, Burbank, Calif.

Daktari (adv) .... Jenny Jones (1968–69)
The Don Rickles Show (com)
.... Janie Robinson (1972)
Happy Days (com)
.... Joanie Cunningham (1974–84)
Joanie Loves Chachi (com)
.... Joanie Cunningham (1982–83)

Cute and bubbly Erin Moran is one of those young performers who can legitimately claim to have grown up in front of the cameras. She was making commercials at the age of six, and had her first regular role, as a little orphan named Jenny, at seven during the last season of *Daktari*.

Many more winsome-tyke roles followed, in series as varied as *My Three Sons* and *Death Valley Days*. She was also Don Rickles' daughter (talk about handling stress!) on his series in early 1972. However, it was her supporting role in the dramatic TV movie *Lisa, Bright and Dark* in 1973 that caught the attention of Anson Williams, who got her an audition for the part of little sister Joanie on *Happy Days*. That role was a young girl's dream come true; a happy, loving cast, a TV mom (Marion Ross) and brother (Ron Howard) with whom she was close, and the chance to flirt with the Fonz! Eventually Erin got her own TV boyfriend, Scott Baio, and co-starred with him in an unsuccessful spin-off called *Joanie Loves Chachi*—which was built around their attempts to launch singing careers.

Erin's real family, which was close-knit, encouraged her all the way. "Not everyone has the good fortune of growing up with two loving and caring families," she says. "I'm glad I did."

MORAN, JIM—

What's in a Word? (quiz) ... panelist (1954)

MORAN, LOIS—actress
b: Mar 1, 1907, Pittsburgh, Pa.

Waterfront (adv)
.... May (Mom) Herrick (1953–56)

MORANIS, RICK—comedian
b: Apr 18, Toronto, Canada

Second City TV (com)
.... Rabbi Karlov, others (1980–81)
SCTV Network 90 (com)
.... regular (1981–82)

Emmy Award: Best Writing for a Comedy Program, for *SCTV Network 90* (1982)

MORDENTE, LISA—actress
b: Jul 30, New Hyde Park, N.Y.

Doc (com) .... Teresa Ortega (1976)
Viva Valdez (com) ... Connie Valdez (1976)

MORDENTE, TONY, DANCERS—

The Jimmy Dean Show (var)
.... dancers (1965–66)
The Jim Nabors Hour (var)
.... dancers (1969–71)

The Sonny and Cher Comedy Hour (var)
.... dancers (1971–74)
The Burns and Schreiber Comedy Hour (var)
.... dancers (1973)
The Mac Davis Show (var)
.... dancers (1974–75)

MORECAMBE, ERIC—comedian
b: May 14, 1926, England d: May 29, 1984

The Piccadilly Palace (var) .. cohost (1967)

Half of the British comedy team of Morecambe and (Ernie) Wise. They had been performing together since 1941, but gained their greatest popularity on television in the '60s.

MORENO, RITA—actress
b: Dec 11, 1931, Humacao, Puerto Rico

9 to 5 (com)..... Violet Newstead (1982–83)

Emmy Awards: Best Supporting Actress in an Appearance on a Variety Show, for *The Muppet Show* (1977); Best Actress in an Appearance on a Dramatic Show, for *The Rockford Files* (1978)

A fiery, energetic Latin actress who is a showstopper wherever she appears. Though primarily a stage performer (since the mid-1940s), she has made guest appearances in television dramas since the early '50s, and was a regular in the '70s on the acclaimed PBS children's series *The Electric Company*. She is one of the few entertainers who has won all of show business's "Big Four" awards: an Oscar for *West Side Story*, a Tony for *The Ritz*, a Grammy for the music from *The Electric Company*, and two Emmys.

MOREY, BILL—actor
b: Dec 13, Framingham, Mass.

Tucker's Witch (drama)
.... Lt. Sean Fisk (1982–83)
The Thorn Birds (drama)
.... Angus MacQueen (1983)

MORGAN BROTHERS, THE—singers

The Jaye P. Morgan Show (music)
.... quartet (1956)

Jaye P. Morgan's real-life brothers (Bob, Charlie, Dick, and Duke), once part of the

601

family stage act and later featured on her television series.

MORGAN, AL—singer, pianist

Al Morgan (music) .... host (1949–51)

MORGAN, CINDY—actress
b: Sep 29, Chicago, Ill.

Bring 'Em Back Alive (adv)
.... Gloria Marlowe (1982–83)

MORGAN, DEBBI—black actress
b: Sep 20, Dunn, N.C.

Roots: The Next Generations (drama)
.... Elizabeth Harvey (1979)
Behind the Screen (drama)
.... Lynette Porter (1981–82)

MORGAN, DENNIS—actor
b: Dec 10, 1910*, Prentice, Wis.

21 Beacon Street (drama)
.... Dennis Chase (1959)

Handsome singer-actor in movies during the '40s, and on television occasionally in the '50s. His one series was a summer replacement detective show in 1959. He remained mostly retired after that, devoting much of his time to the American Cancer Society and to singing in his church choir. Though seldom seen on screen after 1963, he did turn up once on *The Love Boat*, in 1980.

MORGAN, EDWARD P.—newscaster

CBS Weekend News (news)
.... anchorman (1951)
Chronoscope (int) .... moderator (1953)

Newsman prominent in the '50s and '60s, known as "The Voice of Labor" for his regular radio-commentary show sponsored by the AFL-CIO. In the late '60s he was senior correspondent for the Public Broadcast *Laboratory* series on PBS. He retired in 1975.

MORGAN, GEORGE—actor

*M*A*S*H* (com)
.. Father John Mulcahy (pilot only) (1972)
*Some sources give Dec 20 or Dec 30.

MORGAN, HALLIE—juvenile actress

Sara (wes).......... Emma Higgins (1976)

MORGAN, HARRY—actor
b: Apr 10, 1915, Detroit, Mich.

December Bride (com)
.... Pete Porter (1954–59)
Pete and Gladys (com)
.... Pete Porter (1960–62)
The Richard Boone Show (drama)
.... regular (1963–64)
Kentucky Jones (drama)
.... Seldom Jackson (1964–65)
Dragnet (police). Off. Bill Gannon (1967–70)
The D.A. (drama)
.... Chief Dep. D.A. "Staff" Stafford (1971–72)
Hec Ramsey (wes)
.... Doc. Amos Coogan (1972–74)
*M*A*S*H* (com)
.... Col. Sherman Potter (1975–83)
Backstairs at the White House (drama)
.... Pres. Harry S. Truman (1979)
Roots: The Next Generations (drama)
.... Bob Campbell (1979)
AfterMASH (com)
.... Dr. Sherman Potter (1983–84)
Blacke's Magic (drama)
.... Leonard Blacke (1986)

Emmy Award: Best Supporting Actor, for *M*A*S*H* (1980)

This diminutive actor has proven quite popular over the years in roles calling for a touch of sardonic humor. He began acting in movies in 1942 (he was the wisecracking soda jerk in *Orchestra Wives*, starring the Glenn Miller Orchestra, that year) and played many character parts before he moved into television in the mid-1950s. Since then he has had major roles in more different series—ten, up to 1985—than perhaps anyone in TV history. He also has the unique distinction of twice having been spun off from one hit series into another series of his own.

Harry's initial TV venture was the very popular '50s comedy *December Bride*, in which he played Spring Byington's next-door neighbor Pete. Pete was constantly complaining about his wife Gladys, who was never seen until she appeared in the spin-off series, *Pete and Gladys*, in 1960; this was, in fact, the first comedy spin-off ever attempted on TV. Harry was seen in a succession of other series after that, including a three-year run as Jack Webb's partner on *Dragnet* and guest appearances on series as varied as *Gunsmoke* (several times) and *The Partridge Family*. In 1974 he played a memorable onetime role in a *M*A*S*H* episode called "The General Flipped at Dawn." This led to his joining the cast the following year as Col. Sherman Potter. After the long run of *M*A*S*H*, Harry starred in another spin-off, *AfterMASH*, in which he was united with still another previously unseen wife, Mildred.

Harry originally studied to become a lawyer, a vocation which two of his sons have followed. Another son, Chris, is a successful TV producer (*Police Story*, *Quincy, M.E.*, etc.). Prior to entering television, Harry was known in films under the name Henry Morgan, but he changed his billing to avoid confusion with the well-known comedian (see below).

MORGAN, HENRY—comedian
b: Mar 31, 1915, New York City, N.Y.

On the Corner (var) .... host (1948)
Henry Morgan's Great Talent Hunt (var)
.... host (1951)
Draw to Win (quiz).......... emcee (1952)
I've Got a Secret (quiz) .. panelist (1952–67)
That Was the Week That Was (com)
.... regular (1964)
My World and Welcome to It (com)
.... Philip Jensen (1969–70)
I've Got a Secret (quiz) ..... panelist (1976)

Henry Morgan, "the bad boy of radio," earned his nickname in the '40s by hurling sarcastic barbs at practically every hallowed institution of broadcasting. A weather report might be delivered straightforwardly as "snow tomorrow, followed by small boys on sleds, followed by dignified old men getting conked on the bean by small boys on sleds following snow." Sponsors were mercilessly drubbed. Shoes might be described in terms of how much chewing gum had been scraped off their soles; Life Savers were derided for cheating consumers by leaving holes in their middle. Many an outraged advertiser canceled its ads in his show, but others were always waiting to get in.

Henry's vitriolic humor went over less well on television. He hosted a couple of early and short-lived variety shows, including *On the Corner*, which is said to have been ABC's first network series. It was canceled after 13 weeks by an unamused Admiral Corporation. His *Great Talent Hunt* was an early version of *The Gong Show*, with ludicrous "talent" competing. Henry became better-known as a sarcastic panelist for many years on *I've Got a Secret*. Later, he was heard mostly on radio.

MORGAN, JANE—actress
b: 1880 d: Jan 1, 1972

Our Miss Brooks (com)
.... Mrs. Margaret Davis (1952–56)

MORGAN, JAYE P.—singer, panelist
b: Dec 3, 1931, Mancos, Colo.

Stop the Music (quiz)
.... vocalist (1954–55)
The Jaye P. Morgan Show (music)
.... hostess (1956)
Perry Presents (var) .... regular (1959)
The Gong Show (com) ... panelist (1976–80)
The Chuck Barris Rah Rah Show (var)
.... regular (1978)
The $1.98 Beauty Show (com)
.... frequent panelist (1978–80)

A husky-voiced singer who was popular in the '50s, with record hits including "The Longest Walk" and "That's All I Want from You." A former vocalist with the Frank DeVol Orchestra (at age 18), she appeared as a regular on a number of TV programs, including Robert Q. Lewis's daytime series, and had her own summer show in 1956. After years of obscurity she re-emerged in the '70s as a fun-loving comedy game-show panelist.

MORGAN, MARION—singer
b: Dec 14, 1924

Stop the Music (quiz).... vocalist (1950–51)

MORGAN, MICHAEL—juvenile actor

Sons and Daughters (drama)
.... Danny Reed (1974)
Rich Man, Poor Man—Book I (drama)
.... Wesley (1976)

MORGAN, NANCY—actress

The San Pedro Beach Bums (com)
.... Julie (1977)

MORGAN, RAY—host, announcer
d: Jan 5, 1975

I'd Like to See (info)........ host (1948–49)
American Inventory (pub aff)
.... host (1951–52)

MORGAN, READ—actor

The Deputy (wes)
.... Sgt. Hapgood Tasker (1960–61)

MORGAN, ROBIN—juvenile actress
b: Jan 29, 1942, Lake Worth, Fla.

Mama (com) .... Dagmar (1950–56)

MORGAN, RUSS—orchestra leader, songwriter
b: Apr 29, 1904, Scranton, Pa. d: Aug 7, 1969

Welcome Aboard (var)
.... host/orch. leader (1948)
In the Morgan Manner (var)
.... host/orch. leader (1950)
The Russ Morgan Show (music)
.... host (1956)

The '40s bandleader/songwriter who wrote "Somebody Else Is Taking My Place," "You're Nobody Till Somebody Loves You" and other hits. His slogan was "Music in the Morgan Manner." He appeared on numerous TV shows in the '50s, representing a brand of sedate, conventional music that rapidly passed from favor.

MORGAN, SEAN—actor

The Adventures of Ozzie & Harriet (com)
.... Sean (1965–66)

MORGAN, TERENCE—actor
b: Dec 8, 1921, London, England

The Adventures of Sir Francis Drake (adv)
.... Sir Francis Drake (1962)

MORGAN, WESLEY—juvenile actor

The Life of Riley (com)
.... Junior (1953–58)

MORIARTY, MICHAEL—actor
b: Apr 5, 1941, Detroit, Mich.

Holocaust (drama) .... Erik Dorf (1978)

Emmy Awards: Best Supporting Actor in a Drama, for "The Glass Menagerie" (1974); Supporting Actor of the Year (1974); Best Actor in a Limited Series, for *Holocaust* (1978)

An intense, versatile actor, active primarily on the stage; despite his awards he has not become a major star in either films or TV.

MORICK, DAVE—actor

The Queen and I (com)
.... Max Kowalski (1969)

MORIN, ALBERTO—actor
b: Nov 26, 1902*, Puerto Rico

Dallas (drama).. Armando Sidoni (1983–84)

MORITA, PAT—actor
b: 1930, California

The Queen and I (com) ...... Barney (1969)
Sanford and Son (com)
.... Ah Chew (1974–75)
Happy Days (com)
.... Arnold (Matsuo Takahashi) (1975–76)
Mr. T and Tina (com)
.... Taro Takahashi ("Mr. T") (1976)
Blansky's Beauties (com) .... Arnold (1977)
Happy Days (com) .... Arnold (1982–83)

Interned in the U.S. as a youth during World War II, Pat later drifted through several jobs before becoming a comedian and actor in TV commercials. He has been appearing in series and series episodes since the '60s, including multiple appearances on *M*A*S*H, Sanford and Son,* and *The Love Boat.*

MORRILL, PRISCILLA—actress
b: Jun 4, Medford, Mass.

The Mary Tyler Moore Show (com)
.... Edie Grant (1973–74)
A Year at the Top (com)
.... Miss Worley (1977)
In the Beginning (com).. Sister Lillian (1978)
Dorothy (com) ...... Lorna Cathcart (1979)
*Some sources give 1912.

Bret Maverick (wes)
.... Mrs. Springer (1981–82)
Baby Makes Five (com)
.... Edna Kearney (1983)

MORRIS, ANITA—actress

Berrengers (drama).. Babs Berrenger (1985)

MORRIS, CHESTER—actor
b: Feb 16, 1901, New York City, N.Y. d: Sep 11, 1970

Diagnosis: Unknown (drama)
.... Det. Capt. Max Ritter (1960)

The movie's (but not TV's) Boston Blackie. Morris was practically a 1940s B movie stereotype, with his slicked-down hair and jut-jaw. He did appear frequently on television during the '50s and early '60s, on *Studio One, The Defenders,* and other dramas. On *Diagnosis: Unknown* he played the supporting role of the hero's police contact. Ill during his last years, he died of an overdose of medication.

MORRIS, GARRETT—black comedian
b: Feb 1, 1937, New Orleans, La.

Roll Out (com)........ "Wheels" (1973–74)
NBC's Saturday Night Live (com)
.... regular (1975–80)
It's Your Move (com)
.... Principal Dwight Ellis (1984–85)

Garrett Morris was a 38-year-old show business veteran when he joined the cast of NBC's youth-oriented *Saturday Night Live* in 1975. He was originally trained as a singer and had studied at the Juilliard School of Music and other leading schools; for a time he was a singer and arranger for the Harry Belafonte Folk Singers, appearing with them on tour and on television.

During the 1960s Garrett played supporting roles in several Broadway plays. He also did some television work, including a regular part in the 1973 black series *Roll Out,* before gaining his greatest fame as one of the "Not Ready for Prime Time Players" on *SNL.*

MORRIS, GARY—actor

Dynasty II: The Colbys (drama)
.... Wayne Masterson (1986–)

MORRIS, GREG—black actor
b: Sep 27, 1934, Cleveland, Ohio

Mission: Impossible (drama)
.... Barney Collier (1966–73)
Vega$ (drama) .. Lt. David Nelson (1979–81)

Handsome Greg Morris was one of the first black actors to star in a major hit series during the '60s, shortly after Bill Cosby paved the way in *I Spy.* He came to Hollywood in the early '60s, after some minor stage experience in Seattle, and had small guest roles in such series as *Dr. Kildare, The Dick Van Dyke Show* (as one of Dick's Army buddies), and *The Twilight Zone,* all during 1963–65. Then he was cast as the quiet, efficient electronics expert on *Mission: Impossible,* and overnight he became one of the most famous black actors in America.

The exposure brought Greg work in a steady stream of series episodes and TV movies during the following years, although he never seemed to rise above the ranks of supporting actor. Among his roles have been those of Robert Urich's police contact on *Vega$,* a passenger (twice) on *The Love Boat,* and a small part in the *Roots* sequel.

MORRIS, HOWARD—actor, director
b: Sep 4, 1919, New York City, N.Y.

Your Show of Shows (var)
.... regular (1951–54)
Caesar's Hour (var)
.... Fred Brewster (1954–57)
The Jetsons (cartn) . various roles (1962–63)
The Famous Adventures of Mr. Magoo (cartn)
.... voices (1964–65)

Howard Morris, the little guy who was part of so many sight gags on *Your Show of Shows,* has proven to be quite versatile as an actor, writer, and director. His first experience was onstage in the '40s, and he moved naturally into early, live TV—as did many New York actors of the period. On Sid Caesar's shows he was both a writer and an on-camera sidekick, following big Sid around like a yelping puppy and participating in scores of memorable skits (remember "The Haircuts," the parody rock 'n' roll trio with their towering pompadours—Morris, Caesar, and Carl Reiner?).

In the '60s and later, Howard turned to directing and was quite successful both on television *(The Andy Griffith Show, Get Smart)* and in films *(With Six You Get Eggroll)*. He also did voices for many TV cartoons and acted occasionally in comedies, including *The Dick Van Dyke Show, The Danny Thomas Show,* and *The Bob Newhart Show.* Unfortunately, there never was a *Howard Morris Show.* In 1981 he was reunited with Sid Caesar in the TV movie *The Munsters' Revenge* (in which Sid played a mad professor and Howard his henchman). Howard has in recent years concentrated on the lucrative field of directing TV commercials.

MORRIS, WOLFE—actor

The Six Wives of Henry VIII (drama)
.... Oliver Cromwell (1971)

MORRISON, BRIAN—juvenile actor

Maude (com).............. Phillip (1972–77)

MORRISON, SHELLY—actress
b: c. 1937, The Bronx, N.Y.

The Flying Nun (com)
.... Sister Sixto (1967–70)

MORRISS, ANN—actress

The Brothers (com)
.... Dr. Margaret Kleeb (1956–57)

MORROW, BUDDY—orchestra leader
b: Feb 8, 1919, New Haven, Conn.

The Jimmie Rodgers Show (var)
.... orch. leader (1959)

MORROW, BYRON—actor
b: Sep 8, Chicago, Ill.

The New Breed (police)
.... Capt. Keith Gregory (1961–62)
Executive Suite (drama)
.... Pearce Newberry (1976–77)
The Winds of War (drama)
.... Adm. Preble (1983)

MORROW, DON—announcer, host
b: Stamford, Conn.

Martin Kane, Private Eye (drama)
.... as himself (1954)

MORROW, JEFF—actor
b: Jan 13, 1913*, New York City, N.Y.

Union Pacific (wes)
.... Bart McClelland (1958–59)
Temperatures Rising (com)
.... Dr. Lloyd Axton (1973–74)

MORROW, KAREN—actress
b: Dec 15, Chicago, Ill. r: Des Moines, Iowa

The Jim Nabors Hour (var)
.... regular (1969–71)
Tabitha (com)..... Aunt Minerva (1977–78)
Friends (com). Mrs. Pamela Richards (1979)
Ladies' Man (com) .... Betty Brill (1980–81)

MORROW, PATRICIA—actress
b: c. 1943

I Led Three Lives (drama)
Constance Philbrick (occasional) (1953–56)
Peyton Place (drama)
.... Rita Jacks/Harrington (1965–69)

Patricia later gave up acting and became a lawyer.

MORROW, VIC—actor, director
b: Feb 14, 1932**, The Bronx, N.Y. d: Jul 23, 1982

Combat (drama)
.... Sgt. Chip Saunders (1962–67)
Captains and the Kings (drama)
.... Tom Hennessey (1976)
Roots (drama)............... Ames (1977)
B.A.D. Cats (police)
.... Capt. Eugene Nathan (1980)

To his dismay, Vic Morrow was typecast early in his career as a young tough. The pattern was set by his first film, *The Blackboard Jungle* (1955), in which he played one of the surly students. Similar movie roles followed in the late '50s, and by 1960 Vic was looking for a way out; he turned to directing and to television—which often makes heroes out of screen villains. On a 1960 episode of *Bonanza* he helped rescue Ben and Adam Cartwright from a lynch mob, not a bad start in endearing himself to TV viewers. Two years later he starred in his most famous role—still tough, but at least sympathetic—Sgt. Chip Sanders in the wartime adventure *Combat.*

*Some sources give 1917.
**Some sources give 1931.

Vic appeared in many series episodes and TV movies during the '70s and '80s; among his TV films were Truman Capote's *The Glass House, Tom Sawyer* (as Injun Joe), and *The Night That Panicked America*. Later, he began to appeared further down the cast list, in smaller supporting roles (e.g., in *Roots*). Vic Morrow was killed in a freak on-set accident during the filming of the movie *The Twilight Zone* in 1982.

MORSE, BARRY—actor
b: 1919, London, England

The Fugitive (drama)
.... Lt. Philip Gerard (1963–67)
The Adventurer (drama)
.... Parminter (1972–73)
Space 1999 (sci fi)
.... Prof. Victor Bergman (1975–76)
The Winds of War (drama)
.... Wolf Stoller (1983)
Master of the Game (drama)
.... Dr. Harley (1984)

MORSE, DAVID—actor
b: Oct 11, 1953, Beverly, Mass.

St. Elsewhere (drama)
.... Dr. Jack Morrison (1982–)

A youthful, curly-haired actor who was on-stage throughout the '70s, in Boston and later New York. His first major TV break was on *St. Elsewhere,* although he has also appeared in a few TV movies—notably in *Prototypes* (1983) as a cute-looking Frankenstein monster being reprogrammed for destructive purposes.

MORSE, ROBERT—actor
b: May 18, 1931, Newton, Mass.

That's Life (com). Robert Dickson (1968–69)

A gap-toothed, mischievous-looking comic actor who has appeared on television occasionally since the mid-1950s. Even when he turned up in a drama he usually did so with a twinkle in his eye. In a 1960 episode of *Alfred Hitchcock Presents,* for example, he played a trouble-prone young hitchhiker who gets a motorist stopped for speeding, but then turns the tables by picking the cop's pocket and stealing back the ticket.

Morse's principal career has been on Broadway, where he scored his greatest triumph in the 1961 musical *How to Succeed in Business Without Really Trying*—as the self-absorbed young corporate climber who sings "I Believe in You" to his own reflection in a mirror!

MORTON, BOB—
Wayne King (music)
.... regular (1951–52)

MORTON, GREG—juvenile actor
b: Jan 12, 1973, Milwaukee, Wis.

Scarecrow and Mrs. King (adv)
.... Jamie King (1983–)

MORTON, HOWARD—actor
Gimme a Break (com)
.... Off. Ralph Simpson (1981–86)

MORTON, JOE—black actor
b: Oct 18, 1947, New York City, N.Y.

Grady (com) .... Hal Marshall (1975–76)

MORTON, TOMMY—dancer
The College Bowl (com)
.... regular (1950–51)
Upbeat (music)............. dancers (1955)

MOSCHITTA, JOHN—comedian
The Half Hour Comedy Hour (var)
.... regular (1983)
Zorro and Son (com)
.... Corporal Cassette (1983)

One of television's novelty acts; a small, mousy man whose chief talent is his ability to talk incredibly fast. He became briefly famous via his appearances in commercials during the early '80s.

MOSES, DAVID—actor
The New People (drama)
.... Gene Washington (1969–70)

MOSES, RICK—actor
b: Sep 5, Washington, D.C. r: Calif.

Young Dan'l Boone (adv)
.... Daniel Boone (1977)

MOSES, WILLIAM R.—actor
b: Nov 17, 1959, Los Angeles, Calif.

Falcon Crest (drama)
.... Cole Gioberti (1981–   )

Rick and William Moses are brothers.

MOSLEY, ROGER E.—black actor
r: Los Angeles, Calif.

Roots: The Next Generations (drama)
.... Lee Garnett (1979)
Magnum, P.I. (drama)
.... Theodore Calvin (T.C.) (1980–   )

Tom Selleck's pal on *Magnum, P.I.* is a product of the Watts ghetto of Los Angeles, and remains active in community affairs there. Among other things, he founded the Watts Repertory Company in 1974. His social concern has not prevented him from enjoying the fruits of stardom, however; he lives in Beverly Hills and drives to the slums in a blue Rolls Royce. "My philosophy," he says, "is the best way to help poor people is not to be one of them."

MOSS, BILL—orchestra leader

The Skip Farrell Show (music)
.... orch. leader (1949)

MOSS, STEWART—actor

Fay (com) ...... Dr. Elliott Baines (1975–76)

MOSSMAN, DOUG—actor

Hawaiian Eye (drama)..... Moke (1960–63)

MOST, DONNY—actor
b: Aug 8, 1953, Brooklyn, N.Y.

Happy Days (com) . Ralph Malph (1974–80)

MOSTEL, JOSHUA—actor
b: Dec 21, 1957, New York City, N.Y.

Delta House (com)
.... Jim "Blotto" Blutarsky (1979)
At Ease (com)............ Maxwell (1983)

The chubby son of the late stage and screen star Zero Mostel, whom he strongly resembles. Once a boy soprano in major operatic productions, Josh has in more recent years played numerous supporting roles on stage, screen, and television. He

was the John Belushi clone in *Delta House,* ABC's rip-off of Belushi's hit movie *Animal House.*

MOTTOLA, TONY—guitarist, host
b: Apr 18, 1918, Kearney, N.J.

Face the Music (music)...... trio (1948–49)
The Cliff Edwards Show (music)
.... trio (1949)
Manhattan Showcase (var)...... trio (1949)
Melody Street (music) .... host (1954)

A familiar and often-featured musician on TV variety shows of the '50s (Perry Como, Sid Caesar); he later spent 12 years in *The Tonight Show* band.

MOULTRIE, EMILY—juvenile actress

Baby Makes Five (com)
.... Laura Riddle (1983)

MOUNTAIN, JOHNNY—host, announcer
b: Middlesboro, Ky.

Eye on Hollywood (mag)
.... correspondent (1983–86)

MOUNTBATTEN, LADY IRIS—hostess, socialite

Versatile Varieties (child) ... hostess (1951)

Royalty on TV: the third cousin of King George VI of Great Britain.

MOWBRAY, ALAN—actor
b: Aug 18, 1896*, London, England d: Mar 25, 1969

Colonel Humphrey Flack (com)
.... Col. Humphrey Flack (1953–54)
The Mickey Rooney Show (com)
.... the drama instructor (1954–55)
Colonel Flack (com)
.... Col. Humphrey Flack (1958)
Dante (adv)....... Stewart Styles (1960–61)

A well-known British character actor of the stiff-upper-lip school, who often played stuffy butlers or distinguished personages (including George Washington). He is estimated to have made between 200 and 400 movies. He was seen on television rather frequently in the '50s, in dramatic produc-

*Some sources give 1893.

608

tions and in his own briefly popular detective series *Colonel Flack*. He turned up less often in the '60s, mainly in comedies, including a couple episodes of *The Flying Nun* in 1968–69.

MOYER, PAUL—host

Eye on Hollywood (mag)........ host (1984)

MOYERS, BILL—newscaster
b: Jun 5, 1934, Hugo, Okla.

Our Times with Bill Moyers (doc)
.... host/correspondent (1983)
The American Parade (pub aff)
.... anchorman (1984)

Emmy Awards: Best News Segments, for "A Question of Impeachment" (1974), interview with Henry Steele Commager (1974), essay on Watergate (1974), "Battle for South Africa" (writer, 1979), "Our Times" (writer, 1980), interview with Clark Clifford on presidents and power (1981), interview with George Steiner on literature, language, and culture (1981); *A Walk Through the Twentieth Century* segments "Marshall, Texas, Marshall, Texas" (writer, 1984) and "World War II Propaganda Battle" (interviewer, 1985); "Star Wars" (1985), "India Broadcast" (1985), interview with Liz Carpenter (1986), "Africa: Struggle for Survival" (1986); Achievement in Broadcast Journalism (1978)

A thoughtful news commentator who has alternated between CBS, PBS, and government service for 25 years. He began in government during the Kennedy and Johnson administrations, serving as deputy director of the Peace Corps and later White House press secretary (1965–67). He then became publisher of a major New York newspaper, *Newsday,* from 1967–70, before turning to television. His quiet, didactic style has prevented him from becoming a news "superstar," but he is widely respected within the industry. For the record, his tours of duty have been: PBS (1971–76), CBS (1976–79), PBS (1979–81, as host of *Bill Moyers' Journal*), CBS (1981–86), and PBS (since 1987). He sometimes appeared on CBS and PBS simultaneously.

Bill is an ordained minister.

MOYNIHAN, MAURA—comedienne

The New Show (var) .... regular (1984)

MUDD, ROGER—newscaster
b: Feb 9, 1928, Washington, D.C.

CBS Weekend News (Sat) (news)
.... anchorman (1966–73)
CBS Weekend News (Sun) (news)
.... anchorman (1970–71)
NBC Evening News (news)
.... anchorman (1982–83)
1986 (pub aff) .... anchor (1986–)

Emmy Awards: Best News Segments, for "The Shooting of Governor Wallace" (1973), "The Agnew Resignation" (1974), "Watergate: The White House Transcripts" (1974), "The Senate and the Watergate Affair" (1974); Best Interviewer, for *CBS Reports: Teddy* (Kennedy) (1980)

Roger Mudd has been rooted in Washington for his entire life. He began as a local newsman there in the '50s and learned the city well. When he joined CBS in 1961 he was immediately named congressional correspondent and later became the network's chief national affairs (i.e., political) reporter. The first attempt to groom him for the network's top anchor spot was in 1964, when he was teamed with Robert Trout as a temporary replacement for Walter Cronkite. Mudd-Trout, an obvious imitation of NBC's successful Huntley-Brinkley pairing, did not click, however. (Wags around the network suggested he might be tried with Hughes Rudd; then it would be *The Mudd-Rudd Report*).

Roger was nevertheless seen as Uncle Walter's eventual successor, and he served long years as Cronkite's substitute anchor on the *CBS Evening News,* waiting for his chance. When it finally came, in 1980, Dan Rather got the job instead, whereupon Roger quit in disgust and joined NBC. NBC had promised him its anchor position when John Chancellor stepped down; what he got was a co-anchor role with Tom Brokaw, who eventually supplanted him altogether as sole anchor.

These disappointments have not diminished Mudd's contributions to TV news. His lack of interest in broadening his experience to include other areas of news (e.g., international) is what probably cost him the anchor position—he is widely seen as TV's "Mr. Washington, D.C." However, he remains the dean of network reporters in the capital, and a key figure when major news breaks there.

MUIR, GAVIN—actor
b: Sep 8, 1907*, Chicago, Ill. d: May 24, 1972

The Betty Hutton Show (com)
.... Hollister (1959–60)

MULDAUR, DIANA—actress
b: Aug 19, 1943, New York City r: Edgartown, Mass.

The Survivors (drama)...... Belle (1969–70)
McCloud (police).. Chris Coughlin (1970–77)
Born Free (adv) .... Joy Adamson (1974)
The Tony Randall Show (com)
.... Judge Eleanor Hooper (1976–78)
Hizzonner (com) .... Ginny (1979)
Fitz and Bones (com) . Terri Seymour (1981)

Diana is best known for the recurring role of Dennis Weaver's girlfriend on *McCloud*.

MULGREW, KATE—actress
b: Apr 29, 1955, Dubuque, Iowa

Kate Loves a Mystery (drama)
.... Kate Columbo/Callahan (1979)

Kate got her start on television as the original Mary Ryan on the daytime serial *Ryan's Hope*, from 1975–77. Since her short-lived prime time series *Kate Loves a Mystery* (also known as *Kate Columbo*), she has appeared on stage and in occasional TV movies.

MULHALL, JACK—actor
b: Oct 7, 1887**, Wappingers Falls, N.Y. d: Jun 1, 1979

The Ken Murray Show (var)
.... regular (1950–51)

MULHARE, EDWARD—actor
b: Apr 8, 1923, Cork, Ireland

The Ghost and Mrs. Muir (com)
.... Capt. Daniel Gregg (1968–70)
Knight Rider (adv)
.... Devon Miles (1982–86)

*Some sources give 1909.
**Some sources give 1888, 1891 or 1894.

MULHERN, SCOTT—actor

Behind the Screen (drama)
.... Jordan Willow (1981–82)

MULL, MARTIN—actor
b: Aug 18, 1943, Chicago, Ill.

Mary Hartman, Mary Hartman (com)
.... Garth Gimble (1976–77)
Fernwood 2-Night (com)
.... Barth Gimble (1977–78)
Domestic Life (com) ... Martin Crane (1984)

This bland-looking, sandy-haired actor became one of the hip TV comics of the late '70s on the strength of his role as the mock talk show host on *Fernwood 2-Night*. Actually, Martin has been a bit off-center for most of his professional career. Trained as a painter, he went to work instead as a songwriter for Warner Brothers Records in 1968. His first and only "hit" was a song called "A Girl Named Johnny Cash" (an answer, evidently, to Cash's hit "A Boy Named Sue"). Later, in the '70s, he took to recording albums with titles such as "Martin Mull and His Fabulous Furniture in Your Living Room," "Days of Wine and Neuroses," and "Sex and Violins." A single called "Dueling Tubas" actually made the charts in 1973.

Martin's first major acting exposure was on *Mary Hartman, Mary Hartman*, where his character Garth Gimble met an unfortunate end (he impaled himself on an aluminum Christmas tree in the closet). However, Garth's "identical brother" Barth was soon on hand and hosting a mind-numbing talk show called *Fernwood 2-Night*. After that, Martin was much in demand for real talk shows (he even hosted *The Tonight Show*), variety specials and TV movies. In 1984 he tried his hand at producing and starring in his own situation comedy, *Domestic Life*, but it was unsuccessful.

MULLALLY, MEGAN—actress
b: Nov 12, Los Angeles, Calif.

The Ellen Burstyn Show (com)
.... Molly (1986–)

MULLANEY, JACK—actor
b: Sep 18, 1932, Pittsburgh, Pa. d: Jun 27, 1982

The Ann Sothern Show (com)
.... Johnny Wallace (1958–60)

Ensign O'Toole (com)
.... Lt. (jg) Rex St. John (1962–63)
My Living Doll (com)
.... Peter Robinson (1964–65)
It's About Time (com) .... Hector (1966–67)

MULLAVEY, GREG—actor
b: Sep 10, 1939, Buffalo, N.Y.

Mary Hartman, Mary Hartman (com)
.... Tom Hartman (1976–78)
Number 96 (drama)
.... Max Quintzel (1980–81)
Rituals (drama)
.... Eddie Gallagher (1984–85)

Mary Hartman's hapless factory-worker husband on TV. In real life he is married to Meredith MacRae.

MULLEN, SUSAN—actress

The San Pedro Beach Bums (com)
.... Suzi (1977)

MULLIGAN, RICHARD—actor
b: Nov 13, 1932, The Bronx, N.Y.

The Hero (com) ..... Sam Garret (1966–67)
Diana (com) .... Jeff Harmon (1973–74)
Soap (com) ...... Burt Campbell (1977–81)
Reggie (com)......... Reggie Potter (1983)

Emmy Award: Best Actor in a Comedy Series, for *Soap* (1980)

Richard Mulligan originally set out to become a playwright but found he had better luck getting acting roles in local stage plays. By the early '60s the lanky actor had gained a foothold in three media: the New York stage (in *Nobody Loves an Albatross*), movies *(One Potato, Two Potato)*, and television (episodes of *The Defenders, Route 66,* etc.). A major break came with his own comedy series in 1966, about a TV cowboy star who was a total klutz off-camera. It was not a hit, however, and for the next ten years Richard settled down to guest roles, plus a short run on a Diana Rigg series. Then *Soap* made him a star. He has since worked rather steadily in series and TV movies, although a new series of his own —*Reggie*—was a flop.

MULLINS, MICHAEL—actor

Studs Lonigan (drama)....... Paulie (1979)

MULLUZZO, RONNIE—juvenile panelist
b: c. 1944

Wisdom of the Ages (info)
.... panelist (1952–53)

MULQUEEN, KATHLEEN—actress

Dennis the Menace (com)
.... Grandma Mitchell (1961)

MUMY, BILLY—juvenile actor
b: 1954

Lost in Space (sci fi)
.... Will Robinson (1965–68)
Sunshine (com)............ Weaver (1975)

MUNI, SCOTT—disc jockey

Friday Night Videos (music)
.... announcer (1985–)

MUNRO, C. PETE—actor

Enos (com) .... Det. Bigalow (1980)

MUNSEL, PATRICE—singer
b: May 14, 1925, Spokane, Wash.

The Patrice Munsel Show (var)
.... hostess (1957–58)

A beautiful Metropolitan Opera diva (she made her debut there at the age of 17) who also appeared occasionally in films, on Broadway, and on television. Among her splashy TV specials in the '50s were productions of *The Merry Widow* and *Naughty Marietta.* In 1969 she played a rare guest-starring role on an episode of *The Wild, Wild West,* as a temperamental opera star who is stalked by the secret and deadly "Order of Lucia"—a group dedicated to kidnapping anyone who sings the "Mad Scene" from that opera one more time!

MUNSON, WARREN—actor

Father Murphy (drama)
.... Dr. Thompson (1981–82)

MURDOCK, GEORGE—actor

No Time for Sergeants (com)
.... Capt. Krupnick (1964–65)
Barney Miller (com).. Lt. Scanlon (1978–82)
The Winds of War (drama)
.... Gen. Fitzgerald (1983)

MURDOCK, JACK—actor

Operation Petticoat (com)
.. chief machinist's Mate Tostin (1977–78)
Flatbush (com) . . . . Det Bosko (1979)

MURDOCK, JAMES—actor

Rawhide (wes) . . . . Mushy (1959–65)

MURNEY, CHRISTOPHER—actor

The San Pedro Beach Bums (com)
. . . . Buddy (1977)

MURPHY, ALMA—

Turn-On (var) . . . . regular (1969)

MURPHY, AUDIE—actor

b: Jun 20, 1924, Kingston, Texas d: May 28, 1971

Whispering Smith (wes)
. . . . . Det. Tom "Whispering" Smith (1961)

This much-decorated World War II hero made his name in action films during the 1950s. He appeared only occasionally on television, in a few dramatic productions (*General Electric Theater, Ford Startime*) and as the star of a short-lived western in 1961. He died in a private-plane crash.

MURPHY, BEN—actor

b: Mar 6, 1941*, Jonesboro, Ark.

The Name of the Game (adv)
. . . . Joe Sample (1968–71)
Alias Smith and Jones (wes)
. . . . . Thaddeus Jones/Kid Curry (1971–73)
Griff (drama)
. . . . S. Michael (Mike) Murdoch (1973–74)
Gemini Man (adv) . . . . Sam Casey (1976)
The Chisholms (wes)
. . . . Will Chisholm (1979–80)
The Winds of War (drama)
. . . . Warren Henry (1983)
Lottery (drama)
. . . . Patrick Sean Flaherty (1983–84)
Berrengers (drama) . . . Paul Berrenger (1985)

Ben Murphy made his film debut shortly after graduation from college with a small part in *The Graduate* in 1967. His principal career has been on television, however. In 1968 he was signed to a contract by Uni-

*Some sources give 1942.

versal Studios and appeared in episodes of several of their series, including *The Virginian, It Takes a Thief,* and *The Name of the Game* (in which he played the recurring part of a young reporter). He has worked steadily in series since that time, usually as star or costar, although none of his shows has become a big enough hit to propel him to major stardom.

MURPHY, BOB—host

b: c. 1917 d: Oct 25, 1959

R.F.D. America (info) . . . . emcee (1949)

MURPHY, EDDIE—black comedian, actor

b: Apr 3, 1961, Brooklyn, N.Y.* r: Roosevelt, N.Y.

NBC's Saturday Night Live (com)
. . . . regular (1981–84)

"It scares me sometimes. I think, hey, this is happening too fast, I'm getting old when I don't have to." Then Eddie Murphy adds, "I'm a cocky kid, too. I know I'm just scratching the surface. I'm going to be a millionaire when I'm 22, maybe sooner."

Eddie Murphy's rise to fame was certainly meteoric, but, unlike many of TV's overnight sensations, he seems to have the talent—and the sense—to make it last. When he auditioned for *Saturday Night Live* in 1980, he was totally unknown, a local kid who had done standup routines in his high school cafeteria and at some small clubs around the New York area. After a year as an occasional player during the 1980–81 season, he joined the *SNL* cast full-time in 1981 and immediately became the star of the show with skits such as "Little Richard Simmons"—a hilarious combination of frenetic rock star Little Richard and exercise guru Richard Simmons.

Much of Eddie's material was pretty raunchy, and would have been overtly racist if performed by a white man (e.g., Little Rascal Buckwheat hawking his unintelligible "Greatest Hits" LP in ghetto dialect). But outrageousness was *SNL*'s, and Eddie's, stock in trade. Eddie soon left the show that made him a star, and television

*Some sources give nearby Hempstead, Long Island, N.Y.

itself, for even greater success (and his first million) in hit movies such as *48 Hours* and *Beverly Hills Cop.*

MURPHY, ERIN AND DIANE—juvenile actresses (Twins)
b: June 1964

Bewitched (com)
. . . . Tabitha Stephens (1966–72)

MURPHY, GEORGE—actor
b: Jul 4, 1902, New Haven, Conn.

MGM Parade (doc) . . . . host (1955–56)

The dapper song-and-dance man of '30s and '40s movie musicals was seen only briefly on TV, as a host and spokesman for MGM. He was very active in Republican politics at the time and later (1964–71) served as a U.S. senator from California. His autobiography: *Say . . . Didn't You Used to Be George Murphy?* (1970).

MURPHY, HARRY—
The Nashville Palace (var)
. . . . regular (1981–82)

MURPHY, MARY—actress
b: 1931, Washington, D.C.

The Investigators (drama)
. . . . Maggie Peters (1961)

MURPHY, MICHAEL—actor
b: May 5, 1949*, Los Angeles, Calif.

Two Marriages (drama)
. . . . Dr. Art Armstrong (1983–84)

MURPHY, PAMELA—actress
Our Private World (drama)
. . . . Franny Martin (1965)

MURPHY, ROSEMARY—actress
b: Jan 13, 1925, Munich, Germany

Lucas Tanner (drama)
. . . . Margaret Blumenthal (1974–75)

Emmy Award: Best Supporting Actress in a Drama Special, for *Eleanor and Franklin* (1976)

*Some sources give 1938.

MURPHY, TIMOTHY PATRICK—actor
b: Nov 3, 1959, Hartford, Conn.

Dallas (drama) . . . . Mickey Trotter (1982–83)
Glitter (drama)
. . . . . . Chester "Chip" Craddock (1984–85)

MURRAY SISTERS—
Hayloft Hoedown (music) . . . . regular (1948)

MURRAY, ARTHUR—host
b: Apr 4, 1895, New York City, N.Y.

The Arthur Murray Party (var)
. . . . regular (1950–60)

The famous dancing instructor, who was immortalized in a 1940s popular song ("Arthur Murray Taught Me Dancing in a Hurry"). He had a long run on television in the '50s, though he said little on the show; his vivacious wife Kathryn did all the talking. She ended each episode with "Till then, to put a little fun in your life, try dancing." Business at their dance studios boomed. In 1964 the couple sold their national chain of 452 studios and retired to Hawaii.

MURRAY, BILL—comedian, actor
b: Sep 21, 1950, Evanston, Ill.

NBC's Saturday Night Live (com)
. . . . regular (1977–80)

Emmy Award: Best Writing for a Comedy Series, for *NBC's Saturday Night Live* (1977)

Another of the hip young stars created by *Saturday Night Live.* Bill had early experience in the Second City comedy troupe and in National Lampoon's productions off-Broadway and on radio. Once he became famous on NBC's late-night comedy showcase he quickly branched into movies, scoring with such youth-oriented hits as *Stripes* and *Ghostbusters.*

MURRAY, DON—actor
b: Jul 31, 1929, Hollywood, Calif.,r: East Rockaway, N.Y.

Made in America (quiz) . . . . . panelist (1964)
The Outcasts (wes) . . . Earl Corey (1968–69)
How the West Was Won (miniseries) (drama)
. . . . Anderson (1977)

Knots Landing (drama)
.... Sid Fairgate (1979–81)

Don began making films in 1948 and appeared on television in the early '50s; his most famous role was opposite Marilyn Monroe in the 1956 movie *Bus Stop.* Don's TV work since the '50s has been sporadic. Known as a highly principled man (he refused military service during the Korean War as a conscientous objector), he in later years turned down scripts that clashed with his social or political beliefs and endorsed others that were in line with his views. *The Outcasts,* for example, was an appeal for racial equality. It is not known how Don stood on the morality of *Knots Landing.*

MURRAY, JAN—host
b: Oct 4, 1917, The Bronx, N.Y.

Songs for Sale (music)..... emcee (1950–51)
Go Lucky (quiz)............. emcee (1951)
Sing It Again (quiz).......... emcee (1951)
Blind Date (aud par)......... emcee (1953)
Dollar a Second (quiz)..... emcee (1953–57)
Jan Murray Time (var)......... host (1955)
Treasure Hunt (quiz) ...... emcee (1956–58)

This handsome game show host was a former stand-up comic. After making his name on TV quiz programs in the '50s, he turned to acting in the '60s but found only a few roles in scattered films and TV series. Among the latter were episodes of *Zane Grey Theater* (his TV acting debut, in 1960), *Burke's Law,* and *The Lucy Show.* He was seen even less often in later years; for example, in a small part in the 1980 miniseries *The Dream Merchants.*

MURRAY, KATHRYN—hostess
b: Sep 15, 1906, Jersey City, N.J.

The Arthur Murray Party (var)
.... hostess (1950–60)

The wife of dancing master Arthur Murray.

MURRAY, KEN—host, comedian, producer
b: Jul 14, 1903, New York City, N.Y.

The Ken Murray Show (var)
.... host (1950–53)
The Judy Garland Show (var)
.... regular (1964)

The crew-cut showman who is chiefly remembered for his candid home movies of Hollywood stars at play. These films were often shown on his own programs as well as during his appearances on other shows. His autobiography: *Life on a Pogo Stick* (1960).

MURRAY, PEG—actress
b: Feb 14, Denver, Colo.

Me & Mrs. C. (com)
.... Ethel Conklin (Mrs. C.) (1986–)

A veteran stage and daytime soap opera actress (on *Love of Life* in the '70s and *All My Children* in the '80s) who won a Tony Award for her role in the musical *Cabaret.* "I seem to go back and forth from playing strippers and porno queens to mothers," she says.

MURRAY, WYNN—

The Fifty-Fourth Street Revue (var)
.... regular (1949)

MURROW, EDWARD R.—newscaster
b: Apr 25, 1908, Greensboro, N.C. d: Apr 27, 1965

See It Now (doc) .... host (1952–55)
Person to Person (int)........ host (1953–59)
Small World (info) .... moderator (1958–60)

Emmy Award: Outstanding Personality (1953); Best News Commentator (1955, 1956, 1957, 1959); Trustees' Award (1966)

Probably the most venerated newsman in the history of the television medium. His style would sound a bit stilted and pompous today, but there is no doubting the high principles, courage, and dedication to truth that underlay his career.

Murrow joined CBS in 1935, when broadcast journalist scarcely existed; the networks did little news-gathering of their own then, relying on the wire services for their short bulletins. Ed helped found CBS News, then became known for his own dramatic reports from Europe during World War II ("This . . . is London"). By the late 1940s he was radio's premiere commentator. Always fascinated by and adept at using technology, he adapted to television immediately. Some of his telecasts of the 1950s have become legendary: the live linking of the east and west coasts on a split screen via coaxial cable in 1951; his dramatic Christmas reports from the trenches of Korea; his daring 1954 exposé of the methods of Senator Joseph McCarthy, which helped bring an end to the political witch hunts of the McCarthy Era.

Murrow was seen principally on two series during these years: *See It Now,* which addressed public issues, and *Person to Person,* a lighter program in which he electronically visited the homes of celebrities and public figures. The latter drew the largest audiences, but the former was undoubtedly the most influential. By the late '50s, prime time public-affairs programming was being cut back by CBS in the quest for higher profits, a disturbing setback for someone with Murrow's noncommercial goals. He produced a few fine documentaries during this period, notably *Harvest of Shame* (1960), concerning the plight of migrant workers, but his air time had been sharply curtailed.

In 1961, Ed left CBS to enter government service as director of the United States Information Agency in the Kennedy administration. He resigned in 1964 due to ill health. Always a heavy smoker (he was often seen on-camera enveloped in a cloud of smoke), he died of lung cancer the following year. Many eulogized him, both during and after his lifetime. Here are four quotes:

"He is a man fitted to his time and to his task; a student, a philosopher, at heart a poet of mankind and, therefore, a great reporter." (William Paley, Chairman of CBS, in 1941).

"To Ed—reporter, historian, inquirer, actor, ponderer, seeker." (Carl Sandburg, after a 1954 interview).

"When the record is finally written, as it will be one day, it will answer the question, who has helped the Communist cause and who has served his country better, Senator McCarthy or I. I would like to be remembered by the answer to that question." (Murrow himself, after the McCarthy telecast).

"All I can say I've done is agitate the air for 10 or 15 minutes and then *boom!* . . . it's gone." (Murrow).

Not at all.

MURTAUGH, JAMES—actor

The Roller Girls (com)
.... Howie Devine (1978)
Number 96 (drama).. Roger Busky (1980–81)

MURTAUGH, KATE—actress

It's a Man's World (com)
.... Mrs. Iona Dobson (1962–63)

MURTON, LIONEL—actor
b: 1915, London, England r: Canada

O.S.S. (drama) .... the chief (1957–58)

MUSANTE, TONY—actor
b: Jun 30, 1936, Bridgeport, Conn.

Toma (police) ... Det. David Toma (1973–74)

A feisty little actor, in films and on television (occasionally) since the mid-1960s. He had his chance to gain series stardom in the well-received 1973 detective show *Toma,* but after a year he walked away from it because he didn't like the grind of weekly production. The series was recast and retitled *Baretta,* and made Robert Blake a star instead. Tony appeared in some episodes of other series after that (*Police Story, Medical Story*) and later was seen mostly in nondescript TV movies.

MUSCAT, ANGELO—actor

The Prisoner (adv) .... the butler (1968)

Patrick McGoohan's silent butler in the cult classic *The Prisoner.*

MUSE, CLARENCE—black actor
b: Oct 7, 1889, Baltimore, Md. d: Oct 13, 1979

Casablanca (drama) .... Sam (1955–56)

MUSIC, LORENZO—producer, actor
b: May 2, 1937, Brooklyn, N.Y.

Rhoda (com)
Carlton the doorman (voice only) (1974–78)

Emmy Award: Producer, Best Animated Program, for *Carlton, Your Doorman* (1980)

A writer and producer for several hit programs, including *The Smothers Brothers Comedy Hour* and *Rhoda.*

MUSTIN, BURT—actor

b: Feb 18, 1884, Pittsburgh, Pa. d: Jan 28, 1977

Date with the Angels (com)
.... Mr. Finley (1957–58)
Ichabod and Me (com)...... Olaf (1961–62)
The Andy Griffith Show (com)
.... Jud Crowley (1961–66)
The Funny Side (var)........ regular (1971)
All in the Family (com)
.... Justin Quigley (1973–76)
Phyllis (com)......... Arthur Lanson (1976)

A former automobile salesman who entered films at the age of 67, after he had retired from a normal full life's work. He then had an acting career lasting more than 20 years, playing old (and very old) parts in films and on television, including numerous appearances on *The Tonight Show.* He was in his nineties during his tenure on *Phyllis,* making him possibly the oldest regular actor ever on a TV series; he was "married" on the show to 87-year-old Judith Lowry shortly before his death.

MYERS, CARMEL—actress

b: Apr 4, 1901*, San Francisco, Calif. d: Nov 9, 1980

The Carmel Myers Show (talk)
.... hostess (1951–52)

A former silent-movie queen, in the "vamp" style. She hosted a New York–based celebrity interview show in the early 1950s.

MYERS, PAMELA—comedienne

Sha Na Na (var)........ regular (1977–81)
The Big Show (var)......... regular (1980)

*Some sources give 1899.

MYERS, PAULINE—black actress

b: Nov 9, Ocilla, Ga. r: New Jersey

Storefront Lawyers (drama)
.... Gloria Byrd (1970–71)

MYERS, SUSAN—juvenile actress

James at 15 (drama)
.... Marlene Mahoney (1977–78)

MYERSON, BESS—hostess

b: Jul 16, 1924, New York City, N.Y.

The Big Payoff (quiz)..... hostess (1952–53)
The Name's the Same (quiz)
.... panelist (1954–55)
I've Got a Secret (quiz).. panelist (1958–67)
Candid Camera (aud par). cohost (1966–67)

Bess Myerson, Miss America of 1945, was the first of that pageant's winners to be judged on both beauty and talent. She subsequently had a lengthy career as a TV personality, serving as cohost or panelist on game shows of the '50s and '60s—notably a nine-year run on *I've Got a Secret.* She was also a commentator for various events, including the Miss America Pageant. Bess later took up the cause of consumers, becoming New York City's commissioner of consumer affairs in 1969 and later a commentator on consumer matters on radio and in magazines.

MYERSON, JESSICA—actress

Thicker Than Water (com)...... Lily (1973)

MYLES, HOWARD—actor

Roller Derby (sport)... announcer (1950–51)

MYLES, JOHN—orchestra leader

The Marilyn McCoo & Billy Davis, Jr. Show (var)................... orch. leader (1977)

N

NABORS, JIM—actor
b: Jun 12, 1932, Sylacauga, Ala.

Andy Griffith Show (com)
.... Gomer Pyle (1963–64)
Gomer Pyle, U.S.M.C. (com)
.... Pvt. Gomer Pyle (1964–69)
The Jim Nabors Hour (var)... host (1969–71)

Jim Nabors was America's favorite yokel during the "rural comedy" vogue of the '60s; he not only sounded like a hayseed ("Gawl-ee!"), he looked like one, with a face somewhat resembling a dried prune. Jim's big break came when Andy Griffith spotted him performing in a Los Angeles cabaret in the early '60s and signed him to play the naive gas-station attendant Gomer Pyle on *The Andy Griffith Show.* After only a single season, Gomer was spun off into a series of his own, which was a major hit.

Despite his rural twang, Jim had a fine, booming singing voice and he developed a second career on records. Between 1966 and 1972, 12 of his LPs made the best-sellers chart. His musical abilities led him to host a variety show after *Gomer Pyle* left the air, but this was only briefly successful. During the '70s, Jim gradually faded from prominence. He costarred with Ruth Buzzi in a live-action Saturday morning children's show in 1975–76 *(Lost Saucer)* and had his own syndicated talk show in 1978. Neither lasted long. He also appeared in a couple of Burt Reynolds movies in the early '80s, but when he showed up on the top-rated *Return to Mayberry* reunion special in 1986, it was the first time many TV viewers had seen him in years.

NADER, GEORGE—actor
b: Oct 19, 1921, Los Angeles, Calif.

Adventures of Ellery Queen (drama)
.... Ellery Queen (1958–59)
Man and the Challenge (adv)
.... Dr. Glenn Barton (1959–60)
Shannon (drama).... Joe Shannon (1961–62)

After appearing in dramatic shows of the 1950s (numerous times on *The Loretta Young Show*) and starring in three series

between 1958–61, George left for Germany in the early '60s to pursue a film career there.

NADER, MICHAEL—actor
b: Feb 18, 1945, St. Louis, Mo. r: Beverly Hills, Calif.

Gidget (com)
.... Peter "Siddo" Stone (1965–66)
Dynasty (drama)
...... Farnsworth "Dex" Dexter (1983–   )

Handsome Michael Nader, Joan Collins's dashing lover on *Dynasty,* has had two Hollywood careers. The first was as a tawny surfer in the '60s, seen in the background in such "beach" movies as *Beach Blanket Bingo* and *How to Stuff a Wild Bikini,* as well as in Sally Fields' fun-in-the-sun TV series, *Gidget.* He then moved to New York to learn how to act, and after ten rocky years there returned to the West Coast and TV as Kevin Thompson in the daytime soap opera *As the World Turns* (1976–78). Small roles followed, including a brief stint in the prime time serial *Bare Essence* in 1983, before he struck gold as slippery Dex Dexter.

Michael is the nephew of '50s TV star George Nader (Ellery Queen).

NAGEL, CONRAD—actor, host
b: Mar 16, 1896*, Keokuk, Iowa d: Feb 24, 1970

The Silver Theater (drama) .. host (1949–50)
Celebrity Time (quiz)...... emcee (1949–52)
Broadway to Hollywood—Headline Clues (news)...................... host (1953–54)

NAISH, J. CARROL—actor
b: Jan 21, 1897**, New York City, N.Y. d: Jan 24, 1973

Life with Luigi (com) .... Luigi Basco (1952)
The Adventures of Charlie Chan (drama)
.... Charlie Chan (1956–57)
Guestward Ho! (com)... Hawkeye (1960–61)

One of Hollywood's most versatile character actors and dialecticians, Naish was equally convincing as the naive Italian immigrant Luigi (on radio and TV) or the wise, aphorism-spouting Chinaman, Char-

*Some sources give 1897.
**Some sources give 1900.

lie Chan. In still another TV season he became a canny American Indian with one eye on the trinket shop and another on *The Wall Street Journal,* in the comedy *Guestward Ho!*.

Naish was actually of Irish descent, but he rarely portrayed that nationality because of his swarthy complexion. He entered films in the late '20s and branched into television in the '50s, playing every conceivable sort of foreigner over the years. He finally went into semiretirement during the last ten years of his life, although he was seen as late as 1968 in an episode of *Get Smart* and in 1970 in the TV movie *Cutter's Trail* (as a Mexican).

NAISMITH, LAURENCE—actor
b: Dec 14, 1908, Ditton, Surrey, England

The Persuaders (adv)
.... Judge Fulton (1971–72)

NAKAHARA, KELLYE—actress

M*A*S*H (com).... Nurse Kellye (1974–83)

NAKAMOTO, ED—

Pink Lady (var) .... regular (1980)

NALLE, BILL—pianist
b: Fort Myers, Fla.

Glamour-Go-Round (int) ..... pianist (1950)

NAMATH, JOE—sportscaster, actor (?)
b: May 31, 1943, Beaver Falls, Pa.

The Waverly Wonders (com)
.... Joe Casey (1978)
Monday Night Football (sport)
.... sportscaster (1985)

This hulking football superstar (with the New York Jets and later the Los Angeles Rams, from 1965–77) became quite a media celebrity during the late '60s and early '70s. His easy grin and infectious personality made him a welcome guest on most of the top variety shows of the day, including those of Perry Como, Flip Wilson, and Sonny and Cher; he was a frequent guest host on *The Tonight Show.*

"Broadway Joe" had a few walk-ons on comedies such as *Here's Lucy* and *The Brady Bunch* during the early '70s, and when his playing days ended someone

thought it would be a great idea to give him his own comedy series as a high-school basketball coach saddled with a bunch of inept kids. Wrong. Joe as an actor was a little hard to take, so he eventually returned to talk shows and later did commentary on ABC's *Monday Night Football,* in 1985.

NAPIER, ALAN—actor
b: Jan 7, 1903, Birmingham, England

Don't Call Me Charlie (com)
.... Gen. Steele (1962–63)
Batman (adv)
.... Alfred Pennyworth (1966–68)

The tall (6'5"), elegant Englishman who played butlers in many films of the '40s and '50s, and was also Batman's in the hit 1966 series.

NAPIER, CHARLES—actor

The Oregon Trail (wes)
.... Luther Sprague (1977)
The Blue and the Gray (drama)
.... Major Harrison (1982)

NARDINI, JAMES—actor

Fast Times (com)..... Brad Hamilton (1986)

NARDINI, TOM—actor
b: 1945

Cowboy in Africa (adv)
.... John Henry (1967–68)

NARZ, JACK—host, announcer
b: Nov 13, 1922, Louisville, Ky.

Life with Elizabeth (com)
.... announcer (1953–55)
The College of Musical Knowledge (quiz)
.... announcer and "dean" (1954)
The Gisele MacKenzie Show (var)
.... announcer (1957–58)
Dotto (quiz)................. emcee (1958)
Video Village (quiz) .... emcee (1960)
Beat the Clock (quiz) ...... emcee (1969–72)

Jack comes from a family of smiling game show hosts; he is the older brother of Tom Kennedy, and the brother-in-law of Bill Cullen. Although he has never been associated with any one major hit, Jack did host a long string of daytime and nighttime quiz programs in the '50s, '60s, and '70s, among them *Top Dollar, Seven Keys, Now You See It,* and *Beat the Clock.*

NASH, BRIAN—juvenile actor
b: 1956, Glendale, Calif.

Mickey (com) . . . . . . Buddy Grady (1964–65)
Please Don't Eat the Daisies (com)
. . . . Joel Nash (1965–67)

NASH, JOE—actor
Flash Gordon (sci fi)
. . . . Dr. Zharkov (1953–54)

NASH, NOREEN—actress
The Charlie Farrell Show (com)
. . . . Doris Mayfield (1956)

NASH, OGDEN—poet
b: Aug 19, 1902, Rye, N.Y. d: May 19, 1971

Masquerade Party (quiz)
. . . . panelist (1953–57)

NASHVILLE, EDITION, THE—
Hee Haw (var) . . . . regulars (1969–)

NATHAN, STEVE—actor
b: Aug 21, Buffalo, N.Y.

Busting Loose (com)
. . . . Allan Simmonds (1977)

NATOLI, SARAH—juvenile actress
Fish (com) . . . . Diane Pulaski (1977–78)

NATWICK, MILDRED—actress
b: Jun 19, 1908, Baltimore, Md.

The Snoop Sisters (drama)
. . . . Gwen Snoop (1973–74)
Little Women (drama)
. . . . Aunt Kathryn March (1979)

Emmy Award: Best Actress in a Limited Series, for *The Snoop Sisters* (1974)

This delightful actress of stage (in the '30s) and film (from the '40s) played frequent character roles on television dramas of the '50s, usually eccentric older women. She was not seen as much in the '60s, but returned in the '70s in a variety of series episodes and TV movies. She costarred with another old-timer, Helen Hayes, in the 1973 *NBC Mystery Movie* segment *The Snoop Sisters.*

NAUD, MELINDA—actress
b: Feb 24, New York City, N.Y.

Operation Petticoat (com)
. . . . Lt. Dolores Crandell (1977–79)
Detective School (com)
. . . . Maggie Ferguson (1979)

Melinda played Fonzie's first love interest, Paula Petralunga, on several episodes of *Happy Days.*

NAUGHTON, DAVID—actor
b: Feb 13, 1951, Hartford, Conn.

Makin' It (adv) . . . . sang theme (1979)
Makin' It (adv) . . . . Billy Manucci (1979)
At Ease (com) . . . . . P.F.C. Tony Baker (1983)
My Sister Sam (com) . . . . Jack (1986–)

David is perhaps better known as the singing and dancing star of those elaborate "mini-musical" Dr. Pepper soft drink commercials of the late '70s and early '80s, than for his short-lived series.

NAUGHTON, JAMES—actor
b: Dec 6, 1945, Middletown, Conn., r: West Hartford, Conn.

Faraday and Company (drama)
. . . . Steve Faraday (1973–74)
The Planet of the Apes (sci fi)
. . . . Pete Burke (1974)
Making the Grade (com)
. . . . Harry Barnes (1982)
Trauma Center (drama)
. . . . Dr. Michael "Cutter" Royce (1983)

NAVIN, JOHN P., JR.—juvenile actor
b: Jul 24, 1968, Philadelphia, Pa.

Jennifer Slept Here (com)
. . . . Joey Elliot (1983–84)

"My whole life, I've played geeks, nerds, or chubbies," said chubby teenager John P. Navin when he got the leading role in *Jennifer Slept Here.* "Joey's more like me. He's a normal guy!" Though John was clearly delighted, "normal" didn't help his career much; the series lasted only a single season.

The young actor had previously played juvenile roles onstage for several years and had small parts in a few TV episodes. Among other things, he spoke the first line on the first episode of *Cheers:* "How 'bout a beer, chief?"

NEALON, KEVIN—comedian
b: Bridgeport, Conn.

NBC's Saturday Night Live (var)
.... regular (1986–   )

NEDWELL, ROBIN—actor
b: 1946

Doctor in the House (com)
.... Dr. Duncan Waring (1970–73)

NEEDHAM (NEWTON), CONNIE— juvenile actress
b: Dec 5, 1962, Anaheim, Calif.

Eight Is Enough (com)
.... Elizabeth Bradford (1977–81)

Connie, the youngest daughter on *Eight Is Enough,* was married in real life (at age 16) while she was appearing on the show, and changed her professional name from Newton to Needham.

NEENAN, AUDRIE J.—actress

Comedy Zone (com) .... regular (1984)

NEGRON, TAYLOR—actor
b: Aug 1, Los Angeles, Calif.

Detective School (com)
.... Silvio Galindez (1979)

A former comic with the "L.A. Connection" comedy troupe.

NEHER, SUSAN—actress

To Rome with Love (com)
.... Penny Endicott (1969–71)
Getting Together (com)
.... Jennifer Conway (1971–72)

NEIL, GLORIA—actress
b: c. 1941, Palm Springs, Calif.

The Lively Ones (var) .... Melvin (1963)

One of the two sexy "dates" (Smitty and Melvin) who accompanied Vic Damone on the 1963 summer series *The Lively Ones.* Gloria was the 36-23-35 blonde. She was a former Miss America runner-up.

NEILL, NOEL—actress
r: Minneapolis, Minn.

The Adventures of Superman (adv)
.... Lois Lane (1953–57)

Noel was the second and most familiar Lois Lane on the syndicated *Superman* series of the 1950s (the first was Phyllis Coates). The daughter of a Minneapolis newspaperman, Noel had appeared in B films during the 1940s, including the *Superman* serials. She retired when the television series ended, but in later years took to the lecture circuit with clips from the shows. In 1978 she had a cameo role in the big-budget *Superman* movie, as a woman on a train.

NEISE, GEORGE—actor

Wichita Town (wes)
.... Dr. Nat Wyndham (1959–60)

NELKIN, STACEY—actress

The Chisholms (wes)
.... Bonnie Sue Chisholm (1979)
The Last Convertible (drama)
.... Sheilah Garrigan (1979)

NELSON, ANN—actress

Fame (drama).......... Mrs. Berg (1982–   )

NELSON, BARRY—actor
b: Apr 16, 1920, Oakland, Calif.

The Hunter (drama) . Bart Adams (1952–54)
My Favorite Husband (com)
.... George Cooper (1953–55)

A chunky stage and screen actor, active since the 1940s, who appeared in numerous TV dramas from the 1950s on. *The Hunter* was a Cold War adventure in which he rescued innocent people from the clutches of the Communists; *My Favorite Husband* a situation comedy in which he was the levelheaded hubby saddled with a scatterbrained wife (played for most of the series by Joan Caulfield).

Barry was seen after that in various series, including several times on *Alfred*

Hitchcock Presents. In a famous *Twilight Zone* episode called "Stopover in a Quiet Town," he played a man who awoke after a party and found himself in a bizarre, deserted town where nothing seemed to be real (and, as it turned out, nothing was). Among Barry's TV movies have been *The Borgia Stick* (1967) and *Washington: Behind Closed Doors* (1977).

NELSON, BEK—actor
b: Goin, Tenn. r: Canton, Ohio

The Lawman (wes).... Dru Lemp (1958–59)

NELSON, CHRISTINE—actress

The Ray Bolger Show (com)
.... Katie Jones (1954–55)

NELSON, CHRISTOPHER S.—actor
b: Apr 5, 1954, New Orleans, La.

Sons and Daughters (drama) ... Cody (1974)
Co-ed Fever (com)............. Doug (1979)

The son of actor Ed Nelson.

NELSON, CRAIG RICHARD—actor

Paul Sand in Friends and Lovers (com)
.... Mason Woodruff (1974–75)
The Carol Burnett Show (var)
.... regular (1979)

NELSON, CRAIG T.—actor
b: Apr 4, 1946, Spokane, Wash.

Chicago Story (drama)
.... Kenneth A. Dutton (1982)
Call to Glory (drama)
.... Col. Raynor Sarnac (1984–85)

Despite his rather stolid, humorless appearance (he played heavies for many years on TV crime shows), Craig T. Nelson started out, around 1970, as a comedy writer for Tim Conway, Lohman and Barkley, and others. After a few years fighting the Hollywood rat race he and his family decided to retreat to a wilderness cabin near Mount Shasta, Calif., to live a simpler life. Four years of living *au naturel* finally convinced Craig to return to civilization, or Hollywood's approximation thereof. Since 1978 he has worked fairly steadily on TV in supporting, and occasionally leading, roles in dramas and comedies. He also produced a number of half-hour films for the *America Still* syndicated series documenting the experiences of artists like himself who gave up city living for a more primitive lifestyle.

NELSON, DAVID—actor
b: Oct 24, 1936, New York City, N.Y.

The Adventures of Ozzie & Harriet (com)
.... as himself (1952–66)

When last seen in *Ozzie and Harriet* days, younger son Ricky wanted to be a rock 'n' roll musician and older son David an actor. Rick succeeded beyond anyone's wildest dreams, but David has had a less notable career. He has acted a bit in movies *(Cheech and Chong's Up in Smoke, Smashup on Interstate 5),* directed a bit *(Last Plane Out, A Rare Breed),* and turned up once in a while on TV episodes and specials *(The Love Boat, Circus of the Stars).* He also produced a documentary about his brother Rick on tour. David and Rick were close; David and Ozzie were not.

Today David works mostly, and only occasionally, as a producer/director. He inherited a sizable trust fund from his years on *Ozzie & Harriet.*

NELSON, ED—actor
b: Dec 21, 1928, New Orleans, La. r: North Carolina

Peyton Place (drama)
.... Dr. Michael Rossi (1964–69)
The Silent Force (police)
.... Ward Fuller (1970–71)
Doctors' Private Lives (drama)
.... Dr. Michael Wise (1979)

NELSON, FRANK—actor
b: c. 1911 d: Sep 12, 1986

The Hank McCune Show (com)
.... regular (1950)
The Jack Benny Show (com)
.... regular (1950–65)
I Love Lucy (com).... Ralph Ramsey (1957)
The Betty White Show (var) . regular (1958)
The Jetsons (cartn) . various roles (1962–63)

The overbearing guy in Benny's skits—usually playing a clerk or official—who always greeted Jack with an exaggerated

"Yeeessssss?" He also did voices for Saturday morning cartoons in the '60s and '70s.

NELSON, HARRIET—mom
b: Jul 18, 1914, Des Moines, Iowa

The Adventures of Ozzie & Harriet (com)
.... as herself (1952–66)
Ozzie's Girls (com) .... as herself (1973)

Ozzie's wife, and formerly a singer with his band. They were married in 1935. She was a starlet in movies of the '30s and '40s, under the name Harriet Hilliard.

NELSON, HAYWOOD—black juvenile actor
b: Mar 25, 1960, New York City, N.Y.

Grady (com) .. Haywood Marshall (1975–76)
What's Happening!! (com)
.... Dwayne (1976–79)
What's Happening Now!! (com)
.... Dwayne Clemens (1985–)

NELSON, JERRY—puppeteer

The Muppet Show (var)
.... Dr. Strangepork (1976–81)
The Muppet Show (var).... Floyd (1976–81)
The Muppet Show (var)..... Pops (1980–81)
The Muppet Show (var)
.... Lew Zealand (1980–81)

Emmy Awards: As Performer (Puppeteer) in the Best Children's Program, for *Sesame Street* (1974, 1976); and Best Comedy-Variety Series, for *The Muppet Show* (1978)

NELSON, JESSICA—actress

Archie Bunker's Place (com)
.... Marsha (1982–83)

NELSON, JIMMY—ventriloquist
b: Dec 15, 1928, Chicago, Ill.

The Milton Berle Show (var)
.... commercial announcer (1952–53)
Quick As a Flash (quiz).. panelist (1953–54)
Bank on the Stars (quiz) ..... emcee (1954)
Come Closer (quiz) .... emcee (1954)
Down You Go (quiz)
.... regular panelist (1956)

This youthful ventriloquist rocketed to fame on Milton Berle's show in 1952–53,

and was subsequently seen on variety and quiz shows of the 1950s. He was for many years in the late '50s and early '60s the commercial spokesman for Nestle's Chocolate; he has been inactive on TV since then, but continues to make personal appearances. His most famous dummies: the rather crude-looking Danny O'Day (whom he labeled "a blasphemous piece of balsam") and Farfel the dog.

NELSON, JOHN—host

Live Like a Millionaire (talent)
.... emcee (1951–53)

NELSON, KENNETH—actor
b: Mar 24, 1930, Rocky Mount, N.C.

The Aldrich Family (com)
.... Henry Aldrich (1952)

NELSON, KRISTIN—

see Harmon, Kristin

NELSON, LINDSEY—sportscaster
b: May 25, 1919, Pulaski, Tenn.

Sportsreel (sport)...... commentator (1955)

Television play-by-play commentator, most familiar covering college football for NBC in the '50s and CBS since 1963.

NELSON, LORI—actress
b: Aug 15, 1933, Santa Fe, N.M.

How to Marry a Millionaire (com)
.... Greta (1957–58)

Lori, a sexy blonde who had appeared in a number of films and TV productions during the 1950s, landed her first series role in *How to Marry a Millionaire.* She quit after a year to "find better roles." Instead, she virtually dropped out of show business. She was married in the '60s to musician Johnny Mann; later, she ran a cosmetics company.

Trivia buffs will long remember her, however, as the bosomy object of the creature's affections in the sci-fi classic *Revenge of the Creature* (1955).

NELSON, MIRIAM—choreographer

Away We Go (var)........ dancers (1967)

NELSON, NOVELLA—black actress
b: Dec 17, 1939, Brooklyn, N.Y.

Chiefs (drama) . . . . Nellie Cole (1983)

NELSON, OZZIE—actor, producer, director
b: Mar 20, 1906, Jersey City, N.J. d: Jun 3, 1975

The Adventures of Ozzie & Harriet (com)
. . . . as himself (1952–66)
Ozzie's Girls (com) . . . . . . as himself (1973)

Ozzie Nelson is remembered today as a virtual caricature of the 1950s TV dad: diffident, amiable, always getting into little scrapes, and with no visible means of support, in spite of his family's comfortable middle-class lifestyle. The real Ozzie was about as far from that as could be. A hard-driving overachiever since his youth, he had been the nation's youngest Eagle Scout at 13, a honor student and star quarterback at Rutgers, and a nationally known bandleader in his twenties. The vocalist on his early (and now collectible) records was a young film starlet named Harriet Hilliard, who in 1935 became Mrs. Ozzie Nelson.

Ozzie himself branched into movies in 1940, with his band, and in 1944 began a highly popular radio series called *The Adventures of Ozzie & Harriet,* about his idealized family life. Joining him on the show, after a few years, were his real-life sons David and Ricky. The series transferred to ABC-TV in 1952 and had an extraordinarily long (14 year) run—by which time the boys were grown and married. It was never a monster hit, but stayed on the air for other reasons. Ozzie was an astute businessman who produced and directed the show himself and who used simple plots and a small cast to keep costs low (the stars, of course, were his own family). It was just the kind of series financially strapped ABC needed.

Ozzie also realized the potential in son Ricky's musical proclivities and guided his career firmly in the late '50s. Ricky's songs were promoted on every show and care was taken to ensure that he did not become a mere flash-in-the-pan; he was given first-class backing musicians and songwriters to work with (Ozzie was hip to that business, too!). Ricky became one of the

biggest-selling rock singers in America, giving the TV show a further boost.

When *Ozzie & Harriet* finally ran its course in 1966, Ozzie and his wife toured for a few years in regional theater productions and also appeared in episodes of scattered TV shows, including *Love, American Style* and *Night Gallery* (as a wacky inventor and his obliging wife). In 1973 he produced the syndicated series *Ozzie's Girls,* a sort of sequel to *O&H,* but it was not successful. Ozzie had also produced the 1950s hit *Our Miss Brooks.*

His autobiography: *Ozzie* (1973).

NELSON, PETER—actor

V (movie) (sci fi) . . . . Brian (1983)
V: The Final Battle (miniseries) (sci fi)
. . . . Brian (1984)

NELSON, RICK—singer
b: May 8, 1940, Teaneck, N.J. d: Dec 31, 1985

The Adventures of Ozzie & Harriet (com)
. . . . as himself (1952–66)
Malibu U (music) . . . . host (1967)

Singer-son of Ozzie Nelson. Rick was in show business for practically his entire life, from age nine (when he and David persuaded dad to let them appear on the "family" radio show) until his death in a plane crash at age 45, en route to a concert.

As a crew-cut youngster, Ricky provided much of the comic spark for the TV series; he was a highly natural, rambunctious kid who made a very believable TV teenager (zippy one-liners were not the style on *Ozzie & Harriet*). As an adult he proved rather wooden as an actor, but he more than made up for that by becoming one of the biggest rock stars in music history, with 18 top-ten hits between 1957 ("A Teenager's Romance") and 1972 ("Garden Party"). At first, he admitted, his music career was part hype. "Sure, in the beginning I used to fake it on the guitar," he told the *New York Times* in 1972. "I was scared to play, and anyhow, no one could hear you with everyone screaming. But in time I learned to play and enjoy it." Most critics grudgingly agreed that in later years Rick did indeed become quite good.

At the time *Ozzie & Harriet* ended, Rick's music career was in a temporary downswing. Besides hosting the summer musical series *Malibu U* in 1967, he made sporadic acting appearances in such series as *Hondo, Owen Marshall, McCloud,* and *Tales of the Unexpected.* He appeared as a father in the pilot for a proposed series called *Fathers and Sons* (starring Merlin Olsen) in 1985, shortly before his death.

NELSON, TRACY—actress
b: Oct 25, 1963, Santa Monica, Calif.

Square Pegs (com)
.... Jennifer DeNuccio (1982–83)
Glitter (drama).... Angela Timini (1984–85)

The daughter of Rick Nelson and actress Kris Harmon. "Tracy really pursued this on her own," said a surprised Rick, when his daughter landed her first TV role in *Square Pegs.*

NESBITT, CATHLEEN—actress
b: Nov 24, 1888*, Belfast, Northern Ireland**
d: Aug 2, 1982

The Farmer's Daughter (com)
.... Agatha Morley (1963–66)

Emmy Award: Best Actress in a Daytime Drama, and Daytime Actress of the Year, both for *ABC Matinee Today:* "The Mask of Love" (1974)

An aristocratic British character actress, most active on U.S. television in the '50s and '60s, although she was still performing in her nineties. Her autobiography: *A Little Love and Good Companions* (1973).

NESBITT, JOHN—writer, host
b: 1909, California d: 1960

Telephone Time (drama)..... host (1956–57)

NESBITT, SUSAN—
Easy Does It...Starring Frankie Avalon (var)
.... regular (1976)

NESMITH, MICHAEL—actor, musician
b: Dec 30, 1942, Houston r: Farmer's Branch, Texas

The Monkees (com) .... Mike (1966–68)
Michael Nesmith in Television Parts (var)
.... host (1985)

*Some sources give 1889.
**Some sources give Cheshire, England.

"Wool Hat" of *The Monkees* has come a long way since his days as one of television's "imitation Beatles." Raised in a black suburb of Dallas, he was interested in blues and folk music from his youth. In the early '60s he was an itinerant guitarist working the fringes of the folk/rock music scene in Los Angeles. Then, one day in 1965, he answered that famous casting ad in *Variety* looking for "four insane boys, aged 17–21," for a new TV series. So did 400 others, but Mike got one of the parts and the Monkees were born.

The sensational success of the program was gratifying but galling at the same time because the group was being passed off as musicians when in fact studio players made all their records. Mike eventually led a group revolt against this practice and got things changed, but their fame soon blew over anyway; by 1969 the show was off the air and The Monkees disbanded. Mike then pursued his own musical career, planning an ambitious nine-LP project on different American musics with a group he called The First National Band. He was more successful as a songwriter, having previously penned Linda Ronstadt's hit "Different Drum" and later his own "Joanne." In the mid-1970s he founded his own label, Pacific Arts, which became one of the pioneers in the field of music videos. One of the first was "Rio" in 1976; later, he produced clips for *Fridays* and *Saturday Night Live.* His strikingly original video "Elephant Parts" won the first Grammy Award for video in 1982 and led to a short-lived avant-garde TV series called *Television Parts* in 1985. Its offbeat, visual humor was somewhat reminiscent of, guess what —*The Monkees!*

A Monkees reunion tour was announced for 1986, but Mike said he wasn't interested. Besides his many music and video projects, he inherited a great deal of money from his mother, who had invented a widely used office product called "Liquid Paper" and made her own fortune.

NETHERLY, PENDRANT—actor
Room 222 (drama)..... Al Cowley (1969–71)

NETHERTON, TOM—singer
b: Jan 11, 1949, Munich, Germany

The Lawrence Welk Show (music)
.... regular (1973–81)

NETTLETON, LOIS—actress
b: c. 1929, Oak Park, Ill.

Accidental Family (com)
.... Sue Kramer (1967–68)
All That Glitters (com)
.... Christina Stockwood (1977)
Centennial (drama)
.... Maude Wendell (1978–79)

Emmy Awards: Performer, Best Daytime Drama Special, for *The American Woman: Portraits of Courage* (1977); Best Performer in a Religious Program, for *Insight* (1983)

NEUHAUS, LACEY—actress

From Here to Eternity (drama)
.... Emily Austin (1980)

NEUMANN, DOROTHY—actress

Hank (com)...... Miss Mittleman (1965–66)

NEUN, MIKE—

Dinah and Her New Best Friends (var)
.... regular (1976)

NEVARD, BILLIE—juvenile actor

Wesley (com).............. Alvin (1949)

NEVIL, STEVE—actor

The McLean Stevenson Show (com)
.... Chris (1976–77)

NEVINS, CLAUDETTE—actress

The Headmaster (drama)
.... Margaret Thompson (1970–71)
Husbands, Wives & Lovers (com)
.... Courtney Fielding (1978)
Married: The First Year (drama)
.... Barbara Huffman (1979)
Behind the Screen (drama)
.... Angela Aries (1981–82)

NEVINS, NATALIE—singer

The Lawrence Welk Show (music)
.... regular (1965–69)

**NEW CHRISTY MINSTRELS, THE—
singers**
Leader: Randy Sparks, b: Jul 29, 1933, Leavenworth, Kans.

The Andy Williams Show (var)
.... regulars (1962–63)
The New Christy Minstrels (var)
.... stars (1964)

A popular, folk-oriented singing group of the '60s, organized and led by Randy Sparks. There were approximately eight to ten members, although personnel changed frequently. Barry McGuire, who later had a solo hit with the antiwar song "Eve of Destruction," was the lead singer in the early '60s; country crooner Kenny Rogers was a member later on.

**NEW DOODLETOWN PIPERS, THE—
singers**

Make Your Own Kind of Music (var)
.... regulars (1971)

A 16-person singing group, successor to The Doodletown Pipers (Q.V.).

NEW FACES, THE—

Kraft Music Hall Presents The Des O'Connor Show (var)............... regulars (1971)

NEW SEEKERS, THE—singers

The Ken Berry "Wow" Show (var)
.... regulars (1972)

A folk-rock group founded in England in 1969 by Keith Potger (one of the "old" Seekers), and popular in the U.S. during the early '70s. Their biggest hit was based on a Coca-Cola TV commercial called "I'd Like to Teach the World to Sing in Perfect Harmony."

NEWBORN, IRA—orchestra leader
b: Dec 26, 1949, New York City, N.Y.

Manhattan Transfer (var)
.... orch. leader (1975)

NEWELL, PATRICK—actor

The Avengers (drama).. "Mother" (1968–69)
Kraft Music Hall Presents the Des O'Connor Show (var)................ regular (1970)

NEWHART, BOB—comedian, actor
b: Sep 5, 1929, Oak Park, Ill.

The Bob Newhart Show (var)
.... host (1961–62)

The Entertainers (var) .... costar (1964)

The Bob Newhart Show (com)
.... Robert (Bob) Hartley (1972–78)

Newhart (com) ...... Dick Loudon (1982–)

Bob Newhart is perhaps the most popular of television's "quiet comics," a master of double-takes and pauses. A rather meek-looking, unassuming chap, he started out in the '50s as an accountant ("because I *looked* like an accountant") but soon, out of boredom, began writing comedy material reflecting on life's little absurdities. His specialty was the one-way phone call. Bob would talk to an unheard second party, in ever-escalating tones, leaving listeners in hysterics wondering what the person on the other end must be saying.

Bob found few takers for his written efforts, but he did land a short-term job as a "man on the street" interviewer at a Chicago TV station, which led in 1960 to a recording contract for a comedy album. The resulting LP, "The Button-Down Mind of Bob Newhart," was a smash hit. Combined with Bob's exposure on the 1960 Emmy Awards telecast, it made him suddenly a hot property. TV first tried to make Bob into a variety show host, with little success. Not until he began a regular situation comedy in 1972 as a psychologist with a cast of slightly offbeat characters to play off of, did he become a major TV star. Four years after this highly successful series ended he began another one with a similar theme, this time as the owner of a small country inn in Vermont. It, too, was a hit. In between these series, Bob was most frequently seen as a popular guest host on *The Tonight Show*.

NEWLAN, PAUL—actor
b: 1903, Plattsburgh, Nebr. r: Kansas City, Mo.
d: Nov 23, 1973

M Squad (police) ..... Capt. Grey (1957–60)

NEWLAND, JOHN—actor, director, host
b: Nov 23, 1917, Cincinnati, Ohio

One Man's Family (drama)
.... Danny Frank (1950)

Robert Montgomery Presents (summer) (drama). .... repertory player (1952–54)

Alcoa Presents (One Step Beyond) (drama)
.... host (1959–61)

The Next Step Beyond (drama). . host (1978)

This tall, rather reserved actor is best remembered as the host and director of the creepy anthology series *One Step Beyond*. Surprisingly, he had begun as a song and dance man in vaudeville (with Milton Berle) and on Broadway. "I've sung a thousand fair and carnival dates," he lamented in 1952. During the '50s he was very frequently seen in TV dramas, especially on *Philco Playhouse, Kraft Television Theatre, The Loretta Young Show,* and *Robert Montgomery Presents*. In the '60s he turned full-time to directing, carving out another successful career, this time behind the scenes on such series as *Route 66, Dr. Kildare, Star Trek, The Man from U.N.C.L.E.,* and *Harry-O*. Much of his directing work, however, has been in the supernatural genre, with episodes of *Night Gallery*, The *Sixth Sense,* and *Thriller* (including the classic story "Pigeons from Hell"). You might call it the song-and-dance man's revenge.

NEWMAN, BARRY—actor
b: Nov 7, 1938*, Boston, Mass.

Petrocelli (drama)
.... Tony Petrocelli (1974–76)

A curly-haired, dynamic actor who has appeared since the '60s in occasional series episodes and TV movies. He is best remembered as the dedicated big city lawyer who moved to the rural southwest in *Petrocelli*. More recently, he again played a lawyer, in the hit TV movie *Fatal Vision*.

NEWMAN, EDWIN—newscaster
b: Jan 25, 1919, New York City, N.Y.

Edwin Newman Reporting (news)
.... host (1960)

The Nation's Future (pub aff)
.... moderator (1961)

What's Happening to America (info)
.... moderator (1968)

Comment (pub aff) .... host (1971–72)

Emmy Award: Host, Best Religious Program, for "Kids, Drugs and Alcohol" (1983)

Grumpy, heavyset news commentator, who was known as one of the most literate members of the TV news fraternity. He began his career as a wire-service reporter

*Some sources give 1940.

in 1941, joining NBC part-time in 1949 and full-time, in London, in 1952. Many foreign assignments, many special reports, and a great many words later he authored two witty, best-selling books lamenting (hilariously) the misuse of the English language by public figures: *Strictly Speaking* (1974) and *A Civil Tongue* (1976). He retired from NBC in 1984.

NEWMAN, ELMER—host

Hayloft Hoedown (music)
.... emcee/"Pancake Pete" (1948)

NEWMAN, LARAINE—comedienne
b: Mar 2, 1952, Los Angeles, Calif.

Manhattan Transfer (var) .... regular (1975)
NBC's Saturday Night Live (com)
.... regular (1975–80)

NEWMAN, PHYLLIS—actress
b: Mar 19, 1935, Jersey City, N.J.

Diagnosis: Unknown (drama)
.... Doris Hudson (1960)
That Was the Week That Was (com)
.... regular (1964–65)

NEWMAR, JULIE—actress
b: Aug 16, 1935*, Hollywood, Calif.

My Living Doll (com)
.... Rhoda Miller (1964–65)

Julie later turned up as the alluring but deadly Catwoman on *Batman*.

NEWMARK, MATTHEW—actor

Knots Landing (drama)
.... Jason Avery (1986–   )

NEWSOM, TOMMY—orchestra leader, saxophonist
b: Feb 25, 1929, Portsmouth, Va.

The Tonight Show Starring Johnny Carson (talk) .... regular (1968–   )

The bland-looking assistant conductor of *The Tonight Show* orchestra who takes over when Doc Severinsen is away. His milquetoast looks make him often the good-natured butt of Johnny's jokes ("Newsom's been dead for years").

*Some sources give 1930.

NEWTON, CONNIE—
see Needham, Connie

NICASSIO, JOEAL—actor
240-Robert (adv)
.... Deputy Roverino (1979–80)

NICASTRO, MICHELLE—actress
Suzanne Pleshette Is Maggie Briggs (com)
.... Diana Barstow (1984)

NICHOLAS, DENISE—black actress
b: 1944, Detroit, Mich.

Room 222 (drama) ... Liz McIntyre (1969–74)
Baby, I'm Back (com) .... Olivia Ellis (1978)

NICHOLLS, ANTHONY—actor
b: 1902 d: March 1977

The Champions (adv) ..... Tremayne (1968)

NICHOLS, BARBARA—actress
b: Dec 30, 1929, Jamaica, N.Y. d: Oct 5, 1976

Broadway Open House (talk)
.... Agathon (1951)
Caesar Presents (var)
.... Barbara Williams (1955)
Love That Jill (com) .... Ginger (1958)

NICHOLS, NICHELLE—black actress
b: 1936, Chicago, Ill.*

Star Trek (sci fi) .... Uhura (1966–69)

NICHOLSON, CAROL—juvenile actress
Room for One More (com)
.... Laurie Rose (1962)

NICKERSON, DAWN—actress
r: Atlantic City, N.J.

Harry's Girls (com) .... Lois (1963–64)

NIELSEN, LESLIE—actor
b: Feb 11, 1922**, Regina, Saskatchewan, Canada

The New Breed (police)
.... Lt. Price Adams (1961–62)
Peyton Place (drama)
.... Dr. Vincent Markham (1965)

*Some sources give the Chicago suburb of Robbins, Ill.
**Some sources give 1925 or 1926.

The Protectors (police)
.... Sam Danforth (1969–70)
Bracken's World (drama)
.... John Bracken (1970)
The Explorers (doc) .... host (1972–73)
Backstairs at the White House (drama)
.... Ike Hoover (1979)
Police Squad (com)
.... Det. Frank Drebin (1982)
Shaping Up (com) .... Buddy Fox (1984)

It is remarkable that after 35 years of TV leading roles, wide recognition, and many fans, Leslie Nielsen has yet to star in a hit series of his own. He has been one of the most prolific actors in TV, in hundreds of series, series episodes, and TV movies. He often plays distinguished but untrustworthy authority figures but is equally adept at deadpan comedy, as in the lunatic *Police Squad*.

Leslie was born in Canada, the son of a Royal Canadian mounted policeman. After wartime service in the Canadian Air Force, he worked for a time as a disc jockey, then enrolled in Lorne Greene's Academy of Radio Arts in Toronto. Soon he moved to New York, making his television debut in the 1949 *Studio One* production "Battleship Bismarck," alongside a young Charlton Heston. He clearly remembers receiving seventy-five dollars for ten days of work.

At those rates, Leslie took all the work he could get, which was plenty in those days of numerous live playhouse series. In 1950 he appeared in 45 live TV shows; by the time he moved to Hollywood in 1954, he had been in more than 400. During the late '50s, Leslie abandoned television and attempted to build a movie career; among his early films were *The Vagabond King* and the sci-fi classic *Forbidden Planet* in 1956 and *Tammy and the Bachelor* in 1957. However, he did not achieve stardom, and in 1959 returned to TV for his most prominent role to date, that of General Francis Marion in the multipart Disney saga *The Swamp Fox*.

Throughout the '60s and '70s Leslie was seen regularly in action series, including *Wagon Train, The Fugitive, The Virginian, Cannon,* and numerous others. He also played in occasional dramas, such as *Dr. Kildare*. He starred in several drama series of his own, but none clicked. Following his success in the riotous movie *Airplane*

in 1980, he began to turn more toward TV comedy.

NIGH, JANE—actress
b: Feb 25, 1927, Hollywood, California

Big Town (drama)
.... Lorelei Kilbourne (1952–53)

NILES, MARY-ANN—

see Fosse, Bob

NILES, WENDELL—announcer
b: Dec 29, Twin Valley, Minn. r: Livingston, Mont.

It Could Be You (quiz).. assistant (1958–61)

NIMMO, BILL—host

Keep It in the Family (quiz)
.... emcee (1957–58)

NIMOY, LEONARD—actor
b: Mar 26, 1931, Boston, Mass.

Star Trek (sci fi) ...... Mr. Spock (1966–69)
Mission: Impossible (drama)
.... Paris (1969–71)
In Search Of (doc) . host/narrator (1976–82)

Dark, sharp-featured Leonard Nimoy seems well cast as a man of mystery, and it was in such a role—that of half Earthling, half Vulcan Mr. Spock on *Star Trek*—that he became famous.

Leonard began as a bit player in the '50s and early '60s, with small roles on such series as *Dragnet* and *Sea Hunt*. Often he played a villain, either a murderous thug, as on *Laramie,* or (less often) a comic one, as on *Get Smart*. A guest role in 1964 on *The Lieutenant,* which was produced by Gene Roddenberry, led to his most famous part. "Someday I'm going to put ears on you," said Roddenberry to the gaunt actor, "and star you in a science fiction series." Two years later he did.

After *Star Trek* Leonard moved immediately into *Mission: Impossible,* replacing Martin Landau as the team's master of disguises. However, further good roles were hard to find, given his rather special image. Later years brought a grab bag of parts— narrator of the Saturday morning cartoon version of *Star Trek,* host of the syndicated freak show *In Search Of . . .,* roles in occasional TV movies (including a well-received performance in *A Woman Named Golda*) and in miniseries (he was Achmet in 1982's *Marco Polo*). Aside from his acting, he authored five books of poetry, illustrated with his own photographs. Most of all, though, he is and will always be the slightly mysterious Mr. Spock.

NIRVANA, YANA—actress, comedienne

The Last Precinct (com)
.... Sgt. Martha Haggerty (1986)

NIVEN, DAVID—actor
b: Mar 1, 1909*, Kirriemuir, Scotland d: Jul 29, 1983

Four Star Playhouse (drama)
.... costar (1952–56)
Alcoa Theatre (drama)
.... recurring star (1957–58)
David Niven Show (drama) ..... host (1959)
The Rogues (com) .. Alec Fleming (1964–65)

This suave Hollywood star hosted his own dramatic anthology series during the '50s and appeared in a number of productions on others. He also filled in as host of *The Dick Powell Theatre* in early 1963, after Powell's death. The only regular series role Niven ever essayed, however, was in *The Rogues,* a stylish continental comedy/adventure costarring Gig Young and Charles Boyer. Talk about class!

In later years, David was rarely seen on TV; his last major appearance was as a World War II spymaster in the 1979 TV film *A Man Called Intrepid*. He authored two entertaining, and best-selling, reminiscences, *The Moon's a Balloon* (1972) and *Bring on the Empty Horses* (1975). During the '50s David was a co-founder of Four Star Television, which produced several popular series.

NIVERSON, ELAINE—dancer

The Lawrence Welk Show (music)
.... regular (1979–82)

NIX, MARTHA—juvenile actress
b: Sep 26, 1967, Orange County, Calif. r: Fullerton, Ca.

The Waltons (drama)
.... Serena Burton (1979–81)

*Some sources give 1910.

NOBLE, JAMES—actor
b: Mar 5, 1922, Dallas, Texas

Benson (com)
.... Gov. James Gatling (1979–86)

NOBLE, TRISHA—actress
b: Feb 3, Sydney, Australia

Executive Suite (drama)
.... Yvonne Holland (1976–77)
Strike Force (police)
.... Det. Rosie Johnson (1981–82)

NOEL, CHRIS—actress
b: 1941, West Palm Beach, Fla.

The Lieutenant (drama)
.... various roles (1963–64)
Occasional Wife (com)
.... Marilyn (1966–67)

NOEL, DICK—host
b: May 30, 1927, Brooklyn, N.Y.

It's a Small World (doc) .... host (1953)

NOEL, FRANK—actor

The Chisholms (wes) ...... McVeety (1980)

NOEL, HENRI—singer

The Music Show (music) .. regular (1953–54)

NOLAN, JAMES—actor
b: c. 1916, San Francisco, Calif. d: Jul 29, 1985

Dante (adv) .... Insp. Loper (1960–61)

NOLAN, JEANETTE—actress
b: Dec 30, 1911, Los Angeles, Calif.

Hotel De Paree (wes)
.... Annette Deveraux (1959–60)
The Richard Boone Show (drama)
.... regular (1963–64)
The Virginian (wes)
.... Holly Grainger (1967–68)
Dirty Sally (wes) .... Sally Fergus (1974)

The wife of actor John McIntire, with whom she appeared on *The Virginian*.

NOLAN, KATHY—actress
b: Sep 27, 1933, St. Louis, Mo.

Jamie (com) .... Cousin Liz (1953–54)

The Real McCoys (com)
.... Kate McCoy (1957–62)
Broadside (com)
.... Lt. (j.g.) Anne Morgan (1964–65)

Kathy, who was Richard Crenna's pretty young bride on *The Real McCoys*, has made only sporadic acting appearances on TV, stretching from the '50s to the '80s. She has been quite active in Hollywood politics, however. In 1975 she was elected the first woman president of the powerful actors union the Screen Actors Guild.

NOLAN, LLOYD—actor
b: Aug 11, 1902, San Francisco, Calif. d: Sep 27, 1985

Martin Kane, Private Eye (drama)
.... Martin Kane (1951–52)
Special Agent 7 (drama)
.... Special Agent Conroy (1958–59)
Julia (com)... Dr. Morton Chegley (1968–71)

Emmy Award: Best Actor in a Single Performance, for the *Ford Star Jubilee* production of *The Caine Mutiny Court-Martial* (1955)

This gruff but likable actor was a reliable character player in movies for more than 40 years, from the mid-1930s to the late '70s. He often played tough guys, including detective Michael Shayne in B films of the '40s. Lloyd entered television around 1950 and was seen in many TV dramas over the following years; his greatest triumph was in the 1955 telecast of "The Caine Mutiny Court-Martial" as Captain Queeg—a role he had originated on stage. Viewers of the '60s remember him as Diahann Carroll's irascible boss on *Julia*.

NOLAN, TOM—actor
b: Indianapolis, Ind.

Jessie (police)....... Officer Hubbell (1984)

NOLAN, TOMMY—juvenile actor
b: Jan 15, 1948, Montreal, Canada

Buckskin (wes)... Jody O'Connell (1958–59)

After his brief moment of fame as the child star of *Buckskin*, Tommy Nolan pursued acting for another ten years, with steadily diminishing success. Later, he turned to writing, and he now supports himself with articles and columns for *Los Angeles* magazine, *The Los Angeles Times*, *Playboy*, and other publications, as well as by writing books on popular music stars.

NOLTE, NICK—actor
b: Feb 8, 1934*, Omaha, Neb.

Rich Man, Poor Man—Book I (drama)
.... Tom Jordache (1976)

The tough guy movie star of the '70s and '80s got his first major break as the rebellious co-lead in the top-rated miniseries *Rich Man, Poor Man*. He has since abandoned television in favor of the big screen.

NOMKEENA, KEENA—juvenile actor
b: c. 1942

Brave Eagle (wes)........ Keena (1955–56)

NORBERT, GREG—

Marie (var) .... regular (1980–81)

NORDEN, TOMMY—juvenile actor
b: Sep 25, New York City, N.Y.

Flipper (adv)......... Bud Ricks (1964–68)

Tommy was quite active as a child performer, appearing during the early '60s onstage *(Greenwillow, The Music Man)* as well as on TV (*Sing Along with Mitch, Naked City, Route 66*, etc.). The role of ten-year-old Bud on *Flipper* was his favorite, though, as it allowed him to indulge in his favorite sports of swimming and skindiving. It was his last major role in prime time, although he was seen for a bit in the early '70s in the daytime soap opera *Search for Tomorrow*.

NORDINE, KEN—announcer
b: Cherokee, Iowa

Chicago Symphony Chamber Orchestra (music) .... announcer (1951–52)

NORELL, HENRY—actor

Oh, Those Bells (com)
.... Henry Slocum (1962)

*Some sources give 1941.

NORELL, MICHAEL—actor

Emergency (drama)
.... Captain Stanley (1973–77)

NORMAN, B.G.—juvenile actor

Life with Father (com)
.... Whitney Day (1954–55)

NORMAN, RALPH—musician

Manhattan Maharaja (var)
.... regular (1950–51)

NORRIS, CHRISTOPHER—actress
b: Oct 7, 1953, New York City, N.Y.

Trapper John, M.D. (drama)
    Nurse Gloria Brancusi (Ripples) (1979–85)

NORRIS, JAN—actress

It's a Man's World (com)
.... Irene Hoff (1962–63)

NORRIS, KATHI—hostess
b: Jun 1, Newark, Ohio

Spin the Picture (quiz) ..... emcee (1949–50)

NORTH, ALAN—actor
b: Dec 23, New York City, N.Y.

Love, Sidney (com)
.... Judge Mort Harris (1981–82)
Police Squad (com)
.... Capt. Ed Hocken (1982)
Tough Cookies (com)
.... Father McCaskey (1986)

Alan has been active as a TV character actor since the "Golden Age" of live dramas, in the 1950s. Of his chosen profession he has said, "I wanted a job that allowed me to sleep late ... so I went into the theater."

NORTH, JAY—juvenile actor
b: Aug 3, 1952, North Hollywood, Calif.

Dennis the Menace (com)
.... Dennis Mitchell (1959–63)
Maya (adv) .... Terry Bowen (1967–68)

Jay North, the tow-headed star of *Dennis the Menace,* is one of the legion of Hollywood child performers who is warmly remembered as a child but practically ig-

nored as an adult. Jay's mother pushed him into television before he could even say "residuals"; his first appearance was on *Queen for a Day* at age six, followed by commercials and then a supercute acting role. On a December 1958 episode of *Wanted: Dead or Alive,* he played a kid who gave Steve McQueen eight cents to lasso the most elusive quarry of all—Santa Claus! That role was quickly followed by others in *Sugarfoot* and *Desilu Playhouse* in early '59. Then in the fall, at age seven, he began his own series, *Dennis the Menace.*

Four years as the malevolent moppet made Jay one of television's most recognizable kids, and for a time afterward roles came easily, in *Wagon Train, The Lucy Show, My Three Sons,* and other series. He also made a few films; one of them, *Maya,* shot in India in 1965, even led to a second series. During the late '60s and early '70s Jay worked mostly doing voices for Saturday morning cartoons, including three years as Bamm Bamm on *The Flintstones* and *Pebbles and Bamm Bamm* (1971–74). Then, as he later told a reporter, "my career just sort of dried up." He did some local theater, served an enlistment in the navy, and worked as a prison guard. He had a small part in a 1980 movie that starred a more recent child discovery—*Scouts Honor,* with Gary Coleman. However, Jay's acting days, for the most part, seem to be over.

NORTH, SHEREE—actress
b: Jan 17, 1933*, Los Angeles, Calif.

Big Eddie (com) .... Honey Smith (1975)
I'm a Big Girl Now (com)
.... Edie McKendrick (1980–81)
The Bay City Blues (drama)
.... Lynn Holtz (1983)

This energetic blonde actress-dancer starred in a number of films during the 1950s. Touted as "the next Marilyn Monroe," she wound up instead on television, where in the '60s she was finally able to play gutsier roles. Film historian David Quinlan observed that, like Angie Dickinson and Dorothy Malone, she was at her best playing "ladies just a little past their prime, but not their pride."

Sheree was later nominated for Emmy

*Some sources give 1930.

Awards for appearances on *Marcus Welby* and *Archie Bunker's Place*. She was most interesting, perhaps, as Marilyn Monroe's mentally disturbed mother in the 1980 TV movie *Marilyn: The Untold Story*.

NORTH, ZEME—actress

Double Life of Henry Phyfe (com)
.... Judy Kimball (1966)

NORTHROP, WAYNE—actor
b: Apr 12, Sumner, Wash.

Dynasty (drama) .... Michael (1981)
Dynasty (drama)
.... Michael Culhane (1986–   )

Wayne was best known to daytime viewers of the 1980s as Roman Brady on the soap opera *Days of Our Lives*.

NORTHUP, HARRY—actor

Knots Landing (drama)
.... Wayne Harkness (1982)

NORTON, CLIFF—comedian, actor
b: Chicago, Ill.

Garroway at Large (var).. regular (1949–51)
The Public Life of Cliff Norton (com)
.... host (1952)
The Dave Garroway Show (var)
.... regular (1953–54)
What's Going On? (quiz).... panelist (1954)
Caesar Presents (var).. various roles (1955)
It's About Time (com) ...... Boss (1966–67)
Where's Huddles? (cartn)
.... Ed Huddles (voice) (1970)

NORTON, DEBORAH—actress

Holocaust (drama) ...... Marta Dorf (1978)

NORTON, JOHN K.—educator

Answers for Americans (pub aff)
.... panelist (1953–54)

NORTON, KEN—black actor, boxer
b: Aug 9, 1945

The Gong Show (com) ... panelist (1976–80)

The former heavyweight boxing champ. He was also a boxing commentator for CBS and NBC.

NORTON-TAYLOR, JUDY—actress
b: Jan 29, 1958, Santa Monica, Calif.

The Waltons (drama)
.... Mary Ellen Walton Willard (1972–81)

NOTABLES, THE—singers

The Dinah Shore Show (music)
.... vocalists (1951–55)

NOURI, MICHAEL—actor
b: Dec 9, 1945, Washington, D.C. r: Alpine, N.J.

Beacon Hill (drama)
.... Giorgio Bellonci (1975)
The Curse of Dracula (adv)
.... Count Dracula (1979)
The Last Convertible (drama)
.... Jean R.G.R. desBarres (1979)
The Gangster Chronicles (drama)
.... Charles "Lucky" Luciano (1981)
Bay City Blues (drama).. Joe Rohner (1983)
Downtown (police)
.... Det. John Forney (1986–   )

This tall, swarthy actor (of Middle Eastern descent) got his start with a supporting role in the film *Goodbye Columbus* in 1969. He moved into soap operas during the mid-1970s, with featured parts in *Beacon Hill* in prime time and *Somerset* and *Search for Tomorrow* in daytime. He then briefly played an odd, campy version of Count Dracula before hitting his stride playing aggressive young men in prime time drama series and movies.

NOVACK, SHELLY—actor

The F.B.I. (police)
.... agent Chris Daniels (1973–74)
Most Wanted (police)
.... Sgt. Charlie Benson (1976–77)

Lanky pro football player who turned to character acting in 1969, and during the '70s was seen in supporting roles on many action shows.

NOVELITES, THE—singers

Jan Murray Time (var)
.... musical group (1955)

NOVELLO, DON—comedian, writer
b: Jan 1, 1943, Ashtabula, Ohio

The Smothers Brothers Show (var)
.... regular (1975)
NBC's Saturday Night Live (com)
.... regular (1978–80)

Don's best known character—in fact, his only known character to most—is Father Guido Sarducci, rock critic, and gossip columnist for *L'Osservatore Romano,* the Vatican newspaper. Don was formerly an ad agency copywriter, then a stand-up comic; he created his famous character in clubs around 1973.

NOVELLO, JAY—actor
b: 1904 d: Sep 2, 1982

McHale's Navy (com)
.... Mayor Mario Lugatto (1965–66)

NOVINS, STUART—newscaster

Face the Nation (int)
.... moderator (1960–61)

Emmy Award: Best On-the-Spot Coverage of a News Event, for an interview with Fidel Castro (1959)

A newsman with CBS from 1940–1975, Novins scored many scoops in his interviews with world figures. Among them: the first Western interview inside the Kremlin, with Nikita Krushchev in 1957; and the first with a triumphant Fidel Castro, in Cuba in 1959. Novins was moderator of *Face the Nation* on Sunday afternoons from 1953–1960.

NUCKOLS, WILLIAM—actor

Supertrain (drama) .... Wally (1979)

NUGENT, JUDY—juvenile actress

The Ruggles (com)
.... Donna Ruggles (1949–52)

NUNEZ, CHARLES—juvenile actor

The Bad News Bears (com)
.... Miguel Agilar (1979–80)

NUNEZ, DANNY—juvenile actor

The Bad News Bears (com)
.... Jose Agilar (1979–80)

NUNN, ALICE—actress
b: Jacksonville, Fla.

Camp Runamuck (com)
...... Mahala May Gruenecker (1965–66)
Tony Orlando and Dawn (var)
.... regular (1974–76)
Westside Medical (drama)
.... Carrie (1977)

NUSSER, JAMES—actor

Gunsmoke (wes)
.... Louie Pheeters (1955–75)

NUTT, REV. GRADY—actor
b: c. 1935 d: Nov 23, 1982

Hee Haw (var)
.... regular (1979–83)

NYDELL, KEN—actor

Roller Derby (sport)
.... announcer (1949–51)

NYE, LOUIS—comedian
b: May 1, Hartford, Conn.

The Steve Allen Show (var)
.... regular (1956–61)
The Ann Sothern Show (com)
.... Dr. Delbert Gray (1960–61)
The Beverly Hillbillies (com)
.... Sonny Drysdale (1962)
The Steve Allen Comedy Hour (var)
.... regular (1967)
Happy Days (var)
.... host (1970)
Needles and Pins (com)
.... Harry Karp (1973)
The $1.98 Beauty Show (com)
.... frequent panelist (1978–80)

Middle-aged Louis Nye was one of a group of talented character comics who became famous on *The Steve Allen Show* in the late '50s. Among the others: Tom Poston, Don Knotts, Pat Harrington, and Bill Dana. Louis' character, with which he will always be associated, was that of smug Gordon Hathaway ("Hi-ho, Steverino!").

Louis began on radio and stage in the '40s, but did not attract much attention until he became a regular on Jack Paar's morning TV show in the mid-1950s.

After his success with Steve Allen he continued to turn up occasionally on various TV series, played supporting roles in some rather embarrassing movies (e.g., *Sex Kittens Go to College*), and worked the personal appearance circuit.

NYMAN, BETTY ANNE—juvenile actress

School House (var).......... regular (1949)

NYPE, RUSSELL—actor, singer
b: Apr 26, 1924, Zion, Ill.

Dorothy (com) .... Burton Foley (1979)

O

OAKES, RANDI—actress
b: Aug 19, 1951, Randalia, Iowa

CHiPs (police) . Off. Bonnie Clark (1979–82)

Pretty Randi Oakes was one of the earliest of the female "Chippies" (policepersons), who were brought in to dress up the popular police show CHiPs. She had previously made a guest appearance in an episode of the series as a car thief. Before joining CHiPs, Randi worked as a model, and was seen as a semiregular on Rosetti and Ryan.

OAKLAND, SIMON—actor
b: 1922, New York City, N.Y. d: Aug 29, 1983

Toma (police) . . . . . . Insp. Spooner (1973–74)
Kolchak: The Night Stalker (drama)
. . . . Tony Vincenzo (1974–75)
Baa Baa Black Sheep (drama)
. . . . Gen. Moore (1976–78)
David Cassidy—Man Undercover (police)
. . . . Sgt. Walt Abrams (1978)

A burly, authoritative character actor, much on television in supporting roles from the early '60s until his death.

OAKLAND, SUSAN—panelist

What's Going On? (quiz) . . . . panelist (1954)

OATES, WARREN—actor
b: Jul 5, 1928, Depoy, Ky. d: Apr 3, 1982

Stoney Burke (wes) . . . Ves Painter (1962–63)
East of Eden (drama) . . . Cyrus Trask (1981)
The Blue and the Gray (drama)
. . . . Maj. Welles (1982)

This rowdy, rough-edged actor got his start in television in New York in the '50s, pretesting stunts for CBS's Beat the Clock (he replaced another aspiring young actor in the job—James Dean). Warren eventually landed some roles in live TV dramas, but he really hit his stride—or gallop—during the 1960s in TV westerns. He played scores of idiosyncratic villains in Rawhide, Gunsmoke, Trackdown, The Virginian, and similar shows, and was a particular favorite on Wanted: Dead or Alive, where Steve McQueen had to track him down repeatedly! He also appeared in several dozen action films, "dyin' in darn near every one of them," as he later said. Several of these films, including The Wild Bunch and Dillinger (in which he played the title role) have become minor classics of the violence genre.

Warren continued active on television until his untimely death at the age of 53, shortly after he had completed filming the miniseries The Blue and the Gray—in which, of course, he played a villain.

OBER, PHILIP—actor
b: Mar 23, 1902, Fort Payne, Ala. d: Sep 13, 1982

I Dream of Jeannie (com)
. . . . Gen. Wingard Stone (1965–66)

Once married to actress Vivian Vance (of I Love Lucy); after his tour of duty on I Dream of Jeannie, Ober retired from acting and became a consular official in Puerto Vallarta, Mexico.

OBERDIEAR, KAREN—juvenile actress

The Texas Wheelers (com)
. . . . Boo Wheeler (1974–75)

O'BERLIN, BILL—

Happy Days (var) . . . . regular (1970)

OBERON, MERLE—actress
b: Feb 19, 1911, Calcutta, India* d: Nov 23, 1979

Assignment Foreign Legion (drama)
. . . . host (1957)

The regal Hollywood beauty of the '30s and '40s, a stylish member of the international jet set before it was even called that; she appeared fleetingly on television during the mid-1950s in a few dramatic productions.

*Most biographies list Hobart, Tasmania, but author David Ragan in Movie Stars of the '30s claims that this was a fraud, as was the story of her very proper English upbringing, concocted by studio publicists to hide her true origins; she was born in Calcutta, the illegitimate half-caste daughter of an Indian girl and a British soldier (who abandoned them).

O'BOURNE, BRYAN—actor

Blondie (com) . . . . Mr. Beasley (1968–69)

O'BRIAN, HUGH—actor
b: Apr 19, 1925, Rochester, N.Y. r: Chicago, Ill.

The Life and Legend of Wyatt Earp (wes)
. . . . Wyatt Earp (1955–61)
Search (adv) . . . . Hugh Lockwood (1972–73)

Dark, rugged Hugh O'Brian developed his macho image naturally. Enlisting in the marine corps during World War II, at the age of 18, he became the youngest drill instructor in the history of the corps. Later, he planned to study law, but was sidetracked into acting, making his television debut in 1948 and his movie debut in 1950. For the next half-dozen years he played small parts, mostly villains, appearing on such series as *Fireside Theatre* and *The Loretta Young Show*. *Wyatt Earp* in 1955 finally made him both a hero and a star; it remains the role with which he is most closely identified.

Hugh made a good deal of money from this long-running series, and he invested it wisely. Since the '60s he has been active in charitable endeavors in addition to making periodic appearances in TV movies and a few series episodes, including several on *Police Story* and *Fantasy Island* in the '70s. His only subsequent series, a high-tech adventure called *Search,* was unsuccessful.

O'BRIEN, CLAY—juvenile actor
b: May 6, 1961, Ray, Ariz.

The Cowboys (wes) . . . . Weedy (1974)

O'BRIEN, DAVID—actor
b: Oct 1, Chicago, Ill.

Our Private World (drama)
. . . . Dr. Tony Larson (1965)

This handsome soap opera star was best known for his 15-year run as Dr. Steve Aldrich on *The Doctors* (1967–82). He was also seen during the early and mid-1960s in *The Secret Storm* and *Search for Tomorrow,* and in the '80s on *Ryan's Hope*. He is not to be confused with the movie and early television actor and comedy writer (for Red Skelton) Dave O'Brien, who died in 1969.

O'BRIEN, EDMOND—actor
b: Sep 10, 1915, New York City, N.Y. d: May 9, 1985

Johnny Midnight (drama)
. . . . Johnny Midnight (1960)
Sam Benedict (drama)
. . . . Sam Benedict (1962–63)
The Long Hot Summer (drama)
. . . . "Boss" Will Varner (1965)

Edmond O'Brien, a serious-looking and (in his later years) rather heavyset character actor, was seen frequently on television dramas in the '50s and '60s. His first two series were standard action fare, while the third—*The Long Hot Summer*—was the TV adaptation of Faulkner's torrid melodrama, with O'Brien playing the ruthless small-town patriarch. O'Brien began to experience health problems during the '60s but continued to act until the mid-1970s (e.g., *Police Story* in 1974), when advancing Alzheimer's disease made it no longer possible for him to remember his lines. His movie career extended from 1939 to 1974.

O'BRIEN, HUGH—
see O'Brian, Hugh

O'BRIEN, LEO—actor
Chiefs (drama) . . . . Joshua Cole (1983)

O'BRIEN, LOUISE—singer
r: Oklahoma

The Pat Boone-Chevy Showroom (var)
. . . . regular (1959)
Sing Along with Mitch (var)
. . . . regular (1961–64)

Miss Oklahoma of 1952.

O'BRIEN, MARIA—actress
b: 1950

Number 96 (drama)
. . . . Ginny Ramirez (1980–81)

The daughter of actor Edmond O'Brien.

O'BRIEN, PAT—actor
b: Nov 11, 1899, Milwaukee, Wis. d: Oct 15, 1983

Harrigan and Son (com)
. . . . James Harrigan, Sr. (1960–61)

Emmy Awards: Best Actor in a Daytime Special, and Daytime Actor of the Year, for *ABC Matinee Today: The Other Woman* (1974)

Rotund Irish-American charactor actor, popular in films of the '30s (often as a cop or priest, but most memorably as Knute Rocke in *Knute Rockne—All American*). He was also quite busy on television in the '50s and early '60s. He continued to be seen occasionally after that and was always a favorite guest on St. Patrick's Day telecasts. His autobiography: *The Wind at My Back* (1964).

O'BRIEN, RORY—juvenile actor
b: 1955

The Farmer's Daughter (com)
.... Danny Morley (1963–66)

O'BRIEN, THOMAS—actor

Call to Glory (drama)
.... Patrick Thomas (1984–85)

O'BRIEN-MOORE, ERIN—actress
b: 1902, Los Angeles, Calif. r: Tucson, Ariz. d: May 3, 1979

The Ruggles (com)
.... Margaret Ruggles (1950–52)
Peyton Place (drama)
.... Nurse Choate (1965–68)

O'BYRNE, BRYAN—actor

Occasional Wife (com)
.... Man-in-Middle (1966–67)

O'CONNELL, ARTHUR—actor
b: Mar 29, 1908, New York City, N.Y. d: May 18, 1981

Mr. Peepers (com).... Mr. Hansen (1953–54)
The Second Hundred Years (com)
.... Edwin Carpenter (1967–68)

O'CONNELL, HELEN—singer
b: May 23, 1920, Lima, Ohio

TV's Top Tunes (music) ..... hostess (1953)
The Russ Morgan Show (music)
.... regular (1956)
The Helen O'Connell Show (music)
.... hostess (1957)

This famous big-band singer scored several enduring song hits with the Jimmy Dorsey Orchestra early in her career, among them "Green Eyes," "Amapola," and other romantic duets with Bob Eberle. She was with Dorsey from 1939–43. During the '50s, still beautiful, Helen was a popular guest on prime time variety shows, had her own summer show, and was for a time Dave Garroway's cohost on the *Today* show. Later, she was most often seen as a television beauty-pageant host and on occasional big-band nostalgia specials.

O'CONNELL, TAAFFE—actress

Blansky's Beauties (com)
.... Hillary S. Prentiss (1977)

O'CONNER, JINI BOYD—hostess

Scrapbook Junior Edition (child)
.... hostess (1948)

O'CONNOR, CARROLL—actor
b: Aug 2, 1922*, New York City, N.Y.

All in the Family (com)
.... Archie Bunker (1971–79)
Archie Bunker's Place (com)
.... Archie Bunker (1979–83)

Emmy Awards: Best Actor in a Comedy Series, for *All in the Family* (1972, 1977, 1978, 1979)

Carroll O'Connor toiled in semiobscurity for a very long time before, nearing the age of 50, he suddenly became one of TV's biggest stars. His is a story that should give encouragement to all aging character actors who yearn, someday, for greater renown.

Carroll had a hard time even getting into acting. Born of Irish descent in New York, he served for four years in the merchant marine during the mid-1940s and did not become interested in the theater until his (delayed) college days, in his midtwenties. His professional debut was in Ireland, where he was attending college, around 1950. He acted in Europe for several years before returning to New York in 1954, but the pickings there proved slim. It was not until 1958 that he made his Broadway debut and also gained some small television roles on *The Rifleman* and, later, *Armstrong Circle Theatre.*

By the 1960s Carroll had established

*Some sources give 1924 or 1925.

himself as a movie and TV supporting player. His pudgy countenance and blustery manner often got him villainous roles; for example, on *Bonanza* in 1963 he played the crooked boss of Virginia City who had Michael Landon shot, and on *I Spy* in 1966 he was an evil scientist who abducted Robert Culp. Sometimes the parts were a little more wistful; on *Voyage to the Bottom of the Sea* he was "Old John," an enigmatic stranger found floating placidly in a rowboat in the middle of the Pacific.

Carroll might have remained in such roles forever had it not been for a most unusual comedy pilot he made in 1968 for Norman Lear. The networks were highly skeptical (who wants a show about a bigot?), but Lear finally convinced CBS to try it and when it finally went on the air, as a midseason replacement in early 1971, *All in the Family* became one of the biggest and most influential hits in the history of television. The show's extraordinary 12-year run made Carroll rich, famous—and bitter at the dummies who ran CBS (because they eventually canceled the show). Carroll starred in a few specials during the series run (*Of Thee I Sing,* 1972; *The Last Hurrah,* 1977) and has since been seen in occasional TV movies.

O'CONNOR, DES—comedian
b: 1932, Stepney, England

Kraft Music Hall Presents The Des O'Connor Show (var).................. host (1970–71)

English comedian and television star, who twice fronted a summer variety show on the U.S., but never really caught on here.

O'CONNOR, DONALD—actor
b: Aug 28, 1925*, Chicago, Ill.

The Colgate Comedy Hour (var)
.... rotating host (1951–54)
Donald O'Connor Texaco Show (com)
.... as himself (1954–55)

Emmy Award: Best Actor in a Regular Series, for *The Colgate Comedy Hour* (1953)

This ever-youthful Hollywood song-and-dance man was a popular TV variety show

*Some sources give August 30.

638

host in the '50s. He also headlined his own situation comedy in 1954, in which he and his partner Sid Miller played struggling songwriters. Donald's banner years were 1952–53, during which he starred in two of his most famous movies (*Singing in the Rain* and *Call Me Madame)* and won an Emmy Award for his appearances on the top-rated *Colgate Comedy Hour.* After 1955 he was seen less often on television, mostly in prestige productions on *Playhouse 90, Chrysler Theatre,* etc., though in 1966 he made a pilot for a series to be called *The Hoofer.* He also turned up on specials such as the Academy Awards show.

O'CONNOR, GLYNNIS—actress
b: Nov 19, 1955, New York City, N.Y. r: New Rochelle, N.Y.

Sons and Daughters (drama)
.... Anita Cramer (1974)

O'CONNOR, TIM—actor
b: c. 1927

Peyton Place (drama)
.... Elliott Carson (1965–68)
Wheels (drama)...... Hub Hewitson (1978)
Buck Rogers in the 25th Century (sci fi)
.... Dr. Huer (1979–80)

This lean, rather threatening character actor has had a busy career on television since the early '60s. He has appeared mostly in crime dramas such as *The F.B.I., Cannon,* and *Barnaby Jones,* though he was also a leading character (as Mia Farrow's ex-con father) on *Peyton Place.*

O'CONOR, SEN. HERBERT R.— politician
b: Nov 7, 1896, Baltimore, Md. d: Mar 4, 1960

Crime Syndicated (police)
.... narrator (1951–53)

U.S. Senator from Maryland, and former chairman of the Senate crime investigating committee.

O'DELL, BRYAN—actor
What's Happening!! (com)
.... Marvin (1976–77)

O'DELL, DELL—lady magician

The Dell O'Dell Show (var) ... emcee (1951)

O'DELL, TONY—actor
b: Jan 30, Pasadena, Calif.

Otherworld (sci fi).... Trace Sterling (1985)
Head of the Class (com)
.... Alan Pinkard (1986–   )

O'DONNELL, GENE—actor

Barney Blake, Police Reporter (drama)
.... Barney Blake (1948)

O'DONNELL, JACKLYN—actress

The Ed Wynn Show (com)
.... Laurie (1958–59)
Westinghouse Playhouse (com)
.... Nancy (1961)

OFARIM, ESTHER & ABI—

Continental Showcase (var) . regulars (1966)

O'FARRELL, BERNADETTE—actress
b: 1926

The Adventures of Robin Hood (adv)
.... Maid Marian (1955–57)

O'FLYNN, DAMIAN—actor

The Life and Legend of Wyatt Earp (wes)
.... Doc Goodfellow (1959–61)

OGILVY, IAN—actor
b: 1943

Return of the Saint (adv)
.... Simon Templar (1978)

O'GRADY, LANI—actress
b: Oct 2, Walnut Creek, Calif.

The Headmaster (drama) ... Judy (1970–71)
Eight Is Enough (com)
.... Mary Bradford (1977–81)

The daughter of one of Hollywood's most powerful children's talent agents, and the sister of *My Three Sons* star Don Grady.

OH, SOON-TECK—actor
b: Korea

East of Eden (drama).......... Lee (1981)

O'HALLORAN, HAL—host

ABC Barn Dance (music) ..... emcee (1949)

The veteran emcee of radio's long-running *National Barn Dance* from Chicago, which was seen briefly on television in 1949, as the *ABC Barn Dance.*

O'HALLORAN, MICHAEL—actor

Live Like a Millionaire (talent)
.... Merton the butler (1951)

O'HANLON, GEORGE—actor, writer
b: Nov 23, 1917, Brooklyn, N.Y.

The Life of Riley (com)
.... Calvin Dudley (1955–56)
The Jetsons (cartn)
.... George Jetson (voice) (1962–63)
The Reporter (drama).... Artie Burns (1964)

O'HANLON, GEORGE, JR.—actor

The Nancy Drew Mysteries (adv)
.... Ned Nickerson (1977)

The son of actor-writer George O'Hanlon, listed above.

O'HARA, CATHERINE—comedienne, writer
b: Mar 4, 1954, Toronto, Canada

Second City TV (com)
.... Lola Heatherton/others (1977–80)
The Steve Allen Comedy Hour (var)
.... regular (1980–81)
SCTV Network 90 (com)
.... regular (1981–82)

Emmy Award: Best Writing for a Comedy Program, for *SCTV Network* (1982)

O'HARA, JENNY—actress
b: Feb 24, Sonora, Calif.

The Facts of Life (com)
.... Miss Emily Mahoney (1979)
Highcliffe Manor (com)..... Rebecca (1979)
Secrets of Midland Heights (drama)
.... Lucy Dexter (1980–81)
My Sister Sam (com) .... Dixie (1986–   )

O'HARA, QUINN—actress
b: c. 1941, Edinburgh, Scotland

The Lively Ones (var) .... Smitty (1963)

A former Miss Universe contestant, and one of Vic Damone's sexy "dates" on his 1963 summer show. She decorated episodes of a number of prime time series during the 1960s.

OHBAYASHI, TAKESHI—actor

Shogun (drama) ...... Brother Urano (1980)

O'HEANEY, CAITLIN—actress
b: Aug 16, 1953, Whitefish Bay, Wis.

Apple Pie (com)
.... Anna Marie Hollyhock (1978)
Tales of the Gold Monkey (adv)
.... Sarah Stickney White (1982–83)

O'HERLIHY, DAN—actor
b: May 1, 1919, Wexford, Ireland

The Travels of Jaimie McPheeters (wes)
..... "Doc" Sardius McPheeters (1963–64)
The Long Hot Summer (drama)
.... "Boss" Will Varner (1966)
A Man Called Sloane (drama)
.... the director (1979–80)
Whiz Kids (drama)
.... Carson Marsh (1984)

A tall, taciturn Irish actor, much on television from the early '50s onward.

O'HERLIHY, GAVAN—actor

Happy Days (com)
.... Chuck Cunningham (1974)
Rich Man, Poor Man—Book I (drama)
.... Phil McGee (1976)

This unfortunate young actor made his only regular series appearance in a role that has become one of TV's ultimate bits of trivia. Whatever *did* become of Richie Cunningham's older brother, Chuck? According to the *Happy Days* script he went off to college after the first season, but he was never heard from or referred to again during the series' ten-year run. Even his TV parents forgot him; in the series' final episode in 1984 they referred to Richie and Joanie as their only children.

Actor O'Herlihy fared little better, playing tousle-haired young men in a succession of TV movies of the '70s and early '80s.

OKAZAKI, BOB—actor

Archie Bunker's Place (com)
.... Bruce (1982–83)

O'KEEFE, DENNIS—actor, writer
b: Mar. 29, 1908, Ft. Madison, Iowa r: on the road d: Aug 31, 1968

Suspicion (drama) .... host (1957)
The Dennis O'Keefe Show (com)
.... Hal Towne (1959–60)

O'KEEFE, PAUL—actor

The Patty Duke Show (com)
.... Ross Lane (1963–66)

O'KEEFE, WALTER—host, songwriter
b: Aug 18, 1900, Hartford, Conn. d: Jun 26, 1983

Mayor of Hollywood (var)
.... as himself (1952)
Two for the Money (quiz) ..... emcee (1954)

OKLAHOMA WRANGLERS, THE—

Ozark Jubilee (music) .... regulars (1955)

OKUN, MILT—orchestra leader
b: Dec 23, 1923, Brooklyn, N.Y.

The Starland Vocal Band Show (var)
.... orch. leader (1977)

OLAF, PIERRE—actor
b: Jul 14, 1928, Cauderan, France

The Kraft Music Hall (var)
.... regular (1962–63)

OLFSON, KEN—actor

The Nancy Walker Show (com)
.... Terry Folson (1976)
Flying High (adv)
.... Raymond Strickman (1978–79)

Ken's role on *The Nancy Walker Show* was one of the earlier portrayals of a gay male in a television comedy.

OLIN, KEN—actor
b: Jul 30, 1954, Chicago, Ill.

Bay City Blues (drama)
.... Rocky Padillo (1983)
Hill Street Blues (police)
.... Det. Harry Garibaldi (1984–85)

Falcon Crest (drama)
.... Father Christopher (1985–86)

OLIVER, STEPHEN—actor

Peyton Place (drama)
.... Lee Webber (1966–68)
Bracken's World (drama)
.... Tom Hudson (1970)

OLIVER, SUSAN—actress

b: Feb 13, 1937, New York City, N.Y.

Peyton Place (drama).. Ann Howard (1966)

One of television's most familiar supporting actresses, in hundreds of series episodes from the mid-1950s to the mid-1970s,
ranging from *Father Knows Best* to *Night
Gallery*. She was also a regular on the daytime serial *Days of Our Lives* in the mid-
1970s.

OLIVIERI, DENNIS—actor

The New People (drama)
.... Stanley Gabriel (1969–70)

OLKEWICZ, WALTER—actor

b: May 14, Bayonne, N.J.

The Last Resort (com)
.... Zach Comstock (1979–80)
The Blue and the Gray (drama)
.... Big Bear (1982)
Wizards and Warriors (adv) . Marko (1983)
Partners in Crime (drama)
.... Harmon Shain (1984)

Heavyweight actor, often seen as the
dense, clumsy helper in comedies and
comedy/adventures.

OLMOS, EDWARD JAMES—actor

b: Feb 24, 1947, East Los Angeles, Calif.

Miami Vice (police)
.... Lt. Martin Castillo (1984–)

Emmy Award: Best Supporting Actor in a
Drama Series, for *Miami Vice* (1985)

The brooding, mysterious police lieutenant in *Miami Vice*—a man who looks like
he might have an interesting past—is
played by an actor who spent many years
on the fringes of show business, hardly noticed. During his teens (around 1960) he
fronted a rock group, Eddie James and the

Pacific Coast, in Los Angeles; from the
early '60s to the mid-1970s he appeared in
amateur theater productions in the area.
His first professional role did not come
until 1978, in the play *Zoot Suit*, which
brought him several awards and more
work. He has since appeared in a scattering of TV movies (e.g., *Three Hundred
Miles for Stephanie*) and series episodes
(Hill Street Blues).

O'LOUGHLIN, GERALD S.—actor

b: Dec 23, 1921, New York City, N.Y.

Storefront Lawyers (drama)
.... Devlin McNeil (1970–71)
The Rookies (police)
.... Lt. Eddie Ryker (1972–76)
Wheels (drama)....... Rusty Horton (1978)
The Blue and the Gray (drama)
.... Sgt. O'Toole (1982)
Automan (police)..... Capt. Boyd (1983–84)
Our House (drama)
.... Joe Kaplan (1986–)

This mature character actor is most often
seen on television action shows playing
the tough, by-the-book boss to whom the
young heroes report. He was, for example,
the senior cop in charge of *The Rookies*
and *Automan,* and the senior lawyer on
The Storefront Lawyers. He has played
supporting roles on stage, screen, and television since the 1950s.

OLSEN & JOHNSON—comedians

John Sigvard "Ole" Olsen, b: Nov 6, 1892, Wa-
bash, Ind. d: Jan 26, 1963
Harold Ogden "Chic" Johnson, b: Mar 5, 1891,
Chicago, Ill. d: Feb 28, 1962

Fireball Fun-for-All (var)
.... cohosts (1949)

A highly popular knockabout comedy
team, Olsen & Johnson began in vaudeville
in 1914 but scored their greatest hit in 1938
in the long-running Broadway smash *Hellzapoppin*—a frenetic mélange of pie
throwing, seltzer bottles, leggy show girls,
and frantic midgets running about the theater. They produced variations on the
show for many years thereafter, on tour
and in a 1949 television free-for-all. Olsen
was the thin one, Johnson (whose nickname "Chic" came from his birthplace,
Chicago) was the fat one.

OLSEN, J.C.—comedian

Fireball Fun-for-All (var). . . . . regular (1949)

The son of Ole Olsen, of Olsen & Johnson.

OLSEN, JOHNNY—announcer

b: c. 1910, Windon, Minn. d: Oct 12, 1985

Doorway to Fame (talent). . . . host (1947–49)
Fun for the Money (quiz) . . . . . emcee (1949)
The Strawhatters (var). . . . . . . emcee (1953)
Hold That Note (quiz)
 . . . . announcer/host (1957)
Keep It in the Family (quiz)
 . . . . announcer (1957–58)
Play Your Hunch (quiz). . . announcer (1960)
Play Your Hunch (quiz). . . announcer (1962)
The Jackie Gleason Show (var)
 . . . . announcer (1962–70)

One of daytime television's best known announcers, the man who cheerfully intoned the introductions on *What's My Line?, I've Got a Secret,* and *The Price Is Right* ("Come on *down!*"). In addition to his work on dozens of game shows, he hosted children's programs in the late '40s and '50s, including *Johnny Olsen's Rumpus Room* and *Kids & Company,* and also did prime time announcing and hosting. In the 1940s he was a radio announcer on such noisy shows as *Break the Bank.*

OLSEN, MERLIN—actor, sportscaster

b: Sep 15, 1940, Logan, Utah

Little House on the Prairie (adv)
 . . . . Jonathan Garvey (1977–81)
Father Murphy (drama)
 . . . . John Michael Murphy (1981–82)
Fathers and Sons (com)
 . . . . Buddy Landau (1986)

Big, bearded Merlin Olsen, the "gentle giant" of the NFL, had a stellar career in football before turning to acting. During his 15 years with the Los Angeles Rams (1962–77) he was selected for the Pro Bowl 14 times and was named most valuable player in 1974.

After his football retirement in 1977, Merlin began a dual television career as a football commentator for NBC and an actor on the popular *Little House on the Prairie* series. He later starred as a bogus (but kindly) priest in another series produced by *Little House* star Michael Landon, *Father Murphy.* Despite his towering bulk (6'5"), Merlin is quite effective at conveying warmth and sentimentality and is often featured with kids and dogs; indeed, he was even seen as a commercial spokesman for florists during the 1980s.

He is a phi beta kappa graduate of Utah State.

OLSEN, SUSAN—juvenile actress

b: 1961, Santa Monica, Calif.

The Brady Bunch (com)
 . . . . Cindy Brady (1969–74)
The Brady Bunch Hour (var)
 . . . . Cindy Brady (1977)

OLSON, ERIC—juvenile actor

b: Nov 17, 1962, Santa Monica, Calif.

Apple's Way (drama)
 . . . . Steven Apple (1974–75)
Swiss Family Robinson (adv)
 . . . . Ernie Robinson (1975–76)

OLSON, NANCY—actress

b: Jul 14, 1928, Milwaukee, Wis.

Kingston: Confidential (drama)
 . . . . Jessica Frazier (1977)
Paper Dolls (drama)
 . . . . Marjorie Harper (1984)

O'MALLEY, J. PAT—actor

b: 1901, Burnley, England d: Feb 27, 1985

Alarm (drama) . . . . Fireman (1954)
My Favorite Martian (com)
 . . . . Mr. Harry Burns (1963–64)
Wendy and Me (com) . Mr. Bundy (1964–65)
The Rounders (com). . . . . . . Vince (1966–67)
A Touch of Grace (com)
 . . . . Herbert Morrison (1973)
Maude (com). . . . . . . Bert Beasley (1975–77)

Not to be confused with veteran character actor Pat O'Malley (1891–1966), who appeared in films from 1907 to the late '50s and in some early TV productions. Pat was a hawk-nosed, rather determined looking gent; J. Pat a beaming, cherubic, elderly "Irishman," who was much on TV in the '60s and '70s and who also appeared in the '80s in TV movies such as *A Small Killing* (1981). On *Maude* he played the elderly suitor who married Bea Arthur's second maid, Mrs. Naugatuck.

O'MARA, KATE—actress
b: Aug 10, 1939, Leicester, England

Dynasty (drama) .. Caress Morell (1986–)

O'MORRISON, KEVIN—actor

Charlie Wild, Private Detective (drama)
.... Charlie Wild (1950–51)

O'NEAL, ANN—actress
b: Dec 23, 1893, Missouri d: Nov 24, 1971

Professional Father (com)..... Nana (1955)

O'NEAL, FREDERICK—black actor
b: Aug 27, 1905, Brooksville, Miss.

Car 54, Where Are You? (com)
.... Off. Wallace (1962–63)

O'NEAL, KEVIN—actor

No Time for Sergeants (com)
.... airman Ben Whitledge (1964–65)

The younger brother of Ryan O'Neal.

O'NEAL, PATRICK—actor
b: Sep 26, 1927, Ocala, Fla.

Dick and The Duchess (com)
.... Dick Starrett (1957–58)
Diagnosis: Unknown (drama)
.... Dr. Daniel Coffee (1960)
Kaz (drama) ..... Samuel Bennett (1978–79)
Emerald Point N.A.S. (drama)
.... Harlan Adams (1983)

O'NEAL, RON—black actor
b: Sep 1, 1937, Utica, N.Y. r: Cleveland, Ohio

Bring 'Em Back Alive (adv)
.... Sultan of Johore (1982–83)
The Equalizer (drama)
.... Lt. Isadore Smalls (1986–)

The black actor who became famous as "Superfly" in movies of the early '70s.

O'NEAL, RYAN—actor
b: Apr 20, 1941, Los Angeles, Calif.

Empire (wes) .... Tal Garret (1962–63)
Peyton Place (drama)
.... Rodney Harrington (1964–69)

Blonde, boyish, charming Ryan O'Neal spent a rather rebellious and wandering boyhood before becoming a television heartthrob in the 1960s. The son of a screenwriter and an actress, he spent nearly two months in jail as a youth for assault and battery. In 1958 he joined his parents in Germany, where they were working on a film. Ryan got his first exposure there as a stuntman and bit player in the TV series *Tales of the Vikings*, which was filmed in Germany and later syndicated in the U.S. He then returned to America and landed small parts in such series as *Dobie Gillis, Leave It to Beaver,* and *Bachelor Father* in the early '60s. His first regular role was that of Tal, heir to the giant Garret ranch on *Empire*, but the part that made him famous was that of wealthy Rodney Harrington, who loved and lost Mia Farrow on *Peyton Place*.

Ryan was with that multiweekly, prime time serial for its entire five-year run, appearing in more than 500 episodes. When it ended, he appeared in pilots for two new series, in 1968–69. However, before he could land another television series he scored a sudden and spectacular success in the movie melodrama *Love Story* and was lost to TV forever. He later appeared in such hit films as *What's Up Doc* and *Paper Moon*, the latter being made into a TV series (without him).

O'NEIL, CATHRYN—actress

Co-ed Fever (com)......... Elizabeth (1979)

O'NEIL, DANNY—

Windy City Jamboree (music)
.... regular (1950)

O'NEILL DANCERS, THE—

This Is Music (music)..... regular (1958–59)

O'NEILL, DICK—actor
b: Aug 29, The Bronx, N.Y.

Rosetti and Ryan (drama)
.... Judge Hardcastle (1977)
Kaz (drama) .... Malloy (1978–79)
Empire (com) ...... Arthur Broderick (1984)
Better Days (com)
.... Harry Clooney (1986–)

O'NEILL, EILEEN—actress
b: Philadelphia, Pa.

Burke's Law (police)... Sgt. Ames (1964–65)

O'NEILL, JENNIFER—actress

b: Feb 20, 1947, Rio de Janeiro, Brazil r: U.S.A.

Bare Essence (drama)
.... Lady Bobbi Rowan (1983)
Cover Up (drama)
.... Danielle Reynolds (1984–85)

A dark-haired, strikingly beautiful film star of the '70s, formerly a model. She usually portrays independent-minded women (not unrepresentative of Jennifer herself, evidently; her own production company is called Point of View Productions). Rarely seen on TV in the '70s, she became increasingly active in the medium in the '80s.

O'NEILL, JIMMY—host, disc jockey

Shindig (music) .... regular (1964–66)

O'NEILL, KATIE—actress

b: Feb 26, 1970, Los Angeles, Calif.

Together We Stand (com)
.... Amy Randall (1986–)

O'NEILL, PAMELA—hostess

The Fashion Story (misc)
.... fashion commentator (1948–49)

ONTKEAN, MICHAEL—actor

b: Jan 24, 1946, Vancouver, B.C., Canada

The Rookies (police)
.... Off. Willie Gillis (1972–74)

OPATOSHU, DAVID—actor

b: Jan 30, 1918, New York City, N.Y.

Bonino (com) .... Walter Rogers (1953)
The Secret Empire (drama)
.... Hator (1979)
Masada (drama) .... Shimon (1981)

A product of New York's Yiddish theater in the '30s, David played character parts for many years in movies (from 1939) and on television (from c. 1950). He was most often seen in crime or adventure shows such as *Perry Mason, Mission: Impossible,* and *Kojak,* in either villainous or kindly older roles. On *Bonino,* however, he played Ezio Pinza's comically frustrated manager.

OPPENHEIMER, ALAN—actor

b: Apr 23, New York City, N.Y.

The Six Million Dollar Man (adv)
.... Dr. Rudy Wells (1974–75)
Big Eddie (com) .... Jessie Smith (1975)
Eischied (police)
.... Capt. Finnerty (1979–80)

Besides originating the role of Dr. Rudy Wells, the bald, mousy scientist who built the Six Million Dollar Man, Alan provided voices for numerous Saturday morning cartoons in the '70s and '80s, including *Mighty Mouse* (as Mighty Mouse), *Flash Gordon* (as Ming the Merciless), and *The Smurfs.*

ORCHARD, JOHN—actor

M*A*S*H (com) .... Ugly John (1972–73)

ORKIN, DICK—actor

b: Jun 9, 1933*, Williamsport, Pa.

The Tim Conway Show (var)
.... regular (1980–81)

Half of the radio comedy team of Dick and Bert (Berdis), who were often heard in humorous commercials in the late '70s and '80s. Earlier, in the '60s and early '70s, Dick originated such syndicated radio comedy characters as "Chickenman" and "The Tooth Fairy."

ORLANDO, TONY—singer, host

b: Apr 3, 1944, New York City, N.Y.

Tony Orlando and Dawn (var)
.... host (1974–76)

Tony Orlando, the singer who looks a lot like the late comedian Freddie Prinze—and who was profoundly affected by him—has had a career full of bizarre turns. Tony's musical talents were discovered at age 15 by music impresario Don Kirshner, who hired him as a staff songwriter. Two years later, at 17, Tony was allowed to record one of the firm's songs himself. "Halfway to Paradise" became a best-seller, and for the next few months Tony was a hot popular singer (he also had a second whiney hit, "Bless You"). After that, his singing career ended as quickly as it had begun, and he went to work behind the

*Some sources give July 9th.

scenes as a music promotion man.

In 1970, Tony was approached to dub a vocal on to a previously made recording of a song called "Candida"; the original vocalist was not what the producers wanted. The record became a surprise best-seller, but Tony was sure it was another fluke (once burned . . .). So, he stayed with his behind the scenes job. Then a follow-up record called "Knock Three Times" went to number one on the charts, and he was finally persuaded to get a group together and go on tour (up to that time he had used studio singers for his back up). A succession of relative flops followed, confirming his worst fears. However, their stage act was good, and in 1973 they broke through with an enormous seller that has become Tony's trademark song—"Tie a Yellow Ribbon Round the Old Oak Tree." CBS offered the group a summer show in 1974, and it did so well that they were given a regular-season variety hour which lasted two years.

Prinze's *Chico and the Man* was one of TV's top hits at the time, and the two young, hirsute, mustachioed ethnic performers were often mistaken for each other. They became friends, and in 1976 Tony appeared in an episode of *Chico and the Man,* as Prinze's look-alike rival for a young girl's affections. When Prinze shot himself in January 1977, Tony was devastated; he withdrew from show business for nearly two years. Finally, in early 1979, he returned in a "comeback" special for NBC. Subsequently, he produced and starred in an emotional TV movie called *Three Hundred Miles for Stephanie* (1981) and portrayed José Ferrer in *The Rosemary Clooney Story* (1982). He continues to be seen periodically on television but spends much of his time in Las Vegas and on tour with his high energy nightclub act, always remembering the lesson about life learned from his close friend Freddie.

"I've been down," he says. "It seems that every entertainer spends time in those valleys. But things are together now . . . I've gotten my life priorities together. There's a plan, and I'm following it."

ORLANDT, KEN—actor

Riptide (drama)
.... Kirk "The Dool" Dooley (1984–85)

O'ROURKE, HEATHER—juvenile actress

b: Dec 27, 1975, San Diego, Calif.

Happy Days (com)
.... Heather Pfister (1982–83)

The tyke who was kidnapped by angry spirits in the movie *Poltergeist.* On *Happy Days,* she played the cute daughter of Ashley Pfister, the first woman to win Fonzie's heart.

ORRISON, JACK—actor

The Plainclothesman (police)
.... Sgt. Brady (1949–54)

ORTH, FRANK—actor

b: Feb 21, 1880, Philadelphia, Pa. d: Mar 17, 1962

Boston Blackie (drama)
.... Insp. Faraday (1951–53)
The Brothers (com)
.... Capt. Sam Box (1956)

A veteran character actor, in vaudeville from 1897 and in films from 1929, who must have played literally hundreds of Irish bartenders and cops.

OSBORN, LYN—actor

b: c. 1922, Detroit, Mich. d: 1958

Space Patrol (child)
.... Cadet Happy (1951–52)

OSGOOD, CHARLES—newscaster

b: Jan 8, 1933, New York City, N.Y.

CBS Weekend News (news)
.... anchorman (1981–)

A whimsical newsman who is known as CBS's "poet in residence." He was in local broadcasting, and briefly with ABC radio, in the '50s and '60s, before joining CBS-TV in 1971. He is also heard on the CBS radio network, where his *Newsbreak* feature regularly includes the news-related doggerel for which he is famous. His best pieces have been collected in two books: *Nothing Could Be Finer Than a Crisis That Is Minor in the Morning* (1979) and *There's Nothing I Wouldn't Do If You Would Be My POSSLQ* (1981).

O'SHEA, MICHAEL—actor
b: Mar 17, 1906, Hartford, Conn. d: Dec 3, 1973

It's a Great Life (com)
.... Denny David (1954–56)

Genial Irish actor, husband of film beauty Virginia Mayo from 1947 until his death.

O'SHEA, TESSIE—actress
b: Mar 13, 1917, England

The Entertainers (var) ...... regular (1964)

OSMOND BROTHERS, THE—singers
The Andy Williams Show (var)
.... regulars (1962–67)
The Travels of Jaimie McPheeters (wes)
.... Kissel Brothers (1963–64)
The Andy Williams Show (var)
.... regulars (1969–71)

The original Osmond Brothers quartet—Alan, Jay, Merrill, and Wayne—began by singing barbershop songs at social functions and churches in 1959. In 1962 they were invited on a church-sponsored tour of the West Coast and performed at Disneyland, where they were spotted by Andy Williams' father. Andy was looking for a youthful, middle-of-the-road (read: "square") group for his new variety show premiering in the fall, and he signed the boys—then aged eight to 13—as regulars. Their first telecast was in December, 1962; introduced as "the Ogden Brothers from Osmond, Utah," they sang "I'm a Ding Dong Daddy from Dumas" and "Side by Side." Six-year-old Donny joined the act a year later, and for the rest of the '60s the group received regular television exposure with Williams and, during two years in which he was off the air (1967–69), as semiregulars on *The Jerry Lewis Show.* The original four also acted for a season on *The Travels of Jaimie McPheeters* as the God-fearin' Kissel Brothers—Micah, Leviticus, Deuteronomy, and Lamentations. Later, from 1972–74, various members of the family did voices for an ABC cartoon series called *The Osmonds.*

In 1971 the quintet's recording career suddenly took off with a hit called "One Bad Apple" (which many people mistook for a Jackson 5 record). More hits followed, as well as solo successes by individual members of the family. The Osmonds dis-banded as a group in the mid-1970s in order to allow each to follow his own career. The family's story was told in the syrupy 1982 TV movie *Side by Side,* starring sister Marie.

Individual listings follow.

OSMOND, ALAN—singer
b: Jun 22, 1949, Ogden, Utah

Donny and Marie (var) ... regular (1976–79)

See also The Osmond Brothers.

OSMOND, DONNY—singer
b: Dec 9, 1957, Odgen, Utah

Donny and Marie (var) ... cohost (1976–79)

The toothy male "star" of the Osmond family. On television since the early '60s with his brothers, he also cohosted (with Marie) a squeaky-clean variety show in the late '70s and has appeared in musical specials and a few acting roles (e.g., *The Wild Women of Chastity Gulch*).

Musically, he says he came into his own at the ripe old age of 12. "I don't know where we were playing," he says, "but when I came onstage that night, the screaming began in a way I'd never heard before. Eventually, I learned to like that sound." See also The Osmond Brothers.

OSMOND, JAY—singer
b: Mar 2, 1955, Ogden, Utah

Donny and Marie (var) ... regular (1976–79)

See also The Osmond Brothers.

OSMOND, JIMMY—singer
b: Apr 16, 1963, Canoga Park, Calif.

Donny and Marie (var) ... regular (1976–79)

Little Jimmy was the Osmond family's biggest star in Japan, where screaming subteenagers dubbed him "Jimmy-boy" in the early '70s.

OSMOND, KEN—actor
Leave It to Beaver (com)
.... Eddie Haskel (1957–63)

Not a member of the singing Osmond family, by any stretch of the imagination. Ken played Eddie Haskell, the troublemaking "teenage rat" on *Leave It to Beaver*. He later became a Los Angeles motorcycle cop. He still acts occasionally, and was seen in the '80s in *Still the Beaver* (in which Eddie Haskell had grown up to be a crooked contractor) and *High School U.S.A.*

OSMOND, MARIE—singer, actress
b: Oct 13, 1959, Ogden, Utah

Donny and Marie (var) ... cohost (1976–79)
Marie (var) .... hostess (1980–81)
Ripley's Believe It or Not (var)
.... cohost (1985–86)

Peaches-sweet Marie, who made her TV debut at age three on Andy Williams' lap, performed off and on with her brothers during the '60s, but really came into her own with several preteen hit records in the early '70s (e.g., "Paper Roses"). She cohosted the *Donny and Marie* show with her brother in the late '70s, and even had her own sweetness-and-light hour on NBC in 1980–81. Mostly, however, she has been seen on musical specials with Bob Hope, Doug Henning, and others. She has made a number of acting appearances, including one as her own mother in the TV biography of her family, *Side by Side*.

OSMOND, MERRILL—singer
b: Apr 30, 1953, Ogden, Utah

Donny and Marie (var)
.... regular (1976–79)

See also The Osmond Brothers.

OSMOND, WAYNE—singer
b: Aug 28, 1951, Ogden, Utah

Donny and Marie (var) ... regular (1976–79)

See also The Osmond Brothers.

OSOBA, TONY—actor

Dempsey and Makepeace (police)
.... Det. Sgt. Charles Jarvis (1984–)

OSSER, GLENN—orchestra leader
b: Aug 28, 1914, Munising, Mich.

Paul Whiteman's Goodyear Revue (var)
.... orch. leader (1951)

The Vaudeville Show (var)
.... orch. leader (1953)
Music for a Summer Night (music)
.... orch. leader (1959–60)

OSTERWALD, BIBI—actress
b: Feb 3, 1920, New Brunswick, N.J.

Captain Billy's Mississippi Music Hall (var)
.... regular (1948)
Front Row Center (var)
.... regular (1949–50)
Starlit Time (var) .... regular (1950)
The Imogene Coca Show (var)
.... Helen Milliken (1955)
Bridget Loves Bernie (com)
.... Sophie Steinberg (1972–73)

OSTERWALD, HAZY—

Continental Showcase (var)
.... led musical combo (1966)

OSTRANDER, WILLIAM—actor

North and South (drama)
.... Forbes LaMotte (1985)

O'SULLIVAN, RICHARD—actor
b: 1943

Doctor in the House (com)
.... Dr. Bingham (1970–73)

This youthful-looking British actor starred in several TV comedies in that country during the 1970s, including *Man About the House*—the series on which the U.S. hit *Three's Company* was based.

OSWALD, VIRGINIA—singer

Jack Leonard (music) .... vocalist (1949)

O'TOOLE, PETER—actor
b: Aug 2, 1932, Connemara, Galway, Ireland

Masada (drama)
.... Gen. Flavius Silva (1981)

British actor famed for his striking and often eccentric stage and screen roles (*Lawrence of Arabia, Becket*). He was rarely seen on television until the 1980s, when he began to turn up in some of the medium's more prestigious productions, among them *Masada, Svengali,* and Kipling's *Kim*.

OTWELL, DAVID AND ROGER—singers (Twins)

The Lawrence Welk Show (music)
.... regulars (1977–82)

OUSLEY, DINA—actress

Bronk (police)..... Ellen Bronkov (1975–76)

OVERTON, BILL—black actor
b: c. 1947

Firehouse (adv) .... Cal Dakin (1974)
Backstairs at the White House (drama)
.... Jackson (1979)

OVERTON, FRANK—actor
b: 1918 d: Apr 24, 1967

Twelve O'Clock High (drama)
.... Maj. Harvey Stovall (1964–67)

OWEN, BEVERLY—actress
b: c. 1939, Iowa

The Munsters (com)
.... Marilyn Munster (1964)

OWEN, JASON—sportscaster

Tuesday Night Fights (sport)
.... sportscaster (1953)

OWEN, JAY—host

Doctor I.Q. (quiz)......... emcee (1953–54)

OWEN, STEVE—coach

New York Giants Quarterback Huddle (sport)
.... host (1952–53)

The coach of the New York Giants football team.

OWENS, BUCK—singer
b: Aug 12, 1929, Sherman, Texas

Hee Haw (var).............. host (1969–86)

The number-one country music star of the 1960s; during that decade alone he had 30 top-ten records on the country charts—19 of which went to number one. Even the Beatles recorded his songs ("Act Naturally"). Buck and his Buck-aroos have headlined several syndicated country music shows, but he is best

known as cohost of the enormously popular *Hee Haw.*

OWENS, GARY—host, disc jockey
b: May 10, 1936, Mitchell, S.D.

Rowan & Martin's Laugh-In (var)
.... regular (1968–73)
The Hudson Brothers Show (var)
.... regular (1974)
The Gong Show (com) ...... host (1976–77)
Games People Play (sport)
.... announcer (1980–81)

Gary Owens first became known to most Americans as the cupped-hand-to-ear, outrageously overmodulated "announcer" on *Laugh-In.* However, he was, and is, a very popular radio personality in Los Angeles, as well as a familiar voice on network television. Beginning in the mid-1960s, Gary was heard on many Saturday morning cartoon series, including *The Banana Splits, Penelope Pitstop, Space Ghost,* and *Yogi Bear;* he also served as announcer for the prime time *Green Hornet* series. Briefly, in 1969, he hosted a daytime game show called *Letters to Laugh-In,* on which people submitting the best jokes could win—what else?—a trip to beautiful, downtown Burbank!

Aside from his television work, Gary has narrated several comedy LPs, among them *Themes Like Old Times* and *Gary Owens Presents the Funny Side of Bonnie and Clyde.*

OWENS, JILL—actress

Blansky's Beauties (com)
.... Misty Karamazov (1977)

OXENBERG, CATHERINE—actress
b: Sep 22, 1961, New York City, N.Y. r: London, England

Dynasty (drama)
.... Amanda Carrington (1984–86)

This sensuous actress is a real-life child of royalty—the daughter of an exiled Yugoslav princess and a wealthy American businessman, the granddaughter of the former Regent of Yugoslavia, and related to the royal families of England and Greece. Raised among the international jet set (and tutored as a child by family friend Richard

Burton), Catherine first became a model. She made her acting debut, appropriately, as Lady Di in the 1983 TV movie *The Royal Romance of Charles and Diana.* (Prince Charles, whom she knows, sent her a note saying that since the film was going to be made anyway, it was just as well that she should play the part.)

Though she is certainly well-connected, Catherine does not put on royal airs. "Like anyone else, I take my father's name. So the only kind of princess that makes me is a JAP (Jewish American Princess)."

OZ, FRANK—puppeteer

b: May 25, 1944, Hereford, England

The Muppet Show (var)
.... Fozzie Bear (1976–81)

The Muppet Show (var)
.... Animal (1976–81)

The Muppet Show (var)
.... Miss Piggy (1976–81)

The Muppet Show (var)
.... Sam the Eagle (1976–81)

The Muppet Show (var)
.... The Swedish Chef (1976–81)

Emmy Awards: As Performer (Puppeteer) In the Best Children's Program, for *Sesame Street* (1974, 1976); and Best Comedy-Variety Series, for *The Muppet Show* (1978)

OZORIO, CECILE—

Turn-On (var).............. regular (1969)

P

PAAR, JACK—host
b: May 1, 1918, Canton, Ohio

Up to Paar (quiz)............. emcee (1952)
Bank on the Stars (quiz)...... emcee (1953)
The Jack Paar Program (var).... host (1954)
The Jack Paar Show (talk)
.... host (1957–62)
The Jack Paar Program (var)
.... host (1962–65)
ABC Late Night (certain weeks) (talk)
.... host (1973)

In a world of seemingly interchangeable talk show hosts, Jack Paar was an original. Not a singer, not a comic, he made his name by being himself—witty, irreverent, emotions on his sleeve. Love him or hate him (many did both), there was no mistaking him for Johnny-Joey-Mike-Merv.

Jack began as a local radio announcer in the late '30s but first showed his individuality in the army during World War II, where he was assigned to entertain the troops. The target of his gibes was invariably "the brass," and the enlisted men ate it up. After the war, he got into network radio with a 1947 comedy show that was the summer replacement for Jack Benny's; later he hosted the game show Take It or Leave It. He also had a brief fling in movies in the early '50s, appearing with a not-yet-famous Marilyn Monroe in Love Nest and with Lucille Ball in Easy Living. However, it was the new medium of television that would make him famous.

TV has a hard time simply letting performers be themselves, and at first Jack was misused as a game show host, on summer series in 1952 and 1953. Finally, in the fall of '53, he landed a daytime variety show, and from then on his principal activity was to talk. He assembled a changing company of regulars (including his army buddy/pianist Jose Melis, Jack Haskell, Betty Clooney, Edie Adams, and others), who followed him back to prime time in the summer of 1954, to CBS's Morning Show (an early competitor of Today) in 1954–55, and to daytime again in 1955–56. Then, in 1957, Jack began the role for which most remember him, host of The Tonight Show. There he was in his prime, joking, baiting,

feuding, laughing—viewers never knew what to expect next, a celebrity interview or an emotional telecast from the Berlin Wall. At one point he tried to arrange an on-air swap of tractors for prisoners taken by Cuba in the Bay of Pigs invasion; at another, he walked off the show for a month because NBC had censored a mildly off-color "water closet" joke he had wanted to tell. The show made headlines, and got big ratings.

Jack finally left the nightly grind in 1962, emotionally drained. The following fall he began a somewhat tamer prime time variety hour that lasted for three years. Then he retired from the scene to manage his own local television station in Maine. In 1973 ABC brought him back, briefly, to host a once-a-month talkfest as part of its late night lineup, but by that time the spark was gone.

Jack once said, while at the height of his fame, "I don't really do anything, and have no talent. Having finally discovered that, I decided to get out of show business. But I can't, because I'm a star."

PACE, JUDY—black actress
b: 1946, Los Angeles, Calif.

The Young Lawyers (drama)
.... Pat Walters (1970–71)

PACKER, DAVID—actor

V (movie) (sci fi) ... Daniel Bernstein (1983)
V: The Final Battle (miniseries) (sci fi)
.... Daniel Bernstein (1984)
The Best Times (drama)
.... Neil "Trout" Troutman (1985)

PACKER, DORIS—actress
deceased

The Many Loves of Dobie Gillis (com)
.... Clarice Armitage (1959–60)
Happy (com)....... Clara Mason (1960–61)
The Many Loves of Dobie Gillis (com)
.. Mrs. Chatsworth Osborne, Sr. (1960–63)
Tammy (com)........ Mrs. Brent (1965–66)

PACKER, JERRY, SINGERS—

The Patti Page Olds Show (var)
.... regulars (1958–59)
Kraft Music Hall Presents The Dave King Show (var)................ regulars (1959)

PADILLA, MANUEL, JR.—juvenile actor
b: 1956

Tarzan (adv)................ Jai (1966–68)
The Flying Nun (com) .. Marcello (1969–70)

PADILLA, ROBERT—actor

How the West Was Won (miniseries) (drama)
.... Mountain-Is-Long (1977)

PAGANO, GIULIA—actress

Masada (drama) .... Mimiam (1981)

PAGE, GERALDINE—actress
b: Nov 22, 1924, Kirksville, Mo. d: Jun 13, 1987

The Blue and the Gray (drama)
.... Mrs. Lovelace (1982)

Emmy Awards: Best Actress in a Single
Performance in a Drama, for the ABC Spe-
cial *A Christmas Memory* (1967); and for
The Thanksgiving Visitor (1969)

PAGE, HARRISON—black actor
b: Aug 27, Atlanta, Ga.

Love Thy Neighbor (com)
.... Ferguson Bruce (1973)
C.P.O. Sharkey (com)
.... Chief Robinson (1976–78)
Supertrain (drama)
.... porter George Boone (1979)
Sledge Hammer! (com)
.... Capt. Trunk (1986–)

PAGE, LAWANDA—black actress
b: Oct 19, 1920, Cleveland, Ohio

Sanford and Son (com)
.... Aunt Esther Anderson (1973–77)
The Sanford Arms (com)
.... Esther Anderson (1977)
Detective School (com)
.... Charlene Jenkins (1979)
B.A.D. Cats (police) .... Ma (1980)

LaWanda Page, the fearsome, Bible-toting
Aunt Esther of *Sanford and Son,* auditioned unsuccessfully for a part in the series during its first season but was finally
added to the cast in the second when a
producer caught her nightclub act. She had
previously spent many years on the small-
time club circuit, originally billed as "The
Bronze Goddess of Fire"—she lit cigarettes

with her fingertips, swallowed fire, and
touched burning torches to her body. No
wonder ol' Fred Sanford was scared of her!

PAGE, PATTI—singer
b: Nov 8, 1927, Claremore, Okla. r: Tulsa,
Okla.

Music Hall (music)......... hostess (1952)
Scott Music Hall (var).... hostess (1952–53)
The Patti Page Show (var) ... hostess (1956)
The Big Record (music)... hostess (1957–58)
The Patti Page Olds Show (var)
.... hostess (1958–59)

Patti Page, "the Singing Rage," was one of
the most popular recording artists of the
early 1950s, with top hits including "The
Tennessee Waltz," "Cross over the
Bridge," and the unforgettable (even if you
try) "How Much Is That Doggie in the Window?" Her specialty was country-flavored
tunes, on which she employed an usual recording technique that allowed her to sing
in harmony with herself, or even with
whole choruses of her own voice.
   Despite a great deal of television exposure in the '50s, Patti never became a TV
personality of the magnitude of Dinah
Shore; in fact she lost out to Dinah for an
Emmy Award in 1959. In the '60s, with her
singing career on the wane, she turned
briefly to acting (she had previously appeared in a few episodes of *Appointment
with Adventure, The U.S. Steel Hour,* and
Bachelor Father) and then to club work. In
recent years she has been active primarily
in the country music field.

PAGETT, GARY—actor

Lou Grant (drama)
.... financial editor (1978–79)

PAHL, MEL, CHORUS—

Perry Presents (var) .... regulars (1959)

PAICH, MARTY—orchestra leader
b: Jan 23, 1925, Oakland, Calif.

The Glen Campbell Goodtime Hour (var)
.... orch. leader (1969–72)
The Sonny and Cher Comedy Hour (var)
.... orch. leader (1973–74)
The Smothers Brothers Show (var)
.... orch. leader (1975)

Emmy Award: Best Song or Theme, for "Light the Way" (used in an Episode of *Ironside*) (1974)

PAIGE, JANIS—actress

b: Sep 16, 1922, Tacoma, Wash.

It's Always Jan (com)
.... Janis Stewart (1955–56)
Lanigan's Rabbi (police)
.... Kate Lanigan (1977)
Gun Shy (com)........ Nettie McCoy (1983)
Baby Makes Five (com)
.... Blanche Riddle (1983)
Trapper John, M.D. (drama)
.,.......... Catherine Hackett (1985–86)

The vivacious, red-haired costar of movie musicals in the '40s and '50s, and later a major star on Broadway in *The Pajama Game* (1954). Janis entered television at the peak of her fame, in a situation comedy called *It's Always Jan,* on which she played a widowed show-biz mom with a cute kid. (Arte Johnson played a neighborhood delivery boy in the series.) It was not successful. She returned to TV only occasionally afterward, sometimes in dramatic roles on such shows as *Schlitz Playhouse, Wagon Train,* and *The Fugitive,* but more often in musical specials, including the 1958 and 1969 productions of *Roberta.*

Long and happily married to songwriter Ray Gilbert, Janis did not step up her TV activity until after his death, in 1976. During the late '70s and early '80s she played guest roles on *All in the Family, Eight Is Enough, Fantasy Island,* and other series, as well as regular roles on *Lanigan's Rabbi* (as Art Carney's wife) and *Gun Shy* (as the hotel keeper).

PAIGE, ROBERT—actor

b: Dec 2, 1910, Indianapolis, Ind.

The Colgate Comedy Hour (var)
.... rotating host (1955)

This film star of the 1940s became in the '50s a television variety and game show host, seen (among other places) on the daytime versions of *The Big Payoff* and *Bride and Groom.* Later, he was a Los Angeles TV newscaster for many years, then a public relations executive.

PAINTER, WALTER—choreographer

Presenting Susan Anton (var)
.... dancers (1979)

Emmy Award: Best Choreography, for a Lynda Carter special (1981)

Walter was also the choreographer for many of the Academy Awards telecasts.

PALANCE, HOLLY—actress

b: Aug 5, 1950, Los Angeles, Calif.

The Thorn Birds (drama)
.... Miss Carmichael (1983)
Ripley's Believe It or Not (var)
.... cohost (1983–85)

The daughter of Jack Palance. She spent nearly nine years in England during the 1970s, acting on stage and television there, before returning to Hollywood to advance her career here.

PALANCE, JACK—actor

b: Feb 18, 1920, Lattimer, Pa.

The Greatest Show on Earth (drama)
.... Johnny Slate (1963–64)
Bronk (police)... Lt. Alex Bronkov (1975–76)
Ripley's Believe It or Not (var)
.... host (1982–86)

Emmy Award: Best Actor in a Single Performance, for the *Playhouse 90* production "Requiem for a Heavyweight" (1956)

That gaunt, macabre face could have made Jack Palance one of the best one-note villains in screen history. He was chillingly effective in such 1950s movies as *Shane* and *Sudden Fear.* However, a depth of emotion, even anguish, beneath his cadaverous, taut skin won him wider roles; he could even be effective at self-parody (imagine him as Lurch in *The Addams Family*).

Jack's hatchet-face looks like it was built, not born. Indeed, press agents long promoted the story that it was the result of plastic surgery necessitated by terrible burns suffered in a bomber crash during World War II. Jack vehemently denies this; he admits, however, to having his nose broken during an early and brief career as a boxer. Jack turned his appearance to advantage in stage, film, and television work beginning in the late 1940s. His most famous TV role was in the teleplay "Requiem for a Heavyweight," but he also appeared in many other dramatic productions during the Golden Age on *Suspense, Lights Out,* etc.

During the '60s and '70s Jack was only an occasional visitor to TV, playing a circus boss in *The Greatest Show on Earth* and a detective on *Bronk.* Neither was successful; Jack's menacing quality made him a bit hard to take as a sympathetic hero. He finally found his mark as the storytelling host of the '80s freak show *Ripley's Believe It or Not,* on which he could prowl and growl and overact to his heart's content—the subjects were invariably more grotesque than he was.

PALILLO, RON—actor
b: Apr 2, 1954, Conn.

Welcome Back, Kotter (com)
.... Arnold Horshack (1975–79)

The little guy with the hacking laugh ("Aawwk, aawwk, aawwk") on *Kotter.*

PALLADINI, JEFFREY—juvenile actor
b: c. 1968

The Montefuscos (com)
.... Anthony Carmine Montefusco (1975)

PALMER, ANTHONY—actor

Supertrain (drama) .... engineer T.C. (1979)

PALMER, BETSY—actress, panelist
b: Nov 1, 1929, East Chicago, Ind.

Masquerade Party (quiz)
.... panelist (1956–57)
What's It For? (quiz) .... panelist (1957–58)
I've Got a Secret (quiz) .. panelist (1957–67)
Number 96 (drama)
.... Maureen Galloway (1980–81)

Pert Betsy Palmer is an actress who has TV game shows to thank for her fame. She arrived in New York in 1951, after a few years in local theater in the Midwest, and soon began playing roles on the many live TV playhouse series being produced then. Though she was seen often on *Studio One, Goodyear Playhouse, The U.S. Steel Hour* and the like, she did not become a major name until she began appearing on panel shows in the mid-1950s. A ten-year run on *I've Got a Secret* made her less an actress than a TV "personality," the perfect accompaniment for light entertainment. She also became a regular on the *Today* show for a time, as its women's editor.

By the time *I've Got a Secret* ended in 1967, Betsy had practically abandoned her TV acting career. She was seldom seen by a national audience again until the 1980s. Then, determined to change once and for all her '50s image of sweetness and light, she made a most unexpected comeback as Jason's murderous mom in the 1980 theatrical horror movie *Friday the 13th.* (During the filming of one particularly gruesome scene, she turned to the director and asked, "Are you *sure* Bette Davis and Joan Crawford made their comebacks this way?") Soon Betsy was also back on TV, as an uninhibited widow out for some sex on *Number 96* and as a divorcée with a knack for enjoying life on daytime's *As the World Turns.* In addition, she began a cable-TV talk show for women called *Wifeline.*

PALMER, BUD—sportscaster
b: Sep 14, c. 1920, Hollywood, Calif.

It Happened in Sports (sports)
.... host (1953–54)
The Big Moment (drama) .... host (1957)
Fight Beat (sport) .... host (1958)
Jackpot Bowling Starring Milton Berle (sports) .... host (1959)
The Summer Sports Spectacular (sport)
.... host (1961)

A former professional basketball player with the New York Knicks during the late '40s. He began his sportscasting career in 1949 and was a familiar voice for NBC and later ABC in the '50s, '60s, and '70s.

PALMER, GREGG—actor
b: Jan 25, 1927, San Francisco, Calif.

Run Buddy Run (com) ..... Harry (1966–67)

PALMER, JIM—sportscaster
b: Oct 15, 1945, New York City, N.Y.

Monday Night Baseball (sport)
.... sportscaster (1984–)

A former major-league pitcher, with the Baltimore Orioles for 19 years from the mid-1960s to the mid-1980s. He also achieved a certain notoriety during that time as a model for men's underwear. He turned to sportscasting in 1984.

PALMER, JOHN—newscaster
b: Sep 10, 1935, Kingsport, Tenn.

NBC Weekend News (news)
.... anchorman (1984–86)

Emmy Award: Reporter, Best News Segment, for the *NBC Nightly News* report on world hunger (1974)

Palmer joined NBC in 1963 after a brief career in local news. He has been the newscaster on the *Today* show since 1982.

PALMER, LELAND—actress
Manhattan Transfer (var).... regular (1975)
Dinah and Her New Best Friends (var)
.... regular (1976)

PALMER, LIZA—singer
Kay Kyser's Kollege of Musical Knowledge (quiz).................... regular (1949–50)
Chance of a Lifetime (quiz)
.... vocalist (1950–51)

PALMER, PETER—actor
b: 1931

Custer (wes)..... Sgt. James Bustard (1967)
The Kallikaks (com).... Oscar Heinz (1977)

Lanky actor who scored an early hit as "L'il Abner" on stage (1956) and screen (1959), but has since been relegated mostly to supporting roles.

PALUZZI, LUCIANA—actress
b: 1939, Rome, Italy

Five Fingers (drama)
.... Simone Genet (1959–60)

PANKIN, STUART—actor
The San Pedro Beach Bums (com)
.... Stuf (1977)
No Soap, Radio (com) .... Tuttle (1982)

PANTOLIANO, JOE—actor
Free Country (com)
.... Louis Peschi (1978)

From Here to Eternity (drama)
.... Pvt. Angelo Maggio (1979)

PAPAS, IRENE—actress
b: Mar 9, 1926, Corinth, Greece*

Moses—The Lawgiver (drama)
.... Zipporah (1975)

PAPENFUSS, TONY—actor
b: Mar 26, 1950, Minneapolis, Minn.

Newhart (com)....... First Darryl (1982–   )

PARADY, HERSHA—actress
Little House on the Prairie (adv)
.... Alice Garvey (1977–80)

PARAGON, JOHN—actor
The Half Hour Comedy Hour (var)
.... regular (1983)

PARDO, DON—announcer
b: Feb 22, Westfield, Mass.

The Jonathan Winters Show (var)
.... announcer (1956–57)
NBC's Saturday Night Live (com)
.... announcer (1975–   )

Don has been an NBC staff announcer since 1944 and was heard on dozens of daytime game shows, including *Jeopardy* and *The Price is Right*, as well as on many live prime time series of the '50s.

PARE, MICHAEL—actor
b: Oct 9, 1959, Brooklyn, N.Y.

The Greatest American Hero (adv)
.... Tony Villicana (1981–83)

PARFEY, WOODROW—actor
b: c. 1923, New York City, N.Y. d: Jul 29, 1984

Time Express (drama) .. Ticket Clerk (1979)

PARIS, JERRY—actor, director
b: Jul 25, 1925, San Francisco, Calif. d: Mar 31, 1986

Those Whiting Girls (com)..... Artie (1957)
Steve Canyon (adv)
.... Maj. "Willie" Williston (1959)

*Some sources give Khilomodhion, which is a few miles south of Corinth.

654

The Untouchables (police)
.... agent Martin Flaherty (1959–60)
Michael Shayne (drama)
.... Tim Rourke (1960–61)
The Dick Van Dyke Show (com)
.... Jerry Helper (1961–66)

Emmy Award: Best Comedy Direction, for *The Dick Van Dyke Show* (1964)

One of the top TV comedy directors of the '60s and '70s. Among his credits: *That Girl; The Partridge Family; Love, American Style; The Odd Couple;* and *Happy Days.* Previously, in the '50s, he was a TV and movie supporting actor.

PARIS, NORMAN—trio, orchestra leader
b: c. 1926 d: Jul 10, 1977

For Your Pleasure (music) ... trio (1948–49)
Girl About Town (music) .... trio (1948–49)
The Earl Wrightson Show (music)
.... trio and orch. leader (1949–51)
The Patricia Bowman Show (music)
.... trio (1951)
The Martha Wright Show (music)
.... regular (1954)
The Blue Angel (var) .... trio (1954)
That Was the Week That Was (com)
.... orch. leader (1964–65)

PARIS, ROBBY—juvenile actor
The Montefuscos (com)
.... Jerome Montefusco (1975)

PARKE, DOROTHY—actress
b: Feb 24, Toronto, Canada

Hot Shots (drama)
.... Amanda Reed (1986–)

A graduate of the *Star Search* syndicated talent show, on which she was the 1984 grand champion in the "leading lady" category.

PARKER, ANDY & THE PLAINSMEN— country singers
The Marshal of Gunsight Pass (wes)
.... music (1950)

PARKER, DEE—hostess
Rehearsal Call (var) .... hostess (1949)

PARKER, ELEANOR—actress
b: Jun 26, 1922, Cedarville, Ohio

Bracken's World (drama)
.... Sylvia Caldwell (1969–70)

PARKER, ELLEN—actress
Caesar's Hour (var)
.... Alice Brewster (1954–56)

PARKER, FESS—actor
b: Aug 16, 1925*, Fort Worth, Texas r: San Angelo, Texas

Disneyland (misc) . Davy Crockett (1954–55)
Mr. Smith Goes to Washington (com)
.... Sen. Eugene Smith (1962–63)
Daniel Boone (wes)
.... Daniel Boone (1964–70)

At a time when television portrayed the American frontier as a place of blazing guns and impossible superheroes, this soft-spoken Texan carved out quite a career playing quieter, much more realistic frontiersmen. He won his first famous role quite by accident. A former college athlete, Fess studied drama in the early '50s and made his debut in B films in 1952. Walt Disney was asked to screen one of these to watch a potential candidate for his upcoming *Davy Crockett* miniseries; the film was the sci-fi thriller *Them* and the candidate was James Arness. However, Walt spotted Fess in the supporting cast and wanted him instead. Buddy Ebsen was also being considered for the role, but he was eventually cast as Davy's sidekick, George Russell.

Both Arness and Ebsen would find TV fame eventually, but Fess became a superstar almost immediately. *Davy Crockett* was practically a national disease in 1954–55, with huge audiences, a hit song which was being played everywhere, and coonskin caps on the head of every little boy in America. Unfortunately, the series ended with Davy being killed at the Alamo (as he had been in real life). Although Fess made a couple of follow-up episodes about Davy's earlier days, there was no way to prolong the mania.

Fess appeared in other Disney TV productions during the late '50s, and in Disney's film *Westward Ho, The Wagons* in 1956, but nothing could match Crockett. The actor was also seen on other series,

*Some sources give 1924 or 1926.

including *My Little Margie, Death Valley Days,* and *Playhouse 90.* In 1962 he tried to break the Crockett mold by playing a modern-day (but still homespun) politician in *Mr. Smith Goes to Washington.* It flopped, but a couple of years later he did better by reviving, in a way, his original hit. Fess later explained that he very much wanted to do a series based on Crockett, but "Mr. Disney said he wasn't interested. My lawyers told me Disney might sue if we proceeded . . . (so) we fastened on Daniel Boone." As the Kentucky frontiersman, Fess had a highly successful six-year run.

Fess was seldom seen on television after that; he made a pilot for a modern-day family show to be called *The Fess Parker Show* in 1974, but it did not make the schedule. He spent his later years involved with real estate and other business ventures.

PARKER, FRANK—singer
b: Apr 29, 1903, New York City, N.Y.

Arthur Godfrey and His Friends (var)
.... singer (1950–56)
Masquerade Party (quiz).... panelist (1957)

A popular radio tenor of the '30s and '40s, whose career was given a late boost by the Arthur Godfrey show, on which he often sang romantic duets with the much younger Marion Marlowe.

PARKER, JAMESON—actor
b: Nov 18, 1947, Baltimore, Md.

Simon & Simon (drama)
.. Andrew Jackson (A.J.) Simon (1981–)

TV Guide called him "the ultimate WASP, sort of a Robert Redford playing F. Scott Fitzgerald." Female viewers called him gorgeous, whether he was playing a romantic cad on daytime soap operas or the fair-haired, preppy younger brother on the prime time action show *Simon & Simon.* Jameson Parker did in fact come from an upper-class background; his father was a career foreign service officer who later became the curator of a museum in Virginia. Jameson was a bit of a hell-raiser as a young man, but eventually settled down enough to gain his college degree and begin an acting career in local theater in Washington and New York.

Jameson's first big break came in the mid-1970s as a regular on the daytime soap operas *Somerset* and *One Life to Live* (on which he played the slippery Brad Vernon). He then began playing supporting parts in TV movies and prime time series episodes (*Family, Hart to Hart,* etc.), before being cast as A.J. on *Simon & Simon.*

PARKER, LARA—actress

Jessica Novak (drama)
.... Katie Robbins (1981)

This actress is fondly remembered as Angelique, the bizarre, scheming witch who turned Barnabas into a vampire on *Dark Shadows* in the 1960s. She has since been seen in less spectacular roles, in daytime and prime time, and in a few films.

PARKER, LEW—actor
b: Oct 28, 1907 d: Oct 27, 1972

Star Time (var) .... regular (1950–51)
That Girl (com) .... Lou Marie (1966–71)

PARKER, MAGGI—actress
b: 1934, Nashua, N.H.

Hawaii Five-O (police) ..... May (1968–69)

PARKER, PENNEY—actress

The Danny Thomas Show (com)
.... Terry Williams (1959–60)
Margie (com) .. Maybelle Jackson (1961–62)

PARKER, SARAH JESSICA—actress
b: Mar 25, 1965, Nelsonville, Ohio r: Cincinnati, Ohio

Square Pegs (com).. Patty Greene (1982–83)

A former child ballet dancer, Sarah played the title role in the hit Broadway play *Annie* for a time during the late '70s. On *Square Pegs* she was the skinny girl with glasses.

PARKER, SUNSHINE—

AfterMASH (com)........ Sunshine (1984)

PARKER, WARREN—actor

The Growing Paynes (com)
.... regular (1948–49)

PARKER, WILLARD—actor

b: Feb 5, 1912, New York City, N.Y.

Tales of the Texas Rangers (wes)
.... ranger Jace Pearson (1958–59)

PARKHURST, HELEN—educator

Child's World (child) ..... hostess (1948–49)

PARKINS, BARBARA—actress

b: May 22, 1942, Vancouver, B.C., Canada

Peyton Place (drama)
Betty Anderson/Harrington/Cord (1964–69)
Captains and the Kings (drama)
.... Martinique (1976)

PARKS, BERNICE—

Once Upon a Tune (music)... regular (1951)

PARKS, BERT—host

b: Dec 30, 1914, Atlanta, Ga.

Party Line (quiz) .... emcee (1947)
Break the Bank (quiz) .... host (1948–57)
Stop the Music (quiz)...... emcee (1949–52)
Balance Your Budget (quiz)
.... emcee (1952–53)
Double or Nothing (quiz)...... emcee (1953)
Two in Love (quiz) .... emcee (1954)
Stop the Music (quiz)...... emcee (1954–56)
Giant Step (quiz) .... emcee (1956–57)
Hold That Note (quiz) .... emcee (1957)
Bid 'n Buy (quiz) .... emcee (1958)
Masquerade Party (quiz)... emcee (1958–60)
Yours for a Song (quiz) .... emcee (1961–62)
Circus (var)................. host (1971–73)
Strike It Rich (quiz) .... host (1973)

Smiling, exuberant Bert Parks hosted a great many programs during his long career, including major hits on both radio and TV, but he is most remembered for the one he was fired from—*Miss America.* Bert first made his way to New York at the age of 19, during the Depression, in hopes of finding something more lucrative than the fifteen-dollars per week he was making at a local station in Atlanta. His first job was that of a singer and straight man on *The Eddie Cantor Show.* He worked as a staff announcer for CBS for the next several years, but his major break did not come until 1945, when his infectious enthusiasm won him the emcee's spot on a new radio quiz, *Break the Bank.* This was one of the first "big money" radio quiz shows (winners took home as much as $9,000), and it was an immediate smash; Bert later emceed an even bigger hit on radio, *Stop the Music,* beginning in 1948.

Both these hits soon moved to television, establishing the dark, handsome emcee in that medium as well. During the 1950s Bert was everywhere—in daytime, both on quiz shows and in his own variety series (1950–52), and in prime time on nine different programs. He was seen less often in the 1960s, although by then he had begun to act occasionally, on *Burke's Law* and (in the '70s) on *Ellery Queen* and *The Bionic Woman.* He also appeared as ringmaster of the syndicated *Circus* series in the early '70s.

Bert's chief activity during these later years was as the singing host of the *Miss America Pageant.* This annual fall event had come to TV in 1954 with John Daly as its first host; Bert took over in 1955 and remained for the next 25 years. His singing of the theme song at the finale, "There She Is, Miss America," became a tradition. It came as a distinct shock when, in 1980, he was unceremoniously dumped in an effort to increase the youth appeal of the show. His "young" successor, 42-year-old Ron Ely, was dismissed after only two years, however.

PARKS, CATHERINE—actress

Behind the Screen (drama)
.... Sally Dundee (1981–82)
Zorro and Son (com)
.... Senorita Anita (1983)

PARKS, HILDY—writer, producer, actress

b: Mar 12, 1926, Washington, D.C.

Down You Go (quiz)
.... regular panelist (1956)
To Tell the Truth (quiz)
.... panelist (1956–57)

Emmy Awards: Producer, Best Special Events Program, for *The Tony Awards* (1980); Producer, Best Variety Program, for *Night of 100 Stars* (1982)

The noted Broadway producer, formerly an actress. Hildy has been involved with the production of the annual Tony Awards telecast since its inception.

PARKS, MICHAEL—actor
b: Apr 4, 1938, Corona, Calif.

Then Came Bronson (adv)
.... Jim Bronson (1969–70)

The brooding, motorcycle-riding hero of *Then Came Bronson* spent a youth as wandering and aimless as that of the character he played. The son of a truck driver, Michael left home as a teenager and spent much of the 1950s moving about, working at odd jobs, and getting a toehold in the theater on the West Coast. In the early '60s, the tousle-haired, darkly handsome young man began to be seen in alienated-youth (or villainous) roles on numerous prime time series, including *The Detectives, Asphalt Jungle, Bus Stop, Wagon Train,* and others. In 1966 he bared all as Adam in the movie spectacular *The Bible.*

Alienation was "in" during the turbulent '60s, and when NBC wanted a TV series similar to the hit 1969 movie *Easy Rider,* Michael was a natural for the lead. Since then he has continued to be seen in TV movies and series episodes, including a movie pilot in 1980 called *Reward* that would have had him back in a series as a disillusioned ex-cop. By then, however, alienation was "out."

PARKS, VAN DYKE—actor, musician
b: Jan 3, c. 1941, Alabama? r: McKeesport, Pa.

Bonino (com) .... Andrew (1953)
The Billy Crystal Comedy Hour (var)
.... orch. leader (1982)

This juvenile actor, who played one of Ezio Pinza's sons on *Bonino,* went on to become a noted, if somewhat eccentric, folk/rock singer and songwriter in the '60s and '70s. *Rolling Stone* magazine referred to him as a "mad genius" following his musical contributions to (and appearance in) the 1980 movie *Popeye.*

PARNELL, EMORY—actor
b: 1894, St. Paul, Minn. d: Jun 22, 1979

The Life of Riley (com)
.... Riley's Boss (1953–58)

PARNELL, JACK—orchestra leader
b: Aug 6, 1923, London, England

The Piccadilly Palace (var)
.... orch. leader (1967)
Spotlight (var) .... orch. leader (1967)
Showtime (var)........ orch. leader (1968)
The John Davidson Show (var)
.... orch. leader (1969)
Kraft Music Hall Presents Sandler & Young (var)................... orch. leader (1969)
The Liberace Show (var)
.... orch. leader (1969)
This Is Tom Jones (var)
.... orch. leader (1969–70)
Dean Martin Presents the Golddiggers (var)
.... orch. leader (1970)
Engelbert Humperdinck Show (var)
.... orch. leader (1970)
Kraft Music Hall Presents The Des O'Connor Show (var)......... orch. leader (1970–71)

Emmy Awards: Best Music Direction, and Musician of the Year, both for the special *Barbra Streisand . . . and Other Musical Instruments* (1974)

This popular British bandleader provided music for a spate of U.S. variety shows, all of them produced in London in the late '60s and early '70s.

PARRISH, HELEN—actress
b: Mar 12, 1922*, Columbus, Ga. d: Feb 22, 1959

Hour Glass (var) .... emcee (1946)
Show Business, Inc. (var) .... regular (1947)

A sweet-faced young lass who ought to be remembered—but isn't—for being the host of television's very first major variety show (it was, in fact, the first major network series of any kind). *Hour Glass* was a true video pioneer, paving the way for all kinds of TV extravaganzas that would follow. Unfortunately, it was seen by only the few thousand people who had sets in 1946, in three interconnected East Coast cities. Helen, its first permanent host, had been a child actress in the '20s, appearing in several *Our Gang* comedies; later, she played everyone's kid (it seemed) in films of the '30s. She continued to appear on TV occasionally in the '50s, in series including *Racket Squad, Cavalcade of America, Fireside Theatre,* and, the year before she died (of cancer), in an episode of *Leave It to Beaver.*

*Some sources give 1924.

658

PARRISH, JUDY—actress

Barney Blake, Police Reporter (drama)
.... Jennifer Allen (1948)
The Growing Paynes (com)
.... Mrs. Payne (1948–49)

PARRISH, JULIE—actress
b: Oct 21, Middlesboro, Ky.

Good Morning, World (com)
.... Linda Lewis (1967–68)

PARROS, PETER—actor

Knight Rider (drama)
Reginald Cornelius III ("RC3") (1985–86)

PARSONS, ESTELLE—actress
b: Nov 20, 1927, Lynn, Mass.*

Backstairs at the White House (drama)
.... Bess Truman (1979)

A noted character actress of stage (from the '50s on) and screen ('60s on) who started out as an on-camera helper and production assistant on the *Today* show in 1952. She has been seen infrequently on TV since her movie career went into high gear following her Academy Award–winning performance in *Bonnie and Clyde* (1967).

PARSONS, NICHOLAS—actor
b: 1928

The Ugliest Girl in Town (com)
.... David Courtney (1968–69)
The Benny Hill Show (com)
.... regular (1969–82)

PARTON, DOLLY—country singer, songwriter
b: Jan 19, 1946, Sevierville, Tenn.

Dolly (music) .... hostess (1976)
9 to 5 (com)......... sang theme (1982–83)

The pulchritudinous country star, who got her start on Porter Wagoner's syndicated country music show in the late '60s. She became a national media celebrity in the late '70s via prime time specials and appearances on *The Tonight Show,* and has been the target of more bust jokes than anyone since Jayne Mansfield. Dolly is ac-

*Some sources give nearby Marblehead, Mass.

tually a very intelligent lady whose on-camera image is very much part of a plan. "If I could get (viewers') attention long enough, I felt they would see beneath the boobs and find the heart, and that they would see beneath the wig and find the brains. I think one big part of whatever appeal I possess is the fact that I look totally one way and that I am totally another."

PASTENE, ROBERT—actor

Buck Rogers (sci fi).. Buck Rogers (1950–51)

PASTERNAK, MICHAEL—actor
b: Sep 10, Brooklyn, N.Y. r: Florida

Co-ed Fever (com)........... Gobo (1979)

PATAKI, MICHAEL—actor
b: Jan 16, 1938, Youngstown, Ohio

Paul Sand in Friends and Lovers (com)
.... Charlie Dreyfuss (1974–75)
Get Christie Love (police)
.... Sgt. Pete Gallagher (1975)
The Amazing Spider-Man (adv)
.... Capt. Barbera (1978–79)
Phyl & Mikhy (com)
.... Vladimir Gimenko (1980)

PATCHETT, TOM—comedian, writer, producer

Make Your Own Kind of Music (var)
.... regular (1971)

Emmy Award: Best Writing for a Variety Series, for *The Carol Burnett Show* (1973)

Half of the comedy team of Patchett and (Jay) Tarses. Later they became a successful TV comedy producing team, responsible for *The Bob Newhart Show, The Tony Randall Show,* and *Buffalo Bill,* among others.

PATE, MICHAEL—actor, writer, producer
b: 1920, Sydney, Australia

Hondo (wes).......... Chief Vittoro (1967)

PATRICK, BUTCH—juvenile actor
b: Jun 2, Inglewood, Calif.

The Real McCoys (com)
.... Greg Howard (1963)

The Munsters (com)
  Edward Wolfgang (Eddie) Munster (1964–66)

PATRICK, DENNIS—actor
b: Mar 14, 1918, Philadelphia, Pa.

Bert D'Angelo/Superstar (police)
  .... Capt. Jack Breen (1976)
Dallas (drama)... Vaughn Leland (1979–84)
Rituals (drama) ... Patrick Chapin (1984–85)

PATRICK, JOAN—actress
b: c. 1937, Windsor, Ont., Canada

Dr. Kildare (drama)
  ...... receptionist Susan Deigh (1961–62)

Miss Canada of 1957.

PATRICK, LEE—actress
b: Nov 22, 1906*, New York City, N.Y. d: Nov 21, 1982

Boss Lady (com) .... Aggie (1952)
Topper (com) .. Henrietta Topper (1953–55)

A character actress who played many a hardened blonde onstage and in films of the '30s and '40s, most memorably as Bogart's gal Friday in *The Maltese Falcon.* She is remembered by TV viewers as Cosmo Topper's chirpy wife on *Topper.*

PATRICK, LORY—actress
b: Apr 8, 1938, Beckley, W. Va.

Tales of Wells Fargo (wes) . Tina (1961–62)

The wife of actor Dean Jones.

PATTEN, BART—actor
Riverboat (adv) ...... Terry Blake (1959–60)

PATTERN, EDWARD—black singer
b: Aug 2, 1939 r: Atlanta, Ga.

The Gladys Knight & the Pips Show (var)
  .... regular (1975)

A cousin of Gladys Knight, and a member of the Pips.

PATTERSON, HANK—actor
b: Oct 9, 1888, Alabama d: Aug 23, 1975

*Some sources give 1911.

Gunsmoke (wes) .... Hank (1957–75)
Green Acres (com) .... Fred Ziffel (1965–71)

PATTERSON, LEE—actor
b: Mar 31, 1929, Vancouver, B.C., Canada

Surfside Six (drama)
  .... Dave Thorne (1960–62)

This handsome Canadian leading man of the '50s and '60s later went into soap operas, where he had a ten-year run in the late '60s and early '70s as Joe Riley on *One Life to Live.*

PATTERSON, LORNA—actress
b: Jul 1, 1956, Whittier, Calif.

Working Stiffs (com)
  .... Nikki Evashevsky (1979)
Goodtime Girls (com)
  .... Betty Crandall (1980)
Private Benjamin (com)
  .... Pvt. Judy Benjamin (1981–83)

Actors get their big breaks in many different ways; petite blonde Lorna Patterson was the closest thing the producers could find to film star Goldie Hawn when Hawn's hit movie *Private Benjamin* was being made into a TV series. Before that she had had a brief but whirlwind Hollywood career. Arriving in town only a couple of years earlier, following some local stage work, Lorna promptly won giggly parts in episodes of several shows, two failed series *(Working Stiffs* and *Goodtime Girls),* and the hit movie *Airplane* (as Randi, the singing stewardess). She also starred opposite Tony Randall in the 1981 TV movie *Sidney Shorr,* the pilot for *Love, Sidney.*

PATTERSON, MELODY—actress
b: 1947, Los Angeles, Calif.

F Troop (com)..... Wrangler Jane (1965–67)

Married to actor James MacArthur.

PATTERSON, NEVA—actress
b: Feb 10, 1925, Nevada, Iowa

The Governor & J.J. (com)
  .... Maggie McLeod (1969–70)
Nichols (wes) .... Ma Ketcham (1971–72)
Doc Elliot (drama) .... Mags Brimble (1974)

V (movie) (sci fi) .. Eleanor Donovan (1983)
V: The Final Battle (miniseries) (sci fi)
.... Eleanor Donovan (1984)

PATTON, PHIL—producer, cohost

Ladies Be Seated (quiz).... assistant (1949)

PAUL, EUGENIA—actress
b: Dearborn, Mich.

Zorro (wes)........ Elena Torres (1957–59)

PAUL, P.R.—juvenile actor

Fame (drama). Montgomery MacNeil (1982)

PAUL, RICHARD—actor
b: Jun 6, Los Angeles, Calif.

Match Game P.M. (quiz). panelist (1975–82)
Carter Country (com)
.... Mayor Teddy Burnside (1977–79)
One in a Million (com)
.... Barton Stone (1980)
Herbie, The Love Bug (com)
.... Bo Phillips (1982)
Hail to the Chief (com)
.... Rev. Billy Joe Bickerstaff (1985)

Roly-poly comic actor, perhaps most perfectly cast as W. C. Fields in the stage play, *W.C. Fields, 80 Proof.* He was a practicing psychologist before taking up acting.

PAULEY, JANE—newscaster
b: Oct 31, 1950, Indianapolis, Ind.

NBC Weekend News (news)
.... anchor (1980–83)

The pretty and capable cohost of the *Today* show, which she joined in 1976 upon the departure of Barbara Walters. Jane was a local newscaster in Indianapolis and Chicago from 1972–76 before joining *Today*—just four years after she graduated from college.

Jane's maternity leave from *Today* in 1983, after two miscarriages, was one of the most widely publicized pregnancies in recent TV history (she had twins). She promptly returned to the show and then hosted a prime time special called *Women, Work and Babies: Can America Survive?*

She is married to cartoonist Garry Trudeau.

PAULSEN, ALBERT—actor
b: Dec 13, 1929, Guayaquil, Ecuador

Doctors' Hospital (drama)
.... Janos Varga (1975–76)
Stop Susan Williams (drama)
.... Anthony Korf (1979)

Emmy Award: Best Supporting Actor, for the *Bob Hope Chrysler Theatre* production, *One Day in the Life of Ivan Denisovich* (1964)

PAULSEN, PAT—comedian
b: South Bend, Washington r: Calif.

The Smothers Brothers Comedy Hour (var)
.... regular (1967–69)
The Summer Smothers Brothers Show (var)
.... regular (1968)
Pat Paulsen's Half a Comedy Hour (var)
.... host (1970)
The Smothers Summer Show (var)
.... regular (1970)
Joey & Dad (var) .... regular (1975)
The Smothers Brothers Show (var)
.... regular (1975)

Emmy Award: Special Award for Individual Achievement, for *The Smothers Brothers Comedy Hour* (1968)

The sad-faced comedian of *The Smothers Brothers Comedy Hour* describes his career thusly:

"I first did takeoffs on folk singers. Later, several of us bought a barn to put on skits and blackouts but nobody came to see us. When the cows started giving us funny looks we sold the barn."

Next, Pat wrangled a job at the San Francisco night spot The Purple Onion where, one day, he watched two newcomers breaking in their act. Afterward, he went up to Tommy and Dickie Smothers and said, "You guys would be great if you had a little comedy in your act." The brothers, whose entire act was comedy, gave him a strange look.

A few years later, broke and out of work, Pat moved his family to Los Angeles, "for one last run at a show business career. I had a wife and three children and I was knocking on doors all over town looking for a break. I got a few small bookings at various clubs in town. But I wasn't making enough money to support my family, so I took a job as a window washer. I was broke; I couldn't make my house payment . . . and then Tommy called. Tommy and Dick had a show on CBS and Tommy offered me a job. I didn't really have anything to do at first. He just gave me the job to help me make a living. Gradually, he started giving me things to do on the show and then, when they came up with the idea of doing weekly comedy editorials, he pushed me into the spot and things have been fine ever since."

Is Pat appreciative? "I owe a lot to Tom. He not only gave me my push but he taught me never to be jealous of another comedian. He said that I should enjoy any man's talent; that there's room in the world for twice as many comedians as we have at present."

PAYNE, BENNY—black pianist, combo leader

b: Jun 18, 1907, Philadelphia, Pa.

The Billy Daniels Show (music)
. . . . trio (1952)

PAYNE, JACK—writer

Stump the Authors (talk). . . . , author (1949)

PAYNE, JOHN—actor

b: May 23, 1912, Roanoke, Va.

The Restless Gun (wes)
. . . . Vint Bonner (1957–59)

Dark, rugged John Payne, star of Hollywood musicals in the '40s and action flicks in the '50s, was lured into television only occasionally. During the '50s he made a few appearances on *Schlitz Playhouse, General Electric Theater, Hallmark Hall of Fame,* and other dramatic showcases, and in 1957 he launched his own western series, called *The Restless Gun,* which he produced and owned. Like many of his films, it was good entertainment at the time and made a lot of money, but is little remembered today.

In later years Payne was rarely seen, appearing a few times on *Gunsmoke* and also on scattered episodes of *The Name of the Game, Cade's County,* and (in 1975) *Columbo.* He is an extremely wealthy man, having invested his money in California real estate.

PAYNE, JULIE—actress

b: Sep 11, Terre Haute, Ind.

Wizards and Warriors (adv)
. . . . Queen Lattinia (1983)
The Duck Factory (com)
. . . . Aggie Aylesworth (1984)
Leo & Liz in Beverly Hills (com)
. . . . Lucille Trumbley (1986)

PAYTON, JO MARIE—actress

The New Odd Couple (com)
. . . . Mona (1982–83)

PEABODY, DICK—actor

Combat (drama). . . . . . . Littlejohn (1963–67)

PEACHES, THE—singers

The Bobby Vinton Show (var)
. . . . regulars (1976–78)

PEACOCK DANCERS—

Pink Lady (var) . . . . regulars (1980)

PEAKER, E.J.—actress

That's Life (com)
. . . . Gloria Quigley Dickson (1968–69)

A shapely female who was also a frequent player on *Love, American Style.* The "E.J." is short for Edra Jeanne.

PEANUTS, THE—

Continental Showcase (var) . regulars (1966)

PEARCE, ALICE—comedienne, actress

b: Oct 16, 1919*, New York City, N.Y. d: Mar 3, 1966

Alice Pearce (var). . . . . hostess (1949)
Jamie (com). . . . . . Annie Moakum (1953–54)
One Minute Please (quiz)
. . . . panelist (1954–55)
Bewitched (com) . Gladys Kravitz (1964–66)

Emmy Award: Best Supporting Actress in a Comedy, for *Bewitched* (1966)

A homely, rubber-faced, thoroughly delightful comic actress, in movies since 1949; she is best remembered by TV viewers as the befuddled neighbor Gladys on *Bewitched,* her last role.

*Some sources give 1913 or 1921.

PEARL, BARRY—actor

C.P.O. Sharkey (com)... Mignone (1976–77)

PEARL, MINNIE—country comedienne
b: Oct 25, 1912, Centerville, Tenn.

Grand Ole Opry (music) .. regular (1955–56)
Hee Haw (var).......... regular (1970–)

PEARLMAN, MICHAEL—juvenile actor
b: c. 1974, New York City, N.Y.

Charles in Charge (com)
.... Jason Pembroke (1984–85)

PEARLMAN, STEPHEN—actor

Husbands, Wives & Lovers (com)
.... Murray Zuckerman (1978)

PEARSON, DREW—newscaster, columnist
b: Dec 13, 1897, Evanston, Ill. d: Sep 1, 1969

Drew Pearson (news)
.... commentator (1952–53)

The controversial columnist is better known for his radio work in the 1930s and '40s than for his appearances on television.

PEARSON, LEON—newscaster

NBC Weekend News (news)
.... anchorman (1949–50)

PEARSON, MAURICE—singer

The Lawrence Welk Show (music)
.... regular (1957–60)

PEARTHREE, PIPPA—juvenile actress

Buffalo Bill (com)
.. Melanie Bittinger (occasional) (1983–84)

PEARY, HAROLD—actor
b: 1908 r: San Leandro, Calif. d: Mar 30, 1985

Willy (drama)....... Perry Bannister (1955)
Blondie (com)....... Herb Woodley (1957)
Fibber McGee and Molly (com)
.... Mayor La Trivia (1959–60)

Hal Peary created one of the most popular comic characters on radio during the 1940s, that of pompous but lovable old windbag Throckmorton P. Gildersleeve on *Fibber McGee and Molly* and later *The Great Gildersleeve.* Hal's TV career was more limited. Among other things, he recreated one of his other radio roles, that of neighbor Herb on the short-lived 1957 revival of *Blondie,* and he also played pompous Mayor La Trivia (originated on radio by Gale Gordon) on the televersion of *Fibber McGee.* However, Hal's most famous character, Gildersleeve, had been taken over on radio by Willard Waterman in 1950, and it was Waterman who brought it to TV (briefly) in 1955.

Peary later did commercials and provided voices for Saturday morning cartoons, as late as the 1970s.

PECK, ED—actor

Major Dell Conway of the Flying Tigers (adv)
.... Maj. Dell Conway (1951)
The Super (com) .... Off. Clark (1972)
Happy Days (com)
.... Off. Kirk (occasional) (1974–84)
Semi-Tough (com)..... coach Cooper (1980)

PECK, ERIN LEIGH—actress

Hometown (drama).. Jennifer Abbott (1985)

PECK, FLETCHER—pianist

Jan Murray Time (var)....... pianist (1955)

PECK, GREGORY—actor
b: Apr 5, 1916, La Jolla, Calif.

The Blue and the Gray (drama)
.... Pres. Abraham Lincoln (1982)

The famous movie star, whose chisled features could well be placed on Mount Rushmore along with Lincoln's, has rarely been seen on TV, aside from a few movie projects in the 1980s. *The Blue and the Gray* was his first television acting appearance. Why did he wait so long? "There's nothing complicated about my holding out," he says. "I've always been as busy as I wanted to be in features because it's well-known we have more time for rehearsal and a longer shooting schedule. And I'm the kind of bird who likes a lot of rehearsal and a lot of takes."

His autobiography: *An Actor's Life* (1978).

PECK, J. EDDIE—actor
b: Oct 10, c. 1962, Lynchburg, Va. r: Joplin, Mo.

Wildside (wes)...... Sutton Hollister (1985)

PECK, JIM—host

You Don't Say (quiz) ...... emcee (1978–79)

PEDI, TOM—actor

The Stage Door (drama) ...... Rocco (1950)
Arnie (com)............. Julius (1970–72)

PEEPLES, NIA—actress
b: Dec 10, 1961

Fame (drama)... Nicole Chapman (1984–)

PEINE, JOSH—actor

Don't Call Me Charlie (com)
.... Judson McKay (1962–63)

PEINE, VIRGINIA—hostess

The Stork Club (talk)..... cohost (1950–51)
Guess What (quiz) .... panelist (1952)

The wife of author Quentin Reynolds.

PEIRCE, ROBERT—actor
b: Oct 1, Santa Monica, Calif.

Joanie Loves Chachi (com). Bingo (1982–83)

PELIKAN, LISA—actress
b: Jul 12, Paris, France

Studs Lonigan (drama)
.... Lucy Scanlon (1979)

PELLETIER, WILFRED—symphony conductor
b: Jun 30, 1896, Montreal, Canada d: Apr 9, 1982

The Voice of Firestone (music)
.... conductor (occasional) (1962–63)

PELUCE, MEENO—juvenile actor
b: Feb 26, 1970, Amsterdam, The Netherlands r: Los Angeles

The Bad News Bears (com)
.... Tanner Boyle (1979–80)
Best of the West (com)
.... Daniel Best (1981–82)

Voyagers (sci fi)..... Jeffrey Jones (1982–83)
Detective in the House (drama)
.... Todd Wyman (1985)

This irrepressible, pint-sized actor, the son of a Hollywood film caterer ("Mother Moon, Inc."), is the older brother of juvenile TV star Soleil Moon Frye *(Punky Brewster)*. His unusual first name derived from his mispronounciation as a child of his given name, Miro.

PENA, ELIZABETH—actress
b: Sep 23, New Jersey r: Cuba

Tough Cookies (com)
.... Off. Connie Rivera (1986)

PENHALL, BRUCE—actor
b: 1958, Balboa, Calif.

CHiPs (police)
.... cadet Bruce Nelson (1982–83)

A blond, handsome look-alike for Robert Redford, who also happens to be a former world champion motorcycle racer. What better replacement could the producers of the motorcycle show *CHiPs* have found for Erik Estrada's partner, Larry Wilcox, when Wilcox left the show? Much to Penhall's chagrin, however, he was not allowed to do any of his own motorcycle stunt work, or even ordinary scenes on the open highway—they were all done by doubles. "Too dangerous," the producers said. How to explain *that* to his macho friends back on the racing circuit?

PENN, LEO—actor, director

The Gertrude Berg Show (com)
.... Jerry Green (1961)

One of the most prolific directors of television drama series in the '50s and '60s.

PENNELL, LARRY—actor

Ripcord (adv)..... Ted McKeever (1961–63)
The Beverly Hillbillies (com)
.... Dash Riprock (1965–69)
Lassie (adv) .... Keith Holden (1973–74)

PENNINGTON, MARLA—actress

Soap (com) .... Leslie Walker (1979–81)
Small Wonder (com)
.... Joan Lawson (1985–)

PENNY, DON—actor

The Steve Allen Show (var)
.... regular (1961)
The Lieutenant (drama)
.... Lt. Harris (1963–64)
The Wackiest Ship in the Army (adv)
...... ship's cook Charles Tyler (1965–66)
That Girl (com)
.... Seymour Schwimmer (1967–68)

PENNY, JOE—actor
b: Sep 14, 1956, London, England

The Gangster Chronicles (drama)
.... Benjamin "Bugsy" Siegel (1981)
Riptide (drama)
.... Nick Ryder (1984–86)

A tough-looking, scrappy actor who broke into television in 1977, on the premiere episode of *The Nancy Drew Mysteries*. The son of an American airman, he moved around quite a bit as a child and left home at age 15, after his parents divorced. He appeared in supporting roles on various series before advancing to starring roles in the 1980s.

PENNY, SYDNEY—juvenile actress
b: c. 1972

The Thorn Birds (drama)
.... Meggie Cleary (as a girl) (1983)

PENTECOST, GEORGE—actor

Blansky's Beauties (com)
..... Horace "Stubbs" Wilmington (1977)

PEPPARD, GEORGE—actor
b: Oct 1, 1928, Detroit, Mich.

Banacek (drama)
.... Thomas Banacek (1972–74)
Doctors' Hospital (drama)
.... Dr. Jake Goodwin (1975–76)
The A-Team (adv)
.... Col. John "Hannibal" Smith (1983–   )

"Well, you know me," George Peppard once told a group of friends. "I'm easygoing." Great laughter immediately broke out; one man fell off his chair. The fact is, George has been a scrapper from the beginning, which has made for both a rocky career in Hollywood and perfect casting as the cigar-chomping, tough-with-a-twinkle leader of the macho team of do-gooders on *The A-Team*.

The square-jawed actor was considered quite a find during his early days in film. His breakthrough came after a half dozen years of struggle in the theater in New York, during the 1950s. By 1956 he had won his first small role on Broadway (in *The Beautiful Changes*) and in 1957–58 was appearing in episodes of TV series ranging from *Lamp Unto My Feet* to *Kraft Theatre*, *Studio One*, and *Alfred Hitchcock Presents*. He remained fairly active in the medium until the early 1960s, when his career really took off with films such as *Breakfast at Tiffany's* (opposite Audrey Hepburn) and *The Carpetbaggers*. Pursuing movie stardom, he was seldom seen on TV during the '60s. However, as he gained a reputation around Hollywood as a very hard man to work with, his film career soon degenerated into a succession of routine action thrillers.

When George reentered TV in the early '70s, he quickly scored an important success with the popular detective series *Banacek*. However, he walked out of the show after his friend, the producer, left. Next, he landed the lead in *Doctors' Hospital*, but he left that too, after a year. During the rest of the 1970s he appeared only occasionally in TV movies, most notably as Dr. Sam Sheppard in *Guilty or Innocent: The Sam Sheppard Murder Case* (1975). A film he financed and directed himself, *Five Days from Home* (1978), was a failure. By the early '80s George's career was in a slump. He was considered for the role of Blake Carrington on *Dynasty,* but, after arguing with the producers over how the role should be played, was dropped. The *A-Team* was his career saver.

PEPPER, BARBARA—actress
b: May 31, 1912, New York City, N.Y. d: Jul 18, 1969

Green Acres (com) ... Doris Ziffel (1965–69)

PEPPER, CYNTHIA—actress
b: 1940

My Three Sons (com)
.... Jean Pearson (1960–61)
Margie (com)
.... Margie Clayton (1961–62)

PERA, RADAMES—juvenile actor

Kung Fu (wes)
.... Caine (as a youth) (1972–75)

PERETZ, SUSAN—actress

A.E.S. Hudson Street (com)
.... ambulance driver Foshko (1978)

PEREZ, ANTHONY—juvenile actor

Popi (com)........ Junior Rodriguez (1976)

PEREZ, JOSE—actor
b: 1940, New York City, N.Y.

Calucci's Department (com)
.... Ramon Gonzales (1973)
On the Rocks (com)
.... Hector Fuentes (1975–76)

PEREZ, RAUL—singer

CBS Newcomers (var) .... regular (1971)

PERITO, JENNIFER—actress

Makin' It (adv)...... Ivy Papastegios (1979)

PERITO, NICK—orchestra leader
b: Apr 7, 1924, Denver, Colo.

The Don Knotts Show (var)
.... orch. leader (1970–71)
The Big Show (var)
.... orch. leader (1980)

PERKINS, CARL—singer, songwriter
b: Apr 9, 1932, Jackson, Tenn.

The Johnny Cash Show (var)
.... regular (1969–71)

Although he is known to most music fans for just one hit record, "Blue Suede Shoes," in 1956 (can you name anything else by him?), guitarist Carl Perkins was quite an influential figure in the world of country rock. From the mid-1960s to the mid-1970s he worked as a backup musician for Johnny Cash, on tour, on record, and on Cash's popular ABC variety show, on which he was often given a featured solo spot.

PERKINS, GAY—singer

CBS Newcomers (var) .... regular (1971)

PERKINS, JACK—newscaster
b: Dec 28, 1933, Cleveland, Ohio r: Wooster, Ohio

Prime Time Sunday (pub aff)
.... correspondent (1979–80)
NBC Magazine with David Brinkley (pub aff)
.... correspondent (1980–82)

Emmy Awards: Best News Segments, for the *Prime Time Sunday* report "Heart Transplant" (1980); and for the *NBC Magazine* report "Teen Models" (1981)

Perkins joined NBC in 1961, after a brief career in local news.

PERKINS, KENT—

The Nashville Palace (var)
.... regular (1981–82)

PERKINS, MARLIN—host
b: Mar 28, 1905, Carthage, Mo. r: Pittsburg, Kans. d: Jun 14, 1986

Wild Kingdom (doc)........ host (1968–85)

Comics mimicked his loyalty to his sponsor: "The mother rhino stomps the cobra to protect her young . . . just like Mutual of Omaha will stomp your cobra . . ." Johnny Carson had a running bit in which the learned animal expert invariably stepped aside to "take notes" whenever a dangerous animal appeared, leaving his hapless assistant, Jim Fowler, to wrestle the beast to the ground.

The lore surrounding Marlin Perkins and his animal shows is the result of his incredible 40-year run as television's favorite zoologist. A kindly, mild-looking man with an unexpected flair for showmanship, Marlin left college in 1926 to become a laborer at the St. Louis zoo, where he soon advanced to curator of reptiles. In 1938 he moved to the Buffalo Zoo, and in 1944 to the Lincoln Park Zoo in Chicago, as its director.

Chicago was one of the earliest cities to have television, and the 40-year-old zookeeper quickly recognized the new medium's potential. "One of the duties of a zoo director is to publicize the zoo," he said. "There were about 300 TV sets in Chicago at the time (1945), and I would get frequent calls to bring some animals down to the studio. There were no time problems —we'd just stay on until we or the animals had had enough." *Zoo Parade,* with Marlin as its enthusiastic host, began regular live telecasts from the Lincoln Park Zoo locally in 1949 and moved on to the NBC network in 1950; it remained a Sunday afternoon fixture for the next seven years. Marlin took the show to Africa, the Amazon, and every major animal habitat in the U.S.

In 1960, Marlin accompanied Sir Edmund Hillary on an expedition to locate the abominable snowman of the Himalayas (they didn't). Two years after that, he became director of the St. Louis Zoo, and in early 1963 began his second great animal show, *Mutual of Omaha's Wild Kingdom.* The series was seen on Sunday afternoon from 1963–68, had a prime time run from 1968–71, and has been in syndication with a mix of original and repeat episodes ever since. In 1985, during a bout with cancer, the kindly 80-year-old zookeeper finally retired. Faithful Jim Fowler at last took the helm, and could now take the notes while somebody *else* wrestled the alligator into the boat.

PERKINS, MILLIE—actress
b: May 12, 1938, Passaic, N.J.

Knots Landing (drama)
.... Jane Sumner (1983–84)

PERLMAN, RHEA—actress
b: Mar 31, 1948, Brooklyn, N.Y.

Cheers (com)...... Carla Tortelli (1982–   )

Emmy Awards: Best Supporting Actress in a Comedy, for *Cheers* (1984, 1985, 1986)

The peppery, tough-looking waitress on *Cheers.* Rhea is married to actor Danny DeVito, who is even shorter (5′) than she is (5′1″); they met while they were both struggling actors in New York in the early '70s. The two of them have appeared together onstage, and Rhea was occasionally seen as Danny's girlfriend, Zena, on *Taxi.*

PERLOW, BOB—writer, cohost
b: Dec 28, Pawtucket, R.I.

People Do The Craziest Things (aud par)
.... assistant (1984–85)

Bob served as writer and studio warm-up man for numerous television comedies in the '70s and '80s. Among his other writings

is a book called *At the Sound of the Beep* —about answering services. People write about the craziest things.

PERPICH, JONATHAN—actor

The Last Precinct (com)
.... Sgt. Price Pascall (1986)

PERREAU, GIGI—actress
b: Feb 6, 1941, Los Angeles, Calif.

The Betty Hutton Show (com)
.... Pat Strickland (1959–60)
Follow the Sun (adv)
.... Katherine Ann Richards (1961–62)

A popular child actress of the '40s and '50s, whose career fizzled as an adult.

PERRINE, VALERIE—actress
b: Sep 3, 1944, Galveston, Texas

Leo & Liz in Beverly Hills (com)
.... Liz Green (1986)

A tall, sexy leading lady of movies, seen only occasionally on television—mostly in TV films. She started as a topless showgirl in Las Vegas.

PERRY, BARBARA—actress

The Marge and Gower Champion Show (com)
.... Miss Weatherly (1957)
The Hathaways (com)
.... Thelma Brockwood (1961–62)

PERRY, FELTON—black actor

Matt Lincoln (drama)...... Jimmy (1970–71)

PERRY, JAMILLA—actress

Melba (com)........ Tracy Patterson (1986)

PERRY, JOHN BENNETT—actor, singer
b: Jan 4, 1941, Williamstown, Mass.

240-Robert (adv)
   Dep. Theodore Roosevelt Applegate III ("Trap") (1979–81)
Paper Dolls (drama)
.... Michael Caswell (1984)
Falcon Crest (drama)
.... Sheriff Gilmore (1985–   )

A former lead singer of the popular 1960s folk group the Serendipity Singers.

PERRY, JOSEPH—actor

The Bill Cosby Show (com)
.... Max Waltz (1969–71)

PERRY, ROD—black actor
b: c. 1941, Coatesville, Pa.

S.W.A.T. (police)
...... Sgt. David "Deacon" Kay (1975–76)

PERRY, ROGER—actor

Harrigan and Son (com)
.... James Harrigan, Jr. (1960–61)
Arrest and Trial (drama)
.... Det. Sgt. Dan Kirby (1963–64)
The Facts of Life (com)
.... Mr. Charles Parker (1981–83)
Falcon Crest (drama)
.... John Costello (1982–85)

PERRY, WOLFE—black actor
b: Dec 22, New Orleans, La. r: Oakland, Calif.

The White Shadow (drama)
.... Teddy Rutherford (1980–81)

PERSONS, FERN—actress

Those Endearing Young Charms (com)
.... Abbe Charm (1952)

PESCI, JOE—actor
b: Feb 9, 1943, Newark, N.J. r: The Bronx, N.Y.

Half Nelson (drama)... Rocky Nelson (1985)

A diminutive actor who made a virtue out of his short stature, playing a TV detective who got a lot done because the crooks didn't take a little guy seriously. He was previously best known for his supporting role in the movie *Raging Bull*. His name is pronounced "Peshy."

PESCOW, DONNA—actress
b: Mar 24, 1954, Brooklyn, N.Y.

Angie (com)....... Angie Benson (1979–80)

Donna Pescow began her career with a splash in 1977 as John Travolta's loyal Brooklyn goilfriend Annette in the hit film *Saturday Night Fever*. (The role presented something of a problem, as Donna had just spent two years trying to get rid of her na-

tive Brooklyn accent.) She promptly went on to appear in two TV movies in 1978 and then star in her own 1979 comedy series, *Angie,* about a waitress who marries Mr. (Rich and) Wonderful. After this stellar start, however, Donna was seen mostly in TV-movie supporting roles.

PETAL, ERICA—actress

The Bob Crane Show (com)
.... Pam Wilcox (1975)

PETERMAN, STEVEN—actor

Good Time Harry (com)
.... Martin Springer (1980)
Making the Grade (com).. Jeff Kelton (1982)
Square Pegs (com).. Mr. Donovan (1982–83)

PETERS, BERNADETTE—actress
b: Feb 28, 1944*, Ozone Park, N.Y.

All's Fair (com)
..... Charlotte (Charley) Drake (1976–77)

Bubbly comic actress and dancer Bernadette Peters has been seen occasionally on television since the late '60s, but she is better known for her Broadway musicals. As a child she appeared on such TV shows as *Juvenile Jury* and *Name That Tune*.

PETERS, CHRIS—actor

Morningstar/Eveningstar (drama)
.... Kevin Murphy (1986)

PETERS, DEEDY—actress
b: Aug 30, Hartford City, Ind.

House Calls (com)....Mrs. Phipps (1979–82)

PETERS, KELLY JEAN—actress

Hank (com).............. Franny (1965–66)
*M*A*S*H* (com)
.... Nurse Louise Anderson (1973)

PETERS, KEN—actor

Life with Luigi (com) .... Olson (1952)

PETERS, SCOTT—actor

Get Christie Love (police)
.... Det. Valencia (1974–75)

*Some sources give 1948.

PETERSEN, CHRIS—juvenile actor

The Baxters (com).. Jonah Baxter (1979–80)

PETERSEN, PAT—juvenile actor
b: Aug 9, 1966, Los Angeles, Calif.

Knots Landing (drama)
.... Michael Fairgate (1979–)

Chris and Pat Petersen are brothers.

PETERSEN, PATTY—juvenile actress
b: c. 1955

The Donna Reed Show (com)
.... Trisha Stone (1963–66)

Paul Petersen's sister.

PETERSEN, PAUL—actor
b: Sep 23, 1945, Glendale, Calif. r: Iowa

The Donna Reed Show (com)
.... Jeff Stone (1958–66)

"Fame is not a career. It's a sentence." Those are words from one who ought to know, a now older and wiser Paul Petersen, who was once one of the most popular teens in America. A few years after *The Donna Reed Show* left the air, however, he was persona unknown in Hollywood.

Paul came from a non–show business family, but he had a backstage mother who pushed him into the limelight at an early age. At nine, he was hired as one of the original Mouseketeers on *The Mickey Mouse Club;* he claims he was fired after three weeks for punching a fat casting agent who insisted that his name on the show would be "Mouse." Despite this display of juvenile temperament, Paul went on to play roles on *Playhouse 90, Lux Video Theatre, General Electric Theater* and other series, often as a homeless waif. In 1958 he was trundled off to another "cattle call" (mass audition) and got the plum role of Jeff, Donna Reed's TV son, on her upcoming TV series.

The show was a major hit, and it even led to a brief but spectacular recording career for Paul in 1962. He had two top-ten hits that year, "She Can't Find Her Keys" and "My Dad." The former, he says, was once voted the "Worst Record of 1962"; the latter, a paean to his TV dad, was better, but Paul freely admits that he was not really a serious recording artist. When *Donna Reed* left the air, Paul's career slide began. Squeaky-clean TV teens were not exactly in vogue in the late '60s, nor did that image reflect Paul's own personality. He got into drugs, fast cars, and social protest. Pretty soon he could find no acting work at all, and the money he had saved was nearly gone. He turned to writing, beginning with a *Marcus Welby* script that, to his surprise, was accepted. He then began turning out paperback novels, and during the '70s enjoyed substantial success with a series of them featuring a James Bond–type hero named Eric Saveman ("The Smuggler"). Later, he wrote a book about the Disney empire, tellingly titled *Walt, Mickey and Me* (1977).

Paul is today philosophical about his youthful stardom, his years of rejection and drugs ("a purple haze"), and his new career as a writer. "It's difficult to explain to civilians what happens when your circle of effect contracts rather than expands as you grow older, especially when you start young. It's difficult to explain to an ordinary person, an outsider, what being famous is all about." Then, he adds, "Have some consideration for the people who served. There's nothing more painful than someone looking at you and saying, 'Gee, I used to love you.' It's the most distant phrase in the human vocabulary."*

PETERSON, AMANDA—juvenile actress

Boone (drama) .... Squirt Sawyer (1983–84)

PETERSON, ARTHUR—actor
b: Nov 18, 1912, Mandan, N.D.

Crisis (drama) .... the "director" (1949)
Soap (com) .... the major (1977–81)

A prominent actor on radio in the '40s, most famous as Rev. John Ruthledge, the kindly, small-town minister who was the central character on *The Guiding Light* from its inception in 1938 until the late '40s. Forty years later, the actor became known to a new generation—who had never heard of Ruthledge—as the senile major on *Soap*.

*From an interview quoted in *Where Have They Gone*, by Bruce McColm and Doug Payne (Tempo Books, 1979).

PETERSON, DOLORES—singer

The Music Show (music)..... regular (1954)

PETERSON, DR. HOUSTON— psychologist

Theater of the Mind (info)
.... moderator (1949)

PETERSON, EUGENE—actor

Medical Center (drama)
.... Dr. Weller (1970–74)

PETERSON, HANK—actor

The Adventures of Kit Carson (wes)
.... Sierra Jack (occasional) (1951–55)

PETERSON, LENKA—actress

Bonino (com) .... Doris (1953)

The mother of Glynnis and Kevin O'Connor, seen mostly in soap operas *(Young Doctor Malone, A Time for Us, Another World)* from the '50s to the '80s.

PETERSON, MAGGIE—actress

The Bill Dana Show (com).. Susie (1963–65)

PETERSON, PATRICK J.—juvenile actor

The Kallikaks (com)
.... Junior Kallikak (1977)

PETERSON, ROBYN—actress

It's a Living (com)......... Frisco (1986–)

PETERSON, VIRGILIA—host

b: May 16, 1904, New York City, N.Y.

Author Meets the Critics (int)
.... moderator (1952–54)

PETRIE, GEORGE O.—actor

Dallas (drama).. Harve Smithfield (1978–)

PETRILLO, SAMMY—

Seven at Eleven (var)........ regular (1951)

PETTET, JOANNA—actress

b: Nov 16, 1944, London, England r: Montreal, Canada

Captains and the Kings (drama)
.... Katherine Hennessey (1976)
Knots Landing (drama) . Janet Baines (1983)

PEYSER, PENNY—actress

b: Feb 9, 1951, Irvington, N.Y.

Rich Man, Poor Man—Book II (drama)
.... Ramona Scott (1976–77)
The Tony Randall Show (com)
..... Roberta "Bobby" Franklin (1977–78)
The Blue and the Gray (drama)
....................Emma Geyser (1982)
Crazy Like a Fox (drama)
.... Cindy Fox (1984–86)

The daughter of New York congressman Peter Peyser.

PFEIFFER, BOB—host

Operation Success (info)..... host (1948–49)

PFEIFFER, MICHELLE—actress

b: Apr 29, 1962*, Orange County, Calif.

Delta House (com) ... the bombshell (1979)
B.A.D. Cats (police)
.... Off. Samantha Jensen (1980)

PFLUG, JO ANN—actress

b: May 2, Atlanta, Ga.

Candid Camera (aud par). cohost (1974–78)
Operation Petticoat (com)
.... Lt. Katherine O'Hara (1978–79)
The Fall Guy (adv)
..... Samantha "Big Jack" Jack (1981–82)
Rituals (drama)
.... Taylor Chapin (1984–85)

The sexy actress with the cute name and the cute little pug nose made her professional debut on *The Tonight Show* in the '60s, then began to get small parts in TV movies and series episodes. Also during this period she provided the voice of "The Invisible Girl" (what a waste!) for the Saturday morning cartoon *The Fantastic Four.* Jo Ann's first major break was in the movie version of *M*A*S*H* in 1970, as the aptly named Lt. Dish—the one who brings Painless back from the brink of suicide with her tender ministrations. Later, she was seen as a guest in numerous TV series, including *Quincy; Love, American Style;* and *The*

*Some sources give 1957.

Love Boat, as well as in regular supporting roles on several series.

In 1972 Jo Ann married game show host Chuck Woolery.

PHELPS, CLAUDE "JACKIE"—

Hee Haw (var) . . . . regular (1969–)

PHILBIN, REGIS—host

The Joey Bishop Show (talk)
. . . . announcer (1967–69)
Almost Anything Goes (aud par)
. . . . field interviewer (1976)

PHILBROOK, JAMES—
b: c. 1924 d: Oct 24, 1982

The Islanders (adv)
. . . . Zack Malloy (1960–61)
The Investigators (drama)
. . . . Steve Banks (1961)
The New Loretta Young Show (drama)
. . . . Paul Belzer (1962–63)

PHILIPP, KAREN—actress, singer
b: c. 1947, Abilene, Kans. r: Covina, Calif.

M*A*S*H (com)
. . . . Lt. Maggie Dish (1972)

A svelt vocalist formerly with the pop group Sergio Mendez and Brazil '66.

PHILIPS, LEE—actor, director
b: Jan 10, 1927, Brooklyn, N.Y.

The Adventures of Ellery Queen (drama)
. . . . Ellery Queen (1959)

A promising young New York actor of the '50s, Lee appeared in such famous TV dramas as *Marty* and *Twelve Angry Men,* as well as starring as the 1959 version of Ellery Queen. Shortly thereafter he gave up acting in favor of a highly successful career as a TV director, working behind the scenes on *The Andy Griffith Show, The Dick Van Dyke Show, The Waltons,* and others, as well as directing TV movies, including *Mae West* and *Space.*

PHILLIPPE, ANDRE—actor

Mr. Novak (drama)
. . . . Mr. Everett Johns (1963–65)

PHILLIPS, BARNEY—actor
b: Oct 20, 1913, St. Louis, Mo. d: Aug 17, 1982

Dragnet (police) . . . . . . Sgt. Ed Jacobs (1952)
Johnny Midnight (drama) . . Lt. Geller (1960)
Twelve O'Clock High (drama)
. . . . Maj. ("Doc") Kaiser (1964–67)
Felony Squad (police)
. . . . Capt. Franks (1967–68)
The Betty White Show (com)
. . . . Fletcher Huff (1977–78)

PHILLIPS, CARMEN—actress

The Lieutenant (drama) . . . . . . Lily (1963–64)

PHILLIPS, ETHAN—actor

Benson (com) . . . . . . Pete Downey (1980–85)

PHILLIPS, HARRY GEORGE—actor

Hotel (drama)
. . . . Harry the bartender (1984–)

PHILLIPS, KATHY—actress

The RCA Victor Show (com) . . Kathy (1952)

PHILLIPS, MACKENZIE—actress
b: Nov 10, 1959, Alexandria, Va.

One Day at a Time (com)
. . . . Julie Cooper Horvath (1975–83)

MacKenzie Phillips represents one of the most widely publicized examples of the disastrous effects that drugs can have on a performer's career. As a young teenager from a broken family, thrust into the high-pressure world of Hollywood with too much money and not enough control, it is a wonder she survived to age 20.

MacKenzie's father is John Phillips, a member of the very popular '60s rock group the Mamas and the Papas. Her parents were divorced when she was a baby, and she was raised by an aunt, bitterly resentful of the time her father spent away on the road. (John subsequently married a singer in the group, Michele Phillips.) Spoiled and rich, the young girl was smoking marijuana at 12 and drinking heavily at 14. Nevertheless, she landed her first acting role at 13 in the movie *American Graffiti* (1973), and in the years that followed played guest roles on *Movin' On, Baretta,* and *The Mary*

Tyler Moore Show, among others. In the 1976 TV film *Eleanor and Franklin* she portrayed the young (and somewhat homely, as was MacKenzie) Eleanor Roosevelt.

MacKenzie's major break was as one of Bonnie Franklin's daughters in *One Day at a Time.* After four years in the series, however, she became increasingly erratic and unreliable as a performer; heavy use of cocaine and other drugs resulted in severe weight loss and a sickly appearance. In 1980 she and her father (who was addicted to heroin) together entered a drug rehabilitation clinic in New Jersey. MacKenzie was off the series entirely for the 1980–81 season, but by the fall of 1981 was well enough to return on a semiregular basis. In 1983, she again showed signs of severe weight loss and exhaustion—not, this time, from drugs, the producers insisted—and she left the show for good.

During the 1980s, MacKenzie toured periodically with her father as part of a group called the New Mamas and Papas, and has also accompanied him on lecture tours speaking out on the dangers of drug abuse.

PHILLIPS, MICHELLE—actress, singer
b: Apr 6, 1944, Long Beach, Calif.

Aspen (drama) ...... Gloria Osborne (1977)

Glamorous second wife of John Phillips, and a former model. She was the stepmother of MacKenzie for a time. She later married actor Dennis Hopper.

PHILLIPS, NANCIE—actress
b: Louisville, Ky.

Rowan & Martin's Laugh-In (var)
.... regular (1970–71)

PHILLIPS, TACEY—actress
b: Apr 4, Montclair, N.J.

Co-ed Fever (com)............. Hope (1979)

PHILLIPS, WENDY—actress
b: Jan 2, 1952, Brooklyn, N.Y.

Executive Suite (drama)
.... Stacey Walling (1976–77)
Eddie Capra Mysteries (drama)
.... Lacey Brown (1978–79)

PHIPPS, WILLIAM (WILLIAM EDWARD PHIPPS)—actor

The Life and Legend of Wyatt Earp (wes)
.... Curley Bill Brocius (1959–61)
Sara (wes)......... Claude Barstow (1976)
Time Express (drama)
.... Engineer Callahan (1979)
Boone (drama) .... Uncle Link (1983–84)

PHOENIX, LEAF—juvenile actor
b: Oct 28, 1974, Puerto Rico

Morningstar/Eveningstar (drama)
.... Doug Roberts (1986)

The younger brother of child actor River Phoenix.

PHOENIX, RIVER—juvenile actor
b: Aug 23, 1970, Madras, Ore.

Seven Brides for Seven Brothers (adv)
.... Guthrie McFadden (1982–83)

This young actor-singer is from what a press release delicately calls a "free-spirited family." His brother is named Leaf, and his sisters, Rain, Liberty, and Summer. During his childhood, the family lived in various parts of the U.S. and South America, giving young River a rather varied cultural background.

PIAZZA, BEN—actor
b: Jul 30, 1934, Little Rock, Ark.

Ben Casey (drama) . Dr. Mike Rogers (1965)
The Waverly Wonders (com)
.... George Benton (1978)
Dallas (drama)..... Walt Driscoll (1982–83)
The Winds of War (drama)
.... Whitman (1983)

PIAZZA, MARGUERITE—concert singer
b: May 6, 1926, New Orleans, La.

Your Show of Shows (var)
...../.................... regular (1950–53)

PICARD, JOHN—actor

Gunslinger (wes) . Sgt. Maj. Murdock (1961)

PICERNI, PAUL—actor
b: Dec 1, 1922, New York City, N.Y.

The Untouchables (police)
.... agent Lee Hobson (1960–63)

PICK AND PAT—comedians

American Minstrels of 1949 (var)
.... regulars (1949)

A minor radio comedy team of the '30s and '40s, who had some exposure on early television. Their full names: Pick Malone and Pat Padgett.

PICKARD FAMILY, THE—singers

Leader: Obey ("Dad"), d. 1958
Others: Mom, Obey Jr. ("Bubb"), Charlie, Ruth, Ann

Sunday at Home (music).... regulars (1949)

PICKENS, JANE—singer

b: Macon, Ga.

The Jane Pickens Show (music)
.... hostess (1954)

A radio and stage singer of the '30s and '40s, originally part of a trio with her sisters. She later married a millionaire and became a New York socialite.

PICKENS, SLIM—actor

b: Jun 29, 1919, Kingsburg, Calif. d: Dec 8, 1983

The Outlaws (wes)........ Slim (1961–62)
Custer (wes)... California Joe Milner (1967)
B.J. and the Bear (adv)
.... Sgt. Beauregard Wiley (1979)
The Nashville Palace (var)
.... regular (1981–82)
Hee Haw (var).......... regular (1981–83)
Filthy Rich (com)
.... Big Guy Beck (1982)

A lanky, slow-talking character actor, who looked as rustic as they come (hawklike features, no chin); he started out on the rodeo circuit at age 15 and was one of the top rodeo clowns in the country during the late '30s and '40s. He segued easily into western films in the '40s and western TV series in the '50s, with guest appearances on *Wagon Train, Wide Country, Bonanza, Gunsmoke,* and *Alias Smith and Jones,* among others. Once in a while he would turn up in a comedy *(That Girl, The Mary Tyler Moore Show, Best of the West).* One of his best such performances, the year before he died, was in the *Dallas* spoof *Filthy Rich,* in which he played family patriarch Big Guy—who was already dead when the series began, but lived on to torment his greedy heirs via a videotaped will.

PICKETT, CINDY—actress

b: Apr 18, 1947, Norman, Okla. r: Houston, Texas

Call to Glory (drama)
.... Vanessa Sarnac (1984–85)

PICKLES, CHRISTINA—actress

b: Feb 17, Yorkshire, England

St. Elsewhere (drama)
.... Nurse Helen Rosenthal (1982–)

PIDGEON, WALTER—actor

b: Sep 23, 1897, East St. John, New Brunswick, Canada d: Sep 25, 1984

MGM Parade (doc)............ host (1956)

This distinguished-looking star was a major name in movies during the '40s, particularly in "pipe and slippers" romantic roles opposite Greer Garson. Long associated with MGM, he hosted the studio's initial venture into television, an anthology called *MGM Parade,* in 1956. Later, he made periodic guest appearances in a variety of television drama series, including *Zane Grey Theater, Checkmate, Perry Mason, Dr. Kildare, Marcus Welby,* and *Ellery Queen* (1976). He was also in a number of TV movies during the 1970s. Walter retired from acting in 1978 after an extraordinarily long movie career (1925–78), as well as several dozen gentlemanly visits to the TV medium.

PIECARSKI, JULIE—juvenile actress

The Facts of Life (com)
.... Sue Ann Weaver (1979–82)

A former *Mickey Mouse Club* Mouseketeer during that series' revival in the late 1970s. Her name is sometimes spelled Piekarski.

PIERCE, MAGGIE—actress

b: Oct 24, Detroit, Mich.

My Mother the Car (com)
.... Barbara Crabtree (1965–66)

PIERCE, WEBB—country singer
b: Aug 8, 1926, West Monroe, La.

Ozark Jubilee (music)
.... occasional host (1955–56)

An enormously popular country music star during the 1950s, with many top hits in that field (although most were so twangy that he never became well known on the popular charts). He's the one who has a guitar-shaped swimming pool at his Nashville mansion. He has been a guest on many country music TV series.

PIERPOINT, ERIC—actor
Hot Pursuit (drama) ...... Jim Wyler (1984)

PIERSON, RICHARD—actor
Masada (drama) .... Ephraim (1981)

PIERSON, WILLIAM—actor
The Cop and the Kid (com)
.... Sgt. Zimmerman (1975–76)

PIGEON, CORKY—juvenile actor
Silver Spoons (com)
......: Freddy Lippincottleman (1983–85)

PIGUERON, REV. GEORGE—clergyman
Circuit Rider (misc) ...... moderator (1951)

PILON, DANIEL—actor
b: Nov 13, Montreal, Canada

The Hamptons (drama)
.... Nick Atwater (1983)

A tall, swarthy actor who was a French Canadian matinee idol in the '70s before he learned English and began to appear in U.S. soap operas *(Dallas, The Hamptons, Ryan's Hope)* during the 1980s.

PINASSI, DOMINIQUE—juvenile actress
b: c. 1964

The Montefuscos (com)
.... Gina Montefusco (1975)

PINCHOT, BRONSON—actor
b: May 20, 1959, New York City r: South Pasadena, Calif.

Sara (com)......... Dennis Kemper (1985)
Perfect Strangers (com)
.... Balki Bartokomous (1986–)

The odd-talking Mediterranean shepherd of *Perfect Strangers* is a somewhat eccentric actor who first attracted attention in the cameo role of the haughty art-gallery clerk in the movie *Beverly Hills Cop.* After a short, unnoticed run as fourth banana on the 1985 comedy *Sara,* he suddenly became quite popular in his own show—his worldly innocence and strange accent reminding many of vintage Andy Kaufman (Latka) in *Taxi.*

Bronson is of Italian and Russian descent; he got his start on stage in New York in the early '80s, and made his film debut in *Risky Business* in 1983.

PINE, PHILLIP—actor
b: Jul 16, 1925, Hanford, Calif.

The Blue Knight (police)
.... Sgt. Newman (1975–76)

PINE, ROBERT—actor
b: Jul 10, 1941, Scarsdale, N.Y.

Bert D'Angelo/Superstar (police)
.... Insp. Larry Johnson (1976)
CHiPs (police) ... Sgt. Joe Getraer (1977–83)

One of television's perennial supporting players, familiar as the affable stationhouse sergeant on *CHiPs.* During the '60s he often played "the kid" in episodes of TV westerns. He is the scion of a wealthy New York family who decided to take up acting instead of becoming a surgeon. His anonymity, compared to the fame of stars he supports, does not seem to bother him, though it produces funny moments. "People do recognize me and call me 'Sarge' and ask for my autograph," he says. "But when I sign my name they sometimes look at it like maybe they've made a mistake."

PINK LADY—singers
Pink Lady (var) .... regular (1980)

One of television's most notorious examples of hype, the Japanese rock duo Pink Lady came to the screen in early 1980 after a heavy promotion campaign that netted them one moderately popular record in the

U.S., in 1979 ("Kiss in the Dark"). The joke was supposed to be that these two pretty young things didn't even speak English, and America would watch while they learned. We didn't.

Their full names: Mie Nemoto and Kei Masuda.

PINKHARD, RON—actor

Emergency (drama)
.... Dr. Morton (1972–77)

PINTAURO, DANNY—juvenile actor
b: Jan 6, 1976, Milltown, N.J.

Who's the Boss? (com)
.... Jonathan Bower (1984–)

Little Danny made his first network TV commercial when he was three. Later, he appeared in spots with Bob Hope and skater Peggy Fleming and had a five-year recurring run (1979–84) as diminutive millionaire Paul Stenbeck on the daytime serial *As the World Turns.*

PINTER, MARK—actor
b: Mar 7, Decorah, Iowa

Secrets of Midland Heights (drama)
.... Calvin Richardson (1980–81)
Behind the Screen (drama)
.... Karl Madison (1981–82)

PINZA, EZIO—singer
b: May 8, 1892, Rome, Italy d: May 9, 1957

The RCA Victor Show (var)
.... as himself (1951–52)
Bonino (com) .... Bonino (1953)

This handsome operatic basso had a long career at La Scala and New York's Metropolitan Opera from the 1910s to the 1940s, before he suddenly became a multimedia star in his late fifties via his performance in the smash hit Broadway musical *South Pacific* (1949). In the years that followed, Ezio was seen in films and on TV, including starring roles in a music and drama anthology series in 1951–52 and in his own family situation comedy in 1953. He also turned up on variety shows and dramatic productions (on *Robert Montgomery Presents, General Electric Theater,* etc.). He died of a stroke at age 65.

PIOLI, JUDY—actress, writer, producer
b: Mar 3, Brooklyn, N.Y. r: Floral Park, N.Y.

Star of the Family (com)..... Moose (1982)

The former head writer for *Laverne & Shirley,* and the producer of several 1980s situation comedies.

PISANI, REMO—actor

The Reporter (drama)... Ike Dawson (1964)

PISCOPO, JOE—comedian
b: Jun 17, 1951, Passaic, N.J.

NBC's Saturday Night Live (com)
.... regular (1980–84)

Impish, curly-haired Joe Piscopo spent most of the 1970s as a stand-up comedian in clubs such as New York's Improvisation and Los Angeles' Improv West and Laugh Stop, before he won a spot in the cast of *Saturday Night Live* in 1980. Though not one of the show's superstars, he was one of its consistently engaging players during the '80s, with characters such as his loud, monosyllabic sportscaster, "presidential adviser" Frank Sinatra, and querulous commentator Andy Rooney ("Ever notice how annoying my voice is?").

PISIER, MARIE-FRANCE—actress
b: May 10, 1944, Vietnam

Scruples (drama)
.... Valentine O'Neill (1980)

PITHEY, WENSLEY—actor
b: Jan 20, 1914, Cape Town, South Africa

Ike (drama)...... Winston Churchill (1979)

PITLIK, NOAM—actor, director
b: Nov 4, 1932, Philadelphia, Pa.

Sanford and Son (com)
.... Off. Swanhauser (1972)
The Bob Newhart Show (com)
.... Mr. Gianelli (1972–73)

Emmy Award: Best Director of a Comedy Series, for *Barney Miller* (1979)

PITONIAK, ANN—actress

AfterMASH (com).... Mildred Potter (1984)

PITTMAN, ROBERT JOHN—juvenile actor

Dennis the Menace (com)
.... Seymour (1962–63)

PITTS, ZASU—actress
b: Jan 3, 1898, Parsons, Kansas r: Santa Cruz, Calif. d: Jun 7, 1963

The Gale Storm Show (com)
.... Esmerelda Nugent (1956–60)

Gale Storm's delightfully fluttery, ever-flustered companion on Gale's 1950s situation comedy. Though ZaSu started out as a straight dramatic actress in silent films, she found lasting fame in a long series of "Oh, dear me" comedy roles during later years. She made only a few other TV appearances, in dramas such as *Perry Mason* and *Burke's Law*. Her unusual first name is a combination of the names of two relatives, Eli*za* and *Su*san.

PIUTE PETE (MORRIS KAUFMAN)—comedian, square-dance caller
b: Mar 14, 1911, New York City, N.Y.

Village Barn (var) .... regular (1948–49)

PLACE, MARY KAY—actress, writer
b: Sep 23, 1947, Tulsa, Okla.

Mary Hartman, Mary Hartman (com)
.... Loretta Haggers (1976–78)

Emmy Award: Best Supporting Actress in a Comedy Series, for *Mary Hartman, Mary Hartman* (1977)

An authentic country singer who played a burlesque on the type, twangy Loretta Haggers, on *Mary Hartman, Mary Hartman*. She is also quite an accomplished comedy writer, having contributed scripts for *M*A*S*H, Maude, Phyllis,* and other series of the '70s. Her television singing debut was on *All in the Family,* doing a song that Archie must have loved: "If Communism Comes Knocking at Your Door, Don't Answer It."

PLATO, DANA—juvenile actress
b: Nov 7, 1964, Maywood, Calif.

Diff'rent Strokes (com)
.... Kimberly Drummond (1978–84)

PLATT, EDWARD—actor
b: Feb 14, 1916, Staten Island, N.Y. d: Mar 20, 1974

Get Smart (com)
.... Thaddeus (the chief) (1965–70)

The bald, ever-frustrated "Chief" on *Get Smart* started out as a singer and radio actor during the 1940s, and was for a time a vocalist with the Paul Whiteman Orchestra. Jose Ferrer saw him on Broadway in the musical *Allegro* in 1947 and eventually helped introduce him to Hollywood, where he gained supporting roles in films and TV dramas during the 'late '50s and '60s. Prior to *Get Smart* he had appeared in more than 100 television roles, on series including *Dr. Kildare, The Dick Van Dyke Show, Mr. Novak,* and *Wagon Train.*

PLATT, HOWARD—actor
b: Jun 5, Chicago, Ill.

Sanford and Son (com)
.... Off. Hopkins ("Hoppy") (1972–76)
Flying High (adv)
.... Capt. Doug March (1978–79)
Empire (com) ...... Roger Martinson (1984)

PLEASENCE, ANGELA—actress
b: Chapeltown, Yorkshire, England

The Six Wives of Henry VIII (drama)
.... Catherine Howard (1971)

The daughter of actor Donald Pleasence.

PLEASENCE, DONALD—actor
b: Oct 5, 1919, Worksop, England

The Adventures of Robin Hood (adv)
.... Prince John (1955–56)
Master of the Game (drama)
.... Salomon Van der Merwe (1984)

One of the screen's fine villains, who fixed many a hero with his unblinking pale blue eyes and dominant manner. He has appeared periodically in TV movies, series, and miniseries from the '50s to the '80s, among them *The Count of Monte Cristo, The Bastard, All Quiet on the Western Front,* and *The Defection of Simas Kudirka* (for which he received an Emmy nomination).

PLEDGER, COURTNEY—actress

Walking Tall (police)
.... Dep. Joan Litton (1981)

PLESHETTE, JOHN—actor
b: Jul 27, 1942, New York City, N.Y.

Doctors' Hospital (drama)
.... Dr. Danvers (1975–76)
Seventh Avenue (drama)
.... Marty Cass (1977)
Knots Landing (drama)
.... Richard Avery (1979–83)

PLESHETTE, SUZANNE—actress
b: Jan 31, 1937, New York City, N.Y.

The Bob Newhart Show (com)
.... Emily Hartley (1972–78)
Suzanne Pleshette Is Maggie Briggs (com)
.... Maggie Briggs (1984)
Bridges to Cross (drama)
.... Tracy Bridges (1986)

A talented and intelligent actress who, most critics agree, has never realized her full potential in either her film or TV careers. She began appearing on television right out of college, in the late '50s, and played supporting roles in episodes of scores of dramas—*Route 66, Dr. Kildare* (an Emmy nominated performance), *The Fugitive, The Name of the Game, Ironside,* and *Bonanza,* to name a few. She is probably best-remembered as Bob Newhart's sensible wife on *The Bob Newhart Show;* an attempt to launch a comedy of her own in the '80s, in which she played a Mary Tyler Moore–ish reporter, was a failure. Lately, she has been seen in a succession of routine TV movies such as *Help Wanted: Male* and *One Cooks, the Other Doesn't.*

PLUMB, EVE—actress
b: c. 1957, Burbank, Calif.

The Brady Bunch (com)
.... Jan Brady (1969–74)
Little Women (drama)
.... Melissa Jane ("Lissa") Driscoll (1979)
The Brady Brides (com)
.... Jan Brady Covington (1981)

PLUMMER, CHRISTOPHER—actor
b: Dec 13, 1927, Toronto, Canada

The Thorn Birds (drama)
..... Archbishop Contini–Verchese (1983)

Emmy Award: Best Actor in a Limited Series, for *The Moneychangers* (1977)

A prominent actor of stage and screen, often in literate roles derived from history or the classics. He appeared on television dramas from the early 1950s onward, at first mostly in high-class productions on *Hallmark Hall of Fame, Omnibus, DuPont Show of the Month,* etc. After a ten-year period of reduced TV activity he returned to the small screen in the mid-1970s, apparently willing to take on some potboilers such as *The Moneychangers* and *Little Gloria, Happy at Last,* along with the classier stuff (*Dial M for Murder, Jesus of Nazareth* [as Herod], etc.).

POGUE, KEN—actor

Adderly (adv)....... Major Clack (1986–)

POINDEXTER, RON, DANCERS—

The Smothers Brothers Comedy Hour (var)
.... regulars (1968–69)
The Glen Campbell Goodtime Hour (var)
.... regulars (1969–71)

POINTER, PRISCILLA—actress
b: May 18, New York City, N.Y.

From Here to Eternity (drama)
.... Mrs. Austin (1980)
Dallas (drama)
.... Rebecca Wentworth (1981–83)
Call to Glory (drama)....... Lillie (1984–85)

Married to actor Robert F. Simon, and the mother (by a previous marriage) of young actress Amy Irving. Priscilla has been active onstage since the late '50s, and in TV movies since 1971.

POLESIE, HERB—producer, playwright
b: c. 1900 d: Jun 8, 1979

Charade Quiz (quiz)..... panelist (1947–49)
Twenty Questions (quiz). panelist (1949–55)

POLGAR, DR. FRANZ—hypnotist

The Amazing Polgar (misc) ..... host (1949)

POLIC, HENRY, II—actor
b: Feb 20, Pittsburgh, Pa.

When Things Were Rotten (com)
.... the Sheriff of Nottingham (1975)

The Late Summer Early Fall Bert Convy Show
(var)....................... regular (1976)
Webster (com) .... Jerry Silver (1983–)

POLITO, JON—actor

The Gangster Chronicles (drama)
.... Thomas "Three Finger Brown"
Lucchese (1981)

POLK, GORDON—actor
b: c. 1924 d: 1960

The Jerry Colonna Show (var)
.... regular (1951)

POLKA ROUNDERS, THE—dancers

Polka-Go-Round (music) . regulars (1958–59)

POLLACK, ROBERT—drama critic

Super Ghost (quiz) ...... panelist (1952–53)
It's About Time (quiz) ...... panelist (1954)

POLLAN, TRACY—actress

Family Ties (com).... Ellen Reed (1985–86)

POLLARD, MICHAEL J.—actor
b: May 30, 1939, Passaic, N.J.

Leo & Liz in Beverly Hills (com)
.... Leonard (1986)

POLLOCK, DEE—actor

Gunslinger (wes) .... Billy Urchin (1961)

POMERANTZ, EARL—writer, comedian

The Bobbie Gentry Show (var)
.... regular (1974)

Emmy Award: Best Writing for a Comedy-
Variety Special, for *Lily Tomlin* (1976)

PONCE, DANNY—actor
b: Sep 4, 1972, Waltham, Mass.

Knots Landing (drama)
.... Jason Avery (1983–85)
Valerie (com) ...... Willie Hogan (1986–)

PONCE, PONCIE—actor
b: Apr 10, 1933, Maui, Hawaii

Hawaiian Eye (drama)
.... Kazuo Kim (1959–63)

Poncie provided the native comic relief on
the *Hawaiian Eye* detective series. He
now has a nightclub act with his daughters,
and appears in commercials.

PONS, BEA—actress
b: Rhode Island

Car 54, Where Are You? (com)
.... Lucille Toody (1961–63)

PONTEROTTO, DONNA—actress
b: The Bronx, N.Y.

The Late Summer Early Fall Bert Convy Show
(var)....................... regular (1976)
Joe & Valerie (com)
.... Thelma Medina (1978–79)
Report to Murphy (com) .... Lucy (1982)

PONZINI, ANTONY—actor
b: Jun 1, Brooklyn, N.Y.

Flatbush (com)............ Esposito (1979)
Rituals (drama) .. Lt. Lucas Gates (1984–85)

A tough-looking actor, seen mostly in daytime soap operas from the 1960s to the '80s
—including a seven-year run as Vince
Wolek on *One Life to Live* (1968–75).

POOLE, LYNN—educator

The Johns Hopkins Science Review (info)
........................host (1948–49)
Tomorrow's Careers (info) ... host (1955–56)

A member of the faculty of Johns Hopkins
University.

POOLE, ROY—actor
b: c. 1924, San Bernadino, Calif. d: Jul 1, 1986

Andros Targets (drama)
.... Chet Reynolds (1977)
The Winds of War (drama)
.... Harry Hopkins (1983)

POPE, CARMELITA—hostess

Down You Go (quiz)
.... regular panelist (1951–54)

POPE, PEGGY—actress
b: May 15, Montclair, N.J.

Calucci's Department (com)
.... Elaine Fusco (1973)

Billy (com). . . . . Alice Fisher (1979)
Soap (com) . . . . Mrs. David (1979–81)

POPWELL, ALBERT—black actor
b: New York City, N.Y.

Search (adv). . . . . Griffin (1972–73)

PORTER, ARTHUR GOULD—actor
b: 1905, England d: Jan 2, 1987

The Beverly Hillbillies (com)
. . . . . . Ravenswood, the butler (1962–65)

PORTER, BOBBY—actor
b: c. 1953

Quark (com) . . . . Andy the Robot (1978)

A midget actor who works as a supporting player and stunt double for juveniles; among other things, he doubled for Meeno Peluce in *Voyagers*.

PORTER, DON—actor
b: Sep 24, 1912, Miami, Okla.

Private Secretary (com)
. . . . Peter Sands (1953–57)
The Ann Sothern Show (com)
. . . . James Devery (1959–61)
Gidget (com)
. . . . Prof. Russ Lawrence (1965–66)

Don Porter was one of those smiling, fatherly types who seemed born to inhabit TV sitcoms. In fact, he began his career in B movie potboilers of the 1940s *(Night Monsters, She Wolf of London, Eyes of the Underworld)* before advancing to lighter roles a few years later. He was Ann Sothern's boss on both of her early series, and Sally Fields' dad on *Gidget*. He remained quite busy on TV during the '70s and into the '80s playing guest roles in episodes of series as varied as *Happy Days, Barnaby Jones, The Bionic Woman,* and *Dallas*.

PORTER, NYREE DAWN—actress
b: 1940, New Zealand

The Protectors (adv)
. . . . Contessa di Contini (1972–73)

A young New Zealand–born actress who came to notice in the role of Irene in *The Forsyte Saga* (1969–70), which, like *The Protectors,* was a British import to American TV.

PORTER, ROBIE—singer

Malibu U (music)
. . . . regular (1967)

PORTER, TODD—juvenile actor
b: May 15, 1968, New Jersey

Whiz Kids (drama)
. . . . Hamilton Parker (1983–84)

PORTILLO, ROSE—actress

Born to the Wind (adv)
. . . . Star Fire (1982)

POST, MARKIE—actress
b: Nov 4, 1950, Palo Alto, Calif. r: Walnut Creek, Ca.

Semi-Tough (com)
. . . . Barbara Jane Bookman (1980)
The Gangster Chronicles (drama)
. . . . Chris Brennan (1981)
The Fall Guy (adv)
. . . . . . Terri Shannon/Michaels (1982–85)
Night Court (com)
. . . . Christine Sullivan (1985–   )

POST, MIKE—orchestra leader, songwriter

The Andy Williams Show (var)
. . . . orch. leader (1969–71)
The Mac Davis Show (var)
. . . . orch. leader (1974–76)

A conductor/composer who has long been associated with television. Among other things, he produced hit records of the theme songs from *The Rockford Files, Magnum P.I.,* and *Hill Street-Blues,* and contributed music used on the soundtracks of those and many other series, including *The A-Team, The Greatest American Hero, CHiPs,* etc.

POST, WILLIAM, JR.—actor

Beulah (com)
. . . . Harry Henderson (1950–52)

POSTON, TOM—actor
b: Oct 17, 1927*, Columbus, Ohio

The Steve Allen Show (var)
.... regular (1956–59)
To Tell the Truth (quiz).. panelist (1958–67)
The Steve Allen Show (var).. regular (1961)
On the Rocks (com) . Mr. Sullivan (1975–76)
We've Got Each Other (com)
.... Damon Jerome (1977–78)
Mork & Mindy (com)
.... Franklin Delano Bickley (1978–82)
Newhart (com)..... George Utley (1982–   )

Emmy Award: Best Supporting Actor in a Comedy Series, for *The Steve Allen Show* (1959)

"Gee, I don't remember. Golly, is that so? My name? Uh . . ." Tom Poston first became famous on *The Steve Allen Show* as the "man on the street," giving responses like that to an eager interviewer, in a hilarious burlesque of man-on-the-street interviews with people who know nothing about anything. Tom, it seemed, couldn't even remember his own name.

Tom started out with more serious theatrical goals, as a New York stage actor in the late '40s. He made his Broadway debut with a small part in José Ferrer's 1947 production of *Cyrano de Bergerac*. During the following years he played more small stage roles, and found TV work on such early live series as *Tom Corbett—Space Cadet* and the soap opera *Hawkins Falls*. Later, he got better roles in television dramatic productions on *Goodyear Playhouse, Robert Montgomery Presents,* and *The U.S. Steel Hour,* among others. It was as a comedian that he struck gold, however. Although he continued to appear for a time in high-class dramas (such as *The Tempest* with Richard Burton, on *The Hallmark Hall of Fame* in 1963), his image was irrevocably that of the funny, forgetful, and maybe a bit irritable comedian. As the '60s wore on he gradually gave in to the inevitable and began appearing mostly on comedy series such as *The Good Guys* and *Get Smart*. In the '70s he guest-starred on

*By 1944 Poston had attended some college and served as an air force pilot in Europe, so it seems likely that he was born earlier than this commonly given year (some sources give 1921). Also, some biographies claim that he was born on a boat off the coast of North Carolina, and raised in Ohio. If you asked him, he probably wouldn't remember.

The Bob Newhart Show as Bob's fun-loving college chum. Since the mid-1970s, he has played regular supporting roles in several comedies, including that of the rustic handyman in Newhart's hit 1982 series.

POTTER, CAROL—actress
b: May 21, c. 1948, New York City, N.Y. r: Tenafly, N.J.

Today's F.B.I. (police)
.... Maggie Clinton (1981–82)

POTTER, CLIFF—actor

The Name of the Game (adv)
.... Andy Hill (1968–71)

POTTER, JERRY—actor

Alice (com)................ Jerry (1981–82)

POTTER, PETER—disc jockey
b: c. 1904 d: Apr 17, 1983

The Peter Potter Show (music)
.... host (1953–54)

Potter's record-rating show, better known as *Juke Box Jury*, was seen locally in Los Angeles for a number of years and was nationally syndicated later in the 1950s.

POTTS, ANNIE—actress
b: Oct 28, Nashville, Tenn. r: Franklin, Ky.

Goodtime Girls (com)
.... Edith Bedelmeyer (1980)
Designing Women (com)
.... Mary Jo Shively (1986–   )

POTTS, CLIFF—actor
b: Jan 5, c. 1942, Glendale, Calif.

Once an Eagle (drama)
.... Courtney Massengale (1976–77)
Big Hawaii (drama) .... Mitch Fears (1977)
Little Women (drama)
.... John Brooke (1979)
Lou Grant (drama)
.... Ted McCovey (1981–82)
For Love and Honor (drama)
.... 1st Sgt. Eugene Allard (1983)

POWELL, ANGELA—juvenile actress

The New Dick Van Dyke Show (com)
.... Annie Preston (1971–74)

POWELL, BUDDY—comedian

Presenting Susan Anton (var)
.... regular (1979)

POWELL, DICK—actor, producer
b: Nov 14, 1904, Mountain View, Ark. d: Jan 2, 1963

Four Star Playhouse (drama)
.... costar (1952–56)
Dick Powell's Zane Grey Theater (wes)
.... host/star (1956–61)
The Dick Powell Show (drama)
.... host/star (1961–63)

Emmy Award: Trustees' Award, "in grateful memory of his conspicuous contributions to and reflections of credit upon the industry as an actor, director, producer, and executive" (1963)

Dick Powell is forever frozen in time and celluloid as the oh-so-boyish tenor crooning love songs to Ruby Keeler in some of the brightest and most popular movie musicals of the 1930s. Although such roles made him a star, Dick complained in the late '30s that he would never escape from such a well-loved image; but he did, turning to tough-guy detective roles in the '40s, both on-screen *(Phillip Marlowe)* and on radio *(Richard Diamond)*.

Dick was one of the first major Hollywood stars to embrace television, and he became a steady and reliable TV performer during the last decade of his life. First came *Four Star Playhouse,* followed by *Zane Grey Theater* (based on the writings of the famous western author), and finally *The Dick Powell Show.* All were anthologies, which Dick hosted and in which he sometimes starred. The latter also served as a showcase for pilots for prospective series; two series which resulted were *Burke's Law* and *Saints and Sinners.* Dick's costar, on occasion, was his wife June Allyson, and he also appeared in episodes of her dramatic anthology in 1959 and 1960. All of his series were produced by his own firm, Four Star Television, which became one of the most prosperous TV production houses of the 1950s.

Although Dick may be best remembered for his musicals, he was a much-beloved star of early TV and was sorely missed when he passed away of cancer in 1963.

POWELL, JANE—actress
b: Apr 1, 1929, Portland, Ore.

Alcoa/Goodyear Theatre (drama)
.... recurring star (1957–58)

The sweet-faced young star of movie musicals of the '40s and '50s was seen only rarely on television, principally in the *Alcoa/Goodyear* alternate week anthologies in 1957–58, and in a few musical specials of the same period. She made a nostalgic visit to *Fantasy Island* in 1978 and sailed on *The Love Boat* in 1981, a sure sign she had joined the ranks of yesterday's stars.

POWELL, RANDOLPH—actor
b: Apr 14, 1950, Iowa City, Iowa

Logan's Run (sci fi) ...... Francis (1977–78)
Doctors' Private Lives (drama)
.... Dr. Rick Calder (1979)
Dallas (drama) .... Alan Beam (1979–80)

POWELL, SUE—singer

Nashville on the Road (music)
.... regular (1981–83)

POWERS, BEN—black actor

Laugh-In (revival) (var) ... regular (1977–78)
Good Times (com)
.... Keith Anderson (1978–79)
Mickey Spillane's Mike Hammer (drama)
.... Moochie (1984–)

POWERS, JIMMY—sportscaster

Bowling Headliners (sport)
.... announcer (1949)
Gillette Cavalcade of Sports (Friday Night Fights) (sport) .... sportscaster (1949–60)
Sports Newsreel (sport)
.... commentator (1951)
Famous Fights (sport).. commentator (1952)

POWERS, LEONA—actress
b: c. 1897 d: 1970

The Aldrich Family (com)
.... Mrs. Brown (1949–53)
My Son Jeep (com) ...... Mrs. Bixby (1953)

POWERS, MALA—actress
b: Dec 20, 1931*, San Francisco, Calif.

*Some sources give Dec. 29.

Hazel (com) ..... Mona Williams (1965–66)
The Man and the City (drama)
.................Marian Crane (1971–72)

POWERS, PEGGY—singer

The Sammy Kaye Show (var)
.... regular (1953)

POWERS, STEFANIE—actress
b: Nov 2, 1942, Hollywood, Calif.

The Girl from U.N.C.L.E. (drama)
.... April Dancer (1966–67)
The Feather and Father Gang (drama)
.... Toni "Feather" Danton (1977)
Hart to Hart (adv).. Jennifer Hart (1979–84)

One of the mainstays of the scandal sheets in the '80s, a glamorous, globe-trotting lady, with glamorous lovers, in a glamorous series—but oh, what an up and down career! Stefanie was a budding starlet as soon as she graduated from Hollywood High, making her debut in a little-known feature called *Among the Thorns* and moving on to such popular early '60s films as *Tammy Tell Me True* and *Experiment in Terror.* She did a little television, including a 1963 comedy pilot with Bobby Rydell called *Swingin' Together* and a 1963 episode of *Bonanza* in which she played Calamity Jane; however, it represented a major break when, in 1966, she was signed to star in her first TV series, *The Girl from U.N.C.L.E.* "As far as I'm concerned," she said at the time, "my (movie) career was going nowhere. The studio had absolutely no plans for me ... I consider television to be my savior. Ten months of it will do my career more good than years of features." Words she would learn to eat.

The Girl From U.N.C.L.E. was a bomb, and Stefanie was out of work for the next two years. "In this business," she ruefully admitted later, "a failed series is the kiss of death . . . it was a baptism of fire, both coming and going. I was sort of shell-shocked by it. So I left the country." She traveled for a time with her new husband, actor Gary Lockwood; then, after a couple of years doing penance in the theatrical hinterlands, she began to worm her way back on TV, doing guest shots on such series as *Lancer; Love, American Style; Medical Center;* and *Marcus Welby* ("I've had every disease known to man on every

medical series that was ever done—even a few *not* known to man," she complained). Finally, she attempted a full-fledged series comeback in a father-and-daughter crime show called *The Feather and Father Gang,* with Harold Gould. It failed, but two years later a husband-and-wife crime show, co-starring handsome Robert Wagner, did much better. *Hart to Hart* may have been just an updated *Mr. & Mrs. North* (or even *McMillan and Wife*), but a new generation didn't seem to notice, and Stefanie had her hit series at last.

By the time *Hart to Hart* was riding high, the actress had begun a second career, to which she is intensely committed. After her divorce from Gary Lockwood in the early '70s she became the "constant companion" of aging screen idol William Holden, and he introduced her to his dream of a big-game preserve and study center in Kenya. Following his death in 1981, Stefanie carried on with The William Holden Wildlife Foundation, in his memory. On-screen she has turned increasingly to TV movies and miniseries, among them *Washington: Behind Closed Doors* and *Family Secrets.*

PRADOR, IRENE—actress

Holocaust (drama) .... Maria Kalova (1978)

PRAED, MICHAEL—actor

Dynasty (drama) .. Prince Michael (1985–)

PRAGER, STANLEY—comedian, director
b: Jan 8, 1917, New York City, N.Y. d: Jan 18, 1972

The College Bowl (com) .. regular (1950–51)

PRATHER, JOAN—actress

Executive Suite (drama)
.... Glory Dalessio (1976–77)
Eight Is Enough (com)
.... Janet Bradford (1979–81)

One of the Bradford family in-laws on *Eight Is Enough;* she married eldest son David.

PRATT, DEBORAH—actress

Phyl & Mikhy (com) .... Connie (1980)
Airwolf (adv) .... Marella (1984–85)

PRAVDA, GEORGE—actor

b: 1918, Prague, Czechoslovakia d: Apr 30, 1985

Holocaust (drama) .... Felscher (1978)

PREMINGER, MICHAEL—actor

Dinah and Her New Best Friends (var)
.... regular (1976)

PRENDERGAST, GARY—actor

Makin' It (adv)....... Bernard Fusco (1979)

PRENTIS, LOU—actress

Buck Rogers (sci fi)
.... Wilma Deering (1950–51)

PRENTISS, ANN—actress

b: 1941, San Antonio r: Houston, Texas

Captain Nice (com)
.... Sgt. Candy Kane (1967)

The younger sister of actress Paula Prentiss.

PRENTISS, ED—host, actor

Action Autographs (doc)..... host (1949–50)
Dr. Fix-Um (info)........... host (1949–50)
Majority Rules (quiz)...... emcee (1949–50)

A radio actor famous as "Captain Midnight" during the 1940s. After a busy season hosting various informational shows in 1949–50, he went on to play small parts on numerous series, including doctors, bankers, and bartenders on such 1960s westerns as *Wanted: Dead or Alive, Laramie,* and *Bonanza.*

PRENTISS, PAULA—actress

b: Mar 4, 1939, San Antonio, Texas

He & She (com) ... Paula Hollister (1967–68)

The wife of actor Richard Benjamin, and sister of Ann Prentiss. She appears mostly in movies, TV, and otherwise. On-screen since 1961.

PRESCOTT, ALLEN—host

The Wife Saver (info) .... host (1947)
Quizzing the News (quiz) .. emcee (1948–49)
Starlit Time (var) .... regular (1950)

PRESLEY, PRISCILLA—actress

b: May 24, 1945, Brooklyn, N.Y. r: Connecticut

Those Amazing Animals (doc)
.... host (1980–81)
Dallas (drama)...... Jenna Wade (1983–)

The widow of Elvis Presley, whose career has been bathed in the very bright light of constant media attention due to her connection to the King of Rock 'n' Roll. They were married from 1967–73; subsequently, Priscilla, who got $2 million in the divorce settlement, dabbled in karate and dress designing. She then became a television spokesperson for beauty products.

Priscilla's much-publicized series debut was on *Those Amazing Animals,* which failed nevertheless. She costarred with Michael Landon in the 1983 TV movie *Love Is Forever* (aka *Comeback*) and then found steady employment as Bobby Ewing's girlfriend Jenna on *Dallas.*

PRESSMAN, LAWRENCE—actor

b: Jul 10, 1939, Cynthiana, Ky.

Rich Man, Poor Man—Book I (drama)
.... Bill Denton (1976)
Mulligan's Stew (drama)
.... Michael Mulligan (1977)
Ladies' Man (com)
.... Alan Thackeray (1980–81)
The Winds of War (drama)
.... Bunky Thurston (1983)

PRESTIDGE, MEL—actor

Hawaiian Eye (drama)..... Quon (1960–63)

PRESTON, J.A.—black actor

b: Nov 13, Washinton, D.C.

All's Fair (com)
.... Allen Brooks (1976–77)
Hill Street Blues (police)
.... Mayor Ozzie Cleveland (1982–)

PRESTON, KELLY—actress

For Love and Honor (drama)
.... Mary Lee (1983)

PRESTON, MIKE—actor

Hot Pursuit (drama) ..... Alec Shaw (1984)

PRESTON, ROBERT—actor

b: Jun 8, 1918*, Newton Highlands, Mass. d: Mar 21, 1987

Man Against Crime (drama)
.... Pat Barnett (1951)
Anywhere, U.S.A. (doc)
.... the doctor (occasional) (1952)
The Chisholms (wes)
.... Hadley Chisholm (1979–80)

Robert Preston was a rugged, forceful ball of energy—not unlike his most famous character, Professor Harold Hill of *The Music Man*. Only a small part of his long and successful acting career was on television. Preston made his movie debut in 1938, shortly after graduation from high school, and he appeared during the next two decades in a long series of action films such as *Union Pacific* and *Northwest Passage*—usually in supporting roles, sometimes (in B films) as the lead. As one of Hollywood's lesser names, he became fairly active in television in the early 1950s, mostly in playhouse productions on *Pulitzer Prize Playhouse, The U.S. Steel Hour, Climax*, etc., but also fleetingly in a couple of series roles. He was Ralph Bellamy's summer replacement on *Man Against Crime* in 1951, and a doctor on the medical docudrama *Anywhere, U.S.A.*, which lasted one month in 1952.

Preston appeared onstage throughout this period and finally struck gold in the hit 1957 Broadway musical *The Music Man* as the fast-talking con man who boomed out "76 Trombones" and "There's Trouble Right Here in River City." This led to bigger and better screen roles (*The Dark at the Top of the Stairs*, the film version of *The Music Man*, etc.), and for the next 19 years (1960–79) he was scarcely seen on TV at all, aside from a couple of dramas in 1975. In early 1979 he returned, big as life, in the sprawling miniseries *The Chisholms* (as Pa Chisholm), followed by a starring role in the series the following season. He occasionally appeared in TV movies during the 1980s.

PRESTON, WAYDE—actor

b: Laramie, Wyo.

Colt .45 (wes) ... Christopher Colt (1957–60)

*Some sources give 1913 or 1917.

A curly-haired young actor of the '50s, whose promise never really materialized. He moved to Rome in later years and made a good deal of money starring in "spaghetti westerns" that were seldom seen in the U.S.

PREVILLE, ANNE—actress

Foreign Intrigue (drama)
.... Patricia Bennett (1953–54)

PRIBOR, RICHARD—orchestra leader

The Marge and Gower Champion Show (com)
.... orch. leader (1957)

PRICE, ALLEN—actor

The Practice (com). Paul Bedford (1976–77)

PRICE, KENNY—country singer

b: May 27, 1931, Florence, Ky.*

Hee Haw (var) .... regular (1974–   )
Hee Haw Honeys (com)
.... Kenny Honey (1978–79)

A heavyweight (300 pounds) country crooner known as "the Round Mound of Sound." He was long a regular on radio's *Midwestern Hayride*.

PRICE, MARC—juvenile actor

b: Feb. 23, 1968

Family Ties (com)
.... Irwin "Skippy" Handelman (1982–   )
Condo (com) .... Billy Kirkridge (1983)

PRICE, PAUL B.—actor

b: Oct 7, 1933, Carteret, N.J.

Busting Loose (com) ... Ralph Cabell (1977)

PRICE, ROGER—actor, writer

b: Mar 6, 1920, Charleston, W. Va.

School House (var) .... regular (1949)
How To (info) .... moderator (1951)
What Happened? (quiz) ..... panelist (1952)
Who's There? (quiz) .... panelist (1952)
Droodles (quiz) .... emcee (1954)
The Name's the Same (quiz)
.... panelist (1954–55)

This mild-looking young man in horn-rimmed glasses enjoyed quite a vogue

*Some sources give nearby Covington, Ky.

during the early 1950s as the author of "droodles"—simple little line drawings with clever captions (for example, four squares, two black and two white, labeled "chessboard for beginners"). He published a whole series of books of them, appeared on panel shows with them, and even hosted a 1954 summer game show in which contestants thought up their own captions. "It's an old art form," he said. "I just boxed it and gave it a name. All it takes is an adequate minimum of drawing talent, something I have plenty of."

In later years, after "Droodles" blew over, Roger was seen occasionally in minor supporting roles in films and on TV.

PRICE, VINCENT—actor
b: May 27, 1911, St. Louis, Mo.

Pantomime Quiz (quiz) ... regular (1950–52)
E.S.P. (aud par) .... emcee (1958)
The Chevy Mystery Show (drama)
.... Host (1960)
Time Express (drama) .... Jason (1979)

Vincent Price seems to have created an image that is both scary and reassuring at the same time. He may be the "Master of Menace," but he is so cultivated you know he wouldn't really hurt anyone.

Vincent was born in privileged circumstances and exposed to the fine arts as a youth. He traveled to England to get his start as an actor, then returned to the U.S. as a "brilliant English discovery" and broke into films here in 1938. By the time television came along he was well-established in suave romantic roles as well as in horror films. He was quite busy on TV during the '50s, appearing on many major anthologies including *Schlitz Playhouse, Climax,* and *Alfred Hitchcock Presents.* He also briefly hosted two summer series on eerie themes *(E.S.P.* and *The Chevy Mystery Show)* while showing a lighter side on game and panel shows such as *Pantomime Quiz.*

Vincent was seen less often after 1960, and when he did appear it was often in lighter roles, or burlesques of his former scary persona. On *Batman* he was the cartoonish "Egghead," and on *Voyage to the Bottom of the Sea,* the sneaky Professor Multiple, whose puppet show came to life and almost overran the Seaview. Later, in

the '70s, he made stops on *Love, American Style; The Brady Bunch;* and *The Love Boat* ("Ship of Ghouls"), as well as on a few traditional thrillers such as *Night Gallery.* Beginning in 1981 he was the host, with a twinkle in his eye, of the PBS anthology *Mystery.*

Vincent's other well-known passions are connoisseur cooking and fine art; he is a recognized authority in, and has written several books on, both fields. His autobiography: *I Like What I Know* (1959). A biography, *Vincent Price Unmasked,* by J. R. Parish and Steven Whitney, was published in 1976.

PRICKETT, MAUDIE—actress
b: 1915 d: Apr 14, 1976

Date with the Angels (com)
.... Mrs. Cassie Murphy (1957–58)
Hazel (com) .... Rosie (1961–66)
The Tammy Grimes Show (com)
.... Mrs. Ratchett (1966)

PRIEST, PAT—actress
b: c. 1936, Bountiful, Utah

The Munsters (com)
.... Marilyn Munster (1964–66)

The "normal" niece on *The Munsters.* She is the daughter of Ivy Baker Priest, the treasurer of the United States during the Eisenhower administration, and the name that appeared on countless dollar bills of the period. Pat's advice to aspiring actresses? "I'd tell them to have two things—plenty of money and a loyal husband."

PRIMUS, BARRY—actor
b: Feb 16, 1938, New York City, N.Y.

Cagney & Lacey (police)
.... Sgt. Dory McKenna (1984–85)

PRINCE, BOB—sportscaster
b: 1917 d: Jun 10, 1985

Monday Night Baseball (sport)
.... sportscaster (1976)

PRINCE, JACK—singer

The Johnny Carson Show (var)
.... vocalist (1955–56)

PRINCE, JONATHAN—actor

b: Aug 16, c. 1958, Beverly Hills, Calif.

Mr. Merlin (com).... Leo Samuels (1981–82)
Alice (com) .... Danny (1984–85)

PRINCE, RON—

What's It All About, World? (var)
.... regular (1969)

PRINCE, WILLIAM—actor

b: Jan 26, 1913, Nichols, N.Y.

The Mask (drama) ... Peter Guilfoyle (1954)
Justice (drama)... Richard Adams (1955–56)
Aspen (drama) ...... Judge Kendrick (1977)
The American Girls (adv)
.... Jason Cook (1978)

A distinguished-looking character actor who played a great many roles on TV in the 1950s, and some thereafter; unfortunately, none were particularly memorable. He deserves a footnote, at least, as the co-star of the first hour-long drama series with a continuing cast—*The Mask,* in 1954.

From the late '50s to the early '70s Prince was active mostly on daytime soap operas, including a five-year run as the father on *Young Dr. Malone.*

PRINCIPAL, VICTORIA—actress

b: Jan 3, 1945*, Fukuoka, Japan

Dallas (drama)
.... Pamela Barnes Ewing (1978–)

Patrick Duffy's sexy young bride on *Dallas* was born to an air force father and moved around quite a lot as a child. She took up acting studies in her teens, then headed for New York, but made little headway on the Broadway stage. For a time she supported herself as a model. Trying her luck in Hollywood in the early '70s, she began to get roles in a few films and TV episodes (*Love, American Style; Banacek; Love Story;* etc.).

Dissatisfied with the slow progress of her career, and being an extremely ambitious woman, Victoria dropped out of acting in the mid-1970s to become an agent for other actors, including comedian Dick Martin ("For about a year I had the prettiest agent in town," he recalls). Finally, she found the role she wanted for herself, as

*Some sources give 1950.

one of the central characters on the new prime time soap *Dallas.* Good choice. After a modest start, the series went on to become the number-one program on television.

PRINE, ANDREW—actor

b: Feb 14, 1936, Jennings, Fla.

The Wide Country (wes)
.... Andy Guthrie (1962–63)
The Road West (wes)
.... Timothy Pride (1966–67)
W.E.B. (drama)....... Dan Costello (1978)
V (movie) (sci fi) .... Steven (1983)
V: The Final Battle (miniseries) (sci fi)
.... Steven (1984)

A lanky actor, active since the late 1950s, often seen in westerns of the '60s. He co-starred in two short-lived western series *(Wide Country* and *The Road West),* representing the "younger generation" in each.

PRINE, JOHN—singer, songwriter

b: 1946, Maywood, Ill.

The Texas Wheelers (com)
.... sang theme (1974–75)

PRINGLE, JOAN—black actress

b: Jun 2, Harlem, New York City, N.Y.

Ironside (police).... Diana Sanger (1974–75)
That's My Mama (com)
.... Tracy Curtis Taylor (1975)
Rafferty (drama) ...... Nurse Keynes (1977)
The White Shadow (drama)
.... Sybil Buchanan (1978–81)

PRINZE, FREDDIE—actor

b: Jun 22, 1954, New York City, N.Y. d: Jan 29, 1977

Chico and the Man (com)
.... Chico Rodriguez (1974–77)

One of the most famous shooting stars of the television firmament, a brilliant young comic who blazed brightly for just two years, then killed himself at the age of 22. What happened?

Freddie was raised in a poor, heavily ethnic area of New York City, the son of a Puerto Rican mother and a Hungarian father (which, Freddie cracked, made him a

"Hungarican"). A chubby kid who had trouble fitting in, he developed a knack for comedy in school as a way of gaining acceptance; he was so good in his washroom and lunch-hour routines that friends urged him to try to make it as a professional comic. Freddie graduated from New York's High School for the Performing Arts in 1973 and began to click almost immediately. He did stand-up routines at local improvisational clubs (for free), relying on hip, heavily ethnic material ("my neighborhood is a suburb of Harlem—slums with trees!"). Only a few months out of high school, he made his television debut on *The Jack Paar Show;* however, the break that really made a difference was an appearance on *The Tonight Show* in December 1973. In the audience was producer Jimmy Komack, who was looking for a young ethnic comic to star with old pro Jack Albertson in a new series about a Chicano and a grouchy old garage owner. Freddie tested against several others and won the role.

Chico and the Man premiered in September 1974 and was an immediate smash hit. Freddie Prinze, a kid who had been nearly broke and riding the New York City subways a year before, was suddenly catapulted into the Hollywood fast lane, a swirl of cars, sex, money, big deals—and drugs. As soon as the first season's taping was completed, this unseasoned street kid went straight into club work, at the top, playing Las Vegas and packing the house. He appeared on TV specials and made his first TV movie, a crime caper called *The Million Dollar Rip-Off.* Almost on impulse he married a young Las Vegas travel agent in September 1975, a move he would later regret.

Soon he was popping pills at an alarming rate to keep up with the pressure. His fragile marriage hit the rocks after only a few months; his wife, Kathy, filed for divorce and took their infant son with her, a move that devastated Freddie. At the same time he was locked in a bitter legal battle with a former agent. Drugs, especially Quaaludes, began taking over his life. Despondent, confused, with demands on him from all sides, he became increasingly erratic and developed a fixation on guns, often waving a pistol and mock-shooting himself. Friends tried to take the gun and the drugs away, but it was always easy to get them back. Finally, on one incredible night

in January 1977, Freddie called several people, including his mother, pouring out his pain and saying that he was going to end it. They'd heard it many times before, but his manager stayed with him, talking and reassuring him long into the night. Then, suddenly, to the man's horror, Freddie pulled a pistol from the cushions of the couch, put it to his temple and fired.

Freddie was rushed into surgery. He lingered for 33 hours, but he was brain dead. At his funeral a bitter and stunned costar Jack Albertson and best friend Tony Orlando read eulogies. Freddie's anguished mother, a simple woman, then launched a lonely crusade, and even wrote a book, in an effort to clear his name. She said that he had not committed suicide—he was under the influence of drugs, showing off, and unaware that the gun would actually go off. Eventually the courts agreed.

"If anyone killed him, it was Hollywood and all the things that made him show off," she tearfully told a reporter. "He lost contact with himself ... People who made a lot of money out of my boy, they are very rich. What my boy got? Just a grave and people who say he killed himself. He wouldn't do that to me."

PRITCHETT, FLORENCE—panelist
Leave It to the Girls (talk)
.... panelist (1949–54)

PROCTOR, PHIL—actor, writer
The Starland Vocal Band Show (var)
.... regular (1977)

PROFANATO, GENE—juvenile actor
Mr. T and Tina (com) .... Aki (1976)

PROFT, PAT—comedian, writer
b: Apr 3, Minneapolis r: Columbia Heights, Minn.

Joey & Dad (var) .... regular (1975)
Van Dyke and Company (var)
.... regular (1976)
Detective School (com) .... Leo Frick (1979)

PROHASKA, JANOS—actor
b: 1921, Budapest, Hungary d: Mar 13, 1974
The Andy Williams Show (var)
.... regular (1969–71)

A stuntman who (in costume) impersonated various animals on a number of prime time shows. On *The Andy Williams Show* he was the cookie-mooching bear.

PROHUT, LOU—

Polka-Go-Round (music) .. regular (1958–59)

PROMENADERS, THE—dancers

Ozark Jubilee (music).... regulars (1959–60)
Five Star Jubilee (var) ...... regulars (1961)

PROSKY, ROBERT—actor
b: Dec 13, 1930, Philadelphia, Pa.

Hill Street Blues (police)
.... Sgt. Stanislaus Jablonski (1984–)

A veteran actor of Polish extraction, who spent 23 years as a member of the Arena Stage in Washington, D.C. He began playing character roles (usually as a villain) in films and on television around 1980.

PROVINE, DOROTHY—actress
b: Jan 20, 1937, Deadwood, S.D.

The Alaskans (adv) . Rocky Shaw (1959–60)
The Roaring Twenties (drama)
.... Pinky Pinkham (1960–62)

An energetic singer and dancer who seems to have become identified with Gay '90s/Roaring '20s "flapper" roles.

PROVOST, JON—juvenile actor
b: 1949, Pomona, Calif.

Lassie (adv) .... Timmy (1957–64)

Lassie's second TV master, little Jon Provost appeared in small roles in a number of movies before his seven-year run as "Timmy" on the famous series. Afterward, he had a guest shot on *Mr. Ed,* played a bit part in a 1966 Natalie Wood–Robert Redford movie called *This Property Is Condemned,* and then virtually disappeared from show business. In later years he sold real estate.

PROWSE, JULIET—actress, dancer
b: Sep 25, 1936, Bombay, India r: South Africa

Mona McCluskey (com)
.... Mona McCluskey (1965–66)

A stage and screen dancer infrequently seen on television. She starred in her own situation comedy, playing a nutty Hollywood starlet, in 1965–66. George Burns produced the series.

PRUD'HOMME, CAMERON—actor
b: 1892, Auburn, Calif. d: Nov 27, 1967

Young Mr. Bobbin (com)
.... Mr. Deacon (1951–52)

PRYOR, AINSLIE—actor
b: c. 1921 d: May 27, 1958

Adventures of Hiram Holiday (com)
.... Joel Smith (1956–57)

PRYOR, JOE, GROUP—singers

The Gisele MacKenzie Show (var)
.... regulars (1957–58)

PRYOR, NICHOLAS—actor
r: Baltimore, Md.

East of Eden (drama) ...... Mr. Grew (1981)

PRYOR, RICHARD—black comedian
b: Dec 1, 1940, Peoria, Ill.

The Richard Pryor Show (var)
.... host (1977)

Emmy Award: Best Writing for a Comedy Special, for *Lily* (1974)

Richard Pryor, the bad boy of black comedy in the '70s and '80s, has had his run-ins with managers, audiences, and the law—so why not with television? NBC should have known better than to think he would fit in on "the family medium."

Pryor was born to a poor family in Peoria, in seedy surroundings of poolhalls and whorehouses. He dropped out of junior high school, served an enlistment in the army, and in 1960 began trying to make a living as a stand-up comedian and writer. Although he eventually landed performing spots on *The Ed Sullivan Show* and *The Tonight Show,* as well as bit parts in films, his material was pretty tame and he didn't make much of an impression until the early '70s, when he took on a much harsher, ghetto edge. The most famous of his routines was his wino versus junkie bit, but he also lampooned hustlers, card sharks, and pimps, as well as ghetto dialect. He soon built a reputation for vivid and funny characterizations of street people—and also for total unpredictability and even offensiveness. His first hit album, in 1972, was titled *That Nigger's Crazy*. "Pryor horror stories" are legion in the business—the *Mike Douglas Show* on which he insulted an outraged Milton Berle; the *Donahue* show on which he insulted Phil and the audience, and closed the program by suggesting the host have sex with himself; the 1977 Hollywood Bowl benefit at which, irritated by his increasingly hostile reception, he dropped his trousers, taunted "kiss my happy, rich black ass," and walked off the stage.

Despite, or because of, his reputation, Pryor was much in demand on television during the 1970s, both as a writer and comedian. He contributed scripts for *Sanford and Son* and *The Flip Wilson Show* (on which he also appeared) and won an Emmy for his writing for a Lily Tomlin special in 1974. He was a smash hit as a guest on *NBC's Saturday Night Live*, where his raunchy humor fit right in. NBC managed to sign him for a series in 1977, supposedly to run at 9 P.M., where he could use his "adult" material. However, at the last minute the show was inexplicably moved to 8 P.M.—kiddie time—opposite the powerhouse *Happy Days*. An incensed Pryor opened his first show with a shot of himself stating that he had lost nothing in his battles with the network censors, whereupon the camera panned down to reveal him both nude and emasculated (he was actually wearing a body stocking). The censors had cardiac arrest and clipped the segment before telecast, resulting in a battle royal between Pryor and the network. Eventually, only five episodes of the series were telecast.

Since that time Pryor has had little to do with TV, aside from occasional guest appearances; he has gained much greater fame in movies. An incident in 1980 in which he nearly burned himself to death free-basing cocaine seems to have chastened him somewhat. In 1984 he agreed to host a remarkably gentle Saturday morning children's program called *Pryor's Place*, built around educational themes.

PULLIAM, KESHIA KNIGHT—juvenile actress
b: Apr 9, 1979, Newark, N.J.

The Cosby Show (com)
.... Rudy Huxtable (1984–)

PURCELL, SARAH—hostess
b: Oct 8, 1948, Richmond, Ind. r: San Diego, Calif.

Real People (aud par) .... regular (1979–84)

Sarah Purcell, the poised but fun-loving hostess with girl-next-door good looks, started out as a weather girl and movie host on local television in San Diego in the early '70s. In 1975 she moved up to cohost the local TV talk show *A.M. Los Angeles*, where she remained until 1979 and the debut of *Real People*. She has also appeared as an actress in a few films and TV series, including *Wonder Woman* and *Charlie's Angels*.

PURCILL, KAREN—actress
A Man Called Sloane (drama)
.... Kelly (1979–80)

PURL, LINDA—actress
b: Sep 2, 1955, Greenwich, Conn. r: Japan

Happy Days (com) .... Gloria (1974–75)
Beacon Hill (drama)... Betsy Bullock (1975)
Happy Days (com)
.... Ashley Pfister (1982–83)
Matlock (drama)
.... Charlene Matlock (1986–)

PUSTIL, JEFF—actor
Check It Out (com)
.... Jack Christian (1985–)

PUTNAM, GEORGE F.—host, announcer
Television Screen magazine (mag)
.... emcee/"editor" (1948)
Broadway to Hollywood—Headline Clues (quiz)....................... host (1949–51)

PYLE, DENVER—actor
b: May 11, 1920, Bethune, Colo.

The Life and Legend of Wyatt Earp (wes)
.... Ben Thompson (1955–56)
Code 3 (police)....... Sgt. Murchison (1957)
Tammy (com).. Grandpa Tarleton (1965–66)

The Doris Day Show (com)
.... Buck Webb (1968–70)
Karen (com)
.... Dale Busch (first telecast) (1975)
The Life & Times of Grizzly Adams (adv)
.... Mad Jack (1977–78)
The Dukes of Hazzard (com)
.... Uncle Jesse Duke (1979–85)

A lanky, bearded character actor, often in western or other down-home roles. He was a frequent supporting actor on *The Roy Rogers Show, The Gene Autry Show,* and *You Are There* in the 1950s, though he is best known to younger viewers as Uncle Jesse Duke on *The Dukes of Hazzard.*

Q

QUADE, JOHN—actor

Flatbush (com).......... Clean Otto (1979)

QUAID, RANDY—actor
b: Oct 1, 1950*, Houston, Texas

NBC's Saturday Night Live (var)
.... regular (1985–86)

The "graying" of television in the 1980s even seemed to hit that bastion of youth, *Saturday Night Live.* Randy Quaid was in his midthirties and a veteran of 15 years in films and TV when he joined the cast in 1985; a year before that, the cast included 37-year-old Billy Crystal, who had rejuvenated his career—and the show itself. All of which proves that you don't have to be under 25 to be hip these days. Randy was previously known more for dramatic than comic roles, attracting attention in his very first film *The Last Picture Show* (1971) and winning an Academy Award nomination for *The Last Detail* and an Emmy nomination for the 1984 television production of *A Streetcar Named Desire.* A lanky 6'5", he specialized in simple, often pathetic characters. But, as he gamely said upon joining *SNL,* "I consider myself a comedian at heart."

QUAN, KE HUY—juvenile actor
b: Aug 20, 1971, Saigon, Vietnam

Together We Stand (com)
.... Sam (1986–)

Quan is a Vietnamese youth who immigrated to the U.S. with his family in 1977, after the Communist takeover of South Vietnam. He made his acting debut in the hit film *Indiana Jones and the Temple of Doom* (1984), as the hero's young sidekick, Short Round.

QUARRY, ROBERT—actor
b: 1923

Hollywood Screen Test (talent)
.... assistant (1949)

*Some sources give 1948 or 1953.

QUAYLE, ANTHONY—actor
b: Sep 7, 1913, Ainsdale, Lancashire, England

The Six Wives of Henry VIII (drama)
.... narrator (1971)
Strange Report (drama)
.... Adam Strange (1971)
Moses—The Lawgiver (drama)
.... Aaron (1975)
Masada (drama) ..... Rubrius Gallus (1981)

Emmy Award: Best Supporting Actor in a Drama Special, for *QB VII* (1975)

The distinguished and authoritative British actor, at first a star onstage and later (from the late '50s) an important supporting actor in films. His television appearances have been primarily in TV movies and miniseries, although he did star briefly in the British-produced, high-tech crime series *Strange Report.*

QUENTIN, JOHN—actor

The Search for the Nile (drama)
.... John Hanning Speke (1972)

QUILLAN, EDDIE—actor
b: Mar 31, 1907, Philadelphia, Pa.

Valentine's Day (com)
.... Grover Cleveland Fipple (1964–65)
Julia (com).......... Eddie Edson (1968–71)
Hell Town (drama)....... Poco Loco (1985)

QUILLEY, DENIS—actor
b: Dec 26, 1927, London, England

Masada (drama) .... Quadratus (1981)

QUINE, DON—actor
b: c. 1939, Fenville, Mich.

Peyton Place (drama)... Joe Chernak (1965)
The Virginian (wes)
.... Stacy Grainger (1966–68)

QUINLAN, ROBERTA—singer
b: c. 1923, St. Louis, Md.

Song and Dance (music) ... emcee (1948–49)
Mohawk Showroom (music)
.... hostess (1949–51)

QUINLAN, SIOBHAN—actress
b: c. 1948

Doctor in the House (com) . Nurse (1970–73)

QUINLIVAN, CHARLES—actor

b: 1924 d: Nov 12, 1974

Mr. Garlund (adv)
.... Frank Garlund (1960–61)

QUINN, ANTHONY—actor

b: Apr 21, 1915, Chihuahua, Mexico r: Los Angeles

The Man and the City (drama)
.... Mayor Thomas Jefferson Alcala
(1971–72)

This powerful, flamboyant actor, born of Irish and Mexican stock, broke into films in the mid-1930s playing Indians, Mexicans, and other ethnics. Stardom did not come until 20 years later, when he won two Academy Awards during the 1950s, for *Viva Zapata* and *Lust for Life.* Quinn brought his forceful, slightly mystic style to television in the early '50s, appearing in live dramas on *Schlitz Playhouse, Ford Theatre,* and *Lights Out,* among others. After 1955 he disappeared from the small screen for 16 years—until lured back for a TV movie called *The City* in 1971. This led to a short-lived series, *The Man and the City,* in which he played the earthy, caring mayor of a Southwestern metropolis. He has rarely been seen on TV since then, although he did narrate the syndicated *Ten Who Dared* documentary in 1977 and also appeared in the 1977 TV movie *Jesus of Nazareth.* He is, perhaps, a bit overpowering for such a close-up medium as television.
  Autobiography: *The Original Sin* (1972).

QUINN, BILL—actor

b: May 6, 1912, New York City, N.Y.

The Rifleman (wes)
.... Sweeney, the bartender (1958–63)
Please Don't Eat the Daisies (com)
.... Dean Gerald Carter (1966–67)
All in the Family (com)
.... Mr. Van Ranseleer (1978–83)

QUINN, CARMEL—singer

b: 1931, Dublin, Ireland

Arthur Godfrey and His Friends (var)
.... singer (1954–57)

QUINN, LOUIS—actor

b: Mar 1915, Chicago, Ill.

77 Sunset Strip (drama)... Roscoe (1958–63)

QUINN, SPENCER—

The Summer Smothers Show (var)
.... regular (1970)
The Jerry Reed When You're Hot You're Hot Hour (var).................. regular (1972)

QUINN, TEDDY—juvenile actor

b: 1959 r: Los Angeles, Calif.

Karen (com) .... Peter (1964–65)
Accidental Family (com)
.... Sandy Webster (1967–68)

QUINN, THOMAS—actor

Baker's Dozen (com)
.... Desk Sgt. Martin (1982)

QUINONES, ADOLFO—dancer

The Big Show (var)......... dancer (1980)

R

RABY, JOHN—actor

A Woman to Remember (drama)
.... Steve Hammond (1949)

RACE, CLARK—host

The Parent Game (quiz) ..... host (1972–74)

RACHINS, ALAN—actor
b: Oct 10, Cambridge, Mass.

L.A. Law (drama)
.... Douglas Brackman, Jr. (1986–   )

RACIMO, VICTORIA—actress
b: Dec 26, New York City, N.Y.

The Chisholms (wes)
.... Kewedinok (1979–80)
Falcon Crest (drama)
.... Corene Powers (1983–84)

An actress of Filipino, English, Irish, Spanish, and American Indian descent, active since the late '60s.

RADNER, GILDA—comedienne
b: Jun 28, 1946, Detroit, Mich.

NBC's Saturday Night Live (com)
.... regular (1975–80)

Emmy Award: Best Supporting Actress in a Variety Series, for *NBC's Saturday Night Live* (1978)

Gilda Radner is a bawdy, physical comedienne who might be considered the 1970s version of Imogene Coca. An alumnus of Chicago's Second City comedy troup, and of several National Lampoon productions during the early '70s, she was chosen in 1975 to become one of the original Not Ready for Prime Time Players on *Saturday Night Live.* There she created some memorable characters: the lisping Barbara Walters (Ba Ba Wawa), the confused Emily Litella making editorial replies on "Weekend Update," and rambling, loudmouthed newscaster Rosanne Rosanna-Dana. Gilda later appeared in several comedy films and starred in the Broadway show *Gilda Live!*

RAE, CHARLOTTE—actress
b: Apr 22, 1926, Milwaukee, Wis.

Car 54, Where Are You? (com)
.... Sylvia Schnauser (1961–63)
Hot L Baltimore (com).. Mrs. Bellotti (1975)
The Rich Little Show (var)... regular (1976)
Diff'rent Strokes (com)
.... Mrs. Edna Garrett (1978–79)
The Facts of Life (com)
.... Edna Garrett (1979–86)

Rubber-faced comedienne Charlotte Rae has been playing delightfully zany roles on television since the 1950s, although she has shown on occasion that she is capable of a much wider range as an actress. She came to New York around 1950, shortly after graduation from Northwestern University, and got her first break singing and doing satire at the Village Vanguard and Blue Angel nightclubs. Shortly thereafter, she began to land comic supporting roles on Broadway, including that of Mammy Yokum in the 1956 musical *Li'l Abner.* Later, during the '60s, she received two Tony Award nominations for her stage work.

Charlotte's television appearances during the '50s were mostly in comedic playhouse productions, such as "30, Honey, 30" on *Ponds Theatre* and "Harvey" on *The DuPont Show of the Month.* In 1961 she took on her first series role, the recurring part of Officer Schnauser's wife on *Car 54, Where Are You?* Among her other TV credits were a stint on the daytime soap opera *From These Roots,* the role of Molly the Mailman on *Sesame Street,* and an Emmy-nominated dramatic performance in the 1975 TV movie *Queen of the Stardust Ballroom.* She remains best known for comedy, however, particularly as the flaky but vulnerable Mrs. Garrett on both *Diff'rent Strokes* and *The Facts of Life.*

RAFFERTY, BILL—host, comedian
b: Jun 17, 1944, Queens, N.Y.

Laugh-In (revival) (var)... regular (1977–78)
Real People (aud par) .... regular (1979–84)

A stand-up comic and amiable roving reporter on *Real People.*

RAFFERTY, FRANCES—actress
b: Jun 26, 1922, Sioux City, Iowa

December Bride (com)
.... Ruth Henshaw (1954–59)
Pete and Gladys (com) ... Nancy (1961–62)

Spring Byington's TV daughter on *December Bride*. She played supporting roles in many films of the '40s and TV dramas of the '50s and early '60s, but was mostly inactive after that.

RAFFIN, DEBORAH—actress
b: Mar 13, 1953, Los Angeles, Calif.

The Last Convertible (drama)
.... Chris Farris (1979)
Foul Play (drama)... Gloria Munday (1981)

RAFT, GEORGE—actor
b: Sep 26, 1895*, New York City, N.Y. d: Nov 25, 1980

I'm the Law (police)
.... Lt. George Kirby (1952–53)

A famous—and authentic—movie tough guy, who by his own account once had real-life ties to top racketeers. A slick and menacing character, he enjoyed considerable popularity in gangster movies of the '30s and '40s, but his career was on the decline in the '50s, when he starred in the rather violent crime show *I'm The Law*. Television did not rescue him, as it did some other movie has-beens; the series was unsuccessful and lost him a great deal of money. He did little other TV work.

Raft fell upon hard times in his later years, pursued by the IRS for back taxes, suffering the expropriation of his Havana gambling casino by Fidel Castro, and barred from working in England due to his gangland associations. However, friends took care of him. He could be glimpsed in the '70s as the convict who starts a riot in a prison mess-hall in an oft-seen Alka Seltzer commercial. Raft's colorful life was chronicled in the 1961 film *The George Raft Story*, as well as in the books *The George Raft File: An Unauthorized Biography*, by J.R. Parish and Steven Whitney (1973), and *George Raft* by Lewis Jablonsky (1974).

RAGGIO, LISA—actress
b: May 12, New York City, N.Y.

Private Benjamin (com)
.... Pvt. Maria Gianelli (1981–83)

*Some sources give 1903.

694

RAGIN, JOHN S.—actor
b: May 5, 1929, Newark, N.J. r: Irvington, N.J.

Sons and Daughters (drama)
.... Walter Cramer (1974)
Quincy, M.E. (police)
.... Dr. Robert Astin (1976–83)

RAGLAND, LARRY—black comedian
b: Feb 21, 1948, Richmond, Va.

Keep On Truckin' (var)
.... regular (1975)

RAILSBACK, STEVE—actor
b: Dallas, Texas

From Here to Eternity (drama)
.... Pvt. Robert E. Lee Prewitt (1979)

RAINES, CRISTINA—actress
b: Feb 28, 1952, Manila, Philippines r: Florida

Centennial (drama)...... Lucinda (1978–79)
Flamingo Road (drama)
.... Lane Ballou (1981–82)

RAINES, ELLA—actress
b: Aug 6, 1921, Snoqualmie Falls, Wash.

Janet Dean, Registered Nurse (drama)
.... Janet Dean (1953–55)

RAINES, STEVE—actor

Rawhide (wes)....... Jim Quince (1959–66)

RAINEY, DR. FROELICH—museum director
b: Jun 18, 1907, Black Riverfalls, Wis.

What in the World (quiz)
.... moderator (1953)

The director of the University of Pennsylvania Museum; the series was a quiz based on the museum's exhibits.

RAINEY, FORD—actor
b: 1908, Mountain Home, Idaho

Window on Main Street (com)
.... Lloyd Ramsey (1961–62)
The Richard Boone Show (drama)
.... regular (1963–64)
Search (adv)............. Dr. Barnett (1972)
The Manhunter (drama)
.... James Barrett (1974–75)
The Bionic Woman (adv) .. Jim Elgin (1976)

RAINWATER, MARVIN—country singer
b: Jul 2, 1925, Wichita, Kan.

Ozark Jubilee (music)....... regular (1957)

An American Indian who got his big break on *Arthur Godfrey's Talent Scouts* in 1957 and a few months later scored his first and only hit record with his own composition, "Gonna Find Me a Bluebird." He appeared on stage in Indian dress, a practice he later abandoned due to complaints from his fellow Native Americans.

RAISCH, BILL—actor
b: Apr 5, 1905 d: Jul 31, 1984

The Fugitive (drama)
.... Fred Johnson (1963–67)

The mysterious one-armed man who had actually committed the murder for which David Janssen was convicted on *The Fugitive,* and whom Janssen pursued relentlessly to prove his innocence. The actor did, in real life, have only one arm.

RAITT, JOHN—actor, singer
b: Jan 29, 1917*, Santa Ana, Calif.

The Buick Circus Hour (drama)
.... Bill Sothern (1952–53)
The Chevy Show (music)
.... host (1958–59)

A musical comedy stage star who appeared occasionally on television, mostly in the 1950s. His daughter Bonnie Raitt became a popular rock singer in the 1970s.

RALPH, SHERYL LEE—black actress
b: Waterbury, Conn. r: Jamaica

Codename: Foxfire (drama)
.... Maggie Bryan (1985)
It's A Living (com) .... Ginger (1986–)

RALSTON, BOB—pianist, organist

The Lawrence Welk Show (music)
.... regular (1963–82)

RAMBO, DACK—actor
b: Nov 13, 1941, Delano, Calif.

The New Loretta Young Show (drama)
.... Dack Massey (1962–63)
*Some sources give Jan 19.

The Guns of Will Sonnett (wes)
.... Jeff Sonnett (1967–69)
Dirty Sally (wes)....... Cyrus Pike (1974)
Sword of Justice (adv) .. Jack Cole (1978–79)
Paper Dolls (drama) . Wesley Harper (1984)
Dallas (drama)....... Jack Ewing (1985–)

A darkly handsome actor who entered television right out of school, before he had any professional training, on *The New Loretta Young Show*. Dack and his twin brother Dirk played Miss Young's twin sons. Later, the brothers went their separate ways, with Dack building a solid if unexceptional career in soap operas *(Never Too Young, All My Children)*, dramas, and adventure series.

RAMBO, DIRK—actor
b: Nov 13, 1941, Delano, Calif. d: Feb 5, 1967

The New Loretta Young Show (drama)
.... Dirk Massey (1962–63)

Twin brother of Dack; he was killed in a traffic accident in 1967.

RAMIREZ, CONNIE—actress

Berrengers (drama).. Connie Morales (1985)

RAMIREZ, FRANK—actor

Paris (police) .... Ernie Villas (1979–80)

RAMIS, HAROLD—actor

Second City TV (com)
.... Moe Green (1977–78)

RAMOS, RUDY—actor
b: Sep 19, 1950, Lawton, Okla.

The High Chaparral (wes)
.... Wind (1970–71)

RAMSEN, BOBBY—actor

The Mary Tyler Moore Hour (var)
.... Mort Zimmick (1979)

RAMSEY, LOGAN—actor
b: Mar 21, 1921, Long Beach, Calif.

On the Rocks (com) .. the warden (1975–76)
The Winds of War (drama)
.... Congressman LaCouture (1983)

695

RAMSEY, MARION—

Keep On Truckin' (var) . . . . . . regular (1975)
Cos (var) . . . . regular (1976)

RAMUS, NICK—actor
b: Sep 9, Seattle, Wash.

The Chisholms (wes) . . . . . Tehohane (1980)
Falcon Crest (drama)
. . . . Gus Nunouz (1981–82)

An actor of part Blackfoot Indian descent, who often played Indian or mixed-breed roles.

RANDALL, ANN—actress

Hee Haw (var) . . . . regular (1972–73)

RANDALL, BOB—actor

On Our Own (com). J. M. Bedford (1977–78)

RANDALL, CHARLOTTE "REBEL"—actress

Auction-Aire (aud par). . assistant (1949–50)

RANDALL, FRANKIE—singer
b: c. 1937, Clifton, N.J.

The Dean Martin Summer Show (var)
. . . . regular (1966)

RANDALL, STUART—actor

Cimarron City (wes)
. . . . Art Sampson (1958–59)
Laramie (wes) . . . . Mort Corey (1960–63)

RANDALL, SUE—actress
b: c. 1935, Philadelphia, Pa. d: Oct 26, 1984

Leave It to Beaver (com)
. . . . Miss Landers (1958–62)

RANDALL, TONY—actor
b: Feb 26, 1920, Tulsa, Okla.

One Man's Family (drama). . Mac (1950–52)
Mr. Peepers (com)
. . . . Harvey Weskit (1952–55)
The Odd Couple (com)
. . . . Felix Unger (1970–75)
The Tony Randall Show (com)
. . . . Judge Walter Franklin (1976–78)
Love, Sidney (com). Sidney Shorr (1981–83)

Emmy Award: Best Actor in a Comedy Series, for *The Odd Couple* (1975)

Some actors peak early; Tony Randall seemed to get better with age, scoring his most memorable role at 50 in *The Odd Couple,* and another that will not soon be forgotten at 61 in *Love, Sidney.*

The son of an art dealer, Tony came to New York in the 1940s and worked steadily in small roles in important plays such as *The Corn Is Green, Antony and Cleopatra,* and *Inherit the Wind.* He broke into television around 1950 and served his video apprenticeship in such live New York–based series as *One Man's Family* and *Captain Video* (where he met another young unknown, Jack Klugman). His first really important role was that of Wally Cox's best friend, the self-confident history teacher, in *Mr. Peepers.* Tony also appeared rather often in playhouse productions on *Philco Playhouse, Kraft Theatre, Studio One,* etc., until the early '60s, when he began to concentrate on a blossoming film career.

The chance to star in *The Odd Couple* as feisty, fastidious Felix Unger (opposite Klugman's sloppy Oscar Madison) brought Tony back to TV in 1970, and he seldom left after that. In addition to his TV movie and series roles, he became a frequent and witty guest on talk shows, where he left no doubt about his strong opinions on all things. His great love of opera led him to serve as a host of PBS's *Live from the Met* telecasts, as well as a commentator on opera performances.

RANDELL, RON—actor
b: Oct 8, 1918*, Sydney, Australia

The Vise (drama) . . . . host (1954–55)
O.S.S. (drama)
. . . . Capt. Frank Hawthorn (1957–58)

RANDOLPH, AMANDA—black actress
b: 1902, Louisville, Ky. d: Aug 24, 1967

The Laytons (com) . . . . regular (1948)
Amos 'n' Andy (com)
. . . . . Sapphire's mama (Ramona Smith) (1951–53)
The Danny Thomas Show (com)
. . . . Louise (1953–64)

This actress played minor roles from the 1920s onward on stage, radio, and in films

*Some sources give 1920 or 1923.

696

—usually portraying servants—before she got her chance to achieve video immortality during the 1950s. On *Amos 'n' Andy* she gave new meaning to the word "battle-ax" as the Kingfish's fearsome mother-in-law, with her domineering manner and huge hats; on *The Danny Thomas Show* she was a bit less overpowering as Danny's longtime, loyal housekeeper.

One other role of Amanda's deserves notice, even though relatively little is known about the show. *The Laytons,* a domestic comedy seen briefly in the fall of 1948, was by dint of her presence in the cast the first network series to star a black actor in a continuing role.

Amanda was the sister of actress Lillian Randolph.

RANDOLPH, BILL—actor
b: Oct 11, Detroit, Mich.

Trauma Center (drama)
.... Dr. "Beaver" Bouvier (1983)
Comedy Zone (com) .... regular (1984)

RANDOLPH, CHASE—

Hee Haw (var).......... regular (1981–82)

RANDOLPH, ISABEL—actress
b: 1890 d: Jan 11, 1973

Meet Millie (com).... Mrs. Boone (1953–55)
Our Miss Brooks (com)
...................Mrs. Nestor (1955–56)

RANDOLPH, JOHN—actor
b: 1917

Lucas Tanner (drama)
.... John Hamilton (1975)
Lucan (adv)........ Dr. Hoagland (1977–78)
Angie (com)...... Randall Benson (1979–80)

RANDOLPH, JOYCE—actress
b: Oct 21, 1925, Detroit, Mich.

The Jackie Gleason Show (var)
.... regular (1952–55)
The Honeymooners (series) (com)
.... Trixie Norton (1955–56)
The Jackie Gleason Show (var)
.... regular (1956–57)

The original Trixie Norton—Art Carney's TV wife—in "The Honeymooners" sketches on *The Jackie Gleason Show.*

Joyce had been active on television since its experimental days in the mid-1940s, appearing in both dramatic and variety shows. Following her five years with Gleason, she virtually retired from acting, and thereafter was seen primarily in commercials. She was married in later years to a New York advertising executive.

RANDOLPH, LILLIAN—black actress
b: c. 1915 d: Sep 12, 1980

Amos 'n' Andy (com)
.... Madame Queen (1951–53)
The Great Gildersleeve (com)
.... Birdie Lee Coggins (1955–56)
The Bill Cosby Show (com)
.... Rose Kincaid (1969–70)
Roots (drama).......... Sister Sara (1977)

The sister of actress Amanda Randolph. Lillian had a busy career in films and radio during the 1940s, playing, among other things, Birdie the maid on *The Great Gildersleeve* and Beulah on *Beulah.* On TV's *Amos 'n' Andy* she played the occasional role of Andy's girlfriend, and on *The Bill Cosby Show* that of Cosby's mother. She remained active in TV and films until the time of her death.

RANDOM, BOB—actor

The Iron Horse (wes)
.... Barnabas Rogers (1966–68)

RANEY, WALT—host

What's the Story? (quiz) . moderator (1951)

RANKIN, GIL—actor

Tombstone Territory (wes)
.... Dep. Riggs (1957)

RANNOW, JERRY—comedian, writer

The Jonathan Winters Show (var)
.... regular (1968–69)

RAPPAPORT, DAVID—actor
b: Nov 23, London, England

The Wizard (adv) . Simon McKay (1986–)

Diminutive (3'11") English actor, known to U.S. audiences for his role in the movie *Time Bandits.*

RASCHE, DAVID—actor
b: Aug 7, Illinois

Sledge Hammer! (com)
.... Det. Sledge Hammer (1986–)

Pronounced "Rah-she."

RASEY, JEAN—actress

The Nancy Drew Mysteries (adv)
.... George Fayne (1977)

RASH, BRYSON—newscaster
b: c. 1914, Los Angeles, Calif.

All Star News (news)
.... correspondent (1952–53)

A onetime child actor on radio who became a radio newsman in the '30s and later moved to television, where he was seen on both ABC and NBC.

RASHAD, PHYLICIA—

see Ayers-Allen, Phylicia

RASKIN, DAMON—juvenile actor
b: c. 1968, Beverly Hills, Calif.

The Montefuscos (com)
.... Anthony Patrick Cooney (1975)
The Practice (com)
.... Tony Bedford (1976–77)

RASSULO, JOE—actor

Miss Winslow and Son (com)
.... Angelo Vallone (1979)

RASTATTER, WENDY—actress

David Cassidy—Man Undercover (police)
.... Joanne Shay (1978–79)

RASULALA, THALMUS—black actor
b: Nov 15, 1939, Miami, Fla.

What's Happening!! (com)
.... Bill Thomas (1976–77)
Roots (drama).............. Omoro (1977)

RATHBONE, BASIL—actor
b: Jun 13, 1892, Johannesburg, South Africa r: England d: Jul 21, 1967

Your Lucky Clue (quiz) .... emcee (1952)

A lean, debonair film star of the '30s and '40s, most famous as the swashbuckling foe in costume dramas and later as Sherlock Holmes, whom he played in a total of 14 films. Rathbone was seen rather often on television in the 1950s, on *Kraft Theatre, Suspense, The Hallmark Hall of Fame,* etc., but he appeared as a regular in a series only once—as, of all things, a quiz-show host! The series, a summer replacement, was at least appropriate to his image. *Your Lucky Clue* pitted two detectives against two amateur criminologists trying to solve a mystery that they had just seen dramatized. The solutions were, well, elementary, my dear Watson.

Rathbone's autobiography: *In and Out of Character* (1962).

RATHER, DAN—newscaster
b: Oct 31, 1931, Wharton, Texas

CBS Weekend News (Sun) (news)
.... anchorman (1970–75)
CBS Weekend News (Sat) (news)
.... anchorman (1973–76)
60 Minutes (pub aff)
.... correspondent (1975–81)
Who's Who? (pub aff) ...... reporter (1977)
CBS Evening News (news)
.... anchorman (1981–)
Campaign '84 (news) .... anchorman (1984)

Emmy Awards: Best News Segments, for the *CBS Evening News* reports "The Watergate Affair" (1973), "The Shooting of Governor Wallace" (1973), "The Agnew Resignation" (1974), "Afghanistan" (1985), "Mexican Earthquake" (1986); for the news specials *Watergate, The White House Transcripts* (1974), and *The Senate and the Watergate Affair* (1974); for the *60 Minutes* report "Onward Christian Voters" (1980)

Possibly the most ballyhooed ascension since the naming of the last Pope was the announcement that Dan Rather would succeed Walter Cronkite—"the Most Trusted Man in America"—as the anchor of the top-rated *CBS Evening News.* Cronkite had held the post for 19 years, and replacing him was an event worthy of the cover of *Time* magazine (which it got).

The anchor position represented the culmination of a 19-year career at CBS for the feisty, dapper Rather, who, ironically, had joined the network the year Cronkite became anchor. The son of a Texas ditchdigger and his waitress wife, Dan began his professional career as a reporter for the A.P. and U.P.I. wire services and for the *Houston Chronicle,* then moved into local radio and TV in 1956. His dramatic coverage of Hurricane Carla in 1961—literally in the teeth of the gale—caught the attention of CBS, which hired him as chief of its southwestern bureau in 1962. That in turn led to his next major coup, his marathon coverage of the assassination of President John F. Kennedy in Dallas in 1963. CBS shunted Dan between domestic and overseas bureaus during the following years, and his reputation for aggressiveness and sometime combativeness grew. In 1968 he took a nationally televised punch to the midsection from a security guard on the floor of the Democratic National Convention in Chicago. A few years later he was in the thick of the Watergate uproar, pursuing a beleaguered President Nixon as the coverup unraveled. At one memorable press conference in 1974, the president responded to one of Rather's aggressive questions by asking, "Are you running for something?" "No, sir, Mr. President," Dan shot back, "Are you?" In the eyes of many, Dan had come to epitomize the cocky, Eastern liberal press. He himself felt that he was becoming, in his own words, "the most hated White House correspondent."

By the mid-1970s the national turmoil had begun to subside, but Dan's career continued to grow apace, as anchor of CBS's weekend newscasts and then as one of the principal anchors of the top-rated *60 Minutes.* It was for the latter program that he pulled off one of his most daring, and some say melodramatic, coups. In April 1980 he slipped into war-torn Afghanistan in peasant's garb to report on the Soviet invasion from behind the lines. He had at the time already signed a much-publicized $8 million, five-year contract naming him as Cronkite's successor, a position he assumed the following March.

Dan's autobiography: *The Camera Never Blinks: Adventures of a TV Journalist* (with Mickey Herskowitz, 1977).

RATRAY, PETER—actor
b: Kingston, Canada r: Bay Village, Ohio

The New People (drama)
.... George Potter (1969–70)

RATZENBERGER, JOHN—actor
b: Apr 6, 1947, Bridgeport, Conn.

Cheers (com)........ Cliff Clavin (1982–)

RAWLINSON, BRIAN—actor

The Buccaneers (adv)
.... crewman Gaff (1956–57)

RAWLS, LOU—black singer
b: Dec 1, 1936, Chicago, Ill.

Dean Martin Presents the Golddiggers (var)
.... regular (1969)

RAY, GENE ANTHONY—black actor, dancer
b: May 24, 1963, Harlem, N.Y.

Fame (drama)..... Leroy Johnson (1982–)

RAY, MARGUERITE—black actress
b: New Orleans, La. r: Oakland, Calif.

Sanford (com)
.... Evelyn "Eve" Lewis (1980–81)

RAYBURN, GENE—host, announcer
b: Dec 22, 1917, Christopher, Ill. r: Chicago, Ill.

The Name's the Same (quiz)
.... panelist (1953–55)
Tonight (talk) .... announcer (1954–57)
Make the Connection (quiz)
.... moderator (1955)
The Steve Allen Show (var)
.... regular (1956–59)
The Steve Lawrence-Eydie Gorme Show (var)
.... announcer (1958)
Match Game P.M. (quiz)..... host (1975–82)

Gene Rayburn, the tall, angular, slightly menacing-looking game show host is most famous for his many years on *Match Game.* His original goal, however, was to become an actor. He arrived in New York in the mid-1930s, after dropping out of college, and got his first job in broadcasting as a page at NBC. He later became a successful announcer and gained local fame, at least, as half of the popular Rayburn and Finch comedy team on New York radio in the late '40s and early '50s. He then entered television, becoming a member of Steve Allen's repertory company of comics on Allen's *Tonight Show* and on his prime time variety series.

Gene finally began to get acting roles in the 1950s on such series as *Robert Montgomery Presents* and *Kraft Theatre*, as well as in regional stage productions. However, it was neither acting nor comedy that made him a star, but game shows. After a succession of lesser efforts, he hit the jackpot with *The Match Game*, which ran in various daytime, nighttime, and syndicated versions from 1962 until the mid-1980s. Other shows he hosted included, in chronological order, *The Sky's the Limit, Make the Connection, Choose Up Sides, Tic Tac Dough, Dough Re Mi, Play Your Hunch, Snap Judgment,* and *Amateur's Guide to Love.*

RAYBURN, RANDY, SINGERS—

The Edie Adams Show (var)
.... regulars (1963–64)

RAYE, MARTHA—actress
b: Aug 27, 1916, Butte, Mont.

All Star Revue (var)
.... alternating host (1951–53)
The Martha Raye Show (var)
.... hostess (1955–56)
McMillan and Wife (police)
.... Agatha (1976–77)
Alice (com)...... Carrie Sharples (1982–84)

"Martha the Mouth" was one of the best known comic actresses in America from the mid-1930s to the mid-1950s. Her trademarks were a raucous laugh and a cavernous oral cavity; energetic, knockabout comedy was her style.

The yelling began at the age of three, when Martha first joined her parents' vaudeville act as they crisscrossed small-town America. Eventually, she struck out on her own, then crashed movies in the '30s as comic support to Bob Hope and others. By the time television came along, she was an established film and radio star, and she shone brightly on the new medium during the early and mid 1950s. She guest-starred on all the major variety shows, co-hosted the *All Star Revue* from 1951–53, starred in a series of top-rated specials from 1953–55, and finally got her own weekly comedy hour from 1955–56. Appearing with her in many of these was ex-boxer Rocky Graziano, as her muscular boyfriend.

After *The Martha Raye Show* left the air, Martha's career went into a long slide. She made only rare appearances during the '60s (e.g., on *Burke's Law* in 1965); in 1970–71 she appeared as Benita the Witch on *The Bugaloos*, a live-action Saturday morning kid's show about a quartet of insect musicians. Martha had spent much time entertaining the troops during World War II, in Korea and Vietnam, but her outspoken views on the Vietnam War caused her to be virtually blacklisted in Hollywood. She credits Rock Hudson with reviving her career by casting her as his wisecracking housekeeper during the final season of *McMillan*, replacing the departed Nancy Walker. After that, Martha was seen in series including *The Love Boat* and as a regular on *Alice*, as Vic Tayback's mother. "God, it's good to be working again," she *loudly* proclaimed.

RAYE, SUSAN—singer

Susan Raye (music) .... hostess (1950)

RAYE, TISCH—actress

W.E.B. (drama)........... Christine (1978)

RAYMOND, GARY—English actor
b: 1935, London, England

The Rat Patrol (adv)
.... Sgt. Jack Moffitt (1966–68)

RAYMOND, GENE—actor
b: Aug 13, 1908, New York City, N.Y.

Fireside Theatre (drama)
.... host (1953–55)
What's Going On? (quiz).... panelist (1954)
Hollywood Summer Theatre (drama)
.... host (1956)
TV Reader's Digest (drama)..... host (1956)
Paris 7000 (adv)..... Robert Stevens (1970)

A handsome, breezy character actor, in films from the '30s and quite busy on television from the '50s to the early '70s—although he did not make a major impact in either medium. He is best remembered as the husband of movie star Jeanette MacDonald in one of Hollywood's storybook marriages, which lasted nearly 30 years, until her death in 1965.

RAYMOND, GUY—actor

Ichabod and Me (com)
.... Martin Perkins (1961–62)

RAZ, KAVI—actor
b: Aug 13, Dhugga, India

St. Elsewhere (drama)
.... Dr. V. J. Kochar (1982–84)

REA, PEGGY—actress
b: Mar 31, Los Angeles, Calif.

The Red Skelton Show (var)
.... regular (1970–71)
The Waltons (drama)
.... Rose Burton (1979–81)
The Dukes of Hazzard (com)
.... Lulu Hogg (1979–85)

READ, JAMES—actor
b: Jul 31, c. 1952, Buffalo, N.Y. r: Schenectady, N.Y.

Remington Steele (drama)
.... Murphy Michaels (1982–83)
North and South (drama)
.... George Hazard (1985)

READE, FLIP—

Shields and Yarnell (var) .... regular (1978)

READING, DONNA—actress
b: c. 1949

Doctor in the House (com) . nurse (1970–73)

REAGAN, RONALD—actor, politician
b: Feb 6, 1911, Tampico, Ill.

The Orchid Award (var) ... emcee (1953–54)
General Electric Theater (drama)
.... host/star (1954–62)
Death Valley Days (wes) .... host (1965–66)

The fortieth president of the United States was most famous, prior to his entry into politics, for his film career, which began in 1937. During the 1950s he was frequently seen on TV playhouse series such as *Ford Theatre* and *Lux Video Theatre,* sometimes costarring with his wife Nancy Davis; he was also the regular host of three different series, including a short-lived variety show called *The Orchid Award.* During his long run on *General Electric Theater* he became familiar as the commercial spokesman for G.E. His final movie role was in what was supposed to be the very first made-for-television movie, *The Killers* (1964), in an uncharacteristic portrayal of a brutal mobster. The film was so violent that it was withheld from TV and released in theaters instead.

Reagan was married to actress Jane Wyman (of *Falcon Crest*) from 1940–48, and to Nancy Davis in 1952. His autobiography: *Where's the Rest of Me?* (1965).

REASON, REX—actor
b: Nov 20, 1928, Berlin, Germany

Man Without a Gun (wes)
.... Adam MacLean (1957–59)
The Roaring Twenties (drama)
.... Scott Norris (1960–62)

REASON, RHODES—actor
b: Nov 20, 1928, Berlin, Germany

White Hunter (adv) . John Hunter (1958–59)
Bus Stop (drama).. Will Mayberry (1961–62)

The twin brother of Rex Reason.

REASONER, HARRY—newscaster
b: Apr 17, 1923, Dakota City, Iowa

CBS Weekend News (news)
.... anchorman (1963–70)
60 Minutes (pub aff)
.... correspondent (1968–70)
ABC Evening News (news)
.... anchorman (1970–78)
The Reasoner Report (ABC Weekend News)
(news).............. anchorman (1973–75)
60 Minutes (pub aff)
.... correspondent (1978–   )

Emmy Awards: Best News Writing, for *CBS Reports,* "What About Ronald Reagan?" (1968); As Reporter for *CBS Reports,* "The Defense of the United States—Nuclear Battlefield" (1981); As Reporter for *60 Minutes,* "Welcome to Palermo" (1982); Television News Broadcaster of the Year (1974)

This amiable newscaster was once considered the likely heir to Walter Cronkite at CBS and was Cronkite's regular substitute anchor on *The CBS Evening News.* Harry did get his chance to become a national anchorman, but on another network; he proved in the long run to be better suited to the role of roving reporter on the top-rated *60 Minutes.*

Harry began his journalism career while in his teens, as a reporter for *The Minneapolis Times* in 1941. Following military service, he returned to become the paper's drama critic (1946), then moved into radio (1950), and then, after a stint with the U.S. Information Agency in Manila, into local television in Minneapolis (1954). In July 1956 the rising young reporter—who by then had 15 years of experience—was hired by CBS in New York. He became nationally prominent during the 1960s as anchor of the weekend news and as one of "Cronkite's boys," destined, it seemed, to inherit Uncle Walter's mantle. But Walter stayed on and on, and Harry grew increasingly restless, despite the unusual assignments CBS gave him. He was frequent anchor of *CBS Reports,* host of unique audience participation "tests" (*The National Driving Test,* etc.), and narrator of a series of whimsical essays on such subjects as bridges, doors, hotels, women, etc. (These essays were written by a then unknown CBS staffer named Andy Rooney).

In 1970, in a move that rocked the industry, Harry defected to ABC, the also-ran of TV news. He became its most prestigious anchorman, at first paired with Howard K. Smith (1970–75) and later as sole anchor (1975–76). ABC's ratings did not increase, however, and in 1976 the network boldly stole another big name—Barbara Walters —from NBC, and paired her with Harry. The aggressive lady reporter and easygoing "Harry Reasonable" did not get along at all. In 1978 he returned to CBS, which welcomed him with open arms and reinstalled him on *60 Minutes,* where he has held forth ever since.

REDD, VERONICA—actress

Making the Grade (com)
.... Janice Reeves (1982)

REDDICK, GERRI—actress

Blansky's Beauties (com)
.... Jackie Outlaw (1977)

REDDIN, ELIZABETH—actress

David Cassidy—Man Undercover (police)
.... Cindy Shay (1978–79)

REDDING, CHAD—actor

The Gangster Chronicles (drama)
.... Joy Osler (1981)

REDDING, EARL—

Your Show of Shows (var)
.... regular (1950–51)

REDDY, HELEN—singer

b: Oct 25, 1941, Melbourne, Australia

The Helen Reddy Show (var)
.... hostess (1973)

The Midnight Special (music)
.... hostess (1975–76)

Australian singer Helen Reddy was something of a symbol of the women's liberation movement in the '70s as a result of her best-selling record, "I Am Woman" ("I am strong . . . I am invincible!"). She hosted her own summer variety series in 1973 and in 1975 became the first (and only) permanent host of NBC's late-night rock concert, *The Midnight Special.*

Helen's most famous quote, perhaps, was made on the 1973 Grammy Awards telecast, as she accepted the award for Best Female Vocalist: "I want to thank everyone concerned . . . my husband and manager Jeff Wald, because he makes my success possible; and God—because She makes everything possible."

REDEKER, QUINN—actor

b: May 2, 1936, Woodstock, Ill. r: Seattle, Wash.

Dan Raven (police) . . . Perry Levitt (1960–61)

Quinn is well-known to daytime viewers for his long run in the 1980s as scheming Alex Marshall on *Days of Our Lives.*

REDFEARN, LINDA—actress

Born to the Wind (adv)
.... Prairie Woman (1982)

REDFIELD, DENNIS—actor

Friends (com) . . . . Mr. Charley Wilks (1979)

REDFIELD, WILLIAM—actor

b: Jan 26, 1927, New York City, N.Y. d: Aug 17, 1976

Jimmy Hughes, Rookie Cop (police)
.... Off. Jimmy Hughes (1953)
The Marriage (com) ... Bobby Logan (1954)

A youthful-looking former juvenile actor who played many supporting roles on stage, film and television. He was also a writer, co-authoring a book version of the *Mr. Peepers* series with Wally Cox and authoring a book about his own experiences, called *Letters from an Actor*.

REDGRAVE, LYNN—actress
b: Mar 8, 1943, London, England

Centennial (drama)
Charlotte Buckland Lloyd Seccombe (1978–79)
House Calls (com)
.... Ann Anderson (1979–81)
Teachers Only (com)
.... Diana Swanson (1982–83)

Ruddy-cheeked Lynn Redgrave shot to fame in the mid-1960s as an awkward English girl in the hit movie *Georgy Girl*. After several years concentrating on stage and movies, she began to turn up on television in the 1970s in TV films such as *Turn of the Screw* (1974) and on many talk shows, including *Not for Women Only*, which she hosted for a time. Many of her TV roles were quite distinctive; on *Centennial* she aged from 18 to 85; in the miniseries *Beggarman, Thief* she was Kate, the widow of protagonist Tom Jordache. Lynn was quite successful in her first regular series, *House Calls*, as the hospital administrator in love with Wayne Rogers. However, she was fired from the show after two years, in a contract dispute with the producers (either over money or the studio's refusal to let her breast-feed her newborn baby on the set, depending on whom you believe). Her next series, *Teachers Only*, was a failure.

Lynn is from a famous acting family. Her father, Sir Michael Redgrave, and mother, Rachel Kempson, were both actors, as are her brother Corin and her sister Vanessa.

REDMAN, DON—black orchestra leader
b: Jul 29, 1900, Piedmont, W. Va. d: Nov 30, 1964

Sugar Hill Times (var)
.... orch. leader (1949)

A highly respected jazz arranger and bandleader, active since the 1920s. *Sugar Hill Times* was one of television's earliest black variety shows.

REDMOND, MARGE—actress
b: Lakewood, Ohio

The Double Life of Henry Phyfe (com)
.... Mrs. Florence Kimball (1966)
The Flying Nun (com)
.... Sister Jacqueline (1967–70)

REED, ALAINA—black actress
b: Nov 10, 1946, Springfield, Ohio

227 (com).... Rose Lee Holloway (1985–)

Before *227* Alaina was best known as Olivia on *Sesame Street*, a role she has played since the late 1970s.

REED, ALAN—actor
b: Aug 20, 1907, New York City, N.Y. d: Jun 14, 1977

Life with Luigi (com) ...... Pasquale (1952)
Duffy's Tavern (com)
.... Clifton Finnegan (1953–54)
Mr. Adams and Eve (com)
.... J. B. Hafter (1957–58)
Peter Loves Mary (com)
.... Happy Richman (1960–61)
The Flintstones (cartn)
.... Fred Flintstone (voice) (1960–66)
Mickey (com)....... Mr. Swidler (1964–65)
Where's Huddles? (cartn)
.... Mad Dog Maloney (voice) (1970)

A very busy "voice man" in radio days, who played poet Falstaff Openshaw on *The Fred Allen Show*, Clancy the cop on *Duffy's Tavern* and Pasquale on radio's *Life with Luigi*, among others. Although he was seen in many supporting roles on television comedies, he is best known for TV voices too—especially that of the original Fred Flintstone.

REED, ALBERT—black actor

Chase (police)
.... Insp. Frank Dawson (1973–74)

REED, CAROL—singer

Melody, Harmony & Rhythm (music)
.... regular (1949–50)

Rendezvous with Music (music)
.... emcee (1950)

REED, DONNA—actress
b: Jan 27, 1921, Denison, Iowa d: Jan 14, 1986

The Donna Reed Show (com)
.... Donna Stone (1958–66)
Dallas (drama)
.... Miss Ellie Ewing (1984–85)

A wholesome actress popular in movies of the '40s and '50s, Donna achieved fame (and an Academy Award) playing against type as the prostitute Alma in *From Here to Eternity* in 1953. She appeared occasionally in TV dramas of the mid-1950s, on *Ford Theatre, Suspense,* etc., but it was the long-running comedy *The Donna Reed Show* that made her a superstar, and a millionaire.

Despite her success, and image as the idealized all-American mom (her show was nicknamed *Mother Knows Best* and *The Madonna Reed Show*), Donna despised her role, considering it a two-dimensional fantasy invented by the MEN who controlled TV. She took their money but retired from acting when the series ended, with nothing but bitter words for the male Hollywood power structure and for TV's image of women—which she had helped to create. Her roles afterward were infrequent; she guested on *The Love Boat,* played the mother of a rebellious son and hippie daughter in the 1979 TV film *The Best Place to Be,* and was the headmistress of a girls' school where murder headed the curriculum in *Deadly Lessons* (1983). In 1984 she surprised everyone by taking over the role of Miss Ellie on *Dallas,* replacing an ill Barbara Bel Geddes. It was her last major role—once again as a peacemaking mother.

REED, JERRY—country singer, actor
b: Mar 20, 1937, Atlanta, Ga.

The Glen Campbell Goodtime Hour (var)
.... regular (1970–72)
The Jerry Reed When You're Hot You're Hot Hour (var) .... host (1972)
Dean Martin Presents Music Country (var)
.... regular (1973)
Nashville 99 (police)
.... Det. Trace Mayne (1977)

Concrete Cowboys (adv)
.... Jimmy Lee (J.D.) Reed (1981)

A popular country guitar picker and singer ("When You're Hot You're Hot") who turned to acting in Burt Reynolds movies of the mid-1970s. He later costarred in two short-lived TV action series, in good ol' boy roles.

REED, LUCILLE—singer

This Is Music (music)..... regular (1951–52)

REED, LYDIA—actress

The Real McCoys (com)
.... Aunt Hassie (1957–63)

REED, MARSHALL—actor
b: May 28, 1917, Englewood, Calif. d: Apr 15, 1980

The Lineup (police)
.... Insp. Fred Asher (1954–59)

REED, MARSHALL AND MICHAEL—juvenile actors

The Waltons (drama)
.... John Willard (1978–81)

The Reed twins alternated as Mary Ellen's baby, John, on *The Waltons.*

REED, PAMELA—actress
b: 1953, Tacoma, Wash.

Andros Targets (drama)
.... Sandi Farrell (1977)

REED, PAUL—comedian, actor

Caesar's Hour (var) ...... regular (1955–57)
Sid Caesar Invites You (var) . regular (1958)
Car 54, Where Are You? (com)
.... Capt. Martin Block (1961–63)
The Cara Williams Show (com)
.... Damon Burkhardt (1964–65)

REED, PHILIP—actor
b: 1908, New York City, N.Y.

Ruthie on the Telephone (com)
.... Richard (1949)

REED, RALPH—actor

Life with Father (com)
.... Clarence Day, Jr. (1953–54)

REED, REX—critic

b: Oct 2, 1938*, Fort Worth, Texas

The Gong Show (com)... panelist (1976–80)
At the Movies (misc) ..... cohost (1986–)

REED, ROBERT—actor

b: Oct 19, 1932, Highland Park, Ill. r: Muskogee, Okla.

The Defenders (drama)
.... Kenneth Preston (1961–65)
The Brady Bunch (com)
.... Mike Brady (1969–74)
Mannix (drama)
.... Lt. Adam Tobias (1969–75)
Rich Man, Poor Man—Book I (drama)
.... Teddy Boylan (1976)
The Brady Bunch Hour (var)
.... Mike Brady (1977)
Roots (drama)
.... Dr. William Reynolds (1977)
The Runaways (drama)
.... David McKay (1978)
Scruples (drama) ...... Josh Hillman (1980)
Nurse (drama) ... Dr. Adam Rose (1981–82)

Tall, earnest-looking Robert Reed is best known for playing decent middle-class types, especially in his long-running roles as the father on *The Brady Bunch* and the headstrong young lawyer on *The Defenders*. Robert studied drama in both the U.S. and England before getting his start onstage in New York in the mid-1950s. Late in the decade he moved to Hollywood and began landing small parts in TV series including *The Lawman, The Danny Thomas Show,* and *Men into Space.* He credits a guest role as a lawyer on an episode of *Father Knows Best* in 1959 as being the turning point in his career. It resulted in his winning, two years later, the role of E. G. Marshall's son in the much-acclaimed lawyer series *The Defenders,* which ran for four years.

Robert appeared in guest roles for a few years after *The Defenders,* then in 1969 began two regular series roles concurrently (a rarity)—the father on the family comedy *The Brady Bunch* and the recurring part of Mike Connors' police contact on *Mannix.* Despite this display of versatility, and occasional later portrayals of less than honorable types (a slave owner on *Roots,* a family man who makes ob-

*Some sources give 1939 or 1940.

scene phone calls in the TV film *Secret Night Caller*), his basic good-guy image persisted. In *The Runaways* he helped teens come home, and on *Nurse* he provided a shoulder for Michael Learned to cry on. Robert appeared in quite a few other series and TV movies during the '70s and '80s, winning Emmy Award nominations for three—a 1975 episode of *Medical Center* (as a transsexual doctor) and the miniseries *Rich Man Poor Man* and *Roots.*

REED, SHANNA—actress

For Love and Honor (drama)
.... Phyllis Wiecek (1983)
I Had Three Wives (drama)...... Liz (1985)

REED, SUSANNE—actress

Code R (adv) .... Suzy (1977)

REED, TOBY—host, announcer

Top Dollar (quiz)............ emcee (1958)

REED, TRACY—black actress

b: 1949, Fort Benning, Ga.

Love, American Style (com)
.... repertory player (1969–70)
Barefoot in the Park (com)
.... Corie Bratter (1970–71)
Love, American Style (com)
.... repertory player (1972–74)

REES, ANGHARAD—Welsh actress

b: 1949

Master of the Game (drama)
.... Marianne (1984)

REES, LANNY—juvenile actor

The Life of Riley (com) .... Junior (1949–50)

REESE, DELLA—black singer, actress

b: Jul 6, 1932, Detroit, Mich.

Chico and the Man (com)
.... Della Rogers (1976–78)
It Takes Two (com)
.... Judge Caroline Phillips (1982–83)
Charlie & Company (com)
.... Aunt Rachel (1986)

A popular singer of the '50s, first in gospel music with Mahalia Jackson's troupe, and later on the pop charts with soaring, semi-operatic songs such as "Don't You Know." She later turned to acting and has guested on many series, including *Sanford and Son, McCloud, The Rookies,* and *The A-Team* (as Mr. T's mother!).

REESE, JOY—juvenile actress

Wesley (com)... Elizabeth Eggleston (1949)

REESE, ROY—actor

Mr. Roberts (com)
.... Seaman Reber (1965–66)

REESE, TOM—actor
b: 1930

The Adventures of Ellery Queen (drama)
.... Sgt. Velie (1975–76)

REEVE, MARY ANN—actress

School House (var)......... regular (1949)

REEVES, GEORGE—actor
b: Apr 6, 1914, Ashland, Ky. d: Jun 16, 1959

The Adventures of Superman (adv)
.... Superman/Clark Kent (1951–57)

One of Hollywood's most famous, and ironic, violent deaths was that of George Reeves, TV's *Superman.* The actor who played the indestructible "Man of Steel" died from a bullet through the head—but who pulled the trigger is still a matter of controversy.

Reeves was an athletic youth and Golden Gloves boxer who turned to acting while in junior college. Noticed by a talent scout, he was signed to a movie contract and appeared in several minor films of the '30s before landing the choice role of one of the Tarleton twins in *Gone with the Wind,* in 1939. It didn't help his career much, however; though he worked steadily during the 1940s, the roles got worse, until he was reduced to low-budget serials by the end of the decade. Television seemed an opportunity to revive his fortunes. He appeared in a number of TV playhouse productions during the early '50s *(Silver Theater, Kraft Theatre, Fireside Theatre)* and took the role of Superman in both a 1950 movie and in a low-budget TV series which began filming in 1951.

Superman was a smash hit that finally gave Reeves an identity, but it was a rather extreme one (how many heroes are supposed to fly?). It also typecast him severely. When he appeared elsewhere it was invariably in costume. A most memorable occasion was a 1957 episode of *I Love Lucy* in which Lucy did a hilarious imitation of the Man of Steel, then ran into the real thing! Nevertheless, kids around America worshipped him, and George gave the role his all.

Much has been made of Reeves' inability to find other work once *Superman* went out of production. True to a point, but he had made a great deal of money and was actively involved in producing films; he had an acting role in *Westward Ho, the Wagons* in 1956 and several offers of series roles, including, reportedly, a *Dick Tracy* series and a revival of *Superman.* He was planning to begin a film in Spain during the summer of 1959. He was also planning to be married.

On an evening in June 1959, Reeves, his fiancée, and two friends spent some time celebrating his upcoming marriage. The actor, tired, on medication (due to injuries received in a recent auto accident), and drinking, retired to his upstairs bedroom alone. A few minutes later his guests heard a single shot; they found him sprawled across the bed, a pistol at his feet. The police ruled suicide, but many who knew him insisted that this was very unlikely. George had given no signs of suicidal tendencies—quite the opposite—and was not noticeably depressed about his career. He had, they said, no reason to do such a thing days before he was to be married. Did a mind-numbing combination of medication, alcohol, and a nearby pistol suddenly push him over the edge? Was there more going on in his life than friends knew, or were willing to talk about? (He had reportedly been seen with some rather unsavory characters, and some suspected murder.) Did the odd state of his will, which left the bulk of his estate to a former lady acquaintance, have something to do with it? We will never know.

REEVES, LISA—actress

The San Pedro Beach Bums (com)
.... Margie (1977)

REEVES, RICHARD—actor
b: Aug 10, 1912, New York City, N.Y. d: Mar 17, 1967

Date with the Angels (com)
.... Mr. Murphy (Murph) (1957–58)

REGALBUTO, JOE—actor
b: Aug 24, Brooklyn, N.Y. r: New Milford, N.J.

The Associates (com)
.... Eliot Streeter (1979–80)
Ace Crawford, Private Eye (com)
.... Toomey (1983)
Knots Landing (drama)
.... Harry Fisher (1985)
Street Hawk (police).. Norman Tuttle (1985)

REGAN, ELLEN—actress
b: Apr 27, Long Island, N.Y.

The Ted Knight Show (com) ... Irma (1978)
Me & Mrs. C. (com)
.... Kathleen Conklin (1986–)

REGAN, MARGIE—actress

Michael Shayne (drama)
.... Lucy Hamilton (1961)

REGAS, JACK, DANCERS—

The John Gary Show (var) .. dancers (1966)
The Beautiful Phyllis Diller Show (var)
.... dancers (1968)
Jimmy Durante Presents the Lennon Sisters (var).................... dancers (1969–70)
The Flip Wilson Show (var)
.... dancers (1970–74)

REGAS, PEDRO—actor
b: Apr 12, 1882, Sparta, Greece d: Aug 10, 1974

Pat Paulsen's Half a Comedy Hour (var)
.... regular (1970)

REGEHR, DUNCAN—actor
b: Oct 5, 1954, Alberta, Canada r: Victoria, B.C., Canada.

The Blue and the Gray (drama)
.... Capt. Randolph (1982)
Wizards and Warriors (adv)
.... Prince Dirk Blackpool (1983)

REGINA, PAUL—actor
b: Oct 25, Brooklyn, N.Y.

Joe & Valerie (com)...... Joe Pizo (1978–79)
Zorro and Son (com)
Don Carlos de la Vega (Zorro Jr.) (1983)

REID, CARL BENTON—actor
b: 1893, Lansing, Mich. d: Mar 15, 1973

Burke's Law (police)... "the Man" (1965–66)

REID, ELLIOT—actor
b: Jan 16, 1920, New York City, N.Y.

That Was the Week That Was (com)
............................host (1964)
Miss Winslow and Son (com)
.... Warren Winslow (1979)

REID, KATE—actress
b: Nov 4, 1930, London, England

Gavilan (adv)... Marion Jaworski (1982–83)
Dallas (drama)... Aunt Lil Trotter (1983–84)
Morningstar/Eveningstar (drama)
.... Martha Cameron (1986)

REID, MILTON—actor
b: 1917, India

The Adventures of Sir Francis Drake (adv)
.... Diego (1962)

REID, TIM—black actor
b: Dec 19, 1944, Norfolk, Va.

Easy Does It...Starring Frankie Avalon (var)
.... regular (1976)
The Marilyn McCoo and Billy Davis Jr. Show (var)........................ regular (1977)
The Richard Pryor Show (var)
.... regular (1977)
WKRP in Cincinnati (com)
.. Gordon Sims (Venus Flytrap) (1978–82)
Teachers Only (com)
.... Michael Horne (1983)
Simon & Simon (drama)
Det. Marcel "Downtown" Brown (1983–)

Tim Reid plays his comic roles with a certain bite, and no wonder. Born in impoverished circumstances, of parents who separated before his birth, he grew up in several households. When he began to fall in with teenage gangs he was packed off to live with his remarried father, who provided a better role model. During the 1960s the young black teenager vented his frustrations in civil rights protests, including some violent confrontations; at the same time, he became a model student, and, when he graduated, went straight into the corporate world as a junior executive with DuPont.

That only got him an ulcer, so in 1969 he teamed up with another restless young businessman named Tom Dreesen in a topical comedy act called Tim and Tom, which played clubs around the country until 1975. Tim then did solo stand-up work and began to play guest roles on such series as *Rhoda, Lou Grant, What's Happening?*, and *Fernwood 2-Nite.* The role that made him famous was that of the hip, smooth-talking DJ Venus Flytrap on *WKRP;* he has since become equally known as the tough but cool cop Downtown Brown on *Simon & Simon.*

Reid is quite active in industry antidrug programs. There is also a quiet side to him, as evidenced by his book *As I Find It,* a collection of his poetry and photography, published in 1982. He is married to actress Daphne Maxwell.

REILLY, CHARLES NELSON—actor
b: Jan 13, 1931, New York City, N.Y.

The Steve Lawrence Show (var)
.... regular (1965)
The Ghost and Mrs. Muir (com)
.... Claymore Gregg (1968–70)
Dean Martin Presents the Golddiggers (var)
.... regular (1970)
Arnie (com)..... Randy Robinson (1971–72)
Match Game P.M. (quiz). panelist (1975–82)

Charles Nelson Reilly is best known for playing fussy, excitable characters, notably Claymore Gregg, the nephew of the ghost on *The Ghost and Mrs. Muir.* His principal career has been on Broadway, where in the '50s and '60s he appeared in such hits as *Bye Bye Birdie, Hello Dolly,* and *How to Succeed in Business Without Really Trying* (for which he received a Tony Award nomination). On television he has most often been seen on variety and game shows. He appeared on Saturday morning during the early 1970s, playing the role of Horatio J. Hoo Doo, the nutty magician, in the whimsical fantasy *Lidsville* (set in a land of oversized hats).

REILLY, HUGH—actor
b: c. 1920, Newark, N.J.

Claudia, The Story of a Marriage (drama)
.... David Naughton (1952)
TV Reader's Digest (drama)..... host (1955)
Lassie (adv) .... Paul Martin (1958–64)

REILLY, JOHN—actor
b: Nov 11, Chicago, Ill.

Number 96 (drama)
.... Chick Walden (1980–81)
Dallas (drama)........ Roy Ralston (1983)
The Hamptons (drama)
.... Jay Mortimer (1983)

An imposing actor who has spent most of his career in soap operas, including daytime's *As the World Turns* in the '70s and *General Hospital* in the '80s. He was an aggressive businessman for ten years before turning to acting and playing pushy characters on TV.

REILLY, MIKE—orchestra leader

A Couple of Joes (var)
.... orch. leader (1949–50)

REILLY, SUSAN—actress

Love & Marriage (com)
.... Susan Baker (1959–60)

REILLY, TOM—actor
b: Jun 18, Fort Riley, Kan. r: Bergenfield, N.J.

CHiPs (police)
.... Off. Bobby Nelson (1982–83)

REIMERS, ED—announcer

Do You Trust Your Wife? (quiz)
.... announcer (1956–57)

Known in the 1970s as the TV spokesman for Allstate Insurance.

REINER, CARL—actor, writer, director
b: Mar 20, 1922, The Bronx, N.Y.

The Fashion Story (misc)
.... "photographer" (1948–49)
The Fifty-Fourth Street Revue (var)
.... regular (1949)
Eddie Condon's Floor Show (music)
.... cohost (1950)
Your Show of Shows (var)
.... regular (1950–54)
Droodles (quiz)............ panelist (1954)

Caesar's Hour (var)
.... George Hansen (1954–57)
Sid Caesar Invites You (var) . regular (1958)
Keep Talking (quiz) .... emcee (1958–59)
Take a Good Look (quiz)
.... panelist (1960–61)
The Dick Van Dyke Show (com)
.... Alan Brady (1961–66)
The Art Linkletter Show (quiz)
.... regular (1963)
The Celebrity Game (quiz)
.... emcee (1964–65)
Good Heavens (com) ..... Mr. Angel (1976)

Emmy Awards: Best Supporting Actor, for *Caesar's Hour* (1956, 1957); Best Writing for a Comedy, for *The Dick Van Dyke Show* (1962, 1963, 1964); Producer, Best Comedy Series, for *The Dick Van Dyke Show* (1965, 1966); Best Writing for a Variety Program, for *The Sid Caesar, Imogene Coca, Carl Reiner, Howard Morris Special* (1967)

Tall, balding Carl Reiner has one of the most creative minds in TV comedy, though he has spent much of his career behind the scenes creating comedy vehicles for others. Originally, he wanted to become a serious actor, but army service during World War II intervened. He wanted to act, not fight, but, as he later put it, "you couldn't act in the army. You couldn't get a bunch of actors together and put on a (serious) play. So I developed a stand-up comedy routine." After several years entertaining the troops, Carl was discharged and began to win roles in Broadway revues; this led to TV, and Sid Caesar's ambitious new comedy series, *Your Show of Shows*. In all, he was with Caesar doing sketch comedy for nine years.

At the same time the genial Reiner was entertaining viewers on variety and panel shows, he was exploring new areas for himself. During the late '50s he developed the idea for a series about a TV comedy writer, to be called *Head of the Family*, and filmed a pilot with himself in the leading role of Rob Petrie. The networks weren't interested ("it was the year for horses and guns," he later remarked). The single episode was telecast in July 1960 as a "busted pilot," normally the kiss of death for proposed shows that didn't make it. However, producer Sheldon Leonard saw it and liked it. He arranged to have the

episode refilmed with a whole new cast, including Dick Van Dyke as Rob; Carl became the shows' *real* head writer. The resulting series, *The Dick Van Dyke Show*, became a huge hit. Carl got to play the recurring supporting role of the egotistical TV star Alan Brady.

On the heels of this great success, Carl went on to do more behind-the-scenes work, including directing the hit movies *Oh God!* and *The Jerk*. Not everyone appreciated his sometimes daring humor, however. In a well-publicized tiff with CBS he quit *The New Dick Van Dyke Show* in the early '70s when the network refused to allow a scene in which a child opened the bedroom door and saw his parents making love (leading to a story in which Dick explained to the boy the realities and responsibilities of parenting). Carl then worked mostly as a producer-director, acting only occasionally. He was seen briefly as an angel in the short-lived comedy *Good Heavens*. He finally got his chance to play straight drama in the 1981 TV movie *Skokie*.

Carl is also well-remembered for the 1960s comedy routine "The 2,000 Year Old Man," with Mel Brooks, which has had several incarnations on television and records. Carl's semiautobiographical novel *Enter Laughing* (1958) was made into a play and a movie during the 1960s.

REINER, FRITZ—symphony conductor
b: Dec 19, 1888, Budapest, Hungary d: Nov 15, 1963

Chicago Symphony (music)
.... conductor (1954–55)

REINER, ROB—actor
b: Mar 6, 1947, New York City, N.Y.

All in the Family (com)
.... Mike Stivic (Meathead) (1971–78)
Free Country (com)... Joseph Bresner (1978)

Emmy Award: Best Supporting Actor in a Comedy, for *All in the Family* (1974, 1978)

The son of Carl Reiner, also a comic actor (on *Gomer Pyle, That Girl, The Partridge Family*, etc.) as well as a writer (*The Smothers Brothers Comedy Hour*, etc.). Rob has been active on TV since the '60s. Following his great success as son-in-law Mike ("Meathead") on *All in the Family*, he created and starred in his own comedy series, *Free Country,* in 1978. Though certainly unusual—he played a Lithuanian immigrant as a young man and at age 89—it was short-lived. In the '80s he wrote and directed movies including *This Is Spinal Tap* and *Stand by Me,* which did better.

REISCHL, GERI—actress

The Brady Bunch Hour (var)
.... Jan Brady (1977)

REKERT, WINSTON—actor
b: Jun 10, British Columbia, Canada

Adderly (adv)...... V. H. Adderly (1986–)

REMES, JORIE—comedienne

Melody Tour (var).......... regular (1954)

REMICK, LEE—actress
b: Dec 14, 1935, Boston, Mass.

Wheels (drama)...... Erica Trenton (1978)
Ike (drama)........ Kay Summersby (1979)

This cool, sensual leading lady of movies appeared periodically on television during the 1950s, mostly on *Robert Montgomery Presents;* she was seldom seen in the 1960s, as she concentrated on film work. Lee began to favor the small screen again in the '70s, appearing in important TV movies, dramatic specials, and miniseries, the latter including *QB VII, The Blue Knight, Wheels, Ike,* and *Mistral's Daughter.*

REMSEN, BERT—actor
b: Feb 25, 1925, Glen Cove, N.Y.

Gibbsville (drama) .... Pell (1976)
It's a Living (com)........ Mario (1980–81)

RENALDO, DUNCAN—actor
b: Apr 23, 1904, Valladolid, Spain* d: Sep 3, 1980

The Cisco Kid (wes)
.... the Cisco Kid (1950–56)

Duncan Renaldo, the dashing Latin hero of *The Cisco Kid,* had an interesting personal history. He was born Renaldo Duncan, of

*Spain is often given, but Rumania is also a possibility; his official studio biography listed Camden, N.J.! His date of birth is also uncertain.

a Scottish father and Rumanian mother, apparently somewhere in Europe, but was abandoned by them as a child. He never knew either his parents or place of birth. Raised as a foundling in various parts of Europe, he shipped out as a seaman as a young man and arrived in the U.S. in the early 1920s, hoping to find work as a portrait painter. He failed at that, then drifted into the silent movie industry as a set designer, director of short films, and finally an actor. By 1932 he had been in several important features when, suddenly, his career was cast in jeopardy. He was imprisoned by immigration authorities on a charge of illegal entry; this was due, he later revealed, to a feud with movie mogul Louis B. Mayer, who engineered the arrest. After 18 months in prison he was pardoned by President Franklin D. Roosevelt and resumed work (despite Mayer's efforts to blacklist him) in a long series of western second features and low-budget serials. His greatest fame came in the late '40s, when he played the Cisco Kid in 12 films (he was the fifth screen actor to play the role, and the most successful); that led to the television series, which was one of the very first syndicated films made for sale to TV stations.

Cisco was a major hit on TV and Renaldo—who was then around 50—was identified with the character ever after. In later years he made many personal appearances as the Kid, worked on scripts for a proposed revival (which was to star his son), and was active in the annual Santa Barbara "Old Spanish Days" festival. He lived out his life at his Rancho Mi Amigo near there, white-haired, charming, and forever—in his own heart—the embodiment of the chivalrous tradition represented by the character for which he will always be known.

RENELLA, PAT—actor

The New Phil Silvers Show (com)
.... Roxy (1963–64)

RENNARD, DEBBIE—actress

Dallas (drama).............. Sly (1983–)

RENNICK, NANCY—actress

Rescue 8 (adv)..... Patty Johnson (1958–59)

Kentucky Jones (drama)
. . . . Edith Thorncroft (1964–65)

RENNIE, MICHAEL—actor
b: Aug 25, 1909, Bradford, Yorkshire, England
d: Jun 10, 1971

The Third Man (drama)
. . . . Harry Lime (1959–62)

The tall, gaunt English actor was a frequent guest star on television from the mid-1950s until the late '60s, with multiple appearances on *Climax, Alfred Hitchcock Presents, Zane Grey Theater, The Invaders,* and *The F.B.I.,* among others. He was usually seen in dramas, but did turn up twice on *Batman*—as the shifty Sandman.

RENZI, EVA—German actress
b: 1944

Primus (adv) . . . . Toni Hayden (1971)

REPP, STAFFORD—actor
b: Apr 26, 1918, California d: Nov 5, 1974

The Thin Man (drama)
. . . . Lt. Ralph Raines (1957–58)
The New Phil Silvers Show (com)
. . . . Brink (1963–64)
Batman (adv) . . . . . . Chief O'Hara (1966–68)

RESCHER, DEE DEE—
Dinah and Her New Best Friends (var)
. . . . regular (1976)

RESER, HARRY—banjoist, orchestra leader
b: Jan 17, 1896, Piqua, Ohio r: Dayton, Ohio d: Sep 27, 1965

The Sammy Kaye Show (var)
. . . . regular (1958–59)

Reser was popular music's premiere banjo virtuoso during the 1920s, and sold millions of records then, both as a banjoist and bandleader. Unfortunately, when the banjo faded from favor, so did he, and he spent later years as a much-respected (but little known to the public) studio conductor and sideman. Sammy Kaye, at least, gave him a featured spot on his television series.
Reser died performing, in the orchestra pit of the Broadway show *Fiddler on the Roof.* His biography: *The Great Harry*

Reser by W. W. Triggs (Waker, London, 1978).

RESIN, DAN—actor
On Our Own (com)
. . . . Craig Boatwright (1977–78)

RESNICK, AMY—actress
Paper Dolls (drama) . . . . Jenna (1984)

RETTIG, TOMMY—juvenile actor
b: Dec 10, 1941, Jackson Heights, N.Y.

Lassie (adv) . . . . Jeff Miller (1954–57)

Tommy Rettig is widely believed to be one of Hollywood's child-actor horror stories; "Didn't he go to prison or die of an drug overdose or something?" The truth is a bit more complicated than that.
Tommy was a major child star in the 1950s. He began onstage at the age of five, touring with Mary Martin in the road company of *Annie Get Your Gun.* That led to many roles in films of the early 1950s, including *Panic in the Streets, The 5,000 Fingers of Dr. T,* and *River of No Return* with Marilyn Monroe. Tommy was also seen on early television dramas, on *Your Play Time, Ford Theatre,* and *Omnibus,* among others. In 1954 he began the role that made him famous, that of Lassie's original young master in the long-running series about a child and his dog.
When, after three seasons, he was thought to have outgrown the role, 15-year-old Tommy was overjoyed; the constant filming had put a real crimp in his social life. For the next several years he played guest roles in various series, including *Lawman, The Fugitive,* and *Mr. Novak.* In 1965–66 he had a leading role in the youth-oriented daytime serial *Never Too Young,* which was, however, a flop. After that, in his midtwenties, the work just petered out. Tommy retired to his farm with his wife and began to find other ways to occupy his time. That is when the trouble began.
In 1972 Tommy Rettig was arrested for possession of marijuana and received a suspended sentence; in 1975 he was arrested again, this time on the much more serious charge of smuggling cocaine into the U.S. for resale. He was sentenced to five and a half years in prison, but ap-

pealed the conviction and eventually got the charges dropped. In 1980 he was arrested again ("I was at a cocaine laboratory at Lake Arrowhead," he says matter-of-factly, "and some of the neighbors there called the police"); again the authorities could not prove his complicity, and the charges were dropped. He has not—at least as of this writing—served time on any of these charges, nor has his admitted use of drugs noticeably impaired his health. In more recent years he has been a computer programmer and run a unique drug-counseling service in Los Angeles that, according to its publicity, "helps you learn to manage drugs in ways that support your physical and emotional well-being."

Little Jeff, the boy with a dog, seems to have found a new career.

REVERE, PAUL—pianist
b: Jan 7, 1938, Harvard Neb. r: Boise, Idaho

Rock 'n' Roll Summer Action (var)
.... regular (1985)

The leader of the rock group Paul Revere and the Raiders, which was a semiregular attraction on this 1985 summer show. The band's lead singer for many years was Mark Lindsay.

REVILL, CLIVE—actor
b: Apr 18, 1930, Wellington, New Zealand

Wizards and Warriors (adv)
.... Wizard Vector (1983)

REY, ALEJANDRO—actor
b: Feb 8, 1930, Buenos Aires, Argentina d: May 21, 1987

Slattery's People (drama)
.... Mike Valera (1965)
The Flying Nun (com)
.... Carlos Ramirez (1967–70)
Dallas (drama) .... Luis Rueda (1986–87)

REY, ALVINO—orchestra leader
b: Jul 1, 1911, Cleveland, Ohio*

The King Family Show (var)
.... musical director (1965–66)
The King Family Show (var)
.... musical director (1969)

A pioneer in the use of electric guitars during the big-band era. The King Sisters were
*Some sources give Oakland, Calif.

712

vocalists with his band, and he married one of them (Louise); after years of obscurity he returned to the spotlight in their 1960s television series.

REYES, ERNIE, JR.—juvenile actor
b: Jan 15, 1972, San Jose, Calif.

Sidekicks (adv) .... Ernie Lee (1986–)

A pint-sized black belt in karate, who was competing in adult martial arts tournaments by the time he was ten. His father, also a black belt, is a martial arts instructor.

REYNOLDS, BURT—actor
b: Feb 11, 1936, Waycross, Ga. r: Palm Beach, Fla.

Riverboat (adv) ...... Ben Frazer (1959–60)
Gunsmoke (wes) .... Quint Asper (1962–65)
Hawk (police) .... Lt. John Hawk (1966)
Dan August (police)
.... Det. Lt. Dan August (1970–71)

Handsome, virile, fun-loving Burt Reynolds had a considerable career on television before reaching superstardom in movies during the 1970s. The son of a Florida police chief, he excelled at football in college until an auto accident ended his plans to turn pro. He became an actor instead, moving to New York in the mid-1950s and winning his first supporting role on Broadway (as "Buddy Reynolds") in a revival of *Mr. Roberts* in 1956. He also began to get bit parts on television, most of them villainous, on *General Electric Theater, Schlitz Playhouse, M Squad,* and other series. A major break was his casting as Darren McGavin's costar in the 1959 adventure series *Riverboat*. He was dropped after a year, but continued to play guest roles on *The Aquanauts, Michael Shayne, Alfred Hitchcock Presents, Route 66,* and others. One of his rare humorous roles (though many didn't get it) was in a bitingly satirical episode of *The Twilight Zone,* in which Shakespeare comes back to life and is made to write for TV—whereupon his golden words are of course savaged by pea-brained TV producers and actors. Burt played an egotistical method actor—a riotous takeoff on Marlon Brando —who so infuriated the Bard that he finally decked Burt with one swift punch.

In 1962 Burt began the continuing role of Quint Asper, the half-breed blacksmith on *Gunsmoke;* later in the '60s he starred in two series of his own, *Hawk,* as a New York detective who is a full-blooded Indian, and *Dan August,* as a California cop. (Burt is in real life part Indian.) In addition, he filmed an unsuccessful pilot for another series, called *Lassiter,* in which he was cast as an investigative reporter.

Burt's so-so career suddenly exploded in the early '70s, due to several factors: (1) his 1972 box-office smash *Deliverance;* (2) his frequent appearances on TV talk shows, especially *The Tonight Show,* where he proved an usually glib and humorous guest; and (3) the April 1972 issue of *Cosmopolitan* magazine, which readers opened to find Burt spread out as the first male centerfold—wearing a mustache, a cigar, a smile, and nothing else at all! CBS quickly reran *Dan August* and NBC repeated *Hawk* to capitalize on the Reynolds mania, but Burt had clearly moved beyond TV into movie superstardom.

Burt was married in the 1960s to *Laugh-In's* Judy Carne. He has also had well-publicized relationships with Dinah Shore, Sally Field, Chris Evert, and, probably, by the time you read this, others.

REYNOLDS, DEBBIE—actress
b: Apr 1, 1932, El Paso, Texas r: Burbank, Calif.

The Debbie Reynolds Show (com)
............Debbie Thompson (1969–70)
Aloha Paradise (com)
.... Sydney Chase (1981)

Pert, pretty Debbie Reynolds has spent the major portion of her career onstage and in films, rather than on television. In movies since 1948, she was a major star when NBC lured her onto TV in 1969 to appear in her own situation comedy, an unabashed knockoff of *I Love Lucy* (it was even called *Here's Debbie* at one point, aping Lucy's *Here's Lucy*). She played a wacky suburban housewife who constantly cooked up crazy schemes in an effort to crash her husband's glamorous world of newspaper reporting. Sound familiar?

It flopped, and Debbie departed TV for a decade, returning in 1980 for a guest shot on *The Love Boat* and then starring in another series knockoff, *Aloha Paradise* (a sort of landlocked *Love Boat*). It, too, failed. Thereafter, Debbie confined herself to occasional variety specials, such as *The All Star Salute to Mother's Day.*

REYNOLDS, FRANK—newscaster
b: Nov 29, 1923, East Chicago, Ind. d: Jul 20, 1983

ABC Evening News (news)
.... anchorman (1968–70)
ABC Evening News (news)
.... anchorman (1978–83)

Emmy Award: Best News Segment, for *Nightline:* "Post Election Special Edition" (1980)

Frank Reynolds began his career in Chicago as a radio reporter in the late 1940s, moving into television there in 1950. During the next 15 years he became one of the city's most familiar local newscasters, and in 1965 ABC-TV recruited him to become its White House correspondent. ABC ran through anchors rather rapidly in those days, and Frank had his turn at bat from 1968–70 (teamed with Howard K. Smith) but was bumped when a bigger name came to the network in the person of Harry Reasoner. Frank then reverted to political reporting until 1978, when he was once again tapped as part of a new evening anchor team—this time with *three* others (Max Robinson, Peter Jennings, Barbara Walters). Never a colorful type, Reynolds seemed on his way to becoming one of ABC's gray eminences. He died unexpectedly in 1983, of what was first said to be hepatitus, but was in fact bone cancer.

REYNOLDS, JAMES—actor
Time Express (drama)
.... conductor R. J. Walker (1979)

REYNOLDS, KATHRYN—actress
Soap (com) .... Claire (1977–78)

REYNOLDS, MARJORIE—actress
b: Aug 12, 1921, Buhl, Idaho
The Life of Riley (com)
.... Peg Riley (1953–58)

**REYNOLDS, QUENTIN—newscaster,
writer**
b: Apr 11, 1902, New York City, N.Y. d: Mar 17,
1965

It's News to Me (quiz)... panelist (1951–54)
Guess What (quiz) .... panelist (1952)

REYNOLDS, SIMON—actor

Check It Out (com)....... Murray (1985–)

REYNOLDS, WILLIAM—actor
b: 1931, Los Angeles, Calif.

Pete Kelly's Blues (drama)
.... Pete Kelly (1959)
The Islanders (adv)
.... Sandy Wade (1960–61)
The Gallant Men (drama)
.... Capt. Jim Benedict (1962–63)
The F.B.I. (police)
..... special agent Tom Colby (1967–73)

RHOADES, BARBARA—actress
b: Mar 23, 1947, Poughkeepsie, N.Y.

Busting Loose (com)
.... Melody Feebeck (1977)
Celebrity Challenge of the Sexes (sport)
.... Women's Coach (1978)
Hanging In (com).. Maggie Gallagher (1979)
Soap (com) ..... Maggie Chandler (1980–81)

RHOADS, CHERYL—

Motown Revue (var)........ regular (1985)

RHODES, DONNELLY—actor
b: Dec 4, Winnipeg, Canada

Soap (com) .... Dutch (1978–81)
Report to Murphy (com) ..... Charlie (1982)
Double Trouble (com) .... Art Foster (1984)

RHODES, GEORGE—orchestra leader
b: 1919, Chicago, Ill. d: Dec 25, 1985

The Sammy Davis Jr. Show (var)
.... orch. leader (1966)
Sammy and Company (talk)
.... orch. leader (1975–77)

RHODES, HARI—black actor
b: Apr 10, 1932, Cincinnati, Ohio

Daktari (adv) .... Mike (1966–69)
The Protectors (police)
.... D.A. William Washburn (1969–70)

Most Wanted (police)
.... Mayor Dan Stoddard (1976–77)
Roots (drama)......... Brima Cesay (1977)
Backstairs at the White House (drama)
.... Coates (1979)

Also known as Harry Rhodes. He has been
active as a supporting player on television
since 1957, with his most prominent role
being that of the native zoologist on *Daktari.*

RHUE, MADLYN—actress
b: Oct 3, 1934, Washington, D.C.

Bracken's World (drama)
.... Marjorie Grant (1969–70)
Executive Suite (drama)
.... Hilary Madison (1976–77)

Born Madeline Roche; Miss Rhue says her
stage name is a play on the name of the
Paris boulevard, Rue de la Madeline. She
has been quite active as an all-purpose
supporting actress in TV dramas since the
late 1950s.

RHYS-DAVIES, JOHN—actor
b: England

Shogun (drama) .... Vasco Rodrigues (1980)

**RIBEIRO, ALFONSO—black juvenile
actor**
b: Sep 21, 1971, New York City, N.Y.

Silver Spoons (com)
.... Alfonso Spears (1984–86)

A young dancer who got his start onstage
in Broadway's *The Tap Dance Kid,* and on
television in a famous Pepsi commercial in
which he danced right into Michael Jackson.

RICARD, ADRIAN—actress

Doctors' Hospital (drama)
.... Nurse Hester Stanton (1975–76)

RICE, GREG—midget actor

Foul Play (drama).............. Ben (1981)

RICE, HOWARD—black juvenile actor

Room 222 (drama)
.... Richie Lane (1969–71)

RICE, JOHN—midget actor

Foul Play (drama)............. Beau (1981)

RICE, ROSEMARY—actress

Mama (com).............. Katrin (1949–57)

RICH, ADAM—juvenile actor
b: Oct 12, 1968, New York City, N.Y.

Eight Is Enough (com)
.... Nicholas Bradford (1977–81)
Code Red (adv) ..... Danny Blake (1981–82)
Gun Shy (com).............. Clovis (1983)

RICH, BUDDY—drummer, orchestra leader
b: Jun 30, 1917, Brooklyn, N.Y. d: Apr 2, 1987

The Marge and Gower Champion Show (com)
.... Cozy (1957)
Away We Go (var)
.... orch. leader (1967)

RICH, DON—country singer, guitarist
b: Aug 15, 1941, Olympia, Wash. d: 1974

Hee Haw (var).......... regular (1969–75)

The lead guitarist of Buck Owens' backup band The Buckaroos, and a close associate of Buck's from the 1950s on.

RICH, MICHAEL—

The Ted Steele Show (music)
.... regular (1948–49)

RICHARD & MILDRED—

Polka Time (music)...... regulars (1956–57)

Richard Hodyl and Mildred Lawnik, for those who are interested.

RICHARD, DARRYL—actor

The Donna Reed Show (com)
.... Smitty (1965–66)

RICHARDS, ADDISON—actor
b: Oct 20, 1887*, Zanesville, Ohio d: Mar 22, 1964

Pentagon U.S.A. (drama)
.... the Colonel (1953)

*Some sources give 1902.

Cimarron City (wes)
.... Martin Kingsley (1958–59)
Fibber McGee and Molly (com)
.... Doc Gamble (1959–60)

RICHARDS, BEAH—black actress
b: Vicksburg, Miss.

The Bill Cosby Show (com)
.... Rose Kincaid (1970–71)
Sanford and Son (com) .. Aunt Ethel (1972)
Roots: The Next Generations (drama)
.... Cynthia Harvey Palmer (1979)

RICHARDS, BERYL—

A Couple of Joes (var) .... regular (1950)

RICHARDS, CAROL—actress, singer
r: Indiana

The RCA Victor Show (com)
.... Marian (1953–54)

This pretty vocalist had a minor career on television and records in the 1950s, but she lives on as the voice that sings duet with Bing Crosby on his evergreen Christmas recording "Silver Bells." She was Dennis Day's girlfriend on *The RCA Victor Show*.

RICHARDS, CULLY—actor
b: 1910 d: Jun 17, 1978

Don't Call Me Charlie (com)
.... First Sgt. Wozniak (1962–63)

RICHARDS, DEAN—host

Midwestern Hayride (var) .... emcee (1959)

RICHARDS, DENNY, JR.—actor

Willy (drama)... Franklin Dodger (1954–55)

RICHARDS, DON—singer

The Jack Carter Show (var)
.... vocalist (1950–51)

RICHARDS, EVAN—juvenile actor
b: Mar 26, 1970, Los Angeles, Calif.

Mama Malone (com)
.... Frankie Karamakopoulos (1984)

RICHARDS, GRANT—actor
b: 1916, New York City, N.Y. d: Jul 4, 1963

Doorway to Danger (drama)
.... Doug Carter (1951)

RICHARDS, JEFF—actor
b: Nov 1, 1922, Portland, Ore.

Jefferson Drum (wes)
.... Jefferson Drum (1958–59)

Formerly a professional baseball player. One of his first films, in 1950, was called *Kill the Umpire*. In *Jefferson Drum* he was somewhat more peaceful, as a frontier newspaper editor.

RICHARDS, KIM—juvenile actress
b: Sep 19, 1964, Long Island, N.Y.

Nanny and the Professor (com)
.... Prudence Everett (1970–71)
Here We Go Again (com)....... Jan (1973)
James at 15 (drama)
.... Sandy Hunter (1977–78)
Hello, Larry (com)... Ruthie Adler (1979–80)

RICHARDS, LOU—actor
b: Sep 3, Terrytown, Texas r: Hawaii

Gloria (com)
.... Clark V. Uhley, Jr. (1982–83)

RICHARDS, MICHAEL—comedian
b: Jul 24, Los Angeles, Calif.

Fridays (var)............. regular (1980–82)

RICHARDS, PAUL—actor
b: 1924, Hollywood, Calif. d: Dec 10, 1974

Breaking Point (drama)
.... Dr. McKinley Thompson (1963–64)

RICHARDSON, IAN—actor
b: Apr 7, 1934, Edinburgh, Scotland

Ike (drama)
...... Field Marshall Montgomery (1979)

RICHARDSON, JAMES G.—actor
b: Aug 22, 1945, Gainesville, Fla. d: Feb 20, 1983

Sierra (adv)..... ranger Tim Cassidy (1974)

This actor fell in love with mountain climbing while playing the park ranger in *Sierra*, and that proved to be his undoing. The year after the series left the air, he fell off a cliff while climbing in Yosemite National Park and was nearly killed. After a long recuperation he returned to acting, and in 1982 he starred in a *CBS Afternoon Playbreak* drama called "Journey to Survival," which stressed the need for safe climbing practices. Ironically, he died at age 37 in a skiing accident.

RICHARDSON, MICHAEL—actor
b: Dec 23, Riverside, Calif.

Chase (police)
.... Off. Steve Baker (1973–74)

RICHARDSON, PATRICIA—actress
b: Feb 23, Bethesda, Md.

Double Trouble (com)
.... Beth McConnell (1984)

RICHARDSON, SUSAN—actress
b: Mar 11, 1952, Coatesville, Pa.

Eight Is Enough (com)
..... Susan Bradford Stockwell (1977–81)

RICHFIELD, EDWIN—actor

The Buccaneers (adv)
.... crewman Armando (1956–57)

RICHMAN, JEFFREY—actor

Paper Dolls (drama)........ Conrad (1984)

RICHMAN, PETER MARK—actor
b: Apr 16, 1927, Philadelphia, Pa.

Cain's Hundred (police)
.... Nicholas "Nick" Cain (1961–62)
Longstreet (drama)
.... Duke Paige (1971–72)
Dynasty (drama)
.... Andrew Laird (1981–84)

A cold-looking, tight-lipped actor who has been one of television's most familiar supporting players, in hundreds of series episodes from the 1950s to the '80s. He excels at ruthless crime lords and similar villains; even in the one series in which he starred, *Cain's Hundred*, he played an underworld lawyer who had decided to prosecute his former associates (20 years later, curiously, he was Blake Carrington's lawyer on *Dynasty*). Early in his career he was known simply as Mark Richman.

RICHMOND, BRANSCOMBE—actor

b: Aug 8, Los Angeles, Calif. r: Tahiti, Hawaii

Hawaiian Heat (police) . . . . . . Harker (1984)
Heart of the City (drama)
. . . . Sgt. Halui (1986–)

Actor and stuntman of Polynesian ancestry.

RICHMOND, STEVE—actor

Baa Baa Black Sheep (drama)
. . . . Cpl. Stan Richards (1977–78)

RICHTER, DEBI—actress

Aspen (drama) . . . . Angela Morelli (1977)
All Is Forgiven (com) . . . Sherry Levy (1986)

A former beauty queen; Miss California of 1975.

RICHWINE, MARIA—actress

b: Jun 22, Cali, Colombia

a.k.a. Pablo (com) . . . Carmen Rivera (1984)

RICKLES, DON—comedian

b: May 8, 1926, Queens, N.Y.

The Don Rickles Show (var)
. . . . host (1968–69)
The Don Rickles Show (com)
. . . . Don Robinson (1972)
C.P.O. Sharkey (com)
. . . . C.P.O. Otto Sharkey (1976–78)
Foul-Ups, Bleeps & Blunders (com)
. . . . host (1984–85)

Don Rickles, an elfish, balding little man with a malicious grin and a steady stream of put-downs of all around him, is television's leading purveyor of insult comedy. He got off to a slow start in show business and did not begin to play the more important nightclubs until the late 1950s. Trained as an actor, he appeared in some TV dramas during the 1950s, on *Stage 7, Four Star Playhouse,* and other series, and during the 1960s supplemented his club work with numerous appearances in drama and comedy supporting roles. On *The Addams Family* he played a burglar who didn't know what he was getting into when he tried to rob the Addams manse; on *The Dick Van Dyke Show* he was a stickup man who robbed Rob and Laura in an elevator, then got stuck with them there; in *The Wild Wild West* he was one of that series' parade of mad scientists (Asmodeus the Magician).

Don believes that his real breakthrough came on the night of October 7, 1965, when he made his first appearance on *The Tonight Show* and brought down the house with his freewheeling, rapid-fire barbs (everyone is a "dummy" to Don). His reputation was solidified by frequent guest shots on other talk and variety shows, especially *The Dean Martin Show*—where, in his first appearance, he skewered a bewildered Roy Rogers and Dale Evans. Don made a pilot for a situation comedy in 1965, called *Kibbee Hates Finch,* in which he played a fire captain with a jealous subordinate, but it did not make the schedule. Two versions of *The Don Rickles Show* later did, but both were unsuccessful; the first was a combination variety show and roast, the second a situation comedy with Don as a family man beset by life's aggravations. Guest appearances seemed to suit him better (a little Don goes a long way . . .), although *C.P.O. Sharkey,* in which he played a navy man, lasted for two years.

As might be expected, Don is a favorite on "roast" telecasts.

RIDDLE, JIMMY—

Hee Haw (var) . . . . regular (1969–83)

RIDDLE, NELSON—orchestra leader

b: Jun 1, 1921, Oradell, N.J.* d: Oct 6, 1985

The Nat "King" Cole Show (var)
. . . . orch. leader (1956–57)
The Rosemary Clooney Show (var)
. . . . orch. leader (1956–57)
The Frank Sinatra Show (var)
. . . . orch. leader (1957–58)
The Smothers Brothers Comedy Hour (var)
. . . . orch. leader (1967–69)
The Summer Smothers Brothers Show (var)
. . . . orch. leader (1968)
The Leslie Uggams Show (var)
. . . . orch. leader (1969)
The Tim Conway Comedy Hour (var)
. . . . orch. leader (1970)
CBS Newcomers (var) . . orch. leader (1971)
The Julie Andrews Hour (var)
. . . . orch. leader (1972–73)

*Some sources give Hackensack, N.J.

The Helen Reddy Show (var)
.... orch. leader (1973)

RIDDLERS, THE—

Sing It Again (quiz)...... regulars (1950–51)

RIDGELY, ROBERT—actor

The Gallant Men (drama)
.... Lt. Frank Kimbro (1962–63)
Domestic Life (com).. Cliff Hamilton (1984)

Ridgely was a familiar voice on Saturday morning cartoons during the '70s and '80s, providing voices for Tarzan, Flash Gordon, Thundarr the Barbarian, and other superheroes.

RIDGEWAY, FREDDY—actor

Life with Father (com)
.... Whitney Day (1955)

RIFKIN, RON—actor
b: New York City, N.Y.

Adam's Rib (com)
.... Asst. D.A. Roy Mendelsohn (1973)
When Things Were Rotten (com)
.... Prince John (1975)
Husbands, Wives & Lovers (com)
.... Ron Willis (1978)
One Day at a Time (com)
.... Nick Handris (1980–81)
The Winds of War (drama)
.... Mark Hartley (1983)
Falcon Crest (drama).. Dr. Lantry (1983–84)

RIGG, DIANA—actress
b: Jul 20, 1938, Doncaster, England r: Jodhpur, India

The Avengers (drama)
.... Emma Peel (1966–68)
Diana (com) ...... Diana Smythe (1973–74)

The image of Diana Rigg most viewers have—a coolly beautiful, athletic young woman clad in black leather, karate-chopping her way through a forest of bad guys —is so striking that it's unlikely to ever be eradicated, no matter what else she does. Who could forget *that*?

The actress who played Mrs. Peel to perfection was a trained Shakespearean performer, a member of the Royal Shakespeare Company who had made her name onstage in London in the late '50s and early '60s doing distinctly heavier stuff. When *The Avengers'* first lady agent (Honor Blackman) left the show, Diana was signed as her replacement, and it was she who American viewers saw when the series was exported to the U.S. in 1966. Diana attempted a U.S. situation comedy in 1973, a rather routine affair about an English divorcée living in New York, but it failed. Otherwise, she has done little U.S. television—only an occasional TV movie or special—though she bridles at the suggestion that *The Avengers* is the sum total of her career. Her other appearances, though infrequent, have generally been more substantial (*Witness for the Prosecution,* 1982; *King Lear,* 1984; etc.).

RIGHTEOUS BROTHERS, THE—singers
Bill Medley, b: Sep 19, 1940, Santa Ana, Calif.
Bobby Hatfield, b: Aug 10, 1940, Beaver Dam, Wis. r: Anaheim, Calif.

Shindig (music) .. frequent guests (1964–66)

RIHA, BOBBY—juvenile actor
b: 1958, Flushing, N.Y.

The Debbie Reynolds Show (com)
.... Bruce Landers (1969–70)

RILEY, JACK—actor
b: Dec 30, Cleveland, Ohio

Occasional Wife (com)
.... Wally Frick (1966–67)
The Bob Newhart Show (com)
.... Elliot Carlin (1972–78)
Keep On Truckin' (var) ...... regular (1975)
The Tim Conway Show (var)
.... regular (1980)

RILEY, JEANNINE—actress
b: 1939, Madera, Calif.

Petticoat Junction (com)
.... Billie Jo Bradley (1963–65)
Hee Haw (var).......... regular (1969–71)
Dusty's Trail (com)
.... Lulu McQueen (1973)

RILEY, LARRY—black actor
b: Jun 20, Memphis, Tenn.

Stir Crazy (adv)
.... Harry Fletcher (1985–86)

RINARD, FLORENCE—panelist
b: c. 1902 d: Oct 18, 1984

Twenty Questions (quiz). panelist (1949–55)

The wife of Fred Van De Venter, and co-creator with him of *Twenty Questions,* which they began on radio in the late 1940s.

RINGWALD, MOLLY—juvenile actress
b: Feb 16, 1968, Sacramento, Calif.

The Facts of Life (com)
.... Molly Parker (1979–80)

RINKER, JULIA—singer

Three's Company (com)
.... sang theme (1977–84)

RIPLEY, JOE—host

Armstrong Circle Theatre (drama)
.... host/narrator (1952–53)

RIPLEY, ROBERT L.—host, writer
b: Dec 25, 1893, Santa Rosa, Calif. d: May 27, 1949

Believe It or Not (var) .... host (1949)

The cartoonist who created "Ripley's Believe It or Not" for newspapers in 1918, and who spent the rest of his life single-mindedly tracking down bizarre and sometimes grotesque curiosities around the world to fill its columns. He brought the feature to public exhibitions, to radio, to film shorts, and finally to television in March 1949. Less than three months later, while preparing to host a telecast, he died suddenly of a heart attack. The show survived him by about a year and was brought back successfully in the 1980s with Jack Palance as host.

RISLEY, ANN—comedienne

NBC's Saturday Night Live (com)
.... regular (1980–81)

RIST, ROBBIE—juvenile actor

Lucas Tanner (drama)
.... Glendon Farrell (1974–75)
The Mary Tyler Moore Show (com)
.... David Baxter (1976–77)
Battlestar Galactica (sci fi) .. Dr. Zee (1980)

RITCH, STEVEN—actor

Broken Arrow (wes)..... Nukaya (1956–58)

RITTER, JOHN—actor
b: Sep 17, 1948, Burbank, Calif.

The Waltons (drama)
.... Rev. Matthew Fordwick (1972–77)
Three's Company (com)
.... Jack Tripper (1977–84)
Three's a Crowd (com)
.... Jack Tripper (1984–85)

Emmy Award: Best Actor in a Comedy Series, for *Three's Company* (1984)

It hardly seemed likely that the son of one of country music's most famous western singers—a burly baritone who strummed his way through scores of sagebrush film classics in the '40s—would become a first-rank TV comedian in the '70s and '80s. Such a possibility didn't occur to Tex Ritter's son John either, as he pursued a psychology degree in college. However, halfway through his college years, John was invited to take part in a U.S.-British theatrical exchange program, and the acting bug bit. Upon graduation he immediately went into stage work, largely in classics such as *The Glass Menagerie* and works by Shakespeare. Barely a year out of college he appeared in his first movie, Disney's *The Barefoot Executive* (about a chimpanzee who picks hit TV shows) and he also began to play guest roles in TV series—*Hawaii Five-O, Medical Center, M*A*S*H, The Mary Tyler Moore Show,* and others. His most familiar role during the mid '70s was the recurring part of young Rev. Fordwick on *The Waltons.*

In 1977 John began the role that fit him perfectly, that of the high-spirited, slapstick Jack Tripper (who did in fact trip a lot) on the sexy comedy *Three's Company.* Critics lambasted the show as "jiggle" TV at its worst, but it was an enormous hit, and John was singled out as a major comic "find." During and after the run of the series and its spin-off he appeared in a steady stream of TV movies and specials, some of them dramas (e.g., *Pray TV,* 1982), but mostly light romantic comedies.

RITTER, TEX—country singer, actor
b: Jan 12, 1906, Panola County, Texas d: Jan 2, 1974

Five Star Jubilee (var)
.... host (1961)

The legendary western singer, a burly, well-educated folklorist who appeared with guitar and horse (White Flash) in innumerable second features of the '30s and '40s; it was also he who sang, in a rumbling, haunting baritone, the title theme in the Gary Cooper western classic *High Noon.* Tex's television appearances were few, aside from country music shows—an episode of *Zane Grey Theater* in the '50s, one of *The Rebel* in 1961. He later became involved in politics, running unsuccessfully for senator and governor in Tennessee. His son is TV star John Ritter.

RIVERA, CHITA—Broadway actress, dancer
b: Jan 23, 1933, Washington, D.C.

The New Dick Van Dyke Show (com)
.... Connie Richardson (1973–74)

RIVERA, GERALDO—newscaster
b: Jul 4, 1943, New York City, N.Y.

20/20 (mag) .... correspondent (1978–85)

Emmy Awards: Best News Segment, for the *20/20* reports "Arson for Profit" (1980) and "Formula for Disaster" (1981)

Geraldo Rivera is perhaps television's extreme example of advocacy journalism; his energetic aggressiveness and commitment in pursuing social welfare exposés is so transparent that he is practically a caricature of the genre. He may not have invented "ambush journalism" (e.g., chasing important people through the parking lot to their limos, with microphone in hand, shouting incriminating questions), but he certainly refined it to a high art.

Geraldo's dedication to righting social wrongs springs from his own background. A graduate of Brooklyn Law School, he practiced law representing the poor people on New York's Lower East Side during the late 1960s. In 1970 he became an investigative reporter for WABC-TV in New York and soon gained considerable attention (and results) from a headline-making exposé of the dreadful conditions at Willowbrook, a state mental institution. During the mid-1970s, he hosted more than 30 editions of ABC's late-night program *Good Night, America* and was also a regular contributor to *Good Morning, America.* In 1978 he became *20/20*'s equivalent of CBS's Mike Wallace, pinning malefactors to the wall with his often sensational—but always thoroughly researched—reports.

RIVERS, JOAN—comedienne
b: Jun 8, 1933*, Brooklyn, N.Y.

The Tonight Show Starring Johnny Carson (talk) .... regular guest host (1983–86)
The Late Show (talk) .... host (1986–   )

"Can we talk?" she rasps, launching into a stream of chatter about obesity, infidelity, gynecology, fertility, and what's wrong with just about everyone ("Rod Stewart a sex symbol? I mean—the man has got acne—you could play connect-the-dots for a year on his head! And Mick Jagger? He could French-kiss a moose!"). Nor does she spare herself ("I was the ugliest child ever born in Larchmont, New York . . . oh, please! The doctor looked at me and slapped my mother!"). Joan Rivers is America's leading outrageous dame of the 1980s, familiar and controversial from her many appearances on late-night TV.

Joan started as a writer and stand-up comic in "dives and strip joints" (as she puts it). After a long apprenticeship, including a stint with Chicago's Second City troupe, she made her first big splash in a guest shot on *The Tonight Show* in February 1965. Johnny Carson had her back many times, made her one of his most frequent guest hosts, and finally the *only* guest host (in 1983). Along the way she scripted a TV movie (*The Girl Most Likely To,* 1973), wrote a best-selling book (*Having a Baby Can Be a Scream,* 1974), created a sitcom (*Husbands, Wives & Lovers,* 1978), and did guest shots on such shows as *Saturday Night Live.* Finally, doing what she does best, she launched her own highly publicized late-night talk show in competition with Carson in 1986. "Shocking people is my job," she told *TV Guide.* "If I'm vulgar, the whole country's vulgar."

*Some sources—including Joan herself at times—give 1935 or 1937. Ask her and she'll probably bite your head off.

RIZZUTO, PHIL—sportscaster
b: Sep 25, 1918, New York City, N.Y.

Down You Go (quiz)
.... regular panelist (1954–55)

A former major-league baseball player.

ROAD, MIKE—actor

Buckskin (wes)
.... Marshal Tom Sellers (1958–59)
The Roaring Twenties (drama)
.... Lt. Joe Switolski (1960–62)
Jonny Quest (cartn)
.... Race Bannon (voice) (1964–65)

ROARKE, JOHN—comedian
b: Feb 29, Providence, R.I.

Fridays (var)............ regular (1980–82)

ROAT, RICHARD—actor
b: Hartford, Conn.

From Here to Eternity (drama)
.... Mr. Austin (1980)

ROBARDS, GLENN—actor

Flamingo Road (drama)
.... Jasper, the butler (1981–82)

ROBARDS, JASON, SR.—actor
b: Dec 31, 1892, Hillsdale, Mich. d: Apr 4, 1963

Acapulco (adv)............... Max (1961)

A prominent character actor in films from
the silent era to 1961, and the father of
Jason Robards, Jr.; the latter is perhaps
more familiar to TV viewers for his many
appearances over the years in TV dramas.

ROBBINS, BARBARA—actress

The Aldrich Family (com)
.... Mrs. Alice Aldrich (1951–53)

ROBBINS, BRIAN—actor
b: Nov 22, Brooklyn, N.Y.

Head of the Class (com)..... Eric (1986–)

ROBBINS, CINDY—actress

The Tom Ewell Show (com)
.... Carol Potter (1960–61)

ROBBINS, FRED—host, disc jockey
b: Sep 28, 1923, Baltimore, Md.

Adventures in Jazz (music)...... host (1949)
Cavalcade of Bands (music)... emcee (1950)
The Robbins Nest (var)........ host (1950)
Kreisler Bandstand (music) ... emcee (1951)
Coke Time with Eddie Fisher (music)
.... host (1953–57)

Jive-talking New York disc jockey, a popular host of nighttime music and variety
shows during the 1950s. He was known, by
his press agent, at least, as "The Man with
the Spectacular Vernacular."

ROBBINS, GALE—actress, singer
b: May 7, 1922*, Chicago, Ill. d: Feb 18, 1980

Hollywood House (var) ... regular (1949–50)

ROBBINS, JANE MARLA—actress

79 Park Avenue (drama) .... Frannie (1977)

ROBBINS, MARTY—singer, songwriter
b: Sep 26, 1925, Glendale, Ariz. d: Dec 8,
1982

Grand Ole Opry (music) .. regular (1955–56)
Marty Robbins' Spotlight (var) .. host (1977)

The famous singer ("A White Sport Coat,"
"El Paso") was a popular guest star on both
country and popular music shows from the
1950s on—including even the rock-ori-
ented *Midnight Special.* He also hosted his
own syndicated series. In addition to his
musical career, Marty was a top-rated race
car driver on the NASCAR circuit.

ROBBINS, PETER—actor

Blondie (com)
.... Alexander Bumstead (1968–69)

ROBBINS, REX—actor

Nurse (drama) . Dr. Greg Manning (1981–82)

ROBERTO & ALICIA—dancers

Starlit Time (var) .... regulars (1950)

ROBERTS, ANDY—singer

Broadway Open House (talk)
.... regular (1950–51)

*Some sources give 1924.

The Ted Mack Family Hour (var)
.... regular (1951)

ROBERTS, DAVIS—black actor
b: Mar 7, 1917, Mobile, Ala.

Boone (drama)
.... Mr. Johnson (1983–84)

ROBERTS, DORIS—actress
b: Nov 4, 1930, St. Louis, Mo. r: N.Y.C., N.Y.

Angie (com)....... Theresa Falco (1979–80)
Maggie (com) .... Loretta (1981–82)
Remington Steele (drama)
.... Mildred Krebs (1983–86)

Emmy Award: Best Supporting Actress in a Drama, for an episode of *St. Elsewhere* (1983)

A frumpy, dumpy character actress familiar for her many supporting appearances over the years, mostly in comedies. She was the outrageous evangelist Dorelda Doremus on *Mary Hartman, Mary Hartman,* and Flo Flotsky on *Soap,* but she won her Emmy Award for a poignant portrayal of a bag lady on *St. Elsewhere.*

ROBERTS, EWAN—actor
b: Apr 29, 1914, Edinburgh, Scotland

Adventures of Sir Francis Drake (adv)
.... Morton, Earl of Lenox (1962)

ROBERTS, FRANCESCA—actress
b: Louisiana

Private Benjamin (com)
.... Pvt. Harriet Dorsey (1981)

ROBERTS, HOLLY—actress
b: McAllen, Texas

The Hamptons (drama)
.... Tracy Mortimer (1983)

ROBERTS, HOWARD—choral director
b: Jul 18, 1924, Burlington, N.J.

The Leslie Uggams Show (var)
.... singers (1969)

ROBERTS, JIM—singer

The Lawrence Welk Show (music)
.... regular (1955–82)

ROBERTS, JOAN—actress

Private Benjamin (com)
.... Pvt. Barbara Ann Glass (1981)

ROBERTS, KEN—host, announcer

Where Was I? (quiz) .... emcee (1952)

A leading announcer of the radio era, and the father of actor Tony Roberts.

ROBERTS, LOIS—actress

Broadside (com)
machinist's mate Molly McGuire (1964–65)

ROBERTS, LYNN—singer

The Sammy Kaye Show (var)
.... regular (1958–59)

ROBERTS, MARK—actor

The Front Page (drama)
.... Hildy Johnson (1949–50)
The Brothers Brannagan (drama)
.... Bob Brannagan (1960)

ROBERTS, MICHAEL D.—black actor

Baretta (police) .... Rooster (1975–78)
Manimal (police).......... Ty Earle (1983)
Double Trouble (com)
.... Mr. Arrechia (1984–85)

ROBERTS, PERNELL—actor
b: May 18, 1928*, Waycross, Ga.

Bonanza (wes) . Adam Cartwright (1959–65)
Trapper John, M.D. (drama)
Dr. John McIntyre (Trapper John) (1979–86)

Pernell Roberts is one of Hollywood's most celebrated examples of the dangers of walking out on a hit series. Quitting *Bonanza* is said to have cost him upwards of a million dollars. He did it to teach Hollywood a lesson about "junk TV," but instead it seems to have taught him one.

Pernell's lifelong war against authority and the status quo began in college, where he flunked out three times during the late 1940s when he wouldn't pay attention to his studies (a recent network biography discreetly says that he was "persuaded to leave college and begin working"). He joined the Arena Stage in Washington in

*Some sources give 1930.

1950 and for the next seven years played many serious stage roles up and down the East Coast, including several minor productions on Broadway. In 1955 he won a Drama Desk Award as the season's best off-Broadway actor for his performance in *Macbeth*.

Pernell moved west in 1957 to take a supporting role in the movie *Desire Under the Elms*, and stayed on to find more film and TV work. His big break came with the role of eldest son Adam in *Bonanza*, a series that became a megahit—and one that the former "serious" actor came to despise. Producers were the main target of his ire. "Give the silly asses half of what the scene requires and they think it's great," he complained. As for the show, it was all a Lie— wealthy men beating up on people and being made to look like heroes, when there was so much real misery in the world. After six years, he quit. "Don't be a damn fool, Pernell," argued costar Lorne Greene. "Take their money and buy your own studio." Instead, Pernell took a hike, convinced that his newly enhanced reputation would allow him to pick more meaningful roles.

What followed was 14 years in purgatory, playing regional theater and frequent but unrewarding guest roles on dozens of action shows not much different from the one he had left. Among them: *The Wild Wild West, Mission: Impossible, Marcus Welby, The Six Million Dollar Man, The Hardy Boys, Alias Smith and Jones* (a series that apparently drove its star, Peter Deuel, to suicide), and many others. Just before winning his comeback role in *Trapper John*, he was reduced to playing a town sheriff in a TV movie gem called *Hot Rod* ("Lots of revving engines and screeching tires drown out the dumb dialogue" observed one critic).

Pernell presumably thought *Trapper John* was pretty thin stuff too, but it paid well and this time he stuck with it. Complaining all the way. "Ah, that's Pernell for you," commented a friend. "He's teed off because they won't let him bring Chekov to City Hospital."

ROBERTS, RACHEL—actress
b: Sep 20, 1927, Llanelly, Wales d: Nov 26, 1980

The Tony Randall Show (com)
.... Mrs. Bonnie McClellan (1976–78)

ROBERTS, RANDOLPH—actor

Happy Days (com)
.... Chuck Cunningham (1974–75)

The second—and last—actor to play Chuck, the "lost brother" on *Happy Days*.

ROBERTS, ROY—actor
b: Mar 19, 1900, Tampa, Fla. d: May 28, 1975

The Gale Storm Show (com)
.... Capt. Huxley (1956–60)
Petticoat Junction (com)
.... Norman Curtis (1963–64)
The Beverly Hillbillies (com)
.... John Cushing (1964–67)
The Lucy Show (com)
.... Harrison Cheever (1965–68)
Gunsmoke (wes) ..... Mr. Bodkin (1965–75)

ROBERTS, STEPHEN—actor

Mr. Novak (drama)
.... Mr. Stan Peeples (1963–65)
Ike (drama)
.... Pres. Franklin D. Roosevelt (1979)

ROBERTS, TANYA—actress
b: Oct 15, 1955, The Bronx, N.Y.

Charlie's Angels (drama)
.... Julie Rogers (1980–81)

ROBERTS, TONY—actor
b: Oct 22, 1939, New York City, N.Y.

Rosetti and Ryan (drama)
.... Joseph Rosetti (1977)
The Four Seasons (com) .. Ted Bolen (1984)
The Lucie Arnaz Show (com)
.... Jim Gordon (1985)

The curly-haired son of veteran radio and television announcer Ken Roberts. Tony has been active on television since the 1960s, in both nighttime and daytime (*The Edge of Night*, 1965–67).

ROBERTSON, CLIFF—actor
b: Sep 9, 1925, La Jolla, Calif.

Robert Montgomery Presents (summer) (drama) .... repertory player (1954)
Falcon Crest (drama)
.... Dr. Michael Ranson (1983–84)

Emmy Award: Best Actor in a Single Performance in a Drama, for *The Bob Hope*

Chrysler Theatre production "The Game" (1966)

A handsome, personable star of movies *(P.T. 109, Charly)* who has had an off-and-on television career. He was seen quite a bit in the early 1950s, while he was a struggling stage actor in New York. Among other things, he was Rod Brown on Saturday morning's *Rod Brown of the Rocket Rangers* (1953–54) and a repertory player on *Robert Montgomery Presents* (1954). He appeared in various TV dramatic productions during the later 1950s and early '60s, but was seen less often after that as his movie career took off. The few roles he did play were often memorable, however. He won an Emmy for a guest role on *Chrysler Theatre* in 1966 and then appeared on *Batman*—as cowboy criminal Shame with his wife Dina Merrill playing his accomplice, Calamity Jan.

During the late 1970s Cliff began to appear in TV movies and miniseries, including *Washington: Behind Closed Doors,* but his career was suddenly hobbled when he publicly accused Columbia Pictures mogul David Begelman of forging his name on a check. The accusation touched off a large-scale embezzlement scandal that rocked Hollywood and received a thorough airing in the best-selling book *Indecent Exposure.* Cliff is certain that he was blacklisted for several years as a result of his speaking up, but by the early 1980s he was working again, in films (*Brainstorm,* produced by Begelman's studio) and on television, including a regular role on *Falcon Crest.*

ROBERTSON, DALE—actor
b: Jul 14, 1923, Harrah, Okla. r: Oklahoma City, Okla.

Tales of Wells Fargo (wes)
.... Jim Hardie (1957–62)
The Iron Horse (wes)
.... Ben Calhoun (1966–68)
Death Valley Days (wes) .... host (1968–72)
Dynasty (drama)
.... Walter Lankershim (1981)

A tall, rugged star of movie and television westerns, including the top-rated 1950s hit *Tales of Wells Fargo.* An all-star athlete in college, Dale entered films in 1949 and quickly gained attention for his macho roles. His TV work in the '50s and '60s was

limited mostly to his three western series (listed above). He was later seen in occasional guest roles, including that of G-man Melvin Purvis in two TV films in 1974–75, and on *The Love Boat* in 1980.

ROBERTSON, DENNIS—actor
Tammy (com)
.... cousin Cletus Tarleton (1965–66)
The Tim Conway Show (com)
.... Sherman Bell (1970)

ROBIN, DIANE—actress
b: Jul 22, Los Angeles, Calif.

Makin' It (adv)............... Felice (1979)
Angie (com)........ Didi Malloy (1979–80)

ROBIN, TINA—singer
Sing Along (music) .... regular (1958)

ROBINSON, AL—ventriloquist
Alkali Ike (com)........ voice of Ike (1950)

ROBINSON, BARTLETT—actor
b: c. 1912, New York City, N.Y. d: Mar 26, 1986

Wendy and Me (com)
.... Willard Norton (1964–65)
Mona McCluskey (com)
.... Frank Caldwell (1965–66)

A prominent radio actor of the '30s and '40s; radio's original Perry Mason, among other roles.

ROBINSON, BUMPER—actor
Night Court (com) .... Leon (1985–86)

ROBINSON, CAROL—
Andy Williams Presents Ray Stevens (var)
.... regular (1970)

ROBINSON, CHARLES—black actor
b: Nov 9, Houston, Texas

Buffalo Bill (com) .... Newdell (1983–84)
Night Court (com)
..... court clerk Mac Robinson (1984–)

Charlie started out as a musician, and while still in grade school formed a group

724

called the Drells (later to gain fame, without him, as Archie Bell & the Drells). He performed in rock, rhythm and blues, and gospel groups until he was 21 and then turned to acting, first in regional theater and then (c. 1971) in Hollywood. He has played supporting roles in many TV movies and series episodes in the '70s and '80s.

ROBINSON, CHRIS—actor
b: Nov 5, 1938, Fort Lauderdale, Fla.

Twelve O'Clock High (drama)
... Tech. Sgt. Sandy Komansky (1965–67)

A veteran of more than 150 television roles, from the 1960s onward, Chris has starred since 1978 as Dr. Rick Webber on the daytime soap opera *General Hospital.*

ROBINSON, DOUG—actor
Alice (com) .... Doug (1984–85)

ROBINSON, FRAN—black actress
b: Apr 16, 1970, Vallejo, Calif. r: Charleston, S.C.

Charlie & Company (com)
.... Lauren Richmond (1985–86)

ROBINSON, JOHN MARK—actor
The San Pedro Beach Bums (com)
.... dancer (1977)

ROBINSON, LARRY—actor
The Goldbergs (com)
.... Sammy Goldberg (1949–52)

ROBINSON, MAX—black newscaster
b: May 1, 1939, Richmond, Va.

ABC Evening News (news)
.... anchorman (1978–83)
ABC Weekend News (news)
.... anchorman (1983–84)

Emmy Award: Best News Segment, for *Nightline:* "Post Election Special Edition" (1980)

Max Robinson was the first black anchor of a major network newscast, but he proved to be a thorn in the side of the white management that hired him. Robinson began his journalist career in Washington, D.C., where he joined WTOP-TV in 1965 and rose to become the anchor of that station's popular *Eyewitness News* from 1969–78. In 1978 he was hired by ABC to anchor the national desk (from Chicago) of the network's new, four-anchor *World News Tonight.*

A handsome man, with a fairly aggressive reporting style, Robinson proved a popular, mainstream reporter—until 1981, when, in a widely publicized speech at Smith College in Massachussets, he suddenly and bitterly denounced his network for practicing unconscious racism. He singled out his exclusion from the recent coverage of the Iranian hostage return and the inauguration of President Reagan, calling it an "orgy of . . . white patriotism" in which black people might "interfere." Further, he said, "I bring something more to ABC than the color on my face. I bring my history, my culture, my perspectives, which I insist are very important to all Americans." He then asserted that people in his position had been "courted, seduced, cajoled, intimidated to take one position, and that is of white men or women in blackface. I think that is demeaning to white people. I know it is demeaning to me."

Although Robinson later apologized (saying he had been referring to all of society, not just to ABC), ABC was outraged. He left the network in 1984 to return to local television.

ROBINSON, ROGER—black actor
b: May 2, 1940, Seattle, Wash.

Friends (com)
.... Mr. Warren Summerfield (1979)

ROBINSON, RUSSELL PHILLIP—black actor
The White Shadow (drama)
.... Manager Phil Jefferson (1979–81)

ROBINSON, SMOKEY—black singer
b: Feb 19, 1940, Detroit, Mich.

Motown Revue (var)........... host (1985)

The founder and lead singer for many years of the Miracles ("Shop Around," etc.), who became a solo star in the '80s. He is a key performer, songwriter, and executive of the Motown record empire.

ROBLE, CHET—pianist
b: c. 1908 d: Oct 31, 1962

Tin Pan Alley TV (var) ...... pianist (1950)
Stud's Place (var) .... pianist (1950–52)

ROCCO, ALEX—actor
b: Feb 29, 1936, Cambridge, Mass.

Three for the Road (adv)
.... Pete Karras (1975)
79 Park Avenue (drama)
.... Frank Millerson (1977)

ROCHE, EUGENE—actor
b: Sep 22, 1928, Boston, Mass.

The Corner Bar (com) .. Frank Flynn (1973)
Soap (com)
.... atty. E. Ronald Mallu (1978–81)
Good Time Harry (com)
.... Jimmy Hughes (1980)
Webster (com) .... Bill Parker (1984–86)

ROCK, BLOSSOM—actress
b: Aug 21, 1896, Philadelphia, Pa. d: Jan 14, 1978

The Addams Family (com)
.... Grandmama Addams (1964–66)

A veteran comic supporting actress in movies of the '30s and '40s (under the name Marie Blake). She was the sister of actress-singer Jeanette MacDonald.

ROCKET, CHARLES—comedian

NBC's Saturday Night Live (com)
.... regular (1980–81)

ROCKWELL, ROBERT—actor
b: Oct 5, 1921, Chicago, Ill. r: Lake Bluff, Ill.

Our Miss Brooks (com)
.... Philip Boynton (1952–56)
The Man from Blackhawk (wes)
.... Sam Logan (1959–60)

Robert Rockwell is best remembered as the handsome, impossibly dense biology teacher who was the object of Eve Arden's affections in *Our Miss Brooks.* He began the role on radio in the late 1940s, while he was a struggling actor in B films. When the series moved to television, so did he, and he became closely identified with it.

Rockwell played other roles on TV in the '50s and '60s. On the very first episode of *Superman* in 1951 he portrayed Jor-El, Superman's father on the doomed planet Krypton. He also made multiple appearances on *The Loretta Young Show* (usually as Loretta's husband), *Perry Mason,* and *Lassie,* and starred in his own western series in 1959–60, *The Man From Blackhawk* —as a frontier insurance investigator. Since the 1970s Rockwell has been less active on TV. He played Bill Cosby's boss, the head coach, on a few episodes of *The Bill Cosby Show* in 1969–70 and was briefly a regular on daytime's *Search for Tomorrow* in 1977–78. In the '80s he has turned up only occasionally, on series such as *Benson, Dallas,* and *Dynasty.* When he is recognized, however, it is almost invariably as "Mr. Boynton."

ROCKWELL, ROCKY—singer, trumpeter
b: c. 1927, St. Joseph, Mo.

The Lawrence Welk Show (music)
.... regular (1955–62)

RODD, MARCIA—actress
b: Jul 8, 1940, Lyons, Kansas

The David Frost Revue (com)
.... regular (1971–73)
The Dumplings (com) ..... Stephanie (1976)
13 Queens Boulevard (com)
.... Elaine Dowling (1979)
Flamingo Road (drama)
.... Alice Kovacs (1981–82)
Trapper John, M.D. (drama)
.... E. J. Riverside (1983–86)
The Four Seasons (com)
.... Claudia Zimmer (1984)

RODGERS, JIMMIE—singer
b: Sep 18, 1933*, Camas, Wash.

The Jimmie Rodgers Show (var)
.... host (1959)
The Jimmie Rodgers Show (var)
.... host (1969)

The tousle-haired, shy-looking young singer who scored a major hit in the late 1950s with a number of catchy, folk-oriented songs, including "Honeycomb" and "Kisses Sweeter Than Wine." Close on the heels of this success, he appeared on all the top variety shows, had his own sum-

*Some sources give Sept. 19th.

mer series in 1959, and even had his life recounted on *This Is Your Life*. After ten years on the popular music circuit, and several acting roles, Jimmie was involved in a mysterious December 1967 accident that almost claimed his life. He was discovered unconscious and bleeding in his car beside the road; according to conflicting accounts, he had either fallen or been struck on the head by an off-duty police officer who had pulled him over for a traffic violation. For several weeks he hovered between life and death; he eventually recovered sufficiently to resume some activities, including another summer show in 1969, but his career has been relatively low-key ever since.

RODGERS, PAMELA—actress
b: c. 1944, Houston, Texas

Hey Landlord (com)
.... Timothy Morgan (1966–67)
The Jonathan Winters Show (var)
.... regular (1968)
Rowan & Martin's Laugh-In (var)
.... regular (1969–70)

A former Miss Texas. Wa-Hoo!

RODMAN, VIC—actor

Noah's Ark (drama)
.... Dr. Sam Rinehart (1956–57)

RODRIGUES, PERCY—black actor
b: Jun 13, 1924, Montreal, Canada

Peyton Place (drama)
.... Dr. Harry Miles (1968–69)
The Silent Force (police)
.... Jason Hart (1970–71)
Executive Suite (drama)
.... Malcolm Gibson (1976–77)
Sanford (com).......... Winston (1980–81)

RODRIGUEZ, MARCO—actor

Bay City Blues (drama)........ Bird (1983)

RODRIGUEZ, PAUL—actor
b: Jan 19, Mazatlan, Mexico

a.k.a. Pablo (com)
.... Paul (Pablo) Rivera (1984)

Mexican-American comedian, the son of immigrant farm workers.

ROE, CHUBBY CHUCK—comedian

Saturday Night Jamboree (music)
.... regular (1948–49)

ROGERS, CHARLES "BUDDY"—actor, singer
b: Aug 13, 1904, Olathe, Kan.

Cavalcade of Bands (music)... emcee (1951)

A handsome, friendly matinee idol of the '20s and '30s, long married to silent movie queen Mary Pickford. Graying but still good-looking, he made a few appearances on television later in life—including *The Cavalcade of Bands* (and other music shows, leading his own orchestra) in the 1950s; two episodes of *The Lucy Show* in 1967; and *Petticoat Junction* in 1968. An extremely wealthy man, he was long one of Hollywood's most beloved senior citizens.

ROGERS, JAIME—choreographer

The Andy Williams Show (var)
.... dancers (1969–70)
The Ken Berry "Wow" Show (var)
.... dancers (1972)
The Helen Reddy Show (var)
.... dancers (1973)
The Hudson Brothers Show (var)
.... dancers (1974)

ROGERS, JESSE—country singer

Hayloft Hoedown (music).... regular (1948)

"Ranger Joe" on radio and early television.

ROGERS, KASEY—actress

Peyton Place (drama)
.... Julie Anderson (1964–69)
Bewitched (com) ..... Louise Tate (1966–72)

ROGERS, KENNY—singer, actor
b: Aug 21, 1937, Houston, Texas*

Rollin' on the River (music).. host (1971–73)

The bearded music superstar of the '80s started out as a jazz artist, then switched to pop-folk music as a member of The New Christy Minstrels, then to rock 'n' roll as leader of the First Edition. It was with the

*Some sources give Crocket, Texas.

latter group that he appeared on the syndicated series *Rollin' on the River*. After that he switched again, with even greater success, to syrupy country ballads that became huge sellers in the late '70s and '80s. He has appeared in quite a few specials and TV movies, some of them based on his story songs *The Gambler* and *Coward of the County*.

ROGERS, MARIANNE GORDON—

Hee Haw (var) .... regular (1972–)

The wife of Kenny Rogers.

ROGERS, MIMI—actress
b: Jan 27, Coral Gables, Fla.

The Rousters (adv) ... Ellen Slade (1983–84)
Paper Dolls (drama)
.... Blair Harper Fenton (1984)

ROGERS, ROY—cowboy actor
b: Nov 5, 1911*, Cincinnati, Ohio

The Roy Rogers Show (wes)
.... as himself (1951–57)
The Roy Rogers & Dale Evans Show (var)
.... cohost (1962)

Roy Rogers, "the King of the Cowboys," is less a performer than a cultural artifact, an icon of Americana that will be remembered long after the titles of his western movies and songs have been forgotten (most of them already have been). He came to California in 1930 as a fruit picker, but soon gained attention as a western singer, especially after forming a group called the Sons of the Pioneers. His boyish good looks and sincerity began to win him small film roles in 1935; by the 1940s he was the number-one western box-office star, displacing Gene Autry.

When cowboy films declined and television came on the scene, Roy moved easily into the new medium, as did Autry, producing simple little B films for TV as he had for the Saturday matinees. All of them featured the wonder horse Trigger and Roy's charming wife Dale Evans ("the Queen of the West"). Roy and Dale hosted a wholesome variety show in the fall of 1962, after their western series had left the air, but it was short-lived. In later years they were

*Some sources give 1912.

seen almost exclusively in guest appearances, always warmly received, always to the strains of their famous theme song "Happy Trails to You" (written by Dale). Although wealthy beyond counting (worth an estimated $100 million), Roy was not above an occasional cameo appearance in which he was least expected—as when he played a drunk in the 1983 Kenny Rogers TV movie *The Gambler—The Adventure Continues*. However, he knows his place in history, having said that when his time comes he expects to be stuffed and mounted on ol' Trigger (who is already stuffed) in his museum out West.

ROGERS, STEPHEN—actor

Chiefs (drama) .... Sonny Butts (1983)

ROGERS, STEVEN—actor

Combat (drama)
.... Doc Walton (1962–63)

ROGERS, TIMMIE—black singer
b: Jul 4, 1915, Detroit, Mich.

Sugar Hill Times (var) ...... regular (1949)
The Melba Moore-Clifton Davis Show (var)
.... regular (1972)

A veteran vaudeville performer on the black circuit; his trademark was an enthusiastic "Oh yeah!"

ROGERS, VANETTA—

Pat Paulsen's Half a Comedy Hour (var)
.... regular (1970)

ROGERS, WAYNE—actor
b: Apr 7, 1933, Birmingham, Ala.

Stagecoach West (wes)
.... Luke Perry (1960–61)
*M*A*S*H* (com)
.... Capt. John McIntyre (1972–75)
City of Angels (drama)
.... Jake Axminster (1976)
House Calls (com)
.... Dr. Charley Michaels (1979–82)
Chiefs (drama)
.... Chief Will Henry Lee (1983)

Handsome, wavy-haired Wayne Rogers has long been known as one of television's "nice guys." He started out in New York in the late 1950s, after service in the navy, and gained his first experience in small parts onstage and on such TV shows as *Kraft Theatre, Lamp Unto My Feet,* and the daytime serial *The Edge of Night.* For a time he roomed with another struggling young actor, Peter Falk, in a fifth floor walk-up; the two have remained lifelong friends.

Wayne moved to Hollywood in 1959 and scored an early break as a regular in *Stagecoach West,* but the series was short-lived. He played many guest parts during the 1960s, in series ranging from *Combat* to *Gomer Pyle,* and was frequently seen in supporting roles on *The F.B.I.* However, he did not attract much notice until 1972, when, as Trapper John in *M*A*S*H,* he suddenly became an "overnight" star.

Wayne is a perfectionist, and by that time he was feeling more and more strongly that he should have some say over scripts and production. *M*A*S*H* allowed him none, so in 1975 he quit—resulting in multiple lawsuits—and moved on to his own starring series, a detective show set in the 1930s and called *City of Angels.* TV in 1976 was moving toward contemporary jiggle, not period drama, however, and the series quickly sank. Wayne missed out on the chance to reprise his role of Trapper John in a new medical drama (Pernell Roberts got the role instead), but he wound up with something even better—the opportunity to costar with Lynn Redgrave in, and have total creative control over, a medical comedy called *House Calls.*

In addition to his acting career, Wayne is one of Hollywood's financial wizards, handling investments and finances for many Hollywood celebrities, including his old friend Peter Falk.

ROKER, RENNIE—black actor
b: Sep 6, New York City, N.Y.

Nobody's Perfect (com)
.... Det. Ramsey (1980)

A heavyset former record-promotion man and label executive (he still produces concerts), who got into TV acting during the 1960s. Among other things, he had a recurring role on *Gomer Pyle* for a season or two.

ROKER, ROXIE—black actress
b: Aug 28, 1929, Miami, Fla. r: Brooklyn, N.Y.

The Jeffersons (com)
.... Helen Willis (1975–85)

Stylish black actress who played one half of the first integrated couple on a major nighttime series—opposite white actor Franklin Cover (Roxie has long been married to a white husband in real life). She was a secretary and administrator for NBC in New York for many years before becoming a full-time actress in 1969.

ROLAND, WILL—orchestra leader

Arthur Godfrey and His Friends (var)
.... orch. leader (1955–58)
Arthur Godfrey's Talent Scouts (talent)
.... orch. leader (1955–58)

ROLIKE, HANK—black actor

The Last Precinct (com) .. Sundance (1986)

ROLIN, JUDI—singer, actress
b: c. 1947, Lake Villa, Ill.

The Dean Martin Summer Show (var)
.... regular (1966)

ROLLE, ESTHER—black actress
b: Nov 8, 1922*, Pompano Beach, Fla.

Maude (com)....... Florida Evans (1972–74)
Good Times (com)
.... Florida Evans (1974–79)

Emmy Award: Best Supporting Actress in a Drama Special, for *Summer of My German Soldier* (1979)

Hefty actress, active on the New York stage in the 1960s; she was an original member of the Negro Ensemble Company.

ROLLINS, HOWARD E., JR.—black actor
b: Oct 17, 1952, Baltimore, Md.

Wildside (wes)..... Bannister Sparks (1985)

ROMAN, GREG—actor

The New Breed (police)
.... Ptlmn. Pete Garcia (1961–62)

*Some sources give 1933.

ROMAN, JOSEPH—actor
b: May 23, South Philadelphia, Pa.

Quincy, M.E. (police) ... Sgt. Brill (1976–83)

ROMAN, LULU—comedienne
b: c. 1947 r: Dallas, Texas

Hee Haw (var).......... regular (1969–)
Hee Haw Honeys (com)
.... Lulu Honey (1978–79)

Corpulent (c. 275-pound) comedienne seen
on *Hee Haw*. A former comic go-go dancer
in Dallas, Lulu had a serious drug problem
during the 1970s and was dropped from the
show for a time, but she found religion and
mended her ways. She now tours as a gospel singer.

ROMAN, PAUL REID—black host

The Music Scene (music)
.... rotating host (1969)

ROMAN, RUTH—actress
b: Dec 23, 1923*, Boston, Mass.

The Long Hot Summer (drama)
.... Minnie Littlejohn (1965–66)
Knots Landing (drama)
.... Sylvia Lean (1986–)

ROMANO, ANDY—actor

Get Christie Love (police)
.... Det. Joe Caruso (1974–75)
79 Park Avenue (drama) .. Hal Roper (1977)
Friends (com) ... Mr. Frank Richards (1979)

ROMANUS, RICHARD—actor
b: Feb 28, Barre, Vt.

Foul Play (drama)
.... Capt. Vito Lombardi (1981)
Strike Force (police)
.... Lt. Charlie Gunzer (1981–82)

ROMAY, LINA—singer, actress

Mayor of Hollywood (var) . secretary (1952)

Latin singer long associated with the
Xavier Cugat Orchestra.

ROMERO, CARLOS—actor

Wichita Town (wes)
.... Rico Rodriguez (1959–60)
*Some sources give 1922 or 1924.

Falcon Crest (drama)
.... Carlo Agretti (1982)

ROMERO, CESAR—actor
b: Feb 15, 1907, New York City, N.Y.

Your Chevrolet Showroom (var)
.... emcee (1953–54)
Passport to Danger (drama)
.... Steve McQuinn (1954–56)
Take a Good Look (quiz)
.... panelist (1959–61)
Falcon Crest (drama)
.... Peter Stavros (1985–)

One of Hollywood's most suave, charming
"Latin lovers" of the '30s and '40s (though
he never married in real life). He was also
at one time the big screen's Cisco Kid.
Cesar appeared often in television dramas
during the '50s and '60s and starred as a
diplomatic courier in the syndicated *Passport to Danger*. However, he is probably
best remembered as Batman's number-one
archenemy, the garish, giggling "Joker," in
many episodes of that hit series. A fine fate
for a onetime Latin lover!

ROMERO, NED—actor

Dan August (police)
.... Sgt. Joe Rivera (1970–71)
The D.A. (drama)
...... investigator Bob Ramirez (1971–72)

ROMINE, CHARLES—narrator

The Search (doc).......... narrator (1955)

ROMOFF, COLIN—orchestra leader
b: Oct 15, 1924, New York City, N.Y.

The Andy Williams Show (var)
.... orch. leader (1962–63)

ROONEY, ANDY—writer, commentator
b: Jan 14, 1920, Albany, N.Y.

60 Minutes (pub aff)
.... correspondent (1978–)

Emmy Awards: Best News Writing, for
the *CBS News Hour* presentation "Black
History: Lost, Stolen or Strayed" (1969);
as writer and reporter for the *60 Minutes*
segments "Who Owns What in Amer-
ica" (1979), "Grain" (1981), and "Tanks"
(1982)

CBS News seems to nurture offbeat correspondents, whether it is Charles Kuralt and his "On the Road" wanderings, Charles Osgood and his news related poetry, or Andy Rooney and his whimsical "essays." Rooney is primarily a writer, one with a long and varied career. During World War II he served for three years as a reporter for the military newspaper *Stars and Stripes,* covering a number of dangerous missions. After the war he had a fling at writing for Hollywood (MGM optioned a book he had written), but that didn't pan out, so he turned to radio and television, writing for Arthur Godfrey from 1949–55 and for Garry Moore from 1959–65. He also free-lanced for magazines and for CBS news, contributing scripts for *Adventure, The Twentieth Century,* and—from 1962 to 1968—a series of inventive TV "essays" narrated by Harry Reasoner. These were idiosyncratic looks at such commonplace subjects as bridges, hotels, chairs, doors—and women. Though Andy clearly excelled at the offbeat, he won his first Emmy Award for a straightforward 1968 documentary on black America, narrated by Bill Cosby.

Andy began to appear on-camera during the 1970s, an impish, curmudgeonly little fellow, in such CBS news specials as "Mr. Rooney Goes to Washington" and "Mr. Rooney Goes to Work." In 1978 he became the regular essayist for *60 Minutes,* given a few minutes at the end of the show to expound on all sorts of things that irked or amused him. Mostly, that meant the little inconsistencies of everyday life. Take clothing sizes. "Why do I wear a size 7-½ hat but a size 16-½ shirt collar?" he asks. "Doesn't that sound as though I could put my shirt on over my hat with my collar buttoned?"

ROONEY, MICKEY—actor
b: Sep 23, 1920, Brooklyn, N.Y.

The Mickey Rooney Show (com)
.... Mickey Mulligan (1954–55)
Mickey (com) ..... Mickey Grady (1964–65)
NBC Follies (var) .... regular (1973)
One of the Boys (com)
.... Oliver Nugent (1982)

Emmy Award: Best Actor in a Dramatic Special, for *Bill* (1982)

This pint-sized bundle of energy is living proof that child actors *can* succeed as adults, if they work hard enough at it. Mickey has been performing—acting, singing, dancing, ad-libbing, hamming it up (whoa ... !)—since he was an infant in his parents' vaudeville act. From 1927–33 he romped, cigar in hand, through scores of *Mickey McGuire* comedy shorts; in 1937 he began the well-remembered *Andy Hardy* pictures, playing America's ultimate, exuberant teenager; and, shortly thereafter, he starred with Judy Garland in a series of memorable teen musicals.

After World War II, Mickey's movie career began to slow down, despite his prodigious efforts to keep it alive, and he plunged early into television. In 1954 he starred in his own comedy series about a young man trying to break into show business (subtitled *Hey, Mulligan!*). He appeared in numerous TV dramatic productions too, and was several times nominated for an Emmy Award. In the '60s he made multiple appearances on *Dick Powell Theatre,* as well as on *Wagon Train, Naked City, The Twilight Zone, The Fugitive, The Lucy Show,* and others. He also headlined another short-lived comedy, this one about a young man who inherited a marina.

Mickey's TV appearances were somewhat less frequent in the '70s, and in 1978, on *The Tomorrow Show,* he announced his retirement. No one believed him for a minute. Sure enough, the following year he was back on Broadway scoring one of the greatest triumphs of his career in the high-energy musical *Sugar Babies.* Not long after that, he had another very different success in the dramatic TV movie *Bill,* playing a retarded older man. He also plunged into his third situation comedy, *One of the Boys,* which was no more successful than the previous two. No matter. "You never stop learning. You never stop paying your dues," he enthused. "You do the best you can, and after you're finished, you ... try and do better next time."

Mickey's autobiography: *I.E.* (1965).

ROONEY, TIM—actor
b: 1947

Room for One More (com)
.... Jeff Rose (1962)
Mickey (com) ...... Timmy Grady (1964–65)

The son of Mickey Rooney, by the star's second (out of eight) marriages. Tim was at one time a *Mickey Mouse Club* Mouseketeer.

ROPER, ELMO—pollster
b: Jul 31, 1900 d: Apr 30, 1971

Presidential Straws in the Wind (pub aff)
.... regular (1948)

RORKE, HAYDEN—actor
b: Oct 23, 1910*, Brooklyn, N.Y.

Mr. Adams and Eve (com) . Steve (1957–58)
No Time for Sergeants (com)
.... Col. Farnsworth (1964–65)
I Dream of Jeannie (com)
.... Dr. Alfred Bellows (1965–70)

ROSARIO, BERT—actor
b: Nov 17, Juncos, Puerto Rico r: The Bronx, N.Y.

Sword of Justice (adv)
.... Hector Ramirez (1978–79)
a.k.a. Pablo (com) .... Manuel Rivera (1984)

ROSARIO, JOE—actor

Archie Bunker's Place (com)
.... Raoul (1980–83)

ROSATO, TONY—comedian
b: Dec 26, 1954, Naples, Italy r: Toronto, Canada

Second City TV (com) .. Marcello (1980–81)
NBC's Saturday Night Live (com)
.... regular (1981–82)
Amanda's (com).............. Aldo (1983)
Night Heat (police) .. Whitey Low (1985–   )

Another graduate of Toronto's Second City Comedy troupe.

ROSE MARIE—actress
b: Aug 15, 1923, New York City, N.Y.

My Sister Eileen (com) ... Bertha (1960–61)
The Dick Van Dyke Show (com)
.... Sally Rogers (1961–66)
The Doris Day Show (com)
.... Myrna Gibbons (1969–71)

Rose Marie had two distinct but widely separated careers. She was a sensation on

*Some sources give Oct. 24th.

732

radio at the age of three, billed as "Baby Rose Marie," and during the 1930s starred in her own network variety show, singing adult pop songs of the day. She then mostly faded from view, appearing only occasionally onstage (e.g., *Top Banana* with Phil Silvers, in 1951), in a few films, and on television during the 1940s and '50s. Just when her career seemed to have come to a halt she suddenly became a star all over again as the wisecracking, man hungry, seen-it-all comedy writer Sally on *The Dick Van Dyke Show*. She later played other comic supporting roles and was a regular panelist on the daytime comedy quiz *The Hollywood Squares*. It was for her, you might say, a second childhood.

Rose Marie's maiden name was Rose Marie Mazetta, but she dropped the surname when she began performing in the '20s.

ROSE, CHARLIE—newscaster
b: Jan 5, 1942, Henderson, N.C.

CBS News Nightwatch (news)
.... Anchor (1984–   )

ROSE, DAVID—orchestra leader, composer
b: Jun 15, 1910, London, England r: Chicago, Ill.

The Red Skelton Show (var)
.... orch. leader (1951–71)
The Tony Martin Show (music)
.... orch. leader (1955–56)

Emmy Awards: Best Musical Direction, for "An Evening with Fred Astaire" (1959); Best Music for a Series, for *Bonanza* (1971) and for *Little House on the Prairie* (1979, 1982)

A noted composer-conductor, long with Red Skelton on radio and television, and more recently associated with Michael Landon's series *(Bonanza, Little House, Father Murphy, Highway to Heaven)*. David was married in the late 1930s to Martha Raye and in the early 1940s to Judy Garland. His theme, and most famous song: "Holiday for Strings."

ROSE, GEORGE—actor
b: Feb 19, 1920, Bicester, England

Beacon Hill (drama)..... Mr. Hacker (1975)
Holocaust (drama) .... Lowy (1978)

ROSE, JAMIE—actress
b: Nov 26, 1959, New York City r: Los Angeles

Falcon Crest (drama)
...... Victoria Gioberti Hogan (1981–83)
Lady Blue (police)
.... Det. Katy Mahoney (1985–86)
St. Elsewhere (drama)
.... Dr. Susan Birch (1986–   )

ROSE, JANE—actress
b: Feb 7, 1912, Spokane, Wash. d: Jun 29, 1979

The Wonderful John Acton (drama)
.... Aunt Bessie (1953)
Phyllis (com)...... Audrey Dexter (1975–77)
Co-ed Fever (com)....... Mrs. Selby (1979)

ROSE, LINDA—actress
Stockard Channing in Just Friends (com)
.... Miss Yarnell (1979)

ROSE, MARGOT—actress
Report to Murphy (com) ...... Baker (1982)
He's the Mayor (com)
.... Kelly Enright (1986)

ROSE, NORMAN—host, actor, announcer
Police Story (police)....... narrator (1952)
The Man Behind the Badge (police)
.... host/narrator (1953–54)
The Big Story (drama)... narrator (1954–55)

ROSE, POLLY—actress
d: Feb 13, 1971

Love That Jill (com) .... Myrtle (1958)

ROSE, REVA—actress
b: Jul 30, 1940, Chicago, Ill.

Temperatures Rising (com)
..... Nurse Mildred MacInerny (1972–73)

ROSE, ROBIN—actress
The White Shadow (drama)
.... Katie Donahue (1978–79)

ROSEN, LEONARD—host
What's Your Bid? (aud par) ..... host (1953)

ROSENBERG, ARTHUR—actor
Hunter (police).... Capt. Lester Cain (1984)

ROSENFIELD, "BIG" JOE—host
A Couple of Joes (var) ..... costar (1949–50)

ROSENGARDEN, BOBBY—orchestra leader
The Dick Cavett Show (talk)
.... orch. leader (1969–72)

ROSS, ANTHONY—actor
b: 1906, New York City, N.Y. d: Oct 26, 1955

The Telltale Clue (police)
.... Det. Lt. Richard Hale (1954)

ROSS, CHRISTOPHER—actor
The Music Scene (music)
.... rotating host (1969)

ROSS, DAVID—host, announcer
b: c. 1891 d: Nov 12, 1975

Time for Reflection (misc) ..... host (1950)

A holdover from radio, where he was known for his poetry readings.

ROSS, DUNCAN—actor
Tucker's Witch (drama)
.... Stucky, the mortician (1982–83)

ROSS, EARL—actor
Meet Millie (com) ..... Mr. Boone (1952–53)
The Great Gildersleeve (com)
.... Judge Hooker (1955–56)

ROSS, JERRY—dancer
Your Show of Shows (var)
.... regular (1950–52)

ROSS, JOE E.—actor, comedian
b: Mar 15, 1905*, New York City, N.Y. d: Aug 13, 1982

The Phil Silvers Show (com)
.... Mess Sgt. Rupert Ritzik (1955–59)
Car 54, Where Are You? (com)
.... Off. Gunther Toody (1961–63)
It's About Time (com) ..... Gronk (1966–67)

*Some sources give 1914.

Short, pudgy comedian, a veteran of many years of club work.

ROSS, KATHERINE—actress
b: Jan 29, 1942*, Los Angeles, Calif.

Dynasty II: The Colbys (drama)
Francesca Scott Colby Hamilton (1985–)

Despite her current publicity that she long avoided television prior to joining *The Colbys*, Katherine Ross in fact did quite a bit of small-screen work in the early and mid 1960s, before her movie career took off. Between 1962 and 1968 she appeared in numerous westerns, including *Gunsmoke, Wagon Train*, and *Big Valley;* dramas, including *Alfred Hitchcock Hour* and *The Lieutenant;* and even a pilot called *Seven Rich Years*. Since the late '60s her appearances have indeed been rare, consisting of a few TV movies such as *The Legend of the Black Hand* and *Murder in Texas*.

ROSS, LANNY—singer
b: Jan 19, 1906, Seattle, Wash.

The Swift Show (var) . . . . host (1948–49)

A popular radio singer of the '30s and '40s. His theme song: "Moonlight and Roses." Lanny became a radio disc jockey during the 1950s and in later years devoted his time to actors union affairs.

ROSS, MARION—actress
b: Oct 25, 1928, Albert Lea, Minn.

Life with Father (com) . . . . . . Nora (1953–55)
Gertrude Berg Show (com)
. . . . Susan Green (1961)
Mr. Novak (drama)
. . . . Nurse Bromfield (1963–64)
Happy Days (com)
. . . . Marion Cunningham (1974–84)
Pearl (drama) . . . . Mary North (1978)

Need a mom? Need a best friend? Need a maid? Marion Ross spent most of her career playing such roles, many of them the scatterbrained types often seen on TV. Her first major break, after some local theater work on the West Coast, was the role of the cute Irish maid on *Life with Father*. She later played Gertrude Berg's daughter on Berg's 1961 comedy, the school nurse on

*Some sources give 1943.

734

Mr. Novak, as well as a succession of guest roles on such series as *The Outer Limits, Ironside,* and *Mannix*. She also had a regular part in the mid-1960s daytime serial *Paradise Bay*. A sketch on *Love, American Style* in 1972 provided the role for which she is best remembered, however. Once the sketch was spun off into the series *Happy Days,* Marion was firmly entrenched as the all-American sitcom mom of the '70s.

ROSS, SHAVAR—juvenile actor
Diff'rent Strokes (com)
. . . . Dudley Ramsey (1981–86)

ROSS, STAN—actor, writer
b: Jul 22, 1940, New York City, N.Y.

The New Bill Cosby Show (var)
. . . . regular (1972–73)

ROSS, TED—black actor
b: Ohio

Sirota's Court (com)
. . . . Sawyer Dabney (1976–77)
MacGruder & Loud (police)
. . . . Det. Sgt. Debbin (1985)

ROSS-LEMING, EUGENIE—writer, actress
b: Chicago, Ill.

Highcliffe Manor (com)
. . . . Frances Kiskadden (1979)

Eugenie was co-creator, producer, and author of this short-lived gothic comedy, as well as one of its cast members. She was formerly with the Chicago Second City Comedy troupe.

ROSSI, LEO—actor
Partners in Crime (drama)
. . . . Lt. Ed Vronsky (1984)

ROSSINGTON, NORMAN—actor
b: 1928, Liverpool, England

The Search for the Nile (drama)
. . . . Samuel Baker (1972)

ROSSOVICH, RICK—actor
MacGruder & Loud (police)
. . . . Geller (1985)

ROSSOVICH, TIM—actor
b: Mar 14, Palo Alto, Calif.

When the Whistle Blows (com)
.... Martin "Hunk" Kincaid (1980)

A 6'5" former pro football player for the Philadelphia Eagles, San Diego Chargers, and Houston Oilers.

ROSWELL, MAGGIE—actress, singer
b: Nov 14, Los Angeles, Calif.

The Tim Conway Show (var)
.... regular (1980–81)

ROTER, DIANE—actress

The Virginian (wes) ..... Jennifer (1965–66)

ROTH, ALAN—orchestra leader
b: c. 1904 d: Oct 30, 1972

The Milton Berle Show (var)
.... orch. leader (1948–55)

ROTH, JACK—actor, drummer

The Jimmy Durante Show (var)
.... regular (1954–56)

ROTH, PHIL—comedian

Sha Na Na (var) .... regular (1977–78)

ROTHSCHILD, SIGMUND—antique appraiser

What's It Worth? (misc)
.... appraiser (1948–49)
Trash or Treasure (misc)
.... appraiser (1952–53)

ROUNDS, DAVID—actor
b: Oct 9, 1930, Bronxville, N.Y. d: Dec 9, 1983

Beacon Hill (drama)
.... Terence O'Hara (1975)

ROUNDTREE, RICHARD—black actor
b: Jul 9, 1937*, New Rochelle, N.Y.

Shaft (drama) .... John Shaft (1973–74)
Roots (drama) .... Sam Bennett (1977)

Hip, black hero of the rather violent *Shaft* movies of the 1970s, which he also brought

*Some sources give 1942.

to television. He has done relatively little TV other than that, aside from a few TV movies and miniseries (e.g., *Roots, A.D.*).

ROUNTREE, MARTHA—moderator, writer
b: 1916, Gainesville, Fla.

Meet the Press (int)
.... moderator (1947–53)
Keep Posted (pub aff)
.... moderator (1951–53)
The Big Issue (pub aff)
.... moderator (1953–54)
Press Conference (int) . moderator (1956–57)

A former free-lance writer who, with Lawrence Spivak, created television's longest-running series of any kind, *Meet the Press*. The news interview show began on radio in 1945 and moved to TV in 1947, where it has remained ever since, first in prime time and later on Sunday afternoons. Martha was also responsible for several other public affairs series in the 1950s, as well as the lightweight chatter show *Leave It to the Girls*.

ROWAN, DAN—comedian
b: Jul 2, 1922, Beggs, Okla.

The Chevy Show (music) .... regular (1958)
The Dean Martin Summer Show (var)
.... cohost (1966)
Rowan & Martin's Laugh-In (var)
.... cohost (1968–73)

Emmy Award: costar, Best Variety Show, for *Rowan and Martin's Laugh-In* (1969)

The "smarter" half of the Rowan and Martin comedy team—the one with the mustache and frustrated look. Before meeting Martin in 1952 he was an unsuccessful screenwriter and a car salesman for Madman Muntz. (See Dick Martin for more on their career together.)

ROWE, MISTY—actress

Hee Haw (var) .... regular (1972–)
Happy Days (com) .... Wendy (1974–75)
When Things Were Rotten (com)
.... Maid Marian (1975)
Hee Haw Honeys (com)
.... Misty Honey (1978–79)
Joe's World (com) ... Judy Wilson (1979–80)

ROWE, RED—host

Tell It to the Camera (int) ... host (1963–64)

ROWE, VERNE—actor
b: c. 1922 d: Sep 4, 1981

Fernwood 2-Night (com)
.... Verne Taylor (1977–78)

ROWLAND, JADA—actress
b: Feb 23, 1943, New York City, N.Y.

The Hamptons (drama)
.... Penny Drake (1983)

Virtually all of Jada Rowland's acting career has been, you might say, a soap opera. She began as tragedy-beset 11-year-old Amy Ames on *The Secret Storm* in 1954 and stayed with that serial for nearly its entire 20-year run, through romances and deaths, seductions, and artificial insemination. On the serial's last episode, her paralyzed lover of many years lurched out of his wheelchair and finally walked into her arms! Jada then spent six years on *The Doctors* (1976–82), until it, too, expired. She was then murdered at the outset of the short-lived prime time soap opera *The Hamptons*. What a life!

ROWLANDS, GENA—actress
b: Jun 19, 1934, Cambria, Wis.

Top Secret U.S.A. (adv) ...... Powell (1954)
87th Precinct (police)
.... Teddy Carella (1961–62)
Peyton Place (drama)
.... Adrienne Van Leyden (1967)

The wife of actor-director John Cassavetes (since 1954). Gena was active in TV drama supporting roles, principally from the mid-1950s to the mid-1970s, including several appearances on *Alfred Hitchcock Presents*.

ROWLES, POLLY—actress
b: Jan 10, 1914, Philadelphia, Pa.

Jamie (com)........ Aunt Laurie (1953–54)
The Defenders (drama)
.... Helen Donaldson (1961–62)

ROXBY, RODDY-MAUDE—

Rowan & Martin's Laugh-In (var)
.... regular (1968)

ROYAL, ALLAN—Canadian actor
b: c. 1944, Montreal, Canada

Night Heat (police)
.... Tom Kirkwood (1985–)

ROYLANCE, PAMELA—actress
b: Mar 27, 1953, Seattle, Wash. r: Portland, Ore.

Little House on the Prairie (adv)
.... Sarah Carter (1982–83)

ROZARIO, BOB—orchestra leader
b: Jun 2, 1933, Shanghai, China

Tony Orlando and Dawn (var)
.... orch. leader (1974–76)
Marie (var) .... orch. leader (1980–81)

RUBEN, TOM—actor

C.P.O. Sharkey (com)... Kowalski (1976–78)

RUBENSTEIN, PHIL—actor

Working Stiffs (com) . Frank Falzone (1979)
No Soap, Radio (com) .... Rico (1982)

RUBES, JAN—actor
b: c. 1920, Volyne, Czechoslovakia

Kay O'Brien (drama)
.... Dr. Josef Wallach (1986–)

RUBIN, ANDREW—actor
b: Jun 22, 1946, New Bedford, Mass.

Jessica Novak (drama)
.... Phil Bonelli (1981)
Hometown (drama)
.... Christopher Springer (1985)
Joe Bash (com)..... Off. Willie Smith (1986)

RUBIN, BENNY—actor, comedian
b: Feb 2, 1899, Boston, Mass. d: Jul 15, 1986

Stop Me If You've Heard This One (quiz)
.... panelist (1948–49)
The Benny Rubin Show (com)
.... host (1949)

Scrawny, sad-eyed comic who was in vaudeville in the 1910s and 1920s, in scattered films from 1929 to the late '70s (e.g., *Coma*), and on television, off and on, as well. He even cracked 'em up for a while on a daytime soap opera (*The Brighter Day*, 1962).

RUBINSTEIN, JOHN—actor, composer
b: Dec 8, 1946, Los Angeles, Calif.

Family (drama) .... Jeff Maitland (1976–80)
Crazy Like a Fox (drama)
.... Harrison K. Fox (1984–86)

This eager, curly-haired actor is the son of the great classical pianist Artur Rubinstein. John is also a composer, responsible for the music for *Family*, among other things. From 1970 on, he has starred in Broadway musicals (e.g., *Pippin*) as well as in numerous TV movies and series episodes.

RUBIO, EDIE MARIE—actress

a.k.a. Pablo (com) ..... Linda Rivera (1984)

RUCKER, BARBARA—actress

Temperatures Rising (com)
.... Nurse Amanda Kelly (1974)

Barbara later went into soap operas, appearing for several years in the '70s on *As the World Turns* and in the '80s on *Texas*.

RUCKER, DENNIS—actor

Hec Ramsey (wes)
.... Arne Tornquist (1972–74)
Get Christie Love (police)
.... Det. Steve Belmont (1974–75)

RUDD, PAUL—actor
b: May 15, 1940, Boston, Mass.

Beacon Hill (drama)... Brian Mallory (1975)
Knots Landing (drama)
.... Earl Trent (1980–81)

RUDLEY, HERBERT—actor
b: 1911

The Californians (wes)
.... Sam Brennan (1957–58)
Michael Shayne (drama)
.... Will Gentry (1960–61)
Mona McCluskey (com)
.... Gen. Crone (1965–66)
The Mothers-in-Law (com)
.... Herb Hubbard (1967–69)

RUGGLES, CHARLIE—actor
b: Feb 8, 1886, Los Angeles, Calif. d: Dec 23, 1970

The Ruggles (com) .... as himself (1949–52)
The World of Mr. Sweeney (com)
.... Cicero P. Sweeney (1954)
The Bullwinkle Show (cartn)
.... Aesop (voice) (1961–62)

Charming, dapper Charlie Ruggles projected an air of friendliness and warmth that wore well on stage and screen for more than 60 years. He began as a stage actor in San Francisco in 1905 and made his first movie in 1915; during the '30s and '40s he was a familiar and much-loved star in a long series of popular film comedies (*The Ruggles of Red Gap, Bringing Up Baby,* etc.).

When television arrived, Ruggles was already in his sixties, but charm grows with age, and he soon turned up in one of the earliest warm family comedies, *The Ruggles*. Unfortunately, since it was produced live on the West Coast, it could be seen in the rest of the country only via poor-quality kinescopes. Although it ran for three years, it was never a major hit, as filmed shows such as *Ozzie and Harriet* and *Father Knows Best* later became. Charlie then originated a regular sketch on *The Kate Smith TV Hour* in 1953–54 in which he played small-town general store proprietor Cicero P. Sweeney, who offered homespun observations on life. This was spun off into a prime time summer show in 1954 and a regular daytime series in 1954–55. Charlie also played many guest roles on TV dramas of the '50s and '60s, with occasional visits on sitcoms ranging from *The Real McCoys* to *The Munsters*. His chuckling narration of bogus "Aesop's Fables" on the *Bullwinkle* cartoon was replayed for many years. As late as 1968 he played a role on *The Danny Thomas Hour;* he was also, in the '60s, a standby in Disney films.

Charlie was, to TV at least, a charming old-timer to the end.

RUICK, BARBARA—actress, singer
b: 1932, Pasadena, Calif. d: Mar 2, 1974

The College Bowl (com) .. regular (1950–51)
The Jerry Colonna Show (var)
.... regular (1951)
The RCA Victor Show (com)
.... Peggy (1953–54)
The Johnny Carson Show (var)
.... regular (1955–56)

The lovely blonde daughter of actors Lurene Tuttle and Melville Ruick; married at one time to actor Robert Horton, and later to composer John Williams.

RUICK, MELVILLE—actor, announcer
b: Jul 8, 1898, Boise, Idaho d: 1972

Doorway to Danger (drama)
.... John Randolph (1951)
City Hospital (drama)
.... Dr. Barton Crane (1952–53)

Radio and stage actor and announcer; father of Barbara Ruick.

RUIZ, ISAAC—actor

Chico and the Man (com)
.... Mando (1974–77)

RUMAN, SIG—actor
b: 1884, Hamburg, Germany d: Feb 14, 1967

Life with Luigi (com) .... Schultz (1952)

Bushy-browed German comic actor, very busy in films from the 1930s on, usually playing the dummkoff (as in several Marx Brothers movies). On *Life with Luigi* he was one of Luigi's fellow immigrants.

RUNDLE, CIS—actress

Matt Houston (drama) ...... Chris (1982–84)

RUNDLE, ROBBIE—juvenile actor

Code R (adv) ...... Bobby Robinson (1977)

RUNYON, JENNIFER—actress

Charles in Charge (com)
.... Gwendolyn Pierce (1984–85)

RUPPERT, DONNA—actress

Michael Nesmith in Television Parts (var)
.... regular (1985)

RUSCIO, AL—actor
b: Jun 2, Salem, Mass.

Shannon (police) ... Paul Locatelli (1981–82)

RUSH, BARBARA—actress
b: Jan 4, 1927, Denver, Colo. r: Santa Barbara, Calif.

Saints and Sinners (drama)
.... Lizzie Hogan (1962–63)
Peyton Place (drama)
.... Marsha Russell (1968–69)
The New Dick Van Dyke Show (com)
.... Margot Brighton (1973–74)
Flamingo Road (drama)
.... Eudora Weldon (1981–82)

An elegant movie starlet of the '50s (when she was fresh out of college) who has had a respectable though not spectacular career in films and TV since then. She played supporting roles in many TV dramas from the '50s to the '80s, ranging from *Lux Video Theatre* to *Flamingo Road,* with a few stops along the way for comedy as well. "Acting makes me happy," she says simply, "and I love it."

RUSHMORE, KAREN—actress

13 Queens Boulevard (com)
.... Camille (1979)

RUSKIN, SHIMEN—actor
b: 1907, Vilna, Poland d: Apr 23, 1976

The Corner Bar (com)
.... Meyer Shapiro (1972–73)

RUSSEL, DEL—actor
b: Sep 27, 1952, Pasadena, Calif.

Arnie (com)........ Richard Nuvo (1970–72)

RUSSELL & AURA—dancers

Garroway at Large (var)
.... dancers (1950–51)

RUSSELL, ANDY—singer
b: Sep 16, Los Angeles, Calif.

Andy and Della Russell (music)
.... as himself (1950–51)

A popular radio crooner of the '40s, who in his vocals often alternated between English and Spanish (he is of Mexican descent). Later in the 1950s Andy moved to Mexico and then to Buenos Aires, where he spent nearly 20 years as a popular TV host and recording artist, a Latin star long after his U.S. fame had ended. He returned to the U.S.—and to obscurity—in the 1970s. His 1950 TV series featured love duets with his then-wife Della.

RUSSELL, BOB—host, announcer

Versatile Varieties (var) . . . emcee (1950–51)
Time Will Tell (quiz) . . . . . announcer (1954)

RUSSELL, CONNIE—singer
b: May 9, 1924, New York City, N.Y.

Garroway at Large (var) . . regular (1949–51)
Club Embassy (var) . . . . vocalist (1953)

RUSSELL, DEL—

see Russel, Del

RUSSELL, DELLA—singer

Andy and Della Russell (music)
. . . . as herself (1950–51)

The wife of Andy Russell. She later married a wealthy Mexican.

RUSSELL, DON—host

Guide Right (var) . . . . emcee (1952–53)
Stars on Parade (var) . . . . emcee (1953)

RUSSELL, JACK—singer
b: Sep 22, 1919, Saratoga Springs, N.Y. r: Palm Beach, Fla

Your Show of Shows (var)
. . . . regular (1950–54)

RUSSELL, JEANNIE—actress

Dennis the Menace (com)
. . . . Margaret Wade (1959–63)

RUSSELL, JOHN—actor
b: Jan 3, 1921, Los Angeles, Calif.

Soldiers of Fortune (adv)
. . . . Tim Kelly (1955–56)
The Lawman (wes)
. . . . Marshal Dan Troop (1958–62)

The tough, humorless "Lawman" was John Russell, a movie stalwart since the 1930s, who was seen in two TV series and in occasional guest appearances during the late 1950s (mostly in westerns). After *The Lawman* left the air in 1962 he was hardly seen at all, though he did return for a few episodes of *Alias Smith and Jones* in 1971–72 and for a season as the "commander" on the Saturday morning live action series *Jason of Star Command* in 1979–81.

RUSSELL, KURT—actor
b: Mar 17, 1951*, Springfield, Mass. r: Los Angeles

The Travels of Jaimie McPheeters (wes)
. . . . Jaimie McPheeters (1963–64)
The New Land (adv) . . . . Bo (1974)
The Quest (wes) . . Morgan Beaudine (1976)

Square-jawed Kurt Russell began as a juvenile performer, with a busy career both on television and in movies. He was born the son of a former baseball player turned actor (Bing Russell for years played the occasional role of the deputy sheriff on *Bonanza*); young Kurt got his big break at the age of 12 as the lead in the TV series *The Travels of Jaimie McPheeters*. During the remainder of the 1960s he played juvenile roles in various series, including multiple appearances on *Daniel Boone,* and also in quite a few films, many of them for Disney.

Young adult roles began to come his way in the '70s, including those of a deranged student/mass murderer in the TV docudrama *The Deadly Tower* and a young man raised by Indians in *The Quest.* However, most viewers did not really notice that Kurt Russell had grown up until his stunning portrayal of Elvis Presley in the TV biography *Elvis,* in 1979—for which he received an Emmy nomination. (Kurt's movie debut, incidentally, had been as a kid who kicked the real Elvis in the shin in Presley's 1963 film *It Happened at the World's Fair*). Kurt has since concentrated primarily on feature films.

RUSSELL, LEE—singer
b: Feb 16, 1920, Cleveland, Ohio

Vincent Lopez (var) . . . . regular (1950)

RUSSELL, MARK—actor

Kojak (police) . . . . Det. Saperstein (1974–77)

RUSSELL, MARK—satirist
b: Aug 23, 1932, Buffalo, N.Y.

The Starland Vocal Band Show (var)
. . . . regular (1977)
Real People (aud par) . . . . regular (1979–84)

Mark Russell has long been a favorite stand-up comic in the Washington area, known for poking fun at the capital and its

*Some sources give 1947.

739

denizens. He was resident comedian at D.C.'s Shoreham Hotel for 20 years, from 1961–81. He also writes a syndicated column of political satire, has appeared on numerous TV talk shows, and has recorded a number of comedy LPs, whose titles suggest his usual subject matter. Among them: "The Wild, Weird, Wired World of Watergate," "The Face on the Senate Floor," and "Up the Potomac Without a Canoe." Mark modestly says, "I credit my success to a staff of the top gag writers in the country—435 in the House and 100 in the Senate!"

RUSSELL, NIPSEY—black comedian
b: Oct 13, 1920*, Atlanta, Ga.

Car 54, Where Are You? (com)
.... Off. Anderson (1961–62)
ABC's Nightlife (talk)....... regular (1965)
Barefoot in the Park (com)
.... Honey Robinson (1970–71)
The Dean Martin Show (var)
.... regular (1972–73)
The Dean Martin Comedy World (var)
.... host (1974)
Masquerade Party (quiz)
.... regular panelist (1974–75)

Nipsey, the "poet laureate of comedy," with his easy wit and comic doggerel, seems to have been around as long as anyone can remember. Legend has it that he was dancing and ad-libbing in grade school and used his talents to work his way through college (he is a well-educated man, able to quote easily from the classics). After service in World War II (emerging as a captain), Nipsey toured with Billy Eckstein and then played clubs in the New York area, holding forth in Harlem for 20 years. His first major national break came in 1959, when he was repeatedly featured by Jack Paar on *The Tonight Show;* he later turned up in both acting roles and as a stand-up comic, on everything from Arthur Godfrey's program to *The Mouse Factory.*

Nipsey's humor is not generally racial, but he knows where it's at. "The American motto seems to be," he grins, "when you're white, you're right; when you're brown, stick around; but when you're black, get *way, way* back!"

*Some sources give 1924 or 1925.

RUSSELL, TODD—host
Wheel of Fortune (quiz)........ host (1953)

Best known, perhaps, as "Masterootie," the host of the afternoon kid's show *Rootie Kazootie* from 1951–54. The version of *Wheel of Fortune* that he hosted bore no resemblance to the similarly-named hit quiz show of the 1980s.

RUSSELL, WILLIAM—English actor
The Adventures of Sir Lancelot (adv)
.... Sir Lancelot (1956–57)

Also known as Russell Enoch.

RUST, RICHARD—actor
Sam Benedict (drama)
.... Hank Tabor (1962–63)

RUTHERFORD, ANGELO—black juvenile actor
b: c. 1954, Miami, Fla. d: Jan 30, 1987

Gentle Ben (adv).......... Willie (1968–69)

RUTHERFORD, ANN—actress
b: Nov 2, 1917*, Toronto, Canada r: San Francisco, Calif

Leave It to the Girls (talk)
.... panelist (1949–54)

Ann is best remembered as Polly, Mickey Rooney's perennial girlfriend in the *Andy Hardy* pictures of the '30s and '40s. She acted in occasional television dramas during the '50s and early '60s, including several appearances on *Perry Mason,* but was rarely seen after that.

RUTHERFORD, DEAN—
Music Hall America (music) . regular (1976)

RUTHERFORD, LORI—juvenile actress
The New Andy Griffith Show (com)
.... Lori Sawyer (1971)

RUYMEN, AYN—actress
b: Jul 18, 1947, Brooklyn, N.Y.

The McLean Stevenson Show (com)
.... Janet (1976–77)

*Some sources give 1920.

740

RYAN, BILL—newscaster
b: Apr 4, 1926, Brooklyn, N.Y.

The Smithsonian (doc).......... host (1967)

RYAN, FRAN—actress
b: Nov 29, Los Angeles, Calif.

The Doris Day Show (com)
.... Aggie Thompson (1968)
Green Acres (com) ... Doris Ziffel (1969–70)
Gunsmoke (wes) ... Miss Hannah (1974–75)
No Soap, Radio (com) . Mrs. Belmont (1982)
The Wizard (adv) .. Tillie Russell (1986–)

RYAN, IRENE—actress
b: Oct 17, 1903, El Paso, Texas d: Apr 26, 1973

The Beverly Hillbillies (com)
.... Daisy (Granny) Moses (1962–71)

Irene Ryan was one actress whose best role was certainly saved until last. A small, wiry woman, she was in her fifties when cast as the feisty, pipe-smoking old granny on *The Beverly Hillbillies,* but the show was such an enormous hit it carried her nearly to the end of her career. Irene had been onstage since the age of ten and had toured in vaudeville with her husband Tim Ryan as "Tim and Irene." She appeared in quite a few B films during the '40s and early '50s, generally as a wisecracking dame, and also played occasional supporting roles on television. Among her series credits: *Front Row Center, The Ray Bolger Show, Make Room for Daddy, Bringing Up Buddy,* and *Restless Gun.* Her obscurity ended, abruptly, with *The Beverly Hillbillies,* which shot to number one in the ratings during the early 1960s. Remarkably, even after that series' long run ended, she had time to score one more triumph, during the last months of her life, as the lusty, medieval grandmother in the Broadway hit *Pippin.* It brought her a Tony Award nomination in 1973.

RYAN, JOHN P.—actor
b: 1938

Archer (drama) . Lt. Barney Brighton (1975)

RYAN, MEG—actress
b: c. 1962, Fairfield, Conn.

One of the Boys (com)........ Jane (1982)
Wildside (wes)......... Cally Oaks (1985)

RYAN, MITCHELL—actor
b: Jan 11, 1928*, Cincinnati, Ohio r: Louisville, Ky.

Chase (police)
.... Capt. Chase Reddick (1973–74)
Executive Suite (drama)
.... Don Walling (1976–77)
Having Babies (drama)
.... Dr. Blake Simmons (1978–79)
The Chisholms (wes)
.... Cooper Hawkins (1980)
High Performance (adv)
.... Brennan Flannery (1983)

This stolid but authoritative-looking performer entered acting following service in the navy during the Korean War. It proved a long climb; he worked mostly onstage in the '50s and '60s, with his first continuing TV role being that of Burke Devlin on *Dark Shadows* in the late '60s. In the '70s he turned up more often in prime time, cast mostly as authority figures and men-in-charge in a number of routine series. His own police show, *Chase,* was short-lived. He has also appeared in many TV movies, none of them particularly notable.

RYAN, NATASHA—juvenile actress
b: May 14, 1970, Los Angeles, Calif.

Ladies' Man (com)
.... Amy Thackeray (1980–81)

Although she has played guest roles on a number of prime time series, and was briefly a regular on *Ladies' Man* (as Lawrence Pressman's pigtailed daughter), little Natasha is best remembered for the role of Hope Williams on the daytime serial *Days of Our Lives,* which she played for more than six years, beginning in 1974.

RYAN, PEGGY—actress
b: Aug 28, 1924, Long Beach, Calif.

Hawaii Five-O (police)
.... Jenny (1969–76)

Donald O'Connor's pretty, teenaged dancing partner in musicals of the World War II era. She later went into semi-retirement in Hawaii, emerging years later to play Jack Lord's secretary in *Hawaii Five-O* (which was filmed there).

*Some sources give 1934.

RYAN, ROBERT—actor
b: Nov 11, 1909, Chicago, Ill. d: Jul 11, 1973

Alcoa/Goodyear Theatre (drama)
.... recurring star (1957–58)
World War I (doc) ...... narrator (1964–65)

RYAN, ROZ—black singer, actress
b: Jul 7, 1951, Detroit, Mich.

Amen (com).... Amelia Hetebrink (1986–)

RYAN, STEVE—actor

Teachers Only (com)
.... Spud Le Boone (1983)
Crime Story (police)
.... Det. Nate Grossman (1986–)

RYDELL, BOBBY—singer
b: Apr 26, 1942, Philadelphia, Pa.

Paul Whiteman's TV Teen Club (talent)
.... regular (1951–53)
The Milton Berle Show (var)
.... regular (1966)

The sunny, toothsome pop singer of the early 1960s ("Wild One," "Swingin'

School," "I Dig Girls," etc.). He became familiar via a great many appearances on Dick Clark's *American Bandstand,* on which he was practically Dick's standby performer. Bobby was actually an old pro by then; he had gotten his start at the age of nine as a regular on *Paul Whiteman's TV Teen Club,* which had also originated from Philadelphia. It was Whiteman, in fact, who suggested that he change his name from Ridarelli to Rydell. Since the '60s, Bobby has been active primarily on the concert and club circuit.

RYDER, EDDIE—actor

The Dennis O'Keefe Show (com)
.... Eliot (1959–60)
Dr. Kildare (drama)
.... Dr. Simon Agurksi (1961–62)

RYERSON, ANN—actress
b: Aug 15, 1949, Fond du Lac, Wis. r: Minneapolis, Minn.

Private Benjamin (com)
.... Pvt. Carol Winter (1981–82)

S

SAAM, BYRUM—sportscaster

Sportsreel (sport)...... commentator (1954)

SABATINO, MICHAEL—actor

Behind the Screen (drama)
.... Brian Holmby (1981–82)
Knots Landing (drama)
.... Chip Roberts (1982–83)

SABELLA, ERNIE—actor

b: Sep 19, Westchester, N.Y.

It's Your Move (com)
.... Lou Donatelli (1984–85)
Perfect Strangers (com)
.. Donald "Twinkie" Twinkacetti (1986–)

SABIN, DAVID—actor

When Things Were Rotten (com)
.... Little John (1975)

SABO, SHARI—actress

M*A*S*H (com)... various nurses (1980–83)

SACINO, ANDREA—juvenile actress

Many Happy Returns (com)
.... Laurie Randall (1964–65)

SADDLER, DON—dancer

b: Jan 24, 1920, Van Nuys, Calif.

Holiday Hotel (var) .... regular (1950)

SADOWSKY, ADAM—juvenile actor

It's Your Move (com) .... Eli (1984–85)

SAFER, MORLEY—newscaster

b: Nov 8, 1931, Toronto, Canada

60 Minutes (pub aff)
.... correspondent (1970–)

Emmy Awards: Best News Segments, For the *60 Minutes* Reports "Teddy Kolleck's Jerusalem" (1979), "Pops" (Arthur Fiedler) (1979), "Air Force Surgeon" (1982), "It Didn't Have to Happen" (1982); "Ronald Reagan—The Movie" (1986); "The Beeb" (1986).

When historians look back at how the news media turned Vietnam into "The Living Room War"—and in the process turned Americans against U.S. involvement there—they will most likely look at Morley Safer's vivid battlefront reports on *The CBS Evening News*. This was Safer's first big assignment, and it made him both famous and controversial; there was no doubt where he stood on the war.

Safer, a Canadian, had been a reporter and producer for the CBC before joining CBS News in April 1964. He was sent to Saigon to open CBS's bureau there in 1965 and stayed until 1967, a period of rapid and critical escalation in the American involvement. It was Morley who filmed the memorable report showing U.S. marines setting fire to the thatch-roofed huts of poor villagers with their cigarette lighters, in Cam Ne. In the fall of 1967 he scored a major coup when he and a cameraman were allowed into mainland China—which was then closed to most Americans—to film a CBS special which aired as "Morley Safer's Red China Diary."

Morley spent the next three years as chief of CBS's London bureau. One of his major beats was an exclusive 1969 interview with Soviet writer Anatoly Kuznetsov, who had defected to the West; this also aired as a prime time CBS special. In 1970 he was thrown out of Nigeria for reporting on the pilfering of refugee supplies there.

With the South Vietnamese, the Nigerians, the Russians, and no doubt others none too happy with Safer, CBS brought its controversial correspondent back to New York in 1970 to become one of the four anchors on *60 Minutes,* replacing Harry Reasoner (who had left for ABC). Morley quickly became a key contributor to the show, reporting both soft and hard news stories, including many an exposé. Among the latter were the headline-making "Air Force Surgeon" (about the cover-up of the alleged incompetence of the air force's chief heart surgeon) and "It Didn't Have to Happen" (about Massachusetts' release of a mental patient who subsequently killed a child).

SAFRANSKI, EDDIE—orchestra leader

b: Dec 25, 1918, Pittsburgh, Pa.

The Jonathan Winters Show (var)
.... orch. leader (1956–57)
Georgia Gibbs and Her Million Record Show
(music) .... orch. leader (1957)

SAGAL, JEAN—actress
b: Oct 9, 1961, Los Angeles, Calif.

Double Trouble (com)
.... Kate Foster (1984–85)

SAGAL, KATEY—actress

Mary (com)............ Jo Tucker (1985–86)

SAGAL, LIZ—actress
b: Oct 9, 1961, Los Angeles, Calif.

Double Trouble (com)
.... Allison Foster (1984–85)

Jean and Liz are identical twins, daughters
of the prominent TV director Boris Sagal.
They first attracted attention as the bubbly
twin cheerleaders in the movie *Grease II.*

SAGAN, DR. CARL—astronomer
b: Nov 9, 1934, New York City, N.Y.

20/20 (mag)....... correspondent (1978–80)
Cosmos (doc) .... host (1980–81)

SAGAPHI, PRINCESS ANNETTE—
  hostess

Princess Sagaphi (doc).... hostess (1948–49)

The Princess narrated films of the Far East.

SAINT, EVA MARIE—actress
b: Jul 4, 1924, Newark, N.J., r: Albany, N.Y.

One Man's Family (drama)
...... Claudia Barbour Roberts (1950–52)
How the West Was Won (miniseries) (drama)
.... Kate Macahan (1977)

The wispy, intelligent star of some superb
films of the 1950s spent her formative years
on early live TV. She recalls starting out by
doing the singing commercials on a primitive NBC variety show called *Campus
Hoopla* in 1946–47. That was followed by
small acting assignments on radio and TV
dramas and, in 1950, her first major break
—the role of Claudia, the romantic lead on
the prime time soap opera *One Man's Family* (actually, Eva Marie had first appeared

as Claudia's bitchy rival, Judith Richardson, but the producers soon made her the
sympathetic heroine; wonder what the
viewers thought of *that* abrupt change of
personality?).

During the next few years Eva Marie
played increasingly prominent roles on
theater series such as *Philco Playhouse,
The Web,* and *Producers' Showcase.*
Then, in 1954, she suddenly rocketed to
stardom in her first feature film, *On the
Waterfront,* as Marlon Brando's sensitive
girlfriend. It won her an Academy Award
and launched a film career that removed
her from television (except for very rare
appearances) for the next 20 years. In the
late '70s and '80s she returned to the medium to star in occasional TV movies and
miniseries, including *How the West Was
Won, When Hell Was in Session,* and
Fatal Vision.

ST. JACQUES, RAYMOND—black actor
b: 1930, Hartford, Conn.

Rawhide (wes)..... Solomon King (1965–66)
Roots (drama)........ The Drummer (1977)
Falcon Crest (drama).. Dr. Hooks (1983–84)

SAINT JAMES, SUSAN—actress
b: Aug 14, 1946, Los Angeles, Calif. r: Rockford, Ill.

The Name of the Game (adv)
.... Peggy Maxwell (1968–71)
McMillan and Wife (police)
.... Sally McMillan (1971–76)
Kate & Allie (com) .. Kate McArdle (1984–)

Emmy Award: Best Supporting Actress in
a Series, for *The Name of the Game* (1969)

Susan Saint James is a perky, upbeat actress who scored strongly in her first television exposure and has remained a popular
leading lady ever since. After a brief career as a model during her teens, in the U.S.
and France, she headed for Hollywood in
the late 1960s and promptly landed a seven-year contract with Universal Studios.
They put her into episodes of several of
their TV series in 1967–68 *(Ironside, It
Takes a Thief),* as well as in the TV movie
Fame Is the Name of the Game. The latter
lead to her first regular series role, at age
22. Susan was an immediate hit as the
bright, offbeat secretary to *The Name of*

the *Game's* three leads (who played reporters), winning an Emmy Award as best supporting actress. As soon as that series left the air, she went into an even bigger hit, *McMillan and Wife,* as Rock Hudson's meddlesome wife.

After eight years of series work, Susan turned to TV movies in the late '70s and early '80s, but none of them measured up to the standards of her previous hits (among them: *Sex and the Single Parent, S.O.S. Titanic, The Kid from Left Field).* In 1984 she returned to a regular series, as the bright, contemporary roommate of the somewhat more conservative Jane Curtin in *Kate & Allie*—and scored hit number three.

ST. JOHN, AL "FUZZY"—actor
b: Sep 10, 1893, Santa Ana, Calif. d: Jan 21, 1963

Lash of the West (wes)
.... Dep. Fuzzy Q. Jones (1952–53)

A colorful, bewiskered, pop-eyed little sidekick for many western movie heroes of the '30s and '40s—including Lash La Rue, whose B films were reedited and shown as part of the syndicated TV series *Lash of the West* in the early '50s. Fuzzy started out in silent films in 1914, often serving as hayseed comic support for his uncle Fatty Arbuckle; he appeared in hundreds of features, shorts, and serials until his retirement in 1950.

ST. JOHN, HOWARD—actor
b: 1905, Chicago, Ill. d: Mar 13, 1974

The Investigator (drama)
.... Lloyd Prior (1958)
Hank (com) ...... Dr. Lewis Royal (1965–66)

Big, sandy-haired actor who usually played an executive, determined father, or political big shot. He was General Bullmoose in the stage and screen versions of *Li'l Abner.*

ST. JOHN, JANICE—actress
Palmerstown, U.S.A. (drama)
.... Coralee Hall (1980–81)

ST. JOHN, JILL—actress
b: Aug 19, 1940, Los Angeles, Calif.

Emerald Point N.A.S. (drama)
.... Deanna Kincaid (1983–84)

Spirited, vivacious leading lady of '60s films. Jill began as a child actress, making her TV debut in a production of "A Christmas Carol" in 1948, and was later seen in guest roles on series of the '60s through the '80s, including several excursions on *The Love Boat.*

ST. JOHN, KRISTOFF—black juvenile actor
b: Jul 15, 1966, New York City, N.Y.

The San Pedro Beach Bums (com)
.... Ralphie (1977)
Roots: The Next Generations (drama)
.... Alex Haley (as a child) (1979)
The Bad News Bears (com)
.... Ahmad Abdul Rahim (1979–80)
Charlie & Company (com)
.... Charlie Richmond, Jr. (1985–86)

This young actor formerly spelled his first name Christoff.

ST. JOHN, MARCO—actor
b: May 7, 1939, New Orleans, La.

Ball Four (com) .... Rayford Plunkett (1976)

ST. JOHN, ROBERT—host, newscaster

Believe It or Not (var) .... host (1949)

SAJAK, PAT—host
b: Oct 26, Chicago, Ill.

Wheel of Fortune (quiz) .... host (1983–)

One of the more deadpan wits on television is Pat Sajak, the impish host of the phenomenally popular quiz show *Wheel of Fortune.* "As far as I'm concerned, the game is the main thing," he grins, but some would disagree. Pat began as a radio newsman in his native Chicago and served four years in Vietnam (1968–72) as a disc jockey with the army's radio station in Saigon (where they kept a .45-caliber gun beside the microphone and guards outside the door); he then returned to become a local DJ and TV weatherman in Nashville and Los Angeles. He began hosting *Wheel of Fortune* in daytime in 1981, adding a syndicated nighttime version to his schedule in 1983.

SAKAI, FRANKIE—actor

Shogun (drama) . . . . Lord Yabu (1980)

SAKATA, HAROLD—actor
b: 1920, Kona, Hawaii d: Jul 29, 1982

Sarge (drama) . . . . . . Kenji Takichi (1971–72)
Highcliffe Manor (com) . . . . Cheng (1979)

A bull-necked, 225-pound professional wrestler; he was the mute killer Odd Job in the James Bond movie *Goldfinger.* He crushed bones professionally under the name "The Great Tosh Togo."

SALATA, GREGORY—actor

Kate & Allie (com) . . . Ted Bartelo (1984–85)

SALCIDO, MICHAEL A.—actor

David Cassidy—Man Undercover (police)
. . . . Off. Paul Sanchez (1978–79)

SALE, VIRGINIA—actress

Wren's Nest (com) . . . . as herself (1949)
Petticoat Junction (com)
. . . . Selma Plout (1964–65)

The wife of Sam Wren, her costar on *The Wren's Nest.* Virginia appeared in movies from the 1920s to the 1960s.

SALEM, JESSICA—actress

The Paper Chase (drama)
. . . . Mallison (1978–79)

SALEM, KARIO—actor

Centennial (drama)
. . . . Mike Pasquinel (1978–79)
Heart of the City (drama) . . . . Arno (1986–)

SALEM, MURRAY—actor

Holocaust (drama) . . . . Analevitz (1978)

SALERNO, CHARLENE—actress

The Adventures of Ozzie & Harriet (com)
. . . . Ginger (1962–65)

SALES, CLIFFORD—juvenile actor

Beulah (com)
. . . . Donnie Henderson (1950–52)

SALES, SOUPY—comedian
b: Jan 8, 1926, Franklinton, N.C.

Soupy Sales (child) . . . . host (1955)
The Soupy Sales Show (child)
. . . . host (1962)
The Soupy Sales Show (child)
. . . . host (1965–67)
What's My Line (quiz) . . . panelist (1968–75)
The Soupy Sales Show (child)
. . . . host (1978–79)
Sha Na Na (var)
. . . . regular (1978–81)

Soupy Sales found his life's calling when he was hit in the face with a pie. And then another, and another . . . Few entertainers would even want the title of "World's Leading Authority on Pie Throwing," but Soupy is it. He estimates he's been smacked in the kisser by as many as 400 in a single telecast and 14,000 over a seven-year period.

Milton "Soupbone" Hines started out as a DJ and served up his first local TV comedy show in Detroit in 1953. It proved so popular, in both daytime (for the kids) and nighttime (for grown-up kids) versions, ABC picked it up for a network summer run in 1955. Since then, Soupy has been seen in a succession of daytime, evening, and syndicated series: *Lunch with Soupy Sales,* from 1959–61; a Friday night show in 1962 (live from Hollywood); a local New York show in 1964; a syndicated series in 1965; and another in 1978. In between he did local TV and radio programs on the East and West coasts and found time to expound on his specialty in other forums as well; he was once called as an expert witness on pie throwing in a nationally publicized trial. "Mr. Sales, er, could you explain the difference in impact coefficient of custard versus meringue?"

Many of Soupy's shows featured a cast of nutty puppets, including White Fang, the meanest dog in the world, Black Tooth, the nicest (only their giant paws were seen), Herman the Flea, Pookie the Lion, Willie the Worm, and Hippy the Hippo—not to mention curvaceous Marilyn Monwolf, for the big boys in the audience. The gags were slapstick and corny, but the antic comedian kept up the pace for more than 30 years. Watch out, Soupy, here comes another one!

SALMI, ALBERT—actor
b: Mar 11, 1928, Brooklyn, N.Y.

Daniel Boone (wes) ...... Yadkin (1964–65)
Petrocelli (drama) ..... Pete Ritter (1974–76)
79 Park Avenue (drama)
.... Peter Markevich (1977)

"I'm a 'what's-his-name' when it comes to public recognition," says burly Albert Salmi, with a laugh. "They know they know me, but they have trouble putting a name on the face." The beefy, imposing, often mustachioed actor may not be known by name, but he has had a very busy career in television for more than 30 years—as henchman, villain, and sometime sidekick (for both Daniel Boone and Petrocelli). His credits include theater series of the '50s (*The U.S. Steel Hour, Studio One,* etc.), most of the major westerns of the '60s (*Bonanza, Rawhide, The Virginian, Gunsmoke,* etc.), and crime shows after that (*The F.B.I., Ironside,* etc.). "As long as they remember the role, then I sort of feel it's a tribute to me as a performer," he says, twirling his mustache.

SALT, JENNIFER—actress
b: Sep 4, 1944, Los Angeles, Calif.

Soap (com) .... Eunice Tate (1977–81)

SALTER, HARRY—orchestra leader
b: c. 1898 d: Mar 5, 1984

Stop the Music (quiz)
.... orch. leader (1949–52)
Stop the Music (quiz)
.... orch. leader (1954–56)

SALUGA, BILL—comedian

The Steve Allen Comedy Hour (var)
.... regular (1980–81)

SAMMES, MIKE—singers

The Piccadilly Palace (var)
.... singers (1967)
Spotlight (var) .... singers (1967)
Showtime (var)............. singers (1968)
Kraft Music Hall Presents The Des O'Connor Show (var)............. singers (1970–71)
The Val Doonican Show (var)
.... singers (1971)

SAMMS, EMMA—actress
b: Aug 28, 1961, London, England

Dynasty (drama)
.... Fallon Carrington Colby (1985)
Dynasty II: The Colbys (drama)
.... Fallon Carrington Colby (1985–)

This porcelain-pretty young actress has had a rapid rise in show business. She pursued a career as a ballet dancer in her native England until a hip ailment sidelined her at age 16. She made her British film debut in 1979 (in *Arabian Adventure*), then moved to Hollywood, where she landed the plum role of Tony Geary's love interest on the top-rated daytime serial *General Hospital.* After three years of heating up daytime, Emma moved on to the even juicier role of Fallon on the prime time hit *Dynasty* and its spin-off *The Colbys.* She is still in her twenties, and most critics see a bright future for her, perhaps even as bright as that of a fresh, young British-born starlet of the '40s with whom she is sometimes compared—Elizabeth Taylor.

SAMPLES, ALVIN "JUNIOR"—country comedian
b: Apr 10, 1926, Cumming, Ga. d: Nov 13, 1983

Hee Haw (var).......... regular (1969–84)

SAMPSON, ROBERT—actor

Bridget Loves Bernie (com)
.... Father Mike Fitzgerald (1972–73)
Falcon Crest (drama)
.... Sheriff Turk Tobias (1981–82)

SAMPSON, WILL—actor
b: c. 1933, Okmulgee, Okla. d: Jun 3, 1987

From Here to Eternity (drama)
.... Sgt. Cheney (1979–80)
Born to the Wind (adv)
.... Painted Bear (1982)
The Yellow Rose (drama)
.... John Stronghart (1983–84)

Large-size American Indian actor who came to notice in the 1975 movie *One Flew over the Cuckoo's Nest.* He also had a recurring role on *Vega$* as Robert Urich's friend, Chief Harlon Two-Feather.

SAMUELS, JIM—

The Jacksons (var) .... regular (1976)

SAND, PAUL—actor
b: Mar 5, 1944, Los Angeles, Calif.

Paul Sand in Friends and Lovers (com)
.... Robert Dreyfuss (1974–75)
St. Elsewhere (drama)
.... Dr. Michael Ridley (1983–84)

A light comic actor who received a big buildup in the early 1970s, following his 1970 Tony Award–winning performance in the Broadway show *Story Theatre* (which was made into a syndicated TV series in 1971). Despite most advantageous scheduling, in between the top hits *All in the Family* and *The Mary Tyler Moore Show* on Saturday night, his own situation comedy flopped in 1974, and he has been relegated to supporting roles ever since.

SANDE, WALTER—actor
b: 1906, Denver, Colo. r: Portland, Ore. d: Feb 22, 1972

The Adventures of Tugboat Annie (adv)
.... Capt. Horatio Bullwinkle (1956)

SANDERS, BEVERLY—actress
b: Sep 2, 1940, Hollywood, Calif.

Lotsa Luck (com)... Olive Swann (1973–74)
C.P.O. Sharkey (com)
.... Chief Gypsy Koch (1976–78)

SANDERS, GEORGE—actor
b: Jul 3, 1906, St. Petersburg, Russia d: Apr 25, 1972

The George Sanders Mystery Theater (drama)....................... host (1957)

One of the movies' classiest scoundrels, a suave, icy-cold actor whose screen persona is best described by the title of his 1960 autobiography: *Memoirs of a Professional Cad.* One critic observed that he could "sneer in five languages." Sanders made occasional television appearances in the '50s and '60s, hosting his own summer anthology in 1957 and appearing on *General Electric Theater, The Man from U.N.C.L.E., The Rogues* (of course), and *Checkmate,* among others. He was an early villain on *Batman,* as—what else?—Mr. Freeze, a knave who could live in only the coldest of temperatures.

The man who was ever-supercilious toward all fellow mortals committed suicide in 1972; he left a note stating simply that he was bored. Sanders was married in the '50s to Zsa Zsa Gabor (and later to her sister Magda Gabor); his brother was actor Tom Conway.

SANDERS, JAY O.—actor

AfterMASH (com)
.... Dr. Gene Pfeiffer (1983–84)

SANDERS, KELLY—actress

Fathers and Sons (com)
.... Ellen Landau (1986)

SANDERS, LUGENE—actress
b: c. 1934, Oklahoma City, Okla.

Meet Corliss Archer (com)
.... Corliss Archer (1951–52)
The Life of Riley (com)
.... Babs Riley Marshall (1953–58)

SANDERS, RAY—

Hee Haw (var).......... regular (1971–72)

SANDERS, RICHARD—actor, writer
b: Aug 23, 1940, Harrisburg, Pa.

WKRP in Cincinnati (com)
.... Les Nessman (1978–82)
Spencer (com).. Benjamin Beanley (1984–85)
Berrengers (drama)
.... Frank Chapman (1985)

SANDERS, STACIE—actress

Chiefs (drama)............ Ellie Lee (1983)

SANDERSON, WILLIAM—actor
b: Jan 10, Memphis, Tenn.

Newhart (com).............. Larry (1982–)

SANDLER, BOBBY—actor

On the Rocks (com)
.... Nicky Palik (1975–76)

SANDLER, TONY—singer, comedian
b: c. 1934, Kortrjk, Belgium

Kraft Music Hall Presents Sandler & Young (var)....................... cohost (1969)

The younger, continental half of the '60s singing duo Sandler & (Ralph) Young.

SANDOR, STEVE—actor

Amy Prentiss (police)
.... Det. Tony Russell (1974–75)

SANDS, BERNIE—orchestra leader

Versatile Varieties (var)
.... orch. leader (1950–51)

SANDS, BILLY—actor
b: c. 1911 d: Aug 27, 1984

The Phil Silvers Show (com)
.... Pvt. Dino Paparelli (1955–59)
McHale's Navy (com)
.... Harrison "Tinker" Bell (1962–66)
Big Eddie (com)
.... Monte "Bang Bang" Valentine (1975)

SANDY, GARY—actor
b: Dec 25, 1945, Dayton, Ohio

All That Glitters (com) . Dan Kincaid (1977)
WKRP in Cincinnati (com)
.... Andy Travis (1978–82)

Gary Sandy, the hunk-ish, jeans-clad program director on *WKRP*, spent most of his early career in soap operas. During the early 1970s he was seen for varying periods on *As the World Turns, Somerset,* and *The Secret Storm,* seducing the leading ladies; he then played one of the sexually exploited men (role reversal!) on Norman Lear's 1977 soap opera spoof *All That Glitters;* his female bosses at the office were always ordering him to take his shirt off.
　Gary also made a few appearances on prime time series in the late '70s, including *Movin' On, Barnaby Jones,* and *Starsky and Hutch,* before beginning his most famous role, on *WKRP.*

SANFORD, CHARLES—orchestra leader
b: c. 1905, New York City, N.Y. d: Apr 22, 1977

Fireball Fun-for-All (var)
.... orch. leader (1949)
Your Show of Shows (var)
.... orch. leader (1950–54)
Max Liebman Presents (var)
.... orch. leader (1954–56)
The Patrice Munsel Show (var)
.... orch. leader (1957–58)
The Keefe Brasselle Show (var)
.... orch. leader (1963)

SANFORD, ISABEL—black actress
b: Aug 29, 1917, New York City, N.Y.

All in the Family (com)
.... Louise Jefferson (1971–75)
The Jeffersons (com)
.... Louise Jefferson (1975–85)

Emmy Award: Best Actress in a Comedy Series, for *The Jeffersons* (1981)

This hefty black actress had a long career onstage before coming to television. She was a member of New York's American Negro Theater in the 1930s and later performed with YMCA drama troupes, off-Broadway, and finally in supporting roles on Broadway. Her Broadway debut was in *The Amen Corner* in 1965. She then decided, after 30 years in the theater, to try to make it in films and TV. She traveled to the West Coast, where she gained small roles in movies *(Guess Who's Coming to Dinner?)* and in TV series episodes *(Mod Squad, Bewitched).* She was also a semiregular on *The Carol Burnett Show* for two years before landing the role of Sherman Hemsley's no-nonsense wife Louise on *All in the Family* in 1971. The role made her famous and kept her busy for the next 14 years.

SANFORD, RALPH—actor
b: May 21, 1899, Springfield, Mass. d: Jun 20, 1963

The Life and Legend of Wyatt Earp (wes)
.... Jim "Dog" Kelly (1958–59)

SAN JUAN, GUILLERMO—actor

Born to the Wind (adv) . Two Hawks (1982)

SANSBERRY, HOPE—actress

The Phil Silvers Show (com)
.... Nell Hall (1955–59)

SANTANA, ARNALDO—actor
b: Sep 1, El Paso, Texas r: Juarez, Mexico

a.k.a. Pablo (com) .. Hector Del Gato (1984)

SANTIAGO, SAUNDRA—actress
b: Apr 13, 1957, The Bronx, N.Y.

Miami Vice (police)
.... Det. Gina Navarro Calabrese (1984–)

SANTON, PENNY—actress
b: Sep 2, 1916, Greenwich Village, N.Y.

Don't Call Me Charlie (com)
.... Madame Fatima (1962–63)
Roll Out (com)
.... Madame Delacort (1973–74)
Matt Houston (drama)
.... Mama Novelli (1982–83)

SANTONI, RENI—actor

Owen Marshall, Counselor at Law (drama)
.... Danny Paterno (1973–74)
Manimal (police).. Capt. Nick Rivera (1983)

SANTOS, JOE—actor
b: Jun 9, 1934, Brooklyn, N.Y.

The Rockford Files (drama)
.... Det. Dennis Becker (1974–80)
Me and Maxx (com).. Norman Davis (1980)
a.k.a. Pablo (com)...Domingo Rivera (1984)
Hardcastle & McCormick (drama)
.... Lt. Frank Harper (1985–86)

Despite a rather late start as an actor, Joe Santos has carved out a successful career as a Hispanic supporting actor on television in the '70s and '80s. Joe was a football "jock" while in college; however, a career in professional sports didn't pan out, so he worked at odd jobs while bumming around the U.S. and Cuba for the next 16 years. Finally, in 1968, while working in construction, he accompanied a friend to an acting class; this led to his winning the role of a boxer (because of his "tough guy" looks) in the daytime soap opera *The Doctors.* His first major break came in 1973, when he won the part of William Holden's police sergeant boss in the miniseries *The Blue Knight.* The following year he was cast as James Garner's ever-frustrated police contact on *The Rockford Files,* his best known role.

Since *Rockford* ended its run, Santos has played support in a variety of series and TV movies, usually as a cynical official or "average Joe." In his only starring vehicle, *Me and Maxx,* he was horribly miscast as a middle-aged swinger with a cute little daughter to look after.

SANTUCCI, JOHN—actor

Crime Story (police)...Pauli Taglia (1986–)

SARAFIAN, RICHARD C.—director, actor
b: Apr 28, 1925, New York City, N.Y.

Foley Square (com)
.... Spiro Papadopolis (1985–86)

A veteran television and movie director, who took up acting at age 60.

SARGENT, ANNE—actress

My Son Jeep (com)
.... Barbara Miller (1953)

SARGENT, DICK—actor
b: Apr 19, 1933, Carmel, Calif.

One Happy Family (com)
.... Dick Cooper (1961)
Broadside (com)
.... Lt. Maxwell Trotter (1964–65)
The Tammy Grimes Show (com)
.... Terrence Ward (1966)
Bewitched (com)
.... Darrin Stephens (1969–72)

SARTAIN, GAILARD—comedian

Hee Haw (var)............ regular (1972–)
Keep On Truckin' (var)
.... regular (1975)
Cher (var) .... regular (1975–76)
The Sonny and Cher Show (var)
.... regular (1976)
Shields and Yarnell (var)
.... regular (1978)
Hee Haw Honeys (com)
.... Willie Billie Honey (1978–79)

A hefty "good ol' boy" comic, popular on *Hee Haw* and other variety shows of the 1970s.

SATISFIERS, THE—vocal group

The Vaughn Monroe Show (var)
.... regulars (1954)

SAUNDERS, J. JAY—black actor

Salvage 1 (adv) .... Mack (1979)

SAUNDERS, LEW—actor

CHiPs (police) .... Off. Gene Fritz (1977–81)
240-Robert (adv) .... Dep. C.B. (1979–80)

SAUNDERS, LORI—actress
b: c. 1941

Petticoat Junction (com)
.... Bobbie Jo Bradley (1965–70)
Dusty's Trail (com).......... Betsy (1973)

SAUNDERS, MARY JANE—actress

Tales of Wells Fargo (wes)
.... Mary Gee (1961–62)

SAUNDERS, NICHOLAS—actor

Martin Kane, Private Eye (drama)
.... Sgt. Ross (1950–52)

SAUTER-FINEGAN BAND—
Eddie Sauter, b: Dec 2, 1914, Brooklyn, N.Y.
Bill Finegan, b: Apr 3, 1917, Newark, N.J.

Saturday Night Revue (var)
.... orchestra (1954)

One of the most progressive, driving, and well-regarded big bands of the 1950s was that of Sauter-Finegan, formed in 1952 by two arrangers with many years of experience in the great swing bands of the '40s (Dorsey, Goodman, Miller, etc.). The 1950s not being a particularly propitious time for big bands—even good ones—they broke up in 1957, though Eddie and Bill continued to write and arrange, separately and together, for television and other media.

SAVAGE, BOOTH—actor
b: May 21, Frederickton, New Brunswick, Canada

Hot Shots (drama)..... Jason West (1986–)

SAVAGE, BRAD—juvenile actor
b: Dec 9, 1965, Livdnia, Mich. r: Hollywood, Calif.

Bob & Carol & Ted & Alice (com)
.... Sean Sanders (1973)
The Tony Randall Show (com)
.... Oliver Wendell Franklin (1976–78)

SAVAGE, FRED A.—actor

Morningstar/Eveningstar (drama)
.... Alan Bishop (1986)

SAVAGE, JOHN—actor
b: Aug 25, 1954, Old Bethpage, N.Y.

Gibbsville (drama) ...... Jim Malloy (1976)

SAVALAS, GEORGE—actor
b: Dec 5, 1926, The Bronx, N.Y. d: Oct 2, 1985

Kojak (police)....... Det. Stavros (1973–78)

The plump, bushy-haired brother of Telly Savalas. Of his character Det. Stavros, he said, "Stavros is a must, because you can't start stacking bodies up to the ceiling without some kind of comic relief. That's the purpose of Stavros—someone to laugh at in the midst of tough drama."

Also sometimes billed as Demosthenes.

SAVALAS, TELLY—actor
b: Jan 21, 1924, Garden City, N.Y.

Acapulco (adv).......... Mr. Carver (1961)
Kojak (police)..... Lt. Theo Kojak (1973–78)

Emmy Award: Best Actor in a Drama Series, for *Kojak* (1974)

"Who loves ya, baby?" grins the big, bald, powerfully built man. You know he means *he* does, but the vague air of menace behind that tough face makes you wonder. Telly is one of television's most distinctive actors, and all because of one role; his Det. Kojak was as tough and gritty as the New York streets he policed.

Telly did not start out to be an actor. He worked first, after service in World War II, for the U.S. Information Agency and then for ABC, where he rose to become director of news and special events. It was not until 1959—in his midthirties—that he first faced a camera, in small roles that made use of his unique look of "power, menace, and sexuality" (as one critic put it). Mostly that meant brutal villains, on *Armstrong Circle Theatre* (his TV debut), *Naked City*, and *The Witness* (as Lucky Luciano, in 1960). During the first half of the 1960s he was a frequent player on such crime shows as *The Untouchables, Cain's Hundred, Burke's Law*, and *The Fugitive*, almost always getting killed before the fadeout. In his first continuing role, on *Acapulco*, he was a retired crime-busting lawyer who had to be protected by the series leads.

Telly was seen less often on TV once his movie career began to heat up in the mid-1960s with such films as *The Birdman of Alcatraz* and *The Dirty Dozen*, but there, too, he was almost always a threat to someone. The image crystallized once he shaved his head, for his role as Pontius Pilate in *The Greatest Story Ever Told* in 1965. Telly sometimes tried to lighten the image, as in *On Her Majesty's Secret Service* (1969), but a critic nevertheless described him as "the international cinema's bullet-headed sadomachochistic symbol with a special twist of cheerful malevolence."

When *Kojak* came along, Telly was reluctant to play another tough guy, but at least he was on the right side of the law and could introduce some humanizing elements (such as his famous lollipop and his banter with brother George). The series certainly turned the trick in one regard. "People used to say 'There goes what's-his-name,' " he said. "Two weeks on television as Kojak and the whole world knows you." Though he has appeared in a number of TV movies and miniseries since those days (including the pilot *Hellinger*, as a lawyer), he has essentially been Kojak ever since.

SAVIDGE, JENNIFER—actress

St. Elsewhere (drama)
.... Nurse Lucy Papandrao (1982–)

SAVITCH, JESSICA—newscaster
b: 1947, Margate, N.J. r: Kennett Square, Pa. d: Oct 23, 1983

NBC Weekend News (news)
.... anchor (1977–83)
Prime Time Sunday (pub aff)
.... correspondent (1979–80)

This glamorous and intelligent newscaster was just beginning a highly promising career in network news when she was killed in an automobile accident. Had fate not intervened she might well have become one of the major names in television news. Savitch entered journalism during high school and worked at local radio stations throughout her college years in the 1960s. In 1970 she joined a local TV station in Houston, then moved to Philadelphia's KYW-TV in 1972, where she soon became anchor of the popular *Eyewitness News*. Her star rose quickly. NBC hired her as its Senate correspondent in 1977, and also made her anchor of its weekend news and substitute anchor on both the *Today* Show and *NBC Nightly News*. She was a regular

on the network's 1979 newsmagazine, appeared in NBC's prime time newsbreaks, and hosted the PBS series *Frontline* (1983). At the time of her death, PBS had renewed *Frontline* and NBC was considering her for co-anchor of another newsmagazine.

Savitch had faced tragedy in her personal life; her second husband, a victim of kidney disease, committed suicide in 1981, and she suffered a miscarriage the same year. "I chose to go on. I chose to survive. And that's no braver than anybody else," she later said. Her bright career ended suddenly when her car plunged into a river. But the lesson of her career remains. Commented the head of NBC News, "She played a uniquely important role . . . as a symbol of the gradual disappearance of the obstacles to women in broadcast journalism."

Her autobiography: *Anchorwoman* (1982).

SAVO, JIMMY—comedian
b: 1895, New York City, N.Y. d: Sep 6, 1960

Through the Crystal Ball (dance)
.... host (1949)

A rotund little comic, long on Broadway, who specialized in pantomime and song parodies.

SAVOYS, THE—

The Ray Anthony Show (var)
.... regulars (1956–57)

SAWYER, DIANE—newscaster
b: Dec 22, 1945, Glasgow, Ky.

The American Parade (pub aff)
.... correspondent (1984)
60 Minutes (pub aff)
.... correspondent (1984–)

A blonde, brainy newscaster who looks a bit like Meryl Streep, and who has a reputation as one of the most tenacious reporters on television. Her route to the TV big time was unusual—in effect, she came over from the enemy camp.

Diane is the daughter of a county judge and was America's Junior Miss of 1963. She began her professional career as a weather girl on local television in the late 1960s but found that wasn't really suited to her talents ("I knew it was time to try something else," she says, "when I signed off one night with 'The high for today was 68. The current temperature is 73.' "). She went to Washington, D.C., in 1970 and landed a job in the Nixon administration, first in the press office and later as a staff assistant to the president himself. She was intensely loyal to Nixon, and he to her; when he resigned in 1974 she was one of a small group of loyalists who accompanied him to San Clemente, where for the next four years she assisted him in the writing of his memoirs.

When Diane joined CBS in 1978 it was over strong opposition from some correspondents (including, reportedly, Dan Rather, one of Nixon's chief antagonists in the press corps). She had, they argued, insufficient journalistic experience and was closely linked to the discredited administration. However, she proved herself by dint of extraordinarily hard work and unparalled sources within the bureaucracy. Her "rite of passage" came in 1981, when she interviewed Nixon himself on the *CBS Morning News* and grilled him relentlessly about his misdeeds. Even Rather was won over. Diane was co-anchor on the *Morning News* from 1981–84; she then became the first female correspondent on the top-rated *60 Minutes*.

SAWYER, HAL—host
b: 1914 d: Jan 9, 1977

Sawyer Views Hollywood (var)
.... host (1951)

SAWYER, JOE—actor
b: 1901, Canada d: Apr 21, 1982

Adventures of Rin Tin Tin (wes)
.... Sgt. Biff O'Hara (1954–59)

SAXON, DON—

The Fashion Story (misc) . regular (1948–49)

SAXON, JOHN—actor
b: Aug 5, 1935, Brooklyn, N.Y.

The New Doctors (drama)
.... Dr. Ted Stuart (1969–72)
79 Park Avenue (drama) . Harry Vito (1977)

A dark, baby-faced actor of Italian extraction who attracted much attention in the

'50s in juvenile delinquent roles. On television he played supporting parts on quite a few series, especially *Gunsmoke* and *Bonanza,* and starred in his own occasional series *The New Doctors* (part of the *Bold Ones* anthology) in 1969. His youthful promise unrealized, he has since reverted mostly to playing support in TV movies, miniseries, and series episodes, among the latter *Fantasy Island, Dynasty,* and *Scarecrow and Mrs. King.*

SAYLES, FRED—sportscaster

Monday Night Fights (sport)
.... sportscaster (1954–55)

SAYLOR, KATIE—actress

Fantastic Journey (sci fi) ...... Liana (1977)

SAYLOR, SID—actor
b: Mar 24, 1895, Chicago, Ill. d: Dec 21, 1962

Waterfront (adv) .... Wally (1953–56)

SBARGE, RAPHAEL—actor
b: Feb 12, New York City, N.Y.

Better Days (com) .. Brian McGuire (1986–)

SCALIA, JACK—actor
b: Nov 10, 1951, Brooklyn, N.Y.

The Devlin Connection (drama)
.... Nick Corsello (1982)
High Performance (adv)
.... Blue Stratton (1983)
Berrengers (drama) ... Danny Krucek (1985)
Hollywood Beat (police)
.... Det. Nick McCarren (1985)

Sylvester Stallone-ish young "Italian Stallion" actor, who was preposterously cast as Rock Hudson's son in *The Devlin Connection.* He was formerly a male model.

SCANNELL, KEVIN—actor

Harper Valley P.T.A. (com)
.... coach Burt Popwell (1981)

SCANNELL, SUSAN—actress
b: Feb 24, 1958, Lexington, Mass.

Dynasty (drama)
.... Nicole Simpson (1984–85)

SCARBURY, JOEY—singer
b: Jun 7, 1955, Ontario, Calif.

The Greatest American Hero (adv)
.... sang theme (1981–83)

A young singer easily mistaken for Glen Campbell, in sound at least. His recording of the theme from *The Greatest American Hero* ("Believe It or Not") was inescapable on beach radios during the summer of 1981.

SCARPELLI, GLENN—juvenile actor
b: Jul 6, 1966, Staten Island, N.Y.

One Day at a Time (com)
.... Alex Handris (1980–83)
Jennifer Slept Here (com) ... Marc (1983–84)

SCARWID, DIANA—actress
b: Savannah, Ga.

Studs Lonigan (drama)
.... Catherine Banahan (1979)

SCHAAF, LILLIAN—actress
One Man's Family (drama)
.... Hazel Barbour Herbert (1949–52)

SCHAAL, RICHARD—actor
b: May 5, Chicago, Ill.

Phyllis (com)..... Leo Heatherton (1975–76)
Please Stand By (com)
.... Frank Lambert (1978–79)
Trapper John, M.D. (drama)
.... Dr. Sandler (1980–84)
Just Our Luck (com) .... Chuck (1983)

The father of Wendy Schaal; he was an interior designer and homebuilder in Chicago until a friend asked him to design the set for a stage play and he consequently became fascinated with acting. He was later married to actress Valerie Harper.

SCHAAL, WENDY—actress
b: Jul 2, 1954, Chicago, Ill.

The Life and Times of Eddie Roberts (com)
.... Cynthia Lombocker (1980)
It's a Living (com).... Vicki Allen (1980–81)
Fantasy Island (drama) ..... Julie (1981–82)
AfterMASH (com)
.... Bonnie Hornbeck (1983–84)

SCHACHTER, FELICE—juvenile actress
The Facts of Life (com)
.... Nancy Olson (1979–82)

SCHACKELFORD, MICHAEL DAVID—infant actor
Family (drama) . Timmy Maitland (1978–80)

SCHAEFFER, LYDIA—juvenile actress
Leave It to Larry (com)
.... Harriet Tucker (1952)

SCHAEFFER, REBECCA—actress
b: Nov 6, 1967, Eugene, Ore.

My Sister Sam (com) . Patti Russell (1986–)

SCHAFER, NATALIE—actress
b: Nov 5, 1912, Rumson, N.J.

Gilligan's Island (com)
.... Mrs. Lovey Howell, III (1964–67)
The Survivors (drama)
.... Eleanor Carlyle (1969–70)

The widow of film actor Louis Calhern; on television in matronly supporting roles from the late 1950s onward.

SCHALLERT, WILLIAM—actor
b: Jul 6, 1922, Los Angeles, Calif.

The Many Loves of Dobie Gillis (com)
.... Mr. Leander Pomfritt (1959–63)
The Patty Duke Show (com)
.... Martin Lane (1963–66)
The Nancy Walker Show (com)
.... Teddy Futterman (1976)
The Hardy Boys Mysteries (adv)
.... Carson Drew (1977–78)
The Nancy Drew Mysteries (adv)
.... Carson Drew (1977–78)
Little Women (drama)
.... Rev. John March (1979)
Ike (drama) .... Gen. Mark Clark (1979)

A pleasant enough actor who has done a great deal of unexceptional television supporting work from the '50s to the '80s, often as an understanding dad. On *Dobie Gillis* he was Dobie's English teacher and on later series he was almost always a smiling father—Patty Duke's *(The Patty Duke Show),* Sparky Marcus's *(The Nancy Walker Show),* Pamela Sue Martin's *(Nancy Drew Mysteries),* or everybody's

(Little Women). A partial list of the series on which he has made multiple guest appearances over the years reads like a history of TV: *Loretta Young; Perry Mason; Gunsmoke; Have Gun Will Travel; The Wild Wild West; Get Smart; Owen Marshall, Counselor at Law; The F.B.I.; Little House on the Prairie; The Waltons;* et al.

SCHANLEY, TOM—actor

The Yellow Rose (drama)
.... Whit Champion (1983–84)

SCHECHNER, BILL—newscaster
b: c. 1941, Newark, N.J.

NBC News Overnight (news)
.... anchor (1982–83)

SCHEDEEN, ANN—actress
b: Jan 8, Portland, Ore. r: Gresham, Ore.

Marcus Welby, M.D. (drama)
.... Sandy Porter (1975–76)
Paper Dolls (drama)..... Sara Frank (1984)
Alf (com) .... Kate Tanner (1986–)

SCHEFTEL, STUART—newscaster

The Hot Seat (int).............. host (1952)

SCHELL, CATHERINE—actress

The Search for the Nile (drama)
.... Florence Baker (1972)
The Adventurer (drama)
.... Diane Mash (1972–73)
Space 1999 (sci fi) .... Maya (1976–77)

Swiss actress, of moviedom's famed Schell family—which includes Maria, Maxmillian, and Karl.

SCHELL, RONNIE—actor, comedian
b: Dec 23, 1931, Richmond, Calif. r: San Francisco area

Gomer Pyle, U.S.M.C. (com)
.... Duke Slater (1964–69)
That Girl (com) ..... Harvey Peck (1966–67)
Good Morning, World (com)
.... Larry Clarke (1967–68)
The Jim Nabors Hour (var)
.... regular (1969–71)

Ronnie, who billed himself as "America's Slowest Rising Comedian," was among

other things the voice of Peter Puck in the animated "NHL Hockey Hints," seen during NBC's hockey telecasts in the 1970s. He also did voices for assorted Saturday morning cartoon series.

SCHENKEL, CHRIS—sportscaster
b: Aug 21, 1923, Bippus, Ind.

Monday Night Fights (sport)
.... sportscaster (1953–56)

After the demise of the DuMont *Monday Night Fights* (the last regular series on that ill-fated network), Chris worked steadily as a sportscaster for NBC, CBS, and then exclusively for ABC. He began his network career in 1947, covering college football.

SCHERER, RAY—newscaster
b: Fort Wayne, Ind.

This Is NBC News (news)...... host (1962)
Ray Scherer's Sunday Report (news)
.... host (1963)
NBC Weekend News (news)
.... anchorman (1965–67)

SCHIAVELLI, VINCENT—actor

The Corner Bar (com)
.... Peter Panama (1972)
Fast Times (com)
.... Mr. Hector Vargas (1986)

SCHICK, GEORGE—symphony conductor
b: Apr 5, 1908, Prague, Czechoslavakia d: Mar 7, 1985

Chicago Symphony (music)
.... conductor (1954–55)

SCHIEFFER, BOB—newscaster
b: Feb 25, 1937, Austin, Texas

CBS Weekend News (Sun) (news)
.... anchorman (1973–74)
CBS Weekend News (Sun) (news)
.... anchorman (1976)
CBS Weekend News (Sat) (news)
.... anchorman (1976–)

Emmy Awards: Best News Segment, for the *CBS Evening News* Reports "The Air War" (1972) and "TV Campaigning" (1985); Best News Special, for "Watergate—The White House Transcripts" (1974); Best

Newswriting, for *CBS Reports:* "The Defense of the U.S.—Ground Zero" (1981)

Bob has been with CBS News since 1969; for 12 years prior to that, he was a local newspaper and television reporter in the Dallas–Fort Worth area.

SCHILDKRAUT, JOSEPH—actor
b: Mar 22, 1895, Vienna, Austria d: Jan 21, 1964

Joseph Schildkraut Presents (drama)
.... host/star (1953–54)

Autobiography: *My Father and I* (1959).

SCHILLING, WILLIAM G.—actor
b: Aug 30, Philadelphia, Pa.

E/R (com) ... Richard, the orderly (1984–85)
Head of the Class (com)
.... Dr. Samuels (1986–)

A cherubic, middle-aged actor who accurately describes himself (visually, at least) as "a cross between Charles Durning and W. C. Fields." He began on the New York stage, and has been concentrating on TV work since the early '80s.

SCHMOCK, JONATHAN—actor
b: Feb 26, La Jolla, Calif.

Double Trouble (com)
.... Billy Batalato (1984–85)

With James Vallely, half of the "Funny Boys" comedy team.

SCHNECKLEGRUBER—comedian

Dean Martin Presents Bobby Darin (var)
.... regular (1972)

SCHNEIDER, DANIEL J.—actor
b: Jan 14, 1966, Memphis, Tenn.

Head of the Class (com)
.... Dennis Blunden (1986–)

SCHNEIDER, JOHN—actor
b: Apr 8, 1954, Mt. Kisco, N.Y.

The Dukes of Hazzard (com)
.... Bo Duke (1979–85)

One of television's blond hunks, who shot to fame as a "good ol' boy" on *The Dukes*

of Hazzard. He reportedly showed up for his audition for the series wearing a dirty T-shirt and old jeans, with a week's growth of beard, and carrying a can of beer—just to look the part. Before *Dukes,* John was active mostly in theater, clubs, and commercials in the Atlanta area; since then, he has worked very hard to promote for himself a recording career, with only middling results.

He is married to newscaster Tawny Schneider.

SCHNEIDER, TAWNY—newscaster
b: Sep 15, 1956, Portland, Me. r: New York, N.Y.

Eye on Hollywood (mag)..... host (1983–84)

Miss America of 1976.

SCHOEN, VIC—orchestra leader
b: Mar 26, 1916, Brooklyn, N.Y. r: Los Angeles, Calif.

The Dinah Shore Show (music)
.... orch. leader (1951–54)
The Patti Page Olds Show (var)
.... orch. leader (1958–59)
Kraft Music Hall Presents The Dave King Show (var)............ orch. leader (1959)

SCHORR, LONNIE—comedian
b: Zebulon, N.C.

Tony Orlando and Dawn (var)
.... regular (1974–76)

SCHRECK, VICKI—juvenile actress

How the West Was Won (miniseries) (drama)........................ Jessie (1977)
How the West Was Won (wes)
.... Jessie Macahan (1978–79)

SCHREIBER, AVERY—comedian
b: Apr 9, 1935, Chicago, Ill.

My Mother the Car (com)
.... Capt. Mancini (1965–66)
Our Place (var) .... regular (1967)
The Burns and Schreiber Comedy Hour (var)
.... costar (1973)
Ben Vereen ... Comin' at Ya (var)
.... regular (1975)
Sammy and Company (talk)
.... regular (1975–77)
Sha Na Na (var) .... regular (1977–78)

A portly, mustachioed comedian, with Chicago's Second City troupe in the early 1960s. He then joined with natty Jack Burns to form the comedy team of Burns and Schreiber, which was much-seen on variety shows of the '60s and '70s. (*TV Guide* called them "Natty and the Beanbag.") Later, he was familiar crunching his way through corn chip commercials.

SCHRODER, RICKY—juvenile actor
b: Apr 13, 1970, Staten Island, N.Y.

Silver Spoons (com)
.... Ricky Stratton (1982–86)

Some people think it's the tears; he summoned up a river of them in his first film. Others say it's that look of incredible innocence, so refreshing in a day when kids seem to be smarter (or think they are) than the adults around them. Whatever it is, winsome, blond Ricky Schroder was one of the most popular "TV kids" of the 1980s. Ricky, accompanied by his ever-present mother, was in show business from the age of three months, when he began modeling diapers. After approximately 50 commercials, he got his first big acting assignment, with Jon Voight in the tear-stained film *The Champ* ("It's not all that hard," Ricky says. "I do what a lot of actors do. I just think about something sad and cry.") The movie led to other film roles (he cried in all of them) and, in 1982, to the popular situation comedy *Silver Spoons*.

SCHRUM, PETE—actor

Gimme a Break (com)
.... Uncle Ed Kanisky (1982–83)

SCHUBB, MARK—actor

Condo (com) .... Scott Kirkridge (1983)

SCHUCK, JOHN—comedian, actor
b: Feb 4, 1940, Boston, Mass.

McMillan and Wife (police)
.... Sgt. Charles Enright (1971–77)
Holmes and Yoyo (com)
...... Gregory "Yoyo" Yoyonovich (1976)
Roots (drama)............... Ordell (1977)
Turnabout (com) .... Sam Alston (1979)
The New Odd Couple (com)
.... Murray (1982–83)

Tall, gangly John Schuck is best known for his "dumb" roles, particularly that of dim-witted Sgt. Enright (later promoted to lieutenant!) on *McMillan and Wife.* Following graduation from college, John spent the '60s in regional theater and, late in the decade, did a few TV guest roles on *Gunsmoke, NET Playhouse,* etc. The turning point in his career came in 1970, when he was spotted onstage by director Robert Altman, who cast him in the hit movie *M*A*S*H* as Painless, the sexually frustrated dentist. More films and episodic TV followed, and, in 1971, his role in *McMillan.* His subsequent series have been less successful—notably the gimmicky *Holmes and Yoyo,* in which he played a robot, and *Turnabout,* in which he was a woman inside a man's body.

SCHUCK, PETER—actor

Operation Petticoat (com)
.... Seaman Horwich (1977–78)

SCHULMAN, EMILY—actress

Small Wonder (com)
.... Harriet Brindle (1985–)

SCHULTZ, DWIGHT—actor
b: Nov 24, 1947, Baltimore, Md.

The A-Team (adv)
H. M. "Howling Mad" Murdock (1983–)

Married to actress Wendy Fulton. Dwight was primarily a stage actor before his phenomenal success as the wild-eyed "Howling Mad" on *The A-Team.*

SCHULTZ, KEITH—juvenile actor

The Monroes (wes)
.... Jefferson Monroe (1966–67)

SCHULTZ, KEVIN—juvenile actor

The Monroes (wes)
.... Fennimore Monroe (1966–67)
The New Adventures of Huck Finn (adv)
.... Tom Sawyer (1968–69)

Keith and Kevin are twins.

SCHULTZ, LENNY—comedian
b: Dec 13, The Bronx, N.Y.

Ball Four (com)
.... Lenny "Birdman" Siegel (1976)
The Late Summer Early Fall Bert Convy Show (var)....... Lenny the Bionic Chicken (1976)
Laugh-In (revival) (var) ... regular (1977–78)

A former physical education teacher (for 14 years), who gave up making funny faces and sounds for his students and started doing it for the TV cameras.

SCHUMANN, WALTER—choral director
b: Oct 8, 1913, New York City, N.Y. d: Aug 21, 1958

The Ford Show (var) ..... chorus (1956–57)

Emmy Award: Best Original Music, for *Dragnet* (1954).

SCHUYLER, ANN—actress

It's a Man's World (com) ... Nora (1962–63)

SCHWARTZ, AARON—actor

Check It Out (com)........ Leslie (1985–)

SCHWARTZ, NEIL J.—actor

Happy Days (com) .... Bag (1974–75)

SCOGGINS, TRACY—actress
b: Nov 13, Galveston, Texas

Renegades (police) .... Tracy (1983)
Hawaiian Heat (police)
.... Irene Gorley (1984)
Dynasty II: The Colbys (drama)
.... Monica Colby (1985–)

SCOLARI, PETER—actor
b: Sep 12, 1954, New Rochelle, N.Y.

Goodtime Girls (com).. Benny Loman (1980)
Bosom Buddies (com)
.. Henry Desmond (Hildegarde) (1980–82)
Baby Makes Five (com)
.... Eddie Riddle (1983)
Newhart (com)..... Michael Harris (1984–)

SCOTT, ADELE, TRIO—

The Skip Farrell Show (music)
.... regular (1949)

SCOTT, ALAN—host, songwriter
b: Oct 13, 1922, Haddonfield, N.J.

Television Screen Magazine (mag)
.... emcee/"editor" (1948–49)
Spin the Picture (quiz)....... trio (1949–50)

Among other things, Alan composed a bit of television music that probably every viewer has heard at least once—"Smile, You're on Candid Camera!"

SCOTT, BILL—actor
b: c. 1920, r: New Jersey d: Nov 29, 1985

The Bullwinkle Show (cartn)
.... Mr. Peabody (voice) (1961–62)
The Bullwinkle Show (cartn)
.... Dudley Doright (voice) (1961–62)
The Bullwinkle Show (cartn)
.... Bullwinkle J. Moose (voice) (1961–62)

SCOTT, BONNIE—actress

That Girl (com) .. Judy Bessemer (1966–67)

SCOTT, BRENDA—actress
b: Mar 15, 1943, Cincinnati, Ohio

The Road West (wes)
.... Midge Pride (1966–67)

Brenda was married to actor Andrew Prine in 1965, divorced him, and then costarred with him (as his younger sister) in the 1966 western *The Road West*. She was quite active as a guest actress in many other series of the '60s and early '70s as well, including *Dr. Kildare, The Fugitive, The Virginian,* etc.

SCOTT, DEBRALEE—actress
b: Apr 2, 1953, Elizabeth, N.J.

Sons and Daughters (drama)
.... Evie Martinson (1974)
Welcome Back, Kotter (com)
.... Rosalie Totzie (1975–76)
Mary Hartman, Mary Hartman (com)
.... Cathy Shumway (1976–78)
Angie (com)........ Marie Falco (1979–80)

SCOTT, DEVON—actress

We'll Get By (com)..... Andrea Platt (1975)
The Tony Randall Show (com)
..... Roberta "Bobby" Franklin (1976–77)

SCOTT, DIANA—

Hee Haw (var).......... regular (1969–70)

SCOTT, DONOVAN—actor
b: Sep 29, Chico, Calif.

Presenting Susan Anton (var)
.... regular (1979)
Life with Lucy (com)
.... Leonard Stoner (1986–)

SCOTT, ERIC—juvenile actor
b: Oct 20, 1958, Hollywood, Calif.

The Waltons (drama)
.... Ben Walton (1972–81)

SCOTT, EVELYN—actress

Bachelor Father (com)
.... Adelaide Mitchell (1960–62)
Peyton Place (drama).. Ada Jacks (1965–69)

SCOTT, FRANK—pianist, arranger
b: Jun 21, 1921, Fargo, N.D.

The Lawrence Welk Show (music)
.... regular (1956–69)

SCOTT, FRED—actor, singer
b: Feb 14, 1902, Fresno, Calif.

Vincent Lopez (var) ... announcer (1949–50)

A popular cowboy star of the 1940s, billed then as "The Silvery-Voiced Buckaroo."

SCOTT, GEOFFREY—actor
b: Feb 22, Hollywood, Calif.

The Secret Empire (drama)
.... Marshal Jim Donner (1979)
Concrete Cowboys (adv)
.... Will Ewbanks (1981)
Dynasty (drama) .. Mark Jennings (1982–84)

SCOTT, GEORGE C.—actor
b: Oct 18, 1926*, Wise, Va. r: Detroit, Mich.

East Side/West Side (drama)
.... Neil Brock (1963–64)

Emmy Award: Best Actor in a Single Performance, for the *Hallmark Hall of Fame* Production *The Price* (1971) (refused award)

He denounced television as cowardly pap, and refused its highest award. TV acting was merely "garbaging lines," he said, and anyone with any legitimate desires

*Some sources give 1927.

and aspirations as an actor should go elsewhere. Scott, one of Hollywood's great rebels, has had the same tempestuous relationship with TV that he has had with movies. On both screens he could be gruff, intensely powerful, absolutely spellbinding, and his offscreen behavior reflected a similarly demanding temperament.

Scott's TV appearances have been mostly in prestigious dramatic specials. He came to the medium in the late '50s, before he entered films; viewers first saw him on live playhouse series such as *DuPont Show of the Month* ("A Tale of Two Cities," 1958), *Kraft Theatre,* and *Omnibus.* He played guest roles on a few continuing series in the early '60s—*Ben Casey, Naked City, The Virginian*—and then agreed to star in his own one and only regular series, *East Side/West Side.* TV at the time was overwhelmingly dominated by escapist comedies such as *The Beverly Hillbillies* and *My Favorite Martian,* and Scott's was one of the few hard-hitting, realistic dramas on the air. In it, he played a social worker fighting ignorance and bureaucracy in the New York ghettos. It was a noble experiment, but ultimately a frustrating one. CBS continually meddled with the show, he claimed, completely destroying its dramatic thrust in order to avoid offending anyone. For example, network censors insisted on deleting shots of rats in a story about a baby that had been killed by them, and, on another occasion, cut a sequence in which Scott impulsively danced with a black woman.

East Side/West Side was canceled after a single season, and Scott strongly intimated that he would never do another series ("those quivering masses waiting for my return can relax and forget it"). He made only occasional TV appearances thereafter, though they were often notable. Two episodes of *The Road West,* in which he appeared in 1966, were combined and released as a theatrical movie, and he received much acclaim for his dramatic specials, including *The Crucible* (1967), *Jane Eyre* (1971), *Fear On Trial* (1975), and *Beauty and the Beast* (1976)—in which he played the beast, wearing a boar's head for the entire story. In 1970 he made headlines by becoming the first actor in history to refuse an Academy Award (for *Patton*) and a few months later he turned down an Emmy Award as well. He continues to go very much his own way, appearing in the '80s in such highly regarded TV productions as *Oliver Twist* (1982), *A Christmas Carol* (1984)—as Scrooge, of course—and *Mussolini* (1985).

SCOTT, HAZEL—black singer, pianist
b: Jun 11, 1920, Port of Spain, Trinidad r: U.S.A. d: Oct 2, 1981

Hazel Scott (music)......... hostess (1950)

A stylish jazz pianist and cabaret singer who was the first black woman to host a network series. In the mid-1950s her career was hobbled by McCarthy-era political blacklisting and she moved to Paris, where she continued to perform until the early '70s. She was married in the '40s and '50s to activist congressman Adam Clayton Powell.

SCOTT, JACQUELINE—actress
b: Sikeston, Md.

The Fugitive (drama)
.... Donna Taft (1963–67)

The actress who played the understanding married sister of Dr. Richard Kimble (David Janssen), the man on the run on *The Fugitive.*

SCOTT, JACQUES—actor
The Ann Sothern Show (com)
.... Paul Martine (1958–59)

SCOTT, JANE—
Seven at Eleven (var)....... regular (1951)

SCOTT, JEAN BRUCE—actress
b: Feb 25, Monterey, Calif.

Magnum, P.I. (drama)
.... Lt. Poole (1982–84)
Airwolf (adv)
.... Caitlin O'Shannessy (1984–86)

SCOTT, JOE—actor
Mr. Lucky (adv)....... maitre d' (1959–60)

SCOTT, JOSEPH (JOEY)—juvenile actor
National Velvet (adv)
.... Donald Brown (1960–62)

SCOTT, JUDSON—actor
The Phoenix (sci fi)
.... Bennu of the Golden Light (1982)

SCOTT, KATHRYN LEIGH—actress
b: Jan 26, Robbinsdale, Minn.

Big Shamus, Little Shamus (drama)
.... Stephanie Marsh (1979)

Kathryn's first major role, upon graduating from acting school, was in the daytime soap opera *Dark Shadows.* It was she who, in 1966, spoke the unforgettable first words on the first episode of the series—"You're a jerk!" After four years on the famous serial she moved to Europe, where she spent most of the '70s as a stage and film actress. She later returned to the U.S. and played guest roles on *Dynasty* and others, and had a continuing part on the short-lived *Big Shamus, Little Shamus.*

SCOTT, LORENE—actress
b: c. 1908 d: Apr 19, 1983

Faraway Hill (drama) .... regular (1946)

SCOTT, LUCIEN—actor
The Bob Newhart Show (com)
.... Mr. Vickers (1974–75)

SCOTT, MARTHA—actress
b: Sep 22, 1914, Jamesport, Mo.

The Bionic Woman (adv)
.... Helen Elgin (1976)
Dallas (drama)
.... Mrs. Patricia Shepard (1979)
Secrets of Midland Heights (drama)
.... Margaret Millington (1980–81)
Dallas (drama)
.... Mrs. Patricia Shepard (1985)

Martha's most famous role came early in her career—that of Emily in *Our Town,* which she played both onstage in 1938 and in the film version in 1940, the latter bringing her an Academy Award nomination. After that, she moved rather quickly into supporting roles, often of the motherly sort. She was seen quite a bit on television, beginning around 1950, on series including *Lux Video Theatre, Robert Montgomery Presents, Route 66,* etc. She was Bob Newhart's dippy mom in occasional appearances on *The Bob Newhart Show,* Lee Major's honest one on *The Six Million Dollar Man* and *The Bionic Woman,* and Jordan Christopher's scheming one on *Secrets of Midland Heights.*

SCOTT, NORMAN—singer

Melody Tour (var).......... regular (1954)

SCOTT, PAUL C.—actor

Small Wonder (com) .... Reggie (1985–)

SCOTT, PIPPA—actress
b: Nov 10, 1935, Los Angeles, Calif.

Mr. Lucky (adv)
..... Maggie Shank-Rutherford (1959–60)
The Virginian (wes)
.... Molly Wood (1962–63)
Jigsaw John (police)
.... Maggie Hearn (1976)

SCOTT, RAYMOND—orchestra leader
b: Sep 10, 1909, Brooklyn, N.Y.

Your Hit Parade (music)
.... orch. leader (1950–57)

A quintet and orchestra leader of the '30s and '40s, well-known for his offbeat arrangements—and titles ("The Toy Trumpet," "Dinner Music for a Pack of Hungry Cannibals," etc.). Scott was the brother of radio orchestra leader Mark Warnow, whom he succeeded, after the latter's death, on *Your Hit Parade.* He was married to *Hit Parade* singer Dorothy Collins.

SCOTT, SIMON—actor
b: Monterey Park, Calif.

Markham (drama)....... John Riggs (1959)
McHale's Navy (com)
.... Gen. Bronson (1965–66)
Trapper John, M.D. (drama)
.... Arnold Slocum (1979–85)

SCOTT, SYNDA—actress
b: Chicago, Ill.

Foreign Intrigue (drama)
.... Helen Davis (1951–53)

SCOTT, TIMOTHY—actor

Wildside (wes).............. Skillet (1985)

SCOTT, VERNON—cohost

Tonight! America After Dark (talk)
.... regular (1957)

SCOTT, ZACHARY—actor
b: Feb 24, 1914, Austin, Texas d: Oct 3, 1965

Spotlight Playhouse (drama) .... host (1959)

A lean, handsome actor of films, who often portrayed a charming villain. He did quite a bit of television work on playhouse series of the 1950s, including *Robert Montgomery Presents, Science Fiction Theater,* etc. He continued active up to the time of his death, appearing in an episode of *The Rogues* in early 1965.

SCOTTI, VITO—actor
b: Jan 26, 1918, San Francisco, Calif. r: Italy

Mama Rosa (com)........... Nikolai (1950)
The Flying Nun (com)
Police Capt. Gaspar Formento (1968–69)
To Rome with Love (com)
.... Gino Mancini (1969–71)
Barefoot in the Park (com)
.... Mr. Velasquez (1970–71)

SCRIBNER, JIMMY—actor
b: Norfolk, Va.

Sleepy Joe (child) .... host (1949)

A white actor who made his name on radio telling "Darky Stories." He later hosted a children's TV puppet show built around a similar theme. It would probably be considered rather offensive today.

SCROGGINS, BOBBY—juvenile actor

The Adventures of Sir Lancelot (adv)
.... Brian (1956–57)

SCRUGGS, LANGHORN—actress

The Corner Bar (com) .... Mary Ann (1972)

SCRUGGS, LINDA—actress

Whiz Kids (drama).... Ms. Vance (1983–84)

SEAGRAM, LISA—actress

The Beverly Hillbillies (com)
.... Edythe Brewster (1965–66)

SEAGREN, BOB—actor

b: Oct 17, 1946, Pomona, Calif.

Soap (com) .... Dennis Phillips (1978)

A handsome former Olympic pole-vaulting champion, who later turned to acting.

SEAGULL, BARBARA

See HERSHEY BARBARA

SEALES, FRANKLYN—black actor

b: Jul 15, St. Vincent, West Indies

Silver Spoons (com)
.... Dexter Stuffins (1982–86)

The prissy business manager on *Silver Spoons.*

SEALS AND CROFTS—singers

James Seals, b: Oct 17, 1941, Sidney, Texas
Dash Crofts, b: Aug 14, 1940, Cisco, Texas

The Paper Chase (drama)
.... sang theme (1978–79)

SEARS, BILL—host

Kid Gloves (sport)....... announcer (1951)

SEARS, PEGGY—singer

CBS Newcomers (var) .... regular (1971)

SEATLE, DIXIE—actress

Adderly (adv)............. Mona (1986–)

SEBASTIAN, JOHN—singer, songwriter

b: Mar 17, 1944, New York City, N.Y.

Welcome Back, Kotter (com)
.... sang theme (1975–79)

Onetime leader of the 1960s rock group the Lovin' Spoonful.

SEBESKY, DON—orchestra leader

b: Dec 10, 1937, Perth Amboy, N.J.

The Jimmy Dean Show (var)
.... orch. leader (1965–66)

A well-known jazz bandleader and arranger.

SECONDARI, JOHN—producer, newscaster

b: Nov 1, 1919, Rome, Italy r: U.S.A. d: Feb 3, 1975

Open Hearing (pub aff)
.... host/moderator (1957–58)

Emmy Award: Best News Documentary, for *I, Leonardo da Vinci* (1965)

One of television's leading documentary producers of the '60s, specializing in historical subjects such as ABC's *Saga of Western Man* series. He began as a writer (one of his novels was made into the motion picture *Three Coins in the Fountain*), then became a CBS news correspondent, and from 1956–60 was ABC's bureau chief in Washington, D.C. During the latter period he hosted the interview program *Open Hearing.* After spending the 1960s in executive capacities with ABC, he became an independent producer in 1969.

SEDAN, ROLFE—actor

b: Jan 20, 1896, New York City, N.Y. d: Sep 15, 1982

The George Burns and Gracie Allen Show (com)... Mr. Beasley, the mailman (1950–58)

SEEGER, SARA—actress

Dennis the Menace (com)
.... Eloise Wilson (1962–63)
Occasional Wife (com)
.... Mrs. Christopher (1966–67)

SEEL, CHARLES—actor

b: c. 1897, The Bronx, N.Y.

Gunsmoke (wes)
.... Barney (1955–75)
The Road West (wes)
.... Grandpa Pride (1966–67)

A character actor periodically seen as the Dodge City telegraph agent on *Gunsmoke.* He is also remembered for his occasional appearances as Mr. Krinkle on *Dennis the Menace.*

SEER, RICHARD—actor

Delta House (com)
.... Larry ("Pinto") Kroger (1979)

SEFF, RICHARD—actor

Charade Quiz (quiz)
.... repertory player (1947–49)

SEGAL, JONATHAN—actor
b: Jul 8, 1953, New York City, N.Y.

The Paper Chase (drama)
.... Jonathan Brooks (1978)

SEGALL, PAMELA—juvenile actress

The Facts of Life (com)
.... Kelly Affinado (1983–84)
The Redd Foxx Show (com)
.... Toni Rutledge (1986)

SEGALL, RICKY—juvenile actor

The Partridge Family (com)
.... Ricky Stevens (1973–74)

SEGERS, HARRY—orchestra leader

Continental Showcase (var)
.... orch. leader (1966)

SEIGEL, IRMA—actress

Fernwood 2-Night (com)
.... Aunt Edity (1977–78)

SEKKA, JOHNNY—black actor
b: 1939, Dakar, Senegal r: Paris, France

Master of the Game (drama)
.... Banda (1984)

SELBY, DAVID—actor
b: Feb 5, 1941, Morgantown, W. Va.

Flamingo Road (drama)
.... Michael Tyrone (1981–82)
Falcon Crest (drama)
.... Richard Channing (1982–)

This tall, sinewy soap-opera actor got his start as one of television's most famous vampires—Quentin, on *Dark Shadows* in the late '60s. He later played guest roles on various TV dramas *(The Waltons, Family, Washington: Behind Closed Doors)* before becoming a scheming regular on the nighttime serials *Flamingo Road* and *Falcon Crest* in the '80s.

SELBY, SARAH—actress
b: 1906, St. Louis, Mo. d: Jan 7, 1980

Father Knows Best (com)
.... Miss Thomas (1954–60)
Gunsmoke (wes) .... Ma Smalley (1962–75)

As Ma Smalley, Sarah ran the boardinghouse in *Gunsmoke*'s Dodge City.

SELLECCA, CONNIE—actress
b: May 25, 1955, The Bronx, N.Y.

Flying High (adv) ... Lisa Benton (1978–79)
Beyond Westworld (sci fi)
.... Pamela Williams (1980)
The Greatest American Hero (adv)
.... Pam Davidson (1981–83)
Hotel (drama).... Christine Francis (1983–)

This stylish actress began attracting attention almost as soon as she entered acting, right out of high school. Forgoing college, she worked briefly as a model and then, with her very first screen test in 1977, won a costarring role in the TV movie *The Bermuda Depths.* From then on she became known mostly for portraying attractive and self-assured professional women. She was a stewardess in the TV movie (and subsequent series) *Flying High,* the assistant to a security chief in *Beyond Westworld,* a lady lawyer (and William Katt's girlfriend) in *The Greatest American Hero,* and the canny assistant hotel manager in *Hotel.* She is married to actor Gil *(Buck Rogers)* Girard.

SELLECK, TOM—actor
b: Jan 29, 1945, Detroit, Mich. r: Los Angeles, Calif.

The Rockford Files (drama)
...... Lance White (occasional) (1979–80)
Magnum, P.I. (drama)
.... Tom Magnum (1980–)

Emmy Award: Best Actor in a Dramatic Series, for *Magnum, P.I.* (1984)

No doubt the most famous mustache of the '80s adorns Tom Selleck, the commanding (6' 4"), likable star of *Magnum, P.I.* Selleck has managed to develop a type of appeal enjoyed by few other actors (Clark Gable and Burt Reynolds come to mind)— among women for his obvious sex appeal, and among men for his offhanded, "one of the guys," robust sense of humor.

Tom did not come to this happy state overnight. In college he was a star athlete who turned to acting in commercials to help pay the bills. By 1970 he had graduated to TV guest roles, including a recurring part in *Bracken's World*. In that same year he made his movie debut (sans mustache) as one of Mae West's studs in *Myra Breckinridge*. The early and mid 1970s brought a succession of secondary parts in TV movies and series episodes, including roles on *Sarge; Owen Marshall Counselor at Law; Lucas Tanner;* and *Charlie's Angels*. During 1974–75 he was Jamie Lyn Bauer's love interest on daytime's *The Young and the Restless* (still no mustache). His first really major role was in the miniseries *The Sacketts* in 1977, as one of the three Sackett brothers.

Tom also made several pilots in hopes of landing a series of his own, and if things had worked out a bit differently we might have first seen him in a series as a Los Angeles bunco cop partnered with Robert Urich (*Bunco*, 1977), as a World War II commando partnered with James Whitmore, Jr. (*The Gypsy Warriors*, 1978), or as a globe-trotting detective, also with Whitmore (*Boston and Kilbride*, 1979). Instead, a couple of guest shots on *The Rockford Files* as Lance White, the insufferably perfect private eye who drove James Garner up the wall, showed a different side of Tom's talents—action played with humor. It was this approach that made a smash hit out of *Magnum, P.I.*.

SELTZER, WILL—actor

Karen (com) ...... Adam Cooperman (1975)
Hizzonner (com) ...... James Cooper (1979)

SELZER, MILTON—actor

Needles and Pins (com)
.... Julius Singer (1973)
Scruples (drama) .... Sid Amos (1980)

SEMON, LARRY—narrator

The Clock (drama) ...... narrator (1949–52)

SENNETT, SUSAN—actress

Ozzie's Girls (com).. Susie Hamilton (1973)

SENNO, HIROMI—actor

Shogun (drama) .... Fujiko (1980)

SENPORTY, NINO—

The Smothers Brothers Show (var)
.... regular (1975)

SERLING, ROD—writer, host
b: Dec 25, 1924, Syracuse, N.Y. d: Jun 28, 1975

The Twilight Zone (sci fi).... host (1959–64)
The Undersea World of Jacques Cousteau (doc) .... narrator (1968–74)
Liar's Club (quiz).............. host (1969)
Night Gallery (drama) .... host (1970–73)

Emmy Awards: Best Original Teleplay, for the *Kraft Television Theatre* Production "Patterns" (1955); the *Playhouse 90* Productions "Requiem for a Heavyweight" (1956) and "The Comedian" (1957); for Various Episodes of *The Twilight Zone* (1960, 1961); Best Dramatic Adaptation, for the *Chrysler Theatre* Production "It's Mental Work" (1964)

"Before a script goes before the cameras, the networks, the sponsors, and the Madison Avenue ad agency men tinker with it. By the time it's seen on the home screen, a great deal or all of the real life juices have been squeezed out of it . . . No wonder almost everything that passes through the tube is monumentally forgettable."

Those bitter words, ironically, were from a man who did more to raise the standards of television drama—to show what *could* be done—than almost anyone in the medium's history. Rod Serling was a pugnacious little man, and he fought for much of his career to maintain his artistic integrity in the face of overwhelming commercial pressures. Sometimes he won.

Serling had a rugged youth. He was a paratrooper in the Pacific during World War II and a Golden Gloves boxer. He began writing for radio in the late '40s—winning a prize for a script for the *Dr. Christian* series—and moved into TV a few years later. Although his name was unknown to the general public, he wrote for many of the top series of the day, including *Kraft Theatre, The U.S. Steel Hour, Studio One, The Elgin TV Hour, Fireside Theatre, Center Stage, Lux Video Theatre, Suspense, Playhouse 90, Danger, General Electric Theater, Climax,* and *Desilu Playhouse*. Several of his works (see Emmy list above) were among the most honored TV plays ever. His work is often identified with science fiction but actually has a very strong human element, often man in a large, frightening, and not always rational world. In 1959, with traditional playhouse series on the wane, Rod expanded on this theme by creating what became perhaps the most successful and unique anthology series of all, *The Twilight Zone,* which is still widely rerun. He also hosted it, and viewers for the first time became familiar with his dark, tough features and clipped speech—which was widely mimicked.

After five glorious years on *The Twilight Zone,* Rod went on to write for other series (e.g., *The Loner*) and even turned up as an actor once in a while—as on a *Jack Benny Show* episode in which Jack tried to convince Rod to write for him (what a series that would have been!). In the early '70s he was frequently seen in commercials, in addition to hosting his own new series, *Night Gallery.* The latter was a major frustration for him, however, as he had very little creative control over it, serving mainly as the on-camera "front man." Rod's last project was even stranger; he planned to host a 1975 summer comedy variety series called *Keep On Truckin'.* However, he died of complications from open heart surgery shortly before the premiere.

Rod Serling will be remembered not for these later projects but for his massive contribution to quality television in the '50s, and especially for *The Twilight Zone.* As *TV Guide* commented on his passing, "We are all in his debt."

SERVER, ERIC—actor

Buck Rogers in the 25th Century (sci fi)
.... Dr. Theopolis (voice) (1979–80)
B.J. and the Bear (adv)
.... Lt. Jim Steiger (1981)

SEVAREID, ERIC—newscaster
b: Nov 26, 1912, Velva, N.D.

Capitol Cloak Room (pub aff)
.... panelist (1949–50)
The American Week (news)
.... anchorman (1954)
The March of Medicine (doc)
.... narrator (1958)
CBS Weekend News (news)
.... anchorman (1962–63)

Conversations with Eric Sevareid (int)
.... host (1975)

Emmy Awards: Best News Segments, for *CBS Evening News:* "LBJ—The Man and the President" (1973) and coverage of the Agnew Resignation (1974); Special Award for Achievement in Broadcast Journalism (1977)

To younger viewers in the '60s, Eric Sevareid seemed to be CBS's gray eminence, always commenting sagely (and sometimes ponderously) on the Great Events of the Day; to older ones, he was a visible reminder of the continuity of CBS news, "harking" back to the days when Edward R. Murrow began the network's tradition of excellence during World War II.

Sevareid was in fact one of "Murrow's boys," part of the original team assembled by the legendary correspondent at the beginning of World War II. Eric was even then known as an internationalist; he had begun as a reporter for the *Minneapolis Journal* but soon moved to Europe, where he worked for the *Paris Herald Tribune* and United Press. He became a very familiar voice on radio during the war, covering both the European and Pacific campaigns (where he was once shot down in the jungle and forced to live for a month with a tribe of headhunters). After the war he shifted more toward political reporting from Washington and in 1964 was named CBS national correspondent there. As CBS said at the time, "we felt his place is more properly where the great decisions of our day are being made." He was often seen as a commentator on Walter Cronkite's *CBS Evening News*—gruff, forceful, and always with a global perspective. Eric also hosted numerous news specials of the essay/philosophical type, including an acclaimed session with longshoreman-philosopher Eric Hoffer. In 1975, CBS telecast a series of his interviews with world figures under the title *Conversations with Eric Sevareid.*

Sevareid reached CBS's mandatory retirement age in 1977 but continued thereafter as a consultant to the network and was seen in occasional network, syndicated, and PBS news-analysis programs. In 1982 he hosted the 24-part syndicated series *Eric Sevareid's Chronicle.*

SEVEN, JOHNNY—actor

b: Feb 23, 1930, New York City, N.Y.

Ironside (police)
.... Lt. Carl Reese (1969–75)
Amy Prentiss (police)
.... Det. Contreras (1974–75)

SEVERINSEN, DOC—orchestra leader

b: Jul 7, 1927, Arlington, Ore.

The Tonight Show Starring Johnny Carson
(talk) .... orch. leader (1967–)

Carl H. (Doc) Severinsen spent quite a few years as an obscure studio trumpet player before Johnny Carson made him a celebrity on *The Tonight Show*. Doc was a musical prodigy as a child, egged on by his father, who was a physician (hence the nickname; originally dad was "Big Doc" and Carl was "Little Doc"—later shortened to just "Doc"). Doc began touring with the Ted Fio Rito Orchestra in the mid-1940s before he graduated from high school and later played with the postwar bands of Tommy Dorsey, Benny Goodman, Charlie Barnet, and Vaughn Monroe. In 1949 he became a staff musician at NBC in New York, working on Steve Allen's original *Tonight Show*, among other programs. He joined *The Tonight Show* band permanently in 1962 and, when Milton DeLugg left in 1967, Carson put him in charge. He has become known not only for his musicianship but for his flamboyant clothes ("I like my elegant funk," he says) and his ability to trade quips with Carson.

SEVILLE, DAVID—

see Bagdasarian, Ross

SEWELL, GEORGE—British actor

b: 1924

UFO (sci fi) ...... Col. Alec Freeman (1970)
Special Branch (police)
.... Insp. Craven (1973–74)

SEYMOUR, ANNE—actress

b: Sep 11, 1909, New York City, N.Y.

Robert Montgomery Presents (summer) (drama)................ repertory player (1954)
Empire (wes) ...... Lucia Garret (1962–63)
The Tim Conway Show (com)
.... Mrs. K. J. Crawford (1970)

A mature character actress with long experience on stage and radio (she claims to have appeared on approximately 5,000 network radio shows in the '30s and '40s). She made a good stoic mother or lady-in-charge in both drama and comedy.

SEYMOUR, DAN—actor, host

b: Feb 22, 1915, Chicago, Ill. d: Jul 27, 1982

Sing It Again (quiz)........ emcee (1950–51)
We, the People (int) .... host (1950–52)
Where Was I? (quiz) .... emcee (1952)
Casablanca (drama) ...... Ferrari (1955–56)

A scowling, heavyweight movie villain (serious or comic) who became a quiz show host on early television. He was in the film version of *Casablanca* as Abdul.

SEYMOUR, JANE (1950s)—actress

b: 1899 d: Jan 30, 1956

Young Mr. Bobbin (com)
.... Aunt Clara (1951–52)

SEYMOUR, JANE (1970s–80s)—actress

b: Feb 15, 1951, Wimbledon, England

Captains and the Kings (drama)
.... Marjorie Chisholm Armagh (1976)
Seventh Avenue (drama)
.... Eva Meyers (1977)
East of Eden (drama)
.... Cathy/Kate Ames (1981)

A coldly beautiful British leading lady who specializes in glamorous bitches and calculating villainesses. She was originally trained as a dancer and performed with England's Royal Festival Ballet at the age of 13, but a knee injury ended her dancing career at 16. She then became an actress in film and TV in England. She came to the U.S. in the '70s, where she has had leading roles in a number of big, glossy, romantic TV productions.

SEYMOUR, RALPH—actor

Makin' It (adv)
.... Al "Kingfish" Sorrentino (1979)

SHA NA NA—vocal group

Jon "Bowzer" Bauman, b: Sep 14, 1947, Queens, N.Y.
Lennie Baker, b: Apr 18, 1946, Whitman, Mass.

Johnny Contardo, b: Dec 23, 1951, Boston, Mass.
Frederick "Dennis" Greene, b: Jan 11, 1949, New York City, N.Y.
"Dirty Dan" McBride, b: Nov 20, 1945, Boston, Mass.
John "Jocko" Marcellino, b: May 12, 1950, Boston, Mass.
Dave "Chico" Ryan, b: Apr 9, 1948, Arlington, Mass.
"Screamin' Scott" Simon, b: Dec 9, 1948, Boston, Mass.
Tony Santini (Scott Powell), b: Apr 13, 1948, Dallas, Texas
Donald "Donny" York, b: Mar 13, 1949, Boise, Idaho

Sha Na Na (var) .... hosts (1977–81)

A rock group organized at Columbia University in 1969 that became a surprise hit with the acid-rock generation, doing a cappella oldies from the '50s and early '60s. Their name was taken from the background chant on one of those old hits, the Silhouettes' 1957 recording of "Get a Job." Their recording career was in decline by the late '70s, when their manager pushed them into television—and a whole new comedy/rock career on their own very popular syndicated show.

See also separate entry for group leader Jon Bauman.

SHABBA-DOO—

The Big Show (var)........ dancers (1980)

SHACKELFORD, TED—actor
b: Jun 23, 1946, Oklahoma City, Okla r: Tulsa, Okla.

Knots Landing (drama)
.... Gary Ewing (1979–)
Dallas (drama)...... Gary Ewing (1979–81)

Television's most famous soap opera drunk was a rather obscure supporting actor before *Knots Landing* made him a star as the rugged but weak-willed "black sheep" of the Ewing clan. Ted spent most of the '70s in New York, trying to get a foothold in the theater; during 1975–76 he had a regular role on the New York–originated daytime soap *Another World*. He then moved to Hollywood and began to get scattered parts in series (e.g., *Big Hawaii*) and TV films *(The Defection of Simas Kudirka, The Jordan Chance)* be-

fore his big break on *Dallas* and its spin-off *Knots Landing.*

SHACKLEFORD, LYNN—commentator
Almost Anything Goes (aud par)
.... color commentator (1975–76)

SHAD, JERRY, QUARTET—
Spin the Picture (quiz)... regulars (1949–50)

SHADEL, BILL—newscaster
Capitol Cloak Room (pub aff)
.... panelist (1949–50)
The Facts We Face (doc) . moderator (1950)
Focus on America (doc)........ host (1962)

SHAFFER, PAUL—orchestra leader, comedian
b: Nov 28, 1949, Thunder Bay, Ont., Canada

A Year at the Top (com)...... Paul (1977)
NBC's Saturday Night Live (com)
.... regular (1978–80)
Late Night with David Letterman (talk)
.... bandleader (1982–)

The small, bespectacled, spaced-out bandleader on David Letterman's *Late Night* show has been on the hip fringes of bigtime comedy for a number of years. A keyboard artist, he got his start with the Toronto production of *Godspell* in the early '70s, then came to New York and became a member of the original *Saturday Night Live* band in 1975. He was later a writer and sometimes performer on that show, before joining Letterman in 1982.

SHAGINYAN, ANATOLY—actor
The Winds of War (drama)
.... Josef Stalin (1983)

SHAHAN, ROCKY—actor
Rawhide (wes)....... Joe Scarlett (1959–64)

SHANE, JIM—actor
The New Phil Silvers Show (com)
.... Lester (1963–64)

SHANKS, DON—actor
The Life and Times of Grizzly Adams (adv)
.... Nakuma (1977–78)

767

SHANNON, MICHAEL—actor

Riker (police) . . . . Brice Landis (1981)

SHARALEE—

see Sheralee

SHARBUTT, DEL—announcer

b: Feb 16, 1912, Cleburne, Texas

Your Hit Parade (music)
. . . . announcer (1957–58)

SHARMA, BARBARA—actress

b: Sep 14, Dallas, Texas r: Miami, Fla.

Rowan & Martin's Laugh-In (var)
. . . . regular (1970–72)
Rhoda (com) . Myrna Morgenstein (1974–76)
Glitter (drama) . . . . . . Shelly Sealy (1984–85)

SHARP, SAUNDRA—black actress

b: 1943, Cleveland, Ohio

Wonder Woman (adv) . . . . Eve (1977–78)
St. Elsewhere (drama)
. . . . Nurse Peggy Shotwell (1984–)

SHARP, THOM—actor

The Half Hour Comedy Hour (var)
. . . . host (1983)
TV's Bloopers & Practical Jokes (com)
. . . . regular (1984–86)

SHARPE, KAREN—actress

b: c. 1935, Texas

Johnny Ringo (wes)
. . . . Laura Thomas (1959–60)
I Dream of Jeannie (com)
. . . . Melissa Stone (1965–66)

The wife of moviemaker Stanley Kramer.

SHARRETT, MICHAEL—juvenile actor

Joe's World (com)
. . . . Jimmy Wabash (1979–80)

SHATNER, WILLIAM—actor

b: Mar 22, 1931, Montreal, Canada

For the People (police)
. . . . David Koster (1965)
Star Trek (sci fi)
. . . . Capt. James T. Kirk (1966–69)
The Barbary Coast (wes)
. . . . Jeff Cable (1975–76)

T. J. Hooker (police)
. . . . Sgt. T. J. Hooker (1982–86)

A citizen of Canada, Shatner broke into television in the mid-1950s, during the age of live New York–based dramas, and appeared on many of the playhouse series of that day (*Studio One, Omnibus*, etc.). During the early '60s he was seen in straight police series (e.g. *Naked City*) and in a few westerns, along with some science fiction dramas that presaged his future success on *Star Trek*. In the 1963 *Twilight Zone* episode "Nightmare at 20,000 Feet" he convincingly played an airline passenger who doubted his own sanity when he saw a strange creature on the wing outside his window; in a 1964 *Outer Limits* telecast he was an astronaut who returned to earth only to find that he had inexplicably brought the deep cold of outer space back with him.

Shatner was a busy and familiar guest player on TV by the time he landed his first series in 1965. However, *For the People,* in which he portrayed a strong-willed assistant district attorney, was canceled after only three months. That, ironically, meant that he was available the following year when *Star Trek* was being cast, and it was the role of the commanding yet complex captain of the starship Enterprise—"going where no man has gone before"—that secured his niche in TV history. The role did not seem very historic at the time; *Star Trek* was not successful in its original run, and only in repeats did it gradually become a cult phenomenon.

During the '70s Shatner continued to play guest roles, primarily on crime shows such as *Ironside* and *Hawaii Five-O.* He also appeared in a TV movie that was strangely reminiscent of that *Twilight Zone* episode (*The Horror at 37,000 Feet*—this time it was ghosts in the baggage compartment). He had a short run in a latter-day western called *The Barbary Coast,* then found renewed success in the '80s in a genre with which he had had much experience—police shows—as *T. J. Hooker.*

SHAUGHNESSY, MICKEY—actor

b: 1920, New York City, N.Y. d: Jul 23, 1985

The Chicago Teddy Bears (com)
. . . . Duke (1971)

A pugnacious little comic actor, skilled at playing dumb tough guys; a former boxer.

SHAVER, HELEN—actress
b: Feb 24, 1951, St. Thomas, Ont., Canada

United States (com)
., ... Libby Chapin (1980)
Jessica Novak (drama)
. . . . Jessica Novak (1981)

SHAW, BOB—actor

The Steve Allen Comedy Hour (var)
. . . . regular (1980–81)

SHAW, FRANK—

The New Bill Cosby Show (var)
. . . . regular (1972–73)

SHAW, MARK—correspondent
b: Auburn, Ind.

People (mag) . . . . correspondent (1978)

SHAW, MARTIN—British actor
b: 1945

Doctor in the House (com)
. . . . Huw Evans (1970–73)

SHAW, RETA—actress
b: Sep 13, 1912, South Paris, Me. d: Jan 8, 1982

Mr. Peepers (com) . . . . Aunt Lil (1954)
The Betty White Show (var)
. . . . regular (1958)
The Ann Sothern Show (com)
. . . . Flora Macauley (1958–59)
The Tab Hunter Show (com)
. . . . Thelma (1960–61)
Ichabod and Me (com)
. . . . Aunt Lavinia (1961–62)
Oh, Those Bells (com)
. . . . Mrs. Stanfield (1962)
The Cara Williams Show (com)
. . . . Mrs. Burkhardt (1964–65)
The Ghost and Mrs. Muir (com)
. . . . Martha Grant (1968–70)

An amply proportioned comic actress on-stage in the '40s and later seen in Disney movies. She was familiar to television viewers in a succession of roles as aunts, housekeepers, and landladies.

SHAW, ROBERT—actor, writer
b: Aug 9, 1927, Westhoughton, England r: Scotland d: Aug 27, 1978

The Buccaneers (adv)
. . . . Capt. Dan Tempest (1956–57)

A popular, robust British actor who was seen in the U.S. mostly in movies, notably *A Man for All Seasons* (as the king), *The Sting,* and *Jaws.*

SHAW, STAN—black actor
b: Jul 14, 1952, Chicago, Ill.

Roots: The Next Generations (drama)
. . . . Will Palmer (1979)
The Mississippi (drama)
. . . . Lafayette "Lafe" Tate (1983–84)

SHAW, STEVE—actor

Knots Landing (drama)
. . . . Eric Fairgate (1979–)

SHAW, SUSAN—actress

The Swift Show (var) . . . . regular (1948)
One Man's Family (drama)
. . . . Beth Holly (1951–52)

This, presumably, is not the British film actress of the same name (1929–1978).

SHAWLEE, JOAN—actress
b: Mar 5, 1929*, Forest Hills, N.Y. d: Mar 22, 1987

The Abbott and Costello Show (com)
. . . . various roles (1951–52)
The Betty Hutton Show (com)
. . . . Lorna (1959–60)
The Feather and Father Gang (drama)
. . . . Margo (1977)

SHAWLEY, BOB—actor

The Hartmans (com) . . . . the nephew (1949)

SHAWN, DICK—actor, comedian
b: Dec 1, 1923**, Buffalo, N.Y. r: Lackawanna, N.Y. d: Apr 17, 1987

Mary (var) . . . . regular (1978)
Hail to the Chief (com)
. . . . . . Premier Dmitri/Ivan Zolotov (1985)

*Some sources give 1926.
**Some sources give 1928 or 1929.

Dark, large-sized comic actor, most familiar in fairly manic roles. He was active on television from the 1950s, when he got his start as a "discovery" on *Arthur Godfrey's Talent Scouts.* Perhaps his most memorable role was in Mel Brooks' farcical film *The Producers,* as a cavorting Adolf Hitler appearing in a musical comedy.

SHAYNE, ROBERT—actor
b: 1908, Yonkers, N.Y.

The Adventures of Superman (adv)
...... Insp. William Henderson (1951–57)

This actor, who always seemed a little on the dense side in his *Superman* role, later became a successful financier.

SHEA, CHRISTOPHER—juvenile actor

Shane (wes) .... Joey Starett (1966)

Christopher was the original voice of Linus in the *Peanuts* cartoons of the late 1960s.

SHEA, ERIC—juvenile actor

Anna and the King (com)
.... Louis Owens (1972)

SHEA, JOHN—actor
b: Apr 14, 1949, North Conway, N.H.

The Last Convertible (drama)
.... Terry Garrigan (1979)

SHEA, MICHAEL—actor
b: Nov 4, 1952, Glendale, N.Y.

The New Adventures of Huck Finn (adv)
.... Huck Finn (1968–69)
The New Dick Van Dyke Show (com)
.... Lucas Preston (1971–73)

SHEARER, HARRY—comedian, writer

NBC's Saturday Night Live (com)
.... regular (1984–85)

SHEARIN, JOHN—actor
b: Sep 27, Charlotte, N.C., r: Chapel Hill, N.C.

Bret Maverick (wes)
.... Sheriff Mitchell Dowd (1981–82)
Flamingo Road (drama)
.... Dep. Tyler (1981–82)
Hunter (police)... Lt. Ambrose Finn (1985–)

SHEEHAN, DOUGLAS—actor
b: Apr 27, 1949, Santa Monica, Calif. r: Redding, Calif.

Knots Landing (drama)
.... Ben Gibson (1983–)

SHEEN, BISHOP FULTON J.—Catholic priest
b: May 8, 1895, El Paso, Ill. d: Dec 10, 1979

Life Is Worth Living (misc) .. host (1952–57)
The Bishop Sheen Program (misc)
.... host (1961–68)

How many television stars could honestly say, "I certainly did not go on television in order that people might know me, but rather that they would know Him Whom I have the honor so feebly to represent"? This witty, middle-level Catholic cleric was surely one of the most unusual "personalities" in TV history, and the only religious figure ever to have his own prime time network series—which ran for five years in the '50s on the DuMont network and ABC. Sheen was born to a farming family, ordained in 1919, and soon proved himself one of the church's most skilled orators. His style combined imaginative writing, a folksy quality, and a hypnotic, forceful delivery as he made his points. He was often heard on radio and, when TV arrived in the '50s, he made use of that medium with a popular program designed to help people cope with life. Later, in the '60s, he continued with a syndicated series.

Throughout his little talks Sheen always showed a warm sense of humor. Of his chief TV competition he said, "I bear the deepest affection for Milton Berle, and I love his program intensely." (Berle replied by lovingly dubbing him "Uncle Fulty," and remarking that "We work for the same sponsor—Sky Chief.")

Here is a sample Sheenism: "There is a difference between blarney and baloney. Blarney is the varnished truth, baloney is the unvarnished lie . . . To tell a women who is 40, 'You look like 16' is baloney. The blarney way of saying it is, 'Tell me how old you are. I should like to know at what age women are the most beautiful.' "

SHEFFER, CRAIG—actor
b: York, Pa.

The Hamptons (drama)
.... Brian Chadway (1983)

SHEFFIELD, JAY—actor

Tammy (com)...... Steven Brent (1965–66)

SHEFFIELD, JEANNE—

The Jim Stafford Show (var)
.... regular (1975)

SHEINER, DAVID—actor
b: Jan 13, 1928, New York City, N.Y.

Mr. Novak (drama)... Paul Webb (1964–65)
Diana (com) .... Norman Brodnik (1973–74)

SHELDON, GENE—actor
b: 1909 d: May 1, 1982

Zorro (wes)........... Bernardo (1957–59)

Zorro's ostensibly deaf-mute helper/spy in the fight for justice in old California.

SHELDON, JACK—actor
b: Nov 30, 1931, Jacksonville, Fla.

The Cara Williams Show (com)
.... Fletcher Kincaid (1964–65)
Run Buddy Run (com)
.... Buddy Overstreet (1966–67)
The Girl with Something Extra (com)
.... Jerry Burton (1973–74)

A hip comic who started out as a professional trumpet player, working in the *Merv Griffin Show* band, among other gigs. Of his role on *The Girl with Something Extra,* he said, "I'm just playing me, man. I'm not really acting. I just hope they don't find out and stop paying me."

SHELLABARGER, JILL—actress

Chicago Story (drama)........ Carol (1982)

SHELLEY, JOSHUA—actor

Holiday Hotel (var) .... regular (1951)
B.J. and the Bear (adv) ... Bullets (1979–80)

SHELLEY, PAUL—

The Patricia Bowman Show (music)
.... regular (1951)

SHELLY, CAROL—actress

The Odd Couple (com)
.... Gwendolyn Pigeon (1970–71)

SHELTON, DEBORAH—actress
b: Nov 21, 1952, Washington, D.C. r: Norfolk, Va.

The Yellow Rose (drama)
.... Juliette Hollister (1983–84)
Dallas (drama)..... Mandy Winger (1984–)

A 1970 Miss U.S.A., and runner-up in the Miss Universe Pageant. She is also a successful popular-song lyricist, primarily for her husband's music.

SHELTON, EARL—orchestra leader

For Your Pleasure (music)
.... orch. leader (1949)

SHELTON, GEORGE—actor
b: c. 1884 d: Feb 12, 1971

It Pays to Be Ignorant (quiz)
.... panelist (1949–51)

SHENAR, PAUL—actor
b: Feb 12, 1936, Milwaukee, Wis.

Roots (drama)........... Carrington (1977)

SHEPARD, BOB—panelist

Charade Quiz (quiz)..... panelist (1947–49)

SHEPARD, DICK—announcer

What's Your Bid? (aud par)
.... announcer (1953)

SHEPARD, JEAN—country singer
b: Nov 21, 1933, Pauls Valley, Okla.

Ozark Jubilee (music)........ regular (1955)

SHEPHERD, CYBILL—actress
b: Feb 18, 1949*, Memphis, Tenn.

The Yellow Rose (drama)
.... Colleen Champion (1983–84)
Moonlighting (drama)
.... Maddie Hayes (1985–)

Cybill was a model, and a former Miss Teenage Memphis, when she was discovered by producer Peter Bogdanovich and given a prominent role in his 1971 film *The Last Picture Show,* as the high school flirt. Known as Bogdanovich's protégée, she appeared in several more of his movies be-

*Some sources give 1950.

771

fore moving into television. An extremely glamorous woman with an air of fun about her, she scored a major hit in the 1985 series *Moonlighting*. Among her TV films have been *A Guide for the Married Woman, The Long Hot Summer,* and *Seduced*.

SHEPLEY, MICHAEL—actor
b: Sep 29, 1907, Plymouth, England d: Sep 28, 1961

Dick and the Duchess (com)
.... Insp. Stark (1957–58)

SHEPODD, JON—actor
Lassie (adv) .... Paul Martin (1957–58)

SHERA, MARK—actor
b: Jul 10, 1949, Bayonne, N.J.

S.W.A.T. (police)
.... Off. Dominic Luca (1975–76)
Barnaby Jones (drama)
.. Jedediah Romano (J.R.) Jones (1976–80)

SHERALEE—singer
b: Aug 13, 1949, Fort Lauderdale, Fla.

Your Hit Parade (music) .... vocalist (1974)

Also spelled Sharalee; her full name is Sharalee Lucas.

SHERIDAN, ANN—actress
b: Feb 21, 1915, Dallas, Texas r: Denton, Texas d: Jan 21, 1967

Pistols 'n' Petticoats (com)
.... Henrietta Hanks (1966–67)

This pretty, fun-loving movie star of the '40s—once billed as Hollywood's "Oomph Girl"—turned to television in the early 1950s as her film career went into decline. She appeared in a number of the playhouse series of that period, including *Ford Theatre* and *Lux Video Theatre,* then became less active in the early 1960s. By mid-decade, her career was beginning to pick up again; she appeared for a year in the daytime serial *Another World* (1965–66) and then starred in the comedy western *Pistols 'n' Petticoats,* about a rough, tough frontier family of women. She died of cancer during the latter program's first season.

SHERIDAN, ARDELL—actress
The Super (com) ... Francesca Girelli (1972)

SHERIDAN, DAN—actor
The Lawman (wes)......... Jake (1961–62)

SHERIDAN, NICOLLETTE—actress
b: Nov 21, 1963, Worthing, England r: London, Los Angeles

Paper Dolls (drama).... Taryn Blake (1984)
Knots Landing (drama)
.... Paige Matheson (1986–)

SHERMAN, BOBBY—singer, actor
b: Jul 18, 1943*, Santa Monica, Calif. r: Van Nuys, Calif

Shindig (music) ... frequent guest (1964–66)
Here Come the Brides (adv)
.... Jeremy Bolt (1968–70)
Getting Together (com)
.... Bobby Conway (1971–72)

Bobby Sherman was King of the Bubble Gum Set for a few minutes in the late '60s. A pleasant young chap with a great deal of neatly trimmed hair, he looked a lot like David Cassidy (who was King for a few minutes in 1971). Bobby had not intended to go into show business, but he was spotted by an agent while fooling around with a teenage band and signed for several appearances on the rock show *Shindig*. Bobby went along with this; he had been majoring in psychology in college, however, and he later said, "I gave [it] up because I realized that I was a schizo and belonged in show business with the rest of them."

The *Shindig* exposure did not produce any hit records, and Bobby moved on to acting roles *(The Monkees, The F.B.I.),* ultimately landing the one that made him a star, that of the young brother on *Here Come the Brides*. In 1970 his music career exploded with hits such as "Easy Come, Easy Go" and "Julie, Do Ya Love Me." Magazines such as *Sixteen* and *Tiger Beat* couldn't get enough of him; there were photographs, jewelry, pinup posters and a book called *The Secrets of Bobby Sherman*.

Predictably, it all cooled off after about a year. Bobby went into another series,

*Some sources give July 22, 1945.

Getting Together (playing a young song-writer), but it was short-lived. He has since been seen in occasional guest roles on shows including *Emergency, Fantasy Island,* and *Lobo,* and spends the rest of his time polishing the gold records in his den.

SHERMAN, ELLEN—actress

Miss Winslow and Son (com)
.... Rosa Vallone (1979)

SHERMAN, FRED—actor
b: c. 1905 d: 1969

Cimarron City (wes)... Burt Purdy (1958–59)

SHERMAN, HIRAM—actor
b: Feb 11, 1908, Boston, Mass.

The Tammy Grimes Show (com)
.... Uncle Simon (1966)

SHERMAN, MELISSA—actress

Joe's World (com)
.... Maggie Wabash (1979–80)

SHERMAN, RANSOM—host, comedian
b: c. 1898, Appleton, Wis. d: Nov 26, 1985

The Ransom Sherman Show (var)
.... host (1950)
And Here's the Show (var)...... host (1955)
Father of the Bride (com)
.... Herbert Dunston (1961–62)

SHERRY, BILL—

The Little Revue (music).. regular (1949–50)

SHERRY, BOB—announcer, host

Armstrong Circle Theatre (drama)
.... host/narrator (1953–54)

SHERRY, DIANE—juvenile actress

The Bing Crosby Show (com)
.... Joyce Collins (1964–65)

SHERWOOD, BOBBY—orchestra leader, actor, host
b: May 30, 1914, Indianapolis, Ind. d: Jan 23, 1981

A Couple of Joes (var).. orch. leader (1950)
The Milton Berle Show (var)
.... regular (1952–53)

Quick as a Flash (quiz)
.... moderator (1953–54)
Stars on Parade (var)......emcee (1953–54)
Masquerade Party (quiz)
.... panelist (1954–57)
Caesar Presents (var).......... host (1955)
The Red Buttons Show (var) . regular (1955)

A versatile musician (guitar, trumpet, trombone, vocals) who was quite active on radio in the '30s and '40s, backing Bing Crosby and other major stars. His most famous record, made with his own band: "The Elk's Parade." Bobby was just as versatile on early television, appearing as a musician, host, and actor, but somehow he never caught on as a major personality in any of these fields.

SHERWOOD, MADELEINE—actress
b: Nov 13, 1922*, Montreal, Canada

The Flying Nun (com)
.... Mother Superior (1967–70)

SHEYBAL, VLADEK—actor
b: 1932, Kremieniec, Poland

Shogun (drama) .... Capt. Ferriera (1980)

A Polish film actor, often in menacing roles; he defected to the West in 1958.

SHIELDS & YARNELL—mimes
Robert Shields, b: Mar 26
Lorene Yarnell, b: Mar 21 r: Los Angeles, Calif.

The Mac Davis Show (var)
.... regulars (1976)
The Sonny and Cher Show (var)
.... regulars (1976–77)
Shields and Yarnell (var)
.... cohosts (1977–78)

This young husband-and-wife team began as a street mime duo in San Francisco (they were married in a mime ceremony there, in Union Square). After winning a Ted Mack amateur contest, they were signed for a revue in Las Vegas, for concerts, top variety shows, and finally their own summer series in 1977. It was the first (and only) mime series in network history and it was a surprise hit, but its novelty was short-lived. When it was brought back

*Some sources give 1926.

the following winter, it found few viewers opposite the more traditional comedy of *Laverne & Shirley*.

Shields and Yarnell have since been seen in occasional guest spots, with Yarnell sometimes appearing alone.

SHIELDS, AINA—

The Fashion Story (misc) . regular (1948–49)

SHIELDS, ARTHUR—actor
b: 1896, Dublin, Ireland d: Apr 27, 1970

Your Show Time (drama) .... host (1949)

A very Irish character actor, and the brother of film star Barry Fitzgerald. *Your Show Time* is notable as the first network program to receive an Emmy Award, for its debut presentation, "The Necklace."

SHIELDS, FRED—actor

Meet Corliss Archer (com)
.... Mr. Harry Archer (1951–52)

SHILLO, MICHAEL—actor

Masada (drama) .... Ezra (1981)

SHIMADA, YOKO—actress

Shogun (drama)
.... Lady Mariko Toda (1980)

Richard Chamberlain's young lady love in *Shogun;* not to be confused with the well-known Japanese character actor Yuki Shimoda (1922–1981).

SHIPP, MARY—actress

Life with Luigi (com)
.... Miss Spalding (1952)
My Friend Irma (com)
.... Kay Foster (1953–54)

SHIRE, TALIA—actress
b: Apr 25, 1946*, Lake Success, Long Island, N.Y.

Rich Man, Poor Man—Book I (drama)
.... Teresa Sanjoro (1976)

Film actress and sister of moviemaker Francis Ford Coppola.

*Some sources give 1945 or 1947.

SHIRLEY, TOM—actor, announcer
b: c. 1899 d: Jan 24, 1962

They're Off (quiz) .... emcee (1949)

SHIRRIFF, CATHERINE—actress, model
b: Apr 11, Toronto, Ont., Canada

Ripley's Believe It or Not (var)
.... cohost (1982–83)
Shaping Up (com) ... Zoya Antonova (1984)

One of the top international fashion models of the 1970s.

SHOCKLEY, SALLIE—actress
b: Sep 16, Neenah, Wis.

Sarge (drama)........... Valerie (1971–72)

SHOLDAR, MICKEY—actor
b: 1949

The Farmer's Daughter (com)
.... Steve Morley (1963–66)

SHOR, DAN—actor
b: Nov 16, New York City, N.Y.

The Blue and the Gray (drama)
.... Luke Geyser (1982)
Cagney & Lacey (police)
.... Det. Jonah Newman (1985–86)

Shor had his first major exposure as the young Studs Lonigan in the 1979 miniseries of the same name.

SHORE, DANNY—

Front Row Center (var) ... regular (1949–50)

SHORE, DINAH—singer
b: Mar 1, 1917, Winchester, Tenn. r: Nashville, Tenn.

The Dinah Shore Show (music)
.... hostess (1951–57)
The Dinah Shore Chevy Show (var)
.... hostess (1956–63)
Dinah and Her New Best Friends (var)
.... hostess (1976)

Emmy Awards: Best Female Singer (1954, 1955); Best Female Personality (1956, 1957); Best Actress in a Musical or Variety Series, for *The Dinah Shore Chevy Show* (1959); Star, Best Daytime Non-Dramatic Program, for *Dinah's Place* (1973, 1974);

Best Host of a Daytime Talk or Variety Series, for *Dinah!* (1976)

It's hard not to like Dinah—she fairly oozes Southern charm and graciousness, without ever being sticky about it. The two trademarks of her 1950s variety series were the sponsor's bright theme song ("See the U.S.A./In your Chevrolet!"), and the big smooch she would throw to the audience at the end of every show.

Things were not always so bright and sunny for Dinah. A victim of polio as a child, she got her start on local radio in Nashville and came to New York in the late 1930s. She only found doors slamming in her face. Benny Goodman, Tommy and Jimmy Dorsey all turned her down as a vocalist, and she struggled for several years before slow gaining a foothold on radio as a solo singer (not easy in those days; she is one of the few from that era who were never associated with a big band). Her radio and record careers began to gain momentum in the early '40s, and in time she became one of the top vocalists of the day—and a favorite with GIs.

When television came along, Dinah made the transition graciously, appearing on variety shows (including Ed Wynn's, c. 1950) and on her own 15-minute early-evening musical interlude from 1951–57. In 1956 NBC began to feature her in monthly prime time specials, and the following year she began her famous nighttime variety hour. Her slightly husky voice, sparkle, and down-home friendliness made hers one of the most relaxing hours on TV. Loving fans voted her "Woman of the Year," "Mother of the Year," "Best Dressed Woman on TV," and one of the "Ten Most Admired Women in the World" in various polls.

When *The Dinah Shore Chevy Show* finally ended in the early '60s, Dinah reduced her activities for a time and was seen only in specials and guest appearances. She began a new career in 1970 as the hostess of an NBC daytime talk show called *Dinah's Place,* which became a 90-minute daily syndicated series in 1974 and continued until 1980. In addition, she hosted a prime time summer series in 1976.

Dinah was married from 1943-1962 to actor George Montgomery and made one of her few TV acting appearances on his western *Cimarron City* in 1958. In later years she had a much-publicized relationship with Burt Reynolds, who was nearly 20 years younger than she.

SHORE, ELAINE—actress

Arnie (com)....... Felicia Farfiss (1970–72)

SHORE, ROBERTA—actress, singer
b: Apr 7, 1943, Monterey Park, Calif.

Father Knows Best (com)
.... Joyce Kendall (1958–59)
The Bob Cummings Show (adv)
.... Hank Gogerty (1961–62)
The Virginian (wes)....... Betsy (1962–65)

SHORT, MARTIN—actor, comedian, writer
b: Mar 26, Hamilton, Ont., Canada

The Associates (com)
.... Tucker Kerwin (1979–80)
I'm a Big Girl Now (com)
.... Neal Stryker (1980–81)
SCTV Network 90 (com).. regular (1982–83)
NBC's Saturday Night Live (com)
.... regular (1984–85)

Emmy Award: Best Writing for a Variety Program, for *SCTV Network 90* (1983)

SHORTRIDGE, STEPHEN—actor

Welcome Back, Kotter (com)
.... Beau De Labarre (1978–79)
Aloha Paradise (com).. Richard Bean (1981)

SHOWALTER, MAX—actor, composer
b: Jun 2, 1917, Caldwell, Kansas

The Swift Show (var)........ regular (1949)
The Stockard Channing Show (com)
.... Gus Clyde (1980)

Also known as Casey Adams (during the 1950s). Among other things, he is said to have composed the first television musical, "Time for Love," telecast by NBC in 1939.

SHREDE, BOB—host

Midwestern Hayride (var) .... emcee (1951)

SHREEVE, BOB—singer

This Is Music (music).... regular (1958–59)

SHRINER, HERB—host, humorist
b: May 29, 1918, Toledo, Ohio r: Indiana d: Apr 23, 1970

The Herb Shriner Show (var)
..........................host (1949–50)
Herb Shriner Time (var).....host (1951–52)
Two for the Money (quiz).. emcee (1952–56)
The Herb Shriner Show (var) ... host (1956)

This rustic humorist of the '40s and '50s was often compared to the late Will Rogers, though he was less political and probably closer in spirit to Cliff Arquette. His radio and television shows consisted of folksy monologues about rural life back home in Indiana, interspersed with snatches of music on his harmonica. Although he hosted several such programs during the '50s, he was best known as emcee of *Two for the Money*, a comedy quiz show that served more as a vehicle for his gentle witticisms than for the game. Always easy going and low-keyed, he drifted from sight in the late '50s as TV shifted toward bigtime, high-energy Hollywood fare. He died in an auto accident in 1970.

Shriner on Shriner: "Hoosiers are congenitally inquisitive. That means nosy, in a nice sort of way."

SHRINER, WIL—humorist
b: Dec 6, 1953, New York City, N.Y.

Television: Inside & Out (mag)
......................regular (1981–82)
TV's Bloopers & Practical Jokes (com)
......................regular (1985–86)

The son of Herb Shriner, and a humorist who works in a similar, homespun vein. Wil's twin brother, Kin Shriner, is an actor in daytime soap operas.

SHRIVER, MARIA—newscaster
b: Nov 6, 1955, Chicago, Ill.

The American Parade (pub aff)
.... correspondent (1984)

The niece of Senator Edward Kennedy. Prior to joining CBS news in 1983, she was a roving reporter for the syndicated *PM Magazine* series.

SHROYER, SONNY—actor
b: Aug 28, Valdosta, Ga.

The Dukes of Hazzard (com)
.... Dep. Enos Strate (1979–80)
Enos (com) ...... Off. Enos Strate (1980–81)
The Dukes of Hazzard (com)
.... Dep. Enos Strate (1982–85)

SHRYER, BRET—juvenile actor
Shirley (com) ...... Hemm Miller (1979–80)

SHUE, ELISABETH—actress
Call to Glory (drama)
.... Jackie Sarnac (1984–85)

SHULL, RICHARD B.—actor
b: Feb 24, 1929, Evanston, Ill.

Diana (com) ... Howard Tolbrook (1973–74)
Holmes and Yoyo (com)
.... Det. Alexander Holmes (1976)

SHULTZ, LEONARD—comedian
The Marty Feldman Comedy Machine (var)
.... regular (1972)

SHUSTER, FRANK—comedian, actor
r: Canada

Holiday Lodge (com) ... Frank Boone (1961)
Wayne & Shuster Take an Affectionate Look At ... (doc)................... host (1966)

Comedy partner of Johnny Wayne, with whom he appeared in two series and numerous TV guest appearances during the 1960s.

SHUTAN, JAN—actress
b: Nov 5, Los Angeles, Calif.

Sons and Daughters (drama)
.... Ruth Cramer (1974)

SIBBALD, LAURIE—actress
No Time for Sergeants (com)
.... Millie Anderson (1964–65)

SIDNEY, ROBERT, DANCERS—
The Pearl Bailey Show (var)
.... regulars (1971)

SIDNEY, SYLVIA—actress
b: Aug 8, 1910, The Bronx, N.Y.

WKRP in Cincinnati (com)
Lillian "Mama" Carlson (pilot only) (1978)

Morningstar/Eveningstar (drama)
.... Binnie Byrd Baylor (1986)

SIEBERT, CHARLES—actor
b: Mar 9, 1938, Kenosha, Wis.

The Blue Knight (police) ... Sgt. Cabe (1976)
One Day at a Time (com)
.... Mr. Jerry Davenport (1976–79)
Husbands, Wives & Lovers (com)
.... Dixon Carter Fielding (1978)
Trapper John, M.D. (drama)
.... Dr. Stanley Riverside II (1979–86)

The actor who played the naive, officious, preppy chief of emergency services on *Trapper John* had a long career in serious drama before finding success in lighter roles. He began onstage in the 1960s, mostly in classical dramas in the U.S. and England; and from 1967–75 worked steadily in daytime soap operas, including regular roles on *Search for Tomorrow, As the World Turns,* and *Another World*. In 1976, Siebert and his family moved permanently to Hollywood, where his first regular role was that of a cop on *The Blue Knight*. After that, the parts became more comedic, leading to his most successful one to date, on *Trapper John*.

SIEGEL, BARBARA—actress
b: c. 1950, r: Rosemont, Pa.

San Francisco International Airport (drama)
.... Suzie Conrad (1970–71)

SIEGEL, DONNA—

The Nashville Palace (var)
.... regular (1981–82)

SIEGEL, LAURA—actress

Sons and Daughters (drama)
.... Mary Anne (1974)

SIERRA, GREGORY—actor

Sanford and Son (com)
.... Julio Fuentes (1972–75)
Barney Miller (com)
.... Det. Sgt. Chano Amenguale (1975–76)
A.E.S. Hudson Street (com)
.... Dr. Tony Menzies (1978)
Soap (com)
.... Carlos "El Puerco" Valdez (1980–81)
Zorro and Son (com)
.... Commandante Paco Pico (1983)

A tall, hawklike actor who has been a familiar face on television comedies since the late 1960s. Usually his characters have a frustrated or slightly angry edge to them; and, indeed, his scowl has played just as effectively on crime series such as *Columbo* and *Police Story*.

SIERRA, MARGARITA—actress
b: 1936, Madrid, Spain d: Sep 6, 1963

Surfside Six (drama)
.... Cha Cha O'Brien (1960–62)

This sexy actress played the Spanish dancer Cha Cha, who entertained at the Boom Boom Room on *Surfside Six*. She died following heart surgery at the age of 26.

SIKES, CYNTHIA—actress
b: Jan 3, Coffeyville, Kan.

Captains and the Kings (drama)
.... Claudia Desmond (1976)
Big Shamus, Little Shamus (drama)
.... Jingles Lodestar (1979)
Flamingo Road (drama)
.... Sande Swanson (1981–82)
St. Elsewhere (drama)
.... Dr. Annie Cavanero (1982–85)

A former Miss Kansas (1972), who got her show biz start on the 1972 Bob Hope Christmas tour of Southeast Asia, then moved to Hollywood.

SIKKING, JAMES—actor
b: Mar 5, 1934, Los Angeles, Calif.

Turnabout (com)
.... Geoffrey St. James (1979)
Hill Street Blues (police)
.... Lt. Howard Hunter (1981–)

This tall, calm, intelligent-looking actor plied his trade without much fuss for more than 20 years before *Hill Street Blues* lifted him to fame as the pompous S.W.A.T. team leader Hunter. He had been playing small roles in films since the early 1960s and was in more than a dozen TV movies of the '70s and '80s, virtually all of them forgettable. Most often he was seen as an authority figure of some kind—a police official, priest, or aide to somebody important. He was hardly noticed on daytime's *General Hospital,* where he played a doctor for three years (1973–76), nor on *Turnabout,* where he was Sharon Gless's business-man-boss. "I'm just an actor who blends in with the scenery," he says. "I'm happy the way I am."

SILLA, FELIX—midget actor

The Addams Family (com)
.... Cousin Itt (1964–66)
Buck Rogers in the 25th Century (sci fi)
.... Twiki (1979–81)

Cousin Itt was the *Addams Family* relative who stood about four feet tall, had long, flowing blond hair that completely covered him from head to toe, and wore a derby hat.

SILO, JON—actor

Not for Publication (drama).. Luchek (1952)

SILO, SUSAN—actress

The Sammy Kaye Show (var)
.... regular (1958–59)
Harry's Girls (com)........ Rusty (1963–64)
Occasional Wife (com) ..... Vera (1966–67)

SILVA, HENRY—actor
b: 1928, Brooklyn, N.Y.

Buck Rogers in the 25th Century (sci fi)
.... Kane (1979)

A gaunt, high cheekboned actor of Puerto Rican parentage, who looks extremely menacing—and usually plays roles to match. On television from the '50s to the '80s.

SILVA, TRINIDAD—actor

Hill Street Blues (police)
.... Jesus Martinez (1981–)

SILVER, DANIEL—actor

Medical Center (drama)
.... anesthesiologist (1969–70)

SILVER, JEFF—actor

The Charlie Farrell Show (com)
.... Rodney (1956)

SILVER, JOE—actor
b: Sep 28, 1922, Chicago, Ill.

The Fifty-Fourth Street Revue (var)
.... regular (1949–50)
Mr. I Magination (child) .. regular (1949–52)
Joey Faye's Frolics (var)..... regular (1950)
Ad Libbers (var) .... regular (1951)
The Red Buttons Show (var)
.... regular (1952–55)
Coronet Blue (drama)..... Max Spier (1967)
Fay (com) .... Jack Stewart (1975–76)

Long-faced comic actor, often with horn-rimmed glasses; he looks a bit like Richard Deacon with hair.

SILVER, MARC—actor

Stir Crazy (adv).......... Crawford (1985)

SILVER, RON—actor
b: Jul 2, 1946, New York City, N.Y.

The Mac Davis Show (var)... regular (1976)
Rhoda (com).......... Gary Levy (1976–78)
Dear Detective (police)
.... Det. Schwartz (1979)
The Stockard Channing Show (com)
.... Brad Gabriel (1980)
Baker's Dozen (com).. Mike Locasale (1982)

A slightly built young actor, who often wears a neatly trimmed beard.

SILVERA, FRANK—black actor
b: Jul 24, 1914, Kingston, Jamaica, West Indies
d: Jun 11, 1970

The High Chaparral (wes)
.... Don Sebastian Montoya (1967–70)

This Jamaican actor tended to play Hispanic and Mexican more than black roles. He had much stage experience and was seen fairly often in TV dramas and westerns of the '50s and '60s—*Alfred Hitchcock Presents, Bonanza, Rawhide,* etc. He died accidentally when he was electrocuted by a household appliance.

SILVERHEELS, JAY—actor
b: 1919*, Six Nations Indian Reservation, Ont., Canada d: Mar 5, 1980

The Lone Ranger (wes) .... Tonto (1949–57)
*Some sources give 1918 or 1920.

Sometimes it seems that television goes out of its way to see that no one plays what he really is—Puerto Ricans play Chicanos (Freddie Prinze on *Chico and the Man*), Irishmen play Italians (J. Carrol Naish on *Life with Luigi*), Jews play God-fearin' Christians (Michael Landon on *Little House on the Prairie*). However, Jay Silverheels was exactly what he purported to be, an authentic Indian as well as TV's most famous Indian character. Born the son of a Mohawk chief on a reservation in Canada, the handsome, athletic young man was a star lacrosse player and boxer, before entering films in the 1940s. His movie roles were predictable, as was the TV part for which he was signed in 1949. As Tonto, the Lone Ranger's faithful Indian companion, he became the medium's most famous (and least threatening) red man.

When *The Lone Ranger* finally reached the end of its long trail, Jay found his acting opportunities somewhat limited, although he did continue to appear in occasional films and on series including *Frontier Circus, Gentle Ben,* and *Pistols 'n' Petticoats*. During the '60s he became increasingly dissatisfied with the portrayal of Indians on TV and spoke out against the subservient parts he had played. His main interest turned to horse breeding and racing, and in 1974 he began a new career as a professional harness racer. His son, Jay Jr., did voices for Saturday morning cartoons in the 1970s.

SILVERMAN, JONATHAN—actor
b: Aug 5, 1966, Los Angeles, Calif.

Gimme a Break (com)
.... Jonathan Maxwell (1985–86)

SILVERN, BEA—actress

Secrets of Midland Heights (drama)
.... Etta Bormann (1980–81)

SILVERS, CATHY—actress
b: May 27, 1961, New York City r: Los Angeles, Calif.

Happy Days (com) . Jenny Piccalo (1980–83)
Foley Square (com)
.... Asst. D.A. Molly Dobbs (1985–86)

The daughter of comedian Phil Silvers.

SILVERS, PHIL—actor, comedian
b: May 11, 1912, Brooklyn, N.Y. d: Nov 1, 1985

The Arrow Show (var)....... host (1948–49)
The Phil Silvers Show (com)
.... M/Sgt. Ernie Bilko (1955–59)
The New Phil Silvers Show (com)
.... Harry Grafton (1963–64)
The Beverly Hillbillies (com)
.... Shifty Shafer (1969–71)

Emmy Awards: Best Actor in a Continuing Performance, for *The Phil Silvers Show* (1955); Best Comedian (1955)

This burlesque comic created one of the most memorable characters in the annals of TV—the brash, beaming, fast-talking con man Sgt. Ernie Bilko, star of *You'll Never Get Rich* (later retitled *The Phil Silvers Show*). Never out to hurt anyone, Bilko perpetrated his money-making, work-avoiding schemes on the system, or on its more pompous representatives, such as his incompetent superior, Col. Hall. Bilko's horn-rimmed glasses and owlish appearance were a clue to his true nature, however—he was a cream-puff underneath.

Silvers got his start in vaudeville in the 1920s as a member of Gus Edwards' famous all-child "School Days Revue." By the 1940s he was playing comic supporting roles in films, but his first major success was onstage, in the Broadway hits *High Button Shoes* (1947) and *Top Banana* (1951). The latter was a slapstick farce about a vaudeville comic who made it big on television. Silvers himself did just that a few years later, as his Bilko character became a smash hit in the late '50s (earlier he had briefly hosted a live variety series, *The Arrow Show*). When *The Phil Silvers Show* ended, Phil moved on to some colorful specials, including *The Ballad of Louie the Louse* in 1959 and *The Slowest Gun in the West* in 1960, then began a "new" *Phil Silvers Show* in 1963. This time he played a straw boss and small-time con man in a civilian factory, but this rehash of Bilko was not successful. Silvers made periodic appearances after that, mostly in comedies ranging from *Gilligan's Island* and *Julia* to *The Love Boat* and *Happy Days;* he also had a recurring role in *The Beverly Hillbillies* from 1969–71. A pilot for a new series called *Eddie,* in which he would have played a conniving security guard in a posh residential area (Bilko again!), did not make the schedule in 1971.

Phil's autobiography: *The Laugh's on Me* (1973).

SIMCOX, TOM—actor

Code R (adv) . . . . Walt Robinson (1977)

SIMEONE, HARRY—choral director
b: May 9, 1911, Newark, N.J.

The Swift Show (var)
. . . . orch. leader (1948–49)
The Kate Smith Show (var)
. . . . chorus (1960)

This musician is most famous for his classic 1958 Christmas recording, "The Little Drummer Boy."

SIMMONDS, NICHOLAS—actor

The Strauss Family (drama). . . . Josef (1973)

SIMMONS, JEAN—actress
b: Jan 31, 1929, Crouch Hill, London, England

The Thorn Birds (drama)
. . . . Fiona (Fee) Cleary (1983)
North and South (drama)
. . . . Clarissa Main (1985)

Emmy Award: Best Supporting Actress in a Limited Series, for *The Thorn Birds* (1983)

Noted film actress, occasionally on television in plays, movies, and miniseries.

SIMMONS, RICHARD—actor
b: 1918, St. Paul, Minn.

Sergeant Preston of the Yukon (police)
. . . . Sgt. Preston (1955–58)

SIMMS, LU ANN—singer
b: c. 1933, Rochester, N.Y.

Arthur Godfrey and His Friends (var)
. . . . singer (1952–55)

The fresh-faced "youth appeal" member of the Godfrey cast in the mid-50s. A modest, unassuming girl with few show business aspirations, she said she owed all to "Mr. G." (she had originally come to his atten-

tion as a winner on his *Talent Scouts* show).

SIMMS, PHILIP—actor

C.P.O. Sharkey (com). . . Apodaca (1977–78)

SIMON, LEONARD—actor
b: Dec 9, Norristown, Pa.

Just Our Luck (com) . . . . . . Jim Dexter (1983)

SIMON, ROBERT F.—actor
b: Dec 2, Mansfield, Ohio

Saints and Sinners (drama)
. . . . Dave Tabak (1962–63)
Custer (wes)
. . . . Brig. Gen. Alfred Terry (1967)
Nancy (com) . . . . Uncle Everett (1970–71)
M*A*S*H (com). . . . Gen. Mitchell (1973–74)
The Amazing Spider-Man (adv)
. . . . J. Jonah Jameson (1978–79)

SIMPSON, JIM—sportscaster
b: Dec 20, 1927, Washington, D.C.

NBC Sports in Action (sport)
. . . . host (1965–66)
Monday Night Baseball (sport)
. . . . sportscaster (1972–75)

SIMPSON, O.J.—black sportscaster, actor, producer
b: Jul 9, 1947, San Francisco, Calif.

Roots (drama). . . . . Kadi Touray (1977)
Monday Night Football (sport)
. . . . announcer (1983–85)

Former football superstar O.J. (Orenthal James) Simpson has long been a familiar face on television, although his career in the medium hardly matches the one he had on the gridiron. O.J. was a star athlete in college, in both track and football, leading the University of Southern California to two Rose Bowls in the late '60s. Upon graduation in 1969 he joined the Buffalo Bills, where he remained until 1977, setting several records and winning numerous awards. His last two seasons were with the San Francisco 49ers.

O.J. began broadcasting for ABC, off-season, at the same time he began his professional playing career, in 1969. He switched to NBC from 1978–82, but then returned to ABC. In addition to sportscasting, he has appeared in a number of series episodes and TV movies, ranging from *Cade's County* and *Owen Marshall, Counselor at Law* in the early '70s to the *Goldie and the Boxer* movies (as the boxer) in 1979–81, as well as *Cocaine and Blue Eyes* (a detective series pilot) in 1983. He also is frequently seen in commercials.

SIMS, ED—host

Dancing on Air (info) . . . . emcee (1947)

SINATRA, FRANK—singer, actor
b: Dec 12, 1915, Hoboken, N.J.

The Frank Sinatra Show (var)
. . . . host (1950–52)
The Frank Sinatra Show (var)
. . . . host (1957–58)

Emmy Award: Star, Best Musical Program, for *Frank Sinatra: A Man and His Music* (1966)

He calls himself a "saloon singer," but few would deny that he is the greatest American popular singer of the mid–twentieth century—and a show business legend. Frank Sinatra has been a superstar on records and radio and in movie musicals, dramas, and comedies, but, curiously, he has been much less successful on television.

At the time television was spreading across the U.S., in the early 1950s, Sinatra appeared to be a man whose career had already come and gone. He had first shot to stardom as a gaunt, hollow-cheeked bobby-soxers' idol in the early '40s, crooning love songs such as "All or Nothing At All" and "I'll Never Smile Again" with the Harry James and Tommy Dorsey bands. He went solo in 1942 and was a major star on radio, as well as in a series of bright movie musicals. By 1950, however, the hit movies and records were becoming rather sparse. His arrival on TV received a great deal of publicity; would this revive his sagging career? Would he be the next major star in the video medium? The answer was no. The first *Frank Sinatra Show*, a straight variety hour, was a flop opposite the Sid Caesar and (in its second season) Milton Berle shows. By the time it left the air, Sinatra was a "has-been." His record company dropped him and he had to practically beg for his next movie role.

That role, the out-of-character dramatic part of Maggio in *From Here to Eternity,* turned his career around. Following his 1954 Academy Award–winning performance, Frank's record career also began to revive, and in 1955 he had a long-awaited success on TV in the acclaimed *Producer's Showcase* musical production "Our Town." Sinatra was hot once again, and in 1957 ABC paid a reported $3 million to lure him back to series TV. Unfortunately, the second *Frank Sinatra Show,* a mixture of music and drama (on alternate weeks), was an even bigger flop than the first. Thereafter, Frank limited his appearances to specials, some of them quite notable. In May 1960 he played host to Elvis Presley, who had just returned from the army; from 1965–69 he starred in a series of highly acclaimed, big, glossy musical extravaganzas (one a year). In 1971 Frank announced his retirement from show business, but few believed him. Sure enough, he was back in 1973, in another top-rated special called, appropriately, "Ol' Blue Eyes Is Back." More specials followed, along with his first dramatic TV movie, *Contract on Cherry Street* (1977), in which he played a hard-bitten New York cop.

SINATRA, FRANK, JR.—singer
b: Jan 10, 1944, Jersey City, N.J.

Dean Martin Presents the Golddiggers (var)
. . . . regular (1968)

Son of the famous singer. He has made a few acting appearances, on *Adam 12, Marcus Welby, The Love Boat,* etc.

SINATRA, RICHARD—actor

Mr. Roberts (com)
. . . . Seaman D'Angelo (1965–66)

SINBAD—actor

The Redd Foxx Show (com)
. . . . Byron Lightfoot (1986)

SINCLAIR, DIANE—dancer

Kay Kyser's Kollege of Musical Knowledge (quiz) . . . . regular (1949–50)
The Paul Winchell-Jerry Mahoney Show (var) . . . . regular (1951–53)
Garroway at Large (var) . . dancer (1953–54)

Dancing partner of Ken Spaulding.

SINCLAIR, ERIC—actor

Robert Montgomery Presents (summer)
(drama)........... repertory player (1955)

SINCLAIR, MADGE—black actress

b: Apr 28, 1938, Kingston, Jamaica, West Indies

Roots (drama)................. Bell (1977)
Grandpa Goes to Washington (com)
.... Madge (1978–79)
Trapper John, M.D. (drama)
.... Nurse Ernestine Shoop (1980–86)

SING, MAI TAI—actress

b: Oakland, Calif. r: San Francisco, Hong Kong

Hong Kong (adv)...... Ching Mei (1960–61)

SINGER, LORI—actress

b: Nov 6, 1962, Corpus Christi, Texas

Fame (drama)........ Julie Miller (1982–83)

SINGER, MARC—actor

b: Jan 29, Vancouver, Canada r: Corpus Christi, Texas

79 Park Avenue (drama)
.... Ross Savitch (1977)
Roots: The Next Generations (drama)
.... Andy Warner (1979)
The Contender (drama)
.... Johnny Captor (1980)
V (movie) (sci fi)..... Mike Donovan (1983)
V: The Final Battle (miniseries) (sci fi)
.... Mike Donovan (1984)
V (sci fi).......... Mike Donovan (1984–85)
Dallas (drama)...... Matt Cantrell (1986–)

Lori and Marc are brother and sister; their father is symphony conductor Jacques Singer.

SINGER, RAYMOND—actor

b: Dec 21, New York City, N.Y.

Operation Petticoat (com)
.... Lt. Watson (1977–78)
Mama Malone (com) .... Austin (1984)

SINGER, STUFFY—juvenile actor

Beulah (com)
.... Donnie Henderson (1952–53)
Blondie (com).. Alexander Bumstead (1957)

SINGING WAITERS, THE—

Polka-Go-Round (music) . regulars (1958–59)

SINGLETON, DORIS—actress

The Great Gildersleeve (com)
.... Lois (1955–56)
Angel (com)............... Susie (1960–61)

SINGLETON, EDDIE—black actor

Harris and Company (drama)
.... Tommy Harris (1979)

SINGLETON, PENNY—actress

b: Sep 15, 1908, Philadelphia, Pa.

The Jetsons (cartn)
.... Jane Jetson (voice) (1962–63)

The actress most famous as Blondie in the movie series of the same name, during the late '30s and '40s (she was in 28 *Blondie* films altogether). She was only occasionally seen on television. In later years Penny became quite active in actor's union affairs.

SIROLA, JOSEPH—actor

b: Oct 7, New York City, N.Y.

The Magician (adv) .... Dominick (1973–74)
The Montefuscos (com)
.... Tony Montefusco (1975)

SIROTT, BOB—newscaster

b: Chicago, Ill.

West 57th (pub aff)... correspondent (1985)

SISKEL, GENE—movie critic

Sneak Previews (misc).... cohost (1977–82)
At the Movies (misc) ..... cohost (1982–86)
Siskel & Ebert & The Movies (misc)
.... cohost (1986–)

Movie critic for the *Chicago Tribune.*

SKALA, LILIA—actress

b: Vienna, Austria

Claudia, The Story of a Marriage (drama)
.... Bertha (1952)

Motherly actress, seen over the years in occasional series episodes and TV movies, including the films *Eleanor and Franklin*

(1976) and *Sooner or Later* (1979), in the latter as Grandma.

SKELTON, RED—comedian
b: July 18, 1910*, Vincennes, Ind.

The Red Skelton Show (var)
.... host (1951–71)

Emmy Awards: Best Comedian (1951); Best Comedy Writing, for *The Red Skelton Show* (1961); Academy Governor's Award (1986)

One of television's great institutions during the '50s and '60s was a gentle clown named Red Skelton. Because his shows were seldom rerun, and he is no longer in the public eye, we tend to forget how enormously popular he was. Based on actual audience size and longevity, *The Red Skelton Show* was in fact the second most popular series in the history of TV, right after *Gunsmoke* (and ahead of all the Lucys, *Laugh-In*s, Archie Bunkers and everything else that has ever graced the tube).

Red was the son of a circus clown who died before Red was born. He was raised in dire poverty by his mother, and set out at age 12 to join a medicine show. He later performed as a circus clown and on Mississippi riverboats before gaining his first real fame on radio in the late 1930s. He became a major star in that medium during the 1940s, while also appearing in quite a few comedy films, and he easily transferred to television in 1951.

Red's comedy was highly visual—goofy, childlike, and always with a lot of heart. He created a wide range of comic characters, including Clem Kadiddlehopper, the befuddled country bumpkin; Sheriff Deadeye, the scourge of the west; boxer Cauliflower McPugg; Willie Lump Lump, the drunk; San Fernando Red, the con man; the Mean Widdle Kid ("I dood it!"); and Bolivar Shagnasty, among others. A regular and unusual (for TV) highlight of his shows was "The Silent Spot," a mime sketch that often featured the wordless, and poignant, Freddie the Freeloader.

Red remained popular for many years by changing with the times. During the '60s his shows featured many of the top rock acts of the day, in order to bring in younger viewers. Inevitably, though, his audience

*Some sources give 1913.

tended to become older as time went by. When CBS canceled his show, it was not due to any decline in his popularity—incredibly, he was still in the top ten!—but because its advertisters wanted to reach only young, hip urbanites.

In the years after *The Red Skelton Show* ended, Red generally kept a low profile, playing clubs and making other personal appearances. In 1973 he was married for the third time—to a woman 25 years his junior. He was also a successful painter and composer.

SKERRITT, TOM—actor
b: Aug 25, 1933, Detroit, Mich.

Ryan's Four (drama)
.... Dr. Thomas Ryan (1983)

SKILES & HENDERSON—
Dean Martin Presents the Golddiggers (var)
.... regulars (1968)

SKINNER, EDITH—hostess
Children's Sketch Book (child)
.... storyteller (1950)

SKINNER, EDNA—actress
Topper (com) ... Maggie, the cook (1954–55)
Mr. Ed (com)...... Kay Addison (1961–64)

SKIP JACKS, THE—singers
Music on Ice (var).......... regular (1960)

SKLAR, MICHAEL—comedian
b: c. 1944, California d: Mar 5, 1984

Laugh-In (revival) (var) ... regular (1977–78)
Sha Na Na (var) .... regular (1978–79)

SKOV, KENT—actor
Thicke of the Night (talk)
.... recurring player (1983–84)

SKULNIK, MENASHA—comedian
b: 1892, Russia d: Jun 4, 1970

Menasha the Magnificent (com)
.... Menasha (1950)

A Yiddish comedian and actor, heard on radio in the 1940s; he played a little fellow much under life's thumb in the 1950 summer series *Menasha the Magnificent*. He was also briefly seen as Uncle David on *The Goldbergs*.

SKYLARKS, THE—singers

Judge for Yourself (quiz)
.... regulars (1954)
The Dinah Shore Show (music)
.... regulars (1955–57)
The Dinah Shore Chevy Show (var)
.... regulars (1956–57)

SKYLINERS, THE—singers

TV's Top Tunes (music) .... regulars (1954)

SLADE, MARK—actor
b: Salem, Mass.

The Wackiest Ship in the Army (adv)
.... radioman Patrick Hollis (1965–66)
The High Chaparral (wes)
.... Billy Blue Cannon (1967–70)
Salty (adv).......... Taylor Reed (1974–75)

SLATE, HENRY—actor

Adventures in Paradise (adv)
.... Bulldog Lovey (1960–61)

SLATE, JEREMY—actor
b: 1925

The Aquanauts (aka Malibu Run) (adv)
.... Larry Lahr (1960–61)

Jeremy was seen in daytime soap operas, in later years, including *One Life to Live* and *The Guiding Light*, in the 1980s.

SLATEN, TROY—juvenile actor

Cagney & Lacey (police)
.... Michael Lacey (1982–)

SLATER, BILL—host, announcer, sportscaster

Birthday Party (child) .... host (1947)
Charade Quiz (quiz) .... emcee (1947–49)
Fishing and Hunting Club (sport)
.... host (1949–50)
Twenty Questions (quiz) ..... host (1949–52)
With This Ring (quiz) .... host (1951)
Broadway To Hollywood—Headline Clues (news)..................... host (1951–53)

A sportscaster and quiz and panel-show host often heard on radio during the '30s and '40s.

SLATTERY, RICHARD X.—actor
r: The Bronx, N.Y.

The Gallant Men (drama)
.... 1st Sgt. John McKenna (1962–63)
Mr. Roberts (com)
.... Captain John Morton (1965–66)
Switch (drama)...... Lt. Modeer (1976–77)
C.P.O. Sharkey (com)
.... Capt. "Buck" Buckner (1977–78)

A "take charge" type who was a New York City policeman for 12 years before he entered acting full-time in 1958.

SLAVIN, MILLIE—actress
b: Jul 2, New York City, N.Y.

Rafferty (drama)
.... Nurse Vera Wales (1977)
Struck by Lightning (com)...... Nora (1979)

SLEEPY HOLLOW GANG, THE—country band

Hayloft Hoedown (music)... regulars (1948)

SLEZAK, WALTER—actor
b: May 3, 1902, Vienna, Austria d: Apr 21, 1983

This Is Show Business (var)
.... panelist (1956)
High-Low (quiz)............ panelist (1957)
The Chevy Mystery Show (drama)
.... host (1960)
Made in America (quiz)..... panelist (1964)

One of Hollywood's grand old character actors, a heavyset man who was the son of the great opera tenor Leo Slezak and the father of soap opera queen Erika Slezak (Victoria on *One Life to Live*). Walter appeared often on TV playhouse series during the '50s, especially *Danger, Studio One*, and *The U.S. Steel Hour*, but was only occasionally seen in later years. He did turn up in the '60s on *Batman* as the Clock King, who entombed the Dynamic Duo in a giant hourglass so that they would be slowly buried in the sands of time! Later, in 1974, he was seen briefly with daughter Erika on *One Life to Live*, as her godfather. He committed suicide in 1983.

His autobiography: *What Time's the Next Swan?* (1962).

SLOANE, BOB—narrator

The Big Story (drama)
.... narrator (1949–54)

SLOANE, ESTELLE—dancer

American Minstrels of 1949 (var)
.... dancer (1949)
Broadway Open House (talk)
.... regular (1951)

SLOYAN, JAMES—actor
b: Feb 24, Indianapolis, Ind. r: Europe

Westside Medical (drama)
.... Dr. Sam Lanagan (1977)
Oh Madeline (com)
.... Charlie Wayne (1983–84)

SMALL, MARY—singer

American Minstrels of 1949 (var)
.... singer (1949)

This child radio star of the '30s was once known only by the name of her most famous sponsor—"Little Miss Bab-O."

SMALLEY, VIC—orchestra leader

Captain Billy's Mississippi Music Hall (var)
.... orch. leader (1948)

SMANIOTTO, SOLOMON—actor

Dallas (drama)............. Tony (1986–)

SMART, JEAN—actress
b: Sep 13, Seattle, Wash.

Reggie (com)........ Joan Reynolds (1983)
Teachers Only (com) .... Shari (1983)
Designing Women (com)
.... Charlene Frazier (1986–)

SMIGHT, JOYCE—actress

The Donald O'Connor Texaco Show (com)
.... Doreen (1954–55)

SMIKA, GINA MARIE—juvenile actress

The Oregon Trail (wes)
.... Rachel Thorpe (1977)

SMITH, ALEXIS—actress
b: Jun 8, 1921, Penticton, B.C., Canada r: Los Angeles

Dallas (drama)..... Jessica Montford (1984)

Tall, resourceful blonde leading lady in films of the '40s and '50s, who also appeared in some TV dramas during the '50s. She retired from acting in the '60s but returned in character parts following a triumph on Broadway in the 1971 musical *Follies.* She has long been married to actor Craig Stevens.

SMITH, ALLISON—juvenile actress
b: Dec 9, 1969, The Bronx, N.Y.

Kate & Allie (com) .. Jennie Lowell (1984–)

Allison's first major break came at the age of ten, when she won the title role in the Broadway musical *Annie.* She remained with the show for three years.

SMITH, ANDREA—juvenile actress

American Dream (drama)
.... Jennifer Novak (1981)

SMITH, ARCHIE—actor

Crime Photographer (drama)
.... Jack Lipman (1951–52)

SMITH, BILL—actor

The Asphalt Jungle (police)
.... Sgt. Danny Keller (1961)

SMITH, BOB—Chicago actor

Chicagoland Mystery Players (police)
.... Sgt. Holland (1949–50)
This Is Music (music)..... regular (1958–59)

SMITH, BOB—New York host
b: Nov 27, 1917, Buffalo, N.Y.

The Gulf Road Show Starring Bob Smith (var)
.... host (1948–49)

"Buffalo Bob" Smith is best known, by far, as the upbeat host of the famous daytime kiddie show *Howdy Doody* (1947–1960). He was originally a radio singer, however, and in addition to his kid's show he attempted to launch a career as an adult variety show host.

Buffalo Bob got his nickname from his many years on local radio in Buffalo in the '30s and '40s—although the kids on *Howdy Doody* were told that it was given to him by a tribe of Sycapoose Indians living near Doodyville. On radio he sang, played numerous instruments, and hosted musical shows. He moved to New York in 1946 as a radio personality but got his big break the following year, when he was tapped to do a Saturday morning kid's show. This evolved into the Monday through Friday *Hoody Doody Show* in December 1947. A few months later Bob attempted to establish himself with adults on the prime time *Gulf Road Show,* a mixture of variety and talent elements, but this was much less successful. Realizing on which side his bread was peanut-buttered, Bob decided to stick with the kids and went on to become the most famous small-fry entertainer of the 1950s.

Bob retired in 1960 to attend to his business interests, which by then included ownership of three radio stations and a liquor store. He returned to the campus nostalgia circuit (with Howdy) in the '70s and even hosted a syndicated *Howdy Doody* revival series in 1976, but basically his later years were spent quietly because of heart trouble.

SMITH, BUBBA—black actor
b: Feb 28, 1945, Beaumont, Texas

Semi-Tough (com) . . . . Puddin (1980)
Open All Night (com) . . . . . . Robin (1981–82)
Blue Thunder (police)
. . . . Lyman "Bubba" Kelsey (1984)
Half Nelson (drama) . . . . Beau (1985)

An awesome (6'8", 248 pounds) former football great, often teamed with fellow footballer Dick Butkus. An All-American in college in the '60s, Bubba spent ten years with the Baltimore Colts, Oakland Raiders, and Houston Oilers before turning to acting in the late '70s. Although he looks like a bulldozer, his roles tend to be comedic.

SMITH, CARL—country singer
b: Mar 15, 1927, Maynardville, Tenn.

Grand Ole Opry (music)
. . . . regular (1955–56)
Five Star Jubilee (var) . . . . host (1961)

SMITH, CAROLINE—actress
The Last Convertible (drama)
. . . . Nancy Van Breymer (1979)

SMITH, CHARLES—actor
b: c. 1920

Boss Lady (com) . . . . . . Chester Allen (1952)
Holiday Lodge (com)
. . . . Woodrow (1961)

SMITH, CYRIL—actor
b: Apr 4, 1892, Peterhead, Scotland d: Mar 5, 1963

The Adventures of Sir Lancelot (adv)
. . . . Merlin (1956–57)

SMITH, DWAN—black actress
b: Jan 22, Jackson, Tenn.

Joe Forrester (police)
. . . . Jolene Jackson (1975–76)

SMITH, EBONIE—actress
The Jeffersons (com)
. . . . Jessica Jefferson (1984–85)
Morningstar/Eveningstar (drama)
. . . . Eugene Waters (1986)

SMITH, EDWIN—accordion player
Saturday Night Jamboree (music)
. . . . regular (1948–49)

SMITH, ELIZABETH—actress
Big Hawaii (drama)
. . . . Lulu Kalahani (1977)

SMITH, GIL—juvenile actor
Dennis the Menace (com)
. . . . Joey McDonald (1959–60)
Peter Loves Mary (com)
. . . . Steve Lindsey (1960–61)

SMITH, H. ALLEN—host
b: Dec 19, 1907, McLeansboro, Ill. d: Feb 24, 1976

Armchair Detective (drama)
. . . . Mr. Crime Authority (1949)

A humorist, member of the California State Legislature and, evidently, an authority on crime.

SMITH, HAL—actor

b: 1917, Petosky, Mich.

The Andy Griffith Show (com)
.... Otis Campbell (1960–67)
Pat Paulsen's Half a Comedy Hour (var)
.... regular (1970)

A veteran character actor, best known for his cartoon voice work both in movies (with Disney's Goofy, Jiminy Cricket, Winnie the Pooh, etc.) and on many Saturday morning TV shows of the '50s, '60s, and '70s. He played Otis the town drunk on *The Andy Griffith Show.*

SMITH, HILLARY BAILEY—

see Bailey, Hillary

SMITH, HOWARD—actor

b: Aug 12, 1893, Attleboro, Mass. d: Jan 10, 1968

The Aldrich Family (com)
.... Mr. Brown (1949–53)
Peter Loves Mary (com)
.... Horace Gibney (1960–61)
Hazel (com) ...... Harvey Griffin (1961–66)

Heavyweight character actor.

SMITH, HOWARD—orchestra leader, pianist

b: Oct 19, 1910, Ardmore, Okla.

The Garry Moore Show (var)
.... orch. leader (1958–59)

SMITH, HOWARD K.—newscaster

b: May 12, 1914, Ferriday, La.

Behind the News With Howard K. Smith (news).........................host (1959)
Howard K. Smith—News and Comment (news)............ commentator (1962–63)
ABC Evening News (news)
.... anchorman (1969–75)
V (sci fi)............. as himself (1984–85)

Emmy Award: Best Writing for a Documentary, for *CBS Reports:* "The Population Explosion" (1960)

This feisty, independent-minded newsman quit two networks in protest over principles during his career. A Rhodes scholar, Smith began as a newspaper reporter in New Orleans in 1936 and went to Europe in 1939 to cover the initial stages of World War II for the United Press. There, in 1941, he was hired by Edward R. Murrow to be part of CBS's crack (radio) news team; he stayed with the network for 20 years, becoming chief European correspondent after the war and Washington correspondent in 1957. One of the highlights of his career with CBS came when he moderated the historic first presidential debate between Kennedy and Nixon in 1960.

Smith was one of CBS's brightest stars until he quit abruptly in 1961, after a fight with CBS chairman William Paley. Smith described this celebrated incident in an interview with Tom Snyder on *The Tomorrow Show* in 1979. It resulted, he said, from a documentary called "Who Speaks for Birmingham?", in which Smith compared black-baiting racists with Nazi storm troopers. "I finished up the documentary with the famous Edmund Burke quotation, 'All that is necessary for the triumph of evil in the world is for good men to do nothing.' And the (CBS) lawyers came to me and said, 'We can't allow that." I said, 'I didn't say that, Edmund Burke did.' They said, 'You'll have to do another close.' I said, 'I refuse.' Later, Paley asked me to write down what I thought his policy was, and I wrote it down and sent it to him. He invited me to lunch; and halfway through the lunch he pulled out my document, threw it across the table, and said, 'I've read junk like this before. Maybe you ought to try somewhere else.' And so, I pushed my chair away from the table and said, 'I think this lunch is over,' and walked out and that was the end."

ABC welcomed Smith with open arms, gave him his own commentary show, and made him the regular commentator on its evening newscast. One of the resulting reports, "The Political Obituary of Richard Nixon," kicked up a storm when Smith dared to allow Alger Hiss a minute of airtime to attack his arch-foe Nixon. Sponsors ran for cover and lawsuits flew, but Smith stood firm. "Mr. Hiss is news and we're in the news business. I'm not running a Sunday school program." Smith had always been known as a strong political liberal, but as the Vietnam protests mounted he became more and more a defender of administration policies—so much so that ABC became jokingly known as the "Administration Broadcasting Company." "I'm a hawk on most foreign policy issues, and a liberal on domestic issues," he said simply. During the Nixon years he ruffled still more feathers by being one of the few newsman to agree that Vice President Agnew was at least partially correct in his allegations of media bias.

During the early 1970s Smith was co-anchor of ABC's principal evening newscast, but after sports showman Roone Arledge took over ABC News in 1977—with a mandate to "glitz" things up—his role was progressively reduced. Smith quit in disgust in 1979. His career then took a curious turn. Instead of retiring to write books or narrate occasional weighty specials, he moved over to the entertainment side of show business, playing a newsman in such movies as *Close Encounters of the Third Kind* and *The Candidate,* and in the TV series *V.* He enjoyed it immensely, although he admitted in 1984, "I seem to be in a kind of rut, always playing a reporter. I suspect that's because a thing called talent would be required for me to play anything else."

SMITH, J. BRENNAN—juvenile actor
b: c. 1970, Sylmar, Calif.

The Bad News Bears (com)
.... Mike Engelberg (1979–80)

SMITH, JACK—singer, host
b: c. 1919

Place the Face (quiz) .... emcee (1953)
You Asked for It (aud par) ... host (1958–59)
You Asked for It (aud par) ... host (1971–77)
You Asked for It (aud par)
.... narrated clips (1981–83)

A former popular singer, who had several minor record hits in the late 1940s but then drifted into obscurity until his stints on *You Asked for It* (on which he replaced original host Art Baker). The series gave him a pleasant new career; he said of his globe-trotting duties, "It's like a vacation."

SMITH, JACLYN—actress
b: Oct 26, 1947, Houston, Texas

Charlie's Angels (drama)
.... Kelly Garrett (1976–81)

This brown-haired beauty was the only one of Charlie's three angels to last for that series' entire five-year run. She got her start in commercials on the East Coast around 1970, in which she was, among other things, "The Breck Girl." Occasional acting appearances followed, wherever a "knockout" was needed, on *The Partridge Family* (in 1970), *McCloud, The Rookies, Switch,* and others. During and since the run of *Charlie's Angels* she has appeared in quite a few TV movies, playing the leading roles in *Jacqueline Bouvier Kennedy* (1981) and *Rage of Angels* (1983), as well as portraying Sally Fairfax, the true love of the father of our country, in 1984's *George Washington.* George had good taste.

SMITH, JEFF—
Hee Haw (var) .... regular (1984–)

SMITH, JOHN—actor
b: Mar 6, 1931, Los Angeles, Calif.

That's My Boy (com) .. Bill Baker (1954–55)
Cimarron City (wes)
.... Lane Temple (1958–59)
Laramie (wes) ..... Slim Sherman (1959–63)

Blond, boyishly handsome star of the '50s and '60s. His first break was as one of the airline passengers in the 1954 film *The High and the Mighty;* later, he played supporting roles in other films, and in TV action and comedy series, before his two costarring westerns, *Cimarron City* and *Laramie.* These did not lead to greater things, however. He made a few minor movies afterward and then dropped from sight.

SMITH, KATE—singer
b: May 1, 1907*, Greenville, Va. d: Jun 17, 1986

The Kate Smith Evening Hour (var)
.... star (1951–52)
The Kate Smith Show (var) ..... host (1960)

Another of the great radio stars of the '30s and '40s who had a successful career on early television. A hefty woman with a voice to match, Kate started out in the '20s

*Most sources give 1909, but *Variety,* in its obituary, insisted that the correct year is 1907.

singing with jazz bands as "The Songbird of the South" (or, "Kate Smith and Her Swanee Music"). She was at first the butt of so many "fat" jokes that she almost left show business, but in time she became known for her good-hearted, all-American, almost motherly personality. She was the virtual personification of mom and apple pie during the World War II years, an image bolstered by her close identification with the Irving Berlin flag-waver "God Bless America." Her work on behalf of the war effort was prodigious; she reportedly sold $600 million in war bonds, including nearly $40 million in one extraordinary, 17-hour radio marathon.

Kate's initial foray into TV was a popular Monday through Friday daytime hour, which ran from 1950 to 1954. She also hosted a prime time variety series in 1951–52, and another in 1960. She continued to appear as a guest on specials and other shows, often to sing "God Bless America" or her theme song, "When the Moon Comes over the Mountain," until the mid-1970s, when deteriorating health forced her into virtual retirement. One of her last public appearances was at the 1982 Emmy Awards telecast, when she appeared in a wheelchair.

Despite her motherly image, Kate never married. Virtually her entire career was guided by her close friend, manager, and mentor, Ted Collins, who was devoted to her (and she to him) from 1931 until his death in 1964. Kate's autobiographies: *Living in a Great Big Way* (1938), and *Upon My Lips a Song.*

SMITH, KENT—actor
b: Mar 19, 1907, New York City, N.Y. d: Apr 23, 1985

Peyton Place (drama)
.... Dr. Robert Morton (1964–65)
The Invaders (sci fi)
.... Edgar Scoville (1967–68)

A distinguished-looking character actor, very active in supporting roles on television in the '50s and '60s. His favorite role was that of jurist Charles Evans Hughes in the documentary series *Profiles in Courage,* but he is probably better remembered as the industrialist who helped Roy Thinnes battle the aliens in the science-fiction series *Invaders.*

SMITH, KURTWOOD—actor
b: Jul 3, New Lisbon, Wis.

The Renegades (police)
.... Capt. Scanlon (1983)

SMITH, LANE—actor
b: Apr 29, Memphis, Tenn.

Chiefs (drama)......... Hoss Spense (1983)
V (sci fi).......... Nathan Bates (1984–85)
Kay O'Brien (drama)
.... Dr. Robert Moffitt (1986–)

SMITH, LELAND—actor

What's Happening!! (com)
.... "the Snake" (1978–79)

SMITH, LEONARD—actor

Our Miss Brooks (com)
.... Stretch Snodgrass (1952–55)

SMITH, LEWIS—actor

North and South (drama)
.... Charles Main (1985)

SMITH, LIONEL—black actor

Park Place (com)
.... Aaron "Mac" MacRae (1981)

SMITH, LIZ—New York gossip columnist
b: Feb 2, 1923, Fort Worth, Texas

Headliners with David Frost (talk)
.... regular (1978)

SMITH, LORING—actor
b: 1895*, Stratford, Conn. d: Jul 8, 1981

The Hartmans (com)
.... the brother-in-law (1949)

SMITH, MADELINE—actress
b: c. 1950

Doctor in the House (com)
.... Nurse (1970–73)

SMITH, MARTHA—actress
b: Cleveland, Ohio r: Farmington, Mich.

Scarecrow and Mrs. King (adv)
.... Francine Desmond (1983–)

*Some sources give 1900.

Sexy actress often seen as The Dizzy Blonde (or, Girl-in-a-Bikini) on various crime series of the late '70s and '80s. She got her start as a model at auto shows ("Miss Parts") and landed her first major acting role in the TV movie *Ebony, Ivory and Jade* in 1979. She plays a wisecracking agent on *Scarecrow and Mrs. King*.

SMITH, MICHELLE—actress

a.k.a. Pablo (com) ... Elena Del Gato (1984)

SMITH, PATRICIA—actress
b: Feb 20, New Haven, Conn.

The Debbie Reynolds Show (com)
.... Charlotte Landers (1969–70)
The Bob Newhart Show (com)
.... Margaret Hoover (1972–73)

SMITH, PAUL—actor

Fibber McGee and Molly (com)
.... Roy Norris (1959–60)
The Gertrude Berg Show (com)
.... George Howell (1961–62)
No Time for Sergeants (com)
.... Capt. Martin (1964–65)
Mr. Terrific (com) ..... Harley Trent (1967)
The Doris Day Show (com)
.... Ron Harvey (1969–71)

Tall, tough-looking actor who seems best in comic supporting roles.

SMITH, PAUL L.—actor

Masada (drama) .... Gideon (1981)

SMITH, QUEENIE—actress, dancer
b: Sep 8, 1898, New York City, N.Y. d: Aug 5, 1978

The Funny Side (var) .... regular (1971)

SMITH, RAY—actor

Masada (drama) .... Lentius (1981)
Dempsey and Makepeace (police)
.... Chief Sup. G. Spikings (1984–)

SMITH, RED—sportscaster
b: Sep 25, 1905, Green Bay, Wis. d: Jan 15, 1982

Fight Talk (sport)
.... commentator (1953–54)

SMITH, REID—actor
b: May 8, Burbank, Calif.

Chase (police)
.... Off. Norm Hamilton (1973–74)
The Chisholms (wes)
.... Lester Hackett (1980)

SMITH, REX—singer, actor
b: Sep 19, 1956, Jacksonville, Fla.

Solid Gold (music) .... host (1982–83)
Street Hawk (police)
.... Off. Jesse Mach (1985)

This hirsute young singer made a big splash in 1979 in his first acting role, that of a 17-year-old rock idol who falls in love with a 13-year-old fan (who he thinks is 16) in the TV movie *Sooner or Later*. The theme song from the film, "You Take My Breath Away," was a top-ten hit, but Rex's subsequent career did not develop as quickly as expected. His later credits include the leads in the Broadway productions of *Grease* and *The Pirates of Penzance* (with Linda Ronstadt), a season hosting the syndicated rock show *Solid Gold*, and a lightweight—and short-lived—crime series called *Street Hawk*.

SMITH, ROGER—actor
b: Dec 18, 1932, South Gate, Calif.

Father Knows Best (com)
.... Doyle Hobbs (1957–58)
77 Sunset Strip (drama)
.... Jeff Spencer (1958–63)
Mr. Roberts (com)
.... Lt. (j.g.) Douglas Roberts (1965–66)

A handsome actor—in a rather standard 1950's way—who had a successful ten-year career on television, before retiring to manage his wife's career. Roger was serving in the navy in Hawaii when he was spotted by James Cagney, who helped him land a contract with Warner Brothers. The studio put him in a number of harmless films of the late '50s, featured him in episodes of several TV series, and finally gave him the costarring role (with Efrem Zimbalist, Jr.) in a new detective series called *77 Sunset Strip*—which became a major hit. Roger went on to more guest roles and then another series lead, as *Mr. Roberts*. He then left the medium abruptly to manage the career of his wife, singer Ann Margaret, for whom he has produced several highly acclaimed specials. He appeared in one of them, called *Ann Margret Smith*, in 1975, with the comment "This is definitely just a onetime appearance for me."

SMITH, SAMANTHA—juvenile actress
b: Jun 29, 1972, Houlton, Me. d: Aug 25, 1985

Lime Street (drama)
.... Elizabeth Culver (1985)

Samantha Smith was the young schoolgirl who captured the imagination of America —and the world—when, in 1983, she wrote a letter to Soviet leader Yuri Andropov urging peace and was invited to visit the Soviet Union. The journey became a media event of the first magnitude, and the once-obscure 11-year-old became an instant celebrity. She proved quite articulate on talk shows (she was the daughter of an English professor) and soon accepted offers to write a book, host a cable TV show, and even appeared in an episode of the prime time series *Charles in Charge* (in 1984).

Amid much publicity she was then signed for the regular role of Robert Wagner's daughter in the 1985 series *Lime Street*. Unfortunately, she and her father were killed in a plane crash after only a few episodes had been filmed.

SMITH, SANDRA—actress
Our Private World (drama)
.... Sandy Larson (1965)
The Interns (drama)
.... Dr. Lydia Thorpe (1970–71)

SMITH, SCOTT—actor
Firehouse (adv) .... Scotty Smith (1974)

SMITH, SHAWNEE—actress
All Is Forgiven (com) .. Sonia Russell (1986)

SMITH, SHELLEY—actress
b: Oct 25, Princeton, N.J. r: Memphis, Tenn.

The Associates (com)
.... Sara James (1979–80)
For Love and Honor (drama)
.... Capt. Carolyn Engel (1983)

A top fashion model of the 1970s; she has appeared in a number of TV movies of the 1980s, including part two of *Scruples*.

SMITH, SOMETHIN'—singer
Sing Along (music) .... regular (1958)

A 1946 winner (on radio) of *Arthur Godfrey's Talent Scouts*, who formed a group called the Redheads while in college and had a hit record in 1955 called "It's a Sin to Tell a Lie."

SMITH, STEVE—singer
The Lawrence Welk Show (music)
.... regular (1965–69)

SMITH, WILLIAM—actor
b: Mar 24, 1932, Columbia, Mo. r: Burbank, Calif.

Laredo (wes)........... Joe Riley (1965–67)
Rich Man, Poor Man—Book I (drama)
.... Arthur Falconetti (1976)
Rich Man, Poor Man—Book II (drama)
.... Arthur Falconetti (1976–77)
Hawaii Five-O (police)
.... James "Kimo" Carew (1979–80)
Wildside (wes)
.... Brodie Hollister (1985)

A Russian language scholar, who was working on his Ph.D. in languages when he dropped out of academia (in 1957), won a screen test, and began appearing in TV episodes. "I had no acting background," he says, "but this was at the height of television's western binge, and I squinted well and sat tall in the saddle."

After appearing in a 1961 British TV series called *Zero-1*, he returned to the U.S. and had his major break as one of the leads in *Laredo*. Ten years later he starred as the vicious Falconetti, the nemesis of the Jordaches, in the top-rated miniseries and series *Rich Man, Poor Man*.

SMITHERS, JAN—actress
b: Jul 3, 1949, North Hollywood, Calif.

WKRP in Cincinnati (com)
.... Bailey Quarters (1978–82)

SMITHERS, WILLIAM—actor
b: Jul 10, 1927, Richmond, Va.

The Witness (drama)
.... committee member (1960–61)
Peyton Place (drama)
.... David Schuster (1965–66)

Executive Suite (drama)
.... Anderson Galt (1976–77)
Dallas (drama)...... Jeremy Wendell (1981)
Dallas (drama)... Jeremy Wendell (1984–85)

This fair-haired actor is perhaps more notable for what he did offscreen in Hollywood than on. When MGM failed to give him the star billing he'd been promised in his contract for *Executive Suite,* he complained. MGM responded in vintage Hollywood fashion: "Shut up kid, you'll never work in this town again" (or words to that effect). Smith sued, a judged concurred (accusing MGM of taking "outrageous . . . advantage of their superior economic position") and the actor was awarded $1.8 million in damages. That *that,* you big moguls!

SMITROVICH, BILL—actor

Crime Story (police) ·
.... Det. Danny Krychek (1986–)

SMITS, JIMMY—actor
b: Jul 9, c. 1958, New York City r: Brooklyn, N.Y.

L.A. Law (drama) . Victor Sifuentes (1986–)

SMOOT, FRED—actor

The Wackiest Ship in the Army (adv)
    machinist's mate Seymour Trivers (1965–66)
The Marty Feldman Comedy Machine (var)
.... regular (1972)
The Steve Allen Comedy Hour (var)
.... regular (1980–81)

SMOTHERS, DICK—comedian
b: Nov 20, 1939, New York City, N.Y.

The Steve Allen Show (var).. regular (1961)
The Smothers Brothers Show (com)
.... as himself (1965–66)
The Smothers Brothers Comedy Hour (var)
.... cohost (1967–69)
The Smothers Brothers Summer Show (var)
.... cohost (1970)
The Smothers Brothers Show (var)
.... cohost (1975)
Fitz and Bones (com)
.... Ryan Fitzpatrick (1981)

"We were sure (the audience) would like the irreverence of these apple-cheeked fellows," said the CBS executive, "but they turned out to be a little more topical than we had envisioned. The network is for what they are doing. It merely becomes a matter of degree."

The "apple-cheeked fellows" the executive was warily referring to in a 1968 *TV Guide* interview were Tom and Dick Smothers, two coffeehouse comics whose rambunctious 1967 variety show touched off the biggest debate on network censorship in the medium's history. They hardly seemed candidates to challenge the limits of what could be said on TV. Tom and Dick had begun as a youthful folk song act with a little brotherly comedy banter mixed in ("Mom always liked you best!"). After attracting attention at some of the hipper West Coast clubs, they began to appear on network TV, on Jack Paar's *Tonight Show, The Jack Benny Show* and, in the fall of 1961, as regulars on Steve Allen's Wednesday night hour. A series of best-selling albums followed from 1962–65, all using noncontroversial material; the first had comedy routines on one side and straight singing on the other.

The Smothers' first series was a standard-issue situation comedy, concocted by Four Star TV in a traditional TV mold—Dick played a young executive and Tom his deceased brother, a bumbling angel sent to earth to do good deeds. It was a quick and well-deserved flop. In the middle of the following season CBS brought them back in a variety format, expecting to attract the younger viewers with an innocent hour of youth-oriented fun. It started out that way, but the brothers soon began to react to the social turmoil spreading across the country by injecting more and stronger topical material in their skits—almost all of it heavily antiestablishment, antiadministration, and antiwar. Young viewers, the ones doing the protesting, loved it, and the show shot into the top 20. Behind-the-scenes battles raged with the CBS censors over what could and could not be said—politicians, policies, sex, religion, social mores of all kinds were fair game as far as the Smothers were concerned. Worse yet, the brothers turned to the public and to Washington for support. Their dispute with CBS grew more and more bitter (as did the content of the show) until finally, in April 1969, CBS simply canceled them. A great uproar resulted, but the decision stuck.

Tom and Dick were back in the summer of 1970, on ABC, but their time, and their biting edge, seemed to be gone and the show did not make it to the fall. Thereafter, they were seen only occasionally, usually together, sometimes separately, in guest appearances and in a 1975 NBC series that also failed. An attempt to revive their career in a 1981 adventure/comedy series (as TV reporters) was no more successful. Tom and Dick may have fired the opening salvo in the war to bring social relevance to TV, but they themselves did not survive the initial battle.

SMOTHERS, TOM—comedian

b: Feb 2, 1937, New York City, N.Y.

The Steve Allen Show (var).. regular (1961)
The Smothers Brothers Show (com)
.... as himself (1965–66)
The Smothers Brothers Comedy Hour (var)
.... cohost (1967–69)
The Smothers Summer Show (var)
.... cohost (1970)
Tom Smothers' Organic Space Ride (com)
.... host (1971)
The Smothers Brothers Show (var)
.... cohost (1975)
Fitz and Bones (com)
.... Bones Howard (1981)

Brother of Dick. Tom was the seemingly dull, slow-talking one (actually he was the more politically active of the two); Dick was the dark-haired, good looking, always frustrated straight man. See above for details on their joint career.

SNARY, BILL—actor

This Is Music (music)..... regular (1951–52)

SNIDER, BARRY—actor

b: Sep 29, Salinas, Calif.

Beacon Hill (drama)... Harry Emmet (1975)

SNOW, HANK—country singer

b: May 9, 1914, Liverpool, Nova Scotia, Canada

Grand Ole Opry (music) .. regular (1955–56)

SNOW, PHOEBE—singer

b: Jul 17, 1952, New York City, N.Y. r: Teaneck, N.J.

9 to 5 (com)............ sang theme (1982)

SNYDER, ARLEN DEAN—actor

b: Mar 5, Rice, Kan.

Dear Detective (police)
.... Prof. Richard Weyland (1979)
Trauma Center (drama)
.... Dr. Charles Sternhauser (1983)

SNYDER, TOM—newscaster

b: May 12, 1936, Milwaukee, Wis.

The Tomorrow Show (talk)... host (1973–82)
NBC Weekend News (news)
.... anchorman (1975–76)
Prime Time Sunday (pub aff)
.... host (1979–80)

Emmy Award: Outstanding Individual Achievement, as Host, The Tomorrow Show (1974)

Tom Snyder, the brash, aggressive interviewer on The Tomorrow Show, was the first star of late-late-night (after the Tonight Show) TV. Although his audience was small by network standards, numbering "only" about three million per night, his pushy, news-making style was widely talked about, sometimes acclaimed, and even parodied.

Tom spent many years in local news before making it to the network. He began on radio in Milwaukee in 1957, while still in college, and later had TV anchor jobs in Philadelphia and Los Angeles. He had been anchor of the top-rated local newscast in Los Angeles for three years when NBC tapped him for The Tomorrow Show in 1973. The NBC brass had great plans for him, trying him out on a weekend newscast in 1975, in prime time celebrity interview specials (à la Barbara Walters) in 1978–79, and in a unique, live, prime time newsmagazine in 1979–80. However, his abrasiveness did not sit well with the general public and he reverted to his late night show, which was expanded to 90 minutes in 1980. At the same time, gossip columnist Rona Barrett was added as co-host, but Tom and Rona did not get along at all, and, after contract disputes and walkouts the series was finally canceled in January 1982. Tom has since returned to local newscasting.

SNYDERS, SAMMY—juvenile actor

The Baxters (com).. Gregg Baxter (1980–81)

SOBEL, REBECCA—newscaster
b: c. 1950, Brooklyn, N.Y.

Monitor (pub aff).. correspondent (1983–84)

SOBLE, RON—actor

The Monroes (wes)..... Dirty Jim (1966–67)

SODE, LAURA—actress

Hawaii Five-O (police) .... Luana (1978–80)

SODSAI, SONDI—actress

Adventures in Paradise (adv)
.... Sondi (1960–61)

Miss Thailand of 1960.

SOKOL, MARILYN—actress

Van Dyke and Company (var)
.... regular (1976)

SOLARI AND CARR—

Andy Williams Presents Ray Stevens (var)
.... the Sacks (1970)

SOLARI, RUDY—actor

Redigo (wes)........ Frank Martinez (1963)
The Wackiest Ship in the Army (adv)
    gunner's mate Sherman Nagurski (1965–66)
Garrison's Gorillas (drama)
.... Casino (1967–68)

SOLARI, TOM—actor

The Sonny and Cher Comedy Hour (var)
.... regular (1971–72)

SOLDER, FLO—dancer

Dance Fever (dance) ..... dancer (1980–81)

SOLOMON, BRUCE—actor
b: 1944, New York City, N.Y.

Mary Hartman, Mary Hartman (com)
.... Sgt. Dennis Foley (1976–77)
Lanigan's Rabbi (police)
.... Rabbi David Small (1977)

SOLOMON, GEORGE—actor

Motown Revue (var)........ regular (1985)

SOMACK, JACK—actor
b: Sep 14, 1918, Chicago, Ill. d: Aug 24, 1983

Ball Four (com) .. "Cap" Capogrosso (1976)
The Stockard Channing Show (com)
.... Mr. Kramer (1980)

SOMERS, BRETT—actress
b: Jul 11, New Brunswick, Canada r: Portland, Me.

The Odd Couple (com)
.. Blanche Madison (occasional) (1970–75)
Perry Mason (revival) (drama)
.... Gertrude Lade (1973–74)
Match Game P.M. (quiz) . panelist (1975–82)

The former wife of Jack Klugman, with whom she occasionally appeared on *The Odd Couple* (as Oscar's ex).

SOMERS, SUZANNE—actress
b: Oct 16, 1946, San Bruno, Calif.

Three's Company (com)
.... Chrissy Snow (1977–81)

"It's all such a mess," cried Suzanne Somers in 1981, referring to her unraveling career. With only modest acting ability and less-than-classic beauty, but a great deal of sexiness and drive, she had ridden a skyrocket to fame in the hit comedy *Three's Company*. Then it all evaporated.

Suzanne was a minor sex symbol in the '60s and early '70s, appearing in movies and occasional TV episodes—including an early role in *Lassie* in 1965. She began to attract attention in the early '70s, with a small part in *American Graffiti* (1973) and appearances on *The Tonight Show* and elsewhere. She also posed for some nude photo layouts for magazines, which would later come back to haunt her. Then, in 1976, ABC program chief Fred Silverman spotted her and cast her as the dumb blonde in *Three's Company*, which became an enormous hit. Suzanne began making TV movies and starring in Las Vegas; she also got a new manager (her husband), who promptly demanded an enormous increase in pay for her work on *Three's Company* and a piece of the show as well. The producers refused, and after bitter negotiations she was fired.

Suzanne later made occasional appearances in specials and TV movies (e.g., *Hollywood Wives*), but—as of the mid-1980s

—her career just hasn't been the same since.

SOMERVILLE, DAVE—singer
b: Canada

The Tim Conway Comedy Hour (var)
.... regular (1970)

Singing partner of Bruce Belland. In the 1950s Dave was the lead singer of the very popular group the Diamonds, and Bruce was with the Four Preps.

SOMMARS, JULIE—actress
b: Apr 15, Fremont, Neb.

The Governor & J.J. (com)
.... Jennifer Jo (J.J.) Drinkwater (1969–70)

SOMMERS, JIMMY—actor

A Date with Judy (com)
.... Oogie Pringle (1952–53)

SONG SPINNERS, THE—vocal group

Break the Bank (quiz) .... singers (1948–57)

A rather popular vocal group on records during the 1940s.

SONGSMITHS QUARTET, THE—vocal group

Garroway at Large (var).... regulars (1949)

SONNY & CHER—

see entries for Bono, Sonny; and for Cher

SONS OF THE PIONEERS, THE—singers

The Roy Rogers & Dale Evans Show (var)
.... regulars (1962)

Probably the most famous western singing group, formed in the early 1930s by a then-unknown Roy Rogers and several others, and frequently featured in cowboy films and on radio. Their best known songs: "Tumbling Tumbleweeds" and "Cool Water." Key members over the years have been Bob Nolan (who wrote many of their songs), Tim Spencer, and Lloyd Perryman. Among the other alumni have been Pat Brady and Ken Curtis. Although member-

ship has changed over the years, the group is still active today.

Roy Rogers always retained his ties with the group that gave him his start and featured them in many of his movies and TV shows, including his 1962 variety series.

SOO, JACK—actor
b: 1915*, Oakland, Calif. d: Jan 11, 1979

Valentine's Day (com)
.... Rockwell "Rocky" Sin (1964–65)
Barney Miller (com)
.... Det. Nick Yemana (1975–78)

SOODIK, TRISH—juvenile actress

Lucas Tanner (drama)
.... Cindy Damon (1974–75)

SOPER, TONY—actor
b: Nov 20, Yakima, Wash.

Kay O'Brien (drama)
.... Dr. Cliff Margolis (1986–)

SOREL, LOUISE—actress
b: Aug 6, c. 1940, Los Angeles, Calif.

The Survivors (drama)
.... Jean Vale (1969–70)
The Don Rickles Show (com)
.... Barbara Robinson (1972)
Curse of Dracula (adv)
.... Amanda Gibbons (1979)
Ladies' Man (com)
.... Elaine Holstein (1980–81)

A television supporting actress, best at stylish, hard-bitten roles. She has played guest roles on many series since the mid-1960s and has been a regular on several; she was Don Rickles' long-suffering wife on *The Don Rickles Show*, a vampiress on *Curse of Dracula*, and the domineering boss on *Ladies' Man*. In the mid-1980s she was playing one of the rich, bitchy residents on the daytime soap opera *Santa Barbara*. Louise is the daughter of film producer Albert H. Cohen and Egyptian-born actress Jeanne Sorel.

SORENSEN, RICKIE—juvenile actor

Father of the Bride (com)
.... Tommy Banks (1961–62)

*Some sources give 1916 or 1917.

SORG, ANN—actress

The Aldrich Family (com)
.... Anna Mitchell (1949–53)

SORKIN, DAN—announcer

The Bob Newhart Show (var)
.... regular (1961–62)

SORRELLS, BOB—actor

Ensign O'Toole (com)
.... seaman Claude White (1962–63)

SORVINO, PAUL—actor
b: 1939, Brooklyn, N.Y.

We'll Get By (com)..... George Platt (1975)
Bert D'Angelo/Superstar (police)
.... Sgt. Bert D'Angelo (1976)
Chiefs (drama)
.... Sheriff Skeeter Willis (1983)

A tall, dark, heavyset character actor, seen with equal frequency in dramas and comedies. His two starring vehicles in the mid-1960s—*We'll Get By*, a family comedy, and *Bert D'Angelo*, a cop show—were not successful, and he has since concentrated on guest roles and TV movies, among the latter *Seventh Avenue, Dummy,* and *Chiefs.*

SOSEBEE, TOMMY—

Ozark Jubilee (music)........ regular (1955)

SOSNIK, HARRY—orchestra leader
b: Jul 13, 1906, Chicago, Ill.

The Fifty-Fourth Street Revue (var)
.... orch. leader (1949–50)
By Popular Demand (var)
.... orch. leader (1950)
The Jack Carter Show (var)
.... orch. leader (1950–51)
Musical Comedy Time (com)
.... orch. leader (1950–51)
Melody Tour (var)...... orch. leader (1954)
Sing Along (music) ..... orch. leader (1958)
Your Hit Parade (music)
.... orch. leader (1958–59)

SOTHERN, ANN—actress
b: Jan 22, 1909*, Valley City, N.D.

Private Secretary (com)
.... Susie McNamera (1953–57)
*Some sources give 1907.

The Ann Sothern Show (com)
.... Katy O'Connor (1958–61)
My Mother the Car (com)
.... voice of the car (1965–66)

After a long movie career that began in 1929—under her real name, Harriet Lake—Ann came to television quite successfully as the meddlesome Susie McNamera in the 1950s hit *Private Secretary*. The role was not unlike that of the brassy showgirl she had played in several *Mazie* movies made between 1939 and 1947. She is quite proud of the series, saying that it "established on TV the liberated woman that people carry on so much about today. I *always* played independent women!"

After *Private Secretary,* Ann went on to star in another series, as an assistant hotel manager; she also made guest appearances on selected series of the '60s and early '70s, including several on her idol Lucille Ball's shows as "the Countess." Ann's last regular role, and surely her most unusual, was that of the voice of a 1928 Porter automobile in the infamous 1965 sitcom *My Mother the Car* ("I don't even *admit* to doing that series!" she exclaims today). She has been generally inactive since the mid-1970s, although she did return in 1985 for a TV remake of her 1949 movie classic, *A Letter to Three Wives.*

SOTHERN, HARRY—actor
b: Apr 26, 1884 d: Feb 22, 1957

Buck Rogers (sci fi)..... Dr. Huer (1950–51)

SOTO, ROSANA—actress

A.E.S. Hudson Street (com)
.... Nurse Rosa Santiago (1978)

SOTOS, GEORGE—host

Sit or Miss (quiz)............. emcee (1950)

SOUL SISTERS, THE—singers

The Wacky World of Jonathan Winters (var)
.... regulars (1972–73)

SOUL, DAVID—actor
b: Aug 28, 1943, Chicago, Ill.

Here Come the Brides (adv)
.... Joshua Bolt (1968–70)
Owen Marshall, Counselor at Law (drama)
.... Ted Warrick (1974)

Starsky and Hutch (police)
.. Det. Ken "Hutch" Hutchinson (1975–79)
Casablanca (drama)..... Rick Blaine (1983)
The Yellow Rose (drama)
.... Roy Champion (1983–84)

This fair-haired, slightly shifty-looking actor is the son of a minister who was an advisor to the U.S. State Department and so, as a youth, lived in various parts of the U.S. and Mexico. David dropped out of college in the mid-1960s with the intention of becoming a folk singer and got his first, rather bizarre, break on *The Merv Griffin Show* in 1966–67 as the hooded "Mystery Singer." Finally unmasked, he began to get small acting roles (including one on an episode of *Star Trek* in '67) and then his first major break, as costar of *Here Come the Brides.*

David's career languished during the early '70s, with guest roles and a brief run during the last few months of *Owen Marshall.* Squealing tires and screaming sirens rescued him when he was signed to costar with Paul Michael Glaser in one of the most violent—and popular—"buddy" cop shows of the '70s, *Starsky and Hutch.* Since then, David has made his surly, macho presence known in a number of short-lived series and TV movies, among the latter *Salem's Lot, Rage, The Manions of America,* and *World War III.*

SOULE, OLAN—actor
b: Feb 28, 1909, La Harpe, Ill.

My Three Sons (com)
.... Mr. Pfeiffer (1961–63)
Arnie (com)....... Fred Springer (1970–72)

The voice of Batman on Saturday morning cartoons in the 1970s.

SOUTHERNAIRES, THE—black quartet
Roy Yeates, b: Hartford County, N.C.
Lowell Peters, b: Mar 5, 1903, Cleveland, Tenn.
Jay Stone Toney, b: Sep 1896, Columbia, Tenn.
William Edmunson, b: Oct 15, 1902, Spokane, Wash.
Clarence Jones (pianist), b: c. 1890, Wilmington, Ohio
(all are believed to be now deceased)

Southernaires Quartet (music)
.... regulars (1948)

A famous gospel quartet, heard on radio during the '30s and '40s. Their prime time program on ABC in the fall of 1948 was one of the earliest network TV series to star black performers.

SPACE, ARTHUR—actor
b: 1908, New Brunswick, N.J. d: Jan 13, 1983

Lassie (adv) .... Doc Weaver (1954–64)
National Velvet (adv)
.... Herbert Brown (1960–62)

SPADER, JAMES—actor
The Family Tree (drama)
.... Jake Nichols (1983)

SPANG, LAURETTE—actress
Battlestar Galactica (sci fi)
.... Cassiopea (1978–79)

SPANO, JOE—actor
b: Jul 7, 1946, San Francisco, Calif.

Hill Street Blues (police)
.... Sgt./Lt. Henry Goldblume (1981–)

SPARKLERS QUARTET—singers
The Lawrence Welk Show (music)
.... regulars (1955–57)

SPARKS, DANA—actress
Cover Up (drama)........ Ashley (1984–85)

SPARKS, DON—actor
Operation Petticoat (com)
.... seaman Horner (1978–79)

SPARKS, RANDY—
see New Christy Minstrels, The

SPAULDING, KEN—dancer
Kay Kyser's Kollege of Musical Knowledge (quiz).................... regular (1949–50)
The Paul Winchell–Jerry Mahoney Show (var).................... dancer (1951–53)
Garroway at Large (var)
.... dancer (1953–54)

Dance partner of Diane Sinclair.

SPEAR, CHARLIE—orchestra leader

Cavalcade of Stars (var)
.... orch. leader (1949–52)

SPEAR, SAMMY—orchestra leader
b: c. 1909 d: Mar 11, 1975

Front Row Center (var)
.... orch. leader (1949–50)
Cavalcade of Stars (var)
.... orch. leader (1949–52)
The Jackie Gleason Show (var)
.... orch. leader (1962–70)
The John Gary Show (var)
.... orch. leader (1968)
Dom DeLuise Show (var)
.... orch. leader (1968)

SPELL, GEORGE—black actor

Pat Paulsen's Half a Comedy Hour (var)
.... regular (1970)

SPELLBINDERS, THE—singers

The Julius La Rosa Show (var)
.... regulars (1956)
The Patti Page Show (var) .. regulars (1956)
The Tony Bennett Show (var)
.... regulars (1956)
The Vic Damone Show (var)
.... regulars (1957)

SPELMAN, SHARON—actress
b: May 1, Los Angeles, Calif. r: Sioux City, Iowa

The Cop and the Kid (com)
.... Mary Goodhew (1975–76)
Angie (com)........ Joyce Benson (1979–80)

SPENCE, JOHNNIE—orchestra leader

This Is Tom Jones (var)
.... orch. leader (1970–71)

SPENCE, SANDRA—actress

Terry and the Pirates (adv) .. Burma (1953)
The Whirlybirds (adv)
.... Janet Culver (1956–57)

SPENCER, DANIELLE—black juvenile actress
b: Jun 24, 1965

What's Happening!! (com)
.... Dee Thomas (1976–79)

What's Happening Now!! (com)
.... Dee Thomas (1986–)

SPERBER, WENDIE JO—actress
b: Sep 15, Glendale, Calif.

Bosom Buddies (com)
.... Amy Cassidy (1980–82)
Private Benjamin (com)
.... Pvt. Stacy Kouchalakas (1982–83)

SPIELBERG, DAVID—actor
b: Mar 6, 1939, Weslaco, Texas

Bob & Carol & Ted & Alice (com)
.... Ted Henderson (1973)
The Practice (com)
.... Dr. David Bedford (1976–77)
The American Girls (adv)
.... Francis X. Casey (1978)
From Here to Eternity (drama)
.... Lt./Capt. Ross (1979–80)
Jessica Novak (drama).. Max Kenyon (1981)

Mild-looking supporting actor, with stage experience (from the '60s on); he has been active in TV movies and series episodes since the early '70s. David often plays doctors, lawyers, or other buttoned-down types. Among his TV films have been *Judgment: The Trial of Julius and Ethel Rosenberg, In the Matter of Karen Ann Quinlan, Act of Love,* and *Policewoman Centerfold.*

SPIES, ADRIAN—host, writer

Crisis (drama) .... interviewer (1949)

SPIRIDAKIS, TONY—actor

Bay City Blues (drama).. Lee Jacoby (1983)

SPIVAK, LAWRENCE E.—panelist, producer
b: 1900, Brooklyn, N.Y.

Meet the Press (int)
.... regular panelist (1947–75)
Keep Posted (pub aff).... panelist (1951–53)
The Big Issue (pub aff) ... regular (1953–54)

Emmy Award: Executive Producer, Best News Special, for *A Day for History: The Supreme Court and the Pentagon Papers* (1972)

Spivak, the co-founder (with Martha Rountree) of TV's longest-running program, *Meet the Press*, spent the first 20 years of his career as a very successful publisher. He was, among other things, assistant publisher of *National Sportsman* and *Hunting and Fishing* magazines, founder and publisher of both *Ellery Queen's Mystery Magazine* and *The Magazine of Fantasy and Science Fiction*, and a pioneer in the introduction of paperback books. At the time *Meet the Press* began on radio in 1945, he was editor and publisher of *American Mercury*, the famous literary magazine. He became so taken with broadcasting that he sold his interests in that publication in 1950 and spent the rest of his years as a TV interviewer and producer.

SPOUND, MICHAEL—actor
b: Apr 8, Santa Monica, Calif. r: Concord, Mass.

Hotel (drama)....... Dave Kendall (1983–)

SPRADLIN, G.D.—actor
b: c. 1925, Oklahoma

Rich Man, Poor Man—Book II (drama)
.... Senator Dillon (1976–77)

This tough-looking actor has an unusual background; he was a successful attorney, then became a millionaire in the oil business, then was active in politics, all before catching the acting bug via a local Tulsa play. He generally plays ruthless tycoons (naturally!) and has been seen in such TV productions as *Robert Kennedy and His Times* (as L.B.J.) and *Space* (as a publishing mogul); in the movie *Apocalypse Now* he was the general who sent Martin Sheen into the jungle to kill Marlon Brando.

STAAHL, JIM—actor
Mork & Mindy (com)
.... Nelson Flavor (1979–81)
Goodnight, Beantown (com)
.... Frank Fletcher (1983–84)

STAATS, BOB—
Turn-On (var).............. regular (1969)

STACK, ROBERT—actor
b: Jan 13, 1919, Los Angeles, Calif.

The Untouchables (police)
.... Eliot Ness (1959–63)

The Name of the Game (adv)
.... Dan Farrell (1968–71)
Most Wanted (police)
.... Capt. Linc Evers (1976–77)
Strike Force (police)
.... Capt. Frank Murphy (1981–82)

Emmy Award: Best Actor in a Series, for *The Untouchables* (1960)

Watching Robert Stack act, you may find yourself wondering what he's thinking about. He is undeniably tall, ruggedly handsome, and determined, a hero in Hollywood's classic mold—but somehow those blue eyes often seem rather distant.

Presumably his mind was on the matter at hand when he first gained notice in the 1939 film *First Love*, giving lovely young Deanna Durbin her first on-screen kiss. Many more films followed, some fairly notable, such as *The High and the Mighty* and *Written on the Wind*, but it was television that brought Stack his greatest fame. He appeared in a number of dramatic productions during the '50s, on *Lux Video Theatre*, *Producers Showcase*, *Ford Theatre*, and other playhouses. One of these, a *Desilu Playhouse* dramatization of the battle against organized crime in Chicago, led to Stack's first and biggest hit, *The Untouchables*. His upright, humorless, determined portrayal of crimebuster Eliot Ness set his TV image for years.

Stack appeared only occasionally during the mid-1960s, then returned in 1968 as one of the several stars of *The Name of the Game*. His subsequent series efforts have been less successful, and he is now known mostly for melodramatic TV movies and miniseries such as *The Honorable Sam Houston* (title role), *Murder on Flight 502*, *George Washington*, and *Hollywood Wives*.

His autobiography: *Straight Shooting* (1980).

STACK, TIMOTHY—actor
Reggie (com)........... Tom Lockett (1983)
Our Time (var)............. regular (1985)

STACY, JAMES—actor
b: Dec 23, 1936, Los Angeles, Calif.

The Adventures of Ozzie & Harriet (com)
.... Fred (1958–64)

Lancer (wes)
.... Johnny Madrid Lancer (1968–70)

Once married to actress Connie Stevens. Stacy was seriously injured in a motorcycle accident in 1973, losing an arm and a leg; he returned to acting a few years later in the TV films *Just a Little Inconvenience* (playing a Vietnam double amputee) and *My Kidnapper, My Love.*

STADLEN, LEWIS J.—actor
b: Mar 7, 1947, Brooklyn, N.Y.

Benson (com) .... John Taylor (1979–80)

A stage actor known for his portrayal of Groucho Marx in both the Broadway production *Minnie's Boys* and a traveling one-man show.

STAFFORD, JIM—singer, host
b: Jan 16, 1944, Eloise, Fla.

The Jim Stafford Show (var)..... host (1975)
Those Amazing Animals (doc)
.... host (1980–81)
Nashville on the Road (music)
.... host (1981–83)

Amiable, down-home singer and host, known for his peculiar 1970s song hits, which included "My Girl Bill," "Spiders and Snakes," and "Your Bulldog Drinks Champagne."

STAFFORD, JO—singer
b: Nov 12, 1918, Coalinga, Calif. r: Long Beach, Calif.

The Jo Stafford Show (music)
.... hostess (1954–55)

One of the great popular singers of the '40s and '50s, and one with a lively sense of humor; she recorded country music parodies in the late '40s under the pseudonym Cinderella Q. Stump and later masqueraded as half of the music-mangling duo of Jonathan and Darlene Edwards, with her husband, orchestra leader Paul Weston. Jo is even better known, though, for her "straight" song hits, ranging from "I'll Never Smile Again" with the Tommy Dorsey Orchestra in 1940 to "Shrimp Boats" and "You Belong to Me" in the '50s. She was a favorite guest star on variety shows of the

'50s and had her own early-evening musical series in 1954–55.

STAFFORD, MARIAN—hostess
Treasure Hunt (quiz)
.... "Pirate Girl" (1956–58)

STAFFORD, NANCY—actress
b: Jun 5, Wilton Manors, Fla.

St. Elsewhere (drama)
.... Joan Halloran (1983–84)
Sidekicks (adv) ..... Patricia Blake (1986–)

Miss Florida of 1977—and a striking beauty.

STAHL, RICHARD—actor
b: Jan 4, c. 1932, Detroit, Mich.

The Jim Stafford Show (var).. regular (1975)
Struck by Lightning (com)
.... Walt Calvin (1979)
Turnabout (com) .... Jack Overmeyer (1979)
It's a Living (com).. Howard Miller (1985–)

STALEY, JAMES—actor
Mary Hartman, Mary Hartman (com)
.... Dr. Szymon (1977–78)
The Waverly Wonders (com)
.... Alan Kerner (1978)

STALEY, JOAN—actress
b: c. 1940, Minneapolis, Minn.

The Beachcomber (adv).... Linda (1960–61)
The Lively Ones (var) .... Tiger (1962)
77 Sunset Strip (drama).. Hannah (1963–64)
Broadside (com)
    machinist's mate Roberta Love (1964–65)

STALLYBRASS, ANNE—British actress
The Six Wives of Henry VIII (drama)
.... Jane Seymour (1971)
The Strauss Family (drama)
.... Anna Strauss (1973)

STALMASTER, LYN—actor
Big Town (drama)......... Rush (1954–55)

STAMOS, JOHN—actor
b: Aug 19, 1963, Cypress, Calif.

Dreams (com)........ Gino Minnelli (1984)
You Again? (com) ... Matt Willows (1986–)

This dark, energetic teen favorite got his first big acting break just a few months after graduating from high school, when he was signed for the role of trouble-prone Blackie Parrish on the daytime soap opera *General Hospital* (beginning January 1982). He was an immediate sensation with younger viewers, and, after a year and a half—and tons of fan mail—Blackie was packed off to prison so that John could move on to his own prime time series, called *Dreams,* a comedy about an aspiring rock musician. (John is in fact just that and has toured with his own group, John Stamos and the Bad Boyz.) *Dreams* had only a short run; John later had a costarring role in *You Again?*, as Jack Klugman's restless teenage son.

STAMPER, PETE—country comedian

Ozark Jubilee (music)........ regular (1956)

STANDER, LIONEL—actor
b: Jan 11, 1908, New York City, N.Y.

Hart to Hart (adv)......... Max (1979–84)

Gravel-voiced movie character actor with a bulldog face who played many a thug in the '30s and '40s. His career was nearly wrecked by McCarthy-era political blacklisting in the '50s; he later moved to Italy, where they didn't care, and resumed making films. Television viewers finally discovered him in 1979 (at the age of 71) as the delightfully eccentric chauffeur with a shady past in *Hart to Hart.* Still full of fun, vitality, and firm opinions in his seventies, he is one of Hollywood's authentic, larger-than-life characters.

STANDING, JOHN—actor
b: Aug 16, 1934, London, England

Lime Street (drama)
.... Edward Wingate (1985)

The scion of a famous British acting family, which included the eminent Sir Guy Standing (his grandfather) and Kay Hammond (his mother), both prominent onstage and in films of the '30s; John is, he says, a seventh-generation actor.

STANG, ARNOLD—actor, comedian
b: Sep 28, 1925, Chelsea, Mass.

School House (var)......... regular (1949)
Henry Morgan's Great Talent Hunt (var)
.... Gerard (1951)
Doc Corkle (com) ..... Winfield Dill (1952)
The Milton Berle Show (var)
.... Francis, the stagehand (1953–55)
Top Cat (cartn)
.... Top Cat (voice) (1961–62)
Broadside (com)
..... ship's cook 1st class Stanley Stubbs (1965)

Arnold Stang has been compared to a nearsighted chipmunk just dragged out of the rain. A small, owlish, little man with a high-pitched nasal voice, horn-rimmed glasses, and a bow tie, he has been one of television's most unmistakable characters for more than 30 years. Arnold was on radio and in films during the 1940s and he has appeared on every sort of TV show, from *Milton Berle* to *Chico and the Man.* He has also provided voices for a good many theatrical and TV cartoons, including *Top Cat* (a feline parody of Phil Silvers' Sgt. Bilko). Among his other notable roles have been that of a klutzy space villain on *Captain Video* in the early '50s, Milton Berle's pestiferous stagehand Francis, and —in an unusual change of pace—the pathetic junkie Sparrow in the dramatic movie *Man with a Golden Arm* (1955). Although he never had a hit series of his own, he continued to appear, occasionally, into the '80s.

STANIS, BERNNADETTE—black actress
b: Dec 22, 1953, Brooklyn, N.Y.

Good Times (com)
.... Thelma Evans Anderson (1974–79)

STANLEY, AILEEN, JR.—singer

School House (var)......... regular (1949)

A young blonde singer who was the protégée of (but apparently not related to) Aileen Stanley, one of the most popular vocalists on stage and records during the 1920s.

STANLEY, FLORENCE—actress
b: Jul 1, Chicago, Ill.

Joe and Sons (com)
.... Aunt Josephine (1975–76)

Barney Miller (com)
.... Bernice Fish (1975–77)
Fish (com)......... Bernice Fish (1977–78)

STANLEY, LEONARD, TRIO—

Rehearsal Call (var)........ regulars (1949)

STANLEY, RALPH—actor
b: c. 1914 d: 1972

Starlit Time (var) .... regular (1950)

STANTON, BOB—sportscaster, host

Campus Hoopla (var)........ host (1946–47)
Gillette Cavalcade of Sports (aka Friday Night Fights) (sport). sportscaster (1946–49)
Television Screen Magazine (mag)
.... emcee/"editor" (1948)
Saturday Night Basketball (sport)
.... sportscaster (1948–49)
Village Barn (var)........... emcee (1949)
Mohawk Showroom (music)
.... announcer (1949–51)
Around the Town (doc)........ host (1950)

"NBC now televises an average of 28 hours a week," commented *Time* magazine in 1947, "and about 23 of them have the same announcer." *Time* was referring to Bob Stanton, a onetime band singer (in the early 1930s) and assistant to sportscaster Bill Stern who had long been on radio, and who became NBC's principal TV announcer during the medium's formative years. He was pressed into service to handle everything from boxing matches to a newsmagazine to variety shows; then, in the early 1950s, just when things began to get interesting, he disappeared without a trace.

STANTON, JACK—singer

Sing It Again (quiz)....... regular (1950–51)
Seven at Eleven (var)........ regular (1951)

STANWYCK, BARBARA—actress
b: Jul 16, 1907, Brooklyn, N.Y.

The Barbara Stanwyck Show (drama)
.... hostess/star (1960–61)
The Big Valley (wes)
.... Victoria Barkley (1965–69)
The Thorn Birds (drama)
.... Mary Carson (1983)

Dynasty II: The Colbys (drama)
.... Constance Colby (1985–86)

Emmy Awards: Best Actress in a Series, for *The Barbara Stanwyck Show* (1961); Best Actress in a Dramatic Series, for *The Big Valley* (1966); Best Actress in a Limited Series, for *The Thorn Birds* (1983)

Barbara Stanwyck has been called "the best actress never to win an Oscar" for her long, distinguished career in movies, lasting from 1927 to 1965 (they finally gave her an honorary one in 1981). A versatile actress, she often played tough, strong-willed women, but could also be quite adept at comedy. She brought her special magic to television only occasionally in the 1950s, including several appearances each on *The Loretta Young Show* and *Zane Grey Theater*. In 1960 she hosted and starred in her own anthology series, which included the pilot for a continuing series in which she was to star as an American adventuress in Hong Kong—however, that project never made it to the regular schedule. After a few more guest appearances in the early '60s (*Wagon Train, The Untouchables*) she finally found the right vehicle, as the iron-willed matriarch of the Barkley clan on *The Big Valley* (among her offspring on the series were Linda Evans and Lee Majors). She made three TV movies in the early 1970s and then retired in 1973. She has been lured back only twice since then, for an Emmy-winning performance in the 1983 miniseries *The Thorn Birds*— playing, once again, a woman of strength and determination; and in 1986 for the first season of *Dynasty II: The Colbys.*

STAPLETON, JEAN—actress
b: Jan 19, 1923, New York City, N.Y.

All in the Family (com)
.... Edith Bunker (Dingbat) (1971–80)

Emmy Awards: Best Actress in a Comedy Series, for *All in the Family* (1971, 1972, 1978)

Jean Stapleton arrived on television after a long apprenticeship in supporting roles onstage during the '40s and '50s. During the '50s she combined her stage work with periodic appearances on TV playhouse series, including *Studio One, Philco Playhouse,* and *Omnibus;* in the '60s she turned up in such dramas as *Dr. Kildare* and *The Defenders.* Only infrequently did she play comedy. She was most adept at honest, simple women who knew right from wrong. The role that lifted her out of obscurity, of course, was that of Edith (Dingbat) Bunker on the trailblazing *All in the Family,* proving that those same qualities worked just as well in comedy as in drama. She has since had similar roles in several dramatic TV movies, including *Aunt Mary* (as a neighborhood activist), *Angel Dusted* (an anguished mother), *Eleanor, First Lady of the World* (Eleanor Roosevelt) and *A Matter of Sex* (a woman fighting for her job rights).

STAPLETON, MAUREEN—actress
b: Jun 21, 1925, Troy, N.Y.

What Happened? (quiz)..... panelist (1952)

Emmy Award: Best Actress in a Single Performance in a Drama, for *Among the Paths to Eden* (1968)

Maureen Stapleton has not been associated with a famous series—at least nobody I know remembers the 1952 summer panel show *What Happened?;* however, she has starred in quite a few first-rate dramatic productions over the years. Like Jean Stapleton (no kin), Maureen usually plays frumpy, matronly types. She began on stage in the '40s and has had a rather prominent career there and in movies, winning an Oscar (for *Reds,* in 1981) and two Tony Awards. Among the TV dramas in which she has appeared have been *For Whom the Bell Tolls* (on *Playhouse 90,* in 1959), *Among the Paths to Eden* (1967), *Queen of the Stardust Ballroom* (1974), *Cat on a Hot Tin Roof* (1976), *The Gathering* (1977, 1979), *The Electric Grandmother* (1981), *Little Gloria, Happy at Last* (1982), and *Family Secrets* (1984).

STAR NOTERS, THE—singers
Rhythm Rodeo (music).. regulars (1950–51)

STARBUCK, JAMES—choreographer
Your Show of Shows (var)
.... regular (1950–54)
Frankie Laine Time (var) ... dancers (1955)
Sing Along with Mitch (var)
.... dancers (1961–64)

The Andy Williams Show (var)
.... dancers (1966–67)

STARK, CHARLES—announcer
The Jacques Fray Music Room (music)
.... emcee (1949)
Kraft Television Theatre (drama)
.... announcer (1955)

STARK, DOLLY—sportscaster
Your Sports Special (sport)
.... reporter (1948–49)

A former major league umpire.

STARK, LENNY—orchestra leader
The John Davidson Show (var)
.... orch. leader (1976)

STARK, RICHARD (DICK)—announcer
b: c. 1911
Danger (drama) .... host/narrator (1950–55)
The Perry Como Show (var)
.... announcer (1951–55)

STARKE, TOD—juvenile actor
The Doris Day Show (com)
.... Toby Martin (1968–71)

STARLAND VOCAL BAND, THE—vocal group
Bill Danoff, b: May 7, 1946, Springfield, Mass.
Kathy "Taffy" Danoff, b: Oct 25, 1944, Washington, D.C.
Margot Chapman, b: Sep 7, 1957, Honolulu, Hawaii
Jon Carroll, b: Mar 1, 1957, Washington, D.C.

The Starland Vocal Band Show (var)
.... hosts (1977)

A pop vocal group formed in the Washington area in the early 1970s by Bill Danoff and his wife Taffy. They scored a major record hit in 1976 with a song called "Afternoon Delight," which led to a 1977 summer series, but little has been heard of them since.

STARLIGHTERS, THE—singers
The Jo Stafford Show (music)
.... regulars (1954–55)

STARR, DON—actor

Dallas (drama)......... Jordan Lee (1979–)

STARR, RONALD—actor

Mr. Roberts (com)
.... Seaman Mannion (1965–66)

STATLER BROTHERS—country singers

Don Reid, b: Jun 5, 1945, Staunton, Va.
Harold Reid, b: Aug 21, 1939, Augusta County, Va.
Lew DeWitt, b: Mar 8, 1938, Roanoke County, Va.
Phil Balsley, b: Aug 8, 1939, Augusta County, Va.

The Johnny Cash Show (var)
.... regulars (1969–71)

As you will note, only two members of this group are brothers, and none are named Statler. They took their name from a box of tissues. The group was originally formed in the '50s and toured with Johnny Cash through much of the '60s and early '70s, singing both pop and gospel material. Their first and biggest hit was an upbeat number called "Flowers on the Wall" in 1966.

STEARNS, CHRISTOPHER WILLIAM— juvenile actor

b: Dec 1948, New York City, N.Y.

Mary Kay and Johnny (com)
.... as himself (1949–50)

Mary Kay and Johnny's real-life baby, who appeared, in his bassinet, on their family comedy series less than a month after he was born. This would quite possibly make him the youngest regular cast member in TV history. Mary Kay's pregnancy had been incorporated into the script during the preceding months.

STEARNS, JOHNNY—actor

Mary Kay and Johnny (com)
.... as himself (1947–50)

STEARNS, MARY KAY—actress

b: Oct 27, 1925, Glendale, Calif.

Mary Kay and Johnny (com)
.... as herself (1947–50)

STEARNS, ROGER—pianist

The Fashion Story (misc)
.... piano (1948–49)

STEEL, AMY—actress

The Powers of Matthew Star (sci fi)
.... Pam Elliott (1982)
For Love and Honor (drama)
.... Sharon (1983)

STEEL, JEAN—

The Ted Mack Family Hour (var)
.... regular (1951)

STEELE, BOB—actor

b: Jan 23, 1906, Pendleton, Ore.

F Troop (com)..... Trooper Duffy (1965–67)

A pint-sized but energetic cowboy star of the '30s and '40s. He is said to have appeared in more than 400 films over 50 years.

STEELE, RICHARD—juvenile actor

Julia (com)............. Richard (1970–71)

STEELE, STEPHANIE—juvenile actress

Arnie (com)........ Andrea Nuvo (1970–72)

STEELE, TED—host, orchestra leader

b: Jul 9, 1917, Hartford, Conn. r: Boston, Mass.

The Ted Steele Show (music)
.... host (1948–49)
Cavalcade of Bands (music)
.... emcee (1950–51)

Ted Steele was a versatile young musician who had a rapidly rising career in the 1940s. He was the orchestra leader on Perry Como's radio show, a composer of some note ("Smoke Rings"), and also a singer, pianist, and leading performer on a new instrument called the Novachord (an electronic keyboard). Ted was given his own show on NBC-TV in 1948 and later turned up on both the CBS and DuMont networks, including a stint as host of the latter's *Cavalcade of Bands*. He also had a daytime series and hosted a TV dance party for teenagers. His TV career lasted for only a couple of busy years, however;

he later became a radio executive and sometime radio personality.

STEEN, NANCY—

Tony Orlando and Dawn (var)
.... regular (1976)
The Steve Allen Comedy Hour (var)
.... regular (1980–81)

STEFAN, VIRGINIA—actress
b: c. 1926, r: Buffalo, N.Y. d: 1964

I Led Three Lives (drama)
.... Eva Philbrick (1953–56)

STEFFANY, MICHAEL—actor

Manhunt (police).. Det. Paul Kirk (1960–61)

STEFFEN, SIRRY—actress

The Beverly Hillbillies (com)
.... Marie, the maid (1962–63)

STEIN, FRED—panelist, realtor
b: c. 1868, d: Jan 28, 1957

Life Begins at Eighty (talk)
.... panelist (1950–56)

STEIN, LOU—pianist, combo leader
b: Apr 22, 1922, Philadelphia, Pa.

Tonight! America After Dark (talk)
.... trio (1957)

STEINBERG, DAVID—comedian, director
b: Aug 9, 1942, Winnipeg, Canada

The Music Scene (music) .... host (1969–70)
The David Steinberg Show (var)
.... host (1972)

This irreverent young comic rose to national fame in the late '60s, after sharpening his skills during five years with Chicago's famous Second City comedy troupe. He was a guest on many top variety and talk shows, with his most famous routines being his hilarious (and to some, blasphemous) mock sermons—one of which is said to have been the immediate cause of the cancellation of *The Smothers Brothers Comedy Hour*. David was creator and host of *The Music Scene* and had his own summer show in 1972. His star faded with the decline of the "youth era" and he became a film director in the '80s (e.g., *Paternity*).

STEINFELD, JERRY—actor

Benson (com) .... Frankie (1980–81)

STELL, ANN—actress

Faraway Hill (drama) .... regular (1946)

STELLA, ANTOINETTE—actress

Curse of Dracula (adv) ... Antoinette (1979)

STEPHENS, GARN—actress

Phyllis (com).... Harriet Hastings (1976–77)

STEPHENS, JAMES—actor
b: May 18, 1951, Mount Kisco, N.Y. r: Mexico City, Mexico

The Paper Chase (drama)
.... James T. Hart (1978–79)
The Paper Chase (drama)
.... James T. Hart (1983–84)

STEPHENS, LARAINE—actress
b: Oakland, Calif.

O. K. Crackerby (com)
.... Susan Wentworth (1965–66)
Bracken's World (drama)
.... Diane Waring (1969–70)
Matt Helm (drama)
.... Claire Kronski (1975–76)
Rich Man, Poor Man—Book II (drama)
.... Claire Estep (1976–77)

A delicate young actress, much seen on television crime shows of the '70s (*Hawaii Five-O, Mannix, Police Story*, etc.). In the '80s she graced such TV films as *The Dallas Cowboy Cheerleaders II* and *Scruples*.

STEPHENS, ROBERT—actor
b: Jul 14, 1931, Bristol, England

Holocaust (drama) .. Uncle Kurt Dorf (1978)

STEPHENSON, JOHN—actor

Bold Journey (doc) .... host (1955–57)
The People's Choice (com)
.... Roger Crutcher (1955–57)
Top Cat (cartn)
.... Fancy-Fancy (voice) (1961–62)

805

Jonny Quest (cartn)
.... Dr. Benton Quest (voice) (1964)

One of the busiest Saturday morning "voice men," heard on dozens of cartoons of the '60s and '70s—generally in supporting roles, such as Doggie Daddy on a segment of *Yogi Bear.*

STEPHENSON, PAMELA—actress
b: 1951, Auckland, N.Z. r: Sydney, Australia

NBC's Saturday Night Live (com)
.... regular (1984–85)

A popular British TV comedienne, who has done less well—so far—in the U.S.A. She became famous in England on the TV series *Not the Nine O'Clock News*, impersonating such celebrities as Princess Diana, Queen Elizabeth, the Queen Mother, Margaret Thatcher, Sheena Easton, Debbie Harry, and Olivia Newton-John.

STEPHENSON, SKIP—host, comedian
b: Apr 18, 1948, Omaha, Neb.

Real People (aud par) .... regular (1979–84)

STERLING, JACK—host
b: Baltimore, Md.

The Fifty-Fourth Street Revue (var)
.... host (1949)
Big Top (var) .... ringmaster (1950–51)

STERLING, JAN—actress
b: Apr 3, 1923, New York City, N.Y.

You're in the Picture (quiz).. panelist (1961)
Made in America (quiz)..... panelist (1964)
Backstairs at the White House (drama)
.... Lou Hoover (1979)

Cool, rather hard-looking actress who often played tough cookies in films and on television. She was seen on many dramatic series of the '50s and '60s, including multiple episodes of *Lux Video Theatre, Alfred Hitchcock Presents,* and *Wagon Train* and was a regular on daytime's *The Guiding Light* in 1969–70. She has for many years lived in England.

STERLING, PHILIP—actor

City of Angels (drama)
.... Michael Brimm (1976)

STERLING, ROBERT—actor
b: Nov 13, 1917, Newcastle, Pa.

Topper (com) ...... George Kerby (1953–55)
The 20th Century-Fox Hour (drama)
.... host (1956–57)
Love That Jill (com)
.... Jack Gibson (1958)
Ichabod and Me (com)
.... Robert Major (1961–62)

He looked a little like a male Barbie Doll—handsome, but rather bland—and played roles to match: pleasant, popular, but not particularly memorable. Bob's film debut was in 1938; he came to television around 1950 and appeared on *Studio One, Robert Montgomery Presents,* and other playhouse series before gaining greater fame as the dear, dead hubby (a ghost) on *Topper.* His costar in that and in his later series *Love That Jill* was his real-life wife, actress Anne Jeffreys. He had previously been married to Ann Sothern.

Bob was seen quite a bit on TV until the early '60s, and seldom after that. He put in a rare appearance in the TV movie *Beggarman, Thief* in 1979 (again with Miss Jeffreys). In his later years he became a computer expert. His daughter is actress Tisha Sterling.

STERN, BILL—sportscaster
b: Jul 1, 1907, Rochester, N.Y. d: Nov 19, 1971

Harness Racing (sport)
.... host, quiz segment (1950)
Spotlight on Sports (sport) ...... host (1950)
Are You Positive? (quiz) ...... emcee (1952)
Saturday Night Fights (sport)
.... sportscaster (1953)
The Name's the Same (quiz)
.... panelist (1953–54)

The famous showman-sportscaster, whose colorful sports-related yarns were heard on radio for more than 20 years, from the '30s to the '50s (e.g., the tale of the baseball player who suffered a heart attack between third and home and was dead as he slid in to home plate). Bill's play-by-play coverage was highly popular but so melodramatic that it was said a fan listening to a radio in the stands would not know that Stern was describing the same game he was seeing!

STERN, DANIEL—actor
b: Aug 28, 1957, Stamford, Conn.

Hometown (drama)..... Joey Nathan (1985)

STERN, LEONARD—writer, producer
b: Dec 23, 1923

How To (info)............. panelist (1951)

Emmy Awards: Best Writing for a Comedy, for *The Phil Silvers Show* (1956); and for *Get Smart* (1967)

A leading TV comedy writer-producer, one of those responsible (as writer, producer, creator, or all of the aforementioned) for *The Honeymooners, The Steve Allen Show, Get Smart, The Governor & J.J., McMillan and Wife, The Snoop Sisters* and many others. *How To* was an inane little comedic panel-show seen during the summer of 1951.

STERN, SHERL—panelist

Super Ghost (quiz) ...... panelist (1952–53)
It's About Time (quiz) ...... panelist (1954)
Down You Go (quiz)
.... regular panelist (1955)

Reputedly a "local Chicago housewife" who became quite adept as a TV game show panelist in the early 1950s.

STERN, WES—actor

Getting Together (com)
.... Lionel Poindexter (1971–72)

STERNHAGEN, FRANCES—actress
b: Jan 13, 1930, Washington, D.C.

Under One Roof (com)
.... Millie Sprague (1985)

STEVENS, ANDREW—actor
b: Jun 10, 1955, Memphis, Tenn.

The Oregon Trail (wes)
.... Andrew Thorpe (1977)
Code Red (adv) ..... Ted Rorchek (1981–82)
Emerald Point N.A.S. (drama)
.... Lt. Glenn Matthews (1983–84)

The son of actress Stella Stevens. Among his TV films: *The Bastard; The Rebels; Once an Eagle; Beggarman, Thief;* and *Hollywood Wives.*

STEVENS, CONNIE—actress
b: Aug 8, 1938, Brooklyn, N.Y.

Hawaiian Eye (drama)
.... Cricket Blake (1959–63)
Wendy and Me (com)
.... Wendy Conway (1964–65)
Kraft Music Hall Presents The Des O'Connor Show (var)................. regular (1971)
Scruples (drama).. Maggie McGregor (1980)

A pert and pretty young starlet who made her debut in films before she was 20 (in *Young and Dangerous*) and was also seen on TV as a teenager, in *Sugarfoot, The Bob Cummings Show,* etc. She rocketed to stardom at the age of 21 as the goofy photographer-sidekick in *Hawaiian Eye* and appeared in several more regular and guest roles in the early '60s before fading from sight in the late '60s. She was back in periodic TV movies from the '70s on, including *The Sex Symbol, Love's Savage Fury, Scruples, Murder Can Hurt You,* and others; she was also a frequent passenger on *The Love Boat.* Connie had an active recording career in the early '60s, beginning with her duet with *77 Sunset Strip* star Edd Byrnes on the immortal "Kookie, Kookie Lend Me Your Comb" (she's the one who wanted the comb).

Connie was once married to crooner Eddie Fisher. Her real name is Concetta Rosalie Ann Ingolia.

STEVENS, CRAIG—actor
b: Jul 8, 1918, Liberty, Mo.

Peter Gunn (drama) .. Peter Gunn (1958–61)
Man of the World (adv)
.... Michael Strait (1962)
Mr. Broadway (drama) .... Mike Bell (1964)
The Invisible Man (adv)
.... Walter Carlson (1975–76)
Rich Man, Poor Man—Book I (drama)
.... Asher Berg (1976)
Dallas (drama)........ Craig Stewart (1981)

A slick, buttoned-down second lead in movies, who finally made it big—at age 40 —as one of the first of TV's "smooth operator" private eyes. Darkly handsome, in a Cary Grant mold, Craig began his film career in 1941 and entered TV in the early '50s, appearing in many of the lighter dramatic playhouse series (*Fireside Theatre, Four Star Playhouse*). Fame came with the role of the suave lady-killer star of *Peter Gunn*, which was a series known as much for its driving, jazzy music (by Henry Mancini) as for Craig's acting. After its run, he moved to England for a couple of years and starred in the British adventure series *Man of the World* and then returned to the U.S. to portray another smoothie, *Mr. Broadway*. Neither recaptured the hip flavor of *Peter Gunn*, and, thereafter, in the '70s and '80s, he reverted to supporting roles in series, TV movies, and guest spots on episodes.

Craig has been married since 1944 to actress Alexis Smith.

STEVENS, FRANK—

Campus Corner (music)...... regular (1949)

STEVENS, INGER—actress
b: Oct 18, 1934*, Stockholm, Sweden d: Apr 30, 1970

The Farmer's Daughter (com)
.... Katrin "Katy" Holstrum (1963–66)

The Farmer's Daughter was about a sexy farm girl who moved to Washington to become governess for a congressman's children and wound up happily married to the man. Actress Inger Stevens' real life was far less rosy; so much so, in fact, that she ended it a few years later by suicide.

The product of a broken home, Inger had come to the U.S. from Sweden at age 13 with her father. They settled in Iowa, but she hated farm country and ran away, eventually making it to New York. There she began the long struggle to establish a modest show business career, including parts in TV plays of the '50s. A first marriage failed, and a later relationship with Bing Crosby (after the death of his first wife) fell apart; in 1959 she attempted suicide for the first time. She survived and found more frequent work in the '60s, mostly on dramas such as *Checkmate* and *Route 66*. In one of the classic *Twilight Zone* episodes she played a lone driver stalked by a mysterious hitchhiker who proved to be Mr. Death.

Inger's personal problems did not abate with the success of *The Farmer's Daughter* or several films she made thereafter (including two TV movies aired in 1970). She

*Some sources give 1935.

died in 1970 of an overdose of barbiturates; after her death it was revealed that she had been secretly married during the '60s to black musician Isaac Jones.

STEVENS, JULIE—actress
b: c. 1917, St. Louis, Mo. d: Aug 26, 1984

Big Town (drama)
.... Lorelei Kilbourne (1951–52)

STEVENS, MARK—actor
b: Dec 13, 1915, Cleveland, Ohio r: Montreal, Canada

Martin Kane, Private Eye (drama)
.... Martin Kane (1953–54)
Big Town (drama)
.... Steve Wilson (1954–56)

This handsome actor, active in many dramas of the '50s, deserted Hollywood in the mid-1960s to run a bar in Majorca. He returned a decade later for a few more roles on *Police Story*, *S.W.A.T.*, etc. Not to be confused (please!) with the porno star Marc (aka Mark) Stevens.

STEVENS, MORGAN—actor
b: Oct 16, Knoxville, Tenn.

Fame (drama).... David Reardon (1982–83)
Bare Essence (drama) . Larry DeVito (1983)

STEVENS, NAOMI—actress
b: Nov 29, Trenton, N.J.

The Doris Day Show (com)
.... Juanita (1968–69)
The Montefuscos (com)
.... Rose Montefusco (1975)
Vega$ (drama) .. Sgt. Bella Archer (1978–79)

STEVENS, ONSLOW—actor
b: Mar 29, 1902, Los Angeles, Calif. d: Jan 5, 1977

This Is the Life (drama)
.... Mr. Fisher (1952–56)

Dour character actor in many films (from 1932–62) and routine TV dramas. He was murdered in a convalescent home by person or persons unknown.

STEVENS, PATRICIA—actress

*M*A*S*H* (com)... various nurses (1974–78)

STEVENS, RAY—singer
b: Jan 24, 1939, Clarksdale, Ga.

The Andy Williams Show (var)
.... regular (1969–71)
Andy Williams Presents Ray Stevens (var)
.... host (1970)
Dean Martin Presents Music Country (var)
.... regular (1973)

A singer of the 1960s and '70s who was known for his offbeat novelty songs, with titles such as "Ahab the Arab," "Gitarzan," "The Streak," and (take a deep breath!) "Jeremiah Peabody's Poly Unsaturated Quick Dissolving Fast Acting Pleasant Tasting Green and Purple Pills."

STEVENS, RONNIE—actor
b: Sep 2, 1925, London, England

Dick and the Duchess (com)
.... Rodney (1957–58)

STEVENS, RUSTY—juvenile actor
Leave It to Beaver (com)
.... Larry Mondello (1958–60)

STEVENS, SHAWN—actor
b: Apr 5, Morristown, N.J.

The Last Convertible (drama)
.... Rob Dalrymple (1979)
The Mackenzies of Paradise Cove (adv)
.... Kevin Mackenzie (1979)

STEVENS, STELLA—actress
b: Oct 1, 1936, Hot Coffee, Miss.

Ben Casey (drama).... Jane Hancock (1965)
Flamingo Road (drama)
.... Lute-Mae Sanders (1981–82)

A middle-aged but still delicious sexpot, who got her start in the '50s as a *Playboy* centerfold and in the role of Appassionata von Climax in the movie *Li'l Abner* (1959). She was scarcely less outrageous as the flamboyant Lute-Mae, owner of a local bar, 22 years later on TV's *Flamingo Road*. She says her favorite heroine is Scheherazade of *The Arabian Nights*. Stella was quite active in TV guest appearances during the early '60s, and, as Ben Casey's love interest, almost snared the famous doctor. Since then she has been seen mostly in TV movies—approximately two dozen of them, from *Honky Tonk* and *Murder in Peyton Place* to 1984's *No Man's Land* (in which she played a feisty mother with three sexpot daughters).

Stella is the mother of actor Andrew Stevens.

STEVENS, TONY—choreographer
Mary (var)................ dancers (1978)

STEVENS, WARREN—actor
b: Nov 2, 1919, Clark's Summit, Pa.

Tales of the 77th Bengal Lancers (adv)
.... Lt. William Storm (1956–57)
The Richard Boone Show (drama)
.... regular (1963–64)
Bracken's World (drama)
.... John Bracken (voice only) (1969–70)
Behind the Screen (drama)
.... Merritt Madison (1981–82)

STEVENS, WILLIAM—actor
Adam 12 (police)
.... Off. Jerry Walters (1968–69)

STEVENSON, JIM—narrator
Greatest Fights of the Century (sport)
.... narrator (1948–54)

STEVENSON, MCLEAN—actor
b: Nov 14, 1929, Normal, Ill.

The Doris Day Show (com)
.... Michael Nicholson (1969–71)
The Tim Conway Comedy Hour (var)
.... regular (1970)
M*A*S*H (com)
.... Lt. Col. Henry Blake (1972–75)
The McLean Stevenson Show (com)
.... Mac Ferguson (1976–77)
Celebrity Challenge of the Sexes (sport)
.... regular (1978)
In the Beginning (com)
.... Daniel M. Cleary (1978)
Hello, Larry (com)
.... Larry Adler (1979–80)
Condo (com)........ James Kirkridge (1983)

Here's a trivia miniquiz for you. McLean Stevenson is surely in the running for the title of Actor Who Starred in the Most Flop Series in a Row.

Q: What *occupations* did he have in each of the five failed series he starred in following *M*A*S*H?* (shows listed above)

Bonus question: What occupation did McLean's real-life father have?

McLean was born in Illinois and was a relative of that state's political favorite son, Adlai Stevenson. Shortly after graduation from college he campaigned for Uncle Adlai by organizing Young Democrats for Stevenson across the country. He drifted into the theater during the 1950s, appearing in clubs and finally making his stage debut in a 1962 production of *The Music Man*. During the '60s he had small guest roles in a number of TV series, including *Naked City, The Defenders,* and *Car 54, Where Are You?,* but it was as a comedy writer that he made his name. He wrote for *That Was the Week That Was* and *The Smothers Brothers Comedy Hour,* and both allowed him to do occasional on-air bits. His first major acting break was as Doris Day's magazine editor boss on *The Doris Day Show;* his greatest success, however, was as the off-the-wall commanding officer during the first three seasons of *M*A*S*H.* When he left the show, his character was killed off.

Then McLean started starring in his own series, and it has been all downhill from there.

Answers to the quiz: In *The McLean Stevenson Show* he owned a hardware store; in *Celebrity Challenge of the Sexes* he was the men's coach; in *In the Beginning* he was an inner-city priest; in *Hello, Larry* a radio talk show host; in *Condo* an insurance salesman. If you can think of anything else he might play, more successfully, write him. McLean's father was a cardiologist, and McLean himself once worked as a salesman for a hospital supply firm.

STEVENSON, PARKER—actor

b: Jun 4, 1952, Philadelphia, Pa.

The Hardy Boys Mysteries (adv)
.... Frank Hardy (1977–79)
Falcon Crest (drama)
.... Joel McCarthy (1984–85)

STEVENSON, ROBERT—actor

b: c. 1915 d: 1975

Jefferson Drum (wes) ..... Big Ed (1958–59)

STEVENSON, VALERIE—actress, country singer

b: Philadelphia, Pa.

Dreams (com)......... Lisa Copley (1984)

STEWART, BYRON—black actor

b: May 1, c. 1956, Baxter Springs, Kan. r: Marin County Calif.

The White Shadow (drama)
.... Warren Coolidge (1978–81)
St. Elsewhere (drama)
.... orderly Warren Coolidge (1984–)

STEWART, CHARLOTTE—actress

Little House on the Prairie (adv)
.... Eva Beadle Simms (1974–78)

STEWART, HORACE—black actor

see Stewart, Nick

STEWART, JAMES—actor

b: May 20, 1908, Indiana, Pa.

The Jimmy Stewart Show (com)
.... Prof. James K. Howard (1971–72)
Hawkins (drama)
.... Billy Jim Hawkins (1973–74)

One of the great legends of the silver screen—an aw-shucks "Mr. Sincerity" since his film debut in 1935. Jimmy made only rare TV acting appearances during the '50s and '60s, including several on *General Electric Theater*. In 1971 he decided to enter series TV, in a family comedy in which he played a college professor. NBC was ecstatic to have been picked as his network, and, assuming the show to be a guaranteed blockbuster, placed it in one of its toughest Sunday-night time periods. To everybody's surprise, *The Jimmy Stewart Show* was a failure.

Jimmy starred in a TV production of his famous film hit *Harvey* in early 1972 (having just revived it on Broadway as well) and then went into production on his first TV movie, *Hawkins on Murder,* which was telecast in March 1973. This led to his second series, in which he played a country lawyer–sleuth named Hawkins and which was aired on a rotating basis with two other series. This was not successful either. Jimmy has since been seen only in occasional specials, living proof that even movie megastardom is not necessarily transferable to the small screen.

STEWART, JAY—announcer

Let's Make a Deal (quiz)
.... announcer (1967–71)

One of the networks' top announcers (and on-camera cut-ups), active on radio and then TV from the early 1940s to the '80s; latterly on daytime quiz shows.

STEWART, JOHNNY—juvenile actor

Wesley (com)..... Wesley Eggleston (1949)

STEWART, LYNNE MARIE—actress

Husbands, Wives & Lovers (com)
.... Joy Bellini (1978)

STEWART, MARGARET—actress

Operation Neptune (sci fi).... Thirza (1953)

STEWART, MARTHA—singer, actress
b: Oct 7, 1922, Bardwell, Ky.

Those Two (com)........ regular (1952–53)

STEWART, MEL—black actor
b: Sep 19, Cleveland, Ohio

All in the Family (com)
.... Henry Jefferson (1971–73)
Roll Out (com)... Sgt. B. J. Bryant (1973–74)
On the Rocks (com) .. Mr. Gibson (1975–76)
Tabitha (com)..... Marvin Decker (1977–78)
One in a Million (com) .... Raymond (1980)
Freebie and the Bean (police)
.... Rodney ("Axle") Blake (1980–81)
Scarecrow and Mrs. King (adv)
.... Billy Melrose (1983–)

STEWART, NICK—black actor
b: New York City, N.Y. r: Barbados, British West Indies

Amos 'n' Andy (com) ... Lightnin' (1951–53)
Ramar of the Jungle (adv)
.... regular (1952–54)

This radio and TV actor went under several names; he was billed as Nicodemus Stewart on radio in the '40s (on *The Alan Young Show* and *Beulah*), as "Nick O'Demus" in the credits for TV's *Amos 'n'*

Andy, and as Nick (or Horace) Stewart elsewhere. His most famous role was that of the slow-moving janitor Lightnin' on *Amos 'n' Andy,* a black stereotype he was forced many times to explain in later interviews about the controversial series. In later years, Stewart operated the all-Black Ebony Showcase Theatre in Los Angeles.

STEWART, PAUL—actor, director
b: Mar 13, 1908, New York City, N.Y. d: Feb 17, 1986

Top Secret U.S.A. (adv).. Prof. Brand (1954)
Deadline (drama).............. host (1959)
The Man Who Never Was (drama)
.... Paul Grant (1966–67)

A veteran character actor, much on radio during the '30s and '40s (including an important stint with Orson Welles' *Mercury Theatre*), in films, and later on television. He usually played cold-eyed, menacing, untrustworthy types. He was also quite busy as a TV director from the early 1950s onward, directing episodes of such series as *King's Row, Peter Gunn, Philip Marlowe, Michael Shayne, 87th Precinct, The Twilight Zone, Going My Way, Bob Hope Presents the Chrysler Theatre,* and many others. In addition, he did cartoon voice work during the 1960s.

STEWART, RAY—actor

A.E.S. Hudson Street (com)
.... Nurse Newton (1978)

STEWART, REDD—country guitarist, pianist
b: May 27, 1921, Ashland City, Tenn.

The Pee Wee King Show (var)
.... regular (1955)

STEWART, SANDY—singer
b: Jul 10, 1937, Philadelphia, Pa.

Kraft Music Hall (var).... regular (1961–63)
Sing Along with Mitch (var)
.... regular (1963–64)

STEWART, TRISH—actress
b: Jun 14, Hot Springs, Ark.

Salvage 1 (adv) ..... Melanie Slozar (1979)

A young soap opera queen of the '70s, most famous as Chris Brooks on *The Young and the Restless* (1973–78); she also played supporting roles in numerous prime time series episodes and TV movies.

STICH, PATRICIA—actress
b: Manchester, Conn.

Griff (drama).. Gracie Newcombe (1973–74)

STIERS, DAVID OGDEN—actor
b: Oct 31, 1942, Peoria, Ill.

Doc (com) .... Stanley Moss (1976)
M*A*S*H (com)
.... Maj. Charles Emerson Winchester
(1977–83)
North and South (drama)
.... Congressman Sam Greene (1985)

The tall, balding, rather pompous Major Winchester of *M*A*S*H* was portrayed by an actor who spent many years onstage playing noble Shakespearean roles. Stiers performed with West Coast theater groups from 1960–69, then came East to study at Juilliard and win his first Broadway supporting roles, notably that of Feldman the Magnificent in the musical *The Magic Show*. He also studied with John Houseman, some of whose huffy mannerisms he seems to have picked up.

Stiers entered TV in the 1970s, mostly via such TV movies as the *Charlie's Angels* pilot, *A Circle of Children,* and *The Eleanor and Lou Gehrig Story.* A stint as the head of a clinic on *Doc* didn't do much for his career, but some appearances on *The Mary Tyler Moore Show* as a network TV executive caught the eye of the producers of *M*A*S*H* (then looking for a replacement for Major Burns) and brought him his role of a lifetime. Stiers later appeared in miniseries including *The First Olympics* and *North and South;* he also conducts and narrates for symphony orchestras.

STILLER, JERRY—actor
b: Jun 8, 1929, Brooklyn, N.Y.

The Paul Lynde Show (com)
.... Barney Dickerson (1972–73)
Joe and Sons (com)
.... Gus Duzik (1975–76)

The dumpy, grumpy very Jewish half of the Jewish husband/Irish wife comedy team

Stiller and Meara. They were married in 1954 and have been performing together since 1962; before that, Jerry was primarily a dramatic stage actor, usually in—believe it or not—Shakespearean plays. See under Anne Meara for details on their career together.

STILLWELL, JACK—host

ABC Barn Dance (mus)
.... emcee (1949)

STILWELL, DIANE—actress

The Half Hour Comedy Hour (var)
.... regular (1983)

STOCK, ALAN—juvenile actor

The Contender (drama)
.... Brian Captor (1980)

STOCK, BARBARA—actress
b: May 26, Downers Grove, Ill.

Spenser: For Hire (drama)
.... Susan Silverman (1985–86)

STOCKDALE, JULIAN—orchestra leader

Windy City Jamboree (music)
.... orch. leader (1950)

STOCKWELL, GUY—actor
b: Nov 16, 1933, New York City, N.Y.

Adventures in Paradise (adv)
.... Chris Parker (1961–62)
The Richard Boone Show (drama)
.... regular (1963–64)

The son of stage actors Harry Stockwell and Betty Veronica, and the older brother of familiar movie and TV actor Dean Stockwell. Both brothers have been seen often on television since the late 1950s.

STOCKWELL, JOHN—actor

North and South (drama)
.... Billy Hazard (1985)

STOKER, MIKE—actor

Emergency (drama)
.... Fireman Stoker (1973–77)

STOKEY, MIKE—producer, host

Pantomime Quiz (quiz) ...... host (1950–59)
Pantomime Quiz (quiz) ...... host (1962–63)

STOLER, SHIRLEY—actress

Skag (drama) .... Dottie Jessup (1980)

STONE, CAROL—actress
b: 1915, New York City, N.Y.

The Life and Legend of Wyatt Earp (wes)
.... Kate Holliday (1957–58)

STONE, CHRISTOPHER—actor
b: Oct 4, Manchester, N.H.

The Interns (drama)
.... Dr. Pooch Hardin (1970–71)
Spencer's Pilots (adv)... Cass Garrett (1976)
Harper Valley P.T.A. (com)
.... Tom Meechum (1981–82)
The Blue and the Gray (drama)
.... Major Fairbairn (1982)
Dallas (drama)........ Dave Stratton (1984)

STONE, CYNTHIA—actress
b: Feb 26, 1926, Peoria, Ill.

That Wonderful Guy (com)
.... Harold's girlfriend (1949–50)
Ad Libbers (var) .... regular (1951)
Heaven for Betsy (com)... Betsy Bell (1952)

The wife of Jack Lemmon (during the 1950s), with whom she appeared in the three series listed above. She had no known career of her own after she and Lemmon split up.

STONE, DEE WALLACE—actress
b: Dec 14, Kansas City, Mo.

Together We Stand (com)
.... Lori Randall (1986–)

STONE, GAIL—juvenile actress

The Eve Arden Show (com)
.... Jenny (1957–58)

STONE, HAROLD J.—actor
b: 1911, New York City, N.Y.

The Hartmans (com) . the handyman (1949)
The Goldbergs (com) . Jake Goldberg (1952)
The Grand Jury (drama)
.... John Kennedy (1958–59)

My World and Welcome to It (com)
.... Hamilton Greeley (1969–70)
Bridget Loves Bernie (com)
.... Sam Steinberg (1972–73)

STONE, KAREN—newscaster
b: c. 1949, Roaring Springs, Pa. r: Senecca Falls, N.Y.

CBS News Nightwatch (news)
.... anchor (1982–84)

STONE, KIRBY—combo leader
b: Apr 27, 1918, New York City, N.Y.

Strictly for Laughs (music)
.... quintet (1949–50)
Broadway Open House (talk)
.... quintet (1951)
The Jimmie Rodgers Show (var)
.... quartet (1959)

Well-known jazz oriented combo leader ("The Kirby Stone Four") whose most famous recording was "Baubles, Bangles and Beads," from the Broadway show *Kismet*, in 1958.

STONE, LEONARD—actor
b: Nov 3, Salem, Ore.

Camp Runamuck (com)
.... Doc Joslyn (1965–66)
The Jean Arthur Show (com)
.... Morton (1966)

STONE, MILBURN—actor
b: Jul 5, 1904, Burrton, Kan. d: Jun 12, 1980

Gunsmoke (wes)
.... Dr. Galen (Doc) Adams (1955–75)

Emmy Award: Best Supporting Actor in a Drama, for *Gunsmoke* (1968)

Milburn Stone realized every character actor's fondest dream. After scuffling for 20 years in endless B films—westerns, serials, crime flicks, you name it—and playing every sort of villainous or background role imaginable, he latched on to a single, simple part in a TV western that kept him steadily employed for the next 20 years. His crusty, gruff but wise Doc Adams ("Now, Matt . . .") was a TV standby, beloved and eventually honored with an Emmy Award. Milburn did play guest roles on a few other series during the '50s (*Dragnet, Front Row Center, Climax*) but they are long since forgotten. His movie career had begun in 1935.

After *Gunsmoke* finally ended its extraordinary run, Milburn retired to his ranch in Santa Fe and raised livestock during his last few years.

STONE, PADDY—choreographer
b: Sep 16, 1924, Winnipeg, Canada

The Piccadilly Palace (var)
.... dancers (1967)

STONE, ROB—actor
b: Sep 22, 1962, Chicago, Ill. r: Dallas, Texas

Mr. Belvedere (com)
.... Kevin Owens (1985–)

STONE, SHARON—actress

Bay City Blues (drama)
.... Cathy St. Marie (1983)

STONE, SID—comedian
b: 1903 d: Feb 12, 1986

The Milton Berle Show (var)
.... commercial announcer (1948–51)

The fast-talking "Tell ya what I'm gonna do" pitchman who delivered the commercials on Milton Berle's *Texaco Star Theater*—until chased off the stage by a whistle-blowing policeman. More commercials should end that way.

STONE, STEVE—sportscaster
b: Jul 14, 1947, Cleveland, Ohio

Monday Night Baseball (sport)
.... sportscaster (1983)

From 1970–1982, major-league pitcher with the San Francisco Giants, Chicago White Sox, Chicago Cubs, and Baltimore Orioles.

STONE, SUZANNE—black actress

Sanford (com)....... Cissy Lewis (1980–81)

STONEMAN, RONI—comedienne

Hee Haw (var)........... regular (1973–)

Gap-toothed corn-pone comedienne, a member of country music's illustrious Stoneman family.

STORCH, LARRY—comedian
b: Jan 8, 1923, New York City, N.Y.

Cavalcade of Stars (var)... emcee (1951–52)
The Larry Storch Show (var).... host (1953)
F Troop (com)
.... Cpl. Randolph Agarn (1965–67)
The Queen and I (com)
.... Charles Duffy (1969)

A sharp-featured, manic little comic with a knack for dialects, Larry Storch played clubs in New York after World War II, working his way up to TV guest spots and small parts in movies in the '50s. He had a couple of good breaks in the early '50s, including his own live summer show in 1953 (the summer replacement for Jackie Gleason) but it did not seem to lead anywhere until ten years later, when he scored a major hit as the nutty corporal on *F Troop*. He later turned up in assorted series and TV movies, including the live action Saturday morning *Ghost Busters* (1975–78) and the 1981 TV film *The Adventures of Huckleberry Finn*, both costarring his *F Troop* sergeant, Forrest Tucker.

STORDAHL, AXEL—orchestra leader
b: Aug 8, 1913, Staten Island, N.Y. d: Aug 30, 1963

The Frank Sinatra Show (var)
.... orch. leader (1950–52)
Coke Time with Eddie Fisher (music)
.... orch. leader (1953–57)
The Gisele MacKenzie Show (var)
.... orch. leader (1957–58)

STORM, GALE—actress
b: Apr 5, 1922, Bloomington, Texas

My Little Margie (com)
.... Margie Albright (1952–55)
NBC Comedy Hour (var)..... hostess (1956)
The Gale Storm Show (com)
.... Susanna Pomeroy (1956–60)

One of the most popular TV comediennes of the 1950s, a pert and peppy rival to Lucy then, Gale is now a dim figure of nostalgia, even though she has long wanted to get back into the medium. Gale broke into movies in 1939 when she won a "Gateway to Hollywood" talent contest while still in high school. After a series of cheerful but minor films during the '40s, including several westerns with Roy Rogers, she moved to TV circa 1950, appearing first in playhouse productions. In 1952 she scored her first major hit as the trouble-prone daughter on *My Little Margie;* a year after it ended she was back in the equally popular *Gale Storm Show* (aka *Oh! Susanna*), playing the social director of an ocean liner who was always cooking up schemes with her confidante ZaSu Pitts.

At the same time she was a major star on television, Gale launched a remarkably successful recording career—perhaps the first TV star to do so—with teen hits including "I Hear You Knocking," "Ivory Tower," and "Dark Moon." Youthful rock 'n' rollers apparently didn't realize that she was by then in her (gasp!) midthirties. During the '60s and '70s, Gale was rarely seen on television, appearing instead onstage in summer stock. When she turned up on *The Love Boat* in 1979 it was the first time many viewers had seen her in nearly 20 years. She then began to hit the talk show circuit, revealing that in later years she had developed a very serious drinking problem, licked only after a long and difficult struggle which included commitment to a tough treatment center. She described it all in her 1981 autobiography, *I Ain't Down Yet.*

STORRS, SUZANNE—actress
b: 1934, Salt Lake City, Utah

Naked City (police)
.... Janet Halloran (1958–59)

STORY, RALPH—host
b: 1920, Kalamazoo, Mich.

What Do You Have in Common? (quiz)
.... emcee (1954)
The $64,000 Challenge (quiz)
.... emcee (1956–58)
Alias Smith and Jones (wes)
.... narrator (1972–73)

STOSSEL, JOHN—newscaster
b: c. 1947

20/20 (mag)........ correspondent (1981–)

Consumer affairs reporter for *Good Morning, America* and *20/20.*

STOSSEL, LUDWIG—actor
b: Feb 12, 1883, Lockenhaus, Austria d: Jan 29, 1973

Casablanca (drama)...... Ludwig (1955–56)
Man with a Camera (drama)
.... Anton Kovac (1958–60)

One of Hollywood's "German colony," Stossel only occasionally appeared on television as an actor. He was most familiar, toward the end of his years, as the kindly "Little Old Winemaker, Me" in TV commercials.

STOUT, PAUL—juvenile actor
b: May 12, 1972, Saugus, Calif.

Scarecrow and Mrs. King (adv)
.... Philip King (1983–)

STOWE, MADELINE—actress

The Gangster Chronicles (drama)
.... Ruth Lasker (1981)

STRACKE, WIN—actor, folksinger

Hawkins Falls, Population 6,200 (com)
.... Laif Flaigle (1950)
Stud's Place (var)........ Wynn (1950–52)

STRAIGHT, BEATRICE—actress
b: Aug 2, 1916*, Old Westbury, N.Y.

Beacon Hill (drama).... Mrs. Hacker (1975)
King's Crossing (drama)
.... Louisa Beauchamp (1982)

Veteran character actress active on television during the 1950s, often in heavy dramas and classical plays. She was seen less often after the "Golden Age," although she has appeared in a couple of short-lived series and in a few TV movies and miniseries, including *Killer on Board* and *The Dain Curse.*

STRALSER, LUCIA—actress

Big Hawaii (drama)
.... Karen "Keke" Fears (1977)

STRAND, ROBIN—actor

Berrengers (drama)... Billy Berrenger (1985)

STRANGE, GLENN—actor
b: Aug 16, 1899, Weed, N.M. d: Sep 20, 1973

Gunsmoke (wes)
.... Sam the bartender (1962–74)

*Some sources give 1918.

A big, solid man with a commanding presence, who nevertheless played supporting roles throughout his long film career (1931–59). He was seen mostly in westerns, often as a villain, but gained fame among horror fans by portraying Frankenstein in several 1940s films. Glenn was a convincing adversary on television as well; he was, for example, the outlaw Butch Cavendish, who wiped out all of the members of a Texas Rangers patrol—except for one—in the premiere episode of *The Lone Ranger* in 1950. Later, he was best known as *Gunsmoke*'s Sam the bartender, a man you suspected had an interesting past.

STRANGIS, JUDY—actress

Room 222 (drama).. Helen Loomis (1969–74)

Judy was quite busy on Saturday morning TV during the 1970s, providing voices for several cartoons and appearing in a live action series as Dyna Girl. She was one of the students in the school series *Room 222.*

STRASBERG, SUSAN—actress
b: May 22, 1938, New York City, N.Y.

The Marriage (com) .. Emily Marriott (1954)
Toma (police) .... Patty Toma (1973–74)

The petite daughter of famed and controversial acting teacher Lee Strasberg, co-founder of New York's Actor's Studio and chief advocate of "method" acting. Susan did not study with her father until long after she had made her debut, at age 14, in an off-Broadway play. She appeared in a number of TV productions while still a teenager, including the 1954 summer series *The Marriage,* as Hume Cronyn and Jessica Tandy's daughter. During the '60s and '70s she worked rather steadily in westerns, dramas, and crime shows, including multiple episodes of *The F.B.I.; Night Gallery; Owen Marshall; Counselor at Law;* and *The Rockford Files.* On *Toma* she played Tony Musante's worried wife.

Everywhere Susan went, the shadow of her father's theories followed her, even though she insisted she was by no means an extension of them. "My father and I quarrel often," she once said. "We wouldn't enjoy each other if we couldn't argue over everything."

816

STRASSMAN, MARCIA—actress
b: Apr 28, 1948, New York City, N.Y.

*M*A*S*H* (com)
.... Nurse Margie Cutler (1972–73)
Welcome Back, Kotter (com)
.... Julie Kotter (1975–79)
Good Time Harry (com)
.... Carol Younger (1980)
E/R (com)
...... Dr. Eve Sheridan (pilot only) (1984)

STRATFORD, TRACY—juvenile actress
b: c. 1954

The New Loretta Young Show (drama)
.... Maria Massey (1962–63)
The John Forsythe Show (com)
.... Susan (1965–66)

STRATTON, ALBERT—actor
b: Oct 23, Hubbard, Ohio

Perry Mason (revival) (drama)
.... Paul Drake (1973–74)
Sara (wes) .... Martin Pope (1976)

STRATTON, GIL, JR.—actor

That's My Boy (com)
.... Junior Jackson (1954–55)

Later a TV sportscaster in Los Angeles.

STRATTON, W.K.—actor
b: Aug 2, Front Royal, Va.

Baa Baa Black Sheep (drama)
.... Lt. Lawrence Casey (1976–78)

STRAUSS, PETER—actor
b: Feb 20, 1942*, Croton-on-Hudson, N.Y.

Rich Man, Poor Man—Book I (drama)
.... Rudy Jordache (1976)
Rich Man, Poor Man—Book II (drama)
.... Sen. Rudy Jordache (1976–77)
Masada (drama)
.... Eleazar ben Yair (1981)

Emmy Award: Best Actor in a Special, for *The Jericho Mile* (1979)

A rather intense actor who has appeared mostly in TV movies and miniseries, including *Rich Man, Poor Man* (the role that made him famous), *Young Joe, the Forgotten Kennedy* (title role), *The Jericho Mile,*

*Some sources give 1947.

A Whale for the Killing, Masada, Kane and Abel, and Under Siege.

STRAUSS, ROBERT—actor
b: Nov 8, 1913, New York City, N.Y. d: Feb 20, 1975

Mona McCluskey (com)
.... Sgt. Gruzewsky (1965–66)

STREEP, MERYL—actress
b: Jun 22, 1949*, Summit, N.J.*

Holocaust (drama)
.... Inga Helms Weiss (1978)

Emmy Award: Best Actress in a Limited Series, for *Holocaust* (1978)

Plain-looking but extremely talented movie star who appeared in two TV dramatic productions early in her career (*The Deadliest Season,* 1977, and *Holocaust,* 1978) but has had little to do with TV since then.

STREET, DAVE—actor, singer
b: Dec 13, 1917, Los Angeles, Calif. d: Sep 3, 1971

Broadway Open House (talk)
.... regular (1950–51)

STRICKLAND, AMZIE—Actress
Carter Country (com)
.... Julia Mobey (1978–79)

STRICKLAND, GAIL—Actress
b: May 18, Birmingham, Ala.

The Insiders (drama) . Alice West (1985–86)

STRIDERS, THE—vocal quartet
Hotel Broadway (var) ...... regulars (1949)

STRIMPELL, STEPHEN—actor
b: c. 1939, New York City, N.Y.

Mr. Terrific (com) .. Stanley Beamish (1967)

STRINGBEAN (DAVID AKEMAN)— country comedian, banjoist
b: Jun 17, 1915, Annville, Ky. d: Nov 11, 1973

Hee Haw (var) .... regular (1969–74)

*Some sources give 1950 or 1951, and indicate nearby Bernardsville, N.J. as the place of birth.

Nashville has still not gotten over the sudden and senseless murder of this much-loved comedian and his wife one night in 1973 as they returned home from a performance on The *Grand Ole Opry* (and apparently surprised a burglar). The very tall, gangling banjo player had built up a loyal following both for his solid musicianship and his "rube" comedy; he often appeared in a long shirt extending down to his knees, with short pants picking up from there.

STRITCH, ELAINE—actress
b. Feb 2, 1926, Detroit, Mich.

The Growing Paynes (com)
.... Mrs. Payne (1949)
Pantomime Quiz (quiz) ... regular (1953–55)
Pantomime Quiz (quiz) ...... regular (1958)
My Sister Eileen (com)
.... Ruth Sherwood (1960–61)
The Trials of O'Brien (drama)
.... Miss G. (1965–66)
The Ellen Burstyn Show (com)
.... Sydney Brewer (1986–)

Raspy-voiced comic actress of the '50s and '60s, who married (for the first time) at the age of 48 and moved to London, where she starred in the 1976 British TV comedy *Two's Company.*

STROLL, EDSON—actor
McHale's Navy (com)
.... Virgil Farrell (1962–66)

STROMSOE, FRED—actor
Adam 12 (police) .. Officer Woods (1974–75)

STROMSTEDT, ULLA—actress
b: Sweden

Flipper (adv) ...... Ulla Norstrand (1965–66)

A blonde Swedish knockout who was introduced into the *Flipper* kids' show (as a "visiting oceanographer") to add a little, er, adult appeal.

STROOCK, GLORIA—actress
The Girls (com)
.... Cornelia Otis Skinner (1950)
McMillan and Wife (police)
.... Maggie (1976–77)

The sister of actress Geraldine Brooks. Gloria has been on television in minor roles since the 1950s; she played herself in the 1981 TV movie *The Patricia Neal Story*.

STROUD, CLAUDE—actor
b: c. 1907 d: Oct 16, 1985

The Peter Lind Hayes Show (com)
.... regular (1950)
The Duke (com)..... Rudy Cromwell (1954)
The Ted Knight Show (com)
.... Hobart Nalven (1978)

STROUD, DON—actor
b: 1937, Honolulu, Hawaii

Kate Loves a Mystery (drama)
.... Sgt. Mike Varrick (1979)
Mickey Spillane's Mike Hammer (drama)
.... Capt. Pat Chambers (1984–)

Tough, pugnacious, fair-haired character actor who got his start as Troy Donahue's stunt double in *Hawaiian Eye*. He holds a black belt in karate.

STRUNK, JUD—singer, comedian
b: Jun 11, 1933, Jamestown, N.Y. r: Farmington, Maine d: Oct 5, 1981

Rowan & Martin's Laugh-In (var)
.... regular (1972–73)

STRUTHERS, SALLY—actress
b: Jul 28, 1947, Portland, Oregon

The Summer Smothers Show (var)
.... regular (1970)
The Tim Conway Comedy Hour (var)
.... regular (1970)
All in the Family (com)
.... Gloria Bunker Stivic (1971–78)
Gloria (com)
.... Gloria Bunker Stivic (1982–83)
9 to 5 (com)..... Marsha Shrimpton (1986–)

Emmy Awards: Best Supporting Actress in a Comedy, for *All in the Family* (1972, 1979)

Archie Bunker's beloved, vulnerable-looking "little goil" on *All in the Family* has had an up-and-down career on TV. She entered acting straight out of high school in the mid-1960s and after two years of study made her first TV appear-ance as a dancer on a Herb Alpert special. She then toured briefly with the Spike Jones, Jr., band, did some stage work, and landed a few small roles on TV and in films (including 1970's *Five Easy Pieces*). Her career really began to take off in 1970; in that year she was a regular on two variety series and in the fall won the role (over 200 others) of Archie Bunker's addle-brained daughter. *All in the Family* made Sally and the rest of the cast major stars; however, she still pursued other roles as time permitted. On Saturday mornings during the early '70s she was the voice of teenager Pebbles Flintstone on *The Flintstones* and *Pebbles and Bamm Bamm;* she also starred in several TV movies, including *Aloha Means Goodbye* (1974), *Hey I'm Alive* (1975), and *Intimate Strangers* (1977).

As soon as her *All in the Family* contract ran out, Sally quit the series, determined to overcome the "dumb little blonde" image she had acquired. Her later projects had mixed success, however. Her first two post-Gloria TV movies *(My Husband Is Missing* and *And Your Name Is Jonah*) did well, but the later *A Gun in the House* did not. A proposed new series called *Me on the Radio* fell through, and her debut on Broadway (in the short-lived *Wally's Cafe*) ended quickly. A 1982 series called *Gloria,* in which she returned in her familiar role (something she swore she'd never do)—this time as Gloria the divorced single parent—lasted only one season. Sally now spends much of her time working on behalf of the International Christian Children's Fund.

STUART, BARBARA—actress
b: Paris, Ill r: Hume, Ill.

The Great Gildersleeve (com)
.... Bessie, the secretary (1955–56)
Pete and Gladys (com) ..... Alice (1960–61)
Gomer Pyle, U.S.M.C. (com)
.... Bunny Harper (1964–69)
The Queen and I (com)
.... Wilma Winslow (1969)
The McLean Stevenson Show (com)
.... Peggy Ferguson (1976–77)
Our Family Honor (drama)
.... Marianne Danzig (1985–86)
Gomer Pyle (com)
.... Sgt. Carter's girlfriend

STUART, MAXINE—actress
b: Jun 28, Deal, N.J. r: Lawrence, N.Y.

Norby (com) . . . . Maureen (1955)
Room for One More (com)
. . . . Ruth Burton (1962)
Slattery's People (drama)
. . . . B. J. Clawson (1964–65)
Doctors' Hospital (drama)
. . . . Scotty (1975–76)
Executive Suite (drama)
. . . . Marge Newberry (1976–77)
The Rousters (adv)
. . . . Amanda Earp (1983–84)
Hail to the Chief (com) . . . . . Lenore (1985)

Maxine Stuart's acting career is said to go back to one of the first plays ever televised, in 1940. She has played innumerable TV supporting roles since then (also onstage and in films), latterly as a gray-haired, rambunctious old granny on such series as *The Rousters* and *Hail to the Chief.*

STUART, MEL—

Turn-On (var) . . . . regular (1969)

STUART, PATRICK—juvenile actor

Battlestar Galactica (sci fi) . . Dr. Zee (1980)

STUART, RANDY—actress

Biff Baker U.S.A. (adv)
. . . . Louise Baker (1952–53)
This Is the Life (drama)
. . . . Emily Fisher (1952–56)
The Life and Legend of Wyatt Earp (wes)
. . . . Nellie Cashman (1959–60)

STUART, ROY—actor

Gomer Pyle, U.S.M.C. (com)
. . . . Corp. Boyle (1965–68)

STUDER, HAL—actor

Faraway Hill (drama) . . . . regular (1946)

STUMPF, RANDY—actor
b: Sep 9, Belleville, Ill.

Flatbush (com) . . . . Joey Dee (1979)

STUTHMAN, FRED—actor
b: c. 1919, California d: Jul 7, 1982

Hello, Larry (com) . . . . . . Henry Adler (1980)

STYLES, SUSAN—actress
b: Jun 18, Ventura, Calif.

Cutter to Houston (drama)
. . . . Nurse Patty Alvarez (1983)

SUAREZ, OLGA—

The Vaughn Monroe Show (var)
. . . . regular (1950–51)

SUBER, RAY—puppeteer, host

Sandy Strong (child)
. . . . Mr. Mack (1950)

SUBLETTE, LINDA—actress
b: Homewood, Ill.

The John Byner Comedy Hour (var)
. . . . regular (1972)

SUCHET, DAVID—actor

Master of the Game (drama)
. . . . D'Usseau (1984)

SUES, ALAN—comedian
b: Mar 8, Ross, Calif.

Rowan & Martin's Laugh-In (var)
. . . . regular (1968–72)

A lightweight comedian best known as the garrulous sportscaster "Big Al" on *Laugh-In,* who gave newsworthy athletes little "dingdongs" on his bell. He has also been seen on other variety and talk shows, notably *Shindig* in the '60s and *The Merv Griffin Show* in later years.

SUITS, WENDY—

The Nashville Palace (var)
. . . . regular (1981–82)

SULLIVAN, ANN—actress

The Growing Paynes (com)
. . . . regular (1948–49)

SULLIVAN, BARRY—actor
b: Aug 29, 1912, New York City, N.Y.

The Man Called X (drama)
. . . . agent Ken Thurston (1955–56)
Harbourmaster (adv)
. . . . Capt. David Scott (1957–58)
The Tall Man (wes)
. . . . Dep. Sheriff Pat Garrett (1960–62)

The Road West (wes)
.... Benjamin Pride (1966–67)
Rich Man, Poor Man—Book II (drama)
.... Sen. Paxton (1976–77)

Tall, rugged, dour actor who is in the running for the title of Actor Who Has Had the Longest Career on Television Without Ever Smiling. He began onstage in the mid-1930s, moved to Hollywood in the early '40s, and has been on television since the early '50s. He is, in fact, one of the busiest actors on TV, having appeared in many hundreds of episodes and starred in four series, generally as a solid, unsmiling authority figure. Perhaps the highlight of his career was the role of the defense attorney in *The Caine Mutiny Court Martial*, on Broadway and TV in the '50s. Among the many TV series in which he has made multiple appearances are *Ford Theatre*, *Playhouse 90*, *Bonanza*, *The Name of the Game*, *The High Chaparral*, *The Streets of San Francisco*, and *Cannon;* among his TV movies are *The Bastard*, *The Immigrants*, *Casino*, and *Once an Eagle*.

SULLIVAN, BIG JIM—

This Is Tom Jones (var)... regular (1970–71)

SULLIVAN, ED—host, columnist
b: Sep 28, 1901, New York City r: Port Chester, N.Y. d: Oct 13, 1974

The Ed Sullivan Show (var).. host (1948–71)

Emmy Award: Trustees' Award (1971)

"The Great Stone Face" of Sunday nights, the awkward, wooden, word-mangling newspaper columnist who confounded the experts by becoming the most famous variety show host in the history of television. Ed was no slick TV host in the usual mold, but rather an authentic showman, one of the greatest of the age—a sort of twentieth century P. T. Barnum who not only had his finger on the pulse of what was hot at the moment but could get his whole hand on it for his "really big shew." It's no accident that Dean Martin and Jerry Lewis made their TV debut on his first telecast, or that Bob Hope, Dinah Shore, Eddie Fisher, Walt Disney, the Beatles, and countless others were introduced to viewers by him. Elvis Presley had been seen elsewhere before, but for him, too, the Sullivan debut was the one that mattered.

Ed was born one of seven children of a New York customs inspector (he had a twin brother, Daniel, who died in his first year). Ed became a newspaper reporter immediately after graduating from high school and during the 1920s was one of the city's top sports reporters. He began a Broadway column in 1931 and soon his syndicated "Little Old New York" feature was bringing him into contact with the most important names in show business. Ed branched into radio and even films (*Mr. Broadway*, 1933) as a host/impresario, and when television began to spread he immediately saw a good thing there as well. An old photo buried in the NBC files shows him snooping around backstage on the set of the primitive, pioneering 1946 variety series *Hour Glass;* you can almost see the idea germinating in his head for his own show. *The Toast of the Town* (later called *The Ed Sullivan Show*) debuted two years later and became a 23-year TV institution. Throughout its run, and until his death, Ed continued to write his column; it kept him "in touch."

In 1971 the National Academy of TV Arts and Sciences presented Ed with a Special Emmy Award, the text of which is as follows.

"For serving as a founder of the National Academy and its first National President; for pioneering in the variety format which has become a backbone of television programming; for having the foresight and courage to provide network exposure for minority performers; for bringing to millions of Americans cultural performances from ballet to opera to legitimate drama; for introducing performers from throughout the world to audiences who would otherwise never have known them; and, finally, for his showmanship, taste and personal commitment in entertaining a nation for 23 years."

SULLIVAN, FRANCIS C.—host

Destiny (drama)............ host (1957–58)

SULLIVAN, JENNY—actress
b: c. 1947

Me and Maxx (com)........ Barbara (1980)
V (movie) (sci fi) ..... Kristine Walsh (1983)

V: The Final Battle (miniseries) (sci fi)
..................Kristine Walsh (1984)

The daughter of actor Barry Sullivan.

SULLIVAN, KATHLEEN—newscaster
b: 1953, Pasadena, Calif.

ABC Weekend News (news)
.... anchor (1985–)

A glamorous young newscaster who, despite a certain lack of journalistic experience "in the trenches," has had a meteoric rise in TV news. She began as an unpaid intern at KNXT-TV in Los Angeles in 1977, quickly progressed to local reporter, became the first anchor of Cable News Network from 1980–82, and then joined ABC. By 1985 her salary was in the $300,000 range and she was anchor of both the network's early morning and Saturday newscasts. She was, her superiors said, a "natural communicator."

SULLIVAN, KATHY—

The Lawrence Welk Show (music)
.... regular (1976–82)

SULLIVAN, KITTY—actress

The Patty Duke Show (com)
.... Sue Ellen (1963–65)

SULLIVAN, LIAM—actor
b: May 18, 1923, Jacksonville, Ill.

The Monroes (wes).. Maj. Mapoy (1966–67)

SULLIVAN, MADY—actress

The Benny Rubin Show (com)
.... the secretary (1949)

SULLIVAN, OWEN—

The Big Show (var)......... regular (1980)

SULLIVAN, ROBERT—New York newspaper columnist

What's the Story? (quiz) . panelist (1952–53)

SULLIVAN, SUSAN—actress
b: Nov 18, 1944, New York City, N.Y.

Rich Man, Poor Man—Book II (drama)
................Maggie Porter (1976–77)

Having Babies (drama)
.... Dr. Julie Farr (1978–79)
It's a Living (com)... Lois Adams (1980–81)
Falcon Crest (drama)
................Maggie Gioberti (1981–)

Cool, intelligent-looking actress who often plays doctors, lawyers, or scientists (she tried to break the mold playing a waitress in *It's a Living* but she looked as if she owned the place). Susan has been seen on television since the late '60s and from 1971–1976 was Lenore on the daytime soap opera *Another World.* A major break was the role of Peter Strauss's lawyer-lover on *Rich Man, Poor Man;* following that, she was cast as Dr. Julie Farr in the movie and spin-off series, *Having Babies* (aka *Julie Farr, M.D.*).

SUMMERS, HOPE—actress
b: 1901, Mattoon, Ill. d: Jul 22, 1979

Hawkins Falls, Population 6,200 (com)
.... Mrs. Catherwood (1950)
The Rifleman (wes)
.... Hattie Denton (1958–63)
The Andy Griffith Show (com)
................Clara Edwards (1960–68)
Another Day (com)... Olive Gardner (1978)

SUMMERS, YALE—actor
b: New York City, N.Y.

Daktari (adv) .... Jack Dane (1966–68)

A handsome blond six-footer, also seen in daytime soap operas in the '60s and '70s *(General Hospital, Return to Peyton Place).*

SUN, IRENE YAH-LING—actress

Khan (drama)........... Anna Khan (1975)

SUNDSTROM, FLORENCE—actress

The Life of Riley (com)
..................Belle Dudley (1955–56)

SUNG, RICHARD LEE—

Keep On Truckin' (var) ..... regular (1975)

SUPIRAN, JERRY—actor

Small Wonder (com)
.... Jamie Lawson (1985–)

SUROVY, NICHOLAS—actor

Bridges to Cross (drama)
.... Peter Cross (1986)

The son of opera diva Rise Stevens; he has had minor roles on daytime and nighttime television.

SUSANN, JACQUELINE—author, actress

b: Aug 20, 1921, Philadelphia, Pa. d: Sep 21, 1974

The Morey Amsterdam Show (var)
.... Lola (1948–50)

Yes, Jacqueline Susann, the famous sex-and-sleaze novelist (*Valley of the Dolls*, etc.) played a regular role on this early variety show, as Lola the wide-eyed cigarette girl. The show's producer was her husband Irving Mansfield. Jackie also played guest roles on occasional later series, including *Suspense* and *Mannix*.

SUSI, CAROL ANN—actress

Kolchak: The Night Stalker (drama)
.... Monique Marmelstein (1974–75)

SUSMAN, TODD—actor

b: Jan 17, 1947, St. Louis, Mo.

The Bob Crane Show (com)
.... Marvin Susman (1975)
Spencer's Pilots (adv).... Stan Lewis (1976)
Number 96 (drama)
.... Nathan Sugarman (1980–81)
Star of the Family (com)... Feldman (1982)
Goodnight, Beantown (com)
.... Augie Kleindab (1983–84)

Gawky, grinning, curly-haired comic actor, who appeared in a number of comedies (and a few dramas) during the '70s and '80s. *M*A*S*H* fans will remember him from a episode called "Operation Nose-lift," in which he played the G.I. with a huge nose on whom the surgeons of the 4077th performed compassionate plastic surgery.

SUSSKIND, DAVID—producer, host

b: Dec 19, 1920, New York City, N.Y. d: Feb 22, 1987

The David Susskind Show (talk)
.... host (1958–1987)

Emmy Awards: Producer, Best Dramatic Program, for *The Ages of Man* (1966), *Death of a Salesman* (1967), *ABC Theatre:* "Eleanor and Franklin" (1976) and *ABC Theatre:* "Eleanor and Franklin, The White House Years" (1977)

Allan Sherman once sang, to the tune of "Little David Play On Your Harp": "Little David Susskind, *shut up!*"

The reference was to Susskind's famous talk show, which, as originally conceived, was called *Open End* and was just that—it continued on and on into the night until the participants were exhausted and went home. Or perhaps it was a reference to his propensity to make headlines by constantly lambasting television for its poor quality, while at the same time selling it dozens of programs.

Susskind was certainly one of TV's originals. A small, wiry hustler with boundless energy, he began as a talent agent in Hollywood after World War II, then set up his own production company, Talent Associates, in 1948. Sensing the potential of TV, he moved immediately into the medium and soon became a major independent packager and producer of shows—including, it should be said, some of the finest dramas and documentaries ever telecast (he was always associated with quality TV). Among the series with which he was associated were *Mr. Peepers, Philco Playhouse, The DuPont Show of the Week, Armstrong Circle Theatre, Play of the Week, East Side/West Side, Get Smart, The Good Guys, Mr. Broadway,* and *People.* In addition, David produced scores of individual plays, specials, and TV movies and continued quite active into the 1980s—though his greatest achievements were in the '50s and '60s.

David's constant barrage of opinion and criticism may have made him many enemies, but there is no denying his prolific contributions to the medium. Still, watching TV made him nervous. "If it's bad, I hate it," he said. "If it's good I can't stand it because it isn't mine."

SUTORIUS, JAMES—actor

The Bob Crane Show (com)
.... Jerry Mallory (1975)
Andros Targets (drama)
.... Mike Andros (1977)

SUTTON, FRANK—actor
b: Oct 23, 1923, Clarksville, Tenn. d: Jun 28, 1974

Gomer Pyle, U.S.M.C. (com)
.... Sgt. Vince Carter (1964–69)
The Jim Nabors Hour (var)
.... regular (1969–71)

Gruff, crew-cut actor who became most famous as *Gomer Pyle*'s ever-frustrated sergeant, in the 1960s. He had been active on television since the early '50s, when he appeared on such series as *Captain Video* and *Tom Corbett, Space Cadet*. Later, in 1960–61, he was a regular on daytime's *The Secret Storm*.

SUTTON, GRADY—actor
b: Apr 5, 1908, Chattanooga, Tenn.

The Pruitts of Southampton (com)
.... Sturgis, the butler (1966–67)

Plump character comedian adept at simple-minded yokels and flustered desk clerks. He has done a great deal of TV work.

SUTTON, HORACE—

Who's the Boss? (quiz)...... panelist (1954)

SUTTON, LISA—actress

Hill Street Blues (police)
.... Off. Robin Tataglia (1983–)

SUZARI MARIONETTES, THE—

The Singing Lady (child)
.... regulars (1948–50)

SUZUKI, PAT—actress, singer
b: 1931, Cressey, Calif.

Mr. T and Tina (com) .... Michi (1976)

Asian-American actress best known as the star of the 1958 Broadway musical *The Flower Drum Song*.

SVENSON, BO—actor
b: Feb 13, 1941, Goteborg, Sweden

Here Come the Brides (adv)
.... Big Swede (1968–70)
Walking Tall (police)
.... Sheriff Buford Pusser (1981)

SWAIM, CASKEY—actor
b: Jan 11, Lexington, N.C.

Project U.F.O. (drama)
.... Staff Sgt. Harry Fitz (1978–79)

SWAN, MICHAEL—actor
b: Jun 11, Palo Alto, Calif.

Stop Susan Williams (drama)
.... Jack Schoengarth (1979)

SWARTZ, TONY—actor

Battlestar Galactica (sci fi)
.... Flight Sgt. Jolly (1978–79)

SWASEY, NIKKI—actress

Diff'rent Strokes (com)
.... Lisa Hayes (1982–83)

SWAYZE, JOHN CAMERON—newscaster
b: Apr 4, 1906, Wichita, r: Atchison, Kansas City, Kan.

Who Said That? (quiz)... panelist (1948–51)
Camel News Caravan (news)
.... anchorman (1948–56)
Armstrong Circle Theatre (drama)
.... host/narrator (1955–57)
The Steve Allen Show (var)
.... regular (1957–58)
ABC Evening News (news)
.... anchorman (1960)

Television's first superstar news anchorman, and the first to popularize such news catchphrases as the cheery "And a good evening to you" (his opening) and "Glad we could get together" (close). Swayze was really more of a newsreader than a field reporter, but his crisp, precise diction and his natty appearance (he always wore a boutonniere) made him instantly recognizable.

John originally intended to become an actor but soon diverted into newswriting for the Kansas City *Journal* (c. 1930). He was assigned to read the news on the paper's radio station—such work was considered beneath the dignity of the more experienced reporters—and eventually became a full-time Kansas City newscaster. NBC began using him on network radio in 1947 and in the following year assigned him to its principal TV evening newscast,

The Camel News Caravan. At first he was only heard, since the program was produced in the style of a movie newsreel, but later he appeared on camera.

News and entertainment were closely allied in those days, and John appeared on panel shows and also hosted a Sunday afternoon documentary series, *Watch the World*, with his wife and two children (later, the family joined him in a syndicated travelogue series called *Sightseeing with the Swayzes*). After he was replaced on NBC's evening newscast by Huntley-Brinkley in 1956, he appeared on a number of varied series and switched briefly to ABC as its anchorman. He was best known in later years for his 20-year role as commercial spokesman for Timex watches.

SWAYZE, PATRICK—actor, dancer
b: Aug 18, 1954, Houston, Texas

Renegades (police) . . . . Bandit (1983)
North and South (drama)
. . . . Orry Main (1985)

SWEENEY, BOB—actor

My Favorite Husband (com)
. . . . Gillmore Cobb (1953–55)
Our Miss Brooks (com)
. . . . Mr. Oliver Munsey (1955–56)
The Brothers (com) . . Gilmore Box (1956–57)
Fibber McGee and Molly (com)
. . . . Fibber McGee (1959–60)

A small, balding comic actor from radio, where, in the late '40s, he formed a comedy team with Hal March. Sweeney later became a successful TV producer-director, working behind-the-scenes on such series as *Hawaii Five-O, The Love Boat, The Andros Targets, Dynasty,* and *Fantasy Island.*

SWEENEY, JOE—actor
b: c. 1890 d: 1963

Wesley (com) . . . . Grandpa (1949)

SWEENEY, ROBERT—actor

The Life of Riley (com) . . . Dangle (1953–58)

SWEENEY, TERRY—writer, comedian
b: Mar 23, 1960, St. Albans, N.Y.

NBC's Saturday Night Live (var)
. . . . regular (1985–86)

SWEENEY, JOAN—actress

AfterMASH (com) . . . . . Nurse Parker (1984)

SWEET, DOLPH—actor
b: Jul 18, 1920, New York City, N.Y. d: May 8, 1985

The Trials of O'Brien (drama)
. . . . Lt. Garrison (1965–66)
When the Whistle Blows (com)
. . . . Norm Jenkins (1980)
Gimme a Break (com)
. . . . Chief Carl Kanisky (1981–85)

A burly, gruff actor who started out as a drama teacher in the '40s and eventually became head of the drama department at Barnard College, where he taught for 12 years. Dolph turned to Broadway stage work in the '60s and only gradually made his way into television with supporting roles in TV movies and series of the '60s and '70s. Mostly, he appeared in dramas; from 1967–68 he was a regular on daytime's *The Edge of Night* and from 1972–77 on *Another World* (as Gil, a role originated by the similarly proportioned Charles Durning). In the late '70s Dolph began playing comedy, which led to his last and most famous role, on *Gimme a Break*.

SWEET, KATIE—juvenile actress
b: 1957

Hank (com) . . . . Tina Dearborn (1965–66)

SWENSON, INGA—actress
b: Dec 29, 1932, Omaha, Neb.

Benson (com) . . . . Gretchen Kraus (1979–86)
North and South (drama)
. . . . Maude Hazard (1985)

Inga Swenson, the Teutonic terror on *Benson,* had a successful career on Broadway before moving West to sitcom land. Born of Swedish and German parents, she came to New York in the early '50s to study at the Actor's Studio and immediately began playing Shakespeare on the New York stage. In the early '60s she scored a bona fide hit in the musical *110 in the Shade* (she is a lyric soprano).

Simultaneously with her stage career,

Inga began to appear in '50s TV plays, on *Playhouse 90, The DuPont Show of the Month, Hallmark Hall of Fame,* and similar series. During the '60s and '70s she was seen occasionally in *The Defenders, Medical Center,* and *Bonanza* (as Hoss's mother, Inga, in flashbacks). In the late 1970s her TV career remained low-key; if you looked closely you saw her in the miniseries *Testimony of Two Men,* or playing turn-of-the-century musical star Nora Bayes in *Ziegfeld: The Man and His Women.* The role that made a difference was a guest part on *Soap,* where she portrayed Ingrid, the Swedish maid who ran off with Jessica's brother. Ingrid was such a hit that Swenson was carried over into the spin-off series *Benson,* as the tart-tongued foil for Robert Guillaume.

SWENSON, KARL—actor
b: Jul 23, 1908, Brooklyn, N.Y. d: Oct 8, 1978

Little House on the Prairie (adv)
.... Lars Hanson (1974–78)

A very busy actor in radio during the '30s and '40s, best known as the whimsical inventor of impractical gadgets, Lorenzo Jones.

SWIFT, SUSAN—actress
b: Jul 21, 1964, Houston, Texas

The Chisholms (wes)
.... Annabelle Chisholm (1979)
The Chisholms (wes)
.... Mercy Hopwell (1980)

Susan's character died in an Indian attack during the original *Chisholms* miniseries, but the producers liked her so much they brought her back for the subsequent series.

SWIRE, SYDNEY—actress
b: Apr 13, Los Angeles r: Westchester County, N.Y.

Beacon Hill (drama)........ Eleanor (1975)

SWIT, LORETTA—actress
b: Nov 4, 1937, Passaic, N.J.

*M*A*S*H* (com)
.... Maj. Margaret Houlihan (1972–83)

Emmy Awards: Best Supporting Actress in a Comedy Series, for *M*A*S*H* (1980, 1982)

"Hot Lips" Houlihan went through an interesting metamorphosis during the 11-year run of *M*A*S*H,* progressing from a rigid, regulation-obsessed, secretly sex-starved head nurse to a woman with much more dimension and feeling (she was not even called "Hot Lips" in later years). Much of this change was due to actress Loretta Swit, who didn't want her character to become a one-note stereotype. The role represented the culmination of 15 years of show-biz struggle for Loretta. She had spent most of the 1960s touring in regional theater, until arriving in 1969 in Hollywood, where she won guest roles in *Hawaii Five-O, Gunsmoke, Mannix,* and other series. Then came "Hot Lips."

During and since the long run of *M*A*S*H,* Loretta played guest parts on numerous other series and in TV movies. Among her TV films have been *The Hostage Heart; Mirror, Mirror; Friendships; Secrets and Lies; Cagney & Lacey* (the original pilot, as Chris Cagney); *Games Mother Never Taught You,* and *The Execution.* She has won several awards from the Polish-American Congress for her enhancement of the image of Polish-Americans.

SWOFFORD, KEN—actor
b: Jul 25, DuQuoin, Ill.

Switch (drama)........ Lt. Griffin (1975–76)
The Adventures of Ellery Queen (drama)
.... Frank Flannigan (1975–76)
Rich Man, Poor Man—Book II (drama)
.... Al Barber (1976–77)
Eddie Capra Mysteries (drama)
.... J. J. Devlin (1978–79)
Fame (drama)
.... Quentin Morloch (1983–85)

A burly, sandy-haired supporting actor who often plays a boss or important contact. He has been active on television since the '60s and was seen often on *Gunsmoke, Petrocelli,* and *The Rockford Files.*

SWOPE, TRACY BROOKS—actress

The Last Convertible (drama)
.... Liz Baynor (1979)

SYDES, CAROL—juvenile actress
b: c. 1944

The New Loretta Young Show (drama)
.... Binkie Massey (1962–63)

SYKES, BRENDA—black actress
b: Jun 25, c. 1949, Shreveport, La.

Ozzie's Girls (com)
..... Brenda (Jennifer) MacKenzie (1973)
Executive Suite (drama)
.... Summer Johnson (1976–77)

SYLVAN, PAUL—actor
b: Jul 29, New York City, N.Y.

Busting Loose (com)
.... Woody Warshaw (1977)

SYLVERN, HANK—orchestra leader
b: Mar 26, 1908, Brooklyn, N.Y. d: Jul 4, 1964

Jane Froman's U.S.A. Canteen (var)
.... orch. leader (1953–54)

SYLVESTER, HAROLD—black actor
Wheels (drama)....... Rollie Knight (1978)
Walking Tall (police)
.... Dep. Aaron Fairfax (1981)
Today's F.B.I. (police)
.... Dwayne Thompson (1981–82)
Mary (com)....... Harry Dresden (1985–86)

SYLVESTER, WILLIAM—actor
b: Jan 31, 1922, Oakland, Calif.

Gemini Man (adv).. Leonard Driscoll (1976)

SYMONDS, ROBERT—actor
b: Dec 1, 1926, Bristow, Okla.

The Blue and the Gray (drama)
.... Gen. Robert E. Lee (1982)

SZARABAJKA, KEITH—actor
The Equalizer (drama)
.... Mickey Kostmayer (1986–)

T

T, MR.—black actor
b: May 21, 1952, Chicago, Ill.

The A-Team (adv)
.... Sgt. Bosco "B.A." Baracus (1983–)

Few actors have traveled so far on a sneer as Lawrence Tero*, onetime wrestler and product of the Chicago tenements. The youngest of 11 children, he was raised by his single mother on welfare and determined early in life to make something of himself. He was a three-time city wrestling champion and star football player in high school, but a knee injury aborted a planned tryout with the Green Bay Packers. T joined the army as a military policeman, then became a celebrity bodyguard in the mid '70s—employed by the likes of Muhammed Ali, Leon Spinks (they need bodyguards?), LeVar Burton, and Michael Jackson.

Viewers caught an early glimpse of T as the winner of the "Toughest Bouncer" contest on *Games People Play* in 1980, but his major acting break was as the growling, sneering Clubber Lang, Sylvester Stallone's adversary in the movie *Rocky III* (1982). Shortly thereafter, he brought the same fierce presence—a bit toned down for TV (B.A. was afraid of flying and loved little kids)—to the hit series *The A-Team*.

TA-TANISHA—actress

Room 222 (drama) .... Pam (1970–72)

TABORI, KRISTOFFER—actor
b: Aug 4, 1955**, Los Angeles, Calif.

Seventh Avenue (drama)
.... Al Blackman (1977)
Chicago Story (drama)
.... Dr. Max Carson (1982)

A young actor in movies since the age of five, who has appeared in TV plays and episodes of dramatic series. Among his TV films: *QB VII, Black Beauty, Seventh Avenue,* and *Brave New World.* He is the son of director Don Siegel and actress Viveca Lindfors.

*Also given as Tureaud.
**Some sources give 1952.

TACKER, FRANCINE—actress
b: Sep 15, Flushing, N.Y.

The Paper Chase (drama)
.... Elizabeth Logan (1978–79)
Dallas (drama)
.... Jenna Wade (occasional) (1980)
Goodtime Girls (com)
.... Camille Rittenhouse (1980)
Oh Madeline (com)
.... Annie McIntyre (1983–84)
Empire (com) .... Amelia Lapidus (1984)

Statuesque blonde who had her first TV exposure as an aspiring lawyer in *The Paper Chase.*

TACKITT, WESLEY—actress

Margie (com) ...... Nora Clayton (1961–62)

TAEGER, RALPH—actor
b: Jul 30, 1936, Richmond Hill, N.Y.

Klondike (adv) .... Mike Halliday (1960–61)
Acapulco (adv)...... Patrick Malone (1961)
Hondo (wes).......... Hondo Lane (1967)

This "strong, silent type" was a hot property in the 1960s, but a hit series somehow eluded him, despite three tries and many guest appearances. Richard Lamparski, in one of his *Whatever Became of . . .* books, reports that Taeger now makes his living as a wholesaler of firewood in north-central California.

TAILGATE SEVEN, THE—dixieland combo

Chicago Jazz (music) .... regulars (1949)

TAKAMATSU, HIDEO—actor

Shogun (drama) .... Buntaro (1980)

TAKAYO—actress

The Devlin Connection (drama)
.... Mrs. Watanabe (1982)

TAKEI, GEORGE—actor
b: Apr 20, 1940, Los Angeles, Calif.

Star Trek (sci fi) .... Sulu (1966–69)

George Takei, the loyal helmsman of the starship Enterprise, had previously played

roles on a number of series of the 1960s—
I Spy, The John Forsythe Show, and *Perry
Mason* among them. His subsidiary part
on *Star Trek* was by far the biggest thing
that ever happened to him.

TALBOT, GLORIA—actress
b: Glendale, Calif.

The Life and Legend of Wyatt Earp (wes)
.... Abbie Crandall (1955–56)

TALBOT, LYLE—actor
b: Feb 8, 1902, Pittsburgh, Pa.

The Bob Cummings Show (com)
.... Paul Fonda (1955–59)
The Adventures of Ozzie & Harriet (com)
.... Joe Randolph (1956–66)

TALBOT, NITA—actress
b: Aug 8, 1930, New York City, N.Y.

Joe & Mabel (com)
.... Mabel Spooner (1956)
The Thin Man (drama)
.... Beatrice Dane (1958–59)
The Jim Backus Show (com)
.... Dora (1960)
Here We Go Again (com)
.... Judy Evans (1973)
Supertrain (drama) ...... Rose Casey (1979)

Wisecracking blonde comic actress, much
seen on television from the early '50s to the
'80s. She received an Emmy nomination for
one of her several appearances on *Hogan's
Heroes* in the 1960s.

TALBOT, STEPHEN—juvenile actor
b: c. 1948

Leave It to Beaver (com)
.... Gilbert Bates (1959–63)

The son of actor Lyle Talbot.

TALBOTT, MICHAEL—actor
b: Feb 2, 1955, Waverly, Iowa

Miami Vice (police)
.... Det. Stan Switek (1984–)

TALENT, ZIGGY—singer
b: Jun 25, 1925, Manchester, N.H.

The Vaughn Monroe Show (var)
.... regular (1950–51)

TALKINGTON, BRUCE—actor

Billy (com)......... Arthur Milliken (1979)

TALL TIMBER TRIO, THE—

Talent Varieties (var) ...... regulars (1955)
Ozark Jubilee (music).... regulars (1957–60)
Five Star Jubilee (var) ..... regulars (1961)

TALMAN, WILLIAM—actor
b: Feb 4, 1915, Detroit, Mich. d: Aug 30, 1968

Perry Mason (drama)
.... Hamilton Burger (1957–66)

Talman was the gaunt, unsmiling district
attorney who seemed to be television's
most frustrated man—he lost every case to
Perry Mason! That didn't phase Talman
the actor, however, since the steady work
(even with egg on his face) was welcome.
The actor had managed only small stage
roles when he was in his twenties and did
not make it into films until his midthirties,
also in minor roles (mostly villains). He
turned up periodically on TV dramas during the 1950s, on *Lux Video Theatre, Climax,* etc., before *Perry Mason* rescued his
career.

After *Perry Mason* finally ended, Talman played a few guest roles, on *The Invaders* and *The Wild Wild West,* but his
last appearance was unquestionably his
most meaningful. When the actor, who had
long been a heavy smoker, learned that he
had lung cancer he filmed a short message
to be shown only after his death—urging
others to stop smoking. It was widely telecast after he died.

TALTON, ALIX—actress

My Favorite Husband (com)
.... Myra Cobb/Shepard (1953–55)

A former Miss Georgia (in the 1930s).

TALTON, REEDY—actor

Stanley (com)........... Marvin (1956–57)

TAMBOR, JEFFREY—actor
b: Jul 8, San Francisco, Calif.

The Ropers (com)
.... Jeffrey P. Brookes III (1979–80)
Hill Street Blues (police)
.... Alan Wachtel (1981–)

9 to 5 (com)........... Franklin Hart (1982)
Mr. Sunshine (com).. Prof. Paul Stark (1986)

TANDY, JESSICA—actress
b: Jun 7, 1909, London, England

The Marriage (com) .... Liz Marriott (1954)

This dramatic actress is a leading light of the Broadway stage, best known for crafty, intelligent, or neurotic roles. She appeared on a number of television playhouse series during the 1950s—*Studio One* and *Omnibus* among them—but was rarely seen on TV after that. Since 1942 she has been married to, and has often appeared with, actor Hume Cronyn. They played husband and wife in the 1954 summer comedy series *The Marriage.*

TANNEN, STEVE—actor
240-Robert (adv) .... Kestenbaum (1979–81)

TANNEN, WILLIAM—actor
b: 1911, New York City, N.Y. d: Dec 2, 1976

The Life and Legend of Wyatt Earp (wes)
.... Dep. Hal Norton (1957–58)

TANNER, GORDON—British actor
Saber of London (drama)
.... Pete Paulson (1958)

TAPLEY, COLIN—actor
b: 1911

Saber of London (drama)
.... Insp. Parker (1957–60)

TAPP, GORDIE—
Hee Haw (var)............. regular (1969–)

TARI, LE—actor
Diff'rent Strokes (com)
.... Mr. Ted Ramsey (1981–85)

TARKENTON, FRAN—sportscaster, host
b: Feb 3, 1940, Richmond, Va.

Monday Night Football (sport)
.... announcer (1979–82)
That's Incredible (aud par)... host (1980–84)

Fran is one of the sports superstars who found a comfortable home on television after his playing days were over. He first gained fame on the gridiron during his years at the University of Georgia, which he led to the Orange Bowl in 1959, and then, from 1961–1979 went on to an extraordinary 18-year career with the Minnesota Vikings and the New York Giants. He was the top-ranked passer in NFL history.

Fran joined NBC Sports in the mid-1970s, reporting on off-season events, including gymnastics and golf. He later switched to ABC, where his amiable Southern drawl provided a friendly counterpoint to Howard Cosell in the *Monday Night Football* booth. Fran has also become a highly successful businessman; a consulting firm he founded in 1972 is now a worldwide operation.

TARR, JUSTIN—actor
The Rat Patrol (adv)
.... Pvt. Tully Pettigrew (1966–68)

TARSES, JAY—actor, writer
b: Jul 3, 1939, Baltimore, Md.

Make Your Own Kind of Music (var)
.... regular (1971)
Open All Night (com)
.... Off. Steve (1981–82)
The Duck Factory (com)
.... Marty Fenneman (1984)

Emmy Award: Best Writing for a Variety Series, for *The Carol Burnett Show* (1973)

Jay is half of one of television's hottest comedy writing teams, (Tom) Patchett and Tarses. They met while both were working in the advertising department of the Armstrong Cork Company in the '60s, formed a stand-up comedy team in 1966, and began playing clubs. A chance meeting with Carl Reiner on a talk show led to Reiner's helping them crash Hollywood. Both have appeared occasionally on-screen, but their main success has come as writers for such series as *The Carol Burnett Show, The Bob Newhart Show,* and *The Tony Randall Show.*

TATA, JOEY—actor
No Time for Sergeants (com)
.... Pvt. Mike Neddick (1964–65)

TATE, CHARLES—choreographer

Holiday Hotel (var) .... dancers (1951)

TATE, NICK—actor

Space 1999 (sci fi)
.... Capt. Alan Carter (1975–77)

TATE, SHARON—actress
b: 1943, Dallas, Texas d: Aug 9, 1969

The Beverly Hillbillies (com)
.... Janet Trego (1963–65)

The ill-fated blonde beauty who was the most famous victim in one of Hollywood's most sensational murders—the Manson "cult killings," which were later dramatized in the TV movie *Helter Skelter*. Her only major TV role was on *The Beverly Hillbillies,* where she played a shapely bank secretary. She was in real life the bride of filmmaker Roman Polanski.

TATUM, VERA—actress

The Laytons (com) .... regular (1948)

TAYBACK, VIC—actor
b: Jan 6, 1930, Brooklyn, N.Y.

Griff (drama)
.... Capt. Barney Marcus (1973–74)
Khan (drama)........... Lt. Gubbins (1975)
Alice (com) .... Mel Sharples (1976–85)

A gruff-heavyset supporting actor who is best known as the hash-house owner in both the movie and television versions of *Alice* (for years his entire wardrobe seemed to consist of a white T-shirt and rolled-back sailor cap). Vic had a lengthy TV career before that, however, beginning in 1958 and including guest appearances on series ranging from *MacKenzie's Raiders* in the '50s to *Star Trek, Bonanza, The Rookies, Emergency, Barney Miller, Supertrain,* and many others. He has also appeared in several dozen stage plays and films in supporting roles.

**TAYLOR, BILLY—black orchestra
   leader**
b: Jul 21, 1921, Greenville, N.C.

The David Frost Show (talk)
.... orch. leader (1969–72)

Pianist and a leading figure in the jazz world.

TAYLOR, BUCK—actor
b: May 13, 1938, Hollywood, Calif.

The Monroes (wes)
.... John (Brad) Bradford (1966–67)
Gunsmoke (wes)
.... Newly O'Brien (1967–75)

The burly young gunsmith on *Gunsmoke.* An expert gymnast, former stuntman, and true lover of the Old West, he had been playing minor roles on television since 1958. *Gunsmoke* was his favorite role. "I think I've got one o' the better jobs in Hollywood," he drawled in 1973. "I don't work very hard, I'm not overexposed, and I'm not typed. If I never did anything but *Gunsmoke* I'd be happy." Buck was the son of cowboy actor Dub Taylor, and the husband of onetime juvenile actress Judy Nugent.

TAYLOR, CALEB—actor

V (movie) (sci fi) .... Jason (1983)

TAYLOR, CHARLES—actor

Dalton's Code of Vengeance (adv)
.... David Dalton (1986)

TAYLOR, CLARICE—black actress
b: Sep 20, 1927, Buckingham County, Va.

Nurse (drama) .... Nurse Bailey (1981)

TAYLOR, CLIFF—actor

Lash of the West (wes)
.... Flapjack (1952–53)

TAYLOR, DUB—actor
b: 1908

Casey Jones (adv)
.... Willie Sims (1957–58)
Please Don't Eat the Daisies (com)
.... Ed Hewley (1965–66)
Hee Haw (var)........... regular (1985–)

Dumpy, grizzled character actor, in films since the 1930s. In later years he was best known as the sidekick of various B-movie western heroes. Real name: Walter Clarence Taylor, Jr.

TAYLOR, ELIZABETH—actress
b: Feb 27, 1932, London, England

North and South (drama)
.... Madame Conti (1985)

A Hollywood legend whose television acting appearances have been few, highly publicized, and rather eclectic. Among them: an episode of *Here's Lucy* in 1970, with Richard Burton and the couple's huge diamond ring, and the TV movies *Divorce His/Divorce Hers* (1973, also with Burton), *Victory at Entebbe* (1976), *Between Friends* (1983), and *Malice in Wonderland* (1985, as Louella Parsons). She has also been seen in a few specials, ranging from *Elizabeth Taylor in London* in 1963 to Bob Hope's 60th Anniversary of the NFL special in 1981. In 1984, the great lady paid a visit to the prime time series *Hotel,* and in 1985 she was a bordello madam in *North and South.* Perhaps her most memorable TV appearance, though, was her week on the top-rated daytime soap opera *General Hospital* in November 1981, as the glamorous and evil Helena Cassadine, who was out to sabotage the wedding of Luke and Laura. Miss Taylor apparently enjoyed the lark, as she turned up two years later on another soap, *All My Children*—this time as a charwoman!
Biographies: take your pick.

TAYLOR, FORREST—actor
b: 1883 d: Feb 19, 1965

This Is the Life (drama)
.... Grandpa Fisher (1952–56)
Man Without a Gun (wes)
.... Doc Brannon (1957–59)

TAYLOR, GRANT—actor

UFO (sci fi) .... Gen. Henderson (1970)

TAYLOR, HOLLAND—actress
b: Jan 14, Philadelphia, Pa.

Beacon Hill (drama)
.... Marilyn Gardiner (1975)
Bosom Buddies (com)
.... Ruth Dunbar (1980–82)
Me and Mom (drama)
.... Zena Hunnicutt (1985)

Soap opera actress of the '70s (*Somerset, The Edge of Night*), who later blossomed into comedy.

TAYLOR, JOAN—actress
b: c. 1928, Geneva, Ill.

The Rifleman (wes)
.... Miss Milly Scott (1960–62)

TAYLOR, JOSH—actor
b: Sep 25, Princeton, Ill.

Riker (police) .... Frank Riker (1981)
Valerie (com) ...... Michael Hogan (1986–)

Easygoing actor who played a busted cop on *Riker,* and an often absent pilot/husband on *Valerie.* He is probably better known as nice guy Chris Kostichek on daytime's *Days of Our Lives.*

TAYLOR, JUD—actor, director
b: Feb 25, 1940

Dr. Kildare (drama)
.... Dr. Thomas Gerson (1961–62)

A minor actor of the '50s and '60s, who went on to become one of TV's major directors of drama series (including several episodes of *Star Trek*) and more than twenty TV movies.

TAYLOR, JUNE—choreographer
b: Chicago, Ill.

The Ed Sullivan Show (var)
.... dancers (1948–71)
Broadway Spotlight (var) ... dancers (1949)
Cavalcade of Stars (var) . dancers (1950–52)
The Jackie Gleason Show (var)
.... dancers (1952–55)
Stage Show (var) .... dancers (1954–56)
The Jackie Gleason Show (var)
.... dancers (1956–59)
The Jackie Gleason Show (var)
.... dancers (1962–70)
The Dom DeLuise Show (var)
.... dancers (1968)

Emmy Award: Best Choreography, for *The Jackie Gleason Show* (1954)

TAYLOR, KATHY—

The Roy Rogers & Dale Evans Show (var)
.... regular (1962)

TAYLOR, KEITH—juvenile actor

McKeever & the Colonel (com)
.... Tubby (1962–63)

TAYLOR, KENT—actor
b: May 11, 1907*, Nashua, Iowa d: Apr 11, 1987

Boston Blackie (drama)
.... Boston Blackie (1951–53)
The Rough Riders (wes)
.... Capt. Jim Flagg (1958–59)

A slick B movie actor with a pencil-thin mustache, who carved out a nice living via two popular syndicated series of the 1950s. He was not seen much after that, although he did turn up (with a host of other TV old-timers) in the 1974 TV movie *The Phantom of Hollywood*. He was in films from 1931 to the early 1970s.

TAYLOR, MARC L.—actor
b: Oct 25, Houston, Texas

House Calls (com)
.... Conrad Peckler (1980–82)

TAYLOR, MARC SCOTT—scientist, actor
b: 1949

Quincy, M.E. (police)
.... Marc (1978–83)

A bona fide young forensic scientist, hired by Jack Klugman to ensure authenticity in *Quincy*'s lab scenes. In addition to serving as a technical advisor for the series (he came well-equipped, having solved several real-life murders for the L.A. coroner's office), Marc was given an on-camera role during the series' later seasons. Among other things, he could deliver a line like "Wait a sec, Dr. Quincy, this material shows an ultraviolet absorption rate of 280 nanometers—could it possibly be proteinacious?" as if he knew what it meant.

TAYLOR, MARY—
Hee Haw (var).......... regular (1969–70)

TAYLOR, MESHACH—actor
Buffalo Bill (com) .... Tony (1983–84)

TAYLOR, NANCY—
Hee Haw (var).......... regular (1981–82)

*Some sources give 1906.

TAYLOR, NATHANIEL—black actor
b: Mar 31, 1938, St. Louis, Mo.

Sanford and Son (com)
.... Rollo Larson (1972–77)
Sanford (com)....... Rollo Larson (1980–81)
The Redd Foxx Show (com). Jim-Jam (1986)

TAYLOR, RENÉE—writer, actress
b: Mar 19, 1935, New York City, N.Y. r: Miami, Fla.

The Jack Paar Show (talk)
.... semiregular (1959–62)
Mary Hartman, Mary Hartman (com)
.... Annabelle (1977–78)

Emmy Award: Best Writing for a Comedy Special, for *Acts of Love . . . and Other Comedies* (1973)

A comic actress who is also a successful writer, generally in collaboration with her husband, actor Joseph Bologna. Among other things, she and Bologna created the situation comedy *Calucci's Department*.

TAYLOR, RIP—comedian, host
b: Jan 13, 1934

The Beautiful Phyllis Diller Show (var)
.... regular (1968)
Dean Martin Presents Bobby Darin (var)
.... regular (1972)
The Gong Show (com) ... panelist (1976–80)
The $1.98 Beauty Show (com)
.... host (1978–80)

Portly, walrus-mustached comic, mostly in outrageous roles.

TAYLOR, ROBERT—actor
b: Aug 5, 1911, Filley, Neb. r: Beatrice, Neb. d: Jun 8, 1969

The Detectives, Starring Robert Taylor (police) .... Capt. Matt Holbrook (1959–62)
Death Valley Days (wes) .... host (1966–68)

This darkly handsome Hollywood star had ladies swooning in '30s romances (e.g., *Camille*) before turning to rugged westerns and costume dramas (*Quo Vadis, Ivanhoe*). By the time he made his TV series debut in 1959 in *The Detectives*, he was grim-faced and gimlet-eyed—though the famous "perfect profile" remained. In the series he played a rather humorless, hard-nosed cop, although he was allowed a brief romantic interlude with a police reporter played by his real-life wife-actress Ursula Thiess. (Taylor had previously been married to Barbara Stanwyck.) Aside from a stint as host of *Death Valley Days* and a single TV movie in 1967 (*Return of the Gunfighter*), he did little other TV work.

TAYLOR, ROD—actor

b: Jan 11, 1929, Sydney, Australia

Hong Kong (adv).... Glenn Evans (1960–61)
Bearcats (adv) .... Hank Brackett (1971)
The Oregon Trail (wes)
.... Evan Thorpe (1977)
Masquerade (drama) ... Lavender (1983–84)

Square-jawed, rugged, slightly chunky Australian leading man who was trained as a painter but turned to acting and appeared rather often on TV playhouse series of the late '50s, especially *Playhouse 90*. He did little television in the '60s, when his movie career was booming (*The Birds*, etc.), but returned in the '70s and '80s for several more unsuccessful tries at series stardom. Among his TV movies have been *Powderkeg* (pilot for *The Bearcats*), *A Matter of Wife and Death, Cry of the Innocent,* and *Jacqueline Bouvier Kennedy.*

TAYLOR, RON—cinematographer

b: Mar 8, 1934, Sydney, Australia

Those Amazing Animals (doc)
.... regular (1980–81)

A leading underwater and shark photographer, responsible for NBC's 1971 Saturday morning series *Barrier Reef* as well as for gripping underwater footage in such films as *Blue Water-White Death, Jaws* (I and II), and *Orca.*

TAYLOR, TOM—actor

The Goldbergs (com)
.... Sammy Goldberg (1954–55)

TAYLOR, VALERIE—cinematographer

Those Amazing Animals (doc)
.... regular (1980–81)

Petite blonde wife and co-worker of undersea wizard Ron Taylor; she is an accred-

ited skin-diver and spearfishing champion, and "has no fear of predators of the sea."

TAYLOR, VAUGHN—actor

b: 1910, Boston, Mass. d: Apr 26, 1983

Robert Montgomery Presents (summer) (drama)........ repertory player (1952–54)
Johnny Jupiter (child)
.... Ernest P. Duckweather (1953)

Slight, worried-looking actor who was very active on live television in the late '40s and '50s.

TAYLOR-YOUNG, LEIGH—actress

b: Jan 25, 1944, Washington, D.C. r: Bloomfield Hills, Mich.

Peyton Place (drama)
.... Rachael Welles (1966–67)
The Devlin Connection (drama)
.... Lauren Dane (1982)
The Hamptons (drama)
.... Lee Chadway (1983)

Onetime wife of Ryan O'Neal, with whom she appeared in *Peyton Place.*

TAYRI, ANDRE—choreographer

The Andy Williams Show (var)
.... dancers (1970–71)

TEAL, RAY—actor

b: Jan 12, 1902, Grand Rapids, Mich. d: Apr 2, 1976

Bonanza (wes)
.... Sheriff Roy Coffee (1961–71)

A solidly built, fatherly man with a thick mustache; he looked like the town sheriff, and was, in scores of movies from the '30s to the '70s. In films his lawmen were usually corrupt, but TV, being what it is, made an honest man out of him as the sheriff on *Bonanza.*

TEDROW, IRENE—actress

b: Aug 3, 1907, Denver, Colo.

The Ruggles (com)
.... Margaret Ruggles (1949)
Meet Corliss Archer (com)
.... Mrs. Janet Archer (1952)
Dennis the Menace (com)
.... Mrs. Lucy Elkins (1959–63)

Mr. Novak (drama)
.......................Mrs. Ring (1965)

This veteran actress came to television in the late '40s, after a long career on radio (notably as the mom on *Meet Corliss Archer*). She has been active in the video medium right up through the 1980s. Among her later TV films are *Isabel's Choice* and *Family Secrets*.

TEFKIN, BLAIR—actress

V (movie) (sci fi) .... Robin Maxwell (1983)
V: The Final Battle (miniseries) (sci fi)
.... Robin Maxwell (1984)
V (sci fi)........ Robin Maxwell (1984–85)

TEICHER, ROY—actor

Brothers and Sisters (com). Seymour (1979)

TEMPLE, RENNY—actor

Easy Does It ... Starring Frankie Avalon (var)
.... regular (1976)
The Life and Times of Eddie Roberts (com)
.... Eddie Roberts (1980)

TEMPLE, SHIRLEY—actress
b: Apr 23, 1928, Santa Monica, Calif.

Shirley Temple's Storybook (child)
.... hostess (1958–61)

Hollywood's little sweetheart of the 1930s, an incredibly talented child who entered films at age three and received an Academy Award at six. Her singing, dancing, and sunny disposition brightened the Depression years. By age ten she was already "over the hill" in popularity (though she made some fine films later), and her movie career ended in 1949. Shirley had little involvement with television, appearing in only one series, *Shirley Temple's Storybook,* which consisted of dramatizations (often musical) of classic children's stories. She hosted and sometimes starred in these. The program began as a series of specials in 1958 and then ran more regularly between 1959 and 1961.

During the later 1960s Shirley became active in Republican politics, running unsuccessfully for Congress and then serving as a U.S. representative to the United Nations and U.S. Ambassador to Ghana during the Nixon administration. She then became U.S. Chief of Protocol. She is now known as Shirley Temple Black.

TEMPLETON, ALEC—pianist
b: Jul 4, 1910, Cardiff, Wales d: Mar 28, 1963

It's Alec Templeton Time (music)
............................host (1955)

A famous blind concert pianist of the '30s and '40s, also known for his witty jazz and satirical numbers.

TENDLER, JESSE—juvenile actor
b: Apr 16, 1980, Madison, Wis.

The Ellen Burstyn Show (com)
.... Nick (1986–)

TENNANT, DON—singer, puppeteer

The Carolyn Gilbert Show (music)
.... regular (1950)

TENNANT, VICTORIA—actress
b: Sep 30, 1950*, London, England

The Winds of War (drama)
.... Pamela Tudsbury (1983)
Chiefs (drama)............ Trish Lee (1983)

TENNILLE, TONI—singer, host
b: May 8, 1943, Montgomery, Ala.

The Captain and Tennille (music)
.... cohost (1976–77)

The pretty wife of rock keyboard-artist Daryl Dragon ("The Captain"), with whom she starred in a much-hyped but unsuccessful 1976 variety show. Later, in 1980, Toni hosted her own syndicated daytime talk show, which fared little better.

TENORIO, JOHN, JR.—actor

Nakia (police)............ Half Cub (1974)

TERKEL, STUDS—author, host
b: May 16, 1912, New York City, N.Y.

Stud's Place (var) ..... as himself (1949–52)

TERLESKY, J.T.—actor

Legmen (drama)....... David Taylor (1984)
*Some sources give 1953.

834

TERRELL, STEVEN—actor

Life with Father (com)
.... Clarence Day, Jr. (1954–55)

TERRIO, DENEY—host

Dance Fever (dance) .... host (1979–85)

TERRY, ARLENE AND ARDELLE—
actresses
b: Jun 1931, Hawkinsville, Ga.

Toni Twin Time (var)
.... The Toni Twins (1950)

TERRY, MARY ELLEN—dancer

Scott Music Hall (var).... regular (1952–53)
The Paul Winchell–Jerry Mahoney Show
(var)..................... regular (1953–54)

TERZIEFF, LAURENT—actor
b: Jul 25, 1935, Paris, France

Moses—The Lawgiver (drama)
.... Pharaoh (1975)

TESH, JOHN—sportscaster, host
b: Garden City, N.Y.

Entertainment Tonight (news)
.... host (1986–)

Emmy Award: Best Music Composition for
a Sports Program, for *The World University Games* (1983)

A tall, rugged-looking sports and investigative reporter, with local stations in the
'70s, and CBS in the early '80s. In 1986 he
shifted to entertainment reporting as cohost of *Entertainment Tonight.* He is also
a Juilliard-trained pianist and has composed theme music for various sportscasts.

TESSIER, MICHAEL—actor

Barney Miller (com).... David Miller (1975)

Barney Miller's son, who disappeared from
the series (along with the rest of Barney's
family) early in its run.

TETLEY, WALTER—actor
b: c. 1915 d: Sep 4, 1975

The Bullwinkle Show (cartn)
.... Sherman (voice) (1961–62)

TEWES, LAUREN—actress
b: Oct 28, 1953, Trafford, Pa r: Whittier, Calif.

The Love Boat (com)
.... cruise director Julie McCoy (1977–84)

TEXAS WILDCATS, THE—

The Jimmy Dean Show (var)
.... regulars (1957)

THALER, ROBERT—actor
b: Oct 15, Cedar Rapids, Iowa

Renegades (police) .... Dancer (1983)

THALL, BILL—host

Midwestern Hayride (var) . emcee (1951–54)

THAXTON, LLOYD—host

Showcase '68 (var) .... host (1968)

An Ohio TV personality who had a brief
run of national popularity in the '60s hosting rock music programs and daytime
game shows. His most successful effort
was *The Lloyd Thaxton Show*, a syndicated rock show that premiered in 1964.
Showcase '68 was a network summer talent competition on which the grand prize
winner was the then-new Sly and the Family Stone. Lloyd later went into TV production.

THIBAULT, CONRAD—host, singer
b: Nov 13, 1906*, Northbridge, Mass.

The Jacques Fray Music Room (music)
.... emcee (1949)

THICKE, ALAN—actor, host
b: Mar 1, 1947, Kirkland Lake, Ont., Canada

Thicke of the Night (talk).... host (1983–84)
Growing Pains (com)
.... Jason Seaver (1985–)

Caught one night on *Thicke of the Night*:
Alan: "Your dad was such a great actor,
we're all saddened by his passing."
Keith Carradine: "My father's still
alive."
Alan: "Oh, how's he feeling?"
You've got to hand it to Alan Thicke; the
man has a sense of humor to be able to
*Some sources give 1898.

835

tell stories like that on himself when reminiscing about his disastrous 1983 talk show. It wasn't only inane interviews that killed the much-publicized show that was supposed to topple Johnny Carson from his late-night throne. *Thicke of the Night* was over-hyped, under-produced and a total embarrassment when it debuted. By the time the producers got their act together, the audience had long gone. Thicke himself wrote a hilarious postmortem for *TV Guide* in 1984 (titled "Why I Took the Country by Drizzle—Instead of by Storm"), concluding, "I am now forced to regard the show as a stumbling stone to bigger things."

Before and after that debacle, Alan's career was quite successful. He got his start as a disc jockey, emcee, and comedy writer in his native Canada, appearing on a number of CBC programs; later, he became one of that country's most popular talk show hosts. He first broke into the U.S. market as a writer for the *Lohman and Barkley Show* in Los Angeles, and during the '70s he became one of the top comedy writers for TV specials, including those of Barry Manilow, Flip Wilson, Richard Pryor, Glen Campbell, Kenny Rogers, and Bill Cosby. In the late '70s he was writer-producer of the zany *Fernwood 2-Night* and *America 2-Night* series. Alan's U.S. acting debut was on an episode of *The Love Boat* and was followed by appearances on *Masquerade, Scene of the Crime,* and others. Having survived (and even laughed at) the megaflop *Thicke of the Night,* he finally found series success as the amiable but hip dad on the comedy *Growing Pains.*

Alan is also a rock singer and songwriter and has written the title songs for such shows as *The Facts of Life* and *Diff'rent Strokes.*

THIESS, URSULA—actress
b: May 15, 1924*, Hamburg, Germany

The Detectives, Starring Robert Taylor (police) .... Lisa Bonay (1960–61)

The gorgeous wife of actor Robert Taylor, with whom she appeared on *The Detectives.*

*Some sources give 1929.

THIGPEN, LYNNE—black actress, singer
b: Dec 22, Joliet, Ill.

Love, Sidney (com) .... Nancy (1982–83)
The News Is the News (var) . regular (1983)

THINNES, ROY—actor
b: Apr 6, 1938, Chicago, Ill.

The Long Hot Summer (drama)
.... Ben Quick (1965–66)
The Invaders (sci fi)
.... David Vincent (1967–68)
The Psychiatrist (drama)
.... Dr. James Whitman (1971)
From Here to Eternity (drama)
...... Capt./Maj. Dana Holmes (1979–80)
Falcon Crest (drama)
.... Nick Hogan (1982–83)

A rugged, rather intense actor who seemed to be on his way to major stardom in the '60s, but never quite made it. He broke into acting as a teenager, fresh out of high school, and made his network debut as a juvenile on *DuPont Theater* in 1957. A number of guest appearances followed, including several on *The Untouchables,* before his first continuing role as Dr. Phil Brewer during the first two years of the daytime soap opera *General Hospital* (1963–65). It was a short jump from that to playing the young-stud-just-come-to-town on ABC's *Long Hot Summer;* however, the role for which he is best known was quite different, that of a young architect who discovers the world is being taken over by aliens, on *The Invaders.*

Roy made one more stab at series stardom, as *The Psychiatrist,* then turned mainly to TV movies and miniseries. Among them have been *Code Name: Diamond Head, From Here to Eternity, Scruples,* and *Sizzle.*

THOMA, MICHAEL—actor
b: c. 1927 d: Sep 3, 1982

Eight is Enough (com)
.... Dr. Maxwell (1977–79)
Fame (drama)......... Mr. Crandall (1982)

THOMAS, BETTY—actress
b: Jul 27, 1948, St. Louis, Mo.

Hill Street Blues (police)
.... Off./Sgt. Lucy Bates (1981–)

Emmy Award: Best Supporting Actress in a Drama Series, for *Hill Street Blues* (1985)

A six-foot, one-inch "tough" actress, formerly with Chicago's Second City comedy troupe in the early '70s. She was a regular on the 1976 daytime game show *The Fun Factory,* then played a few supporting roles before landing her most famous part as the leather-jacketed, no-nonsense policewoman on *Hill Street Blues.*

THOMAS, CALVIN—actor
b: c. 1885 d: Sep 26, 1964

One Man's Family (drama)
.... Judge Hunter (1949)

THOMAS, DAMIEN—actor
Shogun (drama) .... Father Alvito (1980)

THOMAS, DANNY—comedian
b: Jan 6, 1914, Deerfield, Mich. r: Toledo, Ohio

All Star Revue (var)
.... alternating host (1950–52)
The Danny Thomas Show (com)
.... Danny Williams (1953–64)
The Danny Thomas Hour (misc)
.... host/star (1967–68)
Make Room for Granddaddy (com)
.... Danny Williams (1970–71)
The Practice (com)
.... Dr. Jules Bedford (1976–77)
I'm a Big Girl Now (com)
.... Dr. Benjamin Douglass (1980–81)

Emmy Award: Best Actor in a Regular Series, for *Make Room for Daddy* (aka *The Danny Thomas Show*) (1954)

Early television was filled with nightclub comics, mostly named Jerry, Joey, Johnny, or something similar; none lasted as long as Danny Thomas, the brash, cigar-puffing, super-sincere family man. Born one of nine children to a Lebanese-American family, he worked for seven years during his teens as a "candy butcher" in a burlesque theater, and the experience convinced him he wanted to be in show business. He started out playing clubs in the '30s, but the going was so tough that at one point, with a wife and baby to support and practically no money, he made a deal with his patron saint: if he made it as an enter-

tainer he would someday build a shrine to St. Jude. Years later Danny did just that, endowing the multimillion dollar St. Jude's Children's Research Hospital in Memphis, Tennessee.

Danny's career slowly gained ground in the 1940s, with radio work and a few movie parts, but when television arrived he was still in the second (or third) rank of personalities. He first tried out his nightclub act on *The All Star Revue,* and bombed. Blasting TV as suitable "only for idiots," he vowed never to return. However, a year later he swallowed his pride and tried again, this time in a family comedy in which he played—what else?—a nightclub entertainer. *Make Room for Daddy* (later renamed *The Danny Thomas Show*) was a substantial hit, running for eleven years on ABC and CBS.

By the early 1960s Danny had branched into production, forming partnerships with Sheldon Leonard and, later, Aaron Spelling. Among the series for which his company was responsible were *The Andy Griffith Show* (whose pilot ran as an episode of *The Danny Thomas Show,* in which Danny stopped off in the little southern town of Mayberry), *The Dick Van Dyke Show, Gomer Pyle, U.S.M.C., The Mod Squad,* and others. Danny's company also produced *The Danny Thomas Hour,* an anthology series in 1967–68 with Danny as host and sometimes star. He also appeared in specials and played scattered guest roles in the '60s and '70s, including several on daughter Marlo's hit series *That Girl.* An attempt to revive *Make Room for Daddy* in 1970 was unsuccessful, as were two subsequent series. In later years Danny was semiretired from acting, puffing on his stogie and managing his vast production empire.

THOMAS, DAVE—writer, comedian
b: May 20, St. Catherines, Ont., Canada

Second City TV (com)
.... Angus Crock/others (1977–81)
SCTV Network 90 (com) .. regular (1981–82)
The New Show (var) .... regular (1984)

Emmy Award: Best Writing for a Comedy Program, for *SCTV Network* (1982)

Dave is best known as half of the McKenzie Brothers, Bob (Rick Moranis) and Doug (Dave), two bozos from the far Canadian north.

THOMAS, DICK—host
b: Sep 4, 1915, Philadelphia, Pa.

Village Barn (var)......... emcee (1948–49)

THOMAS, ERNEST—black actor
b: Mar 26, 1950, Gary, Ind.

What's Happening!! (com)
.... Roger Thomas ("Raj") (1976–79)
What's Happening Now!! (com)
.... Roger Thomas ("Raj") (1985–)

THOMAS, FRANK—actor
b: 1889, St. Joseph, Mo.

Wesley (com)......... Mr. Eggleston (1949)
The Black Robe (aud par).. Judge (1949–50)
Martin Kane, Private Eye (drama)
.... Capt. Burke (1951–52)

The husband of soap opera actress Mona Bruns, and father of Frankie Thomas. The Thomas family was busy indeed on early live television, with dad as the captain on *Martin Kane*, mom as Aunt Emily on *The Brighter Day*, and Frankie as *Tom Corbett, Space Cadet*. Frank and Mona also co-starred as a rural mom and dad (with a different son) on the 1949 comedy *Wesley*.

THOMAS, FRANKIE—actor
b: Apr 9, 1921, New York City, N.Y.

One Man's Family (drama)
.... Cliff Barbour (1949)
A Woman to Remember (drama)
.... Charley Anderson (1949)
Tom Corbett, Space Cadet (child)
.... Tom Corbett (1950–55)

Frankie played juveniles on-screen beginning in the early 1930s, including the role of Nancy Drew's boyfriend Ted in a series of teenage detective films. He was still playing youths in the '50s on television, mostly notably in a five-year run (including daytime) as *Tom Corbett, Space Cadet*. By the time the series left the air in 1955, the "teenager" was 34 years old.

After taking a stab at a youth-oriented daytime soap opera in the mid-1950s (*First Love*), Frankie left acting to concentrate on writing and producing. He also became an expert on bridge and has authored several books on that subject.

THOMAS, HEATHER—actress
b: Sep 8, 1957, Greenwich, Conn. r: California

Co-ed Fever (com)........... Sandi (1979)
The Fall Guy (adv)... Jody Banks (1981–86)

Gorgeous blonde, often seen scantily clad on *The Fall Guy*.

THOMAS, HOWARD—actor

Mary Kay and Johnny (com)
.... Howie (1947–50)

THOMAS, J. ALAN—actor

Domestic Life (com)
.... Jeff, the floor manager (1984)

THOMAS, JAY—actor
b: Jul 12, Kermit, Texas r: New Orleans, La.

Mork & Mindy (com)
.... Remo DaVinci (1979–81)

THOMAS, JOHN JOSEPH—juvenile actor
b: Nov 9, 1964, Arcadia, Calif.

Young Dan'l Boone (adv)
.... Peter Dawes (1977)

THOMAS, LOWELL—newscaster, host
b: Apr 6, 1892, Woodington, Ohio d: Aug 29, 1981

High Adventure with Lowell Thomas (doc)
.... host (1964)

This legendary commentator and adventurer was better known on radio than on TV, although he was seen periodically. He was one of the first major newscasters to appear on experimental television in 1939–40; his later video efforts were mostly travelogues to exotic places, packaged in a series of specials in the late 1950s (rerun during the summer of '64 as *High Adventure*) and in the syndicated *World of Lowell Thomas* in 1966.

Lowell was also a very successful businessman. He was chairman of the Cinerama Corporation and narrated its early exhibition films; and was a co-founder of Capital Cities Broadcasting Corp., one of the largest owners of TV and radio stations across the U.S. (This was the company that bought the ABC network in 1985.) He was also a prolific author. Among his 54 books was his autobiography, *Good Evening, Everybody* (1976).

THOMAS, MARLO—actress

b: Nov 21, 1938*, Detroit, Mich. r: Los Angeles, Calif.

The Joey Bishop Show (com)
.... Stella Barnes (1961–62)
That Girl (com) ...... Ann Marie (1966–71)

Emmy Awards: Star and Producer, Best Children's Special, for *Free To Be . . . You and Me* (1974); Best Performer in a Children's Program, for *The Body Human: Facts for Girls* (1981); Best Actress in a Special, for *Nobody's Child* (1986)

Danny Thomas's perky, stylish daughter Marlo (born Margaret) plunged into acting as soon as she graduated from college, playing roles in the early '60s in such series as *Dobie Gillis, Zane Grey Theater,* and *Thriller.* An early break was the role of Joey Bishop's TV sister, an aspiring actress, on *The Joey Bishop Show.* However, the part that made her famous was that of Ann Marie (also an aspiring actress) on the first major TV series built around the idea of an "independent woman"—*That Girl.*

Since then, Marlo has been seen only occasionally in TV movies and specials, three of which won her Emmy Awards. She has also been active as a producer; in 1984 she produced and starred in the dramatic TV movie *The Lost Honor of Kathryn Beck.* Marlo is married to talk show host Phil Donahue.

THOMAS, MICHAEL—actor

Combat Sergeant (drama)
.... Sgt. Nelson (1956)

THOMAS, MONA—

see Bruns, Mona

THOMAS, PHILIP MICHAEL—black actor

b: May 26, 1949, Columbus, Ohio r: California

*Some sources give 1934 or 1937.

Miami Vice (police)
.... Det. Ricardo Tubbs (1984–)

"Yesterday's a canceled check, tomorrow's a promissory note, and today is cash in hand" laughs Philip Michael Thomas. He should know; the baby-faced actor bumped around show business for more than 15 years, playing small roles on TV, stage *(Hair),* and in minor films *(Black Fist; Sparkle)* before he suddenly hit it big in the mid-1980s with the smash-hit cop show *Miami Vice.* He enjoyed the sudden notoriety and the perks it brought for all they were worth.

Among Thomas's TV movies (during his "canceled check" days in the '70s) are *Toma, The Beasts Are on the Streets, This Man Stands Alone,* and *Valentine.*

THOMAS, RICHARD—actor

b: Jun 13, 1951, New York City, N.Y.

1,2,3, Go (child) .... regular (1961–62)
The Waltons (drama)
.... John Boy Walton (1972–77)
Roots: The Next Generations (drama)
.... Jim Warner (1979)

Emmy Award: Best Actor in a Drama Series, for *The Waltons* (1973)

Richard Thomas is the son of balletdancer parents who introduced him to acting as a child. In the late 1950s he appeared on Broadway in *Sunrise at Campobello* (1958) and shortly thereafter he made his TV debut in the *Hallmark Hall of Fame* holiday special "The Christmas Tree." During the early '60s, young Richard had roles on series including *Way Out* and *Great Ghost Tales;* in 1961–62 (at age ten) he costarred with Jack Lescoulie in the Sunday evening children's show *1,2,3, Go,* traveling the world on "learning adventures."

Richard was seen principally on daytime soap operas during his teens, including stints on *From These Roots, A Time for Us,* and *As the World Turns.* By the early 1970s he had graduated to prime time series episodes (*Medical Center; Love, American Style; Bonanza*). His first TV movie, *The Homecoming,* led to his most famous role, as super-sincere John Boy on the spin-off series *The Waltons.*

Well aware of the dangers of juvenile stardom, Richard has attempted to make the transition to more adult roles. He has appeared in numerous TV movies including *The Red Badge of Courage, All Quiet on the Western Front, Living Proof: The Hank Williams, Jr., Story* (title role), *Johnny Belinda, The Master of Ballantrae* (recreating the role played on-screen by Errol Flynn), and *Getting Married*.

THOMAS, SCOTT—actor

The New Land (adv)
.... Christian Larsen (1974)

THOMERSON, TIM—actor

Cos (var) .... regular (1976)
Quark (com) .... Gene/Jean (1978)
Angie (com)............. Gianni (1979–80)
The Associates (com)
.... Johnny Danko (1979–80)
The Two of Us (com)
.... Reggie Cavanaugh (1981–82)
Gun Shy (com)
.... Theodore Ogilvie (1983)

THOMPSON, BILL—singers

The Eddie Fisher Show (var)
.... singers (1957–58)

THOMPSON, CHARLES—actor

The Aquanauts (Malibu Run) (adv)
.... the captain (1961)

THOMPSON, CHUCK—sportscaster

Prime Time Football (sport)
.... announcer (1954)
Prime Time Football (sport)
.... announcer (1959)

THOMPSON, ERNEST—actor, writer
b: Nov 6, 1950, Bellows Falls, Vt.

Sierra (adv)..... Ranger Matt Harper (1974)
Westside Medical (drama)
.... Dr. Philip Parker (1977)

After acting in TV soap operas (*Somerset*) and prime time series during the 1970s, Thompson went on to greater things as a stage and movie writer. In 1981 he won an Academy Award for his screenplay for *On Golden Pond*.

THOMPSON, HILARY—actress

The Young Rebels (adv)
.... Elizabeth Coates (1970–71)
The Manhunter (drama)
.... Lizabeth Barrett (1974–75)
Operation Petticoat (com)
.... Lt. Betty Wheeler (1978–79)
Number 96 (drama)
.... Sharon St. Clair (1980–81)

THOMPSON, JENN—juvenile actor
b: Dec 13, 1967, New York City, N.Y.

Harper Valley P.T.A. (com)
.... Dee Johnson (1981–82)

THOMPSON, JOANN—actress

M*A*S*H (com)... various nurses (1981–83)

THOMPSON, JOHNNY—singer

Club Seven (music)...... regular (1948–49)

THOMPSON, MARSHALL—actor, writer
b: Nov 27, 1925, Peoria, Ill.

The World of Giants (adv)
.... Mel Hunter (1960)
Angel (com).......... John Smith (1960–61)
Daktari (adv) ... Dr. Marsh Tracy (1966–69)

Lanky, clean-cut actor who turned up rather often in both dramas and comedies during the 1950s, including several appearances on *Science Fiction Theater*. In *World of Giants* he played a six-inch-high spy, but mostly he was cast as an amiable nice guy, as in his most famous role, the veterinarian on *Daktari*. (The "act" was for real—his fellow actors on that series called him "the original Boy Scout.") Marshall has been seen only rarely since then, including a small role in *Centennial* in 1978.

THOMPSON, SADA—actress
b: Sep 27, 1929, Des Moines, Iowa r: Fanwood, N.J.

Family (drama) .. Kate Lawrence (1976–80)

Emmy Award: Best Actress in a Drama Series, for *Family* (1978)

A gentle, motherly woman who is usually cast in just that sort of role. Sada became an actress immediately upon graduation from college in the 1950s and, with her principal career being on the stage, has won many theatrical awards, including the Tony. Onstage she generally appears in high-class dramas, and her early television appearances went along similar lines; e.g., in '70s TV productions of *Sandburg's Lincoln* (as Mrs. Lincoln), *Our Town,* and *The Entertainer,* among others. Although theater remains her first love, she is well-known as the mother on *Family.*

THOMPSON, WESLEY—black actor
b: Oct 2, Chicago, Ill.

He's the Mayor (com)
.... Wardell Halsey (1986)

THOMSON, DORRIE—actress

Operation Petticoat (com)
.... Lt. Ruth Colfax (1977–78)

THOMSON, GORDON—actor
b: Mar 2, 1951*, Ottawa, Canada r: Montreal, Canada

Dynasty (drama)
.... Adam Carrington (1982–)

THOMSON, PATRICIA AYAME—actress

Crazy Like a Fox (drama)
.... Allison Ling (1985–86)

THOR, JEROME—actor
b: 1915, Brooklyn, N.Y.

Foreign Intrigue (drama)
.... Robert Cannon (1951–53)

THORNBURY, BILL—actor

Secrets of Midland Heights (drama)
.... Mark Hudson (1980–81)

THORNE, TERESA—actress

The Vise (Mark Saber) (drama)
.... Judy (1956)

THORNE-SMITH, COURTNEY—actress

Fast Times (com).... Stacy Hamilton (1986)

THORSON, LINDA—actress
b: c. 1947, Toronto, Canada

The Avengers (drama) . Tara King (1968–69)
*Some sources give 1945.

THORSON, RUSSELL—actor
b: c. 1910 d: Jul 6, 1982

One Man's Family (drama)
.... Paul Barbour (1949–52)
The Detectives, Starring Robert Taylor (police) .... Lt. Otto Lindstrom (1959–61)

A radio veteran of the '40s, often heard in mystery series, who played one of the grim-faced cops on *The Detectives.* He later had minor supporting roles in TV movies of the '60s and '70s.

THREE FLAMES, THE—black jazz combo
Tiger Haynes, guitar, b: Dec 13, 1907, St. Croix, Virgin Islands
Roy Testamark, piano, b: St. Croix, Virgin Islands d: 1954
Averill "Rill" Pollard, bass, b: Barbados, d: 1977

The Three Flames Show (music)
.... regulars (1949)

A hip black combo, popular in the 1940s with novelty numbers such as "Open the Door, Richard." They were among the first black performers to have a regular network series. The trio lasted until 1964 (with personnel changes); however, beginning in the '50s, leader Tiger Haynes branched out into a successful career as an actor and dancer in Broadway shows. He later appeared onstage in *Two Gentlemen of Verona* and *The Wiz* (as the Tin Man) as well as in such movies as *All That Jazz* and the 1982 TV film *Benny's Place.*

THRONE, MALACHI—actor

It Takes a Thief (drama)
.... Noah Bain (1968–69)

THULIN, INGRID—actress
b: Jan 27, 1929, Solleften, Sweden

Moses—The Lawgiver (drama)
.... Miriam (1975)

THURMAN, TEDI—actress, model
b: 1928, Midville, Ga.

The Jack Paar Show (talk) ... regular (1957)

THURSTON, CAROL—actress
b: c. 1921 d: 1969

The Life and Legend of Wyatt Earp (wes)
. . . . Emma Clanton (1959–60)

THYSSEN, GRETA—actress

Treasure Hunt (quiz)
. . . . "Pirate Girl" (1957–58)

TICOTIN, RACHEL—actress
b: Nov 1, 1958, New York City, N.Y.

For Love and Honor (drama)
. . . . Cpl. Grace Pavlik (1983)

Hispanic actress and dancer who first came to notice as Paul Newman's heroin-addicted girlfriend in the movie *Fort Apache, The Bronx* in 1981.

TIERNEY, GENE—actress
b: Nov 20, 1920, Brooklyn, N.Y.

Scruples (drama)
. . . . Harriet Toppingham (1980)

Hollywood lovely of the '40s and '50s *(Laura, Leave Her to Heaven),* who suffered a mental breakdown in 1955 and was out of show business for five years; its effects lingered for many years afterward. Her rare TV appearances included a very few series episodes in the '60s (e.g., *The F.B.I.*), the 1969 TV movie *Daughter of the Mind,* and the role of the ruthless fashion editor in *Scruples.* Her autobiography: *Self Portrait* (1979).

TIGAR, KENNETH—actor

The Gangster Chronicles (drama)
. . . . Thomas E. Dewey (1981)

TIGHE, KEVEN—actor
b: Aug 13, 1944, Los Angeles, Calif.

Emergency (drama)
. . . . paramedic Roy DeSoto (1972–77)

TILL, JENNY—actress

The Ugliest Girl in Town (com)
. . . . Sondra Wolston (1968–69)

TILLER, TED—actor

Mr. I Magination (child)
. . . . regular (1949–52)

TILLOTSON, JOHNNY—singer
b: Apr 20, 1938, Jacksonville, Fla.

Gidget (com) . . . . sang theme (1965–66)

TILLSTROM, BURR—puppeteer
b: Oct 13, 1917, Chicago, Ill. d: Dec 6, 1985

Kukla, Fran & Ollie (child)
. . . . puppeteer (1948–57)
That Was the Week That Was (com)
. . . . puppeteer (1964–65)
Kukla, Fran & Ollie (child)
. . . . puppeteer (1969–71)
Kukla, Fran & Ollie (child)
. . . . puppeteer (1975–76)

Emmy Awards: Special Award for His "Berlin Wall" Hand Ballet on *That Was the Week That Was* (1966); Best Performer in a Children's Series, for *Kukla, Fran & Ollie* (1971)

Although viewers never saw his face, the gentle, expressive hands and witty, flexible voice of Burr Tillstrom were familiar to several generations of TV kids. Burr was, of course, the creator, voice, and soul of Kukla, Ollie, and all the rest of the Kuklapolitan puppets. He began in puppetry as a teenager, performing in the parks and playgrounds of Chicago. Kukla, the little bulb-nosed fellow with a quizzical air, was born in 1936, when Burr was 19. Ollie, the one-toothed dragon, came along three years later, in time for a performance at the 1939 World's Fair.

Burr and his troupe were Chicago favorites and performed on early television there around 1940. By 1947 they had a regular local show and were joined by actress Fran Allison, who stood in front of the little stage and acted as a sort of human interlocutor. The program was picked up by the NBC network in 1948. *Kukla, Fran & Ollie* was seen off and on for the next 30 years, sometimes in their own show, sometimes in guest appearances on other series, including the *Today* show (they were guest hosts), *Your Show of Shows,* several Perry Como specials, and even *Your Hit Parade.* During the late '60s and '70s they were regular hosts of the *CBS Children's Film Festival* on Saturdays.

Burr occasionally performed in other settings, including an acting appearance in the *Hallmark Hall of Fame* production of "Alice in Wonderland." He won an Emmy for a poignant hand ballet, about the recently constructed Berlin Wall, on *That Was the Week That Was.* For the record, on *Kukla, Fran & Ollie,* Kukla was on Burr's right hand, Ollie on his left. The dialogue, though mapped out in general terms beforehand, was all extemporaneous and voiced by Burr himself.

TILLY, JENNIFER—actress

Shaping Up (com) . Shannon Winters (1984)

TILTON, CHARLENE—actress
b: Dec 1, 1958, San Diego, Calif. r: Hollywood, Calif.

Dallas (drama)
.... Lucy Ewing Cooper (1978–85)

TIMES SQUARE TWO, THE—comedy duo

Dean Martin Presents the Golddiggers (var)
.... regulars (1968)

TINNEY, CAL—comedian
b: Feb 2, 1908, Oklahoma

Stop Me If You've Heard This One (quiz)
.... panelist (1948–49)

Drawling, Will Rogers-esque humorist of the '30s and '40s ("I talk so . . . slow . . . so I can get home . . . and catch my own broadcast").

TIPPEN, DON—pianist

The Nick Kenny Show (talk)
.... pianist (1951–52)

TIRELLI, JAIME—actor
b: Mar 4, 1945, New York City, N.Y.

Ball Four (com) ...... Orlando Lopez (1976)

TOBEN, JOHN—orchestra leader

Thicke of the Night (talk)
.... orch. leader (1984)

TOBEY, KEN—actor
b: 1919

The Whirlybirds (adv)
.... Chuck Martin (1956–59)
Our Private World (drama)
.... Dick Robinson (1965)

TOBIAS, GEORGE—actor
b: Jul 14, 1901, New York City, N.Y. d: Feb 27, 1980

Hudson's Bay (adv) ...... regular (1959–60)
Adventures in Paradise (adv)
.... Trader Penrose (1960–61)
Bewitched (com) .. Abner Kravitz (1964–72)

TOBIN, DAN—actor
b: 1909 d: Nov 26, 1982

I Married Joan (com)
.... Kerwin Tobin (1954–55)
My Favorite Husband (com)
.... Oliver Shepard (1955)
Perry Mason (drama)
.... Terrence Clay (1965–66)

TOBIN, MICHELE—actress
b: Jan 25, 1961, Chicago, Ill. r: Los Angeles, Calif.

The Fitzpatricks (drama)
...... Maureen (Mo) Fitzpatrick (1977–78)
Grandpa Goes to Washington (com)
.... Kathleen Kelley (1978–79)
California Fever (adv)
.... Laurie Newman (1979)

TOCHI, BRIAN—actor
b: May 2, 1959, Los Angeles, Calif.

Anna and the King (com)
...... Crown Prince Chulalongkorn (1972)
Renegades (police) .... Dragon (1983)
St. Elsewhere (drama)
.... Dr. Alan Poe (1984–85)

This young Asian-American actor was quite busy during his teenage years, co-starring in the Saturday morning series *Space Academy* (1977–79) and hosting the children's video magazine *Razzmatazz* (1978); he also had a recurring role on *Hawaii Five-O* as Joey Lee. His network debut was as the adopted TV son of Richard Benjamin and Paula Prentiss on *He & She* in 1968.

TODD, ANN—actress
b: 1932

The Stu Erwin Show (com)
.... Joyce Erwin (1950–54)

A moderately popular child actress of the late '30s and '40s, not to be confused with (but often is) the blonde British leading lady of the same name (b. 1909). Also known as Ann E. Todd.

TODD, BEVERLY—black actress
b: Jul 11, 1946, Ohio

Roots (drama)............... Fanta (1977)
Having Babies (drama) ..... Kelly (1978–79)
The Redd Foxx Show (com)
.... Felicia Clemmons-Hughes (1986)

TODD, BOB—British comedian
b: 1922

The Benny Hill Show (com)
.... regular (1969–82)
The Val Doonican Show (var)
.... regular (1971)

TODD, DANIEL—juvenile actor
My Three Sons (com)
.... Robbie Douglas II (1970–72)

TODD, JAMES—actor
d: 1968

The Halls of Ivy (com)
.... Dr. Merriweather (1954–55)

TODD, JOSEPH—juvenile actor
My Three Sons (com)
.... Steve Douglas, Jr. (1970–72)

TODD, LISA—actress
b: Santa Barbara, Calif.

Hee Haw (var).. Sunshine Cornsilk (1970–)
The Burns and Schreiber Comedy Hour (var)
.... regular (1973)

A micro-miniskirted *Hee Haw* sexpot described by one columnist as "stacked like a pile of hay never was." She was hired for the show after the producer saw her do a walk-on on *The Jonathan Winters Show.* "It was the kind of walk you don't easily forget," he murmured later.

TODD, MICHAEL—juvenile actor
My Three Sons (com)
.... Charley Douglas (1970–72)

Daniel, Joseph, and Michael Todd played the triplets born into the *My Three Sons*

TV family during the 1968–69 season (to Don Grady's character, Robbie).

TOKUDA, MARILYN—actress
b: Seattle, Wash.

The Roller Girls (com)
.... Shana "Pipeline" Akira (1978)

Marilyn played the pretty Japanese-Eskimo member of the *Roller Girls* team, who was constantly uttering obscure native maxims such as "If the whale may blubber, then even the salmon may roe."

TOLAN, MICHAEL—actor
b: Nov 27, 1925, Detroit, Mich.

The Nurses (drama)
.... Dr. Alex Tazinski (1964–65)
The Senator (drama)
.... Jordan Boyle (1970–71)

TOLBERT, BERLINDA—black actress
b: Nov 4, 1949, Charlotte, N.C.

The Jeffersons (com)
.... Jenny Willis Jefferson (1975–85)

TOLENTINO, JOAN—actress
Stockard Channing in Just Friends (com)
.... Mrs. Fischer (1979)

TOLKAN, JAMES—actor
Mary (com)........ Lester Mintz (1985–86)

TOLSKY, SUSAN—actress
b: Apr 6, 1943, Houston, Texas

Here Come the Brides (adv)
.... Biddie Cloom (1968–70)
The New Bill Cosby Show (var)
.... regular (1972–73)
Madame's Place (com)... Bernadette (1982)

TOMACK, SID—actor
b: 1907, Brooklyn, N.Y. d: Nov 12, 1962

The Life of Riley (com)
.... Jim Gillis (1949–50)
My Friend Irma (com)....... Al (1952–53)
Joe Palooka Story (drama)
.... Knobby Walsh (1954)

TOMARKEN, PETER—host, actor
b: Olean, N.Y. r: California

The Secret Empire (drama) ..... Roe (1979)

Peter Tomarken has done a little of everything—acted on television and in movies *(Secrets, Heaven Can Wait);* hosted daytime game shows *(Hit Man, Press Your Luck);* written screenplays; produced several films; created and produced TV commercials (he dreamed up the talking beavers used in a famous chain saw ad); and held the positions of clothing editor for *Woman's Wear Daily* and associate editor of *Business Week* magazine. He was also a cohost of The Playboy Channel (on cable TV). "I love diversity," he says.

TOMLIN, LILY—comedienne, writer
b: Sep 1, 1939, Detroit, Mich.

The Music Scene (music)
.... rotating host (1969)
Rowan & Martin's Laugh-In (var)
.... regular (1969–73)

Emmy Awards: Star, Best Comedy Special, for *Lily* (1974); Best Writing for a Comedy Special, for *Lily* (1974), *Lily Tomlin* (1976), and *The Paul Simon Special* (1978); Producer and Star, Best Comedy Program, for the Special *Lily: Sold Out* (1981)

"One ringy-dingy . . . two ringy-dingy . . . (pause) Is this the party to whom I am speaking?"

Lily Tomlin's hilarious characterization of the overbearing, nasal, spinsterish telephone operator Ernestine was one of the comic sensations of the early '70s. It was a great bit of social satire ("We are the PHONE COMPANY . . . we are omnipotent"), but it was only a part of her comic talents. Lily began appearing in coffeehouses in Detroit during her college days, eventually making her way to New York in the mid-1960s to crash the big time. She won a recurring spot on *The Garry Moore Show* in the fall of 1966, but was little seen (as was the program, running opposite *Bonanza*). Club work and commercials followed. Then, in 1969, her career suddenly began to take off; two off-Broadway shows in the spring, a regular spot on *The Music Show* in September, and in December her first appearance on *Laugh-In.*

Lily developed a wide range of off-the-wall characters: Ernestine, Tess the bag lady, Sister Boogie-Woman, Edith Ann the brat, even Crystal the quadraplegic. Many of these were carried over into a series of highly regarded specials during the 1970s. However, it was Ernestine who was best loved. She was featured on a best-selling comedy LP, titled, of course, *This Is a Recording,* and then made news when she (Ernestine) turned down a half-million-dollar offer to appear in commercials for the phone company!

As for Lily, she has demonstrated her versatility in a variety of hit movies, including *Nashville, The Late Show,* and *9 to 5,* as well as in one-woman shows on Broadway.

TOMLIN, PINKY—singer, actor
b: Sep 9, 1907, Eureka Springs, Ark. r: Durant, Okla.

Waterfront (adv) . . . Tip Hubbard (1953–56)

A red-haired, bumptious singer and supporting actor, active since the 1930s. He got his start in 1934, when he wrote and performed the popular song "The Object of My Affection"—which was inspired by his girlfriend, and future wife, Miss Oklahoma of 1933. Pinky's autobiography was called (what else!): *The Object of My Affection* (1981).

TOMME, RON—actor
b: Oct 24, Chicago, Ill.

Dallas (drama) . . . . . . Charles Eccles (1982)

Soap opera matinee idol, on *Love of Life* as Bruce Sterling for more than 20 years (1959–1980).

TOMPKINS, ANGEL—actress
b: Dec 20, 1943, Albany, Calif.

Search (adv) . . . . . Gloria Harding (1972–73)

TOMPKINS, JOAN—actress

Sam Benedict (drama)
. . . . Trudy Wagner (1962–63)
Occasional Wife (com)
. . . . Mrs. Brahms (1966–67)

TONE, FRANCHOT—actor
b: Feb 27, 1905, Niagara Falls, N.Y. d: Sep 18, 1968

Ben Casey (drama)
. . . . . . Dr. Daniel Niles Freeland (1965–66)

Debonair leading man of '30s and '40s movies, often cast as an effete playboy. He appeared on television a great deal during the 1950s, on playhouse series including *Suspense, Studio One,* and *Playhouse 90.* He continued to be active until shortly before his death (of lung cancer), appearing with James Franciscus in the TV movie *Shadow over Elveron* in early 1968.

TONG, KAM—actor
b: 1907 d: Nov 8, 1969

Have Gun Will Travel (wes)
.... Hey Boy (1957–63)
Mr. Garlund (adv).... Kam Chang (1960–61)

TONG, SAMMEE—actor
b: 1901, San Francisco, Calif. d: Oct 27, 1964

Bachelor Father (com)
.... Peter Tong (1957–62)
Mickey (com)....... Sammy Ling (1964–65)

This small Oriental actor had a rather busy career in films and TV during the '50s and '60s playing houseboys and cooks. He had just begun filming the comedy series *Mickey*—as Mickey Rooney's nemesis, a hotel manager—when he committed suicide in late 1964.

TONGE, PHILIP—actor
b: c. 1893 d: 1959

Northwest Passage (adv)
.... Gen. Amherst (1958–59)

TOOMEY, MARILYN—assistant

Win with a Winner (quiz)
.... "Post Card Girl" (1958)

TOOMEY, REGIS—actor
b: Aug 13, 1902, Pittsburgh, Pa

The Mickey Rooney Show (com)
.... Mr. Mulligan (1954–55)
Richard Diamond, Private Detective (drama)
.... Lt. McGough (1957–58)
Shannon (drama).... Bill Cochran (1961–62)
Burke's Law (police)
.... Det. Sgt. Les Hart (1963–65)
Petticoat Junction (com)
.... Dr. Barton Stuart (1968–69)

A solid, unexceptional supporting actor—usually cast as an official of some sort—

who was all over television in the '50s and '60s, in regular parts and a great many guest roles. He had been similarly busy in movies since the late 1920s (in more than 200 films). Although his roles were many, they are little remembered today.

TOP TWENTY, THE—singers

The Ford Show (var) ..... chorus (1957–61)

TOPOL—actor
b: Sep 9, 1935, Tel Aviv, Palestine

The Winds of War (drama)
.... Berel Jastrow (1983)

Energetic leading Israeli film actor, sometimes seen in TV movies and miniseries. He is best known for the role of Tevye in the stage and screen versions of *Fiddler on the Roof.*

TOPPER, TIM—actor
b: Feb 27, Baltimore, Md.

Seven Brides for Seven Brothers (adv)
.... Evan McFadden (1982–83)

TOPPERS, THE—singers

Arthur Godfrey and His Friends (var)
.... singers (1955–57)

TORK, PETER—singer, actor
b: Feb 13, 1944, Washington, D.C.

The Monkees (com) .... Peter (1966–68)

One of the four Monkees, the sensationally popular TV rock group of the late '60s (he was the poker-faced one). Peter was the son of an economics professor at the University of Connecticut but had flunked out of college, then turned to music. He was a member of a folk group called The Phoenix Singers in the mid-1960s, and after the Monkees phenomenon subsided he tried to continue his music career in the '70s with a succession of groups—without much luck. Instead, he was busted on a drug rap in the early '70s and spent four months in prison, emerging long-haired and bearded to begin a new career teaching eastern philosophy and other subjects. In 1986 Peter and two of the other Monkees regrouped for a widely publicized revival tour.

TORME, MEL—singer
b: Sep 13, 1925, Chicago, Ill.

TV's Top Tunes (music) . . . . host (1951)
Summertime U.S.A. (music) . . cohost (1953)
It Was a Very Good Year (doc)
. . . . host (1971)

One of the great classy popular singers of
the twentieth century (known as "the Velvet Fog"), Mel was seen on television
mainly in guest appearances. He was also
"musical advisor" to his friend Judy Garland for her 1963–64 variety series.

TORN, RIP—actor
b: Feb 6, 1931, Temple, Texas

The Blue and the Gray (drama)
. . . . Gen. Ulysses S. Grant (1982)

Explosive leading man, seen quite a bit in
guest roles on TV dramas from 1955–1965,
and more recently in TV movies and miniseries. Among his TV films have been *Betrayal, Steel Cowboy, Blind Ambition* (as
Richard Nixon), *Sophia Loren: Her Own
Story* (as husband Carlo Ponti), and the
controversial *Atlanta Child Murders.*

TORRES, ANTONIO—actor

a.k.a. Pablo (com) . . . Nicholas Rivera (1984)

TORRES, LIZ—actress
b: Sep 27, 1947, The Bronx, N.Y.

The Melba Moore-Clifton Davis Show (var)
. . . . regular (1972)
Ben Vereen . . . Comin' At Ya (var)
. . . . regular (1975)
Phyllis (com) . . . . Julie Erskine (1975–76)
All in the Family (com)
. . . . Teresa Betancourt (1976–77)
Checking In (com) . . . . . Elena Beltran (1981)
The New Odd Couple (com)
. . . . Maria (1982–83)

TORREY, ROGER—actor

The Iron Horse (wes)
. . . . Nils Torvald (1966–67)
The Beverly Hillbillies (com)
. . . . Mark Templeton (1970–71)

TOTTER, AUDREY—actress
b: Dec 20, 1918, Joliet, Ill.

Cimarron City (wes)
. . . . Beth Purcell (1958–59)
Our Man Higgins (com)
. . . . Alice MacRoberts (1962–63)
Medical Center (drama)
. . . . Nurse Wilcox (1972–76)

Blonde actress of the hard-boiled school,
who got her start on radio in the late '30s
and appeared in many movies from the
mid-1940s on. Her first opportunity for TV
stardom was scuttled when her movie studio refused to let her recreate her popular
radio show *Meet Millie* on television
(Elena Verdugo got the part). Instead, Audrey was limited to guest appearances on
various dramatic shows, until she began a
costarring role with George Montgomery
on *Cimarron City,* as the tough-cookie
boardinghouse owner. In the '60s she made
more guest appearances, including several
each on *Alfred Hitchcock Presents* and *Dr.
Kildare* and played the housewife who inherited an English butler on *Our Man Higgins.* She then reduced her activities for
several years to raise a family but was
lured back for the recurring role of Nurse
Wilcox on *Medical Center.*

TOWNSEND, BARBARA—actress

AfterMASH (com)
. . . . Mildred Potter (1983–84)

TOWNSEND, JILL—English actress

Cimarron Strip (wes)
. . . . Dulcey Coopersmith (1967–68)

**TOYOSHIMA, TIFFANY—juvenile
actress**

Two Marriages (drama)
. . . . Kim Daley (1983–84)

TOZERE, FREDERIC—actor
b: c. 1901 d: Aug 5, 1972

Stanley (com) . . . . Mr. Phillips (1956–57)

TRACY, LEE—actor
b: Apr 14, 1898, Atlanta, Ga. d: Oct 18, 1968

The Amazing Mr. Malone (drama)
. . . . John J. Malone (1951–52)
Martin Kane, Private Eye (drama)
. . . . Martin Kane (1952–53)
New York Confidential (drama)
. . . . Lee Cochran (1958–59)

A bright, wisecracking, fast-talking actor with a distinctive nasal delivery, who was seen quite a bit in the early '50s and had another spurt of activity in the '60s in older roles. He was a lawyer in *Mr. Malone,* a private eye in *Martin Kane,* and a reporter (his most frequent role in '30s movies) in *New York Confidential.*

TRACY, STEVE—actor
b: c. 1952 d: Nov 27, 1986

Little House on the Prairie (adv)
. . . . Percival Dalton (1980–81)

TRANUM, CHUCK—announcer, host

Manhattan Spotlight (int) . . . . host (1949–51)

TRASK, DIANA—singer
b: Jun 23, 1940, Warburton, Australia

Sing Along with Mitch (var)
. . . . regular (1961–62)

Australian-born jazz and pop singer who gained fame in the U.S. on *Sing Along with Mitch.* Then, surprisingly, she switched to country music in the late '60s and scored an even greater success on the *Grand Ole Opry.*

TRAVALENA, FRED—comedian, impressionist
b: Oct 6, 1942, New York City, N.Y.

ABC Comedy Hour (com) . . . . regular (1972)
Keep On Truckin' (var) . . . . . . regular (1975)

TRAVANTI, DANIEL J.—actor
b: Mar 7, 1940, Kenosha, Wis.

Hill Street Blues (police)
. . . . Capt. Frank Furillo (1981–)

Emmy Awards: Best Actor in a Drama Series, for *Hill Street Blues* (1981, 1982)

"I'm having the time of my life," says Daniel J. Travanti. "I once felt that it was never going to happen. Now it seems too good to be true."

Few actors have paid so many dues before it "came true" as has Travanti, the quiet but commanding actor who played Capt. Furillo on *Hill Street Blues.* A hotshot drama major in college, Travanti was winning important stage roles on tour and

in New York almost as soon as he graduated from the Yale School of Drama; among other things, he costarred with James Earl Jones in *Othello* in 1965. He began doing TV guest roles in the mid-1960s, but the parts—on such series as *Route 66, The Defenders, The Man from U.N.C.L.E.,* and *Perry Mason*—were disappointingly limited ("dumb and/or bad guys," he says). As the years went by the actor increasingly turned to drink to dull his fears that fame was not coming quickly, and maybe not at all. In January 1973 he fell to the nadir of his career when he suffered a breakdown onstage while playing opposite Sada Thompson in *Twigs;* by the end of the year he had finally acknowledged the obvious ("I was a goddamned alcoholic") and begun a long and uncertain process of rehabilitation.

Television work came intermittently during the mid-1970s, including several episodes each of *Gunsmoke, Kojak,* and *Barnaby Jones,* and quite a few commercials. In 1979 he began a regular part on daytime's *General Hospital* as an ex-football star, but it lasted only six months. As of 1980, after 20 years as an actor, he was still virtually unknown. Then came *Hill Street Blues*—a role he won over 50 others—and stardom. Travanti's newfound fame won him parts in some notable TV movies, including *Adam, Aurora* (with Sophia Loren), and a cable TV biography of Edward R. Murrow (as Murrow).

TRAVOLTA, ELLEN—actress
b: Oct 6, Englewood, N.J.

Makin' It (adv)
. . . . Dorothy Manucci (1979)
Number 96 (drama)
. . . . Rita Sugarman (1980–81)
Joanie Loves Chachi (com)
. . . . Louisa Delvecchio (1982–83)

The sister of John Travolta, with whom she appeared in the movie *Grease* and, occasionally, in the hit series *Welcome Back, Kotter* (as Horshack's mother).

TRAVOLTA, JOHN—actor
b: Feb 18, 1954, Englewood, N.J.

Welcome Back, Kotter (com)
. . . . Vinnie Barbarino (1975–79)

This tall, loose-limbed, very Italian actor (actually he's of Italian-Irish stock) dropped out of high school at the age of 16 to follow his sister and parents into the theater. The early start helped; over a period of five years, the engaging, energetic youth worked his way up from summer stock in New Jersey to the New York stage (in *Grease* and *Over Here!*) and small roles in episodes of TV series, including *Owen Marshall, Counselor at Law; The Rookies,* and *Medical Center.* In 1975 he won a supporting role as one of the high school students (the "sweathogs") on *Welcome Back, Kotter.* The show became a major hit and John emerged from the supporting cast to become its biggest star. Capitalizing on this sudden fame, he starred in the TV movie *The Boy in the Plastic Bubble* (1976) and in the theatrical film hits *Carrie* and *Saturday Night Fever.* As his movie career soared, he cut back on his appearances on the *Kotter* series, and by the age of 25 he had left television entirely.

While filming his only TV movie, John met the much older actress Diana Hyland (who played his mother); they were immediately attracted to one another and began living together. John credits Diana with helping him get a grip on his life during the tumultuous time when many suddenly successful but still immature young actors see their careers—and sometimes their lives—fly out of control. Unfortunately, Diana died less than a year later of cancer, leaving her young lover devastated. She won a posthumous Emmy Award for her performance in *The Boy in the Plastic Bubble,* and at the awards ceremony, John— the young man she had touched so profoundly—accepted it in her memory, saying in an emotional voice, "Here's to you, Diana...wherever you are."

TREACHER, ARTHUR—actor
b: Jul 23, 1894, Brighton, England d: Dec 14, 1975

Down You Go (quiz)
.... regular panelist (1956)
You're in the Picture (quiz).. panelist (1961)
The Merv Griffin Show (talk)
.... regular (1969–72)

The perfect English butler in many films of the '30s and '40s, icy and distainful; he ap-

peared in some TV plays of the '50s too, but was mostly known as a "veddy British" talk and game show personality. Arthur achieved an unique sort of immortality by lending his name to a national chain of fish and chips fast-food restaurants.

TREAS, TERRI—actress
b: Jul 19, 1959, Kansas City, Kan.

Seven Brides for Seven Brothers (adv)
.... Hannah McFadden (1982–83)

Rhymes with "peace."

TREBEK, ALEX—host
b: Jul 22, 1940, Sudbury, Ontario, Canada

The $128,000 Question (quiz)
.... host (1977–78)

The handsome quiz show host (*High Rollers, Jeopardy!* etc.) who introduced the mustache to the world of daytime game shows.

TREEN, MARY—actress
b: Mar 27, 1907, St. Louis, Mo. r: California

Willy (drama)...... Emily Dodger (1954–55)
The Joey Bishop Show (com)
.... Hilda (1962–65)

TREMAYNE, LES—actor
b: Apr 16, 1913, London, England r: U.S.A.

One Man's Family (drama)
.... Bill Herbert (1950)
The Adventures of Ellery Queen (drama)
.... Insp. Richard Queen (1958–59)

This actor is most famous still as a suave, romantic leading man on radio in the '30s and '40s, on *The First Nighter, Grand Hotel,* etc. He was once voted one of the three most distinctive voices in America, along with President Roosevelt and Bing Crosby. Les played supporting roles on television and in the '70s was appearing in (or heard as a voice for) Saturday morning children's shows, including *Shazam.*

TRENDLER, ROBERT—orchestra leader

This Is Music (music)
.... orch. leader (1951–52)
The Music Show (music)
.... orch. leader (1953–54)

TRENNER, DONN—orchestra leader
b: Mar 10, 1927, New Haven, Conn.

ABC's Nightlife (talk)... orch. leader (1965)

TRENT, BUCK—banjoist, singer
b: Feb 17, c. 1932, Spartanburg, S.C.

Hee Haw (var).......... regular (1975–82)

TRINKA, PAUL—actor

Voyage to the Bottom of the Sea (sci fi)
.... crewman Patterson (1964–68)

TRIPP, PAUL—host
b: Feb 20, 1916, New York City, N.Y.

Mr. I Magination (child)
.... Mr. I Magination (1949–52)
It's Magic (misc) .... host (1955)

A gentle children's show host, most famous as Mr. I Magination. He was also the author of the 1940s classic children's story "Tubby the Tuba."

TROTTER, JOHN SCOTT—orchestra leader
b: Jun 14, 1908, Charlotte, N.C. d: Oct 29, 1975

The George Gobel Show (var)
.... orch. leader (1954–60)
And Here's the Show (var)
.... orch. leader (1955)

Noted orchestra leader associated with Bing Crosby on radio and records during the '30s and '40s. He also composed George Gobel's distinctive TV theme song, "Gobelues," and served as musical director for Charlie Brown and Babar the Elephant TV specials.

TROUGHTON, PATRICK—British actor
b: 1920, London, England d: Mar 28, 1987

Doctor Who (sci fi).. Doctor Who (1966–69)
The Six Wives of Henry VIII (drama)
.... Duke of Norfolk (1971)

TROUP, BOBBY—pianist, actor
b: Oct 18, 1918, Harrisburg, Pa.

Musical Chairs (quiz)...... panelist (1955)
Stars of Jazz (music)........... host (1958)
Acapulco (adv).............. Bobby (1961)

Emergency (drama)
.... Dr. Joe Early (1972–77)

Married to sultry singer/actress Julie London (lucky guy!), with whom he appeared in *Emergency*. Bobby was also the composer of such pop-song standards as "Daddy" and "(Get Your Kicks on) Route 66"—the latter written while he was driving to Hollywood in the '40s to look for a break into show business.

TROUP, RONNE—actress

My Three Sons (com)
.... Polly Williams Douglas (1970–72)

The daughter of actor-musician Bobby Troup.

TROUT, ROBERT—newscaster
b: Oct 15, 1909, Wake County, N.C.

Who Said That? (quiz)..... emcee (1948–51)
Presidential Timber (pub aff)
.... moderator (1952)

You think that Walter Cronkite has been around forever? Robert Trout began his radio reporting career in 1928 and was still at it in the mid-1980s as a "special correspondent" (mostly on radio) for ABC news.

TRUEMAN, PAULA—actress
b: Apr 25, 1907, New York City, N.Y.

Billy (com).................... Gran (1979)

TRUEX, ERNEST—actor
b: Sep 19, 1889*, Kansas City, Mo. d: Jun 27, 1973

Mr. Peepers (com)
.... Mr. Remington (1952–55)
Jamie (com)............ Grandpa (1953–54)
The Ann Sothern Show (com)
.... Jason Macauley (1958–59)
Pete and Gladys (com) .... Pop (1961)

A mild-mannered, grandfatherly type, much on television during the 1950s and early '60s. He even played Caspar Milquetoast in one of his earliest TV appearances, on *Program Playhouse* in 1949.

TRUSEL, LISA—juvenile actress
b: Oct 25, 1968, Hollywood, Calif.

*Some sources give 1890.

Father Murphy (drama)
.... Lizette Winkler (1981–82)

Lisa played one of daytime's most popular young heroines, Melissa Anderson, on *Days of Our Lives* in the mid-1980s.

TUBB, BARRY—actor

Bay City Blues (drama)
.... Mickey Wagner (1983)

TUBB, ERNEST—country singer
b: Feb 9, 1914, Crisp, Texas d: Sep 6, 1984

Grand Ole Opry (music) .. regular (1955–56)

A legendary country star, but practically unknown outside of that field. He opened the first-ever country concert at Carnegie Hall with the words, "My, my, this place sure could hold a lot of hay."

TUBB, JUSTIN—country singer
b: Aug 20, 1935, San Antonio, Texas

Grand Ole Opry (music) .. regular (1955–56)

The eldest son of Ernest Tubb, also a successful country singer.

TUCCI, MICHAEL—actor

Trapper John, M.D. (drama)
.... Dr. Charlie Nichols (1980–84)

TUCKER, FORREST—actor
b: Feb 12, 1919*, Plainfield, Ind. d: Oct 25, 1986

Crunch and Des (adv)
.... Crunch Adams (1955–56)
F Troop (com)
.... Sgt. Morgan O'Rourke (1965–67)
Dusty's Trail (com).... Mr. Callahan (1973)
Filthy Rich (com)... Big Guy Beck (1982–83)

A burly character actor who appeared in numerous dead-serious film westerns in the '40s and '50s, then became famous starring in a hilarious TV send-up of the whole genre, *F Troop* (he played the gruff top-sergeant who had struck a secret deal with the local Indians and had the exclusive franchise to sell their souvenirs to tourists). Forrest entered films in 1940, and in the '50s and '60s he played guest roles on

*Some sources give 1915.

various TV action shows (he was a particular favorite on *Gunsmoke*). In *Crunch and Des* he played a charter-boat captain and adventurer in the Bahamas; his later series were more comedic, including *Dusty's Trail* and the Saturday morning *Ghost Busters* (1975–76). He continued to be active, in series episodes (*Fantasy Island, Police Woman*) and occasional TV movies into the 1980s. Among his TV films and miniseries were *Black Beauty, The Rebels,* and 1983's *Blood Feud* (as Lyndon B. Johnson).

TUCKER, JOHN BARTHOLOMEW—host
b: Apr 8

Candid Camera (aud par). cohost (1974–78)

TUCKER, MICHAEL—actor
b: Feb 6, c. 1944, Baltimore, Md.

L.A. Law (drama)
.... Stuart Markowitz (1986–)

The husband of actress Jill Eikenberry, with whom he appeared in *L.A. Law*.

TUCKER, NANA—actress

Ivan the Terrible (com).... Svetlana (1976)

TUFELD, DICK—announcer

Lost in Space (sci fi)
.... the Robot's voice (1965–68)

TULLEY, PAUL—actor

Harry-O (drama)
.... Sgt. Don Roberts (1975–76)

TULLY, TOM—actor
b: 1896*, Durango, Colo. d: Apr 27, 1982

The Lineup (police)
.... Insp. Matt Grebb (1954–59)
Shane (wes) .... Tom Starett (1966)

A supporting actor who played tough but fair authority figures in quite a few movies of the '40s and '50s, and in television dramas of the '50s and '60s—including a long run on the semidocumentary cop show *The Lineup*. He was also seen in '50s theater series, including *Ford Theatre* and *Zane Grey Theater,* and in later dramas,

*Some sources give 1908.

including *Perry Mason* and *Bonanza*. Tully retired in the early 1970s, returning just once for a cameo role (his last performance) in the 1981 TV movie *Madame X*.

TUNE, TOMMY—actor, dancer, director
b: Feb 28, 1939, Wichita Falls, Texas

Dean Martin Presents the Golddiggers (var)
.... regular (1969–70)

Tall (6'7"), Tony-winning Broadway hoofer; occasionally on television.

TURKUS, BURTON—lawyer, author
b: 1902, Brooklyn, N.Y. d: Nov 22, 1982

Mr. Arsenic (talk) .... host (1952)

New York proscecutor of, and authority on, "Murder, Inc."

TURMAN, GLYNN—black actor
b: Jan 31, 1946, New York City, N.Y.

Peyton Place (drama)
.... Lew Miles (1968–69)
Centennial (drama).. Nate Person (1978–79)
Manimal (police)
.... Ty Earle (pilot only) (1983)
Hail to the Chief (com)
...... Sec. of State LaRue Hawkes (1985)

TURNBEAUGH, BRENDA & WENDY—juvenile actresses

Little House on the Prairie (adv)
.... Grace Ingalls (1978–82)

TURNER, DAIN—black juvenile actor

Harris and Company (drama)
.... Richard Allen Harris (1979)

TURNER, DAVE—black actor

The Barbary Coast (wes)
...... Thumbs, the piano player (1975–76)

TURNER, JACQUELINE—singer

At Liberty Club (music)...... hostess (1948)

Known professionally simply as "Jacqueline," Parisian chanteuse.

TURNER, JANINE—actress
b: Dec 6, Lincoln, Neb. r: Fort Worth, Texas

Behind the Screen (drama)
.... Janie-Claire Willow (1981–82)

TURNER, JIM—singer

The Lawrence Welk Show (music)
.... regular (1979–82)

TURNER, LANA—actress
b: Feb 8, 1920, Wallace, Idaho

The Survivors (drama)
.... Tracy Carlyle Hastings (1969–70)
Falcon Crest (drama)
.... Jacqueline Perrault (1982–83)

The legendary Hollywood "sweater girl" of the '40s finally arrived on television in 1969, amid considerable hoopla, to headline a big, steamy, Harold Robbins soap opera called *The Survivors*. It was one of the grandest big-name flops in TV history, and Lana, her sense of humor strained, abandoned the medium for another decade. She turned up for a season in the early '80s in another soap, *Falcon Crest*. Lana had made her (nonacting) TV debut in the mid-1950s on Bob Hope's show.

In 1981 Lana published her autobiography, detailing her scandal-ridden life (seven husbands, numerous lovers, murders, a suicide attempt, etc.); it was called *Lana Turner: The Lady, The Legend, The Truth*.

TURNER, ROBERT—announcer

Champagne and Orchids (music)
.... announcer (1948–49)

TURNER, TIERRE—black juvenile actor
b: Jan 7, 1960, Detroit, Mich.

The Cop and the Kid (com)
.... Lucas Adams (1975–76)
The Waverly Wonders (com)
.... Hasty Parks (1978)

The son of actor Dave Turner.

TURNER, ZEKE—

Midwestern Hayride (var)
.... regular (1951–59)

TURQUAND, TODD—juvenile actor

Rhoda (com)........ Donny Gerard (1974)

TUTIN, DOROTHY—actress
b: Apr 8, 1930, London, England

The Six Wives of Henry VIII (drama)
.... Anne Boleyn (1971)

TUTTLE, LURENE—actress
b: Aug 29, 1906, Pleasant Lake, Ind. r: California d: May 28, 1986

Life with Father (com)
.... Vinnie Day (1953–55)
Father of the Bride (com)
.... Doris Dunston (1961–62)
Julia (com)....... Hannah Yarby (1968–70)

An engaging actress who got her start on radio in the '30s playing opposite Dick Powell on *Hollywood Hotel;* later, listeners knew her as Sam Spade's adoring secretary, Effie. On television, Lurene played many guest roles and appeared in three series, lastly as the sarcastic head nurse on *Julia.* She continued to be active until shortly before her death, appearing in the '80s in such series as *Murder She Wrote; Trapper John, M.D.,* and *Dynasty.*

TUTTLE, WESLEY—

Hayloft Hoedown (music)
.... regular (1948)

TWEED, SHANNON—actress
b: Mar 10, 1857, St. John's, Newfoundland, Canada

Falcon Crest (drama)
.... Diana Hunter (1982–83)

A former "Miss Canada" runner-up, and *Playboy* magazine's 1982 "Playmate of the Year."

TWEED, TERRY—actress

The Baxters (com)
.... Susan Baxter (1980–81)

TWOMEY, JOHN—novelty performer

The Jerry Reed When You're Hot You're Hot Hour (var)................. regular (1972)

A Chicago attorney who made music with his bare hands.

TYLER, BEVERLY—actress
b: Jul 5, 1924*, Scranton, Pa.

Big Town (drama)
.... Lorelei Kilbourne (1953–54)

TYLER, JANET—assistant

Kuda Bux, Hindu Mystic (misc)
.... assistant (1950)

TYLER, JUDY—actress
b: c. 1932, Milwaukee, Wis. d: Jul 4, 1957

Caesar Presents (var)
.... various roles (1955)

Fondly remembered as Princess Summerfall Winterspring of the Tinka Tonka tribe, on daytime's *Howdy Doody Show* from 1952–57. The pert young actress also appeared on such prime time series as *The Milton Berle Show, The Colgate Comedy Hour,* and *All Star Revue.* She died at the age of 24 in an automobile accident.

TYLER, KIM—juvenile actor
b: Apr 17, 1954, Hollywood, Calif.

Please Don't Eat the Daisies (com)
.... Kyle Nash (1965–67)

TYLER, RICHARD—actor
b: Sep 3, 1932, New York City, N.Y.

The Aldrich Family (com)
.... Henry Aldrich (1950–51)

TYLER, WILLIE—black ventriloquist
b: Sep 8, c. 1940, Red Level, Ala.**

Rowan & Martin's Laugh-In (var)
.... regular (1972–73)

Ventriloquist of the '60s and '70s; his smart-aleck dummy was named Lester.

TYNER, CHARLES—actor
b: 1925

Father Murphy (drama)
.... Howard Rodman (1981–82)

TYRELL, DAVID—actor

Mr. Peepers (com)...... Charlie Burr (1952)

*Some sources give 1928.
**Some sources give Detroit, Mich.

853

TYRRELL, ANN—actress

Private Secretary (com)
.... Vi Praskins (1953–57)
The Ann Sothern Show (com)
.... Olive Smith (1958–61)

A minor stage and screen actress of the '40s and '50s who was Ann Sothern's sidekick and confidante in both of her 1950s comedy series.

TYRRELL, SUSAN—actress
b: 1946, San Francisco r: New Canaan, Conn.

Open All Night (com)
.... Gretchen Feester (1981–82)

TYSON, CECILY—black actress
b: Dec 19, 1933, Harlem, New York City, N.Y.

East Side/West Side (drama)
.... Jane Foster (1963–64)
Roots (drama)................ Binta (1977)

Emmy Awards: Best Actress in a Drama Special and Actress of the Year in a Special, for *The Autobiography of Miss Jane Pittman* (1974)

"I decided long ago never to walk in anyone's shadow" says Cecily Tyson, quoting from a favorite song. Indeed, the small, wispy but determined black actress has made a career out of spunky, idealistic roles—women who made a difference, despite the barriers of race and sex.

Cecily was born to West Indian immigrant parents and raised on welfare in Harlem. She began modeling in her twenties and then began a minor acting career in black-oriented stage dramas in New York. She was appearing in the play *Blue Boy in Black* when George C. Scott tapped her to play his secretary in *East Side/West Side,* one of the few hard-hitting "relevant" dramas on TV in the early '60s. Cecily then played guest roles on various series, including *Slattery's People, I Spy, The F.B.I.* and even *Here Come the Brides;* however, her reputation was made by her films of the late '60s and early '70s (*The Heart Is a Lonely Hunter, Sounder*) and subsequent high-class TV movies and miniseries. Among the latter have been *The Autobiography of Miss Jane Pittman* (a determined woman who lived from the days of slavery to those of the civil rights movement), *Roots* (as Kunta Kinte's mother), *King* (as Coretta King), *A Woman Called Moses* (an escaped slave who fights to free others), and *The Marva Collins Story* (a teacher working with "unteachable" youngsters).

U

UECKER, BOB—sportscaster, actor
b: Jan 26, 1935, Milwaukee, Wis.

Monday Night Baseball (sport)
.... sportscaster (1976–82)
Mr. Belvedere (com)
.... George Owens (1985–)

A former major-league baseball player turned comic. He calls himself "the worst player in baseball history," though in fact he spent six years with the Braves, Cardinals, and Phillies in the '60s. In the '80s Uecker was familiar in Lite Beer commercials as the also-ran who got stomped on by fans, locked out of bars, and left to sit alone in the upper reaches of the stadium.

UGGAMS, LESLIE—black singer, actress
b: May 25, 1943, New York City, N.Y.

Sing Along with Mitch (var)
.... regular (1961–64)
The Leslie Uggams Show (var)
.... hostess (1969)
Roots (drama)............... Kizzy (1977)
Backstairs at the White House (drama)
.... Lillian Rogers Parks (1979)

Emmy Award: Best Hostess of a Daytime Variety Series, for *Fantasy* (1983)

This cheerful lady has been singing, dancing and acting on television since she was a child. At age seven she auditioned for *Paul Whiteman's TV Teen Club* and won a five-week engagement; in the years immediately following, she was seen on Johnny Olsen's Saturday morning *Kids and Company, The Milton Berle Show,* and *Beulah* (as Ethel Waters' niece), among others.

While appearing on *Name That Tune,* at age 14, Leslie was spotted by impressario Mitch Miller; he signed her for his upcoming *Sing Along with Mitch,* which first brought her national fame. She had a few acting roles in the '60s, on *I Spy, The Girl from U.N.C.L.E.,* etc., but was better known as a singer-hostess, a role she fulfilled most famously on her own variety hour in the fall of 1969. She turned more toward acting in the '70s and '80s, notably with the central role in the 1979 miniseries *Backstairs at the White House.*

UMEKI, MIYOSHI—actress
b: 1929, Otaru, Hokaido, Japan

Arthur Godfrey and His Friends (var)
.... singer (1955)
The Courtship of Eddie's Father (com)
.... Mrs. Livingston (1969–72)

A Japanese actress who came to the U.S. in the '50s and won an Academy Award for her performance in the movie *Sayonara* (1957). Besides the *Eddie* series, she has only occasionally been seen on TV.

UNDERWOOD, BLAIR—actor
b: Aug 25, Tacoma, Wash.

Downtown (police) .. Terry Corsaro (1986–)

UNDERWOOD, RAY—actor

The Last Resort (com)
.... Jeffrey Barron (1979–80)

UNTERMEYER, LOUIS—poet, critic
b: Oct 1, 1885, New York City, N.Y. d: Dec 18, 1977

What's My Line (quiz)... panelist (1950–51)

URECAL, MINERVA—actress
b: 1894, Eureka, Calif. d: Feb 26, 1966

The RCA Victor Show (com)
.... Mrs. Pratt (1952–53)
The Ray Milland Show (com)
.... Dean Josephine Bradley (1953–54)
The Adventures of Tugboat Annie (adv)
.... Tugboat Annie (1956)
Peter Gunn (drama) .... "Mother" (1959–61)

Hawk-nosed, amply proportioned character actress (in fact, she was built like a tank)—a formidable grande *dame*. She was well-cast as Tugboat Annie. Her stage surname was formed from that of her birthplace, Eureka, California.

URICH, ROBERT—actor
b: Dec 19, 1946, Toronto, Ohio

Bob & Carol & Ted & Alice (com)
.... Bob Sanders (1973)
S.W.A.T. (police) .. Off. Jim Street (1975–76)
Soap (com) .... Peter Campbell (1977)

Tabitha (com)..... Paul Thurston (1977–78)
Vega$ (drama) .... Dan Tanna (1978–81)
Gavilan (adv) .... Robert Gavilan (1982–83)
Spenser: For Hire (drama)
.... Spenser (1985–)

This handsome TV hunk started out as a radio station time salesman in Chicago in the early '70s, but soon realized he belonged in front of the cameras. He acted in local theater for a few months, then ran into fellow Florida State University alumnus Burt Reynolds, who helped open doors for him in Hollywood. Bob's first TV roles were in episodes of such early '70s series as *Marcus Welby, The F.B.I.*, and *Kung Fu*, along with regular supporting roles in two series. However, it was the part of the sexy tennis pro who was murdered during the first season of *Soap* that gave his career a major boost.

Bob's biggest starring vehicle to date has been the routine but glamorous private eye series *Vega$;* in the mid-1980s he had another successful series along similar lines called *Spenser: For Hire.* He has also appeared in a number of TV movies and miniseries, including *Fighting Back, Princess Daisy,* and *Invitation to Hell.* He is married to actress Heather Menzies.

URQUHART, GORDON—actor

Chicagoland Mystery Players (police)
.... Jeffrey Hall (1949–50)

URSETH, BONNIE—actress

We Got It Made (com)
.... Beth Sorenson (1983–84)

UTAY, WILLIAM—actor

Night Court (com)
.... Phil the derelict (1985–)

UTLEY, GARRICK—newscaster
b: Nov 19, 1939, Chicago, Ill.

First Tuesday (news)
.... anchorman (1971–72)
NBC Weekend News (news)
.... anchorman (1971–75)
NBC Magazine with David Brinkley (pub aff)
.... correspondent (1980–82)

Emmy Awards: Best News Segments, for the *NBC Magazine* Reports "Inside AWACS" and "Rockets for Sale" (1981); for the *NBC Nightly News* Report "The New Cold War" (1985)

Long-faced NBC correspondent, with the network since 1963. He has had several tours of duty overseas, including Vietnam in both the '60s and '70s. His father, Clifton Utley, was an NBC newsman in Chicago and his mother was also an NBC reporter.

UTMAN, BRYAN—actor
b: Jun 6, Hartford, Conn.

Herbie, The Love Bug (com)... Jason (1982)
Seven Brides for Seven Brothers (adv)
.... Ford McFadden (1982–83)

UTTAL, FRED—announcer, host
b: c. 1908 d: Nov 28, 1963

Q.E.D. (quiz)............. moderator (1951)

V

VACCARO, BRENDA—actress
b: Nov 18, 1939, Brooklyn, N.Y. r: Dallas, Texas

Sara (wes)............. Sara Yarnell (1976)
Dear Detective (police)
.... Det. Sgt. Kate Hudson (1979)
Paper Dolls (drama)..... Julia Blake (1984)

Emmy Award: Best Supporting Actress in a Variety Program, for *The Shape of Things* (1974)

A leading lady who often plays strong-willed roles. Brenda had a busy stage career in the '60s, winning Tony Award nominations for *Cactus Flower, How Now Dow Jones,* and *The Goodbye People.* She made occasional television appearances during those years, but became more active in the medium in the '70s, in episodes of *The Name of the Game, Marcus Welby, McCloud,* etc. In her own series, *Sara,* she played a spunky frontier schoolteacher. In recent years, Brenda has alternated between series and TV movies, the latter including *The Star Maker, A Long Way Home,* and *The Pride of Jesse Hallam* (again, as a schoolteacher).

VAGUE, VERA—actress
b: Sep 2, 1904*, New York City, N.Y. d: Sep 14, 1974

Ford Festival (var) .... regular (1951–52)
Follow the Leader (quiz).... hostess (1953)
The Greatest Man on Earth (quiz)
.... emcee (1953)

Vera was well-known for her dizzy-dame routine in the '40s and '50s, on radio (with Bob Hope, etc.) and in movies. Her television appearances were few. Also known by her real name, Barbara Jo Allen.

VALDEZ, MIGUELITO—orchestra leader

Flight to Rhythm (music)
.... orch. leader (1949)

VALDIS, SIGRID—actress
b: c. 1941, Los Angeles, Calif.

Hogan's Heroes (com) ..... Hilda (1966–70)
*Some sources give 1905.

The widow of Bob Crane, star of *Hogan's Heroes.*

VALENTE, CATERINA—singer
b: Jan 14, 1931, Paris, France

The Entertainers (var) ..... costar (1964–65)

VALENTINE, ANTHONY—British actor
b: 1939

Masada (drama) .... Merovius (1981)

VALENTINE, KAREN—actress
b: May 25, 1947, Sebastopol, Calif.

Room 222 (drama).. Alice Johnson (1969–74)
Karen (com) .... Karen Angelo (1975)
Our Time (var)................ host (1985)

Emmy Award: Best Supporting Actress in a Comedy, for *Room 222* (1970)

Perky actress of the '70s, who starred in some of television's truly campy movies (*Gidget Grows Up, The Girl Who Came Gift Wrapped, Coffee, Tea or Me?)* as well as in two series and innumerable *Love, American Style* sketches. In the early '80s, sick and tired of constantly being called "cute" ("I hate that word—it's the most awful word in the language"), she attempted to change her image with harder-edged roles in films such as *Muggable Mary* and *Money on the Side.*

VALENTINE, SCOTT—actor
b: Jun 3, 1958

Family Ties (com)..... Nick Moore (1985–)

VALENTINO, BARRY—actor

Valentino (talk)............. host (1952–53)

VALLANCE, LOUISE—actress

The Ropers (com) ... Jenny Ballinger (1980)
Knots Landing (drama) .... Sylvie (1980–81)
Night Heat (police)
... Det. Stephanie "Stevie" Brody (1985–)

VALLEE, RUDY—singer, actor
b: Jul 28, 1901, Island Pond, Vt. r: Westbrook, Maine d: Jul 3, 1986

On Broadway Tonight (var)
.... emcee (1964–65)

The famous radio crooner of the '20s and '30s appeared occasionally on television during the '50s, '60s, and '70s, in both dramas and comedies. Among the latter were episodes of Lucille Ball's shows, *December Bride,* and *Batman* (as evil Lord Phogg). In 1964, following his surprise comeback on Broadway in *How to Succeed in Business Without Really Trying,* Rudy hosted a CBS talent competition called *On Broadway Tonight,* which showcased such up-and-coming performers as Rich Little and Richard Pryor. Ever the ham, Rudy was seen as late as 1984 in a rock-music video, *Girls Talk.*

Rudy was his own best press agent, writing no fewer than three outspoken autobiographies: *Vagabond Dreams Come True,* (1930) *My Time Is Your Time* (with Gil McKean, 1962), and *Let the Chips Fall* (1975).

VALLELY, JAMES—actor
b: Aug 30, New Brunswick, N.J.

Double Trouble (com)
.... Charles Kincaid (1984–85)

Partnered with Jonathan Schmock in the stand-up comedy team "the Funny Boys."

VALLELY, TANNIS—juvenile actress
b: Dec 28, 1975, New York City, N.Y.

Head of the Class (com)
.... Janice Lazorotto (1986–)

The daughter of actor James Vallely.

VALLI, JUNE—singer
b: Jun 30, 1930, The Bronx, N.Y.

Stop the Music (quiz)....... vocalist (1952)
Your Hit Parade (music)
.... vocalist (1952–53)
Let's Dance (music) .... regular (1954)
The Andy Williams and June Valli Show (music) .... cohost (1957)

A pop vocalist of the 1950s who was discovered on *Arthur Godfrey's Talent Scouts,* where she won first prize.

VAN, BILLY—comedian
Andy Williams Presents Ray Stevens (var)
.... regular (1970)

The Ken Berry "Wow" Show (var)
.... regular (1972)
The Sonny and Cher Comedy Hour (var)
.... regular (1973–74)
The Sonny Comedy Revue (var)
.... regular (1974)
The Bobby Vinton Show (var)
.... regular (1975–76)
The Sonny and Cher Show (var)
.... regular (1976–77)

VAN, GLORIA—singer
The Little Revue (music).. regular (1949–50)
Windy City Jamboree (music)
.... regular (1950)
Tin Pan Alley TV (var) ...... regular (1950)
Wayne King (music)...... regular (1951–52)

VAN, JACKIE—singer
This Is Music (music)........ regular (1952)
The Music Show (music)
.... regular (1953–54)

VAN ARK, JOAN—actress
b: Jun 16, 1943, New York City, N.Y. r: Boulder, Colo.

Temperatures Rising (com)
.... Nurse Annie Carlisle (1972–73)
We've Got Each Other (com)
.... Dee Dee Baldwin (1977–78)
Dallas (drama)..... Valene Ewing (1978–81)
Knots Landing (drama)
.... Valene Ewing (1979–)

Joan Van Ark (who was named, believe it or not, after Joan of Arc) began her career on stage in the early '60s, scoring her first major break in the touring company of *Barefoot in the Park.* She played many guest roles on TV in the late '60s and '70s, on series ranging from *The F.B.I.* to *The Girl with Something Extra* and *Quark.* In addition, she has done a good deal of Saturday morning cartoon voice work on series including *Tarzan and the Super Seven,* *Heathcliff and Dingbat,* and *Spider Woman* (in the title role). Joan was a regular on two comedies in the '70s, but is best known today as Gary Ewing's long-suffering wife on *Knots Landing.*

VANCE, CHRISTIAN—actor
Pearl (drama)........... Pvt. Finger (1978)

VANCE, DANITRA—black comedienne
b: Jul 13, Chicago, Ill.

NBC's Saturday Night Live (var)
.... regular (1985–86)

VANCE, VIVIAN—actress
b: Jul 26, 1907*, Cherryvale, Kan. r: Independence, Kan d: Aug 17, 1979

I Love Lucy (com).... Ethel Mertz (1951–57)
The Lucy-Desi Comedy Hour (specials) (com)
.... Ethel Mertz (1957–60)
The Lucy Show (com)
.... Vivian Bagley (1962–65)

Emmy Award: Best Supporting Actress in a Series, for *I Love Lucy* (1953)

"For years I've heard from my family and friends, 'Don't make a fool of yourself, Vivian,'" said Vivian Vance in later life. "And look how rich I got making a fool of myself!" Vivian was Lucille Ball's cheery, lovable, muddling-through sidekick in a thousand wacky schemes—generations of viewers knew her in no other role. Her career apart from Lucy was indeed minor. The folks in her hometown in Kansas had taken up a collection to send her to study drama in New York when she was young, and Vivian got her first break there singing "Japanese Sandman" in the musical *Music in the Air*. She remained a New York stage actress through the '30s and '40s in productions ranging from the 1934 musical *Anything Goes* to a 1947 revival of the social protest play *The Cradle Will Rock*. In the late '40s she suffered a nervous breakdown and was just recovering when the producers of *I Love Lucy* saw her in a local West Coast play and offered her the role of Ethel. She didn't want it at first, as she had just begun to get small parts in movies, but Desi Arnaz talked her into it. It was one sales pitch she never regretted accepting.

After six classic years on *I Love Lucy* and more on the Lucy-Desi specials that followed, Vivian was induced to film a pilot for a series of her own in 1959. However, when *Guestward Ho!* eventually went on the air it was with a different actress in the leading role. Vivian then married a wealthy publishing executive and retired happily to Connecticut. Lucy managed to get her out of mothballs to do three seasons of her new *Lucy Show* in the

*Some sources give 1911, 1912, or 1913. Take your pick.

early '60s ("I don't believe I'd have started the show without Vivian," she later said), but after that, Vivian returned to Connecticut for good, emerging only on rare occasions. Among these were annual visits to Lucy's series (right up to 1972) and rare appearances on *Love, American Style* and *Rhoda*. She also appeared in two TV movies: *Getting Away from It All* in 1972, and *The Great Houdinis* (the life of Harry Houdini) in 1976. Her last years, it is said, were low-key and pleasant.

VAN CLEEF, LEE—actor
b: Jan 9, 1925, Somerville, N.J.

The Master (adv)
.... John Peter McAllister (1984)

Rangy, mean-looking actor seen quite a bit in television westerns during the '50s and early '60s; then he departed for Europe to star as the cruel villain (and sometimes cruel hero) of numerous "spaghetti westerns." Lee returned to TV in 1984 in the rather surprising role of a heroic ninja martial-arts master in *The Master*. He was, it must be said, in remarkably good shape at the age of 59.

VAN DAMME, ART—jazz accordionist
b: Apr 9, 1920, Norway, Mich. r: Chicago, Ill.

Chicago Jazz (music) .... quintet (1949)
The Ransom Sherman Show (var)
.... quintet (1950)

VANDER PYL, JEAN—actress
The Flintstones (cartn)
...... Wilma Flintstone (voice) (1960–66)
The Flintstones (cartn)
.... Pebbles (voice) (1962–66)
Please Don't Eat the Daisies (com)
.... Ethel Carter (1966–67)
Where's Huddles? (cartn)
.... Marge Huddles (voice) (1970)

VANDERS, WARREN—actor
Empire (wes) .... Chuck Davis (1963)

VAN DE VENTER, FRED—newscaster, host
Twenty Questions (quiz)
.... panelist (1949–55)

VAN DOREN, JOHN—panelist

High-Low (quiz)............ panelist (1957)

VAN DYKE, BARRY—actor

b: Jul 31, 1951, Atlanta, Ga. r: New York and Los Angeles

The Harvey Korman Show (com)
.... Stuart Stafford (1978)
Battlestar Galactica (sci fi)
.... Lt. Dillon (1980)
Gun Shy (com)..... Russell Donovan (1983)
The Redd Foxx Show (com)
.... Sgt. Dwight Stryker (1986)

The son of actor Dick Van Dyke. Barry made his acting debut at age nine on *The Dick Van Dyke Show* and later had bit parts on *The New Dick Van Dyke Show* before striking out on his own.

VAN DYKE, DICK—actor

b: Dec 13, 1925, West Plains, Mo. r: Danville, Ill.

CBS Cartoon Theatre (cartn).... host (1956)
The Chevy Showroom (var).. regular (1958)
Pantomime Quiz (quiz) ... regular (1958–59)
Laugh Line (quiz)............. emcee (1959)
The Dick Van Dyke Show (com)
.... Rob Petrie (1961–66)
The New Dick Van Dyke Show (com)
.... Dick Preston (1971–74)
Van Dyke and Company (var)... host (1976)
The Carol Burnett Show (var)
.... regular (1977)

Emmy Awards: Best Actor in a Series, for *The Dick Van Dyke Show* (1964, 1965); Best Actor in a Comedy Series, for *The Dick Van Dyke Show* (1966); Star, Best Comedy-Variety Series, for *Van Dyke and Company* (1977); Best Performer in a Children's Program, for the *CBS Library* Presentation "The Wrong Way Kid" (1984).

"I never think of myself as having a career," says lanky comic Dick Van Dyke. "Things happen to me, some good, some not so . . . I go with the flow, wherever it takes me." Life has taken Dick down some strange paths since the day, in 1945, when he was discharged from the service and had to decide what to do with his life. First he opened an advertising agency in his hometown of Danville, but it folded in a year. Then he teamed with a friend in a nightclub act called Eric and Van, The Merry Mules. They wandered the country for six long years doing a routine in which they pantomimed and lip-synched to records ("And boy did we stink!").

By 1953, tired of travel and obscurity, Dick settled in Atlanta, where he hosted a local TV show, followed by a similar program in New Orleans. In 1956 an air force buddy, then a television producer, lured him to New York, where he began getting summer replacement assignments on the networks—as host of a prime time cartoon show in 1956 and then, in 1958, on Andy Williams' summer show. Dick was soon recognized as an up-and-coming talent and filled in for Jack Paar and Garry Moore as well as guested on the Ed Sullivan, Dinah Shore, and Perry Como shows. He made his Broadway debut in 1958 and in 1960 scored a major hit in the musical *Bye Bye Birdie.*

Dick's star was rising very fast indeed, and when he began *The Dick Van Dyke Show* in the fall of 1961, his fame was assured. The program shot into the top ten and won a slew of Emmy Awards as the best comedy of the period. Dick soon moved into films with such '60s hits as *Mary Poppins* and *Chitty Chitty Bang Bang,* as well as the movie version of *Bye Bye Birdie.* When he closed down *The Dick Van Dyke Show* (still top-rated) to concentrate on films, it appeared there was little he couldn't do.

However, Dick's type of light fluffy film was already going out of vogue and in 1971 he was back on TV, attempting to rekindle his success with a "new" Dick Van Dyke show. This time he played a talk show host in Arizona. The series limped along for three years, as did Dick's movie career. His time seemed to have passed, and Dick began a very difficult bout with alcoholism. He made headlines when he entered a clinic in 1973 to dry out; he later went on the road as a reformed alcoholic to help others fight the disease and played an alcoholic in the much-publicized TV movie *The Morning After* (1974), his first dramatic film.

After a short-lived variety series in 1976 (which included many mime routines) and a brief stint as Carol Burnett's costar, Dick decided to concentrate on specials and occasional TV movies. Among the films were *Dropout Father* and *Found Money,* the latter costarring another TV comedy legend, Sid Caesar. A 1981 pilot for a new situation comedy with Connie Stevens, *Harry's Battles,* did not make it to the fall schedule.

VAN DYKE, JERRY—actor
b: Jul 27, 1931, Danville, Ill.

Picture This (quiz)........... emcee (1963)
The Judy Garland Show (var)
.... regular (1963)
My Mother the Car (com)
.... Dave Crabtree (1965–66)
Accidental Family (com)
.... Jerry Webster (1967–68)
The Headmaster (drama)
.... Jerry Brownell (1970–71)
13 Queens Boulevard (com)
.... Steven Winters (1979)

Dick Van Dyke's brother, like Dick, started out on the club circuit (often using a banjo as his prop). Jerry was intermittently active on television in the '60s and '70s, but will always be remembered for one infamous role—the male lead in what many consider to be TV's All-Time Most Idiotic Comedy Series, *My Mother the Car.*

VAN DYKE, LEROY—country singer
b: Oct 4, 1929, Spring Fork, Mo.*

Ozark Jubilee (music)....... regular (1958)

Country performer best known for the fast-talking novelty "The Auctioneer," and one of country's classic cheatin' songs, "Walk on By."

VAN DYKE, MARCIA—
Wisdom of the Ages (info)
.... panelist (1952–53)

VAN EMAN, CHARLES—actor
b: May 26, Pittsburgh, Pa.

Dynasty II: The Colbys (drama)
.... Sean McAllister (1985–)

VAN GYSEGHEM, ANDRE—actor
b: Aug 18, 1906, Eltham, Kent, England

The Search for the Nile (drama)
.... Sir Roderick Murchison (1972)

*Some sources give Mississippi.

VAN HORNE, HARRIET—New York newspaper columnist
b: May 17, 1920, Syracuse, N.Y.

Leave It to The Girls (talk)
.... panelist (1949–54)
What's the Story? (quiz)
.... panelist (1952–55)

VAN HORNE, RANDY—singers
b: Feb 10, 1924, El Paso, Texas

The Nat "King" Cole Show (var)
.... singers (1957)

VAN KAMP, MERETE—actress
b: c. 1962, Kolding/Jutland, Denmark

Dallas (drama)............. Grace (1985–)

She was tall and blonde and possessed a regal beauty some compared to that of the young Grace Kelly. She was also, they said, of real-life aristocratic blood—a Danish countess, no less—when, in 1983, NBC announced her "discovery" after a worldwide talent search and cast her in the lead in the miniseries *Princess Daisy.* The press soon debunked the royalty bit ("Countess who?" sniffed the Danish embassy). " 'Countess' was a nickname given to me by my family," she admitted lamely at a press conference. "My father is in the aluminum business in Denmark."
Princess Daisy was a disappointment in the ratings, but the inexperienced actress did better than many expected and has since been seen in other roles, including a continuing part in *Dallas.*

VANOCUR, SANDER—newscaster
b: Jan 8, 1928, Cleveland, Ohio

NBC Weekend News (news)
.... anchorman (1961–65)
First Tuesday (news) . anchorman (1969–70)

This opinionated newsman started out as a newspaper reporter in England and New York in the mid-1950s and joined NBC in 1957. After 14 years with the network, he switched to public television in 1971 but soon came under fire from the Nixon administration for his liberal views. After two years he left TV to teach and become a columnist for *The Washington Post.* He joined ABC News in 1977 as a political and international affairs reporter.

VAN PATTEN, DICK—actor

b: Dec 9, 1928, Richmond Hill, Queens, N.Y.

Mama (com) .... Nels (1949–57)
The Partners (com)
.... Sgt. Higgenbottom (1971–72)
The New Dick Van Dyke Show (com)
.... Max Mathias (1973–74)
When Things Were Rotten (com)
.... Friar Tuck (1975)
Eight Is Enough (com)
.... Tom Bradford (1977–81)

Pudgy, now-balding Dick Van Patten began as a "show biz kid" and has been 50 years in the public eye. His mother pushed him into an MGM audition when he was six; although it resulted in a contract and a trip to Hollywood, he did not enter films at that time. Instead, he got his first role onstage, at seven, as Melvyn Douglas's son in the 1935 play *Tapestry in Gray*. For the next dozen years little Dickie Van Patten (as he was billed) was one of New York's busiest juvenile actors, appearing with the great stars of the day in such plays as George Kaufman's *The American Way* (for two years), *The Skin of Our Teeth,* and *Oh Mistress Mine*, the latter beginning a long association with Alfred Lunt and Lynn Fontanne. Dickie's only movie as a juvenile was the obscure but appropriately titled 1941 release *Reg'lar Fellers*.

At twenty, when many child actors find their careers evaporating, Dick won the role of eldest son Nels in the TV family show *Mama,* which ran for eight long years. So grateful was he that he named his first born son Nels, after the character he played (Nels is now a tennis pro). Dick's career did slow down in the '60s, when he made only occasional appearances onstage, in films (e.g., *Charly*), and in episodes of such series as *I Dream of Jeannie* and *That Girl.* He also had a short stint on the daytime serial *Young Doctor Malone.* During the '70s he was busier, playing amiable but often flustered middled-aged men, notably the dad on *Eight Is Enough*.

VAN PATTEN, JAMES—actor

b: Oct 7, 1956, Brooklyn, N.Y.

The Chisholms (wes)
.... Bo Chisholm (1979–80)

The middle son of Dick Van Patten. He began acting a little later than his dad, at age nine, and has been seen most often in series episodes and Disney movies.

VAN PATTEN, JOYCE—actress

b: Mar 9, 1934, Queens, N.Y.

The Danny Kaye Show (var)
.... regular (1964–67)
The Good Guys (com)
.... Claudia Gramus (1968–70)
The Don Rickles Show (com)
.... Jean Benedict (1972)
The Mary Tyler Moore Hour (var)
.... Iris Chapman (1979)

The sister of Dick Van Patten. As did Dick, she began acting as a child, winning a Shirley Temple look-alike contest at age two and debuting on Broadway at six. She was once married to Martin Balsam.

VAN PATTEN, TIMOTHY—actor

b: Jun 10, 1959 Brooklyn, N.Y.

The White Shadow (drama)
.... Mario Pettrino (Salami) (1978–81)
The Master (adv)
.... Max Keller (1984)

Young half brother of Dick Van Patten.

VAN PATTEN, VINCENT—actor

b: Oct 17, 1957, Bellrose, N.Y.

Apple's Way (drama)
.... Paul Apple (1974–75)
Three for the Road (adv)
.... John Karras (1975)

Son of Dick Van Patten

VAN ROOTEN, LUIS—actor

b: Nov 29, 1906, Mexico City, Mexico d: Jun 17, 1973

One Man's Family (drama)
.... Dr. Thompson (1949–50)
Major Dell Conway of the Flying Tigers (adv)
.... Caribou Jones (1951)
The Wonderful John Acton (drama)
.... narrator (1953)

Small, balding character actor, often a villain in films. He was also a published expert on horticulture.

VAN STEEDEN, PETER—orchestra leader
b: Apr 3, 1904*, Amsterdam, Holland r: U.S.A.

Break the Bank (quiz)
.... orch. leader (1948–57)

VAN VALKENBURGH, DEBORAH—actress
b: Aug 29, 1952, Schenectady, N.Y.

Too Close for Comfort (com)
.... Jackie Rush (1980–85)

VAN VOORHIS, WESTBROOK—announcer
b: 1904 d: Jul 14, 1968

Crusade in Europe (doc) .... narrator (1949)
Doorway to Danger (drama)
.... narrator (1951)
Panic (drama)............. narrator (1957)
No Warning (drama) .... narrator (1958)

The stentorian, oft-parodied voice of radio's *March of Time.*

VARDEN, NORMA—actress
b: 1898, England

Hazel (com) ..... Harriet Johnson (1961–65)

VARELA, JAY—actor

Delvecchio (police)... Sgt. Rivera (1976–77)

VARGAS, JOHN—actor
b: Apr 24, The Bronx, N.Y.

At Ease (com)............. Cardinel (1983)

VARLEY, BEATRICE—actress
b: 1896 d: 1969

Dick and the Duchess (com)
.... Mathilda (1957–58)

VARNEY, JIM—actor
b: Jun 15, Lexington, Ky.

The Johnny Cash Show (var)
.... regular (1976)
Fernwood 2-Night (com)
.... Virgil Sims (1977–78)
Operation Petticoat (com)
.... seaman Broom (1977–79)
Pink Lady (var) .... regular (1980)

*Some sources give Apr 13.

Pop! Goes the Country (music)
.... regular (1982)
The Rousters (adv) .... Evan Earp (1983–84)

VASQUEZ, DENNIS—juvenile actor

Popi (com).......... Luis Rodriguez (1976)

VAUGHN, DENNY—orchestra leader
d: Oct 3, 1972

What's It All About, World? (var)
.... orch. leader (1969)
The Glen Campbell Goodtime Hour (var)
.... singers (1969–70)
The Summer Smothers Show (var)
.... orch. leader (1970)
Pat Paulsen's Half a Comedy Hour (var)
.... orch. leader (1970)

VAUGHN, ROBERT—actor
b: Nov 22, 1932, New York City r: Minneapolis, Minn.

The Lieutenant (drama)
.... Capt. Ray Rambridge (1963–64)
The Man from U.N.C.L.E. (drama)
.... Napoleon Solo (1964–68)
The Protectors (adv).. Harry Rule (1972–73)
Captains and the Kings (drama)
.... Charles Desmond (1976)
Centennial (drama)
.... Morgan Wendell (1978–79)
Backstairs at the White House (drama)
.... Pres. Woodrow Wilson (1979)
The Blue and the Gray (drama)
.... Sen. Reynolds (1982)
Emerald Point N.A.S. (drama)
.... Harlan Adams (1983–84)
The A-Team (adv)
.... Gen. Hunt Stockwell (1986–)

Emmy Award: Best Supporting Actor in a Drama Series, for *Washington: Behind Closed Doors* (1978)

One of television's actor/intellectuals, Robert Vaughn has often chastised the medium for its low quality, while contributing more than his share of potboilers to the schedule. Despite the complaints, and occasional vows never to do another series 'like the last one,' he has remained one of TV's busiest supporting players for more than 30 years.

A dark, suspicious-looking man with a rather superior air, Vaughn has portrayed a splendidly villainous "Mr. Big" on many dramas. Though he was born of theatrical parents, he originally intended to pursue a career in journalism. He began acting to pay his way through graduate school in the mid-1950s and, gradually, acting took over. Vaughn was in many series episodes in the late '50s, from *Dragnet* to *Father Knows Best,* and on even more numerous crime shows and westerns of the '60s. He also began a busy movie career, which peaked early with an Academy Award–nominated performance in *The Young Philadelphians* in 1959.

Vaughn's first regular series role had him cast as Gary Lockwood's tough commanding officer in *The Lieutenant;* however, it was *The Man from U.N.C.L.E.* the following season that made him a star. Although he said he would not do another series, he was back a few years later in the similarly stylish espionage series *The Protectors,* filmed in Europe, and thereafter in many miniseries and TV movies, mostly dramas of intrigue or historical epics of one kind or another. Among them: *The Rebels; Mirror, Mirror; Dr. Franken* (as a modern day Dr. Frankenstein); *The Gossip Columnist; City in Fear; Inside the Third Reich* (as a Nazi field marshal); *Evergreen;* and *Intimate Agony*—the last-named an exploitation film about herpes!

Vaughn continued his academic studies in the '60s, even while busy acting, and eventually earned his Ph.D. in political science. A political activist, he has often worked on behalf of liberal causes and in the '70s authored a book called *The Victims,* about the political blacklisting of the McCarthy Era.

VEAZIE, CAROL—actress
b: c. 1895 d: Jul 19, 1984

Norby (com) .... Mrs. Maude Endles (1955)

VELEZ, EDDIE—actor
b: Jun 4, New York City, N.Y.

Berrengers (drama).... Julio Morales (1985)
Charlie & Company (com)
.... Miguel Santana (1985–86)
The A-Team (adv)
..... "Dishpan" Frankie Sanchez (1986–)

VELEZ, MARTHA—actress
b: Aug 25, The Bronx, N.Y.

a.k.a. Pablo (com)
.... Lucia Rivera Del Gato (1984)

VELVETEERS, THE—

Music in Velvet (music) ..... regular (1949)

VENNERA, CHICK—actor
b: Mar 27, Herkimer, N.Y.

Hail to the Chief (com)
.... Raoul the butler (1985)

VENTURE, RICHARD—actor
b: Nov 12, West New York, N.J.

Street Hawk (police)
.... Capt. Leo Altobelli (1985)

VERA, RICKY—juvenile actor
b: c. 1945

Our Miss Brooks (com)
.... Ricky Velasco (1954–55)
Our Miss Brooks (com)
.... Benny Romero (1955–56)

VERBIT, HELEN—actress

Flatbush (com)....... Mrs. Fortunato (1979)

VERDUGO, ELENA—actress
b: 1926, Hollywood, Calif.

Meet Millie (com)
.... Millie Bronson (1952–56)
Redigo (wes)................. Gerry (1963)
The New Phil Silvers Show (com)
.... Audrey (1964)
Many Happy Returns (com)
.... Lynn Hall (1964–65)
Mona McCluskey (com)
.... Alice Henderson (1965–66)
Marcus Welby, M.D. (drama)
.... Consuelo Lopez (1969–76)

This pert and pretty Spanish-American actress broke into films as a teenager, in 1940, and made her first big splash on TV in the 1950's "other" secretary show, *Meet Millie* (Ann Sothern's *Private Secretary* premiered a few months later). Elena concentrated mostly on series work in the '60s, while making occasional guest appearances on *The Bob Cummings Show, Route 66, 77 Sunset Strip,* etc. She has been seen very little since her long-running role as mature, efficient Nurse Lopez on *Marcus*

Welby. She did come back, however, for the reunion movie *The Return of Marcus Welby, M.D.* in 1984.

VEREEN, BEN—black actor, dancer
b: Oct 10, 1946, Miami, Fla. r: Brooklyn, N.Y.

Ben Vereen . . . Comin' At Ya (var)
.... host (1975)
Roots (drama)....... Chicken George (1977)
Tenspeed and Brown Shoe (drama)
.... E. L. "Tenspeed" Turner (1980)
Webster (com)
.. Uncle Phillip Long (occasional) (1984–)

Energetic song and dance man who rose to fame onstage in the late '60s and early '70s in musicals such as *Hair, Jesus Christ Superstar,* and *Pippin* (for which he won a Tony Award). His television career has been erratic, perhaps because of a lack of focus—he seems to do a little of everything, without really sticking with anything. Ben received much acclaim for his dramatic role in *Roots,* but a 1975 summer song-and-dance series went nowhere, and a 1980 cop show was a bust. His one TV movie of the '70s was the low-rated *Louis Armstrong—Chicago Style,* in which he played the famous jazzman.

In the '80s Ben was seen to better advantage in the series *Webster,* in the sensitive role of Webster's uncle, who wanted to reclaim him from his white adoptive parents.

VERNON, HARVEY—actor
b: Jun 30, Flint, Mich.

Carter Country (com)
.... Dep. Jasper DeWitt, Jr. (1977–79)

VERNON, IRENE—actress

Bewitched (com) ..... Louise Tate (1964–66)

VERNON, JACKIE—actor
b: 1929, New York City, N.Y.

The Garry Moore Show (var)
.... regular (1966–67)

VERNON, JOHN—actor
b: Feb 24, 1932, Regina, Sask., Canada

Delta House (com)
.... Dean Vernon Wormer (1979)

The Blue and the Gray (drama)
.... Sec. of State Seward (1982)
Hail to the Chief (com)
.... Gen. Hannibal Stryker (1985)

A tall, cold-eyed Canadian actor, often a villain but also fine as a pompous bureaucrat—as in the movie *Animal House* and its short-lived TV spin-off.

VERNON, KATE—actress

Falcon Crest (drama)
.... Lorraine Prescott (1984–85)

The daughter of character actor John Vernon.

VICTOR, JAMES—actor
b: Jul 27, 1939, Santiago, Dominican Republic

Viva Valdez (com)
.... Victor Valdez (1976)
Condo (com) .... Jose Montoya (1983)

VIEIRA, MEREDITH—newscaster
b: Providence, R.I.

West 57th (pub aff).. correspondent (1985–)

VIGODA, ABE—actor
b: Feb 24, 1921, New York City, N.Y.

Barney Miller (com)
.... Det. Phil Fish (1975–77)
Fish (com) .... Det. Phil Fish (1977–78)

A hawk-nosed, decrepit-looking actor who labored long onstage during the '60s (and also, for a time, on TV's *Dark Shadows*), then suddenly attracted attention as the ruthless Mafia leader Tessio in the 1971 movie smash *The Godfather.* Vigoda's newfound notoriety, in his fifties, brought him guest roles in a number of TV crime shows (*Kojak, Toma*); then, in another strange twist, he became a comic sensation as the elderly, complaining cop on *Barney Miller* and its spin-off *Fish.*

The novelty of the Fish character soon subsided and Vigoda returned to supporting roles in a wide range of series episodes. He has also appeared in some rather forgettable TV movies, including *How to Pick Up Girls* and *Death Car on the Freeway.*

VIGRAN, HERB—actor
b: 1910, Fort Wayne, Ind. d: Nov 28, 1986

The Ed Wynn Show (com)
.... Ernest Henshaw (1958–59)

VIHARO, ROBERT—actor

The Survivors (drama)
.... Miguel Santerra (1969–70)

VIKINGS, THE—singers

The Jane Pickens Show (music)
.... regulars (1954)

VILLARD, TOM—actor

We Got It Made (com)
.... Jay Bostwick (1983–84)

VILLECHAIZE, HERVE—actor
b: Apr 23, 1943, Paris, France

Fantasy Island (drama) ... Tattoo (1978–83)

Black actors complain about not having enough roles; other ethnic groups do the same; the handicapped have trouble—but none of them face as many barriers in the entertainment world as the midget. Tiny (3′ 10″) Herve Villechaize is one exception to the rule, costarring for five years on the hit series *Fantasy Island,* although he often had little more to do than ring the island's bells or run after white-suited Ricardo Montalban while yelling "Yes, boss!"

Herve was born in Paris to a French surgeon father and English mother and had originally studied to become an artist (he still paints professionally). Newly arrived in New York, he answered an ad seeking "a small person for workshop theater" and launched a second career. He was a supporting player onstage and in films during the '60s and '70s, landing a role in the original *Fantasy Island* TV movie in 1977, which led to the series.

VINCENT, JAN-MICHAEL—actor
b: Jul 15, 1944, Denver, Colo. r: Hanford, Calif.

The Survivors (drama)
.... Jeffrey Hastings (1969–70)
The Winds of War (drama)
.... Byron Henry (1983)
Airwolf (adv)
.... Stringfellow Hawke (1984–86)

A quiet, moody, boyishly handsome actor who has had a rather low-key career in Hollywood, despite his obvious magnetic attraction for women. That is by choice; he is by his own admission basically lazy and would rather "chase a wave" (he is an expert surfer) than toil under hot studio lights.

Because of his youthful looks, Jan initially found work in kid's shows in the late '60s, including episodes of *Lassie* and the Saturday morning adventure serial "Danger Island" on *The Banana Splits Hour.* He also had bits on episodes of *Dragnet* and *Bonanza,* but his major break was a romantic lead in the steamy soap opera *The Survivors,* as Lana Turner's son. Throughout the '70s he continued to appear, without much effort, in a score of movies and hundreds of TV episodes, often portraying a rebellious young man. Though familiar, he never really attained stardom until he portrayed the son of Robert Mitchum (another Hollywood rebel, and Jan's idol) in the miniseries *The Winds of War.* A curiously low-key helicopter adventure series, *Airwolf,* followed. Jan still lives in Malibu, near those waves.

VINCENT, ROMO—comedian, host

You're Invited (var).......... emcee (1948)

VINCENT, VIRGINIA—actress

Meet Millie (com) .... Gladys (1956)
The Joey Bishop Show (com)
.... Betty (1961–62)
The Super (com) .... Dottie Clark (1972)
Eight Is Enough (com)
.... Daisy Maxwell (1977–79)

VINE, BILLY—actor
b: c. 1915 d: Feb 10, 1958

The Fifty-Fourth Street Revue (var)
.... host (1949–50)

VINSON, GARY—actor
b: El Segundo, Calif.

The Roaring Twenties (drama)
.... Chris Higbee (1960–62)
McHale's Navy (com)
.... Christy (1962–66)
Pistols 'n' Petticoats (com)
.... Sheriff Harold Sikes (1966–67)

VINTON, BOBBY—singer

b: Apr 16, 1935*, Pittsburgh, Pa. r: Canonsburg, Pa.

The Bobby Vinton Show (var)
.... host (1975–78)

A multi-talented young musician who originally tried to launch a big band "with a young sound for young people" (inspired by his father's dance band) but soon found that the younger set liked his nasal crooning better. His hits of the '60s included "Roses Are Red" and "Blue on Blue." Bobby remained popular into the '70s and had his own syndicated TV series, whose chief elements were "Polish power" jokes (he is of Polish extraction) and his "sentimental and sincere" songs.

VISCUSO, SAL—actor

b: Oct 5, c. 1948, Brooklyn, N.Y. r: Sacramento, Calif.

The Montefuscos (com)
.... Nunzio Montefusco (1975)
Soap (com)
.... Father Timothy Flotsky (1978–79)

VISO, MIKEY—actor

Hometown (drama)... Dylan Nathan (1985)

VITTE, RAY—black actor

b: Nov 20, 1949, New York City, N.Y. r: Pasadena, Calif. d: Feb 20, 1983

Doc (com) ...... Woody Henderson (1976)
David Cassidy—Man Undercover (police)
.... Off. T. J. Epps (1978–79)
The Quest (adv)....... Cody Johnson (1982)

This young actor died in a scuffle with police.

VIVINO, DONNA—actress

Hometown (drama)..... Tess Abbott (1985)

VIVYAN, JOHN—actor

b: May 31, 1916**, Chicago, Ill. d: Dec 20, 1983

Mr. Lucky (adv)....... Mr. Lucky (1959–60)

John Vivyan became one of television's "lost stars." He had his moments of glory

*Some sources give 1941.
**Some sources give 1923.

in 1959–60 when he appeared in the movie *Imitation of Life,* starred in his own adventure series as a smooth-talking gambler, and played a few guest roles—then he disappeared. What happened to him? According to celebrity-chaser Richard Lamparski, Vivyan returned to regional stage work (from whence he had come) and then suffered a severe heart attack which left him out of commission for quite a while and turned his hair a distinguished white. In his later years he ran an answering service in Los Angeles.

VOGEL, MITCH—juvenile actor

b: Jan 17, 1956, Alhambra, Calif.

Bonanza (wes)
.... Jamie Hunter (1970–73)

The orphaned teenager taken in by the Cartwrights during the final seasons of *Bonanza.*

VOGEL, PETER—actor

Holocaust (drama)
.... Frey Kalova (1978)

VOHS, JOAN—actress

b: Jul 30, 1931, St. Albans, N.Y.

Bachelor Father (com)
.... Elaine Meechim (1959)

VOLA, VICKI—actress

b: Denver, Colo. d: Jul 21, 1985

Mr. District Attorney (police)
.... Miss Miller (1951–52)

VOLAND, HERB—actor

Love on a Rooftop (com)
.... Fred Hammond (1966–67)
Mr. Deeds Goes to Town (com)
.... Henry Masterson (1969–70)
Arnie (com)........ Neil Ogilvie (1970–72)
*M*A*S*H* (com)
.... Gen. Brandon Clayton (1972–73)
The Paul Lynde Show (com)
.... T. J. McNish (1972–73)

VOLDSTAD, JOHN—actor

b: Feb 20, 1950, Oslo, Norway r: U.S.A.

Newhart (com)...... second Darryl (1982–)

VOLZ, NEDRA—actress

A Year at the Top (com)
............Grandma Belle Durbin (1977)
Hanging In (com)....... Pinky Nolan (1979)
Diff'rent Strokes (com)
.... Adelaide Brubaker (1980–82)
The Dukes of Hazzard (com)
.... Miz Tisdale (1981–83)
Filthy Rich (com)
...... Winona "Mother B" Beck (1982–83)
The Fall Guy (drama)
.... Pearl Sperling (1985–86)

Feisty little woman much in demand for "grandma" roles in the late '70s and '80s.

VON HOFFMAN, BRANT—actor

240-Robert (adv) .... Dep. Bottendott (1981)

VON HOFFMAN, NICHOLAS—liberal commentator

b: Oct 16, 1929, New York City, N.Y.

60 Minutes (pub aff)..... debater (1971–74)

VON ZELL, HARRY—announcer

b: Jul 11, 1906, Indianapolis, Ind. d: Nov 21, 1981

The George Burns and Gracie Allen Show (com)................ as himself (1951–58)

The George Burns Show (com)
.... as himself (1958–59)
The George Gobel Show (var)
.... regular (1959–60)

Familiar, imposing announcer and comic foil of radio days, best known to TV viewers as Burns and Allen's longtime sidekick.

VOORHEES, DONALD—conductor

b: Jul 26, 1903, Allentown, Pa.

The Bell Telephone Hour (music)
.... conductor (1959–68)

VORGAN, GIGI—actress

Married: The First Year (drama)
.... Cookie Levin (1979)
Knots Landing (drama) .... Carol (1984)

VOSKOVEC, GEORGE—actor

b: Jun 19, 1905, Sazava, Czechoslovakia d: Jul 1, 1981

Skag (drama) .... Petar Skagska (1980)
Nero Wolfe (drama)... Fritz Brenner (1981)

VYE, MURVYN—actor

b: Jul 15, 1913, Quincy, Mass. d: Aug 17, 1976

The Bob Cummings Show (adv)
.... Lionel (1961–62)

W

WADDELL, JACKIE—

Hee Haw (var) . . . . regular (1984–)

WADE, ADAM—black singer
b: Mar 17, 1935, Pittsburgh, Pa.

Tony Orlando and Dawn (var)
. . . . regular (1976)

Ever wonder what happens to all those pop singers who had one or two hits a long time ago? Adam, who had several best-selling records in the early '60s ("Take Good Care of Her," "The Writing on the Wall"), dabbled in several other fields during the '70s. Among them: acting in movies (*Shaft, Claudine*) and on television (*Search for Tomorrow*); doing voice work for Saturday morning cartoons (*The Harlem Globetrotters Show*); and, most notably, becoming the first black to ever host a daytime network game show, *Musical Chairs,* in 1975.

WADE, ERNESTINE—black actress
b: Jackson, Miss.

Amos 'n' Andy (com)
. . . . Sapphire Stevens (1951–53)

WAGENHEIM, CHARLES—actor
b: 1895*, Newark, N.J. d: Mar 6, 1979

Gunsmoke (wes) . . . . Halligan (1967–75)

WAGGONER, LYLE—actor
b: Apr 13, 1935, Kansas City, Kan. r: St. Louis, Mo.

The Carol Burnett Show (var)
. . . . regular (1967–74)
The Jimmie Rodgers Show (var)
. . . . regular (1969)
Wonder Woman (adv)
. . . . Maj. Steve Trevor (1976–77)
The New Adventures of Wonder Woman (adv) . . . . Steve Trevor, Jr. (1977–79)

The tall, rugged "Rock Hudson" type on *The Carol Burnett Show* and other series, including *Wonder Woman*—on which he played Wonder Woman's love interest. He

*Some sources give 1901.

has also appeared in episodic TV and briefly hosted the syndicated quiz show *It's Your Bet* (1970).

WAGNER, CHUCK—actor
b: Jun 20, Nashville, Tenn.

Automan (police) . . . . Automan (1983–84)

WAGNER, HELEN—actress
b: Sep 3, Lubbock, Texas

The World of Mr. Sweeney (com)
. . . . Marge Franklin (1954)

One of the long-distance champs of daytime soap operas. After her brief stint as Charlie Ruggles' grown daughter on *The World of Mr. Sweeney* (which ran in daytime until 1955), Helen joined the cast of the new daytime serial *As the World Turns* at its premiere in April 1956, in the role of Nancy Hughes. She was still playing the role 30 years later.

WAGNER, JACK—actor

The Adventures of Ozzie & Harriet (com)
. . . . Jack (1961–66)

WAGNER, LINDSAY—actress
b: Jun 22, 1949, Los Angeles, Calif.

The Bionic Woman (adv)
. . . . Jaime Sommers (1976–78)
Scruples (drama) . . . . . . Billie Ikehorn (1980)
Jessie (police) . . . . . Dr. Jessie Hayden (1984)

Emmy Award: Best Actress in a Drama Series, for *The Bionic Woman* (1977).

What has two legs of incredible speed, ears which can hear for miles around, a right arm of unbelievable strength, and a boyfriend with similar attributes? The *Bionic Woman,* of course, ABC's mate for its popular superhero *The Six Million Dollar Man.*

Beautiful Lindsay Wagner began her career in somewhat more prosaic fashion, as a teenage model and a singer with a rock group, before she entered acting in the late '60s. A stylish young woman with an authoritative air, she won roles in episodes of a number of series, including *Marcus Welby* and *The Rockford Files.* She also got her movie career off to an auspicious start with a leading part in the 1973 film

The Paper Chase. However, it was a guest shot on *The Six Million Dollar Man* in 1975 that made her famous; she played Lee Major's doomed sweetheart, who died in the final act. TV moguls liked her so well they literally brought her character back to life for her own spin-off series, which ran first on ABC and then on NBC. Lindsay has since starred in several big, glossy TV movies and miniseries, including *Scruples, Princess Daisy,* and *Passions.* She has also attempted to build a more serious reputation in such "meaningful" films as *The Incredible Journey of Dr. Meg Laurel, Callie and Son,* and *I Want to Live,* as well as in the series *Jessie*—in which she played a police psychiatrist.

WAGNER, LOU—actor

CHiPs (police) .... Harlan (1978–83)

One of the most essential characters on *CHiPs*—the motorcycle repairman!

WAGNER, MIKE—actor

Camp Runamuck (com) .. Malden (1965–66)

WAGNER, ROBERT—actor
b: Feb 10, 1930, Detroit, Mich. r: California

It Takes a Thief (drama)
.... Alexander Mundy (1968–70)
Switch (drama)....... Pete Ryan (1975–78)
Pearl (drama)......... Cal Lanford (1978)
Hart to Hart (adv)
.... Jonathan Hart (1979–84)
Lime Street (drama)
.... James Greyson Culver (1985)

A TV Prince Charming, usually seen in dashing roles of wealth, elegance, and romance. Wagner was the son of a wealthy steel executive, educated in private schools and intended for a business career. However, his boyish good looks led him into acting in the early '50s and he built up quite a following among young moviegoers over the next dozen years in such films as *With a Song in My Heart, Prince Valiant,* and *All the Fine Young Cannibals.*

Wagner did little television in the '50s. His rare appearances included dramatizations of two of his films, *The Ox Bow Incident* and *Gun in His Hand,* on *The 20th Century–Fox Hour* in 1955–56. In the mid-1960s his film career began to drift and he thereafter made a conscious effort to establish himself in TV, starring in three classy series: *It Takes a Thief* (with Fred Astaire), *Colditz* (seen only in Britain, 1972–73), and *Switch.* He was also seen in TV movies and miniseries, mostly mysteries, and in the 1976 special *Cat on a Hot Tin Roof.* No doubt his best remembered role was that of the dashingly handsome detective and husband on *Hart to Hart.*

Offscreen, R.J. (as he is known to friends) had one of Hollywood's storybook marriages, although it ended in tragedy. He was married from 1957 to 1963 to beautiful young starlet Natalie Wood, divorced, then married her again in 1972. They were considered one of the film community's most glamorous and happy couples at the time of her accidental death in 1981.

WAGNER, WENDE—actress

The Green Hornet (drama)
.... Lenore "Casey" Case (1966–67)

WAGON WHEELERS, THE—

Five Star Jubilee (var) ...... regulars (1961)

WAGONER, PORTER—country singer
b: Aug 12, 1927, West Plains, Mo.

Ozark Jubilee (music)..... regular (1955–56)

Porter, a major country star, hosted his own widely syndicated country music series for more than 20 years, beginning in 1960. His costar and duet partner during the late '60s was the then little known Dolly Parton.

WAHL, KEN—actor
b: 1953, Chicago, Ill.

Double Dare (police) ..... Ken Sisko (1985)

WAHL, WALTER DARE—actor
b: c. 1896 d: 1974

Holiday Hotel (var) .... regular (1950)

WAINWRIGHT, JAMES—actor
b: Mar 5, 1938, Danville, Ill.

Jigsaw (police) .... Lt. Frank Dain (1972–73)
Beyond Westworld (sci fi)
.... Simon Quaid (1980)

WAITE, JACQUELINE—actress

Faraway Hill (drama) .... regular (1946)

WAITE, RALPH—actor
b: Jun 22, 1928, White Plains, N.Y.

The Waltons (drama)
.... John Walton (1972–81)
Roots (drama)...... third mate Slater (1977)
The Mississippi (drama)
.... Ben Walker (1983–84)

A big, shirt-sleeved salt-of-the-earth type who began his adult life as a social worker and then became an ordained minister at the United Church of Christ in Garden City, N.Y. Eventually the acting bug bit him and, in the '60s, pastor Waite began to find roles in Broadway and off-Broadway plays. Late in the decade he moved to Los Angeles, where at first he landed only small parts in movies and TV ("I got two lines on *Bonanza,*" he says). His career was stalled until he auditioned for the role of the father on *The Waltons* and, to his surprise, got it—he usually played much harsher cowpoke types. With his success on the series he was able to obtain starring roles in a number of TV movies, among them *The Secret Life of John Chapman, Red Alert, OHMS* and *The Gentleman Bandit,* usually in sympathic, honest workin' man parts. At the same time he fought and eventually overcame the alcoholism that had overtaken him during his long years of struggle.

Since *The Waltons* ended, Waite has continued to play solid, down-home characters both in his own series *The Mississippi* (about an itinerant lawyer) and in movies. His onetime goal to become one of acting's explosive, angry young men has mellowed. "Life isn't a war," he now says. "It's a gift."

WAITRESSES, THE—rock group
(Patty Donahue, Chris Butler, Dan Klayman, Mars Williams, Tracy Wormworth, Billy Ficca)

Square Pegs (com).... sang theme (1982–83)

WAKELY, JIMMY—country singer
b: Feb 16, 1914, Mineola, Ark. d: Sep 23, 1982

Five Star Jubilee (var) .... host (1961)

Popular singer-songwriter of the '40s, whose country hits dealt both with cheatin' ("Slipping Around") and its consequences ("I'll Never Slip Around Again"). He also starred in a large number of low-budget western films during the 1940s.

WALBERG, GARRY—actor
b: Jun 10, Buffalo, N.Y.

The Odd Couple (com)..... Speed (1970–74)
Quincy, M.E. (police)
.... Lt. Frank Monahan (1976–83)

WALCOTT, GREGORY—actor
b: Jan 13, 1928, Wilson, N.C.

87th Precinct (police)
.... Det. Roger Havilland (1961–62)

WALDEN, LOIS—actress

Harris and Company (drama)
.... Louise Foreman (1979)

WALDEN, ROBERT—actor
b: Sep 25, 1943, New York City, N.Y.

The New Doctors (drama)
.... Dr. Martin Cohen (1972–73)
Lou Grant (drama) ..... Joe Rossi (1977–82)

A compact, intense young actor best known as reporter Joe Rossi, who often gave editor Lou Grant heartburn on *Lou Grant.* Walden got his start onstage in the '60s and has appeared in small but notable supporting roles in such films as *Bloody Mama, Hospital,* and *All the President's Men.* His TV movies have included *The Great Ice Ripoff, Enola Gay* (as J. Robert Oppenheimer), and *Memorial Day.*

Walden's experiences on *Lou Grant* so affected him that he began to write real-life articles for major newspapers and magazines as well as speak at college seminars on journalism.

WALDEN, SUSAN—actress

Little Women (drama)
.... Meg March Brooke (1979)
The Contender (drama)
.... Lucinda (Lou) Waverly (1980)

WALDO, JANET—actress
b: c. 1930

The Jetsons (cartn)
.... Judy Jetson (voice) (1962–63)
Valentine's Day (com)
................Libby Freeman (1964–65)

A juvenile actress in movies and on radio in the '40s. She is most famous, perhaps, as radio's *Corliss Archer*. On television, she is best known for her extensive Saturday morning cartoon voice work on series including *The Addams Family* (as Morticia), *Cattanooga Cats, Josie and the Pussycats* (Josie), and *The Perils of Penelope Pitstop* (Penelope).

WALDRIP, TIM—actor
b: May 19, Spokane, Wash. r: Texas

American Dream (drama)
.... Casey Novak (1981)

A.k.a. Timothy Owen; later a regular on daytime's *One Life to Live.*

WALKEN, GLENN—actor
b: Nov 18, 1945, Astoria, Queens, N.Y.

Leave It to Larry (com)
.... Stevie Tucker (1952)
The World of Mr. Sweeney (com)
.... Kippy Franklin (1954)

Juvenile actor of the '50s, who was also a regular on the daytime soap opera *The Guiding Light* in the mid-1950s. He now runs a bakery in Queens, N.Y. Glenn is the brother of Academy Award–winning actor Christopher Walken.

WALKEN, RONNIE—juvenile actor

The Wonderful John Acton (drama)
.... Kevin Acton (1953)

WALKER, ALLAN—actor, writer
b: Jan 28, 1906 d: Sep 2, 1970

The Red Buttons Show (var)
.... regular (1952–53)

WALKER, AMANDA—actress

The Strauss Family (drama)
.... Theresa (1973)

WALKER, BETTY—actress
b: c. 1928 d: Jul 26, 1982

The Steve Lawrence Show (var)
.... regular (1965)

WALKER, BILL—orchestra leader

The Johnny Cash Show (var)
.... orch. leader (1969–71)
The Johnny Cash Show (var)
.... orch. leader (1976)

WALKER, BILLY—country singer
b: Jan 14, 1929, Ralls, Texas

Ozark Jubilee (music)....... regular (1957)

WALKER, CAROLSUE—actress

AfterMASH (com)............ Sarah (1984)

WALKER, CLINT—actor
b: May 30, 1927, Hartford, Ill.

Cheyenne (wes)
.... Cheyenne Bodie (1955–62)
Kodiak (police)
.... Cal "Kodiak" McKay (1974)

As tall and massive as an oak tree (and about as animated), this 6'6" actor was one of television's more imposing figures during the western era. He had no acting training. After serving in the merchant marine during World War II, Clint worked in a number of occupations, including oil worker in Texas, bouncer in Long Beach, and deputy sheriff in Las Vegas, before he met Van Johnson and decided to give acting a try. Warner Brothers just happened to be looking for strong, silent types just then, and Clint was promptly cast in the role that would make him famous—that of the brooding cowpoke who drifted from job to job, enforcing justice, in *Cheyenne.*

Clint was a tough customer offscreen as well as on. He walked off the show in 1958 in a contract dispute (Warner's contracts, signed when actors were unknown, were notoriously one-sided). He returned in 1959 but was afraid that the *Cheyenne* role was typecasting him and yearned to be free of it. Warners, protecting its hit series, would not let him go. "I am like a caged animal," he complained to reporters. Finally, in 1962, both the series and Clint's contract expired and he departed Hollywood for an extended period to hunt sharks in Mexico and tramp the backcountry of the Rockies. He made a few guest appearances in 1963–65, on *77 Sunset Strip, Kraft Suspense Theatre* (in the somewhat autobiographical role of a mysterious hermit), and even *The Jack Benny Show* (singing and clowning!)—then dropped out of sight for seven years. He returned in the early '70s to appear in some rather forgettable TV westerns and horror films, including *The Bounty Man, Scream of the Wolf* (hunting a killer wolfman), *Killdozer* (battling a murderous bulldozer), *Snow Beast* (a beast that stalked skiers), and *The Mysterious Island of Beautiful Women*. A second series, *Kodiak,* in which he played an Alaskan backcountry lawman, was short-lived.

WALKER, DANTON—Broadway columnist
b: Jul 26, 1899, Marietta, Ga. d: Aug 8, 1960

Broadway Spotlight (var) . . . . . . host (1949)

WALKER, ELIZABETH (TIPPY)—actress
b: c. 1947

Peyton Place (drama)
. . . . Carolyn Russell (1968–69)

WALKER, JIMMIE—black actor
b: Jun 25, 1949, The Bronx, N.Y.

Good Times (com)
. . . . James (J.J.) Evans, Jr. (1974–79)
B.A.D. Cats (police)
. . . . Rodney Washington (1980)
At Ease (com)
. . . . Sgt. Val Valentine (1983)

"A bug-eyed young comic of the ghetto with spasms of supercool blowing through his nervous system, a kind of ElectraGlide strut."—*Time* magazine
"Here was the coon character, that rascalish, loud, pushy and conniving stereotype . . ."—J. Fred MacDonald in *Blacks and White TV*

Jimmie "DYN-O-MITE!" Walker, the tall, spindly comic with a wide toothy grin and lots of nervous energy, was one of the more controversial blacks on TV during the "relevance" era of programming. Not everyone approved of the ghetto-hustler role model he seemed to provide to black youths on the hit series *Good Times;* the actress playing his mother on the series (Esther Rolle) actually walked out in protest. Jimmie was a product of the ghetto himself,

born in New York's notorious South Bronx, and was a high school dropout who managed to get two years of college under a poverty program. After an undetermined period of odd jobs (he refuses to reveal his age), Jimmie broke in a stand-up comedy routine, consisting of of the ghetto humor he knew so well, at clubs like New York's Catch a Rising Star. His contemporaries there included such other newcomers as David Brenner and Freddie Prinze. His first network TV exposure was on *The Jack Paar Show,* which led to a job warming up studio audiences for the CBS series *Calucci's Department.* Then came the role of the eldest son in Norman Lear's comedy *Good Times.*

Jimmie continued to play the same shuckin' and jivin' character in TV movies and series of the 1980s and made only occasional forays into more serious roles—notably that of the young leukemia victim in the 1977 TV film *The Greatest Thing That Almost Happened.* In *B.A.D. Cats* he was a street hustler and in *At Ease* an updated Sergeant Bilko–style army con man.

WALKER, KATHRYN—actress
b: Jan 9, Philadelphia, Pa.

Beacon Hill (drama). . Fawn Lassiter (1975)

Emmy Award: Best Actress in a Single Performance, for *The Adams Chronicles* (1976)

WALKER, NANCY—actress
b: May 10, 1921, Philadelphia, Pa.

Family Affair (com)
. . . . Emily Turner (1970–71)
McMillan and Wife (police)
. . . . Mildred (1971–76)
Rhoda (com). . . . Ida Morgenstern (1974–78)
The Nancy Walker Show (com)
. . . . Nancy Kitteridge (1976)
Blansky's Beauties (com)
. . . . Nancy Blansky (1977)

The tiny (4'11"), red-haired, wisecracking, archetypal Jewish mother of the '70s, who loudly doted over Valerie Harper on *The Mary Tyler Moore Show* and *Rhoda* (as her mom) and over Brian Keith and Rock Hudson on *Family Affair* and *McMillan and Wife* (as their housekeepers). Born of vaudeville parents, Nancy was primarily a

New York stage actress for the first 30 years of her career, appearing in her first stage show *(Best Foot Forward)* at 19 and in comic roles in many other musicals thereafter, including *On the Town; Look Ma, I'm Dancing;* and *Do Re Mi.* She made a few appearances in TV plays of the '50s but then largely disappeared from sight and was practically a new face when she burst upon the TV screen once again in 1970 in a whirlwind of renewed activity. Besides her series, Nancy was familiar from Bounty paper towel commercials and guest roles in such series as *Love, American Style* and *Bridget Loves Bernie.* ABC program chief Fred Silverman was so taken with her that he signed her for her own show in the fall of 1976 (as a wisecracking Hollywood talent agent), and when that failed, immediately put her into another in February 1977, *Blansky's Beauties* (as a wisecracking Las Vegas landlady). The latter also failed, making Nancy one of the few TV stars to ever have two flops in a single season.

Nancy's appearances since then have been infrequent. She played God, about to smite Las Vegas, in the 1978 TV film *Human Feelings* (an appropriate follow-up to her failed *Blansky's Beauties!*). How does she describe herself? "I'm filled with rages. I'm the most irate woman I've ever known," she told *TV Guide.* "Most of the time I'm quiet. You would never know I could kill. Oh yes. I explode."

WALKER, PEGGY—actress

The Lazarus Syndrome (drama)
.... Virginia Hamill (1979)

WALLACE, BILLY—actor

One in a Million (com) ...... Dennis (1980)

WALLACE, CHRIS—newscaster
b: Oct 12, 1947, Chicago, Ill.

Prime Time Sunday (pub aff)
.... correspondent (1979–80)
NBC Weekend News (news)
.... anchorman (1982–83)
NBC Weekend News (news)
.... anchor (1986–)

Emmy Award: Best Writing for a News Documentary, for *NBC Reports:* "The Migrants, 1980" (1980)

The son of CBS newscaster Mike Wallace. Chris was a local reporter in Boston, Chicago, and New York during the '70s; he joined the NBC network in 1978 and has since specialized in the Washington political beat.

WALLACE, JANE—newscaster
b: c. 1955, St. Paul, Minn.

West 57th (pub aff)
.... correspondent (1985–86)

WALLACE, MARCIA—actress
b: Nov 1, 1942, Creston, Iowa

The Bob Newhart Show (com)
.... Carol Kester Bondurant (1972–78)

Bob Newhart's dippy receptionist on *The Bob Newhart Show.*

WALLACE, MARJORIE—host

Entertainment Tonight (news) ... host (1981)

WALLACE, MIKE—newscaster
b: May 9, 1918, Brookline, Mass.

Stand by for Crime (police)
.... Lt. Anthony Kidd (1949)
Majority Rules (quiz) ...... emcee (1949–50)
Guess Again (quiz) .... moderator (1951)
All Around the Town (int)
.... cohost (1951–52)
What's in a Word? (quiz) ... panelist (1954)
Who's the Boss? (quiz) .... emcee (1954)
The Big Surprise (quiz) .... emcee (1956–57)
Mike Wallace Interviews (int)
.... host (1957–58)
Who Pays? (quiz) .... emcee (1959)
Biography (doc) .... narrator (1961–64)
60 Minutes (pub aff)
.... correspondent (1968–)

Emmy Awards: Outstanding Achievement on a Magazine Program, for *60 Minutes* (1971, 1972, 1973); Best News Segments, for the following *60 Minutes* Reports: "The Selling of Col. Herbert" (1973); "Misha" (1979); "Bette Davis" and "Here's . . . Johnny" (both 1980); "Killer Wheels," "The Last Mafioso (Jimmy Fratianno)," and "Wanted (Terpil/Korkala Interview)," (all 1981); "The Nazi Connection" (1982)

Few viewers now remember that TV's most famous inquisitor began his network career as an actor, first in Detroit in 1940 and later in Chicago, where he lived for most of the '40s. Among his early jobs were narrating such network radio series as *The Lone Ranger* and *The Green Hornet* and appearing on leading daytime serials including *The Road of Life, Ma Perkins,* and *The Guiding Light.* After service in the navy, Mike returned to Chicago radio and was first seen by TV viewers playing Lieutenant Kidd on the live, Chicago-originated police show *Stand by for Crime.* Mike later had roles in several TV plays during the 1950s, cohosted (with his then-wife, Buff Cobb) the New York–based features program *All Around the Town,* and was emcee or panelist on half a dozen network quiz shows.

Although he had previously done some news reporting, including coverage of the 1952 political conventions, Mike's news career did not begin to take off until the mid-1950s, when he evolved the controversial, hard-driving interviewing style for which he has become famous. He first tried this on a local New York show called *Nightbeat,* which led to a similar but unsuccessful ABC network series called *Mike Wallace Interviews.* By 1961 his half entertainment/half news career was in decline and he was reduced to narrating an innocuous syndicated documentary series called *Biography.* To everyone's surprise, this became quite a hit, reviving Mike's sagging fortunes. He then joined CBS News (in 1963) and for a time anchored its unsuccessful early morning competitor to the *Today* show. In 1968 he was made one of the original team of correspondents on *60 Minutes.* No one expected that to attract much of an audience either, but it went on to become the number-one rated program on television —the first news program ever to do so.

Mike has narrated hundreds of investigative reports over the years, and his bare-knuckles style has been legendary. Perhaps the most notorious example was his *CBS Reports* telecast "The Uncounted Enemy—A Vietnam Deception" in January 1982, which engendered a $120 million lawsuit over its assertion that General William Westmoreland had lied about enemy troop strength in Vietnam. The suit was eventually settled in CBS's favor, although testimony revealed that CBS had indeed "stacked the deck" against the general in producing the program.

Mike's memoirs: *Close Encounters* (with Gary P. Gates, 1984).

WALLACE, PAUL—actor

Father Knows Best (com)
.... Kippy Watkins (1954–59)

WALLACH, ELI—actor
b: Dec 7, 1915, Brooklyn, N.Y.

Our Family Honor (drama)
.... Vincent Danzig (1985–86)

Emmy Award: Best Supporting Actor in a Drama, for the Special *The Poppy Is Also a Flower* (1967)

A veteran actor, onstage since 1945 and in films since the '50s, with a specialty in dapper but ruthless criminals. He was fine as the crime boss in the otherwise forgettable 1985 series *Our Family Honor.* His other TV roles have included sturdy support in many live teleplays of the '50s, some dramatic series episodes in the '60s and '70s, and nearly a dozen TV movies and miniseries, including *Seventh Avenue, Skokie, The Executioner's Song,* and *Christopher Columbus.* He is not above tweaking his own image, either; he was one of the actors camping it up as the evil "Mr. Freeze" on *Batman* in the '60s.

Wallach has been married for many years to actress Anne Jackson.

WALLEY, DEBORAH—actress
b: Aug 12, 1943, Bridgeport, Conn.

The Mothers-in-Law (com)
.... Susie Hubbard Buell (1967–69)

Daughter of the famous skating team, The Walleys, long with the Ice Capades. Deborah was a leading "beach bunny" in such frothy 1960s teen surfing movies as *Gidget Goes Hawaiian* (as Gidget), *It's a Bikini World,* and the classic *Beach Blanket Bingo.*

WALMSLEY, JON—juvenile actor
b: Feb 6, 1956, Lancashire, England r: California

The Waltons (drama)
.... Jason Walton (1972–81)

WALSH, IRENE—actress

The Nick Kenny Show (talk)
.... assistant (1951–52)

WALSH, JOEY—actor

The Frank Sinatra Show (var)
.... regular (1950–51)

WALSH, LORY—actress

The Mackenzies of Paradise Cove (adv)
.... Bridget Mackenzie (1979)

WALSH, M. EMMET—actor
b: 1935

The Sandy Duncan Show (com)
.... Alex Lembeck (1972)
Dear Detective (police)
.... Capt. Gorcey (1979)
East of Eden (drama).. Sheriff Quinn (1981)

WALSTON, RAY—actor
b: Nov 2, 1917*, New Orleans, La.

My Favorite Martian (com)
.... Uncle Martin (1963–66)
Stop Susan Williams (drama)
.... Bob Richards (1979)
Fast Times (com).. Mr. Arnold Hand (1986)

A small, irritated-looking hobgoblin of a man who has been popping up in comic supporting roles on television since the mid-1950s. He was first a stage actor, making his debut in Houston in 1938 and moving to New York in 1945 to appear in such hits as The Front Page, South Pacific, and Me and Juliet. His major break, however, came with the role of the devil in both the stage (1955) and screen (1958) versions of Damn Yankees, which led to a long movie career in comic parts.

Ray began doing television on playhouse series of the '50s but made TV his principal acting venue during the '60s, when he scored his most famous hit as the irritable alien (complete with antenna on his head) in My Favorite Martian. He has also played guest roles on a wide variety of series, from Custer to Code Red and was a regular in the short-lived series-within-a-series Stop Susan Williams (part of Cliffhangers). Among the unsuccessful pilots

*Some sources give 1914 or 1918; also, some indicate Laurel, Miss., as his birth place.

for a series of his own was something called Satan's Waitin', in which he played the devil—again. Ray's TV movies include Institute for Revenge, The Kid With a Broken Halo, and The Jerk, Too.

WALTER, CY—pianist
b: Sep 16, 1915, Minneapolis, Minn. d: Aug 18, 1968

Three's Company (music).... pianist (1950)

WALTER, JESSICA—actress
b: Jan 31, 1940*, Brooklyn, N.Y.

For the People (police)
.... Phyllis Koster (1965)
Amy Prentiss (police)
.... Amy Prentiss (1974–75)
All That Glitters (com)
.... Joan Hamlyn (1977)
Wheels (drama)............. Ursula (1978)
Bare Essence (drama) . Ava Marshall (1983)

Emmy Award: Best Actress in a Limited Series, for Amy Prentiss (1975)

This stylish actress is most often seen in aggressive, sometimes neurotic, roles. A graduate of New York's High School of the Performing Arts (the Fame school), she began her career onstage in the early '60s and learned the art of on-screen conniving during a three-year run on the daytime soap opera Love of Life (1962–65). Much prime time work followed, including guest roles on Route 66, East Side/West Side, The F.B.I., and even Flipper. In 1965 she had a series role as lawyer William Shatner's independent wife on For the People, but it was in the occasional series Amy Prentiss (part of NBC's Sunday Mystery Movie), as San Francisco's first lady chief of detectives, that she gained TV fame.

Jessica has remained busy in many episode, TV movie, and miniseries roles befitting her elegance. Among her TV films have been Secrets of Three Hungry Wives, She's Dressed to Kill, Scruples, and The Execution. Perhaps her best known theatrical film role was that of the beautiful psychotic killer in Clint Eastwood's Play Misty for Me.

WALTER, TRACEY—actor
b: Nov 25, Jersey City, N.J.

Best of the West (com) ..... Frog (1981–82)
*Some sources gallantly give 1944.

WALTERS, BARBARA—newscaster
b: Sep 25, 1931, Boston, Mass.

ABC Evening News (news)
.... anchor (1976–78)
20/20 (mag)...... correspondent (1981–84)
20/20 (mag)............... cohost (1984–)

Emmy Awards: Best Host of a Talk Show, for *Today* (1975); Best News Program Segment, for the *Nightline* Report "Post Election Special Edition" (1980); Best Interviewer, for *The Barbara Walters Special*s (1982, 1983)

"I don't know what people expected," said Barbara Walters shortly after becoming the first female co-anchor of a principal network newscast [with Harry Reasoner] ... that I would come out in tap shoes and wear short skirts and nudge Harry and say cutesy things and bat my eyes?"

The publicity that accompanied Barbara's move from NBC to ABC in 1976—for a record one-million dollars per year—was certainly intensive, and not always flattering. It was the big-bucks, show business angle that upset most. Walter Cronkite's first reaction was "nausea" (she was making twice as much as he did); former CBS News chief Fred Friendly fumed, "This isn't journalism, this is a minstrel show ... is Barbara a journalist or is she Cher?"; *New Yorker* magazine published a cartoon of her doing a show business–style newscast with chorus girls high-kicking in the background; and her former network labeled her a "movie queen." Perhaps most cutting of all was the *Saturday Night Live* lampoon of a certain lisping newswoman named "Baba Wawa" (Barbara has a slight but noticeable lisp).

For all that, Barbara has proven herself one of the most remarkable newscasters in the history of the medium. She was born with a show business background (her father, Lou Walters, ran New York's famed Latin Quarter nightclub) and began working in TV as soon as she graduated from college in the early '50s. After a stint with CBS's morning show, she joined NBC's *Today* in 1961 as a writer, in 1963 was made an on-air personality, and in 1964 was promoted to the position of the regular "Today girl." Over the next dozen years, via *Today,* Barbara gradually became one of the best known newswomen on TV, respected especially for her probing interviews. She simultaneously began to host the syndicated *Not for Women Only* interview series in the early '70s and appeared in occasional prime time interview specials.

Barbara's defection to ABC in 1976 was a blow to *Today* (the show eventually developed a replacement in Jane Pauley) but did little to help third-place ABC News climb out of the ratings cellar. One commentator called her "a million dollar baby in a five and dime store." Her pairing with Harry Reasoner did not work out at all and she soon shifted to the network's prime time newsmagazine *20/20.* She also made use of her fabled interviewing skills in several high-rated prime time specials each year, with a bizarre mix of subjects ranging from Yasir Arafat to Boy George.

WALTERS, BETTY LOU—
The Ken Murray Show (var)
.... regular (1950–51)

WALTERS, LAURIE—actress
b: Jan 8, San Francisco, Calif.

Eight Is Enough (com)
.... Joannie Bradford (1977–81)

WALTHER, SUSAN—actress
Petticoat Junction (com)
.... Henrietta Plout (1965–66)

WANAMAKER, SAM—actor, director
b: Jun 14, 1919, Chicago, Ill.

Holocaust (drama) .... Moses Weiss (1978)
Berrengers (drama)
.... Simon Berrenger (1985)

WAPNER, JUDGE JOSEPH A.—judge
b: c. 1920

The People's Court (misc).... judge (1981–)

Probably more people know the name of this once-obscure local judge than that of the Chief Justice of the United States. The handsome, silver-haired, kindly Judge Wapner once had acting aspirations and is said to have dated Lana Turner. Show business apparently runs in his family—his father, also a lawyer, used to appear on *Divorce Court.* Wapner followed a career in law instead, serving as a small-claims serving as a small-claims court judge and in both municipal and superior courts for 20 years. Then, in his retirement years, *The People's Court* suddenly made him a media star.

WAR BABIES, THE—comedy troupe

Easy Does It... Starring Frankie Avalon (var)
.... regulars (1976)

WARD, BURT—actor
b: Jul 6, 1945, Los Angeles, Calif.

Batman (adv)
.... Dick (Robin) Grayson (1966–68)

The answer to "Whatever happened to Batman's sidekick, Robin?" is, "Not much." Burt Ward was a bright young man who dropped out of college to sell real estate in the mid-1960s. He had no acting experience at all when the producers of *Batman* hired him to play Robin—at actors' union minimum wages. Two seasons of saying "Holy moly, Batman" didn't do much to establish him as a serious actor, and when the series left the air he could find no other work. In the years that followed, Burt lent his voice to a 1977 cartoon revival of *Batman* and turned up occasionally in personal appearances to sign autographs. "The kids go crazy," he said. "They come up and hug me and ask when I'm going to be on television again. It's sad not to be able to tell them." Burt spent the rest of his time in his Malibu apartment studying the occult, dreaming of a comeback, and trying to make a fortune marketing felt-tip pens.

Burt's father, incidentally, was the owner of the Rhapsody in Ice show.

WARD, EVELYN—actress
b: West Orange, N.J.

Manhattan Showcase (var)... regular (1949)
The College Bowl (com)
.... regular (1950–51)

WARD, JONATHAN—juvenile actor
b: Feb 24, 1970, Baltimore, Md. r: Elkridge, Md.

Charles in Charge (com)
.... Douglas Pembroke (1984–85)
Heart of the City (drama)
.... Kevin Kennedy (1986–)

WARD, LARRY—actor
b: c. 1915, Columbus, Ohio d: Feb 16, 1985

The Dakotas (wes)
.... Marshal Frank Ragan (1963)

WARD, RACHAEL—actress
b: 1957, near Chipping-Norton, England

The Thorn Birds (drama)
.... Meggie Cleary (1983)

WARD, RICHARD—black actor
b: Mar 15, 1915, Glenside, Pa. d: Jul 1, 1979

Beacon Hill (drama)... William Piper (1975)

WARD, SANDY—actor

Dallas (drama)........ Jeb Amos (1978–79)

WARD, SELA—actress
b: Jul 11, c. 1956, Meridian, Miss.

Emerald Point N.A.S. (drama)
.... Hilary Adams (1983–84)

WARD, SKIP—actor

The Lineup (police)
.... Off. Pete Larkin (1959–60)
Gertrude Berg Show (com)
.... Joe Caldwell (1961–62)

WARD, WALLY—actor

Fast Times (com)....... Mark Ratner (1986)

WARDEN, JACK—actor
b: Sep 18, 1920, Newark, N.J.

Mr. Peepers (com)
.... coach Frank Whip (1953–55)
Norby (com) .... Bobo (1955)
The Asphalt Jungle (police)
.... Matthew Gower (1961)
The Wackiest Ship in the Army (adv)
.... Maj. Simon Butcher (1965–66)
N.Y.P.D. (police)
.... Det. Lt. Mike Haines (1967–69)
Jigsaw John (police)
.... John (Jigsaw John) St. John (1976)
The Bad News Bears (com)
.... Morris Buttermaker (1979–80)
Crazy Like a Fox (drama)
.... Harry Fox (1984–86)

Emmy Award: Best Supporting Actor in a Drama, for *Brian's Song* (1972)

"Retire? Who, me?" Carrot-topped, irascible Jack Warden has been one of television's standbys since the early days of the medium, and, after 30 years and eight series, he finally had the satisfaction of scoring a hit of his own in *Crazy Like a Fox*. He packed a lot into his 64 years of life before that. Born near the Newark docks to a broken family without much money, Jack became a teenaged professional boxer in the 1930s to earn some pocket change, then served successively in the navy, the merchant marine, and the army (as a paratrooper) in the late '30s and during World War II. He shattered a leg in a parachute jump and spent a year in hospitals, during which time he became acquainted with plays and the theater. Liking what he saw, he used his G.I. benefits after the war to study acting, and began to get roles onstage, in films and on early live TV.

Jack's burly, paratrooper physique and energetic manner (not to mention his boxer's broken nose) typed him early on. He was a boxer on a *Philco Playhouse* drama and the coach on *Mr. Peepers*. By 1960 he had begun to move up the cast list, and during the '60s and '70s he was the star of five different series—only one of which lasted more than a year. He has also appeared over the years in quite a few TV movies and miniseries, including *Brian's Song* (as the coach), *Lieutenant Schuster's Wife, Remember When, Raid on Entebbe, Topper* (the 1979 remake, as Cosmo Topper), *Robert Kennedy and His Times,* and —perhaps his most bizarre role—as a Bronx-talking advisor to the Roman emperor Tiberius in *A.D.*

WARE, MIDGE—actress

Gunslinger (wes) .... Amby Hollister (1961)

WARFIELD, MARLENE—black actress
b: Jun 19, 1941, Queens, N.Y.

Maude (com)
.... Victoria Butterfield (1977–78)

WARFIELD, MARSHA—actress
b: Chicago, Ill.

The Richard Pryor Show (var)
.... regular (1977)
Night Court (com) ..... Roz Russell (1986–)

WARING, FRED—orchestra leader
b: Jun 9, 1900, Tyrone, Pa. d: Jul 29, 1984

The Fred Waring Show (var)
.... host (1949–54)

The famous orchestra and choral director (with his "Pennsylvanians"), popular since the 1920s. He hosted a successful, if sedate, variety series immediately following Ed Sullivan on Sunday nights. Fred devoted his later years to music and youth, running a musical training camp and workshop in Pennsylvania and touring with an ever-changing chorus of young singers; he remained active into his eighties. He was also a mechanical tinkerer and was responsible for the Waring blender.

WARING, TODD—actor

The Lucie Arnaz Show (com)
.... Larry Love (1985)

WARLOCK, BILLY—actor
b: Mar 26, c. 1960, Hawthorne, Calif.

Happy Days (com) ..... Flip Phillips (1982)

WARNER, DAVID—actor
b: Jul 29, 1941, Manchester, England

Holocaust (drama)
.... Reinhard Heydrich (1978)
Masada (drama)
.... Gen. Pomponious Falco (1981)

Emmy Award: Best Supporting Actor in a Limited Series, for *Masada* (1981)

WARNER, ELEANOR—singer

The Music Show (music)
.... regular (1953–54)

WARNER, JODY—actress
b: c. 1934, Seattle r: Orcas Island, Wash.

One Happy Family (com)
.... Penny Cooper (1961)

WARNER, MALCOLM JAMAL—black juvenile actor
b: Aug 18, 1970, Jersey City, N.J. r: Los Angeles, Calif

The Cosby Show (com)
.... Theodore Huxtable (1984–)

WARNER, RICHARD—English actor

The Adventures of Sir Francis Drake (adv)
.... Walsingham (1962)

WARNER, SANDRA—actress

Mr. Smith Goes to Washington (com)
.... Pat Smith (1962–63)

WARNICK, CLAY—choral director
b: Dec 14, 1915, Tacoma, Wash.

The Bob Crosby Show (var).. singers (1958)
The Jimmie Rodgers Show (var)
.... singers (1959)

WARREN, ANN—singer

Vincent Lopez (var) .... regular (1950)

WARREN, BOB—announcer

Broadway Open House (talk)
.... regular (1951)
This Is Your Life (misc)
.... announcer (1952–61)

WARREN, JASON—actor

Check It Out (com).......... Marvin (1986)

WARREN, JENNIFER—actress
b: Aug 12, 1941, Greenwich Village, New York
City, N.Y.

The Smothers Brothers Comedy Hour (var)
.... regular (1967–69)
Paper Dolls (drama).. Dinah Caswell (1984)

WARREN, JOE—actor

Car 54, Where Are You? (com)
.... Off. Steinmetz (1961–63)

WARREN, KENNETH J.—actor
b: 1926 d: 1973

Court-Martial (drama)
.... M/Sgt. John MacCaskey (1966)

WARREN, LESLEY ANN—actress
b: Aug 16, 1946, New York City, N.Y.

Mission: Impossible (drama)
.... Dana Lambert (1970–71)
79 Park Avenue (drama)
. Marja Fludjicki/Marianne Morgan (1977)
Pearl (drama).......... Karel Lang (1978)

This leading lady of the '70s and '80s began acting as a teenager, making her Broadway debut in 1963 in *110 in the Shade*. Shortly thereafter she played the title role in the 1966 television production of *Cinderella*. In the late '60s and early '70s she did some TV series work, including a season on *Mission: Impossible*, a 1971 pilot for a proposed series based on the movie *Cat Ballou* (in the Jane Fonda role), and guest appearances on *The Mod Squad; Night Gallery; Love, American Style; Harry O;* and others. In more recent years Lesley has shifted to big, glossy, soap opera–ish TV movies such as *Betrayal, 79 Park Avenue, Portrait of a Stripper,* and *Evergreen*. Meanwhile, her big-screen career received a major boost with her nomination for an Academy Award for *Victor/Victoria*.

WARREN, MICHAEL—black actor
b: Mar 5, 1946, South Bend, Ind.

Sierra (adv)....... ranger P.J. Lewis (1974)
Paris (police) .... Willie Miller (1979–80)
Hill Street Blues (police)
.... Off. Bobby Hill (1981–)

Michael Warren was an All-American basketball star at UCLA in the late 1960s who got his first break when he was hired as a technical advisor for the 1972 basketball film *Drive, He Said,* which led to a small acting part in the movie. He remained on the fringes of TV throughout the '70s, playing mostly athletic roles in scattered episodes of *Adam 12, Marcus Welby M.D., Mod Squad, The White Shadow,* and *Days of Our Lives*. He also had regular parts on two short-lived series: *Sierra,* as a park ranger, and *Paris,* as a young policeman. But old reputations die hard. Even as Mike began *Hill Street Blues,* 13 years after his college glory days, costar Charles Haid grumbled aloud, "Here's some basketball player trying to be an actor." Mike's work on the top-rated series, for which he received an Emmy nomination, finally began to change his image from that of an athlete to that of an actor.

WARRENSKJOLD, DOROTHY—singer

Ford Festival (var)
.... regular (1951–52)

WARRICK, RUTH—actress
b: Jun 29, 1915, St. Joseph, Mo.

Father of the Bride (com)
.... Ellie Banks (1961–62)
Peyton Place (drama)
.... Hannah Cord (1965–67)

A TV soap opera queen who made her movie debut as Orson Welles' first wife in *Citizen Kane* (1941). On television she starred in *The Guiding Light* and *As the World Turns* in the '50s, in *Peyton Place* in the '60s, and as the formidable matriarch Phoebe Tyler on *All My Children* since 1970.
Her autobiography: *The Confessions of Phoebe Tyler* (1980).

WARWICK, DIONNE—black singer, host
b: Dec 12, 1940, East Orange, N.J.

Solid Gold (music) .... host (1980–81)
Solid Gold (music) .... host (1985–86)
The Love Boat (drama)
.... sang theme (1985–86)

WASHBROOK, JOHNNY—juvenile actor
b: Oct 16, 1944, Toronto, Canada

My Friend Flicka (adv)
.... Ken McLaughlin (1956–57)

WASHBURN, BEVERLY—juvenile actress
b: c. 1943

Professional Father (com)
.... Kathryn (Kit) Wilson (1955)
The New Loretta Young Show (drama)
.... Vickie Massey (1962–63)

WASHINGTON, DENZEL—black actor
b: Dec 28, 1954, Mount Vernon, N.Y.

St. Elsewhere (drama)
.... Dr. Phillip Chandler (1982–)

WASHINGTON, KENNETH—black actor
b: 1918 d: Jun 24, 1971

Hogan's Heroes (com)
.... Sgt. Richard Baker (1970–71)

WASS, TED—actor
b: Oct 27, Lakewood, Ohio

Soap (com) .... Danny Dallas (1977–81)

WASSON, CRAIG—actor, composer
b: Mar 15, 1954, Eugene, Ore.

Phyllis (com)......... Mark Valenti (1977)
Skag (drama) .... David Skagska (1980)

WATERMAN, DENNIS—juvenile actor
b: Feb 24, 1948, Clapham, London, England

Fair Exchange (com)
.... Neville Finch (1962–63)
The Sweeney (police)..... Sgt. Carter (1976)

Cheeky English juvenile actor, quite popular on British television in action series of the '70s and '80s.

WATERMAN, WILLARD—actor

The Great Gildersleeve (com)
.. Throckmorton P. Gildersleeve (1955–56)
Dennis the Menace (com)
.... Mr. Quigley (1959–63)

A portly, moon-faced actor who will forever be enshrined as pompous, delightful Throckmorton P. Gildersleeve on radio and TV (although he was the second actor to play the role; Hal Peary was the first). Willard was very busy on radio in the '30s and '40s, but in later years he turned largely to stage work.

WATERS, ETHEL—black singer, actress
b: Oct 31, 1900*, Chester, Pa. d: Sep 1, 1977

Beulah (com) .... Beulah (1950–52)

Legendary American jazz and blues singer and actress, who is said to have been the first black woman to receive star billing on Broadway and in movies. Born in abject poverty, Ethel began in vaudeville and worked her way up to hit Broadway musicals in the 1920s. Among the songs she made famous, via soulful recordings, were "Stormy Weather," "Heat Wave," and "Dinah." Her many films included *Cabin in the Sky* and *Pinky*. In the early 1950s she scored another major triumph in the stage and screen versions of the drama *The Member of the Wedding*.

*Many sources give 1896, but Ethel insisted in *His Eye Is on the Sparrow* that the correct date was 1900. She says she was 17 and underage when she first went on the stage and that her mother had to sign a paper saying she was four years older than in reality so that Ethel could get the job.

By the time television came along, Ethel was mostly playing large black mammies—a somewhat demeaning characterization for a woman of her stature—and it was in such a role that she starred as *Beulah*. She also appeared in a number of TV playhouse productions of the '50s but attracted more attention when she turned up on the quiz show *Break the $250,000 Bank* in 1956, hoping to win money to pay back taxes. She was seldom seen in later years, although a rare guest role on *Route 66* in 1961 brought an Emmy nomination. Instead, she devoted the remainder of her life to religion, becoming closely associated with the Revernd Billy Graham and singing on his evangelical telecasts. Reflecting back on her long and eventful career, and her turn to God, she once said "When I had everything, I had nothing. Now I have nothing, but I have everything."

Autobiographies: *His Eye Is on the Sparrow* (1951), *To Me It's Wonderful* (1972).

WATERS, REBA—juvenile actress

Peck's Bad Girl (com) .... Francesca (1959)

WATERSTON, SAM—actor
b: Nov 15, 1940, Cambridge, Mass.

Q.E.D. (adv) ..... Quentin E. Deverill (1982)

A sensitive leading man of stage and screen, who has occasionally dabbled in TV. His most notable roles have been in the TV movie *Friendly Fire* and the PBS miniseries *Oppenheimer* (title role).

WATKINS, CARLENE—actress
b: Jun 4, 1952, Hartford, Conn. r: Houston, Texas

The Secret Empire (drama) ... Millie (1979)
Best of the West (com)
.... Elvira Best (1981–82)
It's Not Easy (com)
.... Sharon Long Townsend (1983)
Mary (com)........ Susan Wilcox (1985–86)

WATKINS, JIM—black actor
b: Nov 7, 1944, Philadelphia, Pa.

The Magician (adv)
.... Jerry Wallace (1973–74)

WATLING, DEBORAH—juvenile actress

The Invisible Man (drama)
.... Sally Brady (1958–60)

WATSON, DAVID—actor

Rawhide (wes)........ Ian Cabot (1965–66)

WATSON, DEBBIE—actress
b: Jan 17, 1949, r: La Mirada, Calif.

Karen (com) .... Karen Scott (1964–65)
Tammy (com)... Tammy Tarleton (1965–66)

WATSON, JAMES A., JR.—black actor

Love, American Style (com)
.... repertory player (1972–74)

WATSON, JUSTICE—actor

Holiday Lodge (com)
.... J. W. Harrington (1961)

WATSON, LARRY—actor

Doctor's Hospital (drama)
.... Barney (1975–76)

WATSON, MILLS—actor
b: Jul 10, 1940, Oakland, Calif.

B.J. and the Bear (adv) . Dep. Perkins (1979)
Lobo (com) .... Dep. Perkins (1979–81)
Harper Valley P.T.A. (com)
.... Winslow Homer (Uncle Buster)
Smith (1981–82)

A chubby, balding comic bumbler who attracted attention on *Lobo* for his rubber face and pratfalls. Ironically, he had received his training at England's prestigious Royal Academy of Dramatic Arts and, for many years in the '60s and '70s, specialized almost exclusively in vicious killers on a wide variety of TV action shows. He was a particular favorite on *Gunsmoke* and later on *The Rockford Files*. "They even had me kicking dogs and punching kids," he lamented later. "Today people recognize me as Perkins and they smile ... I've been hated and I've been liked, and being liked is better."

WATSON, VERNEE—black actress

Welcome Back, Kotter (com)
.... Verna Jean (1975–77)

Carter Country (com)
.... Lucille Banks (1977–79)
Foley Square (com)
.... Denise Willums (1985–86)

WATSON, WILLIAM—actor

Roots (drama)............ Gardner (1977)
The Contender (drama)....... Andy (1980)

WATTIS, RICHARD—actor
b: 1912, England d: Feb 1, 1975

Dick and the Duchess (com)
.... Peter Jamison (1957–58)
The Liberace Show (var)..... regular (1969)

WATTRICK, DON—sportscaster

Thursday Night Fights (sport)
.... sportscaster (1953)

WAXMAN, AL—actor
b: Mar 2, 1935, Toronto, Canada

Cagney & Lacey (police)
.... Lt. Albert Samuels (1982–)

Heavyset actor who was a star on Canadian series TV in the '70s before making his mark in the U.S. on *Cagney & Lacey*.

WAYANS, DAMON—comedian

NBC's Saturday Night Live (var)
.... regular (1985–86)

WAYANS, KEENAN IVORY—black actor

For Love and Honor (drama)
.... Pvt. Duke Johnson (1983)

WAYLAND, LEN—actor

Sam (police)..... Capt. Tom Clagett (1978)

WAYNE, DAVID—actor
b: Jan 30, 1914, Traverse City, Mich.

Norby (com)......... Pearson Norby (1955)
The Good Life (com)
.... Charles Dutton (1971–72)
The Adventures of Ellery Queen (drama)
.... Insp. Richard Queen (1975–76)
Dallas (drama)
.... Willard "Digger" Barnes (1978)
House Calls (com)
.... Dr. Amos Weatherby (1979–82)

This impish little actor has had long and successful careers in three major fields of show business. First came the stage, where he made his debut in 1936 and scored triumphs in the '40s, '50s, and '60s, including Tony Awards for *Finian's Rainbow* in 1947 (as a singing leprechaun!) and *Teahouse of the August Moon* in 1954. Next were movies, which he entered in the late 1940s and where he has appeared in such delights as *Adam's Rib, How to Marry a Millionaire,* and *The Apple Dumpling Gang.*

Television came last, but David has been quite active there, too, starting with a *Studio One* appearance in 1950. He has since been seen in both dramas and comedies, from *Omnibus* in the '50s to *House Calls* in the '80s. Some of the highlights along the way: his debut series *Norby* (as a small-town banker), the first TV series filmed in color; productions of *The Ruggles of Red Gap* in 1957 and *The Devil and Daniel Webster* (as the devil!) in the '60s; a 1959 episode of *The Twilight Zone* called "Escape Clause," in which he struck a deal with Lucifer; several hilarious appearances on *Batman* in 1967 as the Mad Hatter; the TV movie *The FBI vs. Alvin Karpis* in 1974, as Ma Barker's boyfriend; *Benjamin Franklin, Statesman* in 1975; and the miniseries *Black Beauty* and *Loose Change,* both in 1978.

WAYNE, JOHNNY—comedian
r: Canada

Holiday Lodge (com) .. Johnny Miller (1961)
Wayne and Shuster Take an Affectionate Look At . . . (doc) .... host (1966)

Half of the Canadian comedy team of Wayne and (Frank) Shuster, popular in the '50s and '60s.

WAYNE, NINA—actress
b: 1943, Chicago, Ill.

Camp Runamuck (com)
.... Caprice Yeudleman (1965–66)

WAYNE, PATRICK—actor
b: Jul 15, 1939, Los Angeles, Calif.

The Rounders (com)
.... Howdy Lewis (1966–67)
Shirley (com) ..... Lew Armitage (1979–80)
The Monte Carlo Show (var).... host (1980)

The son of movie great John Wayne; seen occasionally in TV movies and series episodes.

WEARY, A.C.—actor

Q.E.D. (adv) . . . . . . Charlie Andrews (1982)

WEATHERLY, SHAWN—actress

b: c. 1960, Sumter, S.C.

Shaping Up (com)
. . . . Melissa McDonald (1984)
oceanQuest (adv) . . . . regular (1985)

A former Miss Universe (1980) who tried hard to get a toehold in acting. One must give her credit for spunk; she spent a year under the most arduous conditions traveling on (and under) the six oceans of the world filming the 1985 documentary miniseries *oceanQuest.*

WEATHERS, CARL—black actor

b: Jan 14, New Orleans, La.

Fortune Dane (police). . Fortune Dane (1986)

A former pro football player, with the Oakland Raiders for a couple of years in the early '70s, who has doubled as an actor since his school days. His big breakthrough came as Apollo Creed in the *Rocky* movies beginning in 1976.

WEATHERWAX, KEN—juvenile actor

The Addams Family (com)
. . . . Pugsley Addams (1964–66)

The nephew of famed animal trainer Rudd Weatherwax *(Lassie).*

WEAVER, CHARLIE—

see Arquette, Cliff

WEAVER, DENNIS—actor

b: Jun 4, 1924, Joplin, Mo.

Gunsmoke (wes) . . Chester Goode (1955–64)
Kentucky Jones (drama)
. . . . "Kentucky" Jones (1964–65)
Gentle Ben (adv) . . . Tom Wedloe (1967–69)
McCloud (police)
. . . Dep. Marshal Sam McCloud (1970–77)
Pearl (drama) . . . . Col. Forrest (1978)

Centennial (drama) . . . R. J. Poteet (1978–79)
Stone (police) . Det. Sgt. Daniel Stone (1980)
Emerald Point N.A.S. (drama)
. . . Rear Adm. Thomas Mallory (1983–84)

Emmy Award: Best Supporting Actor in a Drama Series, for *Gunsmoke* (1959)

Dennis Weaver is one 1950s western star who outlived the TV western era very nicely, thank you. He has become one of television's most popular actors. The lanky, drawling midwesterner was a navy flyer during World War II, a star track and field athlete when he returned to college after the war, and a runner-up for the 1948 Olympic track team. He turned to acting in the early '50s, playing supporting roles on stage, in films, and on TV *(Schlitz Playhouse, Dragnet).*

It was on *Gunsmoke* that he first became famous, as the limping, laconic ("Missster Dilllon!") but loyal deputy, Chester. After nine years in the role he left to try his luck in his own series, *Kentucky Jones,* in which he played a modern-day rancher with a small child. This was not successful, but the subsequent *Gentle Ben* (in which he had a young son *and* a 650-pound bear) did much better.

A 1970 TV movie called *McCloud* led to Dennis's third famous role, as a downhome southwestern sheriff transferred to big city police work in New York. Since then he has appeared in two other series and quite a few TV movies. Among the latter have been *Duel,* Steven Spielberg's 1971 small-screen classic about a man versus a giant truck; *The Great Man's Whiskers,* as Abraham Lincoln; *Intimate Agony; Ishi: The Last of His Tribe; The Ordeal of Patty Hearst; Amber Waves; The Ordeal of Dr. Mudd;* and *Cocaine: One Man's Seduction.*

Weaver served for two years as president of the Screen Actors Guild. He is also active in religious pursuits.

WEAVER, DOODLES—comedian

b: May 11, 1911*, Los Angeles, Calif. d: Jan 13, 1983

Doodles Weaver (var) . . . . host (1951)

A lunatic comic who was with the Spike Jones City Slickers in the late '40s. Doodles

*Some sources give 1914.

was the one who delivered the outrageously overmodulated horse-race narration ending with, "and the winnah is . . . Feedelbaum!" He was also—believe it or not—the brother of NBC president Sylvester "Pat" Weaver. Doodles' real name was Winstead Sheffield Weaver. He changed it, he said, because Doodles sounded more dignified (his mother disagreed, saying *she* nicknamed him that because his big ears made him look like a doodlebug).

After his heyday in the '40s and early '50s, Doodles retired to the West Coast, where he hosted local children's shows for several years and had small parts in movies and TV episodes. Despondent over a worsening heart condition, he died by his own hand in 1983.

WEAVER, EARL—sportscaster
b: Aug 14, 1930, St. Louis, Mo.

Monday Night Baseball (sport)
.... sportscaster (1983–84)

The manager of the Baltimore Orioles baseball team, from 1968–1982.

WEAVER, FRITZ—actor
b: Jan 19, 1926, Pittsburgh, Pa.

Holocaust (drama)
.... Josef Weiss (1978)

WEAVER, LEE—black actor
b: Apr 10, Fort Lauderdale, Fla.

Bill Cosby Show (com)
.... Brian Kincaid (1969–71)
Easy Street (com)
.... Ricardo Williams (1986–)

WEAVER, ROBBY—actor
b: Apr 8, 1953

Stone (police) ...... Det. Buck Rogers (1980)

The son of actor Dennis Weaver. He made his acting debut (in a speaking role) in dad's series *Kentucky Jones,* in 1965.

WEAVER, SYLVESTER L. "PAT"—TV executive
b: Dec 21, 1908, Los Angeles, Calif.

Television: Inside and Out (mag)
.... regular (1981–82)

Emmy Awards: Trustees' and Governor's Award (1967); Governor's Award (1983)

One of the most innovative top executives in the history of American television, and the only one to have ever been a regular on a prime time series—albeit briefly, and 25 years after he headed the NBC network. Weaver got his start on Madison Avenue as an advertising executive with Young and Rubicam and the American Tobacco Company during the '30s and '40s. He joined NBC in 1949 as its "vice president in charge of television" (NBC now has 150 VPs and half a dozen presidents). Weaver ran the network for only a few years, but they came during the medium's formative period, and his ideas and determination in forging quality programming during that time are legendary. Among other things, he was the father of the TV talk/service program, founding both the *Tonight* and *Today* shows; of the rotating, multi-star anthology series so popular in the '50s; of the globe-trotting, cultural *Wide Wide World* series; and of the concept of the TV "special," an unusual event preempting regular programming.

Despite his great contributions to NBC, and to viewers, Weaver was "kicked upstairs" to chairman of the board in December 1955 because General Sarnoff, the man who ran NBC's parent corporation, wanted to put his son in charge of the network. Weaver left NBC in 1956 and later worked with two advertising agencies; he also heading his own ill-fated pay-TV service in California in the mid-1960s—an idea clearly ahead of its time.

Weaver's role on *Television: Inside and Out* was to offer expert commentary on the medium. He certainly was qualified to do that. His 1967 Trustees' Award citation read, in part, "For his constant conviction that the American public deserves better than it gets on the television screen . . . [and] for the imagination, leadership, courage and integrity which he has brought to our medium."

Weaver was the brother of comic Doodles Weaver, and the father of 1980's movie actress Sigourney Weaver.

WEBB, CHLOE—actress

Thicke of the Night (talk) .... regular (1983)

WEBB, GREG—actor
b: Murfreesboro, Tenn.

Boone (drama) .... Rome Hawley (1983–84)

WEBB, JACK—actor, producer
b: Apr 2, 1920, Santa Monica, Calif. d: Dec 23, 1982

Dragnet (police)... Sgt. Joe Friday (1952–59)
General Electric True (drama)
.... host/narrator (1962–63)
Dragnet (police)... Sgt. Joe Friday (1967–70)
Escape (adv).............. narrator (1973)

If instant recognizability is the hallmark of a television superstar, Jack Webb had it in spades. There was no mistaking a show he produced or starred in—no romance, no gimmicks, hardly a smile . . . just urgent realism so intense it almost crackled. On *Dragnet* viewers followed the log of a cop's day, delivered in a clipped, down-to-business tone. There were plenty of catch-prases and schtick:
"My name's Friday. I'm a cop."
"Just the facts, ma'am."
"Book him on a 502."
"The story you are about to hear is true; only the names have been changed to protect the innocent."
(Music:) "DUM-DE-DUM-DUM!"
Webb's distinctive Sgt. Joe Friday is still being parodied, long after the show has departed the airwaves and Webb himself is dead and buried.

The grim, dark, crew-cut actor who created all this began in radio in the late '30s. After a stint as a World War II bomber pilot he resumed his career in San Francisco in 1946 with an interesting anti-bigotry series called *One out of Seven*. Then he played a succession of radio private eyes variously named Pat Novak, Johnny Madero, and Jeff Regan—all wise-cracking, smart-mouthed, chip-on-the-shoulder types quite different from Joe Friday. Jack had an idea for a more authentic series based on real police files, however, and in 1949 he persuaded NBC to carry it on radio. *Dragnet* made him a star, running for a phenomenally successful seven years on radio and seven on television in its original run.

Jack produced the show himself, via his Mark VII Productions (the name stood for nothing). He soon began producing other

semidocumentary series as well. Over the years these included *The D.A.; Pete Kelly's Blues; O'Hara, U.S. Treasury; Hec Ramsey; Emergency;* and *Adam 12.* In 1967 *Dragnet* was revived with Webb again in the lead and Harry Morgan as his partner; it ran for three more years, making it the most successful revival of a former hit series in TV history. Webb did no further acting after that, but he continued to produce series bearing his authentic stamp, including *Mobile One* (1975) and *Project U.F.O.* (1979). His ex-wives include a Miss U.S.A., Jackie Loughery, and singer-actress Julie London.

WEBB, LUCY—actress

Private Benjamin (com)
.... Pvt. Luanne Hubble (1981–82)

WEBBER, ROBERT—actor
b: Oct 14, 1924, Santa Ana, Calif.

79 Park Avenue (drama)
.... District Attorney DeWitt (1977)

WEBER, BILL—puppeteer

The Little Revue (music)
.... marionettes (1949–50)

WEBER, LAURA—juvenile actress
b: c. 1937

Young Mr. Bobbin (com) .... Susie (1951–52)

WEBSTER, CHUCK—actor

Photocrime (drama)
.... Insp. Hannibal Cobb (1949)

WEDDLE, VERNON—actor

East of Eden (drama) ..... Mr. Ames (1981)
Filthy Rich (com)
.... George Wilhoit (1982–83)

WEDEMEYER, HERMAN—actor
b: May 20, 1924, Hilo, Hawaii

Hawaii Five-O (police)
.... Duke Lukela (1972–80)

A Hawaiian businessman and politician with no prior acting experience who became a regular on *Hawaii Five-O* in the early '70s. He was a star athlete and football All-American during his college days in the 1940s.

WEDGEWORTH, ANN—actress
b: Jan 21, 1935, Abilene, Texas

Three's Company (com)
.... Lana Shields (1979–80)
Filthy Rich (com)
.... Bootsie Weschester (1982–83)

Once married to Rip Torn; she was active in daytime soap operas in the '60s and '70s, including six years on *Another World* and its spin-off *Somerset* (on both as Lahoma Lucas).

WEED, BUDDY—pianist
b: Jan 6, 1918, Ossining, N.Y.

The Earl Wrightson Show (music)
.... regular (1948–49)
Penthouse Party (var)....... trio (1950–51)
Jimmy Blaine's Junior Edition (music)
.... trio (1951)
The Henny and Rocky Show (var)
.... regular (1955)

WEEKS, ALAN—black actor
Baker's Dozen (com)
.... O. K. Otis Kelly (1982)

WEIGEL, JOHN—host
Treasure Quest (quiz) .... host (1949)

WEIL, LISL—artist
b: Austria

Children's Sketch Book (child)
.... illustrator (1950)

A tiny lady who specialized in giant sketches, typically done with chalk on 20-foot panels and gracefully executed in time with an orchestra playing such works as "Peter and the Wolf" or "The Sorcerer's Apprentice."

WEINBERGER, ED—producer, writer
Mr. Smith (com).. voice of Mr. Smith (1983)

Emmy Awards: Producer, Best Comedy Series, for *The Mary Tyler Moore Show* (1975, 1976, 1977); Best Writing for a Comedy Series, for *The Mary Tyler Moore Show* (1975, 1977); Executive Producer, Best Comedy Series, for *Taxi* (1979, 1980, 1981); Best Writing for a Comedy Series, for *The Cosby Show* (1985)

A leading television comedy writer/producer, also responsible for *The Dean Martin Show, Phyllis,* and *The Associates.* His reputation was temporarily tarnished when he produced and provided the off-screen voice for NBC's notorious monkey-comedy, *Mr. Smith.*

WEINRIB, LEN—comedian, writer
b: Apr 29, 1935, New York City, N.Y.

The Spike Jones Show (var).. regular (1960)

A young comic of the 1950s who was given his start by Bill Dana (Dana was then a writer for Steve Allen). Lennie later became one of the leading Saturday morning voice specialists and was heard on many animated cartoons of the '60s, '70s, and '80s.

WEINTRAUB, CARL—actor
b: Mar 27, 1946

Executive Suite (drama)
.... Harry Ragin (1976–77)

WEINTRAUB, CINDY—actress
b: Apr 5, New York City, N.Y. r: Seattle, Wash.

Baker's Dozen (com).. Terry Munson (1982)

WEIS, GARY—filmmaker
NBC's Saturday Night Live (com)
.... regular (1976–77)

WEISMAN, SAM—actor
Studs Lonigan (drama)
.... Davey Cohen (1979)

WEISS, FRED—actor
Secrets of Midland Heights (drama)
.... Eric Dexter (1980–81)

WEISSMULLER, JOHNNY—actor
b: Jun 2, 1904, Windber, Pa. d: Jan 20, 1984

Jungle Jim (adv)......... Jungle Jim (1955)

The movies' most famous Tarzan (in 12 films of the '30s and '40s). He did relatively little television work, although he did star in an early syndicated series based on one of his other film characters, *Jungle Jim*. Weissmuller was an Olympic champion swimmer in the 1920s. His autobiography: *Water, World and Weissmuller* (1967).

WEIST, DWIGHT—host, actor,
announcer

We, the People (int) . . . . host (1948–50)

"Mister District Attorney" (among many other roles) on radio in the '40s.

WEITZ, BRUCE—actor
b: May 27, 1943, Norwalk, Conn.

Hill Street Blues (police)
. . . . Det. Mick Belker (1981–)

Emmy Award: Best Supporting Actor in a Drama Series, for *Hill Street Blues* (1984)

A small, ferretlike actor, who played the scruffy and somewhat off-center Detective Belker on *Hill Street Blues* (he's the one that growled at dogs and supposedly bit off a criminal's ear). Weitz spent the late '60s and most of the '70s onstage in several cities, moving to Los Angeles in 1977 to get into TV episode work. His two big breaks both came in 1981: a costarring role in his first TV movie, *Death of a Centerfold: The Dorothy Stratton Story*, as Stratton's husband, a seedy promoter; and a regular part on *Hill Street Blues*.

WELCH, LOREN—

Admiral Broadway Revue (var)
. . . . regular (1949)

WELD, TUESDAY—actress
b: Aug 27, 1943, New York City, N.Y.

The Many Loves of Dobie Gillis (com)
. . . . Thalia Menninger (1959–60)

This pretty, vulnerable-looking teenager was known more for her films and for her gossip column coverage than for her television career, although she was quite active in TV in the late '50s and early '60s. Born Susan Weld, she began as a child model at age three (to support her widowed mother), had her first nervous breakdown at nine, and was drinking heavily soon

thereafter. During the late '50s she appeared in several exploitation movies, usually as a sex kitten, and was also seen on such TV series as *Ozzie and Harriet* and *77 Sunset Strip*. On *Dobie Gillis* she played the uppity rich girl sought after by both Dobie (Dwayne Hickman) and his chief rival, Milton Armitage (Warren Beatty).

Tuesday continued to appear in series episodes for a time—*The Millionaire, Bus Stop, Naked City, The Fugitive*, etc.—but by the middle of the decade she had drifted out of TV in favor of movies. She has since been seen in a few TV films, including *Mother and Daughter: The Loving War, Madame X*, and Steinbeck's *The Winter of Our Discontent*.

WELDON, ANN—black actress

One in a Million (com) . . . . Edna (1980)
9 to 5 (com). . . . . Clair (1982–83)

WELK, LAWRENCE—orchestra leader
b: Mar 11, 1903, Strasburg, N.D.

The Lawrence Welk Show (music)
. . . . host (1955–82)
Lawrence Welk's Top Tunes and New Talent (talent) . . . . host (1956–59)

"Music changes, but I don't," Lawrence Welk once said, explaining his remarkable longevity on TV. The old-fashioned, cornball, squarer-than-square bandleader confounded the experts, who gave him no chance of surviving past his initial summertime run in 1955. *The Lawrence Welk Show* lasted for an incredible 27 years. His stock in trade was simple: melodic, easy-listening music ("Champagne Music," he called it), and a large, wholesome "family" of well-scrubbed musicians, dancers, and singers who remained with him year after year.

Welk was born on a farm in North Dakota to immigrant parents and formed his first band in the mid-1920s. He remained a minor league attraction in the Midwest for 25 years before he was booked into a West Coast ballroom in the early '50s. There, a Los Angeles station, hungry for cheap programming, began to telecast his performances. (Years later, he recalled asking the TV people, "What do I do?" "Nothing," they said, "just *play*."

"Well I just played, and the first thing I knew, 26 years had gone by.") The ABC network picked him up as a Saturday night replacement in 1955 and for a time in the late '50s had him hosting a Monday night show as well *(Top Tunes and New Talent)*. His program was finally canceled in 1971, not because the audience was too small but because it was too old to suit advertisers. Welk simply continued producing new episodes and syndicated them to local stations himself, with the result that he was seen on even more stations than when he was on ABC. Obviously, a lot of people appreciated wholesomeness and consistency.

His autobiographies: *Wunnerful, Wunnerful!* (1971), *Ah One, Ah Two: Life With My Musical Family* (1974), and *You're Never Too Young* (1981), all written with Bernice McGeehan.

WELK, TANYA FALAN—singer

The Lawrence Welk Show (music)
.... regular (1968–77)

A young member of Welk's troupe, who married the maestro's son, Lawrence, Jr.

WELKER, FRANK—actor

The Don Knotts Show (var)
.... regular (1970–71)
The Burns and Schreiber Comedy Hour (var)
.... regular (1973)

A comic actor who was a leading voice on Saturday morning caroons during the '70s and '80s. Among his many roles: Dynomut, Jabberjaw, and Dinky Dog.

WELLER, ROBB—host

Entertainment Tonight (news)
.... Host (1984–)

The nephew of veteran announcer Art Gilmore.

WELLES, JESSE—actress

Husbands, Wives & Lovers (com)
.... Helene Willis (1978)
Good Time Harry (com)
.... Billie Howard (1980)
Soap (com) .... Gwen (1980–81)
Oh Madeline (com).. Doris Leone (1983–84)

WELLES, ORSON—actor, producer
b: May 6, 1915, Kenosha, Wis., r: Chicago, Ill.
d: Oct 10, 1985

The Marty Feldman Comedy Machine (var)
.... frequent guest (1972)
Great Mysteries (drama)........ host (1973)
Shogun (drama) .... narrator (1980)
Magnum, P.I. (drama)
.... Robin Masters (voice) (1981–85)
Scene of the Crime (drama)..... host (1985)

"We all have only so much luck," Orson Welles once told an interviewer, "and all of mine came early in life." Early in life was, of course, before television and so Hollywood's maverick genius will be most remembered for daring films such as *Citizen Kane* and *The Magnificent Ambersons*, and for his shattering 1938 radio broadcast *War of the Worlds*, rather than for his later, occasional work on TV.

Welles was a child prodigy, born to a wealthy inventor father and artistic mother. He was playing the violin, painting, and reciting Shakespeare before most children are past comic books. He skipped college (didn't need it) and wandered the world for a time, seeking adventure. His stage debut was in Ireland. In the late '30s he teamed with actor John Houseman to found the Mercury Theatre, which mounted innovative productions onstage and then on radio (including *War of the Worlds*). A tumultuous movie career followed in the '40s, during which he was ultimately rejected by Hollywood as too unconventional and noncommercial.

Welles made occasional appearances on TV in the '50s; for example, in *King Lear* on *Omnibus* and *Twentieth Century* on *Ford Star Jubilee*. His marvelous sense of humor was showcased on a memorable *I Love Lucy* episode in 1956 in which he performed a magic act at Desi's nightclub, levitating Lucy while she thought she was supposed to be doing a Shakespearean scene ("Romeo, Romeo, wherefore art thou. . . . Get me down from here, Romeo!").

In later years Welles was primarily heard as a narrator, his rumbling, godlike tones lending stature to *The Name of the Game* and *Night Gallery* episodes, the TV movie *A Woman Called Moses*, NBC's fiftieth anniversary special, and the miniseries *Shogun*. He acted only rarely, as in the 1972 *Hallmark Hall of Fame* production of *The Man Who Came to Dinner* and the 1977 TV film *It Happened One Christmas*. In addition, he hosted (but did not act in) a rather disappointing syndicated dramatic anthology series called *Great Mysteries*. His most mimicked line, no doubt, came from his oft-seen wine commercials, in which he appeared bearded and corpulent: "We shall sell no wine . . . before its time." And, he might have added, "We shall tolerate no creative geniuses after theirs."

WELLINGTONS, THE—rock group

Shindig (music) .. frequent guests (1964–66)

WELLS, AARIKA—actress

Supertrain (drama) . . . . Gilda (1979)

WELLS, CAROLE—actress
b: Aug 31, 1942, Shreveport, La. r: California

National Velvet (adv)
. . . . Edwina Brown (1960–62)
Pistols 'n' Petticoats (com)
. . . . Lucy Hanks (1966–67)

WELLS, CLAUDETTE—actress
b: Feb 20, St. Louis, Mo.

Square Pegs (com)
. . . . LaDonna Fredericks (1982–83)

WELLS, CLAUDIA—actress
b: Jul 5, Kuala Lumpur, Malaysia r: San Francisco

Herbie, The Love Bug (com)
. . . . Julie MacLane (1982)
Off the Rack (com)
. . . . Shannon Halloran (1985)
Fast Times (com). . . . . . Linda Barrett (1986)

WELLS, DANNY—actor

The Jeffersons (com). . . . . . Charlie (1984–85)

WELLS, DAWN—actress
r: Reno, Nev.

Gilligan's Island (com)
. . . . Mary Ann Summers (1964–67)

A former Miss Nevada, who played the sweet, naive country girl on *Gilligan's Is-*

land. In recent years she has tried to launch a career as a country singer.

WELLS, DEREK—black juvenile actor
b: Aug 2, 1967, Los Angeles, Calif.

The Fitzpatricks (drama)
. . . . R.J. (1977–78)

WELLS, MARY K.—actress
b: Omaha, Neb. r: Long Beach, Calif.

Big Town (drama)
. . . . Lorelei Kilbourne (1950–51)
Robert Montgomery Presents (summer) (drama). . . . . repertory player (1956)

Emmy Award: Best Writing for a Daytime Drama, for *All My Children* (1985)

A prominent actress on daytime soap operas in the '50s, '60s, and early '70s, including a nine-year run on *The Edge of Night* in the '60s. She then became a soap opera writer for the top-rated *All My Children*.

WELLS, MRS. CARVETH—host

Geographically Speaking (doc)
. . . . hostess (1946)

WELLS, TRACY—juvenile actress
b: Mar 13, 1971, Encino, Calif.

Mr. Belvedere (com)
. . . . Heather Owens (1985–)

WELSH, JOHN—actor

What's Happening!! (com)
. . . . Big Earl Babcock/Barnett/Barrett (1978–79)

WELSH, JONATHAN—actor

Adderly (adv)
. . . . Melville Greenspan (1986–)

WENDELL, BILL—announcer, host
b: Mar 22, 1924, New York City, N.Y.

Stage a Number (talent) . . . emcee (1952–53)
Trash or Treasure (misc) . . . . . emcee (1953)
The Ernie Kovacs Show (var)
. . . . regular (1956)
Tonight (talk) . . . . announcer (1956–57)
Late Night with David Letterman (talk)
. . . . announcer (1982–)

A familiar network announcer, on many daytime and nighttime shows since the 1950s—occasionally as an on-camera comic foil.

WENDT, GEORGE—actor
b: Oct 17, 1948, Chicago, Ill.

Making the Grade (com)
.... Gus Bertoia (1982)
Cheers (com)...... Norm Peterson (1982–)

A portly comic actor who spent six years with Chicago's Second City troupe, before breaking into television in the early '80s.

WERLE, BARBARA—actress
San Francisco International Airport (drama)
.... June (1970–71)

WERTIMER, NED—actor
b: Buffalo, N.Y.

The Jeffersons (com)
.... Ralph the doorman (1975–85)

WESSELL, RICHARD—actor
b: 1910* d: Apr 20, 1965

Riverboat (adv) .... Carney (1959–61)

WESSON, DICK—actor, writer, producer
b: Feb 20, 1919, Idaho d: Jan 27, 1979

Hollywood House (var) ... regular (1949–50)
The People's Choice (com) .. Rollo (1956–58)
Paul Sand in Friends and Lovers (com)
.... Jack Riordan (1974–75)

Long-faced comic actor, who was also an announcer *(The Wonderful World of Disney)*, a producer *(Petticoat Junction, Tammy)*, and a writer (for *The Bob Cummings Show*, on which he occasionally played Schultzy's friend).

WEST, ADAM—actor
b: Sep 19, 1928, Walla Walla, Wash.

The Detectives, Starring Robert Taylor (police) .... Sgt. Steve Nelson (1961–62)
Batman (adv)
.... Bruce (Batman) Wayne (1966–68)
The Last Precinct (com)
.... Capt. Rick Wright (1986)

*Some sources give 1913.

"When you wear a mask and create a character, nothing will pigeonhole you faster," laments Adam West. The actor, who was born William West Anderson, did in fact have an active career apart from *Batman*, but few know of it. He began acting shortly after he graduated from college in the '50s and soon won a contract with Warner Brothers. The studio put him into several quickie movies, as well as in episodes of its TV shows; during 1959 alone he could be seen in *Maverick, Sugarfoot, 77 Sunset Strip,* and *Hawaiian Eye,* among others. His first regular role was as one of Robert Taylor's young *Detectives,* during that series' last season. He also played guest parts in *Perry Mason, The Outer Limits, The Real McCoys, Bewitched,* and many others before the campy *Batman*—probably the least demanding role of his career—catapulted him to cult stardom.

It did not catapult him to greater career heights, however. Adam spent the '70s playing occasional roles on *Love, American Style; Alias Smith and Jones; Emergency;* and similar lightweight series. He also made pilots for several new series that did not make it to the schedule. Finally, one of them did, however. *The Last Precinct,* a slapstick comedy about a bunch of bumbling cops, was short-lived. West has also appeared in an assortment of minor TV movies, including *For the Love of It* and *I Take These Men,* usually in roles just as straight as that of *Batman.*

There was a time, West says, "when I retreated to the beach, licked my wounds, and hit the bottle too much" in despair over the *Batman* typecasting. However, he decided to live with the image and take whatever money it could bring from personal appearances, etc. After all, he says, "in this business you're either sipping the champagne or stomping the grapes."

WEST, ALVY—orchestra leader
b: Jan 19, 1915, Brooklyn, N.Y.

Country Style (var) ..... band leader (1950)
The Andy Williams and June Valli Show (music) .... orch. leader (1957)

WEST, BROOKS—actor
b: c. 1916 d: Feb 7, 1984

My Friend Irma (com)
.... Richard Rhinelander III (1952–53)

The husband of actress Eve Arden.

WEST, JANE—actress, writer

The O'Neills (drama)
.... Mrs. Bailey (1949–50)

WEST, MADGE—actress
b: c. 1891, New York City, N.Y. d: May 29, 1985

The McLean Stevenson Show (com)
.... Grandma (1976–77)

WEST, MARY JO—newscaster
b: c. 1949, Atlanta, Ga.

CBS News Nightwatch (news)
.... anchor (1982–84)

WEST, RED—actor
b: c. 1936

Baa Baa Black Sheep (drama)
.... Sgt. Andy Micklin (1977–78)
The Duke (drama)
.... Sgt. Mick O'Brien (1979)

A tall, rugged, red-haired actor who has had—to put it mildly—an interesting life. A high school buddy of Elvis Presley, Red spent most of the following 25 years as one of Presley's small inner circle of friends (the "Memphis Mafia"), as well as his bodyguard. He also did some songwriting for Pat Boone and others and some Hollywood stunt work, including stunts for the series *The Wild Wild West,* where he met and became close friends with actor Robert Conrad.

When Elvis abruptly fired most of his hangers-on in 1976, Red and two other casualties co-authored the sensational *Elvis—What Happened?*, the first of the flood of Presley drugs-and-degradation exposés. They called it "a desperate effort to communicate to Elvis one last time" about what was happening to him, but, unfortunately, the book came out only a few days before Presley's death. Red then went on to pursue his acting career with numerous supporting roles, mostly in Conrad's series and TV movies.

WEST, TIMOTHY—actor
b: Oct 20, 1934, Yorkshire, England

Masada (drama) .... Vespasian (1981)

WESTBROOK, FRANK—choreographer

Arthur Godfrey and His Friends (var)
.... dancers (1958–59)

WESTERFIELD, JAMES—actor
b: 1912, Tennessee d: Sep 20, 1971

The Travels of Jaimie McPheeters (wes)
.... John Murrel (1963–64)

WESTERN, JOHNNY—singer

Have Gun Will Travel (wes)
.... sang theme song (1957–63)

WESTFALL, KAY—actress

Sit or Miss (quiz)............. emcee (1950)
Ask Me Another (quiz) ..... panelist (1952)
The Bob Newhart Show (var)
.... regular (1961)

WESTMAN, NYDIA—actress
b: Feb 19, 1902, New York City, N.Y. d: May 23, 1970

Mary Kay and Johnny (com)
.... Mary Kay's mother (1947–50)
Young Mr. Bobbin (com)
.... Aunt Bertha (1951–52)
Going My Way (com)
.... Mrs. Featherstone (1962–63)

A pudgy, dumpling-cheeked little woman who often played nervous, giggly old maids.

WESTMORE, ERN—makeup artist
b: 1904 d: Feb 1, 1967

Hollywood Backstage (info)..... host (1955)

A member of Hollywood's most celebrated family of makeup artists, Ern demonstrated his secrets of glamorizing women in a series of daytime and nighttime programs in the '50s. Another family member, Frank Westmore, recorded the family's colorful chronicles in the 1976 book *The Westmores of Hollywood.*

WESTMORELAND, JIM—actor

The Monroes (wes)... Ruel Jaxon (1966–67)

WESTON, CELIA—actress
b: Dec 14, Spartanburg, S.C.

Alice (com) ..... Jolene Hunnicutt (1981–85)

WESTON, ELLEN—actress
b: Apr 19, 1939, New York City, N.Y.

S.W.A.T. (police)
.... Betty Harrelson (1975–76)

WESTON, JACK—actor
b: Aug 21, 1925*, Cleveland, Ohio

My Sister Eileen (com)
.... Chick Adams (1960–61)
The Hathaways (com)
.... Walter Hathaway (1961–62)
79 Park Avenue (drama)
.... Joker Martin (1977)
The Four Seasons (com)
.... Danny Zimmer (1984)

A plump, balding character actor often in clumsy or ne'er do well roles. Jack got his start on the New York stage in 1950 and appeared in early live TV dramas as well. His first regular role was as "Wormsey," one of the sidekicks on the Saturday morning kids' show *Rod Brown of the Rocket Rangers* (1953–54). He moved to Hollywood in 1956 and has been a standby there ever since, in roles ranging from the dad in a house full of chimpanzees in *The Hathaways* ("It's the last series I'll ever do without script approval," he huffed at the time) to the worrywart dentist in *The Four Seasons*. He has played support in numerous programs and TV movies, the latter including *Now You See It, Now You Don't; I Love a Mystery;* and *79 Park Avenue*.

Jack is married to actress Marge Redmond, Sister Jacqueline from *The Flying Nun*.

WESTON, JIM—actor
Me and Maxx (com)......... Mitch (1980)

WESTON, PAUL—orchestra leader
b: Mar 12, 1912, Springfield, Mass.

The Orchid Award (var)
.... orch. leader (1953–54)
The Jo Stafford Show (music)
.... orch. leader (1954–55)
The Bob Newhart Show (var)
.... orch. leader (1961–62)
The Danny Kaye Show (var)
.... orch. leader (1963–67)
The Jonathan Winters Show (var)
.... orch. leader (1967–69)
The Jim Nabors Hour (var)
.... orch. leader (1969–71)

*Some sources give 1915.

A noted orchestra leader and arranger for many pop singers, including his wife, Jo Stafford. Most of his own recordings are soft and rather unmemorable; he is said to have originated the concept of "mood music". Paul was a founder and the first West Coast president of the National Academy of Recording Arts and Sciences, which presents the Grammy Awards.

WEXLER, BERNARD—actor
Calucci's Department (com).. Frohler (1973)

WHATLEY, DIXIE—host
Entertainment Tonight (news)
.... host/reporter (1981–84)

WHEATLEY, ALAN—English actor
b: Apr 19, 1907, Tolworth, Surrey, England

The Adventures of Robin Hood (adv)
.... sheriff of Nottingham (1955–56)

WHEEL, PATRICIA—actress
b: c. 1924, New York City, N.Y. d: Jun 3, 1986

A Woman to Remember (drama)
.... Christine Baker (1949)

WHEELER, BERT—comedian
b: Apr 7, 1895, Paterson, N.J. d: Jan 18, 1968

Brave Eagle (wes).... Smokey Joe (1955–56)

Half of the famous slapstick comedy team of Wheeler and (Robert) Woolsey, who made their name on Broadway and in movies in the late '20s and '30s. Woolsey died in 1938. One of Bert's earliest television appearances was in a 1950 *Robert Montgomery Presents* staging of the 1927 Ziegfeld musical *Rio Rita*—the show in which Wheeler and Woolsey had first been teamed.

WHEELER, JACK—teenage cohost
Tell It to Groucho (com)..... regular (1962)

WHEELER, MARK—actor
Mobile One (adv) ... Doug McKnight (1975)

WHELAN, JILL—juvenile actress
b: Sep 29, 1966, Oakland, Calif.

Friends (com) . . . . Nancy Wilks (1979)
The Love Boat (com)
. . . . Vicki Stubing (1979–86)

WHELCHEL, LISA—actress
b: May 29, 1963, Fort Worth, Texas

The Facts of Life (com)
. . . . Blair Warner (1979–)

Lisa Whelchel, the rich kid on *Facts of Life,* is a Texas girl who began as a child actor in local Fort Worth theaters and won her first Hollywood role as a Mouseketeer on *The New Mickey Mouse Club* in 1977. Her career moved quickly after that, with a couple of minor films (*The Double McGuffin, The Magician of Lublin*), some series appearances (*Family, The Mary Tyler Moore Show*), and then the long-running role of Blair. She has also appeared in a number of TV movies, including *Twirl* and *The Wild Women of Chastity Gulch.*

Despite bouts of homesickness and recurrent weight problems, young Lisa believes that crashing Hollywood at age 12 was the right move. Her mother isn't so sure. "I'm very proud of my daughter," she told a reporter in 1982, "but I have some regrets, both for myself and for Lisa, that she came to Hollywood so young . . . If she was talented at 12 she'd be just as talented at 21, and we wouldn't have missed so much of her growing up."

WHINNERY, BARBARA—actress
b: Jul 1, Berkeley, Calif.

St. Elsewhere (drama)
. . . . Dr. Cathy Martin (1982–85)

WHIPPLE, RANDY—juvenile actor
My Mother the Car (com)
. . . . Randy Crabtree (1965–66)

WHIPPLE, SAM—actor
b: Sep 28, Venice, Calif.

Open All Night (com)
. . . . Terry Feester (1981–82)

WHITAKER, JACK—sportscaster
b: May 18, 1924, Philadelphia, Pa.

The Face Is Familiar (quiz) . . . emcee (1966)

Emmy Award: Best Sports Personality (1978)

A veteran sports commentator, with CBS from 1961–81 and ABC since then. He has also hosted a number of entertainment shows, including the daytime *The Verdict Is Yours* and the nighttime summer series *The Face Is Familiar.* He has been in broadcasting since 1947.

WHITAKER, JOHNNIE—juvenile actor
b: Dec 13, 1959, Van Nuys, Calif.

Family Affair (com) . . . . Jody (1966–71)

Redheaded Johnnie Whitaker was one of the cutest of TV's "cute kids" in the '60s: fresh-faced, curly-haired, and positively angelic—especially when his "uncle" Brian Keith was around. He began appearing in commercials at age three, was the little kid in a custody case on *Day in Court,* then had parts on such series as *Bonanza, Gunsmoke, Bewitched,* and daytime's *General Hospital* (as the original Scotty Baldwin). His movie debut was in the 1966 film *The Russians Are Coming, The Russians Are Coming,* on the set of which he met Brian Keith, who liked him so much he cast him as one of the twins in his upcoming series, *Family Affair.* During the series' run Johnnie made occasional other appearances, notably in the title role of the *Hallmark Hall of Fame* Christmas special "The Littlest Angel."

Unlike his cute TV sister Anissa Jones (Buffy), who later died of a drug overdose, Johnnie stayed on a relatively even keel after *Family Affair* left the air. Looking younger than his age, he had several more successful years playing juveniles, including two seasons as star of the Saturday morning *Sigmund and the Sea Monsters* (1973–75); he also appeared in a number of Disney films. Johnnie then changed his name to John and became a Mormon lay missionary in Portugal for two years, after which he returned to college to complete his education.

WHITE, AL—actor
Wheels (drama) . . . . Newkirk (1978)

WHITE, AL—choreographer
b: 1877, d: Jan 7, 1957

NBC Comedy Hour (var) . . . . dancers (1956)

WHITE, BETTY—actress
b: Jan 17, 1924*, Oak Park, Ill. r: California

Life with Elizabeth (com)
.... Elizabeth (1953–55)
Make the Connection (quiz). panelist (1955)
Date with the Angels (com)
.... Vicki Angel (1957–58)
The Betty White Show (var)
.... hostess (1958)
The Jack Paar Show (talk)
.... semiregular (1959–62)
The Mary Tyler Moore Show (com)
.... Sue Ann Nivens (1973–77)
Match Game P.M. (quiz). panelist (1975–82)
Liar's Club (quiz)........ panelist (1976–78)
The Betty White Show (com)
.... Joyce Whitman (1977–78)
Mama's Family (com)
..... Ellen Jackson (occasional) (1983–84)
Golden Girls (com)... Rose Nylund (1985–)

Emmy Awards: Best Supporting Actress in a Comedy Series, for *The Mary Tyler Moore Show* (1975, 1976); Best Hostess of a Daytime Game Show, for *Just Men!* (1983); Best Actress in a Comedy Series, for *The Golden Girls* (1986)

TV Guide in the '50s called her a candidate for "America's Sweetheart." Her fresh, girl-next-door good looks and cheerful personality made her a TV version of Doris Day, but, despite a lot of exposure, including several pleasant series at the time, Betty White had to wait 20 years for major TV stardom as a mature comic actress in the '70s.

A graduate of Beverly Hills High School, Betty entered radio in Los Angeles around 1940 and was a local personality there on TV in the early '50s. Her domestic comedy *Life with Elizabeth* began on KLAC-TV in 1952 and was syndicated the following year, giving Betty her first national exposure. Game show appearances and two network series followed, but by the early '60s she was one of those '50s personalities-without-portfolio (Faye Emerson, Wendy Barrie, Ilka Chase, etc.) whose TV careers seemed to have passed with the days of live TV. Her principal appearances became hosting the Tournament of Roses Parade (for 20 years) and the Macy's Thanksgiving Day Parade (for ten). In 1971 she in-

*Some sources give 1922.

dulged her love for animals with a syndicated show called *The Pet Set*.

Betty's casting as the dippy, man-hungry Sue Ann on *The Mary Tyler Moore Show* in 1973 turned things around. Suddenly she was in great demand again, and in the years that followed she appeared in a variety of series, specials, and TV movies, culminating with the mid-'80s hit *The Golden Girls*. One of her pilots that did not become a series was *Snavely* (1978), an American version of the British TV hit *Fawlty Towers*, in which she played the wife of a daffy hotel manager. Ironically, Betty's *Golden Girls* costar Bea Arthur did get on the schedule with her own *Fawlty Towers* copy in 1983 (called *Amanda's*), and it was a flop.

WHITE, BILL—sportscaster
b: Lakewood, Fla.

Monday Night Baseball (sport)
.... sportscaster (1977–79)

A former major-league player with the New York Giants, the St. Louis Cardinals, and the Philadelphia Phillies.

WHITE, CAROLE ITA—actress
b: Aug 24, New York City, N.Y.

Laverne & Shirley (com)
.... Rosie Greenbaum (1976–77)

The daughter of actor Jesse White; she played "Big Sal" in the TV movie *Helter Skelter* in 1976. On *Laverne & Shirley* she was the girls' uppity friend. Not to be confused with a sexy British ingenue of the '60s, Carol White (b. 1941).

WHITE, CHRISTINE—actress
b: Washington, D.C.

Ichabod and Me (com)
.... Abigail Adams (1961–62)

WHITE, DAVID—actor

Bewitched (com)
.... Larry Tate (1964–72)

WHITE, JALEEL—black juvenile actor
b: Nov 27, 1976, Los Angeles, Calif.

Charlie & Company (com)
.... Robert Richmond (1985–86)

WHITE, JESSE—actor

b: Jan 3, 1918, Buffalo, N.Y. r: Akron, Ohio

Private Secretary (com)
.... Cagey Calhoun (1953–57)
The Danny Thomas Show (com)
.... Jesse Leeds (1955–57)
The Ann Sothern Show (com)
.... Oscar Pudney (1960–61)

Everybody's favorite fast talking, cigar chomping, raspy voiced schemer in comedies of the '50s. Jesse began his career onstage in the '40s and scored his first major success supporting Jimmy Stewart in the whimsical *Harvey*, both onstage (1947) and in the movie (1950). He went on to play many comic supporting parts in films and on TV, including that of a show-biz agent on both *Private Secretary* and *The Danny Thomas Show*—simultaneously!

As he played only one basic role, Jesse was seen only occasionally in later years, in guest appearances and some childrens shows. He was best known in the '70s and '80s as the "lonely Maytag repairman" in oft-seen appliance commercials.

WHITE, JOHN SYLVESTER—actor

Welcome Back, Kotter (com)
.... Mr. Michael Woodman (1975–79)

WHITE, KENNETH—actor

Palmerstown, U.S.A. (drama)
.... the sheriff (1980–81)

WHITE, MORGAN—actor

Hawaii Five-O (police)
.... the attorney general (1968–69)

WHITE, PETER—actor

Dynasty II: The Colbys (drama)
.... Arthur Cates (1985–)

WHITE, SCOTT—actor

It's a Man's World (com)
.... Virgil Dobson (1962–63)

WHITE, SLAPPY—black comedian

Sanford and Son (com) ...... Melvin (1972)

Redd Foxx's former nightclub comedy partner, from the '50s.

WHITE, VANNA—hostess

b: Feb 18, 1957, North Myrtle Beach, S.C.

Wheel of Fortune (quiz)... assistant (1983–)

The clotheshorse on *Wheel of Fortune*. She had small roles in a number of films of the early '80s, including *Looker* and *Graduation Day*, and the TV movie *Midnight Offerings*.

WHITEMAN, MARGO—hostess

b: c. 1932

Paul Whiteman's TV Teen Club (talent)
.... cohost (1949–50)

The adopted daughter of bandleader Paul Whiteman. A vivacious teenager, she cohosted her dad's *TV Teen Club* during its first year, leaving when she was married and became pregnant in early 1950. She briefly attempted a show-biz comeback on local TV in the late 1950s, to no avail. In recent years she has been a certified health aide caring for the elderly in the Princeton, New Jersey, area.

WHITEMAN, PAUL—orchestra leader

b: Mar 28, 1890, Denver, Colo. d: Dec 29, 1967

Paul Whiteman's Goodyear Revue (var)
.... host (1949–52)
Paul Whiteman's TV Teen Club (talent)
.... host (1949–54)
On the Boardwalk with Paul Whiteman (var)
.... emcee (1954)
America's Greatest Bands (music)
.... host (1955)

Paul Whiteman was a rotund, mustachioed bandleader who had been a major name in American music for 30 years by the time TV arrived in the late 1940s. His jazz-oriented dance band, founded in 1919, was sensationally successful during the 1920s; among his protégés were composer George Gershwin, who wrote his immortal "Rhapsody in Blue" for Whiteman; Bing Crosby; and many jazz notables. Always wanting to stay with the times, Whiteman starred in one of the earliest movie musicals (*The King of Jazz*, 1930), was heard on several radio shows during the '30s and '40s, and was featured on the inaugural telecast of the ABC television network in 1948. A few months later he began his own long-running TV series, the Saturday night *TV Teen Club,* a talent competition originating from Philadelphia and based on an antidelinquency program Whiteman had sponsored in his own hometown. He also hosted a flashy Sunday night variety show for three seasons, as well as summer music series in 1954 and 1955.

Whiteman continued to conduct in the later '50s and '60s (frequently in Gershwin tribute concerts) and he never lost his taste for new trends in music. In early 1967, shortly before his death, he was quoted as saying that contemporary pop music had gotten rather good, that the Beatles were turning out some "lovely things," and that "If I started life again, I'd probably let my hair grow long and form a rock group."

A biography of Whiteman, including information on his lifelong drinking problem and his four marriages, appeared in 1983 titled *Pops: Paul Whiteman, The King of Jazz,* by Thomas A. DeLong.

WHITING, ARCH—actor
b: Sep 29, Larchmont, N.Y.

Voyage to the Bottom of the Sea (sci fi)
.... Crewman Sparks (1964–68)

WHITING, BARBARA—actress, singer
b: c. 1932

Those Whiting Girls (com)
.... as herself (1955)
Those Whiting Girls (com)
.... as herself (1957)

The sister of Margaret Whiting.

WHITING, JACK—actor, singer
b: Jun 22, 1901, Philadelphia, Pa. d: Feb 15, 1961

The Marge and Gower Champion Show (com)
.... Marge's Father (1957)

WHITING, MARGARET—singer, actress
b: Jul 22, 1924, Detroit, Mich. r: California

Those Whiting Girls (com)
.... as herself (1955)
Those Whiting Girls (com)
.... as herself (1957)
The Strauss Family (drama).... Hetti (1973)

A popular singer of the '40s and '50s, and the daughter of one of Tin Pan Alley's all-time top songwriters, Richard Whiting.

WHITING, NAPOLEON—black actor
b: c. 1909, Mississippi d: Oct 22, 1984

The Big Valley (wes)....... Silas (1965–69)

WHITMAN, STUART—actor
b: Feb 1, 1926, San Francisco, Calif.

Cimarron Strip (wes)
.... U.S. Marshal Jim Crown (1967–68)

A rugged Hollywood also-ran, who appeared in many action films but never quite made it to the top. A former boxer, he was seen fairly often on television during the mid and late 1950s, mostly in westerns, and returned to the medium to star in his own short-lived western series in 1967. Since then he has played supporting roles in series episodes (*The F.B.I., Night Gallery, Fantasy Island*) and second-rate TV movies, the latter including *The Seekers* and *Condominium.*

WHITMIRE, STEVE—puppeteer

The Muppet Show (var)
.... Rizzo the Rat (1980–81)

WHITMORE, JAMES—actor
b: Oct 1, 1921, White Plains, N.Y.

The Law and Mr. Jones (drama)
.... Abraham Lincoln Jones (1960–62)
My Friend Tony (drama)
.... Prof. John Woodruff (1969)
Temperatures Rising (com)
.... Dr. Vincent Campanelli (1972–73)

This gruff, craggy character actor was one of television's most familiar faces during the '50s and '60s, in scores of drama series ranging from *Playhouse 90* (often) to *Cowboy in Africa.* He starred in series too, as an attorney in *The Law and Mr. Jones,* an investigator in *My Friend Tony,* and a no-nonsense chief of surgery in *Temperatures Rising;* but none of these caught on. Whitmore became somewhat less active after the early '70s. He has had leading roles in several TV movies, among them *I Will Fight No More Forever, The Word, Rage,* and *Celebrity.* He is also known for his one-man shows impersonating historical figures, including Harry Truman and Will Rogers.

WHITMORE, JAMES, JR.—actor
b: Oct 24, New York City, N.Y.

Baa Baa Black Sheep (drama)
.... Capt. James W. Gutterman (1976–77)
Hunter (police)
.... Det. Bernie Terwilliger (1984–)

The son of the above.

WHITNEY, GRACE LEE—actress, singer
b: Apr 1, 1930, Ann Arbor, Mich. r: Detroit

Star Trek (sci fi)
.... Yeoman Janice Rand (1966–67)

Grace is also a singer and songwriter, having composed such numbers as "Disco Trekkin'," "Star Child," and "USS Enterprise." Wonder where she got the inspiration for titles like those?

WHITNEY, JASON—juvenile actor

The McLean Stevenson Show (com)
.... Jason (1976–77)

WHITNEY, PETER—actor
b: 1916, Long Branch, N.J. d: Mar 30, 1972

The Rough Riders (wes)
.... Sgt. Buck Sinclair (1958–59)

WHITSON, SAMUEL—actor

Traffic Court (drama). court clerk (1958–59)

WHITTINGTON, DICK—comedian

Rowan & Martin's Laugh-In (var)
.... regular (1968–69)
Almost Anything Goes (aud par)
.... field interviewer (1975)

WHITTON, MARGARET—actress
b: Nov 30, Baltimore, Md. r: Haddonfield, N.J.

Hometown (drama)
.... Barbara Donnelly (1985)

WHOLEY, DENNIS—host

The Generation Gap (quiz).... emcee (1969)

WHYTE, PATRICK—actor

Tales of the 77th Bengal Lancers (adv)
.... Col. Standish (1956–57)

Peyton Place (drama)
.... Theodore Dowell (1965)

A former British army major who had served in India and who was involved in the creation of *Tales of the 77th Bengal Lancers*, as well as portraying its colonel.

WICKER, IREENE—hostess
b: Quincy, Ill.

The Singing Lady (child).. hostess (1948–50)

A children's show host, prominent on radio in the '30s and '40s with her gentle songs and stories for the little ones. She was one of the most unfortunate victims of political blacklisting in the 1950s, her career being virtually ruined when she was erroneously identified as having supported leftist causes years before. After the furor died down she was briefly seen on a Sunday-morning ABC show in 1953–54, and thereafter on New York radio. She was married for many years to a wealthy New York art dealer, Victor Hammer.

WICKERT, ANTHONY—actor

Whiplash (wes) .... Dan (1960–61)

WICKES, MARY—actress
b: Jun 13, 1912*, St. Louis, Mo.

Inside U.S.A. with Chevrolet (var)
.... regular (1949–50)
The Peter Lind Hayes Show (com)
.... the housekeeper (1950)
Bonino (com) ..... Martha, the maid (1953)
The Halls of Ivy (com)...... Alice (1954–55)
Dennis the Menace (com)
.... Miss Esther Cathcart (1959–61)
The Gertrude Berg Show (com)
.... Maxfield (1961–62)
Julia (com)........ Melba Chegley (1968–71)
Doc (com) .... Miss Tully (1975–76)

A favorite character comedienne, skinny and hook-nosed, usually playing gawky, squawky busybodies. She was the original Mary Poppins in a 1949 TV production of the work on *Studio One;* years later she played Lloyd Nolan's wife on *Julia;* and years after that, she had a role in the 1979 TV movie *Willa.*

*Some sources give 1916.

898

WIDDOES, JAMES—actor
b: Nov 15, Pittsburgh, Pa.

Delta House (com) ... Robert Hoover (1979)
Park Place (com)...... Brad Lincoln (1981)
Charles in Charge (com)
.... Stan Pembroke (1984–85)

The tall (6'6"), blond, handsome Widdoes also played Hoover in the movie *Animal House,* from which *Delta House* was adapted.

**WIDDOWSON-REYNOLDS, ROSINA—
actress**

Number 96 (drama)
................Anthea Bryan (1980–81)

WIDMARK, RICHARD—actor
b: Dec 26, 1914, Sunrise, Mich. r: Chicago, Ill.

Madigan (police)
.... Sgt. Dan Madigan (1972–73)

The famous movie actor has rarely been seen on television, apart from his one series, in which he played a New York City police detective, and a few recent TV films. The films have included *Vanished* (which brought him an Emmy Award nomination for his role as the president), *Mr. Horn, All God's Children,* and *A Whale for the Killing.*
  Although 1971's *Vanished* marked Widmark's TV dramatic debut, he had in fact appeared once before, on a 1955 *I Love Lucy* episode in which Lucy was, as usual, willing to do anything to get a celebrity autograph.

WIERE BROTHERS, THE—comedians
Harry Wiere, b: 1908, Berlin, Germany
Herbert Wiere, b: 1909, Vienna, Austria
Sylvester Wiere, b: 1910, Prague, Czechoslovakia, d: Jul 7, 1970

Ford Festival (var) .... regulars (1951)
Oh, Those Bells (com)
.... the Bell brothers (1962)

Knockabout comedy team, along the lines of a slightly toned-down Three Stooges.

WIGGIN, TOM—actor
b: Jul 6, Alexandria, Va.

Breaking Away (com)...... Mike (1980–81)

WIGGINTON, RICHARD—juvenile actor

One Man's Family (drama)
.... Jack Barbour (1951–52)
My Son Jeep (com).......... Boots (1953)

WIGHTMAN, ROBERT—actor

The Waltons (drama)
.............John Boy Walton (1979–81)

WILCOX, CLAIRE—juvenile actress
b: 1956

Harris Against the World (com)
.... Deedee Harris (1964–65)

WILCOX, FRANK—actor
b: Mar 13, 1907, DeSoto, Mo. d: Mar 3, 1974

The Beverly Hillbillies (com)
.... John Brewster (1962–66)
It's About Time (com) .. Gen. Morley (1967)

WILCOX, LARRY—actor
b: Aug 8, 1947, San Diego, Calif.

Lassie (adv) .... Dale Mitchell (1972–74)
CHiPs (police) .... Off. Jon Baker (1977–82)

Larry Wilcox was the blond, handsome, all-American half of the Jon and Ponch team of motorcycle cops on *CHiPs* (the Hispanic half being Erik Estrada). Wilcox was the more experienced actor of the two, having begun his career in the early '70s after serving in the Vietnam War. In the years that followed, he played the role of *Lassie*'s last owner for two seasons, appeared in a number of drama series episodes (*Police Story, Streets of San Francisco,* etc.) and was seen in several *World of Disney* segments.
  Although *CHiPs* represented Larry's big break, he left the series after five years, reportedly because of differences with Estrada. He has been seen in several TV movies in the '70s and '80s, among them *Sky Heist, The Last Ride of the Dalton Gang, Deadly Lessons,* and *The Dirty Dozen—The Next Mission.*

**WILCOX, MARY CHARLOTTE—
comedienne**

SCTV Network 90 (com) .. regular (1982–83)

Emmy Award: Best Writing for a Variety Program, for *SCTV Network* (1983)

WILCOX, NINA—actress
b: Jan 17, New York City, N.Y.

Harbourmaster (adv)
.... Anna Morrison (1957–58)
Jessica Novak (drama)
.... Audrey Stiles (1981)

WILCOX, RALPH—black actor
b: Jan 30, Milwaukee, Wis.

Big Eddie (com)... Raymond McKay (1975)
Busting Loose (com)
.... Raymond St. Williams (1977)
One in a Million (com) .... Duke (1980)

WILD WEST & FANCI, THE—

Hee Haw (var).......... regulars (1980–)

WILD, EARL—pianist
b: Nov 26, 1915, Pittsburgh, Pa.

Caesar's Hour (var) ...... regular (1955–57)

WILDER, YVONNE—actress
b: Sep 20, New York City, N.Y.

Operation Petticoat (com)
.... Maj. Edna Howard (1977–78)
Condo (com)...... Maria Rodriguez (1983)

WILEY, BILL—actor

All Is Forgiven (com)
.... Wendell Branch (1986)

WILKE, ROBERT—actor
b: 1911

The Legend of Jesse James (wes)
.... Marshall Sam Corbett (1965–66)

WILKES, DONNA—actress

Hello, Larry (com)...... Diane Adler (1979)

WILKINS, GEORGE—orchestra leader

Our Place (var) .... orch. leader (1967)

WILKOF, LEE—actor
b: Jun 25, Canton, Ohio

W.E.B. (drama)
.... Harvey Pearlstein (1978)
Delta House (com) .... Einswine (1979)
Newhart (com)
.... Elliot Gabler (1984–85)

WILLARD, FRED—actor, comedian
b: Sep 18, 1939, Shaker Heights, Ohio

The Burns and Schreiber Comedy Hour (var)
.... regular (1973)
Sirota's Court (com) .. Bud Nugent (1976–77)
Fernwood 2-Night (com)
.... Jerry Hubbard (1977–78)
Real People (aud par) .... regular (1979)
Real People (aud par) .... regular (1981–83)
Thicke of the Night (talk)
.... recurring player (1983–84)

This square-jawed, rather dense-looking
comic actor rose to fame as the gullible
sidekick on the talk show parody *Fernwood 2-Night* (later called *America 2-
Night*). During the '60s he had been with
Chicago's Second City and San Francisco's
Ace Trucking Company improvisational
groups; he also appeared in a number of
off-Broadway productions, including *Little
Murders* and Second City's *20,000 Frozen
Grenadiers* (1966).

Fred has also appeared from time to time
in various series episodes and in lightweight TV movies of the caliber of *Flatbed
Annie and Sweetie Pie.*

WILLCOX, PETE—Elvis Presley
   impersonator

The Last Precinct (com)
.... the King (1986)

WILLIAMS, ALLEN—actor

Lou Grant (drama)
.... Adam Wilson (1978–82)

WILLIAMS, ANDY—singer, host
b: Dec 3, 1930*, Wall Lake, Iowa

The College Bowl (com) .. regular (1950–51)
Tonight (talk) .... regular (1954–57)
The Andy Williams and June Valli Show
(music) .... cohost (1957)
The Chevy Showroom (var) ..... host (1958)
The Andy Williams Show (var)
.... host (1959)
The Andy Williams Show (var)
.... host (1962–67)
The Andy Williams Show (var)
.... host (1969–71)
The Andy Williams Show (var)
.... host (1976–77)

*Some sources give 1927, 1928 or 1932.

Emmy Award: Star, Best Variety Series, for *The Andy Williams Show* (1966, 1967)

Smooth-voiced crooner Andy Williams was one of the most popular musical hosts of the 1960s, the high point of a show business career that stretched back to his childhood. Andy began singing as part of a church choir with his brothers in Iowa. The boys were so good they progressed to radio shows in Des Moines, Chicago, and Cincinnati and, when the family moved to Los Angeles in the early '40s, they found work there as well. The Williams Brothers' first recording (and thus Andy's) was in 1944, when they provided a "children's chorus" backing for Bing Crosby's "Swinging on a Star"—one of the biggest selling records of the '40s. During that same year, young Andy did voice work for the movies, including, incredibly, dubbing the singing voice for Lauren Bacall in her debut film *To Have and Have Not*!

The Williams Brothers teamed up with cabaret entertainer Kay Thompson in 1946 and toured for six years, but by 1952 brothers Bob, Dick, and Don had wearied of traveling and settled down with their families. Andy, now in his twenties, struck out on his own (he had previously had a solo spot on a youth-oriented TV variety show called *College Bowl*). He attracted wide attention on Steve Allen's *Tonight Show* and, in 1956, his recording career took off with hits such as "Canadian Sunset," "Butterfly," and "Hawaiian Wedding Song." Andy's easygoing stage presence and ingratiating manner made him a natural as a young variety show host. He headed summer shows in 1957, 1958, and 1959 before returning in 1962 with a weekly show on NBC that lasted, off and on, until 1971. Among the highlights of those '60s shows were comic Jonathan Winters, "The Williams Weirdoes" (Little General, Walking Suitcase, Big Bird, and the Bear), and the singing Osmond Brothers—who must have reminded Andy of his own Williams Brothers background. Andy's theme song is "Moon River."

Apart from a short-lived syndicated series in 1976, Andy has since concentrated on specials, especially his annual Christmas show.

WILLIAMS, ANSON—actor, producer
b: Sep 25, 1949, Los Angeles, Calif.

Happy Days (com)
.... Warren "Potsie" Weber (1974–83)

A compact, energetic performer who has done a little bit of everything in show business—act, write, sing, produce. His first appearance was on an episode of *Owen Marshall, Counselor at Law*, c. 1971, and he has since turned up in a variety of series episodes, specials, and TV movies. His most famous role has, of course, been "Potsie," on *Happy Days*.

Anson conceived and coproduced (with Ron Howard) the 1980 TV movie *Skyward*, about a paraplegic who dreams of becoming a pilot.

WILLIAMS, BARRY—actor
b: Sep 30, 1954, Santa Monica, Calif.

The Brady Bunch (com)
.... Greg Brady (1969–74)
The Brady Bunch Hour (var)
.... Greg Brady (1977)

Barry, the "teen dream" of *The Brady Bunch*, has remained active in small TV roles and in touring stage productions.

WILLIAMS, BILL—actor
b: May 15, 1916, Brooklyn, N.Y.

Adventures in Jazz (music)...... host (1949)
Starlit Time (var) .... host (1950)
The Adventures of Kit Carson (wes)
.... Kit Carson (1951–55)
Music at the Meadowbrook (var)
.... host (1953)
Music at the Meadowbrook (var)
.... host (1956)
Date with the Angels (com)
.... Gus Angel (1957–58)
Assignment Underwater (adv)
.... Bill Greer (1960)

"I never want to see or hear of Kit Carson again!" insisted Bill Williams in the late '50s. One hundred and four episodes of the syndicated TV western had made him a kid's favorite, but he was sick of dusty trails and six-guns. The handsome, blond all-American "good guy" had been a star athlete in his teens and got his show-biz start as a professional swimmer in aquatic revues in the '30s. He broke into movies in the mid-'40s, mostly in action flicks such as *Thirty Seconds over Tokyo*—with whose star, Van Johnson, he was often compared.

During the early days of live television, Bill hosted a number of music shows, appeared in some dramatic productions, and costarred as Betty White's husband in the 1957 domestic comedy *Date with the Angels*. He turned down the lead in *Sea Hunt* —a natural for him—because he didn't think an underwater show would work on TV. When Lloyd Bridges proved him wrong, Bill belatedly tried a watery series of his own, which demonstrated only that the public would not accept *two* such series.

Since then, Bill, still handsome but now graying, has played occasional roles in TV episodes (*Lassie, Perry Mason, Police Woman*). As recently as 1981 he had a small part in the TV movie *Goldie and the Boxer Go to Hollywood*. He has been married since 1946 to actress Barbara Hale (Della Street of *Perry Mason*), and the couple takes great pride in the booming career of their son, actor William Katt.

WILLIAMS, BILLY—black singer
b: Dec 28, 1909, Waco, Texas d: Jul 16, 1984

Your Show of Shows (var)
.... quartet (1950–54)

Best known in the '50s for his version of the song "I'm Gonna Sit Right Down and Write Myself a Letter."

WILLIAMS, BILLY DEE—black actor
b: Apr 6, 1937, Harlem, New York City, N.Y.

Chiefs (drama) .... Chief Tyler Watts (1983)
Double Dare (police) . Billy Diamond (1985)

A suave black actor who has been in and out of television since the '50s, concurrent with an increasingly successful movie career. He made his stage debut at age seven, and his first film, *The Last Angry Man*, in 1959. His TV credits have included bit parts in the '50s, a stint on *The Guiding Light* in the '60s, and a number of TV movies since 1970; among the latter have been the acclaimed *Brian's Song* in 1971 (the costarring role, and his first big break) and featured parts in *The Hostage Tower, Shooting Stars, Chiefs,* and *Time Bomb.* By the 1980s he had become a major name. Despite that fact, his first starring series, *Double Dare,* was a flop.

WILLIAMS, BOB—actor

Double or Nothing (quiz)... assistant (1953)
The New Phil Silvers Show (com)
.... Bob (1963–64)
The Don Knotts Show (var)
.... regular (1970–71)

WILLIAMS, BRANDON—juvenile actor
b: Oct 20, Paramount, Calif.

Greatest American Hero (adv)
.... Kevin Hinkley (1981)

WILLIAMS, CARA—actress
b: Jun 29, 1925*, Brooklyn, N.Y.

Pete and Gladys (com)
.... Gladys Porter (1960–62)
The Cara Williams Show (com)
.... Cara Bridges/Wilton (1964–65)
Rhoda (com)............... Mae (1974–75)

A feisty, redheaded comedienne, once considered a "second Lucy," who appeared in films from the '40s onward. Cara did occasional television work in the '50s, but her TV heyday was in the early '60s, when she starred as Harry Morgan's wife on *Pete and Gladys* and then on her own sitcom, *The Cara Williams Show*. Aside from a recurring part on *Rhoda* in 1974–75, she has not been seen much since.

Not to fret, however. Cara is comfortably married to a Beverly Hills realtor (a tumultuous marriage to John Drew Barrymore in the '50s ended in divorce). She occupies herself as a successful interior designer and champion high-stakes poker player.

WILLIAMS, CHINO—actor

Baretta (police) .... Fats (1975–78)

WILLIAMS, CINDY—actress
b: Aug 22, 1947, Van Nuys, Calif. r: Irving, Texas

The Funny Side (var)....... regular (1971)
Laverne & Shirley (com)
.... Shirley Feeney (1976–82)

The saga of "Laverne vs. Shirley" has been amply documented elsewhere (check any back issue of *The National Enquirer*); suffice it to say that the feud that brought

*She says 1933.

down one of TV's greatest hits of the '70s did little to further the career that Cindy Williams really wanted—in movies.

Cindy began acting on television shortly after graduation from Los Angeles City College, with bits in *Room 222*, *Nanny and the Professor*, *Police Story*, and *Love, American Style*. She played the teenage ingenue in *Funny Side* sketches (opposite Michael Lembeck), but her first major break was as Ron Howard's cheerleader girlfriend in the 1973 theatrical film *American Graffiti*. Cindy agreed to do *Laverne & Shirley* only because her movie career wasn't developing as fast as anticipated; the hit series, however, seems to have given her the bright and wacky role with which she will always be identified. Her first and most successful starring role in a TV movie came during L & S's run, in 1978's *Suddenly, Love*. Since quitting the series, she has been seen mostly in specials and less successful TV films, e.g., *When Dreams Come True*.

WILLIAMS, CLARENCE, III—black actor
b: Aug 21, 1939, New York City, N.Y.

The Mod Squad (police)
.... Linc Hayes (1968–73)

The angry, afro-ed young black member of *The Mod Squad* team was primarily a stage actor before his most famous television role; he has been infrequently seen on TV since it left the air. He did turn up in the '80s in the Prince movie *Purple Rain*, however.

WILLIAMS, DIAHN—actress

Harry's Girls (com)........ Terry (1963–64)

WILLIAMS, DICK—choral director
b: Jun 7, 1926, Wall Lake, Iowa

The Andy Williams Show (var)
.... singers (1959)
The Steve Lawrence Show (var)
.... singers (1965)
The Julie Andrews Hour (var)
.... singers (1972–73)

Andy's brother.

WILLIAMS, DICK ANTHONY—black actor
b: Aug 9, 1938, Chicago, Ill.

Our Family Honor (drama)
.... Jonas Jones (1985–86)
Heart of the City (drama)
.... Lt. Ed Van Duzer (1986–)

WILLIAMS, ED—actor

Police Squad (com)....... Ted Olson (1982)

WILLIAMS, GRANT—actor
b: Aug 18, 1930, New York City, N.Y. d: Jul 28, 1985

Hawaiian Eye (drama)
.... Greg MacKenzie (1960–63)

An actor best known for the title role in the cult film classic *The Incredible Shrinking Man* (1957).

WILLIAMS, GUINN—actor
b: Apr 26, 1899, Decatur, Texas d: Jun 6, 1962

Circus Boy (adv)........ Big Boy (1956–58)

WILLIAMS, GUY—actor
b: Jan 14, 1924, New York City, N.Y.

Zorro (wes)
.. Don Diego de la Vega (Zorro) (1957–59)
Lost in Space (sci fi)
.... Prof. John Robinson (1965–68)

WILLIAMS, HAL—black actor
b: Dec 14, 1938, Columbus, Ohio

Sanford and Son (com)
.... Officer Smith (Smitty) (1972–76)
On The Rocks (com)...... DeMott (1975–76)
Private Benjamin (com)
.... Sgt. Ted Ross (1981–83)
227 (com).......... Lester Jenkins (1985–)

A husky but gentle black actor who started out in amateur theater in Ohio in the '60s, while working for the Ohio Youth Commission. He decided to try acting as a career and moved to Hollywood in 1968, making the rounds of auditions while working a regular job with the California Youth Authority to support his family. A number of TV roles eventually came his way, including the recurring parts of Smitty the cop on *Sanford and Son*, Harley Foster the neighbor on *The Waltons*, and Clarence the mechanic on *Harry-O*. He also had guest roles on other series, including *Good*

Times and *Cannon,* and was one of the actors who played Alex Haley (at various stages of his life) in *Roots: The Next Generations.* After regular roles in some unsuccessful series, he finally landed in his first major hit as Marla Gibbs' down-to-earth husband in *227.*

WILLIAMS, JOHN—actor
b: Apr 15, 1903, Chalfont St. Giles, Bucks., England d: May 5, 1983

The Rogues (com) . . . Insp. Briscoe (1964–65)
Family Affair (com) . Niles French (1966–67)

A suave British film actor, remembered for his role as the inspector in *Dial M for Murder;* not the famous composer.

WILLIAMS, KEN—announcer
b: c. 1914 d: Feb 16, 1984

Video Village (quiz) . . . . . . announcer (1960)

WILLIAMS, KENT—actor
b: New York City, N.Y.

Mickey Spillane's Mike Hammer (drama)
Asst. D.A. Lawrence D. Barrington (1984–)

WILLIAMS, LOUISE—actress
b: Feb 25, Scranton, Pa.

Busting Loose (com) . . Jackie Gleason (1977)
13 Queens Boulevard (com) . . . . . . Jill (1979)
Baby Makes Five (com)
. . . . Jennie Riddle (1983)

WILLIAMS, MASON—writer, musician
b: Aug 24, 1938, Abilene, Texas

The Smothers Brothers Comedy Hour (var)
. . . . regular (1967–69)

Emmy Award: Best Writing for a Variety Show, for *The Smothers Brothers Comedy Hour* (1969)

A close friend of Tommy Smothers, Mason started out in the Smothers Brothers backup band and emerged as one of the key creative forces behind their landmark counterculture series in the late '60s. He also achieved personal fame with his unusual rock/classical recording, "A Classical Gas," in 1968. In later years he was in and out of show business, writing for such TV personalities as Andy Williams, Petula

Clark, Glen Campbell, Pat Paulsen, and his old friends the Smothers Brothers. He was also, for a time around 1980, the head writer for *NBC's Saturday Night Live.* The "Bluegrass Symphony" he composed for the nation's bicentennial in 1976 didn't catch on, however.

WILLIAMS, PAT—orchestra leader

The Music Scene (music)
. . . . orch. leader (1969–70)

WILLIAMS, R.J.—actor

Detective in the House (drama)
. . . . Dunc Wyman (1985)

WILLIAMS, RHODA—actress

Mixed Doubles (drama)
. . . . Elaine Coleman (1949)

WILLIAMS, RICHARD—actor

Love, American Style (com)
. . . . repertory player (1970–72)
Man from Atlantis (adv) . . . . Jomo (1977–78)

WILLIAMS, ROBERT B.—actor

Fernwood 2-Night (com)
. . . . Garth Gimble, Sr. (1977–78)

WILLIAMS, ROBIN—actor, comedian
b: Jul 21, 1952, Chicago, Ill.

The Richard Pryor Show (var)
. . . . regular (1977)
Laugh-In (revival) (var) . . . regular (1977–78)
Mork & Mindy (com) . . . . . . Mork (1978–82)

Steve Allen, in trying to describe what it is that makes Robin Williams so funny, commented, "With other comedians one can discuss the characters they do, their personalities or mannerisms or quirks. But Williams' public persona seems practically all quirk. He moves too fast, and is so slippery, so perpetually 'on,' that it is almost impossible to pin him down . . ."* Another writer described Williams as "an astonishing lunar wild man out of Jonathan Winters by way of Lenny Bruce with a touch of Richard Burton thrown in."

Robin Williams was one of the most remarkable comic discoveries of the '70s, a

*Steve Allen in *Funny People* (Stein and Day, 1981).

bizarre, mugging, chameleonlike ball of energy who constantly slipped into and out of one character after another, almost daring the audience to keep up. His unconventional, stream-of-consciousness style took TV audiences by storm. He is one of the few major stars who could legitimately be called an "overnight sensation."

Robin was the son of a vice president of the Ford Motor Company, and, much the youngest in his family, grew up pretty much alone with his fantasies. After high school and a couple of stabs at college he decided to become an entertainer and enrolled at New York's Juilliard School, where he studied under, of all people, John Houseman. He augmented his income as a street mime in Manhattan. In 1976 he moved to San Francisco and then to Los Angeles to perform in clubs and was almost immediately spotted and given bits in *The Richard Pryor Show* and an ill-fated revival of *Laugh-In*. Producer Garry Marshall signed him for a single guest spot on *Happy Days* in early 1978 as "Mork from Ork," and the character proved so popular that Robin won his own series the following fall—little more than a year after arriving in town. It was an enormous hit.

For reasons best known to their psychiatrists, ABC's executives began to meddle with the hit show after only its first season, changing its time period and diluting its zany, childlike quality. Although the series lingered on for three more years, its audience declined substantially. Meanwhile, Robin began a rather uneven movie career, trying to transfer his improvisational genius to more structured film vehicles such as *Popeye* and *The World According to Garp*. He remains at his best, however, in specials and variety show appearances where you—and he—are never quite sure what insanity will pop out of his fertile brain next.

WILLIAMS, SPENCER—black actor
b: Jul 14, 1893, Vidalia, La. d: Dec 13, 1969

Amos 'n' Andy (com)
.... Andy Brown (1951–53)

The big dumb guy on *Amos 'n' Andy*. Spencer was a veteran character actor in "blacks only" films of the '30s and '40s, the type that played only in black theaters and bore titles such as *Harlem on the Prairie*,

The Bronze Buckaroo, and *Dirtie Gertie from Harlem*. Aside from his single series, he did little television.

WILLIAMS, STEVEN—actor
The Equalizer (drama).. Lt. Burnett (1985–)

WILLIAMS, TIGER—actor
The Secret Empire (drama) .... Billy (1979)

WILLIAMS, TOM—actor
b: Aug 15, Chicago, Ill.

Nobody's Perfect (com) .. Det. Grauer (1980)

WILLIAMS, TONYA—black actress
Check It Out (com)
.... Jennifer Woods (1985–)

WILLIAMS, VAN—actor
b: Feb 27, 1934, Fort Worth, Texas

Bourbon Street Beat (drama)
.... Kenny Madison (1959–60)
Surfside Six (drama)
.... Ken Madison (1960–62)
The Tycoon (com)..... Pat Burns (1964–65)
The Green Hornet (drama)
.. Britt Reid (the Green Hornet) (1966–67)

Van Williams, a hunky hero of the '60s, began his adult life as the operator of a salvage business and skin-diving school in Hawaii in the mid-1950s. Advised by visiting producer Mike Todd to try a screen test, he arrived in Hollywood with no acting experience at all and was promptly cast in a *General Electric Theater* drama with Ronald Reagan. Shortly thereafter, he won a contract with Warner Brothers, which had him play the same role—private eye Ken Madison—in two different series, *Bourbon Street Beat* and *Surfside Six*. He then became Walter Brennan's private pilot in the comedy *The Tycoon*. His most famous role, however, was that of comic book crimefighter *The Green Hornet*.

Van guest-starred in other series, including *The Big Valley* and *Mission: Impossible*, and starred in a Saturday morning adventure series called *Westwind*, set in Hawaii, in 1975–76. By the end of the '70s his career was pretty much out of steam. Always the astute businessman, he pursued assorted business interests, including real estate and law enforcement supplies. He is said to have turned down a recurring role on *Falcon Crest* in the '80s in order to concentrate on his new, non–show business activities.

WILLIAMS, WILLIAM B.—announcer, disc jockey
b: Aug 6, 1923, Babylon, N.Y. d: Aug 3, 1986

ABC's Nightlife (talk) . . . . regular (1965)
Sammy and Company (talk)
. . . . regular (1975–77)

A leading New York disc jockey for more than 40 years, on station WNEW; he long championed the music of Frank Sinatra and gave the singer the nickname "the Chairman of the Board." Williams was married for many years to early TV personality Dottie Mack.

WILLIAMSON, FRED—black actor
b: Mar 5, 1938, Gary, Ind.

Julia (com) . . . . Steve Bruce (1970–71)
Monday Night Football (sport)
. . . . announcer (1974)
Wheels (drama)
. . . . Leonard Wingate (1978)
Half Nelson (drama) . . . Chester Long (1985)

A former pro football star, known as "the Hammer" during his years with the Kansas City Chiefs in the 1960s. He made his film debut in the movie *M*A*S*H* in 1970 and scored his first major TV success in the same year as Diahann Carroll's boyfriend in *Julia*. Fred compares acting and football thusly: "When acting, if something gets rough, I call for a stuntman. But in football that's just what you are—a stuntman."

WILLIAMSON, MYKEL T.—actor

Bay City Blues (drama)
. . . . Deejay Cummingham (1983)
Cover Up (drama) . . . . Rick (1984–85)

WILLINGHAM, NOBLE—actor
b: Aug 31, Mineola, Texas

When the Whistle Blows (com)
. . . . Bulldog (1980)
Cutter To Houston (drama)
. . . . Mayor Warren Jarvis (1983)

WILLIS, ANDRA—singer

The Lawrence Welk Show (music)
. . . . regular (1967–69)

WILLIS, BRUCE—actor
b: Mar 19, 1955, Penns Grove, N.J.

Moonlighting (drama)
. . . . David Addison (1985–)

A rather obscure New York stage actor in off-Broadway productions of the late '70s and early '80s, Willis began doing television supporting work in the '80s (*Hart to Hart, Miami Vice*). He suddenly rocketed to stardom as the flippant, unconventional private-eye teamed with Cybill Shepherd on *Moonlighting* in 1985.

WILLIS, CURTIZ—juvenile actor

The Cop and the Kid (com)
. . . . Shortstuff (1975–76)

WILLOCK, DAVE—actor
b: 1909, Chicago, Ill.

Pantomime Quiz (quiz) . . . regular (1953–54)
Do It Yourself (com) . . . . host (1955)
Boots and Saddles—The Story of the 5th Cavalry (wes) . . . . Lt. Binning (1957–58)
Margie (com) . . . . Harvey Clayton (1961–62)
The Beautiful Phyllis Diller Show (var)
. . . . regular (1968)
The Queen and I (com) . . . . Ozzie (1969)

Skinny comic actor, from films of the '40s.

WILLOCK, MARGARET—actress

Fay (com) . Linda Stewart Baines (1975–76)

WILLS, ANNEKE—actress

Strange Report (drama)
. . . . Evelyn McLean (1971)

WILLS, BEVERLY—actress
b: 1934 d: Oct 24, 1963

I Married Joan (com) . . . . Beverly (1953–55)

The daughter of actress Joan Davis, the star of *I Married Joan*.

WILLS, CHILL—actor
b: Jul 18, 1903, Seagoville, Texas d: Dec 15, 1978

Frontier Circus (drama)
.... Col. Casey Thompson (1961–62)
The Rounders (com). Jim Ed Love (1966–67)

An easygoing supporting actor with an honest, open face, and a gravelly voice, in scores of Hollywood westerns of the '30s and '40s; he was also the voice of the movies' Francis the Talking Mule. He appeared periodically on television, mostly in westerns of the '60s, and was seen as late as 1978 in the *Hallmark Hall of Fame* special "Stubby Pringle's Christmas"—which aired two days after his death.

Wills was said to have been named "Chill" because he was born on the hottest day of the year in Seagoville, Texas.

WILLS, LOU, JR.—actor

Hank (com)
.... Asst. Coach Gazzari (1965–66)

WILLS, MAURY—black actor, sportscaster

b: Oct 2, 1932, Washington, D.C.

Monday Night Baseball (sport)
.... sportscaster (1973–75)

A former baseball star, in the major leagues from 1959–1973, mostly with the Los Angeles Dodgers.

WILLS, TERRY—actor

Flo (com) .... Wendell Tubbs (1980)

WILLSON, MEREDITH—composer, conductor

b: May 18, 1902, Mason City, Iowa d: Jun 15, 1984

The Meredith Willson Show (music)
.... host (1949)
The Name's the Same (quiz)
.... panelist (1951–53)

The witty composer who gave us such all-time hits as *The Music Man* (which was based on his own boyhood memories) and *The Unsinkable Molly Brown.* During the 1950s, he was a TV talk show raconteur.

Autobiographies: *And There I Stood with My Piccolo* (1948); *Eggs I Have Laid* (1955); *But He Doesn't Know the Territory* (1959).

WILSON, BOB—sportscaster

Sportsreel (sport)... commentator (1953–55)

WILSON, BRIAN GODFREY—juvenile actor

Palmerstown, U.S.A. (drama)
.... David Hall (1980–81)

WILSON, CAL—actor

The Jerry Reed When You're Hot You're Hot Hour (var) .... regular (1972)

WILSON, DAVID—actor

Studs Lonigan (drama)....... Weary (1979)
The Gangster Chronicles (drama)
.... Vincent "Mad Dog" Coll (1981)

WILSON, DEMOND—black actor

b: Oct 13, 1946, Valdosta, Ga.

Sanford and Son (com)
.... Lamont Sanford (1972–77)
Baby, I'm Back (com)
.... Raymond Ellis (1978)
The New Odd Couple (com)
.... Oscar Madison (1982–83)

Demond Wilson was a Vietnam veteran, fresh out of the service, when he entered acting in the late 1960s. After a short period with touring stage companies, he headed for Hollywood, where he promptly landed a role in the 1971 Sidney Poitier movie *The Organization* and, later, the same year, a part in an episode of *All in the Family,* as a burglar. The latter won him an audition for the part of Redd Foxx's son in *Sanford and Son*—and stardom.

Although *Sanford* became one of the biggest hits of the 1970s, both Foxx and Wilson announced in 1977 that they were quitting the show. Demond's subsequent career has been less than spectacular. He costarred in two failed comedies and has appeared in guest roles in a number of other series, including *The Love Boat* and *Today's F.B.I.* He now tours in stage and nightclub shows.

WILSON, DICK—actor

The Better Home Show (info)
.... regular (1951–52)
McHale's Navy (com)
.... Dino Baroni (1965–66)

Presenting Susan Anton (var)
.... regular (1979)
Small & Frye (com)
.... the drunken barfly (1983)

WILSON, DON—announcer
b: 1900, Denver, Colo.* d: Apr 25, 1982

The Jack Benny Show (com)
.... as himself (1950–65)

Jack Benny's portly announcer and comic foil, with him for 33 years.

WILSON, DOOLEY—black actor
b: Apr 3, 1894, Tyler, Texas d: May 30, 1953

Beulah (com) .... Bill Jackson (1951–53)

A minor-league actor (and onetime drummer) who will always be remembered for one brief scene in the movie *Casablanca,* in which Ingrid Bergman said "Play it, Sam ... play 'As Time Goes By' "—and Dooley did. Ironically, in reality he couldn't play a note; the music was dubbed. Dooley's only major television role was as Beulah's boyfriend on *Beulah.*

WILSON, DOREEN—hostess
The Better Home Show (info)
.... regular (1951–52)

The wife of Dick Wilson, with him on *The Better Home Show.*

WILSON, EARL—columnist
b: May 3, 1907, Rockford, Ohio d: Jan 16, 1987

Stage Entrance (int) .... host (1951–52)
Tonight! America After Dark (talk)
.... regular (1957)

Longtime New York show-business columnist, known as "The Midnight Earl."

WILSON, EILEEN—singer
Your Hit Parade (music) . vocalist (1950–52)

WILSON, ELIZABETH—actress
b: Apr 4, 1925, Grand Rapids, Mich.

East Side/West Side (drama)
.... Frieda Hechlinger (1963–64)

*Some sources give Lincoln, Neb.

Doc (com) .... Annie Bogert (1975–76)
Morningstar/Eveningstar (drama)
.... Kathy Kelly (1986)

WILSON, ETHEL—actress
b: c. 1891, Baltimore, Md. d: Apr 19, 1980

The Aldrich Family (com)
.... Aunt Harriet (1949–53)

WILSON, FLIP—black comedian
b: Dec 8, 1933, Jersey City, N.J.

The Flip Wilson Show (var) . . host (1970–74)
People Are Funny (quiz) ...... emcee (1984)
Charlie & Company (com)
.... Charlie Richmond (1985–86)

Emmy Award: Star, Best Variety Series, for *The Flip Wilson Show* (1971); Best Writing for a Variety Series, for *The Flip Wilson Show* (1971).

Flip Wilson was a hip comedian who rose to fame during TV's "minority explosion" in the late '60s. Bill Cosby had been the first black to star in a dramatic series *(I Spy);* Diahann Carroll the first to star in a "respectable" comedy *(Julia);* Flip was the first to headline a successful variety show. *The Flip Wilson Show* also opened another door, for better or worse. While *I Spy* and *Julia* had played down their stars' blackness, Flip thrived on ethnic humor with such outrageous stereotypes as his Revernd Leroy of "the Church of What's Happening Now," Geraldine the black hussy, and shrieking catchphrases such as "The devil made me do it!" All of this somehow seemed acceptable coming from a black comedian—in fun, not anger.

Flip knew what it was like to make it the hard way. Born in deep poverty and raised in foster homes, he quit school at 16 to try to make something of himself ("I guess hungry guys make the best prizefighters and the best comics," he later said). During a four-year hitch in the air force, he began entertaining the troops, who nicknamed him "Flip" for his irreverent, "flip" humor (his real name is Clerow). He was discharged in 1954 and began 12 long years of working odd jobs and small clubs, developing an act. Suddenly, in 1966, black was "in," and Flip's career began to take off. He made his TV debut on *The Tonight Show* and appeared frequently on *Ed Sullivan, Laugh-In,* and in sketches on such series as

That's Life and Love, American Style. In September 1969 he starred in a variety special which led the following year to his hit series.

"My goal was to make it, and I think I've made it. Now I'm going to enjoy it," he said at the time. His career did indeed begin to drift in the later '70s, with only occasional appearances on specials and series episodes (e.g., The Six Million Dollar Man, The Love Boat). A 1980 pilot for a new Wilson series based on the movie The Cheap Detective didn't make it to the schedule, and two others that did in the '80s were unsuccessful.

WILSON, GERALD—orchestra leader
b: Sep 4, 1918, Shelby, Miss.

Redd Foxx (var)..... orch. leader (1977–78)

WILSON, IRON JAW—black performer
The Redd Foxx Show (com).... Duds (1986)

An old friend of Redd Foxx's from the comic's club days. Wilson's act was to lift heavy objects using his mouth.

WILSON, JANE—singer
Celebrity Time (quiz).... panelist (1951–52)

WILSON, JEANNIE—actress
b: Feb 4, Memphis, Tenn.

Simon & Simon (drama)
.... Janet Fowler (1981–83)
Street Hawk (police).. Rachel Adams (1985)
Stir Crazy (adv)....... Captain Betty (1985)

A former Miss Texas. She appeared in commercials for four years as "The Dodge Girl" ("Tell 'em Honey sent ya"), and has been playing guest roles in series since the late 1970s.

WILSON, JIM—
Ozark Jubilee (music)........ regular (1957)

WILSON, JOE ("WHISPERING" JOE)—sportscaster
National Bowling Champions (sport)
.... commentator (1956–57)

WILSON, JOYCE VINCENT—black singer
b: Dec 14, 1946, Detroit, Mich.

Tony Orlando and Dawn (var)
.... member of Dawn (1974–76)

WILSON, LESTER—choreographer
The Sammy Davis Jr. Show (var)
.... dancers (1966)
Marie (var)............. dancers (1980–81)

WILSON, LIONEL—actor
The Aldrich Family (com)
.... George Bigelow (1949–53)

WILSON, LISLE—black actor
That's My Mama (com)
.... Leonard Taylor (1974–75)

WILSON, LOIS—actress
b: Jun 28, 1894*, Pittsburgh, Pa. r: Birmingham, Ala. d: Jan 8, 1983

The Aldrich Family (com)
.... Mrs. Alice Aldrich (1949–51)

WILSON, MARIE—actress
b: Aug 19, 1916, Anaheim, Calif. d: Nov 23, 1972

My Friend Irma (com)
.... Irma Peterson (1952–54)
Where's Huddles? (cartn)
.... Penny McCoy (voice) (1970)

Marie Wilson was Hollywood's archetypal dumb blonde—giggly, innocent, and extremely sexy. She started out in movies at age 18 and played much the same role for most of her life in films, on radio, and finally on TV. My Friend Irma, in which she played a kooky, endearing secretary, capped her career. The show began as a radio show that ran for seven years (1947–54), expanded into two motion pictures in 1949 and 1950, and finally became the TV series for which she is most famous. Some sample Irma-isms, delivered with wide-eyed innocence:

On military service: "A girl shouldn't have to go out with a sailor unless she wants to . . ."
On a friend becoming a man's third wife:

*Some sources give 1895 or 1896.

"The third? What good will that do if he's got two other wives?"

On being told that her no-good boyfriend has no job, no money, no clothes, no car, no prospects, and no future: "I know, but I have to stick with him in case things get tough."

Marie's later career was pretty spotty, consisting of a couple more movies, a few TV appearances, and (mostly) stage work. She provided the voice of housewife Penny in *Where's Huddles?* and appeared in a *Love, American Style* sketch telecast only a few days before she died. She once wistfully said of her image, "It has been very good to me and I'm not complaining . . . but someday I just wish someone would offer me a different kind of role."

WILSON, MARY LOUISE—actress
b: Nov 12, New Haven, Conn. r: New Orleans, La.

One Day at a Time (com)
.... Ginny Wrobliki (1976–77)

WILSON, PAUL—actor

Empire (com) .... Bill (1984)
Fast Times (com)..... Dennis Taylor (1986)

WILSON, ROBIN—actress

Hot L Baltimore (com)........ Jackie (1975)

WILSON, ROGER—actor
b: Oct 8, New Orleans, La.

Seven Brides for Seven Brothers (adv)
.... Daniel McFadden (1982–83)

WILSON, SHEREE J.—actress

Our Family Honor (drama)
.... Rita Danzig (1985–86)

WILSON, SLIM—host, bandleader

Talent Varieties (var) .... emcee (1955)
Ozark Jubilee (music)
.... bandleader (1958–60)
Five Star Jubilee (var)
.... bandleader (1961)

WILSON, STUART—actor

The Strauss Family (drama)
.... Johann Strauss, Jr. (1973)

WILSON, TERRY—actor
b: Sep 3, 1923, Huntington Park, Calif.

Wagon Train (wes)... Bill Hawks (1957–65)

WILSON, THEODORE—black actor
b: Dec 10, 1943, New York City, N.Y.

Roll Out (com) ...... High Strung (1973–74)
That's My Mama (com)
.... Earl Chambers (1974–75)
The Sanford Arms (com)
.... Phil Wheeler (1977)
Good Times (com).. Sweet Daddy (1978–79)
Crazy Like a Fox (drama)... Ernie (1985–86)
The Redd Foxx Show (com). Jim-Jam (1986)

WILSON, TREY—actor

The News Is the News (var) . regular (1983)

WILSON, WARD—host

Can You Top This? (com).. emcee (1950–51)

WILZAK, CRISSY—actress
b: Mar 24, Elyria, Ohio

Mork & Mindy (com)
  Glenda Faye "Crissy" Comstock (1980–81)

WIMBERLY, BILL, COUNTRY RHYTHM BOYS—

Ozark Jubilee (music).... regulars (1956–57)

WINCHELL, PAUL—ventriloquist, actor
b: Dec 21, 1922, New York City, N.Y.

The Bigelow Show (var) ..... host (1948–49)
The Paul Winchell–Jerry Mahoney Show
(var).......................host (1950–54)
Circus Time (var) ..... ringmaster (1956–57)
Keep Talking (quiz) ...... regular (1958–60)

Paul Winchell was the second most popular ventriloquist of the '50s, after the acknowledged master, Edgar Bergen. (Winchell and several others were actually better ventriloquists, but Bergen had superb comic material.) A polio victim as a child, Paul overcame the disease and became an ambitious juvenile performer, making his national debut at age 13 as a winner on radio's *Amateur Hour.* He had his own show in the early '40s and made his TV debut in 1947 on an early variety series called *Show Business Inc.;*

a year later he was starring in his own show.

Paul's heyday was in the '50s, when he was a familiar nighttime TV personality with his bow-tied, wisecracking dummy Jerry Mahoney as well as Knucklehead Smith and others. He was also seen in daytime, where he had a popular kids' show from 1954–61. By the '60s he was devoting all his time to children's shows, including a syndicated series in 1964 and the kids' quiz *Runaround* in 1972. He became a very active "voice man" for Saturday morning cartoons in the '60s, '70s, and '80s; among other things he was the voice of Dastardly of *Dastardly and Muttley* and Goober of *Goober and the Ghost Chasers* and also did voices on the Dr. Seuss and Smurfs specials.

In addition to his entertainment career, Paul made news in 1975 as the inventor of an artificial heart.

WINCHELL, WALTER—columnist
b: Apr 7, 1897, Harlem, N.Y. d: Feb 20, 1972

The Walter Winchell Show (news)
.... reporter (1952–55)
The Walter Winchell Show (var)
.... host (1956)
The Walter Winchell File (drama)
.... host/narrator (1957–58)
The Untouchables (police)
.... narrator (1959–63)
The Walter Winchell Show (news)
.... reporter (1960)

Who could forget Walter Winchell and his rat-tat-tat, crime and scandal gossip bulletins:

Good evening Mr. and Mrs. North and South America and all the ships at sea, let's go to press. FLASH!

Winchell was a onetime vaudevillian who was very popular on radio in the '30s and '40s, with his sensational show biz scoops, feuds, and fast paced, highly theatrical delivery. By the time television came along, that sort of rumor-mongering was becoming a bit old-hat, but his first, 15-minute show nevertheless lasted for three years on ABC, until he got into a fight with the network (Walter got into fights with everyone). He then tried an Ed Sullivan–style variety show and a dramatic series based on some of his scoops before becoming known to a younger audience as the stac-

cato narrator of the period crime show *The Untouchables*.

WINCOTT, JEFF—actor
b: May 8, Toronto, Canada

Night Heat (police)
.... Det. Frank Giambone (1985–)

WINDOM, WILLIAM—actor
b: Sep 28, 1923, New York City, N.Y.

The Farmer's Daughter (com)
..... Congressman Glen Morley (1963–66)
My World and Welcome to It (com)
.... John Monroe (1969–70)
The Girl with Something Extra (com)
.... Stuart Kline (1973–74)
Brothers and Sisters (com)
.... Larry Krandall (1979)
Murder, She Wrote (drama)
.... Dr. Seth Hazlitt (1985–)

Emmy Award: Best Actor in a Comedy Series, for *My World and Welcome to It* (1970)

A frumpy, middle-aged actor who seemed to shamble in and out of guest roles on every drama series, and half the comedies, of the '60s and '70s. He started acting after military service in World War II and was seen mostly onstage in the '50s. Since shifting his allegiance to television in the early '60s, he has appeared in hundreds of episodes and several series, most notably as the widower congressman who eventually married Inger Stevens on *The Farmer's Daughter* and the daydreaming husband on the whimsical *My World and Welcome to It*.

Windom has also played supporting roles in quite a few TV movies and miniseries, among them *Escape*, *The Homecoming* (pilot for *The Waltons*), *Once an Eagle*, *Blind Ambition*, and *Desperate Lives*.

WINFIELD, PAUL—black actor
b: May 22, 1941, Los Angeles, Calif.

Julia (com)........ Paul Cameron (1968–70)
Roots: The Next Generations (drama)
.... Dr. Horace Huguley (1979)
The Blue and the Gray (drama)
.... Jonathan (1982)

WINFIELD, RODNEY—comedian

CBS Newcomers (var) . . . . . . regular (1971)

WINGREEN, JASON—actor
b: Oct 9, Brooklyn, N.Y.

The Rounders (com)
. . . . Shorty Dawes (1966–67)
All in the Family (com)
. . . . Harry Snowden (1977–83)

WINKLEMAN, MICHAEL—juvenile actor

The Real McCoys (com)
. . . . Little Luke (1957–62)

WINKLER, HENRY—actor, producer
b: Oct 30, 1945, New York City, N.Y.

Happy Days (com)
. . . . . Arthur "Fonzie" Fonzarelli (1974–84)

Emmy Award: Executive Producer, Best Children's Special, for the *CBS School-break Special* "All the Kids Do It" (1985)

"What do they want with a short Jewish kid with a big nose?" said Henry Winkler, when his manager urged him to move to Hollywood to get into television. Henry was indeed a smallish (5'6") actor, well educated (a master's in drama from Yale), versed in the classics, and oriented toward the stage. Little did he know that he would find fame as television's ultimate 1950s "greaser"—Fonzie.

The son of the president of an international lumber company, Henry attended private schools in the U.S. and Switzerland before graduating from Yale in 1970. He first did some New York stage work and commercials and appeared occasionally on PBS's *The Great American Dream Machine*. Then, in 1973, came the fateful advice to go west. His movie debut was in *The Lords of Flatbush*, where he played a character not unlike the Fonz; there were bits on episodes of the series *The Mary Tyler Moore Show* and *The Bob Newhart Show;* and then his big break, on *Happy Days*. At first Fonzie was a subsidiary character on the show, providing counterpoint to the Richie-Potsie middle class kids' story. Soon it grew to become the center of the show, making Henry a major TV star.

Henry used his newfound "clout" in Hollywood to expand his horizons, breaking into TV movies (in the Sissy Spacek film *Katherine* in 1975) and especially into production. He was executive producer of the series *Ryan's Four* and of the award-winning documentary *Who Are the DeBolts—and Where Did They Get 19 Kids?* He has also produced children's specials and several TV movies, including *The Plane That Couldn't Land* and *When Your Lover Leaves*. Among his more interesting acting roles have been the lead in the children's special *Henry Winkler Meets William Shakespeare* in 1976, composer Lorenz Hart in the special *America Salutes Richard Rodgers* in 1976, and the "Scrooge" character in an updated *American Christmas Carol* in 1979.

As if to retire his past, Henry took part in a ceremony in 1980 in which Fonzie's original leather jacket was deposited in the Smithsonian Institution. As for Henry himself, his costar Marion Ross once said it best on the set of *Happy Days:* "I'm watching a young actor who's going to be famous."

WINKWORTH, MARK—actor

Sugar Time! (com) . . Paul Landson (1977–78)

WINMILL, SAMMIE—actress
b: c. 1948

Doctor in the House (com) . Nurse (1970–73)

WINN, KITTY—actress
b: Feb 21, 1944, Washington, D.C.

Beacon Hill (drama)
. . . . Rosamond Lassiter (1975)

WINNINGER, CHARLES—actor
b: May 26, 1884, Athens, Wis. d: Jan 27, 1969

The Charlie Farrell Show (com)
. . . . Dad Farrell (1956)

A jovial, portly old-timer from movies who also played Fred Mertz's ex-vaudeville partner ("Mertz and Kurtz—Laugh Till It Hurts") on a 1954 episode of *I Love Lucy*.

WINNINGHAM, MARE—actress
b: May 1959

The Thorn Birds (drama)
. . . . Justine O'Neill (1983)

Emmy Award: Best Supporting Actress in a Special, for *Amber Waves* (1980)

A determined-looking young lady seen mostly in rebellious youth roles in TV movies, including *The Women's Room, Helen Keller—The Miracle Continues* (title role), and *Freedom*. Believe it or not, she made her TV debut as a singer on *The Gong Show* at age 16—and won!

WINONA, KIM—actress
b: c. 1933, Rosebud Reservation, S.D.

Brave Eagle (wes).. Morning Star (1955–56)

A young actress of Sioux indian descent.

WINSLOWE, PAULA—actress

Our Miss Brooks (com)
.... Mrs. Martha Conklin (1953–56)

WINSTON, HATTIE—black actress
b: Mar 3, 1945, Greenville, Miss.

Nurse (drama)
.... Nurse Toni Gilette (1981–82)

Formerly "Valerie the Librarian" on PBS's *The Electric Company*.

WINSTON, LESLIE—actress
b: May 13, Austin, Texas

The Waltons (drama)
.... Cindy Brunson Walton (1979–81)

WINTER, EDWARD—actor
b: Ventura, Calif.

Adam's Rib (com)... atty. Kip Kipple (1973)
Project U.F.O. (drama)
.... Capt. Ben Ryan (1978–79)
Empire (com) .... T. Howard Daniels (1984)
Hollywood Beat (police)
.... Capt. Wes Biddle (1985)
9 to 5 (com)
.... William "Bud" Coleman (1986–)

WINTER, LYNETTE—actress

Gidget (com)............. Larue (1965–66)
Petticoat Junction (com)
.... Henrietta Plout (1966–70)

WINTERS, DAVID—choreographer
b: Apr 5, 1939, London, England

The Steve Allen Comedy Hour (var)
.... dancers (1967)

WINTERS, GLORIA—juvenile actress
b: Nov 28, Los Angeles, Calif.

The Life of Riley (com)..... Babs (1949–50)
Sky King (wes)........... Penny (1951–54)

WINTERS, JONATHAN—comedian
b: Nov 11, 1925, Dayton, Ohio

And Here's the Show (var)... regular (1955)
NBC Comedy Hour (var)..... regular (1956)
The Jonathan Winters Show (var)
.... host (1956–57)
Masquerade Party (quiz).... panelist (1958)
The Andy Williams Show (var)
.... regular (1965–67)
The Jonathan Winters Show (var)
.... host (1967–69)
The Andy Williams Show (var)
.... regular (1970–71)
The Wacky World of Jonathan Winters (var)
.... host (1972–74)
Mork & Mindy (com) ..... Mearth (1981–82)
Hee Haw (var)........... regular (1983–84)

It is often said that there is a fine line between genius and mental instability; Jonathan Winters is living proof. The rotund, unconventional comedian has had a peculiar TV career. Widely acclaimed as one of the funniest, most inventive talents in the medium (and an inspiration to many younger comics), he has had both mental problems and uneven success in his own career.

Jonathan was born the only son of a banker in Dayton and began in local radio after service in World War II. He claims he could not get guests for his show and so created his own, mimicking "the hip rubes, the Babbits, the pseudointellectuals, the little politicians." By 1950 he had moved to New York and into nightclub work. He made his first attempt at television as a contestant on *Arthur Godfrey's Talent Scouts*—and lost! Daunted, he nevertheless began to get guest spots on Steve Allen's *Tonight Show* (Steve loved him) and subsequently guested with Garry Moore, Jack Paar, and others. The critics raved, but Jonathan himself said in 1957, "I think a guy has only two good seasons, three at the most. What a frightening thing to think that in 1958 I'll be washed up."

Washed up he wasn't, but Jonathan continued to appear mostly as a guest on other people's shows. His own CBS variety series in the late '60s fared poorly against the *ABC Wednesday Night Movie,* and a syndicated show in 1972 was only marginally successful. Still, he was a familiar figure, especially in his most popular character, doddering old Maudie Frickert. In between periods of hospitalization as a manic-depressive (which he jokes about), he was also seen on the Saturday morning kids' shows *Linus the Lionhearted* and *Hot Dog* and costarred with Jack Klugman in a memorably chilling 1961 episode of *The Twilight Zone,* a story about winning and losing entitled "A Game of Pool."

In the 1980s, Jonathan found a new lease on live, and popularity with the younger set, as Robin Williams' full-grown "son" on *Mork & Mindy.* Robin, like Steve Allen 30 years before, was a Winters fan. Jonathan then turned up on a series he had once lambasted as one of the worst on television—*Hee Haw* ("That humor is, to me, 50 years old"). He claims he is writing his autobiography, to be titled *I Couldn't Wait for Success—I Went on Ahead Without It.*

WINTERS, ROLAND—actor
b: Nov 22, 1904, Boston, Mass.

Mama (com)......... Uncle Chris (1951–52)
Doorway to Danger (drama)
.... John Randolph (1952)
Meet Millie (com)..... Mr. Boone (1953–56)
The Smothers Brothers Show (com)
.... Leonard J. Costello (1965–66)

Winters, who played Charlie Chan in films of the late '40s, was a familiar character actor playing older, distinguished roles on TV in the '50s and early '60s. He was seen less often after that, although he did appear in *The Dain Curse* in 1978 and the TV movie version of *You Can't Go Home Again* in 1979.

WINTERSOLE, WILLIAM—actor

Sara (wes).......... George Bailey (1976)

WIRGES, BILL—pianist, orchestra leader
b: Jun 26, 1894, Buffalo, N.Y. d: Sep 28, 1971

The Growing Paynes (com)
.... musician (1948–49)

WISBAR, FRANK—director
b: 1899 d: Mar 17, 1967

Fireside Theatre (drama) .... host (1952–53)

WISDOM, NORMAN—British comedian, actor
b: Feb 4, 1918*, London, England

Kraft Music Hall Presents Sandler & Young (var)...................... regular (1969)

WISE, ALFIE—actor
b: Nov 17, Altoona, Pa.

Trauma Center (drama)
.... Sidney "Hatter" Pacelli (1983)

A cherubic little actor who is one of Burt Reynolds' pals, and seen in many of his movies. Alfie also had a recurring role as one of Sandy Duncan's bosses on *The Sandy Duncan Show* and was Uncle Croc's helper (Mr. Rabbit Ears) on the *Uncle Croc's Block* cartoon in the mid-1970s.

WISE, ERNIE—comedian
b: Nov 27, 1925, England

The Piccadilly Palace (var) .. cohost (1967)

Half of the British comedy team of (Eric) Morecambe and Wise.

WISE, RAY—actor

Dallas (drama)........ Blair Sullivan (1982)

WISEMAN, JOSEPH—actor
b: May 15, 1918, Montreal, Canada

Masada (drama) .... Jerahmed (1981)

Sharp-featured villain of stage and screen, much on television dramas since the 1950s. He is perhaps best known as "Dr. No" in the James Bond movie of that name. His recent TV work includes *Rage of Angels* and *The Ghost Writer.*

WISMER, HARRY—sportscaster
b: Jun 30, 1913, Port Huron, Mich. d: 1967

Football Sidelines (sport) .... host (1952)
Prime Time Football (sport)
.... announcer (1953)

*Some sources give 1920 or 1925.

Wismer was, in the early 1960s, the first owner of the New York Titans football team, which later became the New York Jets.

WITHERS, BERNADETTE—juvenile actress

Bachelor Father (com)
   Ginger Farrell/Loomis/Mitchell (1957–62)
Peck's Bad Girl (com) . . . . Jeannie (1959)
Karen (com) . . . . Janis (1964–65)

WITHERS, MARK—actor
b: Jun 5, Nimmonsberg, N.Y.

Kaz (drama) . . . . . . Peter Colcourt (1978–79)

WITHERSPOON, "DETROIT" JOHN— black actor

The Richard Pryor Show (var)
   . . . . regular (1977)

WITNEY, MICHAEL—actor

The Travels of Jaimie McPheeters (wes)
   . . . . Buck Coulter (1963)

Married to the model Twiggy. Michael was the original wagonmaster on *The Travels of Jaimie McPheeters,* but his stay on the show was unfortunately short; he was written out by having his character trampled while saving Jaimie's life.

WITT, HOWARD—actor

W.E.B. (drama)
   . . . . Walter Matthews (1978)

WITT, KATHRYN—actress
b: Nov 30, Miami, Fla.

Flying High (adv)
   . . . . Pam Bellagio (1978–79)

WIXTED, MICHAEL-JAMES—juvenile actor
b: 1961

The Smith Family (drama)
   . . . . Brian Smith (1971–72)

WOLDERS, ROBERT—actor
b: Sep 28, Rotterdam, Netherlands

Laredo (wes). . . . . Erik Hunter (1966–67)

At the time he was starring in *Laredo,* NBC pointed out that Wolders was "the only Dutchman to be cast as a Texas lawman." He was also probably the only TV actor who was a psychology graduate specializing in psychodrama.

WOLF, WARNER—sportscaster
b: c. 1938, Washington, D.C.

Monday Night Baseball (sport)
   . . . . sportscaster (1976–77)

The prototypical loud, jokester sportscaster, a major figure on local television in Washington, D.C. and New York since the mid-1960s.

WOLFE, IAN—actor
b: 1896, Canton, Ill.

Wizards and Warriors (adv)
   . . . . Wizard Tranquil (1983)

WOLFE, JANICE—assistant

Break the Bank (quiz)
   . . . . paying teller (1949–53)

WOLFMAN JACK—disc jockey
b: Jan 21, 1939, Brooklyn, N.Y.

The Midnight Special (music)
   . . . . announcer (1973–81)

One of the more bizarre refugees from the world of radio, this hairy, wild-eyed character is given—true to his name—to baying like a wolf when one of his favorite rock records is playing. He began on radio stations in Newport News, Virginia, and Shreveport, Louisiana, in the '50s, but gained fame as "the Wolfman" on high-powered Mexican station XERF, Tijuana (later on XERB), from 1957 on, when he could be heard throughout the southwestern United States. The Wolfman has become something of a cult figure in the rock world, making cameo appearances in movies (e.g., *American Graffiti*) and mentioned in the lyrics of hit songs ("Clap for the Wolfman," by Guess Who). During his stint on *The Midnight Special* it was said that he could be heard on 2,200 radio stations in more than 42 countries around the world.

His real name is the rather prosaic Bob Smith.

WOLFSON, CARL—comedian
b: Mar 21, 1953, Washington, D.C.

Thicke of the Night (talk)
.... recurring player (1983–84)

**WOLOWIC, STAN, POLKA CHIPS—
polka bandleader**

Polka Time (music)....... regular (1956–57)

WOLTER, SHERILYN—actress
b: Nov 30, Clarksburg, W. Va. r: Sacramento, Calif.

B.J. and the Bear (adv) . Cindy Grant (1981)

WONG, ANNA MAY—actress
b: Jan 3, 1907, Chinatown, Los Angeles, Calif.
d: Feb 3, 1961

Gallery of Mme. Lui-Tsong (drama)
.... Mme. Lui-Tsong (1951)

A delicate Hollywood star of the 1930s, one of the few Chinese-Americans to attain such stature. She appeared infrequently on television but was becoming more active in the medium at the time of her death (she was in episodes of *Wyatt Earp, The Barbara Stanwyck Show,* and *Danger Man* in 1960–61). Her real name was Wong Lui-Tsong—note the similarity to the title of her short-lived series—which means "Frosted Yellow Willow."

WONG, ARTHUR—actor

Kentucky Jones (drama) .. Mr. Ng (1964–65)

WONG, JOE—actor
b: 1903, Philippines d: Nov 9, 1978

The Ken Murray Show (var)
.... regular (1950–51)

WOOD, BARRY—singer, producer
b: Feb 12, 1909, New Haven, Conn. d: Jul 19, 1970

Places Please (var).......... host (1948–49)
Backstage with Barry Wood (var)
.... host (1949)

A radio crooner of the '30s and '40s (on *Your Hit Parade,* etc.), whose singing career was just about over when television arrived. He later became a very successful TV producer of such shows as *Wide*

Wide World and *The Bell Telephone Hour.*

WOOD, CYNDI—

The Jim Stafford Show (var)
.... regular (1975)

WOOD, DEE DEE—choreographer

The Billy Crystal Comedy Hour (var)
.... dancers (1982)

WOOD, DOUGLAS—

Motown Revue (var)........ regular (1985)

WOOD, GENE—host

Beat the Clock (quiz)
.... announcer/emcee (1969–75)

WOOD, HELEN—actress

The Ted Steele Show (music)
.... regular (1948–49)
Broadway Open House (talk)
.... regular (1951)

WOOD, KELLY—actress

The Patty Duke Show (com)
.... Gloria (1964–65)

Later a daytime soap opera actress for many years, on *Search for Tomorrow* and *As the World Turns.*

WOOD, LANA—actress
b: Mar 1, 1946, Santa Monica, Calif.

The Long Hot Summer (drama)
.... Eula Harker (1965–66)
Peyton Place (drama)
.... Sandy Webber (1966–67)

The sister of Natalie Wood, in movies as a child in the '50s. She has been seen sporadically in TV movies and series episodes since her leading roles as the sultry siren in two nighttime soap operas of the mid-1960s. In the mid-1980s she appeared for a time in the daytime soap *Capitol.*

WOOD, LYNN—actress

Dusty's Trail (com)
.... Mrs. Brookhaven (1973)

WOOD, NATALIE—actress

b: Jul 20, 1938, San Francisco, Calif. d: Nov 29, 1981

The Pride of the Family (com)
.... Ann Morrison (1953–54)
From Here to Eternity (drama)
.... Karen Holmes (1979)

A delicately beautiful Hollywood star, in movies from the age of five. As a teenager in the early '50s, Natalie appeared in a number of TV theater productions, was Paul Hartman and Fay Wray's daughter in *Pride of the Family,* and starred in the 1955 special *Heidi.* After she was nominated for an Academy Award for her role as James Dean's girlfriend in the movie *Rebel Without a Cause* in 1955, her film career went into high gear, and she was seldom seen on television again until the mid-1970s. At that time she began to appear in occasional TV movies, often with her husband Robert Wagner. They were seen together in *The Affair* (1973), episodes of his series *Switch* and *Hart to Hart,* and in the 1976 special *Cat on a Hot Tin Roof.* Natalie appeared sans hubby in *From Here to Eternity, The Cracker Factory,* and *The Memory of Eva Ryker.* The last-named movie was telecast the year before she died in a tragic drowning accident.

WOOD, PEGGY—actress

b: Feb 9, 1892, Brooklyn, N.Y. d: Mar 18, 1978

Mama (com)
.... "Mama" Marta Hansen (1949–57)

A kind, motherly actress with an extraordinarily long career, from the chorus of *Naughty Marietta* in 1910 to the play *The Madwoman of Chaillot* in 1970. Peggy was a singer in musical comedies in her early days; later, she became known for her dramatic stage work. She made a few films and had a long and successful run on TV in the '50s in the series *(I Remember) Mama.* Her other TV work was scattered, but included a few playhouse productions in the '50s and '60s and several months on the daytime soap opera *One Life to Live* in 1969.

WOOD, RAY—

The Big Idea (info) .... regular (1952–53)

WOOD, TERRI LYNN—juvenile actress

The Baxters (com)
.... Rachael Baxter (1979–80)

WOODARD, ALFRE—black actress

b: Nov 2, 1953, Tulsa, Okla.

Tucker's Witch (drama)
.... Marcia Fulbright (1982–83)
Sara (com)......... Rozalyn Dupree (1985)
St. Elsewhere (drama)
.... Dr. Roxanne Turner (1985–)

Emmy Award: Best Supporting Actress in a Drama Series, for *Hill Street Blues* (1984)

WOODELL, PAT—actress

b: 1944, Winthrop, Mass.

Petticoat Junction (com)
.... Bobbie Jo Bradley (1963–65)

WOODMAN, KENNY—orchestra leader

The Val Doonican Show (var)
.... orch. leader (1971)

WOODS, DONALD—actor

b: Dec 2, 1904, Brandon, Manitoba, Canada r: California

Craig Kennedy, Criminologist (drama)
.... Craig Kennedy (1952)
The Orchid Award (var) ... emcee (1953–54)
Damon Runyon Theatre (drama)
.... host (1955–56)
Tammy (com)......... John Brent (1965–66)

A B-movie "good guy" of the '30s and '40s, who has played occasional roles on television over the years, from *The U.S. Steel Hour* in the '50s ("A Wind from the South," opposite Julie Harris) to an episode of *The Mississippi* in early 1984.

WOODS, GRANT—actor

Custer (wes) ..... Capt. Miles Keogh (1967)

WOODS, JAMES—actor

b: Apr 18, 1947, Warwick, R.I.

Holocaust (drama) ...... Karl Weiss (1978)

WOODS, LESLEY—actress

Dear Detective (police)
.... Mrs. Hudson (1979)

A prominent daytime actress, on many soap operas of the '50s, '60s, and '70s.

WOODS, MICHAEL—actor
b: Jul 10, Detroit, Mich.

Bare Essence (drama)
.... Sean Benedict (1983)
Our Family Honor (drama)
.... Jerry Cole (Danzig) (1985–86)

WOODS, REN—black actress
b: Jan 1, 1958, Portland, Ore.

Roots (drama)............... Fanta (1977)
We've Got Each Other (com)
.... Donna (1977–78)

WOODS, ROSLYN—model

What's Your Bid? (aud par)
.... model (1953)

WOODS, RUTH—host, model

Short Short Dramas (drama)
.... hostess (1952–53)

WOODWARD, EDWARD—actor
b: Jun 1, 1930, Croydon, Surrey, England

Callan (drama)..... David Callan (1970–72)
The Equalizer (drama)
.... Robert McCall (1985–)

A rather quiet, forceful English actor who seems more imposing than his 5'10" height. He began playing supporting roles on stage and screen in the '50s but did not score major success even in his native country until he starred in the 1967 British espionage series *Callan*, playing a singularly ruthless lone wolf agent. The series was later syndicated in the U.S., but Woodward had to wait almost 20 years before making a major impact here. Then it was as another menacing lone wolf, *The Equalizer*. His other U.S. television appearances have been infrequent, including PBS telecasts of British productions such as *Winston Churchill: The Wilderness Years* and the 1983 Michael Landon movie *Love Is Forever*.

In contrast to his stark screen persona, Woodward is an accomplished singer who has recorded a dozen albums in Britain, plays piano, and imitates musical instruments such as the trumpet.

WOODWARD, MORGAN—actor

The Life and Legend of Wyatt Earp (wes)
.... Shotgun Gibbs (1958–61)
Dallas (drama).... Punk Anderson (1980–)

WOOLERY, CHUCK—singer, host
b: Mar 16, Ashland, Ky.

Your Hit Parade (music).... vocalist (1974)

Tall, smiling Chuck Woolery went through several careers before settling in as one of the top game-show hosts of the 1980s. First he was a songwriter in Nashville in the mid-1960s, composing material for such stars as Ray Price ("Forgive Me, Heart") and Tammy Wynette ("For the Love of My Child"). He then became a singer himself, on *The Jimmy Dean Show* (his debut), *The New Zoo Revue* in 1973, and the summer revival of *Your Hit Parade* in 1974. Chuck also tried acting, in an obscure 1974 film called *Treasure of Jamaica Reef;* his costar was a pre–*Charlie's Angels* Cheryl Ladd. However, it was while singing on *The Merv Griffin Show* that Merv offered him the job of host of a new daytime game show he was producing—*Wheel of Fortune.* Chuck stayed with *Wheel* for six years (1975–81) and later went on to such popular shows as *Scrabble* and *The Love Connection.*

WOOLEY, SHEB—country singer, actor
b: Apr 10, 1921, Erick, Okla.

Rawhide (wes)....... Pete Nolan (1959–65)
Hee Haw (var)............. regular (1969)

A dark, slightly worried-looking character actor who has had an unusual dual career. In movies he would sometimes play villains (most notably, one of the thugs out to gun down Gary Cooper in *High Noon*); on the stage of the Grand Ole Opry he was a leading country comedian, famous for his cornball comedy songs. One of these songs, "The Purple People Eater," was a multimillion-selling pop novelty in the late '50s.

On television, Sheb played occasional guest roles in westerns of the '50s, including *The Lone Ranger,* but he is best known by far as trail scout Pete Nolan on *Rawhide* for six years. He was also an early regular on *Hee Haw* and wrote that show's theme song.

WOOLFE, ERIC—actor

The Strauss Family (drama)
.... Johann Strauss, Sr. (1973)

WOPAT, TOM—actor
b: Sep 9, 1950, Lodi, Wis.

The Dukes of Hazzard (com)
.... Luke Duke (1979–85)

The dark-haired half of the pair of pretty boys on *The Dukes of Hazzard.* The star of the show, many thought, was actually their souped up car, the General Lee. Wopat is also a singer.

WORLEY, JO ANNE—comedienne
b: 1942*, Lowell, Ind.

Rowan & Martin's Laugh-In (var)
.... regular (1968–70)

A comedienne of the screwball variety, with an enormous mouth and raucous laugh; she most often turns up in comedy sketches (she was frequently on *Love, American Style*) and on celebrity game shows.

WORTHINGTON, CAROL—actress

The Red Skelton Show (var)
.... regular (1970–71)

WRAY, FAY—actress
b: Sep 15, 1907**, Alberta, Canada r: Salt Lake City and Los Angeles

The Pride of the Family (com)
.... Catherine Morrison (1953–54)

The actress who will always be remembered as the terrified young beauty in *King Kong* (1933), screaming and thrashing in the monster's giant paw as he climbed the Empire State Building. She made quite a few more films after that (often in "screaming" roles) and when television arrived had an active career there, too, in the '50s and early '60s. She appeared in many drama series, including *Perry Mason* and *Alfred Hitchcock Presents.* In the comedy *Pride of the Family,* she played Paul Hartman's wife—and young Natalie Wood's mother.

*Some sources give 1937.
**Some sources give Sept. 10.

Fay retired from acting in 1965 but was lured back 15 years later, lovely and mature, for a onetime appearance as Henry Fonda's landlady in the acclaimed TV film *Gideon's Trumpet* (1980). She still receives much fan mail—all of it for *King Kong.*

WRAY, PAULA—singer

Rhythm Rodeo (music).... regular (1950–51)

WREN, BOBBY—orchestra leader

Gulf Road Show Starring Bob Smith (var)
.... orch. leader (1949)

WREN, SAM—actor
b: c. 1897 d: Mar 15, 1962

Wren's Nest (com) .... as himself (1949)

WRIGHT, JACKIE—British comedian

The Benny Hill Show (com)
.... regular (1969–82)

WRIGHT, JOHN—actor

McHale's Navy (com)
.... Willy Moss (1964–66)

The son of country superstar Kitty Wells.

WRIGHT, MARTHA—singer, hostess
b: Mar 23, 1926, Seattle, Wash.

The Swift Show (var)........ regular (1949)
Three's Company (music) .... regular (1950)
Celebrity Time (quiz).... panelist (1950–51)
Let's Dance (music) ..... interviewer (1954)
The Martha Wright Show (music)
.... hostess (1954)

WRIGHT, MAX—actor
b: Aug 2, Detroit, Mich.

Buffalo Bill (com) ..... Karl Shub (1983–84)
Misfits of Science (adv)
.... Richard Stetmeyer (1985–86)
Alf (com) .... Willie Tanner (1986–)

WRIGHT, MICHAEL—actor

V (movie) (sci fi) .... Elias Taylor (1983)
V: The Final Battle (miniseries) (sci fi)
.... Elias Taylor (1984)
V (sci fi)........... Elias Taylor (1984–85)

WRIGHT, NANCY—singer

The Ransom Sherman Show (var)
.... regular (1950)

WRIGHT, ROY—actor

The Islanders (adv)
.... Shipwreck Callahan (1960–61)

WRIGHT, SAMUEL E.—black actor
b: Nov 20, 1948, Camden, S.C.

Ball Four (com) .... C. B. Travis (1976)
Enos (com) ..... Off. Turk Adams (1980–81)

WRIGHTSON, EARL—singer
b: Jan 1, 1916, Baltimore, Md.

Girl About Town (music) . cohost (1948–49)
The Earl Wrightson Show (music)
.... host (1948–52)
Paul Whiteman's Goodyear Revue (var)
.... regular (1950–52)

WROE, TRUDY—actress

Big Town (drama)
.... Lorelei Kilbourne (1954–55)

WULFF, KAI—actor

Casablanca (drama) .... Lt. Heinz (1983)

WUN, LONNIE—actor

Wizards and Warriors (adv)
.... oriental guard (1983)

WYATT, JACK—host

Confession (int) .... host (1958–59)

WYATT, JANE—actress
b: Aug 12, 1912*, Campgaw, N.J.

Father Knows Best (com)
.... Margaret Anderson (1954–60)

Emmy Awards: Best Actress in a Continuing Role in a Series, for Father Knows Best (1957, 1959, 1960)

A calm, understanding lady, pretty and proper, who could project a great deal of warmth. Perfect for a TV mom, you say? That's just what she played for six years on the 1950's leading family show, Father Knows Best. Jane had a long but unexcit-

*Some sources give 1911 or 1913.

ing movie and stage career before that, beginning in the early '30s (look for her as Sondra in the 1937 film Lost Horizon). However, it was television that made her famous. She appeared regularly in TV playhouse series of the early '50s, especially Robert Montgomery Presents, and after the run of Father Knows Best resumed periodic guest appearances in dramas including The Virginian, Alfred Hitchcock Presents, and Star Trek—on which she played Mr. Spock's mother!

Jane continued to be seen in the '70s and '80s, primarily in supporting roles in TV movies and in a few series episodes (e.g., The Love Boat). Among her TV films have been 1973's Tom Sawyer (as Aunt Polly), Katherine, Amelia Earhart, Missing Children: A Mother's Story, and, of course, the two Father Knows Best reunion specials in 1977.

WYCHERLY, MARGARET—actress
b: 1881, London, England r: U.S.A. d: Jun 6, 1956

Claudia, The Story of a Marriage (drama)
.... Mrs. Brown (1952)

WYENN, THAN—actor
b: May 2, 1919, New York City, N.Y.

Pete Kelly's Blues (drama)
.... George Lupo (1959)

WYLE, GEORGE—orchestra leader, choreographer
b: Mar 22, 1916, New York City, N.Y.

The Jerry Lewis Show (var)
.... singers (1967–69)
Jimmy Durante Presents The Lennon Sisters
(var)............... orch. leader (1969–70)
The Flip Wilson Show (var)
.... orch. leader (1970–74)
The Jerry Reed When You're Hot You're Hot Hour (var) .... orch. leader (1972)
The Mac Davis Show (var)
.... dancers (1974)
The Gladys Knight & the Pips Show (var)
.... orch. leader (1975)

The musical director—on and off camera—for many television shows since the 1950s. He is also the man who gave us "The Ballad of Gilligan's Island" theme song.

WYLER, GRETCHEN—actress
b: Feb 16, 1932, Bartlesville, Okla.

The Bob Crosby Show (var).. regular (1958)
On Our Own (com).. Toni McBain (1977–78)

A musical comedy stage star of the '50s and '60s *(Silk Stockings)*, occasionally on television.

WYLER, RICHARD—actor
b: 1934

Man from Interpol (police)
.... Anthony Smith (1960)

WYLLIE, MEG—actress

Hennesey (com)...... Mrs. Shafer (1959–62)
The Travels of Jaimie McPheeters (wes)
.... Mrs. Kissel (1963–64)

WYMAN, JANE—actress
b: Jan 4, 1914, St. Joseph, Mo.

Fireside Theatre (drama) . hostess (1955–58)
Summer Playhouse (drama) .. hostess (1957)
Falcon Crest (drama)
.... Angela Channing (1981–)

"My name is Bessie Fuffnik. I swim, ride, dive, imitate birds, and play the trombone!" With that oft-quoted line, eagerly delivered to Dick Powell in the 1936 film *Stage Struck*, Jane Wyman launched her movie career. She was at first cast as brassy (or dumb) blondes in light features of the '30s and '40s. Not until her sensitive performance in the 1945 drama *The Lost Weekend* did she begin to get more varied parts. After she won an Academy Award as the deaf-mute rape victim in *Johnny Belinda* in 1948 she became known primarily for the "Wyman weepies," tearjerkers such as *The Glass Menagerie* and *Magnificent Obsession*. However, she could still cut up occasionally, as in her duet with Bing Crosby singing "In the Cool, Cool, Cool of the Evening" in 1951's *Here Comes the Groom*.

Jane has had, essentially, two television careers. The first was in the '50s, when she was hostess of the very popular *Fireside Theatre* (former husband Ronald Reagan was at the same time hosting the even more popular *General Electric Theater* on another network); and the second in the '80s, as the fearsome matriarch of the prime time soap opera *Falcon Crest*. In between, her appearances were relatively rare. She was seen in a few dramas of the late '50s and early '60s, including *General Electric Theater* in 1961, and then retired for few years. She returned in the early '70s for the TV film *The Failing of Raymond;* two pilots for a series called *Amanda Fallon,* in which she would have starred as a pediatrician; and a few series episodes. In 1979, after another five-year absence, she was seen as Granny the "folk doctor" in the Lindsay Wagner TV film *The Incredible Journey of Dr. Meg Laurel.*

Jane was married to B-movie actor Ronald Reagan from 1940 to 1948, and by most contemporary accounts it was a relatively happy marriage. She said in the '40s, "He was such a sunny person . . . I had never felt free to talk to anyone before I met Ronnie"; politics, she said, had simply stolen him away from her. She has since demurred from commenting on the man who would become president, however, saying only "It's bad taste to talk about ex-husbands or ex-wives."

WYNDHAM, ANNE—actress

Barney Miller (com).. Rachael Miller (1975)

WYNER, GEORGE—actor

Delvecchio (police)
.... Asst. D.A. Dorfman (1976–77)
Kaz (drama) ... D.A. Frank Revko (1978–79)
Big Shamus, Little Shamus (drama)
.... George Korman (1979)
Nero Wolfe (drama).... Saul Panzer (1981)
Hill Street Blues (police)
...... Asst. D.A. Irwin Bernstein (1982–)
Matt Houston (drama)
.... Murray Chase (occasional) (1982–85)
At Ease (com)......... Cpl. Wessel (1983)

WYNN, ED—comedian
b: Nov 9, 1886, Philadelphia, Pa. d: Jun 19, 1966

The Ed Wynn Show (var).... host (1949–50)
All Star Revue (var)
.... alternating host (1950–52)
The Ed Wynn Show (com)
.... John Beamer (1958–59)

Emmy Awards: Star, Best Live Series, for *The Ed Wynn Show* (1949); Outstanding Live Personality (1949)

This giggly, baggy-pants, tragicomic clown was one of the great stars of vaudeville and Broadway in the 1910s and 1920s, and of radio in the early '30s (where he was the "Texaco Fire Chief"). His was a very old fashioned style of slapstick and silly jokes, and by the end of the '30s he was already considered out-of-date and "washed up."

Television helped Ed make a comeback, at least briefly. He had a face only a comic could love—long, silly-looking, with saucer eyes and arching eyebrows. His original 1949 variety series was practically a clubhouse for old-time gags and gangsters, with Ed doing his "Perfect Fool" character and guests such as Buster Keaton, Ben Blue, and the Three Stooges. He wore out as fast on television as he had on radio, however, and by the early '50s his career was once again on the skids. Then his son Keenan helped him make a remarkable transformation. Beginning with the *Playhouse 90* drama "Requiem for a Heavyweight" in 1956, in which Keenan also appeared, Ed began a series of affecting characterizations of old men touched with sadness. From then on, the aging clown alternated between dramatic roles and a quieter style of comedy. A 1958 sitcom, with Ed as a grandpa raising his grandchildren alone, was short-lived; however, he won much acclaim for dramatic appearances on *The Twilight Zone, Hallmark Hall of Fame,* and *Desilu Playhouse.* He continued to be active until shortly before his death, in Disney movies and episodes of series including *Slattery's People* and *Bonanza* (as "The Ponderosa Birdman" in 1965).

Some "Perfect Fool" humor:

Justice of the Peace: "Do you take this woman for your wife?"
Groom: "I do."
J.P.: "That's funny, I took her for your mother."

WYNN, KEENAN—actor
b: Jul 27, 1916, New York City, N.Y. d: Oct 14, 1986

Troubleshooters (adv) .... Kodiak (1959–60)
You're in the Picture (quiz).. panelist (1961)
Dallas (drama)
.... Willard "Digger" Barnes (1979–80)
Call to Glory (drama)
.... Carl Sarnac (1984–85)
The Last Precinct (com) ...... Butch (1986)

A large, walrus-mustached character actor, the son of the great comic Ed Wynn. Keenan was a prolific supporting actor on television, lending his imposing presence to hundreds of dramas from *The U.S. Steel Hour* in 1955 to *Fantasy Island* in the '80s. He also appeared in approximately 20 TV movies, mostly routine schedule-stuffers.

Autobiography: *Ed Wynn's Son* (1960).

WYNN, MAY—actress
b: Jan 8, 1931

Noah's Ark (drama) .... Liz Clark (1956–57)

WYNTER, DANA—actress
b: Jun 8, 1930*, London, England r: Rhodesia

The Man Who Never Was (drama)
.... Eva Wainwright (1966–67)

WYRTZEN, JACK—evangelist

Songtime (misc)............ host (1951–52)

*Some sources give 1927 or 1932.

Y

YAGHER, JEFF—actor

V (sci fi)............ Kyle Bates (1984–85)

YAMA, MICHAEL—actor

Hotel (drama)................ Kei (1984–)

YARBOROUGH, BARTON—actor
b: 1900 d: Dec 19, 1951

Dragnet (police).... Sgt. Ben Romero (1951)

A man who just missed TV immortality. Yarborough was Jack Webb's original sidekick on the radio version of *Dragnet* and was scheduled to repeat the role in the television series. He died suddenly of a heart attack a few days after the first episode, in December 1951.

YARDUM, JET—actress

Dear Detective (police) .... Lisa (1979)

YARLETT, CLAIRE—actress
b: Feb 15, Los Angeles, Calif. r: England

Rituals (drama) ..... Dakota Lane (1984–85)
Dynasty II: The Colbys (drama)
.... Bliss Colby (1985–)

YARNELL, BRUCE—actor
b: c. 1938, Los Angeles, Calif. d: Nov 30, 1973

The Outlaws (wes)
... Dep. Marshal Chalk Breeson (1961–62)

YARNELL, LORENE—

see Shields & Yarnell

YASHIMA, MOMO—actress

Behind the Screen (drama)
.... Jeanne (1981–82)

YATES, CASSIE—actress
b: Mar 2, 1951, Macon, Ga.

Rich Man, Poor Man—Book II (drama)
.... Annie Adams (1976–77)
Nobody's Perfect (com)
.... Det. Jennifer Dempsey (1980)

Detective in the House (drama)
.... Diane Wyman (1985)

YELM, SHIRLEY—actress
b: 1939, Des Moines, Iowa r: Fairoaks, Calif.

The Lively Ones (var) ..... Charley (1962)

YERXA, FENDALL—newscaster

Editor's Choice (news)......... host (1961)

YNIGUEZ, RICHARD—actor
b: Dec 8, Firebaugh, Calif. r: Sacramento, Calif.

Mama Malone (com)
.... Father Jose Silva (1984)

YODA, YOSHIO—actor

McHale's Navy (com)
.... Fuji Kobiaji (1962–66)

YOHN, ERICA—actress

Secrets of Midland Heights (drama)
.... Serena Costin (1980–81)
Behind the Screen (drama)
.... Joyce (1981–82)

YORK, DICK—actor
b: Sep 4, 1928, Fort Wayne, Ind.

Going My Way (com)
.... Tom Colwell (1962–63)
Bewitched (com)
.... Darrin Stephens (1964–69)

This busy actor of the '50s and '60s had his career cut short at the height of his success. Dick entered television in the mid-1950s and worked steadily in episodes of many series, including multiple appearances on *Kraft Theatre, The Twilight Zone, The Millionaire, Wagon Train,* and *Alfred Hitchcock Presents* (in which he was a particularly frequent player). His best known role was that of Elizabeth Montgomery's distressed hubby on *Bewitched*. A drug related illness forced his retirement from acting in 1969.

YORK, FRANCINE—actress
b: Aug 26, 1938, Aurora, Minn.

Slattery's People (drama)
.... Wendy Wendkowski (1965)

YORK, JEFF—actor
b: 1912

The Alaskans (adv) . Reno McKee (1959–60)

YORK, KATHLEEN—actress

Dallas (drama) . . . . Betty (1984–85)

YORK, REBECCA—actress

Newhart (com)
. . . . Cindy Parker Devane (1984)

YOTHERS, COREY—juvenile actor
b: Apr 13, 1971, Los Angeles, Calif.

Off the Rack (com)
. . . . Timothy Halloran (1985)

The older brother of child actress Tina Yothers *(Family Ties).*

YOTHERS, TINA—juvenile actress
b: May 5, 1973, Whittier, Calif.

Family Ties (com)
. . . . Jennifer Keaton (1982–)

YOUNG, ALAN—comedian, actor
b: Nov 19, 1919, North Shields, Northumberland, England r: Vancouver, Canada

The Alan Young Show (var) . . host (1950–53)
Saturday Night Revue (var) . . regular (1954)
Mr. Ed (com). . . . . . . Wilbur Post (1961–66)

Emmy Award: Best Actor (1950)

Alan Young was one of the freshest, most promising faces in early television comedy, a relatively quiet, intelligent funnyman (in those days of loud slapstick) whom many considered destined for superstardom. His basic character was the shy little guy (or rube) much put-upon by the world, and his thoughtful, witty humor led *TV Guide* to acclaim him as "the Charlie Chaplin of TV. Without benefit of purloined gags, squirting seltzer, bad grammar, insults, references to family, worn-out guest stars, or women's hats, [he has] quietly become the rave of a growing legion of loving fans."

Alan broke into radio as a teenager in Canada and came to the U.S. in 1944 to headline the first of a series of network radio shows. He was quite popular in the late '40s, and, when television arrived,

was among the first to be lured into the new medium. *The Alan Young Show* was only moderately successful, however. After two seasons as a variety show the format was changed to situation comedy in 1953; Alan then shifted back to variety on the 1954 summer series *Saturday Night Revue.* Later, he appeared in a TV variety show in England and made guest appearances in the U.S. on *Studio One* and *Ford Startime* ("Tennessee Ernie Meets King Arthur").

Alan had been approached in the mid-1950s to star in a comedy about a talking horse, but he wanted no part of it. But by 1961, with few other offers, he agreed and became the straight man on *Mr. Ed,* a rather simple-minded comedy that ran for a remarkable five years. It is for this —hardly his greatest achievement—that he is most remembered today. He left show business in the late '60s to work full-time for his church, the Christian Scientists. He was back on-screen in the mid-1970s for occasional stage and TV appearances, including *The Love Boat* (1978), and to do voice work for children's cartoons such as *Vampire Rabbit, Mr. T,* and *The Smurfs.*

YOUNG, BOB—newscaster
b: c. 1923, Covington, Ky. r: Cincinnati, Ohio

ABC News Reports (doc)
. . . . anchorman (1963)
ABC Late News (news)
. . . . anchorman (1964–65)
ABC Weekend News (news)
. . . . anchorman (1965–66)
ABC Evening News (news)
. . . . anchorman (1968)

YOUNG, BRUCE A.—actor
b: St. Louis, Mo.

E/R (com) . . . . . Off. Fred Burdock (1984–85)
Lady Blue (police). . . . . . . Cassady (1985–86)

YOUNG, CARLETON—actor
b: 1907 d: Jul 11, 1971

Court of Last Resort (drama)
. . . . Harry Steeger (1957–58)

Suave supporting actor of movies, radio, and TV; he was the father of actor Tony Young.

YOUNG, DONNA JEAN—comedienne
b: May 29, East McKeesport, Pa.

Rowan & Martin's Laugh-In (var)
- .... regular (1972–73)

Billed as "the sex symbol of East McKeesport, Pennsylvania."

YOUNG, EVE—singer

Musical Merry-Go-Round (music)
.... regular (1947)
The Gulf Road Show Starring Bob Smith (var)
.... regular (1949)

YOUNG, GIG—actor
b: Nov 4, 1913, St. Cloud, Minn. r: Washington, D.C. d: Oct 19, 1978

Warner Brothers Presents (misc)
.... host/narrator (1955–56)
The Rogues (com) .. Tony Fleming (1964–65)
Gibbsville (drama) .. Ray Whitehead (1976)

A debonair second lead (and sometime star) in films, who often played sardonic or tipsy bons vivants, the one who didn't get the girl. Gig began in films in 1940 (his stage name was adopted from a character he played in an early film) and was an early, if not frequent, visitor to TV. He appeared on *Robert Montgomery Presents* and *Producers' Showcase* in the early '50s and was selected by Warner Bros. to host its initial foray into the medium, a drama series in 1955. Among his later appearances were roles in: the *Twilight Zone,* as a world-weary advertising executive who steps back into his youth; *Shirley Temple's Storybook,* in its production of "The Prince and the Pauper"; the 1959 special *Philadelphia Story;* and *Alfred Hitchcock Presents,* as a gambler who teaches young Robert Redford a lesson. He was perfectly cast as one of the elegant international con artists in *The Rogues.*

After *The Rogues,* Gig gave up series appearances in favor of an occasional TV movie. He returned to series TV only once, for 1976's *Gibbsville,* in which he played an alcoholic former star-reporter who returned to his hometown in a last attempt to salvage his career. The role was strangely prophetic. Gig, who had been through several failed marriages and an up-and-down career, was said to be a "Jekyll and Hyde" when drunk. He died in a bizarre murder-suicide in 1978, in which he apparently shot his young bride of three weeks and then turned the gun on himself.

YOUNG, HEATHER—actress
b: Apr 1, Bremerton, Wash.

Land of the Giants (sci fi)
.... Betty Hamilton (1968–70)

YOUNG, JOHN S.—

Masquerade Party (quiz).... panelist (1952)

YOUNG, KEONE—actor
b: Sep 6, Honolulu, Hawaii

Kay O'Brien (drama)
.... Dr. Michael Kwan (1986–)

YOUNG, LORETTA—actress
b: Jan 6, 1913*, Salt Lake City, Utah r: Los Angeles

The Loretta Young Show (drama)
.... hostess/star (1953–61)
The New Loretta Young Show (drama)
.... Christine Massey (1962–63)

Emmy Awards: Best Actress in a Continuing Role in a Drama Series, for *The Loretta Young Show* (1954, 1956, 1959)

"I grew up in, of, and with Hollywood," Loretta Young once commented. "Acting is my job. It has responsibilities and obligations which I understand and respect." A determined lady, known offscreen as "the Iron Butterfly," Loretta also understood the value of a star's image. To supplement her somewhat modest acting talents she developed one—as one of the most glamorous and fashionable women in movies and, later, television.

Loretta began acting at the age of four as an extra in silents to help support her mother, who had been abandoned by her husband and who ran a boardinghouse in Hollywood. Loretta's 25 years of leading roles (beginning in 1927) produced no real classics but did bring steady popularity and, in time, an Academy Award for the 1947 comedy *The Farmer's Daughter* (accepting the award, she looked at the statuette and said, "What took you so long?")

In 1953 Loretta abruptly ended her long movie career and plunged wholeheartedly

*Some sources give 1911 or 1912.

into TV, hosting and frequently starring in a dramatic anthology series. In its first season it was called *Letter to Loretta;* Loretta would open by reading a letter from a fan and then transform the writer's request into a story that would follow. Later, the letter and title were dropped in favor of a straight anthology, but the stories remained basically uplifting and cheerful. Often, Loretta would close with some poetry or a quotation from the Bible to reinforce the story's message. For many viewers, however, the chief attraction was Loretta herself. Her swirling entrance, always wearing the latest of fashions, was widely mimicked. Years later, when NBC attempted to rerun these shows, Loretta sued to stop them, claiming that the by-then dated fashions would ruin her image. She won.

After her first famous series ended, Loretta returned in 1962 in a continuing drama called *The New Loretta Young Show,* as the widowed mother of seven, but this was not successful. She then retired from acting to devote the rest of her life to Catholic charities and to live the high-style life of a former movie queen in her Beverly Hills mansion.

Her autobiography: *The Things I Had to Learn* (1961).

YOUNG, OTIS—black actor

b: 1932, Providence, R.I.

The Outcasts (wes).. Jemal David (1968–69)

YOUNG, RALPH—singer

b: c. 1919, The Bronx, N.Y.

Kraft Music Hall Presents Sandler & Young (var)....................... cohost (1969)

One half of the 1960s singing team of (Tony) Sandler & Young. Young had started as a big band singer with Les Brown and Shep Fields in the early '40s.

YOUNG, ROBERT—actor

b: Feb 22, 1907, Chicago, Ill. r: California

Father Knows Best (com)
.... Jim Anderson (1954–60)
Window on Main Street (com)
...... Cameron Garrett Brooks (1961–62)
Marcus Welby, M.D. (drama)
.... Dr. Marcus Welby (1969–76)

Little Women (drama)
.... Mr. James Laurence (1979)

Emmy Awards: Best Actor in a Continuing Performance in a Drama Series, for *Father Knows Best* (1957, 1957); Best Actor in a Dramatic Series, for *Marcus Welby, M.D.* (1970)

One look at that gentle face, with its ready smile and kind, understanding expression, should have convinced cold-hearted TV executives that Robert Young was a surefire bet for a long run in the "living room medium." But Young's was a TV career that almost didn't happen.

Robert got his start in films in the early '30s and for years played bland, amiable roles in B-features ("He has no sex appeal," thundered studio mogul Louis B. Mayer, so he usually didn't get the girl). Somewhat better roles came in the '40s, but, at the time he launched his warm family comedy *Father Knows Best* on radio in 1949, he was still known primarily as one of the movies' many minor league "nice guys."

Practically everything about *Father Knows Best* was maddeningly average— average town in the Midwest, average kids, average occupation (insurance)—but it was a perfect role for Young. The show ran for five successful years on radio, always promoting solid all-American values. However, when CBS moved it to television in 1954 it was inexplicably scheduled at 10 P.M., following a Celeste Holm "swinging single" comedy (*Honestly Celeste*), hardly the place for all-family viewing. Ratings were low and CBS canceled the show, but a flood of viewer protests convinced NBC to pick it up and schedule it in a more sensible, early-evening time slot. It was one of the first instances of viewer mail saving a series. *Father Knows Best* became so popular that when Young finally ceased production of the series in 1960 (he had been playing the role for 11 years), the networks continued to air reruns in prime time for three more years!

Young went on to star in *Window on Main Street,* as a writer in small-town America, but this was short-lived. For the next few years his appearances were limited to a few guest parts on *Dr. Kildare* (shades of things to come!), *Chrysler Theatre* and *The Name of the Game.* Then, in 1969, he made his first TV movie, *Marcus Welby, M.D.,* which led to his second long-running series. After that ended, Young, in his seventies, became less active. There were two *Father Knows Best* reunion specials in 1977, and a movie and short-run series based on the classic *Little Women* in 1978–79 (as Grandpa). In 1984 he starred in a second nostalgic reunion special, this one for *Marcus Welby.*

Young fought a 30-year battle with alcoholism, finally overcoming the disease in the '70s with the help of his loving wife of four decades. Appropriately, after *Welby* left the air he became known as the TV spokesman for Sanka decaffeinated coffee.

YOUNG, SKIP—actor

The Adventures of Ozzie & Harriet (com)
.... Wally (1957–66)

YOUNG, STEPHEN—actor
b: c. 1931, Toronto, Ont., Canada

Seaway (adv) .... Nick King (1965)
Judd, for The Defense (drama)
.... Ben Caldwell (1967–69)

YOUNG, TONY—actor
b: 1932, New York City, N.Y.

Gunslinger (wes) .... Cord (1961)

YOUNG, VICTOR—orchestra leader, composer
b: Aug 8, 1900, Chicago, Ill r: Warsaw, Poland
d: Nov 11, 1956

The Milton Berle Show (var)
.... orch. leader (1955–56)

Emmy Award: Best Scoring of a Variety Program, for the Four-Network Special "Diamond Jubilee of Light" (1954)

An eminent Hollywood composer-conductor, who won an Academy Award posthumously for *Around the World in 80 Days.* He also composed the pretty theme for TV's *Medic* series.

YOUNG, VICTORIA—actress
b: Honolulu, Hawaii

The Brian Keith Show (com)
.... Nurse Puni (1972–74)

The oriental wife of actor Brian Keith.

YOUNGER, BEVERLY—actress

Stud's Place (var)
.... Grace the waitress (1950)

YOUNGFELLOW, BARRIE—actress
b: Oct 22, Cleveland, Ohio

Fernwood 2-Night (com)
.... Linda Barry (1977–78)
It's a Living (com)
.... Jan Hoffmeyer (1980–82)
It's a Living (com)
.... Jan Hoffmeyer (1985–)

YOUNGMAN, HENNY—comedian
b: Jan 12, 1906, Liverpool, England r: Brooklyn, N.Y.

The Henny and Rocky Show (var)
.... cohost (1955)
Joey & Dad (var) .... regular (1975)

The rapid-fire, joke-a-second old-timer, always armed with a fiddle that he would occasionally scrape; he became a surprising running gag on TV variety shows and specials of the '70s and '80s. The more ancient the material, it seemed, the better. "I haven't spoken to my wife in three weeks —I didn't want to interrupt her . . . Zsa Zsa Gabor's been married six times now; she's got rice marks on her face . . . Wanna drive a friend crazy? Send him a telegram saying 'Ignore the first wire' . . . She wasn't a Lana Turner; more of a stomach turner."* And, of course, "Take my wife—*please!*"

YOUNGQUIST, ARTHUR—host

Dr. Fix-Um (info) .... host (1949–50)

YOUNGS, JIM—actor
b: Oct 16, Old Bethpage, N.Y.

Secrets of Midland Heights (drama)
.... John Grey (1980–81)

The younger brother of actor John Savage.

YUE, MARION—actress

Trapper John, M.D. (drama)
.... Nurse Shapiro (1979–80)

*Quoted in Joe Franklin, *Encyclopedia of Comedians* (1979).

YUNG, VICTOR SEN—actor

b: Oct 18, 1915, San Francisco, Calif. d: Nov 9, 1980

Bonanza (wes) . . . . Hop Sing (1959–73)
Bachelor Father (com)
. . . . cousin Charlie Fong (1961–62)

YUSKIS, ANTOINETTE (TONI)—actress, dancer

Blansky's Beauties (com)
. . . . Sylvia Silver (1977)
Dance Fever (dance) . . . . . dancer (1979–80)

Z

ZABACH, FLORIAN—violinist
b: Aug 15, 1921, Chicago, Ill.

Club Embassy (var)
.... featured soloist (1952–53)
The Florian Zabach Show (var)
.... host (1956)

Most famous in the early 1950s for his showpiece number "The Hot Canary."

ZABKA, WILLIAM—actor

The Equalizer (drama)
.... Scott McCall (1986–)

ZACHA, W.T.—actor

Code R (adv) .... Harry (1977)

ZAPATA, CARMEN—actress
b: Jul 15, 1927, New York City, N.Y.

The Man and the City (drama)
.... Josefina (1971–72)
Viva Valdez (com) ... Sophia Valdez (1976)
Hagen (drama) .... Mrs. Chavez (1980)

Carmen appeared as the mayor on the PBS daytime children's series *Villa Alegre* ("Happy Village") throughout most of the '70s. She has played Hispanic supporting roles in many series and TV movies of the '70s and '80s.

ZAPPA, MOON—actress

Fast Times (com)
.... Barbara DeVilbiss (1986)

The daughter of rock musician Frank Zappa; she first impressed herself on the American consciousness with the 1982 novelty hit "Valley Girl."

ZARA, LOU—writer
b: Aug 2, 1910, New York City, N.Y.

Stump the Authors (talk) ..... author (1949)

ZAREMBA, JOHN—actor
b: 1908, Chicago d: Dec 15, 1986

I Led Three Lives (drama)
.... special agent Jerry Dressler (1953–56)

The Time Tunnel (sci fi)
.... Dr. Raymond Swain (1966–67)

ZARIT, PAM—actress

The Sandy Duncan Show (com)
.... Hilary (1972)

ZEE, JOHN—actor
b: May 21, New York City r: New Rochelle, N.Y.

Bring 'Em Back Alive (adv)
.... G. B. VonTurgo (1982–83)

ZEIGLER, TED—comedian, writer

The Sonny and Cher Comedy Hour (var)
.... regular (1971–74)
The Ken Berry "Wow" Show (var)
.... regular (1972)
The Sonny Comedy Revue (var)
.... regular (1974)
The Sonny and Cher Show (var)
.... regular (1976–77)
Shields and Yarnell (var)
.... regular (1977)

ZELTNER, ARI—juvenile actor

Joe's World (com) .. Rick Wabash (1979–80)

ZERBE, ANTHONY—actor
b: 1936 r: California

Harry-O (drama)
.... Lt. K. C. Trench (1975–76)
How the West Was Won (miniseries) (drama)
.... Capt. Martin Grey (1977)
Centennial (drama)
.... Mervin Wendell (1978–79)

Emmy Award: Best Supporting Actor in a Drama Series, for *Harry-O* (1976)

TV Guide said of Zerbe that he was "born with an actor's face, lean, saturnine, half-starved, villainous." After a few starving years onstage in New York he began to earn a good living on television from the mid-1960s on, often in "authority" roles on action shows such as *Mission: Impossible, Gunsmoke,* and *Mannix.* His name is pronounced "ZER-bee."

ZIELINSKI, BRUNO (aka JUNIOR)—host

Polka Time (music)
.... regular (1956–57)

ZIEN, CHIP—actor

b: Mar 20, Milwaukee, Wis.

Love, Sidney (com).. Jason Stoller (1981–83)
Reggie (com).......... C. J. Wilcox (1983)

ZIMBALIST, EFREM, JR.—actor

b: Nov 30, 1918*, New York City, N.Y.

77 Sunset Strip (drama)
.... Stuart Bailey (1958–64)
The F.B.I. (police)
.... Insp. Lewis Erskine (1965–74)
Scruples (drama)....... Ellis Ikehorn (1980)

A self-assured, businesslike actor who, despite a notable lack of screen charisma, had 15 successful years starring in two very popular crime shows—*77 Sunset Strip* (six years) and *The F.B.I.* (nine).

Efrem was born into an illustrious musical family, the son of concert violinist Efrem Zimbalist and opera singer Alma Gluck. Both were major classical stars of the early 1900s. He entered acting after service in World War II and had his first major television role in the daytime soap opera *Concerning Miss Marlowe* in 1954–55. A few TV plays followed, as well as a guest shot on *The Phil Silvers Show*, before he began his first hit series as the suave private eye with an Ivy-League Ph.D. in *77 Sunset Strip*. He also made guest appearances on other Warner Brothers–produced series of the period, including *Maverick, Sugarfoot,* and *Hawaiian Eye.*

Since *The F.B.I.* left the air, Efrem has been seen mostly in TV movies and miniseries, including A *Family Upside Down, The Gathering Part II, Scruples,* and *Shooting Stars.* He is the father of actress Stephanie Zimbalist.

ZIMBALIST, STEPHANIE—actress

b: Oct 8, 1956, New York City, N.Y. r: Encino, Calif.

Centennial (drama).... Elly Zahm (1978–79)
Remington Steele (drama)
.... Laura Holt (1982–86)

"My father didn't influence me to get into the business," says Efrem Zimbalist's

*Most sources give 1923; however, I have recently seen a very old record catalog (of 78s), dated April 1919, which lists new releases by Efrem Sr. and Alma. It contains a picture of the proud artists showing off their brand-new baby boy (they had only one). Efrem, is that you?

pretty, brown-eyed daughter. *"Poor pop!* I remember saying to him, 'I don't want to do television.' " But a stage career didn't work out for Stephanie, so television it was, beginning in TV movies of the late '70s. She was a kidnap victim in *Yesterday's Child,* a grieving family member in *In the Matter of Karen Ann Quinlan,* and a lovelorn teenager in *Forever.* Quite a few more TV flicks followed, including one with her father (*The Best Place to Be,* in 1979); most had her portray the sympathetic heroine type. In *Elvis and the Beauty Queen* Stephanie got to fall in love with Don Johnson (as Elvis); however, in her first series, *Remington Steele,* her relationship with detective-partner Pierce Brosnan was kept deliberately less clear.

ZIMMER, NORMA—singer, hostess

b: Larsen, Idaho

The Meredith Willson Show (music)
.... regular (1949)
The Lawrence Welk Show (music)
.... Champagne Lady (1960–82)

Lawrence Welk's lovely "Champagne Lady" has also toured widely with Billy Graham's evangelical crusades. Prior to joining Welk she was a member of Eddie Fisher's backup group the Echoes.

ZIMMERMAN, CAPT. CARL—narrator

The Big Picture (doc).... narrator (1953–59)

ZIMMERMAN, HARRY—orchestra leader

The Dinah Shore Show (music)
.... orch. leader (1954–57)
The Dinah Shore Chevy Show (var)
.... orch. leader (1957–63)
The Chevy Show (music)
.... orch. leader (1958–59)
The Entertainers (var)
.... orch. leader (1964–65)
The Carol Burnett Show (var)
.... orch. leader (1967–71)

ZIPP, DEBBIE—actress

Small & Frye (com).... Phoebe Small (1983)

ZIPPI, DANIEL—actor

b: Apr 28, Los Angeles, Calif.

930

Secrets of Midland Heights (drama)
.... Teddy Welsh (1980–81)
King's Crossing (drama)
.... Billy McCall (1982)

ZMED, ADRIAN—actor
b: Mar 14, 1954, Chicago, Ill.

Flatbush (com) .... Socks Palermo (1979)
Goodtime Girls (com)
.... Frankie Millardo (1980)
T. J. Hooker (police)
.... Off. Vince Romano (1982–85)
Dance Fever (quiz) .... host (1985–)

A swarthy, sexy, baby-faced young actor who came to notice in the late '70s in the stage musical *Grease,* and later appeared in the movie *Grease II* (1982). He is the son of a Romanian Orthodox priest.

ZORBAUGH, HARVEY, DR.—host
b: c. 1896 d: Jan 21, 1965

Play the Game (quiz) .... host (1946)

A Professor of Sociology at New York University who was a minor celebrity on early live television, due to his talent for charades. He was seen locally on New York TV, off and on, from 1941 until the late '40s.

ZUCKERT, WILLIAM—actor

Mr. Novak (drama)
.... Mr. Arthur Bradwell (1964–65)
The Wackiest Ship in the Army (adv)
.... Gen. Cross (1965–66)
Captain Nice (com)...... Chief Segal (1967)

ZULU—actor
Real name: Gilbert Kauhi
b: Oct 17, Hilo, Hawaii

Hawaii Five-O (police)
.... Det. Kono (1968–72)

A Hawaiian-based disc jockey and character actor seen in 1960s movies of that (or similar) locales, such as *Gidget, Diamond Head,* and *Hawaii.*

Appendix 1
Extremes and Oddities

In poring over 9,000 actor biographies one is bound to encounter some oddities, performers who were "the most" or "the least" or who distinguished themselves in novel ways. Here are some of my favorites among prime time series regulars; your candidates and suggestions are welcome! Answers are on the following page.

1. Who has been a regular in the most prime time series?
   a. As an actor or comedian
   b. As a host or panelist
   c. As a newsman
2. Who starred in the most flops in a row?
3. Who was the tallest regular in TV history?
4. Who was the shortest (adult)?
5. Who was the youngest star of his or her own series? (Note: not a supporting actor, but the one who played the lead.)
6. Who was the youngest star of his own variety series?
7. Who was the oldest star of his own series?
8. Who was TV's oldest teenager? (Hint: be careful!)
9. Who was the youngest regular cast member in TV history?
10. Who got the latest start in life as an actor (age 67) yet became very successful?
11. Some actors deserve an authenticity award. Name:
    a. Two real-life cops who starred in TV cop shows.
    b. The real-life police dispatcher who played the dispatcher on one of TV's most popular police series.
    c. The 14-year-old karate black belt (he looked even younger) who played the same role on a prime time action show.
    d. The most authentic Indian in a TV Western.
12. Marital ironies:
    a. Who costarred with her new husband on a hit series produced by her ex-husband?
    b. Who continued to coo love songs to her husband on their joint series after their acrimonious real-life divorce, even while she was carrying another man's baby?

c. Who married an actor in 1965, divorced him, and then co-starred with him as his kid sister in a 1966 western?

13. Many actors are typecast forever by their first hit role. What well-known actors, who might well have suffered this fate, instead managed the following nifty escapes from typecasting?

a. From hayseed comic on one big hit to clever sleuth on another.

b. From diver-adventurer to pin-striped power broker.

c. From "human fish" to landlocked businessman (and lover).

d. From good guy in a hit '60s comedy to leading villain in one of the biggest hit dramas of the '80s.

ANSWERS

1. Performer who has been a regular in the most prime time series:

ACTORS AND COMEDIANS:

	No. of Series
Paul Lynde	11
John Dehner	10
Harry Morgan	10
Marian Mercer	9
Jonathan Winters	9
Richard Anderson	8
Henry Beckman	8
Tim Conway	8
Alice Ghostley	8
Gale Gordon	8
Reta Shaw	8
Jack Warden	8
Mary Wickes	8

HOSTS/PANELISTS:

Steve Allen	14
Bert Parks	13
Bill Cullen	12
Jack Barry	11
Bud Collyer	10
Dick Clark	10
Dennis James	9
Ernie Kovacs	9

NEWSMEN:

Walter Cronkite	13
John Daly	11
Mike Wallace	11
Quincy Howe	9

MULTITALENTED PERSONALITIES:

	Total Series	Actor	As . . . Host/Panelist
Carl Reiner	13	7	6
Hans Conreid	11	5	6
Betty White	11	6	5
Pat Carroll	10	7	3
Audrey Meadows	10	5	5
Johnny Desmond	9	7	2
Arte Johnson	9	7	2

2. Actor who starred in the most flops in a row:

Without a doubt, the Golden Turkey goes to McLean Stevenson. *M*A*S*H* was certainly a hit, but remember *The McLean Stevenson Show, Celebrity Challenge of the Sexes, In the Beginning, Hello, Larry* and *Condo* after that?

Big Guys, Little Guys

3. TV's tallest regular:

Men: Kevin Peter Hall of *Misfits of Science*–7'2"
Richard Kiel of *The Barbary Coast*–7'2"

Woman: Little Eller Long of *The Pee Wee King Show*–6'5"

Some you may have thought of, who weren't even close:

Ted Cassidy of *The Addams Family*–6'9"
Richard Moll of *Night Court*–6'8"
Ben Davidson of *Code R* (and the NFL)–6'8"
John Matuszak of *Hollywood Beat* (and the NFL)–6'8"
Bubba Smith of *Blue Thunder* (and the NFL)–6'8"
Tommy Tune of *The Golddiggers* (and Broadway)–6'7"
James Arness of *Gunsmoke*–6'6"
Fred Dryer of *Hunter* (and the NFL)–6'6"
Peter Isacksen of *C.P.O. Sharkey*–6'6"
Clint Walker of *Cheyenne*–6'6"
Fred Gwynne of *The Munsters*–6'5" (he wore 5" elevator shoes in his role as Herman Munster).

Among the ladies,

Rhonda Bates of *Speak Up, America*–6'2"
Hope Emerson ("Mother") of *Peter Gunn*–6'2"

4. The shortest adult regular:

Billy Barty of *The Spike Jones Show*–3'9"

Some runners-up:

Herve Villechaize of *Fantasy Island*–3'10"
David Rappaport of *The Wizard*–3'11"
Felix Silla of *The Addams Family*–4' (?)

Not even close:

Danny DeVito of *Taxi*–5'

The "Age Makes No Difference" Awards

5. Youngest star of his own series:

Jay North of *Dennis the Menace*–age 7
John Provost of *Lassie*–age 7

(Note: This refers to the youngest actor to actually play the lead in his own series. It does not count the infants in the titles of such shows as *Happy* and *Baby Makes Five* or the many youngsters who were supporting players for older actors; for example, 7-year-old Brandon Cruz in *The Courtship of Eddie's Father*).

Some runners-up (some not as young as they looked!):

Soleil Moon Frye of *Punky Brewster*–age 8
Jerry Mathers of *Leave It to Beaver*–age 9
Gary Coleman of *Diff'rent Strokes*–age 10
Scott Lane of *McKeever & the Colonel*–age 11
Brandon DeWilde of *Jamie*–age 11
Emmanuel Lewis of *Webster*–age 12
Tommy Rettig of *Lassie*–age 12
Ricky Schroder of *Silver Spoons*–age 12

6. Youngest stars of their own variety series:

The Keane Brothers of *The Keane Brothers Show* (aged 12 and 13)

7. Oldest star of his own series:

George Burns of *George Burns Comedy Week*–age 89

Other oldsters:

John Houseman of *The Paper Chase*–age 83
Joe Howard of *The Gay Nineties Revue*–age 81
Lawrence Welk of *The Lawrence Welk Show*–age 79

8. Oldest teenager:

No, it's not Dick Clark (who never claimed he was a teen). Frankie Thomas played "curly-haired teenager" *Tom Corbett—Space Cadet* until he was 34; Richard Crenna was still playing squeaky-voiced high school student Walter Denton on *Our Miss Brooks* at 28. He never did graduate.

9. The Early Start Award goes to:

Christopher William Stearns, who became a regular cast member of his parents' comedy *Mary Kay and Johnny* in January 1949, less than a month after his birth—debuting in his bassinet! This straight-from-the-womb introduction to show business did little good, however. Where is he now?

10. The Late Start Award belongs to:

Burt Mustin, who spent a lifetime as a salesman, retired, and then—at age 67—decided to become a professional actor. This new career lasted for 25 years and was highly successful; he was a regular on several series, including *All in the Family,* and was a frequent and funny guest on *The Tonight Show.* He died at age 92, while a regular on *Phyllis.* (Other older actors, such as John Houseman, gained fame late in life but had acted professionally before that.)

11. Authenticity Awards:

1. Dennis Farina of *Crime Story* and Eddie Egan of numerous police shows, real-life cops for many years before they moved their beat to TV.

2. Shaaron Claridge, the police dispatcher's voice on *Adam 12*, who was in real life . . . a police dispatcher with the L.A.P.D.

3. Fourteen-year-old Ernie Reyes, Jr., who portrayed a pint-sized karate expert high-kicking burly bad guys on *Sidekicks*, was in real life a black belt.

4. Jay Silverheels ("Tonto"), who was in fact the son of a Mohawk chief and born on a reservation in Canada.

12. Most bizarre marital arrangements:

1. Sexy Julie London costarred with her husband Bobby Troup on *Emergency*, which was owned and produced by none other than her former husband Jack Webb. No hard feelings, apparently.

2. The inimitable Cher was still singing "I Got You, Babe" to ex-husband Sonny Bono on the 1976 *Sonny and Cher Show* after their bitter divorce—even while she was pregnant with Greg Allman's baby.

3. Brenda Scott married Andrew Prine in 1965, promptly divorced him, and the very next year agreed to costar as his kid sister on *The Road West*. For actors and actresses, a good role—not love—conquers all.

13. Nifty escapes from typecasting:

Typecasting is the bane of television actors. Many new stars-of-the-moment have found themselves locked into images they could not escape for the rest of their careers. Will Bob Denver ever be anyone but Gilligan, Leonard Nimoy anyone but Mr. Spock, or Lynda Carter anyone but Wonder Woman? A few, however, have managed the hat trick and gone on to further success in roles very different from their first.

1. Buddy Ebsen—from hayseed comic on *The Beverly Hillbillies* to clever sleuth on *Barnaby Jones*.

2. Lloyd Bridges—from waterlogged diver-adventurer on *Sea Hunt* to pin-striped power broker on *Paper Dolls* and other series.

3. Patrick Duffy did practically the same thing in moving from *Man from Atlantis* to *Dallas*, although he remained a good guy.

4. Larry Hagman made the difficult transition from hit comedy *(I Dream of Jeannie)* to hit drama *(Dallas)*. Or is *Dallas* really a comedy?

Appendix 2
The TV Academy Hall of Fame

In 1984 the Academy of Television Arts and Sciences, which is best known for its annual Emmy Awards, at last instituted a permanent means of honoring those who have made historic contributions to the medium. Both performers and those working behind the scenes are eligible, but the club is an exclusive one. Each year only seven people are inducted, based on their lifelong contributions to TV. They are selected by the academy's board of governors and a blue-ribbon committee drawn from all areas of the industry. Here are the inductees of the first three years, with the year of induction for each. Principal professions are given for nonperformers.

Steve Allen (1986)
Lucille Ball (1984)
Milton Berle (1984)
Carol Burnett (1985)
Sid Caesar (1985)
Paddy Chayefsky, playwright (1984)
Fred Coe, director (1986)
Walter Cronkite (1985)
Walt Disney, producer (1986)
Joyce C. Hall, sponsor, *Hallmark Hall of Fame* (1985)
Jackie Gleason (1986)
Norman Lear, producer (1984)
Mary Tyler Moore (1986)
Edward R. Murrow (1984)
William S. Paley, who built CBS (1984)
David Sarnoff, who built NBC (1984)
Rod Serling (1985)
Frank Stanton, former president of CBS (1986)
Ed Sullivan (1985)
Burr Tillstrom (1986)
Sylvester "Pat" Weaver, former president of NBC (1985)

Appendix 3
TV Stars' Birthday Calendar

Jan 1:   Andrews, Dana
        Bickford, Charles (d. 1967)
        Cugat, Xavier
        Faracy, Stephanie
        Greaza, Walter (d. 1973)
        Hardin, Ty
        Hurst, Rick
        Novello, Don
        Woods, Ren
        Wrightson, Earl

Jan 2:   Bedford-Lloyd, John
        Caine, Howard
        Coleman, Dabney
        Evers, Jason
        LaRosa, Julius
        Lee, Anna
        Miller, Roger
        Phillips, Wendy

Jan 3:   Borge, Victor
        Bower, Tom
        Egan, Eddie
        Furness, Betty
        Loggia, Robert
        McNeeley, Larry
        Milland, Ray (d. 1986)
        Parks, Van Dyke
        Pitts, ZaSu (d. 1963)
        Principal, Victoria
        Russell, John
        Sikes, Cynthia
        White, Jesse
        Wong, Anna May (d. 1961)

Jan 4:   Booke, Sorrell
        Cannon, Dyan

Clark, Oliver
Collins, Al "Jazzbo"
Curreri, Lee
Holloway, Sterling
Kennedy, Lindsay
Licht, Jeremy
Perry, John Bennett
Rush, Barbara
Stahl, Richard
Wyman, Jane

Jan 5:   Dolenz, George
           (d. 1963)
        Duvall, Robert
        Earle, Robert
        Goldin, Ricky Paull
        Hayes, Richard
        Lange, Ted
        Martin, Pamela Sue
        Potts, Cliff
        Rose, Charlie

Jan 6:   Adams, Joey
        Bressler, Brian
        Brown, Tom
        Bruce, David (d. 1976)
        Franklin, Bonnie
        Greene, Billy (d. 1973)
        Lord, Bobby
        Pintauro, Danny
        Tayback, Vic
        Thomas, Danny
        Weed, Buddy
        Young, Loretta

Jan 7:   Baker, Art (d. 1966)
        Gardenia, Vincent

Gray, Erin
Moore, Terry
Napier, Alan
Revere, Paul
Turner, Tierre
Jan 8: Eubanks, Bob
Ferrer, Jose
Gray, Alexander (d. 1976)
Lewis, Jenny
McQueen, Butterfly
Mimieux, Yvette
Moody, Ron
Osgood, Charles
Prager, Stanley (d. 1972)
Sales, Soupy
Schedeen, Ann
Storch, Larry
Vanocur, Sander
Walters, Laurie
Wynn, May
Jan 9: Beck, Kimberly
Boyd, Jimmy
Callan, K
Denver, Bob
Enberg, Dick
Gayle, Crystal
Louise, Anita (d. 1970)
Mizzy, Vic
Van Cleef, Lee
Walker, Kathryn
Jan 10: Bolger, Ray (d. 1987)
Graves, Teresa
Hellman, Bonnie
MacKenzie, Gisele
Philips, Lee
Rowles, Polly
Sanderson, William
Sinatra, Frank, Jr.
Jan 11: Barash, Olivia
Barry, Donald (d. 1980)
Cherry, Don
Greene, Dennis (Sha Na Na)
Hall, Ed
Hill, Goldie
Ivar, Stan
Jacobs, Christian
Lawson, Linda
Netherton, Tom
Ryan, Mitchell
Stander, Lionel

Swaim, Caskey
Taylor, Rod
Jan 12: Alley, Kirstie
Burrud, Bill
Green, Dorothy
Harper, Ron
Kelly, Patsy (d. 1981)
Kreskin
Morton, Greg
Ritter, Tex (d. 1974)
Teal, Ray (d. 1976)
Youngman, Henny
Jan 13: Dunne, Steve (d. 1977)
Gray, Billy
Louis-Dreyfus, Julia
Mitchell, Keith
Moll, Richard
Morrow, Jeff
Murphy, Rosemary
Reilly, Charles Nelson
Sheiner, David
Stack, Robert
Sternhagen, Frances
Taylor, Rip
Walcott, Gregory
Jan 14: Aletter, Frank
Bateman, Jason
Belford, Christine
Bendix, William (d. 1964)
Daly, Jonathan
Gortner, Marjoe
Jones, Jack
Lawrence, Mark
Rooney, Andy
Schneider, Daniel J.
Taylor, Holland
Valente, Caterina
Walker, Billy
Weathers, Carl
Williams, Guy
Jan 15: Ace, Goodman (d. 1982)
Bridges, Lloyd
Brown, Charles
Campos, Victor
Carpenter, Thelma
Charo
Hoving, Thomas
King, Regina
Lowe, Chad
Martin, Andrea

Nolan, Tommy
Reyes, Ernie, Jr.
Jan 16: Allen, Debbie
Boucher, Bob
Jurado, Katy
Lester, Buddy
Pataki, Michael
Reid, Elliot
Stafford, Jim
Jan 17: Boone, Randy
Carrey, Jim
Elliot, Jane
Fogel, Jerry
Gateson, Marjorie (d. 1977)
Herron, Joel
Hull, Warren (d. 1974)
Jones, James Earl
Kaufman, Andy (d. 1984)
North, Sheree
Reser, Harry (d. 1965)
Susman, Todd
Vogel, Mitch
Watson, Debbie
White, Betty
Wilcox, Nina
Jan 18: Chandler, Chick
Goldsboro, Bobby
Hudson, Brett (Hudson
Brothers)
Kaye, Danny (d. 1987)
Moore, Constance
Jan 19: Arnaz, Desi, Jr.
Colasanto, Nicholas (d. 1985)
Crawford, Michael
Everly, Phil
Fabares, Shelley
Jaffe, Taliesin
Kabbible, Ish
MacNeil, Robert
Madison, Guy
Parton, Dolly
Rodriguez, Paul
Ross, Lanny
Stapleton, Jean
Weaver, Fritz
West, Alvy
Jan 20: Ames, Leon
Anthony, Ray
Ates, Roscoe (d. 1962)
Burns, George

Donat, Peter
Johnson, Arte
Kelley, DeForest
Lamas, Lorenzo
Pithey, Wensley
Provine, Dorothy
Sedan, Rolfe (d. 1982)
Jan 21: Bara, Fausto
Benson, Robby
Burke, Paul
Davis, Geena
Davis, Mac
Doucette, John
Eikenberry, Jill
Falkenburg, Jinx
George, John (d. 1968)
Hewitt, Alan (d. 1986)
Hill, Benny
Naish, J. Carrol (d. 1973)
Savalas, Telly
Wedgeworth, Ann
Wolfman Jack
Jan 22: Bixby, Bill
Cooper, Roy
Douglas, Diana
Laurie, Piper
Lemmon, Chris
Smith, Dwan
Sothern, Ann
Jan 23: Anderson, Richard Dean
Antonio, Lou
Duryea, Dan (d. 1968)
Gerard, Gil
Gilliland, Richard
Girardin, Ray
Golonka, Arlene
Halop, Florence (d. 1986)
Hargitay, Mariska
Kovacs, Ernie (d. 1962)
McK, Misha
Paich, Marty
Rivera, Chita
Steele, Bob
Jan 24: Belushi, John (d. 1982)
Borgnine, Ernest
Crowe, Tonya
Hudson, William (d. 1974)
Kaplan, Marvin
Kiernan, Walter (d. 1978)
McLiam, John

Ontkean, Michael
Saddler, Don
Stevens, Ray
Jan 25: Allen, Elizabeth
Jones, Dean
Manoff, Dinah
Maugham, W. Somerset
(d. 1965)
Newman, Edwin
Palmer, Gregg
Taylor-Young, Leigh
Tobin, Michele
Jan 26: Ballantine, Eddie
Cooper, Wyllis (d. 1955)
Cully, Zara
Hill, Richard
Hopper, William (d. 1970)
Jeffreys, Anne
Lonow, Claudia
Prince, William
Redfield, William (d. 1976)
Scott, Kathryn Leigh
Scotti, Vito
Uecker, Bob
Jan 27: Bagdasarian, Ross (d. 1972)
Cohoon, Patty
Cromwell, James
Donahue, Troy
Henderson, Skitch
Kennedy, Sarah
Kondazian, Karen
Lane, Scott
Reed, Donna (d. 1986)
Rogers, Mimi
Thulin, Ingrid
Jan 28: Alda, Alan
Banner, John (d. 1973)
Beck, John
Benton, Barbi
Buckner, Susan
Caliri, Jon
Howard, Susan
Jarrett, Renne
Walker, Allan (d. 1970)
Jan 29: Corey, Irwin
Forsythe, John
George, Anthony
Harrison, Noel
Jillian, Ann
Mandrell, Irlene
Moore, Barbara

Morgan, Robin
Norton-Taylor, Judy
Raitt, John
Ross, Katherine
Selleck, Tom
Singer, Marc
Jan 30: Ashbrook, Daphne
Brooks, Randy
Brown, Ruth
Grimes, Tammy
Ireland, John
Jean, Norma
Leighton, Bernie
Malone, Dorothy
Marlowe, Hugh (d. 1982)
Martin, Dick
O'Dell, Tony
Opatoshu, David
Wayne, David
Wilcox, Ralph
Jan 31: Aidman, Charles
Bankhead, Tallulah (d. 1968)
Cantor, Eddie (d. 1964)
Carlin, Lynn
Dru, Joanne
Franciscus, James
Hackett, Bobby
Joy, Nicholas (d. 1964)
Loftin, Carey
Margolin, Stuart
Moore, Garry
Pleshette, Suzanne
Simmons, Jean
Sylvester, William
Turman, Glynn
Walter, Jessica

Feb 1: Amendolia, Don
Besch, Bibi
Braverman, Bart
Burmester, Leo
Everly, Don
Hart, John—newsman
Hemsley, Sherman
Kemp, Brandis
Leyden, Bill
Morris, Garrett
Whitman, Stuart
Feb 2: Antonacci, Greg
Fawcett, Farrah
Gordon, Gale

Hopkins, Bo
Lewis, Wanda
Mandan, Robert
McGrath, Frank (d. 1967)
Rubin, Benny (d. 1986)
Smith, Liz
Smothers, Tom
Stritch, Elaine
Talbott, Michael
Tinney, Cal
Feb 3: Arms, Russell
Berman, Shelley
Bishop, Joey
Case, Nelson
Correll, Charles (d. 1972)
Costello, Mariclare
Danner, Blythe
Fairchild, Morgan
Fiedler, John
Greene, Michele
Hanley, Bridget
Kemp, Jeremy
Kenny, Nick (d. 1975)
Lane, Nathan
McHattie, Stephen
Noble, Trisha
Osterwald, Bibi
Tarkenton, Fran
Feb 4: Bain, Conrad
Beck, Michael
Conway, Gary
Coote, Robert (d. 1982)
Ferdin, Pamelyn
Foy, Eddie, Jr. (d. 1983)
Fraser, Gordon
Lupino, Ida
Miller, Cheryl
Schuck, John
Talman, William (d. 1968)
Wilson, Jeannie
Wisdom, Norman
Feb 5: Buttons, Red
Carradine, John
Damon, Stuart
Georgiade, Nick
Guest, Christopher
Hershey, Barbara
Parker, Willard
Selby, David
Feb 6: Brokaw, Tom
Farrell, Mike

Lerman, April
Macnee, Patrick
Perreau, Gigi
Reagan, Ronald
Torn, Rip
Tucker, Michael
Walmsley, Jon
Feb 7: Bracken, Eddie
Brand, Oscar
Brasselle, Keefe (d. 1981)
Hoffman, Harold (d. 1954)
Mahoney, Jock
Rose, Jane (d. 1979)
Feb 8: Adams, Brooke
Coleman, Gary
Giambalvo, Louis
Klein, Robert
Larson, Jack
Lemmon, Jack
Meadows, Audrey
Miller, Barry
Morrow, Buddy
Nolte, Nick
Rey, Alejandro
Ruggles, Charlie (d. 1970)
Talbot, Lyle
Turner, Lana
Feb 9: Bullock, JM J.
Colman, Ronald (d. 1958)
Donlevy, Brian (d. 1972)
Edwards, Ronnie Claire
Farrow, Mia
Fridell, Squire
Herman, Ralph
Lee, Gypsy Rose (d. 1970)
Light, Judith
Mudd, Roger
Pesci, Joe
Peyser, Penny
Tubb, Ernest (d. 1984)
Wood, Peggy (d. 1978)
Feb 10: Beller, Kathleen
Bromfield, Valri
Chaney, Lon, Jr. (d. 1973)
Durante, Jimmy (d. 1980)
Howlin, Olin (d. 1959)
Patterson, Neva
Van Horne, Randy
Wagner, Robert
Feb 11: Anglim, Philip
Beckham, Brice

Bobo, Natasha
Dennis, Matt
Fink, John
Freeman, Deena
Gabor, Eva
Halop, Billy (d. 1976)
Janis, Conrad
Kolden, Scott
Lawrence, Matthew
Louise, Tina
Nielsen, Leslie
Reynolds, Burt
Sherman, Hiram
Feb 12: Adams, Maud
Baker, Joe Don
Bellaver, Harry
Clark, Ernest
DeYoung, Cliff
Ford, Wallace (d. 1966)
Garagiola, Joe
Greene, Lorne
Hall, Arsenio
Howard, Joe (d. 1961)
Kerns, Joanna
Kilpatrick, Lincoln
Lehman, Lillian
MacCorkindale, Simon
Mack, Ted (d. 1976)
Sbarge, Raphael
Shenar, Paul
Stossel, Ludwig (d. 1973)
Tucker, Forrest (d. 1986)
Wood, Barry (d. 1970)
Feb 13: Bettger, Lyle
Channing, Stockard
Edwards, Joan (d. 1981)
Ford, Tennessee Ernie
Griffith, James
Lynley, Carol
Manley, Stephen
McGuire, Dotty (McGuire
Sisters)
Moody, Sen. Blair
(d. 1954)
Naughton, David
Oliver, Susan
Svenson, Bo
Tork, Peter
Feb 14: Allen, Mel
Benny, Jack (d. 1974)
Chamberlin, Lee

Corrigan, Ray "Crash"
(d. 1976)
Downs, Hugh
Erwin, Stu (d. 1967)
Henderson, Florence
Kelly, Brian
Lawrence, Elliot
McGuire, Phyllis (McGuire
Sisters)
Morrow, Vic (d. 1982)
Murray, Peg
Platt, Edward (d. 1974)
Prine, Andrew
Scott, Fred
Feb 15: Arbus, Alan
Bloom, Claire
Curtis, Keene
Edwards, Geoff
Hamer, Rusty
Korman, Harvey
McCarthy, Kevin
Romero, Cesar
Seymour, Jane
Yarlett, Claire
Feb 16: Beaumont, Hugh (d. 1982)
Bedford, Brian
Bergen, Edgar (d. 1978)
Block, Hunt
Bono, Sonny
Brook, Faith
Burton, LeVar
Katt, William
Kenin, Alexa (d. 1985)
King, Peggy
King, Wayne (d. 1985)
Loring, Lisa
Lynn, Jeffrey
Morris, Chester (d. 1970)
Primus, Barry
Ringwald, Molly
Russell, Lee
Sharbutt, Del
Wakely, Jimmy (d. 1982)
Wyler, Gretchen
Feb 17: Barber, Red
Bethune, Zina
Freeman, Kathleen
Hagman, Heidi
Holbrook, Hal
Kennedy, Arthur
Mobley, Mary Ann

Pickles, Christina
Trent, Buck
Feb 18: Clark, Dane
Cullen, Bill
DeWolfe, Billy (d. 1974)
Kennedy, George
King, Pee Wee
Melvin, Allan
Menjou, Adolphe (d. 1963)
Mustin, Burt (d. 1977)
Nader, Michael
Palance, Jack
Shepherd, Cybill
Travolta, John
White, Vanna
Feb 19: Bateman, Justine
Hardwicke, Sir Cedric
(d. 1964)
Kenton, Stan (d. 1979)
Marvin, Lee
Oberon, Merle (d. 1979)
Robinson, Smokey
Rose, George
Westman, Nydia (d. 1970)
Feb 20: Albert, Edward
Atterbury, Malcolm
Blake, Amanda
Daly, John
Duncan, Sandy
Dusay, Marj
Hovis, Larry
O'Neill, Jennifer
Polic, Henry, II
Smith, Patricia
Strauss, Peter
Tripp, Paul
Voldstad, John
Wells, Claudette
Wesson, Dick (d. 1979)
Feb 21: Atkins, Christopher
Benoit, Patricia
Beymer, Richard
Brown, Woody
Coleman, Jack
Daly, Tyne
Ebersole, Christine
Fann, Al
Lockwood, Gary
McClanahan, Rue
Orth, Frank (d. 1962)
Ragland, Larry

Sheridan, Ann (d. 1967)
Winn, Kitty
Feb 22: Benjamin, Susan
Chagrin, Julian
Dooley, Paul
Leonard, Sheldon
Markey, Enid (d. 1981)
May, Donald
Mills, John
Pardo, Don
Scott, Geoffrey
Seymour, Dan (d. 1982)
Young, Robert
Feb 23: Barrett, Majel
Chase, Sylvia
Keller, Jason
Keller, Shane
Price, Marc
Richardson, Patricia
Rowland, Jada
Seven, Johnny
Feb 24: Bostwick, Barry
Cristal, Linda
Diener, Joan
Farentino, James
Hill, Steven
Lytell, Bert (d. 1954)
Naud, Melinda
O'Hara, Jenny
Olmos, Edward James
Parke, Dorothy
Scannell, Susan
Scott, Zachary (d. 1965)
Shaver, Helen
Shull, Richard B.
Sloyan, James
Vernon, John
Vigoda, Abe
Ward, Jonathan
Waterman, Dennis
Feb 25: Backus, Jim
Baker, Diane
Browning, Susan
Fenwick, Millicent
George, Christopher (d. 1983)
Grassle, Karen
Holland, Kristina
Jones, Dick
Newsom, Tommy
Nigh, Jane
Remsen, Bert

Schieffer, Bob
Scott, Jean Bruce
Taylor, Jud
Williams, Louise
Feb 26: Adams, Mason
Alda, Robert (d. 1986)
Belack, Doris
Cash, Johnny
Fithian, Jeff
Fithian, Joe
Frawley, William (d. 1966)
Freeman, Damita Jo
Gleason, Jackie
Hall, Jon (d. 1979)
Hutton, Betty
Kennedy, Tom
Knight, Jack
Lopez, Priscilla
Meek, Barbara
O'Neill, Katie
Peluce, Meeno
Randall, Tony
Schmock, Jonathan
Stone, Cynthia
Feb 27: Babcock, Barbara
Bennett, Joan
Demarest, William (d. 1983)
Frann, Mary
Fudge, Alan
Gardiner, Reginald (d. 1980)
Hesseman, Howard
Jackson, Stoney
Melis, Jose
Mitchell, Guy
Taylor, Elizabeth
Tone, Franchot (d. 1968)
Topper, Tim
Williams, Van
Feb 28: Ackerman, Bettye
Beacham, Stephanie
Bird, Billie
Bobo, Willie (d. 1983)
Boles, Jim (d. 1977)
Bonner, Frank
Durning, Charles
Francks, Don
Graff, Ilene
Hecht, Ben (d. 1964)
Lohman, Rick
Lynn, Jennie
MacLeod, Gavin

Peters, Bernadette
Raines, Cristina
Romanus, Richard
Smith, Bubba
Soule, Olan
Tune, Tommy
Feb 29: Dorsey, Jimmy (d. 1957)
Roarke, John
Rocco, Alex
Mar 1: Bach, Catherine
Belafonte, Harry
Benedict, Dirk
Brown, Jim Ed
Carroll, Jon (Starland Vocal
Band)
Clary, Robert
Conrad, Robert
Danova, Cesare
De Marney, Terence (d. 1971)
Hartman, Paul (d. 1973)
Howard, Ron
Mason, Tom
Moran, Lois
Niven, David (d. 1983)
Shore, Dinah
Thicke, Alan
Wood, Lana
Mar 2: Arnaz, Desi (d. 1986)
Carpenter, Karen (d. 1983)
Crawford, Katherine
Mones, Paul
Newman, Laraine
Osmond, Jay
Thomson, Gordon
Waxman, Al
Yates, Cassie
Mar 3: Cheshire, Elizabeth
Conley, Joe
Dandridge, Ruby
Doohan, James
Kazurinsky, Tim
Lowe, Edmund (d. 1971)
Pioli, Judy
Winston, Hattie
Mar 4: Bono, Chastity
Cumbuka, Ji-Tu
Garas, Kaz
Haney, Anne
Lenz, Kay
McNair, Barbara

946

O'Hara, Catherine
Prentiss, Paula
Tirelli, Jaime
Mar 5: Cassidy, Jack (d. 1976)
Christine, Virginia
De Winter, Jo
Eggar, Samantha
Gibb, Andy
Johnson, Chic (Olsen & John-
son) (d. 1962)
Noble, James
Peters, Lowell (Southern-
aires)
Sand, Paul
Shawlee, Joan (d. 1987)
Sikking, James
Snyder, Arlen Dean
Wainwright, James
Warren, Michael
Williamson, Fred
Mar 6: Costello, Lou (d. 1959)
Elson, Andrea
Flippen, Jay C. (d. 1971)
Hayes, Allison (d. 1977)
Horsford, Anna Maria
Hudson, Rochelle (d. 1972)
Kilian, Victor (d. 1979)
Kove, Martin
Kupcinet, Karyn (d. 1963)
McMahon, Ed
Murphy, Ben
Price, Roger
Reiner, Rob
Smith, John
Spielberg, David
Mar 7: Broderick, James
(d. 1982)
Eisner, Michael
Lawson, Richard
Loren, Donna
Marlowe, Marion
Pinter, Mark
Roberts, Davis
Stadlen, Lewis J.
Travanti, Daniel J.
Mar 8: Beavers, Louise (d. 1962)
Bouton, Jim
Clark, Susan
Colman, Booth
DeWitt, Lew (Statler
Brothers)

Dolenz, Mickey
Ewing, Oscar (d. 1980)
Hale, Alan, Jr.
Johnson, Judy
Langdon, Sue Ane
McClory, Sean
Redgrave, Lynn
Sues, Alan
Taylor, Ron
Mar 9: Bauer, Jaime Lyn
Betz, Carl (d. 1978)
Clark, Fred (d. 1968)
Cullen, William Kirby
Geer, Will (d. 1978)
Ingels, Marty
Lewis, Emmanuel
Lindsay, Mark
Papas, Irene
Siebert, Charles
Van Patten, Joyce
Mar 10: Anderson, Warner (d. 1976)
Coates, Paul
Jaffe, Sam (d. 1984)
Kendall, Cy (d. 1953)
Kennedy, Adam
Trenner, Donn
Tweed, Shannon
Mar 11: Alexander, Terry
Donaldson, Sam
Eben, Al
Richardson, Susan
Salmi, Albert
Welk, Lawrence
Mar 12: Dobyns, Lloyd
Feldon, Barbara
Jackson, Marlon
Kaye, Caren
Lane, Sara
MacRae, Gordon (d. 1986)
Mitchlll, Scoey
Parks, Hildy
Parrish, Helen (d. 1959)
Weston, Paul
Mar 13: Berry, Fred
Duke, Robin
Fix, Paul (d. 1983)
Hutton, Ina Ray (d. 1984)
Kaye, Sammy
O'Shea, Tessie
Raffin, Deborah
Stewart, Paul (d. 1986)

Wells, Tracy
Wilcox, Frank (d. 1974)
York, Donny (Sha Na Na)
Mar 14: Brown, Les
Crystal, Billy
Henderson, Luther, Jr.
Jones, Quincy
Kanaly, Steve
Patrick, Dennis
Piute Pete (Morris Kaufman)
Rossovich, Tim
Zmed, Adrian
Mar 15: Baio, Jimmy
Brent, George (d. 1979)
Carey, Macdonald
Gregson, John (d. 1975)
Hirsch, Judd
Maxey, Paul (d. 1963)
Ross, Joe E. (d. 1982)
Scott, Brenda
Smith, Carl
Ward, Richard (d. 1979)
Wasson, Craig
Mar 16: Estrada, Erik
Johnson, Betty
Lewis, Jerry
Nagel, Conrad (d. 1970)
Woolery, Chuck
Mar 17: Cole, Nat "King" (d. 1965)
Down, Lesley-Anne
Duffy, Patrick
Lowe, Rob
McCambridge, Mercedes
Mitchell, Don
O'Shea, Michael (d. 1973)
Russell, Kurt
Sebastian, John
Wade, Adam
Mar 18: Burnette, Smiley
(d. 1967)
Cara, Irene
Dobson, Kevin
Dourif, Brad
Gottlieb, Carl
Graves, Peter
Horton, Edward Everett
(d. 1970)
Mar 19: Andrews, Tige
Case, Russ (d. 1964)
Hayward, Louis (d. 1985)
Henderson, Bill
McGoohan, Patrick

Metcalfe, Burt
Newman, Phyllis
Roberts, Roy (d. 1975)
Smith, Kent (d. 1985)
Taylor, Renee
Willis, Bruce
Mar 20: Barry, Jack (d. 1984)
Bessell, Ted
Buchanan, Edgar (d. 1979)
Corey, Wendell (d. 1968)
Goulding, Ray (Bob and Ray)
Klemperer, Werner
Kruschen, Jack
Linden, Hal
Nelson, Ozzie (d. 1975)
Reed, Jerry
Reiner, Carl
Zien, Chip
Mar 21: Abbott, Philip
Castle, Nick (d. 1968)
Coco, James (d. 1987)
Collier, Lois
Dalton, Timothy
Freeman, Al, Jr.
Hall, Brad
Hon, Jean Marie
LeBeauf, Sabrina
Lindsey, Mort
Ramsey, Logan
Wolfson, Carl
Yarnell, Lorene (Shields &
Yarnell)
Mar 22: Brown, James
Malden, Karl
Martin, Ross (d. 1981)
Marx, Chico (d. 1961)
Schildkraut, Joseph (d. 1964)
Shatner, William
Wendell, Bill
Wyle, George
Mar 23: Allen, Marty
Berdis, Bert
Ganzel, Teresa
Glenn, Christopher
Guarnieri, Johnny (d. 1985)
Ober, Philip (d. 1982)
Rhoades, Barbara
Sweeney, Terry
Wright, Martha
Mar 24: Brown, Vanessa
Campbell, Nicholas
Carradine, Robert

Conte, Richard (d. 1975)
Fell, Norman
Hamilton, Murray (d. 1986)
McQueen, Steve (d. 1980)
Nelson, Kenneth
Pescow, Donna
Saylor, Sid (d. 1962)
Smith, William
Wilzak, Crissy
Mar 25: Axton, Hoyt
Bedelia, Bonnie
Begley, Ed (d. 1970)
Blackton, Jay
Bryant, Anita
Carle, Frankie
Clyde, Andy (d. 1967)
Cosell, Howard
Glaser, Paul Michael
Gross, Mary
Haigh, Kenneth
Hale, Lee
Nelson, Haywood
Parker, Sarah Jessica
Mar 26: Allen, Phillip R.
Brown, Philip
Crawford, Johnny
Elliott, Bob (Bob and Ray)
Hayden, Sterling (d. 1986)
Lawrence, Vicki
Martin, Strother (d. 1980)
Nimoy, Leonard
Papenfuss, Tony
Richards, Evan
Schoen, Vic
Shields, Robert
Short, Martin
Sylvern, Hank (d. 1964)
Thomas, Ernest
Warlock, Billy
Mar 27: Cheek, Molly
Denning, Richard
Glover, Julian
Hayman, Richard
Janssen, David (d. 1980)
Lanson, Snooky
Roylance, Pamela
Treen, Mary
Vennera, Chick
Weintraub, Carl
Mar 28: Clausen, Alf
Dunnam, Stephanie
Ferrell, Conchata

Howard, Ken
Lovejoy, Frank (d. 1962)
McCoy, Charlie
Perkins, Marlin (d. 1986)
Whiteman, Paul (d. 1967)
Mar 29: Ann, Philip (d. 1978)
Bailey, Pearl
Foster, Phil (d. 1985)
Heckart, Eileen
Kay, Dianne
O'Connell, Arthur
(d. 1981)
O'Keefe, Dennis (d. 1968)
Stevens, Onslow (d. 1977)
Mar 30: Astin, John
Beatty, Warren
Cali, Joseph
Dysart, Richard
Laine, Frankie
Macintosh, Jay W.
Marshall, Peter
Mar 31: Cadorette, Mary
Chamberlain, Richard
Cohen, Evan
Curtin, Valerie
Daniels, William
Jones, Shirley
Kaplan, Gabe
Kiley, Richard
Marinaro, Ed
McClure, Marc
Morgan, Henry
Patterson, Lee
Perlman, Rhea
Quillan, Eddie
Rea, Peggy
Taylor, Nathaniel
Walken, Glenn (Christopher)

Apr 1: Andrews, Johnny
Biberman, Abner (d. 1977)
Glass, Ned (d. 1984)
Hastings, Don
Janney, Leon (d. 1980)
Jump, Gordon
Lund, Art
MacGraw, Ali
Mifune, Toshiro
Powell, Jane
Reynolds, Debbie
Whitney, Grace Lee
Young, Heather

Apr 2:	Acker, Sharon
	Ebsen, Buddy
	Greer, Dabbs
	Palillo, Ron
	Scott, Debralee
	Webb, Jack (d. 1982)
Apr 3:	Baldwin, Alec
	Brando, Marlon
	Day, Doris
	Finegan, Bill (of Sauter-Finegan)
	Freeman, Stan
	Gaunt, William
	Jessel, George (d. 1981)
	Landers, Harry
	Laughlin, John
	Lynn, Jonathan
	Murphy, Eddie
	Orlando, Tony
	Proft, Pat
	Sterling, Jan
	Van Steeden, Peter
	Wilson, Dooley (d. 1953)
Apr 4:	Angelou, Maya
	Benaderet, Bea (d. 1968)
	Carmen, Julie
	Coogan, Richard
	Downey, Robert
	Halpin, Luke
	Langford, Frances
	McKeon, Nancy
	McWilliams, Caroline
	Murray, Arthur
	Myers, Carmel (d. 1980)
	Nelson, Craig T.
	Parks, Michael
	Phillips, Tacey
	Ryan, Bill
	Smith, Cyril (d. 1963)
	Swayze, John Cameron
	Wilson, Elizabeth
Apr 5:	Chi, Chou-Li
	Douglas, Melvyn (d. 1981)
	Gail, Max
	Gorshin, Frank
	Hewett, Christopher
	Jones, Gordon (d. 1963)
	Lewis, Robert Q.
	Moriarty, Michael
	Nelson, Christopher S.
	Peck, Gregory

	Raisch, Bill (d. 1984)
	Schick, George (d. 1985)
	Stevens, Shawn
	Storm, Gale
	Sutton, Grady
	Weintraub, Cindy
	Winters, David
Apr 6:	Actman, Jane
	Dixon, Ivan
	Haggard, Merle
	Henner, Marilu
	Lansing, Joi (d. 1972)
	Meyers, Ari
	Phillips, Michelle
	Ratzenberger, John
	Reeves, George (d. 1959)
	Thinnes, Roy
	Thomas, Lowell (d. 1981)
	Tolsky, Susan
	Williams, Billy Dee
Apr 7:	Armstrong, R.G.
	Flanagan, Ralph
	Frost, David
	Garner, James
	Howard, Ronald
	Hucko, Peanuts
	Lime, Yvonne
	Perito, Nick
	Richardson, Ian
	Rogers, Wayne
	Shore, Roberta
	Wheeler, Bert (d. 1968)
	Winchell, Walter (d. 1972)
Apr 8:	Chase, Ilka (d. 1978)
	Gavin, John
	Greene, Shecky
	Keeler, Donald
	Lampley, Jim
	Lennon, Peggy (Lennon Sisters)
	Mulhare, Edward
	Patrick, Lory
	Schneider, John
	Spound, Michael
	Tucker, John Bartholomew
	Tutin, Dorothy
	Weaver, Robby
Apr 9:	Bond, Ward (d. 1960)
	Bufano, Vincent
	Cook, Nathan
	De Wilde, Brandon (d. 1972)

Fowler, Jim
Jenkins, Allen (d. 1974)
Learned, Michael
Perkins, Carl
Pulliam, Keshia Knight
Ryan, Dave "Chico" (Sha Na
  Na)
Schreiber, Avery
Thomas, Frankie
Van Damme, Art
Apr 10: Adams, Jeb
Bergere, Lee
Brown, Olivia
Connors, Chuck
Fulton, Julie
Jacoby, Billy
Meredith, Don
Morgan, Harry
Ponce, Poncie
Rhodes, Hari
Samples, Alvin "Junior"
  (d. 1983)
Weaver, Lee
Wooley, Sheb
Apr 11: Douglas, Paul (d. 1959)
Franklin, Carl
Larkin, John (d. 1965)
Lasser, Louise
Reynolds, Quentin
  (d. 1965)
Shirriff, Catherine
Apr 12: Bank, Frank
Cassidy, David
Clooney, Betty
Doherty, Shannen
Leeds, Elissa
Letterman, David
McCarren, Fred
Northrop, Wayne
Regas, Pedro (d. 1974)
Apr 13: Adams, Don
Blanchard, Mari (d. 1970)
Dow, Tony
Hannah, Page
Karron, Richard
Keel, Howard
Kroeger, Gary
Santiago, Saundra
Santini, Tony (Sha Na Na)
Schroder, Ricky
Swire, Sydney

Waggoner, Lyle
Yothers, Corey
Apr 14: Darling, Joan
DiAquinto, John
Dillman, Bradford
Griffeth, Simone
Hall, Anthony Michael
Healy, Mary
Howard, John
Lynn, Loretta
Powell, Randolph
Shea, John
Tracy, Lee (d. 1968)
Apr 15: Ansara, Michael
Clark, Roy
Conried, Hans (d. 1982)
Ford, Art
Maury, Derrel
McCary, Rod
Montgomery, Elizabeth
Sommars, Julie
Williams, John (d. 1983)
Apr 16: Adams, Edie
Botkin, Perry, Jr.
Cross, Milton J. (d. 1975)
Graff, David
Milligan, Spike
Nelson, Barry
Osmond, Jimmy
Richman, Peter Mark
Robinson, Fran
Tendler, Jesse
Tremayne, Les
Vinton, Bobby
Apr 17: Austin, Teri
Bega, Leslie
Cherry, Byron
Frank, Charles
Genevieve
Gibbs, Timothy
Heydt, Louis Jean (d. 1960)
Lake, Arthur
Langton, Paul (d. 1980)
Reasoner, Harry
Tyler, Kim
Apr 18: Baker, Lennie (Sha Na Na)
Barrie, Wendy (d. 1978)
Drury, James
Hale, Barbara
Hastings, Bob
Hodge, Al (d. 1979)

Hooks, Robert
James, John
Kinskey, Leonid
Lazarus, Bill
Lyman, Dorothy
Markham, Pigmeat
  (d. 1981)
Martin, Lori
Moranis, Rick
Mottola, Tony
Pickett, Cindy
Revill, Clive
Stephenson, Skip
Woods, James
Apr 19: Barbour, Don (Four Fresh-
  men)
Donahue, Elinor
Fontaine, Frank (d. 1978)
Mansfield, Jayne
  (d. 1967)
O'Brian, Hugh
Sargent, Dick
Weston, Ellen
Wheatley, Alan
Apr 20: Braun, Bob
Foch, Nina
Howard, Clint
Lawrence, Joey
Miller, Lara Jill
O'Neal, Ryan
Takei, George
Tillotson, Johnny
Apr 21: Clute, Sidney (d. 1985)
Danza, Tony
Fletcher, Jack
Kay, Beatrice (d. 1986)
Louvin, Ira (d. 1965)
May, Elaine
Mayer, Christopher
Quinn, Anthony
Apr 22: Albert, Eddie
Allen, Byron
Bottoms, Joseph
Byrd, Ralph (d. 1952)
Campbell, Alan
Campbell, Glen
Dudley, Dick
Hendler, Lauri
March, Hal (d. 1970)
Rae, Charlotte
Stein, Lou

Apr 23: Andrews, Tina
Bertinelli, Valerie
Birney, David
Blair, Janet
DeWitt, Joyce
Frischman, Dan
Hillaire, Marcel
Hubbard, John
Johnston, Lionel
Oppenheimer, Alan
Renaldo, Duncan (d. 1980)
Temple, Shirley
Villechaize, Herve
Apr 24: Barbour, John
Cannon, J.D.
Erskine, Marilyn
Ireland, Jill
Leonard, Jack E. (d. 1973)
MacLaine, Shirley
Vargas, John
Apr 25: Brundin, Bo
Conway, Russ
Hamilton, Lynn
Lemon, Meadowlark
Mack, Dotty
Miller, Denny (Scott)
Murrow, Edward R. (d. 1965)
Shire, Talia
Trueman, Paula
Apr 26: Bass, Tod
Burnett, Carol
Kellin, Mike (d. 1983)
McLarty, Ron
Nype, Russell
Repp, Stafford (d. 1974)
Rydell, Bobby
Sothern, Harry (d. 1957)
Williams, Guinn (d. 1962)
Apr 27: Donner, Robert
Gordon, Colin (d. 1972)
Gower, Andre
Klugman, Jack
Regan, Ellen
Sheehan, Douglas
Stone, Kirby
Apr 28: Cornthwaite, Robert
Dunninger, Joseph (d. 1975)
Jones, Carolyn (d. 1983)
Mara, Adele
Sarafian, Richard C.
Sinclair, Madge

Strassman, Marcia
Zippi, Daniel
Apr 29: Carlson, Richard (d. 1977)
Dunn, Nora
Ewell, Tom
Guzaldo, Joseph
Holm, Celeste
Kline, Richard
Lynch, Richard
Morgan, Russ (d. 1969)
Mulgrew, Kate
Parker, Frank
Pfeiffer, Michelle
Roberts, Ewan
Smith, Lane
Weinrib, Len
Apr 30: Arden, Eve
Bray, Thom
King, Perry
Leachman, Cloris
Osmond, Merrill

May 1: Barlow, Howard (d. 1972)
Barr, Douglas
Beradino, John
Diehl, John
Fleming, Art
Ford, Glenn
Hackett, Joan (d. 1983)
Macht, Stephen
Nye, Louis
O'Herlihy, Dan
Paar, Jack
Robinson, Max
Smith, Kate (d. 1986)
Spelman, Sharon
Stewart, Byron
May 2: Alexander, Van
Bakewell, William
Browne, Roscoe Lee
Music, Lorenzo
Pflug, Jo Ann
Redeker, Quinn
Robinson, Roger
Tochi, Brian
Wyenn, Than
May 3: Bal, Jeanne
Carver, Mary
Crosby, Bing (d. 1977)
Humperdinck, Engelbert
La Rue, Jack (d. 1984)

Miller, Mark Thomas
Slezak, Walter (d. 1983)
Wilson, Earl (d. 1987)
May 4: Adler, Luther (d. 1984)
Barbutti, Pete
Brown, Lou
Da Silva, Howard (d. 1986)
Garrett, Patsy
Hicks, Hilly
Jackson, Jackie
McDonough, Mary Elizabeth
May 5: Carroll, Pat
Culea, Melinda
Davies, John Rhys
Davis, Ann B.
Eilbacher, Lisa
Gordon, Phil
Gosden, Freeman (d. 1982)
Hutchins, Will
Murphy, Michael
Ragin, John S.
Schaal, Richard
Yothers, Tina
May 6: Cox, Richard
Eyer, Richard
Granger, Stewart
Hill, Dana
King, Tony
O'Brien, Clay
Piazza, Marguerite
Quinn, Bill
Welles, Orson (d. 1985)
May 7: Baxter, Anne (d. 1985)
Bisoglio, Val
Brewer, Teresa
Danoff, Bill (Starland Vocal Band)
Hegyes, Robert
Jackson, Selmer (d. 1971)
Lowe, Jim
MacDonald, Ed (d. 1951)
McGavin, Darren
Robbins, Gale (d. 1980)
St. John, Marco
May 8: Blankfield, Mark
Furst, Stephen
Gilbert, Melissa
Jens, Salome
Keith, David
Nelson, Rick (d. 1985)
Pinza, Ezio (d. 1957)

Rickles, Don
Sheen, Bishop Fulton J.
  (d. 1979)
Smith, Reid
Tennille, Toni
Wincott, Jeff
May 9: Hall, Kevin Peter
Michaels, Jeanna
Mills, Alley
Russell, Connie
Simeone, Harry
Snow, Hank
Wallace, Mike
May 10: Astaire, Fred
Blacque, Taurean
Carter, Mother Maybelle
  (d. 1978)
Jenkins, Larry Flash
McGraw, Charles (d. 1980)
Owens, Gary
Pisier, Marie-France
Walker, Nancy
May 11: Brooks, Foster
Camarata, Tutti
Gaines, Boyd
Igus, Darrow
McClure, Doug
McGovern, Terry
Pyle, Denver
Silvers, Phil (d. 1985)
Taylor, Kent (d. 1987)
Weaver, Doodles (d. 1983)
May 12: Boxleitner, Bruce
Carlin, George
Carlson, Linda
Fields, Kim
Hyde-White, Wilfred
Jenkins, Gordon (d. 1984)
Marcellino, Jocko (Sha Na
  Na)
Perkins, Millie
Raggio, Lisa
Smith, Howard K.
Snyder, Tom
Stout, Paul
May 13: Ajaye, Franklyn
Arthur, Beatrice
Broekman, David (d. 1958)
Campos, Rafael (d. 1985)
Cellini, Karen
Craig, Helen (d. 1986)

Crawford, Bobby, Jr.
Lampert, Zohra
Middleton, Robert (d. 1977)
Taylor, Buck
Winston, Leslie
May 14: Darin, Bobby (d. 1973)
Flavin, James (d. 1976)
Foster, Meg
Hubley, Season
Lehr, Lew (d. 1950)
Morecambe, Eric (d. 1984)
Munsel, Patrice
Olkewicz, Walter
Ryan, Natasha
May 15: Arnold, Eddy
Cotten, Joseph
D'Andrea, Tom
Fadiman, Clifton
Heslov, Grant
Horsley, Lee
Hutton, Gunilla
Kazan, Lainie
Mason, James (d. 1984)
Pope, Peggy
Porter, Todd
Rudd, Paul
Thiess, Ursula
Williams, Bill
Wiseman, Joseph
May 16: Brosnan, Pierce
Dodson, Jack
Fonda, Henry (d. 1982)
Gaynes, George
Gold, Tracey
Jackson, Janet
Liberace (d. 1987)
Peterson, Virgilia
Turkel, Studs
May 17: Backes, Alice
McMahon, Horace (d. 1971)
Van Horne, Harriet
May 18: Azzara, Candy
Como, Perry
Hickman, Dwayne
Macy, Bill
Morse, Robert
Pointer, Priscilla
Roberts, Pernell
Stephens, James
Strickland, Gail
Sullivan, Liam

Whitaker, Jack
Willson, Meredith (d. 1984)
May 19: Hartman, David
Lenihan, Deirdre
McLean, David
Waldrip, Tim
May 20: Burrell, Maryedith
Butler, Dean
Cher
Cohn, Mindy
Gobel, George
Hedison, David
McEachin, James
Pinchot, Bronson
Stewart, James
Thomas, Dave
Wedemeyer, Herman
May 21: Burr, Raymond
Cass, Peggy
Day, Dennis
Greene, Lynnie
Groh, David
Hatch, Richard
Heidt, Horace (d. 1986)
Jason, Rick
Libertini, Richard
Montgomery, Robert (d. 1981)
Potter, Carol
Sanford, Ralph (d. 1963)
Savage, Booth
T, Mr.
Zee, John
May 22: Benjamin, Richard
Constantine, Michael
Converse, Frank
Corley, Al
Heyes, Douglas, Jr.
Parkins, Barbara
Strasberg, Susan
Winfield, Paul
May 23: Adair, Deborah
Barrie, Barbara
Carson, Jeannie
Chapin, Lauren
Clooney, Rosemary
Collins, Joan
Crothers, Scatman (d. 1986)
Davenport, Nigel
Garrett, Betty
Goring, Marius
McCutcheon, Bill

McHugh, Frank (d. 1981)
Melton, Sid
Michelman, Ken
O'Connell, Helen
Payne, John
Roman, Joseph
May 24: Burghoff, Gary
Kahan, Judy
Maxwell, Elsa (d. 1963)
Presley, Priscilla
Ray, Gene Anthony
May 25: Akins, Claude
Bowen, Roger
Carter, Dixie
Carver, Randall
Cerf, Bennett (d. 1971)
Greenbush, Lindsay
Greenbush, Sidney
Hall, Tom T.
Harsch, Joseph C.
Kallen, Kitty
Nelson, Lindsey
Oz, Frank
Sellecca, Connie
Uggams, Leslie
Valentine, Karen
May 26: Alexander, Ben (d. 1979)
Arness, James
Dotrice, Roy
Duncan, Archie (d. 1979)
Francis, Genie
Gregory, Benji
Lee, Peggy
Stock, Barbara
Thomas, Philip Michael
Van Eman, Charles
Winninger, Charles (d. 1969)
May 27: Best, Willie (d. 1962)
Bridges, Todd
Carmichael, Ralph
Fong, Kam
Foster, Susan
Gossett, Louis, Jr.
Meriwether, Lee
Price, Kenny
Price, Vincent
Silvers, Cathy
Stewart, Redd
Weitz, Bruce
May 28: Ayres, Leah
Cruz, Brandon

Howland, Beth
Karlen, John
Knight, Gladys
McKay, Scott (d. 1987)
Reed, Marshall (d. 1980)

May 29: Adrian, Iris
Berger, Helmut
Bresler, Jerry
Helberg, Sandy
Hope, Bob
Jackson, Rebie (Maureen)
James, Clifton
McQuade, Arlene
Shriner, Herb (d. 1970)
Whelchel, Lisa
Young, Donna, Jean

May 30: Ackroyd, David
Blanc, Mel
Carter, Ralph
Fowley, Douglas
Goodman, Benny (d. 1986)
Lydon, Jimmy
McGinley, Ted
Noel, Dick
Pollard, Michael J.
Sherwood, Bobby (d. 1981)
Walker, Clint

May 31: Allen, Fred (d. 1956)
Ameche, Don
Antonini, Alfredo (d. 1983)
Eastwood, Clint
Gless, Sharon
Harrison, Gregory
Hutton, Jim (d. 1979)
Kampmann, Steven
Namath, Joe
Pepper, Barbara (d. 1969)
Vivyan, John (d. 1983)

Jun 1: Auberjonois, Rene
Boone, Pat
Canova, Diana
Caulfield, Joan
Erdman, Richard
Fairchild, Edgar "Cookie"
(d. 1975)
Griffith, Andy
Hartman, Lisa
Little, Cleavon
Monkhouse, Bob
Norris, Kathi

Ponzini, Antony
Riddle, Nelson (d. 1985)
Woodward, Edward

Jun 2: Farber, Bert
Gleason, Joanna
Grauer, Ben (d. 1977)
Guest, William
Haid, Charles
Haysbert, Dennis
Hill, Tom
Keach, Stacy
Kellerman, Sally
Mathers, Jerry
McKenzie, Richard
Patrick, Butch
Pringle, Joan
Rozario, Bob
Ruscio, Al
Showalter, Max
Weissmuller, Johnny (d. 1984)

Jun 3: Barris, Chuck
Corby, Ellen
Curtis, Tony
Dewhurst, Colleen
Evans, Maurice
Gross, Dr. Mason (d. 1977)
Valentine, Scott

Jun 4: Barrymore, John, Jr.
Collingwood, Charles (d.1985)
Dern, Bruce
Impert, Margaret
Leslie, Nan
Merrill, Robert
Morrill, Priscilla
Stevenson, Parker
Velez, Eddie
Watkins, Carlene
Weaver, Dennis

Jun 5: Allen, Chad
Boyd, William (d. 1972)
Hayes, Bill
Jones, Stan (d. 1963)
Lansing, Robert
Moyers, Bill
Platt, Howard
Reid, Don (Statler Brothers)
Stafford, Nancy

Jun 6: Abel, Walter (d. 1987)
Carvey, Dana
Crane, Richard (d. 1969)
Dukes, David

Englund, Robert
Gart, John
Jones, Marilyn
Paul, Richard
Utman, Bryan
Jun 7: Gray, Dolores
Jeffries, Lang (d. 1987)
Jones, Tom
Kellems, Vivien (d. 1975)
Marcantel, Christopher
Scarbury, Joey
Tandy, Jessica
Williams, Dick
Jun 8: Allman, Sheldon
Casey, Bernie
Clinger, Debra
Darren, James
Healey, Myron
Hirschfield, Robert
Kirby, George
Martin, Millicent
Maxted, Ellen
Preston, Robert (d. 1987)
Rivers, Joan
Smith, Alexis
Stiller, Jerry
Wynter, Dana
Jun 9: Bazlen, Brigid
Cummings, Robert
Fox, Michael J.
Orkin, Dick
Santos, Joe
Waring, Fred (d. 1984)
Jun 10: Bailey, F. Lee
Friedman, David
Garland, Judy (d. 1969)
Gill, Rusty
Heller, Randee
McKay, Gardner
McKeon, Doug
Rekert, Winston
Stevens, Andrew
Van Patten, Timothy
Walberg, Garry
Jun 11: Barbeau, Adrienne
Bergman, Peter
Bromfield, John
Brown, Johnny
Charmoli, Tony
Cousteau, Capt. Jacques-Yves
Everett, Chad

Hodges, Russ
Kiger, Robby
Mohr, Gerald (d. 1968)
Scott, Hazel (d. 1981)
Strunk, Jud (d. 1981)
Swan, Michael
Jun 12: Baker, David Lain
Bleyer, Archie
Busfield, Timothy
Damone, Vic
Foster, Linda
Gallo, Lew
Hamilton, Bernie
Harrison, Jenilee
Hayden, Russell "Lucky"
    (d. 1981)
Holden, Rebecca
Jones, Peter
Link, Michael
Lundigan, William (d. 1975)
Nabors, Jim
Jun 13: Edwards, Ralph
Hallick, Tom
Hunter, Ian (d. 1975)
Johnson, Ben
Lynde, Paul (d. 1982)
Mears, Deann
Rathbone, Basil (d. 1967)
Rodrigues, Percy
Thomas, Richard
Wickes, Mary
Jun 14: Bannon, Jack
Barry, Gene
Coleman, Cy
Davidson, Ben
Edwards, Cliff "Ukulele Ike"
    (d. 1971)
Gibbs, Marla
Hunter, Ronald
Ives, Burl
La Rue, Lash
Lankford, Kim
McGuire, Dorothy
Mekka, Eddie
Stewart, Trish
Trotter, John Scott (d. 1975)
Wanamaker, Sam
Jun 15: Belushi, Jim
Cox, Courteney
Hunt, Helen
Jennings, Waylon

	Kincaid, Aron		Marchand, Nancy
	Rose, David		Marshall, Sean
	Varney, Jim		Natwick, Mildred
Jun 16:	Albertson, Jack (d. 1981)		Rowlands, Gena
	Dizon, Jesse		Voskovec, George (d. 1981)
	Finn, Mickie		Warfield, Marlene
	Lane, Nancy	Jun 20:	Aiello, Danny
	Massey, Ilona (d. 1974)		Atkins, Chet
	Van Ark, Joan		Gordon, Bruce
Jun 17:	Bellamy, Ralph		Halsey, Brett

Kincaid, Aron
Rose, David
Varney, Jim
Jun 16: Albertson, Jack (d. 1981)
Dizon, Jesse
Finn, Mickie
Lane, Nancy
Massey, Ilona (d. 1974)
Van Ark, Joan
Jun 17: Bellamy, Ralph
Cotler, Kami
Fielding, Jerry (d. 1980)
Foley, Red (d. 1968)
Fox, Sonny
Koehler, Frederick
Larsen, Keith
Linn-Baker, Mark
Lucking, William
Martin, Dean
Piscopo, Joe
Rafferty, Bill
Stringbean (David Akeman)
   (d. 1973)
Jun 18: Benben, Brian
Boone, Richard (d. 1981)
Brandt, Mel
Carroll, Bob
Collyer, Bud (d. 1969)
Dale, Jimmy
Ebert, Roger
Flynn, Miriam
Foran, Dick (d. 1979)
Kane, Carol
Kyser, Kay (d. 1985)
Long, Avon (d. 1984)
Luke, Keye
Marshall, E.G.
McCashin, Constance
McKinley, Ray
Payne, Benny
Rainey, Dr. Froelich
Reilly, Tom
Styles, Susan
Jun 19: Ayers-Allen, Phylicia
Coleman, Emil (d. 1965)
Gabel, Martin (d. 1986)
Hobson, Laura (d. 1986)
Jerome, Jerry
Jourdan, Louis
Lauter, Harry
Lombardo, Guy (d. 1977)

Marchand, Nancy
Marshall, Sean
Natwick, Mildred
Rowlands, Gena
Voskovec, George (d. 1981)
Warfield, Marlene
Jun 20: Aiello, Danny
Atkins, Chet
Gordon, Bruce
Halsey, Brett
Howard, Bob
Kreppel, Paul
Landau, Martin
McCook, John
Murphy, Audie (d. 1971)
Riley, Larry
Wagner, Chuck
Jun 21: Baxter-Birney, Meredith
Compton, John
Copage, Marc
Douglass, Robyn
Ely, Ron
Flaherty, Joe
Gross, Michael
Hartley, Mariette
Kent, Jean
Kopell, Bernie
Markham, Monte
McCloskey, Leigh
Scott, Frank
Stapleton, Maureen
Jun 22: Bradley, Ed
Burns, David (d. 1971)
Champion, Gower (d. 1980)
Costa, Cosie
Cross, Murphy
Eastham, Richard
Frees, Paul (d. 1986)
Lander, David L.
Osmond, Alan
Prinze, Freddie (d. 1977)
Richwine, Maria
Rubin, Andrew
Streep, Meryl
Wagner, Lindsay
Waite, Ralph
Whiting, Jack (d. 1961)
Jun 23: Carter, June
Coon, Dr. Carleton (d. 1981)
Fosse, Bob
King, Dave

Metzler, Jim
Shackelford, Ted
Trask, Diana
Jun 24: Brown, Georg Stanford
Carter, Jack
Lee, Michele
Molinaro, Al
Spencer, Danielle
Jun 25: Abbott, George
Bayer, Gary
Crosby, Gary
George, Phyllis
Hayes, Peter Lind
Holliday, Kene
Lembeck, Michael
Lockhart, June
Mayer, Ken (d. 1985)
Montgomery, Barbara
Sykes, Brenda
Talent, Ziggy
Walker, Jimmie
Wilkof, Lee
Withers, Mark
Jun 26: Bellwood, Pamela
Davis, Billy, Jr.
Dreier, Alex
Francis, Clive
Maltby, Richard
Parker, Eleanor
Rafferty, Frances
Wirges, Bill (d. 1971)
Jun 27: Christie, Audrey
Cossart, Valerie
Duffy, Julia
McIntire, John
Jun 28: Barber, Ava
Brisebois, Danielle
Bunce, Alan (d. 1965)
Radner, Gilda
Stuart, Maxine
Wilson, Lois (d. 1983)
Jun 29: Busey, Gary
Davis, Joan (d. 1961)
Fujioka, John
Grandy, Fred
Hardin, Melora
Inescort, Frieda (d. 1976)
Kubelik, Rafael
Pickens, Slim (d. 1983)
Smith, Samantha
   (d. 1985)

Warrick, Ruth
Williams, Cara
Jun 30: Chandler, George
   (d. 1985)
Dussault, Nancy
Foster, Stuart (d. 1968)
Funk, Terry
Musante, Tony
Pelletier, Wilfred (d. 1982)
Rich, Buddy (d. 1987)
Valli, June
Vernon, Harvey
Wismer, Harry (d. 1967)

Jul 1: Anderson, Daryl
Aykroyd, Dan
Black, Karen
Caron, Leslie
De Havilland, Olivia
Evans, Madge (d. 1981)
Eve, Trevor
Farr, Jamie
Hemphill, Shirley
Marsh, Jean
Patterson, Lorna
Rey, Alvino
Stanley, Florence
Stern, Bill (d. 1971)
Whinnery, Barbara
Jul 2: Bradford, Johnny
Curtis, Ken
David, Larry
Holliday, Polly
Ito, Robert
Ladd, Cheryl
McMillan, Kenneth
McNichol, Jimmy
Rainwater, Marvin
Rowan, Dan
Schaal, Wendy
Silver, Ron
Slavin, Millie
Jul 3: Allbritton, Louise (d. 1979)
Brown, John Mason
Buckley, Betty
Fong, Brian
Fountain, Pete
Houlihan, Keri
Kilgallen, Dorothy (d. 1965)
Sanders, George (d. 1972)
Smith, Kurtwood

Smithers, Jan
Tarses, Jay
Jul 4: Bernard, Ed
Davis, Buster
Graham, Virginia
Lee, Johnny (d. 1965)
Lollobrigida, Gina
Miller, Mitch
Murphy, George
Rivera, Geraldo
Rogers, Timmie
Saint, Eva Marie
Templeton, Alec (d. 1963)
Jul 5: Goddard, Don
Helmond, Katherine
Oates, Warren (d. 1982)
Stone, Milburn (d. 1980)
Tyler, Beverly
Wells, Claudia
Jul 6: Beasley, Allyce
Beatty, Ned
Cabot, Sebastian (d. 1977)
Dryer, Fred
Goodeve, Grant
Griffin, Merv
Hack, Shelley
Kirsten, Dorothy
McKayle, Don
Mitchell, Gwenn
Reese, Della
Scarpelli, Glenn
Schallert, William
Ward, Burt
Wiggin, Tom
Jul 7: Britt, Elton (d. 1972)
Brock, Stanley
Eilbacher, Cindy
Harris, Arlene
Louvin, Charlie
Malvin, Artie
Mayehoff, Eddie
Moore, Charlotte
Ryan, Roz
Severinsen, Doc
Spano, Joe
Jul 8: Darby, Kim
Emerson, Faye (d. 1983)
Feldman, Marty (d. 1982)
Henry, Carol
Langan, Glenn
Lawrence, Steve

Rodd, Marcia
Ruick, Melville (d. 1972)
Segal, Jonathan
Stevens, Craig
Tambor, Jeffrey
Jul 9: Ames, Ed
Bregman, Buddy
Burns, Ronnie
Dale, Alan
Dennehy, Brian
Edwards, Vince
Grimes, Scott
Hairston, Jester
Hampton, James
Hanks, Tom
Kaltenborn, H.V. (d. 1965)
Roundtree, Richard
Simpson, O.J.
Smits, Jimmy
Steele, Ted
Jul 10: Adams, Nick (d. 1968)
Allen, Dennis
Anderson, Sheila
Brinkley, David
Donnell, Jeff
Glass, Ron
Gwynne, Fred
Hamner, Earl, Jr.
Herbert, Don
Kerr, Jean
Pine, Robert
Pressman, Lawrence
Shera, Mark
Smithers, William
Stewart, Sandy
Watson, Mills
Woods, Michael
Jul 11: Brynner, Yul (d. 1985)
Bryson, Dr. Lyman
Evans, Gene
Gold, Brandy
Hervey, Irene
Hunter, Tab
Johnson, Jay
Jordan, Bobbi
Mitchell, Thomas
    (d. 1962)
Somers, Brett
Todd, Beverly
Von Zell, Harry (d. 1981)
Ward, Sela

Jul 12:	Andes, Keith		Grant, Faye
	Baker, Jim B.		Hughes, Barnard
	Berle, Milton		Hylton, Jane (d. 1979)
	Bryson, Lyman (d. 1959)		Merrill, Buddy
	Cosby, Bill		Myerson, Bess
	Faye, Joey		Pine, Phillip
	Foster, Buddy		Stanwyck, Barbara
	Gordon, Gerald	Jul 17:	Arnaz, Lucie
	Pelikan, Lisa		Barnes, George
	Thomas, Jay		Bellamy, Ralph
Jul 13:	Bond, Sudie (d. 1984)		Benson, Lucille (d. 1984)
	Conn, Didi		Carroll, Diahann
	Crane, Bob (d. 1978)		Carter, Thomas
	Forster, Robert		Dalio, Marcel (d. 1983)
	Garroway, Dave (d. 1982)		Davis, Phyllis
	Mandrell, Louise		Diller, Phyllis
	Sosnik, Harry		Gargan, William (d. 1979)
	Vance, Danitra		Hasselhoff, David
Jul 14:	Bergen, Polly		Hayman, Lillian
	Chancellor, John		Linkletter, Art
	Edwards, Douglas		McCormick, Pat
	Gold, Missy		Miller, Denise
	Grier, Roosevelt		Monroe, Bill
	Haley, Jackie Earle		Snow, Phoebe
	Houser, Jerry	Jul 18:	Allen, Jonelle
	Lambert, Gloria		Brolin, James
	Laneuville, Eric		Cronyn, Hume
	Murray, Ken		Frazee, Jane (d. 1985)
	Olaf, Pierre		Holliday, Art
	Olson, Nancy		Landers, Audrey
	Robertson, Dale		Leach, Britt
	Shaw, Stan		Miller, Marvin (d. 1985)
	Stephens, Robert		Nelson, Harriet
	Stone, Steve		Roberts, Howard
	Tobias, George (d. 1980)		Ruymen, Ayn
	Williams, Spencer (d. 1969)		Sherman, Bobby
Jul 15:	Aames, Willie		Skelton, Red
	Carey, Philip		Sweet, Dolph (d. 1985)
	Karras, Alex		Wills, Chill (d. 1978)
	Kercheval, Ken	Jul 19:	Archer, Beverly
	Kramer, Jeffrey		Barton, Peter
	Seales, Franklyn		Carr, Vikki
	St. John, Kristoff		Cole, Dennis
	Vincent, Jan-Michael		Edwards, Anthony
	Vye, Murvyn (d. 1976)		Gallagher, Helen
	Wayne, Patrick		Hingle, Pat
	Zapata, Carmen		Jordan, Richard
Jul 16:	Barr, Ray		Medina, Patricia
	Bishop, William (d. 1959)		Treas, Terri
	Carson, Mindy	Jul 20:	Albright, Lola
	Feldman, Corey		Bennett, Elizabeth

	Dixon, Donna		McGuire, Maeve
	Felton, Verna (d. 1966)		Navin, John P., Jr.
	Rigg, Diana		Richards, Michael
	Wood, Natalie (d. 1981)		Silvera, Frank (d. 1970)
Jul 21:	Burton, Wendell	Jul 25:	Brennan, Walter (d. 1974)
	Downing, David		Dumke, Ralph (d. 1964)
	Eisenmann, Ike		Getty, Estelle
	Elliott, Patricia		Gilford, Jack
	Guest, Lance		Margolin, Janet
	Herrmann, Edward		Paris, Jerry (d. 1986)
	Hindle, Art		Swofford, Ken
	Joslyn, Allyn (d. 1981)		Terzieff, Laurent
	Knotts, Don	Jul 26:	Allen, Gracie (d. 1964)
	Lovitz, Jon		Bellson, Louis
	Swift, Susan		Best, James
	Taylor, Billy		Colbert, Robert
	Williams, Robin		Harrison, Linda
Jul 22:	Bean, Orson		Lord, Marjorie
	Brooks, Albert		Martin, Kiel
	Cassey, Chuck		Vance, Vivian (d. 1979)
	Henderson, Marcia		Voorhees, Donald
	Koock, Guich		Walker, Danton
	Laborteaux, Patrick	Jul 27:	Durocher, Leo
	Robin, Diane		Eilber, Janet
	Ross, Stan		Galloway, Don
	Trebek, Alex		Gentry, Bobbie
	Whiting, Margaret		Gilford, Gwynne
Jul 23:	Browne, Coral		Gilliam, Stu
	Convy, Bert		Jones, Simon
	Cornell, Lydia		Lowry, Judith (d. 1976)
	Cox, Ronny		Pleshette, John
	DeForest, Calvert		Thomas, Betty
	DeHaven, Gloria		Van Dyke, Jerry
	Drysdale, Don		Victor, James
	Flippin, Lucy Lee		Wynn, Keenan (d. 1986)
	Freedman, Winifred	Jul 28:	Brown, Joe E. (d. 1973)
	Harrelson, Woody		Doran, Ann
	Manetti, Larry		Engel, Georgia
	Martin, Helen		Goodwin, Bill (d. 1958)
	Montgomery, Belinda		Hickman, Darryl
	Siegel, Janis (Manhattan		Kelsey, Linda
	Transfer)		Leary, Brianne
	Swenson, Karl (d. 1978)		McCain, Frances Lee
	Treacher, Arthur (d. 1975)		Struthers, Sally
Jul 24:	Brookes, Jacqueline		Vallee, Rudy (d. 1986)
	Buzzi, Ruth	Jul 29:	Arnette, Jeannetta
	Carter, Lynda		Belli, Melvin
	Eberly, Bob (d. 1981)		Blessing, Jack
	Goddard, Mark		Bochner, Lloyd
	Hays, Robert		Easterbrook, Leslie
	McAfee, Johnny		Egan, Richard

	Fuller, Robert		Pattern, Edward
	Horton, Robert		Straight, Beatrice
	Jennings, Peter		Stratton, W.K.
	McNally, Stephen		Wells, Derek
	Redman, Don (d. 1964)		Wright, Max
	Sparks, Randy (New Christy Minstrels)		Zara, Lou
	Sylvan, Paul	Aug 3:	Bennett, Tony
	Warner, David		Bloch, Ray
Jul 30:	Atherton, William		Cord, Alex
	Burke, Delta		Femia, John
	Byrnes, Edd		Hagen, Jean (d. 1977)
	Krofft, Sid		Haines, Larry
	McGuire, Chris (McGuire Sisters)		Hendren, Ron
	Mordente, Lisa		Karnilova, Maria
	Olin, Ken		Komack, James
	Piazza, Ben		Laire, Judson (d. 1979)
	Rose, Reva		Leslie, Bethel
	Taeger, Ralph		Maxwell, Marilyn (d. 1972)
	Vohs, Joan		Memmoli, George (d. 1985)
Jul 31:	Bargy, Roy (d. 1974)		North, Jay
	Blocker, Dirk		Tedrow, Irene
	Cutter, Lise	Aug 4:	Buntrock, Bobby
	Flannery, Susan		Fields, Irving
	Gowdy, Curt		Tabori, Kristoffer
	Kupcinet, Irv	Aug 5:	Anderson, Loni
	Lewis, Geoffrey		Brian, David
	Liberace, George (d. 1983)		Colby, Anita
	Murray, Don		Dancy, John
	Read, James		Diamond, Selma (d. 1985)
	Roper, Elmo (d. 1971)		DuBois, Ja'net
	Van Dyke, Barry		Huston, John
			Matheson, Don
Aug 1:	Bledsoe, Tempestt		Palance, Holly
	Clarke, Brian Patrick		Saxon, John
	DeLuise, Dom		Silverman, Jonathan
	Hill, Arthur		Taylor, Robert (d. 1969)
	Johnson, Laura	Aug 6:	Anderson, Michael, Jr.
	Jones, Henry		Augustain, Ira
	Lambert, Paul		Ball, Lucille
	Negron, Taylor		Bates, Barbara (d. 1969)
Aug 2:	Cassidy, Joanna		Bonerz, Peter
	Dunigan, Tim		Buktenica, Ray
	Goodwin, Kia		Carrillo, Leo (d. 1961)
	Harrold, Kathryn		Drier, Moosie
	Kieran, John (d. 1981)		Frye, Soleil Moon
	Kotero, Patricia "Apollonia"		Harewood, Dorian
	Merrill, Gary		Hicks, Catherine
	O'Connor, Carroll		Kelk, Jackie
	O'Toole, Peter		Kramer, Stepfanie
			Mitchum, Robert
			Parnell, Jack

Raines, Ella
Sorel, Louise
Williams, William B. (d. 1986)
Aug 7: Burke, Billie (d. 1970)
Freberg, Stan
Hollander, David
Mason, Marlyn
Rasche, David
Aug 8: Anderson, Richard
Balsley, Phil (Statler Brothers)
Boen, Earl
Calhoun, Rory
Carradine, Keith
Clark, Doran
Francine, Anne
Keen, Malcolm (d. 1970)
Most, Donny
Pierce, Webb
Richmond, Branscombe
Sidney, Sylvia
Stevens, Connie
Stordahl, Axel (d. 1963)
Talbot, Nita
Wilcox, Larry
Young, Victor (d. 1956)
Aug 9: Elliott, Sam
Farrell, Charles
Griffith, Melanie
McCormick, Robert (d. 1985)
Norton, Ken
Petersen, Pat
Shaw, Robert (d. 1978)
Steinberg, David
Williams, Dick Anthony
Aug 10: Alda, Beatrice
Arquette, Rosanna
Beery, Noah, Jr.
Corey, Jeff
Dean, Jimmy
Fisher, Eddie
Haley, Jack (d. 1979)
Hatfield, Bobby (Righteous Brothers)
Hugh-Kelly, Daniel
O'Mara, Kate
Reeves, Richard (d. 1967)
Aug 11: Charleson, Ian
Dahl, Arlene
Douglas, Mike
Jensen, Sanford

King, Kip
Kulky, Henry (d. 1965)
Nolan, Lloyd (d. 1985)
Aug 12: Derek, John
Goodman, Al (d. 1972)
Hamilton, George
Ivey, Dana
Jones, Sam J.
Kasznar, Kurt (d. 1979)
Kerr, Elizabeth
Landsburg, Valerie
Maisnik, Kathy
Owens, Buck
Reynolds, Marjorie
Smith, Howard (actor) (d. 1968)
Wagoner, Porter
Walley, Deborah
Warren, Jennifer
Wyatt, Jane
Aug 13: Bonaduce, Danny
Brand, Neville
Burton, Robert (d. 1964)
Corbett, Gretchen
Cuervo, Alma
Cummings, Quinn
Harrington, Pat, Jr.
Hitchcock, Alfred (d. 1980)
Raymond, Gene
Raz, Kavi
Rogers, Charles "Buddy"
Sheralee
Tighe, Kevin
Toomey, Regis
Aug 14: Crofts, Dash (Seals & Crofts)
Fargas, Antonio
Ghostley, Alice
Gilmour, Sandy
Greco, Buddy
Harry, Jackee
Saint James, Susan
Weaver, Earl
Aug 15: Baird, Bil (d. 1987)
Connors, Mike
Dalton, Abby
Ellerbee, Linda
Johnson, Georgiann
Lange, Jim
Mathews, Larry
Nelson, Lori
Rich, Don (d. 1974)

Rose Marie
Ryerson, Ann
Williams, Tom
Zabach, Florian
Aug 16: Clarke, Gary
Culp, Robert
Gifford, Frank
Gillette, Anita
Gorme, Eydie
Lester, Ketty
Littlefield, Lucien (d. 1960)
Newmar, Julie
O'Heaney, Caitlin
Parker, Fess
Prince, Jonathan
Standing, John
Strange, Glenn (d. 1973)
Warren, Lesley Ann
Aug 17: Allen, Chet (d. 1984)
Gibbs, Georgia
Howe, Quincy (d. 1977)
Killum, Guy
Marshall, Mort (d. 1979)
Moore, Robert (d. 1984)
Aug 18: Fisher, Gail
Jensen, Karen
Jones, Christopher
Light, Enoch (d. 1978)
Mowbray, Alan (d. 1969)
Mull, Martin
O'Keefe, Walter (d. 1983)
Swayze, Patrick
Van Gyseghem, Andre
Warner, Malcolm Jamal
Williams, Grant (d. 1985)
Aug 19: Arkin, Adam
Collyer, June (d. 1968)
Dauphin, Claude (d. 1978)
Goodwin, Michael
Hinton, Darby
Marshall, William
McRaney, Gerald
Muldaur, Diana
Nash, Ogden (d. 1971)
Oakes, Randi
St. John, Jill
Stamos, John
Wilson, Marie (d. 1972)
Aug 20: Acovone, Jay
Alda, Elizabeth
Booth, Shirley

Chung, Connie
Horton, Peter
Manz, Linda
Melville, Sam
Quan, Ke Huy
Reed, Alan (d. 1977)
Susann, Jacqueline (d. 1974)
Tubb, Justin
Aug 21: Cattrall, Kim
Hadley, Nancy
Henry, Bill
McCormack, Patty
Nathan, Steve
Reid, Harold (Statler Brothers)
Rock, Blossom (d. 1978)
Rogers, Kenny
Schenkel, Chris
Weston, Jack
Williams, Clarence, III
Aug 22: Atwater, Edith (d. 1986)
Dean, Morton
Flanigan, Bob (Four Freshmen)
Harper, Valerie
Lennon, Kathy (Lennon Sisters)
Lupton, John
McDonald, Francis (d. 1968)
Richardson, James G. (d. 1983)
Williams, Cindy
Aug 23: Allen, Rex, Jr.
Bill, Tony
Crosby, Bob
Davis, Michael
Diamond, Bobby
Eden, Barbara
Holmes, Jennifer
Hudson, Mark
Kelly, Gene
Long, Shelley
Majors, Lee
Phoenix, River
Russell, Mark (satirist)
Sanders, Richard
Aug 24: Baker, Phil (d. 1963)
Foster, Preston (d. 1970)
Guttenberg, Steve
Hanks, Steve
James, Dennis

Keep, Stephen
Kirby, Durward
Regalbuto, Joe
White, Carole Ita
Williams, Mason
Aug 25: Archer, Anne
Brull, Pamela
Canary, David
DeFore, Don
Ferrer, Mel
Greene, Richard (d. 1985)
Hall, Monty
Jarvis, Graham
Johnson, Van
Rennie, Michael (d. 1971)
Savage, John
Skerritt, Tom
Underwood, Blair
Velez, Martha
Aug 26: Clayton, Jan (d. 1983)
Cullen, Brett
Davis, Jim (d. 1981)
Graham, Ronny
Kantor, Richard
York, Francine
Aug 27: Bailey, G.W.
Dragon, Daryl
Fleischer, Charles
Leahy, Frank (d. 1973)
Meredith, Charles (d. 1964)
O'Neal, Frederick
Page, Harrison
Raye, Martha
Weld, Tuesday
Aug 28: Boyer, Charles (d. 1978)
Gazzara, Ben
Kulp, Nancy
O'Connor, Donald
Osmond, Wayne
Osser, Glenn
Roker, Roxie
Ryan, Peggy
Samms, Emma
Shroyer, Sonny
Soul, David
Stern, Daniel
Aug 29: Geer, Ellen
Gould, Elliott
Gray, Charles
Jackson, Michael
Macready, George (d. 1973)

Montgomery, George
O'Neill, Dick
Sanford, Isabel
Sullivan, Barry
Tuttle, Lurene (d. 1986)
Van Valkenburgh, Deborah
Aug 30: Bishop, Julie
Blondell, Joan (d. 1979)
Bottoms, Timothy
Bryant, Willie (d. 1964)
Ciannelli, Eduardo (d. 1969)
Daily, Bill
Delaney, Steve
Gunther, John (d. 1970)
Jones, Ben
MacMurray, Fred
Mann, Johnny
Massey, Raymond (d. 1983)
Peters, Deedy
Schilling, William G.
Vallely, James
Aug 31: Basehart, Richard (d. 1984)
Berlinger, Warren
Coburn, James
Dennison, Rachel
Godfrey, Arthur (d. 1983)
Hackett, Buddy
Little, Tiny, Jr.
Wells, Carole
Willingham, Noble

Sep 1: DeCarlo, Yvonne
Gorman, Mari
Hawkins, Jack (d. 1973)
Maharis, George
O'Neal, Ron
Santana, Arnaldo
Tomlin, Lily
Sep 2: Amory, Cleveland
Avalos, Luis
Champion, Marge
Chastain, Don
DeSoto, Rosana
Gray, Michael
Harmon, Mark
McCann, Chuck
Purl, Linda
Sanders, Beverly
Santon, Penny
Stevens, Ronnie
Vague, Vera (d. 1974)

Sep 3:	Brennan, Eileen		Feinstein, Alan
	Butrick, Merritt		Michel, Franny
	Canfield, Mary Grace		Morrow, Byron
	Carlisle, Kitty		Muir, Gavin (d. 1972)
	Eiseley, Dr. Loren (d. 1977)		Smith, Queenie (d. 1978)
	Perrine, Valerie		Thomas, Heather
	Richards, Lou		Tyler, Willie
	Tyler, Richard	Sep 9:	Cartwright, Angela
	Wagner, Helen		Desiderio, Robert
	Wilson, Terry		Hamilton, Neil (d. 1984)
Sep 4:	Castellano, Richard		Keaton, Michael
	Frey, Leonard		Ramus, Nick
	Harvey, Paul		Robertson, Cliff
	Jacobs, Lawrence-Hilton		Stumpf, Randy
	Knight, Merald		Tomlin, Pinky
	Morris, Howard		Topol
	Ponce, Danny		Wopat, Tom
	Salt, Jennifer	Sep 10:	Burkley, Dennis
	Thomas, Dick		Feliciano, Jose
	Wilson, Gerald		Irving, Amy
	York, Dick		Kuralt, Charles
Sep 5:	Cronkite, Kathy		Mullavey, Greg
	Devane, William		O'Brien, Edmond (d. 1985)
	Gear, Luella (d. 1980)		Palmer, John
	Lawrence, Carol		Pasternak, Michael
	Moses, Rick		Scott, Raymond
	Newhart, Bob		St. John, Al "Fuzzy" (d. 1963)
Sep 6:	Beatty, Morgan (d. 1975)	Sep 11:	Badel, Alan (d. 1982)
	Cannon, Katherine		Damon, Cathryn
	Curtin, Jane		Dierkop, Charles
	Kruger, Otto (d. 1974)		Falana, Lola
	Kurtz, Swoosie		Fascinato, Jack
	Lavalle, Paul		Holliman, Earl
	McCrea, Jody		McNichol, Kristy
	Roker, Rennie		Payne, Julie
	Young, Keone		Seymour, Anne
Sep 7:	Bernsen, Corbin	Sep 12:	Blue, Ben (d. 1975)
	Blakely, Susan		Daniels, Billy
	Chapman, Margot (Starland Vocal Band)		Gray, Linda
			Holm, Ian
	Karns, Roscoe (d. 1970)		Mahler, Bruce
	Kavner, Julie		McCracken, Jeff
	Lawford, Peter (d. 1984)		McGee, Frank (d. 1974)
	McKenna, T.P.		Scolari, Peter
	Messick, Don	Sep 13:	Alden, Norman
	Milford, John		Bain, Barbara
	Quayle, Anthony		Brady, Scott (d. 1985)
Sep 8:	Askin, Leon		Carter, Nell
	Brooke, Hillary		Charles, Ray
	Caesar, Sid		Dusenberry, Ann
	Darcel, Denise		Engle, Roy (d. 1980)

Estabrook, Christine
Fulton, Eileen
Kiel, Richard
Kusatsu, Clyde
Mathews, Carole
McDevitt, Ruth (d. 1976)
Shaw, Reta (d. 1982)
Smart, Jean
Torme, Mel
Sep 14: Bauman, Jon "Bowser"
Crosby, Mary
Green, Bernie (d. 1975)
Heatherton, Joey
Koenig, Walter
Medford, Kay (d. 1980)
Moore, Clayton
Palmer, Bud
Penny, Joe
Sharma, Barbara
Somack, Jack (d. 1983)
Sep 15: Acuff, Roy
Bailey, Jack (d. 1980)
Compton, Forrest
Conte, John
Conway, Tom (d. 1967)
Cooper, Jackie
Crosby, Norm
Darrow, Henry
Murray, Kathryn
Olsen, Merlin
Schneider, Tawny
Singleton, Penny
Sperber, Wendie Jo
Tacker, Francine
Wray, Fay
Sep 16: Begley, Ed, Jr.
Chakiris, George
Falk, Peter
Fields, Charlie
Francis, Anne
Funt, Allen
Kelly, Jack
King, B.B.
Kurtzman, Katy
McCall, Shalane
Miller, Linda G.
Paige, Janis
Russell, Andy
Shockley, Sallie
Stone, Paddy
Walter, Cy (d. 1968)

Sep 17: Benedict, Paul
Bennett, Peter
Crowley, Patricia
Huddleston, David
Loudon, Dorothy
McDowall, Roddy
Ritter, John
Sep 18: Anderson, Eddie "Roches-
ter" (d. 1977)
Avalon, Frankie
Blake, Robert
Brazzi, Rossano
Brogan, Jimmy
Kirk, Phyllis
Mullaney, Jack (d. 1982)
Rodgers, Jimmie
Warden, Jack
Willard, Fred
Sep 19: Brandt, Victor
Colomby, Scott
Danton, Ray
Elliot, "Mama" Cass
(d. 1974)
Evans, Dr. Bergen (d. 1978)
Garde, Betty
Harris, Rosemary
Hooks, Kevin
Lindsay, Margaret (d. 1981)
Mantooth, Randolph
McCallum, David
McCormick, Carolyn
Medley, Bill (Righteous
Brothers)
Ramos, Rudy
Richards, Kim
Sabella, Ernie
Smith, Rex
Stewart, Mel
Truex, Ernest (d. 1973)
West, Adam
Sep 20: Banas, Bob
Brothers, Dr. Joyce
Comstock, Frank
DeVol, Frank
Maynard, Kermit
(d. 1971)
Meara, Anne
Morgan, Debbi
Roberts, Rachel (d. 1980)
Taylor, Clarice
Wilder, Yvonne

Sep 21: Addams, Dawn (d. 1985)
Balding, Rebecca
Brooks, Rand
Elder, Ann
Flagg, Fannie
Gibson, Henry
Gough, Lloyd (d. 1984)
Hagman, Larry
Kurtis, Bill
Mengatti, John
Murray, Bill
Ribeiro, Alfonso
Sep 22: Anderson, Larry
Baio, Scott
Belafonte-Harper, Shari
Holmes, LeRoy (d. 1986)
Houseman, John
Lane, Allan "Rocky" (d. 1973)
Metrano, Art
Oxenberg, Catherine
Roche, Eugene
Russell, Jack
Scott, Martha
Stone, Rob
Sep 23: Charles, Ray (R&B singer)
Jensen, Maren
Pena, Elizabeth
Petersen, Paul
Pidgeon, Walter (d. 1984)
Place, Mary Kay
Rooney, Mickey
Sep 24: Aaker, Lee
Allen, Dayton
Gates, Larry
Henson, Jim
Jeffries, Herb
Lindley, Audra
MacRae, Sheila
McKay, Jim
Merritt, Theresa
Porter, Don
Sep 25: Douglas, Michael
Ericson, John
Hamill, Mark
Kennedy, Mimi
Locklear, Heather
Madsen, Michael
Norden, Tommy
Prowse, Juliet
Rizzuto, Phil
Smith, Red (d. 1982)

Taylor, Josh
Walden, Robert
Walters, Barbara
Williams, Anson
Sep 26: Anderson, Lynn
Anderson, Melissa Sue
Britton, Barbara (d. 1980)
Cook, Donald (d. 1961)
Hamilton, Linda
Herd, Richard
Jacobs, Rachael
Jameson, Joyce (d. 1987)
Keane, James
London, Julie
McCord, Kent
Michael, Ralph
Nix, Martha
O'Neal, Patrick
Raft, George (d. 1980)
Robbins, Marty (d. 1982)
Sep 27: Brimley, Wilford
Cassidy, Shaun
Conrad, William
Edwards, Gail
Howar, Barbara
Martinez, A
McCallion, James
McCarty, Mary (d. 1980)
Meadows, Jayne
Morris, Greg
Nolan, Kathy
Russel, Del
Shearin, John
Thompson, Sada
Torres, Liz
Sep 28: Breeding, Larry (d. 1982)
Capp, Al (d. 1979)
Casados, Eloy Phil
Clower, Jerry
Higgins, Joel
Hogan, Robert
Jefferson, Herbert, Jr.
Lee, Fran
Marlowe, Christian
Robbins, Fred
Silver, Joe
Stang, Arnold
Sullivan, Ed (d. 1974)
Whipple, Sam
Windom, William
Wolders, Robert

Sep 29: Autry, Gene
Barth, Eddie
DeCorsia, Ted (d. 1973)
Forrest, Steve
Gumbel, Bryant
Harkness, Richard
Hogestyn, Drake
Kahn, Madeline
Lederer, Suzanne
Linville, Larry
McShane, Ian
Morgan, Cindy
Scott, Donovan
Shepley, Michael (d. 1961)
Snider, Barry
Whelan, Jill
Whiting, Arch
Sep 30: Allen, Deborah
Bernard, Crystal
Brewton, Maia
Corey, Jill
Dickinson, Angie
McCoo, Marilyn
Tennant, Victoria
Williams, Barry

Oct 1: Andrews, Julie
Bosley, Tom
Chapman, Lonny
Collins, Stephen
Holloway, Stanley (d. 1982)
Kostal, Irwin
Matthau, Walter
O'Brien, David
Peirce, Robert
Peppard, George
Quaid, Randy
Stevens, Stella
Untermeyer, Louis (d. 1977)
Whitmore, James
Oct 2: Abbott, Bud (d. 1974)
Brooks, Avery
Drake, Charles
Gunn, Moses
Kennedy, Betty
Marx, Groucho (d. 1977)
McAllister, Chip
O'Grady, Lani
Reed, Rex
Thompson, Wesley
Wills, Maury

Oct 3: Berg, Gertrude (d. 1966)
Butterworth, Shane
Dotson, Bob
Hensley, Pamela
Hordern, Michael
Irving, Jay (d. 1970)
Rhue, Madlyn
Oct 4: Applegate, Eddie
Davis, Clifton
Hall, Cliff (d. 1972)
Harper, David W.
Heston, Charlton
Kilpatrick, Eric
Murray, Jan
Stone, Christopher
Van Dyke, Leroy
Oct 5: Allen, Karen
Banfield, Bever-Leigh
Brown, Peter
Conaway, Jeff
Dana, Bill
Davis, Gail
Homeier, Skip
Hoyt, John
Johns, Glynis
Ludden, Allen (d. 1981)
Marvin, Tony
Pleasence, Donald
Regehr, Duncan
Rockwell, Robert
Viscuso, Sal
Oct 6: Alexander, Shana
Copeland, Alan
Cowan, Jerome (d. 1972)
Durrell, Michael
Travalena, Fred
Travolta, Ellen
Oct 7: Allyson, June
Dantine, Helmut (d. 1982)
Dell, Gabriel
Devine, Andy (d. 1977)
Fee, Melinda
Landers, Judy
Monroe, Vaughn (d. 1973)
Mulhall, Jack (d. 1979)
Muse, Clarence (d. 1979)
Norris, Christopher
Price, Paul B.
Sirola, Joseph
Stewart, Martha
Van Patten, James

Oct 8:   Barrett, Rona
          Carradine, David
          Chase, Chevy
          Dudikoff, Michael
          Purcell, Sarah
          Randell, Ron
          Schumann, Walter (d. 1958)
          Wilson, Roger
          Zimbalist, Stephanie
Oct 9:   Andrews, Edward (d. 1985)
          Boomer, Linwood
          Brown, Wally (d. 1961)
          Frank, Gary
          Hanna, Phil (d. 1957)
          Pare, Michael
          Patterson, Hank (d. 1975)
          Rounds, David (d. 1983)
          Sagal, Jean
          Sagal, Liz
          Wingreen, Jason
Oct 10:   Byrne, Bobby
          Downs, Johnny
          Elcar, Dana
          Hayes, Helen
          Holmes, Dennis
          Jaeckel, Richard
          Keen, Noah
          Kramer, Bert
          Peck, J. Eddie
          Rachins, Alan
          Vereen, Ben
Oct 11:   Adams, Catlin
          Belasco, Leon
          Cusack, Joan
          Guild, Nancy
          Landon, Leslie
          Leibman, Ron
          Morse, David
          Randolph, Bill
Oct 12:   Anton, Susan
          Cameron, Kirk
          Douglas, Ronalda
          McKrell, Jim
          McWhirter, Julie
          Rich, Adam
          Wallace, Chris
Oct 13:   Colvin, Jack
          Day, Laraine
          Dumbrille, Douglas (d. 1974)
          Freeman, Ticker (d. 1986)
          Gibbs, Terry

          Hague, Albert
          Hershfield, Harry (d. 1974)
          Jordan, William
          Kerr, Anita
          MacKay, Harper
          McMullan, Jim
          Osmond, Marie
          Russell, Nipsey
          Scott, Alan
          Tillstrom, Burr (d. 1985)
          Wilson, Demond
Oct 14:   Anderson, Harry
          Corcoran, Noreen
          Evigan, Greg
          Finley, Pat
          Hume, Benita (d. 1967)
          Kelton, Pert (d. 1968)
          King, Rori
          Leopold, Thomas
          Moore, Roger
          Webber, Robert
Oct 15:   Carpenter, Richard
          Cooper, Melville (d. 1973)
          Edmunson, William (South-
              ernaires)
          Getz, John
          Haskell, Peter
          Jackson, Tito
          Jacquet, Jeffrey
          Lavin, Linda
          Lenard, Mark
          Leroy, Philippe
          Marshall, Penny
          Miner, Jan
          Modean, Jayne
          Palmer, Jim
          Roberts, Tanya
          Romoff, Colin
          Thaler, Robert
          Trout, Robert
Oct 16:   Bell, Rex (d. 1962)
          Conrad, Michael (d. 1983)
          Corrigan, Lloyd (d. 1969)
          Lansbury, Angela
          McCarver, Tim
          Montague, Lee
          Pearce, Alice (d. 1966)
          Powell, Angela
          Somers, Suzanne
          Stevens, Morgan
          Van Hoffman, Nicholas

Washbrook, Johnny
Youngs, Jim
Oct 17: Adams, Julie
Arthur, Jean
Bottoms, Sam
Breslin, Jimmy
Byington, Spring (d. 1971)
Cole, Carol
Colonna, Jerry (d. 1986)
Garland, Beverly
Hearn, Connie Ann
Hudson, Bill (Hudson Brothers)
Hunt, Marsha
Kidder, Margot
McKean, Michael
Poston, Tom
Rollins, Howard E., Jr.
Ryan, Irene (d. 1973)
Seagren, Bob
Seals, James (Seals & Crofts)
Van Patten, Vincent
Wendt, George
Zulu
Oct 18: Boyle, Peter
Dawber, Pam
Ferguson, Allyn
Jackson, Keith
Martin, Merry
Moran, Erin
Morton, Joe
Scott, George C.
Stevens, Inger (d. 1970)
Troup, Bobby
Yung, Victor Sen (d. 1980)
Oct 19: Cates, George
Cobb, Buff
Dreyfuss, Richard
Garrison, Sean
Haynes, Lloyd (d. 1986)
Hepton, Bernard
Klous, Pat
Linker, Amy
Lo Bianco, Tony
Nader, George
Page, LaWanda
Reed, Robert
Smith, Howard (orch. leader)
Oct 20: Anderson, John
Buchwald, Art
Christopher, William

Diffring, Anton
DonHowe, Gwyda
Dumont, Margaret (d. 1965)
Francis, Arlene
Jackson, Wanda
Jones, Louis M. "Grandpa"
MacKay, Jeff
Phillips, Barney (d. 1982)
Richards, Addison (d. 1964)
Scott, Eric
West, Timothy
Williams, Brandon
Oct 21: Bronson, Lillian
Farrell, Shea
Kelly, Paula
Miller, Jeremy
Parrish, Julie
Randolph, Joyce
Oct 22: Funicello, Annette
Goldblum, Jeff
Green, Mitzi (d. 1969)
Hickox, Harry
Jacobi, Derek
Lloyd, Christopher
Martinelli, Giovanni
(d. 1969)
Miller, Sid
Roberts, Tony
Youngfellow, Barrie
Oct 23: Arliss, Dimitra
Bray, Robert (d. 1983)
Carson, Johnny
Christopher, Jordan
Dabney, Augusta
Daly, James (d. 1978)
Gray, Coleen
Kiff, Kaleena
Rorke, Hayden
Stratton, Albert
Sutton, Frank (d. 1974)
Oct 24: Austin, Karen
Crespi, Todd
Finn, Fred E.
Hart, Moss (d. 1961)
Nelson, David
Pierce, Maggie
Tomme, Ron
Whitmore, James, Jr.
Oct 25: Barty, Billy
Bissel, Whit (d. 1981)
Brauner, Asher

Danoff, Taffy (Starland Vocal
   Band)
Franciosa, Anthony
Kerwin, Brian
King, John Reed (d. 1979)
Matuszak, John
McGuire, Biff
Nelson, Tracy
Pearl, Minnie
Reddy, Helen
Regina, Paul
Ross, Marion
Smith, Shelley
Taylor, Marc L.
Trusel, Lisa
Oct 26: Belland, Bruce
Colt, Marshall
Coogan, Jackie (d. 1984)
Garrett, Hank
Sajak, Pat
Smith, Jaclyn
Oct 27: Carson, Jack (d. 1963)
Connell, Jane
Dee, Ruby
Erickson, Leif (d. 1986)
Fabray, Nanette
Kennedy, Jayne
Moore, Melba
Stearns, Mary Kay
Wass, Ted
Oct 28: Fitzsimmons, Tom
Franz, Dennis
Gertz, Jami
Goodman, Dody
Hopkins, Telma
Lanchester, Elsa (d. 1986)
Parker, Lew (d. 1972)
Potts, Annie
Tewes, Lauren
Oct 29: Brooks, Geraldine (d. 1977)
Emerson, Hope (d. 1960)
Hefti, Neal
Hughes, Robert E.
Jackson, Kate
Jackson, Randy
Kemmer, Ed
Oct 30: Bernardi, Herschel (d. 1986)
Camp, Hamilton
Campbell, William
Cesana, Renzo (d. 1970)
Flatt, Ernest

Gautier, Dick
Goldman, Danny
Hamlin, Harry
Lauter, Ed
Marta, Lynne
Mitchell, Andrea
Winkler, Henry
Oct 31: Bel Geddes, Barbara
Candy, John
Dinsdale, Shirley
Ellerbee, Bobby
Evans, Dale
Franz, Eduard (d. 1983)
Goodfriend, Lynda
Grant, Lee
Hall, Deidre
Landon, Michael
Mitchell, Brian
Pauley, Jane
Rather, Dan
Stiers, David Ogden
Waters, Ethel (d. 1977)
Nov 1: Bosson, Barbara
Foxworth, Robert
Irving, George S.
Kilpatrick, James J.
Palmer, Betsy
Richards, Jeff
Secondari, John (d. 1975)
Ticotin, Rachel
Wallace, Marcia
Nov 2: Ames, Rachel
Charles, Lewis (d. 1979)
Cooksey, Danny
Dunn, James (d. 1967)
Ford, Paul (d. 1976)
Lancaster, Burt
Powers, Stefanie
Rutherford, Ann
Stevens, Warren
Walston, Ray
Woodard, Alfre
Nov 3: Amelio, Philip J., II
Berry, Ken
Bronson, Charles
Corsaut, Aneta
Evans, Mike
Freed, Bert
Landesberg, Steve
Lulu

Michaelsen, Kari
Miller, Dennis
Murphy, Timothy Patrick
Stone, Leonard
Nov 4: Balsam, Martin
Carney, Art
Considine, Bob (d. 1975)
Cronkite, Walter
Hood, Darla (d. 1979)
Howard, Barbara
Macchio, Ralph
Mitchell, Cameron
Pitlik, Noam
Post, Markie
Reid, Kate
Roberts, Doris
Shea, Michael
Swit, Loretta
Tolbert, Berlinda
Young, Gig (d. 1978)
Nov 5: Abernethy, Robert
Davalos, Dick
Edelman, Herb
Floren, Myron
Harty, Patricia
Hexum, Jon-Erik (d. 1984)
McCrea, Joel
McGiver, John (d. 1975)
Robinson, Chris
Rogers, Roy
Schafer, Natalie
Shutan, Jan
Nov 6: Davis, Brad
Field, Sally
Hall, Juanita (d. 1968)
Kerwin, Lance
Matz, Peter
Meyer, Dorothy
Olsen, Ole (Olsen & Johnson) (d. 1962)
Schaeffer, Rebecca
Shriver, Maria
Singer, Lori
Thompson, Ernest
Nov 7: Barnes, C.B.
Bushkin, Joe
Graham, Rev. Billy
Hirt, Al
Houghton, James
Jagger, Dean
Kaye, Lila

LeRoy, Gloria
Michaux, Elder (d. 1968)
Newman, Barry
Plato, Dana
Watkins, Jim
Nov 8: Brooks, Randi
Colorado, Hortensia
Day, Dorothy (d. 1980)
Flynn, Joe (d. 1974)
Garrett, Leif
Harris, Bob
Havoc, June
Ladd, Margaret
Lloyd, Norman
Page, Patti
Rolle, Esther
Safer, Morley
Strauss, Robert (d. 1975)
Nov 9: Darden, Severn
Ferrigno, Lou
Jones, Charlie
Myers, Pauline
Robinson, Charles
Sagan, Dr. Carl
Thomas, John Joseph
Wynn, Ed (d. 1966)
Nov 10: Beaudine, Deka
Burton, Richard (d. 1984)
Froman, Jane (d. 1980)
Hall, Albert
May, Billy
McCoy, Jack
Phillips, Mackenzie
Reed, Alaina
Scalia, Jack
Scott, Pippa
Nov 11: Kaye, Stubby
Longden, John (d. 1971)
Martin, Anne-Marie
McKeon, Philip
O'Brien, Pat (d. 1983)
Reilly, John
Ryan, Robert (d. 1973)
Winters, Jonathan
Nov 12: Clair, Dick
Gaffin, Melanie
Hunter, Kim
Mullally, Megan
Stafford, Jo
Venture, Richard
Wilson, Mary Louise

Nov 13: Atkins, Tom
Baddeley, Hermione (d. 1986)
Elam, Jack
Frazier, Sheila
Mantegna, Joe
Mulligan, Richard
Narz, Jack
Pilon, Daniel
Preston, J.A.
Rambo, Dack
Rambo, Dirk (d. 1967)
Scoggins, Tracy
Sherwood, Madeleine
Sterling, Robert
Thibault, Conrad
Nov 14: Avery, Phyllis
Carson, Ken
DeCamp, Rosemary
Desmond, Johnny (d. 1985)
Downey, Morton (d. 1985)
Ginty, Robert
Grubbs, Gary
Keith, Brian
Powell, Dick (d. 1963)
Roswell, Maggie
Stevenson, McLean
Nov 15: Adams, Franklin P. (d. 1960)
Asner, Edward
Barnes, Joanna
Bruce, Carol
Burns, Jack
Cason, Barbara
Hammond, Peter
Kerr, John
Kotto, Yaphet
Large, Don
Lennon, Janet (Lennon Sisters)
Mantovani (d. 1980)
Mayo, Whitman
Rasulala, Thalmus
Waterston, Sam
Widdoes, James
Nov 16: Barry, Patricia
Bonet, Lisa
Butler, Daws
Cast, Tricia
Condon, Eddie (d. 1973)
Dano, Royal
Gulager, Clu
Kaufman, George S. (d. 1961)

Kerr, Jay
Lauren, Tammy
McBride, Mary Margaret
(d. 1976)
Meredith, Burgess
Pettet, Joanna
Shor, Dan
Stockwell, Guy
Nov 17: Campbell, Archie
Cook, Peter
DeVito, Danny
Hudson, Rock (d. 1985)
Hutton, Lauren
Lescoulie, Jack
Martin, Dean Paul (d. 1987)
Mathias, Bob
Maxwell, Frank
Moses, William R.
O'Connor, Sen. Herbert
(d. 1960)
Olson, Eric
Rosario, Bert
Wise, Alfie
Nov 18: Buffano, Jules (d. 1960)
Coca, Imogene
Collins, Dorothy
Evans, Linda
Gallup, Dr. George (d. 1984)
Marcovicci, Andrea
Mercer, Johnny (d. 1976)
Parker, Jameson
Peterson, Arthur
Sullivan, Susan
Vaccaro, Brenda
Nov 19: Carroll, Nancy (d. 1965)
Cavett, Dick
Dorsey, Tommy (d. 1956)
Farrell, Terry
Fenneman, George
Foster, Jodie
Haggerty, Dan
Jacoby, Scott
O'Connor, Glynnis
Utley, Garrick
Young, Alan
Nov 20: Allison, Fran
Ballard, Kaye
Cooke, Alistair
Cotler, Jeff
Cover, Franklin
Dawson, Richard

Dick, Douglas
Einstein, Bob
Frazer, Dan
Hamel, Veronica
Linkletter, Jack
Lipton, Robert
Masur, Richard
McBride, Dirty Dan (Sha Na
    Na)
Miller, Mark
Parsons, Estelle
Reason, Rex
Reason, Rhodes
Smothers, Dick
Soper, Tony
Tierney, Gene
Vitte, Ray (d. 1983)
Wright, Samuel E.
Nov 21: Blaine, Vivian
Campanella, Joseph
Cavanaugh, Michael
Drivas, Robert (d. 1986)
Hawn, Goldie
Johnson, Cherie
Lenz, Richard
Luckinbill, Laurence
Luft, Lorna
Mills, Juliet
Shelton, Deborah
Shepard, Jean
Sheridan, Nicollette
Thomas, Marlo
Nov 22: Callan, Michael
Carmichael, Hoagy (d. 1981)
Curtis, Jamie Lee
Dangerfield, Rodney
Jackson, Mary
Page, Geraldine
Patrick, Lee (d. 1982)
Robbins, Brian
Vaughn, Robert
Winters, Roland
Nov 23: Caulfield, Maxwell
Dehner, John
Deloy, George
Gordon, Don
Gough, Michael
Karloff, Boris (d. 1969)
Newland, John
O'Hanlon, George
Rappaport, David

Nov 24: Barkley, Alben W. (d. 1956)
Barton, Eileen
Born, Roscoe
Carter, Ray
Duff, Howard
Evans, Damon
Fitzgerald, Geraldine
Fouts, Tom "Stubby"
Grant, Kirby (d. 1985)
Hogan, Jack
Jenkins, Carol Mayo
Nesbitt, Cathleen (d. 1982)
Schultz, Dwight
Nov 25: Applegate, Christina
Baldwin, Curtis
Brodie, Steve
Enriquez, Rene
Harden, Ernest, Jr.
Hunter, Jeffrey (d. 1969)
Husain, Jory
Larroquette, John
Maupin, Rex (d. 1966)
Montalban, Ricardo
Walter, Tracey
Nov 26: Carter, John
Cole, Olivia
Goulet, Robert
Jergens, Adele
Little, Rich
Mercer, Marian
Morin, Alberto
Rose, Jamie
Sevareid, Eric
Wild, Earl
Nov 27: Anderson, Barbara
Elliott, Stephen
Givens, Robin
Husing, Ted (d. 1962)
Lee, Bruce (d. 1973)
McPherson, Patricia
Smith, Bob (New York host)
Thompson, Marshall
Tolan, Michael
White, Jaleel
Wise, Ernie
Nov 28: Grahame, Gloria (d. 1981)
Hewitt, Virginai (d. 1986)
Jory, Victor (d. 1982)
Lange, Hope
Shaffer, Paul
Winters, Gloria

Nov 29: Calvin, John
Crosse, Rupert (d. 1973)
Dagmar
Gary, John
Ladd, Diane
Mandel, Howie
Reynolds, Frank (d. 1983)
Ryan, Fran
Stevens, Naomi
Van Rooten, Luis (d. 1973)
Nov 30: Clark, Dick
Crenna, Richard
Ging, Jack
Guillaume, Robert
McCaffrey, John K.M.
(d. 1983)
Sheldon, Jack
Whitton, Margaret
Witt, Kathryn
Wolter, Sherilyn
Zimbalist, Efrem, Jr.

Dec 1: Doyle, David
Johnston, Johnny
Keith, Richard
Lennon, Dianne (Lennon Sisters)
Manza, Ralph
McLerie, Allyn Ann
Michell, Keith
Picerni, Paul
Pryor, Richard
Rawls, Lou
Shawn, Dick (d. 1987)
Symonds, Robert
Tilton, Charlene
Dec 2: Crosby, Cathy Lee
Delugg, Milton
Erwin, Bill
Gaxton, William (d. 1963)
Gordon, Leo V.
Harris, Julie
Paige, Robert
Sauter, Eddie (Sauter-Finegan)
Simon, Robert F.
Woods, Donald
Dec 3: Anderson, Melody
Boswell, Connee (d. 1976)
Keale, Moe
Matthews, Lester (d. 1975)

Menzies, Heather
Morgan, Jaye P.
Williams, Andy
Dec 4: Baer, Max, Jr.
Dietrich, Dena
French, Victor
Jackson, Allan (d. 1976)
Martindale, Wink
Rhodes, Donnelly
Dec 5: Brittany, Morgan
Disney, Walt (d. 1966)
Hansen, Peter
Hayes, Margaret (d. 1977)
Kirby, Randy
Needham (Newton), Connie
Savalas, George (d. 1985)
Dec 6: Brown, Chelsea
Cornelius, Helen
Cox, Wally (d. 1973)
Hecht, Gina
Marcus, Sparky
Moorehead, Agnes (d. 1974)
Naughton, James
Shriner, Wil
Turner, Janine
Dec 7: Baggetta, Vincent
Barnes, Priscilla
Burstyn, Ellen
Cameron, Rod (d. 1983)
Howell, C. Thomas
Knight, Ted (d. 1986)
Minor, Mike
Wallach, Eli
Dec 8: Basinger, Kim
Cobb, Lee J. (d. 1976)
Davis, Sammy, Jr.
Faylen, Frank (d. 1985)
Laborteaux, Matthew
MacArthur, James
Morgan, Terence
Rubinstein, John
Wilson, Flip
Yniguez, Richard
Dec 9: Bridges, Beau
Butkus, Dick
Cassavetes, John
Crawford, Broderick
(d. 1986)
Fairbanks, Douglas, Jr.
Foxx, Redd
Gingold, Hermione

Hamilton, Margaret (d. 1985)
Martin, Freddy (d. 1983)
Merrill, Dina
Nouri, Michael
Osmond, Donny
Savage, Brad
Simon, Leonard
Simon, Scott (Sha Na Na)
Smith, Allison
Van Patten, Dick
Dec 10: Blocker, Dan (d. 1972)
Brooks, Joel
Colicos, John
Considine, Tim
Dey, Susan
Flanagan, Fionnula
Gould, Harold
Huntley, Chet (d. 1974)
Lewis, George J.
Mako
Morgan, Dennis
Peeples, Nia
Rettig, Tommy
Sebesky, Don
Wilson, Theodore
Dec 11: Armstrong, Bess
Baur, Elizabeth
Birch, Peter
Carey, Ron
Dowling, Eddie (d. 1976)
Firestone, Eddy
Fuccello, Tom
Garr, Teri
Gayle, Tina
George, Lynda Day
Irwin, Wynn
Isacksen, Peter
Mills, Donna
Moreno, Rita
Dec 12: Alicia, Ana
Barker, Bob
Blair, Lionel
Dickinson, Hal (Moder-
naires) (d. 1970)
Douglas, Sarah
Francis, Connie
Francis, Missy
Harrington, Al
Hauser, Tim (Manhattan
Transfer)
Maggart, Brandon

Sinatra, Frank
Warwick, Dionne
Dec 13: Carroll, Jimmy (d. 1972)
Connelly, Marc (d. 1980)
Davidson, John
Harmon, Steve
Haynes, Tiger (Three
Flames)
Heflin, Van (d. 1971)
Malick, Wendie
Morey, Bill
Paulsen, Albert
Pearson, Drew (d. 1969)
Plummer, Christopher
Prosky, Robert
Schultz, Lenny
Stevens, Mark
Street, Dave (d. 1971)
Thompson, Jenn
Van Dyke, Dick
Whitaker, Johnnie
Dec 14: Amsterdam, Morey
Astin, Patty Duke
Brophy, Sallie
Carter, T.K.
Dailey, Dan (d. 1978)
Furth, George
Gibb, Cynthia
Jones, Spike (d. 1965)
Lane, Abbe
Leigh-Hunt, Barbara
Lussier, Robert
Morgan, Marion
Naismith, Laurence
Remick, Lee
Stone, Dee Wallace
Warnick, Clay
Weston, Celia
Williams, Hal
Wilson, Joyce Vincent
Dec 15: Bohay, Heidi
Chartoff, Melanie
Conway, Tim
DuBois, Marta
Freed, Alan (d. 1965)
Johnson, Don
Morrow, Karen
Nelson, Jimmy
Dec 16: Brenner, Dori
Bulifant, Joyce
Carter, Terry

Deutsch, Patti
Greer, Michael
Knox, Terence
Dec 17: Brown, Eric
Cazenove, Christopher
Fiedler, Arthur (d. 1979)
Levy, Eugene
Livingston, Barry
Long, Richard (d. 1974)
Nelson, Novella
Dec 18: Bari, Lynn
Burrows, Abe (d. 1985)
Cooper, Gladys (d. 1971)
Liotta, Ray
Maltin, Leonard
Mann, Larry D.
Smith, Roger
Dec 19: Dickens, Jimmy
Fremin, Jourdan
Hastings, Hal (d. 1973)
Joyce, Elaine
Locane, Amy
Milano, Alyssa
Reid, Tim
Reiner, Fritz (d. 1963)
Smith, H. Allen (d. 1976)
Susskind, David (d. 1987)
Tyson, Cecily
Urich, Robert
Dec 20: Baker, Blanche
Bauer, Charita (d. 1985)
Callas, Charlie
Dunne, Irene
Hillerman, John
Powers, Mala
Simpson, Jim
Tompkins, Angel
Totter, Audrey
Dec 21: Donahue, Phil
Ericson, Devon
Gerritsen, Lisa
Gordon, Barry
Haje, Khrystyne
Kaczmarek, Jane
Martin, Jared
Mostel, Joshua
Nelson, Ed
Singer, Raymond
Weaver, Sylvester L.
  "Pat"
Winchell, Paul

Dec 22: Billingsley, Barbara
Carney, Alan (d. 1973)
Castle, Peggy (d. 1973)
Elizondo, Hector
Garvey, Steve
Hawkins, Hawkshaw
  (d. 1963)
Luz, Franc
Perry, Wolfe
Rayburn, Gene
Sawyer, Diane
Stanis, BernNadette
Thigpen, Lynne
Dec 23: Argo, Allison
Brown, Mitch
Callahan, John
Contardo, Johnny (Sha Na
  Na)
Gregory, James
Guardino, Harry
Kalber, Floyd
McNeill, Don
North, Alan
O'Loughlin, Gerald S.
O'Neal, Ann (d. 1971)
Okun, Milt
Richardson, Michael
Roman, Ruth
Schell, Ronnie
Stacy, James
Stern, Leonard
Dec 24: Ayres, Mitchell (d. 1969)
Billington, Michael
Curb, Mike
Farrell, Sharon
Gardner, Ava
Gilyard, Clarence, Jr.
Dec 25: Ashley, John
Brown, Earl
Cameron, Dean
Ferguson, Frank (d. 1978)
Hillebrand, Fred (d. 1963)
King, Mabel
MacLane, Barton (d. 1969)
Mandrell, Barbara
Martin, Tony
Mazurki, Mike
McCalla, Irish
Ripley, Robert L.
  (d. 1949)
Safranski, Eddie

979

Sandy, Gary
Serling, Rod (d. 1975)
Dec 26: Allen, Steve
Brissette, Tiffany
Cook, Elisha
King, Alan
Moffat, Donald
Newborn, Ira
Quilley, Denis
Racimo, Victoria
Rosato, Tony
Widmark, Richard
Dec 27: Amos, John
Feldshuh, Tovah
Levant, Oscar (d. 1972)
O'Rourke, Heather
Dec 28: Arquette, Cliff (d. 1974)
Ayres, Lew
Bowman, Lee (d. 1979)
Duggan, Andrew
Jacobi, Lou
Levenson, Sam (d. 1980)
Milner, Martin
Perkins, Jack
Perlow, Bob
Vallely, Tannis
Washington, Denzel
Williams, Billy (d. 1984)
Dec 29: Cribbins, Bernard
Danson, Ted
Flanders, Ed
Garrett, Susie
Jarriel, Tom

Masse, Laurel (Manhattan Transfer)
Moore, Mary Tyler
Niles, Wendell
Swenson, Inga
Dec 30: Brandon, Clark
Burns, Michael
Coster, Nicolas
Hartford, John
Jones, David
Kalember, Patricia
Koufax, Sandy
Litel, John (d. 1972)
Lopez, Vincent (d. 1975)
Lord, Jack
Nesmith, Michael
Nichols, Barbara (d. 1976)
Nolan, Jeanette
Parks, Bert
Riley, Jack
Dec 31: Adlam, Buzz
Allen, Rex
Barbour, Ross (Four Freshmen)
Brady, Pat (d. 1972)
Dallesandro, Joe
Graziano, Rocky
Kollmar, Dick (d. 1971)
Matheson, Tim
McCracken, Joan (d. 1961)
Robards, Jason, Sr. (d. 1963)

Appendix 4
Index of TV Stars' Birthplaces

Was one of the TV performers listed in this book born in your hometown, or nearby? All fifty states and many foreign countries have produced actors and others who have been regulars on prime time series; their birthplaces range from Kankakee (Fred MacMurray) to Keokuk (which can claim both Conrad Nagel and Elsa Lanchester) to Kuala Lumpur (Claudia Wells of *Herbie, The Love Bug*). The following is a birthplace index for many of those in the main listings. Notes in parentheses indicate that the performer was raised but not necessarily born in the given location ("raised"), or was born there but brought up elsewhere ("r:" followed by the place where raised).

ALABAMA

City Not Known:
  Parks, Van Dyke (r: McKeesport, Pa.)
  Patterson, Hank
Addison:
  Buttram, Pat
Alabaster:
  Holcombe, Wendy
Birmingham:
  Allen, Mel
  Armstrong, R.G.
  Carter, Nell
  Cox, Courteney
  Flagg, Fannie
  Jackson, Kate
  Lewis, James O. (of the Mariners)
  Rogers, Wayne
  Strickland, Gail
Boothton:
  Hall, Albert
Decatur:
  Jones, Dean
Fort Payne:
  Ober, Philip

Gadsden:
  Leach Britt
Helena:
  Cumbuka, Ji-Tu
Huntsville:
  Bankhead, Tallulah
Jasper:
  Holliday, Polly
  Lindsey, George
Mobile:
  Roberts, Davis
Montgomery:
  Cole, Nat "King"
  Tennille, Toni
Rainsville:
  Louvin, Charlie
  Louvin, Ira
Red Level:
  Tyler, Willie
Scottsboro:
  Benson, Lucille
Selma:
  Lehman, Lillian (r: Buffalo, N.Y.)
Sylacauga:
  Nabors, Jim

Talladega:
 Brown, Charles

ALASKA

Anchorage:
 Hearn, Connie Ann (r: California)

ARIZONA

City Not Known:
 Biehn, Michael
Douglas:
 Jones, Stan
Flagstaff:
 Devine, Andy
Glendale:
 Robbins, Marty
Holbrook:
 Evans, Gene
Miami:
 Elam, Jack (r: Phoenix, Ariz., and Los Angeles)
Phoenix:
 Bauer, Jaime Lyn
 Brophy, Sallie
 Carter, Lynda
 Kay, Dianne
Prescott:
 DeCamp, Rosemary
Ray:
 O'Brien, Clay
Scottsdale:
 Hicks, Catherine
Tucson:
 Dusenberry, Ann
 Eden, Barbara (r: San Francisco, Calif.)
Wilcox:
 Allen, Rex

ARKANSAS

City Not Known:
 Carter, Conlan
Camden:
 Brickell, Beth
Center Ridge:
 Carter, John
Delight:
 Campbell, Glen

Eureka Springs:
 Tomlin, Pinky (r: Durant, Okla.)
Fort Smith:
 Jones, Charlie
 Luckinbill, Laurence
Hope:
 Lester, Ketty (raised)
Hot Springs:
 Jackson, Allan
 Stewart, Trish
Jonesboro:
 Murphy, Ben
Kingsland:
 Cash, Johnny (r: Dyess, Ark.)
Little Rock:
 Balding, Rebecca
 Beatty, Morgan
 Bonner, Frank
 Davis, Gail
 Flippen, Jay C.
 Gerard, Gil
 McKrell, Jim
 Piazza, Ben
Marshall:
 Britt, Elton
Mineola:
 Wakely, Jimmy
Mountain View:
 Powell, Dick
Rector:
 Copeland, Maurice
Sparkman:
 Brown, Jim Ed

CALIFORNIA

City Not Known:
 Corcoran, Brian
 Corcoran, Kelly
 Crosby, Gary
 Elliott, Sam (r: Oregon)
 Hudson, William
 Lor, Denise
 McCormick, Maureen
 Morita, Pat
 Nesbitt, John
 Nigh, Jane
 Repp, Stafford
 Sklar, Michael
 Stuthman, Fred
 Zerbe, Anthony (raised)

Alameda:
  Erickson, Leif
  Heidt, Horace
Albany:
  Tompkins, Angel
Alhambra:
  Vogel, Mitch
Anaheim:
  Needham (Newton), Connie
  Wilson, Marie
Arcadia:
  Jensen, Maren
  Thomas, John Joseph
Atwater:
  Hutchins, Will
Auburn:
  Prud'homme, Cameron
Avalon, Catalina Island:
  Harrison, Gregory
Bakersfield:
  Cruz, Brandon
  Haggard, Merle
  Madison, Guy
Balboa:
  Penhall, Bruce
Berkeley:
  Anderson, Melissa Sue
  Arms, Russell
  Culp, Robert
  Dabney, Augusta
  Grassle, Karen
  McGovern, Terry (r: Pittsburgh, Pa.)
  Whinnery, Barbara
Beverly Hills:
  Barrymore, John, Jr.
  Chamberlain, Richard
  Prince, Jonathan
  Raskin, Damon
Burbank:
  Cheshire, Elizabeth
  Gibbs, Timothy
  Harmon, Mark
  Howard, Clint
  Johnson, Laura
  Kanaly, Steve
  Maisnik, Kathy
  Mathews, Larry
  Moran, Erin
  Plumb, Eve
  Ritter, John
  Smith, Reid

Canoga Park:
  Furlong, Kirby (raised)
  Marshall, Sean
  Osmond, Jimmy
Carmel:
  Sargent, Dick
Cerritos:
  Allen, Chad
Chico:
  Harriman, Fawne (raised)
  Hayden, Russell "Lucky"
  Scott, Donovan
Claremont:
  Hewitt, Martin
Coalinga:
  Brown, Philip
  Stafford, Jo (r: Long Beach, Calif.)
Concord:
  Hanks, Tom
Corona:
  Parks, Michael
Cressey:
  Suzuki, Pat
Culver City:
  Gower, Andre
  Lennon, Janet (Lennon Sisters)
Cypress:
  Stamos, John
Delano:
  Rambo, Dack
  Rambo, Dirk
East Los Angeles:
  Olmos, Edward James
El Centro:
  Cher
  Howard, Ken (r: Manhasset, N.Y.)
El Monte:
  Corbett, Glenn
El Segundo:
  Vinson, Gary
Encino:
  Gregory, Benji
  Kiger, Robby
  Wells, Tracy
Englewood:
  Reed, Marshall
Eureka:
  Urecal, Minerva
Firebaugh:
  Yniguez, Richard (r: Sacramento, Calif.)

Fresno:
  Bagdasarian, Ross
  Connors, Mike
  Hall, Jon
  Scott, Fred
Glendale:
  Angustain, Ira
  Beck, Kimberly
  Englund, Robert
  Harrison, Jenilee (r: Northridge,
    Calif.)
  Lime, Yvonne
  MacGregor, Katherine (r: Wyoming,
    Colo.)
  Martin, Lori
  Martinez, A
  Matheson, Tim
  McClure, Doug
  Nash, Brian
  Petersen, Paul (r: Iowa)
  Potts, Cliff
  Sperber, Wendie Jo
  Stearns, Mary Kay
  Talbot, Gloria
Glendora:
  Frye, Soleil Moon
Grass Valley:
  Costa, Cosie
Hanford:
  Pine, Phillip
Hawthorne:
  Dryer, Fred
  Warlock, Billy
Hollywood:
  Adams, Jeb
  Applegate, Christina
  Baker, Diane
  Bank, Frank
  Bridges, Beau
  Brittany, Morgan
  Burrud, Bill
  Carradine, David
  Cole, Tina
  Dow, Tony
  Garrett, Leif
  Haggerty, Dan
  Heasley, Marla
  Hershey, Barbara
  Hickman, Darryl
  Marcus, Sparky
  Murray, Don (r: East Rockaway,
    N.Y.)

Newmar, Julie
Nigh, Jane
Palmer, Bud
Powers, Stefanie
Richards, Paul
Sanders, Beverly
Scott, Eric
Scott, Geoffrey
Taylor, Buck
Trusel, Lisa
Tyler, Kim
Verdugo, Elena
Huntington Park:
  Wilson, Terry
Inglewood:
  Bonne, Shirley
  Collier, Don
  DeYoung, Cliff
  Lawrence, Vicki
  Patrick, Butch
Kingsburg:
  Pickens, Slim
La Jolla:
  Peck, Gregory
  Robertson, Cliff
  Schmock, Jonathan
La Mirada:
  Watson, Debbie (raised)
Lincoln:
  Clark, Fred
Loma Linda:
  Lawson, Richard
Long Beach:
  Ashbrook, Daphne
  Baker, David Lain
  Beckham, Brice
  Blanchard, Mari
  Britton, Barbara
  Casados, Eloy Phil
  Case, Nelson
  Colbert, Robert (r: Santa Barbara,
    Calif.)
  Cotler, Jeff
  Cotler, Kami
  Crowe, Tonya
  Garver, Kathy
  Gortner, Marjoe
  Harris, Bob
  Houston, Thelma
  Jones, Spike
  Kellerman, Sally
  Linville, Joanne (raised)

Phillips, Michelle
Ramsey, Logan
Ryan, Peggy
Los Angeles:
Aaker, Lee
Adams, Catlin
Adrian, Iris
Ahn, Philip
Albert, Edward
Alexander, Rod
Archer, Anne
Arnaz, Desi, Jr.
Arnaz, Lucie
Bakewell, William
Baldwin, Curtis
Bannon, Jack
Bass, Tod
Baur, Elizabeth
Baxter-Birney, Meredith
Bega, Leslie
Begley, Ed, Jr.
Beradino, John
Billingsley, Barbara
Blake, Whitney
Blocker, Dirk
Boone, Richard
Brand, Jolene
Brandt, Victor
Braverman, Bart
Brennan, Eileen
Brewton, Maia
Brolin, James
Brooks, Albert
Brooks, Rand
Byron, Carol
Calhoun, Rory (r: Santa Cruz, Calif.)
Carlin, Lynn
Carradine, Robert
Carrillo, Leo
Carter, T.K.
Carver, Mary
Cassidy, Shaun
Champion, Marge
Chao, Rosalind (r: Orange County, Calif.)
Chapin, Lauren
Clarke, Gary
Cobb, Julie
Cohen, Evan
Cohn, Mindy
Coogan, Jackie
Cooper, Jackie

Copage, Marc
Copeland, Alan
Crawford, Johnny
Crawford, Katherine
Crenna, Richard
Cromwell, James
Crosby, Cathy Lee
Crosby, Mary
Cummings, Quinn
Curtis, Jamie Lee
Cutter, Lise
Darby, Kim
Davidson, Ben
DeHaven, Gloria
Delugg, Milton
Derek, John
Diamond, Bobby
Dolenz, Mickey
Douglas, James
Easterbrook, Leslie (r: Kearney, Neb.)
Einstein, Bob
Elhardt, Kay
Eyer, Richard
Farrow, Mia
Fee, Melinda
Fields, Kim
Fontane, Char
Francis, Missy
Freberg, Stan
Friedman, David
Gautier, Dick
Gavin, John
Gerritsen, Lisa
Gilbert, Melissa
Gilford, Gwynne
Gillespie, Gina
Gless, Sharon
Gordon, Don
Grahame, Gloria
Gray, Billy
Green, Dorothy
Greenbush, Sidney and Lindsey
Griffith, James
Guild, Nancy
Hadley, Nancy
Hale, Alan, Jr.
Hamilton, Bernie
Hargitay, Mariska
Hart, John (actor)
Henry, Chuck
Hensley, Pamela

Hervey, Irene
Heslov, Grant
Heyes, Douglas, Jr.
Hickman, Dwayne
Hicks, Hilly
Hill, Craig
Hollander, David
Horton, Robert
Houghton, James
Houser, Jerry
Howell, C. Thomas
Hunt, Helen
Jones, Jack
Katt, William
Kavner, Julie
Keeler, Donald
Killum, Guy
Kincaid, Aron
King, Regina
King, Rori
Kramer, Stepfanie
Laborteaux, Matthew
Laborteaux, Patrick
Lamas, Lorenzo
Landon, Leslie
Larson, Jack
Lee, Michele
Lemmon, Chris
Lennon, Dianne (Lennon Sisters)
Lennon, Peggy (Lennon Sisters)
Lenz, Kay
Leslie, Nan
Licht, Jeremy
Lindley, Audra
Livingston, Barry
Livingston, Stanley
Locklear, Heather
Luft, Lorna
MacArthur, James (r: Nyack, N.Y.)
Macklin, Albert
Manley, Stephen
Marlowe, Christopher
Maury, Derrel
McCloskey, Leigh
McCord, Kent
McCrea, Jody (r: Camarillo, Calif.)
McCullen, Kathy
McNear, Howard
McNichol, Jimmy
McNichol, Kristy
Meriwether, Lee

Mimieux, Yvette
Montgomery, Elizabeth
Moore, Terry
Moses, William R.
Mosley, Roger E. (raised)
Mullally, Megan
Murphy, Michael
Nader, George
Negron, Taylor
Newman, Laraine
Nolan, Jeanette
North, Sheree
O'Brien-Moore, Erin (r: Tucson, Ariz.)
O'Neal, Ryan
O'Neill, Katie
Pace, Judy
Palance, Holly
Patterson, Melody
Paul, Richard
Perreau, Gigi
Petersen, Pat
Quinn, Teddy (raised)
Raffin, Deborah
Rash, Bryson
Rea, Peggy
Reynolds, William
Richards, Evan
Richards, Michael
Richmond, Branscombe (r: Tahiti, Hawaii)
Robin, Diane
Ross, Katherine
Roswell, Maggie
Rubinstein, John
Ruggles, Charlie
Russell, Andy
Russell, John
Ryan, Fran
Ryan, Natasha
Sagal, Jean
Sagal, Liz
Saint James, Susan (r: Rockford, Ill.)
Salt, Jennifer
Sand, Paul
Schallert, William
Scott, Pippa
Shutan, Jan
Sikking, James
Silverman, Jonathan
Smith, John

Sorel, Louise
Spelman, Sharon (r: Sioux City, Iowa)
St. John, Jill
Stack, Robert
Stacy, James
Stevens, Onslow
Street, Dave
Swire, Sydney (r: West Chester, N.Y.)
Tabori, Kristoffer
Takei, George
Tighe, Kevin
Tochi, Brian
Valdis, Sigrid
Wagner, Lindsay
Ward, Burt
Wayne, Patrick
Weaver, Doodles
Weaver, Sylvester L. "Pat"
Wells, Derek
White, Jaleel
Williams, Anson
Winfield, Paul
Winters, Gloria
Wong, Anna May (in Chinatown)
Yarlett, Claire (r: England)
Yarnell, Bruce
Yarnell, Lorene (raised)
Yothers, Corey
Zippi, Daniel
Madera:
Riley, Jeannine
Maywood:
Plato, Dana
Mill Valley:
Arden, Eve
Montebello:
Lankford, Kim (r: Orange County)
Monterey Park:
Brull, Pamela
Scott, Simon
Shore, Roberta
Monterey:
Scott, Jean Bruce
Newport Beach:
Aames, Willie
Kerwin, Lance
McGinley, Ted
North Hollywood:
Bayer, Gary

Bernsen, Corbin
North, Jay
Smithers, Jan
Northridge:
Gold, Brandy
Haley, Jackie Earle
Oak Glen:
Anton, Susan
Oakland:
Anderson, Eddie "Rochester"
Baer, Max, Jr.
Burrell, Maryedith (r: Gilroy, Calif.)
Connell, Jane
Fridell, Squire
Gibson, John (raised)
Hamill, Mark
Hansen, Peter
Lange, Ted
Larkin, John
Martin, Tony
Nelson, Barry
Paich, Marty
Sing, Mai Tai (r: San Francisco; Hong Kong)
Soo, Jack
Stephens, Laraine
Sylvester, William
Watson, Mills
Whelan, Jill
Oceanside:
Dizon, Jesse
Ojai:
Linville, Larry
Ontario:
Scarbury, Joey
Orange County:
Nix, Martha (r: Fullerton, Calif.)
Pfeiffer, Michelle
Oxnard:
Hoff, Carl
Palm Springs:
Mitchell, Keith
Neil, Gloria
Palo Alto:
Freeman, Deena
Irving, Amy
Kemp, Brandis
Post, Markie (r: Walnut Creek, Calif.)
Rossovich, Tim
Swan, Michael

Panorama City:
  Cameron, Kirk
Paramount:
  Williams, Brandon
Pasadena:
  Dragon, Daryl
  Field, Sally
  Hamlin, Harry
  Hotchkis, Joan
  Lockard, Tom (Mariners, Calif.)
  Moll, Richard
  O'Dell, Tony
  Ruick, Barbara
  Russel, Del
  Sullivan, Kathleen
Petaluma:
  Healey, Myron
Pomona:
  Provost, Jon
  Seagren, Bob
Redondo Beach:
  Dudikoff, Michael
Reseda:
  Feldman, Corey
Richmond:
  Franklin, Carl
  Schell, Ronnie (r: San Francisco,
    Calif.)
Riverside:
  Butterworth, Shane (r: Simi Valley,
    Calif.)
  Richardson, Michael
Ross:
  Sues, Alan
Sacramento:
  Barbeau, Adrienne
  Benton, Barbi
  Collins, Ray
  De Winter, Jo (r: New Orleans)
  Larson, Dennis
  Lescoulie, Jack
  Mantooth, Randolph
  Ringwald, Molly
Salinas:
  Felton, Verna
  Snider, Barry
San Bernadino:
  Karns, Roscoe
  Poole, Roy
San Bruno:
  Somers, Suzanne

San Diego:
  Bill, Tony
  Buono, Victor
  Comstock, Frank
  Danson, Ted (r: Flagstaff, Ariz.)
  DeVarona, Donna (r: Lafayette,
    Calif.)
  Duvall, Robert
  Embrey, Joan
  Fabray, Nanette
  Kramer, Bert
  Lansing, Robert
  Lauren, Tammy
  Lynn, Jennie
  O'Rourke, Heather
  Tilton, Charlene (r: Hollywood,
    Calif.)
  Wilcox, Larry
San Fernando:
  Mason, Marlyn
San Francisco:
  Allen, Gracie
  Anglim, Philip
  Bailey, Raymond
  Bixby, Bill
  Blanc, Mel
  Bonet, Lisa
  Borelli, Carla (raised)
  Bridges, Todd
  Clair, Dick
  Cook, Elisha
  Corrigan, Lloyd
  Davis, Michael
  Der, Ricky (raised in Chinatown)
  Dillman, Bradford
  Dukes, David
  Eastwood, Clint
  Egan, Richard
  Enriquez, Rene
  Finn, Fred E.
  Firestone, Eddy
  Fitzsimmons, Tom
  Gaxton, William
  Goldin, Ricky Paull
  Goodwin, Bill
  Haid, Charles (r: Palo Alto, Calif.)
  Hamilton, Bobb
  Hammer, Jay
  Hartman, Paul
  Hayes, Peter Lind
  Hellman, Bonnie (r: Palo Alto, Calif.)

Henry, Bill
Hon, Jean Marie (r: Los Angeles)
Jensen, Karen
Kerns, Joanna
King, Walter Woolf
Lane, Charles
Lee, Bruce
Linkletter, Jack
Lord, Marjorie
Manza, Ralph
March, Hal
McGee, Vonetta
Minor, Mike
Myers, Carmel
Nolan, James
Nolan, Lloyd
Palmer, Gregg
Paris, Jerry
Powers, Mala
Scotti, Vito (r: Italy)
Simpson, O.J.
Spano, Joe
Tambor, Jeffrey
Tong, Sammee
Tyrrell, Susan (r: New Canaan,
   Conn.)
Walters, Laurie
Whitman, Stuart
Wood, Natalie
Yung, Victor Sen
San Jose:
   DeSoto, Rosana
   Ferguson, Allyn
   Lowe, Edmund
   Reyes, Ernie, Jr.
San Leandro:
   Bridges, Lloyd
   Peary, Harold (raised)
San Mateo:
   Bostwick, Barry
   Carradine, Keith
   Griffin, Merv
   Haysbert, Dennis
   McClure, Marc (r: Glendale, Calif.)
San Rafael:
   Brown, Candy Ann
Santa Ana:
   Cullen, William Kirby
   Halsey, Brett
   Medley, Bill (Righteous Brothers)
   Raitt, John

St. John, Al "Fuzzy"
Webber, Robert
Santa Barbara:
   Bottoms, Joseph
   Bottoms, Sam
   Bottoms, Timothy
   Edwards, Anthony
   French, Victor
   Hall, Brad
   Todd, Lisa
Santa Clara:
   Haje, Khrystyne
Santa Cruz:
   Garland, Beverly
Santa Maria:
   Miyori, Kim
Santa Monica:
   Bal, Jeanne
   Claridge, Shaaron
   Fabares, Shelley
   Franklin, Bonnie
   Gaffin, Melanie
   Gardner, Craig
   Gifford, Frank
   Gray, Linda
   Hatch, Richard
   Hinton, Darby
   Kiff, Kaleena
   Kotero, Patricia "Apollonia"
   Lennon, Kathy (Lennon Sisters)
   Martin, Dean Paul
   Nelson, Tracy
   Norton-Taylor, Judy
   Olsen, Susan
   Olson, Eric
   Peirce, Robert
   Sheehan, Douglas (r: Redding,
      Calif.)
   Sherman, Bobby (r: Van Nuys,
      Calif.)
   Spound, Michael (r: Concord,
      Mass.)
   Temple, Shirley
   Webb, Jack
   Williams, Barry
   Wood, Lana
Santa Paula:
   Fleming, Eric
Santa Rosa:
   London, Julie
   Ripley, Robert L.

Saratoga:
  Guest, Lance
Saugus:
  Stout, Paul
Sebastopol:
  Valentine, Karen
Sherman Oaks:
  Miller, Cheryl
Sonora:
  Belli, Melvin
  O'Hara, Jenny
South Gate:
  Smith, Roger
South Pasadena:
  McCrea, Joel
Squaw Valley:
  Erwin, Stu
Susanville:
  Cady, Frank
Sylmar:
  Smith, J. Brennan
Taft:
  Cooper, Jeanne
Toluca Lake:
  Kaye, Linda
Torrance:
  Foster, Susan
  Kolden, Scott
Tarzana:
  Lovitz, Jon
Tulare:
  Mathias, Bob
Vallejo:
  Robinson, Fran (r: Charleston, S.C.)
Van Nuys:
  Burkley, Dennis
  Drysdale, Don
  Hill, Dana
  Lockwood, Gary
  McDonough, Mary Elizabeth
  Saddler, Don
  Whitaker, Johnnie
  Williams, Cindy (r: Irving, Tex.)
Venice:
  Collins, Gary
  Jaffe, Taliesin
  Whipple, Sam
Ventura:
  McCook, John
  Styles, Susan
  Winter, Edward

990

Walnut Creek:
  O'Grady, Lani
Watsonville:
  Bobo, Natasha
West Covina:
  Miller, Jeremy
Whittier:
  Cohoon, Patti
  Patterson, Lorna
  Yothers, Tina

COLORADO

City Not Known:
  Culver, Howard (r: Los
    Angeles)
  Langland, Liane
  Michael, Mary
Bethune:
  Pyle, Denver
Colorado Springs:
  Byington, Spring
Denver:
  Bates, Barbara
  Bishop, Julie
  Bond, Ward
  Bower, Tom
  Buntrock, Bobby
  Catlett, Mary Jo (raised)
  Gaye, Lisa
  Hart, John (newsman)
  Hingle, Pat
  Howlin, Olin
  Langan, Glenn
  Mack, Ted
  Murray, Peg
  Perito, Nick
  Rush, Barbara (r: Santa Barbara,
    Calif.)
  Sande, Walter (r: Portland, Ore.)
  Tedrow, Irene
  Vincent, Jan-Michael (r: Hanford,
    Calif.)
  Vola, Vicki
  Whiteman, Paul
  Wilson, Don
Dillon:
  Markey, Enid
Durango:
  Tully, Tom
Gunnison:
  Elliott, Patricia

Lamar:
  Curtis, Ken
Mancos:
  Morgan, Jaye P.
Merino:
  Edwards, Ralph
Pueblo:
  Boen, Earl

CONNECTICUT

City Not Known:
  Foster, Meg (raised)
  Palillo, Ron
Bridgeport:
  Dennehy, Brian (r: Long Island, N.Y.)
  Mitchum, Robert
  Musante, Tony
  Nealon, Kevin
  Ratzenberger, John
  Walley, Deborah
Bristol:
  Burghoff, Gary
East Hartford:
  Cadorette, Mary
Fairfield:
  Ryan, Meg
Greenwich:
  Hack, Shelley
  Purl, Linda (r: Japan)
  Thomas, Heather (r: California)
Hamden:
  Borgnine, Ernest
Hartford:
  Begley, Ed
  Cannon, Katherine
  Evans, Linda
  Holliday, Art
  Karnilova, Maria
  Kean, Betty
  Kean, Jane
  Kellin, Mike
  Merrill, Gary
  Modean, Jayne
  Murphy, Timothy Patrick
  Naughton, David
  Nye, Louis
  O'Keefe, Walter
  O'Shea, Michael
  Roat, Richard
  St. Jacques, Raymond
  Steele, Ted (r: Boston, Mass.)

Utman, Bryan
Watkins, Carlene (r: Houston, Tex.)
Manchester:
  Stich, Patricia
Middletown:
  Naughton, James (r: West Hartford, Conn.)
New Haven:
  Atherton, William
  Bedford-Lloyd, John
  Capp, Al
  Carpenter, Karen
  Carpenter, Richard
  Chartoff, Melanie
  Eikenberry, Jill
  Goodeve, Grant (r: Middlebury, Conn.)
  Kiernan, Walter
  McGuire, Biff
  Moody, Sen. Blair
  Morrow, Buddy
  Murphy, George
  Smith, Patricia
  Trenner, Donn
  Wilson, Mary Louise (r: New Orleans, La.)
  Wood, Barry
New London:
  Michaels, Jeanna
Norwalk:
  Weitz, Bruce
Redding Ridge:
  Lange, Hope
Sharon:
  Amelio, Philip J., II
South Norwalk:
  McMahon, Horace
Stamford:
  Dante, Michael
  Lloyd, Christopher
  Morrow, Don
  Stern, Daniel
Stratford:
  Smith, Loring
Terryville:
  Knight, Ted
Wallingford:
  Downey, Morton
Waterbury:
  Crane, Bob
  Freeman, Stan

Ralph, Sheryl Lee (r: Jamaica, West Indies)
West Hartford:
　Mascolo, Joseph
West Haven:
　Leighton, Bernie
Westport:
　Martin, Pamela Sue

DELAWARE

Wilmington:
　Bertinelli, Valerie

DISTRICT OF COLUMBIA

Washington, D.C.:
　Ames, Nancy
　Arnette, Jeannetta
　Birney, David
　Block, Hunt (r: New England)
　Brown, Blair
　Burke, Billie
　Carroll, Jon (Starland Vocal Band)
　Chung, Connie
　Colby, Anita
　Danoff, Taffy (Starland Vocal Band)
　Engel, Georgia
　Fleischer, Charles
　Garner, Mousie
　Harty, Patricia
　Hawn, Goldie
　Hayes, Helen
　Herrmann, Edward
　Hooks, Robert
　Kennedy, Jayne
　Kurtzman, Katy
　Lawrence, Mark
　Lazarus, Bill
　Learned, Michael
　Moses, Rick (r: Calif.)
　Mudd, Roger
　Murphy, Mary
　Nouri, Michael (r: Alpine, N.J.)
　Parks, Hildy
　Preston, J.A.
　Rhue, Madlyn
　Rivera, Chita
　Shelton, Deborah (r: Norfolk, Va.)
　Simpson, Jim
　Sternhagen, Frances
　Taylor-Young, Leigh (r: Bloomfield Hills, Mich.)

Tork, Peter
White, Christine
Wills, Maury
Winn, Kitty
Wolf, Warner
Wolfson, Carl

FLORIDA

Blountstown:
　Loftin, Carey
Coral Gables:
　Edwards, Gail
　Rogers, Mimi
Eloise:
　Stafford, Jim
Fort Lauderdale:
　Robinson, Chris
　Sheralee
　Weaver, Lee
Fort Myers:
　Nalle, Bill
Gainesville:
　Butrick, Merritt (r: California)
　Richardson, James G.
　Rountree, Martha
Homestead:
　Campbell, Alan
Jacksonville:
　Boone, Pat (r: Nashville, Tenn.)
　Daniels, Billy
　Freeman, Sandy
　Kelly, Paula
　Nunn, Alice
　Sheldon, Jack
　Smith, Rex
　Tillotson, Johnny
Jennings:
　Prine, Andrew
Lake Worth:
　Hall, Deidre
　Morgan, Robin
Lakeland:
　Langford, Frances
Lakewood:
　White, Bill
Manatee:
　Markham, Monte
Marianna:
　Goldsboro, Bobby
Miami:
　Barash, Olivia
　Betts, Jack

Garber, Terri
Goodfriend, Lynda
Jackson, Victoria
Leopold, Thomas
Rasulala, Thalmus
Roker, Roxie (r: Brooklyn, N.Y.)
Rutherford, Angelo
Vereen, Ben (r: Brooklyn, N.Y.)
Witt, Kathryn
Ocala:
O'Neal, Patrick
Orlando:
Burke, Delta
Pensacola:
Dallesandro, Joe (r: New York City)
Dussault, Nancy
Kurtis, Bill (r: Kansas)
Pompano Beach:
Rolle, Esther
Sanford:
Lord, Bobby
St. Petersburg:
Brown, Johnny
Tallahassee:
Davis, Brad
Tampa:
Cuervo, Alma
McQueen, Butterfly
Roberts, Roy
West Palm Beach:
Canova, Diana (r: Hollywood, Calif.)
Noel, Chris
Wilton Manors:
Stafford, Nancy

GEORGIA

Albany:
Charles, Ray (R&B singer)
Fowler, Jim
Athens:
Basinger, Kim
Atlanta:
Cherry, Byron
Gaines, Boyd
Guest, William (raised)
Hooks, Jan
Ivey, Dana
Jeter, Felicia
Kelley, DeForest
Kennedy, Lindsay
Knight, Gladys

Knight, Merald
Lenihan, Deirdre (r: New York City)
Marash, Dave (r: Richmond, Va.)
Page, Harrison
Parks, Bert
Pattern, Edward (raised)
Pflug, Jo Ann
Reed, Jerry
Russell, Nipsey
Tracy, Lee
Van Dyke, Barry (r: New York City; Los Angeles)
West, Mary Jo
Augustus:
Johnston, Lionel
Carrollton:
Jackson, Keith
Cedartown:
Holloway, Sterling
Clarksdale:
Stevens, Ray
Columbus:
Parrish, Helen
Cumming:
Samples, Alvin "Junior"
Cuthbert:
Grier, Roosevelt
Fort Benning:
Reed, Tracy
Gainesville:
Macintosh, Jay W.
Griffin:
Andrews, Edward
Kiker, Douglas
Hawkinsville:
Terry, Arlene and Ardelle
LaGrange:
Jarriel, Tom
Macon:
Douglas, Melvyn
Pickens, Jane
Yates, Cassie
Marietta:
Walker, Danton
Midville:
Thurman, Tedi
Moultrie:
Melton, James
Nelson:
Akins, Claude
Ocilla:
Myers, Pauline (r: New Jersey)

Savannah:
  Curb, Mike
  Griffeth, Simone
  Keach, Stacy
  Mercer, Johnny
  Scarwid, Diana
Upson County:
  Ellerbee, Robby
Valdosta:
  Shroyer, Sonny
  Wilson, Demond
Waycross:
  Dickerson, Nathaniel (of the Mariners)
  Reynolds, Burt (r: Palm Beach, Fla.)
  Roberts, Pernell

HAWAII

City Not Known:
  Abellira, Remi (raised)
  Haleloke
Hilo:
  Wedemeyer, Herman
  Zulu
Honolulu:
  Chapman, Margot (Starland Vocal Band)
  Dreier, Alex
  Fong, Kam
  Gray, Erin
  Keale, Moe
  Kusatsu, Clyde
  Miles, Sherry
  Stroud, Don
  Young, Keone
  Young, Victoria
Kona:
  Sakata, Harold
Lihue, Kauai:
  D'Orso, Wisa
Maui:
  Ponce, Poncie
Oahu:
  Fong, Brian
Olaa:
  Fujioka, John

IDAHO

City Not Known:
  Wesson, Dick

Boise:
  Ruick, Melville
  York, Donny (Sha Na Na)
Buhl:
  Reynolds, Marjorie
Larsen:
  Zimmer, Norma
Moscow:
  McCaffrey, John K.M.
Mountain Home:
  Rainey, Ford
Pocatello:
  Bird, Billie
Rexburg:
  Jacobs, Christian
Ririe:
  Jacobs, Rachael
Salmon:
  Cannon, J.D.
Wallace:
  Turner, Lana
Wendell:
  Jackson, Sherry (r: Hollywood, Calif.)

ILLINOIS

City Not Known:
  Coffield, Peter
  Rasche, David
Avon:
  Carpenter, Ken
Belleville:
  Ebsen, Buddy
  Stumpf, Randy
Bloomington:
  Higgins, Joel
Blue Island:
  Colorado, Hortensia
Canton:
  Wolfe, Ian
Centralia:
  Blake, Oliver
Chicago Heights:
  Barnes, George
Chicago:
  Adams, Franklin P.
  Allen, Rex, Jr.
  Allman, Sheldon
  Amsterdam, Morey
  Andrews, Tina
  Armen, Kay

Atwater, Edith
Bain, Barbara
Ballantine, Carl (raised)
Ballantine, Eddie
Barrie, Barbara (r: Corpus Christi, Texas)
Barton, Dan (raised)
Beck, John
Bell, Rex
Bellamy, Ralph
Belland, Bruce (r: Los Angeles)
Belushi, Jim (r: Wheaton, Ill.)
Belushi, John (r: Wheaton, Ill.)
Bergen, Edgar
Berman, Shelley
Bledsoe, Tempestt
Bosley, Tom
Brauner, Asher
Bregman, Buddy
Bresler, Jerry
Brill, Marty (raised)
Brown, Chelsea (r: Los Angeles)
Brown, Timothy
Butkus, Dick
Carr, Darleen
Carter, Ray
Cassey, Chuck
Chancellor, John
Charles, Ray
Christie, Audrey
Conrad, Robert
D'Andrea, Tom
Daly, Jonathan
Davis, Clifton
Devon, Laura
Disney, Walt
Douglas, Mike
Drier, Moosie
Drivas, Robert
Dunn, Nora
Farina, Dennis
Fosse, Bob
Freeman, Kathleen
Frees, Paul
Furth, George
Gertz, Jami (r: Glenview, Ill.)
Gibbs, Marla
Gobel, George
Golonka, Arlene
Goodman, Benny
Gordon, Gerald
Graham, Virginia
Gray, Dolores (r: Los Angeles)
Gray, Michael (r: Miami)
Greene, Shecky
Gross, Mary
Gross, Michael
Gunther, John
Guzaldo, Joseph
Hagen, Jean
Hager, Jim & Jon
Hannah, Page
Harper, Jessica
Henderson, Bill
Henner, Marilu
Herron, Joel
Homeier, Skip
Howard, Barbara
Hunt, Marsha
Hutton, Ina Ray
Jacoby, Scott
Jameson, Joyce
Johnson, Arte
Johnson, Chic (Olsen & Johnson)
Jones, Quincy (r: Seattle, Wash.)
Jones, Sam J. (r: West Palm Beach, Fla.)
Kelley, Barry
Kerwin, Brian
Kiley, Richard
Kilgallen, Dorothy (r: Brooklyn, N.Y.)
King, Kip
Kirby, George
Kirby, Randy
Koenig, Walter
Korman, Harvey
Kostal, Irwin
Kupcinet, Irv
Ladd, Hank
Laine, Frankie
Lenard, Mark (r: South Haven, Mich.)
Leonard, Jack E.
Lerman, April (r: New York City)
Lester, Buddy
Lester, Jerry
Leyden, Bill
Long, Richard
MacGibbon, Harriet
Madsen, Michael

Mahoney, Jock
Malden, Karl (r: Gary, Ind.)
Malone, Dorothy (r: Dallas, Tex.)
Maltby, Richard
Mantegna, Joe
Mars, Kenneth
May, Donald
McCashin, Constance (r: Greenwich, Conn.)
McCoy, Sid
McCracken, Jeff
McGrath, Paul
McNellis, Maggi
Mills, Alley (r: New York)
Mills, Donna
Moore, Clayton
Morgan, Cindy
Morrow, Byron
Morrow, Karen (r: Des Moines, Iowa)
Muir, Gavin
Mull, Martin
Nelson, Jimmy
Nichols, Nichelle
Norton, Cliff
O'Brien, David
O'Connor, Donald
Olin, Ken
Platt, Howard
Quinn, Louis
Rawls, Lou
Reilly, John
Rhodes, George
Robbins, Gale
Rockwell, Robert (r: Lake Bluff, Ill.)
Rose, Reva
Ross-Leming, Eugenie
Ryan, Robert
Sajak, Pat
Saylor, Sid
Schaal, Richard
Schaal, Wendy
Schreiber, Avery
Scott, Synda
Seymour, Dan
Shaw, Stan
Shriver, Maria
Silver, Joe
Sirott, Bob
Somack, Jack
Sosnik, Harry
Soul, David

St. John, Howard
Stanley, Florence
Stone, Rob (r: Dallas, Tex.)
T, Mr.
Taylor, June
Thinnes, Roy
Thompson, Wesley
Tillstrom, Burr
Tobin, Michele (r: Los Angeles)
Tomme, Ron
Torme, Mel
Utley, Garrick
Vance, Danitra
Vivyan, John
Wahl, Ken
Wallace, Chris
Wanamaker, Sam
Warfield, Marsha
Wayne, Nina
Wendt, George
Williams, Dick Anthony
Williams, Robin
Williams, Tom
Willock, Dave
Young, Robert (r: California)
Young, Victor (r: Warsaw, Poland)
Zabach, Florian
Zaremba, John
Zmed, Adrian
Christopher:
  Rayburn, Gene (r: Chicago)
Clayton:
  Anderson, John
Danville:
  Van Dyke, Jerry
  Wainwright, James
DeKalb:
  Hale, Barbara
Downers Grove:
  Stock, Barbara
DuQuoin:
  Swofford, Ken
East St. Louis:
  Lawrence, Bill
El Paso:
  Sheen, Bishop Fulton J.
Elgin:
  Boxleitner, Bruce (r: Mt. Prospect, Ill.)
Evanston:
  Burns, Ronnie
  Christopher, William

Cusack, Joan
Fulton, Julie
Heston, Charlton
Marshall, Joan
Murray, Bill
Pearson, Drew
Shull, Richard B.
Galena:
McNeill, Don
Geneva:
Champion, Gower
Taylor, Joan
Gillespie:
Keel, Howard
Granite City:
Freedman, Winifred
Hartford:
Walker, Clint
Harvey:
Hayes, Bill
Herin:
Moore, Charlotte
Highland Park:
Lupton, John (r: Milwaukee, Wis.)
Reed, Robert (r: Muskogee, Okla.)
Homewood:
Sublette, Linda
Hunt Township:
Ives, Burl
Jacksonville:
Sullivan, Liam
Joliet:
McCambridge, Mercedes
Thigpen, Lynne
Totter, Audrey
Kankakee:
Bruce, David
MacMurray, Fred (r: Beaver Dam, Wis.)
Kewanee:
Brand, Neville
La Harpe:
Soule, Olan
Lake Villa:
Rolin, Judi
Mattoon:
Summers, Hope
Maywood:
Franz, Dennis
Prine, John
McLeansboro:
Smith, H. Allen

Melrose Park:
Lawrence, Carol
Moline:
Berry, Ken
Luchsinger, Chuck and Jack (raised)
Montgomery:
Mathews, Carole
Morrison:
Cameron, Dean (r: Oklahoma)
Normal:
Stevenson, McLean
Oak Park:
Archer, Beverly (r: Temple City, LA)
Bishop, William
DonHowe, Gwyda
Lund, Deanna
Nettleton, Lois
Newhart, Bob
White, Betty (r: California)
Paris:
Stuart, Barbara (r: Hume, Ill.)
Park Forest:
Ebersole, Christine
Park Ridge:
Black, Karen
Pekin:
Cooper, Wyllis
Dey, Susan (r: Mt. Kisco, N.Y.)
Peoria:
Correll, Charles
Costello, Mariclare
Pryor, Richard
Stiers, David Ogden
Stone, Cynthia
Thompson, Marshall
Princeton:
Hays, Kathryn
Taylor, Josh
Quincy:
Carmichael, Ralph
Ketchum, Dave
Wicker, Ireene
River Forest:
Hanna, Phil
Rock Falls:
Bellson, Louis
Rock Island:
Albert, Eddie
Moore, Tim
Savannah, Ill:
King, Wayne

Springfield:
  Lenz, Richard (r: Jackson, Mich.)
Summum:
  Burnette, Smiley
Tampico:
  Reagan, Ronald
Taylorville:
  Craig, Yvonne
Urbana:
  Ebert, Roger
Waukegan:
  Benny, Jack
  Chandler, George
Western Springs:
  Culea, Melinda
Wheaton:
  Dugan, Dennis
  Maxey, Paul
Winchester:
  Breeding, Larry
Winnetka:
  Dern, Bruce
  Hudson, Rock
Woodstock:
  Redeker, Quinn (r: Seattle, Wash.)
Zion:
  Coleman, Gary
  Nype, Russell

INDIANA

City Not Known:
  Dumke, Ralph
  Richards, Carol (raised)
Auburn:
  Shaw, Mark
Bippus:
  Schenkel, Chris
Bloomington:
  Carmichael, Hoagy
  Miller, Denny (a.k.a. Scott)
Carroll County:
  Fouts, Tom "Stubby"
Columbus:
  Barbour, Ross (Four Freshmen)
Dale:
  Henderson, Florence
East Chicago:
  Palmer, Betsy
  Reynolds, Frank
Elwood:
  Canary, David (r: Massilon,
    Ohio)

Evansville:
  Bates, Rhonda (raised)
  Brooks, Avery (r: Gary, Ind.)
  Glass, Ron
Fort Wayne:
  Hogestyn, Drake
  Long, Shelley
  Scherer, Ray
  Vigran, Herb
  York, Dick
Frankfort:
  Aidman, Charles
  Geer, Will
Gary:
  Jackson, Jackie (raised)
  Jackson, Janet (raised)
  Jackson, Marlon (raised)
  Jackson, Michael
  Jackson, Randy (raised)
  Jackson, Rebie (Maureen) (raised)
  Jackson, Tito (raised)
  Karras, Alex
  Marshall, William
  Thomas, Ernest
  Williamson, Fred
Goodland:
  Condon, Eddie
Greencastle:
  Barbour, Don (Four Freshmen)
  Flanigan, Bob (Four Freshmen)
Hammond:
  Funk, Terry (r: Amarillo, Tex.)
Hartford City:
  Peters, Deedy
Indiana Harbor:
  Hubbard, John
Indianapolis:
  Kirby, Durward (r: Covington, Ky.)
  Letterman, David
  McWhirter, Julie
  Meyer, Dorothy
  Nolan, Tom
  Paige, Robert
  Pauley, Jane
  Sherwood, Bobby
  Sloyan, James (r: Europe)
  Von Zell, Harry
Kokomo:
  Martin, Strother
Lafayette:
  Kennedy, Adam
  McNeeley, Larry

Lowell:
Worley, Jo Anne
Michigan City:
Baxter, Anne (r: Bronxville, N.Y.)
Milan:
Jordan, William
Mishawaka:
Lane, Allan "Rocky"
Newcastle:
Crane, Richard
Plainfield:
Tucker, Forrest
Pleasant Lake:
Tuttle, Lurene (r: California)
Plymouth:
Bergman, Richard
Portland:
Ames, Leon
Richmond:
Purcell, Sarah (r: San Diego, Calif.)
South Bend:
Bromfield, John
Everett, Chad
Haynes, Lloyd
Warren, Michael
Terre Haute:
Crothers, Scatman
Payne, Julie
Vevey:
Maynard, Kermit
Vincennes:
Skelton, Red
Wabash:
Olsen, Ole (Olsen & Johnson)
Warsaw:
McMartin, John
Wolcottville:
Kercheval, Ken (r: Clinton, Ind.)

IOWA

City Not Known:
Dale, Dick
Jackson, Selmer
Owen, Beverly
Alden:
Jones, Gordon
Avoca:
Beymer, Richard
Burlington:
Frawley, William
Cedar Falls:
Kroeger, Gary

Cedar Rapids:
Barr, Douglas
DeFore, Don
Farrell, Terry
Hershfield, Harry
Thaler, Robert
Cherokee:
Nordine, Ken
Clarinda:
Maxwell, Marilyn
Corning:
Carson, Johnny (r: Norfolk, Neb.)
Council Bluffs:
Freeman, Joan (r: Burbank, Calif.)
Creston:
Wallace, Marcia
Dakota City:
Reasoner, Harry
Davenport:
Barry, Patricia
Getz, John
Margolin, Stuart
Decorah:
Johnson, Georgiann
Pinter, Mark
Denison:
Reed, Donna
Des Moines:
Collins, Stephen
Daily, Bill
Jenks, Frank
Leachman, Cloris
Nelson, Harriet
Thompson, Sada (r: Fanwood,
N.J.)
Yelm, Shirley (r: Fairoaks, Calif.)
Dubuque:
Bueno, Delora (r: Brazil)
Lindsay, Margaret
Mulgrew, Kate
Ft. Madison:
O'Keefe, Dennis (r: on the road)
Hamburg:
Case, Russ
Hampton:
Bailey, Jack
Hawarden:
Emerson, Hope
Iowa City:
Powell, Randolph
Jefferson:
Gallup, Dr. George

Keokuk:
  Maxwell, Elsa
  Nagel, Conrad
LaPorte City:
  Allison, Fran
Mason City:
  Willson, Meredith
Nashua:
  Taylor, Kent
Nevada:
  Patterson, Neva
Pleasantville:
  McKay, Scott
Randalia:
  Oakes, Randi
Sioux City:
  Carey, Macdonald
  Farrell, Sharon
  Grandy, Fred
  Mathers, Jerry (r: Tarzana,
    Calif.)
  Moore, Constance
  Rafferty, Frances
Stanton:
  Christine, Virginia
Wall Lake:
  Williams, Andy
  Williams, Dick
Waterloo:
  Adams, Julie
Waverly:
  Talbott, Michael

KANSAS

City Not Known:
  Brewster, Diane
Abilene:
  Philipp, Karen (r: Covina, Calif.)
Altoona:
  Moore, Ida
Baxter Springs:
  Stewart, Byron (r: Marin County,
    Calif.)
Burrton:
  Stone, Milburn
Caldwell:
  Showalter, Max
Cherryvale:
  Vance, Vivian (r: Independence,
    Kan.)
Coffeyville:
  Sikes, Cynthia

Eldorado:
  Brodie, Steve
Fort Riley:
  Reilly, Tom (r: Bergenfield, N.J.)
Hutchinson:
  Corsaut, Aneta
  Klous, Pat (r: Texas)
Kansas City:
  Asner, Edward
  Brands, X. (r: Los Angeles)
  Treas, Terri
  Waggoner, Lyle (r: St. Louis, Mo.)
Lawrence:
  Beaumont, Hugh
Leavenworth:
  Sparks, Randy (New Christy Min-
    strels)
Lyndon:
  Colvin, Jack
Lyons:
  Rodd, Marcia
Olathe:
  Rogers, Charles "Buddy"
Parsons:
  Pitts, ZaSu (r: Santa Cruz, Calif.)
Rice:
  Snyder, Arlen Dean
Russell:
  Dusay, Marj
Topeka:
  Born, Roscoe
Varner's Forge:
  Gnagy, John
Wichita:
  Alley, Kirstie
  Corley, Al
  Fudge, Alan
  Kenton, Stan (r: Los Angeles)
  Rainwater, Marvin
  Swayze, John Cameron (r: Atchison,
    Kansas City, Kansas)
Winfield:
  McCarty, Mary (r: Los Angeles)

KENTUCKY

City Not Known:
  Karnes, Robert
Annville:
  Stringbean (David Akeman)
Ashland:
  Reeves, George
  Woolery, Chuck

Bardwell:
  Stewart, Martha
Blue Lick (or Berea):
  Foley, Red
Bowling Green:
  McDonald, Francis
Brooksville:
  Galloway, Don
Brownie:
  Everly, Don and Phil
Butchers Hollow:
  Lynn, Loretta
Corbin:
  Lake, Arthur
Covington:
  Young, Bob (r: Cincinnati,
    Ohio)
Cynthiana:
  Pressman, Lawrence
Danville:
  McCormick, Robert
Depoy:
  Oates, Warren
Dickeyville:
  Foster, Bill
Florence:
  Price, Kenny
Glasgow:
  Sawyer, Diane
Graves County:
  Barkley, Alben W.
Hardensburg:
  Jordan, Bobbi
Harlan:
  Hill, Richard (r: Toledo, Ohio)
Lexington:
  Beatty, Ned
  Varney, Jim
Louisville:
  Bond, Sudie (r: Hendersonville,
    N.C.)
  Brooks, Foster
  Brown, John Mason
  Burmester, Leo
  Conrad, William (r: Calif.)
  Considine, Tim
  Dunne, Irene
  Hopkins, Telma (r: Detroit)
  Kennedy, Tom
  Link, Frank
  Miller, Mark Thomas
  Narz, Jack

Phillips, Nancie
Randolph, Amanda
Ludlow:
  Braun, Bob
Maysville:
  Clooney, Betty
  Clooney, Rosemary
Middlesboro:
  Mountain, Johnny
  Parrish, Julie
Niagra:
  Jones, Louis M. "Grandpa"
Olive Hill:
  Hall, Tom T.
Owensboro:
  Ewell, Tom
Paintsville:
  Gayle, Crystal
Powderly:
  Best, James (r: Corydon, Ind.)
Russell:
  McCutcheon, Bill

LOUISIANA

City Not Known:
  Howell, Arlene
  Roberts, Francesca
Baywood:
  Douglas, Donna
Delhi (Tensas Swamp):
  Holliman, Earl
Elizabeth:
  Emerson, Faye
Ferriday:
  Smith, Howard K.
Gretna:
  La Rue, Lash
Lafayette:
  Keith, Richard
Metairie:
  Gennaro, Peter
Monroe:
  McGee, Frank
New Orleans:
  Boswell, Connee
  Bryant, Willie
  Burke, Paul
  Carlisle, Kitty
  Carr, Paul
  Clark, Doran
  Colt, Marshall
  Fountain, Pete

Fremin, Jourdan
Gumbel, Bryant (r: Chicago)
Healy, Mary
Hirt, Al
Laneuville, Eric
Larroquette, John
LeBeauf, Sabrina
Monroe, Bill
Morris, Garrett
Nelson, Christopher S.
Nelson, Ed (r: North Carolina)
Perry, Wolfe (r: Oakland, Calif.)
Piazza, Marguerite
Ray, Marguerite (r: Oakland, Calif.)
St. John, Marco
Walston, Ray
Weathers, Carl
Wilson, Roger
Opelousas:
Douglas, Ronalda
Eastham, Richard
Orleans:
Hunter, Jeffrey
Shreveport:
Carroll, Pat (r: Los Angeles)
Connelly, Peggy (r: Texas)
Hewitt, Virginia (r: Kansas City, Mo.)
Sykes, Brenda
Wells, Carole (r: California)
Vidalia:
Williams, Spencer
West Monroe:
Pierce, Webb

MAINE

City Not Known:
Fahey, Myrna
Fort Fairfield:
Mears, Deann
Houlton:
Smith, Samantha
Northeast Harbor:
Fennelly, Parker
Portland:
Barnes, C.B.
Flavin, James
Lavin, Linda
MacVane, John

Martin, Andrea
Schneider, Tawny (r: New York City)
South Paris:
Shaw, Reta
South Windham:
Donnell, Jeff

MARYLAND

City Not Known:
Allen, Karen
Baltimore:
Armstrong, Bess
Astin, John
Ayres, Leah
Blessing, Jack
Conried, Hans
Elliot, "Mama" Cass
Evans, Damon
Ford, Paul
Gillette, Anita (raised)
Hasselhoff, David
Hayes, Margaret
Hayman, Lillian
Long, Avon
Mackin, Catherine
Mann, Johnny
Mayehoff, Eddie
Moore, Garry
Muse, Clarence
Natwick, Mildred
O'Conor, Sen. Herbert
Parker, Jameson
Pryor, Nicholas (raised)
Robbins, Fred
Rollins, Howard E., Jr.
Schultz, Dwight
Sterling, Jack
Tarses, Jay
Topper, Tim
Tucker, Michael
Ward, Jonathan (r: Elkridge, Md.)
Whitton, Margaret (r: Haddonfield, N.J.)
Wilson, Ethel
Wrightson, Earl
Berlin:
Harrison, Linda
Bethesda:
Hays, Robert
Richardson, Patricia

Havre 'de Grace:
  Cross, Murphy (r: Laurel, Md.)
Salisbury:
  Hamilton, Linda
Sikeston:
  Scott, Jacqueline

MASSACHUSETTS

Andover:
  Henderson, Marcia
Arlington:
  Ryan, Dave "Chico" (Sha Na Na)
Attleboro:
  Bowen, Roger (r: Providence, R.I.)
  Smith, Howard (actor)
Auburn:
  Lynn, Jeffrey
Beverly:
  Morse, David
Boston:
  Andrews, Johnny
  Bailey, Hillary
  Barnes, Joanna
  Brogan, Jimmy
  Burns, Jack
  Cass, Peggy
  Casson, Mel (r: New York City)
  Colonna, Jerry
  Contardo, Johnny (Sha Na Na)
  Conway, Gary
  Crosby, Norm
  Darling, Joan
  Delmar, Kenny
  Elliott, Bob (Bob and Ray) (r: Win-
    chester, Mass.)
  Fiedler, Arthur
  Francis, Arlene
  Greene, Lynnie (r: Newton, Mass.)
  Grove, Betty Ann
  Groves, Regina
  Haley, Jack
  Hall, Anthony Michael
  Hall, Thurston
  Haskell, Peter
  Howe, Quincy
  Howland, Beth
  Hunter, Ronald
  Indrisano, John
  Kahn, Madeline
  Kondazian, Karen (r: California)
  La Centra, Peg

Lemmon, Jack
Lewis, Marcia (r: Cincinnati, Ohio)
Loren, Donna
MacKay, Harper
Marcellino, Jocko (Sha Na Na)
McBride, Dirty Dan (Sha Na Na)
Miner, Jan
Newman, Barry
Nimoy, Leonard
Remick, Lee
Roche, Eugene
Roman, Ruth
Rubin, Benny
Rudd, Paul
Schuck, John
Sherman, Hiram
Simon, Scott (Sha Na Na)
Taylor, Vaughn
Walters, Barbara
Winters, Roland
Brighton:
  Dysart, Richard (r: Augusta, Me.)
  Herd, Richard
Brockton:
  Doucette, John
Brookline:
  Gordon, Barry
  Wallace, Mike
Cambridge:
  Allen, Fred
  Bickford, Charles
  Curtin, Jane
  Fontaine, Frank
  Glaser, Paul Michael
  Hayman, Richard
  Jillian, Ann
  Libertini, Richard
  Loudon, Dorothy
  Luz, Franc
  Rachins, Alan
  Rocco, Alex
  Waterston, Sam
Chelsea:
  Stang, Arnold
Clinton:
  Moorehead, Agnes
Dedham:
  Hines, Connie
Dorchester:
  Bolger, Ray
  Herlihy, Ed

Dracut:
  Corey, Wendell
Everett:
  Elliot, Win (raised)
Fall River:
  Dean, Morton
  Holmes, Jennifer (r: Seekonk, Mass.)
Framingham:
  Morey, Bill
Lawrence:
  Fraser, Gordon
  Goulet, Robert
Lexington:
  Scannell, Susan
Lowell:
  Ansara, Michael
  Goddard, Mark (r: Scituate, Mass.)
  Goulding, Ray (Bob and Ray)
  Grimes, Scott (r: Dracut, Mass.)
  Mooney, Art
Lynn:
  Gilman, Sam
  Grimes, Tammy
  Hamilton, Neil
  Parsons, Estelle
Malden:
  Albertson, Jack
  Ames, Ed
  Brown, Wally
  Keim, Betty Lou
Medford:
  Morrill, Priscilla
Nahant:
  Amory, Cleveland
New Bedford:
  Haney, Carol
  Rubin, Andrew
Newton Highlands:
  Preston, Robert
Newton:
  Howard, Bob
  Morse, Robert
Northampton:
  Dunne, Steve
Northbridge:
  Thibault, Conrad
Northfield:
  Edwards, Rick
Onset Bay, Cape Cod:
  Farrell, Charles
Palmer:
  Conte, John (r: Los Angeles)

Pittsfield:
  Giftos, Elaine
Quincy:
  Corcoran, Noreen (r: California)
  Dana, Bill
  Vye, Murvyn
Revere:
  Macy, Bill (r: Brooklyn, N.Y.)
Roxbury:
  Hall, Ed
Salem:
  Larch, John (r: Brooklyn, N.Y.)
  Ruscio, Al
  Slade, Mark
Somerville:
  Knight, Jack
Springfield:
  Danoff, Bill (Starland Vocal Band)
  Foray, June
  Irving, George S.
  Russell, Kurt (r: Los Angeles)
  Sanford, Ralph
  Weston, Paul
Swampscott:
  Brennan, Walter
Wakefield:
  Girardin, Ray
Waltham:
  Bailey, F. Lee
  Ponce, Danny
Wareham:
  Davis, Geena
West Medford:
  Cole, Carol
West Springfield:
  Durocher, Leo
Westfield:
  Pardo, Don
Whitman:
  Baker, Lennie (Sha Na Na)
Williamstown:
  Perry, John Bennett
Winthrop:
  Woodell, Pat
Wollaston:
  DeWolfe, Billy
Worcester:
  Cully, Zara
  Gibbs, Georgia
  Kennedy, Arthur
  Lambert, Gloria
  Mekka, Eddie

MICHIGAN

Ann Arbor:
- Lawson, Linda
- Whitney, Grace Lee (r: Detroit, Mich.)

Battle Creek:
- Hutton, Betty

Birmingham:
- Maxted, Ellen

Camden:
- Martin, Merry

Coldwater:
- McDevitt, Ruth

Dearborn:
- Mara, Adele
- Matheson, Don
- Paul, Eugenia

Deerfield:
- Thomas, Danny (r: Toledo, Ohio)

Detroit:
- Allen, Byron (r: Los Angeles)
- Andre, E.J.
- Arlen, Roxanne
- Bono, Sonny
- Borden, Lynn
- Bryant, William (r: Bogalusa, La.)
- Burstyn, Ellen
- Cole, Dennis
- Cox, Wally
- Desmond, Johnny
- Eilber, Janet
- Fink, John
- Foy, Fred
- Garrett, Susie
- Garvey, Cyndy
- Gilliam, Stu
- Grant, Faye
- Harden, Ernest, Jr.
- Hunter, Kim
- Jeffries, Herb
- Kelly, Brian
- Kiel, Richard
- Laurie, Piper
- Martin, Dick
- McMahon, Ed (r: Lowell, Mass.)
- Meek, Barbara
- Milner, Martin (r: Wash., Calif.)
- Mitchell, Guy (r: California)
- Moody, Lynne (r: Evanston, Ill.)
- Moore, Robert
- Morgan, Harry
- Moriarty, Michael
- Nicholas, Denise
- Osborn, Lyn
- Peppard, George
- Pierce, Maggie
- Radner, Gilda
- Randolph, Bill
- Randolph, Joyce
- Reese, Della
- Robinson, Smokey
- Rogers, Timmie
- Ryan, Roz
- Selleck, Tom (r: Los Angeles)
- Skerritt, Tom
- Stahl, Richard
- Stritch, Elaine
- Talman, William
- Thomas, Marlo (r: Los Angeles)
- Tolan, Michael
- Tomlin, Lily
- Turner, Tierre
- Wagner, Robert (r: California)
- Whiting, Margaret (r: California)
- Wilson, Joyce Vincent
- Woods, Michael
- Wright, Max

East Lansing:
- Busfield, Timothy

Farmington Hills:
- Dawber, Pam

Fenville:
- Quine, Don

Ferndale:
- Elcar, Dana

Flint:
- Eubanks, Bob (r: Los Angeles)
- Vernon, Harvey

Grand Rapids:
- Teal, Ray
- Wilson, Elizabeth

Grosse Pointe Park:
- Harris, Julie

Grosse Pointe:
- Gail, Max

Hillsdale:
- Robards, Jason, Sr.

Holland:
- Masse, Laurel (Manhattan Transfer)

Kalamazoo:
- Powell, Angela
- Story, Ralph

Lansing:
- Reid, Carl Benton

Livonia:
  Savage, Brad (r: Hollywood)
Milford:
  Jackson, Mary
Mt. Clemens:
  Enberg, Dick
Munising:
  Osser, Glenn
Newaygo:
  Bargy, Roy (r: Toledo, Ohio)
Norway:
  Van Damme, Art (r: Chicago, Ill.)
Petosky:
  Smith, Hal
Port Huron:
  Wismer, Harry
South Haven:
  Jensen, Sanford
Sunrise:
  Widmark, Richard (r: Chicago)
Three Rivers:
  Collingwood, Charles
Traverse City:
  Wayne, David
Vicksburg:
  Lucking, William
Wyandotte:
  Majors, Lee

MINNESOTA

Albert Lea:
  Carlson, Richard
  Ross, Marion
Aurora:
  York, Francine
Duluth:
  Frazee, Jane
  Knudsen, Peggy
Grand Rapids:
  Garland, Judy
Minneapolis:
  Anderson, Larry
  Anderson, Richard Dean
  Arness, James
  Averback, Hy (r: Los Angeles)
  Ayres, Lew
  Clausen, Alf
  Dahl, Arlene
  Duffy, Julia
  Flanders, Ed
  Graves, Peter

Guilbert, Ann Morgan
Hanley, Bridget (r: Edmonds, Wash.)
Hong, James
James, John (r: New Canaan, Conn.)
Johnson, Arch
Kelsey, Linda
Lyman, Dorothy
Neill, Noel (raised)
Papenfuss, Tony
Proft, Pat (r: Columbia Heights,
  Minn.)
Staley, Joan
Walter, Cy
Mountain Iron:
  Charmoli, Tony
Northfield:
  Chase, Sylvia
Owatonna:
  Marshall, E.G.
Robbinsdale:
  Scott, Kathryn Leigh
Royal Oak:
  George, Christopher
St. Cloud:
  McCary, Rod
  Young, Gig (r: Washington, D.C.)
St. Paul:
  Abel, Walter
  Alexander, Joan
  Anderson, Loni
  Davis, Joan
  Demarest, William
  Farrell, Mike (r: Los Angeles)
  Gates, Larry
  Greaza, Walter
  Keating, Larry
  Lange, Jim
  Lee, Pinky
  Parnell, Emory
  Simmons, Richard
  Wallace, Jane
Twin Valley:
  Niles, Wendell (r: Livingston,
    Mont.)
Virginia:
  Goodwin, Michael (r: Washington
    State)
Waconia:
  Herbert, Don
Windon:
  Olsen, Johnny

Worthington:
  Little, Tiny, Jr.

MISSISSIPPI

City Not Known:
  Best, Willie
  Whiting, Napoleon
Amite County:
  Clower, Jerry
Amory:
  Grubbs, Gary
Arkabutla:
  Jones, James Earl (r: Manistee,
    Mich.)
Biloxi:
  Mobley, Mary Ann
Brooksville:
  O'Neal, Frederick
Chickasaw County:
  Gentry, Bobbie
Collins:
  Andrews, Dana
  McRaney, Gerald
Columbus:
  Barber, Red
Grange:
  Ates, Roscoe
Greenville:
  Henson, Jim
  Winston, Hattie
Greenwood:
  Butler, Johnny
Hot Coffee:
  Stevens, Stella
Itta Bena (near Indianola):
  King, B.B.
Jackson:
  Lester, Tom
  Wade, Ernestine
Meridian:
  Childress, Alvin
  Gordon, Phil
  Ladd, Diane
  Ward, Sela
Shelby:
  Wilson, Gerald
Smithville:
  Brasfield, Rod
Vicksburg:
  Richards, Beah

Yazoo City:
  Hamilton, Lynn

MISSOURI

City Not Known:
  Engle, Roy
  Lee, Johnny (r: Pueblo, Colo.)
  O'Neal, Ann
Bevier:
  Fascinato, Jack
Carthage:
  Kaye, Celia (r: Wilmington, Del.)
  Perkins, Marlin (r: Pittsburg, Kan.)
Clayton:
  Franciscus, James
Clever:
  Mandan, Robert
Columbia:
  Smith, William (r: Burbank, Calif.)
DeSoto:
  Wilcox, Frank
Edgerton:
  Davis, Jim
Eve:
  Ghostley, Alice (r: Henryetta, Okla.)
Fairview:
  Greer, Dabbs (r: Anderson, Mo.)
Flatt Creek:
  Johnson, Don
Fulton:
  Ferrugia, John
Hannibal:
  Cornelius, Helen
  Edwards, Cliff "Ukulele Ike"
Humansville:
  Buchanan, Edgar
Jamesport:
  Scott, Martha
Joplin:
  Carr, Betty Ann (raised)
  Cummings, Robert
  Weaver, Dennis
Kansas City:
  Ace, Goodman
  Allen, Dennis
  Ashley, John
  Bannon, Jim
  Devore, Cain
  Harrison, Gracie
  Henderson, Luther, Jr.
  Kerr, Elizabeth

Lowery, Robert
McClurg, Edie
McConnell, Lulu
Melvin, Allan (r: New York City)
Stone, Dee Wallace
Truex, Ernest
Kirksville:
Page, Geraldine
Liberty:
Stevens, Craig
McComb:
Boyd, Jimmy
Mound City:
McGrath, Frank
Nevada:
Huston, John
Paris:
McBride, Mary Margaret
Sedalia:
Baker, Ann
Slater:
McQueen, Steve
Spring Fork:
Van Dyke, Leroy
Springfield:
Lowe, Jim
St. Joseph:
Cronkite, Walter (r: Houston, Tex.)
Garrett, Betty (r: Seattle, Wash.)
Maupin, Rex
Rockwell, Rocky
Thomas, Frank
Warrick, Ruth
Wyman, Jane
St. Louis:
Angelou, Maya
Arthur, Maureen
Berry, Fred
Buffano, Jules
Chiles, Linden (r: Barrington, Ill.)
Converse, Frank
Convy, Bert
Davis, Billy, Jr.
Dotson, Bob
Dunigan, Tim
Faylen, Frank
Foley, Ellen (raised)
Foxx, Redd
Frann, Mary
Froman, Jane
Garagiola, Joe

Gill, Rusty
Guillaume, Robert
Gunn, Moses
Harrison, Ray
Johnston, Johnny
Kendall, Cy
Kilpatrick, Eric
Kilpatrick, Lincoln
Linn-Baker, Mark (r: Wethersfield, Conn.)
Marlowe, Marion
Martin, Helen
McAllister, Chip (r: Los Angeles, .Calif.)
Miller, Marvin
Monica, Corbett
Nader, Michael (r: Beverly Hills, Calif.)
Nolan, Kathy
Phillips, Barney
Price, Vincent
Quinlan, Roberta
Roberts, Doris (r: New York City)
Selby, Sarah
Stevens, Julie
Susman, Todd
Taylor, Nathaniel
Thomas, Betty
Treen, Mary (r: California)
Weaver, Earl
Wells, Claudette
Wickes, Mary
Young, Bruce A.
Stanberry:
Karl, Martin (Mariners)
Wardell:
Moore, Barbara
Webster Groves:
Jenkins, Gordon
West Plains:
Van Dyke, Dick (r: Danville, Ill.)
Wagoner, Porter

MONTANA

Brady:
Montgomery, George
Butte:
Grant, Kirby
Raye, Martha
Cardwell:
Huntley, Chet

Great Falls:
  Baker, Jim B. (r: Conrad, Mont.)
  Gold, Missy (r: California)
  Kelton, Pert
Helena:
  Benedict, Dirk (r: White Sulphur
    Springs, Mont.)
Kalispell:
  Bray, Robert
Missoula:
  Carvey, Dana (r: San Carlos, Calif.)
Townsend:
  Duffy, Patrick

NEBRASKA

Filley:
  Taylor, Robert (r: Beatrice, Neb.)
Fremont:
  Sommars, Julie
Grand Island:
  Baird, Bil
  Fonda, Henry
Harvard:
  Revere, Paul
Hastings:
  Hefti, Neal
Kearney:
  Cavett, Dick
Laurel:
  Coburn, James
Lincoln:
  Abbott, Philip
  Lawrence, Bill
  Lynch, Peg (r: Minnesota)
  Turner, Janine (r: Fort Worth, Tex.)
Naponee:
  Janssen, David
O'Neill:
  Leahy, Frank
Omaha:
  Astaire, Fred
  Bloom, Lindsay
  Brando, Marlon
  Doyle, David
  Givot, George
  Kalber, Floyd
  Kurtz, Swoosie
  McGuire, Dorothy
  Nolte, Nick
  Stephenson, Skip
  Swenson, Inga

Wells, Mary K. (r: Long Beach,
  Calif.)
Pawnee City:
  McCalla, Irish
Plattsburgh:
  Newlan, Paul (r: Kansas City, Mo.)
Staplehurst:
  Gray, Coleen
Valentine:
  Bryson, Dr. Lyman
Wahoo:
  Akune, Shuko (r: Chicago, Ill.)

NEVADA

Goldfield:
  Alexander, Ben
Las Vegas:
  Copley, Teri
  Dalton, Abby (r: Los Angeles, Calif.)
  Greene, Michele
  Lewis, Jenny
Reno:
  Wells, Dawn (raised)

NEW HAMPSHIRE

Charleston:
  Broderick, James
Dixville Notch:
  Kallman, Dick
Dover:
  Isacksen, Peter (r: California)
Manchester:
  Stone, Christopher
  Talent, Ziggy
Nashua:
  Parker, Maggi
North Conway:
  Shea, John
Portsmouth:
  Bonerz, Peter (r: Milwaukee, Wis.)

NEW JERSEY

City Not Known:
  Ackerman, Leslie (raised)
  Dhiegh, Khigh
  Hegyes, Robert
  King, Zalman
  Maher, Bill (raised)
  Pena, Elizabeth (r: Cuba)
  Porter, Todd
  Scott, Bill (raised)

Asbury Park:
  Abbott, Bud
Atlantic City:
  De Witt, George
  Garrett, Patsy
  King, John Reed
  Nickerson, Dawn (raised)
Bayonne:
  Keith, Brian
  Olkewicz, Walter
  Shera, Mark
Burlington:
  Roberts, Howard
Camden:
  Bray, Thom
  Falana, Lola
Campgaw:
  Wyatt, Jane
Carteret:
  Price, Paul B.
Clifton:
  Randall, Frankie
Collingwood:
  Brown, Ted
Deal:
  Stuart, Maxine (r: Lawrence, N.Y.)
East Orange:
  Caulfield, Joan
  MacRae, Gordon (r: Syracuse, N.Y.)
  McK, Misha
  Montgomery, Barbara
  Warwick, Dionne
Elberon:
  Ferrer, Mel
Elizabeth:
  Mitchell, Thomas
  Scott, Debralee
Englewood:
  Francis, Genie (r: Los Angeles)
  Travolta, Ellen
  Travolta, John
Flemington:
  Foran, Dick
Fort Dix:
  Barnes, Priscilla
Glassboro:
  Amendolia, Don
Glen Ridge:
  Camarata, Tutti
Green Bank, Egg Harbor:
  Crowley, Kathleen

Hackensack:
  Carey, Philip
  Dow, Harold
  Karabatsos, Ron (r: Union City,
    N.J.)
Haddonfield:
  Cassidy, Joanna
  Scott, Alan
Harrington Park:
  Lydon, Jimmy
Hasbrouck Heights:
  Godfrey, Kathy
Hoboken:
  Hugh-Kelly, Daniel (r: Elizabeth,
    N.J.)
  Sinatra, Frank
Jersey City:
  Allen, Elizabeth
  Conte, Richard
  James, Dennis
  Jefferson, Herbert, Jr.
  Kilian, Victor
  Lane, Nathan
  Lloyd, Norman
  McCoo, Marilyn
  Murray, Kathryn
  Nelson, Ozzie
  Newman, Phyllis
  Sinatra, Frank, Jr.
  Walter, Tracey
  Warner, Malcolm Jamal (r: Los
    Angeles, Calif.)
  Wilson, Flip
Kearney:
  Mottola, Tony
Keyport:
  Hall, Juanita
Livingston:
  Goodwin, Kia
Long Branch:
  Anderson, Richard (r: Los Angeles,
    Calif.)
  Bradford, Johnny
  Whitney, Peter
Margate:
  Savitch, Jessica (r: Kennett Square,
    Pa.)
Millburn:
  Carmen, Julie
Milltown:
  Pintauro, Danny

Montclair:
  Brookes, Jacqueline
  Gilmour, Sandy
  Hayden, Sterling
  Heydt, Louis Jean
  Kirsten, Dorothy
  Kreskin
  Phillips, Tacey
  Pope, Perry
Morristown:
  Mitchell, Gwenn
  Stevens, Shawn
Neptune:
  DeVito, Danny (r: Asbury Park, N.J.)
New Brunswick:
  Douglas, Michael
  Osterwald, Bibi
  Space, Arthur
  Vallely, James
New Milford:
  Fontane Sisters, The (raised)
Newark:
  Amos, John (r: Orange, N.J.)
  Bauer, Charita
  Blacque, Taurean
  Blaine, Vivian
  Bouton, Jim
  Campbell, William
  Carey, Ron
  Finegan, Bill (of Sauter-Finegan)
  Francis, Connie
  Fuccello, Tom
  Henry, Carol
  Igus, Darrow
  Lewis, Jerry
  Lindsey, Mort
  Liotta, Ray
  Mones, Paul (r: West Orange, N.J.)
  Pesci, Joe (r: The Bronx, N.Y.)
  Pulliam, Keshia Knight
  Ragin, John S. (r: Irvington, N.J.)
  Reilly, Hugh
  Saint, Eva Marie (r: Albany, N.Y.)
  Schechner, Bill
  Simeone, Harry
  Wagenheim, Charles
  Warden, Jack
Nutley:
  Blake, Robert
Ocean City:
  Andes, Keith

Foster, Preston
Oradell:
  Riddle, Nelson
Orange:
  Ackroyd, David
  Fisher, Gail
Palisades:
  Bennett, Joan
Passaic:
  Hayes, Richard
  Lane, Nancy (r: Clifton, N.J.)
  Perkins, Millie
  Piscopo, Joe
  Pollard, Michael J.
  Swit, Loretta
Paterson:
  Baggetta, Vincent
  Costello, Lou
  Freeman, Ticker
  Langdon, Sue Ane (r: Kingsville,
    Tex.)
  Wheeler, Bert
Penn's Grove:
  Forsythe, John
  Willis, Bruce
Perth Amboy:
  Sebesky, Don
Pittman:
  Albers, Ken (Four Freshmen)
Plainfield:
  Lewis, Geoffrey
Pompton Plains:
  McKeon, Doug (r: Oakland, N.J.)
Princeton:
  Smith, Shelley (r: Memphis,
    Tenn.)
Ridgewood:
  Kollmar, Dick
Rumson:
  Schafer, Natalie
Short Hills:
  Coogan, Richard
Somerset County:
  Bohay, Heidi
Somerville:
  Van Cleef, Lee
South Amboy:
  Evigan, Greg
  Hoffman, Harold
Summit:
  Streep, Meryl

Teaneck:
  Nelson, Rick
Tenafly:
  Hamer, Rusty
  Hexum, Jon-Erik
Trenton:
  Kovacs, Ernie
  Light, Judith
  Locane, Amy
  Stevens, Naomi
West New York:
  Venture, Richard
West Orange:
  Ward, Evelyn
Westfield:
  Bunce, Alan
  Edwards, Geoff
Whippany:
  Frischman, Dan
Woodbury:
  Browne, Roscoe Lee

NEW MEXICO

City Not Known:
  Ego, Sandra
Cloudcroft:
  Cox, Ronny
Roswell:
  Brookshier, Tom
  Kennedy, Betty
Santa Fe:
  Hamilton, Ray (r: Seattle, Wash.)
  Nelson, Lori
Silver City:
  Benedict, Paul (r: Boston, Mass.)
  Graves, Leslie (r: New York City)
Tularosa:
  Clayton, Jan
Weed:
  Strange, Glenn

NEW YORK

City Not Known:
  Breslin, Pat
  Mayo, Whitman
Albany:
  Devane, William
  Rooney, Andy
Amityville:
  Baldwin, Alec
  Belford, Christine

Armonk:
  Gallagher, Peter
Astoria:
  Bracken, Eddie
  Brooke, Hillary
  Halpin, Luke
  Kelly, Jack
  Kenny, Nick
  Maharis, George
  McGoohan, Patrick (r: England)
Babylon:
  Dangerfield, Rodney
  Williams, William B.
Baldwin:
  Browning, Susan
  Earle, Robert
Bayside:
  Drake, Charles (r: New London,
    Conn.)
Beacon:
  Lavalle, Paul
  Montgomery, Robert
Bedford Hills:
  Hughes, Barnard
Bellrose:
  Van Patten, Vincent
Binghamton:
  Foster, Stuart
  Goddard, Don
  Hutton, Jim (r: Albany, N.Y.)
Bronx:
  Allan, Jed
  Allyson, June
  Birch, Peter
  Bishop, Joey (r: Philadelphia, Pa.)
  Brooks, Randy
  Brown, Mitch
  Buttons, Red
  Cara, Irene
  Carlin, George
  Carroll, Diahann
  Castellano, Richard
  Coco, James
  Curtis, Tony
  Dale, Jimmy
  Darin, Bobby
  Davalos, Dick
  Denison, Anthony
  Desiderio, Robert
  Egan, Eddie
  Fargas, Antonio
  Fleming, Art

Foster, Jodie
Gorme, Eydie
Gregory, James (r: New Rochelle, N.Y.)
Hart, Moss
Keats, Steven
Klein, Robert
Landesberg, Steve
Linden, Hal
Lopez, Priscilla (r: Brooklyn, N.Y.)
Lovejoy, Frank
Marshall, Penny
Maxwell, Frank
Morrison, Shelly
Morrow, Vic
Mulligan, Richard
Murray, Jan
O'Neill, Dick
Ponterotto, Donna
Reiner, Carl
Roberts, Tanya
Santiago, Saundra
Savalas, George
Schultz, Lenny
Seel, Charles
Sellecca, Connie
Sidney, Sylvia
Slattery, Richard X. (raised)
Smith, Allison
Torres, Liz
Valli, June
Vargas, John
Velez, Martha
Walker, Jimmie
Young, Ralph
Bronxville:
Cheek, Molly
Hoyt, John
Rounds, David
Brooklyn:
Adams, Joey
Ajaye, Franklyn
Anderson, Barbara
Anderson, Warner
Andrews, Tige
Arkin, Adam
Azzara, Candy
Baio, Jimmy
Baio, Scott
Baron, Sandy (raised)
Beasley, Allyce
Berlinger, Warren

Brady, Scott
Brandon, Michael
Brandt, Mel
Brisebois, Danielle
Brock, Stanley (r: The Bronx, N.Y.)
Brown, Lou
Burrows, Abe
Callahan, John (r: Long Island)
Callas, Charlie
Carmel, Roger C.
Carney, Alan
Carpenter, Thelma
Carter, Terry
Castle, Nick
Clark, Dane
Clute, Sidney
Colomby, Scott
Conn, Didi
Connors, Chuck
Corey, Irwin
Dale, Alan
Damon, Stuart
Damone, Vic
Daniels, William
Danza, Tony
David, Larry
DeCorsia, Ted
DeForest, Calvert
DeLuise, Dom
De Wilde, Brandon
DiAquinto, John (r: Ft. Lauderdale, Fla.)
Diamond, Don
Dishy, Bob
Downs, Johnny
Dreyfuss, Richard
Durrell, Michael
Edelman, Herb
Edwards, Vince
Fadiman, Clifton
Faracy, Stephanie
Farber, Bert
Farentino, James
Femia, John
Ferrigno, Lou
Fields, Charlie
Ford, Ed ("Senator Ed")
Foster, Phil
Fox, Sonny
Franken, Steve
Fraser, Elisabeth (r: Haiti)
Frey, Leonard

Funt, Allen
Gallagher, Helen
Gallo, Maria
Gargan, William
Gateson, Marjorie
Giambalvo, Louis
Gibbs, Terry
Ginty, Robert
Gleason, Jackie
Glickman, Marty
Gossett, Louis, Jr.
Gould, Elliott
Gould, Sandra
Graff, Ilene
Groh, David
Guttenberg, Steve
Hackett, Buddy
Hall, Cliff
Handleman, Stanley Myron
Harmon, Steve
Haskell, Jimmie
Hastings, Bob
Hastings, Don
Hawkins, Dolores
Heller, Randee (r: West Hempstead, N.Y.)
Hillebrand, Fred
Horton, Edward Everett
Ingels, Marty
Ivar, Stan
Jackson, Eddie
Jarrett, Art
Jergens, Adele
Jerome, Jerry
Jones, Edgar Allan, Jr.
Kantor, Richard
Kaplan, Gabe
Karlen, John
Kaye, Danny
Kazan, Lainie
Kelk, Jackie
Kelly, Patsy
King, Alan
Koufax, Sandy
Kove, Martin
LaRosa, Julius
Landau, Martin
Lander, David L.
Lane, Abbe
Lane, Ken
Larkin, Sheila

Lawrence, Steve
Lembeck, Harvey
Lembeck, Michael
Lewis, Emmanuel
Linker, Amy
Linn, Bambi
Lo Bianco, Tony
Logan, Robert
Lonow, Mark
Lopez, Vincent
Mann, Iris
Marvin, Tony
Mason, Tom
Mathews, George
McBride, Don
McCann, Chuck
McCormack, Patty
McMillan, Kenneth
Meara, Anne
Melton, Sid
Merrill, Robert
Metrano, Art
Michaels, Al
Michel, Franny
Milano, Alyssa
Miller, Denise
Mizzy, Vic
Moore, Mary Tyler
Most, Donny
Murphy, Eddie (r: Roosevelt, Long Island)
Music, Lorenzo
Nelson, Novella
Noel, Dick
O'Hanlon, George
Okun, Milt
Pare, Michael
Pasternak, Michael (r: Florida)
Perlman, Rhea
Pescow, Donna
Philips, Lee
Phillips, Wendy
Pioli, Judy (r: Floral Park, Long Island)
Ponzini, Antony
Presley, Priscilla (r: Connecticut)
Regalbuto, Joe (r: New Milford, N.J.)
Regina, Paul
Rich, Buddy
Rivers, Joan
Robbins, Brian

Rooney, Mickey
Rorke, Hayden
Ruymen, Ayn
Ryan, Bill
Salmi, Albert
Santos, Joe
Sauter, Eddie (of Sauter-Finegan)
Saxon, John
Scalia, Jack
Schoen, Vic (r: Los Angeles, Calif.)
Scott, Raymond
Silva, Henry
Silvers, Phil
Sobel, Rebecca
Sorvino, Paul
Spivak, Lawrence E.
Stadlen, Lewis J.
Stanis, BernNadette
Stanwyck, Barbara
Stevens, Connie
Stiller, Jerry
Swenson, Karl
Sylvern, Hank
Tayback, Vic
Thor, Jerome
Tierney, Gene
Tomack, Sid
Turkus, Burton
Vaccaro, Brenda (r: Dallas, Texas)
Van Patten, James
Van Patten, Timothy
Viscuso, Sal (r: Sacramento, Calif.)
Wallach, Eli
Walter, Jessica
West, Alvy
Williams, Bill
Williams, Cara
Wingreen, Jason
Wolfman Jack
Wood, Peggy
Buffalo:
Andrews, Tod
Blake, Amanda
Booke, Sorrell
Clark, Oliver
Conley, Joe
Dickinson, Hal (Modernaires)
Hallick, Tom
Jewell, Geri
Keane, James
Malick, Wendie

Marchand, Nancy
Messick, Don
Mullavey, Greg
Nathan, Steve
Read, James (r: Schenectady, N.Y.)
Russell, Mark (satirist)
Shawn, Dick (r: Lackawanna, N.Y.)
Smith, Bob (Howdy Doody host)
Stefan, Virginia (raised)
Walberg, Garry
Wertimer, Ned
White, Jesse (r: Akron, Ohio)
Wirges, Bill
College Point, Long Island:
Aletter, Frank
Cornwall:
Farrell, Shea
Corona:
Bleyer, Archie
Croton-on-Hudson:
Strauss, Peter
Dobbs Ferry:
Delaney, Steve
Fix, Paul
Endicott:
George, Anthony
Floral Park:
Cord, Alex
Flushing:
Bessell, Ted
Jacoby, Billy
Riha, Bobby
Tacker, Francine
Forest Hills:
Aaron, Betsy (raised)
Fletcher, Jack (r: Calif. and Ill.)
Landon, Michael (r: Collingswood, N.J.)
Shawlee, Joan
Forestville:
Abbott, George
Franklinville:
Conway, Shirl
Garden City:
Savalas, Telly
Tesh, John
Gasport:
Hull, Warren
Glen Cove:
Remsen, Bert

Glendale:
  Shea, Michael
Great Neck:
  Bruce, Carol
  Lederer, Suzanne
Greenwich Village, New York
  City:
  Buktenica, Ray
  Carradine, John
  Fowley, Douglas
  Santon, Penny
  Warren, Jennifer
Harlem, New York City:
  Belafonte, Harry (r: Jamaica, West
    Indies)
  Berg, Gertrude
  Berle, Milton
  Pringle, Joan
  Ray, Gene Anthony
  Tyson, Cecily
  Williams, Billy Dee
  Winchell, Walter
Hastings-on-the-Hudson:
  Kulky, Henry
Herkimer:
  Vennera, Chick
Highland Falls:
  Durning, Charles
Horseheads:
  Impert, Margaret
Huntington:
  Macchio, Ralph
Hurleyville:
  Kamen, Milt
Irvington:
  Peyser, Penny
Jackson Heights:
  Curtin, Valerie
  Dobson, Kevin
  Rettig, Tommy
Jamaica, New York City:
  Nichols, Barbara
Jamestown:
  Ball, Lucille
  Strunk, Jud (r: Farmington, Me.)
Johnstown:
  Milford, John
Kingston:
  Chandler, Chick
  Kreppel, Paul

Lake Success:
  Beyers, Bill (r: Babylon, Long Island)
  Shire, Talia
Larchmont:
  Whiting, Arch
Lawrence:
  Lipton, Peggy
Lindenhurst:
  Barry, Jack
Lockport:
  Bronson, Lillian
Long Beach:
  Crystal, Billy
  Jaeckel, Richard
  Lauter, Ed
  McMullan, Jim
Long Island:
  Badler, Jane (raised)
  Jenkins, Larry Flash (r: Chicago)
  Regan, Ellen
  Richards, Kim
Mahopac:
  Acovone, Jay
Manhattan, New York City:
(see also New York City)
  Collyer, Bud
  Cox, Richard
  Evans, Madge
  Fields, Chip
  Frazer, Dan
  Gimpel, Erica
  Sanford, Charles
  Stone, Harold J.
Mechanicsville:
  Eberly, Bob
Medford:
  Cast, Tricia
Mineola:
  Burns, Michael
Monticello:
  Garrett, Hank
Mt. Kisco:
  Gallo, Lew
  MacLeod, Gavin
  Schneider, John
  Stephens, James (r: Mexico)
Mt. Vernon:
  Buchwald, Art
  Carney, Art
  Clark, Dick

Haines, Larry
Washington, Denzel
New Hyde Park:
Mordente, Lisa
New Rochelle:
Denver, Bob
Foy, Eddie, Jr.
Mercer, Frances
Roundtree, Richard
Scolari, Peter
New York City:
(See also the city's boroughs of Manhattan, The Bronx, Brooklyn, Queens and Staten Island, and many locally named communities within them.)
Actman, Jane
Adams, Brooke
Adams, Don
Adams, Mason
Adler, Luther
Aiello, Danny
Aladdin
Alda, Alan
Alda, Robert
Alexander, Shana
Alexander, Van
Allen, Dayton (r: Mt. Vernon, N.Y.)
Allen, Jonelle
Allen, Steve
Anderson, Sheila
Anspach, Susan
Antonacci, Greg
Arbus, Alan
Arngrim, Alison (r: Los Angeles, Calif.)
Arquette, Rosanna
Arthur, Beatrice (r: Cambridge, Md.)
Arthur, Jean
Astin, Patty Duke
Auberjonois, Rene
Avery, Phyllis
Baker, Art
Baker, Blanche
Balsam, Martin
Banas, Bob, Dancers
Banfield, Bever-Leigh
Barr, Ray
Barrett, Rona
Barry, Gene

Barton, Eileen
Bavier, Frances
Beck, Jackson
Becker, Sandy
Bedelia, Bonnie
Beery, Noah, Jr. (r: California)
Bel Geddes, Barbara
Belack, Doris
Belafonte-Harper, Shari
Bellwood, Pamela
Benaderet, Bea
Bendix, William
Benjamin, Richard
Bergere, Lee
Bernardi, Herschel
Bethune, Zina
Billingsley, Peter
Bisoglio, Val
Bissel, Whit
Blackton, Jay
Blondell, Joan
Bobo, Willie
Bond, Sheila
Booth, Shirley
Botkin, Perry, Jr.
Bower, Roger
Brandon, Clark
Brandt, Janet
Brenner, Dori (r: Lawrenceville, N.Y.)
Brian, David
Brooks, Geraldine
Brooks, Joel
Brooks, Randi (r: France and California)
Brothers, Dr. Joyce
Brown, Eric
Brown, Peter
Brown, Tom
Bufano, Vincent
Burns, David
Burns, George
Bushkin, Joe
Byrnes, Edd
Cali, Joseph
Campanella, Joseph
Campos, Victor
Cantor, Eddie
Carleton, Claire
Carroll, Jimmy

Carroll, Nancy
Carson, Mindy
Carter, Jack
Carter, Ralph
Cassavetes, John
Cassidy, David
Cates, George
Cavanaugh, Michael (r: San Francisco, Calif.)
Cerf, Bennett
Chamberlin, Lee
Channing, Stockard
Charles, Lewis
Chase, Chevy
Chase, Ilka
Coates, Paul
Cobb, Lee J.
Coleman, Cy
Colin, Margaret (raised)
Collins, Al "Jazzbo"
Collins, Ted
Collyer, June
Conaway, Jeff
Corey, Jeff
Cowan, Jerome
Cross, Milton J.
Crosse, Rupert
Curreri, Lee
Dailey, Dan
Dano, Royal
Danton, Ray
Darrow, Henry
Davis, Sammy, Jr.
Day, Dennis
DeSantis, Joe
Dixon, Ivan
Donahue, Troy
Donner, Robert
Downey, Robert
Downing, David
Drury, James
Duddy, Lynn
Dunn, James
Dunninger, Joseph
Dunphy, Don
Durante, Jimmy
Edwards, Joan
Eisner, Michael
Elizondo, Hector
Elliot, Jane
Elliott, David (r: Spring Valley, N.Y.)

Elliott, Stephen
Elson, Andrea
Estrada, Erik
Evers, Jason
Fairbanks, Douglas, Jr.
Fairchild, Edgar "Cookie"
Falk, Peter
Faye, Joey
Feinstein, Alan
Feldshuh, Tovah
Fenwick, Millicent
Fields, Irving
Flannery, Susan
Ford, Art
Franciosa, Anthony
Frank, Allan
Frazier, Sheila
Freed, Bert
Furness, Betty
Gardner, Hy
Garrison, Sean
Gaynor, Jock
Gazzara, Ben
Gear, Luella
Georgiade, Nick
Getty, Estelle
Gilford, Jack
Givens, Robin
Glenn, Christopher
Gluskin, Lud
Godfrey, Arthur
Gold, Tracey (r: California)
Goldman, Danny
Goldnoni, Lelia
Gordon, Gale
Gordon, Leo V.
Gorman, Mari
Grant, Lee
Grauer, Ben
Graziano, Rocky
Green, Bernie
Green, Mitzi
Greene, Dennis (Sha Na Na)
Griffith, Melanie
Guardino, Harry
Guarnieri, Johnny
Guest, Christopher
Gwynne, Fred
Hackett, Joan
Hall, Huntz
Halop, Billy

Hardin, Ty (r: Texas)
Harrington, Pat, Jr.
Harris, Jonathan
Hartford, John (r: St. Louis, Mo.)
Hartley, Mariette (r: Weston, Conn.)
Hastings, Hal
Hecht, Ben
Helton, Percy
Henry, Buck
Hewitt, Alan
Hirsch, Judd
Hirschfield, Robert
Hobson, Laura (r: Long Island)
Hogan, Robert
Holliday, Kene
Holm, Celeste
Hopper, William
Horsford, Anna Maria
Hoving, Thomas
Howard, Joe
Huber, Harold
Hubley, Season
Hughes, Robert E.
Hunter, Tab
Husing, Ted
Irving, Jay
Irwin, Wynn
Jacobs, Lawrence-Hilton
Jaffe, Sam
James, Clifton
Janis, Conrad
Jarrett, Renne
Jason, Rick
Jenkins, Allen
Jessel, George
Jordan, Richard
Kaplan, Marvin
Karron, Richard
Kaufman, Andy (r: Great Neck, Long Island)
Kay, Beatrice
Kaye, Caren
Kaye, Stubby
Kenin, Alexa
Kennedy, George
Kerr, John
Kieran, John
Kline, Richard
Knight, Christopher (r: Los Angeles, Calif.)
Komack, James
Kopell, Bernie
Kotto, Yaphet
Kramer, Jeffrey
La Rue, Jack
Laire, Judson (r: Pleasantville, N.Y.)
Lampert, Zohra
Lancaster, Burt
Landers, Harry
Landsburg, Valerie
Lane, Don (raised)
Lane, Sara
Lane, Scott
Lang, Stephen
Lasser, Louise
Lee, Fran
Leeds, Elissa
Leibman, Ron
Leonard, Sheldon
Leslie, Bethel
Levenson, Sam
Lewis, Robert Q.
Lipton, Robert
Lockhart, June
Lonow, Claudia
Lord, Jack
Louis-Dreyfus, Julia
Louise, Anita
Louise, Tina
Lynley, Carol
Lytell, Bert
Mahler, Bruce
Malone, Nancy
Maltin, Leonard
Malvin, Artie
Manoff, Dinah
Manz, Linda
Marcovicci, Andrea
Margolin, Janet
Marinaro, Ed (r: New Milford, N.J.)
Marshall, Mort
Martin, Jared
Marvin, Lee
Marx, Chico
Marx, Groucho
Masur, Richard
Matthau, Walter
Mayer, Christopher (r: Ridgewood, N.J.)
McCay, Peggy
McGiver, John
McGraw, Charles (r: Akron, Ohio)

McKay, Gardner
McKayle, Don
McKean, Michael (r: Sea Cliff, N.J.)
McNally, Stephen
McQuade, Arlene
Medford, Kay
Memmoli, George
Mengatti, John
Merrill, Dina
Michaelsen, Kari
Michelman, Ken
Miller, Barry
Miller, Linda G.
Millerick, Kerry
Mitchell, Andrea (r: New Rochelle, N.Y.)
Mohr, Gerald
Moore, Melba
Morgan, Henry
Morris, Chester
Morris, Howard
Morrow, Jeff
Morton, Joe
Mostel, Joshua
Muldaur, Diana (r: Edgartown, Mass.)
Murray, Arthur
Murray, Ken
Myerson, Bess
Naish, J. Carrol
Naud, Melinda
Nelson, David
Nelson, Haywood
Newborn, Ira
Newman, Edwin
Norden, Tommy
Norris, Christopher
North, Alan
O'Brien, Edmond
O'Connell, Arthur
O'Connor, Carroll
O'Connor, Glynnis (r: New Rochelle, N.Y.)
O'Loughlin, Gerald S.
Oakland, Simon
Oliver, Susan
Opatoshu, David
Oppenheimer, Alan
Orlando, Tony
Osgood, Charles

Oxenberg, Catherine (r: London, England)
Palmer, Jim
Parfey, Woodrow
Parker, Frank
Parker, Willard
Patrick, Lee
Pearce, Alice
Pearlman, Michael
Pepper, Barbara
Perez, Jose
Peterson, Virgilia
Picerni, Paul
Pinchot, Bronson (r: South Pasadena, Calif.)
Piute Pete (Morris Kaufman)
Pleshette, John
Pleshette, Suzanne
Pointer, Priscilla
Popwell, Albert
Potter, Carol (r: Tenafly, N.J.)
Prager, Stanley
Primus, Barry
Prinze, Freddie
Quinn, Bill
Racimo, Victoria
Raft, George
Raggio, Lisa
Raymond, Gene
Redfield, William
Reed, Alan
Reed, Philip
Reeves, Richard
Reid, Elliot
Reilly, Charles Nelson
Reiner, Rob
Reynolds, Quentin
Ribeiro, Alfonso
Rich, Adam
Richards, Grant
Rifkin, Ron
Rivera, Geraldo
Rizzuto, Phil
Roberts, Tony
Robinson, Bartlett
Roker, Rennie
Romero, Cesar
Romoff, Colin
Rose Marie
Rose, Jamie (r: Los Angeles, Calif.)

Ross, Anthony
Ross, Joe E.
Ross, Stan
Rowland, Jada
Russell, Connie
Sagan, Dr. Carl
Sanford, Isabel
Sarafian, Richard C.
Savo, Jimmy
Sbarge, Raphael
Schumann, Walter
Sebastian, John
Sedan, Rolfe
Segal, Jonathan
Seven, Johnny
Seymour, Anne
Shaughnessy, Mickey
Sheiner, David
Shor, Dan
Shriner, Wil
Siegel, Janis (Manhattan Transfer)
  (raised)
Silver, Ron
Silvers, Cathy (r: Los Angeles,
  Calif.)
Singer, Raymond
Sirola, Joseph
Slavin, Millie
Smith, Kent
Smith, Queenie
Smits, Jimmy (r: Brooklyn, N.Y.)
Smothers, Dick
Smothers, Tom
Snow, Phoebe (r: Teaneck, N.J.)
Solomon, Bruce
St. John, Kristoff
Stander, Lionel
Stapleton, Jean
Stearns, Christopher William
Sterling, Jan
Stewart, Nick (r: Barbados)
Stewart, Paul
Stockwell, Guy
Stone, Carol
Stone, Kirby
Storch, Larry
Strasberg, Susan
Strassman, Marcia
Strauss, Robert
Strimpell, Stephen

Sullivan, Barry
Sullivan, Ed (r: Port Chester, N.Y.)
Sullivan, Susan
Summers, Yale
Susskind, David
Sweet, Dolph
Sylvan, Paul
Talbot, Nita
Tannen, William
Taylor, Renee (r: Miami, Fla.)
Terkel, Studs
Thomas, Frankie
Thomas, Richard
Thompson, Jenn
Ticotin, Rachel
Tirelli, Jaime
Tobias, George
Travalena, Fred
Tripp, Paul
Trueman, Paula
Turman, Glynn
Tyler, Richard
Uggams, Leslie
Untermeyer, Louis
Vague, Vera
Valley, Tannis
Van Ark, Joan (r: Boulder, Colo.)
Vaughn, Robert (r: Minneapolis,
  Minn.)
Velez, Eddie
Vernon, Jackie
Vigoda, Abe
Vitte, Ray (r: Pasadena, Calif.)
Van Hoffman, Nicholas
Walden, Robert
Warren, Lesley Ann
Weinrib, Len
Weintraub, Cindy (r: Seattle, Wash.)
Weld, Tuesday
Wendell, Bill
West, Madge
Westman, Nydia
Weston, Ellen
Wheel, Patricia
White, Carole Ita
Whitmore, James, Jr.
Wilcox, Nina
Wilder, Yvonne
Williams, Clarence, III
Williams, Grant

Williams, Guy
Williams, Kent
Wilson, Theodore
Winchell, Paul
Windom, William
Winkler, Henry
Wyenn, Than
Wyle, George
Wynn, Keenan
Young, Tony
Zapata, Carmen
Zara, Lou
Zee, John (r: New Rochelle, N.Y.)
Zimbalist, Efrem, Jr.
Zimbalist, Stephanie (r: Encino, Calif.)

Newburgh:
Metzler, Jim
Mitchill, Scoey

Niagara Falls:
Tone, Franchot

Nichols:
Prince, William

Nimmonsberg:
Withers, Mark

Old Bethpage:
Savage, John
Youngs, Jim

Old Westbury:
Avedon, Doe
Straight, Beatrice

Olean:
Tomarken, Peter (r: California)

Ossining:
Francis, Anne
Mercer, Tommy
Weed, Buddy

Ozone Park, New York City:
Peters, Bernadete

Poughkeepsie:
Denning, Richard
Rhoades, Barbara

Pound Ridge:
MacGraw, Ali

Queens:
Bauman, Jon "Bowser"
Beller, Kathleen
Bennett, Tony
Breslin, Jimmy
Halop, Florence
Koehler, Frederick

Rafferty, Bill
Rickles, Don
Van Patten, Joyce
Walken, Glenn
Warfield, Marlene

Richmond Hill, Queens:
Cassidy, Jack
Taeger, Ralph
Van Patten, Dick

Rochester:
Breck, Peter
Canfield, Mary Grace
Deuel, Peter
Erskine, Marilyn
Fogel, Jerry
Forster, Robert
Kennedy, Mimi
LaRoche, Mary
Miller, Mitch
O'Brian, Hugh (r: Chicago)
Simms, Lu Ann
Stern, Bill

Rockville Centre:
Heatherton, Joey

Roslyn Heights:
Kahan, Judy

Rye:
Atkins, Christopher
Bateman, Jason
Bateman, Justine
Nash, Ogden

Saratoga Springs:
Russell, Jack (r: Palm Beach, Fla.)

Scarsdale:
Keller, Jason
Keller, Shane
Pine, Robert

Schenectady:
Davis, Ann B.
Garroway, Dave
Gould, Harold
Kalember, Patricia (r: Louisville, Ky.)
Van Valkenburgh, Deborah

Smithtown:
Marcantel, Christopher

St. Albans:
Sweeney, Terry
Vohs, Joan

Staten Island:
Calvin, John

Dehner, John
Loggia, Robert
Platt, Edward
Scarpelli, Glenn
Schroder, Ricky
Stordahl, Axel
Suffern:
Harper, Valerie
Syracuse:
Hucko, Peanuts
Kirk, Phyllis
Lundigan, William
Serling, Rod
Van Horne, Harriet
Troy:
Fuller, Robert
Stapleton, Maureen
Utica:
Funicello, Annette (r: Los Angeles, Calif.)
O'Neal, Ron (r: Cleveland, Ohio)
Valley Stream:
Barton, Peter
Wappingers Falls:
Mulhall, Jack
Washington Heights, New York City:
Conrad, Michael
Watertown:
Gary, John
West Nyack:
Geer, Ellen
Westbury:
McKeon, Nancy
McKeon, Philip
Westchester:
Sabella, Ernie
White Plains:
Duryea, Dan
Lauter, Harry (r: Colorado)
Waite, Ralph
Whitmore, James
Williston Park:
Fiore, Bill
Yonkers:
Caesar, Sid
Lambert, Jack
Shayne, Robert

NORTH CAROLINA

City Not Known:
Hairston, Jester

Asheville:
Finley, Pat (r: Washington State)
Fulton, Eileen
Hemphill, Shirley
Camp LeJeune:
Bohrer, Corinne
Chapel Hill:
Hogan, Jack
Charlotte:
Graham, Rev. Billy
Shearin, John (r: Chapel Hill, N.C.)
Tolbert, Berlinda
Trotter, John Scott
Dunn:
Morgan, Debbi
Durham:
Fuller, Penny
Greer, Michael
Markham, Pigmeat
Edgecombe County:
Jones, Ben
Fayetteville:
Boone, Randy
Holland, Kristina
Franklinton:
Sales, Soupy
Goldsboro:
Jeffreys, Anne
Grabtown:
Gardner, Ava (r: Smithfield, N.C.)
Greensboro:
Murrow, Edward R.
Greenville:
Taylor, Billy
Guilford County:
Johnson, Betty
Hartford County:
Yeates, Roy (Southernaires)
Henderson:
Jackson, Sammy
Rose, Charlie
Hendersonville:
Lampley, Jim
Lexington:
Swaim, Caskey
Marion:
Loden, Barbara
Mount Airy:
Griffith, Andy

Pennert:
  McEachin, James (r: Hackensack, N.J.)
Pinehurst:
  Hendren, Ron
Rocky Mount:
  Kyser, Kay
  Nelson, Kenneth
Salisbury:
  Evans, Mike
Spencer:
  Allman, Elvia
Wake County:
  Trout, Robert
Washington:
  Hamilton, Murray
Wilmington:
  Brinkley, David
  Kuralt, Charles
Wilson:
  Walcott, Gregory
Winston-Salem:
  Cosell, Howard
  Harry, Jackee
  Hayes, Harold
Zebulon:
  Schorr, Lonnie

NORTH DAKOTA

City Not Known:
  Dollar, Lynn (raised)
Fargo:
  Scott, Frank
Grand Forks:
  Anderson, Lynn
Jamestown:
  Lee, Peggy
Kulm:
  Dickinson, Angie (r: Edgelev, N.D.)
Mandan:
  Peterson, Arthur
Strasburg:
  Welk, Lawrence
Valley City:
  Sothern, Ann
Velva:
  Sevareid, Eric

OHIO

City Not Known:
  Craig, Col. John D.

Earle, Merie
Evans, Dr. Bergen
Ross, Ted
Todd, Beverly
Akron:
  Albright, Lola
  Downs, Hugh
  McCoy, Jack
  McLean, David
  Mercer, Marian
  Monroe, Vaughn
Alliance:
  King, Perry
Ashtabula:
  Bennett, Donn
  Novello, Don
Bucyrus:
  Le Roy, Gloria (r: Bronx, N.Y.)
Cambridge:
  Boyd, William
Canton:
  King, Tony
  Light, Enoch
  Paar, Jack
  Wilkof, Lee
Cedarville:
  Parker, Eleanor
Cincinnati:
  Beavers, Louise
  Bowman, Lee
  Bryant, Nana
  Day, Doris
  Diehl, John
  Keen, Noah
  Mack, Dotty
  Middleton, Robert
  Newland, John
  Rhodes, Hari
  Rogers, Roy
  Ryan, Mitchell (r: Louisville, Ky.)
  Scott, Brenda
Circleville:
  Jordan, Ted
Cleveland Heights:
  Hyland, Diana
Cleveland:
  Backus, Jim
  Ballard, Kaye
  Beutel, Bill
  Cover, Franklin
  Da Silva, Howard
  Dee, Ruby (r: Harlem, N.Y.)

Diener, Joan
Donahue, Phil
Dunn, Elaine
Elder, Ann
Fann, Al
Flynn, Miriam
Greene, Laura
Hall, Arsenio
Hamilton, Margaret
Hart, Dorothy
Holbrook, Hal (r: S. Weymouth,
    Mass.)
Howard, John
Joyce, Elaine (r: Beverly Hills, Calif.)
Kane, Carol
Kolb, Clarence
Lohman, Rick
Martin, Freddy
McGuire, Maeve
Meredith, Burgess
Morris, Greg
Page, LaWanda
Perkins, Jack (r: Wooster, Ohio)
Rey, Alvino
Riley, Jack
Russell, Lee
Sharp, Saundra
Smith, Martha (r: Farmington, Mich.)
Stevens, Mark (r: Montreal, Canada)
Stewart, Mel
Stone, Steve
Vanocur, Sander
Weston, Jack
Youngfellow, Barrie
Columbus:
  Barrett, Majel
  Benson, Red (r: Philadelphia,
    Pa.)
  Brooks, Stephen
  Byrne, Bobby
  D'Angelo, Beverly
  Goodman, Dody
  Harper, John
  Heckart, Eileen
  Poston, Tom
  Thomas, Philip Michael (r: Califor-
    nia)
  Ward, Larry
  Williams, Hal
Dayton:
  Brown, Woody
  Byrd, Ralph

Harewood, Dorian
Jump, Gordon
Lowe, Chad
Sandy, Gary
Winters, Jonathan
Elyria:
  Brasselle, Keefe
  Wilzak, Crissy
Holgate:
  Brown, Joe E.
Hubbard:
  Stratton, Albert
Kent:
  Adamle, Mike
  Boucher, Bob
Lakewood:
  Garr, Teri (r: Hollywood, Calif.)
  Redmond, Marge
  Wass, Ted
Lancaster:
  Graff, David
Lima:
  Diller, Phyllis
  Jagger, Dean
  O'Connell, Helen
Loraine:
  Flanagan, Ralph
Mansfield:
  Simon, Robert F.
Middletown:
  McGuire Sisters, The
Mt. Vernon:
  Lynde, Paul
Nelsonville:
  Parker, Sarah Jessica (r: Cincinnati,
    Ohio)
Newark:
  Norris, Kathi
Norwalk:
  Gandolf, Ray
Norwood:
  Chakiris, George
Piqua:
  Reser, Harry (r: Dayton, Ohio)
Plain City:
  Barlow, Howard
Rockford:
  Wilson, Earl
Rocky River:
  Kaye, Sammy
Shaker Heights:
  Willard, Fred

Springfield:
Reed, Alaina
Steubenville:
Martin, Dean
Martin, Gail
Struthers:
Lewis, Wanda
Toledo:
Arquette, Cliff
Brady, Pat
Brewer, Teresa
Butler, Daws (r: Oak Park, Ill.)
Farr, Jamie
Ganzel, Teresa
Harsch, Joseph C.
Kruger, Otto
Shriner, Herb (r: Indiana)
Toronto:
Urich, Robert
Wadsworth:
Hanks, Steve
Warren:
Bach, Catherine
Willoughby:
Conway, Tim
Wilmington:
Jones, Clarence (Southernaires)
Woodington:
Thomas, Lowell
Youngstown:
Christopher, Jordan
Flynn, Joe
Pataki, Michael
Zanesville:
Basehart, Richard
Richards, Addison

OKLAHOMA

City Not Known:
O'Brien, Louise (raised)
Spradlin, G.D.
Tinney, Cal
Ada:
Edwards, Douglas
Alva:
Ging, Jack
Ardmore:
Smith, Howard (orch. leader)
Barnsdall:
Bryant, Anita
Bartlesville:
Wyler, Gretchen

Beggs:
Rowan, Dan
Bristow:
Symonds, Robert
Chickasha:
Allen, Chet
Little, Cleavon
Claremore:
Page, Patti (r: Tulsa, Okla.)
Coalgate:
Carson, Ken
Dinson:
Davis, Rufe
Duncan:
Axton, Hoyt
Howard, Ron
Enid:
Erdman, Richard
Erick:
Wooley, Sheb
Foraker:
Johnson, Ben
Ft. Sill:
Lowry, Judith
Harrah:
Robertson, Dale (r: Oklahoma City, Okla.)
Healdton:
McClanahan, Rue
Holdenville:
Gulager, Clu (r: Muskogee, Okla.)
Hugo:
Finn, Mickie
Moyers, Bill (r: Texas)
Indian Territory:
Harvey, Harry, Sr.
Lawton:
Crosby, Lou
Ramos, Rudy
Leedey:
Hood, Darla
Maud:
Jackson, Wanda
Miami:
Porter, Don
Moore:
Cooksey, Danny
Norman:
Garner, James
Pickett, Cindy (r: Houston, Tex.)

Oklahoma City:
  Allbritton, Louise (r: Wichita Falls, Tex.)
  Antonio, Lou
  Chaney, Lon, Jr.
  Chastain, Don
  Edwards, Ronnie Claire
  Hampton, James (r: Dallas, Tex.)
  Hudson, Rochelle
  Kilpatrick, James J.
  Sanders, Lugene
  Shackelford, Ted (r: Tulsa, Okla.)
Okmulgee:
  Sampson, Will
Pauls Valley:
  Shepard, Jean
Tulsa:
  Chapman, Lonny (r: Joplin, Mo.)
  Harvey, Paul
  James, Sheila (r: Los Angeles, Calif.)
  Place, Mary Kay
  Randall, Tony
  Woodward, Alfre
Walters:
  Heflin, Van
Wellston:
  Jean, Norma

OREGON

Arlington:
  Severinsen, Doc
Camp Sherman:
  Corbett, Gretchen
Coquille:
  Kennedy, Sarah
Eugene:
  Lindsay, Mark
  Schaeffer, Rebecca
  Wasson, Craig
Madras:
  Phoenix, River
Pendleton:
  Manetti, Larry (r: Chicago, Ill.)
  Steele, Bob
Portland:
  Ames, Rachel
  Colman, Booth
  Cook, Donald
  Hudson Brothers, The
  McMillan, Gloria
  Meredith, Judi (raised)
  Powell, Jane

Richards, Jeff
Schedeen, Ann (r: Gresham, Ore.)
Struthers, Sally
Woods, Ren
Salem:
  Hesseman, Howard
  Stone, Leonard
St. Helens:
  Cornthwaite, Robert

PENNSYLVANIA

City Not Known:
  Binns, Edward
  Houlihan, Keri
  Kabbible, Ish (r: Erie, Pa.)
Abington:
  Errickson, Krista
Allentown:
  Miller, Lara Jill
  Voorhees, Donald
Altoona:
  Blair, Janet
  Wise, Alfie
Ashley:
  Johnson, Russell
Avonmore:
  Corey, Jill
Beaver Falls:
  Namath, Joe
Belle Vernon:
  Bosson, Barbara
Bentleyville:
  Anthony, Ray (r: Cleveland, Ohio)
Bethlehem:
  Frakes, Jonathan (raised)
Bryn Mawr:
  Mansfield, Jayne
Butler:
  McCarren, Fred
Canonsburg:
  Como, Perry
Carlisle:
  Beaudine, Deka
Chester:
  Waters, Ethel
Clark's Summit:
  Stevens, Warren
Coatesville:
  Perry, Rod
  Richardson, Susan
Dallastown:
  Mitchell, Cameron

East McKeesport:
  Young, Donna Jean
Easton:
  Coleman, Jack
Ehrenfield:
  Bronson, Charles
Elkins Park:
  Burns, Stephan (r: Chew's Landing, N.J.)
Erie:
  Estabrook, Christine (r: East Aurora, N.Y.)
Ford City:
  Core, Natalie
Gallitzin:
  Frederick, Pauline (r: Harrisburg, Pa.)
Germantown:
  Gibson, Henry
Gettysburg:
  Clarke, Brian Patrick
Glenside:
  Ward, Richard
Greensburg:
  King, Peggy
Harrisburg:
  Kulp, Nancy
  Sanders, Richard
  Troup, Bobby
High Spire:
  Keefer, Don
Homestead:
  McHugh, Frank
Indiana:
  Stewart, James
Johnstown:
  Davis, Buster
  Freed, Alan
  Kazurinsky, Tim (r: Australia)
Kingston:
  Adams, Edie
Knoxville:
  Meredith, Charles
Lattimer:
  Palance, Jack
Mahanoy Plane:
  Dorsey, Tommy
McKeesport:
  Connelly, Marc
Milford:
  Joslyn, Allyn (r: New York City)

Millsboro:
  Barty, Billy
Montgomery:
  Lawrence, Joey
  Lawrence, Matthew
Nanticoke:
  Adams, Nick
Newcastle:
  Sterling, Robert
Norristown:
  Lake, Janet
  Simon, Leonard
Olyphant:
  Crowley, Patricia
Philadelphia:
  Agronsky, Martin
  Atterbury, Malcolm
  Avalon, Frankie
  Baker, Phil
  Barris, Chuck
  Barth, Eddie
  Bernard, Ed
  Bettger, Lyle
  Boyle, Peter
  Bradley, Ed
  Callan, Michael
  Casnoff, Phil
  Cellini, Karen
  Coca, Imogene
  Cook, Nathan
  Cosby, Bill
  Crawford, Broderick
  Danner, Blythe
  Darren, James
  Davison, Bruce
  De Gore, Janet (raised)
  Deacon, Richard
  Douglas, Paul
  DuBois, Ja'net (r: Brooklyn, N.Y.)
  Eben, Al
  Eisley, Anthony (Fred)
  Englund, Pat
  Fell, Norman
  Fisher, Eddie
  Flippin, Lucy Lee
  Flood, Dick (Country Lads)
  Francine, Anne
  Gabel, Martin
  Garde, Betty
  Graham, Ronny
  Greco, Buddy

Hamel, Veronica
Hemsley, Sherman
Henry, Emmaline
Hooks, Kevin
Jenner, Barry
Jones, Henry
Kallen, Kitty
Kampmann, Steven
Landers, Audrey (r: Valley Cottage, N.Y.)
Landers, Judy (r: Valley Cottage, N.Y.)
Lawrence, Elliot
Lehr, Lew
Loeb, Philip
Macht, Stephen
Marks, Guy
Marlowe, Hugh
Marta, Lynne
May, Elaine
McCracken, Joan
McKay, Jim
Navin, John P., Jr.
O'Neill, Eileen
Orth, Frank
Patrick, Dennis
Payne, Benny
Pitlik, Noam
Prosky, Robert
Quillan, Eddie
Randall, Sue
Richman, Peter Mark
Rock, Blossom
Rowles, Polly
Rydell, Bobby
Schilling, William G.
Singleton, Penny
Stein, Lou
Stevenson, Parker
Stevenson, Valerie
Stewart, Sandy
Susann, Jacqueline
Taylor, Holland
Thomas, Dick
Walker, Kathryn
Walker, Nancy
Watkins, Jim
Whitaker, Jack
Whiting, Jack
Wynn, Ed
Pittsburgh:
  Allen, Marty

Allen, Phillip R.
Atkins, Tom
Berdis, Bert
Betz, Carl
Cassidy, Ted
Cullen, Bill
Davidson, John
Deutsch, Patti
Dietrich, Dena
Dodson, Jack
Feldon, Barbara
Fielding, Jerry
Flaherty, Joe
Goldblum, Jeff
Gorshin, Frank
Hall, Kevin Peter
Holmes, LeRoy
Johnson, Cherie
Jones, Marilyn (r: Grosse Pointe, Mich.)
Kaufman, George S.
Keaton, Michael
Kelly, Gene
Kurty, Lee
Levant, Oscar
Lyons, Gene
Martin, Kiel (r: Miami, Fla.)
Matz, Peter
May, Billy
McQuade, John
Menjou, Adolphe
Miller, Dennis
Moran, Lois
Mullaney, Jack
Mustin, Burt
Polic, Henry, II
Safranski, Eddie
Talbot, Lyle
Toomey, Regis
Van Eman, Charles
Vinton, Bobby (r: Canonsburg, Pa.)
Wade, Adam
Weaver, Fritz
Widdoes, James
Wild, Earl
Wilson, Lois (r: Birmingham, Ala.)
Reading:
  Compton, Forrest
  Constantine, Michael
  Kemmer, Ed
Reinerton:
  Brown, Les

Roaring Springs:
 Stone, Karen (r: Seneca Falls, N.Y.)
Rosemont:
 Sigel, Barbara (raised)
Scranton:
 Barbutti, Pete
 Kerr, Jean
 Morgan, Russ
 Tyler, Beverly
 Williams, Louise
Shenandoah:
 Dorsey, Jimmy
 Miller, Sid
Smithton:
 Jones, Shirley
South Philadelphia:
 Klugman, Jack
 Roman, Joseph
Stewartstown:
 Fulton, Wendy
Titusville:
 Dunn, Ralph
Trafford:
 Tewes, Lauren (r: Whittier, Calif.)
Turtle Creek:
 Harper, Ron
Tyrone:
 Waring, Fred
Wilkes-Barre:
 Fluegel, Darlanne
 Karen, James
 Lorne, Marion
 McDonnell, Mary (r: Ithaca, N.Y.)
Williamsport:
 Orkin, Dick
Windber:
 Weissmuller, Johnny
Wrightsville:
 Gray, Alexander
Wyncote:
 Applegate, Eddie
York:
 McCain, Francis Lee
 Sheffer, Craig

PUERTO RICO

City Not Known:
 Morin, Alberto
 Phoenix, Leaf
Humacao:
 Moreno, Rita

Juncos:
 Rosario, Bert (r: The Bronx, N.Y.)
Lares:
 Feliciano, Jose
San Juan:
 Meyers, Ari
Santurce:
 Ferrer, Jose

RHODE ISLAND

City Not Known:
 Ladd, Margaret
 Pons, Bea
Cranston:
 Jillson, Joyce
Newport:
 Anderson, Harry
 Johnson, Van
Pawtucket:
 Hartman, David
 Perlow, Bob
Providence:
 Caliri, Jon
 Carle, Frankie
 Colasanto, Nicholas
 Hackett, Bobby
 Hedison, David
 Leary, Brianne (r: Tucson, Ariz.)
 Macready, George
 McLarty, Ron
 Roarke, John
 Vieira, Meredith
 Young, Otis
Warwick:
 Woods, James
West Warwick:
 Lussier, Robert
Westerly:
 Buzzi, Ruth (r: Wequetequock,
  Conn.)
Woonsocket:
 Dowling, Eddie

SOUTH CAROLINA

Camden:
 Keep, Stephen
 Wright, Samuel E.
Charleston:
 Compton, Walter
 Hutton, Lauren
 King, Mabel

Columbia:
  MacLane, Barton
Cottageville:
  Ackerman, Bettye
Greenville:
  Cunningham, Sarah
  Hopkins, Bo
Lexington County:
  Lemon, Meadowlark (r: Wilmington,
    N.C.)
North Myrtle Beach:
  White, Vanna
Salley:
  Collier, Lois
Spartanburg:
  Trent, Buck
  Weston, Celia
Sumter:
  Weatherly, Shawn
Yemassee:
  Blair, Frank

SOUTH DAKOTA

Artesian:
  Harkness, Richard
Deadwood:
  Provine, Dorothy
Huron:
  Ladd, Cheryl
Mitchell:
  Owens, Gary
Rosebud Reservation:
  Winona, Kim
Sioux Falls:
  Hart, Mary
Webster:
  Floren, Myron
Yankton:
  Brokaw, Tom

TENNESSEE

City Not Known:
  Dudley, Dick (raised)
  Westerfield, James
Ashland City:
  Stewart, Redd
Bristol:
  Ford, Tennessee Ernie
Bullsgap:
  Campbell, Archie

Carthage:
  Maggart, Brandon
Centerville:
  Pearl, Minnie
Chattanooga:
  McKenzie, Richard
  Sutton, Grady
Clarksville:
  Sutton, Frank
Cleveland:
  Peters, Lowell (Southernaires)
Columbia:
  Toney, Jay S. (Southernaires)
Dayton:
  Hodges, Russ (r: Danville, Ky.)
Goin:
  Nelson, Bek (r: Canton, Ohio)
Henderson:
  Arnold, Eddy
Jackson:
  Dancy, John
  Jones, Christopher
  Martindale, Wink
  Perkins, Carl
  Smith, Dwan
Johnson City:
  Hickman, Herman
Kingsport:
  Palmer, John
Knoxville:
  Barber, Ava
  Bergen, Polly
  Carlson, Linda (r: Sioux Falls, S.D.)
  Costa, Mary (raised)
  Dennison, Rachel
  Jenkins, Carol Mayo
  Keith, David
  Stevens, Morgan
Luttrell:
  Atkins, Chet
Lynchburg:
  Compton, John
Maynardville:
  Acuff, Roy
  Smith, Carl
McLemoresville:
  Carter, Dixie
Memphis:
  Allen, Deborah
  Beck, Michael
  Cason, Barbara

Cole, Olivia (r: New York City)
Dandridge, Ruby
Dees, Rick
Doherty, Shannen
Fidler, Jimmy
Hamilton, George
Haney, Anne
Kerr, Anita
Lanson, Snooky
Laughlin, John
McCarver, Tim
Riley, Larry
Sanderson, William
Schneider, Daniel J.
Shepherd, Cybill
Smith, Lane
Stevens, Andrew
Wilson, Jeannie
Murfreesboro:
    Webb, Greg
Nashville:
    Caine, Howard
    Cherry, Hugh
    Howar, Barbara
    Potts, Annie (r: Franklin, Ky.)
    Wagner, Chuck
Pine Bluff:
    Davis, Janette (r: Memphis, Tenn.)
Possum Hollow (sic):
    Cousin Jody
Pulaski:
    Nelson, Lindsey
Sevierville:
    Parton, Dolly
Winchester:
    Shore, Dinah (r: Nashville, Tenn.)

TEXAS

City Not Known:
    Chamblis, Woody
    Corley, Pat (r: California)
    Jameson, House
    Sharpe, Karen
Abernathy:
    Johnson, Jay
Abilene:
    Harper, David W.
    Wedgeworth, Ann
    Williams, Mason
Alice:
    Chiles, Lois

Amarillo:
    Doran, Ann
    Jones, Carolyn
Austin:
    Coleman, Dabney (r: Corpus Christi)
    Holden, Rebecca
    Koock, Guich
    MacDonnell, Kyle (r: Larnard, Kan.)
    Schieffer, Bob
    Scott, Zachary
    Winston, Leslie
Bay City:
    Jacquet, Jeffrey
Beaumont:
    Godkin, Paul
    Jones, L.Q.
    Smith, Bubba
Big Spring:
    Buckley, Betty
    Hickox, Harry
Bloomington:
    Storm, Gale
Bowie County:
    Blocker, Dan (r: O'Donnell, Texas)
Bryan:
    Ellerbee, Linda
Calvert:
    McCrary, Tex
Cisco:
    Crofts, Dash (Seals & Crofts)
Cleburne:
    Sharbutt, Del
Corpus Christi:
    Fawcett, Farrah
    Mandrell, Irlene
    Mandrell, Louise
    Singer, Lori
Crisp:
    Tubb, Ernest
Dallas:
    Benson, Robby
    Bernard, Crystal
    Callan, K
    Case, Allen
    Fairchild, Morgan
    MacKay, Jeff
    McAfee, Johnny
    Noble, James
    Railsback, Steve
    Roman, Lulu (raised)
    Santini, Tony (Sha Na Na)

Sharma, Barbara (r: Miami, Fla.)
Sheridan, Ann (r: Denton)
Tate, Sharon
Decatur:
  Williams, Guinn
Del Rio:
  Kerr, Jay
Denison:
  Hillerman, John
Denton:
  George, Phyllis
Desdemona:
  Brown, James
El Paso:
  Beaird, Betty (r: Houston)
  Carr, Vikki (r: Rosemead, Calif.)
  Cornell, Lydia
  Cort, Bill
  Donaldson, Sam
  Lambert, Paul (r: Kansas City, Kan.)
  Reynolds, Debbie (r: Burbank, Calif.)
  Ryan, Irene
  Santana, Arnaldo (r: Juarez, Mexico)
  Van Horne, Randy
Fort Worth:
  Alden, Norman
  Benoit, Patricia
  Blair, Patricia (r: Dallas, Texas)
  Carver, Randall
  Gilbert, Jody
  Gilliland, Richard
  Hagman, Larry (r: Weatherford, Texas)
  McKinley, Ray
  Miller, Roger (r: Erick, Okla.)
  Parker, Fess (r: San Angelo, Texas)
  Reed, Rex
  Smith, Liz
  Whelchel, Lisa
  Williams, Van
Galveston:
  Hanson, Marcy
  Helmond, Katherine
  Perrine, Valerie
  Scoggins, Tracy
Goose Creek:
  Busey, Gary
Groesbeck:
  Baker, Joe Don

Henderson:
  Duncan, Sandy
Hereford:
  Ely, Ron
Honey Grove:
  Erwin, Bill
Houston:
  Allen, Debbie
  Barry, Donald
  Blyden, Larry
  Cullen, Brett
  Eisenmann, Ike
  Foxworth, Robert
  Graves, Teresa (r: Los Angeles, Calif.)
  Hardin, Melora (r: Los Angeles, Calif.)
  Hartman, Lisa
  Hecht, Gina
  Hurst, Rick
  MacRae, Meredith
  Mandrell, Barbara
  Miller, Mark
  Mitchell, Don
  Nesmith, Michael (r: Farmer's Branch)
  Quaid, Randy
  Rashad, Phylicia
  Robinson, Charles
  Rodgers, Pamela
  Rogers, Kenny
  Smith, Jaclyn
  Swayze, Patrick
  Swift, Susan
  Taylor, Marc L.
  Tolsky, Susan
Huntsville:
  Forrest, Steve
Karnes County:
  Hill, Goldie
Kermit:
  Thomas, Jay (r: New Orleans, La.)
Kilgore:
  Lon, Alice
Kingston:
  Murphy, Audie
Littlefield:
  Jennings, Waylon
Lubbock:
  Boles, Jim

Davis, Mac
Wagner, Helen
Lufkin:
Martin, Murphy
Marshall:
Howard, Susan
McAllen:
Roberts, Holly
Midland:
Harrelson, Woody
McCormick, Carolyn (r: Houston, Texas)
Mineola:
Willingham, Noble
Mount Vernon:
Meredith, Don
Muleshoe:
Horsley, Lee
Palestine:
Freeman, Damita Jo
Panola County:
Ritter, Tex
Pasadena:
Blankfield, Mark
Petrolia:
Hadley, Reed
Plainview:
Dean, Jimmy
Port Arthur:
Bailey, G.W.
Davis, Phyllis (r: Nederland, Texas)
Posey:
Dean, Eddie
Ralls:
Walker, Billy
San Antonio:
Burnett, Carol (r: Los Angeles, Calif.)
Burton, Wendell
Craig, Helen
Freeman, Al, Jr.
Littlefield, Lucien
Prentiss, Ann (r: Houston, Texas)
Prentiss, Paula
Tubb, Justin
San Marcos:
George, Lynda Day
Seagoville:
Wills, Chill
Sherman:
Owens, Buck

Sidney:
Seals, James (Seals & Crofts)
Snyder:
Boothe, Powers
Jones, Dick
Temple:
Torn, Rip
Terrytown:
Richards, Lou (r: Hawaii)
Tioga:
Autry, Gene
Tyler:
Wilson, Dooley
Uvalde:
Evans, Dale
Waco:
Beaird, Barbara
Martin, Steve (r: Calif.)
Williams, Billy
Weslaco:
Spielberg, David
Wharton:
Rather, Dan
Wichita Falls:
Tune, Tommy
Wichita:
Cherry, Don

UTAH

City Not Known:
Melville, Sam
Bountiful:
Priest, Pat
Logan:
Olsen, Merlin
Mount Pleasant:
Lookinland, Mike
Ogden:
Janney, Leon
Osmond, Alan
Osmond, Donny
Osmond, Jay
Osmond, Marie
Osmond, Merrill
Osmond, Wayne
Provo:
Link, Michael (r: Los Angeles, Calif.)
Roosevelt:
Day, Laraine
Salt Lake City:
Backes, Alice

Brimley, Wilford (r: Santa Monica, Calif.)
Brown, Earl
Clinger, Debra
Curtis, Keene
Ericson, Devon
Kearns, Joseph
Langton, Paul
Lansing, Joi
Larsen, Keith
Lund, Art
Storrs, Suzanne
Young, Loretta (r: Los Angeles, Calif.)
Torrey:
Merrill, Buddy

VERMONT

Barre:
Romanus, Richard
Bellows Falls:
Thompson, Ernest
Bennington:
Gibb, Cynthia
Burlington:
Bean, Orson
Island Pond:
Vallee, Rudy (r: Westbrook, Me.)

VIRGIN ISLANDS

St. Croix:
Haynes, Tiger (Three Flames)
Testamark, Roy (Three Flames)
St. Thomas:
Grammer, Kelsey

VIRGINIA

Alexandria:
Dixon, Donna (r: Europe)
Phillips, Mackenzie
Wiggin, Tom
Appalachia:
Castle, Peggy
Augusta County:
Balsley, Phil (Statler Brothers)
Reid, Harold (Statler Brothers)
Buckingham County:
Taylor, Clarice
Charlottesville:
Lowe, Rob

Emporia:
Harding, June
Front Royal:
Stratton, W.K.
Ft. Belvoir:
Hendler, Lauri
Greenville:
Smith, Kate
Lynchburg:
Adair, Deborah
Peck, J. Eddie (r: Joplin, Mo.)
Maces Spring:
Carter, June
Meherrin:
Clark, Roy
Newport News:
Bailey, Pearl
Bulifant, Joyce
Dobyns, Lloyd
Merritt, Theresa
Nickelsville:
Carter, Mother Maybelle
Norfolk:
Furst, Stephen
Johnson, Judy
Reid, Tim
Scribner, Jimmy
Petersburg:
Cotten, Joseph
Portsmouth:
Brown, Ruth
Newsom, Tommy
Quantico:
Crawford, Bobby, Jr.
Richmond:
Argo, Allison
Beatty, Warren
Gosden, Freeman
Jackson, Stoney
MacLaine, Shirley
Ragland, Larry
Robinson, Max
Smithers, William
Tarkenton, Fran
Roanoke County:
DeWitt, Lew (Statler Brothers)
Roanoke:
Bari, Lynn
Payne, John
Schuyler:
Hamner, Earl, Jr.

Staunton:
Reid, Don (Statler Brothers)
Tazewell:
Harrold, Kathryn
Vinton:
Huddleston, David
Winchester:
Benben, Brian (r: Marlboro, N.Y.)
Wise:
Scott, George C. (r: Detroit, Mich.)

WASHINGTON

Bellevue:
Horton, Peter
Bremerton:
Duff, Howard
Young, Heather
Camas:
Rodgers, Jimmie
Darrington:
Barker, Bob
Forks:
Hunley, Leann
Moses Lake:
Gilyard, Clarence, Jr.
Oak Harbor:
Dunnam, Stephanie (r: Dallas, Tex.)
McPherson, Patricia
Olympia:
Frank, Charles
Rich, Don
Richland:
Knox, Terence
Seattle:
Anderson, Daryl
Buckner, Susan (r: Burien, Wash.)
Damon, Cathryn
Dennis, Matt
Havoc, June
Hill, Steven
Lee, Gypsy Rose
Livingstone, Mary
McCarthy, Kevin
McWilliams, Caroline (r: Barrington, R.I.)
Mitchell, Brian
Osborne, Jinny (Chordettes) (r: Sheboygan, Wis.)
Ramus, Nick
Robinson, Roger
Ross, Lanny

Roylance, Pamela (r: Portland, Ore.)
Smart, Jean
Tokuda, Marilyn
Warner, Jody (r: Orcas Island, Wash.)
Wright, Martha
Snoqualmie Falls:
Raines, Ella
South Bend:
Paulsen, Pat (r: California)
Spokane:
Crosby, Bob
Edmunson, William (Southernaires)
Frank, Gary (r: Los Angeles, Calif.)
Jamison, Mikki
Lewis, Cathy
McGavin, Darren (r: Galt, Calif.)
McIntire, John
Munsel, Patrice
Nelson, Craig T.
Rose, Jane
Waldrip, Tim (r: Texas)
Sumner:
Northrop, Wayne
Tacoma:
Cannon, Dyan
Crosby, Bing (r: Spokane, Wash.)
Donahue, Elinor
Grayco, Helen
Hale, Lee
Millar, Marjie
Paige, Janis
Reed, Pamela
Underwood, Blair
Warnick, Clay
Walla Walla:
West, Adam
Wapito:
Hovis, Larry (r: Houston, Tex.)
Yakima:
Soper, Tony

WEST VIRGINIA

Beckley:
Patrick, Lory
Bolt:
Dickens, Jimmy
Charles Town:
Dick, Douglas (r: Versailles, Ky.)
Charleston:
Carson, Jean

Ferrell, Conchata (r: Cane Fork, W. Va.)
Hayes, Allison
Price, Roger
Clarksburg:
Wolter, Sherilyn (r: Sacramento, Calif.)
Huntington:
Dagmar
Dourif, Brad
Hartzell, Clarence
Hawkins, Hawkshaw
Marshall, Peter
Logan:
Dru, Joanne
Morgantown:
Knotts, Don
Selby, David
Moundsville:
DeVol, Frank
Oak Hill:
McCoy, Charlie
Parkersburg:
Dooley, Paul
Piedmont:
Redman, Don
Welch:
Austin, Karen
Wheeling:
DeWitt, Joyce (r: Speedway, Ind.)
Wyco:
Casey, Bernie

WISCONSIN

Albany:
Litel, John
Appleton:
Sherman, Ransom
Athens:
Winninger, Charles
Beaver Dam:
Hatfield, Bobby (Righteous Brothers)
Black River Falls:
Rainey, Dr. Froelich
Cambria:
Rowlands, Gena
Fond du Lac:
Bazlen, Brigid
Ryerson, Ann (r: Minneapolis, Minn.)
Green Bay:
Smith, Red
Kenosha:
Ameche, Don
Molinaro, Al
Siebert, Charles
Travanti, Daniel J.
Welles, Orson (r: Chicago)
LaCrosse:
Dierkop, Charles
Lodi:
Wopat, Tom
Madison:
Cole, Michael
Daly, Tyne
Tendler, Jesse
Menasha:
Liberace, George
Milwaukee:
Ayres, Mitchell (r: New York City)
Biberman, Abner
Britton, Pamela
Corrigan, Ray "Crash"
Franz, Eduard
Herman, Ralph
Husain, Jory
Jens, Salome
Kaczmarek, Jane (r: Greendale, Wis.)
Kaltenborn, H.V.
King, Pee Wee
Kubek, Tony
Liberace
Matuszak, John
Morton, Greg
O'Brien, Pat
Olson, Nancy
Rae, Charlotte
Shenar, Paul
Snyder, Tom
Tyler, Judy
Uecker, Bob
Wilcox, Ralph
Zien, Chip
Mineral Point:
Ludden, Allen
Neenah:
Shockley, Sallie
New Lisbon:
Smith, Kurtwood

Platville:
  Fiedler, John
Prentice:
  Morgan, Dennis
Racine:
  Corby, Ellen (r: Philadelphia, Pa.)
  McNair, Barbara
Sheboygan:
  Ertel, Janet (Chordettes)
  Hagendorn, Carol (Chordettes)
  Lau, Wesley
  Schwartz, Dorothy (Chordettes)
Whitefish Bay:
  O'Heaney, Caitlin
Wisconsin Rapids:
  Daly, James

WYOMING

Casper:
  Bullock, JM J. (r: Texas)
Goose Egg:
  Anders, Laurie
Green River:
  Gowdy, Curt
Laramie:
  Preston, Wayde

NORTH AMERICA:

CANADA

City Not Known:
  Atkin, Harvey
  Holmes, Ed
  Large, Don
  Maunder, Wayne (r: Bangor, Me.)
  Sawyer, Joe
  Shuster, Frank (raised)
  Somerville, Dave
  Wayne, Johnny (raised)
Alberta:
  McLiam, John
  Regehr, Duncan (r: Victoria, B.C.)
  Wray, Fay (r: Salt Lake City, Utah
    and Los Angeles, Calif.)
Antigonish, Nova Scotia:
  McHattie, Stephen
Big Timber, Quebec:
  Harris, Stacy
Brandon, Manitoba:
  Conway, Russ
  Woods, Donald (r: California)

British Columbia:
  Rekert, Winston
Calgary, Alberta:
  Cameron, Rod
  Jenson, Roy
Carmen, Manitoba:
  Carson, Jack
Dawson City, Yukon:
  Jory, Victor
East St. John, New Brunswick:
  Pidgeon, Walter
Edmonton, Alberta:
  Anderson, Melody
  Fox, Michael J.
Frederickton, New Brunswick:
  Savage, Booth
Grand'Mere, Quebec:
  McLerie, Allyn Ann (r: Brooklyn,
    N.Y.)
Halifax, Nova Scotia:
  Hindle, Art
Hamilton, Ont.:
  Dumbrille, Douglas
  Levy, Eugene
  Short, Martin
Jacksons Point, Ont.:
  Carrey, Jim
Kentville, Nova Scotia:
  Donat, Peter
Kingston, Ont.:
  Ratray, Peter (r: Bay Village, Ohio)
Kirkland Lake, Ont.:
  Thicke, Alan
Lethbridge, Alberta:
  Bain, Conrad
Liverpool, Nova Scotia:
  Snow, Hank
London, Ont.:
  Cronyn, Hume
  Diamond, Selma
  Lombardo, Guy
Melfort, Sask.:
  Hill, Arthur
Montreal:
  Blair, Lionel
  Blue, Ben
  Dewhurst, Colleen
  Krofft, Marty
  MacNeil, Robert
  Nolan, Tommy
  Pelletier, Wilfred
  Pilon, Daniel

Rodrigues, Percy
Royal, Allan
Shatner, William
Sherwood, Madeleine
Wiseman, Joseph
Moose Jaw, Sask.:
Linkletter, Art (r: San Diego, Calif.)
New Brunswick:
Somers, Brett (r: Portland, Me.)
New Westminister, B.C.:
Burr, Raymond
Newmarket, Ont.:
Candy, John
Ontario:
Jeffries, Lang
Hartman, Phil (r: Conn., Calif.)
Oshawa, Ont.:
Harmer, Shirley
Ottawa:
Aykroyd, Dan
Greene, Lorne
Little, Rich
Thomson, Gordon (r: Montreal, Can.)
Penticton, B.C.:
Smith, Alexis (r: Los Angeles, Calif.)
Prince George, B.C.:
Butler, Dean (r: San Francisco, Calif.)
Quebec:
Ford, Glenn
Regina, Sask.:
Nielsen, Leslie
Vernon, John
Sarnia, Ont.:
Clark, Susan
Madden, Dave (r: Terre Haute, Ind.)
Saskatchewan:
Cochran, Ron (r: Fairfield, Iowa)
McCallum, Neil
Metcalfe, Burt
Six Nations Indian Reservation, Ontario:
Silverheels, Jay
St. Catherines, Ont.:
Thomas, Dave
St. John's, Newfoundland:
Tweed, Shannon
St. Thomas, Ont.:
Shaver, Helen
Sudbury, Ont.:
Trebek, Alex

Sydney, Nova Scotia:
Cleveland, George
Thunder Bay, Ont.:
Shaffer, Paul
Toronto:
Acker, Sharon
Austin, Teri
Barbour, John
Bochner, Hart (r: Los Angeles, Calif.)
Bochner, Lloyd
Bromfield, Valri
Brooks, Elisabeth (raised)
Campbell, Nicholas
Colicos, John
Duke, Robin
Francis, Ivor
Gleason, Joanna
Harris, Arlene
Jacobi, Lou
Jarvis, Graham
Jennings, Peter
Mandel, Howie
Mann, Larry D.
Martin, Anne-Marie
Massey, Raymond
Menzies, Heather
Moranis, Rick
O'Hara, Catherine
Parke, Dorothy
Plummer, Christopher
Rutherford, Ann (r: San Francisco, Calif.)
Safer, Morley
Shirriff, Catherine
Thorson, Linda
Washbrook, Johnny
Waxman, Al
Wincott, Jeff
Young, Stephen
Vancouver, B.C.:
Boomer, Linwood (r: San Francisco, Calif.)
Bressler, Brian
DeCarlo, Yvonne
Doohan, James
Francks, Don
Greenwood, Bruce
Hylands, Scott
Ireland, John (r: New York City)
Ito, Robert

Ontkean, Michael
Parkins, Barbara
Patterson, Lee
Singer, Marc (r: Corpus Christi, Tex.)
Windsor, Ont.:
Collins, Dorothy
Patrick, Joan
Winnipeg:
Brand, Oscar
Hall, Monty
Kruschen, Jack
Kuzyk, Mimi
MacKenzie, Gisele
Montgomery, Belinda
Rhodes, Donnelly
Steinberg, David
Stone, Paddy
Yellowknife:
Kidder, Margot

MEXICO

City Not Known:
Allende, Fernando
Chihuahua:
Quinn, Anthony (r: Los Angeles, Calif.)
Guadalajara:
Jurado, Katy
Lewis, George J.
Mazatlan:
Rodriguez, Paul
Mexicali, Baja California:
Bara, Fausto
Mexico City:
Alicia, Ana (r: El Paso, Tex.)
Montalban, Ricardo
Van Rooten, Luis

CENTRAL AND SOUTH AMERICA

ARGENTINA

Buenos Aires:
Cristal, Linda
Rey, Alejandro

BRAZIL

Rio de Janeiro:
O'Neill, Jennifer (r: U.S.A.)

COLOMBIA

Cali:
Richwine, Maria

EQUADOR

Guayaquil:
Paulsen, Albert

NICARAGUA

Managua:
Carrera, Barbara

PANAMA

David:
DuBois, Marta

URUGUAY

Canelones:
Deloy, George (r: Salt Lake City, Utah)

WEST INDIES:

West Indies (Location not known):
Longden, John

BARBADOS

Dell, Gabriel
Pollard, Rill (Three Flames)

BERMUDA

Devonshire:
Douglas, Diana

CUBA

Guantanamo Bay:
Bergman, Peter
Havana:
Avalos, Luis (r: New York City)
Brown, Georg Stanford (r: Harlem, N.Y.)
Melis, Jose
Santiago:
Arnaz, Desi

DOMINICAN REPUBLIC

Santiago:
Campos, Rafael
Victor, James

JAMAICA

Jamaica:
  Lumbly, Carl (r: Minneapolis,
    Minn.)
Kingston:
  Silvera, Frank
  Sinclair, Madge

ST. VINCENT

City Not Known:
  Seales, Franklyn

TRINIDAD

Port of Spain:
  Scott, Hazel (r: U.S.A.)

EUROPE:

AUSTRIA

City Not Known:
  Weil, Lisl
Lemberg:
  Mintz, Eli
Lockenhaus:
  Stossel, Ludwig
Salzburg:
  Berger, Helmut
Tarnopal:
  Mazurki, Mike (r: Cohoes, N.Y.)
Vienna:
  Askin, Leon
  Banner, John
  Besch, Bibi (r: Westchester, N.Y.)
  Brown, Vanessa
  Dantine, Helmut
  Kasznar, Kurt
  Schildkraut, Joseph
  Skala, Lilia
  Slezak, Walter
  Wiere, Herbert (Wiere Brothers)

BELGIUM

Kortrjk:
  Sandler, Tony

CZECHOSLOVAKIA

Batchory:
  Kubelik, Rafael
Prague:
  Pravda, George

  Schick, George
  Wiere, Sylvester (Wiere Brothers)
Sazava:
  Voskovec, George
Volyne:
  Rubes, Jan

DENMARK

Copenhagen:
  Borge, Victor
Kolding/Jutland:
  Van Kamp, Merete

ENGLAND (see also Scotland, Wales, Ireland)

City Not Known:
  Crosbie, Annette
  Crutchley, Rosalie
  Cutts, Patricia
  Daniely, Lisa
  De Marney, Terence
  Dean, Ivor
  Delevanti, Cyril
  Graham, Sheilah
  Mattingly, Hedley
  Morecambe, Eric
  O'Shea, Tessie
  Porter, Arthur Gould
  Rhys-Davies, John
  Varden, Norma
  Wattis, Richard
  Wise, Ernie
Ainsdale, Lancashire:
  Quayle, Anthony
Anerley:
  Howard, Ronald
Ashby, Suffolk:
  Harris, Rosemary
Bath, Somerset:
  Leigh-Hunt, Barbara
  Lynn, Jonathan
Batton:
  Ford, Wallace
Beckenham, Kent:
  Monkhouse, Bob
Berkhampstead:
  Hordern, Michael
Bicester:
  Rose, George
Birmingham:
  Cooper, Melville

Henderson, Skitch (r: Halstad, Minn.)
Napier, Alan
Blackburn, Lancashire:
Billington, Michael (r: London)
McShane, Ian
Bournemouth:
Gray, Charles
Bourton-on-the-Water, Glouces-ter:
Hyde-White, Wilfred
Bow, London:
Montague, Lee
Bradford, Yorkshire:
Hepton, Bernard
Rennie, Michael
Brighton:
Treacher, Arthur
Bristol:
Cartwright, Veronica
Donald, Peter
Keen, Malcolm
Stephens, Robert
Broseley, Shropshire:
Baddeley, Hermione
Burnley:
O'Malley, J. Pat
Cambridge:
Davenport, Nigel
Chalfont St. Giles, Bucks:
Williams, John
Chapeltown, Yorkshire:
Pleasence, Angela
Chelmsford:
Adlam, Buzz
Cheshire:
Cartwright, Angela
Chesterfield:
Kemp, Jeremy
Chipping-Norton:
Ward, Rachael
Clapham, London:
Waterman, Dennis
Crouch Hill, London:
Simmons, Jean
Croydon, Surrey:
Woodward, Edward
Derbyshire:
Caulfield, Maxwell
Ditton, Surrey:
Naismith, Laurence

Doncaster:
Rigg, Diana (r: Jodhpur, India)
Dorchester:
Evans, Maurice
Dulwich:
Karloff, Boris
Eltham, Kent:
Hope, Bob (r: Cleveland, Ohio)
Van Gyseghem, Andre
Ely, Cambridge:
MacCorkindale, Simon
Felixstowe, Suffolk:
Addams, Dawn
Mills, John
Gosport, Hampshire:
Dawson, Richard
Guernsey, Channel Islands:
Dotrice, Roy
Hereford:
Oz, Frank
Hertfordshire:
Beacham, Stephanie
Huddersfield:
Mason, James
Ightham, Kent:
Lee, Anna
Ilford, Essex:
Holm, Ian
Lancashire:
Koppel, Ted
Walmsley, Jon (r: California)
Lancaster:
Foster, Linda
Lee-on-Solvent:
Malet, Arthur (r: Wales)
Leeds:
Gaunt, William
Leicester:
Chapman, Graham
O'Mara, Kate
Lewisham, London:
Cooper, Gladys
Lanchester, Elsa
Liverpool:
Bell, Tom
Cattrall, Kim
Gregson, John
Hamilton, Antony (r: Australia)
Medina, Patricia
Rossington, Norman
Youngman, Henny (r: Brooklyn, N.Y.)

London:
Alexander, Terry
Anderson, Michael, Jr.
Bennett, Peter
Bloom, Claire
Bryne, Barbara
Cabot, Sebastian
Camp, Hamilton
Chagrin, Julian
Collins, Joan
Cooper, Roy
Coote, Robert
Cossart, Valerie
Coster, Nicolas
Down, Lesley-Anne
Eggar, Samantha
Feldman, Marty
Ferris, Barbara
Francis, Clive
Freeman, J. Paul
Gingold, Hermione
Glover, Julian
Gordon, Bruce
Granger, Stewart
Hammond, Peter
Harrison, Noel
Hawkins, Jack
Hitchcock, Alfred
Holloway, Stanley
Hume, Benita
Hylton, Jane
Ireland, Jill
Jacobi, Derek
Jason, Harvey
Kaye, Lila
Kent, Jean
Lansbury, Angela
Lawford, Peter
Leach, Robin
Lunghi, Cherie
Lupino, Ida
MacRae, Sheila
Macnee, Patrick
Marshall, Sarah
McDowall, Roddy
Michael, Ralph
Mills, Juliet
Moody, Ron
Moore, Roger
Morgan, Terence
Morse, Barry

Mowbray, Alan
Murton, Lionel (r: Canada)
Parnell, Jack
Penny, Joe
Pettet, Joanna (r: Montreal, Can.)
Quilley, Denis
Rappaport, David
Raymond, Gary
Redgrave, Lynn
Reid, Kate
Rose, David (r: Chicago)
Samms, Emma
Standing, John
Stevens, Ronnie
Tandy, Jessica
Taylor, Elizabeth
Tennant, Victoria
Tremayne, Les (r: U.S.A.)
Troughton, Patrick
Tutin, Dorothy
Winters, David
Wisdom, Norman
Wycherly, Margaret (r: U.S.A.)
Wynter, Dana (r: Rhodesia)
Maida Vale, London:
Clark, Ernest
Manchester:
Badel, Alan
Cooke, Alistair
Gibb, Andy (r: Brisbane,
Australia)
Jones, David
Warner, David
Morley, Yorkshire:
Bedford, Brian
Newport, Isle of Wight:
Goring, Marius
North Shields, Northumberland:
Young, Alan
Northhampton:
Carne, Judy
Nottingham:
Matthews, Lester
Oldham, Lancaster:
Cribbins, Bernard
Plymouth:
Greene, Richard
Moffat, Donald
Shepley, Michael
Richmond-Surrey:
Colman, Ronald

Romford:
  Martin, Millicent
Salisbury:
  Crawford, Michael
  Davies, John Rhys
Southampton:
  Hill, Benny
Stepney:
  O'Connor, Des
Stoke Newington, London:
  Marsh, Jean
Stourbridge:
  Hardwicke, Sir Cedric
Stratford-on-Avon:
  Douglas, Sarah
Surbiton:
  McNaughton, Harry
Sutton Coldfield:
  Court, Hazel
Tenterden:
  Frost, David
Tolworth, Surrey:
  Wheatley, Alan
Torquay:
  Cook, Peter
Twickenham:
  King, Dave
Walton-on-Thames:
  Andrews, Julie
Warwickshire:
  Chadwick, June
Weedon, Northants:
  Carroll, Leo G.
Wem, Shropshire:
  Jones, Peter
Westhoughton:
  Shaw, Robert (r: Scotland)
Wiltshire:
  Jones, Simon
Wimbledon, Surrey:
  Gardiner, Reginald
  Seymour, Jane (1970s–80s)
Winchester:
  Cazenove, Christopher
Worksop:
  Pleasence, Donald
Worthing, Sussex:
  Hewett, Christopher
  Sheridan, Nicollette (r: London and
    Los Angeles, Calif.)
York:
  Brook, Faith

Yorkshire:
  Bennett, Elizabeth
  Carson, Jeannie
  Haigh, Kenneth
  Pickles, Christina
  West, Timothy

FINLAND

Helsinki:
  Gaynes, George

FRANCE

City Not Known:
  Beer, Jacqueline
  Carere, Christine
  Du Bief, Jacqueline
  Farge, Annie
Alsace-Lorraine:
  Bloch, Ray
Avignon:
  Mathieu, Mireille
Bordeaux:
  Carricart, Robert
Cauderan:
  Olaf, Pierre
Corbeil:
  Dauphin, Claude
Figeac:
  Boyer, Charles
La Rochelle:
  Adam, Noelle
Marseilles:
  Jourdan, Louis
Paris:
  Baruch, Andre
  Caron, Leslie
  Clary, Robert
  Dalio, Marcel
  Darcel, Denise
  Genevieve
  Johnson, Kathie Lee (r: Annapolis,
    Md.)
  Joy, Nicholas
  Leroy, Philippe
  Maugham, W. Somerset
  Pelikan, Lisa
  Terzieff, Laurent
  Valente, Caterina
  Villechaize, Herve
Saint Andre:
  Cousteau, Capt. Jacques-Yves

GERMANY

City Not Known:
  Andor, Paul
  Holland, Steve
Berlin:
  Hague, Albert
  Reason, Rex
  Reason, Rhodes
  Wiere, Harry (Wiere Brothers)
Cologne:
  Hillaire, Marcel
  Klemperer, Werner
Dusseldorf:
  Erickson, John
Frankfurt:
  Blakely, Susan
  Brown, Olivia (r: Sacramento, Calif.)
  Crespi, Todd
  Gayle, Tina
  Helberg, Sandy (r: Toledo, Ohio)
Hamburg:
  Arno, Sig
  Ruman, Sig
  Thiess, Ursula
Kiel:
  Gudegast, Hans
Koblenz:
  Diffring, Anton
Landsthul:
  Burton, LeVar
Munich:
  Murphy, Rosemary
  Netherton, Tom
Rhineland:
  Meisner, Gunter
Rosenheim:
  Dzundza, George

GREECE

Athens:
  Krofft, Sid
Corinth:
  Papas, Irene
Sparta:
  Regas, Pedro
Thessaly:
  Dennis, Nick (r: Lowell, Mass.)

HUNGARY

City Not Known:
  Ferraday, Lisa

Budapest:
  Gabor, Eva
  Massey, Ilona
  Prohaska, Janos
  Reiner, Fritz

IRELAND

City Not Known:
  Doonican, Val
Belfast:
  Nesbitt, Cathleen
Connemara, Galway:
  O'Toole, Peter
Cork:
  Driscoll, Patricia
  Mulhare, Edward
County Cavan:
  McKenna, T.P.
County Meath:
  Brosnan, Pierce
  Moore, Tom
Dublin:
  Brent, George
  Fitzgerald, Geraldine
  Flanagan, Fionnula
  McClory, Sean
  Quinn, Carmel
  Shields, Arthur
Portadown County, Armagh:
  Donlevy, Brian (r: Wisconsin)
Wexford:
  O'Herlihy, Dan

ITALY

City Not Known:
  Mancuso, Nick (r: Toronto, Can.)
Alessandria:
  Antonini, Alfredo
Bologna:
  Brazzi, Rossano
Florence:
  Cobb, Buff
Island of Ischia (near Naples):
  Ciannelli, Eduardo
Montagnana:
  Martinelli, Giovanni
Naples:
  Carter, Thomas
  Gardenia, Vincent (r: New York, N.Y.)
  Rosato, Tony (r: Toronto, Can.)
Rome:
  Cerusico, Enzo

Cesana, Renzo
Danova, Cesare
Paluzzi, Luciana
Pinza, Ezio
Secondari, John (r: U.S.A.)
Subiaco:
Lollobrigida, Gina
Trieste:
Dolenz, George
Venice:
Mantovani (r: England)

THE NETHERLANDS

Amsterdam:
Peluce, Meeno (r: Los Angeles, Calif.)
Van Steeden, Peter (r: U.S.A.)
Leiden:
Broekman, David
Foch, Nina
Rotterdam:
Wolders, Robert

NORWAY

City Not Known:
Dahl, Ronald
Kristen, Marta
Oslo:
Lisa, Anna
Voldstad, John (r: U.S.A.)

POLAND

City Not Known:
Glass, Ned
Grodek:
Martin, Ross (r: New York City)
Kremieniec:
Sheybal, Vladek
Vilna:
Ruskin, Shimen

RUMANIA

Bucharest:
Houseman, John

SCOTLAND, U.K.

City Not Known:
Greene, Marge (r: U.S.A.)
Blairgowrie:
Clyde, Andy

Edinburgh:
Charleson, Ian
Inescort, Frieda
O'Hara, Quinn
Richardson, Ian
Roberts, Ewan
Glasgow:
Duncan, Archie
Martin, Ian
McCallion, James
McCallum, David
Hebrides Islands:
Brown, Robert (r: New York City)
Kirriemuir:
Niven, David
Lennoxtown:
Lulu
Peterhead:
Smith, Cyril

SPAIN

Barcelona:
Cugat, Xavier (r: Havana, Cuba)
Falkenburg, Jinx
Madrid:
Sierra, Margarita
Murcia:
Charo
Valladolid:
Renaldo, Duncan

SWEDEN

City Not Known:
Stromstedt, Ulla
Goteborg:
Hutton, Gunilla
Svenson, Bo
Lulea:
Adams, Maud
Sandviken:
Goude, Ingrid
Solleften:
Thulin, Ingrid
Stockholm:
Brundin, Bo
Stevens, Inger

SWITZERLAND

Geneva:
Abernethy, Robert (r: Washington, D.C.)

WALES, U.K.

City Not Known:
  Eve, Trevor (r: Birmingham, Eng.)
Cardiff:
  Templeton, Alec
Colwyn Bay:
  Dalton, Timothy
Llanelly:
  Roberts, Rachel
Neath:
  Milland, Ray
Pontrhydyfen, South Wales:
  Burton, Richard
Pontypridd:
  Jones, Tom

ASIA & AFRICA:

American Samoa:
  Harrington, Al (r: Hawaii)

AUSTRALIA

City Not Known:
  Matheson, Murray
Adelaide:
  Michell, Keith
Melbourne:
  Browne, Coral
  Reddy, Helen
Sydney:
  Brown, Bryan
  Noble, Trisha
  Pate, Michael
  Randell, Ron
  Taylor, Rod
  Taylor, Ron
Warburton:
  Trask, Diana

CEYLON

City Not Known:
  Gordon, Colin

CHINA

Canton:
  Luke, Keye (r: Seattle, Wash.)
Peking:
  Fenneman, George
Shanghai:
  Rozario, Bob

Taiyuan, Shansi:
  Chi, Chou-Li
Tsing-tao:
  Mifune, Toshiro
Wenchow:
  Gauge, Alexander
Wu Chang:
  Meadows, Audrey
  Meadows, Jayne

HONG KONG
  Barrie, Wendy
  Lorring, Joan (r: Shanghai, China)

INDIA

City Not Known:
  Khan, Sajid
  Milligan, Spike
  Reid, Milton
Akhnur, Kashmir:
  Bux, Kuda
Bombay:
  Prowse, Juliet (r: South Africa)
Calcutta:
  Oberon, Merle:
Dhugga:
  Raz, Kavi
Madras:
  Humperdinck, Engelbert (r: Leicester, Eng.)
Mussoorie:
  Hill, Tom

ISRAEL

Tel Aviv:
  Topol

JAPAN

Fukuoka:
  Principal, Victoria
Kobe:
  Mako
Otaru, Hokaido:
  Umeki, Miyoshi
Sakhalin Island:
  Brynner, Yul
Sendai:
  Douglass, Robyn
Tokyo:
  De Havilland, Olivia

KOREA

City Not Known:
  Oh, Soon-Teck

MADAGASCAR

City Not Known:
  Benard, Francois-Marie

MALAYSIA

Kuala Lumpur:
  Wells, Claudia (r: San Francisco,
    Calif.)
Malaya:
  Gough, Michael

NEW ZEALAND

City Not Known:
  Porter, Nyree Dawn
Auckland:
  Stephenson, Pamela (r: Sydney,
    Australia)
Wellington:
  Revill, Clive

PHILIPPINES

City Not Known:
  Wong, Joe
Manila:
  Raines, Cristina (r: Florida)

RUSSIA

City Not Known:
  Gart, John
  Skulnik, Menasha
Kaunas, Lithuania:
  Garas, Kaz
Nikopol, Russia:
  Goodman, Al
Odessa, Russia:
  Belasco, Leon

St. Petersburg, Russia:
  Conway, Tom
  Kinskey, Leonid
  Sanders, George

SAUDI ARABIA

City Not Known:
  Eilbacher, Cindy
Dharan:
  Eilbacher, Lisa

SENEGAL

Dakar:
  Sekka, Johnny (r: Paris,
    France)

SOUTH AFRICA

Cape Province:
  Gray, Donald
Cape Town:
  Forbes, Scott (r: Easton, Pa.)
  Pithey, Wensley
Johannesburg:
  Daly, John
  Hayward, Louis
  Rathbone, Basil (r: England)
Kenilworth:
  Hunter, Ian
Pretoria:
  Johns, Glynis

SYRIA

City Not Known:
  George, John

VIETNAM

City Not Known:
  Pisier, Marie-France
Saigon:
  Quan, Ke Huy

Bibliography

Books:

Allen, Steve. *Funny People* (Stein and Day, 1981)

American Society of Composers, Authors and Publishers. *ASCAP Biographical Dictionary,* 4th edition (Bowker, 1980)

Brooks, Tim, and Earle Marsh. *The Complete Directory to Prime Time Network TV Shows, 1946–Present,* 3rd edition (Ballantine, 1985)

Buxton, Frank, and Bill Owen. *The Big Broadcast* (Viking, 1972)

Claghorn, Charles Eugene. *Biographical Dictionary of American Music* (Parker, 1973)

Current Biography Yearbook (H. W. Wilson, var. editions)

Duning, John. *Tune in Yesterday* (Prentice-Hall, 1976)

Feather, Leonard. *The New Encyclopedia of Jazz* (Bonanza, 1960)

Franklin, Joe. *Joe Franklin's Encyclopedia of Comedians* (Bell, 1985)

Gertner, Richard (ed.). *International Television Almanac* (Quigley, var. editions)

Halliwell, Leslie. *Halliwell's Filmgoer's Companion,* 8th edition (Scribner's, 1985)

———. *Halliwell's Television Companion* (Granada, 1982)

Herbert, Ian (ed.). *Who's Who in the Theatre* (Gale, 1981)

Jones, Ken D. et al. *Character People* (Citadel, 1976)

Kaplan, Mike (ed.). *The Complete Book of Major U.S. Show Business Awards* (Garland, 1985)

———. *Variety Who's Who in Show Business* (Garland, 1983), and rev. edition (1985)

Katz, Ephraim. *The Film Encyclopedia* (Perigee, 1979)

Kinkle, Roger. *The Complete Encyclopedia of Popular Music and Jazz, 1900–1950* (Arlington House, 1974)

Lamparski, Richard. *Whatever Became of . . .?* vol. 1–10 (Crown, 1967–86)

Lloyd, Ann, and Graham Fuller (eds.). *The Illustrated Who's Who of the Cinema* (Macmillan, 1983)

Mapp, Edward. *Directory of Blacks in the Performing Arts* (Scarecrow, 1978)

Marill, Alvin H. *Movies Made for Television: 1964–1984* (Zoetrope, 1984)

McCarty, John, and Brian Kelleher. *Alfred Hitchcock Presents* (St. Martin's, 1985)

McClure, Arthur F. et al. *More Character People* (Citadel, 1984)

McNeil, Alex. *Total Television* (Penguin, 1984)

Metzger, Linda and Deborah Straub (eds.). *Contemporary Authors* (Gale, Var. Editions)

Nite, Norm N. *Rock On: The Illustrated Encyclopedia of Rock n' Roll,* vol. I (Harper & Row, 1982), II (1984), and III (1985)

Parish, James Robert. *Actors' Television Credits* (Scarecrow, 1973), with supps. I (1978) and II (1982)

Quinlan, David. *The Illustrated Directory of Movie Character Actors* (Harmony, 1985)

──────. *The Illustrated Directory of Film Stars* (Hippocrene, 1981)

Ragan, David. *Movie Stars of the '30s* (Prentice-Hall, 1985)

──────. *Movie Stars of the '40s* (Prentice-Hall, 1985)

──────. *Who's Who in Hollywood 1900–1976* (Arlington House, 1976)

Rovin, Jeff. *TV Babylon* (Signet, 1984)

Rust, Brian. *The American Dance Band Discography* (Arlington House, 1975)

Schemering, Christopher. *The Soap Opera Encyclopedia* (Ballantine, 1985)

Shestack, Melvin. *The Country Music Encyclopedia* (Crowell, 1974)

Smith, Ronald Lande. *Stars of Stand Up Comedy* (Garland, 1986)

Stambler, Irwin, and Grelun Landon. *The Encyclopedia of Folk, Country & Western Music* (St. Martin's, 1984)

Stambler, Irwin. *Encyclopedia of Popular Music* (St. Martin's, 1965)

──────. *The Encyclopedia of Pop, Rock and Soul* (St. Martin's 1974)

Terrace, Vincent. *The Complete Encyclopedia of Television Programs, 1947–1979* (Barnes, 1979)

──────. *Encyclopedia of Television Series, Pilots and Specials,* vols. I (Zoetrope, 1985) and II (1986)

Truitt, Evelyn Mack. *Who Was Who on Screen* (Bowker, 1984)

──────. *Who's Who in America* (Macmillan, Var. Editions)

──────. *Who Was Who in America* (Marquis, 1985)

Wicking, Christopher, and Tise Vahimagi. *The American Vein* (Dutton, 1979)

Wlaschin, Ken. *The Illustrated Encyclopedia of the World's Great Movie Stars* (Bonanza, 1979)

Willis, John. *Screen World* (Crown, var. editions)

──────. *Theatre World* (Crown, var. editions)

Woolery, George W., *Children's Television: The First Thirty-Five Years,* parts I (Scarecrow, 1983) and II (1985)

Zicree, Marc Scott. *The Twilight Zone Companion* (Bantam, 1982)

Periodicals:

Emmy magazine. var. issues, 1984–1986
(3500 West Olive Ave., Suite 700, Burbank, Calif. 91505)

Reruns: The Magazine of Television History. var. issues, 1980–1985
(P.O. Box 1057, Safford, Ariz. 85548)

The TV Collector. var. issues, 1982–1987
(P.O. Box 188, Needham, Mass. 02192)

TV Guide. var. issues, 1948–1987

Variety. obits., 1950–1987

INDEX OF TV PRODUCTIONS

A

Abbott and Costello Show, The, 1, 19, 58, 85, 115, 297, 429, 440, 447, 474, 769
ABC Afterschool Special, 7, 26, 498, 499, 577
ABC Barn Dance, 639, 812
ABC Comedy Hour, 53, 141, 351, 474, 515, 586, 848
ABC Evening News, 183, 223, 344, 439, 497, 539, 701, 713, 725, 787, 823, 877, 924
ABC Late News, 183, 550, 924
ABC Late Night, 166, 650
ABC Matinee Today, 624, 637
ABC News Reports, 183, 924
ABC SportsBeat, 204
ABC Stage '67, 246
ABC Television Players, 324
ABC Theatre, 300, 409, 822
ABC Wednesday Night Movie, 914
ABC Weekend News, 86, 172, 253, 437, 479, 725, 821, 924
ABC's Nightlife, 146, 186, 208, 498, 740, 850, 906
ABC's Wide World of Sports, 572
Abe Burrows' Almanac, 132, 240
About Faces, 12
Acapulco, 182, 393, 721, 751, 827, 850
Accent on an American Summer, 176
Accidental Family, 77, 95, 539, 625, 692, 861
Accused, 290, 339, 368, 408, 446
Ace Crawford, Private Eye, 64, 65, 175, 197, 226, 398, 707
Acorn People, The, 84
Act of Love, 798
Action Autographs, 106, 683
Actor's Studio, 106, 193, 424
Acts of Love . . . and Other Comedies, 832
A.D., 326, 735
Ad Libbers, 253, 378, 416, 504, 581, 778, 813
Adam, 291, 848
Adam-12, 105, 143, 160, 163, 177, 213, 277, 382, 409, 436, 443, 564, 590, 591, 781, 809, 817, 880, 886
Adams Chronicles, The, 30, 88, 227, 873
Adam's Rib, 64, 227, 248, 418, 718, 913
Addams Family, The, 42, 49, 164, 198, 201, 310, 378, 445, 460, 522, 652, 717, 726, 778, 872, 884
Adderly, 677, 710, 762, 890
Admiral Broadway Revue, 45, 139, 140, 168, 182, 183, 217, 487, 522, 562, 888

Adventure, 187, 731
Adventure Theater, 256
Adventurer, The, 62, 607, 755
Adventures in Jazz, 721, 901
Adventures in Paradise, 406, 410, 452, 499, 508, 519, 572, 784, 794, 812, 843
Adventures of Champion, The, 45, 57, 218, 567, 592
Adventures of Charlie Chan, The, 413, 617
Adventures of Ellery Queen, The, 21, 69, 103, 323, 387, 404, 406, 427, 518, 544, 617, 657, 671, 673, 706, 825, 849, 883
Adventures of Fu Manchu, The, 54, 333, 351, 420, 525, 556
Adventures of Hiram Holiday, The, 207, 688
Adventures of Huckleberry Finn, The, 814
Adventures of Jim Bowie, The, 203, 304, 380, 563
Adventures of Judge Roy Bean, The, 125, 392, 523
Adventures of Kit Carson, The, 247, 373, 456, 670, 901
Adventures of Oky Doky, The, 13, 59, 61, 405, 580
Adventures of Ozzie & Harriet, The, 6, 49, 74, 91, 97, 120, 139, 210, 234, 238, 282, 301, 302, 382, 383, 447, 544, 564, 604, 621–623, 737, 746, 799, 828, 869, 888, 927
Adventures of Rin Tin Tin, The, 1, 117, 119, 753
Adventures of Robin Hood, The, 214, 259, 264, 330, 361, 424, 639, 676, 893
Adventures of Sir Francis Drake, The, 209, 240, 247, 467, 491, 574, 604, 707, 722, 880
Adventures of Sir Lancelot, The, 78, 427, 503, 740, 761, 786
Adventures of Superman, The, 128, 181, 193, 378, 495, 620, 706, 726, 770
Adventures of the Sea Hawk, The, 418
Adventures of Tugboat Annie, The, 748, 855
Adventures of Wild Bill Hickok, The, 209, 245, 534
A.E.S. Hudson Street, 203, 337, 541, 587, 666, 777, 796, 811
Affair, The, 917
AfterMASH, 3, 170, 175, 208, 289, 304, 340, 346, 465, 491, 524, 602, 603, 656, 676, 748, 754, 824, 847, 872
Afterschool Specials, 51, 468
Ages of Man, The, 822
Agronsky & Company, 7
Ain't Misbehavin', 160
Air Power, 211

Air Time '57, 369, 498, 595
Airwolf, 101, 201, 683, 760, 866
a.k.a. Pablo, 215, 275, 347, 451, 520, 523, 717, 727, 732, 737, 749, 750, 790, 847, 864
Al Morgan, 602
Alan Burke Show, The, 128
Alan Dale Show, The, 222, 305, 360
Alan Young Show, The, 6, 811, 924
Alarm, 642
Alaskans, The, 228, 599, 600, 688, 924
Alcoa Hour, 212
Alcoa Playhouse, 111
Alcoa Premiere, 42, 74
Alcoa Presents, 551
Alcoa Presents (One Step Beyond), 626
Alcoa Theatre, 104, 157, 504, 629
Alcoa/Goodyear Theatre, 681, 742
Aldrich Family, The, 63, 66, 156, 162, 235, 277, 302, 340, 365, 398, 436, 461, 462, 508, 537, 586, 622, 682, 721, 787, 796, 853, 908, 909
Alexander: The Other Side of Dawn, 370
Alf, 277, 362, 755, 919
Alfred Hitchcock Hour, The, 65, 68, 280, 426, 536, 567, 734
Alfred Hitchcock Presents, 43, 55, 62, 72, 86, 110, 131, 137, 139, 148, 153, 163, 168, 176, 182, 189, 208, 246, 248, 273, 307, 311, 340, 349, 358, 361, 381, 385, 407, 415, 434, 447, 461, 500, 516, 527, 530, 534, 540, 545, 556, 584, 607, 620, 665, 685, 711, 712, 736, 778, 806, 847, 919, 920, 923, 925
Alias Smith and Jones, 143, 175, 233, 244, 296, 430, 434, 612, 673, 723, 739, 815, 891
Alice, 13, 16, 36, 55, 97, 144, 156, 175, 208, 267, 332, 391, 411, 420, 453, 486, 497, 508, 520, 534, 563, 573, 680, 686, 700, 725, 830, 892
Alice Pearce, 498, 662
Alkali Ike, 299, 433, 724
All Around the Town, 181, 874, 875
All God's Children, 899
All in One, 246
All in the Family, 39, 109, 113, 123, 211, 235, 249, 263, 283, 326, 328, 376, 391, 398, 515, 538, 567, 581, 616, 637, 638, 652, 676, 692, 709, 748, 749, 802, 803, 811, 818, 847, 907, 912
All Is Forgiven, 35, 80, 362, 453, 478, 490, 717, 791, 900
All My Children, 81, 93, 113, 145, 527, 591, 614, 695, 831, 881, 890

All My Darling Daughters, 343
All Quiet on the Western Front, 677, 840
All Star Blitz, 547
All Star News, 173, 314, 315, 698
All Star Revue, The, 56, 156, 266, 440, 700, 837, 853, 921
All Star Salute to Mother's Day, The, 713
All That Glitters, 109, 122, 263, 338, 359, 561, 625, 749, 876
All's Fair, 168, 209, 251, 452, 460, 668, 684
Almost Anything Goes, 446, 671, 767, 898
Aloha Means Goodbye, 818
Aloha Paradise, 97, 222, 444, 476, 594, 713, 775
Alvin & the Chipmunks, 50
Alvin Show, The, 50, 304, 581
Amanda Fallon, 921
Amanda's, 39, 40, 219, 363, 425, 561, 732, 895
Amateur Night at the Dixie Bar and Grill, 443
Amateur's Guide to Love, 700
Amazing Chan and the Chan Clan, 525
Amazing Dunninger, The, 265
Amazing Mr. Malone, The, 847
Amazing Polgar, The, 678
Amazing Spider-Man, The, 123, 297, 379, 659, 780
Amazing Stories, 140
Amazing World of Kreskin, The, 482, 527
Amber Waves, 884, 913
Amelia Earhart, 179, 920
Amen, 231, 372, 398, 415, 596, 742
America, 199
America Salutes Richard Rodgers, 912
America Song, 38, 298, 386
America Speaks, 325
America Still, 621
America 2-Night, 187, 836, 900
American Bandstand, 177, 178, 363, 742
American Christmas Carol, 912
American Dream, 150, 195, 402, 531, 571, 785, 872
American Forum of the Air, 356
American Girls, The, 60, 180, 686, 798
American Inventory, 604
American Minstrels of 1949, 132, 159, 673, 785
American Parade, The, 125, 237, 483, 484, 486, 609, 752, 776
American Playhouse, 198
American Sportsman, 354
American Week, The, 765
American West, The, 133

American Woman: Portraits of Courage, The, 625
Americana, 120, 357
Americans, The, 230, 403, 404
America's Greatest Bands, 896
America's Town Meeting, 223, 242
Among the Paths to Eden, 803
Amos Burke, 148
Amos 'n' Andy, 173, 352, 502, 600, 696, 697, 811, 869, 905
Amy Prentiss, 424, 585, 592, 749, 766, 876
And David Wept, 32
And Everything Nice, 60
And Here's the Show, 255, 504, 773, 850, 913
And Your Name Is Jonah, 818
Andros Targets, The, 77, 171, 593, 678, 704, 822, 824
Andy and Della Russell, 514, 738, 739
Andy Griffith Show, The, 49, 67, 131, 175, 203, 251, 252, 364, 389, 417, 419, 478, 505, 512, 528, 576, 606, 616, 617, 671, 787, 821, 837
Andy Williams and June Valli Show, The, 858, 891, 900
Andy Williams Presents Ray Stevens, 218, 275, 526, 551, 724, 794, 809, 858
Andy Williams Show, The, 121, 141, 165, 202, 294, 301, 324, 332, 347, 366, 453, 504, 582, 625, 646, 679, 688, 727, 730, 803, 809, 833, 900, 901, 913
Andy's Gang, 245, 304
Angel, 288, 460, 782, 840
Angel Dusted, 803
Angie, 65, 114, 268, 395, 490, 496, 668, 697, 722, 724, 758, 798, 840
Animal Secrets, 274
Animal World, 133
Animals, Animals, Animals, 512
Ann Margret Smith, 791
Ann Sothern Show, The, 55, 83, 610, 633, 679, 760, 769, 796, 850, 854, 896
Anna and the King, 124, 273, 524, 525, 770, 843
Annie Oakley, 45, 231, 232, 392, 443
Another Day, 274, 365, 369, 512, 821
Another World, 3, 17, 145, 171, 268, 386, 397, 494, 527, 541, 545, 562, 583, 591, 670, 767, 772, 777, 821, 824, 887
Answer Yes or No, 311, 387
Answers for Americans, 133, 329, 408, 420, 632
Ant and the Aardvark, The, 137
Antigone, 458
Any Second Now, 356
Anybody Can Play, 56, 294

Anyone Can Win, 147
Anywhere, U.S.A., 257, 684
Apple Pie, 186, 338, 557, 562, 640
Apple's Way, 44, 84, 184, 206, 560, 576, 586, 642, 862
Appointment with Adventure, 651
Aquanauts, The, 277, 495, 712, 784, 840
Aquanauts, The (Malibu Run), 277
Archer, 460, 461, 741
Archie Bunker's Place, 19, 55, 56, 124, 333, 349, 370, 412, 532, 579, 580, 587, 622, 632, 637, 640, 732
Are You Positive?, 146, 192, 298, 806
Armchair Detective, 466, 786
Armstrong Circle Theatre, 14, 43, 70, 161, 163, 183, 214, 271, 377, 637, 719, 751, 773, 822, 823
Arnie, 83, 103, 491, 664, 708, 738, 775, 797, 804, 867
Around the Town, 802
Arrest and Trial, 65, 193, 325, 327, 331, 404, 460, 468, 494, 567, 593, 668
Arrow Show, The, 338, 487, 779
Art Ford on Broadway, 304
Art Ford Show, The, 304
Art Linkletter Show, The, 513, 579, 709
Art Linkletter's House Party, 513
Arthur Godfrey and His Friends, 93, 99, 110, 174, 232, 288, 345, 360, 373, 494, 497, 544, 545, 553, 570, 656, 692, 729, 780, 846, 855, 892
Arthur Godfrey and His Ukulele, 345
Arthur Godfrey Time, 345
Arthur Godfrey's Talent Scouts, 4, 93, 99, 110, 129, 174, 181, 288, 312, 345, 369, 498, 553, 592, 695, 729, 770, 791, 858, 913
Arthur Murray Dance Party, The, 126, 567
Arthur Murray Party, The, 160, 186, 580, 613, 614
Arthur Penn, 1922: Themes and Variants, 423
As the World Turns, 113, 124, 132, 255, 320, 391, 394, 416, 447, 484, 522, 558, 617, 653, 708, 737, 749, 777, 839, 869, 881, 916
Ask Dr. Brothers, 118
Ask Me Another, 97, 122, 263, 525, 892
Aspen, 62, 85, 233, 248, 264, 276, 310, 311, 383, 403, 414, 416, 449, 472, 571, 672, 686, 717
Asphalt Jungle, The, 442, 658, 785, 878

Assignment America, 133
Assignment Foreign Legion, 635
Assignment Underwater, 901
Assignment Vienna, 176, 194, 249
Associates, The, 427, 471, 589, 707, 775, 791, 840, 887
Astaire Time, 42
At Ease, 57, 103, 317, 434, 608, 619, 863, 873, 921
At Home with Tex and Jinx, 287, 566
At Issue, 7
At Liberty Club, 852
At the Movies, 269, 384, 705, 782
A-Team, The, 49, 76, 215, 264, 320, 395, 500, 503, 525, 665, 680, 706, 757, 827, 863, 864
Atlanta Child Murders, 847
Auction-Aire, 362, 696
Aunt Mary, 803
Aurora, 848
Author Meets the Critics, 278, 559, 670
Autobiography of Miss Jane Pittman, The, 854
Automan, 36, 37, 493, 575, 641, 869
Avengers, The, 424, 526, 533, 625, 718, 841
Awakening Land, The, 596
Away We Go, 149, 294, 360, 622, 715

B

Baa Baa Black Sheep, 5, 34, 94, 146, 175, 194, 261, 275, 340, 494, 500, 531, 539, 566, 635, 717, 816, 892, 898
Babe, 179, 455
Baby, I'm Back, 297, 374, 412, 550, 627, 907
Baby Makes Five, 346, 354, 605, 608, 652, 758, 904
Bachelor Father, 48, 54, 104, 201, 282, 306, 471, 491, 540, 592, 598, 599, 643, 651, 759, 846, 867, 915, 928
Back That Fact, 5, 161, 462, 491
Background, 386
Backstage with Barry Wood, 916
Backstairs at the White House, 25, 61, 95, 127, 155, 186, 257, 263, 300, 330, 352, 356, 385, 396, 412, 413, 424, 444, 465, 499, 602, 628, 648, 659, 714, 806, 855, 863
B.A.D. Cats, 108, 379, 606, 651, 670, 873
Bad News Bears, The, 16, 135, 165, 215, 224, 293, 306, 404, 434, 499, 543, 633, 664, 745, 788, 878
Baffle, 279

Baggy Pants and the Nitwits, 136, 442
Baileys of Balboa, The, 107, 120, 151, 239, 305, 412, 417
Baker's Dozen, 73, 240, 575, 692, 778, 887
Balance Your Budget, 657
Ball Four, 102, 155, 230, 566, 745, 758, 794, 843, 920
Ballad of Andy Crocker, The, 237, 543
Ballad of Louie the Louse, The, 779
Banacek, 73, 541, 555, 665, 686
Banana Splits Hour, The, 648, 866
Bank on the Stars, 215, 622, 650
Banyon, 94, 174, 306, 362, 434
Barbara McNair Show, The, 575
Barbara Mandrell & The Mandrell Sisters, 482, 538, 539
Barbara Stanwyck Show, The, 802, 916
Barbara Walters Special, The, 877
Barbary Coast, The, 469, 563, 768, 852
Barbra Streisand: A Happening in Central Park, 513
Barbra Streisand . . . and Other Musical Instruments, 658
Bare Essence, 67, 123, 239, 268, 310, 312, 317, 320, 527, 578, 617, 644, 808, 876, 918
Barefoot in the Park, 152, 410, 593, 705, 740, 761
Baretta, 91, 233, 275, 284, 365, 615, 672, 722, 902
Barnaby Jones, 159, 270, 366, 420, 437, 507, 517, 538, 583, 638, 679, 749, 772, 848
Barney Blake, Police Reporter, 639, 659
Barney Miller, 61, 123, 127, 148, 149, 222, 323, 341, 362, 371, 489, 497, 512, 516, 611, 676, 777, 795, 802, 830, 835, 865, 921
Baron, The, 296, 306, 350, 516
Barrier Reef, 833
Baseball Bunch, The, 76
Baseball Corner, 93
Baseball World of Joe Garagiola, The, 325
Bastard, The, 677, 807, 820
Bat Masterson, 62, 92, 195
Batman, 42, 49, 56, 68, 82, 91, 127, 137, 189, 190, 207, 262, 283, 351, 378, 394, 435, 444, 446, 464, 501, 509, 511, 526, 555, 558, 567, 582, 618, 627, 685, 711, 724, 748, 784, 858, 875, 878, 883, 891
Battered, 290
Battle of the Ages, 22, 472
Battle Report, 565

Battlestar Galactica, 76, 160, 187, 256, 360, 361, 391, 438, 440, 516, 528, 564, 587, 719, 797, 819, 823, 860
Baxters, The, 19, 303, 338, 461, 561, 571, 669, 793, 853, 917
Bay City Blues, 161, 164, 203, 314, 361, 382, 439, 451, 491, 565, 631, 632, 640, 727, 798, 814, 851, 906
Bay City Rollers, The, 65
Be Our Guest, 107, 246, 573, 593
Beach Ball, 137
Beachcomber, The, 139, 591, 800
Beacon Hill, 200, 263, 276, 402, 542, 571, 579, 632, 690, 732, 735, 737, 793, 815, 825, 831, 873, 878, 912
Beany and Cecil, 134, 154
Bearcats, The, 185, 833
Beasts Are on the Streets, The, 839
Beat the Clock, 34, 79, 190, 375, 618, 619, 635, 916
Beatles, The, 317
Beautiful Phyllis Diller Show, The, 213, 218, 249, 276, 439, 450, 707, 832, 906
Beauty and the Beast, 759
Beggarman, Thief, 118, 703, 806, 807
Behind Closed Doors, 349
Behind the News With Howard K. Smith, 787
Behind the Screen, 12, 124, 170, 286, 295, 514, 602, 610, 625, 657, 675, 743, 809, 852, 923
Believe It or Not, 719, 745
Bell Telephone Hour, The, 868, 916
Ben Casey, 3, 61, 66, 177, 216, 242, 273, 356, 434, 446, 488, 509, 554, 575, 672, 759, 809, 845
Ben Grauer Show, The, 357
Ben Vereen . . . Comin' at Ya, 276, 287, 294, 442, 526, 756, 847, 865
Benjamin Franklin, Statesman, 883
Benny and Barney: Las Vegas Undercover, 344
Benny Goodman Story, The, 45
Benny Hill Show, The, 405, 569, 659, 844, 919
Benny Rubin Show, The, 209, 304, 557, 595, 736, 821
Benny's Place, 841
Benson, 44, 88, 192, 346, 367, 578, 629, 671, 726, 800, 805, 824, 825
Bermuda Depths, The, 763
Berrengers, 15, 40, 75, 174, 192, 250, 292, 406, 414, 452, 487, 513, 542, 591, 605, 612, 695, 748, 753, 815, 864, 877

Bert D'Angelo/Superstar, 660, 674, 796
Best Foot Forward, 874
Best of Broadway, The, 321
Best of Everything, The, 299
Best of the West, 115, 284, 318, 405, 516, 561, 664, 673, 876, 882
Best Place to Be, The, 704, 930
Best Times, The, 53, 219, 223, 273, 274, 374, 380, 496, 548, 585, 650
Betrayal, 847, 880
Better Days, 397, 470, 559, 643, 753
Better Home Show, The, 114, 907, 908
Better Living TV Theatre, 90
Betty Hutton Show, The, 157, 198, 426, 442, 587, 610, 667, 769
Betty White Show, The, 220, 245, 279, 401, 406, 433, 457, 598, 621, 671, 769, 895
Between Friends, 831
Between the Laughter, 500
Between Two Women, 246
Beulah, 70, 123, 315, 385, 446, 577, 680, 697, 746, 782, 855, 881, 882, 908
Beulah Land, 9, 443, 491
Beverly Hillbillies, The, 19, 21, 49, 51, 64, 75, 109, 207, 255, 270, 298, 316, 319, 351, 397, 449, 462, 463, 483, 530, 535, 543, 564, 633, 664, 679, 723, 741, 759, 761, 779, 805, 830, 847, 899
Beverly Hills Madam, 340
Bewitched, 167, 183, 283, 297, 309, 332, 334, 335, 353, 451, 479, 497, 522, 527, 528, 589, 596, 600, 613, 662, 727, 749, 750, 843, 865, 891, 894, 895, 923
Beyond Westworld, 229, 450, 566, 575, 763, 870
Beyond Witch Mountain, 9
Bid 'n Buy, 657
Biff Baker U.S.A., 372, 819
Big Beat, The, 316
Big Eddie, 217, 505, 631, 644, 749, 900
Big Game, The, 466
Big Hawaii, 2, 239, 459, 525, 681, 767, 786, 815
Big Idea, The, 77, 917
Big Issue, The, 735, 798
Big Moment, The, 653
Big Party, 422
Big Payoff, The, 584, 616, 652
Big Picture, The, 930
Big Question, The, 187
Big Record, The, 651
Big Shamus, Little Shamus, 242, 399, 573, 760, 777, 921
Big Show, The, 53, 140, 170, 171, 365, 405, 466, 563, 616, 666, 692, 767, 821
Big Story, The, 352, 357, 582, 733, 785

Big Surprise, The, 63, 874
Big Top, 460, 527, 574, 806
Big Town, 45, 128, 255, 462, 477, 578, 628, 800, 808, 853, 890, 920
Big Valley, The, 26, 108, 112, 244, 282, 283, 362, 369, 520, 527, 533, 536, 734, 802, 897, 905
Bigelow Show, The, 265, 910
Bigelow Theatre, 434
Bill, 731
Bill Cosby Show, The, 126, 203, 204, 352, 377, 435, 565, 668, 697, 715, 726, 885
Bill Cosby Special, The, 203
Bill Dana Show, The, 4, 213, 225, 385, 670
Bill Gwinn Show, The, 368
Bill Moyers' Journal, 609
Billy, 8, 324, 368, 679, 828, 850
Billy Boone and Cousin Kib, 185, 589
Billy Crystal Comedy Hour, The, 24, 25, 215, 325, 352, 428, 456, 658, 916
Billy Daniels Show, The, 90, 227, 662
Billy Graham Crusade, The, 355
Billy: Portrait of a Street Kid, 133
Bing Crosby Show, The, 212, 292, 326, 549, 571, 773
Biography, 437, 874, 875
Bionic Woman, The, 26, 116, 297, 657, 679, 694, 760, 761, 869
Birth and Babies, 388
Birthday Party, 44, 121, 784
Bishop Sheen Program, The, 770
B.J. and the Bear, 8, 118, 138, 236, 246, 284, 293, 295, 378, 414, 429, 444, 489, 497, 517, 536, 566, 673, 765, 771, 882, 916
Black Beauty, 827, 851, 883
Black Market Baby, 258
Black Omnibus, 447
Black Robe, The, 360, 838
Black Saddle, 108, 444, 514
Blacke's Magic, 512, 602
Blansky's Beauties, 52, 66, 97, 243, 244, 337, 348, 457, 474, 580, 604, 637, 648, 665, 702, 873, 874, 928
Blind Ambition, 227, 300, 847, 911
Blind Date, 94, 255, 311, 614
Blondie, 19, 21, 48, 59, 113, 294, 389, 426, 449, 487, 501, 515, 636, 663, 721, 782
Blood Feud, 92, 851
Bloody Mama, 871
Blue and the Gray, The, 53, 74, 77, 111, 140, 141, 246, 258, 262, 378, 383, 393, 400, 415, 449, 458, 468, 525, 618, 635, 641, 651, 663, 670, 707,

774, 813, 826, 847, 863, 865, 911
Blue Angel, The, 69, 655
Blue Angels, The, 213, 325, 350, 448, 449
Blue Knight, The, 465, 466, 562, 674, 710, 750, 777
Blue Light, 147, 353, 543
Blue Thunder, 134, 161, 199, 288, 577, 786
Blues by Bargy, 58
Bob & Carol & Ted & Alice, 33, 308, 338, 751, 798, 855
Bob and Ray Show, The, 96, 499, 500, 578
Bob Crane Show, The, 207, 301, 355, 389, 668, 822
Bob Crosby Show, The, 212, 332, 409, 880, 921
Bob Cummings Show, The, 217, 231, 237, 253, 331, 353, 399, 404, 440, 483, 493, 498, 543, 546, 775, 807, 828, 864, 868, 891
Bob Hope, 19
Bob Hope Christmas Special, The, 413
Bob Hope Presents the Chrysler Theatre, 82, 346, 413, 464, 661, 723, 811
Bob Newhart Show, The, 10, 83, 98, 179, 202, 222, 296, 297, 301, 318, 332, 365, 376, 388, 402, 428, 450, 496, 514, 532, 540, 546, 606, 625, 626, 659, 676, 677, 680, 718, 760, 761, 790, 796, 829, 874, 892, 893, 912
Bobbie Gentry Show, The, 114, 333, 362, 678
Bobby Darin Show, The, 19, 52, 229, 272
Bobby Goldsboro Show, The, 347
Bobby Vinton Show, The, 222, 262, 472, 662, 858, 867
Body Human: Facts For Boys, The, 418
Body Human: Facts for Girls, The, 839
Boing Boing Show, The, 349
Bold Journey, 255, 805
Bold Ones, The, 143, 288, 332, 388, 410, 546, 576, 753
Bold Venture, 177, 354, 546
Bonanza, 48, 53, 72, 94, 101, 106, 131, 143, 145, 154, 163, 184, 207, 280, 317, 318, 327, 328, 332, 360–362, 387, 431, 447, 462, 488–490, 555, 606, 638, 673, 677, 682, 683, 722, 723, 732, 739, 747, 753, 778, 820, 825, 830, 833, 839, 845, 852, 866, 867, 871, 894, 922, 928
Bonino, 13, 27, 274, 384, 426, 436, 462, 644, 658, 670, 675, 898
Bonkers, 98, 421, 595
Book of Lists, The, 89

Boone, 137, 201, 272, 369, 396, 421, 515, 594, 669, 672, 722, 886

Boots and Saddles—The Story of the 5th Cavalry, 572, 578, 906

Borgia Stick, The, 621

Born Free, 188, 237, 315, 452, 526, 610

Born Innocent, 29

Born to the Wind, 84, 240, 552, 679, 702, 747, 749

Bosom Buddies, 79, 250, 379, 414, 758, 798, 831

Boss Lady, 59, 323, 450, 491, 660, 786

Boston and Kilbride, 764

Boston Blackie, 187, 645, 832

Both Sides, 420

Bounty Man, The, 873

Bourbon Street Beat, 262, 263, 420, 519, 905

Bowling Headliners, 176, 390, 681

Boy in the Plastic Bubble, The, 427, 849

Boy Who Drank Too Much, The, 52

Bracken's World, 14, 185, 200, 261, 386, 390, 440, 628, 641, 655, 714, 764, 805, 809

Brady Brides, The, 231, 398, 416, 483, 523, 565, 677

Brady Bunch, The, 26, 36, 231, 398, 446, 477, 520, 565, 618, 642, 677, 685, 705, 901

Brady Bunch Hour, The, 231, 398, 477, 520, 565, 642, 705, 710, 901

Brains & Brawn, 231, 506

Brand New Life, A, 499

Branded, 193

Brave Eagle, 494, 630, 893, 913

Brave New World, 827

Break the Bank, 63, 190, 337, 642, 657, 795, 863, 915

Break the $250,000 Bank, 882

Breakaway, 544

Breakfast Club, 18

Breaking Away, 40, 61, 108, 164, 326, 373, 899

Breaking Point, 314, 716

Breaking Up Is Hard to Do, 84

Brenner, 87, 113

Bret Maverick, 87, 123, 134, 153, 240, 267, 327, 328, 363, 378, 477, 543, 605, 770

Brian Keith Show, The, 103, 285, 359, 371, 375, 460, 461, 483, 927

Brian's Song, 161, 285, 878, 879, 902

Bride and Groom, 652

Bridges to Cross, 295, 323, 567, 677, 822

Bridget Loves Bernie, 62, 68, 88, 258, 277, 341, 512, 647, 747, 813, 874

Brief Encounter, 133

Bright Promise, 28, 29, 438, 478

Brighter Day, The, 123, 409, 479, 504, 736, 838

Bring 'Em Back Alive, 103, 104, 172, 438, 484, 563, 602, 643, 929

Bringing Up Buddy, 11, 544, 581, 741

Broadside, 28, 104, 271, 322, 436, 630, 722, 750, 800, 801

Broadway Jamboree, 9

Broadway Open House, 22, 23, 64, 146, 185, 221, 240, 265, 324, 360, 390, 394, 413, 420, 505–507, 537, 580, 627, 721, 785, 813, 817, 880, 916

Broadway Spotlight, 292, 479, 584, 831, 873

Broadway Television Theatre, 69

Broadway to Hollywood—Headline Clues, 617, 690, 784

Broken Arrow, 30, 286, 527, 719

Bronco, 380, 381

Bronk, 71, 88, 473, 553, 648, 652, 653

Brothers, The, 45, 87, 91, 350, 370, 423, 576, 606, 645, 824

Brothers and Sisters, 25, 117, 205, 213, 219, 444, 503, 834, 911

Brothers Brannagan, The, 722

Buccaneers, The, 257, 379, 380, 539, 699, 716, 769

Buck Rogers, 31, 247, 473, 659, 683, 763, 796

Buck Rogers in the 25th Century, 30, 92, 93, 148, 153, 175, 195, 218, 230, 278, 328, 334, 359, 400, 427, 434, 638, 765, 778

Buckskin, 117, 514, 568, 630, 721

Bud and Lou, 369

Buffalo Bill, 164, 186, 232, 296, 446, 659, 663, 724, 832, 919

Buffalo Bill, Jr, 446

Bugaloos, The, 65, 700

Bugs Bunny, 92, 304

Bugs Bunny Show, The, 92

Bugs Bunny/Roadrunner Show, The (prime time), 92

Buick Circus Hour, The, 119, 120, 324, 359, 695

Bullwinkle Show, The, 194, 195, 304, 317, 415, 737, 758, 835

Bunco, 764

Burke's Law, 45, 62, 72, 76, 81, 151, 163, 166, 197, 209, 271, 311, 323, 377, 426, 520, 542, 614, 643, 657, 676, 681, 700, 707, 751, 846

Burning Bed, The, 292

Burns and Allen Show, The, 19, 583

Burns and Schreiber Comedy Hour, The, 131, 276, 294, 328, 513, 601, 756, 844, 889, 900

Bus Stop, 26, 114, 316, 558, 658, 701, 888

Busting Loose, 32, 34, 156, 347, 482, 619, 685, 714, 826, 900, 904

Butterflies Are Free, 9

Buzzy Wuzzy, 81, 182, 183

By Popular Demand, 11, 311, 796

Byline, 321

C

Cabaret, 614

Cactus Jim, 50, 389

Cade's County, 125, 145, 152, 273, 304, 305, 328, 486, 662, 781

Caesar Presents, 238, 308, 353, 393, 627, 632, 773, 853

Caesar's Hour, 39, 91, 139, 156, 197, 219, 238, 258, 285, 453, 510, 605, 655, 704, 709, 900

Cagney & Lacey, 43, 83, 119, 181, 224, 225, 287, 308, 343, 454, 482, 496, 526, 531, 686, 774, 784, 825, 883

Caine Mutiny Court-Martial, The, 630, 820

Cain's Hundred, 217, 716, 751

California Fever, 97, 138, 202, 205, 487, 563, 576, 843

Californians, The, 140, 182, 198, 301, 465, 506, 556, 562, 737

Call to Glory, 53, 146, 225, 410, 621, 637, 673, 677, 776, 922

Callan, 918

Callie and Son, 870

Calucci's Department, 47, 183, 184, 301, 499, 505, 666, 679, 832, 873, 893

Calvin and the Colonel, 203, 317, 352, 362, 457

Camel News Caravan, The, 823, 824

Camille, 294

Camp Runamuck, 49, 265, 442, 468, 534, 633, 813, 870, 883

Campaign and the Candidates, 568

Campaign Countdown, 211

Campaign '84, 698

Campaign Roundup, 420

Campbell Sound Stage, The, 461

Campus Corner, 128, 144, 231, 299, 808

Campus Hoopla, 744, 802

Can Do, 11

Can You Hear the Laughter? —The Freddie Prinze Story, 30

Can You Top This?, 22, 234, 253, 304, 402, 435, 497, 552, 910

Candid Camera, 188, 321, 333, 345, 346, 474, 595, 616, 670, 851

Cannon, 27, 195, 263, 323, 396, 538, 628, 638, 820, 904

Cannonball, 88, 145

Capitol, 5, 141, 446, 573, 916

Capitol Capers, 33, 180

Capitol Cloak Room, 56, 765, 767

Captain and Tennille, The, 259, 834

Captain Billy's Mississippi Music Hall, 110, 258, 264, 374, 438, 647, 785

Captain Kangaroo, 118, 204

Captain Midnight, 285

Captain Nice, 227, 265, 308, 334, 335, 683, 931

Captain Video and His Video Rangers, 192, 198, 391, 408, 476, 696, 801, 823

Captains and the Kings, 43, 118, 209, 226, 266, 267, 403, 438, 449, 472, 606, 657, 670, 766, 777, 863

Captains Courageous, 537

Car 54, Where Are You?, 134, 240, 289, 328, 351, 366, 368, 378, 398, 474, 508, 512, 643, 678, 693, 704, 733, 740, 810, 880

Cara Williams Show, The, 11, 38, 107, 175, 704, 769, 771, 902

Careful, It's My Art, 34

Caribe, 314, 458, 538

Carlton, Your Doorman, 615

Carmel Myers Show, The, 616

Carol and Company, 129

Carol Burnett Show, The, 129, 176, 197, 198, 300, 317, 451, 480, 498, 538, 545, 557, 575, 621, 659, 749, 829, 860, 869, 930

Carolyn Gilbert Show, The, 337, 834

Carson's Cellar, 157

Carter Country, 162, 317, 318, 365, 411, 479, 661, 817, 865, 883

Cartier Affair, The, 391

Cartoon Teletales, 524

Casablanca, 57, 214, 222, 275, 309, 415, 514, 537, 570, 615, 766, 797, 815, 920

Case of Rape, A, 596

Case of the Dangerous Robin, The, 438

Cases of Eddie Drake, The, 370

Casey Jones, 372, 498, 830

Cash and Carry, 435

Casino, 820

Cassie & Company, 110, 201, 248, 429, 552

Cat Ballou, 880

Cat Creature, The, 68

Cat on a Hot Tin Roof, 803, 870, 917

Cattanooga Cats, 142, 872

Cavalcade of America, 521, 658

Cavalcade of Bands, The, 423, 721, 727, 804

Cavalcade of Sports, 266

Cavalcade of Stars, The, 151, 152, 159, 247, 341, 342, 464, 506, 798, 814, 831

Cavalcade Theatre, 70, 209

Cave In, 587

CBS Afternoon Playbreak, 716

CBS Cartoon Theatre, 860

CBS Children's Film Festival, The, 19, 842

CBS Evening News, The, 211, 271, 272, 387, 483, 484, 609, 698, 701, 743, 765

CBS Library, 860

CBS Morning News, 333, 753

CBS Newcomers, The, 16, 34, 141, 180, 329, 330, 347, 666, 717, 762, 912

CBS News Adventure, 483

CBS News Hour, 730

CBS News Nightwatch, 256, 343, 441, 562, 732, 813, 892

CBS News Retrospective, 387

CBS News Sunday Morning, 237

CBS Playhouse, 255

CBS Radio Workshop, 195

CBS Reports, 211, 486, 609, 701, 702, 756, 787, 875

CBS Schoolbreak Special, 912

CBS Sports Spectacular, 117

CBS Television Workshop, The, 127

CBS Weekend News, 105, 211, 223, 237, 411, 420, 602, 609, 645, 698, 701, 755, 765

Celebrity, 897

Celebrity Bowling, 13

Celebrity Challenge of the Sexes, 117, 333, 714, 809, 810

Celebrity Game, The, 709

Celebrity Sweepstakes, 573

Celebrity Talent Scouts, 508

Celebrity Time, 172, 223, 404, 530, 562, 617, 909, 919

Centennial, 30, 43, 132, 145, 154, 168, 194, 209, 223, 247, 283, 343, 364, 382, 386, 437, 455, 460, 462, 492, 495, 552, 571, 573, 625, 694, 703, 746, 852, 863, 884, 929, 930

Center Door Fancy, 95

Center Stage, 764

Champagne and Orchids, 7, 514, 852

Champions, The, 66, 225, 330, 627

Chance of a Lifetime, 35, 89, 155, 187, 435, 472, 503, 654

Channing, 284, 447

Charade Quiz, 70, 294, 313, 510, 678, 763, 771, 784

Charles in Charge, 1, 52, 182, 505, 663, 738, 791, 878, 899

Charlie & Company, 340, 455, 472, 477, 570, 705, 725, 745, 864, 895, 908

Charlie Farrell Show, The, 40, 41, 147, 236, 289, 619, 778, 912

Charlie Wild, Private Detective, 499, 500, 577, 643

Charlie's Angels, 96, 119, 258, 291, 292, 306, 307, 369, 376, 431, 450, 486, 526, 689, 723, 764, 788, 812, 918

Chase, 213, 303, 326, 557, 703, 716, 741, 790

Cheaters, The, 429

Check It Out, 4, 71, 175, 495, 690, 714, 758, 880, 905

Checking In, 121, 189, 205, 335, 336, 514, 847

Checkmate, 85, 139, 333, 563, 673, 748, 808

Cheers, 24, 184, 185, 228, 245, 355, 383, 520, 620, 667, 699, 891

Cher, 9, 171, 172, 222, 281, 499, 539, 750

Chesterfield Sound Off Time, 14, 413, 414, 506

Chesterfield Supper Club, The, 47, 93, 94, 191, 304

Chet Huntley Reporting, 425

Chevrolet on Broadway, 391, 493, 580

Chevy Mystery Show, The, 685, 784

Chevy Show, The, 4, 91, 315, 475, 549, 695, 735, 930

Chevy Showroom, The, 377, 512, 860, 900

Cheyenne, 148, 193, 283, 327, 381, 447, 449, 872

Chicago Jazz, 827, 859

Chicago Story, 6, 50, 172, 288, 307, 314, 422, 499, 536, 621, 771

Chicago Symphony, 484, 709, 755

Chicago Symphony Chamber Orchestra, 482, 630

Chicago Teddy Bears, The, 57, 289, 374, 446, 453, 559, 585, 768

Chicagoland Mystery Players, 785, 856

Chico and the Man, 9, 97, 171, 213, 214, 293, 355, 479, 580, 645, 687, 705, 738, 801

Chiefs, 129, 154, 190, 217, 231, 267, 344, 367, 383, 402, 464, 556, 623, 636, 728, 748, 789, 796, 834, 902

Child Bride of Short Creek, 51

Children's Sketch Book, 783, 887

Child's World, 657

China Smith, 240, 264, 267

CHiPs, 30, 42, 82, 97, 136, 254, 281, 331, 338, 339, 362, 363, 500, 513, 523, 558, 635, 664, 674, 680, 708, 750, 870, 899

Chisholms, The, 128, 216, 280, 313, 385, 468, 479, 492, 612, 620, 629, 684, 693, 696, 741, 790, 825, 862

Choices of the Heart, 290, 338
Choose Up Sides, 700
Chopper One, 76, 318, 388, 575
Christmas Carol, A, 760
Christmas Memory, A, 651
Christopher Columbus, 875
Chronicle, 187
Chronoscope, 423, 477, 507, 602
Chrysler Theatre, 638, 724, 764, 926
Chuck Barris Rah Rah Show, The, 62, 241, 603
Cimarron City, 94, 122, 149, 265, 286, 596, 696, 715, 773, 775, 788, 847
Cimarron Strip, 99, 401, 847, 897
Cinderella, 880
Circle of Children, A, 812
Circle of Fear, 425
Circuit Rider, 547, 674
Circus, 657
Circus Boy, 64, 65, 71, 251, 351, 420, 524, 545, 903
Circus of the Stars, 621
Circus Time, 365, 401, 910
Cisco Kid, The, 154, 710
Cities Service Band of America, 97, 497
City, The, 692
City Detective, 142, 143
City Hospital, 132, 738
City In Fear, 437, 864
City of Angels, 376, 435, 450, 728, 729, 806
Claudia, The Story of a Marriage, 27, 28, 115, 177, 563, 566, 708, 782, 920
Clear and Present Danger, A, 410
Clear Horizon, 465, 583
Cliff Edwards Show, The, 271, 608
Cliffhangers, 31, 876
Climax, 9, 20, 63, 122, 132, 148, 150, 154, 163, 176, 205, 307, 321, 323, 358, 361, 381, 454, 526, 530, 577, 684, 685, 711, 764, 813, 828
Clock, The, 764
Club Embassy, 96, 158, 278, 408, 578, 739, 929
Club Oasis, 64, 65, 359, 436, 449
Club Seven, 67, 137, 269, 840
Club 60, 256
Cocaine and Blue Eyes, 781
Cocaine: One Man's Seduction, 884
Code Name: Diamond Head, 836
Code R, 230, 416, 482, 705, 738, 780, 929
Code Red, 5, 210, 239, 360, 361, 395, 448, 512, 545, 715, 807, 876
Code 3, 690
Codename: Foxfire, 164, 444, 447, 564, 695

Co-ed Fever, 143, 461, 465, 468, 621, 643, 659, 672, 733, 838
Coffee, Tea or Me?, 496, 857
Coke Time with Eddie Fisher, 20, 270, 298, 721, 814
Colbys, The. See Dynasty II: The Colby's
Colditz, 870
Colgate Comedy Hour, The, 1, 14, 73, 147, 214, 266, 413, 414, 509, 534, 548, 638, 652, 853
College Bowl, The, 113, 126, 411, 426, 512, 525, 553, 607, 683, 737, 878, 900, 901
College of Musical Knowledge, The, 172, 245, 305, 618
Collision Course, 303
Colonel Flack, 439, 608, 609
Colonel Humphrey Flack, 439, 608
Colonel March of Scotland Yard, 454
Colt 45, 253, 466, 558, 684
Columbia University Seminar, 87
Columbo, 212, 216, 287, 331, 377, 569, 570, 662, 777
Combat, 143, 158, 244, 284, 290, 313, 361, 409, 434, 438, 524, 606, 662, 728, 729
Combat Sergeant, 177, 240, 839
Come Closer, 622
Comeback, 683
Comeback Story, The, 311, 441
Comedy Factory, The, 103, 519, 567, 570
Comedy Shop, The, 213
Comedy Spot, The, 339
Comedy Tonight, 62, 105, 162, 250, 280, 357, 360, 452, 475, 514
Comedy Zone, 368, 491, 514, 540, 620, 697
Coming Up Rosie, 46
Comment, 626
Concealed Enemies, 198
Concentration, 63, 258, 574
Concerning Miss Marlowe, 13, 930
Concrete Cowboys, 704, 759
Condo, 11, 45, 150, 685, 757, 809, 810, 865, 900
Condominium, 897
Confession, 920
Conflict, 327, 426
Congressional Report, 595
Consult Dr. Brothers, 118
Contender, The, 29, 146, 350, 368, 496, 782, 812, 871, 883
Continental, The, 167
Continental Showcase, 48, 123, 442, 468, 639, 647, 662, 763
Contract on Cherry Street, 781
Conversations with Eric Sevareid, 765
Convoy, 141, 174, 331, 494
Cool Million, 83, 288, 343, 541

Cop and the Kid, The, 266, 267, 464, 491, 674, 798, 852, 906
Copacabana, 334
Corner Bar, The, 62, 148, 240, 298, 469, 579, 726, 738, 755, 761
Coronado 9, 142, 143, 326
Coronet Blue, 10, 71, 196, 778
Cos, 19, 96, 203, 204, 438, 513, 696, 840
Cosby Show, The, 14, 46, 93, 98, 123, 203, 204, 340, 500, 689, 879, 887
Cosmos, 744
Count of Monte Cristo, The, 168, 251, 677
Counterattack: Crime in America, 465, 466
Counterthrust, 29, 440
Country Music Awards, The, 305
Country Style, 3, 44, 60, 249, 277, 891
Couple of Joes, A, 64, 134, 271, 384, 423, 708, 715, 733, 773
Courage and the Passion, The, 275, 375
Court of Last Resort, 27, 85, 88, 385, 496, 551, 558, 563, 583, 924
Court-Martial, 177, 249, 357, 358, 880
Courtship of Eddie's Father, The, 89, 214, 308, 410, 479, 855
Cousteau's Mississippi, 206
Cover Girls, 273
Cover Up, 25, 26, 296, 377, 403, 575, 644, 797, 906
Coward of the County, 728
Cowboy G-Men, 198, 392
Cowboy in Africa, 193, 272, 352, 419, 618, 897
Cowboy Theatre, 375
Cowboys, The, 120, 154, 232, 255, 368, 417, 464, 532, 552, 636
Cowboys & Injuns, 73
Cowtown Rodeo, 344, 384
C.P.O. Sharkey, 14, 69, 224, 411, 429, 490, 651, 663, 717, 736, 748, 780, 784
Cracker Factory, The, 917
Craig Kennedy, Criminologist, 917
Crash Corrigan's Ranch, 203
Crawford Mystery Theatre, 418, 423
Crazy Like a Fox, 380, 470, 503, 670, 737, 841, 878, 879, 910
Crime Photographer, 150, 336, 373, 562, 568, 591, 785
Crime Story, 135, 145, 241, 288, 301, 491, 742, 750, 792
Crime Syndicated, 375, 638
Crime with Father, 490, 516
Crisis, 217, 669, 798
Critic at Large, 120
Cross-Wits, The, 179, 272

Crucible, The, 759
Crunch and Des, 467, 851
Crusade in Europe, 451, 863
Crusader, 115, 460, 461
Cry of the Innocent, 833
Cry Rape, 542
Crystal Room, 576
Current Opinion, 565
Curse of Dracula, The, 56, 68, 444, 596, 632, 795, 805
Curse of the Black Widow, 140
Custer, 228, 557, 654, 673, 780, 876, 917
Cutter to Houston, 54, 141, 369, 585, 819, 906
Cutter's Trail, 618

D

D.A., The, 182, 194, 602, 730, 886
Dagmar's Canteen, 221, 240, 401, 509, 537
Dain Curse, The, 182, 815, 914
Dakotas, The, 274, 283, 361, 878
Daktari, 352, 370, 556, 587, 600, 714, 821, 840
Dallas, 3, 28, 40, 43, 48, 53, 57, 70, 72, 73, 90, 95, 113, 116, 124, 154, 168, 174, 200, 201, 213, 232, 262, 276, 285, 287, 299, 300, 306, 311, 320, 324, 332, 359, 371, 385, 386, 406, 407, 419, 439, 450, 453, 456, 460, 467, 471, 488, 503, 523, 544, 550, 560, 563, 576, 586, 590, 604, 613, 660, 670, 672–674, 677, 679, 681, 683, 686, 695, 704, 707, 708, 710, 712, 726, 760, 767, 771, 782, 785, 792, 804, 807, 813, 827, 843, 845, 858, 861, 878, 883, 914, 918, 922, 924
Dallas Cowboy Cheerleaders II, The, 805
Dalton's Code of Vengeance, 830
Damien, The Leper Priest, 290
Damon Runyon Theatre, 440, 917
Dan August, 26, 30, 293, 294, 389, 712, 713, 730
Dan Raven, 64, 413, 702
Dance Fever, 235, 447, 472, 794, 835, 928, 931
Dancing on Air, 781
Danger, 124, 163, 244, 504, 764, 784, 803
Danger Is My Business, 207
Danger Man, 569, 916
Dangerous Assignment, 253
Daniel Boone, 20, 21, 57, 91, 96, 161, 187, 236, 237, 344, 363, 387, 406, 430, 451, 518, 573, 655, 739, 747
Danny Kaye Show, The, 119, 171, 289, 428, 451, 457, 480, 539, 585, 862, 893

Danny Thomas Hour, The, 546, 737, 837
Danny Thomas Show, The, 23, 55, 156, 160, 195, 226, 266, 320, 349, 370, 376, 384, 414, 419, 433, 505, 506, 521, 548, 575, 580, 581, 606, 656, 696, 697, 705, 741, 837, 896
Dante, 226, 261, 608, 629
Dark Secret of Harvest Home, 3
Dark Shadows, 78, 431, 656, 741, 760, 763, 865
Darkroom, 182
D.A.'s Man, The, 192, 277, 541
Dastardly and Muttley, 911
Date with Judy, A, 46, 74, 144, 214, 336, 795
Date with Life, A, 391
Date with the Angels, 104, 115, 178, 236, 279, 554, 616, 685, 707, 895, 901, 902
Dating Game, The, 62, 491
Daughter of the Mind, 842
Dave and Charley, 39
Dave Garroway Show, The, 329, 390, 632
David Brinkley's Journal, 112
David Cassidy—Man Undercover, 163, 635, 698, 702, 746, 867
David Frost Revue, The, 92, 166, 319, 338, 429, 514, 726
David Frost Show, The, 319, 830
David Letterman Show, The, 375, 507
David Niven Show, 629
David Steinberg Show, The, 805
David Susskind Show, The, 822
Davy Crockett, 270, 393, 655
Day Dreaming with Laraine Day, 235
Day for History: The Supreme Court and the Pentagon Papers, A, 798
Day in Court, 894
Day in the Life, A, 148
Day the Loving Stopped, The, 383
Day the Women Got Even, The, 523
Days of Our Lives, 13, 29, 121, 136, 147, 148, 180, 252, 290, 300, 374, 393, 423, 527, 529, 553, 559, 562, 632, 641, 702, 741, 831, 851, 880
Deadliest Season, The, 817
Deadline, 811
Deadly Game, The, 88
Deadly Lessons, 704, 899
Deadly Tower, The, 739
Dealer's Choice, 179, 391
Dean Martin Comedy World, The, 199, 293, 740
Dean Martin Presents Bobby Darin, 52, 140, 229, 379, 454, 489, 756, 832

Dean Martin Presents Music Country, 25, 529, 704, 809
Dean Martin Presents the Golddiggers, 21, 116, 120, 153, 167, 293, 298, 339, 346, 379, 395, 397, 517, 528, 550, 572, 658, 699, 708, 781, 783, 843, 852
Dean Martin Show, The, 95, 101, 120, 226, 241, 249, 346, 347, 433, 490, 548, 549, 579, 582, 717, 740, 887
Dean Martin Summer Show, The, 120, 173, 225, 241, 255, 458, 497, 549, 550, 696, 729, 735
Dean Martin's Celebrity Roasts, 116
Dear Detective, 339, 445, 577, 778, 793, 857, 876, 917, 923
Dear Phoebe, 202, 289, 398, 490, 497
Dearest Enemy, 438
Death Among Friends, 164
Death Be Not Proud, 79
Death Car on the Freeway, 369, 865
Death of a Centerfold: The Dorothy Stratton Story, 219, 888
Death of a Salesman, 822
Death Valley Days, 29, 74, 141, 370, 451, 572, 601, 656, 701, 724, 832, 833
Deathstalk, 106
Debbie Reynolds Show, The, 101, 172, 713, 718, 790
December Bride, 36, 136, 137, 294, 454, 533, 587, 602, 694, 858
Decision, 260
Decision '80, 2
Decoy, 326
Defection of Simas Kudirka, The, 677, 767
Defenders, The, 41, 51, 61, 82, 83, 127, 146, 193, 246, 268, 288, 356, 369, 371, 476, 545, 546, 605, 611, 705, 736, 803, 810, 825, 848
Dell O'Dell Show, The, 639
Delora Bueno, 126
Delphi Bureau, The, 438, 524
Delta House, 179, 199, 223, 309, 322, 347, 455, 569, 608, 670, 762, 865, 899, 900
Delvecchio, 193, 194, 324, 371, 407, 863, 921
Dempsey and Makepeace, 58, 107, 647, 790
Dennis O'Keefe Show, The, 278, 381, 464, 640, 742
Dennis the Menace, 25, 100, 176, 297, 350, 400, 419, 459, 611, 631, 676, 739, 762, 786, 833, 881, 898
Department S, 285
Deputy, The, 161, 168, 303, 306, 358, 460, 604
Designing Women, 128, 159, 680, 785

Desilu Playhouse. *See* Westinghouse Desilu Playhouse
Desperate Lives, 911
Destiny, 820
Destry, 331
Detective: Bull in a China Shop, 371
Detective in the House, 275, 407, 428, 664, 904, 923
Detective School, 309, 362, 385, 540, 619, 620, 651, 688
Detectives, Starring Robert Taylor, The, 29, 289, 345, 658, 832, 836, 841, 891
Detective's Wife, 59, 218
Devil and Daniel Webster, The, 883
Devlin Connection, The, 335, 422, 438, 753, 827, 833
Diagnosis: Unknown, 74, 426, 605, 627, 643
Diahann Carroll Show, The, 119, 155, 431
Dial M for Murder, 677
Diamond Jubilee of Light, 927
Diana, 29, 61, 265, 599, 611, 718, 771, 776
Diane Doxee Show, 90, 258
Diary of Anne Frank, The, 338
Dick and the Duchess, 206, 643, 772, 809, 863, 883
Dick Cavett Show, The, 107, 166, 273, 310, 317, 733
Dick Clark Presents the Rock and Roll Years, 177, 484
Dick Clark Show, The, 177
Dick Clark's Live Wednesday, 177
Dick Clark's Nighttime, 177
Dick Clark's World of Talent, 177, 505
Dick Haymes Show, The, 39
Dick Powell Show, The, 681
Dick Powell's Zane Grey Theater, 19, 76, 101, 111, 216, 251, 280, 435, 437, 460, 500, 519, 527, 576, 614, 629, 673, 681, 711, 720, 731, 802, 839, 851
Dick Tracy, 137, 245, 706
Dick Van Dyke Show, The, 19, 22, 23, 51, 72, 225, 234, 236, 289, 367, 505, 556, 598, 599, 605, 606, 655, 671, 676, 709, 717, 732, 837, 860
Diff'rent Strokes, 51, 111, 159, 165, 170, 186, 187, 199, 348, 402, 431, 451, 508, 593, 594, 676, 693, 734, 823, 829, 836, 868
Dillinger, 635
Dinah and Her New Best Friends, 146, 238, 287, 471, 625, 654, 683, 711, 774
Dinah Shore Chevy Show, The, 165, 171, 245, 283, 774, 775, 784, 930
Dinah Shore Show, The, 317, 632, 756, 774, 784, 930
Dinah!, 775

Dinah's Place, 774, 775
Dirty Dozen—The Next Mission, The, 899
Dirty Sally, 571, 629, 695
Disney Sunday Movie, 274
Disneyland, 250, 270, 655
Divorce: American Style, 109
Divorce Court, 877
Divorce His/Divorce Hers, 133, 831
Do It Yourself, 38, 906
Do Not Go Gentle into That Good Night, 255
Do You Trust Your Wife?, 80, 81, 708
Dobie Gillis. *See* The Many Loves of Dobie Gillis.
Doc, 202, 292, 382, 422, 452, 512, 601, 812, 867, 898, 908
Doc Corkle, 128, 278, 545, 558, 801
Doc Elliot, 71, 312, 313, 414, 660
Doctor, The, 27
Dr. Christian, 147, 148
Dr. Fix-Um, 683, 927
Dr. Franken, 864
Dr. Hudson's Secret Journal, 92, 142, 418, 463, 464, 581
Doctor in the House, 178, 215, 230, 282, 499, 529, 585, 620, 647, 691, 701, 769, 789, 912
Doctor I.Q., 466, 562, 648
Dr. Kildare, 42, 55, 68, 77, 137, 168, 176, 223, 248, 257, 484, 500, 537, 554, 605, 626, 628, 660, 673, 676, 677, 742, 803, 831, 847, 926
Dr. Seuss, 195
Dr. Simon Locke, 9, 88, 299, 365, 539
Doctor Who, 850
Doctors, The, 49, 184, 350, 506, 636, 736, 750
Doctors' Hospital, 19, 116, 145, 176, 229, 314, 488, 494, 551, 661, 665, 677, 714, 819, 882
Doctors' Private Lives, 79, 331, 423, 508, 621, 681
Dog and Cat, 32, 65, 179
Dollar a Second, 614
$1.98 Beauty Show, The, 15, 62, 289, 492, 603, 633, 832
Dolly, 659
Dom DeLuise Show, The, 40, 241, 254, 333, 528, 566, 582, 798, 831
Domestic Life, 46, 80, 105, 303, 424, 552, 610, 718, 838
Don Adams' Screen Test, 4
Don Ameche's Musical Playhouse, 20
Don Kirshner's Rock Concert, 475
Don Knotts Show, The, 127, 155, 176, 238, 239, 450, 478, 545, 666, 889, 902
Don McNeill TV Club, 18, 55, 206, 243, 502, 576
Don McNeill's Breakfast Club, 18

Don Rickles Show, The, 28, 49, 165, 349, 409, 565, 593, 600, 717, 795, 862
Donahue, 252, 256, 689
Donald O'Connor Texaco Show, The, 589, 638, 785
Donna Reed Show, The, 86, 207, 208, 285, 491, 500, 566, 669, 704, 715
Donny and Marie, 192, 229, 250, 294, 428, 482, 495, 528, 646, 647
Don't Call Me Charlie, 343, 420, 442, 499, 618, 664, 715, 750
Don't Call Me Mama Anymore, 276
Don't Go to Sleep, 383
Doodles Weaver, 185, 226, 240, 540, 547, 884
Doorway to Danger, 106, 386, 716, 738, 863, 914
Doorway to Fame, 390, 642
Doris Day Show, The, 28, 55, 121, 235, 239, 303, 379, 450, 479, 497, 690, 732, 741, 790, 803, 808–810
Dorothy, 108, 339, 361, 502, 522, 541, 604, 634
Dotto, 618
Dotty Mack Show (aka Girl Alone), 108, 531, 537
Double Dare, 155, 535, 870, 902
Double Life of Henry Phyfe, The, 49, 135, 178, 632, 703
Double McGuffin, 894
Double or Nothing, 657, 902
Double Trouble, 61, 141, 442, 714, 716, 722, 744, 756, 858
Dough Re Mi, 700
Douglas Edwards and the News, 272
Douglas Fairbanks, Jr., Presents, 286
Down You Go, 18, 108, 167, 205, 215, 220, 230, 282, 339, 454, 468, 469, 540, 622, 657, 679, 721, 807, 849
Downtown, 280, 381, 550, 632, 855
Dracula, 450
Dragnet, 12, 31, 132, 277, 294, 328, 445, 564, 602, 603, 628, 671, 758, 813, 864, 866, 884, 886, 923
Drak Pack, The, 142, 195, 578
Draw, 182
Draw Me a Laugh!, 106, 112, 165, 425, 429
Draw to Win, 236, 412, 603
Dream House, 229, 282
Dream Merchants, The, 295, 382, 614
Dreams, 246, 316, 334, 398, 453, 532, 800, 801, 810
Dress Rehearsal, 347
Drew Pearson, 663
Droodles, 193, 521, 685, 708
Dropout Father, 860

Duck Factory, The, 154, 325, 338, 339, 490, 584, 662, 829
Duel, 884
Duffy's Tavern, 549, 703
Duke, The, 181, 194, 198, 338, 439, 505, 539, 818, 892
Dukes of Hazzard, The, 48, 85, 99, 173, 187, 240, 336, 425, 440, 445, 467, 558, 690, 701, 756, 776, 868, 919
Dummy, 133, 796
DuMont Evening News, the, 69, 192
Dumplings, The, 9, 116, 183, 184, 192, 322, 429, 546, 726
Dundee and the Culhane, 329, 590
DuPont Show of the Month, The, 28, 182, 223, 311, 385, 567, 677, 693, 759, 825
DuPont Show of the Week, The, 822
DuPont Show with June Allyson, 19
DuPont Theater, 489, 564, 836
Dusty's Trail, 203, 242, 312, 718, 751, 851, 916
Dynasty, 3, 71, 74, 75, 81, 86, 96, 119, 128, 145, 155, 167, 187, 189, 202, 248, 282, 283, 285, 288, 306, 307, 347, 348, 377, 414, 418, 422, 435, 450, 484, 517, 530, 550, 569, 617, 632, 643, 648, 665, 682, 716, 724, 726, 747, 753, 759, 760, 824, 841, 853
Dynasty II: The Colbys, 68, 97, 121, 166, 360, 396, 402, 418, 435, 595, 605, 734, 747, 758, 802, 861, 896, 923

E

Eagle in a Cage, 233
Earl Wrightson Show, The, 655, 887, 920
Earn Your Vacation, 157
East of Eden, 15, 67, 68, 74, 96, 102–104, 111, 134, 261, 554, 635, 639, 688, 766, 876, 886
East Side/West Side, 293, 352, 447, 759, 822, 854, 876, 908
Easy Aces, 2, 326
Easy Does It . . . Starring Frankie Avalon, 45, 320, 341, 585, 624, 707, 834, 878
Easy Street, 25, 211, 275, 430, 537, 885
Ebony, Ivory and Jade, 790
Ed Sullivan Show, The, 73, 84, 94, 107, 250, 312, 400, 509, 545, 547, 579, 689, 820, 831, 908
Ed Wynn Show, The, 8, 344, 555, 639, 866, 921
Eddie, 779
Eddie Cantor Comedy Theatre, 147
Eddie Cantor Show, The, 657

Eddie Capra Mysteries, 50, 415, 567, 672, 825
Eddie Condon's Floor Show, 192, 708
Eddie Fisher Show, The, 109, 298, 344, 539, 840
Eddy Arnold Show, The, 38, 43, 161, 248, 592
Eddy Arnold Time, 38
Edge of Night, The, 1, 46, 144, 192, 359, 371, 391, 424, 494, 498, 527, 538, 558, 571, 723, 729, 824, 831, 890
Edie Adams Show, The, 5, 172, 346, 379, 557, 700
Editor's Choice, 923
Edwin Newman Reporting, 626
Eight Is Enough, 1, 125, 179, 229, 347, 348, 427, 457, 530, 620, 639, 652, 683, 715, 716, 836, 862, 866, 877
87th Precinct, 216, 293, 294, 383, 493, 736, 811, 871
Eischied, 53, 126, 176, 273, 320, 500, 644
Elder Michaux, 586
Eleanor and Franklin, 300, 613, 672, 782, 822
Eleanor and Franklin: The White House Years, 382, 822
Eleanor and Lou Gehrig Story, The, 812
Eleanor, First Lady of the World, 803
Electra Woman & Dyna Girl, 11
Electric Company, The, 45, 204, 601, 913
Electric Grandmother, The, 803
Elephant Man, The, 320
Eleventh Hour, The, 74, 111, 202, 257, 339
Elgin TV Hour, The, 80, 81, 163, 764
Elizabeth Taylor in London, 831
Ellen Burstyn Show, The, 133, 610, 817, 834
Ellery Queen. See The Adventures of Ellery Queen.
Ellis Island, 133
Elvis, 739
Elvis and the Beauty Queen, 443, 930
Emerald Point N.A.S., 6, 26, 27, 107, 161, 178, 199, 247, 265, 313, 518, 643, 745, 807, 863, 878, 884
Emergency, 253, 320, 337, 420, 519, 520, 540, 541, 558, 631, 675, 773, 812, 830, 842, 850, 886, 891
Empire, 40, 73, 115, 262, 273, 276, 457, 533, 554, 571, 600, 643, 676, 766, 827, 859, 910, 913
End of the Rainbow, The, 52, 59

Engelbert Humperdinck Show, The, 230, 423, 658
Enola Gay, 871
Enos, 239, 351, 587, 611, 776, 920
Ensign O'Toole, 9, 111, 301, 446, 503, 611, 796
Entertainer, The, 97, 504, 841
Entertainers, The, 125, 129, 136, 210, 230, 241, 300, 332, 373, 626, 646, 857, 930
Entertainment Tonight, 39, 273, 335, 376, 387, 399, 538, 835, 874, 889, 893
Equalizer, The, 493, 643, 826, 905, 918, 929
E/R, 8, 12, 45, 96, 180, 255, 295, 353, 567, 597, 756, 816, 924
Eric Sevareid's Chronicle, 765
Ernie in Kovacsland, 4, 243, 480, 481
Ernie Kovacs: Between the Laughter, 5
Ernie Kovacs Show, The, 4, 353, 379, 391, 462, 480, 481, 495, 517, 526, 572, 890
Escape, 195, 317, 886, 911
E.S.P., 685
Ethel and Albert, 127, 527
Eve Arden Show, The, 33, 67, 360, 450, 813
Evening Edition, 7
Evening in Byzantium, 305
Evening with Fred Astaire, An, 42, 732
Evening With Julie Andrews and Harry Belafonte, An, 29
Everglades, The, 394
Evergreen, 864, 880
Everybody's Business, 284
Evita Peron, 589
Execution, The, 383, 825, 876
Executioner's Song, The, 39, 875
Executive Suite, 3, 206, 253, 276, 487, 563, 606, 629, 672, 683, 714, 727, 741, 792, 819, 826, 887
Expedition, 207
Experiment, 401
Explorers, The, 628
Exploring the Universe, 329
Eye Guess, 216
Eye on Hollywood, 149, 400, 608, 609, 756
Eye to Eye, 266, 288
Eye Witness, 357
Eyes Have It, The, 575
Eyewitness News, 725, 752
Eyewitness to History, 187, 211, 483, 484

F

F Troop, 45, 82–84, 116, 239, 247, 336, 379, 660, 804, 814, 851
Fabulous '50s, The, 303
Fabulous Funnies, The, 304

Face Is Familiar, The, 894
Face the Music, 184, 186, 243, 608
Face the Nation, 183, 633
Face to Face, 265
Facts of Life, The, 11, 42, 122, 180, 184, 297, 339, 369, 441, 497, 499, 573, 639, 668, 673, 693, 719, 754, 763, 836, 894
Facts We Face, The, 767
Failing of Raymond, The, 921
Fair Exchange, 151, 173, 174, 222, 310, 522, 534, 544, 881
Falcon, The, 570
Falcon Crest, 9, 12, 29, 33, 65, 100, 141, 142, 150, 159, 171, 173, 200, 218, 222, 223, 249, 256, 269, 276, 286, 295, 309, 316, 333, 346, 360, 379, 412, 417, 434, 444, 447, 480, 487, 488, 507, 518, 530, 541, 555, 558, 566, 569, 575, 608, 641, 667, 668, 693, 696, 701, 718, 723, 724, 730, 733, 744, 747, 763, 810, 821, 836, 852, 853, 865, 906, 921
Fall Guy, The, 60, 536, 670, 679, 838, 868
Fame, 14, 101, 149, 169, 218, 289, 335, 339, 362, 371, 377, 380, 422, 428, 431, 438, 439, 490, 620, 661, 664, 699, 782, 808, 825, 836, 876
Fame Is the Name of the Game, 744
Family, 68, 113, 145, 217, 313, 328, 397, 421, 467, 576, 656, 737, 754, 763, 840, 841, 894
Family Affair, 139, 330, 445, 460, 461, 575, 591, 873, 894, 904
Family Feud, 234
Family Holvak, The, 173, 304, 305, 332, 385, 417, 468, 573
Family Secrets, 682, 803, 834
Family Ties, 66, 68, 309, 365, 678, 684, 857, 924
Family Tree, The, 33, 164, 196, 267, 292, 380, 403, 482, 797
Family Upside Down, A, 42, 930
Famous Adventures of Mr. Magoo, The, 48, 317, 588, 605
Famous Fights, 682
Fanfare, 243, 407, 513, 572
Fantastic Four, The, 670
Fantastic Journey, 274, 314, 550, 567, 753
Fantastic Voyage, 589
Fantastic World of D. C. Collins, The, 187, 260
Fantasy, 855
Fantasy Island, 20, 30, 36, 48, 62, 84, 95, 99, 99, 108, 127, 135, 141, 148, 209, 229, 253, 258, 273, 277, 323, 403, 429, 442, 521, 573, 579, 593, 595, 636, 652, 681, 753, 754, 773, 824, 851, 866, 897
Far Out Space Nuts, The, 243

Faraday and Company, 116, 221, 343, 619
Faraway Hill, 107, 144, 175, 251, 323, 324, 376, 473, 523, 578, 585, 760, 805, 819, 871
Farmer's Daughter, The, 199, 243, 435, 555, 624, 637, 774, 808, 911, 925
Farrell for the People, 383
Fashion Story, The, 96, 233, 235, 300, 349, 451, 490, 644, 708, 753, 774, 804
Fashions on Parade, 392
Fast Lane Blues, 228
Fast Times, 142, 241, 402, 567, 618, 755, 841, 876, 878, 890, 910, 929
Fat Albert and the Cosby Kids, 204
Fatal Vision, 364, 536, 537, 626, 744
Father Knows Best, 66, 170, 252, 277, 308, 312, 333, 358, 436, 511, 575, 641, 705, 737, 763, 775, 790, 864, 875, 920, 926, 927
Father Murphy, 81, 85, 146, 199, 336, 368, 490, 514, 580, 611, 642, 732, 851, 853
Father of the Bride, 21, 197, 226, 286, 585, 773, 795, 853, 881
Fathers and Sons, 318, 354, 366, 372, 496, 624, 642, 748
Favorite Story, 581
Fawlty Towers, 895
Fay, 11, 334, 356, 357, 503, 512, 608, 778, 906
Faye Emerson Show, 278
Faye Emerson's Wonderful Town, 278
F.B.I., The, 2, 26, 41, 86, 87, 117, 131, 204, 232, 268, 313, 411, 450, 522, 589, 632, 638, 711, 714, 729, 747, 755, 772, 816, 842, 854, 856, 858, 876, 897, 930
FBI vs. Alvin Karpis, The, 883
F.D.R., 402, 465
Fear On Trial, 759
Fearless Fosdick, 172
Feather and Father Gang, The, 170, 240, 353, 489, 682, 769
Felony Squad, 12, 185, 223, 254, 261, 262, 558, 671
Feminist and the Fuzz, The, 271, 388
Fernwood 2-Night, 245, 474, 610, 708, 736, 763, 836, 863, 900, 904, 927
Fess Parker Show, The, 656
Festival of Stars, 20
Fibber McGee and Molly, 68, 314, 475, 508, 663, 715, 790, 824
Fifth of July, 484
Fifty-Fourth Street Revue, The, 35, 83, 112, 235, 248, 271, 292, 307, 351, 546, 614, 708, 778, 796, 806, 866

$50,000 Pyramid, The, 177
Fight Beat, 653
Fight Talk, 198, 266, 790
Fighting Back, 856
Files of Jeffrey Jones, The, 370, 400
Filthy Rich, 128, 159, 313, 380, 518, 673, 851, 868, 886, 887
Finder of Lost Loves, 3, 311, 348, 438, 439, 453
Fireball Fun-for-All, 348, 393, 444, 558, 641, 642, 749
Firehouse, 230, 239, 260, 273, 434, 648, 791
Fireside Theatre, 76, 92, 170, 273, 276, 448, 521, 525, 537, 636, 658, 700, 706, 764, 807, 914, 921
First Date, 167
First Hundred Years, The, 315
First Ladies Diaries: Martha Washington, 525
First Ladies Diaries: Rachel Jackson, 350
First Love, 838
First Nine Months Are the Hardest, The, 170
First Olympics, The, 812
First Tuesday, 856, 861
First You Cry, 599
Fish, 59, 111, 164, 349, 587, 619, 802, 865
Fishing and Hunting Club, 784
Fitz and Bones, 150, 462, 585, 610, 792, 793
Fitzpatricks, The, 107, 205, 424, 482, 547, 576, 843, 890
Five Days from Home, 665
Five Fingers, 128, 396, 654
Five Star Jubilee, 16, 451, 493, 539, 688, 720, 786, 828, 870, 871, 910
Flamingo Road, 18, 70, 122, 253, 261, 262, 286, 287, 324, 382, 459, 561, 694, 721, 726, 738, 763, 770, 777, 809
Flash Gordon, 169, 410, 619, 644
Flatbed Annie and Sweetie Pie, 900
Flatbush, 126, 141, 397, 612, 678, 691, 819, 864, 931
Flight to Rhythm, 126, 153, 857
Flintstones, The, 75, 76, 92, 151, 444, 518, 560, 584, 631, 703, 818, 859
Flip Wilson Show, The, 131, 184, 689, 707, 908, 920
Flipper, 245, 293, 376, 463, 630, 817, 876
Flo, 53, 98, 126, 129, 301, 411, 448, 460, 509, 907
Florian Zabach Show, The, 929
Flying Doctor, The, 242
Flying High, 476, 640, 676, 763, 915
Flying Nun, The, 226, 252, 292, 296, 606, 609, 651, 703, 712, 761, 773, 893

Focus on America, 344, 767
Foley Square, 187, 275, 440, 451, 503, 523, 750, 779, 883
Follow the Leader, 857
Follow the Sun, 184, 376, 492, 517, 667
Fonz and the Happy Days Gang, 192
Food for Thought, 355
Foot in the Door, 146, 339, 353, 582
Football Sidelines, 914
For Love and Honor, 71, 366, 480, 482, 581, 681, 684, 705, 791, 804, 842, 883
For the Love of It, 891
For the People, 170, 230, 768, 876
For Whom the Bell Tolls, 803
For Your Pleasure, 91, 431, 530, 655, 771
Ford Festival, 64, 580, 857, 880, 899
Ford Show, The, 305, 332, 758, 846
Ford Star Jubilee, 327, 630, 889
Ford Star Revue, 7, 158, 373, 392, 408, 547
Ford Star Time, 219, 612, 924
Ford Theatre, 27, 62, 78, 86, 98, 106, 113, 137, 141, 148, 200, 242, 255, 261, 461, 561, 692, 701, 704, 711, 772, 799, 820, 851
Foreign Intrigue, 223, 594, 684, 761, 841
Forever, 930
Forsyte Saga, The, 679
Fortune Dane, 40, 222, 320, 884
Foul Play, 102, 165, 694, 714, 715, 730
Foul-Ups, Bleeps & Blunders, 271, 498, 717
Found Money, 861
Four Just Men, 196, 221, 392
Four Seasons, The, 10, 11, 33, 48, 154, 467, 723, 726, 893
Four Square Court, 114
Four Star Playhouse, 70, 87, 104, 190, 526, 527, 629, 681, 717, 807
Frances Langford-Don Ameche Show, 501
Frank Leahy Show, The, 500
Frank Sinatra: A Man and His Music, 781
Frank Sinatra Show, The, 95, 297, 331, 502, 717, 781, 814, 876
Frankie Laine Show, The, 487
Frankie Laine Time, 63, 155, 161, 261, 487, 580, 803
Fred Allen Show, The, 240, 703
Fred Waring Show, The, 879
Freddy Martin Show, The, 38, 363, 548, 550
Free Country, 332, 452, 514, 561, 654, 709, 710

Free To Be ... You and Me, 839
Freebie and the Bean, 227, 275, 554, 811
Freedom, 913
French-Atlantic Affair, The, 295
Friday Night Videos, 586, 611
Fridays, 93, 131, 132, 171, 230, 428, 465, 535, 624, 716, 721
Friendly Fire, 16, 129, 882
Friends, 7, 300, 444, 532, 606, 702, 725, 730, 894
Friends and Lovers, 546
Friends of Man, 304
Friendships, 825
From a Bird's Eye View, 167, 297, 413, 448, 550
From Here to Eternity, 65, 105, 142, 244, 270, 280, 351, 402, 440, 443, 537, 625, 654, 677, 694, 721, 747, 798, 836, 917
From These Roots, 17, 538, 693, 839
Front Page, The, 223, 224, 722, 876
Front Page Detective, 259, 524
Front Row Center, 297, 314, 502, 518, 599, 647, 741, 774, 798, 813
Frontier, 207
Frontier Circus, 243, 434, 779, 907
Frontier Doctor, 16
Frontier Gentleman, 239
Frontier Judge, 21
Frontier Justice, 46, 74, 255
Frontline, 752
Fugitive, The, 41, 72, 143, 146, 176, 194, 244, 248, 359, 412, 419, 437, 527, 607, 628, 652, 677, 695, 711, 731, 751, 760, 888
Fun Factory, The, 837
Fun for the Money, 642
Funky Phantom, 251
Funny Face, 35, 71, 264, 316
Funny Side, The, 22, 82, 170, 176, 297, 358, 463, 503, 575, 616, 790, 902, 903
Fury, 357
Future Cop, 22
F.Y.I., 271, 512

G

Gable and Lombard, 114
Gabrielle, 323
Gale Storm Show, The, 193, 287, 315, 563, 676, 723, 814, 815
Galen Drake Show, The, 259, 277, 308
Gallant Men, The, 233, 303, 352, 496, 577, 714, 718, 784
Gallery of Mme. Lui-Tsong, 916
Gamble on Love, 229
Gambler, The, 728

Gambler—The Adventure Continues, The, 209, 728
Games Mother Never Taught You, 825
Games People Play, 4, 76, 244, 330, 367, 442, 648, 827
Gangster Chronicles, The, 29, 33, 57, 76, 165, 230, 335, 415, 516, 545, 553, 632, 665, 678, 679, 702, 815, 842, 907
Garrison's Gorillas, 99, 161, 227, 383, 794
Garroway at Large, 170, 172, 202, 235, 324, 329, 337, 382, 390, 399, 632, 738, 739, 781, 795, 797
Garry Moore Show, The, 58, 70, 129, 137, 158, 231, 241, 300, 321, 346, 360, 377, 400, 474, 478, 480, 521, 522, 561, 598, 787, 845, 865
Gas Company Playhouse, 578
Gathering, The, 803
Gathering Part II, The, 930
Gaugin the Savage, 154
Gavilan, 533, 707, 856
Gay Nineties Revue, The, 66, 94, 301, 417
G.E. College Bowl, The, 269, 525
G.E. Guest House, 474, 507
Gemini Man, 209, 612, 826
Gene Autry Show, The, 44, 135, 690
General Electric Theater, 42, 68, 81, 101, 115, 131, 135, 170, 205, 208, 214, 219, 284, 323, 358, 390, 401, 513, 571, 582, 612, 662, 669, 675, 701, 712, 748, 764, 810, 905, 921
General Electric True, 195, 886
General Hospital, 5, 21, 27, 80, 110, 122, 187, 224, 225, 276, 312, 350, 377, 380, 391, 438, 517, 562, 573, 708, 725, 747, 778, 801, 821, 831, 836, 848, 894
Generation Gap, The, 63, 898
Gentle Ben, 111, 417, 419, 740, 779, 884
Gentleman Bandit, The, 871
Geographically Speaking, 890
George Burns and Gracie Allen Show, The, 15, 75, 76, 120, 130, 131, 178, 349, 459, 541, 583, 762, 868
George Burns Comedy Week, The, 130, 131
George Burns Show, The, 75, 130, 131, 233, 459, 583, 868
George Gobel Show, The, 46, 124, 245, 253, 298, 301, 344, 382, 469, 472, 539, 576, 593, 850, 868
George Jessel Show, The, 441
George Michael Sports Machine, The, 585
George Sanders Mystery Theater, The, 748
George Washington, 43, 410, 554, 788, 799

Georgetown University Forum, 91

Georgia Gibbs and Her Million Record Show, 335, 744

Gertrude Berg Show, The, 80, 203, 381, 483, 664, 734, 790, 878, 898

Get Christie Love, 28, 151, 176, 358, 463, 659, 669, 730, 737

Get It Together, 276

Get Smart, 4, 101, 209, 263, 293, 317, 330, 369, 399, 451, 455, 459, 468, 479, 589, 597, 606, 618, 628, 676, 680, 755, 807, 822

Getting Away from It All, 859

Getting Married, 840

Getting Together, 131, 156, 620, 772, 807

Ghost and Mrs. Muir, The, 154, 299, 466, 491, 610, 708, 769

Ghost Busters, 814, 851

Ghost Dancing, 571

Ghost Story, 7, 139, 308, 388

Ghost Writer, The, 914

Giant Step, 657

Gibbsville, 562, 570, 710, 751, 925

Gideon, C.I.D., 362

Gideon's Trumpet, 919

Gidget, 193, 244, 296, 313, 617, 679, 842, 913

Gidget Grows Up, 857

Gift of Love, The, 506

Gift of Song, A, 320

Gillette Cavalcade of Sports (aka Friday Night Fights), 306, 682, 802

Gillette Summer Sports Reel, 56, 60, 561

Gilligan's Island, 48, 242, 372, 444, 523, 754, 779, 890

Gimme a Break, 160, 189, 263, 399, 414, 420, 490, 498, 586, 588, 607, 757, 779, 824

Girl About Town, 258, 530, 655, 920

Girl From U.N.C.L.E., The, 156, 386, 474, 507, 682, 855

Girl Most Likely To, The, 720

Girl Talk, 355

Girl Who Came Gift Wrapped, The, 857

Girl with Something Extra, The, 230, 272, 296, 328, 447, 488, 771, 858, 911

Girls, The, 304, 506, 537, 817

Girls of Huntington House, The, 550

Girls Talk, 858

Gisele MacKenzie Show, The, 218, 466, 532, 618, 688, 814

Gladys Knight & The Pips Show, The, 366, 477, 660, 920

Glamour-Go-Round, 172, 474, 618

Glen Campbell Goodtime Hour, The, 144, 218, 241, 576, 651, 677, 704, 863

Glen Campbell Music Show, The, 144

Glencannon, 592

Glenn Miller Time, 165, 179, 243, 573

Glitter, 88, 113, 215, 381, 405, 442, 457, 558, 613, 624, 768

Gloria, 246, 433, 582, 716, 818

Glynis, 27, 442, 556

Go Lucky, 614

Godzilla Power Hour, The, 11

Going My Way, 155, 156, 463, 811, 892, 923

Going Places with Betty Betz, 86

Goldbergs, The, 80, 285, 385, 517, 577, 591, 725, 784, 813, 833

Golddiggers, The, 346

Golden Girls, The, 39, 40, 334, 357, 562, 895

Golden Touch of Frankie Carle, The, 149

Goldie and the Boxer, 781

Goldie and the Boxer Go to Hollywood, 902

Goliath Awaits, 9, 382

Gomer Pyle, U.S.M.C., 58, 84, 175, 192, 417, 505, 581, 617, 709, 729, 755, 818, 819, 823, 837

Gong Show, The, 62, 118, 241, 249, 289, 330, 442, 603, 632, 648, 705, 832, 913

Goober and the Ghost Chasers, 911

Good Company, 50

Good Guys, The, 242, 270, 322, 339, 372, 553, 680, 822, 862

Good Heavens, 709

Good Life, The, 49, 347, 371, 590, 883

Good Morning, America, 50, 61, 337, 388, 444, 569, 720, 815

Good Morning, World, 53, 246, 392, 659, 755

Good News, 348

Good Night, America, 720

Good Time Harry, 84, 85, 349, 455, 540, 668, 726, 816, 889

Good Times, 22, 120, 160, 174, 187, 261, 283, 368, 431, 507, 681, 729, 801, 873, 903, 910

Goodbye Raggedy Ann, 290

Goodnight, Beantown, 50, 89, 184, 288, 346, 387, 388, 508, 799, 822

Goodtime Girls, 279, 347, 510, 543, 660, 680, 758, 827, 931

Goodyear Playhouse, 55, 207, 311, 385, 546, 653, 680

Goodyear Theatre, 294, 352, 504

Goodyear/Philco Playhouse, 556

Gordon MacRae Show, The, 12, 172, 534

Gossip Columnist, The, 864

Governor & J.J., The, 141, 214, 221, 545, 660, 795, 807

Grady, 185, 275, 301, 455, 559, 607, 622

Grambling's White Tiger, 73, 119, 133

Grand Jury, The, 85, 264, 813

Grand Ole Opry, The, 3, 16, 43, 107, 159, 206, 248, 405, 448, 523, 663, 721, 786, 793, 848, 851

Grandpa Goes to Washington, 9, 491, 514, 542, 554, 782, 843

Gray Ghost, The, 29, 168

Grease, 58

Great Adventure, The, 396

Great American Dream Machine, The, 171, 912

Great American Traffic Jam, The, 37, 574

Great Escape, 577

Great Ghost Tales, 839

Great Gildersleeve, The, 461, 509, 592, 697, 733, 782, 818, 881

Great Houdinis, The, 341, 859

Great Ice Rip-Off, The, 182, 871

Great Man's Whiskers, The, 884

Great Mysteries, 889, 890

Great Performances, 230

Great Talent Hunt, 603

Greatest American Hero, The, 167, 216, 217, 346, 356, 373, 456, 654, 680, 754, 763, 902

Greatest Fights of the Century, 809

Greatest Gift, The, 132, 476, 579

Greatest Heroes of the Bible, The, 450

Greatest Man on Earth, The, 122, 197, 857

Greatest Moments in Sports, 469

Greatest Show on Earth, The, 281, 652, 653

Greatest Sport Thrills, 344, 518

Greatest Thing That Almost Happened, The, 873

Green Acres, 8, 9, 57, 135, 139, 145, 310, 323, 484, 507, 564, 580, 594, 597, 660, 665, 741

Green Hornet, The, 116, 353, 407, 501, 558, 648, 870, 905

Griff, 360, 361, 612, 812, 830

Grindl, 182, 183, 589

Growing Pains, 142, 346, 467, 588, 835, 836

Growing Paynes, The, 24, 390, 412, 519, 656, 659, 817, 819, 914

Guess Again, 292, 458, 548, 874

Guess What, 174, 380, 479, 664, 714

Guestward Ho!, 106, 260, 408, 544, 588, 596, 617, 618, 859

Guide for the Married Woman, A, 772
Guide Right, 497, 739
Guiding Light, The, 66, 85, 124, 314, 330, 378, 447, 478, 578, 669, 784, 806, 872, 875, 881, 902
Guild Playhouse, 132
Guilty or Innocent: The Sam Sheppard Murder Case, 665
Guinness Game, The, 325
Gulf Road Show Starring Bob Smith, The, 366, 396, 511, 785, 786, 919, 925
Gun in His Hand, 870
Gun in the House, A, 818
Gun Shy, 23, 447, 509, 565, 592, 652, 715, 840, 860
Guns of Will Sonnett, The, 109, 695
Gunslinger, 308, 358, 672, 678, 879, 927
Gunsmoke, 30, 37, 40, 49, 53, 63, 72, 91, 94, 98, 103, 122, 131, 139, 141, 168, 194, 195, 205, 215, 217, 219, 232, 260, 270, 275, 284, 308, 317, 328, 337, 357, 362, 383, 397, 426, 447, 450, 466, 536, 576, 578, 590, 603, 633, 635, 660, 662, 673, 712, 713, 723, 734, 741, 747, 753, 755, 757, 762, 763, 783, 813–816, 825, 830, 848, 851, 869, 882, 884, 894, 929
Guy Lombardo & His Royal Canadians, 518
Guy Lombardo's Diamond Jubilee, 518
Guy Mitchell Show, The, 12, 147, 392, 592
Guyana Tragedy: The Story of Jim Jones, 100
Guys and Dolls, 90
Gypsy In My Soul, 171, 186, 532
Gypsy Warriors, The, 764

H

Hagen, 283, 284, 405, 471, 929
Haggis Baggis, 513
Hail the Champ, 15
Hail to the Chief, 43, 83–85, 116, 217, 347, 377, 378, 434, 661, 769, 819, 852, 864, 865
Hal Linden's Big Apple, 512
Half Hour Comedy Hour, The, 247, 264, 373, 413, 429, 433, 607, 654, 768, 812
Half Nelson, 134, 366, 433, 548, 668, 786, 906
Hallmark Hall of Fame, The, 15, 65, 223, 283, 294, 307, 312, 335, 385, 388, 405, 424, 662, 677, 680, 698, 759, 825, 839, 842, 890, 894, 907, 922
Halls of Ivy, The, 135, 189, 190, 423, 844, 898

Hamptons, The, 84, 134, 150, 162, 247, 349, 674, 708, 722, 736, 770, 833
Handyman, 114
Hanging In, 129, 534, 556, 714, 868
Hank, 115, 203, 308, 362, 452, 625, 668, 745, 824, 907
Hank McCune Show, The, 83, 124, 459, 474, 566, 621
Hansel and Gretel, 135
Happening, 178
Happiness Is a Warm Clue, 551
Happy, 101, 131, 203, 241, 511, 650
Happy Days, 52, 73, 83, 96, 101, 102, 180, 187, 200, 246, 251, 255, 276, 294, 348, 419, 486, 561, 569, 578, 594, 600, 601, 604, 608, 619, 633, 635, 640, 645, 655, 663, 679, 689, 690, 723, 734, 735, 758, 779, 879, 901, 905, 912
Harbor Command, 202
Harbourmaster, 128, 276, 460, 819, 900
Hardcastle & McCormick, 288, 379, 422, 432, 460, 461, 750
Hardy Boys Mysteries, The, 15, 16, 28, 44, 126, 138, 164, 206, 274, 337, 444, 463, 487, 550, 723, 754, 810
Harlem Globetrotters, The, 214
Harlem Globetrotters on Gilligan's Island, The, 488
Harlem Globetrotters Show, The, 869
Harness Racing, 60, 561, 806
Harper Valley P.T.A., 15, 237, 264, 270, 271, 299, 310, 344, 351, 359, 379, 562, 563, 753, 813, 840, 882
Harrigan and Son, 229, 475, 636, 668
Harris Against the World, 19, 63, 246, 476, 532, 899
Harris and Company, 57, 121, 161, 339, 420, 432, 525, 782, 852, 871
Harry S Truman: Plain Speaking, 300
Harry-O, 229, 291, 437, 492, 525, 626, 851, 880, 903, 929
Harry's Battles, 861
Harry's Girls, 95, 627, 778, 903
Hart to Hart, 656, 682, 801, 870, 906, 917
Hartmans, The, 178, 205, 388, 389, 769, 789, 813
Harvey Korman Show, The, 860
Hatfields and the McCoys, The, 166
Hathaways, The, 145, 163, 503, 597, 667, 893
Have Gun, Will Travel, 92, 100, 115, 222, 239, 270, 312, 466, 524, 755, 846, 892

Having Babies, 43, 58, 417, 741, 821, 844
Hawaii Five-O., 7, 23, 85, 146, 168, 242, 247, 263, 269, 279, 281, 290, 303, 383, 425, 459, 521, 530, 533, 656, 719, 741, 768, 791, 794, 805, 824, 825, 843, 886, 896, 931
Hawaiian Eye, 51, 194, 253, 274, 283, 483, 599, 608, 678, 684, 807, 818, 891, 903, 930
Hawaiian Heat, 340, 536, 565, 717, 758
Hawk, 344, 362, 436, 712, 713
Hawkeye, 169, 387
Hawkins, 552, 810
Hawkins Falls, Population 6,200, 226, 521, 680, 815, 821
Hawkins on Murder, 810
Hayloft Hoedown, 235, 613, 627, 727, 784, 853
Hazel, 12, 77, 92, 100, 127, 238, 307, 320, 441, 508, 511, 682, 685, 787, 863
Hazel Scott, 760
He & She, 77, 143, 164, 353, 545, 683, 843
Head of the Class, 38, 72, 318, 340, 372, 402, 425, 639, 721, 756, 858
Head of the Family, 709
Headliners with David Frost, 319, 328, 789
Headmaster, The, 294, 364, 625, 639, 861
Heart of the City, 32, 122, 243, 717, 746, 878, 903
Heathcliff and Dingbat, 858
Heaven for Betsy, 504, 813
Hec Ramsey, 7, 100, 505, 602, 737, 886
Hee Haw, 3, 25, 53, 79, 87, 88, 131, 144, 179, 185, 191, 291, 348, 370, 376, 386, 427, 439, 448, 499, 512, 539, 565, 573, 587, 619, 633, 648, 663, 671, 673, 684, 696, 697, 715, 717, 718, 728, 730, 735, 747, 748, 750, 758, 788, 814, 817, 829, 830, 832, 844, 850, 869, 900, 913, 914, 918
Hee Haw Honeys, 444, 684, 730, 735, 750
Helen Keller—The Miracle Continues, 913
Helen Morgan Story, The, 81
Helen O'Connell Show, The, 637
Helen Reddy Show, The, 702, 718, 727
Hell Town, 91, 92, 202, 251, 355, 458, 520, 559, 569, 691
Hello Larry, 121, 280, 294, 343, 504, 581, 716, 809, 810, 819, 900
Hellzapoppin, 641
Help Wanted: Male, 677
Helter Skelter, 830, 895
Hennesey, 11, 199, 200, 222, 277, 340, 442, 454, 479, 483, 921

Henny and Rocky Show, The, 185, 359, 369, 887, 927
Henry Fonda and the Family, 303
Henry Morgan's Great Talent Hunt, 55, 151, 176, 360, 437, 464, 603, 801
Henry Winkler Meets William Shakespeare, 912
Herb Shriner Show, The, 776
Herb Shriner Time, 776
Herbie, The Love Bug, 202, 278, 389, 446, 456, 514, 661, 856, 890
Here and Now, 568
Here Come the Brides, 71, 94, 95, 121, 150, 172, 184, 379, 408, 420, 501, 504, 772, 796, 797, 823, 844, 854
Here We Go Again, 53, 69, 330, 357, 371, 716, 828
Here's Debbie, 713
Here's Lucy, 36, 37, 54, 55, 133, 210, 319, 350, 460, 558, 618, 713, 831
Heritage, 90
Herman Hickman Show, The, 404, 547
Hero, The, 52, 317, 387, 388, 414, 519, 611
He's All Yours, 34
He's the Mayor, 113, 203, 288, 351, 354, 413, 733, 841
Hey I'm Alive, 818
Hey Jeannie, 157, 263, 439
Hey Landlord, 60, 196, 426, 543, 558, 727
Hey, Mulligan!, 731
High Adventure, 838
High Adventure with Lowell Thomas, 838
High Button Shoes, 20
High Chaparral, The, 187, 196, 210, 229, 280, 420, 544, 591, 695, 778, 784, 820
High Finance, 435
High Ice, 437
High Performance, 83, 272, 389, 741, 753
High Rollers, 849
High School U.S.A., 160, 243, 404, 647
Highcliffe Manor, 45, 137, 285, 350, 421, 488, 544, 571, 639, 734, 746
Higher and Higher, 10
High-Low, 63, 95, 430, 579, 784, 860
Highway Patrol, 208, 209, 339
Highway to Heaven, 317, 318, 489, 490, 732
Hill Street Blues, 48, 90, 102, 119, 180, 194, 220, 280, 314, 324, 371, 372, 376, 380, 407, 451, 485, 543, 550, 640, 641, 680, 684, 688, 777, 778, 797, 823, 828, 836, 837, 848, 880, 888, 917, 921
Hiram Holiday. See Adventures of Hiram Holiday

Hit Man, 845
Hizzonner, 211, 238, 325, 396, 421, 610, 764
Hobby Lobby, 38
Hogan's Heroes, 41, 57, 180, 207, 208, 234, 250, 297, 417, 474, 475, 528, 828, 857, 881
Hold It Please, 291, 499, 546, 570
Hold That Camera, 90, 530, 584
Hold That Note, 642, 657
Holiday Hotel, 20, 110, 207, 355, 360, 362, 376, 383, 415, 519, 743, 771, 830, 870
Holiday Lodge, 40, 776, 786, 882, 883
Hollywood and the Stars, 205
Hollywood Backstage, 892
Hollywood Beat, 3, 557, 753, 913
Hollywood Hotel, 853
Hollywood House, 48, 721, 891
Hollywood Opening Night, 296
Hollywood Palace, The, 47, 120, 212, 327, 473
Hollywood Screen Test, 378, 529, 691
Hollywood Squares, The, 38, 39, 67, 207, 344, 528, 547, 573, 732
Hollywood Squares/Match Game Hour, The, 547
Hollywood Summer Theatre, 700
Hollywood Talent Scouts, 513
Hollywood Teen, 576
Hollywood Wives, 794, 799, 807
Holmes and Yoyo, 42, 417, 474, 757, 776
Holocaust, 52, 53, 64, 70, 73, 102, 222, 293, 351, 385, 394, 412, 434, 500, 508, 573, 585, 595, 604, 632, 682, 683, 732, 746, 805, 817, 867, 877, 879, 885, 917
Home, 258, 311
Homecoming, The, 839, 911
Hometown, 71, 281, 452, 527, 663, 736, 807, 867, 898
Hondo, 71, 122, 124, 179, 307, 624, 659, 827
Honestly Celeste, 298, 412, 462, 526, 572, 926
Honey Boy, 281
Honey West, 280, 311, 402
Honeymooners, The, 9, 151, 152, 341–343, 464, 578, 697, 807
Hong Kong, 96, 303, 436, 482, 782, 833
Hong Kong Phooey, 214
Honky Tonk, 809
Honorable Sam Houston, The, 799
Hoofer, The, 638
Hootenanny, 513
Hopalong Cassidy, 104, 125
Horace Heidt Show, The, 396
Horizon, 67

Horror at 37,000 Feet, The, 522, 768
Hospital, 871
Hostage Heart, The, 825
Hostage Tower, The, 286, 902
Hot Dog, 914
Hot L Baltimore, 81, 142, 211, 295, 316, 353, 505, 513, 554, 693, 910
Hot Off the Wire, 48
Hot Pursuit, 459, 584, 674, 684
Hot Rod, 723
Hot Seat, The, 755
Hot Shots, 128, 443, 655, 751
Hotel, 67, 68, 73, 96, 114, 198, 290, 671, 763, 799, 831, 923
Hotel Broadway, 817
Hotel de Paree, 411, 552, 583, 629
Hound of the Baskervilles, The, 356
Hour Glass, 558, 658
Hour Magazine, 188, 189
Hour of Decision, 355
House Calls, 126, 203, 343, 387, 424, 433, 488, 668, 703, 728, 729, 832, 883
House Party, 513
How Did They Get That Way?, 503
How the West Was Won, 29, 37, 103, 195, 216, 227, 239, 275, 299, 379, 410, 421, 511, 613, 651, 744, 756, 929
How the West Was Won Part II, 595
How To, 6, 548, 685, 807
How to Marry a Millionaire, 23, 270, 271, 331, 622
How to Pick Up Girls, 865
How to Stay Young and Vital, 217
How to Survive a Marriage, 587
Howard K. Smith—News and Comment, 787
Howard Morris Show, 606
Howdy Doody Show, The, 13, 122, 279, 562, 786, 853
Howling in the Woods, A, 271
How's Your Mother-in-Law?, 62
Hudson Brothers Razzle Dazzle Comedy Show, 421
Hudson Brothers Show, The, 273, 281, 355, 421, 423, 563, 648, 727
Hudson's Bay, 843
Hullabaloo, 557
Human Feelings, 874
110 in the Shade, 824
Hunter, 22, 74, 234, 260, 282, 283, 312, 313, 375, 446, 482, 733, 770, 898
Hunter, The, 494, 620
Huntley-Brinkley Report, The, 112, 211, 425
Husbands, Wives & Lovers, 64, 384, 397, 520, 625, 663, 718, 720, 777, 811, 889

I

I, Claudius, 433, 530
I Cover Times Square, 421
I Dream of Jeannie, 137, 222,
243, 270, 271, 370, 371, 395,
400, 532, 553, 578, 635, 732,
768, 862
I Dream of Jeannie, 15 Years
Later, 271
I Had Three Wives, 45, 200,
201, 291, 325, 705
I Led Three Lives, 80, 150,
407, 422, 557, 606, 805, 929
I, Leonardo da Vinci, 762
I Love a Mystery, 893
I Love Lucy, 35, 36, 54, 55,
105, 176, 210, 232, 271, 305,
314, 315, 336, 350, 364, 414,
422, 444, 461, 621, 635, 706,
713, 859, 889, 899, 912
I Love to Eat, 69
I Married Joan, 48, 115, 153,
212, 232, 233, 278, 843, 906
I Remember Mama. See
Mama.
I Spy, 27, 167, 203, 216, 217,
488, 505, 554, 605, 828, 854,
855, 908
I Take These Men, 891
I Want to Be a Star, 252
I Want to Live, 870
I Will Fight No More Forever,
897
Ichabod and Me, 169, 392, 509,
555, 616, 701, 769, 806, 895
I'd Like to See, 136, 604
Identify, 277
Igor Cassini Show, The, 164
Ike, 28, 146, 250, 267, 343, 401,
524, 568, 675, 710, 716, 723,
754
Ilona Massey Show, The, 297,
554
I'm a Big Girl Now, 56, 146,
267, 473, 631, 775, 837
I'm Dickens—He's Fenster, 42,
71, 245, 400, 428, 468
I'm The Law, 694
Immigrants, The, 820
Immortal, The, 111, 333, 477,
528
Imogene Coca Show, The, 130,
182, 409, 541, 647
In Concert, 475
In Search Of ... , 628
In the Beginning, 58, 251, 275,
520, 604, 809, 810
In the First Person, 142, 420
In the Kelvinator Kitchen, 475
In the Matter of Karen Ann
Quinlan, 798, 930
In the Morgan Manner, 604
Ina Ray Hutton Show, The,
26, 110, 427
Incredible Hulk, The, 89, 191,
295, 387, 388
Incredible Journey of Dr. Meg
Laurel, The, 870, 921
Information Please, 5, 286, 469
Inherit the Wind, 72

Inmates: A Love Story, 448
Inside America, 177
Inside Detective, 378
Inside the Third Reich, 864
Inside U.S.A. with Chevrolet,
90, 97, 394, 395, 898
Insiders, The, 144, 433, 817
Insight, 625
Institute for Revenge, 876
International Detective, 301
International Showtime, 20
Interns, The, 68, 117, 208, 289,
290, 315, 337, 413, 791, 813
Intimate Agony, 864, 884
Intimate Strangers, 224, 818
Invaders, The, 711, 789, 828,
836
Invasion of Privacy, An, 383
Investigator, The, 170, 745
Investigators, The, 44, 312,
613, 671
Invisible Man, The, 30, 209,
227, 292, 560, 807, 882
Invisible Woman, The, 243
Invitation to Hell, 561, 856
Iron Horse, The, 133, 188, 254,
697, 724, 847
Ironside, 11, 23, 26, 27, 30, 36,
67, 68, 132, 143, 153, 154,
156, 177, 200, 325, 362, 411,
424, 448, 501, 529, 591, 592,
652, 677, 687, 734, 744, 747,
766, 768
Isabel's Choice, 834
Ishi: The Last of His Tribe, 884
Islanders, The, 110, 554, 671,
714, 920
It Could Be You, 272, 510, 628
It Happened in Sports, 653
It Happened One Christmas,
890
It Pays to Be Ignorant, 419,
564, 576, 771
It Takes a Thief, 42, 45, 87,
612, 744, 841, 870
It Takes Two, 43, 88, 209, 259,
271, 424, 573, 705
It Was a Very Good Year, 847
It's a Business, 241, 394, 522
It's a Great Life, 66, 67, 89,
265, 646
It's a Living, 83, 96, 272, 441,
475, 482, 495, 582, 670, 695,
710, 754, 800, 821, 927
It's a Man's World, 84, 99,
131, 162, 201, 390, 615, 631,
758, 896
It's a Small World, 629
It's About Time, 11, 18, 147,
182, 183, 246, 267, 282, 316,
353, 354, 559, 611, 632, 678,
733, 807, 899
It's Alec Templeton Time, 834
It's Always Jan, 23, 112, 435,
442, 580, 652
It's Anybody's Guess, 375
It's Magic, 850
It's News to Me, 211, 223, 291,
302, 420, 501, 714
It's Not Easy, 184, 196, 418,
433, 434, 579, 882

It's Time for Ernie, 481
It's Your Bet, 869
It's Your Move, 66, 165, 329,
457, 605, 743
Ivan the Terrible, 63, 166, 244,
403, 433, 454, 457, 502, 552,
851
Ivanhoe, 121, 599, 600
I've Got a Secret, 13, 16, 17,
69, 105, 149, 189, 200, 215,
216, 234, 235, 278, 408, 450,
469, 579, 598, 603, 616, 642,
653
Izzy and Moe, 152

J

Jack and Mike, 116, 265, 320,
369, 554
Jack and the Beanstalk, 463
Jack Benny Show, The, 24, 44,
56, 78, 92, 213, 234, 245, 349,
515, 621, 765, 792, 873, 908
Jack Carter and Company, 159
Jack Carter Show, The, 108,
141, 159, 715, 796
Jack Drees Sports Show, The,
259
Jack Leonard, 218, 505, 647
Jack Paar Program, The, 145,
180, 243, 580, 650
Jack Paar Show, The, 38, 52,
88, 163, 195, 258, 332, 340,
348, 369, 384, 398, 443, 471,
557, 580, 650, 687, 832, 841,
873, 895
Jackie Gleason Show, The, 94,
123, 151, 218, 297, 303, 334,
335, 341, 349, 369, 397, 441,
459, 491, 506, 534, 575, 578,
642, 697, 798, 831
Jackpot Bowling, 346
Jackpot Bowling Starring
Milton Berle, 15, 81, 267, 653
Jackson 5ive, The, 432
Jacksons, The, 40, 87, 184, 229,
431–433, 538, 747
Jacqueline Bouvier Kennedy,
313, 788, 833
Jacqueline Susann's Valley of
the Dolls, 182
Jacques Fray Music Room,
The, 315, 329, 803, 835
James at 15, 84, 149, 174, 420,
468, 477, 616, 716
Jamie, 191, 246, 629, 662, 736,
850
Jan Murray Time, 523, 614,
632, 663
Jane Eyre, 759
Jane Froman's U.S.A. Canteen,
32, 88, 318, 826
Jane Pickens Show, The, 673,
866
Janet Dean, Registered Nurse,
694
Jason of Star Command, 254,
739
Jaye P. Morgan Show, The,
402, 601, 603

Jayne Mansfield Story, The, 25, 540
Jean Arthur Show, The, 40, 196, 383, 813
Jefferson Drum, 94, 240, 549, 716, 810
Jeffersons, The, 21, 77, 174, 187, 206, 216, 282, 283, 335, 336, 378, 380, 398, 729, 749, 786, 844, 890, 891
Jennifer Slept Here, 8, 279, 441, 535, 619, 754
Jeopardy!, 301, 363, 654
Jericho, 313, 510, 554
Jericho Mile, The, 816
Jerk, Too, The, 876
Jerry Colonna Show, The, 190, 286, 678, 737
Jerry Lewis Show, The, 120, 165, 509, 598, 646, 920
Jerry Reed When You're Hot You're Hot Hour, The, 29, 269, 692, 704, 853, 907, 920
Jessica Novak, 339, 471, 656, 736, 769, 798, 900
Jessie, 407, 412, 429, 448, 516, 525, 630, 869, 870
Jesus of Nazareth, 288, 447, 458, 554, 677, 692
Jetsons, The, 83, 92, 134, 576, 584, 605, 621, 639, 782, 872
Jigsaw, 870
Jigsaw John, 292, 413, 761, 878
Jim Backus Show, The, 48, 828
Jim Henson's Muppet Babies, 400
Jim Nabors Hour, The, 601, 606, 617, 755, 823, 893
Jim Stafford Show, The, 14, 87, 170, 218, 454, 532, 771, 800, 916
Jimmie Rodgers Show, The, 44, 128, 192, 210, 288, 312, 498, 606, 726, 813, 869, 880
Jimmy Blaine's Junior Edition, 90, 213, 887
Jimmy Breslin's People, 110
Jimmy Dean Show, The, 163, 206, 210, 232, 236, 251, 400, 475, 557, 601, 762, 835, 918
Jimmy Durante Presents The Lennon Sisters, 266, 504, 707, 920
Jimmy Durante Show, The, 58, 126, 248, 266, 431, 735
Jimmy Hughes, Rookie Cop, 259, 436, 490, 703
Jimmy Stewart Show, The, 5, 12, 224, 321, 332, 431, 495, 569, 810
Jo Stafford Show, The, 800, 803, 893
Joan Edwards Show, The, 272
Joanie Loves Chachi, 52, 316, 557, 585, 594, 600, 601, 664, 848
Joe & Mabel, 95, 197, 293, 294, 332, 540, 828
Joe and Sons, 51, 165, 449, 587, 801, 812

Joe & Valerie, 8, 79, 86, 205, 276, 304, 347, 678, 707
Joe Bash, 105, 736
Joe Dancer, 92
Joe Forrester, 111, 214, 273, 486, 786
Joe Palooka Story, 844
Joe's World, 56, 87, 141, 201, 312, 477, 735, 768, 773, 929
Joey & Dad, 237, 274, 395, 661, 688, 927
Joey Bishop Show, The, 82, 85, 88, 89, 91, 222, 301, 302, 306, 336, 365, 370, 539, 544, 595, 671, 839, 849, 866
Joey Faye's Frolics, 174, 235, 292, 458, 778
John Byner Comedy Hour, The, 121, 137, 170, 244, 300, 588, 819
John Davidson Show, The, 58, 230, 515, 530, 556, 658, 803
John Forsythe Show, The, 153, 231, 294, 306, 307, 488, 514, 544, 816, 828
John Gary Show, The, 47, 330, 451, 707, 798
John Gunther's High Road, 368
Johnny Belinda, 290, 840
Johnny Carson Show, The, 157, 202, 336, 344, 686, 737
Johnny Cash Presents The Everly Brothers Show, 284, 405, 566
Johnny Cash Show, The, 25, 158, 159, 162, 539, 551, 666, 804, 863, 872
Johnny Come Lately, 158
Johnny Goes Home, 158
Johnny Johnston Show, The, 181
Johnny Jupiter, 531, 833
Johnny Mann's Stand Up and Cheer, 539
Johnny Midnight, 636, 671
Johnny Olsen's Rumpus Room, 642
Johnny Ringo, 241, 266, 345, 768
Johnny Staccato, 163, 176
Johns Hopkins Science Review, The, 183, 678
Joker! Joker! Joker!, 63
Joker's Wild, The, 63, 215
Jonathan Winters Show, The, 38, 56, 60, 119, 171, 218, 222, 223, 255, 281, 334, 420, 528, 654, 697, 727, 744, 844, 893, 913
Jonny Quest, 108, 555, 584, 721, 806
Jordan Chance, The, 767
Joseph Cotten Show, The, 205
Joseph Schildkraut Presents, 756
Josie and the Pussycats, 8, 486, 872
Judd, for the Defense, 86, 927

Judge for Yourself, 14, 155, 240, 435, 444, 452, 784
Judge Horton and the Scottsboro Boys, 405
Judge Roy Bean. See The Adventures of Judge Roy Bean.
Judgment: The Trial of Julius and Ethel Rosenberg, 798
Judy Garland Show, The, 165, 300, 327, 332, 512, 515, 614, 861
Judy Splinters, 249
Juke Box Jury, 680
Julia, 12, 69, 107, 155, 200, 341, 394, 406, 436, 513, 553, 590, 630, 691, 779, 804, 853, 898, 906, 908, 911
Julie and Carol at Carnegie Hall, 28, 129
Julie Andrews Hour, The, 28, 171, 334, 515, 717, 903
Julie Andrews' Invitation to the Dance with Rudolf Nureyev, 29
Julie Andrews Show, The, 463
Julie Farr, M.D., 821
Julius La Rosa Show, The, 47, 161, 228, 237, 409, 494, 509, 538, 798
June Allyson Show, The, 108
Jungle Book, The, 304
Jungle Jim, 315, 426, 887
Junior Press Conference, 371
Just a Little Inconvenience, 800
Just Me and You, 496
Just Men!, 895
Just Our Luck, 118, 143, 160, 339, 557, 562, 754, 780
Justice, 584, 686
Juvenile Jury, 62, 63, 668

K

Kallikaks, The, 179, 270, 421, 563, 654, 670
Kane and Abel, 817
Karen, 22, 179, 242, 248, 259, 275, 338, 471, 490, 494, 533, 690, 692, 764, 857, 882, 915
Kate & Allie, 218, 396, 478, 585, 744–746, 785
Kate Loves a Mystery, 393, 447, 610, 818
Kate McShane, 371, 563, 579
Kate Smith Evening Hour, The, 19, 134, 190, 588, 788
Kate Smith Hour, The, 127, 737
Kate Smith Show, The, 396, 780, 788
Katherine, 912, 920
Kay Kyser's Kollege of Musical Knowledge, 78, 256, 357, 408, 413, 452, 485, 547, 654, 781, 797
Kay O'Brien, 76, 452, 520, 736, 789, 795, 925

Kaz, 44, 150, 503, 505, 643, 915, 921
Keane Brothers Show, The, 139, 200, 404, 459, 539
Keefe Brasselle Show, The, 4, 107, 231, 307, 359, 458, 749
Keep It In the Family, 107, 628, 642
Keep On Truckin', 8, 66, 67, 130, 192, 286, 300, 301, 694, 696, 718, 750, 765, 821, 848
Keep Posted, 735, 798
Keep Talking, 22, 69, 88, 156, 163, 172, 235, 363, 375, 558, 578, 709, 910
Kelly Monteith Show, The, 74, 202, 596
Ken Berry "Wow" Show, The, 83, 222, 328, 353, 450, 467, 486, 490, 551, 584, 625, 727, 858, 929
Ken Murray Show, The, 23, 81, 85, 197, 279, 289, 349, 413, 445, 486, 526, 610, 614, 877, 916
Kennedy, 299
Kentucky Jones, 243, 501, 525, 602, 711, 884, 885, 916
Key to the Ages, 524
Key to the Missing, 445
Khan, 247, 471, 821, 830
Kid from Left Field, The, 187, 574, 745
Kid from Nowhere, The, 260
Kid Gloves, 238, 348, 762
Kid with the Broken Halo, The, 19, 187, 876
Kid with the 200 I.Q., The, 187
Kids & Company, 642, 855
Kids Say the Darndest Things, 513
Kieran's Kaleidoscope, 469
Kiernan's Corner, 469
Kildare, 168
Kill Me if You Can, 10
Killdozer, 873
Killer in the Family, A, 543
Killer on Board, 815
Killers, The, 195, 701
Kim, 647
King, 123, 854
King Family Show, The, 47, 151, 473, 712
King Lear, 718, 889
King of Diamonds, 208, 378
Kingdom of the Sea, 207
King's Crossing, 178, 249, 314, 378, 448, 585, 815, 931
Kings Row, 115, 134, 415, 450, 463, 506, 811
Kingston: Confidential, 132, 400, 406, 642
Kit Carson. See The Adventures of Kit Carson.
Kitty Foyle, 43
Klondike, 93, 182, 195, 493, 827
Knight Rider, 227, 273, 390, 391, 410, 577, 610, 659
Knots Landing, 44, 54, 73, 93, 113, 170, 184, 214, 220, 226, 244, 250, 261, 262, 276, 286,

309, 324, 326, 332, 340, 347, 369, 385, 389, 407, 414, 416, 434, 452, 467, 468, 492, 502, 520, 531, 554, 562, 580, 587, 590, 614, 627, 632, 667, 669, 670, 677, 678, 707, 730, 737, 743, 767, 769, 770, 772, 857, 858, 868
Knute Rockne—All American, 637
Kobb's Korner, 278, 318, 326, 425
Kodak Request Performance, 179
Kodiak, 86, 95, 872, 873
Kojak, 196, 214, 250, 281, 315, 366, 467, 488, 644, 739, 751, 752, 848, 865
Kolchak: The Night Stalker, 296, 365, 567, 568, 635, 822
Kovacs on the Korner, 481
Kraft Music Hall, The, 4, 25, 38, 47, 55, 131, 137, 170, 191, 262, 324, 332, 401, 471, 528, 557, 574, 640, 811
Kraft Music Hall Presents Sandler & Young, 151, 658, 748, 914, 926
Kraft Music Hall Presents: The Dave King Show, 97, 307, 324, 361, 406, 471, 530, 548, 650, 756
Kraft Music Hall Presents the Des O'Connor Show, 53, 205, 255, 531, 625, 638, 658, 747, 807
Kraft Mystery Theater, 324
Kraft Summer Music Hall, The, 149, 230, 390, 431, 473, 515
Kraft Suspense Theatre, 82, 553, 872
Kraft Television Theatre, 43, 69, 72, 85, 127, 151, 152, 352, 356, 366, 389, 401, 411, 447, 463, 476, 491, 504, 542, 546, 564, 626, 665, 696, 698, 700, 706, 729, 759, 764, 803, 923
Kreisler Bandstand, 721
Krofft Superstars, The, 65
Krypton Factor, The, 177
Kuda Bux, Hindu Mystic, 136, 547, 853
Kukla, Fran & Ollie, 18, 258, 279, 290, 400, 481, 842, 843
Kung Fu, 7, 153, 154, 215, 232, 421, 525, 526, 536, 666, 856

L

L.A. Law, 83, 247, 268, 273, 361, 378, 693, 792, 851
Laboratory, 602
Ladies Be Seated, 600, 661
Ladies' Man, 34, 270, 363, 465, 606, 683, 741, 795
Lady Blue, 7, 237, 733, 924
Lady's Not for Burning, The, 168
Lamp Unto My Feet, 665, 729

Lancer, 53, 67, 112, 263, 557, 682, 800
Land of the Giants, 38, 197, 370, 455, 526, 545, 555, 925
Lanigan's Rabbi, 151, 152, 259, 543, 652, 794
Laramie, 85, 101, 136, 137, 143, 150, 151, 208, 320, 412, 519, 535, 628, 683, 696, 788
Laredo, 106, 121, 148, 288, 791, 915
Larry Storch Show, The, 94, 814
Lash of the West, 495, 550, 745, 830
Lassie, 8, 13, 102, 108, 134, 169, 180, 181, 241, 290, 294, 295, 394, 460, 499, 500, 516, 517, 555, 557, 567, 664, 688, 708, 711, 726, 772, 794, 797, 866, 899, 902
Lassiter, 713
Last Convertible, The, 9, 103, 104, 229, 343, 472, 561, 620, 632, 694, 770, 786, 809, 825
Last Days of Pompeii, The, 257
Last Hurrah, The, 638
Last Precinct, The, 35, 117, 261, 276, 301, 392, 421, 629, 667, 729, 891, 900, 922
Last Resort, The, 108, 205, 288, 320, 479, 495, 641, 855
Last Ride of the Dalton Gang, The, 899
Last Word, The, 252, 282, 431
Late Night with David Letterman, 238, 353, 507, 767, 890
Late Show, The, 720
Late Summer Early Fall Bert Convy Show, The, 62, 102, 196, 436, 678, 758
Laugh Line, 522, 860
Laugh Trax, 538
Laugh-In. See Rowan and Martin's Laugh-In.
Laugh-In (revival), 33, 43, 93, 95, 105, 291, 301, 323, 340, 681, 693, 758, 783, 904, 905
Laughs for Sale, 541
Laverne & Shirley, 269, 308, 328, 360, 402, 488, 543, 546, 573, 580, 675, 774, 895, 902, 903
Law, The, 407, 510
Law and Mr. Jones, The, 158, 238, 287, 897
Law of the Plainsman, 30, 338, 526, 545
Lawbreaker, 553
Lawless Years, The, 362, 454
Lawman, The, 121, 165, 182, 621, 711, 739, 772
Lawrence Welk Show, The, 8, 11, 23, 25, 40, 58, 93, 105, 127, 128, 165, 222, 237, 264, 292, 301, 302, 308, 334, 386, 413, 416, 417, 421, 428, 440, 468, 471, 504, 511, 515, 516, 519, 584, 624, 625, 629, 648,

663, 695, 722, 726, 759, 791, 797, 821, 852, 888, 889, 906, 930

Lawrence Welk's Top Tunes and New Talent, 888

Lawyers, The, 143, 288, 430

Laytons, The, 696, 697, 830

Lazarus Syndrome, The, 315, 352, 424, 572, 874

Leave It to Beaver, 56, 60, 70, 87, 110, 203, 236, 257, 286, 344, 555, 643, 646, 647, 658, 696, 809, 828

Leave It to Larry, 8, 9, 72, 459, 754, 872

Leave It to the Girls, 91, 122, 291, 295, 568, 576, 687, 735, 740, 861

Legend of Jesse James, The, 161, 254, 446, 571, 587, 900

Legend of Lizzie Borden, The, 596

Legend of the Black Hand, The, 734

Legmen, 8, 140, 362, 834

Leo & Liz in Beverly Hills, 55, 382, 471, 480, 662, 667, 678

Leo and Me, 309

Leslie Uggams Show, The, 14, 22, 120, 394, 471, 572, 590, 717, 722, 855

Let My People Go, 65

Let's Dance, 18, 299, 494, 597, 858, 919

Let's Make a Deal, 375, 811

Let's Rhumba, 230

Let's See, 472

Let's Take a Trip, 309

Letter to Loretta, 926

Letter to Three Wives, A, 796

Letters to Laugh-In, 648

Lewis & Clark, 301, 354, 410, 435, 453, 479, 513, 575

Liar's Club, 35, 88, 213, 299, 330, 348, 417, 525, 764, 895

Liberace Show, The, 510, 511, 597, 658, 883

Lidsville, 708

Lie Detector, 50

Lieutenant, The, 26, 71, 313, 477, 517, 587, 628, 629, 665, 671, 734, 863, 864

Lieutenant Schuster's Wife, 879

Life and Legend of Wyatt Earp, The, 25, 58, 68, 112, 114, 203, 249, 277, 309, 370, 386, 395, 432, 495, 519, 636, 639, 672, 690, 749, 813, 819, 828, 829, 842, 916, 918

Life and Times of Eddie Roberts, The, 56, 170, 416, 754, 834

Life and Times of Grizzly Adams, The, 89, 370, 690, 767

Life Begins at Eighty, 62, 63, 149, 805

Life Is Worth Living, 770

Life of Leonardo da Vinci, The, 506

Life of Riley, The, 76, 94, 120, 226, 237, 264, 302, 341, 342, 412, 483, 546, 590, 604, 639, 658, 705, 713, 748, 821, 824, 844, 913

Life with Elizabeth, 111, 280, 330, 598, 618, 895

Life with Father, 21, 83, 163, 356, 461, 503, 590, 631, 704, 718, 734, 835, 853

Life with Linkletter, 513, 541

Life with Lucy, 20, 25, 54, 267, 350, 509, 759

Life with Luigi, 307, 337, 617, 668, 703, 738, 774, 779

Life with Snarky Parker, 124

Lifeline, 70

Life's Most Embarrassing Moments, 16

Lifestyles of the Rich and Famous, 499

Lights, Camera, Action, 473

Lights Out, 76, 154, 307, 324, 495, 551, 582, 592, 653, 692

Like Mom, Like Me, 577

Lily, 275, 689, 845

Lily: Sold Out, 845

Lily Tomlin, 275, 366, 678, 845

Lime Street, 46, 110, 320, 379, 791, 801, 870

Lineup, The, 21, 27, 64, 248, 506, 704, 851, 878

Linus the Lionhearted, 914

Lisa, Bright and Dark, 601

Listen to Your Heart, 432

Little Gloria, Happy at Last, 493, 677, 803

Little House: A New Beginning, 338

Little House on the Prairie, 26, 38, 53, 56, 64, 66, 99, 126, 134, 251, 301, 312, 317, 318, 332, 337, 357, 360, 362, 370, 430, 466, 486, 489, 490, 507, 531, 642, 654, 732, 736, 755, 779, 810, 825, 848, 852

Little Mo, 500

Little Moon of Alban, 385

Little People, The, 461

Little Revue, The, 254, 283, 443, 494, 557, 773, 858, 886

Little Women, 3, 267, 339, 362, 383, 398, 538, 571, 619, 677, 681, 754, 871, 926, 927

Live from the Met, 696

Live Like a Millionaire, 180, 565, 622, 639

Lively Ones, The, 225, 297, 620, 639, 800, 923

Living Proof: The Hank Williams, Jr., Story, 840

Liza With a "Z," 307

Lloyd Bridges Show, The, 111

Lloyd Thaxton Show, The, 835

Lobo, 8, 102, 126, 140, 160, 205, 207, 219, 423, 468, 773, 882

Lock Up, 147, 148, 255

Logan's Run, 160, 386, 581, 594, 681

Lohman and Barkley Show, 836

Lone Ranger, The, 30, 37, 131, 310, 387, 404, 521, 590, 597, 778, 779, 816, 918

Lone Wolf, The, 395

Loneliest Runner, The, 490

Loner, The, 111, 765

Long Hot Summer, The, 332, 537, 636, 640, 730, 772, 836, 916

Long Way Home, A, 857

Longstreet, 254, 312, 313, 501, 554, 716

Loose Change, 883

Loretta Young Show, The, 20, 27, 62, 70, 95, 143, 198, 209, 214, 247, 284, 315, 535, 595, 617, 626, 636, 726, 755, 802, 925

Lorne Greene's Last of the Wild, 360

Lost Honor of Kathryn Beck, The, 839

Lost in Space, 160, 345, 385, 482, 517, 558, 611, 851, 903

Lost Saucer, 136, 617

Lotsa Luck, 241, 316, 429, 477, 748

Lottery, 191, 612

Lou Grant, 5, 23, 41, 54, 57, 70, 76, 181, 240, 270, 302, 309, 366, 369, 422, 464, 542, 651, 681, 708, 871, 900

Louis Armstrong—Chicago Style, 865

Love, American Style, 13, 45, 55, 82, 84, 101, 126, 131, 141, 142, 151, 183, 197–199, 208, 217, 231, 233, 241, 243, 249, 276, 285, 286, 330, 336, 344, 365, 379, 419, 428, 446, 496, 528, 543, 548, 571, 576, 591, 623, 655, 662, 671, 682, 685, 686, 705, 734, 839, 857, 859, 874, 880, 882, 891, 903, 904, 909, 910, 919

Love & Marriage, 35, 53, 241, 378, 458, 528, 708

Love at First Bite, 377

Love Boat, The, 19, 20, 23, 34, 55, 62, 82, 84, 97, 99, 102, 127, 135, 218, 239, 249, 252, 273, 286, 323, 330, 346, 350, 355, 363, 381, 390, 396, 398, 425, 447, 476, 479, 491, 492, 497, 533, 565, 569, 571, 579, 593, 602, 604, 605, 621, 671, 681, 685, 700, 713, 724, 745, 779, 781, 807, 815, 824, 835, 836, 881, 894, 907, 909, 920, 924

Love Connection, The, 918

Love Is a Many Splendored Thing, 50, 88, 341, 542, 590

Love Is Forever, 683, 918

Love Is Not Enough, 161

Love of Life, 13, 85, 86, 144, 171, 227, 341, 404, 542, 562, 614, 845, 876

Love on A Rooftop, 44, 102, 151, 244, 467, 515, 867

Love, Sidney, 124, 469, 484, 631, 660, 696, 836, 930

Love Story, 686
Love That Bob, 217
Love That Jill, 275, 370, 438, 527, 528, 627, 733, 806
Love Thy Neighbor, 126, 292, 453, 532, 547, 553, 651
Loves Me, Loves Me Not, 247, 339, 343, 585
Love's Savage Fury, 807
Loving, 121, 221, 541
Lucan, 117, 350, 697
Lucas Tanner, 2, 70, 268, 388, 613, 697, 719, 764, 795
Lucie Arnaz Show, The, 37, 124, 431, 723, 879
Lucky Pup, 119
Lucy Moves to NBC, 350
Lucy Show, The, 27, 37, 54, 55, 94, 198, 208, 210, 266, 310, 315, 328, 346, 350, 369, 387, 454, 464, 490, 542, 549, 597, 614, 631, 723, 731, 859
Lucy-Desi Comedy Hour, The, 35, 54, 314, 461, 533, 859
Lunch with Soupy Sales, 746
Lux Show Starring Rosemary Clooney, The, 181, 245, 445, 593
Lux Video Theatre, 5, 21, 37, 68, 152, 209, 404, 412, 461, 477, 482, 534, 554, 555, 669, 701, 738, 760, 764, 772, 799, 806, 828

M

M Squad, 553, 626, 712
Ma Perkins, 875
Mac Davis Show, The, 66, 233, 601, 679, 773, 778, 920
Macahans, The, 37, 103
Macbeth, 458
MacGruder & Loud, 102, 237, 334, 357, 386, 561, 734
MacGyver, 26, 27, 275
Mackenzies of Paradise Cove, The, 169, 367, 375, 397, 459, 470, 547, 592, 809, 876
Mackenzie's Raiders, 150, 340, 830
MacNeil-Lehrer Report, 534
Madame X., 852, 888
Madame's Place, 293, 301, 394, 489, 844
Made in America, 195, 613, 784, 806
Madigan, 899
Madison Square Garden Highlights, 344, 518
Mae West, 671
Mafia Princess, 219
Maggie, 80, 302, 379, 428, 433, 434, 722
Maggi's Private Wire, 576
Magic Cottage, 580
Magician, The, 89, 166, 210, 219, 782, 882
Magician of Lublin, The, 894

Magnum, P.I., 198, 250, 406, 415, 511, 516, 531, 539, 608, 680, 760, 763, 764, 889
Main Street, 368
Major Dell Conway of the Flying Tigers, 24, 301, 355, 409, 473, 501, 663, 862
Majority Rules, 600, 683, 874
Make Me Laugh, 510, 538
Make Mine Manhattan, 140
Make Room for Daddy. See Danny Thomas Show.
Make Room for Granddaddy, 160, 195, 363, 376, 379, 423, 433, 521, 580, 837
Make That Spare, 276, 445
Make the Connection, 105, 239, 475, 572, 699, 700, 895
Make Your Own Kind of Music, 152, 276, 294, 407, 512, 625, 659, 829
Makin' It, 32, 54, 409, 587, 619, 666, 683, 724, 766, 848
Making a Living, 496
Making of a Male Model, The, 403, 522, 561
Making the Grade, 438, 495, 532, 589, 619, 668, 702, 891
Malibu, 182, 253
Malibu Run, 840
Malibu U, 56, 623, 624, 679
Malice in Wonderland, 831
Mama, 144, 205, 313, 319, 330, 460, 487, 539, 564, 604, 715, 862, 914, 917
Mama Malone, 20, 27, 120, 365, 397, 451, 458, 541, 715, 782, 923
Mama Rosa, 26, 144, 241, 761
Mama's Family, 33, 34, 83, 84, 119, 129, 480, 498, 499, 527, 562, 895
Man About the House, 647
Man Against Crime, 74, 521, 523, 684
Man and the Challenge, The, 340, 617
Man and the City, The, 289, 290, 682, 692, 929
Man Behind the Badge, The, 86, 733
Man Called Intrepid, A, 629
Man Called Shenandoah, A, 415
Man Called Sloane, A, 148, 194, 217, 640, 689
Man Called X, The, 819
Man from Atlantis, 127, 257, 262, 320, 413, 520, 527, 596, 904
Man From Blackhawk, The, 726
Man from Interpol, 520, 921
Man from UNCLE, The, 96, 155, 156, 176, 384, 429, 560, 597, 626, 748, 848, 863, 864
Man in a Suitcase, 105
Man in the Iron Mask, The, 168, 570
Man of the Week, 183, 211
Man of the World, 807, 808

Man on the Moon, 211
Man Who Came to Dinner, The, 890
Man Who Never Was, The, 231, 378, 493, 811, 922
Man with a Camera, 115, 300, 815
Man Without a Country, 2
Man Without a Gun, 390, 590, 701, 831
Manhattan Maharaja, 31, 89, 631
Manhattan Showcase, 258, 324, 351, 608, 878
Manhattan Spotlight, 848
Manhattan Transfer, 371, 391, 539, 625, 627, 654
Manhunt, 35, 66, 209, 329, 398, 450, 578, 805
Manhunter, The, 124, 409, 418, 419, 694, 840
Manimal, 26, 530, 722, 750, 852
Manions of America, The, 117, 530, 573, 797
Mannix, 70, 96, 143, 177, 193, 194, 281, 298, 397, 424, 523, 705, 734, 805, 822, 825, 929
Mantovani, 196, 541
Many Happy Returns, 187, 252, 292, 345, 540, 569, 743, 864
Many Loves of Dobie Gillis, The, 51, 69, 78, 89, 131, 138, 176, 242, 247, 290, 292, 313, 318, 403, 404, 436, 511, 643, 650, 754, 839, 888
March of Medicine, The, 357, 765
Marco Polo, 629
Marcus Welby, M.D., 11, 67, 68, 109, 114, 184, 277, 292, 343, 400, 405, 424, 632, 669, 673, 682, 723, 755, 781, 856, 857, 864, 869, 880, 926, 927
Marge and Gower Champion Show, The, 168, 486, 667, 684, 715, 897
Marge and Jeff, 140, 361
Margie, 56, 334, 429, 430, 656, 665, 827, 906
Marie, 60, 66, 168, 301, 358, 402, 421, 428, 429, 593, 630, 647, 736, 909
Marilyn McCoo and Billy Davis, Jr. Show, The, 39, 231, 504, 564, 616, 707
Marilyn: The Untold Story, 632
Mark Saber, 128, 198
Markham, 587, 761
Marriage, The, 114, 212, 703, 816, 829
Married: The First Year, 73, 141, 280, 365, 366, 482, 539, 559, 563, 625, 868
Marshal of Gunsight Pass, The, 7, 43, 236, 392, 655
Martha Raye Show, The, 227, 359, 409, 700
Martha Wright Show, The, 369, 655, 919
Martian Chronicles, The, 422

Martin Kane, Private Eye, 140, 326, 359, 406, 473, 574, 606, 630, 751, 808, 838, 847, 848

Marty, 671

Marty Feldman Comedy Machine, The, 293, 417, 589, 776, 792, 889

Marty Robbins' Spotlight, 721

Marva Collins Story, The, 854

Mary, 42, 137, 180, 288, 379, 452, 460, 484, 507, 570, 598, 744, 769, 809, 826, 844, 882

Mary Hartman, Mary Hartman, 11, 69, 82, 90, 123, 129, 161, 186, 229, 285, 348, 391, 402, 425, 438, 452, 470, 487, 495, 496, 542, 582, 610, 611, 676, 722, 758, 794, 800, 832

Mary Kay and Johnny, 804, 838, 892

Mary Margaret McBride, 559

Mary Tyler Moore Hour, The, 348, 460, 518, 598, 695, 862

Mary Tyler Moore Show, The, 22, 41, 103, 126, 164, 218, 279, 334, 383, 451, 477, 499, 500, 533, 546, 598, 599, 604, 672, 673, 719, 748, 812, 873, 887, 894, 895, 912

Masada, 93, 154, 180, 230, 250, 292, 312, 426, 644, 647, 651, 674, 691, 774, 790, 816, 817, 857, 879, 892, 914

M*A*S*H, 6, 10, 11, 33, 45, 50, 122, 127, 170, 175, 180, 200, 232, 289, 290, 347, 353, 382, 394, 430, 449, 467, 514, 527, 546, 558, 580, 585, 591, 602–604, 618, 644, 668, 670, 671, 676, 719, 728, 729, 743, 757, 780, 808–810, 812, 816, 822, 825, 840, 867

Mask, The, 584, 686

Masquerade, 18, 284, 331, 833, 836

Masquerade Party, 89, 103, 105, 156, 172, 181, 190, 221, 234, 253, 271, 278, 283, 288, 395, 445, 508, 510, 578, 583, 619, 653, 656, 657, 740, 773, 913, 925

Master, The, 480, 859, 862

Master of Ballantrae, The, 840

Master of the Game, 18, 88, 146, 152, 171, 221, 247, 378, 492, 526, 545, 607, 676, 705, 763, 819

Masterpiece Theatre, 199, 257, 385, 545

Masters of Magic, 65

Match Game, The, 699, 700

Match Game P.M., 234, 299, 549, 661, 699, 708, 794, 895

Match Game/Hollywood Squares Hour, The, 67

Matinee Theatre, 63, 196, 426, 462

Mating Season, The, 37

Matlock, 364, 411, 690

Matt Dennis Show, The, 242

Matt Helm, 253, 282, 310, 311, 805

Matt Houston, 32, 112, 270, 318, 400, 415, 471, 738, 750, 921

Matt Lincoln, 118, 273, 381, 494, 667

Matter of Life or Death, A, 224

Matter of Sex, A, 803

Matter of Wife and Death, A, 833

Maude, 22, 39, 49, 51, 58, 303, 355, 534, 538, 562, 585, 606, 642, 676, 729, 879

Maverick, 48, 110, 185, 193, 222, 327, 328, 463, 464, 599, 600, 891, 930

Max Liebman Presents, 514, 749

Maya, 469, 631

Mayberry R.F.D., 67, 83, 84, 251, 307, 308, 332, 334, 335, 347, 389, 474, 512

Mayor of Hollywood, 54, 213, 268, 640, 730

Mayor of the Town, 138, 316, 592

Mazie, 19

McClain's Law, 37, 191, 248, 295, 314

McCloud, 32, 146, 160, 343, 527, 610, 624, 706, 788, 857, 884

McCoy, 122, 123, 219

McHale's Navy, 55, 71, 101, 197, 263, 301, 302, 391, 527, 532, 533, 594, 633, 749, 761, 817, 866, 907, 919, 923

McKeever & The Colonel, 198, 274, 314, 450, 490, 831

McLean Stevenson Show, The, 410, 625, 740, 809, 810, 818, 892, 898

McMillan and Wife, 30, 32, 263, 297, 339, 384, 422, 682, 700, 744, 745, 757, 807, 817, 873

Me and Maxx, 282, 586, 750, 820, 893

Me and Mom, 229, 274, 447, 831

Me & Mrs. C., 68, 571, 614, 707

Me and the Chimp, 84, 205, 338, 478

Me on the Radio, 818

Medic, 100, 927

Medical Center, 10, 54, 116, 128, 142, 168, 223, 224, 263, 283, 298, 374, 392, 411, 412, 426, 579, 670, 682, 705, 719, 778, 825, 839, 847, 849

Medical Horizons, 344, 420

Medical Story, 615

Meet Corliss Archer, 52, 277, 428, 748, 774, 833

Meet McGraw, 248, 523, 570

Meet Millie, 305, 376, 453, 697, 733, 864, 866, 914

Meet the Boss, 217

Meet the Champions, 506

Meet the Press, 116, 595, 735, 798, 799

Meet the Veep, 59, 346

Meet Your Congress, 597

Meeting of Minds, 16, 17, 579

Melba, 386, 433, 580, 591, 599, 667

Melba Moore-Clifton Davis Show, The, 148, 186, 231, 511, 599, 728, 847

Melody, Harmony & Rhythm, 60, 243, 250, 703

Melody Street, 118, 136, 335, 497, 567, 608

Melody Tour, 298, 316, 341, 467, 524, 710, 761, 796

Memorial Day, 871

Memory of Eva Ryker, The, 917

Men at Law, 558

Men From Shiloh, The, 175, 356, 536, 574

Men into Space, 340, 526, 705

Men of Annapolis, 563

Men of Tomorrow, 592

Menasha the Magnificent, 218, 783, 784

Mercury Theatre, 189, 416, 811

Meredith Willson Show, The, 907, 930

Merry Widow, The, 611

Merv Griffin Show, The, 142, 363, 513, 771, 797, 819, 849, 918

Metropolitan Opera Auditions of the Air, 213

MGM Parade, 613, 673

Miami Undercover, 103, 359

Miami Vice, 120, 248, 443, 641, 749, 828, 839, 906

Michael Nesmith in Television Parts, 408, 624, 738

Michael Shayne, 179, 242, 252, 655, 707, 712, 737, 811

Mickey, 400, 619, 703, 731, 846

Mickey Mouse Club, The, 8, 127, 209, 271, 285, 321, 338, 354, 669, 673, 732

Mickey Rooney Show, The, 54, 149, 306, 420, 608, 731, 846

Mickey Spillane's Mike Hammer, 64, 79, 95, 130, 273, 347, 458, 568, 681, 818, 904

Mickie Finn's, 193, 228, 297, 540

Midnight Offerings, 896

Midnight Special, The, 702, 721, 915

Midwestern Hayride, 173, 206, 250, 284, 413, 473, 586, 715, 775, 835, 852

Mighty Mouse, 644

Mike Douglas Show, The, 215, 256, 689

Mike Wallace Interviews, 874, 875

Million Dollar Face, The, 219, 374

Million Dollar Rip-Off, The, 687

Millionaire, The, 30, 86, 122, 241, 317, 437, 588, 888, 923
Milton Berle in the Kraft Music Hall, 81
Milton Berle Show, The, 47, 79, 81, 189, 319, 338, 506, 521, 542, 558, 622, 735, 742, 773, 801, 814, 853, 855, 927
Miracle Worker, The, 43, 338, 564
Mirror, Mirror, 825, 864
Misadventures of Sheriff Lobo. See Lobo.
Misfits of Science, 176, 206, 374, 412, 549, 588, 919
Miss All American Beauty, 500
Miss America Pageant, The, 189, 277, 333, 657
Miss Winslow and Son, 96, 123, 153, 297, 547, 698, 707, 773
Mrs. Columbo, 216
Mrs. G. Goes to College, 80
Missiles of October, The, 239, 500
Missing Children: A Mother's Story, 920
Missing Links, 574
Mission: Impossible, 23, 51, 86, 96, 143, 167, 223, 276, 333, 357, 358, 406, 443, 488, 527, 605, 628, 644, 723, 880, 905, 929
Mississippi, The, 588, 769, 871, 917
Mr. Adams and Eve, 148, 261, 262, 526, 703, 732
Mr. & Mrs. North, 113, 242, 243, 682
Mr. Arsenic, 852
Mr. Belvedere, 71, 354, 403, 814, 855, 890
Mr. Black, 175
Mr. Broadway, 293, 575, 593, 807, 808, 822
Mr. Citizen, 271
Mr. Deeds Goes to Town, 62, 384, 544, 867
Mr. District Attorney, 111, 259, 450, 523, 867
Mr. Dugan, 515
Mr. Ed, 21, 310, 406, 459, 490, 533, 688, 783, 924
Mr. Garlund, 692, 846
Mr. Horn, 154, 899
Mr. I Magination, 279, 778, 842, 850
Mr. Lucky, 11, 122, 551, 760, 761, 867
Mr. Malone, 848
Mr. Merlin, 107, 422, 450, 686
Mr. Mom, 522
Mr. Novak, 46, 54, 62, 187, 202, 251, 257, 277, 312, 313, 380, 399, 419, 434, 582, 671, 676, 711, 723, 734, 771, 834, 931
Mr. Peepers, 79, 178, 207, 208, 273, 297, 302, 444, 522, 566, 637, 696, 703, 769, 822, 850, 853, 878, 879

Mr. Roberts, 336, 382, 430, 706, 781, 784, 790, 804
Mr. Smith, 264, 318, 325, 434, 543, 887
Mr. Smith Goes to Washington, 302, 429, 529, 655, 656, 880
Mr. Sunshine, 48, 318, 386, 477, 550, 829
Mr. T, 924
Mr. T and Tina, 29, 93, 137, 320, 492, 604, 688, 823
Mr. Terrific, 330, 569, 790, 817
Mr. Wizard Close-Ups, 401
Mistral's Daughter, 710
Misunderstood Monsters, The, 154
Mitzi, 171
Mixed Doubles, 52, 298, 318, 428, 904
Mobile One, 199, 362, 886, 893
Mod Squad, The, 29, 185, 233, 352, 514, 558, 749, 837, 880, 903
Modern Romances, 391
Mohawk Showroom, 179, 257, 691, 802
Moment of Crisis, 438
Mona McCluskey, 588, 688, 724, 737, 817, 864
Monday Night Baseball, 113, 162, 204, 260, 325, 336, 354, 432, 480, 482, 488, 562, 585, 653, 686, 780, 814, 855, 885, 895, 907, 915
Monday Night Fights, 518, 753, 755
Monday Night Football, 204, 337, 432, 455, 583, 618, 780, 829, 906
Money on the Side, 857
Moneychangers, The, 189, 300, 361, 677
Monitor, 239, 250, 794
Monkees, The, 251, 446, 475, 507, 542, 624, 772, 846
Monroes, The, 26, 114, 402, 443, 516, 586, 757, 794, 821, 830, 892
Monte Carlo Show, The, 883
Montefuscos, The, 32, 148, 203, 227, 254, 653, 655, 674, 698, 782, 808, 867
Monty Nash, 366
Moon for the Misbegotten, A, 300
Moonlighting, 69, 771, 772, 906
Morey Amsterdam Show, The, 22, 151, 366, 822
Mork & Mindy, 116, 234, 253, 396, 434, 436, 467, 468, 680, 799, 838, 904, 910, 913, 914
Morning, 484
Morning After, The, 860
Morning Court, 368
Morning Show, 291, 363, 650
Morningstar/Eveningstar, 5, 202, 214, 312, 347, 425, 495, 497, 507, 668, 672, 707, 751, 777, 786, 908

Moses—The Lawgiver, 488, 654, 691, 835, 841
Most Deadly Game, The, 74, 535, 591
Most Important People, The, 155, 156
Most Wanted, 384, 632, 714, 799
Mother and Daughter: The Loving War, 888
Mothers-in-Law, The, 33, 34, 36, 55, 150, 236, 302, 737, 875
Motown Revue, 373, 714, 725, 794, 916
Motown 25th Anniversary Special, 432
Mouse Factory, The, 740
Movie Game, The, 95
Movieland Quiz, 112, 124, 264
Movin' On, 8, 196, 363, 370, 431, 585, 672, 749
Moviola, 219
Muggable Mary, 857
Mulligan's Stew, 8, 176, 214, 252, 254, 369, 478, 502, 548, 683
Munsters, The, 237, 340, 368, 445, 508, 648, 660, 685, 737
Munsters' Revenge, The, 368, 606
Muppet Show, The, 346, 400, 401, 424, 601, 622, 649, 897
Murder Can Hurt You, 807
Murder in Coweta County, 162
Murder in Peyton Place, 290, 809
Murder in Texas, 364, 734
Murder on Flight 502, 799
Murder, She Wrote, 101, 348, 492, 493, 525, 853, 911
Music at the Meadowbrook, 90, 222, 401, 901
Music Bingo, 337
Music Country, 25
Music 55, 467
Music for a Summer Night, 647
Music Hall, 408, 651
Music Hall America, 130, 740
Music in Velvet, 405, 512, 557, 864
Music on Ice, 102, 226, 243, 256, 261, 783
Music Scene, The, 96, 379, 730, 733, 805, 845, 904
Music Shop, The, 109
Music Show, The, 256, 629, 670, 845, 849, 858, 879
Musical Almanac, 381
Musical Chairs, 92, 172, 510, 582, 850, 869
Musical Comedy Time, 175, 449, 796
Musical Merry-Go-Round, 246, 334, 471, 925
Mussolini, 760
Mutual of Omaha's Wild Kingdom. See Wild Kingdom.
M.V.P., 76

My Darling Daughters Anniversary, 343
My Eyes Are In My Heart, 426
My Favorite Husband, 122, 130, 166, 193, 620, 824, 828, 843
My Favorite Martian, 89, 113, 279, 282, 403, 545, 642, 759, 876
My Friend Flicka, 69, 282, 295, 523, 567, 881
My Friend Irma, 38, 120, 154, 264, 284, 351, 508, 541, 559, 774, 844, 891, 909
My Friend Tony, 167, 897
My Hero, 89, 217, 514
My Husband Is Missing, 818
My Kidnapper, My Love, 800
My Little Margie, 85, 115, 289, 392, 409, 478, 656, 814, 815
My Living Doll, 217, 257, 611, 627
My Mother the Car, 58, 274, 674, 756, 796, 861, 894
My Name Is Barbra, 557
My Partner the Ghost, 236
My Sister Eileen, 51, 73, 98, 458, 732, 817, 893
My Sister Sam, 116, 234, 619, 639, 754
My Son Jeep, 426, 460, 487, 528, 682, 750, 899
My Sweet Charlie, 43, 316
My Three Sons, 16, 21, 72, 116, 186, 196, 241, 247, 264, 311, 314, 315, 326, 344, 354, 418, 511, 515, 527, 533, 534, 555, 575, 591, 601, 631, 647, 665, 797, 844, 850
My World and Welcome to It, 334, 416, 505, 603, 813, 911
Mysteries of Chinatown, 86, 465, 530, 588
Mysteries of the Sea, 336
Mysterious Island of Beautiful Women, The, 873
Mystery, 685
Mystic Warrior, 480

N

Naked City, 55, 61, 74, 83, 128, 155, 195, 268, 287, 288, 312, 366, 476, 537, 558, 567, 571, 575, 630, 731, 751, 759, 768, 810, 815, 888
Nakia, 239, 306, 465, 486, 834
Name of the Game, The, 30, 55, 62, 68, 72, 123, 143, 209, 216, 310, 311, 385, 447, 516, 588, 612, 662, 677, 680, 744, 799, 820, 857, 889, 926
Name That Tune, 79, 215, 246, 272, 394, 435, 466, 668, 855
Name's the Same, The, 12, 96, 132, 286, 435, 510, 578, 616, 685, 699, 806, 907
Nancy, 11, 32, 66, 297, 412, 437, 531, 780
Nancy Drew Mysteries, The, 126, 207, 218, 550, 639, 665, 698, 754

Nancy Walker Show, The, 33, 211, 227, 542, 640, 754, 873
Nanny and the Professor, 58, 254, 328, 488, 503, 520, 590, 716, 903
Nash Airflyte Theater, 331
Nashville 99, 8, 79, 704
Nashville on the Road, 16, 119, 165, 181, 203, 287, 410, 681, 800
Nashville Palace, The, 127, 143, 250, 326, 379, 565, 613, 666, 673, 777, 819
Nat "King" Cole Show, The, 95, 172, 185, 354, 565, 717, 861
National Barn Dance, 344
National Bowling Champions, 909
National Driving Test, The, 702
National Geographic Special, The, 546
National Velvet, 214, 254, 464, 550, 560, 760, 797, 890
Nation's Future, The, 560, 626
Nature of Things, The, 547
Naughty Marietta, 611
Navy Log, 269, 462
NBC Action Playhouse, 547
NBC Adventure Theatre, 301, 574
NBC Comedy Hour, 45, 171, 348, 439, 814, 894, 913
NBC Comedy Playhouse, 375, 463
NBC Comedy Theater, 463
NBC Evening News, 112, 169, 568, 609
NBC Follies, 233, 431, 531, 731
NBC Magazine, 666, 856
NBC Magazine with David Brinkley, 1, 112, 470, 666, 856
NBC Mystery Movie, 619
NBC News Encore, 2
NBC News Overnight, 250, 275, 755
NBC Nightly News, 114, 387, 654, 752, 856
NBC Playhouse, 54
NBC Reports, 874
NBC Sports in Action, 780
NBC Weekend News, 114, 175, 387, 452, 532, 533, 568, 654, 661, 663, 752, 755, 793, 856, 861, 874
NBC's Saturday Night Live, 12, 24, 46, 75, 116, 118, 149, 161, 171, 215, 218, 219, 233, 249, 256, 257, 259, 263, 265, 269, 308, 313, 352, 365, 366, 373, 375, 389, 400, 401, 413, 433, 442, 456, 458, 475, 482, 523, 551, 556, 588, 605, 612, 613, 620, 624, 627, 633, 654, 675, 689, 691, 693, 719, 720, 726, 732, 767, 770, 775, 806, 824, 859, 877, 883, 887, 904
Needles and Pins, 238, 293, 332, 401, 479, 504, 633, 764
Neon Ceiling, The, 356

Nero Wolfe, 195, 200, 415, 587, 868, 921
NET Playhouse, 757
Network, 404
Never Late Than Better, 344
Never Too Young, 257, 695, 711
New Adventures of Huck Finn, The, 164, 390, 757, 770
New Adventures of Martin Kane. See Martin Kane, Private Eye.
New Adventures of Wonder Woman. See Wonder Woman.
New Andy Griffith Show, The, 40, 233, 364, 367, 560, 583, 740
New Avengers. See The Avengers.
New Bill Cosby Show, The, 116, 203, 204, 239, 275, 287, 355, 441, 448, 565, 734, 769, 844
New Breed, The, 80, 179, 606, 627, 729
New Christy Minstrels, The, 625
New Dick Van Dyke Show, The, 112, 134, 229, 234, 258, 267, 299, 349, 491, 681, 709, 720, 738, 770, 860, 862
New Doctors, The, 388, 545, 546, 753, 871
New Fat Albert Show, The, 203, 204
New Kind of Family, A, 109, 338, 395, 399, 410, 414, 431, 524, 561
New Land, The, 37, 71, 318, 520, 529, 594, 739, 840
New Loretta Young Show, The, 243, 457, 671, 695, 816, 826, 881, 925, 926
New Mickey Mouse Club, The, 894
New Odd Couple, The, 27, 108, 256, 341, 450, 662, 757, 847, 907
New Original Wonder Woman, The, 500
New People, The, 97, 375, 437, 607, 641, 699
New Phil Silvers Show, The, 228, 243, 264, 292, 354, 506, 592, 710, 711, 767, 779, 864, 902
New Show, The, 115, 399, 434, 609, 837
New Treasure Hunt. See Treasure Hunt.
New York Confidential, 847, 848
New York Giants Quarterback Huddle, 390, 648
New Zoo Revue, The, 142, 918
Newhart, 32, 150, 255, 262, 314, 412, 453, 541, 626, 654, 680, 748, 758, 867, 900, 924
Newlywed Game, The, 62, 282
News and Views, 67, 335

News At Sunrise, 176
News Is the News, The, 233,
    449, 597, 836, 910
Newsbreak, 645
Newsweek Analysis, 512
Next Step Beyond, The, 626
NFL Action, 286
NFL Today, The, 333
Nicholas Nickleby, 458
Nichols, 70, 327, 328, 334, 335,
    469, 543, 660
Nick Kenny Show, The, 467,
    843, 876
Nightbeat, 875
Night Court, 24, 25, 44, 247,
    302, 376, 464, 475, 483, 494,
    594, 679, 724, 856, 879
Night Editor, 127
Night Gallery, 23, 42, 127, 143,
    202, 280, 577, 623, 626, 641,
    685, 764, 765, 816, 880, 889,
    897
Night Heat, 178, 210, 360, 365,
    409, 427, 561, 581, 732, 736,
    857, 911
Night of 100 Stars, 498, 657
Night Partners, 565
Night Stalker, The, 7, 281
Night the Bridge Fell Down,
    The, 37, 530
Nightline, 479, 480, 713, 725,
    877
Nightside, 563
9 to 5, 46, 98, 218, 240, 242,
    270, 496, 545, 601, 659, 793,
    818, 829, 888, 913
1986, 175, 609
No Holds Barred, 596
No Man's Land, 809
No Soap, Radio, 50, 225, 368,
    543, 564, 654, 736, 741
No Time for Sergeants, 77,
    181, 364, 404, 432, 478, 567,
    611, 643, 732, 776, 790, 829
No Warning, 863
Noah's Ark, 128, 727, 922
Nobody Loves an Albatross,
    611
Nobody's Child, 839
Nobody's Perfect, 107, 267,
    597, 729, 905, 923
N.O.P.D., 386
Norby, 265, 276, 375, 522, 545,
    819, 864, 878, 883
North and South, 18, 119, 153,
    154, 162, 186, 257, 286, 310,
    312, 325, 367, 384, 409, 410,
    463, 470, 585, 593, 647, 701,
    780, 789, 812, 824, 831
Northwest Passage, 130, 270,
    495, 846
Not for Hire, 11, 277
Not for Publication, 7, 206,
    778
Not for Women Only, 703, 877
Not the Nine O'Clock News,
    806
Not Without Honor, 567
Nothing But the Best, 8, 399
Notorious Woman, 385
Now You See It, 619

Now You See It, Now You
    Don't, 893
Number 96, 64, 95, 174, 218,
    397, 425, 446, 548, 569, 611,
    615, 636, 653, 708, 822, 840,
    848, 899
Nurse, 103, 191, 397, 500, 541,
    705, 721, 830, 913
Nurses, The, 85, 87, 117, 143,
    197, 356, 844
N.Y.P.D., 196, 413, 878

O

O. Henry Playhouse, 592
Occasional Wife, 141, 189,
    389, 543, 629, 637, 718, 762,
    778, 845
OceanQuest, 336, 884
Odd Couple, The, 127, 152,
    252, 283, 328, 332, 371, 380,
    416, 476, 546, 567, 594, 655,
    696, 771, 794, 871
Of Lands and Seas, 207
Of Many Things, 282
Of Mice and Men, 92
Of Thee I Sing, 638
Off the Rack, 41, 109, 123, 395,
    890, 924
Oh, Boy, 375
Oh Madeline, 335, 452, 785,
    827, 889
Oh, Susanna!, 23
Oh, Those Bells, 138, 630, 769,
    899
O'Hara, U.S. Treasury, 437, 886
OHMS, 871
O. K. Crackerby, 4, 22, 126,
    201, 234, 304, 428, 430, 805
Okay, Mother, 435
Old American Barn Dance, 50,
    305
Oldest Living Graduate, The,
    303
Oldsmobile Music Theatre,
    393, 398
Oliver Twist, 760
Omnibus, 199, 212, 223, 378,
    394, 463, 516, 677, 711, 759,
    768, 802, 829, 883, 889
On Broadway Tonight, 857,
    858
On Our Own, 35, 158, 361,
    447, 696, 711, 921
On the Boardwalk with Paul
    Whiteman, 896
On the Corner, 603
On the Line with Considine,
    196
On the Road with Charles
    Kuralt, 483
On the Rocks, 208, 365, 425,
    666, 680, 695, 748, 811, 903
On Trial, 508
On Your Mark, 309
On Your Way, 190, 346, 472
Once an Eagle, 153, 225, 276,
    304, 305, 365, 367, 429, 681,
    807, 820, 911
Once Upon a Dead Man, 422

Once Upon a Fence, 396, 452
Once Upon a Mattress, 129
Once Upon a Tune, 69, 380,
    384, 412, 657
One Cooks, the Other Doesn't,
    677
One Day at a Time, 84, 285,
    286, 313, 324, 384, 402, 503,
    538, 554, 671, 672, 718, 754,
    777, 910
One Day in the Life of Ivan
    Denisovich, 661
One Happy Family, 169, 314,
    475, 583, 750, 879
One in a Million, 55, 219, 297,
    397, 661, 811, 874, 888, 900
One Life to Live, 46, 49, 118,
    148, 171, 221, 233, 316, 333,
    348, 511, 587, 656, 660, 678,
    784, 872, 917
One Man's Family, 73, 96, 97,
    116, 123, 163, 314, 330, 360,
    405, 410, 428, 502, 516, 521,
    529, 540, 545, 559, 561, 626,
    696, 744, 754, 769, 837, 838,
    841, 849, 862, 899
One Minute Please, 22, 193,
    271, 340, 480, 560, 662
One Night in the Tropics, 1
One of the Boys, 71, 161, 214,
    490, 731, 741
One on One, 431
One Out of Seven, 886
One Potato, Two Potato, 611
One Shoe Makes It Murder, 593
One Step Beyond, 626
One Touch of Venus, 331
100 Grand, 179
$100,000 Name That Tune, 492
$100,000 Pyramid, The, 177
$128,000 Question, The, 229,
    849
O'Neills, The, 17, 126, 298,
    337, 499, 550, 892
1,2,3, Go, 506, 839
Open All Night, 56, 268, 786,
    829, 854, 894
Open End, 822
Open Hearing, 211, 223, 762
Opening Night, 221
Opera Cameos, 56, 552
Opera vs. Jazz, 467
Operation Entertainment, 62,
    336
Operation Neptune, 84, 192,
    232, 364, 410, 490, 811
Operation Petticoat, 42, 82,
    110, 119, 165, 218, 219, 250,
    337, 339, 409, 454, 520, 540,
    544, 559, 569, 612, 619, 670,
    757, 782, 797, 840, 841, 863,
    900
Operation Success, 670
Oppenheimer, 882
Orchid Award, The, 529, 701,
    893, 917
Ordeal of Dr. Mudd, The, 884
Ordeal of Patty Hearst, The,
    274, 884
Oregon Trail, The, 71, 153,
    618, 785, 807, 833

Original Amateur Hour, The, 349, 435, 477, 531, 546
Orville and Wilbur, 458
Osmonds, The, 646
O.S.S., 324, 615, 696
Otherworld, 57, 201, 208, 365, 502, 639
Our Family Honor, 40, 444, 453, 514, 535, 554, 575, 818, 875, 903, 910, 918
Our House, 13, 112, 251, 334, 373, 374, 416, 641
Our Man Higgins, 136, 366, 412, 464, 558, 847
Our Miss Brooks, 33, 34, 36, 45, 62, 124, 174, 209, 210, 292, 350, 351, 459, 575, 603, 623, 697, 726, 789, 824, 864, 913
Our Place, 131, 254, 358, 756, 900
Our Private World, 205, 260, 265, 299, 320, 365, 543, 613, 636, 791, 843
Our Secret Weapon—The Truth, 173, 244
Our Time, 24, 136, 282, 389, 502, 799, 857
Our Times with Bill Moyers, 609
Our Town, 841
Our World, 275, 325
Out of the Blue, 58, 107, 114, 158, 236, 396, 462, 496
Outcasts, The, 613, 614, 926
Outer Limits, The, 216, 477, 560, 734, 768, 891
Outlaws, The, 187, 331, 385, 510, 532, 673, 923
Outside U.S.A., 420
Outsider, The, 568
Over Easy, 91, 258
Over the Hill Gang, The, 109, 245
Overland Trail, The, 76, 563
Owen Marshall, Counselor At Law, 32, 128, 143, 150, 229, 292, 377, 384, 405, 536, 555, 624, 750, 755, 764, 781, 796, 797, 816, 849, 901
Ox Bow Incident, The, 870
Ozark Jubilee, 34, 107, 130, 173, 298, 300, 302, 392, 429, 433, 438, 521, 575, 640, 674, 688, 695, 771, 796, 801, 828, 861, 870, 872, 909, 910
Ozzie & Harriet. See The Adventures of Ozzie & Harriet.
Ozzie's Girls, 146, 258, 382, 622, 623, 764, 826

P

Palmerstown, U.S.A., 15, 96, 155, 263, 309, 444, 480, 745, 896, 907
Panic, 863
Pantomime Quiz, 63, 129, 180, 195, 198, 253, 359, 379, 384, 387, 440, 453, 458, 506, 685, 813, 817, 860, 906
Paper Chase, The, 69, 243, 299, 340, 347, 375, 381, 416, 459, 540, 746, 762, 763, 805, 827, 869
Paper Dolls, 86, 91, 101, 103, 111, 286, 287, 290, 310, 320, 340, 427, 514, 556, 642, 667, 695, 711, 716, 728, 755, 772, 857, 880
Paper Moon, 192, 308
Paradise Bay, 27, 123, 734
Parent Game, The, 693
Paris, 168, 328, 386, 447, 592, 695, 880
Paris Cavalcade of Fashions, 278, 336
Paris Precinct, 230, 450
Paris 7000, 44, 377, 700
Park Place, 140, 180, 260, 336, 353, 597, 789, 899
Partners, The, 4, 213, 255, 455, 862
Partners In Crime, 25, 159, 160, 396, 641, 734
Partridge Family, The, 97, 133, 163, 197, 214, 247, 306, 332, 378, 448, 451, 534, 603, 655, 709, 763, 788
Party Line, 657
Party Time at Club Roma, 11, 12, 172, 253, 279, 505
Passions, 870
Passport to Danger, 730
Password, 525
Pat Boone-Chevy Showroom, The, 99, 512, 538, 636
Pat Paulsen's Half a Comedy Hour, 121, 138, 274, 334, 587, 661, 707, 728, 787, 798, 863
Paternity, 805
Patrice Munsel Show, The, 553, 611, 749
Patricia Bowman Show, The, 103, 655, 771
Patricia Neal Story, The, 818
Patti Page Olds Show, The, 186, 557, 650, 651, 756
Patti Page Show, The, 409, 509, 651, 798
Patty Duke Show, The, 12, 32, 42, 43, 138, 356, 406, 569, 581, 589, 640, 754, 821, 916
Paul Arnold Show, The, 38
Paul Dixon Show, The, 250, 349, 510, 531
Paul Harvey News, 390
Paul Lynde Comedy Hour, The, 507
Paul Lynde Show, The, 3, 14, 142, 294, 362, 528, 572, 579, 812, 867
Paul Sand in Friends and Lovers, 338, 489, 546, 621, 659, 748, 891
Paul Simon Special, The, 171, 233, 313, 845
Paul Whiteman's Goodyear Revue, 146, 647, 896, 920
Paul Whiteman's TV Teen Club, 178, 355, 460, 475, 510, 574, 742, 855, 896
Paul Winchell-Jerry Mahoney Show, The, 121, 177, 329, 378, 781, 797, 835, 910
Pauline Frederick's Guestbook, 315
Peak of the Sports News, 58
Pearl, 12, 26, 34, 242, 248, 304, 323, 397, 400, 734, 858, 870, 880, 884
Pearl Bailey Show, The, 51, 75, 230, 776
Pebbles and Bamm Bamm, 631, 818
Peck's Bad Girl, 202, 295, 424, 564, 882, 915
Pee Wee King Show, The, 132, 472, 519, 811
Penelope Pitstop, 648, 872
Penny to a Million, 349
Pentagon U.S.A., 715
Penthouse Party, 173, 321, 887
People, 333, 769, 822
People Are Funny, 513, 908
People Do the Craziest Things, 196, 219, 667
People's Choice, The, 19, 110, 199, 200, 210, 429, 473, 474, 557, 805, 891
People's Court, The, 132, 272, 516, 877, 878
People's Platform, 420
Pepsi-Cola Playhouse, 81, 185, 221, 445, 463, 553
Perfect Strangers, 220, 514, 674, 743
Perry Como Show, The, 47, 170, 191, 228, 304, 324, 332, 395, 400, 401, 474, 803
Perry Mason, 2, 26, 51, 110, 126, 127, 132, 150, 177, 189, 197, 198, 248, 281, 340, 366, 372, 373, 397, 414, 456, 494, 496, 534, 544, 545, 560, 588, 644, 673, 676, 726, 740, 755, 794, 816, 828, 843, 848, 852, 891, 902, 919
Perry Presents, 47, 78, 110, 228, 309, 593, 603, 651
Person to Person, 107, 187, 188, 614, 615
Personality, 95
Personality Puzzle, 11, 295
Persuaders, The, 219, 600, 618
Pet Set, The, 895
Pet Shop, 192, 581
Pete and Gladys, 30, 294, 350, 478, 502, 540, 592, 602, 694, 818, 850, 902
Pete Kelly's Blues, 102, 274, 351, 714, 886, 920
Peter Gunn, 10, 31, 83, 278, 807, 808, 811, 855
Peter Lind Hayes Show, The, 394, 395, 818, 898
Peter Loves Mary, 75, 394, 395, 442, 550, 703, 786, 787
Peter Marshall Variety Show, The, 170, 200, 282, 340, 547

Peter Pan, 290, 457
Peter Potter Show, The, 680
Petrified Forest, The, 303
Petrocelli, 419, 421, 626, 747, 825
Petticoat Junction, 19, 57, 70, 75, 76, 100, 125, 130, 139, 224, 233, 272, 308, 389, 420, 427, 458, 484, 490, 507, 517, 534, 591, 718, 723, 727, 746, 751, 846, 877, 891, 913, 917
Peyton Place, 10, 27, 70, 71, 90, 110, 145, 174, 192, 237, 251, 255, 267, 283, 290, 295, 350, 356, 387, 394, 409, 427, 441, 462, 468, 478, 491, 492, 534, 537, 545, 606, 621, 627, 637, 638, 641, 643, 657, 691, 727, 736, 738, 759, 789, 791, 833, 852, 873, 881, 898, 916
Phantom of Hollywood, The, 832
Phantom Pilot, 261
Phil Silvers Show, The, 10, 28, 29, 55, 160, 212, 264, 292, 305, 314, 316, 352, 368, 466, 503, 515, 523, 581, 733, 749, 779, 807, 930
Philco TV Playhouse, 55, 74, 294, 323, 356, 463, 500, 529, 551, 583, 626, 696, 744, 802, 822, 879
Philip Marlowe, 148, 811
Phoenix, The, 528, 760
Photocrime, 243, 255, 886
Photographic Horizons, 60, 202, 205
Phyl & Mikhy, 213, 251, 372, 518, 659, 683
Phyllis, 149, 334, 447, 497, 499, 500, 524, 616, 676, 733, 754, 805, 847, 881, 887
Piccadilly Palace, The, 550, 601, 658, 747, 814, 914
Pick the Winner, 211
Picture This, 61, 861
Pine Canyon Is Burning, 564
Pink Lady, 19, 273, 556, 618, 662, 675, 863
Pink Panther Show, The, 137, 384
Pinky Lee Show, The, 53, 502
Pinocchio, 457
Pirate, The, 313
Pistols 'n Petticoats, 166, 169, 309, 401, 524, 566, 772, 779, 866, 890
Place the Face, 50, 215, 788
Places Please, 916
Plainclothesman, The, 338, 527, 645
Plane That Couldn't Land, The, 912
Planet of the Apes, The, 190, 383, 504, 567, 619
Play of the Week, 95, 822
Play the Game, 931
Play Your Hunch, 363, 510, 642, 700
Playboy After Dark, 79
Playhouse, 182

Playhouse 90, 28, 63, 65, 68, 81, 86, 95, 100, 152, 157, 198, 251, 255, 396, 406, 416, 419, 424, 430, 434, 451, 476, 491, 493, 546, 554, 564, 567, 638, 652, 656, 669, 764, 803, 820, 825, 833, 846, 897, 922
Playing With Fire, 187
Please Don't Eat the Daisies, 201, 214, 253, 299, 313, 404, 544, 588, 592, 619, 692, 830, 853, 859
Please Don't Hit Me, Mom, 43
Please Stand By, 252, 556, 600, 754
Pleasure Cove, 391
Plot to Overthrow Christmas, The, 49
Plymouth Playhouse, 198
PM Magazine, 776
Police Squad, 261, 628, 631, 903
Police Story, 86, 88, 106, 126, 128, 164, 177, 198, 200, 202, 215, 216, 252, 258, 262, 280, 352, 366, 382, 390, 517, 523, 583, 590, 603, 615, 636, 733, 777, 805, 808, 899, 903
Police Woman, 11, 83, 89, 138, 248, 411, 851, 902
Policewoman Centerfold, 798
Polka Time, 247, 338, 425, 600, 715, 916, 929
Polka-Go-Round, 140, 247, 259, 309, 508, 678, 688, 782
Polly Bergen Show, The, 80, 81, 332, 398
Ponds Theatre, 693
Pop 'n' Rocker Game, The, 67
Pop! Goes the Country, 279, 375, 863
Popi, 210, 247, 275, 666, 863
Poppa and Me, 486
Poppy Is Also a Flower, The, 875
Portia Faces Life, 437
Portrait, 187
Portrait of a Rebel: Margaret Sanger, 313
Portrait of a Stripper, 880
Portrait of America, 63
Powderkeg, 833
Power of Women, The, 462, 502
Powers of Matthew Star, The, 12, 64, 320, 352, 454, 804
Practice, The, 137, 192, 248, 283, 285, 499, 684, 698, 798, 837
Practice Tee, 58
Prescription: Murder, 287
Presenting Susan Anton, 31, 301, 477, 552, 570, 652, 681, 759, 908
Presidential Countdown, 211
Presidential Straws in the Wind, 125, 732
Presidential Timber, 850
Press Conference, 735
Press Your Luck, 845

Preview with Tex and Jinx, 288, 566
Price, The, 130, 759
Price Is Right, The, 59, 215, 216, 435, 642, 654
Pride of Jesse Hallam, The, 162, 857
Pride of the Family, The, 389, 427, 917, 919
Prime of Your Life, The, 312
Prime Suspect, 290
Prime Time Baseball, 266, 297, 299
Prime Time Boxing, 435
Prime Time Football, 97, 204, 298, 395, 840, 914
Prime Time Saturday, 226
Prime Time Sunday, 226, 255, 339, 666, 752, 793, 874
Primus, 121, 483, 711
Princess Daisy, 341, 856, 861, 870
Princess Sagaphi, 744
Prisoner, The, 569, 615
Private Benjamin, 109, 116, 316, 515, 538, 660, 694, 722, 742, 798, 886, 903
Private Secretary, 57, 679, 796, 854, 864, 896
Private Sessions, 290
Prize Performance, 4, 253, 311
Producer's Showcase, 303, 590, 744, 781, 799, 925
Professional Father, 87, 181, 265, 541, 643, 881
Profiles in Courage, 146, 789
Program Playhouse, 850
Project U.F.O., 450, 471, 823, 886, 913
Protectors, The, 30, 628, 679, 714, 863, 864
Prototypes, 607
Prudential Playhouse, 561
Pruitts of Southampton, The, 42, 236, 246, 249, 316, 326, 428, 490, 501, 528, 823
Pryor's Place, 689
Psychiatrist, The, 6, 836
Public Defender, The, 370, 404
Public Life of Cliff Norton, The, 632
Pueblo, 410
Pulitzer Prize Playhouse, 59, 684
Punky Brewster, 160, 238, 277, 307, 320, 328, 331, 443, 664

Q

QB VII, 331, 590, 691, 710, 827
Q.E.D., 119, 123, 302, 344, 409, 428, 492, 856, 882, 884
Quark, 60, 77, 140, 436, 464, 679, 840, 858
Queen and I, The, 55, 246, 265, 604, 814, 818, 906
Queen for a Day, 50, 631
Queen of the Stardust Ballroom, 168, 693, 803

Quest, The, 44, 71, 87, 230, 460, 472, 473, 555, 585, 739, 867
Quick As a Flash, 190, 278, 622, 773
Quick on the Draw, 169, 265
Quincy, M.E., 3, 7, 11, 89, 143, 218, 280, 328, 338, 363, 369, 429, 476, 544, 585, 603, 671, 694, 730, 832, 871
Quiz Kids, 286, 464
Quizzing the News, 683

R

Racket Squad, 370, 658
Rafferty, 79, 180, 334, 569, 570, 687, 784
Rage, 797, 897
Rage of Angels, 419, 788, 914
Raggedy Ann and Andy, 192
Raid on Entebbe, 55, 879
Rainbow, 159
Ramar of the Jungle, 287, 374, 521, 563, 596, 811
Range Rider, The, 45, 446, 535
Rango, 11, 197, 487, 544
Ransom Sherman Show, The, 105, 773, 859, 920
Rape of Richard Beck, The, 210
Rat Patrol, The, 162, 333, 366, 700, 829
Rawhide, 30, 63, 106, 112, 139, 222, 269–271, 280, 301, 358, 429, 487, 535, 612, 635, 694, 744, 747, 767, 778, 882, 918
Ray Anthony Show, The, 31, 75, 153, 266, 301, 308, 500, 584, 752
Ray Bolger Show, The, 97, 146, 280, 450, 510, 528, 587, 621, 741
Ray Milland Show, The, 46, 447, 587, 855
Ray Scherer's Sunday Report, 755
Razzmatazz, 401, 843
RCA Victor Show, The, 38, 39, 134, 234, 294, 435, 541, 598, 671, 675, 715, 737, 855
Reach for the Sun, 594
Real McCoys, The, 45, 91, 94, 109, 181, 209, 210, 238, 326, 553, 630, 659, 704, 737, 891, 912
Real People, 13, 58, 87, 589, 689, 693, 739, 806, 900
Real Tom Kennedy Show, The, 466
Reason to Live, A, 374
Reasoner Report, The, 701
Rebel, The, 5, 6, 92, 194, 260, 289, 720
Rebels, The, 95, 443, 807, 851, 864
Red Alert, 871
Red Badge of Courage, The, 840
Red Barber's Clubhouse, 58
Red Barber's Corner, 58

Red Buttons Show, The, 135, 156, 242, 365, 445, 474, 497, 528, 773, 778, 872
Red Ryder, 490
Red Skelton Show, The, 16, 40, 105, 128, 263, 289, 373, 419, 483, 517, 701, 732, 783, 919
Redd Foxx Show, The, 244, 310, 763, 781, 832, 844, 860, 909, 910
Redigo, 233, 273, 552, 794, 864
Reel Game, The, 63
Reggie, 61, 134, 457, 611, 785, 799, 930
Rehearsal Call, 655, 802
Remember When, 79, 879
Remembrance of Love, 180
Remington Steele, 117, 241, 701, 722, 930
Rendezvous, 554, 572
Rendezvous with Music, 243, 324, 704
Renegades, 57, 117, 525, 594, 758, 824, 835, 843
Renegades, The, 789
Report On .., 408
Report to Murphy, 186, 306, 460, 678, 714, 733
Reporter, The, 107, 366, 584, 639, 675
Requiem for a Heavyweight, 652, 922
Rescue 8, 232, 439, 710
Restless Gun, The, 94, 182, 489, 662, 741
Return of Marcus Welby, M.D., The, 865
Return of Perry Mason, 373
Return of the Beverly Hillbillies, The, 183, 475
Return of the Gunfighter, 833
Return of the Man from U.N.C.L.E., 560
Return of the Saint, 639
Return of the World's Greatest Detective, The, 371
Return to Mayberry, 478, 617
Return to Peyton Place, 821
Revenge of the Cheerleaders, 391
Revlon Mirror Theatre, 169
Reward, 658
R.F.D. America, 612
Rheingold Theatre, 261
Rhinemann Exchange, The, 8, 123, 190, 273, 295, 426, 427, 465, 475, 567
Rhoda, 11, 47, 126, 145, 239, 353, 365, 383, 402, 457, 490, 575, 579, 593, 615, 708, 768, 778, 852, 859, 873, 902
Rhythm Rodeo, 437, 803, 919
Rich Little Show, The, 53, 89, 121, 423, 515, 578, 693
Rich Man, Poor Man—Book I, 16, 41, 64, 89, 92, 134, 147, 207, 228, 262, 263, 283, 293, 299, 333, 355, 378, 384, 438, 440, 444, 505, 535, 537, 563, 570, 571, 587, 603, 630, 640,

683, 705, 774, 791, 807, 816, 821
Rich Man, Poor Man—Book II, 2, 25, 35, 70, 99, 253, 331, 390, 400, 449, 505, 670, 791, 799, 805, 816, 820, 821, 825, 923
Richard Boone Show, The, 91, 92, 96, 100, 245, 381, 506, 602, 629, 694, 809, 812
Richard Diamond, Private Detective, 51, 117, 197, 437, 454, 598, 599, 846
Richard Pryor Show, The, 18, 57, 83, 264, 377, 552, 597, 688, 707, 879, 904, 905, 915
Richard Pryor Special, 30
Richie Brockelman, Private Eye, 102, 262, 409
Richie Rich, 142
Richie Rich/Scooby Doo, 543
Rifleman, The, 91, 193, 208, 209, 217, 233, 260, 299, 451, 637, 692, 821, 831
Riker, 768, 831
Rin Tin Tin. See The Adventures of Rin Tin Tin.
Ring of Passion, 161
Rio Rita, 893
Ripcord, 191, 219, 298, 664
Ripley's Believe It or Not, 647, 652, 653, 774
Riptide, 108, 167, 311, 339, 340, 380, 381, 472, 473, 645, 665
Rituals, 117, 290, 316, 324, 348, 390, 446, 523, 544, 611, 660, 670, 678, 923
Rivals, The, 573
Riverboat, 71, 351, 487, 568, 570, 593, 660, 712, 891
Road of Life, The, 504, 875
Road West, The, 201, 394, 686, 758, 759, 762, 820
Roaring Twenties, The, 239, 300, 558, 688, 701, 721, 866
Robbins Nest, The, 147, 362, 721
Robert Kennedy and His Times, 799, 879
Robert Montgomery Presents, 72, 90, 103, 113, 200, 221, 259, 299, 336, 394, 403, 436, 492, 517, 582, 586, 591, 596, 626, 675, 680, 700, 710, 723, 724, 760, 761, 766, 782, 806, 833, 890, 893, 920, 925
Robert Q. Lewis Show, The, 363, 510
Roberta, 414, 652
Rock Concert, 475
Rock 'n' Roll Summer Action, 43, 712
Rockford Files, The, 44, 71, 200, 201, 262, 327, 328, 388, 414, 424, 525, 543, 601, 680, 750, 763, 764, 816, 825, 869, 882
Rocky King, Inside Detective, 152, 378, 454, 455

Rod Brown of the Rocket Rangers, 724, 893
Roger Miller Show, The, 454, 589
Rogues, The, 104, 105, 199, 200, 629, 748, 761, 904, 925
Roll Out, 72, 89, 339, 340, 404, 428, 605, 750, 811, 910
Roller Derby, 72, 390, 616, 633
Roller Girls, The, 66, 118, 164, 380, 475, 615, 844
Rollin' on the River, 727, 728
Romance Theatre, 450
Ron LeFlore Story, The, 133
Rookies, The, 119, 286, 411, 431, 581, 641, 644, 706, 788, 830, 849
Room for One More, 9, 154, 228, 262, 263, 562, 627, 731, 819
Room 222, 29, 72, 160, 196, 394, 402, 445, 491, 624, 627, 714, 816, 827, 857, 903
Rootie Kazootie, 740
Roots, 14, 22, 29, 30, 41, 87, 106, 111, 119, 133, 147, 148, 185, 186, 188, 193, 213, 217, 231, 264, 297, 303, 333, 352, 360, 361, 368, 377, 404, 430, 433, 445, 448, 563, 578, 597, 605–607, 697, 698, 705, 714, 735, 744, 757, 771, 780, 782, 844, 854, 855, 865, 871, 883, 918
Roots: The Next Generations, 14, 56, 106, 119, 147, 223, 238, 239, 282, 303, 316, 363, 364, 378, 381, 447, 480, 519, 597, 602, 608, 715, 745, 769, 782, 839, 904, 911
Ropers, The, 184, 185, 248, 293, 294, 512, 564, 565, 828, 857
Rosemary Clooney Show, The, 181, 717
Rosetti and Ryan, 276, 318, 547, 635, 643, 723
Rosie: The Rosemary Clooney Story, 181, 645
Rough Riders, The, 583, 832, 898
Roughnecks, 13
Rounders, The, 271, 380, 394, 449, 642, 883, 907, 912
Rousters, The, 46, 283, 284, 336, 728, 819, 863
Route 66, 10, 55, 83, 85, 201, 268, 311, 358, 389, 535, 537, 590, 591, 611, 626, 630, 677, 712, 760, 808, 848, 864, 876, 882
Rowan & Martin's Laugh-In, 14, 65, 79, 109, 110, 112, 118, 120, 136, 151, 234, 244, 259, 275, 290, 336, 339, 358, 392, 417, 438, 442, 466, 516, 519, 534, 544, 549, 560, 585, 648, 672, 713, 727, 735, 736, 768, 818, 819, 845, 853, 898, 908, 919, 925

Roy Rogers & Dale Evans Show, The, 38, 106, 125, 151, 282, 728, 795, 831
Roy Rogers Show, The, 105, 282, 690, 728
Royal Canadian Mounted Police, 313
Royal Romance of Charles and Diana, The, 356, 649
Ruby and Oswald, 451
Ruff & Ready, 90, 585
Ruggles, The, 83, 392, 468, 633, 637, 737, 833
Ruggles of Red Gap, The, 883
Run Buddy Run, 192, 333, 350, 653, 771
Run, Don't Walk, 52
Run for Your Life, 148, 184, 189, 331, 497, 564, 576
Runaround, 911
Runaways, The, 87, 141, 184, 207, 292, 531, 705
Russ Hodges' Scoreboard, 408
Russ Morgan Show, The, 604, 637
Ruthie on the Telephone, 338, 704
Ryan's Four, 94, 205, 224, 274, 373, 783, 912
Ryan's Hope, 13, 83, 160, 324, 422, 610, 636, 674

S

Saber of London, 34, 561, 829
Sacketts, The, 13, 305, 764
Sadat, 352
Safari to Adventure, 133
Saga of Western Man, 762
Sailor of Fortune, 360, 361
Saint, The, 236, 600
St. Elsewhere, 50, 64, 72, 88, 123, 183, 227, 240, 300, 322, 362, 376, 380, 382, 478, 491, 510, 516, 538, 558, 593, 607, 673, 701, 722, 733, 748, 752, 768, 777, 800, 810, 843, 881, 894, 917
Saints and Sinners, 6, 91, 280, 290, 494, 681, 738, 780
Sale of the Century, 325, 464
Salem's Lot, 554, 797
Sally, 166, 243, 350, 442, 522
Salty, 254, 784
Salvage 1, 237, 364, 405, 434, 750, 811
Sam, 382, 883
Sam and Friends, 400
Sam Benedict, 636, 740, 845
Sam Levenson Show, The, 508
Sammy and Company, 233, 714, 756, 906
Sammy Davis Jr. Show, The, 233, 714, 909
Sammy Kaye Show, The, 8, 79, 97, 277, 444, 453, 458, 559, 586, 682, 711, 722, 778
Sammy Kaye's Music from Manhattan, 458

Sam's Son, 490
San Francisco International Airport, 111, 367, 777, 891
San Pedro Beach Bums, The, 243, 417, 566, 604, 611, 612, 654, 706, 725, 745
Sandburg's Lincoln, 409, 841
Sandy Duncan Show, The, 101, 175, 264, 582, 876, 914, 929
Sandy Strong, 509, 819
Sanford, 129, 199, 243, 310, 699, 727, 814, 832
Sanford and Son, 16, 29, 86, 174, 179, 209, 310, 378, 448, 559, 604, 651, 675, 676, 689, 706, 715, 777, 832, 896, 903, 907
Sanford Arms, The, 16, 29, 86, 259, 269, 559, 589, 651, 910
Santa Barbara, 128, 552, 795
Sara, 205, 232, 272, 421, 482, 496, 498, 529, 535, 585, 602, 672, 674, 816, 857, 914, 917
Sarge, 87, 465, 466, 746, 764, 774
Satan's Waitin', 876
Satins and Spurs, 426
Saturday Night Basketball, 329, 354, 802
Saturday Night Dance Party, 506
Saturday Night Fights, 362, 806
Saturday Night Jamboree, 113, 259, 326, 357, 392, 395, 417, 727, 786
Saturday Night Live. *See* NBC's Saturday Night Live.
Saturday Night Live with Howard Cosell, 204, 498
Saturday Night Revue, 8, 95, 150, 156, 344, 751, 924
Saturday Prom, 363
Saturday Roundup, 559
Saturday Sports Final, The, 382
Saturday Sports Mirror, 259, 403
Saturday/Friday Night Fights, 266
Sawyer Views Hollywood, 159, 753
Say It with Acting, 190, 576
Scalplock, 254
Scarecrow and Mrs. King, 103, 104, 326, 431, 432, 607, 753, 789, 790, 811, 815
Scarlet Pimpernell, The, 351
Scene of the Crime, 836, 889
Schlitz Playhouse of Stars, 9, 72, 81, 87, 98, 106, 150, 193, 208, 222, 252, 265, 307, 381, 394, 412, 463, 652, 662, 685, 692, 712, 884
School House, 3, 35, 103, 146, 207, 240, 250, 259, 299, 369, 634, 685, 706, 801
Science Circus, 118

Science Fiction Theater, 59, 62, 105, 262, 761, 840

Scooby Doo, Where Are You?, 276, 584

Scotland Yard, 527

Scott Music Hall, The, 303, 408, 651, 835

Scout's Honor, 160, 187, 631

Scrabble, 918

Scrapbook Junior Edition, 531, 637

Scream of the Wolf, 873

Screen Actors' Guild 50th Anniversary Celebration, The, 499

Screen Director's Playhouse, 141

Scruples, 76, 102, 141, 153, 166, 331, 332, 347, 355, 379, 496, 501, 533, 538, 547, 675, 705, 764, 791, 805, 807, 836, 842, 869, 870, 876, 930

SCTV Network 90, 145, 299, 508, 548, 601, 639, 775, 837, 899

Sea Hunt, 111, 340, 371, 628, 902

Sealab 2000, 551

Search, 27, 165, 175, 237, 289, 310, 311, 347, 376, 448, 563, 582, 636, 679, 694, 845

Search, The, 730

Search for the Nile, The, 3, 126, 353, 372, 503, 514, 554, 566, 691, 734, 755, 861

Search for Tomorrow, 17, 79, 121, 184, 286, 333, 372, 389, 435, 467, 478, 512, 522, 538, 630, 632, 636, 726, 777, 869, 916

Seaway, 927

Second City TV, 145, 263, 299, 508, 548, 601, 639, 695, 732, 837

Second Hundred Years, The, 90, 379, 544, 558, 637

Secret Agent, 569

Secret Empire, The, 108, 123, 329, 482, 504, 544, 644, 759, 844, 882, 905

Secret File, U.S.A., 11

Secret Life of John Chapman, The, 871

Secret Night Caller, 705

Secret Storm, The, 3, 13, 82, 144, 253, 330, 467, 506, 590, 636, 736, 749, 823

Secrets and Lies, 825

Secrets of Midland Heights, 39, 84, 175, 178, 179, 378, 380, 409, 448, 487, 539, 639, 675, 760, 761, 779, 841, 887, 923, 927, 931

Secrets of Three Hungry Wives, 876

Seduced, 772

See How She Runs, 390

See It Now, 411, 457, 614, 615

Seekers, The, 541, 591, 897

Seeking Heart, The, 144

Semi-Tough, 165, 339, 390, 391, 472, 569, 573, 663, 679, 786

Senate and the Watergate Affair, The, 698

Senator, The, 2, 274, 409, 410, 844

Sensitive, Passionate Man, A, 437

Sergeant Preston of the Yukon, 780

Serpico, 44, 88

Serving Through Science, 562

Sesame Street, 240, 400, 424, 622, 649, 693, 703

Seven at Eleven, 240, 246, 292, 317, 353, 462, 521, 523, 527, 670, 760, 802

Seven Brides for Seven Brothers, 26, 27, 409, 415, 475, 672, 846, 849, 856, 910

Seven Keys, 619

Seven Rich Years, 734

Seventh Avenue, 33, 81, 83, 110, 249, 460, 462, 471, 677, 766, 796, 827, 875

79 Park Avenue, 61, 81, 132, 196, 263, 286, 324, 376, 394, 397, 434, 486, 547, 721, 726, 730, 747, 753, 782, 880, 886, 893

77 Sunset Strip, 71, 128, 137, 195, 197, 253, 283, 288, 435, 461, 518, 519, 560, 692, 790, 800, 807, 864, 872, 888, 891, 930

Sex and the Single Parent, 745

Sex Symbol, The, 159, 807

Sha Na Na, 67, 118, 171, 263, 323, 388, 545, 616, 735, 746, 756, 767, 783

Shadow Chasers, 262, 283, 302

Shadow of the Cloak, 228

Shadow Over Elveron, 281, 846

Shaft, 26, 64, 323, 735, 869

Shampoo, 357

Shane, 153, 316, 339, 428, 652, 770, 851

Shannon, 250, 267, 297, 474, 479, 525, 617, 738, 846

Shape of Things, The, 857

Shaping Up, 304, 628, 774, 843, 884

Shazam, 849

She Waits, 571

Sheena, Queen of the Jungle, 259, 560

Sheilah Graham in Hollywood, 355

Sheriff of Cochise, The, 114, 123, 364, 449

Sherlock Holmes, 264, 419

Sherlock Holmes in New York, 600

She's Dressed to Kill, 876

Shields and Yarnell, 164, 539, 701, 750, 773, 929

Shindig, 144, 284, 521, 644, 718, 772, 819, 890

Shirley, 39, 64, 254, 274, 346, 448, 571, 776, 883

Shirley MacLaine . . . Every Little Movement, 442

Shirley MacLaine: If They Could See Me Now, 186

Shirley Temple's Storybook, 139, 198, 834, 925

Shirley's World, 362, 532

Shogun, 49, 168, 414, 428, 453, 514, 580, 586, 640, 714, 746, 764, 773, 774, 827, 837, 889

Shooting Stars, 902, 930

Short Short Dramas, 918

Short Story Playhouse, 108

Shotgun Slade, 106

Show Business, Inc, 355, 658, 910

Show Goes On, The, 510

Showcase '68, 835

Shower of Stars, 78, 315, 526

Showoffs, 95

Showtime, 519, 658, 747

Showtime at the Apollo, 124

Showtime, U.S.A., 316

Sid Caesar, Imogene Coca, Carl Reiner, Howard Morris Special, The, 709

Sid Caesar Invites You, 139, 182, 360, 453, 704, 709

Sid Caesar Show, The, 139, 306, 380, 532

Side by Side, 646

Sidekicks, 98, 334, 712, 800

Sidney Shorr, 527, 660

Sierra, 308, 409, 716, 840, 880

Sightseeing with the Swayzes, 824

Sigmund and the Sea Monsters, 65, 543, 894

Silent Force, The, 194, 333, 621, 727

Silent Night, Lonely Night, 448

Silent Service, The, 268, 462

Silent Victory: The Kitty O'Neill Story, 32

Silent Witness, 84

Silents Please, 480

Silver Spoons, 51, 66, 299, 359, 405, 416, 434, 511, 674, 714, 757, 762

Silver Theater, The, 315, 617, 706

Simon & Simon, 3, 64, 161, 577, 656, 707, 708, 909

Sing Along, 398, 524, 724, 791, 796

Sing Along with Mitch, 197, 487, 524, 589, 630, 636, 803, 811, 848, 855

Sing It Again, 94, 222, 417, 527, 529, 614, 718, 766, 802

Sing-co-pation, 60, 106, 290, 545

Singing Lady, The, 187, 250, 365, 823, 898

Singles Bars, Single Women, 369

Sirota's Court, 134, 196, 384, 588, 734, 900

Siskel & Ebert & The Movies, 270, 782

Sister, Sister, 174

Sit or Miss, 395, 796, 892

Six Million Dollar Man, The, 26, 116, 283, 292, 416, 536, 644, 723, 761, 869, 870, 909
6 Rms Riv Vu, 10
Six Wives of Henry VIII, The, 212, 214, 373, 401, 586, 606, 676, 691, 800, 850, 853
Sixth Sense, The, 188, 280, 295, 341, 626
$64,000 Challenge, The, 118, 309, 815
$64,000 Question, The, 53, 61, 118, 251, 282, 293, 541, 542
60 Minutes, 12, 105, 471, 698, 699, 701, 702, 730, 731, 743, 752, 753, 868, 874, 875
Sizzle, 522, 836
Skag, 3, 100, 143, 324, 410, 497, 536, 813, 868, 881
Skatebirds, 251
Skip Farrell Show, The, 60, 290, 413, 435, 608, 758
Skokie, 300, 457, 709, 875
Sky Heist, 583, 899
Sky King, 356, 370, 472, 913
Sky's the Limit, The, 375, 700
Slattery's People, 41, 46, 122, 209, 210, 293, 332, 712, 819, 854, 922, 923
Sledge Hammer!, 548, 651, 698
Sleepy Joe, 761
Slowest Gun in the West, The, 779
Small & Frye, 82, 93, 156, 222, 568, 908, 930
Small Fry Club, 279
Small Killing, A, 642
Small Wonder, 113, 175, 664, 757, 761, 821
Small World, 614
Smile Jenny, You're Dead, 542
Smilin' Ed McConnell and His Buster Brown Gang, 564
Smith Family, The, 91, 153, 159, 303, 419, 570, 591, 915
Smithsonian, The, 741
Smothers Brothers Comedy Hour, The, 73, 228, 274, 317, 353, 387, 451, 467, 615, 661, 677, 709, 717, 792, 793, 805, 810, 880, 904
Smothers Brothers Show, The, 2, 171, 274, 275, 317, 530, 551, 633, 651, 661, 764, 792, 793, 914
Smothers Summer Show, The, 661, 792, 793
Smurfs, The, 304, 584, 644, 924
Snap Judgment, 574, 700
Snavely, 895
Sneak Preview, 161
Sneak Previews, 269, 782
Snoop Sisters, The, 32, 196, 393, 619, 807
Snow Beast, 873
So This Is Hollywood, 336, 360, 447, 478, 527
Soap, 47, 51, 54, 123, 137, 146, 176, 215, 225, 357, 367, 397, 444, 511, 538, 540, 578, 587,

597, 611, 664, 669, 679, 713, 714, 722, 726, 747, 762, 777, 825, 855, 867, 881, 889
Soldiers, The, 226, 541
Soldiers of Fortune, 169, 739
Solid Gold, 19, 184, 238, 301, 335, 531, 564, 790, 881
Some Kind of Miracle, 542
Somerset, 228, 437, 632, 656, 749, 831, 840, 887
Somerset Maugham TV Theatre, 78, 557
Something Else, 137, 387
Something for Joey, 32
Song and Dance, 277, 545, 691
Songs at Twilight, 28, 155, 360
Songs for Sale, 16, 17, 78, 94, 181, 358, 394, 502, 589, 614
Songtime, 922
Sonny and Cher Comedy Hour, The, 98, 119, 153, 172, 216, 222, 274, 328, 472, 492, 551, 601, 651, 794, 858, 929
Sonny and Cher Show, The, 66, 98, 172, 173, 383, 750, 773, 858, 929
Sonny Comedy Revue, The, 98, 99, 216, 237, 328, 472, 492, 858, 929
Sonny Kendis Show, The, 267, 465
Sons and Daughters, 190, 313, 445, 515, 531, 603, 621, 638, 694, 758, 776, 777
Sooner or Later, 783, 790
Sophia Loren: Her Own Story, 847
Sophisticated Gents, 161, 363
Sorting It Out, 520
S.O.S. Titanic, 500, 745
Sound of Burt Bacharach, The, 557
Sound of Music, The, 160
Soupy Sales Show, The, 6, 746
Southernaires Quartet, 797
Space, 671
Space Academy, 843
Space Ghost, 648
Space 1999, 30, 51, 189, 379, 446, 488, 584, 607, 755, 830
Space Patrol, 57, 403, 445, 465, 480, 559, 588, 645
Sparring Partners with Walter Kiernan, 469
Speak Up, America, 33, 66, 351, 466
Special Agent 7, 630
Special Branch, 766
Special Bulletin, 300
Special Edition, 293
Spencer, 33, 142, 206, 402, 466, 516, 524, 748
Spencer's Pilots, 282, 428, 499, 813, 822
Spenser: For Hire, 116, 434, 565, 574, 812, 856
Spider Woman, 858
Spike Jones Show, The, 64, 225, 359, 436, 449, 887
Spin the Picture, 161, 184, 249, 265, 631, 758, 767

Splendor in the Grass, 338
Sports Focus, 204
Sports Illustrated, 117
Sports Newsreel, 682
Sports Showcase, 118
Sports Spot, 15, 572
Sports with Joe Hasel, 390
Sportsman's Quiz, 53, 261
Sportsreel, 147, 375, 463, 500, 622, 743, 907
Sportswoman of the Week, 199
Spotlight, 91, 658, 747
Spotlight on Sports, 806
Spotlight Playhouse, 523, 578, 761
Square Pegs, 4, 135, 141, 294, 334, 409, 513, 624, 656, 668, 871, 890
Staccato, 163
Stage a Number, 890
Stage Door, The, 13, 572, 664
Stage Entrance, 908
Stage 7, 492, 717
Stage Show, 159, 254, 255, 342, 831
Stage Two Revue, 6, 155, 384, 501
Stagecoach West, 108, 284, 521, 728, 729
Stand By for Crime, 32, 176, 874, 875
Stanley, 129, 192, 369, 528, 828, 847
Star and the Story, The, 303
Star Maidens, 6
Star Maker, The, 574, 857
Star of the Family, 240, 242, 257, 261, 394, 395, 408, 536, 600, 675, 822
Star Search, 574, 655
Star Spangled Girl, 77
Star Stage, 361, 528
Star Time, 348, 349, 492, 502, 656
Star Trek, 23, 60, 189, 209, 252, 254, 462, 478, 526, 595, 626–628, 768, 797, 827, 828, 830, 831, 898, 920
Starland Vocal Band Show, The, 19, 81, 507, 640, 688, 739, 803
Starlit Time, 69, 186, 219, 249, 380, 384, 412, 502, 647, 683, 721, 802, 901
Starman, 59, 166, 395
Starring Boris Karloff, 399, **454**
Stars of Jazz, 850
Stars on Parade, 497, 739, 773
Stars Over Hollywood, 132
Starsky and Hutch, 119, 184, 288, 341, 376, 377, 749, 797
State Trooper, 142, 143
Steel Cowboy, 847
Steve Allen Comedy Hour, The, 16, 53, 55, 116, 136, 137, 253, 306, 335, 336, 402, 505, 526, 579, 633, 639, 747, 769, 792, 805, 913
Steve Allen Show, The, 13, **16**, 120, 197, 225, 240, 306, 384,

399, 417, 433, 478, 579, 633, 665, 680, 699, 792, 793, 807, 823

Steve Allen's Laugh-Back, 16, 17, 579

Steve and Eydie Celebrate Irving Berlin, 351, 498

Steve Canyon, 237, 295, 315, 353, 420, 599, 654

Steve Lawrence Show, The, 300, 366, 498, 708, 872, 903

Steve Lawrence-Eydie Gorme Show, The, 351, 453, 498, 538, 699

Steve Randall, 255

Still the Beaver, 70, 257, 555, 647

Stingray, 538

Stir Crazy, 368, 718, 778, 909

Stock Car Races, 395

Stockard Channing in Just Friends, 169, 210, 310, 347, 355, 466, 733, 844

Stockard Channing Show, The, 169, 347, 775, 778, 794

Stone, 406, 573, 884, 885

Stoned, 52

Stonestreet, 271

Stoney Burke, 243, 257, 284, 386, 521, 635

Stop Me If You've Heard This One, 22, 103, 340, 436, 503, 736, 843

Stop Susan Williams, 31, 267, 379, 591, 661, 823, 876

Stop the Music, 90, 365, 522, 603, 657, 747, 858

Storefront Lawyers, The, 34, 309, 494, 552, 616, 641

Stories of the Century, 232

Stork Club, The, 87, 394, 395, 445, 664

Story of the Week, 382

Story Theatre, 383, 748

Straightaway, 40, 463

Strange Report, 325, 691, 906

Stranger, The, 155

Stranger Who Looks Like Me, The, 68, 262

Strauss Family, The, 30, 296, 380, 433, 780, 800, 872, 897, 910, 919

Strawhatters, The, 642

Street Hawk, 707, 790, 864, 909

Streetcar Named Desire, A, 106

Streets of Los Angeles, 18

Streets of San Francisco, The, 88, 131, 153, 184, 256, 385, 391, 468, 536, 537, 820, 899

Strictly for Laughs, 813

Strike Force, 270, 349, 381, 629, 730, 799

Strike It Rich, 120, 375, 423, 464, 657

Struck by Lightning, 205, 275, 281, 482, 784, 800

Stu Erwin Show, The, 23, 85, 190, 281, 392, 436, 590, 843

Studio 57, 461

Studio One, 9, 48, 51, 65, 69, 124, 135, 148, 150, 152, 200, 212, 223, 287, 294, 307, 312, 321, 333, 361, 362, 378, 403, 521, 542, 551, 554, 577, 592, 605, 628, 653, 665, 696, 747, 764, 768, 784, 802, 806, 829, 846, 883, 898, 924

Studs Lonigan, 200, 246, 256, 266, 267, 280, 318, 378, 383, 397, 611, 664, 754, 887, 907

Stud's Place, 410, 521, 726, 815, 834, 927

Stump the Authors, 108, 161, 235, 662, 929

Stumpers, 525

Subways Are for Sleeping, 383

Sudden Fear, 652

Suddenly, Love, 903

Sugar Hill Times, 73, 124, 451, 703, 728

Sugar Time!, 79, 90, 153, 429, 912

Sugarfoot, 381, 426, 466, 631, 807, 891, 930

Summer Holiday, 363, 365

Summer in the Park, 355

Summer of My German Soldier, 577, 729

Summer Playhouse, 161, 921

Summer Smothers Brothers Show, The, 144, 317, 387, 451, 661, 692, 717, 818, 863

Summer Solstice, 303

Summer Sports Spectacular, The, 653

Summer Sunday U.S.A., 275, 591

Summertime U.S.A., 94, 110, 413, 847

Sunday at Home, 673

Sunday Morning, 484

Sunday Mystery Movie, 100, 876

Sunrise at Campobello, 74

Sunshine, 173, 247, 298, 308, 576, 611

Super, The, 65, 107, 165, 474, 591, 663, 772, 866

Super Circus, 191

Super Ghost, 282, 678, 807

Super Night of Rock 'n' Roll, 402

Super Password, 197

Superfriends, 477

Superman. See The Adventures of Superman.

Supertrain, 11, 28, 34, 112, 189, 239, 354, 633, 651, 653, 828, 830, 890

Surfside Six, 62, 208, 252, 283, 328, 483, 559, 660, 777, 905

Survivors, The, 48, 74, 108, 146, 163, 367, 377, 395, 514, 561, 610, 754, 795, 852, 866

Susan Raye, 700

Suspense, 105, 139, 143, 317, 454, 653, 698, 704, 764, 822, 846

Suspicion, 2, 69, 154, 640

Suzanne Pleshette Is Maggie Briggs, 103, 226, 334, 493, 502, 575, 627, 677

Svengali, 308, 647

Swamp Fox, 70

S.W.A.T., 4, 187, 306, 382, 590, 668, 772, 808, 855, 893

Sweeney, The, 881

$weepstake$, 138, 198

Swift Show, The, 64, 303, 323, 378, 449, 518, 734, 769, 775, 780, 919

Swift Show Wagon, The, 396

Swingin' Country, 178

Swingin' Together, 682

Swiss Family Robinson, 1, 239, 424, 590, 591, 642

Switch, 8–10, 124, 141, 142, 343, 413, 487, 589, 784, 788, 825, 870, 917

'S Wonderful, 'S Marvelous, 'S Gershwin, 442, 498, 504

Sword of Justice, 173, 206, 695, 732

Sybil, 296

Sylvester & Tweety, 76

Szysznyk, 60, 69, 160, 185, 190, 444, 492, 587

T

Tab Hunter Show, The, 206, 280, 424, 769

Tabitha, 30, 389, 606, 811, 856

Tag the Gag, 93

Tail Gunner Joe, 582

Take a Chance, 20

Take a Good Look, 5, 12, 106, 193, 195, 480, 496, 709, 730

Take a Guess, 169, 195, 209, 387, 480, 512, 560

Take It from Me, 151, 155, 522

Take It or Leave It, 650

Take Me Along, 383

Talent Jackpot, 190, 316

Talent Patrol, 16, 17, 84, 190, 311, 394

Talent Scouts, 48, 120, 363

Talent Varieties, 828, 910

Tales from the Dark Side, 525

Tales of the Gold Monkey, 142, 190, 261, 320, 531, 567, 640

Tales of the 77th Bengal Lancers, 148, 809, 898

Tales of the Texas Rangers, 497, 657

Tales of the Unexpected, 195, 624

Tales of the Vikings, 60, 643

Tales of Wells Fargo, 85, 175, 241, 339, 489, 660, 724, 751

Tall Man, The, 367, 819

Tallahassee 7000, 556

Tammy, 322, 360, 532, 546, 570, 650, 690, 724, 771, 882, 891, 917

Tammy Grimes Show, The, 365, 685, 750, 773

Target, 581

Target: The Corruptors, 382, 575, 576

Tarzan, 277, 283, 385, 394, 447, 530, 535, 536, 565, 651

Tarzan and the Super Seven, 858

Tate, 574

Tattletales, 196, 197

Taxi, 161, 192, 228, 245, 399, 407, 453, 456, 516, 667, 674, 887

Teachers Only, 34, 64, 116, 180, 293, 325, 455, 567, 703, 707, 742, 785

Ted Knight Show, The, 7, 31, 104, 127, 133, 156, 191, 267, 382, 383, 467, 477, 505, 707, 818

Ted Mack Family Hour, The, 137, 531, 722, 804

Ted Steele Show, The, 124, 715, 804, 916

Teen Time Tunes, 78, 517

Telephone Time, 68, 500, 624

Television: Inside and Out, 61, 238, 776, 885

Television Parts, 624

Television Screen Magazine, 83, 294, 306, 559, 690, 758, 802

Tell It to Groucho, 294, 382, 553, 893

Tell It to the Camera, 736

Tell Me, Dr. Brothers, 118

Telltale Clue, The, 733

Temperatures Rising, 50, 98, 162, 229, 239, 309, 334, 514, 528, 606, 733, 737, 858, 897

Tempest, The, 680

Temple Houston, 195, 274, 424, 527

Tempo, 329

Ten Who Dared, 692

Tenafly, 208, 337, 421, 422, 432, 503, 568

Tenspeed and Brown Shoe, 346, 865

$10,000 Pyramid, The, 178

Terrible Joe Moran, 151

Terror on the 40th Floor, 583

Terry and the Pirates, 798

Testimony of Two Men, 88, 825

Texaco Star Theater, The, 38, 51, 82, 159, 814

Texan, The, 140, 141, 489

Texas, 3, 14, 378, 558, 737

Texas John Slaughter, 449

Texas Rodeo, 214

Texas Wheelers, The, 71, 128, 134, 274, 275, 377, 471, 635, 686

Thanksgiving Visitor, The, 651

That Certain Summer, 410, 434, 491

That Girl, 10, 84, 100, 136, 149, 186, 227, 237, 466, 479, 655, 656, 665, 673, 709, 755, 758, 837, 839, 862

That Reminds Me, 382, 409, 469

That Thing on ABC, 520

That Was the Week That Was, 10, 21, 60, 101, 225, 250, 279, 319, 365, 399, 581, 603, 627, 655, 707, 810, 842, 843

That Wonderful Guy, 378, 503, 504, 813

That's Hollywood, 101

That's Incredible, 213, 230, 490, 829

That's Life, 528, 607, 662, 909

That's My Boy, 10, 422, 558, 788, 816

That's My Line, 59, 174, 503, 589

That's My Mama, 206, 231, 372, 492, 584, 597, 687, 909, 910

T.H.E. Cat, 35, 154, 518

Theater of the Mind, 670

Theater Time, 523

Then Came Bronson, 658

They're Off, 296, 774

Thicke of the Night, 75, 145, 261, 300, 318, 352, 355, 373, 421, 575, 783, 835, 836, 843, 885, 900, 916

Thicker Than Water, 44, 288, 385, 520, 616

Thin Ice, 432

Thin Man, The, 9, 46, 252, 474, 497, 572, 711, 828

Think Fast, 114, 365, 436, 501, 568

Third Barry Manilow Special, The, 149

Third Man, The, 385, 711

13 Queens Boulevard, 109, 143, 276, 560, 726, 738, 861, 904

This for Remembrance, 181

This House Possessed, 78

This Is Alice, 181

This Is Music, 130, 153, 171, 302, 304, 358, 435, 436, 443, 510, 537, 643, 704, 775, 785, 793, 849, 858

This Is NBC News, 755

This Is Show Business, 132, 286, 457, 508, 784

This Is the Life, 95, 374, 434, 455, 503, 808, 819, 831

This Is the NFL, 117

This Is Tom Jones, 2, 449, 535, 658, 798, 820

This Is Your Life, 143, 272, 396, 727, 880

This Is Your Life Thirtieth Anniversary Show, 320

This Man Dawson, 27

This Man Stands Alone, 839

This Week in Country Music, 171, 212

This Week with David Brinkley, 113

Thorn Birds, The, 30, 118, 119, 132, 168, 201, 216, 288, 318, 411, 418, 419, 470, 497, 574, 601, 652, 665, 677, 780, 802, 878, 912

Those Amazing Animals, 206, 278, 582, 683, 800, 833

Those Endearing Young Charms, 200, 303, 330, 390, 668

Those Two, 90, 333, 502, 811

Those Whiting Girls, 10, 654, 897

Three About Town, 18

Three Flames Show, The, 841

Three for the Money, 279

Three for the Road, 328, 726, 862

3 Girls 3, 14, 137, 179, 302, 442, 466, 487

Three Hundred Miles for Stephanie, 641, 645

Three Musketeers, The, 139

Three Robonic Stooges, The, 551

Three Steps to Heaven, 123

Three's a Crowd, 139, 144, 538, 719

Three's Company, 60, 91, 171, 246, 293, 294, 316, 386, 429, 475, 478, 512, 529, 647, 719, 794, 876, 887, 919

Thrill Seekers, 193

Thriller, 154, 168, 454, 626, 839

Through the Crystal Ball, 752

Through the Curtain, 191, 366

Thursday Night Basketball, 15

Thursday Night Fights, 135, 883

Tic Tac Dough, 140, 276, 431, 552, 700

Tightrope, 193

Tim Conway Comedy Hour, The, 74, 97, 197, 380, 451, 585, 717, 795, 809, 818

Tim Conway Show, The, 57, 80, 95, 189, 197, 210, 236, 301, 302, 480, 538, 557, 644, 718, 724, 735, 766

Time Bomb, 902

Time Express, 122, 654, 672, 685, 713

Time for Beany, 315

Time for Love, 775

Time for Reflection, 733

Time for Us, A, 670, 839

Time Tunnel, The, 89, 185, 229, 583, 929

Time Will Tell, 480, 739

Tin Pan Alley TV, 243, 557, 726, 858

T. J. Hooker, 124, 181, 229, 348, 401, 517, 768, 931

To Rome with Love, 109, 167, 306, 320, 579, 581, 586, 594, 620, 761

To Tell the Truth, 69, 74, 81, 149, 163, 190, 215, 325, 326, 598, 657, 680

To the Queen's Taste, 524

Toast of the Town, The, 42, 820. See also Ed Sullivan Show.

Today, 2, 91, 114, 160, 169, 252, 258, 291, 310, 311, 322,

325, 329, 367, 368, 388, 400, 506, 569, 583, 637, 650, 653, 654, 659, 661, 752, 842, 875, 877, 885
Today's F.B.I., 118, 141, 184, 193, 406, 680, 826, 907
Together We Stand, 96, 353, 365, 644, 691, 813
Tom and Jerry, 304
Tom Corbett, Space Cadet, 123, 124, 327, 390, 476, 544, 583, 680, 823, 838
Tom, Dick and Mary, 126, 313, 325, 420, 573
Tom Ewell Show, The, 8, 10, 173, 280, 284, 721
Tom Horn, 283
Tom Sawyer, 920
Tom Smothers' Organic Space Ride, 793
Toma, 214, 341, 515, 540, 615, 635, 816, 839, 865
Tombstone Territory, 197, 269, 697
Tomorrow Show, The, 61, 318, 731, 787, 793
Tomorrow's Careers, 678
Toni Twin Time, 94, 504, 835
Tonight on Broadway, 120, 278
Tonight Show, The, 13, 16, 17, 23, 25, 38–40, 45, 75, 95, 149, 157–159, 166, 197, 215, 241, 258, 311, 348, 351, 356, 363, 379, 390, 398–401, 412, 429, 433, 455, 471, 474, 475, 480, 489, 498, 507, 509, 515, 517, 546, 547, 551, 574, 583, 585, 595, 608, 610, 616, 618, 626, 627, 650, 659, 670, 687, 689, 699, 713, 717, 720, 740, 766, 792–794, 885, 890, 900, 901, 908, 913
Tonight with Belafonte, 73
Tonight! America After Dark, 181, 188, 196, 326, 340, 366, 444, 483, 506, 512, 761, 805, 908
Tony Awards, The, 657
Tony Bennett Show, The, 78, 409, 509, 798
Tony Martin Show, The, 102, 428, 552, 732
Tony Orlando and Dawn, 149, 412, 414, 431, 492, 552, 563, 633, 644, 736, 756, 805, 869, 909
Tony Randall Show, The, 195, 495, 548, 574, 610, 659, 670, 696, 723, 751, 758, 829
Too Close for Comfort, 126, 143, 146, 203, 247, 267, 316, 349, 477, 578, 579, 863
Too Young to Go Steady, 68, 77, 78, 198, 338, 426
Top Cat, 241, 352, 439, 453, 801, 805
Top Dollar, 619, 705
Top Pro Golf, 226
Top Secret U.S.A., 736, 811
Top Tunes and New Talent), 889

Topper, 155, 156, 316, 375, 432, 438, 660, 783, 806, 879
Touch of Grace, A, 82, 100, 582, 642
Tough Cookies, 34, 79, 208, 458, 585, 631, 664
Tour of the White House with Mrs. John F. Kennedy, A, 188
Trackdown, 216, 217, 577, 635
Trackdown—Finding the Goodbar Killer, 369
Traffic Court, 446, 563, 898
Trap, The, 243
Trapper John, M.D., 5, 55, 128, 134, 217, 309, 358, 386, 426, 428, 462, 525, 542, 562, 579, 591, 631, 652, 722, 723, 726, 754, 761, 777, 782, 851, 853, 927
Trash or Treasure, 161, 735, 890
Trauma Center, 57, 295, 296, 381, 396, 537, 593, 619, 697, 793, 914
Travels of Jaimie McPheeters, The, 15, 17, 24, 115, 467, 556, 560, 640, 646, 739, 892, 915, 921
Treasure Hunt, 272, 614, 800, 842
Treasure of Jamaica Reef, 918
Treasure Quest, 887
Treasury Men in Action, 115, 359, 445, 551
Trial of Lee Harvey Oswald, The, 331
Trials of O'Brien, The, 60, 130, 172, 287, 332, 817, 824
Tribute to the American Housewife, A, 171
Trouble with Father, The, 281
Trouble with Harry, The, 555
Troubleshooters, The, 13, 307, 384, 517, 556, 922
Truth or Consequences, 50, 59, 265, 272, 321
Try and Do It, 112, 449
Tucker's Witch, 61, 404, 555, 601, 733, 917
Tuesday Night Fights, 277, 648
Tuesday/Monday Night Fights, 298
Turn of the Screw, 703
Turnabout, 343, 449, 474, 757, 777, 778, 800
Turn-On, 97, 143, 358, 361, 362, 540, 561, 569, 612, 649, 799, 819
TV Reader's Digest, 700, 708
TV's Bloopers and Practical Jokes, 158, 167, 177, 178, 238, 475, 574, 768, 776
TV's Top Tunes, 31, 47, 269, 304, 494, 502, 582, 590, 637, 784, 847
Tweety and Sylvester, 304
Twelfth Night, 335, 458
Twelve Angry Men, 294, 671

Twelve O'Clock High, 74, 128, 244, 262, 263, 324, 493, 494, 648, 671, 725
Twentieth Century, 889
20th Century, The, 211, 731
20th Century-Fox Hour, The, 205, 806, 870
Twenty Questions, 386, 431, 570, 577, 678, 719, 784, 859
$25,000 Pyramid, The, 177, 215, 562
Twenty-One, 63
21 Beacon Street, 60, 463, 538, 602
26 Men, 184, 398
20/20, 118, 172, 258, 309, 393, 417, 423, 437, 532, 541, 720, 744, 815, 877
Twilight, The, 133
Twilight Theater, 552
Twilight Zone, The, 7, 61, 65, 69, 94, 95, 129, 152, 154, 157, 194, 236, 311, 312, 387, 411, 476, 488, 526, 551, 555, 561, 582, 605, 607, 621, 712, 731, 764, 765, 768, 808, 811, 883, 914, 922, 923
Twirl, 894
Two Faces West, 66, 191
Two Fathers' Justice, 377
Two for the Money, 14, 365, 508, 640, 776
Two Girls Named Smith, 302
Two in Love, 657
Two Marriages, 142, 150, 274, 318, 420, 522, 554, 574, 613, 847
Two of a Kind, 79, 441
Two of Us, The, 179, 198, 405, 466, 840
240-Robert, 48, 131, 164, 382, 400, 627, 667, 750, 829, 868
Two's Company, 817
227, 54, 335, 336, 349, 386, 473, 550, 703, 903, 904
Tycoon, The, 109, 206, 487, 543, 577, 905

U

UFO, 87, 88, 259, 349, 766, 831
Ugliest Girl in Town, The, 106, 455, 546, 659, 842
Ultra Quiz, 549
U.N. Casebook, 125, 420
Uncle Croc's Block, 914
Under One Roof, 33, 142, 353, 386, 402, 466, 807
Under Siege, 410, 817
Underdog, 207
Undersea World of Jacques Cousteau, The, 143, 206, 764
Union Pacific, 606
United or Not, 534
United States, 111, 226, 386, 769
Universe, 211, 212
Untamed World, 148
Untouchables, The, 36, 55, 106, 127, 177, 273, 287, 295, 333,

349, 367, 500, 519, 655, 673,
751, 799, 802, 836, 911
Up to Paar, 650
Upbeat, 161, 413, 607
Upstairs, Downstairs, 49,
545
U.S. Royal Showcase, The, 2,
156
U.S. Steel Hour, The, 43, 68,
69, 74, 80, 85, 94, 95, 104,
148, 157, 158, 278, 312, 364,
371, 381, 430, 476, 493, 651,
653, 680, 684, 747, 764, 784,
917

V

V, 40, 49, 145, 167, 176, 199,
267, 279, 356, 401, 429, 471,
623, 650, 661, 686, 782,
787–789, 820, 830, 834, 919,
923
V: The Final Battle, 49, 256,
267, 279, 356, 401, 429, 445,
448, 623, 650, 661, 686, 782,
821, 834, 919
Vacation in Hell, 542
Vagabond, 133
Val Doonican Show, The, 210,
254, 535, 747, 844, 917
Valentine, 839
Valentine Magic on Love
Island, 58
Valentine's Day, 249, 310, 311,
392, 691, 795, 872
Valentino, 857
Valerie, 66, 269, 383, 511, 564,
678, 831
Valiant Lady, 144
Vampire Rabbit, 924
Van Camp's Little Show, 105,
196
Van Dyke and Company, 274,
456, 469, 486, 561, 688, 794,
860
Vanished, 899
Vaudeo Varieties, 420
Vaudeville Show, The, 647
Vaughn Monroe Show, The,
184, 233, 394, 538, 595, 750,
819, 828
Vega$, 19, 108, 135, 219, 229,
233, 237, 489, 549, 605, 747,
808, 856
Vegetable Soup, 447
Verdict Is Yours, The, 572,
894
Verna: U.S.O. Girl, 230
Versatile Varieties, 62, 311,
340, 440, 608, 739, 749
Very Private Person, A, 190
Vic Damone Show, The, 142,
225, 288, 798
Victims for Victims, 334
Victor Borge Show, The, 100,
428
Victoria Regina, 385
Victory at Entebbe, 488, 831
Video Village, 200, 375, 618,
904

Village Barn, The, 161, 244,
261, 306, 419, 519, 676, 802,
838
Vincent Lopez Show, The, 60,
520, 739, 759, 880
Virginia Graham Show, The,
355
Virginian, The, 70, 86, 99, 126,
143, 148, 150, 179, 182, 194,
224, 246, 260, 276, 280, 356,
367, 388, 447, 490, 500, 555,
563, 564, 571, 612, 628, 629,
635, 691, 735, 747, 758, 759,
761, 775, 920
Vise, The, 54, 237, 359, 570,
696, 841
Viva Valdez, 167, 215, 420,
552, 601, 865, 929
Voice of Firestone, The, 59,
119, 223, 296, 664
Volume One, 200
Voyage to the Bottom of the
Sea, 65, 71, 126, 257, 396,
423, 483, 595, 638, 685, 850,
897
Voyagers, 403, 664, 679

W

Wackiest Ship in the Army,
The, 188, 429, 462, 665, 784,
792, 794, 878, 931
Wacky World of Jonathan
Winters, The, 12, 346, 362,
582, 796, 913
Wagon Train, 51, 76, 98, 101,
131, 141, 177, 253, 320, 361,
415, 527, 530, 570, 571, 588,
595, 628, 631, 652, 658, 673,
676, 731, 734, 802, 806, 910,
923
Wait Till Your Father Gets
Home, 101, 102, 131, 334,
373, 395, 410
Waiting for the Break, 487
Walk Through the Twentieth
Century, A, 609
Walking Tall, 60, 224, 506, 559,
677, 823, 826
Wallenberg, 168
Wally's Cafe, 818
Walter Winchell File, The, 911
Walter Winchell Show, The,
911
Waltons, The, 39, 103, 192,
201, 205, 209, 253, 269, 272,
309, 332, 339, 341, 378, 379,
383, 386, 432, 475, 500, 545,
567, 592, 629, 632, 671, 701,
704, 719, 755, 759, 763, 839,
871, 875, 899, 903, 911, 913
Wanderlust, 133
Wanted, 570
Wanted: Dead or Alive, 473,
489, 577, 631, 635, 683
War as It Happens, The, 18,
306
Warner Brothers Presents,
925
Warren Hull Show, The, 423

Washington Behind Closed
Doors, 16, 364, 416, 468, 621,
682, 724, 763, 863
Washington Exclusive, 576
Washington Report, 184
Watch Mr. Wizard, 401
Watch the World, 344, 824
Waterfront, 85, 214, 248, 308,
369, 376, 403, 439, 497, 601,
753, 845
Watergate, The White House
Transcripts, 698
Waverly Wonders, The, 95,
338, 362, 492, 618, 672, 800,
852
Way It Was, The, 279
Way Out, 221, 839
Wayne & Shuster Take an
Affectionate Look At .., 776,
883
Wayne King, 70, 283, 374, 473,
494, 607, 858
We Got It Made, 201, 482, 565,
856, 866
We Take Your Word, 125,
132, 223, 559
We, the People, 766, 888
W.E.B., 65, 75, 184, 201, 686,
700, 900, 915
Web, The, 91, 124, 127, 223,
744
Webster, 179, 225, 455, 482,
508, 678, 726, 865
Wednesday Night Fights, 259,
408
Wednesday/Monday Night
Fights, 426
Weekend, 250, 275
Weekend Special, 573
Welcome Aboard, 520, 604
Welcome Back, Kotter, 39,
103, 167, 300, 375, 380, 396,
433, 453, 479, 503, 653, 758,
762, 775, 816, 848, 849, 882,
896
We'll Get By, 1, 10, 408, 416,
758, 796
Wendy and Me, 130, 141, 383,
642, 724, 807
Wendy Barrie Show, The, 61,
231
We're Movin', 1, 52
Wesley, 123, 245, 625, 706, 811,
824, 838
West 57th, 296, 782, 865, 874
West Point, 269
West Point Story, The, 558
Westerner, The, 239, 460, 461
Westinghouse Desilu
Playhouse, 35, 36, 321, 631,
764, 799, 922
Westinghouse Playhouse, 202,
247, 285, 465, 639
Westside Medical, 150, 633,
785, 840
Westward Ho, the Wagons,
706
Westwind, 905
We've Got Each Other, 33,
131, 179, 482, 680, 858,
918

Whale for the Killing, A, 817, 899

What Do You Have in Common?, 815

What Happened?, 295, 324, 357, 685, 803

What in the World, 143, 199, 694

What Really Happened to the Class of '65?, 87, 489

Whatever Happened to Dobie Gillis?, 404, 487

What's Going On?, 103, 149, 326, 578, 632, 635, 700

What's Happening Now!!, 83, 398, 442, 473, 622, 798, 838

What's Happening to America, 626

What's Happening!!, 83, 397, 410, 472, 589, 622, 638, 698, 708, 789, 798, 838, 890

What's in a Word?, 278, 286, 578, 601, 874

What's It All About, World?, 14, 40, 149, 176, 259, 355, 443, 446, 575, 593, 686, 863

What's It For?, 132, 195, 295, 339, 541, 653

What's It Worth?, 291, 735

What's My Line?, 14, 16, 17, 93, 95, 167, 223, 224, 311, 323, 327, 470, 595, 642, 746, 855

What's the Story?, 146, 147, 469, 560, 697, 821, 861

What's Your Bid?, 11, 472, 733, 771, 918

Wheel of Fortune, 363, 740, 745, 896, 918

Wheels, 74, 118, 274, 310, 311, 422, 449, 541, 569, 638, 641, 710, 826, 876, 894, 906

When Dreams Come True, 903

When Havoc Struck, 304, 305

When Hell Was in Session, 410, 744

When the West Was Fun, 305

When the Whistle Blows, 15, 60, 121, 126, 407, 491, 735, 824, 906

When Things Were Rotten, 249, 330, 445, 479, 678, 718, 735, 743, 862

When Your Lover Leaves, 912

Where Are You?, 378

Where Have I Been?, 140

Where the Action Is, 178

Where the Heart Is, 562

Where Was I?, 215, 253, 355, 361, 367, 399, 472, 532, 722, 766

Where's Everett?, 10

Where's Huddles?, 92, 279, 439, 528, 584, 632, 703, 859, 909, 910

Whiplash, 357, 358, 898

Whirlybirds, The, 373, 405, 798, 843

Whispering Smith, 126, 592, 612

White Hunter, 701

White Shadow, The, 30, 83, 160, 198, 200, 302, 411, 413, 418, 419, 433, 439, 471, 496, 581, 586, 668, 687, 725, 733, 810, 862, 880

Whiz Kids, 140, 277, 323, 434, 486, 552, 640, 679, 761

Who Am I?, 375

Who Are the De Bolts and Where Did They Get 19 Kids?, 371, 912

Who Do You Trust?, 157, 574

Who in the World?, 423

Who Is the Black Dahlia?, 37

Who Pays?, 381, 412, 475, 874

Who Said That?, 22, 120, 196, 223, 344, 399, 452, 469, 517, 823, 850

Whodunnit?, 50, 74, 574

Who's the Boss?, 228, 397, 469, 479, 511, 529, 572, 587, 675, 823, 874

Who's There?, 200, 215, 315, 685

Who's Watching the Kids?, 52, 75, 97, 108, 348, 457, 474, 496, 510, 535

Who's Who?, 417, 483, 698

Who's Whose, 53, 169, 230, 304, 471

Why?, 215, 472

Wichita Town, 23, 308, 566, 620, 730

Wide Country, The, 126, 411, 673, 686

Wide Wide World, 329, 885, 916

Wide World of Sports, 337, 572

Widow, 500

Wife Saver, The, 683

Wifeline, 653

Wild Bill Hickok. See The Adventures of Wild Bill Hickok.

Wild Bunch, The, 635

Wild Kingdom, 113, 309, 666, 667

Wild Wild West, The, 127, 194, 198, 202, 477, 488, 526, 551, 565, 600, 611, 717, 723, 755, 828, 892

Wild, Wild World of Animals, The, 195

Wild Women of Chastity Gulch, The, 646, 894

Wildside, 247, 303, 320, 321, 402, 409, 577, 664, 729, 741, 761, 791

Will the Real Jerry Lewis Please Sit Down?, 509

Willa, 898

Willy, 193, 203, 392, 412, 663, 715, 849

Willys Theatre Presenting Ben Hecht's Tales of the City, 396

Win with a Winner, 70, 276, 394, 846

Window on Main Street, 84, 138, 230, 359, 449, 555, 598, 694, 926

Window on the World, 465

Winds of War, The, 74, 81, 106, 159, 165, 239, 249, 263, 274, 339, 340, 351, 357, 369, 381, 409, 416, 454, 465, 479, 491, 518, 530, 562, 568, 571, 580, 593, 606, 607, 611, 612, 672, 679, 683, 695, 718, 767, 834, 846, 866

Windy City Jamboree, 643, 812, 858

Wingo, 465

Winky Dink and You, 14, 63

Winner Take All, 190, 448

Winnie the Pooh, 139, 412

Winston Churchill: The Wilderness Years, 918

Winston Churchill: The Valiant Years, 133, 584

Winter of Our Discontent, The, 888

Wire Service, 110, 177, 489, 561

Wisdom of the Ages, 63, 173, 179, 452, 611, 861

With This Ring, 323, 784

Witness, The, 187, 364, 393, 570, 586, 751, 791

Witness for the Prosecution, 718

Wizard, The, 60, 255, 697, 741

Wizards and Warriors, 117, 192, 262, 264, 406, 456, 468, 641, 662, 707, 712, 915, 920

WKRP in Cincinnati, 25, 98, 123, 402, 451, 707, 708, 748, 749, 776, 791

Woman Called Moses, A, 854, 889

Woman Named Golda, A, 629

Woman to Remember, A, 123, 166, 566, 693, 838, 893

Woman Who Willed a Miracle, The, 177

Women in White, 3, 300

Women, Work and Babies: Can America Survive?, 661

Women's Room, The, 43, 224, 228, 913

Wonder Woman, 133, 159, 187, 269, 336, 482, 595, 689, 768, 869

Wonderama, 309

Wonderful John Acton, The, 268, 384, 410, 550, 585, 733, 862, 872

Wonderful Women of the World, The, 133

Wonderful World of Disney, The, 891

Word, The, 897

Word, The, 437

Word of Honor, 537

Words and Music, 440, 545

Working Stiffs, 33, 75, 89, 460, 660, 736

World Apart, A, 88

World News Tonight, 440, 725

World of Disney, The, 139, 899

World of Giants, The, 840
World of Lowell Thomas, 838
World of Mr. Sweeney, The, 737, 869, 872
World of Survival, The, 306, 307
World University Games, The, 835
World War I, 742
World War III., 422, 797
World Wide 60, 568
Wrangler, 284
Wren's Nest, 746, 919
Wuthering Heights, 133
Wyatt Earp. *See* The Life and Legend of Wyatt Earp.

X

Xavier Cugat Show, The, 215, 490

Y

Yancy Derringer, 5, 81, 107, 370, 535
Year at the Top, A, 182, 240, 284, 404, 604, 767, 868
Yellow Rose, The, 9, 31, 71, 78, 193, 219, 276, 459, 747, 755, 771, 797
Yesterday's Child, 930
Yogi Bear, 584, 648, 806
You Again?, 77, 476, 800, 801
You Are an Artist, 344
You Are There, 211, 352, 361, 411, 462, 690
You Asked for It, 52, 466, 515, 788

You Bet Your Life, 294, 369, 553
You Can't Go Home Again, 914
You Don't Say, 466, 664
You'll Never Get Rich, 779
You'll Never See Me Again, 388
Young and the Restless, The, 3, 67, 83, 121, 185, 200, 274, 366, 374, 376, 390, 392, 764, 811
Young Dan'l Boone, 161, 217, 280, 607, 838
Young Dr. Kildare, 439, 584
Young Doctor Malone, 85, 127, 221, 276, 670, 686, 862
Young Joe, the Forgotten Kennedy, 816
Young Lawyers, The, 68, 179, 182, 473, 650
Young Marrieds, The, 583
Young Maverick, 93, 239, 313, 328, 464
Young Mr. Bobbin, 79, 416, 461, 688, 766, 886, 892
Young Philadelphians, The, 864
Young Rebels, The, 277, 306, 352, 401, 840
Your All-American College Show, 346
Your Chevrolet Showroom, 730
Your Funny, Funny Films, 294
Your Hit Parade, 35, 65, 78, 81, 171, 188, 200, 202, 241, 243, 272, 307, 328, 332, 336, 380, 493, 505, 532, 761, 768, 772, 796, 842, 858, 908, 918
Your Lucky Clue, 698

Your Pet Parade, 65
Your Play Time, 711
Your Show of Shows, 45, 139, 140, 159, 182, 183, 238, 298, 377, 393, 444, 478, 514, 555, 584, 605, 672, 702, 708, 709, 733, 739, 749, 803, 842, 902
Your Show Time, 774
Your Sports Special, 4, 803
Your TV Baby Sitter, 580
Your Witness, 524
You're in the Picture, 156, 341, 342, 806, 849, 922
You're Invited, 866
You're on Your Own, 265
You're Putting Me On, 95
Yours for a Song, 657
Youth on the March, 209
Youth Takes a Stand, 207, 431
Youth Wants to Know, 356

Z

Zane Grey Theater. *See* Dick Powell's Zane Grey Theater.
Zero-1, 791
Ziegfeld: The Man and His Women, 825
Zoo Gang, The, 461
Zoo Parade, 667
Zoot Suit, 224
Zorro, 40, 106, 142, 247, 314, 321, 395, 509, 519, 661, 771, 903
Zorro and Son, 69, 225, 229, 500, 548, 607, 657, 707, 777

ABOUT THE AUTHOR

Tim Brooks is Director of Program Research for NBC-TV, in which capacity he tests new program ideas and promotional strategies for the network. (To those who ask, "With all that testing, how do so many lousy programs get on the air?," he replies: "You should see the ones that don't.") Fascinated with the broadcasting industry since childhood, he has held positions with CBS, Westinghouse Broadcasting Co., and local stations. A media historian, he is the coauthor of several books, including (with Earle Marsh) the best-selling *Complete Directory to Prime Time Network TV Shows, 1946–Present*. He has also written numerous articles about the history of the recording industry, and teaches communications courses at C.W. Post Center, Long Island University.

Mr. Brooks is a native of Hampton, N.H., and a graduate of Dartmouth College and Syracuse University. He lives in New York.